Directory of Grant Making Trusts

2003–04
18TH EDITION

CAF

Published by
Directory of Social Change
24 Stephenson Way
London NW1 2DP

Tel: 020 7209 5151
Fax: 020 7391 4804
e-mail: books@dsc.org.uk
Website: www.dsc.org.uk

from whom further copies and a full publications list are available

on behalf of
Charities Aid Foundation (CAF)
Kings Hill
West Malling
Kent ME19 4TA

Tel: 01732 520000
Fax: 01732 520001
e-mail:
enquiries@caf.charitynet.org
Website: www.CAFonline.org

Directory of Social Change is a registered charity no. 800517

Charities Aid Foundation is a registered charity no. 268369

Copyright © Directory of Social Change 2003
Reprinted 2003

Cover and text design
Eugenie Dodd Typographics

Typesetting
Tradespools Ltd, Frome

Printed and bound by
Antony Rowe, Chippenham

A catalogue record for this book is available from the British Library

ISBN 1 903991 33 1

Editorial team
Dave Casson
John Smyth

Additional research
Alan French
Dave Griffiths
Tom Traynor

Contents

Foreword   v

Introduction   vii

How to use the *DGMT*   ix

A typical trust entry   xvii

A list of the top 150 trusts   xviii

Other publications   xx

INDEXES   Trusts by geographical area   1

Trusts by field of interest and type of beneficiary   29

Trusts by type of grant   225

REGISTER   The alphabetical register of grant making trusts   261

Foreword

CAF's strategy is to provide high quality information to donors, with the aim of increasing the flow of funds to charities and NGOs. In recent years, the trends towards both globalisation and online delivery have added exciting new dimensions to our activities in this respect.

Sitting alongside this is the clear need to provide accurate and timely information to help charities and NGOs – in this case, in order to access the community of trusts and foundations in a targeted and effective way. Over the years, nothing has done this better than the *Directory of Grant Making Trusts (DGMT)* and I am delighted that the Directory of Social Change has done so much to ensure that its reputation and impact are unsurpassed.

CAF first published the *DGMT* in 1968 and, in truth, we probably didn't realise quite what a critical role it would play at the fulcrum of the funder/fundraiser relationship – and, what's more, that it would still be going strong 35 years later.

As all readers of the *DGMT* know, we are living in an increasingly frenzied and transactional world – in almost every area of activity that you can imagine. Whether it is money, information, contacts or advice, the growing thirst for more, faster and better, seems to be relentless.

The main purpose of the *DGMT* is clear and has never been more important: it enables charities to target sympathetic grant-making trusts and foundations, at a time when the demands on charities' time and money are increasing. For funders, on the other hand, it reduces the level of ill-targeted applications at a time when they risk becoming beleaguered by the volume and strength of requests for support. On both sides of the funding fence, time and money have become increasingly important commodities.

In this increasingly frenzied and transactional world, the *DGMT* has the ability to save time and increase money for fundraisers, across the spectrum of charitable activity. A rare commodity indeed.

Stephen Ainger CEO
Charities Aid Foundation *14 March 2003*

Introduction

This book covers the largest 2,500 grant-making trusts in the UK which give grants to organisations. The amounts given by individual funders range from £20,000 up to £388 million. The top 150 are listed at the end of this introduction and include the national arts boards and Community Fund, as well as more 'traditional' grant-making trusts.

The companion *Grant-making Trusts CD-ROM* also covers these 2,500 trusts, plus a further 1,500 smaller, local trusts. The same 4,000 trusts' details are available, and regularly updated, on the subscription website *trustfunding.org.uk*. See page xx for further information.

CAF published the first edition of *The Directory of Grant Making Trusts (DGMT)* in 1968. Since that time, the title has gained a notable reputation as a comprehensive guide to UK grant-making trusts and their funding policies. It is designed to provide a bridge between the foundation and fundraising communities in the UK. Today it is hard to imagine the difficulties which must have been encountered in trying to obtain funds from trusts before the *DGMT* threw a spotlight on their existence.

The *DGMT* is a key source of information on how trusts see themselves and their grantmaking. Each entry aims to reflect the trust's own view of its policies, priorities and exclusions. Other guides include independent, sometimes critical comment on and analysis of trust activities. The *DGMT* does not. Rather, it is the trusts' guide to grant-making trusts.

The research carried out has resulted in over 250 trusts appearing in this edition that were not included previously. On average it appears that about 50 new trusts are established each year that at a later date make it into this directory.

The major difference in the indexing of this edition compared to the previous one is the adoption of the increasingly used classification developed by ACF and others. This has resulted in the addition, merger or removal of some categories, perhaps most noticeably in the *Types of Grant* index. We trust these refinements will make these indexes more useful and easier to follow.

We value your comments on any aspect of the directory, from format to content. Please contact us at DGMT Editorial, c/o DSC, Federation House, Hope Street, Liverpool L1 9BW or e-mail us at north@dsc.org.uk

The trusts we have listed This directory aims to include all UK-based trusts capable of giving at least £20,000 a year to organisations. Every trust included was asked to update the information contained in its entry and to classify its grant-making activities.

Many of the trusts are extremely helpful and provide us with comprehensive information on their current policies. However, not all trusts are so open. Where a trust did not respond to our request to amend its entry, the details have been updated where possible using the information on file at the Charity Commission. In addition, all contact details were checked.

Some trusts continue to state their wish not to be included in this book. However, we believe that trust directories provide an invaluable bridge between the trust community and the rest of the voluntary sector, and that trusts in receipt of public funds through tax relief should not attempt to draw a veil of secrecy over their activities. Consequently, we have declined the majority of requests from trusts to be excluded from this directory.

In general we have included:

■ trusts with an income of £20,000 or over that make grants to charities and voluntary organisations, including the Community Fund, national arts councils and the Foundation for Sport and the Arts.

We have excluded:

■ trusts which fund individuals only;

■ trusts which fund one organisation exclusively;

■ trusts which have an income of less than £20,000 (smaller local trusts are included on the companion *Grant-Making Trusts CD-ROM* and on *trustfunding.org.uk*);

■ trusts which have ceased to exist or are being wound down with remaining funds fully committed.

We continue to include trusts which state that they do not respond to unsolicited applications. We believe their inclusion gives fundraisers a broader overview of the grant-making community and that the information could be important in supporting relationship fundraising activity.

Information about trusts which give grants to individuals can be found in *A Guide to Grants for Individuals in Need* and *The Educational Grants Directory*. See page xxi for further information.

How to use the *DGMT*

The directory starts with three indexes:

- Trusts by geographical area;
- Trusts by field of interest and type of beneficiary;
- Trusts by grant type.

There is an alphabetical listing of the top 150 trusts by grant total.

Using these indexes, users should end up with a shortlist of trusts whose funding policies match their needs.

Trusts by geographical area

This index enables you to see which trusts will consider applications from a charity or project in a particular geographical area. It contains two separate listings:

LIST OF GEOGRAPHICAL AREA HEADINGS

This is a complete list of all the geographical area headings used in the *DGMT*. The page numbers relate to the second listing. There is a small new section at the start of this index, headed *Type of place*. This includes four categories.

LIST OF TRUSTS BY GEOGRAPHICAL AREA

These pages list trusts under the geographical areas from which they will consider applications for funding.

Trusts by field of interest and type of beneficiary

This index enables you to see which trusts are likely to fund projects doing a particular type of work to benefit a particular type of person. It lists trusts according to:

- the type of activity or work they are willing to fund – their 'fields of interest';
- who they want to benefit – their preferred 'beneficiaries'.

These pages contain two separate listings:

CATEGORISATION OF FIELDS OF INTEREST AND TYPES OF BENEFICIARY

This lists all of the headings used in the *DGMT* to categorise fields of interest and types of beneficiary. This listing should help you match your project with one – or more – of the categories used. The page numbers relate to the second listing.

LIST OF TRUSTS BY FIELD OF INTEREST AND TYPE OF BENEFICIARY

These pages list trusts under the fields of interest and types of beneficiary they have indicated they might be willing to support.

Trusts were asked to indicate whether projects working in a field of interest/for a type of beneficiary:

- are a **funding priority**, i.e. the area is one which the trust is particularly interested in funding;
- **will be considered**, i.e. the trust may consider funding in the area but it is not one of their priorities.

The index is structured hierarchically. This means that the general heading comes first, followed by more specific subject areas. For example, *Education and training* is split into eight sub-headings, including *Education policy, Pre-school education, Primary and secondary education* and so on. Some of these are then split further. For example, *Primary and secondary education* contains a further five categories, including *Choir schools, Faith schools* and *Special needs schools*.

So, if your project falls under a specific heading, such as *Special needs schools*, it may also be worth looking at the trusts which have expressed a general interest in funding primary and secondary education and, above that, education and training.

Trusts by type of grant

This index enables you to see which trusts will consider making the types of grant you are looking for. Trusts are listed under the types of grant that they have indicated they are willing to make. These pages contain two separate listings:

LIST OF GRANT TYPES

This lists all of the headings used in the *DGMT* to categorise grant types. Page numbers relate to the second listing.

LIST OF TRUSTS BY GRANT TYPE

These pages list trusts under the types of grant that they are willing to make.

Trusts were asked to indicate whether the grant types:

- are a **funding priority**, i.e. the type of grant the trust prefers to give;
- **will be considered**, i.e. the trust may consider making this type of grant.

The largest trusts

At the end of the introduction, we have listed the largest 150 trusts by grant total. This is because we have dispensed with some of the very general index categories, such as Worldwide and UK-wide under the lists of trusts by geographical area, and General under the lists of trusts by field of interest. We felt that these headings were so general as to be effectively useless. For example, over half the trusts in the book are UK-wide

As a compromise, however, we decided to provide a separate list of the top 150 trusts. Between them they account for about £2.1 billion, or 83% of the income in the book. Please do not use this as a simple mailing list. These trusts cover a very wide range of specialist interests. Most of them will never fund your work.

However, we do recommend that you read each entry carefully and compile your own list of the major trusts relevant to you. You can then set this list alongside the other lists generated from the other indexes in the directory. It is, we believe, the most effective way of ensuring that you do not omit any major trusts.

How to use the *DGMT*
Key steps

STEP 1

Define the project, programme or work for which you are seeking funding.

▼

STEP 2

Geographical area: find the area most local to your requirements. Note down the names of the trusts listed here.

▼

STEP 3

Field of interest and type of beneficiary: identify the categories that match your project. Note down the names of trusts listed here.

▼

STEP 4

Type of grant: identify the type of grant you are looking for. Note down the names of the trusts listed here.

▼

STEP 5

Compare the three lists of trusts to produce a list whose funding policies most closely match the characteristics of the project for which you are seeking funding.

▼

STEP 6	**STEP 7**
If your list of trusts is **too short** you could include trusts that have a general interest in funding in your area.	If your list of trusts is **too long** you could limit yourself to trusts that regard your area of work as a 'Funding priority', and leave out those that 'Will consider' applications.

▼

STEP 8

Look up the entries for the trusts identified, studying their details carefully and paying particular attention to 'What is funded' and 'What is not funded'.

▼

STEP 9

Look at the list of the **top 150 trusts**. Look up the entries for the trusts identified, studying their details carefully, once again paying particular attention to 'What is funded' and 'What is not funded'.

Checklist

STEP 1

The following checklist will help you assemble the information you need:

- What is the geographical location of the people who will benefit from any funding received?
- What facilities or services will the funding provide?
- What are the characteristics which best describe the people who will benefit from any funding received?
- What type of grant are you looking for?

EXAMPLE

Funding is being sought for a project in Merseyside to enable unemployed young people to take part in an employment training scheme.

- *The geographical location is:*

*England → North West → **Merseyside***

- *The service to be provided is: **Vocational training***
- *The key characteristic of the people to benefit is that they are: **Unemployed***
- *The type of grant being sought is: **Project***

STEP 2

Look up the area where your project is based in the list of geographical area headings on page 2.

- Turn to the relevant pages in the list of trusts by geographical area and note down the names of the trusts which have stated that they will consider funding projects in your area.

EXAMPLE

Look up the area most local to your requirements (Merseyside) in the list of geographical area headings. Then turn to the relevant page in the list of trusts by geographical area and look up the names of the trusts listed under Merseyside. You may want to look at the trusts listed under the broader region (North West) as well. Note down the names so that they can be compared with the lists produced through the indexes by type of grant and by field of interest and type of beneficiary.

It is also worth looking at trusts listed under England, as a trust listed under a more general heading may be just as willing to fund activity in a specific region as another which states that it has a specific interest in that region.

STEP 3 Using the categorisation of fields of interest and types of beneficiary on page 30, identify all the categories that match the project, programme or work for which you are seeking funding.

Turn to the relevant pages in the list of trusts by field of interest and type of beneficiary and look up the headings identified. Look first at the trusts that appear under the heading 'Funding priority', then look under the heading 'Will consider'.

Note down the names of the trusts appearing under these headings so that you can compare them with the names identified through the indexes by geographical area and by type of grant.

EXAMPLE *With a project to provide training for work, you will probably look first under the main heading 'Education & training'. Under this heading you will find the sub-heading 'Informal & continuing education' and under this you will find the heading 'Vocational education and training'. Note down the page numbers beside 'Informal & continuing education' and 'Vocational education and training'. Trusts that have expressed an interest in funding vocational training may represent your best prospects, but trusts with a more general interest in funding informal education and training might be worth approaching – particularly if they like to fund projects in your area.*

If you look under 'Beneficiaries' you will find 'People who are unemployed' under 'Social and economic circumstances'. Note down this page number too.

STEP 4 Look up the type of grant that you are seeking in the list of grant types on page 226.

Turn to the relevant pages in the list of trusts by types of grant and note down the names of the trusts that will consider giving the type of grant that you are seeking so that you can compare them with the names identified through the indexes by geographical area and by field of interest and type of beneficiary.

EXAMPLE *Look up the type of grant you are seeking (project) in the list of types of grant. Then turn to the relevant page of the list of trusts by types of grant and look at the names of the trusts listed under 'Project'. Note down the names of all these trusts.*

STEP 5 Compare the lists of trust names produced via steps 2, 3 and 4, and make a list of all the trusts which appear on more than one list. This will produce a list of trusts whose funding policies most closely match the characteristics of the project for which you are seeking funding.

STEP 6 If the list turns out to be too short it can easily be adjusted.

EXAMPLE *You may find that you have ended up with a list of five trusts. Going back to step 3, you could include the trusts which come under 'Education & training', or, going back to step 2, you could include trusts which will consider funding projects in the North West.*

STEP 7 If your list turns out to be too long it can easily be adjusted.

EXAMPLE *You may find that you have ended up with a list of 150 trusts. Going back to step 3, you could limit yourself to trusts that regard your particular area of activity as a 'Funding priority' and leave out those that 'Will consider' applications. You could also discard the names of trusts that have a general interest in funding education and training and confine your list to trusts that are interested in funding vocational education and training.*

STEP 8 Look up the entries for the trusts identified and study their details carefully, paying particular attention to 'What Is Funded' and 'What Is Not Funded'.

If you feel that there is a good match between the characteristics of the project for which you require support and the funding policies of the trust identified, you could submit an application.

STEP 9 Look at the list of the top 150 trusts.

Check that you have not missed any of the major funders because you have made your search too specific. Some of the largest foundations give to a wide range of organisations and projects, and they tend to give the largest grants. They are also the most over-subscribed.

Look up the entries for each trust and study their details carefully, paying particular attention to 'What Is Funded' and 'What Is Not Funded'. If you feel that there is a good match between the characteristics of the project for which you require support and the funding policies of the trust identified, you could submit an application.

However, make sure that there is a good reason for writing to any trust that you select; do not just send off indiscriminate applications to the whole list!

A typical trust entry

A complete entry should contain information under the headings listed below. An explanation of the information which should appear in these fields is given alongside.

WHERE FUNDING CAN BE GIVEN
The village, town, borough, parish or other geographical area the trust is prepared to fund

WHAT IS FUNDED
Details of the types of project or activity the trust plans to fund in 2003–2004

WHAT IS NOT FUNDED
The types of project the trust will definitely not fund, e.g. expeditions, scholarships

SAMPLE GRANTS
The main grants given by the trust in the last financial year

TRUSTEES
Names of the trustees

PUBLICATIONS
Titles of publications the trust has produced which are of interest to grantseekers

WHO TO APPLY TO
The name and address of the person to whom applications should be sent

CC NO
Charity Commission number

WHO CAN BENEFIT
The kinds of people, animals, etc., the trust wishes ultimately to benefit

TYPE OF GRANT
The types of grant or loan the trust is prepared to give, e.g. one-off, recurring, running costs

RANGE OF GRANTS
The smallest, largest and typical size of grant normally given

FINANCES
The most recent financial information, including the total amount of grants given

OTHER INFORMATION
Any other information which might be useful to grantseekers

HOW TO APPLY
Useful information to those preparing their grant application

ESTABLISHED
Year established

■ The Fictitious Trust

WHERE FUNDING CAN BE GIVEN UK.

WHO CAN BENEFIT Charities benefiting children.

WHAT IS FUNDED Education and training.

WHAT IS NOT FUNDED No grants to individuals.

TYPE OF GRANT One-off, capital, running costs.

RANGE OF GRANTS £250–£5,000.

SAMPLE GRANTS £5,000 to a school; £1,000 to a university; £800 to a school library; £600 to a school; £500 each to a grammar school, a further education college and for classroom equipment; £400 to a university appeal; £250 for a wheelchair ramp.

FINANCES *Year* 2002 *Income* £55,000 *Grants* £50,000 *Assets* £800,000

TRUSTEES Peter Brown, Chair; Mrs Mary Brown; Alistair Johnson; Lord Great; Lady Good.

PUBLICATIONS Annual report and accounts. *The Fictitious Trust – The First 20 Years.*

OTHER INFORMATION This trust recently merged with the Fictional Trust.

HOW TO APPLY In writing to the address below. An sae should be enclosed if an acknowledgement is required.

WHO TO APPLY TO A Grant, Secretary, The Old Barn, Main Street, New Town ZC48 2QQ *Tel* 020 7012 3456 *Fax* 020 7123 4567 *E-mail* trust@abc.co.uk *Website* www.abc.co.uk

CC NO 123456   **ESTABLISHED** 1993

A list of the top 150 trusts by grant total

This is a list of the largest 150 trusts by grant total. Between them they account for just under £2 billion, or about 80% of the total in the book. **Please do not use this simply as a mailing list.** These trusts cover a wide range of specialist interests. Most of them will never fund your work. However, we do recommend that you read each entry carefully and compile your own list of major trusts relevant to you. You can then send this list alongside the other lists generated from the other indexes in the directory. It is, we believe, the most effective way of ensuring that you do not omit any major trusts.

The 29th May 1961 Charitable Trust

Abbey National Charitable Trust Ltd

Achisomoch Aid Company

Aid to the Church in Need (UK)

Allchurches Trust Ltd

The Arbib Foundation

ARK (Absolute Return for Kids)

The Army Benevolent Fund

Arthritis Research Campaign

The Arts Council of England

Arts Council of Northern Ireland

Arts Council of Wales

The Lord Ashdown Charitable Trust

AW Charitable Trust

The Baily Thomas Charitable Fund

The Balcraig Foundation

The Baring Foundation

The BBC Children in Need Appeal

The Beit Trust

BibleLands

The Birmingham Foundation

The Bridge House Estates Trust Fund

British Heart Foundation

The Barrow Cadbury Trust and the Barrow Cadbury Fund

The Cadogan Charity

CAFOD

The Childwick Trust

CHK Charities Limited

Christian Aid

The Church Urban Fund

The City Parochial Foundation

The Clore Duffield Foundation

The Clothworkers' Foundation and other Trusts

Comic Relief

The Community Foundation for Northern Ireland

Community Foundation Serving Tyne & Wear and Northumberland

The Community Fund

Consortium on Opportunities for Volunteering

Cumbria Community Foundation

Cystic Fibrosis Trust

Diabetes UK

The Diana, Princess of Wales Memorial Fund

The Dulverton Trust

The Dunhill Medical Trust

The John Ellerman Foundation

The Equitable Charitable Trust

The Eveson Charitable Trust

Esmée Fairbairn Foundation

Allan and Nesta Ferguson Charitable Settlement

The Football Association Youth Trust

The Foyle Foundation

The Freshfield Foundation

The Gannochy Trust

The Gatsby Charitable Foundation

The Gertner Charitable Trust

J Paul Getty Jr Charitable Trust

The Glencore Foundation for Education and Welfare

The Goldsmiths' Company's Charity

The Gosling Foundation Ltd

The Grand Charity of Freemasons

The Gulbenkian Foundation

The Paul Hamlyn Foundation

The Peter Harrison Foundation

The Headley Trust

Help the Aged

Historic Churches Preservation Trust

Isle of Dogs Community Foundation

The ITF Seafarers Trust

The Jerusalem Trust

The Jerwood Foundation and the Jerwood Charitable Foundation

The Elton John Aids Foundation

The Jordan Charitable Foundation

The Ian Karten Charitable Trust

Keren Association

King George's Fund for Sailors

The King's Fund (King Edward's Hospital Fund for London)

The Mary Kinross Charitable Trust

The Kreitman Foundation

The Maurice Laing Foundation

The John and Rosemary Lancaster Charitable Foundation

The Lankelly Foundation

The Law Society Charity

Leukaemia Research Fund

The Leverhulme Trust

The Linbury Trust

Lloyds TSB Foundation for England and Wales

Lloyds TSB Foundation for Northern Ireland

Lloyds TSB Foundation for Scotland

The Lord's Taverners

John Lyon's Charity

Mayfair Charities Ltd

Medical Research Council

The Mercers' Charitable Foundation

The Monument Trust

The Peter Moores Foundation

Muslim Hands

The National Art Collections Fund

National Asthma Campaign

The National Kidney Research Fund Limited

The Northern Rock Foundation

The Nuffield Foundation

Oxfam (GB)

The P F Charitable Trust

The Parthenon Trust

The Peacock Charitable Trust

The Jack Petchey Foundation

The Pilgrim Trust

PPP Foundation

The Rank Foundation

The Joseph Rank Trust

The Ruben and Elisabeth Rausing Trust

The Rayne Foundation

Reuters Foundation

The Robertson Trust

The Joseph Rowntree Charitable Trust

The Joseph Rowntree Foundation

Royal British Legion

The Rufford Foundation

The Robert and Lisa Sainsbury Charitable Trust

The Schreib Trust

Sir Samuel Scott of Yews Trust

The Scottish Arts Council

The Scottish Community Foundation

The Sheffield Church Burgesses Trust

The Shetland Islands Council Charitable Trust

The Shirley Foundation

The Henry Smith Charity

The Sobell Foundation

The South Yorkshire Community Foundation

Foundation for Sport and the Arts

The Stewards Company

The Bernard Sunley Charitable Foundation

Tearfund

Tesco Charity Trust

The Sir Jules Thorn Charitable Trust

The Trusthouse Charitable Foundation

The Tudor Trust

The United Society for the Propagation of the Gospel

The Variety Club Children's Charity

The Vodafone UK Foundation

Wales Council for Voluntary Action

The Waterside Trust

The Weinstock Fund

The Wellcome Trust

The Westminster Foundation

The Garfield Weston Foundation

The Charles Wolfson Charitable Trust

The Wolfson Family Charitable Trust

The Wolfson Foundation

Zurich Financial Services Community Trust

Other publications

The following publications may also be of interest to readers of the *DGMT*. They are all available from the Publications department of the Directory of Social Change. Phone 020 7209 5151 or visit www.dsc.org.uk for more information or to place an order. Prices were correct at the time of writing, but may be subject to change.

The Grant-making Trusts CD-ROM

Software development by FunderFinder
DSC/CAF 2003

£115 + VAT = £135.13

£85 + VAT = £99.88
for existing users

This CD-ROM combines the trusts databases of the Directory of Social Change and the Charities Aid Foundation to provide the most comprehensive and up-to-date information ever on grant-making trusts. The improved search facilities ensure fast, easy and effective searching across the whole database.

CONTENTS

- Around 4,000 trusts, with full details as listed in the *Directory of Grant Making Trusts 2003–04* (CAF), the three *Guides to Major Trusts 2003/2004* and *2002/2003* (DSC), and the four *Guides to Local Trusts 2002/2003* (DSC).

SEARCH FACILITIES

- Powerful combined search by geographical area, type of activity and type of beneficiary.
- Search by name of trust, location, or trustee.
- Search by key word.

SOFTWARE

- PC format only.
- Runs on Windows 95 and higher.
- Network capability.
- 'Getting started' tutorial.
- Hyperlinks to trust websites.
- Facility to bookmark selected trusts, add your own notes, and tag for printing or export.

www.trustfunding.org.uk
Annual subscription:

£115 + VAT = £135.13
to charities and voluntary organisations

£160 + VAT = £188
to statutory and commercial organisations

This new internet-based service contains all the same data as the CD but is regularly updated throughout the year.

Funding for Change

Editor: Susan Forrester
Deputy editor: Nicola Hill
Annual subscription:

£40 to voluntary and
community organisations

£50 to statutory and
commercial organisations

A must for all serious fundraisers, this popular journal is the only way to keep fully up-to-date with funding sources across the board.

- Special section on newly identified sources of support and policy changes of top funders.

- Published four times a year: January, April, July and October.

A Guide to Grants for Individuals in Need 2002/03

Alan French, Dave Griffiths,
Tom Traynor & Sarah Wiggins
8th edition, DSC 2002
£20.95

This best-selling guide, now in its eighth edition, includes even more sources of financial help for individuals. It remains a key reference book for advice and social workers, as well as individuals themselves and those concerned for their welfare.

- Contains details of over 2,400 national and local trusts which make grants to individuals, including over 226 new to this guide.

- Lists sources of funds for the relief of individual poverty and hardship totalling over £289 million a year.

- Includes service and ex-service charities, sickness and disability charities and occupational charities.

- Provides a model of how to make an effective application.

The Educational Grants Directory 2002/03

Alan French, Dave Griffiths,
Tom Traynor & Sarah Wiggins
7th edition, DSC 2002
£20.95

This popular guide, now in its seventh edition, uncovers even more sources of funding for schoolchildren and students in need, adding up to £3.3 million of new support. This comprehensive listing of educational charities is an invaluable aid for educational social workers, student welfare officers, teachers, and advice agencies.

- Includes sources of funding up to and including first degree level.

- Lists 1,600 local and national charities, with over 170 new to this guide.

- Charities listed give a total of more than £50 million a year.

- Contains a basic guide to welfare benefits, statutory funding, loans and sponsorship.

- Provides a model of how to make an effective application.

Fundraising from Grant-Making Trusts and Foundations
Karen Gilchrist &
Margo Horsley
DSC/CAF 'How to' guide,
2000
£10.95

Grant-making trusts and foundations are set up to give money to charitable activities. The challenge for any fundraiser is to put an effective case for support by showing how their project matches the aims of the trust. This book takes you through:

- the origins and work of grant-making trusts
- putting together a project proposal and researching appropriate trusts
- the application and assessment processes
- working with trusts that have agreed to fund you.

Trusts by geographical area

This index contains two separate listings:

Geographical area headings: This lists all of the geographical area headings used in the *DGMT*.

Trusts by geographical area: This lists the trusts appearing in the *DGMT* under the geographical area for which they have expressed a funding preference.

Geographical area headings

Type of place

- **Developing world 4**

- **Areas of social deprivation 4**

- **Urban areas, inner cities 5**

- **Rural areas 6**

Worldwide

- **Europe (outside UK) 8**
  Republic of Ireland 8

- **Asia 8**

- **Africa 9**

- **Australasia 9**

- **Americas and the West Indies 9**

United Kingdom
England 10

- **North Eastern England 10**
  Cleveland 10
  Durham County 10
  Northumberland 10
  Tyne & Wear 11

- **North Western England 11**
  Cheshire 11
  Cumbria 11
  Greater Manchester 11
  Lancashire 12
  Merseyside 12

- **Yorkshire & the Humber 12**
  Humberside, East Riding 12
  North Yorkshire 13
  South Yorkshire 13
  West Yorkshire 13

- **East Midlands Region 13**
  Derbyshire 14
  Leicestershire 14
  Lincolnshire 14
  Northamptonshire 14
  Nottinghamshire 14

- **West Midlands Region 15**
  Herefordshire 15
  Shropshire 15
  Staffordshire 15
  Warwickshire 15
  West Midlands 15
  Worcestershire 16

- **Eastern England 16**
  Bedfordshire 16
  Cambridgeshire 16
  Essex 16
  Hertfordshire 17
  Norfolk 17
  Suffolk 17

- **South Eastern England 17**
  Berkshire 18
  Buckinghamshire 18
  East Sussex 18
  Hampshire 18
  Isle of Wight 19
  Kent 19
  Oxfordshire 19
  Surrey 19
  West Sussex 19

- **South Western England 20**
  Avon 20
  Cornwall & Scilly Isles 20
  Devon 20
  Dorset 21
  Gloucestershire 21
  Somerset 21
  Wiltshire 21

■ **London 21**

Barking & Dagenham 22
Barnet 22
Bexley 22
Brent 22
Bromley 22
Camden 22
City of London 22
City of Westminster 22
Croydon 22
Ealing 23
Enfield 23
Greenwich 23
Hackney 23
Hammersmith & Fulham 23
Haringey 23
Harrow 23
Havering 23
Hillingdon 23
Hounslow 23
Islington 23
Kensington & Chelsea 23
Kingston upon Thames 23
Lambeth 23
Lewisham 23
Merton 23
Newham 23
Redbridge 23
Richmond upon Thames 24
Southwark 24
Sutton 24
Tower Hamlets 24
Waltham Forest 24
Wandsworth 24

Northern Ireland 24

Belfast City 24
County Antrim 24
County Armagh 24
County Down 24

Scotland 24

Highlands & Islands 25
Grampian Region 25
Tayside & Fife Region 25
Central Region 25
Strathclyde Region 25
Lothian Region 26
Southern Scotland 26

Wales 26

North Wales 26
Mid and West Wales 26
South Wales 26

Channel Islands 26

Isle of Man 27

Type of place

■ Developing world

Funding priority

Allavida
Veta Bailey Charitable Trust
Enid Blyton Trust for Children
Body Shop Foundation
Bower Trust
BP Conservation Programme
Burdens Charitable Foundation
CAFOD
Casey Trust
Comic Relief
Commonwealth Relations
 Trust
Cowley Charitable Foundation
Miriam K Dean Refugee Trust
 Fund
Alex Deas Charitable Trust
Dickon Trust
Allan and Nesta Ferguson
 Charitable Settlement
Four Acre Trust
Four Winds Trust
Sydney E Franklin Deceased's
 New Second Charity
Global Care
Philip Henman Trust
Joanna Herbert-Stepney
 Charitable Settlement
Hesed Trust
Highmoor Hall Charitable Trust
Hilden Charitable Fund
Hinchley Charitable Trust
Homeless International
ITF Seafarers Trust
Eric and Dorothy Leach
 Charitable Trust
Marchig Animal Welfare Trust
Mitsubishi Corporation Fund
 for Europe and Africa
Oliver Morland Charitable Trust
Muslim Hands
Nchima Trust
Noel Buxton Trust
Onaway Trust
Parthenon Trust
PPP Foundation
Ruben and Elisabeth Rausing
 Trust
Edwin George Robinson
 Charitable Trust
Rufford Foundation
Tinsley Foundation
Tisbury Telegraph Trust
TRAID
Ulting Overseas Trust
Wyndham Charitable Trust

Will consider

Sylvia Aitken Charitable Trust
Ardwick Trust
Bay Tree Charitable Trust
Beit Trust

Morgan Blake Charitable Trust
Viscountess Boyd Charitable
 Trust
Carpenter Charitable Trust
Charities Advisory Trust
Lance Coates Charitable Trust
 1969
Cornwell Charitable Trust
Cotton Trust
Criffel Charitable Trust
Cumber Family Charitable
 Trust
Dinam Charity
Douglas Charitable Trust
Fairbairn Charitable Trust
Gretna Charitable Trust
H C D Memorial Fund
Haramead Trust
Dorothy Hay-Bolton Charitable
 Trust
Hedley Denton Charitable
 Trust
J G Hogg Charitable Trust
Jephcott Charitable Trust
Beatrice Laing Trust
Kirby Laing Foundation
Maurice and Hilda Laing
 Charitable Trust
William & Katherine Longman
 Trust
Margaret Foundation
Marr-Munning Trust
Edgar Milward Charity
New Durlston Trust
Panton Trust
David Pickford Charitable
 Foundation
Ranworth Trust
Karim Rida Said Foundation
Simpson Education &
 Conservation Trust
Staples Trust
Treeside Trust
Douglas Turner Trust
Scurrah Wainwright Charity

....

■ Areas of social deprivation

Funding priority

29th May 1961 Charitable
 Trust
Abbey National Charitable
 Trust Ltd
Sylvia Aitken Charitable Trust
Barbour Trust
Paul Bassham Charitable Trust
BBC Children in Need Appeal
Thomas Betton's Charity
 (Educational)
Thomas Betton's Charity for
 Pensions and Relief-in-Need
Birmingham Foundation
Enid Blyton Trust for Children
Body Shop Foundation
Boots Charitable Trust

Bramble Charitable Trust
Butchers' Company General
 Charities
Cadbury Schweppes
 Foundation
William A Cadbury Charitable
 Trust
Camelot Foundation
Casey Trust
Chapman Charitable Trust
Chelsea Building Society
 Charitable Foundation
Stephen Clark 1957
 Charitable Trust
Cobb Charity
Colchester & Tendring
 Community Trust
Comic Relief
Community Foundation Serving
 Tyne & Wear and
 Northumberland
Consortium on Opportunities
 for Volunteering
Coutts & Co. Charitable Trust
Cowley Charitable Foundation
Lord Cozens-Hardy Trust
John Grant Davies Trust
Denton Charitable Trust
Derbyshire Community
 Foundation
Devon Community Foundation
Dickon Trust
Digbeth Trust
City of Edinburgh Charitable
 Trusts
W G Edwards Charitable
 Foundation
Esmée Fairbairn Foundation
Roy Fletcher Charitable Trust
Football Association National
 Sports Centre Trust
Four Acre Trust
J Paul Getty Jr Charitable Trust
E C Graham Belford Charitable
 Settlement
Greater Bristol Foundation
J C Green Charitable
 Settlement
Bishop of Guildford's
 Foundation
Paul Hamlyn Foundation
Harrow Community Trust
Heart of England Community
 Foundation
Simon Heller Charitable
 Settlement
Heritage of London Trust Ltd
Hilden Charitable Fund
Hospital of God at Greatham
Clifford Howarth Charity
 Settlement
Hyde Charitable Trust
Ironmongers' Quincentenary
 Charitable Fund
Boris Karloff Charitable
 Foundation

Peter Kershaw Trust
Laing's Charitable Trust
Kathleen Laurence Trust
Leeds & Holbeck Building
  Society Charitable
  Foundation
John Spedan Lewis Foundation
Lloyds TSB Foundation for the
  Channel Islands
Lynn Foundation
Magdalen Hospital Trust
Marchig Animal Welfare Trust
Peter Minet Trust
John Moores Foundation
Oliver Morland Charitable Trust
Noel Buxton Trust
Northern Rock Foundation
Patients' Aid Association
  Hospital & Medical
  Charities Trust
Jack Petchey Foundation
Pyke Charity Trust
Fanny Rapaport Charitable
  Settlement
Ruben and Elisabeth Rausing
  Trust
Ripple Effect Foundation
Rosca Trust
Cecil Rosen Foundation
Rothley Trust
Scottish Churches Community
  Trust
Swan Mountain Trust
Tinsley Foundation
Tisbury Telegraph Trust
VEC Acorn Trust
Scurrah Wainwright Charity
Weavers' Company Benevolent
  Fund
Webb Memorial Trust
Welsh Church Fund –
  Carmarthenshire area
Wentwood Education Trust
Lionel Wigram Memorial Trust
Yorkshire Building Society
  Charitable Foundation

Will consider

Abel Charitable Trust
Ardwick Trust
Arts Council of Wales
Barclays Stockbrokers
  Charitable Trust
Morgan Blake Charitable Trust
Viscountess Boyd Charitable
  Trust
Richard Cadbury Charitable
  Trust
Carpenter Charitable Trust
Chase Charity
Childwick Trust
Church Urban Fund
Lance Coates Charitable Trust
  1969
Cornwell Charitable Trust
Cotton Trust

County of Gloucestershire
  Community Foundation
Baron Davenport's Charity
DLA Charitable Trust
Douglas Charitable Trust
Dumfries and Galloway Council
  Charitable Trusts
Elmgrant Trust
Fairbairn Charitable Trust
Fidelity UK Foundation
Forte Charitable Trust
Gannochy Trust
Gatwick Airport Community
  Trust
Girdlers' Company Charitable
  Trust
GMC Trust
Gretna Charitable Trust
Haramead Trust
Kenneth Hargreaves Charitable
  Trust
Gay & Peter Hartley's Hillards
  Charitable Trust
N & P Hartley Memorial Trust
Dorothy Hay-Bolton Charitable
  Trust
Hedley Denton Charitable
  Trust
Help the Aged
Hinchley Charitable Trust
Worshipful Company of
  Innholders General Charity
  Fund
Beatrice Laing Trust
Christopher Laing Foundation
Kirby Laing Foundation
Maurice and Hilda Laing
  Charitable Trust
Lankelly Foundation
Leathersellers' Company
  Charitable Fund
Lewis Family Charitable Trust
Lloyds TSB Foundation for
  England and Wales
Lloyds TSB Foundation for
  Northern Ireland
Lloyds TSB Foundation for
  Scotland
William & Katherine Longman
  Trust
Marie Helen Luen Charitable
  Trust
Lyndhurst Settlement
Margaret Foundation
Millfield House Foundation
Mitsubishi Corporation Fund
  for Europe and Africa
Moss Family Charitable Trust
Newby Trust Limited
Norman Family Charitable
  Trust
North British Hotel Trust
Odin Charitable Trust
Old Enfield Charitable Trust
Panton Trust
Parthenon Trust

Persula Foundation
Peugeot Charity Trust
David Pickford Charitable
  Foundation
Pilgrim Trust
Col W W Pilkington Will Trusts
Princess Anne's Charities
Joseph Rank Trust
Saddlers' Company Charitable
  Fund
Karim Rida Said Foundation
Sherburn House Charity
Steinberg Family Charitable
  Trust
Tory Family Foundation
Treeside Trust
Douglas Turner Trust
Florence Turner Trust
Vale of Glamorgan Welsh
  Church Fund
Charity of Thomas Wade &
  Others
Ward Blenkinsop Trust
William Webster Charitable
  Trust

....

■ Urban areas, inner cities

Funding priority

1970 Trust
Abel Charitable Trust
Aberbrothock Charitable Trust
Sylvia Aitken Charitable Trust
Ashden Trust
Barbour Trust
Paul Bassham Charitable Trust
Birmingham Foundation
Birmingham Hospital Saturday
  Fund Medical Charity &
  Welfare Trust
Enid Blyton Trust for Children
Bramble Charitable Trust
Butchers' Company General
  Charities
Casey Trust
Chapman Charitable Trust
Church Urban Fund
Cobb Charity
Comic Relief
Community Foundation Serving
  Tyne & Wear and
  Northumberland
Consortium on Opportunities
  for Volunteering
Coutts & Co. Charitable Trust
Cowley Charitable Foundation
John Grant Davies Trust
Denton Charitable Trust
Denton Wilde Sapte Charitable
  Trust
Devon Community Foundation
Digbeth Trust
City of Edinburgh Charitable
  Trusts

W G Edwards Charitable
  Foundation
Esmée Fairbairn Foundation
Football Association National
  Sports Centre Trust
Four Acre Trust
Glass-House Trust
E C Graham Belford Charitable
  Settlement
Grantham Yorke Trust
J C Green Charitable
  Settlement
Paul Hamlyn Foundation
Kenneth Hargreaves Charitable
  Trust
Heart of England Community
  Foundation
Hedgcock Bequest
Simon Heller Charitable
  Settlement
Hilden Charitable Fund
Homeless International
Clifford Howarth Charity
  Settlement
Peter Kershaw Trust
Laing's Charitable Trust
Leeds & Holbeck Building
  Society Charitable
  Foundation
John Spedan Lewis Foundation
Lloyds TSB Foundation for the
  Channel Islands
Lynn Foundation
Marchig Animal Welfare Trust
Keith and Joan Mindelsohn
  Charitable Trust
Peter Minet Trust
Oliver Morland Charitable Trust
Mugdock Children's Trust
Noel Buxton Trust
Northern Rock Foundation
Ogilvie Charities Deed 2
Jack Petchey Foundation
Fanny Rapaport Charitable
  Settlement
Ruben and Elisabeth Rausing
  Trust
Rosca Trust
Sir Walter St John's
  Educational Charity
Swan Mountain Trust
Thames Community
  Foundation
Wakeham Trust
Weavers' Company Benevolent
  Fund
Welsh Church Fund –
  Carmarthenshire area
Wentwood Education Trust
Woodlands Trust (1015942)
Yorkshire Building Society
  Charitable Foundation

Will consider

29th May 1961 Charitable
  Trust

Ardwick Trust
Arts Council of Wales
Ashby Charitable Trust
BBC Children in Need Appeal
Morgan Blake Charitable Trust
Body Shop Foundation
Boots Charitable Trust
Viscountess Boyd Charitable
  Trust
Richard Cadbury Charitable
  Trust
Mauritis Mulder Canter Charity
Casey Trust
Chase Charity
Childwick Trust
Colchester & Tendring
  Community Trust
Cotton Trust
County of Gloucestershire
  Community Foundation
Lord Cozens-Hardy Trust
Demigryphon Trust
Derbyshire Community
  Foundation
DLA Charitable Trust
Douglas Charitable Trust
Fairbairn Charitable Trust
Fidelity UK Foundation
Forte Charitable Trust
Gannochy Trust
Gatwick Airport Community
  Trust
J Paul Getty Jr Charitable Trust
Girdlers' Company Charitable
  Trust
GMC Trust
Barry Green Memorial Fund
Gretna Charitable Trust
Haramead Trust
Harbour Foundation
Gay & Peter Hartley's Hillards
  Charitable Trust
Hedley Denton Charitable
  Trust
Help the Aged
Hinchley Charitable Trust
Worshipful Company of
  Innholders General Charity
  Fund
Beatrice Laing Trust
Christopher Laing Foundation
Kirby Laing Foundation
Maurice and Hilda Laing
  Charitable Trust
Lankelly Foundation
Mason Le Page Charitable
  Trust
Leathersellers' Company
  Charitable Fund
Lewis Family Charitable Trust
Lincolnshire Old Churches
  Trust
Lloyds TSB Foundation for
  England and Wales
Lloyds TSB Foundation for
  Northern Ireland

Lloyds TSB Foundation for
  Scotland
William & Katherine Longman
  Trust
Marie Helen Luen Charitable
  Trust
Lyndhurst Settlement
Margaret Foundation
Gerald Micklem Charitable
  Trust
Millfield House Foundation
Mitsubishi Corporation Fund
  for Europe and Africa
Moss Family Charitable Trust
Newby Trust Limited
North British Hotel Trust
Odin Charitable Trust
Panton Trust
Jack Patston Charitable Trust
Peugeot Charity Trust
David Pickford Charitable
  Foundation
Pilgrim Trust
Mr and Mrs J A Pye's
  Charitable Settlement
Joseph Rank Trust
Saddlers' Company Charitable
  Fund
Karim Rida Said Foundation
Scottish Churches Community
  Trust
Steinberg Family Charitable
  Trust
Tisbury Telegraph Trust
Treeside Trust
Douglas Turner Trust
Florence Turner Trust
Vale of Glamorgan Welsh
  Church Fund
Charity of Thomas Wade &
  Others
Robert and Felicity Waley-
  Cohen Charitable Trust
Ward Blenkinsop Trust
Webb Memorial Trust
William Webster Charitable
  Trust
Wixamtree Trust

....

■ Rural areas

Funding priority

Aberbrothock Charitable Trust
Sylvia Aitken Charitable Trust
Ashby Charitable Trust
Ashe Park Charitable Trust
Paul Bassham Charitable Trust
Enid Blyton Trust for Children
Bramble Charitable Trust
Carnegie United Kingdom Trust
Chapman Charitable Trust
Chase Charity
CLA Charitable Trust
Lance Coates Charitable Trust
  1969
Cobb Charity

Comic Relief
Community Foundation Serving
Tyne & Wear and
Northumberland
Consortium on Opportunities
for Volunteering
Countryside Trust
Cowley Charitable Foundation
Cranbury Foundation
William Dean Countryside and
Educational Trust
William Delafield Charitable
Trust
Demigryphon Trust
Denton Charitable Trust
Devon Community Foundation
W G Edwards Charitable
Foundation
Ellis Campbell Charitable
Foundation
Esmée Fairbairn Foundation
Samuel William Farmer's Trust
Football Association National
Sports Centre Trust
Four Acre Trust
Angela Gallagher Memorial
Fund
E C Graham Belford Charitable
Settlement
J C Green Charitable
Settlement
Heart of England Community
Foundation
Simon Heller Charitable
Settlement
Hilden Charitable Fund
Clifford Howarth Charity
Settlement
Kelsick's Educational
Foundation
Leeds & Holbeck Building
Society Charitable
Foundation
John Spedan Lewis Foundation
Lloyds TSB Foundation for the
Channel Islands
Llysdinam Trust
LSA Charitable Trust
Lynn Foundation
Marchig Animal Welfare Trust
Oliver Morland Charitable Trust
Mugdock Children's Trust
Noel Buxton Trust
Norfolk Churches Trust Ltd
Northern Rock Foundation
Ogilvie Charities Deed 2
Jack Patston Charitable Trust
Mrs C S Heber Percy
Charitable Trust
Rooke Atlay Charitable Trust
Rural Trust
Swan Mountain Trust
VEC Acorn Trust
Vincent Wildlife Trust
Wakeham Trust

Weavers' Company Benevolent
Fund
Welsh Church Fund –
Carmarthenshire area
Wentwood Education Trust
Yorkshire Building Society
Charitable Foundation

Will consider
Ardwick Trust
Arts Council of Wales
Barbour Trust
Barclays Stockbrokers
Charitable Trust
BBC Children in Need Appeal
Morgan Blake Charitable Trust
Body Shop Foundation
Boots Charitable Trust
Viscountess Boyd Charitable
Trust
Richard Cadbury Charitable
Trust
Mauritis Mulder Canter Charity
Childwick Trust
Colchester & Tendring
Community Trust
Cornwell Charitable Trust
Cotton Trust
County of Gloucestershire
Community Foundation
Lord Cozens-Hardy Trust
Cray Trust
Derbyshire Community
Foundation
Dumfries and Galloway Council
Charitable Trusts
Elmgrant Trust
Fairbairn Charitable Trust
Farmers Company Charitable
Fund
Forte Charitable Trust
Gannochy Trust
Gatwick Airport Community
Trust
J Paul Getty Jr Charitable Trust
Girdlers' Company Charitable
Trust
Barry Green Memorial Fund
Gretna Charitable Trust
Haramead Trust
Hedley Denton Charitable
Trust
Help the Aged
Hinchley Charitable Trust
Worshipful Company of
Innholders General Charity
Fund
Peter Kershaw Trust
Beatrice Laing Trust
Christopher Laing Foundation
Kirby Laing Foundation
Maurice and Hilda Laing
Charitable Trust
Lankelly Foundation
Leathersellers' Company
Charitable Fund

Lewis Family Charitable Trust
Lincolnshire Old Churches
Trust
Lloyds TSB Foundation for
England and Wales
Lloyds TSB Foundation for
Northern Ireland
Lloyds TSB Foundation for
Scotland
William & Katherine Longman
Trust
Marie Helen Luen Charitable
Trust
Lyndhurst Settlement
Margaret Foundation
Gerald Micklem Charitable
Trust
Mitsubishi Corporation Fund
for Europe and Africa
Newby Trust Limited
Norman Family Charitable
Trust
North British Hotel Trust
Odin Charitable Trust
Panton Trust
David Pickford Charitable
Foundation
Pilgrim Trust
Princess Anne's Charities
Mr and Mrs J A Pye's
Charitable Settlement
Joseph Rank Trust
Fanny Rapaport Charitable
Settlement
Saddlers' Company Charitable
Fund
Karim Rida Said Foundation
Scottish Churches Community
Trust
Steinberg Family Charitable
Trust
M J C Stone Charitable Trust
Summerfield Charitable Trust
Tisbury Telegraph Trust
Tory Family Foundation
Florence Turner Trust
R D Turner Charitable Trust
Vale of Glamorgan Welsh
Church Fund
Robert and Felicity Waley-
Cohen Charitable Trust
Ward Blenkinsop Trust
William Webster Charitable
Trust
Wixamtree Trust

Geographical area

■ Europe

Aid to the Church in Need (UK)
All Saints Educational Trust
Allavida
Anglo-German Foundation for the Study of Industrial Society
Ardwick Trust
Andrew Balint Charitable Trust
George Balint Charitable Trust
Paul Balint Charitable Trust
Barber Charitable Trust
Beacon Trust
British Institute of Archaeology at Ankara
Audrey & Stanley Burton Charitable Trust
Catholic Charitable Trust
Chandris Foundation
Lord Cozens-Hardy Trust
Feed the Minds
Fidelity UK Foundation
Global Care
Grahame Charitable Foundation
Kathleen Hannay Memorial Charity
Headley Trust
Huxham Charitable Trust
Elton John Aids Foundation
Mayfair Charities Ltd
Mitsubishi Corporation Fund for Europe and Africa
Morris Family Israel Trust
Ruth and Conrad Morris Charitable Trust
Elani Nakou Foundation
National Power Charitable Trust
Novi Most International
Oxfam (GB)
Márit and Hans Rausing Charitable Foundation
William Arthur Rudd Memorial Trust
Rufford Foundation
Jean Sainsbury Animal Welfare Trust
Staples Trust
Walter Swindon Charitable Trust
Sylvanus Charitable Trust
Tinsley Foundation
Ulting Overseas Trust
Veneziana Fund
Bertie Watson Foundation
Webb Memorial Trust
Michael and Anna Wix Charitable Trust

Republic of Ireland

Carnegie United Kingdom Trust
Ernest Cook Trust

Lord Cozens-Hardy Trust
Fidelity UK Foundation
Follett Trust
Isaac and Freda Frankel Memorial Charitable Trust
Jill Franklin Trust
Gulbenkian Foundation
Hospital Saturday Fund Charitable Trust
Rita Lila Howard Foundation
Inland Waterways Association
Ireland Fund of Great Britain
Irish Youth Foundation (UK) Ltd
Elton John Aids Foundation
Graham Kirkham Foundation
Late Sir Pierce Lacy Charity Trust
Allen Lane Foundation
Lauchentilly Charitable Foundation 1988
Lawlor Foundation
Esmé Mitchell Trust
Horace Moore Charitable Trust
Mr and Mrs F E F Newman Charitable Trust
Oakdale Trust
Ouseley Trust
Queen Mary's Roehampton Trust
Peggy Ramsay Foundation
Joseph Rank Trust
Joseph Rowntree Charitable Trust
Joseph Rowntree Foundation
Jean Sainsbury Animal Welfare Trust
C B & H H Taylor 1984 Trust
H D H Wills 1965 Charitable Trust

....

■ Asia

A B Charitable Trust
Acacia Charitable Trust
Sylvia Adams Charitable Trust
AIM Foundation
Ambika Paul Foundation
Anglo Hong Kong Trust
Ardwick Trust
Andrew Balint Charitable Trust
George Balint Charitable Trust
Balmore Trust
Barber Charitable Trust
Bestway Foundation
BibleLands
Neville & Elaine Blond Charitable Trust
A Bornstein Charitable Settlement
British Institute of Archaeology at Ankara
Mrs E E Brown Charitable Settlement
R M 1956 Burton Charitable Trust

CAFOD
Charity Association Manchester Ltd
Christian Aid
Clark Charitable Trust
Col-Reno Ltd
E Alec Colman Charitable Fund Ltd
Comic Relief
Lord Cozens-Hardy Trust
Daiwa Anglo-Japanese Foundation
Miriam K Dean Refugee Trust Fund
Dollond Charitable Trust
Doughty Charity Trust
Douglas Charitable Trust
George Elias Charitable Trust
Elman Charitable Trust
Federation of Jewish Relief Organisations
Feed the Minds
Isaac and Freda Frankel Memorial Charitable Trust
Jill Franklin Trust
Robert Gavron Charitable Trust
Global Care
Great Britain Sasakawa Foundation
N and R Grunbaum Charitable Trust
Paul Hamlyn Foundation
Hilden Charitable Fund
Homeless International
India Foundation (UK)
INTACH (UK) Trust
International Bar Association Educational Trust
JCA Charitable Foundation
Jeffrey Charitable Trust
Jerwood Foundation and the Jerwood Charitable Foundation
J G Joffe Charitable Trust
Elton John Aids Foundation
J E Joseph Charitable Fund
Bernard Kahn Charitable Trust
Kasner Charitable Trust
Katzauer Charitable Settlement
Kidani Memorial Trust
Kreitman Foundation
Neil Kreitman Foundation
Kennedy Leigh Charitable Trust
Loseley & Guildway Charitable Trust
Luck-Hille Foundation
M D & S Charitable Trust
Hilda & Samuel Marks Foundation
Matliwala Family Charitable Trust
Methodist Relief and Development Fund
Midhurst Pensions Trust

National Power Charitable
   Trust
Oakdale Trust
Oxfam (GB)
Philanthropic Trust
Porter Foundation
PPP Foundation
Simone Prendergast Charitable
   Trust
Puri Foundation
Rhodes Trust Public Purposes
   Fund
M K Rose Charitable Trust
Cecil Rosen Foundation
Rowan Charitable Trust
J B Rubens Charitable
   Foundation
Rufford Foundation
Michael Sacher Charitable
   Trust
Karim Rida Said Foundation
L H Silver Charitable Trust
Sino-British Fellowship Trust
Sobell Foundation
Solo Charitable Settlement
Songdale Ltd
Staples Trust
Cyril & Betty Stein Charitable
   Trust
Tajtelbaum Charitable Trust
C B & H H Taylor 1984 Trust
Rosanna Taylor's 1987 Charity
   Trust
Tilda Foundation
Tinsley Foundation
TRAID
TUUT Charitable Trust
Ulting Overseas Trust
United Society for the
   Propagation of the Gospel
War on Want
Westcroft Trust
Harold Hyam Wingate
   Foundation
Charles Wolfson Charitable
   Trust
Wolfson Family Charitable
   Trust
Wolfson Foundation
Zurich Financial Services
   Community Trust

■ Africa

A B Charitable Trust
Sylvia Adams Charitable Trust
AIM Foundation
Ardwick Trust
Balcraig Foundation
Balmore Trust
Barber Charitable Trust
Baring Foundation
Beit Trust
BibleLands
Audrey & Stanley Burton
   Charitable Trust

CAFOD
Childwick Trust
Christian Aid
Comic Relief
Commonwealth Relations
   Trust
Lord Cozens-Hardy Trust
Cumberland Trust
Miriam K Dean Refugee Trust
   Fund
Douglas Charitable Trust
Dulverton Trust
Feed the Minds
Jill Franklin Trust
Gibbs Charitable Trusts
Global Care
Kathleen Hannay Memorial
   Charity
Headley Trust
Hilden Charitable Fund
Homeless International
International Bar Association
   Educational Trust
Jeffrey Charitable Trust
J G Joffe Charitable Trust
Elton John Aids Foundation
Loseley & Guildway Charitable
   Trust
Marie Helen Luen Charitable
   Trust
Lord and Lady Lurgan Trust
Methodist Relief and
   Development Fund
Mitsubishi Corporation Fund
   for Europe and Africa
National Power Charitable
   Trust
Nchima Trust
Noel Buxton Trust
Oakdale Trust
Oxfam (GB)
Philanthropic Trust
PPP Foundation
Rhodes Trust Public Purposes
   Fund
Rowan Charitable Trust
Joseph Rowntree Charitable
   Trust
J B Rubens Charitable
   Foundation
Rufford Foundation
SEM Charitable Trust
Bishop Simeon CR Trust
Staples Trust
Sir Halley Stewart Trust
C B & H H Taylor 1984 Trust
Rosanna Taylor's 1987 Charity
   Trust
Tinsley Foundation
TRAID
TUUT Charitable Trust
Ulting Overseas Trust
United Society for the
   Propagation of the Gospel
Scurrah Wainwright Charity
War on Want

Alexander Pigott Wernher
   Memorial Trust
Westcroft Trust

■ Australasia

C Alma Baker Trust
Feed the Minds
Elton John Aids Foundation
Mount Everest Foundation
Rowan Charitable Trust
J B Rubens Charitable
   Foundation
Alexander Pigott Wernher
   Memorial Trust

■ Americas and the West Indies

A B Charitable Trust
Sylvia Adams Charitable Trust
Balmore Trust
Barber Charitable Trust
Baring Foundation
Beacon Trust
Beaverbrook Foundation
George W Cadbury Charitable
   Trust
CAFOD
Catholic Charitable Trust
Christian Aid
Col-Reno Ltd
Comic Relief
Douglas Charitable Trust
Evergreen Foundation
Feed the Minds
Global Care
Christina Mary Hendrie Trust
   for Scottish & Canadian
   Charities
Hilden Charitable Fund
Homeless International
International Bar Association
   Educational Trust
Inverclyde Bequest Fund
Loseley & Guildway Charitable
   Trust
Mackintosh Foundation
Mayfair Charities Ltd
Methodist Relief and
   Development Fund
Peter Moores Foundation
NAM Charitable Trust
National Power Charitable
   Trust
Oxfam (GB)
Rhodes Trust Public Purposes
   Fund
Rowan Charitable Trust
J B Rubens Charitable
   Foundation
Staples Trust
Sylvanus Charitable Trust
Tinsley Foundation
TRAID

TUUT Charitable Trust
Ulting Overseas Trust
United Society for the
   Propagation of the Gospel
War on Want
G R Waters Charitable Trust
   2000

England

ADAPT Trust
AF Trust Company
AIM Foundation
Arts Council of England
Laura Ashley Foundation
Baring Foundation
Bedford Charity
Bergqvist Charitable Trust
Thomas Betton's Charity
   (Educational)
Bothwell Charitable Trust
Palgrave Brown Foundation
Carmichael-Montgomery
   Charitable Trust
Malcolm Chick Charity
Church Urban Fund
CLA Charitable Trust
Consortium on Opportunities
   for Volunteering
Countryside Trust
Sir William Coxen Trust Fund
Peter De Haan Charitable
   Trust
Doughty Charity Trust
Dulverton Trust
English Schools' Football
   Association
Fishmongers' Company's
   Charitable Trust
Joyce Fletcher Charitable Trust
Fox Memorial Trust
Joseph Strong Frazer Trust
General Nursing Council for
   England and Wales Trust
Girdlers' Company Charitable
   Trust
Reginald Graham Charitable
   Trust
Grand Charity of Freemasons
Hampstead Wells and
   Campden Trust
Hedley Foundation
Joseph & Mary Hiley Trust
Lady Hind Trust
Historic Churches Preservation
   Trust
John & Ruth Howard
   Charitable Trust
Hyde Charitable Trust
Incorporated Church Building
   Society
Rachel & Jack Lass Charities
   Ltd
Licensed Trade Charities Trust
Lloyds TSB Foundation for
   England and Wales

Loseley & Guildway Charitable
   Trust
Paul Lunn-Rockliffe Charitable
   Trust
Mackintosh Foundation
Merthyr Charitable Trust
Moss Family Charitable Trust
National Catholic Fund
National Power Charitable
   Trust
Noel Buxton Trust
Noon Foundation
Norwood & Newton Settlement
Kate Wilson Oliver Trust
Ouseley Trust
Oxfam (GB)
J S F Pollitzer Charitable
   Settlement
Queen Mary's Roehampton
   Trust
Märit and Hans Rausing
   Charitable Foundation
Albert Reckitt Charitable Trust
Max Reinhardt Charitable Trust
Royal British Legion
Royal London Aid Society
Jean Sainsbury Animal Welfare
   Trust
St Christopher's College
   Educational Trust
R H Scholes Charitable Trust
Sharon Trust
Sobell Foundation
Adrienne and Leslie Sussman
   Charitable Trust
Walter Swindon Charitable
   Trust
Tinsley Foundation
Tufton Charitable Trust
Vintners Company Charitable
   Trust
Wentwood Education Trust
A H and B C Whiteley
   Charitable Trust
Francis Winham Foundation
Woo Charitable Foundation
Miss Hazel M Wood Charitable
   Trust

....

■ North Eastern England

1989 Willan Charitable Trust
Ballinger Charitable Trust
Barbour Trust
John Bell Charitable Trust
Benfield Motors Charitable
   Trust
Audrey & Stanley Burton
   Charitable Trust
Century Radio Limited
   Charitable Trust
Chase Charity
De Clermont Charitable
   Company Ltd

Charity of Theresa Harriet
   Mary Delacour
J Paul Getty Jr Charitable Trust
Goshen Trust
Greggs Trust
N & P Hartley Memorial Trust
Hedley Denton Charitable
   Trust
Kreditor Charitable Trust
Allen Lane Foundation
Lankelly Foundation
William Leech Charity
M K (Mendel Kaufman)
   Charitable Trust
Leslie & Lilian Manning Trust
Millfield House Foundation
Normanby Charitable Trust
Northern Electric Employees
   Charity Association
Northern Rock Foundation
Northumberland Village Homes
   Trust
Penny in the Pound Fund
   Charitable Trust
Roman Catholic Diocese of
   Hexham and Newcastle
Mrs L D Rope Third Charitable
   Settlement
Rothley Trust
Storrow Scott Will Trust
Patricia and Donald Shepherd
   Trust
Nigel Vinson Charitable Trust
William Webster Charitable
   Trust
Yorkshire Agricultural Society
Yorkshire Bank Charitable
   Trust

Cleveland

Anglian Water Trust Fund
Cleveland Community
   Foundation
Eleanor Hamilton Educational
   and Charitable Trust
Yorkshire Historic Churches
   Trust

Durham County

County Durham Foundation
Hadrian Trust
Hospital of God at Greatham
Ruth & Lionel Jacobson Trust
   (Second Fund) No 2
Sir James Knott Trust
Northumbria Historic Churches
   Trust
Sir John Priestman Charity
   Trust
Shears Charitable Trust
Sherburn House Charity

Northumberland

Community Foundation Serving
   Tyne & Wear and
   Northumberland

Cumberland Building Society
   Charitable Foundation
Dickon Trust
E C Graham Belford Charitable
   Settlement
Hadrian Trust
W A Handley Charitable Trust
Hospital of God at Greatham
Ruth & Lionel Jacobson Trust
   (Second Fund) No 2
Joicey Trust
Sir James Knott Trust
Northumbria Historic Churches
   Trust
Christopher Rowbotham
   Charitable Trust
St Hilda's Trust
Shaftoe Educational
   Foundation
Shears Charitable Trust
Sherburn House Charity
Smith (Haltwhistle & District)
   Charitable Trust

Tyne & Wear

Cannop Trust
Community Foundation Serving
   Tyne & Wear and
   Northumberland
Hadrian Trust
W A Handley Charitable Trust
Hathaway Trust
Hospital of God at Greatham
Ruth & Lionel Jacobson Trust
   (Second Fund) No 2
Joicey Trust
J E Joseph Charitable Fund
Sir James Knott Trust
Leeds & Holbeck Building
   Society Charitable
   Foundation
R W Mann Trustees Limited
Victor Mann Trust
Newcastle Diocesan Society
Northumbria Historic Churches
   Trust
Sir John Priestman Charity
   Trust
Christopher Rowbotham
   Charitable Trust
St Hilda's Trust
Shears Charitable Trust
Sherburn House Charity
SO Charitable Trust
Tyneside Charitable Trust

....

■ North Western England

Green & Lilian F M Ainsworth
   & Family Benevolent Fund
Barnabas Charitable Trust
Bowland Charitable Trust
Burdens Charitable Foundation
Chase Charity

Duchy of Lancaster Benevolent
   Fund
Eventhall Family Charitable
   Trust
J Paul Getty Jr Charitable Trust
Granada Foundation
Gurunanak
N & P Hartley Memorial Trust
Allen Lane Foundation
Lankelly Foundation
Oglesby Trust
Oldham Foundation
Penny in the Pound Fund
   Charitable Trust
Charles Plimpton Foundation
Ravensdale Trust
John Rayner Charitable Trust
Mrs L D Rope Third Charitable
   Settlement
Patricia and Donald Shepherd
   Trust
Steinberg Family Charitable
   Trust
United Trusts
Yorkshire Bank Charitable
   Trust

Cheshire

Philip Barker Charity
Britannia Building Society
   Foundation
Charles Brotherton Trust
Cheshire Provincial Fund of
   Benevolence
Chester Diocesan Moral Aid
   Charity
Robert Clutterbuck Charitable
   Trust
Congleton Inclosure Trust
William Dean Countryside and
   Educational Trust
Ferguson Benevolent Fund Ltd
Healthsure Group Ltd
Peter Kershaw Trust
Ursula Keyes Trust
Lord Leverhulme Charitable
   Trust
North West Cancer Research
   Fund
Patients' Aid Association
   Hospital & Medical
   Charities Trust
Pennycress Trust
Christopher Rowbotham
   Charitable Trust
Rowley Trust
Rycroft Children's Fund
Warrington Church of England
   Educational Trust
Westminster Foundation

Cumbria

Harold and Alice Bridges
   Charity
Cumberland Building Society
   Charitable Foundation

Cumbria Community
   Foundation
Eden Arts Trust
Sir John Fisher Foundation
Hadfield Trust
Clifford Howarth Charity
   Settlement
Kelsick's Educational
   Foundation
Bryan Lancaster's Charity
Herd Lawson Charitable Trust
Manchester Airport Community
   Trust Fund
Sir George Martin Trust
North West Cancer Research
   Fund
Northern Rock Foundation
Northumbria Historic Churches
   Trust
Proven Family Trust
Rawdon-Smith Trust
Christopher Rowbotham
   Charitable Trust
Francis C Scott Charitable
   Trust
Frieda Scott Charitable Trust
Sellafield Charity Trust Fund
Ulverston Town Lands Charity
Norman Whiteley Trust
Yorkshire Dales Millennium
   Trust

Greater Manchester

Lord Barnby's Foundation
Beauland Ltd
Bonamy Charitable Trust
Booth Charities
Ida Carroll Trust
Community Foundation for
   Greater Manchester
Coutts & Co. Charitable Trust
D C Trust
John Grant Davies Trust
Eagle Charity Trust
George Elias Charitable Trust
F P Limited Charitable Trust
Ferguson Benevolent Fund Ltd
Florence's Charitable Trust
Eleanor Hamilton Educational
   and Charitable Trust
Gay & Peter Hartley's Hillards
   Charitable Trust
Hathaway Trust
Healthsure Group Ltd
Holden Charitable Trust
Edward Holt Trust
Hoover Foundation
Clifford Howarth Charity
   Settlement
Hulme Trust Estates
N B Johnson Charitable
   Settlement
Peter Kershaw Trust
P Leigh-Bramwell Trust 'E'
Jack Livingstone Charitable
   Trust

Localtrent Ltd
Manchester Airport Community Trust Fund
Manchester Guardian Society Charitable Trust
Lord Mayor of Manchester's Charity Appeal Trust
Mole Charitable Trust
Oizer Charitable Trust
Fanny Rapaport Charitable Settlement
Christopher Rowbotham Charitable Trust
Rycroft Children's Fund
Scott Bader Commonwealth Ltd
Sir James & Lady Scott Trust
Searchlight Electric Charitable Trust
J Shine Charities Ltd
Stanley Charitable Trust
Stoller Charitable Trust
Mayoress of Trafford's Charity Fund
Treeside Trust
W Wing Yip & Bros Charitable Trust

Lancashire
BNFL Springfields Medical Research & Charity Trust Fund
Harold and Alice Bridges Charity
Charles & Edna Broadhurst Charitable Trust
Coward Trust
Cumberland Building Society Charitable Foundation
William Dean Countryside and Educational Trust
Ferguson Benevolent Fund Ltd
Florence's Charitable Trust
Barry Green Memorial Fund
Harris Charity
Gay & Peter Hartley's Hillards Charitable Trust
M A Hawe Settlement
Healthsure Group Ltd
Clifford Howarth Charity Settlement
John and Rosemary Lancaster Charitable Foundation
W M & B W Lloyd Trust
Lofthouse Foundation
North West Cancer Research Fund
Dowager Countess Eleanor Peel Trust
Pilkington Charities Fund
Riverside Charitable Trust Limited
Christopher Rowbotham Charitable Trust
Rycroft Children's Fund

Francis C Scott Charitable Trust
Shepherd Street Trust
Skelton Bounty
John Slater Foundation
Mrs Waterhouse Charitable Trust
Westminster Foundation
Yorkshire Dales Millennium Trust

Merseyside
'A' Foundation
Baring Foundation
Philip Barker Charity
Bonamy Charitable Trust
Charles & Edna Broadhurst Charitable Trust
Charles Brotherton Trust
Amelia Chadwick Trust
Chrimes Family Charitable Trust
Lord Cozens-Hardy Trust
William Dean Countryside and Educational Trust
Earl of Derby's Charitable Trust
Dock Charitable Fund
Sir John Fisher Foundation
Ford of Britain Trust
Hemby Trust
P H Holt Charitable Trust
J P Jacobs Charitable Trust
Johnson Foundation
Johnson Group Cleaners Charity
Lord Leverhulme Charitable Trust
Liverpool Queen Victoria District Nursing Association
Liverpool Sailors' Home Trust
Merseyside Police and High Sheriff's Charitable Fund
John Moores Foundation
Nigel Moores Family Charitable Trust
Morgan Crucible Company plc Charitable Trust
Mushroom Fund
Newstead Charity
North West Cancer Research Fund
Cecil Pilkington Charitable Trust
Pilkington Charities Fund
Col W W Pilkington Will Trusts
Proven Family Trust
Rainford Trust
E L Rathbone Charitable Trust
Eleanor Rathbone Charitable Trust
Ravensdale Trust
Nathaniel Reyner Trust Fund
Rowan Charitable Trust
Sefton Community Foundation

Tillotson Bradbery Charitable Trust
Ward Blenkinsop Trust
West Derby Wastelands Charity
Westminster Foundation
Mayor of Wirral's Charity Trust

....
■ Yorkshire and the Humber
Sir Alec Black's Charity
Tony Bramall Charitable Trust
Arnold James Burton 1956 Charitable Settlement
Audrey & Stanley Burton Charitable Trust
Chase Charity
Manny Cussins Foundation
J Paul Getty Jr Charitable Trust
Barry Green Memorial Fund
Constance Green Foundation
Gay & Peter Hartley's Hillards Charitable Trust
N & P Hartley Memorial Trust
Joseph & Mary Hiley Trust
Allen Lane Foundation
Lankelly Foundation
Leeds & Holbeck Building Society Charitable Foundation
Paul Lunn-Rockliffe Charitable Trust
George A Moore Foundation
Nestlé Rowntree York Employees Community Fund Trust
Penny in the Pound Fund Charitable Trust
John Rayner Charitable Trust
Mrs L D Rope Third Charitable Settlement
Patricia and Donald Shepherd Trust
W W Spooner Charitable Trust
Samuel Storey Family Charitable Trust
Charles and Elsie Sykes Trust
C Paul Thackray General Charitable Trust
Scurrah Wainwright Charity
Yorkshire Bank Charitable Trust
Yorkshire County Cricket Club Charitable Youth Trust

Humberside, East Riding
Anglian Water Trust Fund
Peter Birse Charitable Trust
Harry Bottom Charitable Trust
R M 1956 Burton Charitable Trust
Joseph & Annie Cattle Trust
Sandy Dewhirst Charitable Trust
Hesslewood Children's Trust

Hull & East Riding Charitable
Trust
Sir James Reckitt Charity
J S & E C Rymer Charitable
Trust
Scots Trust
Severn Trent Water Charitable
Trust
Sylvia & Colin Shepherd
Charitable Trust
C Paul Thackray General
Charitable Trust
Yorkshire Agricultural Society
Yorkshire Historic Churches
Trust

North Yorkshire

G C Armitage Charitable Trust
Harry Bottom Charitable Trust
British Sugar Foundation
Charles Brotherton Trust
Jack Brunton Charitable Trust
R M 1956 Burton Charitable
Trust
Cadbury Schweppes
Foundation
Century Radio Limited
Charitable Trust
Norman Collinson Charitable
Trust
Coutts & Co. Charitable Trust
Sandy Dewhirst Charitable
Trust
A M Fenton Trust
Earl Fitzwilliam Charitable
Trust
Kenneth Hargreaves Charitable
Trust
Yvette and Hermione Jacobson
Charitable Trust
Leeds Hospital Fund
Charitable Trust
Sir George Martin Trust
North British Hotel Trust
Frederic William Plaxton
Charitable Trust
W L Pratt Charitable Trust
Sir John Priestman Charity
Trust
Rooke Atlay Charitable Trust
Joseph Rowntree Charitable
Trust
Shears Charitable Trust
Sylvia & Colin Shepherd
Charitable Trust
Noel Goddard Terry Charitable
Trust
C Paul Thackray General
Charitable Trust
York Children's Trust
Yorkshire Agricultural Society
Yorkshire Dales Millennium
Trust
Yorkshire Historic Churches
Trust
I A Ziff Charitable Foundation

South Yorkshire

Barnabas Charitable Trust
Harry Bottom Charitable Trust
Cadbury Schweppes
Foundation
Church Burgesses Educational
Foundation
Marjorie Coote Old People's
Charity
Earl Fitzwilliam Charitable
Trust
Freshgate Trust Foundation
J G Graves Charitable Trust
Hallam FM – Help a Hallam
Child Appeal
May Hearnshaw's Charity
Leeds Hospital Fund
Charitable Trust
Mayfield Valley Arts Trust
Zachary Merton & George
Woofindin Convalescent
Trust
James Neill Trust Fund
Ronald & Kathleen Pryor
Charitable Trust
Rainford Trust
Rycroft Children's Fund
Shaw Lands Trust
Sheffield Bluecoat & Mount
Pleasant Educational
Foundation
Sheffield Church Burgesses
Trust
Sheffield Town Trust
South Yorkshire Community
Foundation
Hugh & Ruby Sykes Charitable
Trust
Talbot Trusts
C Paul Thackray General
Charitable Trust
Ruth Walker Charitable Trust
Whitecourt Charitable Trust
Yorkshire Agricultural Society
Yorkshire Historic Churches
Trust
I A Ziff Charitable Foundation

West Yorkshire

G C Armitage Charitable Trust
Lord Barnby's Foundation
Bearder Charity
Bishop's Development Fund
Harry Bottom Charitable Trust
Charles Brotherton Trust
R M 1956 Burton Charitable
Trust
Cadbury Schweppes
Foundation
Community Foundation for
Calderdale
Denton Charitable Trust
Emmandjay Charitable Trust
Hammond Suddards Edge
Charitable Trust

Kenneth Hargreaves Charitable
Trust
Harrison & Potter Trust
Joseph & Mary Hiley Trust
Huddersfield Common Good
Trust
Incorporated Leeds Church
Extension Society
Lord Mayor of Leeds Appeal
Fund
Leeds Hospital Fund
Charitable Trust
Linden Charitable Trust
Sir George Martin Trust
Mirfield Educational Charity
Horace Moore Charitable Trust
Morgan Crucible Company plc
Charitable Trust
Joseph Rowntree Charitable
Trust
Rycroft Children's Fund
Salt Foundation
Scott Bader Commonwealth
Ltd
Shanti Charitable Trust
Shears Charitable Trust
Barbara A Shuttleworth
Memorial Trust
L H Silver Charitable Trust
C Paul Thackray General
Charitable Trust
Fred Towler Charity Trust
Charity of Thomas Wade &
Others
Yorkshire Agricultural Society
Yorkshire Historic Churches
Trust
I A Ziff Charitable Foundation

■ East Midlands Region

Aylesford Family Charitable
Trust
Michael Bishop Foundation
Burdens Charitable Foundation
Christopher Cadbury Charitable
Trust
Chase Charity
Coventry Building Society
Charitable Foundation
J Paul Getty Jr Charitable Trust
GNC Trust
May Hearnshaw's Charity
Allen Lane Foundation
Lankelly Foundation
Mercers' Charitable
Foundation
Patients' Aid Association
Hospital & Medical
Charities Trust
Patrick Charitable Trust
Penny in the Pound Fund
Charitable Trust
Ratcliff Foundation

Mrs L D Rope Third Charitable
    Settlement
Severn Trent Water Charitable
    Trust
Sir John Sumner's Trust
Warwickshire Masonic
    Charitable Association Ltd
Whitaker Charitable Trust
David Wilson Foundation
Yorkshire Bank Charitable
    Trust

Derbyshire
Ashby Charitable Trust
Bamford Charitable Foundation
Barnabas Charitable Trust
Bingham Trust
Harry Bottom Charitable Trust
Britannia Building Society
    Foundation
Burton Breweries Charitable
    Trust
Chetwode Foundation
Chetwode Samworth
    Charitable Trust
Helen Jean Cope Trust
Derbyshire Community
    Foundation
Duke of Devonshire's
    Charitable Trust
Griffith UK Foundation
Hallam FM – Help a Hallam
    Child Appeal
Gay & Peter Hartley's Hillards
    Charitable Trust
Leeds & Holbeck Building
    Society Charitable
    Foundation
Zachary Merton & George
    Woofindin Convalescent
    Trust
Provincial Grand Charity of the
    Province of Derbyshire
Rowley Trust
Rycroft Children's Fund
Shakespeare Temperance
    Trust
Hugh & Ruby Sykes Charitable
    Trust

Leicestershire
Anglian Water Trust Fund
Chelsea Building Society
    Charitable Foundation
Chetwode Foundation
Chetwode Samworth
    Charitable Trust
Coates Charitable Settlement
Helen Jean Cope Trust
J Reginald Corah Foundation
    Fund
William Dean Countryside and
    Educational Trust
Maud Elkington Charitable
    Trust
Everard Foundation

Earl Fitzwilliam Charitable
    Trust
Joanna Herbert-Stepney
    Charitable Settlement
P & C Hickinbotham Charitable
    Trust
Kirby & West Charitable Trust
Leeds & Holbeck Building
    Society Charitable
    Foundation
Leicester and Leicestershire
    Historic Churches
    Preservation Trust
Leicester Charity Link
John Longwill's Agricultural
    Scheme
Market Harborough and The
    Bowdens Charity
Alderman Newton's
    Educational Foundation
Jack Patston Charitable Trust
Rowley Trust
Shuttlewood Clarke Foundation
Henry Smith Charity
Florence Turner Trust
Howard Watson Symington
    Memorial Charity

Lincolnshire
Anglian Water Trust Fund
Dorothy Bayles Trust
BBC Radio Lincolnshire Charity
    Trust
Peter Birse Charitable Trust
Sir Alec Black's Charity
Earl Fitzwilliam Charitable
    Trust
Robert Hall Charity
Gay & Peter Hartley's Hillards
    Charitable Trust
Lincolnshire Old Churches
    Trust
Medlock Charitable Trust
Zachary Merton & George
    Woofindin Convalescent
    Trust
Mary Elizabeth Siebel Charity
John and Lucille van Geest
    Foundation
John Warren Foundation

Northamptonshire
Ammco Trust
Anglian Water Trust Fund
Becketts & Sargeants
    Educational Foundation
Benham Charitable Settlement
Francis Coales Charitable
    Foundation
Cripps Foundation
Alicia Duchess Dudleys Charity
Maud Elkington Charitable
    Trust
Earl Fitzwilliam Charitable
    Trust
Ford of Britain Trust

Gay & Peter Hartley's Hillards
    Charitable Trust
Healthsure Group Ltd
Horne Foundation
Macdonald-Buchanan
    Charitable Trust
Northampton Municipal Church
    Charities
Northampton Queen's Institute
    Relief in Sickness Fund
Northamptonshire Historic
    Churches Trust
Nottinghamshire Miners'
    Welfare Trust Fund
Phillips Charitable Trust
Christopher H R Reeves
    Charitable Trust
Scott Bader Commonwealth
    Ltd
Sudborough Foundation
Constance Travis Charitable
    Trust

Nottinghamshire
Anglian Water Trust Fund
Boots Charitable Trust
British Sugar Foundation
Chetwode Foundation
Chetwode Samworth
    Charitable Trust
Helen Jean Cope Trust
Coutts & Co. Charitable Trust
J N Derbyshire Trust
Djanogly Foundation
Harry Dunn Charitable Trust
Sir John Eastwood Foundation
Thomas Farr Charitable Trust
Fifty Fund
Forman Hardy Charitable Trust
Gray Trust
Gay & Peter Hartley's Hillards
    Charitable Trust
Charles Littlewood Hill Trust
Lady Hind Trust
Jones 1986 Charitable Trust
Leeds & Holbeck Building
    Society Charitable
    Foundation
Linmardon Trust
Zachary Merton & George
    Woofindin Convalescent
    Trust
Horace Moore Charitable Trust
New Appeals Organisation for
    the City & County of
    Nottingham
North British Hotel Trust
Nottingham General
    Dispensary
Nottinghamshire Community
    Foundation
Nottinghamshire Historic
    Churches Trust
J D Player Endowment Fund
Mary Potter Convent Hospital
    Trust

Puri Foundation
Mary Elizabeth Siebel Charity
Skerritt Trust
Jessie Spencer Trust
Thoresby Charitable Trust
A H and B C Whiteley
    Charitable Trust

■ West Midlands Region

29th May 1961 Charitable
    Trust
Lord Austin Trust
Aylesford Family Charitable
    Trust
Michael Bishop Foundation
Burdens Charitable Foundation
Christopher Cadbury Charitable
    Trust
Edward Cadbury Charitable
    Trust
Edward & Dorothy Cadbury
    Trust
George Cadbury Trust
William A Cadbury Charitable
    Trust
Cash for Kids
Chase Charity
George Henry Collins Charity
Coventry Building Society
    Charitable Foundation
Dumbreck Charity
W E Dunn Trust
J Paul Getty Jr Charitable Trust
GMC Trust
GNC Trust
Grantham Yorke Trust
Sir Barry Jackson Trust and
    County Fund
Johnnie Johnson Trust
Allen Lane Foundation
Lankelly Foundation
Edgar E Lawley Foundation
Michael Marsh Charitable
    Trust
James Frederick & Ethel Anne
    Measures Charity
Mercers' Charitable
    Foundation
Oakley Charitable Trust
Parivar Trust
Patients' Aid Association
    Hospital & Medical
    Charities Trust
Patrick Charitable Trust
Pedmore Sporting Club Trust
    Fund
Penny in the Pound Fund
    Charitable Trust
Peugeot Charity Trust
Ratcliff Foundation
Mrs L D Rope Third Charitable
    Settlement
M K Rose Charitable Trust
Rowlands Trust

St Peter's Saltley Trust
Severn Trent Water Charitable
    Trust
Sir John Sumner's Trust
C B & H H Taylor 1984 Trust
United Reformed Church (West
    Midlands) Trust Ltd
Warwickshire Masonic
    Charitable Association Ltd
Yorkshire Bank Charitable
    Trust

Herefordshire
Rt Hon Else Countess
    Beauchamp Deceased
    Charitable Trust
E F Bulmer Benevolent Fund
Chelsea Building Society
    Charitable Foundation
Elmley Foundation
Eveson Charitable Trust
Herefordshire Historic
    Churches Trust
Antony Hornby Charitable Trust
Clive Richards Charity Ltd
St Andrews Conservation Trust
Stephen R and Philippa H
    Southall Charitable Trust

Shropshire
P B Dumbell Charitable Trust
Roy Fletcher Charitable Trust
Mrs H R Greene Charitable
    Settlement
Millichope Foundation
North West Cancer Research
    Fund
Owen Family Trust
St Andrews Conservation Trust
Shropshire Historic Churches
    Trust
Walker Trust
Westcroft Trust

Staffordshire
Bamford Charitable Foundation
Barracks Trust of Newcastle-
    under-Lyme
Beacon Centre for the Blind
Britannia Building Society
    Foundation
Swinfen Broun Charitable Trust
Burton Breweries Charitable
    Trust
Consolidated Charity of Burton
    Upon Trent
Clarke Charitable Settlement
Baron Davenport's Charity
William Dean Countryside and
    Educational Trust
Wilfred & Elsie Elkes Charity
    Fund
Alfred Haines Charitable Trust
Harding Trust
Imerys South West Charitable
    Trust

Jarman Charitable Trust
Michael Lowe's & Associated
    Charities
Owen Family Trust
Harry Payne Trust
Charles Plimpton Foundation
Rowley Trust
Rycroft Children's Fund
Second Quothquan Charitable
    Trust
Staffordshire Historic
    Churches Trust
Strasser Foundation

Warwickshire
Ammco Trust
Birmingham International
    Airport Community Trust
Anthony Bourne Foundation
Wilfrid & Constance Cave
    Foundation
College Estate Charity
Baron Davenport's Charity
Alicia Duchess Dudleys Charity
William Edwards Educational
    Charity
Ford of Britain Trust
Mrs Godfrey-Payton Trust
Alfred Haines Charitable Trust
Heart of England Community
    Foundation
Heart of England Radio
    Charitable Trust
Jarman Charitable Trust
Keith and Joan Mindelsohn
    Charitable Trust
Norton Foundation
Owen Family Trust
Park Hill Charitable Trust
Harry Payne Trust
C A Rookes Charitable Trust
Rowley Trust
Second Quothquan Charitable
    Trust
Sheldon Trust
Snowball Trust
Warwick Municipal Charities –
    Charity of King Henry VIII,
    Warwick
Warwickshire Masonic
    Charitable Association Ltd
Wilmcote Charitrust

West Midlands
Aston Villa Charitable Trust
John Avins Trustees
Badley Memorial Trust
Beacon Centre for the Blind
James Beattie Charitable Trust
Birmingham District Nursing
    Charitable Trust
Birmingham Foundation
Birmingham Hospital Saturday
    Fund Medical Charity &
    Welfare Trust

Birmingham International
  Airport Community Trust
Lord Mayor of Birmingham's
  Charity
Charles Brotherton Trust
Bryant Trust
E F Bulmer Benevolent Fund
Richard Cadbury Charitable
  Trust
Cadbury Schweppes
  Foundation
Chatwin Trust
Cole Charitable Trust
Baron Davenport's Charity
Digbeth Trust
William Dudley Trust
P B Dumbell Charitable Trust
Wilfred & Elsie Elkes Charity
  Fund
Eveson Charitable Trust
John Feeney Charitable
  Bequest
George Fentham Birmingham
  Charity
Charles Henry Foyle Trust
General Charities of the City of
  Coventry
L & R Gilley Charitable Trust
Grimmitt Trust
Alfred Haines Charitable Trust
Hammond Suddards Edge
  Charitable Trust
Harborne Parish Lands Charity
Heart of England Community
  Foundation
Heart of England Radio
  Charitable Trust
Alan Edward Higgs Charity
Joseph Hopkins Charity
Jarman Charitable Trust
Lillie Johnson Charitable Trust
Leeds & Holbeck Building
  Society Charitable
  Foundation
Limoges Charitable Trust
Keith and Joan Mindelsohn
  Charitable Trust
Owen Family Trust
Harry Payne Trust
Peugeot Charity Trust
Bernard Piggott Trust
Rainford Trust
Roughley Charitable Trust
Rowley Trust
St Thomas' Dole Charity
Saintbury Trust
Henry James Sayer Charity
Scott Bader Commonwealth
  Ltd
Second Quothquan Charitable
  Trust
Sheldon Trust
Snowball Trust
Sutton Coldfield Municipal
  Charities
Douglas Turner Trust

R D Turner Charitable Trust
Eric W Vincent Trust Fund
R H Willis Charitable Trust
Wilmcote Charitrust
Woodlands Trust (259569)
Yardley Great Trust
W Wing Yip & Bros Charitable
  Trust

Worcestershire
Rt Hon Else Countess
  Beauchamp Deceased
  Charitable Trust
British Sugar Foundation
E F Bulmer Benevolent Fund
Richard Cadbury Charitable
  Trust
Baron Davenport's Charity
Elmley Foundation
Eveson Charitable Trust
Charles Henry Foyle Trust
Grimley Charity
HopMarket Charity
Judge Charitable Foundation
Laslett's (Hinton) Charity
John Martin's Charity
Tony Metherell Charitable
  Trust
Millichope Foundation
Morgan Crucible Company plc
  Charitable Trust
Harry Payne Trust
St Andrews Conservation Trust
Saintbury Trust
R D Turner Charitable Trust
Eric W Vincent Trust Fund
Wilmcote Charitrust
Woodlands Trust (259569)
Worcester Municipal Charities
Worcestershire & Dudley
  Historic Churches Trust

■ Eastern England
Sylvia Adams Charitable Trust
Anglian Water Trust Fund
Chamberlain Foundation
Chase Charity
J Paul Getty Jr Charitable Trust
Antony Hornby Charitable Trust
Nancy Kenyon Charitable Trust
Allen Lane Foundation
Lankelly Foundation
Lynwood Trust
Mrs L D Rope Third Charitable
  Settlement
Royal Eastern Counties
  Schools Limited
South Square Trust
Yorkshire Bank Charitable
  Trust

Bedfordshire
Balney Charitable Trust
Bedford Charity

Bedfordshire & Hertfordshire
  Historic Churches Trust
Peter Boizot Foundation
Carlton Television Trust
Francis Coales Charitable
  Foundation
William Delafield Charitable
  Trust
Horace & Marjorie Gale
  Charitable Trust
House of Industry Estate
Ibbett Trust
Robert Kiln Charitable Trust
Neighbourly Charitable Trust
Christopher H R Reeves
  Charitable Trust
Steel Charitable Trust
Trust Sixty Three
Voluntary Action Luton
John Warren Foundation
Wixamtree Trust

Cambridgeshire
BAA 21st Century
  Communities Trust
BBC Radio Cambridgeshire –
  Trustline
Peter Boizot Foundation
British Sugar Foundation
Burall Charitable Trust
Cambridgeshire Historic
  Churches Trust
Chapman Charitable Trust
Cole Charitable Trust
Cripps Foundation
Earl Fitzwilliam Charitable
  Trust
Charles S French Charitable
  Trust
Simon Gibson Charitable Trust
Robert Hall Charity
Hudson Foundation
Judge Charitable Foundation
Frank Litchfield Charitable
  Trust
D G Marshall of Cambridge
  Trust
Jack Patston Charitable Trust
Pye Foundation
Scott Bader Commonwealth
  Ltd
Mrs Smith & Mount Trust
Foundation of Edward Storey

Essex
A J H Ashby Will Trust
BAA 21st Century
  Communities Trust
Hervey Benham Charitable
  Trust
Buckle Family Charitable Trust
Carlton Television Trust
Leslie Mary Carter Charitable
  Trust
Chapman Charitable Trust
Christabella Charitable Trust

Colchester Catalyst Charity
Colchester & Tendring
    Community Trust
Augustine Courtauld Trust
D J H Currie Memorial Trust
Essex Community Foundation
Essex Fairway Charitable Trust
Essex Heritage Trust
Essex Provincial Charity Fund
Essex Youth Trust
Walter Farthing (Trust) Limited
Ford of Britain Trust
Fowler Memorial Trust
Charles S French Charitable
    Trust
Friends of Essex Churches
Hockerill Educational
    Foundation
Antony Hornby Charitable Trust
Edward Cecil Jones Settlement
Leeds & Holbeck Building
    Society Charitable
    Foundation
Mercers' Charitable
    Foundation
Ogilvie Charities Deed 2
Jack Petchey Foundation
Douglas Prestwich Charitable
    Trust
Rosca Trust
Albert & Florence Smith
    Memorial Trust
Mrs Smith & Mount Trust
Perry Watlington Trust

Hertfordshire
A J H Ashby Will Trust
BAA 21st Century
    Communities Trust
Bartle Family Charitable Trust
Bedfordshire & Hertfordshire
    Historic Churches Trust
Peter Boizot Foundation
Cadbury Schweppes
    Foundation
Carlton Television Trust
Carpenter Charitable Trust
Chapman Charitable Trust
Chelsea Building Society
    Charitable Foundation
Robert Clutterbuck Charitable
    Trust
Francis Coales Charitable
    Foundation
William Delafield Charitable
    Trust
Charles S French Charitable
    Trust
Gretna Charitable Trust
Hertfordshire Community
    Foundation
Hitchin Educational Foundation
Hockerill Educational
    Foundation
Robert Kiln Charitable Trust
Christopher Laing Foundation

Leeds & Holbeck Building
    Society Charitable
    Foundation
Tony Metherell Charitable
    Trust
Neighbourly Charitable Trust
Mrs Smith & Mount Trust
Stevenage Community Trust
Trust Sixty Three
Wellfield Trust

Norfolk
Adnams Charity
Paul Bassham Charitable Trust
Bethesda Community
    Charitable Trust
Peter Boizot Foundation
British Sugar Foundation
Palgrave Brown Foundation
Leslie Mary Carter Charitable
    Trust
Chelsea Building Society
    Charitable Foundation
Lord Cozens-Hardy Trust
Dawe Charitable Trust
Anne French Memorial Trust
Charles S French Charitable
    Trust
Simon Gibson Charitable Trust
Mrs H R Greene Charitable
    Settlement
Robert Hall Charity
Healthsure Group Ltd
Charles Littlewood Hill Trust
Lady Hind Trust
John Jarrold Trust
Leeds & Holbeck Building
    Society Charitable
    Foundation
Mercers' Charitable
    Foundation
Horace Moore Charitable Trust
Norfolk Churches Trust Ltd
Alderman Norman's
    Foundation
Norwich Consolidated
    Charities
Norwich Historic Churches
    Trust Ltd
Norwich Town Close Estate
    Charity
Pennycress Trust
Mr & Mrs Philip Rackham
    Charitable Trust
Ranworth Trust
Sandringham Estate Cottage
    Horticultural Society Trust
Mrs Smith & Mount Trust

Suffolk
Adnams Charity
Beccles Town Lands Charity
Bethesda Commuhity
    Charitable Trust
Peter Boizot Foundation
British Sugar Foundation

Palgrave Brown Foundation
Buckle Family Charitable Trust
Geoffrey Burton Charitable
    Trust
Leslie Mary Carter Charitable
    Trust
Chelsea Building Society
    Charitable Foundation
Dawe Charitable Trust
Charles S French Charitable
    Trust
Ganzoni Charitable Trust
Simon Gibson Charitable Trust
Haymills Charitable Trust
Healthsure Group Ltd
D C Moncrieff Charitable Trust
Music Sales Charitable Trust
Ogilvie Charities Deed 2
Late Barbara May Paul
    Charitable Trust
Mrs L D Rope Third Charitable
    Settlement
Scarfe Charitable Trust
Henry Smith Charity
Mrs Smith & Mount Trust
Southwold Trust
Suffolk Historic Churches Trust
William and Ellen Vinten Trust

....

■ South Eastern
   England

Bellinger Donnay Trust
Rowan Bentall Charitable Trust
Bothwell Charitable Trust
Chamberlain Foundation
Chase Charity
Chelsea Square 1994 Trust
John Coates Charitable Trust
EBM Charitable Trust
E F & M G Hall Charitable
    Trust
Peter Harrison Foundation
Antony Hornby Charitable Trust
Allen Lane Foundation
Lankelly Foundation
Lawson Charitable Foundation
Elaine & Angus Lloyd
    Charitable Trust
Loseley & Guildway Charitable
    Trust
Paul Lunn-Rockliffe Charitable
    Trust
Mercers' Charitable
    Foundation
John Pitman Charitable Trust
Prince Foundation
SHINE
South Square Trust
Tenovus Scotland
Miss Hazel M Wood Charitable
    Trust
Worshipful Company of
    Founders Charities

Berkshire

Ammco Trust
Ashendene Trust
BAA 21st Century
    Communities Trust
Bartle Family Charitable Trust
Louis Baylis (Maidenhead
    Advertiser) Charitable Trust
Berkshire Community
    Foundation
Herbert & Peter Blagrave
    Charitable Trust
Carlton Television Trust
Wilfrid & Constance Cave
    Foundation
Chelsea Building Society
    Charitable Foundation
Colefax Charitable Trust
Cumber Family Charitable
    Trust
Earley Charity
Greenham Common
    Community Trust Limited
Henley Educational Charity
Hitachi Europe Charitable
    Trust
Antony Hornby Charitable Trust
Imerys South West Charitable
    Trust
C L Loyd Charitable Trust
Midhurst Pensions Trust
Mobbs Memorial Trust Ltd
Horace Moore Charitable Trust
Gerald Palmer Trust
Prince Philip Trust Fund
Reading St Laurence Church
    Lands & John Johnson's
    Estate Charities
St Laurence Charities for the
    Poor
Peter Samuel Charitable Trust
Sarum St Michael Educational
    Charity
Yorkshire Bank Charitable
    Trust

Buckinghamshire

Alice Trust
Ammco Trust
Anglian Water Trust Fund
Balney Charitable Trust
Bartle Family Charitable Trust
Bergqvist Charitable Trust
Charles Boot Trust
Buckingham & Gawcott
    Charitable Trust
Buckinghamshire Foundation
Buckinghamshire Historic
    Churches Trust
Buckinghamshire Masonic
    Centenary Fund
Carlton Television Trust
Carrington Charitable Trust
Francis Coales Charitable
    Foundation
Cowley Charitable Foundation

William Delafield Charitable
    Trust
William Harding's Charity
Hitachi Europe Charitable
    Trust
Antony Hornby Charitable Trust
Marchday Charitable Fund
Milton Keynes Community
    Foundation
Mobbs Memorial Trust Ltd
Horace Moore Charitable Trust
Powell Foundation
Roger Vere Foundation
Woburn 1986 Charitable Trust
Woodcote Trust
Yorkshire Bank Charitable
    Trust

East Sussex

Dorothy Askew Trust
Ian Askew Charitable Trust
BAA 21st Century
    Communities Trust
Isabel Blackman Foundation
Brighton District Nursing
    Association Trust
Carlton Television Trust
Chapman Charitable Trust
Chelsea Building Society
    Charitable Foundation
Demigryphon Trust
Fidelity UK Foundation
Friarsgate Trust
Hale Trust
Dorothy Hay-Bolton Charitable
    Trust
Hyde Charitable Trust
Raymond & Blanche Lawson
    Charitable Trust
Magdalen & Lasher Charity
Moss Charitable Trust
North British Hotel Trust
Pallant Charitable Trust
Poling Charitable Trust
Douglas Prestwich Charitable
    Trust
Elise Randall Educational Trust
Märit and Hans Rausing
    Charitable Foundation
Violet M Richards Charity
River Trust
E E Roberts Charitable Trust
Rotherwick Foundation
Henry Smith Charity
Southover Manor General
    Education Trust
Sussex Historic Churches
    Trust
Swan Trust
Mrs A Lacy Tate Trust
Thompson Fund

Hampshire

Ashe Park Charitable Trust
BAA 21st Century
    Communities Trust

Peter Barker-Mill Memorial
    Charity
Bergqvist Charitable Trust
Herbert & Peter Blagrave
    Charitable Trust
Charlotte Bonham-Carter
    Charitable Trust
Bonhomie United Charity
    Society
Roger Brooke Charitable Trust
Burry Charitable Trust
George Cadbury Trust
Wilfrid & Constance Cave
    Foundation
Chapman Charitable Trust
Chelsea Building Society
    Charitable Foundation
Colefax Charitable Trust
John & Freda Coleman
    Charitable Trust
Sir Jeremiah Colman Gift Trust
Alderman Joe Davidson
    Memorial Trust
Dibden Allotments Charity
Ellis Campbell Charitable
    Foundation
Fawcett Charitable Trust
Ford of Britain Trust
Four Lanes Trust
GNC Trust
Greenham Common
    Community Trust Limited
Bishop of Guildford's
    Foundation
Hampshire & Islands Historic
    Churches Trust
Hare of Steep Charitable Trust
Hayden Charitable Trust
Hyde Charitable Trust
Richard Kirkman Charitable
    Trust
Leeds & Holbeck Building
    Society Charitable
    Foundation
Leonard Trust
Gerald Micklem Charitable
    Trust
Midhurst Pensions Trust
Moss Charitable Trust
Pallant Charitable Trust
William Price Charitable Trust
John Rayner Charitable Trust
Rotherwick Foundation
Late St Patrick White
    Charitable Trust
Sarum St Michael Educational
    Charity
Scott Bader Commonwealth
    Ltd
Henry Smith Charity
E J H Stephenson Deceased
    Charitable Trust
VEC Acorn Trust
F J Wallis Charitable
    Settlement
Wessex Cancer Trust

James Wise Charitable Trust

Isle of Wight
Ashe Park Charitable Trust
BAA 21st Century
  Communities Trust
Hampshire & Islands Historic
  Churches Trust
Pallant Charitable Trust
Daisy Rich Trust
Wessex Cancer Trust

Kent
Appleton Trust
Astor of Hever Trust
William Brake Charitable Trust
Carlton Television Trust
Chapman Charitable Trust
Chelsea Building Society
  Charitable Foundation
Cleary Foundation
Cobtree Charity Trust Ltd
Cole Charitable Trust
Sir James Colyer-Fergusson's
  Charitable Trust
Ronald Cruickshanks
  Foundation
Culra Charitable Trust
Sarah D'Avigdor Goldsmid
  Charitable Trust
Earmark Trust
Fidelity UK Foundation
Friends of Kent Churches
Gatwick Airport Community
  Trust
Godinton Charitable Trust
Great Stone Bridge Trust of
  Edenbridge
H & M Charitable Trust
Hale Trust
Dorothy Hay-Bolton Charitable
  Trust
Antony Hornby Charitable Trust
Hyde Charitable Trust
Sir Charles Jessel Charitable
  Trust
Miss A M Johns Charitable
  Trust
Raymond & Blanche Lawson
  Charitable Trust
Moulton Charitable Trust
David Pickford Charitable
  Foundation
Douglas Prestwich Charitable
  Trust
Märit and Hans Rausing
  Charitable Foundation
Violet M Richards Charity
E E Roberts Charitable Trust
Rochester Bridge Trust
Henry Smith Charity
Mrs Smith & Mount Trust
Swan Trust
Company of Tobacco Pipe
  Makers and Tobacco
  Blenders Benevolent Fund

Tory Family Foundation

Oxfordshire
Ammco Trust
Arbib Foundation
Ashendene Trust
Banbury Charities
Barnsbury Charitable Trust
Bartle Family Charitable Trust
Bartlett Taylor Charitable Trust
Bergqvist Charitable Trust
Charles Boot Trust
Carlton Television Trust
Wilfrid & Constance Cave
  Foundation
Chelsea Building Society
  Charitable Foundation
Church Houses Relief in Need
  Charity
Cumber Family Charitable
  Trust
Charity of Thomas Dawson
William Delafield Charitable
  Trust
DLM Charitable Trust
Doris Field Charitable Trust
Henley Educational Charity
Leeds & Holbeck Building
  Society Charitable
  Foundation
Thomas Lilley Memorial Trust
C L Loyd Charitable Trust
Marchday Charitable Fund
Oxford Preservation Trust
Oxfordshire Community
  Foundation
Oxfordshire Historic Churches
  Trust
Cecil Pilkington Charitable
  Trust
Mr and Mrs J A Pye's
  Charitable Settlement
Sandford Trust
Sarum St Michael Educational
  Charity
Souldern Trust
Stanton Ballard Charitable
  Trust
Steventon Allotments & Relief-
  in-Need Charity
Rosanna Taylor's 1987 Charity
  Trust
Tolkien Trust
Tubney Charitable Trust
Robert and Felicity Waley-
  Cohen Charitable Trust
Yorkshire Bank Charitable
  Trust

Surrey
BAA 21st Century
  Communities Trust
Lord Barnby's Foundation
Bergqvist Charitable Trust
Carlton Television Trust
Chapman Charitable Trust

Chelsea Building Society
  Charitable Foundation
John & Freda Coleman
  Charitable Trust
Demigryphon Trust
Fidelity UK Foundation
Gatwick Airport Community
  Trust
Bishop of Guildford's
  Foundation
Hale Trust
Dorothy Hay-Bolton Charitable
  Trust
Antony Hornby Charitable Trust
Hyde Charitable Trust
Ingram Trust
Ian Karten Charitable Trust
Leeds & Holbeck Building
  Society Charitable
  Foundation
Erica Leonard Trust
Sir Edward Lewis Foundation
Elaine & Angus Lloyd
  Charitable Trust
Loseley & Guildway Charitable
  Trust
Midhurst Pensions Trust
Horace Moore Charitable Trust
Rotherwick Foundation
R C Sherriff Rosebriars Trust
Henry Smith Charity
Mrs Smith & Mount Trust
Surrey Historic Buildings Trust
  Ltd
Swan Trust
Albert Van Den Bergh
  Charitable Trust
F J Wallis Charitable
  Settlement
James Wise Charitable Trust

West Sussex
Ashe Park Charitable Trust
Dorothy Askew Trust
Ian Askew Charitable Trust
BAA 21st Century
  Communities Trust
Bowerman Charitable Trust
Carlton Television Trust
Chapman Charitable Trust
Chelsea Building Society
  Charitable Foundation
Demigryphon Trust
Louise Dobson Charitable
  Trust
Fawcett Charitable Trust
Fidelity UK Foundation
Friarsgate Trust
Gatwick Airport Community
  Trust
Hale Trust
Dorothy Hay-Bolton Charitable
  Trust
Hyde Charitable Trust
Lauchentilly Charitable
  Foundation 1988

Marchday Charitable Fund
Midhurst Pensions Trust
Moss Charitable Trust
Lavinia Norfolk's Family
    Charitable Trust
Pallant Charitable Trust
Poling Charitable Trust
Douglas Prestwich Charitable
    Trust
Märit and Hans Rausing
    Charitable Foundation
Violet M Richards Charity
River Trust
Bassil Shippam and Alsford
    Trust
Henry Smith Charity
Southover Manor General
    Education Trust
Sussex Historic Churches
    Trust
Swan Trust
Rosanna Taylor's 1987 Charity
    Trust
Thompson Fund
Three Oaks Trust

....

■ South Western England

Viscount Amory's Charitable
    Trust
Rowan Bentall Charitable Trust
Viscountess Boyd Charitable
    Trust
Chase Charity
Chelsea Square 1994 Trust
J A Clark Charitable Trust
John Coates Charitable Trust
G F Eyre Charitable Trust
Joyce Fletcher Charitable Trust
Angela Gallagher Memorial
    Fund
Garnett Charitable Trust
J Paul Getty Jr Charitable Trust
Imerys South West Charitable
    Trust
Allen Lane Foundation
Lankelly Foundation
Lawson Charitable Foundation
Leach Fourteenth Trust
Elaine & Angus Lloyd
    Charitable Trust
Mrs L D Rope Third Charitable
    Settlement
St Andrews Conservation Trust
Verdon-Smith Family Charitable
    Settlement
Wentwood Education Trust
Elizabeth & Prince Zaiger Trust

Avon

Almondsbury Charity
Ammco Trust
John & Celia Bonham Christie
    Charitable Trust
Bramble Charitable Trust

Bristol Archdeaconry Charities
Bristol Charities
J & M Britton Charitable Trust
Rosemary Bugden Charitable
    Trust
Burdens Charitable Foundation
Chelsea Building Society
    Charitable Foundation
Chipping Sodbury Town Lands
    Charity
Stephen Clark 1957
    Charitable Trust
Coutts & Co. Charitable Trust
Harry Crook Foundation
Richard Davies Charitable
    Foundation
Denman Charitable Trust
Fast Track Trust Limited
Fortuna Charitable Trust
Gibbs Charitable Trusts
Gloucestershire Historic
    Churches Trust
Good Neighbours Trust
Greater Bristol Foundation
M V Hillhouse Trust
John James Bristol Foundation
Lark Trust
Lawlor Foundation
Leeds & Holbeck Building
    Society Charitable
    Foundation
A M McGreevy No 5 Charitable
    Settlement
Medlock Charitable Trust
Merchant Venturers' Charity
Oliver Morland Charitable Trust
Mount 'A' Charitable Trust
Mount 'B' Charitable Trust
Norman Family Charitable
    Trust
Oldham Foundation
Pontin Charitable Trust
Portishead Nautical Trust
Mr and Mrs J A Pye's
    Charitable Settlement
Roman Research Trust
St Thomas Ecclesiastical
    Charity
Sarum St Michael Educational
    Charity
Ralph and Irma Sperring
    Charity
Starfish Trust
Leonard Laity Stoate
    Charitable Trust
Verdon-Smith Family Charitable
    Settlement
Dame Violet Wills Will Trust
Dame Violet Wills Charitable
    Trust

Cornwall & Scilly Isles

B-C H 1971 Charitable Trust
Baring Foundation
Blanchminster Trust

Wilfrid & Constance Cave
    Foundation
Cornwall Historic Churches
    Trust
Cornwall Independent Trust
    Fund
Cornwell Charitable Trust
Wilfrid Bruce Davis Charitable
    Trust
Elmgrant Trust
GNC Trust
J C Green Charitable
    Settlement
Clare Milne Trust
Norman Family Charitable
    Trust
Patrick Charitable Trust
Carew Pole Charitable Trust
St Luke's College Foundation
SPIRAX
Leonard Laity Stoate
    Charitable Trust
Wakefield Trust

Devon

Viscount Amory's Charitable
    Trust
Sir John & Lady Amory's
    Charitable Trust
B-C H 1971 Charitable Trust
Albert Casanova Ballard
    Deceased Trust
Baring Foundation
Bideford Bridge Trust
Bridge Trust
Wilfrid & Constance Cave
    Foundation
Lord Clinton's Charitable Trust
Community Foundation in
    Wales
Dr & Mrs A Darlington
    Charitable Trust
Community Council of Devon
Devon Community Foundation
Devon Educational Trust
Devon Historic Churches Trust
Elmgrant Trust
L & R Gilley Charitable Trust
Heathcoat Trust
Lesley Lesley and Mutter Trust
Clare Milne Trust
Oliver Morland Charitable Trust
Norman Family Charitable
    Trust
Northcott Devon Foundation
Northcott Devon Medical
    Foundation
Patrick Charitable Trust
J B Pelly Charitable Settlement
Claude & Margaret Pike
    Charity
Plymouth Sound Trust
Ripple Effect Foundation
St Luke's College Foundation
Sarum St Michael Educational
    Charity

Scott Bader Commonwealth
    Ltd
Second Sidbury Trust
Leonard Laity Stoate
    Charitable Trust
Wakefield Trust
Dame Violet Wills Will Trust

Dorset
Bisgood Charitable Trust
Wilfrid & Constance Cave
    Foundation
Chelsea Building Society
    Charitable Foundation
Clover Trust
Alice Ellen Cooper-Dean
    Charitable Foundation
Simon Digby (Sherborne)
    Memorial Trust
Dorset Historic Churches Trust
Dorothy Holmes Charitable
    Trust
Oliver Morland Charitable Trust
Moss Charitable Trust
Norman Family Charitable
    Trust
Oldham Foundation
Roman Research Trust
Sarum St Michael Educational
    Charity
Leonard Laity Stoate
    Charitable Trust
Talbot Village Trust
Valentine Charitable Trust
Wessex Cancer Trust
William Williams Charity
Elizabeth & Prince Zaiger Trust

Gloucestershire
Ammco Trust
Barnwood House Trust
George Cadbury Trust
Chelsea Building Society
    Charitable Foundation
CHK Charities Limited
Stephen Clark 1957
    Charitable Trust
County of Gloucestershire
    Community Foundation
Denman Charitable Trust
Gloucestershire Historic
    Churches Trust
M V Hillhouse Trust
Charles Irving Charitable Trust
Langtree Trust
Leeds & Holbeck Building
    Society Charitable
    Foundation
Sylvanus Lyson's Charity
Macfarlane Walker Trust
Medlock Charitable Trust
Notgrove Trust
Oldham Foundation
Mrs C S Heber Percy
    Charitable Trust
Ratcliff Foundation

Roman Research Trust
Rowlands Trust
Saintbury Trust
Sedbury Trust
Henry Smith Charity
Philip Smith's Charitable Trust
SPIRAX
June Stevens Foundation
M J C Stone Charitable Trust
Summerfield Charitable Trust
Colonel W H Whitbread
    Charitable Trust

Somerset
Bramble Charitable Trust
Wilfrid & Constance Cave
    Foundation
Roger & Sarah Bancroft Clark
    Charitable Trust
Stephen Clark 1957
    Charitable Trust
Community Council of Devon
Dorothy Whitney Elmhirst Trust
Medlock Charitable Trust
Oliver Morland Charitable Trust
Ninesquare Charitable Trust
Norman Family Charitable
    Trust
Roman Research Trust
Sarum St Michael Educational
    Charity
Friends of Somerset Churches
    & Chapels
Leonard Laity Stoate
    Charitable Trust
Verdon-Smith Family Charitable
    Settlement
Wakefield Trust
Elizabeth & Prince Zaiger Trust

Wiltshire
Ammco Trust
Herbert & Peter Blagrave
    Charitable Trust
Wilfrid & Constance Cave
    Foundation
Chippenham Borough Lands
    Charity
Stephen Clark 1957
    Charitable Trust
Samuel William Farmer's Trust
Thomas Freke & Lady Norton
    Charity
Fulmer Charitable Trust
Walter Guinness Charitable
    Trust
GWR Community Trust
R J Harris Charitable
    Settlement
Lauchentilly Charitable
    Foundation 1988
Medlock Charitable Trust
Oliver Morland Charitable Trust
John Rayner Charitable Trust
Roman Research Trust

Sarum St Michael Educational
    Charity
Julius Silman Charitable Trust
Underwood Trust
Verdon-Smith Family Charitable
    Settlement
Weinstock Fund
Wiltshire and Swindon
    Community Foundation

■ London
John Apthorp Charitable Trust
Ashendene Trust
BAA 21st Century
    Communities Trust
Baring Foundation
Bellinger Donnay Trust
Thomas Betton's Charity
    (Educational)
Bridge House Estates Trust
    Fund
Broderer's Charity Trust
Butchers' Company General
    Charities
Cadogan Charity
Carlton Television Trust
Chamberlain Foundation
Chapman Charitable Trust
Chasah Trust
Chelsea Building Society
    Charitable Foundation
Chelsea Square 1994 Trust
City and Metropolitan Welfare
    Charity
City Educational Trust Fund
City Parochial Foundation
Cooks Charity
Biss Davies Charitable Trust
Denton Wilde Sapte Charitable
    Trust
Essex Fairway Charitable Trust
Worshipful Company of
    Gardeners of London
Hale Trust
Help a London Child
Heritage of London Trust Ltd
Antony Hornby Charitable Trust
Mrs E G Hornby's Charitable
    Settlement
Humanitarian Trust
Ingram Trust
Inverforth Charitable Trust
IPE Charitable Trust
Jacksons Charitable Trust
Yvette and Hermione Jacobson
    Charitable Trust
J E Joseph Charitable Fund
Ian Karten Charitable Trust
William Kendall's Charity
King's Fund
Robert Kitchin
Kreditor Charitable Trust
Lawlor Foundation
Lawson Charitable Foundation
Lazard Charitable Trust

Mason Le Page Charitable
   Trust
Leach Fourteenth Trust
Elaine & Angus Lloyd
   Charitable Trust
London Youth Trust
Mercers' Charitable
   Foundation
Metropolitan Hospital-Sunday
   Fund
Mitchell Charitable Trust
Moore Stephens Charitable
   Foundation
Morgan Crucible Company plc
   Charitable Trust
Morris Charitable Trust
Music Sales Charitable Trust
Chevras Ezras Nitzrochim Trust
Ogilvie Charities Deed 2
Palmer Foundation
Peabody Community Fund
David Pickford Charitable
   Foundation
John Pitman Charitable Trust
Nyda and Oliver Prenn
   Foundation
Douglas Prestwich Charitable
   Trust
John Rayner Charitable Trust
Mrs L D Rope Third Charitable
   Settlement
Rose Foundation
Royal Victoria Hall Foundation
SHINE
Barnett & Sylvia Shine No 2
   Charitable Trust
Mrs Smith & Mount Trust
South Square Trust
Sparquote Limited
Stanley Foundation Ltd
Adrienne and Leslie Sussman
   Charitable Trust
Walter Swindon Charitable
   Trust
Triangle Trust (1949) Fund
Underwood Trust
Robert and Felicity Waley-
   Cohen Charitable Trust
Warbeck Fund Ltd
Lionel Wigram Memorial Trust
Worshipful Company of
   Founders Charities
William Allen Young Charitable
   Trust

Barking and Dagenham
Christabella Charitable Trust
Essex Fairway Charitable Trust
Ford of Britain Trust
Charles S French Charitable
   Trust
Friends of Essex Churches
Edward Cecil Jones Settlement
London North East Community
   Foundation
Jack Petchey Foundation

Barnet
Sylvia Adams Charitable Trust
Milly Apthorp Charitable Trust
Fidelity UK Foundation
Edward Harvist Trust Fund
Hathaway Trust
Haymills Charitable Trust
Jesus Hospital Charity
Knowles Charitable Trust
John Lyon's Charity
Marchday Charitable Fund
North London Charities Limited
North London Islamic
   Association Trust
Eleanor Palmer Trust
Saint Edmund, King & Martyr
   Trust
Adrienne and Leslie Sussman
   Charitable Trust

Bexley
Hyde Charitable Trust
William Kendall's Charity
South East London Community
   Foundation
Trust Thamesmead Limited

Brent
Edward Harvist Trust Fund
Haymills Charitable Trust
Knowles Charitable Trust
John Lyon's Charity
Marchday Charitable Fund
Saint Edmund, King & Martyr
   Trust
W Wing Yip & Bros Charitable
   Trust

Bromley
Fidelity UK Foundation
Hyde Charitable Trust
South East London Community
   Foundation

Camden
Sir John Cass's Foundation
Coutts & Co. Charitable Trust
Hampstead Wells and
   Campden Trust
Edward Harvist Trust Fund
Haymills Charitable Trust
Knowles Charitable Trust
John Lyon's Charity
Marchday Charitable Fund
Philological Foundation
Saint Edmund, King & Martyr
   Trust

City of London
Aldgate and All Hallows
   Barking Exhibition
   Foundation
Aldgate Freedom Foundation
Baltic Charitable Fund
Worshipful Company of
   Carmen Benevolent Trust

Sir John Cass's Foundation
Coutts & Co. Charitable Trust
Fidelity UK Foundation
Charles S French Charitable
   Trust
Simon Gibson Charitable Trust
Girdlers' Company Charitable
   Trust
Kenneth Hargreaves
   Charitable Trust
Kleinwort Benson Charitable
   Trust
John Lyon's Charity
Marchday Charitable Fund
Charity Fund of the Worshipful
   Company of Paviors
Saint Edmund, King & Martyr
   Trust
Salters' Charities
Wakefield Trust
Woolnoth Society Charitable
   Trust

City of Westminster
Sir John Cass's Foundation
Coutts & Co. Charitable Trust
Simon Gibson Charitable Trust
Edward Harvist Trust Fund
Haymills Charitable Trust
Hyde Park Place Estate Charity
Knowles Charitable Trust
Lauchentilly Charitable
   Foundation 1988
John Lyon's Charity
Marchday Charitable Fund
Midhurst Pensions Trust
Philological Foundation
Simone Prendergast Charitable
   Trust
Saint Edmund, King & Martyr
   Trust
St Martin-in-the-Fields' Vicar's
   General Charity
St Mary-le-Strand Charity
Saint Marylebone Educational
   Foundation
Rosanna Taylor's 1987 Charity
   Trust
Mrs S H Troughton Charity
   Trust
West London Synagogue
   Charitable Fund
Westminster Amalgamated
   Charity
Westminster Foundation
City of Westminster Charitable
   Trust

Croydon
Abel Charitable Trust
Croydon Relief in Need
   Charities
Fidelity UK Foundation
Ford of Britain Trust
Hyde Charitable Trust

W Wing Yip & Bros Charitable
Trust

Ealing
Haymills Charitable Trust
Eleemosynary Charity of
William Hobbayne
John Lyon's Charity
Saint Edmund, King & Martyr
Trust

Enfield
Mayor of the London Borough
of Enfield Appeal Fund
Ford of Britain Trust
Charles S French Charitable
Trust
North London Charities Limited
Old Enfield Charitable Trust
Saint Edmund, King & Martyr
Trust

Greenwich
Abel Charitable Trust
Victor Adda Foundation
Sir William Boreman's
Foundation
Sir John Cass's Foundation
Sir John Evelyn's Charity
Hyde Charitable Trust
St Olave, St Thomas and St
John United Charity
South East London Community
Foundation
Trust Thamesmead Limited

Hackney
Arsenal Charitable Trust
Sir John Cass's Foundation
Coutts & Co. Charitable Trust
Fidelity UK Foundation
Ford of Britain Trust
Charles S French Charitable
Trust
Simon Gibson Charitable Trust
Hackney Parochial Charities
Hornsey Parochial Charities
Kleinwort Benson Charitable
Trust
Knowles Charitable Trust
Marchday Charitable Fund
Jack Petchey Foundation
Saint Edmund, King & Martyr
Trust

Hammersmith & Fulham
Sir John Cass's Foundation
Coutts & Co. Charitable Trust
Simon Gibson Charitable Trust
Girdlers' Company Charitable
Trust
Haymills Charitable Trust
John Lyon's Charity
Saint Edmund, King & Martyr
Trust

Haringey
Coutts & Co. Charitable Trust
Marchday Charitable Fund
North London Charities Limited
Saint Edmund, King & Martyr
Trust

Harrow
Coutts & Co. Charitable Trust
Harrow Community Trust
Edward Harvist Trust Fund
Haymills Charitable Trust
Knowles Charitable Trust
John Lyon's Charity
Saint Edmund, King & Martyr
Trust

Havering
Coutts & Co. Charitable Trust
Essex Fairway Charitable Trust
Ford of Britain Trust
Charles S French Charitable
Trust
Friends of Essex Churches
Edward Cecil Jones Settlement
Jack Petchey Foundation

Hillingdon
Fassnidge Memorial Trust
Haymills Charitable Trust
Hillingdon Partnership Trust
Saint Edmund, King & Martyr
Trust
A P Taylor Fund

Hounslow
Coutts & Co. Charitable Trust
Haymills Charitable Trust
Saint Edmund, King & Martyr
Trust
Thames Community
Foundation

Islington
Arsenal Charitable Trust
Sir John Cass's Foundation
Richard Cloudesley's Charity
Cripplegate Foundation
Hornsey Parochial Charities
Hyde Charitable Trust
Morris Charitable Trust
North London Charities Limited
Saint Edmund, King & Martyr
Trust

Kensington & Chelsea
Cadogan Charity
Campden Charities
Sir John Cass's Foundation
Simon Gibson Charitable Trust
Haymills Charitable Trust
Kensington District Nursing
Trust
John Lyon's Charity
Marchday Charitable Fund
Midhurst Pensions Trust

Horace Moore Charitable Trust
Saint Edmund, King & Martyr
Trust

Kingston upon Thames
Haymills Charitable Trust
Thames Community
Foundation

Lambeth
Abel Charitable Trust
Sir John Cass's Foundation
Coutts & Co. Charitable Trust
Fidelity UK Foundation
Gibbs Charitable Trusts
Simon Gibson Charitable Trust
Haymills Charitable Trust
Hyde Charitable Trust
Lambeth Endowed Charities
Peter Minet Trust
St Gabriel's Trust
Sir Walter St John's
Educational Charity
Sheepdrove Trust
South East London Community
Foundation

Lewisham
Abel Charitable Trust
Sir William Boreman's
Foundation
Sir John Cass's Foundation
Coutts & Co. Charitable Trust
Hyde Charitable Trust
St Gabriel's Trust
South East London Community
Foundation

Merton
Vernon N Ely Charitable Trust
Haymills Charitable Trust

Newham
Aston Charities Trust Limited
Sir John Cass's Foundation
Essex Fairway Charitable Trust
Fidelity UK Foundation
Ford of Britain Trust
Charles S French Charitable
Trust
Friends of Essex Churches
Kleinwort Benson Charitable
Trust
London North East Community
Foundation
Marchday Charitable Fund
Morgan Stanley International
Foundation
Jack Petchey Foundation

Redbridge
Ford of Britain Trust
Charles S French Charitable
Trust
Friends of Essex Churches

London North East Community
Foundation
Jack Petchey Foundation

Richmond upon Thames
Barnes Workhouse Fund
Hampton Fuel Allotment
Charity
Haymills Charitable Trust
Richmond Parish Lands Charity
Thames Community
Foundation

Southwark
Abel Charitable Trust
Sir John Cass's Foundation
Coutts & Co. Charitable Trust
Fidelity UK Foundation
Simon Gibson Charitable Trust
Girdlers' Company Charitable
Trust
Hyde Charitable Trust
Peter Minet Trust
Newcomen Collett Foundation
South East London Community
Foundation
United St Saviour's Charities
Wakefield Trust

Sutton
Fidelity UK Foundation
Haymills Charitable Trust
Hyde Charitable Trust

Tower Hamlets
Abel Charitable Trust
Aldgate and All Hallows
Barking Exhibition
Foundation
Sir John Cass's Foundation
Coutts & Co. Charitable Trust
Fidelity UK Foundation
Ford of Britain Trust
Charles S French Charitable
Trust
Simon Gibson Charitable Trust
Girdlers' Company Charitable
Trust
Hornsey Parochial Charities
Isle of Dogs Community
Foundation
Kleinwort Benson Charitable
Trust
Marchday Charitable Fund
Morgan Stanley International
Foundation
Jack Petchey Foundation
Saint Edmund, King & Martyr
Trust
St Katharine & Shadwell Trust
Spitalfields Market Community
Trust
Tower Hill Improvement Trust
Wakefield Trust

Waltham Forest
Ford of Britain Trust
Charles S French Charitable
Trust
Friends of Essex Churches
O-Regen
Jack Petchey Foundation

Wandsworth
Sir John Cass's Foundation
Coutts & Co. Charitable Trust
Simon Gibson Charitable Trust
Haymills Charitable Trust
Miles Trust for the Putney and
Roehampton Community
Sir Walter St John's
Educational Charity
Tay Charitable Trust

Northern Ireland

Arts Council of Northern
Ireland
William A Cadbury Charitable
Trust
Camelot Foundation
Carnegie United Kingdom Trust
Celtic Charity Fund
Community Foundation for
Northern Ireland
Ernest Cook Trust
Enkalon Foundation
Fidelity UK Foundation
Follett Trust
Isaac and Freda Frankel
Memorial Charitable Trust
Jill Franklin Trust
Garnett Charitable Trust
J Paul Getty Jr Charitable Trust
Gulbenkian Foundation
Hedley Foundation
Hospital Saturday Fund
Charitable Trust
Inverclyde Bequest Fund
Ireland Fund of Great Britain
Elton John Aids Foundation
Graham Kirkham Foundation
Late Sir Pierce Lacy Charity
Trust
Allen Lane Foundation
Lawlor Foundation
Lloyds TSB Foundation for
Northern Ireland
Paul Lunn-Rockliffe Charitable
Trust
Esmé Mitchell Trust
Horace Moore Charitable Trust
John Moores Foundation
Mr and Mrs F E F Newman
Charitable Trust
Oakdale Trust
Ouseley Trust
Penny in the Pound Fund
Charitable Trust
PPP Foundation

Mr and Mrs J A Pye's
Charitable Settlement
Queen Mary's Roehampton
Trust
Peggy Ramsay Foundation
Mrs L D Rope Third Charitable
Settlement
Joseph Rowntree Foundation
Royal British Legion
Jean Sainsbury Animal Welfare
Trust
C B & H H Taylor 1984 Trust
Triangle Trust (1949) Fund
Ultach Trust
Victoria Homes Trust
Westcroft Trust
Whitaker Charitable Trust
Harold Hyam Wingate
Foundation
Women Caring Trust

Belfast City
Ford of Britain Trust
Leeds & Holbeck Building
Society Charitable
Foundation

County Antrim
Ford of Britain Trust

County Armagh
Ford of Britain Trust

County Down
Ford of Britain Trust

Scotland

1970 Trust
Aberbrothock Charitable Trust
ADAPT Trust
Age Concern Scotland
Enterprise Fund
Sylvia Aitken Charitable Trust
AMW Charitable Trust
Baird Trust
Balcraig Foundation
Miss Marion Broughton's
Charitable Trust
Camelot Foundation
D W T Cargill Fund
W A Cargill Charitable Trust
Carnegie Trust for the
Universities of Scotland
Cash for Kids
Celtic Charity Fund
Chase Charity
Chest Heart and Stroke
Scotland
John Christie Trust
Martin Connell Charitable
Trust
Craignish Trust
Cruden Foundation Ltd
Cunningham Trust

Dickon Trust
Douglas Charitable Trust
Dulverton Trust
Dunard Fund
Erskine Cunningham Hill Trust
Ferguson Bequest Fund
Elizabeth Hardie Ferguson
   Charitable Trust Fund
Fox Memorial Trust
Emily Fraser Trust
Hugh Fraser Foundation
Angela Gallagher Memorial
   Fund
Gamma Trust
Gannochy Trust
J Paul Getty Jr Charitable Trust
Gough Charitable Trust
Gunter Charitable Trust
Dr Guthrie's Association
Hedley Foundation
Christina Mary Hendrie Trust
   for Scottish & Canadian
   Charities
Anne Herd Memorial Trust
Hope Trust
Miss Agnes H Hunter's Trust
Inchrye Trust
Lady Eda Jardine Charitable
   Trust
Jeffrey Charitable Trust
Allen Lane Foundation
Lankelly Foundation
R J Larg Family Charitable
   Trust
Rachel & Jack Lass Charities
   Ltd
Lethendy Charitable Trust
Lintel Trust
Lloyds TSB Foundation for
   Scotland
R S MacDonald Charitable
   Trust
Mackintosh Foundation
MacRobert Trust
W M Mann Foundation
Martin Charitable Trust
Hugh and Mary Miller Bequest
   Trust
Mitchell Trust
Morton Charitable Trust
Mount Everest Foundation
Mugdock Children's Trust
Noel Buxton Trust
North British Hotel Trust
Northwood Charitable Trust
Orrin Charitable Trust
Oxfam (GB)
Pastoral Care Trust
Mrs M E S Paterson's
   Charitable Trust
Andrew Paton's Charitable
   Trust
Penny in the Pound Fund
   Charitable Trust
A M Pilkington's Charitable
   Trust

Priory of Scotland of the Order
   of St John of Jerusalem
Albert Reckitt Charitable Trust
Robertson Trust
Russell Trust
St Andrew Animal Fund Ltd
Saltire Society
Scotbelge Charitable Trust
Scots Trust
John Scott Trust
Scottish Arts Council
Scottish Churches
   Architectural Heritage Trust
Scottish Churches Community
   Trust
Scottish Community
   Foundation
Scottish Hospital Endowments
   Research Trust
Scottish International
   Education Trust
Sportsman's Charity
Talteg Ltd
Tay Charitable Trust
Templeton Goodwill Trust
Tenovus Scotland
Len Thomson Charitable Trust
Trades House of Glasgow
Triangle Trust (1949) Fund
Tunnell Trust
Unemployed Voluntary Action
   Fund
A F Wallace Charity Trust
Walton Foundation
Western Recreation Trust
Whitaker Charitable Trust
A H and B C Whiteley
   Charitable Trust
J and J R Wilson Trust
Edith & Isaac Wolfson
   (Scotland) Trust
John K Young Endowment
   Fund

Highlands & Islands

W A Cargill Fund
Culra Charitable Trust
Davidson (Nairn) Charitable
   Trust
Mackintosh Foundation
Shetland Amenity Trust
Shetland Islands Council
   Charitable Trust

Grampian Region

Astor of Hever Trust
BAA 21st Century
   Communities Trust
Demigryphon Trust
Kintore Charitable Trust
Lauchentilly Charitable
   Foundation 1988
Leeds & Holbeck Building
   Society Charitable
   Foundation
A F Wallace Charity Trust

Tayside & Fife region

Appletree Trust
Caring for Kids
Carnegie Dunfermline Trust
Cray Trust
Ellis Campbell Charitable
   Foundation
Gannochy Trust
Guildry Incorporation of Perth
R J Larg Family Charitable
   Trust
Leng Charitable Trust
Lethendy Charitable Trust
Mathew Trust
Melville Trust for Care and
   Cure of Cancer
Northwood Charitable Trust
Radio Forth Help a Child
   Appeal
Arthur & Margaret Thompson
   Charitable Trust
Mrs S H Troughton Charity
   Trust
James Wood Bequest Fund

Central region

W A Cargill Fund
Row Fogo Charitable Trust
Radio Forth Help a Child
   Appeal
South Ayrshire Council
   Charitable Trusts
James Wood Bequest Fund

Strathclyde region

BAA 21st Century
   Communities Trust
Balmore Trust
Bellahouston Bequest Fund
Blair Foundation
W A Cargill Fund
Celtic Charity Fund
M V Hillhouse Trust
Hoover Foundation
James Thom Howat Charitable
   Trust
Leeds & Holbeck Building
   Society Charitable
   Foundation
Martin Charitable Trust
Merchants House of Glasgow
Mickel Fund
Miller Foundation
Stanley Morrison Charitable
   Trust
Mrs L D Rope Third Charitable
   Settlement
Rosemary Scanlan Charitable
   Trust
Scott Bader Commonwealth
   Ltd
Hugh Stenhouse Foundation
Trades House of Glasgow
Mrs S H Troughton Charity
   Trust
James Weir Foundation

J and J R Wilson Trust
James Wood Bequest Fund

Lothian region
BAA 21st Century
   Communities Trust
Miss Marion Broughton's
   Charitable Trust
Cray Trust
Edinburgh Children's Holiday
   Fund
Edinburgh Voluntary
   Organisations' Trust Funds
Row Fogo Charitable Trust
Miss Agnes H Hunter's Trust
Nancie Massey Charitable
   Trust
Melville Trust for Care and
   Cure of Cancer
Mickel Fund
Ponton House Trust
Radio Forth Help a Child
   Appeal
John Watson's Trust
John Wilson Bequest Fund
James Wood Bequest Fund
John K Young Endowment
   Fund

Southern Scotland
W A Cargill Fund
Cray Trust
Cumberland Building Society
   Charitable Foundation
Dumfries and Galloway Council
   Charitable Trusts
Holywood Trust
Lockerbie Trust
Melville Trust for Care and
   Cure of Cancer
Hugh Stenhouse Foundation

Wales

ADAPT Trust
Arts Council of Wales
Laura Ashley Foundation
Atlantic Foundation
Baring Foundation
Thomas Betton's Charity
   (Educational)
Bower Trust
Camelot Foundation
Carmichael-Montgomery
   Charitable Trust
Chapman Charitable Trust
Chase Charity
CLA Charitable Trust
Community Foundation in
   Wales
Gwendoline & Margaret Davies
   Charity
Peter De Haan Charitable
   Trust
Dinam Charity
Duis Charitable Trust

Dulverton Trust
Joseph Strong Frazer Trust
General Nursing Council for
   England and Wales Trust
J Paul Getty Jr Charitable Trust
Grand Charity of Freemasons
Hedley Foundation
Lady Hind Trust
Historic Churches Preservation
   Trust
Jane Hodge Foundation
Mary Homfray Charitable Trust
Incorporated Church Building
   Society
James Pantyfedwen
   Foundation
Jenour Foundation
Allen Lane Foundation
Lankelly Foundation
Rachel & Jack Lass Charities
   Ltd
Eric and Dorothy Leach
   Charitable Trust
Licensed Trade Charities Trust
Lloyds TSB Foundation for
   England and Wales
Llysdinam Trust
Merthyr Charitable Trust
Nigel Moores Family Charitable
   Trust
Mr and Mrs J T Morgan
   Foundation
Mount Everest Foundation
National Catholic Fund
National Power Charitable
   Trust
Noel Buxton Trust
Noon Foundation
Norwood & Newton Settlement
Oakdale Trust
Kate Wilson Oliver Trust
Ouseley Trust
Oxfam (GB)
Albert Reckitt Charitable Trust
Mrs L D Rope Third Charitable
   Settlement
Royal British Legion
St Christopher's College
   Educational Trust
Triangle Trust (1949) Fund
Wentwood Education Trust
A H and B C Whiteley
   Charitable Trust

North Wales
Cemlyn-Jones Trust
Chrimes Family Charitable
   Trust
Gwynedd Council Welsh
   Church Fund
May Hearnshaw's Charity
Isle of Anglesey Charitable
   Trust
Newstead Charity
North West Cancer Research
   Fund

Owen Family Trust
Payne Charitable Trust
Penny in the Pound Fund
   Charitable Trust
Bernard Piggott Trust
Rainford Trust
Ratcliff Foundation
Severn Trent Water Charitable
   Trust

Mid and West Wales
Simon Gibson Charitable Trust
Hoover Foundation
Morgan Crucible Company plc
   Charitable Trust
Powys Welsh Church Fund
Severn Trent Water Charitable
   Trust
Sobell Foundation
Welsh Church Fund –
   Carmarthenshire area

South Wales
City and County of Swansea
   Welsh Church Act Fund
Cwmbran Trust
Ford of Britain Trust
Gibbs Charitable Trusts
Simon Gibson Charitable Trust
Hoover Foundation
Huggard Charitable Trust
Monmouthshire County Council
   Welsh Church Act Fund
Morgan Crucible Company plc
   Charitable Trust
Newport County Borough
   Welsh Church Fund
Red Dragon Radio Trust
Rhondda Cynon Taff Welsh
   Church Acts Fund
Sobell Foundation
Vale of Glamorgan Welsh
   Church Fund
Welsh Church Act Fund –
   Neath Port Talbot County
   Borough Council

Channel Islands

BBC Children in Need Appeal
Comic Relief
Joseph Fattorini Charitable
   Trust 'B' Account
Ferguson Benevolent Fund Ltd
Hampshire & Islands Historic
   Churches Trust
Incorporated Church Building
   Society
Allen Lane Foundation
Lloyds TSB Foundation for the
   Channel Islands
Mount 'A' Charitable Trust
Mount 'B' Charitable Trust
Mr and Mrs F E F Newman
   Charitable Trust
Oakley Charitable Trust

Sarnia Charitable Trust
Wessex Cancer Trust

Isle of Man

BBC Children in Need Appeal
Blair Foundation
Comic Relief
Incorporated Church Building
    Society
Allen Lane Foundation
Thomas Lilley Memorial Trust
George A Moore Foundation
North West Cancer Research
    Fund

Trusts by field of interest and type of beneficiary

This index contains two separate listings:

Categorisation of fields of interest and type of beneficiary: This lists all of the headings used in the *DGMT* to categorise fields of interest and types of beneficiary.

Trusts by field of interest and type of beneficiary: This lists trusts under the fields of interest and types of beneficiary for which they have expressed a funding preference.

Fields of interest and type of beneficiary

Arts, culture, sport and recreation

Arts and culture 37

- Combined arts 39

- Crafts 39

- Literature 39

- Performing arts 40
  Dance 40
  Music 40
  Opera 41
  Theatre 42

- Visual arts 42

- Touring 43

- Amateur and community arts 43

- Access to the arts 44

- Arts and culture of specific communities 44

- Arts management 44

- Libraries 44

- Museums and galleries 44

Media and communications 45

Heritage and the built environment 45

- Arts and the environment 46

- Architecture 46

- Heritage 46

- Maintenance and preservation of buildings 47

- Religious buildings 48

- Restoration and maintenance of inland waterways 49

Humanities 49

- Archaeology 49

- Art history 49

- History 49

- International understanding 49

- Philosophy and ethics 49

Recreation and sport 49

- Parks, open spaces 50

- **Recreational facilities 50**

- **Sports 51**

- **Sport for people with a disability 51**

Development, housing and employment

Community and economic development 52

- **Community/ neighbourhood development 52**

- **Employment, job creation schemes 52**

- **Regeneration schemes 54**

Housing 55

- **Hostels, night shelters 56**

- **Housing advice services 57**

- **Social housing 58**

- **Supported accommodation 58**

Education & training

Education policy 61

Pre-school education, nursery schools 61

Primary & secondary education 63

- **Choir schools 64**

- **Faith schools 64**

- **Public and independent schools 65**

- **Special needs schools 65**

- **Education for excluded pupils and other non-attenders 67**

Higher education 67

Informal & continuing education 68

- **Adult and community education 69**

- **Supplementary schools 69**

- **Vocational education and training 70**

Management of schools 70

Teacher training & development 71

Particular subjects 71

- **Arts education & training 71**

- **Architecture education and training 71**

- **Business education 71**

- **Citizenship, personal & social education 72**

- **Domestic/lifeskills education 72**

- **Engineering education 72**

- **Hospitality education 72**

- **IT education 72**

- **Language teaching 73**

- **Legal education 73**

- **Literacy 73**

- **Printing education 74**

- Religious education 74

- Science education 75

- Social science 75

- Sports education 75

- Textiles & upholstery 75

Environment & animals
Agriculture and fishing 76

- Farming and food production 76

- Fishing and fisheries 77

- Forestry 77

- Horticulture 77

Animal conservation 77

- Endangered species 78

- Birds 79

- Fishes 79

- Land animals in the wild 79

Animal care 79

- Cats 80

- Dogs 80

- Horses 80

Non-animal research 80

Countryside 80

- Access to the countryside 81

- Maintenance and preservation of the countryside 81

Environmental education & research 82

- Environmental education 82

- Environmental research 82

Natural environment 82

- Fauna and flora 84

- Water resources 84

- Wild places, wilderness 84

Pollution abatement and control 84

Sustainable environment 84

- Energy issues 85

Transport 85

Faith activities
Inter-faith activities 86

Religious understanding 86

Christianity 86

- Christian causes, work 87

- Christian churches 88
  Anglican 89
  Roman Catholic 90
  Society of Friends, Quakers 90

- Christian social thought 90

- Ecumenicalism 90

- Missionary work, evangelism 90

Hinduism 91

Islam 91

Judaism 91

- Jewish causes, work 92

- Orthodox Judaism 93

Sikhism 93

Health
Alternative, complementary medicine 94

Health care 94

- General practice 97

- Health training 98

- Medical equipment 98

- Medical institutions 98
  Hospices 101
  Hospice at home 102
  Hospitals 103
  Nursing homes 104

- Medical transport 104

- Nursing 105

- Primary health care 105

- Speech therapy 105

Medical research & clinical treatment 106

- Dentistry 109

- Immune system, allergies 109

- Neurological and brain disorders 109

- Oncology 110

- Ophthalmology 111

- Paediatrics and foetal medicine 111

Health education/ prevention/ development 111

- Environmental health 112

- Health promotion 112

- Occupational health & safety 112

- Well women clinics, centres 112

Philanthropy and voluntary sector
Philanthropic intermediaries 113

Voluntarism 113

Voluntary sector capacity building 114

Rights, law and conflict
Citizen participation 114

Conflict resolution 115

- Cross-border initiatives 115

- Cross-community work 115

- Mediation 115

- Peace and disarmament 115

Legal & advice services 115

- Advice services 116

- Law services 116

Rights, equity and justice 116

- Civil liberties 117

- Cultural equity 117

- Disability rights 117

- Economic justice 117

- The right to employment 117

- Human rights 117

- Rights of people with mental health problems 118

- Older people's rights 118

- Racial justice 118

- Sexuality 118

- Social justice 118

- Women's rights 119

- Young people's rights 119

Science & technology
Engineering/ technology 119

Life sciences 120

- Botany 120

- Ecology 120

- Zoology 121

Social sciences, policy and research
Economics 121

Political science 121

Social policy 121

Social welfare
Community care services 122

- Activities & relationships between generations 125

- Services for carers 125

- Services for and about children and young people 127

  Adoption 128
  Childcare 128
  Family welfare 128
  Parenting 129
  Playschemes 129
  Trips, outings 129
  Youth work 129

- Services for and by older people 131

  Almshouses 132
  Homes for the elderly, sheltered accommodation 132
  Holidays & outings for older people 133

- Services for victims of crime 134

- Services for and by vulnerable/ill people 134

  Care in the community 134
  Counselling services for adults 136
  Day centres 137
  Drug and alcohol rehabilitation 138
  Self-help groups, support groups 139
  Convalescent homes 140
  Holidays for convalescents 140

- Services for women 140

Social preventive schemes 140

- Crime prevention 140

- Family planning and sex education 141

- Prisons, penal reform 142

Community centres and activities 142

- Community and social centres 142

- Community outings and holidays 145

- Community transport 146

Emergency response 146

- Rehabilitation 147

- Relief assistance 147

Beneficial groups
Age 148

- Children (up to 11) 148

- Young people (12–25) 152

- Older people 157

Class, group, occupation or ex-occupation 160

- Armed forces 160

- Art, culture 160

- Education and training 161

- The environment, agriculture 162

■ **Law, mediation and advice services 162**

■ **Manufacturing and service industries 162**

■ **Medicine and health 162**

■ **Religion 163**

■ **Science, technology and engineering 163**

■ **Seafarers & fishermen 164**

■ **Social sciences 164**

■ **Social welfare and public services 164**

■ **Sporting or social clubs, including masons 164**

■ **Textile workers & designers 164**

■ **Transport 164**

■ **Voluntary sector or doing voluntary work 165**

Disability 165

■ **People with a mental impairment 170**
People with autism 170
Brain damaged people 170
People with dyslexia 170

People with learning difficulties 170

■ **People with a physical impairment 171**
Cerebral palsy 171
Spina bifida & Hydrocephalus 171

■ **People with a sensory impairment 172**
Hearing loss 172
Sight loss 172

Ethnicity 173

■ **Ethnic minority groups 173**

Gender and relationships 173

■ **Adopted or fostered children 173**

■ **Bereaved 174**

■ **Carers 175**

■ **Lesbians and gay men 177**

■ **Orphans 177**

■ **Parents 177**

■ **Lone parents 178**

■ **Women 179**

Faith 180

■ **Buddhists 180**

■ **Christians 180**
Anglicans 181
Baptists 182
Evangelists 182
Methodists 182
Quakers 183
Roman Catholics 183
Unitarians 183

■ **Hindus 183**

■ **People of the Jewish faith 183**

■ **Muslims 185**

■ **Sikhs 185**

Ill health 185

■ **Alzheimer's disease 185**

■ **Arthritis & rheumatism 187**

■ **Asthma 188**

■ **Cancers 188**

■ **Cystic fibrosis 190**

■ **Diabetes 191**

■ **Epilepsy 192**

■ **Haematological disorders 192**

■ **Heart disease 193**

■ **HIV & AIDS 194**

■ **Kidney disease 195**

■ **Leprosy 195**

■ **Mental health impairment 196**

■ **Motor neurone disease 197**

■ **Multiple sclerosis 198**

■ **Muscular dystrophy 199**

■ **Parkinson's disease 200**

■ **Polio 201**

■ **Stroke-related disorders 201**

■ **Substance misuse 202**

■ **Terminally ill 203**

■ **Tuberculosis 204**

Social or economic circumstances 204

■ **Disadvantaged and socially excluded people 204**
People who are educationally disadvantaged 205
People who are homeless 205
People leaving care or in care 208
People living in rural areas 208
People living in urban areas 209
Ex-offenders & those at risk of offending 210
Migrants 211

People who are poor 211
Refugees and asylum seekers 215
People with an alternative lifestyle, including travellers 216
People who are unemployed 217

■ **Victims, oppressed people 217**
Victims of abuse 217
Victims of crime 219
Victims of domestic violence 220
Victims of disasters 221
People suffering from famine 222
People suffering injustice 223
People suffering from racism or other discrimination 223
People who have been tortured 223
Victims of war or conflict 223

Arts, culture, sport and recreation

Funding priority

Aberbrothock Charitable Trust
Paul Bassham Charitable Trust
Earl of Derby's Charitable Trust
Dickon Trust
Dorset Historic Churches Trust
Foyle Foundation
Hitachi Europe Charitable Trust
Kathleen Trust
Ian Mactaggart Fund
Market Harborough and Bowdens Charity
Paul Charitable Trust
Radcliffe Trust
Ward Blenkinsop Trust
Warwickshire Masonic Charitable Association Ltd

Will consider

Amberstone Trust
Bedford Charity
Bingham Trust
Morgan Blake Charitable Trust
Roger Brooke Charitable Trust
Mrs E E Brown Charitable Settlement
Bryant Trust
Edward Cadbury Charitable Trust
Edward & Dorothy Cadbury Trust
Carter's Educational Foundation
Chippenham Borough Lands Charity
Community Fund
Gwendoline & Margaret Davies Charity
DLA Charitable Trust
Englefield Charitable Trust
Thomas Farr Charitable Trust
Anne French Memorial Trust
Jacqueline and Michael Gee Charitable Trust
G C Gibson Charitable Trust
Girdlers' Company Charitable Trust
Glass-House Trust
Godinton Charitable Trust
Gretna Charitable Trust
Sue Hammerson's Charitable Trust
R J Harris Charitable Settlement
Headley Trust
Hedley Denton Charitable Trust
Clifford Howarth Charity Settlement
Jacobs Charitable Trust
Anton Jurgens Charitable Trust

Christopher Laing Foundation
Leathersellers' Company Charitable Fund
Lethendy Charitable Trust
G M Morrison Charitable Trust
Stanley Morrison Charitable Trust
Norton Foundation
Pontin Charitable Trust
Powys Welsh Church Fund
Eleanor Rathbone Charitable Trust
Archie Sherman Cardiff Charitable Foundation
Shetland Islands Council Charitable Trust
A R Taylor Charitable Trust
Constance Travis Charitable Trust
Douglas Turner Trust
R D Turner Charitable Trust
Vale of Glamorgan Welsh Church Fund
Valentine Charitable Trust
F J Wallis Charitable Settlement
Howard Watson Symington Memorial Charity
Mary Webb Trust
Webb Memorial Trust
Welsh Church Fund – Carmarthenshire area
David Wilson Foundation
Wixamtree Trust
I A Ziff Charitable Foundation

Arts and culture

Funding priority

'A' Foundation
Arts Council of Northern Ireland
Arts Council of Wales
Baring Foundation
Rt Hon Else Countess Beauchamp Deceased Charitable Trust
Sydney Black Charitable Trust
T B H Brunner Charitable Settlement
Bulldog Trust
R M 1956 Burton Charitable Trust
P H G Cadbury Trust
Elizabeth Cayzer Charitable Trust
Clore Duffield Foundation
Crescent Trust
Eden Arts Trust
Elmley Foundation
Eranda Foundation
Freshgate Trust Foundation
Garrick Charitable Trust
Garthgwynion Charities
Simon Gibson Charitable Trust

Goldschmied Charitable Settlement
Golsoncott Foundation
Great Britain Sasakawa Foundation
Gulbenkian Foundation
William Harding's Charity
Kenneth Hargreaves Charitable Trust
Horne Foundation
John Jarrold Trust
Kobler Trust
Jack Livingstone Charitable Trust
Lord and Lady Lurgan Trust
Lynn Foundation
Manifold Trust
Network for Social Change
Odin Charitable Trust
Ofenheim Charitable Trust
Peltz Trust
J S F Pollitzer Charitable Settlement
Powys Welsh Church Fund
Quercus Trust
Märit and Hans Rausing Charitable Foundation
Rayne Trust
Rooke Atlay Charitable Trust
Willy Russell Charitable Trust
Saltire Society
Scottish Arts Council
Samuel Storey Family Charitable Trust
Walter Swindon Charitable Trust
John Swire (1989) Charitable Trust
Tedworth Trust
Trusthouse Charitable Foundation
Warbeck Fund Ltd
Mrs Wingfield's Charitable Trust
Wixamtree Trust
Maurice Wohl Charitable Trust

Will consider

29th May 1961 Charitable Trust
Acacia Charitable Trust
H B Allen Charitable Trust
Milly Apthorp Charitable Trust
Armenian General Benevolent Union London Trust
Arts Council of England
Ashendene Trust
Laura Ashley Foundation
Astor of Hever Trust
Atlantic Foundation
Richard Attenborough Charitable Trust
Peter Barker-Mill Memorial Charity
Barnsbury Charitable Trust

Barracks Trust of Newcastle-under-Lyme
Bearder Charity
E M Behrens Charitable Trust
Benham Charitable Settlement
Bergqvist Charitable Trust
Birmingham Foundation
Michael Bishop Foundation
Blanchminster Trust
Patsy Bloom & Robert Blausten Charitable Trust
Bowerman Charitable Trust
Viscountess Boyd Charitable Trust
British Record Industry Trust
Charles & Edna Broadhurst Charitable Trust
Charles Brotherton Trust
Arnold James Burton 1956 Charitable Settlement
Burton Breweries Charitable Trust
Edward Cadbury Charitable Trust
Edward & Dorothy Cadbury Trust
William A Cadbury Charitable Trust
Cairns Charitable Trust
Carlton Television Trust
Carnegie Dunfermline Trust
Cemlyn-Jones Trust
Chapman Charitable Trust
Charities Advisory Trust
Chippenham Borough Lands Charity
Chipping Sodbury Town Lands Charity
Cinderford Charitable Trust
City Educational Trust Fund
John Coates Charitable Trust
Denise Cohen Charitable Trust
Community Foundation Serving Tyne & Wear and Northumberland
Congleton Inclosure Trust
Cooper Charitable Trust
Coppings Trust
Duke of Cornwall's Benevolent Fund
Sidney & Elizabeth Corob Charitable Trust
Craignish Trust
Cranbury Foundation
Cripplegate Foundation
Harry Crook Foundation
Cwmbran Trust
Daiwa Anglo-Japanese Foundation
David Charitable Trust
Leopold De Rothschild Charitable Trust
Denton Charitable Trust
Derbyshire Community Foundation
Community Council of Devon

Djanogly Foundation
DLM Charitable Trust
Dunard Fund
Dyers' Company Charitable Trust
Earley Charity
City of Edinburgh Charitable Trusts
Elmgrant Trust
Douglas Heath Eves Charitable Trust
Lord Faringdon Charitable Trust
John Feeney Charitable Bequest
Earl Fitzwilliam Charitable Trust
Oliver Ford Charitable Trust
Donald Forrester Trust
Fortuna Charitable Trust
Hugh Fraser Foundation
Maurice Fry Charitable Trust
Gannochy Trust
Garnett Charitable Trust
Gatwick Airport Community Trust
Mrs Godfrey-Payton Trust
Meir Golda Trust
Granada Foundation
J G Graves Charitable Trust
Grocers' Charity
Mrs Margaret Guido's Charitable Trust
GWR Community Trust
Hadfield Trust
Hampton Fuel Allotment Charity
Harding Trust
Hawthorne Charitable Trust
Hemby Trust
Hobart Charitable Trust
P H Holt Charitable Trust
Homestead Charitable Trust
Mary Homfray Charitable Trust
Sir Harold Hood's Charitable Trust
Antony Hornby Charitable Trust
Clifford Howarth Charity Settlement
Inverforth Charitable Trust
Lady Eileen Joseph Foundation
Jungels-Winkler Charitable Foundation
Stanley Kalms Foundation
Kohn Foundation
Neil Kreitman Foundation
David Laing Foundation
Lauffer Family Charitable Foundation
Carole & Geoffrey Lawson Foundation
Lawson Charitable Foundation
Lawson-Beckman Charitable Trust
Morris Leigh Foundation
Linbury Trust

Linden Charitable Trust
Enid Linder Foundation
Lloyds TSB Foundation for England and Wales
London North East Community Foundation
Marie Helen Luen Charitable Trust
John Lyon's Charity
Sir Jack Lyons Charitable Trust
Macfarlane Walker Trust
Helen Isabella McMorran Charitable Foundation
MacRobert Trust
Michael Marks Charitable Trust
Marsh Christian Trust
D G Marshall of Cambridge Trust
Anthony and Elizabeth Mellows Charitable Settlement
Merchant Taylors' Company Charities Fund
Millichope Foundation
Esmé Mitchell Trust
Monmouthshire County Council Welsh Church Act Fund
Monument Trust
Nigel Moores Family Charitable Trust
Peter Moores Foundation
Morel Charitable Trust
J P Morgan Fleming Educational Trust and Foundation
Morris Charitable Trust
Alderman Newton's Educational Foundation
Noswad Charity
Notgrove Trust
Oakley Charitable Trust
Old Broad Street Charity Trust
Raymond Oppenheimer Foundation
Owen Family Trust
P F Charitable Trust
Park Hill Trust
Personal Assurance Charitable Trust
Ruth & Michael Phillips Charitable Trust
Cecil Pilkington Charitable Trust
Porter Foundation
John Porter Charitable Trust
Nyda and Oliver Prenn Foundation
Prince Philip Trust Fund
Rank Foundation
Rayne Foundation
Reuters Foundation
Richmond Parish Lands Charity
Robertson Trust
Helen Roll Charitable Trust
C A Rookes Charitable Trust
Rowlands Trust

Joseph Rowntree Foundation
Russell Trust
Dr Mortimer and Theresa
    Sackler Foundation
Raymond & Beverley Sackler
    Foundation
Alan and Babette Sainsbury
    Charitable Fund
St Katharine & Shadwell Trust
Basil Samuel Charitable Trust
Coral Samuel Charitable Trust
Sarnia Charitable Trust
Scotbelge Charitable Trust
Frieda Scott Charitable Trust
John Scott Trust
Scottish Community
    Foundation
Scottish International
    Education Trust
Sefton Community Foundation
Shears Charitable Trust
Archie Sherman Charitable
    Trust
E C Sosnow Charitable Trust
W W Spooner Charitable Trust
Foundation for Sport and Arts
Stanley Foundation Ltd
Steel Charitable Trust
E J H Stephenson Deceased
    Charitable Trust
Stevenson Family's Charitable
    Trust
Stoller Charitable Trust
Stone-Mallabar Charitable
    Foundation
Summerfield Charitable Trust
Sutton Coldfield Municipal
    Charities
Swann-Morton Foundation
Swire Charitable Trust
Stella Symons Charitable Trust
Tay Charitable Trust
C B & H H Taylor 1984 Trust
Douglas Turner Trust
R D Turner Charitable Trust
VEC Acorn Trust
Eric W Vincent Trust Fund
Nigel Vinson Charitable Trust
Vodafone UK Foundation
Charity of Thomas Wade &
    Others
Wales Council for Voluntary
    Action
Mrs Waterhouse Charitable
    Trust
Weinstock Fund
Weldon UK Charitable Trust
Westminster Foundation
Garfield Weston Foundation
Whitaker Charitable Trust
A H and B C Whiteley
    Charitable Trust
Kay Williams Charitable
    Foundation
Maurice Wohl Charitable
    Foundation

Wolfson Family Charitable
    Trust
Worcester Municipal Charities
Fred & Della Worms Charitable
    Trust
Wyseliot Charitable Trust
Yorkshire Bank Charitable
    Trust
Zochonis Charitable Trust

....

■ Combined arts

Funding priority
Arts Council of England
Chase Charity
Earmark Trust
Elephant Trust
Esmée Fairbairn Foundation
Harrow Community Trust
Minge's Gift
Northern Rock Foundation
R C Sherriff Rosebriars Trust
Woo Charitable Foundation

Will consider
Arts Council of Wales
Astor Foundation
Britten-Pears Foundation
J A Clark Charitable Trust
Joyce Fletcher Charitable Trust
Four Lanes Trust
Charles Hayward Foundation
James Thom Howat Charitable
    Trust
Idlewild Trust
Jerwood Foundation and
    Jerwood Charitable
    Foundation
Sir James Knott Trust
Leche Trust
Linda Marcus Charitable Trust
Milton Keynes Community
    Foundation
Peter Minet Trust
Mobbs Memorial Trust Ltd
Music Sound Foundation
Northcott Devon Foundation
Norwich Town Close Estate
    Charity
Patrick Charitable Trust
John Rayner Charitable Trust
South Square Trust
Bernard Sunley Charitable
    Foundation
Marie-Louise Von Motesiczky
    Charitable Trust
Woodward Trust

....

■ Crafts

Funding priority
Ashendene Trust
Carpenters' Company
    Charitable Trust

Wilfrid & Constance Cave
    Foundation
Demigryphon Trust
Esmée Fairbairn Foundation
Ironmongers' Quincentenary
    Charitable Fund
Minge's Gift
Morris Charitable Trust
Northern Rock Foundation
Radcliffe Trust
R C Sherriff Rosebriars Trust
Woo Charitable Foundation

Will consider
D'Oyly Carte Charitable Trust
Sir James Knott Trust
Baily Thomas Charitable Fund
Holywood Trust
James Thom Howat Charitable
    Trust
Jerwood Foundation and
    Jerwood Charitable
    Foundation
J A Clark Charitable Trust
Norman Collinson Charitable
    Trust
Ernest Cook Trust
Cray Trust
Derbyshire Community
    Foundation
Arts Council of Wales
Four Lanes Trust
Nicholas & Judith Goodison's
    Charitable Settlement
Charles Hayward Foundation
Girdlers' Company Charitable
    Trust
Idlewild Trust
INTACH (UK) Trust
Mercers' Charitable
    Foundation
Milton Keynes Community
    Foundation
Norman Family Charitable
    Trust
South Square Trust
Bernard Sunley Charitable
    Foundation
Wates Foundation
Marie-Louise Von Motesiczky
    Charitable Trust

....

■ Literature

Funding priority
Arts Council of England
Ashendene Trust
Chase Charity
Esmée Fairbairn Foundation
Jerwood Foundation and
    Jerwood Charitable
    Foundation
Northern Rock Foundation
Pilgrim Trust
R C Sherriff Rosebriars Trust
Swan Trust

....

Woo Charitable Foundation
Wyseliot Charitable Trust

Will consider
Arts Council of Wales
Ashby Charitable Trust
Astor Foundation
British Institute of Archaeology
   at Ankara
Ernest Cook Trust
D'Oyly Carte Charitable Trust
John Ellerman Foundation
Elmgrant Trust
Joyce Fletcher Charitable Trust
Robert Gavron Charitable Trust
Reginald Graham Charitable
   Trust
James Thom Howat Charitable
   Trust
Idlewild Trust
INTACH (UK) Trust
Graham Kirkham Foundation
Sir James Knott Trust
Kreitman Foundation
Leverhulme Trust
John Lyon's Charity
Linda Marcus Charitable Trust
Milton Keynes Community
   Foundation
Oakdale Trust
Oldham Foundation
Peggy Ramsay Foundation
Ravensdale Trust
Roman Research Trust
St Katharine & Shadwell Trust
Scarfe Charitable Trust
South Square Trust
Bernard Sunley Charitable
   Foundation

■ Performing arts
Funding priority
Eric Anker-Petersen Charity
Chase Charity
Esmée Fairbairn Foundation
Harrow Community Trust
Idlewild Trust
Jerwood Foundation and
   Jerwood Charitable
   Foundation
Marina Kleinwort Charitable
   Trust
Lynn Foundation
Minge's Gift
Horace Moore Charitable Trust
Northern Rock Foundation
Austin & Hope Pilkington Trust
R C Sherriff Rosebriars Trust
Skinners' Company Lady
   Neville Charity
Swan Trust
Woo Charitable Foundation

Will consider
Arts Council of Wales
Ashby Charitable Trust
Astor Foundation
BBC Children in Need Appeal
George Henry Collins Charity
Holbeche Corfield Charitable
   Settlement
Coutts & Co. Charitable Trust
D'Oyly Carte Charitable Trust
Daily Telegraph Charitable
   Trust
Duis Charitable Trust
W E Dunn Trust
Robert Gavron Charitable Trust
Paul Hamlyn Foundation
Henley Educational Charity
Ingram Trust
Sir James Knott Trust
Kreitman Foundation
Leche Trust
John Lyon's Charity
Sir George Martin Trust
Mercers' Charitable
   Foundation
Merchants House of Glasgow
Miles Trust for Putney and
   Roehampton Community
Milton Keynes Community
   Foundation
Keith and Joan Mindelsohn
   Charitable Trust
Peter Minet Trust
Music Sound Foundation
Oakdale Trust
Parthenon Trust
Patrick Charitable Trust
Jack Petchey Foundation
Mr and Mrs J A Pye's
   Charitable Settlement
Ravensdale Trust
John Rayner Charitable Trust
Sir Walter St John's
   Educational Charity
South Square Trust
W W Spooner Charitable Trust
Bernard Sunley Charitable
   Foundation
Sutton Coldfield Municipal
   Charities
C B & H H Taylor 1984 Trust
Robert and Felicity Waley-
   Cohen Charitable Trust
Wates Foundation
Wolfson Foundation

■ Dance
Funding priority
Arts Council of England
Audrey & Stanley Burton
   Charitable Trust
R M 1956 Burton Charitable
   Trust
Cleary Foundation
Denton Wilde Sapte Charitable
   Trust

Dorothy Whitney Elmhirst Trust
Geoffrey C Hughes Charitable
   Trust
Marina Kleinwort Charitable
   Trust
Kennedy Leigh Charitable
   Trust
Newcomen Collett Foundation
Quercus Trust

Will consider
Adnams Charity
Bamford Charitable Foundation
James Beattie Charitable Trust
Hervey Benham Charitable
   Trust
Peter Black Charitable Trust
Swinfen Broun Charitable Trust
W A Cargill Fund
Norman Collinson Charitable
   Trust
County of Gloucestershire
   Community Foundation
Cray Trust
John Grant Davies Trust
Derbyshire Community
   Foundation
Joyce Fletcher Charitable Trust
Four Lanes Trust
Girdlers' Company Charitable
   Trust
Robert Hall Charity
Charles Hayward Foundation
Hesslewood Children's Trust
Hilden Charitable Fund
Hinrichsen Foundation
Holywood Trust
James Thom Howat Charitable
   Trust
Joicey Trust
Leverhulme Trust
Mackintosh Foundation
R W Mann Trustees Limited
Simone Prendergast Charitable
   Trust
York Children's Trust

■ Music
Funding priority
Angus Allnatt Charitable
   Foundation
Arts Council of England
Ashendene Trust
E M Behrens Charitable Trust
Britten-Pears Foundation
Rosemary Bugden Charitable
   Trust
R M 1956 Burton Charitable
   Trust
P H G Cadbury Trust
Ida Carroll Trust
Stephen Clark 1957
   Charitable Trust
Cleary Foundation
Delius Trust
Gerald Finzi Charitable Trust

Joyce Fletcher Charitable Trust
Four Lanes Trust
Gatsby Charitable Foundation
J C Green Charitable
　Settlement
Kathleen Hannay Memorial
　Charity
Kenneth Hargreaves Charitable
　Trust
Harris Charitable Trust
Hinrichsen Foundation
Holst Foundation
Ian Karten Charitable Trust
Kathleen Trust
Robert Kiln Charitable Trust
Kohn Foundation
Lauchentilly Charitable
　Foundation 1988
Kennedy Leigh Charitable
　Trust
Mayfield Valley Arts Trust
Morris Charitable Trust
Music Sales Charitable Trust
Music Sound Foundation
Newcomen Collett Foundation
Pallant Charitable Trust
Ronald & Kathleen Pryor
　Charitable Trust
Quercus Trust
R V W Trust
Radcliffe Trust
Rivendell Trust
Tillett Trust
Tinsley Foundation
Tunnell Trust
Miss S M Tutton Charitable
　Trust
Verdon-Smith Family Charitable
　Settlement
Whitaker Charitable Trust
Miss E B Wrightson's
　Charitable Settlement

Will consider
Adnams Charity
Ammco Trust
G C Armitage Charitable Trust
Baily Thomas Charitable Fund
Bamford Charitable Foundation
James Beattie Charitable Trust
Hervey Benham Charitable
　Trust
Peter Black Charitable Trust
Bridge Trust
British Record Industry Trust
Swinfen Broun Charitable Trust
Audrey & Stanley Burton
　Charitable Trust
W A Cargill Fund
Clark Charitable Trust
Norman Collinson Charitable
　Trust
Ernest Cook Trust
Coppings Trust
County of Gloucestershire
　Community Foundation

Lord Cozens-Hardy Trust
Cranbury Foundation
Derbyshire Community
　Foundation
P B Dumbell Charitable Trust
John Ellerman Foundation
Emerton-Christie Charity
Sir John Fisher Foundation
Timothy Franey Charitable
　Foundation
Charles S French Charitable
　Trust
Reginald Graham Charitable
　Trust
Hadrian Trust
Robert Hall Charity
Hare of Steep Charitable Trust
Hedley Denton Charitable
　Trust
Hedley Foundation
Hesslewood Children's Trust
Holywood Trust
James Thom Howat Charitable
　Trust
Huddersfield Common Good
　Trust
Inchrye Trust
Joicey Trust
Michael & Ilse Katz Foundation
Nancy Kenyon Charitable Trust
Graham Kirkham Foundation
Marina Kleinwort Charitable
　Trust
R J Larg Family Charitable
　Trust
Linden Charitable Trust
Lloyds TSB Foundation for
　Northern Ireland
Lofthouse Foundation
Sir Jack Lyons Charitable Trust
Mackintosh Foundation
MacRobert Trust
John Martin's Charity
Nigel Moores Family Charitable
　Trust
Norwich Town Close Estate
　Charity
Oakmoor Trust
Oldham Foundation
Ouseley Trust
Pennycress Trust
Persula Foundation
Simone Prendergast Charitable
　Trust
Rainford Trust
Cliff Richard Charitable Trust
Scarfe Charitable Trust
R H Scholes Charitable Trust
Servite Sisters' Charitable
　Trust Fund
Triangle Trust (1949) Fund
Florence Turner Trust
Welton Foundation
Harold Hyam Wingate
　Foundation
York Children's Trust

■ Opera
Funding priority
Angus Allnatt Charitable
　Foundation
Bergqvist Charitable Trust
Britten-Pears Foundation
R M 1956 Burton Charitable
　Trust
P H G Cadbury Trust
Delius Trust
Joyce Fletcher Charitable Trust
Kenneth Hargreaves Charitable
　Trust
Harris Charitable Trust
Heritage of London Trust Ltd
Geoffrey C Hughes Charitable
　Trust
Kathleen Trust
Peter Moores Foundation
Ronald & Kathleen Pryor
　Charitable Trust
Quercus Trust
R V W Trust
Walter Swindon Charitable
　Trust
Tillett Trust
Tinsley Foundation
Miss S M Tutton Charitable
　Trust
Weldon UK Charitable Trust
Whitaker Charitable Trust

Will consider
G C Armitage Charitable Trust
Audrey & Stanley Burton
　Charitable Trust
W A Cargill Fund
Stephen Clark 1957
　Charitable Trust
Ernest Cook Trust
John Ellerman Foundation
Four Lanes Trust
Charles S French Charitable
　Trust
Nicholas & Judith Goodison's
　Charitable Settlement
Charles Hayward Foundation
Hedley Foundation
Hesslewood Children's Trust
Hinrichsen Foundation
James Thom Howat Charitable
　Trust
Inchrye Trust
Marina Kleinwort Charitable
　Trust
Linden Charitable Trust
Linda Marcus Charitable Trust
Nigel Moores Family Charitable
　Trust
Newcomen Collett Foundation
Norwich Town Close Estate
　Charity
Royal Victoria Hall Foundation
R H Scholes Charitable Trust
Harold Hyam Wingate
　Foundation

Woodward Trust

■ Theatre
Funding priority
Arts Council of England
BBC Radio Cambridgeshire –
  Trustline
P H G Cadbury Trust
Wilfrid & Constance Cave
  Foundation
Cleary Foundation
Equity Trust Fund
Four Lanes Trust
Gatsby Charitable Foundation
Kenneth Hargreaves Charitable
  Trust
Heritage of London Trust Ltd
Sir Barry Jackson Trust and
  County Fund
Mackintosh Foundation
Newcomen Collett Foundation
Ronald & Kathleen Pryor
  Charitable Trust
Peggy Ramsay Foundation
Royal Victoria Hall Foundation
Leslie Smith Foundation
Walter Swindon Charitable
  Trust
Weldon UK Charitable Trust

Will consider
Adnams Charity
Richard Attenborough
  Charitable Trust
BBC Children in Need Appeal
Hervey Benham Charitable
  Trust
Peter Black Charitable Trust
Swinfen Broun Charitable Trust
Bryant Trust
Audrey & Stanley Burton
  Charitable Trust
J A Clark Charitable Trust
Stephen Clark 1957
  Charitable Trust
Norman Collinson Charitable
  Trust
Cray Trust
John Grant Davies Trust
Derbyshire Community
  Foundation
P B Dumbell Charitable Trust
John Ellerman Foundation
Sir John Fisher Foundation
Joyce Fletcher Charitable Trust
Greggs Trust
Hadrian Trust
Hedley Foundation
Holywood Trust
Huddersfield Common Good
  Trust
Isle of Dogs Community
  Foundation
Joicey Trust
Boris Karloff Charitable
  Foundation

Marina Kleinwort Charitable
  Trust
Leng Charitable Trust
Linden Charitable Trust
Lloyds TSB Foundation for
  Northern Ireland
Lofthouse Foundation
R W Mann Trustees Limited
Linda Marcus Charitable Trust
Nigel Moores Family Charitable
  Trust
Norwich Town Close Estate
  Charity
Oldham Foundation
Pennycress Trust
Bernard Piggott Trust
Simone Prendergast Charitable
  Trust
Cliff Richard Charitable Trust
Sir James Roll Charitable Trust
Scarfe Charitable Trust
Triangle Trust (1949) Fund
Whitaker Charitable Trust
Harold Hyam Wingate
  Foundation
Woodward Trust
York Children's Trust

....

■ Visual arts
Funding priority
Eric Anker-Petersen Charity
Arts Council of England
British Institute of Archaeology
  at Ankara
P H G Cadbury Trust
Wilfrid & Constance Cave
  Foundation
J A Clark Charitable Trust
Elephant Trust
Esmée Fairbairn Foundation
Jack Goldhill Charitable Trust
Granada Foundation
Kenneth Hargreaves Charitable
  Trust
Idlewild Trust
Jerwood Foundation and
  Jerwood Charitable
  Foundation
Lauchentilly Charitable
  Foundation 1988
Lynn Foundation
Minge's Gift
Henry Moore Foundation
Northern Rock Foundation
Pilgrim Trust
Austin & Hope Pilkington Trust
Rootstein Hopkins Foundation
R C Sherriff Rosebriars Trust
Swan Trust
Veneziana Fund
Verdon-Smith Family Charitable
  Settlement
Marie-Louise Von Motesiczky
  Charitable Trust
Woo Charitable Foundation

Wyseliot Charitable Trust

Will consider
Arts Council of Wales
Astor Foundation
Barbour Trust
Hervey Benham Charitable
  Trust
British Record Industry Trust
Swinfen Broun Charitable Trust
Audrey & Stanley Burton
  Charitable Trust
Chase Charity
Clark Charitable Trust
Norman Collinson Charitable
  Trust
Ernest Cook Trust
Cray Trust
Daily Telegraph Charitable
  Trust
Duis Charitable Trust
John Ellerman Foundation
Emerton-Christie Charity
Joyce Fletcher Charitable Trust
Four Lanes Trust
Glaziers' Trust
Nicholas & Judith Goodison's
  Charitable Settlement
Reginald Graham Charitable
  Trust
Paul Hamlyn Foundation
Charles Hayward Foundation
Hedley Denton Charitable
  Trust
Holywood Trust
James Thom Howat Charitable
  Trust
Geoffrey C Hughes Charitable
  Trust
Inchrye Trust
INTACH (UK) Trust
Graham Kirkham Foundation
Marina Kleinwort Charitable
  Trust
Sir James Knott Trust
Kreitman Foundation
Raymond & Blanche Lawson
  Charitable Trust
Leverhulme Trust
Linbury Trust
John Lyon's Charity
R W Mann Trustees Limited
John Martin's Charity
Mercers' Charitable
  Foundation
Milton Keynes Community
  Foundation
Peter Minet Trust
Nigel Moores Family Charitable
  Trust
Northcott Devon Foundation
Norwich Town Close Estate
  Charity
Oldham Foundation
J B Pelly Charitable Settlement
Pennycress Trust

Jack Petchey Foundation
Simone Prendergast Charitable
   Trust
Rainford Trust
Ravensdale Trust
John Rayner Charitable Trust
Scarfe Charitable Trust
Scouloudi Foundation
South Square Trust
Bernard Sunley Charitable
   Foundation
Sutton Coldfield Municipal
   Charities
Robert and Felicity Waley-
   Cohen Charitable Trust
Wolfson Foundation
Woodward Trust

....

■ Touring

Funding priority
Esmée Fairbairn Foundation
Harrow Community Trust
Sir Barry Jackson Trust and
   County Fund
Northern Rock Foundation

Will consider
Arts Council of Wales
Chase Charity
Patrick Charitable Trust

....

■ Amateur and community arts

Funding priority
Ashden Trust
Cleary Foundation
Community Foundation for
   Northern Ireland
County Durham Foundation
Joyce Fletcher Charitable Trust
Gerald Fogel Charitable Trust
Four Lanes Trust
Greater Bristol Foundation
Harrow Community Trust
Macfarlane Walker Trust
Minge's Gift
Oppenheimer Charitable Trust
Austin & Hope Pilkington Trust
Frieda Scott Charitable Trust
R C Sherriff Rosebriars Trust
Woo Charitable Foundation

Will consider
Adnams Charity
Arts Council of Wales
Aston Charities Trust Limited
Astor Foundation
Barnes Workhouse Fund
BBC Children in Need Appeal
BBC Radio Cambridgeshire –
   Trustline
Hervey Benham Charitable
   Trust

Birmingham International
   Airport Community Trust
Enid Blyton Trust for Children
Bridge House Estates Trust
   Fund
Harold and Alice Bridges
   Charity
Swinfen Broun Charitable Trust
Bryant Trust
Rosemary Bugden Charitable
   Trust
Audrey & Stanley Burton
   Charitable Trust
Geoffrey Burton Charitable
   Trust
Chase Charity
Church Urban Fund
Cole Charitable Trust
Norman Collinson Charitable
   Trust
Cray Trust
John Grant Davies Trust
Helen and Geoffrey de Freitas
   Charitable Trust
Derbyshire Community
   Foundation
W E Dunn Trust
Earth Love Fund
Gilbert & Eileen Edgar
   Foundation
Ericson Trust
Ford of Britain Trust
Timothy Franey Charitable
   Foundation
Greggs Trust
Walter Guinness Charitable
   Trust
Hackney Parochial Charities
Hadrian Trust
Robert Hall Charity
Paul Hamlyn Foundation
Hampstead Wells and
   Campden Trust
Kenneth Hargreaves Charitable
   Trust
Charles Hayward Foundation
Heart of England Community
   Foundation
Hedley Denton Charitable
   Trust
Hesslewood Children's Trust
Hobson Charity Ltd
Holywood Trust
John & Ruth Howard
   Charitable Trust
James Thom Howat Charitable
   Trust
Huddersfield Common Good
   Trust
Idlewild Trust
Imerys South West Charitable
   Trust
Inchrye Trust
INTACH (UK) Trust
Isle of Dogs Community
   Foundation

R J Larg Family Charitable
   Trust
Lark Trust
Raymond & Blanche Lawson
   Charitable Trust
Kennedy Leigh Charitable
   Trust
Levy Foundation
Lintel Trust
Lloyds TSB Foundation for
   Northern Ireland
Lockerbie Trust
Lofthouse Foundation
Mackintosh Foundation
Manchester Airport Community
   Trust Fund
R W Mann Trustees Limited
John Martin's Charity
Mercers' Charitable
   Foundation
Milton Keynes Community
   Foundation
Peter Minet Trust
Mobbs Memorial Trust Ltd
NAM Charitable Trust
Newcomen Collett Foundation
Newport County Borough
   Welsh Church Fund
Northcott Devon Foundation
Oakdale Trust
Pastoral Care Trust
Jack Petchey Foundation
Peugeot Charity Trust
Bernard Piggott Trust
Powell Foundation
Puri Foundation
Mr and Mrs J A Pye's
   Charitable Settlement
Radio Forth Help a Child
   Appeal
Rainford Trust
Red Dragon Radio Trust
Rhondda Cynon Taff Welsh
   Church Acts Fund
St James' Trust Settlement
St Thomas Ecclesiastical
   Charity
Scarfe Charitable Trust
Sir James & Lady Scott Trust
South Square Trust
South Yorkshire Community
   Foundation
Spitalfields Market Community
   Trust
W W Spooner Charitable Trust
Bernard Sunley Charitable
   Foundation
Thoresby Charitable Trust
Triangle Trust (1949) Fund
Vale of Glamorgan Welsh
   Church Fund
Marie-Louise Von Motesiczky
   Charitable Trust
Wakeham Trust
Westminster Amalgamated
   Charity

Woodward Trust

■ Access to the arts
Funding priority
ADAPT Trust
Esmée Fairbairn Foundation
Paul Hamlyn Foundation
Harrow Community Trust
Tubney Charitable Trust
Marie-Louise Von Motesiczky Charitable Trust

Will consider
Abbey National Charitable Trust Ltd
Arts Council of Wales
Ashby Charitable Trust
BBC Children in Need Appeal
BBC Radio Cambridgeshire – Trustline
County of Gloucestershire Community Foundation
Coutts & Co. Charitable Trust
D'Oyly Carte Charitable Trust
Charles Hayward Foundation
Heart of England Community Foundation
Alan Edward Higgs Charity
Ingram Trust
Linbury Trust
Lloyds TSB Foundation for Scotland
John Lyon's Charity
Mercers' Charitable Foundation
Miles Trust for Putney and Roehampton Community
Keith and Joan Mindelsohn Charitable Trust
Music Sound Foundation

■ Arts and culture of specific communities
Funding priority
British Institute of Archaeology at Ankara
Sir James Colyer-Fergusson's Charitable Trust
Gwynedd Council Welsh Church Fund
Paul Hamlyn Foundation
Elani Nakou Foundation
Northern Rock Foundation
Onaway Trust
Yamanouchi European Foundation

Will consider
Arts Council of Wales
BBC Children in Need Appeal
Mihran Essefian Charitable Trust

Esmée Fairbairn Foundation
Heart of England Community Foundation
Hellenic Foundation
Ireland Fund of Great Britain
Kennedy Leigh Charitable Trust
Lloyds TSB Foundation for Scotland
Linda Marcus Charitable Trust
Mercers' Charitable Foundation
Miles Trust for Putney and Roehampton Community
Keith and Joan Mindelsohn Charitable Trust
Peter Minet Trust
Music Sound Foundation
Newport County Borough Welsh Church Fund
Pastoral Care Trust
Marie-Louise Von Motesiczky Charitable Trust

■ Arts management
Funding priority
Eric Anker-Petersen Charity

Will consider
Arts Council of Wales
Esmée Fairbairn Foundation
Miles Trust for Putney and Roehampton Community
Marie-Louise Von Motesiczky Charitable Trust

■ Libraries
Funding priority
Eric Anker-Petersen Charity
R M 1956 Burton Charitable Trust
Paul Hamlyn Foundation
Heritage of London Trust Ltd
Pilgrim Trust

Will consider
Arts Council of Wales
Viscountess Boyd Charitable Trust
Esmée Fairbairn Foundation
Ford of Britain Trust
W M Mann Foundation
Linda Marcus Charitable Trust
National Manuscripts Conservation Trust
Helen Roll Charitable Trust
Scouloudi Foundation
Wolfson Foundation

■ Museums and galleries
Funding priority
Eric Anker-Petersen Charity
Ashworth Charitable Trust
R M 1956 Burton Charitable Trust
P H G Cadbury Trust
Chase Charity
Stephen Clark 1957 Charitable Trust
Crescent Trust
Esmée Fairbairn Foundation
Simon Gibson Charitable Trust
Heritage of London Trust Ltd
Idlewild Trust
Henry Moore Foundation
National Art Collections Fund
Northern Rock Foundation
Pilgrim Trust
Ronald & Kathleen Pryor Charitable Trust
Quercus Trust
Skinners' Company Lady Neville Charity
Swan Trust
Walter Swindon Charitable Trust
Mrs S H Troughton Charity Trust
Veneziana Fund
Marie-Louise Von Motesiczky Charitable Trust
Weldon UK Charitable Trust

Will consider
Viscount Amory's Charitable Trust
Arts Council of England
Arts Council of Wales
Laura Ashley Foundation
Astor Foundation
Barbour Trust
Lord Barnby's Foundation
Hervey Benham Charitable Trust
British Institute of Archaeology at Ankara
Audrey & Stanley Burton Charitable Trust
Geoffrey Burton Charitable Trust
Richard Cadbury Charitable Trust
Carlton Television Trust
Carron Charitable Trust
Clark Charitable Trust
Cobb Charity
Holbeche Corfield Charitable Settlement
County Durham Foundation
Coutts & Co. Charitable Trust
Denman Charitable Trust
Derbyshire Community Foundation

Community Council of Devon
Duis Charitable Trust
P B Dumbell Charitable Trust
Eden Arts Trust
Fidelity UK Foundation
Fishmongers' Company's
　Charitable Trust
Earl Fitzwilliam Charitable
　Trust
Joyce Fletcher Charitable Trust
Worshipful Company of
　Furniture Makers Charitable
　Fund
Garnett Charitable Trust
Girdlers' Company Charitable
　Trust
Great Britain Sasakawa
　Foundation
Hadrian Trust
Paul Hamlyn Foundation
Hampstead Wells and
　Campden Trust
Kathleen Hannay Memorial
　Charity
Lennox Hannay Charitable
　Trust
Kenneth Hargreaves Charitable
　Trust
Charles Hayward Foundation
Ingram Trust
Isle of Anglesey Charitable
　Trust
Isle of Dogs Community
　Foundation
James Pantyfedwen
　Foundation
Jerwood Foundation and
　Jerwood Charitable
　Foundation
Lauffer Family Charitable
　Foundation
Leche Trust
Kennedy Leigh Charitable
　Trust
Leng Charitable Trust
Leverhulme Trust
Linbury Trust
Linden Charitable Trust
Lyndhurst Settlement
John Lyon's Charity
Helen Isabella McMorran
　Charitable Foundation
Manifold Trust
W M Mann Foundation
Linda Marcus Charitable Trust
Sir George Martin Trust
Mercers' Charitable
　Foundation
Mickel Fund
Peter Minet Trust
J P Morgan Fleming
　Educational Trust and
　Foundation
National Manuscripts
　Conservation Trust
Newby Trust Limited

Northcott Devon Medical
　Foundation
Norwich Town Close Estate
　Charity
Oakmoor Trust
Oldham Foundation
Oxford Preservation Trust
A M Pilkington's Charitable
　Trust
Austin & Hope Pilkington Trust
Rawdon-Smith Trust
Helen Roll Charitable Trust
Roman Research Trust
Karim Rida Said Foundation
Scarfe Charitable Trust
Scouloudi Foundation
South Square Trust
Roama Spears Charitable
　Settlement
W W Spooner Charitable Trust
Stanley Foundation Ltd
Steinberg Family Charitable
　Trust
Summerfield Charitable Trust
C B & H H Taylor 1984 Trust
Tisbury Telegraph Trust
Ulverscroft Foundation
Robert and Felicity Waley-
　Cohen Charitable Trust
Thomas Wall Trust
Wates Foundation
Whitaker Charitable Trust
Michael and Anna Wix
　Charitable Trust
Charles Wolfson Charitable
　Trust
Wolfson Foundation
Woo Charitable Foundation

Media and communications

Funding priority
BBC Radio Cambridgeshire –
　Trustline
Chase Charity
Matthew Hodder Charitable
　Trust
Jerwood Foundation and
　Jerwood Charitable
　Foundation
Boris Karloff Charitable
　Foundation
Heinz & Anna Kroch
　Foundation
Network for Social Change
Austin & Hope Pilkington Trust
R C Sherriff Rosebriars Trust
Leslie Smith Foundation

Will consider
Arts Council of Wales
Astor Foundation
Barracks Trust of Newcastle-
　under-Lyme

Birmingham Foundation
J A Clark Charitable Trust
Derbyshire Community
　Foundation
Four Lanes Trust
Holywood Trust
James Thom Howat Charitable
　Trust
Sir James Knott Trust
Leverhulme Trust
Mackintosh Foundation
Mercers' Charitable
　Foundation
Milton Keynes Community
　Foundation
Music Sound Foundation
Servite Sisters' Charitable
　Trust Fund
Bernard Sunley Charitable
　Foundation
Sutton Coldfield Municipal
　Charities

Heritage and the built environment

Funding priority
Sydney Black Charitable Trust
T B H Brunner Charitable
　Settlement
R M 1956 Burton Charitable
　Trust
Golsoncott Foundation
Manifold Trust
Oxford Preservation Trust
Rothschild Foundation
Saltire Society
Shetland Amenity Trust
Surrey Historic Buildings Trust
　Ltd
Connie and Albert Taylor
　Charitable Trust
Miss Hazel M Wood Charitable
　Trust
Yorkshire Dales Millennium
　Trust

Will consider
Arts Council of England
Arts Council of Wales
Barracks Trust of Newcastle-
　under-Lyme
Lord Cozens-Hardy Trust
Cumber Family Charitable
　Trust
Derbyshire Community
　Foundation
City of Edinburgh Charitable
　Trusts
Maud Elkington Charitable
　Trust
Elmgrant Trust
Lord Faringdon Charitable
　Trust

Gatwick Airport Community
   Trust
Great Britain Sasakawa
   Foundation
Hadfield Trust
Kenneth Hargreaves Charitable
   Trust
Hedley Denton Charitable
   Trust
Hobart Charitable Trust
Mary Homfray Charitable Trust
Marie Helen Luen Charitable
   Trust
Sir James Reckitt Charity
Russell Trust
South Square Trust
Summerfield Charitable Trust

....

■ Arts and the environment

Funding priority

British Institute of Archaeology
   at Ankara
Garrick Charitable Trust
Harrow Community Trust
Lynn Foundation
Northern Rock Foundation
R C Sherriff Rosebriars Trust

Will consider

Arts Council of Wales
Chapman Charitable Trust
D'Oyly Carte Charitable Trust
Eden Arts Trust
Paul Hamlyn Foundation
Richmond Parish Lands Charity
Marie-Louise Von Motesiczky
   Charitable Trust
Robert and Felicity Waley-
   Cohen Charitable Trust

....

■ Architecture

Funding priority

British Institute of Archaeology
   at Ankara
Chase Charity
Stephen Clark 1957
   Charitable Trust
Demigryphon Trust
Glasgow Conservation Trust
Glass-House Trust
Heritage of London Trust Ltd
Lauchentilly Charitable
   Foundation 1988
Leche Trust
Midhurst Pensions Trust
Northern Rock Foundation
Austin & Hope Pilkington Trust
Mrs S H Troughton Charity
   Trust
Verdon-Smith Family Charitable
   Settlement

Will consider

Arts Council of Wales
Astor Foundation
Barbour Trust
Viscountess Boyd Charitable
   Trust
Clark Charitable Trust
Ernest Cook Trust
Holbeche Corfield Charitable
   Settlement
Cray Trust
D'Oyly Carte Charitable Trust
Eden Arts Trust
Fidelity UK Foundation
Earl Fitzwilliam Charitable
   Trust
Hadrian Trust
Robert Hall Charity
Paul Hamlyn Foundation
John & Ruth Howard
   Charitable Trust
Idlewild Trust
INTACH (UK) Trust
Jerwood Foundation and
   Jerwood Charitable
   Foundation
Kirby Laing Foundation
Raymond & Blanche Lawson
   Charitable Trust
Leng Charitable Trust
Lofthouse Foundation
Lyndhurst Settlement
Monmouthshire County Council
   Welsh Church Act Fund
Oakmoor Trust
Oldham Foundation
Prince of Wales's Charitable
   Foundation
Märit and Hans Rausing
   Charitable Foundation
Bernard Sunley Charitable
   Foundation
Sutton Coldfield Municipal
   Charities
Robert and Felicity Waley-
   Cohen Charitable Trust
Wates Foundation
Woodward Trust

....

■ Heritage

Funding priority

Birmingham International
   Airport Community Trust
Charlotte Bonham-Carter
   Charitable Trust
British Institute of Archaeology
   at Ankara
Chase Charity
Stephen Clark 1957
   Charitable Trust
Demigryphon Trust
Essex Heritage Trust
Esmée Fairbairn Foundation
Garrick Charitable Trust
Simon Gibson Charitable Trust

Harebell Centenary Fund
Heritage of London Trust Ltd
Iliffe Family Charitable Trust
Inland Waterways Association
Sir James Knott Trust
Midhurst Pensions Trust
Horace Moore Charitable Trust
Northern Rock Foundation
Oxfordshire Historic Churches
   Trust
Rural Trust
Peter Stormonth Darling
   Charitable Trust
Thoresby Charitable Trust
Mrs S H Troughton Charity
   Trust
Weinstock Fund
Wolfson Foundation

Will consider

Adnams Charity
Ammco Trust
Viscount Amory's Charitable
   Trust
Mary Andrew Charitable Trust
Armenian General Benevolent
   Union London Trust
Arts Council of Wales
A J H Ashby Will Trust
Astor Foundation
Lord Barnby's Foundation
Hervey Benham Charitable
   Trust
Bryant Trust
Arnold James Burton 1956
   Charitable Settlement
William A Cadbury Charitable
   Trust
Chapman Charitable Trust
Charities Advisory Trust
Chipping Sodbury Town Lands
   Charity
Clark Charitable Trust
Coutts & Co. Charitable Trust
Cranbury Foundation
Cripplegate Foundation
Sarah D'Avigdor Goldsmid
   Charitable Trust
D'Oyly Carte Charitable Trust
Helen and Geoffrey de Freitas
   Charitable Trust
William Dean Countryside and
   Educational Trust
Duke of Devonshire's
   Charitable Trust
Dulverton Trust
Earley Charity
Eden Arts Trust
Gilbert & Eileen Edgar
   Foundation
Fidelity UK Foundation
Fishmongers' Company's
   Charitable Trust
Earl Fitzwilliam Charitable
   Trust

Charles S French Charitable
   Trust
Freshgate Trust Foundation
Frognal Trust
Gamma Trust
Gannochy Trust
Great Britain Sasakawa
   Foundation
Grocers' Charity
Hadrian Trust
Robert Hall Charity
Lennox Hannay Charitable
   Trust
Harrow Community Trust
Charles Hayward Foundation
Dorothy Holmes Charitable
   Trust
P H Holt Charitable Trust
Idlewild Trust
INTACH (UK) Trust
Isle of Anglesey Charitable
   Trust
Ruth & Lionel Jacobson Trust
   (Second Fund) No 2
Jeffrey Charitable Trust
Leach Fourteenth Trust
Linbury Trust
Lyndhurst Settlement
Helen Isabella McMorran
   Charitable Foundation
R W Mann Trustees Limited
Anthony and Elizabeth Mellows
   Charitable Settlement
Mercers' Charitable
   Foundation
Mickel Fund
Gerald Micklem Charitable
   Trust
Miles Trust for Putney and
   Roehampton Community
Esmé Mitchell Trust
Monmouthshire County Council
   Welsh Church Act Fund
Peter Moores Foundation
Newport County Borough
   Welsh Church Fund
Oakmoor Trust
Oldham Foundation
Owen Family Trust
Pilgrim Trust
Richmond Parish Lands Charity
Robertson Trust
Roman Research Trust
Royal Docks Trust (London)
Peter Samuel Charitable Trust
Scarfe Charitable Trust
Frieda Scott Charitable Trust
Scouloudi Foundation
Shipwrights Company
   Charitable Fund
Stanley Foundation Ltd
Steinberg Family Charitable
   Trust
Summerfield Charitable Trust
Bernard Sunley Charitable
   Foundation

Sutton Coldfield Municipal
   Charities
Swire Charitable Trust
Charles and Elsie Sykes Trust
Noel Goddard Terry Charitable
   Trust
Mrs Maud Van Norden's
   Charitable Foundation
Robert and Felicity Waley-
   Cohen Charitable Trust
Woodward Trust

■ Maintenance and preservation of buildings

Funding priority

Adnams Charity
Architectural Heritage Fund
Ian Askew Charitable Trust
Astor of Hever Trust
Rt Hon Else Countess
   Beauchamp Deceased
   Charitable Trust
Chase Charity
Stephen Clark 1957
   Charitable Trust
Demigryphon Trust
Ellis Campbell Charitable
   Foundation
Esmée Fairbairn Foundation
Glasgow Conservation Trust –
   West
Heritage of London Trust Ltd
Idlewild Trust
Lauchentilly Charitable
   Foundation 1988
Leche Trust
Manchester Airport Community
   Trust Fund
Midhurst Pensions Trust
Monmouthshire County Council
   Welsh Church Act Fund
Northern Rock Foundation
Nottinghamshire Historic
   Churches Trust
Oxfordshire Historic Churches
   Trust
Pilgrim Trust
Ronald & Kathleen Pryor
   Charitable Trust
Skinners' Company Lady
   Neville Charity
Swan Trust
Noel Goddard Terry Charitable
   Trust
Thoresby Charitable Trust
Mrs S H Troughton Charity
   Trust
Vale of Glamorgan Welsh
   Church Fund
Mrs Maud Van Norden's
   Charitable Foundation
Veneziana Fund
Wolfson Foundation

Will consider

Alice Trust
Ammco Trust
AMW Charitable Trust
Arts Council of Wales
Ashby Charitable Trust
Balney Charitable Trust
Viscountess Boyd Charitable
   Trust
Bridge Trust
British Institute of Archaeology
   at Ankara
Swinfen Broun Charitable Trust
Audrey & Stanley Burton
   Charitable Trust
Carnegie Dunfermline Trust
Leslie Mary Carter Charitable
   Trust
Chapman Charitable Trust
Clark Charitable Trust
Francis Coales Charitable
   Foundation
Cray Trust
Cripps Foundation
Sarah D'Avigdor Goldsmid
   Charitable Trust
De Clermont Charitable
   Company Ltd
DLM Charitable Trust
Duis Charitable Trust
Dulverton Trust
Essex Heritage Trust
Alan Evans Memorial Trust
Norman Evershed Trust
Fairway Trust
Fidelity UK Foundation
Earl Fitzwilliam Charitable
   Trust
Jill Franklin Trust
Charles S French Charitable
   Trust
Frognal Trust
Gannochy Trust
J Paul Getty Jr Charitable Trust
Glaziers' Trust
Meir Golda Trust
Golden Charitable Trust
Reginald Graham Charitable
   Trust
J G Graves Charitable Trust
Grocers' Charity
Hadrian Trust
Robert Hall Charity
Charles Hayward Foundation
Historic Churches Preservation
   Trust
John & Ruth Howard
   Charitable Trust
Inland Waterways Association
INTACH (UK) Trust
Ruth & Lionel Jacobson Trust
   (Second Fund) No 2
John Jarrold Trust
Jeffrey Charitable Trust
Joicey Trust
Robert Kiln Charitable Trust

Graham Kirkham Foundation
Kleinwort Benson Charitable
  Trust
Lauffer Family Charitable
  Foundation
Raymond & Blanche Lawson
  Charitable Trust
Leach Fourteenth Trust
Leng Charitable Trust
Lyndhurst Settlement
Helen Isabella McMorran
  Charitable Foundation
W M Mann Foundation
Marsh Christian Trust
Sir George Martin Trust
Mercers' Charitable
  Foundation
Mickel Fund
Miles Trust for Putney and
  Roehampton Community
Milton Keynes Community
  Foundation
Horace Moore Charitable Trust
Newport County Borough
  Welsh Church Fund
Norwich Town Close Estate
  Charity
Oakmoor Trust
Late Barbara May Paul
  Charitable Trust
Powys Welsh Church Fund
Simone Prendergast Charitable
  Trust
Proven Family Trust
Mr and Mrs J A Pye's
  Charitable Settlement
Rawdon-Smith Trust
Richmond Parish Lands Charity
Royal Docks Trust
Rural Trust
St Andrews Conservation Trust
Scarfe Charitable Trust
Scouloudi Foundation
Leslie Smith Foundation
W W Spooner Charitable Trust
Stevenson Family's Charitable
  Trust
Summerfield Charitable Trust
Sutton Coldfield Municipal
  Charities
Stella Symons Charitable Trust
Florence Turner Trust
Robert and Felicity Waley-
  Cohen Charitable Trust
Woo Charitable Foundation
Woodward Trust

....

■ Religious buildings

Funding priority

Allchurches Trust Ltd
Almondsbury Charity
Architectural Heritage Fund
Barron Bell Trust and
  Additional Fund

Rt Hon Else Countess
  Beauchamp Deceased
  Charitable Trust
Bedfordshire & Hertfordshire
  Historic Churches Trust
Benham Charitable Settlement
Buckinghamshire Historic
  Churches Trust
Chase Charity
Francis Coales Charitable
  Foundation
Community Foundation in
  Wales
Cornwall Historic Churches
  Trust
Demigryphon Trust
Devon Historic Churches Trust
Sandy Dewhirst Charitable
  Trust
Dorset Historic Churches Trust
Jill Franklin Trust
Friends of Essex Churches
Friends of Kent Churches
Gloucestershire Historic
  Churches Trust
Hampshire & Islands Historic
  Churches Trust
Kathleen Hannay Memorial
  Charity
Herefordshire Historic
  Churches Trust
Heritage of London Trust Ltd
Historic Churches Preservation
  Trust
Idlewild Trust
Incorporated Church Building
  Society
Incorporated Leeds Church
  Extension Society
James Pantyfedwen
  Foundation
Edward Cecil Jones Settlement
Laslett's (Hinton) Charity
Lauchentilly Charitable
  Foundation 1988
Leicester and Leicestershire
  Historic Churches
  Preservation Trust
Lincolnshire Old Churches
  Trust
Lyndhurst Trust
Minge's Gift
Monmouthshire County Council
  Welsh Church Act Fund
Horace Moore Charitable Trust
Norfolk Churches Trust Ltd
Northamptonshire Historic
  Churches Trust
Norwich Historic Churches
  Trust Ltd
Nottinghamshire Historic
  Churches Trust
Oxfordshire Historic Churches
  Trust
Mrs M E S Paterson's
  Charitable Trust

Scottish Churches
  Architectural Heritage Trust
Shropshire Historic Churches
  Trust
Skinners' Company Lady
  Neville Charity
Friends of Somerset Churches
  & Chapels
Staffordshire Historic
  Churches Trust
Suffolk Historic Churches Trust
Swan Trust
Rosanna Taylor's 1987 Charity
  Trust
Thoresby Charitable Trust
Mrs S H Troughton Charity
  Trust
Vale of Glamorgan Welsh
  Church Fund
Wakefield Trust
John Warren Foundation
James Wood Bequest Fund
Worcestershire & Dudley
  Historic Churches Trust
Yorkshire Historic Churches
  Trust

Will consider

Mary Andrew Charitable Trust
Bamford Charitable Foundation
Viscountess Boyd Charitable
  Trust
British Institute of Archaeology
  at Ankara
Coutts & Co. Charitable Trust
Earl Fitzwilliam Charitable
  Trust
Girdlers' Company Charitable
  Trust
Dorothy Hay-Bolton Charitable
  Trust
Hedley Denton Charitable
  Trust
Kirby Laing Foundation
Mercers' Charitable
  Foundation
Miles Trust for Putney and
  Roehampton Community
Newport County Borough
  Welsh Church Fund
Privy Purse Charitable Trust
Rawdon-Smith Trust
Richmond Parish Lands Charity
Rufford Foundation
Scarfe Charitable Trust
Steinberg Family Charitable
  Trust
Florence Turner Trust

■ Restoration and maintenance of inland waterways

Funding priority
Robert Clutterbuck Charitable Trust
Inland Waterways Association
Jeffrey Charitable Trust
Northern Rock Foundation
Swan Trust

Will consider
Ammco Trust
Carnegie Dunfermline Trust
Chapman Charitable Trust
Cranbury Foundation
DLM Charitable Trust
Fishmongers' Company's Charitable Trust
Charles Hayward Foundation
Idlewild Trust
INTACH (UK) Trust
Lyndhurst Settlement
Shipwrights Company Charitable Fund

Humanities

Funding priority
British Institute of Archaeology at Ankara
R M 1956 Burton Charitable Trust
Norman Evershed Trust
Goldschmied Charitable Settlement
Great Britain Sasakawa Foundation
Peltz Trust

Will consider
Elmgrant Trust
Golsoncott Foundation
Mary Homfray Charitable Trust
Marie Helen Luen Charitable Trust
Northern Rock Foundation
C A Rookes Charitable Trust
Russell Trust
Robert and Lisa Sainsbury Charitable Trust
Wolfson Family Charitable Trust

■ Archaeology

Funding priority
Marc Fitch Fund
Roman Research Trust

Will consider
Laura Ashley Foundation
Ernest Cook Trust

Earl Fitzwilliam Charitable Trust
John & Ruth Howard Charitable Trust
Humanitarian Trust
Idlewild Trust
INTACH (UK) Trust
Robert Kiln Charitable Trust
Sir James Knott Trust
Leverhulme Trust
Macfarlane Walker Trust
Oxford Preservation Trust
Summerfield Charitable Trust
Thomas Wall Trust

■ Art history

Funding priority
Henry Moore Foundation
Mrs S H Troughton Charity Trust
Marie-Louise Von Motesiczky Charitable Trust
Woo Charitable Foundation

Will consider
Eden Arts Trust
Oxford Preservation Trust
Scouloudi Foundation
Summerfield Charitable Trust

■ History

Funding priority
Mrs S H Troughton Charity Trust

Will consider
Hervey Benham Charitable Trust
Dove-Bowerman Trust
Scouloudi Foundation
Summerfield Charitable Trust

■ International understanding

Funding priority
Anglo Hong Kong Trust
Kitty and Daniel Nabarro Charitable Trust
Tinsley Foundation

Will consider
Altajir Trust
Arts Council of Wales
Dulverton Trust

■ Philosophy and ethics

Will consider
Douglas Charitable Trust

Recreation and sport

Funding priority
Sydney Black Charitable Trust
Denton Wilde Sapte Charitable Trust
Football Foundation
Gannochy Trust
Simon Gibson Charitable Trust
ITF Seafarers Trust
Northern Rock Foundation
Saltire Society
Charity of Thomas Wade & Others
Kay Williams Charitable Foundation

Will consider
Alexandra Rose Day
Milly Apthorp Charitable Trust
Barracks Trust of Newcastle-under-Lyme
Bearder Charity
James Beattie Charitable Trust
Blanchminster Trust
Burton Breweries Charitable Trust
Lord Cozens-Hardy Trust
Cripplegate Foundation
Derbyshire Community Foundation
W E Dunn Trust
Earley Charity
Gilbert & Eileen Edgar Foundation
City of Edinburgh Charitable Trusts
Maud Elkington Charitable Trust
Lord Faringdon Charitable Trust
Gatwick Airport Community Trust
Girdlers' Company Charitable Trust
Great Britain Sasakawa Foundation
GWR Community Trust
Hadfield Trust
Robert Hall Charity
Hedley Denton Charitable Trust
Hobart Charitable Trust
Mary Homfray Charitable Trust
David Laing Foundation
Leeds Hospital Fund Charitable Trust
John Lyon's Charity
Monmouthshire County Council Welsh Church Act Fund
Nigel Moores Family Charitable Trust
Sir James Reckitt Charity
Foundation for Sport and Arts

Bernard Sunley Charitable
   Foundation
VEC Acorn Trust
Robert and Felicity Waley-
   Cohen Charitable Trust
York Children's Trust

....

■ Parks, open spaces

Funding priority

Birmingham International
   Airport Community Trust
P H G Cadbury Trust
Cleary Foundation
Worshipful Company of
   Gardeners of London
Heritage of London Trust Ltd
Ronald & Kathleen Pryor
   Charitable Trust
Stanley Smith UK Horticultural
   Trust
Samuel Storey Family
   Charitable Trust
Tower Hill Improvement Trust
Charity of Thomas Wade &
   Others

Will consider

Astor Foundation
Astor of Hever Trust
Barclays Stockbrokers
   Charitable Trust
W A Cargill Charitable Trust
County Durham Foundation
William Dean Countryside and
   Educational Trust
DLM Charitable Trust
Eden Arts Trust
John Feeney Charitable
   Bequest
Fidelity UK Foundation
Earl Fitzwilliam Charitable
   Trust
Four Lanes Trust
Frognal Trust
Greater Bristol Foundation
Isle of Anglesey Charitable
   Trust
Graham Kirkham Foundation
Lyndhurst Settlement
Sir George Martin Trust
Peter Minet Trust
Horace Moore Charitable Trust
Peter Moores Foundation
Norman Family Charitable
   Trust
Oxford Preservation Trust
Proven Family Trust
Christopher Rowbotham
   Charitable Trust
J B Rubens Charitable
   Foundation
Spitalfields Market Community
   Trust
Sportsman's Charity
Summerfield Charitable Trust

Sutton Coldfield Municipal
   Charities
Thomas Wall Trust

....

■ Recreational facilities

Funding priority

Arsenal Charitable Trust
Birmingham International
   Airport Community Trust
Palgrave Brown Foundation
Davidson (Nairn) Charitable
   Trust
Demigryphon Trust
English Schools' Football
   Association
Football Association National
   Sports Centre Trust
Hale Trust
Kathleen Hannay Memorial
   Charity
Lennox Hannay Charitable
   Trust
William Harding's Charity
Harrow Community Trust
Lord's Taverners
Clive Richards Charity Ltd
Scottish Coal Industry Special
   Welfare Fund
Ralph and Irma Sperring
   Charity
Stewards' Charitable Trust
Walter Swindon Charitable
   Trust
Charity of Thomas Wade &
   Others
Yorkshire County Cricket Club
   Charitable Youth Trust

Will consider

Adnams Charity
Ammco Trust
Ardwick Trust
Astor Foundation
Astor of Hever Trust
Bamford Charitable Foundation
Barbour Trust
Barclays Stockbrokers
   Charitable Trust
BBC Children in Need Appeal
Birmingham Foundation
Herbert & Peter Blagrave
   Charitable Trust
Peter Boizot Foundation
Boots Charitable Trust
Bryant Trust
Geoffrey Burton Charitable
   Trust
W A Cargill Charitable Trust
Caring for Kids
Carlton Television Trust
Chamberlain Foundation
Clover Trust
Cobb Charity

Colchester & Tendring
   Community Trust
George Henry Collins Charity
Norman Collinson Charitable
   Trust
County Durham Foundation
John Grant Davies Trust
De Clermont Charitable
   Company Ltd
William Dean Countryside and
   Educational Trust
Devon Community Foundation
Duis Charitable Trust
Wilfred & Elsie Elkes Charity
   Fund
Samuel William Farmer's Trust
John Feeney Charitable
   Bequest
Finnart House School Trust
Earl Fitzwilliam Charitable
   Trust
Florence's Charitable Trust
Football Association Youth
   Trust
Ford of Britain Trust
Four Lanes Trust
Fox Memorial Trust
Thomas Freke & Lady Norton
   Charity
Charles S French Charitable
   Trust
Greater Bristol Foundation
Constance Green Foundation
Greggs Trust
Hadrian Trust
Harborne Parish Lands Charity
Gay & Peter Hartley's Hillards
   Charitable Trust
Hedley Denton Charitable
   Trust
Hertfordshire Community
   Foundation
Hesslewood Children's Trust
Hobson Charity Ltd
Holywood Trust
Huddersfield Common Good
   Trust
Isle of Anglesey Charitable
   Trust
Isle of Dogs Community
   Foundation
Jeffrey Charitable Trust
Joicey Trust
Edward Cecil Jones Settlement
Anton Jurgens Charitable Trust
Graham Kirkham Foundation
Bryan Lancaster's Charity
Lauffer Family Charitable
   Foundation
Kennedy Leigh Charitable
   Trust
Levy Foundation
Enid Linder Foundation
Lintel Trust
Lloyds TSB Foundation for
   England and Wales

Lloyds TSB Foundation for
    Northern Ireland
Lofthouse Foundation
Mackintosh Foundation
Sir George Martin Trust
Medlock Charitable Trust
Mercers' Charitable
    Foundation
Mickel Fund
Middlesex County Rugby
    Football Union Memorial
    Fund
Peter Moores Foundation
Stanley Morrison Charitable
    Trust
Newport County Borough
    Welsh Church Fund
Norman Family Charitable
    Trust
Northcott Devon Foundation
Norwich Town Close Estate
    Charity
Oxfordshire Community
    Foundation
Parivar Trust
Pennycress Trust
Peugeot Charity Trust
Bernard Piggott Trust
Proven Family Trust
Radio Forth Help a Child
    Appeal
Rawdon-Smith Trust
John Rayner Charitable Trust
Cliff Richard Charitable Trust
Richmond Parish Lands Charity
Rotherwick Foundation
Rothley Trust
Christopher Rowbotham
    Charitable Trust
J B Rubens Charitable
    Foundation
Sir Walter St John's
    Educational Charity
John Scott Trust
Scouloudi Foundation
Sherburn House Charity
Skelton Bounty
Leslie Smith Foundation
South Square Trust
South Yorkshire Community
    Foundation
Spitalfields Market Community
    Trust
Sportsman's Charity
Summerfield Charitable Trust
Sutton Coldfield Municipal
    Charities
Tesco Charity Trust
Tisbury Telegraph Trust
Tompkins Foundation
Tower Hill Improvement Trust
Toy Trust
Variety Club Children's Charity
VEC Acorn Trust
Wakefield Trust
Thomas Wall Trust

Wates Foundation
Western Recreation Trust
Woodward Trust
Worcester Municipal Charities
Yardley Great Trust

....

■ Sports

Funding priority

Football Association National
    Sports Centre Trust
William Harding's Charity
Harrow Community Trust
Jack Petchey Foundation

Will consider

BBC Children in Need Appeal
Peter Boizot Foundation
Colchester & Tendring
    Community Trust
Douglas Charitable Trust
Florence's Charitable Trust
Football Association Youth
    Trust
Heart of England Community
    Foundation
Kirby Laing Foundation
Richard Langhorn Trust
Levy Foundation
W M Mann Foundation
Medlock Charitable Trust
Mercers' Charitable
    Foundation
Middlesex County Rugby
    Football Union Memorial
    Fund
Rawdon-Smith Trust
Richmond Parish Lands Charity
Christopher Rowbotham
    Charitable Trust
Searle Charitable Trust
Shipwrights Company
    Charitable Fund
Charity of Thomas Wade &
    Others

....

■ Sport for people
with a disability

Funding priority

Abbey National Charitable
    Trust Ltd
Aston Villa Charitable Trust
Birmingham Hospital Saturday
    Fund Medical Charity &
    Welfare Trust
CLA Charitable Trust
Lance Coates Charitable Trust
    1969
Football Association National
    Sports Centre Trust
Greater Bristol Foundation
Harrow Community Trust

Leeds & Holbeck Building
    Society Charitable
    Foundation
Northumberland Village Homes
    Trust
Jack Petchey Foundation
Ronald & Kathleen Pryor
    Charitable Trust
Mr and Mrs J A Pye's
    Charitable Settlement
Christopher Rowbotham
    Charitable Trust
Saddlers' Company Charitable
    Fund
Sportsman's Charity
Thames Community
    Foundation
Yorkshire Building Society
    Charitable Foundation

Will consider

Ardwick Trust
Ashby Charitable Trust
BBC Children in Need Appeal
BBC Radio Cambridgeshire –
    Trustline
Birmingham Foundation
Peter Boizot Foundation
Bothwell Charitable Trust
Wilfrid & Constance Cave
    Foundation
Chapman Charitable Trust
Colchester & Tendring
    Community Trust
George Henry Collins Charity
Consortium on Opportunities
    for Volunteering
County of Gloucestershire
    Community Foundation
Coutts & Co. Charitable Trust
Denman Charitable Trust
Duis Charitable Trust
Erskine Cunningham Hill Trust
Florence's Charitable Trust
Ford of Britain Trust
Constance Green Foundation
Kenneth Hargreaves Charitable
    Trust
Gay & Peter Hartley's Hillards
    Charitable Trust
N & P Hartley Memorial Trust
Dorothy Hay-Bolton Charitable
    Trust
Heart of England Community
    Foundation
Hedley Denton Charitable
    Trust
Alan Edward Higgs Charity
Huddersfield Common Good
    Trust
Jewish Child's Day
Edward Cecil Jones Settlement
Kidani Memorial Trust
Kirby Laing Foundation
Richard Langhorn Trust

Lauffer Family Charitable
    Foundation
Levy Foundation
Lloyds TSB Foundation for
    England and Wales
Lloyds TSB Foundation for
    Northern Ireland
Lloyds TSB Foundation for
    Scotland
Ronald McDonald Children's
    Charities Limited
W M Mann Foundation
Medlock Charitable Trust
Mercers' Charitable
    Foundation
Merchants House of Glasgow
Middlesex County Rugby
    Football Union Memorial
    Fund
Keith and Joan Mindelsohn
    Charitable Trust
Peter Minet Trust
Newport County Borough
    Welsh Church Fund
Norman Family Charitable
    Trust
Northcott Devon Foundation
Pastoral Care Trust
Patrick Charitable Trust
Peugeot Charity Trust
Fanny Rapaport Charitable
    Settlement
John Rayner Charitable Trust
Cliff Richard Charitable Trust
Rothley Trust
SEM Charitable Trust
Shipwrights Company
    Charitable Fund
Sobell Foundation
South Square Trust
Steinberg Family Charitable
    Trust
Tesco Charity Trust
Eric W Vincent Trust Fund
Charity of Thomas Wade &
    Others

Development, housing and employment

Funding priority
Paul Bassham Charitable Trust

Will consider
Alexandra Rose Day
James Beattie Charitable Trust
Beaufort House Trust
Bedford Charity
Thomas Betton's Charity for
    Pensions and Relief-in-Need
Bingham Trust
Bryant Trust
Arnold James Burton 1956
    Charitable Settlement
Community Fund
Gwendoline & Margaret Davies
    Charity
Englefield Charitable Trust
Thomas Farr Charitable Trust
Fast Track Trust Limited
G C Gibson Charitable Trust
Girdlers' Company Charitable
    Trust
Gretna Charitable Trust
Christopher Laing Foundation
Lethendy Charitable Trust
Margaret Foundation
G M Morrison Charitable Trust
National Catholic Fund
Norton Foundation
A R Taylor Charitable Trust
Constance Travis Charitable
    Trust
Douglas Turner Trust
Valentine Charitable Trust
Webb Memorial Trust
Welsh Church Fund –
    Carmarthenshire area
David Wilson Foundation
Wixamtree Trust

Community and economic development

Funding priority
Aberbrothock Charitable Trust
Sydney Black Charitable Trust
Community Foundation for
    Calderdale
Criffel Charitable Trust
Fast Track Trust Limited
Bishop of Guildford's
    Foundation
Hospital of God at Greatham
Ironmongers' Quincentenary
    Charitable Fund
O-Regen
Rosca Trust
Triodos Foundation

Will consider
Armourers and Brasiers'
    Gauntlet Trust
Barracks Trust of Newcastle-
    under-Lyme
C J M Charitable Trust
Cattanach Charitable Trust
Comic Relief
Miriam K Dean Refugee Trust
    Fund
Denton Charitable Trust
Derbyshire Community
    Foundation
Lord Faringdon Charitable
    Trust
Joseph Hopkins Charity
Methodist Relief and
    Development Fund
Monmouthshire County Council
    Welsh Church Act Fund
Newby Trust Limited
Norman Family Charitable
    Trust
Northampton Municipal Church
    Charities
Eleanor Rathbone Charitable
    Trust
Sir James Reckitt Charity
Scurrah Wainwright Charity

....

■ Community/ neighbourhood development
Funding priority
Allachy Trust
Anglo-German Foundation for
    Study of Industrial Society
AS Charitable Trust
Ashby Charitable Trust
BBC Radio Cambridgeshire –
    Trustline
James Beattie Charitable Trust
Charles Brotherton Trust
Buckinghamshire Foundation
J A Clark Charitable Trust
Cleary Foundation
Cobb Charity
Community Foundation for
    Northern Ireland
County Durham Foundation
Cumber Family Charitable
    Trust
John Grant Davies Trust
Essex Community Foundation
Esmée Fairbairn Foundation
Fifty Fund
Football Association National
    Sports Centre Trust
Four Lanes Trust
Gatsby Charitable Foundation
Greater Bristol Foundation
J C Green Charitable
    Settlement
Hampton Fuel Allotment
    Charity

Kathleen Hannay Memorial
  Charity
Lord and Lady Haskel
  Charitable Foundation
Hyde Park Place Estate Charity
Isle of Dogs Community
  Foundation
John Jarrold Trust
Sir James Knott Trust
Allen Lane Foundation
Leeds & Holbeck Building
  Society Charitable
  Foundation
Lofthouse Foundation
Milton Keynes Community
  Foundation
Minge's Gift
John Moores Foundation
Morgan Stanley International
  Foundation
Morris Charitable Trust
Kitty and Daniel Nabarro
  Charitable Trust
Noon Foundation
Novi Most International
Oxfordshire Community
  Foundation
Peabody Community Fund
J D Player Endowment Fund
Puebla Charitable Trust
St Thomas' Dole Charity
Sir James & Lady Scott Trust
Scottish Churches Community
  Trust
South Yorkshire Community
  Foundation
C Paul Thackray General
  Charitable Trust
Thames Community
  Foundation
Trust Thamesmead Limited
VEC Acorn Trust
Waterside Trust
Wiltshire and Swindon
  Community Foundation

Will consider
AIM Foundation
Viscount Amory's Charitable
  Trust
Arkleton Trust
Aston Charities Trust Limited
Astor Foundation
BAA 21st Century
  Communities Trust
Barbour Trust
Barclays Stockbrokers
  Charitable Trust
Baring Foundation
Berkshire Community
  Foundation
Blanchminster Trust
Body Shop Foundation
Boots Charitable Trust
Britannia Building Society
  Foundation

E F Bulmer Benevolent Fund
Richard Cadbury Charitable
  Trust
Cadbury Schweppes
  Foundation
William A Cadbury Charitable
  Trust
Carnegie Dunfermline Trust
Wilfrid & Constance Cave
  Foundation
Chase Charity
Chipping Sodbury Town Lands
  Charity
Chrimes Family Charitable
  Trust
Church Urban Fund
City Parochial Foundation
John & Freda Coleman
  Charitable Trust
George Henry Collins Charity
Norman Collinson Charitable
  Trust
Community Foundation Serving
  Tyne & Wear and
  Northumberland
Congleton Inclosure Trust
Consortium on Opportunities
  for Volunteering
County of Gloucestershire
  Community Foundation
Cripplegate Foundation
Cwmbran Trust
Helen and Geoffrey de Freitas
  Charitable Trust
Demigryphon Trust
Devon Community Foundation
Douglas Charitable Trust
Dulverton Trust
W E Dunn Trust
Earley Charity
Eden Arts Trust
Wilfred & Elsie Elkes Charity
  Fund
John Ellerman Foundation
Enkalon Foundation
Ericson Trust
Ferguson Benevolent Fund Ltd
Fidelity UK Foundation
Earl Fitzwilliam Charitable
  Trust
Roy Fletcher Charitable Trust
Florence's Charitable Trust
Four Acre Trust
Gatwick Airport Community
  Trust
Robert Gavron Charitable Trust
GMC Trust
Greater Bristol Foundation
Greggs Trust
Walter Guinness Charitable
  Trust
Gulbenkian Foundation
GWR Community Trust
Hadrian Trust
Paul Hamlyn Foundation

Lennox Hannay Charitable
  Trust
Harborne Parish Lands Charity
Gay & Peter Hartley's Hillards
  Charitable Trust
Charles Hayward Foundation
Headley Trust
Hedgcock Bequest
Hertfordshire Community
  Foundation
Hilden Charitable Fund
Dorothy Holmes Charitable
  Trust
Holywood Trust
Hyde Charitable Trust
James Pantyfedwen
  Foundation
J G Joffe Charitable Trust
Johnson Foundation
Edward Cecil Jones Settlement
Kleinwort Benson Charitable
  Trust
Late Sir Pierce Lacy Charity
  Trust
Laing's Charitable Trust
Lankelly Foundation
Leathersellers' Company
  Charitable Fund
Lintel Trust
Lloyd's Charities Trust
Lloyds TSB Foundation for
  England and Wales
Lloyds TSB Foundation for
  Northern Ireland
London Law Trust
London Youth Trust
Lyndhurst Settlement
R W Mann Trustees Limited
Marsh Christian Trust
Mercers' Charitable
  Foundation
Methodist Relief and
  Development Fund
Peter Minet Trust
Mobbs Memorial Trust Ltd
George A Moore Foundation
Newport County Borough
  Welsh Church Fund
Northern Rock Foundation
Norwich Town Close Estate
  Charity
Notgrove Trust
Jack Petchey Foundation
Peugeot Charity Trust
Pilkington Charities Fund
J S F Pollitzer Charitable
  Settlement
Powell Foundation
Powys Welsh Church Fund
Prairie Trust
Ravensdale Trust
Richmond Parish Lands Charity
Rothley Trust
Christopher Rowbotham
  Charitable Trust

Joseph Rowntree Charitable
   Trust
Joseph Rowntree Foundation
Royal Docks Trust
Russell Trust
St Hilda's Trust
St James' Trust Settlement
Scott Bader Commonwealth
   Ltd
Francis C Scott Charitable
   Trust
Sheldon Trust
Bishop Simeon CR Trust
SMB Trust
Sportsman's Charity
Stanley Foundation Ltd
Summerfield Charitable Trust
Tesco Charity Trust
Tudor Trust
Florence Turner Trust
Van Neste Foundation
Voluntary Action Luton
Weavers' Company Benevolent
   Fund
Wellfield Trust
Westcroft Trust
Westminster Amalgamated
   Charity
Woodroffe Benton Foundation
Worcester Municipal Charities
Worshipful Company of
   Founders Charities
W Wing Yip & Bros Charitable
   Trust
Yorkshire Agricultural Society

■ Employment, job creation schemes

Funding priority

Four Acre Trust
Greater Bristol Foundation
Harrow Community Trust
Mathew Trust
Minge's Gift
Morgan Stanley International
   Foundation
Morris Charitable Trust
Kitty and Daniel Nabarro
   Charitable Trust
Peabody Community Fund
Mrs C S Heber Percy
   Charitable Trust
Jack Petchey Foundation
South Yorkshire Community
   Foundation
Peter Stebbings Memorial
   Charity
Woodlands Trust (1015942)

Will consider

Abbey National Charitable
   Trust Ltd
Milly Apthorp Charitable Trust
Ardwick Trust
Astor Foundation

BAA 21st Century
   Communities Trust
Barbour Trust
Barclays Stockbrokers
   Charitable Trust
Britannia Building Society
   Foundation
R S Brownless Charitable
   Trust
E F Bulmer Benevolent Fund
William A Cadbury Charitable
   Trust
Wilfrid & Constance Cave
   Foundation
Church Urban Fund
John & Freda Coleman
   Charitable Trust
Community Foundation for
   Northern Ireland
Congleton Inclosure Trust
Cray Trust
Douglas Charitable Trust
W E Dunn Trust
Earley Charity
Enkalon Foundation
Essex Fairway Charitable Trust
Esmée Fairbairn Foundation
Fifty Fund
Earl Fitzwilliam Charitable
   Trust
Gatwick Airport Community
   Trust
Robert Gavron Charitable Trust
J Paul Getty Jr Charitable Trust
Greggs Trust
H C D Memorial Fund
Hadfield Trust
Hampstead Wells and
   Campden Trust
Harborne Parish Lands Charity
Hertfordshire Community
   Foundation
Holywood Trust
Hyde Charitable Trust
Isle of Dogs Community
   Foundation
J G Joffe Charitable Trust
Edward Cecil Jones Settlement
Anton Jurgens Charitable Trust
Sir James Knott Trust
Lankelly Foundation
Lawlor Foundation
Leathersellers' Company
   Charitable Fund
Lintel Trust
Lloyds TSB Foundation for
   Northern Ireland
Mercers' Charitable
   Foundation
Methodist Relief and
   Development Fund
Miles Trust for Putney and
   Roehampton Community
George A Moore Foundation
Peter Moores Foundation
Northcott Devon Foundation

Northern Rock Foundation
Notgrove Trust
Oxfordshire Community
   Foundation
Pilkington Charities Fund
J D Player Endowment Fund
Rainford Trust
E L Rathbone Charitable Trust
Rothley Trust
Christopher Rowbotham
   Charitable Trust
Royal Docks Trust
Russell Trust
Scott Bader Commonwealth
   Ltd
Francis C Scott Charitable
   Trust
Bishop Simeon CR Trust
Henry Smith Charity
Sportsman's Charity
Summerfield Charitable Trust
Tudor Trust
Wates Foundation
Wellfield Trust
Worshipful Company of
   Founders Charities
Yorkshire Agricultural Society

■ Regeneration schemes

Funding priority

Anglo-German Foundation for
   Study of Industrial Society
BAA 21st Century
   Communities Trust
County Durham Foundation
Gatsby Charitable Foundation
Greater Bristol Foundation
Hampton Fuel Allotment
   Charity
Minge's Gift
Morgan Stanley International
   Foundation
Morris Charitable Trust
Oxfordshire Community
   Foundation
Peabody Community Fund
Scottish Churches Community
   Trust
South Yorkshire Community
   Foundation

Will consider

Ardwick Trust
Aston Charities Trust Limited
Astor Foundation
Barbour Trust
Barclays Stockbrokers
   Charitable Trust
Britannia Building Society
   Foundation
William A Cadbury Charitable
   Trust
Church Urban Fund

Colchester & Tendring
  Community Trust
John & Freda Coleman
  Charitable Trust
Norman Collinson Charitable
  Trust
Community Foundation Serving
  Tyne & Wear and
  Northumberland
County of Gloucestershire
  Community Foundation
John Grant Davies Trust
Devon Community Foundation
W E Dunn Trust
Eden Arts Trust
Enkalon Foundation
Essex Fairway Charitable Trust
Esmée Fairbairn Foundation
Ferguson Benevolent Fund Ltd
Fishmongers' Company's
  Charitable Trust
Earl Fitzwilliam Charitable
  Trust
Florence's Charitable Trust
Four Acre Trust
Gatwick Airport Community
  Trust
J Paul Getty Jr Charitable Trust
Greater Bristol Foundation
Greggs Trust
Gulbenkian Foundation
Charles Hayward Foundation
Hedgcock Bequest
Hertfordshire Community
  Foundation
Holywood Trust
Hyde Charitable Trust
Joicey Trust
Kleinwort Benson Charitable
  Trust
Sir James Knott Trust
Laing's Charitable Trust
Lankelly Foundation
Linden Charitable Trust
Lintel Trust
Lloyd's Charities Trust
Lyndhurst Settlement
Marchday Charitable Fund
Marr-Munning Trust
Medlock Charitable Trust
Milton Keynes Community
  Foundation
Northern Rock Foundation
Rothley Trust
Joseph Rowntree Foundation
Royal Docks Trust
Francis C Scott Charitable
  Trust
Sir James & Lady Scott Trust
South Square Trust
Sportsman's Charity
Summerfield Charitable Trust
Bernard Sunley Charitable
  Foundation
Triangle Trust (1949) Fund
Voluntary Action Luton

Wates Foundation
Wellfield Trust
Woodroffe Benton Foundation
W Wing Yip & Bros Charitable
  Trust

Housing

Funding priority

Aberbrothock Charitable Trust
Adint Charitable Trust
Bergqvist Charitable Trust
Sydney Black Charitable Trust
Charles Boot Trust
Oliver Borthwick Memorial
  Trust
Bramble Charitable Trust
William A Cadbury Charitable
  Trust
Cattanach Charitable Trust
Chelsea Building Society
  Charitable Foundation
Cole Charitable Trust
Criffel Charitable Trust
Oliver Ford Charitable Trust
Simon Gibson Charitable Trust
Glass-House Trust
Bishop of Guildford's
  Foundation
Homeless International
Hospital of God at Greatham
Housing Associations
  Charitable Trust
Huddersfield Common Good
  Trust
John Jarrold Trust
Beatrice Laing Trust
Northampton Municipal Church
  Charities
Rank Foundation
Richard Rogers Charitable
  Settlement
Rosca Trust

Will consider

Ardwick Trust
Herbert & Peter Blagrave
  Charitable Trust
E F Bulmer Benevolent Fund
Richard Cadbury Charitable
  Trust
Harborne Parish Lands Charity
Inchrye Trust
Lloyds TSB Foundation for
  England and Wales
M N R Charitable Trust
Sir James & Lady Scott Trust
Wellfield Trust
Worshipful Company of
  Founders Charities
Alfred Haines Charitable Trust
Dr & Mrs A Darlington
  Charitable Trust
Alchemy Foundation
Chase Charity
H B Allen Charitable Trust

Milly Apthorp Charitable Trust
Armourers and Brasiers'
  Gauntlet Trust
Army Benevolent Fund
Lord Austin Trust
Berkshire Community
  Foundation
Boots Charitable Trust
Britannia Building Society
  Foundation
British Humane Association
Charles & Edna Broadhurst
  Charitable Trust
Charles Brotherton Trust
R S Brownless Charitable
  Trust
Cadbury Schweppes
  Foundation
A B Charitable Trust
Hadfield Trust
Hampstead Wells and
  Campden Trust
N & P Hartley Memorial Trust
Heart of England Community
  Foundation
Hemby Trust
Hesslewood Children's Trust
Hilden Charitable Fund
Edward Sydney Hogg
  Charitable Settlement
Sir Harold Hood's Charitable
  Trust
Antony Hornby Charitable Trust
Hyde Charitable Trust
Ingram Trust
Ireland Fund of Great Britain
Emmanuel Kaye Foundation
Knowles Charitable Trust
Langdale Trust
Langley Charitable Trust
Lankelly Foundation
Lazard Charitable Trust
Elaine & Angus Lloyd
  Charitable Trust
Lloyds TSB Foundation for
  Scotland
Wilfrid & Constance Cave
  Foundation
Charities Advisory Trust
Chippenham Borough Lands
  Charity
City and Metropolitan Welfare
  Charity
Derbyshire Community
  Foundation
W E Dunn Trust
DLA Charitable Trust
Mayor of London Borough of
  Enfield Appeal Fund
Earley Charity
Ericson Trust
Emmandjay Charitable Trust
John Feeney Charitable
  Bequest
Fiat Auto (UK) Charity

Fishmongers' Company's
  Charitable Trust
Ford of Britain Trust
Lord Ashdown Charitable Trust
ATP Charitable Trust
Barnes Workhouse Fund
Bates Charitable Trust
Morgan Blake Charitable Trust
Salo Bordon Charitable Trust
Consolidated Charity of Burton
  Upon Trent
Cranbury Foundation
Cairns Charitable Trust
W A Cargill Charitable Trust
W A Cargill Fund
Chelsea Square 1994 Trust
Coates Charitable Settlement
Comic Relief
Coutts & Co. Charitable Trust
Lord Cozens-Hardy Trust
Croydon Relief in Need
  Charities
David Charitable Trust
Helen and Geoffrey de Freitas
  Charitable Trust
Denton Charitable Trust
Grocers' Charity
Djanogly Foundation
Dorcas Trust
Douglas Charitable Trust
Exilarch's Foundation
Doris Field Charitable Trust
Gannochy Trust
J Paul Getty Jr Charitable Trust
Girdlers' Company Charitable
  Trust
Grand Charity of Freemasons
Grimsdale Charitable Trust
Hanley Trust (1987)
M A Hawe Settlement
Haymills Charitable Trust
Higgs Charitable Trust
Hillingdon Partnership Trust
Hobart Charitable Trust
Hobson Charity Ltd
J G Hogg Charitable Trust
Mary Homfray Charitable Trust
Joseph Hopkins Charity
Hornsey Parochial Charities
House of Industry Estate
Albert Hunt Trust
Hyde Park Place Estate Charity
  – civil trustees
Isle of Anglesey Charitable
  Trust
J A R Charitable Trust
Ursula Keyes Trust
Graham Kirkham Foundation
Kirkley Poor's Land Estate
Maurice and Hilda Laing
  Charitable Trust
Kirby Laing Foundation
Laslett's (Hinton) Charity
Lord Leverhulme Charitable
  Trust

Harry Livingstone Charitable
  Trust
Jack Livingstone Charitable
  Trust
Lyndhurst Trust
Francis Winham Foundation
Woburn 1986 Charitable Trust
Maurice Wohl Charitable Trust
Woolnoth Society Charitable
  Trust
Mrs A Lacy Tate Trust
Len Thomson Charitable Trust
A F Wallace Charity Trust
West Derby Wastelands
  Charity
Macfarlane Walker Trust
Mackintosh Foundation
R W Mann Trustees Limited
Hilda & Samuel Marks
  Foundation
D G Marshall of Cambridge
  Trust
Sir George Martin Trust
Helen Isabella McMorran
  Charitable Foundation
Mercers' Charitable
  Foundation
Merchant Taylors' Company
  Charities Fund
Tony Metherell Charitable
  Trust
Gerald Micklem Charitable
  Trust
Millichope Foundation
Monument Trust
Newby Trust Limited
Laurie Nidditch Foundation
Norman Family Charitable
  Trust
P F Charitable Trust
Gerald Palmer Trust
Constance Paterson Charitable
  Trust
Arthur James Paterson
  Charitable Trust
Pennycress Trust
Personal Assurance Charitable
  Trust
Persula Foundation
Philanthropic Trust
Cecil Pilkington Charitable
  Trust
J E Posnansky Charitable Trust
Eleanor Rathbone Charitable
  Trust
E L Rathbone Charitable Trust
Sir James Reckitt Charity
Rhododendron Trust
Richmond Parish Lands Charity
Rothley Trust
Royal Docks Trust
J S & E C Rymer Charitable
  Trust
Alan and Babette Sainsbury
  Charitable Fund
Frieda Scott Charitable Trust

Scottish Community
  Foundation
Sedbury Trust
Sefton Community Foundation
SMB Trust
South Square Trust
St Thomas Ecclesiastical
  Charity
Peter Stebbings Memorial
  Charity
Tay Charitable Trust
C B & H H Taylor 1984 Trust
Florence Turner Trust
United St Saviour's Charities
Eric W Vincent Trust Fund
Victor Mann Trust
Mary Webb Trust
Garfield Weston Foundation
Sheila Whitley Trust
Wiltshire and Swindon
  Community Foundation
Matthews Wrightson Charity
  Trust
Zephyr Charitable Trust
Northmoor Trust
Rayne Foundation
Rest Harrow Trust
Ripple Effect Foundation
Robertson Trust
Joseph Rowntree Foundation
Scotbelge Charitable Trust
Ralph and Irma Sperring
  Charity
Spitalfields Market Community
  Trust
St Jude's Trust
St Olave, St Thomas and St
  John United Charity
Stella Symons Charitable Trust
C A Rookes Charitable Trust
Lord Faringdon Charitable
  Trust
Roger Brooke Charitable Trust
City of Edinburgh Charitable
  Trusts
Barracks Trust of Newcastle-
  under-Lyme
St Laurence Charities for Poor

....

■ Hostels, night
  shelters

Funding priority
1970 Trust
Adnams Charity
Ashby Charitable Trust
Aston Villa Charitable Trust
BBC Radio Cambridgeshire –
  Trustline
James Beattie Charitable Trust
Bothwell Charitable Trust
Butchers' Company General
  Charities
Calypso Browning Trust
Cleopatra Trust
Dorus Trust

Epigoni Trust
Eveson Charitable Trust
Greater Bristol Foundation
Constance Green Foundation
Harrow Community Trust
Help Homeless Ltd
Hesslewood Children's Trust
Thomas J Horne Memorial
    Trust
Anton Jurgens Charitable Trust
Peter Kershaw Trust
King George's Fund for Sailors
Leathersellers' Company
    Charitable Fund
Leeds & Holbeck Building
    Society Charitable
    Foundation
Lintel Trust
Lloyds TSB Foundation for
    Channel Islands
Paul Lunn-Rockliffe Charitable
    Trust
Lynwood Trust
Magdalen Hospital Trust
Marchday Charitable Fund
Minge's Gift
Kitty and Daniel Nabarro
    Charitable Trust
Odin Charitable Trust
Philanthropic Trust
Austin & Hope Pilkington Trust
Ponton House Trust
South Yorkshire Community
    Foundation
Third House Trust
Tower Hill Improvement Trust
Wakefield Trust
Warwickshire Masonic
    Charitable Association Ltd
Woodroffe Benton Foundation
Yorkshire Building Society
    Charitable Foundation

Will consider
29th May 1961 Charitable
    Trust
Aston Charities Trust Limited
Astor Foundation
Bamford Charitable Foundation
Barbour Trust
Lord Barnby's Foundation
Barnwood House Trust
BBC Children in Need Appeal
Birmingham Hospital Saturday
    Fund Medical Charity &
    Welfare Trust
Anthony Bourne Foundation
Bridge House Estates Trust
    Fund
Britannia Building Society
    Foundation
Bryant Trust
Church Urban Fund
Colchester & Tendring
    Community Trust
George Henry Collins Charity

Community Foundation Serving
    Tyne & Wear and
    Northumberland
Congleton Inclosure Trust
Coppings Trust
County Durham Foundation
Cripplegate Foundation
Harry Crook Foundation
Denman Charitable Trust
Derbyshire Community
    Foundation
Devon Community Foundation
Double 'O' Charity Ltd
Duis Charitable Trust
Wilfred & Elsie Elkes Charity
    Fund
John Ellerman Foundation
Erskine Cunningham Hill Trust
Essex Community Foundation
Earl Fitzwilliam Charitable
    Trust
Forte Charitable Trust
Robert Gavron Charitable Trust
Girdlers' Company Charitable
    Trust
Godinton Charitable Trust
Greggs Trust
Hadrian Trust
Hampton Fuel Allotment
    Charity
Lennox Hannay Charitable
    Trust
Haramead Trust
R J Harris Charitable
    Settlement
Harrison & Potter Trust
Gay & Peter Hartley's Hillards
    Charitable Trust
Charles Hayward Foundation
Hemby Trust
Hertfordshire Community
    Foundation
Alan Edward Higgs Charity
Hilden Charitable Fund
Dorothy Holmes Charitable
    Trust
Holywood Trust
Hospital Saturday Fund
    Charitable Trust
James Thom Howat Charitable
    Trust
Miss Agnes H Hunter's Trust
Hyde Charitable Trust
Inverforth Charitable Trust
Charles Irving Charitable Trust
Joicey Trust
Edward Cecil Jones Settlement
Boris Karloff Charitable
    Foundation
Sir James Knott Trust
Late Sir Pierce Lacy Charity
    Trust
Laing's Charitable Trust
Mrs F B Laurence Charitable
    Trust
Leach Fourteenth Trust

Lloyds TSB Foundation for
    Northern Ireland
Lyndhurst Settlement
John Lyon's Charity
Sir George Martin Trust
Medlock Charitable Trust
Milton Keynes Community
    Foundation
John Moores Foundation
Morgan Stanley International
    Foundation
Northcott Devon Foundation
Oakdale Trust
Ogilvie Charities Deed 2
Oxfordshire Community
    Foundation
Pastoral Care Trust
Patients' Aid Association
    Hospital & Medical
    Charities Trust
Harry Payne Trust
Jack Petchey Foundation
Peugeot Charity Trust
Pilkington Charities Fund
John Pitman Charitable Trust
Simone Prendergast Charitable
    Trust
Pye Foundation
Mr and Mrs J A Pye's
    Charitable Settlement
Rainford Trust
Ravensdale Trust
Cliff Richard Charitable Trust
Mrs L D Rope Third Charitable
    Settlement
Rothley Trust
Christopher Rowbotham
    Charitable Trust
Russell Trust
St James' Trust Settlement
St Mary-le-Strand Charity
Francis C Scott Charitable
    Trust
Sir James & Lady Scott Trust
Servite Sisters' Charitable
    Trust Fund
Skelton Bounty
Henry Smith Charity
Sobell Foundation
Stanley Foundation Ltd
Summerfield Charitable Trust
Swan Trust
Tisbury Telegraph Trust
Triangle Trust (1949) Fund
Tudor Trust
Scurrah Wainwright Charity
Michael and Anna Wix
    Charitable Trust
Yapp Charitable Trust

....

■ Housing advice
services
Funding priority
BBC Radio Cambridgeshire –
    Trustline

Calypso Browning Trust
Greater Bristol Foundation
Thomas J Horne Memorial
   Trust
Peter Kershaw Trust
Leeds & Holbeck Building
   Society Charitable
   Foundation
Lintel Trust
Philanthropic Trust
Austin & Hope Pilkington Trust
South Yorkshire Community
   Foundation
Woodroffe Benton Foundation

Will consider
Abel Charitable Trust
Age Concern Scotland
   Enterprise Fund
Dorothy Gertrude Allen
   Memorial Fund
Aston Charities Trust Limited
Astor Foundation
Barbour Trust
BBC Children in Need Appeal
James Beattie Charitable Trust
Bisgood Charitable Trust
Bridge House Estates Trust
   Fund
Church Urban Fund
City Parochial Foundation
Community Foundation for
   Northern Ireland
Coppings Trust
County Durham Foundation
County of Gloucestershire
   Community Foundation
Derbyshire Community
   Foundation
Devon Community Foundation
Wilfred & Elsie Elkes Charity
   Fund
Fifty Fund
J G Graves Charitable Trust
Greggs Trust
Hadrian Trust
Haramead Trust
R J Harris Charitable
   Settlement
Gay & Peter Hartley's Hillards
   Charitable Trust
Charles Hayward Foundation
Hedgcock Bequest
Help Homeless Ltd
Hertfordshire Community
   Foundation
Alan Edward Higgs Charity
Hilden Charitable Fund
Dorothy Holmes Charitable
   Trust
Miss Agnes H Hunter's Trust
Hyde Charitable Trust
Elton John Aids Foundation
Joicey Trust
Sir James Knott Trust
Bryan Lancaster's Charity

Mrs F B Laurence Charitable
   Trust
Lloyd's Charities Trust
Lloyds TSB Foundation for
   Northern Ireland
Lyndhurst Settlement
Marchday Charitable Fund
Marsh Christian Trust
Milton Keynes Community
   Foundation
Northern Rock Foundation
Oxfordshire Community
   Foundation
Eleanor Palmer Trust
Pastoral Care Trust
Jack Petchey Foundation
Pilkington Charities Fund
J D Player Endowment Fund
Mrs L D Rope Third Charitable
   Settlement
St James' Trust Settlement
Francis C Scott Charitable
   Trust
Sir James & Lady Scott Trust
Henry Smith Charity
Sobell Foundation
Summerfield Charitable Trust
Tisbury Telegraph Trust
Triangle Trust (1949) Fund
Scurrah Wainwright Charity
Worcester Municipal Charities
Yorkshire Building Society
   Charitable Foundation

....

■ Social housing
Funding priority
R M 1956 Burton Charitable
   Trust
Greater Bristol Foundation

Will consider
Adnams Charity
Hemby Trust
Leathersellers' Company
   Charitable Fund
Medlock Charitable Trust
Northcott Devon Foundation
Christopher Rowbotham
   Charitable Trust

....

■ Supported
accommodation
Funding priority
Calypso Browning Trust
Eveson Charitable Trust
Greater Bristol Foundation
Leathersellers' Company
   Charitable Fund
Third House Trust

Will consider
Wilfrid & Constance Cave
   Foundation

County of Gloucestershire
   Community Foundation
Cripplegate Foundation
Duis Charitable Trust
Erskine Cunningham Hill Trust
Forte Charitable Trust
Girdlers' Company Charitable
   Trust
Harborne Parish Lands Charity
Charles Hayward Foundation
Lloyds TSB Foundation for
   Northern Ireland
Peter Minet Trust
Northcott Devon Foundation
Northern Rock Foundation
Pastoral Care Trust
Sherburn House Charity
Tudor Trust
Weavers' Company Benevolent
   Fund
Yapp Charitable Trust

Education & training

Funding priority

Almondsbury Charity
Altajir Trust
Band (1976) Trust
Paul Bassham Charitable Trust
Blanchminster Trust
Bowland Charitable Trust
British Sugar Foundation
Britten Foundation
Charles Brotherton Trust
Burall Charitable Trust
Carron Charitable Trust
Clore Duffield Foundation
Commonwealth Relations Trust
Alex Deas Charitable Trust
Dickon Trust
Edith M Ellis 1985 Charitable Trust
F P Limited Charitable Trust
Allan and Nesta Ferguson Charitable Settlement
Jacqueline and Michael Gee Charitable Trust
Goldschmied Charitable Settlement
Gosling Foundation Ltd
Griffith UK Foundation
Guildry Incorporation of Perth
Harbo Charities Limited
Harbour Foundation
William Harding's Charity
Heart of England Radio Charitable Trust
Simon Heller Charitable Settlement
Hitachi Europe Charitable Trust
Sir Julian Hodge Charitable Trust
Horne Foundation
Worshipful Company of Innholders General Charity Fund
Kass Charitable Trust
Kathleen Trust
Robert Kitchin
Arnold Lee Charitable Trust
MacRobert Trust
Ian Mactaggart Fund
Medlock Charitable Trust
Mitsubishi Corporation Fund for Europe and Africa
Oliver Morland Charitable Trust
Morris Charitable Trust
Mutual Trust Group
Padwa Charitable Foundation
Personal Assurance Charitable Trust
Rothley Trust
Sarum St Michael Educational Charity
Second Sidbury Trust

Sudborough Foundation
Connie and Albert Taylor Charitable Trust
Thompson Family Charitable Trust
Tompkins Foundation
Trusthouse Charitable Foundation •
Underwood Trust
Warwickshire Masonic Charitable Association Ltd
Howard Watson Symington Memorial Charity
Lionel Wigram Memorial Trust
Maurice Wohl Charitable Trust
Worshipful Company of Chartered Accountants General Charitable Trust

Will consider

Acacia Charitable Trust
Aldgate and All Hallows Barking Exhibition Foundation
Alliance Family Foundation
Ambika Paul Foundation
Sir John & Lady Amory's Charitable Trust
Mary Andrew Charitable Trust
Anglo Hong Kong Trust
Armenian General Benevolent Union London Trust
A J H Ashby Will Trust
Lord Ashdown Charitable Trust
Ashworth Charitable Trust
Associated Country Women of World
Astor of Hever Trust
Atlantic Foundation
ATP Charitable Trust
Balcombe Charitable Trust
Bearder Charity
James Beattie Charitable Trust
Beaufort House Trust
John Beckwith Charitable Trust
Bedford Charity
Rowan Bentall Charitable Trust
Bergqvist Charitable Trust
Bintaub Charitable Trust
Isabel Blackman Foundation
Neville & Elaine Blond Charitable Trust
Booth Charities
Sir William Boreman's Foundation
Viscountess Boyd Charitable Trust
Bristol Charities
Britannia Building Society Foundation
British Record Industry Trust
Mrs E E Brown Charitable Settlement
Burden Trust
Arnold James Burton 1956 Charitable Settlement

R M 1956 Burton Charitable Trust
Cadbury Schweppes Foundation
William A Cadbury Charitable Trust
Cairns Charitable Trust
Campden Charities
Carlton House Charitable Trust
Sir Ernest Cassel Educational Trust
Wilfrid & Constance Cave Foundation
Cemlyn-Jones Trust
Chamberlain Foundation
Chapman Charitable Trust
Charitworth Limited
Chippenham Borough Lands Charity
Chipping Sodbury Town Lands Charity
Chownes Foundation
Hilda & Alice Clark Charitable Trust
Cleveland Community Foundation
Coates Charitable Settlement
John Coates Charitable Trust
Denise Cohen Charitable Trust
Col-Reno Ltd
E Alec Colman Charitable Fund Ltd
Sir Jeremiah Colman Gift Trust
Sir James Colyer-Fergusson's Charitable Trust
Comino Foundation
Community Foundation for Greater Manchester
Community Foundation Serving Tyne & Wear and Northumberland
Gordon Cook Foundation
Cooper Charitable Trust
Alice Ellen Cooper-Dean Charitable Foundation
Duke of Cornwall's Benevolent Fund
Corona Charitable Trust
Craignish Trust
Cranbury Foundation
Crescent Trust
Cripplegate Foundation
Cumber Family Charitable Trust
Dennis Curry Charitable Trust
Cwmbran Trust
Daily Telegraph Charitable Trust
Daiwa Anglo-Japanese Foundation
David Charitable Trust
De La Rue Charitable Trust
Richard Desmond Charitable Trust
Devon Educational Trust

Duke of Devonshire's
    Charitable Trust
Djanogly Foundation
Dorcas Trust
Drapers' Charitable Fund
Gilbert & Eileen Edgar
    Foundation
William Edwards Educational
    Charity
George Elias Charitable Trust
Ellinson Foundation Ltd
Emerging Markets Charity for
    Children
Emmandjay Charitable Trust
Englefield Charitable Trust
Eranda Foundation
Mihran Essefian Charitable
    Trust
Douglas Heath Eves Charitable
    Trust
Thomas Farr Charitable Trust
Farthing Trust
Doris Field Charitable Trust
Florence's Charitable Trust
Flow Foundation
Forbesville Limited
Forte Charitable Trust
Foyle Foundation
Charles Henry Foyle Trust
Isaac and Freda Frankel
    Memorial Charitable Trust
Mejer and Gertrude Miriam
    Frydman Foundation
Fulmer Charitable Trust
Gannochy Trust
G C Gibson Charitable Trust
Girdlers' Company Charitable
    Trust
GNC Trust
Golsoncott Foundation
Grantham Yorke Trust
Great Stone Bridge Trust of
    Edenbridge
J C Green Charitable
    Settlement
Gretna Charitable Trust
Guardian Foundation
Walter Guinness Charitable
    Trust
Gur Trust
Hackney Parochial Charities
Hadfield Trust
Eleanor Hamilton Educational
    and Charitable Trust
Hampton Fuel Allotment
    Charity
Harbour Charitable Trust
Hare of Steep Charitable Trust
Kenneth Hargreaves Charitable
    Trust
Harris Charity
R J Harris Charitable
    Settlement
Maurice Hatter Foundation
Dorothy Hay-Bolton Charitable
    Trust

Haymills Charitable Trust
May Hearnshaw's Charity
Michael & Morven Heller
    Charitable Foundation
Hemby Trust
Henley Educational Charity
Philip Henman Trust
Highcroft Charitable Trust
Hillingdon Partnership Trust
Hitchin Educational Foundation
Hobart Charitable Trust
Hobson Charity Ltd
Jane Hodge Foundation
J G Hogg Charitable Trust
P H Holt Charitable Trust
Sir Harold Hood's Charitable
    Trust
Hoover Foundation
Clifford Howarth Charity
    Settlement
Hyde Park Place Estate Charity
Iliffe Family Charitable Trust
Imerys South West Charitable
    Trust
Isle of Anglesey Charitable
    Trust
J A R Charitable Trust
Jephcott Charitable Trust
Jerwood Foundation and
    Jerwood Charitable
    Foundation
Bernard Kahn Charitable Trust
Keren Association
E & E Kernkraut Charities
    Limited
Kidani Memorial Trust
Mary Kinross Charitable Trust
Graham Kirkham Foundation
Kobler Trust
Kohn Foundation
Neil Kreitman Foundation
Rachel & Jack Lass Charities
    Ltd
Lauchentilly Charitable
    Foundation 1988
Lauffer Family Charitable
    Foundation
Carole & Geoffrey Lawson
    Foundation
Lawson Charitable Foundation
Lawson-Beckman Charitable
    Trust
P Leigh-Bramwell Trust 'E'
Mark Leonard Trust
Lethendy Charitable Trust
Lord Leverhulme Charitable
    Trust
Ralph Levy Charitable
    Company Ltd
Linbury Trust
Lindale Educational
    Foundation
Elaine & Angus Lloyd
    Charitable Trust
W M & B W Lloyd Trust
Localtrent Ltd

Lotus Foundation
Luck-Hille Foundation
Ruth & Jack Lunzer Charitable
    Trust
Mackintosh Foundation
Magdalen Hospital Trust
R W Mann Trustees Limited
Marchig Animal Welfare Trust
Margaret Foundation
Hilda & Samuel Marks
    Foundation
Marr-Munning Trust
Marsh Christian Trust
Charlotte Marshall Charitable
    Trust
Sir George Martin Trust
John Martin's Charity
Matliwala Family Charitable
    Trust
Maxwell Family Foundation
Mayfair Charities Ltd
Merchant Taylors' Company
    Charities Fund
Merchants House of Glasgow
Miller Foundation
Edgar Milward Charity
Monmouthshire County Council
    Welsh Church Act Fund
Peter Moores Foundation
Morel Charitable Trust
J P Morgan Fleming
    Educational Trust and
    Foundation
Mr and Mrs J T Morgan
    Foundation
G M Morrison Charitable Trust
Stanley Morrison Charitable
    Trust
Music Sales Charitable Trust
Newcomen Collett Foundation
Laurie Nidditch Foundation
Noon Foundation
Alderman Norman's
    Foundation
Northmoor Trust
Northumberland Village Homes
    Trust
Norton Foundation
Old Broad Street Charity Trust
Old Possum's Practical Trust
Raymond Oppenheimer
    Foundation
Pastoral Care Trust
Porter Foundation
John Porter Charitable Trust
J E Posnansky Charitable Trust
Nyda and Oliver Prenn
    Foundation
Privy Purse Charitable Trust
Puri Foundation
Pye Foundation
Rank Foundation
Eleanor Rathbone Charitable
    Trust
Rayne Foundation
Rest Harrow Trust

Rhodes Trust Public Purposes
Fund
Richmond Parish Lands Charity
Ridgesave Limited
Rivendell Trust
Riverside Charitable Trust
Limited
Rotherwick Foundation
Rowan Charitable Trust
J B Rubens Charitable
Foundation
Rural Trust
Karim Rida Said Foundation
Alan and Babette Sainsbury
Charitable Fund
St Jude's Trust
St Katharine & Shadwell Trust
Saint Marylebone Educational
Foundation
Salt Foundation
Basil Samuel Charitable Trust
Coral Samuel Charitable Trust
Scots Trust
Scottish Community
Foundation
Scottish International
Education Trust
Samuel Sebba Charitable
Trust
Sefton Community Foundation
Ayrton Senna Foundation
Shaftoe Educational
Foundation
Shears Charitable Trust
Archie Sherman Cardiff
Charitable Foundation
Archie Sherman Charitable
Trust
Bishop Simeon CR Trust
E C Sosnow Charitable Trust
Souldern Trust
Southover Manor General
Education Trust
Spitalfields Market Community
Trust
W W Spooner Charitable Trust
Rosalyn and Nicholas Springer
Charitable Trust
Stanley Foundation Ltd
Stervon Ltd
Stevenson Family's Charitable
Trust
M J C Stone Charitable Trust
Peter Stormonth Darling
Charitable Trust
Peter Storrs Trust
W O Street Charitable
Foundation
Sueberry Ltd
Sutton Coldfield Municipal
Charities
John Swire (1989) Charitable
Trust
Stella Symons Charitable Trust
Tallow Chandlers Benevolent
Fund

Talteg Ltd
Tay Charitable Trust
A R Taylor Charitable Trust
C B & H H Taylor 1984 Trust
Tesco Charity Trust
Thompson Charitable Trust
Sue Thomson Foundation
Tilda Foundation
Company of Tobacco Pipe
Makers and Tobacco
Blenders Benevolent Fund
Tower Hill Improvement Trust
Towry Law Charitable Trust
Constance Travis Charitable
Trust
Triangle Trust (1949) Fund
Truedene Co. Ltd
Douglas Turner Trust
R D Turner Charitable Trust
Vale of Glamorgan Welsh
Church Fund
Valentine Charitable Trust
Bernard Van Leer Foundation
Vardy Foundation
Roger Vere Foundation
Nigel Vinson Charitable Trust
William and Ellen Vinten Trust
Robert and Felicity Waley-
Cohen Charitable Trust
Walton Foundation
Sir Siegmund Warburg's
Voluntary Settlement
Mary Webb Trust
Weinstock Fund
Weldon UK Charitable Trust
Welsh Church Fund –
Carmarthenshire area
Garfield Weston Foundation
David Wilson Foundation
Wixamtree Trust
Maurice Wohl Charitable
Foundation
Charles Wolfson Charitable
Trust
Worcester Municipal Charities
Fred & Della Worms Charitable
Trust
Yorkshire Bank Charitable
Trust
Elizabeth & Prince Zaiger Trust

Education policy

Funding priority
Ashe Park Charitable Trust
Sydney Black Charitable Trust
Cadbury Schweppes
Foundation
City of Edinburgh Charitable
Trusts
Football Association National
Sports Centre Trust
Lynn Foundation

Will consider
Arts Council of Wales
Maud Elkington Charitable
Trust
Ellis Campbell Charitable
Foundation
Mary Homfray Charitable Trust
Laing's Charitable Trust
Marie Helen Luen Charitable
Trust
Millfield House Foundation
Monmouthshire County Council
Welsh Church Act Fund
Nuffield Foundation
Steinberg Family Charitable
Trust
I A Ziff Charitable Foundation

Pre-school education, nursery schools

Funding priority
Aberbrothock Charitable Trust
Sir John & Lady Amory's
Charitable Trust
Bergqvist Charitable Trust
BibleLands
Broadfield Trust
Childwick Trust
Charity of Thomas Dawson
Demigryphon Trust
Esmée Fairbairn Foundation
Football Association National
Sports Centre Trust
Four Lanes Trust
Angela Gallagher Memorial
Fund
Simon Gibson Charitable Trust
Glencore Foundation for
Education and Welfare
Gulbenkian Foundation
Hale Trust
Kenneth Hargreaves Charitable
Trust
Harrow Community Trust
Hedley Foundation
Hornsey Parochial Charities
Huddersfield Common Good
Trust
John Jarrold Trust
Judge Charitable Foundation
Anton Jurgens Charitable Trust
Kelsick's Educational
Foundation
King George's Fund for Sailors
Kennedy Leigh Charitable
Trust
Lynn Foundation
John Lyon's Charity
Muslim Hands
J F Newsome Charitable Trust
Oxfordshire Community
Foundation
William Price Charitable Trust

St Peter's Saltley Trust
St Thomas' Dole Charity
Bishop Simeon CR Trust
Sutton Trust
Walter Swindon Charitable
Trust
Ulverston Town Lands Charity
Bernard Van Leer Foundation
Woo Charitable Foundation

Will consider
Adnams Charity
Alexandra Rose Day
Pat Allsop Charitable Trust
Viscount Amory's Charitable
Trust
Anglian Water Trust Fund
Ardwick Trust
Ashby Charitable Trust
Paul Balint Charitable Trust
Balmore Trust
Bamford Charitable Foundation
Barbour Trust
Barnabas Charitable Trust
Barracks Trust of Newcastle-
under-Lyme
James Beattie Charitable Trust
Benham Charitable Settlement
Thomas Betton's Charity
(Educational)
Bingham Trust
Birmingham Foundation
Enid Blyton Trust for Children
Boots Charitable Trust
Bridge Trust
Charles & Edna Broadhurst
Charitable Trust
Edward Cadbury Charitable
Trust
Edward & Dorothy Cadbury
Trust
Richard Cadbury Charitable
Trust
Caring for Kids
Carlton Television Trust
Carnegie Dunfermline Trust
Carpenters' Company
Charitable Trust
John & Freda Coleman
Charitable Trust
George Henry Collins Charity
Congleton Inclosure Trust
Holbeche Corfield Charitable
Settlement
Coutts & Co. Charitable Trust
Lord Cozens-Hardy Trust
Cranbury Foundation
William Dean Countryside and
Educational Trust
DLA Charitable Trust
Double 'O' Charity Ltd
Dumfries and Galloway Council
Charitable Trusts
Earley Charity
Eden Arts Trust

Maud Elkington Charitable
Trust
Elmgrant Trust
Equitable Charitable Trust
Essex Community Foundation
Fairway Trust
Lord Faringdon Charitable
Trust
Samuel William Farmer's Trust
Earl Fitzwilliam Charitable
Trust
Football Association Youth
Trust
Ford of Britain Trust
Thomas Freke & Lady Norton
Charity
Gatwick Airport Community
Trust
Bishop of Guildford's
Foundation
GWR Community Trust
Hadfield Trust
Hadrian Trust
Robert Hall Charity
Hallam FM – Help a Hallam
Child Appeal
Paul Hamlyn Foundation
Harborne Parish Lands Charity
Charles Hayward Foundation
Headley Trust
Heart of England Community
Foundation
H J Heinz Company Limited
Charitable Trust
Hemby Trust
Henley Educational Charity
Hertfordshire Community
Foundation
Alan Edward Higgs Charity
Clifford Howarth Charity
Settlement
Isle of Dogs Community
Foundation
Sir Barry Jackson Trust and
County Fund
Jewish Child's Day
William Kendall's Charity
Sir James Knott Trust
Kreitman Foundation
Late Sir Pierce Lacy Charity
Trust
Laing's Charitable Trust
Christopher Laing Foundation
Laslett's (Hinton) Charity
William Leech Charity
Lloyds TSB Foundation for
England and Wales
Lloyds TSB Foundation for
Northern Ireland
Lockerbie Trust
Mercers' Charitable
Foundation
Miles Trust for Putney and
Roehampton Community
Mirfield Educational Charity
Mobbs Memorial Trust Ltd

Monmouthshire County Council
Welsh Church Act Fund
John Moores Foundation
Nigel Moores Family Charitable
Trust
Music Sound Foundation
NAM Charitable Trust
Newby Trust Limited
Noel Buxton Trust
Northampton Municipal Church
Charities
Northcott Devon Foundation
Norwich Town Close Estate
Charity
Oakley Charitable Trust
Old Enfield Charitable Trust
P F Charitable Trust
Palmer Foundation
Payne Charitable Trust
Harry Payne Trust
Pennycress Trust
A M Pilkington's Charitable
Trust
J S F Pollitzer Charitable
Settlement
Simone Prendergast Charitable
Trust
Prince Foundation
Mr and Mrs J A Pye's
Charitable Settlement
Rawdon-Smith Trust
Sir James Reckitt Charity
Sir James Roll Charitable Trust
Cecil Rosen Foundation
Rothley Trust
Joseph Rowntree Foundation
Saddlers' Company Charitable
Fund
Karim Rida Said Foundation
St James' Trust Settlement
St Olave, St Thomas and St
John United Charity
Salt Foundation
Annie Schiff Charitable Trust
Sherburn House Charity
Barnett & Sylvia Shine No 2
Charitable Trust
Steinberg Family Charitable
Trust
Sir Sigmund Sternberg
Charitable Foundation
Steventon Allotments & Relief-
in-Need Charity
Stone-Mallabar Charitable
Foundation
A B Strom & R Strom
Charitable Trust
Summerfield Charitable Trust
Bernard Sunley Charitable
Foundation
Sutton Coldfield Municipal
Charities
Charles and Elsie Sykes Trust
Tesco Charity Trust
Thames Community
Foundation

Tisbury Telegraph Trust
Tory Family Foundation
Towry Law Charitable Trust
Toy Trust
Florence Turner Trust
Miss S M Tutton Charitable
  Trust
Variety Club Children's Charity
Wakefield Trust
Warrington Church of England
  Educational Trust
William Williams Charity
Edith & Isaac Wolfson
  (Scotland) Trust
Women Caring Trust
Woodroffe Benton Foundation
Woodward Trust
Worcester Municipal Charities
York Children's Trust
Yorkshire Agricultural Society

Primary & secondary education

Funding priority

Aberbrothock Charitable Trust
Adnams Charity
Sir John & Lady Amory's
  Charitable Trust
Armourers and Brasiers'
  Gauntlet Trust
BAA 21st Century
  Communities Trust
Beaurepaire Trust
Bergqvist Charitable Trust
Thomas Betton's Charity
  (Educational)
BibleLands
Broadfield Trust
Cadbury Schweppes
  Foundation
Carter's Educational
  Foundation
Sir John Cass's Foundation
CfBT Education Services
Church Burgesses Educational
  Foundation
Charity of Thomas Dawson
Football Association National
  Sports Centre Trust
Gatsby Charitable Foundation
Simon Gibson Charitable Trust
Glencore Foundation for
  Education and Welfare
Great Britain Sasakawa
  Foundation
Gulbenkian Foundation
Hale Trust
Hedley Foundation
Henley Educational Charity
Hornsey Parochial Charities
Hulme Trust Estates
  (Educational)

Isle of Dogs Community
  Foundation
Sir Barry Jackson Trust and
  County Fund
John Jarrold Trust
Judge Charitable Foundation
Kelsick's Educational
  Foundation
King George's Fund for Sailors
Lambeth Endowed Charities
Lawlor Foundation
John Lyon's Charity
Magdalen & Lasher Charity
D G Marshall of Cambridge
  Trust
Mercers' Charitable
  Foundation
Morgan Stanley International
  Foundation
Muslim Hands
J F Newsome Charitable Trust
Philological Foundation
William Price Charitable Trust
Clive Richards Charity Ltd
Rooke Atlay Charitable Trust
Karim Rida Said Foundation
St Peter's Saltley Trust
St Thomas' Dole Charity
Salt Foundation
SEM Charitable Trust
Sheffield Bluecoat & Mount
  Pleasant Educational
  Foundation
Bishop Simeon CR Trust
Sutton Trust
Walter Swindon Charitable
  Trust
Thoresby Charitable Trust
Ulverston Town Lands Charity
Bernard Van Leer Foundation
Vandervell Foundation
Edith & Isaac Wolfson
  (Scotland) Trust
Woo Charitable Foundation
Woodroffe Benton Foundation

Will consider

Pat Allsop Charitable Trust
Viscount Amory's Charitable
  Trust
Anglian Water Trust Fund
Arts Council of Wales
Balmore Trust
Bamford Charitable Foundation
Barracks Trust of Newcastle-
  under-Lyme
James Beattie Charitable Trust
Beit Trust
Benham Charitable Settlement
Bingham Trust
Boots Charitable Trust
Bridge Trust
Charles & Edna Broadhurst
  Charitable Trust
Bryant Trust

Edward Cadbury Charitable
  Trust
Edward & Dorothy Cadbury
  Trust
W A Cargill Charitable Trust
W A Cargill Fund
Caring for Kids
Carlton Television Trust
Carnegie Dunfermline Trust
Carpenters' Company
  Charitable Trust
John & Freda Coleman
  Charitable Trust
Holbeche Corfield Charitable
  Settlement
Criffel Charitable Trust
Cripps Foundation
William Dean Countryside and
  Educational Trust
DLA Charitable Trust
Dumfries and Galloway Council
  Charitable Trusts
W E Dunn Trust
Earley Charity
Eden Arts Trust
Maud Elkington Charitable
  Trust
Essex Youth Trust
Fairway Trust
Lord Faringdon Charitable
  Trust
Samuel William Farmer's Trust
Football Association Youth
  Trust
Ford of Britain Trust
Four Lanes Trust
Thomas Freke & Lady Norton
  Charity
Gatwick Airport Community
  Trust
Bishop of Guildford's
  Foundation
Hadrian Trust
Robert Hall Charity
Paul Hamlyn Foundation
Harborne Parish Lands Charity
Kenneth Hargreaves Charitable
  Trust
Headley Trust
H J Heinz Company Limited
  Charitable Trust
Hesslewood Children's Trust
Alan Edward Higgs Charity
Clifford Howarth Charity
  Settlement
William Kendall's Charity
Sir James Knott Trust
Kreitman Foundation
Late Sir Pierce Lacy Charity
  Trust
William Leech Charity
Leverhulme Trade Charities
  Trust
Lockerbie Trust
Macfarlane Walker Trust
W M Mann Foundation

....

63

Sir George Martin Trust
Nancie Massey Charitable
   Trust
Matliwala Family Charitable
   Trust
Medlock Charitable Trust
Miles Trust for Putney and
   Roehampton Community
Minge's Gift
Mirfield Educational Charity
Mobbs Memorial Trust Ltd
Monmouthshire County Council
   Welsh Church Act Fund
Nigel Moores Family Charitable
   Trust
Music Sound Foundation
NAM Charitable Trust
Newby Trust Limited
Northampton Municipal Church
   Charities
Norwich Town Close Estate
   Charity
Notgrove Trust
Nuffield Foundation
Oakley Charitable Trust
Old Enfield Charitable Trust
P F Charitable Trust
Palmer Foundation
Charity Fund of Worshipful
   Company of Paviors
Payne Charitable Trust
Pennycress Trust
A M Pilkington's Charitable
   Trust
Prince Foundation
Mr and Mrs J A Pye's
   Charitable Settlement
Rawdon-Smith Trust
Sir James Reckitt Charity
Robertson Trust
Sir James Roll Charitable Trust
Mrs L D Rope Third Charitable
   Settlement
Cecil Rosen Foundation
Joseph Rowntree Foundation
St Mary-le-Strand Charity
St Olave, St Thomas and St
   John United Charity
Scott Bader Commonwealth
   Ltd
Barnett & Sylvia Shine No 2
   Charitable Trust
Steinberg Family Charitable
   Trust
Sir Sigmund Sternberg
   Charitable Foundation
Steventon Allotments & Relief-
   in-Need Charity
Stone-Mallabar Charitable
   Foundation
A B Strom & R Strom
   Charitable Trust
Summerfield Charitable Trust
Bernard Sunley Charitable
   Foundation

Sutton Coldfield Municipal
   Charities
Charles and Elsie Sykes Trust
Tesco Charity Trust
Thames Community
   Foundation
Tory Family Foundation
Towry Law Charitable Trust
Douglas Turner Trust
Florence Turner Trust
Miss S M Tutton Charitable
   Trust
Vodafone UK Foundation
Wakefield Trust
Warrington Church of England
   Educational Trust
Wates Foundation
Wellfield Trust
Westminster Foundation
William Williams Charity
Women Caring Trust
Worcester Municipal Charities
Worshipful Company of
   Founders Charities
York Children's Trust
Yorkshire Agricultural Society

....

■ Choir schools

Funding priority

Becketts & Sargeants
   Educational Foundation
Sir John Cass's Foundation
Church Burgesses Educational
   Foundation
Charity of Thomas Dawson
Demigryphon Trust
Famos Foundation Trust
Simon Gibson Charitable Trust
Lynn Foundation
Ouseley Trust
Panahpur Charitable Trust
Clive Richards Charity Ltd
St Mary-le-Strand Charity
St Peter's Saltley Trust
St Thomas' Dole Charity
Sheffield Bluecoat & Mount
   Pleasant Educational
   Foundation
Thoresby Charitable Trust
Verdon-Smith Family Charitable
   Settlement
Woo Charitable Foundation

Will consider

Archbishop of Canterbury's
   Charitable Trust
Paul Balint Charitable Trust
James Beattie Charitable Trust
Britland Charitable Trust
Carlton Television Trust
CfBT Education Services
DLM Charitable Trust
Dugdale Charitable Trust
Elmgrant Trust

Earl Fitzwilliam Charitable
   Trust
Ford of Britain Trust
Constance Green Foundation
Hadrian Trust
Kathleen Hannay Memorial
   Charity
Harborne Parish Lands Charity
Kenneth Hargreaves Charitable
   Trust
Hesslewood Children's Trust
Jerusalem Trust
Sir James Knott Trust
Late Sir Pierce Lacy Charity
   Trust
Christopher Laing Foundation
John Lyon's Charity
Sir George Martin Trust
Mercers' Charitable
   Foundation
Norwich Town Close Estate
   Charity
Notgrove Trust
Owen Family Trust
Mrs L D Rope Third Charitable
   Settlement
St Hilda's Trust
Stanley Foundation Ltd
Summerfield Charitable Trust
Bernard Sunley Charitable
   Foundation
Sutton Coldfield Municipal
   Charities
Thames Community
   Foundation
Tisbury Telegraph Trust
Wellfield Trust
Worcester Municipal Charities
Worshipful Company of
   Founders Charities

....

■ Faith schools

Funding priority

Becketts & Sargeants
   Educational Foundation
Bonamy Charitable Trust
R M 1956 Burton Charitable
   Trust
Charity of Theresa Harriet
   Mary Delacour
Grahame Charitable
   Foundation
Melow Charitable Trust
Miles Trust for Putney and
   Roehampton Community
Fanny Rapaport Charitable
   Settlement
Tomchei Torah Charitable
   Trust
Wychdale Ltd
Wychville Ltd

Will consider

James Beattie Charitable Trust
Demigryphon Trust

Ford of Britain Trust
Stanley Kalms Foundation
Kasner Charitable Trust
Maurice and Hilda Laing
   Charitable Trust
Jack Livingstone Charitable
   Trust
John Lyon's Charity
M D & S Charitable Trust
Magen Charitable Trust
Hilda & Samuel Marks
   Foundation
Melodor Ltd
Vyoel Moshe Charitable Trust
Chevras Ezras Nitzrochim Trust
Cecil Rosen Foundation
Annie Schiff Charitable Trust
Schreib Trust
Bassil Shippam and Alsford
   Trust
Sinclair Charitable Trust
Sparquote Limited
Cyril & Betty Stein Charitable
   Trust
Tajtelbaum Charitable Trust
Tisbury Telegraph Trust

■ Public and independent schools

Funding priority

Palgrave Brown Foundation
Church Burgesses Educational
   Foundation
Demigryphon Trust
Dove-Bowerman Trust
Simon Gibson Charitable Trust
Hulme Trust Estates
Peter Kershaw Trust
Lauchentilly Charitable
   Foundation 1988
Lynn Foundation
Midhurst Pensions Trust
Patrick Charitable Trust
William Price Charitable Trust
Sheffield Bluecoat & Mount
   Pleasant Educational
   Foundation
Mrs S H Troughton Charity
   Trust
Verdon-Smith Family Charitable
   Settlement

Will consider

Ashby Charitable Trust
Audi Design Foundation
Carlton Television Trust
CfBT Education Services
DLM Charitable Trust
Elmgrant Trust
Samuel William Farmer's Trust
Earl Fitzwilliam Charitable
   Trust
Godinton Charitable Trust

Hadrian Trust
Jeffrey Charitable Trust
Sir James Knott Trust
Late Sir Pierce Lacy Charity
   Trust
Christopher Laing Foundation
John Lyon's Charity
Sir George Martin Trust
Mercers' Charitable
   Foundation
Norwich Town Close Estate
   Charity
Notgrove Trust
Oakmoor Trust
Owen Family Trust
J S F Pollitzer Charitable
   Settlement
Rowanville Ltd
Saddlers' Company Charitable
   Fund
Leslie Smith Foundation
Bernard Sunley Charitable
   Foundation
Thoresby Charitable Trust
Welton Foundation
Wolfson Foundation
Worshipful Company of
   Founders Charities

■ Special needs schools

Funding priority

Abbey National Charitable
   Trust Ltd
Pat Allsop Charitable Trust
Ardwick Trust
Ashe Park Charitable Trust
Laura Ashley Foundation
BBC Radio Cambridgeshire –
   Trustline
Becketts & Sargeants
   Educational Foundation
BibleLands
Percy Bilton Charity Ltd
Birmingham Hospital Saturday
   Fund Medical Charity &
   Welfare Trust
Bonamy Charitable Trust
R M 1956 Burton Charitable
   Trust
Carlton Television Trust
Church Burgesses Educational
   Foundation
Cleary Foundation
Charity of Thomas Dawson
Dove-Bowerman Trust
Mayor of London Borough of
   Enfield Appeal Fund
Equitable Charitable Trust
Joyce Fletcher Charitable Trust
Angela Gallagher Memorial
   Fund
Simon Gibson Charitable Trust
Grahame Charitable
   Foundation

Constance Green Foundation
Gulbenkian Foundation
Hale Trust
Lennox Hannay Charitable
   Trust
Harebell Centenary Fund
Harrow Community Trust
Charles Hayward Foundation
May Hearnshaw's Charity
Clifford Howarth Charity
   Settlement
Leeds & Holbeck Building
   Society Charitable
   Foundation
Lloyds TSB Foundation for
   Channel Islands
London Law Trust
Lynn Foundation
Ronald McDonald Children's
   Charities Limited
Magdalen Hospital Trust
Magdalen & Lasher Charity
Medlock Charitable Trust
Miles Trust for Putney and
   Roehampton Community
Minge's Gift
Mugdock Children's Trust
Kitty and Daniel Nabarro
   Charitable Trust
Odin Charitable Trust
Ormsby Charitable Trust
Patients' Aid Association
   Hospital & Medical
   Charities Trust
Patrick Charitable Trust
Philological Foundation
William Price Charitable Trust
Clive Richards Charity Ltd
Karim Rida Said Foundation
Sir Walter St John's
   Educational Charity
St Peter's Saltley Trust
St Thomas' Dole Charity
Salt Foundation
Sheffield Bluecoat & Mount
   Pleasant Educational
   Foundation
Barbara A Shuttleworth
   Memorial Trust
Sobell Foundation
Walter Swindon Charitable
   Trust
C Paul Thackray General
   Charitable Trust
Thoresby Charitable Trust
Three Oaks Trust
Tubney Charitable Trust
John Watson's Trust
Wentwood Education Trust
White Rose Children's Aid
   International Charity
Woo Charitable Foundation
Yorkshire Building Society
   Charitable Foundation

Will consider

Adint Charitable Trust
Adnams Charity
Alchemy Foundation
Alexandra Rose Day
Ammco Trust
Astor Foundation
John Avins Trustees
Badley Memorial Trust
Baily Thomas Charitable Fund
Barbour Trust
Barclays Stockbrokers
    Charitable Trust
Philip Barker Charity
Barnabas Charitable Trust
Bartle Family Charitable Trust
BBC Children in Need Appeal
James Beattie Charitable Trust
Benham Charitable Settlement
Birmingham Foundation
Herbert & Peter Blagrave
    Charitable Trust
Blatchington Court Trust
Enid Blyton Trust for Children
Bonhomie United Charity
    Society
Boots Charitable Trust
Harry Bottom Charitable Trust
Viscountess Boyd Charitable
    Trust
British Humane Association
British Sugar Foundation
Charles & Edna Broadhurst
    Charitable Trust
Bryant Trust
Buckinghamshire Masonic
    Centenary Fund
Burdens Charitable Foundation
Audrey & Stanley Burton
    Charitable Trust
Caring for Kids
Carlton Television Trust
Carnegie Dunfermline Trust
Casey Trust
Wilfrid & Constance Cave
    Foundation
CfBT Education Services
Childwick Trust
City Parochial Foundation
Clover Trust
Community Fund
Congleton Inclosure Trust
Ernest Cook Trust
Coutts & Co. Charitable Trust
Lord Cozens-Hardy Trust
Cranbury Foundation
Harry Crook Foundation
D'Oyly Carte Charitable Trust
Baron Davenport's Charity
De Clermont Charitable
    Company Ltd
Double 'O' Charity Ltd
Dulverton Trust
Earley Charity
Ellis Campbell Charitable
    Foundation

Elmgrant Trust
Mayor of London Borough of
    Enfield Appeal Fund
Esmée Fairbairn Foundation
Samuel William Farmer's Trust
Ferguson Benevolent Fund Ltd
Fidelity UK Foundation
Finnart House School Trust
Fishmongers' Company's
    Charitable Trust
Ford of Britain Trust
Four Lanes Trust
Thomas Freke & Lady Norton
    Charity
Gannochy Trust
Girdlers' Company Charitable
    Trust
Godinton Charitable Trust
Good Neighbours Trust
Reginald Graham Charitable
    Trust
Greater Bristol Foundation
Greggs Trust
GWR Community Trust
Hadrian Trust
Robert Hall Charity
Hallam FM – Help a Hallam
    Child Appeal
Hampstead Wells and
    Campden Trust
Kathleen Hannay Memorial
    Charity
Harborne Parish Lands Charity
Kenneth Hargreaves Charitable
    Trust
Harrison & Potter Trust
Hartley Charitable Trust
N & P Hartley Memorial Trust
Hertfordshire Community
    Foundation
Hesslewood Children's Trust
Hilden Charitable Fund
Dorothy Holmes Charitable
    Trust
Holywood Trust
James Thom Howat Charitable
    Trust
Miss Agnes H Hunter's Trust
Inchrye Trust
Inverforth Charitable Trust
Isle of Dogs Community
    Foundation
Ruth & Lionel Jacobson Trust
    (Second Fund) No 2
Jarman Charitable Trust
Jeffrey Charitable Trust
Jewish Child's Day
Johnson Foundation
Joicey Trust
Edward Cecil Jones Settlement
Anton Jurgens Charitable Trust
Robert Kiln Charitable Trust
Sir James Knott Trust
Late Sir Pierce Lacy Charity
    Trust
Christopher Laing Foundation

Mrs F B Laurence Charitable
    Trust
Raymond & Blanche Lawson
    Charitable Trust
Lazard Charitable Trust
Leach Fourteenth Trust
Leathersellers' Company
    Charitable Fund
Kennedy Leigh Charitable
    Trust
Leng Charitable Trust
Levy Foundation
Lloyd's Charities Trust
Lloyds TSB Foundation for
    Northern Ireland
Lloyds TSB Foundation for
    Scotland
M N R Charitable Trust
Macfarlane Walker Trust
Helen Isabella McMorran
    Charitable Foundation
Marchday Charitable Fund
Sir George Martin Trust
Nancie Massey Charitable
    Trust
Mercers' Charitable
    Foundation
Gerald Micklem Charitable
    Trust
Milton Keynes Community
    Foundation
George A Moore Foundation
Morgan Stanley International
    Foundation
Music Sound Foundation
Newby Trust Limited
Alderman Newton's
    Educational Foundation
Norman Family Charitable
    Trust
North British Hotel Trust
Northcott Devon Foundation
Norwich Town Close Estate
    Charity
Notgrove Trust
Oakdale Trust
Old Enfield Charitable Trust
Parivar Trust
Harry Payne Trust
A M Pilkington's Charitable
    Trust
J S F Pollitzer Charitable
    Settlement
Powell Foundation
Rainford Trust
Fanny Rapaport Charitable
    Settlement
Märit and Hans Rausing
    Charitable Foundation
John Rayner Charitable Trust
Red Dragon Radio Trust
Cliff Richard Charitable Trust
Sir James Roll Charitable Trust
Mrs L D Rope Third Charitable
    Settlement
Cecil Rosen Foundation

Rothley Trust
Christopher Rowbotham
   Charitable Trust
Royal Eastern Counties
   Schools Limited
Russell Trust
Saddlers' Company Charitable
   Fund
St Hilda's Trust
St James's Place Foundation
St Mary-le-Strand Charity
R H Scholes Charitable Trust
Scott Bader Commonwealth
   Ltd
Sellafield Charity Trust Fund
SEM Charitable Trust
Simpson Education &
   Conservation Trust
Henry Smith Charity
Leslie Smith Foundation
Sobell Foundation
South Yorkshire Community
   Foundation
Sportsman's Charity
Peter Stebbings Memorial
   Charity
Strangward Trust
Summerfield Charitable Trust
Bernard Sunley Charitable
   Foundation
Sutton Coldfield Municipal
   Charities
Swann-Morton Foundation
Charles and Elsie Sykes Trust
Tesco Charity Trust
Sir Jules Thorn Charitable
   Trust
Tisbury Telegraph Trust
Tudor Trust
Ulverscroft Foundation
Variety Club Children's Charity
VEC Acorn Trust
Voluntary Action Luton
Wates Foundation
William Webster Charitable
   Trust
Wellfield Trust
Harold Hyam Wingate
   Foundation
Women at Risk
Woodward Trust
Worcester Municipal Charities
York Children's Trust

....

■ Education for excluded pupils and other non-attenders

Funding priority
Esmée Fairbairn Foundation
Greater Bristol Foundation
Paul Hamlyn Foundation
Harrow Community Trust
Hilden Charitable Fund
Kitty and Daniel Nabarro
   Charitable Trust

William Price Charitable Trust
Royal Eastern Counties
   Schools Limited
Sir Walter St John's
   Educational Charity
Weavers' Company Benevolent
   Fund

Will consider
Barbour Trust
BBC Children in Need Appeal
Boots Charitable Trust
Cadbury Schweppes
   Foundation
Casey Trust
Dulverton Trust
Equitable Charitable Trust
Ford of Britain Trust
Girdlers' Company Charitable
   Trust
Godinton Charitable Trust
Hadrian Trust
Harborne Parish Lands Charity
Charles Hayward Foundation
Laing's Charitable Trust
Christopher Laing Foundation
Leathersellers' Company
   Charitable Fund
London Law Trust
John Lyon's Charity
Mercers' Charitable
   Foundation
Miles Trust for Putney and
   Roehampton Community
Saddlers' Company Charitable
   Fund
Worcester Municipal Charities

Higher education

Funding priority
Aberbrothock Charitable Trust
AF Trust Company
Sylvia Aitken Charitable Trust
Ambrose & Ann Appelbe Trust
Armourers and Brasiers'
   Gauntlet Trust
Ashworth Charitable Trust
Audi Design Foundation
BibleLands
Sydney Black Charitable Trust
Broadfield Trust
Carnegie Trust for Universities
   of Scotland
Carter's Educational
   Foundation
Sir Ernest Cassel Educational
   Trust
Elizabeth Casson Trust
Church Burgesses Educational
   Foundation
City Educational Trust Fund
Biss Davies Charitable Trust
City of Edinburgh Charitable
   Trusts
Ellinson Foundation Ltd

Football Association National
   Sports Centre Trust
Oliver Ford Charitable Trust
Worshipful Company of
   Furniture Makers Charitable
   Fund
Gatsby Charitable Foundation
Simon Gibson Charitable Trust
Glencore Foundation for
   Education and Welfare
Great Britain Sasakawa
   Foundation
Hedley Foundation
Hockerill Educational
   Foundation
Hornsey Parochial Charities
James Thom Howat Charitable
   Trust
Hulme Trust Estates
International Bar Association
   Educational Trust
John Jarrold Trust
Judge Charitable Foundation
Kathleen Trust
Kelsick's Educational
   Foundation
Kirkley Poor's Land Estate
Lawlor Foundation
Leverhulme Trust
John Lyon's Charity
D G Marshall of Cambridge
   Trust
Migraine Trust
Miller Foundation
Minge's Gift
Muslim Hands
National Kidney Research
   Fund Limited
Richard Newitt Fund
Philological Foundation
William Price Charitable Trust
Christopher H R Reeves
   Charitable Trust
Rhodes Trust Public Purposes
   Fund
Helen Roll Charitable Trust
Rubin Foundation
Karim Rida Said Foundation
St Gabriel's Trust
St Peter's Saltley Trust
St Thomas' Dole Charity
Salt Foundation
SEM Charitable Trust
Sheffield Bluecoat & Mount
   Pleasant Educational
   Foundation
Sutton Trust
Thriplow Charitable Trust
Ulverston Town Lands Charity
Vandervell Foundation
Thomas Wall Trust
Webb Memorial Trust
Wellcome Trust
Edith & Isaac Wolfson
   (Scotland) Trust

Wolfson Family Charitable
Trust

Will consider
All Saints Educational Trust
Pat Allsop Charitable Trust
Viscount Amory's Charitable
Trust
Anglian Water Trust Fund
Fagus Anstruther Memorial
Trust
Ove Arup Foundation
Ashby Charitable Trust
Laura Ashley Foundation
Balmore Trust
Bamford Charitable Foundation
Barracks Trust of Newcastle-
under-Lyme
Beit Trust
Benham Charitable Settlement
Peter Boizot Foundation
Bridge Trust
British Institute of Archaeology
at Ankara
Charles & Edna Broadhurst
Charitable Trust
Edward Cadbury Charitable
Trust
Carpenters' Company
Charitable Trust
CfBT Education Services
John & Freda Coleman
Charitable Trust
Colt Foundation
Holbeche Corfield Charitable
Settlement
Lord Cozens-Hardy Trust
Cripps Foundation
Cunningham Trust
William Dean Countryside and
Educational Trust
Diabetes UK
Douglas Charitable Trust
Dumfries and Galloway Council
Charitable Trusts
Earley Charity
Eden Arts Trust
Elmgrant Trust
Esmée Fairbairn Foundation
Fairway Trust
Lord Faringdon Charitable
Trust
Finnart House School Trust
Football Association Youth
Trust
Gilchrist Educational Trust
Reginald Graham Charitable
Trust
Paul Hamlyn Foundation
Sue Hammerson's Charitable
Trust
Headley Trust
Henley Educational Charity
Holly Hill Charitable Trust
Holywood Trust

Clifford Howarth Charity
Settlement
Humanitarian Trust
James Pantyfedwen
Foundation
Jeffrey Charitable Trust
William Kendall's Charity
King George's Fund for Sailors
Kreitman Foundation
William Leech Charity
Leverhulme Trade Charities
Trust
Lockerbie Trust
London Law Trust
Marie Helen Luen Charitable
Trust
Macfarlane Walker Trust
Linda Marcus Charitable Trust
Nancie Massey Charitable
Trust
Medlock Charitable Trust
Mercers' Charitable
Foundation
Miles Trust for Putney and
Roehampton Community
Mirfield Educational Charity
Mobbs Memorial Trust Ltd
Monmouthshire County Council
Welsh Church Act Fund
Nigel Moores Family Charitable
Trust
Morgan Stanley International
Foundation
Music Sound Foundation
NAM Charitable Trust
Newby Trust Limited
Northampton Municipal Church
Charities
Northcott Devon Foundation
Norwich Town Close Estate
Charity
Nuffield Foundation
Oakley Charitable Trust
Old Enfield Charitable Trust
P F Charitable Trust
Palmer Foundation
Parthenon Trust
Payne Charitable Trust
Michael Peacock Charitable
Foundation
Pennycress Trust
Jack Petchey Foundation
A M Pilkington's Charitable
Trust
Prince Foundation
Mr and Mrs J A Pye's
Charitable Settlement
Rawdon-Smith Trust
Sir James Reckitt Charity
Robertson Trust
Sir James Roll Charitable Trust
Joseph Rowntree Foundation
Saddlers' Company Charitable
Fund
St Olave, St Thomas and St
John United Charity

Sarum St Michael Educational
Charity
Annie Schiff Charitable Trust
Barnett & Sylvia Shine No 2
Charitable Trust
Simpson Education &
Conservation Trust
South Square Trust
Steinberg Family Charitable
Trust
Sir Sigmund Sternberg
Charitable Foundation
Steventon Allotments & Relief-
in-Need Charity
Stone Ashdown Charitable
Trust
Stone-Mallabar Charitable
Foundation
A B Strom & R Strom
Charitable Trust
Bernard Sunley Charitable
Foundation
Sutton Coldfield Municipal
Charities
Swann-Morton Foundation
Charles and Elsie Sykes Trust
Sir Jules Thorn Charitable
Trust
Tory Family Foundation
Florence Turner Trust
Miss S M Tutton Charitable
Trust
VEC Acorn Trust
Wakefield Trust
Warrington Church of England
Educational Trust
Welton Foundation
Westminster Foundation
William Williams Charity
H D H Wills 1965 Charitable
Trust
Wolfson Foundation
Women Caring Trust
Woodroffe Benton Foundation
Worcester Municipal Charities
York Children's Trust
Yorkshire Agricultural Society
I A Ziff Charitable Foundation

Informal & continuing education

Funding priority
Aberbrothock Charitable Trust
Sylvia Aitken Charitable Trust
Sir John & Lady Amory's
Charitable Trust
Association of Colleges
Charitable Trust
Thomas Betton's Charity for
Pensions and Relief-in-Need
Carter's Educational
Foundation
Cheruby Trust

Demigryphon Trust
Fast Track Trust Limited
Minge's Gift
Oizer Charitable Trust
Oxfordshire Community
   Foundation
Paul Charitable Trust
Jack Petchey Foundation
Philological Foundation
William Price Charitable Trust
Rooke Atlay Charitable Trust
St Peter's Saltley Trust
Salt Foundation
Bishop Simeon CR Trust
Thomas Wall Trust
Wentwood Education Trust
Yapp Charitable Trust
Zochonis Charitable Trust

Will consider
Abbey National Charitable
   Trust Ltd
Abbeydale Trust
AF Trust Company
Army Benevolent Fund
Ove Arup Foundation
Laura Ashley Foundation
Barracks Trust of Newcastle-
   under-Lyme
E M Behrens Charitable Trust
Bingham Trust
Michael Bishop Foundation
Blatchington Court Trust
R S Brownless Charitable
   Trust
Arnold James Burton 1956
   Charitable Settlement
C B Trust
Edward Cadbury Charitable
   Trust
Edward & Dorothy Cadbury
   Trust
CfBT Education Services
Christendom Trust
Sidney & Elizabeth Corob
   Charitable Trust
Lord Cozens-Hardy Trust
David Charitable Trust
Derbyshire Community
   Foundation
DLA Charitable Trust
Dumfries and Galloway Council
   Charitable Trusts
Elmgrant Trust
David Finnie & Alan Emery
   Charitable Trust
Ian Fleming Charitable Trust
Hugh Fraser Foundation
Freshgate Trust Foundation
Friarsgate Trust
Gatwick Airport Community
   Trust
Glaziers' Trust
Bishop of Guildford's
   Foundation
Paul Hamlyn Foundation

Higgs Charitable Trust
Hockerill Educational
   Foundation
Holywood Trust
Rita Lila Howard Foundation
Irwin Trust
Isle of Dogs Community
   Foundation
King George's Fund for Sailors
Leverhulme Trade Charities
   Trust
Lintel Trust
London North East Community
   Foundation
Marie Helen Luen Charitable
   Trust
Macfarlane Walker Trust
Linda Marcus Charitable Trust
Nancie Massey Charitable
   Trust
Medlock Charitable Trust
Methodist Relief and
   Development Fund
Monmouthshire County Council
   Welsh Church Act Fund
Morgan Crucible Company plc
   Charitable Trust
Morris Charitable Trust
Moss Charitable Trust
Northampton Municipal Church
   Charities
Norwich Town Close Estate
   Charity
Ormsby Charitable Trust
Parthenon Trust
Payne Charitable Trust
John Porter Charitable Trust
Mr and Mrs J A Pye's
   Charitable Settlement
Reuters Foundation
Rowanville Ltd
Rowlands Trust
Royal Docks Trust
St Gabriel's Trust
Sarum St Michael Educational
   Charity
Shaw Lands Trust
Sheffield Bluecoat & Mount
   Pleasant Educational
   Foundation
Sheffield Church Burgesses
   Trust
Shepherd Street Trust
L H Silver Charitable Trust
Steinberg Family Charitable
   Trust
Stewards' Charitable Trust
Sutton Coldfield Municipal
   Charities
Tillotson Bradbery Charitable
   Trust
Tory Family Foundation
Ullmann Trust
David Uri Memorial Trust
Scurrah Wainwright Charity
Ward Blenkinsop Trust

Mrs Waterhouse Charitable
   Trust
Westcroft Trust
Wiltshire and Swindon
   Community Foundation
Harold Hyam Wingate
   Foundation
Woodroffe Benton Foundation
Worcester Municipal Charities
Worshipful Company of
   Chartered Accountants
   General Charitable Trust

....

■ Adult and community education

Funding priority
Dove-Bowerman Trust
Esmée Fairbairn Foundation
Greater Bristol Foundation
Lynn Foundation
Miles Trust for Putney and
   Roehampton Community

Will consider
Alexandra Rose Day
Ardwick Trust
Ashby Charitable Trust
British Council for Prevention
   of Blindness
County of Gloucestershire
   Community Foundation
Duis Charitable Trust
Dumfries and Galloway Council
   Charitable Trusts
Fidelity UK Foundation
Ford of Britain Trust
GWR Community Trust
Hadfield Trust
Hedgcock Bequest
Leathersellers' Company
   Charitable Fund
Lloyds TSB Foundation for
   England and Wales
Lloyds TSB Foundation for
   Northern Ireland
Methodist Relief and
   Development Fund
John Moores Foundation
Rothley Trust
Christopher Rowbotham
   Charitable Trust
Rural Trust
C B & H H Taylor 1984 Trust
William Webster Charitable
   Trust

....

■ Supplementary schools

Funding priority
Paul Hamlyn Foundation
Hilden Charitable Fund
Peter Minet Trust

....

Will consider

Alexandra Rose Day
Equitable Charitable Trust
Alan Edward Higgs Charity
Lloyds TSB Foundation for
England and Wales
Lloyds TSB Foundation for
Northern Ireland
Thames Community
Foundation

....

■ Vocational education and training

Funding priority

Abbey National Charitable
Trust Ltd
Laura Ashley Foundation
Becketts & Sargeants
Educational Foundation
BibleLands
Britannia Building Society
Foundation
Carlton Television Trust
CLA Charitable Trust
Construction Industry Trust for
Youth
Charity of Thomas Dawson
Community Council of Devon
Dinwoodie Settlement
Dove-Bowerman Trust
Fast Track Trust Limited
Four Acre Trust
Simon Gibson Charitable Trust
Great Britain Sasakawa
Foundation
Greggs Trust
Isle of Dogs Community
Foundation
Kelsick's Educational
Foundation
Peter Kershaw Trust
King George's Fund for Sailors
Leeds & Holbeck Building
Society Charitable
Foundation
London Youth Trust
Paul Lunn-Rockliffe Charitable
Trust
Lynn Foundation
Magdalen Hospital Trust
Mathew Trust
Minge's Gift
Morgan Stanley International
Foundation
Old Enfield Charitable Trust
Ouseley Trust
PPP Foundation
St Thomas' Dole Charity
Bishop Simeon CR Trust
Sobell Foundation
Thomas Wall Trust

Will consider

Alexandra Rose Day
All Saints Educational Trust
Viscount Amory's Charitable
Trust
Milly Apthorp Charitable Trust
Ashby Charitable Trust
Hervey Benham Charitable
Trust
Blatchington Court Trust
Boots Charitable Trust
Bridge House Estates Trust
Fund
Worshipful Company of
Builders Merchants
Geoffrey Burton Charitable
Trust
Camelot Foundation
Wilfrid & Constance Cave
Foundation
Chase Charity
Childwick Trust
John & Freda Coleman
Charitable Trust
Community Fund
Ernest Cook Trust
Holbeche Corfield Charitable
Settlement
County Durham Foundation
Coutts & Co. Charitable Trust
Cray Trust
Helen and Geoffrey de Freitas
Charitable Trust
Duis Charitable Trust
Dulverton Trust
Earley Charity
Emerton-Christie Charity
Equitable Charitable Trust
Ferguson Benevolent Fund Ltd
Fishmongers' Company's
Charitable Trust
Ford of Britain Trust
Lord Forte Foundation
General Nursing Council for
England and Wales Trust
Girdlers' Company Charitable
Trust
Hadfield Trust
Harborne Parish Lands Charity
N & P Hartley Memorial Trust
Charles Hayward Foundation
Hertfordshire Community
Foundation
Holywood Trust
Miss Agnes H Hunter's Trust
Hyde Charitable Trust
J G Joffe Charitable Trust
Edward Cecil Jones Settlement
Judge Charitable Foundation
Sir James Knott Trust
Lankelly Foundation
Lawlor Foundation
Lazard Charitable Trust
Kennedy Leigh Charitable
Trust
Leigh Trust

Leng Charitable Trust
Lintel Trust
Lloyd's Charities Trust
Lloyds TSB Foundation for
England and Wales
Lloyds TSB Foundation for
Northern Ireland
John Lyon's Charity
Marchday Charitable Fund
Mercers' Charitable
Foundation
Methodist Relief and
Development Fund
Miles Trust for Putney and
Roehampton Community
Kitty and Daniel Nabarro
Charitable Trust
Newby Trust Limited
Northcott Devon Foundation
Norwich Town Close Estate
Charity
Parivar Trust
J S F Pollitzer Charitable
Settlement
Rainford Trust
Cliff Richard Charitable Trust
Rothley Trust
Saddlers' Company Charitable
Fund
St Hilda's Trust
Scott Bader Commonwealth
Ltd
Francis C Scott Charitable
Trust
Frieda Scott Charitable Trust
Sir James & Lady Scott Trust
SEM Charitable Trust
Henry Smith Charity
Summerfield Charitable Trust
Charles and Elsie Sykes Trust
C B & H H Taylor 1984 Trust
Tudor Trust
Vale of Glamorgan Welsh
Church Fund
Wates Foundation
Wellfield Trust
Michael and Anna Wix
Charitable Trust
Yorkshire Agricultural Society

Management of schools

Funding priority

Kitty and Daniel Nabarro
Charitable Trust

Will consider

All Saints Educational Trust
Laing's Charitable Trust
Monmouthshire County Council
Welsh Church Act Fund
Jack Petchey Foundation

Teacher training & development

Funding priority
All Saints Educational Trust
Dove-Bowerman Trust
Hockerill Educational
  Foundation
Muslim Hands

Will consider
Esmée Fairbairn Foundation
Great Britain Sasakawa
  Foundation
Paul Hamlyn Foundation
Methodist Relief and
  Development Fund
Monmouthshire County Council
  Welsh Church Act Fund
Jack Petchey Foundation
Elise Randall Educational Trust
Joseph Rank Trust
Fanny Rapaport Charitable
  Settlement
Karim Rida Said Foundation

Particular subjects

■ Arts education & training

Funding priority
Aldgate and All Hallows
  Barking Exhibition
  Foundation
Ashe Park Charitable Trust
Ashendene Trust
Belvedere Trust
British Record Industry Trust
J A Clark Charitable Trust
Else & Leonard Cross
  Charitable Trust
Elmgrant Trust
Esmée Fairbairn Foundation
Four Lanes Trust
Garrick Charitable Trust
Paul Hamlyn Foundation
Matthew Hodder Charitable
  Trust
Clifford Howarth Charity
  Settlement
Idlewild Trust
Lynn Foundation
Minge's Gift
Henry Moore Foundation
Nigel Moores Family Charitable
  Trust
Peter Moores Foundation
Patrick Charitable Trust
Philological Foundation
Austin & Hope Pilkington Trust
Quercus Trust
Rootstein Hopkins Foundation
Willy Russell Charitable Trust
R C Sherriff Rosebriars Trust

Tubney Charitable Trust
Verdon-Smith Family Charitable
  Settlement
Marie-Louise Von Motesiczky
  Charitable Trust
Woo Charitable Foundation

Will consider
Adnams Charity
Fagus Anstruther Memorial
  Trust
Arts Council of Wales
Ashby Charitable Trust
Astor Foundation
Barnabas Charitable Trust
Hervey Benham Charitable
  Trust
Peter Black Charitable Trust
Enid Blyton Trust for Children
British Institute of Archaeology
  at Ankara
Britten-Pears Foundation
Swinfen Broun Charitable Trust
Bryant Trust
Geoffrey Burton Charitable
  Trust
Richard Cadbury Charitable
  Trust
Wilfrid & Constance Cave
  Foundation
Cray Trust
Cripplegate Foundation
D'Oyly Carte Charitable Trust
John Grant Davies Trust
Dove-Bowerman Trust
Duis Charitable Trust
Dorothy Whitney Elmhirst Trust
Joyce Fletcher Charitable Trust
Timothy Franey Charitable
  Foundation
Robert Gavron Charitable Trust
Glaziers' Trust
Golsoncott Foundation
Nicholas & Judith Goodison's
  Charitable Settlement
Greater Bristol Foundation
Greggs Trust
Hadrian Trust
Kenneth Hargreaves Charitable
  Trust
Headley Trust
Holst Foundation
Holywood Trust
Ingram Trust
INTACH (UK) Trust
Isle of Dogs Community
  Foundation
Boris Karloff Charitable
  Foundation
Kleinwort Benson Charitable
  Trust
Marina Kleinwort Charitable
  Trust
Kreitman Foundation
Lankelly Foundation
Lark Trust

Raymond & Blanche Lawson
  Charitable Trust
Kennedy Leigh Charitable
  Trust
Linbury Trust
Marie Helen Luen Charitable
  Trust
R W Mann Trustees Limited
Marchday Charitable Fund
Mayfield Valley Arts Trust
Miles Trust for Putney and
  Roehampton Community
Keith and Joan Mindelsohn
  Charitable Trust
Morgan Stanley International
  Foundation
Music Sound Foundation
Newcomen Collett Foundation
Norwich Town Close Estate
  Charity
Oldham Foundation
Pennycress Trust
John Rayner Charitable Trust
Royal Docks Trust
Sir Walter St John's
  Educational Charity
St Mary-le-Strand Charity
Scarfe Charitable Trust
South Square Trust
Triangle Trust (1949) Fund
Wates Foundation
Whitaker Charitable Trust
Worcester Municipal Charities
York Children's Trust

■ Architecture education and training

Will consider
Ove Arup Foundation
Laura Ashley Foundation
Construction Industry Trust for
  Youth
Duis Charitable Trust
GWR Community Trust
Leverhulme Trust
Lintel Trust
Newby Trust Limited

■ Business education

Funding priority
Anglo-German Foundation for
  Study of Industrial Society
Foundation for Management
  Education
Gatsby Charitable Foundation
McDougall Trust
Patrick Charitable Trust
Philological Foundation

Will consider
Armenian General Benevolent
  Union London Trust

Ashby Charitable Trust
Cadbury Schweppes
    Foundation
Community Fund
Cray Trust
Ellis Campbell Charitable
    Foundation
Fidelity UK Foundation
Houblon-Norman Fund
Humanitarian Trust
Leverhulme Trust
Newby Trust Limited
Norwich Town Close Estate
    Charity
Reuters Foundation
Robert and Lisa Sainsbury
    Charitable Trust
Leslie Smith Foundation
Thomas Wall Trust
Wellfield Trust
Worcester Municipal Charities

■ Citizenship, personal & social education

Funding priority
1970 Trust
Camelot Foundation
Peter Minet Trust
Kitty and Daniel Nabarro
    Charitable Trust
Patrick Charitable Trust
Weavers' Company Benevolent
    Fund

Will consider
Ardwick Trust
Barbour Trust
Roger Brooke Charitable Trust
Cripplegate Foundation
Dove-Bowerman Trust
Dulverton Trust
Elmgrant Trust
Equitable Charitable Trust
Bishop of Guildford's
    Foundation
Paul Hamlyn Foundation
Harborne Parish Lands Charity
Laing's Charitable Trust
Lloyds TSB Foundation for
    Northern Ireland
London Law Trust
Methodist Relief and
    Development Fund
Keith and Joan Mindelsohn
    Charitable Trust
Christopher Rowbotham
    Charitable Trust
Steinberg Family Charitable
    Trust
Thames Community
    Foundation
Webb Memorial Trust

■ Domestic/lifeskills education

Funding priority
All Saints Educational Trust
Ashe Park Charitable Trust
Magdalen Hospital Trust
Peter Minet Trust
Weavers' Company Benevolent
    Fund
Wentwood Education Trust

Will consider
Ardwick Trust
Barbour Trust
Richard Cadbury Charitable
    Trust
Baron Davenport's Charity
Duis Charitable Trust
Equitable Charitable Trust
Girdlers' Company Charitable
    Trust
Bishop of Guildford's
    Foundation
GWR Community Trust
Harborne Parish Lands Charity
Charles Hayward Foundation
Lloyds TSB Foundation for
    Northern Ireland
Lloyds TSB Foundation for
    Scotland
London Law Trust
Methodist Relief and
    Development Fund
Miles Trust for Putney and
    Roehampton Community
Mitsubishi Corporation Fund
    for Europe and Africa
Rothley Trust
Christopher Rowbotham
    Charitable Trust
Whitecourt Charitable Trust

■ Engineering education

Funding priority
Audi Design Foundation
Charles Brotherton Trust
Michael & Morven Heller
    Charitable Foundation
Simon Heller Charitable
    Settlement
Jerwood Foundation and
    Jerwood Charitable
    Foundation
D G Marshall of Cambridge
    Trust
Medlock Charitable Trust
Kitty and Daniel Nabarro
    Charitable Trust
Patrick Charitable Trust
Charity Fund of Worshipful
    Company of Paviors
Philological Foundation

Will consider
Acacia Charitable Trust
Anglo-German Foundation for
    Study of Industrial Society
Ove Arup Foundation
Laura Ashley Foundation
John & Freda Coleman
    Charitable Trust
Construction Industry Trust for
    Youth
Criffel Charitable Trust
Dulverton Trust
Earley Charity
Ford of Britain Trust
Harbour Foundation
Headley Trust
Humanitarian Trust
Newby Trust Limited
Thomas Wall Trust
Wolfson Foundation
Worshipful Company of
    Founders Charities

■ Hospitality education

Funding priority
Clifford Howarth Charity
    Settlement

Will consider
Elise Randall Educational Trust

■ IT education

Funding priority
Carlton Television Trust
Charity of Thomas Dawson
Community Council of Devon
Gatsby Charitable Foundation
IBM United Kingdom Trust
ITF Seafarers Trust
Ian Karten Charitable Trust
Leeds & Holbeck Building
    Society Charitable
    Foundation
Magdalen Hospital Trust
Kitty and Daniel Nabarro
    Charitable Trust
Philological Foundation
Reuters Foundation
SHINE
Weavers' Company Benevolent
    Fund
Yapp Charitable Trust

Will consider
Abbey National Charitable
    Trust Ltd
Ardwick Trust
James Beattie Charitable Trust
Blatchington Court Trust
Swinfen Broun Charitable Trust
Richard Cadbury Charitable
    Trust

John & Freda Coleman
    Charitable Trust
Community Fund
County Durham Foundation
John Grant Davies Trust
Dove-Bowerman Trust
Dulverton Trust
Earley Charity
Equitable Charitable Trust
Esmée Fairbairn Foundation
Ferguson Benevolent Fund Ltd
Fidelity UK Foundation
Ford of Britain Trust
Harbour Foundation
Headley Trust
Holywood Trust
Humanitarian Trust
Isle of Dogs Community
    Foundation
Joicey Trust
Kennedy Leigh Charitable
    Trust
Leigh Trust
Lloyds TSB Foundation for
    England and Wales
Lloyds TSB Foundation for
    Northern Ireland
Mercers' Charitable
    Foundation
Milton Keynes Community
    Foundation
Morgan Stanley International
    Foundation
Newby Trust Limited
Alderman Newton's
    Educational Foundation
Northcott Devon Foundation
Norwich Town Close Estate
    Charity
Nuffield Foundation
Rothley Trust
Scott Bader Commonwealth
    Ltd
Servite Sisters' Charitable
    Trust Fund
Charles and Elsie Sykes Trust
Ulverscroft Foundation
Voluntary Action Luton
Wates Foundation
Wellfield Trust
Harold Hyam Wingate
    Foundation
Yorkshire Agricultural Society

....

■ **Language teaching**
Funding priority
Church Burgesses Educational
    Foundation
ITF Seafarers Trust
Marr-Munning Trust
Sheffield Bluecoat & Mount
    Pleasant Educational
    Foundation
Ultach Trust
Yapp Charitable Trust

Will consider
Ardwick Trust
BBC Children in Need Appeal
Carlton Television Trust
CfBT Education Services
City Parochial Foundation
Community Fund
Dove-Bowerman Trust
Earley Charity
Eden Arts Trust
Hertfordshire Community
    Foundation
Isle of Dogs Community
    Foundation
Lloyds TSB Foundation for
    England and Wales
Morgan Stanley International
    Foundation
Newby Trust Limited
John Rayner Charitable Trust
Servite Sisters' Charitable
    Trust Fund
Thames Community
    Foundation
Wates Foundation
Worcester Municipal Charities
W Wing Yip & Bros Charitable
    Trust

....

■ **Legal education**
Funding priority
International Bar Association
    Educational Trust
Law Society Charity
Philological Foundation

Will consider
Anglo-German Foundation for
    Study of Industrial Society
Baron Davenport's Charity
Humanitarian Trust
Leverhulme Trust
Newby Trust Limited
Nuffield Foundation
C A Rookes Charitable Trust
Thomas Wall Trust

....

■ **Literacy**
Funding priority
Aldgate and All Hallows
    Barking Exhibition
    Foundation
Ambrose & Ann Appelbe Trust
Ashe Park Charitable Trust
Britannia Building Society
    Foundation
Carlton Television Trust
Sir John Cass's Foundation
Community Council of Devon
Esmée Fairbairn Foundation
Matthew Hodder Charitable
    Trust

Clifford Howarth Charity
    Settlement
Isle of Dogs Community
    Foundation
J J Charitable Trust
Magdalen Hospital Trust
Magdalen & Lasher Charity
Morgan Stanley International
    Foundation
Kitty and Daniel Nabarro
    Charitable Trust
SHINE
Bishop Simeon CR Trust
Weavers' Company Benevolent
    Fund
Worshipful Company of
    Chartered Accountants
    General Charitable Trust
Yapp Charitable Trust

Will consider
Abbey National Charitable
    Trust Ltd
Ardwick Trust
Ashendene Trust
BBC Children in Need Appeal
James Beattie Charitable Trust
Enid Blyton Trust for Children
Boots Charitable Trust
British Sugar Foundation
Richard Cadbury Charitable
    Trust
Camelot Foundation
City Parochial Foundation
Community Fund
Ernest Cook Trust
County Durham Foundation
County of Gloucestershire
    Community Foundation
Cripplegate Foundation
Harry Crook Foundation
Roald Dahl Foundation
John Grant Davies Trust
Dove-Bowerman Trust
Duis Charitable Trust
Dulverton Trust
Earley Charity
Elmgrant Trust
Equitable Charitable Trust
Feed Minds
Fidelity UK Foundation
Fishmongers' Company's
    Charitable Trust
Ford of Britain Trust
Robert Gavron Charitable Trust
Godinton Charitable Trust
Bishop of Guildford's
    Foundation
GWR Community Trust
Harborne Parish Lands Charity
Charles Hayward Foundation
Headley Trust
Hertfordshire Community
    Foundation
Holywood Trust
Miss Agnes H Hunter's Trust

Hyde Charitable Trust
J G Joffe Charitable Trust
Joicey Trust
Kleinwort Benson Charitable
    Trust
Laing's Charitable Trust
Lankelly Foundation
Mrs F B Laurence Charitable
    Trust
Kennedy Leigh Charitable
    Trust
Leigh Trust
Linbury Trust
Lloyd's Charities Trust
Lloyds TSB Foundation for
    England and Wales
Lloyds TSB Foundation for
    Northern Ireland
M N R Charitable Trust
Marchday Charitable Fund
Mercers' Charitable
    Foundation
Methodist Relief and
    Development Fund
Miles Trust for Putney and
    Roehampton Community
George A Moore Foundation
Northcott Devon Foundation
Notgrove Trust
John Rayner Charitable Trust
Rothley Trust
Christopher Rowbotham
    Charitable Trust
St Mary-le-Strand Charity
Coral Samuel Charitable Trust
Scott Bader Commonwealth
    Ltd
Frieda Scott Charitable Trust
Sir James & Lady Scott Trust
Servite Sisters' Charitable
    Trust Fund
Sheepdrove Trust
Sportsman's Charity
Sutton Trust
C B & H H Taylor 1984 Trust
Thames Community
    Foundation
Tisbury Telegraph Trust
Tudor Trust
Ulverscroft Foundation
Voluntary Action Luton
Wates Foundation
Wellfield Trust
Whitecourt Charitable Trust
Women at Risk
York Children's Trust

....

■ Printing education
Funding priority
Educational Charity of
    Stationers' and Newspaper
    Makers' Company

Will consider
Fairbairn Charitable Trust
Jack Livingstone Charitable
    Trust
Ulverscroft Foundation
Whitecourt Charitable Trust
Woodlands Trust (259569)

....

■ Religious education
Funding priority
Alexis Trust
All Saints Educational Trust
Archbishop of Canterbury's
    Charitable Trust
Broadfield Trust
Daily Prayer Union Charitable
    Trust Ltd
Dove-Bowerman Trust
Famos Foundation Trust
Gerald Fogel Charitable Trust
Grahame Charitable
    Foundation
Kathleen Hannay Memorial
    Charity
Hockerill Educational
    Foundation
H F Johnson Trust
J E Joseph Charitable Fund
Late Sir Pierce Lacy Charity
    Trust
Lindale Educational
    Foundation
Second Joseph Aaron Littman
    Foundation
Mayfair Charities Ltd
Melow Charitable Trust
Midhurst Pensions Trust
Elani Nakou Foundation
Laurie Nidditch Foundation
Ogle Christian Trust
Payne Charitable Trust
Philological Foundation
Sir John Priestman Charity
    Trust
Rowanville Ltd
St Christopher's College
    Educational Trust
St Gabriel's Trust
St Luke's College Foundation
St Peter's Saltley Trust
St Thomas' Dole Charity
Schreib Trust
Tajtelbaum Charitable Trust
Dame Violet Wills Charitable
    Trust
Benjamin Winegarten
    Charitable Trust
Woo Charitable Foundation

Will consider
Acacia Charitable Trust
Armenian General Benevolent
    Union London Trust
Ashendene Trust
Bamford Charitable Foundation

Barnabas Charitable Trust
Bethesda Community
    Charitable Trust
Britland Charitable Trust
Burdens Charitable Foundation
Wilfrid & Constance Cave
    Foundation
Christendom Trust
Vivienne & Samuel Cohen
    Charitable Trust
Coppings Trust
Criffel Charitable Trust
Charity of Thomas Dawson
Dugdale Charitable Trust
Dulverton Trust
Anne French Memorial Trust
Girdlers' Company Charitable
    Trust
Hinchley Charitable Trust
Holywood Trust
Hope Trust
INTACH (UK) Trust
Ruth & Lionel Jacobson Trust
    (Second Fund) No 2
Stanley Kalms Foundation
Kasner Charitable Trust
Kirby Laing Foundation
Maurice and Hilda Laing
    Charitable Trust
Leverhulme Trust
Levy Foundation
M D & S Charitable Trust
Helen Isabella McMorran
    Charitable Foundation
Hilda & Samuel Marks
    Foundation
Anthony and Elizabeth Mellows
    Charitable Settlement
Melodor Ltd
Miles Trust for Putney and
    Roehampton Community
Vyoel Moshe Charitable Trust
Moss Family Charitable Trust
Muslim Hands
National Committee of
    Women's World Day of
    Prayer for England, Wales,
    and Northern Ireland
Newby Trust Limited
Alderman Newton's
    Educational Foundation
Chevras Ezras Nitzrochim Trust
North London Islamic
    Association Trust
Norwich Town Close Estate
    Charity
A M Pilkington's Charitable
    Trust
Cecil Pilkington Charitable
    Trust
Joseph Rank Trust
Fanny Rapaport Charitable
    Settlement
Cliff Richard Charitable Trust
River Trust
C A Rookes Charitable Trust

Mrs L D Rope Third Charitable
  Settlement
St Hilda's Trust
Annie Schiff Charitable Trust
Sharon Trust
R C Sherriff Rosebriars Trust
Bassil Shippam and Alsford
  Trust
L H Silver Charitable Trust
Sinclair Charitable Trust
Cyril & Betty Stein Charitable
  Trust
Steinberg Family Charitable
  Trust
Sir Sigmund Sternberg
  Charitable Foundation
Tisbury Telegraph Trust
Torchbearer Trust
Trustees of Tzedakah
Vale of Glamorgan Welsh
  Church Fund
Harold Hyam Wingate
  Foundation
W Wing Yip & Bros Charitable
  Trust

■ Science education

Funding priority

Armourers and Brasiers'
  Gauntlet Trust
Charles Brotherton Trust
City Educational Trust Fund
Dove-Bowerman Trust
Gatsby Charitable Foundation
Michael & Morven Heller
  Charitable Foundation
Simon Heller Charitable
  Settlement
Jane Hodge Foundation
Jerwood Foundation and
  Jerwood Charitable
  Foundation
Ian Karten Charitable Trust
Kitty and Daniel Nabarro
  Charitable Trust
John Oldacre Foundation
Philological Foundation
Wilkinson Charitable
  Foundation
Wolfson Foundation

Will consider

Acacia Charitable Trust
Fagus Anstruther Memorial
  Trust
Arthritis Research Campaign
Ove Arup Foundation
Laura Ashley Foundation
Viscountess Boyd Charitable
  Trust
British Institute of Archaeology
  at Ankara
Vivienne & Samuel Cohen
  Charitable Trust

John & Freda Coleman
  Charitable Trust
Ernest Cook Trust
Cripplegate Foundation
Dulverton Trust
Earley Charity
Ford of Britain Trust
Harbour Foundation
Humanitarian Trust
John Jarrold Trust
Lauffer Family Charitable
  Foundation
Kennedy Leigh Charitable
  Trust
Leverhulme Trust
Lindeth Charitable Trust
Macfarlane Walker Trust
Medlock Charitable Trust
Mercers' Charitable
  Foundation
Newby Trust Limited
Nuffield Foundation
Pilkington Charities Fund
Prince Philip Trust Fund
Märit and Hans Rausing
  Charitable Foundation
Mrs L D Rope Third Charitable
  Settlement
Raymond & Beverley Sackler
  Foundation
St Andrew Animal Fund Ltd
Thomas Wall Trust
Michael and Anna Wix
  Charitable Trust
Worshipful Company of
  Founders Charities

■ Social science

Funding priority

Philological Foundation
Sutasoma Trust

Will consider

Laura Ashley Foundation
British Institute of Archaeology
  at Ankara
Cripplegate Foundation
Dove-Bowerman Trust
GWR Community Trust
Kathleen Hannay Memorial
  Charity
Newby Trust Limited
Norwich Town Close Estate
  Charity

■ Sports education

Funding priority

Medlock Charitable Trust

Will consider

Peter Boizot Foundation
Swinfen Broun Charitable Trust
Cripplegate Foundation

Dove-Bowerman Trust
Girdlers' Company Charitable
  Trust
Mercers' Charitable
  Foundation
Fanny Rapaport Charitable
  Settlement
Christopher Rowbotham
  Charitable Trust
Stewards' Charitable Trust
Thames Community
  Foundation

■ Textiles & upholstery

Funding priority

Coats Foundation Trust
Worshipful Company of
  Glovers of London Charity
  Fund
Minge's Gift
R C Sherriff Rosebriars Trust

Will consider

Arts Council of Wales
Lord Barnby's Foundation
County Durham Foundation
Oliver Ford Charitable Trust
Worshipful Company of
  Furniture Makers Charitable
  Fund
Hesslewood Children's Trust
Mercers' Charitable
  Foundation
Elise Randall Educational Trust
Thomas Wall Trust

Environment & animals

Funding priority

Aberbrothock Charitable Trust
Paul Bassham Charitable Trust
Bergqvist Charitable Trust
Chatwin Trust
Robert Clutterbuck Charitable
Trust
Lance Coates Charitable Trust
1969
Freshfield Foundation
Oliver Morland Charitable Trust
Personal Assurance Charitable
Trust
J S F Pollitzer Charitable
Settlement
Privy Purse Charitable Trust
Shetland Amenity Trust
C B & H H Taylor 1984 Trust
Tedworth Trust
Three Oaks Trust
Mrs Waterhouse Charitable
Trust
Miss Hazel M Wood Charitable
Trust
Yorkshire Dales Millennium
Trust

Will consider

Sylvia Aitken Charitable Trust
Dorothy Gertrude Allen
Memorial Fund
H B Allen Charitable Trust
Sir John & Lady Amory's
Charitable Trust
James Beattie Charitable Trust
Belvedere Trust
Benham Charitable Settlement
Bingham Trust
Morgan Blake Charitable Trust
Mrs E E Brown Charitable
Settlement
George W Cadbury Charitable
Trust
Richard Cadbury Charitable
Trust
William A Cadbury Charitable
Trust
Wilfrid & Constance Cave
Foundation
Community Fund
Harry Crook Foundation
Gwendoline & Margaret Davies
Charity
Delves Charitable Trust
Dinam Charity
DLA Charitable Trust
Englefield Charitable Trust
Douglas Heath Eves Charitable
Trust
Earl Fitzwilliam Charitable
Trust
Flow Foundation
Fox Memorial Trust

Hugh Fraser Foundation
Garnett Charitable Trust
G C Gibson Charitable Trust
Girdlers' Company Charitable
Trust
Gretna Charitable Trust
Mrs Margaret Guido's
Charitable Trust
Hamamelis Trust
Kenneth Hargreaves Charitable
Trust
Hawthorne Charitable Trust
Joanna Herbert-Stepney
Charitable Settlement
Higgs Charitable Trust
Holly Hill Charitable Trust
Edward Sydney Hogg
Charitable Settlement
P H Holt Charitable Trust
Sir Harold Hood's Charitable
Trust
Clifford Howarth Charity
Settlement
Miss Agnes H Hunter's Trust
IFAW Charitable Trust
Jephcott Charitable Trust
Jerwood Foundation and
Jerwood Charitable
Foundation
Lady Eileen Joseph Foundation
Kintore Charitable Trust
Graham Kirkham Foundation
David Laing Foundation
Lethendy Charitable Trust
Linbury Trust
Michael Marks Charitable
Trust
Gerald Micklem Charitable
Trust
Mitsubishi Corporation Fund
for Europe and Africa
Nigel Moores Family Charitable
Trust
Morris Charitable Trust
Norman Family Charitable
Trust
Oakley Charitable Trust
Onaway Trust
P F Charitable Trust
A M Pilkington's Charitable
Trust
Cecil Pilkington Charitable
Trust
Pontin Charitable Trust
Clive Richards Charity Ltd
Robertson Trust
Helen Roll Charitable Trust
Rural Trust
Russell Trust
Alan and Babette Sainsbury
Charitable Fund
Sefton Community Foundation
Shetland Islands Council
Charitable Trust
South Square Trust
Steel Charitable Trust

Swire Charitable Trust
Stella Symons Charitable Trust
Tay Charitable Trust
Thoresby Charitable Trust
Constance Travis Charitable
Trust
R D Turner Charitable Trust
Vale of Glamorgan Welsh
Church Fund
Valentine Charitable Trust
Mary Webb Trust
Webb Memorial Trust
Welsh Church Fund –
Carmarthenshire area
Garfield Weston Foundation
David Wilson Foundation
Wixamtree Trust

Agriculture and fishing

Funding priority

Cobb Charity
Gatsby Charitable Foundation
Northern Rock Foundation
John Oldacre Foundation
Jack Patston Charitable Trust
Yorkshire Agricultural Society

Will consider

Balney Charitable Trust
Cranbury Foundation
Lord Faringdon Charitable
Trust
Godinton Charitable Trust
R J Harris Charitable
Settlement
Hemby Trust
Mary Homfray Charitable Trust
MacRobert Trust
Marchig Animal Welfare Trust
Methodist Relief and
Development Fund
Eleanor Rathbone Charitable
Trust
Ripple Effect Foundation
Rural Trust
A R Taylor Charitable Trust
Whitley Animal Protection Trust

■ Farming and food production

Funding priority

Ashden Trust
C Alma Baker Trust
R M 1956 Burton Charitable
Trust
Butchers' Company General
Charities
CLA Charitable Trust
Lance Coates Charitable Trust
1969

Cumber Family Charitable Trust
Demigryphon Trust
Esmée Fairbairn Foundation
J C Green Charitable Settlement
JCA Charitable Foundation
John Longwill's Agricultural Scheme
Marchig Animal Welfare Trust
Midhurst Pensions Trust
Frank Parkinson Agricultural Trust
J B Pelly Charitable Settlement
Austin & Hope Pilkington Trust
Sheepdrove Trust
Whitaker Charitable Trust

Will consider
AIM Foundation
Astor Foundation
Bamford Charitable Foundation
Lord Barnby's Foundation
Charles Brotherton Trust
Charities Advisory Trust
J A Clark Charitable Trust
Sir James Colyer-Fergusson's Charitable Trust
Ecological Foundation
Farmers Company Charitable Fund
H C D Memorial Fund
Hadfield Trust
Lennox Hannay Charitable Trust
Sir James Knott Trust
Leach Fourteenth Trust
M N R Charitable Trust
Methodist Relief and Development Fund
Horace Moore Charitable Trust
Notgrove Trust
Oldham Foundation
Cecil Pilkington Charitable Trust
Polden-Puckham Charitable Foundation
Mr and Mrs J A Pye's Charitable Settlement
Rowan Charitable Trust
Shears Charitable Trust
Staples Trust
Summerfield Charitable Trust
Bernard Sunley Charitable Foundation
Tisbury Telegraph Trust
Westminster Foundation

■ Fishing and fisheries

Funding priority
Demigryphon Trust
Esmée Fairbairn Foundation

Will consider
D'Oyly Carte Charitable Trust
Dulverton Trust
Fishmongers' Company's Charitable Trust

■ Forestry

Funding priority
R M 1956 Burton Charitable Trust
Demigryphon Trust
John Spedan Lewis Foundation

Will consider
Leslie Mary Carter Charitable Trust
Dulverton Trust
Mercers' Charitable Foundation
Methodist Relief and Development Fund
Oakdale Trust
Mr and Mrs J A Pye's Charitable Settlement

■ Horticulture

Funding priority
Viscountess Boyd Charitable Trust
CLA Charitable Trust
Cleary Foundation
Worshipful Company of Gardeners of London
J C Green Charitable Settlement
JCA Charitable Foundation
John Spedan Lewis Foundation
LSA Charitable Trust
Martin McLaren Memorial Trust
Frank Parkinson Agricultural Trust
J B Pelly Charitable Settlement
Sandringham Estate Cottage Horticultural Society Trust
Stanley Smith UK Horticultural Trust

Will consider
Ammco Trust
G C Armitage Charitable Trust
Ashendene Trust
Laura Ashley Foundation
Astor Foundation
C Alma Baker Trust
Sir James Colyer-Fergusson's Charitable Trust
D'Oyly Carte Charitable Trust
Esmée Fairbairn Foundation
Idlewild Trust
Sir James Knott Trust
M N R Charitable Trust
Horace Moore Charitable Trust

Shears Charitable Trust
Bernard Sunley Charitable Foundation

Animal conservation

Funding priority
Ancaster Trust
Birmingham International Airport Community Trust
Boughton Trust
Viscountess Boyd Charitable Trust
R M 1956 Burton Charitable Trust
Charities Advisory Trust
Cleary Foundation
Ernest Cook Trust
Holbeche Corfield Charitable Settlement
Cranbury Foundation
Dr & Mrs A Darlington Charitable Trust
Four Winds Trust
Simon Gibson Charitable Trust
Hamamelis Trust
Lennox Hannay Charitable Trust
Joseph & Mary Hiley Trust
Holly Hill Charitable Trust
Ernest Kleinwort Charitable Trust
John Spedan Lewis Foundation
Lotus Foundation
Manchester Airport Community Trust Fund
Marchig Animal Welfare Trust
Network for Social Change
Oakdale Trust
Panton Trust
Jack Patston Charitable Trust
J B Pelly Charitable Settlement
Cliff Richard Charitable Trust
Rufford Foundation
Rural Trust
Charles and Elsie Sykes Trust
Loke Wan Tho Memorial Foundation
Tubney Charitable Trust
Verdon-Smith Family Charitable Settlement
Woodroffe Benton Foundation

Will consider
Viscount Amory's Charitable Trust
Milly Apthorp Charitable Trust
Ardwick Trust
A J H Ashby Will Trust
Astor Foundation
Astor of Hever Trust
Balcombe Charitable Trust
Lord Barnby's Foundation
E M Behrens Charitable Trust

Beit Trust
Rowan Bentall Charitable Trust
Bergqvist Charitable Trust
Charles Boot Trust
BP Conservation Programme
Bridge House Estates Trust
    Fund
Charles Brotherton Trust
Arnold James Burton 1956
    Charitable Settlement
Edward Cadbury Charitable
    Trust
George W Cadbury Charitable
    Trust
P H G Cadbury Trust
Cadbury Schweppes
    Foundation
Cairns Charitable Trust
Carpenter Charitable Trust
Leslie Mary Carter Charitable
    Trust
Cemlyn-Jones Trust
Chapman Charitable Trust
Chippenham Borough Lands
    Charity
Chipping Sodbury Town Lands
    Charity
John Coates Charitable Trust
Lance Coates Charitable Trust
    1969
Sir James Colyer-Fergusson's
    Charitable Trust
Congleton Inclosure Trust
Conservation Foundation
Duke of Cornwall's Benevolent
    Fund
County Durham Foundation
Lord Cozens-Hardy Trust
Craignish Trust
Criffel Charitable Trust
Dennis Curry Charitable Trust
Cwmbran Trust
D'Oyly Carte Charitable Trust
Daily Telegraph Charitable
    Trust
William Dean Countryside and
    Educational Trust
Community Council of Devon
Dulverton Trust
Dumbreck Charity
Harry Dunn Charitable Trust
Earley Charity
John Ellerman Foundation
Lord Faringdon Charitable
    Trust
Samuel William Farmer's Trust
Donald Forrester Trust
Maurice Fry Charitable Trust
Godinton Charitable Trust
Gough Charitable Trust
Greencard Charitable Trust
Hadfield Trust
Hampton Fuel Allotment
    Charity
R J Harris Charitable
    Settlement

Headley Trust
May Hearnshaw's Charity
Hedley Denton Charitable
    Trust
Mary Homfray Charitable Trust
Cuthbert Horn Trust
Hyde Park Place Estate Charity
IFAW Charitable Trust
J J Charitable Trust
Jephcott Charitable Trust
Sir James Knott Trust
Kreitman Foundation
Kirby Laing Foundation
Maurice Laing Foundation
R J Larg Family Charitable
    Trust
Mrs F B Laurence Charitable
    Trust
Leach Fourteenth Trust
Limoges Charitable Trust
Linden Charitable Trust
Lockerbie Trust
Macfarlane Walker Trust
Mackintosh Foundation
Sir George Martin Trust
Maxwell Family Foundation
Mercers' Charitable
    Foundation
Miller Foundation
Millichope Foundation
Peter Minet Trust
Minos Trust
Esmé Mitchell Trust
Mobbs Memorial Trust Ltd
Monument Trust
Nigel Moores Family Charitable
    Trust
Morel Charitable Trust
Old Possum's Practical Trust
Oldham Foundation
Onaway Trust
Raymond Oppenheimer
    Foundation
Owen Family Trust
Oxford Preservation Trust
Park Hill Trust
Peacock Charitable Trust
Prince of Wales's Charitable
    Foundation
Ravensdale Trust
Rawdon-Smith Trust
Sir James Reckitt Charity
Reuters Foundation
Roman Research Trust
Rotherwick Foundation
Rowlands Trust
St Andrew Animal Fund Ltd
Peter Samuel Charitable Trust
Sandra Charitable Trust
Sarnia Charitable Trust
Scarfe Charitable Trust
Schroder Charity Trust
Scotbelge Charitable Trust
Scottish Community
    Foundation
Shears Charitable Trust

Sylvia & Colin Shepherd
    Charitable Trust
Simpson Education &
    Conservation Trust
Skinners' Company Lady
    Neville Charity
SMB Trust
W F Southall Trust
Spitalfields Market Community
    Trust
W W Spooner Charitable Trust
Peter Stebbings Memorial
    Charity
Leonard Laity Stoate
    Charitable Trust
M J C Stone Charitable Trust
Bernard Sunley Charitable
    Foundation
A R Taylor Charitable Trust
C B & H H Taylor 1984 Trust
Tisbury Telegraph Trust
Douglas Turner Trust
Charity of Thomas Wade &
    Others
Wakefield Trust
Barbara Welby Trust
Westminster Foundation
A H and B C Whiteley
    Charitable Trust
Whitley Animal Protection Trust
Will Charitable Trust
H D H Wills 1965 Charitable
    Trust

....

■ Endangered species

Funding priority
Birmingham International
    Airport Community Trust
Iris Darnton Foundation
Esmée Fairbairn Foundation
Sydney E Franklin Deceased's
    New Second Charity
Millfield House Foundation
Philanthropic Trust
David Shepherd Wildlife
    Foundation
Stanley Foundation Ltd
Roger Vere Foundation

Will consider
Ammco Trust
Body Shop Foundation
William A Cadbury Charitable
    Trust
Mauritis Mulder Canter Charity
Carron Charitable Trust
Marjorie Coote Animal Charity
    Fund
Cray Trust
Community Council of Devon
Earth Love Fund
Fox Memorial Trust
Garnett Charitable Trust
Robert Hall Charity

Lennox Hannay Charitable
Trust
May Hearnshaw's Charity
Ruth & Lionel Jacobson Trust
(Second Fund) No 2
Gerald Micklem Charitable
Trust
Owen Family Trust
Bernard Piggott Trust
Mr and Mrs J A Pye's
Charitable Settlement
Rank Foundation
Rufford Foundation
Simpson Education &
Conservation Trust
Vincent Wildlife Trust
Woodward Trust

■ Birds

Funding priority
Cobb Charity
Charles and Elsie Sykes Trust

Will consider
Mauritis Mulder Canter Charity
Dulverton Trust
Harry Dunn Charitable Trust
Gannochy Trust
William Geoffrey Harvey's
Discretionary Settlement
Graham Kirkham Foundation
Mrs F B Laurence Charitable
Trust
Helen Isabella McMorran
Charitable Foundation
Mercers' Charitable
Foundation
Horace Moore Charitable Trust
Owen Family Trust
Peacock Charitable Trust
Jean Sainsbury Animal Welfare
Trust
Simpson Education &
Conservation Trust
Hugh Stenhouse Foundation
Stella Symons Charitable Trust
J and J R Wilson Trust

■ Fishes

Will consider
Rawdon-Smith Trust

■ Land animals in wild

Funding priority
Adnams Charity
Carron Charitable Trust
Chase Charity
Cobb Charity
Ernest Kleinwort Charitable
Trust

Mr and Mrs J A Pye's
Charitable Settlement
Jean Sainsbury Animal Welfare
Trust
Swan Trust
Thoresby Charitable Trust
Mrs Maud Van Norden's
Charitable Foundation

Will consider
A J H Ashby Will Trust
BBC Radio Lincolnshire Charity
Trust
Blair Foundation
Body Shop Foundation
Charles Boot Trust
British Sugar Foundation
Audrey & Stanley Burton
Charitable Trust
Geoffrey Burton Charitable
Trust
Mauritis Mulder Canter Charity
Vivienne & Samuel Cohen
Charitable Trust
Sir James Colyer-Fergusson's
Charitable Trust
Countryside Trust
Demigryphon Trust
Dulverton Trust
Ecological Foundation
Charles S French Charitable
Trust
Frognal Trust
Gannochy Trust
Meir Golda Trust
J G Graves Charitable Trust
Grocers' Charity
Gunter Charitable Trust
Hadrian Trust
Robert Hall Charity
Harebell Centenary Fund
William Geoffrey Harvey's
Discretionary Settlement
Charles Hayward Foundation
Geoffrey C Hughes Charitable
Trust
Ruth & Lionel Jacobson Trust
(Second Fund) No 2
John Jarrold Trust
Jeffrey Charitable Trust
Joicey Trust
Edward Cecil Jones Settlement
Mrs F B Laurence Charitable
Trust
Helen Isabella McMorran
Charitable Foundation
R W Mann Trustees Limited
Marsh Christian Trust
Sir George Martin Trust
Horace Moore Charitable Trust
Kitty and Daniel Nabarro
Charitable Trust
Norwich Town Close Estate
Charity
Philanthropic Trust
Princess Anne's Charities

Rainford Trust
Märit and Hans Rausing
Charitable Foundation
Sir James Reckitt Charity
Rufford Foundation
Sarnia Charitable Trust
Scott Bader Commonwealth
Ltd
Scouloudi Foundation
Leslie Smith Foundation
South Yorkshire Community
Foundation
Staples Trust
Hugh Stenhouse Foundation
Summerfield Charitable Trust
Sutton Coldfield Municipal
Charities
Swann-Morton Foundation
Sylvanus Charitable Trust
Stella Symons Charitable Trust
Vincent Wildlife Trust
Woodward Trust
Yorkshire Agricultural Society

Animal care

Funding priority
Sylvia Aitken Charitable Trust
Animal Defence Trust
Briggs Animal Welfare Trust
Calypso Browning Trust
CHK Charities Limited
Robert Clutterbuck Charitable
Trust
Marjorie Coote Animal Charity
Fund
Earlsmead Charitable Trust
Garnett Charitable Trust
Simon Gibson Charitable Trust
Barry Green Memorial Fund
Lennox Hannay Charitable
Trust
Harebell Centenary Fund
J G Hogg Charitable Trust
Homelands Charitable Trust
Homestead Charitable Trust
Mrs E G Hornby's Charitable
Settlement
Michael and Shirley Hunt
Charitable Trust
IFAW Charitable Trust
Marchig Animal Welfare Trust
Horace Moore Charitable Trust
Panton Trust
Persula Foundation
Pet Plan Charitable Trust
Phillips Charitable Trust
Rawdon-Smith Trust
Robertson Trust
Jean Sainsbury Animal Welfare
Trust
Loke Wan Tho Memorial
Foundation
Tubney Charitable Trust
Baroness Van Heemstra's
Charitable Trust

Mrs Maud Van Norden's
Charitable Foundation
Verdon-Smith Family Charitable
Settlement
Whitley Animal Protection Trust
Yorkshire Building Society
Charitable Foundation

Will consider
Astor Foundation
Harry Bacon Foundation
Barbour Trust
Lord Barnby's Foundation
BBC Radio Lincolnshire Charity
Trust
Patsy Bloom & Robert
Blausten Charitable Trust
W A Cargill Charitable Trust
Chelsea Square 1994 Trust
Cinderford Charitable Trust
Cray Trust
Cwmbran Trust
De Clermont Charitable
Company Ltd
Double 'O' Charity Ltd
Dumbreck Charity
EBM Charitable Trust
Wilfred & Elsie Elkes Charity
Fund
Beryl Evetts & Robert Luff
Animal Welfare Trust
Lord Faringdon Charitable
Trust
Earl Fitzwilliam Charitable
Trust
Donald Forrester Trust
Meir Golda Trust
Reginald Graham Charitable
Trust
William Geoffrey Harvey's
Discretionary Settlement
Mary Homfray Charitable Trust
Ruth & Lionel Jacobson Trust
(Second Fund) No 2
Sir Charles Jessel Charitable
Trust
Jones 1986 Charitable Trust
Graham Kirkham Foundation
Sir James Knott Trust
Mrs F B Laurence Charitable
Trust
Limoges Charitable Trust
Loseley & Guildway Charitable
Trust
C L Loyd Charitable Trust
R S MacDonald Charitable
Trust
Helen Isabella McMorran
Charitable Foundation
Manchester Airport Community
Trust Fund
Marsh Christian Trust
John Martin's Charity
Maxwell Family Foundation

Metropolitan Drinking Fountain
and Cattle Trough
Association
Minos Trust
Edith Murphy Foundation
Old Possum's Practical Trust
Oldham Foundation
Onaway Trust
Pennycress Trust
Philanthropic Trust
Bernard Piggott Trust
Proven Family Trust
Rank Foundation
Sir James Roll Charitable Trust
St Andrew Animal Fund Ltd
Sandra Charitable Trust
Scots Trust
David Shepherd Wildlife
Foundation
John Slater Foundation
E J H Stephenson Deceased
Charitable Trust
June Stevens Foundation
Bernard Sunley Charitable
Foundation
Sutton Trust
Swann-Morton Foundation
Sylvanus Charitable Trust
Thompson Family Charitable
Trust
Thoresby Charitable Trust
Sir Jules Thorn Charitable
Trust
J and J R Wilson Trust
Yorkshire Agricultural Society
Elizabeth & Prince Zaiger Trust

....

■ **Cats**
Will consider
Tisbury Telegraph Trust

....

■ **Dogs**
Funding priority
Kennel Club Charitable Trust

Will consider
Cranbury Foundation
William Geoffrey Harvey's
Discretionary Settlement
Horace Moore Charitable Trust
Oldham Foundation

....

■ **Horses**
Funding priority
Horace Moore Charitable Trust

Will consider
Ammco Trust
Lord Barnby's Foundation
Cranbury Foundation
Earl Fitzwilliam Charitable
Trust

William Geoffrey Harvey's
Discretionary Settlement
Mrs F B Laurence Charitable
Trust
Willie & Mabel Morris
Charitable Trust
Oldham Foundation
Elsie Pilkington Charitable
Trust
Saddlers' Company Charitable
Fund
Bernard Sunley Charitable
Foundation
Yorkshire Agricultural Society

Non-animal research

Will consider
Body Shop Foundation

Countryside

Funding priority
Ancaster Trust
Ashe Park Charitable Trust
Birmingham International
Airport Community Trust
Boughton Trust
Viscountess Boyd Charitable
Trust
R M 1956 Burton Charitable
Trust
Charities Advisory Trust
Cleary Foundation
Cobb Charity
Ernest Cook Trust
Holbeche Corfield Charitable
Settlement
Countryside Trust
Dr & Mrs A Darlington
Charitable Trust
Ellis Campbell Charitable
Foundation
Four Winds Trust
Simon Gibson Charitable Trust
Hamamelis Trust
Lennox Hannay Charitable
Trust
Joseph & Mary Hiley Trust
Holly Hill Charitable Trust
Ernest Kleinwort Charitable
Trust
Maurice Laing Foundation
John Spedan Lewis Foundation
Manifold Trust
Market Harborough and
Bowdens Charity
Kitty and Daniel Nabarro
Charitable Trust
Network for Social Change
Northern Rock Foundation
Jack Patston Charitable Trust
Rural Trust

Connie and Albert Taylor
   Charitable Trust
Verdon-Smith Family Charitable
   Settlement
Woodroffe Benton Foundation

Will consider
29th May 1961 Charitable
   Trust
Viscount Amory's Charitable
   Trust
Milly Apthorp Charitable Trust
Ardwick Trust
A J H Ashby Will Trust
Astor of Hever Trust
BAA 21st Century
   Communities Trust
Balcombe Charitable Trust
Peter Barker-Mill Memorial
   Charity
Lord Barnby's Foundation
E M Behrens Charitable Trust
Rowan Bentall Charitable Trust
Bergqvist Charitable Trust
Charles Boot Trust
BP Conservation Programme
Bryant Trust
Edward Cadbury Charitable
   Trust
George W Cadbury Charitable
   Trust
P H G Cadbury Trust
Cadbury Schweppes
   Foundation
Cairns Charitable Trust
Mauritis Mulder Canter Charity
Cemlyn-Jones Trust
Chapman Charitable Trust
Chippenham Borough Lands
   Charity
Chipping Sodbury Town Lands
   Charity
John Coates Charitable Trust
Lance Coates Charitable Trust
   1969
Sir James Colyer-Fergusson's
   Charitable Trust
Congleton Inclosure Trust
Conservation Foundation
Duke of Cornwall's Benevolent
   Fund
County Durham Foundation
Craignish Trust
Dennis Curry Charitable Trust
Daily Telegraph Charitable
   Trust
Helen and Geoffrey de Freitas
   Charitable Trust
Derbyshire Community
   Foundation
Community Council of Devon
Dulverton Trust
Dumbreck Charity
Harry Dunn Charitable Trust
Earley Charity
Eden Arts Trust

John Ellerman Foundation
Samuel William Farmer's Trust
Earl Fitzwilliam Charitable
   Trust
Donald Forrester Trust
Maurice Fry Charitable Trust
Gatwick Airport Community
   Trust
Girdlers' Company Charitable
   Trust
Godinton Charitable Trust
Gough Charitable Trust
Great Britain Sasakawa
   Foundation
Greencard Charitable Trust
Hadfield Trust
Hampton Fuel Allotment
   Charity
R J Harris Charitable
   Settlement
Headley Trust
May Hearnshaw's Charity
Hedley Denton Charitable
   Trust
H J Heinz Company Limited
   Charitable Trust
Hobart Charitable Trust
Mary Homfray Charitable Trust
Cuthbert Horn Trust
Hyde Park Place Estate Charity
Ingram Trust
Inverforth Charitable Trust
J J Charitable Trust
Jephcott Charitable Trust
Kreitman Foundation
Kirby Laing Foundation
R J Larg Family Charitable
   Trust
Mrs F B Laurence Charitable
   Trust
Linden Charitable Trust
Lockerbie Trust
Lyndhurst Settlement
Macfarlane Walker Trust
Mackintosh Foundation
Sir George Martin Trust
Mercers' Charitable
   Foundation
Millichope Foundation
Peter Minet Trust
Esmé Mitchell Trust
Mobbs Memorial Trust Ltd
Monument Trust
Nigel Moores Family Charitable
   Trust
Morel Charitable Trust
Raymond Oppenheimer
   Foundation
Owen Family Trust
Park Hill Trust
Peacock Charitable Trust
Prince of Wales's Charitable
   Foundation
Ravensdale Trust
Rawdon-Smith Trust
Sir James Reckitt Charity

Reuters Foundation
Roman Research Trust
Rotherwick Foundation
Rowlands Trust
Peter Samuel Charitable Trust
Sandra Charitable Trust
Sarnia Charitable Trust
Scarfe Charitable Trust
Schroder Charity Trust
Scotbelge Charitable Trust
Scottish Community
   Foundation
Sylvia & Colin Shepherd
   Charitable Trust
Skinners' Company Lady
   Neville Charity
W F Southall Trust
Spitalfields Market Community
   Trust
W W Spooner Charitable Trust
Peter Stebbings Memorial
   Charity
Leonard Laity Stoate
   Charitable Trust
M J C Stone Charitable Trust
A R Taylor Charitable Trust
C B & H H Taylor 1984 Trust
Douglas Turner Trust
Charity of Thomas Wade &
   Others
Wakefield Trust
Barbara Welby Trust
Westminster Foundation
A H and B C Whiteley
   Charitable Trust
Will Charitable Trust
H D H Wills 1965 Charitable
   Trust

....

■ **Access to the
   countryside**

Funding priority
CLA Charitable Trust

Will consider
Esmée Fairbairn Foundation

....

■ **Maintenance and
   preservation of the
   countryside**

Funding priority
Robert Clutterbuck Charitable
   Trust
Cranbury Foundation
Manifold Trust
Oxford Preservation Trust
Rural Trust
Whitaker Charitable Trust

Will consider
Ashby Charitable Trust
Body Shop Foundation
Bothwell Charitable Trust

Arnold James Burton 1956
Charitable Settlement
Leslie Mary Carter Charitable
Trust
Colchester & Tendring
Community Trust
D'Oyly Carte Charitable Trust
Dulverton Trust
Earl Fitzwilliam Charitable
Trust
Gannochy Trust
Hedley Denton Charitable
Trust
Leathersellers' Company
Charitable Fund
Maxwell Family Foundation
Gerald Micklem Charitable
Trust
Miller Foundation
Newport County Borough
Welsh Church Fund
Gerald Palmer Trust
Panton Trust
John Rayner Charitable Trust
Cliff Richard Charitable Trust
Saddlers' Company Charitable
Fund
SMB Trust
Summerfield Charitable Trust
Florence Turner Trust
Eric W Vincent Trust Fund
Woodward Trust

Environmental education & research

Funding priority
Ashe Park Charitable Trust
British Sugar Foundation
Cobb Charity
Cranbury Foundation
Great Britain Sasakawa
Foundation
Hitachi Europe Charitable
Trust
Lindeth Charitable Trust
Market Harborough and
Bowdens Charity
Jack Patston Charitable Trust
Woodroffe Benton Foundation

Will consider
Ardwick Trust
Ove Arup Foundation
Bedford Charity
Beit Trust
Body Shop Foundation
Peter Boizot Foundation
Roger Brooke Charitable Trust
William A Cadbury Charitable
Trust
Duis Charitable Trust
Earley Charity
Eden Arts Trust

Fishmongers' Company's
Charitable Trust
Earl Fitzwilliam Charitable
Trust
Gatwick Airport Community
Trust
R J Harris Charitable
Settlement
Mary Homfray Charitable Trust
Laing's Charitable Trust
Northern Rock Foundation
Porter Foundation
Eleanor Rathbone Charitable
Trust
Ripple Effect Foundation
Summerfield Charitable Trust
Tisbury Telegraph Trust
Charles Wolfson Charitable
Trust

■ Environmental education

Funding priority
BAA 21st Century
Communities Trust
CLA Charitable Trust
John Spedan Lewis Foundation
Kitty and Daniel Nabarro
Charitable Trust
Rural Trust

Will consider
A J H Ashby Will Trust
Barclays Stockbrokers
Charitable Trust
Bedford Charity
Blanchminster Trust
Charles Brotherton Trust
Community Foundation Serving
Tyne & Wear and
Northumberland
County of Gloucestershire
Community Foundation
Helen and Geoffrey de Freitas
Charitable Trust
Derbyshire Community
Foundation
Ford of Britain Trust
Greater Bristol Foundation
Hadfield Trust
Hadrian Trust
Alan Edward Higgs Charity
Leathersellers' Company
Charitable Fund
London Law Trust
Marchig Animal Welfare Trust
Gerald Palmer Trust
Richmond Parish Lands Charity

■ Environmental research

Funding priority
British Institute of Archaeology
at Ankara

Will consider
Sarah D'Avigdor Goldsmid
Charitable Trust
Dulverton Trust
Panton Trust
Rural Trust

Natural environment

Funding priority
Ancaster Trust
Ashe Park Charitable Trust
Birmingham International
Airport Community Trust
Boughton Trust
Viscountess Boyd Charitable
Trust
British Sugar Foundation
R M 1956 Burton Charitable
Trust
Carron Charitable Trust
Charities Advisory Trust
Cleary Foundation
Robert Clutterbuck Charitable
Trust
Cobb Charity
Ernest Cook Trust
Holbeche Corfield Charitable
Settlement
Countryside Trust
Cranbury Foundation
Dr & Mrs A Darlington
Charitable Trust
Esmée Fairbairn Foundation
Four Winds Trust
Simon Gibson Charitable Trust
Hamamelis Trust
Lennox Hannay Charitable
Trust
Joseph & Mary Hiley Trust
Holly Hill Charitable Trust
Hitachi Europe Charitable
Trust
Ernest Kleinwort Charitable
Trust
Maurice Laing Foundation
John Spedan Lewis Foundation
Lindeth Charitable Trust
Manchester Airport Community
Trust Fund
Manifold Trust
Market Harborough and
Bowdens Charity
Mitsubishi Corporation Fund
for Europe and Africa
Network for Social Change
Oakdale Trust

Panton Trust
Jack Patston Charitable Trust
J B Pelly Charitable Settlement
Rufford Foundation
Rural Trust
Loke Wan Tho Memorial
     Foundation
Tubney Charitable Trust
Verdon-Smith Family Charitable
     Settlement
Roger Vere Foundation
Woodroffe Benton Foundation

Will consider
Viscount Amory's Charitable
     Trust
Milly Apthorp Charitable Trust
Ardwick Trust
A J H Ashby Will Trust
Astor of Hever Trust
BAA 21st Century
     Communities Trust
Balcombe Charitable Trust
Peter Barker-Mill Memorial
     Charity
Lord Barnby's Foundation
E M Behrens Charitable Trust
Beit Trust
Rowan Bentall Charitable Trust
Bergqvist Charitable Trust
Charles Boot Trust
BP Conservation Programme
Bridge House Estates Trust
     Fund
British Institute of Archaeology
     at Ankara
Bryant Trust
Geoffrey Burton Charitable
     Trust
Edward Cadbury Charitable
     Trust
George W Cadbury Charitable
     Trust
P H G Cadbury Trust
Cadbury Schweppes
     Foundation
Cairns Charitable Trust
Mauritis Mulder Canter Charity
Leslie Mary Carter Charitable
     Trust
Cemlyn-Jones Trust
Chapman Charitable Trust
Chippenham Borough Lands
     Charity
Chipping Sodbury Town Lands
     Charity
Clothworkers' Foundation and
     other Trusts
John Coates Charitable Trust
Lance Coates Charitable Trust
     1969
Sir James Colyer-Fergusson's
     Charitable Trust
Community Foundation Serving
     Tyne & Wear and
     Northumberland

Congleton Inclosure Trust
Conservation Foundation
Duke of Cornwall's Benevolent
     Fund
County Durham Foundation
Craignish Trust
Dennis Curry Charitable Trust
D'Oyly Carte Charitable Trust
Daily Telegraph Charitable
     Trust
Helen and Geoffrey de Freitas
     Charitable Trust
William Dean Countryside and
     Educational Trust
Community Council of Devon
Dulverton Trust
Dumbreck Charity
Harry Dunn Charitable Trust
Earley Charity
Ecological Foundation
John Ellerman Foundation
Samuel William Farmer's Trust
Donald Forrester Trust
Maurice Fry Charitable Trust
Gatwick Airport Community
     Trust
Girdlers' Company Charitable
     Trust
Godinton Charitable Trust
Meir Golda Trust
Gough Charitable Trust
J G Graves Charitable Trust
Great Britain Sasakawa
     Foundation
Greencard Charitable Trust
Hadfield Trust
Hampton Fuel Allotment
     Charity
R J Harris Charitable
     Settlement
Charles Hayward Foundation
Headley Trust
May Hearnshaw's Charity
Mary Homfray Charitable Trust
Cuthbert Horn Trust
Geoffrey C Hughes Charitable
     Trust
Hyde Park Place Estate Charity
Ingram Trust
Inverforth Charitable Trust
J J Charitable Trust
Jephcott Charitable Trust
Kreitman Foundation
Laing's Charitable Trust
R J Larg Family Charitable
     Trust
Mrs F B Laurence Charitable
     Trust
Leathersellers' Company
     Charitable Fund
Linden Charitable Trust
Lockerbie Trust
Macfarlane Walker Trust
Mackintosh Foundation
Sir George Martin Trust
Maxwell Family Foundation

Mercers' Charitable
     Foundation
Miller Foundation
Millichope Foundation
Peter Minet Trust
Esmé Mitchell Trust
Mobbs Memorial Trust Ltd
Monument Trust
Nigel Moores Family Charitable
     Trust
Morel Charitable Trust
Northern Rock Foundation
Raymond Oppenheimer
     Foundation
Owen Family Trust
Oxford Preservation Trust
Park Hill Trust
Peacock Charitable Trust
Prince of Wales's Charitable
     Foundation
Eleanor Rathbone Charitable
     Trust
Ravensdale Trust
Rawdon-Smith Trust
Sir James Reckitt Charity
Reuters Foundation
Ripple Effect Foundation
Roman Research Trust
Rotherwick Foundation
Rowlands Trust
Peter Samuel Charitable Trust
Sandra Charitable Trust
Sarnia Charitable Trust
Scarfe Charitable Trust
Schroder Charity Trust
Scotbelge Charitable Trust
Scottish Community
     Foundation
Sylvia & Colin Shepherd
     Charitable Trust
Simpson Education &
     Conservation Trust
Skinners' Company Lady
     Neville Charity
W F Southall Trust
Spitalfields Market Community
     Trust
W W Spooner Charitable Trust
Staples Trust
Peter Stebbings Memorial
     Charity
Leonard Laity Stoate
     Charitable Trust
M J C Stone Charitable Trust
Summerfield Charitable Trust
Swann-Morton Foundation
A R Taylor Charitable Trust
C B & H H Taylor 1984 Trust
Tisbury Telegraph Trust
Douglas Turner Trust
Charity of Thomas Wade &
     Others
Wakefield Trust
Barbara Welby Trust
Westminster Foundation

A H and B C Whiteley
   Charitable Trust
Whitley Animal Protection Trust
Will Charitable Trust
H D H Wills 1965 Charitable
   Trust
Charles Wolfson Charitable
   Trust

■ **Fauna and flora**

Funding priority
Ashendene Trust
Blair Foundation
Cobb Charity
Demigryphon Trust
Worshipful Company of
   Gardeners of London
Claude & Margaret Pike
   Woodlands Trust
Ronald & Kathleen Pryor
   Charitable Trust
Mr and Mrs J A Pye's
   Charitable Settlement
David Shepherd Wildlife
   Foundation
Stanley Smith UK Horticultural
   Trust
Swan Trust
Thoresby Charitable Trust
Mrs Maud Van Norden's
   Charitable Foundation
Roger Vere Foundation

Will consider
Adnams Charity
Ammco Trust
Balney Charitable Trust
Bromley Trust
J A Clark Charitable Trust
Iris Darnton Foundation
Earth Love Fund
Alan Evans Memorial Trust
Esmée Fairbairn Foundation
Fishmongers' Company's
   Charitable Trust
Meir Golda Trust
Reginald Graham Charitable
   Trust
J G Graves Charitable Trust
Grocers' Charity
Gunter Charitable Trust
Harebell Centenary Fund
Geoffrey C Hughes Charitable
   Trust
John Jarrold Trust
Edward Cecil Jones Settlement
Lankelly Foundation
Lauffer Family Charitable
   Foundation
Leach Fourteenth Trust
Marchig Animal Welfare Trust
Marsh Christian Trust
Methodist Relief and
   Development Fund
Horace Moore Charitable Trust

Philanthropic Trust
Princess Anne's Charities
Rank Foundation
Märit and Hans Rausing
   Charitable Foundation
Sir James Reckitt Charity
Scott Bader Commonwealth
   Ltd
Scouloudi Foundation
Simpson Education &
   Conservation Trust
Staples Trust
Sutton Coldfield Municipal
   Charities
Swann-Morton Foundation
Charles and Elsie Sykes Trust
Whitaker Charitable Trust
Yorkshire Agricultural Society
John Young Charitable
   Settlement

■ **Water resources**

Funding priority
Cobb Charity
Dock Charitable Fund
J C Green Charitable
   Settlement
Thoresby Charitable Trust

Will consider
1970 Trust
Esmée Fairbairn Foundation
Fishmongers' Company's
   Charitable Trust
Meir Golda Trust
J G Graves Charitable Trust
Gunter Charitable Trust
Geoffrey C Hughes Charitable
   Trust
Lauffer Family Charitable
   Foundation
Methodist Relief and
   Development Fund
Princess Anne's Charities
Mr and Mrs J A Pye's
   Charitable Settlement
Sir James Reckitt Charity
Scott Bader Commonwealth
   Ltd
Staples Trust
Swann-Morton Foundation
Charity of Thomas Wade &
   Others

■ **Wild places,
   wilderness**

Will consider
J Paul Getty Jr Charitable Trust
Girdlers' Company Charitable
   Trust
Leach Fourteenth Trust
Simpson Education &
   Conservation Trust

Pollution abatement and control

Funding priority
Ashden Trust
Countryside Trust
Market Harborough and
   Bowdens Charity
Woodroffe Benton Foundation

Will consider
Ardwick Trust
Body Shop Foundation
British Institute of Archaeology
   at Ankara
British Sugar Foundation
Community Foundation Serving
   Tyne & Wear and
   Northumberland
Cranbury Foundation
Esmée Fairbairn Foundation
Gatwick Airport Community
   Trust
Godinton Charitable Trust
Great Britain Sasakawa
   Foundation
R J Harris Charitable
   Settlement
Mary Homfray Charitable Trust
Leathersellers' Company
   Charitable Fund
Lyndhurst Settlement
Jack Patston Charitable Trust
Porter Foundation
Eleanor Rathbone Charitable
   Trust
Ripple Effect Foundation
Rural Trust
Tisbury Telegraph Trust

Sustainable environment

Funding priority
Ashden Trust
Countryside Trust
Esmée Fairbairn Foundation
Great Britain Sasakawa
   Foundation
Gulbenkian Foundation
Lindeth Charitable Trust
Rufford Foundation

Will consider
Ove Arup Foundation
British Sugar Foundation
Cranbury Foundation
Elmgrant Trust
Gatwick Airport Community
   Trust
Godinton Charitable Trust
R J Harris Charitable
   Settlement
Mary Homfray Charitable Trust

Laing's Charitable Trust
Lyndhurst Settlement
Northern Rock Foundation
Porter Foundation
Eleanor Rathbone Charitable
    Trust
Ripple Effect Foundation
Rural Trust

....

■ Energy issues

Funding priority
Allachy Trust
Cleopatra Trust
Cobb Charity
Dorus Trust
Epigoni Trust
Millfield House Foundation
J B Pelly Charitable Settlement

Will consider
Ajahma Charitable Trust
Anglo-German Foundation for
    Study of Industrial Society
Ardwick Trust
Astor Foundation
BAA 21st Century
    Communities Trust
C Alma Baker Trust
Body Shop Foundation
Bridge House Estates Trust
    Fund
Charities Advisory Trust
Helen and Geoffrey de Freitas
    Charitable Trust
Derbyshire Community
    Foundation
Community Council of Devon
Ecological Foundation
Esmée Fairbairn Foundation
Fiat Auto (UK) Charity
Great Britain Sasakawa
    Foundation
Greater Bristol Foundation
Boris Karloff Charitable
    Foundation
Heinz & Anna Kroch
    Foundation
Mark Leonard Trust
Lintel Trust
Methodist Relief and
    Development Fund
Philanthropic Trust
Polden-Puckham Charitable
    Foundation
Prairie Trust
Joseph Rowntree Charitable
    Trust
Sheepdrove Trust
South Yorkshire Community
    Foundation
Stanley Foundation Ltd
Staples Trust
Summerfield Charitable Trust
Tisbury Telegraph Trust
Webb Memorial Trust

Woodward Trust

Transport

Funding priority
Ashden Trust
Bridge House Estates Trust
    Fund
Rees Jeffreys Road Fund
Millfield House Foundation
J B Pelly Charitable Settlement
RAC Foundation for Motoring
    and Environment Ltd
Tisbury Telegraph Trust

Will consider
Anglo-German Foundation for
    Study of Industrial Society
Astor Foundation
William A Cadbury Charitable
    Trust
Charities Advisory Trust
J A Clark Charitable Trust
John Grant Davies Trust
Helen and Geoffrey de Freitas
    Charitable Trust
Derbyshire Community
    Foundation
Ecological Foundation
Fiat Auto (UK) Charity
Gatwick Airport Community
    Trust
Great Britain Sasakawa
    Foundation
H C D Memorial Fund
Hadrian Trust
Charles Hayward Foundation
Help Aged
Holywood Trust
Leche Trust
Lloyds TSB Foundation for
    Northern Ireland
Macfarlane Walker Trust
Marchday Charitable Fund
Philanthropic Trust
Polden-Puckham Charitable
    Foundation
Eleanor Rathbone Charitable
    Trust
South Yorkshire Community
    Foundation
Summerfield Charitable Trust
Woodward Trust

Faith activities

Funding priority
Bergqvist Charitable Trust
Buckingham Trust
E Alec Colman Charitable Fund
    Ltd
Earl of Derby's Charitable
    Trust
Edith M Ellis 1985 Charitable
    Trust
Harbo Charities Limited
Sir Julian Hodge Charitable
    Trust
Huggard Charitable Trust
John and Rosemary Lancaster
    Charitable Foundation
London Youth Trust
Oliver Morland Charitable Trust
Mutual Trust Group
Rosca Trust
St Peter's Saltley Trust
Moss Spiro Will Charitable
    Foundation
Steinberg Family Charitable
    Trust
Sutton Coldfield Municipal
    Charities
Tompkins Foundation
Tufton Charitable Trust
Van Neste Foundation
Roger Vere Foundation

Will consider
Acacia Charitable Trust
Alexandra Rose Day
Allchurches Trust Ltd
Astor of Hever Trust
Baird Trust
Paul Bassham Charitable Trust
Benham Charitable Settlement
Michael Bishop Foundation
Bowerman Charitable Trust
Mrs E E Brown Charitable
    Settlement
Burdens Charitable Foundation
Edward Cadbury Charitable
    Trust
Edward & Dorothy Cadbury
    Trust
Richard Cadbury Charitable
    Trust
Cairns Charitable Trust
D W T Cargill Fund
Carter's Educational
    Foundation
Chandris Foundation
Church Urban Fund
Sir James Colyer-Fergusson's
    Charitable Trust
Duke of Cornwall's Benevolent
    Fund
County Durham Foundation
Cranbury Foundation
Gwendoline & Margaret Davies
    Charity

DLA Charitable Trust
Esher House Charitable Trust
Fairway Trust
Ferguson Benevolent Fund Ltd
Fiat Auto (UK) Charity
Anne French Memorial Trust
Ganzoni Charitable Trust
G C Gibson Charitable Trust
Girdlers' Company Charitable
   Trust
Gretna Charitable Trust
Hedley Denton Charitable
   Trust
Hesed Trust
Joseph & Mary Hiley Trust
Hobart Charitable Trust
Dorothy Holmes Charitable
   Trust
Homelands Charitable Trust
India Foundation (UK)
Jerusalem Trust
Lauchentilly Charitable
   Foundation 1988
Lethendy Charitable Trust
Ralph Levy Charitable
   Company Ltd
Lyras Family Charitable Trust
M N R Charitable Trust
Market Harborough and
   Bowdens Charity
Michael Marsh Charitable
   Trust
Nigel Moores Family Charitable
   Trust
S C and M E Morland's
   Charitable Trust
Morris Charitable Trust
Laurie Nidditch Foundation
Patients' Aid Association
   Hospital & Medical
   Charities Trust
Jack Patston Charitable Trust
Personal Assurance Charitable
   Trust
Puri Foundation
Joseph Rank Trust
Eleanor Rathbone Charitable
   Trust
Rayne Trust
Sir James Reckitt Charity
Clive Richards Charity Ltd
Sir James Roll Charitable Trust
Cecil Rosen Foundation
Rotherwick Foundation
Royal Docks Trust
Russell Trust
Alan and Babette Sainsbury
   Charitable Fund
Sir Walter St John's
   Educational Charity
St Jude's Trust
St Mary-le-Strand Charity
Leonard Laity Stoate
   Charitable Trust
Summerfield Charitable Trust
Tay Charitable Trust

Constance Travis Charitable
   Trust
Trustees of Tzedakah
Underwood Trust
Vale of Glamorgan Welsh
   Church Fund
Eric W Vincent Trust Fund
Mrs Waterhouse Charitable
   Trust
Mary Webb Trust
Welsh Church Fund –
   Carmarthenshire area
West London Synagogue
   Charitable Fund
Garfield Weston Foundation
Whitaker Charitable Trust
David Wilson Foundation
Wixamtree Trust
I A Ziff Charitable Foundation

Inter-faith activities

Funding priority
Bonamy Charitable Trust
R M 1956 Burton Charitable
   Trust
Inlight Trust
ITF Seafarers Trust
Sir Sigmund Sternberg
   Charitable Foundation

Will consider
Sylvia Aitken Charitable Trust
All Saints Educational Trust
Ardwick Trust
Bedford Charity
Bingham Trust
Arnold James Burton 1956
   Charitable Settlement
CAFOD
Cumber Family Charitable
   Trust
Derbyshire Community
   Foundation
Duis Charitable Trust
Elmgrant Trust
Englefield Charitable Trust
Anne French Memorial Trust
Bishop of Guildford's
   Foundation
Lady Eileen Joseph Foundation
Lawlor Foundation
Levy Foundation
Mercers' Charitable
   Foundation
Keith and Joan Mindelsohn
   Charitable Trust
Moss Family Charitable Trust
Muslim Hands
Pastoral Care Trust
Harry Payne Trust
Alfred and Frances Rubens
   Charitable Trust
Summerfield Charitable Trust

Religious understanding

Funding priority
ITF Seafarers Trust
Padwa Charitable Foundation

Will consider
Sylvia Aitken Charitable Trust
All Saints Educational Trust
Barnabas Charitable Trust
Bingham Trust
Cumber Family Charitable
   Trust
Derbyshire Community
   Foundation
Gilbert & Eileen Edgar
   Foundation
Elmgrant Trust
Englefield Charitable Trust
Anne French Memorial Trust
Great Britain Sasakawa
   Foundation
Hockerill Educational
   Foundation
Lawlor Foundation
Kennedy Leigh Charitable
   Trust
Levy Foundation
Muslim Hands
Steinberg Family Charitable
   Trust
Sir Sigmund Sternberg
   Charitable Foundation
Summerfield Charitable Trust

Christianity

Funding priority
Alexis Trust
Beacon Trust
Sydney Black Charitable Trust
Buckingham Trust
Cannop Trust
Christabella Charitable Trust
John Christie Trust
Earmark Trust
Norman Evershed Trust
F C Charitable Trust
Forest Hill Charitable Trust
Griffith UK Foundation
Matthew Hodder Charitable
   Trust
Huxham Charitable Trust
London Youth Trust
Morgan Williams Charitable
   Trust
Nathan Charitable Trust
New Durlston Trust
Newcastle Diocesan Society
Payne Charitable Trust
Cliff Richard Charitable Trust
Rock Solid Trust
Rooke Atlay Charitable Trust

St Martin-in-the-Fields' Vicar's
General Charity
Shanti Charitable Trust
Theodore Trust
John Wilson Bequest Fund

Will consider

Bingham Trust
D W T Cargill Fund
Joseph & Annie Cattle Trust
George Henry Collins Charity
Coutts & Co. Charitable Trust
Cumber Family Charitable
Trust
Douglas Charitable Trust
Dugdale Charitable Trust
Maud Elkington Charitable
Trust
Emmandjay Charitable Trust
Englefield Charitable Trust
Anne French Memorial Trust
Godinton Charitable Trust
Bishop of Guildford's
Foundation
Mercers' Charitable
Foundation
Miles Trust for Putney and
Roehampton Community
Bassil Shippam and Alsford
Trust
Steinberg Family Charitable
Trust
Leonard Laity Stoate
Charitable Trust
Tay Charitable Trust
A R Taylor Charitable Trust

· ·

■ **Christian causes,
work**

Funding priority

Aid to Church in Need (UK)
Alabaster Trust
Alexis Trust
Almond Trust
André Christian Trust
Archbishop of Canterbury's
Charitable Trust
AS Charitable Trust
Ashburnham Thanksgiving
Trust
Ashendene Trust
Barber Charitable Trust
Dorothy Bayles Trust
Beaufort House Trust
Bellahouston Bequest Fund
Benfield Motors Charitable
Trust
Bethesda Community
Charitable Trust
Thomas Betton's Charity
BibleLands
P G & N J Boulton Trust
William A Cadbury Charitable
Trust
Carpenter Charitable Trust

Childs Charitable Trust
Christabella Charitable Trust
Christian Aid
Church Urban Fund
Clarke Charitable Settlement
Mansfield Cooke Trust
Alice Ellen Cooper-Dean
Charitable Foundation
Corinthian Trust
Criffel Charitable Trust
Cross Trust
Cumberland Trust
Ebenezer Trust
Edwards-Skinner Charitable
Trust
Norman Evershed Trust
Fairbairn Charitable Trust
Farthing Trust
Four Winds Trust
Angela Gallagher Memorial
Fund
Gibbs Charitable Trusts
Global Care
Gough Charitable Trust
Griffith UK Foundation
Grimsdale Charitable Trust
Alfred Haines Charitable Trust
Beatrice Hankey Foundation
Ltd
Kathleen Hannay Memorial
Charity
Harnish Trust
Hinchley Charitable Trust
Incorporated Leeds Church
Extension Society
James Pantyfedwen
Foundation
James Trust
H F Johnson Trust
Edward Cecil Jones Settlement
Maurice and Hilda Laing
Charitable Trust
John and Rosemary Lancaster
Charitable Foundation
William Leech Charity
Paul Lunn-Rockliffe Charitable
Trust
Lyndhurst Trust
Millfield Trust
Millhouses Charitable Trust
Edgar Milward Charity
National Catholic Fund
National Committee of
Women's World Day of
Prayer for England, Wales,
and Northern Ireland
Mr and Mrs F E F Newman
Charitable Trust
Novi Most International
Ogle Christian Trust
Ouseley Trust
Owen Family Trust
Panahpur Charitable Trust
Mrs M E S Paterson's
Charitable Trust
Payne Charitable Trust

William Price Charitable Trust
Sir John Priestman Charity
Trust
Privy Purse Charitable Trust
Nathaniel Reyner Trust Fund
River Trust
Saint Edmund, King & Martyr
Trust
St Gabriel's Trust
St Thomas Ecclesiastical
Charity
Sarum St Michael Educational
Charity
Second Quothquan Charitable
Trust
Seedfield Trust
Simpson Foundation
SMB Trust
Stewards Company
Stobart Newlands Charitable
Trust
Walter Swindon Charitable
Trust
Thornton Trust
Tisbury Telegraph Trust
Vardy Foundation
Wallington Missionary Mart
and Auctions
Waterside Trust
Whitecourt Charitable Trust
Norman Whiteley Trust
Dame Violet Wills Charitable
Trust
Woodlands Trust (1015942)
Woodlands Trust (259569)

Will consider

Viscount Amory's Charitable
Trust
Cwmbran Trust
Emerton-Christie Charity
Hadrian Trust
Sir James Knott Trust
Horace Moore Charitable Trust
Summerfield Charitable Trust
Abel Charitable Trust
Philip Barker Charity
Barnabas Trust
James Beattie Charitable Trust
Bishop's Development Fund
Harry Bottom Charitable Trust
Britland Charitable Trust
Charles & Edna Broadhurst
Charitable Trust
Burden Trust
Jerusalem Trust
CAFOD
Carmichael-Montgomery
Charitable Trust
Hesed Trust
Hockerill Educational
Foundation
Holywood Trust
Sir Harold Hood's Charitable
Trust
John Jarrold Trust

Nancy Kenyon Charitable Trust
Late Sir Pierce Lacy Charity
   Trust
Langley Charitable Trust
P Leigh-Bramwell Trust 'E'
Lynwood Trust
Chasah Trust
Norman Collinson Charitable
   Trust
Congleton Inclosure Trust
Cumber Family Charitable
   Trust
Dulverton Trust
Feed Minds
Earl Fitzwilliam Charitable
   Trust
Fortuna Charitable Trust
Anne French Memorial Trust
Golden Charitable Trust
All Saints Educational Trust
AMW Charitable Trust
Astor Foundation
Beacon Trust
Edward Cadbury Charitable
   Trust
W A Cargill Charitable Trust
W A Cargill Fund
Chownes Foundation
Dugdale Charitable Trust
Daily Prayer Union Charitable
   Trust Ltd
Sir John Evelyn's Charity
Grace Baptist Trust
   Corporation
May Hearnshaw's Charity
Dorcas Trust
Vernon N Ely Charitable Trust
Euroclydon Trust
Ferguson Bequest Fund
Fulmer Charitable Trust
 Girdlers' Company Charitable
   Trust
Goshen Trust
Homestead Charitable Trust
Irwin Trust
Kirby Laing Foundation
Leonard Trust
Jane Hodge Foundation
Tabeel Trust
Tolkien Trust
Albert Waghorn Charitable
   Trust
Marsh Christian Trust
John Martin's Charity
Helen Isabella McMorran
   Charitable Foundation
Mercers' Charitable
   Foundation
Nazareth Trust Fund
Newby Trust Limited
Alderman Newton's
   Educational Foundation
Oikonomia Trust
Gerald Palmer Trust
David Pickford Charitable
   Foundation

Bernard Piggott Trust
Simone Prendergast Charitable
   Trust
Ravensdale Trust
Cliff Richard Charitable Trust
Mrs L D Rope Third Charitable
   Settlement
Sharon Trust
St Hilda's Trust
Sir Halley Stewart Trust
Bernard Sunley Charitable
   Foundation
Torchbearer Trust
United Society for Propagation
   of Gospel
Wates Foundation
Matthews Wrightson Charity
   Trust
Maranatha Christian Trust
Charlotte Marshall Charitable
   Trust
Minos Trust
Nigel Moores Family Charitable
   Trust
Peter Moores Foundation
Mr and Mrs J T Morgan
   Foundation
Pedmore Trust
Rank Foundation
St Mary-le-Strand Charity
Hope Trust

....

■ Christian churches
Funding priority
Allchurches Trust Ltd
Archbishop of Canterbury's
   Charitable Trust
AS Charitable Trust
Baird Trust
Balney Charitable Trust
Dorothy Bayles Trust
Bedfordshire & Hertfordshire
   Historic Churches Trust
 Bellahouston Bequest Fund
Benfield Motors Charitable
   Trust
Benham Charitable Settlement
Rowan Bentall Charitable Trust
Bethesda Community
   Charitable Trust
BibleLands
Isabel Blackman Foundation
A H & E Boulton Trust
Buckinghamshire Historic
   Churches Trust
William A Cadbury Charitable
   Trust
Cambridgeshire Historic
   Churches Trust
Chase Charity
Clarke Charitable Settlement
Cleary Foundation
Richard Cloudesley's Charity
Francis Coales Charitable
   Foundation

Sir Jeremiah Colman Gift Trust
Cornwall Historic Churches
   Trust
Criffel Charitable Trust
Cross Trust
Demigryphon Trust
Sandy Dewhirst Charitable
   Trust
Norman Evershed Trust
F C Charitable Trust
Four Winds Trust
Jill Franklin Trust
Anne French Memorial Trust
Friends of Essex Churches
Friends of Kent Churches
Simon Gibson Charitable Trust
Gloucestershire Historic
   Churches Trust
Gough Charitable Trust
Grace Baptist Trust
   Corporation
Grimsdale Charitable Trust
Hampshire & Islands Historic
   Churches Trust
Kathleen Hannay Memorial
   Charity
Lennox Hannay Charitable
   Trust
Herefordshire Historic
   Churches Trust
Heritage of London Trust Ltd
Historic Churches Preservation
   Trust
Sir Harold Hood's Charitable
   Trust
Huxham Charitable Trust
Incorporated Leeds Church
   Extension Society
James Pantyfedwen
   Foundation
James Trust
Edward Cecil Jones Settlement
Laslett's (Hinton) Charity
Lauchentilly Charitable
   Foundation 1988
Leicester and Leicestershire
   Historic Churches
   Preservation Trust
P Leigh-Bramwell Trust 'E'
Lincolnshire Old Churches
   Trust
Lyndhurst Trust
Midhurst Pensions Trust
Millhouses Charitable Trust
Minge's Gift
Monmouthshire County Council
   Welsh Church Act Fund
Horace Moore Charitable Trust
Norfolk Churches Trust Ltd
Northamptonshire Historic
   Churches Trust
Norwood & Newton Settlement
Oxfordshire Historic Churches
   Trust
Austin & Hope Pilkington Trust
Radcliffe Trust

Joseph Rank Trust
Rawdon-Smith Trust
Nathaniel Reyner Trust Fund
Rhondda Cynon Taff Welsh
  Church Acts Fund
River Trust
Rosca Trust
Saint Edmund, King & Martyr
  Trust
Frieda Scott Charitable Trust
Shropshire Historic Churches
  Trust
Simpson Foundation
SMB Trust
Albert & Florence Smith
  Memorial Trust
Staffordshire Historic
  Churches Trust
Samuel Storey Family
  Charitable Trust
Suffolk Historic Churches Trust
Sussex Historic Churches
  Trust
Sutton Coldfield Municipal
  Charities
Swan Trust
Thoresby Charitable Trust
Mrs S H Troughton Charity
  Trust
United Society for Propagation
  of Gospel
Vale of Glamorgan Welsh
  Church Fund
Verdon-Smith Family Charitable
  Settlement
Wakefield Trust
John Warren Foundation
Welsh Church Fund –
  Carmarthenshire area
Whitecourt Charitable Trust
Dame Violet Wills Charitable
  Trust
Wixamtree Trust
James Wood Bequest Fund
Woodlands Trust (1015942)
Worcestershire & Dudley
  Historic Churches Trust
Yorkshire Historic Churches
  Trust

Will consider
Alabaster Trust
Almond Trust
Viscount Amory's Charitable
  Trust
Mary Andrew Charitable Trust
G C Armitage Charitable Trust
Astor Foundation
Bamford Charitable Foundation
Barbour Trust
Lord Barnby's Foundation
James Beattie Charitable Trust
Bishop's Development Fund
Blanchminster Trust
Harry Bottom Charitable Trust

Charles & Edna Broadhurst
  Charitable Trust
Charles Brotherton Trust
Geoffrey Burton Charitable
  Trust
W A Cargill Charitable Trust
Carmichael-Montgomery
  Charitable Trust
Wilfrid & Constance Cave
  Foundation
Cemlyn-Jones Trust
Childs Charitable Trust
Chipping Sodbury Town Lands
  Charity
Lord Clinton's Charitable Trust
Congleton Inclosure Trust
Holbeche Corfield Charitable
  Settlement
Cumber Family Charitable
  Trust
Daily Prayer Union Charitable
  Trust Ltd
De Clermont Charitable
  Company Ltd
DLM Charitable Trust
Dorcas Trust
Alan Evans Memorial Trust
Fairbairn Charitable Trust
Ferguson Bequest Fund
Earl Fitzwilliam Charitable
  Trust
Forte Charitable Trust
Thomas Freke & Lady Norton
  Charity
Charles S French Charitable
  Trust
Gibbs Charitable Trusts
Girdlers' Company Charitable
  Trust
Meir Golda Trust
Hadrian Trust
E F & M G Hall Charitable
  Trust
Robert Hall Charity
Headley Trust
May Hearnshaw's Charity
Hedley Foundation
Hemby Trust
Hinchley Charitable Trust
Jane Hodge Foundation
Sir Harold Hood's Charitable
  Trust
John & Ruth Howard
  Charitable Trust
Isle of Anglesey Charitable
  Trust
Jarman Charitable Trust
Joicey Trust
Beatrice Laing Trust
Kirby Laing Foundation
Maurice and Hilda Laing
  Charitable Trust
Langley Charitable Trust
R J Larg Family Charitable
  Trust

Lord Leverhulme Charitable
  Trust
Linden Charitable Trust
Elaine & Angus Lloyd
  Charitable Trust
Helen Isabella McMorran
  Charitable Foundation
Manifold Trust
Charlotte Marshall Charitable
  Trust
John Martin's Charity
Mercers' Charitable
  Foundation
Nazareth Trust Fund
Newby Trust Limited
Northumbria Historic Churches
  Trust
Oakley Charitable Trust
Oldham Foundation
Owen Family Trust
Patients' Aid Association
  Hospital & Medical
  Charities Trust
Payne Charitable Trust
Harry Payne Trust
Bernard Piggott Trust
A M Pilkington's Charitable
  Trust
Pilkington Charities Fund
Prince Foundation
Proven Family Trust
Ravensdale Trust
Cliff Richard Charitable Trust
Rotherwick Foundation
Rowlands Trust
Russell Trust
St Hilda's Trust
Saint Sarkis Charity Trust
Sheffield Church Burgesses
  Trust
Shipwrights Company
  Charitable Fund
South Square Trust
Ralph and Irma Sperring
  Charity
Steel Charitable Trust
Steventon Allotments & Relief-
  in-Need Charity
Summerfield Charitable Trust
Bernard Sunley Charitable
  Foundation
Talbot Village Trust
C B & H H Taylor 1984 Trust
Tolkien Trust
Westminster Foundation
Wolfson Foundation
Woodlands Trust (259569)

■ **Anglican**
Funding priority
Benham Charitable Settlement
Bristol Archdeaconry Charities
Richard Cloudesley's Charity
J C Green Charitable
  Settlement

Incorporated Church Building
Society
Nottinghamshire Historic
Churches Trust
William Price Charitable Trust
Sheffield Church Burgesses
Trust

Will consider
Bates Charitable Trust
Cranbury Foundation
Anne French Memorial Trust
Edward Cecil Jones Settlement
Anthony and Elizabeth Mellows
Charitable Settlement
Mercers' Charitable
Foundation
John Pitman Charitable Trust
R H Scholes Charitable Trust
Tisbury Telegraph Trust
Warwick Municipal Charities –
Charity of King Henry VIII,
Warwick

■ **Roman Catholic**
Funding priority
Bisgood Charitable Trust
Catholic Charitable Trust
Charity of Theresa Harriet
Mary Delacour
Joseph Fattorini Charitable
Trust 'B' Account
Angela Gallagher Memorial
Fund
Heagerty Charitable Trust
Edward Cecil Jones Settlement
Kennedy Charitable Foundation
Late Sir Pierce Lacy Charity
Trust
Lindale Educational
Foundation
National Catholic Fund
Nottinghamshire Historic
Churches Trust
Clive Richards Charity Ltd
Roman Catholic Diocese of
Hexham and Newcastle
Rosemary Scanlan Charitable
Trust
Simpson Foundation
Tolkien Trust

Will consider
Catholic Foreign Missions
Chownes Foundation
Nicholas Coote Charitable
Trust
J A R Charitable Trust
Mercers' Charitable
Foundation
Mrs L D Rope Third Charitable
Settlement
St Hilda's Trust
Sylvanus Charitable Trust

■ **Society of Friends,**
Quakers
Funding priority
B C No. 9 1972 Charitable
Trust
Barnabas Charitable Trust
Richard Cadbury Charitable
Trust
William A Cadbury Charitable
Trust
Bryan Lancaster's Charity
Oliver Morland Charitable Trust
S C and M E Morland's
Charitable Trust
Nottinghamshire Historic
Churches Trust
Oakdale Trust
Polden-Puckham Charitable
Foundation
W F Southall Trust

Will consider
William P Bancroft (No 2)
Charitable Trust and
Jenepher Gillett Trust
Hilda & Alice Clark Charitable
Trust
Roger & Sarah Bancroft Clark
Charitable Trust
Marsh Christian Trust
Mercers' Charitable
Foundation
Harry Payne Trust
Joseph Rowntree Charitable
Trust
Joseph Rowntree Foundation
Sarnia Charitable Trust
C B & H H Taylor 1984 Trust
Tisbury Telegraph Trust

■ **Christian social**
thought
Funding priority
ITF Seafarers Trust
Souter Charitable Trust

Will consider
Tisbury Telegraph Trust

■ **Ecumenicalism**
Funding priority
James Pantyfedwen
Foundation

Will consider
All Saints Educational Trust
Carmichael-Montgomery
Charitable Trust
Mercers' Charitable
Foundation

■ **Missionary work,**
evangelism
Funding priority
Aid to Church in Need (UK)
Alabaster Trust
Alexis Trust
Almond Trust
Ashburnham Thanksgiving
Trust
Barber Charitable Trust
Bethesda Community
Charitable Trust
P G & N J Boulton Trust
Catholic Foreign Missions
Chasah Trust
Mansfield Cooke Trust
Criffel Charitable Trust
Cross Trust
Cumberland Trust
Daily Prayer Union Charitable
Trust Ltd
Ebenezer Trust
F C Charitable Trust
Fairbairn Charitable Trust
Farthing Trust
Four Winds Trust
Alfred Haines Charitable Trust
Beatrice Hankey Foundation
Ltd
Kathleen Hannay Memorial
Charity
Highmoor Hall Charitable Trust
Hinchley Charitable Trust
Stuart Hine Trust
Incorporated Leeds Church
Extension Society
James Trust
Kennedy Charitable Foundation
Maurice and Hilda Laing
Charitable Trust
John and Rosemary Lancaster
Charitable Foundation
Paul Lunn-Rockliffe Charitable
Trust
Lynwood Trust
Millfield Trust
Edgar Milward Charity
Nathan Charitable Trust
Mr and Mrs F E F Newman
Charitable Trust
Novi Most International
Ogle Christian Trust
Panahpur Charitable Trust
Payne Charitable Trust
Nathaniel Reyner Trust Fund
Second Quothquan Charitable
Trust
Seedfield Trust
SMB Trust
Souter Charitable Trust
Spring Harvest Charitable
Trust
Stewards Company
Stobart Newlands Charitable
Trust
Tearfund

Thornton Trust
Tisbury Telegraph Trust
Ulting Overseas Trust
Wallington Missionary Mart
  and Auctions
Whitecourt Charitable Trust
Norman Whiteley Trust
Dame Violet Wills Charitable
  Trust
Woodlands Trust (1015942)
Woodlands Trust (259569)

Will consider
Astor Foundation
Barnabas Trust
BibleLands
Britland Charitable Trust
Charles & Edna Broadhurst
  Charitable Trust
Edward Cadbury Charitable
  Trust
Carpenter Charitable Trust
Childs Charitable Trust
Dorcas Trust
Norman Evershed Trust
Feed Minds
Anne French Memorial Trust
Homestead Charitable Trust
Jerusalem Trust
Beatrice Laing Trust
Kirby Laing Foundation
Langley Charitable Trust
Herd Lawson Charitable Trust
Leach Fourteenth Trust
Leonard Trust
Maranatha Christian Trust
Marsh Christian Trust
Mercers' Charitable
  Foundation
Peter Moores Foundation
Nazareth Trust Fund
Oikonomia Trust
Owen Family Trust
Gerald Palmer Trust
Andrew Paton's Charitable
  Trust
Harry Payne Trust
Pedmore Trust
David Pickford Charitable
  Foundation
Cliff Richard Charitable Trust
St Francis Leprosy Guild
Sharon Trust
Summerfield Charitable Trust
Tabeel Trust
United Society for Propagation
  of Gospel
Matthews Wrightson Charity
  Trust

Hinduism

Funding priority
Midhurst Pensions Trust
Sutton Coldfield Municipal
  Charities

Will consider
BBC Children in Need Appeal
William A Cadbury Charitable
  Trust
Joicey Trust
Proven Family Trust
Puri Foundation
Summerfield Charitable Trust
Sussex Historic Churches
  Trust

Islam

Funding priority
London Youth Trust
Muslim Hands
North London Islamic
  Association Trust
Sutton Coldfield Municipal
  Charities

Will consider
William A Cadbury Charitable
  Trust
Joicey Trust
Matliwala Family Charitable
  Trust
Proven Family Trust
Sir Sigmund Sternberg
  Charitable Foundation
Summerfield Charitable Trust
Sussex Historic Churches
  Trust

Judaism

Funding priority
Achiezer Association Ltd
Alba Charitable Trust
Alliance Family Foundation
Altamont Ltd
Amberstone Trust
ATP Charitable Trust
AW Charitable Trust
Beauland Ltd
R J Beecham 1981 Charitable
  Trust
Michael and Leslie Bennett
  Charitable Trust
Bintaub Charitable Trust
Neville & Elaine Blond
  Charitable Trust
Bois Rochel Dsatmar
  Charitable Trust
Bonamy Charitable Trust
A Bornstein Charitable
  Settlement
Briess Family Charitable Trust
R M 1956 Burton Charitable
  Trust
Carlee Ltd
Charitworth Limited
Charity Association
  Manchester Ltd
Chelwood 2000 Settlement

Closehelm Ltd
Clydpride Ltd
Vivienne & Samuel Cohen
  Charitable Trust
Col-Reno Ltd
Cuby Charitable Trust
Debmar Benevolent Trust
Dollond Charitable Trust
Elanore Ltd
Ellador Ltd
Elshore Ltd
Rose Flatau Charitable Trust
Flow Foundation
Gederville Ltd
Jacqueline and Michael Gee
  Charitable Trust
Everard & Mina Goodman
  Charitable Foundation
Grahame Charitable
  Foundation
Harbour Foundation
Hathaway Trust
Haydan Charitable Trust
Heathside Charitable Trust
Bernhard Heuberger Charitable
  Trust
Jacksons Charitable Trust
Bernard Kahn Charitable Trust
Stanley Kalms Foundation
Kass Charitable Trust
Keren Association
Kohn Foundation
Largsmount Ltd
Locker Foundation
London Youth Trust
Malcolm Lyons Foundation
M K (Mendel Kaufman)
  Charitable Trust
Stella and Alexander Margulies
  Charitable Trust
Maypride Ltd
M Miller Charitable Trust
Victor Mishcon Charitable
  Trust
Mole Charitable Trust
Mutual Trust Group
Willie Nagel Charitable Trust
Nesswall Ltd
Laurie Nidditch Foundation
Joseph and Sarah Pearlman
  Jewish Charitable Trust
Peltz Trust
Edith & Ferdinand Porjes
  Charitable Trust
Premierquote Ltd
R S Charitable Trust
Joseph & Lena Randall
  Charitable Trust
Raydan Charitable Trust
Ridgesave Limited
Thomas Roberts Trust
Rothschild Foundation
Joshua and Michelle Rowe
  Charitable Trust
Rubin Foundation

Michael Sacher Charitable
    Trust
Ruzin Sadagora Trust
Schmidt-Bodner Charitable
    Trust
Schreiber Charitable Trust
Searchlight Electric Charitable
    Trust
J Shine Charities Ltd
Shlomo Memorial Fund Limited
Sinclair Charitable Trust
Rosalyn and Nicholas Springer
    Charitable Trust
Jack Steinberg Charitable
    Trust
Sueberry Ltd
Sumray Charitable Trust
Sutton Coldfield Municipal
    Charities
Tajtelbaum Charitable Trust
Talteg Ltd
Tomchei Torah Charitable
    Trust
Tudor Rose Ltd
David Uri Memorial Trust
Weinberg Foundation
Weinstein Foundation
Weinstock Fund
Alfred and Beatrice Weintrop
    Charity
Williams Family Charitable
    Trust
Benjamin Winegarten
    Charitable Trust
Maurice Wohl Charitable
    Foundation
Maurice Wohl Charitable Trust
Woodlands Green Ltd
Wychdale Ltd
Wychville Ltd
I A Ziff Charitable Foundation

Will consider
Andrew Balint Charitable Trust
George Balint Charitable Trust
Paul Balint Charitable Trust
Bear Mordechai Ltd
Blair Foundation
Patsy Bloom & Robert
    Blausten Charitable Trust
Arnold James Burton 1956
    Charitable Settlement
Audrey & Stanley Burton
    Charitable Trust
C B Trust
William A Cadbury Charitable
    Trust
Mauritis Mulder Canter Charity
Childwick Trust
Andrew Cohen Charitable Trust
Denise Cohen Charitable Trust
Manny Cussins Foundation
Davis-Rubens Charitable Trust
Leopold De Rothschild
    Charitable Trust
Djanogly Foundation

Meir Golda Trust
Golden Charitable Trust
Joicey Trust
Kreitman Foundation
Carole & Geoffrey Lawson
    Foundation
Levy Foundation
Loftus Charitable Trust
Keith and Joan Mindelsohn
    Charitable Trust
Vyoel Moshe Charitable Trust
Naggar Charitable Trust
Harry Payne Trust
John Porter Charitable Trust
J E Posnansky Charitable Trust
Proven Family Trust
Cecil Rosen Foundation
Sellata Ltd
Sparquote Limited
Roama Spears Charitable
    Settlement
Stanley Charitable Trust
Steinberg Family Charitable
    Trust
Sir Sigmund Sternberg
    Charitable Foundation
Sussex Historic Churches
    Trust
Ullmann Trust
Charles Wolfson Charitable
    Trust
Wolfson Foundation

....

■ Jewish causes, work

Funding priority
Henry & Grete Abrahams
    Charitable Trust
AM Charitable Trust
Ardwick Trust
Sir Leon Bagrit Memorial Trust
Baker Charitable Trust
Bluston Charitable Settlement
Bonamy Charitable Trust
Salo Bordon Charitable Trust
M Bourne Charitable Trust
Brushmill Ltd
Carroll-Marx Charitable
    Foundation
Muriel and Gershon Coren
    Charitable Foundation
Sidney & Elizabeth Corob
    Charitable Trust
Craps Charitable Trust
Datnow Limited
George Elias Charitable Trust
Elman Charitable Trust
Exilarch's Foundation
Family Foundations Trust
Famos Foundation Trust
Gerald Fogel Charitable Trust
Fordeve Ltd
Forte Charitable Trust
Isaac and Freda Frankel
    Memorial Charitable Trust

Mejer and Gertrude Miriam
    Frydman Foundation
Garvan Limited
Everard & Mina Goodman
    Charitable Foundation
Naomi & Jeffrey Greenwood
    Charitable Trust
GRP Charitable Trust
N and R Grunbaum Charitable
    Trust
Isaacs Charitable Trust
Jacobs Charitable Trust
Susan and Stephen James
    Charitable Settlement
J E Joseph Charitable Fund
Michael & Ilse Katz Foundation
Emmanuel Kaye Foundation
E & E Kernkraut Charities
    Limited
Kobler Trust
Lambert Charitable Trust
Lawson Charitable Foundation
Lawson-Beckman Charitable
    Trust
Arnold Lee Charitable Trust
Kennedy Leigh Charitable
    Trust
Morris Leigh Foundation
Ruth & Stuart Lipton
    Charitable Trust
Second Joseph Aaron Littman
    Foundation
Harry Livingstone Charitable
    Trust
Jack Livingstone Charitable
    Trust
Lolev Charitable Trust
Sir Jack Lyons Charitable Trust
M & C Trust
Magen Charitable Trust
Linda Marcus Charitable Trust
Hilda & Samuel Marks
    Foundation
M Miller Charitable Trust
Laurence Misener Charitable
    Trust
Mitchell Charitable Trust
Morris Family Israel Trust
Ruth and Conrad Morris
    Charitable Trust
Chevras Ezras Nitzrochim Trust
Noswal Charitable Trust
Ruth & Michael Phillips
    Charitable Trust
George & Esme Pollitzer
    Charitable Settlement
Rest Harrow Trust
Rokach Family Charitable Trust
Cissie Rosefield Charitable
    Trust
Schreib Trust
Archie Sherman Charitable
    Trust
L H Silver Charitable Trust
Solo Charitable Settlement
Stervon Ltd

Walter Swindon Charitable
  Trust
Lili Tapper Charitable
  Foundation
Truedene Co. Ltd
Harold Hyam Wingate
  Foundation
Wolfson Family Charitable
  Trust

Will consider
Henry & Grete Abrahams
  Second Charitable
  Foundation
Acacia Charitable Trust
Peter Black Charitable Trust
Dent Charitable Trust
Duis Charitable Trust
Esher House Charitable Trust
Forbesville Limited
Reginald Graham Charitable
  Trust
Ruth & Lionel Jacobson Trust
  (Second Fund) No 2
Sir James Knott Trust
Laufer Charitable Trust
Lauffer Family Charitable
  Foundation
Levy Foundation
John Martin's Charity
Moss Family Charitable Trust
J S F Pollitzer Charitable
  Settlement
Simone Prendergast Charitable
  Trust
Cecil Rosen Foundation
Alfred and Frances Rubens
  Charitable Trust
Summerfield Charitable Trust
Michael and Anna Wix
  Charitable Trust

....
■ **Orthodox Judaism**
  Funding priority
Achisomoch Aid Company
Adenfirst Ltd
Beis Aharon Trust Fund
Alglen Ltd
Becker Family Charitable Trust
Belljoe Tzedoko Ltd
C & F Charitable Trust
Itzchok Meyer Cymerman Trust
  Ltd
Ellinson Foundation Ltd
Entindale Ltd
Friends of Biala Ltd
Gableholt Limited
M & R Gross Charities Limited
Gur Trust
H P Charitable Trust
Highcroft Charitable Trust
Huntingdon Foundation
Hurdale Charity Limited
Invicta Trust
Kasner Charitable Trust

Kermaville Ltd
Localtrent Ltd
M D & S Charitable Trust
Marbeh Torah Trust
Mayfair Charities Ltd
Melodor Ltd
Melow Charitable Trust
Nemoral Ltd
Newpier Charity Ltd
B E Perl Charitable Trust
Premishlaner Charitable Trust
Fanny Rapaport Charitable
  Settlement
Rowanville Ltd
Schapira Charitable Trust
Annie Schiff Charitable Trust
Scopus Jewish Educational
  Trust
Samuel Sebba Charitable
  Trust
SO Charitable Trust
Solev Co Ltd
Songdale Ltd
Cyril & Betty Stein Charitable
  Trust
David Tannen Charitable Trust
Tegham Limited
Trumros Limited
Union of Orthodox Hebrew
  Congregation
Vivdale Ltd
Warbeck Fund Ltd
Stella & Ernest Weinstein
  Trust

Will consider
Lord Ashdown Charitable Trust
Corona Charitable Trust
Ruth & Lionel Jacobson Trust
  (Second Fund) No 2
Menuchar Ltd
MYA Charitable Trust

■ **Sikhism**

  Funding priority
London Youth Trust

  Will consider
William A Cadbury Charitable
  Trust
Summerfield Charitable Trust

Health

  Funding priority
Paul Bassham Charitable Trust
Salo Bordon Charitable Trust
British Sugar Foundation
Church Houses Relief in Need
  Charity
Commonwealth Relations
  Trust
Foyle Foundation
Gatsby Charitable Foundation
Jacqueline and Michael Gee
  Charitable Trust
Hitachi Europe Charitable
  Trust
Clifford Howarth Charity
  Settlement
Margaret Foundation
Willie & Mabel Morris
  Charitable Trust
Oppenheimer Charitable Trust
Second Sidbury Trust
Sheffield and District Hospital
  Services Charitable Fund
Constance Travis Charitable
  Trust
Blyth Watson Charitable Trust
Weinberg Foundation
David Wilson Foundation
John Wilson Bequest Fund
Miss Hazel M Wood Charitable
  Trust
Yamanouchi European
  Foundation

  Will consider
Alexandra Rose Day
Mary Andrew Charitable Trust
Balcombe Charitable Trust
Band (1976) Trust
Misses Barrie Charitable Trust
Batchworth Trust
Peter Beckwith Charitable
  Trust
Bellinger Donnay Trust
Morgan Blake Charitable Trust
Neville & Elaine Blond
  Charitable Trust
David Brooke Charity
Bryant Trust
Campden Charities
Cattanach Charitable Trust
Joseph & Annie Cattle Trust
Chamberlain Foundation
George Henry Collins Charity
  Community Fund
Delves Charitable Trust
Duke of Devonshire's
  Charitable Trust
DLA Charitable Trust
W E Dunn Trust
Dyers' Company Charitable
  Trust
Englefield Charitable Trust
Thomas Farr Charitable Trust

Donald Forrester Trust
G C Gibson Charitable Trust
Godinton Charitable Trust
Grantham Yorke Trust
Gretna Charitable Trust
R J Harris Charitable
    Settlement
Headley Trust
Hedley Denton Charitable
    Trust
Hobart Charitable Trust
Jane Hodge Foundation
J G Hogg Charitable Trust
Joseph Hopkins Charity
Worshipful Company of
    Innholders General Charity
    Fund
King's Fund (King Edward's
    Hospital Fund for London)
Christopher Laing Foundation
Leathersellers' Company
    Charitable Fund
William Leech Charity
Lethendy Charitable Trust
Edgar Milward Charity
G M Morrison Charitable Trust
Stanley Morrison Charitable
    Trust
Janet Nash Charitable Trust
Norton Foundation
Patients' Aid Association
    Hospital & Medical
    Charities Trust
Princess Anne's Charities
Sir James Reckitt Charity
Helen Roll Charitable Trust
Rothley Trust
St Laurence Charities for Poor
Late St Patrick White
    Charitable Trust
Saints & Sinners Trust
Seamen's Hospital Society
Archie Sherman Cardiff
    Charitable Foundation
Archie Sherman Charitable
    Trust
South Yorkshire Community
    Foundation
Sovereign Health Care
    Charitable Trust
A R Taylor Charitable Trust
Thackray Medical Research
    Trust
Tompkins Foundation
Triangle Trust (1949) Fund
Douglas Turner Trust
R D Turner Charitable Trust
Vale of Glamorgan Welsh
    Church Fund
Valentine Charitable Trust
F J Wallis Charitable
    Settlement
Warwickshire Masonic
    Charitable Association Ltd
Welsh Church Fund –
    Carmarthenshire area

Zochonis Charitable Trust

Alternative, complementary medicine

Funding priority
Bothwell Charitable Trust
Lance Coates Charitable Trust
    1969
Elton John Aids Foundation
Ormsby Charitable Trust
J B Pelly Charitable Settlement
Truemark Trust

Will consider
Adint Charitable Trust
AIM Foundation
Sylvia Aitken Charitable Trust
Ashby Charitable Trust
Astor Foundation
Bearder Charity
Birmingham Hospital Saturday
    Fund Medical Charity &
    Welfare Trust
Boots Charitable Trust
Bryant Trust
Chippenham Borough Lands
    Charity
Chipping Sodbury Town Lands
    Charity
J A Clark Charitable Trust
D'Oyly Carte Charitable Trust
Derbyshire Community
    Foundation
Duis Charitable Trust
Elmgrant Trust
Epilepsy Research Foundation
Sir John Fisher Foundation
Hadfield Trust
Charles Hayward Foundation
Mary Homfray Charitable Trust
James Thom Howat Charitable
    Trust
Inchrye Trust
Sir Charles Jessel Charitable
    Trust
Johnson Foundation
Anton Jurgens Charitable Trust
Sir James Knott Trust
Leach Fourteenth Trust
Lloyds TSB Foundation for
    England and Wales
Lloyds TSB Foundation for
    Northern Ireland
M N R Charitable Trust
John Moores Foundation
Norman Family Charitable
    Trust
Northcott Devon Foundation
Norwich Consolidated
    Charities
Austin & Hope Pilkington Trust
PPP Foundation

Mr and Mrs J A Pye's
    Charitable Settlement
Radio Forth Help a Child
    Appeal
Rainford Trust
Christopher H R Reeves
    Charitable Trust
REMEDI
Christopher Rowbotham
    Charitable Trust
Rufford Foundation
Russell Trust
St James' Trust Settlement
Sir James & Lady Scott Trust
Sellafield Charity Trust Fund
Sobell Foundation
South Square Trust
C Paul Thackray General
    Charitable Trust
Tudor Trust
Ward Blenkinsop Trust
Whitaker Charitable Trust

Health care

Funding priority
Aberbrothock Charitable Trust
Airways Charitable Trust
    Limited
Ashe Park Charitable Trust
Sir Leon Bagrit Memorial Trust
Bramble Charitable Trust
Bristol Charities
Burall Charitable Trust
Malcolm Chick Charity
Richard Cloudesley's Charity
Criffel Charitable Trust
Denton Wilde Sapte Charitable
    Trust
Dickon Trust
James Ellis Charitable Trust
Essex Community Foundation
Maurice Fry Charitable Trust
Simon Gibson Charitable Trust
Great Britain Sasakawa
    Foundation
Sue Hammerson's Charitable
    Trust
Hampton Fuel Allotment
    Charity
Kathleen Hannay Memorial
    Charity
Lennox Hannay Charitable
    Trust
Kenneth Hargreaves Charitable
    Trust
N & P Hartley Memorial Trust
Higgs Charitable Trust
Joseph & Mary Hiley Trust
Dorothy Jacobs Charity
Kidani Memorial Trust
King's Fund
Kobler Trust
Kohn Foundation
Arnold Lee Charitable Trust

Leeds Hospital Fund Charitable Trust
Marie Helen Luen Charitable Trust
Lord and Lady Lurgan Trust
Maxwell Family Foundation
Medlock Charitable Trust
Monument Trust
Newstead Charity
Northwood Charitable Trust
Nottingham General Dispensary
Nuffield Trust
Patients' Aid Association Hospital & Medical Charities Trust
Personal Assurance Charitable Trust
Pilkington Charities Fund
Mary Potter Convent Hospital Trust
Richard Radcliffe Charitable Trust
Violet M Richards Charity
Thomas Roberts Trust
Rooke Atlay Charitable Trust
Rosca Trust
Shears Charitable Trust
Stanley Foundation Ltd
Peter Stebbings Memorial Charity
Sutton Coldfield Municipal Charities
Thompson Family Charitable Trust
Tubney Charitable Trust
Ulverston Town Lands Charity
Underwood Trust
Wolfson Family Charitable Trust
Women at Risk
Miss E B Wrightson's Charitable Settlement
John K Young Endowment Fund

Will consider
29th May 1961 Charitable Trust
Henry & Grete Abrahams Charitable Trust
Henry & Grete Abrahams Second Charitable Foundation
Acacia Charitable Trust
Sylvia Aitken Charitable Trust
Alchemy Foundation
H B Allen Charitable Trust
Alliance Family Foundation
Sir John & Lady Amory's Charitable Trust
Appletree Trust
Milly Apthorp Charitable Trust
Armourers and Brasiers' Gauntlet Trust
Army Benevolent Fund

Ashworth Charitable Trust
Astor of Hever Trust
Atlantic Foundation
ATP Charitable Trust
Lord Austin Trust
John Avins Trustees
Balcombe Charitable Trust
Albert Casanova Ballard Deceased Trust
Balmore Trust
Barnes Workhouse Fund
Barracks Trust of Newcastle-under-Lyme
Bates Charitable Trust
BBC Radio Lincolnshire Charity Trust
Bearder Charity
James Beattie Charitable Trust
Beauland Ltd
Peter Beckwith Charitable Trust
Beit Trust
Benfield Motors Charitable Trust
Benham Charitable Settlement
Bergqvist Charitable Trust
Berkshire Community Foundation
Thomas Betton's Charity for Pensions and Relief-in-Need
BibleLands
Bingham Trust
Bintaub Charitable Trust
Birmingham District Nursing Charitable Trust
Peter Birse Charitable Trust
Michael Bishop Foundation
Patsy Bloom & Robert Blausten Charitable Trust
BNFL Springfields Medical Research & Charity Trust Fund
John & Celia Bonham Christie Charitable Trust
Booth Charities
Boots Charitable Trust
Tony Bramall Charitable Trust
Brighton District Nursing Association Trust
British Council for Prevention of Blindness
British Heart Foundation
British Humane Association
British Sugar Foundation
Charles & Edna Broadhurst Charitable Trust
Roger Brooke Charitable Trust
R S Brownless Charitable Trust
Buckle Family Charitable Trust
Burry Charitable Trust
Arnold James Burton 1956 Charitable Settlement
R M 1956 Burton Charitable Trust

Consolidated Charity of Burton Upon Trent
C B Trust
Edward Cadbury Charitable Trust
Edward & Dorothy Cadbury Trust
Cadbury Schweppes Foundation
William A Cadbury Charitable Trust
CAFOD
Cairns Charitable Trust
Calpe Trust
D W T Cargill Fund
Carron Charitable Trust
Wilfrid & Constance Cave Foundation
Chandris Foundation
Chapman Charitable Trust
Charities Advisory Trust
Cheshire Provincial Fund of Benevolence
Chest Heart and Stroke Scotland
Child Growth Foundation
Childwick Trust
Chippenham Borough Lands Charity
Cinderford Charitable Trust
City and Metropolitan Welfare Charity
Classic FM Charitable Trust
Coates Charitable Settlement
John Coates Charitable Trust
Denise Cohen Charitable Trust
Colchester Catalyst Charity
Cole Charitable Trust
George Henry Collins Charity
Norman Collinson Charitable Trust
Commonwealth Relations Trust
Community Foundation Serving Tyne & Wear and Northumberland
Consortium on Opportunities for Volunteering
Cooper Charitable Trust
Duke of Cornwall's Benevolent Fund
Coutts & Co. Charitable Trust
Coward Trust
Lord Cozens-Hardy Trust
Cranbury Foundation
Michael Crawford Children's Charity
Crescent Trust
Cripplegate Foundation
Harry Crook Foundation
Croydon Relief in Need Charities
Cumber Family Charitable Trust
Manny Cussins Foundation
D'Oyly Carte Charitable Trust

Daily Telegraph Charitable Trust
Dr & Mrs A Darlington Charitable Trust
David Charitable Trust
Miriam K Dean Refugee Trust Fund
Richard Desmond Charitable Trust
Diabetes UK
Djanogly Foundation
Double 'O' Charity Ltd
Dunhill Medical Trust
Eagle Charity Trust
Earley Charity
Gilbert Edgar Trust
City of Edinburgh Charitable Trusts
Maud Elkington Charitable Trust
Esher House Charitable Trust
Douglas Heath Eves Charitable Trust
Exilarch's Foundation
Lord Faringdon Charitable Trust
Elizabeth Hardie Ferguson Charitable Trust Fund
Doris Field Charitable Trust
Sir John Fisher Foundation
Rose Flatau Charitable Trust
Ian Fleming Charitable Trust
Forte Charitable Trust
Fortuna Charitable Trust
Isaac and Freda Frankel Memorial Charitable Trust
Freshgate Trust Foundation
Friarsgate Trust
Gamma Trust
Gannochy Trust
Garnett Charitable Trust
L & R Gilley Charitable Trust
Girdlers' Company Charitable Trust
B & P Glasser Charitable Trust
GNC Trust
Sydney & Phyllis Goldberg Memorial Charitable Trust
Gray Trust
Grocers' Charity
Gunter Charitable Trust
Hadfield Trust
E F & M G Hall Charitable Trust
Robert Hall Charity
Hampstead Wells and Campden Trust
Hare of Steep Charitable Trust
Gay & Peter Hartley's Hillards Charitable Trust
Maurice Hatter Foundation
Hawthorne Charitable Trust
Healthsure Group Ltd
H J Heinz Company Limited Charitable Trust

Michael & Morven Heller Charitable Foundation
Hemby Trust
G D Herbert Charitable Trust
Hillingdon Partnership Trust
Edward Sydney Hogg Charitable Settlement
Homelands Charitable Trust
Homestead Charitable Trust
Mary Homfray Charitable Trust
Sir Harold Hood's Charitable Trust
HopMarket Charity
Antony Hornby Charitable Trust
Hospital Saturday Fund Charitable Trust
Clifford Howarth Charity Settlement
HSA Charitable Trust
Hudson Foundation
Human Relief Foundation
Albert Hunt Trust
Hyde Park Place Estate Charity
Iliffe Family Charitable Trust
Ingram Trust
Irwin Trust
Isaacs Charitable Trust
Isle of Anglesey Charitable Trust
ITF Seafarers Trust
John Jarrold Trust
Jephcott Charitable Trust
Sir Charles Jessel Charitable Trust
JMK Charitable Trust
Lillie Johnson Charitable Trust
Jones 1986 Charitable Trust
Lady Eileen Joseph Foundation
Stanley Kalms Foundation
Boris Karloff Charitable Foundation
Michael & Ilse Katz Foundation
William Kendall's Charity
Ursula Keyes Trust
Graham Kirkham Foundation
Kreditor Charitable Trust
Kreitman Foundation
Neil Kreitman Foundation
Maurice and Hilda Laing Charitable Trust
Langdale Trust
Langley Charitable Trust
Laslett's (Hinton) Charity
Lauffer Family Charitable Foundation
Mason Le Page Charitable Trust
Lesley Lesley and Mutter Trust
Linbury Trust
Linden Charitable Trust
Frank Litchfield Charitable Trust
George John Livanos Charitable Trust
Jack Livingstone Charitable Trust

Elaine & Angus Lloyd Charitable Trust
Lockerbie Trust
London North East Community Foundation
Loseley & Guildway Charitable Trust
C L Loyd Charitable Trust
Luck-Hille Foundation
Lyons Charitable Trust
E M MacAndrew Trust
Mackintosh Foundation
Helen Isabella McMorran Charitable Foundation
D D McPhail Charitable Settlement
MacRobert Trust
Magdalen & Lasher Charity
R W Mann Trustees Limited
Leslie & Lilian Manning Trust
Marchday Charitable Fund
Linda Marcus Charitable Trust
Hilda & Samuel Marks Foundation
Erich Markus Charitable Foundation
Marr-Munning Trust
Michael Marsh Charitable Trust
John Martin's Charity
Evelyn May Trust
Mercury Phoenix Trust
Zachary Merton & George Woofindin Convalescent Trust
Tony Metherell Charitable Trust
Methodist Relief and Development Fund
Metropolitan Hospital-Sunday Fund
Gerald Micklem Charitable Trust
Miles Trust for Putney and Roehampton Community
Hugh and Mary Miller Bequest Trust
Millichope Foundation
Peter Minet Trust
Laurence Misener Charitable Trust
Mobbs Memorial Trust Ltd
Monmouthshire County Council Welsh Church Act Fund
Peter Moores Foundation
Morel Charitable Trust
Morgan Crucible Company plc Charitable Trust
S C and M E Morland's Charitable Trust
Morris Charitable Trust
Willie & Mabel Morris Charitable Trust
Moss Charitable Trust
Moulton Charitable Trust
Edwina Mountbatten Trust

Mugdock Children's Trust
Edith Murphy Foundation
Network for Social Change
Newby Trust Limited
Norman Family Charitable
   Trust
Northampton Municipal Church
   Charities
Northampton Queen's Institute
   Relief in Sickness Fund
Northumberland Village Homes
   Trust
Noswad Charity
Father O'Mahoney Memorial
   Trust
Oakley Charitable Trust
Ormsby Charitable Trust
Gerald Palmer Trust
Parthenon Trust
Alan Pascoe Charitable Trust
Arthur James Paterson
   Charitable Trust
Constance Paterson Charitable
   Trust
Late Barbara May Paul
   Charitable Trust
Peacock Charitable Trust
Penny in Pound Fund
   Charitable Trust
Pennycress Trust
Bernard Piggott Trust
A M Pilkington's Charitable
   Trust
J S F Pollitzer Charitable
   Settlement
Porter Foundation
John Porter Charitable Trust
J E Posnansky Charitable Trust
Nyda and Oliver Prenn
   Foundation
Prince of Wales's Charitable
   Foundation
Princess Anne's Charities
Privy Purse Charitable Trust
Mr and Mrs J A Pye's
   Charitable Settlement
Rank Foundation
Rayne Foundation
John Rayner Charitable Trust
Reuters Foundation
Clive Richards Charity Ltd
Richmond Parish Lands Charity
Rivendell Trust
Riverside Charitable Trust
   Limited
C A Rookes Charitable Trust
Rotherwick Foundation
Rowan Charitable Trust
Christopher Rowbotham
   Charitable Trust
Joseph Rowntree Foundation
Royal British Legion
Royal Docks Trust
J B Rubens Charitable
   Foundation
Rubin Foundation

Karim Rida Said Foundation
Alan and Babette Sainsbury
   Charitable Fund
St Mary-le-Strand Charity
Schroder Charity Trust
Scotbelge Charitable Trust
Scots Trust
Scottish Community
   Foundation
Sefton Community Foundation
Ayrton Senna Foundation
Sheffield Church Burgesses
   Trust
Shepherd Street Trust
Sylvia & Colin Shepherd
   Charitable Trust
Bassil Shippam and Alsford
   Trust
Ernest William Slaughter
   Charitable Trust
SMB Trust
Henry Smith Charity
E C Sosnow Charitable Trust
South Square Trust
Spar Charitable Fund
W W Spooner Charitable Trust
Stanton Ballard Charitable
   Trust
Steel Charitable Trust
E J H Stephenson Deceased
   Charitable Trust
Sir Sigmund Sternberg
   Charitable Foundation
Stevenson Family's Charitable
   Trust
Stoller Charitable Trust
M J C Stone Charitable Trust
Stone-Mallabar Charitable
   Foundation
Peter Stormonth Darling
   Charitable Trust
W O Street Charitable
   Foundation
Sueberry Ltd
Bernard Sunley Charitable
   Foundation
Swann-Morton Foundation
Charles and Elsie Sykes Trust
Hugh & Ruby Sykes Charitable
   Trust
Stella Symons Charitable Trust
Talbot Trusts
Mrs A Lacy Tate Trust
Tay Charitable Trust
C B & H H Taylor 1984 Trust
Thompson Charitable Trust
Thornton Trust
Three Guineas Trust
Three Oaks Trust
Tilda Foundation
Tower Hill Improvement Trust
Florence Turner Trust
United Society for Propagation
   of Gospel
Albert Van Den Bergh
   Charitable Trust

Walton Foundation
Warbeck Fund Ltd
Ward Blenkinsop Trust
Warwickshire Masonic
   Charitable Association Ltd
Mrs Waterhouse Charitable
   Trust
Bertie Watson Foundation
Mary Webb Trust
Weinstock Fund
West Derby Wastelands
   Charity
Charity of John West & Others
Westminster Foundation
Garfield Weston Foundation
Colonel W H Whitbread
   Charitable Trust
Sheila Whitley Trust
Maurice Wohl Charitable
   Foundation
Maurice Wohl Charitable Trust
Charles Wolfson Charitable
   Trust
Woodroffe Benton Foundation
Wyseliot Charitable Trust
Xerox (UK) Trust
William Allen Young Charitable
   Trust
Zephyr Charitable Trust
Zurich Financial Services
   Community Trust

....

■ General practice

Funding priority
Gilbert Edgar Trust
Jeffrey Charitable Trust
Judith Trust
Muslim Hands
PPP Foundation
Walter Swindon Charitable
   Trust
Ulverscroft Foundation
Walton Foundation

Will consider
Astor Foundation
John Avins Trustees
Birmingham Hospital Saturday
   Fund Medical Charity &
   Welfare Trust
E F Bulmer Benevolent Fund
Vivienne & Samuel Cohen
   Charitable Trust
Dinwoodie Settlement
Wilfred & Elsie Elkes Charity
   Fund
Earl Fitzwilliam Charitable
   Trust
Four Lanes Trust
Teresa Rosenbaum Golden
   Charitable Trust
Constance Green Foundation
Humanitarian Trust
Edward Cecil Jones Settlement
Sir James Knott Trust

Leukaemia Research Fund
Lloyd's Charities Trust
M N R Charitable Trust
Middlesex County Rugby
    Football Union Memorial
    Fund
Northcott Devon Foundation
John Pitman Charitable Trust
Christopher H R Reeves
    Charitable Trust
Rotherwick Foundation
Karim Rida Said Foundation
Sellafield Charity Trust Fund
Sutton Coldfield Municipal
    Charities
Sir Jules Thorn Charitable
    Trust
Walker Trust
Perry Watlington Trust
Wesleyan Charitable Trust
York Children's Trust

■ Health training

Funding priority

Harrow Community Trust
Judith Trust
PPP Foundation

Will consider

Adnams Charity
Children's Research Fund
John Ellerman Foundation
Medlock Charitable Trust
Mercers' Charitable
    Foundation
Methodist Relief and
    Development Fund
Christopher H R Reeves
    Charitable Trust
Christopher Rowbotham
    Charitable Trust
Saddlers' Company Charitable
    Fund

■ Medical equipment

Funding priority

Harebell Centenary Fund
Healthsure Group Ltd
Clifford Howarth Charity
    Settlement
Anton Jurgens Charitable Trust
Kennedy Leigh Charitable
    Trust
Muslim Hands
Barbara A Shuttleworth
    Memorial Trust
Walker Trust
West London Synagogue
    Charitable Fund
Wolfson Foundation

Will consider

Adint Charitable Trust
Adnams Charity
Ardwick Trust
BibleLands
Blanchminster Trust
Booth Charities
Bothwell Charitable Trust
Harry Bottom Charitable Trust
E F Bulmer Benevolent Fund
Childwick Trust
Epilepsy Research Foundation
Samuel William Farmer's Trust
Fidelity UK Foundation
Earl Fitzwilliam Charitable
    Trust
GWR Community Trust
H C D Memorial Fund
Edward Holt Trust
Holywood Trust
Heinz & Anna Kroch
    Foundation
Leach Fourteenth Trust
Leathersellers' Company
    Charitable Fund
Leng Charitable Trust
Levy Foundation
Lloyd's Charities Trust
Lloyds TSB Foundation for
    Northern Ireland
Lofthouse Foundation
W M Mann Foundation
John Martin's Charity
Medlock Charitable Trust
Mercers' Charitable
    Foundation
North British Hotel Trust
Northcott Devon Foundation
Priory of Scotland of Order of
    St John of Jerusalem
Puri Foundation
Queen Mary's Roehampton
    Trust
Radio Forth Help a Child
    Appeal
Red Dragon Radio Trust
Cliff Richard Charitable Trust
Rothley Trust
Christopher Rowbotham
    Charitable Trust
Russell Trust
Saddlers' Company Charitable
    Fund
Sellafield Charity Trust Fund
Skelton Bounty
Leslie Smith Foundation
Sobell Foundation
Steinberg Family Charitable
    Trust
Tesco Charity Trust
Wellfield Trust
Harold Hyam Wingate
    Foundation
Michael and Anna Wix
    Charitable Trust

■ Medical institutions

Funding priority

Bartholomew Charitable Trust
Bristol Charities
Richard Cloudesley's Charity
Fiat Auto (UK) Charity
Charles Henry Foyle Trust
Maurice Fry Charitable Trust
Grahame Charitable
    Foundation
Sue Hammerson's Charitable
    Trust
Hampton Fuel Allotment
    Charity
Kathleen Hannay Memorial
    Charity
Lennox Hannay Charitable
    Trust
Higgs Charitable Trust
Joseph & Mary Hiley Trust
Clifford Howarth Charity
    Settlement
Dorothy Jacobs Charity
Kobler Trust
Arnold Lee Charitable Trust
W M & B W Lloyd Trust
Medlock Charitable Trust
Monument Trust
Newstead Charity
Nottingham General
    Dispensary
Oppenheimer Charitable Trust
Patients' Aid Association
    Hospital & Medical
    Charities Trust
Personal Assurance Charitable
    Trust
Pilkington Charities Fund
Scouloudi Foundation
Shears Charitable Trust
Stanley Foundation Ltd
Thompson Family Charitable
    Trust
Thoresby Charitable Trust
Ulverston Town Lands Charity
Underwood Trust
Vandervell Foundation
Williams Family Charitable
    Trust
Wolfson Family Charitable
    Trust
Women at Risk

Will consider

29th May 1961 Charitable
    Trust
Henry & Grete Abrahams
    Charitable Trust
Acacia Charitable Trust
Alchemy Foundation
H B Allen Charitable Trust
Sir John & Lady Amory's
    Charitable Trust
Appletree Trust
Ardwick Trust

Armenian General Benevolent
    Union London Trust
Army Benevolent Fund
Astor of Hever Trust
Atlantic Foundation
ATP Charitable Trust
Lord Austin Trust
Balcombe Charitable Trust
Albert Casanova Ballard
    Deceased Trust
Balmore Trust
Bamford Charitable Foundation
David and Frederick Barclay
    Foundation
Barnes Workhouse Fund
BBC Radio Lincolnshire Charity
    Trust
James Beattie Charitable Trust
Beauland Ltd
Peter Beckwith Charitable
    Trust
Bedford Charity
Beit Trust
Benfield Motors Charitable
    Trust
Benham Charitable Settlement
BibleLands
Bingham Trust
Birmingham District Nursing
    Charitable Trust
Peter Birse Charitable Trust
Peter Black Charitable Trust
Herbert & Peter Blagrave
    Charitable Trust
Blanchminster Trust
BNFL Springfields Medical
    Research & Charity Trust
    Fund
John & Celia Bonham Christie
    Charitable Trust
Tony Bramall Charitable Trust
British Council for Prevention
    of Blindness
British Heart Foundation
British Humane Association
Charles & Edna Broadhurst
    Charitable Trust
Charles Brotherton Trust
Burden Trust
Burry Charitable Trust
R M 1956 Burton Charitable
    Trust
Consolidated Charity of Burton
    Upon Trent
C B Trust
Edward & Dorothy Cadbury
    Trust
Cadbury Schweppes
    Foundation
William A Cadbury Charitable
    Trust
Cairns Charitable Trust
Calpe Trust
D W T Cargill Fund
Carron Charitable Trust

Wilfrid & Constance Cave
    Foundation
Chandris Foundation
Chapman Charitable Trust
Charities Advisory Trust
Cheshire Provincial Fund of
    Benevolence
Children's Research Fund
Chippenham Borough Lands
    Charity
Chipping Sodbury Town Lands
    Charity
Cinderford Charitable Trust
Classic FM Charitable Trust
Coates Charitable Settlement
John Coates Charitable Trust
Denise Cohen Charitable Trust
Colchester Catalyst Charity
Norman Collinson Charitable
    Trust
Community Foundation Serving
    Tyne & Wear and
    Northumberland
Congleton Inclosure Trust
Cooper Charitable Trust
Duke of Cornwall's Benevolent
    Fund
Coward Trust
Lord Cozens-Hardy Trust
Cranbury Foundation
Michael Crawford Children's
    Charity
Crescent Trust
Cripplegate Foundation
Harry Crook Foundation
Croydon Relief in Need
    Charities
Cumber Family Charitable
    Trust
D'Oyly Carte Charitable Trust
Daily Telegraph Charitable
    Trust
Dr & Mrs A Darlington
    Charitable Trust
David Charitable Trust
Richard Desmond Charitable
    Trust
Djanogly Foundation
Double 'O' Charity Ltd
P B Dumbell Charitable Trust
Dunhill Medical Trust
Harry Dunn Charitable Trust
Eagle Charity Trust
Earley Charity
Epilepsy Research Foundation
Esher House Charitable Trust
Douglas Heath Eves Charitable
    Trust
Exilarch's Foundation
Fidelity UK Foundation
Doris Field Charitable Trust
Ian Fleming Charitable Trust
Florence's Charitable Trust
Fox Memorial Trust
Isaac and Freda Frankel
    Memorial Charitable Trust

Hugh Fraser Foundation
Friarsgate Trust
Gannochy Trust
L & R Gilley Charitable Trust
Girdlers' Company Charitable
    Trust
B & P Glasser Charitable Trust
GNC Trust
Sydney & Phyllis Goldberg
    Memorial Charitable Trust
Gray Trust
Grocers' Charity
Gunter Charitable Trust
Hadfield Trust
E F & M G Hall Charitable
    Trust
Handicapped Children's Aid
    Committee
Hare of Steep Charitable Trust
Kenneth Hargreaves Charitable
    Trust
N & P Hartley Memorial Trust
Maurice Hatter Foundation
Healthsure Group Ltd
H J Heinz Company Limited
    Charitable Trust
Michael & Morven Heller
    Charitable Foundation
Hemby Trust
G D Herbert Charitable Trust
Hillingdon Partnership Trust
Edward Sydney Hogg
    Charitable Settlement
Homelands Charitable Trust
Homestead Charitable Trust
Sir Harold Hood's Charitable
    Trust
Antony Hornby Charitable Trust
Hospital Saturday Fund
    Charitable Trust
Human Relief Foundation
Albert Hunt Trust
Hyde Park Place Estate Charity
    – civil trustees
Iliffe Family Charitable Trust
Isaacs Charitable Trust
Jephcott Charitable Trust
JMK Charitable Trust
Lillie Johnson Charitable Trust
Lady Eileen Joseph Foundation
Stanley Kalms Foundation
Boris Karloff Charitable
    Foundation
Michael & Ilse Katz Foundation
William Kendall's Charity
Ursula Keyes Trust
Graham Kirkham Foundation
Kreditor Charitable Trust
Heinz & Anna Kroch
    Foundation
Kirby Laing Foundation
Langdale Trust
Langley Charitable Trust
Lauffer Family Charitable
    Foundation

Leathersellers' Company Charitable Fund

Lesley Lesley and Mutter Trust

Linden Charitable Trust

George John Livanos Charitable Trust

Jack Livingstone Charitable Trust

Elaine & Angus Lloyd Charitable Trust

Lloyds TSB Foundation for Scotland

Lockerbie Trust

London North East Community Foundation

Loseley & Guildway Charitable Trust

C L Loyd Charitable Trust

Luck-Hille Foundation

Lyons Charitable Trust

E M MacAndrew Trust

Mackintosh Foundation

Helen Isabella McMorran Charitable Foundation

Magdalen & Lasher Charity

R W Mann Trustees Limited

Leslie & Lilian Manning Trust

Linda Marcus Charitable Trust

Hilda & Samuel Marks Foundation

Michael Marsh Charitable Trust

Evelyn May Trust

Mayfair Charities Ltd

Mercury Phoenix Trust

Metropolitan Hospital-Sunday Fund

Gerald Micklem Charitable Trust

Miles Trust for Putney and Roehampton Community

Millichope Foundation

Laurence Misener Charitable Trust

Mobbs Memorial Trust Ltd

Monmouthshire County Council Welsh Church Act Fund

Peter Moores Foundation

Morel Charitable Trust

Morgan Crucible Company plc Charitable Trust

S C and M E Morland's Charitable Trust

Morris Charitable Trust

Moulton Charitable Trust

Edwina Mountbatten Trust

Mugdock Children's Trust

NAM Charitable Trust

Network for Social Change

Norman Family Charitable Trust

Northampton Queen's Institute Relief in Sickness Fund

Northcott Devon Medical Foundation

Northumberland Village Homes Trust

Father O'Mahoney Memorial Trust

Oakley Charitable Trust

Kate Wilson Oliver Trust

Ormsby Charitable Trust

P F Charitable Trust

Gerald Palmer Trust

Alan Pascoe Charitable Trust

Arthur James Paterson Charitable Trust

Constance Paterson Charitable Trust

Patrick Charitable Trust

Peacock Charitable Trust

Penny in Pound Fund Charitable Trust

Bernard Piggott Trust

A M Pilkington's Charitable Trust

G S Plaut Charitable Trust

J S F Pollitzer Charitable Settlement

Porter Foundation

J E Posnansky Charitable Trust

Powys Welsh Church Fund

Nyda and Oliver Prenn Foundation

Prince of Wales's Charitable Foundation

Proven Family Trust

Rayne Foundation

John Rayner Charitable Trust

Clive Richards Charity Ltd

Violet M Richards Charity

Richmond Parish Lands Charity

Muriel Edith Rickman Trust

Rivendell Trust

Riverside Charitable Trust Limited

C A Rookes Charitable Trust

Rowlands Trust

Alan and Babette Sainsbury Charitable Fund

St Mary-le-Strand Charity

Schmidt-Bodner Charitable Trust

Scotbelge Charitable Trust

Scots Trust

Frieda Scott Charitable Trust

Scottish Community Foundation

Ayrton Senna Foundation

Sheffield Church Burgesses Trust

Sylvia & Colin Shepherd Charitable Trust

Sinclair Charitable Trust

Ernest William Slaughter Charitable Trust

SMB Trust

Henry Smith Charity

Sobell Foundation

David Solomons Charitable Trust

E C Sosnow Charitable Trust

South Square Trust

Sovereign Health Care Charitable Trust

W W Spooner Charitable Trust

Stanton Ballard Charitable Trust

Peter Stebbings Memorial Charity

Steel Charitable Trust

Steinberg Family Charitable Trust

E J H Stephenson Deceased Charitable Trust

Sir Sigmund Sternberg Charitable Foundation

Stevenson Family's Charitable Trust

Stoller Charitable Trust

M J C Stone Charitable Trust

Stone-Mallabar Charitable Foundation

W O Street Charitable Foundation

Sueberry Ltd

Bernard Sunley Charitable Foundation

Sutton Coldfield Municipal Charities

Swann-Morton Foundation

Hugh & Ruby Sykes Charitable Trust

Stella Symons Charitable Trust

Mrs A Lacy Tate Trust

Thompson Charitable Trust

Thornton Trust

Three Guineas Trust

Three Oaks Trust

Tilda Foundation

Tower Hill Improvement Trust

Towry Law Charitable Trust

Florence Turner Trust

Albert Van Den Bergh Charitable Trust

Variety Club Children's Charity

Robert and Felicity Waley-Cohen Charitable Trust

Warbeck Fund Ltd

Sir Siegmund Warburg's Voluntary Settlement

Warwickshire Masonic Charitable Association Ltd

Mrs Waterhouse Charitable Trust

Mary Webb Trust

Welton Foundation

West Derby Wastelands Charity

Garfield Weston Foundation

Colonel W H Whitbread Charitable Trust

Sheila Whitley Trust

Will Charitable Trust

Maurice Wohl Charitable Foundation

Maurice Wohl Charitable Trust

Charles Wolfson Charitable
Trust
William Allen Young Charitable
Trust
Elizabeth & Prince Zaiger Trust
Zephyr Charitable Trust

■ **Hospices**
Funding priority
Ammco Trust
Astor Foundation
BBC Radio Cambridgeshire –
Trustline
Bethesda Community
Charitable Trust
Birmingham Hospital Saturday
Fund Medical Charity &
Welfare Trust
Sir Alec Black's Charity
Bothwell Charitable Trust
R M 1956 Burton Charitable
Trust
Clarke Charitable Settlement
Cleopatra Trust
D'Oyly Carte Charitable Trust
De Clermont Charitable
Company Ltd
De La Rue Charitable Trust
Dorus Trust
Gilbert Edgar Trust
Epigoni Trust
Eveson Charitable Trust
Gerald Fogel Charitable Trust
Simon Gibson Charitable Trust
Grand Charity of Freemasons
Constance Green Foundation
J C Green Charitable
Settlement
Harebell Centenary Fund
Charles Hayward Foundation
Healthsure Group Ltd
Help the Hospices
Dorothy Holmes Charitable
Trust
Mrs E G Hornby's Charitable
Settlement
Clifford Howarth Charity
Settlement
Inman Charity
Anton Jurgens Charitable Trust
Sir James Knott Trust
Edgar E Lawley Foundation
Mason Le Page Charitable
Trust
Leeds & Holbeck Building
Society Charitable
Foundation
Lloyds TSB Foundation for
Channel Islands
Lynn Foundation
D G Marshall of Cambridge
Trust
Mercers' Charitable
Foundation
Tony Metherell Charitable
Trust

Metropolitan Hospital-Sunday
Fund
Mickel Fund
Minge's Gift
Odin Charitable Trust
Ormsby Charitable Trust
Charity Fund of Worshipful
Company of Paviors
Pilkington Charities Fund
Douglas Prestwich Charitable
Trust
Ronald & Kathleen Pryor
Charitable Trust
Märit and Hans Rausing
Charitable Foundation
Cliff Richard Charitable Trust
Rosca Trust
St James's Place Foundation
Scouloudi Foundation
Bishop Simeon CR Trust
Leslie Smith Foundation
Sutton Coldfield Municipal
Charities
Swan Trust
Walter Swindon Charitable
Trust
Tallow Chandlers Benevolent
Fund
Tisbury Telegraph Trust
Mrs S H Troughton Charity
Trust
Trusthouse Charitable
Foundation
Vandervell Foundation
Variety Club Children's Charity
Verdon-Smith Family Charitable
Settlement
Vintners Company Charitable
Trust
Walton Foundation
Warwickshire Masonic
Charitable Association Ltd
West London Synagogue
Charitable Fund
Wolfson Foundation
Yorkshire Building Society
Charitable Foundation

Will consider
Adint Charitable Trust
Adnams Charity
Pat Allsop Charitable Trust
Viscount Amory's Charitable
Trust
Ardwick Trust
G C Armitage Charitable Trust
John Avins Trustees
Andrew Balint Charitable Trust
George Balint Charitable Trust
Paul Balint Charitable Trust
Balney Charitable Trust
Barbour Trust
Philip Barker Charity
Lord Barnby's Foundation
Bartle Family Charitable Trust
BBC Children in Need Appeal

John Bell Charitable Trust
Percy Bilton Charity Ltd
Birmingham Foundation
Bonhomie United Charity
Society
Charles Boot Trust
Booth Charities
Boots Charitable Trust
Harry Bottom Charitable Trust
Anthony Bourne Foundation
Bridge House Estates Trust
Fund
Bridge Trust
R S Brownless Charitable
Trust
E F Bulmer Benevolent Fund
Burdens Charitable Foundation
Audrey & Stanley Burton
Charitable Trust
Geoffrey Burton Charitable
Trust
Richard Cadbury Charitable
Trust
Mauritis Mulder Canter Charity
W A Cargill Charitable Trust
Leslie Mary Carter Charitable
Trust
Chamberlain Foundation
Childwick Trust
Christadelphian Samaritan
Fund
City and Metropolitan Welfare
Charity
Lord Clinton's Charitable Trust
John Cowan Foundation
Cwmbran Trust
Baron Davenport's Charity
Wilfrid Bruce Davis Charitable
Trust
Demigryphon Trust
Denman Charitable Trust
Denton Charitable Trust
Derbyshire Community
Foundation
Duis Charitable Trust
P B Dumbell Charitable Trust
Wilfred & Elsie Elkes Charity
Fund
Elmgrant Trust
Emerton-Christie Charity
Emmandjay Charitable Trust
Samuel William Farmer's Trust
Fidelity UK Foundation
David Finnie & Alan Emery
Charitable Trust
Earl Fitzwilliam Charitable
Trust
Ford of Britain Trust
Four Lanes Trust
Timothy Franey Charitable
Foundation
Charles S French Charitable
Trust
Frognal Trust
Gannochy Trust
Ganzoni Charitable Trust

Garnett Charitable Trust
Gatwick Airport Community
   Trust
Robert Gavron Charitable Trust
Girdlers' Company Charitable
   Trust
Good Neighbours Trust
Greggs Trust
Grimley Charity
GWR Community Trust
Hadrian Trust
Robert Hall Charity
Hampstead Wells and
   Campden Trust
Harborne Parish Lands Charity
Gay & Peter Hartley's Hillards
   Charitable Trust
Hedley Foundation
Hemby Trust
Alan Edward Higgs Charity
Jane Hodge Foundation
Edward Holt Trust
James Thom Howat Charitable
   Trust
Humanitarian Trust
Miss Agnes H Hunter's Trust
Inchrye Trust
Inverforth Charitable Trust
Ruth & Lionel Jacobson Trust
   (Second Fund) No 2
Jarman Charitable Trust
John Jarrold Trust
Jeffrey Charitable Trust
Elton John Aids Foundation
Johnson Foundation
Joicey Trust
Edward Cecil Jones Settlement
Late Sir Pierce Lacy Charity
   Trust
R J Larg Family Charitable
   Trust
Mrs F B Laurence Charitable
   Trust
Kathleen Laurence Trust
Raymond & Blanche Lawson
   Charitable Trust
Lazard Charitable Trust
Leach Fourteenth Trust
Levy Foundation
Enid Linder Foundation
Lloyd's Charities Trust
Lloyds TSB Foundation for
   England and Wales
Lloyds TSB Foundation for
   Northern Ireland
London Law Trust
M N R Charitable Trust
Ronald McDonald Children's
   Charities Limited
MacRobert Trust
Magdalen Hospital Trust
W M Mann Foundation
Marchday Charitable Fund
Erich Markus Charitable
   Foundation
John Martin's Charity

Medlock Charitable Trust
Anthony and Elizabeth Mellows
   Charitable Settlement
Middlesex County Rugby
   Football Union Memorial
   Fund
Keith and Joan Mindelsohn
   Charitable Trust
George A Moore Foundation
Horace Moore Charitable Trust
Morgan Stanley International
   Foundation
North British Hotel Trust
Northcott Devon Foundation
Oakdale Trust
Ogilvie Charities Deed 2
Oldham Foundation
Kate Wilson Oliver Trust
Owen Family Trust
Parivar Trust
Patrick Charitable Trust
Harry Payne Trust
Pennycress Trust
John Pitman Charitable Trust
W L Pratt Charitable Trust
Simone Prendergast Charitable
   Trust
Privy Purse Charitable Trust
Pye Foundation
Mr and Mrs J A Pye's
   Charitable Settlement
Queen Mary's Roehampton
   Trust
Radio Forth Help a Child
   Appeal
Rainford Trust
Fanny Rapaport Charitable
   Settlement
E L Rathbone Charitable Trust
Ravensdale Trust
Rotherwick Foundation
Rothley Trust
Christopher Rowbotham
   Charitable Trust
Russell Trust
Sarnia Charitable Trust
Scarfe Charitable Trust
Sir James & Lady Scott Trust
Search
Sellafield Charity Trust Fund
Sherburn House Charity
L H Silver Charitable Trust
W W Spooner Charitable Trust
Starfish Trust
Summerfield Charitable Trust
Charles and Elsie Sykes Trust
Tay Charitable Trust
Tesco Charity Trust
Sir Jules Thorn Charitable
   Trust
Douglas Turner Trust
John and Lucille van Geest
   Foundation
Vodafone UK Foundation
Walker Trust
Wates Foundation

Perry Watlington Trust
Bertie Watson Foundation
William Webster Charitable
   Trust
James Weir Foundation
Wesleyan Charitable Trust
Michael and Anna Wix
   Charitable Trust
Woodward Trust
Worshipful Company of
   Founders Charities
Xerox (UK) Trust
York Children's Trust

■ **Hospice at home**
   Funding priority
1970 Trust
Ammco Trust
Astor Foundation
Bergqvist Charitable Trust
Birmingham Hospital Saturday
   Fund Medical Charity &
   Welfare Trust
Bothwell Charitable Trust
Elizabeth Clark Charitable
   Trust
De La Rue Charitable Trust
Demigryphon Trust
Fiat Auto (UK) Charity
Constance Green Foundation
J C Green Charitable
   Settlement
Harebell Centenary Fund
Charles Hayward Foundation
Dorothy Holmes Charitable
   Trust
Thomas J Horne Memorial
   Trust
Miss Agnes H Hunter's Trust
Peter Kershaw Trust
Edgar E Lawley Foundation
Lynn Foundation
Mercers' Charitable
   Foundation
Ormsby Charitable Trust
Cliff Richard Charitable Trust
Clive Richards Charity Ltd
Rosca Trust
St James's Place Foundation
Scouloudi Foundation
Swan Trust
Walter Swindon Charitable
   Trust
Mrs S H Troughton Charity
   Trust
Verdon-Smith Family Charitable
   Settlement
Yorkshire Building Society
   Charitable Foundation

   Will consider
Adint Charitable Trust
Adnams Charity
Viscount Amory's Charitable
   Trust
Ardwick Trust

Badley Memorial Trust
Bamford Charitable Foundation
Barbour Trust
Bartle Family Charitable Trust
BBC Children in Need Appeal
Percy Bilton Charity Ltd
Herbert & Peter Blagrave
   Charitable Trust
Charles Boot Trust
Boots Charitable Trust
Bridge House Estates Trust
   Fund
Buckinghamshire Masonic
   Centenary Fund
E F Bulmer Benevolent Fund
Burdens Charitable Foundation
Richard Cadbury Charitable
   Trust
Mauritis Mulder Canter Charity
Chamberlain Foundation
Chipping Sodbury Town Lands
   Charity
Chrimes Family Charitable
   Trust
Lord Clinton's Charitable Trust
Vivienne & Samuel Cohen
   Charitable Trust
Coppings Trust
Holbeche Corfield Charitable
   Settlement
John Cowan Foundation
Cwmbran Trust
Denman Charitable Trust
P B Dumbell Charitable Trust
Elmgrant Trust
Emerton-Christie Charity
Fidelity UK Foundation
David Finnie & Alan Emery
   Charitable Trust
Ford of Britain Trust
Charles S French Charitable
   Trust
Gannochy Trust
Robert Gavron Charitable Trust
Girdlers' Company Charitable
   Trust
Greggs Trust
Hadrian Trust
Harborne Parish Lands Charity
Harrison & Potter Trust
Gay & Peter Hartley's Hillards
   Charitable Trust
Hedley Foundation
Hemby Trust
Alan Edward Higgs Charity
Inchrye Trust
Inman Charity
Ruth & Lionel Jacobson Trust
   (Second Fund) No 2
Jeffrey Charitable Trust
Johnson Foundation
Joicey Trust
Edward Cecil Jones Settlement
Sir James Knott Trust
Heinz & Anna Kroch
   Foundation

Mrs F B Laurence Charitable
   Trust
Raymond & Blanche Lawson
   Charitable Trust
Leach Fourteenth Trust
Kennedy Leigh Charitable
   Trust
Lloyd's Charities Trust
Lloyds TSB Foundation for
   England and Wales
Lloyds TSB Foundation for
   Northern Ireland
London Law Trust
M N R Charitable Trust
Hugh and Mary Miller Bequest
   Trust
Horace Moore Charitable Trust
Morgan Stanley International
   Foundation
Nestlé Rowntree York
   Employees Community Fund
   Trust
Northcott Devon Foundation
Oakdale Trust
Odin Charitable Trust
Oldham Foundation
Kate Wilson Oliver Trust
Parivar Trust
Pilkington Charities Fund
John Pitman Charitable Trust
W L Pratt Charitable Trust
Priory of Scotland of Order of
   St John of Jerusalem
Proven Family Trust
Mr and Mrs J A Pye's
   Charitable Settlement
Radio Forth Help a Child
   Appeal
Christopher Rowbotham
   Charitable Trust
Russell Trust
Sir James & Lady Scott Trust
Sellafield Charity Trust Fund
Sheldon Trust
Sherburn House Charity
Mary Elizabeth Siebel Charity
Leslie Smith Foundation
Starfish Trust
Strangward Trust
Summerfield Charitable Trust
Tesco Charity Trust
Sir Jules Thorn Charitable
   Trust
John and Lucille van Geest
   Foundation
Vodafone UK Foundation
William Webster Charitable
   Trust
James Weir Foundation
Wellfield Trust
Wesleyan Charitable Trust
Michael and Anna Wix
   Charitable Trust
Woodward Trust
Worshipful Company of
   Founders Charities

■ **Hospitals**
   Funding priority
Aldgate Freedom Foundation
Balmore Trust
Rowan Bentall Charitable Trust
Birmingham Hospital Saturday
   Fund Medical Charity &
   Welfare Trust
Isabel Blackman Foundation
BNFL Springfields Medical
   Research & Charity Trust
   Fund
De Clermont Charitable
   Company Ltd
Demigryphon Trust
Eveson Charitable Trust
Family Rich Charities Trust
Gerald Fogel Charitable Trust
Timothy Franey Charitable
   Foundation
Simon Gibson Charitable Trust
Healthsure Group Ltd
Dorothy Holmes Charitable
   Trust
Clifford Howarth Charity
   Settlement
King George's Fund for Sailors
Lauchentilly Charitable
   Foundation 1988
Lofthouse Foundation
Lynn Foundation
Ronald McDonald Children's
   Charities Limited
Metropolitan Hospital-Sunday
   Fund
Minge's Gift
Penny in Pound Fund
   Charitable Trust
Ronald & Kathleen Pryor
   Charitable Trust
Märit and Hans Rausing
   Charitable Foundation
Dr Mortimer and Theresa
   Sackler Foundation
Sutton Coldfield Municipal
   Charities
Walter Swindon Charitable
   Trust
Tajtelbaum Charitable Trust
Trusthouse Charitable
   Foundation
Ulverscroft Foundation
Variety Club Children's Charity
Vintners Company Charitable
   Trust
Walker Trust
Walton Foundation
White Rose Children's Aid
   International Charity

   Will consider
Adint Charitable Trust
Viscount Amory's Charitable
   Trust
Arthritis Research Campaign
Ashby Charitable Trust

John Avins Trustees
Barbour Trust
Philip Barker Charity
Lord Barnby's Foundation
Bartle Family Charitable Trust
Boots Charitable Trust
Bothwell Charitable Trust
Harry Bottom Charitable Trust
E F Bulmer Benevolent Fund
Burdens Charitable Foundation
Mauritis Mulder Canter Charity
Caring for Kids
Childwick Trust
Christadelphian Samaritan
    Fund
Vivienne & Samuel Cohen
    Charitable Trust
Sir William Coxen Trust Fund
Denton Charitable Trust
Diabetes UK
Duis Charitable Trust
Wilfred & Elsie Elkes Charity
    Fund
Elmgrant Trust
Samuel William Farmer's Trust
Earl Fitzwilliam Charitable
    Trust
Four Lanes Trust
Charles S French Charitable
    Trust
Gannochy Trust
Ganzoni Charitable Trust
Teresa Rosenbaum Golden
    Charitable Trust
Constance Green Foundation
GWR Community Trust
H C D Memorial Fund
Robert Hall Charity
Hampstead Wells and
    Campden Trust
Haymills Charitable Trust
Humanitarian Trust
Ruth & Lionel Jacobson Trust
    (Second Fund) No 2
Jarman Charitable Trust
John Jarrold Trust
Jeffrey Charitable Trust
Elton John Aids Foundation
Johnson Foundation
Sir James Knott Trust
Raymond & Blanche Lawson
    Charitable Trust
Leukaemia Research Fund
Levy Foundation
Lloyd's Charities Trust
London Law Trust
M N R Charitable Trust
John Martin's Charity
Medlock Charitable Trust
Anthony and Elizabeth Mellows
    Charitable Settlement
Middlesex County Rugby
    Football Union Memorial
    Fund
Morgan Stanley International
    Foundation

National Asthma Campaign
North British Hotel Trust
Northcott Devon Foundation
Kate Wilson Oliver Trust
Owen Family Trust
Harry Payne Trust
Privy Purse Charitable Trust
Radio Forth Help a Child
    Appeal
Rainford Trust
Rotherwick Foundation
Karim Rida Said Foundation
Samuel Sebba Charitable
    Trust
Sellafield Charity Trust Fund
Sovereign Health Care
    Charitable Trust
W W Spooner Charitable Trust
A B Strom & R Strom
    Charitable Trust
Charles and Elsie Sykes Trust
Tay Charitable Trust
Tesco Charity Trust
Sir Jules Thorn Charitable
    Trust
Vodafone UK Foundation
Wates Foundation
Bertie Watson Foundation
Wesleyan Charitable Trust
Wolfson Foundation
Woodward Trust

■ Nursing homes
Funding priority
Bothwell Charitable Trust
Palgrave Brown Foundation
Dunhill Medical Trust
W G Edwards Charitable
    Foundation
Charles Hayward Foundation
Clifford Howarth Charity
    Settlement
King George's Fund for Sailors
Lynn Foundation
Metropolitan Hospital-Sunday
    Fund
Minge's Gift
Skerritt Trust

Will consider
Adint Charitable Trust
Astor Foundation
John Avins Trustees
Lord Barnby's Foundation
Percy Bilton Charity Ltd
Birmingham Hospital Saturday
    Fund Medical Charity &
    Welfare Trust
Booth Charities
E F Bulmer Benevolent Fund
Mauritis Mulder Canter Charity
Christadelphian Samaritan
    Fund
Baron Davenport's Charity
Samuel William Farmer's Trust
Frognal Trust

Gannochy Trust
Grimley Charity
GWR Community Trust
H C D Memorial Fund
Harborne Parish Lands Charity
Hospital of God at Greatham
Jarman Charitable Trust
Jeffrey Charitable Trust
Joicey Trust
Edward Cecil Jones Settlement
Sir James Knott Trust
Kathleen Laurence Trust
Lloyd's Charities Trust
M N R Charitable Trust
John Martin's Charity
Milton Keynes Community
    Foundation
Kate Wilson Oliver Trust
Queen Mary's Roehampton
    Trust
Rotherwick Foundation
Russell Trust
Sir James & Lady Scott Trust
Sellafield Charity Trust Fund
Sheldon Trust
Sir Jules Thorn Charitable
    Trust
John and Lucille van Geest
    Foundation
Walker Trust
Michael and Anna Wix
    Charitable Trust

■ Medical transport
Funding priority
Birmingham Hospital Saturday
    Fund Medical Charity &
    Welfare Trust
Harebell Centenary Fund
Anton Jurgens Charitable Trust
Kennedy Leigh Charitable
    Trust
Muslim Hands
Rosca Trust
Walton Foundation

Will consider
Astor Foundation
John Bell Charitable Trust
Boots Charitable Trust
Harry Bottom Charitable Trust
Bridge Trust
Swinfen Broun Charitable Trust
E F Bulmer Benevolent Fund
Burdens Charitable Foundation
Lord Clinton's Charitable Trust
John Cowan Foundation
De Clermont Charitable
    Company Ltd
P B Dumbell Charitable Trust
Samuel William Farmer's Trust
Earl Fitzwilliam Charitable
    Trust
Ford of Britain Trust
Robert Gavron Charitable Trust

Constance Green Foundation
H C D Memorial Fund
Charles Hayward Foundation
John Jarrold Trust
Jesus Hospital Charity
Johnson Foundation
Sir James Knott Trust
Heinz & Anna Kroch
    Foundation
Leach Fourteenth Trust
Lloyd's Charities Trust
Lloyds TSB Foundation for
    Northern Ireland
M N R Charitable Trust
John Martin's Charity
Miles Trust for Putney and
    Roehampton Community
George A Moore Foundation
Northcott Devon Foundation
Priory of Scotland of Order of
    St John of Jerusalem
Radio Forth Help a Child
    Appeal
Rainford Trust
Russell Trust
Saddlers' Company Charitable
    Fund
Karim Rida Said Foundation
Sellafield Charity Trust Fund
Sherburn House Charity
Snowball Trust
Steinberg Family Charitable
    Trust
Tesco Charity Trust
Vodafone UK Foundation
York Children's Trust

■ Nursing

Funding priority

Birmingham Hospital Saturday
    Fund Medical Charity &
    Welfare Trust
Bothwell Charitable Trust
Palgrave Brown Foundation
Chest Heart and Stroke
    Scotland
Harebell Centenary Fund
Clifford Howarth Charity
    Settlement
Peter Kershaw Trust
Minge's Gift
Clive Richards Charity Ltd
Rosca Trust
Sobell Foundation

Will consider

Adint Charitable Trust
Astor Foundation
Badley Memorial Trust
Andrew Balint Charitable Trust
George Balint Charitable Trust
Paul Balint Charitable Trust
Herbert & Peter Blagrave
    Charitable Trust
Charles Brotherton Trust

Buckinghamshire Masonic
    Centenary Fund
E F Bulmer Benevolent Fund
Childwick Trust
Chipping Sodbury Town Lands
    Charity
Christadelphian Samaritan
    Fund
Clover Trust
Cwmbran Trust
Wilfrid Bruce Davis Charitable
    Trust
John Ellerman Foundation
Emerton-Christie Charity
David Finnie & Alan Emery
    Charitable Trust
Robert Gavron Charitable Trust
Hadrian Trust
Harborne Parish Lands Charity
Harrison & Potter Trust
Charles Hayward Foundation
Dorothy Holmes Charitable
    Trust
James Thom Howat Charitable
    Trust
Ruth & Lionel Jacobson Trust
    (Second Fund) No 2
Johnson Foundation
Kathleen Laurence Trust
Raymond & Blanche Lawson
    Charitable Trust
Levy Foundation
Lloyd's Charities Trust
London Law Trust
M N R Charitable Trust
Hugh and Mary Miller Bequest
    Trust
Morgan Stanley International
    Foundation
Oldham Foundation
John Pitman Charitable Trust
PPP Foundation
W L Pratt Charitable Trust
Proven Family Trust
Radio Forth Help a Child
    Appeal
Christopher Rowbotham
    Charitable Trust
Russell Trust
Saddlers' Company Charitable
    Fund
Sellafield Charity Trust Fund
David Solomons Charitable
    Trust
Starfish Trust
Strangward Trust
Perry Watlington Trust
Wellfield Trust
Wesleyan Charitable Trust
Harold Hyam Wingate
    Foundation
Woodward Trust

■ Primary health care

Funding priority

Balmore Trust
BibleLands
British Dietetic Association
    General and Education
    Trust Fund
Child Growth Foundation
Harebell Centenary Fund
Clifford Howarth Charity
    Settlement
Judith Trust
Minge's Gift
Monument Trust
Muslim Hands
Karim Rida Said Foundation
Bishop Simeon CR Trust
Sobell Foundation
C Paul Thackray General
    Charitable Trust

Will consider

Alcohol Education and
    Research Fund
Astor Foundation
Badley Memorial Trust
Birmingham Hospital Saturday
    Fund Medical Charity &
    Welfare Trust
E F Bulmer Benevolent Fund
BUPA Foundation
Constance Green Foundation
Harborne Parish Lands Charity
Ruth & Lionel Jacobson Trust
    (Second Fund) No 2
Johnson Foundation
King's Fund
Kathleen Laurence Trust
Lloyd's Charities Trust
Lofthouse Foundation
London Law Trust
M N R Charitable Trust
Methodist Relief and
    Development Fund
Hugh and Mary Miller Bequest
    Trust
Austin & Hope Pilkington Trust
PPP Foundation
Radio Forth Help a Child
    Appeal
Christopher Rowbotham
    Charitable Trust
Saddlers' Company Charitable
    Fund
Woodward Trust
York Children's Trust

■ Speech therapy

Funding priority

BibleLands
Dorothy Whitney Elmhirst Trust
Simon Gibson Charitable Trust
Mercers' Charitable
    Foundation

Patients' Aid Association
Hospital & Medical
Charities Trust
Walter Swindon Charitable
Trust

Will consider
Ardwick Trust
Ashby Charitable Trust
Astor Foundation
John Avins Trustees
BBC Children in Need Appeal
Percy Bilton Charity Ltd
Birmingham Hospital Saturday
Fund Medical Charity &
Welfare Trust
Harry Bottom Charitable Trust
Buckinghamshire Masonic
Centenary Fund
Caring for Kids
Carlton Television Trust
Wilfrid & Constance Cave
Foundation
De Clermont Charitable
Company Ltd
Duis Charitable Trust
John Ellerman Foundation
Equitable Charitable Trust
Essex Fairway Charitable Trust
Fidelity UK Foundation
Finnart House School Trust
Good Neighbours Trust
Greggs Trust
Lennox Hannay Charitable
Trust
Harborne Parish Lands Charity
N & P Hartley Memorial Trust
Charles Hayward Foundation
Hertfordshire Community
Foundation
Hockerill Educational
Foundation
Holywood Trust
Humanitarian Trust
Ruth & Lionel Jacobson Trust
(Second Fund) No 2
Jeffrey Charitable Trust
Jewish Child's Day
Johnson Foundation
Sir James Knott Trust
Lazard Charitable Trust
Leathersellers' Company
Charitable Fund
Leigh Trust
Leng Charitable Trust
Levy Foundation
Lloyd's Charities Trust
Lloyds TSB Foundation for
Northern Ireland
Lloyds TSB Foundation for
Channel Islands
London Law Trust
Gerald Micklem Charitable
Trust
Northcott Devon Foundation
Parivar Trust

A M Pilkington's Charitable
Trust
Red Dragon Radio Trust
Christopher Rowbotham
Charitable Trust
Saddlers' Company Charitable
Fund
Scott Bader Commonwealth
Ltd
Henry Smith Charity
Peter Stebbings Memorial
Charity
Charles and Elsie Sykes Trust
Tesco Charity Trust
Thomas Wall Trust
Wates Foundation
Wellfield Trust
Michael and Anna Wix
Charitable Trust
Woodward Trust
York Children's Trust

Medical research & clinical treatment

Funding priority
Aberbrothock Charitable Trust
Sylvia Aitken Charitable Trust
Arthritis Research Campaign
Ashe Park Charitable Trust
Ian Askew Charitable Trust
Lord Austin Trust
John Avins Trustees
David and Frederick Barclay
Foundation
Bartholomew Charitable Trust
Birmingham Hospital Saturday
Fund Medical Charity &
Welfare Trust
British Heart Foundation
Palgrave Brown Foundation
Malcolm Chick Charity
Children's Research Fund
Colt Foundation
Criffel Charitable Trust
Cunningham Trust
Cystic Fibrosis Trust
Denman Charitable Trust
Denton Wilde Sapte Charitable
Trust
Dickon Trust
Earmark Trust
James Ellis Charitable Trust
Emmandjay Charitable Trust
Epilepsy Research Foundation
Eranda Foundation
Eveson Charitable Trust
Family Rich Charities Trust
Simon Gibson Charitable Trust
Teresa Rosenbaum Golden
Charitable Trust
Everard & Mina Goodman
Charitable Foundation

Grahame Charitable
Foundation
Great Britain Sasakawa
Foundation
Sue Hammerson's Charitable
Trust
Kathleen Hannay Memorial
Charity
Lennox Hannay Charitable
Trust
Harbour Charitable Trust
Kenneth Hargreaves Charitable
Trust
Harris Charitable Trust
Heart of England Radio
Charitable Trust
Simon Heller Charitable
Settlement
Higgs Charitable Trust
Joseph & Mary Hiley Trust
Sir Julian Hodge Charitable
Trust
Homelands Charitable Trust
Dorothy Jacobs Charity
Jeffrey Charitable Trust
Peter Kershaw Trust
Ursula Keyes Trust
Ernest Kleinwort Charitable
Trust
KPR Charitable Trust
Leeds Hospital Fund
Charitable Trust
Kennedy Leigh Charitable
Trust
Enid Linder Foundation
Second Joseph Aaron Littman
Foundation
George John Livanos
Charitable Trust
London Law Trust
Marie Helen Luen Charitable
Trust
Robert Luff Foundation Ltd
Lord and Lady Lurgan Trust
Lynn Foundation
Madeline Mabey Trust
Violet Mauray Charitable Trust
Maxwell Family Foundation
Medical Research Council
Medlock Charitable Trust
Mental Health Foundation
Mercers' Charitable
Foundation
F H Muirhead Charitable Trust
National Asthma Campaign
Newstead Charity
Laurie Nidditch Foundation
Northcott Devon Medical
Foundation
Northwood Charitable Trust
Nottingham General
Dispensary
Oakdale Trust
Ormsby Charitable Trust
Constance Paterson Charitable
Trust

Patients' Aid Association
Hospital & Medical
Charities Trust
Personal Assurance Charitable
Trust
Pilkington Charities Fund
J S F Pollitzer Charitable
Settlement
PPP Foundation
John Pryor Charitable Trust
Max Reinhardt Charitable Trust
Violet M Richards Charity
Thomas Roberts Trust
Edwin George Robinson
Charitable Trust
Basil Samuel Charitable Trust
Camilla Samuel Fund
Sir Samuel Scott of Yews
Trust
Scouloudi Foundation
Shears Charitable Trust
Stanley Foundation Ltd
Peter Stebbings Memorial
Charity
John Swire (1989) Charitable
Trust
Charles and Elsie Sykes Trust
Tallow Chandlers Benevolent
Fund
Tenovus Scotland
Loke Wan Tho Memorial
Foundation
Three Oaks Trust
Trusthouse Charitable
Foundation
Underwood Trust
Roger Vere Foundation
Mrs Waterhouse Charitable
Trust
Weinstein Foundation
Wellcome Trust
Felicity Wilde Charitable Trust
Williams Family Charitable
Trust
Maurice Wohl Charitable Trust
Wolfson Family Charitable
Trust
Yamanouchi European
Foundation
John K Young Endowment
Fund

Will consider
Abbeydale Trust
Henry & Grete Abrahams
Charitable Trust
Acacia Charitable Trust
Adint Charitable Trust
Alchemy Foundation
Alcohol Education and
Research Fund
Dorothy Gertrude Allen
Memorial Fund
H B Allen Charitable Trust
Alliance Family Foundation
Pat Allsop Charitable Trust

Ardwick Trust
Armourers and Brasiers'
Gauntlet Trust
Ashby Charitable Trust
Astor Foundation
Astor of Hever Trust
ATP Charitable Trust
Harry Bacon Foundation
Balcombe Charitable Trust
Paul Balint Charitable Trust
Balney Charitable Trust
Bamford Charitable Foundation
Barbour Trust
Lord Barnby's Foundation
Misses Barrie Charitable Trust
Bearder Charity
John Beckwith Charitable Trust
Peter Beckwith Charitable
Trust
Benham Charitable Settlement
Bergqvist Charitable Trust
Billingsgate Christian Mission
Charitable Trust
Bingham Trust
Birmingham District Nursing
Charitable Trust
Peter Black Charitable Trust
Herbert & Peter Blagrave
Charitable Trust
John & Celia Bonham Christie
Charitable Trust
Harry Bottom Charitable Trust
British Dietetic Association
General and Education
Trust Fund
Charles & Edna Broadhurst
Charitable Trust
David Brooke Charity
Roger Brooke Charitable Trust
Charles Brotherton Trust
Bulldog Trust
E F Bulmer Benevolent Fund
BUPA Foundation
Burden Trust
Burry Charitable Trust
Arnold James Burton 1956
Charitable Settlement
R M 1956 Burton Charitable
Trust
Edward Cadbury Charitable
Trust
Cadbury Schweppes
Foundation
William A Cadbury Charitable
Trust
Cairns Charitable Trust
W A Cargill Charitable Trust
W A Cargill Fund
Carrington Charitable Trust
Carron Charitable Trust
Leslie Mary Carter Charitable
Trust
H and M Castang Charitable
Trust
Wilfrid & Constance Cave
Foundation

Chandris Foundation
Chapman Charitable Trust
Charities Advisory Trust
Chest Heart and Stroke
Scotland
Child Growth Foundation
Children's Liver Disease
Foundation
Childwick Trust
Christadelphian Samaritan
Fund
Cinderford Charitable Trust
Clarke Charitable Settlement
Coates Charitable Settlement
John Coates Charitable Trust
Denise Cohen Charitable Trust
Congleton Inclosure Trust
Cooper Charitable Trust
Holbeche Corfield Charitable
Settlement
Coutts & Co. Charitable Trust
Lord Cozens-Hardy Trust
Cranbury Foundation
Michael Crawford Children's
Charity
Crescent Trust
Cumber Family Charitable
Trust
Daily Telegraph Charitable
Trust
Daiwa Anglo-Japanese
Foundation
Dr & Mrs A Darlington
Charitable Trust
Gwendoline & Margaret Davies
Charity
Denton Charitable Trust
Diabetes UK
Dinwoodie Settlement
Douglas Charitable Trust
Dunhill Medical Trust
Gilbert Edgar Trust
Gilbert & Eileen Edgar
Foundation
City of Edinburgh Charitable
Trusts
Maud Elkington Charitable
Trust
Emerton-Christie Charity
Esher House Charitable Trust
Exilarch's Foundation
Lord Faringdon Charitable
Trust
Elizabeth Hardie Ferguson
Charitable Trust Fund
David Finnie & Alan Emery
Charitable Trust
Sir John Fisher Foundation
Fishmongers' Company's
Charitable Trust
Ian Fleming Charitable Trust
Row Fogo Charitable Trust
Fortuna Charitable Trust
Fox Memorial Trust
Isaac and Freda Frankel
Memorial Charitable Trust

Hugh Fraser Foundation
Maurice Fry Charitable Trust
Mejer and Gertrude Miriam
    Frydman Foundation
Gamma Trust
General Nursing Council for
    England and Wales Trust
Girdlers' Company Charitable
    Trust
B & P Glasser Charitable Trust
GNC Trust
Sydney & Phyllis Goldberg
    Memorial Charitable Trust
Mike Gooley Trailfinders
    Charity
Mrs Margaret Guido's
    Charitable Trust
Walter Guinness Charitable
    Trust
Hadfield Trust
Hamamelis Trust
Hampton Fuel Allotment
    Charity
Hare of Steep Charitable Trust
N & P Hartley Memorial Trust
Hawthorne Charitable Trust
Haymills Charitable Trust
H J Heinz Company Limited
    Charitable Trust
Michael & Morven Heller
    Charitable Foundation
Help Hospices
Hemby Trust
Jane Hodge Foundation
Edward Holt Trust
P H Holt Charitable Trust
Homestead Charitable Trust
Mary Homfray Charitable Trust
Sir Harold Hood's Charitable
    Trust
Hoover Foundation
Antony Hornby Charitable Trust
Hospital Saturday Fund
    Charitable Trust
Clifford Howarth Charity
    Settlement
HSA Charitable Trust
Albert Hunt Trust
Hyde Park Place Estate Charity
Iliffe Family Charitable Trust
India Foundation (UK)
Inman Charity
Inverforth Charitable Trust
Jerwood Foundation and
    Jerwood Charitable
    Foundation
Lillie Johnson Charitable Trust
Jones 1986 Charitable Trust
Lady Eileen Joseph Foundation
Judith Trust
Stanley Kalms Foundation
Boris Karloff Charitable
    Foundation
Michael & Ilse Katz Foundation
Emmanuel Kaye Foundation
Kay Kendall Leukaemia Fund

Mary Kinross Charitable Trust
Graham Kirkham Foundation
Kobler Trust
Kohn Foundation
Kreditor Charitable Trust
Kreitman Foundation
Heinz & Anna Kroch
    Foundation
Kyte Charitable Trust
Kirby Laing Foundation
Rachel & Jack Lass Charities
    Ltd
Lauffer Family Charitable
    Foundation
Edgar E Lawley Foundation
Arnold Lee Charitable Trust
Leng Charitable Trust
Leonard Trust
Lesley Lesley and Mutter Trust
Linbury Trust
Linden Charitable Trust
Elaine & Angus Lloyd
    Charitable Trust
W M & B W Lloyd Trust
Lloyds TSB Foundation for
    Channel Islands
C L Loyd Charitable Trust
Lyons Charitable Trust
M N R Charitable Trust
Robert McAlpine Foundation
E M MacAndrew Trust
R S MacDonald Charitable
    Trust
Mackintosh Foundation
Helen Isabella McMorran
    Charitable Foundation
D D McPhail Charitable
    Settlement
R W Mann Trustees Limited
Leslie & Lilian Manning Trust
Hilda & Samuel Marks
    Foundation
Erich Markus Charitable
    Foundation
Michael Marsh Charitable
    Trust
Nancie Massey Charitable
    Trust
Evelyn May Trust
Anthony and Elizabeth Mellows
    Charitable Settlement
Merchant Taylors' Company
    Charities Fund
Mercury Phoenix Trust
Gerald Micklem Charitable
    Trust
Victor Mishcon Charitable
    Trust
Mobbs Memorial Trust Ltd
Monmouthshire County Council
    Welsh Church Act Fund
Morel Charitable Trust
Morgan Crucible Company plc
    Charitable Trust

J P Morgan Fleming
    Educational Trust and
    Foundation
Morris Charitable Trust
Willie & Mabel Morris
    Charitable Trust
Moulton Charitable Trust
Edith Murphy Foundation
Janet Nash Charitable Trust
National Kidney Research
    Fund Limited
Nestlé Rowntree York
    Employees Community Fund
    Trust
Network for Social Change
Newby Trust Limited
Frances and Augustus
    Newman Foundation
Norman Family Charitable
    Trust
Noswad Charity
Oakley Charitable Trust
Old Possum's Practical Trust
Raymond Oppenheimer
    Foundation
P F Charitable Trust
Gerald Palmer Trust
Parthenon Trust
Alan Pascoe Charitable Trust
Arthur James Paterson
    Charitable Trust
Patrick Charitable Trust
Late Barbara May Paul
    Charitable Trust
Peacock Charitable Trust
Pennycress Trust
Ruth & Michael Phillips
    Charitable Trust
Bernard Piggott Trust
A M Pilkington's Charitable
    Trust
Cecil Pilkington Charitable
    Trust
Porter Foundation
J E Posnansky Charitable Trust
Prince of Wales's Charitable
    Foundation
Privy Purse Charitable Trust
Proven Family Trust
Rank Foundation
Ranworth Trust
E L Rathbone Charitable Trust
Märit and Hans Rausing
    Charitable Foundation
Ravensdale Trust
Rayne Foundation
John Rayner Charitable Trust
Christopher H R Reeves
    Charitable Trust
Reuters Foundation
Muriel Edith Rickman Trust
Robertson Trust
C A Rookes Charitable Trust
Cecil Rosen Foundation
Rowlands Trust
Rubin Foundation

Raymond & Beverley Sackler
　Foundation
Saddlers' Company Charitable
　Fund
Alan and Babette Sainsbury
　Charitable Fund
St Andrew Animal Fund Ltd
Late St Patrick White
　Charitable Trust
Peter Samuel Charitable Trust
Sandra Charitable Trust
Schmidt-Bodner Charitable
　Trust
Scotbelge Charitable Trust
Scottish Hospital Endowments
　Research Trust
Seamen's Hospital Society
Samuel Sebba Charitable
　Trust
Sefton Community Foundation
Sylvia & Colin Shepherd
　Charitable Trust
Simpson Education &
　Conservation Trust
Ernest William Slaughter
　Charitable Trust
SMB Trust
Henry Smith Charity
E C Sosnow Charitable Trust
South Square Trust
Sparks Charity
W W Spooner Charitable Trust
Steel Charitable Trust
E J H Stephenson Deceased
　Charitable Trust
Stevenson Family's Charitable
　Trust
Stewards' Charitable Trust
Stoller Charitable Trust
M J C Stone Charitable Trust
Stone-Mallabar Charitable
　Foundation
Sueberry Ltd
Bernard Sunley Charitable
　Foundation
Swann-Morton Foundation
Swire Charitable Trust
Hugh & Ruby Sykes Charitable
　Trust
Stella Symons Charitable Trust
Tay Charitable Trust
Thompson Charitable Trust
Len Thomson Charitable Trust
Thoresby Charitable Trust
Towry Law Charitable Trust
Douglas Turner Trust
Albert Van Den Bergh
　Charitable Trust
John and Lucille van Geest
　Foundation
Robert and Felicity Waley-
　Cohen Charitable Trust
Sir Siegmund Warburg's
　Voluntary Settlement
Ward Blenkinsop Trust
Perry Watlington Trust

Bertie Watson Foundation
Mary Webb Trust
Weinstock Fund
James Weir Foundation
Welton Foundation
Alexander Pigott Wernher
　Memorial Trust
Wesleyan Charitable Trust
Westminster Foundation
Garfield Weston Foundation
Wilkinson Charitable
　Foundation
Harold Hyam Wingate
　Foundation
Maurice Wohl Charitable
　Foundation
Charles Wolfson Charitable
　Trust
Wolfson Foundation
Woodroffe Benton Foundation
Woodward Trust
Wyseliot Charitable Trust
Yapp Charitable Trust

....

■ Dentistry
Will consider
Astor Foundation
E F Bulmer Benevolent Fund

....

■ Immune system, allergies
Funding priority
Fiat Auto (UK) Charity
Harebell Centenary Fund
Lewis Family Charitable Trust
Frances and Augustus
　Newman Foundation
Mr and Mrs J A Pye's
　Charitable Settlement
Christopher H R Reeves
　Charitable Trust
REMEDI

Will consider
Blair Foundation
E F Bulmer Benevolent Fund
Duis Charitable Trust
Epilepsy Research Foundation
Leach Fourteenth Trust
W M Mann Foundation
Mercury Phoenix Trust
Northcott Devon Foundation
Charity Fund of Worshipful
　Company of Paviors
Austin & Hope Pilkington Trust
Pilkington Charities Fund
Simone Prendergast Charitable
　Trust
Search
Leslie Smith Foundation
Starfish Trust
Steinberg Family Charitable
　Trust

Sir Jules Thorn Charitable
　Trust
Wellcome Trust

....

■ Neurological and brain disorders
Funding priority
Ardwick Trust
Baker Charitable Trust
Barnwood House Trust
Patrick Berthoud Charitable
　Trust
Bothwell Charitable Trust
BUPA Foundation
Burden Trust
De Clermont Charitable
　Company Ltd
Epilepsy Research Foundation
Family Rich Charities Trust
Fiat Auto (UK) Charity
Row Fogo Charitable Trust
Garthgwynion Charities
Harebell Centenary Fund
Charles Hayward Foundation
Edward Holt Trust
International Spinal Research
　Trust
Lewis Family Charitable Trust
Little Foundation
Paul Lunn-Rockliffe Charitable
　Trust
Migraine Trust
Frances and Augustus
　Newman Foundation
REMEDI
Muriel Edith Rickman Trust
Walter Swindon Charitable
　Trust
Tisbury Telegraph Trust
John and Lucille van Geest
　Foundation
Verdon-Smith Family Charitable
　Settlement

Will consider
Ashby Charitable Trust
Andrew Balint Charitable Trust
George Balint Charitable Trust
Blair Foundation
Bonhomie United Charity
　Society
Charles Boot Trust
R S Brownless Charitable
　Trust
E F Bulmer Benevolent Fund
Burdens Charitable Foundation
Cemlyn-Jones Trust
Coward Trust
Duis Charitable Trust
Ferguson Benevolent Fund Ltd
Fidelity UK Foundation
Girdlers' Company Charitable
　Trust
Robert Hall Charity
May Hearnshaw's Charity

Ingram Trust
Ruth & Lionel Jacobson Trust
    (Second Fund) No 2
John Jarrold Trust
Johnson Foundation
David Laing Foundation
R J Larg Family Charitable
    Trust
Kathleen Laurence Trust
Leach Fourteenth Trust
Levy Foundation
Lloyds TSB Foundation for
    Scotland
R S MacDonald Charitable
    Trust
W M Mann Foundation
Medlock Charitable Trust
Mickel Fund
Northcott Devon Foundation
Kate Wilson Oliver Trust
Austin & Hope Pilkington Trust
Pilkington Charities Fund
Mr and Mrs J A Pye's
    Charitable Settlement
Rainford Trust
Fanny Rapaport Charitable
    Settlement
Cliff Richard Charitable Trust
Scarfe Charitable Trust
Search
Starfish Trust
Steinberg Family Charitable
    Trust
Sir Jules Thorn Charitable
    Trust
Alfred and Beatrice Weintrop
    Charity
Wellcome Trust
Michael and Anna Wix
    Charitable Trust
York Children's Trust

....
■ **Oncology**
Funding priority
Sylvia Aitken Charitable Trust
Appletree Trust
Ardwick Trust
Bergqvist Charitable Trust
M Bourne Charitable Trust
Breast Cancer Research Trust
De Clermont Charitable
    Company Ltd
Demigryphon Trust
Denton Charitable Trust
Family Rich Charities Trust
Fiat Auto (UK) Charity
Bud Flanagan Leukaemia Fund
Gerald Fogel Charitable Trust
Garthgwynion Charities
Gould Charitable Trust
Harebell Centenary Fund
Christina Mary Hendrie Trust
    for Scottish & Canadian
    Charities
Edward Holt Trust

Miss Agnes H Hunter's Trust
Kidani Memorial Trust
Lauchentilly Charitable
    Foundation 1988
Mason Le Page Charitable
    Trust
Kennedy Leigh Charitable
    Trust
Leukaemia Research Fund
Lewis Family Charitable Trust
Mandeville Trust
Melville Trust for Care and
    Cure of Cancer
Mickel Fund
Midhurst Pensions Trust
Frances and Augustus
    Newman Foundation
North West Cancer Research
    Fund
Austin & Hope Pilkington Trust
Pilkington Charities Fund
Ronald & Kathleen Pryor
    Charitable Trust
Mr and Mrs J A Pye's
    Charitable Settlement
Muriel Edith Rickman Trust
Swan Trust
Walter Swindon Charitable
    Trust
Rosanna Taylor's 1987 Charity
    Trust
Mrs S H Troughton Charity
    Trust
Verdon-Smith Family Charitable
    Settlement
Walton Foundation
Alfred and Beatrice Weintrop
    Charity
West London Synagogue
    Charitable Fund
Miss E B Wrightson's
    Charitable Settlement
Wyseliot Charitable Trust

Will consider
Adint Charitable Trust
G C Armitage Charitable Trust
Ashby Charitable Trust
Andrew Balint Charitable Trust
George Balint Charitable Trust
Blair Foundation
Charles Boot Trust
British Humane Association
E F Bulmer Benevolent Fund
Burdens Charitable Foundation
Richard Cadbury Charitable
    Trust
Cemlyn-Jones Trust
Lord Clinton's Charitable Trust
Norman Collinson Charitable
    Trust
John Cowan Foundation
Coward Trust
Elmgrant Trust
Samuel William Farmer's Trust

Earl Fitzwilliam Charitable
    Trust
Timothy Franey Charitable
    Foundation
Charles S French Charitable
    Trust
Gannochy Trust
Girdlers' Company Charitable
    Trust
Reginald Graham Charitable
    Trust
Robert Hall Charity
May Hearnshaw's Charity
Dorothy Holmes Charitable
    Trust
James Thom Howat Charitable
    Trust
Ingram Trust
Ruth & Lionel Jacobson Trust
    (Second Fund) No 2
Jarman Charitable Trust
John Jarrold Trust
Johnson Foundation
Nancy Kenyon Charitable Trust
Robert Kiln Charitable Trust
David Laing Foundation
R J Larg Family Charitable
    Trust
Kathleen Laurence Trust
Raymond & Blanche Lawson
    Charitable Trust
Leach Fourteenth Trust
Levy Foundation
Second Joseph Aaron Littman
    Foundation
Lloyds TSB Foundation for
    Scotland
W M Mann Foundation
Medlock Charitable Trust
Tony Metherell Charitable
    Trust
George A Moore Foundation
North British Hotel Trust
Northcott Devon Foundation
Oakmoor Trust
Oldham Foundation
Kate Wilson Oliver Trust
Patrick Charitable Trust
Prince Foundation
Rainford Trust
Fanny Rapaport Charitable
    Settlement
Cliff Richard Charitable Trust
Russell Trust
L H Silver Charitable Trust
Starfish Trust
Sir Jules Thorn Charitable
    Trust
Tisbury Telegraph Trust
Harold Hyam Wingate
    Foundation
Michael and Anna Wix
    Charitable Trust

■ Ophthalmology

Funding priority
BibleLands
British Council for Prevention
 of Blindness
Frognal Trust
T F C Frost Charitable Trust
Garthgwynion Charities
Harebell Centenary Fund
Kennedy Leigh Charitable
 Trust
Frances and Augustus
 Newman Foundation
REMEDI
Muriel Edith Rickman Trust
Ulverscroft Foundation
Alexander Pigott Wernher
 Memorial Trust

Will consider
Andrew Balint Charitable Trust
George Balint Charitable Trust
British Humane Association
E F Bulmer Benevolent Fund
Charles Hayward Foundation
Johnson Foundation
Kathleen Laurence Trust
Leach Fourteenth Trust
Lloyds TSB Foundation for
 Scotland
R S MacDonald Charitable
 Trust
W M Mann Foundation
Northcott Devon Foundation
Kate Wilson Oliver Trust
Austin & Hope Pilkington Trust
Pilkington Charities Fund
Priory of Scotland of Order of
 St John of Jerusalem
Mr and Mrs J A Pye's
 Charitable Settlement
Simpson Education &
 Conservation Trust
Steinberg Family Charitable
 Trust
Sir Jules Thorn Charitable
 Trust
Wellcome Trust
Will Charitable Trust
Michael and Anna Wix
 Charitable Trust
York Children's Trust

■ Paediatrics and foetal medicine

Funding priority
Bergqvist Charitable Trust
Birmingham Hospital Saturday
 Fund Medical Charity &
 Welfare Trust
Children's Research Fund
De Clermont Charitable
 Company Ltd
Demigryphon Trust

Charles Hayward Foundation
Lewis Family Charitable Trust
Little Foundation
REMEDI
Sparks Charity
Sir Halley Stewart Trust
Rosanna Taylor's 1987 Charity
 Trust
Mrs S H Troughton Charity
 Trust
West London Synagogue
 Charitable Fund

Will consider
Adint Charitable Trust
Enid Blyton Trust for Children
E F Bulmer Benevolent Fund
Richard Cadbury Charitable
 Trust
Duis Charitable Trust
Epilepsy Research Foundation
Girdlers' Company Charitable
 Trust
Constance Green Foundation
Harebell Centenary Fund
Ingram Trust
Ruth & Lionel Jacobson Trust
 (Second Fund) No 2
John Jarrold Trust
Jewish Child's Day
Leach Fourteenth Trust
Lloyds TSB Foundation for
 Scotland
M N R Charitable Trust
W M Mann Foundation
Medlock Charitable Trust
North British Hotel Trust
Northcott Devon Foundation
Austin & Hope Pilkington Trust
Pilkington Charities Fund
Priory Foundation
Mr and Mrs J A Pye's
 Charitable Settlement
Cliff Richard Charitable Trust
Search
Ayrton Senna Foundation
Sobell Foundation
Starfish Trust
Steinberg Family Charitable
 Trust
Sir Jules Thorn Charitable
 Trust
Tisbury Telegraph Trust
Perry Watlington Trust
Wellcome Trust
York Children's Trust

Health education/ prevention/ development

Funding priority
Aberbrothock Charitable Trust
Ajahma Charitable Trust

Alcohol Education and
 Research Fund
Birmingham Hospital Saturday
 Fund Medical Charity &
 Welfare Trust
BUPA Foundation
Chest Heart and Stroke
 Scotland
Cleopatra Trust
Cobb Charity
Dorus Trust
Gilbert Edgar Trust
Epigoni Trust
Fiat Auto (UK) Charity
Kathleen Hannay Memorial
 Charity
Lennox Hannay Charitable
 Trust
Haramead Trust
Joseph & Mary Hiley Trust
ITF Seafarers Trust
King's Fund
Lloyds TSB Foundation for
 Channel Islands
Marie Helen Luen Charitable
 Trust
Medlock Charitable Trust
Mercers' Charitable
 Foundation
National Kidney Research
 Fund Limited
Oxfordshire Community
 Foundation
Patients' Aid Association
 Hospital & Medical
 Charities Trust
Personal Assurance Charitable
 Trust
Austin & Hope Pilkington Trust
Prairie Trust
Walter Swindon Charitable
 Trust
Kay Williams Charitable
 Foundation

Will consider
1970 Trust
Adnams Charity
AIM Foundation
Sylvia Aitken Charitable Trust
Arthritis Research Campaign
Bedford Charity
BibleLands
Bingham Trust
Birmingham Foundation
British Council for Prevention
 of Blindness
British Dietetic Association
 General and Education
 Trust Fund
Roger Brooke Charitable Trust
Bryant Trust
Audrey & Stanley Burton
 Charitable Trust
Chippenham Borough Lands
 Charity

Chipping Sodbury Town Lands
   Charity
J A Clark Charitable Trust
Holbeche Corfield Charitable
   Settlement
Coutts & Co. Charitable Trust
Cumber Family Charitable
   Trust
Dunhill Medical Trust
City of Edinburgh Charitable
   Trusts
John Ellerman Foundation
Florence's Charitable Trust
Robert Gavron Charitable Trust
Constance Green Foundation
Holywood Trust
Mary Homfray Charitable Trust
James Thom Howat Charitable
   Trust
Ironmongers' Quincentenary
   Charitable Fund
Isle of Dogs Community
   Foundation
Judith Trust
Boris Karloff Charitable
   Foundation
Sir James Knott Trust
Heinz & Anna Kroch
   Foundation
Frank Litchfield Charitable
   Trust
Lloyd's Charities Trust
Lloyds TSB Foundation for
   England and Wales
Methodist Relief and
   Development Fund
Millfield House Foundation
Milton Keynes Community
   Foundation
Monmouthshire County Council
   Welsh Church Act Fund
John Moores Foundation
National Asthma Campaign
Norwich Town Close Estate
   Charity
PPP Foundation
Violet M Richards Charity
Richmond Parish Lands Charity
Rothley Trust
Christopher Rowbotham
   Charitable Trust
St James' Trust Settlement
Sir Walter St John's
   Educational Charity
Sherburn House Charity
SMB Trust
South Square Trust
Sovereign Health Care
   Charitable Trust
Tesco Charity Trust
Ward Blenkinsop Trust
James Weir Foundation
Wolfson Foundation
Woodroffe Benton Foundation
Yapp Charitable Trust

■ Environmental health

Will consider
Ashby Charitable Trust
Boots Charitable Trust
Cobb Charity
Godinton Charitable Trust
GWR Community Trust
W M Mann Foundation
Medlock Charitable Trust
Search
Thames Community
   Foundation
Tisbury Telegraph Trust
York Children's Trust

■ Health promotion

Funding priority
Alcohol Education and
   Research Fund
Chest Heart and Stroke
   Scotland
Child Growth Foundation
Consortium on Opportunities
   for Volunteering
Derbyshire Community
   Foundation
Harrow Community Trust
ITF Seafarers Trust
Muslim Hands
Austin & Hope Pilkington Trust

Will consider
Adnams Charity
BibleLands
Boots Charitable Trust
British Dietetic Association
   General and Education
   Trust Fund
Audrey & Stanley Burton
   Charitable Trust
Richard Cadbury Charitable
   Trust
Eden Arts Trust
H C D Memorial Fund
Hadrian Trust
Hedgcock Bequest
Alan Edward Higgs Charity
Holywood Trust
India Foundation (UK)
Isle of Dogs Community
   Foundation
Judith Trust
Lloyd's Charities Trust
Lloyds TSB Foundation for
   Northern Ireland
W M Mann Foundation
National Asthma Campaign
Park Hill Trust
Search
Sherburn House Charity
Tesco Charity Trust
Thames Community
   Foundation

Tisbury Telegraph Trust
Wiltshire and Swindon
   Community Foundation
York Children's Trust

■ Occupational health & safety

Funding priority
ITF Seafarers Trust

Will consider
Consortium on Opportunities
   for Volunteering
Harrow Community Trust
Lloyds TSB Foundation for
   Northern Ireland
Search

■ Well women clinics, centres

Funding priority
Harrow Community Trust
Walter Swindon Charitable
   Trust

Will consider
Adnams Charity
Barbour Trust
BibleLands
Birmingham Hospital Saturday
   Fund Medical Charity &
   Welfare Trust
Boots Charitable Trust
E F Bulmer Benevolent Fund
Richard Cadbury Charitable
   Trust
Community Foundation for
   Calderdale
Community Foundation for
   Northern Ireland
Community Fund
Consortium on Opportunities
   for Volunteering
De Clermont Charitable
   Company Ltd
Duis Charitable Trust
Greater Bristol Foundation
GWR Community Trust
Hadrian Trust
Charles Hayward Foundation
Jeffrey Charitable Trust
Sir James Knott Trust
Lawlor Foundation
Lloyds TSB Foundation for
   Northern Ireland
M N R Charitable Trust
Marsh Christian Trust
Parivar Trust
Harry Payne Trust
Austin & Hope Pilkington Trust
Proven Family Trust
E L Rathbone Charitable Trust
Sir James & Lady Scott Trust

*Wiltshire and Swindon
　Community Foundation*

Philanthropy and voluntary sector

Funding priority
Paul Bassham Charitable Trust
Bergqvist Charitable Trust
Sydney Black Charitable Trust
Dickon Trust
Bishop of Guildford's
　Foundation
Harrow Community Trust
Thames Community
　Foundation

Will consider
Alexandra Rose Day
Bedford Charity
Bingham Trust
Boots Charitable Trust
Roger Brooke Charitable Trust
Burton Breweries Charitable
　Trust
Gwendoline & Margaret Davies
　Charity
DLA Charitable Trust
Englefield Charitable Trust
Great Britain Sasakawa
　Foundation
Kenneth Hargreaves Charitable
　Trust
Hitachi Europe Charitable
　Trust
R W Mann Trustees Limited
Eleanor Rathbone Charitable
　Trust
R D Turner Charitable Trust
Vale of Glamorgan Welsh
　Church Fund
VEC Acorn Trust
Webb Memorial Trust
David Wilson Foundation
Wixamtree Trust
I A Ziff Charitable Foundation

Philanthropic intermediaries

Will consider
Sylvia Aitken Charitable Trust
Morgan Blake Charitable Trust
Carpenter Charitable Trust
Esmée Fairbairn Foundation
Samuel William Farmer's Trust
Gannochy Trust
Leathersellers' Company
　Charitable Fund
VEC Acorn Trust

Voluntarism

Funding priority
BBC Radio Cambridgeshire –
　Trustline

Bridge House Estates Trust
　Fund
Criffel Charitable Trust
Edinburgh Voluntary
　Organisations' Trust Funds
Simon Gibson Charitable Trust
GWR Community Trust
Medlock Charitable Trust
Northern Rock Foundation
Patients' Aid Association
　Hospital & Medical
　Charities Trust
Sir James & Lady Scott Trust
South Yorkshire Community
　Foundation
Thames Community
　Foundation

Will consider
Baily Thomas Charitable Fund
Barbour Trust
Blanchminster Trust
Charles Brotherton Trust
Richard Cadbury Charitable
　Trust
Carnegie Dunfermline Trust
City Parochial Foundation
Community Foundation Serving
　Tyne & Wear and
　Northumberland
John Grant Davies Trust
Earley Charity
Wilfred & Elsie Elkes Charity
　Fund
Esmée Fairbairn Foundation
Ford of Britain Trust
Four Lanes Trust
Harrison & Potter Trust
James Thom Howat Charitable
　Trust
Isle of Dogs Community
　Foundation
Joicey Trust
Raymond & Blanche Lawson
　Charitable Trust
Mark Leonard Trust
Lintel Trust
Lloyds TSB Foundation for
　Northern Ireland
Lloyds TSB Foundation for
　Scotland
Lloyds TSB Foundation for
　Channel Islands
London Youth Trust
John Martin's Charity
John Moores Foundation
Newport County Borough
　Welsh Church Fund
Northcott Devon Foundation
Oxfordshire Community
　Foundation
Pastoral Care Trust
Jack Petchey Foundation
St Mary-le-Strand Charity
Francis C Scott Charitable
　Trust

Summerfield Charitable Trust
Triangle Trust (1949) Fund
VEC Acorn Trust
Wakeham Trust
Wates Foundation
Worcester Municipal Charities
York Children's Trust

Voluntary sector capacity building

Funding priority

Berkshire Community
    Foundation
Bridge House Estates Trust
    Fund
Chase Charity
Digbeth Trust
Esmée Fairbairn Foundation
Greater Bristol Foundation
GWR Community Trust
Sir James Knott Trust
Northern Rock Foundation
Privy Purse Charitable Trust
Frieda Scott Charitable Trust
Sir James & Lady Scott Trust
South Yorkshire Community
    Foundation
Thames Community
    Foundation

Will consider

G C Armitage Charitable Trust
Arts Council of Wales
Bingham Trust
Charles Brotherton Trust
Carpenter Charitable Trust
Church Urban Fund
Norman Collinson Charitable
    Trust
Comic Relief
Community Foundation Serving
    Tyne & Wear and
    Northumberland
John Grant Davies Trust
Derbyshire Community
    Foundation
Devon Community Foundation
Dulverton Trust
Earley Charity
Wilfred & Elsie Elkes Charity
    Fund
John Ellerman Foundation
Ford of Britain Trust
Four Lanes Trust
Gatwick Airport Community
    Trust
Greggs Trust
Hertfordshire Community
    Foundation
Joicey Trust
Late Sir Pierce Lacy Charity
    Trust
Laing's Charitable Trust

Lloyds TSB Foundation for
    England and Wales
Lloyds TSB Foundation for
    Northern Ireland
Lloyds TSB Foundation for
    Scotland
London Youth Trust
John Martin's Charity
Medlock Charitable Trust
Milton Keynes Community
    Foundation
John Moores Foundation
Newport County Borough
    Welsh Church Fund
Northcott Devon Foundation
Oxfordshire Community
    Foundation
Patients' Aid Association
    Hospital & Medical
    Charities Trust
Jack Petchey Foundation
Richmond Parish Lands Charity
Rothley Trust
Summerfield Charitable Trust
War on Want
Webb Memorial Trust
Westcroft Trust
Wiltshire and Swindon
    Community Foundation

Rights, law and conflict

Funding priority

Bergqvist Charitable Trust
Commonwealth Relations
    Trust
Webb Memorial Trust

Will consider

Alexandra Rose Day
Bingham Trust
Mrs E E Brown Charitable
    Settlement
Bryant Trust
Comic Relief
DLA Charitable Trust
Englefield Charitable Trust
Ericson Trust
Anne French Memorial Trust
Maurice Fry Charitable Trust
Gretna Charitable Trust
Lethendy Charitable Trust
Eleanor Rathbone Charitable
    Trust
Rothley Trust
Alan and Babette Sainsbury
    Charitable Fund
Sir Halley Stewart Trust
Stone Ashdown Charitable
    Trust
Stella Symons Charitable Trust
A R Taylor Charitable Trust
Constance Travis Charitable
    Trust
Welsh Church Fund –
    Carmarthenshire area
David Wilson Foundation
Wixamtree Trust

Citizen participation

Funding priority

Aberbrothock Charitable Trust
Camelot Foundation
Esmée Fairbairn Foundation
Tinsley Foundation
Webb Memorial Trust

Will consider

Bedford Charity
E F Bulmer Benevolent Fund
Chippenham Borough Lands
    Charity
Community Foundation Serving
    Tyne & Wear and
    Northumberland
Derbyshire Community
    Foundation
Lyndhurst Settlement
Methodist Relief and
    Development Fund
Millfield House Foundation

*Joseph Rowntree Charitable
  Trust*
Summerfield Charitable Trust
Wates Foundation

Conflict resolution

Funding priority
Aberbrothock Charitable Trust
Denton Charitable Trust
Bryan Lancaster's Charity
Tinsley Foundation

Will consider
Barnabas Charitable Trust
E F Bulmer Benevolent Fund
*Edward Cadbury Charitable
  Trust*
*William A Cadbury Charitable
  Trust*
Carpenter Charitable Trust
*Community Foundation Serving
  Tyne & Wear and
  Northumberland*
*Cumber Family Charitable
  Trust*
Four Acre Trust
Ireland Fund of Great Britain
Sir James Reckitt Charity

■ Cross-border initiatives

Will consider
Paul Hamlyn Foundation
Lawlor Foundation
*Mr and Mrs J A Pye's
  Charitable Settlement*

■ Cross-community work

Funding priority
Paul Bassham Charitable Trust
Enkalon Foundation
Esmée Fairbairn Foundation
Harrow Community Trust
Lawlor Foundation
*Kitty and Daniel Nabarro
  Charitable Trust*

Will consider
E F Bulmer Benevolent Fund
Devon Community Foundation
Paul Hamlyn Foundation
*Lloyds TSB Foundation for
  Northern Ireland*
Lyndhurst Settlement
*Mercers' Charitable
  Foundation*
Noon Foundation
*Oxfordshire Community
  Foundation*
Jack Petchey Foundation

Women Caring Trust

■ Mediation

Funding priority
Paul Bassham Charitable Trust

Will consider
Bedford Charity
E F Bulmer Benevolent Fund
Four Acre Trust
Charles Hayward Foundation
Lankelly Foundation
*Lloyds TSB Foundation for
  Northern Ireland*
Lyndhurst Settlement
Peter Minet Trust
Northcott Devon Foundation
Oakdale Trust
*Oxfordshire Community
  Foundation*
Jack Petchey Foundation
Rothley Trust
C B & H H Taylor 1984 Trust
Tudor Trust
*Weavers' Company Benevolent
  Fund*

■ Peace and disarmament

Funding priority
*Community Foundation for
  Northern Ireland*
*Allan and Nesta Ferguson
  Charitable Settlement*
*S C and M E Morland's
  Charitable Trust*
*Polden-Puckham Charitable
  Foundation*
*Joseph Rowntree Charitable
  Trust*
W F Southall Trust
Westcroft Trust

Will consider
Ajahma Charitable Trust
Calpe Trust
J A Clark Charitable Trust
Oakdale Trust
Philanthropic Trust
*A M Pilkington's Charitable
  Trust*
Tisbury Telegraph Trust
Whitaker Charitable Trust

Legal & advice services

Funding priority
Greater Bristol Foundation
ITF Seafarers Trust
John Moores Foundation
Oakdale Trust

*South Yorkshire Community
  Foundation*

Will consider
A B Charitable Trust
Ajahma Charitable Trust
Andrew Anderson Trust
Anglian Water Trust Fund
Ardwick Trust
Baring Foundation
Barnsbury Charitable Trust
James Beattie Charitable Trust
Bedford Charity
Blanchminster Trust
Boots Charitable Trust
*Bridge House Estates Trust
  Fund*
E F Bulmer Benevolent Fund
*William A Cadbury Charitable
  Trust*
*Commonwealth Relations
  Trust*
Congleton Inclosure Trust
Cripplegate Foundation
Harry Crook Foundation
John Grant Davies Trust
*Derbyshire Community
  Foundation*
Earley Charity
J Paul Getty Jr Charitable Trust
J G Graves Charitable Trust
Grocers' Charity
Hadrian Trust
*Hampstead Wells and
  Campden Trust*
*Hampton Fuel Allotment
  Charity*
*Heart of England Community
  Foundation*
*Hertfordshire Community
  Foundation*
Hilden Charitable Fund
*Sir Harold Hood's Charitable
  Trust*
HopMarket Charity
Joicey Trust
Bryan Lancaster's Charity
Lankelly Foundation
*Mrs F B Laurence Charitable
  Trust*
Leigh Trust
*Lloyds TSB Foundation for
  Northern Ireland*
*Lloyds TSB Foundation for
  Scotland*
Lyndhurst Settlement
*Manchester Airport Community
  Trust Fund*
R W Mann Trustees Limited
John Martin's Charity
*Metropolitan Hospital-Sunday
  Fund*
Peter Minet Trust
*Norwich Town Close Estate
  Charity*
Nuffield Foundation

Personal Assurance Charitable
    Trust
Bernard Piggott Trust
Pilkington Charities Fund
Powys Welsh Church Fund
Princess Anne's Charities
Sir James Reckitt Charity
Helen Roll Charitable Trust
Sir James & Lady Scott Trust
Scottish Community
    Foundation
Spitalfields Market Community
    Trust
Peter Stebbings Memorial
    Charity
Sutton Coldfield Municipal
    Charities
Scurrah Wainwright Charity
Wiltshire and Swindon
    Community Foundation

....
■ Advice services
Funding priority
Abel Charitable Trust
Alcohol Education and
    Research Fund
Paul Bassham Charitable Trust
Greggs Trust
Housing Associations
    Charitable Trust
Anton Jurgens Charitable Trust
Peter Kershaw Trust
Allen Lane Foundation
Leeds & Holbeck Building
    Society Charitable
    Foundation
Lloyds TSB Foundation for
    Channel Islands
Market Harborough and
    Bowdens Charity
Rosca Trust
Frieda Scott Charitable Trust
Severn Trent Water Charitable
    Trust

Will consider
1970 Trust
Age Concern Scotland
    Enterprise Fund
Astor Foundation
BAA 21st Century
    Communities Trust
BBC Children in Need Appeal
Berkshire Community
    Foundation
Bingham Trust
Blatchington Court Trust
Britannia Building Society
    Foundation
Bryant Trust
Burdens Charitable Foundation
Audrey & Stanley Burton
    Charitable Trust
Chase Charity

Chippenham Borough Lands
    Charity
Church Urban Fund
Colchester & Tendring
    Community Trust
Community Foundation for
    Northern Ireland
Community Foundation Serving
    Tyne & Wear and
    Northumberland
Coppings Trust
Cwmbran Trust
Helen and Geoffrey de Freitas
    Charitable Trust
Community Council of Devon
Devon Community Foundation
W E Dunn Trust
Emmandjay Charitable Trust
Essex Youth Trust
Fifty Fund
Ford of Britain Trust
Jill Franklin Trust
Constance Green Foundation
Kathleen Hannay Memorial
    Charity
Lennox Hannay Charitable
    Trust
Harborne Parish Lands Charity
Charles Hayward Foundation
Help Aged
Miss Agnes H Hunter's Trust
Hyde Park Place Estate Charity
India Foundation (UK)
Isle of Dogs Community
    Foundation
John Jarrold Trust
Elton John Aids Foundation
Boris Karloff Charitable
    Foundation
Sir James Knott Trust
Heinz & Anna Kroch
    Foundation
Lintel Trust
Lloyds TSB Foundation for
    England and Wales
Medlock Charitable Trust
Milton Keynes Community
    Foundation
Morgan Stanley International
    Foundation
Newby Trust Limited
Northcott Devon Foundation
Northern Rock Foundation
Oxfordshire Community
    Foundation
Harry Payne Trust
A M Pilkington's Charitable
    Trust
Pye Foundation
Richmond Parish Lands Charity
Rothley Trust
Russell Trust
Sir Walter St John's
    Educational Charity
St Katharine & Shadwell Trust
St Mary-le-Strand Charity

Francis C Scott Charitable
    Trust
Scottish Churches Community
    Trust
Sefton Community Foundation
Sellata Ltd
Sheldon Trust
Sherburn House Charity
Bishop Simeon CR Trust
Summerfield Charitable Trust
Charles and Elsie Sykes Trust
Triangle Trust (1949) Fund
Unemployed Voluntary Action
    Fund
Wellfield Trust
Westminster Amalgamated
    Charity
Women at Risk
Worcester Municipal Charities

....
■ Law services
Funding priority
Saint Sarkis Charity Trust

Will consider
Housing Associations
    Charitable Trust
Law Society Charity
Annie Schiff Charitable Trust

Rights, equity and justice
Funding priority
Abbey National Charitable
    Trust Ltd
Ajahma Charitable Trust
Cadbury Schweppes
    Foundation
Community Foundation for
    Northern Ireland
Greggs Trust
Hampton Fuel Allotment
    Charity
Kathleen Hannay Memorial
    Charity
Lennox Hannay Charitable
    Trust
Housing Associations
    Charitable Trust
Lyndhurst Settlement
Millfield House Foundation
Novi Most International
Primrose Hill Trust
C Paul Thackray General
    Charitable Trust
Webb Memorial Trust
Women at Risk
Xerox (UK) Trust

Will consider
A B Charitable Trust
Amberstone Trust

Andrew Anderson Trust
Astor Foundation
Barnabas Charitable Trust
Bedford Charity
Berkshire Community
    Foundation
Blatchington Court Trust
Boots Charitable Trust
Bridge House Estates Trust
    Fund
Barrow Cadbury Trust and
    Barrow Cadbury Fund
Edward Cadbury Charitable
    Trust
Edward & Dorothy Cadbury
    Trust
Richard Cadbury Charitable
    Trust
William A Cadbury Charitable
    Trust
Chase Charity
Coppings Trust
Cripplegate Foundation
Cumber Family Charitable
    Trust
John Grant Davies Trust
Derbyshire Community
    Foundation
Earley Charity
Sydney E Franklin Deceased's
    New Second Charity
Hadrian Trust
Hampstead Wells and
    Campden Trust
Charles Hayward Foundation
Heart of England Community
    Foundation
Help Aged
Holywood Trust
Sir Harold Hood's Charitable
    Trust
Human Relief Foundation
Isle of Dogs Community
    Foundation
John Jarrold Trust
Judith Trust
Sir James Knott Trust
Allen Lane Foundation
Lankelly Foundation
Law Society Charity
Lintel Trust
Lloyds TSB Foundation for
    Northern Ireland
Lloyds TSB Foundation for
    Scotland
Lloyds TSB Foundation for
    Channel Islands
Manchester Airport Community
    Trust Fund
R W Mann Trustees Limited
John Martin's Charity
Milton Keynes Community
    Foundation
Peter Minet Trust
Nuffield Foundation

Oxfordshire Community
    Foundation
Personal Assurance Charitable
    Trust
Prairie Trust
Princess Anne's Charities
Sir James Reckitt Charity
Red Dragon Radio Trust
Joseph Rowntree Charitable
    Trust
Russell Trust
Sir James & Lady Scott Trust
Sherburn House Charity
South Yorkshire Community
    Foundation
Spitalfields Market Community
    Trust
Sportsman's Charity
Peter Stebbings Memorial
    Charity
Summerfield Charitable Trust
Unemployed Voluntary Action
    Fund
Scurrah Wainwright Charity
Garfield Weston Foundation
Wiltshire and Swindon
    Community Foundation

....

■ **Civil liberties**

Funding priority
Tinsley Foundation

Will consider
1970 Trust
Esmée Fairbairn Foundation
Kennedy Leigh Charitable
    Trust
Joseph Rowntree Charitable
    Trust

....

■ **Cultural equity**

Funding priority
Harrow Community Trust
Kitty and Daniel Nabarro
    Charitable Trust
Northern Rock Foundation

Will consider
Body Shop Foundation
Community Foundation Serving
    Tyne & Wear and
    Northumberland
John Moores Foundation
Joseph Rowntree Charitable
    Trust

....

■ **Disability rights**

Funding priority
Harrow Community Trust
Northern Rock Foundation
Karim Rida Said Foundation
Wentwood Education Trust

Will consider
Ardwick Trust
Colchester & Tendring
    Community Trust
Community Foundation Serving
    Tyne & Wear and
    Northumberland
Esmée Fairbairn Foundation
Ford of Britain Trust
Lloyds TSB Foundation for
    Northern Ireland
Mercers' Charitable
    Foundation
John Moores Foundation
Rothley Trust
David Solomons Charitable
    Trust
Yapp Charitable Trust

....

■ **Economic justice**

Funding priority
Northern Rock Foundation
Tinsley Foundation

Will consider
Body Shop Foundation
Esmée Fairbairn Foundation

....

■ **The right to
employment**

Will consider
Esmée Fairbairn Foundation

....

■ **Human rights**

Funding priority
Community Foundation for
    Northern Ireland
Maurice Fry Charitable Trust
Lennox Hannay Charitable
    Trust
Network for Social Change
Onaway Trust
Ruben and Elisabeth Rausing
    Trust
C Paul Thackray General
    Charitable Trust
Tinsley Foundation

Will consider
Richard Attenborough
    Charitable Trust
Beaurepaire Trust
Body Shop Foundation
Boltons Trust
Bromley Trust
Calpe Trust
Chownes Foundation
Coppings Trust
John Grant Davies Trust
W E Dunn Trust
Help Aged

Human Relief Foundation
Law Society Charity
Leigh Trust
Lyndhurst Settlement
Methodist Relief and
    Development Fund
Morel Charitable Trust
Northern Rock Foundation
Persula Foundation
Philanthropic Trust
Rowan Charitable Trust
Joseph Rowntree Charitable
    Trust
St James' Trust Settlement
Woodward Trust

■ Rights of people with mental health problems

Funding priority
Paul Bassham Charitable Trust
BBC Radio Cambridgeshire –
    Trustline
Jill Franklin Trust
Harrow Community Trust
Allen Lane Foundation
Kitty and Daniel Nabarro
    Charitable Trust
Northern Rock Foundation

Will consider
1970 Trust
Abbey National Charitable
    Trust Ltd
Ashby Charitable Trust
Church Urban Fund
Colchester & Tendring
    Community Trust
Community Foundation Serving
    Tyne & Wear and
    Northumberland
Esmée Fairbairn Foundation
Ford of Britain Trust
Lloyds TSB Foundation for
    Northern Ireland
Medlock Charitable Trust
John Moores Foundation
Odin Charitable Trust
Pastoral Care Trust
Persula Foundation
Richmond Parish Lands Charity
Yapp Charitable Trust

■ Older people's rights

Funding priority
Allen Lane Foundation
Northern Rock Foundation

Will consider
Ardwick Trust
BBC Radio Cambridgeshire –
    Trustline

Colchester & Tendring
    Community Trust
Community Foundation Serving
    Tyne & Wear and
    Northumberland
Cripplegate Foundation
Duis Charitable Trust
Esmée Fairbairn Foundation
Lloyds TSB Foundation for
    Northern Ireland
Medlock Charitable Trust
Mercers' Charitable
    Foundation
Thames Community
    Foundation
Yapp Charitable Trust

■ Racial justice

Funding priority
AS Charitable Trust
Barrow Cadbury Trust and
    Barrow Cadbury Fund
Community Foundation for
    Northern Ireland
Dinam Charity
Enkalon Foundation
Paul Hamlyn Foundation
Harrow Community Trust
Hilden Charitable Fund
Housing Associations
    Charitable Trust
Ireland Fund of Great Britain
Allen Lane Foundation
Kennedy Leigh Charitable
    Trust
John Moores Foundation
Morel Charitable Trust
Northern Rock Foundation
Joseph Rowntree Charitable
    Trust
W F Southall Trust
Tinsley Foundation
Webb Memorial Trust

Will consider
Ardwick Trust
Lord Ashdown Charitable Trust
Bryant Trust
Richard Cadbury Charitable
    Trust
Celtic Charity Fund
Church Urban Fund
City Parochial Foundation
Community Foundation Serving
    Tyne & Wear and
    Northumberland
Coppings Trust
Cripplegate Foundation
John Grant Davies Trust
Duis Charitable Trust
Elmgrant Trust
Esmée Fairbairn Foundation
Ford of Britain Trust
Robert Gavron Charitable Trust
GMC Trust

Greggs Trust
Hadrian Trust
Hampstead Wells and
    Campden Trust
Help Aged
Human Relief Foundation
Leigh Trust
Levy Foundation
Lintel Trust
Lloyds TSB Foundation for
    Northern Ireland
Noon Foundation
Novi Most International
Philanthropic Trust
Simone Prendergast Charitable
    Trust
Rothley Trust
St James' Trust Settlement
South Yorkshire Community
    Foundation
Thames Community
    Foundation

■ Sexuality

Funding priority
Community Foundation for
    Northern Ireland
Harrow Community Trust
Northern Rock Foundation

Will consider
Britten-Pears Foundation
Richard Cadbury Charitable
    Trust
Community Foundation Serving
    Tyne & Wear and
    Northumberland
John Grant Davies Trust
Ford of Britain Trust
Greggs Trust
Allen Lane Foundation
Lintel Trust
Rothley Trust
South Yorkshire Community
    Foundation
Summerfield Charitable Trust
Thames Community
    Foundation

■ Social justice

Funding priority
Harrow Community Trust
Northern Rock Foundation
Tinsley Foundation
Webb Memorial Trust

Will consider
1970 Trust
Body Shop Foundation
Church Urban Fund
Duis Charitable Trust
W E Dunn Trust
Esmée Fairbairn Foundation

Hadrian Trust
Lawlor Foundation
Rothley Trust
Joseph Rowntree Charitable
    Trust
Thames Community
    Foundation

....

■ Women's rights
Funding priority
Maurice Fry Charitable Trust
Harrow Community Trust
Northern Rock Foundation
Polden-Puckham Charitable
    Foundation

Will consider
BBC Radio Cambridgeshire –
    Trustline
Body Shop Foundation
Richard Cadbury Charitable
    Trust
Colchester & Tendring
    Community Trust
Community Foundation Serving
    Tyne & Wear and
    Northumberland
Duis Charitable Trust
Esmée Fairbairn Foundation
Ford of Britain Trust
Hadrian Trust
Lloyds TSB Foundation for
    Northern Ireland
Methodist Relief and
    Development Fund
Rothley Trust
Staples Trust
York Children's Trust

....

■ Young people's rights
Funding priority
Paul Bassham Charitable Trust
Camelot Foundation
Harrow Community Trust
Northern Rock Foundation

Will consider
BBC Radio Cambridgeshire –
    Trustline
Colchester & Tendring
    Community Trust
Community Foundation Serving
    Tyne & Wear and
    Northumberland
Duis Charitable Trust
Esmée Fairbairn Foundation
Hadrian Trust
Lloyds TSB Foundation for
    Northern Ireland
Methodist Relief and
    Development Fund
Jack Petchey Foundation

Rothley Trust
Karim Rida Said Foundation
Thames Community
    Foundation
Yapp Charitable Trust
York Children's Trust

Science & technology
Funding priority
Aberbrothock Charitable Trust
Altajir Trust
Bergqvist Charitable Trust
Hitachi Europe Charitable
    Trust
MacRobert Trust
Oliver Morland Charitable Trust
Saltire Society
Roger Vere Foundation
Wolfson Foundation
Yamanouchi European
    Foundation

Will consider
Sylvia Aitken Charitable Trust
Paul Bassham Charitable Trust
Bingham Trust
Arnold James Burton 1956
    Charitable Settlement
Commonwealth Relations
    Trust
Gwendoline & Margaret Davies
    Charity
DLA Charitable Trust
Englefield Charitable Trust
Gannochy Trust
G C Gibson Charitable Trust
Great Britain Sasakawa
    Foundation
Gretna Charitable Trust
R J Harris Charitable
    Settlement
Humanitarian Trust
Graham Kirkham Foundation
Lethendy Charitable Trust
Mercers' Charitable
    Foundation
G M Morrison Charitable Trust
Raymond & Beverley Sackler
    Foundation
Stella Symons Charitable Trust
Constance Travis Charitable
    Trust
Vale of Glamorgan Welsh
    Church Fund
Valentine Charitable Trust
Welsh Church Fund –
    Carmarthenshire area
David Wilson Foundation
Wolfson Family Charitable
    Trust

Engineering/ technology
Funding priority
Armourers and Brasiers'
    Gauntlet Trust
Medlock Charitable Trust
Kitty and Daniel Nabarro
    Charitable Trust

Will consider

Ove Arup Foundation
Charles Brotherton Trust
Edward Cadbury Charitable
    Trust
Lord Cozens-Hardy Trust
Dulverton Trust
Epilepsy Research Foundation
Headley Trust
Kirby Laing Foundation
Patrick Charitable Trust
Vodafone UK Foundation

Life sciences

Funding priority

Ancaster Trust
Boughton Trust
British Institute of Archaeology
    at Ankara
R M 1956 Burton Charitable
    Trust
Robert Clutterbuck Charitable
    Trust
Cobb Charity
Ernest Cook Trust
Cranbury Foundation
Esmée Fairbairn Foundation
Holly Hill Charitable Trust
Märit and Hans Rausing
    Charitable Foundation
Rural Trust
Loke Wan Tho Memorial
    Foundation
Vincent Wildlife Trust

Will consider

Dorothy Gertrude Allen
    Memorial Fund
H B Allen Charitable Trust
Arbib Foundation
Ardwick Trust
A J H Ashby Will Trust
Astor Foundation
Barnsbury Charitable Trust
Benham Charitable Settlement
Bergqvist Charitable Trust
BP Conservation Programme
Charles Brotherton Trust
Edward Cadbury Charitable
    Trust
Richard Cadbury Charitable
    Trust
Cadbury Schweppes
    Foundation
William A Cadbury Charitable
    Trust
Cairns Charitable Trust
Carron Charitable Trust
Leslie Mary Carter Charitable
    Trust
Wilfrid & Constance Cave
    Foundation
Cemlyn-Jones Trust
Chapman Charitable Trust
John Coates Charitable Trust

Lance Coates Charitable Trust
    1969
Community Foundation Serving
    Tyne & Wear and
    Northumberland
Community Fund
Conservation Foundation
Holbeche Corfield Charitable
    Settlement
Dennis Curry Charitable Trust
Sarah D'Avigdor Goldsmid
    Charitable Trust
D'Oyly Carte Charitable Trust
William Dean Countryside and
    Educational Trust
Dinam Charity
Dulverton Trust
Epilepsy Research Foundation
Ericson Trust
Douglas Heath Eves Charitable
    Trust
Samuel William Farmer's Trust
Fishmongers' Company's
    Charitable Trust
Maurice Fry Charitable Trust
Greencard Charitable Trust
Mrs Margaret Guido's
    Charitable Trust
Hamamelis Trust
Hemby Trust
Edward Sydney Hogg
    Charitable Settlement
Sir Harold Hood's Charitable
    Trust
Cuthbert Horn Trust
Geoffrey C Hughes Charitable
    Trust
J J Charitable Trust
Jerwood Foundation and
    Jerwood Charitable
    Foundation
Johnson Foundation
Robert Kiln Charitable Trust
Kintore Charitable Trust
Sir James Knott Trust
David Laing Foundation
Maurice Laing Foundation
Mrs F B Laurence Charitable
    Trust
Leverhulme Trust
Lindeth Charitable Trust
Mackintosh Foundation
R W Mann Trustees Limited
Michael Marks Charitable
    Trust
Marsh Christian Trust
Mobbs Memorial Trust Ltd
Nigel Moores Family Charitable
    Trust
Peter Moores Foundation
Morel Charitable Trust
Norman Family Charitable
    Trust
Onaway Trust
J B Pelly Charitable Settlement

Personal Assurance Charitable
    Trust
A M Pilkington's Charitable
    Trust
Cecil Pilkington Charitable
    Trust
J S F Pollitzer Charitable
    Settlement
Porter Foundation
John Porter Charitable Trust
Helen Roll Charitable Trust
Sir James Roll Charitable Trust
Rufford Foundation
Russell Trust
Peter Samuel Charitable Trust
Schroder Charity Trust
Sefton Community Foundation
Shears Charitable Trust
Sylvia & Colin Shepherd
    Charitable Trust
Simpson Education &
    Conservation Trust
South Square Trust
W F Southall Trust
Steel Charitable Trust
Bernard Sunley Charitable
    Foundation
Swann-Morton Foundation
Stella Symons Charitable Trust
Tay Charitable Trust
C B & H H Taylor 1984 Trust
Mary Webb Trust
Wellcome Trust
Woodroffe Benton Foundation
Zephyr Charitable Trust

....

■ **Botany**

Funding priority

Birmingham International
    Airport Community Trust
Gatsby Charitable Foundation
John Spedan Lewis Foundation
Stanley Smith UK Horticultural
    Trust

Will consider

M N R Charitable Trust
Rural Trust

....

■ **Ecology**

Funding priority

Birmingham International
    Airport Community Trust
Blair Foundation
City Educational Trust Fund
Lance Coates Charitable Trust
    1969
Esmée Fairbairn Foundation
Walter Guinness Charitable
    Trust
Lindeth Charitable Trust
J B Pelly Charitable Settlement
Tisbury Telegraph Trust

Will consider
Arbib Foundation
C Alma Baker Trust
Bridge House Estates Trust
    Fund
Harry Dunn Charitable Trust
Hamamelis Trust
Lennox Hannay Charitable
    Trust
INTACH (UK) Trust
Sir James Knott Trust
Mrs F B Laurence Charitable
    Trust
Leach Fourteenth Trust
Lyndhurst Settlement
M N R Charitable Trust
Rowan Charitable Trust
Rural Trust
Sheepdrove Trust
Summerfield Charitable Trust
United Society for Propagation
    of Gospel
Westminster Foundation
Whitaker Charitable Trust
Charles Wolfson Charitable
    Trust
Yorkshire Agricultural Society

■ Zoology
Funding priority
John Spedan Lewis Foundation
J B Pelly Charitable Settlement
Rural Trust

Will consider
Geoffrey Burton Charitable
    Trust
Iris Darnton Foundation
Leach Fourteenth Trust
Owen Family Trust

Social sciences, policy and research

Funding priority
Bergqvist Charitable Trust
Gatsby Charitable Foundation
Great Britain Sasakawa
    Foundation
Oliver Morland Charitable Trust

Will consider
Sylvia Aitken Charitable Trust
Paul Bassham Charitable Trust
G C Gibson Charitable Trust
Lethendy Charitable Trust
G M Morrison Charitable Trust
Nuffield Foundation
Powys Welsh Church Fund
Eleanor Rathbone Charitable
    Trust
Stella Symons Charitable Trust
Constance Travis Charitable
    Trust
Vale of Glamorgan Welsh
    Church Fund
Welsh Church Fund –
    Carmarthenshire area
David Wilson Foundation

Economics

Funding priority
Anglo-German Foundation for
    Study of Industrial Society

Will consider
British Institute of Archaeology
    at Ankara
Märit and Hans Rausing
    Charitable Foundation
Wolfson Foundation

Political science

Will consider
British Institute of Archaeology
    at Ankara
Tisbury Telegraph Trust

Social policy

Funding priority
Anglo-German Foundation for
    Study of Industrial Society
Kitty and Daniel Nabarro
    Charitable Trust

Will consider
Commonwealth Relations
    Trust
Gulbenkian Foundation

Kenneth Hargreaves Charitable
    Trust
Charles Hayward Foundation
Levy Foundation
Lyndhurst Settlement
Millfield House Foundation
Tisbury Telegraph Trust
Scurrah Wainwright Charity

Social welfare

Funding priority

Almondsbury Charity
Paul Bassham Charitable Trust
Thomas Betton's Charity for
　Pensions and Relief-in-Need
Church Houses Relief in Need
　Charity
D C Trust
Davidson (Nairn) Charitable
　Trust
F C Charitable Trust
Maurice Fry Charitable Trust
Gatsby Charitable Foundation
General Charities of City of
　Coventry
Bishop of Guildford's
　Foundation
Guildry Incorporation of Perth
Gurunanak
Hampton Fuel Allotment
　Charity
Hitachi Europe Charitable
　Trust
Ironmongers' Quincentenary
　Charitable Fund
Lambeth Endowed Charities
Mercers' Charitable
　Foundation
Oliver Morland Charitable Trust
Northwood Charitable Trust
Norton Foundation
Reading St Laurence Church
　Lands & John Johnson's
　Estate Charities
Thomas Roberts Trust
Frieda Scott Charitable Trust
Second Sidbury Trust
South Ayrshire Council
　Charitable Trusts
Thames Community
　Foundation
Constance Travis Charitable
　Trust
Warwickshire Masonic
　Charitable Association Ltd
Blyth Watson Charitable Trust
Howard Watson Symington
　Memorial Charity
John Wilson Bequest Fund
Miss Hazel M Wood Charitable
　Trust

Will consider

29th May 1961 Charitable
　Trust
Sylvia Aitken Charitable Trust
Alexandra Rose Day
Mary Andrew Charitable Trust
Ashworth Charitable Trust
Batchworth Trust
Beaufort House Trust
Peter Beckwith Charitable
　Trust
Bingham Trust

Morgan Blake Charitable Trust
Joseph & Annie Cattle Trust
Sir Jeremiah Colman Gift Trust
　Community Fund
Craignish Trust
Cumbria Community
　Foundation
Baron F A d'Erlanger
　Charitable Trust
Derbyshire Community
　Foundation
Duke of Devonshire's
　Charitable Trust
DLA Charitable Trust
Englefield Charitable Trust
Thomas Farr Charitable Trust
Flow Foundation
Donald Forrester Trust
Jacqueline and Michael Gee
　Charitable Trust
Girdlers' Company Charitable
　Trust
Godinton Charitable Trust
Gretna Charitable Trust
R J Harris Charitable
　Settlement
Dorothy Hay-Bolton Charitable
　Trust
Headley Trust
Jane Hodge Foundation
Ingram Trust
King's Fund
Christopher Laing Foundation
Kathleen Laurence Trust
William Leech Charity
Leeds Hospital Fund
　Charitable Trust
Lethendy Charitable Trust
Linbury Trust
M & C Trust
Margaret Foundation
Merchants House of Glasgow
Edgar Milward Charity
Peter Moores Foundation
National Catholic Fund
Patients' Aid Association
　Hospital & Medical
　Charities Trust
Sir James Reckitt Charity
Robertson Trust
St Laurence Charities for Poor
Saint Sarkis Charity Trust
Saints & Sinners Trust
Seamen's Hospital Society
Souter Charitable Trust
South East London Community
　Foundation
W O Street Charitable
　Foundation
A R Taylor Charitable Trust
Tompkins Foundation
Douglas Turner Trust
R D Turner Charitable Trust
Vale of Glamorgan Welsh
　Church Fund
Valentine Charitable Trust

VEC Acorn Trust
F J Wallis Charitable
　Settlement
Webb Memorial Trust
Weinstock Fund
David Wilson Foundation
Wixamtree Trust
Zochonis Charitable Trust

Community care services

Funding priority

Airways Charitable Trust
　Limited
BBC Radio Cambridgeshire –
　Trustline
Chelsea Building Society
　Charitable Foundation
Cheruby Trust
Commonwealth Relations
　Trust
Community Foundation for
　Northern Ireland
Cornwall Independent Trust
　Fund
Criffel Charitable Trust
Earl of Derby's Charitable
　Trust
Sandy Dewhirst Charitable
　Trust
Dickon Trust
Essex Community Foundation
Freshgate Trust Foundation
Garthgwynion Charities
Grahame Charitable
　Foundation
Hampstead Wells and
　Campden Trust
Hampton Fuel Allotment
　Charity
Kathleen Hannay Memorial
　Charity
Kenneth Hargreaves Charitable
　Trust
Harrow Community Trust
Heart of England Radio
　Charitable Trust
Joseph & Mary Hiley Trust
Clifford Howarth Charity
　Settlement
Miss E M Johnson Charitable
　Trust
Kensington District Nursing
　Trust
King's Fund
Kyte Charitable Trust
Leathersellers' Company
　Charitable Fund
MacRobert Trust
Ian Mactaggart Fund
Medlock Charitable Trust
Oakdale Trust
Oizer Charitable Trust
Pilkington Charities Fund

Rayne Trust
Rosca Trust
Rothley Trust
Sir James & Lady Scott Trust
Sheffield and District Hospital
    Services Charitable Fund
Peter Stebbings Memorial
    Charity
John Swire (1989) Charitable
    Trust
Tolkien Trust
Ulverston Town Lands Charity
Underwood Trust
Weinberg Foundation
Lionel Wigram Memorial Trust
Williams Family Charitable
    Trust

Will consider
29th May 1961 Charitable
    Trust
A B Charitable Trust
Sylvia Adams Charitable Trust
Alchemy Foundation
Allachy Trust
H B Allen Charitable Trust
Sir John & Lady Amory's
    Charitable Trust
Ancaster Trust
Andrew Anderson Trust
Anglian Water Trust Fund
Milly Apthorp Charitable Trust
Army Benevolent Fund
ATP Charitable Trust
Lord Austin Trust
Bacta Charitable Trust
Balcombe Charitable Trust
Albert Casanova Ballard
    Deceased Trust
Barbour Trust
David and Frederick Barclay
    Foundation
Barnes Workhouse Fund
Barnsbury Charitable Trust
Barracks Trust of Newcastle-
    under-Lyme
Bates Charitable Trust
James Beattie Charitable Trust
Peter Beckwith Charitable
    Trust
Bedford Charity
Beit Trust
Benfield Motors Charitable
    Trust
Benham Charitable Settlement
Rowan Bentall Charitable Trust
Berkshire Community
    Foundation
Betard Bequest
Bethesda Community
    Charitable Trust
Bingham Trust
Peter Birse Charitable Trust
Herbert & Peter Blagrave
    Charitable Trust
Blanchminster Trust

Boots Charitable Trust
A Bornstein Charitable
    Settlement
Bridge Trust
Bristol Charities
Britannia Building Society
    Foundation
British Humane Association
British Sugar Foundation
Charles & Edna Broadhurst
    Charitable Trust
Charles Brotherton Trust
R S Brownless Charitable
    Trust
Bryant Trust
Arnold James Burton 1956
    Charitable Settlement
Consolidated Charity of Burton
    Upon Trent
C B Trust
Edward Cadbury Charitable
    Trust
Edward & Dorothy Cadbury
    Trust
George W Cadbury Charitable
    Trust
Cadbury Schweppes
    Foundation
William A Cadbury Charitable
    Trust
CAFOD
Cairns Charitable Trust
Calpe Trust
W A Cargill Charitable Trust
Carnegie Dunfermline Trust
Wilfrid & Constance Cave
    Foundation
Chandris Foundation
Chapman Charitable Trust
Charities Advisory Trust
Chelsea Square 1994 Trust
Chippenham Borough Lands
    Charity
Chipping Sodbury Town Lands
    Charity
Church Urban Fund
Coates Charitable Settlement
Denise Cohen Charitable Trust
Cole Charitable Trust
Sir James Colyer-Fergusson's
    Charitable Trust
Comic Relief
Community Foundation Serving
    Tyne & Wear and
    Northumberland
Congleton Inclosure Trust
Consortium on Opportunities
    for Volunteering
Sidney & Elizabeth Corob
    Charitable Trust
Corona Charitable Trust
Coutts & Co. Charitable Trust
Lord Cozens-Hardy Trust
Cranbury Foundation
Michael Crawford Children's
    Charity

Cripplegate Foundation
Harry Crook Foundation
Croydon Relief in Need
    Charities
Cumber Family Charitable
    Trust
Cwmbran Trust
Dr & Mrs A Darlington
    Charitable Trust
Baron Davenport's Charity
David Charitable Trust
Gwendoline & Margaret Davies
    Charity
John Grant Davies Trust
Denton Charitable Trust
Derbyshire Community
    Foundation
Richard Desmond Charitable
    Trust
Community Council of Devon
Devon Community Foundation
Diana, Princess of Wales
    Memorial Fund
Dinam Charity
Djanogly Foundation
Dorcas Trust
Double 'O' Charity Ltd
Drapers' Charitable Fund
W E Dunn Trust
Eagle Charity Trust
Gilbert & Eileen Edgar
    Foundation
Elanore Ltd
George Elias Charitable Trust
John Ellerman Foundation
Edith M Ellis 1985 Charitable
    Trust
Vernon N Ely Charitable Trust
Emerging Markets Charity for
    Children
Emmandjay Charitable Trust
Enkalon Foundation
Eranda Foundation
Ericson Trust
Sir John Evelyn's Charity
Exilarch's Foundation
Fassnidge Memorial Trust
Elizabeth Hardie Ferguson
    Charitable Trust Fund
Doris Field Charitable Trust
Ian Fleming Charitable Trust
Foresters' Charity Stewards
    UK Trust
Charles Henry Foyle Trust
Isaac and Freda Frankel
    Memorial Charitable Trust
Friarsgate Trust
Fund for Human Need
Gannochy Trust
G C Gibson Charitable Trust
Glass-House Trust
Sydney & Phyllis Goldberg
    Memorial Charitable Trust
Gosling Foundation Ltd
Gough Charitable Trust
Grand Charity of Freemasons

Mrs H R Greene Charitable Settlement
Grimsdale Charitable Trust
Grocers' Charity
Walter Guinness Charitable Trust
Gulbenkian Foundation
Hackney Parochial Charities
Hadfield Trust
Hadley Trust
Hadrian Trust
Alfred Haines Charitable Trust
Hanley Trust
Haramead Trust
Harbour Foundation
Harding Trust
Hare of Steep Charitable Trust
M A Hawe Settlement
Haymills Charitable Trust
Healthsure Group Ltd
Heart of England Community Foundation
Help Aged
Hemby Trust
G D Herbert Charitable Trust
Joanna Herbert-Stepney Charitable Settlement
Alan Edward Higgs Charity
Hillingdon Partnership Trust
Hobart Charitable Trust
Hobson Charity Ltd
Edward Sydney Hogg Charitable Settlement
J G Hogg Charitable Trust
P H Holt Charitable Trust
Holywood Trust
Homelands Charitable Trust
Sir Harold Hood's Charitable Trust
Hoover Foundation
Joseph Hopkins Charity
HopMarket Charity
Antony Hornby Charitable Trust
Hornsey Parochial Charities
Human Relief Foundation
Albert Hunt Trust
Hyde Park Place Estate Charity
Imerys South West Charitable Trust
Inman Charity
Ireland Fund of Great Britain
Ironmongers' Quincentenary Charitable Fund
Irwin Trust
Isle of Anglesey Charitable Trust
Lillie Johnson Charitable Trust
Jones 1986 Charitable Trust
Lady Eileen Joseph Foundation
Kass Charitable Trust
Michael & Ilse Katz Foundation
Emmanuel Kaye Foundation
William Kendall's Charity
Ursula Keyes Trust
Mary Kinross Charitable Trust
Graham Kirkham Foundation

Kirkley Poor's Land Estate
Kreditor Charitable Trust
Neil Kreitman Foundation
Langdale Trust
Langley Charitable Trust
Laslett's (Hinton) Charity
Lauchentilly Charitable Foundation 1988
Lawson Charitable Foundation
Lawson-Beckman Charitable Trust
Morris Leigh Foundation
Lord Leverhulme Charitable Trust
Enid Linder Foundation
Harry Livingstone Charitable Trust
Jack Livingstone Charitable Trust
Elaine & Angus Lloyd Charitable Trust
Lloyds TSB Foundation for Scotland
Localtrent Ltd
Lofthouse Foundation
London North East Community Foundation
Michael Lowe's & Associated Charities
C L Loyd Charitable Trust
Luck-Hille Foundation
Sir Jack Lyons Charitable Trust
Lyons Charitable Trust
Sylvanus Lyson's Charity
Robert McAlpine Foundation
R S MacDonald Charitable Trust
Macfarlane Walker Trust
Mackintosh Foundation
Magdalen Hospital Trust
Magdalen & Lasher Charity
R W Mann Trustees Limited
Victor Mann Trust
Leslie & Lilian Manning Trust
Linda Marcus Charitable Trust
Hilda & Samuel Marks Foundation
Erich Markus Charitable Foundation
Michael Marsh Charitable Trust
D G Marshall of Cambridge Trust
Jim Marshall Charitable Trust
Sir George Martin Trust
John Martin's Charity
Mercers' Charitable Foundation
Merchant Taylors' Company Charities Fund
Tony Metherell Charitable Trust
Metropolitan Hospital-Sunday Fund
Gerald Micklem Charitable Trust

Miles Trust for Putney and Roehampton Community
Miller Foundation
Millichope Foundation
Peter Minet Trust
Victor Mishcon Charitable Trust
Mobbs Memorial Trust Ltd
Monmouthshire County Council Welsh Church Act Fund
Morel Charitable Trust
Morgan Crucible Company plc Charitable Trust
Morris Charitable Trust
G M Morrison Charitable Trust
Peter Morrison Charitable Foundation
Mugdock Children's Trust
Music Sales Charitable Trust
Muslim Hands
Mr and Mrs F E F Newman Charitable Trust
Norman Family Charitable Trust
Northampton Queen's Institute Relief in Sickness Fund
Northumberland Village Homes Trust
Norwich Historic Churches Trust Ltd
Noswad Charity
Father O'Mahoney Memorial Trust
Old Possum's Practical Trust
Oppenheimer Charitable Trust
Ormsby Charitable Trust
P F Charitable Trust
Gerald Palmer Trust
Arthur James Paterson Charitable Trust
Constance Paterson Charitable Trust
Late Barbara May Paul Charitable Trust
Peabody Community Fund
Peacock Charitable Trust
Personal Assurance Charitable Trust
Pilgrim Trust
Cecil Pilkington Charitable Trust
Col W W Pilkington Will Trusts
John Porter Charitable Trust
Sir John Priestman Charity Trust
Princess Anne's Charities
Proven Family Trust
Puebla Charitable Trust
Puri Foundation
Mr and Mrs J A Pye's Charitable Settlement
Joseph & Lena Randall Charitable Trust
Joseph Rank Trust
Ranworth Trust
E L Rathbone Charitable Trust

Eleanor Rathbone Charitable
   Trust
Rayne Foundation
John Rayner Charitable Trust
Sir James Reckitt Charity
Rest Harrow Trust
Reuters Foundation
Rhododendron Trust
Rhondda Cynon Taff Welsh
   Church Acts Fund
Clive Richards Charity Ltd
Richmond Parish Lands Charity
Helen Roll Charitable Trust
Mrs L D Rope Third Charitable
   Settlement
Cecil Rosen Foundation
Rowan Charitable Trust
Royal Docks Trust
J B Rubens Charitable
   Foundation
Russell Trust
Alan and Babette Sainsbury
   Charitable Fund
St Hilda's Trust
St Olave, St Thomas and St
   John United Charity
Late St Patrick White
   Charitable Trust
Saint Sarkis Charity Trust
St Thomas Ecclesiastical
   Charity
Peter Samuel Charitable Trust
Sandra Charitable Trust
Schmidt-Bodner Charitable
   Trust
John Scott Trust
Scottish Community
   Foundation
Scottish International
   Education Trust
Samuel Sebba Charitable
   Trust
Sedbury Trust
Sefton Community Foundation
Shakespeare Temperance
   Trust
Shaw Lands Trust
Shepherd Street Trust
Sylvia & Colin Shepherd
   Charitable Trust
Archie Sherman Cardiff
   Charitable Foundation
Archie Sherman Charitable
   Trust
Sinclair Charitable Trust
John Slater Foundation
SMB Trust
Philip Smith's Charitable Trust
E C Sosnow Charitable Trust
W F Southall Trust
Spitalfields Market Community
   Trust
W W Spooner Charitable Trust
Sportsman's Charity
Spring Harvest Charitable
   Trust

Rosalyn and Nicholas Springer
   Charitable Trust
Stanton Ballard Charitable
   Trust
Steel Charitable Trust
E J H Stephenson Deceased
   Charitable Trust
Steventon Allotments & Relief-
   in-Need Charity
Leonard Laity Stoate
   Charitable Trust
Bernard Sunley Charitable
   Foundation
Swire Charitable Trust
Charles and Elsie Sykes Trust
Stella Symons Charitable Trust
Talteg Ltd
Mrs A Lacy Tate Trust
Tay Charitable Trust
C B & H H Taylor 1984 Trust
Tedworth Trust
Tesco Charity Trust
Thompson Charitable Trust
Len Thomson Charitable Trust
Thornton Trust
Tillotson Bradbery Charitable
   Trust
Truemark Trust
Douglas Turner Trust
Florence Turner Trust
United St Saviour's Charities
United Trusts
David Uri Memorial Trust
Albert Van Den Bergh
   Charitable Trust
Eric W Vincent Trust Fund
William and Ellen Vinten Trust
A F Wallace Charity Trust
Warbeck Fund Ltd
Ward Blenkinsop Trust
Warwickshire Masonic
   Charitable Association Ltd
Bertie Watson Foundation
Weavers' Company Benevolent
   Fund
Mary Webb Trust
Welsh Church Fund –
   Carmarthenshire area
Welton Foundation
West Derby Wastelands
   Charity
Westminster Foundation
Garfield Weston Foundation
Whitaker Charitable Trust
Colonel W H Whitbread
   Charitable Trust
Sheila Whitley Trust
Will Charitable Trust
William Williams Charity
Benjamin Winegarten
   Charitable Trust
Mayor of Wirral's Charity Trust
Maurice Wohl Charitable
   Foundation
Maurice Wohl Charitable Trust

Charles Wolfson Charitable
   Trust
Women Caring Trust
Woodroffe Benton Foundation
Woolnoth Society Charitable
   Trust
Worshipful Company of
   Chartered Accountants
   General Charitable Trust
Wyseliot Charitable Trust
Xerox (UK) Trust
Yorkshire Bank Charitable
   Trust
William Allen Young Charitable
   Trust
Zurich Financial Services
   Community Trust

....

■ Activities & relationships between generations

Funding priority
Bramble Charitable Trust
Denton Wilde Sapte Charitable
   Trust
Hospital of God at Greatham

Will consider
Colchester & Tendring
   Community Trust
Elmgrant Trust
Essex Fairway Charitable Trust
Gannochy Trust
Gatwick Airport Community
   Trust
Greater Bristol Foundation
GWR Community Trust
Heart of England Community
   Foundation
Hedgcock Bequest
Mary Homfray Charitable Trust
Judith Trust
Lloyds TSB Foundation for
   England and Wales
Northern Rock Foundation
Pastoral Care Trust
Jack Petchey Foundation
Christopher Rowbotham
   Charitable Trust
Saddlers' Company Charitable
   Fund
Scottish Churches Community
   Trust
South Square Trust
Charity of Thomas Wade &
   Others

....

■ Services for carers

Funding priority
1970 Trust
Aberbrothock Charitable Trust
Alchemy Foundation

Ammco Trust
Ardwick Trust
Astor Foundation
Astor of Hever Trust
Balney Charitable Trust
Barnwood House Trust
Percy Bilton Charity Ltd
Bramble Charitable Trust
Brighton District Nursing
    Association Trust
Chest Heart and Stroke
    Scotland
Cleopatra Trust
Colchester Catalyst Charity
D'Oyly Carte Charitable Trust
Denton Wilde Sapte Charitable
    Trust
Dorus Trust
Epigoni Trust
Eveson Charitable Trust
Fiat Auto (UK) Charity
Four Acre Trust
Angela Gallagher Memorial
    Fund
Simon Gibson Charitable Trust
Harebell Centenary Fund
Harris Charitable Trust
Charles Hayward Foundation
Headley Trust
Dorothy Holmes Charitable
    Trust
Hospital of God at Greatham
Clifford Howarth Charity
    Settlement
Miss Agnes H Hunter's Trust
Jeffrey Charitable Trust
Anton Jurgens Charitable Trust
Edgar E Lawley Foundation
Levy Foundation
Lloyds TSB Foundation for
    Channel Islands
Lynn Foundation
Lynwood Trust
Mercers' Charitable
    Foundation
Zachary Merton & George
    Woofindin Convalescent
    Trust
Minge's Gift
John Moores Foundation
Odin Charitable Trust
Ogilvie Charities Deed 2
Ormsby Charitable Trust
Patients' Aid Association
    Hospital & Medical
    Charities Trust
Philanthropic Trust
Pilkington Charities Fund
Rawdon-Smith Trust
Christopher Rowbotham
    Charitable Trust
St Thomas' Dole Charity
Scouloudi Foundation
Sobell Foundation
Swan Trust

Walter Swindon Charitable
    Trust
Verdon-Smith Family Charitable
    Settlement
Wakefield Trust
West Derby Wastelands
    Charity
White Rose Children's Aid
    International Charity
Wiltshire and Swindon
    Community Foundation
Woodlands Trust (1015942)
Woodroffe Benton Foundation

Will consider
Abbeydale Trust
Adint Charitable Trust
Viscount Amory's Charitable
    Trust
Ashby Charitable Trust
Aston Charities Trust Limited
Badley Memorial Trust
Baily Thomas Charitable Fund
Band (1976) Trust
Barclays Stockbrokers
    Charitable Trust
Philip Barker Charity
Barnabas Charitable Trust
Bartle Family Charitable Trust
BBC Children in Need Appeal
Bearder Charity
Birmingham Foundation
Birmingham Hospital Saturday
    Fund Medical Charity &
    Welfare Trust
Herbert & Peter Blagrave
    Charitable Trust
Blatchington Court Trust
Charles Boot Trust
Harry Bottom Charitable Trust
Bridge House Estates Trust
    Fund
Roger Brooke Charitable Trust
Charles Brotherton Trust
Bryant Trust
Buckinghamshire Masonic
    Centenary Fund
E F Bulmer Benevolent Fund
Audrey & Stanley Burton
    Charitable Trust
Richard Cadbury Charitable
    Trust
Chamberlain Foundation
Chase Charity
Chipping Sodbury Town Lands
    Charity
Chrimes Family Charitable
    Trust
Christadelphian Samaritan
    Fund
Lord Clinton's Charitable Trust
Clover Trust
Vivienne & Samuel Cohen
    Charitable Trust
Colchester & Tendring
    Community Trust

George Henry Collins Charity
Consortium on Opportunities
    for Volunteering
Cooper Charitable Trust
County of Gloucestershire
    Community Foundation
Cray Trust
Cwmbran Trust
Baron Davenport's Charity
Derbyshire Community
    Foundation
Devon Community Foundation
Dulverton Trust
Dunhill Medical Trust
Earley Charity
Edinburgh Voluntary
    Organisations' Trust Funds
Wilfred & Elsie Elkes Charity
    Fund
Maud Elkington Charitable
    Trust
Elmgrant Trust
Emerton-Christie Charity
Erskine Cunningham Hill Trust
Essex Fairway Charitable Trust
Lord Faringdon Charitable
    Trust
Ferguson Benevolent Fund Ltd
Fidelity UK Foundation
Fifty Fund
Finnart House School Trust
Fishmongers' Company's
    Charitable Trust
Earl Fitzwilliam Charitable
    Trust
Ford of Britain Trust
Forte Charitable Trust
Fox Memorial Trust
Jill Franklin Trust
Frognal Trust
Gannochy Trust
Gatwick Airport Community
    Trust
Robert Gavron Charitable Trust
Girdlers' Company Charitable
    Trust
Good Neighbours Trust
J G Graves Charitable Trust
Greater Bristol Foundation
Greggs Trust
GWR Community Trust
H C D Memorial Fund
Hadrian Trust
Hampton Fuel Allotment
    Charity
Lennox Hannay Charitable
    Trust
Harborne Parish Lands Charity
Harrison & Potter Trust
Gay & Peter Hartley's Hillards
    Charitable Trust
N & P Hartley Memorial Trust
May Hearnshaw's Charity
Heart of England Community
    Foundation
Hedley Foundation

Help the Aged
Hemby Trust
Hertfordshire Community
 Foundation
Holywood Trust
Mary Homfray Charitable Trust
Joseph Hopkins Charity
Hospital Saturday Fund
 Charitable Trust
James Thom Howat Charitable
 Trust
Inchrye Trust
Inverforth Charitable Trust
Ruth & Lionel Jacobson Trust
 (Second Fund) No 2
Jarman Charitable Trust
Elton John Aids Foundation
Johnson Foundation
Joicey Trust
Judith Trust
Peter Kershaw Trust
Kidani Memorial Trust
King George's Fund for Sailors
Kleinwort Benson Charitable
 Trust
Sir James Knott Trust
Knowles Charitable Trust
Kobler Trust
Heinz & Anna Kroch
 Foundation
Beatrice Laing Trust
Bryan Lancaster's Charity
Lankelly Foundation
Mrs F B Laurence Charitable
 Trust
Kathleen Laurence Trust
Lawlor Foundation
Lazard Charitable Trust
Mason Le Page Charitable
 Trust
Leach Fourteenth Trust
Lintel Trust
Lloyd's Charities Trust
Lloyds TSB Foundation for
 England and Wales
Lloyds TSB Foundation for
 Northern Ireland
London Law Trust
Paul Lunn-Rockliffe Charitable
 Trust
Lyndhurst Settlement
M N R Charitable Trust
Marchday Charitable Fund
Gerald Micklem Charitable
 Trust
Middlesex County Rugby
 Football Union Memorial
 Fund
Milton Keynes Community
 Foundation
Keith and Joan Mindelsohn
 Charitable Trust
George A Moore Foundation
Morgan Stanley International
 Foundation
Newby Trust Limited

North British Hotel Trust
Northcott Devon Foundation
Northern Rock Foundation
Norwich Consolidated
 Charities
Kate Wilson Oliver Trust
Oxfordshire Community
 Foundation
Eleanor Palmer Trust
Parivar Trust
Pastoral Care Trust
Patrick Charitable Trust
Jack Petchey Foundation
Bernard Piggott Trust
Austin & Hope Pilkington Trust
John Pitman Charitable Trust
G S Plaut Charitable Trust
J D Player Endowment Fund
Powell Foundation
Simone Prendergast Charitable
 Trust
Priory of Scotland of Order of
 St John of Jerusalem
Proven Family Trust
Queen Mary's Roehampton
 Trust
Radio Forth Help a Child
 Appeal
Rainford Trust
Ravensdale Trust
John Rayner Charitable Trust
Cliff Richard Charitable Trust
Violet M Richards Charity
Rothley Trust
Russell Trust
Saddlers' Company Charitable
 Fund
St Mary-le-Strand Charity
R H Scholes Charitable Trust
Francis C Scott Charitable
 Trust
Sir James & Lady Scott Trust
Sellafield Charity Trust Fund
Servite Sisters' Charitable
 Trust Fund
Sheepdrove Trust
Sheldon Trust
Sherburn House Charity
Shuttlewood Clarke Foundation
Barbara A Shuttleworth
 Memorial Trust
Mary Elizabeth Siebel Charity
Skelton Bounty
Henry Smith Charity
David Solomons Charitable
 Trust
South Square Trust
Starfish Trust
Sir Halley Stewart Trust
Foundation of Edward Storey
Summerfield Charitable Trust
Talbot Trusts
Tesco Charity Trust
Sir Jules Thorn Charitable
 Trust
Triangle Trust (1949) Fund

Tudor Trust
Unemployed Voluntary Action
 Fund
Wakeham Trust
Wates Foundation
William Webster Charitable
 Trust
Wellfield Trust
Wesleyan Charitable Trust
Wessex Cancer Trust
Westminster Amalgamated
 Charity
Whitaker Charitable Trust
Whitecourt Charitable Trust
Harold Hyam Wingate
 Foundation
Michael and Anna Wix
 Charitable Trust
Women at Risk
Woodward Trust
Worshipful Company of
 Founders Charities
Yapp Charitable Trust
Yorkshire Building Society
 Charitable Foundation

....

■ Services for and about children and young people

Funding priority

ARK
Ashe Park Charitable Trust
Balcraig Foundation
Bier Charitable Settlement
Bramble Charitable Trust
Carnegie United Kingdom Trust
Casey Trust
Cash for Kids
Denton Wilde Sapte Charitable
 Trust
Duis Charitable Trust
Emmandjay Charitable Trust
Angela Gallagher Memorial
 Fund
Gatsby Charitable Foundation
Simon Gibson Charitable Trust
Help a London Child
Christina Mary Hendrie Trust
 for Scottish & Canadian
 Charities
Hospital of God at Greatham
Peter Kershaw Trust
Paul Lunn-Rockliffe Charitable
 Trust
Lynn Foundation
John Lyon's Charity
Madeline Mabey Trust
Mandeville Trust
Noel Buxton Trust
Rank Foundation
Rooke Atlay Charitable Trust
Woodroffe Benton Foundation

Will consider

Henry & Grete Abrahams
 Second Charitable
 Foundation
Acacia Charitable Trust
Mary Andrew Charitable Trust
Armourers and Brasiers'
 Gauntlet Trust
Band (1976) Trust
Barclays Stockbrokers
 Charitable Trust
BBC Children in Need Appeal
Bearder Charity
Beit Trust
Belvedere Trust
Roger Brooke Charitable Trust
E F Bulmer Benevolent Fund
R M 1956 Burton Charitable
 Trust
Edward & Dorothy Cadbury
 Trust
D W T Cargill Fund
Colchester & Tendring
 Community Trust
George Henry Collins Charity
Coutts & Co. Charitable Trust
Douglas Charitable Trust
Dumfries and Galloway Council
 Charitable Trusts
Earley Charity
Edinburgh Children's Holiday
 Fund
City of Edinburgh Charitable
 Trusts
Fairbairn Charitable Trust
Lord Faringdon Charitable
 Trust
Charles S French Charitable
 Trust
Grantham Yorke Trust
Hale Trust
Harris Charity
N & P Hartley Memorial Trust
Hedley Denton Charitable
 Trust
H J Heinz Company Limited
 Charitable Trust
Philip Henman Trust
Mary Homfray Charitable Trust
Joseph Hopkins Charity
Rita Lila Howard Foundation
Miss Agnes H Hunter's Trust
Hyde Charitable Trust
Lillie Johnson Charitable Trust
Judith Trust
Anton Jurgens Charitable Trust
Kidani Memorial Trust
Kintore Charitable Trust
Late Sir Pierce Lacy Charity
 Trust
Rachel & Jack Lass Charities
 Ltd
Carole & Geoffrey Lawson
 Foundation
Lotus Foundation
Lyons Charitable Trust

Robert McAlpine Foundation
Gerald Micklem Charitable
 Trust
Victor Mishcon Charitable
 Trust
Willie & Mabel Morris
 Charitable Trust
Newby Trust Limited
North British Hotel Trust
Northern Rock Foundation
Nuffield Foundation
Old Possum's Practical Trust
Ruth & Michael Phillips
 Charitable Trust
Priory Foundation
Privy Purse Charitable Trust
Rothley Trust
Rufford Foundation
Russell Trust
Saddlers' Company Charitable
 Fund
Philip Smith's Charitable Trust
South Square Trust
Spar Charitable Fund
Swire Charitable Trust
Charles and Elsie Sykes Trust
C B & H H Taylor 1984 Trust
Sue Thomson Foundation
Towry Law Charitable Trust
Toy Trust
Bernard Van Leer Foundation
Variety Club Children's Charity
Wakefield Trust

■ **Adoption**
 Funding priority

1970 Trust
Access 4 Trust
Clara E Burgess Charity
Chester Diocesan Moral Aid
 Charity
Lennox Hannay Charitable
 Trust
Peter Kershaw Trust
David Laing Foundation
Lloyds TSB Foundation for
 Channel Islands
Parivar Trust
Austin & Hope Pilkington Trust

Will consider

Astor Foundation
Percy Bilton Charity Ltd
Bridge House Estates Trust
 Fund
E F Bulmer Benevolent Fund
Baron Davenport's Charity
Dulverton Trust
Wilfred & Elsie Elkes Charity
 Fund
Esmée Fairbairn Foundation
Ford of Britain Trust
Greggs Trust
Hadrian Trust
Harborne Parish Lands Charity
Charles Hayward Foundation

Hertfordshire Community
 Foundation
Homelands Charitable Trust
Joicey Trust
Sir James Knott Trust
Lankelly Foundation
Leach Fourteenth Trust
Lloyds TSB Foundation for
 Northern Ireland
John Lyon's Charity
M N R Charitable Trust
Northcott Devon Foundation
Jack Petchey Foundation
Pilgrim Trust
Rothley Trust
SMB Trust
Henry Smith Charity
Mrs Smith & Mount Trust
Sobell Foundation
Stanley Foundation Ltd
Wates Foundation
Woodward Trust
Yapp Charitable Trust

■ **Childcare**
 Funding priority

Eveson Charitable Trust
Lloyds TSB Foundation for
 Channel Islands
Sir James & Lady Scott Trust
Social Education Trust

Will consider

Birmingham Foundation
E F Bulmer Benevolent Fund
Baron Davenport's Charity
Dulverton Trust
Finnart House School Trust
Ford of Britain Trust
Girdlers' Company Charitable
 Trust
Harborne Parish Lands Charity
Harbour Charitable Trust
Gay & Peter Hartley's Hillards
 Charitable Trust
Jewish Child's Day
Laing's Charitable Trust
Lloyds TSB Foundation for
 Northern Ireland
John Lyon's Charity
W M Mann Foundation
Old Enfield Charitable Trust
Jack Petchey Foundation
Mr and Mrs J A Pye's
 Charitable Settlement
Rothley Trust

■ **Family welfare**
 Funding priority

Chase Charity
Eveson Charitable Trust
J Paul Getty Jr Charitable Trust
Glass-House Trust
Leeds & Holbeck Building
 Society Charitable
 Foundation

Lloyds TSB Foundation for
 Channel Islands
Lotus Foundation
Magdalen Hospital Trust
Ronald & Kathleen Pryor
 Charitable Trust
Trusthouse Charitable
 Foundation

Will consider
Adnams Charity
Ardwick Trust
Philip Barker Charity
Birmingham Foundation
Birmingham Hospital Saturday
 Fund Medical Charity &
 Welfare Trust
E F Bulmer Benevolent Fund
Childwick Trust
Consortium on Opportunities
 for Volunteering
Dulverton Trust
Erskine Cunningham Hill Trust
Esmée Fairbairn Foundation
Gatwick Airport Community
 Trust
Girdlers' Company Charitable
 Trust
Gay & Peter Hartley's Hillards
 Charitable Trust
Charles Hayward Foundation
Hemby Trust
Miss Agnes H Hunter's Trust
Edward Cecil Jones Settlement
Beatrice Laing Trust
Maurice Laing Foundation
Maurice and Hilda Laing
 Charitable Trust
Lankelly Foundation
Lawlor Foundation
Lloyds TSB Foundation for
 Northern Ireland
John Lyon's Charity
Old Enfield Charitable Trust
Jack Petchey Foundation
Rothley Trust
Francis C Scott Charitable
 Trust
Mrs Smith & Mount Trust
Tesco Charity Trust
Tisbury Telegraph Trust
Waterside Trust
William Webster Charitable
 Trust
Westminster Amalgamated
 Charity
Whitecourt Charitable Trust
Yapp Charitable Trust
York Children's Trust
Yorkshire Building Society
 Charitable Foundation

■ **Parenting**
 Funding priority
Camelot Foundation
Glass-House Trust

Headley Trust
Lloyds TSB Foundation for
 Channel Islands
Sir James & Lady Scott Trust

Will consider
Birmingham Foundation
Birmingham Hospital Saturday
 Fund Medical Charity &
 Welfare Trust
E F Bulmer Benevolent Fund
Richard Cadbury Charitable
 Trust
Chase Charity
Consortium on Opportunities
 for Volunteering
Dulverton Trust
Edinburgh Voluntary
 Organisations' Trust Funds
Gatwick Airport Community
 Trust
J Paul Getty Jr Charitable Trust
Gay & Peter Hartley's Hillards
 Charitable Trust
Heart of England Community
 Foundation
Hedgcock Bequest
Hemby Trust
Maurice Laing Foundation
Maurice and Hilda Laing
 Charitable Trust
Lankelly Foundation
Lloyds TSB Foundation for
 Northern Ireland
John Lyon's Charity
Keith and Joan Mindelsohn
 Charitable Trust
Old Enfield Charitable Trust
Oxfordshire Community
 Foundation
Harry Payne Trust
Rothley Trust
Christopher Rowbotham
 Charitable Trust
Francis C Scott Charitable
 Trust
Mrs Smith & Mount Trust
Weavers' Company Benevolent
 Fund
Yapp Charitable Trust

■ **Playschemes**
 Funding priority
1970 Trust
Birmingham International
 Airport Community Trust
Chippenham Borough Lands
 Charity
Cripplegate Foundation
Angela Gallagher Memorial
 Fund
Greater Bristol Foundation
Greggs Trust
Hale Trust
Robert Hall Charity

Lennox Hannay Charitable
 Trust
William Harding's Charity
Hilden Charitable Fund
Leeds & Holbeck Building
 Society Charitable
 Foundation
Lloyds TSB Foundation for
 Channel Islands
London Youth Trust
Magdalen Hospital Trust
Magdalen & Lasher Charity
Peter Minet Trust
Mugdock Children's Trust
Patients' Aid Association
 Hospital & Medical
 Charities Trust
Peacock Charitable Trust
Pilkington Charities Fund
Ronald & Kathleen Pryor
 Charitable Trust
Sir Walter St John's
 Educational Charity
St Thomas' Dole Charity
Sir James & Lady Scott Trust
Walter Swindon Charitable
 Trust
Variety Club Children's Charity
Charity of Thomas Wade &
 Others
John Watson's Trust

Will consider
Abbey National Charitable
 Trust Ltd
Ardwick Trust
Ashby Charitable Trust
Baily Thomas Charitable Fund
Balmore Trust
Bamford Charitable Foundation
Barnabas Charitable Trust
BBC Children in Need Appeal
BBC Radio Lincolnshire Charity
 Trust
Birmingham Foundation
Birmingham Hospital Saturday
 Fund Medical Charity &
 Welfare Trust
Enid Blyton Trust for Children
Bonhomie United Charity
 Society
Harry Bottom Charitable Trust
Swinfen Broun Charitable Trust
E F Bulmer Benevolent Fund
Audrey & Stanley Burton
 Charitable Trust
Richard Cadbury Charitable
 Trust
Caring for Kids
Carlton Television Trust
Norman Collinson Charitable
 Trust
Baron Davenport's Charity
Denman Charitable Trust
Derbyshire Community
 Foundation

DLM Charitable Trust
Wilfred & Elsie Elkes Charity Fund
Finnart House School Trust
Florence's Charitable Trust
Ford of Britain Trust
Four Lanes Trust
Gatwick Airport Community Trust
Girdlers' Company Charitable Trust
Good Neighbours Trust
J G Graves Charitable Trust
Constance Green Foundation
GWR Community Trust
Hadrian Trust
Hallam FM – Help a Hallam Child Appeal
Harborne Parish Lands Charity
Harrison & Potter Trust
Gay & Peter Hartley's Hillards Charitable Trust
N & P Hartley Memorial Trust
Charles Hayward Foundation
Heart of England Community Foundation
Hedgcock Bequest
Hemby Trust
Henley Educational Charity
Hertfordshire Community Foundation
Hesslewood Children's Trust
Holywood Trust
Homelands Charitable Trust
Hospital of God at Greatham
James Thom Howat Charitable Trust
Huddersfield Common Good Trust
Isle of Dogs Community Foundation
Ruth & Lionel Jacobson Trust (Second Fund) No 2
Jarman Charitable Trust
Jewish Child's Day
Joicey Trust
Sir James Knott Trust
Laing's Charitable Trust
Bryan Lancaster's Charity
Lankelly Foundation
Mrs F B Laurence Charitable Trust
Lintel Trust
Lloyds TSB Foundation for Northern Ireland
London Law Trust
John Lyon's Charity
Manchester Airport Community Trust Fund
W M Mann Foundation
Middlesex County Rugby Football Union Memorial Fund
Milton Keynes Community Foundation
John Moores Foundation

Morgan Stanley International Foundation
Moss Family Charitable Trust
Northcott Devon Foundation
Old Enfield Charitable Trust
Oxfordshire Community Foundation
Parivar Trust
Harry Payne Trust
Bernard Piggott Trust
John Pitman Charitable Trust
Powell Foundation
Powys Welsh Church Fund
Simone Prendergast Charitable Trust
Prince Philip Trust Fund
Radio Forth Help a Child Appeal
Rawdon-Smith Trust
Red Dragon Radio Trust
Cliff Richard Charitable Trust
Rothley Trust
St Katharine & Shadwell Trust
R H Scholes Charitable Trust
Scott Bader Commonwealth Ltd
Francis C Scott Charitable Trust
Scottish Churches Community Trust
Sylvia & Colin Shepherd Charitable Trust
Sherburn House Charity
Skelton Bounty
Henry Smith Charity
Sobell Foundation
Steinberg Family Charitable Trust
Summerfield Charitable Trust
Sutton Coldfield Municipal Charities
Sutton Trust
Tesco Charity Trust
Tisbury Telegraph Trust
Voluntary Action Luton
Thomas Wall Trust
Wesleyan Charitable Trust
Westminster Amalgamated Charity
Wiltshire and Swindon Community Foundation
Woodward Trust
Worcester Municipal Charities
Yapp Charitable Trust
Yardley Great Trust
York Children's Trust

■ Trips, outings
Funding priority
Astor of Hever Trust
BBC Radio Cambridgeshire – Trustline
Angela Gallagher Memorial Fund
Greater Bristol Foundation
William Harding's Charity

Leeds & Holbeck Building Society Charitable Foundation
London Youth Trust
Peter Minet Trust
Charity of Thomas Wade & Others

Will consider
Ashby Charitable Trust
Birmingham Foundation
Birmingham Hospital Saturday Fund Medical Charity & Welfare Trust
Enid Blyton Trust for Children
Bothwell Charitable Trust
Harry Bottom Charitable Trust
E F Bulmer Benevolent Fund
Childwick Trust
CLA Charitable Trust
County of Gloucestershire Community Foundation
Cray Trust
Denman Charitable Trust
Finnart House School Trust
Girdlers' Company Charitable Trust
Constance Green Foundation
GWR Community Trust
Hedgcock Bequest
Henley Educational Charity
Huddersfield Common Good Trust
Ruth & Lionel Jacobson Trust (Second Fund) No 2
Jewish Child's Day
Lloyds TSB Foundation for Channel Islands
Magdalen Hospital Trust
W M Mann Foundation
Moss Family Charitable Trust
Northcott Devon Foundation
Old Enfield Charitable Trust
Oxfordshire Community Foundation
Harry Payne Trust
Jack Petchey Foundation
Peugeot Charity Trust
Prince Philip Trust Fund
Cliff Richard Charitable Trust
Rothley Trust
Sir Walter St John's Educational Charity
Francis C Scott Charitable Trust
Steinberg Family Charitable Trust
Wakeham Trust
Yapp Charitable Trust
York Children's Trust
Yorkshire Building Society Charitable Foundation

■ Youth work
Funding priority
Arsenal Charitable Trust
BBC Radio Cambridgeshire –
Trustline
Percy Bilton Charity Ltd
Isabel Blackman Foundation
Bonamy Charitable Trust
Sir William Boreman's
Foundation
Bridge House Estates Trust
Fund
Burton Breweries Charitable
Trust
Camelot Foundation
Chase Charity
Construction Industry Trust for
Youth
Cripplegate Foundation
Gilbert Edgar Trust
Essex Youth Trust
J Paul Getty Jr Charitable Trust
Greater Bristol Foundation
Robert Hall Charity
William Harding's Charity
Jewish Youth Fund
Anton Jurgens Charitable Trust
Leeds & Holbeck Building
Society Charitable
Foundation
Lloyds TSB Foundation for
Channel Islands
London Youth Trust
MacRobert Trust
Magdalen Hospital Trust
Miles Trust for Putney and
Roehampton Community
Peter Minet Trust
Peacock Charitable Trust
Jack Petchey Foundation
Ronald & Kathleen Pryor
Charitable Trust
Red Dragon Radio Trust
Christopher Rowbotham
Charitable Trust
Sir Walter St John's
Educational Charity
Sir James & Lady Scott Trust
Leslie Sell Charitable Trust
Shakespeare Temperance
Trust
Skelton Bounty
Tallow Chandlers Benevolent
Fund
Charity of Thomas Wade &
Others
Scurrah Wainwright Charity
Wakefield Trust
Weavers' Company Benevolent
Fund
Earl & Countess of Wessex
Charitable Trust
White Rose Children's Aid
International Charity
William Williams Charity

Yorkshire County Cricket Club
Charitable Youth Trust

Will consider
Ardwick Trust
Astor of Hever Trust
Birmingham Foundation
Birmingham Hospital Saturday
Fund Medical Charity &
Welfare Trust
E F Bulmer Benevolent Fund
Richard Cadbury Charitable
Trust
Lord Clinton's Charitable Trust
John Cowan Foundation
Baron Davenport's Charity
Denman Charitable Trust
Derbyshire Community
Foundation
Dulverton Trust
Eden Arts Trust
Edinburgh Voluntary
Organisations' Trust Funds
Dorothy Whitney Elmhirst Trust
Erskine Cunningham Hill Trust
Esmée Fairbairn Foundation
Samuel William Farmer's Trust
Ford of Britain Trust
Gannochy Trust
Gatwick Airport Community
Trust
Girdlers' Company Charitable
Trust
Mrs Godfrey-Payton Trust
Constance Green Foundation
GWR Community Trust
Paul Hamlyn Foundation
Harborne Parish Lands Charity
Gay & Peter Hartley's Hillards
Charitable Trust
Charles Hayward Foundation
Heart of England Community
Foundation
Hedgcock Bequest
Hemby Trust
Henley Educational Charity
Hertfordshire Community
Foundation
Holywood Trust
Huddersfield Common Good
Trust
Miss Agnes H Hunter's Trust
Ruth & Lionel Jacobson Trust
(Second Fund) No 2
James Pantyfedwen
Foundation
Jarman Charitable Trust
Johnson Foundation
Johnnie Johnson Trust
Joicey Trust
Edward Cecil Jones Settlement
Maurice Laing Foundation
Lankelly Foundation
R J Larg Family Charitable
Trust
Lawlor Foundation

Lloyds TSB Foundation for
Northern Ireland
London Law Trust
Paul Lunn-Rockliffe Charitable
Trust
John Lyon's Charity
Middlesex County Rugby
Football Union Memorial
Fund
Milton Keynes Community
Foundation
Moss Family Charitable Trust
Northcott Devon Foundation
Old Enfield Charitable Trust
Oxfordshire Community
Foundation
Late Barbara May Paul
Charitable Trust
Harry Payne Trust
Peugeot Charity Trust
G S Plaut Charitable Trust
Portishead Nautical Trust
Powys Welsh Church Fund
Prince Philip Trust Fund
Priory Foundation
Mr and Mrs J A Pye's
Charitable Settlement
Radio Forth Help a Child
Appeal
Fanny Rapaport Charitable
Settlement
Cliff Richard Charitable Trust
Rothley Trust
Francis C Scott Charitable
Trust
Scottish Churches Community
Trust
Searle Charitable Trust
Samuel Sebba Charitable
Trust
Sellafield Charity Trust Fund
Mrs Smith & Mount Trust
W W Spooner Charitable Trust
Steinberg Family Charitable
Trust
Summerfield Charitable Trust
Charles and Elsie Sykes Trust
Waterside Trust
William Webster Charitable
Trust
Westminster Amalgamated
Charity
Yapp Charitable Trust
York Children's Trust

....

■ Services for and by older people
Funding priority
Aberbrothock Charitable Trust
Ardwick Trust
Denton Wilde Sapte Charitable
Trust
William Dudley Trust
W G Edwards Charitable
Foundation

Eveson Charitable Trust
Simon Gibson Charitable Trust
Christina Mary Hendrie Trust
for Scottish & Canadian
Charities
Hospital of God at Greatham
Hudson Foundation
Worshipful Company of
Innholders General Charity
Fund
Marie Helen Luen Charitable
Trust
Lynn Foundation
Northampton Municipal Church
Charities
Rooke Atlay Charitable Trust
St Thomas' Dole Charity
Sir James & Lady Scott Trust
Foundation of Edward Storey
Tower Hill Improvement Trust
Wakefield Trust
Francis Winham Foundation
Maurice Wohl Charitable
Foundation
Maurice Wohl Charitable Trust
Woodroffe Benton Foundation
Yapp Charitable Trust

Will consider
Armourers and Brasiers'
Gauntlet Trust
Band (1976) Trust
Barclays Stockbrokers
Charitable Trust
Bearder Charity
Beit Trust
Birmingham Foundation
Roger Brooke Charitable Trust
E F Bulmer Benevolent Fund
Edward & Dorothy Cadbury
Trust
Richard Cadbury Charitable
Trust
D W T Cargill Fund
George Henry Collins Charity
Coutts & Co. Charitable Trust
Douglas Charitable Trust
Dumfries and Galloway Council
Charitable Trusts
City of Edinburgh Charitable
Trusts
Lord Faringdon Charitable
Trust
Forte Charitable Trust
Harrison & Potter Trust
N & P Hartley Memorial Trust
Hedley Denton Charitable
Trust
H J Heinz Company Limited
Charitable Trust
Hobson Charity Ltd
Mary Homfray Charitable Trust
Joseph Hopkins Charity
Kidani Memorial Trust
Lloyds TSB Foundation for
England and Wales

Robert McAlpine Foundation
D D McPhail Charitable
Settlement
Willie & Mabel Morris
Charitable Trust
Newby Trust Limited
North British Hotel Trust
Nuffield Foundation
Kate Wilson Oliver Trust
Late Barbara May Paul
Charitable Trust
Ruth & Michael Phillips
Charitable Trust
Privy Purse Charitable Trust
Riverside Charitable Trust
Limited
Cecil Rosen Foundation
Russell Trust
Saddlers' Company Charitable
Fund
Bassil Shippam and Alsford
Trust
Skelton Bounty
South Square Trust
Charles and Elsie Sykes Trust
C B & H H Taylor 1984 Trust
Towry Law Charitable Trust
William Webster Charitable
Trust

■ **Almshouses**
Funding priority
Almshouse Association
Booth Charities
R M 1956 Burton Charitable
Trust
Chase Charity
Duke of Cornwall's Benevolent
Fund
Baron Davenport's Charity
William Harding's Charity
Harrison & Potter Trust
Help Homeless Ltd
Jesus Hospital Charity
Anton Jurgens Charitable Trust
MacRobert Trust
Norwich Consolidated
Charities
Ogilvie Charities Deed 2
Old Enfield Charitable Trust
Eleanor Palmer Trust
Skerritt Trust
Verdon-Smith Family Charitable
Settlement
Worcester Municipal Charities

Will consider
Pat Allsop Charitable Trust
Viscount Amory's Charitable
Trust
Astor Foundation
Baker Charitable Trust
Balney Charitable Trust
Lord Barnby's Foundation
Percy Bilton Charity Ltd
Burdens Charitable Foundation

County Durham Foundation
John Cowan Foundation
Harry Crook Foundation
Dunhill Medical Trust
Wilfred & Elsie Elkes Charity
Fund
Samuel William Farmer's Trust
Fidelity UK Foundation
Earl Fitzwilliam Charitable
Trust
Mrs Godfrey-Payton Trust
Hampton Fuel Allotment
Charity
Charles Hayward Foundation
Jarman Charitable Trust
Graham Kirkham Foundation
Sir James Knott Trust
Knowles Charitable Trust
Raymond & Blanche Lawson
Charitable Trust
Lintel Trust
Lloyd's Charities Trust
Sir George Martin Trust
Milton Keynes Community
Foundation
Mobbs Memorial Trust Ltd
Northcott Devon Foundation
Pastoral Care Trust
Bernard Piggott Trust
Austin & Hope Pilkington Trust
John Pitman Charitable Trust
John Rayner Charitable Trust
Violet M Richards Charity
St Mary-le-Strand Charity
Scouloudi Foundation
Henry Smith Charity
Sobell Foundation
Summerfield Charitable Trust
Bernard Sunley Charitable
Foundation
Swan Trust
Wakefield Trust
Sheila Whitley Trust

■ **Homes for elderly,**
sheltered
accommodation
Funding priority
Balney Charitable Trust
Barnwood House Trust
BBC Radio Cambridgeshire –
Trustline
Percy Bilton Charity Ltd
R M 1956 Burton Charitable
Trust
Duke of Cornwall's Benevolent
Fund
Lennox Hannay Charitable
Trust
Harrison & Potter Trust
Elton John Aids Foundation
Kass Charitable Trust
King George's Fund for Sailors
Lloyds TSB Foundation for
Channel Islands

Paul Lunn-Rockliffe Charitable
    Trust
Minge's Gift
Ogilvie Charities Deed 2
Eleanor Palmer Trust
Patients' Aid Association
    Hospital & Medical
    Charities Trust
Philanthropic Trust
St Thomas' Dole Charity
Sherburn House Charity
Skerritt Trust
Sobell Foundation
Swan Trust
Mrs S H Troughton Charity
    Trust
Maurice Wohl Charitable
    Foundation
Maurice Wohl Charitable Trust

Will consider
Viscount Amory's Charitable
    Trust
Baily Thomas Charitable Fund
Lord Barnby's Foundation
James Beattie Charitable Trust
Bothwell Charitable Trust
Burdens Charitable Foundation
Audrey & Stanley Burton
    Charitable Trust
Mauritis Mulder Canter Charity
Chamberlain Foundation
Chase Charity
Childwick Trust
Lord Clinton's Charitable Trust
Congleton Inclosure Trust
Cooper Charitable Trust
County Durham Foundation
Cranbury Foundation
Harry Crook Foundation
Baron Davenport's Charity
Double 'O' Charity Ltd
Dunhill Medical Trust
Wilfred & Elsie Elkes Charity
    Fund
Elmgrant Trust
Samuel William Farmer's Trust
Ferguson Benevolent Fund Ltd
Fidelity UK Foundation
Earl Fitzwilliam Charitable
    Trust
Ford of Britain Trust
Frognal Trust
Gannochy Trust
Gatwick Airport Community
    Trust
Girdlers' Company Charitable
    Trust
Constance Green Foundation
Greggs Trust
H C D Memorial Fund
Hampton Fuel Allotment
    Charity
Gay & Peter Hartley's Hillards
    Charitable Trust
Charles Hayward Foundation

May Hearnshaw's Charity
Hedley Foundation
Hemby Trust
Hertfordshire Community
    Foundation
Dorothy Holmes Charitable
    Trust
Edward Holt Trust
James Thom Howat Charitable
    Trust
Charles Irving Charitable Trust
Jarman Charitable Trust
Joicey Trust
Edward Cecil Jones Settlement
Anton Jurgens Charitable Trust
Graham Kirkham Foundation
Sir James Knott Trust
Knowles Charitable Trust
Late Sir Pierce Lacy Charity
    Trust
Beatrice Laing Trust
Maurice Laing Foundation
Bryan Lancaster's Charity
Lankelly Foundation
Mrs F B Laurence Charitable
    Trust
Raymond & Blanche Lawson
    Charitable Trust
Levy Foundation
Lintel Trust
Lloyd's Charities Trust
Lloyds TSB Foundation for
    Northern Ireland
Lyndhurst Settlement
Lynwood Trust
Marsh Christian Trust
Milton Keynes Community
    Foundation
Mobbs Memorial Trust Ltd
George A Moore Foundation
Moss Family Charitable Trust
Notgrove Trust
Oakdale Trust
Oxfordshire Community
    Foundation
Pastoral Care Trust
Patrick Charitable Trust
Ruth & Michael Phillips
    Charitable Trust
A M Pilkington's Charitable
    Trust
Austin & Hope Pilkington Trust
Pilkington Charities Fund
John Pitman Charitable Trust
G S Plaut Charitable Trust
Prince Philip Trust Fund
Pye Foundation
Queen Mary's Roehampton
    Trust
Rainford Trust
Fanny Rapaport Charitable
    Settlement
Ravensdale Trust
John Rayner Charitable Trust
Violet M Richards Charity
Cecil Rosen Foundation

St James' Trust Settlement
St Mary-le-Strand Charity
R H Scholes Charitable Trust
Francis C Scott Charitable
    Trust
Sir James & Lady Scott Trust
Sellafield Charity Trust Fund
Skelton Bounty
Henry Smith Charity
Stanley Foundation Ltd
Steinberg Family Charitable
    Trust
Summerfield Charitable Trust
Bernard Sunley Charitable
    Foundation
Tajtelbaum Charitable Trust
Tesco Charity Trust
Wates Foundation
Westminster Amalgamated
    Charity
Whitecourt Charitable Trust

■ **Holidays & outings for
    older people**
Funding priority
Betard Bequest
Greater Bristol Foundation
William Harding's Charity
Leeds & Holbeck Building
    Society Charitable
    Foundation
Ormsby Charitable Trust
Charity of Thomas Wade &
    Others

Will consider
Ashby Charitable Trust
Birmingham Hospital Saturday
    Fund Medical Charity &
    Welfare Trust
Bonhomie United Charity
    Society
E F Bulmer Benevolent Fund
Childwick Trust
Colchester & Tendring
    Community Trust
County of Gloucestershire
    Community Foundation
D'Oyly Carte Charitable Trust
Elmgrant Trust
Erskine Cunningham Hill Trust
Hedgcock Bequest
Anton Jurgens Charitable Trust
Lloyds TSB Foundation for
    Northern Ireland
Lloyds TSB Foundation for
    Channel Islands
Keith and Joan Mindelsohn
    Charitable Trust
Moss Family Charitable Trust
Northcott Devon Foundation
Old Enfield Charitable Trust
Pastoral Care Trust
Harry Payne Trust
Prince Philip Trust Fund
Rawdon-Smith Trust

Cliff Richard Charitable Trust
Wakeham Trust
Westminster Amalgamated
 Charity

....

■ Services for victims
of crime
Funding priority
Aberbrothock Charitable Trust
Bramble Charitable Trust
R M 1956 Burton Charitable
 Trust
Demigryphon Trust
Denton Wilde Sapte Charitable
 Trust
Simon Gibson Charitable Trust
Charles Hayward Foundation
Hospital of God at Greatham
Anton Jurgens Charitable Trust
Lynn Foundation
Woodroffe Benton Foundation

Will consider
Ardwick Trust
Barclays Stockbrokers
 Charitable Trust
BBC Children in Need Appeal
Bearder Charity
Birmingham Hospital Saturday
 Fund Medical Charity &
 Welfare Trust
Roger Brooke Charitable Trust
E F Bulmer Benevolent Fund
Edward & Dorothy Cadbury
 Trust
Chase Charity
Colchester & Tendring
 Community Trust
George Henry Collins Charity
Dumfries and Galloway Council
 Charitable Trusts
Essex Fairway Charitable Trust
Lord Faringdon Charitable
 Trust
Florence's Charitable Trust
Forte Charitable Trust
Girdlers' Company Charitable
 Trust
Greater Bristol Foundation
GWR Community Trust
Harborne Parish Lands Charity
Heart of England Community
 Foundation
Hemby Trust
Joseph Hopkins Charity
Sir Charles Jessel Charitable
 Trust
Boris Karloff Charitable
 Foundation
Lloyds TSB Foundation for
 England and Wales
Lloyds TSB Foundation for
 Channel Islands
Lyndhurst Settlement
Peter Minet Trust

Newby Trust Limited
Northcott Devon Foundation
Northern Rock Foundation
Old Enfield Charitable Trust
Pastoral Care Trust
Patrick Charitable Trust
Jack Petchey Foundation
David Pickford Charitable
 Foundation
Pye Foundation
Christopher Rowbotham
 Charitable Trust
Rufford Foundation
Francis C Scott Charitable
 Trust
Sir James & Lady Scott Trust
Sellafield Charity Trust Fund
Sherburn House Charity
Wakefield Trust
York Children's Trust
Yorkshire Building Society
 Charitable Foundation

....

■ Services for and by
vulnerable/ill
people
Funding priority
Aberbrothock Charitable Trust
Ashe Park Charitable Trust
Bramble Charitable Trust
Butchers' Company General
 Charities
Denton Wilde Sapte Charitable
 Trust
Eveson Charitable Trust
Family Rich Charities Trust
Simon Gibson Charitable Trust
Hospital of God at Greatham
Liverpool Queen Victoria
 District Nursing Association
Marie Helen Luen Charitable
 Trust
Mandeville Trust
Northampton Municipal Church
 Charities
Patients' Aid Association
 Hospital & Medical
 Charities Trust
Tower Hill Improvement Trust
Trust Sixty Three
Wakefield Trust
Wentwood Education Trust
West Derby Wastelands
 Charity
Maurice Wohl Charitable
 Foundation
Maurice Wohl Charitable Trust
Woodroffe Benton Foundation
Miss E B Wrightson's
 Charitable Settlement

Will consider
Aston Villa Charitable Trust
Band (1976) Trust

Barclays Stockbrokers
 Charitable Trust
BBC Children in Need Appeal
Bearder Charity
Roger Brooke Charitable Trust
E F Bulmer Benevolent Fund
George Henry Collins Charity
Dumfries and Galloway Council
 Charitable Trusts
Earley Charity
City of Edinburgh Charitable
 Trusts
Maud Elkington Charitable
 Trust
Lord Faringdon Charitable
 Trust
Girdlers' Company Charitable
 Trust
Hampton Fuel Allotment
 Charity
N & P Hartley Memorial Trust
May Hearnshaw's Charity
Hedley Denton Charitable
 Trust
H J Heinz Company Limited
 Charitable Trust
Mary Homfray Charitable Trust
Joseph Hopkins Charity
Kidani Memorial Trust
Kirby Laing Foundation
Lankelly Foundation
Mason Le Page Charitable
 Trust
Robert McAlpine Foundation
Matliwala Family Charitable
 Trust
Maxwell Family Foundation
Victor Mishcon Charitable
 Trust
Moss Family Charitable Trust
Edwina Mountbatten Trust
Newby Trust Limited
North British Hotel Trust
Parthenon Trust
Jack Petchey Foundation
Privy Purse Charitable Trust
Rufford Foundation
Russell Trust
Saddlers' Company Charitable
 Fund
Sherburn House Charity
Philip Smith's Charitable Trust
South Square Trust
Sovereign Health Care
 Charitable Trust
W W Spooner Charitable Trust
Steinberg Family Charitable
 Trust
Talbot Trusts
Albert Van Den Bergh
 Charitable Trust

■ Care in the community
Funding priority
1970 Trust
Abel Charitable Trust

AIM Foundation
Percy Bilton Charity Ltd
Cleopatra Trust
Dorus Trust
W G Edwards Charitable
Foundation
Epigoni Trust
Fassnidge Memorial Trust
Gerald Fogel Charitable Trust
Mrs Godfrey-Payton Trust
Constance Green Foundation
Lennox Hannay Charitable
Trust
Hertfordshire Community
Foundation
Clifford Howarth Charity
Settlement
Incorporated Leeds Church
Extension Society
Anton Jurgens Charitable Trust
Peter Kershaw Trust
King George's Fund for Sailors
David Laing Foundation
Leeds & Holbeck Building
Society Charitable
Foundation
Lintel Trust
Lloyds TSB Foundation for
Channel Islands
Lynn Foundation
Tony Metherell Charitable
Trust
Monument Trust
Nestlé Rowntree York
Employees Community Fund
Trust
Ormsby Charitable Trust
Patients' Aid Association
Hospital & Medical
Charities Trust
Austin & Hope Pilkington Trust
Pilkington Charities Fund
Ronald & Kathleen Pryor
Charitable Trust
Sir James & Lady Scott Trust
Skerritt Trust
Sobell Foundation
Walter Swindon Charitable
Trust
Verdon-Smith Family Charitable
Settlement
Wates Foundation
Wiltshire and Swindon
Community Foundation
Yorkshire Building Society
Charitable Foundation

Will consider

Adint Charitable Trust
Adnams Charity
Age Concern Scotland
Enterprise Fund
Viscount Amory's Charitable
Trust
Armenian General Benevolent
Union London Trust

Astor Foundation
Baily Thomas Charitable Fund
Bamford Charitable Foundation
Philip Barker Charity
Barnabas Charitable Trust
Birmingham Foundation
Birmingham Hospital Saturday
Fund Medical Charity &
Welfare Trust
Peter Black Charitable Trust
Bridge House Estates Trust
Fund
British Dietetic Association
General and Education
Trust Fund
Buckinghamshire Masonic
Centenary Fund
E F Bulmer Benevolent Fund
Chamberlain Foundation
Chase Charity
Childwick Trust
Christadelphian Samaritan
Fund
Vivienne & Samuel Cohen
Charitable Trust
Colchester & Tendring
Community Trust
Norman Collinson Charitable
Trust
Derbyshire Community
Foundation
Devon Community Foundation
DLM Charitable Trust
Duis Charitable Trust
Dulverton Trust
Edinburgh Voluntary
Organisations' Trust Funds
Wilfred & Elsie Elkes Charity
Fund
Elmgrant Trust
Esmée Fairbairn Foundation
Samuel William Farmer's Trust
Ferguson Benevolent Fund Ltd
Fidelity UK Foundation
Earl Fitzwilliam Charitable
Trust
Roy Fletcher Charitable Trust
Ford of Britain Trust
Fox Memorial Trust
Sydney E Franklin Deceased's
New Second Charity
Frognal Trust
Gannochy Trust
Gatwick Airport Community
Trust
J Paul Getty Jr Charitable Trust
L & R Gilley Charitable Trust
Good Neighbours Trust
J G Graves Charitable Trust
Greggs Trust
GWR Community Trust
Hadrian Trust
Hallam FM – Help a Hallam
Child Appeal
Harborne Parish Lands Charity
Charles Hayward Foundation

Hemby Trust
Hospital Saturday Fund
Charitable Trust
James Thom Howat Charitable
Trust
Miss Agnes H Hunter's Trust
Inchrye Trust
Isle of Dogs Community
Foundation
Jarman Charitable Trust
John Jarrold Trust
Johnson Foundation
Johnson Group Cleaners
Charity
Joicey Trust
Judith Trust
Boris Karloff Charitable
Foundation
Robert Kiln Charitable Trust
Sir James Knott Trust
Knowles Charitable Trust
Heinz & Anna Kroch
Foundation
Late Sir Pierce Lacy Charity
Trust
Lankelly Foundation
R J Larg Family Charitable
Trust
Lauffer Family Charitable
Foundation
Mrs F B Laurence Charitable
Trust
Raymond & Blanche Lawson
Charitable Trust
Leach Fourteenth Trust
Levy Foundation
Linden Charitable Trust
Lloyd's Charities Trust
Lloyds TSB Foundation for
England and Wales
Lloyds TSB Foundation for
Northern Ireland
Lyndhurst Settlement
M N R Charitable Trust
Helen Isabella McMorran
Charitable Foundation
Marchday Charitable Fund
Methodist Relief and
Development Fund
Mickel Fund
Milton Keynes Community
Foundation
Keith and Joan Mindelsohn
Charitable Trust
George A Moore Foundation
Morgan Stanley International
Foundation
Northcott Devon Foundation
Northern Rock Foundation
Oxfordshire Community
Foundation
Parivar Trust
Pastoral Care Trust
Harry Payne Trust
Bernard Piggott Trust

A M Pilkington's Charitable
   Trust
G S Plaut Charitable Trust
Powell Foundation
Prince Philip Trust Fund
Rainford Trust
Fanny Rapaport Charitable
   Settlement
Rawdon-Smith Trust
Cliff Richard Charitable Trust
Rothley Trust
Rowan Charitable Trust
Christopher Rowbotham
   Charitable Trust
St Mary-le-Strand Charity
R H Scholes Charitable Trust
Scott Bader Commonwealth
   Ltd
Francis C Scott Charitable
   Trust
Scottish Churches Community
   Trust
Sellafield Charity Trust Fund
Sheldon Trust
Mary Elizabeth Siebel Charity
SMB Trust
Henry Smith Charity
Foundation of Edward Storey
Summerfield Charitable Trust
Swann-Morton Foundation
Truemark Trust
Tudor Trust
Unemployed Voluntary Action
   Fund
Voluntary Action Luton
Webb Memorial Trust
William Webster Charitable
   Trust
Wellfield Trust
Wesleyan Charitable Trust
Michael and Anna Wix
   Charitable Trust
Woodward Trust
Worcester Municipal Charities
Yapp Charitable Trust
W Wing Yip & Bros Charitable
   Trust

■ **Counselling services for**
   adults
   Funding priority
1970 Trust
Artemis Charitable Trust
Ashendene Trust
Birmingham Hospital Saturday
   Fund Medical Charity &
   Welfare Trust
Chippenham Borough Lands
   Charity
Cleopatra Trust
Richard Cloudesley's Charity
Cripplegate Foundation
Dorus Trust
Epigoni Trust
J Paul Getty Jr Charitable Trust
Greater Bristol Foundation

Greggs Trust
HopMarket Charity
Clifford Howarth Charity
   Settlement
Peter Kershaw Trust
Lark Trust
Leeds & Holbeck Building
   Society Charitable
   Foundation
Lloyds TSB Foundation for
   Channel Islands
Lynn Foundation
Magdalen Hospital Trust
Metropolitan Hospital-Sunday
   Fund
Nestlé Rowntree York
   Employees Community Fund
   Trust
Novi Most International
Austin & Hope Pilkington Trust
Pilkington Charities Fund
Primrose Hill Trust
Ronald & Kathleen Pryor
   Charitable Trust
Mr & Mrs Philip Rackham
   Charitable Trust
Karim Rida Said Foundation
Sir James & Lady Scott Trust
Three Oaks Trust
Truemark Trust
Victoria Homes Trust
Wates Foundation
Wentwood Education Trust
Wiltshire and Swindon
   Community Foundation
Woodlands Trust (1015942)
Yorkshire Bank Charitable
   Trust

Will consider
Adnams Charity
Ajahma Charitable Trust
Alcohol Education and
   Research Fund
Astor Foundation
Barnabas Charitable Trust
Peter Black Charitable Trust
Bridge House Estates Trust
   Fund
Buckinghamshire Masonic
   Centenary Fund
E F Bulmer Benevolent Fund
Richard Cadbury Charitable
   Trust
Chase Charity
Chownes Foundation
Colchester & Tendring
   Community Trust
Norman Collinson Charitable
   Trust
Coppings Trust
County of Gloucestershire
   Community Foundation
Derbyshire Community
   Foundation
Duis Charitable Trust

Fifty Fund
Earl Fitzwilliam Charitable
   Trust
Ford of Britain Trust
Four Lanes Trust
Gannochy Trust
J G Graves Charitable Trust
GWR Community Trust
Hadrian Trust
Hallam FM – Help a Hallam
   Child Appeal
Harborne Parish Lands Charity
Gay & Peter Hartley's Hillards
   Charitable Trust
Charles Hayward Foundation
Hertfordshire Community
   Foundation
Dorothy Holmes Charitable
   Trust
Holywood Trust
House of Industry Estate
James Thom Howat Charitable
   Trust
Miss Agnes H Hunter's Trust
Inchrye Trust
Charles Irving Charitable Trust
Isle of Dogs Community
   Foundation
Jarman Charitable Trust
Elton John Aids Foundation
Joicey Trust
Judith Trust
Richard Kirkman Charitable
   Trust
Sir James Knott Trust
Bryan Lancaster's Charity
Lankelly Foundation
Mrs F B Laurence Charitable
   Trust
Leigh Trust
Levy Foundation
Lloyd's Charities Trust
Lloyds TSB Foundation for
   England and Wales
Lloyds TSB Foundation for
   Northern Ireland
Lyndhurst Settlement
John Lyon's Charity
M N R Charitable Trust
Helen Isabella McMorran
   Charitable Foundation
Marchday Charitable Fund
Milton Keynes Community
   Foundation
John Moores Foundation
Morgan Stanley International
   Foundation
Northcott Devon Foundation
Northern Rock Foundation
Old Enfield Charitable Trust
Oxfordshire Community
   Foundation
Parivar Trust
Pastoral Care Trust
Harry Payne Trust

A M Pilkington's Charitable Trust
J D Player Endowment Fund
Portishead Nautical Trust
Proven Family Trust
Pye Foundation
Rothley Trust
St Mary-le-Strand Charity
Scott Bader Commonwealth Ltd
Francis C Scott Charitable Trust
Scottish Churches Community Trust
Sheldon Trust
Skelton Bounty
Henry Smith Charity
Leslie Smith Foundation
Mrs Smith & Mount Trust
Sobell Foundation
Summerfield Charitable Trust
Swann-Morton Foundation
C B & H H Taylor 1984 Trust
Sir Jules Thorn Charitable Trust
Triangle Trust (1949) Fund
Voluntary Action Luton
Thomas Wall Trust
Weavers' Company Benevolent Fund
James Weir Foundation
Wellfield Trust
Wesleyan Charitable Trust
Wessex Cancer Trust
Westcroft Trust
Westminster Amalgamated Charity
Wiltshire and Swindon Community Foundation
Michael and Anna Wix Charitable Trust
Woodward Trust
Worcester Municipal Charities
Yapp Charitable Trust
York Children's Trust

■ **Day centres**
Funding priority
Barnwood House Trust
BibleLands
Percy Bilton Charity Ltd
Birmingham International Airport Community Trust
Fassnidge Memorial Trust
Angela Gallagher Memorial Fund
Greater Bristol Foundation
Lennox Hannay Charitable Trust
Charles Hayward Foundation
Help Aged
Hilden Charitable Fund
Peter Kershaw Trust
King George's Fund for Sailors

Leeds & Holbeck Building Society Charitable Foundation
Lloyds TSB Foundation for Channel Islands
Paul Lunn-Rockliffe Charitable Trust
Lynn Foundation
Midhurst Pensions Trust
Patients' Aid Association Hospital & Medical Charities Trust
Powell Foundation
Red Dragon Radio Trust
St Thomas' Dole Charity
Sir James & Lady Scott Trust
Skerritt Trust
Sobell Foundation
Sutton Coldfield Municipal Charities
Swan Trust
Verdon-Smith Family Charitable Settlement
Charity of Thomas Wade & Others
Wentwood Education Trust
Wiltshire and Swindon Community Foundation
Yorkshire Building Society Charitable Foundation

Will consider
1970 Trust
Age Concern Scotland Enterprise Fund
Viscount Amory's Charitable Trust
Ardwick Trust
Baily Thomas Charitable Fund
Balmore Trust
Bamford Charitable Foundation
Barnabas Charitable Trust
Bartle Family Charitable Trust
BBC Radio Lincolnshire Charity Trust
Birmingham Hospital Saturday Fund Medical Charity & Welfare Trust
Peter Black Charitable Trust
Booth Charities
Bridge House Estates Trust Fund
Charles Brotherton Trust
Buckinghamshire Masonic Centenary Fund
E F Bulmer Benevolent Fund
Audrey & Stanley Burton Charitable Trust
Richard Cadbury Charitable Trust
Chamberlain Foundation
Chase Charity
Childwick Trust
Chippenham Borough Lands Charity

Christadelphian Samaritan Fund
Vivienne & Samuel Cohen Charitable Trust
Consortium on Opportunities for Volunteering
County Durham Foundation
County of Gloucestershire Community Foundation
Helen and Geoffrey de Freitas Charitable Trust
Derbyshire Community Foundation
Devon Community Foundation
Dulverton Trust
Dunhill Medical Trust
Edinburgh Voluntary Organisations' Trust Funds
Wilfred & Elsie Elkes Charity Fund
Fairway Trust
Samuel William Farmer's Trust
Ferguson Benevolent Fund Ltd
Fidelity UK Foundation
Fifty Fund
Florence's Charitable Trust
Ford of Britain Trust
Four Lanes Trust
Charles S French Charitable Trust
Frognal Trust
Gannochy Trust
Gatwick Airport Community Trust
J Paul Getty Jr Charitable Trust
Good Neighbours Trust
J G Graves Charitable Trust
Greggs Trust
Hadrian Trust
Harborne Parish Lands Charity
Hemby Trust
Hertfordshire Community Foundation
Homelands Charitable Trust
James Thom Howat Charitable Trust
Miss Agnes H Hunter's Trust
Charles Irving Charitable Trust
Ruth & Lionel Jacobson Trust (Second Fund) No 2
Jarman Charitable Trust
John Jarrold Trust
Elton John Aids Foundation
Joicey Trust
Sir James Knott Trust
Knowles Charitable Trust
Late Sir Pierce Lacy Charity Trust
Beatrice Laing Trust
Laing's Charitable Trust
Bryan Lancaster's Charity
Lankelly Foundation
Mrs F B Laurence Charitable Trust
Levy Foundation
Lintel Trust

Lloyd's Charities Trust
Lloyds TSB Foundation for
England and Wales
Lloyds TSB Foundation for
Northern Ireland
Lyndhurst Settlement
M N R Charitable Trust
Manchester Airport Community
Trust Fund
Marchday Charitable Fund
Marsh Christian Trust
Sir George Martin Trust
Methodist Relief and
Development Fund
Milton Keynes Community
Foundation
George A Moore Foundation
Horace Moore Charitable Trust
Newport County Borough
Welsh Church Fund
Northcott Devon Foundation
Oldham Foundation
Kate Wilson Oliver Trust
Oxfordshire Community
Foundation
Eleanor Palmer Trust
Harry Payne Trust
Bernard Piggott Trust
A M Pilkington's Charitable
Trust
John Pitman Charitable Trust
J D Player Endowment Fund
Prince Philip Trust Fund
Puri Foundation
Pye Foundation
Rainford Trust
Rawdon-Smith Trust
Rothley Trust
Christopher Rowbotham
Charitable Trust
St James' Trust Settlement
St Mary-le-Strand Charity
R H Scholes Charitable Trust
Scott Bader Commonwealth
Ltd
Francis C Scott Charitable
Trust
Scottish Churches Community
Trust
Sellafield Charity Trust Fund
Servite Sisters' Charitable
Trust Fund
Sheldon Trust
Skelton Bounty
SMB Trust
Henry Smith Charity
Mrs Smith & Mount Trust
Summerfield Charitable Trust
Tesco Charity Trust
Sir Jules Thorn Charitable
Trust
Tudor Trust
Unemployed Voluntary Action
Fund
Voluntary Action Luton

Wakeham Trust
Thomas Wall Trust
Wates Foundation
Weavers' Company Benevolent
Fund
William Webster Charitable
Trust
Wellfield Trust
Wesleyan Charitable Trust
Westminster Amalgamated
Charity
Michael and Anna Wix
Charitable Trust
Worcester Municipal Charities
Yapp Charitable Trust
Yardley Great Trust
W Wing Yip & Bros Charitable
Trust
York Children's Trust

■ Drug and alcohol rehabilitation

Funding priority

Christabella Charitable Trust
Richard Cloudesley's Charity
J Paul Getty Jr Charitable Trust
Greater Bristol Foundation
Clifford Howarth Charity
Settlement
Anton Jurgens Charitable Trust
Leeds & Holbeck Building
Society Charitable
Foundation
Lotus Foundation
Paul Lunn-Rockliffe Charitable
Trust
Lynn Foundation
Pilgrim Trust
Ronald & Kathleen Pryor
Charitable Trust
Sir James & Lady Scott Trust
Third House Trust
Scurrah Wainwright Charity

Will consider

Adint Charitable Trust
Adnams Charity
Ardwick Trust
BBC Children in Need Appeal
Birmingham Hospital Saturday
Fund Medical Charity &
Welfare Trust
Charles Boot Trust
E F Bulmer Benevolent Fund
Chase Charity
Colchester & Tendring
Community Trust
Consortium on Opportunities
for Volunteering
Douglas Charitable Trust
Duis Charitable Trust
Elmgrant Trust
Erskine Cunningham Hill Trust
Ford of Britain Trust
Gannochy Trust

Gatwick Airport Community
Trust
GWR Community Trust
H C D Memorial Fund
Gay & Peter Hartley's Hillards
Charitable Trust
Charles Hayward Foundation
Hemby Trust
Hilden Charitable Fund
Jarman Charitable Trust
Edward Cecil Jones Settlement
Peter Kershaw Trust
Graham Kirkham Foundation
Richard Kirkman Charitable
Trust
Beatrice Laing Trust
David Laing Foundation
Maurice and Hilda Laing
Charitable Trust
Lawlor Foundation
Leigh Trust
Linbury Trust
Lloyds TSB Foundation for
England and Wales
Lloyds TSB Foundation for
Northern Ireland
Lyndhurst Settlement
Marchday Charitable Fund
Keith and Joan Mindelsohn
Charitable Trust
John Moores Foundation
Northcott Devon Foundation
Northern Rock Foundation
Oxfordshire Community
Foundation
Pastoral Care Trust
Patrick Charitable Trust
Harry Payne Trust
Portishead Nautical Trust
Simone Prendergast Charitable
Trust
Mr and Mrs J A Pye's
Charitable Settlement
Cliff Richard Charitable Trust
Robertson Trust
Rothley Trust
Christopher Rowbotham
Charitable Trust
Francis C Scott Charitable
Trust
Scottish Churches Community
Trust
Sellafield Charity Trust Fund
Leslie Smith Foundation
Mrs Smith & Mount Trust
Tisbury Telegraph Trust
Weavers' Company Benevolent
Fund
Webb Memorial Trust
Westcroft Trust
Westminster Amalgamated
Charity
Whitecourt Charitable Trust
Yapp Charitable Trust
Yorkshire Building Society
Charitable Foundation

■ Self-help groups, support groups

Funding priority

Ajahma Charitable Trust
Chest Heart and Stroke
    Scotland
Coutts & Co. Charitable Trust
Derbyshire Community
    Foundation
Greater Bristol Foundation
Greggs Trust
Charles Hayward Foundation
Heart of England Community
    Foundation
Hilden Charitable Fund
Clifford Howarth Charity
    Settlement
Jeffrey Charitable Trust
Peter Kershaw Trust
Leeds & Holbeck Building
    Society Charitable
    Foundation
Lintel Trust
Lloyds TSB Foundation for
    Channel Islands
Magdalen Hospital Trust
Kitty and Daniel Nabarro
    Charitable Trust
Oxfordshire Community
    Foundation
Ronald & Kathleen Pryor
    Charitable Trust
Christopher Rowbotham
    Charitable Trust
Sir James & Lady Scott Trust
Third House Trust
Wakeham Trust
Wentwood Education Trust
Earl & Countess of Wessex
    Charitable Trust
Woodlands Trust (1015942)

Will consider

1970 Trust
Adnams Charity
Age Concern Scotland
    Enterprise Fund
Ammco Trust
Ardwick Trust
Ashby Charitable Trust
Astor Foundation
Bamford Charitable Foundation
Bartle Family Charitable Trust
BBC Children in Need Appeal
Percy Bilton Charity Ltd
Birmingham Foundation
Birmingham Hospital Saturday
    Fund Medical Charity &
    Welfare Trust
Charles Boot Trust
Bridge House Estates Trust
    Fund
Charles Brotherton Trust
Bryant Trust
Buckinghamshire Masonic
    Centenary Fund

E F Bulmer Benevolent Fund
Richard Cadbury Charitable
    Trust
Camelot Foundation
Colchester & Tendring
    Community Trust
Community Foundation for
    Northern Ireland
Consortium on Opportunities
    for Volunteering
County of Gloucestershire
    Community Foundation
John Grant Davies Trust
DLM Charitable Trust
Duis Charitable Trust
Dulverton Trust
Edinburgh Voluntary
    Organisations' Trust Funds
Elmgrant Trust
Ferguson Benevolent Fund Ltd
Ford of Britain Trust
Fox Memorial Trust
Gannochy Trust
Gatwick Airport Community
    Trust
GWR Community Trust
Hadrian Trust
Hallam FM – Help a Hallam
    Child Appeal
Harborne Parish Lands Charity
Gay & Peter Hartley's Hillards
    Charitable Trust
Hedgcock Bequest
Hemby Trust
Holywood Trust
James Thom Howat Charitable
    Trust
Miss Agnes H Hunter's Trust
Inchrye Trust
Isle of Dogs Community
    Foundation
Jarman Charitable Trust
Jesus Hospital Charity
Elton John Aids Foundation
King's Fund
Graham Kirkham Foundation
Kleinwort Benson Charitable
    Trust
Sir James Knott Trust
Heinz & Anna Kroch
    Foundation
Bryan Lancaster's Charity
Lankelly Foundation
Lawlor Foundation
Lazard Charitable Trust
Leigh Trust
Levy Foundation
Lloyds TSB Foundation for
    England and Wales
Lloyds TSB Foundation for
    Northern Ireland
London Law Trust
Lyndhurst Settlement
M N R Charitable Trust
Marchday Charitable Fund
Marsh Christian Trust

Medlock Charitable Trust
Mercers' Charitable
    Foundation
Middlesex County Rugby
    Football Union Memorial
    Fund
Hugh and Mary Miller Bequest
    Trust
Milton Keynes Community
    Foundation
Keith and Joan Mindelsohn
    Charitable Trust
George A Moore Foundation
John Moores Foundation
Newport County Borough
    Welsh Church Fund
Northcott Devon Foundation
Northern Rock Foundation
Oakdale Trust
Old Enfield Charitable Trust
Park Hill Trust
Pastoral Care Trust
Peugeot Charity Trust
Austin & Hope Pilkington Trust
Pilkington Charities Fund
John Pitman Charitable Trust
Powell Foundation
Proven Family Trust
Puri Foundation
Pye Foundation
Radio Forth Help a Child
    Appeal
Fanny Rapaport Charitable
    Settlement
E L Rathbone Charitable Trust
Sir James Reckitt Charity
Cliff Richard Charitable Trust
Rothley Trust
Francis C Scott Charitable
    Trust
Scottish Churches Community
    Trust
Servite Sisters' Charitable
    Trust Fund
Sheldon Trust
Sherburn House Charity
Shuttlewood Clarke Foundation
Sobell Foundation
David Solomons Charitable
    Trust
Summerfield Charitable Trust
Tesco Charity Trust
Trust for London
Tudor Trust
Unemployed Voluntary Action
    Fund
Voluntary Action Luton
Webb Memorial Trust
William Webster Charitable
    Trust
James Weir Foundation
Wellfield Trust
Wesleyan Charitable Trust
Westcroft Trust
Westminster Amalgamated
    Charity

Wiltshire and Swindon
  Community Foundation
Michael and Anna Wix
  Charitable Trust
Woodward Trust
Yapp Charitable Trust
Yorkshire Building Society
  Charitable Foundation

■ Convalescent homes
Funding priority
Birmingham Hospital Saturday
  Fund Medical Charity &
  Welfare Trust
Clifford Howarth Charity
  Settlement
King George's Fund for Sailors
Zachary Merton & George
  Woofindin Convalescent
  Trust
Metropolitan Hospital-Sunday
  Fund
Walker Trust
Walton Foundation

Will consider
Astor Foundation
Booth Charities
Boots Charitable Trust
E F Bulmer Benevolent Fund
Christadelphian Samaritan
  Fund
City and Metropolitan Welfare
  Charity
Cranbury Foundation
Baron Davenport's Charity
Wilfred & Elsie Elkes Charity
  Fund
Fox Memorial Trust
GWR Community Trust
Gay & Peter Hartley's Hillards
  Charitable Trust
Charles Hayward Foundation
May Hearnshaw's Charity
Charles Irving Charitable Trust
Jarman Charitable Trust
John Jarrold Trust
Joicey Trust
Sir James Knott Trust
Beatrice Laing Trust
M N R Charitable Trust
Magdalen Hospital Trust
George A Moore Foundation
Ogilvie Charities Deed 2
Kate Wilson Oliver Trust
Queen Mary's Roehampton
  Trust
Sir James & Lady Scott Trust
Sir Jules Thorn Charitable
  Trust
William Webster Charitable
  Trust
Wellfield Trust
Michael and Anna Wix
  Charitable Trust
York Children's Trust

■ Holidays for
convalescents
Funding priority
Badley Memorial Trust
William Harding's Charity
Ormsby Charitable Trust
Charity of Thomas Wade &
  Others

Will consider
Birmingham Hospital Saturday
  Fund Medical Charity &
  Welfare Trust
E F Bulmer Benevolent Fund
Childwick Trust
GWR Community Trust
Keith and Joan Mindelsohn
  Charitable Trust
Peter Minet Trust
Northcott Devon Foundation
Kate Wilson Oliver Trust
Rothley Trust

....

■ Services for women
Funding priority
Aberbrothock Charitable Trust
Bramble Charitable Trust
Hospital of God at Greatham
Lotus Foundation
Eleanor Rathbone Charitable
  Trust
Wakefield Trust

Will consider
Access 4 Trust
Adnams Charity
Bearder Charity
BibleLands
Birmingham Hospital Saturday
  Fund Medical Charity &
  Welfare Trust
Body Shop Foundation
Colchester & Tendring
  Community Trust
Consortium on Opportunities
  for Volunteering
City of Edinburgh Charitable
  Trusts
J Paul Getty Jr Charitable Trust
Gay & Peter Hartley's Hillards
  Charitable Trust
Charles Hayward Foundation
Heart of England Community
  Foundation
Lankelly Foundation
Peter Minet Trust
Newby Trust Limited
Northern Rock Foundation
Jack Petchey Foundation
Rothley Trust
Christopher Rowbotham
  Charitable Trust
Francis C Scott Charitable
  Trust
South Square Trust

Staples Trust

Social preventive schemes
Funding priority
Aberbrothock Charitable Trust
Bramble Charitable Trust
R M 1956 Burton Charitable
  Trust
Commonwealth Relations
  Trust
Denton Wilde Sapte Charitable
  Trust
Harrow Community Trust
Leathersellers' Company
  Charitable Fund
Northern Rock Foundation
Jack Petchey Foundation
Woodroffe Benton Foundation

Will consider
Acacia Charitable Trust
Bearder Charity
Bedford Charity
Boots Charitable Trust
Bryant Trust
Wilfrid & Constance Cave
  Foundation
Coutts & Co. Charitable Trust
Cumber Family Charitable
  Trust
Joseph Hopkins Charity
Kirby Laing Foundation
Lloyds TSB Foundation for
  Scotland
Norman Family Charitable
  Trust
Peugeot Charity Trust
Eleanor Rathbone Charitable
  Trust
Ripple Effect Foundation
Rothley Trust
South Square Trust

....

■ Crime prevention
Funding priority
Britannia Building Society
  Foundation
Demigryphon Trust
Simon Gibson Charitable Trust
Greater Bristol Foundation
Greggs Trust
Charles Hayward Foundation
Hertfordshire Community
  Foundation
Clifford Howarth Charity
  Settlement
Sir James Knott Trust
Lloyds TSB Foundation for
  Channel Islands
Magdalen Hospital Trust
Merseyside Police and High
  Sheriff's Charitable Trust

Tony Metherell Charitable
  Trust
Noel Buxton Trust
Ronald & Kathleen Pryor
  Charitable Trust
St Thomas' Dole Charity
Sir James & Lady Scott Trust
Walter Swindon Charitable
  Trust
Third House Trust
Wates Foundation
Weavers' Company Benevolent
  Fund

Will consider
Adint Charitable Trust
Alcohol Education and
  Research Fund
Ammco Trust
Ardwick Trust
G C Armitage Charitable Trust
Ashby Charitable Trust
Astor Foundation
Bamford Charitable Foundation
John Bell Charitable Trust
Birmingham Foundation
Charles Boot Trust
Bridge House Estates Trust
  Fund
Roger Brooke Charitable Trust
Buckinghamshire Masonic
  Centenary Fund
Richard Cadbury Charitable
  Trust
Chase Charity
Chelsea Building Society
  Charitable Foundation
Chippenham Borough Lands
  Charity
J A Clark Charitable Trust
Cleopatra Trust
Colchester & Tendring
  Community Trust
Norman Collinson Charitable
  Trust
Community Foundation Serving
  Tyne & Wear and
  Northumberland
County Durham Foundation
Cripplegate Foundation
Derbyshire Community
  Foundation
DLM Charitable Trust
Dorus Trust
Dulverton Trust
Earley Charity
Wilfred & Elsie Elkes Charity
  Fund
Maud Elkington Charitable
  Trust
Elmgrant Trust
Epigoni Trust
Esmée Fairbairn Foundation
Lord Faringdon Charitable
  Trust
Fidelity UK Foundation

Earl Fitzwilliam Charitable
  Trust
Florence's Charitable Trust
Ford of Britain Trust
Gannochy Trust
J Paul Getty Jr Charitable Trust
GWR Community Trust
Hadrian Trust
Harborne Parish Lands Charity
Kenneth Hargreaves Charitable
  Trust
N & P Hartley Memorial Trust
Heart of England Community
  Foundation
Hemby Trust
Hilden Charitable Fund
Huddersfield Common Good
  Trust
Hyde Charitable Trust
Inchrye Trust
John Jarrold Trust
Johnson Foundation
Joicey Trust
Boris Karloff Charitable
  Foundation
Laing's Charitable Trust
David Laing Foundation
Maurice Laing Foundation
Lankelly Foundation
Lark Trust
Mrs F B Laurence Charitable
  Trust
Leigh Trust
Levy Foundation
Lloyd's Charities Trust
Lloyds TSB Foundation for
  England and Wales
Lloyds TSB Foundation for
  Northern Ireland
London Law Trust
Lyndhurst Settlement
M N R Charitable Trust
R W Mann Trustees Limited
Marchday Charitable Fund
Milton Keynes Community
  Foundation
George A Moore Foundation
Morgan Stanley International
  Foundation
Newby Trust Limited
Notgrove Trust
Oxfordshire Community
  Foundation
Harry Payne Trust
David Pickford Charitable
  Foundation
Bernard Piggott Trust
Simone Prendergast Charitable
  Trust
Rothley Trust
Christopher Rowbotham
  Charitable Trust
Royal London Aid Society
Shuttlewood Clarke Foundation
Henry Smith Charity

Steinberg Family Charitable
  Trust
Sir Halley Stewart Trust
Summerfield Charitable Trust
Swann-Morton Foundation
Sir Jules Thorn Charitable
  Trust
Wakefield Trust
Thomas Wall Trust
Wellfield Trust
Wesleyan Charitable Trust
Whitecourt Charitable Trust
Yorkshire Agricultural Society

....
■ Family planning and sex education
Funding priority
Ajahma Charitable Trust
George W Cadbury Charitable
  Trust
Camelot Foundation
Richard Cloudesley's Charity
Lloyds TSB Foundation for
  Channel Islands
Lyndhurst Settlement
Kitty and Daniel Nabarro
  Charitable Trust

Will consider
Barclays Stockbrokers
  Charitable Trust
Birmingham Foundation
Birmingham Hospital Saturday
  Fund Medical Charity &
  Welfare Trust
Richard Cadbury Charitable
  Trust
Community Foundation Serving
  Tyne & Wear and
  Northumberland
Consortium on Opportunities
  for Volunteering
Robert Gavron Charitable Trust
Greggs Trust
Harborne Parish Lands Charity
Charles Hayward Foundation
Jeffrey Charitable Trust
Jephcott Charitable Trust
Boris Karloff Charitable
  Foundation
Maurice and Hilda Laing
  Charitable Trust
Lloyds TSB Foundation for
  Northern Ireland
M N R Charitable Trust
Marsh Christian Trust
Milton Keynes Community
  Foundation
Notgrove Trust
Harry Payne Trust
Webb Memorial Trust
York Children's Trust

■ Prisons, penal reform

Funding priority

Ajahma Charitable Trust
Ashendene Trust
Barrow Cadbury Trust and
  Barrow Cadbury Fund
Chase Charity
J Paul Getty Jr Charitable Trust
Paul Hamlyn Foundation
Charles Hayward Foundation
Hilden Charitable Fund
Allen Lane Foundation
Lankelly Foundation
Paul Lunn-Rockliffe Charitable
  Trust
Lyndhurst Settlement
Noel Buxton Trust
Pilgrim Trust
Primrose Hill Trust
Wates Foundation
Weavers' Company Benevolent
  Fund

Will consider

1970 Trust
Alchemy Foundation
Bromley Trust
Carpenter Charitable Trust
Chownes Foundation
Community Foundation Serving
  Tyne & Wear and
  Northumberland
John Grant Davies Trust
Elmgrant Trust
Ericson Trust
Esmée Fairbairn Foundation
Jill Franklin Trust
H C D Memorial Fund
Anton Jurgens Charitable Trust
Beatrice Laing Trust
Maurice Laing Foundation
Mrs F B Laurence Charitable
  Trust
Lloyds TSB Foundation for
  England and Wales
Northmoor Trust
Nuffield Foundation
Odin Charitable Trust
Harry Payne Trust
Persula Foundation
David Pickford Charitable
  Foundation
Joseph Rank Trust
Mrs L D Rope Third Charitable
  Settlement
Royal London Aid Society
Summerfield Charitable Trust
Bernard Sunley Charitable
  Foundation
Tudor Trust
Woodward Trust

Community centres and activities

Funding priority

Aberbrothock Charitable Trust
BBC Radio Cambridgeshire –
  Trustline
R M 1956 Burton Charitable
  Trust
Denton Wilde Sapte Charitable
  Trust
Football Association National
  Sports Centre Trust
Harrow Community Trust
Hospital of God at Greatham
Paul Lunn-Rockliffe Charitable
  Trust
O-Regen
Patients' Aid Association
  Hospital & Medical
  Charities Trust
Paul Charitable Trust
Cliff Richard Charitable Trust
Sir James & Lady Scott Trust
Charity of Thomas Wade &
  Others
Wakefield Trust
Woodroffe Benton Foundation
Yorkshire Dales Millennium
  Trust

Will consider

Acacia Charitable Trust
Aston Villa Charitable Trust
Barclays Stockbrokers
  Charitable Trust
Bedford Charity
Beit Trust
Birmingham Foundation
Boots Charitable Trust
Roger Brooke Charitable Trust
Bryant Trust
E F Bulmer Benevolent Fund
Edward Cadbury Charitable
  Trust
Edward & Dorothy Cadbury
  Trust
Colchester & Tendring
  Community Trust
George Henry Collins Charity
Cumber Family Charitable
  Trust
Devon Community Foundation
William Dudley Trust
City of Edinburgh Charitable
  Trusts
Lord Faringdon Charitable
  Trust
Ganzoni Charitable Trust
Grantham Yorke Trust
GWR Community Trust
Hedgcock Bequest
P H Holt Charitable Trust
Joseph Hopkins Charity
Hyde Charitable Trust

Graham Kirkham Foundation
Lloyds TSB Foundation for
  England and Wales
Lloyds TSB Foundation for
  Scotland
Monmouthshire County Council
  Welsh Church Act Fund
Newby Trust Limited
North British Hotel Trust
Northampton Municipal Church
  Charities
Jack Petchey Foundation
Eleanor Rathbone Charitable
  Trust
Cecil Rosen Foundation
Rothley Trust
Saddlers' Company Charitable
  Fund
SMB Trust
South Yorkshire Community
  Foundation
Foundation of Edward Storey
VEC Acorn Trust
Bertie Watson Foundation

■ Community and social centres

Funding priority

Birmingham International
  Airport Community Trust
Carnegie United Kingdom Trust
Cleary Foundation
County Durham Foundation
Demigryphon Trust
Community Council of Devon
Essex Community Foundation
Four Lanes Trust
Freshgate Trust Foundation
Garthgwynion Charities
Simon Gibson Charitable Trust
Greater Bristol Foundation
Constance Green Foundation
Greggs Trust
Hampstead Wells and
  Campden Trust
Hampton Fuel Allotment
  Charity
Kathleen Hannay Memorial
  Charity
Lennox Hannay Charitable
  Trust
Harborne Parish Lands Charity
Kenneth Hargreaves Charitable
  Trust
Charles Hayward Foundation
Hedley Foundation
Clifford Howarth Charity
  Settlement
Incorporated Leeds Church
  Extension Society
James Pantyfedwen
  Foundation
Anton Jurgens Charitable Trust
Peter Kershaw Trust
Bryan Lancaster's Charity

Lauchentilly Charitable
   Foundation 1988
Leeds & Holbeck Building
   Society Charitable
   Foundation
W M & B W Lloyd Trust
Lockerbie Trust
Paul Lunn-Rockliffe Charitable
   Trust
Lynn Foundation
Macfarlane Walker Trust
Medlock Charitable Trust
Midhurst Pensions Trust
Minge's Gift
John Moores Foundation
Newstead Charity
Oakdale Trust
Park Hill Trust
Pilkington Charities Fund
J S F Pollitzer Charitable
   Settlement
Powys Welsh Church Fund
Ronald & Kathleen Pryor
   Charitable Trust
Puri Foundation
Clive Richards Charity Ltd
Richmond Parish Lands Charity
Rosca Trust
Skelton Bounty
Ralph and Irma Sperring
   Charity
Thoresby Charitable Trust
Tompkins Foundation
Charity of Thomas Wade &
   Others
Wates Foundation

Will consider

1970 Trust
29th May 1961 Charitable
   Trust
Adnams Charity
Alchemy Foundation
Allachy Trust
Dorothy Gertrude Allen
   Memorial Fund
H B Allen Charitable Trust
Ammco Trust
Viscount Amory's Charitable
   Trust
Sir John & Lady Amory's
   Charitable Trust
Ancaster Trust
Andrew Anderson Trust
Milly Apthorp Charitable Trust
Ardwick Trust
Armenian General Benevolent
   Union London Trust
ATP Charitable Trust
Bacta Charitable Trust
Balcombe Charitable Trust
Albert Casanova Ballard
   Deceased Trust
Bamford Charitable Foundation
Barbour Trust

David and Frederick Barclay
   Foundation
Philip Barker Charity
Peter Barker-Mill Memorial
   Charity
Barnes Workhouse Fund
Barnsbury Charitable Trust
BBC Children in Need Appeal
BBC Radio Lincolnshire Charity
   Trust
Bearder Charity
James Beattie Charitable Trust
Peter Beckwith Charitable
   Trust
John Bell Charitable Trust
Benham Charitable Settlement
Berkshire Community
   Foundation
Bingham Trust
Peter Birse Charitable Trust
Peter Black Charitable Trust
Blanchminster Trust
Booth Charities
Boots Charitable Trust
Bridge House Estates Trust
   Fund
Bridge Trust
British Humane Association
Charles Brotherton Trust
Swinfen Broun Charitable Trust
Bryant Trust
Buckinghamshire Masonic
   Centenary Fund
E F Bulmer Benevolent Fund
Burdens Charitable Foundation
Geoffrey Burton Charitable
   Trust
George W Cadbury Charitable
   Trust
Richard Cadbury Charitable
   Trust
William A Cadbury Charitable
   Trust
Cairns Charitable Trust
Carnegie Dunfermline Trust
Wilfrid & Constance Cave
   Foundation
Cemlyn-Jones Trust
Chandris Foundation
Chapman Charitable Trust
Charities Advisory Trust
Chase Charity
Chippenham Borough Lands
   Charity
Chipping Sodbury Town Lands
   Charity
Church Urban Fund
Lord Clinton's Charitable Trust
Robert Clutterbuck Charitable
   Trust
Coates Charitable Settlement
Coats Foundation Trust
Denise Cohen Charitable Trust
Cole Charitable Trust
Norman Collinson Charitable
   Trust

Sir James Colyer-Fergusson's
   Charitable Trust
Community Foundation Serving
   Tyne & Wear and
   Northumberland
Congleton Inclosure Trust
Consortium on Opportunities
   for Volunteering
Construction Industry Trust for
   Youth
County of Gloucestershire
   Community Foundation
John Cowan Foundation
Lord Cozens-Hardy Trust
Cranbury Foundation
Michael Crawford Children's
   Charity
Cray Trust
Criffel Charitable Trust
Cripplegate Foundation
Harry Crook Foundation
Cwmbran Trust
Daily Telegraph Charitable
   Trust
De Clermont Charitable
   Company Ltd
Helen and Geoffrey de Freitas
   Charitable Trust
Derbyshire Community
   Foundation
DLM Charitable Trust
Double 'O' Charity Ltd
Duis Charitable Trust
Dulverton Trust
Earley Charity
Eden Arts Trust
Gilbert & Eileen Edgar
   Foundation
Wilfred & Elsie Elkes Charity
   Fund
Maud Elkington Charitable
   Trust
Edith M Ellis 1985 Charitable
   Trust
Elmgrant Trust
Eranda Foundation
Esmée Fairbairn Foundation
Fairway Trust
Samuel William Farmer's Trust
Fidelity UK Foundation
Doris Field Charitable Trust
Earl Fitzwilliam Charitable
   Trust
Joyce Fletcher Charitable Trust
Florence's Charitable Trust
Ford of Britain Trust
Foresters' Charity Stewards
   UK Trust
Fortuna Charitable Trust
Fox Memorial Trust
Thomas Freke & Lady Norton
   Charity
Charles S French Charitable
   Trust
Fund for Human Need
Gannochy Trust

Gatwick Airport Community Trust
Sydney & Phyllis Goldberg Memorial Charitable Trust
Gosling Foundation Ltd
Gough Charitable Trust
J G Graves Charitable Trust
Mrs H R Greene Charitable Settlement
Grocers' Charity
Walter Guinness Charitable Trust
Hackney Parochial Charities
Hadfield Trust
Hadrian Trust
Robert Hall Charity
Hanley Trust
Hare of Steep Charitable Trust
Gay & Peter Hartley's Hillards Charitable Trust
Haymills Charitable Trust
May Hearnshaw's Charity
Heart of England Community Foundation
Help Aged
Hemby Trust
Hertfordshire Community Foundation
Hesslewood Children's Trust
Hillingdon Partnership Trust
Hobson Charity Ltd
Holywood Trust
Sir Harold Hood's Charitable Trust
Hoover Foundation
HopMarket Charity
James Thom Howat Charitable Trust
Huddersfield Common Good Trust
Human Relief Foundation
Hyde Park Place Estate Charity
Imerys South West Charitable Trust
Inman Charity
Ireland Fund of Great Britain
Ironmongers' Quincentenary Charitable Fund
Charles Irving Charitable Trust
Isle of Dogs Community Foundation
ITF Seafarers Trust
Jarman Charitable Trust
John Jarrold Trust
Jeffrey Charitable Trust
Joicey Trust
Jones 1986 Charitable Trust
Edward Cecil Jones Settlement
Michael & Ilse Katz Foundation
Emmanuel Kaye Foundation
Mary Kinross Charitable Trust
Kirkley Poor's Land Estate
Sir James Knott Trust
Kreditor Charitable Trust
Kirby Laing Foundation
Langdale Trust

Lankelly Foundation
R J Larg Family Charitable Trust
Lawlor Foundation
Raymond & Blanche Lawson Charitable Trust
William Leech Charity
Leng Charitable Trust
Lord Leverhulme Charitable Trust
Ralph Levy Charitable Company Ltd
Linden Charitable Trust
Lintel Trust
Elaine & Angus Lloyd Charitable Trust
Lloyds TSB Foundation for Northern Ireland
Lloyds TSB Foundation for Channel Islands
Lofthouse Foundation
Michael Lowe's & Associated Charities
C L Loyd Charitable Trust
Luck-Hille Foundation
Lyndhurst Settlement
John Lyon's Charity
Lyons Charitable Trust
Mackintosh Foundation
Helen Isabella McMorran Charitable Foundation
Magdalen Hospital Trust
Manchester Airport Community Trust Fund
Manifold Trust
R W Mann Trustees Limited
Victor Mann Trust
Linda Marcus Charitable Trust
Hilda & Samuel Marks Foundation
Michael Marsh Charitable Trust
D G Marshall of Cambridge Trust
Sir George Martin Trust
John Martin's Charity
Merchant Taylors' Company Charities Fund
Tony Metherell Charitable Trust
Methodist Relief and Development Fund
Gerald Micklem Charitable Trust
Middlesex County Rugby Football Union Memorial Fund
Miller Foundation
Milton Keynes Community Foundation
Peter Minet Trust
Mobbs Memorial Trust Ltd
Monmouthshire County Council Welsh Church Act Fund
Horace Moore Charitable Trust

Nigel Moores Family Charitable Trust
Morel Charitable Trust
Morgan Crucible Company plc Charitable Trust
Morris Charitable Trust
Mr and Mrs F E F Newman Charitable Trust
Newport County Borough Welsh Church Fund
Northcott Devon Foundation
Northern Rock Foundation
Norwich Consolidated Charities
Norwich Historic Churches Trust Ltd
Norwich Town Close Estate Charity
Noswad Charity
Oakley Charitable Trust
Old Enfield Charitable Trust
Owen Family Trust
Oxford Preservation Trust
Oxfordshire Community Foundation
Arthur James Paterson Charitable Trust
Constance Paterson Charitable Trust
Pennycress Trust
Personal Assurance Charitable Trust
Bernard Piggott Trust
A M Pilkington's Charitable Trust
Cecil Pilkington Charitable Trust
Col W W Pilkington Will Trusts
John Pitman Charitable Trust
G S Plaut Charitable Trust
Powell Foundation
Prince Philip Trust Fund
Princess Anne's Charities
Proven Family Trust
Puri Foundation
Mr and Mrs J A Pye's Charitable Settlement
Radio Forth Help a Child Appeal
Rank Foundation
Rawdon-Smith Trust
John Rayner Charitable Trust
Sir James Reckitt Charity
Red Dragon Radio Trust
Rhododendron Trust
Rhondda Cynon Taff Welsh Church Acts Fund
Cliff Richard Charitable Trust
Richmond Parish Lands Charity
Helen Roll Charitable Trust
C A Rookes Charitable Trust
Cecil Rosen Foundation
Rothley Trust
Christopher Rowbotham Charitable Trust
Rowlands Trust

Royal Docks Trust
Russell Trust
Alan and Babette Sainsbury
    Charitable Fund
St Hilda's Trust
St James' Trust Settlement
St Katharine & Shadwell Trust
St Mary-le-Strand Charity
St Thomas Ecclesiastical
    Charity
Peter Samuel Charitable Trust
Sandra Charitable Trust
Schroder Charity Trust
Scotbelge Charitable Trust
Francis C Scott Charitable
    Trust
Scottish Churches Community
    Trust
Scottish Community
    Foundation
Scottish International
    Education Trust
Samuel Sebba Charitable
    Trust
Sedbury Trust
Sefton Community Foundation
Sellafield Charity Trust Fund
Shakespeare Temperance
    Trust
Shaw Lands Trust
Shepherd Street Trust
Sherburn House Charity
R C Sherriff Rosebriars Trust
Barnett & Sylvia Shine No 2
    Charitable Trust
Philip Smith's Charitable Trust
Sobell Foundation
E C Sosnow Charitable Trust
W W Spooner Charitable Trust
Foundation for Sport and Arts
Sportsman's Charity
Steel Charitable Trust
Steinberg Family Charitable
    Trust
Steventon Allotments & Relief-
    in-Need Charity
Leonard Laity Stoate
    Charitable Trust
Sueberry Ltd
Summerfield Charitable Trust
Bernard Sunley Charitable
    Foundation
Sutton Coldfield Municipal
    Charities
Charles and Elsie Sykes Trust
Stella Symons Charitable Trust
Tay Charitable Trust
C B & H H Taylor 1984 Trust
Tesco Charity Trust
Thompson Charitable Trust
Len Thomson Charitable Trust
Tory Family Foundation
Tudor Trust
Douglas Turner Trust
Florence Turner Trust
R D Turner Charitable Trust

United St Saviour's Charities
United Trusts
Bernard Van Leer Foundation
Eric W Vincent Trust Fund
Scurrah Wainwright Charity
Wakeham Trust
Thomas Wall Trust
Mrs Waterhouse Charitable
    Trust
Weavers' Company Benevolent
    Fund
Mary Webb Trust
Webb Memorial Trust
William Webster Charitable
    Trust
Barbara Welby Trust
Wellfield Trust
Westcroft Trust
Westminster Amalgamated
    Charity
Garfield Weston Foundation
Sheila Whitley Trust
William Williams Charity
Michael and Anna Wix
    Charitable Trust
Women Caring Trust
Woodward Trust
Woolnoth Society Charitable
    Trust
Worcester Municipal Charities
Wyseliot Charitable Trust
Yardley Great Trust
W Wing Yip & Bros Charitable
    Trust
York Children's Trust
Yorkshire Building Society
    Charitable Foundation
William Allen Young Charitable
    Trust

....

■ Community outings and holidays

Funding priority
Astor of Hever Trust
Angela Gallagher Memorial
    Fund
Greater Bristol Foundation
Alfred Haines Charitable Trust
Leeds & Holbeck Building
    Society Charitable
    Foundation
Lloyds TSB Foundation for
    Channel Islands
London Youth Trust
Lynn Foundation
Pilkington Charities Fund
Ronald & Kathleen Pryor
    Charitable Trust
Stanton Ballard Charitable
    Trust
Charity of Thomas Wade &
    Others

Will consider
Adint Charitable Trust
Adnams Charity
Barbour Trust
BBC Children in Need Appeal
Bryant Trust
Buckinghamshire Masonic
    Centenary Fund
E F Bulmer Benevolent Fund
Chamberlain Foundation
Chippenham Borough Lands
    Charity
CLA Charitable Trust
Lord Clinton's Charitable Trust
County Durham Foundation
County of Gloucestershire
    Community Foundation
De Clermont Charitable
    Company Ltd
Helen and Geoffrey de Freitas
    Charitable Trust
Duis Charitable Trust
Fox Memorial Trust
Timothy Franey Charitable
    Foundation
Charles S French Charitable
    Trust
Constance Green Foundation
Greggs Trust
Hadrian Trust
Harborne Parish Lands Charity
N & P Hartley Memorial Trust
Huddersfield Common Good
    Trust
Isle of Dogs Community
    Foundation
Jarman Charitable Trust
Johnson Group Cleaners
    Charity
Lloyds TSB Foundation for
    Northern Ireland
Paul Lunn-Rockliffe Charitable
    Trust
Magdalen Hospital Trust
R W Mann Trustees Limited
Marsh Christian Trust
Mickel Fund
Middlesex County Rugby
    Football Union Memorial
    Fund
Peter Minet Trust
Northcott Devon Foundation
Norwich Consolidated
    Charities
Old Enfield Charitable Trust
Oxfordshire Community
    Foundation
John Pitman Charitable Trust
Powell Foundation
Powys Welsh Church Fund
Prince Philip Trust Fund
Rainford Trust
Cliff Richard Charitable Trust
Christopher Rowbotham
    Charitable Trust
Russell Trust

St Mary-le-Strand Charity
R H Scholes Charitable Trust
Francis C Scott Charitable
  Trust
Skelton Bounty
Steinberg Family Charitable
  Trust
Sutton Coldfield Municipal
  Charities
Wakeham Trust
Thomas Wall Trust
Westminster Amalgamated
  Charity
Woodward Trust
Yardley Great Trust
Yorkshire Building Society
  Charitable Foundation

....

■ Community transport

Funding priority

Bridge House Estates Trust
  Fund
Simon Gibson Charitable Trust
Greater Bristol Foundation
Greggs Trust
Hertfordshire Community
  Foundation
Ronald & Kathleen Pryor
  Charitable Trust
Sobell Foundation
Thoresby Charitable Trust
Charity of Thomas Wade &
  Others
Wiltshire and Swindon
  Community Foundation

Will consider

Adnams Charity
Age Concern Scotland
  Enterprise Fund
Viscount Amory's Charitable
  Trust
Ashby Charitable Trust
Astor Foundation
BAA 21st Century
  Communities Trust
Badley Memorial Trust
Percy Bilton Charity Ltd
Bryant Trust
Buckinghamshire Masonic
  Centenary Fund
E F Bulmer Benevolent Fund
Norman Collinson Charitable
  Trust
Community Foundation Serving
  Tyne & Wear and
  Northumberland
Consortium on Opportunities
  for Volunteering
County of Gloucestershire
  Community Foundation
Criffel Charitable Trust
Cripplegate Foundation
Demigryphon Trust

Derbyshire Community
  Foundation
Wilfred & Elsie Elkes Charity
  Fund
Elmgrant Trust
Fidelity UK Foundation
Earl Fitzwilliam Charitable
  Trust
Ford of Britain Trust
Four Lanes Trust
Fox Memorial Trust
Frognal Trust
Gannochy Trust
Gatwick Airport Community
  Trust
J G Graves Charitable Trust
Constance Green Foundation
Hadfield Trust
Hadrian Trust
Robert Hall Charity
Hallam FM – Help a Hallam
  Child Appeal
Harborne Parish Lands Charity
Charles Hayward Foundation
Hemby Trust
Holywood Trust
James Thom Howat Charitable
  Trust
Isle of Dogs Community
  Foundation
James Pantyfedwen
  Foundation
John Jarrold Trust
Jeffrey Charitable Trust
Jesus Hospital Charity
Joicey Trust
Anton Jurgens Charitable Trust
Sir James Knott Trust
Beatrice Laing Trust
David Laing Foundation
Mrs F B Laurence Charitable
  Trust
Leach Fourteenth Trust
Lloyd's Charities Trust
Lloyds TSB Foundation for
  Northern Ireland
Lloyds TSB Foundation for
  Channel Islands
M N R Charitable Trust
R W Mann Trustees Limited
Sir George Martin Trust
Middlesex County Rugby
  Football Union Memorial
  Fund
Milton Keynes Community
  Foundation
Morgan Stanley International
  Foundation
North London Islamic
  Association Trust
Old Enfield Charitable Trust
Oxfordshire Community
  Foundation
Patients' Aid Association
  Hospital & Medical
  Charities Trust

Peugeot Charity Trust
A M Pilkington's Charitable
  Trust
John Pitman Charitable Trust
Powell Foundation
Prince Philip Trust Fund
Pye Foundation
Rawdon-Smith Trust
Cliff Richard Charitable Trust
Rothley Trust
Christopher Rowbotham
  Charitable Trust
Francis C Scott Charitable
  Trust
Scottish Churches Community
  Trust
Sellafield Charity Trust Fund
Sherburn House Charity
Shuttlewood Clarke Foundation
Skelton Bounty
Henry Smith Charity
Summerfield Charitable Trust
Tesco Charity Trust
Sir Jules Thorn Charitable
  Trust
Unemployed Voluntary Action
  Fund
Voluntary Action Luton
Thomas Wall Trust
Wates Foundation
Webb Memorial Trust
Wellfield Trust
Wesleyan Charitable Trust
Westminster Amalgamated
  Charity
Woodward Trust
Worcester Municipal Charities
Yardley Great Trust

Emergency response

Funding priority

Aberbrothock Charitable Trust
Huxham Charitable Trust
Trust Sixty Three
Miss E B Wrightson's
  Charitable Settlement

Will consider

Ardwick Trust
Bedford Charity
Birmingham Hospital Saturday
  Fund Medical Charity &
  Welfare Trust
Roger Brooke Charitable Trust
E F Bulmer Benevolent Fund
CAFOD
Wilfrid & Constance Cave
  Foundation
Chippenham Borough Lands
  Charity
George Henry Collins Charity
Coutts & Co. Charitable Trust

City of Edinburgh Charitable
Trusts
Maud Elkington Charitable
Trust
Kenneth Hargreaves Charitable
Trust
Joseph Hopkins Charity
Boris Karloff Charitable
Foundation
Marr-Munning Trust
Monmouthshire County Council
Welsh Church Act Fund
Newby Trust Limited
Pastoral Care Trust
Eleanor Rathbone Charitable
Trust
Saddlers' Company Charitable
Fund
Bernard Sunley Charitable
Foundation

....

■ Rehabilitation

Funding priority

BibleLands
Lloyds TSB Foundation for
Channel Islands
Lynn Foundation

Will consider

E F Bulmer Benevolent Fund
Dunhill Medical Trust
Lloyds TSB Foundation for
Northern Ireland
Paul Lunn-Rockliffe Charitable
Trust
Northcott Devon Foundation
Northern Rock Foundation
William Webster Charitable
Trust

....

■ Relief assistance

Funding priority

Pat Allsop Charitable Trust
BibleLands
Charles Boot Trust
Britten Foundation
Audrey & Stanley Burton
Charitable Trust
Christadelphian Samaritan
Fund
Christian Aid
Miriam K Dean Refugee Trust
Fund
Dinam Charity
Edith M Ellis 1985 Charitable
Trust
Norman Evershed Trust
Family Rich Charities Trust
Fund for Human Need
Harbour Foundation
Joanna Herbert-Stepney
Charitable Settlement
Highmoor Hall Charitable Trust

Human Relief Foundation
Huxham Charitable Trust
Jeffrey Charitable Trust
Lloyds TSB Foundation for
Channel Islands
Magdalen Hospital Trust
Muslim Hands
Nestlé Rowntree York
Employees Community Fund
Trust
Novi Most International
Philanthropic Trust
Sir James & Lady Scott Trust
Shanti Charitable Trust
E C Sosnow Charitable Trust
Stobart Newlands Charitable
Trust
Walter Swindon Charitable
Trust
Charles and Elsie Sykes Trust
Rosanna Taylor's 1987 Charity
Trust
Loke Wan Tho Memorial
Foundation
Three Oaks Trust
TRAID
Trust Sixty Three
Roger Vere Foundation

Will consider

Adint Charitable Trust
Adnams Charity
Lord Ashdown Charitable Trust
Astor Foundation
Peter Black Charitable Trust
E F Bulmer Benevolent Fund
Carpenter Charitable Trust
Coppings Trust
County of Gloucestershire
Community Foundation
Criffel Charitable Trust
Cripplegate Foundation
Helen and Geoffrey de Freitas
Charitable Trust
Derbyshire Community
Foundation
Duis Charitable Trust
Dulverton Trust
Wilfred & Elsie Elkes Charity
Fund
Emmandjay Charitable Trust
Fidelity UK Foundation
Sydney E Franklin Deceased's
New Second Charity
Constance Green Foundation
Greggs Trust
H C D Memorial Fund
Hadrian Trust
Harborne Parish Lands Charity
Harrison & Potter Trust
Hilden Charitable Fund
John Jarrold Trust
Joicey Trust
Bryan Lancaster's Charity
Mrs F B Laurence Charitable
Trust

Leach Fourteenth Trust
Kennedy Leigh Charitable
Trust
Leonard Trust
Linden Charitable Trust
Lintel Trust
Lloyds TSB Foundation for
Northern Ireland
M N R Charitable Trust
Helen Isabella McMorran
Charitable Foundation
Marchday Charitable Fund
Marr-Munning Trust
Marsh Christian Trust
Keith and Joan Mindelsohn
Charitable Trust
Mitchell Trust
Northcott Devon Foundation
Ogle Christian Trust
Parthenon Trust
Harry Payne Trust
A M Pilkington's Charitable
Trust
Puri Foundation
Rainford Trust
Ranworth Trust
Red Dragon Radio Trust
Rufford Foundation
Scott Bader Commonwealth
Ltd
Servite Sisters' Charitable
Trust Fund
SMB Trust
Henry Smith Charity
Stanley Foundation Ltd
Foundation of Edward Storey
Sir Jules Thorn Charitable
Trust
Tisbury Telegraph Trust
Tory Family Foundation
Triodos Foundation
United Society for Propagation
of Gospel
Wellfield Trust
Michael and Anna Wix
Charitable Trust
Yardley Great Trust

Beneficial groups
Age

■ Children (up to 11)
Funding priority
Acacia Charitable Trust
Access 4 Trust
Miss Agnes Gilchrist
 Adamson's Trust
Sylvia Aitken Charitable Trust
Aldgate and All Hallows
 Barking Exhibition
 Foundation
Alliance Family Foundation
Pat Allsop Charitable Trust
Ardwick Trust
ARK
Ashe Park Charitable Trust
Associated Country Women of
 the World
Aston Villa Charitable Trust
Astor of Hever Trust
ATP Charitable Trust
Lord Austin Trust
B-C H 1971 Charitable Trust
BAA 21st Century
 Communities Trust
Balcraig Foundation
Balmore Trust
Bamford Charitable Foundation
Band (1976) Trust
Philip Barker Charity
Bartle Family Charitable Trust
Paul Bassham Charitable Trust
BBC Children in Need Appeal
Beaufort House Trust
Beaurepaire Trust
John Beckwith Charitable Trust
Belvedere Trust
Hervey Benham Charitable
 Trust
Bestway Foundation
Bethesda Community
 Charitable Trust
Thomas Betton's Charity
 (Educational)
BibleLands
Bier Charitable Settlement
Bintaub Charitable Trust
Birmingham Foundation
Birmingham Hospital Saturday
 Fund Medical Charity &
 Welfare Trust
Enid Blyton Trust for Children
Sir William Boreman's
 Foundation
Bowland Charitable Trust
Tony Bramall Charitable Trust
Bramble Charitable Trust
Bridge House Estates Trust
 Fund
Bristol Charities
Charles Brotherton Trust
R S Brownless Charitable
 Trust

Buckinghamshire Masonic
 Centenary Fund
Clara E Burgess Charity
Bill Butlin Charity Trust
Edward & Dorothy Cadbury
 Trust (1928)
Cadbury Schweppes
 Foundation
Caring for Kids
Carlton House Charitable Trust
Carlton Television Trust
Carpenters' Company
 Charitable Trust
Casey Trust
Cash for Kids
Sir John Cass's Foundation
Celtic Charity Fund
Chatwin Trust
Child Growth Foundation
Children's Research Fund
Church Burgesses Educational
 Foundation
Hilda & Alice Clark Charitable
 Trust
Cleary Foundation
Lord Clinton's Charitable Trust
Clover Trust
Coates Charitable Settlement
John Coates Charitable Trust
Cobb Charity
Denise Cohen Charitable Trust
Vivienne & Samuel Cohen
 Charitable Trust
Col-Reno Ltd
Cole Charitable Trust
E Alec Colman Charitable Fund
 Ltd
Community Foundation Serving
 Tyne & Wear and
 Northumberland
Community Fund
Ernest Cook Trust
Gordon Cook Foundation
Sir William Coxen Trust Fund
Michael Crawford Children's
 Charity
Crescent Trust
Cumber Family Charitable
 Trust
Suzanne & Raymond Curtis
 Foundation
Roald Dahl Foundation
Daily Telegraph Charitable
 Trust
Baron Davenport's Charity
David Charitable Trust
Gwendoline & Margaret Davies
 Charity
John Grant Davies Trust
Dawe Charitable Trust
De Clermont Charitable
 Company Ltd
Peter De Haan Charitable
 Trust
De La Rue Charitable Trust
Denton Charitable Trust

Denton Wilde Sapte Charitable
 Trust
Derbyshire Community
 Foundation
Richard Desmond Charitable
 Trust
Devon Community Foundation
Devon Educational Trust
Diamond Industry Educational
 Charity
Dibden Allotments Charity
Dinam Charity
Double 'O' Charity Ltd
Dyers' Company Charitable
 Trust
Gilbert Edgar Trust
Edinburgh Children's Holiday
 Fund
Edinburgh Voluntary
 Organisations' Trust Funds
William Edwards Educational
 Charity
Wilfred & Elsie Elkes Charity
 Fund
Ellis Campbell Charitable
 Foundation
Dorothy Whitney Elmhirst Trust
Emerton-Christie Charity
English Schools' Football
 Association
Famos Foundation Trust
Fassnidge Memorial Trust
Joseph Fattorini Charitable
 Trust 'B' Account
John Feeney Charitable
 Bequest
Fiat Auto (UK) Charity
Doris Field Charitable Trust
Finnart House School Trust
Joyce Fletcher Charitable Trust
Roy Fletcher Charitable Trust
Gerald Fogel Charitable Trust
Football Association National
 Sports Centre Trust
Football Association Youth
 Trust
Forte Charitable Trust
Four Lanes Trust
Timothy Franey Charitable
 Foundation
Isaac and Freda Frankel
 Memorial Charitable Trust
Thomas Freke & Lady Norton
 Charity
Charles S French Charitable
 Trust
Freshgate Trust Foundation
Mejer and Gertrude Miriam
 Frydman Foundation
Angela Gallagher Memorial
 Fund
Gannochy Trust
Gatsby Charitable Foundation
Glass-House Trust
Global Care
Good Neighbours Trust

Gough Charitable Trust
Gould Charitable Trust
Grantham Yorke Trust
Greater Bristol Foundation
Constance Green Foundation
J C Green Charitable
  Settlement
Greggs Trust
Gulbenkian Foundation
Dr Guthrie's Association
Hackney Parochial Charities
Hale Trust
E F & M G Hall Charitable
  Trust
Hallam FM – Help a Hallam
  Child Appeal
Eleanor Hamilton Educational
  and Charitable Trust
Paul Hamlyn Foundation
Handicapped Children's Aid
  Committee
Haramead Trust
Harbour Charitable Trust
William Harding's Charity
Harebell Centenary Fund
Kenneth Hargreaves Charitable
  Trust
Harris Charity
Peter Harrison Foundation
N & P Hartley Memorial Trust
M A Hawe Settlement
Haymills Charitable Trust
Charles Hayward Foundation
H J Heinz Company Limited
  Charitable Trust
Help a London Child
Henley Educational Charity
Joanna Herbert-Stepney
  Charitable Settlement
Hertfordshire Community
  Foundation
Alan Edward Higgs Charity
Joseph & Mary Hiley Trust
Homelands Charitable Trust
Joseph Hopkins Charity
Hospital of God at Greatham
Rita Lila Howard Foundation
Huddersfield Common Good
  Trust
Hyde Charitable Trust
Imerys South West Charitable
  Trust
Irish Youth Foundation (UK)
  Ltd
Ironmongers' Quincentenary
  Charitable Fund
Isle of Dogs Community
  Foundation
J J Charitable Trust
James Pantyfedwen
  Foundation
Jeffrey Charitable Trust
Jewish Child's Day
Jewish Youth Fund
JMK Charitable Trust
Elton John Aids Foundation

Lillie Johnson Charitable Trust
Judith Trust
Anton Jurgens Charitable Trust
David Laing Foundation
Maurice and Hilda Laing
  Charitable Trust
John and Rosemary Lancaster
  Charitable Foundation
Richard Langhorn Trust
Laslett's (Hinton) Charity
Rachel & Jack Lass Charities
  Ltd
Lauchentilly Charitable
  Foundation 1988
Edgar E Lawley Foundation
Lawson Charitable Foundation
Arnold Lee Charitable Trust
Leeds & Holbeck Building
  Society Charitable
  Foundation
Kennedy Leigh Charitable
  Trust
Mark Leonard Trust
Lethendy Charitable Trust
John Spedan Lewis Foundation
John Lewis Partnership
  General Community Fund
Lister Charitable Trust
Elaine & Angus Lloyd
  Charitable Trust
Lloyds TSB Foundation for
  Scotland
Lofthouse Foundation
London Law Trust
London Youth Trust
Lord's Taverners
Lotus Foundation
Paul Lunn-Rockliffe Charitable
  Trust
Lynn Foundation
John Lyon's Charity
Lyons Charitable Trust
Madeline Mabey Trust
E M MacAndrew Trust
R S MacDonald Charitable
  Trust
Ronald McDonald Children's
  Charities Limited
Helen Isabella McMorran
  Charitable Foundation
Magdalen Hospital Trust
Mandeville Trust
Jim Marshall Charitable Trust
Masonic Trust for Girls and
  Boys
Evelyn May Trust
Mayfair Charities Ltd
Medlock Charitable Trust
Anthony and Elizabeth Mellows
  Charitable Settlement
Mickel Fund
Middlesex County Rugby
  Football Union Memorial
  Fund
Miller Foundation
Mole Charitable Trust

Horace Moore Charitable Trust
Morgan Crucible Company plc
  Charitable Trust
J P Morgan Fleming
  Educational Trust and
  Foundation
Morgan Stanley International
  Foundation
Mount 'A' Charitable Trust
Mount 'B' Charitable Trust
Mugdock Children's Trust
Music Sales Charitable Trust
Music Sound Foundation
Muslim Hands
Newcomen Collett Foundation
Newport County Borough
  Welsh Church Fund
J F Newsome Charitable Trust
Noel Buxton Trust
Alderman Norman's
  Foundation
Northampton Queen's Institute
  Relief in Sickness Fund
Northern Rock Foundation
Northumberland Village Homes
  Trust
Norton Foundation
Nova Charitable Trust
Novi Most International
Old Broad Street Charity Trust
Oppenheimer Charitable Trust
Oxfordshire Community
  Foundation
Parivar Trust
Alan Pascoe Charitable Trust
Pastoral Care Trust
Arthur James Paterson
  Charitable Trust
Constance Paterson Charitable
  Trust
Peacock Charitable Trust
Frank Pearson Foundation
Austin & Hope Pilkington Trust
Col W W Pilkington Will Trusts
  – The General Charity Fund
Plymouth Sound Trust – The
  Magic Appeal
John Porter Charitable Trust
Portishead Nautical Trust
Powys Welsh Church Fund
William Price Charitable Trust
Sir John Priestman Charity
  Trust
Princess Anne's Charities
Privy Purse Charitable Trust
Ronald & Kathleen Pryor
  Charitable Trust
Puri Foundation
Mr and Mrs J A Pye's
  Charitable Settlement
Radio Forth Help a Child
  Appeal
Rayne Foundation
Rayne Trust
John Rayner Charitable Trust
Red Dragon Radio Trust

Rhondda Cynon Taff Welsh
   Church Acts Fund
Cliff Richard Charitable Trust
Clive Richards Charity Ltd
Rivendell Trust
Rooke Atlay Charitable Trust
Rothley Trust
Royal Eastern Counties
   Schools Limited
J B Rubens Charitable
   Foundation
Rycroft Children's Fund
Karim Rida Said Foundation
St James's Place Foundation
St James' Trust Settlement
Sir Walter St John's
   Educational Charity
Scott Bader Commonwealth
   Ltd
John Scott Trust
Scouloudi Foundation
Search
Sedbury Trust
SEM Charitable Trust
Ayrton Senna Foundation
Shaftoe Educational
   Foundation
Shakespeare Temperance
   Trust
Shaw Lands Trust
Sheffield Bluecoat & Mount
   Pleasant Educational
   Foundation
Sylvia & Colin Shepherd
   Charitable Trust
SHINE
Barbara A Shuttleworth
   Memorial Trust
Bishop Simeon CR Trust
Skelton Bounty
Snowball Trust
Sobell Foundation
W F Southall Trust
Southover Manor General
   Education Trust
Spitalfields Market Community
   Trust
Stanley Spooner Deceased
   Charitable Trust
Sportsman's Charity
Stanton Ballard Charitable
   Trust
Educational Charity of the
   Stationers' and Newspaper
   Makers' Company
Stewards' Charitable Trust
Peter Stormonth Darling
   Charitable Trust
Sueberry Ltd
Sutton Trust
Walter Swindon Charitable
   Trust
Swire Charitable Trust
Talbot Village Trust
Talteg Ltd

Rosanna Taylor's 1987 Charity
   Trust
Tesco Charity Trust
Thames Community
   Foundation
Sue Thomson Foundation
Tower Hill Improvement Trust
Fred Towler Charity Trust
Towry Law Charitable Trust
Toy Trust
Trades House of Glasgow
Truedene Co. Ltd
Trusthouse Charitable
   Foundation
Ulverston Town Lands Charity
John and Lucille van Geest
   Foundation
Bernard Van Leer Foundation
Mrs Maud Van Norden's
   Charitable Foundation
Variety Club Children's Charity
Victoria Homes Trust
Voluntary Action Luton
Walker Trust
Waterside Trust
John Watson's Trust
West London Synagogue
   Charitable Fund
Western Recreation Trust
Felicity Wilde Charitable Trust
William Williams Charity
Dame Violet Wills Will Trust
Women Caring Trust
Woo Charitable Foundation
Miss Hazel M Wood Charitable
   Trust
Woodward Trust
Woolnoth Society Charitable
   Trust
Xerox (UK) Trust
York Children's Trust
Yorkshire Bank Charitable
   Trust
Yorkshire Building Society
   Charitable Foundation
Yorkshire County Cricket Club
   Charitable Youth Trust

Will consider

Sylvia Adams Charitable Trust
Adint Charitable Trust
Alchemy Foundation
Angus Allnatt Charitable
   Foundation
Ambika Paul Foundation
Ammco Trust
Viscount Amory's Charitable
   Trust
Mary Andrew Charitable Trust
Anglo Hong Kong Trust
Appletree Trust
Arts Council of Wales
A J H Ashby Will Trust
Lord Ashdown Charitable Trust
Ashendene Trust
Balcombe Charitable Trust

Andrew Balint Charitable Trust
George Balint Charitable Trust
Paul Balint Charitable Trust
Albert Casanova Ballard
   Deceased Trust
David and Frederick Barclay
   Foundation
Beacon Trust
Bedford Charity
E M Behrens Charitable Trust
Bergqvist Charitable Trust
Percy Bilton Charity Ltd
Bingham Trust
Peter Birse Charitable Trust
Michael Bishop Foundation
Bishop's Development Fund
Isabel Blackman Foundation
Herbert & Peter Blagrave
   Charitable Trust
Blair Foundation
Morgan Blake Charitable Trust
Blanchminster Trust
Blatchington Court Trust
Harry Bottom Charitable Trust
Anthony Bourne Foundation
Harold and Alice Bridges
   Charity
John Bristow and Thomas
   Mason Trust
British Record Industry Trust
David Brooke Charity
Miss Marion Broughton's
   Charitable Trust
Bulldog Trust
Burden Trust
Edward Cadbury Charitable
   Trust
Richard Cadbury Charitable
   Trust
William A Cadbury Charitable
   Trust
W A Cargill Charitable Trust
Carnegie Dunfermline Trust
Chamberlain Foundation
Chase Charity
Childwick Trust
Chownes Foundation
City and Metropolitan Welfare
   Charity
J A Clark Charitable Trust
Clothworkers' Foundation and
   other Trusts
John & Freda Coleman
   Charitable Trust
George Henry Collins Charity
Norman Collinson Charitable
   Trust
Comino Foundation
Consortium on Opportunities
   for Volunteering
Cooper Charitable Trust
Sidney & Elizabeth Corob
   Charitable Trust
Corona Charitable Trust
County of Gloucestershire
   Community Foundation

Cray Trust
Criffel Charitable Trust
Cripplegate Foundation
Dennis Curry Charitable Trust
Manny Cussins Foundation
D'Oyly Carte Charitable Trust
Alderman Joe Davidson
    Memorial Trust
Miriam K Dean Refugee Trust
    Fund
Community Council of Devon
Duke of Devonshire's
    Charitable Trust
Dorcas Trust
Douglas Charitable Trust
William Dudley Trust
Dulverton Trust
Dumbreck Charity
Dumfries and Galloway Council
    Charitable Trusts
W E Dunn Trust
Earley Charity
Sir John Eastwood Foundation
Eden Arts Trust
City of Edinburgh Charitable
    Trusts
Vernon N Ely Charitable Trust
Englass Charitable Trust
Equitable Charitable Trust
Erskine Cunningham Hill Trust
Mihran Essefian Charitable
    Trust
Essex Fairway Charitable Trust
Sir John Evelyn's Charity
Eveson Charitable Trust
Fairbairn Charitable Trust
Esmée Fairbairn Foundation
Fairway Trust
Samuel William Farmer's Trust
Elizabeth Hardie Ferguson
    Charitable Trust Fund
Fidelity UK Foundation
Earl Fitzwilliam Charitable
    Trust
Forbesville Limited
Donald Forrester Trust
Fortuna Charitable Trust
Charles Henry Foyle Trust
Friarsgate Trust
Girdlers' Company Charitable
    Trust
Godinton Charitable Trust
Gosling Foundation Ltd
Reginald Graham Charitable
    Trust
Grocers' Charity
Guardian Foundation
Bishop of Guildford's
    Foundation
H C D Memorial Fund
Hadfield Trust
Hadrian Trust
Alfred Haines Charitable Trust
Robert Hall Charity
Hampstead Wells and
    Campden Trust

Harborne Parish Lands Charity
Harrison & Potter Trust
Gay & Peter Hartley's Hillards
    Charitable Trust
Hathaway Trust
Maurice Hatter Foundation
Hawthorne Charitable Trust
Dorothy Hay-Bolton Charitable
    Trust
May Hearnshaw's Charity
Heart of England Community
    Foundation
Hedley Foundation
Hemby Trust
Philip Henman Trust
Hesslewood Children's Trust
Hilden Charitable Fund
Hitchin Educational Foundation
Sir Julian Hodge Charitable
    Trust
Mary Homfray Charitable Trust
Horne Foundation
Hospital Saturday Fund
    Charitable Trust
Clifford Howarth Charity
    Settlement
Miss Agnes H Hunter's Trust
Hyde Park Place Estate Charity
    – civil trustees
Idlewild Trust
India Foundation (UK)
Isle of Anglesey Charitable
    Trust
J P Jacobs Charitable Trust
Ruth & Lionel Jacobson Trust
    (Second Fund) No 2
James Trust
JCA Charitable Foundation
Jerusalem Trust
Johnnie Johnson Trust
Ian Karten Charitable Trust
Keren Association
Kidani Memorial Trust
Graham Kirkham Foundation
Kleinwort Benson Charitable
    Trust
Ernest Kleinwort Charitable
    Trust
Neil Kreitman Foundation
Beatrice Laing Trust
Laing's Charitable Trust
Christopher Laing Foundation
Kirby Laing Foundation
Maurice Laing Foundation
R J Larg Family Charitable
    Trust
Carole & Geoffrey Lawson
    Foundation
Lazard Charitable Trust
Levy Foundation
Lindale Educational
    Foundation
Enid Linder Foundation
George John Livanos
    Charitable Trust
Lloyd's Charities Trust

W M & B W Lloyd Trust
Lloyds TSB Foundation for
    England and Wales
Lloyds TSB Foundation for
    Northern Ireland
London North East Community
    Foundation
Ruth & Jack Lunzer Charitable
    Trust
Sir Jack Lyons Charitable Trust
M N R Charitable Trust
Mackintosh Foundation
Magdalen & Lasher Charity
Man Group plc Charitable
    Trust
Michael Marsh Charitable
    Trust
Charlotte Marshall Charitable
    Trust
Sir George Martin Trust
John Martin's Charity
Merchant Taylors' Company
    Charities Fund
Tony Metherell Charitable
    Trust
Metropolitan Hospital-Sunday
    Fund
Miles Trust for the Putney and
    Roehampton Community
Peter Minet Trust
Minge's Gift
George A Moore Foundation
Nigel Moores Family Charitable
    Trust
Peter Moores Foundation
Morris Charitable Trust
G M Morrison Charitable Trust
Moss Family Charitable Trust
Murphy-Newmann Charity
    Company Limited
MYA Charitable Trust
National Power Charitable
    Trust
Laurie Nidditch Foundation
North British Hotel Trust
North London Islamic
    Association Trust
Northcott Devon Foundation
Northmoor Trust
Norwich Town Close Estate
    Charity
Nuffield Foundation
Oakley Charitable Trust
Ogilvie Charities Deed 2
Old Enfield Charitable Trust
Old Possum's Practical Trust
Oldham Foundation
Ouseley Trust
Andrew Paton's Charitable
    Trust
Harry Payne Trust
Pennycress Trust
Peugeot Charity Trust
Philological Foundation
David Pickford Charitable
    Foundation

Bernard Piggott Trust
A M Pilkington's Charitable
    Trust
J S F Pollitzer Charitable
    Settlement
Porter Foundation
W L Pratt Charitable Trust
Simone Prendergast Charitable
    Trust
Nyda and Oliver Prenn
    Foundation
Priory Foundation
Proven Family Trust
Pye Foundation
Joseph Rank Trust
Märit and Hans Rausing
    Charitable Foundation
REMEDI
Rest Harrow Trust
Richmond Parish Lands Charity
Robertson Trust
C A Rookes Charitable Trust
Mrs L D Rope Third Charitable
    Settlement
Rose Foundation
Christopher Rowbotham
    Charitable Trust
Royal Docks Trust
Rufford Foundation
Alan and Babette Sainsbury
    Charitable Fund
St Andrew Animal Fund Ltd
St Hilda's Trust
St Jude's Trust
St Mary-le-Strand Charity
Andrew Salvesen Charitable
    Trust
R H Scholes Charitable Trust
Scottish Community
    Foundation
Scottish International
    Education Trust
Sefton Community Foundation
Archie Sherman Charitable
    Trust
Barnett & Sylvia Shine No 2
    Charitable Trust
Shipwrights Company
    Charitable Fund
Shuttlewood Clarke Foundation
L H Silver Charitable Trust
Leslie Smith Foundation
Philip Smith's Charitable Trust
E C Sosnow Charitable Trust
South East London Community
    Foundation
Spar Charitable Fund
Stanley Foundation Ltd
Starfish Trust
Hugh Stenhouse Foundation
Sir Sigmund Sternberg
    Charitable Foundation
June Stevens Foundation
Leonard Laity Stoate
    Charitable Trust
Stoller Charitable Trust

W O Street Charitable
    Foundation
Bernard Sunley Charitable
    Foundation
Swann-Morton Foundation
Charles and Elsie Sykes Trust
Tajtelbaum Charitable Trust
Tay Charitable Trust
Tedworth Trust
Thompson Charitable Trust
Tisbury Telegraph Trust
Company of Tobacco Pipe
    Makers and Tobacco
    Blenders Benevolent Fund
Douglas Turner Trust
R D Turner Charitable Trust
Albert Van Den Bergh
    Charitable Trust
Scurrah Wainwright Charity
Wakeham Trust
Warrington Church of England
    Educational Trust
Wates Foundation
Bertie Watson Foundation
Weavers' Company Benevolent
    Fund
Mary Webb Trust
Weinstock Fund
Wellfield Trust
Wesleyan Charitable Trust
Charity of John West & Others
Westminster Amalgamated
    Charity
Colonel W H Whitbread
    Charitable Trust
Michael and Anna Wix
    Charitable Trust
Maurice Wohl Charitable
    Foundation
Worcester Municipal Charities
Yapp Charitable Trust
Yardley Great Trust

·······································

■ Young people (12–25)

Funding priority

Abel Charitable Trust
Acacia Charitable Trust
AF Trust Company
Green & Lilian F M Ainsworth
    & Family Benevolent Fund
Sylvia Aitken Charitable Trust
Aldgate and All Hallows
    Barking Exhibition
    Foundation
Allavida
Alliance Family Foundation
Angus Allnatt Charitable
    Foundation
Viscount Amory's Charitable
    Trust
Ambrose & Ann Appelbe Trust
Armourers and Brasiers'
    Gauntlet Trust
Ashby Charitable Trust

Ashe Park Charitable Trust
Associated Country Women of
    the World
Aston Villa Charitable Trust
Astor of Hever Trust
ATP Charitable Trust
Audi Design Foundation
BAA 21st Century
    Communities Trust
Balmore Trust
Bamford Charitable Foundation
Band (1976) Trust
Philip Barker Charity
Paul Bassham Charitable Trust
Beaufort House Trust
Beaurepaire Trust
Becketts & Sargeants
    Educational Foundation
John Beckwith Charitable Trust
Hervey Benham Charitable
    Trust
Bergqvist Charitable Trust
Bestway Foundation
Bethesda Community
    Charitable Trust
Thomas Betton's Charity
    (Educational)
BibleLands
Bier Charitable Settlement
Birmingham Foundation
Birmingham Hospital Saturday
    Fund Medical Charity &
    Welfare Trust
Sir William Boreman's
    Foundation
Anthony Bourne Foundation
Bowland Charitable Trust
Bramble Charitable Trust
Bridge House Estates Trust
    Fund
Bristol Charities
Charles Brotherton Trust
R S Brownless Charitable
    Trust
Buckinghamshire Masonic
    Centenary Fund
Burton Breweries Charitable
    Trust
Edward & Dorothy Cadbury
    Trust
Cadbury Schweppes
    Foundation
Carlton House Charitable Trust
Carlton Television Trust
Carnegie United Kingdom Trust
Carpenters' Company
    Charitable Trust
Casey Trust
Cash for Kids
Sir John Cass's Foundation
Sir Ernest Cassel Educational
    Trust
Elizabeth Casson Trust
Chasah Trust
Chase Charity

Church Burgesses Educational
Foundation
City Educational Trust Fund
CLA Charitable Trust
Hilda & Alice Clark Charitable
Trust
Lord Clinton's Charitable Trust
Coates Charitable Settlement
John Coates Charitable Trust
Cobb Charity
Vivienne & Samuel Cohen
Charitable Trust
Col-Reno Ltd
Cole Charitable Trust
E Alec Colman Charitable Fund
Ltd
Comic Relief
Community Foundation for
Northern Ireland
Community Foundation Serving
Tyne & Wear and
Northumberland
Community Fund
Construction Industry Trust for
Youth
Ernest Cook Trust
Gordon Cook Foundation
Craignish Trust
Michael Crawford Children's
Charity
Cray Trust
Crescent Trust
Cumber Family Charitable
Trust
Suzanne & Raymond Curtis
Foundation
Roald Dahl Foundation
Daily Telegraph Charitable
Trust
Baron Davenport's Charity
Gwendoline & Margaret Davies
Charity
Dawe Charitable Trust
De Clermont Charitable
Company Ltd
Peter De Haan Charitable
Trust
De La Rue Charitable Trust
Denton Charitable Trust
Denton Wilde Sapte Charitable
Trust
Derbyshire Community
Foundation
Devon Community Foundation
Devon Educational Trust
Diamond Industry Educational
Charity
Dickon Trust
Double 'O' Charity Ltd
Dove-Bowerman Trust
Dyers' Company Charitable
Trust
Eden Arts Trust
Edinburgh Voluntary
Organisations' Trust Funds

William Edwards Educational
Charity
Maud Elkington Charitable
Trust
Ellis Campbell Charitable
Foundation
Dorothy Whitney Elmhirst Trust
English Schools' Football
Association
Essex Youth Trust
Famos Foundation Trust
Joseph Fattorini Charitable
Trust 'B' Account
John Feeney Charitable
Bequest
George Fentham Birmingham
Charity
Doris Field Charitable Trust
Finnart House School Trust
Joyce Fletcher Charitable Trust
Roy Fletcher Charitable Trust
Football Association National
Sports Centre Trust
Football Association Youth
Trust
Forte Charitable Trust
Foundation for Management
Education
Four Lanes Trust
Timothy Franey Charitable
Foundation
Isaac and Freda Frankel
Memorial Charitable Trust
Thomas Freke & Lady Norton
Charity
Charles S French Charitable
Trust
Freshgate Trust Foundation
Mejer and Gertrude Miriam
Frydman Foundation
Gannochy Trust
Gatsby Charitable Foundation
J Paul Getty Jr Charitable Trust
Glass-House Trust
Good Neighbours Trust
Gough Charitable Trust
Grantham Yorke Trust
Great Britain Sasakawa
Foundation
Greater Bristol Foundation
Greggs Trust
Gulbenkian Foundation
Dr Guthrie's Association
Hackney Parochial Charities
Hale Trust
Hallam FM – Help a Hallam
Child Appeal
Eleanor Hamilton Educational
and Charitable Trust
Paul Hamlyn Foundation
Harbour Charitable Trust
William Harding's Charity
Harris Charity
Peter Harrison Foundation
Haymills Charitable Trust
Hedley Foundation

H J Heinz Company Limited
Charitable Trust
Henley Educational Charity
Joanna Herbert-Stepney
Charitable Settlement
Hertfordshire Community
Foundation
Alan Edward Higgs Charity
Hockerill Educational
Foundation
Dorothy Holmes Charitable
Trust
Holywood Trust
Hospital of God at Greatham
Hyde Charitable Trust
Imerys South West Charitable
Trust
Worshipful Company of
Innholders General Charity
Fund
Irish Youth Foundation (UK)
Ltd
Ironmongers' Quincentenary
Charitable Fund
Isle of Dogs Community
Foundation
Yvette and Hermione Jacobson
Charitable Trust
James Pantyfedwen
Foundation
James Trust
Jerwood Foundation and the
Jerwood Charitable
Foundation
Jewish Youth Fund
Elton John Aids Foundation
Lillie Johnson Charitable Trust
Edward Cecil Jones Settlement
Anton Jurgens Charitable Trust
Peter Kershaw Trust
Maurice and Hilda Laing
Charitable Trust
John and Rosemary Lancaster
Charitable Foundation
Richard Langhorn Trust
Lankelly Foundation
Lauchentilly Charitable
Foundation 1988
Edgar E Lawley Foundation
Lawlor Foundation
Lawson Charitable Foundation
Arnold Lee Charitable Trust
William Leech Charity
Leeds & Holbeck Building
Society Charitable
Foundation
Kennedy Leigh Charitable
Trust
Mark Leonard Trust
Lethendy Charitable Trust
John Spedan Lewis Foundation
John Lewis Partnership
General Community Fund
Lintel Trust
Lister Charitable Trust

Elaine & Angus Lloyd
   Charitable Trust
Lloyds TSB Foundation for
   Scotland
Lloyds TSB Foundation for the
   Channel Islands
Lofthouse Foundation
London Law Trust
London Youth Trust
Lotus Foundation
Paul Lunn-Rockliffe Charitable
   Trust
Lynn Foundation
John Lyon's Charity
Magdalen Hospital Trust
Magdalen & Lasher Charity
Mandeville Trust
Jim Marshall Charitable Trust
Masonic Trust for Girls and
   Boys
Mathew Trust
Mayfair Charities Ltd
Medlock Charitable Trust
Anthony and Elizabeth Mellows
   Charitable Settlement
Mickel Fund
Miller Foundation
Peter Minet Trust
Minge's Gift
Mole Charitable Trust
Morgan Crucible Company plc
   Charitable Trust
Morgan Stanley International
   Foundation
Stanley Morrison Charitable
   Trust
Mount 'A' Charitable Trust
Mount 'B' Charitable Trust
Mugdock Children's Trust
Music Sales Charitable Trust
Music Sound Foundation
Muslim Hands
Newcomen Collett Foundation
Newport County Borough
   Welsh Church Fund
J F Newsome Charitable Trust
Noel Buxton Trust
Alderman Norman's
   Foundation
Northampton Queen's Institute
   Relief in Sickness Fund
Northern Rock Foundation
Northumberland Village Homes
   Trust
Norton Foundation
Novi Most International
Old Broad Street Charity Trust
Oppenheimer Charitable Trust
Oxfordshire Community
   Foundation
Pastoral Care Trust
Mrs M E S Paterson's
   Charitable Trust
Peacock Charitable Trust
J B Pelly Charitable Settlement

Mrs C S Heber Percy
   Charitable Trust
Jack Petchey Foundation
Austin & Hope Pilkington Trust
Col W W Pilkington Will Trusts
   – The General Charity Fund
Plymouth Sound Trust – The
   Magic Appeal
John Porter Charitable Trust
Portishead Nautical Trust
Powys Welsh Church Fund
William Price Charitable Trust
Princess Anne's Charities
Privy Purse Charitable Trust
Ronald & Kathleen Pryor
   Charitable Trust
Puri Foundation
Mr and Mrs J A Pye's
   Charitable Settlement
Rayne Foundation
Christopher H R Reeves
   Charitable Trust
Rhondda Cynon Taff Welsh
   Church Acts Fund
Richmond Parish Lands Charity
Rivendell Trust
Rooke Atlay Charitable Trust
Mrs L D Rope Third Charitable
   Settlement
Rothley Trust
Christopher Rowbotham
   Charitable Trust
Royal Eastern Counties
   Schools Limited
Royal London Aid Society
J B Rubens Charitable
   Foundation
Rycroft Children's Fund
Karim Rida Said Foundation
St Hilda's Trust
St James's Place Foundation
St James' Trust Settlement
Sir Walter St John's
   Educational Charity
Saint Marylebone Educational
   Foundation
Sarum St Michael Educational
   Charity
Scott Bader Commonwealth
   Ltd
John Scott Trust
Scottish International
   Education Trust
Search
Searle Charitable Trust
Sedbury Trust
SEM Charitable Trust
Shakespeare Temperance
   Trust
Shaw Lands Trust
Sheffield Bluecoat & Mount
   Pleasant Educational
   Foundation
Shepherd Street Trust
SHINE

Shipwrights Company
   Charitable Fund
Bishop Simeon CR Trust
Skelton Bounty
Snowball Trust
Social Education Trust
W F Southall Trust
Southover Manor General
   Education Trust
Spitalfields Market Community
   Trust
W W Spooner Charitable Trust
Sportsman's Charity
Educational Charity of the
   Stationers' and Newspaper
   Makers' Company
Stewards' Charitable Trust
Sir Halley Stewart Trust
Peter Stormonth Darling
   Charitable Trust
Sueberry Ltd
Sutton Trust
Talbot Village Trust
Talteg Ltd
Tesco Charity Trust
Thames Community
   Foundation
Len Thomson Charitable Trust
Sue Thomson Foundation
Thriplow Charitable Trust
Tillett Trust
Torchbearer Trust
Tower Hill Improvement Trust
Towry Law Charitable Trust
Trades House of Glasgow
Truedene Co. Ltd
Trusthouse Charitable
   Foundation
Ulverston Town Lands Charity
VEC Acorn Trust
Victoria Homes Trust
Voluntary Action Luton
Scurrah Wainwright Charity
Walker Trust
Thomas Wall Trust
Waterside Trust
Wates Foundation
John Watson's Trust
Weavers' Company Benevolent
   Fund
Wentwood Education Trust
Earl & Countess of Wessex
   Charitable Trust
Western Recreation Trust
White Rose Children's Aid
   International Charity
William Williams Charity
Wiltshire and Swindon
   Community Foundation
Mayor of Wirral's Charity Trust
Women Caring Trust
Woo Charitable Foundation
Miss Hazel M Wood Charitable
   Trust
Woodlands Trust (1015942)
Woodlands Trust (259569)

Xerox (UK) Trust
W Wing Yip & Bros Charitable
Trust
York Children's Trust
Yorkshire Bank Charitable
Trust
Yorkshire Building Society
Charitable Foundation
Yorkshire County Cricket Club
Charitable Youth Trust

Will consider
Sylvia Adams Charitable Trust
Miss Agnes Gilchrist
Adamson's Trust
Adint Charitable Trust
Ambika Paul Foundation
Ammco Trust
AMW Charitable Trust
Mary Andrew Charitable Trust
Anglo Hong Kong Trust
Ardwick Trust
Arts Council of Wales
A J H Ashby Will Trust
Lord Ashdown Charitable Trust
Balcombe Charitable Trust
David and Frederick Barclay
Foundation
Bartle Family Charitable Trust
BBC Children in Need Appeal
Beacon Trust
Bedford Charity
E M Behrens Charitable Trust
Beit Trust
John Bell Charitable Trust
Bellinger Donnay Trust
Bingham Trust
Bishop's Development Fund
Isabel Blackman Foundation
Morgan Blake Charitable Trust
Blanchminster Trust
Blatchington Court Trust
Enid Blyton Trust for Children
Harry Bottom Charitable Trust
BP Conservation Programme
Harold and Alice Bridges
Charity
John Bristow and Thomas
Mason Trust
British Record Industry Trust
David Brooke Charity
Bulldog Trust
Edward Cadbury Charitable
Trust
Richard Cadbury Charitable
Trust
William A Cadbury Charitable
Trust
Camelot Foundation
W A Cargill Charitable Trust
Carnegie Dunfermline Trust
Carter's Educational
Foundation
Child Growth Foundation
Childwick Trust
Chownes Foundation

City and Metropolitan Welfare
Charity
J A Clark Charitable Trust
Clothworkers' Foundation and
other Trusts
Clover Trust
John & Freda Coleman
Charitable Trust
George Henry Collins Charity
Comino Foundation
Consortium on Opportunities
for Volunteering
Cooper Charitable Trust
Sidney & Elizabeth Corob
Charitable Trust
Corona Charitable Trust
County of Gloucestershire
Community Foundation
Criffel Charitable Trust
Cripplegate Foundation
Dennis Curry Charitable Trust
D'Oyly Carte Charitable Trust
David Charitable Trust
Community Council of Devon
Duke of Devonshire's
Charitable Trust
Dibden Allotments Charity
Dorcas Trust
Douglas Charitable Trust
William Dudley Trust
Dulverton Trust
P B Dumbell Charitable Trust
Dumfries and Galloway Council
Charitable Trusts
W E Dunn Trust
Earley Charity
City of Edinburgh Charitable
Trusts
Wilfred & Elsie Elkes Charity
Fund
Vernon N Ely Charitable Trust
Emerton-Christie Charity
Equitable Charitable Trust
Erskine Cunningham Hill Trust
Mihran Essefian Charitable
Trust
Essex Fairway Charitable Trust
Sir John Evelyn's Charity
Eveson Charitable Trust
Esmée Fairbairn Foundation
Fairway Trust
Ferguson Benevolent Fund Ltd
Elizabeth Hardie Ferguson
Charitable Trust Fund
Fiat Auto (UK) Charity
Fidelity UK Foundation
Earl Fitzwilliam Charitable
Trust
Forbesville Limited
Fortuna Charitable Trust
Charles Henry Foyle Trust
Friarsgate Trust
Girdlers' Company Charitable
Trust
Godinton Charitable Trust
Gosling Foundation Ltd

Reginald Graham Charitable
Trust
Constance Green Foundation
Grimley Charity
Grocers' Charity
Guardian Foundation
Bishop of Guildford's
Foundation
H C D Memorial Fund
Hadfield Trust
Hadrian Trust
Alfred Haines Charitable Trust
Robert Hall Charity
Hampstead Wells and
Campden Trust
Haramead Trust
Harborne Parish Lands Charity
Kenneth Hargreaves Charitable
Trust
Harrison & Potter Trust
Gay & Peter Hartley's Hillards
Charitable Trust
N & P Hartley Memorial Trust
Maurice Hatter Foundation
M A Hawe Settlement
Dorothy Hay-Bolton Charitable
Trust
Charles Hayward Foundation
May Hearnshaw's Charity
Heart of England Community
Foundation
Hemby Trust
Christina Mary Hendrie Trust
for Scottish & Canadian
Charities
Philip Henman Trust
Hesslewood Children's Trust
Hilden Charitable Fund
Hitchin Educational Foundation
Sir Julian Hodge Charitable
Trust
Mary Homfray Charitable Trust
Hoover Foundation
Horne Foundation
Hospital Saturday Fund
Charitable Trust
House of Industry Estate
John & Ruth Howard
Charitable Trust
Clifford Howarth Charity
Settlement
Huddersfield Common Good
Trust
Humanitarian Trust
Miss Agnes H Hunter's Trust
Hyde Park Place Estate Charity
– civil trustees
Idlewild Trust
India Foundation (UK)
Isle of Anglesey Charitable
Trust
Ruth & Lionel Jacobson Trust
(Second Fund) No 2
Jeffrey Charitable Trust
Jerusalem Trust
Johnnie Johnson Trust

Judge Charitable Foundation
Ian Karten Charitable Trust
Keren Association
Kidani Memorial Trust
Kintore Charitable Trust
Graham Kirkham Foundation
Kleinwort Benson Charitable
    Trust
Ernest Kleinwort Charitable
    Trust
Neil Kreitman Foundation
Beatrice Laing Trust
Laing's Charitable Trust
Christopher Laing Foundation
David Laing Foundation
Kirby Laing Foundation
Maurice Laing Foundation
R J Larg Family Charitable
    Trust
Lazard Charitable Trust
Levy Foundation
Lindale Educational
    Foundation
W M & B W Lloyd Trust
Lloyds TSB Foundation for
    England and Wales
Lloyds TSB Foundation for
    Northern Ireland
London North East Community
    Foundation
Lord's Taverners
Ruth & Jack Lunzer Charitable
    Trust
Lyndhurst Settlement
Sir Jack Lyons Charitable Trust
M N R Charitable Trust
Mackintosh Foundation
Helen Isabella McMorran
    Charitable Foundation
Man Group plc Charitable
    Trust
Michael Marsh Charitable
    Trust
Charlotte Marshall Charitable
    Trust
Sir George Martin Trust
John Martin's Charity
Nancie Massey Charitable
    Trust
Tony Metherell Charitable
    Trust
Metropolitan Hospital-Sunday
    Fund
Middlesex County Rugby
    Football Union Memorial
    Fund
Miles Trust for the Putney and
    Roehampton Community
Nigel Moores Family Charitable
    Trust
Peter Moores Foundation
J P Morgan Fleming
    Educational Trust and
    Foundation
Morris Charitable Trust
G M Morrison Charitable Trust

Moss Family Charitable Trust
Mount Everest Foundation
MYA Charitable Trust
National Power Charitable
    Trust
Nazareth Trust Fund
Laurie Nidditch Foundation
North British Hotel Trust
North London Islamic
    Association Trust
Northcott Devon Foundation
Northmoor Trust
Norwich Consolidated
    Charities
Norwich Town Close Estate
    Charity
Nuffield Foundation
Oakley Charitable Trust
Ogilvie Charities Deed 2
Old Enfield Charitable Trust
Old Possum's Practical Trust
Oldham Foundation
Ouseley Trust
Eleanor Palmer Trust
Andrew Paton's Charitable
    Trust
Harry Payne Trust
Pennycress Trust
Peugeot Charity Trust
Philological Foundation
David Pickford Charitable
    Foundation
Bernard Piggott Trust
A M Pilkington's Charitable
    Trust
Porter Foundation
Nyda and Oliver Prenn
    Foundation
Prince Philip Trust Fund
Priory Foundation
Pye Foundation
Joseph Rank Trust
Rayne Trust
REMEDI
Rest Harrow Trust
Rhodes Trust Public Purposes
    Fund
Cliff Richard Charitable Trust
Robertson Trust
C A Rookes Charitable Trust
Royal Docks Trust
Alan and Babette Sainsbury
    Charitable Fund
St Andrew Animal Fund Ltd
St Gabriel's Trust
St Jude's Trust
St Mary-le-Strand Charity
R H Scholes Charitable Trust
Scottish Community
    Foundation
Scouloudi Foundation
Samuel Sebba Charitable
    Trust
Sefton Community Foundation
Leslie Sell Charitable Trust

Shaftoe Educational
    Foundation
Barnett & Sylvia Shine No 2
    Charitable Trust
Shuttlewood Clarke Foundation
Barbara A Shuttleworth
    Memorial Trust
L H Silver Charitable Trust
E C Sosnow Charitable Trust
South Square Trust
Spar Charitable Fund
Stanley Spooner Deceased
    Charitable Trust
Stanley Foundation Ltd
Starfish Trust
Hugh Stenhouse Foundation
Sir Sigmund Sternberg
    Charitable Foundation
Leonard Laity Stoate
    Charitable Trust
Stoller Charitable Trust
W O Street Charitable
    Foundation
Bernard Sunley Charitable
    Foundation
Swann-Morton Foundation
Tajtelbaum Charitable Trust
Tay Charitable Trust
Thompson Charitable Trust
Tisbury Telegraph Trust
Company of Tobacco Pipe
    Makers and Tobacco
    Blenders Benevolent Fund
Tudor Trust
Douglas Turner Trust
R D Turner Charitable Trust
Albert Van Den Bergh
    Charitable Trust
Wakeham Trust
Wallington Missionary Mart
    and Auctions
Warrington Church of England
    Educational Trust
Bertie Watson Foundation
Mary Webb Trust
Weinstock Fund
Wellfield Trust
Charity of John West & Others
Westminster Amalgamated
    Charity
Westminster Foundation
Garfield Weston Foundation
Colonel W H Whitbread
    Charitable Trust
Harold Hyam Wingate
    Foundation
Michael and Anna Wix
    Charitable Trust
Worcester Municipal Charities
Matthews Wrightson Charity
    Trust
Yapp Charitable Trust
Yardley Great Trust

■ Older people

Funding priority

Age Concern Scotland Enterprise Fund
Green & Lilian F M Ainsworth & Family Benevolent Fund
Sylvia Aitken Charitable Trust
Aldgate Freedom Foundation
Almshouse Association
Viscount Amory's Charitable Trust
Ardwick Trust
Lord Austin Trust
Baker Charitable Trust
Paul Bassham Charitable Trust
Beaufort House Trust
Betard Bequest
Mason Bibby 1981 Trust
Birmingham Hospital Saturday Fund Medical Charity & Welfare Trust
Bonhomie United Charity Society
Boughton Trust
Bridge House Estates Trust Fund
Buckingham Trust
Bill Butlin Charity Trust
Elizabeth Casson Trust
Chase Charity
Chatwin Trust
Chelsea Square 1994 Trust
Cleary Foundation
Clore Duffield Foundation
Denise Cohen Charitable Trust
Cole Charitable Trust
George Henry Collins Charity
Community Foundation Serving Tyne & Wear and Northumberland
Marjorie Coote Old People's Charity
Suzanne & Raymond Curtis Foundation
Baron Davenport's Charity
David Charitable Trust
Alderman Joe Davidson Memorial Trust
Davidson (Nairn) Charitable Trust
De Clermont Charitable Company Ltd
Denton Charitable Trust
Dibden Allotments Charity
William Dudley Trust
Dunhill Medical Trust
Eden Arts Trust
Edinburgh Voluntary Organisations' Trust Funds
W G Edwards Charitable Foundation
Wilfred & Elsie Elkes Charity Fund
Maud Elkington Charitable Trust
Emerton-Christie Charity

Eveson Charitable Trust
Fassnidge Memorial Trust
Joseph Fattorini Charitable Trust 'B' Account
Fiat Auto (UK) Charity
Roy Fletcher Charitable Trust
Gerald Fogel Charitable Trust
Football Association National Sports Centre Trust
Foresters' Charity Stewards UK Trust
Foundation for Management Education
Emily Fraser Trust
Frognal Trust
L & R Gilley Charitable Trust
Mrs Godfrey-Payton Trust
Good Neighbours Trust
Gosling Foundation Ltd
Grand Charity of Freemasons
Gray Trust
Greater Bristol Foundation
Greggs Trust
Guildry Incorporation of Perth
Gulbenkian Foundation
E F & M G Hall Charitable Trust
Harebell Centenary Fund
Kenneth Hargreaves Charitable Trust
Harrison & Potter Trust
N & P Hartley Memorial Trust
M A Hawe Settlement
Charles Hayward Foundation
Help the Aged
Joanna Herbert-Stepney Charitable Settlement
Hertfordshire Community Foundation
Joseph & Mary Hiley Trust
Sir Julian Hodge Charitable Trust
Dorothy Holmes Charitable Trust
Edward Holt Trust
Joseph Hopkins Charity
Cuthbert Horn Trust
Mrs E G Hornby's Charitable Settlement
Hospital of God at Greatham
Housing Associations Charitable Trust
Huddersfield Common Good Trust
Hudson Foundation
Huggard Charitable Trust
Inman Charity
Charles Irving Charitable Trust
Yvette and Hermione Jacobson Charitable Trust
Jeffrey Charitable Trust
Edward Cecil Jones Settlement
Anton Jurgens Charitable Trust
Kass Charitable Trust
Peter Kershaw Trust
Kirkley Poor's Land Estate

Ernest Kleinwort Charitable Trust
Knowles Charitable Trust
Lankelly Foundation
Laslett's (Hinton) Charity
Edgar E Lawley Foundation
Leeds & Holbeck Building Society Charitable Foundation
Lintel Trust
Lloyds TSB Foundation for Scotland
Lloyds TSB Foundation for the Channel Islands
Lofthouse Foundation
Paul Lunn-Rockliffe Charitable Trust
Lord and Lady Lurgan Trust
Lynn Foundation
Helen Isabella McMorran Charitable Foundation
Magdalen & Lasher Charity
Victor Mann Trust
Margaret Foundation
Mathew Trust
Maxwell Family Foundation
Evelyn May Trust
Charity of Mary Jane, Countess of Meath
Medlock Charitable Trust
Tony Metherell Charitable Trust
Midhurst Pensions Trust
Miles Trust for the Putney and Roehampton Community
Peter Minet Trust
Newport County Borough Welsh Church Fund
Laurie Nidditch Foundation
Northampton Municipal Church Charities
Northern Rock Foundation
Nuffield Foundation
Ogilvie Charities Deed 2
Oppenheimer Charitable Trust
Oxfordshire Community Foundation
Eleanor Palmer Trust
Park Hill Trust
Pastoral Care Trust
Arthur James Paterson Charitable Trust
Constance Paterson Charitable Trust
Late Barbara May Paul Charitable Trust
Michael Peacock Charitable Foundation
Frank Pearson Foundation
Austin & Hope Pilkington Trust
Elsie Pilkington Charitable Trust
Powell Foundation
Douglas Prestwich Charitable Trust

Sir John Priestman Charity
    Trust
Privy Purse Charitable Trust
Puri Foundation
Rayne Foundation
Rayne Trust
Rest Harrow Trust
Clive Richards Charity Ltd
Violet M Richards Charity
Rooke Atlay Charitable Trust
C A Rookes Charitable Trust
Christopher Rowbotham
    Charitable Trust
J S & E C Rymer Charitable
    Trust
St James' Trust Settlement
Late St Patrick White
    Charitable Trust
Schroder Charity Trust
Scouloudi Foundation
Sylvia & Colin Shepherd
    Charitable Trust
Mary Elizabeth Siebel Charity
Skelton Bounty
Skerritt Trust
Sobell Foundation
Spitalfields Market Community
    Trust
Stanton Ballard Charitable
    Trust
Foundation of Edward Storey
Talbot Village Trust
Tesco Charity Trust
Thames Community
    Foundation
Thriplow Charitable Trust
Tillotson Bradbery Charitable
    Trust
Fred Towler Charity Trust
Towry Law Charitable Trust
Trades House of Glasgow
Triangle Trust (1949) Fund
Mrs S H Troughton Charity
    Trust
Truemark Trust
John and Lucille van Geest
    Foundation
Van Neste Foundation
Mrs Maud Van Norden's
    Charitable Foundation
Vintners Company Charitable
    Trust
Wakefield Trust
Thomas Wall Trust
A F Wallace Charity Trust
Warwickshire Masonic
    Charitable Association Ltd
Waterside Trust
Alfred and Beatrice Weintrop
    Charity
Charity of John West & Others
Western Recreation Trust
Sheila Whitley Trust
J and J R Wilson Trust
Wiltshire and Swindon
    Community Foundation

Francis Winham Foundation
Michael and Anna Wix
    Charitable Trust
Woburn 1986 Charitable Trust
Miss Hazel M Wood Charitable
    Trust
Woodlands Trust (1015942)
Woodlands Trust (259569)
Yapp Charitable Trust
Yorkshire Building Society
    Charitable Foundation

Will consider
Adint Charitable Trust
Ammco Trust
Ambrose & Ann Appelbe Trust
Arts Council of Wales
Audi Design Foundation
BAA 21st Century
    Communities Trust
Andrew Balint Charitable Trust
George Balint Charitable Trust
Paul Balint Charitable Trust
Bamford Charitable Foundation
David and Frederick Barclay
    Foundation
Beacon Trust
Bedford Charity
Beit Trust
John Bell Charitable Trust
BibleLands
Percy Bilton Charity Ltd
Bingham Trust
Birmingham Foundation
Isabel Blackman Foundation
Herbert & Peter Blagrave
    Charitable Trust
Blair Foundation
Morgan Blake Charitable Trust
Blanchminster Trust
Harry Bottom Charitable Trust
BP Conservation Programme
Harold and Alice Bridges
    Charity
John Bristow and Thomas
    Mason Trust
Charles Brotherton Trust
Miss Marion Broughton's
    Charitable Trust
Burden Trust
Richard Cadbury Charitable
    Trust
William A Cadbury Charitable
    Trust
D W T Cargill Fund
Carnegie Dunfermline Trust
Joseph & Annie Cattle Trust
Chamberlain Foundation
Childwick Trust
Chownes Foundation
City and Metropolitan Welfare
    Charity
Hilda & Alice Clark Charitable
    Trust
Lord Clinton's Charitable Trust

John & Freda Coleman
    Charitable Trust
Norman Collinson Charitable
    Trust
Comic Relief
Community Foundation for
    Northern Ireland
Community Fund
Consortium on Opportunities
    for Volunteering
Cooper Charitable Trust
County of Gloucestershire
    Community Foundation
Criffel Charitable Trust
Cripplegate Foundation
Croydon Relief in Need
    Charities
Manny Cussins Foundation
D'Oyly Carte Charitable Trust
Dr & Mrs A Darlington
    Charitable Trust
Miriam K Dean Refugee Trust
    Fund
Derbyshire Community
    Foundation
Community Council of Devon
Duke of Devonshire's
    Charitable Trust
Douglas Charitable Trust
Dove-Bowerman Trust
Dulverton Trust
Dumbreck Charity
Dumfries and Galloway Council
    Charitable Trusts
W E Dunn Trust
Earley Charity
Sir John Eastwood Foundation
City of Edinburgh Charitable
    Trusts
Englass Charitable Trust
Ericson Trust
Erskine Cunningham Hill Trust
Essex Fairway Charitable Trust
Sir John Evelyn's Charity
Fairbairn Charitable Trust
Esmée Fairbairn Foundation
Samuel William Farmer's Trust
Fidelity UK Foundation
Rose Flatau Charitable Trust
Joyce Fletcher Charitable Trust
Donald Forrester Trust
Four Lanes Trust
Hugh Fraser Foundation
Charles S French Charitable
    Trust
Freshgate Trust Foundation
Friarsgate Trust
Gannochy Trust
Girdlers' Company Charitable
    Trust
Great Britain Sasakawa
    Foundation
Constance Green Foundation
Grimley Charity
Grocers' Charity

Bishop of Guildford's
Foundation
H C D Memorial Fund
Hadfield Trust
Hadrian Trust
Alfred Haines Charitable Trust
Hampstead Wells and
Campden Trust
Haramead Trust
Harborne Parish Lands Charity
Gay & Peter Hartley's Hillards
Charitable Trust
Hawthorne Charitable Trust
Dorothy Hay-Bolton Charitable
Trust
May Hearnshaw's Charity
Heart of England Community
Foundation
Hemby Trust
Christina Mary Hendrie Trust
for Scottish & Canadian
Charities
Hilden Charitable Fund
Hobson Charity Ltd
Hockerill Educational
Foundation
Mary Homfray Charitable Trust
Hospital Saturday Fund
Charitable Trust
Clifford Howarth Charity
Settlement
Miss Agnes H Hunter's Trust
India Foundation (UK)
Isle of Dogs Community
Foundation
J A R Charitable Trust
J P Jacobs Charitable Trust
Ruth & Lionel Jacobson Trust
(Second Fund) No 2
James Trust
Elton John Aids Foundation
Kidani Memorial Trust
Beatrice Laing Trust
Christopher Laing Foundation
Kirby Laing Foundation
Maurice Laing Foundation
Maurice and Hilda Laing
Charitable Trust
Lawlor Foundation
Lazard Charitable Trust
Lord Leverhulme Charitable
Trust
Levy Foundation
John Spedan Lewis Foundation
Enid Linder Foundation
George John Livanos
Charitable Trust
Lloyd's Charities Trust
Lloyds TSB Foundation for
England and Wales
Lloyds TSB Foundation for
Northern Ireland
London North East Community
Foundation
LSA Charitable Trust
Lyndhurst Settlement

M N R Charitable Trust
D D McPhail Charitable
Settlement
Sir George Martin Trust
John Martin's Charity
Nancie Massey Charitable
Trust
Merchant Taylors' Company
Charities Fund
Metropolitan Hospital-Sunday
Fund
Mickel Fund
Middlesex County Rugby
Football Union Memorial
Fund
Millfield Trust
Minge's Gift
George A Moore Foundation
John Moores Foundation
J P Morgan Fleming
Educational Trust and
Foundation
Morgan Stanley International
Foundation
Morris Charitable Trust
G M Morrison Charitable Trust
Moss Family Charitable Trust
Mount Everest Foundation
Murphy-Newmann Charity
Company Limited
National Power Charitable
Trust
North British Hotel Trust
Northcott Devon Foundation
Norwich Consolidated
Charities
Norwich Town Close Estate
Charity
Old Enfield Charitable Trust
Old Possum's Practical Trust
Kate Wilson Oliver Trust
Parthenon Trust
Harry Payne Trust
Pennycress Trust
Peugeot Charity Trust
Ruth & Michael Phillips
Charitable Trust
A M Pilkington's Charitable
Trust
J S F Pollitzer Charitable
Settlement
Powys Welsh Church Fund
W L Pratt Charitable Trust
Simone Prendergast Charitable
Trust
Proven Family Trust
Pye Foundation
Mr and Mrs J A Pye's
Charitable Settlement
Joseph Rank Trust
E L Rathbone Charitable Trust
John Rayner Charitable Trust
Christopher H R Reeves
Charitable Trust
REMEDI
Cliff Richard Charitable Trust

Richmond Parish Lands Charity
Riverside Charitable Trust
Limited
Robertson Trust
Mrs L D Rope Third Charitable
Settlement
Rose Foundation
Cecil Rosen Foundation
Royal Docks Trust
Royal London Aid Society
J B Rubens Charitable
Foundation
St Andrew Animal Fund Ltd
Scottish Community
Foundation
Samuel Sebba Charitable
Trust
Sefton Community Foundation
Shaftoe Educational
Foundation
Archie Sherman Charitable
Trust
Shipwrights Company
Charitable Fund
Shuttlewood Clarke Foundation
Ernest William Slaughter
Charitable Trust
Philip Smith's Charitable Trust
E C Sosnow Charitable Trust
South Square Trust
Ralph and Irma Sperring
Charity
Stanley Spooner Deceased
Charitable Trust
Starfish Trust
Sir Halley Stewart Trust
W O Street Charitable
Foundation
A B Strom & R Strom
Charitable Trust
Bernard Sunley Charitable
Foundation
Charles and Elsie Sykes Trust
Tajtelbaum Charitable Trust
Tay Charitable Trust
Tower Hill Improvement Trust
Constance Travis Charitable
Trust
Tudor Trust
Douglas Turner Trust
R D Turner Charitable Trust
Albert Van Den Bergh
Charitable Trust
Scurrah Wainwright Charity
Wakeham Trust
Wallington Missionary Mart
and Auctions
Wates Foundation
Bertie Watson Foundation
Mary Webb Trust
Weinstock Fund
Wellfield Trust
Wesleyan Charitable Trust
West London Synagogue
Charitable Fund

Westminster Amalgamated
    Charity
Garfield Weston Foundation
Wilkinson Charitable
    Foundation
Maurice Wohl Charitable
    Foundation
Worcester Municipal Charities
Yardley Great Trust

Class, group, occupation or ex-occupation

■ Armed forces
Funding priority
Mrs M H Allen Trust
Army Benevolent Fund
Baltic Charitable Fund
Malcolm Chick Charity
Cleary Foundation
Robert Clutterbuck Charitable
    Trust
De Clermont Charitable
    Company Ltd
Dyers' Company Charitable
    Trust
Erskine Cunningham Hill Trust
Gray Trust
Lennox Hannay Charitable
    Trust
Joseph & Mary Hiley Trust
Charles Littlewood Hill Trust
Edward Sydney Hogg
    Charitable Settlement
King George's Fund for Sailors
Sir James Knott Trust
Paul Lunn-Rockliffe Charitable
    Trust
MacRobert Trust
Mountbatten Festival of Music
Noswad Charity
Constance Paterson Charitable
    Trust
Peacock Charitable Trust
Pennycress Trust
Queen Mary's Roehampton
    Trust
Christopher Rowbotham
    Charitable Trust
Royal British Legion
Verdon-Smith Family Charitable
    Settlement
Westminster Foundation

Will consider
Ammco Trust
Viscount Amory's Charitable
    Trust
Sir John & Lady Amory's
    Charitable Trust
Astor Foundation
Astor of Hever Trust
Balney Charitable Trust

Lord Barnby's Foundation
Rowan Bentall Charitable Trust
Charles Brotherton Trust
W A Cargill Fund
Childwick Trust
Lord Clinton's Charitable Trust
Coutts & Co. Charitable Trust
Cwmbran Trust
Dulverton Trust
Sir John Fisher Foundation
Earl Fitzwilliam Charitable
    Trust
Girdlers' Company Charitable
    Trust
Constance Green Foundation
Dorothy Holmes Charitable
    Trust
Mary Homfray Charitable Trust
James Thom Howat Charitable
    Trust
Boris Karloff Charitable
    Foundation
Graham Kirkham Foundation
Heinz & Anna Kroch
    Foundation
Mrs F B Laurence Charitable
    Trust
Limoges Charitable Trust
Liverpool Sailors' Home Trust
C F Lunoe Trust Fund
M N R Charitable Trust
Mercers' Charitable
    Foundation
Minge's Gift
Mobbs Memorial Trust Ltd
George A Moore Foundation
Horace Moore Charitable Trust
Newby Trust Limited
Norman Family Charitable
    Trust
Oldham Foundation
Pastoral Care Trust
Patients' Aid Association
    Hospital & Medical
    Charities Trust
A M Pilkington's Charitable
    Trust
J S F Pollitzer Charitable
    Settlement
W L Pratt Charitable Trust
Simone Prendergast Charitable
    Trust
Pye Foundation
John Rayner Charitable Trust
Mrs L D Rope Third Charitable
    Settlement
Scouloudi Foundation
Shipwrights Company
    Charitable Fund
Henry Smith Charity
Charles and Elsie Sykes Trust
Tay Charitable Trust
Mary Webb Trust
Wellfield Trust
Michael and Anna Wix
    Charitable Trust

■ Art, culture
Funding priority
Angus Allnatt Charitable
    Foundation
Ambrose & Ann Appelbe Trust
Arts Council of England
Arts Council of Wales
Ashendene Trust
Britten-Pears Foundation
Chase Charity
Classic FM Charitable Trust
Criffel Charitable Trust
Delius Trust
Eden Arts Trust
Equity Trust Fund
Ian Fleming Charitable Trust
Joyce Fletcher Charitable Trust
Gulbenkian Foundation
Paul Hamlyn Foundation
Kathleen Hannay Memorial
    Charity
Hinrichsen Foundation
Sir Barry Jackson Trust and
    County Fund
Ian Karten Charitable Trust
Marina Kleinwort Charitable
    Trust
Lawson Charitable Foundation
Lynn Foundation
Macfarlane Walker Trust
Anthony and Elizabeth Mellows
    Charitable Settlement
Nigel Moores Family Charitable
    Trust
Music Sales Charitable Trust
Music Sound Foundation
Noswad Charity
Old Broad Street Charity Trust
John Porter Charitable Trust
R V W Trust
Radcliffe Trust
Peggy Ramsay Foundation
Clive Richards Charity Ltd
Scottish International
    Education Trust
R C Sherriff Rosebriars Trust
Tillett Trust
Tunnell Trust
Miss S M Tutton Charitable
    Trust
Whitaker Charitable Trust
Woo Charitable Foundation
Miss E B Wrightson's
    Charitable Settlement

Will consider
Ammco Trust
Armenian General Benevolent
    Union London Trust
G C Armitage Charitable Trust
Ashby Charitable Trust
Lord Ashdown Charitable Trust
Laura Ashley Foundation
Astor of Hever Trust
Richard Attenborough
    Charitable Trust

BBC Children in Need Appeal
Hervey Benham Charitable
    Trust
Blanchminster Trust
British Record Industry Trust
Swinfen Broun Charitable Trust
R M 1956 Burton Charitable
    Trust
Edward Cadbury Charitable
    Trust
Edward & Dorothy Cadbury
    Trust
W A Cargill Fund
Carnegie Dunfermline Trust
Cinderford Charitable Trust
John Coates Charitable Trust
Denise Cohen Charitable Trust
Duke of Cornwall's Benevolent
    Fund
Coutts & Co. Charitable Trust
Crescent Trust
Harry Crook Foundation
Cwmbran Trust
David Charitable Trust
Elephant Trust
Elmley Foundation
Douglas Heath Eves Charitable
    Trust
Gerald Finzi Charitable Trust
Four Lanes Trust
Freshgate Trust Foundation
Maurice Fry Charitable Trust
Robert Gavron Charitable Trust
Granada Foundation
Harding Trust
May Hearnshaw's Charity
Holst Foundation
Homestead Charitable Trust
Mary Homfray Charitable Trust
Antony Hornby Charitable Trust
James Thom Howat Charitable
    Trust
Geoffrey C Hughes Charitable
    Trust
INTACH (UK) Trust
James Pantyfedwen
    Foundation
Jerwood Foundation and the
    Jerwood Charitable
    Foundation
Boris Karloff Charitable
    Foundation
Robert Kiln Charitable Trust
Heinz & Anna Kroch
    Foundation
Lawson Charitable Foundation
Leche Trust
C F Lunoe Trust Fund
Sir Jack Lyons Charitable Trust
Macfarlane Walker Trust
Mackintosh Foundation
Linda Marcus Charitable Trust
Merchant Taylors' Company
    Charities Fund
Millichope Foundation
Minge's Gift

Esmé Mitchell Trust
Monument Trust
Horace Moore Charitable Trust
Peter Moores Foundation
Music Sound Foundation
Oakley Charitable Trust
Pallant Charitable Trust
Pastoral Care Trust
Bernard Piggott Trust
Cecil Pilkington Charitable
    Trust
J S F Pollitzer Charitable
    Settlement
Porter Foundation
Nyda and Oliver Prenn
    Foundation
Rayne Foundation
John Rayner Charitable Trust
Richmond Parish Lands Charity
Rivendell Trust
Royal Victoria Hall Foundation
Dr Mortimer and Theresa
    Sackler Foundation
Alan and Babette Sainsbury
    Charitable Fund
Robert and Lisa Sainsbury
    Charitable Trust
Scarfe Charitable Trust
Schroder Charity Trust
Skinners' Company Lady
    Neville Charity
E C Sosnow Charitable Trust
Stanley Foundation Ltd
Tay Charitable Trust
Verdon-Smith Family Charitable
    Settlement
Nigel Vinson Charitable Trust
Mary Webb Trust
Weldon UK Charitable Trust
Maurice Wohl Charitable Trust
Wyseliot Charitable Trust
Yorkshire Bank Charitable
    Trust

....

■ Education and training

Funding priority
All Saints Educational Trust
Ambrose & Ann Appelbe Trust
Ashe Park Charitable Trust
Band (1976) Trust
CfBT Education Services
City Educational Trust Fund
Cobb Charity
Vivienne & Samuel Cohen
    Charitable Trust
E Alec Colman Charitable Fund
    Ltd
Crescent Trust
De La Rue Charitable Trust
Dove-Bowerman Trust
Mejer and Gertrude Miriam
    Frydman Foundation
Greater Bristol Foundation
Paul Hamlyn Foundation

Michael & Morven Heller
    Charitable Foundation
Simon Heller Charitable
    Settlement
Hockerill Educational
    Foundation
Arnold Lee Charitable Trust
Muslim Hands
Ogilvie Charities Deed 2
Jack Petchey Foundation
John Porter Charitable Trust
Christopher Rowbotham
    Charitable Trust
Sutton Trust
Yorkshire County Cricket Club
    Charitable Youth Trust

Will consider
Acacia Charitable Trust
Ashby Charitable Trust
BBC Children in Need Appeal
Beit Trust
Bestway Foundation
Bingham Trust
Blanchminster Trust
W A Cargill Charitable Trust
W A Cargill Fund
Ellinson Foundation Ltd
Elmley Foundation
English Schools' Football
    Association
Girdlers' Company Charitable
    Trust
Harbour Charitable Trust
Kenneth Hargreaves Charitable
    Trust
Sir Julian Hodge Charitable
    Trust
Mary Homfray Charitable Trust
Isle of Anglesey Charitable
    Trust
Lord Leverhulme Charitable
    Trust
C F Lunoe Trust Fund
R W Mann Trustees Limited
Linda Marcus Charitable Trust
Minge's Gift
Peter Moores Foundation
Music Sound Foundation
Newby Trust Limited
Pastoral Care Trust
A M Pilkington's Charitable
    Trust
Porter Foundation
PPP Foundation
Rayne Foundation
Richmond Parish Lands Charity
Rothley Trust
Alan and Babette Sainsbury
    Charitable Fund
St Gabriel's Trust
St Luke's College Foundation
Scott Bader Commonwealth
    Ltd
Stewards' Charitable Trust
Tay Charitable Trust

Ulverscroft Foundation

■ The environment, agriculture

Funding priority
Ashe Park Charitable Trust
CLA Charitable Trust
Cobb Charity
Eden Arts Trust
Frank Litchfield Charitable
Trust
John Longwill's Agricultural
Scheme
Yorkshire Dales Millennium
Trust

Will consider
Bingham Trust
Samuel William Farmer's Trust
Earl Fitzwilliam Charitable
Trust
Girdlers' Company Charitable
Trust
Mary Homfray Charitable Trust
Pastoral Care Trust
Christopher Rowbotham
Charitable Trust
Mary Webb Trust

■ Law, mediation and advice services

Funding priority
International Bar Association
Educational Trust
Law Society Charity

Will consider
Ajahma Charitable Trust
Anglo-German Foundation for
the Study of Industrial
Society
BBC Children in Need Appeal
Bingham Trust
May Hearnshaw's Charity
Dorothy Holmes Charitable
Trust
Mary Homfray Charitable Trust
Lloyds TSB Foundation for
Northern Ireland
C F Lunoe Trust Fund
Minge's Gift
Newby Trust Limited
Nuffield Foundation
Pastoral Care Trust
Richmond Parish Lands Charity
Rothley Trust

■ Manufacturing and service industries

Will consider
Mary Homfray Charitable Trust
Leverhulme Trade Charities
Trust
Pastoral Care Trust
Patrick Charitable Trust
Peugeot Charity Trust

■ Medicine and health

Funding priority
Arthritis Research Campaign
Ashby Charitable Trust
Patrick Berthoud Charitable
Trust
BibleLands
Birmingham District Nursing
Charitable Trust
Birmingham Hospital Saturday
Fund Medical Charity &
Welfare Trust
Breast Cancer Research Trust
British Council for Prevention
of Blindness
British Dietetic Association
General and Education
Trust Fund
British Heart Foundation
Buckingham Trust
Carron Charitable Trust
H and M Castang Charitable
Trust
Chest Heart and Stroke
Scotland
Child Growth Foundation
Children's Liver Disease
Foundation
Clarke Charitable Settlement
Vivienne & Samuel Cohen
Charitable Trust
Lord Cozens-Hardy Trust
Crescent Trust
Criffel Charitable Trust
Dinwoodie Settlement
Gilbert Edgar Trust
Gilbert & Eileen Edgar
Foundation
T F C Frost Charitable Trust
Garthgwynion Charities
General Nursing Council for
England and Wales Trust
Teresa Rosenbaum Golden
Charitable Trust
Sue Hammerson's Charitable
Trust
Kathleen Hannay Memorial
Charity
Lennox Hannay Charitable
Trust
Michael & Morven Heller
Charitable Foundation
Simon Heller Charitable
Settlement
India Foundation (UK)

International Spinal Research
Trust
Emmanuel Kaye Foundation
Kyte Charitable Trust
Arnold Lee Charitable Trust
Leukaemia Research Fund
Lyons Charitable Trust
Melville Trust for Care and
Cure of Cancer
Mental Health Foundation
Muslim Hands
Network for Social Change
Patients' Aid Association
Hospital & Medical
Charities Trust
Patrick Charitable Trust
Late Barbara May Paul
Charitable Trust
PPP Foundation
Rubin Foundation
Camilla Samuel Fund
Sandra Charitable Trust
Sir Samuel Scott of Yews
Trust
Starfish Trust
Walter Swindon Charitable
Trust
Tenovus Scotland
Ulverscroft Foundation
Wellcome Trust
Wessex Cancer Trust
Felicity Wilde Charitable Trust

Will consider
Acacia Charitable Trust
Alchemy Foundation
Anglo-German Foundation for
the Study of Industrial
Society
Artemis Charitable Trust
Astor Foundation
John Avins Trustees
B-C H 1971 Charitable Trust
Bamford Charitable Foundation
David and Frederick Barclay
Foundation
Bingham Trust
Burden Trust
W A Cargill Charitable Trust
Children's Research Fund
Childwick Trust
John Coates Charitable Trust
Cooper Charitable Trust
Coutts & Co. Charitable Trust
De Clermont Charitable
Company Ltd
Diabetes UK
DLM Charitable Trust
Dunhill Medical Trust
Ian Fleming Charitable Trust
Isaac and Freda Frankel
Memorial Charitable Trust
Maurice Fry Charitable Trust
Girdlers' Company Charitable
Trust
Harbour Charitable Trust

Kenneth Hargreaves Charitable
   Trust
Hawthorne Charitable Trust
May Hearnshaw's Charity
Help the Hospices
Sir Julian Hodge Charitable
   Trust
Homelands Charitable Trust
Mary Homfray Charitable Trust
Antony Hornby Charitable Trust
HSA Charitable Trust
Human Relief Foundation
Ruth & Lionel Jacobson Trust
   (Second Fund) No 2
Jerwood Foundation and the
   Jerwood Charitable
   Foundation
Johnson Foundation
Judith Trust
Kennel Club Charitable Trust
Leverhulme Trade Charities
   Trust
Lewis Family Charitable Trust
Linden Charitable Trust
London Law Trust
C F Lunoe Trust Fund
M N R Charitable Trust
Mackintosh Foundation
Evelyn May Trust
Merchant Taylors' Company
   Charities Fund
Minge's Gift
George A Moore Foundation
Morgan Crucible Company plc
   Charitable Trust
National Asthma Campaign
National Kidney Research
   Fund Limited
Newby Trust Limited
Frances and Augustus
   Newman Foundation
Laurie Nidditch Foundation
Northcott Devon Foundation
Northcott Devon Medical
   Foundation
Pastoral Care Trust
A M Pilkington's Charitable
   Trust
G S Plaut Charitable Trust
J S F Pollitzer Charitable
   Settlement
Porter Foundation
Simone Prendergast Charitable
   Trust
Märit and Hans Rausing
   Charitable Foundation
Rayne Foundation
John Rayner Charitable Trust
Rhodes Trust Public Purposes
   Fund
Richmond Parish Lands Charity
Cecil Rosen Foundation
Rowan Charitable Trust
Christopher Rowbotham
   Charitable Trust

Alan and Babette Sainsbury
   Charitable Fund
Peter Samuel Charitable Trust
Scouloudi Foundation
Stanley Foundation Ltd
Sir Halley Stewart Trust
Swann-Morton Foundation
Sir Jules Thorn Charitable
   Trust
Tisbury Telegraph Trust
Towry Law Charitable Trust
Underwood Trust
Wallington Missionary Mart
   and Auctions
Bertie Watson Foundation
Mary Webb Trust
Westcroft Trust
Maurice Wohl Charitable Trust
Wolfson Foundation
Women at Risk
Worshipful Company of
   Founders Charities
Wyseliot Charitable Trust

....

■ Religion

Funding priority
Archbishop of Canterbury's
   Charitable Trust
Ashendene Trust
Bellahouston Bequest Fund
Christendom Trust
E Alec Colman Charitable Fund
   Ltd
Criffel Charitable Trust
Anne French Memorial Trust
Grace Baptist Trust
   Corporation
Kathleen Hannay Memorial
   Charity
Joseph & Mary Hiley Trust
Sylvanus Lyson's Charity
Sir John Priestman Charity
   Trust
Leslie Smith Foundation
Stewards Company
Foundation of Edward Storey
Verdon-Smith Family Charitable
   Settlement
Woodlands Trust (259569)

Will consider
Viscount Amory's Charitable
   Trust
Bamford Charitable Foundation
Bingham Trust
British Humane Association
Earl Fitzwilliam Charitable
   Trust
May Hearnshaw's Charity
Hesed Trust
Dorothy Holmes Charitable
   Trust
Homelands Charitable Trust
Mary Homfray Charitable Trust

James Pantyfedwen
   Foundation
Maurice and Hilda Laing
   Charitable Trust
C F Lunoe Trust Fund
M N R Charitable Trust
John Martin's Charity
Minge's Gift
Newby Trust Limited
Pastoral Care Trust
Payne Charitable Trust
A M Pilkington's Charitable
   Trust
Nathaniel Reyner Trust Fund
Richmond Parish Lands Charity
Mrs L D Rope Third Charitable
   Settlement
St Luke's College Foundation
Scouloudi Foundation
Stanley Foundation Ltd
Sir Halley Stewart Trust
Tisbury Telegraph Trust
Wallington Missionary Mart
   and Auctions
Mary Webb Trust
Whitecourt Charitable Trust

....

■ Science,
technology and
engineering

Funding priority
British Council for Prevention
   of Blindness
British Institute of Archaeology
   at Ankara
Charles Brotherton Trust
Children's Liver Disease
   Foundation
Colt Foundation
Garthgwynion Charities
Teresa Rosenbaum Golden
   Charitable Trust
Michael & Morven Heller
   Charitable Foundation
Simon Heller Charitable
   Settlement
International Spinal Research
   Trust
Emmanuel Kaye Foundation
Lindeth Charitable Trust
Macfarlane Walker Trust
Kitty and Daniel Nabarro
   Charitable Trust
North West Cancer Research
   Fund
Ulverscroft Foundation
Wilkinson Charitable
   Foundation
Wolfson Foundation
John K Young Endowment
   Fund

Will consider
Bingham Trust
Childwick Trust
Coutts & Co. Charitable Trust
Diabetes UK
Ian Fleming Charitable Trust
Maurice Fry Charitable Trust
Sue Hammerson's Charitable Trust
Sir Julian Hodge Charitable Trust
Mary Homfray Charitable Trust
C F Lunoe Trust Fund
Minge's Gift
National Asthma Campaign
Newby Trust Limited
Northcott Devon Medical Foundation
Pastoral Care Trust
Patrick Charitable Trust
J S F Pollitzer Charitable Settlement
Märit and Hans Rausing Charitable Foundation
Mrs L D Rope Third Charitable Settlement
Peter Samuel Charitable Trust
Scouloudi Foundation
Sir Halley Stewart Trust
Triangle Trust (1949) Fund

■ Seafarers & fishermen

Funding priority
Billingsgate Christian Mission Charitable Trust
Sir Alec Black's Charity
Cleary Foundation
Criffel Charitable Trust
Dock Charitable Fund
Erskine Cunningham Hill Trust
Fishmongers' Company's Charitable Trust
Simon Gibson Charitable Trust
Inverclyde Bequest Fund
ITF Seafarers Trust
Jeffrey Charitable Trust
King George's Fund for Sailors
Sir James Knott Trust
Liverpool Sailors' Home Trust
MacRobert Trust
Pennycress Trust
Phillips Charitable Trust
Seamen's Hospital Society
Shipwrights Company Charitable Fund
Verdon-Smith Family Charitable Settlement

Will consider
Sir John & Lady Amory's Charitable Trust
G C Armitage Charitable Trust
Astor Foundation
Baltic Charitable Fund

Bingham Trust
Lord Clinton's Charitable Trust
Coutts & Co. Charitable Trust
De Clermont Charitable Company Ltd
Dulverton Trust
Sir John Fisher Foundation
Constance Green Foundation
H & M Charitable Trust
Mary Homfray Charitable Trust
James Thom Howat Charitable Trust
Inverforth Charitable Trust
Joicey Trust
Edward Cecil Jones Settlement
Maurice Laing Foundation
George John Livanos Charitable Trust
C F Lunoe Trust Fund
R W Mann Trustees Limited
Minge's Gift
George A Moore Foundation
Horace Moore Charitable Trust
Norman Family Charitable Trust
Northcott Devon Foundation
Pastoral Care Trust
Bernard Piggott Trust
A M Pilkington's Charitable Trust
J S F Pollitzer Charitable Settlement
John Rayner Charitable Trust
Christopher Rowbotham Charitable Trust
Coral Samuel Charitable Trust
Scouloudi Foundation
Tay Charitable Trust
Mary Webb Trust

■ Social sciences

Will consider
Bingham Trust
Girdlers' Company Charitable Trust
Mary Homfray Charitable Trust
Pastoral Care Trust
Patients' Aid Association Hospital & Medical Charities Trust

■ Social welfare and public services

Funding priority
CLA Charitable Trust
Greater Bristol Foundation

Will consider
Bingham Trust
Coutts & Co. Charitable Trust
Earl Fitzwilliam Charitable Trust

Girdlers' Company Charitable Trust
Mary Homfray Charitable Trust
Northcott Devon Foundation
Pastoral Care Trust
Patients' Aid Association Hospital & Medical Charities Trust
Rothley Trust

■ Sporting or social clubs, including masons

Funding priority
Grand Charitable Trust of the Order of Women Freemasons
Warwickshire Masonic Charitable Association Ltd

Will consider
Cheshire Provincial Fund of Benevolence
May Hearnshaw's Charity
Mary Homfray Charitable Trust
Lynn Foundation
Minge's Gift
Pastoral Care Trust
Jack Petchey Foundation

■ Textile workers & designers

Funding priority
Lord Barnby's Foundation
Coats Foundation Trust
Dyers' Company Charitable Trust
Worshipful Company of Glovers of London Charity Fund

Will consider
Bingham Trust
Eden Arts Trust
Mary Homfray Charitable Trust
Nigel Moores Family Charitable Trust
Northcott Devon Foundation
Pastoral Care Trust
Radcliffe Trust
Riverside Charitable Trust Limited
Scouloudi Foundation

■ Transport

Funding priority
Worshipful Company of Carmen Benevolent Trust

Will consider

Mary Homfray Charitable Trust
Pastoral Care Trust
Patrick Charitable Trust

....

■ **Voluntary sector or doing voluntary work**

Funding priority

R S Brownless Charitable
  Trust
Camelot Foundation
CLA Charitable Trust
Cobb Charity
Consortium on Opportunities
  for Volunteering
Cray Trust
Criffel Charitable Trust
De Clermont Charitable
  Company Ltd
Derbyshire Community
  Foundation
William Dudley Trust
Erskine Cunningham Hill Trust
Essex Community Foundation
Simon Gibson Charitable Trust
Greater Bristol Foundation
J C Green Charitable
  Settlement
Greggs Trust
Kenneth Hargreaves Charitable
  Trust
Joseph & Mary Hiley Trust
Sir James Knott Trust
William Leech Charity
Lintel Trust
Lloyds TSB Foundation for
  Scotland
Lloyds TSB Foundation for the
  Channel Islands
London Law Trust
London Youth Trust
Milton Keynes Community
  Foundation
Patients' Aid Association
  Hospital & Medical
  Charities Trust
Jack Petchey Foundation
Pilkington Charities Fund
Mrs L D Rope Third Charitable
  Settlement
Christopher Rowbotham
  Charitable Trust
St Peter's Saltley Trust
Torchbearer Trust
West Derby Wastelands
  Charity
Whitaker Charitable Trust

Will consider

Adnams Charity
Astor Foundation
Bamford Charitable Foundation
Barbour Trust

Philip Barker Charity
Barnabas Charitable Trust
BBC Children in Need Appeal
Hervey Benham Charitable
  Trust
Berkshire Community
  Foundation
Bingham Trust
Charles Brotherton Trust
Carlton Television Trust
Chase Charity
Chrimes Family Charitable
  Trust
Christendom Trust
Lord Clinton's Charitable Trust
Norman Collinson Charitable
  Trust
County of Gloucestershire
  Community Foundation
Coutts & Co. Charitable Trust
Harry Crook Foundation
Cwmbran Trust
Roald Dahl Foundation
John Grant Davies Trust
Helen and Geoffrey de Freitas
  Charitable Trust
Dove-Bowerman Trust
Dulverton Trust
Eden Arts Trust
Earl Fitzwilliam Charitable
  Trust
Joyce Fletcher Charitable Trust
Ford of Britain Trust
Robert Gavron Charitable Trust
Girdlers' Company Charitable
  Trust
Bishop of Guildford's
  Foundation
Hadrian Trust
Hale Trust
Charles Hayward Foundation
Hilden Charitable Fund
Dorothy Holmes Charitable
  Trust
Holywood Trust
Mary Homfray Charitable Trust
Housing Associations
  Charitable Trust
James Thom Howat Charitable
  Trust
Human Relief Foundation
Hyde Park Place Estate Charity
  – civil trustees
Isle of Dogs Community
  Foundation
Jeffrey Charitable Trust
Jesus Hospital Charity
Lankelly Foundation
Mrs F B Laurence Charitable
  Trust
Leigh Trust
Lloyds TSB Foundation for
  Northern Ireland
C F Lunoe Trust Fund
R W Mann Trustees Limited
John Martin's Charity

Mercers' Charitable
  Foundation
Minge's Gift
John Moores Foundation
Morel Charitable Trust
Newby Trust Limited
Norman Family Charitable
  Trust
Northcott Devon Foundation
Pastoral Care Trust
A M Pilkington's Charitable
  Trust
Powys Welsh Church Fund
Prince Philip Trust Fund
John Rayner Charitable Trust
Reuters Foundation
Richmond Parish Lands Charity
Rothley Trust
Sir Walter St John's
  Educational Charity
Scott Bader Commonwealth
  Ltd
Henry Smith Charity
Leslie Smith Foundation
Tay Charitable Trust
Mary Webb Trust
Whitecourt Charitable Trust
Michael and Anna Wix
  Charitable Trust
Woodlands Trust (259569)
Worshipful Company of
  Founders Charities
Yardley Great Trust

■ **Disability**

Funding priority

Abbey National Charitable
  Trust Ltd
Aberbrothock Charitable Trust
Henry & Grete Abrahams
  Second Charitable
  Foundation
Miss Agnes Gilchrist
  Adamson's Trust
ADAPT Trust
Green & Lilian F M Ainsworth
  & Family Benevolent Fund
Ajahma Charitable Trust
Ammco Trust
Ardwick Trust
Astor Foundation
BAA 21st Century
  Communities Trust
Baily Thomas Charitable Fund
Baker Charitable Trust
Band (1976) Trust
Barbour Trust
Barnes Workhouse Fund
Barnwood House Trust
Bartle Family Charitable Trust
Paul Bassham Charitable Trust
BBC Children in Need Appeal
BBC Radio Cambridgeshire –
  Trustline
Beaurepaire Trust

Benham Charitable Settlement
Rowan Bentall Charitable Trust
Berkshire Community
    Foundation
Bethesda Community
    Charitable Trust
Thomas Betton's Charity for
    Pensions and Relief-in-Need
BibleLands
Percy Bilton Charity Ltd
Birmingham Hospital Saturday
    Fund Medical Charity &
    Welfare Trust
Isabel Blackman Foundation
BNFL Springfields Medical
    Research & Charity Trust
    Fund
Bonhomie United Charity
    Society
A Bornstein Charitable
    Settlement
Boughton Trust
P G & N J Boulton Trust
Bridge House Estates Trust
    Fund
Bridge Trust
Charles Brotherton Trust
R S Brownless Charitable
    Trust
Burton Breweries Charitable
    Trust
Bill Butlin Charity Trust
Barrow Cadbury Trust and the
    Barrow Cadbury Fund
Camelot Foundation
Carlton Television Trust
H and M Castang Charitable
    Trust
Chase Charity
Chelsea Building Society
    Charitable Foundation
Chest Heart and Stroke
    Scotland
Chippenham Borough Lands
    Charity
Cleary Foundation
Cleopatra Trust
Lord Clinton's Charitable Trust
Richard Cloudesley's Charity
Coates Charitable Settlement
Commonwealth Relations
    Trust
Community Foundation Serving
    Tyne & Wear and
    Northumberland
Consortium on Opportunities
    for Volunteering
Construction Industry Trust for
    Youth
Cooper Charitable Trust
Cotton Trust
Coutts & Co. Charitable Trust
Cumber Family Charitable
    Trust
Alex Deas Charitable Trust
Dickon Trust

Dorus Trust
Dumbreck Charity
Dwek Family Charitable Trust
Wilfred & Elsie Elkes Charity
    Fund
Ellis Campbell Charitable
    Foundation
James Ellis Charitable Trust
Emerton-Christie Charity
Mayor of the London Borough
    of Enfield Appeal Fund
Epigoni Trust
Equitable Charitable Trust
Essex Community Foundation
Essex Fairway Charitable Trust
Douglas Heath Eves Charitable
    Trust
Eveson Charitable Trust
Family Rich Charities Trust
Fassnidge Memorial Trust
Fawcett Charitable Trust
Fiat Auto (UK) Charity
Fidelity UK Foundation
Fifty Fund
Ian Fleming Charitable Trust
Joyce Fletcher Charitable Trust
Roy Fletcher Charitable Trust
Oliver Ford Charitable Trust
Foresters' Charity Stewards
    UK Trust
Donald Forrester Trust
Forte Charitable Trust
Frognal Trust
Gatsby Charitable Foundation
Simon Gibson Charitable Trust
L & R Gilley Charitable Trust
B & P Glasser Charitable Trust
Global Care
Good Neighbours Trust
Gray Trust
Greater Bristol Foundation
Constance Green Foundation
Grocers' Charity
Hadley Trust
Alfred Haines Charitable Trust
Hale Trust
E F & M G Hall Charitable
    Trust
Hampstead Wells and
    Campden Trust
Hampton Fuel Allotment
    Charity
Handicapped Children's Aid
    Committee
Kathleen Hannay Memorial
    Charity
Lennox Hannay Charitable
    Trust
William Harding's Charity
Harebell Centenary Fund
Peter Harrison Foundation
N & P Hartley Memorial Trust
M A Hawe Settlement
Charles Hayward Foundation
Healthsure Group Ltd

Heart of England Community
    Foundation
Hedley Foundation
Hertfordshire Community
    Foundation
Joseph & Mary Hiley Trust
Hillingdon Partnership Trust
Sir Julian Hodge Charitable
    Trust
Edward Sydney Hogg
    Charitable Settlement
Dorothy Holmes Charitable
    Trust
Holywood Trust
Antony Hornby Charitable Trust
Mrs E G Hornby's Charitable
    Settlement
Housing Associations
    Charitable Trust
Huggard Charitable Trust
Miss Agnes H Hunter's Trust
Iliffe Family Charitable Trust
Imerys South West Charitable
    Trust
Inman Charity
Ironmongers' Quincentenary
    Charitable Fund
Charles Irving Charitable Trust
J J Charitable Trust
Yvette and Hermione Jacobson
    Charitable Trust
Jeffrey Charitable Trust
Jewish Child's Day
Jones 1986 Charitable Trust
J E Joseph Charitable Fund
Ian Karten Charitable Trust
Kidani Memorial Trust
Ernest Kleinwort Charitable
    Trust
Beatrice Laing Trust
David Laing Foundation
Langdale Trust
Richard Langhorn Trust
Leeds Hospital Fund
    Charitable Trust
John Lewis Partnership
    General Community Fund
Lintel Trust
Lloyds TSB Foundation for
    Scotland
Lloyds TSB Foundation for the
    Channel Islands
Lord's Taverners
Paul Lunn-Rockliffe Charitable
    Trust
Lynn Foundation
MacRobert Trust
Ian Mactaggart Fund
Man Group plc Charitable
    Trust
Marchday Charitable Fund
D G Marshall of Cambridge
    Trust
Jim Marshall Charitable Trust
Maxwell Family Foundation

Charity of Mary Jane,
  Countess of Meath
Mental Health Foundation
Tony Metherell Charitable
  Trust
Metropolitan Hospital-Sunday
  Fund
Gerald Micklem Charitable
  Trust
Miller Foundation
Hugh and Mary Miller Bequest
  Trust
Clare Milne Trust
Milton Keynes Community
  Foundation
Peter Minet Trust
Minge's Gift
John Moores Foundation
Morgan Crucible Company plc
  Charitable Trust
S C and M E Morland's
  Charitable Trust
Mountbatten Memorial Trust
Edith Murphy Foundation
Music Sales Charitable Trust
National Power Charitable
  Trust
Neighbourly Charitable Trust
New Appeals Organisation for
  the City & County of
  Nottingham
Newby Trust Limited
Newport County Borough
  Welsh Church Fund
Newstead Charity
North British Hotel Trust
Norton Foundation
Oakdale Trust
Odin Charitable Trust
Old Enfield Charitable Trust
Pastoral Care Trust
Patients' Aid Association
  Hospital & Medical
  Charities Trust
Patrick Charitable Trust
Peabody Community Fund
Peacock Charitable Trust
Persula Foundation
Austin & Hope Pilkington Trust
Pilkington Charities Fund
Platinum Trust
J D Player Endowment Fund
Portishead Nautical Trust
Powell Foundation
PPP Foundation
Douglas Prestwich Charitable
  Trust
Privy Purse Charitable Trust
Radio Forth Help a Child
  Appeal
Märit and Hans Rausing
  Charitable Foundation
John Rayner Charitable Trust
Red Dragon Radio Trust
Rest Harrow Trust
Clive Richards Charity Ltd

Rivendell Trust
Thomas Roberts Trust
Rooke Atlay Charitable Trust
Rosca Trust
Cecil Rosen Foundation
Rothley Trust
Christopher Rowbotham
  Charitable Trust
Royal Docks Trust
Saddlers' Company Charitable
  Fund
Karim Rida Said Foundation
St James's Place Foundation
Sir Walter St John's
  Educational Charity
St Mary-le-Strand Charity
Late St Patrick White
  Charitable Trust
Saint Sarkis Charity Trust
Francis C Scott Charitable
  Trust
Frieda Scott Charitable Trust
Sir James & Lady Scott Trust
Scouloudi Foundation
Shakespeare Temperance
  Trust
Sylvia & Colin Shepherd
  Charitable Trust
Barbara A Shuttleworth
  Memorial Trust
Skinners' Company Lady
  Neville Charity
Mrs Smith & Mount Trust
Snowball Trust
Sobell Foundation
Solo Charitable Settlement
Stanton Ballard Charitable
  Trust
Starfish Trust
Strangward Trust
Charles and Elsie Sykes Trust
Mrs A Lacy Tate Trust
Tesco Charity Trust
C Paul Thackray General
  Charitable Trust
Thames Community
  Foundation
Thornton Trust
Three Oaks Trust
Tower Hill Improvement Trust
Towry Law Charitable Trust
Trades House of Glasgow
Triangle Trust (1949) Fund
Truemark Trust
Trust Sixty Three
Trusthouse Charitable
  Foundation
Ulverscroft Foundation
Ulverston Town Lands Charity
John and Lucille van Geest
  Foundation
Variety Club Children's Charity
Verdon-Smith Family Charitable
  Settlement
Vintners Company Charitable
  Trust

Thomas Wall Trust
Ward Blenkinsop Trust
Warwickshire Masonic
  Charitable Association Ltd
Perry Watlington Trust
John Watson's Trust
Mary Webb Trust
Weinstock Fund
Alfred and Beatrice Weintrop
  Charity
Charity of John West & Others
White Rose Children's Aid
  International Charity
Sheila Whitley Trust
Lionel Wigram Memorial Trust
Wiltshire and Swindon
  Community Foundation
Mayor of Wirral's Charity Trust
Wixamtree Trust
Maurice Wohl Charitable
  Foundation
Maurice Wohl Charitable Trust
Woodlands Trust (1015942)
Woodlands Trust (259569)
Xerox (UK) Trust
Yorkshire Bank Charitable
  Trust
Yorkshire Building Society
  Charitable Foundation
Elizabeth & Prince Zaiger Trust
Zurich Financial Services
  Community Trust

Will consider
29th May 1961 Charitable
  Trust
Sylvia Adams Charitable Trust
Adint Charitable Trust
Adnams Charity
Alchemy Foundation
Viscount Amory's Charitable
  Trust
Sir John & Lady Amory's
  Charitable Trust
AMW Charitable Trust
Andrew Anderson Trust
Appletree Trust
G C Armitage Charitable Trust
Armourers and Brasiers'
  Gauntlet Trust
Lord Ashdown Charitable Trust
Laura Ashley Foundation
Badley Memorial Trust
Balcombe Charitable Trust
Andrew Balint Charitable Trust
George Balint Charitable Trust
Paul Balint Charitable Trust
Bamford Charitable Foundation
David and Frederick Barclay
  Foundation
Philip Barker Charity
Barnabas Charitable Trust
Lord Barnby's Foundation
Bedford Charity
E M Behrens Charitable Trust
Bingham Trust

Herbert & Peter Blagrave
    Charitable Trust
Morgan Blake Charitable Trust
Blanchminster Trust
Enid Blyton Trust for Children
Charles Boot Trust
Bramble Charitable Trust
John Bristow and Thomas
    Mason Trust
British Humane Association
Roger Brooke Charitable Trust
Miss Marion Broughton's
    Charitable Trust
Bryant Trust
Buckinghamshire Masonic
    Centenary Fund
Arnold James Burton 1956
    Charitable Settlement
R M 1956 Burton Charitable
    Trust
Consolidated Charity of Burton
    Upon Trent
Edward Cadbury Charitable
    Trust
Edward & Dorothy Cadbury
    Trust
William A Cadbury Charitable
    Trust
Caring for Kids
Carnegie Dunfermline Trust
Cattanach Charitable Trust
Wilfrid & Constance Cave
    Foundation
Childwick Trust
Chipping Sodbury Town Lands
    Charity
Chrimes Family Charitable
    Trust
City and Metropolitan Welfare
    Charity
City Parochial Foundation
Clover Trust
John Coates Charitable Trust
Colchester Catalyst Charity
John & Freda Coleman
    Charitable Trust
Norman Collinson Charitable
    Trust
Comic Relief
Community Fund
Congleton Inclosure Trust
Ernest Cook Trust
Coppings Trust
County Durham Foundation
County of Gloucestershire
    Community Foundation
Cranbury Foundation
Criffel Charitable Trust
Cripplegate Foundation
Harry Crook Foundation
Cwmbran Trust
D'Oyly Carte Charitable Trust
Dr & Mrs A Darlington
    Charitable Trust
John Grant Davies Trust

De Clermont Charitable
    Company Ltd
Derbyshire Community
    Foundation
Devon Community Foundation
Douglas Charitable Trust
Drapers' Charitable Fund
Duis Charitable Trust
Dunhill Medical Trust
Earley Charity
Sir John Eastwood Foundation
Eden Arts Trust
City of Edinburgh Charitable
    Trusts
Edinburgh Voluntary
    Organisations' Trust Funds
John Ellerman Foundation
Elmgrant Trust
Vernon N Ely Charitable Trust
Emmandjay Charitable Trust
Enkalon Foundation
Erskine Cunningham Hill Trust
Exilarch's Foundation
Esmée Fairbairn Foundation
Samuel William Farmer's Trust
Finnart House School Trust
David Finnie & Alan Emery
    Charitable Trust
Fishmongers' Company's
    Charitable Trust
Earl Fitzwilliam Charitable
    Trust
Ford of Britain Trust
Fordeve Ltd
Fox Memorial Trust
Charles S French Charitable
    Trust
Angela Gallagher Memorial
    Fund
Gannochy Trust
Robert Gavron Charitable Trust
G C Gibson Charitable Trust
Girdlers' Company Charitable
    Trust
Godinton Charitable Trust
Sydney & Phyllis Goldberg
    Memorial Charitable Trust
J G Graves Charitable Trust
Grimley Charity
Bishop of Guildford's
    Foundation
Walter Guinness Charitable
    Trust
Gulbenkian Foundation
H C D Memorial Fund
Hadfield Trust
Hadrian Trust
Eleanor Hamilton Educational
    and Charitable Trust
Harborne Parish Lands Charity
Harrison & Potter Trust
Gay & Peter Hartley's Hillards
    Charitable Trust
Hemby Trust
Hesslewood Children's Trust
Alan Edward Higgs Charity

Hilden Charitable Fund
Jane Hodge Foundation
Mary Homfray Charitable Trust
Hospital of God at Greatham
Clifford Howarth Charity
    Settlement
James Thom Howat Charitable
    Trust
Huddersfield Common Good
    Trust
Human Relief Foundation
Humanitarian Trust
Inchrye Trust
Inverforth Charitable Trust
Isle of Anglesey Charitable
    Trust
Ruth & Lionel Jacobson Trust
    (Second Fund) No 2
Jarman Charitable Trust
Jephcott Charitable Trust
Jesus Hospital Charity
Johnson Foundation
Johnson Group Cleaners
    Charity
Joicey Trust
Boris Karloff Charitable
    Foundation
King's Fund
Kirkley Poor's Land Estate
Kleinwort Benson Charitable
    Trust
Sir James Knott Trust
Knowles Charitable Trust
Kobler Trust
Kreitman Foundation
Neil Kreitman Foundation
Heinz & Anna Kroch
    Foundation
Late Sir Pierce Lacy Charity
    Trust
Christopher Laing Foundation
Kirby Laing Foundation
Maurice Laing Foundation
Maurice and Hilda Laing
    Charitable Trust
Bryan Lancaster's Charity
Lankelly Foundation
R J Larg Family Charitable
    Trust
Lauffer Family Charitable
    Foundation
Raymond & Blanche Lawson
    Charitable Trust
Leach Fourteenth Trust
Leathersellers' Company
    Charitable Fund
Lord Leverhulme Charitable
    Trust
Levy Foundation
Linbury Trust
Enid Linder Foundation
Lloyd's Charities Trust
Lloyds TSB Foundation for
    England and Wales
Lloyds TSB Foundation for
    Northern Ireland

London Law Trust
London North East Community
    Foundation
C L Loyd Charitable Trust
Luck-Hille Foundation
C F Lunoe Trust Fund
Helen Isabella McMorran
    Charitable Foundation
D D McPhail Charitable
    Settlement
R W Mann Trustees Limited
Leslie & Lilian Manning Trust
Hilda & Samuel Marks
    Foundation
Sir George Martin Trust
John Martin's Charity
Mercers' Charitable
    Foundation
Merchant Taylors' Company
    Charities Fund
Zachary Merton & George
    Woofindin Convalescent
    Trust
Middlesex County Rugby
    Football Union Memorial
    Fund
Miles Trust for the Putney and
    Roehampton Community
Keith and Joan Mindelsohn
    Charitable Trust
Victor Mishcon Charitable
    Trust
Mobbs Memorial Trust Ltd
Monument Trust
George A Moore Foundation
Horace Moore Charitable Trust
J P Morgan Fleming
    Educational Trust and
    Foundation
Morgan Stanley International
    Foundation
Moss Family Charitable Trust
Edwina Mountbatten Trust
Mugdock Children's Trust
NAM Charitable Trust
Nestlé Rowntree York
    Employees Community Fund
    Trust
Norman Family Charitable
    Trust
North London Islamic
    Association Trust
Northcott Devon Foundation
Northmoor Trust
Norwich Consolidated
    Charities
Noswad Charity
Nottingham General
    Dispensary
Nova Charitable Trust
Nuffield Foundation
Oakley Charitable Trust
Old Possum's Practical Trust
Kate Wilson Oliver Trust
Oxfam (GB)
Parivar Trust

Parthenon Trust
Arthur James Paterson
    Charitable Trust
Constance Paterson Charitable
    Trust
Harry Payne Trust
Jack Petchey Foundation
Ruth & Michael Phillips
    Charitable Trust
A M Pilkington's Charitable
    Trust
John Pitman Charitable Trust
J S F Pollitzer Charitable
    Settlement
W L Pratt Charitable Trust
Simone Prendergast Charitable
    Trust
Princess Anne's Charities
Proven Family Trust
Puri Foundation
Pye Foundation
Rainford Trust
Joseph & Lena Randall
    Charitable Trust
Rank Foundation
Eleanor Rathbone Charitable
    Trust
Ravensdale Trust
Rayne Foundation
Reuters Foundation
Rhododendron Trust
Cliff Richard Charitable Trust
Richmond Parish Lands Charity
Robertson Trust
Mrs L D Rope Third Charitable
    Settlement
Rowan Charitable Trust
Rowlands Trust
Joseph Rowntree Foundation
Rufford Foundation
St James' Trust Settlement
St Laurence Charities for the
    Poor
Andrew Salvesen Charitable
    Trust
Basil Samuel Charitable Trust
R H Scholes Charitable Trust
Scottish Community
    Foundation
Sefton Community Foundation
Sellafield Charity Trust Fund
Servite Sisters' Charitable
    Trust Fund
Sheldon Trust
Sherburn House Charity
Shuttlewood Clarke Foundation
Mary Elizabeth Siebel Charity
Bishop Simeon CR Trust
Skelton Bounty
SMB Trust
Henry Smith Charity
Leslie Smith Foundation
David Solomons Charitable
    Trust
South Yorkshire Community
    Foundation

Sovereign Health Care
    Charitable Trust
Stanley Spooner Deceased
    Charitable Trust
W W Spooner Charitable Trust
Sportsman's Charity
Stanley Foundation Ltd
Sir Halley Stewart Trust
Leonard Laity Stoate
    Charitable Trust
Foundation of Edward Storey
W O Street Charitable
    Foundation
Summerfield Charitable Trust
Bernard Sunley Charitable
    Foundation
Talbot Trusts
Sue Thomson Foundation
Sir Jules Thorn Charitable
    Trust
Tisbury Telegraph Trust
Constance Travis Charitable
    Trust
Trust for London
Douglas Turner Trust
Florence Turner Trust
R D Turner Charitable Trust
Ullmann Trust
Underwood Trust
Unemployed Voluntary Action
    Fund
Albert Van Den Bergh
    Charitable Trust
Mrs Maud Van Norden's
    Charitable Foundation
Wakefield Trust
Wates Foundation
Bertie Watson Foundation
Wellfield Trust
Welsh Church Fund –
    Carmarthenshire area
Wesleyan Charitable Trust
Westminster Amalgamated
    Charity
Garfield Weston Foundation
Whitaker Charitable Trust
Whitecourt Charitable Trust
Michael and Anna Wix
    Charitable Trust
Charles Wolfson Charitable
    Trust
Wolfson Family Charitable
    Trust
Wolfson Foundation
Woodward Trust
Worcester Municipal Charities
Worshipful Company of
    Founders Charities
Wyseliot Charitable Trust
Yapp Charitable Trust
Yardley Great Trust
York Children's Trust
Zephyr Charitable Trust

■ People with a mental impairment

Funding priority

Kelsick's Educational Foundation
Leeds & Holbeck Building Society Charitable Foundation
Northern Rock Foundation
Thomson Corporation Charitable Trust
Three Oaks Trust

Will consider

Richard Cadbury Charitable Trust
Gatwick Airport Community Trust
Good Neighbours Trust
Edward Cecil Jones Settlement
Peter Kershaw Trust
Laing's Charitable Trust
Mr and Mrs J A Pye's Charitable Settlement

■ People with autism
Funding priority

Astor of Hever Trust
Baily Thomas Charitable Fund
Birmingham Hospital Saturday Fund Medical Charity & Welfare Trust
Cleopatra Trust
Dorus Trust
Epigoni Trust
Jill Franklin Trust
Teresa Rosenbaum Golden Charitable Trust
Hampton Fuel Allotment Charity
Handicapped Children's Aid Committee
May Hearnshaw's Charity
Kennedy Leigh Charitable Trust
Cliff Richard Charitable Trust
Shirley Foundation
David Solomons Charitable Trust
Stanley Foundation Ltd
Tesco Charity Trust
Three Guineas Trust
Verdon-Smith Family Charitable Settlement
Wentwood Education Trust
West London Synagogue Charitable Fund

Will consider

Adnams Charity
Ardwick Trust
Bonhomie United Charity Society
Chase Charity

Chrimes Family Charitable Trust
Norman Collinson Charitable Trust
Criffel Charitable Trust
Jacqueline and Michael Gee Charitable Trust
Constance Green Foundation
Hallam FM – Help a Hallam Child Appeal
Hampstead Wells and Campden Trust
Hare of Steep Charitable Trust
Charles Hayward Foundation
Heart of England Community Foundation
Edward Holt Trust
Hospital Saturday Fund Charitable Trust
James Thom Howat Charitable Trust
Miss Agnes H Hunter's Trust
Jarman Charitable Trust
Jeffrey Charitable Trust
Anton Jurgens Charitable Trust
London Law Trust
Magdalen Hospital Trust
R W Mann Trustees Limited
Marchday Charitable Fund
Mercers' Charitable Foundation
Tony Metherell Charitable Trust
Metropolitan Hospital-Sunday Fund
Minge's Gift
Horace Moore Charitable Trust
Nestlé Rowntree York Employees Community Fund Trust
Northern Rock Foundation
Oxfordshire Community Foundation
Pilkington Charities Fund
John Pitman Charitable Trust
J S F Pollitzer Charitable Settlement
Ravensdale Trust
John Rayner Charitable Trust
Red Dragon Radio Trust
Rivendell Trust
Rufford Foundation
Saddlers' Company Charitable Fund
Andrew Salvesen Charitable Trust
Frieda Scott Charitable Trust
Sir James & Lady Scott Trust
Scouloudi Foundation
Sefton Community Foundation
Sobell Foundation
W W Spooner Charitable Trust
Charles and Elsie Sykes Trust
Thoresby Charitable Trust
Sir Jules Thorn Charitable Trust

Tisbury Telegraph Trust
Tudor Trust
Perry Watlington Trust
Wellfield Trust
Wesleyan Charitable Trust
Michael and Anna Wix Charitable Trust

■ Brain damaged people
Funding priority

Ardwick Trust
Roald Dahl Foundation
Anton Jurgens Charitable Trust
Cliff Richard Charitable Trust

Will consider

Adnams Charity
Birmingham Hospital Saturday Fund Medical Charity & Welfare Trust
Bothwell Charitable Trust
Sarah D'Avigdor Goldsmid Charitable Trust
Wilfrid Bruce Davis Charitable Trust
Charles Hayward Foundation
Scouloudi Foundation
Steinberg Family Charitable Trust
Tesco Charity Trust
Wentwood Education Trust

■ People with dyslexia
Funding priority

Ashby Charitable Trust
Joseph & Annie Cattle Trust
Anton Jurgens Charitable Trust
Vision Charity

Will consider

Ardwick Trust
Birmingham Hospital Saturday Fund Medical Charity & Welfare Trust
Tesco Charity Trust

■ People with learning difficulties
Funding priority

Ardwick Trust
Cattanach Charitable Trust
Joseph & Annie Cattle Trust
Chase Charity
Child Growth Foundation
Forbes Charitable Trust
Jill Franklin Trust
Judith Trust
Anton Jurgens Charitable Trust
Kitty and Daniel Nabarro Charitable Trust
Northumberland Village Homes Trust
Royal Eastern Counties Schools Limited
Mrs Smith & Mount Trust

David Solomons Charitable
Trust
Wentwood Education Trust
West London Synagogue
Charitable Fund

Will consider
Adnams Charity
Bellinger Donnay Trust
Birmingham Foundation
Birmingham Hospital Saturday
Fund Medical Charity &
Welfare Trust
Bothwell Charitable Trust
Coates Charitable Settlement
Teresa Rosenbaum Golden
Charitable Trust
Charles Hayward Foundation
London Law Trust
Magdalen Hospital Trust
Middlesex County Rugby
Football Union Memorial
Fund
Northern Rock Foundation
Tesco Charity Trust
Scurrah Wainwright Charity
Will Charitable Trust
Harold Hyam Wingate
Foundation

....

■ People with a physical impairment
Funding priority
Birmingham Hospital Saturday
Fund Medical Charity &
Welfare Trust
Cattanach Charitable Trust
Joseph & Annie Cattle Trust
Lance Coates Charitable Trust
1969
Simon Gibson Charitable Trust
Hampton Fuel Allotment
Charity
Anton Jurgens Charitable Trust
Richard Radcliffe Charitable
Trust
Stanley Foundation Ltd
Thomson Corporation
Charitable Trust
West London Synagogue
Charitable Fund
Lionel Wigram Memorial Trust

Will consider
Ardwick Trust
Beit Trust
Bellinger Donnay Trust
Birmingham Foundation
Peter Birse Charitable Trust
Bonhomie United Charity
Society
Bill Butlin Charity Trust
Chase Charity
Coates Charitable Settlement

Norman Collinson Charitable
Trust
Gatwick Airport Community
Trust
Teresa Rosenbaum Golden
Charitable Trust
Good Neighbours Trust
Hallam FM – Help a Hallam
Child Appeal
Hampstead Wells and
Campden Trust
Charles Hayward Foundation
Heart of England Community
Foundation
Hospital Saturday Fund
Charitable Trust
Ruth & Lionel Jacobson Trust
(Second Fund) No 2
Jeffrey Charitable Trust
Peter Kershaw Trust
Raymond & Blanche Lawson
Charitable Trust
London Law Trust
Tony Metherell Charitable
Trust
Metropolitan Hospital-Sunday
Fund
Minge's Gift
Nestlé Rowntree York
Employees Community Fund
Trust
Oxfordshire Community
Foundation
Bernard Piggott Trust
John Pitman Charitable Trust
J S F Pollitzer Charitable
Settlement
Rainford Trust
John Rayner Charitable Trust
Red Dragon Radio Trust
Cliff Richard Charitable Trust
Rivendell Trust
Saddlers' Company Charitable
Fund
Andrew Salvesen Charitable
Trust
Frieda Scott Charitable Trust
Sir James & Lady Scott Trust
Scottish International
Education Trust
Scouloudi Foundation
Sefton Community Foundation
W W Spooner Charitable Trust
Starfish Trust
Steinberg Family Charitable
Trust
Charles and Elsie Sykes Trust
Tesco Charity Trust
Sir Jules Thorn Charitable
Trust
Perry Watlington Trust
Wesleyan Charitable Trust
Harold Hyam Wingate
Foundation

■ Cerebral palsy
Funding priority
James and Grace Anderson
Trust
Baily Thomas Charitable Fund
BibleLands
Audrey & Stanley Burton
Charitable Trust
Norman Evershed Trust
Paul Lunn-Rockliffe Charitable
Trust
R S MacDonald Charitable
Trust
Willie & Mabel Morris
Charitable Trust
Northumberland Village Homes
Trust
Ronald & Kathleen Pryor
Charitable Trust
Sobell Foundation
Verdon-Smith Family Charitable
Settlement

Will consider
Andrew Balint Charitable Trust
George Balint Charitable Trust
Enid Blyton Trust for Children
Clover Trust
Criffel Charitable Trust
Constance Green Foundation
Lennox Hannay Charitable
Trust
Miss Agnes H Hunter's Trust
John Jarrold Trust
Lauffer Family Charitable
Foundation
R W Mann Trustees Limited
Pilkington Charities Fund
Mr and Mrs J A Pye's
Charitable Settlement
Ravensdale Trust
David Solomons Charitable
Trust
Tisbury Telegraph Trust
Triangle Trust (1949) Fund
Michael and Anna Wix
Charitable Trust

■ Spina bifida & Hydrocephalus
Funding priority
Ashby Charitable Trust
Cleopatra Trust
Dorus Trust
Epigoni Trust
Garthgwynion Charities
Handicapped Children's Aid
Committee
Lennox Hannay Charitable
Trust
Clifford Howarth Charity
Settlement
Pilkington Charities Fund
Mr and Mrs J A Pye's
Charitable Settlement

Will consider

Baily Thomas Charitable Fund
Audrey & Stanley Burton
    Charitable Trust
Richard Cadbury Charitable
    Trust
Chownes Foundation
Earl Fitzwilliam Charitable
    Trust
Hadrian Trust
Humanitarian Trust
Jarman Charitable Trust
Loseley & Guildway Charitable
    Trust
Sobell Foundation
Wellfield Trust

....

■ People with a sensory impairment

Funding priority

BibleLands
Birmingham Hospital Saturday
    Fund Medical Charity &
    Welfare Trust
Blair Foundation
Bothwell Charitable Trust
Cleopatra Trust
Lord Clinton's Charitable Trust
Dorus Trust
Epigoni Trust
Timothy Franey Charitable
    Foundation
Simon Gibson Charitable Trust
Teresa Rosenbaum Golden
    Charitable Trust
Hampton Fuel Allotment
    Charity
Handicapped Children's Aid
    Committee
Lennox Hannay Charitable
    Trust
Anton Jurgens Charitable Trust
Peter Kershaw Trust
John Spedan Lewis Foundation
Northumberland Village Homes
    Trust
Oxfordshire Community
    Foundation
Ronald & Kathleen Pryor
    Charitable Trust
Richard Radcliffe Charitable
    Trust
Cecil Rosen Foundation
Stanley Foundation Ltd
Walter Swindon Charitable
    Trust
Variety Club Children's Charity
Alexander Pigott Wernher
    Memorial Trust
West London Synagogue
    Charitable Fund
Lionel Wigram Memorial Trust

Will consider

Ashby Charitable Trust
Birmingham Foundation
Bonhomie United Charity
    Society
Audrey & Stanley Burton
    Charitable Trust
Richard Cadbury Charitable
    Trust
Chase Charity
Chrimes Family Charitable
    Trust
Criffel Charitable Trust
Dunhill Medical Trust
David Finnie & Alan Emery
    Charitable Trust
Good Neighbours Trust
Constance Green Foundation
Hadrian Trust
Hampstead Wells and
    Campden Trust
Hare of Steep Charitable Trust
Dorothy Hay-Bolton Charitable
    Trust
Charles Hayward Foundation
Heart of England Community
    Foundation
Hospital Saturday Fund
    Charitable Trust
Ruth & Lionel Jacobson Trust
    (Second Fund) No 2
John Jarrold Trust
Jeffrey Charitable Trust
Johnson Foundation
Kennel Club Charitable Trust
Raymond & Blanche Lawson
    Charitable Trust
London Law Trust
Tony Metherell Charitable
    Trust
Metropolitan Hospital-Sunday
    Fund
George A Moore Foundation
Nestlé Rowntree York
    Employees Community Fund
    Trust
Bernard Piggott Trust
John Pitman Charitable Trust
Mr and Mrs J A Pye's
    Charitable Settlement
Queen Mary's Roehampton
    Trust
Rainford Trust
Ravensdale Trust
John Rayner Charitable Trust
Cliff Richard Charitable Trust
Rivendell Trust
Saddlers' Company Charitable
    Fund
Andrew Salvesen Charitable
    Trust
Frieda Scott Charitable Trust
Sir James & Lady Scott Trust
Scottish International
    Education Trust
Scouloudi Foundation

Sefton Community Foundation
Sobell Foundation
W W Spooner Charitable Trust
Steinberg Family Charitable
    Trust
Charles and Elsie Sykes Trust
Tesco Charity Trust
Sir Jules Thorn Charitable
    Trust
Tisbury Telegraph Trust
Perry Watlington Trust
Alfred and Beatrice Weintrop
    Charity
Wellfield Trust
Wesleyan Charitable Trust
Michael and Anna Wix
    Charitable Trust
Yardley Great Trust

■ Hearing loss
Funding priority

Astor of Hever Trust
Lance Coates Charitable Trust
    1969
Wilfred & Elsie Elkes Charity
    Fund
Peacock Charitable Trust
Max Reinhardt Charitable Trust
Verdon-Smith Family Charitable
    Settlement

Will consider

Ardwick Trust
Bamford Charitable Foundation
Barnwood House Trust
Ferguson Benevolent Fund Ltd
Fortuna Charitable Trust
Jacqueline and Michael Gee
    Charitable Trust
Hallam FM – Help a Hallam
    Child Appeal
Miss Agnes H Hunter's Trust
Minge's Gift
Pilkington Charities Fund
Coral Samuel Charitable Trust
Mrs Maud Van Norden's
    Charitable Foundation

■ Sight loss
Funding priority

Appletree Trust
Ardwick Trust
Beacon Centre for the Blind
Isabel Blackman Foundation
Blatchington Court Trust
British Council for Prevention
    of Blindness
Palgrave Brown Foundation
Four Acre Trust
Frognal Trust
T F C Frost Charitable Trust
Garthgwynion Charities
Anne Herd Memorial Trust
Joseph & Mary Hiley Trust
Miss Agnes H Hunter's Trust

*Jungels-Winkler Charitable
  Foundation*
*Paul Lunn-Rockliffe Charitable
  Trust*
*R S MacDonald Charitable
  Trust*
Minge's Gift
Laurie Nidditch Foundation
Pilkington Charities Fund
Muriel Edith Rickman Trust
*W O Street Charitable
  Foundation*
*Connie and Albert Taylor
  Charitable Trust*
Ulverscroft Foundation
Vision Charity
Charity of John West & Others

Will consider
Adnams Charity
Lord Ashdown Charitable Trust
Andrew Balint Charitable Trust
George Balint Charitable Trust
Carpenter Charitable Trust
John Cowan Foundation
Coward Trust
Diabetes UK
DLM Charitable Trust
*Boris Karloff Charitable
  Foundation*
*Heinz & Anna Kroch
  Foundation*
*Loseley & Guildway Charitable
  Trust*
R W Mann Trustees Limited
Proven Family Trust
Red Dragon Radio Trust
Reuters Foundation
Rowan Charitable Trust
Starfish Trust
Triangle Trust (1949) Fund
Will Charitable Trust

Ethnicity

■ Ethnic minority groups

Funding priority
CAF (Charities Aid Foundation)
*Community Foundation Serving
  Tyne & Wear and
  Northumberland*
*Consortium on Opportunities
  for Volunteering*
*Derbyshire Community
  Foundation*
Devon Community Foundation
Esmée Fairbairn Foundation
*Football Association National
  Sports Centre Trust*
J Paul Getty Jr Charitable Trust
Global Care
Greater Bristol Foundation
Greggs Trust

Paul Hamlyn Foundation
Hilden Charitable Fund
*Housing Associations
  Charitable Trust*
India Foundation (UK)
Allen Lane Foundation
Lintel Trust
*Lloyds TSB Foundation for
  Scotland*
John Moores Foundation
Northern Rock Foundation
Rosca Trust
*Joseph Rowntree Charitable
  Trust*
*Sir Walter St John's
  Educational Charity*
*Spitalfields Market Community
  Trust*
*Thames Community
  Foundation*
Wates Foundation
*Yorkshire Building Society
  Charitable Foundation*

Will consider
Lord Ashdown Charitable Trust
BBC Children in Need Appeal
*BBC Radio Cambridgeshire –
  Trustline*
Bedford Charity
Birmingham Foundation
*Birmingham Hospital Saturday
  Fund Medical Charity &
  Welfare Trust*
Body Shop Foundation
Bramble Charitable Trust
*Richard Cadbury Charitable
  Trust*
*William A Cadbury Charitable
  Trust*
Chase Charity
Church Urban Fund
CLA Charitable Trust
Comic Relief
Coppings Trust
*County of Gloucestershire
  Community Foundation*
Cripplegate Foundation
William Dudley Trust
*David Finnie & Alan Emery
  Charitable Trust*
Robert Gavron Charitable Trust
Hadrian Trust
*Hampstead Wells and
  Campden Trust*
Help the Aged
Alan Edward Higgs Charity
Hinchley Charitable Trust
Hospital of God at Greatham
Inlight Trust
Sir James Knott Trust
Lankelly Foundation
Leigh Trust
Levy Foundation
*Lloyds TSB Foundation for
  England and Wales*

*Lloyds TSB Foundation for
  Northern Ireland*
Lyndhurst Settlement
John Martin's Charity
*Mercers' Charitable
  Foundation*
Minge's Gift
Peter Moores Foundation
*Northumbria Historic Churches
  Trust*
Old Enfield Charitable Trust
*Oxfordshire Community
  Foundation*
Pastoral Care Trust
Pennycress Trust
Jack Petchey Foundation
Bernard Piggott Trust
*Simone Prendergast Charitable
  Trust*
Richmond Parish Lands Charity
*Mrs L D Rope Third Charitable
  Settlement*
Rothley Trust
St James' Trust Settlement
St Peter's Saltley Trust
*Scottish Churches Community
  Trust*
Sir Halley Stewart Trust
*Walter Swindon Charitable
  Trust*
C B & H H Taylor 1984 Trust
Tudor Trust
R D Turner Charitable Trust
Trustees of Tzedakah
Wellfield Trust
*Westminster Amalgamated
  Charity*
*Wiltshire and Swindon
  Community Foundation*
*Michael and Anna Wix
  Charitable Trust*
Worcester Municipal Charities

Gender and relationships

■ Adopted or fostered children

Funding priority
BBC Children in Need Appeal
BibleLands
Clara E Burgess Charity
Charities Advisory Trust
*Chester Diocesan Moral Aid
  Charity*
Essex Community Foundation
Fiat Auto (UK) Charity
Finnart House School Trust
Gerald Fogel Charitable Trust
*Timothy Franey Charitable
  Foundation*
Simon Gibson Charitable Trust
Greater Bristol Foundation
Greggs Trust

Bishop of Guildford's
   Foundation
Paul Hamlyn Foundation
Lennox Hannay Charitable
   Trust
Charles Hayward Foundation
Joseph & Mary Hiley Trust
Jeffrey Charitable Trust
Anton Jurgens Charitable Trust
David Laing Foundation
Leeds & Holbeck Building
   Society Charitable
   Foundation
Magdalen Hospital Trust
Noel Buxton Trust
Nova Charitable Trust
Austin & Hope Pilkington Trust
Red Dragon Radio Trust
Sir Walter St John's
   Educational Charity
Sedbury Trust
Walter Swindon Charitable
   Trust
Thames Community
   Foundation
Trades House of Glasgow
Variety Club Children's Charity
Walker Trust
Wates Foundation

Will consider
1970 Trust
Viscount Amory's Charitable
   Trust
Ardwick Trust
Bartle Family Charitable Trust
Bingham Trust
Birmingham Foundation
Herbert & Peter Blagrave
   Charitable Trust
Blatchington Court Trust
Enid Blyton Trust for Children
Bramble Charitable Trust
Bryant Trust
Burden Trust
Audrey & Stanley Burton
   Charitable Trust
Richard Cadbury Charitable
   Trust
Carlton Television Trust
Clover Trust
Community Foundation Serving
   Tyne & Wear and
   Northumberland
Cripplegate Foundation
Miriam K Dean Refugee Trust
   Fund
Diana, Princess of Wales
   Memorial Fund
Double 'O' Charity Ltd
Dulverton Trust
Edinburgh Children's Holiday
   Fund
Eveson Charitable Trust
Esmée Fairbairn Foundation
Ferguson Benevolent Fund Ltd

Fidelity UK Foundation
Fifty Fund
Earl Fitzwilliam Charitable
   Trust
Joyce Fletcher Charitable Trust
Robert Gavron Charitable Trust
Girdlers' Company Charitable
   Trust
Constance Green Foundation
Gulbenkian Foundation
Hampstead Wells and
   Campden Trust
Hampton Fuel Allotment
   Charity
Hemby Trust
Hesslewood Children's Trust
Hilden Charitable Fund
Holywood Trust
Mary Homfray Charitable Trust
Hospital of God at Greatham
Clifford Howarth Charity
   Settlement
Miss Agnes H Hunter's Trust
Hyde Charitable Trust
Joicey Trust
Sir James Knott Trust
Beatrice Laing Trust
Christopher Laing Foundation
Lazard Charitable Trust
Leigh Trust
Linbury Trust
Lloyd's Charities Trust
Lloyds TSB Foundation for
   England and Wales
Lloyds TSB Foundation for
   Scotland
C F Lunoe Trust Fund
John Lyon's Charity
Helen Isabella McMorran
   Charitable Foundation
Marchday Charitable Fund
John Martin's Charity
Metropolitan Hospital-Sunday
   Fund
Minge's Gift
Mobbs Memorial Trust Ltd
George A Moore Foundation
Morris Charitable Trust
Laurie Nidditch Foundation
Northcott Devon Foundation
Northern Rock Foundation
Nuffield Foundation
Oxfordshire Community
   Foundation
Parivar Trust
Harry Payne Trust
Proven Family Trust
Puri Foundation
Radio Forth Help a Child
   Appeal
Rank Foundation
John Rayner Charitable Trust
Reuters Foundation
Richmond Parish Lands Charity
Rothley Trust
St Hilda's Trust

Scottish Community
   Foundation
Sefton Community Foundation
Sheffield Bluecoat & Mount
   Pleasant Educational
   Foundation
Sherburn House Charity
Hugh Stenhouse Foundation
Bernard Sunley Charitable
   Foundation
Sue Thomson Foundation
Tisbury Telegraph Trust
John and Lucille van Geest
   Foundation
John Watson's Trust
Wellfield Trust
Wesleyan Charitable Trust
Westminster Amalgamated
   Charity
Woodward Trust

....

■ Bereaved

Funding priority
Fiat Auto (UK) Charity
Grand Charity of Freemasons
Greater Bristol Foundation
Greggs Trust
Hampton Fuel Allotment
   Charity
Lennox Hannay Charitable
   Trust
King George's Fund for Sailors
Leeds & Holbeck Building
   Society Charitable
   Foundation
C F Lunoe Trust Fund
Midhurst Pensions Trust
Old Enfield Charitable Trust
Patients' Aid Association
   Hospital & Medical
   Charities Trust
Rosca Trust
St Mary-le-Strand Charity
Thames Community
   Foundation
Verdon-Smith Family Charitable
   Settlement

Will consider
Ajahma Charitable Trust
Viscount Amory's Charitable
   Trust
Sir John & Lady Amory's
   Charitable Trust
Ardwick Trust
Army Benevolent Fund
Badley Memorial Trust
Bingham Trust
Birmingham Hospital Saturday
   Fund Medical Charity &
   Welfare Trust
Bramble Charitable Trust
Bridge House Estates Trust
   Fund
Bryant Trust

Richard Cadbury Charitable
Trust
Cheshire Provincial Fund of
Benevolence
Norman Collinson Charitable
Trust
Comic Relief
Community Foundation Serving
Tyne & Wear and
Northumberland
Cripplegate Foundation
Baron Davenport's Charity
Earley Charity
Englass Charitable Trust
Fassnidge Memorial Trust
Fifty Fund
Grocers' Charity
Hadfield Trust
Hampstead Wells and
Campden Trust
Charles Hayward Foundation
Hemby Trust
Hertfordshire Community
Foundation
Hilden Charitable Fund
Dorothy Holmes Charitable
Trust
Mary Homfray Charitable Trust
Hospital of God at Greatham
Clifford Howarth Charity
Settlement
Sir James Knott Trust
Christopher Laing Foundation
Leach Fourteenth Trust
Lloyds TSB Foundation for
England and Wales
Lloyds TSB Foundation for
Northern Ireland
Lloyds TSB Foundation for
Scotland
John Martin's Charity
Metropolitan Hospital-Sunday
Fund
Minge's Gift
George A Moore Foundation
Morris Charitable Trust
Northcott Devon Foundation
Northern Rock Foundation
Ogilvie Charities Deed 2
Oxfordshire Community
Foundation
Queen Mary's Roehampton
Trust
John Rayner Charitable Trust
Richmond Parish Lands Charity
Rothley Trust
Scottish Community
Foundation
Sefton Community Foundation
Servite Sisters' Charitable
Trust Fund
Sherburn House Charity
Henry Smith Charity
Bernard Sunley Charitable
Foundation
Triangle Trust (1949) Fund

Wates Foundation
Wellfield Trust
Westminster Amalgamated
Charity
Worcester Municipal Charities
Yardley Great Trust

....

■ **Carers**

Funding priority
Ammco Trust
Astor Foundation
Barbour Trust
Barnwood House Trust
BBC Radio Cambridgeshire –
Trustline
Percy Bilton Charity Ltd
Bothwell Charitable Trust
Bridge House Estates Trust
Fund
Charles Brotherton Trust
Carlton Television Trust
Chest Heart and Stroke
Scotland
Chippenham Borough Lands
Charity
D'Oyly Carte Charitable Trust
Derbyshire Community
Foundation
Diana, Princess of Wales
Memorial Fund
Essex Community Foundation
Fassnidge Memorial Trust
Four Acre Trust
Jill Franklin Trust
Simon Gibson Charitable Trust
Greater Bristol Foundation
Hampton Fuel Allotment
Charity
Harebell Centenary Fund
Charles Hayward Foundation
Hertfordshire Community
Foundation
Joseph & Mary Hiley Trust
Dorothy Holmes Charitable
Trust
Miss Agnes H Hunter's Trust
Jeffrey Charitable Trust
Johnson Group Cleaners
Charity
Judith Trust
Anton Jurgens Charitable Trust
Peter Kershaw Trust
Sir James Knott Trust
Leeds & Holbeck Building
Society Charitable
Foundation
Levy Foundation
Lintel Trust
Lloyds TSB Foundation for the
Channel Islands
Paul Lunn-Rockliffe Charitable
Trust
Mercers' Charitable
Foundation

Zachary Merton & George
Woofindin Convalescent
Trust
Tony Metherell Charitable
Trust
John Moores Foundation
Newby Trust Limited
Northern Rock Foundation
Oakdale Trust
Oxfordshire Community
Foundation
Patients' Aid Association
Hospital & Medical
Charities Trust
Patrick Charitable Trust
Peacock Charitable Trust
Austin & Hope Pilkington Trust
Pilkington Charities Fund
J D Player Endowment Fund
John Porter Charitable Trust
Rosca Trust
Christopher Rowbotham
Charitable Trust
Francis C Scott Charitable
Trust
Frieda Scott Charitable Trust
Sir James & Lady Scott Trust
Sobell Foundation
Tesco Charity Trust
Thames Community
Foundation
Triangle Trust (1949) Fund
West Derby Wastelands
Charity
Wiltshire and Swindon
Community Foundation
Woodlands Trust (1015942)
Woodlands Trust (259569)

Will consider
Adint Charitable Trust
Ajahma Charitable Trust
Alchemy Foundation
Andrew Anderson Trust
Ardwick Trust
Bamford Charitable Foundation
David and Frederick Barclay
Foundation
Philip Barker Charity
BBC Children in Need Appeal
Berkshire Community
Foundation
Bingham Trust
Birmingham Foundation
Birmingham Hospital Saturday
Fund Medical Charity &
Welfare Trust
Bisgood Charitable Trust
Herbert & Peter Blagrave
Charitable Trust
Boltons Trust
P G & N J Boulton Trust
Bramble Charitable Trust
Brighton District Nursing
Association Trust
Bryant Trust

Consolidated Charity of Burton
   Upon Trent
Edward Cadbury Charitable
   Trust
Richard Cadbury Charitable
   Trust
Carnegie Dunfermline Trust
Wilfrid & Constance Cave
   Foundation
Chase Charity
Chrimes Family Charitable
   Trust
Clover Trust
Colchester Catalyst Charity
Norman Collinson Charitable
   Trust
Comic Relief
Community Foundation Serving
   Tyne & Wear and
   Northumberland
Congleton Inclosure Trust
Consortium on Opportunities
   for Volunteering
Cooper Charitable Trust
County Durham Foundation
Cranbury Foundation
Cripplegate Foundation
Harry Crook Foundation
John Grant Davies Trust
Helen and Geoffrey de Freitas
   Charitable Trust
Devon Community Foundation
Dulverton Trust
Dunhill Medical Trust
Earley Charity
Wilfred & Elsie Elkes Charity
   Fund
Emerton-Christie Charity
Emmandjay Charitable Trust
Ericson Trust
Erskine Cunningham Hill Trust
Essex Fairway Charitable Trust
Eveson Charitable Trust
Esmée Fairbairn Foundation
Ferguson Benevolent Fund Ltd
Fiat Auto (UK) Charity
Fidelity UK Foundation
Fifty Fund
David Finnie & Alan Emery
   Charitable Trust
Fishmongers' Company's
   Charitable Trust
Ford of Britain Trust
Fox Memorial Trust
Robert Gavron Charitable Trust
Girdlers' Company Charitable
   Trust
Grocers' Charity
Bishop of Guildford's
   Foundation
Gulbenkian Foundation
Hadfield Trust
Hadrian Trust
Hampstead Wells and
   Campden Trust
Harborne Parish Lands Charity

Harrison & Potter Trust
N & P Hartley Memorial Trust
Headley Trust
Heart of England Community
   Foundation
Hedley Foundation
Help the Aged
Hemby Trust
Joanna Herbert-Stepney
   Charitable Settlement
Holywood Trust
Mary Homfray Charitable Trust
Hospital of God at Greatham
Clifford Howarth Charity
   Settlement
James Thom Howat Charitable
   Trust
Huddersfield Common Good
   Trust
Human Relief Foundation
Inchrye Trust
Inverforth Charitable Trust
Isle of Anglesey Charitable
   Trust
Jarman Charitable Trust
Jephcott Charitable Trust
Johnson Foundation
Joicey Trust
Kidani Memorial Trust
King's Fund
Kobler Trust
Kreitman Foundation
Late Sir Pierce Lacy Charity
   Trust
Beatrice Laing Trust
Christopher Laing Foundation
Bryan Lancaster's Charity
Leach Fourteenth Trust
Lord Leverhulme Charitable
   Trust
Lloyd's Charities Trust
Lloyds TSB Foundation for
   England and Wales
Lloyds TSB Foundation for
   Northern Ireland
Lloyds TSB Foundation for
   Scotland
London Law Trust
London North East Community
   Foundation
C F Lunoe Trust Fund
Lyndhurst Settlement
John Lyon's Charity
R W Mann Trustees Limited
Marchday Charitable Fund
Hilda & Samuel Marks
   Foundation
Sir George Martin Trust
John Martin's Charity
Merchant Taylors' Company
   Charities Fund
Metropolitan Hospital-Sunday
   Fund
Hugh and Mary Miller Bequest
   Trust

Milton Keynes Community
   Foundation
Minge's Gift
George A Moore Foundation
Morgan Stanley International
   Foundation
National Power Charitable
   Trust
Norman Family Charitable
   Trust
Northcott Devon Foundation
Norwich Consolidated
   Charities
Nuffield Foundation
Kate Wilson Oliver Trust
Arthur James Paterson
   Charitable Trust
Constance Paterson Charitable
   Trust
Harry Payne Trust
A M Pilkington's Charitable
   Trust
John Pitman Charitable Trust
J S F Pollitzer Charitable
   Settlement
Porter Foundation
Princess Anne's Charities
Mr and Mrs J A Pye's
   Charitable Settlement
Rainford Trust
Joseph & Lena Randall
   Charitable Trust
Rayne Foundation
John Rayner Charitable Trust
Rhododendron Trust
Cliff Richard Charitable Trust
Richmond Parish Lands Charity
Helen Roll Charitable Trust
Mrs L D Rope Third Charitable
   Settlement
Rothley Trust
Rowan Charitable Trust
Sir Walter St John's
   Educational Charity
St Mary-le-Strand Charity
Basil Samuel Charitable Trust
Scottish Community
   Foundation
Scouloudi Foundation
Sefton Community Foundation
Servite Sisters' Charitable
   Trust Fund
Sheldon Trust
Sherburn House Charity
Shuttlewood Clarke Foundation
Mary Elizabeth Siebel Charity
Skelton Bounty
Henry Smith Charity
Leslie Smith Foundation
David Solomons Charitable
   Trust
South Yorkshire Community
   Foundation
Stanley Spooner Deceased
   Charitable Trust
Sportsman's Charity

Sir Halley Stewart Trust
Bernard Sunley Charitable
  Foundation
Sutton Trust
Talbot Trusts
Tudor Trust
Unemployed Voluntary Action
  Fund
Mrs Maud Van Norden's
  Charitable Foundation
Wakeham Trust
Wates Foundation
Wellfield Trust
Wesleyan Charitable Trust
Westminster Amalgamated
  Charity
Garfield Weston Foundation
Michael and Anna Wix
  Charitable Trust
Woodward Trust
Worcester Municipal Charities
Wyseliot Charitable Trust
Yapp Charitable Trust

■ Lesbians and gay men

Funding priority
Greater Bristol Foundation
Judith Trust
Lintel Trust
Northern Rock Foundation
Frieda Scott Charitable Trust
Sir James & Lady Scott Trust
Stonewall Iris Trust
Thames Community
  Foundation

Will consider
Ajahma Charitable Trust
Alcohol Education and
  Research Fund
Berkshire Community
  Foundation
Bramble Charitable Trust
Bridge House Estates Trust
  Fund
Richard Cadbury Charitable
  Trust
Carlton Television Trust
City Parochial Foundation
Comic Relief
Community Foundation Serving
  Tyne & Wear and
  Northumberland
Consortium on Opportunities
  for Volunteering
County Durham Foundation
Cripplegate Foundation
Harry Crook Foundation
John Grant Davies Trust
Derbyshire Community
  Foundation
Esmée Fairbairn Foundation
Grocers' Charity
Hadrian Trust

Hampton Fuel Allotment
  Charity
Heart of England Community
  Foundation
Hertfordshire Community
  Foundation
Hospital of God at Greatham
Joicey Trust
King's Fund
Sir James Knott Trust
Kobler Trust
Allen Lane Foundation
Lloyds TSB Foundation for
  England and Wales
Lloyds TSB Foundation for
  Northern Ireland
Lloyds TSB Foundation for
  Scotland
London North East Community
  Foundation
C F Lunoe Trust Fund
Lyndhurst Settlement
Milton Keynes Community
  Foundation
Minge's Gift
Northcott Devon Foundation
Oxfordshire Community
  Foundation
Joseph & Lena Randall
  Charitable Trust
Richmond Parish Lands Charity
Rothley Trust
St Mary-le-Strand Charity
Scottish Community
  Foundation
Sefton Community Foundation
Henry Smith Charity
South Yorkshire Community
  Foundation
Stanley Spooner Deceased
  Charitable Trust
Unemployed Voluntary Action
  Fund
Wates Foundation
Wellfield Trust
Wiltshire and Swindon
  Community Foundation
Worcester Municipal Charities

■ Orphans

Funding priority
Greater Bristol Foundation
Hathaway Trust
Thames Community
  Foundation

Will consider
Bingham Trust
Bramble Charitable Trust
Bryant Trust
Community Foundation Serving
  Tyne & Wear and
  Northumberland
Cripplegate Foundation
Baron Davenport's Charity

Erskine Cunningham Hill Trust
Essex Fairway Charitable Trust
Fidelity UK Foundation
Girdlers' Company Charitable
  Trust
Hospital of God at Greatham
Christopher Laing Foundation
Lloyds TSB Foundation for
  Scotland
Northcott Devon Foundation
Northern Rock Foundation
Oxfordshire Community
  Foundation
Harry Payne Trust
Richmond Parish Lands Charity
Rothley Trust
Sue Thomson Foundation

■ Parents

Funding priority
Balmore Trust
BBC Children in Need Appeal
Bridge House Estates Trust
  Fund
John Grant Davies Trust
Essex Community Foundation
Fassnidge Memorial Trust
Bud Flanagan Leukaemia Fund
Glass-House Trust
Greater Bristol Foundation
Greggs Trust
Bishop of Guildford's
  Foundation
Lennox Hannay Charitable
  Trust
Charles Hayward Foundation
Hertfordshire Community
  Foundation
Miss Agnes H Hunter's Trust
Hyde Charitable Trust
Isle of Dogs Community
  Foundation
Judith Trust
King George's Fund for Sailors
David Laing Foundation
Lloyds TSB Foundation for
  England and Wales
Lloyds TSB Foundation for
  Scotland
C F Lunoe Trust Fund
Magdalen Hospital Trust
Minge's Gift
Noel Buxton Trust
Old Enfield Charitable Trust
Oxfordshire Community
  Foundation
J D Player Endowment Fund
Rosca Trust
St Mary-le-Strand Charity
Barbara A Shuttleworth
  Memorial Trust
Mrs Smith & Mount Trust
Stanton Ballard Charitable
  Trust
Sutton Trust

Thames Community
 Foundation
Waterside Trust
Woodlands Trust (259569)
York Children's Trust

Will consider
Viscount Amory's Charitable
 Trust
Sir John & Lady Amory's
 Charitable Trust
Army Benevolent Fund
Artemis Charitable Trust
Badley Memorial Trust
Barbour Trust
Barnabas Charitable Trust
Bartle Family Charitable Trust
Bingham Trust
Birmingham Foundation
Blatchington Court Trust
Bramble Charitable Trust
Bryant Trust
Richard Cadbury Charitable
 Trust
William A Cadbury Charitable
 Trust
W A Cargill Fund
Caring for Kids
Carlton Television Trust
Chase Charity
Cheshire Provincial Fund of
 Benevolence
Chownes Foundation
J A Clark Charitable Trust
Lord Clinton's Charitable Trust
Clover Trust
Norman Collinson Charitable
 Trust
Comic Relief
Community Foundation Serving
 Tyne & Wear and
 Northumberland
Consortium on Opportunities
 for Volunteering
Cripplegate Foundation
Baron Davenport's Charity
Sandy Dewhirst Charitable
 Trust
Double 'O' Charity Ltd
Dulverton Trust
Edinburgh Children's Holiday
 Fund
Esmée Fairbairn Foundation
Fifty Fund
Earl Fitzwilliam Charitable
 Trust
Joyce Fletcher Charitable Trust
J Paul Getty Jr Charitable Trust
Gulbenkian Foundation
Hadfield Trust
Hallam FM – Help a Hallam
 Child Appeal
Hampstead Wells and
 Campden Trust
Hampton Fuel Allotment
 Charity

Handicapped Children's Aid
 Committee
Harbour Charitable Trust
Hemby Trust
Hesslewood Children's Trust
Hilden Charitable Fund
Dorothy Holmes Charitable
 Trust
Holywood Trust
Mary Homfray Charitable Trust
Hospital of God at Greatham
Clifford Howarth Charity
 Settlement
Ruth & Lionel Jacobson Trust
 (Second Fund) No 2
Christopher Laing Foundation
Lankelly Foundation
Lawlor Foundation
Linbury Trust
Lintel Trust
Lloyd's Charities Trust
Lotus Foundation
John Lyon's Charity
Ronald McDonald Children's
 Charities Limited
Marchday Charitable Fund
John Martin's Charity
Metropolitan Hospital-Sunday
 Fund
Mobbs Memorial Trust Ltd
Morris Charitable Trust
Northcott Devon Foundation
Northern Rock Foundation
Norwich Consolidated
 Charities
Nuffield Foundation
Ogilvie Charities Deed 2
Parivar Trust
Harry Payne Trust
Pennycress Trust
Austin & Hope Pilkington Trust
Puri Foundation
Rank Foundation
John Rayner Charitable Trust
Red Dragon Radio Trust
Richmond Parish Lands Charity
Rothley Trust
St James' Trust Settlement
Sir Walter St John's
 Educational Charity
Scottish Community
 Foundation
Sefton Community Foundation
Sheffield Bluecoat & Mount
 Pleasant Educational
 Foundation
Shipwrights Company
 Charitable Fund
Henry Smith Charity
Bernard Sunley Charitable
 Foundation
Tedworth Trust
Tisbury Telegraph Trust
Triangle Trust (1949) Fund
Tudor Trust
Wates Foundation

Wellfield Trust
Westminster Amalgamated
 Charity
Woodward Trust
Worcester Municipal Charities
Yardley Great Trust

....

■ Lone parents
Funding priority
BBC Children in Need Appeal
Clara E Burgess Charity
Camelot Foundation
Essex Community Foundation
Glass-House Trust
Greater Bristol Foundation
Greggs Trust
Bishop of Guildford's
 Foundation
Charles Hayward Foundation
King George's Fund for Sailors
David Laing Foundation
Leeds & Holbeck Building
 Society Charitable
 Foundation
Magdalen Hospital Trust
Old Enfield Charitable Trust
Austin & Hope Pilkington Trust
J D Player Endowment Fund
Rosca Trust
Sir Walter St John's
 Educational Charity
Stanton Ballard Charitable
 Trust
Thames Community
 Foundation
Woodlands Trust (259569)
York Children's Trust

Will consider
1970 Trust
Ajahma Charitable Trust
Viscount Amory's Charitable
 Trust
Army Benevolent Fund
Badley Memorial Trust
Barbour Trust
Barnabas Charitable Trust
Bartle Family Charitable Trust
Bingham Trust
Birmingham Foundation
Blatchington Court Trust
Bramble Charitable Trust
Bridge House Estates Trust
 Fund
Bryant Trust
Audrey & Stanley Burton
 Charitable Trust
Richard Cadbury Charitable
 Trust
William A Cadbury Charitable
 Trust
W A Cargill Fund
Caring for Kids
Carlton Television Trust
Chase Charity

Cheshire Provincial Fund of
  Benevolence
J A Clark Charitable Trust
Norman Collinson Charitable
  Trust
Comic Relief
Community Foundation Serving
  Tyne & Wear and
  Northumberland
Consortium on Opportunities
  for Volunteering
Cripplegate Foundation
Baron Davenport's Charity
John Grant Davies Trust
Double 'O' Charity Ltd
Edinburgh Children's Holiday
  Fund
Esmée Fairbairn Foundation
Fassnidge Memorial Trust
Fidelity UK Foundation
Fifty Fund
Robert Gavron Charitable Trust
J Paul Getty Jr Charitable Trust
Girdlers' Company Charitable
  Trust
Hadfield Trust
Paul Hamlyn Foundation
Hampstead Wells and
  Campden Trust
Hampton Fuel Allotment
  Charity
Handicapped Children's Aid
  Committee
Harbour Charitable Trust
Hemby Trust
Hertfordshire Community
  Foundation
Hesslewood Children's Trust
Hilden Charitable Fund
Dorothy Holmes Charitable
  Trust
Holywood Trust
Hospital of God at Greatham
Clifford Howarth Charity
  Settlement
Miss Agnes H Hunter's Trust
Hyde Charitable Trust
Jarman Charitable Trust
Joicey Trust
Lankelly Foundation
Linbury Trust
Lintel Trust
Lloyds TSB Foundation for
  England and Wales
Lloyds TSB Foundation for
  Scotland
Lotus Foundation
C F Lunoe Trust Fund
Lyndhurst Settlement
John Lyon's Charity
Ronald McDonald Children's
  Charities Limited
Marchday Charitable Fund
John Martin's Charity
Metropolitan Hospital-Sunday
  Fund

Minge's Gift
John Moores Foundation
Morris Charitable Trust
Northcott Devon Foundation
Northern Rock Foundation
Norwich Consolidated
  Charities
Nuffield Foundation
Ogilvie Charities Deed 2
Oxfordshire Community
  Foundation
Constance Paterson Charitable
  Trust
Harry Payne Trust
Pennycress Trust
Puri Foundation
Radio Forth Help a Child
  Appeal
Rank Foundation
Reuters Foundation
Richmond Parish Lands Charity
Rothley Trust
St Mary-le-Strand Charity
Scottish Community
  Foundation
Sefton Community Foundation
Servite Sisters' Charitable
  Trust Fund
Sheffield Bluecoat & Mount
  Pleasant Educational
  Foundation
Sylvia & Colin Shepherd
  Charitable Trust
Henry Smith Charity
Bernard Sunley Charitable
  Foundation
Tedworth Trust
Tisbury Telegraph Trust
Triangle Trust (1949) Fund
Wakeham Trust
Wates Foundation
John Watson's Trust
Wellfield Trust
Westminster Amalgamated
  Charity
Woodward Trust
Worcester Municipal Charities
Yardley Great Trust

....

■ Women
Funding priority
1970 Trust
Access 4 Trust
Barrow Cadbury Trust and the
  Barrow Cadbury Fund
William A Cadbury Charitable
  Trust
Chester Diocesan Moral Aid
  Charity
Community Foundation Serving
  Tyne & Wear and
  Northumberland
Consortium on Opportunities
  for Volunteering
Alex Deas Charitable Trust

Greater Bristol Foundation
Greggs Trust
Jesus Hospital Charity
Judith Trust
Lotus Foundation
John Moores Foundation
Stanley Morrison Charitable
  Trust
E L Rathbone Charitable Trust
Eleanor Rathbone Charitable
  Trust
Rosca Trust
Rowley Trust
Foundation of Edward Storey
Thames Community
  Foundation
Wakefield Trust
John Wilson Bequest Fund
Women at Risk

Will consider
Ajahma Charitable Trust
Ammco Trust
Birmingham Foundation
Bramble Charitable Trust
Bridge House Estates Trust
  Fund
Bryant Trust
Richard Cadbury Charitable
  Trust
Chase Charity
John & Freda Coleman
  Charitable Trust
Comic Relief
County Durham Foundation
Cripplegate Foundation
Baron Davenport's Charity
Equitable Charitable Trust
Ferguson Benevolent Fund Ltd
J Paul Getty Jr Charitable Trust
Hadrian Trust
Hampstead Wells and
  Campden Trust
Charles Hayward Foundation
Hilden Charitable Fund
Hospital of God at Greatham
Nancy Kenyon Charitable Trust
Christopher Laing Foundation
Allen Lane Foundation
Lankelly Foundation
Lloyds TSB Foundation for
  Northern Ireland
Lloyds TSB Foundation for
  Scotland
London North East Community
  Foundation
Mercers' Charitable
  Foundation
Northern Rock Foundation
Oxfordshire Community
  Foundation
Richmond Parish Lands Charity
Rothley Trust
Scottish Community
  Foundation
Sefton Community Foundation

SEM Charitable Trust
Sylvia & Colin Shepherd
    Charitable Trust
Society for the Assistance of
    Ladies in Reduced
    Circumstances
Bernard Sunley Charitable
    Foundation
Tesco Charity Trust
Westminster Amalgamated
    Charity
Worcester Municipal Charities

Faith

■ Buddhists

Will consider
Derbyshire Community
    Foundation
David Finnie & Alan Emery
    Charitable Trust
Great Britain Sasakawa
    Foundation
Inlight Trust
Sir James Knott Trust
John Martin's Charity
Minge's Gift
Northumbria Historic Churches
    Trust
Pastoral Care Trust
Harry Payne Trust
J B Pelly Charitable Settlement
Pennycress Trust
St Peter's Saltley Trust
Walter Swindon Charitable
    Trust
Trustees of Tzedakah
Wellfield Trust

■ Christians

Funding priority
Abel Charitable Trust
Aid to the Church in Need (UK)
Alexis Trust
Allchurches Trust Ltd
Almond Trust
Archbishop of Canterbury's
    Charitable Trust
AS Charitable Trust
Ashburnham Thanksgiving
    Trust
Balney Charitable Trust
Barber Charitable Trust
Bartle Family Charitable Trust
Dorothy Bayles Trust
Beaufort House Trust
Bedfordshire & Hertfordshire
    Historic Churches Trust
Benham Charitable Settlement
Bethesda Community
    Charitable Trust
Isabel Blackman Foundation
Britland Charitable Trust

Charles & Edna Broadhurst
    Charitable Trust
Buckingham Trust
Buckinghamshire Historic
    Churches Trust
Carpenter Charitable Trust
Chasah Trust
Childs Charitable Trust
Christabella Charitable Trust
Clarke Charitable Settlement
Cleary Foundation
Alice Ellen Cooper-Dean
    Charitable Foundation
Criffel Charitable Trust
Cross Trust
Daily Prayer Union Charitable
    Trust Ltd
De Clermont Charitable
    Company Ltd
Dorcas Trust
Dugdale Charitable Trust
Erskine Cunningham Hill Trust
Norman Evershed Trust
Fairbairn Charitable Trust
Feed the Minds
Ferguson Bequest Fund
Four Winds Trust
Thomas Freke & Lady Norton
    Charity
Anne French Memorial Trust
Friends of Essex Churches
Angela Gallagher Memorial
    Fund
Global Care
Grimsdale Charitable Trust
Alfred Haines Charitable Trust
Beatrice Hankey Foundation
    Ltd
Kathleen Hannay Memorial
    Charity
Highmoor Hall Charitable Trust
Hope Trust
James Trust
Edward Cecil Jones Settlement
John and Rosemary Lancaster
    Charitable Foundation
Langley Charitable Trust
William Leech Charity
Erica Leonard Trust
Paul Lunn-Rockliffe Charitable
    Trust
Lyndhurst Trust
Maranatha Christian Trust
John Martin's Charity
Miles Trust for the Putney and
    Roehampton Community
Millfield Trust
Millhouses Charitable Trust
Edgar Milward Charity
Minos Trust
Morgan Williams Charitable
    Trust
National Committee of The
    Women's World Day of
    Prayer for England, Wales,
    and Northern Ireland

Norfolk Churches Trust Ltd
Ogle Christian Trust
Owen Family Trust
Oxfordshire Historic Churches
    Trust
Gerald Palmer Trust
Panahpur Charitable Trust
Mrs M E S Paterson's
    Charitable Trust
Pedmore Trust
David Pickford Charitable
    Foundation
Bernard Piggott Trust
John Pitman Charitable Trust
Rhondda Cynon Taff Welsh
    Church Acts Fund
River Trust
Rosca Trust
Sarum St Michael Educational
    Charity
Second Quothquan Charitable
    Trust
Bassil Shippam and Alsford
    Trust
SMB Trust
Stobart Newlands Charitable
    Trust
Tabeel Trust
Tay Charitable Trust
Thornton Trust
Torchbearer Trust
Tufton Charitable Trust
United Reformed Church (West
    Midlands) Trust Ltd
Albert Waghorn Charitable
    Trust
Wallington Missionary Mart
    and Auctions
Whitecourt Charitable Trust
Norman Whiteley Trust
Dame Violet Wills Charitable
    Trust
John Wilson Bequest Fund
Wolfson Family Charitable
    Trust
Woodlands Trust (1015942)
Yorkshire Historic Churches
    Trust

Will consider
Alabaster Trust
AMW Charitable Trust
Andrew Anderson Trust
Astor Foundation
Baird Trust
Barnabas Trust
Beacon Trust
Benfield Motors Charitable
    Trust
Bingham Trust
Morgan Blake Charitable Trust
Geoffrey Burton Charitable
    Trust
W A Cargill Charitable Trust
W A Cargill Fund

Carmichael-Montgomery
    Charitable Trust
Christendom Trust
Norman Collinson Charitable
    Trust
Cumberland Trust
Derbyshire Community
    Foundation
David Finnie & Alan Emery
    Charitable Trust
Earl Fitzwilliam Charitable
    Trust
Ganzoni Charitable Trust
Hadrian Trust
May Hearnshaw's Charity
Hesed Trust
Hinchley Charitable Trust
Hockerill Educational
    Foundation
Jane Hodge Foundation
Homestead Charitable Trust
Mary Homfray Charitable Trust
Inlight Trust
James Pantyfedwen
    Foundation
Nancy Kenyon Charitable Trust
Sir James Knott Trust
Beatrice Laing Trust
Maurice and Hilda Laing
    Charitable Trust
Kennedy Leigh Charitable
    Trust
Helen Isabella McMorran
    Charitable Foundation
Minge's Gift
Peter Moores Foundation
Moss Charitable Trust
Northumbria Historic Churches
    Trust
Pallant Charitable Trust
Pastoral Care Trust
Payne Charitable Trust
Harry Payne Trust
Pennycress Trust
A M Pilkington's Charitable
    Trust
Simone Prendergast Charitable
    Trust
Puri Foundation
Ravensdale Trust
Nathaniel Reyner Trust Fund
Cliff Richard Charitable Trust
Rock Solid Trust
Mrs L D Rope Third Charitable
    Settlement
Rotherwick Foundation
St Luke's College Foundation
St Peter's Saltley Trust
Saint Sarkis Charity Trust
Seedfield Trust
Sharon Trust
Sheffield Church Burgesses
    Trust
Souter Charitable Trust
Steventon Allotments & Relief-
    in-Need Charity

A B Strom & R Strom
    Charitable Trust
Bernard Sunley Charitable
    Foundation
Walter Swindon Charitable
    Trust
C B & H H Taylor 1984 Trust
Tisbury Telegraph Trust
Trustees of Tzedakah
Ulting Overseas Trust
United Society for the
    Propagation of the Gospel
Van Neste Foundation
Wellfield Trust
Michael and Anna Wix
    Charitable Trust
Worshipful Company of
    Founders Charities
Matthews Wrightson Charity
    Trust

■ **Anglicans**
   Funding priority
Appleton Trust
Archbishop of Canterbury's
    Charitable Trust
Bates Charitable Trust
Beacon Trust
Becketts & Sargeants
    Educational Foundation
Thomas Betton's Charity
    (Educational)
Bristol Archdeaconry Charities
Buckinghamshire Historic
    Churches Trust
Cleary Foundation
Cranbury Foundation
Criffel Charitable Trust
Angela Gallagher Memorial
    Fund
Global Care
Gough Charitable Trust
J C Green Charitable
    Settlement
Kathleen Hannay Memorial
    Charity
Joseph & Mary Hiley Trust
Hockerill Educational
    Foundation
Incorporated Leeds Church
    Extension Society
James Trust
Sylvanus Lyson's Charity
John Martin's Charity
Minge's Gift
Horace Moore Charitable Trust
Ouseley Trust
Oxfordshire Historic Churches
    Trust
Bernard Piggott Trust
William Price Charitable Trust
Rosca Trust
Saint Edmund, King & Martyr
    Trust
St Gabriel's Trust

St Thomas Ecclesiastical
    Charity
Foundation of Edward Storey
Walter Swindon Charitable
    Trust
Tufton Charitable Trust
Verdon-Smith Family Charitable
    Settlement
Yorkshire Historic Churches
    Trust

   Will consider
Aid to the Church in Need (UK)
Alabaster Trust
AMW Charitable Trust
Astor Foundation
Bamford Charitable Foundation
Barber Charitable Trust
Bishop's Development Fund
Burden Trust
W A Cargill Charitable Trust
W A Cargill Fund
Derbyshire Community
    Foundation
David Finnie & Alan Emery
    Charitable Trust
Earl Fitzwilliam Charitable
    Trust
G C Gibson Charitable Trust
Constance Green Foundation
May Hearnshaw's Charity
Hinchley Charitable Trust
Inlight Trust
Sir James Knott Trust
Helen Isabella McMorran
    Charitable Foundation
Minge's Gift
Peter Moores Foundation
Northumbria Historic Churches
    Trust
Norwood & Newton Settlement
Notgrove Trust
Oldham Foundation
Pastoral Care Trust
Harry Payne Trust
Pennycress Trust
A M Pilkington's Charitable
    Trust
Ravensdale Trust
Nathaniel Reyner Trust Fund
Cliff Richard Charitable Trust
Rotherwick Foundation
St Christopher's College
    Educational Trust
St Hilda's Trust
St Luke's College Foundation
St Peter's Saltley Trust
R H Scholes Charitable Trust
Bernard Sunley Charitable
    Foundation
Trustees of Tzedakah
United Society for the
    Propagation of the Gospel
Wallington Missionary Mart
    and Auctions
Wellfield Trust

Worshipful Company of
  Founders Charities
Matthews Wrightson Charity
  Trust

■ **Baptists**
Funding priority
Barber Charitable Trust
Beacon Trust
Buckinghamshire Historic
  Churches Trust
Horace & Marjorie Gale
  Charitable Trust
Global Care
Grace Baptist Trust
  Corporation
Norwood & Newton Settlement
Oxfordshire Historic Churches
  Trust
Rosca Trust
Tufton Charitable Trust
Yorkshire Historic Churches
  Trust

Will consider
Aid to the Church in Need (UK)
Alabaster Trust
AMW Charitable Trust
W A Cargill Charitable Trust
W A Cargill Fund
Derbyshire Community
  Foundation
Ebenezer Trust
David Finnie & Alan Emery
  Charitable Trust
G C Gibson Charitable Trust
Kathleen Hannay Memorial
  Charity
Hinchley Charitable Trust
Inlight Trust
Sir James Knott Trust
John Martin's Charity
Minge's Gift
Peter Moores Foundation
Northumbria Historic Churches
  Trust
Pastoral Care Trust
Payne Charitable Trust
Harry Payne Trust
Pennycress Trust
Nathaniel Reyner Trust Fund
Cliff Richard Charitable Trust
Rotherwick Foundation
St Peter's Saltley Trust
Walter Swindon Charitable
  Trust
Trustees of Tzedakah
United Society for the
  Propagation of the Gospel
Wallington Missionary Mart
  and Auctions
Wellfield Trust

■ **Evangelists**
Funding priority
Almond Trust
Ashburnham Thanksgiving
  Trust
Barber Charitable Trust
Beacon Trust
Bellahouston Bequest Fund
Chasah Trust
Criffel Charitable Trust
Daily Prayer Union Charitable
  Trust Ltd
Global Care
Kathleen Hannay Memorial
  Charity
Hinchley Charitable Trust
Stuart Hine Trust
Lyndhurst Trust
Maranatha Christian Trust
Edgar Milward Charity
Ogle Christian Trust
David Pickford Charitable
  Foundation
Nathaniel Reyner Trust Fund
Tabeel Trust
Thornton Trust
Torchbearer Trust
Tufton Charitable Trust
Norman Whiteley Trust
Dame Violet Wills Charitable
  Trust

Will consider
Aid to the Church in Need (UK)
Alabaster Trust
AMW Charitable Trust
Andrew Anderson Trust
Barnabas Trust
Britland Charitable Trust
W A Cargill Charitable Trust
W A Cargill Fund
Derbyshire Community
  Foundation
Ebenezer Trust
David Finnie & Alan Emery
  Charitable Trust
Hesed Trust
Inlight Trust
Sir James Knott Trust
John Martin's Charity
Minge's Gift
Peter Moores Foundation
Northumbria Historic Churches
  Trust
Norwood & Newton Settlement
Oikonomia Trust
Pastoral Care Trust
Payne Charitable Trust
Pennycress Trust
David Pickford Charitable
  Foundation
Cliff Richard Charitable Trust
Second Quothquan Charitable
  Trust
Seedfield Trust
Sharon Trust

Walter Swindon Charitable
  Trust
Tisbury Telegraph Trust
Trustees of Tzedakah
Ulting Overseas Trust
United Society for the
  Propagation of the Gospel
Wallington Missionary Mart
  and Auctions
Wellfield Trust

■ **Methodists**
Funding priority
Beacon Trust
Buckinghamshire Historic
  Churches Trust
Criffel Charitable Trust
Gibbs Charitable Trusts
Global Care
Kathleen Hannay Memorial
  Charity
P Leigh-Bramwell Trust 'E'
Norwood & Newton Settlement
Oxfordshire Historic Churches
  Trust
Joseph Rank Trust
Rosca Trust
Tufton Charitable Trust
Yorkshire Historic Churches
  Trust

Will consider
Alabaster Trust
AMW Charitable Trust
Bamford Charitable Foundation
W A Cargill Charitable Trust
W A Cargill Fund
Derbyshire Community
  Foundation
Ferguson Benevolent Fund Ltd
David Finnie & Alan Emery
  Charitable Trust
Earl Fitzwilliam Charitable
  Trust
May Hearnshaw's Charity
Hinchley Charitable Trust
Inlight Trust
Sir James Knott Trust
John Martin's Charity
Minge's Gift
Peter Moores Foundation
Northumbria Historic Churches
  Trust
Pastoral Care Trust
Patrick Charitable Trust
Payne Charitable Trust
Harry Payne Trust
Pennycress Trust
Nathaniel Reyner Trust Fund
Cliff Richard Charitable Trust
Rotherwick Foundation
St Peter's Saltley Trust
Leonard Laity Stoate
  Charitable Trust
Bernard Sunley Charitable
  Foundation

Walter Swindon Charitable
Trust
Trustees of Tzedakah
Wallington Missionary Mart
and Auctions
Wellfield Trust

■ Quakers
Funding priority
William P Bancroft (No 2)
Charitable Trust and
Jenepher Gillett Trust
J A Clark Charitable Trust
Global Care
Oliver Morland Charitable Trust
Oakdale Trust
Oxfordshire Historic Churches
Trust
J B Pelly Charitable Settlement
Albert Reckitt Charitable Trust
Sir James Reckitt Charity
Rosca Trust
W F Southall Trust
Tufton Charitable Trust
Westcroft Trust
Yorkshire Historic Churches
Trust

Will consider
Barnabas Charitable Trust
Richard Cadbury Charitable
Trust
Hilda & Alice Clark Charitable
Trust
Derbyshire Community
Foundation
David Finnie & Alan Emery
Charitable Trust
Inlight Trust
Sir James Knott Trust
Bryan Lancaster's Charity
John Martin's Charity
Minge's Gift
Northumbria Historic Churches
Trust
Norwood & Newton Settlement
Pastoral Care Trust
Harry Payne Trust
Pennycress Trust
Joseph Rowntree Charitable
Trust
Joseph Rowntree Foundation
St Peter's Saltley Trust
Walter Swindon Charitable
Trust
C B & H H Taylor 1984 Trust
Tisbury Telegraph Trust
Trustees of Tzedakah
Wellfield Trust
Worshipful Company of
Founders Charities

■ Roman Catholics
Funding priority
Aid to the Church in Need (UK)
Bisgood Charitable Trust

Buckinghamshire Historic
Churches Trust
Catholic Charitable Trust
Catholic Foreign Missions
Nicholas Coote Charitable
Trust
Joseph Fattorini Charitable
Trust 'B' Account
Forte Charitable Trust
Angela Gallagher Memorial
Fund
Global Care
Heagerty Charitable Trust
J A R Charitable Trust
Kennedy Charitable Foundation
Labone Charitable Trust
Late Sir Pierce Lacy Charity
Trust
Lindale Educational
Foundation
Charlotte Marshall Charitable
Trust
Horace Moore Charitable Trust
National Catholic Fund
Oxfordshire Historic Churches
Trust
Clive Richards Charity Ltd
Rosca Trust
Simpson Foundation
Tufton Charitable Trust
Yorkshire Historic Churches
Trust

Will consider
AMW Charitable Trust
Bamford Charitable Foundation
W A Cargill Charitable Trust
W A Cargill Fund
Chownes Foundation
Clover Trust
Derbyshire Community
Foundation
David Finnie & Alan Emery
Charitable Trust
Earl Fitzwilliam Charitable
Trust
G C Gibson Charitable Trust
Constance Green Foundation
Hinchley Charitable Trust
Sir Harold Hood's Charitable
Trust
Inlight Trust
John Martin's Charity
Minge's Gift
Peter Moores Foundation
Northumbria Historic Churches
Trust
Pastoral Care Trust
Pennycress Trust
Rotherwick Foundation
St Peter's Saltley Trust
Bernard Sunley Charitable
Foundation
Sylvanus Charitable Trust
Trustees of Tzedakah
Wellfield Trust

■ Unitarians
Funding priority
Yorkshire Historic Churches
Trust

Will consider
Derbyshire Community
Foundation
David Finnie & Alan Emery
Charitable Trust
Inlight Trust
Sir James Knott Trust
Minge's Gift
Northumbria Historic Churches
Trust
Pastoral Care Trust
Harry Payne Trust
Pennycress Trust
Ravensdale Trust
St Peter's Saltley Trust
Walter Swindon Charitable
Trust
Tufton Charitable Trust
Trustees of Tzedakah
Wellfield Trust

■ Hindus
Funding priority
Puri Foundation

Will consider
Derbyshire Community
Foundation
Inlight Trust
Sir James Knott Trust
John Martin's Charity
Minge's Gift
Northumbria Historic Churches
Trust
Pastoral Care Trust
Harry Payne Trust
Pennycress Trust
St Peter's Saltley Trust
Walter Swindon Charitable
Trust
Trustees of Tzedakah
Wellfield Trust

■ People of the Jewish faith
Funding priority
Henry & Grete Abrahams
Charitable Trust
Acacia Charitable Trust
Achisomoch Aid Company
Adenfirst Ltd
Beis Aharon Trust Fund
Alba Charitable Trust
Alglen Ltd
Alliance Family Foundation
Altamont Ltd
Amberstone Trust
Ardwick Trust

Lord Ashdown Charitable Trust
AW Charitable Trust
Baker Charitable Trust
Bear Mordechai Ltd
Beauland Ltd
Peter Black Charitable Trust
Neville & Elaine Blond
  Charitable Trust
Bois Rochel Dsatmar
  Charitable Trust
Salo Bordon Charitable Trust
A Bornstein Charitable
  Settlement
M Bourne Charitable Trust
Brushmill Ltd
Carlee Ltd
Carlton House Charitable Trust
Carroll-Marx Charitable
  Foundation
Charitworth Limited
Charity Association
  Manchester Ltd
Chelwood 2000 Settlement
Clore Duffield Foundation
Closehelm Ltd
Clydpride Ltd
Vivienne & Samuel Cohen
  Charitable Trust
Col-Reno Ltd
E Alec Colman Charitable Fund
  Ltd
Confidential Fund, Lishkas
  Chasho'in
Sidney & Elizabeth Corob
  Charitable Trust
Corona Charitable Trust
Itzchok Meyer Cymerman Trust
  Ltd
Alderman Joe Davidson
  Memorial Trust
Debmar Benevolent Trust
Dellal Foundation
Dollond Charitable Trust
Doughty Charity Trust
Elanore Ltd
George Elias Charitable Trust
Ellinson Foundation Ltd
Elman Charitable Trust
Elshore Ltd
Entindale Ltd
Esher House Charitable Trust
Exilarch's Foundation
Family Foundations Trust
Famos Foundation Trust
Federation of Jewish Relief
  Organisations
Finnart House School Trust
Gerald Fogel Charitable Trust
Forbesville Limited
Fordeve Ltd
Forte Charitable Trust
Isaac and Freda Frankel
  Memorial Charitable Trust
Friends of Biala Ltd
Mejer and Gertrude Miriam
  Frydman Foundation

Jacqueline and Michael Gee
  Charitable Trust
Gertner Charitable Trust
B & P Glasser Charitable Trust
Joseph & Queenie Gold
  Charitable Trust
Grahame Charitable
  Foundation
M & R Gross Charities Limited
Gur Trust
H P Charitable Trust
Lord and Lady Haskel
  Charitable Foundation
Hathaway Trust
Maurice Hatter Foundation
Bernhard Heuberger Charitable
  Trust
Highcroft Charitable Trust
Holden Charitable Trust
Huntingdon Foundation
Hurdale Charity Limited
P Y N & B Hyams Trust
Invicta Trust
Jacobs Charitable Trust
Dorothy Jacobs Charity
Yvette and Hermione Jacobson
  Charitable Trust
Susan and Stephen James
  Charitable Settlement
Jewish Child's Day
Jewish Youth Fund
Nicholas Joels Charitable Trust
N B Johnson Charitable
  Settlement
J E Joseph Charitable Fund
Bernard Kahn Charitable Trust
Stanley Kalms Foundation
Ian Karten Charitable Trust
Kasner Charitable Trust
Michael & Ilse Katz Foundation
Katzauer Charitable
  Settlement
C S Kaufman Charitable Trust
Geoffrey John Kaye Charitable
  Foundation
Emmanuel Kaye Foundation
Keren Association
Kermaville Ltd
E & E Kernkraut Charities
  Limited
Kessler Foundation
Kohn Foundation
Kreditor Charitable Trust
Largsmount Ltd
Rachel & Jack Lass Charities
  Ltd
Laufer Charitable Trust
Carole & Geoffrey Lawson
  Foundation
Lawson Charitable Foundation
Lawson-Beckman Charitable
  Trust
Arnold Lee Charitable Trust
Kennedy Leigh Charitable
  Trust
Morris Leigh Foundation

Ruth & Stuart Lipton
  Charitable Trust
Jack Livingstone Charitable
  Trust
Localtrent Ltd
Locker Foundation
Loftus Charitable Trust
Lolev Charitable Trust
M & C Trust
M D & S Charitable Trust
M K (Mendel Kaufman)
  Charitable Trust
Magen Charitable Trust
Marbeh Torah Trust
Stella and Alexander Margulies
  Charitable Trust
Hilda & Samuel Marks
  Foundation
Violet Mauray Charitable Trust
Mayfair Charities Ltd
Maypride Ltd
Melodor Ltd
Melow Charitable Trust
Menuchar Ltd
M Miller Charitable Trust
Laurence Misener Charitable
  Trust
Moette Charitable Trust
Mole Charitable Trust
Vyoel Moshe Charitable Trust
MYA Charitable Trust
Willie Nagel Charitable Trust
Nemoral Ltd
Nesswall Ltd
Newpier Charity Ltd
Chevras Ezras Nitzrochim Trust
Noswal Charitable Trust
Joseph and Sarah Pearlman
  Jewish Charitable Trust
Peltz Trust
B E Perl Charitable Trust
Ruth & Michael Phillips
  Charitable Trust
George & Esme Pollitzer
  Charitable Settlement
Edith & Ferdinand Porjes
  Charitable Trust
J E Posnansky Charitable Trust
Premierquote Ltd
Premishlaner Charitable Trust
R S Charitable Trust
Joseph & Lena Randall
  Charitable Trust
Raydan Charitable Trust
Rest Harrow Trust
Ridgesave Limited
Rokach Family Charitable Trust
Cissie Rosefield Charitable
  Trust
Joshua and Michelle Rowe
  Charitable Trust
Rubin Foundation
Michael Sacher Charitable
  Trust
Ruzin Sadagora Trust
Schapira Charitable Trust

Annie Schiff Charitable Trust
Schmidt-Bodner Charitable
　Trust
Schreib Trust
Schreiber Charitable Trust
Scopus Jewish Educational
　Trust
Searchlight Electric Charitable
　Trust
Samuel Sebba Charitable
　Trust
Archie Sherman Charitable
　Trust
J Shine Charities Ltd
Shlomo Memorial Fund Limited
L H Silver Charitable Trust
Sinclair Charitable Trust
SO Charitable Trust
Sobell Foundation
Solev Co Ltd
Solo Charitable Settlement
Songdale Ltd
Cyril & Betty Stein Charitable
　Trust
Jack Steinberg Charitable
　Trust
Stervon Ltd
Sueberry Ltd
Sumray Charitable Trust
Walter Swindon Charitable
　Trust
Tajtelbaum Charitable Trust
Talteg Ltd
David Tannen Charitable Trust
Lili Tapper Charitable
　Foundation
Tegham Limited
Tomchei Torah Charitable
　Trust
Truedene Co. Ltd
Trumros Limited
Tudor Rose Ltd
Trustees of Tzedakah
Union of Orthodox Hebrew
　Congregation
David Uri Memorial Trust
Vivdale Ltd
Warbeck Fund Ltd
Weinberg Foundation
Weinstein Foundation
Stella & Ernest Weinstein
　Trust
Weinstock Fund
Alfred and Beatrice Weintrop
　Charity
Williams Family Charitable
　Trust
Benjamin Winegarten
　Charitable Trust
Harold Hyam Wingate
　Foundation
Michael and Anna Wix
　Charitable Trust
Maurice Wohl Charitable Trust
Aviezer Wolfson Charitable
　Trust

Wolfson Family Charitable
　Trust
Woodlands Green Ltd
Fred & Della Worms Charitable
　Trust
Wychdale Ltd
Wychville Ltd
David Young Charitable
　Settlement

Will consider
Andrew Balint Charitable Trust
George Balint Charitable Trust
Paul Balint Charitable Trust
Boltons Trust
Audrey & Stanley Burton
　Charitable Trust
R M 1956 Burton Charitable
　Trust
Derbyshire Community
　Foundation
David Finnie & Alan Emery
　Charitable Trust
Rose Flatau Charitable Trust
Glencore Foundation for
　Education and Welfare
Reginald Graham Charitable
　Trust
Constance Green Foundation
Inlight Trust
JCA Charitable Foundation
Judith Trust
Sir James Knott Trust
Kobler Trust
Kreitman Foundation
Lambert Charitable Trust
Levy Foundation
Lewis Family Charitable Trust
Harry Livingstone Charitable
　Trust
Linda Marcus Charitable Trust
John Martin's Charity
Minge's Gift
Victor Mishcon Charitable
　Trust
Moss Family Charitable Trust
Naggar Charitable Trust
Northumbria Historic Churches
　Trust
Pastoral Care Trust
Harry Payne Trust
Pennycress Trust
J S F Pollitzer Charitable
　Settlement
Simone Prendergast Charitable
　Trust
Cecil Rosen Foundation
Rowanville Ltd
St Peter's Saltley Trust
Sellata Ltd
Stanley Charitable Trust
Tufton Charitable Trust
Wellfield Trust
Maurice Wohl Charitable
　Foundation

Charles Wolfson Charitable
　Trust

....

■ **Muslims**

Funding priority
Muslim Hands

Will consider
Derbyshire Community
　Foundation
David Finnie & Alan Emery
　Charitable Trust
Inlight Trust
Sir James Knott Trust
Kennedy Leigh Charitable
　Trust
John Martin's Charity
Matliwala Family Charitable
　Trust
Minge's Gift
North London Islamic
　Association Trust
Northumbria Historic Churches
　Trust
Pastoral Care Trust
Harry Payne Trust
Pennycress Trust
St Peter's Saltley Trust
Walter Swindon Charitable
　Trust
Trustees of Tzedakah
Wellfield Trust

....

■ **Sikhs**

Will Consider
Pastoral Care Trust
Harry Payne Trust

Ill health

■ **Alzheimer's disease**
Funding priority
Sylvia Aitken Charitable Trust
Ammco Trust
Ardwick Trust
Ashby Charitable Trust
Astor Foundation
Baily Thomas Charitable Fund
Barnwood House Trust
Birmingham Hospital Saturday
　Fund Medical Charity &
　Welfare Trust
Bothwell Charitable Trust
Palgrave Brown Foundation
Audrey & Stanley Burton
　Charitable Trust
Cleopatra Trust
John Coates Charitable Trust
Cranbury Foundation
Dorus Trust

Wilfred & Elsie Elkes Charity
Fund
Epigoni Trust
Gerald Fogel Charitable Trust
Garthgwynion Charities
Simon Gibson Charitable Trust
Teresa Rosenbaum Golden
Charitable Trust
Hampton Fuel Allotment
Charity
Charles Hayward Foundation
Joseph & Mary Hiley Trust
Clifford Howarth Charity
Settlement
Miss Agnes H Hunter's Trust
Levy Foundation
Lynn Foundation
Laurie Nidditch Foundation
Peacock Charitable Trust
Austin & Hope Pilkington Trust
Pilkington Charities Fund
Mr and Mrs J A Pye's
Charitable Settlement
Cliff Richard Charitable Trust
Christopher Rowbotham
Charitable Trust
Sir Halley Stewart Trust
Walter Swindon Charitable
Trust
Tesco Charity Trust
Mrs Maud Van Norden's
Charitable Foundation
Verdon-Smith Family Charitable
Settlement
Alfred and Beatrice Weintrop
Charity
Yorkshire Building Society
Charitable Foundation

Will consider

Andrew Balint Charitable Trust
George Balint Charitable Trust
John Bell Charitable Trust
Morgan Blake Charitable Trust
Bonhomie United Charity
Society
Charles Boot Trust
British Dietetic Association
General and Education
Trust Fund
Richard Cadbury Charitable
Trust
Chase Charity
Childwick Trust
Chrimes Family Charitable
Trust
Norman Collinson Charitable
Trust
Comic Relief
John Cowan Foundation
Criffel Charitable Trust
Cripplegate Foundation
Harry Crook Foundation
Cumber Family Charitable
Trust
Baron Davenport's Charity

Denton Wilde Sapte Charitable
Trust
Derbyshire Community
Foundation
Douglas Charitable Trust
Dunhill Medical Trust
Eden Arts Trust
City of Edinburgh Charitable
Trusts
W G Edwards Charitable
Foundation
Essex Fairway Charitable Trust
Samuel William Farmer's Trust
Ferguson Benevolent Fund Ltd
Fidelity UK Foundation
David Finnie & Alan Emery
Charitable Trust
Ford of Britain Trust
Fortuna Charitable Trust
Girdlers' Company Charitable
Trust
GMC Trust
Good Neighbours Trust
Gould Charitable Trust
Constance Green Foundation
Bishop of Guildford's
Foundation
Hadfield Trust
Hadrian Trust
Hampstead Wells and
Campden Trust
Harborne Parish Lands Charity
Hare of Steep Charitable Trust
Kenneth Hargreaves Charitable
Trust
May Hearnshaw's Charity
Heart of England Community
Foundation
Hemby Trust
Edward Holt Trust
Mary Homfray Charitable Trust
Hospital of God at Greatham
Hospital Saturday Fund
Charitable Trust
James Thom Howat Charitable
Trust
Inverforth Charitable Trust
Ruth & Lionel Jacobson Trust
(Second Fund) No 2
Jarman Charitable Trust
John Jarrold Trust
Jeffrey Charitable Trust
Johnson Foundation
Edward Cecil Jones Settlement
Anton Jurgens Charitable Trust
Knowles Charitable Trust
Kirby Laing Foundation
Lankelly Foundation
Lauffer Family Charitable
Foundation
Raymond & Blanche Lawson
Charitable Trust
Leach Fourteenth Trust
Lloyds TSB Foundation for
England and Wales

Lloyds TSB Foundation for
Northern Ireland
Lloyds TSB Foundation for
Scotland
Loseley & Guildway Charitable
Trust
Mackintosh Foundation
R W Mann Trustees Limited
Marchday Charitable Fund
Jim Marshall Charitable Trust
Matliwala Family Charitable
Trust
Tony Metherell Charitable
Trust
Metropolitan Hospital-Sunday
Fund
Gerald Micklem Charitable
Trust
Minge's Gift
George A Moore Foundation
Horace Moore Charitable Trust
Nestlé Rowntree York
Employees Community Fund
Trust
Northcott Devon Foundation
Kate Wilson Oliver Trust
Owen Family Trust
Oxfordshire Community
Foundation
Patients' Aid Association
Hospital & Medical
Charities Trust
Charity Fund of the Worshipful
Company of Paviors
Harry Payne Trust
Bernard Piggott Trust
John Pitman Charitable Trust
G S Plaut Charitable Trust
J S F Pollitzer Charitable
Settlement
Simone Prendergast Charitable
Trust
Proven Family Trust
Pye Foundation
Rainford Trust
Ravensdale Trust
John Rayner Charitable Trust
REMEDI
Richmond Parish Lands Charity
Rivendell Trust
Rothley Trust
Rufford Foundation
Saddlers' Company Charitable
Fund
St Laurence Charities for the
Poor
Frieda Scott Charitable Trust
Sir James & Lady Scott Trust
Scouloudi Foundation
Sefton Community Foundation
Sherburn House Charity
Sobell Foundation
Sovereign Health Care
Charitable Trust
W W Spooner Charitable Trust

Steinberg Family Charitable
Trust
Charles and Elsie Sykes Trust
Talbot Trusts
Thoresby Charitable Trust
Sir Jules Thorn Charitable
Trust
Triangle Trust (1949) Fund
Tudor Trust
Perry Watlington Trust
Wellfield Trust
Wesleyan Charitable Trust
Michael and Anna Wix
Charitable Trust
Wolfson Foundation

■ Arthritis & rheumatism

Funding priority

Arthritis Research Campaign
Betard Bequest
Bothwell Charitable Trust
Cleopatra Trust
John Coates Charitable Trust
Dorus Trust
Epigoni Trust
Simon Gibson Charitable Trust
Teresa Rosenbaum Golden
Charitable Trust
Hampton Fuel Allotment
Charity
Lennox Hannay Charitable
Trust
Miss Agnes H Hunter's Trust
Lynn Foundation
Willie & Mabel Morris
Charitable Trust
Laurie Nidditch Foundation
Pennycress Trust
Pilkington Charities Fund
Ronald & Kathleen Pryor
Charitable Trust
Christopher Rowbotham
Charitable Trust
Sir Halley Stewart Trust
Walter Swindon Charitable
Trust
Verdon-Smith Family Charitable
Settlement
Yorkshire Building Society
Charitable Foundation

Will consider

Ammco Trust
Ardwick Trust
Barnwood House Trust
Birmingham Hospital Saturday
Fund Medical Charity &
Welfare Trust
Morgan Blake Charitable Trust
Bonhomie United Charity
Society
Charles & Edna Broadhurst
Charitable Trust

Richard Cadbury Charitable
Trust
Childwick Trust
Chrimes Family Charitable
Trust
John Cowan Foundation
Cray Trust
Criffel Charitable Trust
Cripplegate Foundation
Denton Wilde Sapte Charitable
Trust
Derbyshire Community
Foundation
Dunhill Medical Trust
City of Edinburgh Charitable
Trusts
Samuel William Farmer's Trust
David Finnie & Alan Emery
Charitable Trust
Ford of Britain Trust
Good Neighbours Trust
Bishop of Guildford's
Foundation
Hadfield Trust
Hadrian Trust
Hampstead Wells and
Campden Trust
Harborne Parish Lands Charity
Hare of Steep Charitable Trust
Kenneth Hargreaves Charitable
Trust
Charles Hayward Foundation
May Hearnshaw's Charity
Heart of England Community
Foundation
Hemby Trust
Dorothy Holmes Charitable
Trust
Mary Homfray Charitable Trust
Hospital Saturday Fund
Charitable Trust
Clifford Howarth Charity
Settlement
Inverforth Charitable Trust
Ruth & Lionel Jacobson Trust
(Second Fund) No 2
Jarman Charitable Trust
John Jarrold Trust
Jeffrey Charitable Trust
Johnson Foundation
Anton Jurgens Charitable Trust
Kirby Laing Foundation
R J Larg Family Charitable
Trust
Raymond & Blanche Lawson
Charitable Trust
Leach Fourteenth Trust
Lloyds TSB Foundation for
England and Wales
Lloyds TSB Foundation for
Northern Ireland
Lloyds TSB Foundation for
Scotland
London Law Trust
Loseley & Guildway Charitable
Trust

Jim Marshall Charitable Trust
Matliwala Family Charitable
Trust
Tony Metherell Charitable
Trust
Metropolitan Hospital-Sunday
Fund
Minge's Gift
George A Moore Foundation
Horace Moore Charitable Trust
Moss Family Charitable Trust
Nestlé Rowntree York
Employees Community Fund
Trust
Northcott Devon Foundation
Kate Wilson Oliver Trust
Oxfordshire Community
Foundation
Patients' Aid Association
Hospital & Medical
Charities Trust
John Pitman Charitable Trust
J S F Pollitzer Charitable
Settlement
Proven Family Trust
Pye Foundation
Mr and Mrs J A Pye's
Charitable Settlement
Rainford Trust
Ravensdale Trust
John Rayner Charitable Trust
REMEDI
Cliff Richard Charitable Trust
Richmond Parish Lands Charity
Rivendell Trust
Rothley Trust
Saddlers' Company Charitable
Fund
St Laurence Charities for the
Poor
Andrew Salvesen Charitable
Trust
Frieda Scott Charitable Trust
Sir James & Lady Scott Trust
Scouloudi Foundation
Sefton Community Foundation
Sherburn House Charity
Leslie Smith Foundation
Sobell Foundation
Sovereign Health Care
Charitable Trust
W W Spooner Charitable Trust
Steinberg Family Charitable
Trust
Charles and Elsie Sykes Trust
Talbot Trusts
Tesco Charity Trust
Thoresby Charitable Trust
Sir Jules Thorn Charitable
Trust
Tisbury Telegraph Trust
Perry Watlington Trust
Alfred and Beatrice Weintrop
Charity
Wellfield Trust
Wesleyan Charitable Trust

Michael and Anna Wix
  Charitable Trust
Wolfson Foundation

....

■ Asthma

Funding priority
Palgrave Brown Foundation
Chest Heart and Stroke
  Scotland
Cleopatra Trust
Dorus Trust
Epigoni Trust
Teresa Rosenbaum Golden
  Charitable Trust
Hampton Fuel Allotment
  Charity
Lynn Foundation
Moulton Charitable Trust
National Asthma Campaign
Austin & Hope Pilkington Trust
Pilkington Charities Fund
Mr & Mrs Philip Rackham
  Charitable Trust
Barbara A Shuttleworth
  Memorial Trust
Leslie Smith Foundation
Verdon-Smith Family Charitable
  Settlement
Walton Foundation
Alfred and Beatrice Weintrop
  Charity
Felicity Wilde Charitable Trust
Yorkshire Building Society
  Charitable Foundation

Will consider
Ardwick Trust
Birmingham Hospital Saturday
  Fund Medical Charity &
  Welfare Trust
Morgan Blake Charitable Trust
Richard Cadbury Charitable
  Trust
Childwick Trust
Chownes Foundation
Chrimes Family Charitable
  Trust
Norman Collinson Charitable
  Trust
Criffel Charitable Trust
Cripplegate Foundation
Denton Wilde Sapte Charitable
  Trust
Derbyshire Community
  Foundation
Dunhill Medical Trust
City of Edinburgh Charitable
  Trusts
Samuel William Farmer's Trust
Ferguson Benevolent Fund Ltd
Ford of Britain Trust
Good Neighbours Trust
Bishop of Guildford's
  Foundation
Hadfield Trust

Hallam FM – Help a Hallam
  Child Appeal
Hampstead Wells and
  Campden Trust
Harborne Parish Lands Charity
Kenneth Hargreaves Charitable
  Trust
Charles Hayward Foundation
May Hearnshaw's Charity
Heart of England Community
  Foundation
Hemby Trust
Dorothy Holmes Charitable
  Trust
Mary Homfray Charitable Trust
Hospital Saturday Fund
  Charitable Trust
Clifford Howarth Charity
  Settlement
Inverforth Charitable Trust
Jarman Charitable Trust
John Jarrold Trust
Jeffrey Charitable Trust
Kirby Laing Foundation
R J Larg Family Charitable
  Trust
Lauffer Family Charitable
  Foundation
Leach Fourteenth Trust
Lloyds TSB Foundation for
  England and Wales
Lloyds TSB Foundation for
  Northern Ireland
Lloyds TSB Foundation for
  Scotland
London Law Trust
Jim Marshall Charitable Trust
Matliwala Family Charitable
  Trust
Tony Metherell Charitable
  Trust
Metropolitan Hospital-Sunday
  Fund
Minge's Gift
George A Moore Foundation
Moss Family Charitable Trust
Nestlé Rowntree York
  Employees Community Fund
  Trust
Northcott Devon Foundation
Kate Wilson Oliver Trust
Oxfordshire Community
  Foundation
Patients' Aid Association
  Hospital & Medical
  Charities Trust
Harry Payne Trust
John Pitman Charitable Trust
J S F Pollitzer Charitable
  Settlement
Proven Family Trust
Pye Foundation
Mr and Mrs J A Pye's
  Charitable Settlement
Ravensdale Trust
John Rayner Charitable Trust

REMEDI
Richmond Parish Lands Charity
Rivendell Trust
Rothley Trust
Christopher Rowbotham
  Charitable Trust
Saddlers' Company Charitable
  Fund
St Laurence Charities for the
  Poor
Andrew Salvesen Charitable
  Trust
Frieda Scott Charitable Trust
Sir James & Lady Scott Trust
Scouloudi Foundation
Sefton Community Foundation
Sheldon Trust
Sherburn House Charity
Sobell Foundation
Sovereign Health Care
  Charitable Trust
W W Spooner Charitable Trust
Steinberg Family Charitable
  Trust
Charles and Elsie Sykes Trust
Talbot Trusts
Tesco Charity Trust
Sir Jules Thorn Charitable
  Trust
Tisbury Telegraph Trust
Wellfield Trust
Wesleyan Charitable Trust
Michael and Anna Wix
  Charitable Trust
Wolfson Foundation

....

■ Cancers

Funding priority
Appletree Trust
Ardwick Trust
Ashby Charitable Trust
Ashe Park Charitable Trust
Bergqvist Charitable Trust
Birmingham Hospital Saturday
  Fund Medical Charity &
  Welfare Trust
Blair Foundation
Bothwell Charitable Trust
British Dietetic Association
  General and Education
  Trust Fund
Palgrave Brown Foundation
Audrey & Stanley Burton
  Charitable Trust
Cleopatra Trust
Lord Clinton's Charitable Trust
John Coates Charitable Trust
Denton Charitable Trust
Dorus Trust
Epigoni Trust
Bud Flanagan Leukaemia Fund
Timothy Franey Charitable
  Foundation
Garthgwynion Charities
Simon Gibson Charitable Trust

Teresa Rosenbaum Golden
   Charitable Trust
Hampton Fuel Allotment
   Charity
Lennox Hannay Charitable
   Trust
Dorothy Holmes Charitable
   Trust
Edward Holt Trust
Clifford Howarth Charity
   Settlement
Miss Agnes H Hunter's Trust
Kidani Memorial Trust
Neil Kreitman Foundation
Mason Le Page Charitable
   Trust
Leeds & Holbeck Building
   Society Charitable
   Foundation
Kennedy Leigh Charitable
   Trust
Leukaemia Research Fund
Levy Foundation
Lewis Family Charitable Trust
Second Joseph Aaron Littman
   Foundation
Lord and Lady Lurgan Trust
Lynn Foundation
Mandeville Trust
D G Marshall of Cambridge
   Trust
Melville Trust for Care and
   Cure of Cancer
Tony Metherell Charitable
   Trust
Minge's Gift
Willie & Mabel Morris
   Charitable Trust
Laurie Nidditch Foundation
North West Cancer Research
   Fund
Parthenon Trust
Peacock Charitable Trust
Austin & Hope Pilkington Trust
Pilkington Charities Fund
Ronald & Kathleen Pryor
   Charitable Trust
Mr and Mrs J A Pye's
   Charitable Settlement
John Rayner Charitable Trust
Cliff Richard Charitable Trust
Muriel Edith Rickman Trust
Walter Swindon Charitable
   Trust
Connie and Albert Taylor
   Charitable Trust
Tesco Charity Trust
Mrs Maud Van Norden's
   Charitable Foundation
Verdon-Smith Family Charitable
   Settlement
Walton Foundation
Alfred and Beatrice Weintrop
   Charity
Wessex Cancer Trust

West London Synagogue
   Charitable Fund
Miss E B Wrightson's
   Charitable Settlement
Wyseliot Charitable Trust
Yorkshire Building Society
   Charitable Foundation

Will consider
Adnams Charity
Ammco Trust
G C Armitage Charitable Trust
Andrew Balint Charitable Trust
George Balint Charitable Trust
Bamford Charitable Foundation
Morgan Blake Charitable Trust
Enid Blyton Trust for Children
Charles Boot Trust
Charles & Edna Broadhurst
   Charitable Trust
P H G Cadbury Trust
Richard Cadbury Charitable
   Trust
Childwick Trust
Chrimes Family Charitable
   Trust
Norman Collinson Charitable
   Trust
John Cowan Foundation
Coward Trust
Cray Trust
Criffel Charitable Trust
Cripplegate Foundation
Cumber Family Charitable
   Trust
Baron Davenport's Charity
Wilfrid Bruce Davis Charitable
   Trust
De La Rue Charitable Trust
Denton Wilde Sapte Charitable
   Trust
Derbyshire Community
   Foundation
Douglas Charitable Trust
City of Edinburgh Charitable
   Trusts
Esher House Charitable Trust
Norman Evershed Trust
Samuel William Farmer's Trust
Ferguson Benevolent Fund Ltd
David Finnie & Alan Emery
   Charitable Trust
Earl Fitzwilliam Charitable
   Trust
Gerald Fogel Charitable Trust
Ford of Britain Trust
Fortuna Charitable Trust
Gannochy Trust
Robert Gavron Charitable Trust
Jacqueline and Michael Gee
   Charitable Trust
Girdlers' Company Charitable
   Trust
Good Neighbours Trust
Reginald Graham Charitable
   Trust

Constance Green Foundation
Bishop of Guildford's
   Foundation
Hadfield Trust
Hadrian Trust
Hallam FM – Help a Hallam
   Child Appeal
Hampstead Wells and
   Campden Trust
Harborne Parish Lands Charity
Hare of Steep Charitable Trust
Kenneth Hargreaves Charitable
   Trust
May Hearnshaw's Charity
Heart of England Community
   Foundation
Hemby Trust
Christina Mary Hendrie Trust
   for Scottish & Canadian
   Charities
Sir Julian Hodge Charitable
   Trust
Mary Homfray Charitable Trust
Hospital Saturday Fund
   Charitable Trust
James Thom Howat Charitable
   Trust
Inverforth Charitable Trust
Ruth & Lionel Jacobson Trust
   (Second Fund) No 2
Jarman Charitable Trust
John Jarrold Trust
Jeffrey Charitable Trust
Johnson Foundation
Edward Cecil Jones Settlement
Anton Jurgens Charitable Trust
Boris Karloff Charitable
   Foundation
Kay Kendall Leukaemia Fund
Robert Kiln Charitable Trust
Kirby Laing Foundation
R J Larg Family Charitable
   Trust
Laufer Charitable Trust
Raymond & Blanche Lawson
   Charitable Trust
Leach Fourteenth Trust
Leonard Trust
Lloyds TSB Foundation for
   England and Wales
Lloyds TSB Foundation for
   Northern Ireland
Lloyds TSB Foundation for
   Scotland
London Law Trust
Loseley & Guildway Charitable
   Trust
R W Mann Trustees Limited
Jim Marshall Charitable Trust
Matliwala Family Charitable
   Trust
Metropolitan Hospital-Sunday
   Fund
George A Moore Foundation
Moss Family Charitable Trust

Nestlé Rowntree York
Employees Community Fund
Trust
Northcott Devon Foundation
Kate Wilson Oliver Trust
Owen Family Trust
Oxfordshire Community
Foundation
Patients' Aid Association
Hospital & Medical
Charities Trust
Patrick Charitable Trust
Harry Payne Trust
Persula Foundation
Bernard Piggott Trust
John Pitman Charitable Trust
J S F Pollitzer Charitable
Settlement
Simone Prendergast Charitable
Trust
Prince Foundation
Pye Foundation
Rainford Trust
Ravensdale Trust
Red Dragon Radio Trust
Reuters Foundation
Richmond Parish Lands Charity
Rivendell Trust
Rothley Trust
Christopher Rowbotham
Charitable Trust
Saddlers' Company Charitable
Fund
St Laurence Charities for the
Poor
Andrew Salvesen Charitable
Trust
Frieda Scott Charitable Trust
Sir James & Lady Scott Trust
Scouloudi Foundation
Sefton Community Foundation
Sherburn House Charity
Leslie Smith Foundation
Sobell Foundation
Sovereign Health Care
Charitable Trust
W W Spooner Charitable Trust
Starfish Trust
Steinberg Family Charitable
Trust
Charles and Elsie Sykes Trust
Talbot Trusts
Thoresby Charitable Trust
Tisbury Telegraph Trust
Perry Watlington Trust
Wellfield Trust
Wesleyan Charitable Trust
Westminster Amalgamated
Charity
Will Charitable Trust
Michael and Anna Wix
Charitable Trust
Wolfson Foundation

■ Cystic fibrosis

Funding priority
Ammco Trust
Birmingham Hospital Saturday
Fund Medical Charity &
Welfare Trust
British Dietetic Association
General and Education
Trust Fund
Chest Heart and Stroke
Scotland
Cystic Fibrosis Trust
Simon Gibson Charitable Trust
Teresa Rosenbaum Golden
Charitable Trust
Hampton Fuel Allotment
Charity
Handicapped Children's Aid
Committee
Levy Foundation
Lynn Foundation
Walter Swindon Charitable
Trust
Verdon-Smith Family Charitable
Settlement
Yorkshire Building Society
Charitable Foundation

Will consider
Ardwick Trust
Morgan Blake Charitable Trust
Bonhomie United Charity
Society
Richard Cadbury Charitable
Trust
Childwick Trust
Clover Trust
Norman Collinson Charitable
Trust
Criffel Charitable Trust
Cripplegate Foundation
Denton Wilde Sapte Charitable
Trust
Derbyshire Community
Foundation
City of Edinburgh Charitable
Trusts
Samuel William Farmer's Trust
Ford of Britain Trust
Girdlers' Company Charitable
Trust
Good Neighbours Trust
Reginald Graham Charitable
Trust
Bishop of Guildford's
Foundation
Hadfield Trust
Hallam FM – Help a Hallam
Child Appeal
Hampstead Wells and
Campden Trust
Harborne Parish Lands Charity
Hare of Steep Charitable Trust
Charles Hayward Foundation
Heart of England Community
Foundation

Hemby Trust
Mary Homfray Charitable Trust
Hospital Saturday Fund
Charitable Trust
Clifford Howarth Charity
Settlement
James Thom Howat Charitable
Trust
Inverforth Charitable Trust
Ruth & Lionel Jacobson Trust
(Second Fund) No 2
Jarman Charitable Trust
John Jarrold Trust
Jeffrey Charitable Trust
Anton Jurgens Charitable Trust
Kirby Laing Foundation
Raymond & Blanche Lawson
Charitable Trust
Leach Fourteenth Trust
Lloyds TSB Foundation for
England and Wales
Lloyds TSB Foundation for
Northern Ireland
Lloyds TSB Foundation for
Scotland
London Law Trust
Loseley & Guildway Charitable
Trust
Marchday Charitable Fund
Jim Marshall Charitable Trust
Matliwala Family Charitable
Trust
Tony Metherell Charitable
Trust
Metropolitan Hospital-Sunday
Fund
Minge's Gift
Northcott Devon Foundation
Kate Wilson Oliver Trust
Oxfordshire Community
Foundation
Patients' Aid Association
Hospital & Medical
Charities Trust
Harry Payne Trust
Bernard Piggott Trust
Pilkington Charities Fund
John Pitman Charitable Trust
J S F Pollitzer Charitable
Settlement
Pye Foundation
Mr and Mrs J A Pye's
Charitable Settlement
Rainford Trust
Ravensdale Trust
John Rayner Charitable Trust
Cliff Richard Charitable Trust
Richmond Parish Lands Charity
Rivendell Trust
Rothley Trust
Christopher Rowbotham
Charitable Trust
Saddlers' Company Charitable
Fund
St Laurence Charities for the
Poor

Andrew Salvesen Charitable
Trust
Frieda Scott Charitable Trust
Sir James & Lady Scott Trust
Scouloudi Foundation
Sefton Community Foundation
Sherburn House Charity
Leslie Smith Foundation
Sobell Foundation
Sovereign Health Care
Charitable Trust
W W Spooner Charitable Trust
Starfish Trust
Steinberg Family Charitable
Trust
Talbot Trusts
Tesco Charity Trust
Thoresby Charitable Trust
Sir Jules Thorn Charitable
Trust
Tisbury Telegraph Trust
Mrs Maud Van Norden's
Charitable Foundation
Perry Watlington Trust
Wellfield Trust
Wesleyan Charitable Trust
Wolfson Foundation

....

■ Diabetes

Funding priority

Ashe Park Charitable Trust
British Dietetic Association
General and Education
Trust Fund
Cleopatra Trust
Diabetes UK
Dorus Trust
Epigoni Trust
Simon Gibson Charitable Trust
Teresa Rosenbaum Golden
Charitable Trust
J C Green Charitable
Settlement
Hampton Fuel Allotment
Charity
Jeffrey Charitable Trust
Second Joseph Aaron Littman
Foundation
Lynn Foundation
Cecil Rosen Foundation
Alfred and Beatrice Weintrop
Charity
West London Synagogue
Charitable Fund
Yorkshire Building Society
Charitable Foundation

Will consider

Sir John & Lady Amory's
Charitable Trust
Ardwick Trust
Birmingham Hospital Saturday
Fund Medical Charity &
Welfare Trust
Morgan Blake Charitable Trust

Bonhomie United Charity
Society
Charles Boot Trust
Childwick Trust
Coward Trust
Cray Trust
Criffel Charitable Trust
Cripplegate Foundation
Cumber Family Charitable
Trust
Denton Wilde Sapte Charitable
Trust
Derbyshire Community
Foundation
Dunhill Medical Trust
City of Edinburgh Charitable
Trusts
Esher House Charitable Trust
Samuel William Farmer's Trust
Ferguson Benevolent Fund Ltd
David Finnie & Alan Emery
Charitable Trust
Earl Fitzwilliam Charitable
Trust
Ford of Britain Trust
Girdlers' Company Charitable
Trust
Bishop of Guildford's
Foundation
Hadfield Trust
Hampstead Wells and
Campden Trust
Harborne Parish Lands Charity
Hare of Steep Charitable Trust
Charles Hayward Foundation
May Hearnshaw's Charity
Heart of England Community
Foundation
Hemby Trust
Dorothy Holmes Charitable
Trust
Mary Homfray Charitable Trust
Hospital Saturday Fund
Charitable Trust
Clifford Howarth Charity
Settlement
Humanitarian Trust
Inverforth Charitable Trust
Jarman Charitable Trust
John Jarrold Trust
Anton Jurgens Charitable Trust
Robert Kiln Charitable Trust
Kirby Laing Foundation
R J Larg Family Charitable
Trust
Laufer Charitable Trust
Raymond & Blanche Lawson
Charitable Trust
Leach Fourteenth Trust
Lloyds TSB Foundation for
England and Wales
Lloyds TSB Foundation for
Northern Ireland
Lloyds TSB Foundation for
Scotland
London Law Trust

Jim Marshall Charitable Trust
Matliwala Family Charitable
Trust
Tony Metherell Charitable
Trust
Metropolitan Hospital-Sunday
Fund
Minge's Gift
Nestlé Rowntree York
Employees Community Fund
Trust
Northcott Devon Foundation
Kate Wilson Oliver Trust
Oxfordshire Community
Foundation
Patients' Aid Association
Hospital & Medical
Charities Trust
Pilkington Charities Fund
John Pitman Charitable Trust
J S F Pollitzer Charitable
Settlement
Simone Prendergast Charitable
Trust
Pye Foundation
Mr and Mrs J A Pye's
Charitable Settlement
Ravensdale Trust
John Rayner Charitable Trust
REMEDI
Reuters Foundation
Richmond Parish Lands Charity
Rivendell Trust
Rothley Trust
Christopher Rowbotham
Charitable Trust
Saddlers' Company Charitable
Fund
St Laurence Charities for the
Poor
Andrew Salvesen Charitable
Trust
Frieda Scott Charitable Trust
Sir James & Lady Scott Trust
Scouloudi Foundation
Sefton Community Foundation
Sherburn House Charity
Sovereign Health Care
Charitable Trust
W W Spooner Charitable Trust
Steinberg Family Charitable
Trust
Charles and Elsie Sykes Trust
Talbot Trusts
Tesco Charity Trust
Thoresby Charitable Trust
Sir Jules Thorn Charitable
Trust
Ulverscroft Foundation
Perry Watlington Trust
Wellfield Trust
Wesleyan Charitable Trust
Wolfson Foundation

■ Epilepsy

Funding priority

Ammco Trust
Ardwick Trust
Ashe Park Charitable Trust
Bergqvist Charitable Trust
Roald Dahl Foundation
Dorus Trust
Epigoni Trust
Epilepsy Research Foundation
Simon Gibson Charitable Trust
Teresa Rosenbaum Golden
    Charitable Trust
Constance Green Foundation
Hampton Fuel Allotment
    Charity
Clifford Howarth Charity
    Settlement
Lynn Foundation
Verdon-Smith Family Charitable
    Settlement
Yorkshire Building Society
    Charitable Foundation

Will consider

Baily Thomas Charitable Fund
Birmingham Hospital Saturday
    Fund Medical Charity &
    Welfare Trust
Morgan Blake Charitable Trust
Bonhomie United Charity
    Society
Childwick Trust
Clover Trust
Cripplegate Foundation
Denton Wilde Sapte Charitable
    Trust
Derbyshire Community
    Foundation
City of Edinburgh Charitable
    Trusts
Samuel William Farmer's Trust
Ford of Britain Trust
Girdlers' Company Charitable
    Trust
Good Neighbours Trust
Bishop of Guildford's
    Foundation
Hadfield Trust
Hallam FM – Help a Hallam
    Child Appeal
Hampstead Wells and
    Campden Trust
Harborne Parish Lands Charity
Charles Hayward Foundation
Heart of England Community
    Foundation
Hemby Trust
Edward Holt Trust
Mary Homfray Charitable Trust
Hospital of God at Greatham
Hospital Saturday Fund
    Charitable Trust
Miss Agnes H Hunter's Trust
Inverforth Charitable Trust
Jeffrey Charitable Trust

Anton Jurgens Charitable Trust
Kennel Club Charitable Trust
Heinz & Anna Kroch
    Foundation
Kirby Laing Foundation
R J Larg Family Charitable
    Trust
Leach Fourteenth Trust
Lloyds TSB Foundation for
    England and Wales
Lloyds TSB Foundation for
    Northern Ireland
Lloyds TSB Foundation for
    Scotland
London Law Trust
Loseley & Guildway Charitable
    Trust
Jim Marshall Charitable Trust
Matliwala Family Charitable
    Trust
Tony Metherell Charitable
    Trust
Metropolitan Hospital-Sunday
    Fund
Minge's Gift
Nestlé Rowntree York
    Employees Community Fund
    Trust
Oxfordshire Community
    Foundation
Patients' Aid Association
    Hospital & Medical
    Charities Trust
Pilkington Charities Fund
John Pitman Charitable Trust
G S Plaut Charitable Trust
Pye Foundation
Mr and Mrs J A Pye's
    Charitable Settlement
Rainford Trust
Ravensdale Trust
John Rayner Charitable Trust
Red Dragon Radio Trust
REMEDI
Richmond Parish Lands Charity
Rivendell Trust
Rothley Trust
Christopher Rowbotham
    Charitable Trust
Saddlers' Company Charitable
    Fund
St Laurence Charities for the
    Poor
Andrew Salvesen Charitable
    Trust
Frieda Scott Charitable Trust
Sir James & Lady Scott Trust
Scouloudi Foundation
Sefton Community Foundation
Sherburn House Charity
Sobell Foundation
Sovereign Health Care
    Charitable Trust
W W Spooner Charitable Trust
Steinberg Family Charitable
    Trust

Talbot Trusts
Tesco Charity Trust
Thoresby Charitable Trust
Sir Jules Thorn Charitable
    Trust
Perry Watlington Trust
Wellfield Trust
Wesleyan Charitable Trust
Westcroft Trust
Wolfson Foundation

■ Haematological
disorders

Funding priority

Birmingham Hospital Saturday
    Fund Medical Charity &
    Welfare Trust
Roald Dahl Foundation
Teresa Rosenbaum Golden
    Charitable Trust
Hampton Fuel Allotment
    Charity
Second Joseph Aaron Littman
    Foundation
Lynn Foundation
Walter Swindon Charitable
    Trust
Yorkshire Building Society
    Charitable Foundation

Will consider

Morgan Blake Charitable Trust
Childwick Trust
Cripplegate Foundation
Denton Wilde Sapte Charitable
    Trust
Derbyshire Community
    Foundation
City of Edinburgh Charitable
    Trusts
Samuel William Farmer's Trust
Ford of Britain Trust
Bishop of Guildford's
    Foundation
Hadfield Trust
Hampstead Wells and
    Campden Trust
Harborne Parish Lands Charity
Charles Hayward Foundation
Heart of England Community
    Foundation
Hemby Trust
Mary Homfray Charitable Trust
Hospital Saturday Fund
    Charitable Trust
Clifford Howarth Charity
    Settlement
Miss Agnes H Hunter's Trust
Inverforth Charitable Trust
Jeffrey Charitable Trust
Johnson Foundation
Kirby Laing Foundation
Leach Fourteenth Trust
Lloyds TSB Foundation for
    England and Wales

Lloyds TSB Foundation for
Northern Ireland
Lloyds TSB Foundation for
Scotland
London Law Trust
Jim Marshall Charitable Trust
Matliwala Family Charitable
Trust
Tony Metherell Charitable
Trust
Metropolitan Hospital-Sunday
Fund
Minge's Gift
Nestlé Rowntree York
Employees Community Fund
Trust
Northcott Devon Foundation
Oldham Foundation
Oxfordshire Community
Foundation
Patients' Aid Association
Hospital & Medical
Charities Trust
Pilkington Charities Fund
John Pitman Charitable Trust
J S F Pollitzer Charitable
Settlement
Proven Family Trust
Pye Foundation
Mr and Mrs J A Pye's
Charitable Settlement
Rainford Trust
Ravensdale Trust
John Rayner Charitable Trust
REMEDI
Richmond Parish Lands Charity
Rivendell Trust
Rothley Trust
Christopher Rowbotham
Charitable Trust
Saddlers' Company Charitable
Fund
St Laurence Charities for the
Poor
Andrew Salvesen Charitable
Trust
Frieda Scott Charitable Trust
Sir James & Lady Scott Trust
Scouloudi Foundation
Sefton Community Foundation
Sherburn House Charity
Sovereign Health Care
Charitable Trust
W W Spooner Charitable Trust
Starfish Trust
Talbot Trusts
Tesco Charity Trust
Sir Jules Thorn Charitable
Trust
Perry Watlington Trust
Alfred and Beatrice Weintrop
Charity
Wellfield Trust
Wesleyan Charitable Trust
Wolfson Foundation

■ Heart disease

Funding priority

Appletree Trust
Ardwick Trust
Ashby Charitable Trust
Birmingham Hospital Saturday
Fund Medical Charity &
Welfare Trust
Bothwell Charitable Trust
British Dietetic Association
General and Education
Trust Fund
British Heart Foundation
Palgrave Brown Foundation
Audrey & Stanley Burton
Charitable Trust
Chest Heart and Stroke
Scotland
Cleopatra Trust
Dorus Trust
Epigoni Trust
Simon Gibson Charitable Trust
Teresa Rosenbaum Golden
Charitable Trust
Hampton Fuel Allotment
Charity
Lynn Foundation
Horace Moore Charitable Trust
Willie & Mabel Morris
Charitable Trust
Peacock Charitable Trust
Mr and Mrs J A Pye's
Charitable Settlement
Cliff Richard Charitable Trust
Cecil Rosen Foundation
Walter Swindon Charitable
Trust
Connie and Albert Taylor
Charitable Trust
Tesco Charity Trust
Walton Foundation
Alfred and Beatrice Weintrop
Charity
West London Synagogue
Charitable Fund
Yorkshire Building Society
Charitable Foundation

Will consider

John Bell Charitable Trust
Morgan Blake Charitable Trust
Richard Cadbury Charitable
Trust
Childwick Trust
Norman Collinson Charitable
Trust
John Cowan Foundation
Cray Trust
Criffel Charitable Trust
Cripplegate Foundation
Denton Wilde Sapte Charitable
Trust
Derbyshire Community
Foundation
Diabetes UK
DLM Charitable Trust

Dunhill Medical Trust
City of Edinburgh Charitable
Trusts
Esher House Charitable Trust
Samuel William Farmer's Trust
Ferguson Benevolent Fund Ltd
David Finnie & Alan Emery
Charitable Trust
Ford of Britain Trust
Fortuna Charitable Trust
Gannochy Trust
Girdlers' Company Charitable
Trust
Bishop of Guildford's
Foundation
Hadfield Trust
Hadrian Trust
Hampstead Wells and
Campden Trust
Lennox Hannay Charitable
Trust
Harborne Parish Lands Charity
Hare of Steep Charitable Trust
Heart of England Community
Foundation
Hemby Trust
Mary Homfray Charitable Trust
Hospital Saturday Fund
Charitable Trust
Clifford Howarth Charity
Settlement
Inverforth Charitable Trust
Jarman Charitable Trust
John Jarrold Trust
Jeffrey Charitable Trust
Johnson Foundation
Anton Jurgens Charitable Trust
Kirby Laing Foundation
R J Larg Family Charitable
Trust
Raymond & Blanche Lawson
Charitable Trust
Leach Fourteenth Trust
Lloyds TSB Foundation for
England and Wales
Lloyds TSB Foundation for
Northern Ireland
Lloyds TSB Foundation for
Scotland
London Law Trust
Loseley & Guildway Charitable
Trust
Jim Marshall Charitable Trust
Matliwala Family Charitable
Trust
Tony Metherell Charitable
Trust
Metropolitan Hospital-Sunday
Fund
Gerald Micklem Charitable
Trust
Minge's Gift
George A Moore Foundation
Nestlé Rowntree York
Employees Community Fund
Trust

Northcott Devon Foundation
Kate Wilson Oliver Trust
Oxfordshire Community
 Foundation
Patients' Aid Association
 Hospital & Medical
 Charities Trust
Pilkington Charities Fund
John Pitman Charitable Trust
J S F Pollitzer Charitable
 Settlement
Prince Foundation
Pye Foundation
Rainford Trust
Ravensdale Trust
John Rayner Charitable Trust
REMEDI
Reuters Foundation
Richmond Parish Lands Charity
Rivendell Trust
Rothley Trust
Christopher Rowbotham
 Charitable Trust
Saddlers' Company Charitable
 Fund
St Laurence Charities for the
 Poor
Andrew Salvesen Charitable
 Trust
Frieda Scott Charitable Trust
Sir James & Lady Scott Trust
Scouloudi Foundation
Sefton Community Foundation
Sherburn House Charity
Sobell Foundation
Sovereign Health Care
 Charitable Trust
W W Spooner Charitable Trust
Steinberg Family Charitable
 Trust
Charles and Elsie Sykes Trust
Talbot Trusts
Thoresby Charitable Trust
Sir Jules Thorn Charitable
 Trust
John and Lucille van Geest
 Foundation
Mrs Maud Van Norden's
 Charitable Foundation
Perry Watlington Trust
Wellfield Trust
Wesleyan Charitable Trust
Michael and Anna Wix
 Charitable Trust
Wolfson Foundation

....

■ HIV & AIDS

Funding priority
British Dietetic Association
 General and Education
 Trust Fund
Cleopatra Trust
Dorus Trust
Epigoni Trust

Timothy Franey Charitable
 Foundation
Hampton Fuel Allotment
 Charity
Dorothy Holmes Charitable
 Trust
Elton John Aids Foundation
Leeds & Holbeck Building
 Society Charitable
 Foundation
Lyndhurst Settlement
Mackintosh Foundation
Magdalen Hospital Trust
Mercury Phoenix Trust
Monument Trust
Parthenon Trust
Austin & Hope Pilkington Trust
J E Posnansky Charitable Trust
Mr and Mrs J A Pye's
 Charitable Settlement
Rufford Foundation
West London Synagogue
 Charitable Fund
Yorkshire Building Society
 Charitable Foundation

Will consider
Ashendene Trust
Bamford Charitable Foundation
Beit Trust
Birmingham Hospital Saturday
 Fund Medical Charity &
 Welfare Trust
Morgan Blake Charitable Trust
Audrey & Stanley Burton
 Charitable Trust
Richard Cadbury Charitable
 Trust
John Coates Charitable Trust
Coppings Trust
Criffel Charitable Trust
Cripplegate Foundation
Denton Wilde Sapte Charitable
 Trust
Derbyshire Community
 Foundation
Douglas Charitable Trust
City of Edinburgh Charitable
 Trusts
Samuel William Farmer's Trust
Ford of Britain Trust
Teresa Rosenbaum Golden
 Charitable Trust
Bishop of Guildford's
 Foundation
H C D Memorial Fund
Hampstead Wells and
 Campden Trust
Harborne Parish Lands Charity
Charles Hayward Foundation
Heart of England Community
 Foundation
Hemby Trust
Mary Homfray Charitable Trust
Hospital Saturday Fund
 Charitable Trust

Clifford Howarth Charity
 Settlement
Miss Agnes H Hunter's Trust
Inverforth Charitable Trust
Jeffrey Charitable Trust
Anton Jurgens Charitable Trust
Kirby Laing Foundation
Leach Fourteenth Trust
Lloyds TSB Foundation for
 England and Wales
Lloyds TSB Foundation for
 Northern Ireland
Lloyds TSB Foundation for
 Scotland
London Law Trust
Loseley & Guildway Charitable
 Trust
Marchday Charitable Fund
Jim Marshall Charitable Trust
Matliwala Family Charitable
 Trust
Tony Metherell Charitable
 Trust
Methodist Relief and
 Development Fund
Metropolitan Hospital-Sunday
 Fund
Minge's Gift
Nestlé Rowntree York
 Employees Community Fund
 Trust
Northcott Devon Foundation
Oldham Foundation
Oxfordshire Community
 Foundation
Patients' Aid Association
 Hospital & Medical
 Charities Trust
Harry Payne Trust
Pilkington Charities Fund
John Pitman Charitable Trust
Simone Prendergast Charitable
 Trust
Pye Foundation
Ravensdale Trust
Richmond Parish Lands Charity
Rivendell Trust
Rothley Trust
Saddlers' Company Charitable
 Fund
St Laurence Charities for the
 Poor
Andrew Salvesen Charitable
 Trust
Frieda Scott Charitable Trust
Sir James & Lady Scott Trust
Sefton Community Foundation
Sherburn House Charity
Sovereign Health Care
 Charitable Trust
W W Spooner Charitable Trust
Talbot Trusts
Tearfund
Tesco Charity Trust
Tisbury Telegraph Trust
Perry Watlington Trust

Wellfield Trust
Westminster Amalgamated
 Charity
Wolfson Foundation

....

■ Kidney disease

Funding priority

Birmingham Hospital Saturday
 Fund Medical Charity &
 Welfare Trust
British Dietetic Association
 General and Education
 Trust Fund
Audrey & Stanley Burton
 Charitable Trust
Simon Gibson Charitable Trust
Teresa Rosenbaum Golden
 Charitable Trust
Hampton Fuel Allotment
 Charity
Lynn Foundation
National Kidney Research
 Fund Limited
Laurie Nidditch Foundation
Ronald & Kathleen Pryor
 Charitable Trust
Walter Swindon Charitable
 Trust
Yorkshire Building Society
 Charitable Foundation

Will consider

Ardwick Trust
Andrew Balint Charitable Trust
George Balint Charitable Trust
Morgan Blake Charitable Trust
Richard Cadbury Charitable
 Trust
Childwick Trust
Comic Relief
Criffel Charitable Trust
Cripplegate Foundation
Wilfrid Bruce Davis Charitable
 Trust
Denton Wilde Sapte Charitable
 Trust
Derbyshire Community
 Foundation
Diabetes UK
Dunhill Medical Trust
City of Edinburgh Charitable
 Trusts
Samuel William Farmer's Trust
Ford of Britain Trust
Girdlers' Company Charitable
 Trust
Bishop of Guildford's
 Foundation
Hadfield Trust
Hampstead Wells and
 Campden Trust
Harborne Parish Lands Charity
Hare of Steep Charitable Trust
Charles Hayward Foundation

Heart of England Community
 Foundation
Hemby Trust
Mary Homfray Charitable Trust
Hospital Saturday Fund
 Charitable Trust
Clifford Howarth Charity
 Settlement
Inverforth Charitable Trust
Jeffrey Charitable Trust
Kirby Laing Foundation
R J Larg Family Charitable
 Trust
Raymond & Blanche Lawson
 Charitable Trust
Leach Fourteenth Trust
Kennedy Leigh Charitable
 Trust
Lloyds TSB Foundation for
 England and Wales
Lloyds TSB Foundation for
 Northern Ireland
Lloyds TSB Foundation for
 Scotland
London Law Trust
Jim Marshall Charitable Trust
Matliwala Family Charitable
 Trust
Tony Metherell Charitable
 Trust
Metropolitan Hospital-Sunday
 Fund
Minge's Gift
George A Moore Foundation
Nestlé Rowntree York
 Employees Community Fund
 Trust
Northcott Devon Foundation
Oxfordshire Community
 Foundation
Patients' Aid Association
 Hospital & Medical
 Charities Trust
Bernard Piggott Trust
Pilkington Charities Fund
John Pitman Charitable Trust
J S F Pollitzer Charitable
 Settlement
Pye Foundation
Mr and Mrs J A Pye's
 Charitable Settlement
Rainford Trust
Ravensdale Trust
John Rayner Charitable Trust
REMEDI
Cliff Richard Charitable Trust
Richmond Parish Lands Charity
Rivendell Trust
Rothley Trust
Christopher Rowbotham
 Charitable Trust
Saddlers' Company Charitable
 Fund
St Laurence Charities for the
 Poor

Andrew Salvesen Charitable
 Trust
Frieda Scott Charitable Trust
Sir James & Lady Scott Trust
Scouloudi Foundation
Sefton Community Foundation
Sherburn House Charity
Sobell Foundation
Sovereign Health Care
 Charitable Trust
W W Spooner Charitable Trust
Steinberg Family Charitable
 Trust
Talbot Trusts
Tesco Charity Trust
Thoresby Charitable Trust
Sir Jules Thorn Charitable
 Trust
Tisbury Telegraph Trust
Mrs Maud Van Norden's
 Charitable Foundation
Perry Watlington Trust
Alfred and Beatrice Weintrop
 Charity
Wellfield Trust
Wesleyan Charitable Trust
Wolfson Foundation

....

■ Leprosy

Funding priority

Birmingham Hospital Saturday
 Fund Medical Charity &
 Welfare Trust
Cleopatra Trust
Cumberland Trust
Dorus Trust
Epigoni Trust
Simon Gibson Charitable Trust
Hampton Fuel Allotment
 Charity
Lynn Foundation
Pilkington Charities Fund
St Francis Leprosy Guild
Yorkshire Building Society
 Charitable Foundation

Will consider

Ardwick Trust
Beit Trust
Morgan Blake Charitable Trust
Richard Cadbury Charitable
 Trust
Childwick Trust
Criffel Charitable Trust
Cripplegate Foundation
Cumber Family Charitable
 Trust
Denton Wilde Sapte Charitable
 Trust
Derbyshire Community
 Foundation
City of Edinburgh Charitable
 Trusts
Ferguson Benevolent Fund Ltd

Trusts by fields of interest and types of beneficiary

Earl Fitzwilliam Charitable
  Trust
Teresa Rosenbaum Golden
  Charitable Trust
Bishop of Guildford's
  Foundation
Hampstead Wells and
  Campden Trust
Harborne Parish Lands Charity
Charles Hayward Foundation
Heart of England Community
  Foundation
Hemby Trust
Hinchley Charitable Trust
Mary Homfray Charitable Trust
Hospital Saturday Fund
  Charitable Trust
Clifford Howarth Charity
  Settlement
Inverforth Charitable Trust
Ruth & Lionel Jacobson Trust
  (Second Fund) No 2
John Jarrold Trust
Jeffrey Charitable Trust
Anton Jurgens Charitable Trust
Kirby Laing Foundation
Leach Fourteenth Trust
Lloyds TSB Foundation for
  Northern Ireland
Lloyds TSB Foundation for
  Scotland
London Law Trust
Loseley & Guildway Charitable
  Trust
Jim Marshall Charitable Trust
Matliwala Family Charitable
  Trust
Tony Metherell Charitable
  Trust
Metropolitan Hospital-Sunday
  Fund
Minge's Gift
Nestlé Rowntree York
  Employees Community Fund
  Trust
Northcott Devon Foundation
Oxfordshire Community
  Foundation
Patients' Aid Association
  Hospital & Medical
  Charities Trust
John Pitman Charitable Trust
Pye Foundation
Rainford Trust
John Rayner Charitable Trust
Cliff Richard Charitable Trust
Richmond Parish Lands Charity
Rivendell Trust
Rothley Trust
Andrew Salvesen Charitable
  Trust
Frieda Scott Charitable Trust
Sir James & Lady Scott Trust
Scouloudi Foundation
Sefton Community Foundation
Sherburn House Charity

Sovereign Health Care
  Charitable Trust
W W Spooner Charitable Trust
Steinberg Family Charitable
  Trust
Talbot Trusts
Tesco Charity Trust
Sir Jules Thorn Charitable
  Trust
Perry Watlington Trust
Wellfield Trust
Wesleyan Charitable Trust
Michael and Anna Wix
  Charitable Trust
Wolfson Foundation

....

■ Mental health impairment

Funding priority
Ammco Trust
Ardwick Trust
Ian Askew Charitable Trust
Baily Thomas Charitable Fund
Barnwood House Trust
Bothwell Charitable Trust
British Dietetic Association
  General and Education
  Trust Fund
Audrey & Stanley Burton
  Charitable Trust
Camelot Foundation
Chase Charity
Cleopatra Trust
Community Foundation Serving
  Tyne & Wear and
  Northumberland
Dorus Trust
Epigoni Trust
Oliver Ford Charitable Trust
Jill Franklin Trust
Garthgwynion Charities
Gatsby Charitable Foundation
J Paul Getty Jr Charitable Trust
Simon Gibson Charitable Trust
Teresa Rosenbaum Golden
  Charitable Trust
Hampton Fuel Allotment
  Charity
Handicapped Children's Aid
  Committee
Kathleen Hannay Memorial
  Charity
Charles Hayward Foundation
Heart of England Community
  Foundation
Miss Agnes H Hunter's Trust
Charles Irving Charitable Trust
Judith Trust
Allen Lane Foundation
Lankelly Foundation
Lynn Foundation
Mental Health Foundation
Metropolitan Hospital-Sunday
  Fund
Northern Rock Foundation

Pastoral Care Trust
Peacock Charitable Trust
Pilgrim Trust
Pilkington Charities Fund
Ronald & Kathleen Pryor
  Charitable Trust
Mr and Mrs J A Pye's
  Charitable Settlement
Rivendell Trust
Cecil Rosen Foundation
Christopher Rowbotham
  Charitable Trust
Mrs Smith & Mount Trust
Sobell Foundation
Swan Mountain Trust
Walter Swindon Charitable
  Trust
Tudor Trust
Variety Club Children's Charity
Verdon-Smith Family Charitable
  Settlement
Walton Foundation
Waterside Trust
Alfred and Beatrice Weintrop
  Charity
West London Synagogue
  Charitable Fund
Woodlands Trust (1015942)
Yorkshire Building Society
  Charitable Foundation
Elizabeth & Prince Zaiger Trust

Will consider
Adnams Charity
Birmingham Hospital Saturday
  Fund Medical Charity &
  Welfare Trust
Blair Foundation
Morgan Blake Charitable Trust
Enid Blyton Trust for Children
Bonhomie United Charity
  Society
Charles Boot Trust
Richard Cadbury Charitable
  Trust
Childwick Trust
Chownes Foundation
Norman Collinson Charitable
  Trust
Comic Relief
Criffel Charitable Trust
Cripplegate Foundation
Harry Crook Foundation
Denton Wilde Sapte Charitable
  Trust
Derbyshire Community
  Foundation
Drapers' Charitable Fund
Dunhill Medical Trust
Eden Arts Trust
City of Edinburgh Charitable
  Trusts
Essex Fairway Charitable Trust
Samuel William Farmer's Trust
Earl Fitzwilliam Charitable
  Trust

Ford of Britain Trust
Robert Gavron Charitable Trust
Girdlers' Company Charitable
Trust
GMC Trust
Bishop of Guildford's
Foundation
Hadfield Trust
Hadley Trust
Hadrian Trust
Eleanor Hamilton Educational
and Charitable Trust
Hampstead Wells and
Campden Trust
Harborne Parish Lands Charity
Hare of Steep Charitable Trust
Kenneth Hargreaves Charitable
Trust
Hemby Trust
Edward Holt Trust
Mary Homfray Charitable Trust
Hospital Saturday Fund
Charitable Trust
Clifford Howarth Charity
Settlement
James Thom Howat Charitable
Trust
Humanitarian Trust
Inverforth Charitable Trust
Jeffrey Charitable Trust
Edward Cecil Jones Settlement
Boris Karloff Charitable
Foundation
Knowles Charitable Trust
Kreitman Foundation
Heinz & Anna Kroch
Foundation
Kirby Laing Foundation
R J Larg Family Charitable
Trust
Leach Fourteenth Trust
Leonard Trust
Levy Foundation
Lloyds TSB Foundation for
England and Wales
Lloyds TSB Foundation for
Northern Ireland
Lloyds TSB Foundation for
Scotland
London Law Trust
Loseley & Guildway Charitable
Trust
John Lyon's Charity
R W Mann Trustees Limited
Marchday Charitable Fund
Jim Marshall Charitable Trust
Matliwala Family Charitable
Trust
Tony Metherell Charitable
Trust
Minge's Gift
George A Moore Foundation
Nestlé Rowntree York
Employees Community Fund
Trust
Northcott Devon Foundation

Oldham Foundation
Oxfordshire Community
Foundation
Patients' Aid Association
Hospital & Medical
Charities Trust
Harry Payne Trust
Persula Foundation
Cecil Pilkington Charitable
Trust
John Pitman Charitable Trust
Pye Foundation
Queen Mary's Roehampton
Trust
Rainford Trust
Ravensdale Trust
John Rayner Charitable Trust
Red Dragon Radio Trust
Cliff Richard Charitable Trust
Richmond Parish Lands Charity
Rothley Trust
Saddlers' Company Charitable
Fund
St Laurence Charities for the
Poor
Andrew Salvesen Charitable
Trust
Frieda Scott Charitable Trust
Sir James & Lady Scott Trust
Scouloudi Foundation
Sefton Community Foundation
Sheldon Trust
Sherburn House Charity
David Solomons Charitable
Trust
Sovereign Health Care
Charitable Trust
W W Spooner Charitable Trust
Steinberg Family Charitable
Trust
Talbot Trusts
Tesco Charity Trust
Sir Jules Thorn Charitable
Trust
Triangle Trust (1949) Fund
John and Lucille van Geest
Foundation
Perry Watlington Trust
Wellfield Trust
Wesleyan Charitable Trust
Westminster Amalgamated
Charity
Will Charitable Trust
Michael and Anna Wix
Charitable Trust
Maurice Wohl Charitable
Foundation
Wolfson Family Charitable
Trust
Wolfson Foundation
Yapp Charitable Trust

....

■ Motor neurone disease

Funding priority
Ammco Trust
Ardwick Trust
Birmingham Hospital Saturday
Fund Medical Charity &
Welfare Trust
Blair Foundation
Palgrave Brown Foundation
Cleopatra Trust
Dorus Trust
Epigoni Trust
Timothy Franey Charitable
Foundation
Garthgwynion Charities
Simon Gibson Charitable Trust
Teresa Rosenbaum Golden
Charitable Trust
Hampton Fuel Allotment
Charity
Handicapped Children's Aid
Committee
May Hearnshaw's Charity
Clifford Howarth Charity
Settlement
Lynn Foundation
Mr and Mrs J A Pye's
Charitable Settlement
Mrs Maud Van Norden's
Charitable Foundation
Yorkshire Building Society
Charitable Foundation

Will consider
Morgan Blake Charitable Trust
Bonhomie United Charity
Society
Audrey & Stanley Burton
Charitable Trust
Richard Cadbury Charitable
Trust
Childwick Trust
Norman Collinson Charitable
Trust
John Cowan Foundation
Coward Trust
Cripplegate Foundation
Wilfrid Bruce Davis Charitable
Trust
Denton Wilde Sapte Charitable
Trust
Derbyshire Community
Foundation
Dunhill Medical Trust
City of Edinburgh Charitable
Trusts
Essex Fairway Charitable Trust
Samuel William Farmer's Trust
Ford of Britain Trust
Girdlers' Company Charitable
Trust
Good Neighbours Trust
Bishop of Guildford's
Foundation
Hadfield Trust
Hadrian Trust

....

Hampstead Wells and
    Campden Trust
Harborne Parish Lands Charity
Hare of Steep Charitable Trust
Charles Hayward Foundation
Heart of England Community
    Foundation
Hemby Trust
Dorothy Holmes Charitable
    Trust
Edward Holt Trust
Mary Homfray Charitable Trust
Hospital Saturday Fund
    Charitable Trust
Inverforth Charitable Trust
Jarman Charitable Trust
Jeffrey Charitable Trust
Edward Cecil Jones Settlement
Anton Jurgens Charitable Trust
Kirby Laing Foundation
Raymond & Blanche Lawson
    Charitable Trust
Leach Fourteenth Trust
Lloyds TSB Foundation for
    England and Wales
Lloyds TSB Foundation for
    Northern Ireland
Lloyds TSB Foundation for
    Scotland
London Law Trust
Loseley & Guildway Charitable
    Trust
R W Mann Trustees Limited
Jim Marshall Charitable Trust
Matliwala Family Charitable
    Trust
Tony Metherell Charitable
    Trust
Metropolitan Hospital-Sunday
    Fund
Minge's Gift
George A Moore Foundation
Nestlé Rowntree York
    Employees Community Fund
    Trust
Northcott Devon Foundation
Kate Wilson Oliver Trust
Oxfordshire Community
    Foundation
Patients' Aid Association
    Hospital & Medical
    Charities Trust
Harry Payne Trust
Bernard Piggott Trust
Pilkington Charities Fund
John Pitman Charitable Trust
J S F Pollitzer Charitable
    Settlement
Proven Family Trust
Pye Foundation
Rainford Trust
Ravensdale Trust
John Rayner Charitable Trust
REMEDI
Cliff Richard Charitable Trust
Richmond Parish Lands Charity

Rivendell Trust
Rothley Trust
Christopher Rowbotham
    Charitable Trust
Saddlers' Company Charitable
    Fund
St Laurence Charities for the
    Poor
Frieda Scott Charitable Trust
Sir James & Lady Scott Trust
Scouloudi Foundation
Sefton Community Foundation
Sherburn House Charity
Sobell Foundation
Sovereign Health Care
    Charitable Trust
W W Spooner Charitable Trust
Starfish Trust
Steinberg Family Charitable
    Trust
Charles and Elsie Sykes Trust
Talbot Trusts
Tesco Charity Trust
Thoresby Charitable Trust
Sir Jules Thorn Charitable
    Trust
Tisbury Telegraph Trust
Perry Watlington Trust
Alfred and Beatrice Weintrop
    Charity
Wellfield Trust
Wesleyan Charitable Trust
Michael and Anna Wix
    Charitable Trust
Wolfson Foundation

....

■ Multiple sclerosis

Funding priority
Ammco Trust
Ardwick Trust
Ashby Charitable Trust
Ashe Park Charitable Trust
Birmingham Hospital Saturday
    Fund Medical Charity &
    Welfare Trust
Bothwell Charitable Trust
British Dietetic Association
    General and Education
    Trust Fund
Cleopatra Trust
Lord Clinton's Charitable Trust
Dorus Trust
Harry Dunn Charitable Trust
Epigoni Trust
Garthgwynion Charities
Simon Gibson Charitable Trust
Teresa Rosenbaum Golden
    Charitable Trust
Hampton Fuel Allotment
    Charity
Handicapped Children's Aid
    Committee
May Hearnshaw's Charity
Clifford Howarth Charity
    Settlement

Lynn Foundation
Horace Moore Charitable Trust
Peacock Charitable Trust
Ronald & Kathleen Pryor
    Charitable Trust
Mr and Mrs J A Pye's
    Charitable Settlement
Sobell Foundation
Walter Swindon Charitable
    Trust
Verdon-Smith Family Charitable
    Settlement
West London Synagogue
    Charitable Fund
Miss E B Wrightson's
    Charitable Settlement
Yorkshire Building Society
    Charitable Foundation

Will consider
Adnams Charity
Andrew Balint Charitable Trust
George Balint Charitable Trust
Barnwood House Trust
Morgan Blake Charitable Trust
Bonhomie United Charity
    Society
P H G Cadbury Trust
Richard Cadbury Charitable
    Trust
Childwick Trust
John Coates Charitable Trust
Norman Collinson Charitable
    Trust
Cripplegate Foundation
Cumber Family Charitable
    Trust
Denton Wilde Sapte Charitable
    Trust
Derbyshire Community
    Foundation
Dunhill Medical Trust
City of Edinburgh Charitable
    Trusts
Essex Fairway Charitable Trust
Samuel William Farmer's Trust
Ferguson Benevolent Fund Ltd
Ford of Britain Trust
Girdlers' Company Charitable
    Trust
Good Neighbours Trust
Reginald Graham Charitable
    Trust
Constance Green Foundation
Bishop of Guildford's
    Foundation
Hadfield Trust
Hadrian Trust
Hampstead Wells and
    Campden Trust
Harborne Parish Lands Charity
Hare of Steep Charitable Trust
Kenneth Hargreaves Charitable
    Trust
Charles Hayward Foundation

Heart of England Community
  Foundation
Hemby Trust
Dorothy Holmes Charitable
  Trust
Mary Homfray Charitable Trust
Hospital Saturday Fund
  Charitable Trust
James Thom Howat Charitable
  Trust
Inverforth Charitable Trust
Ruth & Lionel Jacobson Trust
  (Second Fund) No 2
Jarman Charitable Trust
John Jarrold Trust
Jeffrey Charitable Trust
Johnson Foundation
Edward Cecil Jones Settlement
Anton Jurgens Charitable Trust
Kirby Laing Foundation
R J Larg Family Charitable
  Trust
Lauffer Family Charitable
  Foundation
Raymond & Blanche Lawson
  Charitable Trust
Leach Fourteenth Trust
Lloyds TSB Foundation for
  England and Wales
Lloyds TSB Foundation for
  Northern Ireland
Lloyds TSB Foundation for
  Scotland
London Law Trust
Loseley & Guildway Charitable
  Trust
R W Mann Trustees Limited
Marchday Charitable Fund
Jim Marshall Charitable Trust
Matliwala Family Charitable
  Trust
Tony Metherell Charitable
  Trust
Metropolitan Hospital-Sunday
  Fund
Gerald Micklem Charitable
  Trust
Minge's Gift
George A Moore Foundation
Nestlé Rowntree York
  Employees Community Fund
  Trust
Northcott Devon Foundation
Kate Wilson Oliver Trust
Oxfordshire Community
  Foundation
Patients' Aid Association
  Hospital & Medical
  Charities Trust
Patrick Charitable Trust
Harry Payne Trust
Persula Foundation
Bernard Piggott Trust
Pilkington Charities Fund
John Pitman Charitable Trust
G S Plaut Charitable Trust

J S F Pollitzer Charitable
  Settlement
Proven Family Trust
Pye Foundation
Rainford Trust
Ravensdale Trust
John Rayner Charitable Trust
REMEDI
Reuters Foundation
Cliff Richard Charitable Trust
Richmond Parish Lands Charity
Rivendell Trust
Rothley Trust
Christopher Rowbotham
  Charitable Trust
Saddlers' Company Charitable
  Fund
St Laurence Charities for the
  Poor
Andrew Salvesen Charitable
  Trust
Scarfe Charitable Trust
Frieda Scott Charitable Trust
Sir James & Lady Scott Trust
Scouloudi Foundation
Sefton Community Foundation
Sherburn House Charity
Sovereign Health Care
  Charitable Trust
W W Spooner Charitable Trust
Starfish Trust
Steinberg Family Charitable
  Trust
Talbot Trusts
Tesco Charity Trust
Thoresby Charitable Trust
Sir Jules Thorn Charitable
  Trust
Tisbury Telegraph Trust
Triangle Trust (1949) Fund
Mrs Maud Van Norden's
  Charitable Foundation
Perry Watlington Trust
Alfred and Beatrice Weintrop
  Charity
Wellfield Trust
Wesleyan Charitable Trust
Michael and Anna Wix
  Charitable Trust
Wolfson Foundation

....

■ Muscular dystrophy

Funding priority
Ammco Trust
Ashe Park Charitable Trust
Bergqvist Charitable Trust
Birmingham Hospital Saturday
  Fund Medical Charity &
  Welfare Trust
Cleopatra Trust
Cranbury Foundation
Dorus Trust
Epigoni Trust
Simon Gibson Charitable Trust

Teresa Rosenbaum Golden
  Charitable Trust
Hampton Fuel Allotment
  Charity
Handicapped Children's Aid
  Committee
May Hearnshaw's Charity
Lynn Foundation
Patrick Charitable Trust
Barbara A Shuttleworth
  Memorial Trust
Yorkshire Building Society
  Charitable Foundation

Will consider
Ardwick Trust
Morgan Blake Charitable Trust
Bonhomie United Charity
  Society
Childwick Trust
Norman Collinson Charitable
  Trust
Cripplegate Foundation
Denton Wilde Sapte Charitable
  Trust
Derbyshire Community
  Foundation
City of Edinburgh Charitable
  Trusts
Essex Fairway Charitable Trust
Samuel William Farmer's Trust
Ford of Britain Trust
Girdlers' Company Charitable
  Trust
Good Neighbours Trust
Bishop of Guildford's
  Foundation
Hadfield Trust
Hadrian Trust
Hampstead Wells and
  Campden Trust
Harborne Parish Lands Charity
Charles Hayward Foundation
Heart of England Community
  Foundation
Hemby Trust
Dorothy Holmes Charitable
  Trust
Edward Holt Trust
Mary Homfray Charitable Trust
Hospital Saturday Fund
  Charitable Trust
Clifford Howarth Charity
  Settlement
Inverforth Charitable Trust
Jarman Charitable Trust
Jeffrey Charitable Trust
Kirby Laing Foundation
R J Larg Family Charitable
  Trust
Lauffer Family Charitable
  Foundation
Leach Fourteenth Trust
Lloyds TSB Foundation for
  England and Wales

Lloyds TSB Foundation for
Northern Ireland
Lloyds TSB Foundation for
Scotland
London Law Trust
Loseley & Guildway Charitable
Trust
R W Mann Trustees Limited
Jim Marshall Charitable Trust
Matliwala Family Charitable
Trust
Tony Metherell Charitable
Trust
Metropolitan Hospital-Sunday
Fund
Minge's Gift
George A Moore Foundation
Nestlé Rowntree York
Employees Community Fund
Trust
Northcott Devon Foundation
Kate Wilson Oliver Trust
Oxfordshire Community
Foundation
Patients' Aid Association
Hospital & Medical
Charities Trust
Harry Payne Trust
Bernard Piggott Trust
Pilkington Charities Fund
John Pitman Charitable Trust
J S F Pollitzer Charitable
Settlement
Pye Foundation
Mr and Mrs J A Pye's
Charitable Settlement
Rainford Trust
Ravensdale Trust
John Rayner Charitable Trust
REMEDI
Cliff Richard Charitable Trust
Richmond Parish Lands Charity
Rivendell Trust
Rothley Trust
Christopher Rowbotham
Charitable Trust
Saddlers' Company Charitable
Fund
St Laurence Charities for the
Poor
Andrew Salvesen Charitable
Trust
Frieda Scott Charitable Trust
Sir James & Lady Scott Trust
Scouloudi Foundation
Sefton Community Foundation
Sherburn House Charity
Sobell Foundation
Sovereign Health Care
Charitable Trust
W W Spooner Charitable Trust
Steinberg Family Charitable
Trust
Talbot Trusts
Tesco Charity Trust

Sir Jules Thorn Charitable
Trust
Triangle Trust (1949) Fund
Perry Watlington Trust
Alfred and Beatrice Weintrop
Charity
Wellfield Trust
Wesleyan Charitable Trust
Wolfson Foundation

....

■ Parkinson's disease

Funding priority
Ammco Trust
Ashby Charitable Trust
Birmingham Hospital Saturday
Fund Medical Charity &
Welfare Trust
Bothwell Charitable Trust
Dorus Trust
Wilfred & Elsie Elkes Charity
Fund
Epigoni Trust
Garthgwynion Charities
Simon Gibson Charitable Trust
Teresa Rosenbaum Golden
Charitable Trust
Hampton Fuel Allotment
Charity
May Hearnshaw's Charity
Clifford Howarth Charity
Settlement
Paul Lunn-Rockliffe Charitable
Trust
Lynn Foundation
West London Synagogue
Charitable Fund
Yorkshire Building Society
Charitable Foundation

Will consider
Ardwick Trust
Barnwood House Trust
Morgan Blake Charitable Trust
Childwick Trust
John Coates Charitable Trust
Norman Collinson Charitable
Trust
Cripplegate Foundation
Denton Wilde Sapte Charitable
Trust
Derbyshire Community
Foundation
Dunhill Medical Trust
City of Edinburgh Charitable
Trusts
W G Edwards Charitable
Foundation
Essex Fairway Charitable Trust
Samuel William Farmer's Trust
Ford of Britain Trust
Girdlers' Company Charitable
Trust
Good Neighbours Trust
Bishop of Guildford's
Foundation

Hadfield Trust
Hampstead Wells and
Campden Trust
Harborne Parish Lands Charity
Charles Hayward Foundation
Heart of England Community
Foundation
Hemby Trust
Mary Homfray Charitable Trust
Hospital Saturday Fund
Charitable Trust
Inverforth Charitable Trust
Ruth & Lionel Jacobson Trust
(Second Fund) No 2
Jeffrey Charitable Trust
Edward Cecil Jones Settlement
Anton Jurgens Charitable Trust
Kirby Laing Foundation
Raymond & Blanche Lawson
Charitable Trust
Leach Fourteenth Trust
Lloyds TSB Foundation for
England and Wales
Lloyds TSB Foundation for
Northern Ireland
Lloyds TSB Foundation for
Scotland
Loseley & Guildway Charitable
Trust
Jim Marshall Charitable Trust
Matliwala Family Charitable
Trust
Tony Metherell Charitable
Trust
Metropolitan Hospital-Sunday
Fund
Gerald Micklem Charitable
Trust
Minge's Gift
George A Moore Foundation
Horace Moore Charitable Trust
Nestlé Rowntree York
Employees Community Fund
Trust
Northcott Devon Foundation
Kate Wilson Oliver Trust
Oxfordshire Community
Foundation
Patients' Aid Association
Hospital & Medical
Charities Trust
Harry Payne Trust
Bernard Piggott Trust
Pilkington Charities Fund
John Pitman Charitable Trust
J S F Pollitzer Charitable
Settlement
Simone Prendergast Charitable
Trust
Proven Family Trust
Pye Foundation
Mr and Mrs J A Pye's
Charitable Settlement
Ravensdale Trust
John Rayner Charitable Trust
REMEDI

Cliff Richard Charitable Trust
Richmond Parish Lands Charity
Rivendell Trust
Rothley Trust
Christopher Rowbotham
Charitable Trust
Saddlers' Company Charitable
Fund
St Laurence Charities for the
Poor
Frieda Scott Charitable Trust
Sir James & Lady Scott Trust
Scouloudi Foundation
Sefton Community Foundation
Sherburn House Charity
Sobell Foundation
Sovereign Health Care
Charitable Trust
W W Spooner Charitable Trust
Steinberg Family Charitable
Trust
Charles and Elsie Sykes Trust
Talbot Trusts
Tesco Charity Trust
Sir Jules Thorn Charitable
Trust
Triangle Trust (1949) Fund
Perry Watlington Trust
Alfred and Beatrice Weintrop
Charity
Wellfield Trust
Wesleyan Charitable Trust
Wolfson Foundation

■ Polio
Funding priority
Birmingham Hospital Saturday
Fund Medical Charity &
Welfare Trust
Dorus Trust
Epigoni Trust
Teresa Rosenbaum Golden
Charitable Trust
Hampton Fuel Allotment
Charity
Lynn Foundation
Yorkshire Building Society
Charitable Foundation

Will consider
Ardwick Trust
Blair Foundation
Morgan Blake Charitable Trust
Bonhomie United Charity
Society
Childwick Trust
Cripplegate Foundation
Cumber Family Charitable
Trust
Denton Wilde Sapte Charitable
Trust
Derbyshire Community
Foundation
City of Edinburgh Charitable
Trusts

Samuel William Farmer's Trust
Ferguson Benevolent Fund Ltd
Ford of Britain Trust
Good Neighbours Trust
Bishop of Guildford's
Foundation
Hadfield Trust
Hampstead Wells and
Campden Trust
Harborne Parish Lands Charity
Charles Hayward Foundation
May Hearnshaw's Charity
Heart of England Community
Foundation
Hemby Trust
Sir Julian Hodge Charitable
Trust
Mary Homfray Charitable Trust
Hospital Saturday Fund
Charitable Trust
Clifford Howarth Charity
Settlement
Inverforth Charitable Trust
John Jarrold Trust
Jeffrey Charitable Trust
Kirby Laing Foundation
Leach Fourteenth Trust
Lloyds TSB Foundation for
England and Wales
Lloyds TSB Foundation for
Northern Ireland
Lloyds TSB Foundation for
Scotland
London Law Trust
Jim Marshall Charitable Trust
Matliwala Family Charitable
Trust
Tony Metherell Charitable
Trust
Metropolitan Hospital-Sunday
Fund
Minge's Gift
Nestlé Rowntree York
Employees Community Fund
Trust
Northcott Devon Foundation
Oxfordshire Community
Foundation
Patients' Aid Association
Hospital & Medical
Charities Trust
Patrick Charitable Trust
Pilkington Charities Fund
John Pitman Charitable Trust
J S F Pollitzer Charitable
Settlement
Pye Foundation
Mr and Mrs J A Pye's
Charitable Settlement
Rainford Trust
John Rayner Charitable Trust
Richmond Parish Lands Charity
Rivendell Trust
Rothley Trust
Christopher Rowbotham
Charitable Trust

Saddlers' Company Charitable
Fund
St Laurence Charities for the
Poor
Andrew Salvesen Charitable
Trust
Frieda Scott Charitable Trust
Sir James & Lady Scott Trust
Scouloudi Foundation
Sefton Community Foundation
Sherburn House Charity
Sobell Foundation
Sovereign Health Care
Charitable Trust
W W Spooner Charitable Trust
Steinberg Family Charitable
Trust
Talbot Trusts
Tesco Charity Trust
Sir Jules Thorn Charitable
Trust
Perry Watlington Trust
Wellfield Trust
Wesleyan Charitable Trust
Wolfson Foundation

■ Stroke-related disorders
Funding priority
Ardwick Trust
Bergqvist Charitable Trust
Birmingham Hospital Saturday
Fund Medical Charity &
Welfare Trust
Palgrave Brown Foundation
Chest Heart and Stroke
Scotland
Cleopatra Trust
Dorus Trust
Dunhill Medical Trust
Epigoni Trust
Garthgwynion Charities
Simon Gibson Charitable Trust
Teresa Rosenbaum Golden
Charitable Trust
Hampton Fuel Allotment
Charity
Charles Hayward Foundation
Lynn Foundation
Pilkington Charities Fund
Mr and Mrs J A Pye's
Charitable Settlement
Christopher Rowbotham
Charitable Trust
Walter Swindon Charitable
Trust
Verdon-Smith Family Charitable
Settlement
Walton Foundation
Alfred and Beatrice Weintrop
Charity
Yorkshire Building Society
Charitable Foundation

Will consider

Barnwood House Trust
Morgan Blake Charitable Trust
Charles Boot Trust
Audrey & Stanley Burton
    Charitable Trust
Childwick Trust
Norman Collinson Charitable
    Trust
Criffel Charitable Trust
Cripplegate Foundation
Wilfrid Bruce Davis Charitable
    Trust
Denton Wilde Sapte Charitable
    Trust
Derbyshire Community
    Foundation
Diabetes UK
City of Edinburgh Charitable
    Trusts
Samuel William Farmer's Trust
David Finnie & Alan Emery
    Charitable Trust
Ford of Britain Trust
Girdlers' Company Charitable
    Trust
Good Neighbours Trust
Bishop of Guildford's
    Foundation
Hadfield Trust
Hadrian Trust
Hampstead Wells and
    Campden Trust
Lennox Hannay Charitable
    Trust
Harborne Parish Lands Charity
Hare of Steep Charitable Trust
May Hearnshaw's Charity
Heart of England Community
    Foundation
Hemby Trust
Edward Holt Trust
Mary Homfray Charitable Trust
Hospital Saturday Fund
    Charitable Trust
Clifford Howarth Charity
    Settlement
Inverforth Charitable Trust
Ruth & Lionel Jacobson Trust
    (Second Fund) No 2
Jarman Charitable Trust
Jeffrey Charitable Trust
Edward Cecil Jones Settlement
Anton Jurgens Charitable Trust
Kirby Laing Foundation
Raymond & Blanche Lawson
    Charitable Trust
Leach Fourteenth Trust
Levy Foundation
Lloyds TSB Foundation for
    England and Wales
Lloyds TSB Foundation for
    Northern Ireland
Lloyds TSB Foundation for
    Scotland
London Law Trust

Loseley & Guildway Charitable
    Trust
Jim Marshall Charitable Trust
Matliwala Family Charitable
    Trust
Tony Metherell Charitable
    Trust
Metropolitan Hospital-Sunday
    Fund
Minge's Gift
Horace Moore Charitable Trust
Nestlé Rowntree York
    Employees Community Fund
    Trust
Northcott Devon Foundation
Kate Wilson Oliver Trust
Owen Family Trust
Oxfordshire Community
    Foundation
Patients' Aid Association
    Hospital & Medical
    Charities Trust
J S F Pollitzer Charitable
    Settlement
Simone Prendergast Charitable
    Trust
Pye Foundation
Rainford Trust
Ravensdale Trust
John Rayner Charitable Trust
Red Dragon Radio Trust
REMEDI
Cliff Richard Charitable Trust
Richmond Parish Lands Charity
Rivendell Trust
Rothley Trust
Saddlers' Company Charitable
    Fund
St Laurence Charities for the
    Poor
Frieda Scott Charitable Trust
Sir James & Lady Scott Trust
Scouloudi Foundation
Sefton Community Foundation
Sherburn House Charity
Sobell Foundation
Sovereign Health Care
    Charitable Trust
W W Spooner Charitable Trust
Charles and Elsie Sykes Trust
Talbot Trusts
Tesco Charity Trust
Sir Jules Thorn Charitable
    Trust
Tisbury Telegraph Trust
Triangle Trust (1949) Fund
Perry Watlington Trust
Wellfield Trust
Wesleyan Charitable Trust
Wolfson Foundation

....

■ Substance misuse

Funding priority

Cleopatra Trust
Dorus Trust

Epigoni Trust
J Paul Getty Jr Charitable Trust
Charles Hayward Foundation
Richard Kirkman Charitable
    Trust
Lynn Foundation
Oxfordshire Community
    Foundation
Peacock Charitable Trust
Pilkington Charities Fund
Mr and Mrs J A Pye's
    Charitable Settlement
John Rayner Charitable Trust
W F Southall Trust
Tudor Trust
Victoria Homes Trust
Vintners Company Charitable
    Trust
Waterside Trust
Wates Foundation
Yorkshire Building Society
    Charitable Foundation

Will consider

Ardwick Trust
Birmingham Hospital Saturday
    Fund Medical Charity &
    Welfare Trust
Morgan Blake Charitable Trust
British Dietetic Association
    General and Education
    Trust Fund
Richard Cadbury Charitable
    Trust
Comic Relief
Cripplegate Foundation
Denton Wilde Sapte Charitable
    Trust
Derbyshire Community
    Foundation
City of Edinburgh Charitable
    Trusts
Ford of Britain Trust
Bishop of Guildford's
    Foundation
Hadfield Trust
Hadrian Trust
Hampstead Wells and
    Campden Trust
Harborne Parish Lands Charity
Heart of England Community
    Foundation
Hemby Trust
Hilden Charitable Fund
Mary Homfray Charitable Trust
Hospital Saturday Fund
    Charitable Trust
Clifford Howarth Charity
    Settlement
Inverforth Charitable Trust
Jeffrey Charitable Trust
Edward Cecil Jones Settlement
Anton Jurgens Charitable Trust
Graham Kirkham Foundation
Kirby Laing Foundation
Leach Fourteenth Trust

Lloyds TSB Foundation for
England and Wales
Lloyds TSB Foundation for
Northern Ireland
Lloyds TSB Foundation for
Scotland
John Lyon's Charity
Marchday Charitable Fund
Jim Marshall Charitable Trust
Matliwala Family Charitable
Trust
Merchant Taylors' Company
Charities Fund
Tony Metherell Charitable
Trust
Metropolitan Hospital-Sunday
Fund
Minge's Gift
Northcott Devon Foundation
Patients' Aid Association
Hospital & Medical
Charities Trust
Harry Payne Trust
Pye Foundation
Rainford Trust
Ravensdale Trust
Richmond Parish Lands Charity
Rivendell Trust
Robertson Trust
Rothley Trust
Christopher Rowbotham
Charitable Trust
Andrew Salvesen Charitable
Trust
Frieda Scott Charitable Trust
Sir James & Lady Scott Trust
Sefton Community Foundation
Sheldon Trust
Sherburn House Charity
Leslie Smith Foundation
Sovereign Health Care
Charitable Trust
W W Spooner Charitable Trust
Steinberg Family Charitable
Trust
Talbot Trusts
Sir Jules Thorn Charitable
Trust
Trusthouse Charitable
Foundation
Wellfield Trust
Wesleyan Charitable Trust
Westminster Amalgamated
Charity
Michael and Anna Wix
Charitable Trust
Wolfson Foundation
Yapp Charitable Trust

....

■ Terminally ill

Funding priority
Ardwick Trust
Ashe Park Charitable Trust

Birmingham Hospital Saturday
Fund Medical Charity &
Welfare Trust
British Dietetic Association
General and Education
Trust Fund
Palgrave Brown Foundation
Elizabeth Clark Charitable
Trust
Lord Clinton's Charitable Trust
Simon Gibson Charitable Trust
Constance Green Foundation
Hampton Fuel Allotment
Charity
Lennox Hannay Charitable
Trust
Kenneth Hargreaves Charitable
Trust
Charles Hayward Foundation
Dorothy Holmes Charitable
Trust
Kidani Memorial Trust
Mason Le Page Charitable
Trust
Leeds & Holbeck Building
Society Charitable
Foundation
Lynn Foundation
Magdalen Hospital Trust
Laurie Nidditch Foundation
Pilkington Charities Fund
Ronald & Kathleen Pryor
Charitable Trust
Mr and Mrs J A Pye's
Charitable Settlement
Cliff Richard Charitable Trust
Sobell Foundation
Mrs Maud Van Norden's
Charitable Foundation
Verdon-Smith Family Charitable
Settlement
Walton Foundation
Warwickshire Masonic
Charitable Association Ltd
Alfred and Beatrice Weintrop
Charity
West London Synagogue
Charitable Fund
Xerox (UK) Trust
Yorkshire Building Society
Charitable Foundation

Will consider
Adnams Charity
Ammco Trust
G C Armitage Charitable Trust
Andrew Balint Charitable Trust
George Balint Charitable Trust
Paul Balint Charitable Trust
Barnwood House Trust
Blair Foundation
Morgan Blake Charitable Trust
Audrey & Stanley Burton
Charitable Trust
P H G Cadbury Trust

Richard Cadbury Charitable
Trust
Childwick Trust
Chrimes Family Charitable
Trust
Clover Trust
John Coates Charitable Trust
John Cowan Foundation
Coward Trust
Criffel Charitable Trust
Cripplegate Foundation
Harry Crook Foundation
Cumber Family Charitable
Trust
Wilfrid Bruce Davis Charitable
Trust
De La Rue Charitable Trust
Denton Wilde Sapte Charitable
Trust
Derbyshire Community
Foundation
City of Edinburgh Charitable
Trusts
Samuel William Farmer's Trust
Fidelity UK Foundation
David Finnie & Alan Emery
Charitable Trust
Ford of Britain Trust
Gannochy Trust
Girdlers' Company Charitable
Trust
Teresa Rosenbaum Golden
Charitable Trust
Good Neighbours Trust
Bishop of Guildford's
Foundation
Hadfield Trust
Hadrian Trust
Hampstead Wells and
Campden Trust
Harborne Parish Lands Charity
Hare of Steep Charitable Trust
May Hearnshaw's Charity
Heart of England Community
Foundation
Hemby Trust
Mary Homfray Charitable Trust
Hospital Saturday Fund
Charitable Trust
Clifford Howarth Charity
Settlement
Miss Agnes H Hunter's Trust
Inverforth Charitable Trust
Ruth & Lionel Jacobson Trust
(Second Fund) No 2
Jeffrey Charitable Trust
Anton Jurgens Charitable Trust
Kirby Laing Foundation
Raymond & Blanche Lawson
Charitable Trust
Leach Fourteenth Trust
Lloyds TSB Foundation for
England and Wales
Lloyds TSB Foundation for
Northern Ireland

Lloyds TSB Foundation for
Scotland
London Law Trust
Loseley & Guildway Charitable
Trust
R W Mann Trustees Limited
Marchday Charitable Fund
Jim Marshall Charitable Trust
Matliwala Family Charitable
Trust
Tony Metherell Charitable
Trust
Metropolitan Hospital-Sunday
Fund
Minge's Gift
George A Moore Foundation
Nestlé Rowntree York
Employees Community Fund
Trust
Northcott Devon Foundation
Oxfordshire Community
Foundation
Patients' Aid Association
Hospital & Medical
Charities Trust
Harry Payne Trust
J S F Pollitzer Charitable
Settlement
Pye Foundation
Rainford Trust
Ravensdale Trust
John Rayner Charitable Trust
Red Dragon Radio Trust
Richmond Parish Lands Charity
Rivendell Trust
Rothley Trust
Christopher Rowbotham
Charitable Trust
Rufford Foundation
St Laurence Charities for the
Poor
Andrew Salvesen Charitable
Trust
Frieda Scott Charitable Trust
Sir James & Lady Scott Trust
Scouloudi Foundation
Sefton Community Foundation
Sheldon Trust
Sherburn House Charity
Sovereign Health Care
Charitable Trust
W W Spooner Charitable Trust
Starfish Trust
Steinberg Family Charitable
Trust
Sir Halley Stewart Trust
Charles and Elsie Sykes Trust
Talbot Trusts
Tesco Charity Trust
Thoresby Charitable Trust
Sir Jules Thorn Charitable
Trust
Tisbury Telegraph Trust
Triangle Trust (1949) Fund
John and Lucille van Geest
Foundation

Perry Watlington Trust
Wellfield Trust
Wesleyan Charitable Trust
Michael and Anna Wix
Charitable Trust
Wolfson Foundation
Yardley Great Trust

■ Tuberculosis

Funding priority
Ardwick Trust
Birmingham Hospital Saturday
Fund Medical Charity &
Welfare Trust
Chest Heart and Stroke
Scotland
Hampton Fuel Allotment
Charity
Miss Agnes H Hunter's Trust
Lynn Foundation
Pilkington Charities Fund
West London Synagogue
Charitable Fund
Yorkshire Building Society
Charitable Foundation

Will consider
Beit Trust
Morgan Blake Charitable Trust
Childwick Trust
Cripplegate Foundation
Denton Wilde Sapte Charitable
Trust
Derbyshire Community
Foundation
Dunhill Medical Trust
City of Edinburgh Charitable
Trusts
Samuel William Farmer's Trust
Ford of Britain Trust
Teresa Rosenbaum Golden
Charitable Trust
Bishop of Guildford's
Foundation
Hadfield Trust
Hampstead Wells and
Campden Trust
Harborne Parish Lands Charity
Charles Hayward Foundation
Heart of England Community
Foundation
Hemby Trust
Sir Julian Hodge Charitable
Trust
Mary Homfray Charitable Trust
Hospital Saturday Fund
Charitable Trust
Clifford Howarth Charity
Settlement
Inverforth Charitable Trust
Jeffrey Charitable Trust
Kirby Laing Foundation
Leach Fourteenth Trust
Lloyds TSB Foundation for
England and Wales

Lloyds TSB Foundation for
Northern Ireland
London Law Trust
Jim Marshall Charitable Trust
Matliwala Family Charitable
Trust
Tony Metherell Charitable
Trust
Metropolitan Hospital-Sunday
Fund
Minge's Gift
Nestlé Rowntree York
Employees Community Fund
Trust
Northcott Devon Foundation
Oxfordshire Community
Foundation
Patients' Aid Association
Hospital & Medical
Charities Trust
Pye Foundation
Queen Mary's Roehampton
Trust
Ravensdale Trust
John Rayner Charitable Trust
Richmond Parish Lands Charity
Rivendell Trust
Rothley Trust
Saddlers' Company Charitable
Fund
St Laurence Charities for the
Poor
Andrew Salvesen Charitable
Trust
Frieda Scott Charitable Trust
Sir James & Lady Scott Trust
Sefton Community Foundation
Sherburn House Charity
Sovereign Health Care
Charitable Trust
W W Spooner Charitable Trust
Talbot Trusts
Tesco Charity Trust
Tisbury Telegraph Trust
Wellfield Trust
Wesleyan Charitable Trust
Wolfson Foundation

Social or economic circumstances

■ Disadvantaged and socially excluded people

Funding priority
29th May 1961 Charitable
Trust
Adnams Charity
Ajahma Charitable Trust
Barbour Trust
Paul Bassham Charitable Trust
BBC Children in Need Appeal
Beacon Trust

Thomas Betton's Charity for
Pensions and Relief-in-Need
Bramble Charitable Trust
Chase Charity
Chelsea Building Society
Charitable Foundation
Clore Duffield Foundation
Sir James Colyer-Fergusson's
Charitable Trust
Community Foundation Serving
Tyne & Wear and
Northumberland
Criffel Charitable Trust
William Dudley Trust
Esmée Fairbairn Foundation
Roy Fletcher Charitable Trust
J Paul Getty Jr Charitable Trust
Greater Bristol Foundation
William Harding's Charity
Hare of Steep Charitable Trust
Ironmongers' Quincentenary
Charitable Fund
Beatrice Laing Trust
Lankelly Foundation
Lyndhurst Settlement
Northern Rock Foundation
Norton Foundation
Jack Petchey Foundation
Pilgrim Trust
Pyke Charity Trust
Rooke Atlay Charitable Trust
Rothley Trust
Sportsman's Charity
Thames Community
Foundation
Thomson Corporation
Charitable Trust
Wakefield Trust
Lionel Wigram Memorial Trust
Woo Charitable Foundation
Worshipful Company of
Chartered Accountants
General Charitable Trust

Will consider
Miss Agnes Gilchrist
Adamson's Trust
David and Frederick Barclay
Foundation
Bedford Charity
Bingham Trust
Morgan Blake Charitable Trust
Roger Brooke Charitable Trust
William A Cadbury Charitable
Trust
Commonwealth Relations
Trust
Community Fund
County of Gloucestershire
Community Foundation
Cripplegate Foundation
Cumber Family Charitable
Trust
Denton Charitable Trust
Duis Charitable Trust

Dumfries and Galloway Council
Charitable Trusts
Ganzoni Charitable Trust
Girdlers' Company Charitable
Trust
Hadley Trust
Haramead Trust
Hobart Charitable Trust
Clifford Howarth Charity
Settlement
J E Joseph Charitable Fund
King's Fund
Kirby Laing Foundation
Maurice Laing Foundation
Maurice and Hilda Laing
Charitable Trust
Lloyds TSB Foundation for
England and Wales
Mercers' Charitable
Foundation
Keith and Joan Mindelsohn
Charitable Trust
North British Hotel Trust
Northcott Devon Foundation
Nuffield Foundation
Pye Foundation
Eleanor Rathbone Charitable
Trust
Rayne Foundation
Richmond Parish Lands Charity
Ripple Effect Foundation
Rufford Foundation
Sherburn House Charity
SMB Trust
Foundation of Edward Storey
Summerfield Charitable Trust
Constance Travis Charitable
Trust
R D Turner Charitable Trust
Welsh Church Fund –
Carmarthenshire area

■ **People who are
educationally
disadvantaged
Funding priority**
Birmingham Hospital Saturday
Fund Medical Charity &
Welfare Trust
CLA Charitable Trust
Construction Industry Trust for
Youth
Ellis Campbell Charitable
Foundation
Equitable Charitable Trust
Essex Fairway Charitable Trust
Four Acre Trust
Simon Gibson Charitable Trust
Global Care
Jewish Child's Day
Leeds & Holbeck Building
Society Charitable
Foundation
Lynn Foundation
Noon Foundation
Rosca Trust

Rothley Trust
Sir Walter St John's
Educational Charity
Mrs Smith & Mount Trust
Tesco Charity Trust
Thames Community
Foundation
Yapp Charitable Trust
Yorkshire Building Society
Charitable Foundation

Will consider
Abbey National Charitable
Trust Ltd
Adnams Charity
Birmingham Foundation
Church Urban Fund
Coutts & Co. Charitable Trust
Dove-Bowerman Trust
Fidelity UK Foundation
Finnart House School Trust
Girdlers' Company Charitable
Trust
Gay & Peter Hartley's Hillards
Charitable Trust
Kidani Memorial Trust
Laing's Charitable Trust
Christopher Laing Foundation
Kennedy Leigh Charitable
Trust
Lloyds TSB Foundation for
Northern Ireland
Lloyds TSB Foundation for
Scotland
John Lyon's Charity
Middlesex County Rugby
Football Union Memorial
Fund
Northern Rock Foundation
Old Enfield Charitable Trust
Oxfordshire Community
Foundation
Patients' Aid Association
Hospital & Medical
Charities Trust
Peugeot Charity Trust
Christopher Rowbotham
Charitable Trust
Royal Eastern Counties
Schools Limited
St James' Trust Settlement
St Laurence Charities for the
Poor
Whitecourt Charitable Trust

■ **People who are
homeless
Funding priority**
1970 Trust
29th May 1961 Charitable
Trust
Abel Charitable Trust
Ashby Charitable Trust
Ashden Trust
Ashendene Trust
Astor Foundation

Band (1976) Trust
BBC Children in Need Appeal
BBC Radio Cambridgeshire –
    Trustline
Berkshire Community
    Foundation
Birmingham Hospital Saturday
    Fund Medical Charity &
    Welfare Trust
Oliver Borthwick Memorial
    Trust
Burton Breweries Charitable
    Trust
Richard Cadbury Charitable
    Trust
Calypso Browning Trust
Carlton Television Trust
Cattanach Charitable Trust
Celtic Charity Fund
Charities Advisory Trust
Cleopatra Trust
Cole Charitable Trust
Community Foundation for
    Northern Ireland
Coutts & Co. Charitable Trust
Dawe Charitable Trust
De Clermont Charitable
    Company Ltd
Denton Wilde Sapte Charitable
    Trust
Derbyshire Community
    Foundation
Dorus Trust
Epigoni Trust
Essex Community Foundation
Eveson Charitable Trust
Fiat Auto (UK) Charity
Gerald Fogel Charitable Trust
Simon Gibson Charitable Trust
Global Care
Greater Bristol Foundation
Constance Green Foundation
Grocers' Charity
Bishop of Guildford's
    Foundation
Alfred Haines Charitable Trust
Hampton Fuel Allotment
    Charity
Harbour Foundation
Kenneth Hargreaves Charitable
    Trust
M A Hawe Settlement
Charles Hayward Foundation
Help the Homeless Ltd
Hertfordshire Community
    Foundation
Hilden Charitable Fund
Holywood Trust
Homeless International
Thomas J Horne Memorial
    Trust
Housing Associations
    Charitable Trust
Albert Hunt Trust
Miss Agnes H Hunter's Trust
Charles Irving Charitable Trust

Jewish Child's Day
Johnson Group Cleaners
    Charity
Edward Cecil Jones Settlement
Anton Jurgens Charitable Trust
Peter Kershaw Trust
King's Fund
Sir James Knott Trust
Laing's Charitable Trust
Bryan Lancaster's Charity
Leeds & Holbeck Building
    Society Charitable
    Foundation
Lintel Trust
Lloyds TSB Foundation for
    Scotland
Lloyds TSB Foundation for the
    Channel Islands
Paul Lunn-Rockliffe Charitable
    Trust
Lyons Charitable Trust
Marchday Charitable Fund
Miles Trust for the Putney and
    Roehampton Community
Mitchell Charitable Trust
Monument Trust
John Moores Foundation
Kitty and Daniel Nabarro
    Charitable Trust
Newby Trust Limited
Nova Charitable Trust
Odin Charitable Trust
Oxfordshire Community
    Foundation
Persula Foundation
Philanthropic Trust
Austin & Hope Pilkington Trust
Pilkington Charities Fund
Portishead Nautical Trust
J E Posnansky Charitable Trust
John Pryor Charitable Trust
Joseph & Lena Randall
    Charitable Trust
Richard Rogers Charitable
    Settlement
Mrs L D Rope Third Charitable
    Settlement
Rosca Trust
Rothley Trust
Francis C Scott Charitable
    Trust
Frieda Scott Charitable Trust
Sir James & Lady Scott Trust
Mrs Smith & Mount Trust
Sobell Foundation
South Yorkshire Community
    Foundation
Thames Community
    Foundation
Third House Trust
Three Guineas Trust
Tisbury Telegraph Trust
Tower Hill Improvement Trust
Triangle Trust (1949) Fund
Tudor Trust

Verdon-Smith Family Charitable
    Settlement
Victoria Homes Trust
Vintners Company Charitable
    Trust
Scurrah Wainwright Charity
Wakefield Trust
Waterside Trust
Wates Foundation
Westminster Foundation
Wiltshire and Swindon
    Community Foundation
Maurice Wohl Charitable Trust
Miss Hazel M Wood Charitable
    Trust
Woodlands Trust (1015942)
Woodlands Trust (259569)
Woolnoth Society Charitable
    Trust
Yorkshire Building Society
    Charitable Foundation

Will consider

Abbey National Charitable
    Trust Ltd
Adint Charitable Trust
Adnams Charity
Viscount Amory's Charitable
    Trust
Sir John & Lady Amory's
    Charitable Trust
Ardwick Trust
Lord Ashdown Charitable Trust
Bamford Charitable Foundation
Lord Barnby's Foundation
Bartle Family Charitable Trust
Beit Trust
Percy Bilton Charity Ltd
Bothwell Charitable Trust
P G & N J Boulton Trust
Bridge House Estates Trust
    Fund
Bridge Trust
Britannia Building Society
    Foundation
Bryant Trust
Audrey & Stanley Burton
    Charitable Trust
Edward Cadbury Charitable
    Trust
Calpe Trust
Carnegie Dunfermline Trust
Chippenham Borough Lands
    Charity
Christian Aid
Church Urban Fund
City Parochial Foundation
J A Clark Charitable Trust
Clover Trust
Norman Collinson Charitable
    Trust
Comic Relief
Congleton Inclosure Trust
Coppings Trust
Duke of Cornwall's Benevolent
    Fund

County Durham Foundation
Cranbury Foundation
Harry Crook Foundation
Cumber Family Charitable
    Trust
Cwmbran Trust
John Grant Davies Trust
Helen and Geoffrey de Freitas
    Charitable Trust
De La Rue Charitable Trust
Miriam K Dean Refugee Trust
    Fund
Devon Community Foundation
Djanogly Foundation
Douglas Charitable Trust
Dulverton Trust
Wilfred & Elsie Elkes Charity
    Fund
John Ellerman Foundation
Elmgrant Trust
Emmandjay Charitable Trust
Enkalon Foundation
Ericson Trust
Essex Fairway Charitable Trust
Ferguson Benevolent Fund Ltd
Fishmongers' Company's
    Charitable Trust
Ford of Britain Trust
Fordeve Ltd
Charles S French Charitable
    Trust
Patrick Frost Foundation
Fund for Human Need
Robert Gavron Charitable Trust
Girdlers' Company Charitable
    Trust
Gould Charitable Trust
J G Graves Charitable Trust
Gulbenkian Foundation
H C D Memorial Fund
Hadfield Trust
Hadrian Trust
Eleanor Hamilton Educational
    and Charitable Trust
Hampstead Wells and
    Campden Trust
Lennox Hannay Charitable
    Trust
Harborne Parish Lands Charity
Harrison & Potter Trust
Gay & Peter Hartley's Hillards
    Charitable Trust
N & P Hartley Memorial Trust
Heart of England Community
    Foundation
Help the Aged
Hemby Trust
Hesslewood Children's Trust
Higgs Charitable Trust
Alan Edward Higgs Charity
Jane Hodge Foundation
Mary Homfray Charitable Trust
Hospital of God at Greatham
James Thom Howat Charitable
    Trust

Huddersfield Common Good
    Trust
Hyde Charitable Trust
Hyde Park Place Estate Charity
    – civil trustees
Inverforth Charitable Trust
Isle of Anglesey Charitable
    Trust
Ruth & Lionel Jacobson Trust
    (Second Fund) No 2
James Pantyfedwen
    Foundation
Jarman Charitable Trust
Jeffrey Charitable Trust
Joicey Trust
Knowles Charitable Trust
Christopher Laing Foundation
Langdale Trust
Lauffer Family Charitable
    Foundation
Lazard Charitable Trust
Leach Fourteenth Trust
Leonard Trust
Levy Foundation
Linbury Trust
Lloyd's Charities Trust
Lloyds TSB Foundation for
    Northern Ireland
London North East Community
    Foundation
C F Lunoe Trust Fund
John Lyon's Charity
Mackintosh Foundation
Helen Isabella McMorran
    Charitable Foundation
R W Mann Trustees Limited
Victor Mann Trust
Hilda & Samuel Marks
    Foundation
Marr-Munning Trust
Sir George Martin Trust
John Martin's Charity
Mercers' Charitable
    Foundation
Merchant Taylors' Company
    Charities Fund
Tony Metherell Charitable
    Trust
Millfield Trust
Milton Keynes Community
    Foundation
Peter Minet Trust
Minge's Gift
Victor Mishcon Charitable
    Trust
Mobbs Memorial Trust Ltd
J P Morgan Fleming
    Educational Trust and
    Foundation
Morgan Stanley International
    Foundation
National Power Charitable
    Trust
Nestlé Rowntree York
    Employees Community Fund
    Trust

Norman Family Charitable
    Trust
Northern Rock Foundation
Northmoor Trust
Oakdale Trust
Ogilvie Charities Deed 2
Kate Wilson Oliver Trust
Parthenon Trust
Arthur James Paterson
    Charitable Trust
Constance Paterson Charitable
    Trust
Patients' Aid Association
    Hospital & Medical
    Charities Trust
Harry Payne Trust
Bernard Piggott Trust
A M Pilkington's Charitable
    Trust
W L Pratt Charitable Trust
Princess Anne's Charities
Proven Family Trust
Pye Foundation
Rainford Trust
Ravensdale Trust
John Rayner Charitable Trust
Rest Harrow Trust
Reuters Foundation
Rhododendron Trust
Cliff Richard Charitable Trust
Robertson Trust
Rose Foundation
Rowan Charitable Trust
Christopher Rowbotham
    Charitable Trust
Joseph Rowntree Foundation
Royal Docks Trust
St Laurence Charities for the
    Poor
Andrew Salvesen Charitable
    Trust
Scott Bader Commonwealth
    Ltd
Scottish Churches Community
    Trust
Scottish Community
    Foundation
Scouloudi Foundation
Sefton Community Foundation
Servite Sisters' Charitable
    Trust Fund
Sheldon Trust
Bishop Simeon CR Trust
Skelton Bounty
Henry Smith Charity
Stanley Spooner Deceased
    Charitable Trust
Sportsman's Charity
June Stevens Foundation
Summerfield Charitable Trust
Bernard Sunley Charitable
    Foundation
Tinsley Foundation
Douglas Turner Trust
Unemployed Voluntary Action
    Fund

Wellfield Trust
Wesleyan Charitable Trust
Westminster Amalgamated
    Charity
White Rose Children's Aid
    International Charity
Whitecourt Charitable Trust
Michael and Anna Wix
    Charitable Trust
Women at Risk
Woodward Trust
Worcester Municipal Charities
Wyseliot Charitable Trust
Zephyr Charitable Trust

■ **People leaving care or in
    care**
    Funding priority
Birmingham Hospital Saturday
    Fund Medical Charity &
    Welfare Trust
Coutts & Co. Charitable Trust
Essex Fairway Charitable Trust
Four Acre Trust
Anton Jurgens Charitable Trust
Leeds & Holbeck Building
    Society Charitable
    Foundation
Pilgrim Trust
Rosca Trust
Rothley Trust
Sir Walter St John's
    Educational Charity
Social Education Trust
Yorkshire Building Society
    Charitable Foundation

    Will consider
Beit Trust
Church Urban Fund
Comic Relief
Consortium on Opportunities
    for Volunteering
Dulverton Trust
Earley Charity
Ferguson Benevolent Fund Ltd
Fidelity UK Foundation
Girdlers' Company Charitable
    Trust
Harborne Parish Lands Charity
Charles Hayward Foundation
Joanna Herbert-Stepney
    Charitable Settlement
Alan Edward Higgs Charity
Neil Kreitman Foundation
Kyte Charitable Trust
Laing's Charitable Trust
Christopher Laing Foundation
Lloyds TSB Foundation for
    Northern Ireland
Lloyds TSB Foundation for
    Scotland
John Lyon's Charity
Magdalen Hospital Trust
Old Enfield Charitable Trust

Patients' Aid Association
    Hospital & Medical
    Charities Trust
Whitecourt Charitable Trust

■ **People living in rural
    areas**
    Funding priority
Arkleton Trust
Astor Foundation
Balney Charitable Trust
BBC Radio Cambridgeshire –
    Trustline
Berkshire Community
    Foundation
BibleLands
Burton Breweries Charitable
    Trust
CLA Charitable Trust
Community Foundation for
    Northern Ireland
Consortium on Opportunities
    for Volunteering
Construction Industry Trust for
    Youth
Ernest Cook Trust
Cray Trust
Derbyshire Community
    Foundation
Essex Community Foundation
Samuel William Farmer's Trust
Four Acre Trust
J C Green Charitable
    Settlement
Heart of England Community
    Foundation
Holywood Trust
Housing Associations
    Charitable Trust
Sir James Knott Trust
Bryan Lancaster's Charity
Leeds & Holbeck Building
    Society Charitable
    Foundation
Lintel Trust
London Youth Trust
Midhurst Pensions Trust
Newby Trust Limited
Northern Rock Foundation
Oxfordshire Community
    Foundation
Austin & Hope Pilkington Trust
Puebla Charitable Trust
Rothley Trust
J S & E C Rymer Charitable
    Trust
Frieda Scott Charitable Trust
Scottish Churches Community
    Trust
Mrs S H Troughton Charity
    Trust
VEC Acorn Trust
Westminster Foundation
Wiltshire and Swindon
    Community Foundation
Woodlands Trust (1015942)

Yorkshire Agricultural Society

    Will consider
Adnams Charity
Viscount Amory's Charitable
    Trust
Ardwick Trust
BBC Children in Need Appeal
Birmingham Hospital Saturday
    Fund Medical Charity &
    Welfare Trust
Edward Cadbury Charitable
    Trust
Richard Cadbury Charitable
    Trust
Carlton Television Trust
Carnegie Dunfermline Trust
Comic Relief
County Durham Foundation
Cranbury Foundation
Cumber Family Charitable
    Trust
Devon Community Foundation
Dulverton Trust
Eden Arts Trust
Elmgrant Trust
Emmandjay Charitable Trust
Enkalon Foundation
Ferguson Benevolent Fund Ltd
Earl Fitzwilliam Charitable
    Trust
Joyce Fletcher Charitable Trust
Girdlers' Company Charitable
    Trust
Grocers' Charity
Gulbenkian Foundation
Hadfield Trust
Lennox Hannay Charitable
    Trust
Charles Hayward Foundation
Help the Aged
Hemby Trust
Hertfordshire Community
    Foundation
Hesslewood Children's Trust
Alan Edward Higgs Charity
Miss Agnes H Hunter's Trust
Hyde Charitable Trust
Inchrye Trust
Isle of Anglesey Charitable
    Trust
JCA Charitable Foundation
Jephcott Charitable Trust
Joicey Trust
Edward Cecil Jones Settlement
Ursula Keyes Trust
Kyte Charitable Trust
Christopher Laing Foundation
Langdale Trust
Leach Fourteenth Trust
Lloyds TSB Foundation for
    Northern Ireland
Lloyds TSB Foundation for
    Scotland
C F Lunoe Trust Fund
Sir George Martin Trust

Tony Metherell Charitable
   Trust
Millfield House Foundation
Milton Keynes Community
   Foundation
Minge's Gift
Victor Mishcon Charitable
   Trust
Mobbs Memorial Trust Ltd
George A Moore Foundation
National Power Charitable
   Trust
Norman Family Charitable
   Trust
Arthur James Paterson
   Charitable Trust
Constance Paterson Charitable
   Trust
Peugeot Charity Trust
A M Pilkington's Charitable
   Trust
J S F Pollitzer Charitable
   Settlement
Princess Anne's Charities
Pye Foundation
Joseph & Lena Randall
   Charitable Trust
Rhododendron Trust
Robertson Trust
Mrs L D Rope Third Charitable
   Settlement
Rowan Charitable Trust
Christopher Rowbotham
   Charitable Trust
Joseph Rowntree Foundation
Francis C Scott Charitable
   Trust
Sir James & Lady Scott Trust
Scottish Community
   Foundation
Sefton Community Foundation
Skelton Bounty
Henry Smith Charity
Leslie Smith Foundation
Sobell Foundation
South Yorkshire Community
   Foundation
Stanley Spooner Deceased
   Charitable Trust
Summerfield Charitable Trust
Bernard Sunley Charitable
   Foundation
Truemark Trust
Tudor Trust
Unemployed Voluntary Action
   Fund
Wates Foundation
Wellfield Trust
Whitaker Charitable Trust

■ **People living in urban
   areas**
   Funding priority
Berkshire Community
   Foundation

Birmingham Hospital Saturday
   Fund Medical Charity &
   Welfare Trust
Oliver Borthwick Memorial
   Trust
Burton Breweries Charitable
   Trust
Butchers' Company General
   Charities
Church Urban Fund
CLA Charitable Trust
Community Foundation for
   Northern Ireland
Construction Industry Trust for
   Youth
Coutts & Co. Charitable Trust
John Grant Davies Trust
Derbyshire Community
   Foundation
Digbeth Trust
Four Acre Trust
Gatsby Charitable Foundation
Hampton Fuel Allotment
   Charity
Holywood Trust
Homeless International
Isle of Dogs Community
   Foundation
King's Fund
Sir James Knott Trust
Leeds & Holbeck Building
   Society Charitable
   Foundation
Lintel Trust
Paul Lunn-Rockliffe Charitable
   Trust
Millfield House Foundation
Newby Trust Limited
Northern Rock Foundation
Puebla Charitable Trust
Rosca Trust
Rothley Trust
Sir Walter St John's
   Educational Charity
Francis C Scott Charitable
   Trust
Frieda Scott Charitable Trust
Sir James & Lady Scott Trust
Scottish Churches Community
   Trust
Thames Community
   Foundation
Fred Towler Charity Trust
VEC Acorn Trust
Charity of Thomas Wade &
   Others
Wates Foundation
Woodlands Trust (1015942)

Will consider
Pat Allsop Charitable Trust
Ardwick Trust
Astor Foundation
BBC Children in Need Appeal
Birmingham Foundation

Herbert & Peter Blagrave
   Charitable Trust
Bridge House Estates Trust
   Fund
Edward Cadbury Charitable
   Trust
Carlton Television Trust
Carnegie Dunfermline Trust
City Parochial Foundation
Comic Relief
Consortium on Opportunities
   for Volunteering
Ernest Cook Trust
County Durham Foundation
Cranbury Foundation
Helen and Geoffrey de Freitas
   Charitable Trust
Devon Community Foundation
Edinburgh Children's Holiday
   Fund
Elmgrant Trust
Emmandjay Charitable Trust
Enkalon Foundation
Ferguson Benevolent Fund Ltd
Fidelity UK Foundation
Girdlers' Company Charitable
   Trust
Grocers' Charity
Gulbenkian Foundation
Hadfield Trust
Harborne Parish Lands Charity
Harrison & Potter Trust
Gay & Peter Hartley's Hillards
   Charitable Trust
Charles Hayward Foundation
Heart of England Community
   Foundation
Hemby Trust
Hertfordshire Community
   Foundation
Hesslewood Children's Trust
Alan Edward Higgs Charity
Miss Agnes H Hunter's Trust
Hyde Charitable Trust
Isle of Anglesey Charitable
   Trust
Joicey Trust
Neil Kreitman Foundation
Christopher Laing Foundation
Bryan Lancaster's Charity
Leach Fourteenth Trust
Leigh Trust
Lloyds TSB Foundation for
   Northern Ireland
London North East Community
   Foundation
C F Lunoe Trust Fund
R W Mann Trustees Limited
Hilda & Samuel Marks
   Foundation
Sir George Martin Trust
John Martin's Charity
Tony Metherell Charitable
   Trust
Hugh and Mary Miller Bequest
   Trust

Minge's Gift
Victor Mishcon Charitable
    Trust
John Moores Foundation
Morel Charitable Trust
National Power Charitable
    Trust
Norwich Consolidated
    Charities
Oxfordshire Community
    Foundation
Arthur James Paterson
    Charitable Trust
Constance Paterson Charitable
    Trust
Bernard Piggott Trust
Princess Anne's Charities
Joseph & Lena Randall
    Charitable Trust
John Rayner Charitable Trust
Reuters Foundation
Rhododendron Trust
Robertson Trust
Mrs L D Rope Third Charitable
    Settlement
Christopher Rowbotham
    Charitable Trust
Joseph Rowntree Foundation
Scottish Community
    Foundation
Sefton Community Foundation
Henry Smith Charity
Sobell Foundation
South Yorkshire Community
    Foundation
Stanley Spooner Deceased
    Charitable Trust
Summerfield Charitable Trust
Bernard Sunley Charitable
    Foundation
Sir Jules Thorn Charitable
    Trust
Tisbury Telegraph Trust
Truemark Trust
Tudor Trust
Unemployed Voluntary Action
    Fund
Wellfield Trust
Wiltshire and Swindon
    Community Foundation
Worcester Municipal Charities
Wyseliot Charitable Trust

■ **Ex-offenders & those at
    risk of offending
    Funding priority**
1970 Trust
29th May 1961 Charitable
    Trust
Ashendene Trust
Berkshire Community
    Foundation
Burton Breweries Charitable
    Trust
Carlton Television Trust

Community Foundation for
    Northern Ireland
Coutts & Co. Charitable Trust
Derbyshire Community
    Foundation
Essex Community Foundation
Essex Fairway Charitable Trust
Fiat Auto (UK) Charity
Charles Hayward Foundation
Hertfordshire Community
    Foundation
Hilden Charitable Fund
Michael and Shirley Hunt
    Charitable Trust
J J Charitable Trust
Sir James Knott Trust
Allen Lane Foundation
Lawlor Foundation
Lintel Trust
Paul Lunn-Rockliffe Charitable
    Trust
Marchday Charitable Fund
Newby Trust Limited
Noel Buxton Trust
Odin Charitable Trust
Peacock Charitable Trust
Austin & Hope Pilkington Trust
Portishead Nautical Trust
Rosca Trust
Royal London Aid Society
Francis C Scott Charitable
    Trust
Frieda Scott Charitable Trust
Sir James & Lady Scott Trust
Swan Mountain Trust
Third House Trust
Tudor Trust
Waterside Trust
Wates Foundation
Weavers' Company Benevolent
    Fund
Woodlands Trust (1015942)
Woodlands Trust (259569)

Will consider
Adnams Charity
Alchemy Foundation
Alcohol Education and
    Research Fund
Astor Foundation
Barnabas Charitable Trust
Percy Bilton Charity Ltd
Birmingham Hospital Saturday
    Fund Medical Charity &
    Welfare Trust
Bisgood Charitable Trust
Bridge House Estates Trust
    Fund
British Humane Association
Bromley Trust
Edward Cadbury Charitable
    Trust
Richard Cadbury Charitable
    Trust
Carnegie Dunfermline Trust
Church Urban Fund

City and Metropolitan Welfare
    Charity
City Parochial Foundation
J A Clark Charitable Trust
Comic Relief
Congleton Inclosure Trust
Ernest Cook Trust
County Durham Foundation
Cranbury Foundation
Harry Crook Foundation
John Grant Davies Trust
Dulverton Trust
Wilfred & Elsie Elkes Charity
    Fund
Elmgrant Trust
Ericson Trust
Ford of Britain Trust
Fox Memorial Trust
Jill Franklin Trust
Robert Gavron Charitable Trust
Girdlers' Company Charitable
    Trust
Grocers' Charity
Bishop of Guildford's
    Foundation
Gulbenkian Foundation
Hadfield Trust
Hadrian Trust
Eleanor Hamilton Educational
    and Charitable Trust
Paul Hamlyn Foundation
Hampstead Wells and
    Campden Trust
Hampton Fuel Allotment
    Charity
Harborne Parish Lands Charity
Harrison & Potter Trust
Gay & Peter Hartley's Hillards
    Charitable Trust
N & P Hartley Memorial Trust
Heart of England Community
    Foundation
Hemby Trust
Hesslewood Children's Trust
Alan Edward Higgs Charity
Inchrye Trust
Joicey Trust
Edward Cecil Jones Settlement
Anton Jurgens Charitable Trust
Neil Kreitman Foundation
Kyte Charitable Trust
Christopher Laing Foundation
Bryan Lancaster's Charity
Leach Fourteenth Trust
Leigh Trust
Linbury Trust
Lloyds TSB Foundation for
    Northern Ireland
Lloyds TSB Foundation for
    Scotland
London North East Community
    Foundation
C F Lunoe Trust Fund
John Lyon's Charity
R W Mann Trustees Limited

Hilda & Samuel Marks
Foundation
Sir George Martin Trust
Mercers' Charitable
Foundation
Hugh and Mary Miller Bequest
Trust
Minge's Gift
Victor Mishcon Charitable
Trust
Mobbs Memorial Trust Ltd
Monument Trust
J P Morgan Fleming
Educational Trust and
Foundation
National Power Charitable
Trust
Norman Family Charitable
Trust
Northern Rock Foundation
Oakdale Trust
Oxfordshire Community
Foundation
Harry Payne Trust
Bernard Piggott Trust
Princess Anne's Charities
Mr and Mrs J A Pye's
Charitable Settlement
Rainford Trust
Joseph & Lena Randall
Charitable Trust
Rhododendron Trust
Mrs L D Rope Third Charitable
Settlement
Christopher Rowbotham
Charitable Trust
Sir Walter St John's
Educational Charity
Scott Bader Commonwealth
Ltd
Scottish Churches Community
Trust
Scottish Community
Foundation
Sefton Community Foundation
Henry Smith Charity
South Yorkshire Community
Foundation
Stanley Spooner Deceased
Charitable Trust
Staples Trust
Sir Halley Stewart Trust
Summerfield Charitable Trust
Bernard Sunley Charitable
Foundation
Unemployed Voluntary Action
Fund
John and Lucille van Geest
Foundation
Scurrah Wainwright Charity
Wakefield Trust
Wellfield Trust
Westcroft Trust
Whitaker Charitable Trust
Whitecourt Charitable Trust

Wiltshire and Swindon
Community Foundation
Women at Risk
Worcester Municipal Charities
Matthews Wrightson Charity
Trust
Wyseliot Charitable Trust
Yapp Charitable Trust
York Children's Trust

■ **Migrants**
Funding priority
Rosca Trust
Rothley Trust

Will consider
Birmingham Hospital Saturday
Fund Medical Charity &
Welfare Trust
Comic Relief
SEM Charitable Trust

■ **People who are poor**
Funding priority
Abel Charitable Trust
Henry & Grete Abrahams
Second Charitable
Foundation
Alliance Family Foundation
Almshouse Association
Ancaster Trust
Anglian Water Trust Fund
Ambrose & Ann Appelbe Trust
Ashendene Trust
ATP Charitable Trust
Albert Casanova Ballard
Deceased Trust
Balmore Trust
Balney Charitable Trust
Band (1976) Trust
Barnes Workhouse Fund
Barnsbury Charitable Trust
Bartle Family Charitable Trust
BBC Children in Need Appeal
BBC Radio Cambridgeshire –
Trustline
Peter Beckwith Charitable
Trust
Bellahouston Bequest Fund
Benham Charitable Settlement
Berkshire Community
Foundation
Betard Bequest
Bethesda Community
Charitable Trust
BibleLands
Sir William Boreman's
Foundation
A Bornstein Charitable
Settlement
Bothwell Charitable Trust
Bridge House Estates Trust
Fund
Bridge Trust
Bristol Charities
Buckingham Trust

Burton Breweries Charitable
Trust
Consolidated Charity of Burton
Upon Trent
Butchers' Company General
Charities
Richard Cadbury Charitable
Trust
Cadbury Schweppes
Foundation
CAFOD
Carlton Television Trust
Sir John Cass's Foundation
Cattanach Charitable Trust
Joseph & Annie Cattle Trust
Chamberlain Foundation
Chandris Foundation
Chest Heart and Stroke
Scotland
Chippenham Borough Lands
Charity
Church Urban Fund
Classic FM Charitable Trust
Cleary Foundation
Cleopatra Trust
Closehelm Ltd
Richard Cloudesley's Charity
Clydpride Ltd
Coates Charitable Settlement
Vivienne & Samuel Cohen
Charitable Trust
Cole Charitable Trust
E Alec Colman Charitable Fund
Ltd
Community Foundation for
Northern Ireland
Construction Industry Trust for
Youth
Alice Ellen Cooper-Dean
Charitable Foundation
Duke of Cornwall's Benevolent
Fund
Cornwall Independent Trust
Fund
County Durham Foundation
Coutts & Co. Charitable Trust
Lord Cozens-Hardy Trust
Michael Crawford Children's
Charity
Ronald Cruickshanks
Foundation
John Grant Davies Trust
De La Rue Charitable Trust
Denton Charitable Trust
Derbyshire Community
Foundation
Richard Desmond Charitable
Trust
Devon Community Foundation
Dinam Charity
Dorcas Trust
Dorus Trust
Doughty Charity Trust
Dwek Family Charitable Trust
Gilbert & Eileen Edgar
Foundation

Elanore Ltd
George Elias Charitable Trust
Maud Elkington Charitable
    Trust
Edith M Ellis 1985 Charitable
    Trust
Emerging Markets Charity for
    Children
Emerton-Christie Charity
Epigoni Trust
Equitable Charitable Trust
Essex Community Foundation
Euro Charity Trust
Sir John Evelyn's Charity
Farmers Company Charitable
    Fund
Fiat Auto (UK) Charity
Doris Field Charitable Trust
Fifty Fund
Ian Fleming Charitable Trust
Roy Fletcher Charitable Trust
Fordeve Ltd
Four Acre Trust
Timothy Franey Charitable
    Foundation
Isaac and Freda Frankel
    Memorial Charitable Trust
Sydney E Franklin Deceased's
    New Second Charity
Emily Fraser Trust
Hugh Fraser Foundation
Friarsgate Trust
Friends of Biala Ltd
Fund for Human Need
Angela Gallagher Memorial
    Fund
Garthgwynion Charities
Simon Gibson Charitable Trust
Global Care
Gosling Foundation Ltd
Grand Charity of Freemasons
Gray Trust
Mrs H R Greene Charitable
    Settlement
Grimsdale Charitable Trust
Grocers' Charity
Bishop of Guildford's
    Foundation
Gurunanak
Hackney Parochial Charities
Alfred Haines Charitable Trust
Hale Trust
Paul Hamlyn Foundation
Sue Hammerson's Charitable
    Trust
Hanley Trust (1987)
Haramead Trust
Harborne Parish Lands Charity
Harbour Foundation
Harrison & Potter Trust
Hawthorne Charitable Trust
Haymills Charitable Trust
Heart of England Community
    Foundation
Henley Educational Charity

Joanna Herbert-Stepney
    Charitable Settlement
Hertfordshire Community
    Foundation
Alan Edward Higgs Charity
Highcroft Charitable Trust
Hillingdon Partnership Trust
Hobson Charity Ltd
Homeless International
HopMarket Charity
Horne Foundation
Hospital of God at Greatham
Huggard Charitable Trust
Miss Agnes H Hunter's Trust
IBM United Kingdom Trust
Ireland Fund of Great Britain
James Trust
Jeffrey Charitable Trust
Jewish Child's Day
J G Joffe Charitable Trust
Jones 1986 Charitable Trust
Edward Cecil Jones Settlement
Anton Jurgens Charitable Trust
Michael & Ilse Katz Foundation
Emmanuel Kaye Foundation
Peter Kershaw Trust
Kirkley Poor's Land Estate
Sir James Knott Trust
Bryan Lancaster's Charity
Langdale Trust
Richard Langhorn Trust
Laslett's (Hinton) Charity
Lauchentilly Charitable
    Foundation 1988
Lawlor Foundation
Lawson Charitable Foundation
William Leech Charity
Leeds & Holbeck Building
    Society Charitable
    Foundation
Kennedy Leigh Charitable
    Trust
John Lewis Partnership
    General Community Fund
Lintel Trust
Elaine & Angus Lloyd
    Charitable Trust
Lloyds TSB Foundation for the
    Channel Islands
London Youth Trust
Paul Lunn-Rockliffe Charitable
    Trust
C F Lunoe Trust Fund
Lyras Family Charitable Trust
Ian Mactaggart Fund
Magdalen Hospital Trust
Magdalen & Lasher Charity
Man Group plc Charitable
    Trust
Victor Mann Trust
Marchday Charitable Fund
Hilda & Samuel Marks
    Foundation
Michael Marsh Charitable
    Trust

D G Marshall of Cambridge
    Trust
Charity of Mary Jane,
    Countess of Meath
Methodist Relief and
    Development Fund
Gerald Micklem Charitable
    Trust
Miles Trust for the Putney and
    Roehampton Community
Miller Foundation
Millfield House Foundation
Millhouses Charitable Trust
Milton Keynes Community
    Foundation
Peter Minet Trust
Minge's Gift
Victor Mishcon Charitable
    Trust
Mitchell Charitable Trust
Mole Charitable Trust
John Moores Foundation
Morel Charitable Trust
S C and M E Morland's
    Charitable Trust
Moss Charitable Trust
Edith Murphy Foundation
Music Sales Charitable Trust
Muslim Hands
Mutual Trust Group
Kitty and Daniel Nabarro
    Charitable Trust
New Appeals Organisation for
    the City & County of
    Nottingham
Newby Trust Limited
Richard Newitt Fund
Northampton Municipal Church
    Charities
Northampton Queen's Institute
    Relief in Sickness Fund
Northmoor Trust
Nova Charitable Trust
Novi Most International
Father O'Mahoney Memorial
    Trust
Oakdale Trust
Odin Charitable Trust
Ogilvie Charities Deed 2
Old Enfield Charitable Trust
Onaway Trust
Oppenheimer Charitable Trust
Oxfam (GB)
Oxfordshire Community
    Foundation
Padwa Charitable Foundation
Eleanor Palmer Trust
Gerald Palmer Trust
Arthur James Paterson
    Charitable Trust
Constance Paterson Charitable
    Trust
Patients' Aid Association
    Hospital & Medical
    Charities Trust
Peabody Community Fund

Frank Pearson Foundation
Persula Foundation
Philanthropic Trust
Austin & Hope Pilkington Trust
Pilkington Charities Fund
Elsie Pilkington Charitable
 Trust
Col W W Pilkington Will Trusts
 – The General Charity Fund
J D Player Endowment Fund
Portishead Nautical Trust
J E Posnansky Charitable Trust
Premierquote Ltd
Premishlaner Charitable Trust
Sir John Priestman Charity
 Trust
Puebla Charitable Trust
Puri Foundation
R S Charitable Trust
Joseph & Lena Randall
 Charitable Trust
Ruben and Elisabeth Rausing
 Trust
Rayne Trust
Red Dragon Radio Trust
Rest Harrow Trust
Rhondda Cynon Taff Welsh
 Church Acts Fund
Clive Richards Charity Ltd
Ridgesave Limited
Mrs L D Rope Third Charitable
 Settlement
Rosca Trust
Rothley Trust
Royal Docks Trust
Karim Rida Said Foundation
St Hilda's Trust
Sir Walter St John's
 Educational Charity
St Jude's Trust
St Mary-le-Strand Charity
St Olave, St Thomas and St
 John United Charity
Sandra Charitable Trust
Schreib Trust
Schroder Charity Trust
Scott Bader Commonwealth
 Ltd
Francis C Scott Charitable
 Trust
Frieda Scott Charitable Trust
Sir James & Lady Scott Trust
Scottish Churches Community
 Trust
Search
Sedbury Trust
Severn Trent Water Charitable
 Trust
Shepherd Street Trust
Julius Silman Charitable Trust
Bishop Simeon CR Trust
Skelton Bounty
Sobell Foundation
E C Sosnow Charitable Trust
South Yorkshire Community
 Foundation

W F Southall Trust
Stanley Spooner Deceased
 Charitable Trust
Stanton Ballard Charitable
 Trust
Foundation of Edward Storey
Sueberry Ltd
Swann-Morton Foundation
Walter Swindon Charitable
 Trust
Talbot Village Trust
Talteg Ltd
Mrs A Lacy Tate Trust
Tegham Limited
Thames Community
 Foundation
Thornton Trust
Three Guineas Trust
Tower Hill Improvement Trust
Fred Towler Charity Trust
Trades House of Glasgow
Triangle Trust (1949) Fund
Truemark Trust
Tudor Rose Ltd
Trustees of Tzedakah
United St Saviour's Charities
David Uri Memorial Trust
John and Lucille van Geest
 Foundation
VEC Acorn Trust
Voluntary Action Luton
Scurrah Wainwright Charity
Thomas Wall Trust
Walton Foundation
War on Want
Warwickshire Masonic
 Charitable Association Ltd
Waterside Trust
Wates Foundation
John Watson's Trust
West Derby Wastelands
 Charity
White Rose Children's Aid
 International Charity
Sheila Whitley Trust
William Williams Charity
John Wilson Bequest Fund
Wiltshire and Swindon
 Community Foundation
Benjamin Winegarten
 Charitable Trust
Maurice Wohl Charitable Trust
Women at Risk
Woodlands Trust (1015942)
Woodlands Trust (259569)
Woolnoth Society Charitable
 Trust
Worcester Municipal Charities
Xerox (UK) Trust
Yardley Great Trust
Yorkshire Bank Charitable
 Trust
Yorkshire Building Society
 Charitable Foundation
Elizabeth & Prince Zaiger Trust

Will consider
29th May 1961 Charitable
 Trust
A B Charitable Trust
Abbey National Charitable
 Trust Ltd
Sylvia Adams Charitable Trust
Miss Agnes Gilchrist
 Adamson's Trust
Adnams Charity
Alchemy Foundation
Pat Allsop Charitable Trust
Viscount Amory's Charitable
 Trust
Sir John & Lady Amory's
 Charitable Trust
Andrew Anderson Trust
Ardwick Trust
Lord Ashdown Charitable Trust
Laura Ashley Foundation
Aston Charities Trust Limited
Astor Foundation
Bacta Charitable Trust
Badley Memorial Trust
Baker Charitable Trust
Balcombe Charitable Trust
Bamford Charitable Foundation
Lord Barnby's Foundation
Barnwood House Trust
Bates Charitable Trust
Bedford Charity
E M Behrens Charitable Trust
Beit Trust
Belljoe Tzedoko Ltd
Benfield Motors Charitable
 Trust
Percy Bilton Charity Ltd
Birmingham Foundation
Birmingham Hospital Saturday
 Fund Medical Charity &
 Welfare Trust
Body Shop Foundation
Salo Bordon Charitable Trust
Oliver Borthwick Memorial
 Trust
John Bristow and Thomas
 Mason Trust
British Humane Association
Charles & Edna Broadhurst
 Charitable Trust
R S Brownless Charitable
 Trust
Bryant Trust
Audrey & Stanley Burton
 Charitable Trust
Geoffrey Burton Charitable
 Trust
Bill Butlin Charity Trust
Edward Cadbury Charitable
 Trust
George W Cadbury Charitable
 Trust
Calpe Trust
Carnegie Dunfermline Trust
Charities Advisory Trust
Chelsea Square 1994 Trust

Chipping Sodbury Town Lands
  Charity
Chownes Foundation
Christendom Trust
Christian Aid
City and Metropolitan Welfare
  Charity
City Parochial Foundation
J A Clark Charitable Trust
Clover Trust
Denise Cohen Charitable Trust
John & Freda Coleman
  Charitable Trust
Norman Collinson Charitable
  Trust
Comic Relief
Congleton Inclosure Trust
Ernest Cook Trust
Marjorie Coote Old People's
  Charity
Sidney & Elizabeth Corob
  Charitable Trust
Corona Charitable Trust
Cotton Trust
Cranbury Foundation
Harry Crook Foundation
Cumber Family Charitable
  Trust
Cwmbran Trust
Baron Davenport's Charity
David Charitable Trust
De Clermont Charitable
  Company Ltd
Helen and Geoffrey de Freitas
  Charitable Trust
Miriam K Dean Refugee Trust
  Fund
Sandy Dewhirst Charitable
  Trust
Djanogly Foundation
Drapers' Charitable Fund
Dulverton Trust
Earley Charity
EBM Charitable Trust
Edinburgh Children's Holiday
  Fund
Wilfred & Elsie Elkes Charity
  Fund
John Ellerman Foundation
Elmgrant Trust
Emmandjay Charitable Trust
Mayor of the London Borough
  of Enfield Appeal Fund
Enkalon Foundation
Ericson Trust
Essex Fairway Charitable Trust
Exilarch's Foundation
Fassnidge Memorial Trust
George Fentham Birmingham
  Charity
Ferguson Benevolent Fund Ltd
Fidelity UK Foundation
Finnart House School Trust
David Finnie & Alan Emery
  Charitable Trust

Fishmongers' Company's
  Charitable Trust
Ford of Britain Trust
Four Lanes Trust
Fox Memorial Trust
Charles Henry Foyle Trust
Freshgate Trust Foundation
Patrick Frost Foundation
Maurice Fry Charitable Trust
Gannochy Trust
Robert Gavron Charitable Trust
Girdlers' Company Charitable
  Trust
Mrs Godfrey-Payton Trust
Sydney & Phyllis Goldberg
  Memorial Charitable Trust
J G Graves Charitable Trust
Constance Green Foundation
Gulbenkian Foundation
H C D Memorial Fund
Hadfield Trust
Hadrian Trust
Eleanor Hamilton Educational
  and Charitable Trust
Hampstead Wells and
  Campden Trust
Hampton Fuel Allotment
  Charity
Harding Trust
Gay & Peter Hartley's Hillards
  Charitable Trust
N & P Hartley Memorial Trust
M A Hawe Settlement
Charles Hayward Foundation
Healthsure Group Ltd
May Hearnshaw's Charity
Help the Aged
Hemby Trust
Hesslewood Children's Trust
Higgs Charitable Trust
Jane Hodge Foundation
Edward Sydney Hogg
  Charitable Settlement
Homestead Charitable Trust
Joseph Hopkins Charity
Hornsey Parochial Charities
James Thom Howat Charitable
  Trust
Huddersfield Common Good
  Trust
Human Relief Foundation
Hyde Charitable Trust
Hyde Park Place Estate Charity
  – civil trustees
Inchrye Trust
Isle of Anglesey Charitable
  Trust
J A R Charitable Trust
James Pantyfedwen
  Foundation
Jephcott Charitable Trust
Jerusalem Trust
Jesus Hospital Charity
Johnson Foundation
Johnson Group Cleaners
  Charity

Joicey Trust
Lady Eileen Joseph Foundation
Boris Karloff Charitable
  Foundation
Ursula Keyes Trust
King's Fund
Mary Kinross Charitable Trust
Graham Kirkham Foundation
Kleinwort Benson Charitable
  Trust
Knowles Charitable Trust
Kohn Foundation
Kreditor Charitable Trust
Kreitman Foundation
Neil Kreitman Foundation
Heinz & Anna Kroch
  Foundation
Kyte Charitable Trust
Late Sir Pierce Lacy Charity
  Trust
Laing's Charitable Trust
Christopher Laing Foundation
Langley Charitable Trust
Lauffer Family Charitable
  Foundation
Lazard Charitable Trust
Leach Fourteenth Trust
Leigh Trust
Leonard Trust
Lord Leverhulme Charitable
  Trust
Harry Livingstone Charitable
  Trust
Jack Livingstone Charitable
  Trust
Lloyd's Charities Trust
Lloyds TSB Foundation for
  Scotland
London North East Community
  Foundation
C L Loyd Charitable Trust
Luck-Hille Foundation
Sir Jack Lyons Charitable Trust
M & C Trust
Mackintosh Foundation
Helen Isabella McMorran
  Charitable Foundation
R W Mann Trustees Limited
Leslie & Lilian Manning Trust
Marr-Munning Trust
Sir George Martin Trust
John Martin's Charity
Matliwala Family Charitable
  Trust
Mercers' Charitable
  Foundation
Zachary Merton & George
  Woofindin Convalescent
  Trust
Tony Metherell Charitable
  Trust
Metropolitan Hospital-Sunday
  Fund
Middlesex County Rugby
  Football Union Memorial
  Fund

Hugh and Mary Miller Bequest
  Trust
Millfield Trust
Millichope Foundation
Mobbs Memorial Trust Ltd
Monmouthshire County Council
  Welsh Church Act Fund
J P Morgan Fleming
  Educational Trust and
  Foundation
Morgan Stanley International
  Foundation
Peter Morrison Charitable
  Foundation
National Power Charitable
  Trust
Nestlé Rowntree York
  Employees Community Fund
  Trust
Newpier Charity Ltd
Noel Buxton Trust
North London Islamic
  Association Trust
Northern Rock Foundation
Northumberland Village Homes
  Trust
Norwich Consolidated
  Charities
Noswad Charity
Noswal Charitable Trust
Oakley Charitable Trust
Oldham Foundation
Kate Wilson Oliver Trust
Parivar Trust
Parthenon Trust
Harry Payne Trust
Peugeot Charity Trust
Ruth & Michael Phillips
  Charitable Trust
Bernard Piggott Trust
A M Pilkington's Charitable
  Trust
John Pitman Charitable Trust
Ponton House Trust
Prairie Trust
W L Pratt Charitable Trust
Princess Anne's Charities
Privy Purse Charitable Trust
Proven Family Trust
Pye Foundation
Mr and Mrs J A Pye's
  Charitable Settlement
Radio Forth Help a Child
  Appeal
Rainford Trust
Peggy Ramsay Foundation
E L Rathbone Charitable Trust
Ravensdale Trust
John Rayner Charitable Trust
Reuters Foundation
Rhododendron Trust
Cliff Richard Charitable Trust
Richmond Parish Lands Charity
Riverside Charitable Trust
  Limited
Thomas Roberts Trust

Robertson Trust
Christopher Rowbotham
  Charitable Trust
Rowlands Trust
Joseph Rowntree Foundation
St Laurence Charities for the
  Poor
Basil Samuel Charitable Trust
Peter Samuel Charitable Trust
R H Scholes Charitable Trust
John Scott Trust
Scottish Community
  Foundation
Scouloudi Foundation
Searle Charitable Trust
Seedfield Trust
Sefton Community Foundation
Sellata Ltd
Servite Sisters' Charitable
  Trust Fund
Sheffield Church Burgesses
  Trust
Sheldon Trust
Mary Elizabeth Siebel Charity
Henry Smith Charity
Ralph and Irma Sperring
  Charity
W W Spooner Charitable Trust
Sportsman's Charity
Hugh Stenhouse Foundation
E J H Stephenson Deceased
  Charitable Trust
Sir Halley Stewart Trust
Leonard Laity Stoate
  Charitable Trust
W O Street Charitable
  Foundation
Summerfield Charitable Trust
Bernard Sunley Charitable
  Foundation
Tearfund
Thompson Charitable Trust
Sir Jules Thorn Charitable
  Trust
Company of Tobacco Pipe
  Makers and Tobacco
  Blenders Benevolent Fund
Tudor Trust
Douglas Turner Trust
Florence Turner Trust
Unemployed Voluntary Action
  Fund
Albert Van Den Bergh
  Charitable Trust
Variety Club Children's Charity
Wakefield Trust
Wellfield Trust
Wesleyan Charitable Trust
Westminster Amalgamated
  Charity
Colonel W H Whitbread
  Charitable Trust
Whitecourt Charitable Trust
Michael and Anna Wix
  Charitable Trust

Maurice Wohl Charitable
  Foundation
Worshipful Company of
  Founders Charities
Wyseliot Charitable Trust
W Wing Yip & Bros Charitable
  Trust
York Children's Trust

■ Refugees and asylum seekers
Funding priority

BBC Children in Need Appeal
BibleLands
Barrow Cadbury Trust and the
  Barrow Cadbury Fund
Camelot Foundation
Carlton Television Trust
Charities Advisory Trust
Devon Community Foundation
Diana, Princess of Wales
  Memorial Fund
Edith M Ellis 1985 Charitable
  Trust
Fiat Auto (UK) Charity
Jill Franklin Trust
Fund for Human Need
Paul Hamlyn Foundation
Harbour Foundation
Hilden Charitable Fund
Housing Associations
  Charitable Trust
Jewish Child's Day
J G Joffe Charitable Trust
Anton Jurgens Charitable Trust
King's Fund
Allen Lane Foundation
Lintel Trust
Marchday Charitable Fund
Newby Trust Limited
Oakdale Trust
Odin Charitable Trust
Onaway Trust
Philanthropic Trust
Austin & Hope Pilkington Trust
Rosca Trust
Sir Walter St John's
  Educational Charity
Frieda Scott Charitable Trust
Sir James & Lady Scott Trust
Walter Swindon Charitable
  Trust
Tinsley Foundation
Tisbury Telegraph Trust
Walton Foundation
Waterside Trust
Wates Foundation
Women at Risk

Will consider

Adint Charitable Trust
Aid to the Church in Need (UK)
Pat Allsop Charitable Trust
Ardwick Trust
Andrew Balint Charitable Trust
George Balint Charitable Trust

Lord Barnby's Foundation
Berkshire Community
 Foundation
Body Shop Foundation
P G & N J Boulton Trust
Bridge House Estates Trust
 Fund
Edward Cadbury Charitable
 Trust
Calpe Trust
Christian Aid
Church Urban Fund
City Parochial Foundation
Cole Charitable Trust
Comic Relief
Coppings Trust
Cranbury Foundation
John Grant Davies Trust
Helen and Geoffrey de Freitas
 Charitable Trust
Miriam K Dean Refugee Trust
 Fund
Derbyshire Community
 Foundation
Earley Charity
Wilfred & Elsie Elkes Charity
 Fund
John Ellerman Foundation
Ericson Trust
Finnart House School Trust
Fordeve Ltd
Maurice Fry Charitable Trust
Robert Gavron Charitable Trust
J G Graves Charitable Trust
Grocers' Charity
Bishop of Guildford's
 Foundation
H C D Memorial Fund
Hadrian Trust
Hampstead Wells and
 Campden Trust
Hampton Fuel Allotment
 Charity
Harborne Parish Lands Charity
Harrison & Potter Trust
Heart of England Community
 Foundation
Hertfordshire Community
 Foundation
Hinchley Charitable Trust
James Thom Howat Charitable
 Trust
Human Relief Foundation
Humanitarian Trust
Ruth & Lionel Jacobson Trust
 (Second Fund) No 2
Jeffrey Charitable Trust
Joicey Trust
Sir James Knott Trust
Bryan Lancaster's Charity
Leach Fourteenth Trust
Leigh Trust
Lloyds TSB Foundation for
 Scotland
London North East Community
 Foundation

C F Lunoe Trust Fund
Mackintosh Foundation
Marr-Munning Trust
Hugh and Mary Miller Bequest
 Trust
Millfield House Foundation
Minge's Gift
Victor Mishcon Charitable
 Trust
John Moores Foundation
Northern Rock Foundation
Oxfam (GB)
Oxfordshire Community
 Foundation
Parthenon Trust
Pilgrim Trust
Pilkington Charities Fund
Princess Anne's Charities
Mr and Mrs J A Pye's
 Charitable Settlement
Joseph & Lena Randall
 Charitable Trust
Rhododendron Trust
Mrs L D Rope Third Charitable
 Settlement
Rothley Trust
Joseph Rowntree Charitable
 Trust
St Laurence Charities for the
 Poor
Scottish Churches Community
 Trust
Scottish Community
 Foundation
Sefton Community Foundation
Servite Sisters' Charitable
 Trust Fund
Sheldon Trust
Henry Smith Charity
South Yorkshire Community
 Foundation
Stanley Spooner Deceased
 Charitable Trust
Trust for London
Tudor Trust
Unemployed Voluntary Action
 Fund
Wellfield Trust
Westminster Amalgamated
 Charity
Wiltshire and Swindon
 Community Foundation
Michael and Anna Wix
 Charitable Trust
Woodlands Trust (1015942)
Woodlands Trust (259569)
Worcester Municipal Charities
Wyseliot Charitable Trust

■ **People with an**
 alternative lifestyle,
 including travellers
 Funding priority
Community Foundation for
 Northern Ireland
Devon Community Foundation

Allen Lane Foundation
John Moores Foundation
Newby Trust Limited

Will consider
BBC Children in Need Appeal
Berkshire Community
 Foundation
Bridge House Estates Trust
 Fund
Carlton Television Trust
Charities Advisory Trust
City Parochial Foundation
Comic Relief
Derbyshire Community
 Foundation
Elmgrant Trust
Fiat Auto (UK) Charity
Harrison & Potter Trust
Charles Hayward Foundation
Heart of England Community
 Foundation
Hertfordshire Community
 Foundation
Hilden Charitable Fund
Sir James Knott Trust
Bryan Lancaster's Charity
Lintel Trust
Lloyds TSB Foundation for
 Northern Ireland
Lloyds TSB Foundation for
 Scotland
C F Lunoe Trust Fund
John Martin's Charity
Millfield House Foundation
Minge's Gift
Victor Mishcon Charitable
 Trust
Northern Rock Foundation
Odin Charitable Trust
Oxfordshire Community
 Foundation
Joseph & Lena Randall
 Charitable Trust
Rothley Trust
Joseph Rowntree Charitable
 Trust
Francis C Scott Charitable
 Trust
Frieda Scott Charitable Trust
Sir James & Lady Scott Trust
Scottish Churches Community
 Trust
Scottish Community
 Foundation
Servite Sisters' Charitable
 Trust Fund
South Yorkshire Community
 Foundation
Stanley Spooner Deceased
 Charitable Trust
Summerfield Charitable Trust
Tudor Trust
Unemployed Voluntary Action
 Fund
Wates Foundation

Wiltshire and Swindon
   Community Foundation
Worcester Municipal Charities

■ **People who are
unemployed
Funding priority**
Abel Charitable Trust
Carlton Television Trust
Celtic Charity Fund
Community Foundation for
   Northern Ireland
Community Fund
Construction Industry Trust for
   Youth
John Grant Davies Trust
Derbyshire Community
   Foundation
Dove-Bowerman Trust
Enkalon Foundation
Timothy Franey Charitable
   Foundation
Simon Gibson Charitable Trust
Greggs Trust
Hampton Fuel Allotment
   Charity
Holywood Trust
Isle of Dogs Community
   Foundation
Anton Jurgens Charitable Trust
Sir James Knott Trust
Lloyds TSB Foundation for the
   Channel Islands
Paul Lunn-Rockliffe Charitable
   Trust
Millfield House Foundation
Morgan Crucible Company plc
   Charitable Trust
Kitty and Daniel Nabarro
   Charitable Trust
Pilkington Charities Fund
J D Player Endowment Fund
Puri Foundation
Rosca Trust
Rothley Trust
Christopher Rowbotham
   Charitable Trust
Sir Walter St John's
   Educational Charity
St Peter's Saltley Trust
Walter Swindon Charitable
   Trust
Scurrah Wainwright Charity
Waterside Trust
Western Recreation Trust
Worcester Municipal Charities

Will consider
Abbey National Charitable
   Trust Ltd
Adnams Charity
Barnabas Charitable Trust
Church Urban Fund
Norman Collinson Charitable
   Trust
Comic Relief

Consortium on Opportunities
   for Volunteering
Coutts & Co. Charitable Trust
Cwmbran Trust
Charity of Thomas Dawson
Helen and Geoffrey de Freitas
   Charitable Trust
Dibden Allotments Charity
Douglas Charitable Trust
Dulverton Trust
Earley Charity
Essex Fairway Charitable Trust
Ferguson Benevolent Fund Ltd
Ford of Britain Trust
Patrick Frost Foundation
Robert Gavron Charitable Trust
Constance Green Foundation
Bishop of Guildford's
   Foundation
H C D Memorial Fund
Hadfield Trust
Hadrian Trust
Hale Trust
Harborne Parish Lands Charity
Charles Hayward Foundation
Dorothy Holmes Charitable
   Trust
House of Industry Estate
Housing Associations
   Charitable Trust
James Thom Howat Charitable
   Trust
Human Relief Foundation
Jesus Hospital Charity
Bryan Lancaster's Charity
Mrs F B Laurence Charitable
   Trust
Leigh Trust
Lintel Trust
Lloyds TSB Foundation for
   Northern Ireland
Lloyds TSB Foundation for
   Scotland
C F Lunoe Trust Fund
John Lyon's Charity
M N R Charitable Trust
R W Mann Trustees Limited
John Martin's Charity
Minge's Gift
Newby Trust Limited
Northern Rock Foundation
Norwich Consolidated
   Charities
Old Enfield Charitable Trust
Oxfordshire Community
   Foundation
Parthenon Trust
John Rayner Charitable Trust
Richmond Parish Lands Charity
Mrs L D Rope Third Charitable
   Settlement
Rowan Charitable Trust
Scott Bader Commonwealth
   Ltd
Henry Smith Charity
Leslie Smith Foundation

Sportsman's Charity
Wellfield Trust
White Rose Children's Aid
   International Charity
Michael and Anna Wix
   Charitable Trust
Woodlands Trust (1015942)
Woodlands Trust (259569)
Yardley Great Trust

....

■ **Victims, oppressed
people**
Funding priority
Ajahma Charitable Trust
Greater Bristol Foundation
Northern Rock Foundation
Thames Community
   Foundation

Will consider
Beaurepaire Trust
Bedford Charity
Bingham Trust
Morgan Blake Charitable Trust
William A Cadbury Charitable
   Trust
Commonwealth Relations
   Trust
County of Gloucestershire
   Community Foundation
Coutts & Co. Charitable Trust
Cripplegate Foundation
William Dudley Trust
Duis Charitable Trust
W E Dunn Trust
City of Edinburgh Charitable
   Trusts
Fidelity UK Foundation
Girdlers' Company Charitable
   Trust
Haramead Trust
Northcott Devon Foundation
Jack Petchey Foundation
Eleanor Rathbone Charitable
   Trust
Rayne Foundation
Richmond Parish Lands Charity
Sherburn House Charity
SMB Trust
Constance Travis Charitable
   Trust
Douglas Turner Trust

■ **Victims of abuse
Funding priority**
1970 Trust
Ardwick Trust
BBC Radio Cambridgeshire –
   Trustline
Burton Breweries Charitable
   Trust
Richard Cadbury Charitable
   Trust
Chase Charity

Trusts by fields of interest and types of beneficiary

Richard Cloudesley's Charity
Community Foundation for
Northern Ireland
Derbyshire Community
Foundation
Essex Community Foundation
Essex Fairway Charitable Trust
Fiat Auto (UK) Charity
Timothy Franey Charitable
Foundation
Angela Gallagher Memorial
Fund
Simon Gibson Charitable Trust
Global Care
Hampton Fuel Allotment
Charity
Joseph & Mary Hiley Trust
Jeffrey Charitable Trust
Jewish Child's Day
Johnson Group Cleaners
Charity
Sir James Knott Trust
Allen Lane Foundation
Lankelly Foundation
Leeds & Holbeck Building
Society Charitable
Foundation
Lintel Trust
Lloyds TSB Foundation for
Scotland
Lloyds TSB Foundation for the
Channel Islands
Marchday Charitable Fund
Mitchell Charitable Trust
Newby Trust Limited
Nova Charitable Trust
Patients' Aid Association
Hospital & Medical
Charities Trust
Austin & Hope Pilkington Trust
Portishead Nautical Trust
Saint Sarkis Charity Trust
Francis C Scott Charitable
Trust
Frieda Scott Charitable Trust
Sir James & Lady Scott Trust
Trades House of Glasgow
Warwickshire Masonic
Charitable Association Ltd
Wates Foundation
West Derby Wastelands
Charity
Women at Risk

Will consider
Adint Charitable Trust
Adnams Charity
Andrew Anderson Trust
Astor Foundation
Bartle Family Charitable Trust
BBC Children in Need Appeal
Berkshire Community
Foundation
Percy Bilton Charity Ltd
Birmingham Foundation

Birmingham Hospital Saturday
Fund Medical Charity &
Welfare Trust
Body Shop Foundation
Charles Boot Trust
P G & N J Boulton Trust
Bridge House Estates Trust
Fund
Bridge Trust
Buckinghamshire Masonic
Centenary Fund
Caring for Kids
Carlton Television Trust
Carnegie Dunfermline Trust
Wilfrid & Constance Cave
Foundation
Charities Advisory Trust
Chippenham Borough Lands
Charity
Church Urban Fund
City Parochial Foundation
J A Clark Charitable Trust
Clover Trust
Norman Collinson Charitable
Trust
Comic Relief
Congleton Inclosure Trust
County Durham Foundation
Cranbury Foundation
Harry Crook Foundation
Baron Davenport's Charity
Denton Charitable Trust
Emmandjay Charitable Trust
Enkalon Foundation
Esmée Fairbairn Foundation
David Finnie & Alan Emery
Charitable Trust
Earl Fitzwilliam Charitable
Trust
Ford of Britain Trust
Fox Memorial Trust
Charles S French Charitable
Trust
Girdlers' Company Charitable
Trust
Reginald Graham Charitable
Trust
J G Graves Charitable Trust
Grocers' Charity
Bishop of Guildford's
Foundation
Hadfield Trust
Hadrian Trust
Hampstead Wells and
Campden Trust
Harborne Parish Lands Charity
Harrison & Potter Trust
Gay & Peter Hartley's Hillards
Charitable Trust
N & P Hartley Memorial Trust
Charles Hayward Foundation
Heart of England Community
Foundation
Hemby Trust
Hertfordshire Community
Foundation

Hesslewood Children's Trust
Alan Edward Higgs Charity
Holywood Trust
Homelands Charitable Trust
Mary Homfray Charitable Trust
Hospital of God at Greatham
James Thom Howat Charitable
Trust
Hyde Charitable Trust
Inverforth Charitable Trust
Charles Irving Charitable Trust
Isle of Anglesey Charitable
Trust
Johnson Foundation
Joicey Trust
Edward Cecil Jones Settlement
Judith Trust
Boris Karloff Charitable
Foundation
Kleinwort Benson Charitable
Trust
Heinz & Anna Kroch
Foundation
Christopher Laing Foundation
Bryan Lancaster's Charity
Langdale Trust
Lauffer Family Charitable
Foundation
Raymond & Blanche Lawson
Charitable Trust
Lazard Charitable Trust
Leach Fourteenth Trust
Leigh Trust
Lord Leverhulme Charitable
Trust
W M & B W Lloyd Trust
Lloyds TSB Foundation for
England and Wales
Lloyds TSB Foundation for
Northern Ireland
London North East Community
Foundation
Loseley & Guildway Charitable
Trust
C F Lunoe Trust Fund
Lyndhurst Settlement
Mackintosh Foundation
R W Mann Trustees Limited
Hilda & Samuel Marks
Foundation
Sir George Martin Trust
John Martin's Charity
Mercers' Charitable
Foundation
Tony Metherell Charitable
Trust
Metropolitan Hospital-Sunday
Fund
Hugh and Mary Miller Bequest
Trust
Milton Keynes Community
Foundation
Minge's Gift
Victor Mishcon Charitable
Trust
Horace Moore Charitable Trust

J P Morgan Fleming
Educational Trust and
Foundation
Moss Family Charitable Trust
National Power Charitable
Trust
Nestlé Rowntree York
Employees Community Fund
Trust
Norman Family Charitable
Trust
Northern Rock Foundation
Old Enfield Charitable Trust
Kate Wilson Oliver Trust
Oxfordshire Community
Foundation
Parivar Trust
Arthur James Paterson
Charitable Trust
Constance Paterson Charitable
Trust
Harry Payne Trust
Philanthropic Trust
A M Pilkington's Charitable
Trust
Pilkington Charities Fund
Simone Prendergast Charitable
Trust
Princess Anne's Charities
Proven Family Trust
Mr and Mrs J A Pye's
Charitable Settlement
Rainford Trust
Joseph & Lena Randall
Charitable Trust
Ravensdale Trust
John Rayner Charitable Trust
Red Dragon Radio Trust
Rhododendron Trust
Rothley Trust
Christopher Rowbotham
Charitable Trust
Joseph Rowntree Foundation
St Laurence Charities for the
Poor
St Mary-le-Strand Charity
Scottish Community
Foundation
Sefton Community Foundation
Henry Smith Charity
Sobell Foundation
South Yorkshire Community
Foundation
Stanley Spooner Deceased
Charitable Trust
Sportsman's Charity
Staples Trust
Summerfield Charitable Trust
Bernard Sunley Charitable
Foundation
Unemployed Voluntary Action
Fund
War on Want
Wellfield Trust
Wesleyan Charitable Trust
Westcroft Trust

Wiltshire and Swindon
Community Foundation
Woodlands Trust (1015942)
Woodlands Trust (259569)
Woodward Trust
Worcester Municipal Charities
Wyseliot Charitable Trust
Yardley Great Trust
Yorkshire Building Society
Charitable Foundation

■ **Victims of crime**
Funding priority
1970 Trust
Ardwick Trust
BBC Radio Cambridgeshire –
Trustline
Burton Breweries Charitable
Trust
Richard Cadbury Charitable
Trust
Cleopatra Trust
Richard Cloudesley's Charity
Derbyshire Community
Foundation
Dorus Trust
Epigoni Trust
Essex Community Foundation
Essex Fairway Charitable Trust
Fiat Auto (UK) Charity
Simon Gibson Charitable Trust
Hampton Fuel Allotment
Charity
Heart of England Community
Foundation
Joseph & Mary Hiley Trust
Anton Jurgens Charitable Trust
Sir James Knott Trust
Leeds & Holbeck Building
Society Charitable
Foundation
Newby Trust Limited
Oakdale Trust
Ronald & Kathleen Pryor
Charitable Trust
Clive Richards Charity Ltd
Francis C Scott Charitable
Trust
Frieda Scott Charitable Trust
Sir James & Lady Scott Trust
Trades House of Glasgow
Wates Foundation
West Derby Wastelands
Charity

Will consider
Adint Charitable Trust
Adnams Charity
Andrew Anderson Trust
G C Armitage Charitable Trust
Astor Foundation
Lord Barnby's Foundation
Bartle Family Charitable Trust
BBC Children in Need Appeal
Berkshire Community
Foundation

Percy Bilton Charity Ltd
Bridge House Estates Trust
Fund
Bridge Trust
Bryant Trust
Buckinghamshire Masonic
Centenary Fund
Carnegie Dunfermline Trust
Wilfrid & Constance Cave
Foundation
Charities Advisory Trust
Chase Charity
Chippenham Borough Lands
Charity
Church Urban Fund
City Parochial Foundation
Clover Trust
Norman Collinson Charitable
Trust
Comic Relief
Congleton Inclosure Trust
County Durham Foundation
Cranbury Foundation
Harry Crook Foundation
Denton Charitable Trust
Emmandjay Charitable Trust
Enkalon Foundation
Esmée Fairbairn Foundation
Fidelity UK Foundation
David Finnie & Alan Emery
Charitable Trust
Earl Fitzwilliam Charitable
Trust
Ford of Britain Trust
Fox Memorial Trust
Charles S French Charitable
Trust
Girdlers' Company Charitable
Trust
J G Graves Charitable Trust
Grocers' Charity
Bishop of Guildford's
Foundation
Hadfield Trust
Hadrian Trust
Hampstead Wells and
Campden Trust
Harborne Parish Lands Charity
Harrison & Potter Trust
Gay & Peter Hartley's Hillards
Charitable Trust
N & P Hartley Memorial Trust
Charles Hayward Foundation
Hemby Trust
Hertfordshire Community
Foundation
Hesslewood Children's Trust
Joseph Hopkins Charity
James Thom Howat Charitable
Trust
Inverforth Charitable Trust
Charles Irving Charitable Trust
Isle of Anglesey Charitable
Trust
Jeffrey Charitable Trust
Joicey Trust

Boris Karloff Charitable
  Foundation
Kleinwort Benson Charitable
  Trust
Heinz & Anna Kroch
  Foundation
Christopher Laing Foundation
Bryan Lancaster's Charity
Langdale Trust
Lankelly Foundation
Raymond & Blanche Lawson
  Charitable Trust
Leigh Trust
Lord Leverhulme Charitable
  Trust
W M & B W Lloyd Trust
Lloyds TSB Foundation for
  England and Wales
Lloyds TSB Foundation for
  Northern Ireland
Lloyds TSB Foundation for the
  Channel Islands
London North East Community
  Foundation
C F Lunoe Trust Fund
Lyndhurst Settlement
R W Mann Trustees Limited
Hilda & Samuel Marks
  Foundation
Sir George Martin Trust
John Martin's Charity
Tony Metherell Charitable
  Trust
Hugh and Mary Miller Bequest
  Trust
Milton Keynes Community
  Foundation
Minge's Gift
Victor Mishcon Charitable
  Trust
George A Moore Foundation
National Power Charitable
  Trust
Nestlé Rowntree York
  Employees Community Fund
  Trust
Norman Family Charitable
  Trust
Northern Rock Foundation
Old Enfield Charitable Trust
Kate Wilson Oliver Trust
Oxfordshire Community
  Foundation
Arthur James Paterson
  Charitable Trust
Constance Paterson Charitable
  Trust
Harry Payne Trust
Philanthropic Trust
Bernard Piggott Trust
Pilkington Charities Fund
J S F Pollitzer Charitable
  Settlement
Princess Anne's Charities
Rainford Trust

Joseph & Lena Randall
  Charitable Trust
Ravensdale Trust
Rhododendron Trust
Rothley Trust
Christopher Rowbotham
  Charitable Trust
Joseph Rowntree Foundation
St Laurence Charities for the
  Poor
St Mary-le-Strand Charity
Scottish Community
  Foundation
Sefton Community Foundation
Shuttlewood Clarke Foundation
Henry Smith Charity
South Yorkshire Community
  Foundation
Stanley Spooner Deceased
  Charitable Trust
W W Spooner Charitable Trust
Sportsman's Charity
June Stevens Foundation
Summerfield Charitable Trust
Bernard Sunley Charitable
  Foundation
Douglas Turner Trust
Unemployed Voluntary Action
  Fund
War on Want
Mary Webb Trust
Wellfield Trust
Wesleyan Charitable Trust
Wiltshire and Swindon
  Community Foundation
Worcester Municipal Charities
Wyseliot Charitable Trust
Yardley Great Trust
York Children's Trust
Yorkshire Building Society
  Charitable Foundation

■ **Victims of domestic**
  violence
  Funding priority
1970 Trust
Balmore Trust
BBC Radio Cambridgeshire –
  Trustline
Burton Breweries Charitable
  Trust
Richard Cadbury Charitable
  Trust
Chase Charity
Cleopatra Trust
Richard Cloudesley's Charity
Community Foundation for
  Northern Ireland
Derbyshire Community
  Foundation
Dorus Trust
Epigoni Trust
Essex Community Foundation
Essex Fairway Charitable Trust
Fassnidge Memorial Trust
Fiat Auto (UK) Charity

Simon Gibson Charitable Trust
Hampton Fuel Allotment
  Charity
Housing Associations
  Charitable Trust
Johnson Group Cleaners
  Charity
Anton Jurgens Charitable Trust
Sir James Knott Trust
Allen Lane Foundation
Lankelly Foundation
Lawlor Foundation
Leeds & Holbeck Building
  Society Charitable
  Foundation
Lintel Trust
Lloyds TSB Foundation for the
  Channel Islands
Mitchell Charitable Trust
Newby Trust Limited
Nova Charitable Trust
Oxfordshire Community
  Foundation
Patients' Aid Association
  Hospital & Medical
  Charities Trust
Austin & Hope Pilkington Trust
Portishead Nautical Trust
Mr and Mrs J A Pye's
  Charitable Settlement
Rosca Trust
Francis C Scott Charitable
  Trust
Frieda Scott Charitable Trust
Sir James & Lady Scott Trust
Walter Swindon Charitable
  Trust
Trades House of Glasgow
Warwickshire Masonic
  Charitable Association Ltd
Wates Foundation
West Derby Wastelands
  Charity
Women at Risk

Will consider
Adint Charitable Trust
Adnams Charity
Ammco Trust
Andrew Anderson Trust
Ardwick Trust
Bartle Family Charitable Trust
BBC Children in Need Appeal
Berkshire Community
  Foundation
Percy Bilton Charity Ltd
Birmingham Foundation
Birmingham Hospital Saturday
  Fund Medical Charity &
  Welfare Trust
Body Shop Foundation
Charles Boot Trust
Bridge House Estates Trust
  Fund
Carlton Television Trust
Carnegie Dunfermline Trust

Wilfrid & Constance Cave
Foundation
Charities Advisory Trust
Chippenham Borough Lands
Charity
Church Urban Fund
City Parochial Foundation
Comic Relief
Congleton Inclosure Trust
Consortium on Opportunities
for Volunteering
Coppings Trust
County Durham Foundation
Cranbury Foundation
Harry Crook Foundation
Cwmbran Trust
Baron Davenport's Charity
John Grant Davies Trust
Denton Charitable Trust
Wilfred & Elsie Elkes Charity
Fund
Emmandjay Charitable Trust
Enkalon Foundation
Esmée Fairbairn Foundation
Ferguson Benevolent Fund Ltd
Fidelity UK Foundation
David Finnie & Alan Emery
Charitable Trust
Ford of Britain Trust
J Paul Getty Jr Charitable Trust
Girdlers' Company Charitable
Trust
Reginald Graham Charitable
Trust
J G Graves Charitable Trust
Grocers' Charity
Bishop of Guildford's
Foundation
Hadfield Trust
Hadrian Trust
Hampstead Wells and
Campden Trust
Lennox Hannay Charitable
Trust
Harborne Parish Lands Charity
Harrison & Potter Trust
Gay & Peter Hartley's Hillards
Charitable Trust
Charles Hayward Foundation
Heart of England Community
Foundation
Hemby Trust
Hertfordshire Community
Foundation
Alan Edward Higgs Charity
Homelands Charitable Trust
Hospital of God at Greatham
James Thom Howat Charitable
Trust
Huddersfield Common Good
Trust
Charles Irving Charitable Trust
Isle of Anglesey Charitable
Trust
Jeffrey Charitable Trust
Jephcott Charitable Trust

Joicey Trust
Edward Cecil Jones Settlement
Judith Trust
Kleinwort Benson Charitable
Trust
Heinz & Anna Kroch
Foundation
Christopher Laing Foundation
Bryan Lancaster's Charity
Langdale Trust
Lauffer Family Charitable
Foundation
Leach Fourteenth Trust
Kennedy Leigh Charitable
Trust
Lord Leverhulme Charitable
Trust
W M & B W Lloyd Trust
Lloyds TSB Foundation for
England and Wales
Lloyds TSB Foundation for
Northern Ireland
London North East Community
Foundation
C F Lunoe Trust Fund
Lyndhurst Settlement
Mackintosh Foundation
R W Mann Trustees Limited
Hilda & Samuel Marks
Foundation
Marr-Munning Trust
Sir George Martin Trust
John Martin's Charity
Tony Metherell Charitable
Trust
Hugh and Mary Miller Bequest
Trust
Milton Keynes Community
Foundation
Minge's Gift
Victor Mishcon Charitable
Trust
Mobbs Memorial Trust Ltd
John Moores Foundation
Moss Family Charitable Trust
National Power Charitable
Trust
Norman Family Charitable
Trust
Northern Rock Foundation
Norwich Consolidated
Charities
Old Enfield Charitable Trust
Kate Wilson Oliver Trust
Parivar Trust
Arthur James Paterson
Charitable Trust
Constance Paterson Charitable
Trust
Harry Payne Trust
Philanthropic Trust
Bernard Piggott Trust
Pilkington Charities Fund
Princess Anne's Charities
Proven Family Trust

Joseph & Lena Randall
Charitable Trust
Ravensdale Trust
John Rayner Charitable Trust
Red Dragon Radio Trust
Rhododendron Trust
Mrs L D Rope Third Charitable
Settlement
Rothley Trust
Christopher Rowbotham
Charitable Trust
Joseph Rowntree Foundation
St Laurence Charities for the
Poor
St Mary-le-Strand Charity
Scottish Community
Foundation
Sefton Community Foundation
Servite Sisters' Charitable
Trust Fund
Henry Smith Charity
Sobell Foundation
South Yorkshire Community
Foundation
Stanley Spooner Deceased
Charitable Trust
Sportsman's Charity
Staples Trust
Foundation of Edward Storey
Summerfield Charitable Trust
Bernard Sunley Charitable
Foundation
Triangle Trust (1949) Fund
Unemployed Voluntary Action
Fund
Wellfield Trust
Wesleyan Charitable Trust
Wiltshire and Swindon
Community Foundation
Woodlands Trust (1015942)
Woodlands Trust (259569)
Woodward Trust
Worcester Municipal Charities
Wyseliot Charitable Trust
Yardley Great Trust
Yorkshire Building Society
Charitable Foundation

■ Victims of disasters
Funding priority

BibleLands
P G & N J Boulton Trust
Audrey & Stanley Burton
Charitable Trust
Christadelphian Samaritan
Fund
Fiat Auto (UK) Charity
Angela Gallagher Memorial
Fund
Simon Gibson Charitable Trust
Grand Charity of Freemasons
Joanna Herbert-Stepney
Charitable Settlement
Joseph & Mary Hiley Trust
Jewish Child's Day
Anton Jurgens Charitable Trust

Paul Lunn-Rockliffe Charitable Trust
Lyras Family Charitable Trust
Millhouses Charitable Trust
Muslim Hands
Newby Trust Limited
Nova Charitable Trust
Novi Most International
Oakdale Trust
Patients' Aid Association Hospital & Medical Charities Trust
Philanthropic Trust
Austin & Hope Pilkington Trust
Schroder Charity Trust
Scouloudi Foundation
Three Oaks Trust
TRAID
John and Lucille van Geest Foundation
Verdon-Smith Family Charitable Settlement
Walton Foundation

Will consider
Alchemy Foundation
Ardwick Trust
Astor Foundation
Lord Barnby's Foundation
Bartle Family Charitable Trust
Benfield Motors Charitable Trust
Percy Bilton Charity Ltd
Boltons Trust
Bridge House Estates Trust Fund
Richard Cadbury Charitable Trust
Calpe Trust
Wilfrid & Constance Cave Foundation
Charities Advisory Trust
Chipping Sodbury Town Lands Charity
Christian Aid
Lord Clinton's Charitable Trust
Clover Trust
Congleton Inclosure Trust
County Durham Foundation
Cranbury Foundation
Cumber Family Charitable Trust
Helen and Geoffrey de Freitas Charitable Trust
Miriam K Dean Refugee Trust Fund
Denton Charitable Trust
Derbyshire Community Foundation
Diana, Princess of Wales Memorial Fund
Wilfred & Elsie Elkes Charity Fund
Emerton-Christie Charity
Emmandjay Charitable Trust

Earl Fitzwilliam Charitable Trust
Sydney E Franklin Deceased's New Second Charity
Maurice Fry Charitable Trust
Fund for Human Need
Robert Gavron Charitable Trust
Grocers' Charity
H C D Memorial Fund
Hampstead Wells and Campden Trust
Lennox Hannay Charitable Trust
Harrison & Potter Trust
Highmoor Hall Charitable Trust
Hinchley Charitable Trust
Human Relief Foundation
Inchrye Trust
Ruth & Lionel Jacobson Trust (Second Fund) No 2
Jeffrey Charitable Trust
Jerusalem Trust
Edward Cecil Jones Settlement
Sir James Knott Trust
Maurice Laing Foundation
Maurice and Hilda Laing Charitable Trust
Bryan Lancaster's Charity
Lauffer Family Charitable Foundation
Raymond & Blanche Lawson Charitable Trust
Leach Fourteenth Trust
Lintel Trust
Lloyd's Charities Trust
Loseley & Guildway Charitable Trust
C F Lunoe Trust Fund
Mackintosh Foundation
Marr-Munning Trust
Evelyn May Trust
Tony Metherell Charitable Trust
Hugh and Mary Miller Bequest Trust
Minge's Gift
Victor Mishcon Charitable Trust
Monmouthshire County Council Welsh Church Act Fund
Nestlé Rowntree York Employees Community Fund Trust
North London Islamic Association Trust
Oikonomia Trust
Old Enfield Charitable Trust
Oldham Foundation
Oxfam (GB)
Parthenon Trust
Harry Payne Trust
A M Pilkington's Charitable Trust
Pilkington Charities Fund
J S F Pollitzer Charitable Settlement

W L Pratt Charitable Trust
Princess Anne's Charities
Puri Foundation
Rainford Trust
Joseph & Lena Randall Charitable Trust
Rhododendron Trust
Rothley Trust
St Laurence Charities for the Poor
Scott Bader Commonwealth Ltd
Frieda Scott Charitable Trust
Sir James & Lady Scott Trust
Seedfield Trust
Sefton Community Foundation
Servite Sisters' Charitable Trust Fund
Stanley Spooner Deceased Charitable Trust
Tearfund
Tisbury Telegraph Trust
Douglas Turner Trust
Mary Webb Trust
Westcroft Trust
Whitecourt Charitable Trust
Michael and Anna Wix Charitable Trust
Worcester Municipal Charities
Wyseliot Charitable Trust
Zephyr Charitable Trust

■ **People suffering from famine**
Funding priority
P G & N J Boulton Trust
Audrey & Stanley Burton Charitable Trust
Celtic Charity Fund
Christadelphian Samaritan Fund
Dinam Charity
Edith M Ellis 1985 Charitable Trust
Norman Evershed Trust
Fiat Auto (UK) Charity
Fund for Human Need
Angela Gallagher Memorial Fund
Simon Gibson Charitable Trust
Global Care
Grand Charity of Freemasons
Joanna Herbert-Stepney Charitable Settlement
Anton Jurgens Charitable Trust
Paul Lunn-Rockliffe Charitable Trust
Marchday Charitable Fund
Millhouses Charitable Trust
Newby Trust Limited
Nova Charitable Trust
Oakdale Trust
Philanthropic Trust
Austin & Hope Pilkington Trust
Schroder Charity Trust
Sir James & Lady Scott Trust

Scouloudi Foundation
Three Oaks Trust
TRAID

Will consider
Adint Charitable Trust
Pat Allsop Charitable Trust
Ardwick Trust
Astor Foundation
Lord Barnby's Foundation
Bartle Family Charitable Trust
Benfield Motors Charitable
    Trust
Percy Bilton Charity Ltd
Richard Cadbury Charitable
    Trust
Calpe Trust
Wilfrid & Constance Cave
    Foundation
Charities Advisory Trust
Christian Aid
Clover Trust
Congleton Inclosure Trust
Cranbury Foundation
Cumber Family Charitable
    Trust
Helen and Geoffrey de Freitas
    Charitable Trust
Miriam K Dean Refugee Trust
    Fund
Denton Charitable Trust
Diana, Princess of Wales
    Memorial Fund
Wilfred & Elsie Elkes Charity
    Fund
Emmandjay Charitable Trust
Sydney E Franklin Deceased's
    New Second Charity
Maurice Fry Charitable Trust
Robert Gavron Charitable Trust
Constance Green Foundation
H C D Memorial Fund
Hampstead Wells and
    Campden Trust
Highmoor Hall Charitable Trust
Hilden Charitable Fund
Hinchley Charitable Trust
Human Relief Foundation
Ruth & Lionel Jacobson Trust
    (Second Fund) No 2
Jeffrey Charitable Trust
Jerusalem Trust
Sir James Knott Trust
Maurice Laing Foundation
Maurice and Hilda Laing
    Charitable Trust
Bryan Lancaster's Charity
Lauffer Family Charitable
    Foundation
Leach Fourteenth Trust
Levy Foundation
Lloyd's Charities Trust
C F Lunoe Trust Fund
Mackintosh Foundation
Marr-Munning Trust

Tony Metherell Charitable
    Trust
Hugh and Mary Miller Bequest
    Trust
Minge's Gift
Victor Mishcon Charitable
    Trust
Morel Charitable Trust
Nestlé Rowntree York
    Employees Community Fund
    Trust
North London Islamic
    Association Trust
Ogle Christian Trust
Oikonomia Trust
Oxfam (GB)
Parthenon Trust
A M Pilkington's Charitable
    Trust
Pilkington Charities Fund
W L Pratt Charitable Trust
Simone Prendergast Charitable
    Trust
Princess Anne's Charities
Puri Foundation
Rainford Trust
Joseph & Leña Randall
    Charitable Trust
Rhododendron Trust
Scott Bader Commonwealth
    Ltd
Seedfield Trust
Servite Sisters' Charitable
    Trust Fund
Stanley Spooner Deceased
    Charitable Trust
Tearfund
Westcroft Trust
Whitecourt Charitable Trust
Worcester Municipal Charities
Zephyr Charitable Trust

■ **People suffering
    injustice
    Funding priority**
Stephen Clark 1957
    Charitable Trust
Global Care
Tinsley Foundation

Will consider
Church Urban Fund
Comic Relief
Esmée Fairbairn Foundation
Sydney E Franklin Deceased's
    New Second Charity
Lyndhurst Settlement
Millfield House Foundation
Persula Foundation

■ **People suffering from
    racism or other
    discrimination
    Funding priority**
Hilden Charitable Fund
Allen Lane Foundation

John Moores Foundation
Tinsley Foundation

Will consider
Ardwick Trust
Charles Boot Trust
Church Urban Fund
Comic Relief
Esmée Fairbairn Foundation
Paul Hamlyn Foundation
Lawlor Foundation
Kennedy Leigh Charitable
    Trust
Lloyds TSB Foundation for
    England and Wales
Lyndhurst Settlement
Millfield House Foundation
Moss Family Charitable Trust
Oxfordshire Community
    Foundation
Rothley Trust

■ **People who have been
    tortured
    Funding priority**
Stephen Clark 1957
    Charitable Trust
Philanthropic Trust
Tinsley Foundation
TRAID

Will consider
BBC Children in Need Appeal
Charles Boot Trust
Bromley Trust
Comic Relief
Lyndhurst Settlement
Tisbury Telegraph Trust
Westcroft Trust

■ **Victims of war or conflict
    Funding priority**
Celtic Charity Fund
Christadelphian Samaritan
    Fund
Diana, Princess of Wales
    Memorial Fund
Edith M Ellis 1985 Charitable
    Trust
Fiat Auto (UK) Charity
Timothy Franey Charitable
    Foundation
Simon Gibson Charitable Trust
Global Care
Grand Charity of Freemasons
Harebell Centenary Fund
Joanna Herbert-Stepney
    Charitable Settlement
Joseph & Mary Hiley Trust
Jewish Child's Day
Anton Jurgens Charitable Trust
Sir James Knott Trust
Marchday Charitable Fund
Millhouses Charitable Trust
Muslim Hands
Newby Trust Limited

Nova Charitable Trust
Oakdale Trust
Philanthropic Trust
Austin & Hope Pilkington Trust
Queen Mary's Roehampton
    Trust
Schroder Charity Trust
Scouloudi Foundation
Walter Swindon Charitable
    Trust
Tinsley Foundation
Tisbury Telegraph Trust
TRAID

Will consider

Ammco Trust
Ardwick Trust
G C Armitage Charitable Trust
Astor Foundation
Lord Barnby's Foundation
BBC Children in Need Appeal
Benfield Motors Charitable
    Trust
Percy Bilton Charity Ltd
Charles Boot Trust
P G & N J Boulton Trust
Richard Cadbury Charitable
    Trust
Calpe Trust
Charities Advisory Trust
Christian Aid
Clover Trust
Comic Relief
Coppings Trust
Cranbury Foundation
Cumber Family Charitable
    Trust
Helen and Geoffrey de Freitas
    Charitable Trust
Miriam K Dean Refugee Trust
    Fund
Wilfred & Elsie Elkes Charity
    Fund
Emerton-Christie Charity
Emmandjay Charitable Trust
Sydney E Franklin Deceased's
    New Second Charity
Maurice Fry Charitable Trust
Fund for Human Need
Robert Gavron Charitable Trust
Constance Green Foundation
H C D Memorial Fund
Hampstead Wells and
    Campden Trust
Harrison & Potter Trust
Highmoor Hall Charitable Trust
Hinchley Charitable Trust
Mary Homfray Charitable Trust
Human Relief Foundation
Jeffrey Charitable Trust
Jephcott Charitable Trust
Jerusalem Trust
Heinz & Anna Kroch
    Foundation
Bryan Lancaster's Charity

Lauffer Family Charitable
    Foundation
Raymond & Blanche Lawson
    Charitable Trust
Leach Fourteenth Trust
Lintel Trust
C F Lunoe Trust Fund
Mackintosh Foundation
Tony Metherell Charitable
    Trust
Minge's Gift
Victor Mishcon Charitable
    Trust
Nestlé Rowntree York
    Employees Community Fund
    Trust
Oikonomia Trust
Oxfam (GB)
Parthenon Trust
Harry Payne Trust
A M Pilkington's Charitable
    Trust
Pilkington Charities Fund
Prairie Trust
W L Pratt Charitable Trust
Princess Anne's Charities
Puri Foundation
Joseph & Lena Randall
    Charitable Trust
Rothley Trust
Scott Bader Commonwealth
    Ltd
Frieda Scott Charitable Trust
Sir James & Lady Scott Trust
Seedfield Trust
Sefton Community Foundation
Servite Sisters' Charitable
    Trust Fund
Shipwrights Company
    Charitable Fund
Stanley Spooner Deceased
    Charitable Trust
Sportsman's Charity
Tearfund
Mrs Maud Van Norden's
    Charitable Foundation
Wates Foundation
Westcroft Trust
Worcester Municipal Charities
Zephyr Charitable Trust

Trusts by type
of grant

This index contains two separate listings:

List of types of grant: This lists all the headings used in the *DGMT* to categorise types of grant.

Trusts by type of grant: This lists trusts under the types of grant for which they have expressed a funding preference.

List of types of grant

Type of support

Core support 227

■ **Development funding 229**

....

■ **Strategic funding 230**

Capital support 230

■ **Building/renovation and adaption 231**

....

■ **Collections and acquisition 234**

....

■ **Computer systems and equipment 234**

....

■ **Equipment 237**

....

■ **Vehicles 241**

Project support 244

■ **Full project funding 249**

....

■ **Project funding 249**

....

■ **Seed funding 250**

....

■ **Feasibility 252**

Loan finance 253

Duration of grant

We have not listed those trusts that stated they gave one-off grants or grants for one year. Over half the trusts in the guide would have been included in such a list.

■ **Two years 254**

....

■ **Three years 256**

....

■ **Longer than three years 259**

Funding priority

Aberbrothock Charitable Trust
AIM Foundation
Air Charities Trust
Sir John & Lady Amory's
Charitable Trust
André Christian Trust
Ashendene Trust
Baker Charitable Trust
Barber Charitable Trust
Paul Bassham Charitable Trust
BBC Radio Cambridgeshire –
Trustline
Becketts & Sargeants
Educational Foundation
BibleLands
Bideford Bridge Trust
Sydney Black Charitable Trust
Blair Foundation
Charles Boot Trust
Bothwell Charitable Trust
Anthony Bourne Foundation
Roger Brooke Charitable Trust
R M 1956 Burton Charitable
Trust
Butchers' Company General
Charities
Cattanach Charitable Trust
Wilfrid & Constance Cave
Foundation
Chester Diocesan Moral Aid
Charity (St Bridget's Trust)
Cleary Foundation
Richard Cloudesley's Charity
Cobb Charity
Community Foundation Serving
Tyne & Wear and
Northumberland
Community Fund
Lord Cozens-Hardy Trust
Cross Trust
Demigryphon Trust
Earl of Derby's Charitable
Trust
Richard Desmond Charitable
Trust
Devon Community Foundation
Diana, Princess of Wales
Memorial Fund
Douglas Charitable Trust
Duis Charitable Trust
Edinburgh Voluntary
Organisations' Trust Funds
James Ellis Charitable Trust
Essex Community Foundation
Eveson Charitable Trust
Esmée Fairbairn Foundation
Famos Foundation Trust
Fiat Auto (UK) Charity
Four Acre Trust
Jill Franklin Trust
Angela Gallagher Memorial
Fund

E C Graham Belford Charitable
Settlement
Grahame Charitable
Foundation
Greater Bristol Foundation
Barry Green Memorial Fund
Greggs Trust
Kathleen Hannay Memorial
Charity
Lennox Hannay Charitable
Trust
William Harding's Charity
Harebell Centenary Fund
Hedgcock Bequest
Simon Heller Charitable
Settlement
Joseph & Mary Hiley Trust
Charles Littlewood Hill Trust
Lady Hind Trust
Mary Homfray Charitable Trust
Hospital of God at Greatham
Housing Associations
Charitable Trust
James Thom Howat Charitable
Trust
Inverforth Charitable Trust
ITF Seafarers Trust
James Trust
Jeffrey Charitable Trust
J G Joffe Charitable Trust
H F Johnson Trust
Jordan Charitable Foundation
Nancy Kenyon Charitable Trust
King George's Fund for Sailors
Mary Kinross Charitable Trust
Sir James Knott Trust
Allen Lane Foundation
Leathersellers' Company
Charitable Fund
Lethendy Charitable Trust
Lloyds TSB Foundation for the
Channel Islands
Marie Helen Luen Charitable
Trust
Paul Lunn-Rockliffe Charitable
Trust
Lyndhurst Settlement
Lynn Foundation
MacRobert Trust
W M Mann Foundation
Marchig Animal Welfare Trust
Marsh Christian Trust
Mayfield Valley Arts Trust
Mercury Phoenix Trust
Minge's Gift
Mitsubishi Corporation Fund
for Europe and Africa
John Moores Foundation
Oliver Morland Charitable Trust
Mount 'A' Charitable Trust
Mount 'B' Charitable Trust
Nestlé Rowntree York
Employees Community Fund
Trust
New Durlston Trust
P F Charitable Trust

Parivar Trust
Parthenon Trust
Arthur James Paterson
Charitable Trust
Personal Assurance Charitable
Trust
Philanthropic Trust
David Pickford Charitable
Foundation
Pilgrim Trust
A M Pilkington's Charitable
Trust
Austin & Hope Pilkington Trust
Pilkington Charities Fund
Ruben and Elisabeth Rausing
Trust
C A Redfern Charitable
Foundation
Jean Sainsbury Animal Welfare
Trust
Frieda Scott Charitable Trust
Sir James & Lady Scott Trust
SHINE
Bishop Simeon CR Trust
Sobell Foundation
Spitalfields Market Community
Trust
Tedworth Trust
Tinsley Foundation
Trades House of Glasgow
Constance Travis Charitable
Trust
VEC Acorn Trust
Verdon-Smith Family Charitable
Settlement
Vincent Wildlife Trust
Warwickshire Masonic
Charitable Association Ltd
Wentwood Education Trust
Alexander Pigott Wernher
Memorial Trust
West London Synagogue
Charitable Fund
Westminster Foundation
Lionel Wigram Memorial Trust
Women at Risk
Woo Charitable Foundation
Yapp Charitable Trust
I A Ziff Charitable Foundation

Will consider

1970 Trust
Acacia Charitable Trust
Adint Charitable Trust
Sylvia Aitken Charitable Trust
Ajahma Charitable Trust
Alexandra Rose Day
Dorothy Gertrude Allen
Memorial Fund
H B Allen Charitable Trust
Almond Trust
Arts Council of Wales
Aston Villa Charitable Trust
Baily Thomas Charitable Fund
Barracks Trust of Newcastle-
under-Lyme

Bear Mordechai Ltd
Bearder Charity
Beaufort House Trust
Bedford Charity (The Harpur Trust)
Billingsgate Christian Mission Charitable Trust
Bisgood Charitable Trust
Morgan Blake Charitable Trust
Blatchington Court Trust
Body Shop Foundation
Boltons Trust
Harry Bottom Charitable Trust
Bramble Charitable Trust
Bridge House Estates Trust Fund
John Bristow and Thomas Mason Trust
British Institute of Archaeology at Ankara
Britland Charitable Trust
Charles Brotherton Trust
Worshipful Company of Builders Merchants
Clara E Burgess Charity
Barrow Cadbury Trust and the Barrow Cadbury Fund
Cadbury Schweppes Foundation
William A Cadbury Charitable Trust
Carpenter Charitable Trust
Chapman Charitable Trust
Charities Advisory Trust
Chase Charity
Chelsea Building Society Charitable Foundation
Chippenham Borough Lands Charity
Church Urban Fund
Colchester & Tendring Community Trust
John & Freda Coleman Charitable Trust
Sir James Colyer-Fergusson's Charitable Trust
Comic Relief
Cooper Charitable Trust
Coppings Trust
County Durham Foundation
Cripplegate Foundation
Harry Crook Foundation
Cumber Family Charitable Trust
D'Oyly Carte Charitable Trust
Daily Telegraph Charitable Trust
Baron Davenport's Charity
Derbyshire Community Foundation
Community Council of Devon
Duke of Devonshire's Charitable Trust
Dibden Allotments Charity
DLA Charitable Trust
William Dudley Trust

Dumfries and Galloway Council Charitable Trusts
Dunhill Medical Trust
Harry Dunn Charitable Trust
Audrey Earle Charitable Trust
John Ellerman Foundation
Elmgrant Trust
Emerton-Christie Charity
Englefield Charitable Trust
Equitable Charitable Trust
Essex Fairway Charitable Trust
Fairbairn Charitable Trust
Lord Faringdon Charitable Trust
Fifty Fund
Fishmongers' Company's Charitable Trust
Timothy Franey Charitable Foundation
Gordon Fraser Charitable Trust
Worshipful Company of Furniture Makers Charitable Fund
Ganzoni Charitable Trust
Gatwick Airport Community Trust
J Paul Getty Jr Charitable Trust
G C Gibson Charitable Trust
Simon Gibson Charitable Trust
Global Care
Mrs Godfrey-Payton Trust
Golsoncott Foundation
J C Green Charitable Settlement
Gretna Charitable Trust
Grocers' Charity
H C D Memorial Fund
Paul Hamlyn Foundation
Hampstead Wells and Campden Trust
W A Handley Charitable Trust
Haramead Trust
Harborne Parish Lands Charity
R J Harris Charitable Settlement
Harrow Community Trust
N & P Hartley Memorial Trust
Dorothy Hay-Bolton Charitable Trust
May Hearnshaw's Charity
Hedley Denton Charitable Trust
Henley Educational Charity
Philip Henman Trust
Joanna Herbert-Stepney Charitable Settlement
Alan Edward Higgs Charity
Hilden Charitable Fund
Hinchley Charitable Trust
Holywood Trust
Miss Agnes H Hunter's Trust
Hyde Charitable Trust
Hyde Park Place Estate Charity
Idlewild Trust
Ingram Trust

Worshipful Company of Innholders General Charity Fund
Jarman Charitable Trust
Johnson Foundation
Johnson Group Cleaners Charity
Joicey Trust
Boris Karloff Charitable Foundation
Kleinwort Benson Charitable Trust
Marina Kleinwort Charitable Trust
Christopher Laing Foundation
Bryan Lancaster's Charity
Lankelly Foundation
Lauchentilly Charitable Foundation 1988
Lauffer Family Charitable Foundation
Mrs F B Laurence Charitable Trust
Lawlor Foundation
Lazard Charitable Trust
Mason Le Page Charitable Trust
Leach Fourteenth Trust
Kennedy Leigh Charitable Trust
Levy Foundation
Lloyds TSB Foundation for England and Wales
Lloyds TSB Foundation for Northern Ireland
Lloyds TSB Foundation for Scotland
London Law Trust
London North East Community Foundation
William & Katherine Longman Trust
Luck-Hille Foundation
R S MacDonald Charitable Trust
R W Mann Trustees Limited
Hilda & Samuel Marks Foundation
Mercers' Charitable Foundation
Gerald Micklem Charitable Trust
Midhurst Pensions Trust
Hugh and Mary Miller Bequest Trust
Morgan Stanley International Foundation
Morris Charitable Trust
Willie & Mabel Morris Charitable Trust
Stanley Morrison Charitable Trust
National Catholic Fund
Noel Buxton Trust
Norman Family Charitable Trust

Northern Rock Foundation
Oakdale Trust
Eleanor Palmer Trust
Constance Paterson Charitable
   Trust
Harry Payne Trust
Jack Petchey Foundation
Col W W Pilkington Will Trusts
Polden-Puckham Charitable
   Foundation
J S F Pollitzer Charitable
   Settlement
PPP Foundation
Prairie Trust
Primrose Hill Trust
Prince of Wales's Charitable
   Foundation
Princess Anne's Charities
Pyke Charity Trust
R V W Trust
Joseph Rank Trust
Eleanor Rathbone Charitable
   Trust
John Rayner Charitable Trust
Sir James Reckitt Charity
Christopher H R Reeves
   Charitable Trust
Violet M Richards Charity
Richmond Parish Lands Charity
Helen Roll Charitable Trust
Rotherwick Foundation
Joseph Rowntree Charitable
   Trust
Rufford Foundation
Russell Trust
Audrey Sacher Charitable Trust
Saddlers' Company Charitable
   Fund
St Katharine & Shadwell Trust
Scott Bader Commonwealth
   Ltd
Scottish Churches Community
   Trust
Searle Charitable Trust
Sherburn House Charity
Archie Sherman Cardiff
   Charitable Foundation
Shipwrights Company
   Charitable Fund
Skerritt Trust
SMB Trust
Henry Smith Charity
Stanley Smith UK Horticultural
   Trust
Spar Charitable Fund
Jessie Spencer Trust
Peter Stebbings Memorial
   Charity
Talbot Trusts
Tay Charitable Trust
A R Taylor Charitable Trust
Tesco Charity Trust
Third House Trust
Sue Thomson Foundation
Sir Jules Thorn Charitable
   Trust

Tisbury Telegraph Trust
Tory Family Foundation
Treeside Trust
Triangle Trust (1949) Fund
Tudor Trust
Douglas Turner Trust
R D Turner Charitable Trust
Valentine Charitable Trust
Voluntary Action Luton
Charity of Thomas Wade &
   Others
Robert and Felicity Waley-
   Cohen Charitable Trust
Ward Blenkinsop Trust
Wates Foundation
Bertie Watson Foundation
Webb Memorial Trust
Wellfield Trust
Westminster Amalgamated
   Charity
Whitaker Charitable Trust
Whitecourt Charitable Trust
Whitley Animal Protection Trust
Wiltshire and Swindon
   Community Foundation
Wixamtree Trust
Woodroffe Benton Foundation
Worcester Municipal Charities
Yorkshire Agricultural Society

....

■ Development
funding

Funding priority

Ambrose & Ann Appelbe Trust
Beacon Trust
Bristol Archdeaconry Charities
Camelot Foundation
Lance Coates Charitable Trust
   1969
Countryside Trust
Cowley Charitable Foundation
Denton Wilde Sapte Charitable
   Trust
Simon Digby (Sherborne)
   Memorial Trust
Dinwoodie Settlement
Hilden Charitable Fund
Clifford Howarth Charity
   Settlement
India Foundation (UK)
ITF Seafarers Trust
Miles Trust for the Putney and
   Roehampton Community
Ripple Effect Foundation
R C Sherriff Rosebriars Trust
Thames Community
   Foundation
Vincent Wildlife Trust
Weavers' Company Benevolent
   Fund
Welsh Church Fund –
   Carmarthenshire area
Wentwood Education Trust

Will consider
Sylvia Aitken Charitable Trust
Arts Council of Northern
   Ireland
Arts Council of Wales
Ashby Charitable Trust
Barbour Trust
Bingham Trust
Morgan Blake Charitable Trust
Boots Charitable Trust
John Bristow and Thomas
   Mason Trust
Edward Cadbury Charitable
   Trust
Edward & Dorothy Cadbury
   Trust (1928)
Cadbury Schweppes
   Foundation
Chase Charity
County of Gloucestershire
   Community Foundation
Denman Charitable Trust
Dulverton Trust
Edinburgh Voluntary
   Organisations' Trust Funds
Farmers Company Charitable
   Fund
Football Association National
   Sports Centre Trust
Worshipful Company of
   Furniture Makers Charitable
   Fund
Godinton Charitable Trust
H C D Memorial Fund
Hadfield Trust
Harborne Parish Lands Charity
Joseph Hopkins Charity
Christopher Laing Foundation
Lankelly Foundation
Lloyds TSB Foundation for
   Scotland
Margaret Foundation
Market Harborough and The
   Bowdens Charity
Mercers' Charitable
   Foundation
Music Sound Foundation
National Catholic Fund
Newport County Borough
   Welsh Church Fund
Ogle Christian Trust
Old Enfield Charitable Trust
Jack Petchey Foundation
Pilgrim Trust
Col W W Pilkington Will Trusts
Douglas Prestwich Charitable
   Trust
Pye Foundation
Christopher H R Reeves
   Charitable Trust
Cliff Richard Charitable Trust
Joseph Rowntree Charitable
   Trust
Sheldon Trust
Simpson Education &
   Conservation Trust

SMB Trust
Webb Memorial Trust
Whitley Animal Protection Trust
I A Ziff Charitable Foundation

....

■ Strategic funding

Funding priority

Casey Trust
Norman Evershed Trust
Clifford Howarth Charity
  Settlement
ITF Seafarers Trust
Panton Trust
Ripple Effect Foundation
Search
Thames Community
  Foundation
Douglas Turner Trust
Vincent Wildlife Trust

Will consider

Sylvia Aitken Charitable Trust
Arts Council of Wales
Ashby Charitable Trust
Barbour Trust
Bingham Trust
Morgan Blake Charitable Trust
Boots Charitable Trust
Bowerman Charitable Trust
John Bristow and Thomas
  Mason Trust
Chase Charity
Worshipful Company of
  Furniture Makers Charitable
  Fund
Hadfield Trust
Joseph Hopkins Charity
Christopher Laing Foundation
Lankelly Foundation
Lloyds TSB Foundation for
  Scotland
Margaret Foundation
Market Harborough and The
  Bowdens Charity
Mercers' Charitable
  Foundation
Miles Trust for the Putney and
  Roehampton Community
National Catholic Fund
Newport County Borough
  Welsh Church Fund
Jack Petchey Foundation
Pilgrim Trust
Pye Foundation
Christopher H R Reeves
  Charitable Trust
Cliff Richard Charitable Trust
Joseph Rowntree Charitable
  Trust
St Christopher's College
  Educational Trust
Sir Sigmund Sternberg
  Charitable Foundation
Webb Memorial Trust
Wentwood Education Trust

Whitley Animal Protection Trust

Capital support

Funding priority

Ashe Park Charitable Trust
Paul Bassham Charitable Trust
Thomas Betton's Charity
  (Educational)
Thomas Betton's Charity for
  Pensions and Relief-in-Need
Percy Bilton Charity Ltd
Bramble Charitable Trust
Roger Brooke Charitable Trust
E F Bulmer Benevolent Fund
Burton Breweries Charitable
  Trust
Community Foundation for
  Calderdale
John Cowan Foundation
Cross Trust
William Delafield Charitable
  Trust
Demigryphon Trust
Earl of Derby's Charitable
  Trust
Richard Desmond Charitable
  Trust
Douglas Charitable Trust
W G Edwards Charitable
  Foundation
Eveson Charitable Trust
Fairbairn Charitable Trust
Greater Bristol Foundation
Simon Heller Charitable
  Settlement
Hobart Charitable Trust
Mary Homfray Charitable Trust
Huddersfield Common Good
  Trust
Inland Waterways Association
Kidani Memorial Trust
Leeds & Holbeck Building
  Society Charitable
  Foundation
Kennedy Leigh Charitable
  Trust
Marie Helen Luen Charitable
  Trust
Lynn Foundation
MacRobert Trust
W M Mann Foundation
Marchig Animal Welfare Trust
Market Harborough and The
  Bowdens Charity
Monmouthshire County Council
  Welsh Church Act Fund
Oliver Morland Charitable Trust
New Durlston Trust
Parthenon Trust
Jack Patston Charitable Trust
Payne Charitable Trust
Prince Philip Trust Fund
Rooke Atlay Charitable Trust
Constance Travis Charitable
  Trust

VEC Acorn Trust
Warwickshire Masonic
  Charitable Association Ltd
West London Synagogue
  Charitable Fund
Lionel Wigram Memorial Trust
David Wilson Foundation
I A Ziff Charitable Foundation

Will consider

Sylvia Aitken Charitable Trust
Arts Council of Wales
Ashby Charitable Trust
Aston Villa Charitable Trust
Barbour Trust
Barracks Trust of Newcastle-
  under-Lyme
Bearder Charity
Bedford Charity (The Harpur
  Trust)
Billingsgate Christian Mission
  Charitable Trust
Morgan Blake Charitable Trust
Body Shop Foundation
John Bristow and Thomas
  Mason Trust
Bromley Trust
Arnold James Burton 1956
  Charitable Settlement
Carpenter Charitable Trust
Chelsea Building Society
  Charitable Foundation
John Coates Charitable Trust
Colchester & Tendring
  Community Trust
Criffel Charitable Trust
Cumber Family Charitable
  Trust
William Dean Countryside and
  Educational Trust
William Dudley Trust
Dumfries and Galloway Council
  Charitable Trusts
Esmée Fairbairn Foundation
Lord Faringdon Charitable
  Trust
Fishmongers' Company's
  Charitable Trust
Ganzoni Charitable Trust
Gatwick Airport Community
  Trust
G C Gibson Charitable Trust
Global Care
GMC Trust
Grantham Yorke Trust
Gretna Charitable Trust
Grocers' Charity
Hampton Fuel Allotment
  Charity
R J Harris Charitable
  Settlement
Hedgcock Bequest
Hedley Denton Charitable
  Trust
Philip Henman Trust
Alan Edward Higgs Charity

Hinchley Charitable Trust
Ingram Trust
Worshipful Company of
Innholders General Charity
Fund
Jarman Charitable Trust
Boris Karloff Charitable
Foundation
Christopher Laing Foundation
Kirby Laing Foundation
Mason Le Page Charitable
Trust
Lethendy Charitable Trust
William & Katherine Longman
Trust
Lyndhurst Settlement
Northern Rock Foundation
Norton Foundation
Col W W Pilkington Will Trusts
Primrose Hill Trust
Princess Anne's Charities
Pyke Charity Trust
Eleanor Rathbone Charitable
Trust
Sir James Reckitt Charity
Christopher H R Reeves
Charitable Trust
Richmond Parish Lands Charity
Audrey Sacher Charitable Trust
Leonard Laity Stoate
Charitable Trust
A R Taylor Charitable Trust
Tory Family Foundation
Douglas Turner Trust
Valentine Charitable Trust
Scurrah Wainwright Charity
Ward Blenkinsop Trust
Bertie Watson Foundation
Mary Webb Trust
Webb Memorial Trust
Wentwood Education Trust

....

■ Building/renovation and adaption

Funding priority

ADAPT Trust
Appletree Trust
Ashe Park Charitable Trust
Baird Trust
Balney Charitable Trust
BBC Radio Lincolnshire Charity
Trust
Bedfordshire & Hertfordshire
Historic Churches Trust
BibleLands
Birmingham Hospital Saturday
Fund Medical Charity &
Welfare Trust
Bishop's Development Fund
A H & E Boulton Trust
Anthony Bourne Foundation
Swinfen Broun Charitable Trust
Buckinghamshire Historic
Churches Trust
E F Bulmer Benevolent Fund

R M 1956 Burton Charitable
Trust
Cambridgeshire Historic
Churches Trust
Carmichael-Montgomery
Charitable Trust
Cattanach Charitable Trust
Wilfrid & Constance Cave
Foundation
Chase Charity
Stephen Clark 1957
Charitable Trust
Richard Cloudesley's Charity
Francis Coales Charitable
Foundation
Community Fund
Construction Industry Trust for
Youth
Cornwall Historic Churches
Trust
Cowley Charitable Foundation
William Delafield Charitable
Trust
Demigryphon Trust
J N Derbyshire Trust
Dinwoodie Settlement
Dorset Historic Churches Trust
Norman Evershed Trust
Ferguson Bequest Fund
Fiat Auto (UK) Charity
Bud Flanagan Leukaemia Fund
Football Association National
Sports Centre Trust
Four Acre Trust
Friends of Essex Churches
Friends of Kent Churches
Frognal Trust
Glasgow Conservation Trust
Gloucestershire Historic
Churches Trust
Grace Baptist Trust
Corporation
Constance Green Foundation
Kenneth Hargreaves Charitable
Trust
William Geoffrey Harvey's
Discretionary Settlement
Charles Hayward Foundation
Help the Homeless Ltd
Herefordshire Historic
Churches Trust
Heritage of London Trust Ltd
Edward Sydney Hogg
Charitable Settlement
Idlewild Trust
Incorporated Church Building
Society
Incorporated Leeds Church
Extension Society
Ironmongers' Quincentenary
Charitable Fund
James Pantyfedwen
Foundation
John Jarrold Trust
Edward Cecil Jones Settlement
Anton Jurgens Charitable Trust

Kelsick's Educational
Foundation
King George's Fund for Sailors
Leche Trust
Lincolnshire Old Churches
Trust
London Law Trust
Ronald McDonald Children's
Charities Limited
MacRobert Trust
Manifold Trust
Market Harborough and The
Bowdens Charity
Peter Minet Trust
Stanley Morrison Charitable
Trust
Norfolk Churches Trust Ltd
Northumbria Historic Churches
Trust
Norwood & Newton Settlement
Nottinghamshire Historic
Churches Trust
Ogilvie Charities Deed 2
Oxfordshire Historic Churches
Trust
P F Charitable Trust
Parivar Trust
Arthur James Paterson
Charitable Trust
Patrick Charitable Trust
Personal Assurance Charitable
Trust
Pilgrim Trust
Pilkington Charities Fund
Priory of Scotland of the Order
of St John of Jerusalem
Ruben and Elisabeth Rausing
Trust
Rayne Trust
Rochester Bridge Trust
Rosca Trust
Frieda Scott Charitable Trust
Scottish Churches
Architectural Heritage Trust
Scouloudi Foundation
Archie Sherman Charitable
Trust
Leslie Smith Foundation
Sobell Foundation
Foundation for Sport and the
Arts
Suffolk Historic Churches Trust
Tower Hill Improvement Trust
Mrs S H Troughton Charity
Trust
VEC Acorn Trust
Verdon-Smith Family Charitable
Settlement
Nigel Vinson Charitable Trust
Weavers' Company Benevolent
Fund
Welsh Church Fund –
Carmarthenshire area
Westminster Foundation
Edith & Isaac Wolfson
(Scotland) Trust

Wolfson Foundation
Yorkshire Historic Churches
    Trust
I A Ziff Charitable Foundation

Will consider
Adint Charitable Trust
Adnams Charity
AF Trust Company
Aid to the Church in Need (UK)
Sylvia Aitken Charitable Trust
Dorothy Gertrude Allen
    Memorial Fund
H B Allen Charitable Trust
Almond Trust
Ammco Trust
Viscount Amory's Charitable
    Trust
Milly Apthorp Charitable Trust
Ardwick Trust
Arts Council of England
Arts Council of Northern
    Ireland
Arts Council of Wales
Lord Ashdown Charitable Trust
Aston Charities Trust Limited
Astor Foundation
BAA 21st Century
    Communities Trust
Bacta Charitable Trust
Baily Thomas Charitable Fund
Baker Charitable Trust
William P Bancroft (No 2)
    Charitable Trust and
    Jenepher Gillett Trust
Barclays Stockbrokers
    Charitable Trust
Lord Barnby's Foundation
Barnes Workhouse Fund
Barnwood House Trust
Bartle Family Charitable Trust
BBC Children in Need Appeal
James Beattie Charitable Trust
Beaufort House Trust
Beit Trust
Hervey Benham Charitable
    Trust
Berkshire Community
    Foundation
Bingham Trust
Birmingham Foundation
Bisgood Charitable Trust
Herbert & Peter Blagrave
    Charitable Trust
Blanchminster Trust
Blatchington Court Trust
Peter Boizot Foundation
Bonhomie United Charity
    Society
Boots Charitable Trust
Bridge House Estates Trust
    Fund
Bridge Trust
John Bristow and Thomas
    Mason Trust

British Institute of Archaeology
    at Ankara
Britland Charitable Trust
Charles Brotherton Trust
Bryant Trust
Worshipful Company of
    Builders Merchants
Burdens Charitable Foundation
Clara E Burgess Charity
Geoffrey Burton Charitable
    Trust
Edward Cadbury Charitable
    Trust
Edward & Dorothy Cadbury
    Trust
Richard Cadbury Charitable
    Trust
William A Cadbury Charitable
    Trust
Campden Charities
Carnegie Dunfermline Trust
Leslie Mary Carter Charitable
    Trust
Chapman Charitable Trust
Charities Advisory Trust
Childwick Trust
Chippenham Borough Lands
    Charity
Chipping Sodbury Town Lands
    Charity
Chownes Foundation
Church Urban Fund
Cinderford Charitable Trust
CLA Charitable Trust
Clover Trust
Robert Clutterbuck Charitable
    Trust
George Henry Collins Charity
Sir James Colyer-Fergusson's
    Charitable Trust
Community Foundation Serving
    Tyne & Wear and
    Northumberland
Congleton Inclosure Trust
Cooper Charitable Trust
Holbeche Corfield Charitable
    Settlement
Lord Cozens-Hardy Trust
Cray Trust
Cripplegate Foundation
Harry Crook Foundation
D'Oyly Carte Charitable Trust
Baron Davenport's Charity
Gwendoline & Margaret Davies
    Charity
Richard Davies Charitable
    Foundation
Miriam K Dean Refugee Trust
    Fund
William Dean Countryside and
    Educational Trust
Denman Charitable Trust
Community Council of Devon
Duke of Devonshire's
    Charitable Trust
Dibden Allotments Charity

Simon Digby (Sherborne)
    Memorial Trust
Drapers' Charitable Fund
Dulverton Trust
Dunhill Medical Trust
W E Dunn Trust
Earley Charity
Wilfred & Elsie Elkes Charity
    Fund
Maud Elkington Charitable
    Trust
Elmley Foundation
Englass Charitable Trust
Englefield Charitable Trust
Equitable Charitable Trust
Equity Trust Fund
Essex Fairway Charitable Trust
Essex Heritage Trust
Alan Evans Memorial Trust
Samuel William Farmer's Trust
Ferguson Benevolent Fund Ltd
Fidelity UK Foundation
Finnart House School Trust
Earl Fitzwilliam Charitable
    Trust
Joyce Fletcher Charitable Trust
Ford of Britain Trust
Four Lanes Trust
Charles Henry Foyle Trust
Gordon Fraser Charitable Trust
Charles S French Charitable
    Trust
Freshgate Trust Foundation
Gannochy Trust
Gibbs Charitable Trusts
Simon Gibson Charitable Trust
Mrs Godfrey-Payton Trust
Godinton Charitable Trust
Golsoncott Foundation
J G Graves Charitable Trust
Barry Green Memorial Fund
Greggs Trust
Bishop of Guildford's
    Foundation
GWR Community Trust
H C D Memorial Fund
Hadfield Trust
Hadrian Trust
Robert Hall Charity
Hampstead Wells and
    Campden Trust
Hampton Fuel Allotment
    Charity
W A Handley Charitable Trust
Haramead Trust
Harborne Parish Lands Charity
Harrow Community Trust
N & P Hartley Memorial Trust
May Hearnshaw's Charity
Heart of England Community
    Foundation
Hedley Foundation
Hemby Trust
Hertfordshire Community
    Foundation
Hilden Charitable Fund

Edward Holt Trust
Holywood Trust
Joseph Hopkins Charity
Clifford Howarth Charity
   Settlement
Huddersfield Common Good
   Trust
Miss Agnes H Hunter's Trust
Hyde Charitable Trust
ITF Seafarers Trust
Ruth & Lionel Jacobson Trust
   (Second Fund) No 2
Jeffrey Charitable Trust
Jewish Youth Fund
Joicey Trust
Mary Kinross Charitable Trust
Kleinwort Benson Charitable
   Trust
Sir James Knott Trust
Knowles Charitable Trust
Kreitman Foundation
Late Sir Pierce Lacy Charity
   Trust
Beatrice Laing Trust
Laing's Charitable Trust
Maurice Laing Foundation
Maurice and Hilda Laing
   Charitable Trust
Richard Langhorn Trust
Lankelly Foundation
R J Larg Family Charitable
   Trust
Lauchentilly Charitable
   Foundation 1988
Lauffer Family Charitable
   Foundation
Raymond & Blanche Lawson
   Charitable Trust
Lazard Charitable Trust
Leach Fourteenth Trust
Leathersellers' Company
   Charitable Fund
Kennedy Leigh Charitable
   Trust
Leigh Trust
Leng Charitable Trust
Levy Foundation
Linden Charitable Trust
Lloyds TSB Foundation for
   Scotland
Lockerbie Trust
John Lyon's Charity
M N R Charitable Trust
R S MacDonald Charitable
   Trust
R W Mann Trustees Limited
Hilda & Samuel Marks
   Foundation
Sir George Martin Trust
John Martin's Charity
Mercers' Charitable
   Foundation
Mickel Fund
Miles Trust for the Putney and
   Roehampton Community

Hugh and Mary Miller Bequest
   Trust
Milton Keynes Community
   Foundation
Mobbs Memorial Trust Ltd
Monument Trust
George A Moore Foundation
John Moores Foundation
Peter Moores Foundation
Morris Charitable Trust
Moulton Charitable Trust
Edwina Mountbatten Trust
Music Sound Foundation
National Power Charitable
   Trust
Newby Trust Limited
Newport County Borough
   Welsh Church Fund
Norman Family Charitable
   Trust
North British Hotel Trust
Northcott Devon Foundation
Norwich Town Close Estate
   Charity
Notgrove Trust
Oakdale Trust
Oakley Charitable Trust
Odin Charitable Trust
Owen Family Trust
Pastoral Care Trust
Constance Paterson Charitable
   Trust
Harry Payne Trust
Austin & Hope Pilkington Trust
John Pitman Charitable Trust
J S F Pollitzer Charitable
   Settlement
Pontin Charitable Trust
Porter Foundation
Powell Foundation
Powys Welsh Church Fund
Douglas Prestwich Charitable
   Trust
Pye Foundation
Rainford Trust
Rank Foundation
Märit and Hans Rausing
   Charitable Foundation
Rayne Foundation
John Rayner Charitable Trust
Christopher H R Reeves
   Charitable Trust
Clive Richards Charity Ltd
Violet M Richards Charity
Helen Roll Charitable Trust
Rose Foundation
Rotherwick Foundation
Rothley Trust
Rowlands Trust
Royal Eastern Counties
   Schools Limited
Royal Victoria Hall Foundation
Rural Trust
Russell Trust
Karim Rida Said Foundation

Jean Sainsbury Animal Welfare
   Trust
St Andrew Animal Fund Ltd
Sir Walter St John's
   Educational Charity
St Mary-le-Strand Charity
Francis C Scott Charitable
   Trust
Sir James & Lady Scott Trust
Scottish Churches Community
   Trust
Scottish Community
   Foundation
Linley Shaw Foundation
Sheldon Trust
Sherburn House Charity
Shipwrights Company
   Charitable Fund
Shuttlewood Clarke Foundation
Mary Elizabeth Siebel Charity
Bishop Simeon CR Trust
SMB Trust
Henry Smith Charity
Mrs Smith & Mount Trust
Stanley Smith UK Horticultural
   Trust
David Solomons Charitable
   Trust
South Square Trust
Starfish Trust
Steinberg Family Charitable
   Trust
Stoller Charitable Trust
Alan Sugar Foundation
Bernard Sunley Charitable
   Foundation
Sutton Coldfield Municipal
   Charities
Stella Symons Charitable Trust
Talbot Trusts
Tay Charitable Trust
Thriplow Charitable Trust
Tisbury Telegraph Trust
Toy Trust
Tudor Trust
Douglas Turner Trust
R D Turner Charitable Trust
Ulverscroft Foundation
United St Saviour's Charities
Vale of Glamorgan Welsh
   Church Fund
John and Lucille van Geest
   Foundation
Eric W Vincent Trust Fund
Vodafone UK Foundation
Wakefield Trust
Wates Foundation
William Webster Charitable
   Trust
Wellfield Trust
Wentwood Education Trust
Wesleyan Charitable Trust
Westminster Amalgamated
   Charity
Garfield Weston Foundation
Whitaker Charitable Trust

Whitecourt Charitable Trust
Felicity Wilde Charitable Trust
Michael and Anna Wix
   Charitable Trust
Wixamtree Trust
Woodlands Trust (259569)
Worcester Municipal Charities
Yardley Great Trust
York Children's Trust
Yorkshire Agricultural Society

....

■ Collections and acquisition

Funding priority
R M 1956 Burton Charitable
   Trust
Harrow Community Trust
Market Harborough and The
   Bowdens Charity
National Art Collections Fund

Will consider
Sylvia Aitken Charitable Trust
Alexandra Rose Day
John Bristow and Thomas
   Mason Trust
CLA Charitable Trust
William Delafield Charitable
   Trust
Golsoncott Foundation
Charles Hayward Foundation
Newport County Borough
   Welsh Church Fund
Märit and Hans Rausing
   Charitable Foundation

....

■ Computer systems and equipment

Funding priority
Aberbrothock Charitable Trust
Appletree Trust
Ashe Park Charitable Trust
Balney Charitable Trust
Barron Bell Trust and
   Additional Fund
BBC Radio Lincolnshire Charity
   Trust
Bellahouston Bequest Fund
Thomas Betton's Charity
   (Educational)
BibleLands
Birmingham Hospital Saturday
   Fund Medical Charity &
   Welfare Trust
Birmingham International
   Airport Community Trust
Booth Charities
Harry Bottom Charitable Trust
Anthony Bourne Foundation
British Dietetic Association
   General and Education
   Trust Fund
British Humane Association

E F Bulmer Benevolent Fund
Cattanach Charitable Trust
CLA Charitable Trust
Cleopatra Trust
Richard Cloudesley's Charity
Cobb Charity
Cole Charitable Trust
Community Fund
Cooper Charitable Trust
Demigryphon Trust
J N Derbyshire Trust
Diana, Princess of Wales
   Memorial Fund
Dorus Trust
George Elias Charitable Trust
Ellinson Foundation Ltd
Enkalon Foundation
Epigoni Trust
Norman Evershed Trust
John Feeney Charitable
   Bequest
Fiat Auto (UK) Charity
Bud Flanagan Leukaemia Fund
Ford of Britain Trust
Thomas Freke & Lady Norton
   Charity
Frognal Trust
Good Neighbours Trust
GWR Community Trust
Handicapped Children's Aid
   Committee
Kathleen Hannay Memorial
   Charity
Lennox Hannay Charitable
   Trust
William Harding's Charity
Harris Charity
Harrow Community Trust
William Geoffrey Harvey's
   Discretionary Settlement
Charles Hayward Foundation
Headley Trust
Help the Homeless Ltd
Joseph & Mary Hiley Trust
Edward Sydney Hogg
   Charitable Settlement
Horne Foundation
Hospital of God at Greatham
Clifford Howarth Charity
   Settlement
HSA Charitable Trust
ITF Seafarers Trust
John Jarrold Trust
Edward Cecil Jones Settlement
Jordan Charitable Foundation
Kelsick's Educational
   Foundation
Nancy Kenyon Charitable Trust
Mary Kinross Charitable Trust
George John Livanos
   Charitable Trust
Liverpool Sailors' Home Trust
Lloyds TSB Foundation for the
   Channel Islands
London Law Trust
Lynwood Trust

Market Harborough and The
   Bowdens Charity
Mayfair Charities Ltd
James Frederick & Ethel Anne
   Measures Charity
Mercury Phoenix Trust
Metropolitan Hospital-Sunday
   Fund
Peter Minet Trust
F H Muirhead Charitable Trust
Music Sound Foundation
Kitty and Daniel Nabarro
   Charitable Trust
Norwich Town Close Estate
   Charity
Oxfordshire Community
   Foundation
Parivar Trust
Arthur James Paterson
   Charitable Trust
Pedmore Sporting Club Trust
   Fund
Penny in the Pound Fund
   Charitable Trust
Personal Assurance Charitable
   Trust
Pilkington Charities Fund
Powell Foundation
Priory of Scotland of the Order
   of St John of Jerusalem
Joseph & Lena Randall
   Charitable Trust
Muriel Edith Rickman Trust
Rochester Bridge Trust
Rosca Trust
Rothley Trust
Jean Sainsbury Animal Welfare
   Trust
St Francis Leprosy Guild
Saint Sarkis Charity Trust
Frieda Scott Charitable Trust
Sir James & Lady Scott Trust
Archie Sherman Charitable
   Trust
R C Sherriff Rosebriars Trust
Barbara A Shuttleworth
   Memorial Trust
Skelton Bounty
Skerritt Trust
Skinners' Company Lady
   Neville Charity
Leslie Smith Foundation
Snowball Trust
Sobell Foundation
David Solomons Charitable
   Trust
Southover Manor General
   Education Trust
Sportsman's Charity
Stanley Foundation Ltd
Thames Community
   Foundation
Trades House of Glasgow
Mayoress of Trafford's Charity
   Fund
David Uri Memorial Trust

Variety Club Children's Charity
Verdon-Smith Family Charitable
Settlement
Nigel Vinson Charitable Trust
Charity of Thomas Wade &
Others
John Watson's Trust
Weavers' Company Benevolent
Fund
Weldon UK Charitable Trust
Wentwood Education Trust
Westminster Foundation
Norman Whiteley Trust
Wiltshire and Swindon
Community Foundation
Edith & Isaac Wolfson
(Scotland) Trust
Wolfson Family Charitable
Trust
James Wood Bequest Fund
Yorkshire Agricultural Society

Will consider

Abbey National Charitable
Trust Ltd
Adint Charitable Trust
Adnams Charity
Aid to the Church in Need (UK)
Sylvia Aitken Charitable Trust
Alchemy Foundation
Alexandra Rose Day
Dorothy Gertrude Allen
Memorial Fund
H B Allen Charitable Trust
Mrs M H Allen Trust
Almond Trust
Viscount Amory's Charitable
Trust
Anglian Water Trust Fund
Animal Defence Trust
Milly Apthorp Charitable Trust
Ardwick Trust
Arts Council of England
Arts Council of Northern
Ireland
Arts Council of Wales
Lord Ashdown Charitable Trust
Aston Charities Trust Limited
Astor Foundation
BAA 21st Century
Communities Trust
Bacta Charitable Trust
Baily Thomas Charitable Fund
Barber Charitable Trust
Barbour Trust
Barclays Stockbrokers
Charitable Trust
Lord Barnby's Foundation
Barnes Workhouse Fund
Barnwood House Trust
Bartle Family Charitable Trust
BBC Children in Need Appeal
James Beattie Charitable Trust
John Beckwith Charitable Trust
Beit Trust

Berkshire Community
Foundation
Bingham Trust
Birmingham Foundation
Bisgood Charitable Trust
Herbert & Peter Blagrave
Charitable Trust
Blanchminster Trust
Blatchington Court Trust
Bonhomie United Charity
Society
Boots Charitable Trust
Viscountess Boyd Charitable
Trust
Bridge House Estates Trust
Fund
Bridge Trust
John Bristow and Thomas
Mason Trust
Britannia Building Society
Foundation
Britland Charitable Trust
Charles Brotherton Trust
Bryant Trust
Burdens Charitable Foundation
Clara E Burgess Charity
Geoffrey Burton Charitable
Trust
Richard Cadbury Charitable
Trust
William A Cadbury Charitable
Trust
Campden Charities
Carlton Television Trust
Carmichael-Montgomery
Charitable Trust
Carnegie Dunfermline Trust
Carnegie Trust for the
Universities of Scotland
Leslie Mary Carter Charitable
Trust
Joseph & Annie Cattle Trust
Chapman Charitable Trust
Charities Advisory Trust
Chase Charity
Chest Heart and Stroke
Scotland
Childwick Trust
Chippenham Borough Lands
Charity
Chipping Sodbury Town Lands
Charity
Chownes Foundation
Christabella Charitable Trust
Church Urban Fund
Cinderford Charitable Trust
City Parochial Foundation
Elizabeth Clark Charitable
Trust
Clothworkers' Foundation and
other Trusts
Clover Trust
Robert Clutterbuck Charitable
Trust
John & Freda Coleman
Charitable Trust

Sir James Colyer-Fergusson's
Charitable Trust
Comic Relief
Community Foundation Serving
Tyne & Wear and
Northumberland
Congleton Inclosure Trust
Consortium on Opportunities
for Volunteering
Cornwell Charitable Trust
County Durham Foundation
Cripplegate Foundation
Cripps Foundation
Harry Crook Foundation
Cwmbran Trust
D'Oyly Carte Charitable Trust
Baron Davenport's Charity
Gwendoline & Margaret Davies
Charity
John Grant Davies Trust
Richard Davies Charitable
Foundation
William Dean Countryside and
Educational Trust
William Delafield Charitable
Trust
Derbyshire Community
Foundation
Community Council of Devon
Devon Community Foundation
Duke of Devonshire's
Charitable Trust
Dibden Allotments Charity
Simon Digby (Sherborne)
Memorial Trust
Djanogly Foundation
Drapers' Charitable Fund
Duis Charitable Trust
Dulverton Trust
W E Dunn Trust
Earley Charity
Wilfred & Elsie Elkes Charity
Fund
Maud Elkington Charitable
Trust
Elmley Foundation
Englass Charitable Trust
Englefield Charitable Trust
Entindale Ltd
Epilepsy Research Foundation
Equitable Charitable Trust
Eranda Foundation
Ericson Trust
Erskine Cunningham Hill Trust
Essex Community Foundation
Essex Fairway Charitable Trust
Essex Heritage Trust
Feed the Minds
Ferguson Benevolent Fund Ltd
Fidelity UK Foundation
Fifty Fund
Finnart House School Trust
David Finnie & Alan Emery
Charitable Trust
Earl Fitzwilliam Charitable
Trust

Roy Fletcher Charitable Trust
Forte Charitable Trust
Four Lanes Trust
Charles Henry Foyle Trust
Gordon Fraser Charitable Trust
Joseph Strong Frazer Trust
Charles S French Charitable
Trust
Freshgate Trust Foundation
Gannochy Trust
Robert Gavron Charitable Trust
J Paul Getty Jr Charitable Trust
Gibbs Charitable Trusts
G C Gibson Charitable Trust
Simon Gibson Charitable Trust
Mrs Godfrey-Payton Trust
Golsoncott Foundation
Grahame Charitable
Foundation
J G Graves Charitable Trust
Barry Green Memorial Fund
Constance Green Foundation
Greggs Trust
Bishop of Guildford's
Foundation
Hadfield Trust
Hadrian Trust
Robert Hall Charity
Hampstead Wells and
Campden Trust
Hampton Fuel Allotment
Charity
W A Handley Charitable Trust
Harborne Parish Lands Charity
Kenneth Hargreaves Charitable
Trust
Gay & Peter Hartley's Hillards
Charitable Trust
N & P Hartley Memorial Trust
Hedgcock Bequest
Help the Aged
Hemby Trust
Henley Educational Charity
Joanna Herbert-Stepney
Charitable Settlement
Hertfordshire Community
Foundation
Dorothy Holmes Charitable
Trust
Edward Holt Trust
Holywood Trust
Joseph Hopkins Charity
Huddersfield Common Good
Trust
Hull & East Riding Charitable
Trust
Miss Agnes H Hunter's Trust
Hyde Charitable Trust
Hyde Park Place Estate Charity
Incorporated Leeds Church
Extension Society
Charles Irving Charitable Trust
Isle of Dogs Community
Foundation
James Pantyfedwen
Foundation

James Trust
Jeffrey Charitable Trust
Rees Jeffreys Road Fund
Jerusalem Trust
Jewish Child's Day
Jewish Youth Fund
Joicey Trust
Anton Jurgens Charitable Trust
William Kendall's Charity
King George's Fund for Sailors
Sir James Knott Trust
Knowles Charitable Trust
Kreitman Foundation
Neil Kreitman Foundation
Late Sir Pierce Lacy Charity
Trust
Beatrice Laing Trust
Bryan Lancaster's Charity
Lankelly Foundation
Lauchentilly Charitable
Foundation 1988
Lauffer Family Charitable
Foundation
Lazard Charitable Trust
Leach Fourteenth Trust
Leathersellers' Company
Charitable Fund
Kennedy Leigh Charitable
Trust
Leigh Trust
Leng Charitable Trust
Leukaemia Research Fund
Lord Leverhulme Charitable
Trust
Levy Foundation
Lewis Family Charitable Trust
Linden Charitable Trust
Lloyds TSB Foundation for
England and Wales
Lloyds TSB Foundation for
Northern Ireland
Lloyds TSB Foundation for
Scotland
Lockerbie Trust
Lofthouse Foundation
Luck-Hille Foundation
M N R Charitable Trust
R S MacDonald Charitable
Trust
Ronald McDonald Children's
Charities Limited
Mackintosh Foundation
Manchester Airport Community
Trust Fund
R W Mann Trustees Limited
Marchday Charitable Fund
Hilda & Samuel Marks
Foundation
Sir George Martin Trust
John Martin's Charity
Medlock Charitable Trust
Melville Trust for Care and
Cure of Cancer
Mercers' Charitable
Foundation
Mickel Fund

Middlesex County Rugby
Football Union Memorial
Fund
Milton Keynes Community
Foundation
Monument Trust
George A Moore Foundation
John Moores Foundation
Peter Moores Foundation
Morgan Crucible Company plc
Charitable Trust
J P Morgan Fleming
Educational Trust and
Foundation
Morgan Stanley International
Foundation
Morris Charitable Trust
Moulton Charitable Trust
Edwina Mountbatten Trust
National Power Charitable
Trust
Nemoral Ltd
Newby Trust Limited
Newport County Borough
Welsh Church Fund
Northcott Devon Foundation
Norwich Consolidated
Charities
Notgrove Trust
Oakdale Trust
Ogilvie Charities Deed 2
Owen Family Trust
Eleanor Palmer Trust
Pastoral Care Trust
Constance Paterson Charitable
Trust
Harry Payne Trust
Persula Foundation
Jack Petchey Foundation
Bernard Piggott Trust
Austin & Hope Pilkington Trust
John Pitman Charitable Trust
J S F Pollitzer Charitable
Settlement
Pontin Charitable Trust
Portishead Nautical Trust
Powys Welsh Church Fund
PPP Foundation
Prince Foundation
Prince of Wales's Charitable
Foundation
Pye Foundation
Mr and Mrs J A Pye's
Charitable Settlement
Queen Mary's Roehampton
Trust
Radio Forth Help a Child
Appeal
Rainford Trust
Rank Foundation
Märit and Hans Rausing
Charitable Foundation
John Rayner Charitable Trust
Red Dragon Radio Trust
Christopher H R Reeves
Charitable Trust

REMEDI
Violet M Richards Charity
Helen Roll Charitable Trust
Rotherwick Foundation
Christopher Rowbotham
    Charitable Trust
Rowlands Trust
Joseph Rowntree Charitable
    Trust
Royal Eastern Counties
    Schools Limited
Royal Victoria Hall Foundation
J B Rubens Charitable
    Foundation
Russell Trust
Saddlers' Company Charitable
    Fund
Karim Rida Said Foundation
Alan and Babette Sainsbury
    Charitable Fund
Robert and Lisa Sainsbury
    Charitable Trust
St Andrew Animal Fund Ltd
Saint Edmund, King & Martyr
    Trust
Sir Walter St John's
    Educational Charity
St Jude's Trust
St Katharine & Shadwell Trust
St Mary-le-Strand Charity
Salt Foundation
Scarfe Charitable Trust
Scott Bader Commonwealth
    Ltd
Francis C Scott Charitable
    Trust
Scottish Churches Community
    Trust
Scottish Community
    Foundation
Seedfield Trust
Cyril Shack Trust
Sheldon Trust
Sherburn House Charity
Shipwrights Company
    Charitable Fund
Shuttlewood Clarke Foundation
Mary Elizabeth Siebel Charity
Bishop Simeon CR Trust
SMB Trust
Henry Smith Charity
Smith (Haltwhistle & District)
    Charitable Trust
Mrs Smith & Mount Trust
Stanley Smith UK Horticultural
    Trust
South Square Trust
South Yorkshire Community
    Foundation
Jessie Spencer Trust
Foundation for Sport and the
    Arts
Educational Charity of the
    Stationers' and Newspaper
    Makers' Company

Peter Stebbings Memorial
    Charity
Steinberg Family Charitable
    Trust
Stoller Charitable Trust
Strangward Trust
W O Street Charitable
    Foundation
Alan Sugar Foundation
Bernard Sunley Charitable
    Foundation
Sutton Coldfield Municipal
    Charities
Swan Mountain Trust
Swan Trust
Stella Symons Charitable Trust
Talbot Trusts
C Paul Thackray General
    Charitable Trust
Thriplow Charitable Trust
Tisbury Telegraph Trust
Triangle Trust (1949) Fund
Tudor Trust
Douglas Turner Trust
R D Turner Charitable Trust
TUUT Charitable Trust
Ulverscroft Foundation
United St Saviour's Charities
John and Lucille van Geest
    Foundation
Eric W Vincent Trust Fund
Vodafone UK Foundation
Voluntary Action Luton
Wales Council for Voluntary
    Action
Thomas Wall Trust
Wates Foundation
William Webster Charitable
    Trust
Wellfield Trust
Wesleyan Charitable Trust
Charity of John West & Others
Western Recreation Trust
Westminster Amalgamated
    Charity
Garfield Weston Foundation
Whitaker Charitable Trust
Whitecourt Charitable Trust
Felicity Wilde Charitable Trust
Will Charitable Trust
Harold Hyam Wingate
    Foundation
Wixamtree Trust
Wolfson Foundation
Woodlands Trust (259569)
Worcester Municipal Charities
Yardley Great Trust
I A Ziff Charitable Foundation
Zurich Financial Services
    Community Trust

···

■ Equipment
Funding priority
Aberbrothock Charitable Trust
Appletree Trust

Ashe Park Charitable Trust
Balney Charitable Trust
Barron Bell Trust and
    Additional Fund
BBC Radio Lincolnshire Charity
    Trust
Bellahouston Bequest Fund
Thomas Betton's Charity
    (Educational)
BibleLands
Birmingham Hospital Saturday
    Fund Medical Charity &
    Welfare Trust
Birmingham International
    Airport Community Trust
Bishop's Development Fund
Sydney Black Charitable Trust
Booth Charities
Harry Bottom Charitable Trust
Anthony Bourne Foundation
British Humane Association
E F Bulmer Benevolent Fund
Cattanach Charitable Trust
Wilfrid & Constance Cave
    Foundation
CLA Charitable Trust
Cleopatra Trust
Richard Cloudesley's Charity
Cobb Charity
Cole Charitable Trust
Community Foundation for
    Greater Manchester
Community Fund
Cooper Charitable Trust
Demigryphon Trust
Denton Wilde Sapte Charitable
    Trust
J N Derbyshire Trust
Diana, Princess of Wales
    Memorial Fund
Dorus Trust
George Elias Charitable Trust
Ellinson Foundation Ltd
Enkalon Foundation
Epigoni Trust
Norman Evershed Trust
John Feeney Charitable
    Bequest
Fiat Auto (UK) Charity
Bud Flanagan Leukaemia Fund
Ford of Britain Trust
Four Acre Trust
Thomas Freke & Lady Norton
    Charity
Frognal Trust
Good Neighbours Trust
GWR Community Trust
Handicapped Children's Aid
    Committee
Kathleen Hannay Memorial
    Charity
Lennox Hannay Charitable
    Trust
William Harding's Charity
Harris Charity
Harrow Community Trust

William Geoffrey Harvey's
Discretionary Settlement
Charles Hayward Foundation
Headley Trust
Help the Homeless Ltd
Joseph & Mary Hiley Trust
Edward Sydney Hogg
Charitable Settlement
Horne Foundation
Hospital of God at Greatham
Clifford Howarth Charity
Settlement
HSA Charitable Trust
Ironmongers' Quincentenary
Charitable Fund
ITF Seafarers Trust
John Jarrold Trust
Edward Cecil Jones Settlement
Jordan Charitable Foundation
Kelsick's Educational
Foundation
Nancy Kenyon Charitable Trust
Mary Kinross Charitable Trust
George John Livanos
Charitable Trust
Liverpool Sailors' Home Trust
London Law Trust
Lynwood Trust
Market Harborough and The
Bowdens Charity
Mayfair Charities Ltd
James Frederick & Ethel Anne
Measures Charity
Mercury Phoenix Trust
Metropolitan Hospital-Sunday
Fund
Peter Minet Trust
Mugdock Children's Trust
F H Muirhead Charitable Trust
Music Sound Foundation
North West Cancer Research
Fund
Norwich Town Close Estate
Charity
Oxfordshire Community
Foundation
Parivar Trust
Arthur James Paterson
Charitable Trust
Patients' Aid Association
Hospital & Medical
Charities Trust
Pedmore Sporting Club Trust
Fund
Penny in the Pound Fund
Charitable Trust
Personal Assurance Charitable
Trust
Pilkington Charities Fund
Powell Foundation
Priory of Scotland of the Order
of St John of Jerusalem
Elise Randall Educational Trust
Joseph & Lena Randall
Charitable Trust
Muriel Edith Rickman Trust

Rochester Bridge Trust
Rosca Trust
Rothley Trust
Jean Sainsbury Animal Welfare
Trust
St Francis Leprosy Guild
Saint Sarkis Charity Trust
Frieda Scott Charitable Trust
Sir James & Lady Scott Trust
Search
Archie Sherman Charitable
Trust
R C Sherriff Rosebriars Trust
Barbara A Shuttleworth
Memorial Trust
Skelton Bounty
Skerritt Trust
Skinners' Company Lady
Neville Charity
Leslie Smith Foundation
Snowball Trust
Sobell Foundation
David Solomons Charitable
Trust
Southover Manor General
Education Trust
Foundation for Sport and the
Arts
Sportsman's Charity
Stanley Foundation Ltd
Thames Community
Foundation
Trades House of Glasgow
Mayoress of Trafford's Charity
Fund
David Uri Memorial Trust
Variety Club Children's Charity
Verdon-Smith Family Charitable
Settlement
Nigel Vinson Charitable Trust
Charity of Thomas Wade &
Others
John Watson's Trust
Weavers' Company Benevolent
Fund
Weldon UK Charitable Trust
Welsh Church Fund –
Carmarthenshire area
Wentwood Education Trust
Westminster Foundation
Norman Whiteley Trust
Wiltshire and Swindon
Community Foundation
Edith & Isaac Wolfson
(Scotland) Trust
Wolfson Family Charitable
Trust
James Wood Bequest Fund
Yorkshire Agricultural Society
Yorkshire Building Society
Charitable Foundation

Will consider
Abbey National Charitable
Trust Ltd
Adint Charitable Trust

Adnams Charity
Aid to the Church in Need (UK)
Sylvia Aitken Charitable Trust
Alchemy Foundation
Alexandra Rose Day
Dorothy Gertrude Allen
Memorial Fund
H B Allen Charitable Trust
Mrs M H Allen Trust
Almond Trust
Viscount Amory's Charitable
Trust
Anglian Water Trust Fund
Animal Defence Trust
Milly Apthorp Charitable Trust
Ardwick Trust
Arts Council of England
Arts Council of Northern
Ireland
Arts Council of Wales
Lord Ashdown Charitable Trust
Aston Charities Trust Limited
Astor Foundation
BAA 21st Century
Communities Trust
Bacta Charitable Trust
Baily Thomas Charitable Fund
Barber Charitable Trust
Barbour Trust
Barclays Stockbrokers
Charitable Trust
Lord Barnby's Foundation
Barnes Workhouse Fund
Barnwood House Trust
Bartle Family Charitable Trust
BBC Children in Need Appeal
James Beattie Charitable Trust
John Beckwith Charitable Trust
Beit Trust
Hervey Benham Charitable
Trust
Berkshire Community
Foundation
Bingham Trust
Birmingham Foundation
Bisgood Charitable Trust
Herbert & Peter Blagrave
Charitable Trust
Blanchminster Trust
Blatchington Court Trust
Peter Boizot Foundation
Bonhomie United Charity
Society
Boots Charitable Trust
Viscountess Boyd Charitable
Trust
Bridge House Estates Trust
Fund
Bridge Trust
John Bristow and Thomas
Mason Trust
Britannia Building Society
Foundation
Britland Charitable Trust
Charles Brotherton Trust
Bryant Trust

Burdens Charitable Foundation
Clara E Burgess Charity
Geoffrey Burton Charitable Trust
Edward Cadbury Charitable Trust
Edward & Dorothy Cadbury Trust
Richard Cadbury Charitable Trust
William A Cadbury Charitable Trust
Campden Charities
Carlton Television Trust
Carmichael-Montgomery Charitable Trust
Carnegie Dunfermline Trust
Carnegie Trust for the Universities of Scotland
Leslie Mary Carter Charitable Trust
Joseph & Annie Cattle Trust
Chapman Charitable Trust
Charities Advisory Trust
Chase Charity
Chest Heart and Stroke Scotland
Childwick Trust
Chippenham Borough Lands Charity
Chipping Sodbury Town Lands Charity
Chownes Foundation
Christabella Charitable Trust
Church Urban Fund
Cinderford Charitable Trust
City Parochial Foundation
Elizabeth Clark Charitable Trust
Clothworkers' Foundation and other Trusts
Clover Trust
Robert Clutterbuck Charitable Trust
John & Freda Coleman Charitable Trust
Sir James Colyer-Fergusson's Charitable Trust
Comic Relief
Community Foundation Serving Tyne & Wear and Northumberland
Congleton Inclosure Trust
Consortium on Opportunities for Volunteering
Cornwell Charitable Trust
Cotton Trust
County Durham Foundation
County of Gloucestershire Community Foundation
Lord Cozens-Hardy Trust
Cray Trust
Cripplegate Foundation
Cripps Foundation
Harry Crook Foundation
Cwmbran Trust

D'Oyly Carte Charitable Trust
Baron Davenport's Charity
Gwendoline & Margaret Davies Charity
John Grant Davies Trust
Richard Davies Charitable Foundation
William Dean Countryside and Educational Trust
Derbyshire Community Foundation
Community Council of Devon
Devon Community Foundation
Duke of Devonshire's Charitable Trust
Dibden Allotments Charity
Simon Digby (Sherborne) Memorial Trust
Djanogly Foundation
Drapers' Charitable Fund
Dulverton Trust
Dunhill Medical Trust
W E Dunn Trust
Earley Charity
Edinburgh Voluntary Organisations' Trust Funds
Wilfred & Elsie Elkes Charity Fund
Maud Elkington Charitable Trust
Elmley Foundation
Englass Charitable Trust
Englefield Charitable Trust
Entindale Ltd
Epilepsy Research Foundation
Equitable Charitable Trust
Eranda Foundation
Ericson Trust
Erskine Cunningham Hill Trust
Essex Community Foundation
Essex Fairway Charitable Trust
Essex Heritage Trust
Feed the Minds
Ferguson Benevolent Fund Ltd
Fidelity UK Foundation
Fifty Fund
Finnart House School Trust
David Finnie & Alan Emery Charitable Trust
Earl Fitzwilliam Charitable Trust
Roy Fletcher Charitable Trust
Forte Charitable Trust
Four Lanes Trust
Charles Henry Foyle Trust
Gordon Fraser Charitable Trust
Joseph Strong Frazer Trust
Charles S French Charitable Trust
Freshgate Trust Foundation
Gannochy Trust
Robert Gavron Charitable Trust
J Paul Getty Jr Charitable Trust
Gibbs Charitable Trusts
G C Gibson Charitable Trust
Simon Gibson Charitable Trust

Mrs Godfrey-Payton Trust
Godinton Charitable Trust
Golsoncott Foundation
Grahame Charitable Foundation
J G Graves Charitable Trust
Barry Green Memorial Fund
Constance Green Foundation
Greggs Trust
Bishop of Guildford's Foundation
Hadfield Trust
Hadrian Trust
Robert Hall Charity
Hampstead Wells and Campden Trust
Hampton Fuel Allotment Charity
W A Handley Charitable Trust
Haramead Trust
Harborne Parish Lands Charity
Kenneth Hargreaves Charitable Trust
Gay & Peter Hartley's Hillards Charitable Trust
N & P Hartley Memorial Trust
Heart of England Community Foundation
Hedgcock Bequest
Hedley Foundation
Help the Aged
Hemby Trust
Henley Educational Charity
Joanna Herbert-Stepney Charitable Settlement
Hertfordshire Community Foundation
Hilden Charitable Fund
Dorothy Holmes Charitable Trust
Edward Holt Trust
Holywood Trust
Joseph Hopkins Charity
Huddersfield Common Good Trust
Hull & East Riding Charitable Trust
Miss Agnes H Hunter's Trust
Hyde Charitable Trust
Hyde Park Place Estate Charity
Incorporated Leeds Church Extension Society
Charles Irving Charitable Trust
Isle of Dogs Community Foundation
Sir Barry Jackson Trust and County Fund
James Pantyfedwen Foundation
James Trust
Jeffrey Charitable Trust
Rees Jeffreys Road Fund
Jerusalem Trust
Jesus Hospital Charity
Jewish Child's Day
Jewish Youth Fund

Joicey Trust
Anton Jurgens Charitable Trust
William Kendall's Charity
Peter Kershaw Trust
King George's Fund for Sailors
Sir James Knott Trust
Knowles Charitable Trust
Kreitman Foundation
Neil Kreitman Foundation
Late Sir Pierce Lacy Charity
  Trust
Beatrice Laing Trust
Laing's Charitable Trust
Maurice Laing Foundation
Maurice and Hilda Laing
  Charitable Trust
Bryan Lancaster's Charity
Lankelly Foundation
Lauchentilly Charitable
  Foundation 1988
Lauffer Family Charitable
  Foundation
Lawlor Foundation
Lazard Charitable Trust
Leach Fourteenth Trust
Leathersellers' Company
  Charitable Fund
Kennedy Leigh Charitable
  Trust
Leigh Trust
Leng Charitable Trust
Leukaemia Research Fund
Lord Leverhulme Charitable
  Trust
Levy Foundation
Lewis Family Charitable Trust
Linden Charitable Trust
Lloyds TSB Foundation for
  England and Wales
Lloyds TSB Foundation for
  Northern Ireland
Lloyds TSB Foundation for
  Scotland
Lloyds TSB Foundation for the
  Channel Islands
Lockerbie Trust
Lofthouse Foundation
Luck-Hille Foundation
John Lyon's Charity
M N R Charitable Trust
R S MacDonald Charitable
  Trust
Ronald McDonald Children's
  Charities Limited
Mackintosh Foundation
Manchester Airport Community
  Trust Fund
R W Mann Trustees Limited
Marchday Charitable Fund
Hilda & Samuel Marks
  Foundation
Sir George Martin Trust
John Martin's Charity
Medlock Charitable Trust
Melville Trust for Care and
  Cure of Cancer

Mercers' Charitable
  Foundation
Mickel Fund
Gerald Micklem Charitable
  Trust
Middlesex County Rugby
  Football Union Memorial
  Fund
Milton Keynes Community
  Foundation
Monument Trust
George A Moore Foundation
John Moores Foundation
Peter Moores Foundation
Morgan Crucible Company plc
  Charitable Trust
J P Morgan Fleming
  Educational Trust and
  Foundation
Morgan Stanley International
  Foundation
Morris Charitable Trust
Willie & Mabel Morris
  Charitable Trust
Moulton Charitable Trust
Edwina Mountbatten Trust
National Power Charitable
  Trust
Nemoral Ltd
Newby Trust Limited
Newport County Borough
  Welsh Church Fund
North British Hotel Trust
Northcott Devon Foundation
Norwich Consolidated
  Charities
Notgrove Trust
Oakdale Trust
Odin Charitable Trust
Ogilvie Charities Deed 2
Owen Family Trust
Eleanor Palmer Trust
Pastoral Care Trust
Constance Paterson Charitable
  Trust
Harry Payne Trust
Persula Foundation
Jack Petchey Foundation
Bernard Piggott Trust
Austin & Hope Pilkington Trust
John Pitman Charitable Trust
J S F Pollitzer Charitable
  Settlement
Pontin Charitable Trust
Portishead Nautical Trust
Powys Welsh Church Fund
PPP Foundation
Prince Foundation
Prince of Wales's Charitable
  Foundation
Pye Foundation
Queen Mary's Roehampton
  Trust
Radio Forth Help a Child
  Appeal
Rainford Trust

Rank Foundation
Rayne Foundation
John Rayner Charitable Trust
Red Dragon Radio Trust
Christopher H R Reeves
  Charitable Trust
REMEDI
Cliff Richard Charitable Trust
Violet M Richards Charity
Helen Roll Charitable Trust
Rotherwick Foundation
Christopher Rowbotham
  Charitable Trust
Rowlands Trust
Royal Eastern Counties
  Schools Limited
Royal Victoria Hall Foundation
J B Rubens Charitable
  Foundation
Russell Trust
Saddlers' Company Charitable
  Fund
Karim Rida Said Foundation
Alan and Babette Sainsbury
  Charitable Fund
Robert and Lisa Sainsbury
  Charitable Trust
St Andrew Animal Fund Ltd
Saint Edmund, King & Martyr
  Trust
Sir Walter St John's
  Educational Charity
St Jude's Trust
St Katharine & Shadwell Trust
St Mary-le-Strand Charity
Salt Foundation
Scarfe Charitable Trust
Scott Bader Commonwealth
  Ltd
Francis C Scott Charitable
  Trust
Scottish Churches Community
  Trust
Scottish Community
  Foundation
Scottish International
  Education Trust
Seedfield Trust
Cyril Shack Trust
Sheldon Trust
Sherburn House Charity
Shipwrights Company
  Charitable Fund
Shuttlewood Clarke Foundation
Mary Elizabeth Siebel Charity
Bishop Simeon CR Trust
SMB Trust
Henry Smith Charity
Smith (Haltwhistle & District)
  Charitable Trust
Stanley Smith UK Horticultural
  Trust
South Square Trust
South Yorkshire Community
  Foundation
Jessie Spencer Trust

Educational Charity of the
Stationers' and Newspaper
Makers' Company
Peter Stebbings Memorial
Charity
Steinberg Family Charitable
Trust
Stoller Charitable Trust
Strangward Trust
W O Street Charitable
Foundation
Alan Sugar Foundation
Bernard Sunley Charitable
Foundation
Sutton Coldfield Municipal
Charities
Swan Mountain Trust
Swan Trust
Stella Symons Charitable Trust
Talbot Trusts
C Paul Thackray General
Charitable Trust
Sue Thomson Foundation
Treeside Trust
Triangle Trust (1949) Fund
Tudor Trust
Douglas Turner Trust
R D Turner Charitable Trust
TUUT Charitable Trust
Ulverscroft Foundation
United St Saviour's Charities
John and Lucille van Geest
Foundation
Eric W Vincent Trust Fund
Vodafone UK Foundation
Voluntary Action Luton
Wales Council for Voluntary
Action
Thomas Wall Trust
Wates Foundation
Webb Memorial Trust
William Webster Charitable
Trust
Wellfield Trust
Wesleyan Charitable Trust
Charity of John West & Others
Westcroft Trust
Western Recreation Trust
Westminster Amalgamated
Charity
Garfield Weston Foundation
Whitaker Charitable Trust
Whitecourt Charitable Trust
Felicity Wilde Charitable Trust
Will Charitable Trust
Harold Hyam Wingate
Foundation
Wixamtree Trust
Wolfson Foundation
Woodlands Trust (259569)
Worcester Municipal Charities
Yardley Great Trust
I A Ziff Charitable Foundation
Zurich Financial Services
Community Trust

■ Vehicles

Funding priority

Aberbrothock Charitable Trust
Appletree Trust
Ashe Park Charitable Trust
Balney Charitable Trust
Barron Bell Trust and
Additional Fund
BBC Radio Lincolnshire Charity
Trust
Bellahouston Bequest Fund
BibleLands
Birmingham Hospital Saturday
Fund Medical Charity &
Welfare Trust
Birmingham International
Airport Community Trust
Sydney Black Charitable Trust
Booth Charities
Harry Bottom Charitable Trust
Anthony Bourne Foundation
British Humane Association
E F Bulmer Benevolent Fund
Cattanach Charitable Trust
Cleopatra Trust
Richard Cloudesley's Charity
Cobb Charity
Cole Charitable Trust
Community Fund
Cooper Charitable Trust
Demigryphon Trust
J N Derbyshire Trust
Diana, Princess of Wales
Memorial Fund
Dorus Trust
George Elias Charitable Trust
Ellinson Foundation Ltd
Enkalon Foundation
Epigoni Trust
Norman Evershed Trust
John Feeney Charitable
Bequest
Fiat Auto (UK) Charity
Ford of Britain Trust
Thomas Freke & Lady Norton
Charity
Frognal Trust
Good Neighbours Trust
GWR Community Trust
Handicapped Children's Aid
Committee
Kathleen Hannay Memorial
Charity
Lennox Hannay Charitable
Trust
Harris Charity
William Geoffrey Harvey's
Discretionary Settlement
Charles Hayward Foundation
Headley Trust
Help the Homeless Ltd
Joseph & Mary Hiley Trust
Edward Sydney Hogg
Charitable Settlement
Horne Foundation
Hospital of God at Greatham

Clifford Howarth Charity
Settlement
HSA Charitable Trust
John Jarrold Trust
Edward Cecil Jones Settlement
Jordan Charitable Foundation
Nancy Kenyon Charitable Trust
Mary Kinross Charitable Trust
George John Livanos
Charitable Trust
Liverpool Sailors' Home Trust
London Law Trust
Lynwood Trust
Market Harborough and The
Bowdens Charity
Mayfair Charities Ltd
James Frederick & Ethel Anne
Measures Charity
Mercury Phoenix Trust
Metropolitan Hospital-Sunday
Fund
Norwich Town Close Estate
Charity
Oxfordshire Community
Foundation
Parivar Trust
Arthur James Paterson
Charitable Trust
Pedmore Sporting Club Trust
Fund
Penny in the Pound Fund
Charitable Trust
Personal Assurance Charitable
Trust
Pilkington Charities Fund
Powell Foundation
Priory of Scotland of the Order
of St John of Jerusalem
Joseph & Lena Randall
Charitable Trust
Muriel Edith Rickman Trust
Rochester Bridge Trust
Rosca Trust
Rothley Trust
Jean Sainsbury Animal Welfare
Trust
St Francis Leprosy Guild
Saint Sarkis Charity Trust
Frieda Scott Charitable Trust
Sir James & Lady Scott Trust
Archie Sherman Charitable
Trust
R C Sherriff Rosebriars Trust
Barbara A Shuttleworth
Memorial Trust
Skelton Bounty
Skerritt Trust
Skinners' Company Lady
Neville Charity
Leslie Smith Foundation
Snowball Trust
Sobell Foundation
David Solomons Charitable
Trust
Southover Manor General
Education Trust

Foundation for Sport and the
Arts
Sportsman's Charity
Stanley Foundation Ltd
Trades House of Glasgow
Mayoress of Trafford's Charity
Fund
David Uri Memorial Trust
Variety Club Children's Charity
Verdon-Smith Family Charitable
Settlement
Nigel Vinson Charitable Trust
Charity of Thomas Wade &
Others
John Watson's Trust
Weldon UK Charitable Trust
Welsh Church Fund –
Carmarthenshire area
Westminster Foundation
Norman Whiteley Trust
Wiltshire and Swindon
Community Foundation
Edith & Isaac Wolfson
(Scotland) Trust
Wolfson Family Charitable
Trust
James Wood Bequest Fund
Yorkshire Agricultural Society

Will consider

Abbey National Charitable
Trust Ltd
Adint Charitable Trust
Adnams Charity
Aid to the Church in Need (UK)
Sylvia Aitken Charitable Trust
Alchemy Foundation
Dorothy Gertrude Allen
Memorial Fund
H B Allen Charitable Trust
Mrs M H Allen Trust
Almond Trust
Viscount Amory's Charitable
Trust
Anglian Water Trust Fund
Animal Defence Trust
Milly Apthorp Charitable Trust
Ardwick Trust
Arts Council of England
Arts Council of Northern
Ireland
Arts Council of Wales
Lord Ashdown Charitable Trust
Aston Charities Trust Limited
Astor Foundation
BAA 21st Century
Communities Trust
Bacta Charitable Trust
Baily Thomas Charitable Fund
Barber Charitable Trust
Barbour Trust
Barclays Stockbrokers
Charitable Trust
Lord Barnby's Foundation
Barnes Workhouse Fund
Barnwood House Trust

Bartle Family Charitable Trust
BBC Children in Need Appeal
James Beattie Charitable Trust
John Beckwith Charitable Trust
Berkshire Community
Foundation
Bingham Trust
Bisgood Charitable Trust
Herbert & Peter Blagrave
Charitable Trust
Blanchminster Trust
Blatchington Court Trust
Bonhomie United Charity
Society
Viscountess Boyd Charitable
Trust
Bridge House Estates Trust
Fund
Bridge Trust
John Bristow and Thomas
Mason Trust
Britannia Building Society
Foundation
Britland Charitable Trust
Charles Brotherton Trust
Bryant Trust
Burdens Charitable Foundation
Clara E Burgess Charity
Geoffrey Burton Charitable
Trust
Richard Cadbury Charitable
Trust
William A Cadbury Charitable
Trust
Campden Charities
Carlton Television Trust
Carmichael-Montgomery
Charitable Trust
Carnegie Dunfermline Trust
Carnegie Trust for the
Universities of Scotland
Leslie Mary Carter Charitable
Trust
Joseph & Annie Cattle Trust
Chapman Charitable Trust
Charities Advisory Trust
Chest Heart and Stroke
Scotland
Childwick Trust
Chippenham Borough Lands
Charity
Chipping Sodbury Town Lands
Charity
Chownes Foundation
Christabella Charitable Trust
Church Urban Fund
Cinderford Charitable Trust
City Parochial Foundation
Elizabeth Clark Charitable
Trust
Clothworkers' Foundation and
other Trusts
Clover Trust
Robert Clutterbuck Charitable
Trust

John & Freda Coleman
Charitable Trust
Sir James Colyer-Fergusson's
Charitable Trust
Comic Relief
Community Foundation Serving
Tyne & Wear and
Northumberland
Congleton Inclosure Trust
Consortium on Opportunities
for Volunteering
Cornwell Charitable Trust
Cotton Trust
County Durham Foundation
Cripplegate Foundation
Cripps Foundation
Harry Crook Foundation
Cwmbran Trust
D'Oyly Carte Charitable Trust
Baron Davenport's Charity
Gwendoline & Margaret Davies
Charity
John Grant Davies Trust
Richard Davies Charitable
Foundation
William Dean Countryside and
Educational Trust
Derbyshire Community
Foundation
Community Council of Devon
Duke of Devonshire's
Charitable Trust
Dibden Allotments Charity
Simon Digby (Sherborne)
Memorial Trust
Djanogly Foundation
Drapers' Charitable Fund
Dulverton Trust
W E Dunn Trust
Earley Charity
Wilfred & Elsie Elkes Charity
Fund
Maud Elkington Charitable
Trust
Elmley Foundation
Englass Charitable Trust
Englefield Charitable Trust
Entindale Ltd
Eranda Foundation
Ericson Trust
Erskine Cunningham Hill Trust
Essex Community Foundation
Essex Fairway Charitable Trust
Essex Heritage Trust
Feed the Minds
Ferguson Benevolent Fund Ltd
Fidelity UK Foundation
Fifty Fund
Finnart House School Trust
David Finnie & Alan Emery
Charitable Trust
Earl Fitzwilliam Charitable
Trust
Roy Fletcher Charitable Trust
Forte Charitable Trust
Four Lanes Trust

Gordon Fraser Charitable Trust
Joseph Strong Frazer Trust
Charles S French Charitable
   Trust
Freshgate Trust Foundation
Gannochy Trust
Robert Gavron Charitable Trust
J Paul Getty Jr Charitable Trust
Gibbs Charitable Trusts
G C Gibson Charitable Trust
Simon Gibson Charitable Trust
Mrs Godfrey-Payton Trust
Grahame Charitable
   Foundation
J G Graves Charitable Trust
Barry Green Memorial Fund
Constance Green Foundation
Greggs Trust
Bishop of Guildford's
   Foundation
Hadfield Trust
Hadrian Trust
Robert Hall Charity
Hampstead Wells and
   Campden Trust
Hampton Fuel Allotment
   Charity
W A Handley Charitable Trust
Haramead Trust
Harborne Parish Lands Charity
Kenneth Hargreaves Charitable
   Trust
Harrow Community Trust
Gay & Peter Hartley's Hillards
   Charitable Trust
N & P Hartley Memorial Trust
Heart of England Community
   Foundation
Help the Aged
Hemby Trust
Joanna Herbert-Stepney
   Charitable Settlement
Hertfordshire Community
   Foundation
Dorothy Holmes Charitable
   Trust
Holywood Trust
Joseph Hopkins Charity
Huddersfield Common Good
   Trust
Hull & East Riding Charitable
   Trust
Miss Agnes H Hunter's Trust
Hyde Charitable Trust
Hyde Park Place Estate Charity
Incorporated Leeds Church
   Extension Society
Isle of Dogs Community
   Foundation
ITF Seafarers Trust
Sir Barry Jackson Trust and
   County Fund
James Pantyfedwen
   Foundation
James Trust
Jeffrey Charitable Trust

Rees Jeffreys Road Fund
Jerusalem Trust
Jesus Hospital Charity
Jewish Child's Day
Jewish Youth Fund
Joicey Trust
Anton Jurgens Charitable Trust
William Kendall's Charity
King George's Fund for Sailors
Sir James Knott Trust
Knowles Charitable Trust
Kreitman Foundation
Neil Kreitman Foundation
Late Sir Pierce Lacy Charity
   Trust
Beatrice Laing Trust
Maurice Laing Foundation
Maurice and Hilda Laing
   Charitable Trust
Bryan Lancaster's Charity
Lauchentilly Charitable
   Foundation 1988
Lauffer Family Charitable
   Foundation
Lazard Charitable Trust
Leach Fourteenth Trust
Kennedy Leigh Charitable
   Trust
Leigh Trust
Leng Charitable Trust
Leukaemia Research Fund
Lord Leverhulme Charitable
   Trust
Levy Foundation
Lewis Family Charitable Trust
Linden Charitable Trust
Lloyds TSB Foundation for
   England and Wales
Lloyds TSB Foundation for
   Northern Ireland
Lloyds TSB Foundation for
   Scotland
Lloyds TSB Foundation for the
   Channel Islands
Lockerbie Trust
Lofthouse Foundation
Luck-Hille Foundation
M N R Charitable Trust
R S MacDonald Charitable
   Trust
Ronald McDonald Children's
   Charities Limited
Mackintosh Foundation
Manchester Airport Community
   Trust Fund
R W Mann Trustees Limited
Marchday Charitable Fund
Hilda & Samuel Marks
   Foundation
Sir George Martin Trust
John Martin's Charity
Medlock Charitable Trust
Melville Trust for Care and
   Cure of Cancer
Mercers' Charitable
   Foundation

Mickel Fund
Gerald Micklem Charitable
   Trust
Middlesex County Rugby
   Football Union Memorial
   Fund
Milton Keynes Community
   Foundation
Monument Trust
George A Moore Foundation
Peter Moores Foundation
Morgan Crucible Company plc
   Charitable Trust
J P Morgan Fleming
   Educational Trust and
   Foundation
Morgan Stanley International
   Foundation
Morris Charitable Trust
Moulton Charitable Trust
Edwina Mountbatten Trust
Music Sound Foundation
National Power Charitable
   Trust
Nemoral Ltd
Newby Trust Limited
Newport County Borough
   Welsh Church Fund
North British Hotel Trust
Northcott Devon Foundation
Norwich Consolidated
   Charities
Notgrove Trust
Oakdale Trust
Odin Charitable Trust
Ogilvie Charities Deed 2
Owen Family Trust
Eleanor Palmer Trust
Pastoral Care Trust
Constance Paterson Charitable
   Trust
Harry Payne Trust
Persula Foundation
Jack Petchey Foundation
Bernard Piggott Trust
Austin & Hope Pilkington Trust
John Pitman Charitable Trust
J S F Pollitzer Charitable
   Settlement
Pontin Charitable Trust
Portishead Nautical Trust
Prince Foundation
Prince of Wales's Charitable
   Foundation
Pye Foundation
Queen Mary's Roehampton
   Trust
Radio Forth Help a Child
   Appeal
Rainford Trust
Rank Foundation
Märit and Hans Rausing
   Charitable Foundation
John Rayner Charitable Trust
Red Dragon Radio Trust

Christopher H R Reeves
 Charitable Trust
Cliff Richard Charitable Trust
Violet M Richards Charity
Helen Roll Charitable Trust
Rotherwick Foundation
Christopher Rowbotham
 Charitable Trust
Rowlands Trust
Royal Eastern Counties
 Schools Limited
Royal Victoria Hall Foundation
J B Rubens Charitable
 Foundation
Russell Trust
Saddlers' Company Charitable
 Fund
Karim Rida Said Foundation
Alan and Babette Sainsbury
 Charitable Fund
Robert and Lisa Sainsbury
 Charitable Trust
St Andrew Animal Fund Ltd
Saint Edmund, King & Martyr
 Trust
Sir Walter St John's
 Educational Charity
St Jude's Trust
St Katharine & Shadwell Trust
St Mary-le-Strand Charity
Salt Foundation
Scarfe Charitable Trust
Scott Bader Commonwealth
 Ltd
Francis C Scott Charitable
 Trust
Scottish Churches Community
 Trust
Scottish Community
 Foundation
Seedfield Trust
Cyril Shack Trust
Sherburn House Charity
Shipwrights Company
 Charitable Fund
Shuttlewood Clarke Foundation
Mary Elizabeth Siebel Charity
Bishop Simeon CR Trust
SMB Trust
Henry Smith Charity
Smith (Haltwhistle & District)
 Charitable Trust
Stanley Smith UK Horticultural
 Trust
South Yorkshire Community
 Foundation
Jessie Spencer Trust
Educational Charity of the
 Stationers' and Newspaper
 Makers' Company
Peter Stebbings Memorial
 Charity
Steinberg Family Charitable
 Trust
Stoller Charitable Trust
Strangward Trust

W O Street Charitable
 Foundation
Alan Sugar Foundation
Bernard Sunley Charitable
 Foundation
Sutton Coldfield Municipal
 Charities
Swan Trust
Stella Symons Charitable Trust
Talbot Trusts
C Paul Thackray General
 Charitable Trust
Triangle Trust (1949) Fund
Tudor Trust
Douglas Turner Trust
R D Turner Charitable Trust
TUUT Charitable Trust
Ulverscroft Foundation
United St Saviour's Charities
John and Lucille van Geest
 Foundation
Eric W Vincent Trust Fund
Vodafone UK Foundation
Voluntary Action Luton
Wales Council for Voluntary
 Action
Thomas Wall Trust
Wates Foundation
Weavers' Company Benevolent
 Fund
William Webster Charitable
 Trust
Wellfield Trust
Wesleyan Charitable Trust
Charity of John West & Others
Westcroft Trust
Western Recreation Trust
Westminster Amalgamated
 Charity
Garfield Weston Foundation
Whitaker Charitable Trust
Whitecourt Charitable Trust
Felicity Wilde Charitable Trust
Will Charitable Trust
Harold Hyam Wingate
 Foundation
Wixamtree Trust
Wolfson Foundation
Worcester Municipal Charities
Yardley Great Trust
Yorkshire Building Society
 Charitable Foundation
Zurich Financial Services
 Community Trust

Project support

Funding priority
1970 Trust
Aberbrothock Charitable Trust
Adnams Charity
Green & Lilian F M Ainsworth
 & Family Benevolent Fund
Sylvia Aitken Charitable Trust
Ajahma Charitable Trust
Alexis Trust

Allavida
Pat Allsop Charitable Trust
Eric Anker-Petersen Charity
Ambrose & Ann Appelbe Trust
Appletree Trust
Ashendene Trust
Audi Design Foundation
Andrew Balint Charitable Trust
George Balint Charitable Trust
Paul Balint Charitable Trust
Baring Foundation
Barnabas Charitable Trust
Barron Bell Trust and
 Additional Fund
Bartle Family Charitable Trust
Paul Bassham Charitable Trust
BBC Radio Cambridgeshire –
 Trustline
Bergqvist Charitable Trust
Thomas Betton's Charity for
 Pensions and Relief-in-Need
Birmingham Hospital Saturday
 Fund Medical Charity &
 Welfare Trust
Birmingham International
 Airport Community Trust
Blair Foundation
Morgan Blake Charitable Trust
Enid Blyton Trust for Children
Charles Boot Trust
British Dietetic Association
 General and Education
 Trust Fund
British Heart Foundation
British Institute of Archaeology
 at Ankara
Britten-Pears Foundation
Broadfield Trust
Roger Brooke Charitable Trust
Palgrave Brown Foundation
E F Bulmer Benevolent Fund
BUPA Foundation
Audrey & Stanley Burton
 Charitable Trust
William A Cadbury Charitable
 Trust
CAFOD
Camelot Foundation
Carnegie United Kingdom Trust
Carron Charitable Trust
Sir John Cass's Foundation
Elizabeth Casson Trust
Cattanach Charitable Trust
Wilfrid & Constance Cave
 Foundation
Cemlyn-Jones Trust
Chase Charity
Christendom Trust
Christian Aid
Cleopatra Trust
Richard Cloudesley's Charity
Cobb Charity
Commonwealth Relations
 Trust
Community Foundation for
 Calderdale

Community Foundation for Greater Manchester
Community Fund
Cooper Charitable Trust
County Durham Foundation
Coutts & Co. Charitable Trust
Craignish Trust
Cross Trust
Cystic Fibrosis Trust
John Grant Davies Trust
De La Rue Charitable Trust
Miriam K Dean Refugee Trust Fund
Delius Trust
Earl of Derby's Charitable Trust
Richard Desmond Charitable Trust
Devon Community Foundation
Diana, Princess of Wales Memorial Fund
Dorus Trust
Douglas Charitable Trust
Eden Arts Trust
Elephant Trust
Enkalon Foundation
Epigoni Trust
Epilepsy Research Foundation
Essex Community Foundation
Essex Fairway Charitable Trust
Eveson Charitable Trust
Feed the Minds
Fiat Auto (UK) Charity
Fifty Fund
Bud Flanagan Leukaemia Fund
Four Acre Trust
Four Lanes Trust
Four Winds Trust
Charles Henry Foyle Trust
Jill Franklin Trust
Gannochy Trust
Jacqueline and Michael Gee Charitable Trust
Simon Gibson Charitable Trust
Mrs Godfrey-Payton Trust
Golsoncott Foundation
Good Neighbours Trust
Great Britain Sasakawa Foundation
Greater Bristol Foundation
Constance Green Foundation
Greggs Trust
Gulbenkian Foundation
GWR Community Trust
Hadfield Trust
Alfred Haines Charitable Trust
William Harding's Charity
Kenneth Hargreaves Charitable Trust
William Geoffrey Harvey's Discretionary Settlement
Charles Hayward Foundation
Headley Trust
Hedley Foundation
Simon Heller Charitable Settlement

Help the Homeless Ltd
Hertfordshire Community Foundation
Hinchley Charitable Trust
Lady Hind Trust
Hinrichsen Foundation
Hobart Charitable Trust
Edward Sydney Hogg Charitable Settlement
Mary Homfray Charitable Trust
Horne Foundation
Housing Associations Charitable Trust (Hact)
John & Ruth Howard Charitable Trust
James Thom Howat Charitable Trust
HSA Charitable Trust
Hull & East Riding Charitable Trust
Miss Agnes H Hunter's Trust
Idlewild Trust
Incorporated Leeds Church Extension Society
Inland Waterways Association
Inlight Trust
INTACH (UK) Trust
Ironmongers' Quincentenary Charitable Fund
Isle of Dogs Community Foundation
J R S S T Charitable Trust
John Jarrold Trust
Jeffrey Charitable Trust
J G Joffe Charitable Trust
Johnson Foundation
H F Johnson Trust
Edward Cecil Jones Settlement
Judith Trust
Stanley Kalms Foundation
Kidani Memorial Trust
King George's Fund for Sailors
Ernest Kleinwort Charitable Trust
Marina Kleinwort Charitable Trust
Laing's Charitable Trust
David Laing Foundation
Allen Lane Foundation
Lawlor Foundation
Leach Fourteenth Trust
Kennedy Leigh Charitable Trust
Lethendy Charitable Trust
Levy Foundation
John Spedan Lewis Foundation
Lintel Trust
Lister Charitable Trust
Second Joseph Aaron Littman Foundation
Lloyd's Charities Trust
Lloyds TSB Foundation for the Channel Islands
London Youth Trust (W H Smith Memorial)

Marie Helen Luen Charitable Trust
Lynn Foundation
R S MacDonald Charitable Trust
McDougall Trust
Macfarlane Walker Trust
Magdalen Hospital Trust
Manchester Airport Community Trust Fund
W M Mann Foundation
Marchig Animal Welfare Trust
Market Harborough and The Bowdens Charity
Anthony and Elizabeth Mellows Charitable Settlement
Mental Health Foundation
Mercury Phoenix Trust
Migraine Trust
Minge's Gift
Mitsubishi Corporation Fund for Europe and Africa
John Moores Foundation
Morel Charitable Trust
Oliver Morland Charitable Trust
S C and M E Morland's Charitable Trust
Stanley Morrison Charitable Trust
Mount 'A' Charitable Trust
Mount 'B' Charitable Trust
Mount Everest Foundation
Music Sound Foundation
Muslim Hands
National Asthma Campaign
National Kidney Research Fund Limited
National Power Charitable Trust
New Durlston Trust
North West Cancer Research Fund
Northcott Devon Medical Foundation
Nottingham General Dispensary
Novi Most International
Nuffield Trust
Oakdale Trust
Ogilvie Charities Deed 2
Ouseley Trust
Oxfam (GB)
Oxfordshire Community Foundation
P F Charitable Trust
Parivar Trust
Park Hill Trust
Jack Patston Charitable Trust
Frank Pearson Foundation
J B Pelly Charitable Settlement
Personal Assurance Charitable Trust
Philanthropic Trust
David Pickford Charitable Foundation
Pilgrim Trust

Austin & Hope Pilkington Trust
Cecil Pilkington Charitable
  Trust
Pilkington Charities Fund
Portishead Nautical Trust
Powell Foundation
Powys Welsh Church Fund
PPP Foundation
Pyke Charity Trust
Ruben and Elisabeth Rausing
  Trust
Rayne Trust
Sir James Reckitt Charity
Red Dragon Radio Trust
C A Redfern Charitable
  Foundation
Max Reinhardt Charitable Trust
Cliff Richard Charitable Trust
Roman Research Trust
Rooke Atlay Charitable Trust
Rosca Trust
Rural Trust
Jean Sainsbury Animal Welfare
  Trust
St Francis Leprosy Guild
St Hilda's Trust
Sir Walter St John's
  Educational Charity
St Peter's Saltley Trust
Saint Sarkis Charity Trust
Sarum St Michael Educational
  Charity
Henry James Sayer Charity
Scott Bader Commonwealth
  Ltd
Frieda Scott Charitable Trust
Sir James & Lady Scott Trust
Servite Sisters' Charitable
  Trust Fund
David Shepherd Wildlife
  Foundation
Sylvia & Colin Shepherd
  Charitable Trust
Archie Sherman Charitable
  Trust
R C Sherriff Rosebriars Trust
SHINE
Skerritt Trust
Skinners' Company Lady
  Neville Charity
SMB Trust
Mrs Smith & Mount Trust
Stanley Smith UK Horticultural
  Trust
Sobell Foundation
Social Education Trust
South Yorkshire Community
  Foundation
Southover Manor General
  Education Trust
Moss Spiro Will Charitable
  Foundation
Sportsman's Charity
Stanley Foundation Ltd
Stewards' Charitable Trust
Sir John Sumner's Trust

Sutton Trust
Walter Swindon Charitable
  Trust
Charles and Elsie Sykes Trust
Tearfund
Tenovus Scotland
Loke Wan Tho Memorial
  Foundation
Thoresby Charitable Trust
Thriplow Charitable Trust
Constance Travis Charitable
  Trust
Truemark Trust
Tufton Charitable Trust
Ultach Trust
Ulverscroft Foundation
Unemployed Voluntary Action
  Fund
VEC Acorn Trust
Verdon-Smith Family Charitable
  Settlement
Nigel Vinson Charitable Trust
War on Want
Warwickshire Masonic
  Charitable Association Ltd
John Watson's Trust
Wellcome Trust
Wentwood Education Trust
West Derby Wastelands
  Charity
West London Synagogue
  Charitable Fund
Westminster Foundation
Lionel Wigram Memorial Trust
Wiltshire and Swindon
  Community Foundation
Maurice Wohl Charitable
  Foundation
Maurice Wohl Charitable Trust
Woo Charitable Foundation
Yorkshire Agricultural Society
Yorkshire Bank Charitable
  Trust
I A Ziff Charitable Foundation

Will consider

Acacia Charitable Trust
Adint Charitable Trust
Aid to the Church in Need (UK)
Alexandra Rose Day
All Saints Educational Trust
Dorothy Gertrude Allen
  Memorial Fund
H B Allen Charitable Trust
Mrs M H Allen Trust
Almond Trust
James and Grace Anderson
  Trust
Arthritis Research Campaign
Arts Council of England
Arts Council of Wales
Ove Arup Foundation
Lord Ashdown Charitable Trust
Aston Charities Trust Limited
Astor Foundation
Baily Thomas Charitable Fund

Balmore Trust
Barber Charitable Trust
Barbour Trust
David and Frederick Barclay
  Foundation
Philip Barker Charity
Lord Barnby's Foundation
Barnes Workhouse Fund
Barnwood House Trust
Barracks Trust of Newcastle-
  under-Lyme
BBC Children in Need Appeal
Bearder Charity
James Beattie Charitable Trust
Beaufort House Trust
Bedford Charity (The Harpur
  Trust)
Hervey Benham Charitable
  Trust
Berkshire Community
  Foundation
Billingsgate Christian Mission
  Charitable Trust
Percy Bilton Charity Ltd
Bingham Trust
Herbert & Peter Blagrave
  Charitable Trust
Blanchminster Trust
Blatchington Court Trust
Boltons Trust
Booth Charities
Boots Charitable Trust
Sir William Boreman's
  Foundation
Bridge House Estates Trust
  Fund
Bridge Trust
John Bristow and Thomas
  Mason Trust
Britannia Building Society
  Foundation
British Sugar Foundation
Bromley Trust
Mrs E E Brown Charitable
  Settlement
Bryant Trust
Burdens Charitable Foundation
Clara E Burgess Charity
Burton Breweries Charitable
  Trust
Barrow Cadbury Trust and the
  Barrow Cadbury Fund
Edward Cadbury Charitable
  Trust
Cadbury Schweppes
  Foundation
Campden Charities
Carlton Television Trust
Carmichael-Montgomery
  Charitable Trust
Carnegie Dunfermline Trust
Carpenter Charitable Trust
Leslie Mary Carter Charitable
  Trust
Chapman Charitable Trust
Charities Advisory Trust

Chelsea Building Society
Charitable Foundation
Chest Heart and Stroke
Scotland
Children's Liver Disease
Foundation
Chippenham Borough Lands
Charity
Church Urban Fund
Cinderford Charitable Trust
City Parochial Foundation
Elizabeth Clark Charitable
Trust
Lord Clinton's Charitable Trust
Clover Trust
Coats Foundation Trust
Colchester & Tendring
Community Trust
John & Freda Coleman
Charitable Trust
George Henry Collins Charity
Norman Collinson Charitable
Trust
Colt Foundation
Sir James Colyer-Fergusson's
Charitable Trust
Comic Relief
Community Foundation for
Northern Ireland
Community Foundation Serving
Tyne & Wear and
Northumberland
Congleton Inclosure Trust
Consortium on Opportunities
for Volunteering
Ernest Cook Trust
Gordon Cook Foundation
Coppings Trust
Cornwell Charitable Trust
Cotton Trust
County of Gloucestershire
Community Foundation
Criffel Charitable Trust
Cripplegate Foundation
Harry Crook Foundation
Cumber Family Charitable
Trust
Cwmbran Trust
D'Oyly Carte Charitable Trust
Richard Davies Charitable
Foundation
Helen and Geoffrey de Freitas
Charitable Trust
William Dean Countryside and
Educational Trust
Derbyshire Community
Foundation
J N Derbyshire Trust
Community Council of Devon
Duke of Devonshire's
Charitable Trust
Dibden Allotments Charity
DLA Charitable Trust
Drapers' Charitable Fund
Duchy of Lancaster Benevolent
Fund

William Dudley Trust
Dulverton Trust
Dumfries and Galloway Council
Charitable Trusts
Dunhill Medical Trust
W E Dunn Trust
Audrey Earle Charitable Trust
Earley Charity
Ecological Foundation
Wilfred & Elsie Elkes Charity
Fund
Maud Elkington Charitable
Trust
John Ellerman Foundation
Elmley Foundation
Englass Charitable Trust
Englefield Charitable Trust
Equitable Charitable Trust
Eranda Foundation
Ericson Trust
Fairbairn Charitable Trust
Esmée Fairbairn Foundation
Lord Faringdon Charitable
Trust
Samuel William Farmer's Trust
Ferguson Benevolent Fund Ltd
Fidelity UK Foundation
Finnart House School Trust
David Finnie & Alan Emery
Charitable Trust
Fishmongers' Company's
Charitable Trust
Earl Fitzwilliam Charitable
Trust
Joyce Fletcher Charitable Trust
Gordon Fraser Charitable Trust
Hugh Fraser Foundation
Anne French Memorial Trust
Freshgate Trust Foundation
Gamma Trust
Ganzoni Charitable Trust
Garnett Charitable Trust
Gatwick Airport Community
Trust
Robert Gavron Charitable Trust
Gibbs Charitable Trusts
G C Gibson Charitable Trust
Gilchrist Educational Trust
Glaziers' Trust
Glencore Foundation for
Education and Welfare
Global Care
GMC Trust
Teresa Rosenbaum Golden
Charitable Trust
Grantham Yorke Trust
J G Graves Charitable Trust
Gretna Charitable Trust
Grocers' Charity
Bishop of Guildford's
Foundation
Hadrian Trust
Hamamelis Trust
Paul Hamlyn Foundation
Hampton Fuel Allotment
Charity

W A Handley Charitable Trust
Haramead Trust
Harborne Parish Lands Charity
Harrison & Potter Trust
Hartley Charitable Trust
Gay & Peter Hartley's Hillards
Charitable Trust
N & P Hartley Memorial Trust
Dorothy Hay-Bolton Charitable
Trust
Heart of England Community
Foundation
Hedley Denton Charitable
Trust
Philip Henman Trust
Alan Edward Higgs Charity
Hilden Charitable Fund
Hockerill Educational
Foundation
Dorothy Holmes Charitable
Trust
Edward Holt Trust
Holywood Trust
Hyde Charitable Trust
Hyde Park Place Estate Charity
India Foundation (UK)
Ingram Trust
Charles Irving Charitable Trust
ITF Seafarers Trust
Ruth & Lionel Jacobson Trust
(Second Fund) No 2
James Pantyfedwen
Foundation
James Trust
Jarman Charitable Trust
Jephcott Charitable Trust
Jerusalem Trust
Jewish Child's Day
Jewish Youth Fund
Elton John Aids Foundation
Johnson Group Cleaners
Charity
Joicey Trust
Boris Karloff Charitable
Foundation
Ian Karten Charitable Trust
Kay Kendall Leukaemia Fund
King's Fund
Mary Kinross Charitable Trust
Kleinwort Benson Charitable
Trust
Sir James Knott Trust
Knowles Charitable Trust
Kreitman Foundation
Late Sir Pierce Lacy Charity
Trust
Bryan Lancaster's Charity
Lankelly Foundation
Lauffer Family Charitable
Foundation
Mrs F B Laurence Charitable
Trust
Raymond & Blanche Lawson
Charitable Trust
Lazard Charitable Trust

Mason Le Page Charitable
Trust
Leigh Trust
Leverhulme Trust
Linbury Trust
Linden Charitable Trust
Lloyds TSB Foundation for
England and Wales
Lloyds TSB Foundation for
Northern Ireland
Lloyds TSB Foundation for
Scotland
Lofthouse Foundation
London North East Community
Foundation
William & Katherine Longman
Trust
John Lyon's Charity
M N R Charitable Trust
Mackintosh Foundation
Helen Isabella McMorran
Charitable Foundation
R W Mann Trustees Limited
Marchday Charitable Fund
Hilda & Samuel Marks
Foundation
Melville Trust for Care and
Cure of Cancer
Mercers' Charitable
Foundation
Methodist Relief and
Development Fund
Metropolitan Hospital-Sunday
Fund
Mickel Fund
Middlesex County Rugby
Football Union Memorial
Fund
Hugh and Mary Miller Bequest
Trust
Millfield House Foundation
Milton Keynes Community
Foundation
Mobbs Memorial Trust Ltd
Monument Trust
George A Moore Foundation
J P Morgan Fleming
Educational Trust and
Foundation
Morgan Stanley International
Foundation
Willie & Mabel Morris
Charitable Trust
Moulton Charitable Trust
Edwina Mountbatten Trust
Mountbatten Memorial Trust
National Manuscripts
Conservation Trust
Newby Trust Limited
Newstead Charity
Noel Buxton Trust
Norman Family Charitable
Trust
Northcott Devon Foundation
Northern Rock Foundation
Norton Foundation

Norwich Consolidated
Charities
Norwich Town Close Estate
Charity
Nuffield Foundation
Oakley Charitable Trust
Old Broad Street Charity Trust
Old Enfield Charitable Trust
John Oldacre Foundation
Kate Wilson Oliver Trust
Eleanor Palmer Trust
Parthenon Trust
Constance Paterson Charitable
Trust
Harry Payne Trust
Michael Peacock Charitable
Foundation
Persula Foundation
Jack Petchey Foundation
Col W W Pilkington Will Trusts
Polden-Puckham Charitable
Foundation
J S F Pollitzer Charitable
Settlement
Pontin Charitable Trust
Porter Foundation
Prairie Trust
W L Pratt Charitable Trust
Primrose Hill Trust
Princess Anne's Charities
Pye Foundation
Queen Mary's Roehampton
Trust
R V W Trust
Rainford Trust
Peggy Ramsay Foundation
Märit and Hans Rausing
Charitable Foundation
John Rayner Charitable Trust
Rest Harrow Trust
Reuters Foundation
Rhododendron Trust
Clive Richards Charity Ltd
Violet M Richards Charity
Richmond Parish Lands Charity
Helen Roll Charitable Trust
Mrs L D Rope Third Charitable
Settlement
Rothley Trust
Rowlands Trust
Joseph Rowntree Charitable
Trust
Royal Victoria Hall Foundation
J B Rubens Charitable
Foundation
Rufford Foundation
Russell Trust
Audrey Sacher Charitable Trust
Karim Rida Said Foundation
Alan and Babette Sainsbury
Charitable Fund
St Andrew Animal Fund Ltd
Saint Edmund, King & Martyr
Trust
St Gabriel's Trust
St James' Trust Settlement

St Katharine & Shadwell Trust
St Luke's College Foundation
St Mary-le-Strand Charity
St Thomas Ecclesiastical
Charity
Salt Foundation
Scarfe Charitable Trust
R H Scholes Charitable Trust
Francis C Scott Charitable
Trust
Sir Samuel Scott of Yews
Trust
Scottish Churches Community
Trust
Scottish Community
Foundation
Searle Charitable Trust
Seedfield Trust
Sheldon Trust
Archie Sherman Cardiff
Charitable Foundation
Shipwrights Company
Charitable Fund
Bishop Simeon CR Trust
Rita and David Slowe
Charitable Trust
Henry Smith Charity
David Solomons Charitable
Trust
South Square Trust
Spar Charitable Fund
Starfish Trust
Peter Stebbings Memorial
Charity
Sir Halley Stewart Trust
Leonard Laity Stoate
Charitable Trust
Stoller Charitable Trust
W O Street Charitable
Foundation
Alan Sugar Foundation
Summerfield Charitable Trust
Bernard Sunley Charitable
Foundation
Sutton Coldfield Municipal
Charities
Stella Symons Charitable Trust
A R Taylor Charitable Trust
Tesco Charity Trust
Sue Thomson Foundation
Sir Jules Thorn Charitable
Trust
Tisbury Telegraph Trust
Tory Family Foundation
Tudor Trust
United St Saviour's Charities
Valentine Charitable Trust
John and Lucille van Geest
Foundation
Bernard Van Leer Foundation
Van Neste Foundation
Vodafone UK Foundation
Voluntary Action Luton
Charity of Thomas Wade &
Others

Wales Council for Voluntary
  Action
Thomas Wall Trust
Wallington Missionary Mart
  and Auctions
Ward Blenkinsop Trust
Wates Foundation
Bertie Watson Foundation
Mary Webb Trust
Wellfield Trust
Welton Foundation
Westminster Amalgamated
  Charity
Garfield Weston Foundation
Whitaker Charitable Trust
Whitecourt Charitable Trust
Whitley Animal Protection Trust
Harold Hyam Wingate
  Foundation
Woodlands Trust (259569)
Woodroffe Benton Foundation
Yapp Charitable Trust
Yardley Great Trust
W Wing Yip & Bros Charitable
  Trust
Zurich Financial Services
  Community Trust

■ Full project funding
Funding priority
E F Bulmer Benevolent Fund
Camelot Foundation
Consortium on Opportunities
  for Volunteering
Miriam K Dean Refugee Trust
  Fund
Market Harborough and The
  Bowdens Charity
Miles Trust for the Putney and
  Roehampton Community
John Oldacre Foundation
Ruben and Elisabeth Rausing
  Trust
Thames Community
  Foundation

Will consider
Sylvia Aitken Charitable Trust
Arts Council of Wales
Barclays Stockbrokers
  Charitable Trust
Morgan Blake Charitable Trust
BP Conservation Programme
John Bristow and Thomas
  Mason Trust
Cadbury Schweppes
  Foundation
Roald Dahl Foundation
Dulverton Trust
Essex Fairway Charitable Trust
Beatrice Laing Trust
Mercers' Charitable
  Foundation
Märit and Hans Rausing
  Charitable Foundation

Rayne Foundation
Royal Eastern Counties
  Schools Limited
Rita and David Slowe
  Charitable Trust
Swan Mountain Trust
I A Ziff Charitable Foundation

■ Project funding
Funding priority
Abbey National Charitable
  Trust Ltd
Sylvia Aitken Charitable Trust
Morgan Blake Charitable Trust
BP Conservation Programme
Bristol Archdeaconry Charities
E F Bulmer Benevolent Fund
Camelot Foundation
Casey Trust
CLA Charitable Trust
Stephen Clark 1957
  Charitable Trust
Cobb Charity
Consortium on Opportunities
  for Volunteering
Cowley Charitable Foundation
Daily Prayer Union Charitable
  Trust Ltd
Miriam K Dean Refugee Trust
  Fund
Farmers Company Charitable
  Fund
Bud Flanagan Leukaemia Fund
Four Acre Trust
Mrs Godfrey-Payton Trust
Harrow Community Trust
Philip Henman Trust
Hilden Charitable Fund
Sir Barry Jackson Trust and
  County Fund
Kathleen Trust
Kelsick's Educational
  Foundation
Kathleen Laurence Trust
Leathersellers' Company
  Charitable Fund
LSA Charitable Trust
Market Harborough and The
  Bowdens Charity
Methodist Relief and
  Development Fund
Miles Trust for the Putney and
  Roehampton Community
Keith and Joan Mindelsohn
  Charitable Trust
Peter Minet Trust
John Oldacre Foundation
Oxfordshire Historic Churches
  Trust
Panton Trust
Pastoral Care Trust
Pilgrim Trust
Prince Philip Trust Fund
Ruben and Elisabeth Rausing
  Trust

Ripple Effect Foundation
Search
SEM Charitable Trust
R C Sherriff Rosebriars Trust
Swan Mountain Trust
Thames Community
  Foundation
Welsh Church Fund –
  Carmarthenshire area
David Wilson Foundation

Will consider
Arts Council of Northern
  Ireland
Arts Council of Wales
Barclays Stockbrokers
  Charitable Trust
Barnabas Trust
Barnwood House Trust
Bingham Trust
Birmingham Foundation
Peter Boizot Foundation
John Bristow and Thomas
  Mason Trust
Edward & Dorothy Cadbury
  Trust
Cadbury Schweppes
  Foundation
Chase Charity
Childwick Trust
Church Urban Fund
County of Gloucestershire
  Community Foundation
Lord Cozens-Hardy Trust
Roald Dahl Foundation
Simon Digby (Sherborne)
  Memorial Trust
Dinwoodie Settlement
Dulverton Trust
City of Edinburgh Charitable
  Trusts
Essex Fairway Charitable Trust
Forte Charitable Trust
Gannochy Trust
Hadfield Trust
Hampton Fuel Allotment
  Charity
R J Harris Charitable
  Settlement
Heart of England Community
  Foundation
Hedgcock Bequest
Hemby Trust
Henley Educational Charity
Joseph Hopkins Charity
Hospital of God at Greatham
Worshipful Company of
  Innholders General Charity
  Fund
Peter Kershaw Trust
King's Fund
Beatrice Laing Trust
Christopher Laing Foundation
Kirby Laing Foundation
Maurice Laing Foundation

Maurice and Hilda Laing
  Charitable Trust
Lankelly Foundation
Lawlor Foundation
Leche Trust
Levy Foundation
Lyndhurst Settlement
Linda Marcus Charitable Trust
Mercers' Charitable
  Foundation
Gerald Micklem Charitable
  Trust
Moss Family Charitable Trust
Odin Charitable Trust
Ogle Christian Trust
Persula Foundation
Pye Foundation
Elise Randall Educational Trust
Rayne Foundation
Rothley Trust
Joseph Rowntree Charitable
  Trust
Royal Eastern Counties
  Schools Limited
Royal London Aid Society
Rural Trust
Saddlers' Company Charitable
  Fund
Scottish International
  Education Trust
Simpson Education &
  Conservation Trust
Rita and David Slowe
  Charitable Trust
SMB Trust
Steinberg Family Charitable
  Trust
Stoller Charitable Trust
Treeside Trust
Vale of Glamorgan Welsh
  Church Fund
Wentwood Education Trust
Westcroft Trust
Whitecourt Charitable Trust
Yapp Charitable Trust
I A Ziff Charitable Foundation

....

■ Seed funding

Funding priority

Abel Charitable Trust
Age Concern Scotland
  Enterprise Fund
AIM Foundation
Architectural Heritage Fund
Balney Charitable Trust
BBC Radio Cambridgeshire –
  Trustline
Hervey Benham Charitable
  Trust
BibleLands
Birmingham Foundation
Morgan Blake Charitable Trust
Charles Boot Trust
Anthony Bourne Foundation
Bridge Trust

British Dietetic Association
  General and Education
  Trust Fund
E F Bulmer Benevolent Fund
Camelot Foundation
Cattanach Charitable Trust
Chase Charity
CLA Charitable Trust
Richard Cloudesley's Charity
Lance Coates Charitable Trust
  1969
Cobb Charity
Cole Charitable Trust
Community Fund
Cumberland Trust
Daily Prayer Union Charitable
  Trust Ltd
Richard Davies Charitable
  Foundation
Demigryphon Trust
Denman Charitable Trust
J N Derbyshire Trust
Devon Community Foundation
Edinburgh Voluntary
  Organisations' Trust Funds
Enkalon Foundation
Essex Community Foundation
Fiat Auto (UK) Charity
Fifty Fund
Four Acre Trust
Four Lanes Trust
Charles Henry Foyle Trust
Jill Franklin Trust
Frognal Trust
Godinton Charitable Trust
Harrow Community Trust
Charles Hayward Foundation
Heart of England Community
  Foundation
Help the Aged
Hilden Charitable Fund
Charles Littlewood Hill Trust
Hospital of God at Greatham
Housing Associations
  Charitable Trust
James Thom Howat Charitable
  Trust
Miss Agnes H Hunter's Trust
ITF Seafarers Trust
Sir Barry Jackson Trust and
  County Fund
John Jarrold Trust
Peter Kershaw Trust
David Laing Foundation
Allen Lane Foundation
Lawlor Foundation
Leathersellers' Company
  Charitable Fund
Lincolnshire Old Churches
  Trust
Lintel Trust
Lloyds TSB Foundation for the
  Channel Islands
London Law Trust
London Youth Trust
LSA Charitable Trust

Macfarlane Walker Trust
Magdalen Hospital Trust
Market Harborough and The
  Bowdens Charity
D G Marshall of Cambridge
  Trust
Miles Trust for the Putney and
  Roehampton Community
Minge's Gift
Mountbatten Memorial Trust
Mugdock Children's Trust
Nestlé Rowntree York
  Employees Community Fund
  Trust
North West Cancer Research
  Fund
Novi Most International
Oakdale Trust
Ogilvie Charities Deed 2
Onaway Trust
Oxfordshire Community
  Foundation
Parivar Trust
Park Hill Trust
Pastoral Care Trust
J B Pelly Charitable Settlement
Jack Petchey Foundation
Pilgrim Trust
Austin & Hope Pilkington Trust
Powell Foundation
Prince Philip Trust Fund
Mr and Mrs J A Pye's
  Charitable Settlement
Ruben and Elisabeth Rausing
  Trust
REMEDI
Rosca Trust
Joseph Rowntree Foundation
Royal London Aid Society
Saint Edmund, King & Martyr
  Trust
Sir Walter St John's
  Educational Charity
Sir James & Lady Scott Trust
SHINE
Bishop Simeon CR Trust
Stanley Smith UK Horticultural
  Trust
Sutton Trust
Tenovus Scotland
Thames Community
  Foundation
Third House Trust
Ultach Trust
VEC Acorn Trust
Charity of Thomas Wade &
  Others
Wakeham Trust
John Watson's Trust
Weavers' Company Benevolent
  Fund
Welsh Church Fund –
  Carmarthenshire area
David Wilson Foundation
Woodlands Trust (1015942)
Yorkshire Agricultural Society

Will consider

Abbey National Charitable
    Trust Ltd
Adnams Charity
Aid to the Church in Need (UK)
Sylvia Aitken Charitable Trust
Alexandra Rose Day
Angus Allnatt Charitable
    Foundation
Almond Trust
Milly Apthorp Charitable Trust
Ardwick Trust
Arts Council of England
Arts Council of Wales
Ove Arup Foundation
Ashby Charitable Trust
Lord Ashdown Charitable Trust
Astor Foundation
BAA 21st Century
    Communities Trust
Bacta Charitable Trust
Baily Thomas Charitable Fund
Balmore Trust
William P Bancroft (No 2)
    Charitable Trust and
    Jenepher Gillett Trust
Barber Charitable Trust
Barbour Trust
Barnabas Charitable Trust
Barnes Workhouse Fund
Barnwood House Trust
BBC Children in Need Appeal
James Beattie Charitable Trust
Berkshire Community
    Foundation
Bingham Trust
Blanchminster Trust
Body Shop Foundation
Booth Charities
Boots Charitable Trust
Bowerman Charitable Trust
John Bristow and Thomas
    Mason Trust
Britannia Building Society
    Foundation
Bromley Trust
Bryant Trust
Burdens Charitable Foundation
Clara E Burgess Charity
Geoffrey Burton Charitable
    Trust
Barrow Cadbury Trust and the
    Barrow Cadbury Fund
Cadbury Schweppes
    Foundation
William A Cadbury Charitable
    Trust
Campden Charities
Carlton Television Trust
Carmichael-Montgomery
    Charitable Trust
Carnegie Dunfermline Trust
Chapman Charitable Trust
Charities Advisory Trust
Chippenham Borough Lands
    Charity

Christendom Trust
Church Urban Fund
Cinderford Charitable Trust
City Parochial Foundation
J A Clark Charitable Trust
Lord Clinton's Charitable Trust
Clover Trust
John & Freda Coleman
    Charitable Trust
Norman Collinson Charitable
    Trust
Sir James Colyer-Fergusson's
    Charitable Trust
Community Foundation for
    Northern Ireland
Congleton Inclosure Trust
Ernest Cook Trust
Coppings Trust
County Durham Foundation
County of Gloucestershire
    Community Foundation
Cray Trust
Cwmbran Trust
Roald Dahl Foundation
John Grant Davies Trust
Helen and Geoffrey de Freitas
    Charitable Trust
Miriam K Dean Refugee Trust
    Fund
William Dean Countryside and
    Educational Trust
Derbyshire Community
    Foundation
Community Council of Devon
Duke of Devonshire's
    Charitable Trust
Dibden Allotments Charity
DLM Charitable Trust
Duis Charitable Trust
Dulverton Trust
Dunhill Medical Trust
W E Dunn Trust
Earley Charity
Wilfred & Elsie Elkes Charity
    Fund
John Ellerman Foundation
Elmley Foundation
Englefield Charitable Trust
Equitable Charitable Trust
Essex Fairway Charitable Trust
Samuel William Farmer's Trust
Fassnidge Memorial Trust
Ferguson Benevolent Fund Ltd
Joyce Fletcher Charitable Trust
Ford of Britain Trust
Gordon Fraser Charitable Trust
Hugh Fraser Foundation
Freshgate Trust Foundation
Worshipful Company of
    Furniture Makers Charitable
    Fund
Gannochy Trust
Grahame Charitable
    Foundation
J G Graves Charitable Trust

Great Britain Sasakawa
    Foundation
Barry Green Memorial Fund
Greggs Trust
Bishop of Guildford's
    Foundation
Gulbenkian Foundation
H C D Memorial Fund
Hadrian Trust
Robert Hall Charity
Hampstead Wells and
    Campden Trust
W A Handley Charitable Trust
Harborne Parish Lands Charity
R J Harris Charitable
    Settlement
Gay & Peter Hartley's Hillards
    Charitable Trust
N & P Hartley Memorial Trust
Hedgcock Bequest
Hemby Trust
Joanna Herbert-Stepney
    Charitable Settlement
Hertfordshire Community
    Foundation
Dorothy Holmes Charitable
    Trust
Clifford Howarth Charity
    Settlement
Hyde Charitable Trust
Hyde Park Place Estate Charity
Idlewild Trust
India Foundation (UK)
Inland Waterways Association
Worshipful Company of
    Innholders General Charity
    Fund
Isle of Dogs Community
    Foundation
James Pantyfedwen
    Foundation
James Trust
Jeffrey Charitable Trust
Jephcott Charitable Trust
Jewish Child's Day
Jewish Youth Fund
Joicey Trust
King's Fund
Mary Kinross Charitable Trust
Sir James Knott Trust
Knowles Charitable Trust
Late Sir Pierce Lacy Charity
    Trust
Christopher Laing Foundation
Lankelly Foundation
R J Larg Family Charitable
    Trust
Lauffer Family Charitable
    Foundation
Mrs F B Laurence Charitable
    Trust
Lazard Charitable Trust
Leach Fourteenth Trust
Kennedy Leigh Charitable
    Trust
Leigh Trust

Leng Charitable Trust
Lloyds TSB Foundation for
England and Wales
Lloyds TSB Foundation for
Northern Ireland
London North East Community
Foundation
Paul Lunn-Rockliffe Charitable
Trust
Lyndhurst Settlement
Lynwood Trust
John Lyon's Charity
Marchday Charitable Fund
Hilda & Samuel Marks
Foundation
John Martin's Charity
Mercers' Charitable
Foundation
Metropolitan Hospital-Sunday
Fund
Midhurst Pensions Trust
Millfield House Foundation
Milton Keynes Community
Foundation
George A Moore Foundation
John Moores Foundation
J P Morgan Fleming
Educational Trust and
Foundation
Morris Charitable Trust
Moss Family Charitable Trust
Muslim Hands
James Neill Trust Fund
Norman Family Charitable
Trust
Old Enfield Charitable Trust
Harry Payne Trust
Personal Assurance Charitable
Trust
Polden-Puckham Charitable
Foundation
Pontin Charitable Trust
PPP Foundation
Pye Foundation
Rainford Trust
Joseph Rank Trust
John Rayner Charitable Trust
Christopher H R Reeves
Charitable Trust
Reuters Foundation
Violet M Richards Charity
Helen Roll Charitable Trust
Mrs L D Rope Third Charitable
Settlement
Rotherwick Foundation
Rothley Trust
Christopher Rowbotham
Charitable Trust
Joseph Rowntree Charitable
Trust
Russell Trust
Saddlers' Company Charitable
Fund
Karim Rida Said Foundation
St Andrew Animal Fund Ltd

St Christopher's College
Educational Trust
St Gabriel's Trust
St James' Trust Settlement
St Katharine & Shadwell Trust
St Luke's College Foundation
St Mary-le-Strand Charity
St Thomas Ecclesiastical
Charity
Scott Bader Commonwealth
Ltd
Francis C Scott Charitable
Trust
Frieda Scott Charitable Trust
Scottish Churches Community
Trust
Scottish Community
Foundation
Search
Seedfield Trust
Servite Sisters' Charitable
Trust Fund
Sheldon Trust
Sherburn House Charity
Shipwrights Company
Charitable Fund
Skerritt Trust
Rita and David Slowe
Charitable Trust
SMB Trust
Henry Smith Charity
David Solomons Charitable
Trust
South Yorkshire Community
Foundation
Peter Stebbings Memorial
Charity
Steinberg Family Charitable
Trust
Sir Sigmund Sternberg
Charitable Foundation
Sir Halley Stewart Trust
Stoller Charitable Trust
Summerfield Charitable Trust
Sutton Coldfield Municipal
Charities
Swan Mountain Trust
Swan Trust
Stella Symons Charitable Trust
Talbot Trusts
Treeside Trust
Tudor Trust
United St Saviour's Charities
John and Lucille van Geest
Foundation
Voluntary Action Luton
Wales Council for Voluntary
Action
Thomas Wall Trust
Wates Foundation
Wellfield Trust
Wentwood Education Trust
Westcroft Trust
Westminster Amalgamated
Charity
Garfield Weston Foundation

Whitaker Charitable Trust
Whitecourt Charitable Trust
Wiltshire and Swindon
Community Foundation
Women at Risk
Woodlands Trust (259569)
Worcester Municipal Charities
Yapp Charitable Trust
Yardley Great Trust
W Wing Yip & Bros Charitable
Trust
York Children's Trust
I A Ziff Charitable Foundation
Zurich Financial Services
Community Trust

....

■ Feasibility

Funding priority
Abel Charitable Trust
Architectural Heritage Fund
Camelot Foundation
Christendom Trust
Richard Cloudesley's Charity
Cobb Charity
Community Fund
Digbeth Trust
Eden Arts Trust
Essex Community Foundation
Fiat Auto (UK) Charity
Gulbenkian Foundation
Housing Associations
Charitable Trust
Incorporated Leeds Church
Extension Society
Inland Waterways Association
Isle of Dogs Community
Foundation
ITF Seafarers Trust
JCA Charitable Foundation
Rees Jeffreys Road Fund
Macfarlane Walker Trust
Market Harborough and The
Bowdens Charity
Northumbria Historic Churches
Trust
Oakdale Trust
Prince Philip Trust Fund
Sir James & Lady Scott Trust
Sir Halley Stewart Trust
David Uri Memorial Trust
Wakeham Trust
Westminster Foundation

Will consider
Sylvia Aitken Charitable Trust
Milly Apthorp Charitable Trust
Arts Council of England
Arts Council of Wales
Ove Arup Foundation
Lord Ashdown Charitable Trust
Aston Charities Trust Limited
Bacta Charitable Trust
Barnes Workhouse Fund
Barnwood House Trust

Hervey Benham Charitable
Trust
BibleLands
Morgan Blake Charitable Trust
Blanchminster Trust
Viscountess Boyd Charitable
Trust
Bridge House Estates Trust
Fund
John Bristow and Thomas
Mason Trust
Britannia Building Society
Foundation
E F Bulmer Benevolent Fund
William A Cadbury Charitable
Trust
Campden Charities
Carnegie Dunfermline Trust
Carnegie United Kingdom Trust
Chapman Charitable Trust
Chippenham Borough Lands
Charity
Church Urban Fund
Cinderford Charitable Trust
City Parochial Foundation
Clover Trust
Congleton Inclosure Trust
Consortium on Opportunities
for Volunteering
County Durham Foundation
County of Gloucestershire
Community Foundation
Harry Crook Foundation
John Grant Davies Trust
Richard Davies Charitable
Foundation
Helen and Geoffrey de Freitas
Charitable Trust
Miriam K Dean Refugee Trust
Fund
William Dean Countryside and
Educational Trust
Community Council of Devon
Duke of Devonshire's
Charitable Trust
Dibden Allotments Charity
DLM Charitable Trust
Earley Charity
Ecological Foundation
Elmley Foundation
Equitable Charitable Trust
Gordon Fraser Charitable Trust
Anne French Memorial Trust
Freshgate Trust Foundation
Mrs Godfrey-Payton Trust
Great Britain Sasakawa
Foundation
Greggs Trust
Robert Hall Charity
Hampstead Wells and
Campden Trust
W A Handley Charitable Trust
R J Harris Charitable
Settlement
Charles Hayward Foundation

Heart of England Community
Foundation
Holywood Trust
Miss Agnes H Hunter's Trust
Idlewild Trust
Joicey Trust
Peter Kershaw Trust
King George's Fund for Sailors
Mary Kinross Charitable Trust
Sir James Knott Trust
Knowles Charitable Trust
Christopher Laing Foundation
Allen Lane Foundation
Kennedy Leigh Charitable
Trust
Leukaemia Research Fund
Levy Foundation
Lincolnshire Old Churches
Trust
Lintel Trust
London North East Community
Foundation
Lyndhurst Settlement
R W Mann Trustees Limited
Mercers' Charitable
Foundation
Miles Trust for the Putney and
Roehampton Community
Millfield House Foundation
Milton Keynes Community
Foundation
Norfolk Churches Trust Ltd
Norwich Town Close Estate
Charity
John Oldacre Foundation
Oxfordshire Community
Foundation
Personal Assurance Charitable
Trust
Austin & Hope Pilkington Trust
J S F Pollitzer Charitable
Settlement
Pontin Charitable Trust
Powell Foundation
PPP Foundation
Christopher H R Reeves
Charitable Trust
Violet M Richards Charity
Helen Roll Charitable Trust
Joseph Rowntree Charitable
Trust
Royal London Aid Society
Royal Victoria Hall Foundation
Rural Trust
Russell Trust
St Luke's College Foundation
St Mary-le-Strand Charity
Basil Samuel Charitable Trust
Francis C Scott Charitable
Trust
Scottish Churches Community
Trust
Scottish Community
Foundation
Search
R C Sherriff Rosebriars Trust

Henry Smith Charity
Stanley Smith UK Horticultural
Trust
David Solomons Charitable
Trust
South Yorkshire Community
Foundation
Sutton Trust
Triangle Trust (1949) Fund
Unemployed Voluntary Action
Fund
John and Lucille van Geest
Foundation
Voluntary Action Luton
Weavers' Company Benevolent
Fund
Whitaker Charitable Trust
Wiltshire and Swindon
Community Foundation
Worcester Municipal Charities
Yardley Great Trust
Yorkshire Agricultural Society

Loan finance

Funding priority

Architectural Heritage Fund
Cambridgeshire Historic
Churches Trust
Fifty Fund
Four Acre Trust
Grace Baptist Trust
Corporation
Jane Hodge Foundation
Incorporated Church Building
Society
Incorporated Leeds Church
Extension Society
David Laing Foundation
William Leech Charity
Lintel Trust
Lynn Foundation
Norman Family Charitable
Trust
Payne Charitable Trust
Mr and Mrs J A Pye's
Charitable Settlement
Joseph Rowntree Foundation

Will consider

Milly Apthorp Charitable Trust
Arts Council of Wales
Ashby Charitable Trust
Lord Ashdown Charitable Trust
Baily Thomas Charitable Fund
Barnes Workhouse Fund
Barnwood House Trust
Hervey Benham Charitable
Trust
Blanchminster Trust
Peter Boizot Foundation
British Dietetic Association
General and Education
Trust Fund
Britland Charitable Trust
Joseph & Annie Cattle Trust

Charities Advisory Trust
Cinderford Charitable Trust
Harry Crook Foundation
Cwmbran Trust
Gwendoline & Margaret Davies
  Charity
Richard Davies Charitable
  Foundation
Community Council of Devon
Duke of Devonshire's
  Charitable Trust
Dorset Historic Churches Trust
Doughty Charity Trust
Dumfries and Galloway Council
  Charitable Trusts
Ebenezer Trust
Englefield Charitable Trust
Esmée Fairbairn Foundation
Marc Fitch Fund
Gordon Fraser Charitable Trust
Freshgate Trust Foundation
Friends of Kent Churches
Gannochy Trust
Grahame Charitable
  Foundation
Bishop of Guildford's
  Foundation
Hampton Fuel Allotment
  Charity
Harborne Parish Lands Charity
James Pantyfedwen
  Foundation
JCA Charitable Foundation
Jewish Youth Fund
J E Joseph Charitable Fund
Mary Kinross Charitable Trust
Christopher Laing Foundation
Richard Langhorn Trust
Levy Foundation
Lincolnshire Old Churches
  Trust
Lockerbie Trust
William & Katherine Longman
  Trust
R W Mann Trustees Limited
Medlock Charitable Trust
Moss Charitable Trust
Nemoral Ltd
Northern Rock Foundation
Personal Assurance Charitable
  Trust
Pontin Charitable Trust
Clive Richards Charity Ltd
Violet M Richards Charity
Mrs L D Rope Third Charitable
  Settlement
Joseph Rowntree Charitable
  Trust
Seedfield Trust
Bishop Simeon CR Trust
Skerritt Trust
Henry Smith Charity
Stanley Smith UK Horticultural
  Trust
Spitalfields Market Community
  Trust

Foundation for Sport and the
  Arts
Sussex Historic Churches
  Trust
Sutton Trust
United Society for the
  Propagation of the Gospel
United St Saviour's Charities
Valentine Charitable Trust
Charity of Thomas Wade &
  Others
Charles Wolfson Charitable
  Trust
Worcester Municipal Charities

Duration of grant

■ Two years

Funding priority
29th May 1961 Charitable
  Trust
Anglo-German Foundation for
  the Study of Industrial
  Society
Appletree Trust
G C Armitage Charitable Trust
Barber Charitable Trust
BBC Children in Need Appeal
Viscountess Boyd Charitable
  Trust
Breast Cancer Research Trust
British Dietetic Association
  General and Education
  Trust Fund
Camelot Foundation
Carnegie United Kingdom Trust
Casey Trust
Sir John Cass's Foundation
Cattanach Charitable Trust
Chest Heart and Stroke
  Scotland
Child Growth Foundation
Cole Charitable Trust
Cystic Fibrosis Trust
William Delafield Charitable
  Trust
Dinwoodie Settlement
Jill Franklin Trust
Frognal Trust
Grahame Charitable
  Foundation
Simon Heller Charitable
  Settlement
Johnson Foundation
Michael & Ilse Katz Foundation
Nancy Kenyon Charitable Trust
Marina Kleinwort Charitable
  Trust
Allen Lane Foundation
MacRobert Trust
Melville Trust for Care and
  Cure of Cancer
Zachary Merton & George
  Woofindin Convalescent
  Trust
Gerald Micklem Charitable
  Trust
Miles Trust for the Putney and
  Roehampton Community
National Kidney Research
  Fund Limited
Ouseley Trust
Panton Trust
Frank Parkinson Agricultural
  Trust
Personal Assurance Charitable
  Trust
PPP Foundation
Riverside Charitable Trust
  Limited

Dr Mortimer and Theresa
Sackler Foundation
Stanley Smith UK Horticultural
Trust
Sobell Foundation
Sparks Charity
Sportsman's Charity
Suffolk Historic Churches Trust
Tower Hill Improvement Trust
Unemployed Voluntary Action
Fund
VEC Acorn Trust
Wakefield Trust
Wates Foundation
Weavers' Company Benevolent
Fund
Westminster Foundation

Will consider
All Saints Educational Trust
Almond Trust
James and Grace Anderson
Trust
Ardwick Trust
Ove Arup Foundation
Ashburnham Thanksgiving
Trust
Ashby Charitable Trust
Lord Ashdown Charitable Trust
Laura Ashley Foundation
Astor Foundation
Atlantic Foundation
BAA 21st Century
Communities Trust
Bacta Charitable Trust
Philip Barker Charity
Lord Barnby's Foundation
Barracks Trust of Newcastle-
under-Lyme
Bartle Family Charitable Trust
Bedford Charity
Berkshire Community
Foundation
Bingham Trust
Birmingham Foundation
Charles Boot Trust
Bramble Charitable Trust
Britannia Building Society
Foundation
Bromley Trust
Charles Brotherton Trust
BUPA Foundation
Cadbury Schweppes
Foundation
Cadogan Charity
Carlton Television Trust
Charities Advisory Trust
Chase Charity
Chippenham Borough Lands
Charity
Chownes Foundation
Church Burgesses Educational
Foundation
Cinderford Charitable Trust
CLA Charitable Trust
J A Clark Charitable Trust

John & Freda Coleman
Charitable Trust
Colt Foundation
Sir James Colyer-Fergusson's
Charitable Trust
Comic Relief
Community Foundation Serving
Tyne & Wear and
Northumberland
Gordon Cook Foundation
Coutts & Co. Charitable Trust
Cripplegate Foundation
Cumber Family Charitable
Trust
Roald Dahl Foundation
Miriam K Dean Refugee Trust
Fund
William Dean Countryside and
Educational Trust
Denman Charitable Trust
J N Derbyshire Trust
Devon Community Foundation
Dunhill Medical Trust
Ecological Foundation
City of Edinburgh Charitable
Trusts
W G Edwards Charitable
Foundation
Wilfred & Elsie Elkes Charity
Fund
Maud Elkington Charitable
Trust
James Ellis Charitable Trust
Epilepsy Research Foundation
Ericson Trust
Eveson Charitable Trust
Fairbairn Charitable Trust
Esmée Fairbairn Foundation
Fifty Fund
Finnart House School Trust
Timothy Franey Charitable
Foundation
Gordon Fraser Charitable Trust
Anne French Memorial Trust
Freshgate Trust Foundation
Worshipful Company of
Furniture Makers Charitable
Fund
Gannochy Trust
Girdlers' Company Charitable
Trust
Global Care
Teresa Rosenbaum Golden
Charitable Trust
Golsoncott Foundation
Reginald Graham Charitable
Trust
Grand Order of Water Rats
Charities Fund
Greenham Common
Community Trust Limited
Greggs Trust
GWR Community Trust
Paul Hamlyn Foundation
R J Harris Charitable
Settlement

N & P Hartley Memorial Trust
Charles Hayward Foundation
Henley Educational Charity
Hertfordshire Community
Foundation
Hilden Charitable Fund
Hinchley Charitable Trust
Dorothy Holmes Charitable
Trust
Edward Holt Trust
Hospital of God at Greatham
Miss Agnes H Hunter's Trust
Inland Waterways Association
Sir Barry Jackson Trust and
County Fund
James Pantyfedwen
Foundation
Jewish Child's Day
Jewish Youth Fund
Johnson Group Cleaners
Charity
Joicey Trust
Boris Karloff Charitable
Foundation
Ian Karten Charitable Trust
Kidani Memorial Trust
King's Fund
Kleinwort Benson Charitable
Trust
Knowles Charitable Trust
Beatrice Laing Trust
Christopher Laing Foundation
Kirby Laing Foundation
Maurice Laing Foundation
Maurice and Hilda Laing
Charitable Trust
Lankelly Foundation
R J Larg Family Charitable
Trust
Mason Le Page Charitable
Trust
Leathersellers' Company
Charitable Fund
Leng Charitable Trust
Leverhulme Trade Charities
Trust
Leverhulme Trust
John Spedan Lewis Foundation
Lintel Trust
Lloyds TSB Foundation for
England and Wales
Lloyds TSB Foundation for
Northern Ireland
Lloyds TSB Foundation for
Scotland
Lockerbie Trust
Lofthouse Foundation
London Law Trust
William & Katherine Longman
Trust
Marie Helen Luen Charitable
Trust
Manchester Airport Community
Trust Fund
R W Mann Trustees Limited
Marchig Animal Welfare Trust

Market Harborough and The
  Bowdens Charity
Sir George Martin Trust
Mercers' Charitable
  Foundation
Methodist Relief and
  Development Fund
Mitchell Charitable Trust
Esmé Mitchell Trust
Mitsubishi Corporation Fund
  for Europe and Africa
George A Moore Foundation
John Moores Foundation
J P Morgan Fleming
  Educational Trust and
  Foundation
Willie & Mabel Morris
  Charitable Trust
National Power Charitable
  Trust
Noel Buxton Trust
Northern Rock Foundation
Nottingham General
  Dispensary
Nuffield Foundation
Nuffield Trust
Oakdale Trust
Old Enfield Charitable Trust
Patrick Charitable Trust
Mrs C S Heber Percy
  Charitable Trust
Persula Foundation
Col W W Pilkington Will Trusts
  – The General Charity Fund
G S Plaut Charitable Trust
Polden-Puckham Charitable
  Foundation
Pontin Charitable Trust
Mary Potter Convent Hospital
  Trust
Powell Foundation
Primrose Hill Trust
Prince Foundation
Prince Philip Trust Fund
Pye Foundation
Queen Mary's Roehampton
  Trust
Joseph Rank Trust
Eleanor Rathbone Charitable
  Trust
Sir James Reckitt Charity
Christopher H R Reeves
  Charitable Trust
REMEDI
Clive Richards Charity Ltd
Violet M Richards Charity
Richmond Parish Lands Charity
Helen Roll Charitable Trust
Rotherwick Foundation
Christopher Rowbotham
  Charitable Trust
Joseph Rowntree Charitable
  Trust
Russell Trust
Audrey Sacher Charitable Trust
Karim Rida Said Foundation

Jean Sainsbury Animal Welfare
  Trust
St Christopher's College
  Educational Trust
St James's Place Foundation
St Katharine & Shadwell Trust
Sarum St Michael Educational
  Charity
Scottish Churches Community
  Trust
Search
Sefton Community Foundation
Sheffield Bluecoat & Mount
  Pleasant Educational
  Foundation
Sheldon Trust
Rita and David Slowe
  Charitable Trust
Mrs Smith & Mount Trust
Solo Charitable Settlement
Steinberg Family Charitable
  Trust
Swan Trust
Thames Community
  Foundation
Tisbury Telegraph Trust
Treeside Trust
Florence Turner Trust
TUUT Charitable Trust
Ulting Overseas Trust
Ulverscroft Foundation
John and Lucille van Geest
  Foundation
Victoria Homes Trust
Charity of Thomas Wade &
  Others
Wellfield Trust
Westcroft Trust
Whitley Animal Protection Trust
Felicity Wilde Charitable Trust
Will Charitable Trust
Harold Hyam Wingate
  Foundation
Wolfson Foundation
Woodlands Trust (259569)
Yapp Charitable Trust
W Wing Yip & Bros Charitable
  Trust
Elizabeth & Prince Zaiger Trust

....

■ **Three years**
Funding priority
1970 Trust
29th May 1961 Charitable
  Trust
Abel Charitable Trust
Sir John & Lady Amory's
  Charitable Trust
G C Armitage Charitable Trust
Balney Charitable Trust
BBC Children in Need Appeal
BBC Radio Cambridgeshire –
  Trustline
Patrick Berthoud Charitable
  Trust

BibleLands
Anthony Bourne Foundation
Viscountess Boyd Charitable
  Trust
British Dietetic Association
  General and Education
  Trust Fund
Palgrave Brown Foundation
BUPA Foundation
Cambridgeshire Historic
  Churches Trust
Camelot Foundation
Carnegie United Kingdom Trust
Sir John Cass's Foundation
Sir Ernest Cassel Educational
  Trust
Wilfrid & Constance Cave
  Foundation
Cobb Charity
Community Fund
Construction Industry Trust for
  Youth
Cystic Fibrosis Trust
William Delafield Charitable
  Trust
Dove-Bowerman Trust
Edinburgh Voluntary
  Organisations' Trust Funds
Feed the Minds
Bud Flanagan Leukaemia Fund
Jill Franklin Trust
Simon Gibson Charitable Trust
Simon Heller Charitable
  Settlement
Philip Henman Trust
Housing Associations
  Charitable Trust
Ingram Trust
International Spinal Research
  Trust
ITF Seafarers Trust
James Trust
Jordan Charitable Foundation
Judith Trust
Michael & Ilse Katz Foundation
Peter Kershaw Trust
Mary Kinross Charitable Trust
Allen Lane Foundation
Lawlor Foundation
Kennedy Leigh Charitable
  Trust
Levy Foundation
Lloyd's Charities Trust
Lloyds TSB Foundation for the
  Channel Islands
London Youth Trust
MacRobert Trust
W M Mann Foundation
Mayfield Valley Arts Trust
Oliver Morland Charitable Trust
Stanley Morrison Charitable
  Trust
Muslim Hands
National Asthma Campaign
National Kidney Research
  Fund Limited

Frances and Augustus
Newman Foundation
North West Cancer Research
Fund
Northcott Devon Medical
Foundation
P F Charitable Trust
Panton Trust
Parivar Trust
Charity Fund of the Worshipful
Company of Paviors
J B Pelly Charitable Settlement
Austin & Hope Pilkington Trust
Portishead Nautical Trust
PPP Foundation
Mr and Mrs J A Pye's
Charitable Settlement
Peggy Ramsay Foundation
Riverside Charitable Trust
Limited
Dr Mortimer and Theresa
Sackler Foundation
Saint Edmund, King & Martyr
Trust
St Peter's Saltley Trust
St Thomas Ecclesiastical
Charity
Scott Bader Commonwealth
Ltd
Sheepdrove Trust
R C Sherriff Rosebriars Trust
Bishop Simeon CR Trust
Stanley Smith UK Horticultural
Trust
Sobell Foundation
Sparks Charity
Fred Towler Charity Trust
Unemployed Voluntary Action
Fund
David Uri Memorial Trust
Bernard Van Leer Foundation
VEC Acorn Trust
Wates Foundation
Westminster Foundation
Woo Charitable Foundation
Yorkshire Agricultural Society
Yorkshire Historic Churches
Trust

Will consider
Sylvia Aitken Charitable Trust
Ajahma Charitable Trust
All Saints Educational Trust
Allachy Trust
Dorothy Gertrude Allen
Memorial Fund
H B Allen Charitable Trust
Viscount Amory's Charitable
Trust
James and Grace Anderson
Trust
Anglian Water Trust Fund
Milly Apthorp Charitable Trust
Arthritis Research Campaign
Arts Council of England

Arts Council of Northern
Ireland
Arts Council of Wales
Ove Arup Foundation
Ashby Charitable Trust
Lord Ashdown Charitable Trust
Ashendene Trust
Astor Foundation
Atlantic Foundation
BAA 21st Century
Communities Trust
Bacta Charitable Trust
William P Bancroft (No 2)
Charitable Trust and
Jenepher Gillett Trust
Barnabas Charitable Trust
Barnes Workhouse Fund
Barnwood House Trust
Barracks Trust of Newcastle-
under-Lyme
Bedford Charity
Hervey Benham Charitable
Trust
Bisgood Charitable Trust
Herbert & Peter Blagrave
Charitable Trust
Blatchington Court Trust
Body Shop Foundation
Charles Boot Trust
Boots Charitable Trust
Bramble Charitable Trust
Breast Cancer Research Trust
Bridge House Estates Trust
Fund
Britannia Building Society
Foundation
Britland Charitable Trust
Bromley Trust
Charles Brotherton Trust
R S Brownless Charitable
Trust
Bryant Trust
E F Bulmer Benevolent Fund
Clara E Burgess Charity
Barrow Cadbury Trust and the
Barrow Cadbury Fund
Edward Cadbury Charitable
Trust
Cadbury Schweppes
Foundation
Carlton Television Trust
Carnegie Trust for the
Universities of Scotland
Casey Trust
Charities Advisory Trust
Chase Charity
Child Growth Foundation
Children's Liver Disease
Foundation
Chownes Foundation
Christendom Trust
Church Burgesses Educational
Foundation
Church Urban Fund
Cinderford Charitable Trust
City Parochial Foundation

J A Clark Charitable Trust
Clover Trust
Francis Coales Charitable
Foundation
John & Freda Coleman
Charitable Trust
Colt Foundation
Comic Relief
Community Foundation Serving
Tyne & Wear and
Northumberland
Consortium on Opportunities
for Volunteering
Ernest Cook Trust
Gordon Cook Foundation
Cooper Charitable Trust
Coppings Trust
Cornwell Charitable Trust
Cripplegate Foundation
Cumber Family Charitable
Trust
D'Oyly Carte Charitable Trust
Daily Telegraph Charitable
Trust
John Grant Davies Trust
Richard Davies Charitable
Foundation
Wilfrid Bruce Davis Charitable
Trust
Miriam K Dean Refugee Trust
Fund
Denman Charitable Trust
J N Derbyshire Trust
Diabetes UK
Dibden Allotments Charity
DLM Charitable Trust
Drapers' Charitable Fund
Dunhill Medical Trust
W E Dunn Trust
City of Edinburgh Charitable
Trusts
Wilfred & Elsie Elkes Charity
Fund
John Ellerman Foundation
Elmley Foundation
Emerton-Christie Charity
Epilepsy Research Foundation
Equitable Charitable Trust
Eranda Foundation
Eveson Charitable Trust
Fairbairn Charitable Trust
Esmée Fairbairn Foundation
Samuel William Farmer's Trust
Fifty Fund
David Finnie & Alan Emery
Charitable Trust
Florence's Charitable Trust
Four Lanes Trust
Gordon Fraser Charitable Trust
Freshgate Trust Foundation
Worshipful Company of
Furniture Makers Charitable
Fund
Gannochy Trust
Robert Gavron Charitable Trust
J Paul Getty Jr Charitable Trust

Girdlers' Company Charitable
Trust
Teresa Rosenbaum Golden
Charitable Trust
Golsoncott Foundation
Reginald Graham Charitable
Trust
J G Graves Charitable Trust
Great Britain Sasakawa
Foundation
Greater Bristol Foundation
Greenham Common
Community Trust Limited
Greggs Trust
Bishop of Guildford's
Foundation
Gulbenkian Foundation
GWR Community Trust
H C D Memorial Fund
Hadrian Trust
Robert Hall Charity
R J Harris Charitable
Settlement
N & P Hartley Memorial Trust
Charles Hayward Foundation
May Hearnshaw's Charity
Hedley Foundation
Help the Aged
Hertfordshire Community
Foundation
Hilden Charitable Fund
Hinchley Charitable Trust
Hockerill Educational
Foundation
Dorothy Holmes Charitable
Trust
Holywood Trust
Hospital of God at Greatham
Inland Waterways Association
Worshipful Company of
Innholders General Charity
Fund
Isle of Dogs Community
Foundation
Sir Barry Jackson Trust and
County Fund
Rees Jeffreys Road Fund
Jephcott Charitable Trust
J G Joffe Charitable Trust
Elton John Aids Foundation
Joicey Trust
Anton Jurgens Charitable Trust
William Kendall's Charity
Kennel Club Charitable Trust
Kidani Memorial Trust
King's Fund
Kleinwort Benson Charitable
Trust
Marina Kleinwort Charitable
Trust
Sir James Knott Trust
Kreitman Foundation
Beatrice Laing Trust
Christopher Laing Foundation
Kirby Laing Foundation
Maurice Laing Foundation

Maurice and Hilda Laing
Charitable Trust
Lankelly Foundation
Mason Le Page Charitable
Trust
Leathersellers' Company
Charitable Fund
Leigh Trust
Leverhulme Trade Charities
Trust
Leverhulme Trust
Lewis Family Charitable Trust
Linden Charitable Trust
Lloyds TSB Foundation for
England and Wales
Lloyds TSB Foundation for
Northern Ireland
Lloyds TSB Foundation for
Scotland
London Law Trust
William & Katherine Longman
Trust
Marie Helen Luen Charitable
Trust
John Lyon's Charity
R S MacDonald Charitable
Trust
Mackintosh Foundation
Manchester Airport Community
Trust Fund
Marchday Charitable Fund
Marchig Animal Welfare Trust
Market Harborough and The
Bowdens Charity
Sir George Martin Trust
Medlock Charitable Trust
Mercers' Charitable
Foundation
Merchant Taylors' Company
Charities Fund
Methodist Relief and
Development Fund
Miles Trust for the Putney and
Roehampton Community
Millfield House Foundation
Mitchell Charitable Trust
Esmé Mitchell Trust
Mitsubishi Corporation Fund
for Europe and Africa
Mobbs Memorial Trust Ltd
Monument Trust
John Moores Foundation
Morgan Stanley International
Foundation
National Catholic Fund
National Manuscripts
Conservation Trust
National Power Charitable
Trust
Newby Trust Limited
Noel Buxton Trust
Norman Family Charitable
Trust
Northern Rock Foundation
Nottingham General
Dispensary

Nuffield Foundation
Nuffield Trust
Oakdale Trust
Odin Charitable Trust
Old Enfield Charitable Trust
John Oldacre Foundation
Frank Parkinson Agricultural
Trust
Patrick Charitable Trust
Harry Payne Trust
Mrs C S Heber Percy
Charitable Trust
Personal Assurance Charitable
Trust
Jack Petchey Foundation
Cecil Pilkington Charitable
Trust
Col W W Pilkington Will Trusts
– The General Charity Fund
John Pitman Charitable Trust
G S Plaut Charitable Trust
Polden-Puckham Charitable
Foundation
Pontin Charitable Trust
Mary Potter Convent Hospital
Trust
Prairie Trust
Simone Prendergast Charitable
Trust
Primrose Hill Trust
Prince Foundation
Prince Philip Trust Fund
Pye Foundation
R V W Trust
Radcliffe Trust
Rainford Trust
Joseph Rank Trust
E L Rathbone Charitable Trust
Eleanor Rathbone Charitable
Trust
John Rayner Charitable Trust
Sir James Reckitt Charity
Christopher H R Reeves
Charitable Trust
REMEDI
Violet M Richards Charity
Richmond Parish Lands Charity
Ripple Effect Foundation
Helen Roll Charitable Trust
Christopher Rowbotham
Charitable Trust
Joseph Rowntree Charitable
Trust
Royal Docks Trust
Rufford Foundation
Karim Rida Said Foundation
Jean Sainsbury Animal Welfare
Trust
St Andrew Animal Fund Ltd
St Christopher's College
Educational Trust
St James' Trust Settlement
Sir Walter St John's
Educational Charity
St Katharine & Shadwell Trust
St Luke's College Foundation

Camilla Samuel Fund
Sarum St Michael Educational
   Charity
Scarfe Charitable Trust
Francis C Scott Charitable
   Trust
Frieda Scott Charitable Trust
Scottish Churches Community
   Trust
Searle Charitable Trust
Seedfield Trust
Sefton Community Foundation
Sheffield Bluecoat & Mount
   Pleasant Educational
   Foundation
Sheldon Trust
Sherburn House Charity
Simpson Education &
   Conservation Trust
Henry Smith Charity
Mrs Smith & Mount Trust
Solo Charitable Settlement
Staples Trust
Steinberg Family Charitable
   Trust
Stewards' Charitable Trust
Sir Halley Stewart Trust
Stoller Charitable Trust
Alan Sugar Foundation
Summerfield Charitable Trust
Bernard Sunley Charitable
   Foundation
Sutton Coldfield Municipal
   Charities
Sutton Trust
Tearfund
Sir Jules Thorn Charitable
   Trust
Tisbury Telegraph Trust
Triangle Trust (1949) Fund
Florence Turner Trust
TUUT Charitable Trust
Ulting Overseas Trust
Ulverscroft Foundation
Valentine Charitable Trust
John and Lucille van Geest
   Foundation
Vodafone UK Foundation
Charity of Thomas Wade &
   Others
Scurrah Wainwright Charity
Wakefield Trust
Robert and Felicity Waley-
   Cohen Charitable Trust
War on Want
Ward Blenkinsop Trust
Weavers' Company Benevolent
   Fund
Westcroft Trust
Whitaker Charitable Trust
Whitecourt Charitable Trust
Whitley Animal Protection Trust
Wiltshire and Swindon
   Community Foundation
Harold Hyam Wingate
   Foundation

Charles Wolfson Charitable
   Trust
Wolfson Foundation
Woodlands Trust (259569)
Worshipful Company of
   Founders Charities
Yapp Charitable Trust
Zurich Financial Services
   Community Trust

....

■ Longer than three years

Funding priority

G C Armitage Charitable Trust
Bergqvist Charitable Trust
BibleLands
John & Celia Bonham Christie
   Charitable Trust
British Institute of Archaeology
   at Ankara
Broadfield Trust
Commonwealth Relations
   Trust
Cystic Fibrosis Trust
William Delafield Charitable
   Trust
Delius Trust
Diana, Princess of Wales
   Memorial Fund
Fiat Auto (UK) Charity
Fifty Fund
Four Acre Trust
Fund for Human Need
Jacqueline and Michael Gee
   Charitable Trust
Golden Charitable Trust
Simon Heller Charitable
   Settlement
Philip Henman Trust
Mary Homfray Charitable Trust
Hyde Charitable Trust
John Jarrold Trust
Kelsick's Educational
   Foundation
Mary Kinross Charitable Trust
Paul Lunn-Rockliffe Charitable
   Trust
Ronald McDonald Children's
   Charities Limited
Marsh Christian Trust
Migraine Trust
Minge's Gift
G M Morrison Charitable Trust
Nathan Charitable Trust
National Kidney Research
   Fund Limited
Novi Most International
Oxfam (GB)
Pilkington Charities Fund
PPP Foundation
Ronald & Kathleen Pryor
   Charitable Trust
St Laurence Charities for the
   Poor

Rosemary Scanlan Charitable
   Trust
Archie Sherman Charitable
   Trust
Douglas Turner Trust
Vincent Wildlife Trust
Welsh Church Fund –
   Carmarthenshire area
Earl & Countess of Wessex
   Charitable Trust
Westcroft Trust
Westminster Foundation
Women at Risk

Will consider

1970 Trust
Adint Charitable Trust
AIM Foundation
All Saints Educational Trust
James and Grace Anderson
   Trust
Arthritis Research Campaign
Arts Council of England
Ove Arup Foundation
Lord Ashdown Charitable Trust
Bacta Charitable Trust
Barnes Workhouse Fund
Barracks Trust of Newcastle-
   under-Lyme
Beacon Trust
James Beattie Charitable Trust
Bedford Charity
Peter Black Charitable Trust
Charles Boot Trust
Viscountess Boyd Charitable
   Trust
John Bristow and Thomas
   Mason Trust
Britten-Pears Foundation
Bromley Trust
BUPA Foundation
Burden Trust
Mauritis Mulder Canter Charity
Charities Advisory Trust
Chipping Sodbury Town Lands
   Charity
Chownes Foundation
Cinderford Charitable Trust
Stephen Clark 1957
   Charitable Trust
Cleary Foundation
Clothworkers' Foundation and
   other Trusts
John & Freda Coleman
   Charitable Trust
Colt Foundation
Construction Industry Trust for
   Youth
Gordon Cook Foundation
Holbeche Corfield Charitable
   Settlement
Cranbury Foundation
Criffel Charitable Trust
Cripplegate Foundation
Gwendoline & Margaret Davies
   Charity

Richard Davies Charitable
Foundation
Richard Desmond Charitable
Trust
Diabetes UK
City of Edinburgh Charitable
Trusts
Wilfred & Elsie Elkes Charity
Fund
Ellis Campbell Charitable
Foundation
Epilepsy Research Foundation
Esmée Fairbairn Foundation
Feed the Minds
Forman Hardy Charitable Trust
Worshipful Company of
Furniture Makers Charitable
Fund
Gatsby Charitable Foundation
Girdlers' Company Charitable
Trust
Godinton Charitable Trust
Teresa Rosenbaum Golden
Charitable Trust
Golsoncott Foundation
Reginald Graham Charitable
Trust
Barry Green Memorial Fund
J C Green Charitable
Settlement
Greenham Common
Community Trust Limited
Gretna Charitable Trust
GWR Community Trust
R J Harris Charitable
Settlement
N & P Hartley Memorial Trust
Dorothy Hay-Bolton Charitable
Trust
Charles Hayward Foundation
Joanna Herbert-Stepney
Charitable Settlement
Higgs Charitable Trust
Hilden Charitable Fund
Hinchley Charitable Trust
Dorothy Holmes Charitable
Trust
India Foundation (UK)
Inland Waterways Association
Edward Cecil Jones Settlement
Kreitman Foundation
Christopher Laing Foundation
Richard Langhorn Trust
Lark Trust
Lauffer Family Charitable
Foundation
Lawlor Foundation
Lazard Charitable Trust
Leach Fourteenth Trust
Leathersellers' Company
Charitable Fund
Lethendy Charitable Trust
Leverhulme Trust
Levy Foundation
William & Katherine Longman
Trust

Loseley & Guildway Charitable
Trust
Macfarlane Walker Trust
Marchig Animal Welfare Trust
Market Harborough and The
Bowdens Charity
Mickel Fund
Miles Trust for the Putney and
Roehampton Community
Hugh and Mary Miller Bequest
Trust
Millichope Foundation
Mitsubishi Corporation Fund
for Europe and Africa
Stanley Morrison Charitable
Trust
Muslim Hands
Noel Buxton Trust
Northern Rock Foundation
Old Enfield Charitable Trust
Owen Family Trust
Mrs C S Heber Percy
Charitable Trust
Personal Assurance Charitable
Trust
G S Plaut Charitable Trust
Mary Potter Convent Hospital
Trust
Primrose Hill Trust
Prince Foundation
Proven Family Trust
Mr and Mrs J A Pye's
Charitable Settlement
Pyke Charity Trust
Joseph Rank Trust
Sir James Reckitt Charity
Christopher H R Reeves
Charitable Trust
Christopher Rowbotham
Charitable Trust
St Jude's Trust
St Katharine & Shadwell Trust
St Thomas Ecclesiastical
Charity
R H Scholes Charitable Trust
Scott Bader Commonwealth
Ltd
Scottish Churches Community
Trust
Sefton Community Foundation
Bishop Simeon CR Trust
Stanley Smith UK Horticultural
Trust
Sobell Foundation
Sparks Charity
Jessie Spencer Trust
Steinberg Family Charitable
Trust
Hugh Stenhouse Foundation
Sir Sigmund Sternberg
Charitable Foundation
Tay Charitable Trust
Ulverscroft Foundation
Valentine Charitable Trust
John and Lucille van Geest
Foundation

War on Want
Whitley Animal Protection Trust
Harold Hyam Wingate
Foundation
Wixamtree Trust
Wolfson Foundation
Zurich Financial Services
Community Trust

The alphabetical register of grant making trusts

This section lists the individual entries for the grant making trusts.

■ The 1970 Trust

WHERE FUNDING CAN BE GIVEN UK, with an interest in Scotland.

WHO CAN BENEFIT Charities which support disadvantaged minorities.

WHAT IS FUNDED The trust states it supports small UK charities 'doing innovative, educational, or experimental work in the following fields: civil liberties (e.g. freedom of information; constitutional reform; humanising work; children's welfare); the public interest in the face of vested interest groups (such as the advertising, alcohol, road, war, pharmaceuticals, and tobacco industries); disadvantaged minorities, multiracial work, prison reform; new economics ('as if people mattered' – Schumacher) and intermediate technology; public transport, pedestrians, bicycling, road crash prevention, traffic-calming, low-energy lifestyles; preventative health.

WHAT IS NOT FUNDED No support for larger charities, those with religious connections, or individuals (except in rare cases – and then only through registered charities or educational bodies). No support to central or local government agencies.

TYPE OF GRANT Usually one to three years; sometimes longer.

RANGE OF GRANTS Usually £300–£2,000.

SAMPLE GRANTS £3,000 to each of Earth Resources, Make Votes Count and Roadpeace; £2,000 each to Backcare, BADAC, Parent to Parent Adoption, Parents for Children and The Pestices; £1,500 to Concern.

FINANCES *Year* 2001 *Income* £50,000 *Grants* £70,000 *Assets* £1,500,000

TRUSTEES David Rennie.

HOW TO APPLY In writing to the correspondent. Proposals should be summarised on one page with one or two more pages of supporting information. The trust states that it regrettably only has time to reply to the very few applications it is able to fund and that it is fully committed for the next two years.

WHO TO APPLY TO The Trustee, c/o C W Pagan, Messrs Pagan Osborne, 12 St Catherine Street, Cupar, Fife KY15 4HN *Tel* 01334 653777 *Fax* 01334 655063 *E-mail* enquiries@pagan.co.uk *Website* www.pagan.co.uk

SC NO SC008788   **ESTABLISHED** 1970

■ The 1989 Willan Charitable Trust

WHERE FUNDING CAN BE GIVEN Worldwide, but mainly the north east of England.

WHO CAN BENEFIT Registered charities for the benefit of children; disabled people; carers; volunteers; refugees; and offenders.

WHAT IS FUNDED Grants are given to: advance the education of children and help children in need; encourage the study of animals and birds and their protection for the benefit of mankind; benefit people with physical or mental disabilities and alleviate hardship and distress either generally or individually; and further medical research.

WHAT IS NOT FUNDED Grants are not given directly to individuals. Grants for gap years may be considered if the individual will be working for a charity (in this case the grant would be paid to the charity).

RANGE OF GRANTS £500–£10,000.

SAMPLE GRANTS In 2000–01: £20,000 each to Mea Trust and the Community Foundation; £10,000 to Greggs Trust; £5,000 each to Newcastle upon Tyne Church High School, Durham CVS, Tyne and Wear Autistic Society, Salvation Army and Tyne Tees Crimestoppers.

FINANCES *Year* 2001–02 *Income* £590,000 *Grants* £498,300 *Assets* £10,000,000

TRUSTEES Miss E Willan; P R M Harbottle; A Fettes; F A Chapman.

HOW TO APPLY In writing to the correspondent. Grants appear to be given four times a year, in March, June, September and November.

WHO TO APPLY TO A Fettes, Trustee, 8 Kelso Drive, The Priorys, Tynemouth, North Tyneside NE29 9NS *Tel* 0191 258 2533

CC NO 802749   **ESTABLISHED** 1989

■ The 29th May 1961 Charitable Trust

WHERE FUNDING CAN BE GIVEN UK, with a special interest in the Warwickshire/Birmingham/Coventry area.

WHO CAN BENEFIT Charitable organisations in the UK. People who are socially disadvantaged may be favoured.

WHAT IS FUNDED General charitable purposes across a broad spectrum, including: art, leisure and youth; health; social welfare; education and training; homelessness and housing; offenders; and conservation and protection.

WHAT IS NOT FUNDED Grants only to registered charities. No grants to individuals.

TYPE OF GRANT One-off, recurring and some spread over two to three years. Grants are given for capital and revenue purposes.

RANGE OF GRANTS £500–£100,000, but the great majority are less than £10,000.

SAMPLE GRANTS £183,000 to University of Warwick for general running costs of the Arts Centre; £100,000 each to Coventry & Warwickshire Awards Trust towards the running costs of a sports centre providing facilities for under-privileged communities, London Business School towards refurbishing the careers facilities and University of Warwick towards widening access to the University; £93,750 to Federation of London Youth Clubs towards general funds; £75,000 to Prince's Trust; £65,000 to Coventry Day Care Fund for People with Learning Difficulties; £60,000 each to National Portrait Gallery towards refurbishment of the Regency Galleries and West of England School towards the cost of a new hydrotherapy pool; £50,000 to Crisis for core costs.

FINANCES *Year* 2001–02 *Income* £3,178,000 *Grants* £2,971,000 *Assets* £82,289,000

TRUSTEES V E Treves; J H Cattell; P Varney; A J Mead.

HOW TO APPLY To the secretary in writing, enclosing in triplicate the most recent annual report and accounts. Trustees normally meet in March, June, September and December.

WHO TO APPLY TO The Secretary, c/o Macfarlanes, 10 Norwich Street, London EC4A 1BD *Tel* 020 7831 9222 *Fax* 020 7831 9607

CC NO 200198   **ESTABLISHED** 1961

■ The 'A' Foundation

WHERE FUNDING CAN BE GIVEN Liverpool.
WHO CAN BENEFIT Charitable organisations.
WHAT IS FUNDED The arts.
SAMPLE GRANTS £50,000 to Liverpool Biennial of Contemporary Art.
FINANCES *Year* 2000 *Grants* £50,000
TRUSTEES James C S Moore; Jane C Rankin Reid; Portia M Kennaway.
HOW TO APPLY In writing to the correspondent.
WHO TO APPLY TO Jayne Casey, Director, 2nd Floor, Bands Warehouse, 8 Vernon Street, Liverpool L2 2AY *Tel* 0151 236 0446
CC NO 1071488   **ESTABLISHED** 1998

■ The A B Charitable Trust

WHERE FUNDING CAN BE GIVEN UK and developing world.
WHO CAN BENEFIT Institutions and charities benefiting at risk groups and people disadvantaged by poverty.
WHAT IS FUNDED To promote and defend the cause of human dignity.
WHAT IS NOT FUNDED No support for medical research, animal welfare, expeditions, scholarships, conservation and environment.
TYPE OF GRANT Single donations.
RANGE OF GRANTS £1,000–£5,000.
SAMPLE GRANTS £12,000 to Prison Reform Trust; £6,000 to Richmond Fellowship; £5,000 each to Bethany Project, Catholic Housing Aid Society, Comeback, Holy Cross Centre Trust, New Horizon Youth Centre, Prisoners Abroad, Prisoners of Conscience, Respond, Women's Therapy Centre and Youth at Risk.
FINANCES *Year* 2000–01 *Income* £277,987 *Grants* £216,100 *Assets* £199,571
TRUSTEES Y J M Bonavero; D Boehm; Mrs A G M-L Bonavero; Miss C Bonavero; Miss S Bonavero.
HOW TO APPLY In writing to the secretary, up to a maximum of four A4 pages if appropriate, plus the most recent detailed audited accounts. The trustees meet on a quarterly basis in March, June, September and December. Applications should be from UK registered charities only.
WHO TO APPLY TO T M Denham, Secretary, 12 Addison Avenue, London W11 4QR
CC NO 1000147   **ESTABLISHED** 1990

■ Abbey National Charitable Trust Ltd

WHERE FUNDING CAN BE GIVEN UK.
WHO CAN BENEFIT Registered charities which benefit disabled people and disadvantaged and socially isolated groups. Smaller charities and local appeals are favoured.
WHAT IS FUNDED Equal opportunities for disabled people. Education and training, and employment provision and creation for disadvantaged/ socially excluded groups. This includes special needs education, including special schools, training for work, job creation, IT training, literacy, and vocational training. Playschemes are also considered.

WHAT IS NOT FUNDED Registered charities only. Grants are not given to individuals or for the exclusive benefit of a single religious or ethnic group.
TYPE OF GRANT One-off donations. Preference for capital projects and start-up costs.
RANGE OF GRANTS £50–£25,000.
SAMPLE GRANTS £76,500 in total to Prince's Trust; £30,000 to Money Advice Trust; £20,000 each to Milton Keynes Community Foundation, Royal National College for the Blind, Employment for Disabled People and St Mungo Association Charitable Trust; £18,000 each to National Deaf Children's Society and University of Newcastle; £16,000 to Family Policy Studies Centre; £15,000 each to Common Purpose Charitable Trust, Rehab UK, Business in the Community, Shopmobility (in total), Barnados, Toynbee Hall and Bradford Access Action; £10,000 each to Royal Horticultural Society, Centre for Independent Living in Glasgow and Emmaus Gloucestershire; £5,000 each to Dogs for the Disabled, Orchardsville Society, St Georges & St Peters Community Association, Princess Royal Trust for Carers, Safe Anchor Trust and Scottish Council Scout Association.
FINANCES *Year* 2001 *Income* £1,500,746 *Grants* £2,045,744 *Assets* £9,328,380
TRUSTEES J Smart; N Wilkes; M Cooke; T Coops; A Elliott; J Hayhow; B Morrison; T Murley; M Pendle; J Price.
PUBLICATIONS *Abbey National in the Community.*
HOW TO APPLY In writing to the correspondent, with supporting information. The trust does not issue application forms. Applications may be made at any time. Initial telephone enquiries are welcome. Successful applicants are expected to work with local Abbey National managers to obtain mutual publicity.
WHO TO APPLY TO Alan Eagle, Community Partnership Manager, PO Box 911, Milton Keynes, Buckinghamshire MK9 1AD *Tel* 0870 608 0104 *E-mail* alan.eagle@abbeynational.co.uk *Website* www.abbeynational.com
CC NO 803655   **ESTABLISHED** 1990

■ Abbeydale Trust

WHERE FUNDING CAN BE GIVEN UK.
WHO CAN BENEFIT Individuals, and organisations benefiting children, young adults, medical professionals, research workers, students, teachers and governesses.
WHAT IS FUNDED Advancement of medical research, respite and education. Preference is given to projects in which the trustees have special interest or knowledge.
FINANCES *Year* 2001–02 *Income* £24,127
HOW TO APPLY The trust states that all of the income is already allocated. No new applicants can be considered.
WHO TO APPLY TO The Secretary, c/o HSBC plc, 2 Fargate, Sheffield S1 2JS
CC NO 217333   **ESTABLISHED** 1959

■ The Abel Charitable Trust

WHERE FUNDING CAN BE GIVEN London.
WHO CAN BENEFIT Registered charities benefiting young adults, unemployed people, Christians, at risk groups, people disadvantaged by poverty and homeless people. Mainly emergent charities aiming to make the individual more self-sufficient and treating the person as a whole and not a malfunctioning part.

WHAT IS FUNDED Charities working in the fields of: advice and information about housing; care in the community; and Christian outreach. The trust aims to support charities working to resolve rather than alleviate problems.

WHAT IS NOT FUNDED Only registered charities are supported. No grants to individuals, or for building appeals, vehicles, research (including medical research), support services for elderly people or large general appeals. The trust does not make loans or pay off mortgages, bank loans or deficits.

TYPE OF GRANT Recurring costs; feasibility studies; and start-up costs. Funding of up to three years will be considered.

RANGE OF GRANTS £500–£5,000, typical grant £2,000.

SAMPLE GRANTS £3,000 each to Mission in Hounslow towards refurbishment costs, Cricklewood Homeless Concern to fund travel expenses for interviews and so on, Prisons Video Magazine towards the cost of employment and SAMM (South East) towards the cost of information packs; £2,500 to Renewal Turnaround Project towards refurbishment costs; £2,000 each to Centre 70 Counselling Services and Womens Link.

FINANCES *Year* 2001 *Income* £15,000 *Grants* £33,000 *Assets* £511,000

TRUSTEES Canon I Smith-Cameron; Dr P Logan; Mrs H Abrahams; J D Abel; Mrs M Marshall.

HOW TO APPLY In writing to the correspondent, stating the specific purpose for which help is sought, the status of the organisation, membership and accounts, a brief description of the work, the amount sought from the trust and how the figure is derived. Applications should be made in writing from November to January. Trustees consider applications annually in June/July.

WHO TO APPLY TO Revd D J Abel, Administrator, Balcombe Mill, Mill Lane, Balcombe, Haywards Heath, West Sussex RH17 6QT *Tel* 01444 811123 *Fax* 01444 811123

CC NO 288421   **ESTABLISHED** 1983

■ Aberbrothock Charitable Trust

WHERE FUNDING CAN BE GIVEN East of Scotland, north of the firth of Tay.

WHO CAN BENEFIT Organisations benefiting the community with charitable status.

WHAT IS FUNDED Children/young people; disability; environment/conservation; hospitals/hospices; and medical research are all considered.

WHAT IS NOT FUNDED The only exclusions are geographical restrictions.

TYPE OF GRANT One-off, including project, research, capital and core costs.

RANGE OF GRANTS £1,000–£5,000.

SAMPLE GRANTS £2,000 each to Angus Independent Advocacy Services, Arbroath Sea Fest, Angus Mental Health Association, Cornerstone Community Care, Youthlink.

FINANCES *Year* 2001 *Income* £74,000 *Grants* £71,000 *Assets* £1,800,000

TRUSTEES G McNicol; J G Mathieson; Mrs A T L Grant; G N J Smart.

HOW TO APPLY In writing to the correspondent. Trustees meet to consider grants in March, July and November.

WHO TO APPLY TO Messrs Thorntons, Brothockbank House, Arbroath, Angus DD11 1NF *Tel* 01241 872683

SC NO SC003110   **ESTABLISHED** 1971

■ The Henry & Grete Abrahams Charitable Trust

WHERE FUNDING CAN BE GIVEN UK and overseas.

WHO CAN BENEFIT Registered Jewish and medical charities benefiting Jewish people and people who are sick.

WHAT IS FUNDED Jewish organisations and medical charities.

WHAT IS NOT FUNDED No grants to individuals.

TYPE OF GRANT Recurring, though amounts vary greatly from one year to the next.

RANGE OF GRANTS £100–£5,000.

SAMPLE GRANTS 1998–99: £10,000 to Macmillan Cancer Relief; £5,000 each to Cancer Research Campaign and Lewis Hammerson Charitable Trust; £1,000 to Liberal Jewish Synagogue; £500 each to Children's Hospital Trust Fund, Derma Trust, Jessie May Trust, Norwood Ravenswood, and Shepherds Bush Families.

FINANCES *Year* 2000–01 *Income* £25,723

TRUSTEES Mrs G Abrahams; M H Gluckstein; D M Maislish.

HOW TO APPLY In writing to the correspondent.

WHO TO APPLY TO David Maislish, Trustee, Hill Dickinson, 66–67 Cornhill, London EC3V 3RN *Tel* 020 7695 1048 *Fax* 020 7695 1001

CC NO 265517   **ESTABLISHED** 1973

■ The Henry & Grete Abrahams Second Charitable Foundation

WHERE FUNDING CAN BE GIVEN UK.

WHO CAN BENEFIT Charities benefiting young people who are disadvantaged or disabled.

WHAT IS FUNDED General charitable purposes, including Jewish organisations, medical and welfare charities.

WHAT IS NOT FUNDED No grants to individuals or non-registered charities.

RANGE OF GRANTS £25–£20,000.

SAMPLE GRANTS £20,000 to Royal Star & Garter Home; £12,500 to Wizo Charitable Foundation; £10,000 each to St John's Hospice and Wingate Youth Trust; £3,000 to Gurkha Welfare Trust; £2,000 to Nightingale House; £1,000 to Evelina Children's Hospital Appeal.

FINANCES *Year* 1998–99 *Income* £58,000 *Grants* £62,000

TRUSTEES Grete Abrahams; David Maislish; Mark Gluckstein.

HOW TO APPLY The trust states: 'We are fully committed to a number of charities for the next few years, therefore cannot undertake any more appeals'. The trustees meet in November.

WHO TO APPLY TO D Maislish, Trustee, Hill Dickinson, 66–67 Cornhill, London EC3V 3RN *Tel* 020 7695 1048 *Fax* 020 7695 1001

CC NO 298240   **ESTABLISHED** 1987

■ The Acacia Charitable Trust

WHERE FUNDING CAN BE GIVEN UK and Israel.

WHO CAN BENEFIT Registered charities benefiting children, young adults and Jewish people. Support may be given to charities benefiting medical professionals, teachers, governesses and students.

WHAT IS FUNDED Educational and medical charities in the UK. Jewish charities, both in the UK and the State of Israel.

WHAT IS NOT FUNDED No grants to individuals.

TYPE OF GRANT Core and project costs will be considered.

RANGE OF GRANTS £20–£36,000, although most for under £1,000.

SAMPLE GRANTS £36,000 to University of Reading; £26,000 to ORT Trust; £11,500 to World Jewish Relief; £10,000 to Community Security Trust; £9,000 to Jewish Museum; £2,000 each to Centre for Theology and Society and Jewish Care; £1,600 to Spanish and Portuguese Jews Congregation; £1,000 each to British Museum Development Trust, Institute for Jewish Policy Research, Norwood Ltd, JJCT, NSPCC, Royal National Theatre and Spanish and Portugese Jews' Home fir the Aged.

FINANCES *Year* 2000–01 *Income* £87,000 *Grants* £109,000 *Assets* £1,576,789

TRUSTEES K D Rubens; Mrs A G Rubens; S A Rubens.

HOW TO APPLY In writing to the correspondent.

WHO TO APPLY TO Mrs Nora Howland, Secretary, 5 Clarke's Mews, London W1G 6QN *Tel* 020 7486 1884 *Fax* 020 7487 4171

CC NO 274275   **ESTABLISHED** 1977

■ Access 4 Trust

WHERE FUNDING CAN BE GIVEN UK and newly developing countries.

WHO CAN BENEFIT Institutions and registered charities benefiting deprived children and needy families.

WHAT IS FUNDED Trustees focus their grants primarily towards deprived children and needy families, women's organisations and adoption.

WHAT IS NOT FUNDED No grants to individuals.

TYPE OF GRANT Single donations.

RANGE OF GRANTS Up to £3,000.

SAMPLE GRANTS £24,000 to Entebbe All Christian Womens Association; £23,000 to Post Adoption Centre; £20,000 to TRAX Programme Support; £11,400 to Friends of the Centre of the Rehabilitation of the Paralysed; £11,000 to ActionAid; £7,454 to Dharka Ashsania Mission: £7,000 to Rains Appeal – Ghana; £5,000 each to Bartimeus Fund – Ghana, British Agencies for Adoption and Fostering, Commonwork Land Trust and UNIFAT School – Uganda.

FINANCES *Year* 2000–01 *Income* £82,205 *Grants* £215,803 *Assets* £422,460

TRUSTEES Miss S M Wates; J R F Lulham.

HOW TO APPLY In writing to the correspondent.

WHO TO APPLY TO C Sadlow, Slater Maidment, 7 St James's Square, London SW1Y 4JU *Tel* 020 7930 7621

CC NO 267017   **ESTABLISHED** 1973

■ Achiezer Association Ltd

WHERE FUNDING CAN BE GIVEN Worldwide.

WHO CAN BENEFIT Organisations benefiting orthodox Jewish people, elderly people, academics, rabbis, students, teachers and governesses and people disadvantaged by poverty.

WHAT IS FUNDED People and institutions of the orthodox Jewish religion for: the relief of elderly people and people in need; advancement of education; advancement of religion; and general charitable purposes.

SAMPLE GRANTS £49,500 to JET; £47,800 to Gerurch Ari Torah Ac Trust; £36,250 to Menorah Grammar Schoool; £35,000 to Achisomoch Aid; £29,605 to Ohel Shimon Chaim; £20,000 to Be'er Yitzchock Kollel; £15,200 to Beth Jacob Grammar School; £11,613 to Stamford Hill Beth Hamedrash; £11,600 to Torah Teminah Primary School; £7,300 to Emuno Education Ltd; £7,200 to Chested Le Yisroel Trust.

FINANCES *Year* 1999–2000 *Income* £410,341 *Grants* £405,076 *Assets* £1,298,956

TRUSTEES Mrs J A Chontow; D Chontow; S S Chontow; M M Chontow.

HOW TO APPLY The trust states that funds are already committed to existing beneficiaries for the next two years. Unsolicited applications are therefore very unlikely to be successful.

WHO TO APPLY TO David Chontow, Trustee, 132 Clapton Common, London E5 9AG *Tel* 020 8800 5465

CC NO 255031   **ESTABLISHED** 1965

■ Achisomoch Aid Company

WHERE FUNDING CAN BE GIVEN Unrestricted.

WHO CAN BENEFIT Jewish religious charities.

WHAT IS FUNDED The advancement of religion in accordance with the Jewish faith.

SAMPLE GRANTS In 1997–98: £103,338 to Lolev Charitable Trust; £63,490 to Marbeh Torah Trust; £32,033 to Achiezer; £33,002 to Gateshead Talmudical College; £29,781 to WSRT; £21,224 to Jewish Secondary Schools Movement.

FINANCES *Year* 2000–01 *Income* £1,600,000 *Grants* £1,565,000

TRUSTEES Isaac M Katz; D C Chontow.

HOW TO APPLY In writing to the correspondent.

WHO TO APPLY TO Isaac Mark Katz, Secretary, 35 Templars Avenue, London NW11 0NU *Tel* 020 8731 8988 *Fax* 020 8458 1790 *E-mail* admin@achisimoch.org

CC NO 278387   **ESTABLISHED** 1979

■ The Company of Actuaries Charitable Trust Fund

WHERE FUNDING CAN BE GIVEN UK and overseas.

WHO CAN BENEFIT Charitable organisations and individuals.

WHAT IS FUNDED Assistance with actuarial education; to benefit distressed actuaries; and other charitable purposes.

WHAT IS NOT FUNDED No grants for expeditions or parish churches.

TYPE OF GRANT One-off.

RANGE OF GRANTS Largest £10,000; typical £500; one or two small grants of £100.

SAMPLE GRANTS £10,000 to Christ's Hospital 200 Years on Appeal; £2,000 to Lord Mayor's Appeal 2000; £1,000 each to Parkinson's Disease Society, Taylor-Schechter Genizah Research, Tower Hamlets Summer University and YMCA England; £500 each to Action for Blind People, Children Nationwide, Intermediate Technology and Women's Link.

FINANCES *Year* 1999–2000 *Income* £45,000 *Grants* £50,000 *Assets* £170,000

TRUSTEES R Squires, Chair; A Gibson; D Tandy; E S Thomas; G G Bannerman.

HOW TO APPLY In writing to the correspondent. Charitable organisations should supply the latest annual accounts.

WHO TO APPLY TO Graham Lockwood, Almoner, 34 Howe Drive, Beaconsfield, Buckinghamshire HP9 2BD *Tel* 01494 673451

CC NO 280702   **ESTABLISHED** 1980

■ The Sylvia Adams Charitable Trust

WHERE FUNDING CAN BE GIVEN UK, especially the eastern region of England, and Hertfordshire in particular; Africa, the Indian sub-continent and South America.

WHO CAN BENEFIT Projects benefiting children and young people, people living in poverty, and people with disabilities.

WHAT IS FUNDED The trust makes all its grants through UK registered charities and not directly to the country concerned. About 50% of the trust's grant total is given to UK causes, with the remaining 50% going to causes in the developing world. It is particularly interested in helping people to become self-supporting and self-help projects. UK focus is on enabling people to participate fully in society. Worldwide, the focus is on primary healthcare and health education, access to education, appropriate technology and community enterprise schemes.

WHAT IS NOT FUNDED The trust restricts its support to the three key areas shown above. Grants are not given to: individuals; charities only benefiting older people; UK charities benefiting those suffering from AIDS and HIV; medical research; animal charities. Grants are not made in war zones or to emergency relief appeals, nor in Eastern Europe, the former Soviet Union or the Middle East. Grants in the UK are not made to local charities outside the eastern region.

RANGE OF GRANTS £5,000–£20,000.

SAMPLE GRANTS £50,000 each to Deafblind UK as part of a five-year funding programme and to help endow a field hospital treating visual impairment in Pakistan; £25,000 each to Emmaus UK, Intermediate Technology, National Autistic Society, Saracens Foundation and Sense (as part of a £50,000 two-year grant); £21,000 to Hertfordshire Action on Disability for an information display vehicle; £12,000 each to Sight Savers International and UNAIS.

FINANCES *Year* 2000–01 *Income* £517,000 *Grants* £506,000 *Assets* £12,000,000

TRUSTEES A D Morris, Chair; R J Golland.

HOW TO APPLY In writing to the correspondent. Guidelines for applicants are available from the trust, and are quoted below. You are encouraged to contact the trust before applying. Applications should be in your own words, showing why we should support the organisation and which work you would like us to fund. You should enclose: a budget for the work; your latest annual report and accounts. You are actively encouraged to contact the trust to see if the application is well targeted. Deadlines for UK applications are every two months (the last days in February, April, June, August, October and December) and applicants are normally advised of the decision within two months of the deadline. The trust is able to provide a swift response when an urgent need for funding arises. The urgency proceedure will only be initiated if: the need is genuine and was unpredictable; a swift response enables and facilitates important long term planning.

WHO TO APPLY TO Kate Baldwin, Director, Sylvia Adams House, 24 The Common, Hatfield, Hertfordshire AL10 0NB *Tel* 01707 259259

CC NO 1050678   **ESTABLISHED** 1995

■ Miss Agnes Gilchrist Adamson's Trust

WHERE FUNDING CAN BE GIVEN UK, but preference will be given to requests on behalf of Scottish children.

WHO CAN BENEFIT Physically or mentally disabled children aged 16 or under, both groups and individuals.

WHAT IS FUNDED Assistance with holidays for children with a physical or mental disability. Grants may be given to the parent(s) of children or as block grants; for example, to the special needs unit of a school.

WHAT IS NOT FUNDED Anything falling outside of the trust's area of support.

TYPE OF GRANT Usually one-off

SAMPLE GRANTS In 2000: £5,500 to Lake District Calvert Trust; £2,000 each to Sense Scotland and Uphill Ski Club.

FINANCES *Year* 2001 *Income* £66,000 *Grants* £40,000

TRUSTEES A R Muir; R C Farrell; J Allen.

HOW TO APPLY On a form available from the correspondent. A copy of the latest audited accounts should be included together with details of your organisation, the number of children who would benefit and the proposed holiday. Applications are considered in January, May and September.

WHO TO APPLY TO K B Divine, Barnshaw, Comrie Road, Crieff, Perthshire PH7 4BQ *Tel* 01764 656048

SC NO SC016517   **ESTABLISHED** 1946

■ The ADAPT Trust

WHERE FUNDING CAN BE GIVEN UK.

WHO CAN BENEFIT Arts and heritage venues.

WHAT IS FUNDED Improvements in access for disabled people to arts and heritage venues.

WHAT IS NOT FUNDED No grants to: stately homes, heritage centres and crafts centres; halls designed and used for other purposes such as church halls, hospitals or educational establishments even though they sometimes house the arts; or festivals, unless at a permanent arts venue.

TYPE OF GRANT One-off grants for buildings and capital.

RANGE OF GRANTS £500–£5,000. Average £3,000.

SAMPLE GRANTS In 1999: £4,500 each to the following for infra-red audio description equipment: Theatre Royal Windsor, Cottesloe Theatre RNT, Lyceum Theatre Sheffield, Lyric Theatre Hammersmith, Marlowe Theatre Canterbury; £3,500 each to Grosvenor Museum Chester for accessible toilet, Ironbridge Open Air Museum for improved pathways, Wisbech & Fernland Museum for a platform lift, St Margaret's Bay Trust (Devon) for a ramp and accessible toilet; £3,250 to Midland Railway Centre Ripley for ramped access to a car park.

FINANCES *Year* 2001 *Income* £174,739 *Grants* £87,771 *Assets* £346,429

TRUSTEES Michael Cassidy, Chair; Elizabeth Fairbairn; Gary Flather; John C Griffiths; Alison Heath; Trevan Hingston; Robin Hyman; C Wycliffe Noble; Maurice Paterson; Rita Tushingham.

PUBLICATIONS Annual newsletter.

HOW TO APPLY Guidelines and application details are available from the ADAPT office. Applicants for grants have to demonstrate that all aspects of access have been considered, including parking, publicity and staff training.

WHO TO APPLY TO Stewart Coulter, Wellpark, 120 Sydney Street, Glasgow G31 1JF *Tel* 0141 556 2233 *Fax* 0141 556 7799
E-mail adapt.trust@virgin.net
SC NO SC020814   ESTABLISHED 1989

····················

■ The Victor Adda Foundation
WHERE FUNDING CAN BE GIVEN UK, but in practice Greenwich.
WHO CAN BENEFIT Organisations.
WHAT IS FUNDED This trust mainly supports the Fan Museum in Greenwich.
SAMPLE GRANTS £68,000 to The Fan Museum Trust; £250 to Glenurquhart Care Project; £60 to Catford & Bromley Combined Charities Appeal.
FINANCES *Year* 1999–2000 *Income* £307,000 *Grants* £68,000 *Assets* £2,300,000
TRUSTEES Mrs H E Alexander; M I Gee; Mrs B E Hodgkinson.
HOW TO APPLY In writing to the correspondent. Only successful applications are notified of a decision.
WHO TO APPLY TO c/o Kleinwort Benson Trustees, PO Box 191, 10 Fenchurch Street, London EC3M 3LB *Tel* 020 7475 5093
CC NO 291456   ESTABLISHED 1984

····················

■ Adenfirst Ltd
WHERE FUNDING CAN BE GIVEN Worldwide.
WHO CAN BENEFIT Jews.
WHAT IS FUNDED Jewish organisations only.
RANGE OF GRANTS Up to £10,000.
SAMPLE GRANTS £10,000 each to Beis Rachel D'Satmar, Beis Yaakov Institutions, Friends of Harim Establishments and Yesodei Hatorah Grammar School; £9,000 to Yad Eliezer; £8,502 to Emuno Educational Centre Ltd; £8,000 to Ezer Layeled; £7,450 to Colel Polen Kupath Ramban; £7,000 to Ponevez Beth Hamednash; £5,000 each to Gur Trust Building Fund and Keren Hatorah.
FINANCES *Year* 2000 *Grants* £136,177
TRUSTEES Mrs H F Bondi; I M Cymerman; Mrs R Cymerman.
HOW TO APPLY In writing to the correspondent.
WHO TO APPLY TO I M Cymerman, Governor, 479 Holloway Road, London N7 6LE *Tel* 020 7272 2255
CC NO 291647   ESTABLISHED 1984

····················

■ The Adint Charitable Trust
WHERE FUNDING CAN BE GIVEN UK.
WHO CAN BENEFIT Registered charities only, including those benefiting disabled people, homeless people, refugees, and victims of abuse, crime, domestic violence, or famine.
WHAT IS FUNDED General charitable purposes, including accommodation and housing, infrastructure and technical support, special needs education (including special schools), health and community services.
WHAT IS NOT FUNDED Grants can be made to registered charities only and in no circumstances to individuals.
TYPE OF GRANT One-off grants and recurrent grants for more than three years are considered, for capital costs (including buildings) and core costs.
RANGE OF GRANTS £500–£16,000, but over 70 per cent of grants are of £5,000.
SAMPLE GRANTS £16,047 to UCL; £10,000 each to Cancer Bacup, Crisis, Disabled Living

Foundation, NCH Action for Children, NSPCC, Queens Park Family Service Unit, Scope, and Winged Fellowship.
FINANCES *Year* 2001–02 *Income* £332,256 *Grants* £341,917 *Assets* £5,202,656
TRUSTEES Anthony J Edwards; Mrs Margaret Edwards; D R Oram; Brian Pate.
HOW TO APPLY To the correspondent, in writing only. There is no particular form in which applications are required; each applicant should make its own case in the way it considers best. The trust notes that it cannot enter into correspondence.
WHO TO APPLY TO D R Oram, Trustee, BDO Stoy Hayward, 8 Baker Street, London W1U 3LL
CC NO 265290   ESTABLISHED 1973

····················

■ The Adnams Charity
WHERE FUNDING CAN BE GIVEN Southwold in Suffolk, and the area within 25 miles of Southwold Church, excluding Ipswich and Norwich.
WHO CAN BENEFIT Small local projects, and innovative projects benefiting: retired people; people who are unemployed; volunteers; people who are ill or disabled; people disadvantaged by poverty; ex-offenders and those at risk of offending; homeless people; people living in rural areas; or victims of abuse and domestic violence.
WHAT IS FUNDED Welfare, including community facilities and services, well woman clinics, support/self help groups, hostels and hospices; education and training to include pre-school, primary and secondary schools as well as special needs education; humanities covering various arts and cultural activities; conservation; and other charitable purposes.
WHAT IS NOT FUNDED No grants for UK organisations unless they are a local branch in the area of benefit. No grants to individuals.
TYPE OF GRANT One-off, buildings, capital, project, research and start-up costs will be considered. Funding may be given for up to one year.
RANGE OF GRANTS £250–£5,000. No repeat grants within two years.
SAMPLE GRANTS £6,500 to Alfred Corry Project; £5,000 each to Suffolk Wildlife Trust, Aldeborough Foundation, Southwold Sailors' Reading Room and Bungay High School; £4,500 to Benjamin Britten School; £4,420 to Action for Families; £4,000 each to Leiston High School and Denes High School; £3,500 to Kirkley High School.
FINANCES *Year* 2000–2001 *Income* £44,000 *Grants* £32,000
TRUSTEES Bernard Segrave-Daly, Chair; Jonathan Adnams; Melvyn Horn; Andrew Wood; Robert Chase; Simon Loftus.
HOW TO APPLY In writing to the correspondent. Trustees meet quarterly.
WHO TO APPLY TO Rebecca Abraham, Trust Administrator, Sole Bay Brewery, Southwold, Suffolk IP18 6JW *Tel* 01502 727200 *Fax* 01502 727267
CC NO 1000203   ESTABLISHED 1990

····················

■ AF Trust Company
WHERE FUNDING CAN BE GIVEN England and Wales.
WHO CAN BENEFIT Organisations benefiting young adults and students.
WHAT IS FUNDED Charitable purposes connected with the provision of higher education. The company currently provides property services and leasing facilities to educational establishments on an arms length basis.

····················

WHAT IS NOT FUNDED No grants to individuals.
TYPE OF GRANT Buildings will be considered.
FINANCES *Year* 1999–2000 *Income* £254,068
TRUSTEES Keith Blanshard; Roger Clayton; Richard Clarke; Denise Everitt; Miles Hedges; Anthony Knapp; Alison Reid; Jane Ross; Colin Showell; David Savage; Kirsty Gillingham.
HOW TO APPLY The trust does not encourage unsolicited applications.
WHO TO APPLY TO P D Welch, Secretary, 34 Chapel Street, Thatcham, Berkshire RG18 4QL
CC NO 1060319   **ESTABLISHED** 1996

■ The Age Concern Scotland Enterprise Fund

WHERE FUNDING CAN BE GIVEN Scotland.
WHO CAN BENEFIT Age Concern member groups and other voluntary organisations working for the benefit of older people in Scotland.
WHAT IS FUNDED The costs of setting up a new project or service. Equipment or materials for small local groups.
WHAT IS NOT FUNDED No grants to statutory authorities, commercial organisations and individuals. No grants are awarded for minibuses, holidays/outings, dinners/parties, running costs, major building costs and general appeals.
TYPE OF GRANT One-off, project or start-up grants.
RANGE OF GRANTS Up to £300 for equipment; up to £1,000 for new projects or services. A few larger grants, up to £5,000, are awarded to groups which are members of Age Concern Scotland, to start up significant new projects. These are awarded at the beginning of the calendar year.
SAMPLE GRANTS £5,591 to Cumbernauld Action for the Care of the Elderly for a welfare rights outreach service; £4,815 to Talk Lochaber to set up a talking newspaper service; £1,000 each to Alzheimer Scotland Action on Dementia to provide information materials in community languages, Age Concern Orkney for fundraising development, Anderson Mel-milaap Centre for the development of day centre services, Tranent Day Care for the development of day centre services, St Mungo's Day Centre for furniture, Dunoon Senior Citizens Club for set up costs of a lunch club, and Ross of Mull Historical Centre for reminiscence work with older people; £969 to Age Concern Glenrothes for equipment for a day centre.
FINANCES *Year* 1999–2000 *Grants* £48,287
TRUSTEES Members of Age Concern Scotland's Assembly.
PUBLICATIONS Guidelines for applicants and a general leaflet.
HOW TO APPLY An application form and further details are available from the correspondent. Applications are considered every two months, except for the larger grants to Age Concern member organisations which are given in January.
WHO TO APPLY TO The Membership Unit, Suite 1C1, Templeton Business Centre, Templeton Street, Glasgow G40 1DA
SC NO SC010100

■ Beis Aharon Trust Fund

WHERE FUNDING CAN BE GIVEN UK.
WHO CAN BENEFIT Jewish organisations.
WHAT IS FUNDED Advancement of religion in accordance with the Jewish faith.
FINANCES *Year* 1999–2000 *Income* £530,000 *Grants* £470,000 *Assets* £780,000
TRUSTEES D Frand; Y Lipschitz; A Spitzer.
HOW TO APPLY In writing to the correspondent.
WHO TO APPLY TO J Lipschitz, Company secretary, 7 Darenth Road, London N16 6EP *Tel* 020 8806 6248
CC NO 1010420   **ESTABLISHED** 1990

■ Aid to the Church in Need (UK)

WHERE FUNDING CAN BE GIVEN Eastern Europe, Africa, Russia, Asia and South America.
WHO CAN BENEFIT Persecuted, oppressed and poor Christians, especially Roman Catholics, Russian Orthodox and refugees.
WHAT IS FUNDED Religion and pastoral projects.
TYPE OF GRANT Buildings, capital, core costs, endowment, one-off, project, running costs, salaries and start-up costs.
RANGE OF GRANTS Up to £81,103.
SAMPLE GRANTS £81,103 to RVA Foundation; £39,452 to Archdiocese of Liviv; £34,630 to Apostolic Administration of Moscow; £29,990 to Diocese of Lodz; £24,889 to Diocese of Presov; £24,769 to Carmelite Sisters of Mahajanga; £23,541 to Archdiocese of Khartoum; £20,862 to Diocese of Tagum; £20,222 to Diocese of Trnava; £18,887 to Archdiocese of Maputo.
FINANCES *Year* 2001 *Income* £4,043,621 *Grants* £2,854,387 *Assets* £840,788
TRUSTEES Prince Rupert Zu Loewenstein, Chair; Mrs Joanna Bogle; Father Ronald Creighton-Jobe; Maria Carmella Viscountess Hambleden; Philipp Habsburg-Lothringen; Patrick Heren; Piers Paul Read; Peter Williams.
OTHER INFORMATION Please note: the focus of this charity is the church overseas and that individuals without the backing as required may not apply for funding.
HOW TO APPLY All applications by individuals must have the backing of a Catholic Bishop or religious superior.
WHO TO APPLY TO Neville Kyrke-Smith, National Director, 1 Times Square, Sutton, Surrey SM1 1LF *Tel* 020 8642 8668 *Fax* 020 8661 6293 *E-mail* acn@acnuk.org *Website* www.acnuk.org
CC NO 265582   **ESTABLISHED** 1947

■ The AIM Foundation

WHERE FUNDING CAN BE GIVEN UK, with an apparent local interest in Essex, and overseas.
WHO CAN BENEFIT Charitable organisations.
WHAT IS FUNDED Charitable projects, principally in the fields of: care in the community; integrated health; community development; and environmental matters, including organic food production.
WHAT IS NOT FUNDED No grants to individuals.
TYPE OF GRANT Either one-off or three-year grants subject to annual review. Grants are for core costs, start-up costs or endowments.
RANGE OF GRANTS Under £1,000–£1,000,000.
SAMPLE GRANTS £63,000 to Network Foundation; £55,000 to New Economics Foundation; £30,000 each to Antidote and NSPCC; £21,000 to Essex Community Foundation; £20,000 each to Chelmsford and District MIND and Youth at Risk; £13,000 to Foundation for Integrated

Medicine; £10,000 each to Drop the Debt and Berkeley Reafforestation Trust.

FINANCES *Year* 2001–02 *Income* £426,000 *Grants* £420,000 *Assets* £7,000,000

TRUSTEES Ian Roy Marks; Mrs Angela D Marks; Charles F Woodhouse.

HOW TO APPLY It cannot be stressed enough that this foundation does not wish to receive applications.

WHO TO APPLY TO Charles Woodhouse, Trustee, Farrer & Co., 66 Lincoln's Inn Fields, London WC2A 3LH *Tel* 020 7242 2022

CC NO 263294   **ESTABLISHED** 1971

■ The Green & Lilian F M Ainsworth & Family Benevolent Fund

WHERE FUNDING CAN BE GIVEN UK, with some preference for north west England.

WHO CAN BENEFIT Charities benefiting young, elderly and disabled people.

WHAT IS FUNDED The trustees have a comprehensive list of national charities from which they select each year, requesting the money is spent in the North West. Smaller grants are given to local charities.

WHAT IS NOT FUNDED No grants to individuals or non-registered charities.

TYPE OF GRANT Prefers specific projects.

RANGE OF GRANTS £250–£5,000.

SAMPLE GRANTS £5,000 to Chester Diocesan Adoption Services; £4,000 to Arthritis Care in north England; £3,500 to Cooper Housing Trust; £3,000 each to Brain Research Trust and Wirral Autistic Society; £2,400 to St John Ambulance – young carers in Chester; £2,000 to Special Care Baby Unit – Hope Hospital; £1,500 each to National Asthma Campaign and Deafway.

FINANCES *Year* 1999–2000 *Income* £40,765 *Grants* £43,450 *Assets* £1,010,307

TRUSTEES The Royal Bank of Scotland plc.

HOW TO APPLY In writing to the correspondent.

WHO TO APPLY TO Don Henderson, Royal Bank of Scotland plc, Trust and Estate Services, 2 Festival Square, Edinburgh EH3 9SU

CC NO 267577   **ESTABLISHED** 1974

■ The Air Charities Trust

WHERE FUNDING CAN BE GIVEN UK and City of London.

WHO CAN BENEFIT Charities linked with the work of the Guild of Air Pilots and Air Navigators of the City of London.

WHAT IS FUNDED The advancement of education in all branches of aviation, especially the promotion of safety. It is the practice of the trust to make grants only to charities linked with the work of the Guild of Air Pilots and Air Navigators of the City of London.

SAMPLE GRANTS Each year the trust divides its support between Air Safety Trust and Guild of Air Pilots.

FINANCES *Year* 2000–01 *Income* £60,000 *Grants* £60,000

TRUSTEES The Master of the Guild of Air Pilots and Air Navigators; Sir Michael J Cobham; Capt. Christopher Hodgkinson; Capt. R C Owens.

HOW TO APPLY In writing to the correspondent.

WHO TO APPLY TO Capt. Christopher Hodgkinson, Cobham House, 9 Warwick Court, Grays Inn, London WC1R 5DJ *Tel* 020 7404 4032 *Fax* 020 7404 4035 *E-mail* gapan@gapan.org *Website* www.gapan.org

CC NO 286915   **ESTABLISHED** 1983

■ Airways Charitable Trust Limited

WHERE FUNDING CAN BE GIVEN UK.

WHO CAN BENEFIT Health and welfare charities.

WHAT IS FUNDED Grantmaking is only a small part of its work. The trust's priority is to help people to maintain independence within their own home, for example, through providing residential accommodation, and welfare and health services and amenities.

SAMPLE GRANTS £27,000 to Shepperton Parish Church; £15,000 to Woodlands School, Guildford; £10,000 to CONNECT; £9,800 to Spelthorne Farm; £9,000 to Royal Schools for the Deaf; £5,000 to Age Concern; £4,100 to Guildford Voluntary Services; £4,000 to Hillingdon Autistic Care and Support; £3,500 to National Benevolent Fund for the Aged.

FINANCES *Year* 1999–2000 *Income* £1,500,000 *Grants* £105,000 *Assets* £30,000,000

TRUSTEES E P Gostling, Chair; D P Dugard; J J O'Sullivan; D N Taylor; M Street; P Nield.

HOW TO APPLY In writing to the correspondent, stating: the name of your organisation and what you do; what you want the grant for; how much you want; how much of the grant total you have already raised; and who else you are approaching for funds. Individual applicants should contact the correspondent to request an application form.

WHO TO APPLY TO Sandra Fletcher, Grants Coordinator, The Gate House, 2 Park Street, Windsor, Berkshire SL4 1LU *Tel* 01753 753900 *Fax* 01753 753901 *E-mail* sandra.fletcher@actg.co.uk *Website* www.actg.co.uk

CC NO 1068617   **ESTABLISHED** 1998

■ The Sylvia Aitken Charitable Trust

WHERE FUNDING CAN BE GIVEN UK, with a preference for Scotland.

WHO CAN BENEFIT Medical research and welfare charities, and any small local groups – particularly in Scotland. Individuals can not be funded.

WHAT IS FUNDED General charitable purposes, with a preference for medical and welfare organisations.

WHAT IS NOT FUNDED No grants to individuals: the trust can only support UK registered charities.

RANGE OF GRANTS £200–£15,000.

SAMPLE GRANTS £12,000 to Respiratory Diseases; £10,000 to Royal Zoological Society of Scotland, National Counselling Services, and Stirling University; £7,000 to Paths for All Partnerships; £6,000 to Shabbos Youth Club; £5,000 each to National Missing Persons Helpline and Shelter Scotland; £2,500 each to Scottish Bone Bifida and Variety Club.

FINANCES *Year* 2000–01 *Income* £214,076 *Grants* £140,575 *Assets* £3,890,187

TRUSTEES Mrs S M Aitken; Mrs M Harkis; J Ferguson.

HOW TO APPLY In writing to the correspondent. Applicants should outline the charity's objectives and current projects for which funding may be required. The trustees meet at least twice a year, usually in March/April and September/October.

WHO TO APPLY TO Jim Ferguson, Trust Administrator, Fergusons Chartered Accountants, 24 Woodside, Houston, Renfrewshire PA6 7DD *Tel* 01505 610412 *Fax* 01505 614944

SC NO SC010556   **ESTABLISHED** 1985

■ The Ajahma Charitable Trust

WHERE FUNDING CAN BE GIVEN Worldwide.

WHO CAN BENEFIT There are no restrictions on the age or the social circumstances of the beneficiaries.

WHAT IS FUNDED Development; health, especially campaigning, advocacy and counselling; disability; poverty; women's issues; family planning; human rights; and social need.

WHAT IS NOT FUNDED Large organisations with a turnover above £4 million will not normally be considered, nor will applications with any sort of religious bias or those which support animal rights/welfare, arts, medical research, buildings, equipment, local groups or overseas projects where the charity income is less than £500,000 a year. Applications for grants or sponsorship for individuals will not be supported.

TYPE OF GRANT Core and running costs, projects and salaries. Funding is available for up to three years.

SAMPLE GRANTS £59,250 in total to 13 local Headway Groups; £35,000 to Oxfam; £23,000 to Action on Disability & Development; £19,000 to Sudanese Victims of Turture; £15,000 each to CAMFED, Health Unlimited and International Care & Relief; £10,000 each to 14 organisations including Anti-Slavery International, APT Enterprise Development, Marie Stopes International and Who Cares? Trust.

FINANCES *Year* 2000–01 *Income* £194,768 *Grants* £475,000 *Assets* £4,713,987

TRUSTEES Jennifer Sheridan; Elizabeth Simpson; James Sinclair Taylor; Michael Horsman.

HOW TO APPLY The trustees meet in May and November; the closing dates for applications are mid-March and mid-September. Information about applying should be sought first from the administrator.

WHO TO APPLY TO Suzanne Hunt, Administrator, 4 Jephtha Road, London SW18 1QH
CC NO 273823   **ESTABLISHED** 1977

■ The Al Fayed Charitable Foundation

WHERE FUNDING CAN BE GIVEN Mainly UK.

WHO CAN BENEFIT There are no restrictions on the age; professional and economic group; family situation; religion and culture; social circumstances; or disease or medical condition of the beneficiaries.

WHAT IS FUNDED General charitable purposes.

SAMPLE GRANTS £251,000 to West Heath School in Sevenoaks; £70,000 to Zoe's Place, Baby Hospital; £65,000 to Rainbow Family Trust; £24,000 to Thai Football Team; £12,000 to Thailand Orphanage; £6,000 to Kids Company; £5,000 each to Jerusalem 2000 and The Samaritans.

FINANCES *Year* 2001 *Income* £629,000 *Grants* £631,000

TRUSTEES Mohammed Al-Fayed; A Fayed; S Fayed.

HOW TO APPLY In writing to the correspondent.

WHO TO APPLY TO Belinda White, 87–135 Brompton Road, Knightsbridge, London SW1X 7XL *Tel* 020 7225 6673 *Fax* 020 7225 6872
CC NO 297114   **ESTABLISHED** 1987

■ The Alabaster Trust

WHERE FUNDING CAN BE GIVEN UK and overseas.

WHO CAN BENEFIT Organisations benefiting evangelical Christian organisations.

WHAT IS FUNDED General charitable purposes, particularly the advancement of the Christian faith.

WHAT IS NOT FUNDED No grants to individuals.

RANGE OF GRANTS £500.

FINANCES *Year* 2000–01 *Income* £61,000 *Grants* £51,000

TRUSTEES G A Kendrick; M Buchanan; Mrs J Kendrick; Mrs A Sheldrake.

HOW TO APPLY In writing to the correspondent. The trustees meet to consider grants quarterly, in March, June, September and December.

WHO TO APPLY TO J R Caladine, Accountant, 1 The Avenue, Eastbourne, East Sussex BN21 3YA *Tel* 01323 644579 *Fax* 01323 417643 *E-mail* john@caladine.co.uk
CC NO 1050568   **ESTABLISHED** 1995

■ Alba Charitable Trust

WHERE FUNDING CAN BE GIVEN UK and overseas.

WHO CAN BENEFIT Educational institutions.

WHAT IS FUNDED Predominantly Jewish organisations.

SAMPLE GRANTS In 1997–98: £6,000 each to Children's Educational Homes – Sanhedria and Wiodova Charity and Rehabilitation Trust; £5,000 each to Craven Walk Charity, Emuno Educational Centre, Lolev Charitable Trust and SOFT.

FINANCES *Year* 1999–2000 *Income* £42,000 *Grants* £33,000 *Assets* £224,000

TRUSTEES L Glatt, Chair; Mrs R Glatt; Mrs D Kestel.

HOW TO APPLY In writing to the correspondent.

WHO TO APPLY TO Leslie Glatt, Trustee, 3 Goodyers Gardens, London NW4 2HD *Tel* 020 7434 3494
CC NO 276391   **ESTABLISHED** 1978

■ D G Albright Charitable Trust

WHERE FUNDING CAN BE GIVEN UK, with a preference for Gloucestershire.

WHO CAN BENEFIT Registered charities.

WHAT IS FUNDED General charitable purposes.

WHAT IS NOT FUNDED Grants are not usually made to individuals.

TYPE OF GRANT One-off and recurrent.

RANGE OF GRANTS £500–£5,000.

SAMPLE GRANTS £7,000 to Bromesterrow Village Hall Appeal; £5,000 to St Lukes Hospital for the Clergy; £3,000 to the Haven Trust; £2,000 each to Gloucestershire Macmillan Cancer Services, The Children's Society and Gloucestershire Family Support.

FINANCES *Year* 2000–01 *Income* £42,000 *Grants* £40,000 *Assets* £1,200,000

TRUSTEES Hon. Dr G Greenall; R G Wood.

HOW TO APPLY In writing to the correspondent.

WHO TO APPLY TO Richard G Wood, Trustee, Old Church School, Hollow Street, Great Somerford, Chippenham, Wiltshire SN15 5JD
CC NO 277367   **ESTABLISHED** 1978

■ The Alchemy Foundation

WHERE FUNDING CAN BE GIVEN UK and overseas.

WHO CAN BENEFIT Community projects, voluntary organisations and registered charities benefiting children, carers, disabled people, people disadvantaged by poverty, prisoners, victims of natural disasters, medical professionals and research workers.

WHAT IS FUNDED Third world water projects; disability; social welfare; individual enterprises; salary support for a small number of voluntary sector individuals; medical research and aid; respite for carers; penal reform, and work with prisoners and their families; holidays for disadvantaged children.

TYPE OF GRANT Capital; revenue; one-off; salaries.

SAMPLE GRANTS £299,920 to The Orpheus Trust; £18,500 to Bridgets; £6,000 to Weston Spirit; £5,000 to MERU; £2,000 each to Chicken Shed Theatre Company and Sight Savers International; £1,000 each to Apex Trust, Marlborough Brandt Group, Starting Point and Surrey Care Trust.

FINANCES *Year* 2000–01 *Income* £806,066 *Grants* £366,189 *Assets* £2,419,433

TRUSTEES Richard Stilgoe; Annabel Stilgoe; Rev. Donald Reeves; Esther Rantzen; Alex Armitage; Andrew Murison; Holly Stilgoe; Jack Stilgoe; Rufus Stilgoe; Joseph Stilgoe; Dr Jemima Stilgoe.

OTHER INFORMATION The trust gave £20,485 in 144 grants to individuals.

HOW TO APPLY In writing to the correspondent.

WHO TO APPLY TO Annabel Stilgoe, Trevereux Manor, Limpsfield Chart, Oxted, Surrey RH8 OTL

CC NO 292500   **ESTABLISHED** 1985

■ Alcohol Education and Research Fund

WHERE FUNDING CAN BE GIVEN UK.

WHO CAN BENEFIT Small local projects, established organisations, innovative projects and individuals. Main beneficiaries are universities and academic research institutions, educational organisations and students.

WHAT IS FUNDED Alcohol education and research. Original research or novel ways of treating alcohol misuse.

WHAT IS NOT FUNDED No grants to statutory authorities or for service provision.

TYPE OF GRANT Research, educational and other action projects; research and taught course studentships.

SAMPLE GRANTS £132,000 to Centre for Alcohol & Drug Studies, Newcastle upon Tyne to carry out research and develop strategy for implementing brief interventions in primary health care; £102,230 to University of Bath for research on work with relatives of alcohol and drug misusers; £44,900 to TACADE to develop educational materials; £39,322 to Alcohol & Health Research Centre, Edinburgh for epidemiological survey on drug use amongst European students; £30,011 to University College Medical School for an alcohol epidemiological project; £27,561 to University of Nottingham for epidemiological research; £21,790 to National Federation of Young Farmers' Clubs for Theatre-in-Education project on sensible drinking; £6,630 to Addictions Forum to fund conference bursaries. Eight studentships ranged from £12,640 to £2,340.

FINANCES *Year* 1999–2000 *Income* £629,649 *Grants* £482,178 *Assets* £11,681,951

TRUSTEES John Bennett; Dr Jonathan Chick; Dr Robin Davidson; Ms Perminder Dhillon; Alistair Eadie; Dr Roger Farmer; Baroness Flather, Chair; Dr John Kemm; Mrs Gill Mackenzie; Prof Phyllida Parsloe; Mrs Daljit Sidebottom; Dr Betsy Thom; Dr Richard Velleman.

PUBLICATIONS *Alcohol Insights*(summaries of conclusions of recent projects).

HOW TO APPLY An application form is available on request and can be downloaded from the website.

WHO TO APPLY TO Leonard Hay, Secretary to the Council, Room 408, Horseferry House, Dean Ryle Street, London SW1P 2AW *Tel* 020 7271 8896 *Fax* 020 7271 8847 *E-mail* len.hay@aerc.org.uk *Website* www.aerc.org.uk

CC NO 284748   **ESTABLISHED** 1981

■ Aldgate and All Hallows Barking Exhibition Foundation

WHERE FUNDING CAN BE GIVEN City of London and the London borough of Tower Hamlets.

WHO CAN BENEFIT Schools and organisations that benefit children and young people under the age of 25, and students who have lived or worked in the City of London or Tower Hamlets for at least three years, and who are studying for a recognised qualification.

WHAT IS FUNDED Projects which are: initiated by schools that will enhance the National Curriculum; aimed at improving literacy and numeracy; or aimed at promoting the study of science, mathematics and the arts. Preference is given to: original developments which are not yet part of the regular activities of an organisation; developments that are either strategic, such as practical initiatives directed towards addressing the root causes of problems, or seminal, because they seek to influence policy and practice elsewhere.

WHAT IS NOT FUNDED The foundation does not give grants for: the purchase, repair or furnishing of buildings; basic equipment or teachers' salaries, which by law are the responsibility of the education authorities; performances, exhibitions or festivals; youth projects or foreign travel; conferences or seminars; university or medical research; establishing funds for bursary or loan schemes; stage, film or video production costs, or commercial publications; supplementary schools or mother tongue teaching; general fundraising campaigns or appeals; or retrospective grants to help pay off overdrafts or loans. Nor will the foundation remedy the withdrawal or reduction of statutory funding.

SAMPLE GRANTS £25,000 to Bishop Challoner RC Girls' School for sponsorship for the school's application to become a technology centre; £15,000 each to Guildhall School of Music and Drama for a musician in residence project at three secondary schools and St Botolph's Project for employment training for young homeless people; £14,000 each to Tower Hamlets Education Business Partnership towards the cost of the Reading Partners secondary literacy scheme and Spitalfields Festival for 5 artist in residence projects involving 10 schools in Tower Hamlets; £12,000 to Understanding Industry for work experience preparation courses for secondary school children; £9,200 to Leyton Orient Community Sports Programme for a primary schools football programme; £9,000 each to London Enterprise Agency Trust for the implementation of a social and personal skills development programme at four schools and Children's Music Workshop for a music and literacy programme at three schools.

Think carefully about every application. Is it justified?

271

FINANCES *Year* 2000 *Income* £218,000
Grants £210,000 *Assets* £6,300,000

TRUSTEES D Mash, Chair; Mrs I Buckman; Ms S
Barrow; Revd Canon P J Delaney; R Hazelwood;
Ms P Hull; Mrs D Jones; G F Jones; Mrs M W F
Kellett; Revd Dr B J Lee; Ms C McMillen; P
Convery; Cllr S Mizan; M G Delahooke; D J
Ross.

OTHER INFORMATION The foundation will only
consider applications for specific projects where
it is clear for what purposes and activities grant
aid is being sought.

HOW TO APPLY The foundation's assessment
procedure is as follows: 'Applications are
received throughout the year. The foundation's
governors meet three times a year in January,
May and September. Initial approaches are
assessed by the clerk to the governors. If
appropriate, a meeting is then arranged
between the project's sponsors and a member
of the foundation's staff. A report is then
prepared for one of the foundation meetings
where a decision is made. Unsuccessful
applicants are advised that they should not re-
apply for funding from the foundation within a
12 month period. An application is only finalised
when all documentation has been received (see
below), a meeting has taken place and there are
no further questions to raise. All this takes time
and it is the applicant's responsibility to allow
reasonable time for this process to take place.
All applicants are informed of the outcome of
their application immediately after the
appropriate meeting. The decision of the
governors is final.' An application in the form of
a letter should be sent to the foundation
including: a statement about the organisation,
its legal status, aims, brief history, staffing and
management committee and its current
activities; a detailed financial statement for the
current year listing the organisation's main
sources of income and expenditure; the exact
purpose for which funding is being sought,
including information on who would benefit from
the project; the amount required, with a
breakdown of how this amount has been arrived
at; information about other sources of income
for the particular project proposal, if any; and
plans for monitoring and evaluating the project
(the foundation will also require a report on the
project if an applicant is successful). The above
should be accompanied by: a copy of the
organisation's constitution (if applicable); the
most recent annual report and audited
accounts; and a contact name, address and
telephone number.

WHO TO APPLY TO C C Wright, Clerk to the Governors,
31 Jewry Street, London EC3N 2EY *Tel* 020
7488 2518 *Fax* 020 7488 2519

CC NO 312500   **ESTABLISHED** 1893

■ The Aldgate Freedom Foundation

WHERE FUNDING CAN BE GIVEN Freedom part of the
parish of St Botolph, Aldgate.

WHO CAN BENEFIT Organisations benefiting older
people.

WHAT IS FUNDED Hospitals and voluntary
organisations.

TYPE OF GRANT One-off.

RANGE OF GRANTS £100–£250.

SAMPLE GRANTS £18,000 to St Botolphs Church
Project for help for homeless people; £1,000 to
Portsoken Ward Club; £100 to Rectors
Discretionary Fund; £60 to Aldgate Church

Foundation. A total of £2,500 was given to
projects run in local hospitals.

FINANCES *Year* 2000 *Income* £35,000
Grants £33,000 *Assets* £1,117,000

TRUSTEES Revd B J Lee, Chair; W H Dove; S J
Rowbotham; Miss M Everingham; M Levett;
Revd R Trafford-Roberts; E Lord; R Stephenson;
Ms R F Johnson; E Lord; Mrs P Donnellan.

HOW TO APPLY In writing to the correspondent.

WHO TO APPLY TO C C Wright, Clerk to the Governors,
31 Jewry Street, London EC3N 2EY *Tel* 020
7480 5884

CC NO 207046   **ESTABLISHED** 1962

■ Alexandra Rose Day

WHERE FUNDING CAN BE GIVEN UK.

WHO CAN BENEFIT UK registered charities that are
involved in caring for people.

WHAT IS FUNDED Grants to registered charities only,
who take part in the Alexandra Rose Day
collections.

WHAT IS NOT FUNDED Only charities participating in
Flag Days or raffles are eligible to apply. Grants
are not made to individuals or charities
operating overseas.

TYPE OF GRANT Core, capital and project support.
Grants are equivalent to 70% of all monies
collected by participating charities during Flag
Days, through other collections and through
raffles. Further small discretionary grants are
available from Special Appeal Fund, only to
charities working with ARD.

SAMPLE GRANTS £5,796 to League of Friends – St
Helier Hospital; £3,734 to the Shooting Star
Trust; £3,156 to SPHERE; £2,458 to Bishop
Creighton House; £1,863 to Norfolk Association
for the Disabled; £1,767 to League of Friends –
Rutland Hospital; £1,737 to Friends of
Abbeyfield (Orpington) Society; £1,207 to
Friends of Royal Brompton Hospital; £1,049 to
the Shaftsbury Society.

FINANCES *Year* 2001–02 *Income* £379,438
Grants £188,842 *Assets* £542,885

TRUSTEES The Council: Rt Hon. Lord Wakeham,
Chairman; Andrew Mitchell; Lady Grade; Lady
Heald; Lord King of Wartnaby; Mrs Aubrey
Beckham; Peter Beckham; Ms Cecily Engle;
Stephen King; Mrs Katheryn Langridge; Mrs
Morton Neal; Sir Ian Rankin; Peter Russell-
Wood; Raymond Salisbury-Jones; Mrs Diane
Sillem; Mrs Domonic Tayler.

PUBLICATIONS Information sheets on successful
fundraising with ARD.

HOW TO APPLY In writing to the correspondent.

WHO TO APPLY TO Alan Leng, National Director, 2A
Ferry Road, London SW13 9RX *Tel* 0870 770
0275 *Fax* 0870 770 0276
E-mail enquiries@alexandraroseday.org.uk
Website www.alexandraroseday.org.uk

CC NO 211535   **ESTABLISHED** 1912

■ The Alexis Trust

WHERE FUNDING CAN BE GIVEN UK and overseas.

WHO CAN BENEFIT Individuals and organisations.

WHAT IS FUNDED Support for a variety of causes,
principally Christian.

WHAT IS NOT FUNDED No grants for building appeals,
or to individuals for education.

TYPE OF GRANT One-off, project and some recurring
costs will be considered.

FINANCES *Year* 2001–02 *Income* £35,000
Grants £32,000

TRUSTEES Prof. D W Vere; C P Harwood; Mrs E M
Harwood; Mrs V Vere.

272

Does the trust you have chosen match your needs? Haphazard applications waste postage and time

HOW TO APPLY In writing to the correspondent, although the trust states that most of the funds are regularly committed.
WHO TO APPLY TO Prof. D W Vere, Trustee, 14 Broadfield Way, Buckhurst Hill, Essex IG9 5AG
CC NO 262861   **ESTABLISHED** 1971

....

■ Alglen Ltd

WHERE FUNDING CAN BE GIVEN Worldwide.
WHO CAN BENEFIT Jewish organisations.
WHAT IS FUNDED Jewish causes.
RANGE OF GRANTS £150–£36,000.
SAMPLE GRANTS In 1997: £36,000 to Torah Vemmunah Charity Trust; £7,000 each to Torah Vechased Le'ezra Vesad and Beis Yaacov; £5,000 each to SOFT, Gur Trust, and Emuno Educational Centre Ltd; £3,800 to Ponevez Yeshivah; £3,600 to Friends of Harim Establishments; £3,000 to Friends of Achiezer; £2,000 to Hachnasas Kalloh Fund Aguda.
FINANCES *Year* 1999–2000 *Income* £89,000 *Grants* £509,000
TRUSTEES D Schreiber; Mrs E Stieglitz; Mrs R Lipschitz; J A Brunner.
HOW TO APPLY In writing to the correspondent.
WHO TO APPLY TO Mrs R Lipschitz, Governor, Felds, Trustees' Accountants, 5 North End Road, London NW11 7RJ *Tel* 020 8455 6789 *Fax* 020 8455 2277
CC NO 287544   **ESTABLISHED** 1983

....

■ The Alice Trust

WHERE FUNDING CAN BE GIVEN Buckinghamshire.
WHO CAN BENEFIT The trust's giving is focused on its principal beneficiary, but very occasionally grants are made to other organisations.
WHAT IS FUNDED The preservation, protection, maintenance and improvement of Waddesdon Manor, its lands and its contents, for the benefit of the public generally, together with the advancement of education in matters of historic, artistic, architectural or aesthetic interest.
SAMPLE GRANTS £949,841 to The National Trust for Waddesdon Manor running costs, repair and refurbishment.
FINANCES *Year* 2001–02 *Income* £1,145,056 *Grants* £949,841 *Assets* £52,079,617
TRUSTEES Lord Rothschild; Lady Rothschild; Sir Edward Cazalet; Peter Troughton; Hon. Beth Rothschild; SJP Trustee Company Limited.
HOW TO APPLY In view of the trust's commitment to its principal objective, it does not at present invite applications; however, any enquiries are acknowledged.
WHO TO APPLY TO Fiona Sinclair, The Dairy, Queen Street, Waddesdon, Aylesbury, Buckinghamshire
CC NO 290859   **ESTABLISHED** 1984

....

■ All Saints Educational Trust

WHERE FUNDING CAN BE GIVEN Mostly UK.
WHO CAN BENEFIT Ultimately, persons who are or intend to become engaged as teachers or in other capacities connected with education, in particular home economics and religious subjects, and those who teach or intend to teach in multicultural areas.
WHAT IS FUNDED Primarily, the training of Christian teachers. Also the promotion of research in and the development of education, particularly religious education, home economics and kindred subjects, and multicultural and inter-faith education.

WHAT IS NOT FUNDED The trust cannot support: schools by providing grants for buildings, equipment or supplies; the general funds of any organisation; public appeals; the establishment of courses or departments in universities and colleges, which is a prime responsibility of the institutions themselves; chaplaincies; applicants which have already been supported by the trust; overseas applications from individuals (a temporary moratorium until investment returns improve).
Grants are not made retrospectively.
TYPE OF GRANT One-off, project or annual grants for a limited period. Funding may be given for more than three years.
RANGE OF GRANTS £250–£14,000.
SAMPLE GRANTS £35,000 each to RSA 'Focus on Food' Campaign for an issue of a new magazine to be distributed free to 28,000 schools in the UK and Association of Church College Trusts for an extention to the RETRI project; £33,000 to The Patrick V Saxton Fellowship Award for a University of Stirling student to continue her research; £15,000 to The Society for Promoting Christian Knowledge for the final year towards the establishment of a website to provide updated Christian material for use in school assemblies; £10,000 to The Wulugu Project for an educational project in Northern Ghana which involved 'twinning' with UK schools and establishing a science curriculum which is relevant to girls in a developing country; £9,000 to Guildhall School of Music and Drama for bursary funds to be awarded to two students selected by the school on a postgraduate music therapy course; £8,600 to London Diocesan Board for Schools for the final of three grants for a 'Preparation for Headship' course for staff in church schools; £8,500 to Exchange for the continuation of a research and communication network; £7,500 to The National Society for the final year of an on-going grant for a project to set up a website; £5,000 to Southwark Cathedral Education Trust towards the salary and associated costs of an educational officer; £3,000 to Churches' Action for Racial Equality as the last of three grants to enable research and the preparation of teaching materials on 'holy people of the African diaspora'; £2,500 to Ockenden International to provide textbooks, training materials and other supplies to 240 teachers in Sudan.
FINANCES *Year* 2001–02 *Income* £414,359 *Grants* £461,132 *Assets* £8,670,235
TRUSTEES The Rt Revd & Rt Hon. Richard Chartres, Bishop of London, Chair; Revd Prebendary Swan; Mrs M R Behenna; P Chandler; T L Guiver; Revd Canon P Hartley; Dr D W Lankshear; Ms D McCrea; Miss A Philpott; Revd K G Riglin; Mrs A Rose; D Trillo; Ven C Chessun; Mrs B Harvey; J K Hoskin; G King.
OTHER INFORMATION The trust gave 80 new awards to individuals, and continued 59 previous awards to individuals, totalling £281,000. Awards to organisations totalled £180,000.
HOW TO APPLY For applications from organisations (not individuals): applicants are invited to discuss their ideas informally with the clerk before requesting an application form. In some cases, a 'link trustee' is appointed to assist the organisation in preparing the application and who will act in a liaison role with the trust. Completed applications are put before the awards committee in February or May, with final decisions made in June. The trust normally responds to all written enquiries received, but in order to reduce administration costs, the trust cannot guarantee to reply to letters seeking

assistance in respect of projects detailed in Exclusions above.

WHO TO APPLY TO R Poulton, Clerk, St Katherine Cree Church, 86 Leadenhall Street, London EC3A 3DH *Tel* 020 7283 4485 *Fax* 020 7621 9758 *E-mail* enquiries@aset.org.uk *Website* www.aset.org.uk

CC NO 312934   **ESTABLISHED** 1978

■ The Allachy Trust

WHERE FUNDING CAN BE GIVEN Developing countries.

WHO CAN BENEFIT Registered charities.

WHAT IS FUNDED Development projects that emphasise the criteria of sustainable livelihoods within a community context and a developing world, demonstrate clear innovative thinking with an emphasis on appropriate technology, and are conducted by experienced and locally experienced organisations.

WHAT IS NOT FUNDED No grant to individuals, or for general charity funds, provision of health, veterinary, or general education services to end-users, or building projects.

RANGE OF GRANTS £3,000–£22,000.

SAMPLE GRANTS £10,000 to The Kaloko Trust; £9,319 to El Hombre Sobre la Tierra AC; £9,070 to Find Your Feet (two projects); £6,700 to UK for the South Pacific; £5,560 to Nysasdri; £5,000 to Development Organisation for Rural Sichuan; £4,000 to International Service; £2,500 to Action Village India; £2,000 to Centre for Community Development.

FINANCES *Year* 1999–2000 *Income* £50,635 *Grants* £54,148 *Assets* £1,786,907

TRUSTEES A W Layton, Chair; Lord Newby; J R Sandbrook.

OTHER INFORMATION A substantial part of the trust's annual income is fully committed. Grants may be awarded out of any balance of annual income. The trustees will award grants in the manner they think will best benefit the project or community.

HOW TO APPLY Project proposal accompanied by annual report and accounts, and a full estimate of costs with breakdown.

WHO TO APPLY TO Miss E Aspden, Administrator, 3 Endsleigh Street, London WC1H 0DD

CC NO 326237   **ESTABLISHED** 1982

■ Allavida

WHERE FUNDING CAN BE GIVEN South east Europe.

WHO CAN BENEFIT Voluntary organisations, community groups, charities and NGOs. Organisations, both lead and partner, must be based in two different countries/territories from the following – Albania, Bosnia-Herzegovina, Bulgaria, Croatia, Kosovo, Macedonia, Montenegro, Romania and Serbia; be youth-led groups with open membership between the ages of 16 and 30, or have as their main target group young people in the same age range; and clearly have their roots in their local community and operate in that community.

WHAT IS FUNDED The purpose of this grants programme is to support organisation to organisation learning and exchange of skills and knowledge, and to encourage and enable groups from the south east Europe region to acquire meaningful experience. Projects should contain a significant and demonstrable element of transfer and exchange of skills between the applicant and partner organisations. Intended learning outcomes and partnership goals are more important than the precise way of achieving them.

Ways in which this may happen include the following, but do not exclude other ideas: training events, such as workshops and seminars for NGO staff and volunteers of the applicant and partner organisations; exploratory work or study visits to other organisations linked to the partner's mission, in organisational or thematic areas, or supporting youth sector organisational learning and development; short-term (up to three months) volunteer placements within a partner organisation, to allow individuals to 'shadow' the work of staff or key activists; action-oriented joint research; joint activities relating to the principal activities of either partner, such as the organisation of a summer camp, a campaign, publication or other event done as a means of achieving something else, not just for its own sake.

WHAT IS NOT FUNDED Grants are not normally available for the following: retrospective activities; the preparation of funding proposals or applications; the teaching of foreign languages, computer skills training or other student programmes; humanitarian aid or medical equipment or the costs of transporting it; attendance at conferences or meetings of international youth organisations by their national members; activities considered to be for personal rather than institutional or group development; the direct promotion of a particular political view, specific religion or sectarian belief; activities which do not involve person-to-person contact and actual crossing of borders; training courses organised by partners of the third parties or individuals where there is no evident learning process between the partners; joint training or other activity predominantly or substantially carried out on the organisations' behalf by a consultant or other external individuals or organisations.

TYPE OF GRANT Most grants are small, for one-off projects.

RANGE OF GRANTS Up to 3,000.

FINANCES *Year* 2001–02 *Grants* £185,000

TRUSTEES David Carrington, Chair; Steven Burkeman; Duncan Grant; Christine Forrester; Barry Knight; David Bonbright; Bisi Adelaye-Fayemi; Lenka Setkova; Jason Scott.

PUBLICATIONS Guidelines for applicants.

HOW TO APPLY There is a clear application form to which other material can be attached, together with comprehensive guidance notes for applicants. Potential applicants should first read the 'Guidelines for Applicants' available before contacting the trust.

WHO TO APPLY TO The Grants Department, 55 Bondway, London SW8 1SJ *Tel* 020 7735 8006 *Fax* 020 7735 7608 *E-mail* enquiries@allavida.org *Website* www.allavida.org

CC NO 1089984   **ESTABLISHED** 2001

■ Allchurches Trust Ltd

WHERE FUNDING CAN BE GIVEN UK.

WHO CAN BENEFIT Churches and charitable institutions benefiting Christians.

WHAT IS FUNDED Promotion of the Christian religion and contributions to the funds of other charitable institutions.

WHAT IS NOT FUNDED The trustees do not make grants to charities with political associations. They do not generally make grants to national charities, or respond to appeals from individuals.

TYPE OF GRANT Primarily one-off.

RANGE OF GRANTS Usually £100–£5,000.

SAMPLE GRANTS £25,000 each to Council for the Care of Churches and Gloucestershire University; £10,000 Church of England Board of Education; £5,000 each to Diocese of Liverpool Board of Education, Fylde Coast YMCA, National Centre for Deaf Blindness and St George's House; £3,000 each to Cumbria Community Recovery Fund, Sarum College and Thaxted PCC.

FINANCES *Year* 2001 *Grants* £4,023,000

TRUSTEES Sir Alan McLintock, Chair; Viscount Churchill; M R Cornwall-Jones; Rt Revd D G Snelgrove; B V Day; W H Yates; Mrs S Homersham; N Assheton.

HOW TO APPLY Applications should be submitted in writing to the correspondent, on the trust's straightforward, two-side application form. Application should detail charity number, the objectives of the charity, the appeal target, how the funds are to be utilised, funds raised to date and previous support received from the trust. If available, the application should be accompanied by supporting literature and annual report.
Trustees meet quarterly.

WHO TO APPLY TO Mrs R J Hall, Company Secretary, Beaufort House, Brunswick Road, Gloucester GL1 1JZ *Tel* 01452 528533
Website www.allchurches.co.uk

CC NO 263960   **ESTABLISHED** 1972

■ The Dorothy Gertrude Allen Memorial Fund

WHERE FUNDING CAN BE GIVEN UK.

WHO CAN BENEFIT Registered charities only.

WHAT IS FUNDED General charitable purposes including advice and information (housing); community facilities; medical research; and conservation and environment.

WHAT IS NOT FUNDED No grants to individuals (including gap-year students) or to organisations which are not UK-registered charities.

TYPE OF GRANT One-off or recurring up to three years, including capital and core costs.

RANGE OF GRANTS £1,000–£5,000.

SAMPLE GRANTS £5,000 each to Child Hope for street children, International Otter Survival Fund, Royal Society for the Protection of Birds, Send a Cow for work in Africa, Scottish Wildlife Trust, and Wildfowl and Wetlands Trust; £3,000 each to Hearing Research Trust, National Playbus Association, Rural Youth Trust, and St Petroc's Society.

FINANCES *Year* 2001 *Income* £74,888
Grants £99,000 *Assets* £733,071

TRUSTEES Miss Heather B Allen; Peter B Shone.

HOW TO APPLY In writing to the correspondent. Applications should be received by October for consideration in November/December. Due to an increasing number of appeals (the amount has doubled in the last few years) the trustees do not acknowledge them. Applicants are contacted usually only when they are successful or where further information is required.

WHO TO APPLY TO Peter B Shone, Trustee, Teigncombe Barn, Chagford, Devon TQ13 8ET *Tel* 01647 433235
E-mail dgallen.memorialfund@btinternet.com

CC NO 290676   **ESTABLISHED** 1984

■ The H B Allen Charitable Trust

WHERE FUNDING CAN BE GIVEN Worldwide.

WHO CAN BENEFIT Registered charities in the UK.

WHAT IS FUNDED General charitable purposes including accommodation and housing, arts, welfare, health, conservation and environment.

WHAT IS NOT FUNDED No grants to individuals, organisations which are not UK-registered charities or gap-year students (even if payable to a registered charity).

TYPE OF GRANT One-off and recurrent up to three years, revenue and capital including core costs.

RANGE OF GRANTS £5,000–£100,000.

SAMPLE GRANTS £25,000 each to Crisis, The Rowans – Portsmouth Area Hospice and Wildlife Conservation Research Unit; £20,000 each to Children's Society, Dermatrust, Hebridean Trust, Institute of Orthopaedics, Intermediate Technology, Sobriety Project and Save the Children.

FINANCES *Year* 2001 *Income* £791,195
Grants £670,000 *Assets* £15,138,000

TRUSTEES Heather B Allen; P B Shone.

HOW TO APPLY In writing to the correspondent. Almost all grants are decided at a meeting in November or December. It will assist trustees if applications can be submitted by the end of October and if applications are not submitted in November and December.

WHO TO APPLY TO P B Shone, Teigncombe Barn, Chagford, Devon TQ13 8ET *Tel* 01647 433235 *Fax* 01647 433053
E-mail hballen.charitabletrust@btinternet.com
Website www.peter.shone.btinternet.co.uk

CC NO 802306   **ESTABLISHED** 1987

■ Mrs M H Allen Trust

WHERE FUNDING CAN BE GIVEN UK.

WHO CAN BENEFIT Registered military charities.

WHAT IS FUNDED Military charities. The trustees prefer to assist people (disabled, injured and disadvantaged) rather than institutions or the preservation of buildings.

WHAT IS NOT FUNDED No grants to any non-naval or military charities, individuals, scholarships or education generally.

TYPE OF GRANT Capital, one-off, project, research and recurring costs. Funding of up to two years.

RANGE OF GRANTS £500–£25,000, typically £2,500.

SAMPLE GRANTS Grants for general purposes: £5,000 each to St Dunstans and King Edward VII's Hospital for Officers; £3,000 each to St David's Home (Ealing), British Limbless Ex-Servicemens Association, Scottish National Institute for War Blinded, Princess Louise's Scottish Hospital, and Scottish Veteran's Residences; £2,500 each to Ex-services Mental Welfare Society, King George's Fund for Sailors and Royal Star and Garter Home.

FINANCES *Year* 2000 *Income* £49,248
Grants £62,000 *Assets* £1,124,000

TRUSTEES Col. A F Niekirk; A P C Niekirk; W D Niekirk.

HOW TO APPLY In writing to the correspondent at any time.

WHO TO APPLY TO Col. A F Niekirk, Trustee, West Field, Gelt Road, Brampton, Cumbria CA8 1QH

CC NO 211529   **ESTABLISHED** 1924

Think carefully about every application. Is it justified? •

275

■ The Alliance Family Foundation

WHERE FUNDING CAN BE GIVEN UK, with some preference for the Manchester area.

WHO CAN BENEFIT Organisations, particularly Jewish causes, benefiting children, young adults, and people disadvantaged by poverty.

WHAT IS FUNDED The relief of poverty and advancement of religion, education and medical knowledge.

SAMPLE GRANTS £105,000 to Weizman Institute; £75,000 to JFS; £25,000 to United Jewish Israel Appeal; £20,000 to Iranian Jewish Centre; £17,606 to Fariborz Fred Matloob Foundation; £17,361 to Cultural Foundation of Habib Levy; £16,000 each to Manchester University for a chair in modern Jewish studies and Young Israel Synagogue of Ramot Gimmel, Jerusalem; £12,500 to Community Security Trust; £11,000 to Spanish and Portuguese Jews Burial Society.

FINANCES *Year* 2001–02 *Income* £523,000 *Grants* £505,000 *Assets* £16,000,000

TRUSTEES Sir David Alliance; G N Alliance; Mrs S D Esterkin.

OTHER INFORMATION £70,000 of the grant total went to individuals.

HOW TO APPLY In writing to the correspondent at any time.

WHO TO APPLY TO The Trustees, 12th Floor, Bank House, Charlotte Street, Manchester M1 4ET *Tel* 0161 236 8193

CC NO 258721   **ESTABLISHED** 1968

■ Angus Allnatt Charitable Foundation

WHERE FUNDING CAN BE GIVEN UK.

WHO CAN BENEFIT Mostly small organisations which are registered charities benefiting young people who are involved in music or water-based activities, such as sailing and canoeing.

WHAT IS FUNDED Organisations which provide music or water-based activities for young people (13–25). Bursaries and fees will be considered.

WHAT IS NOT FUNDED No grants to individuals, and none to organisations which use music or water-based activities primarily for therapeutic or social purposes.

TYPE OF GRANT One-off for specific needs or start-up costs. Funding is available for up to one year.

RANGE OF GRANTS £250–£1,000 with a maximum of £2,000.

SAMPLE GRANTS £1,200 to Chasetown High School for music software and a computer; £1,000 to Bournemouth Symphony Orchestra towards the EeJay Project; £800 to Jubilee Sailing Trust towards four bursaries for its Youth Leadership at Sea Scheme; £750 to Helensburgh Sea Cadet Unit towards the full cost of a 4.4 metre rib; £650 to Yorkshire Youth Orchestra towards three bursaries; £500 each to Gwyl Gregynog Festival towards a masterclass and 3rd Totnes Sea Scout Group towards replacing rowing boats; £350 to Askham Guide Unit towards the cost of the guides' voyage on the Ocean Youth Trust's James Cook; £300 to Ignite Trust towards the purchase of a bass guitar.

FINANCES *Year* 2002 *Income* £32,192 *Grants* £34,560 *Assets* £541,006

TRUSTEES Rodney Dartnall; Anthony Pritchard; Calton Younger; Marian Durban.

HOW TO APPLY In writing to the correspondent. Trustees meet three times a year to consider applications. The trust has no staff and no telephone. Appeals falling outside the guidelines will not be considered.

WHO TO APPLY TO Calton Younger, Trustee, 34 North End Road, London W14 0SH

CC NO 1019793   **ESTABLISHED** 1993

■ The Pat Allsop Charitable Trust

WHERE FUNDING CAN BE GIVEN UK.

WHO CAN BENEFIT National organisations benefiting: children; people in property management; people disadvantaged by poverty; people living in urban areas; refugees; and the victims of famine.

WHAT IS FUNDED Medicine and health; welfare; and education. Particularly concerned with: almshouses; housing associations; hospices; medical studies and research; schools and colleges; special needs education; and emergency care for refugees and people affected by famine.

WHAT IS NOT FUNDED No grants to individuals.

TYPE OF GRANT One-off, project, research and recurring costs.

SAMPLE GRANTS 1998–99: £10,000 to Annigton Trust; £1,000 plus to each of Babes in Arms, Centrepoint, Cottage Homes Charity, Jewish Care, National Schizophrenia Fellowship, Norwood Ravenswood, NSPCC, Sparks, and The Story of Christmas.

FINANCES *Year* 2000–01 *Income* £52,646

TRUSTEES J P G Randel; A Collett; A G Butler; B C Fowler.

OTHER INFORMATION Trust has historical connections with surveying and estate management.

HOW TO APPLY In writing to the correspondent, but please note, the trust does not accept unsolicited applications.

WHO TO APPLY TO J P G Randel, Trustee, c/o Monier Williams & Boxalls, 71 Lincoln's Inn Fields, London WC2A 3JF *Tel* 020 7405 6195 *Fax* 020 7405 1453

CC NO 1030950   **ESTABLISHED** 1973

■ The Almond Trust

WHERE FUNDING CAN BE GIVEN UK and worldwide.

WHO CAN BENEFIT Mostly individuals or organisations of which the trustees have personal knowledge, particularly those benefiting Christians and evangelists.

WHAT IS FUNDED Support of evangelical Christian projects, Christian evangelism, and advancement of Scripture.

TYPE OF GRANT Buildings, capital, core costs, one-off, project, recurring and running costs, salaries, and start-up costs. Funding is available for up to two years.

SAMPLE GRANTS £100,000 each to All Saints Crawborough and Oasis Trust; £27,000 to Christian Youth and Sports Charitable Company; £25,000 to London Insitute for Contemporary Christianity; £22,000 to Counselling, Consulting Training and Leadership; £20,420 to St Barnabas PCC; £12,000 to Lawyers' Christain Trust, £10,000 each to Christains in Sport and St Peter's Trust; £7,000 to Freemantle PCC; £5,000 to Agape; £3,000 to Great Whyte Baptist Church.

FINANCES *Year* 1999–2000 *Income* £426,143 *Grants* £406,243 *Assets* £247,204

TRUSTEES J L Cooke; Barbara H Cooke.

HOW TO APPLY In writing to the correspondent, but please note that the trust states it rarely responds to uninvited applications.

WHO TO APPLY TO J L Cooke, Trustee, 111 Dulwich Village, London SE21 7BJ

CC NO 328583   **ESTABLISHED** 1990

■ Almondsbury Charity

WHERE FUNDING CAN BE GIVEN The parish of Almondsbury as it existed in 1892, i.e. Almondsbury, Patchway, Easter Compton and parts of Pilning and Bradley Stoke North.

WHO CAN BENEFIT The Church of England; residents and organisations in the beneficial area.

WHAT IS FUNDED Grants are made to maintain and repair churches, to further the religious and charitable work of the Church of England and to support educational requirements and sick and needy residents and organisations within the old parish of Almondsbury.

SAMPLE GRANTS Ecclesiastical fund – £27,000 to Almondsbury Parochial Church Council; £6,700 to Patchway Ecumenical Church Council; £5,800 to Pilning Church Council. Education/and relief fund – £2,200 to Almondsbury Local History Society; £1,000 to Patchwork Festival; £500 each to Coniston Women's Group, and Patchway and Bradley Stoke Play Association; £250 SPACE; £130 to Wesley Pre-School; £40 Patchway Newstart.

FINANCES *Year* 1999–2000 *Income* £46,000 *Grants* £60,000 *Assets* £2,000,000

TRUSTEES A B Gaydon; Dr A G Warner; Revd B E Penn; Mrs S J Cook; I Humphries; L Gray; Mrs H M Denison; K J Beard; R E Davies; Mrs R E Jenkins.

HOW TO APPLY On a form available from the correspondent.

WHO TO APPLY TO T Davies, Secretary, 18 Coape Road, Stockwood, Bristol BS14 8TN *Tel* 01275 833026

CC NO 202263   **ESTABLISHED** 1963

■ The Almshouse Association

WHERE FUNDING CAN BE GIVEN UK.

WHO CAN BENEFIT Almshouse charities benefiting elderly people and people disadvantaged by poverty.

WHAT IS FUNDED Grants and loans to almshouse charities after full advantage has been taken of statutory aid.

WHAT IS NOT FUNDED No grants to individuals.

TYPE OF GRANT Usually a one-off grant or interest-free loan for a specific project.

SAMPLE GRANTS In 1999: £38,000 to Dixon's Almshouses, Christleton (Cheshire); £7,500 to Eight Men of Broadclyst, Devon; £5,200 to Wadham Almshouses, Ilton (Somerset); £5,000 each to Almshouses of Thomas Bell, Kingerby (Lincs), Friskney United Charities (Leics), and Hebden Wright Almshouse Charity, Keighley; £2,500 to Tibbenham Almshouse Charity, Norfolk; £1,750 to Portsmouth & District Friendly Societies Homes, Milton (Hants).

FINANCES *Year* 2002 *Grants* £126,500

TRUSTEES Executive Committee.

PUBLICATIONS Quarterly *Almshouse Gazette*.

HOW TO APPLY In writing to the director at any time.

WHO TO APPLY TO A L Leask, Director, Billingbear Lodge, Carters Hill, Wokingham, Berkshire RG40 5RU *Tel* 01344 452922 *Fax* 01344 862062 *E-mail* naa@almshouses.org.uk

CC NO 245668   **ESTABLISHED** 1965

■ The Altajir Trust

WHERE FUNDING CAN BE GIVEN UK and Arab or Islamic states.

WHO CAN BENEFIT Individuals and organisations.

WHAT IS FUNDED The advancement of science, education and research beneficial to the community in Britain or any Arab or Islamic states. Support is given to students at universities in the UK, USA and Bahrain, and conferences and exhibitions are sponsored which promote understanding and the study of Islamic culture and arts throughout the world.

SAMPLE GRANTS £60,000 to Arab Womens Association; £40,000 to School of Oriental and African Studies – Research Fellowship; £30,070 to Learning Centre – Adu Daubi; £24,000 to Dar Al Hekma; £20,000 to St Catherine's – Cumberland Lodge; £5,000 each to Jubilee Sailing Trust and Royal Collection Trust.

FINANCES *Year* 2000 *Income* £651,284 *Grants* £568,431 *Assets* £77,000

TRUSTEES Sir John Moberly, Chair; Peter Tripp; Prof. Alan Jones; Dr Roger Williams; Dr Charles Tripp.

HOW TO APPLY The trust states that its resources are fully used without receiving applications.

WHO TO APPLY TO A C Duncan, Director, 11 Elvaston Place, London SW7 5QG *Tel* 020 7581 3522 *Fax* 020 7584 1977

CC NO 284116   **ESTABLISHED** 1982

■ Altamont Ltd

WHERE FUNDING CAN BE GIVEN Worldwide.

WHO CAN BENEFIT Organisations benefiting Jewish people.

WHAT IS FUNDED Jewish charitable purposes.

RANGE OF GRANTS £500–£270,000.

FINANCES *Year* 1999–2000 *Grants* £400,000

TRUSTEES D Last; H Last; Mrs H Kon; Mrs S Adler; Mrs G Wiesenfeld.

HOW TO APPLY In writing to the correspondent.

WHO TO APPLY TO The Clerk, Gerald Kreditor & Co, Tudor House, Llan Vanor Road, Finchley Road, London NW2 2AQ *Tel* 020 7247 8376

CC NO 273971   **ESTABLISHED** 1977

■ AM Charitable Trust

WHERE FUNDING CAN BE GIVEN UK and overseas.

WHO CAN BENEFIT Registered charities; Jewish organisations.

WHAT IS FUNDED General charitable purposes, including medical, welfare, arts and conservation charities. The trustees prefer to provide medium-term support for a number of charities already known to them.

WHAT IS NOT FUNDED No grants to individuals.

RANGE OF GRANTS £100–£10,000; mainly £250 or less.

SAMPLE GRANTS £10,000 each to Jerusalem Foundation and World Jewish Relief; £5,000 each to British ORT, British Technion Society and Friends of the Hebrew University of Jerusalem; £3,000 to Friends of Boys Town Jerusalem; £2,500 to Joint Jewish Charitable Trust; £2,225 to Weizmann Institute Foundation; £2,000 each to British Heart Foundation, Cancer Research Campaign and Norwood Ltd.

FINANCES *Year* 1999–2000 *Income* £73,291 *Grants* £58,900 *Assets* £1,610,356

TRUSTEES Kleinwort Benson Trustees Ltd.

HOW TO APPLY Unsolicited applications are not welcomed. The trust stated that its funds are fully committed and only a small percentage of its income is allocated to new beneficiaries. Only successful applications are notified of the trustees' decision. Trustees meet in March and applications need to be received by January.

WHO TO APPLY TO The Secretary, Kleinwort Benson Trustees Ltd, The Trustees Department, 10 Fenchurch Street, London EC3M 3LB *Tel* 020 7475 5086 *Fax* 020 7475 5558
CC NO 256283   ESTABLISHED 1968

■ Amber Trust

WHERE FUNDING CAN BE GIVEN UK.
WHO CAN BENEFIT General, registered charities.
WHAT IS FUNDED General charitable purposes.
SAMPLE GRANTS £5,000 to Corpus Christi College, Cambridge; £4,000 to The Landmark Trust; £3,000 to The Almeida Theatre Co. Ltd; and £1,000 each to Durrell Wildlife Conservation Trust, Handel House Trust Limited, Kings Corner Project, National Trust (Lake District Appeal) and Orchestra of the Age of Englightenment.
FINANCES *Year* 2000 *Income* £26,000 *Grants* £23,000
TRUSTEES Michael Gwinnell; Barbara Mary Gwinnell.
HOW TO APPLY Unsolicited applications are not considered and will not be acknowledged.
WHO TO APPLY TO Mr & Mrs M Gwinnell, 3 Almeida Street, London N1 1TA *Tel* 020 7292 3200
CC NO 802649   ESTABLISHED 1988

■ The Amberstone Trust

WHERE FUNDING CAN BE GIVEN Worldwide.
WHO CAN BENEFIT Registered charities.
WHAT IS FUNDED General charitable purposes; however, all funds are presently committed.
SAMPLE GRANTS £306,000 to Jerusalem Foundation; £69,000 to Barbados Amberstone Trust; £60,000 to One World Broadcasting Trust; £58,000 to Students Partnership Worldwide; £50,000 to Writers and Scholars Educational Trust; £36,846 to Vetiver Network; £33,800 to Family Welfare Association; £33,496 to American Academy of Arts and Science; £25,000 each to Centre for Study of Financial Innovations, Prisoners of Conscience Appeal and V & A Spiral Research Project.
FINANCES *Year* 2000 *Income* £233,000 *Grants* £1,091,000 *Assets* £5,700,000
TRUSTEES David Bernstein; P S Zuckerman.
OTHER INFORMATION The trust's policy is to spend all its resources and then wind up by 2005.
HOW TO APPLY 'The trustees are not accepting applications from the public as all the trust's funds are fully committed.'
WHO TO APPLY TO The Trustees, c/o Buss Murton (ref 46), Wellington Gate, 7–9 Church Road, Tunbridge Wells, Kent TN1 1HT *Tel* 01892 510222
CC NO 279787   ESTABLISHED 1978

■ Ambika Paul Foundation

WHERE FUNDING CAN BE GIVEN UK and India.
WHO CAN BENEFIT Large organisations, registered charities, colleges and universities benefiting children, young adults and students.
WHAT IS FUNDED UK and India. Large organisations, registered charities, colleges and universities benefiting children, young adults and students. Main areas of interest are to do with young people and education.
WHAT IS NOT FUNDED Grants are only available to children and young people's charities. No funding for individuals or DSS requests, nor for individuals' salaries/running costs. Applications from individuals, including students, are mainly ineligible. Funding for scholarships is made

direct to colleges/universities, not to individuals. No expeditions.
TYPE OF GRANT Direct donations; deeds of covenant.
RANGE OF GRANTS £100–£3,000.
FINANCES *Year* 2000–01 *Income* £484,861
TRUSTEES Lord Paul; Lady Paul; Hon. Angad Paul; Hon. Anjli Punn.
HOW TO APPLY In writing to the trustees at the address above. Acknowledgements are sent if an sae is enclosed. However, the trust has no paid employees and the enormous number of requests it receives creates administrative difficulties.
WHO TO APPLY TO Lord Paul, Caparo House, 103 Baker Street, London W1U 6LN
CC NO 276127   ESTABLISHED 1978

■ The Ammco Trust

WHERE FUNDING CAN BE GIVEN Oxfordshire and adjoining counties.
WHO CAN BENEFIT Small local charities and charitable projects based in the area of benefit. Disability is a priority. There is no age restriction.
WHAT IS FUNDED Disability, health, special needs education, ex-services, conservation, music, and cultural heritage.
WHAT IS NOT FUNDED No grants to individuals, students or for research.
TYPE OF GRANT One-off.
RANGE OF GRANTS £50–£2,000, except in exceptional circumstances.
SAMPLE GRANTS £5,000 each to Mulberry Bush School Oxon, Pace Centre Aylesbury and Seven Springs Gloucestershire; £3,000 to Drake Music Project.
FINANCES *Year* 2001–02 *Income* £110,513 *Grants* £100,094 *Assets* £1,219,470
TRUSTEES Mrs E M R Lewis; Mrs R S E Vickers; N P Cobbold.
HOW TO APPLY In writing to the correspondent; there are no application forms. Applications are considered at any time. An sae is appreciated.
WHO TO APPLY TO Mrs E M R Lewis, Trustee, Glebe Farm, Hinton Waldrist, Faringdon, Oxon SN7 8RX *Tel* 01865 820269 *Fax* 01865 821188
CC NO 327962   ESTABLISHED 1988

■ Sir John & Lady Amory's Charitable Trust

WHERE FUNDING CAN BE GIVEN Devon, and elsewhere in the UK.
WHO CAN BENEFIT Local organisations, plus a few national charities, benefiting disabled people, people disadvantaged by poverty, homeless people, ex-service/service people, seafarers, students, parents and children, and widows/ widowers.
WHAT IS FUNDED General charitable purposes, including education, health and welfare; also animals and environment.
TYPE OF GRANT One-off grants for core or running costs.
RANGE OF GRANTS Generally £100 to £350.
SAMPLE GRANTS £3,000 each to Blundells School and Relief for the Elderly and Infirm.
FINANCES *Year* 2000–01 *Grants* £56,000
TRUSTEES Sir John Palmer; Sir Ian Heathcoat Amory; Lady Heathcoat Amory; William Heathcoat Amory.
HOW TO APPLY In writing to the correspondent.

WHO TO APPLY TO Lady Heathcoat Amory, Trustee, Calverleigh Court, Tiverton, Devon EX16 6LT *Tel* 01884 254492
CC NO 203970   **ESTABLISHED** 1961

■ Viscount Amory's Charitable Trust

WHERE FUNDING CAN BE GIVEN UK, primarily in Devon.
WHO CAN BENEFIT Particular favour is given to young adults and elderly people. Charities benefiting people from different family situations, clergy, ex-service and service people, people with disabilities, people disadvantaged by poverty, homeless people and people living in rural areas are also considered.
WHAT IS FUNDED The income is employed mostly in the field of youth service and elderly people. Particularly to help a number of charitable objects with which the trust has been associated for a number of years, mostly within the county of Devon, including education and training for children and young people. Conservation and heritage causes are also considered.
WHAT IS NOT FUNDED No grants to individual applications from outside south west England.
TYPE OF GRANT Usually one-off including capital (including building) costs. Grants for up to three years will be considered.
RANGE OF GRANTS £100–£72,600; typically for £5,000 or less.
SAMPLE GRANTS £72,600 to London Sailing Project; £46,247 to Blundell's School; £20,000 to Blundell's Foundation; £19,035 to Eton College; £10,000 each to Mid Devon Show and Sight Savers International; £7,436 to Queen's College; £7,000 to Sands School; £6,973 to Wellington School; £6,700 to Grenville College.
FINANCES *Year* 2001–02 *Income* £315,694 *Grants* £399,363 *Assets* £9,077,369
TRUSTEES Sir Ian Heathcoat Amory; Sir John Palmer; Mrs D Cavender.
HOW TO APPLY In writing to the correspondent, giving general background information, total costs involved, amount raised so far and details of applications to other organisations.
WHO TO APPLY TO The Trust Secretary, The Island, Lowman Green, Tiverton, Devon EX16 4LA *Tel* 01884 254899 *Fax* 01884 255155
CC NO 204958   **ESTABLISHED** 1962

■ The Ampelos Trust

WHERE FUNDING CAN BE GIVEN UK.
WHO CAN BENEFIT Registered charities.
WHAT IS FUNDED General charitable purposes.
TYPE OF GRANT Usually one-off.
RANGE OF GRANTS £500–£6,000.
SAMPLE GRANTS £6,000 to Refuge; £5,000 each to John Aspinal Appeal Fund and The Smith Institute; £2,000 each to Bexley NSPCC, and Children's Aid Direct; £1,200 to NSPCC.
FINANCES *Year* 1997–98 *Income* £40,000 *Grants* £26,000 *Assets* £41,000
TRUSTEES G W N Stewart; Baroness Rendell of Babergh; A M Witt.
HOW TO APPLY In writing to the correspondent.
WHO TO APPLY TO G W N Stewart, Secretary, 9 Trinity Street, Colchester, Essex CO1 1JN *Tel* 01206 544434
CC NO 1048778   **ESTABLISHED** 1995

■ The AMW Charitable Trust

WHERE FUNDING CAN BE GIVEN Scotland only, with a priority for the West of Scotland.
WHO CAN BENEFIT Organisations benefiting young adults, disabled people and Christians.
WHAT IS FUNDED A broad range of activity is supported including work with the disabled, Christian charities, historic buildings and work with young people.
WHAT IS NOT FUNDED No grants for individuals, or to organisations outside Scotland.
RANGE OF GRANTS £3,000–£8,000.
SAMPLE GRANTS Arthritis Care Scotland, Christian Aid, The Dystonia Society, Greater Glasgow Scout Council, Kelvin School – Glasgow, Scottish Dyslexia Association, Scottish Motor Neurone Disease Association and University of Glasgow.
FINANCES *Year* 2000 *Grants* £220,000
TRUSTEES R W Speirs; C Denholm; Prof. R B Jack.
HOW TO APPLY In writing to the correspondent. Appeals are not acknowledged and the trust only advises successful applications.
WHO TO APPLY TO Campbell Denholm, Trustee, 24 Blythswood Square, Glasgow G2 4QS *Tel* 0141 226 5511
SC NO SC006959   **ESTABLISHED** 1974

■ The Ancaster Trust

WHERE FUNDING CAN BE GIVEN Mainly UK, occasionally overseas.
WHO CAN BENEFIT Registered charities benefiting at risk groups, people disadvantaged by poverty and people who are socially isolated.
WHAT IS FUNDED Welfare and environmental causes.
TYPE OF GRANT Normally small, recurring grants.
RANGE OF GRANTS £10–£300.
SAMPLE GRANTS £1,000 each to Kesteven Blind Society, Lincolnshire Trust, Morrisons Academy, St James' Episcopal Church Muthill, Swinstead Church and The London Library; £300 each to Children's Family Trust, Methodist Homes for the Aged, Royal Commonwealth Society for the Blind and South Lincolnshire Enterprise Agency.
FINANCES *Year* 1999–2000 *Income* £20,000 *Grants* £26,000 *Assets* £1,100,000
TRUSTEES Lady Willoughby de Eresby; Stuart George Kemp; David Boulton Genders.
HOW TO APPLY In writing to the correspondent. Please note that the trust states that available income is fully committed to existing beneficiaries. This entry was not confirmed by the trust, but the information was correct according to the trust's Charity Commission file.
WHO TO APPLY TO The Trustees, c/o Sayers Butterworth, 18–19 Bentinck Street, London W1U 2AR *Tel* 020 7935 8504
CC NO 270822   **ESTABLISHED** 1965

■ The Andrew Anderson Trust

WHERE FUNDING CAN BE GIVEN UK and overseas.
WHO CAN BENEFIT Organisations benefiting: Christians and evangelists; at risk groups; carers; people with disabilities; people disadvantaged by poverty; socially isolated people; and victims of abuse, crime and domestic violence.
WHAT IS FUNDED Grants to evangelical organisations and churches, small grants to health, disability and social welfare causes.
WHAT IS NOT FUNDED Individuals should not apply for travel or education.

FINANCES *Year* 2000–01 *Income* £281,000
Grants £279,000 *Assets* £8,000,000
TRUSTEES Miss A A Anderson; Miss M S Anderson;
Revd A R Anderson; Mrs M L Anderson.
HOW TO APPLY In writing to the correspondent. The
trust states 'we prefer to honour existing
commitments and initiate new ones through our
own contacts rather than respond to
applications'.
WHO TO APPLY TO The Trustees, 84 Uphill Road, Mill
Hill, London NW7 4QE
CC NO 212170   **ESTABLISHED** 1954

■ James and Grace Anderson Trust
WHERE FUNDING CAN BE GIVEN UK.
WHO CAN BENEFIT Organisations and individuals
carrying out research into the causes or
alleviation of cerebral palsy. Organisations
providing special facilities for those suffering
from cerebral palsy.
WHAT IS FUNDED Grants are given for research into
the cure or alleviation of cerebral palsy.
WHAT IS NOT FUNDED No grants are made: to
individuals who do not have cerebral palsy; to
projects not directly related to research into
cure or alleviation of cerebral palsy; or as
sponsorship of individuals.
TYPE OF GRANT At least one grant is recurring.
Project and research grants are considered.
Funding is available for more than three years.
RANGE OF GRANTS Up to £25,000 a year considered.
SAMPLE GRANTS £16,464 to Lothian Primary Care
NHS Trust for Gait Analysis Project; £2,500 to
Sequal Trust for general purposes.
FINANCES *Year* 1999–2000 *Income* £26,000
Grants £18,964 *Assets* £618,748
TRUSTEES I Ritchie, Chair; J Donald; J D M Urquhart;
T D Straton.
HOW TO APPLY In writing to the correspondent.
Trustees meet in May and October. Applications
should be received by the previous month.
WHO TO APPLY TO T D Straton, Trustee, c/o Scott-
Moncrieff, 17 Melville Street, Edinburgh EH3
7PH *Tel* 0131 473 3500 *Fax* 0131 473 3535
E-mail tim.straton@scott-moncrieff.com
SC NO SC004172   **ESTABLISHED** 1974

■ The André Christian Trust
WHERE FUNDING CAN BE GIVEN UK.
WHO CAN BENEFIT Christian organisations.
WHAT IS FUNDED Charities specified in the trust
deed; advancement of the Christian religion.
TYPE OF GRANT Core support.
SAMPLE GRANTS £5,000 each to CARE for the
Family, Overseas Missionary Fellowship, Open
Air Campaigners (West Country), Scripture Gift
Mission, Scripture Union International,
Strangers' Rest Mission and Universities and
Colleges Christian Fellowship; £3,000 to
Scripture Union (England & Wales).
FINANCES *Year* 2001 *Income* £39,047
Grants £38,000 *Assets* £1,088,994
TRUSTEES Christopher M Mowll; Andrew K Mowll.
HOW TO APPLY In writing to the correspondent.
However, the trust states: 'Applications are
discouraged since grants are principally made to
those organisations which are listed in the trust
deed.' Funds are therefore fully committed and
unsolicited requests cannot be supported.
WHO TO APPLY TO Christopher M Mowll, Secretary to
the Trustees, 15 West Hill, Sanderstead, South
Croydon, Surrey CR2 0SB *Tel* 020 8657 1207
CC NO 248466   **ESTABLISHED** 1950

■ Mary Andrew Charitable Trust
WHERE FUNDING CAN BE GIVEN UK, with a preference
for Scotland.
WHO CAN BENEFIT General charitable purposes;
registered charities only.
WHAT IS FUNDED Areas of interest include churches;
health and welfare; education and training;
children and young people; and heritage.
WHAT IS NOT FUNDED No grants to individuals or
registered charities applying on behalf of
individuals.
RANGE OF GRANTS Generally £500–£1,000.
FINANCES *Year* 2000–01 *Income* £30,000
Grants £22,000
TRUSTEES E H Webster; D A R Ballantine; A J
Campbell.
HOW TO APPLY In writing to the correspondent.
WHO TO APPLY TO The Trustees, Mitchells Roberton
Solicitors, George House, 36 North Hanover
Street, Glasgow G1 2AD *Tel* 0141 552 3422
SC NO SC021977

■ The Anglian Water Trust Fund
WHERE FUNDING CAN BE GIVEN Anglian Water region,
i.e. Cambridgeshire, Lincolnshire, North East
Lincolnshire, Norfolk, Suffolk, Peterborough,
Milton Keynes and Hartlepool plus parts of
Bedford, Buckinghamshire, Essex, Hertfordshire,
Leicestershire, Northamptonshire, North
Lincolnshire and Rutland.
WHO CAN BENEFIT Individuals, families and voluntary
sector organisations within the Anglian Water
region.
WHAT IS FUNDED Individuals and families in need;
voluntary sector organisations who wish to
establish or improve the provision of
independent money advice services.
WHAT IS NOT FUNDED No grants for: fines for criminal
offences; educational needs; debts to central
government departments; medical equipment,
aids and adaptations; holidays; business debts;
catalogues; credit cards; personal loans;
deposits for secure accommodation;
overpayment of benefits.
TYPE OF GRANT One-off grants for individuals; one-off
and recurrent capital and revenue grants for
organisations.
RANGE OF GRANTS Grants to individuals will rarely
exceed £2,000 with the average being £400–
£500. Grants to organisations average £15,000
per year per organisation.
SAMPLE GRANTS £41,500 in total to NACAB;
£31,400 to NCH Action for Children – Norfolk/
Suffolk; £29,166 to Mancroft Advice Project;
£19,053 to Wymondham/Norwich CAB and
Norfolk Money Advice; £13,274 in total to
Castle Point CAB; £10,592 in total to Brandon
CAB; £9,951 to Dereham CAB; £6,435 in total
to Great Yarmouth CAB; £5,529 to Marham
CAB; £3,961 to Huntingdon Independent Advice
Centre; £3,628 to Lowestoft CAB; £1,768 to
West Lindsey CAB; £500 to Buckingham CAB.
FINANCES *Year* 2001–02 *Income* £1,581,000
Grants £1,483,000 *Assets* £675,000
TRUSTEES Barbara Ruffell, Chair; Graham Blagden;
Norman Guffick; Elizabeth Ingram; Stuart de
Prochnow; John Sansby; Stephen Harrap;
Valerie Mansfield.
PUBLICATIONS Free quarterly newsletter containing
details of developments to the grants
programmes.
HOW TO APPLY Organisational grants: Unfortunately,
the trust states that until further notice no
applications from organisations can be
considered due to commitments to individuals

and families. Up-to-date information can be found on the trust's website. Individual grants: Applications can be submitted throughout the year. Applications must be made on a standard application form which can be obtained from local advice centres such as citizens advice bureaux or by writing to the trust.

WHO TO APPLY TO Paul Hobbs, Administrator, PO Box 42, Peterborough PE3 8XH *Tel* 01733 331177 *Fax* 01733 334344 *E-mail* admin@awtf.org.uk *Website* www.awtf.org.uk

CC NO 1054026   **ESTABLISHED** 1996

....

■ The Anglo Hong Kong Trust

WHERE FUNDING CAN BE GIVEN UK and Hong Kong.

WHO CAN BENEFIT Institutions or organisations, particularly those benefiting children, young adults and students.

WHAT IS FUNDED To promote the advancement of commerce and industry for the benefit of the UK, Hong Kong and China and to promote mutual educational and cultural activities, in particular through development and improvement of contacts between their respective educational and cultural institutions.

SAMPLE GRANTS In 1997: $244,980 to The South Bank Centre; $16,357 to an individual for educational sponsorship; $12,495 to an individual for educational sponsorship; $12,485 to an individual for educational sponsorship; $12,000 to an individual for art sponsorship; $12,000 to an individual for educational sponsorship; $8,000 to Raleigh International HK Committee.

FINANCES *Year* 2000–01 *Income* £1,881,496

TRUSTEES J G Cluff; D Tang; D J Davies; S Murray.

OTHER INFORMATION All finances are in Hong Kong Dollars.

HOW TO APPLY In writing to the correspondent

WHO TO APPLY TO D Tang, Secretary, Cluff Mining, 29 St James' Place, London SW1A 1NR *Tel* 020 7495 2030

CC NO 328194   **ESTABLISHED** 1989

....

■ Anglo-German Foundation for the Study of Industrial Society

WHERE FUNDING CAN BE GIVEN UK and Germany.

WHO CAN BENEFIT Organisations benefiting academics and research workers in the UK and Germany. Finance for higher degree work is only acceptable as a project.

WHAT IS FUNDED The foundation now concentrates its major resources on four priority topics: the delivery of health care; work-life balance; employment and social policies for an aging society; migration and the labour market. As well as the priority topics listed above, minor grants (up to £4,000 or 6,000) are available for projects in a wider range of fields, such as employment and unemployment, public spending and taxation, the management and promotion of innovation, adjustment to European and global economic change and the environment.

WHAT IS NOT FUNDED The Foundation does not provide grants of any kind for undergraduate or postgraduate study or fund academic posts, or pay overheads.

TYPE OF GRANT One-off, salaries, some administrative support, travel and subsistence, feasibility studies, salaries for research staff, teaching replacements, related conference and

publication costs. Funding for up to two years will be considered.

SAMPLE GRANTS £51,688 for a study into the development of new organisational forms in response to the growth of high-tech business services in Germany and the UK; £45,341 for an examination of regional venture capital in Germany and the UK; £31,000 for an investigation into the development of the relationship between UK subsidiaries and their German parent companies; £21,000 to the Königswinter Conference 2002, an annual event designed to promote British-German understanding and cooperation; £10,000 towards a survey of polices to stimulate biotechnology innovation in Germany and Britain.

FINANCES *Year* 2001 *Income* £751,565 *Grants* £291,295 *Assets* £4,102,812

TRUSTEES Bryan Rigby, Chair; Lord Croham; Simon Broadbent; Prof. Dorothy Wedderburn; Prof. Robert Leicht; Prof. Dr Anita B Pfaff; Dr Jürgen Ruhfus; Prof. Dr Carl-Christian von Weizsacker; John Edmonds; Dr Erika Mezger; Peter von Siemens; Dr Andrew Sentence.

HOW TO APPLY In first instance by letter. Two page outline required before formal application submitted. Decisions on major grants (£4,000+) three times per year, February, June and October. Major applications due three months before these dates.

WHO TO APPLY TO Keith Dobson, Secretary-General, 34 Belgrave Square, London SW1 8DZ *Tel* 020 7823 1123 *Fax* 020 7823 2324 *E-mail* kd@agf.org.uk *Website* www.agf.org.uk

CC NO 266844   **ESTABLISHED** 1973

....

■ The Animal Defence Trust

WHERE FUNDING CAN BE GIVEN UK.

WHO CAN BENEFIT National and established organisations benefiting animals.

WHAT IS FUNDED Capital projects for animal welfare.

WHAT IS NOT FUNDED No grants to individuals.

TYPE OF GRANT One-off and recurrent.

RANGE OF GRANTS Up to £6,000.

SAMPLE GRANTS £6,000 each to Celia Hammond Animal Trust, International League for the Protection of Horses – Glenda Spooner Farm, Ferne Animal Sanctuary and Thoroughbred Rehabilitation Centre; £4,000 to The Society for the Welfare of Horses and Ponies; £2,500 each to The Dartmoor Livestock Protection Society, Brooke Hospital for Animals, Cat Abuse Treatment Society, International Otter Foundation, People and Dogs Society and Essex Horse and Pony Protection Society; £2,000 to Devon Horse and Pony Sanctuary; £1,500 to Prevent Unwanted Pups.

FINANCES *Year* 2000–01 *Income* £52,000 *Grants* £82,000 *Assets* £1,463,401

TRUSTEES Marion Saunders; Alan A Meyer; Vivien McIrvine; Carole Bowles; Paddy Newton.

HOW TO APPLY In writing to the correspondent.

WHO TO APPLY TO A A Meyer, Trustee, c/o Butler Associates, 10 Wales Street, Kings Sutton, Banbury, Oxfordshire OX17 3RR *Tel* 01295 811888 *E-mail* ba@kingssuttonfreeserve.co.uk

CC NO 263095   **ESTABLISHED** 1971

....

■ The Eric Anker-Petersen Charity

WHERE FUNDING CAN BE GIVEN UK.

WHO CAN BENEFIT Charitable causes in the fields of screen and stage.

WHAT IS FUNDED Grants are made towards the conservation of classic films.

....

WHAT IS NOT FUNDED No grants to individuals or for non-charitable purposes.
SAMPLE GRANTS £40,000 to British Film Institute for restoration of the classic film Napoleon vu par Abel Gance by the British Film Institute; £6,000 to Theatrical Ladies Guild.
FINANCES *Year* 1999–2000 *Income* £42,000 *Grants* £48,000 *Assets* £1,100,000
TRUSTEES George Lindsay Duncan; Eric John Noel Anker-Petersen; Shan Warnock-Smith; David Eric Long.
HOW TO APPLY In writing to the correspondent. The trust wished to emphasise that it is always looking for projects to support which meet its criteria, outlined above.
WHO TO APPLY TO D E Long, 8–10 New Fetter Lane, London EC4A 1RS *Tel* 020 7203 5000
CC NO 1061428   **ESTABLISHED** 1997

■ The Annandale Charitable Trust

WHERE FUNDING CAN BE GIVEN UK.
WHO CAN BENEFIT Major UK charities.
SAMPLE GRANTS £7,000 to Victim Support; £6,000 each to Macmillan Cancer Relief and Oxfam; £4,300 to British Red Cross; £4,000 each to Age Concern, Imperial Cancer Research Campaign and RSPCA; £3,000 to National Canine Defence League.
FINANCES *Year* 1999–2000 *Income* £512,234 *Grants* £69,300 *Assets* £3,400,839
TRUSTEES Mrs S M Blofeld; Mrs A Lee; HSBC Trust Company (UK) Ltd.
HOW TO APPLY In writing to the correspondent. The trust stated that it has an ongoing programme of funding for specific charities and all its funds are fully committed.
WHO TO APPLY TO A T Fryers, Trust Officer, HSBC Trust Services, Norwich House, Nelson Gate, Commercial Road, Southampton SO15 1GX *Tel* 023 8072 2244
CC NO 1049193   **ESTABLISHED** 1995

■ Anpride Ltd

WHERE FUNDING CAN BE GIVEN Not known.
WHO CAN BENEFIT Registered charities.
WHAT IS FUNDED Advancement of the Jewish faith and the relief of poverty.
WHAT IS NOT FUNDED Grants to state-aided institutions will generally not be considered.
FINANCES *Year* 1998–99 *Income* £17,000 *Grants* £243,000 *Assets* £19,000
TRUSTEES C Benedikt; G L Benedikt; I M Halpern.
HOW TO APPLY In writing to the correspondent.
WHO TO APPLY TO C Benedikt, Trustee, 99 Geldeston Road, London E5 8RS *Tel* 020 8806 1011
CC NO 288978   **ESTABLISHED** 1984

■ The Fagus Anstruther Memorial Trust

WHERE FUNDING CAN BE GIVEN Overseas.
WHO CAN BENEFIT Organisations only.
WHAT IS FUNDED General charitable purposes, with express powers to make grants for purposes connected with further education in the arts and sciences.
WHAT IS NOT FUNDED No unsolicited applications from individuals will be considered.
TYPE OF GRANT Small grants, not exceeding £500.
FINANCES *Year* 2000–01 *Income* £25,308

TRUSTEES Susan Anstruther; Sebastian Anstruther; George Smith; Katrina Pevsner; Eleanor Anstruther.
HOW TO APPLY In writing to the correspondent.
WHO TO APPLY TO The Trustees, c/o Bircham Dyson Bell, 50 Broadway, London SW1H 0BL *Tel* 020 7227 7047
CC NO 275173   **ESTABLISHED** 1978

■ Ambrose & Ann Appelbe Trust

WHERE FUNDING CAN BE GIVEN UK.
WHO CAN BENEFIT Organisations benefiting students and research workers.
WHAT IS FUNDED Education and training, especially postgraduate education (bursaries and fees), literacy, professional or specialist training.
WHAT IS NOT FUNDED Buildings are not funded.
RANGE OF GRANTS £25–£500.
SAMPLE GRANTS £5,000 to Orchestra of the Age of Enlightenment; £3,000 each to Anatomical Donors Association and Handlines/Red Cross; £2,500 to Save the Elephants; £2,000 each to Emmaus UK, Fulcrum Challenge, RNLI, St Edmund's College for a bursary and Seven Springs Play & Support Centre.
FINANCES *Year* 1998–99 *Income* £32,198 *Grants* £28,960 *Assets* £126,920
TRUSTEES F A Appelbe; V Thomas.
HOW TO APPLY In writing to the correspondent, enclosing an sae. Individuals should apply through their college/university.
WHO TO APPLY TO Mrs V Thomas, Trustee, 28 Maresfield Gardens, London NW3 5SX
CC NO 208658   **ESTABLISHED** 1944

■ The Appleton Trust

WHERE FUNDING CAN BE GIVEN Diocese of Canterbury and the parish of St John the Evangelist, Shirley, Croydon.
WHO CAN BENEFIT Individuals and charitable and religious organisations in the beneficial area.
WHAT IS FUNDED In accordance with the trust deed for the general benefit of the Church of England.
WHAT IS NOT FUNDED No grants to relieve the Diocesan Board of Finance or the parishes in the diocese of normal obligations to provide the money necessary for financing the work of the Church of England in the diocese. No support for building works on church buildings.
SAMPLE GRANTS In 2000: £7,500 to Family Life and Marriage Education; £2,400 to the Rose Trust for clergy wives holidays; £2,000 each to Churches Together in Dover for a youth worker and Cliftonville Community and Training Centre; £1,000 to fund a youth worker for the Thanet Churches.
FINANCES *Year* 2001 *Income* £33,000 *Grants* £28,000 *Assets* £780,000
TRUSTEES R Finlinson; D S Kemp; P Trollope.
HOW TO APPLY In writing to the correspondent.
WHO TO APPLY TO J Hills, Diocesan House, Lady Wootton's Green, Canterbury CT1 1NQ *Tel* 01227 459401 *E-mail* jhills@diocant.org
CC NO 250271   **ESTABLISHED** 1966

■ The Appletree Trust

WHERE FUNDING CAN BE GIVEN UK and overseas, with a preference for the north east Fife district.
WHO CAN BENEFIT Organisations benefiting disabled children, and people suffering from cancer, heart disease and sight loss.

WHAT IS FUNDED Cancer research and care, and organisations which are concerned with disabled children, blind people and heart disease.

WHAT IS NOT FUNDED No grants to individuals.

TYPE OF GRANT Capital, buildings, project, research. Grants can be for up to two years.

RANGE OF GRANTS £250–£10,000.

SAMPLE GRANTS £7,000 to Rymonth Housing Association; £5,000 each to Macmillan Cancer Fund, North East Fife Homestart, and Childrens Hospice Association Scotland; £4,000 to Marie Curie Cancer Care; £3,000 each to Sightsavers, National Institute for the Blind, and Child & Family Trust; £1,860 to Leonard Cheshire; £1,250 to Dundee Society for the Visually Impaired.

FINANCES *Year* 1999–2000 *Income* £48,231 *Grants* £41,205 *Assets* £1,201,545

TRUSTEES The Royal Bank of Scotland plc; Revd W McKane; Revd Dr J D Martin; Revd L R Brown.

HOW TO APPLY In writing to the correspondent. Trustees meet to consider grants in October and November. Applications should be received from July to September.

WHO TO APPLY TO Don Henderson, Royal Bank of Scotland plc, Private Trust & Taxation, 2 Festival Square, Edinburgh EH3 9SU *Tel* 0131 523 2648 *Fax* 0131 228 9889

SC NO SC004851   **ESTABLISHED** 1982

....

■ The John Apthorp Charitable Trust

WHERE FUNDING CAN BE GIVEN UK, with an interest in Greater London.

WHO CAN BENEFIT Organisations, especially in Greater London.

WHAT IS FUNDED General charitable purposes.

SAMPLE GRANTS £23,000 to Aldenham Parish Council for Radlett Gardens; £3,600 to Radlett Art Society; £2,500 to Radlett District Round Table Charitable Trust for Radlett Carnival; £1,500 to Skin Treatment and Research Trust; £1,000 to Radlett Choral Society; £500 to Stanley Bowling Club for a charity day.

FINANCES *Year* 1999–2000 *Income* £20,000 *Grants* £32,000

TRUSTEES John Dorrington Apthorp; Dr D Arnold.

HOW TO APPLY Unsolicited appeals are not welcome and will not be answered. The trustees carry out their own research into prospective grant areas.

WHO TO APPLY TO The Trustees Accountant, BDO Stoy Hayward, 8 Baker Street, London W1U 3LL *Tel* 020 7486 5888

CC NO 289713   **ESTABLISHED** 1983

....

■ The Milly Apthorp Charitable Trust

WHERE FUNDING CAN BE GIVEN North west London, mainly the London borough of Barnet.

WHO CAN BENEFIT Individuals as well as voluntary and charitable organisations.

WHAT IS FUNDED Grants are made to a wide variety of organisations and individuals, providing holidays for disabled people and their carers, sports facilities, subsidised instrumental lessons, and job training and character-building activities for young people. Students receiving grants for educational purposes are required to pay back a proportion of these after completing their courses.

WHAT IS NOT FUNDED The trust states that grants are normally only given to registered charities and that trustees do their own research into areas

of interest; 'unsolicited appeals are not welcome and no reply is given to unsuccessful applicants'.

TYPE OF GRANT Buildings, capital, feasibility studies, start-up costs for up to three years. One-off grants and educational loans.

FINANCES *Year* 2002 *Income* £644,499 *Grants* £571,118 *Assets* £10,159,215

TRUSTEES John D Apthorp; Lawrence S Fenton.

OTHER INFORMATION Applicants to the three Barnet-based funds must be residents of, studying in, or working in the London borough of Barnet.

HOW TO APPLY No applications to the Milly Apthorp Trust are invited. Trustees meet in March, June, September and December. Organisations and individuals in the area of the London borough of Barnet can apply for the three funds administered by the borough. Organisations must be a registered charity or other non-profit making body which provides a service for residents of the borough and its environs and will normally be based in the Barnet area. Grants may be for either capital or revenue projects, which are designed to extend existing levels of provision or to develop new services, and which demonstrate a clearly defined benefit to local people. Awards will not generally be made to support existing activities alone. Projects will be monitored and close attention paid to how the grant awarded is meeting its objectives. UK charities are not eligible to apply but autonomous local branches of UK charities may do so. Applications must be submitted in the approved format and accompanied by latest audited accounts, plus constitution of rules and most recent annual report if one is produced. Projects should not normally exceed three years, and at the end of the funding period should be self financing or have an alternative source of funding available. For fuller details and an application form, contact the Grants Unit, Borough Treasurer's Dept, London Borough of Barnet, Town Hall, Hendon NW4 4BG (020 8359 2092).

WHO TO APPLY TO The Secretary, c/o Myers Clark, Woodford House, Woodford Road, Watford, Hertfordshire WD17 1DL *Tel* 01923 224411 *Fax* 01923 235303

CC NO 284415   **ESTABLISHED** 1982

....

■ The Arbib Foundation

WHERE FUNDING CAN BE GIVEN Unrestricted, but with a special interest in the Henley area.

WHO CAN BENEFIT Registered charities and local organisations with charitable purposes.

WHAT IS FUNDED In particular to establish and maintain a River and Rowing Museum in the Thames Valley for the education of the general public in the history, geography and ecology of the Thames Valley and the River Thames, with some donations for general purposes.

TYPE OF GRANT Recurrent and single donations.

RANGE OF GRANTS £100–£100,000.

SAMPLE GRANTS £3,900,000 to River and Rowing Museum, Henley; £1,037,000 to NSPCC; £100,000 to Institute of Cancer Research; £50,000 to Barbados Community Foundation; £25,000 to Racing Welfare Charities.

FINANCES *Year* 2000–01 *Income* £4,882,033 *Grants* £5,333,548 *Assets* £1,970,000

TRUSTEES Martin Arbib; A H E Arbib; J S Kirkwood.

HOW TO APPLY In writing to the correspondent, but 'funds are targeted to organisations with which the foundation or the trustees have an established connection'. The trust regrets that it cannot respond to unsolicited applications, except in the case of charities local to its address.

WHO TO APPLY TO Linda Sanderson, The Old Rectory, 17 Thameside, Henley-on-Thames, Oxon RG9 1LH

CC NO 296358   **ESTABLISHED** 1987

■ The Archbishop of Canterbury's Charitable Trust

WHERE FUNDING CAN BE GIVEN Worldwide.

WHO CAN BENEFIT Individuals and organisations benefiting the clergy and their dependants and other followers of the Church of England. Named charitable funds have been recipients in the past.

WHAT IS FUNDED The training for the ministry and work of the Church, for the maintenance of the clergy, provision of pensions and for the benefit of ministers, teachers and workers of the Church and their families and dependants. The extension of education in and knowledge of the faith and practice of the Church of England; the development of any work of such Church Union of Churches to further the Christian religion generally.

FINANCES *Year* 2000 *Income* £283,360 *Grants* £198,867 *Assets* £2,544,214

TRUSTEES Archbishop of Canterbury; Miss Sheila Cameron; Rt Revd Richard Llewellin; Jeremy Harris.

HOW TO APPLY Funds are allocated for several years ahead, therefore no new applications can be considered.

WHO TO APPLY TO P F B Beesley, Registrar, 1 The Sanctuary, Westminster, London SW1P 3JT *Tel* 020 7222 5381

CC NO 287967   **ESTABLISHED** 1983

■ The John M Archer Charitable Trust

WHERE FUNDING CAN BE GIVEN UK and overseas.

WHO CAN BENEFIT Registered charities.

WHAT IS FUNDED General charitable purposes, including the prevention or relief of human suffering; welfare of sick and distressed people; alleviation of need; advancement of education; advancement of religious or missionary work; advancement of scientific research and discovery; and preservation of Scottish heritage and the advancement of associated cultural activities.

SAMPLE GRANTS £5,000 to Eastgate Theatre & Arts Centre, Peebles; £3,000 each to the British Red Cross (general appeals overseas) and Merchants Trust for university students bursaries; £2,500 to Liverpool University Hospital (Muscular Degeneration Research); £1,500 to the Castlebrae School Scholarship Fund.

FINANCES *Year* 2001–02 *Income* £65,000 *Grants* £34,850 *Assets* £631,000

TRUSTEES G B Archer; Mrs I Morrison; Mrs A Morgan; Mrs W Grant; Mrs C Fraser; Mrs I C Smith.

HOW TO APPLY In writing to the correspondent at the above address.

WHO TO APPLY TO Mrs Ruth L Lothian, Secretary, 12 Broughton Place, Edinburgh EH1 3RX *Tel* 0131 556 4518

SC NO SC010583   **ESTABLISHED** 1969

■ The Architectural Heritage Fund

WHERE FUNDING CAN BE GIVEN UK.

WHO CAN BENEFIT Any UK charity.

WHAT IS FUNDED Support is given in the form of grants, loans, advice and information for the preservation and sustainable re-use of historic buildings.

WHAT IS NOT FUNDED Applications from private individuals and non-charitable organisations. Applications for projects not involving a change of ownership or of use, or for a building not on a statutory list or in a conservation area.

TYPE OF GRANT Loans; feasibility study grants; project administration grants; project organiser grants; refundable project development grants; refundable working capital grants.

RANGE OF GRANTS Grants up to £25,000; loans up to £500,000 (more in exceptional circumstances).

SAMPLE GRANTS The following were loans rather than grants: £500,000 to Mansfield Traquair Trust for a church in Edinburgh; £344,000 to Fife Historic Buildings Trust; £280,000 to Glasgow Building Preservation Trust for 176 Duke Street; £245,000 to Highland Buildings Preservation Trust for Forss Mill; £220,000 to Museum of Empire and Commonwealth Trust for Bristol Old Station; £210,000 to Suffolk Building Preservation Trust for Pakenham Water Mill Farmhouse; £200,000 each to Ironbridge Gorge Museum Trust Ltd and Sedbergh and District Buildings Preservation Trust for Farfield Mills; £150,000 to Four Acres Charitable Trust for Steeple Phase, former Dowanhill Church; £140,000 to Alexander Greek Thomson Trust for St Vincent Street Church, Glasgow.

FINANCES *Year* 2000–01 *Income* £944,000 *Grants* £746,000 *Assets* £13,346,000

TRUSTEES Jane Sharman, Chair; David Adams; Colin Amery; Nicholas Baring; William Cadell; Robert Clow; Malcolm Crowder; Fionnuala Jay-O'Boyle; Merlin Waterson; Dr Roger Wools; John Pavitt; Roy Dantzic.

OTHER INFORMATION In addition to the amount given in grants, £3,000,000 was given in new loans.

HOW TO APPLY Detailed notes for applicants for loans and feasibility studies are supplied with the application forms. The trustees meet in March, June, September and December; applications must be received six weeks before meetings.

WHO TO APPLY TO Jonathan Thompson, Clareville House, 26–27 Oxendon Street, London SW1Y 4EL *Tel* 020 7925 0199 *Fax* 020 7930 0295 *E-mail* ahf@ahfund.org.uk *Website* www.ahfund.org.uk

CC NO 266780   **ESTABLISHED** 1973

■ The Ardwick Trust

WHERE FUNDING CAN BE GIVEN UK, Israel and the third world.

WHO CAN BENEFIT Institutions and registered charities (mainly national charities) benefiting people of all ages, students and Jews.

WHAT IS FUNDED To support Jewish welfare, along with a wide band of non-Jewish causes to include social welfare, health, education (especially special schools), elderly people, conservation and the environment, child welfare, disability and medical research.

WHAT IS NOT FUNDED No grants to individuals.

TYPE OF GRANT One-off or recurrent grants up to two years. Capital, including buildings, research and start-up costs.

RANGE OF GRANTS £50–£2,000.

SAMPLE GRANTS In 1998–99: £25,000 to Nightingale House for the training fund in memory of Howard Bloch; £2,500 to Nightingale House for the Alzheimer's wing; £2,000 each to British Technion Society and Jewish Care; £1,000 each to Cheltenham Ladies College (Bursaries Fund), Norwood/Ravenswood, and World Jewish Relief.

FINANCES *Year* 2000–01 *Income* £120,000 *Grants* £42,000 *Assets* £969,000

TRUSTEES Mrs J B Bloch; Miss E R Wix; Miss Judith Portrait.

HOW TO APPLY In writing to the correspondent.

WHO TO APPLY TO Mrs J B Bloch, Trustee, 6 Hocroft Avenue, London NW2 2EH

CC NO 266981   **ESTABLISHED** 1975

....

■ ARK (Absolute Return for Kids)

WHERE FUNDING CAN BE GIVEN Unrestricted.

WHO CAN BENEFIT Local and international projects benefiting children who are victims of abuse, disability, illness and poverty.

WHAT IS FUNDED A relatively small number of grants are given in specific areas, to projects comprehensively researched by ARK. The selected 'themes' currently being researched, are child destitution in the UK and deprived children in Eastern Europe.

FINANCES *Year* 2002 *Grants* £2,900,000

TRUSTEES Arpad Busson; Blaine Tomlinson; Kevin Gundle; Ian Wace; Paul Marshall; Paul Dunning; Jennifer Moses.

HOW TO APPLY Unsolicited appeals will not be accepted or acknowledged.

WHO TO APPLY TO Teresa Albor, Director of Projects and Operations, 27 Queen Anne's Gate, London SW1H 9BU *Tel* 020 7222 9272 *Fax* 020 7799 5666 *Website* www.arkonline.org

CC NO 1083567

....

■ The Arkleton Trust

WHERE FUNDING CAN BE GIVEN UK and overseas.

WHO CAN BENEFIT People living in rural areas.

WHAT IS FUNDED The trust itself does not make grants, but administers three grant-making funds.

To study practical ways of improving the conditions of life of rural people particularly through education and rural development. It aims to stimulate discussion between politicians, administrators and practitioners on problems facing rural people throughout the world. To collaborate with other bodies which share its aims and with individuals working in the same field. To hold seminars and undertake research and studies. To publish and disseminate results of research, studies and fellowships.

WHAT IS NOT FUNDED No grants to individuals seeking support for educational purposes. Applicants must conform to the requirements of each fund including closing dates.

TYPE OF GRANT One-off awards from the funds listed in Other Information only are available to applicants after adjudication by a selection committee.

RANGE OF GRANTS £400–£5,000.

FINANCES *Year* 1999 *Income* £34,926 *Grants* £43,028 *Assets* £379,240

TRUSTEES M Galsworthy; D Walton; D C Y Higgs; Lady Higgs; Mrs C A Higgs; Ms C Carlson; Mrs Margaret Clark; Prof. Malcolm Moseley.

OTHER INFORMATION (a) The David Moore Memorial Fund, aimed at young people engaged in the study of rural development and social change in Europe and/or third world countries to enable them to supplement academic course work with some research/practical field investigations. Amount of award between £400 and £800. Closing date: 31 January of each year. (b) The Bernard Conyers Fund seeks to encourage an individual or small organisation to disseminate information, findings or ideas relating to the third world, the links between Europe and the third world, or the lessons which Europe can learn from third world experience. More than one award may be given in any one year. Total to be awarded: £6,000. Closing date: 15 May of each year. (c) John Higgs Fund seeks to identify groups doing specific development, community (not playgroups), or education (not schools) work in rural areas: small awards made on a one-off basis.

HOW TO APPLY Applications in writing, by letter, e-mail or fax. Notes for guidance are available from the trust for The David Moore Memorial Fund and The Bernard Conyers Fund. Full information about the funds is available on the trust's website.

WHO TO APPLY TO The Administrator, Enstone, Chipping Norton, Oxfordshire OX7 4HH *Tel* 01608 677255 *Fax* 01608 677276 *E-mail* arkleton@enstoneuk.demon.co.uk *Website* www.enstoneuk.demon.co.uk/arkleton

CC NO 275153   **ESTABLISHED** 1978

....

■ Armenian General Benevolent Union London Trust

WHERE FUNDING CAN BE GIVEN UK and overseas.

WHO CAN BENEFIT Armenian individuals and organisations, particularly those benefiting students, education, cultural organisations in the Armenian diaspora and within the republic of Armenia.

WHAT IS FUNDED To advance education among Armenians, particularly those in the UK, and to promote the study of Armenian history, literature, language, culture and religion. The trustees may provide grants and scholarships to needy students; assist other Armenian institutions which are registered as exclusively charitable institutions; establish charitable schools and provide facilities for the physical education of those people attending such schools; and establish charitable educational institutes, cultural centres and clinics, and other medical institutions, and provide assistance in the running of such institutions.

WHAT IS NOT FUNDED No support for projects of a commercial nature or for education for individual students.

RANGE OF GRANTS £200–£6,000.

SAMPLE GRANTS £52,100 as student loans and grants; £19,260 for humanitarian and medical aid to Armenia; £9,000 for Armenian culture; £6,000 to Marie Noubar Student Hostel for running costs; £5,000 to AGBU London Branch for youth activities; £4,000 to Armenian schools in London.

FINANCES *Year* 2001 *Income* £115,100 *Grants* £104,134 *Assets* £2,775,364

TRUSTEES G S Kurkjian; L Simone; B Setrakian; A R E Topalian; H Hamparzounian; S Pattie; H Aghajanian.

HOW TO APPLY In writing to the correspondent.

WHO TO APPLY TO H Aghajanian, Trustee, Armenian House, 25 Cheniston Gardens, London W8 6TG

CC NO 282070   **ESTABLISHED** 1981

....

■ The G C Armitage Charitable Trust

WHERE FUNDING CAN BE GIVEN North and West Yorkshire, especially Leeds, Wakefield and York.

WHO CAN BENEFIT Organisations benefiting: musicians; seafarers and fishermen; people with disabilities; victims of crime; victims of war; and people who are terminally ill or have cancer.

WHAT IS FUNDED Charities working in the fields of: churches; music; opera; support to voluntary and community organisations; crime prevention schemes; councils for voluntary service; hospices; cancer research; woodlands; and horticulture. Local or known charities are favoured.

WHAT IS NOT FUNDED No grants to individuals.

TYPE OF GRANT Funding for up to and over three years will be considered.

RANGE OF GRANTS £100–£2,500; average approximately £800.

SAMPLE GRANTS £1,000 each to Martin House Hospice, Oundle School Foundation, RNLI, St Andrew's Church Aldborough, St George's Crypt, St Michael's Hospice and Wheatfields Hospice; £500 each to Friends of North Aldborough Festival, Friends of Opera North and Giving for Sight.

FINANCES *Year* 2001–02 *Income* £28,026 *Grants* £21,700 *Assets* £741,850

TRUSTEES Mrs V M Armitage; Mrs C J Dew; Mrs S M Macleod.

HOW TO APPLY In writing to the correspondent.

WHO TO APPLY TO Mrs V M Armitage, Trustee, Aldborough House, Aldborough, Boroughbridge, North Yorkshire YO51 9EY

CC NO 326418   **ESTABLISHED** 1985

■ The Armourers and Brasiers' Gauntlet Trust

WHERE FUNDING CAN BE GIVEN UK, with some preference for London.

WHO CAN BENEFIT Organisations benefiting young adults, academics, research workers and students.

WHAT IS FUNDED Research and education in materials science.

WHAT IS NOT FUNDED In general grants are not made to: organisations or groups which are not registered; individuals; organisations or groups whose main object is to fund or support other charitable bodies which are in direct relief of any reduction of financial support from public funds; charities with a turnover of over £4 million; charities which spend over 10% of their income on fundraising activities; organisations whose accounts disclose substantial financial reserves. Grants are also not made towards general maintenance, repair or restoration of buildings, including ecclesiastical buildings, unless there is a long standing connection with the Armourers and Brasiers' Company or unless of outstanding importance to the national heritage.

SAMPLE GRANTS £4,750 to UTCS/Rolls-Royce; £3,500 to Royal Society of Chemistry; £2,823 to STA for voyages; £2,640 to Royal Society Award; £1,905 to Royal Armoured Corps for silver statuettes; £1,700 to Guildhall School of Music for a bursary; £1,500 to Cambridge A &B Newton for bursaries; £1,400 to Sheffield Hallam University for scholarships; £1,000 to St Mary's Convent and Nursing Home.

FINANCES *Year* 2001–02 *Income* £335,583 *Grants* £172,239 *Assets* £5,141,828

TRUSTEES Ven. C J H Wagstaff, Chair; Revd P E de D Warburton; R A Crabb; R N Lay; A M R Pontifex.

HOW TO APPLY In writing to the correspondent, with a copy of the latest annual report and audited accounts. Applications are considered quarterly.

WHO TO APPLY TO The Secretary, Armourers' Hall, 81 Coleman Street, London EC2R 5BJ *Tel* 020 7374 4000 *Fax* 202 7606 7481

CC NO 279204   **ESTABLISHED** 1979

■ The Army Benevolent Fund

WHERE FUNDING CAN BE GIVEN Worldwide.

WHO CAN BENEFIT National headquarters of charities and charitable funds of Corps and Regimental Associations benefiting ex-service and service people, and their dependants.

WHAT IS FUNDED Support and benefit of people serving, or who have served, in the British Army, or their families/dependants. The work of the charity/service concerned must be of direct benefit to a number of soldiers, ex-soldiers or their dependants. Not only should this number be considerable but it must also comprise an appreciable portion of the numbers of people who benefit from the work or service of the charity.

TYPE OF GRANT One-off grants.

SAMPLE GRANTS In 1998: £410,000 to British Commonwealth Ex-Services League; £326,086 to SSAFA Forces Help; £300,000 to Haig Homes; £100,000 each to Chaseley Trust and St Dunstan's; £75,750 to Royal Cambridge Home for Soldiers' Widows; £75,000 to Royal Star and Garter Home; £66,000 to Ex-Services Fellowship Centres; £60,000 each to St David's Home, Ealing and St Dunstan's.

FINANCES *Year* 2002 *Income* £4,890,738 *Grants* £2,152,339 *Assets* £34,962,170

TRUSTEES Gen. Sir Jeremy Mackenzie, Chair; Maj. Gen. M A Charlton-Weedy; Maj. Gen. D F E Botting; N A Gold; M B Hockney; Maj. Gen. J Boyne; Sir Paul Newall; Col R R Barkshire; Col T A Hall; D J M Roberts.

OTHER INFORMATION £1,848,402 went to regiments and corps for the benefit of individuals in 2002.

HOW TO APPLY Individual cases should be referred initially to the appropriate Corps or Regimental Association. Charities should apply in writing and enclose the latest annual report and accounts.

WHO TO APPLY TO The Controller, 41 Queen Anne's Gate, London SW7 5HR *Tel* 020 7591 2000 *Fax* 020 7584 0889 *Website* www.armybenevolentfund.com

CC NO 211645   **ESTABLISHED** 1944

■ Arsenal Charitable Trust

WHERE FUNDING CAN BE GIVEN Mainly Greater London.

WHO CAN BENEFIT Social welfare.

WHAT IS FUNDED Youth projects and the provision of recreational facilities for the use of people living in the Greater London boroughs; any charitable purpose for the inhabitants of Islington and Hackney.

SAMPLE GRANTS £29,000 to Gunner's Community Fund; £5,000 to Jack O'Dowd Fund; £4,000 each BCS Disability Group and Kanu Heart Foundation; £2,000 to British Aid for Deprived Families.

FINANCES *Year* 2000–01 *Income* £61,000 *Grants* £54,000 *Assets* £216,000

TRUSTEES K J Friar; D Miles; A Setton.

HOW TO APPLY In writing to the correspondent.

WHO TO APPLY TO The Trustees, Arsenal Stadium, Highbury, London N5 1BU *Tel* 020 7704 4000 *Fax* 020 7704 4001
CC NO 1008024   ESTABLISHED 1992

....

■ The Artemis Charitable Trust

WHERE FUNDING CAN BE GIVEN UK.
WHO CAN BENEFIT Registered charities benefiting parents, counsellors and psychotherapists.
WHAT IS FUNDED Counselling, psychotherapy, parenting, and human relationship training.
TYPE OF GRANT Recurring.
SAMPLE GRANTS £206,000 to Counselling in Primary Care Trust; £166,000 to Metanoia Institute; £84,000 to Parents in Partnership (for Parent Infant Network).
FINANCES *Year* 2000–01 *Grants* £513,000
TRUSTEES Richard Evans; Joyce Gai Evans.
HOW TO APPLY The trust can only give grants to registered charities. 'We cannot entertain applications either from individuals or from organisations which are not registered charities. Applicants should also be aware that most of the trust's funds are committed to a number of major ongoing projects and that spare funds available to meet new applications are very limited.'
WHO TO APPLY TO Richard Evans, Trustee, Brook House, Quay Meadow, Bosham, West Sussex PD18 8LY
CC NO 291328   ESTABLISHED 1985

....

■ Arthritis Research Campaign

WHERE FUNDING CAN BE GIVEN Mainly UK.
WHO CAN BENEFIT Medical schools, hospitals and individual research workers, medical professionals, and those suffering from arthritis, rheumatism and allied diseases.
WHAT IS FUNDED Research into the cause and cure of rheumatic diseases.
WHAT IS NOT FUNDED Applications for welfare and social matters will not be considered.
TYPE OF GRANT One-off, project, recurring, running costs, and salaries. Programme support is for five years; project grants are usually for three years.
RANGE OF GRANTS £1,000–£750,000.
SAMPLE GRANTS £1,557,000 in 11 grants to University College London; £1,341,000 in 10 grants to University of Oxford; £1,286,000 in 9 grants to Imperial Hospital NHS Trust; £1,183,000 in 7 grants to Kings College London; £1,090,000 in 6 grants to Univeristy of Aberdeen; £1,014,000 in 9 grants to University of Manchester; £901,000 in 6 grants to Univeristy of Leeds; £889,000 in 5 grants to University of Birmingham; £871,000 in 7 grants to University of Sheffield; £598,000 in 3 grants to University of Edinburgh.
FINANCES *Year* 2000–01 *Income* £26,480,000 *Grants* £16,605,000 *Assets* £13,832,000
TRUSTEES Lord Lewis of Newnham, President; Prof. R D Sturrock, Chair; J C Maisey; Mrs S Arnott; Sir Richard Butler; Dr Peter Copeman; Dame Mary Glen-Haig; Prof. H J F Hodgson; Sir Peter Lachmann; Prof. George Nuki; Alan Torry.
HOW TO APPLY Application forms and guidelines are available from the research and education department.

WHO TO APPLY TO Debbie Branscombe, PA to Fergus Logan, Copeman House, St Mary's Court, St Mary's Gate, Chesterfield, Derbyshire S41 7TD *Tel* 01246 558033 *Fax* 01246 558007 *Website* www.arc.org.uk
CC NO 207711   ESTABLISHED 1936

....

■ The Arts Council of England

WHERE FUNDING CAN BE GIVEN England.
WHO CAN BENEFIT Non-profit distributing arts organisations; professional creative artists; actors and entertainment professionals; musicians; and writers and poets.
WHAT IS FUNDED Developing, sustaining and promoting the arts. The majority of funding is provided to organisations which are regularly funded by the Arts Council.
WHAT IS NOT FUNDED Applications for individuals, including students, will not be considered.
TYPE OF GRANT One-off and recurrent grants for: buildings; capital; core costs; feasibility studies; project, research; running costs; salaries; and start-up costs.
RANGE OF GRANTS From £500.
SAMPLE GRANTS £13,218,250 to South Bank Board; £11,955,000 to English National Opera; £11,167,000 to Royal National Theatre; £8,470,000 to Royal Shakespeare Company; £7,954,000 to Royal Opera House; £6,455,000 to Royal Ballet; £1,215,200 to Northern Ballet Theatre; £528,000 to Ikon Gallery, Birmingham; £150,280 to Poetry Society.
FINANCES *Year* 1999 *Income* £191,171,000 *Grants* £211,800,000 *Assets* £58,843,000
TRUSTEES Members of the Arts Council of England: Gerry Robinson, Chair; Derrick Anderson; David Brierley; Ms Deborah Bull; Anthony Gormley; Anish Kapoor; Ms Joanna MacGregor; Ms Hilary Strong; Brian McMaster; Dr Janet Ritterman; William Sieghart.
OTHER INFORMATION From 1 April 2002, the Arts Council of England and the Englishh Regional Arts Boards joined to form a single development organisation for the arts in England. ACE plans to devolve more funding responsibility to the regions, for further information, and details, of current regional arts lottery programmes and policies, contact the relevant regional arts office.
HOW TO APPLY The relevant department should be contacted for further information on available funding, including deadline dates and application forms.
WHO TO APPLY TO The Information Department, 14 Great Peter Street, London SW1P 3NQ *Tel* 020 7333 0100 *Fax* 020 7973 6590 *E-mail* emquiries@artscouncil.org.uk *Website* www.artscouncil.org.uk
CC NO 1036733   ESTABLISHED 1994

....

■ Arts Council of Northern Ireland

WHERE FUNDING CAN BE GIVEN UK and Ireland (but projects must benefit people of Northern Ireland).
WHO CAN BENEFIT Applications are welcomed from the widest range of organisations in Northern Ireland, whether community, amateur or professional, or for projects which benefit Northern Ireland. Applicant organisations must have a constitution, set of rules or other legal entity, and should operate on a non-profit distributing basis. Commercial organisations may apply for projects which are for public benefit rather than private gain.

WHAT IS FUNDED The Arts Council of Northern Ireland National Lottery Fund aims to increase opportunities for access to, participation in and practice of the arts by all the people of Northern Ireland.

WHAT IS NOT FUNDED Projects which have commenced, have been completed, or which are for private gain. No grants are made to individuals and no loans are made.

TYPE OF GRANT One-off and development grants (up to three years).

RANGE OF GRANTS (a) Access to the Arts: £5,000 – £40,000 per year for up to three years; (b) Audience Development: £5,000 – £100,000 per year for up to three years; (c) New Work: £5,000 – £50,000; (d) Equipment: from £5,000 – no stated maximum; (e) Buildings: feasibility studies – up to £10,000, design development – £5,000 – £50,000, construction – from £5,000, no stated maximum; (f) Musical Instruments for Bands. (Note: (a), (b) and (c) programmmes suspended in July 2002 – due to be relaunched in March 2003 – financial limits may differ.

SAMPLE GRANTS £4,000,000 to Omagh Distrct Council for a new arts centre; £2,500,000 to Conway Mill Preservation Trust to refurbish existing building to create craft studios; £467,925 to Grand Opera House to refurbish the auditorium and front of house areas; £300,000 to Ulster Orchestra Society for an audience development programme; £75,000 to Feile and Phobail to increase participation by people with disabilities in its festival activities; £23,130 to Old Museum Arts Centre for an exhibition of work by ' Ten Men Artists'; £13,710 to Spanner in the Works Theatre Company produce three short drama pieces for women.

FINANCES *Year* 2001–02 *Income* £9,229,647 *Grants* £5,475,954 *Assets* £5,844,338

TRUSTEES Council Members: Prof. Brian Walker, Chair; Ms Eilis O Baoill, Vice Chair; Ms Maureen Armstrong; David Boyd; Martin Bradley; Dr Maurna Crozier; Ronald Dunn; David Hyndman; Ms Judith Jordan; James Kerr; Dr Tess Maginess; Prof. Brian McClelland; Ms Gerri Moriarty; Aidan Shortt; Mrs Margaret Yeomans.

OTHER INFORMATION We were informed that as of February 2003 the council members listed will come to the end of their term in office. New members will be in place by March/April 2003. Further information will be available on the website.

HOW TO APPLY Guidelines and application forms are available from the address below or from the ACNI website.

WHO TO APPLY TO MacNeice House, 77 Malone Road, Belfast BT9 6AQ *Tel* 028 9038 5200 *Fax* 028 9066 1715 *E-mail* lottery@artscouncil-ni.org *Website* www.artscouncil-ni.org
CC NO Y00118   **ESTABLISHED** 1995

....

■ Arts Council of Wales

WHERE FUNDING CAN BE GIVEN Wales.

WHO CAN BENEFIT Arts organisations benefiting: actors and entertainment professionals; musicians; textile workers and designers; writers and poets. There are residency requirements for some grant schemes: contact the relevant local office for details.

WHAT IS FUNDED Arts activities in Wales through: capital grants for building development and purchase of equipment, such as staging equipment and musical instruments; feature film grants, for script development and production;

Arts for All, non-capital grants in support of projects that encourage people to enjoy the arts or take part in the arts.

WHAT IS NOT FUNDED Individual schemes may stipulate restrictions on the origin of beneficiary organisations or individuals. Applications for funding for projects which have already started will not be considered.

TYPE OF GRANT One-off and recurrent for: capital costs (including buildings); core costs; feasibility studies; loans; project; research; running costs; salaries; and start-up costs.

RANGE OF GRANTS £40–£3,000,000.

SAMPLE GRANTS £2,947 400 to Welsh National Opera; £2,095,902 to Cwmni Tref Caernarfon; £203,920 to Aberrystwyth Arts Centre; £109,290 to Hijinx Theatre; £100,743 to Gwent Theatre; £68,000 to Valley Kids; £59,749 to Rhondda Cyon Taff Community Arts; £47,856 to Glynn Vivian Art Gallery; £43,366 to Welsh Books Council; £41,741 to Welsh Jazz Society.

FINANCES *Year* 2001–02 *Income* £16,926,000 *Grants* £15,171,000 *Assets* £3,128,000

TRUSTEES Sybil Crouch; Roger Davies; Keith Evans; Dewi Walters; Dai Davies; Hazel Walford Davies; Meg Elis; Edmond Fivet; Stephen Garrett; Ellenap Gwynn; Harry James; Daniel Jones; Janet Roberts; Penny Ryan.

HOW TO APPLY Applicants are asked to contact the relevant local office for details of individual grants schemes.

WHO TO APPLY TO The Communications Team, 9 Museum Place, Cardiff CF10 3NX *Tel* 029 2037 6500 *Fax* 029 2022 1447 *Minicom* 029 2039 0027 *E-mail* info@artswales.org.uk *Website* www.artswales.org.uk
CC NO 1034245   **ESTABLISHED** 1994

....

■ The Ove Arup Foundation

WHERE FUNDING CAN BE GIVEN Unrestricted.

WHO CAN BENEFIT Organisations benefiting research workers and designers.

WHAT IS FUNDED Education and research in matters related to the built environment, particularly if related to multi-disciplinary design, through educational institutions and charities.

WHAT IS NOT FUNDED No grants to individuals, including students.

TYPE OF GRANT Research and project, including start-up and feasibility costs. They can be one-off or recurrent.

RANGE OF GRANTS Typically £5,000.

SAMPLE GRANTS £26,569 to Imperial College; £10,000 each to Foundation for Art & Creative Technology and University of Nottingham; £5,000 to @Bristol; £4,000 to XL Wales; £3,525 to The Edge; £3,000 to Museum of Empire & Commonwealth Trust; £2,500 to Architectural Foundation; £2,000 to Space Link Learning Foundation; £1,200 to Anglo-Danish Society.

FINANCES *Year* 2001–02 *Income* £39,000 *Grants* £70,000 *Assets* £2,500,000

TRUSTEES P Ahm; P Dowson; B Perry; M Shears; D Michael; R F Emmerson; R B Haryott.

HOW TO APPLY In writing to the correspondent, with brief supporting financial information. Trustees meet quarterly to consider applications (March, June, September and December).

WHO TO APPLY TO K D Dawson, 13 Fitzroy Street, London W1T 4BQ *Tel* 020 7755 3298 *E-mail* keithdavid@aol.com *Website* www.theovearupfoundation.com
CC NO 328138   **ESTABLISHED** 1989

■ The AS Charitable Trust

WHERE FUNDING CAN BE GIVEN UK and the developing world.

WHO CAN BENEFIT Preference for charities in which the trust has special interest, knowledge of or association with. Christian organisations will benefit. Support may go to victims of famine, man-made or natural disasters, and war.

WHAT IS FUNDED The trust is sympathetic to projects which combine the advancement of the Christian religion with Christian lay leadership, third world development, peacemaking and reconciliation, or other areas of social concern.

WHAT IS NOT FUNDED Grants to individuals or large charities are very rare. Such applications are discouraged.

SAMPLE GRANTS £30,000 to Christian International Peace Service; £1,500 to War on Want; £1,100 each to Barnabas Fund and St Matthew Housing; £1,000 each to Christain Engineers in Development, Corrymeela Community, St Michael's Church – Chester Square and Traidcraft Exchange.

FINANCES *Year* 2000–01 *Income* £167,164 *Grants* £40,600 *Assets* £6,568,765

TRUSTEES R Calvocoressi; C W Brocklebank.

HOW TO APPLY In writing to the correspondent.

WHO TO APPLY TO The Administrator, Bixbottom Farm, Bix, Henley-on-Thames RG9 6BH *Tel* 01491 577745

CC NO 242190   **ESTABLISHED** 1965

■ Ashburnham Thanksgiving Trust

WHERE FUNDING CAN BE GIVEN UK and worldwide.

WHO CAN BENEFIT Individuals and organisations benefiting Christians and evangelists.

WHAT IS FUNDED Only Christian work already known to the trustees is supported, particularly evangelical overseas missionary work.

WHAT IS NOT FUNDED No grants for buildings.

SAMPLE GRANTS £10,990 to Lawrence Barham Memorial Trust; £5,170 to Evangelical Alliance; £4,000 to Genesis Arts Trust; £3,000 to Penhurst Retreat Centre; £2,410 to Ashburnham Village Jubilee Millennium Fund; £2,030 to Ashburnham Christian Trust; £2,000 each to Wycliffe Bible Translators and Youth for Christ; £1,750 to Interserve; £1,400 to Oakhill Bursary Fund.

FINANCES *Year* 2000–01 *Income* £137,305 *Grants* £99,616 *Assets* £4,108,925

TRUSTEES Mrs M Bickersteth; Mrs E M Habershon; E R Bickersteth; R D Bickersteth.

HOW TO APPLY By e-mail only, potential applicants should not send anything by post. The trust has stated that its funds are fully committed to current beneficiaries. Unfortunately it receives far more applications than it is able to deal with.

WHO TO APPLY TO The Trustees, Agmerhurst House, Ashburnham, Battle, East Sussex TN33 9NB *E-mail* att@lookingforward.biz

CC NO 249109   **ESTABLISHED** 1965

■ The Ashby Charitable Trust

WHERE FUNDING CAN BE GIVEN Derbyshire or with a Derbyshire connection.

WHO CAN BENEFIT Individuals and organisations benefiting young people, mature students, research workers and medical professionals. Support may be given to those with a variety of diseases and medical conditions.

WHAT IS FUNDED Educational awards to educational establishments and to individuals, especially to mature students ineligible for state support. Also support for research and help for people with cancer, leukaemia, heart disease, multiple sclerosis, Alzheimer's disease, Parkinson's disease, dyslexia and spina bifida, as well as people who are homeless.

TYPE OF GRANT Research and educational awards are considered.

SAMPLE GRANTS £2,500 educational grant towards fees for a local student to attend the Webber Douglas Academy of Dramatic Art.

FINANCES *Year* 2001–02 *Income* £109,000 *Grants* £32,125 *Assets* £783,000

TRUSTEES Brian Ashby, Chair; Mrs I Ashby; D R Ashby; R Goodwin; C Clements.

HOW TO APPLY In writing to the correspondent.

WHO TO APPLY TO c/o The Old Vicarage, 226 Ashbourne Road, Turnditch, Belper, Derbyshire DE56 2LH

CC NO 276497   **ESTABLISHED** 1978

■ A J H Ashby Will Trust

WHERE FUNDING CAN BE GIVEN Lea Valley area of Hertfordshire.

WHO CAN BENEFIT Small local projects benefiting children and young adults.

WHAT IS FUNDED Education; environmental resources; children in the Lea Valley; wildlife; conservation; English heritage.

WHAT IS NOT FUNDED No grants to individuals or students.

TYPE OF GRANT One-off and recurrent.

FINANCES *Year* 2001 *Income* £76,919 *Grants* £82,822 *Assets* £1,460,257

HOW TO APPLY In writing to the correspondent.

WHO TO APPLY TO S J Gladwell, Trust Manager, HSBC Trust Company (UK) Ltd – Trust Services, Norwich House, Nelson Gate, Commercial Road, Southampton, Hants SO15 1GX *Tel* 023 8072 2243

CC NO 803291   **ESTABLISHED** 1990

■ The Ashden Trust

WHERE FUNDING CAN BE GIVEN UK and overseas.

WHO CAN BENEFIT Registered charities.

WHAT IS FUNDED The environment UK – in the areas of transport policy, sustainable agriculture, energy efficiency and renewable energy technology; Environment overseas – community-based renewable energy projects that aim to help people to help themselves in an environmentally sustainable way; Homelessness – support for organisations that help homeless people to access emergency shelter and support, to secure permanent accommodation and to regain economic independence; Urban rejuvenation – aimed at schemes that help people to develop skills, improve self-esteem and increase employment prospects in areas of urban deprivation, including projects concerning drug misuse and offending through training and education programmes; Community arts – grass-roots arts activities and in particular those groups for which relatively modest grants can have a considerable impact, with an interest in environmental drama; General charitable purposes. The trustees prefer to support innovative schemes that can be successfully replicated or become self-sustaining.

TYPE OF GRANT Primarily project.

SAMPLE GRANTS £123,000 over three years to Cycling Project for the North West for the transfer from London School of Economics and long-term development of the Bike Up Your Life

Initiative; £101,752 to Kenya Schools Programme for the development of a new initiative to promote renewable energy technology in Kenyan schools; £70,000 to Intermediate Technology Development Group towards the development of the Renewable Energy Network in East Africa; £50,000 to Soil Association towards proposed research and farmer education programme based on organic farming; £40,000 to St Mungo's towards the sanctuary appeal; £34,500 to Whitley Laing Foundation for the prizes and administrative costs of the Ashden Award for Renewable Energy; £30,000 each to Community Catalyst Ltd to enable them to become more flexible and broaden the service offered, and SCODE – Kenya for the renewal energy project in Nakuru providing biogas installations on the basis of revolving credit; £29,000 to Thames Reach to enable the Mapping Social Networks Study and toolkit to be researched and disseminated; £25,000 each to Aviation and the Environment seminar – Heathrow and Crime Concern – Wolverhampton to continue support for the neighbourhood safety project on the Bushbury/Lowhill Estate.

FINANCES *Year* 2000–01 *Income* £835,795 *Grants* £873,000 *Assets* £21,981,718

TRUSTEES Mrs S Butler-Sloss; R Butler-Sloss; Miss Judith Portrait.

OTHER INFORMATION The trust is one of the Sainsbury Family Charitable Trusts which share a common administration. An application to one is taken as an application to all.

HOW TO APPLY Proposals are generally invited by the trustees or initiated at their request. Unsolicited applications are nort encouraged and are unlikely to be successful.

WHO TO APPLY TO Michael Pattison, Director, Allington House, 1st Floor, 150 Victoria Street, London SW1E 5AE *Tel* 020 7410 0330 *Fax* 020 7410 0332

CC NO 802623   **ESTABLISHED** 1989

■ The Lord Ashdown Charitable Trust

WHERE FUNDING CAN BE GIVEN UK.

WHO CAN BENEFIT People disadvantaged by poverty and social circumstance including children and young adults; students; artists; musicians; textile workers and designers; writers and poets; ethnic minority groups; at risk groups; disabled people; disaster victims; homeless people; immigrants; socially isolated people; and people with sight loss.

WHAT IS FUNDED Inter-faith work and racial harmony, Jewish education, grass-roots community development.

WHAT IS NOT FUNDED No recent information is available. Before the division of the trust's assets, it reported that 'The trust does not, save in exceptional cases, fund the mainstream arts, large well-established national charities, exploration or adventure projects, purely academic research (although it does assist in medical research with practical objectives); nor does it give grants to enable students to study overseas, support elective periods of medical students, or assist with fees at private schools.'

TYPE OF GRANT Buildings, capital, core costs, endowment, feasibility studies, interest-free loans, one-off, project, research, recurring and running costs, salaries, and start-up costs. Funding may be given for up to and over three years.

SAMPLE GRANTS £241,000 to London School of Jewish Studies; £187,000 to Spiro Institute's London Jewish Cultural Centre; £150,000 to Centre for Advanced Professional Educators; £50,000 to Clore Tivka Primary School; £34,000 to Friends of Israel Education Trust; £27,000 to Limmud.

FINANCES *Year* 1999–2000 *Grants* £3,455,000

TRUSTEES Clive Marks; J M Silver; Dr Richard Stone.

HOW TO APPLY Due to the commitment of nearly all the funds available, the trustees are not likely to respond to unsolicited applications.

WHO TO APPLY TO C M Marks, c/o Clive Marks FCA, 44a New Cavendish Street, London W1M 7LG

CC NO 272708   **ESTABLISHED** 1968

■ The Ashe Park Charitable Trust

WHERE FUNDING CAN BE GIVEN UK possible preference for Hampshire, Isle of Wight and West Sussex.

WHO CAN BENEFIT Registered charities, child-related hospitals and hospices.

WHAT IS NOT FUNDED Anything salary related.

RANGE OF GRANTS £20,000 upwards.

SAMPLE GRANTS £66,000 each to The Rose Road Children's Appeal and The NSPCC Full Stop Appeal; £62,000 to The Leonard Children's Cancer Fund.

FINANCES *Year* 2000 *Income* £276,000 *Grants* £194,000 *Assets* £8,500

TRUSTEES P J Scott; Mrs J M T Scott.

HOW TO APPLY In writing to the correspondent.

WHO TO APPLY TO Mrs Jan Scott, Ashe Park, Steventon, Basingstoke, Hampshire RG25 3AZ *Tel* 01256 771689

CC NO 297647   **ESTABLISHED** 1987

■ The Ashendene Trust

WHERE FUNDING CAN BE GIVEN Oxford, London and Berkshire.

WHO CAN BENEFIT Registered charities benefiting children; clergy; musicians; writers and poets; people disadvantaged by poverty; ex-offenders and those at risk of offending and homeless people.

WHAT IS FUNDED Small organisations, ex-offenders, socially deprived, and the arts. Charities working in the field of the arts and culture; conservation of flora; the purchase of books; clubs, counselling and penal reform. This a small trust that gives to organisations where the grant will really make an impact.

WHAT IS NOT FUNDED No support for large organisations, education or health. No scholarships or individual grants.

TYPE OF GRANT Capital, core costs and project. Funding available for up to three years.

RANGE OF GRANTS £500 up to £25,000 over four years. Average grant £2,500.

SAMPLE GRANTS In 1996–97: £6,500 to Royal Horticultural Society; £5,000 each to Musicians Benevolent Fund, National Literary Trust, Oxford Homeless Medical Fund and St Katharine's House – Wantage; £500 each to SANE and Wantage Parish Appeal 2000; £250 each to Artists Benevolent Association, Ashburton Museum, Christchurch School Garden Project, National Schizophrenia Fellowship Oxford and Oxford Youth Works.

FINANCES *Year* 2000–01 *Income* £40,000 *Grants* £34,000 *Assets* £1,100,000

TRUSTEES Sir Simon Hornby; Sir Edward Cazalet; A D Loehnis.

HOW TO APPLY In writing to the correspondent. Replies are not sent without an sae.

WHO TO APPLY TO Sir Simon Hornby, Trustee, The Ham, Wantage, Oxfordshire OX12 9JA
Tel 01235 770222 *Fax* 01235 768763
CC NO 270749   ESTABLISHED 1975

■ The Laura Ashley Foundation

WHERE FUNDING CAN BE GIVEN England and Wales.
WHAT IS FUNDED Projects in Wales (especially Mid Wales); education – direct to institutions, with emphasis on mature students. Special bursaries set up through institutions of the trustees' choice and knowledge; fellowships – aimed at encouraging individuals with truly innovative and workable ideas, in fields as diverse as music and design, engineering and physics, to bring the ideas to fruition. The awards are made under the heading of science and the arts. Guidance notes are available; the arts – at present there is one pilot scheme in London.
WHAT IS NOT FUNDED The foundation does not fund the following: individuals; new buildings; medical research; overseas travel/exchange visits; private education; purchase cost of property/ land; restoration of historic buildings or churches; university or similar research; projects concerned with domestic violence; penal affairs; sport; youth clubs/projects concerned with 'youth at risk'; general funds; taking projects into schools; outward bound type courses; newspapers/journals/publications/information packs; video projects; safety devices; theatre, dances, shows/touring; internet-related projects.
TYPE OF GRANT One-off and recurring. Funding may be given for up to three years.
RANGE OF GRANTS £500–£15,000.
SAMPLE GRANTS £14,000 to Rhyader School; £10,700 Camberwell Art College; £10,000 each to Family Welfare Association and University of Edinburgh; £8,600 to Live Music Now; £8,713 to National Opera Studio; £8,000 to Rhyader 2000; £6,000 to Merthyr Citizens' Advice Bureau; £5,990 to Virsa Educational Trust; £5,480 to Brunel University; £5,000 each to Age Concern Radnorshire, Honeypot, Mid Wales Opera and Relate Dyfed Powys.
FINANCES *Year* 2000–01 *Income* £277,460 *Grants* £211,259
TRUSTEES Jane Ashley, Chair; Prof. Susan Solombok; Martyn C Gowar; Martin Jones; Emma Shuckburgh; Marquis of Queensbury; Helena Appio.
OTHER INFORMATION The foundation is constantly reviewing its funding policies. For this reason, they tend to be reactive rather than proactive in their grantmaking. Very few unsolicited applications receive funding. Potential applicants are advised to check the website for the latest details.
HOW TO APPLY Potential applicants are encouraged to telephone the trust to discuss eligibility before submitting an application. An initial application should be made in writing to the correspondent. It should include a summary of your activities and work, outline the actual project and for what specific purpose the grant is required and what funds have already been raised. It should be typed on one side of headed note paper.
WHO TO APPLY TO The Administrator, 3 Cromwell Place, London SW7 2JE *Tel* 020 7581 4662 *E-mail* info@laf.uk.net *Website* www.laf.uk.net
CC NO 288099   ESTABLISHED 1985

■ The Ashworth Charitable Trust

WHERE FUNDING CAN BE GIVEN UK and worldwide, with some preference for certain specific needs in Ottery St Mary, Honiton and Sidmouth in Devon.
WHO CAN BENEFIT Individuals (living in the areas covered by the medical practices in Ottery St Mary, Honiton and Sidmouth only) and organisations.
WHAT IS FUNDED General charitable purposes. Particular emphasis is given to support for the Ironbridge Gorge Museum Trust and to humanitarian projects.
WHAT IS NOT FUNDED No grants for research-based charities; animal charities; 'heritage charities' such as National Trust or other organisations whose aim is the preservation of a building, museum, library and so on (with the exception of the Ironbridge Gorge Museum); 'faith-based' charities, unless the project is for primarily humanitarian purposes and is neither exclusive to those of that particular faith or evangelical in its purpose. Grants to individuals are strictly limited to the geographical area and purpose specified in the general section.
RANGE OF GRANTS £200–£10,000.
SAMPLE GRANTS £10,000 each to Iron Bridge Gorge Museum Trust and Hospiscare; £4,000 each to Exeter Women's Aid and Angels International; £3,000 each to The Esther Benjamins Trust and Action on Water; £2,500 to Red Rose Children's Appeal; £2,000 each to Action on Addiction, Relief Fund for Romania, Contact the Elderly, Deafblind UK, Young Minds, Coldingley Welfare Fund, Richmond Fellowship International and Chooselife.
FINANCES *Year* 2000–01 *Income* £131,713 *Grants* £134,000 *Assets* £3,478,517
TRUSTEES C F Bennett, Chair; Miss S E Crabtree; Mrs K A Gray; G D R Cockram.
HOW TO APPLY In writing to the correspondent.
WHO TO APPLY TO Alison Tancock, Administrative Correspondent, Foot Anstey Sargent, 4–6 Barnfield Crescent, Exeter, Devon EX1 1RF *Tel* 01392 411221 *Fax* 01392 218554 *E-mail* ajt@foot-ansteys.co.uk
CC NO 1045492   ESTABLISHED 1995

■ The Dorothy Askew Trust

WHERE FUNDING CAN BE GIVEN UK, with a preference for Sussex-based charities.
WHO CAN BENEFIT Sussex charities, and charities which have previously been supported.
WHAT IS FUNDED General charitable purposes.
WHAT IS NOT FUNDED No grants to individuals.
RANGE OF GRANTS £225–£500.
FINANCES *Year* 1999–2000 *Income* £30,000 *Grants* £28,000 *Assets* £829,000
TRUSTEES I V Askew; Mrs C Pengelley; Mrs D M McAlpine; Mrs M Askew; Mrs P St Q Askew; R A R Askew; B A McAlpine; G B Ackery.
HOW TO APPLY In writing to the correspondent.
WHO TO APPLY TO Christine Wilson, c/o Baker Tilly, Spectrum House, 20–26 Cursitor Street, London EC4A 1HY *Tel* 020 7405 2088
CC NO 286088   ESTABLISHED 1982

■ The Ian Askew Charitable Trust

WHERE FUNDING CAN BE GIVEN UK, with a preference for Sussex and overseas.
WHO CAN BENEFIT Mainly headquarters organisations. There is no restriction on the disease or medical condition.

WHAT IS FUNDED All forms of health research, particularly mental health. Preservation of ancient buildings. Grants are mainly made to headquarters organisations.

WHAT IS NOT FUNDED No grants to individuals.

RANGE OF GRANTS Most grants for £500 or less.

SAMPLE GRANTS £12,000 to Middle East Relief; £2,500 to Ringmer Village Hall Fundraising Appeal; £2,000 to St Peter and St James Hospice Anniversary Appeal; £1,500 to Ringmer Parochial Church Council; £1,000 each to The Salvation Army, British Brain and Spine Foundation, Carl Grace Memorial Foundation, David Tolkien Trust for Stoke Manderville Hospital, The Kingswood Trust, PDSA and Sussex Heritage Trust.

FINANCES *Year* 2000–01 *Income* £213,932 *Grants* £72,261 *Assets* £5,299,363

TRUSTEES J R Rank; Mrs C Pengelley; R A R Askew; R J Wainwright; G B Ackery.

HOW TO APPLY In writing to the correspondent. Applications are considered monthly.

WHO TO APPLY TO Christine Wilson, Baker Tilly, Spectrum House, 20–26 Cursitor Street, London EC4A 1HY *Tel* 020 7405 2088

CC NO 264515   ESTABLISHED 1972

....

■ The Associated Country Women of the World

WHERE FUNDING CAN BE GIVEN Overseas.

WHO CAN BENEFIT Small local projects and established organisations benefiting children, young adults and rural communities in particular.

WHAT IS FUNDED Education, environmental resources and other general charitable purposes will be considered.

WHAT IS NOT FUNDED No grants to individuals or students.

TYPE OF GRANT One-off.

RANGE OF GRANTS £3,000 or less.

SAMPLE GRANTS £3,000 each for a coffee and banana growing project in Africa and education on reproductive processes for adolescents in Bangladesh; £2,980 for a HIV/AIDS awareness programme in India; £2,200 for a rural women's development project in Africa; £2,030 for a milk production project in India.

FINANCES *Year* 2001 *Income* £605,135 *Grants* £84,466 *Assets* £2,184,092

TRUSTEES Mrs Hilda Stewart; Jennifer Mitchell; Louise Nichols.

PUBLICATIONS *All about ACWW; Women Feed the World; Water for All.*

HOW TO APPLY In writing to the correspondent.

WHO TO APPLY TO The General Secretary, Mary Sumner House, 24 Tufton Street, London SW1P 3RB *Tel* 020 7799 3875 *Fax* 020 7340 9950 *E-mail* info@acww.org.uk *Website* www.acww.org.uk

CC NO 290367   ESTABLISHED 1984

....

■ The Association of Colleges Charitable Trust

WHERE FUNDING CAN BE GIVEN UK.

WHO CAN BENEFIT Further educational establishments and sixth form colleges.

WHAT IS FUNDED Further education colleges; fine art students from further education colleges.

WHAT IS NOT FUNDED Applications from individuals. Grants are only awarded through Beacon Awards and Fine Art Awards, both of which are soley open to further education colleges.

TYPE OF GRANT One-off.

RANGE OF GRANTS Generally £4,200.

SAMPLE GRANTS £8,400 in two grants to Telford College of Arts of Technology; £4,200 each to Aberdeen College, Barnsley College, Bournville College of Further Education, Joseph Chamberlain College, Coleg Sir Gâr, Kingston College, Leicester College, North West Consortium, and Pembrokeshire College.

FINANCES *Year* 2001–02 *Income* £198,656 *Grants* £121,695 *Assets* £151,085

TRUSTEES Association of Colleges.

OTHER INFORMATION The charitable trust is responsible for administering four programmes. The largest of these is the Beacon Awards, which provide monetary grants to award-winning initiatives within further education colleges. The other programmes that operate within the trust are the Gold Awards, the Work Shadowing Scheme, and the International Churchill Society for Fine Art Painting.

HOW TO APPLY Potential applicants are advised to look at the Beacon Awards Charitable Trust Zone at the Association of Colleges website, or contact the Beacon Awards office for a prospectus. Applications should be made in writing to the correspondent, with three copies of each application sent. There is an annual deadline, usually in early summer. Contact should be made solely with the trust's office; the individual sponsors should never be approached.

WHO TO APPLY TO Alice Thiagaraj, Trust Manager, 5th Floor, Centre Point, 103 New Oxford Street, London WC1A 1RG *Tel* 020 7827 4600 *Fax* 020 7827 4645 *E-mail* alice_thiagaraj@aoc.co.uk *Website* www.feonline.net

CC NO 1040631   ESTABLISHED 1994

....

■ Aston Charities Trust Limited

WHERE FUNDING CAN BE GIVEN The borough of Newham.

WHO CAN BENEFIT Organisations benefiting people of all ages disadvantaged by poverty.

WHAT IS FUNDED To support, maintain and extend the fund's community development work through its centres and hostel in the London borough of Newham and its holiday hotel for the elderly at Westcliff on Sea. Support is also considered for charities working in the fields of: advice and information on housing; emergency and short-term housing; respite; information technology and computers; publishing and printing; community development; economic regeneration schemes; support to voluntary and community organisations; and community arts and recreation.

WHAT IS NOT FUNDED Revenue funding for salaries and maintenance is unlikely to be given. No national appeals and no grants to individuals.

TYPE OF GRANT Capital (including buildings), feasibility studies, one-off, project and research. Funding of one year or less will be considered.

FINANCES *Year* 1999–2000 *Grants* £47,000

TRUSTEES Directors: Christopher Keen; Andrew West; Bishop of Chelmsford; Patricia Jamal; Alan Shelley, Chair; Alan Siddick.

PUBLICATIONS Occasional papers by Aston Community Involvement Unit.

HOW TO APPLY In writing to the correspondent. No guidelines; no forms. The trust will be making no further grants for the foreseeable future apart from continuing to give some limited help to those it is currently assisting.

WHO TO APPLY TO Geoffrey Wheeler, Company Secretary, Durning Hall, Earlham Grove, Forest Gate, London E7 9AB *Tel* 020 8555 0142 *Fax* 020 8519 5472 *E-mail* gw@aston-mansfield.org.uk *Website* www.aston-mansfield.org.uk
CC NO 208155   **ESTABLISHED** 1930

■ The Aston Villa Charitable Trust

WHERE FUNDING CAN BE GIVEN Mainly the Birmingham area.
WHO CAN BENEFIT Sports groups and children.
WHAT IS FUNDED The trust has general charitable purposes, particularly supporting sport and children who are underprivileged or disadvantaged in the Midlands.
FINANCES *Grants* £30,000
TRUSTEES H D Ellis; J A Alderson; M J Ansell.
HOW TO APPLY In writing to the correspondent.
WHO TO APPLY TO H D Ellis, Trustee, Aston Villa plc, Villa Park, Birmingham B6 6HE *Tel* 0121 327 2299 *Fax* 0121 322 2107
CC NO 327923   **ESTABLISHED** 1998

■ The Astor Foundation

WHERE FUNDING CAN BE GIVEN UK.
WHO CAN BENEFIT Mainly headquarters organisations. Innovatory projects rather than long-established or well-endowed ones (with some exceptions). Organisations benefiting Christians and the Church of England; ex-service and service people; medical professionals; research workers; seafarers and fishermen; and volunteers.
WHAT IS FUNDED Medical research and helping people who are disabled by physical and mental disease. Help for new and imaginative charities in their early days. Funding may be given to charities working in the fields of: accommodation and housing; the advancement of the Christian religion; arts, culture and recreation; health; and conservation and environment. Support may also be considered for infrastructure, support and development; social care and development; and special needs education and speech therapy.
WHAT IS NOT FUNDED No grants to individuals or towards salaries. Grants are given to registered charities only.
TYPE OF GRANT Grants are usually one-off. Buildings, capital, core costs, project, research and start-up costs will be considered. Salaries are rarely given. Funding may be for up to three years.
RANGE OF GRANTS £500–£25,000; mainly £2,000 or less.
SAMPLE GRANTS £25,000 to Royal Free University College Medical School; £4,500 to League of Friends – Middlesex Hospital; £3,500 to Help the Hospices; £3,000 to Samaritans; £2,500 each to Aidis Trust, Council for the Order of St John, Jubilee Sailing Trust, RNLI and Royal National College for the Blind.
FINANCES *Year* 2000–01 *Income* £160,978 *Grants* £148,000 *Assets* £3,382,757
TRUSTEES Sir William Slack; J R Astor, Chair; Lord Astor of Hever; Dr H Swanton; R H Astor; C Money-Coutts.
HOW TO APPLY There are no deadline dates; applications should be in writing to the correspondent. If the appeal arrives too late for one meeting it will automatically be carried over for consideration at the following meeting. The trustees meet twice a year, in March and October. A reply will always be sent irrespective

of whether an appeal is successful. This entry was not confirmed by the trust, but is correct according to information on file at the Charity Commission.
WHO TO APPLY TO Mrs Pam Garraway, Secretary, 2 Kew Gardens, Shalbourne, Wiltshire SN8 3QW *Tel* 01672 870733 *Fax* 01672 870926 *E-mail* pam.garraway@which.net
CC NO 225708   **ESTABLISHED** 1963

■ The Astor of Hever Trust

WHERE FUNDING CAN BE GIVEN UK and worldwide, with a preference for Kent and the Grampian region of Scotland.
WHO CAN BENEFIT Both headquarters and local branches of charities, mainly established organisations with particular emphasis on Kent. To the benefit of: children and young adults; actors and entertainment professionals; musicians; textile workers and designers; writers and poets; students; and sportsmen and women.
WHAT IS FUNDED Charitable bodies in the fields of the arts, medicine, religion, education, conservation, youth and sport.
WHAT IS NOT FUNDED No grants to individuals.
SAMPLE GRANTS £5,000 to Migvie Church; £3,500 to Household Cavelry Museum; £3,000 to Trustees of Uppingham School; Seven grants of £1,000 each including those to Commonwealth Press Union Education and Training Trust, Hospice in the Weald, Jubilee Appeal of Commonwealth Veterans, RAFT and St Mary's Church Restoration Appeal (Westerham – Kent).
FINANCES *Year* 2002 *Income* £39,379 *Grants* £48,300 *Assets* £984,831
TRUSTEES John Jacob, Third Baron Astor of Hever; Irene, Lady Astor of Hever; Hon. Philip D P Astor.
HOW TO APPLY In writing to the correspondent. Unsuccessful applications are not acknowledged.
WHO TO APPLY TO Lord Astor of Hever, Trustee, Frenchstreet House, Westerham, Kent TN16 1PW *Tel* 01959 562051 *Fax* 01959 561286
CC NO 264134   **ESTABLISHED** 1955

■ The Atlantic Foundation

WHERE FUNDING CAN BE GIVEN Worldwide, though with some preference for Wales.
WHO CAN BENEFIT Schools, colleges, registered charities and community organisations.
WHAT IS FUNDED Independent schools and colleges; a wide range of charitable causes including community aid, medical appeals, education, international appeals and religious foundations.
SAMPLE GRANTS £3,300 to The Variety Club; £2,800 to Welsh College of Music and Drama; £2,350 to Royal Academy of Music; £2,000 each to Deafblind UK and London Academy of Music and Dramatic Art; £1,800 to Bristol Old Vic Theatre School; £1,000 each to Alzheimers Research Trust, Llanishen Fach Primary School, Vale View Allotment Association, Welsh Initiative for Conductive Education and Weston Spirit.
FINANCES *Year* 2000–01 *Income* £61,000 *Grants* £75,000 *Assets* £17,332
TRUSTEES P Thomas; Mrs B L Thomas.
HOW TO APPLY In writing to the correspondent. Applications are considered throughout the year.
WHO TO APPLY TO Mrs B L Thomas, Trustee, 7–8 Raleigh Walk, Atlantic Wharf, Cardiff CF10 4LN *Tel* 029 2046 1651
CC NO 328499   **ESTABLISHED** 1989

■ ATP Charitable Trust

WHERE FUNDING CAN BE GIVEN Worldwide.
WHO CAN BENEFIT Organisations benefiting children, young adults and students, at risk groups, people disadvantaged by poverty and socially isolated people.
WHAT IS FUNDED Educational, religious, medical and social care.
WHAT IS NOT FUNDED Expeditions are not funded.
RANGE OF GRANTS £150–£15,000.
SAMPLE GRANTS £15,000 to Jewish Care; £10,000 each to Centre for Jewish Education and Givat Haviva; £5,250 to Nightingale House; £3,000 to Bar Ilan University; £2,250 to JM Trust; £1,300 to Brighton Jewish Film Festival; £1,000 to Hammerson House; £500 each to National Deaf Children's Society, Textile Conservation Centre and Worldwide Volunteers.
FINANCES *Year* 2001–02 *Income* £54,444 *Grants* £50,300 *Assets* £81,937
TRUSTEES M R Bentata; J A Bentata; Mrs S Bentata.
HOW TO APPLY In writing to the correspondent. Individuals who apply must include two personal references and a current CV. Applications are considered throughout the year.
WHO TO APPLY TO M R Bentata, Trustee, 31 Millharbour, Isle of Dogs, London E14 9TX *Tel* 020 7510 0623
CC NO 328408   **ESTABLISHED** 1989

■ The Richard Attenborough Charitable Trust

WHERE FUNDING CAN BE GIVEN UK and developing world with some preference for South Africa.
WHO CAN BENEFIT Organisations benefiting actors; overseas aid organisations; registered charities.
RANGE OF GRANTS £700–£28,000.
SAMPLE GRANTS £28,000 to Royal Academy of Dramatic Art; £13,675 to Waterford School Trust; £10,000 to Bretton Hall; £9,800 to Waterford Kamhlaba; £5,000 to Royal Academy of Arts; £3,000 to The Adapt Trust; £2,000 to Orange Tree Theatre; £1,700 to Muscular Dystrophy; £1,500 to Chicken Shed Theatre Company; £1,000 to Arts Alive.
FINANCES *Year* 2000–01 *Income* £4,128 *Grants* £89,765 *Assets* £326,191
TRUSTEES Lady Attenborough; Lord Attenborough.
HOW TO APPLY The funds of this trust are donated principally to charities with which the trustees are associated. They greatly regret, therefore, that they are unable to reply to any external applications.
WHO TO APPLY TO Lady Attenborough, Trustee, Beaver Lodge, Richmond Green, Surrey TW9 1NQ *Tel* 020 8940 7234
CC NO 259186   **ESTABLISHED** 1969

■ The Audi Design Foundation

WHERE FUNDING CAN BE GIVEN UK.
WHO CAN BENEFIT Young adults between the ages of 18 and 25 and students; both individually and through non-profit organisations and higher education establishments.
WHAT IS FUNDED To advance education and research in engineering and in furtherance of this object to provide bursaries; support research and support charitable organisations with similar objects. All projects must satisfy a number of the following criteria: a demonstration of innovation or new technology; the use of three dimensional design not art; the application of electrical or mechanical engineering;

demonstrate the potential for a commercial application; the project has to be of benefit to the community; the applicant must be a European citizen resident in the UK for the duration of the grant.
WHAT IS NOT FUNDED No grants for paying off debts, i.e. visa card or similar, bank loans or arrears of any description; paying for materials or services which have already been used or paying for the materials used in the production of your application.
TYPE OF GRANT One-off and project. Rolling programme of grants.
SAMPLE GRANTS £17,459 to YMCA Herrington Burn for sectional building development; £5,000 each to Brunel University for fire extinguisher nozzle development, Bolton Institute for bicycle storage unit, and University of Leeds for formula student SAE; £4,800 to an individual for automated train access/egress ramp; £4,750 to Flytech Group, Loughborough University for flywheel assisted scooter; £3,500 to an individual for a sports shoe stud; £3,325 to Cranfield University for a sample holder; £3,250 to an individual for a sport and recreational vehicle; £2,348 to FEWS Group, Bangor University for a foaling early warning system.
FINANCES *Year* 1998 *Income* £42,729 *Grants* £17,050 *Assets* £116,715
TRUSTEES Kevin Rose; Andrea Tarry; Trevor Metcalfe; Richard Taylor; Carole Lowe; Isobell Pollock.
HOW TO APPLY By phone or in writing to the address below, to request criteria and guidance notes.
WHO TO APPLY TO Michael Farmer, Manager, Yeomans Drive, Blakelands, Milton Keynes MK14 5AN *Tel* 01908 601570 *Fax* 01908 601943 *E-mail* audi.foundation@audi.co.uk *Website* www.audi.co.uk/information/foundation
CC NO 1064159   **ESTABLISHED** 1997

■ The Aurelius Charitable Trust

WHERE FUNDING CAN BE GIVEN Generally UK only.
WHO CAN BENEFIT Registered charities, institutions and academic bodies benefiting academics and research workers.
WHAT IS FUNDED Research or publications in the conservation of culture inherited from the past and the humanities field.
WHAT IS NOT FUNDED No grants to individuals.
TYPE OF GRANT Seed-corn or completion funding not otherwise available, usually one-off.
RANGE OF GRANTS Generally £500–£3,000.
SAMPLE GRANTS £10,500 to Oxford University; £10,000 to London Library; £7,500 to British Academy; £5,000 to British Record Society; £2,500 each to Lincoln Cathedral Music Appeal and University of North London; £2,000 each to St Leonard's Church and University of Bristol.
FINANCES *Year* 2001–02 *Income* £74,081 *Grants* £50,920 *Assets* £1,835,731
TRUSTEES W J Wallis; P E Haynes.
HOW TO APPLY In writing to the correspondent. Grants are generally made on the recommendation of the trust's board of advisors. Unsolicited applications will only be responded to if an sae is included. Trustees meet twice a year, in January and July, and applications need to be received by May and November.
WHO TO APPLY TO P E Haynes, Trustee, Briarsmead, Old Road, Buckland, Betchworth, Surrey RH3 7DU *Tel* 01737 842186 *Fax* 01737 842186 *E-mail* haynes@knowall.co.uk
CC NO 271333   **ESTABLISHED** 1975

■ The Lord Austin Trust

WHERE FUNDING CAN BE GIVEN Birmingham and its immediate area.

WHO CAN BENEFIT Charitable institutions or projects in England, restricted to: local charities based in Birmingham and West Midlands; and national organisations (but not their provincial branches).

WHAT IS FUNDED Emphasis on the welfare of children, the care of older people, medical institutions and research.

WHAT IS NOT FUNDED No support for appeals from, or on behalf of, individual applicants.

TYPE OF GRANT One-off.

RANGE OF GRANTS £500–£2,500.

SAMPLE GRANTS In 1998–99 grants were categorised as follows: young people £59,000; older people £33,000; miscellaneous £81,000.

FINANCES *Year* 1999–2000 *Income* £180,000 *Grants* £148,000 *Assets* £4,000,000

TRUSTEES Baring Trust Co Ltd; J M G Fea; R S Kettel.

HOW TO APPLY In writing to the joint correspondents, D L Turfrey and Miss Lucy Chatt, including a set of recent accounts. Trustees meet twice a year in or around May and November to consider grants. The trustees stress that new awards are now severely limited.

WHO TO APPLY TO D L Turfrey, c/o Martineau Johnson, St Phillips House, St Phillips Place, Birmingham B3 2PP *Tel* 0121 200 3300

CC NO 208394   **ESTABLISHED** 1937

■ The Avenue Charitable Trust

WHERE FUNDING CAN BE GIVEN Worldwide.

WHO CAN BENEFIT Registered charities.

WHAT IS FUNDED General charitable purposes.

TYPE OF GRANT One-off and recurrent.

RANGE OF GRANTS Generally £18–£20,000, although larger grants have been given.

SAMPLE GRANTS £103,000 to Anna Freud Centre; £20,000 to Brandon Centre; £17,250 to Progressive Farming Trust; £15,000 to Prisoners Advice; £14,000 to Prisoners Abroad; £10,000 each to Adventure Playground, Lincoln Trust, Youth at Risk, and Waterford School.

FINANCES *Year* 1999–2000 *Income* £6,473 *Grants* £347,960 *Assets* £596,091

TRUSTEES R D L Astor; The Hon. Mrs B A Astor; S G Kemp.

HOW TO APPLY The trust has previously stated that all available income is now committed to existing beneficiaries.

WHO TO APPLY TO Sue Brotherhood, c/o Messrs Sayers Butterworth, 18 Bentinck Street, London W1U 2AR *Tel* 020 7935 8504 *Fax* 020 7487 5621

CC NO 264804   **ESTABLISHED** 1972

■ The John Avins Trustees

WHERE FUNDING CAN BE GIVEN Birmingham and district.

WHO CAN BENEFIT Medical charities. Support may be given to medical professionals and research workers.

WHAT IS FUNDED Medical charities in Birmingham and neighbourhood, and the following charities mentioned in the will of John Avins: Birmingham Blue Coat School; Birmingham Royal Institution for the Blind; and Middlemore Homes, Birmingham.

WHAT IS NOT FUNDED No grants to individuals, non-medical charities or for purposes outside the beneficial area.

TYPE OF GRANT One-off.

RANGE OF GRANTS Up to £5,000.

SAMPLE GRANTS 1998–99: £5,000 each to Birmingham Royal Institution for the Blind and Middlemore Homes; £4,000 to St Mary's Hospice; £2,500 to Birmingham Blue Coat School; £1,000 each to Little Sisters of the Poor, C B and A B Holinsworth Fund for Help, East Birmingham Family Service Unit, Macmillan Good Hope Hospital Appeal, Sir Josiah Mason's Home for Life Appeal, and Salvation Army.

FINANCES *Year* 2001–02 *Income* £55,949

TRUSTEES M B Shaw, Chair; C F Smith; C J Timbrell; Miss A M Grove; I McArdle.

HOW TO APPLY On a form available from the correspondent. Trustees meet in May and November.

WHO TO APPLY TO J M G Fea, Joint Secretary, Martineau Johnson, St Philips House, St Philips Place, Birmingham B3 2PP *Tel* 0121 200 3300

CC NO 217301   **ESTABLISHED** 1931

■ AW Charitable Trust

WHERE FUNDING CAN BE GIVEN Worldwide.

WHO CAN BENEFIT Jewish organisations; registered charities.

WHAT IS FUNDED General charitable purposes.

FINANCES *Year* 1999–2000 *Income* £42,000,000 *Grants* £1,717,000 *Assets* £70,000,000

TRUSTEES A Weis; Mrs R Weis.

HOW TO APPLY In writing to the correspondent.

WHO TO APPLY TO The Secretary, Messrs B Olsberg & Co, 1st Floor, Barclay House, 35 Whitworth Street West, Manchester M1 5NG *Tel* 0161 228 1407

CC NO 283322   **ESTABLISHED** 1961

■ The Aylesford Family Charitable Trust

WHERE FUNDING CAN BE GIVEN West Midlands and Warwickshire.

WHO CAN BENEFIT Registered charities.

WHAT IS FUNDED General charitable purposes.

WHAT IS NOT FUNDED Grants are not normally given to individuals.

SAMPLE GRANTS £10,000 to The Countryside Foundation for Education; £7,500 to Strathconon Social and Recreational Society; £5,000 each to Extra Care Charitable Trust and Hereward College; £3,200 in two grants to Regain; £1,800 to St John Ambulance; £1,400 to Parents for Inclusion; £1,000 each to Acorns Children's Hospice and Birmingham Settlement; £500 each to BTCV and Jump for Joy Appeal; £350 to North Warwickshire Summer Playscheme; £250 each to English Disabled Fly Fishers and Lowbrook Stroke Club.

FINANCES *Year* 1998–99 *Income* £43,000 *Grants* £70,000

TRUSTEES Lord and Lady Guernsey.

HOW TO APPLY In writing to the correspondent at any time.

WHO TO APPLY TO The Trustees, Martineau Johnson, St Philips House, St Philips Place, Birmingham B3 2PP *Tel* 0121 200 3300

CC NO 328299   **ESTABLISHED** 1989

Think carefully about every application. Is it justified?

295

The B C No. 9 1972 Charitable Trust

WHERE FUNDING CAN BE GIVEN Somerset.

WHO CAN BENEFIT Charitable institutions only; particular favour is given to the Society of Friends.

WHAT IS FUNDED General charitable purposes, in particular, donations to the Society of Friends.

WHAT IS NOT FUNDED No grants to individuals.

FINANCES *Year* 2000–01 *Income* £117,000 *Grants* £25,000 *Assets* £2,900,000

TRUSTEES R B Clark; Mrs S M Pedder; J D Clark.

HOW TO APPLY In writing to the correspondent. 'The trustees do not normally reply to correspondence.' Resources are currently fully committed.

WHO TO APPLY TO Mike Haynes, KPMG, 100 Temple Street, Bristol BS1 6AG *Tel* 0117 905 4694

CC NO 264135   **ESTABLISHED** 1972

The B-C H 1971 Charitable Trust

WHERE FUNDING CAN BE GIVEN UK, with preference for Cornwall and Devon.

WHO CAN BENEFIT Registered charities only, benefiting children and sick people. Support may be given to medical professionals and research workers.

WHAT IS FUNDED Children's and medical charities.

WHAT IS NOT FUNDED No grants to individuals.

RANGE OF GRANTS £500–£2,000.

SAMPLE GRANTS 1998–99: £2,000 each to British Red Cross Society, Cornwall Disabled Association, and Macmillan Nursing Fund, Blue Cross, Bolenowe Animal Sanctuary, Breakthrough, Communicability, Invalids At Home, Sense and Trimar Christian Hospice Trust.

FINANCES *Year* 2000–01 *Income* £29,136

TRUSTEES Miss J Holman; M A Hayes; R C Holman.

HOW TO APPLY In writing to the correspondent. Trustees meet twice a year to consider applications.

WHO TO APPLY TO Geraldine Fitzpatrick, c/o Macfarlanes, 10 Norwich Street, London EC4A 1BD *Tel* 020 7831 9222

CC NO 263241   **ESTABLISHED** 1971

The BAA 21st Century Communities Trust

WHERE FUNDING CAN BE GIVEN Local communities around the following BAA run airports: Heathrow, Gatwick, Stansted, Southampton, Edinburgh, Glasgow and Aberdeen. Limited help is available for projects in the area immediately surrounding BAA's HQ in Victoria, London.

WHO CAN BENEFIT Support is concentrated on projects which will be of community benefit in the areas of education, environment and economic regeneration.

WHAT IS FUNDED The trust supports a wide variety of projects but only if they satisfy the criteria above. Proximity to the airports and proven community benefit are essential.

WHAT IS NOT FUNDED Anything which falls outside the criteria will not be considered. In particular, applications which benefit individuals only, whether or not they meet the other criteria, will fail. No support for religious or political projects, the arts, medical research, sickness/disability, animal welfare, or overseas. Grants will not be made to nationally based organisations unless the direct benefit will be felt locally and the other criteria are satisfied.

TYPE OF GRANT One-off, recurring (for up to three years), buildings, start-up costs.

RANGE OF GRANTS £1,000–£50,000, typical grant £5,000–£10,000.

SAMPLE GRANTS £30,000 to Hounslow Sustainable Communities; £17,500 to New Environmental Education Resource Gatwick; £10,000 each to Lampton School Heathrow, Preston Sure Start and Rainbow Services Harlow; £5,000 each to Broomhill Representative Council Edinburgh and Education Centre at Edinburgh Zoo.

FINANCES *Year* 2001–02 *Income* £700,000 *Grants* £600,000

TRUSTEES T Ward; C Green; Ms J Bradley; Miss V Gooding; A B Currie.

HOW TO APPLY Applications should always be made in the first instance to the community relations manager at Gatwick, Heathrow, Southampton and Stansted airports. For Scotland: the community relations manager, Scottish Airports, based at Glasgow Airport. Contact details can be found on the BAA web site (www.baa.com).

WHO TO APPLY TO A B Currie, Community Relations Director, 130 Wilton Road, London SW1V 1LQ *Tel* 01293 503056 *Fax* 01293 503794 *E-mail* Andrew_Currie@baa.com

CC NO 1058617   **ESTABLISHED** 1996

Harry Bacon Foundation

WHERE FUNDING CAN BE GIVEN UK.

WHO CAN BENEFIT Registered charities.

WHAT IS FUNDED Particularly medical charities and animal welfare.

SAMPLE GRANTS £7,950 each to Arthritis Research Campaign, British Heart Foundation, Donkey Sanctuary, ILPH, Imperial Cancer Research, People's Dispensary for Sick Animals and Royal National Lifeboat Institution.

FINANCES *Year* 2002 *Income* £58,855 *Grants* £63,600 *Assets* £1,785,840

TRUSTEES NatWest Bank plc.

HOW TO APPLY In writing to the correspondent.

WHO TO APPLY TO The Manager, NatWest Bank plc, 153 Preston Road, Brighton BN1 6BD *Tel* 01273 545035 *Fax* 01273 545141

CC NO 1056500   **ESTABLISHED** 1996

The Bacta Charitable Trust

WHERE FUNDING CAN BE GIVEN UK.

WHO CAN BENEFIT Usually local charities benefiting at risk groups; people disadvantaged by poverty; and socially isolated people.

WHAT IS FUNDED Welfare charitable purposes. Generally to support causes recommended to it by members of The Amusement Machine Industry.

WHAT IS NOT FUNDED No grants for overseas charities or religious purposes.

TYPE OF GRANT Capital (including buildings), core costs, endowment, feasibility studies, one-off, project, research, recurring costs and running costs. Funding is available for up to and over three years.

RANGE OF GRANTS £500–£3,000.

SAMPLE GRANTS £3,000 each to Alexander School Harrow, BACTA West of England, Disability Sport

England, and Spinal Injuries; £2,000 to Lymphoma & Parkinsons Disease Society, Sandville Court, and South Wales Regional Golf Day; £1,500 each to Royal British Legion, SACRO and Teenage Cancer Trust.

FINANCES *Year* 1997–98 *Income* £75,000 *Grants* £44,000 *Assets* £65,000

TRUSTEES Robert Higgins, Chair; Sonia Meaden; Charles Henry; Simon Thomas; Mark Horwood.

HOW TO APPLY In writing to the correspondent, but via a Bacta member. Applications should be submitted by January, April or August, for trustees' meetings in February, May or September.

WHO TO APPLY TO Linda Malcolm, Clerk, Bacta House, Regents Wharf, 6 All Saints Street, London N1 9RQ *Tel* 020 7713 7144 *Fax* 020 7713 0446

CC NO 328668   **ESTABLISHED** 1991

■ The Badley Memorial Trust

WHERE FUNDING CAN BE GIVEN The former county borough of Dudley as constituted in 1953 and, in exceptional cases, the present metropolitan boroughs of Dudley and Sandwell.

WHO CAN BENEFIT Individuals, and organisations giving help to people in need who are sick, convalescent, disabled or infirm in the former county borough of Dudley, and in certain circumstances, to people who live elsewhere in the present Dudley Metropolitan Borough area or in the borough of Sandwell.

WHAT IS FUNDED Essential items of household or medical equipment, respite care and support for local organisations or charities giving direct help to individuals residing in the area of benefit.

WHAT IS NOT FUNDED Holidays abroad or any request that is outside What is Funded.

TYPE OF GRANT One-off.

FINANCES *Year* 2000–01 *Income* £51,000 *Grants* £39,000 *Assets* £967,000

HOW TO APPLY In writing to the address below. Initial telephone calls welcome. Guidelines and application forms are available. An sae is preferred.

WHO TO APPLY TO D Underwood, Clerk, 23 Water Street, Kingswinford, West Midlands DY6 7QA *Tel* 01384 277463

CC NO 222999   **ESTABLISHED** 1983

■ The Bagri Foundation

WHERE FUNDING CAN BE GIVEN Worldwide.

WHO CAN BENEFIT Institutions and individuals.

WHAT IS FUNDED General charitable purposes.

FINANCES *Year* 1999–2000 *Income* £116,000 *Grants* £70,000 *Assets* £2,200,000

TRUSTEES Lord Bagri; Hon. A Bagri; Lady Bagri; R J Gatehouse.

OTHER INFORMATION A further £11,000 was given in grants to individuals.

HOW TO APPLY In writing to the correspondent.

WHO TO APPLY TO R Gatehouse, Trustee, 3rd Floor, 80 Cannon Street, London EC4N 6EJ *Tel* 020 7280 0000

CC NO 1000219   **ESTABLISHED** 1990

■ The Sir Leon Bagrit Memorial Trust

WHERE FUNDING CAN BE GIVEN UK.

WHO CAN BENEFIT Educational, general.

WHAT IS FUNDED The trust states that it is 'primarily concerned with continuing to support scholarships to the college', i.e Imperial College, London.

WHAT IS NOT FUNDED No grants to individuals.

SAMPLE GRANTS £25,000 to World Jewish Relief; £3,000 to Royal College Radiologists; £1,000 each to Yehudi Menuhin Memorial Trust, Help the Hospices, and Charing Cross Holiday Dialysis Trust.

FINANCES *Year* 1999 *Income* £24,000 *Grants* £31,000 *Assets* £755,000

TRUSTEES Lady Sarah Bagrit; Sir Matthew Farrer; Hon. Mark T Bridges; Lord Rees-Mogg; Lady Rees-Mogg; Lawrence P Fielding.

HOW TO APPLY In writing to the correspondent, although the trust states that it does not respond to unsolicited applications.

WHO TO APPLY TO Hon. Mark T Bridges, Trustee, 66 Lincoln's Inn Fields, London WC2A 3LH *Tel* 020 7242 2022

CC NO 298075   **ESTABLISHED** 1987

■ Veta Bailey Charitable Trust

WHERE FUNDING CAN BE GIVEN Developing countries (generally those with GNP less than US$1,000 a head), or UK for work in developing countries.

WHO CAN BENEFIT Organisations (UK or overseas based) training medical personnel in developing countries.

WHAT IS FUNDED Training of doctors and other medical personnel and the development of good healthcare practices in third world and developing countries.

WHAT IS NOT FUNDED No grants to individuals, unless towards electives for medical students (see above).

TYPE OF GRANT One-off grants.

RANGE OF GRANTS Up to £10,000.

SAMPLE GRANTS In 2000: £9,347 to Voluntary Service Overseas; £7,760 to LEPRA; £6,000 to Centre for Caribbean Medicine; £5,075 to Africa Now; £5,000 each to International Nepal Fellowship, Mildmay and UNA International Service; £4,000 each to Tearfund, Ockenden Venture, a local organisation for work in Cameroon, and a local organisation for work in Kenya.

FINANCES *Year* 2002 *Income* £34,882 *Grants* £73,849 *Assets* £245,879

TRUSTEES Brian Worth; Dr Elizabeth McClatchey; John Humphreys; Sue Yates.

HOW TO APPLY In writing to the correspondent by June, for consideration at a trustees' meeting in August.

WHO TO APPLY TO B L Worth, Trustee, The Cottage, Tiltups End, Horsley, Stroud, Gloucestershire GL6 0QE *Tel* 01453 834914

CC NO 1007411   **ESTABLISHED** 1981

■ The Baily Thomas Charitable Fund

WHERE FUNDING CAN BE GIVEN UK.

WHO CAN BENEFIT Community groups, support groups and organisations benefiting people affected by learning disability.

WHAT IS FUNDED The trustees restrict their remit to learning disability. This can include residential facilities; respite; sheltered accommodation; crafts and music; support to volunteers; special schools and special needs education; care in the community; day centres; holidays and outings; playschemes; and research.

WHAT IS NOT FUNDED The following areas are unlikely to receive funding: mental illness, hospices, minibuses – except those for residential and/or day centres for people with learning disabilities, advocacy projects, arts and theatre projects, physical disabilities unless accompanied by significant learning disabilities.

TYPE OF GRANT Capital and revenue. Loans may be made in certain circumstances. Grants are one-off.

RANGE OF GRANTS £500–£230,000.

SAMPLE GRANTS £500,000 to Mental Health Foundation for research into the emotional wellbeing of young people with learning disabilities and mental health problems; £100,000 to Mental Health Foundation for inquiry into the emotional wellbeing of young people with learning disabilities and mental health problems; £90,000 each to Mencap City Foundation for the special projects fund and Rose Road Association Children's Appeal for a sitting/common room within their new centre; £75,000 each to Autistic Society (Hampshire), Development Trust for children's respite home – Coventry, National Autistic Society for Robert Ogden School project; £62,000 to Wales University Medical College for development of a carer determined screening questionnaire for dementia in people with Down's Syndrome; £50,000 each to Bliss=Ability for information services in the Tyne and Wear area and Contact a Family for the UK Information Centre.

FINANCES *Year* 2000–01 *Income* £2,547,485 *Grants* £2,849,000 *Assets* £61,763,000

TRUSTEES Charles J T Nangle; Prof. W I Fraser; Prof. Michael Gelder; Michael R Macfadyen; Mrs Zira Robertson.

HOW TO APPLY Applications (other than those for research) should be made in writing on the fund's four-page application form. Applications will only be considered from voluntary organisations which are registered charities or are associated with a registered charity. All applications will be subject to independent review. A copy of the applicant's latest annual report and accounts should be submitted with the application form. Do not send architectural drawings, plans or photographs. These are seldom necessary and will be asked for, if required. Research applications should be made in writing in the form of a research plan to include a brief background and a short account of the design of the study and number of subjects, the methods of assessment and analysis, timetable, main outcomes and some indication of other opportunities arising from the support of such research. A detailed budget of costs should be submitted together with details of any other applications for funding which have been made to other funders and their outcomes, if known. The fund does not expect to contribute towards university overheads. A curriculum vitae will be required for each of the personnel actually carrying out the study and for their supervisor. Evidence must be provided of the approval of the ethics committee of the applicant to the study and the approval of the university for the application to the fund. An 80-word lay summary should also be submitted with the detailed research proposal. Before submitting a full application, researchers may submit a one-page summary of the proposed study so that the trustees may indicate whether they are prepared to consider a full application. Meetings of the trustees are usually held in June and early December each year and applications should therefore be submitted no later than 1 May or 1 October for consideration at the next relevant meeting. Late applications will not be considered.

WHO TO APPLY TO Geoffrey R Mean, Ernst & Young, 400 Capability Green, Luton LU1 3LU *Tel* 01582 643125 *Fax* 01582 643006

CC NO 262334   **ESTABLISHED** 1970

....

■ The Baird Trust

WHERE FUNDING CAN BE GIVEN Scotland.

WHO CAN BENEFIT Generally, the Church of Scotland.

WHAT IS FUNDED The trust is chiefly concerned with supporting the repair and refurbishment of the churches and halls belonging to the Church of Scotland. It also endows parishes and gives help to the Church of Scotland in its work.

TYPE OF GRANT Buildings. Funding for up to one year.

SAMPLE GRANTS £10,000 each to Boys Brigade – Carronvale Centre and Church of Scotland for widows of ministers; £9,000 to Lodging House Mission for a joint chaplaincy; £5,000 to Solid Rock Youth Development Project; £4,000 to Church House for its holiday fund; £3,000 to Colston Milton Children's Project; £2,000 to The Stewartry of Strathearn; £1,000 to Licentiates Book Tokens.

FINANCES *Year* 2000 *Income* £316,000 *Grants* £297,000 *Assets* £7,300,000

TRUSTEES D S Erskine, Chair; Alexander W Barbour; Miss Marianne Baird; Lieut Cmdr Edward F B Spragge; Col. Hon. W D Arbuthnott; Hon. Mrs Coltman; Maj. J Henry Callander; Maj. J M K Erskine; Revd J R McKay.

HOW TO APPLY In writing to the correspondent at any time.

WHO TO APPLY TO Ronald D Oakes, Secretary, 182 Bath Street, Glasgow G2 4HG *Tel* 0141 332 0476

SC NO SC016549   **ESTABLISHED** 1873

....

■ The Baker Charitable Trust

WHERE FUNDING CAN BE GIVEN UK and overseas.

WHO CAN BENEFIT Mainly headquarters organisations benefiting older people; Jews; and disabled people.

WHAT IS FUNDED Priority is given to charities concerned with the welfare of Jewish, elderly and disabled people; neurological research; and people with diabetes and epilepsy. Preference is given to charities in which the trust has special interest, knowledge or association.

WHAT IS NOT FUNDED No grants to individuals or non-registered charities.

TYPE OF GRANT Core costs.

RANGE OF GRANTS £250–£10,000; typical grant £500–£3,000.

SAMPLE GRANTS £10,000 to Jewish Care; £6,000 to Norwood Ravenswood; £2,000 to World Jewish Relief; £1,000 each to Bnai Brith Hillel Foundation, Chai Life Line, Diabetes UK, Institute of Jewish Policy Research and National Society for Epilepsy.

FINANCES *Year* 2000–01 *Income* £43,264 *Grants* £40,150 *Assets* £1,402,350

TRUSTEES Dr Harvey Baker; Dr Adrienne Baker.

HOW TO APPLY In writing to the correspondent. The trustees meet to consider applications in January, April, July and October. This entry was not confirmed by the trust, but the information was correct according to the trust's file at the Charity Commission.

WHO TO APPLY TO Dr Harvey Baker, Trustee, 16 Sheldon Avenue, Highgate, London N6 4JT *Tel* 020 8340 5970 *Fax* 020 8347 7017
CC NO 273629   **ESTABLISHED** 1977

■ The C Alma Baker Trust

WHERE FUNDING CAN BE GIVEN UK and overseas, particularly New Zealand.

WHO CAN BENEFIT Individuals or scientific research institutions benefiting young adults, farmers, academics, research workers and students.

WHAT IS FUNDED Agriculture and education with an agricultural connection, particularly in New Zealand and UK. (a) Agricultural research particularly New Zealand. (b) Massey University, New Zealand – Wye College, UK, Undergraduate Scheme. (c) UK YFC Scheme for young farmers to experience New Zealand farming on the trust's property in New Zealand. (d) Annual Travel Fellowship New Zealand-UK, UK-New Zealand. (e) Maori Language Education Scholarship, Wailato University, New Zealand. (f) Postgraduate study grants for agriculture-related subjects in New Zealand.

WHAT IS NOT FUNDED No general education grants.

TYPE OF GRANT Range of grants, though normally one-off annual grants.

RANGE OF GRANTS For agricultural education £200–£15,000; typical grant £1,600. For research £1,000–£5,000.

SAMPLE GRANTS All grants are shown in New Zealand dollars.
$59,000 for postgraduate scholarships; $15,000 for the C Alma Baker fellowship; $10,322 to Waikaretu School; $10,000 to Holy Trinity Cathedral Choral Scholarship; $9,000 Maori Language Scholarships; $7,500 to Tuakau School; $6,660 to Royal Agricultural Society; $5,500 to UK Agricultural College – Massey University Exchange; $760 to Perak Planters' Association; $500 to Countries Rodeo Club; £300 to Auckland Helicopter Trust.

FINANCES *Year* 2000–01 *Grants* £78,000

TRUSTEES C R Boyes; R Moore; S F B Taylor. New Zealand Committee: C T Horton, Chair; Prof. A Frampton; D J Frith; K I Lowe; Prof. B MacDonald; Mrs M Millard; T G Mandeno.

PUBLICATIONS Limestone Downs Annual Report in New Zealand.

OTHER INFORMATION The trust's main asset is Limestone Downs, a sheep and beef property in the North Island, New Zealand utilised for new ideas and development in agriculture to be explored and debated in a working farm environment.

HOW TO APPLY In writing for annual grant review at the end of November each year. The trust only has a limited number of grants available. For New Zealand applicants apply to Prof. B Macdonald, Secretary to New Zealand Committee, The C Alma Baker Trust, Massey University, Bag 11–222, Palmerston North, New Zealand. Fax: 00 64 63 505686.

WHO TO APPLY TO J N Hemens, Clerk to the Trustees, 20 Hartford Road, Huntingdon, Cambridgeshire PE29 3QH *Tel* 01480 411331 *Fax* 01480 459012
E-mail nickhemens@wbalaw.demon.co.uk
CC NO 283015   **ESTABLISHED** 1981

■ The Balcombe Charitable Trust

WHERE FUNDING CAN BE GIVEN UK.

WHO CAN BENEFIT Registered charities benefiting children and young adults, students, at risk groups, disabled people, people disadvantaged by poverty, socially isolated people, and people who are sick.

WHAT IS FUNDED Education; the environment; health and welfare.

WHAT IS NOT FUNDED No grants to individuals or non-registered charities.

RANGE OF GRANTS £1,000–£25,000.

SAMPLE GRANTS £50,000 to Brook Advisory Centres; £25,000 each to British Red Cross, Childline, Durrell Wildlife Conservation Trust and NSPCC; £20,000 to World Wildlife Fund UK; £15,000 to BACUP, Crisis and Parentline; £10,000 each to Friends of the Earth, MIND, Princess Diana Trust for Carers, Samaritans and Who Cares Trust.

FINANCES *Year* 2000–01 *Income* £257,409 *Grants* £409,500 *Assets* £8,196,520

TRUSTEES R A Kreitman; P M Kreitman; Mrs S I Kreitman.

HOW TO APPLY In writing to the correspondent.

WHO TO APPLY TO J Prevezer, c/o Citroen Wells, Devonshire House, 1 Devonshire Street, London W1W 5DR *Tel* 020 7304 2000
CC NO 267172   **ESTABLISHED** 1975

■ The Balcraig Foundation

WHERE FUNDING CAN BE GIVEN Scotland and Africa.

WHO CAN BENEFIT Registered charities.

WHAT IS FUNDED Grants have been given to fund charitable projects in Africa.

FINANCES *Year* 1995–96 *Grants* £2,500,000 *Assets* £8,000,000

TRUSTEES Ann Gloag; David McCleary.

OTHER INFORMATION The trust does not provide its accounts, despite its statutory obligation to do so. We have therefore not been able to update any information on this trust.

HOW TO APPLY As the trust only supports long-time beneficiaries, unsolicited applications will not be considered.

WHO TO APPLY TO David McCleary, Secretary, Balcraig House, Scone, Perth PH2 7PG *Tel* 01738 552303 *Fax* 01738 552101
SC NO SC020037

■ The Andrew Balint Charitable Trust

WHERE FUNDING CAN BE GIVEN UK, Europe, the Soviets, Africa, Middle East, Far East, North America, South America, Australasia.

WHO CAN BENEFIT Charitable organisations.

WHAT IS FUNDED Medical, educational, religious, child, old age, refugee, welfare and benevolent causes.

TYPE OF GRANT Mostly recurrent.

SAMPLE GRANTS £49,033 to welfare causes (including £45,700 in the UK); £30,960 to old age (£11,650 in the UK); £27,950 to education (£13,500 in the UK); £27,750 to benevolent (all in the UK); £9,250 to children (£5,750 in the UK); £9,100 to medical (£3,850 in the UK); £6,585 to individuals (£1,250 in the UK); £5,500 to religion (all in the UK).

FINANCES *Year* 2001–02 *Income* £255,376 *Grants* £166,128 *Assets* £2,573,459

TRUSTEES Agnes Balint; Dr Gabriel Balint-Kurti; Roy David Balint-Kurti.

HOW TO APPLY In writing to the correspondent, although all funds are fully committed.

Think carefully about every application. Is it justified?

299

WHO TO APPLY TO J K Olver, Administrator, Suite A, 4–6 Canfield Place, London NW6 3BT *Tel* 020 7624 2098 *Fax* 020 7624 2076
CC NO 273691   ESTABLISHED 1977

■ The George Balint Charitable Trust

WHERE FUNDING CAN BE GIVEN UK, Europe, the Soviets, Africa, Middle East, Far East, North America, South America, Australasia.
WHO CAN BENEFIT Charitable organisations.
WHAT IS FUNDED Medical, educational, religious, child, old age, refugee, welfare and benevolent causes.
TYPE OF GRANT Mostly recurrent.
SAMPLE GRANTS £131,878 to welfare causes (of which £109,095 was given in the UK); £88,450 to educational (£48,000 in the UK); £51,600 to children (£33,350 in the UK); £42,400 to benevolent (£41,600 in the UK); £35,658 to old age (£15,050 in the UK); £29,050 to medical (£18,800 in the UK); £14,225 to individuals (£8,925 in the UK); £10,185 to religion (£7,135 in the UK); £1,200 to refugee (£1,000 in the UK).
FINANCES *Year* 2001–02 *Income* £285,677 *Grants* £404,646 *Assets* £1,712,788
TRUSTEES Dr Andrew Balint; George Balint; George Rothschild; Marion Farkas-Balint.
HOW TO APPLY In writing to the correspondent, although all funds are fully committed.
WHO TO APPLY TO J K Olver, Administrator, Suite A, 4–6 Canfield Place, London NW6 3BT *Tel* 020 7624 2098 *Fax* 020 7624 2076
CC NO 267482   ESTABLISHED 1974

■ Paul Balint Charitable Trust

WHERE FUNDING CAN BE GIVEN UK, Europe, the Soviets, Africa, Middle East, Far East, North America, South America, Australasia
WHO CAN BENEFIT Charitable organisations.
WHAT IS FUNDED Medical, educational, religious, child, old age, refugee, welfare and benevolent causes.
TYPE OF GRANT Mostly recurrent.
SAMPLE GRANTS £132,734 to welfare causes (£129,400 in the UK); £28,705 to old age (£10,500 in the UK); £26,000 to benevolent (all in the UK); £22,950 to education (£8,500 in the UK); £6,000 to medical (all in the UK); £4,200 to children (£1,700 in the UK); £500 to religion (all in the UK); £300 to refugee (all in the UK); £200 to individuals (all in the UK).
FINANCES *Year* 2001–02 *Income* £234,196 *Grants* £221,589 *Assets* £1,073,245
TRUSTEES Dr Andrew Balint; Dr Gabriel Balint-Kurti; Paul Balint; Marc Balint.
HOW TO APPLY In writing to the correspondent, although all funds are fully committed.
WHO TO APPLY TO J K Olver, Administrator, Suite A, 4–6 Canfield Place, London NW6 3BT *Tel* 020 7624 2098 *Fax* 020 7624 2076
CC NO 273690   ESTABLISHED 1977

■ The Albert Casanova Ballard Deceased Trust

WHERE FUNDING CAN BE GIVEN The Plymouth area only.
WHO CAN BENEFIT Children entering secondary school education, and registered charities benefiting children; at risk groups; people disadvantaged by poverty; and socially isolated people.
WHAT IS FUNDED Local charities and local branches of national organisations working in the Plymouth area in the fields of health, welfare and young people. Children entering secondary school education to assist with school uniform and books.
TYPE OF GRANT Recurrent.
RANGE OF GRANTS Charities: £250–£1,500. Individuals: £100–£200.
SAMPLE GRANTS £2,000 to Ballard Activity Centre; £1,000 each to Dame Hannah Rogers School, Heartswell South West, Plymouth Council of Clubs for Young People and YWCA; £750 each to Plymouth Philharmonic Choir and Relate; £650 to Prince Rock Youth Club; £600 each to Ford Youth & Community Centre and Plymouth & District Disabled Fellowship.
FINANCES *Year* 1999–2000 *Income* £44,644 *Grants* £37,000 *Assets* £848,338
TRUSTEES I D Rendle; K J Banfield; Mrs A B Houston; Mrs M M Pengelly.
HOW TO APPLY In writing to the correspondent. Applications from local charities are considered in November and notices appear in the Western Morning News and Evening Herald at that time. Grants for individuals are made once a year in July. Grants will NOT be entertained outside these periods.
WHO TO APPLY TO Mrs Rendle, Blue Gates, The Glade, Crapstone, Yelverton, Devon PL20 7PR *Tel* 01822 853421
CC NO 201759   ESTABLISHED 1962

■ The Ballinger Charitable Trust

WHERE FUNDING CAN BE GIVEN North east England, Tyne and Wear.
WHO CAN BENEFIT Registered charities only.
WHAT IS FUNDED General charitable purposes.
WHAT IS NOT FUNDED No grants to individuals.
SAMPLE GRANTS £55,000 to The Society of St Vincent de Paul. The remaining £27,000 was given in smaller grants (less than £2,000).
FINANCES *Year* 1999–2000 *Income* £33,000 *Grants* £82,000 *Assets* £967,000
TRUSTEES M S A Ballinger; Mrs D S Ballinger.
OTHER INFORMATION No more up-to-date information was available.
HOW TO APPLY In writing to the correspondent.
WHO TO APPLY TO M S A Ballinger, Trustee, Bolam Hall East, Morpeth NE61 3UA
CC NO 1053273   ESTABLISHED 1994

■ The Balmore Trust

WHERE FUNDING CAN BE GIVEN Developing countries and UK, with a preference for Strathclyde.
WHO CAN BENEFIT Organisations benefiting those in greatest social need, especially children, young adults and women, at risk groups, people disadvantaged by poverty and victims of domestic violence.
WHAT IS FUNDED Two-thirds of grants are given to overseas projects and the remainder to local projects in the UK, working with women or young people in areas of greatest social need. Holiday schemes in the UK are looked on favourably.

Medical/educational projects are favoured overseas, but not generally in the UK.

WHAT IS NOT FUNDED No grants to individuals.

TYPE OF GRANT Grants are one-off. Core costs, project and start-up costs will be considered. Funding may be given for up to one year.

RANGE OF GRANTS £50–£3,000, but larger grants to 'old friends'. New overseas grants maximum £500 and UK £200.

SAMPLE GRANTS £4,000 to Amajuba Education Trust, South Africa for university fees; £2,800 to Child in Need Institute, Calcutta, India for medical aid and malnutrition relief; £2,700 to Sophia Mission Institute, Myanmar for education; £1,160 to Wells for India for water projects; £1,000 each to Braendam Family House towards respite holidays, Church House Bridgeton for youth/community work, and East Dunbarton Women's Aid. £500 each was given to various overseas projects.

FINANCES *Year* 1999 *Income* £26,000 *Grants* £24,500 *Assets* £80,000

TRUSTEES J Riches; Ms R Jarvis; Ms O Beauvoisin; C Brown; Ms J Brown; J Eldridge; Ms R Riches; B Holman.

PUBLICATIONS A twice yearly newsletter is available free from the trust's shop, The Coach House Charity Craft Shop in Balmore, or from the address given upon receipt of an sae.

HOW TO APPLY The trust is run entirely voluntarily and unless the applicant is known to the trust or has a connection with The Coach House and could be categorised as being in great social need, applications are unlikely to succeed. Applications should be made in writing to the correspondent at the above address at the very beginning of the year (main disbursement is made annually in February or March). The following information should be provided: details of the project for which funding is sought; the amount requested; details of past and current funders; an outline of the background and experience of key staff; a copy of the organisation's recent accounts; references; details of other funders the organisation is approaching; any other relevant information. Applications are only acknowledged if an sae is enclosed.

WHO TO APPLY TO The Secretary, Viewfield, Balmore, Torrance, Glasgow G64 4AE *Tel* 01360 620742 *Fax* 01360 620742

SC NO SC008930   **ESTABLISHED** 1980

····································

■ The Balney Charitable Trust

WHERE FUNDING CAN BE GIVEN UK, with a preference for north Buckinghamshire and north Bedfordshire.

WHO CAN BENEFIT Individuals, and registered charities and institutions benefiting Christians and people disadvantaged by poverty.

WHAT IS FUNDED Trustees favour local appeals and ex-servicemen/womens' institutions. Particularly charities working in the fields of residential facilities and services; churches; Anglican bodies; Free Churches; acute health care; hospices; and conservation will be considered.

WHAT IS NOT FUNDED Local community organisations and individuals outside north Buckinghamshire and north Bedfordshire.

TYPE OF GRANT Start-up costs, capital grants (including contributions to building projects, e.g. local churches) and research. Funding for up to three years will be considered.

RANGE OF GRANTS £25–£5,000.

SAMPLE GRANTS £5,000 to Willen Hospice; £2,000 to Macmillan Milton Keynes Appeal; £1,000

each to Emmaus Village and Gurkha Welfare Trust.

FINANCES *Year* 2001–02 *Income* £61,000 *Grants* £50,000 *Assets* £785,000

TRUSTEES Major J G B Chester; R Rucke-Keene.

HOW TO APPLY In writing to the correspondent. Applications are acknowledged if an sae is enclosed, otherwise if the charity has not received a reply within six weeks the application has not been successful.

WHO TO APPLY TO G C W Beazley, Clerk, The Chicheley Estate, Bartlemas Office, Pavenham, Bedford MK43 7PF *Tel* 01234 823663 *Fax* 01234 825058

CC NO 288575   **ESTABLISHED** 1983

····································

■ The Baltic Charitable Fund

WHERE FUNDING CAN BE GIVEN UK, with a preference for the City of London.

WHO CAN BENEFIT Registered charities benefiting residents of the City of London, seafarers, fishermen, and ex-service and service people.

WHAT IS FUNDED Registered charities only which must be connected with the City of London or shipping or the military forces.

WHAT IS NOT FUNDED No support for advertising or charity dinners, and so on.

TYPE OF GRANT One-off.

RANGE OF GRANTS £250–£25,000; typical grant £500.

SAMPLE GRANTS £25,000 to RNLI for lifeboat 'Baltic Exchange III' 2003 Appeal; £6,000 to City of London School for Boys towards a bursary; £5,700 to City of London School for Girls towards a bursary; £5,000 to Lord Mayor of City of London Appeal for British Diabetics Association and NCH Action for Children; £3,500 to City University Business School towards a bursary; £3,000 to SSAFA; £2,600 to Lloyds Officer Cadet Scholarship as part funding; £2,000 each to Royal Merchant Navy School Foundation and King George's Fund for Sailors; £1,000 to Medway Missions to Seamen Trust for Pembroke House.

FINANCES *Year* 1999–2000 *Income* £50,000 *Grants* £52,000 *Assets* £1,200,000

TRUSTEES The Board of Directors.

HOW TO APPLY The fund supports a set list of charities and does not consider unsolicited applications. It stated in 2001 that funds were fully committed until 2005.

WHO TO APPLY TO Mark Soutter, Company Secretary, The Baltic Exchange, 38 St Mary Axe, London EC3A 8BH *Tel* 020 7623 5501

CC NO 279194   **ESTABLISHED** 1979

····································

■ The Bamford Charitable Foundation

WHERE FUNDING CAN BE GIVEN Within a 20-mile radius of Rocester.

WHO CAN BENEFIT Mainly local organisations benefiting children; young adults; older people; clergy; medical professionals; volunteers; Church of England; Methodists; Roman Catholics; at risk groups; carers; disabled people; people disadvantaged by poverty; disaster victims; homeless people; and people with cancers, hearing loss and HIV and AIDS.

WHAT IS FUNDED Particularly charities working in the fields of hostels; support to voluntary and community organisations; churches; Anglican bodies; Catholics; diocesan boards; dance and ballet; music; hospices at home; support; self help groups; health facilities and buildings; medical studies and research; church buildings; agriculture; schools and colleges; cultural and religious teaching; and various community facilities and services.

WHAT IS NOT FUNDED Grants are not normally made to individuals.

TYPE OF GRANT One-off.

RANGE OF GRANTS £100–£3,000; typical £500.

SAMPLE GRANTS Beneficiaries have included All Saints First School, Catholic Youth Association, Denstone College – Language Centre, Dove First School – Uttoxeter, Elton John Aids Foundation, Katherine House Hospice Appeal, Kite Appeal, St George's Hospital Special Trustees for the Hold my Hand Appeal, Shuttlewood Clarke Foundation and Tommy's Campaign.

FINANCES *Year* 1999 *Income* £92,992 *Grants* £205,062

TRUSTEES Sir A P Bamford; Lady C Bamford; E T D Leadbeater.

HOW TO APPLY In writing to the correspondent.

WHO TO APPLY TO S E R Owens, Administrator, J C Bamford Excavators Ltd, Lakeside Works, Denstone Road, Rocester, Uttoxeter, Staffordshire ST14 5JP *Tel* 01889 590312

CC NO 279848   **ESTABLISHED** 1979

....

■ The Banbury Charities

WHERE FUNDING CAN BE GIVEN Banbury or its immediate environs.

WHO CAN BENEFIT Individuals and groups.

WHAT IS FUNDED General charitable purposes.

WHAT IS NOT FUNDED No grants for debts or ongoing expenses.

TYPE OF GRANT One-off grants.

RANGE OF GRANTS £10–£33,000.

SAMPLE GRANTS £33,000 Millennium Book Project – Books for schools; £16,000 Horton General Hospital; £13,000 Cherwell District Council for sports and arts bursaries, a youth forum and a mentoring project. All other grants were for £5,000 or less; recipients included Banbury Rotary Club, Carer's Centre and Sunshine Centre.

FINANCES *Year* 1999 *Income* £324,000 *Grants* £152,000

TRUSTEES Mrs J M Colegrave, Chair; J P Friswell; M Humphris; R L Keys; Mrs J May; R P Walford; C F Blackwell; Mrs J Justice; P M R Helmore; Mrs R Higham; J C Vine.

OTHER INFORMATION The Banbury Charities are The Bridge Estate, Lady Arran's Charity, Banbury Arts and Educational Charity, Banbury Sick Poor Fund, Banbury Almshouse Charity, and the Banbury Welfare Trust.

HOW TO APPLY In writing to the correspondent.

WHO TO APPLY TO A Scott Andrews, Clerk to the Trustees, 36 West Bar, Banbury, Oxfordshire OX16 9RU *Tel* 01295 251234 *Fax* 01295 270948

CC NO 201418   **ESTABLISHED** 1961

....

■ William P Bancroft (No 2) Charitable Trust and Jenepher Gillett Trust

WHERE FUNDING CAN BE GIVEN UK and overseas.

WHO CAN BENEFIT Mainly charities benefiting Quakers.

WHAT IS FUNDED Mainly Quaker charities or projects.

WHAT IS NOT FUNDED No appeals unconnected with Quakers. No support for individual or student grant applications.

TYPE OF GRANT Buildings, core costs, endowment, one-off and start-up costs. Funding of up to three years will be considered.

RANGE OF GRANTS £400–£6,000; average grant £2,200.

SAMPLE GRANTS £6,000 to Woodbrooke College Quaker Study Centre for bursaries; £5,000 to Britain Yearly Meeting, Society of Friends for property maintenance; £4,500 to Sibford School for bursaries; £4,200 to Chainey Manor, Quaker Conference Centre for bursaries and maintenance; £2,000 each to Bookham School for Development Appeal, Glebe House – Friends Therapeutic Community for general purposes, Bedford Institute Association, Quaker Social Action for general purposes, and Quaker Council for European Affairs for general purposes; £1,500 each to Cape Town Quaker Peace Centre for bursaries for staff to attend Woodbrooke College, and Pendle Hill (Quaker College near Philadelphia, USA), a grant to British residents for one seminar.

FINANCES *Year* 2000 *Income* £48,500 *Grants* £40,500

TRUSTEES R Gillett; G T Gillett; D S Gillett; J Moseley; A J Yelloly; C E Gardiner.

OTHER INFORMATION Applications should only come from Quaker charities.

HOW TO APPLY In writing to the correspondent. Trustees meet in May, applications must be received no later than April.

WHO TO APPLY TO Dr Roger Gillett, Fernroyd, St Margaret's Road, Altrincham, Cheshire WA14 2AW *Tel* 0161 928 5112 *Fax* 0161 928 5112

CC NO 288968   **ESTABLISHED** 1984

....

■ The Band (1976) Trust

WHERE FUNDING CAN BE GIVEN UK.

WHO CAN BENEFIT Organisations benefiting children, young adults, students and teachers. Support is also given to people who are disabled, disadvantaged by poverty and socially isolated, and at risk groups.

WHAT IS FUNDED Available income is principally used for assisting people who are disabled and other disadvantaged people, and for education.

RANGE OF GRANTS £190–£105,000.

SAMPLE GRANTS £100,000 to Chelsea and Westminster Hospital; £35,000 to Blond McIndoe Research Centre; £25,750 to NSPCC; £25,000 each to Honoroubale Society Grays Inn, Florence Nightingale Memorial Committee, Royal Free Hospital – Colon Cancer, Samantha Dickinson Research Trust, Shooting Star Trust and Speech Language and Hearing Centre.

FINANCES *Year* 2000–01 *Income* £660,000 *Grants* £639,000 *Assets* £18,500,000

TRUSTEES Hon. Mrs Nicholas Wallop; Hon. Nicholas Wallop; R J S Mason; B G Streather.

HOW TO APPLY In writing to the correspondent, for consideration at trustees' meetings three times a year. However, 'unsolicited applications will not normally be considered'.

WHO TO APPLY TO R J S Mason, Trustee, Macnair Mason, Chartered Accountants, John Stow House, 18 Bevis Marks, London EC3A 7ED *Tel* 020 7469 0550 *Fax* 020 7469 0660

CC NO 279802   **ESTABLISHED** 1976

■ The Barber Charitable Trust

WHERE FUNDING CAN BE GIVEN UK, with some preference for West Sussex, and overseas.

WHO CAN BENEFIT Mainly evangelical Christian causes benefiting people of all ages and races.

WHAT IS FUNDED Evangelical Christian causes, missionary societies, bible societies, Christian radio, Christian relief, Christian education and outreach.

WHAT IS NOT FUNDED Requests from individuals are not considered unless personally known by the trustees. Requests from non-registered charities are not considered. Requests for building construction or renovation are not considered.

TYPE OF GRANT Project, recurring costs, one-off, core costs, certain capital projects.

RANGE OF GRANTS £100–£8,900; typical grant £250.

SAMPLE GRANTS £8,900 to Scripture Union International; £7,500 to Arundel Baptist Church; £5,600 to Hope Now Ministries; £4,400 to Gideons International; £4,000 to Africa Inland Mission; £3,000 to Western Province Baptist Association (South Africa); £2,900 to Christian Ministries; £2,100 to Missionary Aviation Fellowship; £2,000 each to SASRA, Worldshare and Scripture Gift Mission.

FINANCES *Year* 2000–01 *Income* £71,626 *Grants* £68,094 *Assets* £46,220

TRUSTEES E E Barber; Mrs D H Barber.

HOW TO APPLY In writing to the correspondent. Funds tend to be committed several years in advance and therefore unsolicited appeals are unlikely to be considered or acknowledged.

WHO TO APPLY TO E E Barber, Trustee, Tortington Cottage, Tortington, Arundel, West Sussex BN18 0BG *Tel* 01903 882337 *Fax* 01903 882337

CC NO 269544   **ESTABLISHED** 1975

■ The Barbour Trust

WHERE FUNDING CAN BE GIVEN Mainly Tyne & Wear, County Durham, Northumberland and Cleveland.

WHO CAN BENEFIT The trust likes to support local activities, and also supports local branches of national charities benefiting people who are unemployed; volunteers; parents and children; one-parent families; people disadvantaged by poverty; disabled people; at risk groups; carers; victims of abuse, crime and domestic violence; and homeless people. People with various diseases and medical conditions will also be considered.

WHAT IS FUNDED Relief of patients suffering from any form of illness or disease, promotion of research into causes of such illnesses; furtherance of education; preservation of buildings and countryside of environmental, historical or architectural interest; relief of people in need. Charities working in the fields of infrastructure development, religious umbrella bodies and animal welfare will also be considered.

TYPE OF GRANT Capital, core costs, one-off, project, research, running costs, recurring costs, salaries, and start-up costs. Funding for up to one year will be considered.

RANGE OF GRANTS Small grants £50–£500. Main grants £500 upwards.

SAMPLE GRANTS £175,000 to Royal Agricultural Benevolent Institution following the foot and mouth outbreak; £136,000 to Salvation Army; £114,000 to Newcastle Police Aid to Romania; £75,000 to Royal Scottish Agricultural Benevolent Institution; £26,216 to Bede's World; £25,000 each to Mercy Ships and NCHS Development Trust; £10,500 to Tyne & Wear

Museum Service; £10,000 each to Cancer Bridge and Crisis.

FINANCES *Year* 2000–01 *Income* £478,000 *Grants* £931,000 *Assets* £4,963,108

TRUSTEES Dame Margaret Barbour, Chair; Henry Jacob Tavroges; Anthony Glenton; Miss Helen Barbour.

HOW TO APPLY In writing to the correspondent at PO Box 21, Guisborough, Cleveland, TS14 8YH or the address below. The applications should include full back-up information, a statement of accounts and the official charity number of the applicant. A main grants meeting is held every three months to consider grants of £500 plus. Applications are processed and researched by the administrator and secretary and further information may be requested. A small grants meeting is held monthly to consider grants up to £500. The usual budget each meeting is £4,000.

WHO TO APPLY TO Mrs Audrey Harvey, Administrator, J Barbour and Sons, Simonside, South Shields, Tyne and Wear NE34 9PD *Tel* 0191 455 4444 *Fax* 0191 427 4259
E-mail edith.howse@barbour.com

CC NO 328081   **ESTABLISHED** 1988

■ David and Frederick Barclay Foundation

WHERE FUNDING CAN BE GIVEN UK.

WHO CAN BENEFIT Hospitals, medical research bodies, individual medical researchers and registered charities benefiting medical professionals; charities benefiting sick and disabled people, older people and young people.

WHAT IS FUNDED Medical research; welfare and disability.

TYPE OF GRANT Projects and one-off grants.

SAMPLE GRANTS Grants in excess of £20,000 were made to: Cavendish Hip Foundation; FORME; John Grooms Capital Appeal; Moorfields Eye Hospital; Ronald Raven Cancer Research Trust; Rose Road Children's Appeal; Sark School and Community Centre; Glasgow University; Oxford University.

FINANCES *Year* 2001 *Income* £971,645 *Grants* £1,117,685 *Assets* £306,628

TRUSTEES Lord Peyton of Yeovil, Chair; Sir David Barclay; Sir Frederick Barclay; Lord McAlpine of West Green.

OTHER INFORMATION The grant total includes £52,171 to individuals.

HOW TO APPLY Applications should be in writing, clearly outlining the details of the proposed project (if for medical research, so far as possible in lay terms). The total cost and duration should be stated; also the amount, if any, which has already been raised. Following an initial screening, applications are selected according to their merits, suitability and funds available. Visits are usually made to projects where substantial funds are involved. Decisions are normally made as soon as possible following receipt of application. The trustees welcome information as to progress and require this on completion of a project.

WHO TO APPLY TO Lord Peyton, Chairman, 3rd Floor, 20 St James's Street, London SW1A 1ES *Tel* 020 7915 0915

CC NO 803696   **ESTABLISHED** 1990

Think carefully about every application. Is it justified?

303

■ Barclays Stockbrokers Charitable Trust

WHERE FUNDING CAN BE GIVEN UK

WHO CAN BENEFIT Small/medium registered and exempt charities benefiting: physical and mental disability, ill health, relief of suffering, poverty, homelessness, family and social welfare, education and training, children, young people and older people.

WHAT IS FUNDED Capital projects/specific programmes where, if possible, the trustees decision to award a grant will 'make a diffference'.

WHAT IS NOT FUNDED The trust will not consider funding large national charities, and generally will not consider funding individuals, schools, colleges or universities, religious buildings, overseas projects, medical research or animal welfare. Expenses that have already been incurred will not be considered.

TYPE OF GRANT One-off.

RANGE OF GRANTS £10,000–£50,000.

FINANCES *Year* 2002 *Income* £150,000

TRUSTEES Barclays Bank Trust Co. Ltd

OTHER INFORMATION This newly established trust was set up in July 2002. It expects to makes grants totalling around £100,000 a year.

HOW TO APPLY Initially in writing to the correspondent for consideration quarterly in February, May, August and November. If eligibility is established following receipt of an appeal letter, then an application form will be sent.

WHO TO APPLY TO Miss M Y Bertenshaw, Trust Officer, Barclays Bank Trust Co. Ltd, Estates and Trusts, Osbourne Court, Gadbrook Park, Northwich, Cheshire CW4 7UE *Tel* 01606 313173 *Fax* 01606 303000

CC NO 1093833   **ESTABLISHED** 2002

■ The Baring Foundation

WHERE FUNDING CAN BE GIVEN England and Wales, with a special interest in London, Merseyside, Cornwall and Devon; also UK charities working with NGO partners in developing countries.

WHO CAN BENEFIT Varies from programme to programme; please refer to the foundation's guidelines.

WHAT IS FUNDED Grants programmes are Strengthening the Voluntary Sector programme (includes support for mergers), International programme, and Arts programme. Outside these programmes the foundation makes its largest grant to support the work of the Manor Charitable Trust, which manages two residential educational centres.

WHAT IS NOT FUNDED See guidelines for specific programmes. More generally: appeals or charities set up to support statutory organisations; animal welfare charities; grant maintained, private, or local education authority schools or their parent teachers associations; individuals.

TYPE OF GRANT Strengthening the Voluntary Sector – mostly one-off grants for work which will lead to significant change in the effectiveness of an organisation by improvements to its strategy and structure, systems or skills. For example, feasibility studies, business planning, dissemination or replication of effective practice, joint working/mergers.
Arts – one-year grants for the cost of small-scale arts projects taking place in an educational or community context. For example, a participatory activity, an event, a one-off programme of work,

the development of an idea or a learning opportunity such as an exchange with another arts organisation.
International – three-year grants to improve capacity and enhance the effectiveness of UK International NGOs and their partner NGOs and community-based orgnaisations in Sub-Saharan Africa and Latin America.
Core grants – a small number of grants are made for core costs under the Strengthening the Voluntary Sector and Arts programmes, but these are by invitation only.

RANGE OF GRANTS Strengthening the Voluntary Sector – up to £30,000, average grant £8,567; Arts – up to £7,000, average grant £4,055; International – up to £240,000, average grant £166,953.

SAMPLE GRANTS Arts programme – £5,000 to Bamboozle Theatre Company to provide opportunities for young people with mild to severe learning difficulties in Leicester to discover their potential through educational theatre experiences; £3,360 to WOW! – Wales One World Film Festival towards a film education programme for local schools and colleges in Aberystwyth, Newport and Swansea.
Strengthening the Voluntary Sector – £20,000 to Homeless Link towards the cost of work enabling Homeless Network to become part of a new homeless umbrella organisation; £15,000 to New Connection Project to research strategic, partnership and funding opportunities to secure the work of the organisation; £8,500 to Sefton Women's and Children's Aid towards a feasibility study into the development of a new centre; £6,600 to Autism London to undertake strategic and development training for the management committee and staff; £3,440 to Howard League for Penal Reform to establish a network of organisations to develop knowledge and co-ordinate work with disabled prisoners.
International – £238,948 to Pastoral and Environmental Network in the Horn of Africa towards a three-year project aiming to provide capacity building and institutional support to organisations of nomadic pastoralists in Somaliland.

FINANCES *Year* 2001 *Income* £2,150,373 *Grants* £3,473,581 *Assets* £65,547,736

TRUSTEES Nicholas Baring, Chair; Tessa Baring; Martin Findlay; Sir Crispin Tickell; Anthony Loehnis; Janet Lewis-Jones; J R Peers; Dr Ann Buchanan; R D Broadley; C J Steane; Ranjit Sondhi.

HOW TO APPLY See the guidelines for specific programmes. Note that there is no provision for 'general' applications that lie outside the foundation's specific programmes. 'Applications will only be considered if all the supporting information and the completed datasheet are sent to the foundation.'

WHO TO APPLY TO Toby Johns, Director, 60 London Wall, London EC2M 5TQ *Tel* 020 7767 1348 *Fax* 020 7767 7121
E-mail baring.foundation@uk.ing.com
Website www.baringfoundation.org.uk

CC NO 258583   **ESTABLISHED** 1969

■ The Philip Barker Charity

WHERE FUNDING CAN BE GIVEN Cheshire.

WHO CAN BENEFIT Registered charities benefiting children and young adults; carers; disabled people; and volunteers.

WHAT IS FUNDED Principally local youth organisations; medical, health, disability, welfare and educational charities.

WHAT IS NOT FUNDED Grants are only made to individuals sponsored by registered charities.

TYPE OF GRANT Principally one-off grants. Will consider contribution towards recurring costs, core costs, and projects. Funding is available for up to two years.

RANGE OF GRANTS £200–£1,000.

SAMPLE GRANTS Grant distribution was broken down as follows: young people's charitable work (£38,000), medical charities (£17,000), community/homeless families and care/welfare (£31,000) and international (£3,000).

FINANCES *Year* 2000–01 *Income* £81,000 *Grants* £90,000 *Assets* £1,518,135

TRUSTEES Mrs M G Mather; H J Partington; T R A Groves; Mrs J P E Groves; Sir Edmund Burton; Lady Burton.

HOW TO APPLY In writing to the correspondent.

WHO TO APPLY TO Mrs M G Mather, Trustee, 1a Rothesay Road, Curzon Park, Chester CH4 8AJ

CC NO 1000227   **ESTABLISHED** 1990

■ Peter Barker-Mill Memorial Charity

WHERE FUNDING CAN BE GIVEN UK, with a preference for Hampshire, including Southampton.

WHAT IS FUNDED Arts and culture, community facilities and conservation.

WHAT IS NOT FUNDED No grants to individuals.

SAMPLE GRANTS £5,000 to Red Cross Land Mines Appeal; £4,800 to Wessex Children's Hospice; £3,000 to North Kensington Community Care; £2,000 each to RNLI and Chelsea and Westminster Arts Project.

FINANCES *Year* 2000–01 *Income* £84,306

TRUSTEES C Gwyn-Evans; T Jobling; G N Knowles.

HOW TO APPLY In writing to the correspondent.

WHO TO APPLY TO Mrs Annette Todhunter, Administrator, Longdown Management Ltd, The Estate Office, Longdown, Southampton, Hampshire SO40 4UH *Tel* 023 8029 2107

CC NO 1045479   **ESTABLISHED** 1995

■ The Barnabas Charitable Trust

WHERE FUNDING CAN BE GIVEN Preference for North Derbyshire, Sheffield, Greater Manchester and some preference for Liverpool.

WHO CAN BENEFIT Individuals and organisations benefiting: unemployed people; volunteers; parents and children; one parent families; at risk groups; disabled people; and ex-offenders and those at risk of offending.

WHAT IS FUNDED Trustees will consider a wide range of community-based, including inner-city, projects. Children's education including arts education; community services; and bursaries.

WHAT IS NOT FUNDED No grants directly to individuals or for church buildings or fabric. Large UK charities, including their regional branches, are not usually supported.

TYPE OF GRANT One-off and recurrent for: core costs projects; running costs; salaries; and start-up costs. Funding is available for up to three years.

RANGE OF GRANTS £100–£10,000.

SAMPLE GRANTS £6,150 to Furnival Project, Sheffield for the community centre; £3,300 to Brook Centre – Manchester for a drop-in for homeless people; £3,195 to Kinder Children's Choir; £3,000 to Children's Society; £2,000 each to Church Youth Centre and St Wilfreds – Sheffield for a drop-in centre; £1,599 to Wash Nursery School; £1,500 to Whaley Hall Retreat for a non-denominational religious retreat; £1,400

each to Bilston Community Care and Grindleford School.

FINANCES *Year* 1999 *Income* £19,255 *Grants* £38,780 *Assets* £745,753

TRUSTEES D Harding; R L Harding; Mrs R M Harding.

HOW TO APPLY In writing to the correspondent. All applications are acknowledged on receipt, but only successful applicants are notified of the final decision.

WHO TO APPLY TO D Harding, Trustee, Gorsty Low Farm, The Wash, Chapel-en-le-Frith, High Peak SK23 0QL

CC NO 299718   **ESTABLISHED** 1988

■ The Barnabas Trust

WHERE FUNDING CAN BE GIVEN UK and overseas. Overseas projects are supported only if they are personally known by the trustees.

WHO CAN BENEFIT Organisations and individuals benefiting Christians and evangelists.

WHAT IS FUNDED Christian evangelical projects – overtly evangelical, not social, unless for a particular evangelical input. The trust will consider funding Christian theological education and outreach; missionaries and evangelicals; and Anglican and Free Church bodies.

WHAT IS NOT FUNDED 'The trust is no longer able to help with building, refurbishment or equipment for any church, since to be of any value grants need to be large.' On-going revenue costs such as salaries are not supported.

TYPE OF GRANT One-off for one year or less, for project funding.

RANGE OF GRANTS £250–£5,000.

SAMPLE GRANTS In 2000–01: £90,000 to SGM International; £12,000 to Shaftsbury Society; £8,000 to Princess Alice Hospital; £6,000 each to Medical Missionary News and Yeldall Manor; £5,000 each to Bethany Children's Trust, International Fellowship of Evangelical Students and Message to Schools Trust; £4,000 to Redcliffe College; and £3,000 each to Operation Mobilisation and Latin Link.

FINANCES *Year* 2001–02 *Income* £185,914 *Grants* £338,094 *Assets* £3,729,082

TRUSTEES N Brown; K C Griffiths, Chair; D S Helden.

HOW TO APPLY In writing to the correspondent, giving as much detail as possible, and enclosing a copy of the latest audited accounts, if applicable. The trust states: 'Much of the available funds generated by this trust are allocated to existing donees. The trustees are willing to consider new applications, providing they refer to a project which is overtly evangelical in nature.' If in doubt about whether to submit an application, please telephone the secretary to the trust for guidance. The trustees meet four times a year, or more often as required, and applications will be put before the next available meeting.

WHO TO APPLY TO Mrs Doris Edwards, Secretary, 63 Wolsey Drive, Walton-on-Thames, Surrey KT12 3BB *Tel* 01932 220622

CC NO 284511   **ESTABLISHED** 1983

■ Lord Barnby's Foundation

WHERE FUNDING CAN BE GIVEN UK.

WHO CAN BENEFIT Registered charities.

WHAT IS FUNDED The preservation of the environment; heritage; the countryside and ancient buildings, particularly the 'great Anglican cathedrals'; ex-service and service people; Polish people; welfare of horses and those who look after them; youth and other local organisations in Ashtead – Surrey, Blyth – Nottinghamshire and Bradford – Yorkshire; people who are disabled; refugees; technical education for the woolen industry.

WHAT IS NOT FUNDED No grants to individuals.

TYPE OF GRANT One-off, capital (including buildings), core costs, project, research. Funding is up to two years.

RANGE OF GRANTS Grants range from £500 – £50,000; but are generally £1,000 – £2,000.

SAMPLE GRANTS £40,000 to Therfield School; £15,000 each to Country Trust, Sherwood Rangers, and Atlantic College; £10,000 to The Textile Institute; £5,000 each to Animal Health Trust, Ashtead Rotary Club, Fairbridge, Ghurkha Welfare Trust, Langford Trust, Royal Commonwealth Society for the Blind and Volunteer Reading Help.

FINANCES *Year* 2000–01 *Income* £135,944 *Grants* £162,050 *Assets* £4,777,909

TRUSTEES Sir John Lowther; Lord Newall; Sir Michael Farquhar; Hon. George Lopes; Countess Peel.

OTHER INFORMATION Annual review of permanent lists of donations and additions or deletions at trustees' discretion. Appeals are considered three times a year in February, July and November.

HOW TO APPLY Applications will only be considered if received in writing accompanied by a set of the latest accounts. Applicants do not need to send an sae. Appeals are considered three times a year, in February, June and November.

WHO TO APPLY TO Mrs J A Lethbridge, Secretary, PO Box 71, Plymstock, Plymouth PL8 2YF

CC NO 251016   **ESTABLISHED** 1966

■ Barnes Workhouse Fund

WHERE FUNDING CAN BE GIVEN Ancient parish of Barnes only (SW13 postal district in London).

WHO CAN BENEFIT Organisations benefiting at risk groups; people with disabilities; people disadvantaged by poverty; or socially isolated people.

WHAT IS FUNDED The relief of need and sickness; the provision and support (with the object of improving of life for the said inhabitants in the interests of social welfare) of facilities for recreation or other leisure time occupation; the provision and support of educational facilities.

TYPE OF GRANT Capital (including buildings), core costs, endowments, feasibility studies, interest free loans, one-off, project, research, running costs, recurring costs, salaries and start-up costs. Funding for up to and over three years will be considered.

RANGE OF GRANTS £300–£5,500; average grant £450.

SAMPLE GRANTS £5,500 to Strathmore Centre for young offenders; £5,000 to North Barnes Citizen's Advice Bureau; £4,000 to Crossroads Care; £3,500 to Lowther Primary School; £2,500 to Women's Information & Resource Centre; £2,000 each to Ethnic Minorities Advocacy Group and Barnes Music Society; £1,600 to Power Station Youth Club; £500 each to Churches Together in Barnes Refugee Support Group and St Mary Magdalene RC Primary School.

FINANCES *Year* 2000 *Income* £214,000 *Grants* £120,000 *Assets* £5,100,000

TRUSTEES Mrs Veronica Schroter, Chair; Miss B Westmorland; Mrs A Style; Mrs F Hallett; Dr N Boheimer; G Barnett; Revd J Hawes; P Howe.

HOW TO APPLY In writing to the correspondent (no telephone calls to the office). Application forms and guidelines are available. Applications must

state clearly the extent to which any project will benefit residents of Barnes and include details of other sources of funding. Trustees meet to consider grants every two months.

WHO TO APPLY TO Jonathon Walsh, 1 Rocks Lane, Barnes, London SW13 0DE

CC NO 200103   **ESTABLISHED** 1970

■ The Barnsbury Charitable Trust

WHERE FUNDING CAN BE GIVEN UK, but no local charities outside Oxfordshire.

WHO CAN BENEFIT Charitable bodies, particularly those benefiting at risk groups, people disadvantaged by poverty and socially isolated people.

WHAT IS FUNDED The financial support of national charities in the UK and local charities in Oxfordshire in the fields of social welfare, the arts, and the environment.

WHAT IS NOT FUNDED No grants to individuals.

RANGE OF GRANTS £23–£1,000.

SAMPLE GRANTS £2,000 each to Dorchester Abbey Preservation Trust and the Oxfordshire Nature Conservation Forum. Other grants ranged from £23 to £1,000; beneficiaries included: First International, St John Ambulance, Amnesty International, Oxfordshire Army Benevolent Fund, NSPCC, Oxfordshire Common Purpose, Oxfordshire Association for the Blind, Deanery of Oxford and Gatehouse.

FINANCES *Year* 1999–2000 *Income* £34,000 *Grants* £29,000 *Assets* £152,000

TRUSTEES H L J Brunner; M R Brunner; T E Yates.

HOW TO APPLY In writing to the correspondent.

WHO TO APPLY TO H L J Brunner, Trustee, 26 Norham Road, Oxford OX2 6SF

CC NO 241383   **ESTABLISHED** 1964

■ The Barnwood House Trust

WHERE FUNDING CAN BE GIVEN Gloucestershire.

WHO CAN BENEFIT Individuals and organisations who help people, with disabilities. Carers and disabled people are given priority, as well as organisations benefiting people with Alzheimer's disease and mental illness. Organisations benefiting people with arthritis and rheumatism, head and other injuries, hearing loss, multiple sclerosis, and Parkinson's disease, stroke victims, terminally ill people, and people disadvantaged by poverty are also considered.

WHAT IS FUNDED The relief of sickness, poverty and distress affecting people with mental or nervous disorders or with serious physical infirmity or disability. Related research can be national if benefit could cover Gloucestershire.

WHAT IS NOT FUNDED Grants are only made for charitable work undertaken in Gloucestershire. The trust would not normally provide core funding to a statutory body where the public sector had a duty to provide. Grants are not normally made for delivery of health care or counselling services, for building or adapting public sector/social housing or to charities to start up or subsidise services contracted out to them by the public sector. Grants to non-disability organisations to make community buildings more accessible to people with disabilities are only considered where there is evidence of substantial need or regular usage by a large number of people with disabilities. A management charge applied to a project in order to underwrite core costs is not normally supported. Actual costs arising from a new project should be included in the project costs.

TYPE OF GRANT Research, buildings, core costs, feasibility studies, interest-free loans, project, recurring costs, salaries, start-up costs, one-off, capital, revenue and charitable loans. Funding may be given for up to three years.

RANGE OF GRANTS £100–£100,000. Larger grants mainly for research.

SAMPLE GRANTS £44,377 to Action Research for gene therapy; £43,459 to Action Research/BHT Research Training Fellowship; £43,284 to Stroke Association for clinical research at Bristol University with stroke patients; £42,683 to Motor Neurone Disease Association towards understanding the causes of motor neurone disease; £41,152 to Cambridge University for research into repair of the myelin sheath in multiple sclerosis; £33,609 to Dementia Care Trust for relief care in the home; £30,000 each to CareShare – Cirencester for core funding, and Forest of Dean Crossroads for relief care in the home for people with terminal illnesses; £28,500 to EGNHST for a nursing home education project on the care of older people with mental illness; £21,354 to Cystic Fibrosis Trust for a Phd project.

FINANCES *Year* 2001 *Income* £1,993,811 *Grants* £979,000 *Assets* £46,894,577

TRUSTEES The trust is controlled by a board of trustees (maximum 15) drawn from an elected governing council. Members of the grants committee are as follows: K D Anderson; Mrs J E Barclay, Chair; Mrs A L Cadbury; S C Fisher; Mrs S Shipway; D A Ackland; R Ashenden; J H W Davis; Mrs Cole Hann; M B Heywood; Mrs D L Hutton; R H Ker; Mrs S Parsons; Mrs J Whiteman.

HOW TO APPLY The trust advises potential applicants to ring before making an application. On a application form available from: Mrs Christine Ellson, assistant director (grants) or Mrs Gail Rodway, grants administrator, at the trust's address (Tel: 01452 611292). Applications from organisations are investigated by representatives of the trust who then make recommendations to the trustees. Trustees meet every other month. Grantmaking committees meet quarterly. For information about grants for individuals, contact the trust.

WHO TO APPLY TO Paul Guy, Director, The Manor House, 162 Barnwood Road, Gloucester GL4 7JX *Tel* 01452 614429; 01452 611292 (grant enquires) *Website* www.barnwoodhousetrust.org

CC NO 218401   **ESTABLISHED** 1792

······································

■ The Barracks Trust of Newcastle-under-Lyme

WHERE FUNDING CAN BE GIVEN The former borough of Newcastle-under-Lyme.

WHO CAN BENEFIT Organisations and, to a lesser extent, individuals.

WHAT IS FUNDED The trust's objects are as follows: (i) relief of people who are elderly or poor; (ii) relief of distress and sickness; (iii) to improve the quality of life of people in the beneficial area, by the provision and support of facilities for recreation and other leisure-time occupation; (iv) the provision and support of educational facilities.

WHAT IS NOT FUNDED No grants for the relief of public funds, or taxes, rates or other public funds.

TYPE OF GRANT One-off and recurrent grants for up to three years or more for core, capital and project support.

RANGE OF GRANTS £250 – £3,000.

SAMPLE GRANTS Previous beneficiaries included Staffordshire Housing Association Care & Repair, Salvation Army – Newcastle-under-Lyme, CVS, Peter Pan Playgroup, Mediation Advisory Services, Planet Sound Community Arts, Beaver Arts, Elim Church Luncheon Club, Wolstanton Church Regeneration Project, Newcastle Volunteer Bureau, The Lyme Trust, Salvation Army – Chesterton, Wulstan Reyelles Dance Troupe and Local Agenda 21.

FINANCES *Year* 2001–02 *Income* £45,000 *Grants* £22,000 *Assets* £128,000

TRUSTEES R C M Fyson; Mrs A Hammond; Mrs J Pyatt; N Coulton; G Bebbington; M Platt; Cllr Mrs B Cox; Cllr D Clarke.

HOW TO APPLY In writing to the correspondent. Trustees meet twice a year to consider grants, usually in March and September.

WHO TO APPLY TO Mrs D A Dimock, Hon. Secretary, Legal & Support Services, Civic Offices, Merrial Street, Newcastle-under-Lyme, Staffordshire ST5 2AG *Tel* 01782 717717

CC NO 217919   **ESTABLISHED** 1980

······································

■ The Misses Barrie Charitable Trust

WHERE FUNDING CAN BE GIVEN UK.

WHO CAN BENEFIT Registered charities.

WHAT IS FUNDED General charitable purposes.

WHAT IS NOT FUNDED No grants to individuals.

TYPE OF GRANT Mainly one-off.

RANGE OF GRANTS £500–£15,000.

SAMPLE GRANTS £15,000 to University of Dundee for research support; £5,000 to Princess Royal Trust for Carers; £4,000 to Age Concern – Edinburgh and Leith; £3,150 to Surrey Cricket Board; £3,000 each to Company of Hackney Carriage Drivers, Eden Project, Over the Wall Gang and Worcestershire County Cricket Board; £2,500 to SSAFA.

FINANCES *Year* 2001–02 *Income* £218,792 *Grants* £188,150 *Assets* £4,915,057

TRUSTEES R G Carter; R S Waddell; R S Ogg.

HOW TO APPLY In writing to the correspondent. Trustees meet four times a year.

WHO TO APPLY TO Raymond Carter, Trustee, Messrs Raymond Carter & Co, 1b Haling Road, South Croydon CR2 6HS *Tel* 020 8686 1686

CC NO 279459   **ESTABLISHED** 1979

······································

■ Barron Bell Trust and Additional Fund

WHERE FUNDING CAN BE GIVEN UK.

WHO CAN BENEFIT Bell restoration funds.

WHAT IS FUNDED Providing, installing, inspecting, repairing or maintaining carillons of bells in churches in Great Britain. The trust aims to support as many applicants as possible with sums which are an encouragement rather than any great contribution. The fund is administered within the requirements of the trust deed but also within the spirit of Emma Barron's original desires. The trustees also endeavour to support churches where there are a minimum of six bells to form the peal. The trustees are keen to support applications where there is an intention to increase the number of bells up to a minimum of six.

WHAT IS NOT FUNDED Grants are made strictly in respect of the items covered under the objects. There is a restriction that the services held in the church should be Low Church. The trustees also endeavour to support those applicants

Think carefully about every application. Is it justified?

········

307

where at least 50 per cent of the required monies have already been accumulated.

RANGE OF GRANTS £600–£4,000.

FINANCES *Year 2000 Income* £23,565 *Grants* £19,900 *Assets* £709,923

TRUSTEES I H Walrond; N D L Kidson; Mrs A G Bryant-Fenn.

HOW TO APPLY In writing to the correspondent. The trustees meet twice a year to consider applications and there is little correspondence outside these times.

WHO TO APPLY TO I H Walrond, Trustee, 71 Lower Green Road, Pembury, Tunbridge Wells, Kent TN2 4EB

CC NO 228846   **ESTABLISHED** 1925

■ Bartholomew Charitable Trust

WHERE FUNDING CAN BE GIVEN UK.

WHO CAN BENEFIT Registered charities only, for the benefit of people who are sick, disabled or terminally ill.

WHAT IS FUNDED Particularly respite care, hospices, rehabilitation centres and cancer research. Hospices are supported in preference to nursing homes.

WHAT IS NOT FUNDED No grants are made to individuals. Normally grants are not made in response to general appeals from large national charities.

RANGE OF GRANTS £75–£3,500.

SAMPLE GRANTS £3,500 to Guy's Hospital Trust; £3,000 to St Christopher's Hospice; £2,000 each to Brainwave, Camphill Foundation, John Grooms Working with the Disabled, Headway, National Head Injuries Association, Little Haven Children's Hospice and Quidenham.

FINANCES *Year 1999–2000 Grants* £20,000

TRUSTEES Julian Berry; Simon Berry; Rita Kathleen Theresa Berry.

HOW TO APPLY In writing to the correspondent, or via e-mail. No telephone calls will be accepted. This entry was not confirmed by the trust, but the information was correct according to Charity Commission files.

WHO TO APPLY TO J Berry, Trustee, Goddards Farm, Ardingly Road, Lindfield, Haywards Heath, West Sussex RH16 2QX
E-mail charity@bartholomew.co.uk

CC NO 1063797   **ESTABLISHED** 1997

■ The Bartle Family Charitable Trust

WHERE FUNDING CAN BE GIVEN Locally in Buckinghamshire, Berkshire, Hertfordshire and Oxfordshire.

WHO CAN BENEFIT Charities benefiting children with disabilities, especially those which improve the education and the quality of life of the children.

WHAT IS FUNDED Children with disabilities or illness, and those who are disadvantaged. The trustees are more biased to the smaller, less well-known charities with few resources. However, national charities will not be ruled out if the request meets the interest of the trustees. Special consideration is also given to local charities and those where the trustees have a personal interest. With some local charities the trust is building an ongoing relationship.

WHAT IS NOT FUNDED No grants to individuals or to local charities not in the counties listed above.

TYPE OF GRANT Capital (including buildings) and project, usually on a one-off basis. Funding may be given for up to two years.

RANGE OF GRANTS Grants up to £5,000. Larger grants might be considered in exceptional circumstances.

SAMPLE GRANTS £4,000 to Yeldall Manor; £3,600 to SENSE; £3,000 each to NCH Action for Children – The Aylesbury Project, Starlight Children's Foundation and REACT; £2,500 to Make-a-Wish Foundation UK; £2,000 each to Children's Centre Fund, Jessie's Fund, Ataxia-Telangiectasie Society, PACE, Iain Rennie Hospice at Home and Martin House.

FINANCES *Year 2000 Income* £4,600 *Grants* £53,000 *Assets* £217,000

TRUSTEES John Bartle; Mrs Pat Bartle; Mrs Juliet Wraith; Mrs Sarah Walters; Jeremy Blakeley.

HOW TO APPLY In writing to the correspondent, giving details of the particular project area that you want to be considered. Applications are considered in February, May, August and November.

WHO TO APPLY TO Mrs P A Bartle, Trustee, Woodland, 214 Amersham Road, Hazlemere, High Wycombe, Buckinghamshire HP15 7QT *Tel* 01494 521704 *Fax* 01494 558194

CC NO 1069927   **ESTABLISHED** 1998

■ The Bartlett Taylor Charitable Trust

WHERE FUNDING CAN BE GIVEN Preference for Oxfordshire.

WHO CAN BENEFIT Registered charities.

WHAT IS FUNDED General charitable purposes, with grants given in the following catagories: (a) international charities; (b) UK national charities – medical; UK national charities – educational; (c) local organisations – community projects; local organisations – medical; Local organisations – other; (d) individuals – educational; individuals – relief.

RANGE OF GRANTS £35–£5,000.

FINANCES *Year 2001–02 Income* £53,797 *Grants* £50,793 *Assets* £1,559,727

TRUSTEES I O Welch; Mrs B Cook; R Bartlett; P A Burchett; Mrs R Warmer; J W Dingle.

HOW TO APPLY In writing to the correspondent. Trustees meet bi-monthly.

WHO TO APPLY TO I O Welch, Trustee, 24 Church Green, Witney, Oxfordshire OX8 6AT *Tel* 01993 703941 *Fax* 01993 776 071

CC NO 285249   **ESTABLISHED** 1982

■ The Paul Bassham Charitable Trust

WHERE FUNDING CAN BE GIVEN UK, mainly Norfolk.

WHO CAN BENEFIT UK registered charities.

WHAT IS FUNDED General charitable purposes. Preference given to Norfolk charitable causes; if funds permit, other charities with national coverage will be considered.

WHAT IS NOT FUNDED Grant payments will not be made directly to individuals.

SAMPLE GRANTS £50,000 to Norwich Cathedral Millennium Appeal; £11,750 each to National Trust, Great Yarmouth & Waveney MIND and The Great Hospital. All other listed grants were for varying amounts between £1,000 and £5,000; beneficiaries included Age Concern, Motability, Norwich Community Church, Peper Harow Foundation, Scope and Sense.

FINANCES *Year 2000–01 Income* £126,119 *Grants* £162,150 *Assets* £3,140,150

TRUSTEES R Lovett; R J Jacob.

HOW TO APPLY In writing to the correspondent. Telephone enquiries are not invited because of administrative costs. 'The trustees meet quarterly (March, June, September, December) to consider general applications although additional meetings or discussions are held where major projects are the subject of an application or where there is some degree of urgency.'

WHO TO APPLY TO R Lovett, Trustee, Howes Percival, The Guildyard, 51 Colegate, Norwich NR3 1DD

CC NO 266842 **ESTABLISHED** 1973

■ The Batchworth Trust

WHERE FUNDING CAN BE GIVEN Worldwide.

WHO CAN BENEFIT Major UK and international charities.

WHAT IS FUNDED General charitable purposes.

WHAT IS NOT FUNDED No applications from individuals can be considered.

RANGE OF GRANTS £2,000–£10,000.

SAMPLE GRANTS £15,000 to International Red Cross; £1,000 each to Alzheimer's Society, Médicins Sans Frontières, New Hall College, Prisoners of Conscience, RNID, Restore, Royal Commonwealth Society for the Blind and Schizophrenia Research; £750 to Farm Africa.

FINANCES *Year* 2001–02 *Income* £2,527,304 *Grants* £215,000 *Assets* £7,905,089

TRUSTEES Lockwell Trustees Ltd.

HOW TO APPLY In writing to the correspondent. An sae should be included if a reply is required.

WHO TO APPLY TO M R Neve, Administrative Executive, 33–35 Bell Street, Reigate, Surrey RH2 7AW *Tel* 01737 221311

CC NO 245061 **ESTABLISHED** 1965

■ The Bates Charitable Trust

WHERE FUNDING CAN BE GIVEN UK.

WHO CAN BENEFIT Registered charities benefiting the Church of England, at risk groups, people disadvantaged by poverty and socially isolated people.

WHAT IS FUNDED A wide range of humanitarian causes, with particular regard to work which stands within the evangelical tradition of the Church of England.

WHAT IS NOT FUNDED No donations to individuals.

RANGE OF GRANTS £100–£2,500.

SAMPLE GRANTS In 1998–99: £8,000 in four grants to St Nicholas Church, Allestree; £1,000 to DEC Kosova Appeal; £750 each to Children's Aid Direct and Sue Ryder Foundation; £500 each to Blond McIndoe Medical Research, Christchurch Centre, Ex-Services Housing, National Opera Studio, Project Trust and West London Mission.

FINANCES *Year* 2001–02 *Income* £22,000

TRUSTEES Mrs A L Bates; W F Bates; J H Bates; D L Hohnen.

HOW TO APPLY In writing to the correspondent.

WHO TO APPLY TO D L Hohnen, Trustee, Cedars Lodge, Church Road, Windlesham, Surrey GU20 6BL

CC NO 280602 **ESTABLISHED** 1980

■ The Bay Tree Charitable Trust

WHERE FUNDING CAN BE GIVEN UK and overseas.

WHAT IS FUNDED Development work.

WHAT IS NOT FUNDED No grants to individuals.

RANGE OF GRANTS £10,000–£56,250.

SAMPLE GRANTS £56,000 to Crusaid; £25,000 each to Tree Aid and Wateraid; £20,000 to Brtish

Red Cross; £19,000 to Fair Trial Abroad; £10,000 to Save the Children.

FINANCES *Year* 2001 *Income* £105,602 *Grants* £155,000 *Assets* £2,930,492

TRUSTEES I M P Benton; Miss E L Benton; P H Benton.

HOW TO APPLY In writing to the correspondent. No acknowledgements will be made to unsuccessful applications.

WHO TO APPLY TO c/o Payne Hicks Beach, 10 New Square, London WC2A 3QG

CC NO 1044091 **ESTABLISHED** 1994

■ The Dorothy Bayles Trust

WHERE FUNDING CAN BE GIVEN Lincolnshire.

WHO CAN BENEFIT Organisations benefiting Christians.

WHAT IS FUNDED Christian causes and general charitable purposes.

WHAT IS NOT FUNDED Animal and bird welfare societies are not supported.

RANGE OF GRANTS £100–£2,000.

FINANCES *Year* 1999 *Income* £22,924 *Grants* £23,000 *Assets* £775

TRUSTEES M Brant; Mrs C Wheeldon; J B Strawson; H Strawson; R M B Strawson; Mrs A D V F Campbell.

HOW TO APPLY In writing to the correspondent; there are no application forms. The trust stated that no new applications can be considered until October 2007.

WHO TO APPLY TO M Strawson, Secretary, Lings Farmhouse, Croxby, Market Rasen LN7 6BN *Tel* 01472 371561

CC NO 271259 **ESTABLISHED** 1976

■ D H & L H Baylin Charitable Trust

WHERE FUNDING CAN BE GIVEN UK.

WHAT IS FUNDED General charitable purposes.

FINANCES *Year* 1999–2000 *Income* £26,000 *Grants* £28,000 *Assets* £1,800

TRUSTEES D M Baylin; L H Baylin.

HOW TO APPLY In writing to the correspondent.

WHO TO APPLY TO Arram Berlyn Gardner, Holborn Hall, 100 Gray's Inn Road, London WC1X 8BY *Tel* 020 7400 6000 *Fax* 020 7400 6001

CC NO 298708 **ESTABLISHED** 1988

■ The Louis Baylis (Maidenhead Advertiser) Charitable Trust

WHERE FUNDING CAN BE GIVEN Maidenhead and district.

WHO CAN BENEFIT General charitable purposes.

WHAT IS FUNDED The trust states that it was 'established to safeguard the newspaper, The Maidenhead Advertiser, from all outside influence and provide for the newspaper's continuance as part of the civic and social life of the community it serves'. Grants can be given towards any charitable purpose, and from the grants list it appears that all the organisations supported were within the area covered by the newspaper.

SAMPLE GRANTS £26,000 Holyport Manor School; £9,500 People to Places; £5,000 Wrexham Park Heart Trust; £2,500 Salvation Army; and £2,000 Maidenhead CAB.

FINANCES *Year* 1999–2000 *Income* £62,000 *Grants* £62,000 *Assets* £146,000

HOW TO APPLY In writing to the correspondent. The trustees meet twice a year in June and October.
WHO TO APPLY TO A G Baylis, Secretary, Newspaper House, 48 Bell Street, Maidenhead, Berkshire SL6 1HX
CC NO 210533   **ESTABLISHED** 1962

■ The BBC Children in Need Appeal

WHERE FUNDING CAN BE GIVEN UK.
WHO CAN BENEFIT Non-profit making groups and organisations benefiting children in the UK.
WHAT IS FUNDED Practical and lasting support for children disadvantaged by poverty, disability, illness, abuse and neglect.
WHAT IS NOT FUNDED The appeal does not consider applications from private individuals or the friends or families of individual children. In addition, grants will not be given for trips and projects abroad; medical treatment or medical research; unspecified expenditure; deficit funding or repayment of loans; projects which take place before applications can be processed (this takes up to five months from the closing dates); projects which are unable to start within 12 months; distribution to another/other organisation(s); general appeals and endowment funds; the relief of statutory responsibilities.
TYPE OF GRANT Capital, revenue and recurring for up to three years.
RANGE OF GRANTS No fixed upper or lower limit; in practice very few grants over £25,000 a year.
SAMPLE GRANTS £700,000 to Family Welfare Association to provide emergency grants for individual children in need throughout the UK; £152,000 to Circles network over three years for a salary and running costs; £129,000 to NSPCC over three years for a volunteer coordinator; £110,000 to Encephalitis Support Group, North Yorkshire for the recruitment and salary of a family support coordinator plus associated costs; £98,000 to WRVS Glasgow for a salary and individual small grants; £93,000 to Children's Liver Disease foundation for salary costs; £92,000 to Agency for Culture and Change management over three years for a salary and running costs; £90,000 to LOOK for running costs including a salary; £88,808 to National Pyramid Trust for the continued funding of the South West scheme; £85,177 to Women's Aid Delyn over three years for the salary of a child and family worker plus a contribution towards running costs.
FINANCES *Year* 2001–02 *Income* £28,301,266 *Grants* £25,219,523 *Assets* £14,539,305
TRUSTEES Sir Robert Smith, Chair; Will Day; Simon Milner; Diane Louise Jordan; Michelle Kershaw; Neena Mahal; Liz Rylatt; Terry Wogan; Tim Cook; Lorraine Heggessy; Andy Duncan; Yogesh Chauhan; Steve Wood.
HOW TO APPLY Straightforward and excellent application forms and guidelines are available from the website or from the appeal at the following addresses: England: PO Box 76, London W3 6FS. Tel: 020 8576 7788; Textphone: 020 8576 4558; Scotland: BBC Edinburgh, The Tun, Holyrood Road, Edinburgh EH8 8JF. Tel: 0131 248 4225; Wales: Broadcasting House, Llandaff, Cardiff CF5 2YQ, Tel: 029 2032 2383; Northern Ireland: Broadcasting House, Ormeau Avenue, Belfast BT2 8HQ. Tel: 028 9033 8221. There are two closing dates for applications – 30 November and 30 March. Organisations may submit only one application and may apply to only one of these dates. Applicants should allow up to five months after each closing date for notification of a decision. (For summer projects applications must be submitted by the November closing date or will be rejected because they cannot be processed in time.)
WHO TO APPLY TO Martina Milburn, Director, PO Box 76, London W3 6FS *Tel* 020 8576 7788 *Fax* 020 8576 8887 *E-mail* pudsey@bbc.co.uk *Website* www.bbc.co.uk/pudsey
CC NO 802052   **ESTABLISHED** 1989

■ BBC Radio Cambridgeshire – Trustline

WHERE FUNDING CAN BE GIVEN Cambridgeshire only.
WHO CAN BENEFIT Groups and organisations benefiting young, elderly, disadvantaged and disabled people.
WHAT IS FUNDED Particularly charities working in the fields of: residential facilities and services; infrastructure, support and development; hospices and various community services.
WHAT IS NOT FUNDED No grants to individuals.
TYPE OF GRANT Local charities to buy equipment to benefit the largest number of people. Core costs, one-off, project, running costs and start-up costs. Funding for up to three years will be considered.
RANGE OF GRANTS £100–£1,000.
SAMPLE GRANTS In 2000: £2,500 to Cambs City Mayor's Trip for a pensioners' outing; £1,000 each to Association of Wheelchair Children for wheelchairs in Cambridgeshire, and Peterborough Shopmobility for a wheelchair in a car park; £680 to Cambridge OnLine City Pathways Project for disabled access; £600 each to Huntingdonshire Society for the Blind for new equipment, Life Education Centres for set-up costs, and Peterborough & District Talking Newspaper Association for new recording equipment; £500 each to Addenbrookes Sick Children's Trust towards accommodation for families of children with cancer, Age Concern Peterborough for security in homes, and Friends of Samuel Pepys School for music therapy sessions.
FINANCES *Year* 2001 *Income* £45,000 *Grants* £41,000
TRUSTEES James Rone, Archdeacon of Wisbech; Michael J Marshall.
OTHER INFORMATION Only charities/groups in Cambridgeshire need apply.
HOW TO APPLY In writing to the address below in January of each year. Grants allocated in July of each year. Applicants are advised that no initial telephone call is welcome. There is an application form and guidelines are issued. Sae helpful.
WHO TO APPLY TO Mrs Sylvia Green, Administrator, BBC Radio Cambridgeshire, 104 Hills Road, Cambridge CB2 1LD *Tel* 01223 259696 *Fax* 01223 589850 *E-mail* sylvia.green@bbc.co.uk *Website* www.bbc.co.uk/Radio cambridgeshire
CC NO 297555   **ESTABLISHED** 1987

■ The BBC Radio Lincolnshire Charity Trust

WHERE FUNDING CAN BE GIVEN Lincolnshire.
WHO CAN BENEFIT Registered charities.
WHAT IS FUNDED Provision of grant aid for capital items which will benefit people resident in Lincolnshire.
WHAT IS NOT FUNDED No grants to individuals or for charities outside Lincolnshire.
TYPE OF GRANT Capital and one-off funding for one year or less.
SAMPLE GRANTS £40,000 to St Barnabas Hospice Trust for refurbishment of four bedded rooms.
FINANCES Year 1998–99 Income £40,000 Grants £40,000
TRUSTEES John Thomas; David Armes; William Warwick; Betty Joshi.
HOW TO APPLY On a form available from the correspondent.
WHO TO APPLY TO Wendy Trotter, BBC Radio Lincolnshire, PO Box 219, Newport, Lincoln LN1 3XY Tel 01522 511411 Fax 01522 511726 E-mail wendy.trotter@bbc.co.uk
CC NO 1052162   **ESTABLISHED** 1996

■ The Beacon Centre for the Blind

WHERE FUNDING CAN BE GIVEN The boroughs of Dudley, Sandwell and Wolverhampton, and part of the south Staffordshire District Council area.
WHO CAN BENEFIT Organisations and individuals.
WHAT IS FUNDED Day centres, residential homes, employment schemes, socials and outings, holidays, and talking books and newspapers for the benefit of blind and partially sighted people.
TYPE OF GRANT One-off.
FINANCES Year 1999–2000 Income £3,700,000 Grants £92,000 Assets £4,900,000
HOW TO APPLY In writing to the correspondent.
WHO TO APPLY TO The Chief Executive, Wolverhampton Road East, Wolverhampton WV4 6AZ Tel 01902 880111 Fax 01902 671889 E-mail enquiries@beacon4blind.co.uk Website www.beacon4blind.co.uk
CC NO 216092   **ESTABLISHED** 1961

■ The Beacon Trust

WHERE FUNDING CAN BE GIVEN Mainly UK, but also some overseas (usually in the British Commonwealth) and Spain and Portugal.
WHO CAN BENEFIT Organisations benefiting evangelical Protestants, including Baptists, Anglican and Methodists. Funding is usually given to headquarters organisations.
WHAT IS FUNDED Evangelical Protestant causes.
WHAT IS NOT FUNDED Applications from individuals are not considered.
TYPE OF GRANT One-off grants for development funding. Longer-term grants may be considered.
SAMPLE GRANTS £22,000 to Cascadas.
FINANCES Year 1999–2000 Income £59,828 Grants £56,759 Assets £674,875
TRUSTEES Mrs D J Spink; Miss J M Spink; M Spink.
HOW TO APPLY In writing to the correspondent. The trustees normally meet once a year in December and all applications are generally dealt with at that meeting.
WHO TO APPLY TO D J Stacey, 80 Heath Road, Petersfield, Hampshire GU31 4EL
CC NO 230087   **ESTABLISHED** 1963

■ Bear Mordechai Ltd

WHERE FUNDING CAN BE GIVEN Worldwide.
WHO CAN BENEFIT Individuals, small local projects and national organisations benefiting Jewish people.
WHAT IS FUNDED Jewish charities.
TYPE OF GRANT Recurring costs and core costs will be considered.
SAMPLE GRANTS £219,000 to Kollel Bear Mordechy; £130,700 to Agudat Yad Yemin Jerusalem; £88,000 to Kolel Shomrei Hachomoth; £47,710 to Kolel Ohel Elimelech; £25,934 to Almat Limited; £16,000 to Kollel Rabinov; £14,700 to Yedokoh Bechol; £12,500 to Yeshivo Horomo Talmudical College; £12,000 to Ravchested Trust; £10,000 to Orthodox Council of Jerusalem Ltd.
FINANCES Year 2000–01 Income £382,793 Grants £619,064 Assets £832,703
TRUSTEES Y Benedikt; C Benedikt; E S Benedikt.
HOW TO APPLY In writing to the correspondent.
WHO TO APPLY TO Mrs Leah Benedikt, Secretary, 136 Holmleigh Road, London N16 5PY
CC NO 286806   **ESTABLISHED** 1982

■ The Bearder Charity

WHERE FUNDING CAN BE GIVEN Calderdale.
WHO CAN BENEFIT Registered charities and individuals.
WHAT IS FUNDED General charitable purposes, particularly the arts, infrastructure support and development, education and training, and community facilities and services.
FINANCES Year 1999 Income £80,000 Grants £80,000 Assets £3,000,000
TRUSTEES V Shepherd; P W Townend; T Simpson; R D Smithies; Mrs S Gee; L Smith.
HOW TO APPLY In writing to the correspondent.
WHO TO APPLY TO V Shepherd, Secretary, Martin Mill, Walker Lane, Hebden Bridge, West Yorkshire HX7 8SJ Tel 01422 847078 E-mail vivshep@aol.com
CC NO 1010529   **ESTABLISHED** 1992

■ The James Beattie Charitable Trust

WHERE FUNDING CAN BE GIVEN Wolverhampton area.
WHO CAN BENEFIT Local projects and organisations benefiting the people of Wolverhampton.
WHAT IS FUNDED General charitable purposes including accommodation and housing; community development, support to voluntary and community organisations; and social care professional bodies. Also health; conservation and the environment; education; community facilities and services; dance groups and orchestras; volunteer bureaux; Christian education and churches; schools; and youth projects such as scouts and air training corps may be considered.
WHAT IS NOT FUNDED No grants to individuals, organisations outside the West Midlands, or exclusive organisations (e.g. all-white or all-Asian groups).
TYPE OF GRANT Grants awarded for capital including buildings, core costs, project research, running costs, salaries and start-up costs. Grants may be one-off or recurring and funding for a single project may be available for less than one year to more than three.
RANGE OF GRANTS Typical £500.
SAMPLE GRANTS £15,000 to James Beattie House Appeal; £12,000 to Bromford Carinthia Housing

Think carefully about every application. Is it justified?

311

Association; £7,000 to Wolverhampton Grammar School; £5,000 each to Air Bridge Association, Fairbridge, Lichfield Cathedral Trust, Mount Olive Apostolic Church, Orbis, Parkinson Trust Fund, and Urban Adventure Wolverhampton Support.

FINANCES *Year* 1998–99 *Income* £141,829 *Grants* £144,784 *Assets* £3,452,891

TRUSTEES Mrs J V Redshaw; M W Redshaw; K Dolman; Mrs S J Norbury.

HOW TO APPLY In writing to the correspondent, including accounts.

WHO TO APPLY TO Mrs J V Redshaw, Trustee, PO Box 12, Bridgnorth, Shropshire WV15 5LQ

CC NO 265654   **ESTABLISHED** 1961

■ The Rt Hon Else Countess Beauchamp Deceased Charitable Trust

WHERE FUNDING CAN BE GIVEN Herefordshire and Worcestershire.

WHO CAN BENEFIT Charities in the beneficial area.

WHAT IS FUNDED The preservation of buildings and rural scenery. Arts and arts facilities are also considered.

WHAT IS NOT FUNDED No grants to individuals or for endowments.

FINANCES *Year* 2001–02 *Income* £160,000 *Grants* £7,000 *Assets* £3,000,000

TRUSTEES John de la Cour; Diana Johnson; S Driver White.

OTHER INFORMATION The trust's funds are used overwhelmingly to support the Elmley Foundation, which the trustees also control.

HOW TO APPLY In writing to the correspondent. Grants are given only at the trustees' instigation. Also note the comments above.

WHO TO APPLY TO J de la Cour, Trustee, West Aish, Morchard Bishop, Crediton, Devon EX17 6RX *Tel* 01363 877433 *Fax* 01363 877433

CC NO 1042208   **ESTABLISHED** 1994

■ The Beaufort House Trust

WHERE FUNDING CAN BE GIVEN UK.

WHO CAN BENEFIT Organisations benefiting Christians, children and young adults.

WHAT IS FUNDED To support schools, colleges, universities or other charitable bodies engaged in the advancement, promotion and furtherance of education, religion or any other charitable purposes.

WHAT IS NOT FUNDED No grants are made to organisations with political associations, national charities or individuals.

TYPE OF GRANT Some recurring, majority one-off.

RANGE OF GRANTS £100–£5,000.

SAMPLE GRANTS £20,000 to Be Your Best Foundation – Sussex; £5,000 to Queen Margaret School – York; £2,000 to Worshipful Company of Insurers; £1,500 each to St John's College – Nottingham and St Williams Foundation – York; £500 each to Diocese of Southwark, Edgehill Theological College – Belfast and St Martin's School Classroom Appeal – Newbury; £250 each to Deanery Church of England High School – Wigan and St Paul's C of E Primary School – Winchmore Hill.

FINANCES *Year* 2001 *Income* £676,495 *Grants* £78,955 *Assets* £111,117

TRUSTEES Sir Alan McLintock; M R Cornwall-Jones; B V Day; Viscount Churchill; Revd D G Shelgrove; W H Yates; Mrs S Homersham; N Assheton.

HOW TO APPLY In writing to the correspondent detailing: charity number; the objectives of the charity; the appeal target; how the funds are to be utilised; funds raised to date; and previous support received from the trust. If available the application should be accompanied by supporting literature and an annual report.

WHO TO APPLY TO Mrs R J Hall, Company Secretary, Beaufort House, Brunswick Road, Gloucester GL1 1JZ *Tel* 01452 528533 *Website* www.allchurches.co.uk

CC NO 286606   **ESTABLISHED** 1983

■ Beauland Ltd

WHERE FUNDING CAN BE GIVEN Worldwide, possibly with a preference for the Manchester area.

WHO CAN BENEFIT To benefit Jewish people and people who are sick.

WHAT IS FUNDED Healthcare charities and exclusively Jewish projects are supported.

SAMPLE GRANTS £29,000 to Chesed L'Yisroel; £17,350 to Torah V'emunah Charitable Trust; £15,000 to Tomchei Shaarei Zion; £12,625 to Beis Yakov Seminary; £10,675 to Jewish High School; £10,200 to Beis Yakov Institutions; £10,000 to Yeshivas Nitra; £8,770 to Bnos Yisovel School; £5,000 each to Bnei Emes, Kehilla Centre, MALA and yeshivas Ohel Shimon.

FINANCES *Year* 2000–01 *Income* £205,371 *Grants* £196,102 *Assets* £1,355,666

TRUSTEES F Neuman; H Neuman; M Friedlander; H Roseman; J Bleir; R Delange; M Neuman; P Neuman; E Neuman; E Henry.

HOW TO APPLY In writing to the correspondent.

WHO TO APPLY TO The Trustees, 4 Cheltenham Crescent, Salford M7 4FP

CC NO 511374   **ESTABLISHED** 1981

■ The Beaurepaire Trust

WHERE FUNDING CAN BE GIVEN UK.

WHO CAN BENEFIT Charitable organisations.

WHAT IS FUNDED Grants to relieve poverty, advance education, assist people with disabilities, and relieve suffering and sickness.

SAMPLE GRANTS £12,000 to Park Atwood Clinic; £8,000 to British Humanitarian Aid; £5,000 to Human Values Foundation; £2,000 to Sri Sathya Sai Organisation (Trinidad & Tobago); £1,030 to OUDCE (Oxford University Department of Continuing Education); £1,000 to Nuffield Hospitals; £585 to St Charles Catholic Sixth Form College; £500 each to Whitechapel Mission, Sri Sathya Sai Heart Hospital, and REACT.

FINANCES *Year* 2001–02 *Income* £13,000 *Grants* £34,000 *Assets* £198,000

TRUSTEES L J Ralli; Mrs J P Ralli; Mrs Doggart.

HOW TO APPLY In writing to the correspondent, but please note, in July 2001 the trust stated 'the funds available are fully committed for the next five years'.

WHO TO APPLY TO L J Ralli, Trustee, 14 Oxford Square, London W2 2PB

CC NO 248812   **ESTABLISHED** 1966

■ The Beaverbrook Foundation

WHERE FUNDING CAN BE GIVEN UK and Canada.
WHO CAN BENEFIT Mainly headquarters organisations or national charities.
WHAT IS FUNDED General charitable purposes.
WHAT IS NOT FUNDED Only registered charities are supported.
TYPE OF GRANT One-off.
FINANCES *Year* 1999–2000 *Income* £519,328 *Grants* £96,000 *Assets* £18,000,000
TRUSTEES Lord Beaverbrook, Chair; Lady Beaverbrook; Lady Aitken; T M Aitken; Laura Levi; J E A Kidd; M F Aitken.
HOW TO APPLY In writing to the correspondent with an sae. Trustees meet in May and November.
WHO TO APPLY TO Jane Ford, General Secretary, 11 Old Queen Street, London SW1H 9JA *Tel* 020 7222 7474 *Fax* 020 7222 2198 *Website* www.beaverbrookfoundation.org
CC NO 310003   **ESTABLISHED** 1954

■ The Beccles Town Lands Charity

WHERE FUNDING CAN BE GIVEN Beccles.
WHO CAN BENEFIT Organisations and individuals in Beccles.
WHAT IS FUNDED General charitable purposes.
WHAT IS NOT FUNDED Applications from outside of, or not to the benefit of, Beccles and its inhabitants.
FINANCES *Year* 1998–99 *Income* £140,000 *Grants* £100,000 *Assets* £3,200,000
TRUSTEES Miss C M Skippings, Chair; R F H Boyce; R W Garrood; G D Hickman; D L Hipperson; J I Langeskov; K J Leggett; M P Pitkin; C J Savage; R Seppings.
HOW TO APPLY In writing to the correspondent.
WHO TO APPLY TO R W Peck, Secretary, Leman House, Ballygate, Beccles, Suffolk NR34 9ND
CC NO 210714

■ The Becker Family Charitable Trust

WHERE FUNDING CAN BE GIVEN UK and overseas.
WHO CAN BENEFIT Registered charities.
WHAT IS FUNDED General charitable purposes, particularly orthodox Jewish organisations.
FINANCES *Year* 1999–2000 *Income* £41,000 *Grants* £56,000 *Assets* £21,000
TRUSTEES A Becker; L Becker; Ms R Becker; Ms D Fried; C Guttentag.
HOW TO APPLY In writing to the correspondent. However, the trust states that it is fully committed at the moment and no further applications will be considered until further notice.
WHO TO APPLY TO L Becker, Trustee, 7 Riverside Drive, Golders Green Road, London NW11 9PU
CC NO 1047968   **ESTABLISHED** 1995

■ The Becketts & Sargeants Educational Foundation

WHERE FUNDING CAN BE GIVEN The borough of Northampton.
WHO CAN BENEFIT Church schools in the borough, and individuals under 25 years of age and in need of financial assistance, and either a resident in the borough or attending schools or full-time courses of education at any further education establishment in the borough, or a former pupil of All Saints Middle School for at least two years.
WHAT IS NOT FUNDED No grants are given for part-time courses.
TYPE OF GRANT £100–£1,000 plus.
SAMPLE GRANTS In 1998: £15,561 to All Saints Middle School; £7,500 to All Saints Choir Tour; £5,000 to Northamptonshire County Cricket School; £3,719 to Friends of All Saints Music Nurture Programme; £1,000 to St James Middle School; £515 to Billing Brook School; £420 to St Andrew's Pathfinders; £392 to Greenfield School.
FINANCES *Year* 2001 *Income* £163,598
TRUSTEES J R Dove; Revd Simon Godfrey; F A York; Mrs L A Mayne.
HOW TO APPLY On a form available from the correspondent. Applications are considered four times a year, usually in February/March, May, September and December.
WHO TO APPLY TO Mrs G R Evans, Grants Sub-committee Clerk, Hewitson Becke & Shaw, 7 Spencer Parade, Northampton NN1 5AB *Tel* 01604 233233 *Fax* 01604 231053 *E-mail* gillevans@hewitsons.com
CC NO 309766   **ESTABLISHED** 1986

■ The John Beckwith Charitable Trust

WHERE FUNDING CAN BE GIVEN UK and overseas.
WHO CAN BENEFIT Registered charities.
WHAT IS FUNDED General charitable purposes with a preference for sports programmes for young people; education; children's charities; cancer charities; and charities involved with overseas aid.
TYPE OF GRANT Capital, one-off and recurring.
RANGE OF GRANTS £100–£252,000.
SAMPLE GRANTS £128,000 to Youth Sport Trust; £125,000 to Institute of Sport, Loughborough University; £56,000 to Royal Opera House Development Trust; £37,000 to Harrow Development Trust; £25,000 to Colon Cancer Care; £5,000 each to Helen Rollason Cancer Care Centre, Leukaemia Research Fund and Release; £4,000 to National Literacy Trust.
FINANCES *Year* 2000–01 *Income* £1,067,000 *Grants* £474,000
TRUSTEES J L Beckwith; H M Beckwith; C M Meech.
HOW TO APPLY To the correspondent in writing.
WHO TO APPLY TO Irene Crapnell, Administrator, Pacific Investments, 124 Sloane Street, London SW1X 9BW *Tel* 020 8941 7896
CC NO 800276   **ESTABLISHED** 1987

■ The Peter Beckwith Charitable Trust

WHERE FUNDING CAN BE GIVEN UK.
WHO CAN BENEFIT Institutions and registered charities benefiting at risk groups, people disadvantaged by poverty and socially isolated people.
WHAT IS FUNDED A broad range of medical and welfare charities.
FINANCES *Year* 2000–01 *Income* £137,239 *Grants* £121,477 *Assets* £84,300
TRUSTEES P M Beckwith; Mrs P Beckwith; Mrs A Peppiatt.
HOW TO APPLY In writing to the correspondent.
WHO TO APPLY TO P M Beckwith, Trustee, Hill Place House, 55a High Street, Wimbledon Village, London SW19 5BA *Tel* 020 8944 1288
CC NO 802113   **ESTABLISHED** 1989

■ The Bedford Charity (The Harpur Trust)

WHERE FUNDING CAN BE GIVEN The borough of Bedford.

WHO CAN BENEFIT Community groups, schools, individuals (under education object), and organisations. Particularly children and young adults, people with additional support needs, older people, and people disadvantaged by poverty.

WHAT IS FUNDED The promotion of education; the relief of people who are sick or in need, hardship or distress; the provision in the interest of social welfare of facilities for recreation and other leisure-time occupations.

WHAT IS NOT FUNDED No grants to organisations or individuals outside the borough of Bedford, unless the organisation supports a significant proportion of residents of the borough.

TYPE OF GRANT Capital, revenue, salaries, running costs. The very great majority of grant giving is targeted at organisations.

RANGE OF GRANTS £20–£400,000 in the last two years.

SAMPLE GRANTS £30,000 to Children's University; £25,000 each to an Education Action Zone (EAZ) in the Bedford area, the EAZ adminstered Frontier's Club, and The Bedford Players Trust initiated performance and rehearsal facility/community venue at Bradgate Road; £24,707 to Youth Action Bedfordshire; £20,160 to the Volunteer Bureau; £17,800 (each year for three years) for a family support manager at Spurgeon's Child Care; £15,100 to a women's refuge; £15,000 each to Bedford Community Arts, and Young People's Outreach by Alcohol Services for the Community; four awards of £10,000 each including that to Stagsden Village Hall.

FINANCES *Year* 2001–02 *Income* £3,050,000 *Grants* £638,737 *Assets* £103,610,000

TRUSTEES The governing body consists of four university nominations; the nominees of the teaching staff and parents of the trust's four schools; ten co-opted trustees; and two nominees each of Bedford Borough Council and Bedfordshire County Council. Additional memebers with specific skills and experience are co-opted onto the grants committee.

OTHER INFORMATION Website went live in early 2003.

HOW TO APPLY Application forms are available from the trust. They encourage initial telephone enquiries and preliminary proposal letters. Trustees meet throughout the year. Guidance will be provided on the timescales for decision.

WHO TO APPLY TO The Community Grants Executive, Princetown Court, Pilgrim Centre, Brickhill Drive, Bedford MK41 7PZ *Tel* 01234 369500 *Fax* 01234 369505 *E-mail* grants@harpur-trust.org.uk *Website* www.bedfordcharity.org.uk

CC NO 204817   **ESTABLISHED** 1566

■ The Bedfordshire & Hertfordshire Historic Churches Trust

WHERE FUNDING CAN BE GIVEN Bedfordshire and Hertfordshire.

WHO CAN BENEFIT Those entrusted with the upkeep of places of active Christian worship.

WHAT IS FUNDED Work to ensure that places of active Christian worship are maintained in a structurally sound and weatherproof condition.

WHAT IS NOT FUNDED No grants to individuals.

TYPE OF GRANT One-off and buildings. Funding may be given for one year or less.

RANGE OF GRANTS £1,500–£4,000. Average grant £3,000.

SAMPLE GRANTS £4,000 each to St Martins – Knebworth for roof repairs and St Mary the Virgin – Walkern for stone repairs and pointing; £3,000 to St Mary – Shephall towards reroofing of nave; and £2,500 each to St Catherine – Sacombe for flint work on tower, Leaside URC & Methodist Church – Ware for stonework and roof repairs, and to St Giles – Wyddial for roof and window repairs.

FINANCES *Year* 2000–01 *Income* £100,000 *Grants* £37,000

TRUSTEES P F D Lepper; S Y C Farmbrough; R H Tomlins; Dr C P Green; P A Lomax; A J Philpott; S A Russell; A A I Jenkins.

HOW TO APPLY In writing to the correspondent.

WHO TO APPLY TO S A Russell, Trustee, Wychbrook, 31 Ivel Gardens, Biggleswade, Bedfordshire SG18 0AN *Tel* 01767 314513

CC NO 1005697   **ESTABLISHED** 1991

■ R J Beecham 1981 Charitable Trust

WHERE FUNDING CAN BE GIVEN UK.

WHO CAN BENEFIT Registered charities.

WHAT IS FUNDED General charitable purposes, with some preference for Jewish causes.

TYPE OF GRANT One-off.

SAMPLE GRANTS £18,000 to Jewish Child's Day; £10,000 to Friends of the Hebrew University of Jerusalem; £1,000 to Toy Trust; £360 to Royal Albert Hall; £250 each to Joint Jewish Charitable Trust – Kol Nidre Appeal, Juvenile Diabetes Foundation, St Albans Cathedral Trust and St John's Wood United Synagogue; £150 to Badinage.

FINANCES *Year* 1999–2000 *Income* £117,000 *Grants* £30,000

TRUSTEES R S Beecham; Mrs C J Goldstein.

HOW TO APPLY In writing to the correspondent.

WHO TO APPLY TO The Trustees, c/o H W Fisher & Company, Acre House, 11/15 William Road, London NW1 3ER *Tel* 020 7388 7000

CC NO 283262   **ESTABLISHED** 1981

■ The David & Ruth Behrend Fund

WHERE FUNDING CAN BE GIVEN UK, with a preference for Merseyside.

WHO CAN BENEFIT Registered charities.

WHAT IS FUNDED General charitable purposes. The trust only gives funding to charities known to the settlors.

WHAT IS NOT FUNDED Anyone not known to the settlors.

SAMPLE GRANTS £4,000 to Amelia Chadwick Trust; £1,500 each to Ariel Trust, Granby Residents Association and Speke Garston Domestic Violence Project; £1,000 each to Chara Trust, Medical Foundation, Merseyside Holiday Services, PSS, The Missionary Training Service and Toxteth Health & Community Care Forum.

FINANCES *Year* 2000–01 *Income* £37,903 *Grants* £32,131 *Assets* £1,339,665

TRUSTEES Liverpool Council of Social Service (Inc).

HOW TO APPLY This trust states that it does not respond to unsolicited applications.

WHO TO APPLY TO c/o Liverpool Council of Social Service (Inc.), 14 Castle Street, Liverpool L2 0NJ *Tel* 0151 236 7728 *Fax* 0151 258 1153

CC NO 261567   **ESTABLISHED** 1969

■ E M Behrens Charitable Trust

WHERE FUNDING CAN BE GIVEN UK.

WHO CAN BENEFIT UK registered charities.

WHAT IS FUNDED General charitable purposes, especially music, arts and education, but also children and young people, people who are disadvantaged or with special needs, and environment.

WHAT IS NOT FUNDED No grants to non-registered charities, or in response to general appeals from large national charities.

SAMPLE GRANTS 1998–99: £5,000 to Society of London Theatre Bursary Fund; £4,000 to Guildhall School of Music & Drama Foundation; £2,500 each to Dartington International Summer School, and Memorials by Artists; £1,500 to St Nicholas Church, Remenham; £1,250 to Oxford Flute Summer School Bursary Fund; £1,000 to Royal College of Art Travelling Scholarships.

FINANCES Year 2000–01 Income £33,162

TRUSTEES S J Cokburn; C H W Parish; J N Behrens.

HOW TO APPLY In writing to the correspondent. **This trust states that it does not respond to unsolicited applications.**

WHO TO APPLY TO J R Males, Secretary to the Trustees, 3rd Floor, Salisbury House, London EC2M 5QS *Tel* 020 7448 4754

CC NO 266324   **ESTABLISHED** 1973

■ The Beit Trust

WHERE FUNDING CAN BE GIVEN Zimbabwe, Zambia and Malawi.

WHO CAN BENEFIT Individuals and charities benefiting young adults, students, teachers and academics, at risk groups, people disadvantaged by poverty, and homeless and socially isolated people.

WHAT IS FUNDED Post-primary education; health and welfare. Occasionally grants are made for environmental projects.

WHAT IS NOT FUNDED Grants are only given to charities in the areas above and the trust is reluctant to give grants to other grant-making charities.

TYPE OF GRANT Recurring, one-off, capital, bursaries, postgraduate fellowships.

RANGE OF GRANTS Not normally in excess of £30,000.

SAMPLE GRANTS £114,622 for Book Packs to provide 750 books to 15 secondary schools; £88,000 to Book Aid International for books to the countries listed above; £80,000 to Beit Memorial Medical Fellowships for medical research; £45,000 for Nkhamenya Parich, Malawi; £37,500 each for Baobab College, Lusaka, Zambia and Borradaile Trust, Marondera, Zimbabwe; £33,400 for St Albert's Mission Hospital, Zimbabwe; £32,000 for Likuni Mission Hospital, Malawi; £30,000 for CINDI, Kitwe, Zambia.

FINANCES Year 2001 Income £2,081,933 Grants £2,917,577 Assets £62,763,782

TRUSTEES Sir Alan Munro, Chair; Sir Cosmo Haskard; R A C Byatt; Prof. J G G Ledingham; C J Driver; Dame Maeve Fort.

HOW TO APPLY Contact the trust by telephone or in writing for an application form. Grants are approved by trustees at their six-monthly meetings.

WHO TO APPLY TO Brigadier C L G Henshaw, Secretary, Beit House, Grove Road, Woking, Surrey GU21 5JB *Tel* 01483 772575 *Fax* 01483 725833 *E-mail* beit.trust@clara.co.uk

CC NO 232478   **ESTABLISHED** 1906

■ The John Bell Charitable Trust

WHERE FUNDING CAN BE GIVEN Tyne and Wear, Northumberland and County Durham.

WHO CAN BENEFIT Local organisations benefiting young adults and older people. Also people with Alzheimer's disease and heart disease.

WHAT IS FUNDED General charitable purposes with a preference for youth work, older people and medical charities. This trust also considers ambulances and mobile units; hospices; community centres and village halls; crime prevention schemes; and playschemes.

TYPE OF GRANT One-off.

SAMPLE GRANTS £3,000 to Northumberland Scouts; £2,000 each to Brain Injury Vocational Service, British Heart Foundation, and Durham Scouts; £1,000 each to ADAPT, Cedarwood Trust, Cry in the Dark, Fairbridge in Tyne & Wear, Foyer, and Percy Hedley Trust.

FINANCES Year 2001 Income £22,000 Grants £24,000 Assets £212,000

TRUSTEES R I Stewart; N Sherlock; H Straker.

HOW TO APPLY In writing to the correspondent. Applications are not acknowledged.

WHO TO APPLY TO R I Stewart, Trustee, Brockenhurst, 2 The Broadway, Tynemouth, Tyne & Wear NE30 2LD

CC NO 272631   **ESTABLISHED** 1974

■ The Bellahouston Bequest Fund

WHERE FUNDING CAN BE GIVEN Glasgow and district, but not more than five miles beyond the Glasgow City boundary.

WHO CAN BENEFIT Churches and registered charities in Glasgow or within five miles especially those benefiting Protestant evangelical denominations and clergy of such churches, as well as people disadvantaged by poverty.

WHAT IS FUNDED Churches and charitable bodies within Glasgow; the promotion of Protestant religion; and the relief of poverty and disease in Glasgow.

WHAT IS NOT FUNDED No grants to organisations or churches whose work does not fall within the geographical remit of the fund. Overseas projects and political appeals are not supported. No grants to individuals.

TYPE OF GRANT One-off.

RANGE OF GRANTS £150–£5,500

SAMPLE GRANTS In 1999: £5,000 each to Strathbungo Queens Park Church, Glasgow Academy, All Saints Episcopal Church, and St David's Parish Church; £4,000 each to Bridgeton St Frances in the East Church, and Church of Scotland for social work in Glasgow.

FINANCES Year 1999–2000 Income £147,000 Grants £127,000 Assets £3,900,000

TRUSTEES B G Hardie; D H Galbraith; J Forbes MacPherson; E H Webster; Peter C Paisley; Peter L Fairley.

HOW TO APPLY On a form available from the trust for church applications. The trustees meet to consider grants in March, July, October and December.

Think carefully about every application. Is it justified?

315

WHO TO APPLY TO J A M Cuthbert, Administrator, George House, 36 North Hanover Street, Glasgow G1 2 AD *Tel* 0141 552 3422 *Fax* 0141 552 2935 *E-mail* JAMC@Mitchells-Roberton.co.uk
SC NO SC011781   ESTABLISHED 1888

■ The Bellinger Donnay Trust

WHERE FUNDING CAN BE GIVEN London, Buckinghamshire and southern counties.
WHO CAN BENEFIT Registered charities.
WHAT IS FUNDED Charitable projects by organisations.
WHAT IS NOT FUNDED No grants to individuals for education or organised visits abroad.
RANGE OF GRANTS £100–£4,150.
SAMPLE GRANTS £4,200 to Wellbeing; £2,500 to Suport St John; £1,000 each to Christ Church – Flackwell Heath, Riding for the Disabled and Union Baptist Church; £700 to British Red Cross; £500 each to Barnardos, Crisis, London Connection, Norwood Ltd, Shelter, Thames Valley Partnership and Westminster Childrens Society.
FINANCES *Year* 1999–2000 *Income* £97,969 *Grants* £31,905 *Assets* £1,825,809
TRUSTEES Lady C M L Bellinger; Ms L E Spackman; I A Bellinger.
HOW TO APPLY In writing to the correspondent.
WHO TO APPLY TO I A Bellinger, Trustee, 30 Burlington Road, Fulham, London SW6 4NS
CC NO 289462   ESTABLISHED 1984

■ Belljoe Tzedoko Ltd

WHERE FUNDING CAN BE GIVEN UK.
WHO CAN BENEFIT Registered charities and institutions.
WHAT IS FUNDED Advancement of religion in accordance with the orthodox Jewish faith and the relief of poverty.
FINANCES *Year* 2000 *Income* £67,901 *Grants* £71,557 *Assets* £2,262
TRUSTEES H J Lobenstein; Mrs B Lobenstein; D Lobenstein; M Lobenstein.
HOW TO APPLY In writing to the correspondent.
WHO TO APPLY TO H J Lobenstein, Trustee, 27 Fairholt Road, London N16 5EW *Tel* 020 8800 4384
CC NO 282726   ESTABLISHED 1981

■ Belvedere Trust

WHERE FUNDING CAN BE GIVEN Worldwide.
WHAT IS FUNDED Arts education; children at risk, children who are terminally or chronically ill, particularly primary school children; conservation. The trust also supports causes nominated by Newman Ragazzi & Co.
SAMPLE GRANTS £19,000 to Barretstown Gang towards funding work with children and towards the endowment fund; £13,000 to Polka Theatre towards the cost of Up Curtain! and the costs of signed performances for five productions; £11,000 to Starlight towards the Adolescent Centre at the Royal London Hospital and two fun centres at Hammersmith and St Bartholomew's Hospitals; £10,000 to Writernet towards an apprenticeship scheme; £7,000 to Donmar Education Initiative towards educational support for one production; £5,000 to Sophia's Alpine Disabled Adventure; £3,000 to WWF Big Cat Project; £2,000 to David Shepherd Conservation Foundation; £1,000 to 21st Century Tiger.

FINANCES *Year* 2000 *Income* £212,000 *Grants* £141,000
TRUSTEES Richard Mervyn Hughes; Irene Josephene Ann Cerini; Mary Ellen Marziale; Stella Prince-Wright.
HOW TO APPLY In writing to the correspondent.
WHO TO APPLY TO Bridget Cass, PO Box 3145, London SW1X 8WN
CC NO 1078667   ESTABLISHED 1999

■ The Bendixson 1967 Settlement

WHERE FUNDING CAN BE GIVEN UK and worldwide.
WHO CAN BENEFIT Charities specified by the settlor.
RANGE OF GRANTS £640–£3,000.
FINANCES *Year* 2000–01 *Income* £79,854
TRUSTEES Paul G Eaton; Andrew B Tappin; Lt Col. D S Balmain.
HOW TO APPLY The trust does not consider unsolicited applications.
WHO TO APPLY TO Penningtons, Trustees Solicitors, Highfield, Brighton Road, Godalming, Surrey GU7 1NS *Tel* 01483 791800 *Fax* 01483 424177
CC NO 275345   ESTABLISHED 1967

■ The Benfield Motors Charitable Trust

WHERE FUNDING CAN BE GIVEN Worldwide with preferences for north east England, Leeds and Edinburgh.
WHO CAN BENEFIT Neighbourhood-based community projects and national schemes benefiting Christians, at risk groups, people disadvantaged by poverty and socially isolated people. Third world relief will be considered.
WHAT IS FUNDED Grants are given to mainly health and welfare and Christian charities.
WHAT IS NOT FUNDED Expeditions, scholarships and animal charities are not funded.
TYPE OF GRANT One-off.
RANGE OF GRANTS £50–£25,000; typical grant £1,000.
SAMPLE GRANTS £10,000 to Community Foundation (which also received three other grants totalling £480), £7,600 to St Oswald's Hospice, £6,700 to Tyneside Foyer, £3,000 in three grants each to British Red Cross and Christian Aid; £1,000 each to Acorn Centre Youth Project and The Church of St Thomas the Martyr; £500 each to Honeycomb Community Project and Jesmond Swimming Pool
FINANCES *Year* 1999–2000 *Income* £50,000 *Grants* £44,000 *Assets* £30,000
TRUSTEES John Squires, Chair; Malcolm Squires; Stephen Squires; Mrs Lynn Squires.
HOW TO APPLY In writing to the correspondent.
WHO TO APPLY TO Mrs Lynn Squires, Hon. Secretary, c/o Benfield Motor Group, Asama Court, Newcastle Business Park, Newcastle upon Tyne NE4 7YD
CC NO 328149   ESTABLISHED 1989

■ The Benham Charitable Settlement

WHERE FUNDING CAN BE GIVEN UK, with very strong emphasis on Northamptonshire.
WHO CAN BENEFIT Organisations benefiting children, young adults, older people, at risk groups, disabled people, people disadvantaged by poverty and socially isolated people. Most good causes considered, including national appeals, or branches of the same in Northamptonshire.

National cathedrals supported, but only churches in Northamptonshire.

WHAT IS FUNDED The trust's policy is to make a large number of relatively small grants to groups working in many charitable fields, including charities concerned with medical research, disability, older people, children, young people, churches, people who are disadvantaged, wildlife, the environment, education and the arts. The emphasis is very much on activities within Northamptonshire.

WHAT IS NOT FUNDED No grants to individuals.

TYPE OF GRANT One-off and recurring grants will be considered.

RANGE OF GRANTS £100–£35,000; typically £500.

SAMPLE GRANTS £35,000 to Northamptonshire Association of Youth Clubs; £12,000 to The Lambeth Partnership; £8,000 to Coworth Park School; £5,000 each to St George's School, Ascot and St Jude's Church, Plymouth; and £2,000 to Northampton Symphony Orchestra.

FINANCES *Year* 2001–02 *Income* £140,743 *Grants* £177,850 *Assets* £4,646,133

TRUSTEES Mrs M M Tittle; Lady Hutton; E N Langley.

HOW TO APPLY In writing to the correspondent. The trust regrets that it cannot send replies to all applicants, nor will they accept telephone calls. 'Applications will be dealt with promptly at any time of year (no application forms necessary), but no charity will be considered more than once each year (repeated applications are automatically ignored for 12 months).'

WHO TO APPLY TO Mrs M Tittle, Managing Trustee, Hurstbourne, Portnall Drive, Virginia Water, Surrey GU25 4NR

CC NO 239371   **ESTABLISHED** 1964

■ The Hervey Benham Charitable Trust

WHERE FUNDING CAN BE GIVEN Colchester and north east Essex.

WHO CAN BENEFIT Individuals or self-help organisations from Colchester and north east Essex.

WHAT IS FUNDED Artistic (particularly musical) activities which benefit the people of Colchester and district and which would benefit from pump-priming by the trust and/or a contribution which enables self-help to function more effectively; individuals with potential artistic (especially musical) talent who are held back by physical, environmental or financial disability; preservation of Colchester and district's heritage with particular emphasis on industrial heritage and the maritime traditions of the Essex/Suffolk coast; local history and conservation affecting the heritage and environment of the area.

WHAT IS NOT FUNDED No grants to organisations or individuals outside the beneficial area.

TYPE OF GRANT Capital including buildings, feasibility studies, interest-free loans, one-off, and pump-priming costs. Funding is available for up to three years. Tuition fees are normally paid direct to educational institutions.

RANGE OF GRANTS Grants range from £100–£5,000.

SAMPLE GRANTS In 1999–2000: £10,000 to Kingsway Hall Trust, Dovercourt for a property purchase appeal; £2,700 to Colchester Engineering Society for a history of Colchester engineering display at the Museum of East Anglia Life; £500 each to Braintree District Museum Trust for the Ernest Beckwith exhibition programme, and Kingsway Hall Arts & Theatre Community Trust for refurbishment.

FINANCES *Year* 2001–02 *Income* £36,474 *Grants* £41,185 *Assets* £910,687

TRUSTEES M Ellis, Chair; A B Phillips; M R Carr; K E Mirams.

PUBLICATIONS Brochure.

HOW TO APPLY In writing to the correspondent by the normal quarterly dates.

WHO TO APPLY TO John Woodman, Clerk, 3 Cadman House, off Peartree Road, Colchester, Essex CO3 0NW *Tel* 01206 561086 *Fax* 01206 561086

CC NO 277578   **ESTABLISHED** 1978

■ Michael and Leslie Bennett Charitable Trust

WHERE FUNDING CAN BE GIVEN UK.

WHO CAN BENEFIT Jewish organisations.

WHAT IS FUNDED The trust supports a range of causes, but the largest donations were to Jewish organisations.

SAMPLE GRANTS £10,000 each to Jewish Care and World Jewish Relief; £8,000 to Norwood Ravenswood; £2,500 each to UJIA and Mocre Word Fund; £350 to Royal National Theatre; £250 to Mencap; £100 each to Friends of Covent Garden and New Shakespeare Company.

FINANCES *Year* 1999–2000 *Income* £23,000 *Grants* £45,000 *Assets* £682,000

HOW TO APPLY In writing to the correspondent.

WHO TO APPLY TO Michael Bennett, c/o 69–77 Paul Street, London EC2A 4PN

CC NO 1047611   **ESTABLISHED** 1995

■ The Rowan Bentall Charitable Trust

WHERE FUNDING CAN BE GIVEN Southern England.

WHO CAN BENEFIT Charities benefiting children, young adults, older people, those in the armed forces, students, and people with disabilities.

WHAT IS FUNDED Charities in southern England, assisting hospitals, churches, youth organisations, care of elderly people, people with disabilities, education and preservation of the environment.

WHAT IS NOT FUNDED No grants to individuals.

RANGE OF GRANTS £100–£3,000.

SAMPLE GRANTS £3,000 each to Kingston & District Sea Cadets Corps and Kingston Mayor's Charity; £2,500 to Kingston All Saints Parish Church Appea; £1,500 to Shooting Star Trust – Childrens Hospice Appeal.

FINANCES *Year* 2001–02 *Income* £47,472 *Grants* £45,145 *Assets* £1,215,850

TRUSTEES L Edward Bentall; Alastair R Bentall; Kate C Bentall.

HOW TO APPLY In writing to the correspondent. The trustees meet twice a year to consider applications, in February and August.

WHO TO APPLY TO L Edward Bentall, Trustee, PO Box 33438, London SW18 5XJ

CC NO 273818   **ESTABLISHED** 1960

■ The Geoffrey Berger Charitable Trust

WHERE FUNDING CAN BE GIVEN UK and overseas.

WHO CAN BENEFIT Registered charities.

WHAT IS FUNDED General charitable purposes.

WHAT IS NOT FUNDED No grants to individuals.

FINANCES *Year* 2001–02 *Income* £28,048

TRUSTEES G D Berger; N J Berger; I J Brownstein.

HOW TO APPLY The trust has stated that its funds are fully committed and that it does not accept unsolicited applications.

WHO TO APPLY TO G D Berger, Trustee, PO Box 12162, London NW11 7WR

CC NO 1059991   **ESTABLISHED** 1996

■ Bergqvist Charitable Trust

WHERE FUNDING CAN BE GIVEN Buckinghamshire, Hampshire, Oxfordshire and Surrey.

WHO CAN BENEFIT Organisations benefiting people involved in the arts, medical professionals and research workers.

WHAT IS FUNDED Medical research, children and young people, the arts, the preservation of historic buildings and environmental concerns.

WHAT IS NOT FUNDED No grants to individuals, non-registered charities or for animal causes.

TYPE OF GRANT One-off and recurrent grants.

SAMPLE GRANTS £3,000 to Generation Trust for medical research; £2,000 each to Abracadabra – Royal Surrey Hospital Paediatric Unit, and Stoke Mandeville Hospital for MRI scanner appeal; £1,500 each to British Epilepsy Association for general purposes, Cancer Care & Haematology at Stoke Mandeville Hospital, and PACE school for children with cerebral palsy; £1,000 each to British Heart Foundation for research, Church Urban Fund for diocese expenses, Sightsavers for eyesight research, and John Soane Museum for restoration work.

FINANCES *Year* 1998 *Income* £54,000 *Grants* £31,000 *Assets* £1,600,000

TRUSTEES Mrs P A Bergqvist; Philip Bergqvist.

HOW TO APPLY In writing to the correspondent.

WHO TO APPLY TO Mrs P A Bergqvist, Trustee, Moat Farm, Ford, Aylesbury, Buckinghamshire HP17 8XD *Tel* 01296 747212 *E-mail* paberg@quintadelarosa.com

CC NO 1015707   **ESTABLISHED** 1992

■ The Berkshire Community Foundation

WHERE FUNDING CAN BE GIVEN Berkshire, i.e. the unitary authorities of Bracknell, Reading, Slough, Windsor and Maidenhead, West Berkshire and Wokingham.

WHO CAN BENEFIT Voluntary organisations only, locally managed and providing services within Berkshire. Trustees particularly wish to encourage smaller groups. Organisations benefiting: children; young adults; older people; volunteers; people in care, fostered and adopted; parents and children; one-parent families; widows and widowers; at risk groups; carers; disabled people; people disadvantaged by poverty; ex-offenders and those at risk of offending; gays and lesbians; immigrants; refugees; people living in rural areas; socially isolated people; travellers and those living in urban areas; victims of abuse, crime and domestic violence.

WHAT IS FUNDED Local groups in the following categories: community leadership; ethnic minority access; community care; mental health; counselling services; disability; homelessness; rural deprivation; voluntary sector support training; community safety and victim support; addiction and rehabilitation of offenders.

WHAT IS NOT FUNDED No grants to individuals, statutory or public bodies or to appeals or charities for projects supporting statutory organisations. Grants are not made to

education, sport, the arts or environment (unless in the context of tackling wider social need). No grants for religious or political purposes. Grants are not intended to support major capital appeals and groups with more than one year's unrestricted reserves will not be supported. Grants are not made retrospectively.

TYPE OF GRANT Strategic: recurring core or project costs for activities identified as of strategic importance to the local community. Quick response and project support: specifically costed items of expenditure on a non-recurring basis.

RANGE OF GRANTS Three sizes of grants: quick reponse – up to £300; project support – up to £2,000; strategic – up to £15,000 annually for up to two years.

SAMPLE GRANTS £8,070 to Berkshire Association of Clubs for Young People for a mobile activities project to cover isolated rural areas; £7,000 to WEA Womens Learning Centre to help develop the work of the centre; £3,000 to Reading Mental Health Resource Centre to run fortnightly employment dinners and social evenings; £2,000 to Britwell Youth and Community Project towards the cost of sound reproductive equipment and a dance instructor; £1,000 each to Englefield Garden Centre to buy display benches for people with learning disabilities and Be You towards volunteer expensesto encourage more volunteers; £845 to Alzheimer's Society Slough and District towards a reminiscence activity day staging 'Memories are made of this'.

FINANCES *Year* 2001–02 *Income* £598,960 *Grants* £204,600 *Assets* £2,059,326

TRUSTEES Drawn from the local community, including representatives of local voluntary groups.

PUBLICATIONS Newsletters; corporate brochure; grants policy and guidelines; community needs survey.

OTHER INFORMATION The trust also provides a Give a Child a Chance grants programme for individual disadvantaged children and groups that support children in the radio braodcasting area of 2-TEN FM and acts as an intermediary body for ESF Global Grants. These are aimed at enabling people to develop their skills and confidence as a means of progressing towards employment.

HOW TO APPLY On an application form available from the correspondent. A preliminary telephone call to the grants officer is encouraged, to eliminate ineligible applications and to trigger support where required. Quick response grant applications can be made all year round and applicants will receive a response within a month. Deadlines for project support grants are 1 March and 1 October, with decisions being announced around six weeks later. Grants are limited to one per organisation per year. The strategic grant application process is longer. A preliminary phonecall to the grants officer to express an interest is encouraged, followed up by a short written proposal in advance of completion of formal documents. Formal applications are then screened and those selected are invited to make a formal presentation to the grants committee. All applicants are expected to produce substantial evidence of sound management. The application deadline is 1 December.

WHO TO APPLY TO The Grants Officer, Arlington Business Park, Theale, Reading, Berkshire RG7 4SA *Tel* 0118 930 3021 *Fax* 0118 930 4933 *E-mail* grants.bcf@patrol.i-way.co.uk *Website* www.berksfoundation.org.uk

CC NO 294220   **ESTABLISHED** 1985

■ Patrick Berthoud Charitable Trust

WHERE FUNDING CAN BE GIVEN UK.

WHO CAN BENEFIT (a) Individuals who are clinical trainees in all specialities concerned with neurological disease; (b) individuals with at least three years further clinical training before acquiring their CCST who have yet to complete a research training fellowship and wish to spend part of their fellowship leave in the USA; (c) neurological research charities.

WHAT IS FUNDED (a) Full-time three-year fellowships to people in clinical training in the UK who have obtained their MRCP or equivalent for the training in a related discipline and are eligible for training for a specialist, registrar or clinical lecturer; (b) supplementing a newly appointed SpR post with a three-year research level fellowship, preferably to be held in the host department, which the trust anticipates will take place in a clinical training posts to consolidate their area of specialist interest; (c) existing peer-reviewed innovative research projects in the UK to meet, or help to meet, the cost of special equipment or defined medical research project support costs which, for good reason, could not have been anticipated when the grant was made.

WHAT IS NOT FUNDED Applications will not be considered from universities or NHS trusts for retrospective funding; for recurrent funding (at least two years should elapse from the receipt of a grant before a further application will be considered from a successful recipient charity); or for support of salaries, except in exceptional circumstances.

TYPE OF GRANT (a) Research fellowships; (b) research leave fellowships; (c) one-off capital grants.

RANGE OF GRANTS For (a) up to £50,000 per year; for (b) clinical training for up to two session a week during the research leave fellowship; and (c) up to £10,000 per year.

SAMPLE GRANTS Up to £50,000 a year to support Berthaud Fellows; £5,000 to PSP Association for consumables for a research project.

FINANCES *Year* 2000–01 *Income* £160,000 *Grants* £94,000 *Assets* £4,500,000

OTHER INFORMATION Up to two fellowships will be awarded each year. Priority will be given to applications from smaller charities working in less popular fields.

HOW TO APPLY On a form available from the correspondent. Deadline for receipt of applications is 31 December.

WHO TO APPLY TO The Grants Administrator, Charities Aid Foundation, Kings Hill, West Malling, Kent ME19 4TA *Tel* 01732 520334 *Fax* 01732 520159 *E-mail* grants@cafonline.org

CC NO 268369b   **ESTABLISHED** 1994

■ The Bestway Foundation

WHERE FUNDING CAN BE GIVEN UK and overseas.

WHO CAN BENEFIT Individuals and institutions benefiting children, young adults, students, and teachers and governesses.

WHAT IS FUNDED Advancement of education by grants to schoolchildren and students who are of Indian, Pakistani, Bangladeshi or Sri Lankan origin; and relief of sickness, and preservation and protection of health in the UK and overseas, especially in India, Pakistan, Bangladesh and Sri Lanka.

WHAT IS NOT FUNDED No grants for trips/travel abroad.

FINANCES *Year* 1998–99 *Income* £406,160 *Grants* £191,020 *Assets* £2,198,738

TRUSTEES A K Bhatti; A K Chaudhary; M Y Sheikh; Z M Chaudrey; M A Pervez; Z U H Khan.

HOW TO APPLY In writing to the address below, enclosing an sae. Telephone calls are not welcome.

WHO TO APPLY TO Ms D Taylor, Bestway Cash & Carry Ltd, Abbey Road, Park Royal, London NW10 7BW

CC NO 297178   **ESTABLISHED** 1987

■ Betard Bequest

WHERE FUNDING CAN BE GIVEN UK.

WHO CAN BENEFIT Grants are made to welfare charities to distribute to eligible individuals.

WHAT IS FUNDED Holidays, specially adapted furniture, computers and medical aids for people with arthritis and rheumatism and to Scottish and French people who are old and lonely, and resident in the UK. Support is given only where it is not the duty of the DSS and other government departments.

WHAT IS NOT FUNDED Grants are not made directly to individuals but through an appropriate charity or social worker.

TYPE OF GRANT Funding available for one year.

RANGE OF GRANTS Welfare charities (for distribution): up to £5,000.

SAMPLE GRANTS £3,500 to Abilitynet (for individuals); £2,250 each to Arthritis Care for support for people disabled through arthritis and Leicester Charity Organisation Society (for individuals). Previous beneficiaries have included Mobility Trust, Ryder-Cheshire Foundation, Raynauds Scleroderma Association, Lady Hoare Trust, 3H Fund, League of the Helping Hand and National Benevolent Fund for the Aged.

FINANCES *Year* 2001–02 *Income* £38,000 *Grants* £28,000 *Assets* £700,000

HOW TO APPLY Applications can be sent in at any time for quarterly consideration. Initial telephone calls by applicants are welcome. No application forms are necessary, but guidelines are issued. There are no deadlines for applications and no sae is required.

WHO TO APPLY TO CAF Grantmaking, Kings Hill, West Malling, Kent ME19 4TA *Tel* 01732 520334 *Fax* 01732 520159 *E-mail* grants@caf.online.org *Website* www.cafonline.org/grants

CC NO 268369c   **ESTABLISHED** 1985

■ Bethesda Community Charitable Trust

WHERE FUNDING CAN BE GIVEN Norfolk and Suffolk.

WHO CAN BENEFIT Organisations benefiting children; young adults; Christians; at risk groups; people disadvantaged by poverty; and socially isolated people.

WHAT IS FUNDED The advancement of the Christian religion and Christian faith; the relief of poverty, suffering and distress in the community; the advancement of education; and other general charitable purposes.

WHAT IS NOT FUNDED No grants to individuals.

FINANCES *Year* 2001 *Income* £77,000 *Grants* £40,000 *Assets* £500,000

HOW TO APPLY In writing to the address correspondent. However, please note that the trust states that all available funds have been allocated for the foreseeable future.

WHO TO APPLY TO R W Jarritt, 41 Highfield Road, Ipswich, Suffolk IP1 6DD
CC NO 1042816   **ESTABLISHED** 1994

■ Thomas Betton's Charity (Educational)

WHERE FUNDING CAN BE GIVEN England and Wales, especially Greater London.
WHO CAN BENEFIT Diocesan Education Committees for their aided schools. Occasionally independent schools not under the control of Diocesan Education Committees are supported.
WHAT IS FUNDED Grants are given for the reconstruction of schools with charitable status that give religious instruction in accordance with the principles of the Church of England or Church in Wales.
WHAT IS NOT FUNDED No grants to individuals.
TYPE OF GRANT One-off and capital grants will be considered.
RANGE OF GRANTS £1,000–£10,000.
FINANCES Year 1998–99 Income £115,286 Grants £185,735 Assets £823,657
TRUSTEES Ironmongers' Company.
HOW TO APPLY Grants are made via diocesan authorities only, who are invited to submit applications in writing. Applications should arrive by 1 February enclosing an sae.
WHO TO APPLY TO The Charities Administrator, Ironmongers' Hall, Barbican, London EC2Y 8AA *Tel* 020 7606 2725 *Website* www.ironhall.co.uk
CC NO 313632   **ESTABLISHED** 1723

■ Thomas Betton's Charity for Pensions and Relief-in-Need

WHERE FUNDING CAN BE GIVEN UK.
WHO CAN BENEFIT Homelessness, general.
WHAT IS FUNDED The trust makes a block grant to Housing the Homeless which allocates grants to individuals. Other organisations for the relief of need are also supported.
RANGE OF GRANTS £1,000–£5,000.
SAMPLE GRANTS £18,000 to Housing the Homeless.
FINANCES Year 2000–01 Income £52,000 Grants £42,000 Assets £839,000
TRUSTEES The Worshipful Company of Ironmongers.
OTHER INFORMATION Applications for grants to individuals accepted only from registered social workers or other agencies.
HOW TO APPLY In writing to the correspondent.
WHO TO APPLY TO The Charities Administrator, Ironmongers' Hall, Barbican, London EC2Y 8AA *Tel* 020 7606 2725
CC NO 280143   **ESTABLISHED** 1973

■ The Mason Bibby 1981 Trust

WHERE FUNDING CAN BE GIVEN Merseyside and other areas where the company has or had a presence.
WHO CAN BENEFIT Priority to elderly people and employees and ex-employees of J Bibby and Sons Plc.
WHAT IS FUNDED Main area of interest is elderly people but applications are considered from other groups, particularly from areas in which the company has a presence.
WHAT IS NOT FUNDED Apart from employees and ex-employees of J Bibby & Sons PLC, applications are considered from registered charities only.
RANGE OF GRANTS £250–£3,000

SAMPLE GRANTS £1,000 each to St John's Hospice – Thornton, Wheatfield Hospice – Leeds, Thames Valley Hospice, Shropshire & Mid Wales Hospice, Sunny Bank Marie Curie Centre – Liverpool, Abbeyfield North Mersey and Abbeyfield Birkenhead; £500 each to Calibre, Talking Newspapers for the Blind, Action for Blind People, The Claire House Appeal – Clatterbridge, Samaritans of Liverpool and Merseyside, Wirral Society for the Blind & Partially Sighted and The League – Liverpool; £250 each to Bryson House – Belfast, Martin House Hospice – West Yorkshire, Age Concern – Cheshire, Arthritis Care in North England and Ormskirk District Hospital League of Friends.
FINANCES Year 2001–02 Income £84,680 Grants £87,845 Assets £2,208,589
TRUSTEES J B Bibby, Chair; K A Allan; J P Wood; Mrs D M Fairclough; S W Bowman; J McPheat; A S Gresty.
HOW TO APPLY In writing to the correspondent. Trustees meet half yearly. Applications are only acknowledged if a grant is agreed.
WHO TO APPLY TO Mrs D M Fairclough, Trustee, c/o Rathbone Brothers & Co. Ltd, Port of Liverpool Building, Pierhead, Liverpool L3 1NW
CC NO 283231   **ESTABLISHED** 1981

■ BibleLands

WHERE FUNDING CAN BE GIVEN Lands of the Bible, especially Lebanon, the Holy Land and Egypt.
WHO CAN BENEFIT Local organisations working in the beneficial area which benefit people of all ages, faiths and nationalities in the region; those in care, or fostered or adopted; disabled people; people disadvantaged by poverty; or disaster victims and refugees, particularly children. These include people with cerebral palsy, hearing loss, sight loss and a wide range of other disabilities.
WHAT IS FUNDED BibleLands exists to support and encourage local Christians in the lands of the Bible, who are dedicated to fulfilling the compassionate ministry of Christ. Its calling is to encourage work for the welfare of children, young people and others in need, with an emphasis on health and education. BibleLands has special concern for children; education; vocational training (including nurses); special needs; medical care; social care and the support and care of refugees.
WHAT IS NOT FUNDED Grants are confined to Christian-led work, but beneficiaries are helped regardless of faith or nationality. No grants to individuals or UK bodies.
TYPE OF GRANT Capital including buildings, recurring, core costs, one-off, running costs and start-up costs. Funding is for up to or more than three years. Child sponsorship schemes and ongoing grants to specific projects are also in place.
RANGE OF GRANTS £1,000–£350,000
SAMPLE GRANTS £300,000 to Helen Keller School for the Visually Impaired (BibleLand's only wholly owned project partner); £132,000 to Al Kafaat Foundation Lebanon; £118,944 to Nazareth Hospital; £104,487 to Cedar Capabilities Centre Lebanon; £103,021 to Jeel al Amal Bethany; £68,637 to Hebron School for Boys; £54,344 to Rawdat El Zuhur School; £54,041 to Talitha Kumi Beit Jala; £48,616 to Bethany Girls School.
FINANCES Year 2001–02 Income £3,300,000 Grants £2,350,651 Assets £7,702,342
TRUSTEES These include Dr C Young, Chair; H Boulter; K S Mills.

PUBLICATIONS *The Star in the East*, quarterly newsletter.

HOW TO APPLY Apply in writing for an application form, giving brief outline of the support being sought.

WHO TO APPLY TO Miss Mo Burnley, Head of Overseas Programmes, PO Box 50, High Wycombe, Buckinghamshire HP15 7QU *Tel* 01494 897979 *Fax* 01494 897951 *E-mail* info@biblelands.co.uk

CC NO 1076329   **ESTABLISHED** 1854

■ The Bideford Bridge Trust

WHERE FUNDING CAN BE GIVEN The parish of Bideford, Devon and neighbourhood.

WHO CAN BENEFIT Charities and individuals in the area of benefit.

WHAT IS FUNDED General charitable purposes.

TYPE OF GRANT Core and recurring costs.

SAMPLE GRANTS £24,000 each to Bethel Evangelical Free Church, Bideford and Instow Railway Group and Torridge District Council for school swimming lessons.

FINANCES *Year* 2001 *Income* £528,000 *Grants* £310,000

TRUSTEES C Coates; J R Baker; R Chope; R E Day; E A Hubber; P Trapnell; Mrs R Timms; D Vickers; H R Barton; P Christie; D J Daniel; the Mayor of Bideford.

HOW TO APPLY In writing to the correspondent.

WHO TO APPLY TO P R Sims, Steward, 24 Bridgeland Street, Bideford, Devon EX39 2QB *Tel* 01237 473122

CC NO 204536   **ESTABLISHED** 1973

■ Bier Charitable Settlement

WHERE FUNDING CAN BE GIVEN UK.

WHO CAN BENEFIT Children's charities.

WHAT IS FUNDED The trust makes grants to established charities, primarily to help children.

WHAT IS NOT FUNDED Grants are not made to individuals.

FINANCES *Year* 1999–2000 *Income* £22,000 *Grants* £27,000 *Assets* £268,000

TRUSTEES Mrs Lieselotte F Bier, Chair; Jonathan P Davies; Robert A Dolman.

HOW TO APPLY In writing to the correspondent. However, the trust stated that funds are fully committed until 2004.

WHO TO APPLY TO Jonathan P Davies, Trustee, 4 Heath Close, London NW11 7DX *Tel* 020 7242 5905

CC NO 802985   **ESTABLISHED** 1989

■ Billingsgate Christian Mission Charitable Trust

WHERE FUNDING CAN BE GIVEN UK.

WHO CAN BENEFIT Registered charities benefiting people engaged in the fish and fishing industries in the UK who may be sick, in distress or disadvantaged by poverty. Charities involved in medical research may also be considered.

WHAT IS FUNDED Relief of poverty, distress and sickness among people engaged in the fish and fishing industries in the UK. Advancement of religious and social work in accordance with the Christian faith among such people. Advancement of medical science, particularly by way of grants for scholarships.

WHAT IS NOT FUNDED No grants to individuals.

TYPE OF GRANT One-off.

RANGE OF GRANTS £2,000–£10,000.

SAMPLE GRANTS £10,000 each to Fishermen's Mission (Peterhead) and Schizophrenia Association of Great Britain; £8,000 to Fishmongers' & Poulterers' Institution; £7,500 each to Ark Facility at Basingstoke Hospital and Breast Cancer Campaign; £2,500 each to Cancer and Leukaemia in Childhood and Fishermen's Mission (Grimsby); £2,000 to Iris Fund for Prevention of Blindness.

FINANCES *Year* 2001 *Income* £21,000 *Grants* £50,000 *Assets* £667,000

TRUSTEES The Court of the Fishmongers' Company.

HOW TO APPLY In writing to the correspondent, including the latest annual accounts. Trustees meet three times a year.

WHO TO APPLY TO K S Waters, Clerk, Fishmongers' Company, Fishmongers' Hall, London Bridge, London EC4R 9EL *Tel* 020 7626 3531 *Fax* 020 7929 1389

CC NO 1013851   **ESTABLISHED** 1992

■ The Billmeir Charitable Trust

WHERE FUNDING CAN BE GIVEN UK, with a preference for the Surrey area, specifically Elstead, Tilford, Farnham and Frensham.

WHAT IS FUNDED General charitable purposes.

SAMPLE GRANTS £20,000 to Elstead United Reform Church; £10,000 to Reed School – Cobham; £6,000 each to Lord Mayor Treloar School and Meath Home and RNLI; £5,000 each to British Home and Hospital for Incurables, Cancer Vaccine Institute, Homestart, Marlborough College, Old Kiln Museum Ltd, Woodlarks Campsite Trust and Youth Sport Trust.

FINANCES *Year* 2000–01 *Income* £123,312 *Grants* £169,000 *Assets* £3,830,732

TRUSTEES B C Whitaker; M R Macfadyen; S Marriott; J Whitaker.

HOW TO APPLY The trust states that it does not request applications and that its funds are fully committed.

WHO TO APPLY TO T T Cripps, Accountant, Messrs Moore Stephens, 1 Snow Hill, London EC1A 2EN *Tel* 020 7334 9191

CC NO 208561   **ESTABLISHED** 1956

■ Percy Bilton Charity Ltd

WHERE FUNDING CAN BE GIVEN UK (though very occasional response to overseas disaster appeals).

WHO CAN BENEFIT Registered charities and youth organisations. Limited assistance on a one-off basis to individuals and families who fall within the following categories: older people, people with disabilities and people with a medical illness. All applications for individuals to be sent in by the relevant social worker on local or health authority headed notepaper.

WHAT IS FUNDED People who are elderly, disabled, or young and disadvantaged/at risk.

WHAT IS NOT FUNDED If you have already received a grant, please allow at least one year from the date of payment before reapplying. The charity will not consider (the list is not exhaustive): running expenses for the organisation or individual projects; salaries or office equipment/furniture; donations for general funding/circularised appeals; play schemes/summer schemes; holidays or expeditions for individuals or groups; trips, activities or events; community centres or village halls for wider community use; community sports/play area facilities; pre-schools or play groups (other than for children with disabilities); refurbishment or repair of places of worship/church halls; research projects; the arts (theatre, dance, etc.); schools, colleges and universities (other than special schools); welfare funds or other grantmaking bodies for distribution; hospital/medical equipment; disabled access to facilities used predominantly by the able bodied; works to premise used primarily by those not within the criteria; projects that have been completed; or items already purchased.

TYPE OF GRANT One-off.

RANGE OF GRANTS Grants to individuals: up to £200; small grants to organisations: up to £500 towards furnishing and equipment for small projects; main funding single grants for capital expenditure: in excess of £2,000.

SAMPLE GRANTS £15,000 to National Autistic Society for provision of an outdoor multi-sensory environment at Sybil Elgar School; £12,000 to Children's Trust for construction of the technical workshop within the new rehabilitation and therapy centre; £10,800 each to Jigsaw Partnerships for fixtures and fittings for shop promises to provide training opportunities for people with learning difficulties; £10,000 each to Advance for the construction of eight self-contained flats in Redditch for adults with mental health problems, Bobath Children's Therapy Centre Cardiff towards construction of a 2-storey extension and refurbishment, Boys and Girls Welfare Society Cheshire towards construction of a fitness and physiotherapy suite, Cystic Fibrosis Trust towards construction of a 12-bed unit at the Cardiothoracic Centre in Liverpool, Outward Bound Trust London for personal development courses for disadvantaged young people, Stepping Stones for furnishings for two flats and Age Concern Sandwell for refurbishment of new premises.

FINANCES *Year* 2001–02 *Income* £679,304 *Grants* £775,935 *Assets* £16,986,000

TRUSTEES M A Bilton; J R Lee; W J D Moberly; W J Uzielli; S J Paciorek.

OTHER INFORMATION The grant total included £579,000 to organisations.

HOW TO APPLY In writing to the correspondent on headed notepaper, including: a brief history and outline of your charity; a description of the project and its principal aims; building or other plans – does the project have all relevant planning consents; a budget for the project, including details of funds already raised and other sources being approached; for equipment appeals, provide a list of items required with costs; cost or costs involved for building/refurbishment projects – please itemise major items and professional fees (if any); dates when construction/refurbishment is to commence and be completed; whether the project has ongoing revenue funding; plans for monitoring and evaluating the project; and a copy of your latest annual report and accounts.

For a small grant (£500 or less), please supply the following: brief details of your organisation; outline of the project and its principal aims; cost of the item/s required; and a copy of your most recent audited accounts. If your organisation is not a registered charity please obtain a reference from a youth organisation that you work with of or from the Voluntary Service Council. Small grants are dealt with by a committee on an ongoing basis and we aim to let you have decision within two weeks. If in doubt regarding the suitability of an appeal, contact the charity either in writing, or by telephone. Applications are acknowledged within two weeks, giving details of if, and when, the application will be considered. Applications are usually considered in March, June, September and December. Site visits or meetings may be required for certain applications.

WHO TO APPLY TO Miss Priya Ponnaiyah, Secretary, Bilton House, 58 Uxbridge Road, Ealing, London W5 2TL *Tel* 020 8579 2829 *Fax* 020 8567 5459

CC NO 212474   **ESTABLISHED** 1962

■ The Bingham Trust

WHERE FUNDING CAN BE GIVEN Buxton and district.

WHO CAN BENEFIT Primarily charitable organisations benefiting volunteers; people in care, fostered and adopted; parents and children; one-parent families; widows and widowers; at risk groups; carers; disabled people; people disadvantaged by poverty; ex-offenders and those at risk of offending; people living in rural areas; socially isolated people; and victims of abuse, crime and domestic violence. Occasionally individuals.

WHAT IS FUNDED Identifiable community needs in the areas of: accommodation and housing; building services; information and computer technology; infrastructure and development; charity or voluntary umbrella bodies; religion; arts, culture and recreation; health; conservation and environment; education and training; community facilities and services; and other charitable purposes.

WHAT IS NOT FUNDED Generally, limited to the town of Buxton and district.

TYPE OF GRANT One-off, capital including buildings, project, running costs, salaries and start-up costs. Funding is for up to three years.

RANGE OF GRANTS £50–£10,000.

SAMPLE GRANTS £10,000 to Good News Family Care Home, Charis House; £4,300 to Buxton Citizens Advice Bureau; £3,000 each to Buxton Opera House and St Peters Church Fairfield; £2,000 to Buxton Festival; £1,000 each to Marie Curie Cancer Care, Peaks and Dales Advocacy, Samaritans, Tideswell Parish Church Fund and Whaley Hall – King of Love.

FINANCES *Year* 1999–2000 *Income* £53,000 *Grants* £41,000 *Assets* £1,300,000

TRUSTEES Dr R G B Willis; R A Horne; Mrs J H Lawton; Revd P J Meek; Mrs A M Hurst.

HOW TO APPLY In writing to the correspondent on no more than two pages of A4, stating the total cost of the project and sources of other funding. Applications should arrive before the end of February, June, September and December each year.

WHO TO APPLY TO R Horne, Trustee, Brooke-Taylors Solicitors, 4 The Quadrant, Buxton, Derbyshire SK17 6AW *Tel* 01298 22741

CC NO 287636   **ESTABLISHED** 1977

■ The Bintaub Charitable Trust

WHERE FUNDING CAN BE GIVEN Greater London, national and international.

WHO CAN BENEFIT Jewish, health, education, children.

WHAT IS FUNDED Mainly London organisations, towards 'the advancement of education in and the religion of the orthodox Jewish faith'. Grants are also given for other charitable causes, mainly towards medical and children's work.

FINANCES *Year* 1999–2000 *Income* £43,000 *Grants* £35,000 *Assets* £11,000

TRUSTEES James Frohwein; Tania Frohwein; Daniel Frohwein.

HOW TO APPLY In writing to the correspondent. However, the correspondent stated previously that new applications are not being accepted.

WHO TO APPLY TO Mrs D Rosenberg, 29 Woodlands Close, London NW11 9QR *Tel* 020 8455 1874 *Fax* 020 8209 1831

CC NO 1003915   **ESTABLISHED** 1991

■ The Birmingham District Nursing Charitable Trust

WHERE FUNDING CAN BE GIVEN Within a 20-mile radius of the Council House in Birmingham.

WHO CAN BENEFIT Local organisations benefiting medical professionals. Grants may be made to local branches of national organisations.

WHAT IS FUNDED Medical or nursing organisations; convalescent homes; convalescent homes or rest homes for nurses or other medical or nursing institution; amenities for patients or nursing staff of Birmingham Domicilary Nursing Service; amenities for patients or nursing staff of any state hospital.

WHAT IS NOT FUNDED No grants are given to individuals.

RANGE OF GRANTS £500–£8,500.

SAMPLE GRANTS In 1998: £8,500 to Birmingham & Three Counties Trust for Nurses; £7,000 to Age Concern; £5,000 to Macmillan Cancer Relief; £3,500 to Little Sisters of the Poor; £3,000 each to Birmingham PHAB Camps and St Mary's Hospice; £2,600 to Association of Friends of Home Nursing in Birmingham; £2,250 to Akril Day Centre; £2,000 each to Edward's Trust and Huntingdon's Disease Association.

FINANCES *Year* 2000–01 *Income* £60,932

TRUSTEES G De'Ath; Miss B Holmes; Dr J R Mann; A D Martineau; H W Tuckey; Prof. W A Littler.

HOW TO APPLY In writing to the correspondent with a copy of the latest acccounts. Applications should be sent in August/September. Trustees meet to consider grants in the first week of November.

WHO TO APPLY TO Anthony Jones, Shakespeares Solicitors, Somerset House, Temple Street, Birmingham B2 5DJ *Tel* 0121 632 4199 *Fax* 0121 633 2257

CC NO 215652   **ESTABLISHED** 1960

■ The Birmingham Foundation

WHERE FUNDING CAN BE GIVEN Greater Birmingham.

WHO CAN BENEFIT Small community-based groups and organisations involved in activities that regenerate and rebuild communities.

WHAT IS FUNDED Small grants are generally given, focusing support on: initiatives which encourage community responsibility and develop 'community capacity' (such as projects which aim to become sustainable by providing their members with the skills and confidence to carry out its aims); projects which give support in areas not currently served by major initiatives; and projects which benefit children and young people.

WHAT IS NOT FUNDED No funding is available for projects operating outside the Greater Birmingham area; general appeals or large national charities (except for local branches working specifically for local people); individuals – for whatever purpose; organisations and individuals in the promotion of political or religious ideology.

RANGE OF GRANTS £3,000 on average.

SAMPLE GRANTS £6,000 each to Children At Risk Project to run a series of 'Art Afloat ' workshops, ARC (Assisting Retinoblatoma Children) to purchase indoor/outdoor play and activity equipment, electrical items, a karaoke machine and camcorder, and an anti-bullying project for information leaflets and volunteers' travel expenses; £2,500 to Fairway Changeover Group to purchase specialist kitchen equipment for use by disabled people; £650 to Fund & Fitness project to provide young women with the opportunity of taking part in the 'healthy lifestyles for women' project; £500 to Sikh Community and Youth Forum to establish a group that enables Asian women to help themselves, especially those whose first language is not English; £176 to Fundays to provide equipment, toys and collage materials to a small mothers and toddlers group.

FINANCES *Year* 2001–02 *Income* £1,907,240 *Grants* £1,559,636 *Assets* £610,498

TRUSTEES R Taylor, President; P Bache; D J Bucknall, Chair; M Ames; Revd Canon D J Collyer; P Graves; G Gould; Dr J Higgins; Cllr I McArdle; J M Munn; S Saville; C Trixson; T van Beurden; T Watts.

HOW TO APPLY There is an application form which is available from the foundation and can be downloaded from its website (ww.bhamfoundation.co.uk/receivefs.html) which has been designed to enable the foundation to match each application to the most appropriate fund. Some managed funds, however, do require a separate application form to be completed.

WHO TO APPLY TO Harvey Mansfield, Director, St Peter's Urban Village Trust, Bridge Road, Saltley, Birmingham B8 3TE *Tel* 0121 326 6886 *Fax* 0121 328 8575 *E-mail* team@bhamfoundation.co.uk *Website* www.bhamfoundation.co.uk

CC NO 1048160   **ESTABLISHED** 1995

■ The Birmingham Hospital Saturday Fund Medical Charity & Welfare Trust

WHERE FUNDING CAN BE GIVEN UK, but mostly centred around the West Midlands and Birmingham area.

WHO CAN BENEFIT Hospitals and other medical and welfare organisations and charities.

WHAT IS FUNDED To improve the quality of life for those disadvantaged in society; provide comforts and amenities for patients in hospital and medical charities, assist medical research, education and science, and support charitable organisations concerned with people who are sick. The trust will consider funding: health; speech therapy; scholarships; building services; information technology and computers; publishing and printing; and health professional bodies.

WHAT IS NOT FUNDED The trust will not generally fund: direct appeals from individuals or students; administration expenditure including salaries; bank loans/deficits/mortgages; items or services which should normally be publicly funded; large general appeals; vehicle operating costs; or motor vehicles for infrequent use and where subsidised vehicle share schemes are available to charitable organisations.

TYPE OF GRANT One-off grants, capital, project and research, all funded for up to one year.

RANGE OF GRANTS Up to £5,000.

SAMPLE GRANTS £5,100 to West Midlands NHS Trust for three travel scholarships for nurses; £5,000 to Age Concern for a minibus; £4,990 to Foundation for Nursing Studies – London for the Patient Involvement in Care awards scheme for nurses; £4,700 to Friends of Stourbridge Education Centre for computer; £4,500 to City of Birmingham Special Olympics for 2001 Midlands Regional Games; £4,275 to Abbeyfield Stafford Society for air conditioning for a new conservatory; £4,250 to Institute of Ageing and Health for the Excellent Care Award and desk top publishing equipment; £4,000 to The Extra Care Charitable Trust for equipment for a dementia project; £3,715 to The Adis Trust – Dorset for a specialist laptop computer for equipment for a library for people who are disabled; £3,600 to Birmingham Medical Institute for the 2001 and 2002 Gamgee Lecture and library books.

FINANCES *Year* 2001 *Income* £914,300 *Grants* £105,277 *Assets* £928,000

TRUSTEES Dr R P Kanas; S G Hall; E S Hickman; M Malone; D J Read; J Salmons.

HOW TO APPLY On a form available from the correspondent. The form requires basic information and should be submitted with financial details. Evidence should be provided that the project has been adequately considered through the provision of quotes or supporting documents, although the trust dislikes applications which provide too much general information or have long-winded descriptions of projects.

WHO TO APPLY TO Kate Bradshaw, Appeals Administrator, Gamgee House, 2 Darnley Road, Birmingham B16 8TE *Tel* 0121 454 3601

CC NO 502428   **ESTABLISHED** 1972

··

■ Birmingham International Airport Community Trust

WHERE FUNDING CAN BE GIVEN The areas affected by the airport's operation (East Birmingham, Solihull and parts of north Warwickshire).

WHO CAN BENEFIT Local organisations only.

WHAT IS FUNDED Projects that improve the local environment by: building community links through sport and recreation; encouraging and protecting wildlife; improving awareness of environmental issues; heritage conservation and environmental improvement.

WHAT IS NOT FUNDED Grants will not be given to the following: individuals; projects which have already been carried out or paid for; organisations which have statutory responsibilities e.g. hospitals, surgeries, clinics, schools etc. unless the project is clearly not a statutory responsibility. Grants are not normally given towards the purchase of land or buildings. Requests for equipment, fixtures and fittings may be supported. Grants are not normally recurrent.

TYPE OF GRANT One-off, capital and project. Funding may be given for one year or less.

RANGE OF GRANTS Generally up to £3,000.

FINANCES *Year* 2000–01 *Income* £50,000 *Grants* £157,000 *Assets* £130,000

TRUSTEES M Bryant; Elaine Clarke; Cllr M Nangle; Cllr M Ward; Cllr J Ryan; Cllr A Martin; A Middleton; Cllr Don Hitchcock; Marcus Balmforth.

PUBLICATIONS *Birmingham International Airport Community Trust Fund Application Guidelines.*

OTHER INFORMATION Applicants must be able to demonstrate how their project will benefit the area affected by the airport. Priority is given to: groups based locally or under local control; projects which are of benefit to the local community, or a substantial section of it, and not groups of an exclusive nature; projects where the grant will be at least supplemented by a contribution from other sources; projects for which detailed costs, including copies of estimates, are provided (proposals for projects which involve the creation of a physical asset, e.g. a garden requiring ongoing maintenance, must include a maintenance plan). Those in receipt of, or with access to, substantial support from elsewhere will have low priority. The trustees would encourage proposals involving facilities or access to take account of people with special needs and the elderly.

HOW TO APPLY On a form available from the correspondent. Applications should provide the following information: how their project will benefit an area affected by the airport and detailed costs, including copies of estimates. Proposals for projects which involve the creation of a physical asset, e.g. a garden, which require ongoing maintenance, should include a maintenance plan. When the form is sent applicants will be advised when the next grant allocation meeting is being held. The trustees may want to visit the project. All applications will be acknowledged. Applicants will be informed of the trustees' decision by letter. The trust will not discuss their decision with unsuccessful applicants or consider an appeal. Applications can be made at any time. Grants are awarded twice a year, usually in April and October. They should be spent within six months of the receipt, if this timescale cannot be achieved the administrator should be notified as soon as possible. Successful applicants are required to submit a progress report after 6 months, and also after 12 months if it is a longer project. Receipts should be sent to the trust fund administrator when items or equipment have been purchased. The trustees may request to visit projects which have received grants and it states they: 'maintain the right to request their auditors to audit any records held by the organisation for the projects sponsored and to request copies of any relevant documents'.

WHO TO APPLY TO Amy McCandlish, Community Affairs Assistant, Birmingham International Airport Ltd, Birmingham B26 3QJ *Tel* 0121 767 7360 *Fax* 0121 767 7065 *E-mail* trustfund@bhx.co.uk *Website* www.bhx.co.uk

CC NO 1071176   **ESTABLISHED** 1998

··

■ The Lord Mayor of Birmingham's Charity

WHERE FUNDING CAN BE GIVEN Birmingham and West Midlands.

WHO CAN BENEFIT General charitable purposes.

WHAT IS FUNDED Beneficiaries are determined by the Lord Mayor prior to taking up office. Three or four charities/voluntary organisations are usually selected at the beginning of the year. No other donations are made.

TYPE OF GRANT One-off.

SAMPLE GRANTS A total of £50,000 to beneficiaries that will include Acorns Children's Hospice – Birmingham, Alzheimer's Disease Society, MS Research Trust and The Woodlands Hospital – Birmingham for their new children's orthopaedic unit.

FINANCES *Year* 2001–02 *Grants* £50,000

324

Does the trust you have chosen match your needs? Haphazard applications waste postage and time

TRUSTEES Lord Mayor of Birmingham; Deputy Lord Mayor of Birmingham; Hon. Alderman H McCallion.

HOW TO APPLY In writing to the correspondent. Although the beneficiaries are often predetermined, applications can be sent in January/February for the new Lord Mayor to consider.

WHO TO APPLY TO Cathy Dukes, Civic Affairs Manager, Lord Mayor's Parlour, Council House, Birmingham B1 1BB *Tel* 0121 303 2040 *Fax* 0121 303 4809 *E-mail* lord.mayor@birmingham.gov.uk *Website* www.birmingham.gov.uk

CC NO 1036968   **ESTABLISHED** 1994

■ The Peter Birse Charitable Trust

WHERE FUNDING CAN BE GIVEN Worldwide, some preference for the East Riding of Yorkshire and North Lincolnshire.

WHO CAN BENEFIT Mostly national schemes; some local organisations.

WHAT IS FUNDED Virtually all grants are given to health and welfare charities, mostly national, with a preference for those concerned with children.

WHAT IS NOT FUNDED No grants to animal welfare charities or organisations associated with sport or the arts.

TYPE OF GRANT Some recurring; generally one-off.

FINANCES *Year* 2000–01 *Income* £34,754 *Grants* £25,000 *Assets* £519,776

TRUSTEES Peter Birse; Mrs Helen Birse.

HOW TO APPLY In writing to the correspondent. Applications can be considered at any time.

WHO TO APPLY TO The Secretary, c/o Birse Group plc, Humber Road, Barton-on-Humber, North Lincolnshire DN18 5BW *Tel* 01652 633222

CC NO 801611   **ESTABLISHED** 1989

■ The Bisgood Charitable Trust (registered as The Miss Jeanne Bisgood's Charitable Trust)

WHERE FUNDING CAN BE GIVEN UK, overseas and locally in Bournemouth and Dorset, especially Poole.

WHO CAN BENEFIT Registered charities.

WHAT IS FUNDED General charitable purposes. Main grants have been and will be concentrated on the following categories: (a) operating under Roman Catholic auspices; (b) operating in Poole, Bournemouth and the county of Dorset; (c) national (not local) charities concerned with older people.

WHAT IS NOT FUNDED Grants are not given to local charities not fitting categories 1 or 2, see above. Individuals and non-registered charities are not supported.

TYPE OF GRANT One-off, capital and recurring.

RANGE OF GRANTS £25–£2,500.

SAMPLE GRANTS £2,000 each to Intermediate Technology, Impact, Medical Foundation for the Victims of Torture, the Passage, Sight Savers International and the De Paul Trust; and £1,500 each to St Francis Leprosy Guild, Intercare, Shaftesbury Society – Poole and St Barnabas Society.

FINANCES *Year* 2001–02 *Income* £172,118 *Grants* £173,000 *Assets* £4,891,429

TRUSTEES Miss J M Bisgood; P Schulte; P J K Bisgood.

OTHER INFORMATION A sub-fund, the Bertram Fund, had assets in 1998–99 totalling £3.8 million

with an income of £126,000. This fund does not accept applications, and grants are usually made anonymously.

HOW TO APPLY In writing to the correspondent, quoting the UK registration number and registered title of the charity. A copy of the most recent accounts should also be enclosed. Applications should NOT be made directly to the Bertram Fund. Applications for capital projects 'should provide brief details of the main purposes, the total target and the current state of the appeal'. The trustees regret that they are unable to acknowledge appeals. The trustees normally meet in late February/early March and September.

WHO TO APPLY TO Miss J M Bisgood, Trustee, 12 Waters Edge, Brudenell Road, Poole BH13 7NN *Tel* 01202 708460

CC NO 208714   **ESTABLISHED** 1963

■ The Michael Bishop Foundation

WHERE FUNDING CAN BE GIVEN Worldwide with a preference for Birmingham and the Midlands.

WHO CAN BENEFIT Registered charities concerned with arts, health, child welfare, education and religion.

WHAT IS FUNDED The trust currently has a long-term commitment to the D'Oyly Carte Opera Trust, limiting other grants.

WHAT IS NOT FUNDED Due to the long-term commitment to the D'Oyly Carte Opera Trust, the foundation is unable to support new applicants at the present time.

FINANCES *Year* 1999–2000 *Income* £79,000 *Grants* £40,000 *Assets* £982,000

TRUSTEES Sir Michael Bishop, Chair; Grahame N Elliott; John T Wolfe; John S Coulson.

HOW TO APPLY In writing to the correspondent. However, the long-term commitment mentioned above means that new applicants are not supported at present.

WHO TO APPLY TO Mrs P Robinson, Donington Hall, Castle Donnington, Derby BE74 2SB

CC NO 297627   **ESTABLISHED** 1987

■ The Bishop's Development Fund

WHERE FUNDING CAN BE GIVEN The diocese of Wakefield.

WHO CAN BENEFIT Church of England organisations benefiting children, young adults and Christians.

WHAT IS FUNDED The fund will support diocesan mission and seek to specifically encourage: congregational growth – projects which will provide new facilities or initiatives to encourage more people to attend and support church; attracting younger people – new facilities or initiatives to attract and retain young people; community outreach – new projects which will bring benefits to the wider local community. The aim is to support locally-based projects where mission and not maintenance is the keynote of church life.

WHAT IS NOT FUNDED Any application which does not meet the criteria above.

TYPE OF GRANT Capital grants.

RANGE OF GRANTS £200–£5,000.

SAMPLE GRANTS £4,000 to St Botolph's Knottingley; £2,000 to St Philip's Birchencliffe; £1,000 to St Michael's Wakefield; £900 to St Barnabas' Hightown; £300 to St John's Golcar; £250 to St Luke's Whitechapel.

FINANCES *Year* 2001–02 *Income* £24,000 *Grants* £26,500 *Assets* £627,000

TRUSTEES Right Revd Nigel S McCulloch; Ven. Richard Inwood; Ven. Anthony Robinson; Mrs Mary Judkins; Ron Carbutt; Stephen Williamson; Richard Sanderson; Roger Holmes; Mrs Christine Haigh; Mrs Carol Leckie; Kenn Winter.

HOW TO APPLY In writing to the correspondent. Only applications formally approved by the parochial church councils of Church of England churches in the diocese of Wakefield will be considered. The trustees meet four times a year.

WHO TO APPLY TO Revd Ian Gaskell, Church House, 1 South Parade, Wakefield, West Yorkshire WF1 1LP *Tel* 01924 371802

CC NO 700588   **ESTABLISHED** 1988

■ The Bertie Black Foundation

WHERE FUNDING CAN BE GIVEN UK, Israel.

WHO CAN BENEFIT Registered charities.

WHAT IS FUNDED The relief and assistance of people who are in need, the advancement of education and religion, and other charitable purposes.

SAMPLE GRANTS £25,000 to Magen David Adom – UK; £6,000 to Child Resettlement Fund; £5,000 each to Bournemouth Jewish Day School, Community Security Trust, Lanaido Hospital and Norwood Ltd; £2,000 each to Friends of Lubavitch UK and Jewish National Fund; £1,000 each to Bournemouth Hebrew Congregation and Jewish Music Institute.

FINANCES *Year* 2000–01 *Income* £139,507 *Grants* £77,281 *Assets* £2,569,286

TRUSTEES I B Black; Mrs D Black; H S Black; Mrs I R Broido.

HOW TO APPLY In writing to the correspondent, but please note, the trust states it 'supports causes known to the trustees'.

WHO TO APPLY TO Mrs I R Broido, Trustee, Abbots House, 198 Lower High Street, Watford WDI7 2FG

CC NO 245207   **ESTABLISHED** 1965

■ Peter Black Charitable Trust

WHERE FUNDING CAN BE GIVEN UK and overseas.

WHO CAN BENEFIT Regional and UK charities, and Jewish charities.

WHAT IS FUNDED Support for Jewish organisations is favoured.

WHAT IS NOT FUNDED No grants to individuals.

TYPE OF GRANT One-off and recurrent grants.

RANGE OF GRANTS £10–£5,000.

SAMPLE GRANTS £5,000 to AES Tring Park School Trust Ltd; £2,600 to The One to One Project; £2,000 to Yorkshire Ballet Seminars; £1,500 to the Beth Shalom Holocaust Centre; £1,000 each to Bradford Jewish Benevolent Fund, Project Bandstand 2000, The Ashton Trust/Israel Tennis Centre and Martin House.

FINANCES *Year* 2000–01 *Income* £14,000 *Grants* £24,000 *Assets* £39,000

TRUSTEES T S S Black; G L Black; A S Black.

HOW TO APPLY In writing to the correspondent.

WHO TO APPLY TO Kathleen M Bell, Peter Black Holdings plc, Airedale Mill, Lawkholme Lane, Keighley, West Yorkshire BD21 3BB

CC NO 264279   **ESTABLISHED** 1972

■ The Sydney Black Charitable Trust

WHERE FUNDING CAN BE GIVEN UK.

WHO CAN BENEFIT Evangelical Christianity, social welfare, young people, older people and people who are disabled.

WHAT IS FUNDED For the latest year the report stated that support is given to youth organisations, religious, medical and other institutions, such as those helping people who are disadvantaged or disabled.

TYPE OF GRANT One-off grants for core support, equipment and vehicles.

FINANCES *Year* 2000–01 *Income* £49,516

TRUSTEES Mrs J D Crabtree; Mrs H J Dickenson.

OTHER INFORMATION In 2001 The Edna Black Charitable Trust and The Cyril Black Charitable Trust were incorporated into this trust.

HOW TO APPLY Applications, made in writing to the correspondent, will be considered by the appropriate trust.

WHO TO APPLY TO M B Pilcher, Secretary, 6 Leopold Road, London SW19 7BD *Tel* 020 8947 1041

CC NO 219855   **ESTABLISHED** 1949

■ Sir Alec Black's Charity

WHERE FUNDING CAN BE GIVEN UK, with some preference for Grimsby.

WHO CAN BENEFIT Ex-employees of Sir Alec Black, charitable institutions benefiting the sick and infirm including hospices, and poor fishermen and dockworkers of Grimsby.

WHAT IS FUNDED Primarily to benefit former employees of Sir Alec Black and to provide bedlinen and pillows to hospitals. Secondarily to benefit sick poor fishermen and dockworkers of Grimsby.

SAMPLE GRANTS 1999: £7,302 to Hospice in the Weald; £6,575 to St Catherine's Hospice; £4,285 to BLESMA; £3,800 to The Manor; £3,730 to St Joseph's Hospice; £3,586 to St Julian's Hospice; £2,549 to St Peter & St Joseph's Hospice; £2,382 to Phyllis Tuckwell Hospice; £2,322 to Petworth Cottage Nursing Home; £2,229 to St Luke's Hospice.

FINANCES *Year* 2001 *Income* £75,000 *Grants* £73,000 *Assets* £2,500,000

TRUSTEES J N Harrison; P A Mounfield; G H Taylor; Dr D F Wilson; S Wilson.

HOW TO APPLY In writing to the correspondent. Trustees meet in May and in November; applications need to be received in March or September.

WHO TO APPLY TO Stewart Wilson, Trustee, Messrs Wilson Sharpe & Co., 17–19 Osborne Street, Grimsby, North East Lincolnshire DN31 1HA *Tel* 01472 348315

CC NO 220295   **ESTABLISHED** 1942

■ Isabel Blackman Foundation

WHERE FUNDING CAN BE GIVEN UK, but grants are practically all confined to organsiations in the Hastings area.

WHO CAN BENEFIT Organisations benefiting children, young adults, older people, retired people, disabled people, Christians and people suffering from sight loss and blindness.

WHAT IS FUNDED People who are elderly, blind or disabled, hospitals, churches, voluntary charitable bodies, youth organisations, education.

WHAT IS NOT FUNDED Please note only applications from Hastings and district are considered.

Every application represents a cost to you and to the trust

TYPE OF GRANT One-off.

RANGE OF GRANTS £250–£15,000.

SAMPLE GRANTS In 2000: £15,000 to Two Towers Trust; £12,000 to Wellington Square Baptist Church; £10,000 each to Salvation Army and Hastings Old Town Community Centre; £7,000 to Community Action Team Projects – South East; £5,000 to Marie Curie Cancer Care; £4,000 each to Homecall and Hastings Trust; £3,000 to Youth Clubs Sussex Ltd; £2,500 to the Stables Trust Ltd.

FINANCES *Year* 2001 *Income* £203,000 *Grants* £186,000 *Assets* £4,600,000

TRUSTEES Mrs W M Mabbett; R A Vint; R T Mennell; D J Jukes; Mrs M Haley.

HOW TO APPLY In writing to the correspondent. The trustees meet bi-monthly to consider applications.

WHO TO APPLY TO R A Vint, Secretary, 13 Laton Road, Hastings, East Sussex TN34 2ES *Tel* 01424 431 756

CC NO 313577   **ESTABLISHED** 1966

■ The Herbert & Peter Blagrave Charitable Trust

WHERE FUNDING CAN BE GIVEN Hampshire, Wiltshire and Berkshire.

WHO CAN BENEFIT Registered charities only working in the geographical areas stated.

WHAT IS FUNDED Elderly people, children with disabilities and special needs, injured and disabled sportsmen, and medical research.

WHAT IS NOT FUNDED 'Applications are only considered from registered charities. Individuals, including students, are not eligible for grants. Normally, grants are not made in response to general appeals from large national organisations'. No grants may be made where funds from statutory sources can be obtained.

TYPE OF GRANT Usually one-off but can be recurrent.

RANGE OF GRANTS £500–£25,000, but typically £2,500 or more.

SAMPLE GRANTS £30,000 to the Injured Jockeys Fund; £20,000 each to the Wiltshire Community Foundation and HAPA; £10,000 each to Royal Berkshire Community Trust, Enham Trust and Treloar Trust; £7,500 to UBS; £5,000 each to John Simmons Trust and Abilitynet; £4,500 to Disability Aid Fund.

FINANCES *Year* 1999–2000 *Income* £384,000 *Grants* £227,700 *Assets* £15,000,000

TRUSTEES Julian R Whately; Timothy W A Jackson-Stops; Sir P A Neave.

HOW TO APPLY The trustees meet three times a year in March, July and November. Applications should be made using the trust's application form, which can be requested from the trust's offices. Application forms should be received at least six weeks before the next trustees' meeting. Once your application has arrived you will be contacted by the director who will usually organise to visit your project to discuss it in more detail. Successful applicants will be asked to give a report about how a grant has been used within 12 months of receiving it.

WHO TO APPLY TO Jane Love, Director, 142 Buckingham Palace Road, London SW1W 9TR

CC NO 277074   **ESTABLISHED** 1978

■ The Blair Foundation

WHERE FUNDING CAN BE GIVEN UK and overseas.

WHO CAN BENEFIT Organisations, particularly disability and wildlife groups.

WHAT IS FUNDED General, especially conservation and protection of the environment; improving disabled access to wildlife areas; and medical charities.

WHAT IS NOT FUNDED Charities that have objectives the trustees consider harmful to the environment are not supported.

RANGE OF GRANTS £100–£50,000.

SAMPLE GRANTS £50,751 to Ayrshire Wildlife Services; £17,000 to Queen Elizabeth Foundation for the Disabled; £5,000 each to Dailly Amateur Football Club, and Surrey Community Development Trust; £4,000 to Sense; £2,500 each to Help the Aged and National Trust for Scotland for Culzean Castle; £2,000 to Ayrshire Fiddler Orchestra, Manx Wildlife Trust, and Wells Cathedral School.

FINANCES *Year* 2000/01 *Income* £206,443 *Grants* £120,354 *Assets* £1,371,595

TRUSTEES Robert Thornton; Jennifer Thornton; Graham Healy; Alan Thornton; Philippa Thornton.

HOW TO APPLY In writing to the correspondent, for consideration at trustees' meetings held at least once a year. A receipt for donations is requested from all donees. The correspondent stated: 'I have been inundated with appeals for help, which far exceed the resources available ... the costs of administration are now becoming disproportionate to the funds available.'

WHO TO APPLY TO Graham Healy, Trustee, Smith & Williamson, 1 Bishops Wharf, Walnut Tree Close, Guildford, Surrey GU1 4RA *Tel* 01483 407100 *Fax* 01483 407194

CC NO 801755   **ESTABLISHED** 1989

■ The Morgan Blake Charitable Trust

WHERE FUNDING CAN BE GIVEN UK.

WHO CAN BENEFIT Registered charities.

WHAT IS FUNDED General charitable purposes. Most projects will be considered.

WHAT IS NOT FUNDED No grants to individuals.

RANGE OF GRANTS £1,500–£4,000.

SAMPLE GRANTS £4,000 each to East Anglia's Children's Hospices, Soundabout, St Bart's Cancer Centre, and Marie Curie Cancer Care; £2,000 each to Swaffham Hospital League of Friends and Phamly Hamond's School–Tanzania project.

FINANCES *Year* 2000–01 *Grants* £39,000

TRUSTEES J P Hall; J F Whigham.

HOW TO APPLY In writing to the correspondent. (Enquiries by telephone are not accepted.)

WHO TO APPLY TO J F Whigham, Trustee, Hood Vores & Allwood Solicitors, The Priory, Church Street, Dereham, Norfolk NR19 1DW *Tel* 01362 692424 *Fax* 01362 698858 *E-mail* jwhigham@hoodvoreslaw.co.uk

CC NO 293706   **ESTABLISHED** 1985

■ Blakes Benevolent Trust

WHERE FUNDING CAN BE GIVEN UK.

WHO CAN BENEFIT Charities; individuals connected with the J Blake & Co. Ltd Group of companies.

WHAT IS FUNDED General charitable purposes.

FINANCES *Year* 2000–01 *Income* £103,560 *Grants* £74,000 *Assets* £2,062,338

TRUSTEES N K Silk; B Ball; P M Davies.

Think carefully about every application. Is it justified?

327

HOW TO APPLY In writing to the correspondent. However, please note that the trust stated that it only gives to 'private beneficiaries'.

WHO TO APPLY TO Norman Silk, Trustee, Carrickness, Oldfield Drive, Heswall, Wirral CH60 6SS *Tel* 0151 342 3103

CC NO 225268   **ESTABLISHED** 1958

■ The Blanchminster Trust

WHERE FUNDING CAN BE GIVEN The parishes of Bude, Stratton and Poughill (i.e. the former urban district of Bude-Stratton on 31 March 1974).

WHO CAN BENEFIT Organisations or individuals having residential qualifications as above and showing proof of financial need. Organisations benefiting children; young adults; older people; academics; students; actors and entertainment professionals; and musicians may be considered.

WHAT IS FUNDED Charities working in the fields of: infrastructure, support and development; religious buildings; arts, culture and recreation; health facilities and buildings; education and training; community services and facilities; and advice and information. Applicants must reside within the beneficial area and give proof of financial need.

WHAT IS NOT FUNDED Applications from Bude-Stratton only will be considered, or from people who have at least one parent so residing.

TYPE OF GRANT Cash or equipment. Cash may be grant or loan, equipment normally 'permanent loan'. Capital including buildings, core costs, feasibility studies, interest free loans, one-off, project, running costs and start-up costs. Funding will be considered for one year or less.

RANGE OF GRANTS £100–£63,700.

SAMPLE GRANTS £63,700 to Bude Infant School; £6,000 to Bude CAB; £4,000 to Bude Toy Library; £3,000 to Bude Hockey Club.

FINANCES *Year* 2001 *Income* £357,000 *Grants* £276,000 *Assets* £6,190,000

TRUSTEES A N Benney; Miss M H Clowes; C B Cornish; J E Gardiner; W J Keat; Mrs V A Newman; J Richardson; G C Rogers; B C Rowlands; Mrs J M Shepherd; R S Thorn; L M J Tozer; P Truscott.

HOW TO APPLY In writing to the correspondent. Applications are considered at monthly meetings. All applications are acknowledged.

WHO TO APPLY TO O A May, Clerk to the Trustees, Blanchminster Building, 38 Lansdown Road, Bude, Cornwall EX23 8EE *Tel* 01288 352851 *Fax* 01288 352851

CC NO 202118   **ESTABLISHED** 1421

■ Blatchington Court Trust

WHERE FUNDING CAN BE GIVEN UK, preference for Sussex.

WHO CAN BENEFIT Charities and other bodies in the field of education for the under 30 age group who are visually impaired.

WHAT IS FUNDED To provide funding for the education of children and young people under 30 years of age with visual impairment.

RANGE OF GRANTS Up to £250,000.

SAMPLE GRANTS £525,000 to SeeABILITY towards the residential unit and day centre for visually impaired children and young adults at Barclay House; £300,000 to SeeABILITY towards the construction of a new centre for children with Battnes Disease in Hampshire; £40,000 to Dorton House School distance learning project; £16,500 to LOOK for the provision of advocacy

services and costs of producing a newsletter; £6,200 to Eastnet project; £6,000 to Scope; £5,500 to West Sussex Association for the Blind; £3,000 to Berkshire County Blind Association; £1,600 to Fordwater School; £1,534 to Talking Newspapers Association.

FINANCES *Year* 1998–99 *Income* £494,000 *Grants* £1,100,000 *Assets* £11,500,000

TRUSTEES Dr Geoffrey Lockwood, Chair; Roger Jones; Dr Geoffrey Lockwood; Richard Martin; Lady Helen Trafford; Bruce McCleod; Colin Finnerty; Ms Georgina James.

HOW TO APPLY In writing to the correspondent from whom individual or corporate/charity grant application forms can be obtained. Applications can be considered at any time. An application on behalf of a registered charity should include audited accounts and up-to-date information on the charity and its commitments.

WHO TO APPLY TO Dr Geoff Lockwood, Chair, Ridgeland House, 165 Dyke Road, Hove, East Sussex BN3 1TL *Tel* 01273 727222 *Fax* 01273 722244 *E-mail* enquiries@blatchington-court.co.uk *Website* www.blatchington-court.co.uk

CC NO 306350   **ESTABLISHED** 1966

■ The Neville & Elaine Blond Charitable Trust

WHERE FUNDING CAN BE GIVEN Worldwide.

WHO CAN BENEFIT Particularly Jewish charities.

WHAT IS FUNDED General charitable purposes, with particular emphasis on Jewish Charities.

WHAT IS NOT FUNDED Only registered charities are supported.

SAMPLE GRANTS £55,000 to British WIZO; £30,000 to JPAIME; £10,000 each to Weizmann Institute Foundation and World Jewish Relief; £7,000 to GRET; £4,000 to Halle Orchestra; £2,500 to Jerusalem Foundation; £1,000 each to British ORT, Chicken Shed Theatre, Fulcrum Challenge, Institute of Child Health, Jewish Lads and Girls Brigade and Westminster Children's Society.

FINANCES *Year* 2001–02 *Income* £74,037 *Grants* £124,664 *Assets* £1,384,189

TRUSTEES Dame Simone Prendergast; Peter Blond; Mrs A E Susman; S N Susman; Mrs J Skidmore.

HOW TO APPLY In writing to the correspondent. Applications should arrive by 31 January for consideration in late spring.

WHO TO APPLY TO The Trustees, c/o H W Fisher & Co, Chartered Accountants, Acre House, 11–15 William Road, London NW1 3ER *Tel* 020 7388 7000

CC NO 206319   **ESTABLISHED** 1953

■ The Patsy Bloom & Robert Blausten Charitable Trust

WHERE FUNDING CAN BE GIVEN UK.

WHO CAN BENEFIT Registered charities.

WHAT IS FUNDED General charitable purposes, including Jewish organisations, animal welfare, cancer charities and culture.

FINANCES *Year* 2000 *Income* £34,000 *Grants* £36,000

TRUSTEES I A Brecher; Patsy Bloom; A L Bloom; A I Krais; R Blausten.

HOW TO APPLY The trust stated: 'Funds for the next two years are fully committed. Unsolicited applications will not be acknowledged.'

WHO TO APPLY TO Mark Deller, Administrator, PO Box 11217, London NW1 4WE *Tel* 020 7935 4070 *Fax* 020 7935 0766
CC NO 1054034   **ESTABLISHED** 1996

■ The Bluston Charitable Settlement

WHERE FUNDING CAN BE GIVEN Mostly UK.
WHO CAN BENEFIT Registered charities, particularly Jewish organisations.
WHAT IS FUNDED General charitable purposes.
WHAT IS NOT FUNDED No grants to individuals.
SAMPLE GRANTS £100,000 to Jewish Free School; £50,000 to Variety Club Children's Charity; £1,000 to British Friends of the Ohel Sarah.
FINANCES *Year* 2000–01 *Income* £126,223 *Grants* £151,000 *Assets* £225,296
TRUSTEES Edward Langton; M D Paisner.
HOW TO APPLY In writing to the correspondent. The trustees meet annually in March.
WHO TO APPLY TO The Trustees, BDO Stoy Hayward, 8 Baker Street, London W1U 3LL *Tel* 020 7486 5888
CC NO 256691   **ESTABLISHED** 1968

■ Enid Blyton Trust for Children

WHERE FUNDING CAN BE GIVEN UK and overseas.
WHO CAN BENEFIT Children up to the age of 16 years where there is a need not supplied from the non-charitable sector; including children who are in care, sick or disabled.
WHAT IS FUNDED Special schools; some primary schools; literacy; playschemes; arts activities; holidays; some medical support. Particularly small projects or ongoing requirements of small charities.
WHAT IS NOT FUNDED No grants for further education, private education or for the benefit of anyone over the age of 16 years. No grants to individuals.
TYPE OF GRANT One-off and some recurring.
RANGE OF GRANTS £300–£1,200.
SAMPLE GRANTS £1,000 each to Calibre Cassette Library for recording new titles for cassettes for blind and visually impaired children and Children of the Andes for care of street children in Colombia; £800 each to the Bourne Trust for all day children's visits to Holloway Prison and Computer International to supply recycled computers to schools in the third world; £629 to Thrive for St Mary's Garden project in Hackney; £600 to Enuresis Resource and Research Centre for support of children affected by enuresis; £500 to Rainbow Trust for books and videos for children with life threatening illness.
FINANCES *Year* 2001–02 *Income* £27,069 *Grants* £24,656 *Assets* £550,930
TRUSTEES S Smallwood; B Nyman; F Rowett; R Wood; I Smallwood.
HOW TO APPLY In writing to the address above, including annual accounts or at least good financial details. Trustees meet three times a year, usually in March, July and November.
WHO TO APPLY TO Ms S Smallwood, 98 Bomeville Gardens, London SW4 9LE *Tel* 020 8675 6836
CC NO 284999   **ESTABLISHED** 1982

■ The BNFL Springfields Medical Research & Charity Trust Fund

WHERE FUNDING CAN BE GIVEN Lancashire.
WHO CAN BENEFIT Organisations benefiting disabled people.
WHAT IS FUNDED Grants to hospitals and local medical and welfare charities for medical equipment.
TYPE OF GRANT One-off grants.
RANGE OF GRANTS £80–£3,500; typically £1,500.
SAMPLE GRANTS £3,500 each to Lancashire Ambulance Service – First Responders and Little Sisters of the Poor; £2,895 to Sense; £2,700 to Blackpool Bears; £2,645 to National Autistic Association; £2,500 to Blackpool Hospital Radio; and £1,425 Parkinsons Disease Society.
FINANCES *Year* 2001 *Income* £38,976 *Grants* £33,688 *Assets* £54,584
TRUSTEES D J Craig; I R Driver; Miss J A Humphreys.
HOW TO APPLY In writing to the correspondent.
WHO TO APPLY TO Ian R Driver, Welfare Officer, British Nuclear Fuels plc, UK Fuel Business Springfields, Salwick, Preston PR4 0XJ *Tel* 01772 764578 *Fax* 01772 763228
CC NO 518005   **ESTABLISHED** 1985

■ The Body Shop Foundation

WHERE FUNDING CAN BE GIVEN UK and overseas.
WHO CAN BENEFIT Small, grassroots organisations at the forefront of positive social and environmental change; projects that demonstrate some or all of the following: commitment, vision, activism, innovation, sound management, holistic approach, strong volunteer support and risk taking; people of all races, gender, nations and ethnic groups; organisations which demonstrate good financial management; 'advocate' organisations working with policy makers; groups working to increase public awareness.
WHAT IS FUNDED Grants are given to innovative, grassroots organisations working in the field of human and civil rights, and environmental and animal protection.
WHAT IS NOT FUNDED No grants to individuals or for sports, the arts, projects which have a low likelihood of sustainability, grants which create a dependant relationship.
TYPE OF GRANT One-off and recurring grants.
RANGE OF GRANTS £100–£15,000.
SAMPLE GRANTS £25,000 to the Ogoni Foundation for development, education and rehabilitation in Ogoni; £20,000 each to Black Liners for a youth magazine for black and Asian Londoners, Body & Soul – HIV/AIDS support group, Emmaus Project for homeless people, Media House Education to fund a video against the practice of female genital mutilation, and National Missing Persons Helpline to support the telephone helpline; £15,000 to Undercurrents; £10,000 each to Genetics Forum for a magazine to stimulate debate on genetic engineering, ISEC for a conference on anti-globalisation, and Soil Association for sustainable organic farming.
FINANCES *Year* 2001 *Income* £1,355,731 *Grants* £734,749 *Assets* £415,216
TRUSTEES Anita Roddick; Gordon Roddick; Barbara Sharples; Annalisa Nicolora-Cinque; Peter Youngs; Bill Hughes; Josine Martin.
HOW TO APPLY The Body Shop Foundation does not accept unsolicited applications. The trustees research projects which meet their funding criteria and only then invite organisations to make an application.

WHO TO APPLY TO The Grants Manager, Watersmead, Littlehampton, West Sussex BN17 6LS
Tel 01903 731500 *Fax* 01903 844202
E-mail debbie.osborne@the-body-shop.com
Website www.the-body-shop.co.uk
CC NO 802757   ESTABLISHED 1990

....

■ Bois Rochel Dsatmar Charitable Trust

WHERE FUNDING CAN BE GIVEN UK.
WHO CAN BENEFIT Jewish organisations.
WHAT IS FUNDED The advancement of the Jewish religion in general and in particular towards the maintenance of a school that provides Jewish and secular education.
RANGE OF GRANTS £1,000–£12,000.
SAMPLE GRANTS £24,000 to Bois Rochel Yetev Lev Nursery; £12,000 to Craven Walk Charity; £10,000 to Yad Eliezer; £4,700 to Holmleigh Trust; £1,000 to Friends of Horim.
FINANCES *Year* 1999 *Income* £547,000 *Grants* £52,000 *Assets* £963,000
TRUSTEES W Low; J Low; J Frankel.
HOW TO APPLY In writing to the correspondent.
WHO TO APPLY TO The Trustees, 21 Warwick Grove, London E5 9HX *Tel* 020 8806 1549
CC NO 281371   ESTABLISHED 1980

....

■ Peter Boizot Foundation

WHERE FUNDING CAN BE GIVEN UK, with a preference for the Peterborough area.
WHO CAN BENEFIT Charitable organisations.
WHAT IS FUNDED General charitable purposes.
SAMPLE GRANTS £8,000 to Fenland Archaeology Trust; £7,000 to Cancer Research Campaign; £5,000 each to Dean and Chapter of Ely and World Monuments Fund in Britain; £2,000 to University of Westminster; £1,500 to British Museum Development Trust; £1,000 each to British Olympic Medical Trust, Childline, Hackney Trust, Inter-Action Trust and Royal Academy.
FINANCES *Year* 2000–01 *Income* £19,502 *Grants* £39,250 *Assets* £777,838
TRUSTEES P J Boizot, Chair; M C Allen; F S Fowler.
HOW TO APPLY In writing to the correspondent. Applications are considered throughout the year.
WHO TO APPLY TO The Trust Administrator, White Horse Court, North Street, Bishops Stortford, Hertfordshire CM23 2LD
CC NO 1020517   ESTABLISHED 1992

....

■ The Boltons Trust

WHERE FUNDING CAN BE GIVEN Unrestricted.
WHO CAN BENEFIT Organisations benefiting children, young adults, older people, Jewish people, carers, and victims of disaster s.
WHAT IS FUNDED Relief of suffering; cultural and religious teaching; bursaries and fees; international rights of the individual, and other charitable purposes.
TYPE OF GRANT Generally single grants for core costs, project, recurring costs and running costs. Funding is available for one year or less.
SAMPLE GRANTS £50,000 each to Conciliation Resources and Power; £30,000 to Spiro Institute; £20,000 each to Friends of Israel Education Trust and Nightingale House; £10,000 each to Dartington International Summer School, Human Rights Watch and Prisoners Abroad; £5,000 to Family Welfare Association; £2,000 to Macmillan Cancer Relief.

FINANCES *Year* 2000–01 *Income* £74,628 *Grants* £247,000 *Assets* £2,406,688
TRUSTEES Clive Marks; Henry B Levin; Mrs C Albuquerque.
HOW TO APPLY 'Sadly, the trust can no longer respond to unsolicited applications.'
WHO TO APPLY TO Clive Marks, Trustee, 44a New Cavendish Street, London W1G 8TR
CC NO 257951   ESTABLISHED 1967

....

■ The Bonamy Charitable Trust

WHERE FUNDING CAN BE GIVEN UK and overseas, with a preference for Liverpool.
WHO CAN BENEFIT Jewish, general.
WHAT IS FUNDED 'The principal objective of the charity is the distribution of funds to religious, educational and similar charities.'
SAMPLE GRANTS £2,600 to Merseyside Jewish Community Centre; £1,100 to Childwall Hebrew Congregation; £750 to Liverpool Yeshiva and Midrasha; £300 to Merseyside Jewish Welfare Council; £100 each to Liverpool Old Hebrew Congregation and Merseyside Jewish Representative Council; £80 to Childwall Hebrew Congregation; £50 each to Liverpool Hebrew Associated Charities Fund, Liverpool Lubavitch and Liverpool Young Wizo.
FINANCES *Year* 2000 *Income* £55,000 *Grants* £25,000 *Assets* £180,000
TRUSTEES Max Moryoussef; Gillian Moryoussef; R Moryoussef.
HOW TO APPLY In writing to the correspondent.
WHO TO APPLY TO The Trustees, Lowfield Mil, Belfield, Rochdale OL16 3AZ
CC NO 326424   ESTABLISHED 1983

....

■ The John & Celia Bonham Christie Charitable Trust

WHERE FUNDING CAN BE GIVEN UK, with some preference for the former county of Avon.
WHO CAN BENEFIT Local and national organisations.
WHAT IS FUNDED Grants are generally small and made to medical charities and organisations, though smaller grants are made to a wide range of other organisations.
WHAT IS NOT FUNDED No grants to individuals.
TYPE OF GRANT Recurrent; over three to five years.
RANGE OF GRANTS £200–£2,000.
SAMPLE GRANTS 1996–97: £2,000 to Bath Abbey; £1,000 each to Multiple Sclerosis Society and Monkton Combe School; £800 to St Luke's Hospice; £600 each to Hospice of the Good Shepherd, National Eye Research Centre, and Rainbow Trust; £500 each to Devon County Association for Blind, Freeway Association and FWA.
FINANCES *Year* 2000–01 *Income* £36,691
TRUSTEES Mrs J R Bonham Christie; Richard Bonham Christie; Mrs Rosemary Kerr; P R Fitzgerald; Robert Bonham Christie.
HOW TO APPLY In writing to the correspondent. The trustees regret that the income is fully allocated for the foreseeable future. Only a small number of new applications are supported each year.
WHO TO APPLY TO P R Fitzgerald, Trustees, Wilsons, Steynings House, Fisherton Street, Salisbury SP2 7RJ
CC NO 326296   ESTABLISHED 1983

■ The Charlotte Bonham-Carter Charitable Trust

WHERE FUNDING CAN BE GIVEN UK, with some emphasis on Hampshire.

WHO CAN BENEFIT Registered charities.

WHAT IS FUNDED General charitable purposes which were of particular concern to Lady Charlotte Bonham-Carter during her lifetime.

WHAT IS NOT FUNDED No grants to individuals or non-registered charities.

RANGE OF GRANTS £100–£15,000.

SAMPLE GRANTS £15,000 to The National Trust; £5,000 each to Canine Partners for Independence, Fitzwilliam Museum and Tate Gallery; £3,000 to Ashmolean Museum; £2,500 each to British Museum and International Merv Project; £2,000 each to Ballet Rambert, Romsey Hospital Appeal and Sports Trust's Refit 2001 Appeal.

FINANCES *Year* 2000–01 *Income* £99,767 *Grants* £94,511 *Assets* £3,630,861

TRUSTEES Sir Matthew Farrer; Norman Bonham-Carter; Nicolas Wickham-Irving.

HOW TO APPLY In writing to the correspondent, although the trust states that 'unsolicited general applications are unlikely to be successful and only increase the cost of administration'. There are no application forms. Trustees meet in January and July; applications need to be received by May or November.

WHO TO APPLY TO Sir Matthew Farrer, Trustee, 66 Lincoln's Inn Fields, London WC2A 3LH *Tel* 020 7917 7331 *Fax* 020 7831 6301

CC NO 292839　　　　**ESTABLISHED** 1985

■ Bonhomie United Charity Society

WHERE FUNDING CAN BE GIVEN Southampton.

WHO CAN BENEFIT Local organisations benefiting elderly and disabled people.

WHAT IS FUNDED The trust will consider funding hospices, MS research, special schools and special needs education, holidays and outings, and playschemes. The conservation of monuments will also be considered.

WHAT IS NOT FUNDED No grants to individuals directly, only through voluntary organisations or social services.

TYPE OF GRANT One-off for buildings and capital.

RANGE OF GRANTS £100–£5,000.

FINANCES *Year* 1999 *Grants* £54,000

TRUSTEES B J Davies; Mrs S Davies; J Davies; R Davies.

HOW TO APPLY The trust states that funds are fully committed and it does not wish to receive any applications.

WHO TO APPLY TO B J Davies, Trustee, 48 Lingwood Close, Southampton SO16 7GJ

CC NO 247816　　　　**ESTABLISHED** 1966

■ Charles Boot Trust

WHERE FUNDING CAN BE GIVEN Oxfordshire.

WHO CAN BENEFIT Oxfordshire charities.

WHAT IS FUNDED Apart from long-term existing beneficiaries elsewhere in the UK, the trusts now directs any new support to local, Oxfordshire-based charitable organisations or projects.

WHAT IS NOT FUNDED No grants to individuals or from charities outside Oxfordshire.

RANGE OF GRANTS £1,000–£15,000.

SAMPLE GRANTS Prison Phoenix Trust; NSPCC; Coventry Cathedral to benefit local disadvantaged people; Shelter; Extracare; Save The Children; Sense; Trax, to combat car-crime by re-educating offenders; Smart; Mental Health Foundation; IMPS; Sightsavers; RNID; Age Concern; Brainwave.

FINANCES *Year* 2000–01 *Income* £97,162 *Grants* £89,100

TRUSTEES John S Reis; Simon C Hogg; Miss Elizabeth J Reis.

HOW TO APPLY In writing to the correspondent. The trust states that it does not consider unsolicited applications.

WHO TO APPLY TO Miss E J Reis, Trustee, Meadow Cottage, Church Street, Beckley, Oxford OX3 9UT

CC NO 802050　　　　**ESTABLISHED** 1989

■ The Booth Charities

WHERE FUNDING CAN BE GIVEN Salford.

WHO CAN BENEFIT Inhabitants of the City of Salford, especially those over 60 years of age.

WHAT IS FUNDED Relief of elderly people and people in need, including payments of pensions and provision of almshouses; relief of distress and sickness; provision and support of facilities for recreation and other leisure-time occupation (with the aim of improving the conditions of life in the interest of social welfare); provision and support of education facilities; any other charitable purpose.

TYPE OF GRANT Capital, salaries.

SAMPLE GRANTS In 1999: £350,000 to Salford Park Hospitals Trust for a new neurosciences department; £30,000 to Hope Hospital, Salford for a research post in the gerontology department; £26,000 to Hope Hospital for a clinical fellow in stroke research; £25,000 each to Hope Hospital for a stroke department nurse and Booth Centre for the drop-in and activities centre for homeless people; £20,000 to Salford Education Department for a music bursary; £18,500 to YMCA for a youth programme organiser; £15,000 to Princess Royal Trust for Carers for the start-up costs of a new carers centre; £13,500 to Age Concern for an activity organisers post; £10,000 to REHAB UK as part funding for an assistant psychologist's post.

FINANCES *Year* 2000–01 *Income* £1,200,000 *Grants* £1,058,000 *Assets* £24,000,000

TRUSTEES M C Mowat, Chair; R P Kershaw; W Jones; E S Tudor-Evans; R J Weston; E W Hunt; R J Christmas; D J Tully; R C Rees; W T Whittle; A D Ginger.

HOW TO APPLY In writing to the correspondent.

WHO TO APPLY TO Mrs L J Needham, Chief Executive, Midwood Hall, 1 Eccles Old Road, Salford, Manchester M6 7DE *Tel* 0161 736 2989 *Fax* 0161 737 4775

CC NO 221800　　　　**ESTABLISHED** 1963

■ The Boots Charitable Trust

WHERE FUNDING CAN BE GIVEN Nottinghamshire, Nottingham and Erewash.

WHO CAN BENEFIT Groups registered with the Charity Commission or accepted as charitable within the meaning of the act.

WHAT IS FUNDED Health including: community healthcare such as community healthcare services, home care, after care, relief of people who are disabled or have a medical condition and continuing care; and health education and prevention by promoting knowledge and awareness of specific diseases and medical conditions.

Lifelong learning: Helping people of any age to achieve their educational potential, supporting supplementary schools, literacy and numeracy projects, community education, vocational/restart education for the unemployed and alternative education for excluded school pupils.

Community development: Helping groups to organise and respond to problems and needs in their communities or networks. This could include groups such as Councils for Voluntary Services and self-help groups.

Social care including: personal social services – organisations assisting individuals or families to overcome social deprivation, such as people who are homeless or disabled and their carers, lone parent and childcare groups and other family support groups; social preventive schemes – activities preventing crime, dropping out and general delinquency and providing other social care outreach work, social health and safety awareness schemes and so on; and community social activity – activities to promote social engagement for vulnerable people, mitigating against isolation and loneliness.

The trust is especially interested in approaches with the capacity to influence a wide audience within the beneficial area.

WHAT IS NOT FUNDED No grants to individuals, non-registered organisations or private fundraising groups. Projects with a clear statutory obligation are also excluded.

TYPE OF GRANT One-off; recurrent; capital including buildings; core costs; project, salaries and start-up costs. Funding is for up to three years.

SAMPLE GRANTS £15,000 to Bassetlaw Fashion Services for Disabled; £7,500 each to ACET – AIDS Care Information & Training, Metropolitan Housing Trust, NORSACA and VOSE Credit Union Development; £7,000 to Elisabeth Fry Family Centre; £6,000 each to Carers Foundation, Notts Dyslexia Association, Ollerton Youth Project and St Peter's Centre Management Committee.

FINANCES *Year* 2001–02 *Income* £258,719 *Grants* £172,640 *Assets* £10,241

TRUSTEES J J H Watson, Chair; A L Bowe; J A Cohen; K R Whitesides; A P Smith; S Rose.

HOW TO APPLY On a form available, with guidelines, from the website. Completed forms should be sent to the correspondent with the latest annual report and accounts. The trustees meet quarterly.

WHO TO APPLY TO The Systems and Trust Development Manager, The Boots Company PLC, Thane Road, Nottingham NG90 4GR *Tel* 0115 949 2185 *Fax* 0115 949 2120 *E-mail* gary.beharrell@boots-plc.com *Website* www.boots-plc.com/communityinvestment

CC NO 1045927   **ESTABLISHED** 1971

....

■ Salo Bordon Charitable Trust

WHERE FUNDING CAN BE GIVEN Worldwide.

WHO CAN BENEFIT Organisations, primarily Jewish, benefiting at risk groups, people disadvantaged by poverty and socially isolated people.

WHAT IS FUNDED Jewish organisations, religious education and social welfare.

SAMPLE GRANTS £8,500 each to Agudas Israel Housing Association Ltd and MIR Charitable Trust; £5,300 to Gateshead Foundation for Torah; £5,000 each to Gateshead Jewish Primary School, North West London Communal Mikvah and Shaarei Torah Buildings Ltd; £4,400

to Parsha Ltd; £4,875 to Golders Green Beth Hamedrash Congregation; £4,300 to Institute for Higher Rabbinical Studies; £4,220 to Menovah Primary School.

FINANCES *Year* 2000–01 *Income* £219,079 *Grants* £162,565 *Assets* £6,719,009

TRUSTEES S Bordon; Mrs L Bordon; M Bordon; D Bordon; M Bordon.

HOW TO APPLY In writing to the correspondent.

WHO TO APPLY TO S Bordon, Trustee, 78 Corringham Road, London NW11 7EB *Tel* 020 8458 5842

CC NO 266439   **ESTABLISHED** 1973

....

■ Sir William Boreman's Foundation

WHERE FUNDING CAN BE GIVEN Greenwich, Deptford, Lewisham and Woolwich – London boroughs of Greenwich and Lewisham (with a preference for Greenwich).

WHO CAN BENEFIT People/organisations concerned with people under 25, resident in the London boroughs of Lewisham or Greenwich for three years or more, in financial need.

WHAT IS FUNDED Providing educational awards to people under 25, and to organisations benefiting eligible individuals, including youth clubs, colleges and educational projects in the beneficial area.

WHAT IS NOT FUNDED No grants to replace or subsidise statutory funding. Grants to organisations must mainly benefit qualified beneficiaries (under 25, resident in Lewisham or Greenwich, in financial need); any benefit to non-qualified beneficiaries is merely incidental.

TYPE OF GRANT One-off.

FINANCES *Year* 2000–01 *Grants* £60,000

TRUSTEES Drapers' Company.

OTHER INFORMATION Administered by the Draper's Company, the foundation was founded under the will of Sir William Boreman, dated 1684.

HOW TO APPLY In writing to the correspondent. Only one application within a 12-month period is permitted. The application should include the following: an sae; a brief description of your organisation, its work and existing sources of funding; a brief description of the project for which you are applying for funds, with time-scales; costings of the project including details of funds already raised and where else you have or will be applying, and how much you are applying for from the foundation; details of how the project will benefit its intended beneficiaries; details of previous applications to and grants from the foundation; and an annual report and latest set of audited accounts. Individuals should write to or telephone the clerk to the governors for an application form. Evidence of income will need to be provided. Parental joint income must not exceed £17,000 gross per annum. Evidence of age and an academic reference are also required. The governors meet four times a year, in January, April, July and October. Applications are put to the next meeting for consideration and applicants are advised of the outcome in due course.

WHO TO APPLY TO Miss D J Thomas, Clerk to the Governors, The Drapers' Company, Drapers' Hall, London EC2N 2DQ *Tel* 020 7588 5001 *Fax* 020 7628 1988 *E-mail* dthomas@thedrapers.co.uk

CC NO 312796   **ESTABLISHED** 1962

■ The A Bornstein Charitable Settlement

WHERE FUNDING CAN BE GIVEN UK and Israel.

WHO CAN BENEFIT Jewish organisations benefiting disabled people and disadvantaged people.

WHAT IS FUNDED Jewish organisations, mainly in Israel, concentrating on disabled and disadvantaged people of all ages.

WHAT IS NOT FUNDED No grants for non-Jewish organisations.

RANGE OF GRANTS £500–£115,000.

SAMPLE GRANTS £115,000 to Shaare Zedek Hospital in Israel; £23,000 to British Olim Society Charitable Trust; £15,000 to UJA Federation; £12,500 to Friends of Care of the Needy of Jerusalem; £7,500 to Friends of Yad Sarah; £5,000 to National Foundation for Jewish Culture; £2,000 to Chabad House; £500 to Chai Lifeline Cancer Care.

FINANCES *Year* 2000–01 *Income* £244,000 *Grants* £186,000

TRUSTEES N P Bornstein; M Hollander.

HOW TO APPLY In writing to the correspondent.

WHO TO APPLY TO Peter Musgrave, HLB AV Audit plc, 66 Wigmore Street, London W1H 2HQ *Tel* 020 7467 4000 *Fax* 020 7467 4040

CC NO 262472   **ESTABLISHED** 1967

■ The Oliver Borthwick Memorial Trust

WHERE FUNDING CAN BE GIVEN UK.

WHO CAN BENEFIT Registered charities benefiting homeless people and people disadvantaged by poverty. In particular the trustees welcome applications from small but viable charities in deprived inner city areas.

WHAT IS FUNDED Currently the main areas of interest are to provide shelter and help for homeless people.

WHAT IS NOT FUNDED No grants to individuals, including people working temporarily overseas for a charity where the request is for living expenses, together with applications relating to health, disability and those from non-registered charitable organisations.

TYPE OF GRANT One-off.

RANGE OF GRANTS £500–£5,000.

SAMPLE GRANTS £5,000 to Woborn's Almhouses; £1,500 each to Banbury District Housing Coalition, F N Charrington Tower Hamlets Mission, Homerton Space Project and New Horizon Youth Centre; £1,000 each to Alone in London Service and National Association of Almshouses; £500 each to Byker Bridge Housing Association Limited and to Central and Cecil Housing Trust.

FINANCES *Year* 1999–2000 *Income* £32,000 *Grants* £29,000 *Assets* £1,200,000

TRUSTEES Earl Bathurst; R Marriott; H L de Quetteville; M H R Bretherton; R A Graham; I J MacDonald; J R Marriott; Mrs V Wrigley; Mrs J S Mace.

HOW TO APPLY Letters should be set out on a maximum of two sides of A4, giving full details of the project with costs, who the project will serve and the anticipated outcome of the project. Meetings take place once a year in May. Applications should be received no later than April.

WHO TO APPLY TO Sue David, Corporate Appeals Administrator, Information Services Department, Charities Aid Foundation, Kings Hill, West Malling, Kent ME19 4TA *Tel* 01732 520082 *Fax* 01732 520001

CC NO 256206   **ESTABLISHED** 1968

■ The Bothwell Charitable Trust

WHERE FUNDING CAN BE GIVEN England, particularly the South East.

WHO CAN BENEFIT Registered charities benefiting carers, people with disabilities and people disadvantaged by poverty and conservation projects.

WHAT IS FUNDED Health, disability and research.

WHAT IS NOT FUNDED No grants for animal charities, overseas causes, individuals, or charities not registered with the Charity Commission.

TYPE OF GRANT Core costs, running costs and research grants, for one year or less.

RANGE OF GRANTS £1,000–£2,500.

SAMPLE GRANTS £2,500 each to Arthritis & Rheumatism Council, Blackthorn Trust, British Home & Hospital for Incurables, Camphill Village Trust, Cancer Relief Macmillan Fund, Echo International Health Services Ltd, Family Holiday Association, Friends of the Elderly, Invalid Children's Aid Nationwide, Leukaemia Research Fund.

FINANCES *Year* 1999–2000 *Income* £44,000 *Grants* £40,000 *Assets* £350,000

TRUSTEES Mrs Angela J Bothwell, Chair; Paul James; Crispian M P Howard.

HOW TO APPLY In writing to the correspondent. Distributions are usually made in March each year.

WHO TO APPLY TO Angela Bothwell, Chair of Trustees, 14 Kirkly Close, Sanderstead, Surrey CR2 0ET *Tel* 020 8657 3369

CC NO 299056   **ESTABLISHED** 1987

■ The Harry Bottom Charitable Trust

WHERE FUNDING CAN BE GIVEN UK, with a preference for Yorkshire and Derbyshire.

WHO CAN BENEFIT Registered charities.

WHAT IS FUNDED The advancement of religion; relief of older people or people who are sick; advancement of education; relief of chronic diseases and research into the cause, relief or cure of chronic diseases; and general charitable purposes.

WHAT IS NOT FUNDED No grants to individuals.

SAMPLE GRANTS £25,000 to South Yorkshire Baptist Association; £10,000 to Sheffield Kidney Research; £7,500 to University of Sheffield Children's Hospital; £5,500 to University of Sheffield School of Medicine; £5,000 each to Cemetery Road Baptist Association, Macmillan Cancer Relief Fund and Wishbone Trust; £4,500 to St Luke's Hospice; £3,000 each to St Luke's Hospice and Innovations Project; £3,000 to Innovations Project.

FINANCES *Year* 2000–01 *Income* £167,000 *Grants* £137,469 *Assets* £3,504,671

TRUSTEES J G Potter; J M Kilner; H F Woods.

HOW TO APPLY In writing to the correspondent.

WHO TO APPLY TO D R Proctor, Westons, Queen's Buildings, 55 Queen Street, Sheffield S1 2DX *Tel* 0114 273'8341 *Fax* 0114 272 5116

CC NO 204675   **ESTABLISHED** 1960

■ The Boughton Trust

WHERE FUNDING CAN BE GIVEN UK.

WHO CAN BENEFIT Organisations known to the trustees, benefiting elderly people and people with disabilities.

WHAT IS FUNDED All grants have been made to charities known to the trustees that fall within the catergories of the elderly, disability, or the environment.

WHAT IS NOT FUNDED No individuals would be sponsored by the charity. Registered charities only.

TYPE OF GRANT One-off grants.

SAMPLE GRANTS In 1997: £4,000 to Winston Churchill Memorial Trust for travelling scholarship; £2,500 to Hospice in the Weald for Egerton Paragon bed; £1,500 each to St Andrew Church, Compton and Freeway Trust; £1,000 each to London Sailing Trust, Martha Trust, and National Trust for Scotland for Great Gardens Project; £750 to Luxford Day Centre Appeal; £600 to Mount Ephraim House, Amenities Fund.

FINANCES *Year* 1999–2000 *Income* £34,600 *Grants* £30,000 *Assets* £703,000

TRUSTEES P M Williams; G J M Wilding; C J T Harris.

HOW TO APPLY In writing only to the correspondent.

WHO TO APPLY TO R D A Sweeting, Clerk to the Trustees, c/o Kidd Rapinet, Solicitors, 14 and 15 Craven Street, London WC2N 5AD

CC NO 261413   **ESTABLISHED** 1968

■ The A H & E Boulton Trust

WHERE FUNDING CAN BE GIVEN Worldwide.

WHO CAN BENEFIT Particularly Christian charities.

WHAT IS FUNDED The erection of buildings for religious purposes of preaching the gospel and of teaching the doctrines. Other Christian institutions, especially missions.

TYPE OF GRANT Tend to be recurrent.

SAMPLE GRANTS £45,000 to Echoes of Service; £30,000 to Liverpool City Mission; £20,000 each to Bridge Street Chapel and Charles Thompson Mission (£20,000); £4,000 to The Salvation Army; £3,000 each to Open Air Mission, Leprosy Mission and Home Evangelism; £2,000 to Gideons International.

FINANCES *Year* 2000–01 *Income* £166,152 *Grants* £138,200 *Assets* £3,096,838

TRUSTEES Mrs J R Gopsill; F P Gopsill.

HOW TO APPLY In writing to the correspondent. The trust tends to support a set list of charities and applications are very unlikely to be successful.

WHO TO APPLY TO J Glasby, Moore Stephens, 47–49 North John Street, Liverpool L2 6TG *Tel* 0151 236 9044

CC NO 225328   **ESTABLISHED** 1935

■ The P G & N J Boulton Trust

WHERE FUNDING CAN BE GIVEN Worldwide.

WHO CAN BENEFIT Charitable bodies of particular interest to the trustees. Particularly organisations benefiting carers; disabled people; homeless people; refugees; victims of abuse; victims of famine; victims of man-made or natural disasters; and victims of war.

WHAT IS FUNDED Relief work at home and overseas. Christian missionary work.

WHAT IS NOT FUNDED No grants to individuals, environment/conservation, heritage or animal welfare.

TYPE OF GRANT One-off.

SAMPLE GRANTS £65,000 to Shalom Christian Fellowship; £16,000 to Intercessors for Britain; £15,500 to Elim Pentecostal Mission Fund; £6,500 to British Red Cross; £5,000 to Just Care; £3,000 each to Mission Aviation Fellowship and Open Doors; £2,500 each to Elam Ministries, Operation Mobilisation and Ebenezer Emergency Fund; £1,800 to Christian Friends of Israel; £1,600 each to International Gospel Outreach and Southeast Asian Outreach; £1,400 each to four organisations, including Life for the World Trust, and Messianic Testimony.

FINANCES *Year* 2000–01 *Income* £98,000 *Grants* £166,000 *Assets* £1,608,516

TRUSTEES Miss N J Boulton, Chair; Miss L M Butchart; A L Perry; Mrs S Perry.

HOW TO APPLY In writing to the correspondent. Owing to the number of applications received the trustees cannot acknowledge all of them. Successful applicants will be contacted within two months.

WHO TO APPLY TO Miss N J Boulton, Trustee, 28 Burden Road, Moreton, Wirral, Merseyside CH46 6BQ *E-mail* email@boultontrust.org.uk *Website* www.boultontrust.org.uk

CC NO 272525   **ESTABLISHED** 1976

■ The M Bourne Charitable Trust

WHERE FUNDING CAN BE GIVEN UK.

WHO CAN BENEFIT Individuals, and institutions benefiting Jewish people.

WHAT IS FUNDED The trustees favour Jewish causes although a number of cancer charities have also benefited.

RANGE OF GRANTS Less than £100 up to £25,000.

SAMPLE GRANTS £25,000 to Prostate Cancer Charitable Trust; £16,000 to Jewish Care; £2,100 to Chigwell Synagogue; £2,000 to Children with Leukaemia; £1,900 to Teenage Cancer Trust; £1,000 to Chabad Lubavich Foundation; £550 to BACUP; £50 each to Jewish Blind and Disabled Charity and Ovarian Cancer Research.

FINANCES *Year* 1998–99 *Income* £176,000 *Grants* £52,000 *Assets* £2,000,000

TRUSTEES C J Bourne; Mrs J H Bourne; D M Morein.

HOW TO APPLY In writing to the correspondent.

WHO TO APPLY TO David Morein, Trustee, Purlieu House, 11 Station Road, Epping, Essex CM16 4HA *Tel* 01992 560500

CC NO 290620   **ESTABLISHED** 1984

■ The Anthony Bourne Foundation

WHERE FUNDING CAN BE GIVEN UK, especially Warwickshire.

WHO CAN BENEFIT Primarily institutions benefiting children and young people.

WHAT IS FUNDED Youth-related activities.

WHAT IS NOT FUNDED No grants to individuals.

TYPE OF GRANT One-off grants for capital (including buildings), core costs and start-up costs. Funding of up to three years will be considered.

RANGE OF GRANTS £1,000–£15,000.

SAMPLE GRANTS In 1998/99: £15,000 to Bourne Youth Challenge; £4,000 to Weston Spirit; £2,000 to Centrepoint; £1,000 each to Leonora Children's Cancer Fund and Raleigh International.

FINANCES *Year* 2001–02 *Income* £25,000 *Grants* £28,000 *Assets* £673,000

TRUSTEES Mrs V A Bourne; A B V Hughes; R F V Jeune.

HOW TO APPLY In writing to the correspondent, including a full set of accounts and an annual report, for consideration in May and November.
WHO TO APPLY TO G J Harmer, Payne Hicks Beach Solicitors, 10 New Square, Lincoln's Inn, London WC2A 3QG *Tel* 020 7465 4300
CC NO 1015759   **ESTABLISHED** 1992

....

■ The Bower Trust

WHERE FUNDING CAN BE GIVEN Wales and developing countries worldwide.
WHO CAN BENEFIT Generally, registered charities.
WHAT IS FUNDED General charitable purposes, though the trust mostly supported causes in the third world rather than those in Wales.
WHAT IS NOT FUNDED No personal sponsorships.
RANGE OF GRANTS £29–£7,000, but generally £500 or less.
SAMPLE GRANTS £7,000 each to Merlin and United World College of the Atlantic; £5,000 to Rainforest Concern; £2,537 to RSNC; £2,500 to St Catherines College.
FINANCES *Year* 2001–02 *Income* £34,060 *Grants* £36,766 *Assets* £657,082
TRUSTEES Mrs C V E Benfield; G Benfield; R Harriman; F C Slater.
HOW TO APPLY In writing to the correspondent. Trustees meet quarterly to consider grants.
WHO TO APPLY TO Roger Harriman, Trust Administrator, New Guild House, 45 Great Charles Street, Queensway, Birmingham B3 2LX *Tel* 0121 212 2222
CC NO 283025   **ESTABLISHED** 1981

....

■ The Bowerman Charitable Trust

WHERE FUNDING CAN BE GIVEN UK, with a preference for West Sussex.
WHO CAN BENEFIT Registered charities.
WHAT IS FUNDED Church activities, arts, medical, youthwork, relief of poverty and resettlement of offenders.
TYPE OF GRANT One-off.
SAMPLE GRANTS £77,686 to Elgar Foundation; £49,172 to English Chamber Orchestra and Music Society; £25,000 to University of St Andrews; £21,076 to St Margaret's Trust; £17,000 to Chichester Cathedral Trust; £11,840 to British Youth Opera; £10,000 to London Handel Society; £6,000 to Royal College of Music; £5,850 to Chelsea Festival; £5,000 to Titus Trust.
FINANCES *Year* 2000–01 *Income* £327,620 *Grants* £262,735 *Assets* £10,097,774
TRUSTEES D W Bowerman; Mrs C M Bowerman; Mrs J M Taylor; Miss K E Bowerman; Mrs A M Downham; J M Capper.
HOW TO APPLY In writing to the correspondent. The trustees said that they are bombarded with applications and unsolicited applications will not be considered.
WHO TO APPLY TO D W Bowerman, Trustee, Champs Hill, Coldwatham, Pulborough, West Sussex RH20 1LY *Tel* 01798 831205
CC NO 289446   **ESTABLISHED** 1984

....

■ The Bowland Charitable Trust

WHERE FUNDING CAN BE GIVEN UK, with a preference for north west England.
WHO CAN BENEFIT Individuals, institutions, and registered charities benefiting, in general, children and young adults. Students may be considered.

WHAT IS FUNDED Preference to help young people, educational or for leisure.
SAMPLE GRANTS £91,000 to Lancaster University; £27,000 to Brantwood; £10,000 to Unitarian Millennium Appeal; £9,700 to Nazareth Unitarian Chapel; £2,500 to Christie's Hospital; £1,300 to Blackburn Cathedral and Ribblesdale Scouts.
FINANCES *Year* 1999 *Income* £93,000 *Grants* £148,000
TRUSTEES H A Cann; R A Cann; D Walmsley.
HOW TO APPLY In writing to the correspondent, to be considered at any time.
WHO TO APPLY TO Mrs Carol Fahy, TDS House, Whitebirk Estate, Blackburn, Lancashire BB1 5TH *Tel* 01254 676921 *Fax* 01254 676950
CC NO 292027   **ESTABLISHED** 1985

....

■ The Viscountess Boyd Charitable Trust

WHERE FUNDING CAN BE GIVEN Worldwide, with a bias towards south west England, i.e. Devon and Cornwall.
WHO CAN BENEFIT Registered charities.
WHAT IS FUNDED Conservation, horticulture and education.
WHAT IS NOT FUNDED No grants to individuals.
TYPE OF GRANT Flexible.
RANGE OF GRANTS £500–£1,000.
SAMPLE GRANTS £1,000 each to Humphrey Davy School to promote and help fund Shakespeare plays, and Rowing Foundation for the Rupert Guinness Centenary Appeal; £500 each to Endsleigh Charitable Trust to help restore and run an historic house, and Royal Horticultural Society for the Lindley Library.
FINANCES *Year* 1998–99 *Income* £24,300 *Grants* £22,050 *Assets* £811,150
TRUSTEES The Iveagh Trustees Ltd; Viscount Boyd; Viscountess Boyd.
HOW TO APPLY In writing to the correspondent; no application form is used. Please enclose an sae to ensure a reply. Applications are considered four times a year.
WHO TO APPLY TO The Administrator, Ince Castle, Saltash, Cornwall PL12 4QZ *Tel* 01752 842249 *Fax* 01752 847134 *E-mail* boydince@aol.com
CC NO 284270   **ESTABLISHED** 1982

....

■ BP Conservation Programme

WHERE FUNDING CAN BE GIVEN Expeditions to and from anywhere in the world.
WHO CAN BENEFIT International teams of students interested in wildlife conservation.
WHAT IS FUNDED International conservation projects which address globally recognised priorities at a local level; projects must involve local counterparts.
WHAT IS NOT FUNDED Only an entire expedition team will be funded: no applications will be considered from individuals applying for funding to join an expedition.
TYPE OF GRANT One-off.
RANGE OF GRANTS £5,000–£50,000.
SAMPLE GRANTS In 2000: £20,000 to Project Tutururu, Tahiti; £13,000 for Bat Surveys, Madagascar; £12,000 for Operation Tortoise, Malaysia; £10,000 for Chinese Grouse project; £7,000 for Iguana Conservation, Fiji; £5,000 each to Andinoheps 2000 (Ecuador), Amphibian Monitoring (Hungary), Conservation Education (Ecuador), Conservation of Kerita Forest (Kenya), and Wetlands Survey (Madagascar).

Think carefully about every application. Is it justified?

335

FINANCES *Year* 2000 *Income* £4,230,632

TRUSTEES The Council: Dr Enrique Bucher (Argentina); Dr Jon Fjeldsa (Denmark); S A Hussain (India); Petar Iankov (Bulgaria); Anastasios P Leventis (UK); Prof. Yaa Ntiamoa-Baidu (Ghana); Baroness Young of Old Scone (UK).

OTHER INFORMATION The programme is a partnership between Birdlife International, Fauna and Flora International, Conservation International, The Wildlife Conservation Society and BP.

HOW TO APPLY Contact the programme manager for guidelines for applicants and application forms.

WHO TO APPLY TO Marianne Dunn, BP Conservation Programme Manager, Birdlife International/FFI, Wellbrook Court, Girton Road, Cambridge CB3 0NA *Tel* 01223 277318 *Fax* 01223 277200 *E-mail* bp-conservation-programme@birdlife.org.uk *Website* http://conservation.bp.com

CC NO 1042125   ESTABLISHED 1990

■ The William Brake Charitable Trust

WHERE FUNDING CAN BE GIVEN Probably Kent.

WHO CAN BENEFIT Registered charities.

WHAT IS FUNDED General charitable purposes.

RANGE OF GRANTS £1,000–£25,000.

SAMPLE GRANTS £25,000 to The Maidstone Trust; £2,500 to the Weald of Kent Rotary Club; £2,000 to Toxoplasmosis Trust; £1,000 each to National Asthma Campaign, St Anselm's School, RNLI, Samaritans, Heart of Kent Hospital, Mote Cheshire Home, NSPCC, Cancer Research Campaign, RSPCA and DEC Kosovo Crisis Appeal.

FINANCES *Year* 1999–2000 *Grants* £43,000

TRUSTEES Bruce Rylands; Michael Philpott; David Richardson.

HOW TO APPLY In writing to the correspondent.

WHO TO APPLY TO B Rylands, Solicitor, Gill Turner & Tucker, Colman House, King Street, Maidstone, Kent ME14 1JE *Tel* 01622 759051 *Fax* 01622 762792

CC NO 1023244   ESTABLISHED 1984

■ The Tony Bramall Charitable Trust

WHERE FUNDING CAN BE GIVEN UK, with some preference for Yorkshire.

WHO CAN BENEFIT Registered charities.

WHAT IS FUNDED To provide support to local charities within the county of Yorkshire and national medical institutions, in particular those concerned with child health.

RANGE OF GRANTS £100–£5,000.

SAMPLE GRANTS In 1998–99: £7,000 to Bradford Millennium Scanner Appeal; £2,500 to War on Cancer – Silver Jubilee Equipment Appeal; £2,000 to Motor & Allied Trades Benevolent Fund; £1,000 each to Cancer Research Campaign, Marie Curie Bradford Appeal, and Wakefield Hospice.

FINANCES *Year* 2001–02 *Income* £57,000 *Grants* £47,000 *Assets* £588,453

TRUSTEES D C A Bramall; Mrs K S Bramall Odgen; Mrs M J Foody; G M Tate; Miss A Bramall.

HOW TO APPLY In writing to the correspondent.

WHO TO APPLY TO D C A Bramall, 12 Cardale Court, Cardale Park, Harrogate HG3 1RY *Tel* 01423 529888

CC NO 1001522   ESTABLISHED 1990

■ Bramble Charitable Trust

WHERE FUNDING CAN BE GIVEN UK, with a preference for Avon and Somerset.

WHO CAN BENEFIT Organisations benefiting young people who are disadvantaged in the Bristol/Weston-super-Mare area.

WHAT IS FUNDED Local groups, and national organisations working in south west England.

RANGE OF GRANTS £250 – £5,000. It is unlikely that larger grants will be made in future years.

SAMPLE GRANTS £250,000 to North Somerset Council for Churchill Primary School; £51,000 to Knightstone Housing for a foyer; £4,000 to Greater Bristol Foundation for summer activities; £2,000 to Winged Fellowship Trust; £1,000 each to Bristol Children's Help Society, NCH Action for Children, and Windmill City Farm; £500 each to Network Counselling, Salvation Army, and Wheels Project.

FINANCES *Year* 2000–01 *Income* £408,565 *Grants* £428,475 *Assets* £208,164

TRUSTEES Caroline Smallwood; Glenys Parkinson; Graeme Varley.

HOW TO APPLY In writing to the correspondent.

WHO TO APPLY TO Caroline Smallwood, Trustee, Bramble Cottage, Dinghurst Road, Churchill, Winscombe BS25 5PJ *Tel* 01934 852589

CC NO 1028751   ESTABLISHED 1993

■ The Breast Cancer Research Trust

WHERE FUNDING CAN BE GIVEN UK.

WHO CAN BENEFIT National and established organisations for innovative projects benefiting medical professionals, research workers and people with breast cancer.

WHAT IS FUNDED Medical research mainly into breast cancer and diagnosis.

WHAT IS NOT FUNDED No grants to students.

TYPE OF GRANT Research funding of up to three years will be considered.

SAMPLE GRANTS £24,233 to Royal Marsden Hospital; £21,955 to Imperial College; £10,000 each to Institute of Cancer Research, Mount Vernon Hospital and University Hospital Oxford; £9,900 to University of St Andrews; £6,450 to University of Glasgow; £5,000 to an individual for research at Brighton Cancer Care Clinic.

FINANCES *Year* 2001 *Income* £161,733 *Grants* £92,736 *Assets* £704,518

TRUSTEES Vera Lynn; Jean-Claude Gazet.

HOW TO APPLY On a form available from the correspondent.

WHO TO APPLY TO J C Gazet, Trustee, 48 Waynflete Tower Avenue, Esher, Surrey KT10 8QG *Tel* 01372 463235 *Fax* 01372 463235

CC NO 272214   ESTABLISHED 1961

■ The Brewers' Company General Charitable Trust

WHERE FUNDING CAN BE GIVEN UK.

WHO CAN BENEFIT Generally, existing beneficiaries.

WHAT IS FUNDED General charitable purposes. In practice, however, funding is restricted to existing beneficiaries with no scope to support unsolicited applications.

WHAT IS NOT FUNDED No support for unsolicited applications. No grants to individuals.

RANGE OF GRANTS Up to £100 except for existing beneficiaries.

SAMPLE GRANTS £15,000 to Aldenham School for Breweries scholarships; £1,200 each to City

University and City and Guilds of London Institute; £1,000 to St Paul's Cathedral for upkeep; £680 each to nine other existing beneficiaries.

FINANCES *Year* 2001 *Income* £27,373 *Grants* £27,250 *Assets* £165

TRUSTEES The Brewers' Company.

HOW TO APPLY In writing to the correspondent, but please note the above comments. No phone calls can be accepted.

WHO TO APPLY TO The Clerk to the Brewers' Company, Brewers' Hall, Aldermanbury Square, London EC2V 7HR *Tel* 020 7606 1301 *Fax* 020 7796 3557

CC NO 1059811   **ESTABLISHED** 1996

··

■ The Bridge House Estates Trust Fund

WHERE FUNDING CAN BE GIVEN Greater London.

WHO CAN BENEFIT Young people, elderly people and people with disabilities.

WHAT IS FUNDED Access to transport, buildings and opportunities for older people and people with disabilities; environmental conservation; children and young people; technical assistance; older people.

WHAT IS NOT FUNDED The trust cannot fund: political parties; political lobbying; non-charitable activities; statutory or corporate bodies where the body involved is under a statutory or legal duty to incur the expenditure in question; grants which do not benefit the inhabitants of Greater London.

The trust does not fund: individuals; grantmaking bodies to make grants on its behalf; schools, universities or other educational establishments; other statutory bodies; medical or academic research; churches or other religious bodies where the monies will be used for the construction, maintenance and repair of religious buildings and for other religious buildings and for other religious purposes; hospitals.

Grants will not usually be given to: organisations seeking funding to replace cuts by statutory authorities; organisations seeking funding to top up on underpriced contracts.

TYPE OF GRANT Capital and revenue grants. Recurring revenue grants up to three years.

RANGE OF GRANTS No minimum amount but applications over £25,000 need to be accompanied by a detailed proposal. Large grants to small organisations are unlikely to be made. The trust is piloting a small grants scheme for organisations with an annual income of under £50,000. The range of grants available is £500–£5,000. Please contact the trust for further details.

SAMPLE GRANTS £723,000 to East London Partnership towards a building in the extended Mile End Park; £500,000 to Forum for the Future to establish a London Sustainability Exchange; £400,000 to St Mungo's towards hostel refurbishment; £255,000 to Barnardos for services to disabled children and their carers; £177,000 to New Economics Foundation to help improve access to community finance; £165,000 to Outset for a distance learning programme; £150,000 to Community Organisations Forum; £140,000 to Age Concern Waltham Forest; £135,000 to Save the Children to support young Vietnamese people in Deptford; £130,000 to BTCV for a bio-diversity project.

FINANCES *Year* 2000–01 *Grants* £15,724,000

TRUSTEES The Corporation of the City of London. Membership of the grants committee: Sir Alan Traill; Richard Agutter; John Holland; Esmond Roney; John Leslie Bird; Michael Cassidy; Richard Scriven; Wilfred William Archibald; William Fraser; John Barker; Joyce Nash; Barbara Newman; Jonathan Charkham.

PUBLICATIONS Guidelines for applicants.

OTHER INFORMATION The prime objective of the trust is the provision and maintenance of the four bridges across the Thames into the City of London.

HOW TO APPLY There is a detailed eight-page application form, available from the trust or downloadable from its website. It includes a one-page summary which will be seen by members of the grants committee. 'If you need someone to talk to about your application, please get in touch with the Grants Unit. We will be happy to talk to you.'

WHO TO APPLY TO The Chief Grants Officer, PO Box 270, Guildhall, London EC2P 2EJ *Tel* 020 7332 3710 *Minicom* 020 7332 3151 *Website* www.bridgehousegrants.org.uk

CC NO 1035628   **ESTABLISHED** 1995

··

■ The Bridge Trust

WHERE FUNDING CAN BE GIVEN Barnstaple and immediate neighbourhood.

WHO CAN BENEFIT Local organisations benefiting at risk groups; disabled people; people disadvantaged by poverty; homeless people; and victims of crime and abuse.

WHAT IS FUNDED Organisations working in the fields of music, hospices, ambulances and mobile units, and voluntary bodies will be considered. Church and historic buildings, schools and colleges, and community facilities and services and other charitable purposes may also be given funding.

WHAT IS NOT FUNDED No grants to individuals, other than on referral through a caring agency.

TYPE OF GRANT Capital including buildings, core costs, one-off, project, research, running costs, recurring costs and start-up costs will be considered. Funding may be given for up to one year.

RANGE OF GRANTS Up to £15,000, with most under £1,000.

FINANCES *Year* 2000 *Income* £248,000 *Grants* £90,000 *Assets* £411,000

TRUSTEES 16 local trustees, 5 of whom are councillors.

HOW TO APPLY In writing to the correspondent. The trustees meet quarterly to make decisions.

WHO TO APPLY TO C J Bartlett, Clerk, 7 Bridge Chambers, Barnstaple, Devon EX31 1HB *Tel* 01271 343995

CC NO 201288   **ESTABLISHED** 1961

··

■ The Harold and Alice Bridges Charity

WHERE FUNDING CAN BE GIVEN South Cumbria and North Lancashire (as far south as Preston).

WHO CAN BENEFIT Particular favour is given to children, young adults, elderly people and village activities.

WHAT IS FUNDED General charitable purposes, particularly young people, elderly people and supporting village activities.

WHAT IS NOT FUNDED No grants to individuals.

RANGE OF GRANTS £500–£5,000.

SAMPLE GRANTS In 1998–99: £5,000 to St Martins College – Lancashire, £2,000 each to Eden Valley Hospice Carlisle Ltd, Heart of Lancashire Trust, Macmillan Cancer Relief – Furness Appeal, Penwortham Grammar School Foundation, RNLI, St Catherine's Hospice, St Peter's Parish Church; £1,600 to St John's Church (towards churchyard maintenance); £1,500 to 1st Lytham St Anne's (St Cuthbert's) Sea Scout Group.

FINANCES *Year* 2001–02 *Grants* £74,000

TRUSTEES Richard N Hardy; Jeffrey W Greenwood.

OTHER INFORMATION The trustees prefer mainly capital projects which have an element of self help.

HOW TO APPLY In writing to the correspondent, followed by completion of a standard application form.

WHO TO APPLY TO Richard N Hardy, Trustee, Messrs Senior Calveley & Hardy Solicitors, 8 Hastings Place, Lytham FY8 5NA *Tel* 01253 733333 *Fax* 01253 794430 *E-mail* rnh@seniorslaw.co.uk

CC NO 236654   ESTABLISHED 1963

■ The Briess Family Charitable Trust

WHERE FUNDING CAN BE GIVEN UK.

WHAT IS FUNDED Jewish organisations.

SAMPLE GRANTS £6,000 to World Jewish Relief; £3,500 to UJIA; £2,000 to British Ort; £1,500 to Jewish Care; £700 to British Heart Foundation; £600 to NSPCC; £400 to World Wildlife Fund; £200 to North London Hospice.

FINANCES *Year* 2001–02 *Income* £36,000 *Grants* £27,000

TRUSTEES S A Rayner; Peter Briess.

HOW TO APPLY In writing to the correspondent.

WHO TO APPLY TO S A Rayner, Trustee, Royds RDW, 2 Crane Court, Fleet Street, London EC4A 2BL *Tel* 020 7583 2222 *Fax* 020 7583 2034 *E-mail* sar@royds.com

CC NO 272721   ESTABLISHED 1976

■ Briggs Animal Welfare Trust

WHERE FUNDING CAN BE GIVEN UK and overseas.

WHO CAN BENEFIT Charities concerned with animal welfare, particularly animals in distress caused by man including wildlife.

WHAT IS FUNDED Although the original objects of the trust were general, but with particular support for animal welfare, the trust's policy is to support only animal welfare causes.

RANGE OF GRANTS £1,000–£2,000.

SAMPLE GRANTS £2,000 to Society for the Welfare of Horses and Ponies; £1,000 to Bleakholt Animal Sanctuary, Friends of Bristol Horses Society, Sebakwe Black Rhino Trust, Thoroughbred Rehabilitation Centre and Woodgreen Animal Shelters.

FINANCES *Year* 1998–99 *Grants* £32,000 *Assets* £796,000

HOW TO APPLY In writing to the correspondent. This entry was not confirmed by the trust, but the information was correct according to the trust's file at the Charity Commission.

WHO TO APPLY TO Mrs A J Hartnett, Belmoredean, Maplehurst Road, West Grinstead, West Sussex RH13 6RN

CC NO 276459   ESTABLISHED 1978

■ The Brighton District Nursing Association Trust

WHERE FUNDING CAN BE GIVEN Brighton and Hove.

WHO CAN BENEFIT Individuals, organisations benefiting sick people and carers.

WHAT IS FUNDED Health; the relief of sickness; respite.

TYPE OF GRANT One-off and funding for one year or less may be considered.

RANGE OF GRANTS Up to £10,000 to organisations.

FINANCES *Year* 2001 *Income* £59,522

OTHER INFORMATION The amount available for distribution to both individuals and organisations each year is about £50,000.

HOW TO APPLY In writing to the correspondent.

WHO TO APPLY TO Anthony Druce, Secretary, c/o Fitzhugh Gates, 3 Pavilion Parade, Brighton BN2 1RY *Tel* 01273 686811

CC NO 213851   ESTABLISHED 1963

■ Bristol Archdeaconry Charities

WHERE FUNDING CAN BE GIVEN Archdeaconry of Bristol.

WHO CAN BENEFIT Charities and individuals for advancement of the Church of England.

WHAT IS FUNDED Religious and other charitable purposes of the Church of England in the area of benefit.

SAMPLE GRANTS Previous grants include: £70,000 to Bristol Diocesan Board of Finance for stipends; £25,000 to St Stephen's towards its city ministry; £10,000 to Easton Family Centre; £5,000 each to Community Sisters of the Church, and Ministry among Asians; £2,600 to Christ the Servant; £2,500 to East Bristol Team Ministry for secretarial assistance.

FINANCES *Year* 1999 *Grants* £140,000

HOW TO APPLY In writing to the correspondent.

WHO TO APPLY TO Mrs E J Wright, Clerk, All Saints Church, 1 All Saints Court, Bristol BS1 1JN *Tel* 0117 929 2709 *Fax* 0117 929 2709

CC NO 1058853   ESTABLISHED 1996

■ The Bristol Charities

WHERE FUNDING CAN BE GIVEN Within a 10-mile radius of Bristol city centre.

WHO CAN BENEFIT Individuals, and organisations benefiting children, young adults and students, at risk groups, people disadvantaged by poverty and socially isolated people.

WHAT IS FUNDED Education; relief of sickness; and relief of need.

RANGE OF GRANTS £35–£10,000; average grant £200.

SAMPLE GRANTS £61,000 to Bristol Grammar School; £12,000 to Orchard Homes; £10,000 each to Bristol Drugs Project and Bristol Cyrenians.

FINANCES *Year* 1999–2000 *Income* £1,300,000 *Grants* £564,000 *Assets* £9,300,000

OTHER INFORMATION In practice about 85 per cent of funds go to individuals, leaving the remainder for organisations.

HOW TO APPLY In writing to the correspondent.

WHO TO APPLY TO D W Jones, Chief Executive, Orchard Street, Bristol BS1 5EQ *Tel* 0117 929 0084

CC NO 204665   ESTABLISHED 1960

■ John Bristow and Thomas Mason Trust

WHERE FUNDING CAN BE GIVEN Parish of Charlwood (as the boundaries stood in 1926).

WHO CAN BENEFIT Children, people with disabilities and people in need.

WHAT IS FUNDED Churches, community amenities, disability, and education.

WHAT IS NOT FUNDED Any application that will not benefit the residents of the Parish of Charlwood (as the boundaries stood in 1926).

SAMPLE GRANTS £29,000 to St Catherine's Hospice; £11,406 to St Michael & All Angels; £10,000 to Millennium Field – Charlwood; £3,410 to Charlwood Providence Chapel; £1,000 to Charlwood Day Centre; £350 to Horley Playscheme – Surrey; £100 to Charlwood Women's Union.

FINANCES *Year* 2001 *Income* £70,000 *Grants* £38,500 *Assets* £2,000,000

TRUSTEES Mrs Hilary Sewill, Chair; Revd Bill Campen; Martin Cooper; John Daniels; Sir Matthew Farrer; Mrs Jean Smith; Mrs Pat Wilson; Colin Gates; Gavin Purser.

HOW TO APPLY Applications should be made on a form available from the correspondent upon written request, and should include an estimate of the total cost of the project.

WHO TO APPLY TO Mrs P J Assender, Secretary, 54 Churchfield Road, Reigate, Surrey RH2 9RH *Tel* 01737 226008 *Fax* 01737 226008

CC NO 1075971   **ESTABLISHED** 1999

■ Britannia Building Society Foundation

WHERE FUNDING CAN BE GIVEN 'Within 25 miles of Leek, where the society is based, in the counties of Staffordshire, Cheshire and Derbyshire. This area covers the city of Stoke on Trent, and the towns of Stafford, Stone, Uttoxeter, Ashbourne, Buxton, Macclesfield, Congleton and Crewe and the rural communities between them.'

WHO CAN BENEFIT Organisations benefiting homeless people and people in need of training, especially in financial matters.

WHAT IS FUNDED Initiatives and projects that will make a difference to local communities. Priorities are: homelessness, including helping people to stay in their homes; educational achievement and aspirations; community safety, including crime prevention schemes; and encouraging prudent money management, by improving financial literacy and money advice services. Infrastructure development is also considered.

WHAT IS NOT FUNDED The following will not be supported: activities which are mainly the responsibility of the state (unless it is for added support services); hospitals, medical centres, medical treatment or research (except for projects which are clearly extra to statutory responsibilities); grant-making organisations; political or pressure groups; animal welfare organisations; profit-making organisations; individuals or individual fundraising efforts, including expeditions or overseas travel; general fundraising events, activities or appeals; fabric appeals for places of worship; promotion of religion; sponsorship of marketing appeals (including advertising in charity brochures or souvenir programmes); overseas charities.

TYPE OF GRANT Any, but preferably special items, and not general contributions towards large appeals. Funding for core costs normally restricted to one-off grants. Capital including buildings, feasibility studies, one-off, project, research all considered. Recurring costs, running costs, salaries and start-up costs are exceptional.

RANGE OF GRANTS £250–£25,000.

SAMPLE GRANTS Beneficiaries have included: Macmillan Cancer Relief, Comic Relief, Ethiopia Appeal, North Staffordshire Hospital, Ipswich Hospital and Regent Theatre.

FINANCES *Year* 2001 *Income* £296,608

TRUSTEES Elizabeth Walmsley; Graham Stow; Gerald Gregory; John Gifford; Mike Frewer; Carol Connolly; Gill Brown.

PUBLICATIONS Grants and donations policy leaflet.

HOW TO APPLY On a form available from the correspondent. Before making an application a copy of the grants and donations policy should be obtained from the foundation to check eligibility. Initial telephone calls are welcomed. Applications for more than £25,000 will only be considered in exceptional cases. Trustees meet three times a year to approve donations. It may take up to four months before a decision is reached.

WHO TO APPLY TO Christine Massey, Secretary, Britannia House, Leek, Staffordshire ST13 5RG *Tel* 01538 391734 *Fax* 01538 399261

CC NO 1069081   **ESTABLISHED** 1998

■ The British Council for Prevention of Blindness

WHERE FUNDING CAN BE GIVEN Worldwide.

WHO CAN BENEFIT Organisations benefiting people with sight loss, and medical professionals, research workers and scientists in the field.

WHAT IS FUNDED Research into eye disease, sight restoration and prevention of blindness throughout the world. Grants are made to hospitals and research workers investigating the causes of blindness, and to those taking steps to cure blindness caused by malnutrition. Support is also given to the organisation of sight-restoration operations, e.g. for cataracts.

WHAT IS NOT FUNDED 'We do NOT deal with the individual welfare of blind people in the UK.'

TYPE OF GRANT For scientific personnel, consumables and equipment.

RANGE OF GRANTS Usually for a maximum of £40,000

SAMPLE GRANTS £96,527 to International Centre for Eye Health; £123,385 in four grants to International Centre for Eye Health for work related to rapid diagnosis of corneal ulcers (£44,953), rapid pregnancy and childbirth risk factors for cataracts in women (£33,550), factors influencing the outcome of surgery for childhood cataracts in developing countries (£29,480) and evaluation of costs of tele-ophthalmology in South Africa (£15,403); £28,994 to Queens University – Belfast; £28,555 to University of Liverpool; £15,000 to Boulter Fellowship Awards to enable individuals from developing countries to study community eye health; two grants of £5,000 each to British Ophthalmology Surveillance Unit.

FINANCES *Year* 2000–01 *Income* £414,680 *Grants* £302,461 *Assets* £226,077

TRUSTEES Prof. Andrew Elkington; Rolf Blach; William Weisblatt; Mark Thompson; Prof. Alistair Fielder; Lady Wilson; Richard Porter; Jackie Boulter; Raymond Hazan; Margaret Hallendorff; Richard Titley.

Think carefully about every application. Is it justified?

339

HOW TO APPLY Application forms are available from the correspondent. An initial proforma must be completed prior to submission of the formal application and must be received no later than the first Monday in June. The deadline for completed applications is the last Friday in July. All projects are subject to a review process and a shortlist made at a meeting in October. All successful grants are awarded in February, unless otherwise stated.

WHO TO APPLY TO Prof. Andrew Elkington., 296 Montague Street, London WC1B 5BH *Tel* 020 7631 5100

CC NO 270941   **ESTABLISHED** 1976

■ The British Dietetic Association General and Education Trust Fund

WHERE FUNDING CAN BE GIVEN UK.

WHO CAN BENEFIT Individuals/research groups of state registered dietitians (and colleagues in related disciplines); professional bodies concerned with dietetics.

WHAT IS FUNDED The development of the scientific knowledge base for the discipline of dietetics through funding of relevant research; support to the profession's development of pre- and post-registration education structures and standards; and an annual travel bursary for students and newly qualified dietitians.

WHAT IS NOT FUNDED Direct support of dietetic students in training or postgraduate qualifications for individuals, i.e. the trust will not pay postgraduate fees/expenses, or elective/MSc study for doctors.

TYPE OF GRANT Project, one-off, research, recurring costs, salaries, start-up costs, interest-free loans and running costs. Funding can be given for up to three years.

RANGE OF GRANTS £2,000–£30,000.

SAMPLE GRANTS £27,529 (over three years) to The British Dietetic Association for a project on clinical effectiveness for dietitians; £6,200 to State Registered Dietitians for development of a molecular-based behaviour change programme; £5,750 to BDA Education for development of a work-based MSc in dietetics; £2,325 to a dietitian for analysis of research project data.

FINANCES *Year* 1999–2000 *Income* £164,120 *Grants* £49,479 *Assets* £519,760

TRUSTEES P Brindley; Dame Barbara Clayton; Mrs L L Daniels; Mrs Carol Leverkus; Miss E T Elliot; W T Seddon.

HOW TO APPLY Guidelines, the grant-giving policy and an application form are sent to prospective applicants. All applications are acknowledged.

WHO TO APPLY TO J C J Grigg, Secretary to the Trustees, 5th Floor, Charles House, 148–149 Great Charles Street, Queensway, Birmingham B3 3HT *Tel* 0121 200 8080 *Fax* 0121 800 8081 *E-mail* info@bda.uk.com *Website* www.bda.uk.com

CC NO 282553   **ESTABLISHED** 1981

■ British Heart Foundation

WHERE FUNDING CAN BE GIVEN UK.

WHO CAN BENEFIT Organisations which benefit people of all ages; academics; medical professionals; students; and people with heart disease.

WHAT IS FUNDED Medical research into all aspects of heart disease.

WHAT IS NOT FUNDED Applications are accepted only from appropriately qualified individuals.

TYPE OF GRANT Project, programme and fellowship grants.

RANGE OF GRANTS No limit.

SAMPLE GRANTS The following grants were given for research into aspects of heart disease to researchers at the named institutions: £1,107,496 to Queen's Medical Centre, Nottingham; £1,107,496 to St Thomas' Hospital, London; £950,012 to Glasgow Royal Infirmary; £782,445 to University of Cambridge; £684,350 to University of Glasgow; £657,272 to St Mary's Hospital, London; £631,642 to University College London; £594,572 to University of Cambridge; £441,174 to Radcliffe Infirmary, Oxford; £378,215 to Addenbrooke's Hospital, Cambridge.

FINANCES *Year* 2000 *Income* £69,000,000 *Grants* £55,300,000 *Assets* £218,206,000

TRUSTEES The Council.

HOW TO APPLY Application forms and guidelines are available on request.

WHO TO APPLY TO The Research Funds Manager, 14 Fitzhardinge Street, London W1H 6DH *Tel* 020 7487 9408 *Fax* 020 7486 1273 *Minicom* 020 7487 7256 *E-mail* research@bhf.org.uk *Website* www.bhf.org.uk

CC NO 225971   **ESTABLISHED** 1961

■ British Humane Association

WHERE FUNDING CAN BE GIVEN UK.

WHO CAN BENEFIT (a) Charities directly involved in humanitarian activities; (b) charities distributing grants to individuals; (c) charities providing relief of poverty or sickness, or benefit to the community.

TYPE OF GRANT One-off, capital and recurring grants will be considered.

RANGE OF GRANTS £1,000–£10,000; exceptionally higher.

SAMPLE GRANTS £20,000 each to Medical Foundation and Professional Classes Aid Council; £7,500 to Craighead Centre; £7,000 to Ophthalmic Hospital Jerusalem; £5,000 each to Friends of the Elderly, Guild of Aid for Gentlepeople and St Luke's Hospital for Clergy; £2,500 each to Church Lad's and Girl's Brigade and Greater London Central Scout County.

FINANCES *Year* 2001 *Income* £135,942 *Grants* £88,905 *Assets* £3,035,635

TRUSTEES C Campbell-Johnston, Chair; Sir David Floyd Ewin; B Campbell-Johnston; H Gould; A C W Lee; Sir Anthony Grant; J M Huntington-Whiteley; Richard Walduck.

HOW TO APPLY In writing to the correspondent; however, the trust only supports one new cause each year and applications are unlikely to be successful.

WHO TO APPLY TO C A E Butler, 24 Craddocks Avenue, Ashtead, Surrey KT21 1PB *Tel* 01372 813717

CC NO 207120   **ESTABLISHED** 1922

■ British Institute of Archaeology at Ankara

WHERE FUNDING CAN BE GIVEN UK, Turkey and the Black Sea region.

WHO CAN BENEFIT British and UK-resident students and academics of archaeology and associated fields. This includes academics, the retired and scientists.

WHAT IS FUNDED Research into archaeology and associated subjects of Turkey and surrounding areas from prehistoric until modern times.

Grants made to undergraduates and graduates in archaeology wishing to specialise in archaeology and allied subjects, who are studying or travelling in Turkey and surrounding regions. The trust will consider funding: arts, culture and recreation; religious buildings; publishing and printing; professional bodies; charity or voluntary umbrella bodies; conservation; botany; natural history; heritage; postgraduate, tertiary and higher education; fellowships; academic subjects; science and research; and libraries and museums.

TYPE OF GRANT Travel, research, study and conference, capital, feasibility studies, one-off, project, recurring costs, salaries and start-up costs. All funding of up to and over three years.

RANGE OF GRANTS Research grants £450–£25,000. Travel grants £250–£500. Study grants £800–£1,800. Conference grants £500.

FINANCES *Year* 2002 *Income* £369,000 *Grants* £127,000 *Assets* £205,000

TRUSTEES Council of Management.

PUBLICATIONS *Anatolian Studies and Anatolian Archaeology.* Both annual publications.

HOW TO APPLY Initial telephone calls welcome. Application forms and guidelines are available on the website.

WHO TO APPLY TO The London Secretary, 10 Carlton House Terrace, London SW1Y 5AH *Tel* 020 7969 5204 *Fax* 020 7969 5401 *E-mail* biaa@britac.ac.uk *Website* www.biaa.ac.uk

CC NO 313940   **ESTABLISHED** 1948

■ British Record Industry Trust

WHERE FUNDING CAN BE GIVEN UK.

WHO CAN BENEFIT Registered charities benefiting young people involved in the arts.

WHAT IS FUNDED The mission of the British Record Industry Trust (BRIT) is to encourage young people in the exploration and pursuit of educational, cultural or therapeutic benefits emanating from music. The trust has an ongoing commitment to the BRIT School for Performing Arts & Technology, but it has stated that it 'continues to seek other projects where it may be of assistance'.

WHAT IS NOT FUNDED No bursaries or grants to individual. No capital funding projects are considered. Only registered charities are supported.

TYPE OF GRANT One-off and recurring grants.

RANGE OF GRANTS £50–£120,499.

SAMPLE GRANTS £260,000 each to Brit School for the Performing Arts and Technology and Nordoff Robbins; £200,000 to National Foundation of Youth Music; £25,000 to Institute for the Study of Drug Dependency; £7,200 to Heart 'n' Soul; £5,000 each to Avenues Youth Project and Fairbridge in Kent.

FINANCES *Year* 1999 *Income* £1,100,000 *Grants* £762,000 *Assets* £2,000,000

TRUSTEES S Alder; P Burger; J Craig; R Perry; R Dickins; Andrew Yeates.

HOW TO APPLY By application form. Applications which match the trust's mission statement are welcomed.

WHO TO APPLY TO Maggie Crowe, BPI, Riverside Building, County Hall, Westminister Bridge Road, London SE1 7JA *Tel* 020 7803 1300 *Website* www.brittrust.co.uk

CC NO 1000413   **ESTABLISHED** 1989

■ The British Sugar Foundation

WHERE FUNDING CAN BE GIVEN Local to British Sugar operational sites in East Anglia and East Midlands.

WHO CAN BENEFIT Volunteer organisations only.

WHAT IS FUNDED General charitable purposes, but the main areas of interest are environment, education and healthcare. Projects inspired by company employees and benefiting the communities in which company employees and their families live will receive special attention.

WHAT IS NOT FUNDED No funding for the arts, or large national organisations. Applications from individuals, including students, are not eligible. No overseas aid.

TYPE OF GRANT Usually one-off for specific projects.

FINANCES *Year* 2001–02 *Income* £94,984 *Grants* £95,000

PUBLICATIONS Policy and guidelines leaflet.

HOW TO APPLY In writing to the correspondent. Policy and guidelines are available on request.

WHO TO APPLY TO Angela MacDougall, Foundation Secretary, Oundle Road, Peterborough, Cambridgeshire PE2 9QU *Tel* 01733 422902 *Fax* 01733 422487 *E-mail* info@britishsugar.co.uk *Website* www.britishsugar.co.uk

CC NO 290966   **ESTABLISHED** 1984

■ The Britland Charitable Trust

WHERE FUNDING CAN BE GIVEN UK and worldwide, with some preference for London.

WHO CAN BENEFIT Individuals and institutions benefiting Christians and evangelists.

WHAT IS FUNDED People engaged in mission, particularly supporting Christian education and training.

TYPE OF GRANT Grants may be for one year or less or up to three years, and for capital (including buildings) or core costs. Interest-free loans are also considered.

RANGE OF GRANTS £45–£10,000, but mostly £45 – £750.

SAMPLE GRANTS £10,000 to St Mark's Church Millennium Project; £4,000 each to Noah's Ark Bursary Fund and St Mark's Church; £750 to Movement for Christian Democracy; £600 to Regeneration Trust; £500 each to CARE and Derbyshire Dales Christian Centre; £300 to Southwark Cathedral; £250 each to Beesom Foundation and St Gabriel's Health Project.

FINANCES *Year* 2000 *Income* £50,000 *Grants* £21,000

TRUSTEES J M P Colman; Mrs S E Colman; R G O Bell.

HOW TO APPLY In writing to the correspondent, including an sae if a response is required.

WHO TO APPLY TO J M P Colman, Trustee, 20 Henderson Road, Wandsworth, London SW18 3RR *Tel* 020 7353 2500 *E-mail* jcolman@lineone.net

CC NO 1014956   **ESTABLISHED** 1992

■ The Britten Foundation

WHERE FUNDING CAN BE GIVEN UK and overseas.

WHO CAN BENEFIT Disaster relief; education; general.

WHAT IS FUNDED The trust has two main areas of interest: relief for people in need, hardship or distress as a result of local, national or international disaster, or for other welfare needs; the furtherance of education for children and young people at all levels, whether they are permanently resident in the UK or only

temporarily.
Other general causes are also supported by the trust.

RANGE OF GRANTS £500–£20,000.

SAMPLE GRANTS £20,000 to Population Concern; £10,000 to CIWFF; £6,000 to Royal Marsden Hospital Charity; £5,000 to Save the Children Fund; £1,000 each to West Herts Community NHS Trust and International Myeloma Foundation; £500 to St Helen's Parish Community.

FINANCES *Year* 1999–2000 *Income* £48,000 *Grants* £44,000 *Assets* £1,700,000

HOW TO APPLY The trust says it only supports charities it knows. Speculative applications have no possibility whatsoever of being successful.

WHO TO APPLY TO The Trustees, PO Box 8, Chobham, Woking, Surrey GU24 8YE

CC NO 1040558   **ESTABLISHED** 1994

■ The Britten-Pears Foundation

WHERE FUNDING CAN BE GIVEN UK, with a preference for East Anglia.

WHO CAN BENEFIT Registered charities.

WHAT IS FUNDED Promotion of the arts, particularly music for commissions, live performances and occasionally, recordings and innovatory musical education projects; education, environment and peace organisations.

WHAT IS NOT FUNDED No grants for: general charitable projects; general support for festivals other than Aldeburgh; requests from individuals for bursaries and course grants other than for Britten-Pears School; travel costs; or purchase or restoration of musical instruments or equipment, and of buildings other than at Snape Maltings/Aldeburgh. The foundation does not consider applications for support for performances or recordings of the works of Benjamin Britten, of whose estate it is the beneficiary. Subsidy for works by Britten which, in the estate's view, need further promotion, can be sought from The Britten Estate Ltd, which is a subsidiary trading company.

TYPE OF GRANT One-off, some recurring and project. Funding may be given for one year or less, or more than three years.

RANGE OF GRANTS Generally £100–£2,500.

SAMPLE GRANTS £179,000 in total to Aldeburgh Productions; £32,000 to Aldeburgh Primary School; £10,000 to Aldeburgh PCC; £5,000 to Symphony Hall SPNM; £3,000 to Joan Cross Bursary; £2,000 to Nancy Evans Bursary.

FINANCES *Year* 2000–01 *Income* £990,390 *Grants* £304,925 *Assets* £12,252,962

TRUSTEES Lord Justice Carnwath, Chair; Dr Colin Matthews; Noel Periton; Hugh Cobbe; Peter Carter; Michael Berkeley; Mark Fisher; Stephen Oliver; Janice Susskind; John Evans.

HOW TO APPLY In writing to the correspondent. Trustees meet in January, May and October. Applications should be sent for consideration by the middle of the preceding month. Five copies of any application should be sent. Applications should be addressed to Dr Elizabeth Gibson (Tel: 01728 451709; e-mail: e.gibson@britten-pears.co.uk).

WHO TO APPLY TO Dr E Gibson, The Red House, Golf Lane, Aldesburgh, Suffolk IP15 5PZ *Tel* 01728 452615 *E-mail* e.gibson@btinternet.com

CC NO 295595   **ESTABLISHED** 1986

■ The Britto Foundation

WHERE FUNDING CAN BE GIVEN UK.

WHO CAN BENEFIT Children and organisations benefiting the people of Israel.

WHAT IS FUNDED The largest grants were to Israeli organisations, with arts, sporting and children's organisations also supported.

RANGE OF GRANTS £100–£16,000.

SAMPLE GRANTS £16,000 to Tel Aviv Fund; £9,000 to Keshet Eilon; £2,000 to B'nai B'rith Hillel Foundation; £1,600 to UK Friends for Further Education in Israel; £1,300 to Israel Philharmonic Orchestra Fund; £1,000 to Friends of MDA in GB; £700 to Buxinton.

FINANCES *Year* 1999–2000 *Income* £35,000 *Grants* £35,000 *Assets* £602,000

TRUSTEES J C Y P Gommes; C L Corman; H K Lewis; T Gommes.

HOW TO APPLY The trustees stated: 'Applications are not sought at this time – trustees choose causes.' They were also keen to point out that these causes were 'Israeli' rather than 'Jewish'.

WHO TO APPLY TO The Trustees, 14a Eccleston Street, London SW1W 9LT

CC NO 1010897   **ESTABLISHED** 1992

■ The J & M Britton Charitable Trust

WHERE FUNDING CAN BE GIVEN Mainly Bristol and the former county of Avon.

WHO CAN BENEFIT General, education.

WHAT IS FUNDED Local charities such as hospital appeals and other charities that the trustees are involved in.

WHAT IS NOT FUNDED No grants to individuals or to non-registered charities.

FINANCES *Year* 2000–01 *Income* £56,617 *Grants* £49,000

TRUSTEES R E J Bernays; R O Bernays; J E D Wilcox; Lady Merrison; Mrs A Bernays.

HOW TO APPLY In writing to the correspondent enclosing an sae. Charities can apply at any time, but the trust makes distributions twice a year, usually in May and November.

WHO TO APPLY TO R E J Bernays, Trustee, Old Down House, Tockington, Bristol BS32 4PG *Tel* 01454 413605 *Fax* 01454 413955

CC NO 1081979   **ESTABLISHED** 1996

■ The Broadfield Trust

WHERE FUNDING CAN BE GIVEN UK.

WHO CAN BENEFIT Educational establishments only.

WHAT IS FUNDED Educational establishments have been the main recipients.

WHAT IS NOT FUNDED No grants to individuals.

SAMPLE GRANTS £108,000 to Farmington Trust; £13,950 to Rendcomb College; £1,000 to Mill Reef Fund.

FINANCES *Year* 1999 *Income* £200,986 *Grants* £122,950 *Assets* £6,652,945

TRUSTEES Hon. E R H Wills; J R Henderson; Sir Ashley Ponsonby; P N H Gibbs; C A H Wills; P J H Wills.

HOW TO APPLY In writing to the correspondent.

WHO TO APPLY TO Ann Sheldon, Accountant, c/o Baker Tilly, Elgar House, Holmer Road, Hereford HR4 9SF *Tel* 01432 352222

CC NO 206623   **ESTABLISHED** 1959

■ The Charles & Edna Broadhurst Charitable Trust

WHERE FUNDING CAN BE GIVEN Preference for Southport.

WHO CAN BENEFIT Academics; research workers; Christians; at risk groups; people disadvantaged by poverty; socially isolated people; people with arthritis/rheumatism or cancer.

WHAT IS FUNDED Grants are mainly given to social welfare organisations, and medical academic research, arts and Christian causes.

WHAT IS NOT FUNDED No grants to individuals.

RANGE OF GRANTS £250–£4,000.

SAMPLE GRANTS In 2000: £4,000 to Birkdale School for Hearing Impaired Children; £3,000 to Southbank Road Methodist Church; £2,000 each to Macmillan Cancer Relief, RNIB Sunshine House, and Samaritans; £1,500 each to ChildLine North West, Light for Life, and Southport Music Festival.

FINANCES *Year* 2002 *Income* £28,190 *Grants* £33,000 *Assets* £644,660

TRUSTEES Mrs J Carver, Chair; Mrs G Edmondson; Mrs K A Griffith; Cllr T J Francis.

HOW TO APPLY In writing to the correspondent. Applications are considered twice a year, usually in July and November.

WHO TO APPLY TO D H Hobley, Administrator, 11 Silverthorne Drive, Southport PR9 9PF *Tel* 01704 225274

CC NO 702543   **ESTABLISHED** 1988

■ The Broderer's Charity Trust

WHERE FUNDING CAN BE GIVEN UK, with a preference for London.

WHO CAN BENEFIT Textiles and embroidery; general.

RANGE OF GRANTS £500–£5,000.

SAMPLE GRANTS £5,000 to Royal School of Needlework; £4,000 to Embroiderers' Guild; £2,500 to The Grange Centre; £2,000 to the Lord Mayor's Appeal.

FINANCES *Year* 2000–01 *Income* £73,000 *Grants* £24,000 *Assets* £289,000

TRUSTEES S A A Block, Chair; N S Charrington; S G Errington; J A Fooks; K M H Millar.

HOW TO APPLY In writing to the correspondent.

WHO TO APPLY TO P J C Crouch, Ember House, 35–37 Creek Road, East Molesey, Surrey KT8 9BE *Tel* 020 8941 3116 *Minicom* 020 8979 5934

CC NO 275080   **ESTABLISHED** 1977

■ The Bromley Trust

WHERE FUNDING CAN BE GIVEN Worldwide.

WHO CAN BENEFIT UK registered charities only working overseas and benefiting victims of violations of human rights or torture, and the environment.

WHAT IS FUNDED Combat violations of human rights, and help victims of torture and oppression and people who have been falsely imprisoned. Help people who have suffered severe bodily or mental hurt through no fault of their own, and if need be help their dependants; try in some small way to offset man's inhumanity to man. Oppose the extinction of the world's fauna and flora and the destruction of the environment for wildlife and for mankind worldwide. By far the greatest part of the income goes to those charities that are concerned with human rights, a comparatively small proportion being paid to charities concerned with the preservation of the world environment. In general, conservation interests are limited to the preservation of rainforests and national and international conservation issues, not local projects.

WHAT IS NOT FUNDED Grants are only given to UK registered charities. No grants to non-registered charities and individuals, or for expeditions or scholarships, or anything outside the stated objectives.

TYPE OF GRANT Mainly recurrent; one-off grants are occasionally made, but these are infrequent. It is the trust's declared policy to give larger amounts to fewer charities rather than to spread income over a large number of small grants. Consequently they are slow to add new charities to the list. Buildings, capital, project, research, running costs, salaries and start-up costs will be considered. The trust's mainstream charities normally receive their grants in two half-yearly payments for a period of not less than three years, barring unforeseen circumstances.

RANGE OF GRANTS £250–£15,000.

SAMPLE GRANTS £15,000 each to Medical Foundation and Redress Trust; £12,000 each to Amnesty International, Anti-Slavery International, Kings College Institute of Psychiatry and Survival International; £10,000 each to Durrell Wildlife Trust, Greenpeace, Hardman Trust, Ockendon Trust, Prison Reform Trust, Prisoners Abroad and Prisoners of Conscience.

FINANCES *Year* 2001–02 *Income* £310,536 *Grants* £315,450 *Assets* £7,933,886

TRUSTEES Keith Bromley; Anna Home; Peter Edwards; Anne Lady Prance; Ann Lady Wood; Anthony Roberts; Michael Ingall; Bryan Blamey.

HOW TO APPLY In writing to the correspondent in the form of a short letter setting out objectives and achievements and with a copy of summarised accounts. The trustees meet twice a year in April and October; applications should be received the previous month. Urgent appeals may be dealt with at any time.

WHO TO APPLY TO Keith Bromley, Trustee, Ashley Manor, King's Somborne, Stockbridge, Hampshire SO20 6RQ *Tel* 01794 388241 *Fax* 01794 388264

CC NO 801875   **ESTABLISHED** 1989

■ The David Brooke Charity

WHERE FUNDING CAN BE GIVEN UK.

WHO CAN BENEFIT Voluntary and community-based groups, especially those concerned with disadvantaged young people.

WHAT IS FUNDED Preference is given to organisations which provide opportunities for self-help programmes and outdoor activity training. Medical charities are also supported.

RANGE OF GRANTS £500–£4,500.

SAMPLE GRANTS £4,500 to Finchdale Training College; £4,000 to Vandestar (ATSO); £3,500 to Great Ormond St Hospital; £3,000 each to Arthritis Research Trust, Barnardos, British Stammering Association, Camphill Village Trust, Childrens Society, Fairbridge, Fortune Centre of Riding Therapy, NSPCC, RNIB and Salvation Army.

FINANCES *Year* 2000–01 *Income* £84,687 *Grants* £76,750 *Assets* £1,856,769

TRUSTEES D Brooke; D J Rusman; P M Hutt; N A Brooke.

HOW TO APPLY The correspondent stated that the trust's annual income is not for general distribution as it is committed to a limited number of charities on a long-term basis.

Think carefully about every application. Is it justified?

343

WHO TO APPLY TO D J Rusman, Trustee, Windmill House, 37–39 Station Road, Henley-on-Thames, Oxfordshire RG9 1AT
CC NO 283658 **ESTABLISHED** 1961

■ The Roger Brooke Charitable Trust

WHERE FUNDING CAN BE GIVEN UK, with a preference for Hampshire.
WHO CAN BENEFIT Registered charities.
WHAT IS FUNDED General charitable purposes, especially medical research, support for carers and social action.
WHAT IS NOT FUNDED In general, individuals are not supported.
FINANCES Year 2000–01 Income £34,959 Grants £206,100 Assets £1,002,803
TRUSTEES J P Arnold; C R E Brooke; N B Brooke; J R Rousso; S H R Brooke.
HOW TO APPLY In writing to the correspondent. Applications will only be acknowledged if successful.
WHO TO APPLY TO J P Arnold, Trustee, Withers, 16 Old Bailey, London EC4M 7EY
CC NO 1071250 **ESTABLISHED** 1998

■ The Charles Brotherton Trust

WHERE FUNDING CAN BE GIVEN The cities of Birmingham, Leeds, Liverpool, Wakefield, York and Bebington in the borough of Wirral.
WHO CAN BENEFIT Organisations benefiting chemists; ex-service and service people; research workers; scientists; students; volunteers; carers and disabled people. There may be restrictions on the medical condition of the beneficiaries.
WHAT IS FUNDED Advancement of education including the establishment and maintenance of scholarships and the recreational training and education of young people; furtherance of medical and surgical research; support of medical or surgical charities. Charities working in the fields of housing and accommodation, arts, culture and recreation, conservation and environment, and community facilities and services will be considered. Support may also go to community development, volunteers and voluntary organisations, churches and religious ancillary buildings.
WHAT IS NOT FUNDED Grants to registered charities and recognised bodies only. No grants to individuals.
TYPE OF GRANT Capital including buildings, core costs, one-off and research will be considered. Funding may be given for up to three years.
RANGE OF GRANTS £100–£350.
FINANCES Year 1999–2000 Income £92,000 Grants £84,000 Assets £1,500,000
TRUSTEES C Brotherton-Ratcliffe; D R Brotherton; J Riches.
HOW TO APPLY Applicants' annual accounts required. Applications are not acknowledged. Distribution made annually in June for successful applications received by 31 January. Applications for student grants and scholarships should be made to the Bursar at the Universities of Leeds and Liverpool, the Registrar at York University and the Students' Welfare Adviser at Birmingham University.
WHO TO APPLY TO The Secretary, PO Box 374, Harrogate HG1 4YW
CC NO 227067 **ESTABLISHED** 1940

■ Miss Marion Broughton's Charitable Trust

WHERE FUNDING CAN BE GIVEN Scotland, with a preference for Lothians.
WHO CAN BENEFIT Organisations benefiting children, older people and disabled people.
WHAT IS FUNDED Grants are made to charities and organisations which are dedicated to helping elderly and disabled people, and also children.
WHAT IS NOT FUNDED No grants to individuals.
RANGE OF GRANTS £500–£10,000.
SAMPLE GRANTS £10,000 to Marie Curie Cancer Care; £5,000 to Cancer Research Campaign; £1,500 each to Alzheimer's Scotland, Capability Scotland, Drum Riding, Edinburgh & Leith Age Concern and St Mary's Cathedral; £1,000 each to Acredale House, Clackmannanshire Care & Repair, Enable and Scottish Motor Neurone Association.
FINANCES Year 2000 Income £40,000 Grants £40,000 Assets £900,000
TRUSTEES E J Cuthbertson; A M C Dalgleish.
HOW TO APPLY In writing to the correspondent but please note the trust states it is 'overburdened with applications' and not looking for more.
WHO TO APPLY TO A M C Dalgleish, Trustee, Brodies Solicitors, 15 Atholl Crescent, Edinburgh EH3 8HA *Tel* 0131 228 3777
SC NO SC009781 **ESTABLISHED** 1975

■ The Swinfen Broun Charitable Trust

WHERE FUNDING CAN BE GIVEN Lichfield.
WHO CAN BENEFIT People living in Lichfield.
WHAT IS FUNDED Support for public buildings and facilities, and general charitable purposes.
WHAT IS NOT FUNDED No grants for the benefit of ecclesiastical or relief of poverty charities.
SAMPLE GRANTS £12,000 to Darwin Foundation for Erasmus Darwin Room; £5,000 to Lichfield Mysteries for staging; £4,500 to Friary School for a new theatre; £4,000 to Staffordshire Regiment for museum; £3,020 to Lichfield City Band for instruments; £3,000 to Lichfield Gymnastics Club for equipment; £2,000 each to Lichfield District Arts Association for a festival, and The Fringe for the Lichfield Festival; £1,500 to Lichfield and District Voluntary Services; £1,298 to Lichfield Friary Grange Cricket Club for equipment.
FINANCES Year 2000–01 Income £29,000 Grants £55,000 Assets £677,000
TRUSTEES J A Hopping, Chair.
HOW TO APPLY In writing to the correspondent.
WHO TO APPLY TO J A Haggett, Clerk, Moseley Chapman & Skemp, 18 Bore Street, Lichfield, Staffordshire WS13 6LW *Tel* 01543 414100 *Fax* 01543 253721
CC NO 503515 **ESTABLISHED** 1973

■ Mrs E E Brown Charitable Settlement

WHERE FUNDING CAN BE GIVEN UK and Israel.
WHO CAN BENEFIT Registered charities.
WHAT IS FUNDED General charitable purposes.
WHAT IS NOT FUNDED No grants to individuals or to medical research.
TYPE OF GRANT Recurring and one-off.
RANGE OF GRANTS £10–£1,000; typical £500.
SAMPLE GRANTS £1,000 each to Age Concern, Jewish Care, Jewish Museum, Nightingale

House, Royal Star & Garter Home, Victim Support and Youth at Risk.
FINANCES *Year* 1999–2000 *Income* £37,000 *Grants* £29,000 *Assets* £754,000
TRUSTEES M D Brown; Sir Simon Brown.
HOW TO APPLY In writing to the correspondent. However, the trust states that it is not currently considering appeals for assistance, preferring to concentrate on organisations already supported.
WHO TO APPLY TO J Rowan, Barber Harrison & Platt, Accountants, 2 Rutland Park, Sheffield S10 2PD *Tel* 0114 266 7171 *Fax* 0114 266 9846 *E-mail* info@bhp.co.uk
CC NO 261397   **ESTABLISHED** 1970

■ The Palgrave Brown Foundation

WHERE FUNDING CAN BE GIVEN UK, with a preference for the south of England.
WHO CAN BENEFIT Registered charities benefiting sportsmen and women, students, and people with cancer, sight loss and terminal illness.
WHAT IS FUNDED Health, education and sports, particularly medical studies and research; independent schools; costs of study; and sports centres.
WHAT IS NOT FUNDED No grants to individuals.
TYPE OF GRANT Capital, recurring, one-off, endowment and project. Funding is available for up to three years.
RANGE OF GRANTS Up to £125,000, but generally £2,000–£50,000.
SAMPLE GRANTS £125,000 to Shrewsbury School Foundation; £50,000 to The Fettes Foundation; £40,000 to University of Cambridge School of Clinical Medicine; £10,000 each to Macmillan Cancer Relief and Prostate Cancer Charity; £5,000 each to British Limbless Ex-Servicemen's Association, Marie Curie Cancer Care, Greensleeves House Trust and Tapping House Hospice.
FINANCES *Year* 2001–02 *Income* £324,357 *Grants* £291,055 *Assets* £3,535,535
TRUSTEES A P Brown; I P Brown.
HOW TO APPLY Unsolicited applications are not accepted under any circumstances.
WHO TO APPLY TO D Dooley, Trustees' Correspondent, c/o PB Forestry Lands Ltd, 24 Bedford Row, London WC1R 4EH *Tel* 020 7831 6393
CC NO 267848   **ESTABLISHED** 1973

■ Bill Brown's Charitable Settlement

WHERE FUNDING CAN BE GIVEN UK.
WHO CAN BENEFIT Registered charities.
WHAT IS FUNDED Health and welfare charities, including those for older people.
TYPE OF GRANT One-off.
RANGE OF GRANTS £1,000–£10,000.
SAMPLE GRANTS £10,000 each to Macmillan Cancer Relief, Leonard Cheshire Foundation and Salvation Army; £7,500 to Imperial Cancer Research Fund; £6,000 to Alzheimer's Disease Society; £5,000 each to National Association for Colitis and Crohn's Disease, Scout Association and UCL Hospitals Charitable Foundation; £4,000 to John Chilton Charitable Trust; £3,000 to Linton Lodge Charitable Trust; £2,000 to Twickenham & District Mental Health Association.
FINANCES *Year* 2000–01 *Income* £71,000 *Grants* £84,000 *Assets* £1,193,489
TRUSTEES P W E Brown; G S Brown; A J Barnett.

HOW TO APPLY In writing to the correspondent, including as much detail as possible. Applications are considered every six months. The trust states that nearly all of its funds are allocated to charities known to the trust and new applications have little chance of receiving grants.
WHO TO APPLY TO G S Brown, Trustee, Payne Hicks Beach, 10 New Square, Lincoln's Inn, London WC2A 3QG *Tel* 020 7465 4300
CC NO 801756   **ESTABLISHED** 1989

■ R S Brownless Charitable Trust

WHERE FUNDING CAN BE GIVEN Mainly UK and occasionally overseas.
WHO CAN BENEFIT Children, young adults and disabled people will be considered.
WHAT IS FUNDED Disabled, disadvantaged and seriously ill people. Charities working in the fields of accommodation and housing, education, job creation, and voluntary work.
WHAT IS NOT FUNDED Grants are rarely given to individuals for educational projects or to education or conservation causes or overseas aid.
TYPE OF GRANT Usually one-off; sometimes annual.
RANGE OF GRANTS Up to £2,000 (occasionally more); usually £100–£500.
SAMPLE GRANTS £4,000 to Camp Mohawk for maintenance and running costs; £3,500 to UNICEF for Mozambique and Venezuela; £3,014 to Prader-Willi Foundation for research and support; £1,500 to Warfrave PCC for cemetery maintenance; £1,000 each to Casa Allianza UK, Foundation for Study of Infant Deaths, St Andrew's Hall (for maintenance), and Witham on the Hill PCC; £500 each to Alzheimer's Society and Crisis.
FINANCES *Year* 1999–2000 *Income* £67,000 *Grants* £46,000 *Assets* £1,700,000
TRUSTEES Mrs F A Plummer; Mrs P M Nicolai.
HOW TO APPLY In writing to the correspondent. The trustees meet twice a year, but in special circumstances will meet at other times. The trust is unable to acknowledge all requests.
WHO TO APPLY TO Mrs P M A Nicolai, Trustee, Hennerton Holt, Wargrave, Reading RG10 8PD *Tel* 01189 404029
CC NO 1000320   **ESTABLISHED** 1990

■ The T B H Brunner Charitable Settlement

WHERE FUNDING CAN BE GIVEN UK.
WHO CAN BENEFIT Registered charities.
WHAT IS FUNDED Heritage; arts; general charitable purposes.
SAMPLE GRANTS £10,000 to Rotherfield Greys PCC (in 11 grants); £2,000 to Society of Chemical Industry; £1,500 to Friends of Covent Garden; £1,000 each to Care International UK, Minority Rights Group, National Centre for Early Music and Portobello Trust.
FINANCES *Year* 2000–01 *Income* £33,000 *Grants* £29,000 *Assets* £1,800,000
TRUSTEES T B H Brunner; Mrs H U Brunner.
HOW TO APPLY In writing to the correspondent.
WHO TO APPLY TO T B H Brunner, Trustee, 2 Inverness Gardens, London W8 4RN
CC NO 260604   **ESTABLISHED** 1969

■ The Jack Brunton Charitable Trust

WHERE FUNDING CAN BE GIVEN Old North Riding area of Yorkshire.

WHO CAN BENEFIT Registered charities for the benefit of the population of the rural villages and towns within the beneficial area.

WHAT IS FUNDED General charitable purposes. All applications are considered.

WHAT IS NOT FUNDED Grants are made to individuals only in very rare and exceptional circumstances.

TYPE OF GRANT One-off.

SAMPLE GRANTS £25,000 to York Minster; £10,000 to Blind & Partially Sighted Society in Scarborough; £5,000 each to Abbeyfield York Society, Cleveland Communication Aids Fund, Marie Curie Cancer Care Nurses, Nursery Action Group – Hutton Rudby, Risedale Youth and Community Centre, St Augustine's Village Hall – Kirkby in Cleveland, St Botolph's Church – Carlton in Cleveland, St John Ambulance Middlesbrough, and Wensleysdale School Minibus.

FINANCES *Year* 1999–2000 *Income* £133,145 *Grants* £138,000 *Assets* £912,765

TRUSTEES Mrs A J Brunton; J G Brunton; E Marquis; D W Noble; P Reed; J A Lumb; Dr C Bruton.

HOW TO APPLY In writing to the correspondent including full details of costings if relevant.

WHO TO APPLY TO D A Swallow, Administrator, Commercial House, 10 Bridge Road, Stokesley, North Yorkshire TS9 5AA

CC NO 518407   **ESTABLISHED** 1986

■ Brushmill Ltd

WHERE FUNDING CAN BE GIVEN Worldwide.

WHO CAN BENEFIT Organisations benefiting Jewish people.

WHAT IS FUNDED Jewish charitable purposes.

FINANCES *Year* 1996 *Income* £133,561 *Grants* £217,276 *Assets* £22,888

TRUSTEES J Weinberger; Y Getter; Mrs E Weinberger.

HOW TO APPLY In writing to the correspondent.

WHO TO APPLY TO Stanley Davis, Cohen Arnold, 13–17 New Burlington Place, Regent Street, London W1S 2HL *Tel* 020 8731 0777

CC NO 285420   **ESTABLISHED** 1981

■ The Bryant Trust

WHERE FUNDING CAN BE GIVEN Roughly the Birmingham conurbation within about 10 miles of the city centre but only east of the M6 (to include Solihull and Sutton Coldfield).

WHO CAN BENEFIT Registered charities only.

WHAT IS FUNDED General charitable purposes. A large proportion of the trust's income is committed to organisations in which the trustees have a special interest. Charities working in the fields of community arts and recreation, cultural activity, hostels, voluntary and community organisations, respite care, self-help groups, heritage, education, campaigning, advice centres and various community services and facilities will be considered.

WHAT IS NOT FUNDED No grants to non-registered charities, animal welfare or individuals. National charities based outside of Birmingham are rarely funded.

TYPE OF GRANT Capital projects are preferred to core funding. Buildings, project, research, salaries, start-up costs will be considered. Funding is available for up to three years.

RANGE OF GRANTS About 20% of grants are part of a small grants scheme where a typical grant is £200–£500.

SAMPLE GRANTS £30,000 to Birmingham Settlement; £25,000 to YMCA £15,000 to RAPT; £10,000 to Midland Arts Centre.

FINANCES *Year* 1999–2000 *Income* £139,000 *Grants* £145,000 *Assets* £2,594,000

HOW TO APPLY In writing to the correspondent, with a copy of the latest accounts. Applications should be submitted by mid-March (for the spring meeting) and mid-September (for the autumn meeting).

WHO TO APPLY TO W M Galliard, Secretary, PO Box 1624, Shirley, Solihull, West Midlands B90 4QZ

CC NO 501450   **ESTABLISHED** 1972

■ The Buckingham & Gawcott Charitable Trust

WHERE FUNDING CAN BE GIVEN Buckingham and Gawcott.

WHO CAN BENEFIT Organisations benefiting the inhabitants of Buckingham and Gawcott.

WHAT IS FUNDED The preservation, improvement and enhancement of Buckingham and Gawcott and the amenities which benefit the inhabitants.

WHAT IS NOT FUNDED No grants to individuals or for projects which would normally be statutory responsibility.

TYPE OF GRANT One-off; capital.

RANGE OF GRANTS £50–£10,000; typically £1,000–£3,000.

FINANCES *Year* 2001–02 *Grants* £58,000

TRUSTEES H Cadd; R Carey; D Foote; D Isham; K Liverseidge; A Morgan; D Rolands; Mrs P Stevens; T Goodman; Mrs C Stain-Clarke; P Strain-Clarke.

HOW TO APPLY In writing to the correspondent.

WHO TO APPLY TO David Bolton, Clerk to the Trust, c/o Finance Department, County Hall, Aylesbury, Buckinghamshire HP20 1UD *Tel* 01296 382315

CC NO 1010071   **ESTABLISHED** 1992

■ Buckingham Trust

WHERE FUNDING CAN BE GIVEN UK and worldwide.

WHO CAN BENEFIT Individuals and organisations promoting the advancement of religion, Christian charities, missionary organisations, missionaries and churches.

WHAT IS FUNDED Advancement of religion (including missionary activities); relief of people disadvantaged by poverty and people who are ill or elderly.

FINANCES *Year* 2001 *Income* £220,837 *Grants* £154,978 *Assets* £838,078

TRUSTEES D J Hanes; D G Benson; R W D Foot; P R Edwards.

OTHER INFORMATION Preference is given to charities of which the trustees have personal interest, knowledge, or association. The trust acts mainly as an agency charity and in 2001 acted on behalf of 56 donors.

HOW TO APPLY In writing to the address below. However, generally funds are allocated to known organisations and limited funds are available for unsolicited applications. Please enclose an sae.

WHO TO APPLY TO The Secretary, Messrs Foot Davson & Co., 17 Church Road, Tunbridge Wells, Kent TN1 1LG

CC NO 237350   **ESTABLISHED** 1962

■ The Buckinghamshire Foundation

WHERE FUNDING CAN BE GIVEN Buckinghamshire.

WHO CAN BENEFIT Community development.

WHAT IS FUNDED The foundation seeks 'to promote charitable activity in the county and thus improve the quality of life, particularly in areas of social development'. While it exists to help any group, it particularly hopes to support very small organisations working at a grass-roots level.

WHAT IS NOT FUNDED No grants to individuals or to religious causes or projects which are properly the responsibility of local government.

RANGE OF GRANTS Up to £8,000.

FINANCES *Year* 2002–03 *Grants* £100,000

TRUSTEES Martin Jourdan, Chair; Gwyneth Davies; Nick Hamilton; Bill McDonald; Tim May; Gillian Miscampbell; John Prodger; Richard Pushman; Ian Taylor.

HOW TO APPLY Application forms are available from the correspondent.

WHO TO APPLY TO Les Sheldon, Unit 4, Farmbrough Close, Aylesbury Vale Industrial Park, Aylesbury, Buckinghamshire HP20 1DQ *Tel* 01296 330134 *Fax* 01296 330158 *E-mail* tbf@bucksfoundation.f9.co.uk.uk *Website* www.thebucksfoundation.org.uk

CC NO 1073861   **ESTABLISHED** 1998

■ The Buckinghamshire Historic Churches Trust

WHERE FUNDING CAN BE GIVEN The county or archdeaconry of Buckingham.

WHO CAN BENEFIT Parochial church councils or trustees of Christian churches and chapels, including Baptist, Anglican, Methodist and Catholic.

WHAT IS FUNDED The preservation, repair, maintenance and upkeep of the fabric of churches or chapels in Buckinghamshire. Grants are made to churches and chapels embarking upon restoration.

WHAT IS NOT FUNDED Grants cannot be given for repairs to bells, bell frames, bell chambers, window glass, organs, furnishings, work on heating, lighting, decoration or churchyard maintenance. Churches and chapels not in use for public worship are not supported.

TYPE OF GRANT One-off.

FINANCES *Year* 2000–01 *Income* £42,000 *Grants* £48,000

TRUSTEES Lord Lieutenant of Buckinghamshire, President; Suffragan Bishop of Buckingham; up to 20 others appointed by the president.

PUBLICATIONS Newsletter.

HOW TO APPLY An application form is available by writing to the correspondent.

WHO TO APPLY TO Mrs P Keens, Hon. Secretary, 9 St Paul's Court, Stony Stratford, Milton Keynes MK11 1LJ *Tel* 01908 571232 *E-mail* ppkeens@tesco.net

CC NO 206471   **ESTABLISHED** 1957

■ The Buckinghamshire Masonic Centenary Fund

WHERE FUNDING CAN BE GIVEN Buckinghamshire.

WHO CAN BENEFIT Registered charities and institutions, particularly those benefiting children and young adults, disabled people, and victims of crime and abuse.

WHAT IS FUNDED General charitable purposes, in particular health, education, community services, community centres and village halls.

WHAT IS NOT FUNDED No grants to individuals, for expeditions or for youth work overseas. Larger charities which have national appeal capability are unlikely to receive funding.

TYPE OF GRANT One-off.

RANGE OF GRANTS £1,000–£5,000.

SAMPLE GRANTS £4,475 to Stoke Mandeville Hospital Paediatric Unit; £2,500 to Milton Keynes MIND; £2,000 to Heart & Soul, South Bucks; £1,800 to Marlow District Guide Association; £1,000 to Thames Valley & Chiltern Air Ambulance Trust.

FINANCES *Year* 2002 *Income* £57,957 *Grants* £57,454

TRUSTEES D G Varney; Dr E W Hall; Lord Burnham; J H Parkin.

HOW TO APPLY In writing to the correspondent, setting out aims and objectives on one page of A4 with a copy of the latest audited accounts if available. The trustees meet three or four times a year to consider applications. The trust states that some grants are made after the organisation has been visited by a committee member.

WHO TO APPLY TO A R Watkins, Hon. Secretary, 51 Townside, Haddenham, Aylesbury, Buckinghamshire HP17 8AW *Tel* 01844 291275

CC NO 1007193   **ESTABLISHED** 1991

■ The Buckle Family Charitable Trust

WHERE FUNDING CAN BE GIVEN Mainly Suffolk and Essex.

WHO CAN BENEFIT Medical and general charitable causes.

WHAT IS FUNDED This trust has an interest in supporting small charities in the Suffolk/Essex area. It also funds a research fellowship at Charing Cross and Westminster Hospital.

SAMPLE GRANTS £37,000 to Imperial College of Science Technology and Medicine (in two separate donations); £10,000 to Oundle Schools Foundation; £9,200 to Nedging with Naughton Village Hall Committee.

FINANCES *Year* 2000 *Grants* £71,000

TRUSTEES Brian Buckle; Gillian Buckle; James Buckle; Joanna Buckle; Gavin Stewart.

HOW TO APPLY In writing to the correspondent although beneficiaries are normally selected through personal contact.

WHO TO APPLY TO G W N Stewart, Trustee, 9 Trinity Street, Colchester, Essex CO1 1JN *Tel* 01206 544434

CC NO 1001962   **ESTABLISHED** 1990

■ The Rosemary Bugden Charitable Trust

WHERE FUNDING CAN BE GIVEN UK, with a preference for the former county of Avon (in practice Bath and North East Somerset, Bristol, North Somerset and South Gloucestershire).

WHO CAN BENEFIT Arts, education, general charitable causes.

WHAT IS FUNDED Local schools for the purchase musical instruments.

FINANCES *Year* 2001–02 *Income* £32,338 *Grants* £54,389 *Assets* £834,204

TRUSTEES John Wetherherd Sharpe; Mrs Elizabeth Anne Frimston.

Think carefully about every application. Is it justified?

347

HOW TO APPLY In writing to the correspondent. However, the trust states that its funds are fully committed for the forseeable future. No applications will be considered.
WHO TO APPLY TO Miss Anne Tamlyn, Trust Officer, Osborne Clarke, 2 Temple Back East, Temple Quay, Bristol BS1 6EG *Tel* 0117 917 3022 *Fax* 0117 917 3023
CC NO 327626   **ESTABLISHED** 1987

■ The Worshipful Company of Builders Merchants

WHERE FUNDING CAN BE GIVEN City of London, UK and overseas.
WHO CAN BENEFIT Because of the company's specific constitution and ordinances, grants are directed almost entirely to the benefit of builders merchants and the building industry.
WHAT IS FUNDED Emphasis is given to education within the industry and to the relief of people from the builders merchants' industry and their families experiencing hardship. Grants are also given to certain City charities and to charities nominated by the officers of the company.
WHAT IS NOT FUNDED 'The trust does not consider unsolicited applications for sponsorship from individuals.'
SAMPLE GRANTS £9,300 to the Builders Merchants Federation for a Millennium Essay and for distance learning course prizes; £3,200 to the Builders Merchants Federation CRASH Appeal for single homeless people; £3,000 to the Lord Mayor's Charity for Barnardos; £2,500 to the Commonwealth Forestry Association for a scholarship for a Ghanaian postgraduate to take a MSc at Oxford; £1,000 to St Paul's Cathedral for the fabric fund; and £500 to Construction Industry for Youth for retraining.
FINANCES *Year* 1999–2000 *Income* £33,000 *Grants* £28,000 *Assets* £827,000
TRUSTEES The Master & Past Masters: J Faulder; M Pares; B Castledine.
HOW TO APPLY In writing to the correspondent.
WHO TO APPLY TO The Almoner, 4 College Hill, London EC4R 2RB *Tel* 020 7329 2189 *Fax* 020 7329 2190 *E-mail* WCoBM@aol.com
CC NO 235467   **ESTABLISHED** 1964

■ The Bulldog Trust

WHERE FUNDING CAN BE GIVEN Worldwide, with a preference for the south of England.
WHAT IS FUNDED General charitable purposes.
WHAT IS NOT FUNDED No grants are given to individuals or to unsolicited applications.
RANGE OF GRANTS £100–£10,000.
SAMPLE GRANTS £22,000 to Chamraj Children's Home – India; £15,000 to Royal British Legion; £14,000 to Hampshire County Council Project Tahir; £10,000 to Hampshire Gardens Trust.
FINANCES *Year* 1998–99 *Income* £921,000 *Grants* £130,000 *Assets* £4,500,000
TRUSTEES Richard Hoare; Messrs Hoare Trustees; Martin Rupert Riley.
HOW TO APPLY In writing to the correspondent; there are no application forms. However, please note that unsolicited applications are not acknowledged and are unlikely to be successful.
WHO TO APPLY TO Richard Hoare, Trustee, Messrs Hoare Trustees, 37 Fleet Street, London EC4P 4DQ
CC NO 326292   **ESTABLISHED** 1983

■ The E F Bulmer Benevolent Fund

WHERE FUNDING CAN BE GIVEN Preference for west Midlands, particularly Herefordshire.
WHO CAN BENEFIT Organisations benefiting people who are sick or disadvantaged by poverty.
WHAT IS FUNDED Individual employees who are in need, and charities for the relief of sickness and poverty.
WHAT IS NOT FUNDED Large UK charities are unlikely to be supported.
TYPE OF GRANT One-off or recurring. Capital (including buildings), core costs, feasibility studies, project, research, running costs, salaries and start-up costs. Funding may be given for up to three years.
RANGE OF GRANTS £100–£30,000.
SAMPLE GRANTS Grants over £5,000, all in Herefordshire, went to: MIND, NSPCC, Workmatch, WRVS, Royal Orthopaedic Hospital Oswestry, Herefordshire Education Action Zone, Primrose Hospice, Relate, Hereford Hospital Radio, St Michael's Hospice in Bartestree, Holly Bush Family Centre, Hereford Cathedral School, Hope in Bromyard, Plynlimon Trust (Dial-a-Ride), Newton Farm Community Association, St John Ambulance Herefordshire and Worcestershire, Family Mediation, Centre for Independent Living and Community Care Alliance.
FINANCES *Year* 2001–02 *Income* £453,201 *Grants* £380,000 *Assets* £9,000,000
TRUSTEES G M Bulmer; J Bulmer; Wilma Bulmer; A Patten; Jocelyn Harvey Wood.
HOW TO APPLY In writing to the correspondent, although an application form is available and will be sent if requested. Applications should be accompanied by a copy of the latest report and accounts. All applications will be acknowledged. The administrator is very happy to discuss applications by telephone prior to the application being submitted. The trustees usually meet in January, April, July and August; applications should be received the previous month.
WHO TO APPLY TO John Caiger, Administrator, The Old Rectory, Stoke Lacy, Nr Bromyard, Herefordshire HR7 4HH *Tel* 01432 820272 *Fax* 01432 820959 *E-mail* jcaiger@lineone.net
CC NO 214831   **ESTABLISHED** 1938

■ The BUPA Foundation

WHERE FUNDING CAN BE GIVEN UK.
WHO CAN BENEFIT Ultimately, the patients and carers in the areas supported; initially the medical research projects.
WHAT IS FUNDED Three areas of medical research are supported, namely: (a) surgical projects, including the development in surgical practice with particular emphasis on evaluation and economic outcomes, and identification and teaching of new surgical techniques; (b) preventive, epidemiological and health maintenance projects covering all environments, including the workplace, and (c) projects covering health information and communication between health professionals and the public/ patients.
WHAT IS NOT FUNDED No grants are made for applications for general appeals, applications from students for sponsorship through college or applications from other charitable organisations.
TYPE OF GRANT Project, research and salaries funded for up to three years; beyond this, if further funding is required, a review is carried out.

SAMPLE GRANTS In 1999: £200,000 to Oxford Medical Knowledge for a health information project; £135,926 to University of Cambridge (Papworth Hospital) for a lung reduction study; £124,150 to Epidemiology Department at St Bartholomew's Hospital for two projects; £60,154 to Institute of Child Health, London for research in child metabolic diseases; £54,296 to University of Oxford for computer aided communication; £46,050 to Imperial College School of Medicine, St Mary's for assessment of surgical tasks; £44,970 to London School of Hygiene & Tropical Medicine for epidemiology study; £40,000 to University of Bristol for outcomes of CS study; £36,105 to Imperial College, London for aneurysm study; £27,028 to Imperial College Science Technology & Medicine for arterial design.

FINANCES *Year* 2000 *Income* £1,514,000 *Grants* £909,183 *Assets* £195,713,05753

TRUSTEES Prof. Sir Michael Peckham, Chair; Dr A Vallance-Owen; Philip Brett; Prof. Ara Darzi; Dr Ros Eeles; Dr Judy Evans; Prof. Ray Fitzpatrick; P Jones; Prof. Philip Poole-Wilson; Dr Virginia Warren.

HOW TO APPLY An application form is available from the address below.

WHO TO APPLY TO The Administrator, BUPA House, 15–19 Bloomsbury Way, London WC1A 2BA *Tel* 020 7656 2591 *Fax* 020 7656 2708 *E-mail* saunderl@bupa.com *Website* www.bupafoundation.org

CC NO 277598   **ESTABLISHED** 1979

■ The Burall Charitable Trust

WHERE FUNDING CAN BE GIVEN UK, with a preference for Cambridgeshire.

WHO CAN BENEFIT Education, health, and relief of need organisations.

WHAT IS FUNDED The trust supports education, health improvement, relief of financial hardship or other purposes for the benefit of the communities where the Burall companies operate, particularly Cambridgeshire.

FINANCES *Year* 1999–2000 *Income* £56,000 *Grants* £56,000 *Assets* £1,700,000

TRUSTEES S C Burall; K M Burall; J D Burall.

HOW TO APPLY In writing to the correspondent.

WHO TO APPLY TO Stephen Henson, Pond Acre, Russell Close, Thorney, Peterborough PE6 0SW

CC NO 1069455   **ESTABLISHED** 1998

■ The Burden Trust

WHERE FUNDING CAN BE GIVEN UK and overseas.

WHO CAN BENEFIT A bias towards the Anglican church (as laid down in the trust deeds). Beneficiaries include children and older people; medical professionals; Church of England; children in care, fostered and adopted; and at risk groups.

WHAT IS FUNDED Medical research; hospitals; schools and training institutions; homes for and care of elderly, sick and needy people; children's homes and care. There is an overall adherence to the tenets and principles of the Church of England. The priority is to support research in neurosciences.

WHAT IS NOT FUNDED No grants to individuals.

TYPE OF GRANT Recurring and one-off.

RANGE OF GRANTS £1,000–£45,000.

SAMPLE GRANTS £45,000 to Burden Neurological Institute; £17,500 to Trinity College, Bristol; £15,000 to Langham Research Scholarships; £12,000 to Oxford Centre for Mission Studies;

£10,000 each to Association for Theological Education by Extention – Bangalore and Theological College – Vaux-sur-Seine; £9,000 to Union Biblical Seminary – Pune; £6,000 to Home Farm Trust; £5,000 each to All Nations Christian College, Research into Ageing, Dean Close School and Monkton Combe School.

FINANCES *Year* 2001–02 *Income* £170,000 *Grants* £177,000 *Assets* £3,890,657

TRUSTEES Dr M G Barker, Chair; R E J Bernays; A C Miles; Prof. G M Stirrat; Bishop of Southwell; M C Tosh; Mrs Caroline Baker.

HOW TO APPLY In writing to the correspondent to be received before 31 March each year. Financial information is required in support of the project for which help is requested. No application is responded to without an sae. Recipients of recurring grants are notified each year that grants are not automatic and must be applied for annually. Applications are considered at the annual trustees meeting.

WHO TO APPLY TO Malcolm Tosh, Hon. Secretary, Little Clandon, West Clandon, Surrey GU4 7ST *Tel* 01483 222561 *Fax* 01483 224187

CC NO 235859   **ESTABLISHED** 1913

■ Burdens Charitable Foundation

WHERE FUNDING CAN BE GIVEN UK, but mostly overseas, with special interest in West Africa.

WHO CAN BENEFIT Registered charities only.

WHAT IS FUNDED The trustees main emphasis relates to the prevention and relief of poverty with particular reference to people in countries such as those of sub-Saharan Africa, who are substantially less fortunate than those in the UK.Preference is given to the provision of safe water, sanitation and access to information for people who are visually impaired. It is increasingly the case that the trustees most favour the work of highly-focussed overseas projects capable of effective service delivery without incurring significant costs in the UK.

WHAT IS NOT FUNDED Causes which rarely or never benefit include animal welfare (except in less developed countries), the arts and museums, political activities, most medical research, preservation etc. of historic buildings and monuments, individual educational grants and sport, except sport for people with disabilities. No grants are made to individuals.

TYPE OF GRANT Generally one-off grants, exceptionally more than one-year. Capital, project, research, running and recurring costs, salaries and start-up costs will also be considered. No loans are made.

RANGE OF GRANTS Up to £16,000. Most under £2,500.

SAMPLE GRANTS £18,500 to Easton Christian Family Centre; £11,000 to William Hulme Grammar School; £10,000 to Hand in Hand; £7,500 to Manchester Prison Visitors Centre; £6,000 each to International Foundation for Dermatology, and National Library for the Blind for the Books around the World project; £5,000 each to Armitage School – Gambia, Busoga Trust, Gaddum Centre, and Scottish Churches Community Trust.

FINANCES *Year* 2001–02 *Income* £392,070 *Grants* £351,373 *Assets* £11,849,669

TRUSTEES Arthur Burden; Godfrey Burden; Hilary Perkins; Sally Schofield.

HOW TO APPLY In writing to the correspondent, accompanied by recent, audited accounts and statutory reports, coupled with at least an outline business plan where relevant. Trustees usually meet in March, June, September and December.

WHO TO APPLY TO A J Burden, Trustee, St George's House, 215–219 Chester Road, Manchester M15 4JE *Tel* 0161 832 4901 *Fax* 0161 835 3668

CC NO 273535   **ESTABLISHED** 1977

■ The Clara E Burgess Charity

WHERE FUNDING CAN BE GIVEN UK and worldwide.

WHO CAN BENEFIT Registered charities benefiting children.

WHAT IS FUNDED Provision of facilities and assistance to enhance the education, health and physical well-being of children, particularly (but not exclusively) those under the age of 10 who have lost one or both parents.

WHAT IS NOT FUNDED No grants to non-registered charities.

TYPE OF GRANT One-off and recurrent grants (up to three years) for capital costs, core costs, salaries, projects, research, and start-up costs.

RANGE OF GRANTS £100 upwards.

SAMPLE GRANTS £93,000 in total to Winston's Wish; £39,000 in total each to Cheltenham & Gloucester College of Further Education and After Adoption; £35,000 to St Francis Children's Society: The Anancy Project; £28,000 to International Care & Relief; £25,000 each to Little Haven Children's Hospice, Barnardo's Orchard Project Newcastle and NCH Action for Children; £20,000 to Mildmay Mission Hospital; £18,000 to British Agencies for Adoption and Fostering; £15,000 each to DEBRA – Gene Therapy Project and World Medical Fund; £12,000 to Save the Children Fund; £10,000 each to The Royal Schools for the Deaf – Manchester, The Rainbow Trust Children's Charity, Le Jeune Clinic, BREAK, Sierra Leonne War Trust for Children, The Royal Wolverhampton School: The Orphan Foundation, Hope & Homes for Children and The Rainbow Centre; £8,000 to Wigan Mencap; £7,500 to Richard House Trust – Children's Hospice; £5,000 each to Acorn's Children's Hospice, Family Service Units, Children's Aid Direct and Relief Fund for Romania; £3,000 to The Wirral Autistic Society; £2,000 each to Cwm Cynon Women's Aid Children's Playscheme and Motability; £1,000 each to KIND, Berwick Family Centre and Befriend a Child Scheme; £750 to Seaton Delavla Pre-School Playgroup; £500 to Reach.

FINANCES *Year* 2000–01 *Income* £659,196 *Grants* £589,981 *Assets* £10,007,391

TRUSTEES The Royal Bank of Scotland plc

HOW TO APPLY On a form available from the correspondent. The trustees meet to consider grants in February, May, August and November and applications should be received in the month before those meetings. The trust states that applications should be as brief as possible: the trustees will ask for any further information they require.

WHO TO APPLY TO Eileen Kidd, Administrator, The Royal Bank of Scotland plc, Trust and Estate Services, Capital House, 2 Festival Square, Edinburgh EH3 9SU *Tel* 0131 556 8555 *Fax* 0131 228 9889

CC NO 1072546   **ESTABLISHED** 1998

■ The Burry Charitable Trust

WHERE FUNDING CAN BE GIVEN UK, with a preference for Hampshire.

WHO CAN BENEFIT Registered charities.

WHAT IS FUNDED Medicine and health.

WHAT IS NOT FUNDED No grants to individuals or students.

SAMPLE GRANTS £27,000 to Oakhaven Hospice Trust; £13,000 to Wessex Heartbeat; £7,400 to New Milton Health Centres; £5,500 to Not Forgotten Associaton; £5,000 to Life Education Centre Dorset; £4,300 to Salvation Army; £3,000 to Ability Net; £2,000 to Mobility Trust; £1,000 each to Bournemouth & Christchurch Stroke Unit Appeal and John Grooms – Disabled People.

FINANCES *Year* 2000–01 *Income* £67,000 *Grants* £69,000 *Assets* £108,000

TRUSTEES R J Burry; Mrs J A Knight; A J Osman.

HOW TO APPLY **This trust states that it does not respond to unsolicited applications.**

WHO TO APPLY TO R J Burry, 261 Lymington Road, Highcliffe, Christchurch, Dorset BH23 5EE

CC NO 281045   **ESTABLISHED** 1961

■ The Arnold James Burton 1956 Charitable Settlement

WHERE FUNDING CAN BE GIVEN UK and overseas, with preferences for Yorkshire and Israel.

WHO CAN BENEFIT Registered charities.

WHAT IS FUNDED General charitable purposes, especially Jewish charities, medical research and health care, education, social welfare, arts and heritage, animal conservation and inter-faith activities.

WHAT IS NOT FUNDED No grants to individuals.

RANGE OF GRANTS Generally up to £10,000.

SAMPLE GRANTS £52,000 to UJIA; £10,000 each to Lubavitch Centre and Marie Curie Cancer Care; £8,625 to JNF Foundation; £6,000 to Arthritis Research and Care; £5,500 to Beth Shalom; £5,492 to Cambridge Expeditions; £5,000 each to The Heathlands Village, Sustrans and Yorkshire Air Museum.

FINANCES *Year* 2000–01 *Income* £198,667 *Grants* £251,500 *Assets* £4,648,480

TRUSTEES A J Burton; J J Burton; M T Burton.

HOW TO APPLY In writing to the trust managers. The trust states that its funds are fully committed to charities already known to the trustees and new applications will not be invited. Unsuccessful appeals will not necessarily be acknowledged.

WHO TO APPLY TO Keith Pailing, Trustee Management Ltd, 19 Cookridge Street, Leeds LS2 3AG

CC NO 1020986   **ESTABLISHED** 1956

■ The Audrey & Stanley Burton Charitable Trust

WHERE FUNDING CAN BE GIVEN Unrestricted, with a strong special interest in Yorkshire, especially west Yorkshire.

WHO CAN BENEFIT Charitable organisations.

WHAT IS FUNDED Priority for projects concerning health, the arts, education and social needs. Preference is given to charities in Yorkshire. Consideration is given to some medical appeals, but not for research. Developing world donations are only given to major organisations.

WHAT IS NOT FUNDED No grants to individuals.

TYPE OF GRANT Preferably one-off donations and project grants, occasionally for more than three years.

SAMPLE GRANTS In 2000–01: £276,000 to United Joint Jewish Israel Appeal; £50,000 to Oxfam; £31,605 to New Israel Fund; £25,000 to Children in Crisis; £20,000 to Children's Aid Direct; £18,000 to Alzheimer's Research Trust; £12,000 to Leeds International Piano Competition; £10,000 each to Age Concern Knaresborough, Mental Health Foundation and Public Art Development Trust.

FINANCES *Year* 2001–02 *Income* £426,582 *Grants* £484,210 *Assets* £1,136,428

TRUSTEES Audrey Burton; Amanda C Burton; Deborah Hazan; Philip Morris; David Solomon; Raymond Burton.

HOW TO APPLY In writing only to the trust. Unsuccessful applicants will not necessarily be notified.

WHO TO APPLY TO The Secretary, Trustee Management Ltd, 19 Cookridge Street, Leeds LS2 3AG

CC NO 1028430   **ESTABLISHED** 1960

■ The Burton Breweries Charitable Trust

WHERE FUNDING CAN BE GIVEN Burton, East Staffordshire and South Derbyshire district (including a small area of north west Leicestershire).

WHO CAN BENEFIT Young people (11–25 years), education and training for individuals of any age who assist young people and youth/community organisations.

WHAT IS FUNDED Young people and youth organisations. Funding is given in areas such as residential facilities and services, community facilities, and extra-curricular education and training.

WHAT IS NOT FUNDED Beneficiaries must be aged between 11 and 25 – other age-groups are excluded. Organisations and individuals living or in full-time education outside the beneficial area are not supported. No support for education where there is provision by the state.

TYPE OF GRANT Capital including buildings, core costs, interest-free loans, one-off, project, recurring costs, running costs, salaries and start-up costs. Funding is available for up to two years.

RANGE OF GRANTS £100–£5,000.

SAMPLE GRANTS In 1999–2000: £21,000 to East Staffs Youth & Community Service for a minibus.

FINANCES *Year* 2002 *Income* £32,000 *Grants* £25,000 *Assets* £750,000

TRUSTEES Mrs Janet Dean, Chair; Martin Thomas; Lesley Allman; Stephen Oliver; Andrew Knight; Joyce Woodrow; Adrian Wedgwood.

HOW TO APPLY In writing to the correspondent. The trustees meet in February, June and October. Applications should be sent in January, May and September. A copy of the trust's guidelines is available on request or on its website www.burtonbctrust.co.uk

WHO TO APPLY TO B E Keates, Secretary, Gretton House, Waterside Court, Third Avenue, Centrum 100, Burton-on-Trent, Staffordshire DE14 2WQ *Tel* 01283 740600 *Fax* 01283 511899 *E-mail* info@burtonbctrust.co.uk *Website* www.burtonbctrust.co.uk

CC NO 326097   **ESTABLISHED** 1998

■ The Geoffrey Burton Charitable Trust

WHERE FUNDING CAN BE GIVEN UK, especially Suffolk.

WHO CAN BENEFIT Organisations in the UK.

WHAT IS FUNDED General charitable purposes of a welfare nature, and environment. Particularly charities working in the fields of medical research, conservation and community projects.

WHAT IS NOT FUNDED No grants to individuals.

TYPE OF GRANT Buildings and core costs. Funding for one year or less will be considered.

RANGE OF GRANTS £150–£3,000, with one exception.

SAMPLE GRANTS £10,000 to the Blond McIndoe Centre for medical research; £3,000 each to St John's PCC Needham Market and RSPB; £2,200 to Suffolk Wildlife Trust.

FINANCES *Year* 2001–02 *Income* £44,639 *Grants* £39,021 *Assets* £616,420

TRUSTEES E de B Nash; E E Maule.

HOW TO APPLY In writing to the correspondent.

WHO TO APPLY TO Eric Maule, Trustee, Salix House, Falkenham, Ipswich IP10 0QY *Tel* 01394 448339 *Fax* 01394 448339 *E-mail* ericmaule@hotmail.com

CC NO 290854   **ESTABLISHED** 1984

■ The R M 1956 Burton Charitable Trust

WHERE FUNDING CAN BE GIVEN England, with a preference for the Yorkshire and Humber area, particularly Leeds; also Israel.

WHO CAN BENEFIT Organisations benefiting entertainment professionals, musicians, students, retired or orphaned textile workers and designers, writers and poets, Jewish people and people with disabilities.

WHAT IS FUNDED Jewish charities, education (particularly faith schools and special needs schools), the arts, heritage, medicine, services for children, almshouses and sheltered housing, services for victims of crime, community centre and activities, inter-faith activities, Judaism and conservation.

WHAT IS NOT FUNDED Grants are not given to local charities outside Yorkshire or London, individuals or to new charities where their work overlaps with already established organisations that are supported by the trust.

TYPE OF GRANT One-off grants for core support, buildings and collections.

RANGE OF GRANTS £50–£100,000.

SAMPLE GRANTS £250,000 each to Harriet Burton Charitable Trust and The Calmcott Trust; £10,000 to Dean and Chapter of York; £5,500 to Community Security Trust; £5,000 each to Harrogate Community House Trust, and Yorkshire Archaeological Society; £3,520 to Weizmann Institute; £2,000 each to Woodland Trust, and Yorkshire and Humberside Arts; £1,500 to Royal Opera House Trust.

FINANCES *Year* 2000–01 *Income* £124,130 *Grants* £84,004 *Assets* £1,200,859

TRUSTEES Raymond M Burton; Arnold Burton.

OTHER INFORMATION Over the last year the trustees have distributed £4.5 million, making the trust considerably smaller.

HOW TO APPLY In writing to the correspondent at any time. The trustees try to make a decision within a month. Negative decisions are not necessarily communicated.

Think carefully about every application. Is it justified?

351

WHO TO APPLY TO The Trustees, c/o Trustee Management Ltd, 19 Cookridge Street, Leeds LS2 3AG

CC NO 253421   ESTABLISHED 1956

■ Consolidated Charity of Burton Upon Trent

WHERE FUNDING CAN BE GIVEN The former county borough of Burton upon Trent and the parishes of Branston, Stretton and Outwoods.

WHO CAN BENEFIT Individuals, and organisations who benefit people in need, who live in the beneficial area.

WHAT IS FUNDED Benefit of poor, sick and needy residents of Burton on Trent; provision of recreational and educational facilities, including those for social and physical training.

SAMPLE GRANTS £27,000 to SARAC; £25,000 to St Giles Hospice; £21,000 to Burton Caribbean Association; £20,000 each to Shopmobility and Burton Amateur Boxing; £10,000 to Uxbridge Table Tennis Club; £5,200 to Pakistani Community Centre; £1,400 to Burton MIND; £430 to Winshill Tiddler and Tots Group.

FINANCES Year 2000 Income £416,000 Grants £417,000

TRUSTEES Cllr P Beresford; Mrs M P Boyle; Mrs M J Brooks; Mrs V Burton; W V Cook; Cllr P R Davies; Cllr T M Dawn; Mrs G M Foster; Cllr P Haynes; Rev. Preb. E C Hayward; Alderman Mrs P P Hill; A Kabal; Alderman Mrs M L Nash; Mrs A M Parker; J M Peach; Cllr Mrs P J Perry; D E Salter; R D Seabridge; Cllr Mrs P Stokes.

HOW TO APPLY On a form available from the correspondent. Applications from individuals should be on the form available from the correspondent and should include quotations in respect of items required as well as a supporting letter from a social worker, doctor, health visitor, probation officer, priest or some other person in authority. The trustees meet four times a year, in February, May, August and November.

WHO TO APPLY TO T J Bramall, Clerk, Messrs Talbot & Co, 148 High Street, Burton upon Trent, Staffordshire DE14 1JY *Tel* 01283 564716 *Fax* 01283 510861 *E-mail* consolidatedcharity@talbotandco.freeserve.co.uk

CC NO 239072   ESTABLISHED 1981

■ Butchers' Company General Charities

WHERE FUNDING CAN BE GIVEN UK, with a preference for inner city London.

WHO CAN BENEFIT Organisations benefiting people in need.

WHAT IS FUNDED Meat industry related charities. Charities associated with work in inner city London. National charities.

WHAT IS NOT FUNDED No grants to individuals, however, see above if the individual has a connection with the meat industry.

TYPE OF GRANT One-off for core costs.

RANGE OF GRANTS £200–£2,500.

FINANCES Year 2000–01 Income £32,000 Grants £27,000 Assets £651,000

TRUSTEES The members of the court of the Worshipful Company of Butchers.

HOW TO APPLY In many cases a simple letter is sufficient for the committee to make a decision on grants. Applications should be addressed to the chairman of the charities committee. In order to keep costs down, unsuccessful applicants will not be corresponded with. The committee meets monthly.

WHO TO APPLY TO The Chairman of the Charities Committee, Butchers Hall, 87 Bartholomew Close, London EC1A 7EB *Tel* 020 7606 4106 *Fax* 020 7606 4108 *E-mail* clerk@butchershall.com *Website* www.butchershall.com

CC NO 257928   ESTABLISHED 1969

■ The Bill Butlin Charity Trust

WHERE FUNDING CAN BE GIVEN UK.

WHO CAN BENEFIT Registered charities benefiting children, older people, disabled people and people in need.

WHAT IS FUNDED Normally to assist disabled children, and older and needy people through recognised institutions.

RANGE OF GRANTS £500–£20,000.

SAMPLE GRANTS £20,000 to Canadian Veterans Association (UK); £10,000 each to Crowndale Recreational Association and Jessie May Trust; £5,000 each to Home Farm Trust, Liver Research Trust and NSPCC – Full Stop Appeal; £2,500 each to Cup of Kindness Fund and Tresco and Bryher Educational Foundation; £2,000 each to Grand Order of Water Rats, Saints & Sinners Club of London, South Buckinghamshire Riding for the Disabled, The Story of Christmas 2000 and Victims of Violence.

FINANCES Year 2000–01 Income £100,416 Grants £75,700 Assets £2,400,172

TRUSTEES R F Butlin; Lady Sheila Butlin; P A Hetherington; T Watts; F T Devine; S I Meaden; T H North.

HOW TO APPLY In writing to the correspondent. Trustees usually meet twice a year.

WHO TO APPLY TO The Secretary, Eagle House, 110 Jermyn Street, London SW1Y 6RH *Tel* 020 7451 9000

CC NO 228233   ESTABLISHED 1963

■ C & F Charitable Trust

WHERE FUNDING CAN BE GIVEN UK and overseas.
WHO CAN BENEFIT Registered charities.
WHAT IS FUNDED Orthodox Jewish charities.
WHAT IS NOT FUNDED Registered charities only.
FINANCES *Year* 1999–2000 *Income* £57,000
Grants £65,000 *Assets* £683,000
TRUSTEES C S Kaufman; F H Kaufman.
HOW TO APPLY In writing to the correspondent.
WHO TO APPLY TO C S Kaufman, Trustee, c/o New
Burlington House, 1075 Finchley House Road,
London NW11 0PU
CC NO 274529   **ESTABLISHED** 1977

■ The C B Trust

WHERE FUNDING CAN BE GIVEN UK.
WHO CAN BENEFIT Registered charities.
WHAT IS FUNDED Jewish organisations; charities
concerned with health, welfare and education.
SAMPLE GRANTS £6,000 to Genesis Osteopathic
Foundation; £3,500 to Royal Opera Trust;
£3,000 to University of Southampton
Development Trust; £2,000 to UK JAID
Mozambique Appeal; £1,500 to Delamere
Forest School.
FINANCES *Year* 1999–2000 *Income* £27,305
Grants £21,340 *Assets* £614,718
TRUSTEES Harold S Klug; Naomi S Klug; HSBC Trust
Co. Ltd.
HOW TO APPLY In writing to the correspondent.
WHO TO APPLY TO Derek Eyles, HSBC Trust Company
UK Ltd, Trust Services, Norwich House, Nelson
Gate, Southampton SO15 1GX *Tel* 023 8072
2229
CC NO 287180   **ESTABLISHED** 1983

■ The C J M Charitable Trust

WHERE FUNDING CAN BE GIVEN UK and overseas.
WHAT IS FUNDED Social entrepreneurship.
SAMPLE GRANTS £63,000 to Network Foundation;
£8,000 to Ashoka (UK) Trust; £1,000 to
Falkland Community Trust.
FINANCES *Year* 1998–99 *Income* £33,000
Grants £72,000 *Assets* £474,000
TRUSTEES Christopher James Marks; Timothy John
Marks; William Robert Marks; Rupert Philip
Marks; Mary Elizabeth Falk.
HOW TO APPLY In writing to the correspondent.
WHO TO APPLY TO Mrs Jane Leighton, Messrs Farrer
and Co., 66 Lincoln's Inn Fields, London WC2A
3LH *Tel* 020 7242 2022
CC NO 802325   **ESTABLISHED** 1989

■ The Barrow Cadbury Trust and the Barrow Cadbury Fund

WHERE FUNDING CAN BE GIVEN Unrestricted, but
mainly UK.
WHO CAN BENEFIT Charities and voluntary
organisations which benefit causes within the
trust's programmes.
WHAT IS FUNDED In early 2003 the trust was
reviewing its existing programmes; from April it

expected to have new information available. See
website for further details.
WHAT IS NOT FUNDED The trustees rarely respond to
general appeals or applications from local
projects except in the racial justice and gender
programmes.
TYPE OF GRANT Core costs, project, recurring costs,
running costs, salaries and start-up costs.
Funding is usually given for 1–3 years.
RANGE OF GRANTS Smallest £1,000; largest
£166,000; typical £5,000–£20,000.
SAMPLE GRANTS £250,000 to Citizen Organising
Foundation for running costs; £150,000 to
Fermanagh Trust for their endowment and
grants programme; £108,000 to Islamic
Foundation, Markfield for a Cadbury fellow;
£100,000 each to Circles Network for running
costs, Community Resource and Information
Service Trust in Birmingham for running costs
and Committee on the Administration of Justice
(NI) for running costs and endowment; £70,000
to Women Acting in Today's Society for core
costs; £60,000 each to Alliance for Inclusive
Education for running costs, Exeter University for
awards and fees and Forth Spring Community
Group in Belfast for running costs.
FINANCES *Year* 2001–02 *Income* £2,302,000
Grants £4,251,000 *Assets* £80,000,000
TRUSTEES Anna C Southall, Chair; James Cadbury;
Anna Hickinbotham; Roger Hickinbotham;
Richard G Cadbury; Erica R Cadbury; Ruth
Cadbury; Candia Compton; Thomas Cadbury;
Helen Cadbury; Nicola Cadbury.
PUBLICATIONS Guidelines.
HOW TO APPLY Consult the website before contacting
the trust. Trustees meet in March, July and
November. Applications usually have to be
received at least two months before the
meeting, but it can take 6–18 months before
projects are ready to be put forward to the
trustees.
WHO TO APPLY TO Sukhvinder Stubbs, Director, 2
College Walk, Selly Oak, Birmingham B29 6SL
Tel 0121 472 0417
Website www.barrowcadbury.org.uk
CC NO 226331   **ESTABLISHED** 1920

■ C J Cadbury Charitable Trust

WHERE FUNDING CAN BE GIVEN UK.
WHO CAN BENEFIT Registered charitable
organisations.
WHAT IS FUNDED General.
TYPE OF GRANT One-off.
FINANCES *Year* 2001–02 *Income* £32,000
Grants £60,000 *Assets* £596,000
TRUSTEES H B Carslake; Mrs Joy Cadbury; P H G
Cadbury.
HOW TO APPLY In writing to the correspondent.
WHO TO APPLY TO H B Carslake, Trustee, Martineau
Johnson, St Philips House, St Philips Place,
Birmingham B3 2PP *Tel* 0121 200 3300
CC NO 270609   **ESTABLISHED** 1969

■ The Christopher Cadbury Charitable Trust

WHERE FUNDING CAN BE GIVEN UK, with a strong
preference for the Midlands.
WHO CAN BENEFIT Registered charities only.
WHAT IS FUNDED To support approved charities by
annual contribution.
WHAT IS NOT FUNDED No support for individuals.
TYPE OF GRANT Recurring grants up to five years.
RANGE OF GRANTS £200–£15,000.

SAMPLE GRANTS £15,000 to Royal Society for Nature Conservation (various projects); £5,000 to Norfolk Wildlife Trust; £4,000 to Worcestershire Wildlife Trust; £2,000 to Guide Association Beaconsfield Campsites; £1,000 each to Edith Cadbury Nursery School and Ironbridge Gorge Museum Trust; £500 each to Avoncroft Arts Society and Selly Oak Nursery Schoool; £250 to St Augustine's Church – Edgbaston; £200 to St Annes Church – Wyre Piddle.

FINANCES *Year* 2002 *Income* £71,661 *Grants* £59,950 *Assets* £1,731,564

TRUSTEES Roger V J Cadbury; Dr C James Cadbury; Mrs V B Reekie; Dr T N D Peet; P H G Cadbury; Mrs C V E Benfield.

HOW TO APPLY The trustees have fully committed funds for projects presently supported and cannot respond positively to any further applications. Unsolicited applications are unlikely to be successful.

WHO TO APPLY TO Roger Harriman, Administrator, New Guild House, 45 Great Charles Street, Queensway, Birmingham B3 2LX *Tel* 0121 212 2222

CC NO 231859   **ESTABLISHED** 1922

■ The Edward Cadbury Charitable Trust

WHERE FUNDING CAN BE GIVEN UK, mainly in the West Midlands; overseas.

WHO CAN BENEFIT Registered charities benefiting children and young adults, musicians and community projects.

WHAT IS FUNDED Christianity, youth, welfare and education. Also ecumenical movements, inter-faith relations, people who are oppressed or disadvantaged, the arts and the environment.

WHAT IS NOT FUNDED Grants to registered charities only. No student grants or support for individuals.

TYPE OF GRANT One-off and project.

RANGE OF GRANTS £250–£500,000.

SAMPLE GRANTS £300,000 to Worcester Cathedral Chapter House; £123,000 to University of Birmingham; £56,500 to Birmingham Conservation for Back to Back; £40,000 to Woodlands Quaker Home – Wolverhampton; £30,000 to Cataloguing of the Mingana Collection; £25,000 to Elizabeth Fitzroy Support – Malvern; £22,200 to Responding to Conflict; £18,484 to Selly Oak Colleges for the Dorothy Cadbury Fellow; £12,000 to Marie Curie Cancer Care; £10,000 to Police Foundation for research into terrorism.

FINANCES *Year* 2001–02 *Income* £718,529 *Grants* £859,632 *Assets* £23,771,065

TRUSTEES Charles E Gillett, Chair; Christopher Littleboy; Charles R Gillett; Andrew Littleboy; Nigel Cadbury.

HOW TO APPLY At any time, but allow three months for a response. The trust does not have an application form. Applications should be made in writing to the manager. They should clearly and concisely give relevant information concerning the project and its benefits, an outline budget and how the project is to be funded initially and in the future. Up-to-date accounts and the organisation's latest annual report are also required. Applications that do not come within the trust's policy as stated above may not be considered or acknowledged.

WHO TO APPLY TO Sue Anderson, Trust Manager, College Walk, Selly Oak, Birmingham B29 6SL *Tel* 0121 472 1838 *Fax* 0121 472 7013

CC NO 227384   **ESTABLISHED** 1945

■ The Edward & Dorothy Cadbury Trust (1928)

WHERE FUNDING CAN BE GIVEN Preference for the West Midlands area.

WHO CAN BENEFIT Registered charities and community projects, benefiting children, young adults and musicians.

WHAT IS FUNDED The trust continues to support, where appropriate, the interests of the founders and the particular charitable interests of the trustees. A special preference for West Midlands appeals for health, education and the arts.

WHAT IS NOT FUNDED No grants to individuals.

TYPE OF GRANT Ongoing funding commitments rarely considered.

RANGE OF GRANTS Usually £500–£10,000.

SAMPLE GRANTS £10,000 to Countess of Huntingdon Hall; £5,000 each to Bromsgrove Age Concern, Bromsgrove Bereavement Counselling and Dodford Children's Holiday Farm; £3,750 to Bromsgrove Festival; £3,000 to Birmingham Royal Ballet; £2,500 each to Queen Alexandra College and Sunfield Children's Home; £2,000 each to Acorn Children's Hospice and Edwards' Trust.

FINANCES *Year* 2001–02 *Income* £113,758 *Grants* £78,625 *Assets* £3,777,203

TRUSTEES Mrs P A Gillett, Chair; Dr C M Elliott; Mrs P S Ward.

HOW TO APPLY In writing to the correspondent, giving clear, relevant information concerning the project's aims and its benefits, an outline budget and how the project is to be funded initially and in the future. Up-to-date accounts and annual reports, where available, should be included. Applications can be submitted at any time but three months should be allowed for a response. Applications that do not come within the policy as stated above may not be considered or acknowledged.

WHO TO APPLY TO Miss Susan Anderson, Trust Manager, College Walk, Selly Oak, Birmingham B29 6LE *Tel* 0121 472 1838 *Fax* 0121 472 7013

CC NO 221441   **ESTABLISHED** 1928

■ The George Cadbury Trust

WHERE FUNDING CAN BE GIVEN Preference for the West Midlands, Hampshire and Gloucestershire.

WHO CAN BENEFIT UK-based charities.

WHAT IS FUNDED General charitable purposes.

WHAT IS NOT FUNDED No support for individuals for projects, courses of study, expeditions or sporting tours. No support for overseas appeals.

RANGE OF GRANTS Up to £25,000, but mostly for under £1,000.

SAMPLE GRANTS £25,000 to The Michael Cadbury Children's Orthopaedic Assessment Centre; £20,000 to National Youth Ballet; £11,500 to St John Ophthalmic Hospital; £8,000 each to Bower Trust, PHG Cadbury Charitable Trust, RVJ Cadbury Charitable Trust, RA & VB Reekie Charitable Trust, Sarnia Charitable Trust and C James Cadbury Charitable Trust.

FINANCES *Year* 2001/02 *Income* £300,000 *Grants* £256,000 *Assets* £8,300,000

TRUSTEES Peter E Cadbury; Annette L K Cadbury; R N Cadbury; Sir Adrian Cadbury; Roger V J Cadbury.

HOW TO APPLY In writing to the correspondent to be considered quarterly. Please note that very few new applications are supported due to ongoing and alternative commitments.

WHO TO APPLY TO Roger Harriman, Trust Administrator, New Guild House, 45 Great Charles Street, Queensway, Birmingham B3 2LX *Tel* 0121 212 2222 *Fax* 0121 212 2300 CC NO 1040999   ESTABLISHED 1924

■ The George W Cadbury Charitable Trust

WHERE FUNDING CAN BE GIVEN Worldwide.

WHO CAN BENEFIT Organisations benefiting at risk groups, people disadvantaged by poverty, and socially isolated people.

WHAT IS FUNDED General charitable purposes with a bias towards population control and conservation.

WHAT IS NOT FUNDED No grants to individuals or non-registered charities, or for scholarships.

RANGE OF GRANTS Up to £20,000; 18 grants over £5,000 and 73 below £5,000.

SAMPLE GRANTS £20,000 each to Belfast Brook Advisory Centre, The (National) Brook Advisory Centre, Family Planning Association and Friends of the Earth; £16,000 to World Development Movement Trust; £13,500 each to Westchester Children's Association and New York City Ballet Combinations Fund; £12,000 to Sustrans; £10,000 to Maternity Alliance Education and Research Association; £9,000 to Planned Parenthood Federation of Canada.

FINANCES *Year* 2001–02 *Income* £212,475 *Grants* £270,000 *Assets* £5,600,000

TRUSTEES M/s C A Woodroffe; M/s L E Boal; P C Boal; M/s J C Boal; N B Woodroffe; M/s J L Woodroffe.

HOW TO APPLY In writing to the correspondent. However, it should be noted that trustees' current commitments are such that no unsolicited applications can be considered at present.

WHO TO APPLY TO Roger Harriman, Trust Administrator, New Guild House, 45 Great Charles Street, Queensway, Birmingham B3 2LX *Tel* 0121 212 2222 *Fax* 0121 212 2300 CC NO 231861   ESTABLISHED 1922

■ P H G Cadbury Trust

WHERE FUNDING CAN BE GIVEN UK and overseas.

WHO CAN BENEFIT Registered charities.

WHAT IS FUNDED General charitable purposes, particularly the arts; conservation and cancer-related charities also considered.

RANGE OF GRANTS £25–£3,000

SAMPLE GRANTS £3,000 to Royal Academy Trust; £2,500 each to National Art Collections Fund and Victoria & Albert Museum; £2,000 each to English National Opera and Natural History Museum; £1,500 to Trinity Hospice; £1,000 each to Friends of Fairford Church, Garsington Opera, Helen House and Wildfowl & Wetlands Trust.

FINANCES *Year* 2002 *Income* £31,638 *Grants* £23,335 *Assets* £491,545

TRUSTEES D Larder; P H G Cadbury; S Cadbury.

OTHER INFORMATION Unlikely that any new applications can be granted

HOW TO APPLY The trust does not usually respond to unsolicited applications.

WHO TO APPLY TO Derek Larder, Trustee, KS Carmichael , PO Box 4UD, London W1A 4UD *Tel* 020 7258 1577 CC NO 327174   ESTABLISHED 1986

■ The Richard Cadbury Charitable Trust

WHERE FUNDING CAN BE GIVEN UK, but mainly Birmingham, Coventry and Worcester.

WHO CAN BENEFIT Organisations benefiting children, young adults, elderly people, people in care, fostered and adopted, parents and children, and one-parent families.

WHAT IS FUNDED Community centres and village halls; libraries and museums; counselling; crime prevention; play schemes; gay and lesbian rights; racial equality, discrimination and relations; social advocacy; health care; hospices and rehabilitation centres; cancer and prenatal research; health promotion; and health-related volunteer schemes. Grants also for accommodation and housing; infrastructure support and development; conservation and environment; and religion.

WHAT IS NOT FUNDED Grants are only given to organisations with charitable status and not to individuals and students. No grants for running costs.

TYPE OF GRANT One-off for capital and buildings (preferred). Funding is available for one year or less.

RANGE OF GRANTS £400–£1,000.

SAMPLE GRANTS £1,000 each to Barnardos, Birmingham Settlement, Centrepoint Soho, Leukaemia Research Fund, Oxfam, Shelter (national), South Birmingham Family Service Unit, St Mary's Hospice Birmingham, Birmingham; £750 to Children's Family Trust.

FINANCES *Year* 1998–99 *Income* £34,202 *Grants* £57,357 *Assets* £716,658

TRUSTEES R B Cadbury; Mrs M M Eardley; D G Slora; J A Slora.

HOW TO APPLY In writing to the correspondent giving reasons why a grant is needed and including a copy of the latest accounts if possible. Meetings are held in February, June and October.

WHO TO APPLY TO Mrs M M Eardley, Administrator, 26 Randall Road, Kenilworth, Warwickshire CV8 1JY *Tel* 01926 857793 CC NO 224348   ESTABLISHED 1948

■ Cadbury Schweppes Foundation

WHERE FUNDING CAN BE GIVEN UK.

WHO CAN BENEFIT Organisations benefiting children, young adults, at risk groups, people disadvantaged by poverty and socially isolated people.

WHAT IS FUNDED Education and enterprise; health and welfare; the environment; and equal opportunities. The priority theme for the next two to three years will be education and enterprise particularly around Yorkshire, Birmingham and London. Particular focus on projects where company employees are directly involved and in areas where the company has operations.

WHAT IS NOT FUNDED No support for individuals, building and refurbishment projects, product donation, sponsorship or advertising.

RANGE OF GRANTS £1,000–£100,000.

FINANCES *Year* 2001 *Income* £810,438 *Grants* £724,267

TRUSTEES D N Makin; N M Boultwood; D G McCabe; J M Sunderland; K Dennis.

HOW TO APPLY In writing to the correspondent.

■ The William A Cadbury Charitable Trust

WHERE FUNDING CAN BE GIVEN West Midlands, especially Birmingham; to a lesser extent, UK, Ireland and overseas.

WHO CAN BENEFIT Organisations serving Birmingham and the West Midlands; organisations whose work has a national significance; organisations outside the West Midlands where the trust has well-established links; organisations in Northern Ireland, and UK-based charities working overseas. Applications are welcomed from ethnic minority groups and women-led initiatives. All organisations must be registered charities.

WHAT IS FUNDED Birmingham and the West Midlands: social welfare, community and self-help groups working with people who are disadvantaged, counselling and mediation agencies; medical and healthcare projects including medical research; education and training, schools and universities, adult literacy schemes, training for employmemt; Religious Society of Friends; places of religious worship and associated social projects; conservation of the environment including the preservation of listed buildings and monuments; the performing and visual arts, museums and art galleries; penal affairs, work with offenders and ex-offenders, penal reform and police project.
UK: Religious Society of Friends; penal reform.
Ireland: cross community initiatives promoting peace and reconciliation.
International: social welfare, healthcare and environmental projects; sustainable development.

WHAT IS NOT FUNDED The trust does not fund individuals (whether for research, expeditions or educational purposes); projects concerned with travel, adventure, sports or recreation; organisations which do not have UK charity registration (except those legally exempt); overseas charities not registered in the UK. The trust receives many more applications than can be supported.
'Even if your project meets our requirements we may not be able to help, particularly if you are located outside the West Midlands.'

TYPE OF GRANT Specific grant applications are favoured. Grants are generally one-off or for projects of one year or less. The trust will consider building grants, capital, core and running costs, recurring and start-up costs, research, endowment, feasibility studies and salaries. Grants are not usually awarded on an annual basis, except to a small number of charities for revenue costs. Grants are only made to or through registered charities and generally range from £100 to £5,000. Larger grants are seldom awarded. Major appeals are considered by trustees at meetings in May and November. Small grants of up to £1,000 are made on a continuing basis under the trust's Small Grants Programme.

RANGE OF GRANTS £300–£20,000.

SAMPLE GRANTS £90,000 to Concern Universal – the second instalment of a five-year grant; £20,000 to Royal Orthopaedic Charity for Michael Cadbury' Children's Assessment Centre;

£15,000 to United Nation's Childrens Fund for emergency relief in Afghanistan; £10,000 each to Brandon Centre for evaluation of a new treatment programme, CARAD Rhayader as matched funding for the director's salary, Friends of Birmingham Museum and Art Gallery and Quaker Peace and Social Witness for conflict resolution in Gulu – Northern Uganda; £9,000 to Earthwatch Institute for education and training for African environmentalists; £8,000 to Welsh Historic Gardens Trust for the Gateway Project; £6,000 to Humanity at Heart for the Joshua Family Centre.

FINANCES *Year* 2001–02 *Grants* £541,000

TRUSTEES Brandon Cadbury; James Taylor; Rupert Cadbury; Katherine van Hagen Cadbury; Margaret Salmon; Sarah Stafford; Adrian Thomas; John Penny; Sophy Blandy.

PUBLICATIONS Policy statement and guidelines for applicants.

OTHER INFORMATION Telephone calls should only be made in the mornings.

HOW TO APPLY Applications to the correspondent in writing, including the following information: charity registration number; a description of the charity's aims and achievements; a copy of the latest set of accounts; an outline and budget for the project for which funding is sought; details of funds raised and the current shortfall. Alternatively you may fill in and submit a copy of our online application form. Please also forward a copy of your latest set of accounts to the above address. Applications are considered on a continuing basis throughout the year. Small grants (amounts not exceeding £1,000) are assessed each month. Major grants are awarded at the trustees' meetings held twice annually, normally in May and November. Applicants whose appeals are to be considered at one of the meetings will be notified in advance and asked to complete an application form.

WHO TO APPLY TO Carolyn Bettis, Trust Administrator, 2 College Walk, Selly Oak, Birmingham B29 6SL *Tel* 0121 472 1464 *Fax* 0121 472 1464 *Website* www.wa-cadbury.org.uk
CC NO 213629   **ESTABLISHED** 1923

■ The Cadogan Charity

WHERE FUNDING CAN BE GIVEN UK, especially Kensington and Chelsea in London and Scotland.

WHO CAN BENEFIT Charities and organisations benefiting children, especially those in care, fostered and adopted; older people; members of the clergy; ex-service and service people; research workers; seafarers and fishermen; sportsmen and women; unemployed people; people disadvantaged by poverty; disabled people; and victims of crime and abuse.

WHAT IS FUNDED Primarily medical care and research charities, some welfare organisations, children's charities, community organisations, arts organisations and animal welfare charities, as well as local churches, conservation and the environment.

WHAT IS NOT FUNDED No grants to individuals.

TYPE OF GRANT Support is usually given over one to two years, although some one-off grants may be made.

RANGE OF GRANTS Up to £500,000, although mostly for £1,000 and £2,000.

SAMPLE GRANTS £500,000 to NSPCC Full Stop Campaign; £250,000 each to Royal Agricultural Benevolent Institute, Royal Agricultural Scottish Benevolent Institute and Royal Veterinary

College; £100,000 each to Bart's Cancer Centre, Culford Foundation, Dockland Settlement and Guild of Air Pilots and Navigators; £50,000 each to Animal Health Trust and Foundling Museum; £25,000 each to Kensington Housing Trust and Royal Ballet School Floral Street Appeal; £23,000 to Barnados; £15,000 to League of Friends of the Royal Marsden NHS Trust. Grants of £10,000 each included those to Bishop of Kensington's Discretionary Fund, Martin Chateris Memorial Appeal, National Hospital for Neurology and Neurosurgery, St John Ambulance and St Wilfred's.

FINANCES *Year* 2000–01 *Income* £2,800,000 *Grants* £2,372,000 *Assets* £9,700,000

TRUSTEES Earl Cadogan; Countess Cadogan; Viscount Chelsea.

HOW TO APPLY In writing to the correspondent, who states: 'Please note that contributions are given to a regular list of charities.'

WHO TO APPLY TO J L Treves, Secretary, The Cadogan Office, 18 Cadogan Gardens, London SW3 2RP *Tel* 020 7730 4567

CC NO 247773   **ESTABLISHED** 1966

■ CAF (Charities Aid Foundation)

WHERE FUNDING CAN BE GIVEN UK.

WHO CAN BENEFIT Any registered (or Inland Revenue approved) charity anywhere in the UK with an income of less than £1.5 million a year.

WHAT IS FUNDED Funding is offered to improve the finances, governance and infrastructure of small to medium-sized charities. The aim is to provide new and innovative opportunities for small and medium-sized charities to develop their capacity. In 2002–2003 there were the following five funds: minority ethnic fund, supporting small minority or ethnic-led groups, including visible minorities, Jewish and Irish communities, travellers, refugees and faith groups; critical assistance fund, to provide consultancy support to organisations in particularly difficult situations; consultancy fund, providing low-cost, high quality consultancy; fast track fund for specific training needs to strength the organisation; and collaborative fund, for organisations looking to work in partnership with CAF.

WHAT IS NOT FUNDED Grants will not be given for: capital items, buildings, vehicles, maintenance costs; start-up costs of a new charitable organisation; academic or scientific research projects; debt, deficit or loan funding; funding that should properly be the responsibility of statutory agencies; support or services to individuals or other beneficiaries; schools, universities or NHS trusts; religious activities; or work already completed or currently taking place or due to start before the application has been considered.

TYPE OF GRANT One-off.

RANGE OF GRANTS £600–£60,000.

FINANCES *Year* 2001–02 *Income* £6,000,000 *Grants* £1,000,000 *Assets* £163,000,000

TRUSTEES Grants Advisory Council: Kim Lavely (Chair and CAF Trustee); Yogesh Chauhan (Chair of Minority Ethnic Fund); John Bateman (Chair of Short Term Assistance); Jackie Hurst (Chair of International); Gillian Crosby (Chair of Collaborative); David Landon (Medical Adviser); Christopher Phillips (Disability Adviser); Fiona Ellis (Consultancy).

HOW TO APPLY On a form available from the correspondent, or CAF's website, at any time.

Forms can be returned online, via e-mail or by post.

WHO TO APPLY TO CAF Grantmaking, Kings Hill, West Malling, Kent ME19 4TA *Tel* 01732 520334 *E-mail* grants@CAFonline.org *Website* www.CAFonline.org/grants

CC NO 268369   **ESTABLISHED** 1974

■ CAFOD

WHERE FUNDING CAN BE GIVEN Predominantly overseas, with some funding to partners in the UK.

WHO CAN BENEFIT Poorer communities overseas and victims of famine, disasters or war.

WHAT IS FUNDED Long-term development work with some of the world's poorest communities. In almost all cases work overseas is planned and run by local people. Programmes include education and skills training, human rights promotion, healthcare, HIV/AIDS, safe water, agriculture and small businesses. Immediate help for people affected by emergencies such as wars and natural disasters is also funded, as is the analysis of the causes of underdevelopment and campaigns on behalf of the world's poor. All programmes seek to promote gender equality. In England and Wales CAFOD's Development Education Fund makes small grants to local or national groups with young people and adults for projects developing education and action on local-global poverty and injustice issues.

WHAT IS NOT FUNDED No grants to individuals or to organisations whose aims are primarily political.

TYPE OF GRANT Partnership, programme and project.

FINANCES *Year* 2002 *Income* £26,487,086 *Grants* £16,525,000 *Assets* £17,094,000

TRUSTEES Rt Revd John Rawsthorne, Chair; Most Revd Patrick Kelly; Dr Mary Hallaway; Nicholas Warren.

HOW TO APPLY Potential applicants should contact the correspondent for further information.

WHO TO APPLY TO Julian Filochowski, Director, Romero Close, Stockwell Road, London SW9 9TY *Tel* 020 7733 7900 *Fax* 020 7274 9630 *E-mail* hqcafod@cafod.org.uk *Website* www.cafod.org.uk

CC NO 285776   **ESTABLISHED** 1962

■ The Cairns Charitable Trust

WHERE FUNDING CAN BE GIVEN UK and overseas.

WHO CAN BENEFIT Small local projects; new, national and established organisations.

WHAT IS FUNDED Medicine and health; welfare; education; sciences; humanities; religion; environmental resources; international; and other general charitable purposes.

WHAT IS NOT FUNDED No grants to individuals.

TYPE OF GRANT One-off and recurrent.

SAMPLE GRANTS 1998–99: £2,500 each to Lewa Wildlife Conservancy UK, National Council for One Parent Families, Portobello Trust, and Prof. Ray Dowles Leukaemia Research Fund.

FINANCES *Year* 2000–01 *Income* £155,797

TRUSTEES Rt. Hon. Earl Cairns; Countess Cairns; Sir John Palmer.

HOW TO APPLY In writing to the correspondent.

WHO TO APPLY TO The Trustees, c/o Ernst & Young, Broadwalk House, Southernhay West, Exeter, Devon EX1 1LF *Tel* 01392 284300

CC NO 295662   **ESTABLISHED** 1986

■ The Calpe Trust

WHERE FUNDING CAN BE GIVEN Worldwide.

WHO CAN BENEFIT Registered charities benefiting people in need including refugees, homeless people, people who are socially disadvantaged, victims of war, victims of disasters and so on.

WHAT IS FUNDED Grants towards peace, human rights, health and welfare, emergencies and so on.

WHAT IS NOT FUNDED No grants towards animal welfare or to individuals.

SAMPLE GRANTS In 1998–99: £5,000 to Anti-Slavery International; £2,500 to Lansbury Trust Fund; £2,000 each to Chernobyl Children's Project, and CIIR; £1,500 each to Cambodia Trust, ChildLine, Family Rights Group, Howard League, and Trax; £1,250 to Hardman Trust.

FINANCES *Year* 2000–01 *Income* £43,857

TRUSTEES R H L R Norton, Chair; B E M Norton; E R H Parks.

HOW TO APPLY In writing to the correspondent. Applications need to be received by June or December as trustees meet in January and July.

WHO TO APPLY TO R H Norton, Trustee, The Hideaway, Hatford Down, Faringdon, Oxon SN7 8JH *Tel* 01367 870665 *Fax* 01367 870500

CC NO 1004193   **ESTABLISHED** 1990

■ Calypso Browning Trust

WHERE FUNDING CAN BE GIVEN UK.

WHO CAN BENEFIT Organisations benefiting homeless people and animals.

WHAT IS FUNDED Regular grants made to some chosen charities but very occasionally to new charities in line with the trust's objects.

WHAT IS NOT FUNDED No grants to individuals.

TYPE OF GRANT One-off and recurrent.

RANGE OF GRANTS £500–£5,000.

SAMPLE GRANTS In 1998: £4,664 each to Shelter, and Housing Association Charitable Trust; £3,887 to Nottinghill Housing Trust; £2,332 to YMCA; £1,554 each to SPEAR, and Brighton Housing Trust; £1,000 each to Kensington Housing Trust, People's Dispensary for Sick Animals, and RSPCA; £500 to Donkey Sanctuary.

FINANCES *Year* 2000–01 *Income* £34,844

TRUSTEES A B S Weir; Ms A Kapp.

HOW TO APPLY In writing to the correspondent. Please note that most of the beneficiaries are ongoing, as specified in the trust's deed.

WHO TO APPLY TO Michael Knowles, Tweedie & Prideaux Solicitors, 5 Lincoln's Inn Fields, London WC2A 3BT *Tel* 020 7405 1234

CC NO 281986   **ESTABLISHED** 1979

■ The Cambridgeshire Historic Churches Trust

WHERE FUNDING CAN BE GIVEN Cambridgeshire.

WHO CAN BENEFIT Bodies responsible for the upkeep, repair and maintenance of a church, chapel or other building used for public worship.

WHAT IS FUNDED The preservation, repair, maintenance, improvement, upkeep and reconstruction of churches in the county of Cambridge and the monuments, fittings, fixtures, stained glass, furniture, ornaments and chattels in such churches and the churchyards belonging to any such churches.

WHAT IS NOT FUNDED Grants are not available for additional building work, or for redecoration or minor programmes of maintenance.

TYPE OF GRANT The grants scheme is funded from an annual payment made by Waste Recycling Environmental (WREN) and is resourced entirely from Landfill Tax credits assigned by Waste Recycling plc.

RANGE OF GRANTS From £1,000–£7,000 primarily for urgent repairs to fabric or renewal of essential services in churches and chapels.

FINANCES *Year* 2001–02 *Income* £124,706 *Grants* £43,000 *Assets* £215,981

PUBLICATIONS Newsletter.

HOW TO APPLY In writing to the correspondent.

WHO TO APPLY TO J N Cleaver, Hon. Secretary, 18 High Street, Histon, Cambridge CB4 9JD *Tel* 01223 232897 *E-mail* marian@cleaver18.fsnet.co.uk

CC NO 287486   **ESTABLISHED** 1983

■ The Camelot Foundation

WHERE FUNDING CAN BE GIVEN UK.

WHO CAN BENEFIT Registered charities working with young people aged between 11 and 25. Priority groups are young parents or those at risk of becoming young parents, young asylum seekers, young people with mental health problems or young people who are disabled.

WHAT IS FUNDED Through the Transforming Lives Grants Programme: salaries, project costs, running costs and contributions towards management costs for charities working with the above priority groups.

WHAT IS NOT FUNDED The foundation will not fund work with children under 11 or people over 25; large national charities; projects where funding from local or central government has run out; work that is the responsibility of local authorities; capital projects; academic research that is not linked to a development project; overseas travel; playschemes; holidays; after school clubs; individuals; general appeals or any well-established or routine approaches.

TYPE OF GRANT One-off grants and recurrent grants for up to three years. Development funding and project support.

RANGE OF GRANTS £10,000 to £90,000.

SAMPLE GRANTS £90,000 to The British Agencies for Adoption and Fostering for a new project that aims to increase the number of young people in care in the UK who are disabled who are placed successfully in permanent family homes; £90,000 to Refugee Lifeline to provide support services to young asylum seekers in the Sheffield and Rotherham areas; £83,868 to Speaking Up to implement their Big Change project, which aims to make sure young people with learning difficulties in Cambridge achieve a successful transition from school to adult life; £65,000 to Hi8us Projects Ltd to develop an interactive drama using video and the internet to enable 11 to 15 year olds to explore issues relating to relationships, sexual health and pregnancy; £60,000 to The Who Cares? Trust to support their Employability Plus project which will adapt and extend earlier work which assisted young people in care to access training, education or employment; £60,000 over three years to LEAP Confronting Conflict, which addresses issues of conflict in the lives of young people aged 14 to 24; £57,554 to Penarth Youth Project to pay for the development of specialist sexual health services to young people in Penarth and surrounding areas in South Wales; £35,681 to The Children's Foundation to support their Golden Freeway project, which uses web-based 'portal technology' to enable young people with cerebral palsy to access specialised information and support their transition from adolescence to independent adulthood.

FINANCES *Year* 2002 *Income* £2,000,000 *Grants* £1,000,000

TRUSTEES Caroline Pickering, Chair; Robert McGowan; David Bryan; Frances Hasler; Dot Renshaw; Dianne Thompson; Anne Spackman; Neil Wragg; John Graham.

HOW TO APPLY For guidelines and a project proposal form send an A4 sae with 33p postage. Different formats, large print and audiotape are also available. There are usually four deadlines per year. Deadlines in 2003 are 3 January, 31 March and 30 June. Decisions usually take three months.

WHO TO APPLY TO Julie Gilson, Grants Manager, University House, 11–13 Lower Grosvenor Place, London SW1W 0EX *Tel* 020 7828 6085 *Fax* 020 7828 6087 *E-mail* info@camelotfoundation.org.uk *Website* www.camelotfoundation.org.uk

CC NO 1060606   **ESTABLISHED** 1996

■ The Campden Charities

WHERE FUNDING CAN BE GIVEN The former parish of Kensington, London; a north-south corridor, roughly from Earl's Court to the north of Ladbroke Grove.

WHO CAN BENEFIT Individuals and organisations.

WHAT IS FUNDED Individuals and organisations serving deprived people.

WHAT IS NOT FUNDED UK charities or charities outside Kensington, unless they are of significant benefit to Kensington residents; schemes or activities which are generally regarded as the responsibility of the statutory authorities; UK fundraising appeals; environmental projects unless connected with education or social need; medical research or equipment; animal welfare; advancement of religion or religious groups, unless they offer non-religious services to the community; commercial and business activities; endowment appeals; projects of a political nature; retrospective capital grants.

TYPE OF GRANT Buildings, capital, core costs, feasibility studies, one-off, project, recurring and running costs, salaries, and start-up costs. Funding may be given for one year or less. Pensions to older people, grants in cash or in kind to relieve need, bursaries and all kinds of grants to Kensington based organisations.

SAMPLE GRANTS £41,000 to Consortium of Supplementary Schools in North Kensington; £40,000 to Westway Sports Centre; £39,000 to Venture Community Centre towards general running costs; £34,000 to Kensington and Chelsea Pre School Alliance towards running costs for eight playgroups; £20,000 each to Middle Row Primary School for computers and Streetwise Youth.

FINANCES *Year* 2000–01 *Grants* £1,102,000

TRUSTEES Revd Tim Thornton, Chair; D C Banks; M Heald; Dr A Hamilton; Lady Astor; Miss E Christmas; S Dehn; S Hoier; P Kraus; Mrs A Law; Ms S Lockhart; C Marr-Johnson; C McLaren; Mrs C Porteous; E Tomlin; R Tuck; I Weekes; N Wickham-Irving.

HOW TO APPLY Initial enquiries from organisations should be made in writing or by telephone to the grants officer for advice and an application form which must be completed and returned with supporting information as required. Office visits are also encouraged to discuss complex applications, or staff may visit organisations.

The organisations committee, which meets 11 times a year, first considers applications and trustees may decide to visit organisations or invite them to present their requests in person. The committee's recommendations are subsequently approved by the board of trustees. This process can take up to two months. Trustees' decisions are imparted to the applicant by letter, which stipulates the nature and size of the grant, date of payment and follow-up reports required from beneficiaries. Beneficiaries must ensure monies are spent only as intended. The charities' staff monitor grants made by studying annual or follow-up reports and by visits.

WHO TO APPLY TO C Stannard, Clerk to the Trustees, 27a Pembridge Villas, London W11 3EP *Tel* 020 7243 0551 *Website* www.campdencharities.org.uk

CC NO 1003641   **ESTABLISHED** 1629

■ The Canning Trust

WHERE FUNDING CAN BE GIVEN UK and the developing world.

WHO CAN BENEFIT Small concerns.

WHAT IS FUNDED Only donations proposed internally by staff members.

RANGE OF GRANTS £1,000–£6,500.

SAMPLE GRANTS 1997–98: £6,500 to Cara; £5,100 to Tushar Project (Emmanual Hospital Association European Fellowship); £5,000 each to Friends of Hadhramut, Kafue Fisheries Ltd, and St Mary Abbots Rehabilitation and Training; £3,000 to Lawrence Barham Memorial Trust; £2,000 each to Accept and New Life Centre – Dehva Dun; £1,000 to Society for Motivational Training and Action.

FINANCES *Year* 2000–01 *Income* £39,704

TRUSTEES A J MacDonald; A W Reed; P Ong.

HOW TO APPLY Unsolicited applications are not considered. The trust states that it generally only makes grants to charities which staff, ex-staff and friends are directly involved with.

WHO TO APPLY TO The Trustees, 4–6 Abingdon Road, London W8 6AF

CC NO 292675   **ESTABLISHED** 1985

■ The Cannop Trust

WHERE FUNDING CAN BE GIVEN UK, with a preference for Tyne and Wear.

WHO CAN BENEFIT Christian and general charitable causes.

WHAT IS FUNDED The relief of certain poor people, the advancement of the Christian religion and general charitable purposes.

FINANCES *Year* 1999 *Income* £5,600 *Grants* £31,000 *Assets* £23,000

TRUSTEES Pauline Fleming; Richard Fleming.

HOW TO APPLY In writing to the correspondent.

WHO TO APPLY TO K C Cannop, Birney Wood, Stamfordham Road, Newcastle upon Tyne NE15 9RB

CC NO 1068365   **ESTABLISHED** 1997

■ The Mauritis Mulder Canter Charity

WHERE FUNDING CAN BE GIVEN UK.

WHO CAN BENEFIT Individuals and organisations.

WHAT IS FUNDED General charitable purposes, including those purposes connected with Netherlands Benevolent Society.

Think carefully about every application. Is it justified?

359

WHAT IS NOT FUNDED No support for national charities.

RANGE OF GRANTS £275–£2,500.

SAMPLE GRANTS £2,500 to Princess Alice Hospital; £2,000 to Edinburgh Medical Missionary Society for Nazareth Hospital; £1,500 to Snowball Club/Children Nationwide; £1,100 to Nightingale House; £1,000 each to Cancer Research Campaign, Cystic Fibrosis Trust and League of Friends Royal Brompton.

FINANCES *Year* 2000 *Income* £30,000 *Grants* £24,000 *Assets* £744,000

TRUSTEES Mrs Maria Lever; Robert Preece; Mrs Rosalind Woollard.

HOW TO APPLY In writing to the correspondent.

WHO TO APPLY TO Rosalind Woollard, Trustee, 19 Annetyard Drive, Skelmorlie, Ayrshire PA17 5BN *Tel* 01475 520699 *E-mail* rosalind@woollard.org.uk

CC NO 266006   **ESTABLISHED** 1973

....

■ The D W T Cargill Fund

WHERE FUNDING CAN BE GIVEN UK, with a preference for the west of Scotland.

WHO CAN BENEFIT Registered charities.

WHAT IS FUNDED General charitable purposes, particularly religious causes, medical charities and help for older people.

WHAT IS NOT FUNDED No grants are made to individuals.

TYPE OF GRANT One-off and recurrent.

RANGE OF GRANTS Mostly £500–£5,000.

SAMPLE GRANTS £35,000 to Ardgowan Hospice; £23,426 in total to David Cargill House; £15,000 to RUKBA; £9,000 to Marie Curie Cancer Care – Hunter's Hill; £8,000 to Greenock Medical Aid Society; £7,500 to City of Glasgow Society of Social Service; £7,000 to Quarriers Village; £6,000 to Glasgow and West of Scotland Society for the Blind; £5,000 each to Scottish Maritime Museum – Irvine and Scottish Episcopal Church – Eventide Homes; £4,000 each to The Thistle Foundation, Muscular Dystrophy Group and Enable; £3,000 to Colquhoun Bequest Fund for Incurables; £2,000 each to Glasgow City Mission and Scottish Motor Neurone Disease Association; £1,000 each to Bethesda Nursing Home and Hospice – Stornoway and Earl Haig Fund; £500 each to Alzheimer Scotland Action on Dementia and Kennyhill School.

FINANCES *Year* 2000–01 *Income* £193,761 *Grants* £196,000 *Assets* £6,319,998

TRUSTEES A C Fyfe; W G Peacock; N A Fyfe; Mirren Elizabeth Graham.

HOW TO APPLY In writing to the correspondent, supported by up-to-date accounts. Trustees meet quarterly.

WHO TO APPLY TO Norman A Fyfe, Trustee, Miller Beckett & Jackson, 190 St Vincent Street, Glasgow G2 5SP *Tel* 0141 204 2833

SC NO SC012703

....

■ The W A Cargill Charitable Trust

WHERE FUNDING CAN BE GIVEN Scotland.

WHO CAN BENEFIT Children and young adults, medical professionals, teachers and Christians.

WHAT IS FUNDED Social services and relief in a local area; hospices; Christians; medical research and specific conditions; youth recreational organisations; people with visual impairments; primary and secondary education; animals and wildlife; and lifeboat services.

WHAT IS NOT FUNDED No grants are given to individuals or organisations which have been 'nationalised or taken over by state/local authorities'.

SAMPLE GRANTS £9,000 to Church of Scotland (in three grants); £7,000 to Crossroads (Scotland); £6,000 to City of Glasgow Social Services; £3,000 each to Glasgow Braendam Link and Trefoil House; £2,000 each to Cornerstone Community Centre, Scottish Conservation Projects, Glasgow Braendam Link, Possil & Milton Forum on Disability and Stobhill Kidney Patients Association.

FINANCES *Year* 1999–2000 *Income* £97,000 *Grants* £83,000 *Assets* £3,000,000

TRUSTEES A C Fyfe; W G Peacock; N A Fyfe; Mirren Elizabeth Graham.

HOW TO APPLY In writing to the correspondent.

WHO TO APPLY TO Norman A Fyfe, Trustee, Miller Beckett & Jackson , 190 St Vincent Street, Glasgow G2 5SP *Tel* 0141 204 2833

SC NO SC012076   **ESTABLISHED** 1954

....

■ The W A Cargill Fund

WHERE FUNDING CAN BE GIVEN Glasgow and the West of Scotland.

WHO CAN BENEFIT Children, young adults and older people, ex-service and service people, musicians, teachers, parents and children, and one-parent families.

WHAT IS FUNDED Medical associations and societies; welfare of older people, the family, young people and service and ex-service personnel; Christian causes; dance, music and opera; youth recreational organisations; medical research and specific conditions; and primary and secondary education.

WHAT IS NOT FUNDED Individuals are not supported.

TYPE OF GRANT One-off or recurrent.

RANGE OF GRANTS Usually £500–£2,000.

SAMPLE GRANTS £18,000 to Erskine Hospital; £10,000 to Scottish Episcopal Church (for widows and orphans); £8,000 to The Salvation Army; £7,500 each to Glasgow Academy Millennium Appeal (third of four grants) and High School of Glasgow Development Campaign (second of four grants); £6,000 each to Deaf Connections and Church of Scotland Baxter House Eventide Home; £5,000 each to Imperial Cancer Research Fund, Sense in Scotland, Glasgow Academy and High School of Glasgow.

FINANCES *Year* 1999–2000 *Income* £380,000 *Grants* £230,000 *Assets* £10,000,000

TRUSTEES A C Fyfe; W G Peacock; N A Fyfe; Mirren Elizabeth Graham.

HOW TO APPLY In writing to the correspondent, including a copy of the charity's latest accounts or details of its financial position.

WHO TO APPLY TO Norman A Fyfe, Trustee, Miller Beckett & Jackson , 190 St Vincent Street, Glasgow G2 5SP *Tel* 0141 204 2833

SC NO SC008456   **ESTABLISHED** 1962

....

■ Caring for Kids (Radio Tay Charity Auction Trust)

WHERE FUNDING CAN BE GIVEN Tayside, Angus and north east Fife.

WHO CAN BENEFIT Individuals and organisations benefiting children and young people, especially those from one parent families, and those who are at risk, disabled, disadvantaged by poverty, socially isolated or victims of abuse.

WHAT IS FUNDED Children's education, disability and recreation.

WHAT IS NOT FUNDED No grants for staff wages or rent.

RANGE OF GRANTS £30–£2,500.

SAMPLE GRANTS £8,000 to Ninewells Hospital; £2,000 to Strathmore Comfort Fund; £1,000 each to Brechin Youth Project, Special Needs at Play and Youth Care; £800 to Oasis Youth Project.

FINANCES *Year* 2000–01 *Income* £98,458 *Grants* £89,500 *Assets* £43,617

TRUSTEES Moira Naulty, Chair; Arthur Ballingall; Margaret Laird; Boris Klapiscak; Lorraine Stevenson; Paul Smith; Lady Fiona Fraser.

HOW TO APPLY Application forms are available from the correspondent from early December. They must be returned by the end of January for consideration for the distribution in March. Applications from individuals must be recommended from a third party such as a social worker, doctor, head teacher, or charitable organisation and so on.

WHO TO APPLY TO The Coordinator, Radio Tay Ltd, 6 North Isla Street, Dundee DD3 7JQ *Tel* 01382 200800 *Fax* 01382 423252 *E-mail* tay-cfk@radiotay.co.uk

SC NO SC008440

■ Carlee Ltd

WHERE FUNDING CAN BE GIVEN Worldwide.

WHO CAN BENEFIT Talmudical scholars and Jewish people.

WHAT IS FUNDED The advancement of religion in accordance with the orthodox Jewish faith; the relief of poverty; general charitable purposes.

RANGE OF GRANTS £8–£26,000.

SAMPLE GRANTS £26,000 to YHTC; £20,000 Rav Chesed; £17,000 to Tevini; £13,000 to UTA; £12,500 to Telz Academy; £10,000 to Gur Trust; £9,500 each to Gevurath Trust and Egerton Road Building Trust; £8,000 each to Bais Yacob Institution and YHTS.

FINANCES *Year* 2000–01 *Income* £194,255 *Grants* £182,308 *Assets* £798,692

TRUSTEES H Grunhut; Mrs P Grunhut.

HOW TO APPLY In writing to the correspondent. This entry was not confirmed by the trust, but the address was correct according to the Charity Commission database.

WHO TO APPLY TO The Secretary, 6 Grangecourt Road, London N16 5EG

CC NO 282873   **ESTABLISHED** 1981

■ The Carlton House Charitable Trust

WHERE FUNDING CAN BE GIVEN UK and overseas.

WHO CAN BENEFIT Organisations benefiting children and young adults, academics, research workers, students and Jewish people.

WHAT IS FUNDED Mostly Jewish organisations. The advancement of education, research work and fellowships. Most funds are committed to various charitable institutions in the UK and abroad; a limited number of bursaries are given, mainly connected with the professional interests of the trustees and never exceeding £5,000 in total in any one year.

TYPE OF GRANT One-off.

RANGE OF GRANTS £35–£9,000.

SAMPLE GRANTS In 1999–2000: £9,095 to B'nai B'rith District 15 of GB and Ireland; £2,895 to Western Marble Arch Synagogue; £1,500 to

Jewish Care Scotland; £1,000 each to Community Security Trust, Jesus College Cambridge, Jewish Care, Lubavitch Foundation, Nightingale House, North Westminster Victim Support Scheme, and Sayser Charity.

FINANCES *Year* 2000–01 *Income* £35,541 *Grants* £29,140 *Assets* £635,348

TRUSTEES Stewart S Cohen; Pearl C Cohen; Fiona A Stein.

HOW TO APPLY In writing to the correspondent.

WHO TO APPLY TO Stewart S Cohen, Trustee, Craven House, 121 Kingsway, London WC2B 6PA *Tel* 020 7242 5283 *Fax* 020 7831 1162 *E-mail* stewartcohen@carltonconsultants.com

CC NO 296791   **ESTABLISHED** 1986

■ The Carlton Television Trust

WHERE FUNDING CAN BE GIVEN Greater London, and part of the counties of Essex, Hertfordshire, Buckinghamshire, Bedfordshire, Oxfordshire, Berkshire, Surrey, East and West Sussex and Kent.

WHO CAN BENEFIT Properly constituted non profit-making organisations and registered charities. Low priority is given to appeals from statutory services and local authorities. The trust will consider charities benefiting: children, young adults and students; unemployed people; and volunteers. Grants may be considered for individual children and young people if the applications come from organisations which apply on their behalf and which can speak about the family's financial circumstances. (Applications are not accepted from private individuals or parents, nor from teachers or other welfare professionals on behalf of their clients.)

WHAT IS FUNDED Educational projects for children and young people who have special needs or are disadvantaged, within the categories: educational establishments and projects, training and employment projects, arts organisations and projects, play and minded care projects, young people's activities, and support for families. Both organisation and project must be based in the Carlton Television area. Grants are only made to registered charities so non-registered groups must find a charity willing to endorse their application and receive any cheque on their behalf.

WHAT IS NOT FUNDED Very low priority will be given to applications from statutory services and local authorities.

TYPE OF GRANT One-off, capital or project grants. Exceptionally salaries and running costs may be considered for two/three years if this will establish new ways of meeting need or to become more effective. Start-up costs also considered.

RANGE OF GRANTS £200–£30,000, average grant £4,000, mostly £1,000–£5,000.

SAMPLE GRANTS £49,700 to Carers UK the second year of a three year project developing services for children and young people with caring responsibilities; £25,000 to YCTV Foundation towards the salary and costs of its Head of Training for one year; £7,500 to Action for Kids Charitable Trust towards outreach workers' salaries; £6,870 to Mount Bovington Visitors Centre Association towards salary costs of an existing part-time post to concentrate on children's activities; £5,000 each to Hanlon Centre towards salary costs of a Somali Community Development Worker and London Connection towards project costs; £4,455 to Island Neighbourhood Project for a children's adventure service challenge programme; £4,320 each to Greenwich Chinese Community School to fund four tutors' fees for one year and Keen Students School towards an English tutor's fees for one year; £4,160 to Camden People's Theatre for a drama workers' fees for a deaf hearing integrated theatre project.

FINANCES *Year* 2001 *Grants* £251,205

TRUSTEES Nigel Walmsley, Chair; Erica De'Ath; Michael Green; Colin Stanbridge; Karen McHugh; Baroness Jay of Paddington.

HOW TO APPLY Funds are disbursed once a year only. Application forms are available from the correspondent between April and early June ONLY and an A4 sae (postage for 75 grammes) should be included. The closing date for receipt of completed forms is 7 June. Organisations may submit only one application per calendar year for projects due to take place from November onwards. Applications must come from properly constituted non-profit making organisations in the Carlton transmission area. Grants will be made payable only to organisations registered as charities. Each application must be endorsed by a management committee member, and an independent referee, or the registered charity supporting the request and acting as a conduit for the funds. Applications for educational equipment or mobility/communication aids must: enclose a professional assessment from a relevant consultant or therapist; confirm that the organisation will take responsibility for matters relating to safety regulations, insurance and maintenance; explain any loan system and its criteria (if administered). The trustees meet in September to shortlist applications and in November to decide the allocation for grants. Applicants will be advised in writing of the outcome by 30 November.

WHO TO APPLY TO Liz Delbarre, Administrator, 101 St Martin's Lane, London WC2N 4RF *Tel* 020 7615 1641 *E-mail* ctvtrust@carltontv.co.uk *Website* www.carlton.com

CC NO 1019628   **ESTABLISHED** 1993

■ The Worshipful Company of Carmen Benevolent Trust

WHERE FUNDING CAN BE GIVEN City of London and UK.

WHO CAN BENEFIT People connected with transport.

WHAT IS FUNDED Objects of relieving necessitous past or present Liverymen or Freemen of the Company, its employees and servants, or those connected with transport in the UK. The trust is also allowed to made grants to any charitable fund in the City of London or elsewhere.

RANGE OF GRANTS £50–£4,500.

FINANCES *Year* 1999–2000 *Income* £80,000 *Grants* £55,000 *Assets* £708,000

TRUSTEES Sir Christopher Leaver; J P Wells; J A T Saywell; M J Power; Brig. M H Turner; M W J Older; D J Skinner.

HOW TO APPLY In writing to the correspondent.

WHO TO APPLY TO Lt Col G T Pearce, Secretary, Painter's Hall Chambers, 8 Little Trinity Lane, London EC4V 2AN *Tel* 020 7489 8289

CC NO 1050893   **ESTABLISHED** 1995

■ The Carmichael-Montgomery Charitable Trust

WHERE FUNDING CAN BE GIVEN England and Wales.

WHO CAN BENEFIT United Reformed Church.

WHAT IS FUNDED Support is given chiefly to URC or ecumenical projects, with some consideration given to individuals known personally to the trustees. This includes Christian education, Christian outreach and Free Church umbrella bodies.

WHAT IS NOT FUNDED Grants are not made to medical charities or individuals.

TYPE OF GRANT Capital, buildings, one-off, project and start-up costs.

RANGE OF GRANTS £100–£10,000; average £2,500.

SAMPLE GRANTS In 1999–2000: the trust gave 42 grants broken down as follows: 24 grants to United Reform Churches totalling £41,000; 10 grants to trusts and societies ranging from £250 to £5,000 and totalling £14,000; and 8 grants to individuals totalling £7,100.

FINANCES *Year* 2002 *Income* £64,345 *Grants* £74,800

TRUSTEES Mrs B J Baker; D J Carmichael; The Revd B Exley; K Forrest; D M Johnson; Mrs N Johnson; Revd M G Hanson; P J Maskell; Mrs S Nicholson.

HOW TO APPLY In writing to the correspondent. The trustees normally meet in April and October and applications should be submitted in March and September. An sae is not necessary, since the trust does not acknowledge ineligible applications.

WHO TO APPLY TO Mrs N Johnson, Trustee, 3 Bear Close, Henley-in-Arden, Warwickshire B95 5HS *Tel* 01564 793561

CC NO 200842   **ESTABLISHED** 1961

■ The Carnegie Dunfermline Trust

WHERE FUNDING CAN BE GIVEN Dunfermline and Rosyth. Applicants must be based in, or have a strong connection with, this area.

WHO CAN BENEFIT Local clubs and societies.

WHAT IS FUNDED Social, educational, cultural and recreational purposes in Dunfermline and its immediate environs. This includes: sports activities, play, information technology and computers; infrastructure development, voluntary sector activities; arts, culture, recreation; schools and colleges; community facilities and services; and other purposes of charitable or benevolent nature.

WHAT IS NOT FUNDED No grants for individuals; closed clubs (i.e. groups not open to the general public to join – this does not exclude minority groups catering for specialised interests); political organisations or causes, commercial enterprises, religious or sectarian bodies, or military or warlike pursuits; organisations which simply want help with maintenance and running costs; the trustees think these should be met out of subscription income. Exceptions might be made in special cases or for new bodies; projects which have already been started; overseas projects; health and medical organisations.

TYPE OF GRANT Buildings, capital, feasibility studies, one-off and project. Funding is for one year or less.

RANGE OF GRANTS £100–£75,000. Typical grant £500–£1,000.

SAMPLE GRANTS £25,000 to a skate park/youth centre project in Dunfermline Public Park; £15,000 to Dunfermline Centre for a synthetic grass outdoor court; £9,324 to Foxtrot Theatre

Company for a tour of local primary schools; £7,500 to Carnegie Hall for a motorised screen for its cinema; £5,500 to Riding for the Disabled to create an indoor school as part of its outdoor arena; £5,000 each to Carnegie Hall for a programme of dramatic works by artists, and Pittencrieff Park for the 2001 Guy Fawkes Day fireworks; £4,300 to a scout group to replace their kilts; £3,900 to Music Library; £3,200 to Inverkeithing High School to produce a book about Rosyth Dockland.

FINANCES *Year* 2001 *Income* £344,311 *Grants* £199,044 *Assets* £10,160,851

TRUSTEES George R Atkinson, Chair; Dr D M Fraser, Vice-Chair; plus 16 life trustees, 3 trustees appointed by Fife Council and 2 honorary trustees.

HOW TO APPLY By letter at any time. Initial telephone calls are welcome. Application forms and guidelines available. Grants are considered monthly. Sae is not required. 'It is sometimes difficult for the trust to steer the correct course between helping a deserving group and sapping its initiative.' Applicants are always expected to have applied to all relevant statutory bodies 'and to show members' willingness to commit existing reserves or to embark on special fundraising activities'. Applications are considered monthly.

WHO TO APPLY TO Bruce Anderson, Chief Executive, Abbey Park House, Abbey Park Place, Dunfermline KY12 7PB *Tel* 01383 723638 *Fax* 01383 721862 *E-mail* admin@carnegietrust.com
SC NO SC015710   **ESTABLISHED** 1903

....

■ The Carnegie Trust for the Universities of Scotland

WHERE FUNDING CAN BE GIVEN Scotland.

WHO CAN BENEFIT Undergraduates of Scottish birth, Scottish parentage or Scottish schooling; graduates and members of staff of the Scottish universities.

WHAT IS FUNDED Universities in Scotland through the improvement of facilities and support of research. Graduates and members of staff of Scottish universities, and undergraduates of Scottish birth or extraction for fees for first degrees at Scottish universities.

WHAT IS NOT FUNDED Research grants can be made only to members of staff and graduates of Scottish universities; costs of equipment, consumables, bench fees, radiocarbon dating and secretarial, technical and other assistance are specifically excluded. The trust does not give grants to individuals for attendance at conferences, participation in expeditions, travel (other than for research) or attendance at institutions other than Scottish universities. Assistance is not given for the fees for first degree or postgraduate diploma courses at Scottish universities. Only those born in Scotland, with a parent born in Scotland or with at least two years secondary education in Scotland, are eligible to apply to the trust and awards made by other bodies will not be supplemented. Carnegie Scholarships are open only to those holding a degree with first-class honours from a Scottish university and nominated by a member of staff, although final year students who are expected to get first-class honours may also apply.

TYPE OF GRANT Capital for projects of value to the Scottish universities, with wide discretion on what is allowable.

FINANCES *Year* 2000–01 *Income* £1,990,806 *Grants* £1,402,581 *Assets* £49,551,438

TRUSTEES There are 14 appointed trustees. Ex-officio trustees comprise the principals of the Scottish universities, the Lord Provosts of Edinburgh and Glasgow and the Secretary of State for Scotland.

OTHER INFORMATION All of the trust's schemes are described in detail on the internet.

HOW TO APPLY Regulations and application forms can be obtained from the secretary. Preliminary telephone enquiries are welcome. Trustees meet in February, June, and November to consider research grants. Fee assistance is considered from April to 1 October for the coming session. Scholarships close on 15 March. Research grant closing dates are 15 January, 15 February and 15 October.

WHO TO APPLY TO Sir John P Arbuthnott, Secretary and Treasurer, Cameron House, Abbey Park Place, Dunfermline, Fife KY12 7PZ *Tel* 01383 622148 *Fax* 01383 622149 *E-mail* jgray@carnegie-trust.org *Website* www.carnegie-trust.org
SC NO SC015600   **ESTABLISHED** 1901

....

■ The Carnegie United Kingdom Trust

WHERE FUNDING CAN BE GIVEN UK and Eire, with a special interest in Scotland.

WHO CAN BENEFIT Priority to appropriate voluntary agencies with a UK dimension, registered as charitable; local groups only where a project is innovatory with UK implications within a category of policy. Particularly those benefiting young adults, older people, parents and children, and one-parent families.

WHAT IS FUNDED Improvement of the wellbeing of the masses of the people of Great Britain and Ireland through projects which the trustees select as best fitted from age to age for securing these purposes, remembering that new needs are constantly arising as the masses advance. From 2001–2006 grants will be for three purposes: creativity; rural; young people. Principally support for the arts, support for community service and support for heritage projects, (d) support for village halls. The trust will consider funding voluntary and community organisations; voluntary arts groups in the fields of dance and ballet, film, video and multimedia broadcasting, literature, music, opera, theatre and the visual arts; community arts and recreation; community centres and village halls; libraries and museums.

WHAT IS NOT FUNDED Generally, the following are excluded: general appeals; closed societies; endowment funds; debt clearance; individuals; replacement of statutory funding; retrospective appeals. Specifically excluded during this quinquennium 2001–2006: restoration, conservation, repair and purchase of buildings; formal education, schools, college, and universities; students or organisations for personal study, travel or expeditions; research or publications, conferences and exhibitions; animal welfare; sports; medical or related healthcare purposes; holidays, adventure centres and youth hostels; conciliation and counselling services; care in the community; arts centres, professional arts companies and festivals (including performances and workshops; pipe organs; libraries.

TYPE OF GRANT Project, for up to three years. Feasibility studies may also be considered.

....

Think carefully about every application. Is it justified?

363

RANGE OF GRANTS Usually £1,000–£30,000 in total.

SAMPLE GRANTS £30,000 each to Voluntary Action Cumbria supporting a range of village hall initiatives in rural Allerdale, Here We Are – Cairndow for core costs and Article 12 for developing a regional structure in England; £27,000 to Voluntary Arts Network to fund a Scottish Network Officer, development in Northern Ireland and a UK wide officer for organisations and persoanl development; £21,000 to Deveron Arts linking a creative young artist-in-residence project and research into how contemporary art can be made of interest to and be of socio-economic benefit for people in rural and remote areas; £20,000 each to Broli to develop a programme of arts in regeneration projects, Circus Eruption to strengthen and extend outreach to young people, DEMOS to support research which aims to shift the debate about children's needs from problems to opportunities, Greater East Belfast Youth Strategy Group to support a worker to establish a youth assembly and Music Traditions Wales to enable development as the Welsh national umbrella for traditional music.

FINANCES *Year* 2001 *Income* £1,731,000 *Grants* £1,145,000 *Assets* £33,431,000

TRUSTEES William Thomson, Chair; George R Atkinson; Linda P Brown; Sir Neil Cossons; Lady Anthony Hamilton; Joy Kinna; Janet A Lewis-Jones; Paddy Linaker; Rosie Millard; Anthony Pender; Sandy Saddler; David J Stobie; C Roy Woodrow; Millie Banerjee; Dr David Fraser; Jeremy Holmes; Dr David Smith; Bill Livingstone.

HOW TO APPLY Application is usually by letter, except where an application form is indicated. All applications need the following information: brief description of the organisation – its history, work, budget, management and staffing; description of the project including its purpose, time scales incorporating any milestones during the programme; expected outcomes; number of people who will benefit; and how the project with be managed; budget for the project, including details of funds already raised and other sources being approached; amount requested from the Carnegie UK Trust; plans for monitoring and evaluating the project. The Carnegie UK Trust attaches great importance to this; how the work will continue after the Carnegie UK Trust's grant has been completed; if appropriate, how it is proposed to share information about the project and what was learnt from it with others in the field; last annual report, audited accounts, the main part of the signed constitution, charity registration number and committee membership; contact name, postal and e-mail addresses, telephone and fax numbers. This should normally be the person directly responsible for the work, not a fundraiser. The application letter must be signed by the senior person responsible, such as the chairman or the director. Unless otherwise stated, deadlines for applications are 30 January for the March trustees' meeting; 30 April for the June meeting; and 30 September for the November meeting. Applications can be submitted at any time. Early preliminary submissions are recommended so that a comprehensive assessment can be presented to the trustees. Applications which arrive on the deadline and require follow up may not be considered at that meeting. Applications are acknowledged on receipt.

WHO TO APPLY TO John Naylor, Chief Executive, Comely Park House, Dunfermline, Fife KY12 7EJ *Tel* 01383 721445 *Website* www.carnegieuktrust.org.uk

SC NO SC012799   **ESTABLISHED** 1913

■ The Carpenter Charitable Trust

WHERE FUNDING CAN BE GIVEN UK and overseas.

WHO CAN BENEFIT Humanitarian and Christian outreach charities are preferred.

WHAT IS FUNDED General charitable objects with a Christian bias.

WHAT IS NOT FUNDED No grants to individuals or to repair local churches.

TYPE OF GRANT One-off (but some are in practice repeated).

RANGE OF GRANTS £250–£2,500.

SAMPLE GRANTS £2,500 each to British Red Cross and Help in Suffering; £1,500 to Crisis; £1,000 each to Brooks Hospital for Animals, Christians Against Poverty, Merlin, Mission Aviation Fellowship, Orbis, Prison Fellowship and Salvation Army.

FINANCES *Year* 2001–02 *Income* £30,140 *Grants* £45,980 *Assets* £981,460

TRUSTEES M S E Carpenter; Mrs G M L Carpenter.

HOW TO APPLY In writing to the correspondent including sufficient details to enable a decision to be made. However, as about half the donations made are repeat grants, the amount available for unsolicited applications remains small.

WHO TO APPLY TO M S E Carpenter, Trustee, The Old Vicarage, Hitchin Road, Kimpton, Hitchin, Hertfordshire SG4 8EF *E-mail* mcarpent@waitrose.com

CC NO 280692   **ESTABLISHED** 1980

■ The Carpenters' Company Charitable Trust

WHERE FUNDING CAN BE GIVEN UK.

WHO CAN BENEFIT Individuals and schools, colleges, universities and other charitable organisations promoting the craft of carpentry.

WHAT IS FUNDED Grants are given to support the carpentry craft, but also for medical, welfare, restoration and general chartiable purposes.

SAMPLE GRANTS £20,000 to Carpenters and Dockland Centre; £2,000 each to St Paul's Cathedral, Metropolitan Society for the Blind, The PACE Centre, Neonatal Unit at St George's Hospital, Starlight Children's Foundation, Carers First, The Lord Mayor's Appeal, Royal British Legion, Arthritis Care and Sports Aid London.

FINANCES *Year* 2000–01 *Income* £1,211,438 *Grants* £264,000 *Assets* £1,243,490

TRUSTEES V F Browne; M R Francis; P C Osborne.

HOW TO APPLY In writing to the correspondent, although the trust states that unsolicited applications are not invited.

WHO TO APPLY TO The Clerk, Carpenters' Hall, 1 Throgmorton Avenue, London EC2N 2JJ *Tel* 020 7588 7001

CC NO 276996   **ESTABLISHED** 1978

■ The Carrington Charitable Trust

WHERE FUNDING CAN BE GIVEN Preference for Buckinghamshire.

WHO CAN BENEFIT Local branches of a wide range of charities, and local charities.

WHAT IS FUNDED General charitable purposes.

Does the trust you have chosen match your needs? Haphazard applications waste postage and time

WHAT IS NOT FUNDED No grants to individuals.

RANGE OF GRANTS £15–£10,045, mostly under £250.

SAMPLE GRANTS £10,045 to Royal Academy; £10,000 to Duke of Edinburgh's Award, Hope and Homes for Children, and University of Reading Department of Agriculture; £6,000 to Bledlow Church; £5,000 to VSO; £2,150 to Friends of Garsington Opera; £750 to Ryder Cheshire Foundation; £550 to Soldiers', Sailors' and Airmen's Families' Association; £500 to NSPCC.

FINANCES *Year* 1999–2000 *Income* £75,871 *Grants* £63,507 *Assets* £3,598,930

TRUSTEES Rt Hon. Lord Carrington; J A Cloke.

HOW TO APPLY In writing to the correspondent.

WHO TO APPLY TO J A Cloke, Trustee, Messrs Cloke & Co., Warnford, Throgmorton Street, London EC2N 2AT *Tel* 020 7638 8992

CC NO 265824   **ESTABLISHED** 1973

■ **The Ida Carroll Trust**

WHERE FUNDING CAN BE GIVEN UK, particularly Manchester.

WHO CAN BENEFIT Organisations concerned with music.

WHAT IS FUNDED The education of the public in the study, practice, knowledge and appreciation of music.

SAMPLE GRANTS £4,000 to Northern Chamber Orchestra; £3,000 to Rawsthorne Trust; £2,500 to Manchester University – Walter Carroll Lunchtime Concert Series; £2,000 to Chethams School of Music; £1,300 to Royal Northern College of Music – Ida Carroll Research Fellowship; £1,000 to Manchester Musical Heritage Trust.

FINANCES *Year* 1999–2000 *Income* £38,000 *Grants* £22,000

TRUSTEES J B Turner; F P Welton; M Hancock.

HOW TO APPLY This trust does not respond to unsolicited applications.

WHO TO APPLY TO J B Turner, Trustee, 40 Parsonage Road, Heaton Moor, Stockport, Cheshire SK4 4JR

CC NO 1059193   **ESTABLISHED** 1988

■ **The Carroll-Marx Charitable Foundation**

WHERE FUNDING CAN BE GIVEN UK and overseas.

WHO CAN BENEFIT Registered charities, particularly Jewish organisations.

WHAT IS FUNDED General charitable purposes.

RANGE OF GRANTS £500–£6,000.

SAMPLE GRANTS £6,000 to Jewish Care; £5,000 to Nightingale House; £2,500 each to Research into Ageing and Community Society; £1,500 each to the Daily Express Kosovo Appeal and the Motor Neurone Disease Association; £1,000 each the Royal Star and Garter Home and Council of Christians and Jews and Sparks.

FINANCES *Year* 1999 *Income* £38,000 *Grants* £54,000 *Assets* £1,100,000

HOW TO APPLY In writing to the correspondent.

WHO TO APPLY TO C Ward, PO Box 472, St Peter's House, Le Bordage, St Peter Port, Guernsey GY1 6AX *Tel* 01481 707826

CC NO 212605   **ESTABLISHED** 1960

■ **The Carron Charitable Trust**

WHERE FUNDING CAN BE GIVEN UK and overseas.

WHO CAN BENEFIT Organisations benefiting academics, medical professionals, nurses and doctors, research workers and students.

WHAT IS FUNDED Applications from charities linked to wildlife, education, medicine, the countryside, printing and publishing will be considered, including charities working in the fields of health professional bodies, health campaigning and advocacy, conservation, wildlife parks and sanctuaries, natural history, endangered species, education and training, costs of study and academic research.

WHAT IS NOT FUNDED No grants to individuals.

TYPE OF GRANT Project, research, running costs and salaries.

SAMPLE GRANTS £3,793 to Highland News Group for the Inverness Hospital scanner appeal; £2,500 to St Edward's School towards tour costs; £2,389 to Mary How Trust for Cancer Prevention for printing costs; £1,340 to Dornoch Academy for filofaxes; £1,250 to AMREF for general costs; £1,128 to Church of Kincardine; £1,000 each to Covent Garden Cancer Research and Highland Cross, both general donations.

FINANCES *Year* 1999 *Income* £26,789 *Grants* £18,927 *Assets* £338,397

TRUSTEES P G Fowler; Mrs J Wells; W M Allen; D L Morgan.

HOW TO APPLY Almost all of the charity's funds are committed for the foreseeable future and the trustees therefore do not invite applications from the general public.

WHO TO APPLY TO Mrs C S Cox, Messrs Rothman Pantall & Co., 10 Romsey Road, Eastleigh, Hampshire SO50 9AL *Tel* 023 8061 4555

CC NO 289164   **ESTABLISHED** 1984

■ **The Leslie Mary Carter Charitable Trust**

WHERE FUNDING CAN BE GIVEN UK, with a preference for Norfolk and Suffolk.

WHO CAN BENEFIT Registered charities.

WHAT IS FUNDED General charitable purposes. Trustees prefer well thought-out applications for larger gifts, than many applicants for smaller grants. The preferred areas for grant giving are nature conservation and wildlife. Other applications will be considered but acknowledgements may not always be sent.

WHAT IS NOT FUNDED No grants to individuals.

TYPE OF GRANT Capital including buildings, core costs, one-off, project, research, running costs and recurring costs will be considered.

RANGE OF GRANTS £1,000–£10,000; typical grant £5,000.

SAMPLE GRANTS £10,000 each to Multiple Sclerosis Society, Raleigh International, Royal Agricultural Benevolent Institution, Save the Children, Soil Association and YWCA; £7,500 to WWF-UK; £6,000 each to British Trust for Ornithology and Cancer Relief Macmillan Fund.

FINANCES *Year* 2001 *Income* £169,500 *Grants* £122,450

TRUSTEES Miss L M Carter; S R M Wilson.

HOW TO APPLY In writing to the correspondent. Telephone calls are not welcome. There is no need to enclose an sae unless applicants wish to have materials returned.

WHO TO APPLY TO S R M Wilson, Birketts, 24–26 Museum Street, Ipswich IP1 1HZ *Tel* 01473 232300

CC NO 284782   **ESTABLISHED** 1982

■ Carter's Educational Foundation

WHERE FUNDING CAN BE GIVEN The ancient parish of Wilford.

WHO CAN BENEFIT The trust supports the South Wilford Endowed Church of England School. It may also give grants to individuals under 25 living in the ancient parish and organisations for such people, with a broadly educational nature, operating within the beneficial area.

WHAT IS FUNDED Education.

SAMPLE GRANTS £91,000 to South Wilford Endowed Church of England School.

FINANCES *Year* 2001 *Income* £227,085 *Grants* £90,680

TRUSTEES Mrs J A Buckland; Mrs P Hammond; R A D Nettleship; R W Stanley; P Wicks.

HOW TO APPLY Applicants should write to the correspondent for an application form which is available each year at Easter. Completed forms must be returned by 31 May; late applications cannot be considered. More than one member of a family may apply. Grants are awarded for the following academic year. Applicants must be under 25 on 1 September. Applications must be in writing and telephone calls are not welcome.

WHO TO APPLY TO Mrs S A Rodgers, Clerk, Pennine House, 8 Stanford Street, Nottingham NG1 7BQ

CC NO 528161   **ESTABLISHED** 1888

■ The Carvill Trust

WHERE FUNDING CAN BE GIVEN UK.

WHO CAN BENEFIT Registered charities.

WHAT IS FUNDED General charitable purposes.

SAMPLE GRANTS 1997–98: £10,000 to Mary Hare Foundation; £5,000 to Downs Syndrome Association; £750 to Pattaya Orphanage; £115 to Lord's Taverners.

FINANCES *Year* 2000–01 *Income* £128,840

TRUSTEES R K Carvill; R E Pooley; K D Tuson.

HOW TO APPLY In writing to the correspondent, although the trust states that it only supports beneficiaries known to or connected with the trustees. Unsolicited applications from individuals will not be supported.

WHO TO APPLY TO K D Tuson, Trustee, Alto House, 29–30 Newbury Street, London EC1A 7HZ *Tel* 020 7600 0203 *Fax* 020 7600 0795

CC NO 1036420   **ESTABLISHED** 1994

■ The Casey Trust

WHERE FUNDING CAN BE GIVEN UK and developing countries.

WHO CAN BENEFIT Charities benefiting children.

WHAT IS FUNDED Children and young people in the UK and developing countries by supporting new projects.

WHAT IS NOT FUNDED Grants are not given to 'individual applicants requesting funds to continue studies or travel'.

SAMPLE GRANTS UK grants: £14,000 to Borough of Camden Youth Club; £8,000 to Norwood Ravenswood; £5,600 to Child Psychotherapy Trust; £5,000 each to East London Schools Club and Family Welfare Association; £3,500 to BREAK; £3,000 each to Association of Wheelchair Children and Movement Foundation; £2,500 to St Christopher Fellowship; £1,500 to Children's Adventure Farm Trust; £1,000 each to Children with Leukaemia, British Ohel Sarah and Scottish Downs Syndrome; £500 each to CHICKS and Rose Road Association.

FINANCES *Year* 1999–2000 *Income* £95,000 *Grants* £112,000 *Assets* £3,300,000

TRUSTEES Ken; Edwin Green; Judge Leonard Krikler.

HOW TO APPLY In writing to the correspondent. This entry was not confirmed by the trust, but the information was correct according to the trust's file at the Charity Commission.

WHO TO APPLY TO Ken Howard, Trustee, 27 Arkwright Road, London NW3 6BJ

CC NO 1055726   **ESTABLISHED** 1996

■ Cash for Kids

WHERE FUNDING CAN BE GIVEN West Midlands only (within a 50-mile radius of Birmingham).

WHO CAN BENEFIT Organisations benefiting young people.

WHAT IS FUNDED The charity aims to help disadvantaged children and young people (under 18s). It supports relief of poverty or deprivation and the general welfare of children.

WHAT IS NOT FUNDED No grants to organisations outside the West Midlands. No grants to individuals, for research, trips abroad, medical treatment, unspecified expenditure, deficit funding or repayment of loans, for distribution to other organisations or for administration costs.

TYPE OF GRANT One-off.

RANGE OF GRANTS £50–£8,000

FINANCES *Year* 1998–99 *Income* £118,746 *Grants* £67,000 *Assets* £117,210

TRUSTEES Dr Barry Roseman, Chair; John Buckingham; Peter Languard; Mike Owen; Julie Fair; Sir Bernard Ziffman.

PUBLICATIONS Brief guide to Cash for Kids.

HOW TO APPLY On a form available from the correspondent. Applications must be received between 1 March and 1 July. Enclose an sae for receipt of application. Applicants will be informed by letter as to the outcome of their application. Please do not telephone the trust, unless you have a specific enquiry.

WHO TO APPLY TO Pat Short, BRMB Radio Group, Nine Brindley Place, 4 Ooozells Square, Birmingham B1 2DJ *Tel* 0121 245 5314 *Fax* 0121 245 5255 *E-mail* pat.short@brmb.co.uk *Website* www.brmb.co.uk

CC NO 1042820   **ESTABLISHED** 1994

■ Cash for Kids – Radio Clyde

WHERE FUNDING CAN BE GIVEN Radio Clyde transmission area, i.e. west central Scotland.

WHO CAN BENEFIT Children and young adults up to the age of 16, including those in care, fostered and adopted.

WHAT IS FUNDED Christmas presents, food, pantomime trips, clothing and other tangible items are given to sick or underprivileged children via Strathclyde Regional Councils Social Work Department and through community and voluntary groups.

WHAT IS NOT FUNDED The trust does not fund trips in the summer or at Easter, equipment or salaries. Children benefiting must be aged 16 or under.

SAMPLE GRANTS £30,000 to Ronald McDonald House; £25,000 to Craighalbert Centre; £10,000 to Riding for the Disabled; £7,000 to Hamish Allan Centre Children's Fund; £5,851 to SAMH; £5,000 each to Eyeless Trust, Pageot School of Dance and Princess Royal Trust for Carers; £4,000 each to Home-Start Wigtownshire and Kirkcudbright Centipede Playgroup.

FINANCES *Year* 2001–02 *Income* £751,512 *Grants* £592,000 *Assets* £240,477

TRUSTEES Sir John Orr, Chair; Paul Cooney; Robert Caldwell; Kirsty Archer.

HOW TO APPLY On a form available from the correspondent. 'To ensure proper stewardship of the funds raised, all nominations from those who believe the funds should be destined to a particular family or group have to be accompanied by a recommendation from an accredited body such as social work departments, Children 1st, head teachers, members of the clergy and community workers.'

WHO TO APPLY TO Yvonne Wyper, Finance Manager, Clyde Action, 236 Clyde Street, Glasgow G1 4JH *Tel* 0141 204 1025
Website www.cashforkids.net

SC NO SC003334   **ESTABLISHED** 1984

···

■ Sir John Cass's Foundation

WHERE FUNDING CAN BE GIVEN The inner London boroughs – Kensington & Chelsea, Camden, City of London, Greenwich, Hackney, Hammersmith & Fulham, Islington, Lambeth, Lewisham, Newham, Southwark, Tower Hamlets, Wandsworth, Westminster.

WHO CAN BENEFIT Individuals; schools and organisations benefiting young people under the age of 25, who are permanently residents of inner London. The foundation will consider time-limited projects where it is clear for what purpose and activities grant assistance is being sought. The trustees wish to encourage and, where appropriate, support applications which incorporate structures which have educational content relating, where appropriate, to the teaching and learning of the relevant key stage(s) of the national curriculum; demonstrate a realistic likelihood of continuing after expiry of the foundation's grant; are innovative, in the sense of identifying and meeting educational needs not met by other grant-giving bodies. Within these parameters, trustees particularly favour applications which promote the teaching of science, maths, engineering and technology; develop programmes that improve access to the curriculum and prepare beneficiaries for the world of work; and develop curricula or activities outside the normal school day.

WHAT IS FUNDED Education, especially of people in financial need.

WHAT IS NOT FUNDED The governors will not fund basic equipment or teachers' salaries that are the responsibility of the education authorities; the purchase, repair or furnishing of buildings; stage, film or video production costs; performances, exhibitions or festivals; independent schools; local youth and community projects; conferences or seminars; university or medical research; pre-school, nursery education or toy libraries; establishing funds for bursary or loan schemes; supplementary schools or mother tongue teaching; retrospective grants to help pay off overdrafts or loans (nor will the foundation remedy the withdrawal or reduction of statutory funds); the purchase of vehicles, computers or sports equipment; research or publication costs; one-off music, drama, dance or similar productions, or the tours of such productions (nor does the foundation support ticket subsidy schemes); holiday projects, school journeys, trips abroad or exchange visits; school ground improvements; general fundraising campaigns and appeals.

TYPE OF GRANT Recurrent for individuals; project, recurrent or one-off support for groups,

organisations and schools. Funding may be given for up to three years.

RANGE OF GRANTS Usually £5,000–£40,000.

SAMPLE GRANTS £109,098 to Sir John Cass's and Red Coat C of E Secondary School; £100,000 each to Education Action Zone, and St Mary Magdalene C of E School – Peckham Rye; £73,500 to London Guildhall University for A-level Saturday schools; £60,000 to London Diocesan Board for Schools for capital works; £50,000 to City University for development of IT teaching; £35,669 to Newham Training and Education Centre Ltd for IT training courses for young women who are unemployed; £33,962 to Sir John Cass's Foundation Primary School; £30,000 to London Diocesan Board for Schools for New Opportunities Fund partnership funding for 20 C of E primary schools; £25,000 to Camden School for Girls for building costs of a new sixth form block and assembly hall.

FINANCES *Year* 2000–01 *Income* £1,578,541 *Grants* £921,000 *Assets* £39,551,225

TRUSTEES 18 in all, of whom the following are members of the grants committee: M Venn; K M Everett; Revd Dr B J Lee.

OTHER INFORMATION The foundation also committed £5 million over four years to City University to support the development of their new business school.

HOW TO APPLY To apply for a grant you should send an initial letter outlining your application to the correspondent. The letter should include some basic costings for your project and background details on your organisation; if your proposal falls within the current policy and the foundation's basic criteria are satisfied, you will be invited to submit an application under headings that the foundation will provide, together with an annual report and audited accounts; upon receipt of the completed application, foundation staff will discuss your proposal with you and may arrange to visit; completed applications are then considered by governors, who meet quarterly; decisions are conveyed to applicants within seven days of a meeting; throughout the process, the foundation's staff will be happy to clear up any questions you might have and are available to receive initial telephone enquiries. Applicants should note that an application is only finalised when all documentation has been received, a meeting has taken place and there are no further questions to raise. All this takes time and it is the applicant's responsibility to allow a reasonable length of time for this process. Successful projects will include appropriate measures of performance, as the foundation is interested in evaluating the results of funded activities.

WHO TO APPLY TO Colin Wright, Clerk, 31 Jewry Street, London EC3N 2EY *Tel* 020 7480 5884 *Fax* 020 7488 2519

CC NO 312425   **ESTABLISHED** 1748

···

■ Sir Ernest Cassel Educational Trust

WHERE FUNDING CAN BE GIVEN UK.

WHO CAN BENEFIT Institutions of higher education, colleges or organising bodies (e.g. in adult education) benefiting young adults, students and academics.

WHAT IS FUNDED Grants for educational purposes to institutions or organising bodies.

WHAT IS NOT FUNDED No grants to individuals. General appeals will not be funded.

TYPE OF GRANT One-off or recurrent grants will be considered. Funding may be given for up to three years.

RANGE OF GRANTS £500–£5,000.

SAMPLE GRANTS £5,000 to Christ's College Cambridge for a Commonwealth postgraduate; £1,000 to £1,500 each to Centre for Disability and the Arts, Leicester University student support fund, Edinburgh University to support Commonwealth postgraduates and the Marine Society.

FINANCES *Year* 2001–02 *Income* £38,172 *Grants* £39,000 *Assets* £1,249,715

TRUSTEES Countess Mountbatten of Burma, Chair; H J Renton; Lord Sutherland; Ms A S Kennedy; Baroness O'Neill of Bengarve; Lady Amanda Ellingworth; Prof. John Barron.

HOW TO APPLY In writing with supporting documents but not annual accounts.

WHO TO APPLY TO D N Constable, 199 West Malvern Road, Malvern, Worcestershire WR14 4BB *Tel* 01684 572437 *E-mail* casseltrust@sherborn.demon.co.uk **CC NO** 313820   **ESTABLISHED** 1919

■ The Elizabeth Casson Trust

WHERE FUNDING CAN BE GIVEN UK.

WHO CAN BENEFIT Oxford Brookes University, other occupational therapy schools and departments, and individual occupational therapists.

WHAT IS FUNDED 75% to support Oxford Brookes University occupational therapy courses. 25% to support other occupational therapy schools/departments and individual occupational therapists.

WHAT IS NOT FUNDED No support for anything other than occupational therapy education and training.

TYPE OF GRANT Research projects and courses/travel bursaries that will benefit the profession as well as the individual.

RANGE OF GRANTS £100–£65,000.

SAMPLE GRANTS £65,000 to Oxford Brookes University School of Healthcare; £22,000 for a one-year scholarship at Tufts University, Boston, USA; £5,000 to University of Greenwich for wheelchair course accreditation; £1,000 towards MSc course fees.

FINANCES *Year* 2001–02 *Income* £217,563 *Grants* £209,690 *Assets* £3,810,778

TRUSTEES B M Mandlebrote, Chair; Prof. W Couchman; K D Grevling; B E Hulse; Mrs C Rutland; Prof. D T Wade; Lady Williams; Mrs J S Croft; Mrs C A G Gray; Dr P L Aguenic.

OTHER INFORMATION The trust was founded in 1930 as Dorset House School of Occupational Therapy (a registered company). In 1948 the founder Dr Elizabeth Casson, registered this trust and an associated trust, The Casson Trust, under the same number at the Charity Commission. In 1992 Dorset House site was leased to Oxford Brookes University and in 1993 the company changed its name to the Elizabeth Casson Trust.

HOW TO APPLY On the trust's application form which can be obtained from the address below.

WHO TO APPLY TO B A Davies, Secretary, 20 Chaundy Road, Tackley, Kidlington, Oxfordshire OX5 3BJ *Tel* 01869 331379 *E-mail* bernard.davies@btinternet.com **CC NO** 227166   **ESTABLISHED** 1930

■ H and M Castang Charitable Trust

WHERE FUNDING CAN BE GIVEN UK.

WHO CAN BENEFIT Registered charities benefiting medical professionals, research workers and people with physical or mental disabilities.

SAMPLE GRANTS In 1998–99: £40,000 to The Little Foundation for a research project relating to cerebral palsy (£30,000) and for general purposes (£10,000); £5,158 to Neurology and Orthopaedic Development Fund – Royal Hospital for Sick Children Edinburgh for a part-time study assistant for a cerebral palsy study; £600 for travelling expenses for a doctor to attend a meeting at the International Federation of Placental Associations; £498 to fund a trip to Tubingen for a doctor.

FINANCES *Year* 2000–01 *Income* £103,467

TRUSTEES I A Burman; M B Glynn; Dr I StJ Kemm.

HOW TO APPLY In writing to the address below.

WHO TO APPLY TO I A Burman, Trustee, Carmelite House, 50 Victoria Embankment, Blackfriars, London EC4Y OLS **CC NO** 1003867   **ESTABLISHED** 1991

■ The Catholic Charitable Trust

WHERE FUNDING CAN BE GIVEN America and Europe.

WHO CAN BENEFIT Traditional Catholic organisations and Roman Catholics.

WHAT IS FUNDED The traditional teachings of the Roman Catholic faith. The trust income is usually fully committed.

WHAT IS NOT FUNDED No grants to individuals.

RANGE OF GRANTS £1,000–£15,000.

SAMPLE GRANTS 1998: £15,000 to Society of Saint Pius X; £10,000 to Worth School; £4,000 to White Sisters; £3,000 to Carmelite Monastery, Carmel, California; £2,000 each to St Joseph's Catholic Primary School and Society of the Grail; £1,000 to Ealing Abbey.

FINANCES *Year* 2002 *Grants* £35,000

TRUSTEES J C Vernor Miles; R D D Orr; W E Vernor Miles.

HOW TO APPLY In writing to the correspondent.

WHO TO APPLY TO J C Vernor Miles, Trustee, Messrs Vernor, Miles & Noble, 5 Raymond Buildings, Gray's Inn, London WC1R 5DD *Tel* 020 7242 8688 **CC NO** 215553   **ESTABLISHED** 1935

■ Catholic Foreign Missions

WHERE FUNDING CAN BE GIVEN UK and overseas.

WHO CAN BENEFIT Catholic Foreign Missions.

WHAT IS FUNDED Grants are made in support of Catholic Foreign Missions in any part of the world.

WHAT IS NOT FUNDED No grants are made to external applicants.

FINANCES *Year* 2001 *Income* £761,014 *Grants* £766,384 *Assets* £18,844,164

TRUSTEES Council of Management: Desmond Bierne; Jean Marie Lesbats; Abel Maniez; Bernard Meade; Hugh Murnaghan; Eric Saint-Sevin; Philip Walshe; Phillipe Lamblin.

HOW TO APPLY No external applications are considered. The funds are fully committed.

WHO TO APPLY TO The Secretary, 70 St George's Square, London SW1V 3RD *Tel* 020 7821 8211 *Fax* 020 7630 6484 *E-mail* postmaster@wwlaw.co.uk **CC NO** 249252   **ESTABLISHED** 1941

■ The Cattanach Charitable Trust

WHERE FUNDING CAN BE GIVEN UK, with a preference for Scotland.

WHO CAN BENEFIT Recognised charities only.

WHAT IS FUNDED General charitable purposes. Grants are made to a range of charities with the main themes being homelessness and disability.

WHAT IS NOT FUNDED Only registered charities can receive support. Grants will not be given to fund salaries of staff already in post; the trustees also prefer not to commit to permanent funding of any long-term project.

TYPE OF GRANT Capital including buildings, core costs, one-off, project, research, and start-up costs, for up to two years.

SAMPLE GRANTS £11,356 to ECSH; £10,000 each to Ex-Services Mental Health, Glasgow Simon Community, and Lead Scotland; £7,000 to Barnardos; £6,600 to Scottish Dyslexia Association; £5,400 to Motability; £5,000 each to Donaldson's Development Project, Salvation Army, and Shelter Scotland.

FINANCES *Year* 1999 *Income* £239,796 *Grants* £135,560 *Assets* £6,398,939

TRUSTEES Royal Bank of Scotland plc; Colette Douglas Home; Lord MacLay; F W Fletcher; Adam Thomson; William Syson.

HOW TO APPLY A standard application form is available from the correspondent. The trustees meet at the end of June and December and applications together with the charity's latest report and annual accounts must be received not less than three months before each meeting. Applications received after this deadline will only be considered if they are extraordinary, in which case they should be received not less than seven days prior to the meeting at which they are to be considered. Applications are acknowledged upon receipt. The trust may contact the applicant for further information prior to the trustees' meeting. All applicants are informed of the trustees' decision and, if sucessful, any conditions attached to it.

WHO TO APPLY TO Don Henderson, Royal Bank of Scotland plc, Private Trust and Taxation, 2 Festival Square, Edinburgh EH3 9SU *Tel* 0131 523 2648 *Fax* 0131 228 9889 *E-mail* don.henderson@rbs.co.uk

SC NO SC020902   **ESTABLISHED** 1992

■ The Joseph & Annie Cattle Trust

WHERE FUNDING CAN BE GIVEN Worldwide, with a preference for Hull and East Yorkshire.

WHO CAN BENEFIT Disabled, especially aged and young and local charities.

WHAT IS FUNDED General charitable purposes.

WHAT IS NOT FUNDED No grants to individuals, national societies (except for work in North Humberside area) or professional appeals (where agents and appeal staff are employed or paid).

TYPE OF GRANT One-off, capital, recurring and interest-free loans are considered.

RANGE OF GRANTS £200–£20,000.

SAMPLE GRANTS £20,000 to Brocklehurst Neurosurgical Fund for equipment; £17,159 to Dyslexia Institute for pupils' fees; £10,000 each to Cottingham Young People's Sports Foundation for equipment, Holy Trinity Appeal for refurbishment, and Sobriety Project for refurbishment; £8,735 to Hull Grammar School for school fees; £5,000 each to Hull Compact Awards for student fees, Lifestyle for a children's innovation project, North Bransholme

Sports Forum for an all-weather playing facility, and Partially Sighted Society for general needs.

FINANCES *Year* 1998–99 *Income* £396,000 *Grants* £298,000 *Assets* £7,400,000

TRUSTEES J A Collier; M T Gyte; P A Robins.

HOW TO APPLY In writing to the correspondent. Meetings are usually held on the third Monday of each month.

WHO TO APPLY TO R C Waudby, Administrator, Morpeth House, 114 Spring Bank, Hull HU3 1QJ *Tel* 01482 211198 *Fax* 01482 219772

CC NO 262011   **ESTABLISHED** 1970

■ The Thomas Sivewright Catto Charitable Settlement

WHERE FUNDING CAN BE GIVEN Unrestricted, for UK-based registered charities.

WHO CAN BENEFIT Registered charities only.

WHAT IS FUNDED General charitable purposes.

WHAT IS NOT FUNDED The trust does not support non-registered charities, expeditions, travel bursaries and so on, or unsolicited applications from churches of any denomination. Grants are unlikely to be considered in the areas of community care, playschemes and drug abuse, or for local branches of national organisations such as scout groups.

RANGE OF GRANTS £50–£20,000.

SAMPLE GRANTS £20,000 to Oxfam Partners Against Poverty; £10,000 each to King Edward VII's Hospital and London Immunotherapy Cancer Trust; £5,000 each to Disasters Emergency Committee for the Indian Earthquake, Elizabeth Finn Trust, Minchinhampton Centre for the Elderly, Royal Hospital for Neuro-Disability, Royal Scottish Academy of Music and Westbourne House School.

FINANCES *Year* 2000–01 *Income* £267,300 *Grants* £226,210 *Assets* £3,937,144

TRUSTEES Mrs Olivia Marchant; Lord Catto; Miss Zoe Richmond-Watson.

HOW TO APPLY In writing to the correspondent, including an sae.

WHO TO APPLY TO Miss Ann Unwins, Clarebell House, 5–6 Cork Street, London W1S 3NX

CC NO 279549   **ESTABLISHED** 1979

■ The Wilfrid & Constance Cave Foundation

WHERE FUNDING CAN BE GIVEN UK with preference for Berkshire, Cornwall, Devon, Dorset, Hampshire, Oxfordshire, Somerset, Warwickshire and Wiltshire.

WHO CAN BENEFIT Registered charities. Mainly local charities or charities which the trustees have personal knowledge of, interest in, or association with are considered.

WHAT IS FUNDED General charitable purposes.

WHAT IS NOT FUNDED No grants to individuals.

TYPE OF GRANT Buildings, core costs, one-off, project, research, and running costs. Grants may be given for up to three years.

RANGE OF GRANTS £1,000–£25,000.

SAMPLE GRANTS £25,000 to Exford First School; £15,000 to Royal Agricultural Benevolent Institution; £11,000 to British Red Cross; £8,000 to The Farmer's Club Pinnacle Award; £7,500 to Nuneaton Equestrian Centre; £6,000 to Titirheleni Primary School; £5,000 each to Dulverton Town Hall, Lifeline, The Fortune Centre for Riding Therapy and Devon Air Ambulance.

FINANCES *Year* 2000–01 *Income* £107,495 *Grants* £181,178 *Assets* £1,934,243

TRUSTEES F Jones, Chair; Mrs T Jones; Mrs J Pickin; M D A Pickin; Mrs N Thompson; Mrs J Archer; R Walker; Mrs M Waterworth.

HOW TO APPLY In writing to the correspondent a month before trustees' meetings held twice each year, in May and October.

WHO TO APPLY TO Mrs Lorraine Olsen, Secretary, New Lodge Farm, Drift Road, Winkfield, Windsor SL4 4QQ

CC NO 241900   ESTABLISHED 1965

■ The B G S Cayzer Charitable Trust

WHERE FUNDING CAN BE GIVEN UK.

WHO CAN BENEFIT Registered charities.

WHAT IS FUNDED General charitable purposes.

WHAT IS NOT FUNDED No grants to organisations outside the UK. Unsolicited appeals will not be supported.

RANGE OF GRANTS Up to £25,000.

SAMPLE GRANTS £25,000 to Feathers Clubs Association; £10,000 each to Tinsbury Youth Club and Westerkirk Parish Trust; £5,000 each to Game Conservancy Trust, Romsey Hospital Appeal and Tabor Tree Methodist Church; £3,000 to Christchurch; £2,500 to Clan McQuarrie Memorial Hall and C Waller Memorial Trust; and £2,250 to PSP Association.

FINANCES *Year* 1999–2000 *Income* £87,506 *Grants* £87,600 *Assets* £2,182,228

TRUSTEES Peter N Buckley; Peter R Davies.

HOW TO APPLY In writing to the correspondent, although the trust tends to support only people/ projects known to the Cayzer family or the trustees.

WHO TO APPLY TO Ms Jeanne Cook, Cayzer House, 30 Buckingham Gate, London SW1E 6NN *Tel* 020 7802 8080

CC NO 286063   ESTABLISHED 1982

■ Elizabeth Cayzer Charitable Trust

WHERE FUNDING CAN BE GIVEN UK.

WHO CAN BENEFIT Arts.

WHAT IS FUNDED Funds are used in promoting activities related to art.

SAMPLE GRANTS 1998–99: £8,400 to The National Gallery.

FINANCES *Year* 2000–01 *Income* £22,183

TRUSTEES The Hon. Elizabeth Gilmour; Diana Caroline Lloyd; John Ivor Mehrtens.

HOW TO APPLY In writing to the correspondent.

WHO TO APPLY TO Ms Jeanne Cook, The Cayzer Trust, Cayzer House, 30 Buckingham Gate, London SW1E 6NN *Tel* 020 7802 8080

CC NO 1059265   ESTABLISHED 1996

■ Celtic Charity Fund

WHERE FUNDING CAN BE GIVEN Preference for Scotland and Northern Ireland.

WHO CAN BENEFIT Charities benefiting children, homeless people, unemployed people, and victims of famine or war.

WHAT IS FUNDED Promotion of religious and ethnic harmony, drug-related projects, alleviation of suffering.

FINANCES *Year* 1999–2000 *Grants* £100,000

TRUSTEES Eric Riley; Kevin Sweeney; John Maguire.

HOW TO APPLY An application form should be requested in writing from the trust. Trustees meet to consider grants in July each year.

WHO TO APPLY TO The Public Relations Department, Celtic Football Club, Celtic Park, Glasgow G40 3RE *Tel* 0141 556 2611 *Fax* 0141 551 8106 *Website* www.celticfc.co.uk

CC NO Y00119

■ The Cemlyn-Jones Trust

WHERE FUNDING CAN BE GIVEN North Wales and Anglesey.

WHO CAN BENEFIT Small local projects.

WHAT IS FUNDED Conservation and protection of general public amenities, historic or public interests in Wales; medical research; protection and welfare of animals and birds; study and promotion of music; activities and requirements of religious and educational bodies.

WHAT IS NOT FUNDED No grants to individuals or non-charitable organisations.

TYPE OF GRANT One-off.

RANGE OF GRANTS £100 upwards.

SAMPLE GRANTS £20,000 to UCNW Development Trust for various purposes; £11,000 to Macmillan Cancer Relief, North Wales; £4,200 to Beaumaris & District Silver Band; and £3,000 to North Wales Wildlife Trust.

FINANCES *Year* 2000–01 *Income* £41,000 *Grants* £39,000 *Assets* £1,200,000

TRUSTEES P G Brown; Mrs J E Lea; Mrs E G Jones.

HOW TO APPLY In writing to the correspondent.

WHO TO APPLY TO P G Brown, Trustee, 59 Madoc Street, Llandudno LL30 2TW *Tel* 01492 874391

CC NO 1039164   ESTABLISHED 1994

■ The Century Radio Limited Charitable Trust

WHERE FUNDING CAN BE GIVEN The transmission area of Century radio – effectively, North east England.

WHO CAN BENEFIT General charitable purposes.

WHAT IS FUNDED Registered charities and smaller groups, which may not be registered as a charity, provided the purpose for which the grant is required is wholllly charitable.

WHAT IS NOT FUNDED Grants are not given to individuals, major UK fundraising appeals or for ongoing expenses (e.g. rent, telephone, petrol), repeat applications within a 12-month period.

RANGE OF GRANTS £3,000–£5,000

FINANCES *Year* 1999 *Grants* £50,000

TRUSTEES Jeff Stevenson, the managing director of Century Radio; Julian Kenyon from Northern Electric; Jan O'Brian; and a solicitor from Dickenson Dees.

OTHER INFORMATION The trustees choose four charities to support each year. Other grants, drawn from the applications received, are made to a wide range of community and social activities and social issues to benefit those within the station's transmission area.

HOW TO APPLY An application form can be obtained by writing to the correspondent. The trustees meet quarterly, at the end of January, April, July and October to consider grant applications received by the 1st of the month.

WHO TO APPLY TO Jane Spooner, Century House, PO Box 100, Church Street, Gateshead NE8 2YY *Tel* 0191 477 6666

CC NO 1074635   ESTABLISHED 1999

■ CfBT Education Services

WHERE FUNDING CAN BE GIVEN UK and overseas.

WHO CAN BENEFIT Individuals and organisations involved in education, particularly those concerned with the development and management of schools, educational project management, teacher education, careers guidance, accountability and English language teaching.

WHAT IS FUNDED Support from CfBT follows the main theme 'Investments in Ideas' where support is given through: commissioned research and development projects; research awards by competition/tender; and funding for projects in response to applications and invitation.

WHAT IS NOT FUNDED The following are not funded: loans; general appeals; grants to replace statutory funding; buildings or capital costs; projects which have only a local focus; research of a mainly theoretical nature; running costs; the arts, religion, sports and recreation; conservation, heritage or environmental projects; animal rights or welfare; expeditions, travel, adventure/holiday projects; educational exchanges between institutions; or staff salaries.

TYPE OF GRANT One-off and recurring grants.

RANGE OF GRANTS £15,000–£100,000.

SAMPLE GRANTS £50,000 to High Reliability Schools Project; £41,371 to NPHA/Queen's University for improving schools through effective leadership; £40,267 to Banbury School/University of Oxford for a writing skills project; £30,000 to Special Needs Training Consortium for a certificate for SEN workers; £29,936 to Warwick University – Improving Partnerships for consultancy related communication in complex projects; £29,590 to Institute of Public Policy Research for Parents as Partners in Learning; £28,000 to Link Africa for Soshanguve Phase III for training for South African Principals; £22,000 to Changemakers (II) for promoting opportunities for youth; £20,000 to Education Advisory Group for development of new education policies.

FINANCES *Year* 1999 *Income* £16,604,000 *Grants* £489,000 *Assets* £10,847,000

TRUSTEES Thelma Henderson; Dame Mary Richardson; John Webb; Iain MacArthur; Andrew Stuart, Chair; Stephen Yeo.

PUBLICATIONS *Development Funding – Guide to Applicants.*

HOW TO APPLY Individual applicants should write to the development fund manager, stating their personal circumstances and the nature of the assistance sought. They will then be advised whether or not to proceed with a formal application. Organisations must first submit an outline proposal to the development fund manager who will advise them whether the proposal meets the criteria agreed by the trustees, and also on how to proceed. Full applications are considered at the meetings of trustees, in March, June, September and December.

WHO TO APPLY TO The Development Fund Manager, 60 Queens Road, Reading, Berkshire RG1 4BS *Tel* 0118 952 3900 *Fax* 0118 952 3926 *E-mail* gen@cfbt-hq.org.uk *Website* www.cfbt.com

CC NO 270901   **ESTABLISHED** 1965

■ The Amelia Chadwick Trust

WHERE FUNDING CAN BE GIVEN UK, especially Merseyside.

WHO CAN BENEFIT Neighbourhood-based community projects, some UK organisations.

WHAT IS FUNDED Education, health, the arts, social welfare and the environment.

TYPE OF GRANT Recurring.

RANGE OF GRANTS £200–£19,000.

SAMPLE GRANTS £19,000 to Merseyside Development Foundation; £6,500 to Liverpool PSS; £6,000 to St Helens Women's Aid; £2,600 to Garston Adventure Playground; £2,000 each to Centre Point and Sue Ryder Home; £1,500 each to British Red Cross and Merseyside Holiday Service; £1,300 to St John's Service.

FINANCES *Year* 1998–99 *Income* £96,000 *Grants* £74,000 *Assets* £3,600,000

TRUSTEES J R McGibbon; J C H Bibby.

HOW TO APPLY All donations are made through Liverpool Council for Social Services. Grants are only made to charities known to the trustees, and unsolicited applications are not considered.

WHO TO APPLY TO J R McGibbon, Partner, Guy Williams Layton, 1 Union Court, Cook Street, Liverpool L2 4SJ *Tel* 0151 236 7171 *Fax* 0151 236 1129

CC NO 213795   **ESTABLISHED** 1960

■ The Chamberlain Foundation

WHERE FUNDING CAN BE GIVEN UK, with a preference for London and the south east and eastern regions.

WHO CAN BENEFIT Individuals and organisations benefiting people of all ages, who are infirm or disadvantaged by poverty.

WHAT IS FUNDED Relief of poor, older and infirm people, limited educational needs and other general charitable purposes for the benefit of the community, including respite care, sheltered accommodation, recreation grounds, care in the community, day centres, holidays and outings, hospice at home, hospices, and at risk groups.

RANGE OF GRANTS £50–£7,000.

SAMPLE GRANTS £50,000 to The Farmhouse in Bucquay; £5,000 to Birdham C of E School; £3,750 to Seven Rivers Cheshire Home; £3,000 to Winged Fellowship; £2,000 each to Befriending Network, Burns Camp Endowment Fund, Parkinson's Disease Society, Progressive Palsy Association, Ripple Down House Trust, and Tourette Syndrome Association.

FINANCES *Year* 1998–99 *Income* £130,000 *Grants* £140,000 *Assets* £3,149,876

TRUSTEES Mrs M J Spears; Mrs G M Chamberlain; G R Chamberlain; A G Chamberlain; Mrs S J Kent; Mrs C M Lester; Mrs L A Churcher.

OTHER INFORMATION Total amount of gifts and grants to individuals was £59,000 for the year 1998–99. Trustees visit individuals who are shown to have need of support.

HOW TO APPLY In writing to the correspondent. However, the trust states that it is proactive in choosing beneficiaries and the amount available for unsolicited applications is limited. Unsolicited applications are not acknowledged. The trustees meet at least twice a year.

WHO TO APPLY TO C Elmer, 3c Wilson Street, London N21 1BP *Tel* 020 8886 0965

CC NO 1033995   **ESTABLISHED** 1949

Think carefully about every application. Is it justified?

371

■ The Pamela Champion Foundation

WHERE FUNDING CAN BE GIVEN UK, with a preference for Kent.

WHO CAN BENEFIT Registered charities.

WHAT IS FUNDED General charitable purposes. Grants are made to all or any of the following: National Council for the Single Woman and Her Dependants; The Salvation Army; Church Army; Royal United Kingdom Beneficent Association; Wood Green Animal Shelter; Help the Aged; NSPCC; Marie Curie Memorial Foundation; and other charitable causes.

WHAT IS NOT FUNDED No grants to non-registered charities.

FINANCES Year 2001 *Income* £40,354

TRUSTEES M Stanlake; C Winser; J G Bower; J E Richardson.

HOW TO APPLY In writing to the correspondent.

WHO TO APPLY TO The Trustees, Wiltons, Newnham Lane, Eastling, Faversham, Kent ME13 0AS

CC NO 268819   **ESTABLISHED** 1974

■ The Chandris Foundation

WHERE FUNDING CAN BE GIVEN UK and Greece.

WHO CAN BENEFIT Established organisations benefiting at risk groups, and people who are disadvantaged by poverty or socially isolated.

WHAT IS FUNDED Medicine and health; welfare; religion (Greek orthodox charities).

WHAT IS NOT FUNDED No grants to individuals.

TYPE OF GRANT One-off and recurrent.

RANGE OF GRANTS £60–£5,000.

SAMPLE GRANTS 1998: £5,000 each to Action on Addiction, Hellenic College of London, and Cycladic AA Foundation; £1,000 to SMH Special Trustees Fundraising; £970 to Royal Marsden Hospital; £500 each to Frangiskatos Book, St Sophia School, Malcolm Sargent Cancer Fund for Children, Teenage Cancer Trust Appeal, and War on Cancer.

FINANCES Year 2002 *Income* £40,000 *Grants* £40,000

TRUSTEES Chandris Foundation Trustees Ltd.

HOW TO APPLY The trustees allocate grants mainly to their existing beneficiaries, and prefer to seek new beneficiaries through their own research.

WHO TO APPLY TO R H Hall, Director, Chandris Foundation Trustees Ltd, 17 Old Park Lane, London W1K 1QT *Tel* 020 7412 3922

CC NO 280559   **ESTABLISHED** 1980

■ The Chapman Charitable Trust

WHERE FUNDING CAN BE GIVEN Eastern and south east England, including London, and Wales.

WHO CAN BENEFIT Any recognised charity, but mainly those charities in which the late settlor had, or the trustees have, a personal interest or concern.

WHAT IS FUNDED General charitable purposes. Main areas supported are social services, culture and recreation, education and research, health, environment and heritage.

WHAT IS NOT FUNDED No grants to or for the benefit of individuals, local branches of UK charities, animal welfare, sports tours or sponsored adventure holidays.

RANGE OF GRANTS £500–£20,000.

SAMPLE GRANTS £20,000 in two grants to Aldeburgh Productions; £10,000 each, all in two grants, to Methodist Homes – MHA Care Group, NCH Action for Children, Pesticide Action Network UK, Queen Alexandra Hospital Home, and St Bridget's Cheshire Home; £5,000 each to A Rocha, Harington Scheme, Kings Cross Furniture Projects, and Leys and St Faith Foundation.

FINANCES Year 2001–2002 *Income* £194,854 *Grants* £185,000 *Assets* £5,192,609

TRUSTEES Roger S Chapman; Richard J Chapman; Bruce D Chapman; Guy J A Chapman.

HOW TO APPLY In writing at any time. The trustees currently meet to consider grants twice a year at the end of September and March. They receive a large number of applications and regret that they cannot acknowledge receipt of them. The absence of any communication for six months would mean that an application must have been unsuccessful.

WHO TO APPLY TO Roger S Chapman, Trustee, Messrs Crouch Chapman, 62 Wilson Street, London EC2A 2BU *Tel* 020 7782 0007 *Fax* 020 7782 0939 *E-mail* cct@crouchchapman.co.uk

CC NO 232791   **ESTABLISHED** 1963

■ The Charities Advisory Trust

WHERE FUNDING CAN BE GIVEN UK and overseas.

WHO CAN BENEFIT Any charitable purpose is considered, but generally the trust is proactive.

WHAT IS FUNDED General charitable purposes, particularly: income generation projects; homelessness; museums; cancer research and treatment; peace and reconciliation; and refugees.

WHAT IS NOT FUNDED 'We do not have an application form and we accept applications throughout the year. Nearly all our grants are made because we have prior knowledge of the project or area of concern. In most cases the idea for the project comes from us; we work with suitable organisations to achieve our objectives. We rarely respond to unsolicited applications for projects of which we know nothing. In such cases where support is given, the amounts are usually £200 or less. We do not consider grants to individuals in need. Neither do we give to individuals going on gap year trips to the developing world. We are unlikely to give to large fund-raising charities. We do not give for missionary work.'

TYPE OF GRANT Buildings, capital, core costs, endowments, interest-free loans; one-off, project, research, running costs, recurring costs, salaries and start-up costs. Funding is available for up to and over three years.

RANGE OF GRANTS £500–£61,494; typically £5,000 or less.

SAMPLE GRANTS £61,494 to Trees for London; £35,000 to New Israel Fund for nominated projects; £30,000 to Whittington Hospital for cancer research; £20,000 to Friends of Feltham Hardship Fund; £18,670 to Ducane Housing Association; £17,000 to ACCORD Tea Co-operative – India; £12,100 to Vridavan Gujerat; £11,537 to MS Research Trust; £9,012 to NCH Action for Children; £7,700 to Area Youth Foundation – Jamaica.

FINANCES Year 2000–01 *Income* £1,189,075 *Grants* £397,448 *Assets* £1,344,871

TRUSTEES Dr Cornelia Navari; Dr Carolyne Dennis; Prof. J Bob Holman; Ms Dawn Penso.

HOW TO APPLY 'To apply simply send us details of your proposal (no more than two pages in length) in the form of a letter. You might try to include the following information: the aims and objectives of your organisation; the project for which you need money; who benefits from the project and how; breakdown of the costs and total estimated costs; how much money you need from us; other funding secured for the project; a summary of your latest annual accounts.

'If we refuse you it is not because your project is not worthwile – it is because we do not have sufficient funds, or it is simply outside our current area of interest.

'Applications should be addressed to the Director. Good luck!'

WHO TO APPLY TO Hilary Blume, Director, Radius Works, Back Lane, London NW3 1HL *Tel* 020 7794 9835 *Fax* 020 7431 3739 *E-mail* charities.advisory.trust@ukonline.co.uk *Website* www.charitiesadvisorytrust.org.uk
CC NO 1040487   **ESTABLISHED** 1994

■ Charitworth Limited

WHERE FUNDING CAN BE GIVEN UK.
WHO CAN BENEFIT Individuals and organisations benefiting children and young adults.
WHAT IS FUNDED Religious, particularly Jewish causes, and educational charities.
SAMPLE GRANTS £317,000 to Cosmon (Belz) Limited, a charity which promotes the advancement of the Jewish Orthodox faith; £250,000 to Friends of Beis Yaacov; £190,000 to Yeshiva Ohel Shimon Trust; £120,000 to Friends of Horim; £70,000 to Zichron Nachum; £40,000 to Dushinsky Trust; £32,000 to Mercaz Chasidei Buhush; £30,000 to Beth Hayeled Trust; £28,000 to SOFT.
FINANCES *Year* 2000–01 *Income* £345,733 *Grants* £1,172,000 *Assets* £8,586,367
TRUSTEES D M Halpern; Mrs R Halpern; S Halpern; S J Halpern.
HOW TO APPLY In writing to the correspondent.
WHO TO APPLY TO D Halpern, Trustee, c/o Cohen Arnold, Regent Street, 13–17 New Burlington Place, London W1S 2HL *Tel* 020 7734 1362
CC NO 286908   **ESTABLISHED** 1983

■ Charity Association Manchester Ltd

WHERE FUNDING CAN BE GIVEN UK and Israel.
WHO CAN BENEFIT Charities benefiting Jewish people.
WHAT IS FUNDED Jewish charities.
SAMPLE GRANTS £63,000 to Ahavas Chesed Trust; £51,000 to Academy for Rabbinical Research; £28,000 to Tzedoko Charity; £23,000 to Sayser Charity; £15,000 to Friends of Malchus Shomayim.
FINANCES *Year* 1999–2000 *Income* £622,000 *Grants* £643,000
TRUSTEES Peter John Koppenheim and at least one other.
HOW TO APPLY In writing to the correspondent.
WHO TO APPLY TO J Freedman, 134 Leicester Road, Salford, Manchester M7 0HB *Tel* 0161 740 1960
CC NO 257576   **ESTABLISHED** 1969

■ The Charter 600 Charity

WHERE FUNDING CAN BE GIVEN UK.
WHO CAN BENEFIT Registered charities.
WHAT IS FUNDED General charitable purposes.
WHAT IS NOT FUNDED Applications for charitable grants will only be accepted when put forward by a member of the Mercers' Company.
SAMPLE GRANTS £3,000 to Pirate Club; £2,000 each to Bouveirie Hall Committee, City & East London

Bereavement, Rose Road Children's Appeal and Woodland Centre Trust; £1,700 to AMREF; £1,650 to Luton Samaritans; £1,500 to Lochalsh & Skye Housing Trust.
FINANCES *Year* 1999–2000 *Income* £180,538 *Grants* £27,150 *Assets* £584,737
TRUSTEES Not disclosed.
HOW TO APPLY In writing to the correspondent.
WHO TO APPLY TO The Trust Administrator, Mercers' Hall, Ironmongers Lane, London EC2V 8HE *Tel* 020 7726 4991
CC NO 1051146   **ESTABLISHED** 1995

■ The Chasah Trust

WHERE FUNDING CAN BE GIVEN Greater London and UK.
WHO CAN BENEFIT Evangelists and Christians.
WHAT IS FUNDED The encouragement of missionary activity as well as the advancement of the evangelical tenets of Christianity.
WHAT IS NOT FUNDED Buildings or general appeals are not funded.
TYPE OF GRANT Salaries for one year or less.
RANGE OF GRANTS £100–£15,000.
FINANCES *Year* 1999–2000 *Income* £23,000 *Grants* £23,000 *Assets* £4,200
TRUSTEES Karen Collier-Keywood; Richard Collier-Keywood; Glyn Williams.
HOW TO APPLY In writing to the correspondent.
WHO TO APPLY TO R D Collier-Keywood, Trustee, Glydwish Hall, Fontridge Lane, Burwash, East Sussex TN19 7DG
CC NO 294898   **ESTABLISHED** 1986

■ The Chase Charity

WHERE FUNDING CAN BE GIVEN UK, except Northern Ireland and London, with a special interest in rural areas.
WHO CAN BENEFIT Mostly small organisations, particularly those supporting people who are frail and elderly; people with special needs; carers groups; day centres; rural homeless projects only; isolated communities; rural touring groups; and young people at risk of getting into trouble.
WHAT IS FUNDED The trustees work over a wide field but projects in rural areas are of particular interest together with strengthening vulnerable groups. They try to make an impact with each grant so small charities are preferred. Start-up finance, unforeseen capital expenditure, salaries or even help over a bad patch are considered. The charity works in three areas: historic buildings, the arts and social welfare. Historic buildings: the trustees make grants to small rurally situated parish churches and almshouses of architectural merit and to other interesting rural buildings which serve the community. The arts: the trustees will help charities wishing to take the arts to rural areas, such as professional touring groups and also agencies using art forms for their therapeutic properties. Social welfare: the charity will consider projects helping poor, marginalised and vulnerable communities in urban or rural settings in eight categories – older people; families and children; homelessness; mental health; neighbourhood work; penal affairs; physical and learning disabilities; young people.
WHAT IS NOT FUNDED 'We do not contribute to large, widely circulated appeals, nor will we consider retrospective funding for work that has already taken place. More particularly, we do not make grants in support of adaptations to improve

access to buildings; the advancement of religion; animal welfare; conferences or seminars; endowment funds; festivals or theatre productions; hospices; individual needs; individual youth clubs; large capital projects; medical research; other grant making bodies; publications, film or video; schools for people with special needs; sport; travel, expedition or holidays; vehicles. We do not support formal education including institutes of further and higher education, NHS Hospital Trusts and those emanating from associated charities concerned with medical projects. If in doubt, it is probably advisable to contact the office for an informal discussion before spending time putting together a detailed application.'

TYPE OF GRANT Buildings, capital, core costs, one-off, project, research, salaries and start-up costs. Funding is available for up to three years.

RANGE OF GRANTS Social welfare £1,000–£10,000; art and heritage £1,000–£30,000.

SAMPLE GRANTS £45,000 to Geese Theatre Company at Albatross Arts Project – Birmingham for a series of three-day residences in Prisons; £25,000 to Kirckman Concert Society as an annual grant; £20,000 to Trestle Theatre Company Limited – St Albans for conversion of a chapel into a community arts resource centre; £15,500 to Pear Tree Community Group – Rugeley for running costs; £15,000 each to Performing Arts Labs – Kent for a playwrights lab, and Quondam Theatre Company – Penrith towards the cost of a part-time administrator; £11,000 to FWA – London to be distributed as small grants to individuals; £10,000 each to Borders 1996 Company Limited – Peebles, Scotland for capital costs of the Eastgate Arts Centre project, Julia Margaret Cameron Trust – Isle of Wight for roof repairs, and Child Deaf Youth Project – Middlesbrough for running costs.

FINANCES *Year* 2001–02 *Income* £483,000 *Grants* £390,000

TRUSTEES Dodie Carter; Gordon Halcrow, Chair; Mrs R A Moore; Paul Curno; Ninian Perry; Alexander Robertson; Ann Stannard.

PUBLICATIONS How to Apply for a Grant.

HOW TO APPLY 'Your initial letter (by post) should describe who you are; what you do; why you are seeking our help; how you will measure success; how much money you need to raise; how soon you need it ; who else you have asked to help; what support you have already attracted. You should attach brief information about the origins and current company/ charitable status of your organisation; a copy of your most recent annual report and full audited accounts; an itemised income and expenditure budget for your organisation; an itemised income and expenditure budget for the work to be funded; equal opportunities policy. We receive many more applications than we can help, over 1,500 per annum of which approximately 60 will receive support. This inevitably means that we have to disappoint good schemes which meet our criteria. All letters receive a written answer and we attempt to reply to all correspondence within one month. The trustees meet quarterly, in February, May, September and November. Applications may be submitted at any time but you should be aware that agendas are planned well ahead and you should expect a period of six months between an initial application and formal consideration by the trustees. In the period leading up to formal consideration by the trustees one of the staff will arrange to visit you to discuss your application in more detail. You will be notified of the trustees' decision as soon as possible and,

if a grant is agreed, of the conditions that have been attached to its release.'

WHO TO APPLY TO Ailsa Hollond, 2 The Court, High Street, Harwell, Didcot, Oxfordshire OX11 0EY *Tel* 01235 820044 *Website* www.chase-charity.org.uk

CC NO 207108   **ESTABLISHED** 1962

....

■ Chatwin Trust

WHERE FUNDING CAN BE GIVEN UK, with a preference for Coventry and West Midlands.

WHO CAN BENEFIT Registered charities.

WHAT IS FUNDED Older people, children, animals, general.

RANGE OF GRANTS £250–£3,000.

FINANCES *Year* 2000–01 *Income* £23,000 *Grants* £25,000 *Assets* £564,000

TRUSTEES Michael John Pratt, Chair; Dorothy Mary Redgrave; Elizabeth Jean Pratt; Michael John Harris.

HOW TO APPLY In writing to the correspondent, to be considered in May and December.

WHO TO APPLY TO Jean Pratt, Secretary, 9 Moorland Road, Egbaston, Birmingham B16 9JP *Tel* 0121 454 1071

CC NO 1015633   **ESTABLISHED** 1992

....

■ The Chelsea Building Society Charitable Foundation

WHERE FUNDING CAN BE GIVEN UK, with a preference for the south of England, especially Gloucestershire.

WHO CAN BENEFIT Registered charities.

WHAT IS FUNDED 'The primary focus of the Foundations's charitable giving is to help relieve suffering and disadvantage and to benefit local communities.' Its priorities include: (i) homelessness; (ii) housing; (iii) people who are disadvantaged; (iv) vulnerable groups, e.g. elderly people, people with learning difficulties, people who are mentally ill and people who are disabled; (v) health – self-help and voluntary groups; (vi) encouraging prudent money management, e.g. money advice services; (vii) the relief of social exclusion; (viii) security and community safety.

WHAT IS NOT FUNDED The trustees will not usually consider grants for the following: activities which are mainly/normally the statutory responsibilty of central or local government or some other responsible body (except proposals for added support services); hospitals, medical centres, medical treatment research (except projects extra to statutory responsibilities; collecting funds for later distribution to other charities or to individuals; political or pressure groups profit distributing organisations; individuals or individual fund-raising efforts, including expeditions or overseas travel; general fund-raising events, activities or appeals; fabric appeals for places of worship and the promotion of religion; animal welfare or wildlife.

TYPE OF GRANT One-off for core costs, capital or project support.

RANGE OF GRANTS £250–£5,000.

FINANCES *Year* 2000 *Grants* £50,000

TRUSTEES Richard Hombrook; David Porter; Dorothy Anderson; Geoff Divito; Darren Stevens.

HOW TO APPLY Application forms can be downloaded from the website or alternatively obtained on written request from the Secretary of the Foundation. Trustees meet twice a year. Applications must be received in April and

October for consideration in May and November. All applications will be acknowledged. Applicants will be notified of the result of their application as soon as possible but they should appreciate that it may take up to six months for their request to be considered.

WHO TO APPLY TO Gillian Greenwell, Secretary to the Foundation, Administrative Headquarters, Thirlestaine Hall, Thirlestaine Road, Cheltenham, Gloucestershire GL53 7AL *Tel* 01242 283649 *Fax* 01242 271222 *E-mail* charitablefoundation@thechelsea.co.uk *Website* www.thechelsea-charity-foundation.co.uk
CC NO 1079292   **ESTABLISHED** 2000

■ The Chelsea Square 1994 Trust

WHERE FUNDING CAN BE GIVEN Southern England, and to a limited extent, overseas.

WHO CAN BENEFIT Organisations benefiting elderly people, at risk groups, those disadvantaged by poverty and socially isolated people.

WHAT IS FUNDED Chiefly animals, older people and underprivileged people.

WHAT IS NOT FUNDED No grants to individuals.

TYPE OF GRANT One-off grants.

SAMPLE GRANTS £2,100 each to Crossroads, Children's Hospital Trust Chelsea and Westminster, Youth at Risk – London, PDSA and Radar.

FINANCES *Year* 2000 *Income* £65,000 *Grants* £65,000 *Assets* £1,400,000

TRUSTEES J B Talbot; P J Talbot; J T Woods; I Blackwood Burlington.

HOW TO APPLY In writing to the correspondent with report and accounts. Unsuccessful applicants will not receive a reply; send an sae if you wish documents to be returned.

WHO TO APPLY TO The Trustees, Moon Beaver Solicitors, 24–26 Bloomsbury Square, London WC1A 2PL *Tel* 020 7637 0661
CC NO 1040479   **ESTABLISHED** 1994

■ The Chelwood 2000 Settlement

WHERE FUNDING CAN BE GIVEN UK.

WHO CAN BENEFIT Organisations which encourage or demonstrate the application of technology in their work. Also mainstream Jewish charities, most of which have been known to the trustees for a considerable time.

SAMPLE GRANTS £240,000 to Reform Synagogues; £50,000 each to Jewish Care and Oxford Centre for Hebrew Studies; £20,000 to Royal Society of Arts; £15,000 each to British ORT and Cystic Fibrosis Trust; £10,000 to Cancer Treatment and Research Trust; £5,000 each to Brent Adolescent Centre and Tricycle; £2,500 each to Anna Freud Centre and the Royal Academy of Music.

FINANCES *Year* 2000–01 *Grants* £554,000 *Assets* £2,500,000

TRUSTEES Jonathan Bernard Silver; Caroline Lewis; Stephen Thomas Lloyd.

OTHER INFORMATION As all grants are made from the capital base of the trust, the trustees expect the size of the trust to decrease significantly within a short period.

HOW TO APPLY In writing to the correspondent. Please note the trust states that 'all the beneficiaries are known to the trustees... They do not seek unsolicited applications to grants'.

WHO TO APPLY TO The Secretary, 44A New Cavendish Street, London WIM 0LG *Tel* 020 7486 4663
CC NO 1082696   **ESTABLISHED** 2000

■ The Cheruby Trust

WHERE FUNDING CAN BE GIVEN UK and worldwide.

WHO CAN BENEFIT Registered charities.

WHAT IS FUNDED Welfare, education and general charitable purposes.

SAMPLE GRANTS £6,000 each to Crisis at Christmas and Save the Children; £5,000 each to Help the Aged and Shelter; £2,000 each to Amnesty International, Friends of the Earth, Gingerbread Association, National Association for Mental Health, Shelter, and Sight Savers International.

FINANCES *Year* 1999–2000 *Income* £58,000 *Grants* £43,000 *Assets* £88,000

TRUSTEES A L Corob; L E Corob; T A Corob; Mrs S P Berg.

HOW TO APPLY In writing to the correspondent.

WHO TO APPLY TO Mrs Sylvia Berg, Trustee, 62 Grosvenor Street, London W1K 3FJ *Tel* 020 7499 4301
CC NO 327069   **ESTABLISHED** 1986

■ The Cheshire Provincial Fund of Benevolence

WHERE FUNDING CAN BE GIVEN Cheshire.

WHO CAN BENEFIT Individuals and organisations benefiting masons and their families.

WHAT IS FUNDED The relief of masons and their dependants, masonic charities and other charities, especially medical.

FINANCES *Year* 1999–2000 *Income* £357,756 *Grants* £373,901 *Assets* £3,052,703

TRUSTEES C Acton; A Glazier; P E Carroll; D R Hinde.

OTHER INFORMATION In 1999–2000, payments of £150,871 were made to individuals, £140,000 was given to masonic charities, and £83,030 to non-masonic charities.

HOW TO APPLY In writing to the correspondent. Applications for non-masonic charities will be considered in July for approval in October.

WHO TO APPLY TO Peter Carroll, Provincial Grand Secretary, Ashcroft House, 36 Clay Lane, Timperley, Altrincham, Greater Manchester WA15 7AB *Tel* 0161 980 6090
CC NO 219177   **ESTABLISHED** 1963

■ Chest Heart and Stroke Scotland

WHERE FUNDING CAN BE GIVEN Scotland.

WHO CAN BENEFIT Funding is given to academics, research workers and medical professionals living and working in Scotland.

WHAT IS FUNDED Grants are given for medical research into all aspects of the aetiology, diagnosis, prevention, treatment and social impact of chest, heart and stroke illness.

WHAT IS NOT FUNDED Research involving animals is not funded.

TYPE OF GRANT Research fellowships, project grants, travel and equipment grants, career development awards, research secondments, and student electives. Funding may be given for up to two years.

RANGE OF GRANTS Research grants up to £60,000.

SAMPLE GRANTS £59,998 over two years for research at University of Glasgow on caring for informal carers of stroke patients; £58,546 over two years for research at Western General Hospital on reliability of CT scan interpretation; £56,817 over two years for research at Aberdeen Royal Infirmary on factors affecting decline of lung function; £50,038 over two years for research at Royal Infirmary Glasgow on

Think carefully about every application. Is it justified?

375

protocol of care for early stroke subjects trial; £41,327 over two years for research at Western Infirmary on T-cell regulatory cytokines in asthma; £33,538 over two years for research at Western Infirmary on pulse pressure as a predictor of coronary heart disease; £25,932 over two years for research at Royal Infirmary Edinburgh on subacute stent thrombosis.

FINANCES *Year* 1999–2000 *Income* £2,264,750 *Grants* £446,071 *Assets* £2,462,580

TRUSTEES Prof. Charles Forbes, Chair; Dr Gavin Boyd; Colin McLean; Sir John Crofton; Dr Martin Dennis; Kenneth Dick; Dr Peter Langhorne; Miss Valerie Lobban; Alasdair Macdonald; Dr Hazel McHaffie; Dr David Player; Prof. Lewis D Ritchie; Mrs Christina Seiler; Dr Roger G Smith; James Williamson; Prof. David Lidgate; Prof. A R Lorimer; John Moorhouse; Dr Douglas Stuart.

HOW TO APPLY For research grants contact Fiona Swann-Skimming at the address given.

WHO TO APPLY TO 65 North Castle Street, Edinburgh EH2 3LT *Tel* 0131 225 6963 *Fax* 0131 220 6313 *E-mail* admin@chss.org.uk *Website* chss.org.uk

SC NO SC018761   **ESTABLISHED** 1990

■ The Chester Diocesan Moral Aid Charity (St Bridget's Trust)

WHERE FUNDING CAN BE GIVEN Cheshire.

WHO CAN BENEFIT Women (and their children), particularly those in care, fostered and adopted, and victims of abuse.

WHAT IS FUNDED Societies supporting women in moral danger, and their children.

WHAT IS NOT FUNDED No grants to individuals.

TYPE OF GRANT Core costs.

RANGE OF GRANTS £1,100pa–£11,000pa; typical £1,800pa.

SAMPLE GRANTS £11,000 to Chester Diocesan Adoption Service; £8,500 to Committee for Social Responsibility; £1,600 each to Chester Women's Aid and Macclesfield Cradle Concern; £650 each to Save the Family and YWCA Winsford.

FINANCES *Year* 1999–2000 *Income* £25,000 *Grants* £23,000 *Assets* £379,000

TRUSTEES Canon C J Samuels; Revd R M Powley; R L Jones; Mrs Wendy Steadman; The Bishop of Chester; P Collins.

HOW TO APPLY In writing to the correspondent, after an initial telephone call. The trust has stated that all its income is fully committed.

WHO TO APPLY TO Peter Collins, Trustee, Walker Smith & Way, 26 Nicholas Street, Chester CH1 2PQ *Tel* 01244 357400

CC NO 213298   **ESTABLISHED** 1962

■ The Chetwode Foundation

WHERE FUNDING CAN BE GIVEN Nottinghamshire, Leicestershire and Derby.

WHO CAN BENEFIT Registered charities only.

WHAT IS FUNDED General charitable purposes.

RANGE OF GRANTS £50–£10,000.

SAMPLE GRANTS £100,000 to Uppingham School (over four years); £10,000 each to Nottingham Hospitals Concert 2000 and NSPCC; £2,000 to Sue Ryder Foundation; £1,400 to Newark and Nottinghamshire Agricultural Society; £1,000 each to Tythby & Cropwell Butler PCC, Nottingham Royal Society for the Blind and East Holton Charity; £500 each to Sense and CLASP.

FINANCES *Year* 1999–2000 *Income* £72,000 *Grants* £132,000 *Assets* £1,300,000

TRUSTEES J G Ellis; R N J S Price.

HOW TO APPLY In writing to the correspondent.

WHO TO APPLY TO J G Ellis, Samworth Brothers (Holdings) Ltd, Chetwode House, Leicester Road, Melton Mowbray, Leicestershire LE13 1GA *Tel* 01664 414500

CC NO 265950   **ESTABLISHED** 1973

■ The Chetwode Samworth Charitable Trust

WHERE FUNDING CAN BE GIVEN Derby, Leicestershire and Nottinghamshire.

WHO CAN BENEFIT Registered charities only.

WHAT IS FUNDED General charitable purposes.

WHAT IS NOT FUNDED No grants to individuals.

SAMPLE GRANTS £100,000 to Leicester Cathedral; £30,000 to Uppingham School; £11,000 each to Christian Aid and Oundre School; £10,000 to Jed Bentley Trust; £8,000 to Villa Maninga – Mozambique; £3,000 to Animal Health Trust.

FINANCES *Year* 1999–2000 *Income* £44,000 *Grants* £144,000 *Assets* £1,500,000

TRUSTEES Mrs C Frostwick; T J Barker.

HOW TO APPLY In writing to the correspondent. Unsolicited applications are not considered.

WHO TO APPLY TO Mrs C Frostwick, Trustee, Samworth Brothers Ltd, Chetwode House, 1 Samworth Way, Melton Mowbray, Leicestershire LE13 1GA *Tel* 01664 414500 *Fax* 01664 414501

CC NO 265647   **ESTABLISHED** 1973

■ The Malcolm Chick Charity

WHERE FUNDING CAN BE GIVEN England only.

WHO CAN BENEFIT Registered charities.

WHAT IS FUNDED General charitable purposes, but effectively small grants to organisations the trustees are familiar with in the following areas: Youth character building – There is an emphasis on grants towards sailing training; Armed service charities – Grants are limited to those charities supporting ex-army personnel and to charities providing direct care for ex-army personnel, for example grants to homes and charities providing welfare services for such persons; Medical research and care – Grants are made towards research into causes and treatment of heart disease and for buying equipment suitable for the treatment and care of people recovering from coronary heart disease.

SAMPLE GRANTS In 1999–2000: £4,000 each to The Cord Blood Charity and the Children's Heart Foundation; £3,700 to Fairbridge – Freespirit bursary scheme; £1,000 to Barrow and District Council for Voluntary Service Voyager.

FINANCES *Year* 2000–01 *Grants* £31,000

HOW TO APPLY In the first place, applicants should write to ask for a copy of the criteria and application forms. Applicants are then required to complete the form and provide a detailed report on the project, not more than two pages long. Telephone calls are not welcomed. The trustees meet to consider applications twice a year, in March and September. There is a separate application form and guidance notes for individual applicants.

WHO TO APPLY TO Mrs P H Miles, Trust Administrator, White Horse Court, 25c North Street, Bishops Stortford, Hertfordshire CM23 2LD *Tel* 01279 506421 *E-mail* charities@pothecary.co.uk

CC NO 327732   **ESTABLISHED** 1988

■ Child Growth Foundation

WHERE FUNDING CAN BE GIVEN UK

WHO CAN BENEFIT Institutions researching child/adult growth disorders, and people with such diseases.

WHAT IS FUNDED The foundation seeks to: ensure that the growth of every UK child is regularly assessed and that any child growing excessively slowly or fast is referred for medical attention as soon as possible; ensure that no child will be denied the drugs they need to correct their stature; support institutions researching the cause/cures of growth conditions; and maintain a network of families to offer support/advice for any family concerned/diagnosed with a growth problem.

TYPE OF GRANT Research.

SAMPLE GRANTS £44,730 to Imperial College; £34,405 to University of Wales; £21,796 to University of Wales; £20,618 to Institute of Child Health; £18,934 to Edinburgh Hospital for Sick Children; £17,777 to Endocrine Research Nurse – Imperial College; £17,025 to Institute of Child Health; £16,000 to Middlesex Hospital; £8,000 to British Society for Paediatric Endocrinology & Diabetes; £6,000 to Sheffield Children's Hospital.

FINANCES *Year* 1998–99 *Income* £532,617 *Grants* £177,449 *Assets* £125,442

TRUSTEES Tam Fry, Chair; plus one representative from each condition group the foundation supports, e.g. Growth Hormone Deficiency, Premature Sexual Maturation, Turner Syndrome, Sotos Syndrome and Bone Dysplasias.

PUBLICATIONS Patient information booklets and newsletters.

HOW TO APPLY In writing to the correspondent.

WHO TO APPLY TO T Fry, Hon. Chair, 2 Mayfield Avenue, Chiswick W4 1PY *Tel* 020 8995 0257 *Fax* 020 8995 9075 *E-mail* cfglondon@aol.com *Website* www.cgf.org.uk

CC NO 274325   **ESTABLISHED** 1977

■ Children's Liver Disease Foundation

WHERE FUNDING CAN BE GIVEN UK.

WHO CAN BENEFIT Organisations benefiting children (0–18 years) with liver disease; medical professionals; research workers and scientists.

WHAT IS FUNDED Medical research into all aspects of paediatric liver disease and disease of the biliary tract.

WHAT IS NOT FUNDED No grants to individuals, whether medical professionals or patients. No grants for travel or personal education.

TYPE OF GRANT Research and project. Occasionally medical equipment.

SAMPLE GRANTS In 2000–01: £114,171 to University of Southampton; £110,550 to University Birmingham; £109,447 to King's College Hospital, London; £75,067 to University of Newcastle; £28,680 to Birmingham Children's Hospital.

FINANCES *Year* 1998–99 *Income* £604,549 *Grants* £166,917 *Assets* £582,011

TRUSTEES Robert J Benton; Thomas Ross, Chair; David J L Butler; Dr H Richard Maltby; Mrs Ann Mowat; Mrs Michele Hunter; Andrew Sparrow.

PUBLICATIONS *Delivery*magazine published twice yearly.

OTHER INFORMATION The foundation is a member of the Association of Medical Research Charities (AMRC), and adheres to their guidelines.

HOW TO APPLY Applicants are advised to telephone prior to making an application. Research grants

can be applied for via an application form. All grant requests are subject to peer review and are assessed by the Medical Advisory Committee before submission to the trustees.

WHO TO APPLY TO Mrs C Arkley, Chief Executive, 36 Great Charles Street, Queensway, Birmingham B3 3JY *Tel* 0121 212 3839 *Fax* 0121 212 4300 *E-mail* info@childliverdisease.org *Website* www.childliverdisease.org

CC NO 1067331   **ESTABLISHED** 1998

■ The Children's Research Fund

WHERE FUNDING CAN BE GIVEN UK.

WHO CAN BENEFIT Institutes of child health and university child health departments benefiting sick children. Academics, medical professionals, research workers and students may benefit.

WHAT IS FUNDED Promoting, encouraging and fostering research into all aspects of diseases in children, child health and prevention of illness in children. Support of research centres and research units by grants to academic institutions, hospitals and other bodies with similar aims and objects to the fund. Support after the first year is dependent on receipt of a satisfactory report.

WHAT IS NOT FUNDED No grants for capital projects.

TYPE OF GRANT Research.

SAMPLE GRANTS £45,000 to University of Liverpool Department of Paediatrics; £31,500 to Great Ormond Street Hospital; £25,000 each to Great Ormond Street Hospital Institute of Child Health and University of Southampton for a therapist course; £23,000 to University of Glasgow Department of Paediatrics; £17,500 to University of Exeter; £15,400 to University of Wales College of Medicine; £15,000 to Alder Hey Hospital; £3,000 to University of Glasgow; £650 to University of Hull.

FINANCES *Year* 1998–99 *Income* £198,000 *Grants* £216,000 *Assets* £1,300,000

TRUSTEES H Greenwood, Chair; G W Inkin; Dr G J Piller; H E Greenwood; Prof. J Lister; Lord Morris; Elizabeth Theobald.

HOW TO APPLY Applicants from child health research units and university departments are invited to send in an initial outline of their proposal; if it is eligible they will then be sent an application form. Applications are considered in March and November.

WHO TO APPLY TO H Greenwood, Chair, 668 India Buildings, Water Street, Liverpool L2 0RA *Tel* 0151 236 2844 *Fax* 0151 258 1606 *Website* www.crfund.org

CC NO 226128   **ESTABLISHED** 1962

■ The Childs Charitable Trust

WHERE FUNDING CAN BE GIVEN Worldwide.

WHO CAN BENEFIT Churches or Christian organisations.

WHAT IS FUNDED Christian activity at home and overseas, especially the furtherance of the Christian Gospel.

RANGE OF GRANTS Up to £54,000.

SAMPLE GRANTS £54,000 to Home Evangelism; £32,000 to Mission Aviation Fellowship; £19,900 to Latin Link; £13,000 each to Echoes of Service, and Mustard Seed Trust; £12,168 to Russian Ministries; £12,000 to Counties Evangelistic Work; £11,000 to Words of Life Ministry; £10,800 to Scripture Gift Mission; £10,000 to Medical Missionary News.

FINANCES *Year* 2000–01 *Income* £366,566 *Grants* £286,798 *Assets* £7,671,719

TRUSTEES D N Martin; R H Williams; A B Griffiths.

HOW TO APPLY In writing to the correspondent. The trust stated that its funds are fully committed and further applications are not welcomed.

WHO TO APPLY TO D Martin, Trustee, 2–4 Saffrons Road, Eastbourne, East Sussex BN21 1DQ *Tel* 01323 417944
E-mail childs@charitabletrust.fsnet.co.uk
CC NO 234618   **ESTABLISHED** 1962

■ The Childwick Trust

WHERE FUNDING CAN BE GIVEN UK; South Africa.

WHO CAN BENEFIT Registered charities only.

WHAT IS FUNDED Promotion of the health and relief of people with disabilities in the UK; Pre-school education and training in South Africa; charities connected with thoroughbred racing and breeding; Jewish charities.

WHAT IS NOT FUNDED The trust will not fund statutory bodies; replace statutory funding; support students' individual education costs; participate in co-funding projects or match funding.

TYPE OF GRANT Mainly one-off, project and capital for research and medical equipment.

RANGE OF GRANTS £100–£112,000; typical £2,000–£10,000.

SAMPLE GRANTS In 2000–01: £150,000 to Racing Welfare Charities; £130,000 to Northwick Park Institute for Medical Research; £100,000 to Guy's, King's and St Thomas' School of Medicine; £92,780 to Khululeka Community Education Development Centre; £83,502 to West Rand Educare Project; £81,182 to African Self Help Association; £80,000 to Great Ormond Street Hospital; £75,000 to St Raphael's Hospice; £55,000 to Marie Curie Centre, Ardenlea; £50,000 to Paul Strickland Scanner Centre.

FINANCES *Year* 2001–02 *Income* £2,956,115 *Grants* £2,366,000

TRUSTEES C A S Grimston; A R G Cane; J D Wood, Chair; P G Glossop; Mrs S Frost.

OTHER INFORMATION Preference is given to medical equipment and equipment for research.

HOW TO APPLY The trust does not issue application forms but provides the following information for applicants. Applications should be made in writing on the registered charity's official headed notepaper. Ideally, the appeal letter should be not longer than two pages of A4. Detailed costings or a budget for the project or projects referred to in the appeal letter should form a separate appendix or appendices to the appeal letter and should provide the fullest possible financial detail. The latest annual report of the applicant charity, together with the latest available full audited accounts, including a full balance sheet, should also accompany the written application. During the course of the written application letter, applicants should endeavour to introduce the work of the applicant charity, state when the charity was established, describe its aims and objectives, and define precisely what the applicant charity does and who benefits from its activities; comment upon the applicant charity's track record since its inception and refer to its notable achievements and successes to date; endeavour to provide an interesting synopsis of the organisation; describe the project for which a grant is being sought fully, clearly and concisely and comment on the charity's plans for the future; provide full costings or a budget for the project/projects to include a detailed breakdown of the costs involved; give details of all other applications which the applicant charity has made to other

sources of funding, and indicate precisely what funds have already been raised from other sources for the project. Applications for grants for South African beneficiaries should be sent to The Fund Manager, The Jim Joel Education and Training Fund, PO Box 2862, Saxonwold, 2132, South Africa.

WHO TO APPLY TO Karen Groom, Trust Secretary, 9 The Green, Childwick Bury, St Albans, Hertfordshire AL3 6JJ *Tel* 01727 812486 *Fax* 01727 844666
CC NO 326853   **ESTABLISHED** 1985

■ The Chippenham Borough Lands Charity

WHERE FUNDING CAN BE GIVEN Chippenham Parish.

WHO CAN BENEFIT Residents of the parish. Organisations benefiting children, young adults, older people, people disadvantaged by poverty, disabled people, at risk groups, carers, homeless people, socially isolated people, and victims of abuse, crime or domestic violence. Individuals must have lived in the parish for the two years prior to application.

WHAT IS FUNDED Relief of people as stated above, especially people who are older, sick, poor or disabled; provision of facilities for recreation and other leisure time occupation; and advancement of education.

WHAT IS NOT FUNDED Anyone outside Chippenham. No support for religious organisations, individual sports people, or retrospective applications.

TYPE OF GRANT One-off; capital (including buildings); core costs; feasibility study; project; running costs; start-up costs.

SAMPLE GRANTS £27,000 to Schools Millennium Project; £12,000 to Wiltshire NHS Trust; £8,800 to Relate's Relation Service; £6,800 to SPLITZ; £6,200 to St Mary's Primary School; £5,000 each to Kings Lodge School, Queens Crescent School and Central Methodist Church; £4,500 to Hardenhush School; £4,000 to Wiltshire Youth Theatre.

FINANCES *Year* 1999–2000 *Income* £338,000 *Grants* £255,000 *Assets* £12,000,000

TRUSTEES Mrs J M Wood; Mr Dobson; Mrs Woodman; Mr McGregor; Mrs Lloyd; Mr Jenrick; Mrs D Allen; D Ellis.

HOW TO APPLY On a form available from the correspondent, either via an agency or self referral.

WHO TO APPLY TO M Roynon, Administrator, 32 Market Place, Chippenham, Wiltshire SN15 3HP *Tel* 01249 658180 *Fax* 01249 446048
E-mail cblc@lineone.net
CC NO 270062   **ESTABLISHED** 1990

■ The Chipping Sodbury Town Lands Charity

WHERE FUNDING CAN BE GIVEN The parishes of Chipping Sodbury and Old Sodbury.

WHO CAN BENEFIT Both individuals and organisations benefiting one-parent families, widows and widowers, people who are disabled or disadvantaged by poverty, and disaster victims. Support may also go to students, actors and entertainment professionals and musicians.

WHAT IS FUNDED Relief in need and educational purposes. A variety of other fields will be considered, including dance and ballet; music and the theatre; arts education; church buildings and historic buildings; and health education.

TYPE OF GRANT Buildings, capital, one-off and recurring costs will be considered.

SAMPLE GRANTS £10,000 to the local rugby club; £8,000 to St John's Mead Primary School; £7,500 to Chipping Sodbury Endowed School; £6,000 to St John the Baptist Church; £1,000 to Yate Community Transport.

FINANCES *Year* 2000 *Income* £228,000 *Grants* £54,500 *Assets* £8,900,000

HOW TO APPLY In writing to the correspondent. The trustees meet on the third week of each month except August.

WHO TO APPLY TO Mrs Nicola Gideon, Clerk, Town Hall, 57–59 Broad Street, Chipping Sodbury, South Gloucestershire BS37 6AD *Tel* 01454 852223 *E-mail* cstlc.townhall.virgin.net

CC NO 236364   **ESTABLISHED** 1977

■ CHK Charities Limited

WHERE FUNDING CAN BE GIVEN UK, with a special interest in Gloucestershire, especially close to Chipping Norton, and Oxfordshire.

WHO CAN BENEFIT Registered charities benefiting people of all ages, particularly homeless people, disabled people, those suffering from hearing loss or sight loss, those using or exposed to drugs, and ex-offenders and those at risk of offending.

WHAT IS FUNDED There are no restrictions upon the type of project funded, although education, job creation, conservation, arts, population control, crime prevention and youth development are areas of particular interest.

WHAT IS NOT FUNDED No grants to individuals nor to small local charities, such as individual churches or village halls, where there is no special connection to the trust. Appeals from local branches or offshoots of national charitable bodies are normally not considered.

TYPE OF GRANT Start-up capital costs and ongoing expenses (three to five years).

RANGE OF GRANTS Mostly £2,000–£5,000.

SAMPLE GRANTS £150,000 to Life Education Centres UK; £100,000 to Royal Agricultural Benevolent Institution; £67,000 each to Goldsmiths College and Royal National Institute for Deaf People; £63,000 to Charities Aid Foundation; £55,000 to Prince's Trust; £50,000 to Cotswold Enrichment Fund; £30,000 to Prince's Trust; £25,000 each to Chipping Norton Theatre and Spinal Research.

FINANCES *Year* 2001–02 *Income* £2,157,208 *Grants* £1,572,000 *Assets* £59,940,688

TRUSTEES David Peake, Chair; D A Acland; Mrs S E Acland; Mrs K S Assheton; Mrs C S Heber Percy; Mrs L H Morris; Mrs S Peake; Mrs J A S Prest.

HOW TO APPLY To the correspondent. CHK charities say: 'Appeals will usually be considered within three months, but may be referred for further consideration at board meetings which are held twice a year, normally in March and October.'

WHO TO APPLY TO N R Kerr-Sheppard, The Secretary, PO Box 191, 10 Fenchurch Street, London EC3M 3LB *Tel* 020 7475 6246

CC NO 1050900   **ESTABLISHED** 1995

■ The Chownes Foundation

WHERE FUNDING CAN BE GIVEN UK.

WHO CAN BENEFIT Small local projects; UK and established organisations; individuals requiring finance for education or the relief of poverty. This includes: children; young adults; retired people; students; parents and children; Roman Catholics; people disadvantaged by poverty; and people with asthma, mental illness, and spina bifida and hydrocephalus.

WHAT IS FUNDED Medicine and health; welfare; education; and religion. These include: Christian education; catholic bodies; training for personal development; bursaries, fees and scholarships; international rights of the individual; penal reform; and health counselling.

WHAT IS NOT FUNDED Applicant organisations must fit into the above criteria.

TYPE OF GRANT One-off, recurrent, buildings, capital, core costs, research and running costs. Funding is available for up to and over three years.

FINANCES *Year* 1998–99 *Income* £115,000 *Grants* £98,000 *Assets* £34,000

TRUSTEES Charles Stonor; the Abbot of Worth; Mrs U Hazeel.

HOW TO APPLY In writing to the correspondent.

WHO TO APPLY TO Sylvia Spencer, Secretary, The Courtyard, Beeding Court, Steyning, West Sussex BN44 3TN *Tel* 01903 816699 *E-mail* sjs.russellnew@btconnect.com

CC NO 327451   **ESTABLISHED** 1987

■ The Chrimes Family Charitable Trust

WHERE FUNDING CAN BE GIVEN Merseyside, Wirral, Conwy and Gywnedd.

WHO CAN BENEFIT Charities benefiting volunteers, carers, disabled people, and people with Alzheimer's disease, arthritis and rheumatism, asthma, autism, cancer, hearing and sight loss, or a terminal illness.

WHAT IS FUNDED Infrastructure development; hospice at home; and respite and care for carers. The trustees give preference to support of community welfare on Merseyside and in North Wales.

WHAT IS NOT FUNDED No grants to individuals, arts, conservation or education and training.

RANGE OF GRANTS £50–£500.

FINANCES *Year* 2000 *Income* £26,878 *Grants* £20,820 *Assets* £743,426

TRUSTEES Mrs Anne Williams; Mrs Helen Prosser.

HOW TO APPLY In writing (letter or fax) to the correspondent. There are no deadlines. No phone calls.

WHO TO APPLY TO Mrs Anne Williams, Trustee, Northfield, Upper Raby Road, Neston CH64 7TZ

CC NO 210199   **ESTABLISHED** 1955

■ The Christabella Charitable Trust

WHERE FUNDING CAN BE GIVEN Essex and the surrounding areas.

WHO CAN BENEFIT Registered charities, local organisations and individuals.

WHAT IS FUNDED Local projects and causes, in Essex and East London, especially those with Christian associations.

WHAT IS NOT FUNDED No support for UK-wide or international charities or for annual operating costs.

TYPE OF GRANT One-off and capital.

SAMPLE GRANTS £45,000 to London School of Economics; £37,560 to Barking & Dagenham Befrienders; £35,320 to Viz-a-Viz; £20,665 to LDF Charitable Trust; £19,325 to St Francis Church West Horndon; £18,625 to Young People's Counselling Service; £15,000 to Parents of Autistic Children; £12,762 to

Think carefully about every application. Is it justified?

379

Bridget's Trust; £9,185 to Arab Vision Trust Fund; £8,595 to RADA.
FINANCES *Year* 1998–99 *Income* £399,563 *Grants* £451,801 *Assets* £3,838,076
TRUSTEES E B Munroe, Chair; R F Folwell.
HOW TO APPLY In writing to the correspondent, from whom an application form is available. However, very few applications are considered each year.
WHO TO APPLY TO R F Folwell, Trustee, 97–99 High Street, Rayleigh, Essex SS6 7EJ *Tel* 01268 776200 *Fax* 01268 776400 *E-mail* bob.folwell@which.net
CC NO 800610   **ESTABLISHED** 1988

....
■ **Christadelphian Samaritan Fund**
WHERE FUNDING CAN BE GIVEN UK and overseas.
WHO CAN BENEFIT Registered charities and organisations in the third world.
WHAT IS FUNDED Preference is given to human causes and aid to third world.
WHAT IS NOT FUNDED No support to individuals or non-registered charities.
TYPE OF GRANT Single donations.
SAMPLE GRANTS In 1999: £6,000 to Red Cross for the Turkish earthquake appeal; £4,000 to UNICEF for Ethiopia; £1,900 to Red Cross for Columbia; £1,600 to DEC for Kosovo.
FINANCES *Year* 2001 *Grants* £90,515
TRUSTEES K H A Smith; N V Moss.
HOW TO APPLY In writing to the correspondent.
WHO TO APPLY TO K H A Smith, Treasurer, 1 Sherbourne Road, Acocks Green, Birmingham B27 6AB *Tel* 0121 706 6100 *Fax* 0121 706 7193
CC NO 1004457   **ESTABLISHED** 1991

....
■ **The Christendom Trust**
WHERE FUNDING CAN BE GIVEN UK and overseas.
WHAT IS FUNDED Promotion of research and application of research in the area of Christian social thought.
WHAT IS NOT FUNDED Grants are not normally made to individuals pursuing research for university degrees; nor are grants given to maintain already existing projects. No grants for building work, vehicles or equipment.
TYPE OF GRANT Feasibility studies, one-off, project, research, salaries and start-up costs. Funding is considered for up to three years.
RANGE OF GRANTS £500–£20,000.
SAMPLE GRANTS The main beneficiaries during the year were Irish School of Ecumenics – Moving Beyond Sectarianism Project, Changing Attitude – Response to Issues in Human Sexuality Report, Kairos Europa – 'Development Needs a New Financial Order', Bishop Simeon Trust – 'Christian Critique of Global HIV/AIDS Pandemic', Ushaw College – Conference on Alternatives to Global Capitalism. A grant was also awarded for human rights research.
FINANCES *Year* 2001–02 *Income* £15,205 *Grants* £24,200 *Assets* £435,047
TRUSTEES Mrs Angela Cunningham; William Fuge; Revd Ermal Kirby; Dr David Ormrod; Revd Alyson Peberdy; Dr R C Towler; Dr Stephen Yeo; Mrs Angela West.
HOW TO APPLY Applications for guidelines should be sent to the correspondent. The trust meets three times a year to consider applications, which should be sent by the end of January, May and September.

WHO TO APPLY TO Gill & Mike O'Connell, Hon. Secretaries, Sawrey Ground, Hawkshead Hill, Ambleside, Cumbria LA22 0PP *Tel* 01539 436683
CC NO 262394   **ESTABLISHED** 1971

....
■ **Christian Aid**
WHERE FUNDING CAN BE GIVEN Mainly third world. Limited assistance for development education projects in the UK.
WHO CAN BENEFIT Councils of Churches; other ecumenical bodies, development and relief groups; UN agencies which benefit at risk groups; people disadvantaged by poverty; homeless people; refugees; immigrants; socially isolated people; victims of famine, man-made or natural disasters, and war.
WHAT IS FUNDED Organisations which work with the world's poorest people and communities. Funding is given to partner organisations only.
WHAT IS NOT FUNDED No grants are made to individuals. No grants are made towards political causes or to organisations whose aims are primarily political.
TYPE OF GRANT Project.
SAMPLE GRANTS During the year £28.9 million was spent on development and £9.4 million on emergencies, broken down as follows: Africa – 242 partner organisations: £13.9 million; Latin America and the Caribbean – 150 partner organisations: £8.3 million; Asia – 132 partner organisations: £7 million; Eastern Europe and Middle East – 40 partner organisations: £6.5 million; Rest of the world – 41 partner organisations: £2.6 million. The organisation also spent £6.5 million on campaigning and education in the UK and Ireland, and included grants to 90 partner organisations.
FINANCES *Year* 2001–02 *Income* £50,000,000 *Grants* £40,000,000 *Assets* £24,700,000
TRUSTEES Revd Inderjit Bhogal; Revd Tony Burnham; Revd Jim Campbell; Revd Dr Susan Cole King; Revd David Copley; Revd Noel Davies; Ms Val Ferguson; Rt Revd John Gladwin; Dr David Goodbourn; Rt Revd Richard Harries; Michael Hockney; Adam Holloway; Revd Pauline Huggan; Ms Helen Hood; Revd Denzil John; Revd Trefor Lewis; Ms Margaret Macintosh; Rt Revd Michael Mayes; Rt Hon. John Montagu; Earl of Sandwich; David Pocock; Revd Roger Purce; Dr Elizabeth Rhodes; Revd Lindsey Sanderson; Revd Bill Snelson; Michael Soole; Revd Norman Taggart; Revd Anne Wilkinson Hayes.
HOW TO APPLY Initial approaches by potential partner organisations should be made in writing.
WHO TO APPLY TO Roger Ridell, 35–41 Lower Marsh, London SE1 7RL *Tel* 020 7620 4444 *Website* www.christianaid.org.uk
CC NO 258003   **ESTABLISHED** 1945

....
■ **John Christie Trust**
WHERE FUNDING CAN BE GIVEN Scotland.
WHO CAN BENEFIT Religion, missions, welfare of orphans.
WHAT IS FUNDED The same organisations, as listed in the trust deed, are supported each year and receive an income in fixed, but not equal, proportions. Most are concerned with religion, missionary work or the welfare of orphans.
FINANCES *Year* 2001 *Grants* £84,000.
TRUSTEES J D Lennie; D W McLetchie; Ina Rankin; Katherine M B Severn; M J R Simpson; Margaret K Watt; R York.

HOW TO APPLY Due to the nature of this trust unsolicited applications cannot be considered.

WHO TO APPLY TO The Trustees, c/o Tods Murray, 66 Queen Street, Edinburgh EH2 4NE

SC NO SC005291

■ The Church Burgesses Educational Foundation

WHERE FUNDING CAN BE GIVEN Sheffield.

WHO CAN BENEFIT Individuals and schools benefiting children and young adults.

WHAT IS FUNDED Church schools, independent schools, junior schools, language schools, primary and secondary schools, special schools, tertiary and higher education, and youth organisations. Also funded are bursaries, fees, scholarships, and the purchase of books.

TYPE OF GRANT Core costs, one-off and running costs. Funding may be given for up to three years.

SAMPLE GRANTS In 1999: £27,000 to YMCA; £10,000 to Cherrytree; £9,000 to Phoenix House; £8,000 to Youth Associations South Yorkshire; £7,000 each to South Yorkshire Clubs for Young People, the local scouts group and St Leonard's; £6,700 to St John the Baptist – Owlerton; £6,000 to YWCA; £5,500 to Sea Cadets.

FINANCES *Year* 2001 *Income* £274,219 *Grants* £289,764

TRUSTEES Prof. G D Sims; Mrs M Barker; M Robertson; District Judge J F W Peters; Revd Canon Prof. J Atkinson; Revd Canon Dr G Tolley; S A P Hunter; Prof. A G Johnson.

HOW TO APPLY In writing to the correspondent. Trustees meet four times a year in January, April/May, July/August and October. Applications should be sent in December, March, June and September.

WHO TO APPLY TO G J Smallman, Law Clerk, c/o Wrigleys, 4th Floor, Fountain Precinct, Leopold Street, Sheffield S1 2GZ *Tel* 0114 267 5596

CC NO 529357   ESTABLISHED 1963

■ The Church Houses Relief in Need Charity

WHERE FUNDING CAN BE GIVEN City of Oxford.

WHO CAN BENEFIT Health and welfare charities.

WHAT IS NOT FUNDED Individuals are very rarely supported.

SAMPLE GRANTS £5,000 each to Marie Curie Cancer Care and Oxford Mencap; £3,000 to Oxford Victim Support; £2,000 each to Salvation Army, Stroke Association, Citizens Advice Bureau, and St John's Home. All organisations supported were local branches.

FINANCES *Year* 2000 *Income* £105,000 *Grants* £101,000

TRUSTEES Dr E Anderson; C Burton; D Christie; J Cole; R Earl; R Hawes; M Lear; Mrs J McLean; Sir Peter North; Revd Dr S Pix; P Scaden.

HOW TO APPLY In writing to the correspondent.

WHO TO APPLY TO P W Beavis, St Michael at the North Gate, Cornmarket Street, Oxford OX1 3EY *Tel* 01865 240940

CC NO 202750   ESTABLISHED 1980

■ The Church Urban Fund

WHERE FUNDING CAN BE GIVEN Urban priority areas in England.

WHO CAN BENEFIT Community-based projects that tackle issues of disadvantage, poverty and marginalisation in the poorest areas of England's inner cities and outer estates. Projects which work ecumenically and work in partnership with other agencies and faiths in the community.

WHAT IS FUNDED Particularly projects that tackle major problems in their area, such as poverty, unemployment and job scarcity, lack of local social amenities, loneliness and isolation, or housing and homelessness; equip communities to address local needs and issues, and encourage people to make decisions and take control of their lives; empower the faith community to take an active role in wider community development, particularly through interfaith and ecumenical projects; and are innovative, will make a practical impact, and can develop partnerships with other local agencies.

WHAT IS NOT FUNDED The fund does not award local project grants for projects outside England; individuals; clergy stipends; work previously funded by a statutory agency that has ceased because of cutbacks, or activities that should be funded by such sources; projects based in schools which benefit only that school, or which address basic education needs or other services that should be the responsibility of the local education authority or the school itself; voluntary-aided schools eligible for statutory funding; direct support to other grantmaking bodies; general appeals. The fund never makes retrospective grants, nor can it help to pay off deficits or loans.

TYPE OF GRANT Revenue and capital funding. Buildings; core costs; feasibility studies; one-off; project; recurring costs; and start-up costs.

RANGE OF GRANTS Usually £100–£30,000.

SAMPLE GRANTS £100,000 to Community and Race Relations Unit; £47,975 to Coalfield Regeneration Trust; £45,000 each to Faith Works Yorkshire, Greater Manchester Partnership Development Project, Lancashire Community Resettlement project and Lichfield Diocesan Deprivation Team; £30,000 to East London Christian Centre; £25,000 each to Centre Manager – St James Rawthorpe, Horden Churches Together Group and St Peter's Centre.

FINANCES *Year* 2001 *Income* £2,125,000 *Grants* £2,638,000 *Assets* £20,751,000

TRUSTEES The Archbishop of Canterbury, Chair; Peter Doyle, Vice-chair; Mark Cornwall-Jones; Richard Farnell; Ven. Granville Gibson; Chair of Grants Committee; Canon John Stanley; Patrick Coldstream; Dorothy Stewart; Rt Revd John Austin; Rt Revd Pete Broadbent.

HOW TO APPLY Check with the fund whether a project falls into one of the supported areas, and request a formal application form. All applications for grants are first of all sent to the diocesan bishop, who will help put forward applications. They must be approved by the bishop before being sent to the trustees. The bishop is also requested to indicate the priority of projects in relation to the long-term plan for the diocese. Projects which survive this procedure will go to the trustees of the fund who may sanction assistance. Field officers also visit every applicant to help with applications. The grants committee meets in March, June, September and December; applications have to be sent over two months in advance. Contact the fund for details of exact dates and of the relevant diocese contacts. Please remember that the diocese will set its own deadlines in advance of these dates.

WHO TO APPLY TO Fran Beckett, Chief Executive, 1 Millbank, London SW1P 3JZ *Tel* 020 7898 1000 *Website* www.cuf.org.uk

CC NO 297483   **ESTABLISHED** 1988

■ The Cinderford Charitable Trust

WHERE FUNDING CAN BE GIVEN UK.

WHO CAN BENEFIT Registered charities.

WHAT IS FUNDED General charitable purposes, usually in the fields of health, the arts and the environment. The trust usually supports well known and established charitable organisations of personal interest and concern to the trustees.

SAMPLE GRANTS £12,000 each to Barnardos, Musicians' Benevolent Fund, NSPCC, St Wilfred's Hospice, Salvation Army, Save the Children Fund and World Wildlife Fund; £7,500 each to British Stroke Association, King Edward VII Hospital and National Youth Orchestra of Great Britain.

FINANCES *Year* 2000–01 *Income* £281,624 *Grants* £278,480 *Assets* £8,193,805

TRUSTEES Roger J Clark; Rory McLeod.

HOW TO APPLY In writing to the correspondent. The bulk of the income is given to charities supported over a number of years and unsolicited applications will not be acknowledged. The trustees meet in November and applications must be received by October.

WHO TO APPLY TO G Wright, Baker Tilly, 1st Floor, 4b Clarendon Road, Watford, Hertfordshire WD17 1HE *Tel* 01923 816400

CC NO 286525   **ESTABLISHED** 1983

■ City and County of Swansea Welsh Church Act Fund

WHERE FUNDING CAN BE GIVEN Swansea.

WHO CAN BENEFIT Registered charities.

WHAT IS FUNDED General charitable purposes.

WHAT IS NOT FUNDED No grants to individuals.

TYPE OF GRANT Revenue rather than capital.

RANGE OF GRANTS Up to £5,000.

FINANCES *Year* 2001–02 *Income* £50,000 *Grants* £39,000

HOW TO APPLY On a form available from the correspondent. Trustees meet twice a year to consider grants. Applications should be sent by April or the end of September.

WHO TO APPLY TO Mrs Susan Morgan, City and County of Swansea, County Hall, Oystermouth Road, Swansea SA1 3SN *Tel* 01792 636499 *E-mail* susan.morgan@swansea.gov.uk

CC NO 1071913   **ESTABLISHED** 1997

■ The City and Metropolitan Welfare Charity

WHERE FUNDING CAN BE GIVEN London, especially the City of London.

WHO CAN BENEFIT Organisations benefiting older people, at risk groups, people who are disadvantaged by poverty, disabled or ill, and ex-offenders and those at risk of offending.

WHAT IS FUNDED The assistance of deserving people who by reason of age, ill-health, accident, infirmity or straitened financial circumstances are in need. Grants are made to institutions or organisations providing welfare services

established for the care and relief of such people, with a preference for those which are administered in or in connection with the City of London, or are located in Greater London. Funds are fully committed.

WHAT IS NOT FUNDED No grants to individuals or for research purposes.

RANGE OF GRANTS £1,000–£3,000.

SAMPLE GRANTS In 1999: £2,750 each to Homerton Hospital Social Services and New Islington & Hackney Housing Association; £2,500 each to Samaritan Fund of St Thomas Hospital, Sheriff's and Recorder's Fund, and Whittington Hospital Social Services; £2,000 each to Association of Wheelchair Children for wheelchair training courses, Chelsea & Westminster Hospital, Prisoners' Education Trust for distance learning courses and Safe Ground for a new parenting skills programme; £1,500 to City Road Youth Counselling for development work – youth justice panels.

FINANCES *Year* 2000 *Income* £28,000 *Grants* £37,000 *Assets* £703,000

TRUSTEES R A Eve; B C Gothard; Sir Michael Harrison; R A R Hedderwick; Major D Ide-Smith; H S Johnson; W P Martineau; G H J Nicholson; R S Whitmore; J D Hedges.

HOW TO APPLY In writing to the correspondent.

WHO TO APPLY TO H W Truelove, Clerk to the Trustees, Mercers' Company, Mercers' Hall, Ironmonger Lane, London EC2V 8HE *Tel* 020 7726 4991

CC NO 205943   **ESTABLISHED** 1961

■ The City Educational Trust Fund

WHERE FUNDING CAN BE GIVEN Generally Greater London.

WHO CAN BENEFIT Institutions in London benefiting young adults, research workers, students and teachers.

WHAT IS FUNDED A variety of educational groups and institutions to promote study, teaching and training in areas such as science, technology, business management, commerce, biology, ecology and the cultural arts.

WHAT IS NOT FUNDED No grants to individuals.

TYPE OF GRANT One-off, ongoing and fixed period grants.

RANGE OF GRANTS £100–£21,000.

SAMPLE GRANTS £50,000 to Guildhall School of Music and Drama, the final payment of a three-year commitment ; £25,000 to St Paul's Cathedral Choir School, the third payment of a five-year commitment; £500 to Young Vic Theatre Company, the final payment of a three year commitment.

FINANCES *Year* 2001–02 *Income* £89,486 *Grants* £75,500 *Assets* £2,498,060

TRUSTEES Corporation of London.

HOW TO APPLY In writing to the correspondent. Guidelines are available from the trust.

WHO TO APPLY TO The Chamberlain of London, Corporation of London, PO Box 270, Guildhall, London EC2P 2EJ *Tel* 020 7606 3030

CC NO 290840   **ESTABLISHED** 1967

■ The City Parochial Foundation

WHERE FUNDING CAN BE GIVEN The Metropolitan Police District of London and the City of London.

WHO CAN BENEFIT Organisations providing advice, information and individual advocacy, especially those which are user-led or which encourage user involvement, participation and which lead to user empowerment. Organisations developing, promoting and providing education, training and employment schemes. Organisations which are attempting to develop initiatives which tackle violence and hate crimes against the target groups; applications will be considered for work with people who commit crimes and violence as well as work with the victims of it.

WHAT IS FUNDED Work that aims to bring about policy changes relating to discrimination, isolations and violence and improving people's quality of life; second tier and infrastructure organisations which meet the needs of the targeted groups; projects involving working together with others to meet the needs of their members.

WHAT IS NOT FUNDED No grants for endowment appeals; individual members of the public; major expenses for buying or building premises; medical research and equipment; organisations currently receiving funding from Trust for London; replacing public funds; trips abroad.

TYPE OF GRANT Core and management costs; work that aims to change policy.

RANGE OF GRANTS Usually £15,000–£50,000 often up to three years. There is also a small grant programme of up to £10,000 as a one-off.

SAMPLE GRANTS £190,000 to Praxis for its Refugee Awards Scheme; £150,000 each to Employability and the Evelyn Oldfield Unit; £65,000 to Salusbury World over two years; £60,000 to Family Services Unit in Barking and Dagenham over three years; £50,000 each to Chinese Mental Health Association in Tower Hamlets, Disability Advice Service – Lambeth, Status Employment in Croydon and Voluntary Action Lewisham.

FINANCES *Year* 2001 *Income* £10,100,000 *Grants* £4,576,000 *Assets* £182,000,000

TRUSTEES Prof. Gerald Manners, Chair; Maggie Baxter, Vice-chair; John Barnes; the Bishop of Willesden; Peter Dale; William Dove; Prof. Julian Franks; Patrick Haynes; Edward Lord; Ian Luder; John Muir; Miss Jyoti Munsiff; Elahe Panahi; Nigel Pantling; Roger Payton; Gillian Roberts; Robin Sherlock; Lynda Stevens; Albert Tucker; Jane Wilmot.

HOW TO APPLY There are no application forms. The first thing you should do is read the guidelines and check that your organisation and the work that you want the City Parochial Foundation to fund fits into their grantmaking programme. If you feel that your work does fit the guidelines you should follow these stages. Stage 1 – Send written details of your planned work and funding needs (on no more than two sides of A4 paper) along with your organisation's constitution; your most recent financial accounts; your most recent annual report. Or: Telephone a field officer at the foundation to talk about your work and the funding you are looking for. Stage 2 – If CPF feels that your planned work fits their grantmaking criteria, a field officer will arrange to meet you and discuss it further. Stage 3 – Once you and the field officer agree about what you should apply for, you can apply by making a full written application on no more than three sides of A4 paper in a format that the field officer will give to you. Full applications must be received before the relevant deadlines listed below. Stage 4 – The field officer will present this application to the grants committee, which will make the final decision about funding your application. Stage 5 – You will be told about the decision in writing after the foundation's trustee board meeting. If you would like to discuss your proposal before writing to CPF, you should contact them by telephone on 020 7606 6145.

When you should apply – You should contact CPF at least three months before the relevant deadline. The grants committee meets four times a years in January, April, July and October. The deadlines for receiving completed applications are 31 January for the April meeting; 15 April for the July meeting; 15 August for the October meeting; 15 November for the January meeting. An application is completed when you have had a meeting with a field officer, staff have no further questions to raise, and all the necessary papers have been received.

WHO TO APPLY TO Bharat Mehta, Clerk, 6 Middle Street, London EC1A 7PH *Tel* 020 7606 6145 *Fax* 020 7600 1866 *E-mail* info@cityparochial.org.uk *Website* www.cityparochial.org.uk

CC NO 205629

....

■ CLA Charitable Trust

WHERE FUNDING CAN BE GIVEN England and Wales only.

WHO CAN BENEFIT Small local projects, innovative projects and newly established projects to promote recreation, access and education in the countryside benefiting disabled people and disadvantaged young people.

WHAT IS FUNDED Provision of facilities for recreation and leisure in the countryside for people with disabilities. Advancement of education in agriculture and conservation.

WHAT IS NOT FUNDED No grants to individuals.

TYPE OF GRANT Buildings, capital, one-off and project. Funding is available for up to one year.

RANGE OF GRANTS Rarely more than £2,000.

SAMPLE GRANTS £3,000 to Essex Association of Boys Clubs; £2,520 to Yvonne Arnaud Theatre; £2,000 each to Dwyryd Anglers Ltd, and Nancy Oldfield Trust; £1,750 to West Norfolk Riding for the Disabled; £1,000 each to Living Springs, and Royal Bath and West Show.

FINANCES *Year* 2000–01 *Income* £90,445 *Grants* £66,988 *Assets* £310,409

TRUSTEES A Duckworth-Chad; A H Duberly; G E Lee-Strong; G N Mainwaring.

HOW TO APPLY In writing to the correspondent. Trustees meet four times a year.

WHO TO APPLY TO Peter Geldart, Caunton Grange, Caunton, Newark, Nottinghamshire NG23 6AB *Tel* 01636 636171 *Fax* 01636 636171 *Website* www.clacharitabletrust.org

CC NO 280264   **ESTABLISHED** 1980

....

■ Clark Charitable Trust

WHERE FUNDING CAN BE GIVEN UK and Asia.

WHO CAN BENEFIT Charities only.

WHAT IS FUNDED Firstly, the trust responds to emergency relief appeals, then considers general charitable purposes, including architecture, fine art, music, art galleries and cultural amenities, historic and church buildings, and heritage.

WHAT IS NOT FUNDED No grants to individuals or non-charitable bodies.

TYPE OF GRANT One-off.

RANGE OF GRANTS £1,000–£20,000.

SAMPLE GRANTS £20,000 to British Red Cross for the Turkey Earthquake Appeal; £10,000 each to UNICEF for Kosovo Appeal and Christian Aid for Kosovo Appeal; £5,000 to Red Cross for Columbian Earthquake; £3,000 to Stoke Mandeville Hospital.

FINANCES *Year* 1999 *Income* £19,500 *Grants* £34,400 *Assets* £440,000
TRUSTEES Barclays Bank Trust Co Ltd; Revd D E R Isitt.
HOW TO APPLY In writing to the correspondent.
WHO TO APPLY TO Barclays Bank Trust Company Limited, Executorship and Trustee Service, PO Box 15, Northwich, Cheshire CW9 7UR
CC NO 274300   ESTABLISHED 1977

■ The Elizabeth Clark Charitable Trust

WHERE FUNDING CAN BE GIVEN UK.
WHO CAN BENEFIT Registered charities.
WHAT IS FUNDED Improvements in nursing care and developing good practice in palliative care.
WHAT IS NOT FUNDED The trust does not normally support capital or revenue appeals from hospices or make grants to individuals.
TYPE OF GRANT Capital and project grants.
SAMPLE GRANTS £387,943 to University of Sheffield Department of Palliative Medicine for an initiative to design and test a protocol for use in all healthcare settings to measure a patient's current and potential need for palliative care services.
FINANCES *Year* 2001–02 *Income* £42,767 *Grants* £387,943 *Assets* £545,263
TRUSTEES Miss Judith Portrait; Dr Jane Davy; Dr Gillian Ford.
OTHER INFORMATION The trust is one of the Sainsbury Family Charitable Trusts which share a common administration. An application to one is taken as an application to all.
HOW TO APPLY Proposals are generally invited by the trustees or initiated at their request. Unsolicited applications are nort encouraged and are unlikely to be successful.
WHO TO APPLY TO Michael Pattison, Director, Allington House, 1st Floor, 150 Victoria Street, London SW1E 5AE *Tel* 020 7410 0330 *Fax* 020 7410 0322
CC NO 265206   ESTABLISHED 1973

■ The Hilda & Alice Clark Charitable Trust

WHERE FUNDING CAN BE GIVEN Street, Somerset.
WHO CAN BENEFIT There is a preference given to the Society of Friends (Quakers) and to children and young adults.
WHAT IS FUNDED Educational charities. General charitable purposes.
FINANCES *Year* 2001 *Income* £38,000 *Grants* £34,500 *Assets* £1,058,000
TRUSTEES R B Clark; A T Clothier; T A Clark; M Lovell; Alice Clark.
HOW TO APPLY In writing to the correspondent. Trustees meet in December.
WHO TO APPLY TO Michael Haynes, Secretary, c/o KPMG, 100 Temple Street, Bristol BS1 6AG *Tel* 0117 905 4694
CC NO 290916   ESTABLISHED 1953

■ J A Clark Charitable Trust

WHERE FUNDING CAN BE GIVEN UK, with a preference for south west England.
WHO CAN BENEFIT Organisations benefiting children, young adults, parents and children, one-parent families, Quakers, people disadvantaged by poverty, ex-offenders and those at risk of offending, homeless people and victims of abuse.
WHAT IS FUNDED Projects orientated towards social change in areas of health, education, peace, preservation of the earth and the arts. Preference for the work of small, new, innovative projects and for young people. Charities working in the fields of community development, arts and arts facilities, arts education, alternative healthcare, conservation of fauna and flora, organic food production, environmental issues, transport and alternative transport, training for community development, crime prevention schemes, family support and community issues.
WHAT IS NOT FUNDED No support for independent schools (unless they are for special needs), conservation of buildings or for individuals.
TYPE OF GRANT One-off or for up to three years, including start-up costs and research.
RANGE OF GRANTS £800–£27,000.
SAMPLE GRANTS £27,000 to Cyrus Clark Charitable Trust; £14,000 to Inner City Scholarship Fund; £12,000 to QPS; £10,000 to ASHOKA; £6,500 to Watershed Arts Trust; £5,500 to Quaker Peace Studies; £5,000 each to Addiction Recovery Agency, CJC Bursary and Street Theatre Workshop Trust; £4,000 each to Dance United and Jubilee 2000 Coalition; £3,000 to Take Art Ltd; £2,000 each to British Red Cross, New Economics Foundation and Drop The Debt; £1,000 each to Children's Classic Concerts and Hareclive Football Club; £800 to Guild of Psychotherapy.
FINANCES *Year* 2000–01 *Income* £397,134 *Grants* £134,395 *Assets* £8,488,998
TRUSTEES Lancelot Pease Clark; John Cyrus Clark; Thomas Aldham Clark; Caroline Pym; Aidan J R Pelly.
HOW TO APPLY The trust is fundamentally restructuring itself towards the objective of supporting exclusively one or two innovative projects, and so is 'absolutely unable to respond to any unsolicited appeals at this point in time'.
WHO TO APPLY TO Mrs P Grant, Secretary, PO Box 1704, Glastonbury, Somerset BA16 0YB *Tel* 01458 842374 *Fax* 01458 842022 *E-mail* jactrust@ukonline.co.uk
CC NO 1010520   ESTABLISHED 1992

■ The Roger & Sarah Bancroft Clark Charitable Trust

WHERE FUNDING CAN BE GIVEN UK and overseas, preference for Somerset.
WHO CAN BENEFIT Society of Friends, registered charities and individuals. Preference is given to local appeals.
WHAT IS FUNDED General charitable purposes with particular reference to: Religious Society of Friends and associated bodies; charities connected with Somerset; education (for individuals).
TYPE OF GRANT Recurrent grants.
RANGE OF GRANTS £50–£1,000.
SAMPLE GRANTS £24,000 in three grants to Trustees of Long Sutton Courthouse Charity; £2,000 each to Britain Yearly Meeting of Friends – Swarthmoor Hall Appeal, Oxfam, Quaker Peace Service, and The Hickman (Friends Boarding Home).
FINANCES *Year* 2000 *Income* £136,000 *Grants* £140,000 *Assets* £2,500,000

TRUSTEES Eleanor C Robertson; Mary P Lovell; Stephen Clark; S Caroline Gould; Roger S Goldby.

HOW TO APPLY In writing to the correspondent. There is no application form and telephone calls are not accepted. Trustees meet about three times a year. Applications will be acknowledged if an sae is enclosed.

WHO TO APPLY TO Mrs Lynette Cooper, Secretary, C & J Clark Ltd, 40 High Street, Street, Somerset BA16 0YA *Tel* 01458 443131 *E-mail* lynette.cooper@clarks.com

CC NO 211513   **ESTABLISHED** 1960

■ Stephen Clark 1957 Charitable Trust

WHERE FUNDING CAN BE GIVEN Some preference for Bath and Somerset.

WHO CAN BENEFIT Registered charities.

WHAT IS FUNDED The trust's priorities are 'to make donations to charities in respect of the preservation, embellishment, maintenance, improvement or development of any monuments, churches or other buildings'. The trust prefers local charities to national ones.

WHAT IS NOT FUNDED No grants to animal charities or to individuals.

SAMPLE GRANTS £16,000 to Bath Industrial Heritage Trust; £1,000 to Friends to Holbourne Museum; £570 (in two grants) to Dorothy House Foundation; £200 to Médecins Sans Frontières.

FINANCES *Year* 1998 *Income* £29,000 *Grants* £21,000 *Assets* £666,000

TRUSTEES Dr M I H Clark; Mrs M P Lovell.

HOW TO APPLY In writing to the correspondent. Please note, replies are not usually made to unsuccessful applications.

WHO TO APPLY TO Dr Marianna I H Clark, Trustee, 16 Lansdown Place East, Bath BA1 5ET

CC NO 258690   **ESTABLISHED** 1969

■ The Clarke Charitable Settlement

WHERE FUNDING CAN BE GIVEN Staffordshire.

WHO CAN BENEFIT Funding may be considered for Christians, research workers and medical professionals.

WHAT IS FUNDED The advancement of Christian religion, medical research and hospices.

RANGE OF GRANTS £25–£88,125; but mainly under £500.

SAMPLE GRANTS In 1998–99: £88,125 to Animal Health Trust; £40,000 to MRI Scanner Appeal; £20,000 to Lichfield Cathedral Music Campaign; £8,500 to John Taylor High School; £5,000 to St Anselms Millennium Appeal; £1,000 to St Giles Hospice; £1,000 to Litchfield Methodist Church; £500 each to Barnardos – Trek China, Barton Cottage Hospital, and Burton Crime Prevention Panel.

FINANCES *Year* 2000–01 *Income* £107,637 *Grants* £130,000 *Assets* £1,000,000

TRUSTEES S W Clarke; Lady H J Clarke; Ms S A Hayward; Ms M E MacGregor.

HOW TO APPLY In writing to the correspondent, although the trust stated that support is only given to charities known to the trustees or the Clarke family.

WHO TO APPLY TO Lady H J Clarke, Trustee, The Knoll, Main Street, Barton-under-Needwood, Nr Burton, Staffordshire DE13 8AB *Tel* 01283 712294

CC NO 702980   **ESTABLISHED** 1990

■ The Classic FM Charitable Trust

WHERE FUNDING CAN BE GIVEN UK.

WHO CAN BENEFIT Established organisations benefiting musicians and people disadvantaged by poverty.

WHAT IS FUNDED The promotion of education and training of members of the public in music; the relief of financial need and the relief of sickness. The trustees select one grant per year associated with music.

WHAT IS NOT FUNDED No grants to individuals.

TYPE OF GRANT One-off.

SAMPLE GRANTS In 2000: £60,000 to the Master Class Charity (towards the production of a video for the Federation of Music Teachers).

FINANCES *Year* 2001–02 *Income* £60,429

TRUSTEES Mrs V L Duffield; Prof. Stanley Glasser; Robert O'Dowd; John McLaren; Robin Ray; John Spearman; Douglas Thackway; Andrew Tuckey.

HOW TO APPLY In writing to the correspondent.

WHO TO APPLY TO Danny Cooper, Eltham College, Grove Park Road, London SE9 4QF *Tel* 020 8857 7360 *E-mail* bursar@eltham-college.org.uk

CC NO 1028531   **ESTABLISHED** 1993

■ The Cleary Foundation

WHERE FUNDING CAN BE GIVEN UK, with a preference for Kent.

WHO CAN BENEFIT Registered charities benefiting: children; older people; ex-service and service people; seafarers and fishermen; Christians; Church of England; people with disabilities; and people disadvantaged by poverty.

WHAT IS FUNDED Principally to apply the income of the foundation for various selected charities for the relief of pain and hardship, and conservation. These include: civil society development; community development; social care professional bodies; churches; music; visual art; arts activities; dance and ballet; dance groups; theatrical companies and theatre groups; horticulture; special schools; community centres and village halls; and parks.

WHAT IS NOT FUNDED No grants to individuals who require aid with further education.

TYPE OF GRANT Core costs and one-off.

RANGE OF GRANTS £100–£1,000.

SAMPLE GRANTS All the following were for core costs unless stated: £30,000 to Ripple Down House Trust; £750 to Canterbury Festival; £400 to Cruse for Dover Counselling Service; £270 to Canterbury Choral Society; £200 each to Save the Children Fund and National Gardens Scheme.

FINANCES *Year* 2001 *Income* £44,261 *Grants* £33,420 *Assets* £1,162,056

TRUSTEES P M Gould; A T F Gould; K A F Phillips; M R Thody; P A Took.

HOW TO APPLY In writing to the correspondent, although the trust would welcome a preliminary telephone call to check whether they are in the position of being able to offer grants to new beneficiaries.

WHO TO APPLY TO Ms Colette Fronty, Secretary to the Trustees, South Sands Lodge, Beach Road, St Margaret's Bay, Kent CT15 6DZ *Tel* 01304 852764 *Fax* 01304 853626

CC NO 242675   **ESTABLISHED** 1965

■ The Cleopatra Trust

WHERE FUNDING CAN BE GIVEN Mainly UK.

WHO CAN BENEFIT Registered charities within the UK with a national focus, benefiting people of all ages, homeless people, people with addictions, physical disabilities, cancer, diabetes and underprivileged children.

WHAT IS FUNDED Support is given to projects including hostels, hospices, holiday accommodation, respite care, care in the community, health counselling and some environmental issues.

WHAT IS NOT FUNDED No grants to individuals, expeditions, research, scholarships, charities with a local focus, local branches of UK-wide charities or towards running costs.

TYPE OF GRANT Projects and one-off. Funding for one year or less.

RANGE OF GRANTS £500–£16,000.

SAMPLE GRANTS £16,000 to Sight Savers; £10,000 each to Tommy's Campaign, Brick by Brick London Home Activity Group, Couple Counselling Scotland, St Mungo Community Housing Association, Cancer Link, Heal Cancer Charity Ltd and Royal Blind Asylum & School; £8,000 each to Medical Foundation for the Care of Victims of Torture and Claire House; £5,000 each to Cruse Bereavement Care Swindon, Habitat for Humanity Belfast and Fairtrade Foundation; £3,000 to Help the Hospices; £2,500 to Inspire; £2,000 to St Giles Hospice (£2,000).

FINANCES *Year* 2000 *Income* £161,655 *Grants* £162,000 *Assets* £3,125,024

TRUSTEES Charles Peacock; Mrs Bettine Bond; Dr Clare Sellers.

HOW TO APPLY On a 'funding proposal form' available from the correspondent. Applications should include a copy of the latest audited annual report and accounts. They are considered twice a year in mid-summer and mid-winter. Organisations which have received grants from this trust, Dorus Trust or the Epigoni Trust should not reapply in the following two years. Usually, funding will be considered by only one of these trusts.

WHO TO APPLY TO Mrs Sue David, Donor Grants Officer, Charities Aid Foundation, King's Hill, West Malling, Kent ME19 4TA *Tel* 01732 520083 *Fax* 01732 520001

CC NO 1004551   **ESTABLISHED** 1990

■ Cleveland Community Foundation

WHERE FUNDING CAN BE GIVEN The old county of Cleveland, being the local authority areas of Hartlepool, Middlesborough, Redcar and Cleveland and Stockton-on-Tees.

WHO CAN BENEFIT All registered charities or bonafide voluntary/community groups, provided the purpose of the grant is wholly charitable and for the benefit of people in Cleveland. To benefit: young adults and older people; at risk groups; carers and disabled people; those disadvantaged by poverty; socially isolated people; and those living in urban areas.

WHAT IS FUNDED Grants are made through six programmes: Tees Valley TEC Distribution Fund, for the advancement of education and learning; Teesside Youth Development Programme, to address the needs of young people aged 8 to 25 who are in some way disadvantaged; Cleveland Fund which is a general fund; Social Exclusion and Economic Development Fund – a European Community economic development

funding programme; Teesside Power Fund giving grants in the nine wards adjacent to Teesside Power Station; Voluntary Sector Management Training Fund.

WHAT IS NOT FUNDED No grants to individuals or to organisations for major fundraising appeals, sponsored events, promotion of religion, holidays or social outings.

TYPE OF GRANT Capital or revenue.

SAMPLE GRANTS £28,000 to St Michael's School; £25,000 to Tom Leonard Mining Museum; £10,000 each to Eastbourne School, Grangefield School, Northfield School and Ian Ramsey C of E School; £7,000 to Back in the System.

FINANCES *Year* 2001–02 *Grants* £927,000 *Assets* £5,800,000

TRUSTEES Dr Tony Gillham, Chair; Margaret Fay; John Foster; Chris Hope; Marjory Houseman; Alan Kitching; Roberta Ladds; Kate Macnaught; Sir Ronald Norman; Jack Ord; Robert Sale; Mike Scott; Pat Sole; Michael Stewart; Ian Collinson; Geoffrey Crute.

PUBLICATIONS Periodic newsletter.

HOW TO APPLY On application forms, available from the correspondent. If you require advice or have any problems completing the application, please contact Ian Scrutton, principal grants officer, on the number above or e-mail ian@clevelandfoundation.org.uk. There are three grant rounds a year, with deadlines for applications as follows 1 January; 1 May; 1 September.

WHO TO APPLY TO Kevin Ryan, Director, Southlands Business Centre, Ormesby Road, Middlesbrough TS3 0HB *Tel* 01642 314200 *Fax* 01642 313700 *E-mail* office@clevelandfoundation.org.uk

CC NO 700568   **ESTABLISHED** 1988

■ The Clifton Charitable Trust

WHERE FUNDING CAN BE GIVEN UK and overseas, preference for south west England.

WHAT IS FUNDED General charitable purposes.

RANGE OF GRANTS Up to £50,000.

SAMPLE GRANTS £50,000 each to Bristol Cathedral, Bristol Foyer Project, Dorothy House, Farm America, Julian House, Royal United Hospital Charitable Fund, South Mead MRI Scanner Appeal, and Welsh National Opera; £25,000 to National Eye Research Centre.

FINANCES *Year* 2000 *Income* £897,000 *Grants* £702,000 *Assets* £1,800,000

TRUSTEES Avon Executor and Trustee Company.

OTHER INFORMATION The Craig Fund is part of the Clifton Charitable Trust; however, it has separate finances.

HOW TO APPLY In writing to the correspondent. Unsolicited applications cannot be considered.

WHO TO APPLY TO Lisa Mirams, KPMG, 100 Temple Street, Bristol BS1 6AG *Tel* 0117 905 4000

CC NO 285564   **ESTABLISHED** 1970

■ Lord Clinton's Charitable Trust

WHERE FUNDING CAN BE GIVEN North and east Devon.

WHO CAN BENEFIT Registered charities benefiting people of all ages, ex-service and service people, seafarers and fishermen, sportsmen and women, volunteers, parents and children, disabled people, victims of man-made or natural disasters, people with cancer, paediatric diseases, or sight loss, and people who are terminally ill.

WHAT IS FUNDED Young people and the encouragement of youth activities, people who are disabled, support for older people, medical aid and research, maritime charities. Respite and sheltered accommodation; churches; information technology and computers; personnel and human resources; support to voluntary and community organisations and volunteers; professional bodies; community centres and village halls; clubs; holidays and outings are also considered.

WHAT IS NOT FUNDED No support for animal charities. No grants made in response to general appeals from large UK organisations nor to smaller bodies working in areas other than those set out above.

TYPE OF GRANT For projects, recurring costs and start-up costs. Funding is available for one year or less.

SAMPLE GRANTS £2,000 each to St Michael's Church Roof Rescue Fund and Genesis Trust.

FINANCES *Year* 2000–01 *Income* £21,714 *Grants* £22,000

TRUSTEES Hon. Charles Fane Trefusis; John C Varley.

HOW TO APPLY In writing to the correspondent. Applications not falling within the trust's objects and funding priorities will not be considered or acknowledged.

WHO TO APPLY TO John C Varley, Estates Director, Rolle Estate Office, East Budleigh, Budleigh Salterton, Devon EX9 7DP *Tel* 01395 443881 *Fax* 01395 446126 *E-mail* mail@clintondevon.co.uk *Website* www.clintondevon.co.uk **CC NO** 268061   **ESTABLISHED** 1974

....

■ The Clore Duffield Foundation

WHERE FUNDING CAN BE GIVEN UK, but most money goes to London-based institutions.

WHO CAN BENEFIT Charities, particular emphasis on supporting children, young people and society's more vulnerable individuals.

WHAT IS FUNDED Main grants programme, mainly in the fields of arts and museum education; the arts generally; health and social welfare, especially but not only to Jewish charities. Two smaller grants programmes: museum and gallery education, and artworks programme for schools art education.

WHAT IS NOT FUNDED No donations or grants to individuals, whether for education or any other purpose.

SAMPLE GRANTS £1 million to NSPCC over ten years; £170,000 to Royal Opera House; £150,000 each to @ Bristol for an early years touring exhibition and Manchester Art Gallery for Clore Interactive Gallery; £100,000 to Grange Park Opera; £98,000 to Guildhall University for the Clore Education Space and seminar room of the women's library; £50,000 to Almeida for redevelopment; £36,000 to Belcea String Quartet for educational work; £30,000 to Anna Freud Centre over three years towards their family support work; £25,000 to Engage: the National Association for Gallery Education.

FINANCES *Year* 2001 *Grants* £5,245,000

TRUSTEES Dame Vivien Duffield, Chair; Caroline Deletra; David Harrel; Sir Jocelyn Stevens; Michael Trask; Sir Mark Weinberg.

HOW TO APPLY Applicants whose proposals fall within the foundation's defined areas of interest are advised to submit first-stage letters of application, on no more than two sides of A4 (enclosing an stamped addressed envelope and omitting any annual reports or other

enclosures). There are no deadlines for submitting an application. Institutions wishing to apply to the Clore small grants programme for museum and gallery education should contact the foundation to request an application form. There a two grants rounds a year for this programme, with closing dates in mid-March and mid-September.

WHO TO APPLY TO Sally Bacon, Executive Director, Studio 3, Chelsea Manor Studios, Flood Street, London SW3 5SR *Tel* 020 7351 6061 *Fax* 020 7351 5308 *Website* www.cloreduffield.org.uk **CC NO** 1084412

....

■ Miss V L Clore's 1967 Charitable Trust

WHERE FUNDING CAN BE GIVEN UK.

WHO CAN BENEFIT Registered charities.

WHAT IS FUNDED General charitable purposes.

WHAT IS NOT FUNDED No grants are given to individuals.

RANGE OF GRANTS £200–£10,000.

SAMPLE GRANTS £10,000 to English Touring Opera; £4,000 to Starlight Foundation; £3,000 each to Cancer Relief Macmillan Fund and Cancer Research Campaign; £2,000 each to The National Tenants' Resource Centre and NSPCC in London; £1,000 each to Cancerkin – The Royal Free Hospital Appeal Trust, Design Museum, Foundation Friends of Warsaw and Help Poland Fund, and KIDS for work with children with special needs.

FINANCES *Year* 1998–99 *Income* £44,697 *Grants* £35,000 *Assets* £864,520

TRUSTEES Mrs V L Duffield, Chair; David Harrel; Sir Jocelyn Stevens; Caroline Deletra.

HOW TO APPLY In writing to the correspondent. However, only charities personally known to the trustees are considered. Funds are fully allocated and applications are not acknowledged.

WHO TO APPLY TO Miss Sally Bacon, Unit 3 Chelsea Manor Studios, Flood Street, London SW3 5SR *Tel* 020 7351 6061 *Fax* 020 7351 5308 **CC NO** 253660   **ESTABLISHED** 1967

....

■ Closehelm Ltd

WHERE FUNDING CAN BE GIVEN UK.

WHO CAN BENEFIT Individuals and institutions benefiting Jewish people and people disadvantaged by poverty.

WHAT IS FUNDED The advancement of religion in accordance with the Jewish faith; the relief of poverty; and general charitable purposes.

FINANCES *Year* 2000–01 *Income* £433,182

TRUSTEES A Van Praagh; H W Van Praagh; H R Van Praagh.

HOW TO APPLY In writing to the correspondent.

WHO TO APPLY TO A Van Praagh, Trustee, 30 Armitage Road, London NW11 8RD *Tel* 020 8201 8688 **CC NO** 291296   **ESTABLISHED** 1983

....

■ The Clothworkers' Foundation and other Trusts

WHERE FUNDING CAN BE GIVEN UK and overseas.

WHO CAN BENEFIT UK registered charities only.

WHAT IS FUNDED Funding is given in the following areas: medicine and health; clothworking; relief in need and welfare; education and the sciences; children and youth; overseas; heritage and the environment; the church; and the arts.

WHAT IS NOT FUNDED Charitable support is not given in the following cases: to go in direct relief of state aid or in the reduction of financial support from public funds; to go directly to organisations or groups which are not registered charities; in response to applications by, or for the benefit of, individuals; by means of sponsorship for individuals undertaking fundraising activities on behalf of any charity; towards the general maintenance, repair or restoration of cathedrals, abbeys, churches or other ecclesiastical buildings, unless they have an existing and long-standing connection with The Clothworkers' Company, or unless they are appealing for a specific purpose which is considered to be of outstanding importance in relation to the national heritage; to schools/colleges in the primary or secondary sector of education (whether public or private), unless they have an existing and long-standing connection with The Clothworkers' Company; to organisations or groups whose main objects are to fund or support other charitable bodies; to any political, industrial or commercial appeal. It is normally expected that a period of at least five years will elapse before consideration is given to further grants to the same charitable organisation. Assistance to individuals for educational purposes is limited; in London such grants are made through the associated Mary Datchelor Trust, details of which can be found in the companion Educational Grants Directory.

TYPE OF GRANT Capital; one-off; occasionally recurring for more than three years.

SAMPLE GRANTS £1.2 million to St Ethelburga's Centre for Peace and Reconciliation for construction to celebrate the millennium; £250,000 to the Royal College of Obstetricians and Gynaecologists for a training suite; £225,000 (paid in instalments) to Royal Geographical Society towards building environmentally controlled archive storage facilities; £150,000 to St Mungo's; £100,000 each to Craven Trust and Cumbria Community Foundation in response to the foot and mouth crisis; £76,000 to King Edward VII's Hospital Sister Agnes; £60,000 to ECHO Disaster Fund; £53,000 to Fairbridge for training courses around the UK for disadvantaged people and volunteers; £51,000 to Welsh National Opera.

FINANCES *Year* 2001 *Income* £4,617,000 *Grants* £4,450,000 *Assets* £61,535,000

TRUSTEES 37 governors of the foundation including Peter Rawson, chair of the trusts and grants committee; Anthony West, deputy chair.

PUBLICATIONS Annual review; annual report and financial statement.

HOW TO APPLY The Clothworkers' Foundation does not issue application forms. However, all applicants must complete a data information sheet, which should accompany the written application/appeal. The application should be posted; application via fax or e-mail will not be accepted. Applications from registered charities should be made in writing on the applicant charity's official headed notepaper. Ideally, the appeal letter itself should be no longer than two and a half pages of A4. Detailed costings or a budget for the project or projects referred to in the appeal letter should form a separate appendix or appendices to the appeal letter and should provide the fullest possible financial details. The latest annual report of the applicant charity, together with the latest available full audited accounts, including a full balance sheet should also accompany the written application.

During the course of the written application letter, applicants should endeavour to introduce the work of the applicant charity; state when the charity was established; describe its aims and objectives; and define precisely what the applicant charity does and who benefits from its activities; comment upon the applicant charity's track record since its inception, refer to its notable achievements and successes to date and endeavour to provide an interesting synopsis of the organisation; describe the project requiring funding fully, clearly and concisely and comment on the charity's plans for the future; provide full costings or a budget for the project/projects to include a detailed breakdown of the costs involved; give details of all other applications which the applicant charity has made to other sources of funding, and indicate precisely what funds have already been raised from other sources for the project. All applicants are, of course, perfectly at liberty to request a precise sum of money by way of grant. However, it can be more beneficial for the applicant charity to concentrate on providing accurate and detailed costings of the project concerned, thereby enabling the foundation to make its own judgement as to the level of financial support to be considered. Applicants can greatly help their cause by concentrating on clarity of presentation and by providing detailed factual information. The foundation will then do its utmost to ensure that the application receives the fullest and most careful consideration.

The foundation's trusts and grants committee meets on six occasions each year, usually in October, December, January, February, May and July. The committee's recommendations are then placed before a subsequent meeting of the governors. Accordingly, there is a rolling programme of dealing with and processing applications and the foundation prides itself on its flexibility.

The foundation's 'guidelines for grant applicants' clearly indicate the information required for use in the decision-making process. Successful applicants are normally notified of the result of their application within days of the final decision being reached by the governors. All unsuccessful applicants receive a written refusal letter.

WHO TO APPLY TO Andrew Blessley, Secretary, Clothworkers' Hall, Dunster Court, Mincing Lane, London EC3R 7AH *Tel* 020 7623 7041 *Website* www.clothworkers.co.uk

CC NO 274100   **ESTABLISHED** 1977

....

■ Richard Cloudesley's Charity

WHERE FUNDING CAN BE GIVEN North Islington only.

WHO CAN BENEFIT Individuals as well as voluntary and charitable organisations. At risk groups, disabled people, people disadvantaged by poverty, disaster victims, and victims of abuse, crime and domestic violence are given priority.

WHAT IS FUNDED The assistance of people with a financial and a medical need, and Church of England churches. Half of the charity's income is given to medical charities and causes and the other half to local Church of England churches.

WHAT IS NOT FUNDED Applicants must fall within the geographic and purposes scope of the charity.

TYPE OF GRANT One-off grants are preferred; the vast majority of grants are free of restrictions. Grants for capital, core, recurring, running and start-up costs will be considered, as will grants for

388

Does the trust you have chosen match your needs? Haphazard applications waste postage and time

buildings, feasibility studies, project, research and salaries. Funding is for one year or less.

RANGE OF GRANTS £100–£20,000.

SAMPLE GRANTS In 2000–01: £32,000 each to Assisted Living Foundation, St John's District Church and St Mary's Upper Street; £28,000 to St Jude with St Paul, Mildmay Park; £26,000 each to St James with St Peter, prebend Street and St Stephen, Canonbury; £22,000 to Islington MIND; £16,000 each to Islington Community Contact and St Andrew – Whitehall Park; £14,000 to CARIS (Islington) Bereavement Project.

FINANCES *Year* 2001–02 *Income* £514,000 *Grants* £710,000 *Assets* £19,000,000

TRUSTEES Appointed by the local council, the local Church of England churches, and co-opted. The Mayor of Islington and the Vicar of St Mary's, Upper Street are also trustees. The grants committee: J Durdin, Chair; Mayor of Islington; Canon G Kings; W Carter; Mrs S Clark; P Haynes; K Streater; Ms V Lang; J W Wilson.

HOW TO APPLY The guidelines say: 'If you think your charity is going to be able to qualify for consideration of a grant, write first to the clerk to the charity. You will then get an application form. Applications should be timely; in writing; supported by accounts. If you would like us to acknowledge your application, please send a self-addressed envelope. Otherwise, to save expense, we will not confirm safe receipt. Block grants are considered twice a year, around late April and early November at a grants committee meeting. Recommendations are made by the grants committee at these meetings and are reviewed and authorised by the Cloudesley trustees as a whole two weeks later. The trustees normally adopt all the recommendations.

We need to know what work your charity does, how it fits within [our] geographical scope and purpose scope and the purpose for which you are seeking a grant. So long as this is clearly set out, we do not need a great deal of detail. We place a great deal of importance on receiving the accounts of the charities we fund so please be sure to send these each time you apply.

We will give brief reasons with any application that is not successful.

WHO TO APPLY TO Keith Wallace, Clerk, 11th Floor, Beaufort House, 15 St Botolph Street, London EC3A 7EE *Tel* 020 7247 6555 *Fax* 020 7247 5091

CC NO 205959   **ESTABLISHED** 1517

....

■ Clover Trust

WHERE FUNDING CAN BE GIVEN UK and overseas, with a slight preference for West Dorset.

WHO CAN BENEFIT Registered charities benefiting disadvantaged children, people with disabilities and young people.

WHAT IS FUNDED Respite and sheltered accommodation, nursing services, respite care, playgrounds, holidays and outings, special needs education, Cathalic bodies, and personnel and human resources services.

WHAT IS NOT FUNDED The arts, monuments and non-registered charities are not supported.

TYPE OF GRANT Capital, core costs, endowments, feasibility studies, one-off, project, research, recurring and running costs, salaries, and start-up costs. Funding can be given for up to three years.

RANGE OF GRANTS £2,000–£30,000.

SAMPLE GRANTS £30,000 to Downsize Settlement; £15,000 each to Action Research for the Crippled Child, National Society for the Prevention of Cruelty to Children and Friends of Orphanages in Romania; £13,000 to 999 Club; £10,000 each to British Red Cross Society and Cotswold Care.

FINANCES *Year* 2000 *Income* £275,000 *Grants* £330,000 *Assets* £4,900,000

TRUSTEES N C Haydon; S Woodhouse.

HOW TO APPLY In writing to the correspondent. Replies are not given to unsuccessful applications.

WHO TO APPLY TO Nicholas C Haydon, Trustee, c/o Suite 7, Messrs Herbert Pepper and Rudland, Accurist House, 44 Baker Street, London W1U 7BD *Tel* 020 7486 5535

CC NO 213578   **ESTABLISHED** 1961

....

■ The Robert Clutterbuck Charitable Trust

WHERE FUNDING CAN BE GIVEN Mainly UK, with preference for the counties of Cheshire and Hertfordshire.

WHO CAN BENEFIT Registered charities only, benefiting ex-service and service people, and sportsmen and women.

WHAT IS FUNDED Personnel within the armed forces and ex-service men and women; sport and recreational facilities; natural history; the welfare, protection and preservation of animal life.

WHAT IS NOT FUNDED No grants to individuals. The trustees do not favour applications relating to counselling, drug abuse, lone parents and playgroups or for community projects (except in Cheshire or Hertfordshire).

TYPE OF GRANT Payments normally from income, generally for the purchase of specific items.

RANGE OF GRANTS £500–£5,000; typical £2,000–£3,000.

SAMPLE GRANTS £4,000 to Royal Star & Garter Homes; £2,700 to St Johns Ambulance; £2,500 to South Manchester Gymnastics Centre; £1,800 to British Athletics Fellowship Trust.

FINANCES *Year* 2001–02 *Income* £37,017 *Grants* £32,925 *Assets* £1,075,563

TRUSTEES Major R G Clutterbuck; C N Lindsell; I A Pearson.

HOW TO APPLY In writing to the correspondent. There are no application forms. Applications are acknowledged and considered by the trustees twice a year.

WHO TO APPLY TO G A Wolfe, Secretary, 28 Brookfields, Calver, Hope Valley, Derbyshire S32 3XB *Tel* 01433 631308 *Fax* 0870 133 3198 *E-mail* geowolfe@onetel.net.uk *Website* www.clutterbucktrust.org.uk

CC NO 1010559   **ESTABLISHED** 1992

....

■ Clydpride Ltd

WHERE FUNDING CAN BE GIVEN UK.

WHO CAN BENEFIT Individuals and institutions benefiting Jewish people and people disadvantaged by poverty.

WHAT IS FUNDED Advancement of the orthodox Jewish faith; relief of poverty; general charitable purposes.

FINANCES *Year* 2000–01 *Income* £1,300,000 *Grants* £250,000

TRUSTEES L Faust; D Faust; T Faust.

HOW TO APPLY The trust states that unsolicited applications are not entertained.

WHO TO APPLY TO L Faust, Secretary to the Trustees, 1003 Finchley Road, London NW11 7HB *Tel* 020 8731 7744 *Fax* 020 8731 8373
CC NO 295393   **ESTABLISHED** 1982

■ The Francis Coales Charitable Foundation

WHERE FUNDING CAN BE GIVEN UK, with a preference for Bedfordshire, Buckinghamshire, Hertfordshire and Northamptonshire.
WHO CAN BENEFIT Old buildings open to the public, usually churches.
WHAT IS FUNDED The repair/restoration of any ecclesiastical buildings built before 1875; also memorial brasses and monuments.
WHAT IS NOT FUNDED No grants for buildings built after 1875, hospitals or hospices. Ecclesiastical buildings cannot receive grants for 'domestic' items such as electrical wiring, heating, improvements or re-ordering.
TYPE OF GRANT Largely one-off (or recurrent if for an ongoing application).
RANGE OF GRANTS £25–£10,000, typical grant £1,000–£2,500.
SAMPLE GRANTS £25,000 to Northamptonshire VCH Trust for research; £5,000 each to Higham Ferrers – Northamptonshire for repairs to its tower, Sawbridgeworth – Hertfordshire to repair the dry root in the nave roof, Stoneleigh – Warwickshire to conserve a monument, and Thorpe Malsor – Northamptonshire to repairs its tower and spires; £4,000 each to Little Addlington – Northamptonshire for spire repairs, and Marsham – North Yorkshire for the Danby Monument; £3,000 each to Ashby St Ledges – Northamptonshire for roof repairs, Drayton Parslow – Buckinghamshire for general structural repairs and Hulcote – Bedfordshire for roof timbers.
FINANCES *Year* 2001 *Income* £99,670 *Grants* £113,889 *Assets* £1,732,293
TRUSTEES J Coales, Chair; H G M Leighton; A G Harding; Revd B H Wilcox; H M Stuchfield.
HOW TO APPLY On a form available from the correspondent. Applications for buildings or contents should include a copy of the relevant part of the architect/conservator's specification showing the actual work proposed. 'Photographs showing details of the problems often speak louder than words.' The trust also states that receiving six copies of any leaflet or statement of finance is helpful so that each trustee can have a copy in advance of the meeting. Trustees normally meet three times a year to consider grants.
WHO TO APPLY TO T H Parker, Administrator, The Bays, Hillcote, Bleadon Hill, Weston-super-Mare, Somerset BS24 9JS *Tel* 01934 814009 *Fax* 01934 814009 *E-mail* fccf45@hotmail.com
CC NO 270718   **ESTABLISHED** 1975

■ The Coates Charitable Settlement

WHERE FUNDING CAN BE GIVEN UK, with a preference for Leicestershire.
WHO CAN BENEFIT Children and young adults.
WHAT IS FUNDED Medicine and health, welfare, education, humanities.
WHAT IS NOT FUNDED No support for individuals.
SAMPLE GRANTS Previous beneficiaries have included Leicester Action on Domestic Violence, Leicester Children's Asthma Centre and Leicester Royal Infirmary Coronary Care Unit.

FINANCES *Year* 2001–02 *Income* £16,360 *Grants* £35,000 *Assets* £350,000
TRUSTEES W C Coates; Mrs B M Coates; M A Chamberlain.
HOW TO APPLY In writing to the correspondent.
WHO TO APPLY TO M A Chamberlain, Trustee, KPMG, Peat House, 1 Waterloo Way, Leicester LE1 6LP *Tel* 0116 256 6000
CC NO 1015659   **ESTABLISHED** 1992

■ John Coates Charitable Trust

WHERE FUNDING CAN BE GIVEN UK, mainly southern England.
WHO CAN BENEFIT Institutions either national or of personal or local interest to one or more of the trustees.
WHAT IS FUNDED Preference is given to educational foundations, medical charities (especially those sponsoring research into the causes of ankylosing spondylitis, the rheumatic diseases generally, and non-specific back pain), charities associated with preservation of the environment, and heritage.
WHAT IS NOT FUNDED Grants are given to individuals only in exceptional circumstances.
TYPE OF GRANT Capital and recurring.
RANGE OF GRANTS £250–£15,000.
FINANCES *Year* 2001–02 *Income* £286,311 *Grants* £307,000 *Assets* £8,687,532
TRUSTEES Mrs McGregor; Mrs Kesley; Mrs Lawes; Mrs Youngman.
HOW TO APPLY In writing to the correspondent. Small local charities are visited by the trust.
WHO TO APPLY TO Mrs P L Youngman, Trustee, 40 Stanford Road, London W8 5PZ *Tel* 020 7938 1944 *Fax* 020 7938 2390
CC NO 262057   **ESTABLISHED** 1969

■ Lance Coates Charitable Trust 1969

WHERE FUNDING CAN BE GIVEN UK.
WHO CAN BENEFIT Local activities are often preferred.
WHAT IS FUNDED Promotion of biological and ecological approach to food production with the object of: maintaining soil fertility for future generations; improving health; safeguarding scarce resources; and minimising pollution.
WHAT IS NOT FUNDED No grants to individuals.
SAMPLE GRANTS £20,000 to International Therapeutic Institute (UK) Ltd; £10,000 to Country Trust; £500 to Farm Africa; £350 to Whitechurch PCC; £300 to Country Trust; £150 to Overmoigne PCC for the Holocaust Centre.
FINANCES *Year* 1998–99 *Income* £33,594 *Grants* £31,300 *Assets* £1,174,335
TRUSTEES H L T Coates; E P Serjeant.
HOW TO APPLY In writing to the correspondent.
WHO TO APPLY TO H L T Coates, Trustee, Sanilles, Ctra de Lles, Lles de Cerdanya, 25726 Lerida, Spain *E-mail* ecomundi@teleline.es / info@sanilles.com
CC NO 261521   **ESTABLISHED** 1969

■ Coats Foundation Trust

WHERE FUNDING CAN BE GIVEN UK.
WHO CAN BENEFIT Individuals and organisations benefiting students on textile and thread-related training courses and research.
WHAT IS FUNDED Preference is given, but not specifically restricted, to applicants from textile-related training courses.

TYPE OF GRANT One-off grants, project and research will be considered.

RANGE OF GRANTS £520–£5,000.

FINANCES *Year* 2002–03 *Income* £70,000 *Grants* £50,000 *Assets* £1,500,000

TRUSTEES S Dow; A H Macdiamid; C Healy; Jonathon Lea; Keith Merrifield.

HOW TO APPLY Please write, enclosing a cv and an sae, giving details of circumstances and the nature and amount of funding required. There is no formal application form. Only applicants enclosing an sae will receive a reply.

WHO TO APPLY TO Carolyn Houston, Coats plc, Pacific House, 70 Wellington Street, Glasgow G2 6UB *Tel* 0141 207 6821

CC NO 268735   **ESTABLISHED** 1974

■ Cobb Charity

WHERE FUNDING CAN BE GIVEN UK.

WHO CAN BENEFIT Ecological causes in the UK and related educational and cooperative projects.

WHAT IS FUNDED The encouragement of cooperative values and support of a more sustainable environment with eco-friendly technologies and the promotion of education. The charity will consider: research; food/health; recycling; organic food production; country and traditional skills; cycle routes; and educational projects. Support will be given to: publishing and printing; small enterprises; voluntary and community organisations; and volunteers working in these areas. ·

WHAT IS NOT FUNDED Grants are given to registered charities only, not to individuals. No support for medical organisations, student expeditions or building restorations.

TYPE OF GRANT Capital, core costs, feasibility studies, one-off, project, research, running costs, recurring costs, salaries and start-up costs. Funding is available for more than three years.

RANGE OF GRANTS Usually £750.

SAMPLE GRANTS £750 each to Arid Lands Initiative for tree planting, Countryside Restoration Trust for land for a model traditional orchard, Forum for the Future for training for sustainability, FWAG for sustainable growing methods for farmers, Good Gardeners Association for food and health awareness, Green Light for environmental education, Green Network for lobbying parliament about bad practice in cancer research, Groundwork for the production of an environmental education directory, Soil Association for persuading local authorities to buy sustainable timber, and SPARC for distribution of recyclable materials for schools.

FINANCES *Year* 2002 *Income* £24,000 *Grants* £22,500 *Assets* £470,000

TRUSTEES E Allitt; C Cochran; E Cochran; M Wells.

HOW TO APPLY On an application form available from the correspondent, preferably in September or February. Only smaller charities need apply. No phone calls.

WHO TO APPLY TO Eleanor Allitt, Trustee, 108 Leamington Road, Kenilworth, Warwickshire CV8 2AA

CC NO 248030   **ESTABLISHED** 1964

■ The Cobtree Charity Trust Ltd

WHERE FUNDING CAN BE GIVEN Maidstone and district.

WHO CAN BENEFIT Registered charities.

WHAT IS FUNDED The maintenance and development of Cobtree Manor Estate, and other general charitable purposes by other charities in the Maidstone and district area.

WHAT IS NOT FUNDED No support for individuals, non-registered charities and charities outside Maidstone and district.

TYPE OF GRANT Largely recurrent.

SAMPLE GRANTS Previous beneficiaries included Cheshire Homes, Friends of Kent Churches, Friends of Samaritans, Heart of Kent Hospice, Kent Association for the Blind, Kent Youth Music Association, Linton Scout Group, Maidstone Guides Association, Maidstone Organisation for the Disabled, Mute Park Scout Group, NSPCC, Relate, Salvation Army and several churches. A number of these organisations have received support over several years.

FINANCES *Year* 2001–02 *Income* £127,844

TRUSTEES R J Corben; J Fletcher; L J Martin; R N Hext; D T B Wigg; M W Hardcastle.

HOW TO APPLY In writing to the correspondent. The trustees meet quarterly.

WHO TO APPLY TO G M Davis, Secretary, 5 Salts Avenue, Loose, Maidstone, Kent ME15 0AY *Tel* 01622 743566

CC NO 208455   **ESTABLISHED** 1961

■ The Alfred S Cohen Foundation

WHERE FUNDING CAN BE GIVEN UK.

WHO CAN BENEFIT Small registered charities.

WHAT IS FUNDED General charitable purposes. The annual support of a number of registered charities selected by the settlor.

WHAT IS NOT FUNDED No grants to individuals.

RANGE OF GRANTS £50–£2,920.

SAMPLE GRANTS In 1998–99: £2,920 to RACE; £2,737 to The Oratory Preparatory School; £2,000 each to Norwood Ravenswood and National Racehorse Retirement Programme; £1,304 to The Grayson Jockey Club Foundation; £1,000 each to Maidenhead Synagogue building fund and Cookridge Cancer Centre; £550 to Friends of Alyn; £500 each to Wimbledon and District Synagogue and Roy Castle Foundation.

FINANCES *Year* 2001–02 *Income* £30,271

TRUSTEES P C Cohen.

HOW TO APPLY In writing to the correspondent.

WHO TO APPLY TO P C Cohen, Trustee, The Brass Bell, Warren Road, Kingston-upon-Thames KT2 7HR *Tel* 020 8949 2435

CC NO 273879   **ESTABLISHED** 1977

■ The Andrew Cohen Charitable Trust

WHERE FUNDING CAN BE GIVEN UK.

WHO CAN BENEFIT Registered charities.

WHAT IS FUNDED General charitable purposes, particularly Jewish causes.

SAMPLE GRANTS Grants have previously been given to JIA, Oxford University L'Chaim Society, Scope Jewish Trust and Imperial Cancer Research.

FINANCES *Year* 2001–02 *Income* £6,500 *Grants* £90,000 *Assets* £200,000

TRUSTEES Andrew L Cohen; Wendy P Cohen.

HOW TO APPLY The trust does not respond to unsolicited applications. It states that its funds are fully committed for the next couple of years and that generally grants are made to

Think carefully about every application. Is it justified?

391

organisations that have been previously supported. New applications are unlikely to be successful.

WHO TO APPLY TO Mr & Mrs Cohen, c/o Wood Hall Securities Ltd, Wood Hall Lane, Shenley, Hertfordshire WD7 9AA *Tel* 01923 289999 *E-mail* alc@woodhall.com

CC NO 1033283   **ESTABLISHED** 1994

■ The Denise Cohen Charitable Trust

WHERE FUNDING CAN BE GIVEN UK.

WHO CAN BENEFIT Charities benefiting children and older people, actors and entertainment professionals, musicians, textile workers and designers, students, writers and poets, at risk groups, people who are disadvantaged by poverty and socially isolated people.

WHAT IS FUNDED Education; health and welfare of older people, infirm people and children; encouragement of the arts and grants to major UK centres for the performing arts.

SAMPLE GRANTS £10,000 to Norwood Ravenswood Foundation; £8,000 to Royal Opera House Trust; £5,500 to Nightingale House; £2,000 to Donmar; £1,500 to National Gallery Trust; £1,300 to Jewish Care; £1,200 each to Ben Gurion University Foundation, Almedia Theatre Company and Western Marble Arch Synagogue; £1,100 to British EMUNAH Child Resettlement Fund; £1,000 each to Imperial Cancer Research Fund, British Techmon Society, Macmillan Cancer Relief, Royal Academy Exhibition Patrons Group and Royal National Theatre Board.

FINANCES *Year* 2000–01 *Income* £48,222 *Grants* £60,441 *Assets* £902,520

TRUSTEES Mrs Denise Cohen; M D Paisner; Sara Cohen.

HOW TO APPLY In writing to the correspondent.

WHO TO APPLY TO Martin D Paisner, Trustee, Berwin Leighton & Paisner, Bouverie House, 154 Fleet Street, London EC4A 2JD *Tel* 020 7353 0299 *Fax* 020 7583 4897 *E-mail* martin.paisner@blplaw.com

CC NO 276439   **ESTABLISHED** 1977

■ The Vivienne & Samuel Cohen Charitable Trust

WHERE FUNDING CAN BE GIVEN UK and Israel.

WHO CAN BENEFIT Jewish people, people who are disabled, sick, elderly and people who are disadvantaged by poverty. Research workers especially medical.

WHAT IS FUNDED General charitable purposes in Israel and the UK, mainly education, medical causes including research and welfare including student welfare. Particular emphasis is given to Jewish causes.

WHAT IS NOT FUNDED No grants to individuals.

RANGE OF GRANTS £50–£25,000.

SAMPLE GRANTS £75,000 to London School of Jewish Studies; £31,000 to Maaleh Nievo Synagogue; £6,000 to Be'er Hatarah School; £5,000 each to Maaleh Hatorah School and Variety Club; £3,500 to B'Nei B'Rith; £2,000 to Machanim. Smaller grants totalled £57,000.

FINANCES *Year* 2000–01 *Income* £104,102 *Grants* £180,000 *Assets* £2,415,208

TRUSTEES Dr Vivienne Cohen; M Y Ben-Gershon; G Cohen; D H J Cohen; J S Lauffer.

HOW TO APPLY In writing only, to the correspondent.

WHO TO APPLY TO Dr Vivienne Cohen, Trustee, 9 Heathcroft, Hampstead Way, London NW11 7HH

CC NO 255496   **ESTABLISHED** 1965

■ Col-Reno Ltd

WHERE FUNDING CAN BE GIVEN UK, Israel, USA.

WHO CAN BENEFIT Religious and educational institutions benefiting children, young adults, students and Jewish people.

WHAT IS FUNDED Jewish religion and education.

RANGE OF GRANTS £180–£15,000.

SAMPLE GRANTS In 1997–98: £20,000 to Agudas Yisroel of California; £8,100 to JSSM; £6,600 to SOFOT for distribution to Jewish and general charities; £4,000 to Friends of Yeshivas Beis Yisroel.

FINANCES *Year* 2001–02 *Income* £77,699

TRUSTEES M H Stern; A E Stern; Mrs C Stern.

HOW TO APPLY In writing to the correspondent.

WHO TO APPLY TO Mrs C Stern, Trustee, 15 Shirehall Gardens, Hendon, London NW4 2QT *Tel* 020 8202 7013

CC NO 274896   **ESTABLISHED** 1977

■ The Colchester Catalyst Charity

WHERE FUNDING CAN BE GIVEN North east Essex.

WHO CAN BENEFIT Health organisations.

WHAT IS FUNDED Provision of support by direct contributions to health organisations for specific and well-designed projects in order to improve healthcare.

WHAT IS NOT FUNDED No support for general funding, staff or running costs (usually). Retrospective funding is not considered.

TYPE OF GRANT One-off.

RANGE OF GRANTS £95–£27,000.

FINANCES *Year* 1999–2000 *Income* £341,000 *Grants* £503,000 *Assets* £8,900,000

TRUSTEES Director: C F Pertwee, Chairman; R W Whybrow; Dr R W Griffin; A H Frost; P W E Fitt; Dr E Hall; C Hayward.

HOW TO APPLY In writing to the correspondent.

WHO TO APPLY TO P W Fitt, 7 Coast Road, West Mersea, Colchester CO5 8QE

CC NO 228352   **ESTABLISHED** 1959

■ The Colchester & Tendring Community Trust

WHERE FUNDING CAN BE GIVEN Colchester borough and Tendring district only.

WHO CAN BENEFIT Voluntary organisations.

WHAT IS FUNDED General charitable purposes.

WHAT IS NOT FUNDED No grants to individuals.

TYPE OF GRANT One-off for core, capital and project costs.

RANGE OF GRANTS £50–£1,000. Average grant £200–£300.

FINANCES *Year* 2001–02 *Income* £60,465 *Grants* £49,522 *Assets* £51,592

TRUSTEES D Wood; J C Garnett; S A Cuthew; M Hopkins; K Scott; B Davenport; R Roberts; W E Sandford; G A Wallington-Hayes; R Finch; J Nicholls.

HOW TO APPLY On a form available from the correspondent. Applications are considered half yearly; closing dates 30 April and 31 October.

WHO TO APPLY TO G Posner, Director, Colchester Carers Centre, 25 Oaks Drive, Colchester CO3 3PR *Tel* 01206 500443 *Fax* 01206 500446

CC NO 803193   **ESTABLISHED** 1989

■ John Coldman Charitable Trust

WHERE FUNDING CAN BE GIVEN UK, with a preference for Edenbridge in Kent.

WHO CAN BENEFIT Registered charities.

WHAT IS FUNDED General charitable purposes, particularly community and Christian groups and UK organisations whose work benefits the community such as children's and medical charities.

RANGE OF GRANTS £250 upwards.

SAMPLE GRANTS Previous beneficiaries included British Liver Trust, Care and Action for Children with Handicaps, Croydon Colorectal Cancer Appeal, Cypress Junior School, League of Friends – Edenbridge Hospital, Marie Curie Cancer Care, NSPCC, Oasis Trust India and St Peter's Church – Hever.

FINANCES *Year* 2001–02 *Income* £384,796

TRUSTEES D J Coldman; G E Coldman; C J Warner.

OTHER INFORMATION This trust appaers to have grown significantly since the last edition of this guide (income in 2000–01 was £72,777).

HOW TO APPLY In writing to the correspondent.

WHO TO APPLY TO D Coldman, Polebrook, Hever, Edenbridge, Kent TN8 7NJ *Tel* 020 7578 7000

CC NO 1050110   **ESTABLISHED** 1995

■ The Cole Charitable Trust

WHERE FUNDING CAN BE GIVEN Greater Birmingham, Kent and Cambridge.

WHO CAN BENEFIT Individuals, and local community projects or local branches of larger organisations benefiting people who are refugees and people who are disadvantaged by poverty or homeless.

WHAT IS FUNDED The trust supports housing/homelessness, health, community development, opportunities for young people, self-help, promotion of improved quality of life and personal and community empowerment, particularly in the Greater Birmingham area.

WHAT IS NOT FUNDED No grants for national organisations, religion, education, animal welfare, or to individuals not backed by a charity.

TYPE OF GRANT Small capital or project grants; normally one-off.

RANGE OF GRANTS £300–£2,000; mostly £300 or £500.

SAMPLE GRANTS £2,000 each to Rotary Club of Birmingham, CAMFED and Adoption UK Manor Farm; £1,700 to Daneford Trust; £1,500 to Life Education Centre; £1,200 to Raleigh International; £1,000 each to Medical Foundation for the Care of Victims of Torture, Bangladesh Community Development, Birmingham Settlement and Christians Together in Dover.

FINANCES *Year* 2001–02 *Income* £44,000 *Grants* £43,000 *Assets* £1,247,000

TRUSTEES Dr T J Cole; G N Cole; Dr J G Cole; Mrs D M Newton; T E C Cole; A J Buchan.

HOW TO APPLY In writing to the correspondent, and must include recent annual accounts. An sae should not be sent. Three meetings per year; deadlines for applications are mid-April, August and December.

WHO TO APPLY TO The Administrator, PO Box 51, Cambridge CB3 9QL *Tel* 01223 312374 *Fax* 01223 312374

CC NO 264033   **ESTABLISHED** 1972

■ The Colefax Charitable Trust

WHERE FUNDING CAN BE GIVEN Berkshire and Hampshire.

WHO CAN BENEFIT Registered charities.

WHAT IS FUNDED The trust supports charities based in Berkshire and Hampshire, with a preference for the former.

RANGE OF GRANTS £1,000–£15,000

SAMPLE GRANTS In 1999–2000: £15,000 to Newbury Spring Festival; £10,000 each to St Georges Community Hall and Abbeyfield House; £8,000 to Blue Sky Appeal; £7,000 to Multiple Sclerosis Therapy Centre; £5,000 to The Friday People; £4,000 to NSPCC; £3,000 each to Kennet School and Naomi House; £1,000 each to Brainwave, Wessex Children's Hospital and Stroke Care.

FINANCES *Year* 2001–02 *Income* £226,989

TRUSTEES J E Heath; H J Krohn.

HOW TO APPLY In writing to the correspondent.

WHO TO APPLY TO Hans J Krohn, Trustee, Grange Farm House, Grange Farm, Shaw, Nr Newbury, Berkshire RG14 2TF *Tel* 01635 200968

CC NO 1017285   **ESTABLISHED** 1993

■ The John & Freda Coleman Charitable Trust

WHERE FUNDING CAN BE GIVEN Surrey and Hampshire.

WHO CAN BENEFIT Education and training centres benefiting children, young adults, older people, and people who are disabled or disadvantaged by poverty.

WHAT IS FUNDED Training young people to equip them with practical, manual skills and relevant technical knowledge in order to prepare them for employment. Particularly charities working in the fields of economic regeneration; job creation; small enterprises; IT training; training for work; vocational training; engineering research and research into science and technology.

WHAT IS NOT FUNDED No grants are made to students.

TYPE OF GRANT Loans not given. Grants to 'kick start' relevant projects, capital costs other than buildings and core costs are all considered. Recurrent grants are given.

RANGE OF GRANTS £250 to over £20,000.

SAMPLE GRANTS £20,000 to RNIB; £10,000 each to Lord Mayor Treloars Trust, Queen Elizabeth College and Frensham Sailability.

FINANCES *Year* 2000–01 *Income* £74,000 *Grants* £64,000 *Assets* £1,100,000

TRUSTEES P B Spark; Mrs F M K Coleman; L P Fernandez; A J Coleman; P H Coleman; B R Coleman.

OTHER INFORMATION The trust always takes an active interest in the activities of those helped.

HOW TO APPLY In writing to the correspondent. Telephone calls are not welcome.

WHO TO APPLY TO John Round, Administrator, Tanglewood, Bullbeggars Lane, Woking, Surrey GU21 4SH *Tel* 01483 762289 *Fax* 01483 762289 *E-mail* roundjohnround@aol.com

CC NO 278223   **ESTABLISHED** 1979

■ The College Estate Charity

WHERE FUNDING CAN BE GIVEN The town of Stratford-upon-Avon.

WHAT IS FUNDED General charitable purposes to benefit the people of Stratford-upon Avon.

WHAT IS NOT FUNDED Very few grants are made to individuals; no education grants are made to individuals.

TYPE OF GRANT One-off and recurring costs will be considered.

SAMPLE GRANTS In 1996: £46,264 to 50th Anniversary World War II Celebrations; £38,895 for bus passes; £36,001 for educational grants; £26,928 for special grants; £26,215 for grants to local organisations; £22,994 for Christmas lighting and trees; £19,500 to Stratford in Bloom; £19,000 to Stratford-upon-Avon Festival and Carnival; £8,000 to Minor Injuries Unit; £7,000 to Baptist Church.

FINANCES *Year* 2000–01 *Income* £1,341,258

HOW TO APPLY In writing to the correspondent. Applications are considered once a year only at the end of May or early June, and must be on the official application form.

WHO TO APPLY TO Richard Eggington, Town Clerk, Stratford-upon-Avon Town Council, 14 Rother Street, Stratford-upon-Avon CV37 6LU *Tel* 01789 269332 *Fax* 01789 297072 *E-mail* richardeggington@stratfordtowntrust.co.uk

CC NO 217485   **ESTABLISHED** 1911

■ The George Henry Collins Charity

WHERE FUNDING CAN BE GIVEN Within a 50-mile radius of Birmingham.

WHO CAN BENEFIT Local charities and local branches of registered national charities in Birmingham benefiting older people, the socially isolated, or people who are ill.

WHAT IS FUNDED Wide, but the relief of illness, infirmity, old age or loneliness take preference. Trustees will consider donating one-tenth of annual income to charities for use overseas.

WHAT IS NOT FUNDED No grants to individuals.

TYPE OF GRANT One-off.

RANGE OF GRANTS £100–£1,000.

SAMPLE GRANTS £2,000 to Symphony Hall; £1,000 to Castle Bromwich Hall Gardens Trust; £500 each to Acorns Children's Hospice Trust, Birmingham Bach Choir, Birmingham City Mission, Birmingham Settlement, Blakesley Hall – Birmingham, Carrs Lane Counselling Service, Dodford Children's Holiday Farm, Middlemore Homes, MSA for Midland People with Disabilities and St Martins' in the Bullring.

FINANCES *Year* 1999–2000 *Income* £91,000 *Grants* £43,000 *Assets* £1,400,000

TRUSTEES A R Collins, Chair; Mrs E A Davies; A A Waters; M S Hansell; P Coggan; R Otto.

HOW TO APPLY In writing to the joint correspondents, David L Turfrey and Lucy Chatt. The trustees meet in March, July and November.

WHO TO APPLY TO David L Turfrey, c/o Martineau Johnson, St Philips House, St Philips Place, Birmingham B3 2PP *Tel* 0121 200 3300

CC NO 212268   **ESTABLISHED** 1959

■ The Norman Collinson Charitable Trust

WHERE FUNDING CAN BE GIVEN York and district.

WHO CAN BENEFIT Young people; people who are aged, infirm or disabled; or individuals or organisations who provide help for such people. Also considered are: at risk groups; people disadvantaged by poverty; carers; homeless people and victims of abuse.

WHAT IS FUNDED This trust will consider funding: infrastructure and development; charity or voluntary bodies; Christian outreach; arts, culture and recreation; health; and community services. Community centres, village halls, playgrounds and other charitable purposes are also considered.

WHAT IS NOT FUNDED The trustees have found it necessary to place a geographical restriction and confine grants to helping people in York and district. The trust does, however, make a limited number of grants to national charities, particularly where they can demonstrate the beneficiaries reside in the York area. No grants for the repair or maintenance of buildings unless such work would be of direct benefit to people meeting the trust's criteria.

TYPE OF GRANT Core costs, one-off, project and running costs are funded for up to one year. The trust does not enter into ongoing commitments. Grants are reconsidered each year.

RANGE OF GRANTS No upper or lower limit.

SAMPLE GRANTS £5,300 to One Parent Families; £2,000 each to Rawcliffe Recreational Association, Riding Lights Theatre Company, St Michael le Belfry for its church hall extension and York Scout Association.

FINANCES *Year* 2000 *Income* £72,285 *Grants* £147,000 *Assets* £1,600,000

TRUSTEES J M Saville, Chair; B Catton; F E Dennis; D C Fotherington; D B Holman.

HOW TO APPLY In writing to the correspondent. Applications from individuals should be through recognised agencies. Applications from organisations should give details of their officers, recent accounts and/or budget and information on how any grant would be used. The trustees meet monthly to consider applications, normally on the second Tuesday of the month. Deadline is seven days before the meeting.

WHO TO APPLY TO Dianne Hepworth, Clerk, 30 Main Street, Wetwang, Driffield, East Yorkshire YO25 9XJ *Tel* 01377 236262 *Fax* 01377 236175

CC NO 277325   **ESTABLISHED** 1979

■ The E Alec Colman Charitable Fund Ltd

WHERE FUNDING CAN BE GIVEN UK and Israel.

WHO CAN BENEFIT Organisations benefiting children, young adults, students, teachers and governesses. Support is given to people disadvantaged by poverty and to the clergy. Support may also be given to people of various religions and particular favour is given to Jewish people.

WHAT IS FUNDED Relief of poverty; advancement of education; and advancement of religion. The trust aims to pinpoint areas of interest and take the initiative in funding organisations working in these fields.

WHAT IS NOT FUNDED No grants to individuals.

TYPE OF GRANT Recurring.

RANGE OF GRANTS £20–£20,000; mostly under £200.

SAMPLE GRANTS £10,100 to Jewish Care; £6,100 to JNF Charitable Trust; £1,800 to Diana Princess of Wales Children's Hospital, Birmingham; £1,100 each to Royal Star and Garter Home and Fight For Sight; £1,000 each to Birmingham Hebrew Congregation and Salvation Army India Earthquake Appeal.

FINANCES *Year* 2000–01 *Income* £59,000 *Grants* £26,000 *Assets* £1,000,000

TRUSTEES The Council of Management: S H Colman; Mrs E A Colman; M Harris.

HOW TO APPLY In writing to the correspondent; however, the trust has stated that new beneficiaries are only considered in exceptional circumstances.

WHO TO APPLY TO A N Carless, Secretary, 6–10 South Street, Harborne, Birmingham B17 0DB *Tel* 0121 427 7818
CC NO 243817   ESTABLISHED 1965

■ The Sir Jeremiah Colman Gift Trust

WHERE FUNDING CAN BE GIVEN UK, with a preference for Hampshire, especially Basingstoke.
WHO CAN BENEFIT Projects with well-established needs for support; the trust has already established priority beneficiaries.
WHAT IS FUNDED Advancement of education and literary scientific knowledge; moral and social improvement of people; maintenance of churches of the Church of England and gifts and offerings to the churches; financial assistance to past and present employees/members of Sir Jeremiah Colman at Gatton Park or other institutions associated with Sir Jeremiah Colman.
WHAT IS NOT FUNDED Grants are not made to individuals requiring support for personal education, or to individual families for welfare purposes.
SAMPLE GRANTS £5,000 to Ark Facility; £3,000 to The Margaret Mee Fellowship Programme; £2,500 each to All Saints Church Centre in Weston, Judd School Development Fund, Loddon Partnership, Norwich Cathedral, The Anvil, Basingstoke Sports Centre, Gilbert White's House and Oates Museum, and Mercey Ships.
FINANCES *Year* 2001–02 *Income* £92,880 *Grants* £106,564 *Assets* £2,132,953
TRUSTEES Sir Michael Colman; Lady Judith Colman; Oliver J Colman; Cynthia Colman; Jeremiah M Colman.
HOW TO APPLY 'The funds of the trust are fully committed and any unsolicited applications are most unlikely to be successful.'
WHO TO APPLY TO Sir Michael Colman, Trustee, Malshanger, Basingstoke, Hampshire RG23 7EY
CC NO 229553   ESTABLISHED 1920

■ The Colt Foundation

WHERE FUNDING CAN BE GIVEN UK.
WHO CAN BENEFIT Universities and research establishments benefiting research workers and students taking higher degrees.
WHAT IS FUNDED Grants are made for research projects at universities and other independent research institutions into occupational and environmental health.
WHAT IS NOT FUNDED Grants are not made for the general funds of another charity or projects overseas.
TYPE OF GRANT Research, project.
RANGE OF GRANTS £20,000–£100,000.
SAMPLE GRANTS £85,769 to National Heart and Lung Institute; £69,499 to Napier University; £32,805 to Hearing Research Trust; £31,036 to Silsoe Research Institute; £29,832 to University of Manchester; £29,274 to Institute of Occupational Health; £25,000 to University of Edinburgh; £24,247 to University of Southampton; £15,230 to British Occupational Health Research Foundation; £8,487 to St George's Hospital Medical School. Please note that these figures are for payments actually made in 2001 against multi-year awards.
FINANCES *Year* 2001 *Income* £352,442 *Grants* £502,449 *Assets* £11,297,047

TRUSTEES Mrs Patricia Lebus, Chair; Timothy Ault; Prof. David Coggon; Mrs Clare Gilchrist; Ms Natasha Lebus; Walter McD Morison; Alan O'Hea; Jerome O'Hea; Juliette O'Hea; Peter O'Hea. Prof. D Denison and Prof. A J Newman Taylor act as scientific advisors.
HOW TO APPLY In writing to the correspondent. Trustees meet in May and November and applications may be submitted at any time.
WHO TO APPLY TO Mrs Jacqueline Douglas, New Lane, Havant, Hampshire PO9 2LY *Tel* 023 9249 1400 *Fax* 023 9249 1363 *E-mail* jackie.douglas@uk.coltgroup.com *Website* www.coltfoundation.org.uk
CC NO 277189   ESTABLISHED 1978

■ Sir James Colyer-Fergusson's Charitable Trust

WHERE FUNDING CAN BE GIVEN Kent.
WHO CAN BENEFIT Charities and churches in Kent aiming to improve quality of life, tackle poverty, social isolation or exclusion and protect the natural resources and heritage of the local areas for their inhabitants.
WHAT IS FUNDED Current priority areas are projects that involve the utilisation of church buildings or other church resources for the wider community and can demonstrate a practical need; projects that involve the preservation of the natural environment and promote access to these resources; projects that are innovative or developmental and aim to tackle social isolation, exclusion or poverty as they affect the community; and projects that will use the arts to provide the community with a new creative experience or increase access to the arts in locations where access is limited. Extra consideration will be given to projects that encourage self-help; involve users in their management; have built-in evaluation procedures; and will use funds to lever funding from other sources.
WHAT IS NOT FUNDED No grants to churches and charities outside Kent. No grants to individuals or to the following: animal welfare charities; individuals directly; research (except practical research designed to benefit the local community directly); hospitals or schools; political activities; commercial ventures or publications; the purchase of vehicles including minibuses; overseas travel or holidays; retrospective grants or loans; direct replacement of statutory funding or activities that are primarily the responsibility of central or local government; large capital, endowment or widely distributed appeals; applications from churches and charities outside Kent.
TYPE OF GRANT One-off, recurring, capital, core, running and start-up costs will all be considered, as will salaries, buildings, project and research costs. Funding may be given for up to two years.
RANGE OF GRANTS £500–£10,000 and some larger one-off grants.
SAMPLE GRANTS £70,000 to Holy Trinity Church, Margate towards the cost of employing a community development worker; £50,000 to Maidstone YMCA towards a furniture and employment project; £30,000 to Waterside Centre, Gravesend towards the cost of a play therapist; £25,000 to Home Start, Maidstone for providing a rapid response to families with young children needing assistance; £15,000 to Buckmore Park Scout Centre in Chatham towards creating a nature reserve; £10,000 to Canterbury Symphony Orchestra;

£5,000 each to Youthnet UK for web access for disadvantaged young people, Museum of Kent for a multimedia presentation and Trinity Church to improve facilities for community use.

FINANCES *Year* 2001–02 *Grants* £480,000 *Assets* £18,000,000

TRUSTEES Jonathan Monckton; Nicholas Fisher; Simon Buxton; Robert North; Ruth Murphy.

HOW TO APPLY In 2003 the trust is piloting an online application process. During this year applications will be accepted only via the trust's website. Applicants who are not able to use the internet for any reason should contact the trust to make alternative arrangements.

WHO TO APPLY TO Jacqueline Rae, Suite 232–233, Friars House, 157–168 Blackfriars Road, London SE1 8EZ *Tel* 020 7620 1209 *E-mail* jrae@issimo.co.uk *Website* www.colyer-fergusson.org.uk

CC NO 258958   **ESTABLISHED** 1969

■ Comic Relief

WHERE FUNDING CAN BE GIVEN UK and Africa.

WHO CAN BENEFIT UK registered charities; voluntary organisations; and self-help groups.

WHAT IS FUNDED Two-thirds of all money is spent in Africa on long-term development helping people affected by conflict; women and girls; pastoralists; people living in towns and cities; people with disabilities; and people affected by HIV and AIDS. A third is spent in the UK, with priorities from April 2001 until the guidelines for the next cycle are available in May 2003 being fighting for justice; supporting young people; strengthening services – refugees and asylum seekers, and domestic violence; supporting communities. The aims of the UK programme are to: reach the poorest and most disadvantaged people; support people in finding solutions to the problems they face; give a voice to groups who face discrimination so that their views and voices are heard; support groups who encourage users to take part in developing and running their services, or who can show they want to move towards users controlling the service; increase public awareness of the needs, hopes and rights of the disadvantaged people supported; and support work which influences policy at national, regional and local levels.

WHAT IS NOT FUNDED In general, the charity does not fund the following (for UK grants): academic research; general appeals; schools, colleges and hospitals; individuals; promoting religion; trips abroad, holidays and outings; services run by statutory or public authorities; medical research or equipment; minibuses; sporting activities.

TYPE OF GRANT Capital or revenue. One-off or spread over up to three years.

RANGE OF GRANTS UK: Small Grants Programme up to £5,000; Large Grants Programme up to £25,000 each year for up to three years. Africa: up to £1,000,000 over five years.

SAMPLE GRANTS £90,000 over three years to The rainbow Project, Youthreach Greenwich and Newcastle Women's Aid; £20,000 over three years to The Jericho Project; £5,000 to Brent Somali Community Group.

FINANCES *Year* 2001 *Income* £66,666,443 *Grants* £19,038,596 *Assets* £65,766,128

TRUSTEES Peter Benett-Jones, Chair; Richard Curtis; Emma Freud; Matthew Freud; Mike Harris; Lenny Henry; Colin Howes; Melinda Letts; Claudia Lloyd; Laurence Newman; Eric Nicoli; J K Rowling; Albert Tucker; Nalini Varma.

UK grants committee: Nalini Varma, Chair; Dr Dorothy Black; Louise Casey; Jim Deery; Fiona Ellis; Nikhil Gomes; Frances Hasler; David Johnson; Anthony Kendall; Nic Millington; Hannah Murdock; Alison Norman; Saverimuthu Stanislaus; Richard Wood; Zaya Yeebo.

PUBLICATIONS *UK and Africa Grants Programmes*, also available in big print, audiotape and braille.

HOW TO APPLY For details of the latest grant programmes and application procedures, please refer to the website or contact the UK Grants Team at the address belwo.

WHO TO APPLY TO The UK Grants Team, 5th Floor, 89 Albert Embankment, London SE1 7TP *Tel* 020 7820 5555 *Minicom* 020 7820 5570 *Website* www.comicrelief.org.uk

CC NO 326568   **ESTABLISHED** 1985

■ The Comino Foundation

WHERE FUNDING CAN BE GIVEN UK.

WHO CAN BENEFIT Organisations benefiting young adults and academics.

WHAT IS FUNDED Support of educational activities which encourage and enable individuals and groups to motivate and empower themselves; progressively develop their potential for the benefit of themselves and others; and encourage a culture which affirms and celebrates both achievement and responsible practice in industry and commerce.

WHAT IS NOT FUNDED No grants to individuals or general appeals.

TYPE OF GRANT One-off.

RANGE OF GRANTS £1,500–£30,400.

SAMPLE GRANTS £30,400 each to King Alfred's College – Winchester, Liverpool John Moores University, Sheffield Hallam University, University of Warwick, Wigan Borough Partnership, and Wolverhampton Univeristy; £30,000 to Institute for Global Ethics UK Trust.

FINANCES *Year* 2001–02 *Income* £266,646 *Grants* £293,977 *Assets* £6,508,476

TRUSTEES Anna Comino-Jones; J A C Darbyshire; Dr W Eric Duckworth; Prof. John Tomlinson; Mike Tomlinson; Simon Bailey; J E Slater.

HOW TO APPLY By letter, including full details of proposed project and finances. There is no formal application form. Applications are considered at four formal meetings of the trustees each year.

WHO TO APPLY TO A C Roberts, Administrator, 29 Hollow Way Lane, Amersham, Buckinghamshire HP6 6DJ *Tel* 01494 722595 *E-mail* enquire@cominofoundation.org.uk *Website* www.cominofoundation.org.uk

CC NO 312875   **ESTABLISHED** 1971

■ Commonwealth Relations Trust

WHERE FUNDING CAN BE GIVEN Developing Commonwealth countries. Priority to eastern and southern Africa.

WHO CAN BENEFIT UK non-governmental organisations and education providers benefiting children; young adults and older people; legal professionals; medical professionals, nurses and doctors; students; scientists; teachers and governesses; people disadvantaged by poverty; people who are disabled; and refugees.

WHAT IS FUNDED The trust contributes towards a Commonwealth Programme with Nuffield Foundation. The programme funds advanced education and training schemes which support change in developing Commonwealth countries, focusing on education; science; access to

justice; health; child protection; legal services; professional bodies; and advice and information. During 2000 the focus was on southern and eastern Africa. Four projects were supported with grants over a five-year period.
WHAT IS NOT FUNDED No grants to individuals. No grants for formal qualifications. No grants for attendance at conferences. No contributions to appeals.
TYPE OF GRANT Project costs for up to five years.
RANGE OF GRANTS Up to £250,000.
SAMPLE GRANTS Each grant spread over five years: £250,000 to Department of Forensic Medicine, University of Dundee for medico-legal training and education in the Gender and Child project in South Africa; £250,000 to University College London/Royal Free and University College Medical School for a professional development programme for health professionals in Tanzania; £212,000 to International Extention College to improve teacher education through human resource development at ITEK, Uganda; £174,000 to Tropical Health and Education Trust to establish a sustainable training programme in trauma management in Malawi.
FINANCES *Year* 2000–05 *Income* £274,451 *Grants* £885,000 *Assets* £7,000
TRUSTEES Dr Onora O'Neill; Prof. Genevra Richardson; Sir John Banham; Prof. Sir Michael Rutter; Mrs Anne Sofer; Prof. A B Atkinson.
OTHER INFORMATION Each grant.is for the five-year period 2000–05.
HOW TO APPLY The trust states: 'Interested organisations should first approach by telephone or short enquiry letter. Currently applications are considered on a competitive basis every two years but this may be reviewed. Guidelines, including the application timetable will be available prior to each grant-making round'.
WHO TO APPLY TO Anthony Tomei, Nuffield Foundation Commonwealth Programme, 28 Bedford Square, London WC1B 3EG *Tel* 020 7631 0566 *E-mail* atomei@nuffieldfoundation.org *Website* www.nuffieldfoundation.org
CC NO 205551   **ESTABLISHED** 1937

....

■ The Community Foundation for Calderdale

WHERE FUNDING CAN BE GIVEN Calderdale and, to a much lesser extent, west Yorkshire.
WHO CAN BENEFIT Individuals and organisations.
WHAT IS FUNDED Grants are made to families and individuals in need and to community groups and voluntary organisations promoting the arts, education, leisure activities, environmental awareness and support for disabled or disadvantaged people.
WHAT IS NOT FUNDED The foundation will not fund the promotion of political activity or the direct promotion of religious activity. It will not fund projects or activities which replace statutory funding.
TYPE OF GRANT Revenue, capital, one-off.
RANGE OF GRANTS £150–£2,500.
SAMPLE GRANTS £2,000 each to Dodnazr Community Association (towards their summer playscheme) and Stonham Housing Association (for furniture packs and kitchen and bedding packs); £670 to Stainland Playgroup (for educational play equipment); £300 to Calder Valley Single Parents Group (towards weekend breaks for parents and children).
FINANCES *Year* 2001–02 *Grants* £1,300,000

TRUSTEES Les Lawson, Chair; Mohamed Aslam; Malcolm Kielty; Ronika Cunningham; Ian Firth; Mike Payne; Martin Olive; Kate Thornton; Brenda Hodgson; Cllr Peter Coles; Lynda Hanson; Ingrid Holdsworth; Alison Roberts; Rose Wheeler; David Roper; Carol Stevenson.
HOW TO APPLY There is a single initial application process for all grants (except those from the Local Network Fund). Application forms and guidelines are available from the foundation and its website.
WHO TO APPLY TO Christine Harris, Director, Room 158, Dean Clough, Halifax, West Yorkshire HX3 5AX *Tel* 01422 349 700 *Website* www.ccfound.co.uk
CC NO 1002722   **ESTABLISHED** 1991

....

■ The Community Foundation for Greater Manchester

WHERE FUNDING CAN BE GIVEN The ten boroughs of Greater Manchester, i.e. Bolton, Bury, Manchester, Oldham, Rochdale, Salford, Stockport, Tameside, Trafford and Wigan.
WHO CAN BENEFIT Small local projects, new and established organisations and innovative projects benefiting children, young adults and older people, at risk groups, and people who are disabled, disadvantaged by poverty or socially isolated.
WHAT IS FUNDED Health; welfare; education; people with disabilities; older people; youth and children. Other charitable purposes will be considered.
WHAT IS NOT FUNDED The foundation will not support the following: requests for help from organisations outside Greater Manchester; capital building projects; academic research; grants to individuals (except Millenium Awards); overseas travel; medical research and equipment; sponsorship and fundraising events; contributions to major/large/general appeals; the substitution of statutory funding; proposals that fall within the remit of statutory funders; political groups for political purposes; religious groups for religious purposes; projects which have already taken place; organisations trading for profit; organisations intending to redistribute our grant.
TYPE OF GRANT One-off; project. Start-up costs will be considered.
RANGE OF GRANTS Up to £1,000.
FINANCES *Year* 2001–02 *Grants* £1,400,000
TRUSTEES J Sandford; C Smith; I Wicks; W Risby; E Polding; J Buckley; J Hughes Lundy; M Bashir; M Cunningham; A Downie; G Johnson; T Manion; Melinda Beckett-Hughes; A Chaudry; C Hirst; E Bush.
PUBLICATIONS Guidelines; information packs.
HOW TO APPLY Application packs, which include the foundation's grants criteria and help notes on completing the application, are available from the foundation's office. You make a single application to the Community Foundation using the form. Each application is matched to the most appropriate fund and submitted for consideration. If you are applying for a grant for the first time, or if you would like advice before making an application, call the foundation on 061 214 0940. Applications will only be accepted if submitted on the foundation's application form. All sections of the form must be completed even if the information is supplied in the form of a report, leaflet and so on. We prefer not to receive applications by fax; so completed forms should be returned to us by

post. The decision of the foundation's trustees is final and no discussion will be entered into. We will, however, try to provide helpful feedback to both successful and unsuccessful applicants. Applicants are requested to provide copies of the constitution, and a copy of the latest, relevant annual accounts and the last two bank statements with their applications. We aim to give you an answer to your application as soon as possible, almost always within three months but please don't hold us to this literally. The exact time will often depend on a number of factors and not just when the appropriate committee next meets. One of our grants administrators may contact you for further information or to discuss your application with you. The Community Foundation operate a 24-hour grant line where application forms can be obtained at any time. The grant line telephone number is 0161 214 0951.

WHO TO APPLY TO Julie Langford, Grants Manager, 1st Floor, Beswick House, Beswick Row, Manchester M4 4LA *Tel* 0161 214 0944 *Website* www.communityfoundation.co.uk
CC NO 1017504   **ESTABLISHED** 1993

....

■ **The Community Foundation for Northern Ireland** (formerly the Northern Ireland Voluntary Trust)

WHERE FUNDING CAN BE GIVEN Northern Ireland and the six border counties of the Republic of Ireland.
WHO CAN BENEFIT Community groups, self-help organisations and voluntary organisations benefiting young adults, women, and unemployed people.
WHAT IS FUNDED Priority areas: peace-building; community development; social justice; cross-border development; active citizenship; social inclusion.
WHAT IS NOT FUNDED Individuals; ongoing running costs of organisations; major capital building programmes; travel; vehicles; holiday schemes; play groups; sports activities; housing associations; promotion of religion; paying off debts; retrospective grants; general appeals. Neither will the trust fund projects where there is a statutory responsibility or respond to cutbacks in statutory funding.
TYPE OF GRANT One-off.
RANGE OF GRANTS £100–£150,000.
FINANCES *Year* 2001–02 *Grants* £4,658,000
TRUSTEES Mary Black, Chair; Vivienne Anderson; Maureen Armstrong; Baroness May Blood; Mark Conway; Barney Devine; Sammy Douglas; Mari Fitzduff; Jim Flynn; Noreen Kearney; Philip McDonagh; Mike Mills; Angela Paisley; Ben Wilson.
PUBLICATIONS Annual report and accounts; guidelines for grant seekers.
HOW TO APPLY Most of the grant programmes (excluding Peace II) do not have a set application form. Instead applicants should write a letter of request to the correspondent, who will forward it to the appropriate grants officer. This letter should detail the name and address of your group and the lead contact person; background information about your group including why you have set up, what your aims and objectives are, what activities you are currently involved in and who your activities are for or with; a description of your proposed project including where the idea for this project came from, what you hope to achieve through this project, why it is needed; how people who

are often excluded from activities or programmes will be included; the costs of the project and how much is needed (if there are other funders supporting the work as well please say who they are and what they are giving); how you will record and assess the progress of your project. You should also attach a copy of your group's constitution; your latest annual report (if you have one); a copy of your most recent accounts or, for new groups, a current income and expenditure record.

WHO TO APPLY TO Avila Kilmurray, Director, Community House, Citylink Business Park, 6a Albert Street, Belfast BT12 4HQ *Tel* 028 9024 5927 *Website* www.communityfoundationni.org
IR NO XN45242   **ESTABLISHED** 1979

....

■ **The Community Foundation in Wales**

WHERE FUNDING CAN BE GIVEN Wales.
WHO CAN BENEFIT Charitable organisations.
WHAT IS FUNDED The promotion of any charitable purposes for the benefit of communities within Wales. Projects providing worthwhile service to the community.
TYPE OF GRANT Capital, start-up and project support grants.
RANGE OF GRANTS £50–£150,000.
SAMPLE GRANTS £60,000 to Penywaun Enterprise Partnership for running costs; £50,000 to Oasis Youth Drop-in Centre for capital costs; £10,500 to Bethesda Art Works for an environmental project.
FINANCES *Year* 2000–01 *Income* £246,075 *Grants* £151,814 *Assets* £335,151
TRUSTEES Kim Brook, Chair; Ms Barbara Chidgey; John Curteis; Andrew Reid; Prof. John Pathy; Ken Abram; Gloria Jones-Powell; David Dudley; Mrs Elizabeth Murphey; Hon. Antony Lewis; Christopher Last; Richard Tyler.
OTHER INFORMATION The foundation is currently building up its endowment which will ensure a suitable source of grantmaking in Wales. In the meantime, it is managing a range of pass through grant schemes for a number of significant donors.
HOW TO APPLY By contacting the correspondent.
WHO TO APPLY TO D Nigel Griffiths, Chief Executive, 14–16 Merthyr Road, Whitchurch, Cardiff CF14 1DG *Tel* 029 2052 0250 *Fax* 029 2052 1250 *E-mail* mail@cfiw.org.uk
CC NO 1074655   **ESTABLISHED** 1999

....

■ **Community Foundation Serving Tyne & Wear and Northumberland**

WHERE FUNDING CAN BE GIVEN Tyne and Wear and Northumberland.
WHO CAN BENEFIT Voluntary organisations benefiting the local community.
WHAT IS FUNDED The help of those in greatest need. The funds generally have a specific cause as their individual funding priority, but overall the foundation has social welfare as its predominant cause to support. Projects that help communities and individuals who are disadvantaged because of poverty, poor health or disability are of particular interest. Some arts and environment work is funded, but only when it is of direct benefit to those in social need.
WHAT IS NOT FUNDED The foundation does not normally make grants for the following purposes: sponsorship and fundraising events;

small contributions to major appeals; large capital projects; endowments; political or religious groups; work which should be funded by health and local authorities; projects outside it's area (unless funding is made available by a supporter from funds they have contributed to the foundation).

TYPE OF GRANT Mostly single grants, but some grants recurrent for up to three years. Will consider capital, core costs, recurring, running and start-up costs, as well as one-off, feasibility studies and salaries.

RANGE OF GRANTS Usually up to £5,000, exceptionally up to £100,000.

SAMPLE GRANTS £250,000 to Northern Centre for Cancer Treatment; £130,000 in three grants to North Music Trust; £48,000 in two grants to Walker Health Project; £46,000 to Sunderland Age Concern; £39,000 in four grants to Skills for People; £35,000 to Stepping Stones; £32,000 each to Police Foundation and South Tyneside Furniture Recycling Scheme; £29,000 to YMCA Herrington Burn.

FINANCES *Year* 2001–02 *Income* £7,600,000 *Grants* £4,581,000 *Assets* £21,000,000

TRUSTEES Robert Hollinshead, Chair; Joy Higginson; Sally Black; Steve Brown; Alan Ferguson; John Hamilton; Chris Parkin; Colin Sinclair; Derek Smail; Derek Walker; Jan Worters; Mike Worthington; David Barker; Pamela Denham; Pummi Mattu; John Mowbray; Jane Streather; Bill Teasdale; Hugh Welch; Roy McLachlan.

PUBLICATIONS Guidance notes for applicants.

OTHER INFORMATION The grant total includes £1,200,000 administered on behalf of the Henry Smith Charity.

HOW TO APPLY Applicants should obtain a set of the latest guidelines, available from the foundation and downloadable from its website. We recommend that you plan your application well in advance. It can be made at any time. You only need to make one application, which the foundation will match to the appropriate fund or funds. You are welcome to phone to discuss your application at any stage. The following should be enclosed with your application: up-to-date annual accounts; latest annual report; copies of written estimates or catalogue pages if asking the foundation to fund equipment or capital costs. Requests for over £7,000 should also include copies of the minutes of the last three management committee meetings; business plan, if there is one. Your application will be acknowledged within a week, so please contact the foundation if you do not receive an acknowledgement. You may receive a phone call from a member of staff requesting further information or a visit. A decision is normally made within three months. If you are applying for a grant for the first time, or if you would like advice before making an application, do give one of the grants managers a ring. There are also agencies to help you with grant applications and these are listed on the foundation's website. The grants staff are Jane Shewell (grants director) and five grants managers: Khalid Malik, Karen Griffith, Elizabeth Harper, Alison Robinson, Francid Baring.

WHO TO APPLY TO Cale Cross House, 156 Pilgrim Street, Newcastle upon Tyne NE1 6SU *Tel* 0191 222 0945 *Website* www.communityfoundation.org.uk **CC NO** 700510   **ESTABLISHED** 1988

■ The Community Fund

WHERE FUNDING CAN BE GIVEN UK and UK charities working overseas.

WHO CAN BENEFIT Charitable, benevolent and philanthropic organisations benefiting those at greatest disadvantage in society.

WHAT IS FUNDED Projects submitted from registered charities and/or voluntary sector organisations which are charitable, philanthropic or benevolent and based in the UK. There are five grant programmes (with budget figures for 2002/3): Large grants (seldom now for more than £250,000); Medium grants (£5,000 to £60,000); Strategic grants (From £60,000. No upper limit); Research grants (£500 to £500,000, now with continuous application); International grants (£60,000 upwards, now with continual application). Small grants for small organisations (£500 to £5,000) are delivered under the Awards for All programme. For full details see the Community Fund website, or obtain the relevant information from the address given.

WHAT IS NOT FUNDED Organisations must be legally eligible to apply for a grant from the board. No grants to individuals or students. No loans, duplication of existing services or replacement of statutory provision. No grants to local authorities, local education Trusts, to schools or to charities set up to support statutory bodies. Applications will not be accepted from professional fundraisers. No emergency awards. All grants must be in addition to public expenditure.

TYPE OF GRANT Capital grants, revenue grants or a combination of both. Also buildings, feasibility studies, one-off, project, research, recurring and running costs, salaries and start-up costs. Grants are awarded for projects for up to three years for the main grants programmes and up to five years for International awards. Re-applications can be considered.

RANGE OF GRANTS £500 minimum (in main and small grants programmes); no maximum, although the largest grant so far is about £1.5 million.

SAMPLE GRANTS £294,800 to Deptford Action Group for the Elderly; £172,186 to Youth Clubs North Yorkshire; £140,942 to Earls Court Homeless Family Project; £90,000 to Foyle Search and Rescue; £83,479 to Valleys Furniture Recycling; £78,984 to Khilona Toy Library; £59,185 to Wear Valley Disability Access Forum; £57,970 to Dosti Muslim Groups; £53,771 to Alzheimer's Society; £31,861 to Children's Cancer Support Group; £28,905 to Port Carlisle Village Hall;

FINANCES *Year* 2001–02 *Income* £305,051,000 *Grants* £308,233,000

TRUSTEES Board members: Lady Diana Brittan, chair; Dame Valerie Strachan, deputy chair; Richard Martineau, chair, England Committee; Jeff Carroll, chair, Wales Committee; Kay Hampton, chair, Scotland Committee; Professor Jimmy Kearney, chair, Northern Ireland Committee; Elaine Appelbee; Paul Cavanagh; Steve Burkeman; Lorne Macleod; James Strachan; Ben Whitaker; Douglas Graham; Elisabeth Watkins; Sheila Jane Malley; Carole Tongue.

PUBLICATIONS Annual report and accounts which only becomes a public document after it has been formally laid in parliament by the Secretary of State for Culture Media and Sport. *Guide to Eligibility* leaflet. Range of information materials and guidelines for applicants in 12 languages as well as braille, large print, on audio tape and

Think carefully about every application. Is it justified?

399

as a guide for people with learning difficulties available from all board offices.

OTHER INFORMATION The board receives 4.7 pence from every £1 spent on the Lottery. The board is not subject to the control of the Charity Commission.

HOW TO APPLY In all cases, applications can only be made on the appropriate application forms; ring 0845 791 9191 for a pack (or visit the website). For Awards for All small grants, ring 0845 600 2040.

WHO TO APPLY TO The Chief Executive, St Vincent House, 16 Suffolk Street, London SW1Y 4NL *Tel* 020 7747 5300 *Minicom* 020 7747 5347 *Website* www.community-fund.org.uk

CC NO Y00080   **ESTABLISHED** 1994

■ The Confidential Fund, Lishkas Chasho'in

WHERE FUNDING CAN BE GIVEN Worldwide.

WHO CAN BENEFIT Organisations and individuals.

WHAT IS FUNDED General charitable purposes, but there may be a preference for supporting Jewish causes.

FINANCES *Year* 1999–2000 *Income* £36,000 *Grants* £32,000 *Assets* £701

TRUSTEES Rabbi D Kahn; Rabbi M Levy; Rabbi S R Lewis.

HOW TO APPLY In writing to the correspondent.

WHO TO APPLY TO Rabbi D Kahn, Trustee, 25 St Kilda's Road, London N16 5BS *Tel* 020 8809 4770 *Fax* 020 8809 4777

CC NO 1055558   **ESTABLISHED** 1996

■ The Congleton Inclosure Trust

WHERE FUNDING CAN BE GIVEN The town of Congleton and the parishes of Hulme Walfield and Newbold with Astbury.

WHO CAN BENEFIT Local organisations; UK organisations with projects in the area.

WHAT IS FUNDED The relief of people who are older, impotent and poor; the relief of distress and sickness; the provision and support of facilities for recreation or other leisure-time activities; the provision and support of educational facilities; and any other charitable purpose.

WHAT IS NOT FUNDED No grants to individuals outside the beneficial area or to organisations not benefiting exclusively the people in the area of benefit.

TYPE OF GRANT Buildings, capital, core costs, feasibility studies, salaries and start-up costs will be considered. Funding may be given for up to one year.

RANGE OF GRANTS £100–£10,000.

SAMPLE GRANTS £10,000 to New Life Church; £5,000 each to MAST Appeal and 230 Congleton Squadron Air Training Corps; £4,000 to Congleton Edge Methodist Chapel; £3,800 to Congleton Community Trust; £3,250 to Congleton Amateur Operatic Society; £2,200 to Trinity Methodist Church; £2,000 each to Congleton Community Youth Café, North West Air Ambulance and St John Ambulance.

FINANCES *Year* 2001 *Income* £59,076 *Grants* £48,810 *Assets* £1,447,557

TRUSTEES G Taylor, Chair; D Bibbey; K P Boon; C M Brocklehurst; Revd Dr J Cuttell; A Horton; G Humphreys; R Painter; E G Pedley; M A S Roy; E R Tansley; A B Watson; Canon M W Walters.

HOW TO APPLY On a form available from the correspondent. The trustees meet in January, April, July and October. Applications should be submitted by the first day of the month in which the trustees meet.

WHO TO APPLY TO D A Daniel, Clerk, PO Box 138, Congleton, Cheshire CW12 3SZ *Tel* 01260 273180 *Fax* 01260 273180 *E-mail* dad.astbury@tinyworld.co.uk

CC NO 244136   **ESTABLISHED** 1795

■ The Martin Connell Charitable Trust

WHERE FUNDING CAN BE GIVEN Scotland.

WHO CAN BENEFIT Scottish-based local charities.

WHAT IS FUNDED General charitable purposes and religious purposes.

WHAT IS NOT FUNDED No grants to individuals.

RANGE OF GRANTS £1,000–£4,000.

FINANCES *Year* 2000 *Income* £150,000 *Grants* £140,000

HOW TO APPLY In writing to the correspondent. The trustees meet in June and December.

WHO TO APPLY TO The Trustees, Messrs Maclay Murray & Spens, 151 St Vincent Street, Glasgow G2 5NJ *Tel* 0141 248 5011

SC NO SC009842

■ The Conservation Foundation

WHERE FUNDING CAN BE GIVEN UK and overseas.

WHO CAN BENEFIT Registered charities.

WHAT IS FUNDED Creation and management of environmental and conservation orientated projects funded by sponsorship. Income is generated to pay for the costs of managing charitable projects and supporting activities.

TYPE OF GRANT One-off.

FINANCES *Year* 2001 *Income* £177,502 *Grants* £76,760

TRUSTEES J Senior, Chair; D A Shreeve; G W Arthur; Dr B Baxter; Prof. D J Bellamy; J B Curtis; W F Moloney.

PUBLICATIONS *Network 21; Environmental Media Diary.*

OTHER INFORMATION Information about the foundation's current projects can be found on its website.

HOW TO APPLY In writing to the address below.

WHO TO APPLY TO W F Moloney, Trustee, Lowther Lodge, 1 Kensington Gore, London SW7 2AR *Tel* 020 7591 3111 *Fax* 020 7591 3110 *E-mail* info@conservationfoundation.co.uk *Website* www.conservationfoundation.co.uk

CC NO 284656   **ESTABLISHED** 1982

■ Consortium on Opportunities for Volunteering

WHERE FUNDING CAN BE GIVEN England.

WHO CAN BENEFIT Volunteers and volunteer-involving projects working in the fields of health and social care. Priorities include refugees and asylum seekers, women and those living in rural areas.

WHAT IS FUNDED To tackle health inequalities by involving local volunteers in the delivery of health and social care services.

WHAT IS NOT FUNDED Applications from individuals are not considered.

TYPE OF GRANT Capital and revenue. Projects, running costs and salaries will be considered.

RANGE OF GRANTS £10,000–£35,000. Typical grants £25,000–£30,000.

SAMPLE GRANTS £200,000 to Childline; £35,000 to Changing Faces – Newport; £34,945 to Project

V – Brighton; £34,343 to Ovenden Food Co-op Volunteer Project; £32,105 to Mentoring for Independence – London; £28,769 to Reaching Out – London; £24,009 to Kent Carers Group – Dartford; £19,211 to Macclesfield Cradle Concern/Mulberry House; £17,455 to One-to-One Shropshire VA – Ludlow; £1,904 to Ealing Services Volunteers; £857 to Feltham Volunteers Project.

FINANCES *Year* 2001–02 *Income* £2,183,469 *Grants* £1,884,215

TRUSTEES Christina Schwabenland, Chair; Jane Heath; Christopher Penberthy; Janet Harris; David Obaze; Penny Rossetter; John Oliver; Kristina Glen; Tzeggai Yohannes Deres.

HOW TO APPLY Application forms for funding for the period 2004–2007 will be available from April 2003. Applications will be invited at that time. The deadline for grants starting 1 April 2003 was July 2002. The consortium awards grants on a two- or three-year cycle. Further grants are not available until April 2004.

WHO TO APPLY TO Ruth Johnson, Chief Executive, 18 Devonshire Street, London W1G 7AV *Tel* 020 7323 5354 *Fax* 020 7323 5363 *E-mail* consortium.ofv@virgin.net

CC NO 1066973   **ESTABLISHED** 1997

■ The Construction Industry Trust for Youth

WHERE FUNDING CAN BE GIVEN UK.

WHO CAN BENEFIT Any youth organisation for building projects benefiting young people aged 8 to 25 who are unemployed or disadvantaged by poverty, and those living in both rural and urban areas. Individuals under 25 can be considered for sponsorship for training in the construction industry.

WHAT IS FUNDED To improve the condition of life, by sponsorship of youth training in the construction industry and by assisting in providing buildings for recreational use and occupational training. Grants for building projects will only be given to organisations which have no restrictions as to colour, class, creed or sect and only for the provision of permanent buildings for the use of youth between the ages of 8 and 25 years or for sponsorship in training young people under 25 who are disadvantaged and wish to enter the construction industry.

WHAT IS NOT FUNDED No grants for equipment, furniture, maintenance, repairs, decorating, transport or running costs. Training outside the construction industry and associated trades and professions is not considered.

TYPE OF GRANT One-off for buildings. Funding can be given for up to three years for training.

RANGE OF GRANTS £2,000–£5,000.

FINANCES *Year* 2000 *Income* £55,000 *Grants* £68,000 *Assets* £129,000

TRUSTEES Rod Bennion, Chair; Doug Barratt; John Carpenter; Peter G Fearfield; Anthony J Furlong; Rob Oldham; Martin P W Scarth; Ray Squires; Alistair Voaden; Richard Haryott; John Taylor; Martin Davis.

PUBLICATIONS *Building a Fresh Future.*

HOW TO APPLY In writing to the correspondent for an application form, with an outline of the request.

WHO TO APPLY TO The Company Secretary, Construction House, 56–64 Leonard Street, London EC2A 4JX *Tel* 020 7608 5184 *Fax* 020 7608 5001 *E-mail* city@thecc.org.uk *Website* www.charitynet.org/~city

CC NO 1029361   **ESTABLISHED** 1961

■ The Ernest Cook Trust

WHERE FUNDING CAN BE GIVEN UK, but with a special interest in Gloucestershire and in other areas where the trust owns land (Buckinghamshire, Leicestershire, Dorset and Oxfordshire).

WHO CAN BENEFIT Charitable organisations working through education or training to conserve the natural environment, architecture of distinction and traditional skills and to create opportunities for employment, particularly in rural areas. Organisations benefiting children and young adults; unemployed people; at risk groups; people disadvantaged by poverty; ex-offenders and those at risk of offending; and people living in rural and urban areas.

WHAT IS FUNDED Grants are given exclusively for educational work in the fields of countryside and environment, arts, crafts and architecture, research and other educational projects.

WHAT IS NOT FUNDED Projects principally allied to medicine, health or social work are not supported. Awards are not made retrospectively, or for the following: schemes where its input would replace statutory funds; individuals; agricultural colleges; general appeals; building and restoration work; sports and recreational activities; work overseas. Support for wildlife trusts and for farming and wildlife advisory groups is largely restricted to those based in counties in which ECT owns land (Gloucestershire, Buckinghamshire, Leicestershire, Dorset and Oxfordshire).

TYPE OF GRANT Conditional; annual; one-off. Project; research; salaries; and start-up costs. Funding may be given for up to three years.

RANGE OF GRANTS From £100; average grant £5,000.

SAMPLE GRANTS £20,000 each to Eden Project for the Plants in Myth and Folklore exhibition and Whirlow Hall Farm for a training and development manager for NVQ classes; £15,000 each to the National Museum of Wales towards the salary of a full-time interpreter to develop educational potential and for the training of supply teachers in a schools education programme; £12,000 for a part-time teacher to deliver a community empowerment project; £10,000 each to Coventry Cathedral Development Trust for setting up a website to encourage and support school visits and Woodlands Farm Trust towards the salary of an education and outreach officer; £5,000 each to Carmarthen Youth and Children's Association for a rural development worker, Orton Trust for student bursaries and Yorkshire Sculpture Park for classroom equipment.

FINANCES *Year* 2001–02 *Grants* £644,000

TRUSTEES Sir William Benyon, Chair; Sir S A J P Bosanquet; M C Tuely; A W M Christie-Miller; P S W K Maclure; T R E Cook.

PUBLICATIONS Annual report and accounts; leaflet for intending applicants.

HOW TO APPLY Trustees meet in March and October to consider applications and additional meetings are held at more frequent intervals to consider requests for £3,000 or less. Applications for the two main meetings must be finalised by 31 January and 31 August. There is no set form for these but applicants are asked to focus their request on a specific educational need and to present clear and concise proposals on a maximum of four sides of A4 paper. A simple budget for the project and a copy of the latest annual report and accounts should also be enclosed. Applicants are encouraged to contact the grants officer if they require further details.

WHO TO APPLY TO Mrs Antonia Eliot, Grants administrator, Fairford Park, Fairford, Gloucestershire GL7 4JH *Tel* 01285 713273 *Website* www.ernestcooktrust.org.uk
CC NO 313497   **ESTABLISHED** 1952

■ Gordon Cook Foundation

WHERE FUNDING CAN BE GIVEN UK.
WHO CAN BENEFIT Charities benefiting children and young adults.
WHAT IS FUNDED The foundation is dedicated to the advancement of all aspects of education and training which are likely to promote character development and citizenship. In recent years the foundation has adopted the term 'Values Education' to denote the wide range of activity it seeks to support.
WHAT IS NOT FUNDED Individuals are unlikely to be funded.
TYPE OF GRANT One-off and recurring for projects and research. Funding may be given for more than three years.
RANGE OF GRANTS £1,000- £30,000.
SAMPLE GRANTS £30,000 to Norham Foundation; £20,000 to Health Education Board for Scotland; £13,500 to The Citizen Foundation; £10,000 each to Northern College and North Lanarkshire Council.
FINANCES *Year* 2000 *Income* £285,000 *Grants* £214,000 *Assets* £9,000,000
TRUSTEES D A Adams, Chair; Prof. B J McGettrick; Dr P Clarke; Dr W Gatherer; J Marshall; C P Skene; D S C Levie.
HOW TO APPLY The trustees are proactive in looking for projects to support; however, unsolicited applications may be considered if they fall within the foundation's criteria and are in accordance with current programmes. Forms may be obtained from the correspondent.
WHO TO APPLY TO Irene B Brown, Foundation Secretary, Hilton Place, Aberdeen AB24 4FA *Tel* 01224 283704 *Fax* 01224 485457 *E-mail* i.b.brown@norcol.ac.uk *Website* www.norcol.ac.uk
SC NO SC017455   **ESTABLISHED** 1974

■ The Mansfield Cooke Trust

WHERE FUNDING CAN BE GIVEN Worldwide.
WHO CAN BENEFIT Registered charities.
WHAT IS FUNDED Evangelical Christian work known personally to the trustees.
RANGE OF GRANTS £100–£19,000.
SAMPLE GRANTS £19,000 to Worthing Tabernacle; £9,000 to Operation Mobilisation; £7,500 to Haggai Institute; £5,000 to Tear Fund; £2,500 each to Luis Palau Evangelistic Association, Care Trust and Christians in Overseas Services Trust; £2,000 each to Africa Inland Mission, Action Partners, Mission Aviation Fellowship and Micah Trust.
FINANCES *Year* 2000–01 *Income* £143,223 *Grants* £86,147 *Assets* £120,000
TRUSTEES N A M Cooke; B O Chilver.
HOW TO APPLY The correspondent states that the trust is 'established for specific purposes related to the personal contacts of the trustees' and that 'funds are fully committed and that applicants should not waste their time or ours by writing'. There would therefore seem little point in applying to this trust unless you have personal contact with a trustee.
WHO TO APPLY TO Nigel A M Cooke, Trustee, PO Box 201, West Malling, Kent ME19 5RS
CC NO 244493   **ESTABLISHED** 1960

■ The Cooks Charity

WHERE FUNDING CAN BE GIVEN UK and London.
WHAT IS FUNDED Projects concerned with catering. Any charitable purpose in the City of London.
SAMPLE GRANTS £98,000 to Hackney College; £51,000 to Bournemouth University; £20,000 to Academy of Culinary Arts; £7,500 to Cooks Benefactors Charity; £1,000 to St Lawrence Jewry; £800 to City of London Sea Cadets. In previous years beneficiaries have included British Heart Foundation, Broderers Trust, Constable Trust, Friends of Highgate Cemetery, HCBA, St John Ambulance and PM Club.
FINANCES *Year* 2000–01 *Income* £224,000 *Grants* £178,300 *Assets* £3,000,000
TRUSTEES M V Kenyon; A W Murdoch; H F Thornton.
HOW TO APPLY In writing to the correspondent. Applications are considered in spring and autumn.
WHO TO APPLY TO M C Thatcher, Clerk and Solicitor, The Old Deanery, Deans Court, London EC4V 5AA *Tel* 020 7593 5043 *Fax* 020 7248 3221
CC NO 297913   **ESTABLISHED** 1987

■ The Cooper Charitable Trust

WHERE FUNDING CAN BE GIVEN UK.
WHO CAN BENEFIT National charities benefiting people who are disabled or ill, carers, academics, medical professionals, and students.
WHAT IS FUNDED Medical research, healthcare especially acute healthcare, and Jewish charities. The following are also considered: residential facilities, respite, sheltered accommodation, arts, information technology, schools and colleges.
WHAT IS NOT FUNDED No grants to individuals.
TYPE OF GRANT Capital (buildings considered), project and research. Core costs and running costs are considered. Funding available for up to three years.
RANGE OF GRANTS One large grant; the remainder for £1,000 and £2,000.
SAMPLE GRANTS A grant of £108,000 was made to British Heart Foundation, with a further three grants of £2,000 each given to Elimination of Leukaemia Fund, Heathlands Village and Motor Neurone Disease Association. A further 14 grants of £1,000 each were given to Aidis Trust, Aspire, Children's Hospitals Appeals Trust, Disabled Young and Adults Centre, Dystonia Society, Guideposts Trust, Handicapped Children's Action Group, International Spinal Research Trust, Jewish Blind and Disabled, Kidscape, Movement Foundation, Muscular Dystrophy Group, Side by Side and Thrive.
FINANCES *Year* 2000–01 *Income* £145,509 *Grants* £127,700 *Assets* £2,066,477
TRUSTEES Mrs S Roter; Miss Judith Portrait; Ms M Hockley.
HOW TO APPLY In writing to the correspondent; applications are not acknowledged.
WHO TO APPLY TO Miss J S Portrait, Trustee, c/o Portrait Solicitors, 1 Chancery Lane, London WC2A 1LF *Tel* 020 7320 3890
CC NO 206772   **ESTABLISHED** 1962

■ Cooper Gay Charitable Trust

WHERE FUNDING CAN BE GIVEN UK and overseas.
WHO CAN BENEFIT Charitable organisations in the UK.
WHAT IS FUNDED General charitable purposes.
WHAT IS NOT FUNDED No grants for individuals for furthering academic qualifications.

RANGE OF GRANTS £500–£20,000.

SAMPLE GRANTS In 1999–2000: £10,000 to Sierra Leone Mission, made in memory of a deceased trustee who had supported it in the past. There were also ten donations of £2,000 each made including Down's Syndrome Association, RNLI, Saint Francis Hospice, The National Ankylosing Spondylitis Society and Willen Hospice; and 39 doantions of £1,000 each including Cerebral Palsy Care, Counsel & Care, Deafblind UK, King Cross Homelessness Project, Save the Children, Sign, The Cancer Research Campaign, The Dystonia Society, The Rainbow Centre and Tower Hamlets Mission. Most of the other grants made were for £500 each.

FINANCES *Year* 2000–01 *Income* £158,843

TRUSTEES M D Conway, Chair; D A Allen; A A Mason; R C Pickup.

HOW TO APPLY In writing to the correspondent.

WHO TO APPLY TO A A Mason, Trustee/Secretary, c/o Cooper Gay & Co., International House, 26 Creechurch Lane, London EC3A 5JE *Tel* 020 7480 7322

CC NO 327514   ESTABLISHED 1987

■ Mabel Cooper Charity

WHERE FUNDING CAN BE GIVEN UK, with a possible interest in South Devon.

WHO CAN BENEFIT Registered charities.

WHAT IS FUNDED General charitable purposes. Preference is given to projects with low overheads.

WHAT IS NOT FUNDED No grants to individuals.

RANGE OF GRANTS £100–£15,000.

SAMPLE GRANTS In 1996–97: £15,000 to Kingsbridge Methodist Church Building Fund; £11,000 to Kingsbridge Swimming Pool Fund; £5,000 to Sidney Hill Cottage Houses; £3,000 to Crisis; £2,000 to St Martins BBC Christmas Appeal; £1,000 to Christian Aid.

FINANCES *Year* 2000–01 *Income* £61,116

TRUSTEES A E M Harbottle; J Harbottle; I A Harbottle.

HOW TO APPLY In writing to the correspondent, although the trust states that it does not welcome, or reply to, unsolicited applications.

WHO TO APPLY TO A E M Harbottle, Secretary, Lambury Cottage, East Portlemouth, Salcombe, Devon TQ8 8PU *Tel* 01548 842118

CC NO 264621   ESTABLISHED 1972

■ The Alice Ellen Cooper-Dean Charitable Foundation

WHERE FUNDING CAN BE GIVEN UK, with a preference for Dorset.

WHO CAN BENEFIT Charities benefiting people in poverty, in distress or ill, or concerned with the advancement of education and religion.

WHAT IS FUNDED The relief of poverty, distress and sickness, the advancement of education and religion, and other charitable purposes of benefit to the community.

WHAT IS NOT FUNDED No grants to individuals.

TYPE OF GRANT One-off and recurring.

RANGE OF GRANTS £500–£25,000.

SAMPLE GRANTS £25,000 to Bournemouth University; £15,000 to Sheltered Work Opportunities Project for the Chestnut Nursery; £10,000 each to A R C Addington Fund, Cancer Research Campaign, Elimination of Leukaemia Fund, Hyped BCHA Ltd, Prama Care Attendant Scheme, Sheltered Work Opportunities Project for the Cherry Tree Nursery, and West of

England School; £5,000 to Life Education Centres – Dorset.

FINANCES *Year* 2001–02 *Income* £502,704 *Grants* £333,500 *Assets* £707,327

TRUSTEES Miss S A M Bowditch; Rupert J A Edwards; Douglas J E Neville-Jones; Miss E J Bowditch.

HOW TO APPLY In writing to the correspondent. The trust has stated that its funds are fully committed and that unsolicited applications have little chance of success.

WHO TO APPLY TO D J Neville-Jones, Trustee, Hinton House, Hinton Road, Bournemouth BH1 2EN *Tel* 01202 292424

CC NO 273298   ESTABLISHED 1977

■ The Marjorie Coote Animal Charity Fund

WHERE FUNDING CAN BE GIVEN Worldwide.

WHO CAN BENEFIT Registered charities for the benefit of animals.

WHAT IS FUNDED The care and protection of horses, dogs and other animals and birds. It is the policy of the trustees to concentrate on research into animal health problems and on the protection of species, whilst continuing to apply a small proportion of the income to general animal welfare, including sanctuaries.

WHAT IS NOT FUNDED No grants to individuals.

RANGE OF GRANTS £500–£20,000 in one-off grants and £1,000–£25,000 in recurrent grants.

SAMPLE GRANTS £25,000 to Animal Health Trust; £20,000 to Langford Trust; £7,000 to PDSA; £6,000 to Friends of Conservation; £5,500 to World Wide Fund for Nature; £5,000 each to Frame and Guide Dogs for the Blind; £3,500 each to Devon Wildlife Trust and Whitley Wildlife Conservation Trust; £2,500 to Dian Fossey Gorilla Fund.

FINANCES *Year* 2000/01 *Income* £111,272 *Grants* £103,500 *Assets* £2,731,224

TRUSTEES Sir Hugh Neill; Mrs J P Holah; N H N Coote.

HOW TO APPLY In writing to the correspondent. Applications should reach the correspondent during September for consideration in October/ November. Urgent one-off applications for a specific project can be considered between meetings, although most applications are held over until the next meeting.

WHO TO APPLY TO Sir Hugh Neill, Trustee, Barn Cottage, Lindrick Common, Worksop, Nottinghamshire S81 8BA

CC NO 208493   ESTABLISHED 1954

■ The Marjorie Coote Old People's Charity

WHERE FUNDING CAN BE GIVEN South Yorkshire.

WHO CAN BENEFIT Old people of small means.

WHAT IS FUNDED The established charitable organisations which work actively for the benefit of old people in the area of jurisdiction.

WHAT IS NOT FUNDED No grants to individuals.

RANGE OF GRANTS £200–£30,000.

SAMPLE GRANTS £30,000 to Age Concern Sheffield; £23,000 to Sheffield Dial-A-Ride Club; £15,000 each to Cavendish Centre, St Luke's Hospice – Sheffield and Voluntary Action Sheffield; £7,000 to Age Concern Rotherham; £5,000 to Alzheimer's Disease Society (Sheffield Branch); £3,000 to South Yorkshire Community Foundation; £2,000 to Age Concern Barnsley; £1,000 to Contact the Elderly.

Think carefully about every application. Is it justified?

403

FINANCES *Year* 2001–02 *Income* £110,000
Grants £118,000 *Assets* £2,759,904
TRUSTEES Sir Hugh Neill; Mrs J A Lee; Lady Neill.
HOW TO APPLY In writing to the correspondent.
Trustees meet in June each year to consider
grants; organisations must apply in May.
WHO TO APPLY TO Sir Hugh Neill, Trustee, Barn
Cottage, Lindrick Common, Worksop,
Nottinghamshire S81 8BA
CC NO 226747　　　**ESTABLISHED** 1958

■ The Nicholas Coote Charitable Trust

WHERE FUNDING CAN BE GIVEN Sheffield and
(restricted) worldwide.
WHO CAN BENEFIT Charities benefiting people living in
Sheffield, and charities elsewhere connected
with the Catholic religion.
WHAT IS FUNDED Charities for the benefit of the
residents of Sheffield, and charities elsewhere
connected with the Catholic religion.
WHAT IS NOT FUNDED Grants not made to individuals.
RANGE OF GRANTS £500–£16,000.
SAMPLE GRANTS £16,000 to English College in
Rome; £5,000 to South Yorkshire Community
Foundation; £4,000 to Voluntary Action
Sheffield; £2,000 to Cavendish Centre for
Cancer Care; £1,000 to Safe@Last; £500 each
to Carmel Care Centre, Castle Advice Centre,
Childline Yorkshire, Dyslexia Institute (Sheffield
branch) and Home Start Sheffield.
FINANCES *Year* 2001–02 *Income* £33,806
Grants £32,000 *Assets* £811,354
TRUSTEES N H N Coote; Sir Hugh Neill; Mrs P J
Coote.
HOW TO APPLY In writing to the correspondent.
Trustees meet in July each year; applications
must be sent in June.
WHO TO APPLY TO Sir Hugh Neill, Trustee, Barn
Cottage, Lindrick Common, Worksop,
Nottinghamshire S81 8BA
CC NO 241955　　　**ESTABLISHED** 1965

■ The Helen Jean Cope Trust

WHERE FUNDING CAN BE GIVEN East Midlands, with a
preference for Leicestershire.
WHO CAN BENEFIT Registered charities only.
WHAT IS FUNDED General charitable purposes,
supporting single projects.
WHAT IS NOT FUNDED No grants to individuals or
unregistered charities.
TYPE OF GRANT Generally single projects.
SAMPLE GRANTS £12,500 to LOROS; £10,000 to
Loughborough High School and Peter le
Marchant Trust; £5,000 each to Charnwood
Shelter Project, Leicester Children's Holiday
Centre and Redgate Farm Animal Sanctuary;
£1,000 each to Charnwood Stroke Club and
Shepshed Volunteer Centre.
FINANCES *Year* 2001–02 *Income* £135,696
Grants £203,016 *Assets* £2,942,047
TRUSTEES K J Brydson; D N Murphy; J M Savage;
Miss L A Brydson; G S Freckelton.
HOW TO APPLY In writing to the correspondent.
WHO TO APPLY TO Mrs M M Savage, 39 Farndale
Drive, Loughborough, Leicestershire LE11 2RG
Tel 01509 550932 *Fax* 01509 550932
CC NO 1071203　　　**ESTABLISHED** 1998

■ The Coppings Trust

WHERE FUNDING CAN BE GIVEN UK.
WHO CAN BENEFIT Organisations benefiting: people of
all ages; ethnic minority groups; disabled
people; homeless people; immigrants and
refugees; victims of domestic violence, victims
of war; and people with HIV and AIDS.
WHAT IS FUNDED Charities working in the fields of:
advice and information on housing; emergency
and short-term housing; personnel and human
resource services; support to voluntary and
community organisations; orchestras; cultural
activity; health counselling; hospices at home;
cultural and religious teaching; social issues
counselling; emergency care, refugees and
famine and international rights of the individual;
racial equality, discrimination and relations;
advice centres; and other charitable purposes
will be considered.
TYPE OF GRANT Core costs, one-off, projects,
recurring costs, running costs, salaries and
start-up costs. Funding for up to three years
may be considered.
SAMPLE GRANTS £51,000 to Power; £50,000 to
Prisoners Abroad; £35,000 each to 1990 Trust
and Friends of Hebrew University of Jerusalem;
£25,000 to London Jewish Cultural Centre;
£20,000 each to Uniting Britain Trust and Ebony
Steel Band Trust; £15,000 each to Brighton
Islamic Mission, Conciliation Resources, Yakar
Educational Foundationand – Jerusalem and
Yakar Educational Foundation – London.
FINANCES *Year* 2000–01 *Income* £66,807
Grants £388,950 *Assets* £1,735,872
TRUSTEES Clive Marks; Dr R M E Stone; T P Bevan.
HOW TO APPLY The trust has previously stated: 'The
trustees are at present considering a number of
applications already placed before them.
Because of the heavy existing demands made,
the trustees are concentrating on those projects
already known to them'. The trust has previously
stated: 'As funds are not available for new
projects, the trustees do not feel justified in
allocating administrative costs to responding to
applications.'
WHO TO APPLY TO Clive M Marks, Trustee, 44a New
Cavendish Street, London W1G 8TR *Tel* 020
7486 4663
CC NO 1015435　　　**ESTABLISHED** 1966

■ The J Reginald Corah Foundation Fund

WHERE FUNDING CAN BE GIVEN Leicester city and
Leicestershire.
WHO CAN BENEFIT Charitable organisations. However,
particular favour is given to hosiery firms
carrying out their business in the city or county
of Leicester.
WHAT IS FUNDED General charitable purposes,
particularly for the benefit of employees and ex-
employees of hosiery firms carrying on business
in the city or county of Leicester.
WHAT IS NOT FUNDED No grants to individuals for
educational purposes.
SAMPLE GRANTS In 1999: £50,000 to Framework
Knitters Home; £25,000 to Natural Forest
Foundation for a visitors centre; £12,000 to
Leicester Charity Organisation Society for
expenses and grants; £5,200 to LOROS;
£5,000 to Leicester University; £2,500 to
Cruse; £1,000 each to British Polio Fellowship,
Jubilee Sailing, and McIntrye Housing.
FINANCES *Year* 2000–01 *Income* £113,050
TRUSTEES D P Corah; Roger Bowder; G S Makings.

HOW TO APPLY In writing to the corespondent. Trustees meet about every two months.
WHO TO APPLY TO Ms Rawle, Clerk, c/o Harvey Ingram Owston, 20 New Walk, Leicester LE1 6TX *Tel* 0116 254 5454 *Fax* 0116 255 4559
CC NO 220792　　　　**ESTABLISHED** 1953

■ The Muriel and Gershon Coren Charitable Foundation

WHERE FUNDING CAN BE GIVEN UK.
WHO CAN BENEFIT Registered charities, particularly Jewish organisations.
WHAT IS FUNDED General charitable purposes.
RANGE OF GRANTS £60–£5,000; mainly £500 or less.
SAMPLE GRANTS In 1998–99: £5,000 each to Child Mental Health Research Fund and Lubavitch Foundation; £2,000 each to Joint Jewish Charitable Trust and Yesoday Hatorah School; £1,500 to Jewish Blind and Disabled; £1,000 to Israel Free Loan Association; £630 to Community Security Trust; £500 each to Cancer Worldwide, Centrepoint, and Chai Life Line.
FINANCES *Year* 2000–01 *Income* £85,387
TRUSTEES G Coren; Mrs M Coren; A Coren.
HOW TO APPLY In writing to the correspondent.
WHO TO APPLY TO G Coren, Trustee, 3 Albemarle Street, London W1X 4AU *Tel* 020 7499 7558
CC NO 257615　　　　**ESTABLISHED** 1968

■ The Holbeche Corfield Charitable Settlement

WHERE FUNDING CAN BE GIVEN UK and overseas.
WHO CAN BENEFIT Registered charities only.
WHAT IS FUNDED General charitable purposes, with an emphasis on museums, religious bodies and environmental projects.
WHAT IS NOT FUNDED The settlement does not consider unsolicited applications.
RANGE OF GRANTS £100–£25,000.
SAMPLE GRANTS £10,000 to Royal Artillery Museum for funds for a new museum; £7,705 to Coventry University for funding education of an overseas orphan; £7,500 to Rotary Club of Sherbourne for charity work; £2,750 each to National Trust for general funding and Royal Lifeboat Institutes for general funding; £2,350 to Sherbourne Prep School Trust for books for library and computer equipment; £1,600 to NSPCC for general purposes; £1,546 to Mahasarakam University for educational funding; £1,500 to National Artillery Association for general purposes; £1,250 to National Trust of Scotland for general purposes.
FINANCES *Year* 2001 *Income* £44,000 *Grants* £32,000 *Assets* £628,000
TRUSTEES C H Corfield-Moore, Chair; S J H Corfield-Moore.
HOW TO APPLY The trust states that funds are fully committed.
WHO TO APPLY TO C H Corfield-Moore, Chair of the Trustees, Greenoaks, Bradford Road, Sherborne, Dorset DT9 6BW *Tel* 01935 816637 *Fax* 01935 389172 *E-mail* chcm@greenoaks.fsbusiness.co.uk
CC NO 258625　　　　**ESTABLISHED** 1969

■ The Corinthian Trust

WHERE FUNDING CAN BE GIVEN UK and overseas.
WHO CAN BENEFIT Evangelical Christianity.
WHAT IS FUNDED The trust makes grants only to evangelical Christian organisations and individuals who are known to, or recommended to, the trustees. Nearly all the trust's grants are ongoing.
SAMPLE GRANTS In 2000–01: £8,700 to International Nepal Fellowship; £5,600 to Esher Green Baptist Church; £4,400 to Operation Mobilisation; £2,000 to Educate Trust; £1,000 to Children Alone Trust. Grants to Christian workers totalled £600 and grants to other registered charities totalled £780.
FINANCES *Year* 2001–02 *Income* £21,000 *Grants* £21,000 *Assets* £512,000
TRUSTEES John S Bradley; Mrs Judith M Bradley; James N Bradley.
HOW TO APPLY In writing to the correspondent, if recommended to apply.
WHO TO APPLY TO John S Bradley, Trustee, Oregon, Avenue Road, Cobham, Surrey KT11 3HW
CC NO 278531　　　　**ESTABLISHED** 1979

■ Edwin Cornforth 1983 Charity Trust

WHERE FUNDING CAN BE GIVEN UK.
WHO CAN BENEFIT Christian science organisations.
WHAT IS FUNDED Eight charities as stated in the will. Preference is given to certain Christian science organisations and in practice, other charities are not considered.
WHAT IS NOT FUNDED No grants to individuals.
TYPE OF GRANT Recurrent.
SAMPLE GRANTS Charitable expenditure was divided between First Church of Christ – Sutton Coldfield, The Pison Trust, Vermont Trust Ltd, Claremount Fan Court Foundation Ltd and Auxiliary Committee for Retirement Homes.
FINANCES *Year* 2001–02 *Income* £30,000 *Grants* £27,000
TRUSTEES Lloyds TSB Private Banking Ltd.
HOW TO APPLY In writing to the correspondent.
WHO TO APPLY TO Mrs Anita Goodway, Lloyds TSB Private Banking Ltd, UK Trust Centre, The Clock House, 22–26 Ock Street, Abingdon, Oxfordshire OX14 5SW *Tel* 01235 232746
CC NO 287196　　　　**ESTABLISHED** 1983

■ The Duke of Cornwall's Benevolent Fund

WHERE FUNDING CAN BE GIVEN UK.
WHO CAN BENEFIT Organisations benefiting people of all ages, people disadvantaged by poverty, and homeless people. Actors and entertainment professionals, musicians, textile workers and designers, writers and poets will also be considered.
WHAT IS FUNDED The relief of people in need of assistance because of sickness, poverty or age; the provision of almshouses, homes of rest, hospitals and convalescent homes; the advancement of education; the advancement of the arts and religion; and the preservation for the benefit of the public of lands and buildings.
RANGE OF GRANTS £1,000–£100,000, typically under £5,000 each.
SAMPLE GRANTS £100,000 to Prince of Wales Charitable Foundation; £15,000 to Soil Association; £5,500 to Trustees of Edington Foundation; £5,259 to Isles of Scilly

Environmental Trust; £5,000 each to Brownsword Hall Charity and Hereford Cathedral Perpetual Trust; £4,200 to Church of the Archangel Michael and St Piron; £2,000 each to Cornwall Macmillan Service, National Trust and University of Reading; £1,500 to Cornwall Children's Hospital Appeal.

FINANCES *Year* 2000–01 *Income* £98,412 *Grants* £195,508 *Assets* £2,512,864

TRUSTEES Hon. James Leigh-Pemberton; W R A Ross.

HOW TO APPLY In writing to the correspondent. Applicants should give as much detail as possible, especially information on how much money has been raised to date, what the target is and how it will be achieved. Applications can be made at any time.

WHO TO APPLY TO Robert Mitchell, 10 Buckingham Gate, London SW1E 6LA *Tel* 020 7834 7346 *Fax* 020 7931 9541

CC NO 269183   **ESTABLISHED** 1975

■ The Cornwall Historic Churches Trust

WHERE FUNDING CAN BE GIVEN Cornwall and the Scilly Isles.

WHO CAN BENEFIT Places of Christian worship.

WHAT IS FUNDED The repair and restoration of churches, with particular regard to those of architectural or historical merit.

WHAT IS NOT FUNDED The trust is unlikely to consider the following: routine maintenance and repair work which the church community could be expected to deal with themselves; re-decoration – other than when it follows from a major restoration scheme; introduction of domestic or similar facilities within the church building; schemes which damage or adversely affect the basic building, especially its external appearance; replacement or installation of heating systems required for the comfort of the congregations; redesign and layout of the churchyard and work on tombstones – other than the restoration of specific tombstones with some significant historic connections; repair and/or maintenance of associated buildings (e.g. school rooms and church halls).

TYPE OF GRANT One-off grants.

RANGE OF GRANTS £1,000–£4,500.

SAMPLE GRANTS £4,500 each to Lostwithiel Parish Church and St Neot Parish Church; £4,000 to South Hill Parish Church; £2,750 to Illogan Highway Methodist Church; £2,250 to Gwennap Parish Church.

FINANCES *Year* 2000 *Income* £80,000 *Grants* £30,000 *Assets* £218,000

TRUSTEES A Foot, Chair; Viscountess Boyd of Merton; H M Lord Lieutenant for Cornwall, President; Lord Bishop of Truro, Vice-President; C F Hall; G J Holborow; Prof. A C Thomas; Major D G F Hall; Mrs F Briggs.

PUBLICATIONS Leaflet on Cornish church conservation.

HOW TO APPLY In writing to the correspondent for an application form and guidelines. An initial telephone call is welcome.

WHO TO APPLY TO L G Coates, Hon. Secretary, Greenholme, Cambrose, Redruth TR16 4HT *Tel* 01209 891520 *E-mail* lionel@pal, print.freeserve.co.uk

CC NO 218340   **ESTABLISHED** 1955

■ The Cornwall Independent Trust Fund

WHERE FUNDING CAN BE GIVEN Cornwall and the Isles of Scilly.

WHO CAN BENEFIT Registered charities.

WHAT IS FUNDED The trust makes grants to help with the relief of poverty and deprivation.

FINANCES *Year* 2000–01 *Income* £90,000 *Grants* £124,000 *Assets* £200,000

TRUSTEES Revd William Ind, Bishop of Truro; Revd Donald Snelgrove; Lady Mary Holborow; Prof George Giarchi; Dr Clive Gronow; Mrs Jean Redfearn.

OTHER INFORMATION This trust now administers The Community Foundation Network UK's fund in Cornwall.

HOW TO APPLY In writing to the correspondent.

WHO TO APPLY TO Allen Chesney, Secretary, 1 Oaklands, Week St Mary, Holdsworthy, Devon EX22 6XH *Tel* 01288 341298 *Fax* 01288 341298 *E-mail* allen@chesney.fsbusiness.co.uk

CC NO 1071590   **ESTABLISHED** 1998

■ The Cornwell Charitable Trust

WHERE FUNDING CAN BE GIVEN The south west of England, with a preference for Cornwall.

WHO CAN BENEFIT Registered charities.

WHAT IS FUNDED General charitable purposes, funding projects and individuals specifically and primarily in the Cornwall area.

WHAT IS NOT FUNDED No support for travel, expeditions or university grants.

TYPE OF GRANT Project and capital.

FINANCES *Year* 2002 *Income* £48,444 *Grants* £94,246 *Assets* £921,403

TRUSTEES David Cornwell; Valerie Cornwell; Gordon Smith.

HOW TO APPLY In writing to the correspondent.

WHO TO APPLY TO G C Smith, Trustee, Devonshire House, 1 Devonshire Street, London W1N 2DR *Tel* 020 7304 2000

CC NO 1012467   **ESTABLISHED** 1992

■ The Sidney & Elizabeth Corob Charitable Trust

WHERE FUNDING CAN BE GIVEN UK.

WHO CAN BENEFIT At risk groups, people disadvantaged by poverty, socially isolated people and educational institutions benefiting children, and young adults. There may be some preference for Jewish people and Jewish organisations, but not exclusively so.

WHAT IS FUNDED General charitable purposes, supporting a range of causes including education, arts, welfare and Jewish charities.

WHAT IS NOT FUNDED No grants to individuals or non-registered charities.

RANGE OF GRANTS £1,000–£90,000.

SAMPLE GRANTS £90,000 to Oxford Centre for Hebrew and Jewish Studies; £27,000 to University College London; £15,150 to Jewish Care; £10,500 to British Museum Development Trust; £8,500 to British Technion Society; £7,250 to Community Security Trust; £6,000 to Pegasus Scholarship Trust; £5,820 to Royal Opera House; £5,400 to Royal National Theatre; £5,350 to Norwood Ltd; £5,000 to Chief Rabbinate Charitable Trust.

FINANCES *Year* 2000–01 *Income* £86,946 *Grants* £267,927 *Assets* £1,722,121

TRUSTEES S Corob; E Corob; C J Cook; J V Hajnal; Ms S A Wechsler; S Wiseman.

HOW TO APPLY Due to funds being fully committed the trust cannot accept any further applications for at least the next 12, possibly 24, months.
WHO TO APPLY TO Stephen Wiseman, Trustee, 62 Grosvenor Street, London W1K 3JF
CC NO 266606   **ESTABLISHED** 1973

■ The Corona Charitable Trust

WHERE FUNDING CAN BE GIVEN UK and overseas.
WHO CAN BENEFIT Children, young adults, people disadvantaged by poverty, and Jewish people.
WHAT IS FUNDED General charitable purposes, in particular the relief of need and the advancement of education in any part of the world including, without limitation, Jewish religious education.
SAMPLE GRANTS £17,000 to Menorah Foundation School; £4,500 to Hasmonean High School; £3,700 to Woodstock Sinclair Trust; £3,200 to Torah and Chesed Limited; £3,000 each to Friends of Kisharon and Lubavitch Yeshiva; £2,800 to Od Yosef Chai.
FINANCES *Year* 1999–2000 *Income* £39,000 *Grants* £54,000 *Assets* £64,000
TRUSTEES A Levy; A Levy; B Levy.
HOW TO APPLY In writing to the correspondent.
WHO TO APPLY TO A Levy, Trustee and Secretary, 16 Mayfield Gardens, Hendon, London NW4 2QA *Tel* 020 7405 3041
CC NO 1064320   **ESTABLISHED** 1997

■ The Cotton Trust

WHERE FUNDING CAN BE GIVEN UK and overseas.
WHO CAN BENEFIT UK-registered charities concerned with the relief of suffering, the elimination and control of disease and helping disabled and disadvantaged people of all ages.
WHAT IS FUNDED Capital projects and running costs for specific projects.
WHAT IS NOT FUNDED Grants are only given to UK-registered charities that have been registered for at least one year. No grants to animal charities, individuals, students, further education, travel, expeditions, conservation, environment, arts, new building construction or the purchase of new buildings. The trustees will only support the purchase of computer systems and equipment if it is to be directly used by people who are disadvantaged or have disabilities, but not for general IT equipment for the running of organisations.
TYPE OF GRANT Defined capital projects, excluding building construction. Running costs and salaries are only considered in exceptional cases where a charity only incurs such costs.
RANGE OF GRANTS £500–£5,000.
FINANCES *Year* 2001–02 *Income* £200,000 *Grants* £190,000 *Assets* £4,262,239
TRUSTEES Mrs J B Congdon; Mrs T E Dingle; Ms E S Cotton.
HOW TO APPLY In writing to the correspondent with latest accounts, evidence of charitable status, detailed budget, timetable and details of funds raised. Guidelines are available with an sae. Deadlines for applications are the end of July and the end of January, with successful applicants being notified within three months of these dates. It is regretted that only successful applications can be answered. The trustees only accept one application in a 12-month period.
WHO TO APPLY TO Mrs J B Congdon, Trustee, PO Box 6895, Earl Shilton, Leicester LE9 8ZE *Tel* 01455 440917 *Fax* 01455 440917
CC NO 222995   **ESTABLISHED** 1956

■ The Countryside Trust

WHERE FUNDING CAN BE GIVEN England.
WHO CAN BENEFIT Community or voluntary bodies concerned with the care of the local countryside of England.
WHAT IS FUNDED At present the trustees only offer grants for fundraising events where the money raised benefits practical conservation projects of local rather than national significance.
WHAT IS NOT FUNDED Trustees wish to assist small-scale, local initiatives. Capital payments and the labour costs of carrying out conservation work are not funded. Applications from individuals are ineligible. The trust does not give direct contributions towards environmental projects.
TYPE OF GRANT One-off payment towards a specific fundraising event. Core funding and/or salary costs are unlikely to be considered.
RANGE OF GRANTS Up to £5,000.
SAMPLE GRANTS £2,100 to West Country Rivers Trust; £1,300 to Pound for the Peak Appeal; £1,200 to Commonwork Land Trust; £1,000 each to Dorset Wildlife Trust, Wootton Conservation Trust, National Trust Northumbria and Wildfowl and Wetlands Trust.
FINANCES *Year* 1999–2000 *Grants* £242,000 *Assets* £918,000
TRUSTEES Ewen Cameron, Chair; Richard Wakeford; Martin Davis.
HOW TO APPLY On a (simple) standard application form, available from the correspondent or on the website. Application deadlines are the end of April and end of October.
WHO TO APPLY TO Rachel Chitty, Secretary, John Dower House, Crescent Place, Cheltenham, Gloucestershire GL50 3RA *Tel* 01242 533338 *Fax* 01242 584270 *E-mail* countrysidetrust@countryside.gov.uk *Website* www.countrysidetrust.org
CC NO 803496   **ESTABLISHED** 1990

■ County Durham Foundation

WHERE FUNDING CAN BE GIVEN County Durham, Darlington and surrounding areas.
WHO CAN BENEFIT Community groups and grassroots organisations seeking to improve the quality of life in their local area, particularly those aiming to combat poverty and disadvantage or promote a more equitable and just society. Applications from branches of UK organisations will only be considered if they are able to demonstrate financial independence.
WHAT IS FUNDED Accommodation and housing; infrastructure, support and development; arts, culture and recreation; conservation; education and training; bursaries and fees; purchase of books; and community facilities and services.
WHAT IS NOT FUNDED Groups that have substantial free reserves (over £15,000) or are in serious deficit; national charities that have no local office; projects outside County Durham and Darlington (groups from Sunderland can apply for environmental grants); a contribution towards large projects (with a total budget of over £10,000); grants for more than one year (unless you are applying for a Local Network Fund grant which can be for two years in exceptional circumstances); individuals (please telephone the office for information on grants available for individuals); general appeals, sponsorship and marketing appeals; membership applications; expeditions or overseas travel; minibuses or other vehicle purchases; holidays; endowments, loans or guarantee bonds; deficit or retrospective

Think carefully about every application. Is it justified?

407

funding; replacement of statutory funding/ responsibilities, including work on designated footpaths or highways, i.e. roundabouts and verges; excessive overheads; lap top computers (unless for people with special needs); political, exclusively religious activities or funding for the promotion of religion; animal welfare; mainstream education including Parents and Teachers Associations that do not have a strong community involvement (schools can apply for environmental projects); development of any land that is not open to the general public at convenient hours; medical research, hospitals or medical centres; building or buying premises or freehold or leasehold land rights; unpaid or contingent liabilities, bad debts, fines or interest charges; service charges for finance leases, hire purchase or credit arrangements; depreciation of fixed assets; payments for unfair dismissal, redundancy or compensation payments; payments into private pension schemes or unfunded pension payments; gifts, entertaining or travel and subsistence that would give rise to a taxable benefit; reclaimable or refundable VAT . Some of the programmes have other exclusions. If your project is at all unusual please contact the foundation to discuss your application before submitting it.

TYPE OF GRANT Local Network Fund/Investing in Children: up to £7,000 for projects that combat child poverty disadvantage. CDENT/Green Scheme: up to £2,500 for environmental/waste reduction/recycling schemes. Neighbourhood Renewal Community Chest: up to £5,000 for regeneration projects in Derwentside, Easington, Sedgefield or Wear Valley. Community Learning Chest: up to £5,000 for groups or £500 for individuals for training related to projects in Derwentside, Easington, Sedgefield or Wear Valley. Community Action: up to £400 for small organisations especially in Durham City, Chester Le Street, Teesdale and Darlington. Stanhope Castle School: up to £500 education and training grants for individual young people who are or have been in care. Hylton House Fund: up to £500 financial assistance for people with cerebral palsy and their families. John T Shuttleworth Ropner Memorial Fund: up to £1,000 for recuperative care for individuals in the Tees Valley with a preference for Stockton and Thornaby.

RANGE OF GRANTS £50–£7,000.

SAMPLE GRANTS £5,000 to South Moor Partnership towards a community appraisal; £6,524 to Darlington Association on Disability for playcare schemes for children with disabilities; £2,500 to Ponthead Residents Association to create a community garden; £2,150 to Single Homeless Action Initiative Derwentside for a life skills course for young people; £400 to Willington Monarchs Juvenile Jazz Band for a community fun day.

FINANCES *Year* 2001–02 *Income* £2,570,632 *Grants* £940,982 *Assets* £3,299,783

TRUSTEES Bernard Robinson, Chair; Sir Paul Nicholson; Peter Cook; Michele Armstrong; Henry Barrie; David Brown; David L Brown; Prof. John Clarke; Neville Fairclough; John Fitzpatrick; Hilary Florek; Barry Keel; Mark I'Anson; Judith Lund; Alasdair MacConachie; Lady Nicholson; Kevin Richards; John Hamilton; Don Robinson; Mark Lloyd; Robin Todd; Rod Wilkinson; David Watson; Paul Wilding.

PUBLICATIONS Newsletter, information leaflets, grant guidelines and application forms.

OTHER INFORMATION 'County Durham Foundation works with individuals, companies and other charities or trusts to improve the quality of life for local people in County Durham and Darlington. Our support to grassroots organisations ensures that everyone has as full a chance as possible of enjoying and contributing to the development of their local community. We have built a £3,500,000 endowment fund in four years.'

HOW TO APPLY Full guidelines, criteria and application details for each programme are available from the foundation or from its website. For further information please contact Lynsey Jordan, grants officer, on the number above.

WHO TO APPLY TO Lynsey Jordan, Grants Officer, Forster Business Centre, Jordan House , Finchale Road, Durham DH1 5HL *Tel* 0191 383 0055 *Fax* 0191 383 2969 *E-mail* lynsey@countydurhamfoundation.co.uk *Website* www.countydurhamfoundation.co.uk

CC NO 1047625   **ESTABLISHED** 1995

....

■ The County of Gloucestershire Community Foundation

WHERE FUNDING CAN BE GIVEN Gloucestershire.

WHO CAN BENEFIT Charitable organisations in Gloucestershire.

WHAT IS FUNDED The foundation's grant-making policy is to support organisations whose work is in combating disadvantage in Gloucestershire, both in urban and rural areas. Examples of projects which will be considered include: supporting community care; community involvement; and new initiatives/emerging needs. Projects will need to show: that they are a registered charity or are constituted as an organisation with charitable purposes; that the project is well-managed and holds up-to-date financial records which can be made available to the foundation; and that the activity is well-planned, achievable and well-organised. Rapid-response grants: these grants are mainly intended to meet immediate small expenses, including those which have arisen as a result of a crisis or emergency. Strategic grants: these grants are for the support of front line organisations demonstrating that the work they do is alleviating social isolation and poverty.

WHAT IS NOT FUNDED No grants for the following causes: animal welfare; buildings; endowment funding; general appeals; individuals; overseas travel; party political activities; promotion of religious organisations; research and equipment; and sponsored events.

TYPE OF GRANT Feasibility studies, one-off, projects, start-up costs and equipment (not materials, courses, activities, pilot projects or IT) will be considered.

SAMPLE GRANTS In 2000: £2,500 to Gloucestershire Resource Centre; £2,440 to Gloucester FM; £2,240 to Podsmead Neighbourhood Project; £1,000 each to Gloucestershire Chinese Women's Guild and Tewkesbury Young Carers; Matson Community Grants, where each was for less than £1,000 and in all totalled £5,000.

FINANCES *Year* 2001 *Income* £111,987 *Grants* £48,206 *Assets* £550,040

TRUSTEES Graham Bruce; Jane Winstanley; John Downs; David Drew; Mark Gale; Charles Green; Robin Grist; Jane Jennifer Fost; David Seed; Chris Wakeman; Tania Hitchins; Eddie Wilson; Patrick Wood.

PUBLICATIONS *Children in the Community – Making Things Better* teachers' pack.

HOW TO APPLY Please write to the address below for an application form and guidelines. Rapid response grants: Grants of up to £500 are made monthly throughout the year. The deadline for receipt of completed application forms is noon on the last Friday of each month. Applicants will be informed of the result within the following month. If acknowledgement of receipt is required an sae should accompany the application. Strategic grants: As part of its regular programme of grant giving, the programme will consider bids for between £500 and £2,500 three times a year, normally in spring, summer and winter. The first deadline for completed application forms is June, and the second deadline is July with the third in December. Applicants will be informed of the result within two months of the deadline. All applications will be acknowledged. If your application is successful you will receive a letter offering a grant and explaining any conditions. The foundation asks for a report six months after the grant has been paid with details of how the grant has been used (and again after 12 months in the case of strategic grants). A grants monitor will be appointed by the foundation to liaise with organisations receiving strategic grants. The foundation likes to maintain regular contact after a grant has been made. If problems do arise you should contact the foundation to discuss how these might be resolved before any misunderstanding occurs. If you are unable to use the grant for the purposes agreed, the foundation will withdraw the offer or ask for the grant to be returned. If the grant is not taken up within six months of the offer, the offer will be withdrawn unless there are extenuating circumstance.

WHO TO APPLY TO The Director, 3 College Green, Gloucester GL1 2LR *Tel* 01452 522006 *Fax* 01452 522069 *E-mail* darien.parkes@virgin.net mary.applegate@virgin.net *Website* http://beehive.thisisgloucestershire.co.uk/gloscommunityfoundation
CC NO 900239   **ESTABLISHED** 1989

■ The Augustine Courtauld Trust

WHERE FUNDING CAN BE GIVEN UK, with a preference for Essex.

WHO CAN BENEFIT Registered charities benefitting people in Essex and explorers.

WHAT IS FUNDED General charitable purposes, but mostly organisations in Essex working with young people who are disadvantaged and conservation. Exploration of the Arctic and Antarctic regions are also supported. Preference is given to charities which the trust has a special interest in, knowledge of or association with.

WHAT IS NOT FUNDED No grants to individuals. No grants to individual churches for fabric repairs or maintenance.

TYPE OF GRANT One-off grants for projects and core costs, which may be made for multiple years if an application is submitted for each year.

RANGE OF GRANTS £500–£2,000.

SAMPLE GRANTS £10,000 to Friends of Essex Churches; £7,000 to Gino Watkins Memorial Fund; £5,000 to Chelmsford Cathedral; £4,000 to Essex Association of Boys Clubs; £3,000 to Saffron Walden Church; £2,500 each to Bishop of Chelmsford's Discretionary Fund, Lord Lieutenant's Discretionary Fund, and YMCA Chelmsford.

FINANCES *Year* 2000–01 *Income* £97,800 *Grants* £94,250 *Assets* £1,254,781

TRUSTEES Lord Bishop of Chelmsford; Revd A C C Courtauld; Lord Braybrooke; Col. N A C Croft; J Courtauld; Lord Tanlaw; Lady Braybrooke; Derek Fordham.

HOW TO APPLY In writing to the correspondent, or online via the trust's website. Applications are considered in spring.

WHO TO APPLY TO Richard Long, Clerk, Red House, Colchester Road, Halstead, Essex CO9 2DZ *Website* www.augustinecourtauldtrust.org
CC NO 226217   **ESTABLISHED** 1956

■ Coutts & Co. Charitable Trust

WHERE FUNDING CAN BE GIVEN UK, specifically London.

WHO CAN BENEFIT UK registered charities benefiting children and young adults, older people, medical professionals, scientists, unemployed people, substance misusers, at risk groups, disabled people, people disadvantaged by poverty and homeless people.

WHAT IS FUNDED Support is, in the main, directed towards charities involved with people who are homeless, disadvantaged and disabled children and adults, those dealing with rehabilitation and teaching self-help, youth organisations and the relief of poverty. The trustees will also consider applications from special schools and for special needs education, health education, training for community development and work, vocational training and specialist research. Where possible, the trustees continue support for those charities to which they have traditionally given over a number of years. They also prefer to support organisations in areas where Coutts & Co. has a physical presence.

WHAT IS NOT FUNDED No response to circular appeals. No support for appeals from individuals or overseas projects.

TYPE OF GRANT Regular annual grants and one-off for specific projects.

RANGE OF GRANTS £250–£50,000.

SAMPLE GRANTS In 1998–99: £50,000 to Coutts' Foundation; £30,000 to Vine's Centre Trust; £14,650 to St Martin-in-the-Fields; £10,000 to Duke of York's Community initiative; £7,500 to Down's Syndrome Association; £5,000 each to Coutts' Staff Benevolent Fund, Johanna Primary School, Just Ask Counselling and Advice Service, and Prince's Trust; £4,000 to RNIB.

FINANCES *Year* 2000–01 *Income* £235,242 *Grants* £234,050 *Assets* £235,775

TRUSTEES The Earl of Home; Nigel G C P Banbury; Anthony Beale; Mrs Sally Doyle; Terrence Brown.

HOW TO APPLY In writing to the correspondent, at any time. Applications should include clear details of the purpose for which the grant is required. Grants are made regularly where amounts of £500 or less are felt to be appropriate. The trustees meet quarterly to consider larger donations.

WHO TO APPLY TO Mrs C Attwater, Administrator, 440 Strand, London WC2R 0QS *Tel* 020 7753 1000 *Fax* 020 7753 1066 *E-mail* carole.attwater@coutts.com
CC NO 1000135   **ESTABLISHED** 1987

■ Coventry Building Society Charitable Foundation

WHERE FUNDING CAN BE GIVEN The Midlands.
WHO CAN BENEFIT Registered charities.
WHAT IS FUNDED A wide range of causes based, or active, in the Midlands, with a preference for smaller local charities.
WHAT IS NOT FUNDED No grants can be given outside of the Midlands area.
FINANCES *Year* 1999 *Income* £134,000 *Grants* £55,000 *Assets* £79,000
TRUSTEES N J J Wood; Mrs M R Cowan; K Railton; J Rushton.
HOW TO APPLY In writing to the correspondent. The trustees meet quarterly.
WHO TO APPLY TO N J J Wood, Oakfield House, PO Box 600, Binley Business Park, Coventry CV3 2TQ *Tel* 024 7665 3575/024 7665 3510
CC NO 1072244   **ESTABLISHED** 1998

■ The John Cowan Foundation

WHERE FUNDING CAN BE GIVEN UK.
WHO CAN BENEFIT Charitable organisations.
WHAT IS FUNDED The foundation makes grants to purely local causes apart from national established charities. Charitable support will be considered for: oncology, hospices, hospices at home, medical transport, youth work, almshouses, community and social centres, Alzheimer's disease, arthritis and rheumatism, cancers, heart disease, motor neurone disease, terminal illness and sight loss. Grants range from £25 to £20,000.
WHAT IS NOT FUNDED No support for individuals, community projects outside Surrey area, or overseas projects.
RANGE OF GRANTS £25–£20,000.
SAMPLE GRANTS £2,500 to Cancer Bacup; £1,000 each to Barnardos, Children's Trust – Tadworth, CYDT, Jubilee Sailing Trust, and Samaritans.
FINANCES *Year* 1999–2000 *Income* £39,000 *Grants* £14,000 *Assets* £400,000
TRUSTEES C E Foster; S J Arkoulis; J A Schabacker.
HOW TO APPLY In writing to the correspondent.
WHO TO APPLY TO Mrs C E Foster, Trustee, Lane End, Tydcombe Road, Warlingham, Surrey CR6 9LU *Tel* 01883 622417 *Fax* 01883 622417
CC NO 327613   **ESTABLISHED** 1987

■ The Coward Trust

WHERE FUNDING CAN BE GIVEN North of England, particularly Lancashire.
WHO CAN BENEFIT UK and local organisations benefiting people who are visually impaired or disabled.
WHAT IS FUNDED Medical charities.
WHAT IS NOT FUNDED Applications from individuals are not considered.
TYPE OF GRANT One-off grants.
RANGE OF GRANTS £1,000–£3,000
SAMPLE GRANTS £3,000 each to Barnardos, British Diabetic Association for research, Leonard Cheshire Foundation, and Derian House Children's Hospice; £2,000 to Christie Hospital NHS Trust for cancer research; £1,000 each to Henshaws Society for the Blind, Iris Fund for the Prevention of Blindness, RNID, Royal School for the Blind, and St Dunstans.
FINANCES *Year* 1999–2000 *Income* £24,869 *Grants* £26,000 *Assets* £501,601
TRUSTEES Norman Jamieson; Gerald Sharples; David Sharples.

HOW TO APPLY In writing to the correspondent for consideration in December. No application forms or guidelines are available.
WHO TO APPLY TO Norman Jamieson, Trustee, 58 Riverside Mead, Stanground, Peterborough, Cambridgeshire PE2 8JN *Tel* 01733 345800 *Fax* 01733 345800
E-mail normanjamieson@hotmail.com
CC NO 519341   **ESTABLISHED** 1987

■ Cowley Charitable Foundation

WHERE FUNDING CAN BE GIVEN Worldwide, with some preference for south Buckinghamshire and the Aylesbury area.
WHO CAN BENEFIT Registered charities.
WHAT IS FUNDED The foundation was set up in 1973 with funds donated by Lord Hartwell. It now has wide objects, with no particular areas favoured.
WHAT IS NOT FUNDED No grants to non-registered charities. No grants to individuals, or for causes supposed to be serviced by public funds or with a scope considered to be too narrow.
TYPE OF GRANT One-off donations for development, capital projects and project funding.
RANGE OF GRANTS Usually £1,000–£2,000.
SAMPLE GRANTS £2,000 each to Médecins Sans Frontierés and Wordsworth Trust; £1,000 to Friends of War Memorials.
FINANCES *Year* 2001–02 *Income* £83,389 *Grants* £24,000 *Assets* £915,677
TRUSTEES The 140 Trustee Co. Ltd; Miss K Dickson.
HOW TO APPLY The trust states that unsolicited applications are not invited, and that the trustees carry out their own research into charities.
WHO TO APPLY TO The 140 Trustee Co. Ltd, 36 Broadway, London SW1H 0BH
CC NO 270682   **ESTABLISHED** 1973

■ The Sir William Coxen Trust Fund

WHERE FUNDING CAN BE GIVEN England.
WHO CAN BENEFIT Hospitals or charitable institutions carrying out orthopaedic work.
WHAT IS FUNDED Hospitals and other charitable institutions in England carrying out orthopaedic work, particularly in respect of children.
WHAT IS NOT FUNDED No grants to individuals or non-charitable institutions.
TYPE OF GRANT One-off grants and research fellowships.
SAMPLE GRANTS £34,000 to St Bartholomew's Foundation to fund a fellowship. The remaining eight beneficiaries each received £5,000; these were Brittle Bones Society, Claire House, Jennifer Trust, Medical Engineering Resource Unit, Osteopathic Centre for Children, Handicapped Children's Action Group, Brainwave and Simon Paul Foundation.
FINANCES *Year* 2001–02 *Income* £66,435 *Grants* £74,000 *Assets* £1,600,000
TRUSTEES Six Aldermen appointed by the Court of Aldermen, together with the Lord Mayor.
HOW TO APPLY In writing to the correspondent.
WHO TO APPLY TO David Haddon, Clerk to the Trustees, The Town Clerk's Office, Corporation of London, PO Box 270, Guildhall, London EC2P 2EJ *Tel* 020 7332 1432
E-mail david.haddon@corpoflondon.gov.uk
CC NO 206936   **ESTABLISHED** 1940

■ The Lord Cozens-Hardy Trust

WHERE FUNDING CAN BE GIVEN UK and overseas, with a preference for Merseyside and Norfolk.

WHO CAN BENEFIT Registered charities benefiting at risk groups and people who are disadvantaged by poverty or socially isolated. Research workers and medical professionals may be considered.

WHAT IS FUNDED Preference for UK, Norfolk and Merseyside charities in the fields of medicine, health and welfare.

TYPE OF GRANT One-off and recurrent.

RANGE OF GRANTS £100–£12,000.

SAMPLE GRANTS £12,000 to BMA Medical Education Trust Fund; £7,200 to PCC Cley.

FINANCES *Year* 1999–2000 *Income* £75,000 *Grants* £64,000 *Assets* £2,000,000

TRUSTEES Hon. Beryl Cozens-Hardy; Hon. Helen Phelps; J E V Phelps; Mrs L F Phelps.

HOW TO APPLY In writing to the correspondent before December. The main distribution list is prepared in January. Telephone calls are not invited.

WHO TO APPLY TO The Trustees, PO Box 29, Fakenham, Norfolk NR21 9LJ

CC NO 264237   **ESTABLISHED** 1972

■ The Craignish Trust

WHERE FUNDING CAN BE GIVEN UK, with a preference for Scotland.

WHO CAN BENEFIT Charitable organisations concerned with the arts, education and the environment.

WHAT IS FUNDED Projects which promote the welfare of the local community, particularly through the arts, education and the environment. Projects of special interest to the trustees.

WHAT IS NOT FUNDED Running costs are not normally supported.

TYPE OF GRANT Project grants.

SAMPLE GRANTS £5,000 each to Henley Symphony Orchestra and Institute of Economic Affairs; £4,000 to Autonomic Disorders Association; £3,500 to John Muir Trust Appeal; £2,500 each to Boilerhouse Theatre Group, Drug Prevention Group, Edinburgh Common Purpose and Friends of the Earth Scotland; £2,000 each to Edinburgh Cyrenians and Sustrans.

FINANCES *Year* 2000–01 *Income* £151,000 *Grants* £81,750 *Assets* £4,118,765

TRUSTEES Clifford Hastings; Ms Caroline Younger; Ms Margaret Matheson.

HOW TO APPLY There is no formal application form; applicants should write to the correspondent. Details of the project should be included together with a copy of the most recent annual report and accounts.

WHO TO APPLY TO The Secretaries, Messrs Geoghegan & Co., 6 St Colme Street, Edinburgh EH3 6AD *Tel* 0131 225 4681 *Fax* 0131 220 1132

SC NO SC016882

■ The Cranbury Foundation

WHERE FUNDING CAN BE GIVEN USA, British Commonwealth and UK, with a preference for Hampshire.

WHO CAN BENEFIT Small local projects.

WHAT IS FUNDED General charitable purposes including pre-school education and special needs schools, health care and research, community care services, arts particularly music, heritage, environmental causes particularly animal conservation especially endangered species, environmental education and research and natural environment.

WHAT IS NOT FUNDED No grants to individuals or students.

TYPE OF GRANT One-off grants.

RANGE OF GRANTS £10–£1,000.

SAMPLE GRANTS £16,000 to Muscular Dystrophy Trust; £1,000 each to Hampshire Scout Business Trust, Textile Conservation Centre, Hampshire and Isle of Wight Youth Options, NSPCC One Stop appeal and World Wildlife Fund.

FINANCES *Year* 1999–2000 *Income* £52,000 *Grants* £27,000 *Assets* £474,000

TRUSTEES Lord Lifford; Lord Northbrook; Sir Ian MacDonald.

HOW TO APPLY In writing to the correspondent.

WHO TO APPLY TO The Honorary Treasurer, The Chamberlayne Estate, Cranbury Park, Winchester, Hampshire SO21 2HL *Tel* 023 8025 2617 *Fax* 023 8026 2692

CC NO 314105   **ESTABLISHED** 1970

■ The Craps Charitable Trust

WHERE FUNDING CAN BE GIVEN UK, Israel.

WHO CAN BENEFIT Organisations.

WHAT IS FUNDED General charitable purposes, particularly Jewish organisations. It is not the policy of the trustees to make grants in response to appeals addressed to them, and applications will not be acknowledged.

RANGE OF GRANTS £75–£31,000.

SAMPLE GRANTS £30,000 to British Technion Society; £20,000 to Jewish Care; £16,000 each to Friends of the Federation of Women Zionists and Home for Aged Jews; £10,000 each to Joint Jewish Charitable Trust and New Israel Fund; £4,000 each to Amnesty International, Ben-Gurian University Foundation, Friends of the Earth, British Friends of Haifa University, Friends of Israel Educational Trust and Revelswood Foundation.

FINANCES *Year* 2001–02 *Income* £264,015 *Grants* £199,670 *Assets* £3,371,990

TRUSTEES J P M Dent; C S Dent; L R Dent.

HOW TO APPLY The trust states that 'funds of the trust are fully committed and the trust does not invite applications for its funds'.

WHO TO APPLY TO The Trustees, 3rd Floor, Bryanston Court, Selden Hill, Hemel Hempstead, Hertfordshire HP2 4TN

CC NO 271492   **ESTABLISHED** 1976

■ Michael Crawford Children's Charity

WHERE FUNDING CAN BE GIVEN UK.

WHO CAN BENEFIT Children and young adults, especially those disadvantaged by poverty and/or illness.

WHAT IS FUNDED Children and young people, and in particular the relief of sickness and the relief of poverty.

WHAT IS NOT FUNDED No grants for school fees and living expenses, travel and other expenses for 'year out' projects, conferences and so on.

SAMPLE GRANTS £10,000 to Sick Childrens Trust.

FINANCES *Year* 2001–02 *Income* £305,908 *Grants* £15,000 *Assets* £1,788,483

TRUSTEES M P Crawford, Chair; M D Paisner; I B Paul; A Clark.

OTHER INFORMATION The charity is undertaking a substantial capital project with the NSPCC; additional donations are usually to individuals.

HOW TO APPLY In writing to the correspondent. Grants are made half yearly and are considered in April and October of each year. Only successful applicants will be notified.
WHO TO APPLY TO Alan Clark, Regina House, 124 Finchley Road, London NW3 5JS
CC NO 1042211   **ESTABLISHED** 1994

■ The Cray Trust

WHERE FUNDING CAN BE GIVEN Mainly the east of Scotland.
WHO CAN BENEFIT Charities benefiting young people, animals and disadvantaged areas.
WHAT IS FUNDED The trust makes a number of grants to charities supporting young people on GAP years.
WHAT IS NOT FUNDED No support for political appeals and large UK or international charities. No grants to individuals.
RANGE OF GRANTS £100–£20,000; typically £200–£500.
SAMPLE GRANTS £20,000 (exceptionally) to University of Aberdeen for historical research; £1,000 each to Children of Conflict and Strathcarron Hospice; £500 each to Royal Botanic Garden, Sandpiper Trust and Scottish Society for Autism.
FINANCES *Year* 2001–02 *Income* £52,000 *Grants* £52,000 *Assets* £1,000,000
TRUSTEES Mrs S P B Gammell; P R Gammell; J E B Gammell.
HOW TO APPLY In writing to the correspondent. The trust stated: 'applications should be short and to the point. Grants are aimed to make a difference and so will seldom be made to large national charities unless for specific projects in east Scotland.'
WHO TO APPLY TO The Trustees, c/o Springfords, Dundas House, Westfield Park, Eskbank, Midlothian EH22 3FB
SC NO SC005592   **ESTABLISHED** 1976

■ The Crescent Trust

WHERE FUNDING CAN BE GIVEN UK.
WHO CAN BENEFIT Organisations benefiting children, young adults, medical professionals, students, teachers and arts practitioners.
WHAT IS FUNDED Grants to large museums and arts, occasionally to health and education. Only specific charities of which the trustees have personal knowledge are supported.
TYPE OF GRANT One-off and recurrent.
RANGE OF GRANTS £100–£20,000
SAMPLE GRANTS In 1999–2000: £20,000 to the Victoria and Albert Museum; £10,000 to Port Regis 2000; £8,000 to The Wallace Collection; £5,000 St Mary RC Church; £4,600 to The Attingham Trust.
FINANCES *Year* 2000–01 *Income* £137,000
TRUSTEES J C S Tham; R A F Lascelles.
HOW TO APPLY This trust states that it does not respond to unsolicited applications.
WHO TO APPLY TO Ms C Akehurst, 27a Sloane Square, London SW1W 8AB *Tel* 020 7730 5420
CC NO 327644   **ESTABLISHED** 1987

■ Criffel Charitable Trust

WHERE FUNDING CAN BE GIVEN UK and overseas.
WHO CAN BENEFIT Charities benefiting: the clergy; medical professionals; musicians; research workers; seafarers and fisherman; unemployed people; volunteers; Christians; Church of England; Evangelists; and Methodists.
WHAT IS FUNDED Residential facilities and services; building services; infrastructure development; professional bodies; Christian religion; film, video and multimedia broadcasting; music, orchestras, theatres; health; conservation; bird and wildlife sanctuaries; endangered species; heritage; education and training; community centres and village halls; and community services.
WHAT IS NOT FUNDED No grants to individuals.
TYPE OF GRANT Buildings, capital, core costs, one-off, projects, research, recurring costs and running costs. Funding is available for more than three years.
RANGE OF GRANTS £100–£10,000. Typical grant £200–£300.
SAMPLE GRANTS £29,980 towards advancement of Christianity; £14,100 towards relief of sickness; £7,900 towards relief of poor and needy; £5,500 for miscellaneous.
FINANCES *Year* 2001–02 *Income* £55,692 *Grants* £57,480 *Assets* £1,585,701
TRUSTEES J C Lees; Mrs J E Lees; Mrs J I Harvey.
HOW TO APPLY All funds are fully committed. The trust states that no applications are considered or acknowledged. Please do not apply.
WHO TO APPLY TO Mr & Mrs J C Lees, Trustees, 4 Wentworth Road, Sutton Coldfield, West Midlands B74 2SG
CC NO 1040680   **ESTABLISHED** 1994

■ Cripplegate Foundation

WHERE FUNDING CAN BE GIVEN The ancient parish of St Giles, Cripplegate, London, the former parish of St Luke Old Street as constituted in 1732 (broadly speaking, the southern part of Islington and the north of the City of London), and now extended to include the Islington Council wards of Barnsbury, Bunhill, Clerkenwell, Canonbury East, Canonbury West, St Mary, St Peter and Thornhill.
WHO CAN BENEFIT Anyone who lives or works in the area of benefit and can demonstrate that they are in need.
WHAT IS FUNDED The relief of need, hardship and distress of residents of the area; to provide facilities for recreation or leisure-time occupations that promote social welfare; other charitable purposes which are for the general benefit of the area. 30% of the foundation's funding is proactive. Current programes include: assisting schools in raising levels of achievement and to enrich pupils' experience of the curriculum (guidelines have been adopted for the funding of the 30 schools in the area, copies of which are available); the provision of £200,000 over three years to develop a new mental health service for young people aged 16–25 in south Islington. Grants are also given to organisations in the area whose work does not meet the current priorities, but which falls within the general grant-making powers of the foundation.
WHAT IS NOT FUNDED No grants to national charities and organisations, or organisations outside the area of benefit, unless they are carrying out particular pieces of work in the area of benefit; schemes or activities which would be regarded

as relieving either central government or local authorities of their statutory responsibilities; grants to replace cuts in funding made by the local authority or others; medical research or equipment; national fundraising appeals or appeals to provide an endowment; advancement of religion and religious groups, unless they offer non-religious services to the local community; animal welfare; retrospective grants; commercial or business activities; grants for concerts or other events held in the Church of St Giles-without-Cripplegate; grants for students at City University.

TYPE OF GRANT Both capital and revenue grants are made, often over more than one year.

SAMPLE GRANTS £90,000 over four years to London City YMCA towards the slary and running costs of their youth work at The Drum; £75,000 each to Islington Age Concern over three years for a salary to strengthen the management of the organisation and King's Corner Project over three years towards the cost of a worker with young people leaving care and hard to reach young people; £60,000 over three years to Guildhall School Trust for post-graduate bursaries; £50,000 to London Symphony Orchestra towrads completing the refurbishment of St Luke's Church to become the new St Luke's Music Education Centre; £49,425 over two years to Islington Volunteer Centre Ltd for running costs; £36,300 over three years to Finsbury & Clerkenwell Volunteers for slaries and running costs; £36,000 over three years o Thornhill Neighbourhood Project towards the costs of a half-time worker with older people; £28,500 for core costs over three years to the Maya Centre, which provides mental health services to women; £25,200 to Islington Community Transport towards the cost of two new low floor buses for the Islington Playbus Service.

FINANCES *Year* 2001 *Income* £1,080,507 *Grants* £979,000 *Assets* £27,114,000

TRUSTEES Grants committee: Roger Daily-Hunt; John Broadbent; Joseph Trotter; Barbara Riddell; Angela Agard-Brennan; Rosemary Boyes-Watson; Paula Kahn; Rachel Panikker; Jack Sheehan, Chair.

HOW TO APPLY Applicants can either apply by letter or use the charity's application form. The forms can be obtained from the correspondent. They are also available as a Microsoft Word document, which can be supplied on receipt of a formatted 3.5 inch floppy disk, or by e-mail. However, the foundation will not accept completed application forms by e-mail. The foundation welcomes a preliminary approach by telephone from charities, organisations or individuals who are unsure how to complete their application form or if they are eligible for a grant. The best people to speak to are Kristina Glenn, grants manager, or Rachel Ransley, grants officer. Before an application goes to the governors an applicant will normally be visited and you should allow time for this when applying. Applications should be received at least six weeks before the meeting date of each committee to allow time for a visit to your project to be arranged, and to allow for any clarification or discussion of the project that may be needed. We will use our best endeavours to ensure that applications are put to the next committee , but we cannot guarantee that an application will be put to a particular meeting. Applications for less than £25,000 a year are considered at grant committee meetings in January, April, July and October. Applications for £25,000 or more a year are considered by the full board in March, June and December.

WHO TO APPLY TO Christina Glenn, Grants Manager, 76 Central Street, London EC1V 8AG *Tel* 020 7549 8181 *Fax* 020 7549 8180 *E-mail* grants@cripplegate-stlukes.org.uk
CC NO 207499   **ESTABLISHED** 1891

■ The Cripps Foundation

WHERE FUNDING CAN BE GIVEN Northamptonshire, diocese of Peterborough and the University of Cambridge.

WHO CAN BENEFIT Charities concerned with the construction of new buildings and the maintenance of ancient buildings in the beneficial area; education and healthcare.

WHAT IS FUNDED New buildings and the maintenance of ancient buildings connected with education and religion. Support is generally concentrated on, and committed to major single projects which would not otherwise be undertaken. The foundation does not welcome applications generally because it has a long list of projects it would like to support already when funds are available, and as it concentrates on major projects it has few funds for minor purposes.

WHAT IS NOT FUNDED No grants are made to individual applicants or to organisations based outside the beneficial area.

TYPE OF GRANT One-off; normally capital grants.

SAMPLE GRANTS £50,000 to Peterborough Cathedral Trust; £3,000 each to St John the Baptist Church – Boddington, St Andrew's Church and Trinity Centre.

FINANCES *Year* 2001–02 *Income* £30,914 *Grants* £73,000

TRUSTEES Edward J S Cripps, Chair; D J T Cochrane; R W H Cripps.

HOW TO APPLY Applications should be by letter or by direct approach to the trustees. The trustees have a number of projects to which the majority of their funds are committed (see above), but there is a relatively small amount open to unsolicited applications. Applications are filtered by assessing whether or not they strictly fit the areas of interest: Is it local? Is it a religious charity? Is it an educational charity? Suitable applications are then passed on to the council of management (the trustees) for consideration. Both applicants and recipients are visited by the foundation, particularly in the case of larger projects.

WHO TO APPLY TO Ken Clark, Secretary, Mellors Basden and Co., 8th Floor Aldwych House, 81 Aldwych, London WC2B 4HP *Tel* 020 7242 2444
CC NO 212285   **ESTABLISHED** 1955

■ The Harry Crook Foundation

WHERE FUNDING CAN BE GIVEN Bristol.

WHO CAN BENEFIT Registered charities.

WHAT IS FUNDED Older people, homelessness, education, young people, civic, sundry small donations.

WHAT IS NOT FUNDED Medical research charities and charities serving need outside the boundaries of the City of Bristol. No grants to individuals.

TYPE OF GRANT One-off, capital and recurring. Also buildings, core costs, feasibility studies, interest-free loans and project. Funding is given for one year or less.

RANGE OF GRANTS £100–£250,000.

SAMPLE GRANTS In 1998–99: £172,000 to St George's Music Trust; £100,000 to Colston

Collegiative School; £27,000 to Little Brothers of Nazareth; £10,500 to Hanham Folk Centre; £8,000 to Bristol Age Concern; £7,500 to Avon Riding Centre for the Disabled; £7,245 to Manor Farm Boys Club; £5,500 to Game Conservancy Trust; £5,000 each to Cotswold Home and Bristol 5 Boys Club.

FINANCES *Year* 1999–2000 *Income* £107,000 *Grants* £358,000 *Assets* £3,900,000

TRUSTEES J O Gough, Chair; R G West; Mrs I Wollen; D J Bellew.

OTHER INFORMATION Address appeals to D J Bellew c/o Solicitor to the Trustees Miss J Pierce

HOW TO APPLY In writing to the correspondent. The trustees meet twice a year in November and July, but applications can be sent at any time as there is a vetting process prior to the trustees' meetings.

WHO TO APPLY TO D J Bellew, Veale Wasbrough, Solicitors, Orchard Court, Orchard Lane, Bristol BS1 5WS *Tel* 0117 925 2020

CC NO 231470   **ESTABLISHED** 1963

■ The Cross Trust

WHERE FUNDING CAN BE GIVEN UK and overseas.

WHO CAN BENEFIT Individuals, and organisations benefiting Christians.

WHAT IS FUNDED Christian work.

TYPE OF GRANT One-off grants for core, capital and project support.

RANGE OF GRANTS £1,000–£40,000.

SAMPLE GRANTS In 2000–01: £150,000 to Aeropagus Trust for general work; £50,036 to George Whitefield Theological Training College for the new building fund; £25,000 to Rock Foundation; £10,000 to Cornhill Training Courses for overseas students fees; £5,468 to E. Ivor Hughes Education Foundation; £3,295 to Girls' Day School Trust; £3,000 each to Emmanuel College and Gujarat Appeal; £1,496 to Met Clinic.

FINANCES *Year* 2001–02 *Income* £8,337 *Grants* £222,750 *Assets* £151,826

TRUSTEES M S Farmer; Mrs J D Farmer; D J Olsen.

HOW TO APPLY No unsolicited applications are supported, with funds already fully committed.

WHO TO APPLY TO The Trustees, Cansdale's, Bourbon Court, Nightingale Corner, Little Chalfont, Buckinghamshire HP7 9QS *Tel* 01494 765428

CC NO 298472   **ESTABLISHED** 1987

■ The Else & Leonard Cross Charitable Trust

WHERE FUNDING CAN BE GIVEN UK.

WHO CAN BENEFIT Music education.

WHAT IS FUNDED The trust's objects are the advancement of public education in music, and in particular the founding of scholarships and prizes for the encouragement and advancement of musical education; assistance to musicians and students of music to further their musical education; financing of public performances or musical works.

RANGE OF GRANTS £500–£4,000.

SAMPLE GRANTS £4,000 each to Guildhall School of Music and Drama, Royal Northern College of Music and Trinity College of Music – Junior Department.

FINANCES *Year* 1999–2000 *Income* £26,000 *Grants* £42,000 *Assets* £389,000

TRUSTEES Mrs Helen Gillingwater; Brian R Green; Paul D Harris.

HOW TO APPLY The trust writes to the main music institutions once a year requesting applications and makes grants in July. However, it is open to other applications.

WHO TO APPLY TO Mrs H Gillingwater, Trustee, The Wall House, 2 Lichfield Road, Richmond, Surrey TW9 3JR *Tel* 020 8948 4950 *E-mail* helengillingwater@hotmail.com

CC NO 1008038   **ESTABLISHED** 1991

■ The Derek Crowson Charitable Settlement

WHERE FUNDING CAN BE GIVEN UK.

WHO CAN BENEFIT Registered charities.

WHAT IS FUNDED General charitable purposes.

RANGE OF GRANTS £100–£46,000.

SAMPLE GRANTS £19,000 to Helping Children With Leukaemia; £10,000 each to The Orpheus Trust and Stanley Gold Community Trust Fund; £8,000 to St Giles' Church; £5,500 to NSPCC; £3,200 to Cottage Homes; £2,600 to Mencap; £2,300 to Plumpton College Charity Fair; £2,000 to New Sussex Opera; £1,000 each to Connor John Trust Fund and Leukaemia 2000 – Lord Mayor's Appeal.

FINANCES *Year* 1998–99 *Income* £26,000 *Grants* £67,000

TRUSTEES D C Crowson, Chair; J R Hughes; J E Eden.

HOW TO APPLY In writing to the correspondent.

WHO TO APPLY TO J R Hughes, Trustee, Rix & Kay Solicitors, The Courtyard, River Way, Uckfield, East Sussex TN22 1SL *Tel* 01825 761555

CC NO 1027486   **ESTABLISHED** 1993

■ The Croydon Relief in Need Charities

WHERE FUNDING CAN BE GIVEN The borough of Croydon.

WHO CAN BENEFIT Older people.

WHAT IS FUNDED Health and welfare.

TYPE OF GRANT Recurrent.

SAMPLE GRANTS In 1999: £80,000 to Croydon Crossroads; £60,000 to Croydon Youth Information & Counselling Service; £25,000 to Drug Concern (Croydon) Ltd for the '55' Project; £12,000 to Croydon YMCA Housing Association for a cold weather shelter; £10,000 each to Croydon Council on Ageing (Age Concern) and Croydon Opportunity Playgroup; £6,000 to CYDT for CABS Scheme; £5,000 to 6th Croydon St Augustine's Scout Group; £4,000 to Croydon Darby and Joan Club Ltd; £3,000 to Bluebirds Wheelchair Basketball Club.

FINANCES *Year* 2001 *Income* £317,531

TRUSTEES N P Hepworth, Chair; T S Rogers; Mrs B E Cripps; D J Cripps; Mrs D Pickard; D M Rawling; Mrs T G Stewart; Mrs C D A Trower; E N Trower; M A Fowler; J L Aston; C P Clementi; P T Pearce; R J Horden; Mrs P J Cook; Mrs L A Talbot; A J Sharp; Revd C J L Boswell; L P Tasker.

HOW TO APPLY In writing to the correspondent.

WHO TO APPLY TO W B Rymer, Clerk, 74 High Street, Croydon CR9 2UU *Tel* 020 8680 2638

CC NO 810114   **ESTABLISHED** 1962

■ Cruden Foundation Ltd

WHERE FUNDING CAN BE GIVEN Mainly Scotland.
WHO CAN BENEFIT Registered charities.
WHAT IS FUNDED General charitable purposes.
WHAT IS NOT FUNDED No grants to individuals.
TYPE OF GRANT Recurrent and one-off.
RANGE OF GRANTS £100–£7,500.
SAMPLE GRANTS In 2000–01: £7,500 to Scottish
Hospitals Endowments Research Trust; £5,000
each to Pitlochry Festival Theatre and Scottish
Cancer Foundation; £3,000 to Edinburgh
International Festival; £2,550 to Edinburgh
Common Purpose; £2,500 to Edinburgh
Academy Foundation; £2,000 each to Edinburgh
Headway Group, George Watson's Family
Foundation and Scottish Seabird Centre;
£1,700 to St Giles Renewal Appeal.
FINANCES *Year* 1999–2000 *Income* £93,000
Grants £82,500 *Assets* £798,000
TRUSTEES N Lessels, Chair; M R A Matthews; G B R
Gray; J G Mitchell; A Johnston; M J Rowley; D D
Walker.
HOW TO APPLY In writing to the correspondent.
WHO TO APPLY TO M R A Matthews, Secretary,
Baberton House, Juniper Green, Edinburgh
EH14 3HN
SC NO SC004987   **ESTABLISHED** 1956

■ The Ronald Cruickshanks Foundation

WHERE FUNDING CAN BE GIVEN UK, with some
preference for Folkestone, Faversham and the
surrounding area.
WHO CAN BENEFIT Individuals and organisations.
WHAT IS FUNDED General charitable purposes, but
particularly for the benefit of people in financial
and other need within the stated beneficial
area.
TYPE OF GRANT Recurrent
RANGE OF GRANTS £250–£4,000.
SAMPLE GRANTS £4,000 to Pilgrim's Hospice;
£3,000 each to Salvation Army, Kent Air
Ambulance and Age Concern – Folkestone;
£1,000 each to Arthritis Research Campaign,
Cancer Research UK, British Heart Foundation,
Barnados, RNLI and British Red Cross. Grants
were also given to various local churches.
FINANCES *Year* 2001–02 *Income* £185,187
Grants £67,000
TRUSTEES I F Cloke, Chair; Jan Siemen Schilder;
Mrs S Cloke.
HOW TO APPLY In writing to the correspondent.
Applications should be received by the end of
September for consideration on a date
coinciding closely with the anniversary of the
death of the founder, which was 7 December.
WHO TO APPLY TO I F Cloke, Trustee, 34 Cheriton
Gardens, Folkestone, Kent CT20 2AX
Tel 01303 251742 *Fax* 01303 258039
CC NO 296075   **ESTABLISHED** 1987

■ Cuby Charitable Trust

WHERE FUNDING CAN BE GIVEN UK.
WHO CAN BENEFIT Registered charities.
WHAT IS FUNDED Jewish causes.
FINANCES *Year* 1999–2000 *Income* £133,000
Grants £123,000
TRUSTEES S S Cuby; Mrs C B Cuby.
HOW TO APPLY In writing to the correspondent.
WHO TO APPLY TO S S Cuby, Chair, 16 Mowbray
Road, Edgware, Middlesex HA8 8JQ *Tel* 020
7563 6868
CC NO 328585   **ESTABLISHED** 1990

■ The Culra Charitable Trust

WHERE FUNDING CAN BE GIVEN Scottish Highlands and
Kent.
WHO CAN BENEFIT Registered charities only.
WHAT IS FUNDED General charitable purposes with
preference for Highland and Kent charities.
WHAT IS NOT FUNDED Grants are not given to non-
registered charities or individuals.
SAMPLE GRANTS In 1999: £3,000 to Sons of Clergy;
£1,750 to Bedford School Trust; £1,250 to
Hospice in Weald; £1,000 each to Help our
Hospices and Talbat Hospice Trust.
FINANCES *Year* 2001–02 *Income* £30,563
Grants £20,000
TRUSTEES C Byam-Cook; P J Sienesi; G Needham.
HOW TO APPLY In writing to the correspondent.
WHO TO APPLY TO P T Dunkelley, c/o The Hedley
Foundation, 9 Dowgate Hill, London EC4R 2SU
Tel 020 7489 8076 *Fax* 020 7489 8997
CC NO 274612   **ESTABLISHED** 1977

■ The Cumber Family Charitable Trust

WHERE FUNDING CAN BE GIVEN Worldwide, with a
preference for the third world and Berkshire and
Oxfordshire.
WHO CAN BENEFIT Individuals and organisations
benefiting children, young adults and a wide
range of social circumstances are considered
for funding.
WHAT IS FUNDED Health, homelessness, disability
and welfare, rural development, housing,
overseas aid, Christian aid, agricultural
development, youth and children's welfare,
education.
WHAT IS NOT FUNDED No grants for animal welfare.
Only very few to individuals with local
connections and who are personally known to
the trustees are supported. Local appeals
outside Berkshire and Oxfordshire are not
usually supported.
TYPE OF GRANT Usually single grant, not repeated
within three years. Occasionally support up to
three years for a project.
RANGE OF GRANTS £200–£3,000.
SAMPLE GRANTS £3,000 to Mozambique Flood
Appeal; £2,000 to Shelter; £1,500 to MAF
(Chorley Family); £1,000 each to Action against
Breast Cancer, Care, Christian Aid, Farm Africa,
Marcham with Garford PCC for a youth worker,
Ockenden International, and Society of Friends
in Britain.
FINANCES *Year* 1999–2000 *Income* £62,265
Grants £37,500 *Assets* £695,263
TRUSTEES Miss M Cumber; A R Davey; W Cumber;
Mrs M J Cumber; Mrs M J Freeman; Mrs M E
Tearney.
HOW TO APPLY In writing to the correspondent.
Applications are considered in February and
September.
WHO TO APPLY TO Mrs M E Tearney, Trustee, Manor
Farm, Marcham, Abingdon, Oxfordshire OX13
6NZ *Tel* 01865 391327/391840 *Fax* 01865
391164
CC NO 291009   **ESTABLISHED** 1985

■ Cumberland Building Society Charitable Foundation

WHERE FUNDING CAN BE GIVEN Cumbria, Dumfriesshire, Lancashire (Preston area) and Northumberland (Haltwhistle area).

WHO CAN BENEFIT Registered charities.

WHAT IS FUNDED General charitable purposes in areas where the trustees determine Cumberland Building Society operates.

WHAT IS NOT FUNDED Non-registered charities and those working outside the operating area.

RANGE OF GRANTS Up to £1,000.

SAMPLE GRANTS £1,000 each to After Adoption, Alzheimer's Society (Carlisle), Alzheimer Scotland, Epilepsy Action Scotland, Barnardos, Branthwaite & District Fire Responders, DEBRA, National Deaf Children's Society and Whizz-kidz; £750 to Leonard Cheshire North West.

FINANCES *Year* 2001–02 *Income* £147,393 *Grants* £33,600

HOW TO APPLY In writing to the correspondent, including a description of your organisation, what it does, what the grant will be used for and the size of grant requested. Trustees meet about every three months.

WHO TO APPLY TO Judi Thomson, Cumberland House, Castle Street, Carlisle CA3 8RX *Tel* 01228 541341 *Fax* 01228 403111 *E-mail* executives@cumberland.co.uk

CC NO 1072435 **ESTABLISHED** 1998

■ The Cumberland Trust

WHERE FUNDING CAN BE GIVEN UK and Africa.

WHO CAN BENEFIT Registered charities and institutions administered by Christians.

WHAT IS FUNDED Charities working in the fields of Christian education, Christian outreach, mission and evangelism. The trust tends to give to a selected list of beneficiaries. Small grants are also given to enable (Christian) students to spend a year 'out' on medicine, training and Christian projects.

WHAT IS NOT FUNDED In future, the trust will only make grants to organisations and individuals known personally to the trustees.

TYPE OF GRANT Recurrent, occasional single donations and start-up costs, and funding for up to three years will be considered.

SAMPLE GRANTS In 1997: £1,000 to Traidcraft Exchange towards overseas help in village industry; £400 to Willington Baptist Church for general purposes; £250 to World Cancer Research; £200 each to Bible Society, Care Trust, Crossfire Trust, Mission Aviation Fellowship, Save the Children, Tearfund and WEC.

FINANCES *Year* 2000–01 *Income* £32,000 *Grants* £34,000

TRUSTEES B J Hosking; C A Hosking; Mrs E Hosking.

HOW TO APPLY Initial telephone calls are not welcome. No application form, guidelines or deadlines for applications. Applicants should enclose an sae.

WHO TO APPLY TO Mrs E Hosking, Holly Cottage, 34 Tyeford Road, Willington, Derby DE65 6DE *Tel* 01283 704520

CC NO 266475 **ESTABLISHED** 1973

■ Cumbria Community Foundation

WHERE FUNDING CAN BE GIVEN Cumbria.

WHO CAN BENEFIT Organisations and individuals, under several different schemes.

WHAT IS FUNDED Improving the quality of the community life of the people of Cumbria, and in particular those in need by reason of disability, age, financial or other disadvantage.

SAMPLE GRANTS £20,000 each to Cumbris Federation of YFCs and Penrith and Eden CAB; £14,000 each to Age Concern Carlisle and District, Age Concern Eden and Whitehaven CAB; £13,400 each to Age Concern North West Cumbria; £12,000 to North Lakeland Hospice at Home; £10,000 each to Voluntary Action Cumbria, Solway Rural Initiative and Womens' Aid Impact Housing.

FINANCES *Year* 2001–02 *Income* £3,450,542 *Grants* £2,219,857 *Assets* £1,827,282

TRUSTEES Capt John Green; Cllr Jim Musgrave; Dr John Stanforth; Arthur Sanderson; Bob Mather; Glyn Roberts; Henry Bowring; Ian Brown; James Cropper; John Dunning; John Fryer-Spedding; Keith Adamson; Louis Victory; Mark Elliott; Michael Hart; Peter Hensman; Richard Simpson; Robin Burgess; Mr and Mrs Charles Woodhouse; Mrs Margaret Martindale; Mrs Suzie Markham; Ms Chris Coombes; Ms Shirley Williams; Ms Susan Aglionby.

OTHER INFORMATION The foundation allocated £1,824,000 to various organisations under the Cumbria Community Recovery Appeal to alleviate the consequences of the recent outbreak of foot and mouth disease.

HOW TO APPLY For details on how to apply, refer to the foundation's website or contact the foundation on 01900 825 760.

WHO TO APPLY TO Andrew Beeforth, Director, Unit 6b, Lakeland Business Park, Cockermouth, Cumbria CA13 0QT *Tel* 01900 825760 *Website* www.cumbriafoundation.org

CC NO 1075120 **ESTABLISHED** 1999

■ The Cunningham Trust

WHERE FUNDING CAN BE GIVEN Scotland.

WHO CAN BENEFIT Organisations benefiting academics and research workers.

WHAT IS FUNDED Grants are made to university departments which are carrying out academic research in the field of medicine.

WHAT IS NOT FUNDED Grants are unlikely to be made available to non-regular beneficiaries.

TYPE OF GRANT A number of the grants made are recurring.

FINANCES *Year* 2000 *Grants* £270,000 *Assets* £8,538,000

TRUSTEES Prof. C Blake; A C Caithness; Dr D McD Greenhough.

HOW TO APPLY Current information about dates and procedures for submitting applications is supplied to the deans of faculties of medicine of the Scottish universities. Applications need to be received by May and trustees meet in June and November. All applications must be submitted on the standard form, and early admission is advisable.

WHO TO APPLY TO Murray Donald & Caithness, Solicitors, Kinburn Castle, St Andrews, Fife KY16 9DR *Tel* 01334 477107 *Fax* 01334 476862

SC NO SC013499 **ESTABLISHED** 1984

■ The D J H Currie Memorial Trust

WHERE FUNDING CAN BE GIVEN Essex.
WHO CAN BENEFIT Registered charities. No recipient may benefit more than once every four years.
WHAT IS FUNDED General charitable purposes.
WHAT IS NOT FUNDED No grants to individuals.
RANGE OF GRANTS Average £2,500.
FINANCES *Year* 2001–02 *Income* £37,000 *Grants* £28,000
TRUSTEES National Westminster Bank plc.
HOW TO APPLY In writing to the correspondent. The trustees consider applications in June each year and all applications should be submitted by the end of May.
WHO TO APPLY TO John Feeney, Assistant Manager, Natwest Private Banking (Brighton Branch), 153 Preston Road, Brighton, East Sussex BN1 6BD *Tel* 01273 545035 *Fax* 01273 545075
CC NO 802971   **ESTABLISHED** 1990

■ The Dennis Curry Charitable Trust

WHERE FUNDING CAN BE GIVEN UK.
WHAT IS FUNDED Particular interest in conservation/environment and education.
RANGE OF GRANTS £500–£20,000.
SAMPLE GRANTS £10,000 each to Council for National Parks and Galopagos Trust; £2,000 to Forest Stewardship Council; £1,000 to Berkshire, Buckinghamshire and Oxfordshire Wildlife Trust Ltd.
FINANCES *Year* 2001–02 *Income* £110,194 *Grants* £261,400 *Assets* £2,806,676
TRUSTEES M Curry; Mrs A S Curry; Mrs M Curry-Jones; Mrs P Edmond.
HOW TO APPLY In writing to the correspondent.
WHO TO APPLY TO N J Armstrong, Secretary to the Trust, Messrs Alliotts, 5th Floor, 9 Kingsway, London WC2B 6XF *Tel* 020 7240 9971
CC NO 263952   **ESTABLISHED** 1971

■ The Suzanne & Raymond Curtis Foundation

WHERE FUNDING CAN BE GIVEN UK.
WHO CAN BENEFIT Registered charities.
WHAT IS FUNDED Organisations supporting children under 18 and older people.
SAMPLE GRANTS In 1998–99: £5,000 to Nightingale House; £4,200 to Macmillan Cancer Relief (in two payments); £3,500 to Babes in Arms; £2,500 to Variety Club; £600 to Greater London for the Blind; £580 to Duke of Edinburgh Scheme; £500 each to Teenage Cancer Relief, Worshipful Company of Carmen and the Magic Circle.
FINANCES *Year* 2000–01 *Income* £25,915
HOW TO APPLY In writing to the correspondent.
WHO TO APPLY TO R Curtis, Glebe Farm, Island Farm Road, Ufton Nervet, Reading RG7 4EP *Tel* 01189 835486
CC NO 1050295   **ESTABLISHED** 1995

■ The Manny Cussins Foundation

WHERE FUNDING CAN BE GIVEN Mainly UK, with some emphasis on Yorkshire.
WHO CAN BENEFIT Organisations.
WHAT IS FUNDED Welfare and care of older people and children at risk; Jewish causes; healthcare in Yorkshire and overseas; general in Yorkshire and the former county of Humberside.
WHAT IS NOT FUNDED Applications for the benefit of individuals are not supported.
RANGE OF GRANTS £20–£8,000, but mostly under £1,000.
SAMPLE GRANTS In 1998–99: £8,000 to Manny Cussins House; £5,300 to Angels International; £4,000 to Bramley & Rodley Community; £3,600 to St George's Crypt; £2,600 to Leeds Jewish Welfare Board.
FINANCES *Year* 2001–02 *Income* £58,629
TRUSTEES A Reuben, Chair; A Cussins; A J Cussins; J Cussins; Mrs A Reuben.
HOW TO APPLY The correspondent states that applications are not sought as the trustees carry out their own research.
WHO TO APPLY TO Arnold Reuben, Chair, c/o Freedman Ross, 9 Lisbon Square, Leeds LS1 4LY *Tel* 0113 243 3022
CC NO 219661   **ESTABLISHED** 1962

■ The Cwmbran Trust

WHERE FUNDING CAN BE GIVEN Cwmbran.
WHO CAN BENEFIT Neighbourhood-based community projects benefiting people of all ages; ex-service and service people; musicians; retired people; sportsmen and women; students; unemployed people; volunteers; those in care, fostered and adopted; parents and children; one-parent families; widows and widowers; at risk groups; people with disabilities; those disadvantaged by poverty; homeless people; and victims of domestic violence.
WHAT IS FUNDED Grants are made to provide social amenities for the advancement of education and the relief of poverty and sickness in the urban area of Cwmbran town. Particularly charities working in the fields of: community development; support to volunteers, voluntary organisations; Christian education; arts, culture and recreation; health care; hospices; rehabilitation centres; church buildings; memorials and monuments; animal homes and welfare; campaigning for environmental issues; education and training; community facilities and services.
WHAT IS NOT FUNDED No grants are made outside of Cwmbran.
TYPE OF GRANT Capital, core costs, interest-free loans, one-off, project, running costs, and start-up costs.
RANGE OF GRANTS £100–£10,000.
SAMPLE GRANTS £8,919 to MIND; £5,000 to Autistic Society; £2,300 to Toy Time Playgroup; £2,000 each to Fairhill Methodist Church and Children's Hospice for Wales; £1,750 to Gwent Victim Support; £1,710 to Torfaen Women; £1,325 to Torfaen Gymnastics Club; £1,190 to Congress Players; £1,000 to South Gwent Cancer Support.
FINANCES *Year* 2001 *Income* £60,200 *Grants* £53,294 *Assets* £1,640,000
TRUSTEES P M Harris, Chair; K L Maddox; A Rippon; B E Smith; B J Cunningham; D J Bassett.
HOW TO APPLY In writing to the correspondent. Trustees usually meet five times a year in March, May, July, October and December. Where appropriate, applications are investigated by the grants research officer. When the trustees judge it would be helpful, applicants are invited to put their case to the trustees in person. Where an application has to be dealt with urgently, for example, because of the pressure of time or of need, trustees may be contacted by letter or telephone in order that an early decision may be made.

WHO TO APPLY TO K L Maddox, c/o Arvin (UK) Ltd, Meritor H V B S (UK) Ltd, Grange Road, Cwmbran NP44 3XU *Tel* 01633 834040 *Fax* 01633 834051
CC NO 505855   ESTABLISHED 1976

....

■ Itzchok Meyer Cymerman Trust Ltd

WHERE FUNDING CAN BE GIVEN UK and overseas.
WHO CAN BENEFIT Jewish people.
WHAT IS FUNDED To advance religion in accordance with the orthodox Jewish faith and other charitable purposes.
FINANCES *Year* 1999–2000 *Income* £512,000 *Grants* £916,000 *Assets* £1,600,000
TRUSTEES Mrs H L Bondi; I M Cymerman; M D Cymerman; Mrs R Cymerman; Mrs S Heitner.
HOW TO APPLY In writing to the correspondent.
WHO TO APPLY TO I M Cymerman, Trustee, 22 Overlea Road, London E5
CC NO 265090   ESTABLISHED 1972

....

■ Cystic Fibrosis Trust

WHERE FUNDING CAN BE GIVEN UK and worldwide.
WHO CAN BENEFIT Individuals and families coping with cystic fibrosis, directly and via the National Health Service and professionals who offer medical and social care.
WHAT IS FUNDED Research to find better treatments, care and a cure for cystic fibrosis.
WHAT IS NOT FUNDED No grants are made to projects with very little relevance to cystic fibrosis.
TYPE OF GRANT Research projects and programmes. Funding is available for up to and over three years.
RANGE OF GRANTS £100 – £100,000 and more.
SAMPLE GRANTS In previous years major grants have included those to Imperial College London, University of Dundee, University of Oxford, University of Edinburgh, University of Cambridge, University of Wales College of Medicine, University of Manchester, Medical Research Council – Western General Hospital Edinburgh, University of Southampton and Royal Belfast Hospital.
FINANCES *Year* 2001–02 *Income* £6,829,000 *Grants* £3,855,000 *Assets* £2,619,000
TRUSTEES Duncan Black, Chair; Sir Robert Johnson; Peter Levy; Anthony Angel; Sir Peter Cresswell; Dr James Littlewood.
PUBLICATIONS Newsletter – *CF News, CF Talk and Focus on Fundraising.*
HOW TO APPLY Please telephone or e-mail the research administrator for an application form.
WHO TO APPLY TO Mrs Jan Drayton, Research Administrator, 11 London Road, Bromley, Kent BR1 1BY *Tel* 020 8464 7211 *Fax* 020 8313 0472 *E-mail* jdrayton@cftrust.org.uk *Website* www.cftrust.org.uk
CC NO 1079049   ESTABLISHED 1964

■ The D C Trust

WHERE FUNDING CAN BE GIVEN Greater Manchester.
WHO CAN BENEFIT Registered charities.
WHAT IS FUNDED The trust supports the relief of poverty.
FINANCES *Year* 1999–2000 *Income* £65,000 *Grants* £65,000
TRUSTEES S J Mendelson; K S L Trustees Ltd.
HOW TO APPLY In writing to the correspondent.
WHO TO APPLY TO The Trustees, 81 King Street, Manchester M2 4ST *Tel* 0161 950 1999
CC NO 1075748   **ESTABLISHED** 1997

■ The Sarah D'Avigdor Goldsmid Charitable Trust

WHERE FUNDING CAN BE GIVEN Mainly Kent.
WHO CAN BENEFIT Registered charities only.
WHAT IS FUNDED No specific policy, but charities concerned with conservation and environment, and head injuries are of most interest.
WHAT IS NOT FUNDED No grants to individuals.
TYPE OF GRANT One-off.
RANGE OF GRANTS £25–£1,000; typical grant £50–£100.
SAMPLE GRANTS £5,000 each to Lady Margaret Hall Oxford, Lady Raynor Hall and Round House Trust; £2,600 to Headway; £2,500 to Glyndebourne; £2,100 to Royal Engineers' Museum; £1,500 to Haven Trust; and £1,000 each to Badminton Trust, Friends of the Imperial War Museum and Kent Air Ambulance.
FINANCES *Year* 2000 *Income* £135,000 *Grants* £57,000 *Assets* £602,000
TRUSTEES Mrs R C Teacher; A J M Teacher; H D M Teacher.
OTHER INFORMATION The income for the year 2000 was unusually high, more typically it is around £25,000.
HOW TO APPLY In writing to the correspondent. Unsuccessful applications are not acknowledged.
WHO TO APPLY TO Mrs R C Teacher, Trustee, Hadlow Place, Golden Green, Tonbridge, Kent TN11 0BW
CC NO 233083   **ESTABLISHED** 1963

■ The Baron F A d'Erlanger Charitable Trust

WHERE FUNDING CAN BE GIVEN UK.
WHO CAN BENEFIT Organisations and individuals.
WHAT IS FUNDED Relief in need.
SAMPLE GRANTS £10,000 each to Bethany Christain Trust, Crisis, Kidscape, Refresh, Royal Society of Musicians of Great Britain and Shelter; £1,000 each to Brainwave; £500 to Peter Pan Nursery.
FINANCES *Year* 2000–01 *Income* £127,000 *Grants* £187,000 *Assets* £6,000,000
TRUSTEES Peter Frederick Denham; Philip Roderick Denham; Dr David O'Flynn.
OTHER INFORMATION £125,000 was given to 305 individuals.
HOW TO APPLY In writing to the correspondent.

■ The D'Oyly Carte Charitable Trust

WHERE FUNDING CAN BE GIVEN UK.
WHO CAN BENEFIT Registered charities only, or where it is clear the objects of the appeal are for charitable purposes.
WHAT IS FUNDED Mainly the arts, medical/welfare charities and the environment. Priorities for support for the next three years are: the promotion of access, education and excellence in the arts for young people to increase their opportunities to become involved outside school and to build future audiences; access to the arts for people who least have access to them; performance development of graduates in the performing arts in the early stages of their careers and to encourage their involvement in the community through performances and workshops for the benefit of those with special needs and those who would otherwise have no opportunity to hear or particpate in a live performance; promotion and provision of music and art therapy to improve the quality of life for the elderly and the disabled; promotion and provision of music and art therapy in the palliative care of children; support for charities concerned with alleviating the suffering of adults and children with medical conditions who have difficulty finding support through traditional sources; support and respite for carers with emphasis on the provison of holidays for carers who wouldn't normally have a break from their responsibilities – with special emphasis on projects and schemes that allow young carers to enjoy being children; preservation of the countryside and its woodlands – with emphasis on the encouragement of voluntary work and active involvement in hands-on activities; protection of species within the UK and their habitats under threat or in decline; conservation of the marine environment and sustainable fisheries; heritage conservation within the UK based on value to, and use by the local community – the trust favours projects that seek to create a new use for fine buildings of architectural and historic merit to encourage the widest possible cross-section of use.
WHAT IS NOT FUNDED The trust is unlikely to support the following: animal welfare; applications from individuals; charities requiring funding for statutory requirements; charities operating outside the UK; conferences or seminars; exhibitions; expeditions and overseas travel; general appeals; large national charities which enjoy widespread support; maintenance of religious buildings; medical research; NHS trust hospitals for operational or building costs; recordings and commissioning of new works; religious activities; schools, nurseries and playgroups (other than those for special needs children); support and rehabilitation from drug abuse or alcoholism. Because of the volume of appeals received, the trustees have decided not to consider requests from charities that have had an application turned down until two years have elapsed after the date of rejection.
TYPE OF GRANT Mainly one-off.
SAMPLE GRANTS Final instalment of grants totalling £265,000 over three years to National Youth Music; second instalments of grants totalling

£150,000 each to Music for Youth, National children's Orchestra and National Youth Orchestra; £45,000 over three years to Abbotsbury Music Festival; £30,000 each to Guillain-Barre Syndrome Support Group, Norwich Cathedral for its development programme and Painshill Park Trust for running costs; £15,000 to Help the Hospices towards its outreach programme; £15,000 over three years to both Heartlands Cystic Fibrosis Centre for a new centre in Birmingham and National Eczema Society for development of a national telephone helpline.

FINANCES *Year* 2001–02 *Income* £1,000,000 *Grants* £1,425,000 *Assets* £35,600,000

TRUSTEES J Leigh Pemberton, chair; E J P Elliott; Sir John Batten; Mrs F Radcliffe; Mrs J Sibley; Dr R K Knight; H Freeland.

HOW TO APPLY Potential applicants should write to the correspondent with an outline proposal of no more than two A4 pages. This should cover the work of the charity, its beneficiaries and the need for funding. Applicants qualifying for consideration will then be required to complete the trust's two-page application form. The form should be returned with a copy of the latest annual report and accounts. Applications for specific projects should also include clear details of the need the intended project is designed to meet and an outline budget. The trust also requires applicants to provide information on how the work supported will continue after the trust's grant has been completed, with plans for monitoring and evaluation. The trustees usually consider applications in July and December.

WHO TO APPLY TO Mrs J Thorne, Secretary, 1 Savoy Hill, London WC2R 0BP *Tel* 020 7420 2600 *Fax* 020 7240 8561

CC NO 265057   ESTABLISHED 1972

··

■ The Roald Dahl Foundation

WHERE FUNDING CAN BE GIVEN UK.

WHO CAN BENEFIT Individuals as well as voluntary and charitable organisations. In general, the trust aims to provide help to organisations to whom funds are not readily available. Preference for small or new organisations rather than long-established, large or national organisations.

WHAT IS FUNDED Haematology: help for children and young people up to the age of 25 with blood disorders which are not cancer related – most commonly haemophilia, sickle cell and thalassaemia; Neurology: help for children and young people up to the age of 25 who have epilepsy, acquired brain injury or neuro-degenerative conditions where there is progressive intellectual and neurological deterioration; Literacy: work to assist children and young people who may need extra help to achieve this essential basic skill. There is a small grants scheme to give individual assistance to children and young people (and their families) who fall within the medical categories. Within the medical fields specifically, grants may be made for pump-priming funding of specialist paediatric nursing and other care, especially where there is an emphasis on community care, for a maximum of two years; assistance to residential and day care centres for children and young people who come into the above medical categories; small items of medical equipment that will allow the patient to be cared for in the home with community care/hospital back-up.

Within the literacy field the trust is interested in

making grants for: specific literacy work to improve poor literacy skills among children and young people, and their families, in out of school clubs and centres for young people 16–25 years; computer/technological and other assistance to enable children and young people who are visually impaired or head injured to access the written word.

WHAT IS NOT FUNDED The foundation does not consider grant applications for: general appeals from large, well-established charities or national appeals for large building projects; research in any field; any organisations which do not have charitable status or exclusively charitable aims; statutory bodies; projects outside the UK; school or higher education fees.

TYPE OF GRANT One-off, start-up costs, salaries, projects for up to two years; the range is wide

RANGE OF GRANTS Individual: £50–£500. Organisations: up to £25,000. The foundation's largest grants are made to pump prime new nursing posts.

SAMPLE GRANTS £34,308 to Glan Hafren NHS Trust – Newport; £25,000 each to Royal Hospital for Neuro-disability – London and University College London; £20,000 to St Piers – Lingfield, Surrey; £19,917 to Ninewells Hospital – Dundee; £12,000 to Primary Immunodeficiency Association UK; £10,000 to Headway Belfast; £9,000 to Oxford Radliffe Hospital Trust; £7,141 to National Hospital for Neurology and Neurosurgery; £6,250 to Different Strokes; £6,000 to Leeds Teaching Hospitals NHS Trust.

FINANCES *Year* 2000–01 *Income* £673,691 *Grants* £453,400 *Assets* £1,471,690

TRUSTEES Felicity Dahl, Chair; Martin Goodwin; Roger Hills.

HOW TO APPLY On the straightforward form provided, with a covering letter if necessary. Applications are considered throughout the year. Decisions on smaller sums can take as little as a few weeks. Applications for grants of several thousand pounds may take several months to be considered.

WHO TO APPLY TO Linda Lazenby, Deputy Director, 92 High Street, Great Missenden, Bucks HP16 0AN *Tel* 01494 890465 *Fax* 01494 890459 *Website* www.roalddahlfoundation.org

CC NO 1004230   ESTABLISHED 1991

··

■ The Daily Prayer Union Charitable Trust Ltd

WHERE FUNDING CAN BE GIVEN UK.

WHO CAN BENEFIT Christians and evangelists.

WHAT IS FUNDED Evangelical Christian purposes.

WHAT IS NOT FUNDED No grants for bricks and mortar.

RANGE OF GRANTS £1,000–£7,000.

SAMPLE GRANTS £7,000 to Monkton Coombe School; £3,000 to Fan Fare – New Generation; £2,500 to IFES; £2,000 each to Oak Hill College and Society for International Mission; £1,500 to Dagenham Church.

FINANCES *Year* 1998–99 *Income* £60,000 *Grants* £57,000 *Assets* £155,000

TRUSTEES Bishop T Dudley-Smith; Revd G C Grinham; Canon J Tiller; Sir T Hoare; Mrs E Bridger; Mrs A Thompson; Mrs F M Ashton; Mrs R K Harley; Revd D Jackman; R M Horn; Mrs A J I Lines.

HOW TO APPLY The trust supports causes already known to the trustees. Unsolicited applications are unlikely to be successful. Trustees meet at different times throughout the year, usually around March, June and October.

WHO TO APPLY TO Sir Timothy Hoare, Trustee, 10 Belitha Villas, London N1 1PD
CC NO 284857   **ESTABLISHED** 1983

....

■ Daily Telegraph Charitable Trust

WHERE FUNDING CAN BE GIVEN UK, with a preference for East London.

WHO CAN BENEFIT Registered charities benefiting every sector other than animals, especially children, young adults and those working in the newspaper industry.

WHAT IS FUNDED Emphasis is given to charities in the fields of education, the newspaper industry and local projects.

WHAT IS NOT FUNDED No grants to animal charities or individuals.

SAMPLE GRANTS In 1999: £25,000 to Royal Free Hospital; £12,500 to Business for Sterling; £10,000 each to Centre for Policy Studies and Royal Ballet School; £5,000 to Disfigurement Guidance Centre, Isle of Dogs Community Foundation, NewstrAid Benevolent Society, and Sulgrave Manor.

FINANCES *Year* 2001 *Income* £151,378

TRUSTEES D J Alder; A J Davies; C I Dolphin.

HOW TO APPLY In writing to the correspondent.

WHO TO APPLY TO Paul Lotherington, Telegraph Group Ltd, 1 Canada Square, Canary Wharf, London E14 5DT *Tel* 020 7538 7008 *E-mail* paul.lotherington@telegraph.co.uk

CC NO 205296   **ESTABLISHED** 1944

....

■ The Daiwa Anglo-Japanese Foundation

WHERE FUNDING CAN BE GIVEN UK, Japan.

WHO CAN BENEFIT Individuals and institutions (UK or Japanese) benefiting young adults, students and Japanese people.

WHAT IS FUNDED The education of citizens of the UK and Japan in each other's culture, institutions, arts, and so on. Scholarships, bursaries and awards to enable students and academics in the UK and Japan to pursue their education abroad. Grants to charitable institutions promoting education in the UK or Japan, and research. The granting of Daiwa Scholarships to five postgraduates each year to enable them to study Japanese for two years in Japan. Support of Japanese studies in the UK. Activities based at Daiwa Foundation Japan House, a centre for those interested in non-governmental Anglo-Japanese relations.

TYPE OF GRANT Outright or partnership grants, paid in sterling or Japanese yen.

FINANCES *Year* 1999–2000 *Income* £1,640,157 *Grants* £296,352 *Assets* £40,607,327

TRUSTEES Sir David Wright; Yoshitoki Chino; Lady Adrian; Prof. Sir Alec Broers; Lord Carrington; Nicholas Clegg; Hiroaki Fujii; Tomoaki Kusuda; Lord Roll of Opsden.

PUBLICATIONS *Managing Across Borders: Culture and Communications, Issues for British and Japanese Businesses.*

OTHER INFORMATION Average annual grants expected to be approximately £500,000 (exclusive of funds for Daiwa Scholarships and activities based at Daiwa Foundation Japan House).

HOW TO APPLY Forms are available online at www.dajf.org.uk. Deadlines for applications are 31 March and 30 September. Applications originating from the UK should be sent to the address shown. Applications originating from Japan should be sent to The Daiwa Anglo-

Japanese Foundation, TBR Bldg. 810, Nagat-cho2–10-2, Chiyoda-ku, Tokyo 100–0014.

WHO TO APPLY TO Prof. Marie Conte-Helm, Director General, Daiwa Foundation, 'Japan House, 13/14 Cornwall Terrace, London NW1 4QP *Tel* 020 7486 4348 *Fax* 020 7486 2914 *E-mail* office@dajf.org.uk *Website* www.dajf.org.uk

CC NO 299955   **ESTABLISHED** 1988

....

■ Oizer Dalim Trust

WHERE FUNDING CAN BE GIVEN UK.

WHO CAN BENEFIT Registered charities.

WHAT IS FUNDED General charitable purposes.

FINANCES *Year* 1998–99 *Income* £141,377 *Grants* £147,438 *Assets* £7,234

TRUSTEES B Berger; M Freund; N Weinberger.

HOW TO APPLY In writing to the correspondent.

WHO TO APPLY TO M Cik, 68 Osbaldeston Road, London N16 7DR

CC NO 1045296   **ESTABLISHED** 1994

....

■ The Dr & Mrs A Darlington Charitable Trust

WHERE FUNDING CAN BE GIVEN Devon, in particular Sidmouth and east Devon.

WHO CAN BENEFIT Only registered charities.

WHAT IS FUNDED The trust mainly supports medical causes; at risk groups; people who are disabled; older people; and socially isolated people. Grants also given in the fields of nature conservation and preservation.

WHAT IS NOT FUNDED Applications from individuals, including students, are unlikely to be successful.

TYPE OF GRANT One-off, some recurring.

RANGE OF GRANTS £1,000–£30,000.

SAMPLE GRANTS In 1999–2000: £30,000 to Institute of Clinical Science for research; £10,000 to Devon Wildlife Trust for nature reserves; £5,000 to Multiple Sclerosis Therapy Centre for a new building; £4,000 to Sense for general costs; £2,850 to Royal Devon & Exeter Hospital for equipment for the A&E department; £2,000 each to Royal West of England School for the Deaf for a stairlift, Invalids at Home for general costs, RNIB for talking books, and West Country Rivers Trust for general expenses; £1,000 to RUKBA.

FINANCES *Year* 2000–01 *Income* £102,716 *Grants* £105,111 *Assets* £2,204,296

TRUSTEES Lloyds TSB Bank plc; V A Donson.

HOW TO APPLY In writing to the correspondent. The trustees regret that they cannot send replies to unsuccessful applicants. The trustees meet quarterly in March, June, September and December; applications should be received the previous month.

WHO TO APPLY TO V A Donson, Trustee, Ford Simey, 8 Cathedral Close, Exeter EX1 1EW *Tel* 01392 274126 *Fax* 01392 410933

CC NO 283308   **ESTABLISHED** 1981

....

■ The Iris Darnton Foundation

WHERE FUNDING CAN BE GIVEN UK, but preference for overseas.

WHO CAN BENEFIT Institutions benefiting academics and research workers.

WHAT IS FUNDED Educational and research projects only. Research into habitat and species protection and conservation. Promoting by

educational means the aesthetic appreciation of flora and fauna, and to promote public morality and advancement of humanitarian principles in relation to wildlife and its preservation.
WHAT IS NOT FUNDED No grants for expeditions, scholarships or individuals.
RANGE OF GRANTS £500–£10,000.
SAMPLE GRANTS In 1999: £10,000 to Whitley Darnton International Conservation Awards; £5,000 each to Wildfowl and Wetlands Trust (Whooper Swan Research), Oxford Wildlife Conservation Research Unit, Galapagos Conservation Trust, and Dian Fossey Gorilla Fund; £3,000 to FFI-IPE (Brazil Rainforest); £2,500 each to Cheetah Conservation Fund, Cheetah Outreach, and Seub Nakhasthien Foundation; £2,000 to Mauritian Wildlife Appeal (Echo Parakeet).
FINANCES *Year* 2000–01 *Income* £21,329
TRUSTEES J Teacher, Chair; Miss A D Darnton; Mrs C Hardy; Mrs H Robinson.
HOW TO APPLY No written or telephone applications will be accepted. The trust states that new applicants are only considered if proposed by World Wildlife Fund in Nature.
WHO TO APPLY TO James Teacher, Smith & Williamson, 21 Chipper Lane, Salisbury SP1 1BG *Tel* 01722 411881 *Fax* 01722 434813
CC NO 252576   **ESTABLISHED** 1966

....

■ Datnow Limited
WHERE FUNDING CAN BE GIVEN UK and overseas.
WHO CAN BENEFIT Registered charities only.
WHAT IS FUNDED General charitable purposes, particularly Jewish-related causes.
SAMPLE GRANTS £6,600 to National Society for Epilepsy; £5,000 to Eagle Hill Capital Campaign; £3,000 each to Hope Charity and New Israel Fund; £2,900 to Age Endeavour; £2,500 to Consent Medical Society; £1,000 each to University of Liverpool and Royal Hospital for Neurology.
FINANCES *Year* 1999–2000 *Income* £13,000 *Grants* £42,000 *Assets* £448,000
TRUSTEES Mrs E M Datnow; E L Datnow; J A Datnow; A D Datnow.
HOW TO APPLY In writing to the correspondent, but replies will not be sent to unsuccessful applicants. This entry was not confirmed by the trust, but the information was correct according to the trust's file at the Charity Commission.
WHO TO APPLY TO A D Datnow, Trustee, 130 Holland Park Avenue, London W11 4UE *Tel* 020 7243 2416
CC NO 247183   **ESTABLISHED** 1966

....

■ Baron Davenport's Charity
WHERE FUNDING CAN BE GIVEN The counties of Warwickshire, Worcestershire, Staffordshire, Shropshire and West Midlands.
WHO CAN BENEFIT Individuals (as defined by the trust deed) and charitable organisations and institutions, benefiting children, young adults, retired people, widows, and people disadvantaged by poverty.
WHAT IS FUNDED £10,000 annually for charitable purposes nominated between the trustees (excluding any ex-officio trustee); not less than £2,000 and not more than £10,000 to the Bishop of Birmingham and not less than £1,000 and not more than £5,000 to the Chief Minister of the Birmingham Hebrew Congregation. Of the remaining balance, 30% is available to charities benefiting children and young people under 25

years of age, 30% is for almshouses, homes for older people and hospices, and 40% is for the assistance of widows, spinsters and divorced women (aged 60 years and over), and women abandoned by their partners and the children of such people under 25 years of age who are in reduced financial circumstances.
WHAT IS NOT FUNDED None, providing the applications come within the charity's objects and the applying organisation is based within the charity's benefit area, or the organisation's project lies within or helps young people who live in the benefit area.
TYPE OF GRANT One-off or annual grants, for capital or revenue costs.
SAMPLE GRANTS £7,000 to The Stonehouse Gang; £6,000 each to Coventry Church Municipal Charities, and Primrose Hospice – Bromsgrove; £5,000 to Little Sisters of the Poor Nursing Home – Birmingham; £4,500 to Birmingham Jewish Community Care; £4,000 each to Myton Hospice – Warwickshire, St Giles Hospice – Whittington, St Richard's Hospice – Worcester, and Thomas Whites Cottage Homes – Bromsgrove.
FINANCES *Year* 2002 *Income* £827,000 *Grants* £885,000 *Assets* £21,000,000
TRUSTEES A C Hordern; G R Willcox; P A Gough; W M Colacicchi; Mrs S A Wood.
HOW TO APPLY In writing, accompanied by the latest accounts and any project costs. Distributions take place twice a year at the end of May and November and applications should be received at the charity's office by 15 March or 15 September. All applications are acknowledged and those not within the charity's objects are advised.
WHO TO APPLY TO Bernard Cooper, Secretary, Portman House, 5–7 Temple Row West, Birmingham B2 5NY *Tel* 0121 236 8004 *Fax* 0121 233 2500 *E-mail* baron.davenport@virgin.net
CC NO 217307   **ESTABLISHED** 1930

....

■ David Charitable Trust
WHERE FUNDING CAN BE GIVEN UK.
WHO CAN BENEFIT Actors and entertainment professionals, musicians, textile workers and designers, students, writers and poets, at risk groups, people disadvantaged by poverty, and socially isolated people.
WHAT IS FUNDED Health and welfare, children, older and infirm people, educational institutions, the arts.
WHAT IS NOT FUNDED No grants to individuals.
SAMPLE GRANTS £75,000 to Lady Hoare Trust; £10,000 each to Home Farm Trust and Prisoners of Conscience; £5,000 each to Martlet Hospice, Trestle Theatre Company Ltd and Trinity Hospice; £500 to National Endometriosis Society.
FINANCES *Year* 2001 *Income* £13,397 *Grants* £110,500 *Assets* £385,718
TRUSTEES B J David; C M David; G S Brown.
HOW TO APPLY In writing to the correspondent, accompanied by latest annual report and accounts.
WHO TO APPLY TO The Trustees, Payne Hicks Beach, Solicitors, 10 New Square, Lincoln's Inn, London WC2A 3QG *Tel* 020 7465 4300
CC NO 1015509   **ESTABLISHED** 1990

■ Davidson Charitable Trust

WHERE FUNDING CAN BE GIVEN UK.
WHO CAN BENEFIT Jewish organisations.
RANGE OF GRANTS £100–£25,000
SAMPLE GRANTS In 1997–98: £5,300 to Norwood Ravenswood; £3,000 to British Friends of CBI; £2,700 to Joint Jewish Charitable Trust; £2,500 to Imperial War Museum's Holocaust Project; £1,700 to World Jewish Relief.
FINANCES *Year* 1999–2000 *Income* £108,000 *Grants* £64,000 *Assets* £75,000
TRUSTEES G A Davidson; M Y Davidson; Mrs E Winer.
HOW TO APPLY In writing to the correspondent.
WHO TO APPLY TO Mrs E Winer, Trustee, 58 Queen Anne Street, London W1G 8HW *Tel* 020 7224 1030
CC NO 262937   **ESTABLISHED** 1971

■ The Alderman Joe Davidson Memorial Trust

WHERE FUNDING CAN BE GIVEN UK, with a preference for Hampshire.
WHO CAN BENEFIT Local and specific national organisations and individuals benefiting: children; older people, nominated by Age Concern; and Jewish people.
WHAT IS FUNDED The trust deed allows for annual maintenance of one block of flats owned by the trust. The balance of the income is distributed as follows: the provision of homes for people aged over 70 in need; charitable donations to specific organisations as detailed in the trust deed; annual grants to needy people nominated by Age Concern; Christmas parties each year for older people and children; and presentation of watches to schoolchildren for regular attendance.
TYPE OF GRANT Recurring grants given to specific organisations.
FINANCES *Year* 2001–02 *Income* £37,000
TRUSTEES Ald. Mrs M B E Leonard; C Davidson; P Gooch; Miss M A Ashton; K J Veness; J Klein; K Crabbe; M Thomas.
HOW TO APPLY Applications are not accepted if not a regular beneficiary.
WHO TO APPLY TO John Stock, Trustees Secretary, Chief Executive's Office, Civic Offices, Portsmouth PO1 2AL *Tel* 023 9283 4060 *Fax* 023 9283 4076 *E-mail* jstock@portsmouthcc.gov.uk
CC NO 202591   **ESTABLISHED** 1962

■ The Davidson (Nairn) Charitable Trust

WHERE FUNDING CAN BE GIVEN Nairn area.
WHO CAN BENEFIT Social welfare organisations.
WHAT IS FUNDED Grants may be made towards the provision of leisure and recreation facilities, relieving poverty, assisting elderly people, and educational concerns.
WHAT IS NOT FUNDED Only recognised charities are supported.
FINANCES *Grants* £100,000
TRUSTEES Ian A Macgregor and others.
HOW TO APPLY Write to the correspondent for an application form.
WHO TO APPLY TO Ian A Macgregor, Solicitor, Messrs Macgregor & Co., Royal Bank of Scotland Buildings, 20 High Street, Nairn IV12 4AX *Tel* 01667 453278 *Fax* 01667 453499 *E-mail* macgregorco@btinternet.com
SC NO sc024273

■ The Biss Davies Charitable Trust

WHERE FUNDING CAN BE GIVEN London.
WHO CAN BENEFIT Higher education establishments.
WHAT IS FUNDED University departments.
SAMPLE GRANTS £15,000 to London School of Economics; £7,500 to University College London Development Fund; £3,000 to Kings College School of Dentistry; £2,500 to University College Music Department; £1,000 to North London Music Festival; £250 to GDST Prizes and Scholarships Fund.
FINANCES *Year* 1999–2000 *Income* £33,000 *Grants* £32,000 *Assets* £200,000
HOW TO APPLY This trust does its own research and does not seek or respond to unsolicited applications.
WHO TO APPLY TO R O Davies, 7 Elsworthy Road, London NW3 3DS *Tel* 020 7586 3999
CC NO 296824   **ESTABLISHED** 1987

■ The Gwendoline & Margaret Davies Charity

WHERE FUNDING CAN BE GIVEN UK, with particular favour given to Wales.
WHO CAN BENEFIT Registered charities only. Welsh charities are particularly favoured.
WHAT IS FUNDED General charitable purposes, with special consideration given to the arts, health and young people. Organisations in the fields of education, medical research, community care services environment and faith activities may also be considered.
WHAT IS NOT FUNDED Grants are made to registered charities only.
TYPE OF GRANT Mainly one-off, occasionally recurrent for specific capital projects.
RANGE OF GRANTS £100–£100,000, typical grant £5,000–£10,000.
SAMPLE GRANTS Committed funds for 2002–03: £100,000 to MCRA for a gallery; £50,000 to Millennium Centre; £30,000 to Bethshan Nursing Home; £20,000 to University of Wales; £12,000 to Wales Video Press; £10,000 each to Institute of Orthopaedics, and North East Wales NHS Trust; £5,000 each to Powys Challenge Trust and University of Wales.
FINANCES *Year* 2001/02 *Income* £309,496 *Grants* £274,450 *Assets* £5,770,938
TRUSTEES Dr J A Davies; Lord Davies; Dr D Balsom.
HOW TO APPLY The trustees consider appeals on an individual basis. There are no application forms as the trustees prefer to receive letters from applicants setting out the following information: whether the organisation is a registered charity; details of the reason for the application – the type of work and so on; the cost; how much has been raised so far towards the cost; the source of the sums raised; a copy of the last audited accounts if available; and any other information that the applicant may consider would help the application. Unsuccessful appeals are not informed unless an sae is enclosed.
WHO TO APPLY TO Mrs S Hamer, The Offices, Plas Dinam, Llandinam, Powys SY17 5DO *Tel* 01686 689172 *Fax* 01686 689172
CC NO 235589   **ESTABLISHED** 1934

■ The John Grant Davies Trust

WHERE FUNDING CAN BE GIVEN Greater Manchester.
WHO CAN BENEFIT Charitable organisations.
WHAT IS FUNDED Financial support is given for combating poverty to community groups, voluntary organisations and faith communities.

Think carefully about every application. Is it justified?

423

Preference is given to small grassroots organisations. This includes: infrastructure development; charity or voluntary umbrella bodies; community arts and recreation; health counselling; health education; environmental issues; transport and alternative transport; IT training; literacy; training for community development; playgrounds and recreation grounds; community services; campaigning for social issues; equal opportunities; and advice and information.

WHAT IS NOT FUNDED The trust does not fund building or refurbishment projects or medical charity work.

TYPE OF GRANT One-off, capital, core costs, feasibility studies, project, research, salaries and start-up costs. Funding is available for up to three years.

RANGE OF GRANTS £100–£3,000.

SAMPLE GRANTS In 1999: £2,500 each to Dream Scheme Network for children in the inner city, M13 Youth Project for youth work in Brunswick, PJ's Youth Projects for youth clubs in East Manchester, and STEPS (Strategies to Elevate People) for increasing self-esteem among black children; £2,158 to Woodhouse Park Family Centre for core costs of a contact group; £2,000 each to Bolton Neighbourhood Economical Development Agency for computers and core costs and St Mark's Church – Wythershawe for work with children, families and young people; £1,400 to St Brides Church – Old Trafford for community workers' and volunteers' expenses; £1,000 each to AWAB (Calabash) Longsight for a drop-in centre and Junior Day Care Centre – Bury for a minibus for older people.

FINANCES *Year* 2001 *Income* £22,930 *Grants* £35,254 *Assets* £444,909

TRUSTEES Nora Davies; Katherine Davies; Jonathan Dale; Craig Russell.

HOW TO APPLY On a form available from the correspondent. Grants are made quarterly and the deadlines are the middle of March, June, September and December.

WHO TO APPLY TO Nora Davies, Trustee, 1462 Ashton Old Road, Higer Openshaw, Manchester M11 1HL *Tel* 0161 301 5119

CC NO 1041001   **ESTABLISHED** 1994

■ Michael Davies Charitable Settlement

WHERE FUNDING CAN BE GIVEN UK.

WHO CAN BENEFIT Organisations.

WHAT IS FUNDED General charitable purposes.

RANGE OF GRANTS £500–£10,000.

SAMPLE GRANTS In 1996–97: £10,000 each to Camden Arts Centre and North London Hospice; £5,633 to Royal Albert Dock Trust; £5,000 each to Arkwright Arts Trust and Save the Children; £3,000 to Aviation Ball; £2,000 each to Family Holiday Association, St John Ambulance and Uphill Ski Clubs.

FINANCES *Year* 1999–2000 *Income* £5,800 *Grants* £56,000 *Assets* £146,000

TRUSTEES M J P Davies; G H Camamile.

HOW TO APPLY In writing to the correspondent.

WHO TO APPLY TO K Hawkins, Lee Associates, 5 Southampton Place, London WC1A 2DA *Tel* 020 7025 4600

CC NO 1000574   **ESTABLISHED** 1990

■ The Richard Davies Charitable Foundation

WHERE FUNDING CAN BE GIVEN Bristol.

WHAT IS FUNDED General charitable purposes, particular help for small organisations for start-up and self-help.

WHAT IS NOT FUNDED No grants to individuals or for capital projects for buildings.

TYPE OF GRANT The foundation will not enter into long-term funding but will consider recurrent grants for up to five years. Core costs, running costs, recurring costs, salaries and start-up costs.

SAMPLE GRANTS In 1999–2000: £3,500 to Bristol Children's Help Society.

FINANCES *Year* 2000–01 *Income* £32,000 *Grants* £20,000 *Assets* £882,000

TRUSTEES R E Davies; Mrs K M Davies; Mrs J M Coles; T E Pyper; R A Powell; G J Coles.

HOW TO APPLY In writing to the correspondent. There are no formal application procedures/forms. Trustees meet bi-monthly, every second Wednesday.

WHO TO APPLY TO R A Powell, Secretary, 298 Canford Lane, Westbury-on-Trym, Bristol BS9 3PL *Tel* 0117 949 8571

CC NO 279380   **ESTABLISHED** 1979

■ The Wilfrid Bruce Davis Charitable Trust

WHERE FUNDING CAN BE GIVEN UK, but mainly Cornwall; India.

WHO CAN BENEFIT Voluntary groups and registered charities benefiting people with cancer, head and other injuries, kidney disease, motor neurone disease, strokes or people with terminal illnesses.

WHAT IS FUNDED The support of cancer and kidney dialysis patients and others with improved nursing care, counselling and provision of holidays.

WHAT IS NOT FUNDED No applications from individuals are considered.

TYPE OF GRANT All funding is for up to three years.

SAMPLE GRANTS £46,000 to Pain and Palliative Care Society; £35,000 to Royal Cornwall Hospital's Trust; £3,100 to Cornwall Macmillan Service; £3,000 to Pathway; £500 to Nimrod Marching Band; £300 to Woodside St Ives; £250 each to Cornish Talking Newspaper and Magazine Association and Penzance and District Disabled Club.

FINANCES *Year* 2000–01 *Income* £81,000 *Grants* £89,000 *Assets* £702,000

TRUSTEES W B Davis; Mrs D F Davis; Mrs D S Dickens; Mrs C A S Peirce.

HOW TO APPLY No replies are made to unsolicited applications. The correspondent has stated that the budget for many years to come is fully committed and that the trust receives hundreds of applications, none of which can be supported.

WHO TO APPLY TO W B Davis, Trustee, La Feock Grange, Feock, Truro, Cornwall TR3 6RG

CC NO 265421   **ESTABLISHED** 1967

■ Davis-Rubens Charitable Trust

(formerly the Lily and Henry Davis Charitable Foundation)

WHERE FUNDING CAN BE GIVEN UK.

WHO CAN BENEFIT Registered charities with a preference for UK-wide and Jewish charities.

WHAT IS FUNDED General charitable purposes.

WHAT IS NOT FUNDED No grants to individuals.

TYPE OF GRANT Mainly recurrent.

RANGE OF GRANTS £50–£1,000, mostly under £500.

SAMPLE GRANTS £1,300 to Jewish Care; £800 to Winged Fellowship Trust; £600 each to British Diabetic Association, Jewish Care for Lady Sarah Cohen House, Jewish Children's Holiday Fund, Jewish Deaf Association, Jewish Philanthropic Association for Israel & Middle East, and Muscular Dystrophy Group of Great Britain and Northern Ireland.

FINANCES *Year* 2001–02 *Grants* £24,000 *Assets* £632,000

TRUSTEES Mrs E B Rubens; J A Clemence.

HOW TO APPLY In writing to the correspondent, however, the trust states that applications from new charities are rarely considered.

WHO TO APPLY TO Renny Clark, Gilbert Allen & Co., Churchdown Chambers, Bordyke, Tonbridge, Kent TN9 1NR *Tel* 01732 770100 *Fax* 01732 369300

CC NO 263662   **ESTABLISHED** 1971

■ The Dawe Charitable Trust

WHERE FUNDING CAN BE GIVEN Primarily East Anglia.

WHAT IS FUNDED The trust is primarily concerned with homelessness and people under 18.

RANGE OF GRANTS £1,000–£100,000.

SAMPLE GRANTS £100,000 to Centrepoint; £50,000 to Order of St Ethelreda; £10,000 each to Access Partnership, Break and Motability; £1,000 to Camsight.

FINANCES *Year* 2000–01 *Income* £243,416 *Grants* £181,000 *Assets* £4,613,091

TRUSTEES Peter Dawe; Lindsay Dawe.

HOW TO APPLY In writing to the correspondent, outlining ideas and needs.

WHO TO APPLY TO Lisa Baldwin, East View, 5 Coles Lane, Oakington, Cambridge CB4 5BA *Tel* 01223 237700 *Fax* 01223 235870 *E-mail* lisa@dawemedia.co.uk

CC NO 1060314   **ESTABLISHED** 1997

■ The Charity of Thomas Dawson

WHERE FUNDING CAN BE GIVEN The city of Oxford only (postcodes OX1 to OX4).

WHO CAN BENEFIT Individuals and organisations benefiting students and people who are unemployed.

WHAT IS FUNDED General charitable purposes, particularly youth, community projects, and education and training.

WHAT IS NOT FUNDED No expeditions or medical requests are considered. Education grants are only given to individuals who fulfil certain criteria. Contact the trust for further information.

TYPE OF GRANT One-off for up to one year.

SAMPLE GRANTS In 1998–99: £38,583 to St Clements PCC; £19,291 to Parochial Charities of St Clements. A total of £11,130 was given to other organisations.

FINANCES *Year* 2000–01 *Income* £241,507

TRUSTEES Revd J B Gillingham; I R Harris; J L Pain; K R Howson; H H Prickett; J Gray.

HOW TO APPLY In writing to the correspondent, including an sae.

WHO TO APPLY TO Mrs K K Lacey, Clerk, 56 Poplar Close, Garsington, Oxford OX44 9BP *Tel* 01865 368259

CC NO 203258   **ESTABLISHED** 1962

■ The De Clermont Charitable Company Ltd

WHERE FUNDING CAN BE GIVEN UK, with a preference for north east England.

WHO CAN BENEFIT Headquarters organisations, and local organisations in Scotland and the north east of England.

WHAT IS FUNDED General charitable purposes, particularly those charities of special interest to the founders of this company, i.e. medical research, children and young people, service organisations and overseas disaster appeals.

WHAT IS NOT FUNDED No grants for organisations concerned with drugs and alcohol abuse. No grants to individuals.

RANGE OF GRANTS £28–£1,500.

SAMPLE GRANTS In 1996–97: £1,000 to Berwick Preservation Trust; £500 each to Berwick Sailing Club, British Red Cross, Institute of Cancer Research, Northumberland Aged Miners Homes Association, and Percy Hedley Centre; £300 each to CLIC Millennium Cancer Appeal, CARE International, BEN Birch Hill and Royal Star & Garter Home.

FINANCES *Year* 2000–01 *Income* £38,000

TRUSTEES Mrs E K de Clermont; H S Orpwood.

HOW TO APPLY In writing to the correspondent.

WHO TO APPLY TO Mrs E K de Clermont, Trustee, Morris Hall, Norham, Berwick-upon-Tweed TD15 2JY *Tel* 01289 382259

CC NO 274191   **ESTABLISHED** 1977

■ The Helen and Geoffrey de Freitas Charitable Trust

WHERE FUNDING CAN BE GIVEN UK.

WHO CAN BENEFIT Charitable organisations registered in the UK.

WHAT IS FUNDED The trustees wish to benefit other charitable organisations and bodies. Most of the trust income is destined for the conservation of countryside and environment in rural Britain; for the preservation of Britain's cultural heritage; and for the assistance of the underprivileged through community facilities and services, advice centres, and community arts and recreation. Overseas work of UK charities can be supported.

WHAT IS NOT FUNDED No grants to non-registered charities, individuals, or to charities on behalf of individuals. Definitely no support for charities concerned with medical or health matters, or with physical, mental or sensory impairments.

TYPE OF GRANT Feasibility studies, specific or one-off projects. No long-term commitments.

RANGE OF GRANTS £500–£4,000.

SAMPLE GRANTS £3,500 to the Pedestrians Association for special conferences; £3,000 to Victim Support for volunteer training; £2,500 to the Somerset Rural Youth Project for rural skills and work-based training project; £2,000 each to the Thames Explorer Trust for purchase of video camera and laptop for ecology education work; to Tree Aid towards costs of a part-time community liaison officer for woodland project and to Lady Margaret Hungerford Charity towards restoration of a listed Almshouse;

£1,000 each to Tale Valley Trust for setting up a river restoration demonstration site, to Cornwall Rural Community Council for production of information folder on money matters and to Civic Trust for a project to rejuvenate local civic societies.

FINANCES *Year* 2001–02 *Income* £32,000 *Grants* £32,000 *Assets* £550,000

TRUSTEES R C Kirby; Frances de Freitas; Roger de Freitas.

HOW TO APPLY In writing to the address above. Initial telephone calls are not welcome. No application form or guidelines. No sae required. All applications are acknowledged by postcard. Trustees meet four times a year. Unsuccessful applicants are not notified.

WHO TO APPLY TO The Trustees, PO Box 18667, London NW3 5WB

CC NO 258597   **ESTABLISHED** 1969

■ Peter De Haan Charitable Trust

WHERE FUNDING CAN BE GIVEN UK.

WHAT IS FUNDED General charitable purposes, including organisations connected with children and young people.

SAMPLE GRANTS £40,000 to Brandon Centre; £30,000 to Rainbow Centre; £25,000 to National Missing Persons Helpline; £20,000 to CHAS Housing Aid Centre; £15,000 to Kids Company; £8,000 to League of Friends of Hazelhurst Resource Centre; £5,000 each to Apex Leicester, Option 2 and Tenterden Day Care Centre; £4,7850 to KCA; £2,500 to Princes Trust; £2,000 to Demelza House.

FINANCES *Year* 2000–01 *Income* £297,000 *Grants* £174,000 *Assets* £1,309,000

TRUSTEES Peter Charles De Haan; Katherine Cockburn De Haan; Sallie Donaldson; David Peter Davies.

HOW TO APPLY In writing to the correspondent.

WHO TO APPLY TO Peter Charles De Haan, Trustee, 3 Eurogate Business Park, Ashford, Kent TN24 8XW *Tel* 01233 652010

CC NO 1077005   **ESTABLISHED** 1999

■ The De La Rue Charitable Trust

WHERE FUNDING CAN BE GIVEN Internationally, within given categories.

WHO CAN BENEFIT Registered charities benefiting children and young adults, students and teachers, at risk groups, people disadvantaged by poverty and socially isolated people, people who are terminally ill and people with cancer.

WHAT IS FUNDED Allocation of funds to charitable and good causes that fall within policy categories, i.e. education, international understanding, relief of suffering, the hospice movement and for special community projects and institutions close to De La Rue locations and within its national and international markets.

WHAT IS NOT FUNDED No grants to small local charities or interests which are not in the vicinity of De La Rue industrial and business locations. No grants to individuals.

TYPE OF GRANT Usually one-off for a specific project or part thereof.

SAMPLE GRANTS Recent beneficiaries include Whitchurch Silk Mill and Joint Commonwealth Society Council. No further information was available.

FINANCES *Year* 2000–01 *Grants* £132,500

TRUSTEES Michael Pugh, Chair; Steve Brunswick; Nicol Mcgregor; Douglas Denham; Mrs Irene Richards; Mrs Kaajal Kotecha.

HOW TO APPLY In writing to the correspondent.

WHO TO APPLY TO Mrs Teresa Kerr, Appeals Secretary, De la Rue plc, De La Rue House, Jays Close, Basingstoke, Hampshire RG22 4BS *Tel* 01256 329122 *Fax* 01256 351323 *E-mail* teresa.kerr@uk.delarue.com *Website* www.delarue.com

CC NO 274052   **ESTABLISHED** 1977

■ The Leopold De Rothschild Charitable Trust

WHERE FUNDING CAN BE GIVEN UK.

WHO CAN BENEFIT Registered charities only.

WHAT IS FUNDED General charitable purposes, particularly the arts and Jewish organisations.

RANGE OF GRANTS £600–£25,100.

SAMPLE GRANTS £25,100 to English Chamber Orchestra and Music Society; £5,200 to American Museum in Britain; £5,000 each to Sadlers Wells, Jewish Child Day, and Child Southbank Foundation; £4,450 to Royal College of Music; £1,865 to Liberal Jewish Synagogue; £1,550 to Exbury Gardens; £1,000 each to Border Crossings and Merchant Navy.

FINANCES *Year* 1997 *Income* £62,278 *Grants* £78,578 *Assets* £607,879

TRUSTEES Rothschild Trust Corporation Ltd.

HOW TO APPLY In writing to the correspondent.

WHO TO APPLY TO Miss Norma Watson, Rothschild Trust Corporation Ltd, New Court, St Swithin's Lane, London EC4P 4DU

CC NO 212611   **ESTABLISHED** 1959

■ The Miriam K Dean Refugee Trust Fund

WHERE FUNDING CAN BE GIVEN Mainly India (including Tibetan refugees).

WHO CAN BENEFIT Charities benefiting people who are sick or elderly, refugees, and victims of disasters, war and famine will be considered, but excluded UK residents excluded.

WHAT IS FUNDED For the benefit of people abroad whether orphans, sick, aged or otherwise, who are in need of assistance by reason of war, disaster, pestilence or otherwise, or any organisation engaged in the relief of suffering humanity abroad. Projects are usually only considered if personally investigated by trustees.

WHAT IS NOT FUNDED The trust states they are unable to award major block grants to organisations in the UK or Europe. No grants are given to individuals for Operation Raleigh or other overseas trips.

FINANCES *Year* 2000 *Income* £182,453 *Grants* £137,856 *Assets* £304,975

TRUSTEES Trevor Dorey; Val Dorey; Hugh Capon; Jill Budd; Gina Livermore; Brian Tims; Christine Tims.

HOW TO APPLY The trust does not wish to receive any applications. Its funds are fully committed to projects/organisations already known to the trustees.

WHO TO APPLY TO B Tims, St Peter's Vicarage, Shipton Bellinger, near Tidworth, Hampshire SP9 7UF *Tel* 01980 8422244 *Fax* 01980 8422244 *E-mail* brian@timsfamily.com

CC NO 269655   **ESTABLISHED** 1964

■ William Dean Countryside and Educational Trust

WHERE FUNDING CAN BE GIVEN Principally Cheshire; also Derbyshire, Lancashire, Staffordshire and the Wirral.

WHO CAN BENEFIT Individuals and organisations.

WHAT IS FUNDED The trust gives grants towards enterprises in its immediate locality which promote education in natural history, ecology and the conservation of the natural environment. For example, wildlife trusts; schools for ecological and conservation projects; and parks and pleasure grounds for similar purposes.

TYPE OF GRANT Capital, core costs, feasibility studies, one-off, project, research, and start-up costs. Funding may be given for up to two years.

RANGE OF GRANTS £100–£25,000.

SAMPLE GRANTS £25,000 to Cheshire Wildlife Trust; £5,000 to Congleton Museum Trust; £2,500 each to Derbyshire Wildlife Trust and National Trust for Biddulph Grange Gardens; £2,000 to Lower Moss Wood Educational Trust; £1,000 each to British Butterfly Conservation Society, Staffordshire Wildlife Trust and Woodland Trust; £920 to Brereton Health Country Park; £500 each to Daven Primary School, Mid Cheshire Barn Owl Conservation and Plantlife Mosses in Lancashire.

FINANCES *Year* 2001 *Income* £47,000 *Grants* £46,000 *Assets* £1,200,000

TRUSTEES David Daniel, Chair; William Crawford; John Ward; David Crawford; Margaret Williamson.

HOW TO APPLY In writing to the correspondent.

WHO TO APPLY TO Mrs Brenda Bell, St Mary's Cottage, School Lane, Astbury, Congleton, Cheshire CW12 4RG *Tel* 01260 290194 *E-mail* bellstmarys@hotmail.com

CC NO 1044567   **ESTABLISHED** 1995

■ Alex Deas Charitable Trust

WHERE FUNDING CAN BE GIVEN UK and overseas.

WHO CAN BENEFIT Individuals and charities.

WHAT IS FUNDED Causes addressing education, human rights, extreme poverty and injustice.

WHAT IS NOT FUNDED Any activity where any person or officer involved earns more than the lower of the average wage in their country of origin or country of charitable work; genetic or medical research, women's' or homosexual rights, lobbying or any political activity whatsoever; cultural exchanges or other work of a short-term nature (less than five years); young people who wish to visit to third world countries to work in schools or on village projects, typically from six weeks to six months, are not supported as their cost, typically of £4,000, is not economic given the average wage in these countries – £4,000 is a wage for a family for five years for most people in the world!

FINANCES *Grants* £500,000 *Assets* £25,000,000

HOW TO APPLY In writing to the trustees.

WHO TO APPLY TO Dr Alex Deas, King's Gate Lodge, Dalkeith Country Park, Dalkeith, Edinburgh EH22 1ST

SC NO SC023390

■ The Debmar Benevolent Trust

WHERE FUNDING CAN BE GIVEN UK.

WHO CAN BENEFIT Jewish organisations.

WHAT IS FUNDED Jewish charitable purposes.

TYPE OF GRANT Up to £30,000, but mostly under £1,000.

SAMPLE GRANTS £25,000 to Square Foundation; £22,500 each to Gevuras Ari Academy Trust and Telz Talmudical College; £10,525 to Belz – Manchester; £10,120 to Dushinsky Trust; £10,100 to Kollel Shomrei Hachomos; £10,050 to Ozer Dalim Trust; £10,000 each to Ksar Sofer Yeshira – Israel, Ohel Shimon – Jerusalem and Torah V'emurah – Jerusalem.

FINANCES *Year* 1999–2000 *Income* £439,527 *Grants* £358,559 *Assets* £1,864,212

TRUSTEES M Weisz; G Klein; H Olsberg.

HOW TO APPLY In writing to the correspondent.

WHO TO APPLY TO M Weisz, Secretary, 3rd Floor, Manchester House, 86 Princess Street, Manchester M1 6NP *Tel* 0161 236 4107

CC NO 283065   **ESTABLISHED** 1979

■ The Charity of Theresa Harriet Mary Delacour

WHERE FUNDING CAN BE GIVEN North east England.

WHO CAN BENEFIT Catholic organisations.

WHAT IS FUNDED In practice the trustees only give donations to Catholic schools, churches and organisations in the north east of England.

RANGE OF GRANTS Up to £5,000.

FINANCES *Year* 2000 *Grants* £50,000

TRUSTEES Lady Patricia Talbot; Mrs Z F A Richards; Maj. Richard Murphy, S P Weil.

HOW TO APPLY In writing to the correspondent. The trustees meet once every two years, with a meeting in May 2002.

WHO TO APPLY TO S P Weil, Trustee, Bircham Dyson Bell, 50 Broadway, London SW1H 0BL *Tel* 020 7222 8044

CC NO 222292   **ESTABLISHED** 1926

■ William Delafield Charitable Trust

WHERE FUNDING CAN BE GIVEN UK, particularly Oxfordshire, Buckinghamshire, Hertfordshire and Bedfordshire.

WHO CAN BENEFIT Historical societies/bodies.

WHAT IS FUNDED Restoration of records or archives of historical societies/bodies.

TYPE OF GRANT One-off and ongoing.

SAMPLE GRANTS £7,700 to Berkhamsted Collegiate School; £4,000 to Pitt Rivers Museum; £3,500 to Oxfordshire Historic Churches Trust; £400 to Buckinghamshire Archaelogical Society.

FINANCES *Year* 2001–02 *Income* £30,000 *Grants* £20,000 *Assets* £544,000

TRUSTEES William Hugh Delafield; Richard Frederick Bagot Gilman; Christopher John Gee.

HOW TO APPLY In writing to the correspondent.

WHO TO APPLY TO MacIntyre Hudson, 31 Castle Street, High Wycombe, Buckinghamshire HP13 6RU *Tel* 01494 441226

CC NO 328022   **ESTABLISHED** 1988

Think carefully about every application. Is it justified?

427

■ The Delfont Foundation

WHERE FUNDING CAN BE GIVEN UK.
WHO CAN BENEFIT Registered charities.
WHAT IS FUNDED General charitable purposes.
TYPE OF GRANT Usually one-off for specific purposes.
RANGE OF GRANTS £14–£4,500.
SAMPLE GRANTS In 1999: £4,500 to Entertainment Artiste's Benevolent Fund; £2,500 to BSO; £1,100 to JAMI; £1,000 each to LIFT, 'King George VI', World Wildlife Fund and 'Fire Brigade'.
FINANCES *Year* 2001 *Income* £53,421 *Grants* £27,000
TRUSTEES Lady Delfont; D Delfont; Miss J Delfont; Miss S Delfont; G Parsons; Mary Connor.
HOW TO APPLY In writing to the correspondent.
WHO TO APPLY TO The Secretary, 8 Ashburnham Road, Eastbourne, East Sussex BN21 2HU *Tel* 01323 645820
CC NO 298047   **ESTABLISHED** 1987

■ The Delius Trust

WHERE FUNDING CAN BE GIVEN UK and overseas.
WHO CAN BENEFIT Individuals and organisations benefiting young adults, older people and musicians.
WHAT IS FUNDED Promoting the music of Delius by financing recordings; by giving grants for performances where the making of profit is not an object; by financing the issue of a uniform edition of Delius' music; acquiring material for the trust's archives; preserving and making available to the public, improving, and diffusing knowledge of his life and works.
TYPE OF GRANT Project funding for more than three years will be considered.
FINANCES *Year* 2001 *Income* £127,680 *Grants* £76,645
TRUSTEES Musicians Benevolent Fund (Representative: Helen Faulkner); David Lloyd-Jones; Martin Williams.
PUBLICATIONS *A Descriptive Catalogue of the Works of Frederick Delius* by Robert Threlfall. *A Descriptive Catalogue with Checklists of the Letters and Related Documents in the Delius Collection of the Grainger Museum, University of Melbourne, Australia* by Rachel Lowe. A supplementary catalogue by Robert Threlfall, *The Collected Edition of the works of Frederick Delius.* Brochure – *Delius, 1862–1934: A Short Guide to his Life and Works.*
HOW TO APPLY In writing for consideration by the trustees and the advisers (Felix Aprahamian, Dr Lional Carley, Robert Montgomery, Robert Threlfall). Notes on application procedure are available from the secretary.
WHO TO APPLY TO Marjorie Dickinson, Secretary to the Trust, 16 Ogle Street, London W1P 6JB *Tel* 020 7436 4816 *Fax* 020 7637 4307 *E-mail* DeliusTrust@mbf.org.uk *Website* www.delius.org.uk
CC NO 207324   **ESTABLISHED** 1935

■ The Dellal Foundation

WHERE FUNDING CAN BE GIVEN UK.
WHO CAN BENEFIT Registered charities only.
WHAT IS FUNDED Mostly 'the welfare and benefit of Jewish people'.
WHAT IS NOT FUNDED No grants to individuals.
TYPE OF GRANT One-off.
SAMPLE GRANTS £500,000 to Somerset House Arts Fund; £400,000 to Tate Gallery; £50,000 to St John's Hospice; £35,000 to Tel Aviv

Foundation; £33,031 to Hineni Heritage Centre; £25,000 each to Institute for Policy Research and Westminster Synagogue and Community Security Trust; £10,000 each to Anglo-Brazilian Society, Chain of Hope, Charity Challenge, Hadassah Medical Relief Organisation, Leukaemia Research Fund and Norwood Ltd.
FINANCES *Year* 2000–01 *Income* £245,084 *Grants* £1,243,788 *Assets* £2,269,521
TRUSTEES J Dellal; E Azouz; J Azouz; G Dellal.
HOW TO APPLY In writing to the correspondent.
WHO TO APPLY TO S Whalley, Administrator, 14th Floor, Bowater House, 68 Knightsbridge, London SW1X 7LT *Tel* 020 7299 1400
CC NO 265506   **ESTABLISHED** 1973

■ The Delves Charitable Trust

WHERE FUNDING CAN BE GIVEN UK.
WHO CAN BENEFIT General approved charities.
WHAT IS FUNDED General charitable purposes. To support approved charities by annual contributions.
WHAT IS NOT FUNDED The trust does not give sponsorships or personal educational grants.
RANGE OF GRANTS Generally £200–£5,000 to new applicants.
SAMPLE GRANTS £25,000 to British Heart Foundation; £10,000 each to Intermediate Technology, Macmillan Cancer Relief, Médecins Sans Frontierés, Sequel, Survival International, and WaterAid; £9,000 to Liverpool School of Tropical Medicine; £8,000 to Quaker Peace and Service; £6,000 to Woodland Trust.
FINANCES *Year* 2000–01 *Income* £208,529 *Grants* £240,115 *Assets* £6,132,572
TRUSTEES Mary Breeze; John Breeze; George Breeze; Dr Charles Breeze; Elizabeth Breeze; Roger Harriman.
HOW TO APPLY 'The funds of the trust are currently fully committed and no unsolicited requests can therefore be considered by the trustees.' Trustees meet in July and applications should therefore be received by the end of May.
WHO TO APPLY TO Roger Harriman, Trust Administrator, New Guild House, 45 Great Charles Street, Queensway, Birmingham B3 2LX *Tel* 0121 212 2222 *Fax* 0121 212 2300
CC NO 231860   **ESTABLISHED** 1922

■ The Demigryphon Trust

WHERE FUNDING CAN BE GIVEN UK, with a preference for Scotland.
WHO CAN BENEFIT Registered charities only.
WHAT IS FUNDED General charitable purposes. The trust supports a wide range of organisations and appears to have a preference for education, medical, children and Scottish organisations.
WHAT IS NOT FUNDED No grants to individuals; only registered charities are supported.
TYPE OF GRANT Mainly one-off grants.
RANGE OF GRANTS £100–£3,000.
SAMPLE GRANTS £3,000 to The Game Conservancy for its uplands funding appeal; £1,000 each to Cancer & Leukaemia in Childhood, Fergus Macklay Cancer Research Campaign, Friends of King Edward VII Hospital – Midhurst, Macmillan Cancer Relief; £500 each to Aboyne & Deeside Festival, Royal Scottish Agricultural Institution and South of England Agricultural Society.
FINANCES *Year* 2001 *Income* £90,521 *Grants* £66,991 *Assets* £2,466,709
TRUSTEES The Cowdray Trust Ltd.
HOW TO APPLY In writing to the correspondent including an sae. No application forms or

guidelines are issued and there is no deadline. Only successful applications are acknowledged.
WHO TO APPLY TO Alan Winborn, Secretary, Pollen House, 10–12 Cork Street, London W1S 3LW *Tel* 020 7439 9061
CC NO 275821   **ESTABLISHED** 1978

■ The Denman Charitable Trust

WHERE FUNDING CAN BE GIVEN Bristol and South Gloucestershire.
WHO CAN BENEFIT Organisations benefiting research workers, at risk groups, people disadvantaged by poverty, and socially isolated people.
WHAT IS FUNDED Medical research, health and welfare.
TYPE OF GRANT Research.
SAMPLE GRANTS £33,700 to @t Bristol; £17,500 to University of Bristol Research; £2,000 each to Rainbow Centre, Gloucestershire Society and Grateful Society; £1,000 each to BIME, Enuresis Resource Fund and Westcare UK.
FINANCES *Year* 2001–02 *Income* £97,205 *Grants* £70,835
TRUSTEES A G Denman; Mrs D M Denman; D J Marsh.
HOW TO APPLY In writing to the correspondent.
WHO TO APPLY TO Mrs D M Denman, Trustee, Steeple House, 58–59 Old Market Street, Bristol BS2 0HF
CC NO 326532   **ESTABLISHED** 1983

■ The Dent Charitable Trust

WHERE FUNDING CAN BE GIVEN Worldwide.
WHO CAN BENEFIT Registered charities, particularly Jewish organisations.
WHAT IS FUNDED General charitable purposes. The trust regularly supports the following organisations: Friends of the Hebrew University of Jerusalem, Children and Youth Aliyah Committee for Great Britain, Norwood Home for Jewish Children, British Technion Society, Society of Friends of Jewish Refugees, Home and Hospital for Jewish Incurables, Joint Palestine Appeal and Relief of the Jewish Poor.
RANGE OF GRANTS £25–£30,000.
SAMPLE GRANTS £30,000 to British Technion Society; £14,000 to Friends of the Hebrew University; £10,000 each to JNF Charitable Trust and Jerusalem Foundation; £5,000 each to CBF World Jewish Relief, Sarah Herzog Memorial Hospital and Shaare Zedek Medical Centre; £3,000 each to British ORT, MIND and Save the Children Fund.
FINANCES *Year* 2000–01 *Income* £97,714 *Grants* £96,950 *Assets* £1,588,319
TRUSTEES Miss C S Dent; J P M Dent; Miss L Dent.
HOW TO APPLY The trust has previously stated that 'no further applications for funds can be considered'.
WHO TO APPLY TO J P M Dent, Trustee, c/o RSM Robson Rhodes, 186 City Road, London EC1V 2NU *Tel* 020 7251 1644
CC NO 271512   **ESTABLISHED** 1976

■ The Denton Charitable Trust

WHERE FUNDING CAN BE GIVEN UK, with a preference for West Yorkshire.
WHO CAN BENEFIT Small local and UK organisations particularly interested in benefiting children, at risk groups, people disadvantaged by poverty, socially isolated people and people with cancer.

WHAT IS FUNDED In practice, particular interest in children, cancer charities, care, the arts and local causes.
TYPE OF GRANT One-off preferred.
SAMPLE GRANTS In 1999–2000: £5,000 each to Abbeyfield Society – Ilkley, Martin House Children's Hospice – Wetherby, St Michael's Hospice – Harrogate, The Stroke Association – Leeds and Yorkshire Cancer Research Campaign; £1,000 each to A Home for All – Bradford, Church Housing Trust – Leeds, Sail Training Association – Liverpool and Shaftesbury Society – London.
FINANCES *Year* 2001–02 *Income* £33,938 *Grants* £32,500 *Assets* £195,715
TRUSTEES J A J Wood; Mrs S J Wood; T C J Wood; D C Wilson.
HOW TO APPLY In writing to the correspondent. Grants are made in May and November.
WHO TO APPLY TO Mrs S J Wood, Trustee and Secretary, c/o Garbutt & Elliott, Chartered Accountants, Monkgate House, 44 Monkgate, York YO3 7HF *Tel* 01904 654656 *Fax* 01904 610015
CC NO 1054546   **ESTABLISHED** 1996

■ The Denton Wilde Sapte Charitable Trust

WHERE FUNDING CAN BE GIVEN Preference for the City of London.
WHO CAN BENEFIT Normally registered charities.
WHAT IS FUNDED General charitable purposes with a preference for organisations with a legal connection, such as community law centres, or children's charities, medical charities or the arts.
WHAT IS NOT FUNDED No grants to individuals. Education and scholarships will not be funded.
TYPE OF GRANT Recurrent.
RANGE OF GRANTS £250–£1,000.
SAMPLE GRANTS The following organisations have all received large grants over a number of years: City Solicitors Educational Trust, Institute of Advanced Legal Studies, Housing Associations Charitable Trust, Hackney Law Centre and Tower Hamlets Law Centre. Other beneficiaries have included London Federation of Clubs for the Young and The Mayor of Southwark Common Good Trust.
FINANCES *Year* 2001 *Income* £54,737 *Grants* £50,159
TRUSTEES Mark Andrews; Virginia Glastonbury; Alan Williams.
HOW TO APPLY In writing only, to the correspondent. Trustees meet quarterly.
WHO TO APPLY TO Ms K Young, 1 Fleet Place, London EC4M 7WS *Tel* 020 7246 7000
CC NO 1041204   **ESTABLISHED** 1994

■ The Earl of Derby's Charitable Trust

WHERE FUNDING CAN BE GIVEN North west England, predominantly Merseyside.
WHO CAN BENEFIT Local charitable organisations, predominantly within the beneficial area.
WHAT IS FUNDED Grant giving is categorised as follows: (a) age, disablement and sickness; (b) education and youth; (c) religion; (d) racing charities; (e) general.
WHAT IS NOT FUNDED No grants to individuals.
RANGE OF GRANTS £100–£1,000; generally £500.
SAMPLE GRANTS £1,000 each to The Game Conservancy, Newmarket 200 and Racing

Welfare; £850 to Friends of Liverpool Cathedral; £500 each to 32 organisations including Zoe's Place, Anfield Youth Club, Holy Trinity – Bickerstaff, British Racing School, Twig Lane Workshop and Liverpool Family Support Unit.
FINANCES *Year* 1999–2000 *Income* £28,000 *Grants* £22,000 *Assets* £5,698,000
TRUSTEES Rt Hon. The 19th Earl of Derby; C J Allan.
HOW TO APPLY In writing to the correspondent. Trustees meet twice a year in January and July; applicants should apply two months before the meetings.
WHO TO APPLY TO Chris Allan, Trustee, The Estate Office, Thornton Hough, Wirral CH63 1JD *Tel* 0151 336 4828 *E-mail* chris.allan@leverhulmeesates.co.uk
CC NO 515783   **ESTABLISHED** 1984

■ The Derbyshire Community Foundation

WHERE FUNDING CAN BE GIVEN Derbyshire and the city of Derby.
WHO CAN BENEFIT Voluntary groups and volunteers and the people they work with in Derbyshire across a wide spectrum of activity tackling disadvantage and promoting quality of life.
WHAT IS FUNDED Community groups and voluntary organisations working to tackle disadvantage and improve quality of life. Likely priority themes are as follows: supporting families; getting back to work; health and wellbeing; young people; helping groups work; and creative community.
WHAT IS NOT FUNDED No grants to individuals, work which replaces statutory funding, animal welfare, party politics, evangelism, general appeals or UK charities (except independent local branches).
TYPE OF GRANT Usually one-off, though depending on the programme and donor's wishes, the trust may give more than one grant to the same group for different projects or items. Capital, core costs, feasibility studies, research, running costs, salaries and start-up costs. Funding for up to one year will be considered.
RANGE OF GRANTS Up to £1,000 for DCF grants; up to £7,000 for managed programmes depending on their criteria.
SAMPLE GRANTS In 1999–2000: £3,100 to Derbyshire Fire & Rescue Service; £2,400 (in two grants) to Erewash Partnership; £2,000 to The Jericho Café Project; £1,500 each to The Millennium Cellar and Woodville Primary School PTA; £1.300 to High Peaks CAB; £1,000 each to Derbyshire Rural Community Council, Gamesley Food Co-operative and Atlow Mill Centre; £900 to Derby Rainbow.
FINANCES *Year* 2001–02 *Income* £651,000 *Grants* £330,000 *Assets* £800,000
TRUSTEES Brian Ashby, Chair; Helen Bishop; Arthur Blackwood; Andrew Borkowski; Dawn Forman; Roger Hollick; David Moss; Lucy Palmer; Denise Servante; Kultaran Singh; Gersh Subhra; Philip Tregoning; Edward Wilkinson; Robin Wood; Peter Beevers; Nick Mirfin.
HOW TO APPLY Please contact the office. It is worth phoning first to check that the trust has a pot of money suitable for your needs. There is a standard form and the trust will tell you the deadline for current round. Grants are usually made in three annual rounds, with applications invited from April, July and October.
WHO TO APPLY TO Mrs Hilary Gilbert, Director, The Old Nursery, University of Derby, Mickleover, Derby DE3 5GX *Tel* 01332 592050 *Fax* 01332 592200

E-mail infor@derbyshirecommunityfoundation. co.uk
Website www.derbyshirecommunityfoundation. co.uk
CC NO 1039485   **ESTABLISHED** 1996

■ The J N Derbyshire Trust

WHERE FUNDING CAN BE GIVEN Mainly Nottingham and Nottinghamshire.
WHO CAN BENEFIT Organisations with charitable status.
WHAT IS FUNDED General charitable purposes, including: the promotion of health; the development of physical improvement; the advancement of education; and the relief of poverty, distress and sickness. Local charities receive preferential consideration.
WHAT IS NOT FUNDED No grants to individuals. Costs of study are not supported.
TYPE OF GRANT Buildings, capital, core costs, project, research, recurring and running costs, salaries, and start-up costs will be considered. Funding may be given for up to three years.
RANGE OF GRANTS £500–£20,000.
SAMPLE GRANTS £20,000 to the Extracare Charitable Trust; £15,000 to Marie Curie Cancer Care; £10,000 to Nottinghamshire Royal Society for the Blind; £7,000 to Stonebridge City Farm; £6,000 to St Paul's Church – West Bridgford; £5,050 to Elizabeth Finn; £5,000 each to Association for Spina Bifida and Hydrocephalus, Making It! Discovery Centre – Mansfield, MENCAP, Motability, NCH, Southwell Diocesan Council for Family Care, Zone Youth Project and Youth Potential (East Midlands) Ltd.
FINANCES *Year* 2000–01 *Income* £23,000 *Grants* £213,000 *Assets* £4,100,000
TRUSTEES Mrs A L Carver, Chair; Mrs E Cathery; S J Christophers; P R Moore; Mrs L Whittle; C J George.
HOW TO APPLY On a form available from the correspondent. Applications can be made at any time but trustees usually only meet to consider them twice a year in March and September. Details of the project are required. A reply is only given to unsuccessful applicants if they enclose an sae.
WHO TO APPLY TO P R Moore, The Secretary, Foxhall Lodge, Gregory Boulevard, Nottingham NG7 6LH *Tel* 0115 955 2000
CC NO 231907   **ESTABLISHED** 1944

■ The Richard Desmond Charitable Trust

WHERE FUNDING CAN BE GIVEN Worldwide.
WHO CAN BENEFIT Charitable organisations.
WHAT IS FUNDED The relief of poverty and sickness, particularly among children.
TYPE OF GRANT Core, capital and project funding in one-off and recurrent grants.
RANGE OF GRANTS £100–£25,000.
SAMPLE GRANTS Disability Foundation, Variety Club Educational Trust, and World Jewish Relief.
FINANCES *Year* 2001 *Income* £144,186 *Grants* £138,403
TRUSTEES R C Desmond; Mrs J Desmond.
HOW TO APPLY In writing to the correspondent.
WHO TO APPLY TO Gary Suckling, The Northern and Shell Tower, Ludgate House, 245 Blackfriars Road, London SE1 9UX *Tel* 020 7579 4580
CC NO 1014352   **ESTABLISHED** 1992

■ Community Council of Devon

WHERE FUNDING CAN BE GIVEN Devon.

WHO CAN BENEFIT Residents of the county of Devon.

WHAT IS FUNDED (a) Village halls: the Community Council of Devon's Village Halls Service currently administers (on behalf of Devon County Council) three grant schemes for village halls: major capital projects; minor works costing up to £3,000; and small emergency works. (b) Rural Development Programme Small Grants Fund: this fund can provide matched funding of up to £1,000 for community groups in Devon. Funds totalling about £20,000 are usually available for projects in Devon each year for community/social projects. (c) Minor sport and play grants: grants are administered through Devon Playing Fields Association. Financial help can be given to minor projects, either through a grant (maximum £400 or one third of the cost for a single sport or play project; maximum £800 or one-third of the cost for a multi-sport project). The maximum cost of a project should as a rule be less than £10,000 and the association cannot offer matched funding to projects seeking support from the Sports Lottery. (d) Rural Initiatives Loan Fund: loans of up to a maximum of £2,000, or for not more than 50% of project costs.

TYPE OF GRANT One-off and capital grants and interest-free loans.

SAMPLE GRANTS £25,000 to Langtree Village Hall to build a new hall; £16,666 to Ashprington Village Hall to build a new hall; £16,500 to Meldon Village Hall to build a new hall; £11,000 to Buckland Monochorum Village Hall for an extension; £9,502 to Stoke Fleming Village Hall to build a new hall; £7,872 to Newton and Noss Village Hall for refurbishment; £3,915 to Black Torrington Village Hall for refurbishment; £2,493 to Willand Village Hall for refurbishment.

FINANCES *Year* 1999 *Grants* £140,000

HOW TO APPLY Village halls: please contact Peter Harding (Village Halls Advisor) on 01392 383345 for further information. Rural Development Programme Small Grants Fund: please contact Paul Tucker. Minor sports and play grants: potential applicants should write to Peter Harding with the following information: name of the organisation, including contact address and telephone number; brief description of the project; likely cost; other sources of funding; evidence of community support; whether the activity or facility is open to all members of the community, including disadvantaged groups. Rural Initiatives Loan Fund: in writing to the correspondent.

WHO TO APPLY TO Jay Talbot, Chief Executive, County Hall, Topsham Road, Exeter, Devon EX2 4QB *Tel* 01392 383443 *Fax* 01392 382062 *E-mail* info@devonrcc.org.uk *Website* www.devonrcc.org.uk

CC NO 1074047   **ESTABLISHED** 1999

■ Devon Community Foundation

WHERE FUNDING CAN BE GIVEN County of Devon.

WHO CAN BENEFIT Voluntary and community groups.

WHAT IS FUNDED Support primarily for voluntary and community organisations, particularly those working to relieve the effects of poverty and disadvantage.

WHAT IS NOT FUNDED No grants to individuals. No funding for religious causes, statutory agencies or responsibilities, party political activities, medical research, animal welfare, projects outside Devon or village appraisal groups.

TYPE OF GRANT Predominantly one-off small grants for projects. Running costs and start-up costs will be considered. Funding may be given for up to one year, and very occasionally for two years.

RANGE OF GRANTS £50–£7,000.

SAMPLE GRANTS £5,000 to Horizons (Plymouth) for three Pico sailing boats for use by young people; £2,750 to Moretonhampstead Association for Youth for two holiday play schemes; £1,400 to Babes n Us to develop a programme for teenage parents; £1,140 to Mount Wise Towers Residents Association to upgrade their common room; £500 to Monkleigh Village Shop towards stock for a community shop.

FINANCES *Year* 2001–02 *Income* £159,536 *Grants* £85,100 *Assets* £145,854

TRUSTEES E Bourne, Chair; Sir Ian Heathcoat Amory; The Countess of Arran; M H Gee; G Halliday; T Legood; N A Maxwell-Lawford; I Mercer; S Rous; J Trafford; N J Wollen; S Hindley; G Sturtridge; Dr K Gurney; P Thistlethwaite; Mrs M Garton.

OTHER INFORMATION As well as running its own grants programme, the foundation currently manages the Local Network Fund in Devon and the Neighbourhood Renewal Community Chest and the Community Learning Chest in Plymouth.

HOW TO APPLY Telephone calls are welcome. Application forms and current guidelines are available on request. No sae required.

WHO TO APPLY TO The Island, Lowman Green, Tiverton, Devon EX16 4LA *Tel* 01884 235887 *Fax* 01884 243824 *E-mail* grants@devoncf.com *Website* www.devoncf.com

CC NO 1057923   **ESTABLISHED** 1996

■ The Devon Educational Trust

WHERE FUNDING CAN BE GIVEN Devon.

WHO CAN BENEFIT Primarily individuals living in Devon, or whose parents live in Devon. Individuals, and organisations benefiting children, young adults and students.

WHAT IS FUNDED The education of people under the age of 25.

WHAT IS NOT FUNDED No grants for school fees and help is not normally given to people starting a second or higher degree.

RANGE OF GRANTS £35–£900. Average grant £255. Usual maximum of £500.

FINANCES *Year* 2000 *Income* £31,400 *Grants* £46,000

TRUSTEES D R Wakinshaw; Mrs J A E Cook; H B Evans; Prof. W J Forsythe; Dr C M Gillet; F J Rosamond; B W Wills-Pope.

HOW TO APPLY In writing to the correspondent for an application form. The trustees meet three times a year in March, July and November with a closing date four weeks before each meeting.

WHO TO APPLY TO The Clerk, PO Box 298, Exeter EX2 8WG

CC NO 220921   **ESTABLISHED** 1988

■ The Devon Historic Churches Trust

WHERE FUNDING CAN BE GIVEN Devon.

WHO CAN BENEFIT Churches and chapels.

WHAT IS FUNDED The trust gives grants/loans for the preservation, repair, maintenance, beautification and reconstruction of: churches and chapels; and monuments, fittings and fixtures which are mostly in places of worship of historic interest.

WHAT IS NOT FUNDED Redundant churches/chapels and routine maintenance.

TYPE OF GRANT Grants and loans.
RANGE OF GRANTS £500–£3,500
FINANCES *Year* 2001–02 *Income* £49,925
   Grants £50,000
TRUSTEES Lord Lt of Devon; Lord Bishop of Exeter;
   R C M Bass; Lady Anne Boles; J P Cooke-Hurle;
   N A Maxwell-Lawford; P R Plumbley; Mrs Carol
   Plumstead; Maj. T N T Thistlethwayte; Lt Cdr C
   B Tuke; Capt J F R Weir; The Earl of Devon.
HOW TO APPLY In writing to the correspondent.
WHO TO APPLY TO John Malleson, Clifford Lodge,
   Drewsteignton, Exeter EX6 6QE *Tel* 01803
   782444
   Website www.devonhistoricchurches.co.uk
CC NO 265594   **ESTABLISHED** 1973

■ The Duke of Devonshire's Charitable Trust

WHERE FUNDING CAN BE GIVEN UK, with a preference
   for Derbyshire.
WHO CAN BENEFIT Registered charities only.
WHAT IS FUNDED General charitable purposes.
WHAT IS NOT FUNDED Grants are only given to
   registered charities and not to individuals.
TYPE OF GRANT Buildings, capital, core costs,
   endowments, feasibility studies, interest-free
   loans, one-off, project, research, recurring costs,
   running costs, salaries and start-up costs will be
   considered. Funding can be given for any length
   of time.
RANGE OF GRANTS £50–£60,000.
SAMPLE GRANTS £60,000 to Chatsworth House
   Trust; £25,000 to Macmillan Cancer Relief;
   £20,000 to Pilsley Church of England School;
   £14,000 to Bolton Abbey for the vicar's house;
   £10,000 each to Cavendish Disabled Sailing
   Group, Craven Trust, Duke's Barn Trust, and
   Myasthenia Gravis Association; £8,271 to Boyle
   & Petyt Foundation; £5,000 to Countryside
   Foundation for Education.
FINANCES *Year* 2001–02 *Income* £253,994
   Grants £244,541 *Assets* £9,416,420
TRUSTEES Marquess of Hartington; Sir Richard
   Beckett; Nicholas W Smith.
HOW TO APPLY In writing to the correspondent.
WHO TO APPLY TO The Trustee Manager, Currey & Co,
   21 Buckingham Gate, London SW1E 6LS
   Tel 020 7802 2700 *Fax* 020 7828 5049
CC NO 213519   **ESTABLISHED** 1949

■ The Sandy Dewhirst Charitable Trust

WHERE FUNDING CAN BE GIVEN UK, with a strong
   preference for East and North Yorkshire.
WHO CAN BENEFIT To benefit, in particular, those
   connected with I J Dewhirst Holdings Limited
   and their dependants who are in need.
WHAT IS FUNDED Preservation and restoration of
   church buildings; community service; relieving
   people in need, particularly those who are or
   were connected with I J Dewhirst Holdings
   Limited and their dependants.
SAMPLE GRANTS £7,500 (in two grants) to York
   Minster Fund; £5,000 to Driffield PCC; £2,000
   each to Burma Star Association – Bridlington
   branch, Hull Sea Cadets and RNIB; £1,000
   each to Cleveland Alzheimer's Residential
   Centre, Salvation Army, University of Hull
   Concert Fund and YMCA.
FINANCES *Year* 2000–01 *Income* £62,000
   Grants £59,000 *Assets* £638,000
TRUSTEES T C Dewhirst; P J Howell; J A R Dewhirst.

HOW TO APPLY In writing to the correspondent. The
   trust does not accept unsolicited applications.
WHO TO APPLY TO Paul J Howell, Trustees' Solicitor,
   Sovereign House, Sovereign Street, Leeds LS1
   1HQ *Tel* 0113 209 2000
CC NO 279161   **ESTABLISHED** 1979

■ DG Charitable Trust

WHERE FUNDING CAN BE GIVEN UK.
WHO CAN BENEFIT Registered charities.
WHAT IS FUNDED General charitable purposes.
RANGE OF GRANTS £500–£50,000.
SAMPLE GRANTS £50,000 to Amnesty International;
   £27,000 to Terrence Higgins Trust; £25,000
   each to Crisis, Dian Fossey Gorilla Fund, and
   Amnesty International; £15,000 to Petworth
   Cottage Nursing Home; £10,000 each to Great
   Ormond Street Hospital and St Richard's
   Hospital Appeal; £8,000 to The Weald; £1,600
   to Prince of Wales Charitable Foundation.
FINANCES *Year* 1998–99 *Income* £512,996
   Grants £221,800 *Assets* £653,206
TRUSTEES D J Gilmour; P Grafton-Green; Ms P A
   Samson.
HOW TO APPLY This trust does not consider
   unsolicited applications.
WHO TO APPLY TO Joanna Nelson, PO Box 62,
   Heathfield, East Sussex TN21 8ZE *Tel* 01435
   867604 *Fax* 01435 863287
CC NO 1040778   **ESTABLISHED** 1994

■ The Laduma Dhamecha Charitable Trust

WHERE FUNDING CAN BE GIVEN UK and overseas.
WHO CAN BENEFIT Organisations only.
WHAT IS FUNDED General charitable purposes
   including the relief of sickness and education in
   rural areas.
FINANCES *Year* 2000–01 *Income* £330,099
   Grants £100,000
TRUSTEES K R Dhamecha; S R Dhamecha; P K
   Dhamecha.
HOW TO APPLY In writing to the correspondent.
WHO TO APPLY TO Pradip Dhamecha, Trustee,
   Dhamecha Foods Ltd, Wembley Stadium
   Industrial Estate, First Way, Wembly, Middlesex
   HA9 0TU *Tel* 020 8903 8181
CC NO 328678   **ESTABLISHED** 1990

■ Diabetes UK

WHERE FUNDING CAN BE GIVEN UK.
WHO CAN BENEFIT Individuals and organisations
   which benefit: people of all ages; academics;
   medical professionals; research workers and
   scientists; people with diabetes, heart disease,
   kidney disease, paediatric diseases, sight loss,
   and people who have had strokes. Prenatal care
   will also be considered.
WHAT IS FUNDED To promote and fund research into
   the causes and effects of diabetes, and the
   treatment and alleviation of the effects of
   diabetes to minimise the potential serious
   complications that can arise.
TYPE OF GRANT Equipment, fellowships, research
   grants, small grants, and studentships will be
   considered.
RANGE OF GRANTS £5,000–£40,000.
SAMPLE GRANTS Grants were broken down as
   follows: care and information: £7,822,000;
   research: £5,199,000.

FINANCES *Year* 2001 *Income* £17,317,000
Grants £13,021,000
TRUSTEES Dr M Hall, Chair; Dr F Burden; Mrs M
Burden; Sir M Hirst; Mrs M Hunter; M Higgens;
Dr R Bilows; Prof. R Williams; Dr D Carson; D
Banks; Dr D Cavan; B Finney; Mrs W Gane; Lord
Gladwin; J Grainger; Dr R Holland; Prof. S
Howell; Mrs J Tettey; Dr I Jefferson; B Maddox;
Dr D Matthews; Dr M Small; F Millar; Dr J
Peters; Prof. J Tooke; Ms A McNeill; R Anaokar;
Miss J Hoggins; Dr P Tasker.
HOW TO APPLY Please telephone Diabetes UK for an
application form. Resubmission of applications
for project grants, equipment grants or diabetes
development project committee grants is not
permitted. Any future applications must contain
at least 50 per cent new scientific/clinical
investigations.
WHO TO APPLY TO Patrick Stewart, 10 Parkway,
London NW1 7AA *Tel* 020 7424 1000 *Fax* 020
7424 1001 *E-mail* info@diabetes.org.uk
Website www.diabetes.org.uk
CC NO 215199   **ESTABLISHED** 1934

■ Alan and Sheila Diamond Charitable Trust

WHERE FUNDING CAN BE GIVEN UK.
WHO CAN BENEFIT Registered charities only,
particularly Jewish causes.
WHAT IS FUNDED Funds are fully committed to
charities supported for many years.
WHAT IS NOT FUNDED No grants to individuals.
SAMPLE GRANTS Regular beneficiaries include
Community Centre in Israel Project, Youth
Aliyah, Girton College – Cambridge, British
School of Osteopathy, Anglo Israel Association,
Jewish Care, Norwood Ravenswood, Community
Security Trust and Holocaust Educational Trust.
FINANCES *Year* 2000–01 *Income* £49,850
Grants £67,000 *Assets* £1,000,000
TRUSTEES A Diamond, Chair; Mrs S Diamond; P
Rodney; J Kropman.
HOW TO APPLY In writing to the correspondent.
However, the trust states that it will not
consider unsolicited applications. No preliminary
telephone calls. There are no regular trustees'
meetings. The trustees frequently decide how
the funds should be allocated. The trustees
have their own guidelines, which are not
published.
WHO TO APPLY TO Peter Rodney, Trustee, Bright
Grahame Murray, 124–130 Seymour Place,
London W1H 1BG *Tel* 020 7402 5201
E-mail peterrodney@bgm.co.uk
CC NO 274312   **ESTABLISHED** 1977

■ The Diamond Industry Educational Charity

WHERE FUNDING CAN BE GIVEN UK and overseas.
WHO CAN BENEFIT Up to three quarters of the income
and capital in any year can be put towards the
secondary educational needs of children of
those currently or formerly employed in the
mining, cutting, polishing, marketing or
brokering of diamonds. Other small grants are
made to educational establishments.
WHAT IS FUNDED Apart from scholarships, the
trustees will also consider applications for
educational projects.
TYPE OF GRANT One-off grants and recurrent grants
for eligible individuals.
RANGE OF GRANTS £250–£12,000.

SAMPLE GRANTS Previous beneficiaries include
Friends of Guys Hospital, Harrow School, King
Edward's School, Jesus College Cambridge,
Cobham Hall, Modern School in New Delhi,
Charutar Arogya Mandal, London School of
Hygiene and Tropical Medicine and Churchill
College.
FINANCES *Year* 2000–01 *Income* £50,000
Grants £40,000
TRUSTEES Sir Christopher Collet; G L S Rothschild;
G I Watson; Alasdair Adamson.
HOW TO APPLY In writing to the correspondent,
preferably between October and December.
WHO TO APPLY TO Nicholas Stacey, 1 Charterhouse
Street, London EC1P 1BL *Tel* 020 7404 4444
CC NO 277447   **ESTABLISHED** 1979

■ The Diana, Princess of Wales Memorial Fund

WHERE FUNDING CAN BE GIVEN UK, including UK
organisations working overseas.
WHO CAN BENEFIT Organisations working with the
most disadvantaged people.
WHAT IS FUNDED From 2003 to 2005 the theme in
the UK is 'the transition to adulthood and
independence'. Readers should check the
website. In the UK, the intention is to
concentrate on groups and causes that would
otherwise find it difficult to receive recognition
and support. Within this, and within the theme
for the year, the fund prioritises the following
areas: refugees and asylum seekers; prisoners'
families.
Overseas, one-third of the fund's grants go to
international work. From 2002 to 2005, the
specific priority is work to assist communities
affected by landmines and similar devices.
WHAT IS NOT FUNDED The trust will not fund projects
outside its funding priorities; individuals;
services run by statutory or public authorities*;
organisations that are mainly fundraising
bodies; arts and sporting activities which give
little benefit in terms of social inclusion;
academic research; schools, colleges and
hospitals; repayment of loans; promotion of
religious beliefs; rapid response to emergency
situations; retrospective funding; debts; capital
expenditure for religious institutions or
buildings; party political organisations; fees for
professional fundraisers; major capital projects
related to premises or buildings; appeals.
*While the trust will not fund activities which
are the responsibility of any statutory agency,
for example a government department, local
council or health authority, and it will not fund
projects that are direct replacements of
statutory funding, it welcomes applications for
collaborative projects and those involving both
the voluntary and public sectors.
TYPE OF GRANT Revenue grants for running costs will
be considered. Capital grants are given, but not
for building refurbishments or purchase.
RANGE OF GRANTS £15,000–£100,000 a year.
SAMPLE GRANTS £314,000 to Hospice Uganda;
£299,000 to Action Mental health in Down;
£292,000 to NACRO (Wales); £263,000 to
Intermediate Technology; £262,000 to MIND in
Tower Hamlets; £249,000 to Groundwork in
Belfast; £248,000 to Citizen Advocacy and
Training; £240,000 to Council for Disabled
Children; £189,000 to Survivors Fund for work
in Rwanda; £160,000 to Coalition To Stop The
Use Of child Soldiers.
FINANCES *Year* 2001 *Income* £5,910,000
Grants £7,918,000 *Assets* £63,462,000

TRUSTEES Lady Sarah McCorquodale, President; Taheera Aanchawan; Lord Bhatia; Douglas Board; Jenny McAleese; Roger Singleton; Christopher Spence, Chair; Earl Cairns; Andrew Hind; Caroline Whitfield.

HOW TO APPLY An excellent application pack is available from the fund, from which the following information is taken.

What we need from you is an original completed application form and a photocopy of the completed form; a constitution or set of rules (this may be a memorandum of articles or a trust deed). It should include your organisation name, objectives, aims and how they are achieved, details of how the management committee or governing body is elected or appointed and how, if applicable, the organisation admits members. Your management committee must have formally adopted your constitution or set of rules; a set of your latest audited or certified and signed annual accounts; a copy of your equal opportunities policy and/or implementation strategy; an annual report or published information about your organisation; and, if applicable, written approval from your parent organisation. These should be sent to the grants committee (applications) at the address below. In 2003, the deadlines for the receipt of completed application forms fell in March and July, with awards being announced in July and December. Unsuccessful applicants are informed in writing of the broad reason why they were unable to get a grant.

WHO TO APPLY TO The The Grants Department, The County Hall, Westminster Bridge Road, London SE1 7PB *Tel* 020 7902 5500 *Website* www.theworkcontinues.org
CC NO 1064238   **ESTABLISHED** 1997

■ The Dibden Allotments Charity

WHERE FUNDING CAN BE GIVEN Hythe, Fawley and Marchwood.

WHO CAN BENEFIT Grants can be made to individuals as well as organisations, including students and unemployed people.

WHAT IS FUNDED To relieve need, hardship or distress, and to invest in the community's future. Grants are awarded to individuals in need, to voluntary and charitable organisations, and to schemes benefiting children, particularly under-fives, older people and young people.

WHAT IS NOT FUNDED Scholarships to 'Schools of Excellence', e.g. the performing arts.

RANGE OF GRANTS £200–£10,000.

SAMPLE GRANTS £33,000 to Hampshire CC Hythe Library; £10,000 to Waterside Heritage; £6,600 to Hythe 2000; £3,500 to Indigo; £3,757 to 4th NF East Hythe Scout Group; £2,995 to Stonham Housing; £2,388 to Hythe Parish Youth; £2,225 to Honey Pot; £2,000 each to Hythe Dragons and NF & Romsey Mobile Community; £1,500 to Waterside Streetwise Project.

FINANCES *Year* 2001–02 *Income* £361,404 *Grants* £238,919 *Assets* £7,586,886

TRUSTEES Bryan Wilson; Derek Gurney; Keith Carley; Maureen McLean; Judy Saxby; Martin Cox; Malcolm Fidler; Joan Shewry; Robin Watton.

OTHER INFORMATION A total of £145,000 was given to individuals.

HOW TO APPLY In writing to the correspondent who will supply guidelines and application forms. Applications from individuals must be supported by a third party.

WHO TO APPLY TO Barrie Smallcalder, The Grove, 25 St John's Street, Hythe, Hampshire SO45 6BZ *Tel* 023 8084 1305 *Fax* 023 8084 1305 *E-mail* dibdenallotmentscharity@btinternet.com
CC NO 255778   **ESTABLISHED** 1995

■ The Dickon Trust

WHERE FUNDING CAN BE GIVEN UK and overseas, with a preference for Northumberland and Scotland.

WHO CAN BENEFIT UK and overseas organisations and local groups in Northumberland and Scotland.

WHAT IS FUNDED General charitable purposes as the trustees in their absolute discretion determine.

WHAT IS NOT FUNDED No support for individuals.

TYPE OF GRANT One-off.

RANGE OF GRANTS £500–£5,000.

SAMPLE GRANTS £1,000 to Macmillan Cancer Relief and £500 to Norh East Search & Rescue.

FINANCES *Year* 2001–02 *Income* £45,499 *Grants* £35,350 *Assets* £1,103,238

TRUSTEES J R Barrett; Mrs D L Barrett; P J Dudding; Major-General R V Brims; R R V Nicholson; R Y Barrett.

HOW TO APPLY In writing to the correspondent.

WHO TO APPLY TO Helen Tavroges, Dickinson Dees, St Anne's Wharf, 112 Quayside, Newcastle NE99 1SB *Tel* 0191 279 9698
CC NO 327202   **ESTABLISHED** 1986

■ The Digbeth Trust

WHERE FUNDING CAN BE GIVEN West Midlands, principally Birmingham.

WHO CAN BENEFIT Smaller local, new and emerging voluntary and community groups, particularly those addressing exclusion and disadvantage.

WHAT IS FUNDED Feasibility studies for new projects.

WHAT IS NOT FUNDED General appeals, capital core costs, medical research, project running costs and grants for individuals.

TYPE OF GRANT One-off grants to enable groups to access specialist advice and services.

RANGE OF GRANTS £1,000–£5,000 approximately.

SAMPLE GRANTS £10,000 each to Local Community Association Centre for IT training and confidence building project and Coalition of Disabled People – Birmingham for a newsletter and training; * £9,875 to Millennium Volunteers at BVSC for confidence building course for individuals with disablities; £9,700 and £9,338 to Birmingham Disability Resources Centre for vocational training and business start-up; £5,821 to CHANGE for a volunteer co-ordinator position/ expenses and training; £4,199 to MIND – Birmingham for IT equipment and camcorder; £3,510 to Queen Alexandra College for a feasability study of a cycle storage facility; £2,500 each to Arabic Cultural Association for profile raising and Kurdish Development Foundation for a development plan.

FINANCES *Year* 2001–02 *Income* £358,271 *Grants* £122,793 *Assets* £49,099

TRUSTEES Rachel Brackwell; J Burrows; April Hall; Zualfqar Hussain; Grace Macaulay; Ruby Osei; Mike Parker; T Wouhra; Eddie Currall; David Williams-Masinda.

OTHER INFORMATION The trust secures grant funding for groups from regeneration programmes (such as SRB, NDC) and these are generally targeted by area or theme, or both. Call for details of current programmes.

HOW TO APPLY The trust welcomes direct contact with groups. Application forms and guidance

notes are available. Development worker support is offered to eligible groups.
WHO TO APPLY TO Kate Hazlewood, Co-ordinator, Unit 321, The Custard Factory, Gibb Street, Digbeth, Birmingham B9 4AA *Tel* 0121 248 3323/0121 753 0706 *Fax* 0121 248 3323 *E-mail* digbeth_trust@hotmail.com
CC NO 517343　　**ESTABLISHED** 1984

■ The Simon Digby (Sherborne) Memorial Trust

WHERE FUNDING CAN BE GIVEN The town of Sherborne and neighbourhood.
WHO CAN BENEFIT Charitable and voluntary organisations.
WHAT IS FUNDED General charitable purposes for the benefit of those in Sherborne and the neighbourhood.
WHAT IS NOT FUNDED No grants to individuals.
TYPE OF GRANT One-off for development funding. Support for capital costs and for project funding in partnership will be considered.
SAMPLE GRANTS £10,000 to Swim 2000 towards a swimming pool for Sherborne; £5,000 to Friends of Yeatman Hospital to help replace its capital reserves; £3,000 each to 1st Sherborne Scout Group for a new headquarters, Sherborne Age Concern and Sherborne Town Council for heating and ventilation at Digby Hall; £2,500 each to ArtsLink for an arts and music festival and Sherborne ArtsLink Limited; £2,000 each to Sherborne Area Youth and Community Service, Castleton Waterwheel Group, Sherborne West End Community Association, Sherborne Age Concern and RendezVous; £600 to Sherborne House Trust.
FINANCES *Year* 2000–01 *Grants* £40,000
TRUSTEES J Wingfield Digby; Mrs J Wingfield Digby; The Members of Sherborne Town Council (ex-officio): T P Farmer; Mrs L A Ashby; Mrs J Palmer; O M Chisholm; R A S Legg; Mrs M Snowden; R Bygrave; T P Bartle; Mrs J S Greene; V M Clark; P Cliffe.
HOW TO APPLY In writing to the correspondent.
WHO TO APPLY TO Mrs Valerie Todd, Clerk to the Trustees, The Manor House, Newland, Sherborne, Dorset DT9 3JL *Tel* 01935 812807 *Fax* 01935 812611
CC NO 801462　　**ESTABLISHED** 1989

■ The Dinam Charity

WHERE FUNDING CAN BE GIVEN Worldwide.
WHO CAN BENEFIT Registered charities.
WHAT IS FUNDED Support for organisations dealing with international understanding, famine relief, child welfare, environmental protection, and animal welfare.
WHAT IS NOT FUNDED Grants are only given to registered charities. No grants to individuals.
SAMPLE GRANTS £92,000 to David Davies Memorial Institute; £1,000 to St Andrew's Evangelical Mission; £600 to Edinburgh Direct Aid; £500 each to Jubilee Action, Kurdish Disaster Fund, Medical Foundation and NSPCC; £400 to Christain Aid; £300 to Seafront Trust; £200 to Friends of the Earth – Scotland; £150 to World Development Movement.
FINANCES *Year* 1999–2000 *Income* £86,187 *Grants* £97,163 *Assets* £2,736,202
TRUSTEES Hon. Mrs M M Noble; Hon. Mrs G R J Cormack; Mrs A C Weston; Mrs M A M Lovegrove; R D Noble.

HOW TO APPLY Applications can be made at any time. Unsuccessful applicants will not be notified unless an sae is enclosed with the application.
WHO TO APPLY TO Amanda King-Jones, Thomas Eggar, The Corn Exchange, Baffins Lane, Chichester, West Sussex PO19 1GE *Tel* 01243 786111
CC NO 231295　　**ESTABLISHED** 1926

■ The Dinwoodie Settlement

WHERE FUNDING CAN BE GIVEN UK.
WHO CAN BENEFIT Organisations benefiting academics and postgraduate research workers.
WHAT IS FUNDED Postgraduate medical education centres (PMCs) and research fellowships for suitably qualified medical practitioners for registrar status in general medicine or general surgery.
WHAT IS NOT FUNDED Anything falling outside the main areas of work referred to above. The trustees do not expect to fund consumable or equipment costs or relieve the NHS of its financial responsibilities.
TYPE OF GRANT Building projects will be considered.
RANGE OF GRANTS Maximum of £1 million towards no more than one postgraduate medical centre project in an area. No more than the salary of two research workers in any one year.
SAMPLE GRANTS St George's Hospital Medical School for Research Fellowships (£47,623); Ark Centre, North Hampshire Hospital, Basingstoke (£1,000,000); Charles Hastings Education Centre, Worcester Royal Infirmary NHS Trust (£250,000). The figures in brackets refer to the trust's total commitment to each project.
FINANCES *Year* 2001–02 *Income* £485,374 *Grants* £50,623 *Assets* £5,323,782
TRUSTEES W A Fairbairn; Dr J M Fowler; Miss C Webster; E W Gillison; R B N Fisher.
OTHER INFORMATION Annual figures for grants versus income may vary substantially as payments towards building costs of each project usually absorb more than one year's available income.
HOW TO APPLY In writing to the correspondent. The trustees state they are proactive rather than reactive in their grant-giving. Negotiating for new PMCs and monitoring their construction invariably takes a number of years. The trust's funds can be committed for three years when supporting major projects. The accounts contain detailed reports on the development of centres under consideration.
WHO TO APPLY TO The Clerk, c/o Thomas Eggar, The Corn Exchange, Baffins Lane, Chichester PO19 1GK, West Sussex *Tel* 01243 786111
CC NO 255495　　**ESTABLISHED** 1968

■ The Djanogly Foundation

WHERE FUNDING CAN BE GIVEN Unrestricted, with a special interest in Nottingham and Israel.
WHO CAN BENEFIT Registered charities benefiting children, young adults and older people, at risk groups, and people who are disadvantaged by poverty, homeless or socially isolated.
WHAT IS FUNDED Developments in medicine, education, social welfare and the arts; relief of distress and promotion of the welfare of older people and young people. Particularly educational establishments in Nottingham, well-known arts organisations and Jewish charities.
TYPE OF GRANT Capital expenditure and donations.
SAMPLE GRANTS £350,000 to the Tate Gallery; £100,000 to Imperial War Museum; £95,000 to

Nottingham City Technology College; £87,000 to Weizmann Institute Foundation; £85,000 to Royal National Theatre; £53,000 to Nottingham Trent University; £50,000 each to Royal Ballet School and Somerset House Trust; £25,000 each to Israel Philharmonic Orchestra and Leuka 2000.

FINANCES *Year* 2000–01 *Income* £1,438,000 *Grants* £1,454,000

TRUSTEES Sir Harry Djanogly; Michael S Djanogly.

HOW TO APPLY In writing to the correspondent.

WHO TO APPLY TO Mr Christopher Sills, 57 Broadwick Street, London W1F 9QS *Tel* 020 7302 2309

CC NO 280500   **ESTABLISHED** 1980

....

■ DLA Charitable Trust

WHERE FUNDING CAN BE GIVEN UK.

WHO CAN BENEFIT Charitable organisations.

WHAT IS FUNDED General charitable purposes.

WHAT IS NOT FUNDED No grants to individuals.

TYPE OF GRANT Mainly single donations.

RANGE OF GRANTS £50–£5,000.

SAMPLE GRANTS In 1998–99: £5,000 to Carlton Bolling College; £2,500 to Leukaemia Research Fund; £2,000 to Imperial Cancer Research Fund; £1,000 each to Leeds Girls High School and Sheffield Cathedral; £832 to Liverpool Parish Church; £700 to The Prince's Youth Trust and Rainbow Family Trust; £600 each to Carlton Bolling College and Right to Read.

FINANCES *Year* 2001 *Income* £52,066 *Grants* £42,781

HOW TO APPLY In writing to the correspondent, for consideration every three months.

WHO TO APPLY TO G J Smallman, Trustee, DLA, Fountain Precinct, Balm Green, Sheffield S1 1RZ *Tel* 0114 283 3466 *Fax* 0114 278 1158 *E-mail* godfrey.smallman@dla.com

CC NO 327280   **ESTABLISHED** 1986

....

■ The DLM Charitable Trust

WHERE FUNDING CAN BE GIVEN UK, especially the Oxford area.

WHO CAN BENEFIT Organisations benefiting: children; young adults; older people; medical professionals, nurses and doctors; and people with head and other injuries, heart disease or blindness.

WHAT IS FUNDED Charities operating in Oxford and the surrounding areas, particularly charities working in the fields of: arts, culture and recreation; religious buildings; self-help groups; the conservation of historic buildings; memorials; monuments and waterways; schools; community centres and village halls; parks; various community services and other charitable purposes.

WHAT IS NOT FUNDED No grants to individuals.

TYPE OF GRANT Feasibility studies, one-off, research, recurring costs, running costs and start-up costs. Funding of up to three years will be considered.

SAMPLE GRANTS In 1996–97: £10,000 to Cumnor Old School Charity; £5,000 each to Royal National College for the Blind and Friends of Glebe House; £4,500 to New Road Baptist Church; £2,000 to Oxford City Football Club; £1,500 to Crossroads.

FINANCES *Year* 2000–01 *Income* £108,000

TRUSTEES Dr E A de la Mare; Mrs P Sawyer; J A Cloke.

HOW TO APPLY In writing to the correspondent. Trustees meet in February, July and November to consider applications.

WHO TO APPLY TO J A Cloke, Trustee, Messrs Cloke & Co., Warnford Court, Throgmorton Street, London EC2N 2AT *Tel* 020 7638 8992

CC NO 328520   **ESTABLISHED** 1990

....

■ Louise Dobson Charitable Trust

WHERE FUNDING CAN BE GIVEN Some preference for West Sussex.

WHO CAN BENEFIT Children, people with mental disabilities, religious groups and general poverty relief.

WHAT IS FUNDED General charitable purposes with some preference for causes local to the trust.

SAMPLE GRANTS £27,000 to Williamson Charitable Trust; £1,100 to Kosovo Crisis Appeal; £1,000 to A & B Lourdes Fund; £800 to Worth School Appeal; £770 to Worth Abbey Lay Community; £700 to British Red Cross; £530 to Worth Abbey Parish; £500 each to CAFOD, Christian Aid, DCE and HCPT.

FINANCES *Year* 1999–2000 *Income* £40,000 *Grants* £38,000

TRUSTEES Christopher Dobson, Chair; Josephine Dobson; Stephen Leach.

HOW TO APPLY In writing to the correspondent.

WHO TO APPLY TO C N Y Dobson, Sopers Ride, Selsfield Road, Turners Hill, Crawley, West Sussex RH10 4PP *Tel* 01293 521191

CC NO 1022659   **ESTABLISHED** 1986

....

■ The Dock Charitable Fund

WHERE FUNDING CAN BE GIVEN Merseyside.

WHO CAN BENEFIT Seafaring, registered charities on Merseyside.

WHAT IS FUNDED The relief of people who are sick, disabled and retired in the dock service or the families of those who were killed in service; and to benefit charities in the port of Liverpool.

RANGE OF GRANTS £25–£10,000.

SAMPLE GRANTS £10,000 each to Archbishop Beck Catholic High School and Chesterfield High School (to attain sports college status) and to University Hospital – Aintree (for its Clinical Sciences Centre Appea); £5,000 each to Alder Hey Rocking Horse Appeal, Fairbridge in Merseyside, Mersey Mission to Seafarers and Royal Liverpool Philharmonic Society.

FINANCES *Year* 2000 *Income* £71,000 *Grants* £118,000

TRUSTEES Directors of the Mersey Docks & Harbour Company.

HOW TO APPLY In writing to the correspondent.

WHO TO APPLY TO W J Bowley, The Mersey Docks & Harbour Company, Maritime Centre, Port of Liverpool, Liverpool L21 1LA *Tel* 0151 949 6340 *Fax* 0151 949 6338 *Website* www.merseydocks.co.uk

CC NO 206913   **ESTABLISHED** 1811

....

■ The Dollond Charitable Trust

WHERE FUNDING CAN BE GIVEN UK and Israel.

WHO CAN BENEFIT Jewish organisations.

WHAT IS FUNDED Jewish communities; general charitable purposes.

TYPE OF GRANT One-off and recurrent.

SAMPLE GRANTS Beneficiaries included Edgware Synagogue, Jerusalem College of Technology and United Synagogue.

FINANCES *Year* 2001–02 *Income* £750,076
Grants £20,000 *Assets* £3,900,000
TRUSTEES A L Dolland; A Dolland; J Milston.
HOW TO APPLY In writing to the correspondent.
WHO TO APPLY TO J Milston, c/o FMCB, Hathaway
House, Popes Drive, Finchley, London N3 1QF
Tel 020 8346 6446 *Fax* 020 8349 3990
E-mail prof@fmcb.co.uk
CC NO 293459   **ESTABLISHED** 1986

■ The Dorcas Trust

WHERE FUNDING CAN BE GIVEN UK.
WHO CAN BENEFIT Designated charities specified by
the trustees, benefiting children, young adults,
students, Christians, and people disadvantaged
by poverty.
WHAT IS FUNDED Advancement of the Christian
religion, relief of poverty and advancement of
education.
RANGE OF GRANTS £100–£3,500, exceptionally
higher.
SAMPLE GRANTS Regular beneficiaries include Botton
Village, Church Army, Help the Aged, Jubilee
Trust, Krila Riding, Macmillan Cancer Relief,
Mildmay Mission, Navigators, Newmarket Day
Centre, Shaftesbury Society and Treasures in
Heaven Trust.
FINANCES *Year* 2001–02 *Income* £25,447
Grants £35,000
TRUSTEES J C L Broad; J D Broad; P L Butler.
HOW TO APPLY In writing to the correspondent,
although the trust stated that applications
cannot be considered as funds are already
committed.
WHO TO APPLY TO I Taylor, Port of Liverpool Building,
Pier Head, Liverpool L3 1NW *Tel* 0151 236
6666
CC NO 275494   **ESTABLISHED** 1978

■ The Dorema Charitable Trust

WHERE FUNDING CAN BE GIVEN UK.
WHO CAN BENEFIT Organisations benefiting children,
young adults, older people, at risk groups and
socially isolated people.
WHAT IS FUNDED Medicine, health, welfare,
education and religion.
TYPE OF GRANT One off and recurrent.
FINANCES *Year* 2000–01 *Income* £36,000
Grants £23,000 *Assets* £224,000
TRUSTEES D S M Nussbaum; G B Nussbaum; Mrs K
M Nussbaum.
HOW TO APPLY The trust strongly stated that
unsolicited applications are not considered,
describing such appeals as a waste of
charitable resources.
WHO TO APPLY TO D S M Nussbaum, Trustee, 4
Church Grove, Amersham, Buckinghamshire HP6
6SH
CC NO 287001   **ESTABLISHED** 1983

■ The Dorset Historic Churches Trust

WHERE FUNDING CAN BE GIVEN Dorset (including
Bournemouth).
WHO CAN BENEFIT Any church in Dorset.
WHAT IS FUNDED The trust gives grants for 'the
preservation, repair, maintenance, improvement,
upkeep, beautification and reconstruction of
churches in Dorset and of monuments, fittings,
fixtures, stained glass furniture, ornaments and
chattels in such churches and the churchyard

belonging to any such churches'. They state 'no
appropriate application for a grant has been
refused'.
WHAT IS NOT FUNDED No grants towards heating,
electrics, decoration, organs or church halls.
TYPE OF GRANT One-off grants, mainly, but also
interest-free loans for up to four years will be
considered.
RANGE OF GRANTS Governed by funds available and
by need.
SAMPLE GRANTS £10,000 each to Beaminster,
Yetminster and Sherborne Abbey; other lesser
amounts appropriate to the scale of the
problem in each case.
FINANCES *Year* 2002 *Income* £46,500
Grants £104,000 *Assets* £506,000
TRUSTEES Capt. N T L Thimbleby, Chair; Bishop of
Salisbury; Lord Digby; Anthony Pitt-Rivers; Maj. J
C Mansel; C G Dean; Sir Michael Hanham;
Archdeacon of Dorset; Archdeacon of
Sherborne; P F Moule; P Mayne; Lady May; R D
Allan; Sir Philip Williams; Viscount Cranborne; A
C Stuart; Maj. Gen. J O C Alexander; R N R
Peers.
HOW TO APPLY In writing to the appropriate deanery
representative (via secretary if necessary).
WHO TO APPLY TO P F Moule, Ryall's Ground,
Yetminster, Sherborne, Dorset DT9 6LL
Tel 01935 872447
CC NO 282790   **ESTABLISHED** 1960

■ The Dorus Trust

WHERE FUNDING CAN BE GIVEN Mainly UK.
WHO CAN BENEFIT Registered UK charities with a
national focus benefiting people of all ages,
homeless people, people with addictions,
physical disabilities, cancer or diabetes, and
underprivileged children.
WHAT IS FUNDED Support is given to projects
including hostels, hospices, holiday
accommodation, respite care, care in the
community, health counselling and some
environmental issues.
WHAT IS NOT FUNDED No grants to individuals,
expeditions, research, scholarships, charities
with a local focus, local branches of UK
charities or towards running costs.
TYPE OF GRANT Projects and one-off. Funding for one
year or less.
RANGE OF GRANTS £500–£15,000.
SAMPLE GRANTS £18,000 to Royal Commonwealth
Society for the Blind; £10,000 each to Carers
National Association, Contact the Elderly,
Independent Panel for Special Education Advice,
Mentor Foundation (UK) for the Prevention of
Substance Abuse, Refuge and Scottish Council
on Alcohol; £8,000 to Children's Liver Disease
Foundation; £7,000 to Association of
Wheelchair Children; £6,000 each to Action
Cancer, Epilepsy Association of Scotland and
Maternity Alliance.
FINANCES *Year* 2000 *Income* £161,303
Grants £167,500 *Assets* £3,116,428
TRUSTEES C H Peacock; Mrs Bettine Bond; A M
Bond.
HOW TO APPLY On a 'funding proposal form'
available from the correspondent. Applications
should include a copy of the latest audited
annual report and accounts. They are
considered twice a year in mid-summer and mid-
winter. Organisations which have received
grants from this trust, The Cleopatra Trust or
The Epigoni Trust should not reapply in the
following two years. Usually, funding will be
considered from only one of these trusts.

WHO TO APPLY TO Mrs Sue David, Donor Grants Officer, Charities Aid Foundation, King's Hill, West Malling, Kent ME19 4TA *Tel* 01732 520083 *Fax* 01732 520001
CC NO 328724   ESTABLISHED 1990

■ Double 'O' Charity Ltd

WHERE FUNDING CAN BE GIVEN UK and overseas.
WHO CAN BENEFIT Registered charities.
WHAT IS FUNDED Primarily, grants towards the relief of poverty, preservation of health and the advancement of religion. However, the charity considers all requests for aid.
WHAT IS NOT FUNDED No grants to individuals towards education or for their involvement in overseas charity work.
TYPE OF GRANT Preferably one-off.
RANGE OF GRANTS £1,000–£20,000.
SAMPLE GRANTS £20,000 to Lansdowne House Alchohol Advisory Service; £5,000 to Roehampton Priory Hospital; £1,700 to Knee High Theatre; £1,000 each to Breast Cancer Campaign, Howard League for Penal Reform and Vineyard Project.
FINANCES *Year* 1998–99 *Income* £40,000 *Grants* £35,000
TRUSTEES P D B Townshend; Mrs K Townshend.
HOW TO APPLY In writing to the correspondent. This entry was not confirmed by the trust, but the information was correct according to the trust's file at the Charity Commission.
WHO TO APPLY TO The Trustees, 4 Friars Lane, Richmond, Surrey TW9 1NL
CC NO 271681   ESTABLISHED 1976

■ The Doughty Charity Trust

WHERE FUNDING CAN BE GIVEN England, Israel.
WHO CAN BENEFIT Jewish organisations benefiting people who are disadvantaged by poverty or who are sick.
WHAT IS FUNDED To promote (a) the orthodox Jewish Religion, (b) orthodox Jewish education and (c) institutions for Jewish people who are poor, ill and or elderly.
WHAT IS NOT FUNDED No grants to individuals.
TYPE OF GRANT Loan or grant, usually £1,000 or less.
RANGE OF GRANTS £100–£4,500.
SAMPLE GRANTS In 1999: £4,500 to Woodstock Sinclair; £3,500 to Sharreh Torah; £3,000 to Ezras Nitzrochim; £2,700 to Sinai Synagogue; £2,000 each to Menorah Primary School and Ofahim; £1,600 to GGBH; £1,000 each to Gateshead Talmudical College and London Academy of Jewish Studies.
FINANCES *Year* 2001 *Income* £31,607
TRUSTEES G Halibard, Chair; Mrs M Halibard.
HOW TO APPLY In writing to the correspondent. This entry was not confirmed by the trust, but the information was correct according to the trust's file at the Charity Commission.
WHO TO APPLY TO Gerald B Halibard, Trustee, 22 Ravenscroft Avenue, Golders Green, London NW11 0RY *Tel* 020 8209 0500
CC NO 274977   ESTABLISHED 1977

■ The Douglas Charitable Trust

WHERE FUNDING CAN BE GIVEN Scotland and the third world.
WHO CAN BENEFIT Academics, students, young adults, people with disabilities and people who are homeless.

WHAT IS FUNDED Scottish universities and church restoration projects are the main interests. Grants are also made to charities which help people who are disadvantaged or homeless, and people in the third world.
RANGE OF GRANTS £500–£5,000.
SAMPLE GRANTS £5,000 to Save the Children; £2,500 to University of St Andrews; £1,000 to Shelter; £500 each to Age Concern and European Children's Trust.
FINANCES *Year* 2001–02 *Income* £25,000 *Grants* £33,500 *Assets* £455,000
TRUSTEES Revd Prof. D Shaw; D Connell; E Cameron.
HOW TO APPLY In writing to the correspondent. Apply at any time.
WHO TO APPLY TO Lesley Kelly, Turcan Connell, Princes Exchange, 1 Earl Grey Street, Edinburgh EH3 9EE *Tel* 0131 228 8111 *Fax* 0131 228 8118
SC NO SC019840   ESTABLISHED 1992

■ The R M Douglas Charitable Trust

WHERE FUNDING CAN BE GIVEN UK, preference for Staffordshire.
WHO CAN BENEFIT Registered charities already in receipt of support from the trust.
WHAT IS FUNDED The relief of poverty (including provision of pensions) especially for present and past employees (and their families) of Robert M Douglas (Contractors) Ltd, and general charitable purposes especially in the parish of St Mary, Dunstall.
TYPE OF GRANT Mostly small grants, including buildings, capital, core costs, one-off, research, and recurring costs.
RANGE OF GRANTS £200–£5,000. Typically £200–£500.
SAMPLE GRANTS In 1999–2000: £5,000 each to Burton Graduate Medical College for equipment for a new lecture theatre and SAT-7 Trust for Christian outreach; £4,000 to Lichfield Diocesan Urban Fund for Christian mission; £2,000 each to Four Oaks Methodist Church for its centenary appeal and St Giles Hospice – Lichfield for developments; £1,000 each to Bible Explorer for Christian outreach, British Red Cross for general purposes, St Mary's Hospice – Sellyoak for general purposes and John Taylor High School – Barton in Needwood for a performing arts block.
FINANCES *Year* 2001–02 *Income* £51,342
TRUSTEES J R T Douglas; Mrs J E Lees; F W Carder.
HOW TO APPLY The trust states that its funds are fully committed and applications 'are not being sought for the time being'.
WHO TO APPLY TO The Administrator, 68 Liverpool Road, Stoke on Trent ST4 1BG
CC NO 248775   ESTABLISHED 1966

■ Dove-Bowerman Trust

WHERE FUNDING CAN BE GIVEN UK.
WHO CAN BENEFIT Registered charities, involving women in further education.
WHAT IS FUNDED Small grants are made to fund women in further education or vocational training.
WHAT IS NOT FUNDED No loans. No funds for students on gap years such as Operation Raleigh.

TYPE OF GRANT Mostly one-off grants. No loans. Research and running costs are considered. Funding may be given for up to three years.

SAMPLE GRANTS £26,000 to Wycombe Abbey for Seniors Bursaries; £14,000 to Wycombe Abbey for 6th Form Bursaries; £6,000 to Hertford Regional College (Ware site) for individual students; £1,500 to Peckham Settlement; £1,000 to Thames Valley Adventure Playground; £500 to Thomas Coram Foundation.

FINANCES Year 2001–02 *Income* £61,090 *Grants* £54,760 *Assets* £1,544,969

TRUSTEES Revd Mrs C Canti; Mrs K Alderson; W P W Barnes; Mrs G Fletcher-Watson; Mrs C Davis; P Wolton; J Stewart; Mrs C Archer; Mrs L Packman; C Atkins; Mrs V Howes.

HOW TO APPLY Applications close on April 30. Application forms and guidelines will be sent if an sae is enclosed. Please note, however, the trustees are concerned by the number of applications they are not in a position to support according to the terms of the trust deed, resources being limited and virtually all earmarked. Letters will not be acknowledged unless there is a possibility of a grant being given. The trust also states that all resources are likely to be already earmarked for May 2003.

WHO TO APPLY TO Mrs J Kingsley, Fawney, High Street, Whitchurch-on-Thames, Reading RG8 7DD *Tel* 0118 984 2441

CC NO 262888   **ESTABLISHED** 1971

■ The Drapers' Charitable Fund

WHERE FUNDING CAN BE GIVEN UK, with a special interest in the City and adjacent parts of London.

WHO CAN BENEFIT Registered charities, or organisations established for charitable, benevolent or philanthropic purposes benefiting textiles, and people who are disadvantaged by poverty, or disabled or mentally ill.

WHAT IS FUNDED The major charitable themes for considering new proposals should remain: the causes and effects of social exclusion among young people, normally in inner cities and particularly in London, with an emphasis on eduction; causes with strong historic links with the company, including appeals for the support of textiles; and Northern Ireland, particularly the areas of Moneymore and Draperstown.

WHAT IS NOT FUNDED The following will not generally be supported: medical projects; church restoration; running costs; replacement of statutory funding.

TYPE OF GRANT One-off or recurrent grants.

RANGE OF GRANTS £500–£25,000.

SAMPLE GRANTS £100,000 each to Bancrofts School and Queen Mary & Westfield College; £40,300 in four grants to University of Wales, Bangor; £33,000 in two grants over three years to St Anne's College, Oxford; £30,000 to Hertford College, Oxford; £25,000 to Pembroke College, Cambridge; £18,500 in two grants to Moneymore Heritage Trust; £18,200 in two grants to Nottingham Trent University; £15,000 in two grants to Adam's School, Wem; £11,500 to John Taylor High School.

FINANCES Year 2000–01 *Income* £970,789 *Grants* £836,962 *Assets* £18,036,065

TRUSTEES The Drapers' Company. Chair of the charity committee: Richard Beharrell.

HOW TO APPLY Please send in a brief proposal including a copy of your annual report and accounts.

WHO TO APPLY TO Miss Debbie J Thomas, Charities Administrator, The Drapers' Company, Drapers' Hall, Throgmorton Avenue, London EC2N 2DQ *Tel* 020 7588 5001 *Fax* 020 7628 1988 *E-mail* dthomas@thedrapers.co.uk

CC NO 251403   **ESTABLISHED** 1959

■ The Anthony du Boulay Charitable Trust

WHERE FUNDING CAN BE GIVEN UK and Dorset.

WHO CAN BENEFIT Registered charities, mostly on a regular basis.

WHAT IS FUNDED General charitable purposes, but especially research, health care, the arts, and foreign aid.

RANGE OF GRANTS £500–£5,000.

SAMPLE GRANTS £5,000 to Dorset County Museum; £2,500 to St Mary's Church, Frampton; £2,000 each to British Red Cross Dorset Branch, CancerCare Dorset, Family Holiday Association, Family Welfare Association, Orpington Mental Health, and Peper Harrow Foundation; £1,500 to Community APA; £1,000 to SOS Sahel.

FINANCES Year 1999 *Income* £54,586 *Grants* £49,500 *Assets* £1,224,254

TRUSTEES Anthony du Boulay; Judith du Boulay; Michael Edwardes-Evans.

HOW TO APPLY Unsolicited applications cannot be supported as funds are fully committed.

WHO TO APPLY TO Anthony du Boulay, Trustee, Langford Farm, Sydling St Nicholas, Nr Dorchester, Dorset DT2 9TP

CC NO 269513   **ESTABLISHED** 1975

■ Duchy of Lancaster Benevolent Fund

WHERE FUNDING CAN BE GIVEN The county palatine of Lancashire (in Lancashire, Greater Manchester and Merseyside), and elsewhere in the country where the Duchy of Lancaster has historical links such as land interests and church livings.

WHO CAN BENEFIT Individuals and organisations.

WHAT IS FUNDED General charitable causes, but especially youth and education, welfare of people who are disabled or elderly, community help, religion.

TYPE OF GRANT Mainly one-off grants for specific projects. Recurrent grants occasionally given.

RANGE OF GRANTS £50–£5,000 but can be larger.

SAMPLE GRANTS £20,000 to Invalids at Home; £10,000 each to North West ACF Trust Fund and The Magistrates Association; £5,000 each to Imperial War Museum, QuadSquad, Broughton House, Charing Cross, Lister Steps, United Trusts, Wade Hall Family Trust and Wirral CVS; £1,000 each to Emmanuel Community, North West Air Ambulance and Tinytots Vision.

FINANCES Year 2001–02 *Income* £300,944 *Grants* £270,591 *Assets* £10,100,000

TRUSTEES Hon. Justice Blackbourne; R G McCombe; Sir Michael Peat; Lord Shuttleworth; Col. J B Timmins; A W Waterworth; Cllr Mrs I Short.

HOW TO APPLY In writing to the correspondent, at any time. There is no application form. Applications should be by letter, including as much information as possible. All applications are acknowledged.

WHO TO APPLY TO Mrs Lindsay Addison, Duchy of Lancaster Office, 1 Lancaster Place, Strand, London WC2E 7ED *Tel* 020 7836 8277 *Fax* 020 7836 3098

CC NO 1026752   **ESTABLISHED** 1993

Think carefully about every application. Is it justified?

439

■ The William Dudley Trust

WHERE FUNDING CAN BE GIVEN Within the boundaries of the city of Birmingham.

WHO CAN BENEFIT Smaller local charities benefiting older people or alleviating the need, hardship and distress of the general population of Birmingham.

WHAT IS FUNDED (a) Assistance to young people studying or setting up business in Birmingham (restricted area of work – no applications invited). (b) Assistance to older tradespeople who have fallen on hard times (restricted area of work – no applications invited). (c) Grants to charitable organisations in Birmingham towards general alleviation of need, hardship and distress.

WHAT IS NOT FUNDED No grants are given for general appeals, medical research or to individuals. Holidays and outings are not seen as a priority.

TYPE OF GRANT One-off, capital, core costs, project, recurring costs, running costs and start-up costs. Funding is available for up to one year.

RANGE OF GRANTS £500–£1,000.

SAMPLE GRANTS £1,000 to Home from Hospital for worker costs; £950 to Rotton Park Elderly Men's Asian Project for cost of short-term development worker; £900 to Yemeni Elderly in Small Heath & Sparkbrook for a computer; £500 each to 24 organisations including – Midlands Ethnic Albanian Foundation, Special Gymnastics Association, St Luke's Church, Gilgal Project, Highgate Children's Counselling Service, Senior Citizens Ministry and Pancreatitis Supporters Network.

FINANCES *Year* 2001 *Income* £29,281 *Grants* £36,785 *Assets* £828,161

TRUSTEES P H D White; A N Mabe; Cllr M E Scrimshaw; Cllr R H Spector; Dr J Blythe; Anil Bhalla; Cllr L Lawrence; Mrs S Robinson.

HOW TO APPLY The trust welcomes initial telephone calls to discuss applications. There is no application form, but guidance notes are available which include details of application closing dates. Trustees meet five times each year. Applicants will hear whether or not they have been successful within two weeks of the relevant meeting.

WHO TO APPLY TO Ms Kate Hazlewood, Administrator, Unit 321 The Custard Factory, Gibb Street, Digbeth, Birmingham B9 4AA *Tel* 0121 753 0706 *Fax* 0121 248 3323 *E-mail* williamdudleytrust@hotmail.com

CC NO 214752   **ESTABLISHED** 1875

■ Alicia Duchess Dudleys Charity

WHERE FUNDING CAN BE GIVEN Northamptonshire and Warwickshire.

WHO CAN BENEFIT Only local charities and vicars mentioned in Founder's will.

WHAT IS FUNDED Specific charitable purposes.

WHAT IS NOT FUNDED Only the charities mentioned in the will of the Late Duchess Dudley are supported.

FINANCES *Year* 1999–2000 *Income* £94,000 *Grants* £45,000 *Assets* £1,800,000

TRUSTEES A F Birtles; J D S Ainscow; Most Hon. Dowager Marchioness of Hertford; H L Gray-Cheape; Mrs M V Goldberg-Steuart; J Rigg; Hon. Camilla Leigh; Sir John Greenaway; Mrs J Bird; C P Stratton.

HOW TO APPLY No appplications can be considered.

WHO TO APPLY TO R V Stone, 4 Bull Street, Birmingham B4 6AF *Tel* 0121 236 1844 *Fax* 0121 236 1966 *E-mail* roger.stone@btconnect.com

CC NO 244804   **ESTABLISHED** 1962

■ The Dugdale Charitable Trust

WHERE FUNDING CAN BE GIVEN UK and overseas.

WHO CAN BENEFIT Christians and Christian organisations who are personally known to the trustees.

WHAT IS FUNDED General charitable purposes.

SAMPLE GRANTS £24,519 to Waltham Chase Methodist Church; £3,780 to OMS International; £1,300 to Africa Evangelical Fellowship; £1,000 to Prospects; £200 to Sudan Interior Mission.

FINANCES *Year* 1998–99 *Income* £21,383 *Grants* £31,231 *Assets* £182,150

TRUSTEES R A Dugdale; Mrs B Dugdale.

HOW TO APPLY This trust only supports causes known personally to the trustees. Unsolicited applications are not considered.

WHO TO APPLY TO R Dugdale, Trustee, Harmsworth Farm, Botley Road, Curbridge, Hampshire SO30 2HB

CC NO 1052941   **ESTABLISHED** 1995

■ The Duis Charitable Trust

WHERE FUNDING CAN BE GIVEN Worldwide.

WHO CAN BENEFIT Children, medical, general.

WHAT IS FUNDED The trust makes grants benefiting groups largely concerned with Jewish causes, although this incorporates support of social welfare, education, capital library and hospital appeals.

WHAT IS NOT FUNDED No grants to individuals.

SAMPLE GRANTS In 1998–99: £2,800 to Norwood Ravenswood; £2,000 each to Great Ormond Street Hospital, BINOH Norwood Childcare, Dulwich Picture Gallery, National Playing Fields, Downs Syndrome Association and Joint Jewish Charitable Trust; £1,000 each including those to Hillel Special Purposes Fund, Breakaway Charity Committee, Children's Wish Foundation and Jewish Care.

FINANCES *Year* 2001–02 *Income* £38,000 *Grants* £22,700 *Assets* £479,232

TRUSTEES Robert Michael Gore; Julian Michael Fellerman.

HOW TO APPLY In writing to the correspondent.

WHO TO APPLY TO Arshoo Singh,,Prichard Englefield, 14 New Street, London EC2M 4HE *Tel* 020 7972 9720

CC NO 800487   **ESTABLISHED** 1987

■ The Dulverton Trust

WHERE FUNDING CAN BE GIVEN Unrestricted. Mainly UK in practice. An interest in the Cotswolds, and in Scotland. Limited support to parts of Africa. Few grants for work in London or Northern Ireland.

WHO CAN BENEFIT Mainly UK projects, some regional and local projects at a minor level.

WHAT IS FUNDED Youth and education, conservation, general welfare and to a lesser extent activities in religion, peace and security, preservation and industrial understanding.

WHAT IS NOT FUNDED Applications should be made in writing to the director. Trustee meetings are held four times a year – in January, May, July and October (though decisions on small grants can be made more rapidly – if essential, very rapidly). There is no set format for applications, but it is helpful if they can include the background and a clear statement of the aims of the appeal, together with the funding target and any progress made in reaching it. Initial enquiries by telephone, for example to establish eligibility, are welcomed. Applications should, if possible, be restricted to a letter and maximum of two sheets of paper. Initial applications should always include a copy of the previous year's annual report and accounts.

TYPE OF GRANT Project and one-off funding. Also capital and core costs. Funding is rarely given for more than one year.

RANGE OF GRANTS £500–£140,000; typically £20,000.

SAMPLE GRANTS £131,000 to Farmington Trust; £125,000 to Oxford University Dulverton Scholarships; £40,000 each to Oxfordshire Community Foundation and Quaker Social Action; £30,000 each to Building Conservation Centre Trust, Duke of Edinburgh's Award Scheme, and Norwich Cathedral Trust; £28,000 to Farms for City Children; £25,000 to Family Service Units; £21,000 to Computer Aid International; £15,000 each to British Trust for Conservation Volunteers, and Wildfowl and Wetlands Trust.

FINANCES *Year* 2001–02 *Income* £3,180,725 *Grants* £3,175,000 *Assets* £81,482,106

TRUSTEES Colonel David Fanshawe, Chair; Christopher Wills; Sir John Kemp-Welch; Hon. Robert Wills; Rt Hon. Lord Carrington; Lord Dulverton; Earl of Gowrie; Dr Catherine Wills; Richard Fitzalan Howard; Sir Malcolm Rifkind.

HOW TO APPLY Applications should be made in writing to the director. Trustee meetings are held four times a year – in January, May, July and October (though decisions on small grants can be made more rapidly – if essential, very rapidly). There is no set format for applications, but it is helpful if they can include the background and a clear statement of the aims of the appeal, together with the funding target and any progress made in reaching it. Initial enquiries by telephone, for example to establish eligibility, are welcomed. Applications should, if possible, be restricted to a letter and maximum of two sheets of paper. Initial applications should always include a copy of the previous year's annual report and accounts.

WHO TO APPLY TO Col. Christopher Bates, Director, 5 St James's Place, London SW1A 1NP *Tel* 020 7629 9121 *Fax* 020 7495 6201 *E-mail* trust@dulverton.org

CC NO 206426　　**ESTABLISHED** 1949

....

■ **The P B Dumbell Charitable Trust**

WHERE FUNDING CAN BE GIVEN Wolverhampton and surrounding areas.

WHO CAN BENEFIT Institutions and individuals.

WHAT IS FUNDED General charitable purposes.

WHAT IS NOT FUNDED No educational grants are given.

RANGE OF GRANTS £100–£2,500.

SAMPLE GRANTS £2,500 each to Age Concern Wolverhampton, James Beattie House Appeal, Beacon Centre for the Blind, Bromesberrow Church, Clocolan Peace Feeding Scheme, Clunbury Church, Compton Hospice, Ironbridge Gorge Museum, Wolverhampton Multiple Sclerosis Society and Worfield Church, all for running costs/upkeep.

FINANCES *Year* 1999–2000 *Income* £39,365 *Grants* £30,720 *Assets* £963,308

TRUSTEES M H Gilbert; C F Dumbell.

HOW TO APPLY In writing to the correspondent. The trustees meet annually in June when most grants are considered. Some applications will be considered at other times. Telephone calls are not welcomed.

WHO TO APPLY TO C F Dumbell, Trustee, Lower Hall, Worfield, Bridgnorth, Shropshire WV15 5LH

CC NO 232770　　**ESTABLISHED** 1964

....

■ **The Dumbreck Charity**

WHERE FUNDING CAN BE GIVEN Worldwide, especially the Midlands.

WHO CAN BENEFIT UK and West Midlands charities.

WHAT IS FUNDED Animal welfare and conservation; children's welfare; people who are elderly or mentally or physically disabled; medical causes; and general charitable purposes.

WHAT IS NOT FUNDED No grants to individuals.

TYPE OF GRANT Recurring and one-off grants.

RANGE OF GRANTS £500–£3,000, but mainly for amounts under £1,000 each.

SAMPLE GRANTS £3,000 to Brooke Hospital for Animals – Cairo; £2,000 each to International League for the Protection of Horses and Myton Hospice; £1,500 to Warwickshire Association for the Blind; £1,000 each to Birmingham Dogs Home, Greek Animal Welfare Fund, Leamington Boys' Club, Mobility, National Benevolent Fund for the Ages, Pet Care, NSPCC, Save the Children Fund and Warwick Old People's Friendship Circle.

FINANCES *Year* 2001–02 *Income* £97,631 *Grants* £99,500 *Assets* £3,157,740

TRUSTEES A C S Hordern; H B Carslake; Mrs J E Melling.

HOW TO APPLY In writing to the correspondent. The trustees meet annually in April/May. Unsuccessful applications will not be acknowledged.

WHO TO APPLY TO A C S Hordern, Trustee, Church House, North Piddle, Worcestershire WR7 4PR

CC NO 273070　　**ESTABLISHED** 1976

....

■ **Dumfries and Galloway Council Charitable Trusts**

WHERE FUNDING CAN BE GIVEN Dumfries and Galloway.

WHO CAN BENEFIT Individuals and local organisations.

WHAT IS FUNDED Grants were given under the following three categories: social welfare, charitable, education.

WHAT IS NOT FUNDED No support for arts, religious appeals, health/medical appeals, animal welfare or environment/heritage.

TYPE OF GRANT £10–£18,000.

SAMPLE GRANTS £18,000 to Lockerbie Academy for students to attend Syracuse University; £12,600 to Dalbeattie Day Centre; £500 to Sanquhar Academy for sports equipment.

FINANCES *Year* 2001–02 *Income* £92,000 *Grants* £60,000 *Assets* £785,000

TRUSTEES The Members of the Council.

HOW TO APPLY In writing to the correspondent.

WHO TO APPLY TO The Council Secretariat, Dumfries and Galloway Council, Carruthers House, English Street, Dumfries DG1 2HP *Tel* 01387 260000 *Fax* 01387 260034 *Website* www.dumgal.gov.uk

SC NO SC025071

....

■ **Dunard Fund**

WHERE FUNDING CAN BE GIVEN UK, but with a strong interest in Scotland and the north of England.

WHO CAN BENEFIT Arts organisations.

WHAT IS FUNDED Principally to the training for and performance of classical music at the highest standard and to education and display of the visual arts, also at international standard. A small percentage of the fund is dedicated to environmental projects.

WHAT IS NOT FUNDED Grants are only given to charities recognised in Scotland or charities registered in England and Wales. The fund says that it does not consider unsolicited applications or applications from individuals.

SAMPLE GRANTS £200,000 to Monteverdi Choir and Orchestra; £100,000 to London Philharmonic Orchestra; £50,000 to National Trust for Scotland; £20,000 each to Durham Cathedral, St Mary's Music School Development Appeal and Royal Scottish National Opera; £15,000 to Fruitmarket Gallery; £10,000 to Royal Opera House; £8,000 to John Currie Singers Ltd; £5,000 to RSPB Scotland.

FINANCES *Year* 2000–01 *Grants* £712,000

TRUSTEES Carol Colburn Hogel; Elisabeth Norman; Catherine Hogel; Colin Liddell.

HOW TO APPLY Any applications should be in writing only to the Dunard Fund, but see exclusions above.

WHO TO APPLY TO Mrs C Hogel, Trustee, 4 Royal Terrace, Edinburgh EH7 5AB *Tel* 0131 556 4043 *Fax* 0131 556 3969

CC NO 295790   **ESTABLISHED** 1986

■ The Dunhill Medical Trust

WHERE FUNDING CAN BE GIVEN UK.

WHO CAN BENEFIT Registered charities particularly those benefiting older people and academic institutions undertaking medical research.

WHAT IS FUNDED Organisations involved in medical research, furtherance of medical knowledge and care of, and accommodation for, older people.

WHAT IS NOT FUNDED The trustees will not normally approve the use of funds for providing clinical services that, in their opinion, would be more appropriately provided by the National Health Service; sponsorship of individuals; organisations outside the UK; charities representing specific professions or trade associations; institutional overheads; travel/conference fees; hospices.

TYPE OF GRANT Project grants to research groups, as well as some grants for salaries and building or equipment costs for specific projects.

SAMPLE GRANTS £1,065,000 for the endowment of the Herbert Dunhill Chair in Rehabilitation at King's College, London; £600,000 to Connect (The Communication Disability Network) for research, therapy and training; £100,000 each to Guildcare, Newcastle University for rheumatology research, Northwick Park for cardiovascular and other research, Oxford Centre for Diabetes, Endocrinology and Metabolism for equipment and Southampton University for epidemiology/nutrition research; £90,000 to CEDAR (Centre for Diabetes, Endocrinology and Research) for a building; £67,000 to the University of Central Lancashire, part of a £200,000 grant for an evaluation of the work with older people at London's Bromley by Bow Healthy Living Centre; £59,000 to the Dementia Relief Trust.

FINANCES *Year* 2001–02 *Income* £3,423,346 *Grants* £4,113,000 *Assets* £77,997,564

TRUSTEES Ronald E Perry; Timothy Sanderson; Dr Christopher Bateman; Prof. Maurice Lessof; Sir Cyril Chantler.

HOW TO APPLY To the assistant director. Trustees meet in March, May, September and December.

WHO TO APPLY TO Claire Large, Assistant Director, I Fairholt Street, London SW7 1EQ *Tel* 020 7584 7411 *Fax* 0207581 5463 *E-mail* info@dunhillmedical.org.uk *Website* www.dunhillmedical.org.uk

CC NO 294286   **ESTABLISHED** 1951

■ The Harry Dunn Charitable Trust

WHERE FUNDING CAN BE GIVEN UK, with a strong preference for Nottinghamshire.

WHO CAN BENEFIT Organisations benefiting sufferers of multiple sclerosis; environmental charities.

WHAT IS FUNDED Charities working in the fields of health facilities and buildings; support to voluntary and community organisations; MS research; conservation; bird sanctuaries and ecology.

WHAT IS NOT FUNDED Only organisations known to the trustees are supported. No grants to individuals.

TYPE OF GRANT Core costs and one-off; funding for one year or less will be considered.

RANGE OF GRANTS £1,000–£2,000.

SAMPLE GRANTS £2,000 each to Nottingham Friends of ARMS, Disability Aid Fund, Winged Fellowship Trust, and British Disabled Water Ski; £1,500 to Wildfowl and Wetlands Trust; £1,000 each to Support Dogs, Rainbows, Peter Le Merchant Trust, and Multiple Sclerosis Society of Great Britain and Northern Ireland.

FINANCES *Year* 1998–99 *Income* £69,388 *Grants* £29,150 *Assets* £1,028,267

TRUSTEES A H Dunn; Mrs C N Dunn; N A Dunn; R M Dunn.

HOW TO APPLY In writing to the correspondent, but note the comments under exclusions.

WHO TO APPLY TO P Robinson, Rushcliffe Developments, 13–15 Rectory Road, West Bridgford, Nottingham NG2 6BE *Tel* 0115 945 5300

CC NO 297389   **ESTABLISHED** 1987

■ The W E Dunn Trust

WHERE FUNDING CAN BE GIVEN The Midlands.

WHO CAN BENEFIT Charitable organisations and individuals.

WHAT IS FUNDED The funding priorities are to benefit people who are sick or in adversity and resident in the Midlands area, particularly in Wolverhampton, Wednesbury, North Staffordshire and neighbouring localities. The trustees have full discretion and in addition to dealing with local personal requests through social services departments, they make donations to local charities and occasionally to UK charities. The trustees particularly wish to assist older people and the very young, but they will not make grants to settle or reduce debts already incurred. They are prepared to assist students from the Midlands wishing to further their education, but who have special difficulties which prevent them from doing so. The trust will consider funding: accommodation and housing; infrastructure, support and development; community arts and recreation; health; church buildings; environmental issues; education and training; costs of study; community facilities and services; and other charitable purposes.

WHAT IS NOT FUNDED No grants to settle or reduce debts already incurred.

TYPE OF GRANT Buildings, capital, core costs, one-off, project and start-up costs. All funding is for up to three years.

SAMPLE GRANTS £20,000 to Cancer Research UK; £10,000 to Acorns Children's Hospice Trust;

£2,000 each to Kemp Hospice, NSPCC, Parkinson's Disease Society, St Giles Hospice and Summerfield Foundation; £1,000 each to Bethany Trust, Big Issue Foundation, Birmingham Rathbone Society, Good Shepherd Trust, Motability, NSPCC, Royal Orthopaedic Charity, Sandwell Community Caring Trust and Woodrush High School.

FINANCES *Year* 2001–02 *Income* £147,692 *Grants* £169,718 *Assets* £3,825,937

TRUSTEES Charles E Corney, Chair; David J Corney; David F Perkins; Leita H Smethurst; C Paul King.

HOW TO APPLY In writing to the correspondent giving the name and address, some idea of the income/outgoings and any other necessary particulars of the grantee. Organisations should always enclose accounts. Grants to individuals are considered every week; grants to organisations, every three or four months.

WHO TO APPLY TO Alan H Smith, The Trust Office, 30 Bentley Heath Cottages, Tilehouse Green Lane, Knowle, Solihull B93 9EL

CC NO 219418   **ESTABLISHED** 1958

....

■ The Dwek Family Charitable Trust

WHERE FUNDING CAN BE GIVEN UK, with a preference for the Manchester area.

WHO CAN BENEFIT Individuals and small charities without a large fundraising profile. In previous years mainly Jewish charities have been supported.

WHAT IS FUNDED People who are in need, disabled or disadvantaged.

RANGE OF GRANTS £100–£10,000.

SAMPLE GRANTS In 1997: £18,600 to Bodycote Educational Trust; £5,500 to Ta'ali-A History; £5,000 each to JNF Charitable Trust and Manchester Jewish Social Services; £3,000 to North Cheshire Jewish School; £2,694 to Jewish Cultural Centre; £1,850 to Barnardos; £1,500 to Shaare Sedek Synagogue; £1,250 each to Delamere Forest School and Withington Congregation of Spanish and Portuguese Jews.

FINANCES *Year* 2000–01 *Grants* £62,000 *Assets* £523,000

TRUSTEES J C Dwek; J V Dwek; A J Leon.

HOW TO APPLY In writing to the correspondent.

WHO TO APPLY TO J C Dwek, Trustee, Suite One, Courthill House, 66 Water Lane, Wilmslow, Cheshire SK9 5AP *Tel* 01625 549081 *Fax* 01625 530791

CC NO 1001456   **ESTABLISHED** 1989

....

■ The Dyers' Company Charitable Trust

WHERE FUNDING CAN BE GIVEN UK.

WHO CAN BENEFIT Registered charities only.

WHAT IS FUNDED General charitable purposes.

WHAT IS NOT FUNDED No grants to individuals.

SAMPLE GRANTS £123,200 to Norwich School; £10,000 to Textile Conservation Centre, £8,250 to Boucher C of E Primary School – Bermondsey; £9,000 over three years to Heriot-Watt University; £6,000 to St Saviour's and St Olave's Secondary School – Southwark; £3,000 each to Homerton House School – Hackney and UMIST; £2,500 each to Hyde Park Nursery School Charitable Trust and National Maritime Museum; £2,073 to City & Guilds of London Institute.

FINANCES *Year* 1999–2000 *Income* £203,742 *Grants* £240,173 *Assets* £3,429,045

TRUSTEES The court of The Dyers' Company.

HOW TO APPLY The trust does not welcome unsolicited applications.

WHO TO APPLY TO The Clerk, Dyers Hall, Dowgate Hill, London EC4R 2ST *Tel* 020 7236 7197

CC NO 289547   **ESTABLISHED** 1984

Think carefully about every application. Is it justified?

443

■ The Eagle Charity Trust

WHERE FUNDING CAN BE GIVEN UK, in particular Manchester, and overseas.

WHO CAN BENEFIT UK, international and local charities.

WHAT IS FUNDED The trust stated it supports a wide variety of charities, especially those concerned with medicine and welfare.

SAMPLE GRANTS Beneficiaries included Alzheimer's Society, Amnesty International, ASBAH, Children's Society, Esther Benjamin Trust and UNICEF.

FINANCES *Year* 2000 *Grants* £24,500

TRUSTEES Mrs L A Gifford; Miss D Gifford; Mrs E Y Williams; Mrs S A Nowakowski; R M E Gifford.

HOW TO APPLY In writing to the correspondent. However, please note, unsolicited applications are not invited.

WHO TO APPLY TO C Roberts, Accountant, Messrs Nairne Son & Green, 477 Chester Road, Cornbrook, Manchester M16 9HF *Tel* 0161 872 1701

CC NO 802134   **ESTABLISHED** 1989

■ Audrey Earle Charitable Trust

WHERE FUNDING CAN BE GIVEN UK.

WHO CAN BENEFIT Registered charities.

WHAT IS FUNDED General charitable purposes with some preference for animal welfare and conservation charities.

TYPE OF GRANT Mostly recurrent.

SAMPLE GRANTS £3,000 to Burnham Overy Village Hall; £2,500 to British Red Cross; £1,500 each to The League of Friends of Wells Hospital and Oxfam; £1,000 to St Clements Church Fabric Fund.

FINANCES *Year* 1998–99 *Income* £31,000 *Grants* £22,000 *Assets* £848,000

TRUSTEES John Francis Russell Smith; Catherine May Livingston; Roger James Weetch.

HOW TO APPLY In writing to the correspondent.

WHO TO APPLY TO Paul Sheils, 24 Bloomsbury Square, London WC1A 2PL *Tel* 020 7637 0661 *Fax* 020 7436 4663

CC NO 290028   **ESTABLISHED** 1984

■ The Earley Charity

WHERE FUNDING CAN BE GIVEN The liberty of Earley, the central, eastern and southern part of Reading borough, Earley and the immediate surrounding area.

WHO CAN BENEFIT Individuals in need and charitable and community organisations.

WHAT IS FUNDED To give aid to: people who are disabled; those with housing need; those caring for older parents or relatives; widows/widowers, single older people and single parents with families; those undertaking vocational training or apprenticeships; appropriate local charities and community organisations; arts, culture and recreation; health; conservation and campaigning; schools and colleges; and social care and development.

WHAT IS NOT FUNDED No UK or international appeals are considered.

TYPE OF GRANT One-off, project and start-up costs. Funding is available for up to one year.

RANGE OF GRANTS £30–£2,500 for individuals, and £250–£40,000 for organisations.

SAMPLE GRANTS £50,000 to Reading CAB; £41,000 to Garley Crescent; £25,000 to RCWRY; £24,000 to Readibus; £10,000 to CCA; £3,000 each to Age Concern Berks and to Trinity Concert Band; £2,000 each to Wokingham Volunteer Developments and Reading Womens Voluntary Agency; £1,000 to Reading Association of Blind.

FINANCES *Year* 2001 *Income* £388,480 *Grants* £252,828 *Assets* £12,784,557

TRUSTEES R F Ames; Mrs M Eastwell; Dr D G Jenkins; L G Norton; I M Robertson; D C Sutton.

HOW TO APPLY In writing to the correspondent; applications are considered at any time. No response is given to applicants from outside the area. Telephone calls are welcome from applicants who wish to check eligibility.

WHO TO APPLY TO John Evans, Clerk, The Liberty of Earley House, Strand Way, Earley, Reading, Berkshire RG6 4EA *Tel* 0118 975 5663 *Fax* 0118 975 2263

CC NO 244823   **ESTABLISHED** 1820

■ Earlsmead Charitable Trust

WHERE FUNDING CAN BE GIVEN UK.

WHO CAN BENEFIT Registered charities.

WHAT IS FUNDED General charitable purposes with some preference for animal welfare charities.

TYPE OF GRANT Donations at trustees discretion.

RANGE OF GRANTS £30–£3,000 but mostly for £500 or £1,000.

FINANCES *Year* 2002–03 *Income* £49,000 *Grants* £21,000 *Assets* £71,000

TRUSTEES Mrs A M Langley-Hunt; T R Langley-Hunt.

HOW TO APPLY The trust states that it only has very small funds available, since most of its grant total is already committed. Unsolicited applications will not receive a response.

WHO TO APPLY TO Mrs A M Langley-Hunt, Trustee, 53 Ellerby Street, London SW6 6EU *Tel* 020 7736 5120

CC NO 1043766   **ESTABLISHED** 1977

■ The Earmark Trust

WHERE FUNDING CAN BE GIVEN UK, with a preference for charities based in Kent.

WHO CAN BENEFIT Charitable organisations, usually those personally known to the trustees.

WHAT IS FUNDED People with disabilities, children, cancer research, the arts, Christian causes and general charitable purposes.

WHAT IS NOT FUNDED Applications from individuals are seldom considered. Applications from large-scale charities, church/cathedral restoration schemes or organ rebuilding projects are also not considered.

RANGE OF GRANTS £100–£500.

SAMPLE GRANTS In 1999–2000: £500 each to Commonwork, Disability, Great Ormond Street Hospital, Ightham Mote Appeal and RNIB.

FINANCES *Year* 2001–02 *Income* £33,000 *Grants* £25,461 *Assets* £923,000

TRUSTEES F C Raven; A C M Raven.

HOW TO APPLY In writing to the correspondent.

WHO TO APPLY TO F C Raven, Trustee, The Knoll, Ightham, Sevenoaks, Kent TN15 9DY

CC NO 267176   **ESTABLISHED** 1974

■ The Earth Love Fund

WHERE FUNDING CAN BE GIVEN UK and overseas.
WHO CAN BENEFIT Environmental organisations.
WHAT IS FUNDED Community-based rainforest conservation projects; community arts organisations for the annual Artists for the Environment festival.
RANGE OF GRANTS £500 for community arts.
SAMPLE GRANTS £15,014 to Bona Vista Project – Brazil; £11,108 to Rainforest Alliance; £3,034 to Amazon Watch; £2,975 to Gurukula Botanical Project; £1,500 to Kayapo Land Management.
FINANCES *Year* 2000–01 *Income* £32,952 *Grants* £37,481 *Assets* £20,742
TRUSTEES Nicholas H Glennie-Smith; Ivan Hattingh; Ed Posey.
HOW TO APPLY Applications should be made in writing to the correspondent.
WHO TO APPLY TO Paul Antony Denby, Denby Associates, 10 Coldbath Square, London EC1R 5HL *Tel* 020 7837 7200 *Fax* 020 7833 9177 *E-mail* mail@pauldenby.com *Website* www.unisong.com/elf
CC NO 328137   **ESTABLISHED** 1989

■ The Sir John Eastwood Foundation

WHERE FUNDING CAN BE GIVEN UK, but mainly Nottinghamshire in practice.
WHO CAN BENEFIT Local organisations, particularly those concerned with disabled and older people and children with special needs.
WHAT IS FUNDED General charitable purposes.
WHAT IS NOT FUNDED No grants to individuals.
RANGE OF GRANTS Usually £500–£2,500.
FINANCES *Year* 2000–01 *Income* £442,853 *Grants* £394,061 *Assets* £11,182,590
TRUSTEES G G Raymond, Chair; Mrs D M Cottingham; Mrs V A Hardingham; Mrs C B Mudford; P M Spencer.
OTHER INFORMATION £100,000 to Nottingham City Hospital General Fund, Breast Unit Fund; £22,000 in total to Nottingham Hospice; £10,000 each to Royal Life Saving Society Meden School, Newark & Nottinghamshire Agricultural Society, Fountaindale School Trust and Warsop & District Mentally Handicapped Association; £10,000 in total to Jenny Farr Centre; £9,000 to Yeoman Park School Fund; £6,000 to Leonard Cheshire; £5,000 each to Friends of Bramcote School and Disabilities Living Centre.
HOW TO APPLY In writing to the correspondent.
WHO TO APPLY TO Gordon Raymond, Chair, Burns Lane, Warsop, Mansfield, Nottinghamshire NG20 0QG *Tel* 01623 842581 *Fax* 01623 847955
CC NO 235389   **ESTABLISHED** 1964

■ The Ebenezer Trust

WHERE FUNDING CAN BE GIVEN UK and overseas.
WHO CAN BENEFIT Registered charities.
WHAT IS FUNDED Advancement of Protestant and Evangelical tenets of the Christian faith. Activities in which the trustees are personally interested or involved.
WHAT IS NOT FUNDED No grants to individuals.
TYPE OF GRANT Occasionally interest-free loans.
RANGE OF GRANTS £50–£5,000.
SAMPLE GRANTS In 1998–99: £19,649 to Brentwood Baptist Church; £6,700 to Tearfund; £3,300 to Spurgeons College; £3,290 to Pilgrims Hatch Baptist Church; £3,000 to Banchory-Ternan East

Parish Church; £2,766 to Baptist Missionary Society; £2,200 to Scripture Union; £2,000 each to Brentwood Schools Christian Worker Trust and St Francis Hospice; £1,775 to Operation KGRI.
FINANCES *Year* 2000–01 *Income* £124,465
TRUSTEES Nigel Davey; Ruth Davey.
HOW TO APPLY The trust states that they 'are most unlikely to consider unsolicited requests for grants'.
WHO TO APPLY TO N T Davey, Trustee, 180 Strand, London, Essex WC2R 1BL *Tel* 020 7936 3000 *E-mail* nigel.davey@deloitte.co.uk
CC NO 272574   **ESTABLISHED** 1976

■ The EBM Charitable Trust

WHERE FUNDING CAN BE GIVEN UK.
WHAT IS FUNDED General charitable purposes, especially animal welfare and research, youth development and the relief of poverty.
TYPE OF GRANT Recurring and one-off.
RANGE OF GRANTS £1,000–£200,000.
SAMPLE GRANTS In 2000–01: £200,000 to Salvation Army; £100,000 each to Fairbridge, OK Club and SPARKS; £80,000 to Royal Veterinary School; £50,000 to St John's Ambulance; £40,000 to Youth Sport Trust; £33,000 to Community Links; £32,000 to PDSA; £25,000 to Calvert Trust.
FINANCES *Year* 2001–02 *Income* £1,003,373 *Grants* £1,089,187 *Assets* £29,925,795
TRUSTEES Richard Moore; Michael Macfadyen; Stephen Hogg.
HOW TO APPLY In writing to the correspondent, but the trust states that 'unsolicited applications are not requested' and 'the trustees' funds are fully committed'.
WHO TO APPLY TO Richard Moore, Moore Stephens, St Paul's House, Warwick Lane, London EC4P 4BN *Tel* 020 7334 9191
CC NO 326186   **ESTABLISHED** 1982

■ The Ecological Foundation

WHERE FUNDING CAN BE GIVEN Worldwide.
WHO CAN BENEFIT Environmental projects the trust has established itself or decided to sponsor.
WHAT IS FUNDED Conservation, wildlife sanctuaries, organic food production, environmental issues, renewable energy, and transport and alternative transport.
TYPE OF GRANT Feasibility studies, project and research. Funding can be given for up to two years.
SAMPLE GRANTS £110,000 to Trade Investment and Environment Project; £35,199 to Eden Bequest; £29,587 to World Rainforest Project; £22,617 to Outsider's Guide; £20,500 to Global Commons Institute; £8,000 to Chapter Seven; £5,070 to Rural Futures.
FINANCES *Year* 2001 *Income* £181,327 *Grants* £231,853 *Assets* £62,455
TRUSTEES Marquis of Londonderry; R Hanbury-Tenison; Edward Goldsmith.
HOW TO APPLY Unsolicited applications are not entertained, as the foundation has no unrestricted funds.
WHO TO APPLY TO J Faull, Director, Lower Bosneives, Withiel, Bodmin, Cornwall PL30 5NQ *Tel* 01208 831236 *Fax* 01208 831083 *E-mail* ojfaull@gn.apc.org
CC NO 264947   **ESTABLISHED** 1972

■ Eden Arts Trust

WHERE FUNDING CAN BE GIVEN The Eden district of Cumbria.

WHO CAN BENEFIT Individuals and organisations benefiting: young adults and older people; artists; actors and entertainment professionals; musicians; textile workers and designers; volunteers; and writers and poets.

WHAT IS FUNDED To promote and develop the arts and art projects involving the community, and to encourage new groups.

WHAT IS NOT FUNDED Only projects/groups in Eden district can be funded.

TYPE OF GRANT Local arts and crafts projects, days and events, feasibility studies.

RANGE OF GRANTS £50–£2,000, average grant £250.

SAMPLE GRANTS In 2000–01: £7,385 to Millennium Arts Projects; £2,000 each to Appleby Jazz Society and North Pennine Highlights for a rural touring theatre; £1,000 each to Eden Millennium Festival, North Pennine Storytelling and Penrith Music Festival; £500 to Penrith Music Club.

FINANCES *Year* 2001–02 *Income* £108,393 *Grants* £30,000 *Assets* £58,000

TRUSTEES Nancy Walker; Lady Inglewood.

HOW TO APPLY Telephone the trust for further information.

WHO TO APPLY TO Irene Faith, 2 Sandgate, Penrith, Cumbria CA11 7TP *Tel* 01768 899444 *Fax* 01768 895920 *E-mail* edenarts@aol.com *Website* www.edenarts.co.uk

CC NO 1000476   **ESTABLISHED** 1990

■ Gilbert Edgar Trust

WHERE FUNDING CAN BE GIVEN Predominantly UK, limited overseas.

WHO CAN BENEFIT Registered charities, educational or cultural bodies benefiting children, medical professionals and research workers.

WHAT IS FUNDED Only charities which the trustees find worthwhile will be supported. Grants are given in the following categories: homeless; hospice; medical; overseas; research; social; youth.

WHAT IS NOT FUNDED No grants to individuals or non-registered charities.

RANGE OF GRANTS £250–£1,000.

SAMPLE GRANTS £1,000 each to British Red Cross, Cancer Relief Macmillan Fund, Centrepoint Soho, Mind, Notting Hill Housing Trust, Samaritans, and Shelter; £500 each to Myton Hamlet Hospice, Save the Children, and YMCA.

FINANCES *Year* 1999–2000 *Income* £41,000 *Grants* £38,000 *Assets* £1,000,000

TRUSTEES S C E Gentilli; A E Gentilli; Dr R E B Solomons.

HOW TO APPLY In writing to the correspondent, with a copy of a brochure describing your work.

WHO TO APPLY TO The Trustees, c/o Cave Harper & Co., North Lee House, 66 Northfield End, Henley-on-Thames, Oxfordshire RG9 2BE *Tel* 01491 572565

CC NO 213630   **ESTABLISHED** 1955

■ The Gilbert & Eileen Edgar Foundation

WHERE FUNDING CAN BE GIVEN UK (and a few international appeals).

WHO CAN BENEFIT Smaller organisations.

WHAT IS FUNDED The trust supports: medical and surgical science; people who are young, old or in need; the artistic taste of the public in music, drama, opera, painting, sculpture and the fine arts; education in the fine arts; academic education; religion; and conservation and heritage, recreation and other leisure-time activities.

WHAT IS NOT FUNDED Grants for education in the fine arts are made by way of scholarships awarded by academies and no grants are made directly to individuals in this regard.

RANGE OF GRANTS Usually £250–£5,000.

SAMPLE GRANTS £9,000 to a Royal Academy for scholarships; £5,000 to two Royal Academies, both for scholarships, £3,000 to Royal National Theatre; £2,000 to Holy Cross Church – Ramsbury; £1,500 to Wolverhampton Grammar School; £1,000 each to Disasters Emergency Committee for the Kosovo crisis and English National Ballet; £500 each to Breast Cancer Campaign and Women Caring Trust for Children in Northern Ireland.

FINANCES *Year* 1999 *Income* £92,000 *Grants* £71,000 *Assets* £1,800,000

TRUSTEES A E Gentilli; J G Matthews.

OTHER INFORMATION The total grants given in 1999 were: medical and surgical research – £10,000; care and support – £27,000; fine arts – £6,800; education in the fine arts – £19,000; academic education – £2,500; and religion, recreation, conservation and heritage – £6,500.

HOW TO APPLY In writing to the correspondent. There are no application forms.

WHO TO APPLY TO Penny Tyson, c/o Chantrey Vellacott DFK, Prospect House, 58 Queens Road, Reading RG1 4RP *Tel* 0118 952 4700 *Website* www.cvdfk.com

CC NO 241736   **ESTABLISHED** 1965

■ Edinburgh Children's Holiday Fund

WHERE FUNDING CAN BE GIVEN Edinburgh and the Lothians.

WHO CAN BENEFIT Children.

WHAT IS FUNDED Grants are awarded to charitable and voluntary organisations which are concerned with children's welfare and provide holidays for disadvantaged children.

WHAT IS NOT FUNDED No grants directly to individuals.

TYPE OF GRANT One-off grants funded for up to one year.

RANGE OF GRANTS £250–£7,000.

SAMPLE GRANTS £7,000 to Children 1st; £3,000 to Greendykes Primary School; £2,500 to Stepping Stones; £2,000 to Midlothian Women's Aid; £1,500 to Craigmuir Primary School; £1,000 each to Hopscotch, Fort Primary School and Edinburgh University Children's Holiday Venture.

FINANCES *Year* 2001 *Income* £72,000 *Grants* £77,000 *Assets* £1,500,000

TRUSTEES W G Waterson, Chair; Lady Clerk; Mrs P Balfour.

HOW TO APPLY On a form available from the correspondent. Trustees meet to consider grants in January and May. Applications should be sent in mid-December and mid-April respectively.

WHO TO APPLY TO The Secretaries, Bryce, Wilson & Co., Chartered Accountants, 13a Manor Place, Edinburgh EH3 7DH *Tel* 0131 225 5111 *Fax* 0131 220 0283

SC NO SC010312

Every application represents a cost to you and to the trust

■ City of Edinburgh Charitable Trusts

WHERE FUNDING CAN BE GIVEN Edinburgh.

WHO CAN BENEFIT Individuals and organisations. The same beneficiaries are supported each year; only occasionally will outside organisations be considered.

WHAT IS FUNDED Arts; children and young people; education/training; hospitals/hospices; older people; religious appeals; social welfare; and sports/recreation.

WHAT IS NOT FUNDED The trust does not support: animal welfare; buildings; disability; environment/conservation; heritage; medical/ health, including medical research; overseas projects; or political appeals.

TYPE OF GRANT One-off and recurrent.

RANGE OF GRANTS £10–£100.

FINANCES *Year* 2001–02 *Income* £881,000 *Grants* £406,000 *Assets* £14,750,000

HOW TO APPLY The application procedure varies with each individual trust. Contact the correspondent for further details.

WHO TO APPLY TO Susan Sharkie, Investment and Treasury Department, Edinburgh City Council, 12 St Giles Street, Edinburgh EH1 1PT *Tel* 0131 469 3895 *Fax* 0131 225 6356 *E-mail* susan.sharkie@edinburgh.gov.uk **SC NO** SC006504

■ The Edinburgh Trust, No 2 Account

WHERE FUNDING CAN BE GIVEN UK and worldwide.

WHO CAN BENEFIT Registered charities only.

WHAT IS FUNDED General charitable purposes, but the trust fund and the income may be applied for the promotion and advancement of education and of the efficiency of the armed services.

WHAT IS NOT FUNDED No grants to individuals; only scientific expeditions are considered with the backing of a major society. No grants to non-registered charities.

SAMPLE GRANTS In 1998–99: £2,700 to Edwina Mountbatten Trust; £2,500 each to British Commonwealth Ex-Serviceman's League, King George Fund for Sailors and Royal Marines General Fund, The Award Scheme, London Federation of Clubs for Young People, Outward Bound Trust and PPT for Windsor and Maidenhead; £2,000 to St George's House and International Sacred Literature Trust; £1,750 to King Edward VII Hospital for Officers.

FINANCES *Year* 1999–2000 *Income* £64,000 *Grants* £66,000

TRUSTEES Sir Brian McGrath; C Woodhouse; M Hunt-Davis.

HOW TO APPLY In writing to the correspondent. The trustees meet to consider grants in April each year, and applications must be submitted by January.

WHO TO APPLY TO P Hughes, Secretary, Buckingham Place, London SW1A 1AA *Tel* 020 7930 4832 **CC NO** 227897   **ESTABLISHED** 1959

■ Edinburgh Voluntary Organisations' Trust Funds

WHERE FUNDING CAN BE GIVEN Edinburgh and the Lothians.

WHO CAN BENEFIT Organisations and individuals.

WHAT IS FUNDED The trustees have revised their grant-making policy with effect from April 2001

in recognition of the difficulty that local voluntary organisations face in attaining regular funding for their main activites. During the period 2001 to 2005 the trust is looking to support social welfare causes, especially local initiatives which benefit people in Edinburgh and the Lothians. Applicant organsiations must: be properly constituted and registered charities; be solvent and not have any debts; have an imaginative and 'sound' plan; have a turnover of less than £250,000; and show that they have made progress in the past or formative year, by providing accounts and report and particular examples of activity and tasks undertaken. Priority is given to: local organisations – national organisations must indicate need in Edinburgh and the Lothians and have an independent local committee and accounts so the responsibiltiy is with the local initiative (financial restrictions above will apply only to the local unit); organisations that are not eligible for large sums of statutory or Community Fund funding; organisations providing social service activties that assist people most in need; and organisations involving appropriate participation of volunteers. Examples of activities that will be considered include: support groups for carers, older people, single parents, homeless young people, young people's clubs and work with, and by, people who are disabled. Arts or environmental tasks will only be considered when a social service or therapeutic service is the main aim. Small grants (up to a maximum of £200, annually) are made to recognised social work or voluntary agencies to assist individuals in need.

WHAT IS NOT FUNDED No grants are given to or for: non-registered charities; general appeals; statutory agencies or to replace statutory funding; commercial organisations or purposes; private schools and colleges; distribution by other agencies; or repairs, extensions and alterations for property or for new buildings (grants can be given for essential equipment as part of a project).

RANGE OF GRANTS Organisations: up to £3,000 annually; organisations on behalf of individuals: up to a maximum of £200 annually.

SAMPLE GRANTS £3,000 to Edinburgh Central CAB; £2,000 each to Enlighten – Action on Eplilepsy and Multi Cultural Family Base; £1,000 each to Homelink and Scotland Yard Adventure Play Centre.

FINANCES *Year* 2001–02 *Income* £155,287 *Grants* £104,415 *Assets* £3,436,727

TRUSTEES Penny Richardson; Helen Berry; Graeme Thom; Geoffrey Lord; Monica Langa.

OTHER INFORMATION At present the Edinburgh Voluntary Organisations Council is the administrative structure for the following trusts: Miss A Beveridge's Trust, William Thyne Trust and Edinburgh Voluntary Organisations' Trust. It now administers these together and there is one application form for organisations. The trustees then decide which fund is most appropriate. In addition, the Children in Need and the Ponton House are reserved funds.

HOW TO APPLY On a form available from the correspondent. Applications must be submitted to Edinburgh Voluntary Organisations Trust (EVOT) and not to the individual trusts. (If an applicant wishes to prepare an application by computer, the headings and respective information should be entered in the order and style of the application form.) A copy of the latest annual report and audited accounts must be included otherwise the application will not be considered (if not available a copy of the most

Think carefully about every application. Is it justified?

447

recent unaudited accounts with an explanation). Only one application for a particular project will be considered in a 12-month period, whether successful or not. Deadlines for applications are the end of February, May, August or November. Guidelines and application forms are available in large print and on tape.

WHO TO APPLY TO Janette Scappaticcio, Trust Fund Administrator, 14 Ashley Place, Edinburgh EH6 5PX *Tel* 0131 555 9109 *Fax* 0131 555 9101 *E-mail* janettescappaticco@evoc.org.uk
SC NO SC031561   **ESTABLISHED** 1868

■ The W G Edwards Charitable Foundation

WHERE FUNDING CAN BE GIVEN UK.
WHO CAN BENEFIT Neighbourhood-based community projects benefiting older people.
WHAT IS FUNDED The care of older people.
WHAT IS NOT FUNDED No grants to individuals.
TYPE OF GRANT Capital.
SAMPLE GRANTS Large grants have previously been made to Lillian Faithful Homes, Age Concern in Tower Hamlets and Friends of the Elderly.
FINANCES *Year* 2001–02 *Grants* £201,000
TRUSTEES Mrs Margaret E Offley Edwards; Prof. Wendy D Savage; Mrs G Shepherd Coates.
HOW TO APPLY In writing to the correspondent.
WHO TO APPLY TO Janet Brown, Clerk to the Trustees, Wedge Property Co. Ltd, 123a Station Road, Oxted, Surrey RH8 0QE *Tel* 01883 714412 *Fax* 01883 714433
CC NO 293312   **ESTABLISHED** 1985

■ The William Edwards Educational Charity

WHERE FUNDING CAN BE GIVEN Kenilworth.
WHO CAN BENEFIT Schools and colleges benefiting children, young adults, academics and students under the age of 25.
TYPE OF GRANT One-off and recurrent grants.
SAMPLE GRANTS In 1998–99: £24,500 to Kenilworth School; £13,977 to Clinton Primary School; £11,461 to St John's County Primary School; £9,800 to St Nicholas' Community Primary School; £8,046 to Park Hill Junior School; £7,830 to Prior's Field County Primary School; £6,722 to St Augustine's Roman Catholic School; £6,247 to Kenilworth Nursery School; £5,374 to St Joseph's School; £5,150 to Thorn's Infant School.
FINANCES *Year* 1999–2000 *Income* £207,451 *Grants* £173,000
TRUSTEES K Rawsley; J Halfield; Dr R L J Lovick; P W Martin; Dr G Raper; Cllr Mrs P Edwards; Cllr S C Harrison; Cllr H A Thomas; Cllr L G Windybank; Cllr R R Wooller.
OTHER INFORMATION In 1998–99: grants were broken down as follows: £109,121 to schools, £42,175 for individuals and £21,537 for postgraduate bursaries.
HOW TO APPLY In writing to the correspondent. Trustees meet four times a year.
WHO TO APPLY TO J M P Hathaway, Clerk to the Trustees, Messrs Heath and Blenkinsop, 42 Brook Street, Warwick CV34 4BL *Tel* 01926 492407
CC NO 528714   **ESTABLISHED** 1981

■ Edwards-Skinner Charitable Trust

WHERE FUNDING CAN BE GIVEN UK and overseas.
WHO CAN BENEFIT Christan organisations.
WHAT IS FUNDED The trust works for the promotion of the Christian faith, particularly supporting those charities it already has links with.
TYPE OF GRANT Almost half are recurrent.
RANGE OF GRANTS Mostly £500–£1,000.
SAMPLE GRANTS £1,000 each to Hope Now Ministries, London City Mission, On the Move and Uganda Development Services.
FINANCES *Year* 2000 *Income* £38,000 *Grants* £28,000 *Assets* £1,500,000
TRUSTEES P J Stanford, Chair; W Richards; E D Anstead; Mrs B O'Driscoll; J A Anstead.
HOW TO APPLY In writing to the correspondent.
WHO TO APPLY TO P J Stanford, Trustee, 15 Wilman Road, Tunbridge Wells, Kent TN4 9AJ *Tel* 01892 537301
CC NO 258519   **ESTABLISHED** 1968

■ The Eeman Charitable Trust

WHERE FUNDING CAN BE GIVEN UK and overseas.
WHO CAN BENEFIT National charities and international emergencies.
WHAT IS FUNDED Established national charities and international emergencies, whilst maintaining the interest in theological projects with which the settlor or her advisor had already established connection.
SAMPLE GRANTS In 1998–99: £10,000 each to Y Care International and Central American Hurricane Appeal; £7,000 to Dorothy Kerin Trust; £3,600 to Community of St John the Baptist; £2,000 to Task Brasil Trust; £1,000 each to British Red Cross, RNLI and Salvation Army.
FINANCES *Year* 1999–2000 *Income* £126,000 *Grants* £37,000 *Assets* £333,000
HOW TO APPLY In writing to the correspondent.
WHO TO APPLY TO R Hutchinson, Green Cottage, Ward Green, Old Newton, Stowmarket, Suffolk IP14 4EZ *Tel* 01449 673650
CC NO 261972   **ESTABLISHED** 1969

■ Elanore Ltd

WHERE FUNDING CAN BE GIVEN UK.
WHO CAN BENEFIT Jewish people and educational establishments and people disadvantaged by poverty.
WHAT IS FUNDED Advancement of religion in accordance with the orthodox Jewish faith and the relief of poverty.
FINANCES *Year* 2001–02 *Income* £37,500 *Grants* £23,000
TRUSTEES J Beck; Mrs D Beck.
HOW TO APPLY In writing to the correspondent.
WHO TO APPLY TO J Beck, 25 Highfield Gardens, London NW11 9HD *Tel* 020 8455 7173
CC NO 281047   **ESTABLISHED** 1980

■ The Elephant Trust

WHERE FUNDING CAN BE GIVEN UK.
WHO CAN BENEFIT Individual artists, arts organisations and publications concerned with the visual arts.
WHAT IS FUNDED Visual arts. The priorities are to extend the frontiers of creative endeavour, to promote the unconventional and the imaginative and, within its limited resources, to make it

possible for artists and arts organisations to realise and complete specific projects.

WHAT IS NOT FUNDED No education or other study grants. No travel grants.

TYPE OF GRANT One-off contributions to specific projects.

RANGE OF GRANTS Usually modest. In 2001–02, grants awarded ranged between £1,000 and £5,000.

SAMPLE GRANTS £5,000 to Camden Arts Centre; £2,000 each to Harris Museum & Art Gallery – Preston and Wapping Project; £1,500 each to Cubitt Gallery and Gainsborough House.

FINANCES *Year* 2001–02 *Income* £66,508 *Grants* £23,477 *Assets* £1,550,000

TRUSTEES Dawn Ades; Antony Forwood; Matthew Slotover; Nikos Stangos; Richard Wentworth; Sarah Whitfield, Chair.

OTHER INFORMATION The trustees also administer the George Melhuish Bequest which has similar objectives.

HOW TO APPLY In writing to the correspondent. Guidelines are available. The trustees normally meet four times a year.

WHO TO APPLY TO Ruth Rattenbury, Bankside Lofts, 65 Hopton Street, London SE1 9GZ *Tel* 020 7922 1160 *E-mail* ruth@banksidelofts.freeserve.co.uk

CC NO 269615   **ESTABLISHED** 1975

■ The George Elias Charitable Trust

WHERE FUNDING CAN BE GIVEN Some preference for Manchester.

WHO CAN BENEFIT Mostly Jewish organisations.

WHAT IS FUNDED Mainly Jewish causes, some smaller donations (£100–£750) to more general charitable causes, including educational needs and the fight against poverty.

TYPE OF GRANT Capital.

SAMPLE GRANTS £26,511 to Bet Hatfusot; £10,000 to South Manchester Mikua Trust; £8,725 to Hoba; £8,500 to Yad Eli Ezer; £6,500 to Parkhill Charity Trust; £4,500 to Associaion Chested; £4,000 each to Craven Charities and Ponovez Congregation; £3,500 to CST; £3,250 each to Aish Hatorah and Belz Advertising Agency; £3,200 to Lubavitch – South Manchester.

FINANCES *Year* 2000–01 *Income* £67,435 *Grants* £116,945 *Assets* £312,557

TRUSTEES G H Elias; Mrs D Elias; E C Elias; S E Elias.

HOW TO APPLY In writing to the correspondent. Trustees meet monthly.

WHO TO APPLY TO N G Denton, Charity Accountant, Elitex House, Moss Lane, Hale, Altrincham, Cheshire WA15 8AD *Tel* 0161 928 7171

CC NO 273993   **ESTABLISHED** 1977

■ The Wilfred & Elsie Elkes Charity Fund

WHERE FUNDING CAN BE GIVEN Staffordshire and especially Uttoxeter, although grants to UK charities including this area will be considered.

WHO CAN BENEFIT Organisations benefiting children and elderly people.

WHAT IS FUNDED The trustees have a particular interest in child welfare, the welfare of older people, organisations working with deaf people, and medical charities involved with deafness, Alzheimer's disease, Parkinson's disease and a range of other diseases. Animal welfare;

infrastructure development; charity or voluntary umbrella bodies; accommodation and housing; and community facilities and services, are also considered.

WHAT IS NOT FUNDED Grants are normally made to other organisations rather than to individuals.

TYPE OF GRANT Recurrent grants are given in a number of cases but more normally the grant is a one-off payment. Grants can be made for buildings, capital, core costs, project, research, running costs, salaries and start-up costs. Funding is available for up to and over three years.

SAMPLE GRANTS In 1998–99: £6,000 to Uttoxeter Health Community Centre; £3,000 each to Alton Castle Appeal and Marchington Chawner Almshouses; £2,500 to Cheadle & District Home Link Scheme; £2,000 to Oxfam, WaterAid, Leukaemia Research Fund, Alzheimer's Disease Society, BASIC, and Queen's Hospital MRI Scanner Appeal.

FINANCES *Year* 1999–2000 *Income* £82,000 *Grants* £121,000 *Assets* £3,000,000

TRUSTEES Royal Bank of Scotland plc; F A Barnes.

HOW TO APPLY In writing to the correspondent. Trustees meet at least quarterly.

WHO TO APPLY TO The Senior Trust Officer, Royal Bank of Scotland Private Banking, Trust and Estate Services, Eden, Lakeside, Chester Business Park, Wrexham Road, Chester CH4 9QT *Tel* 01244 625813

CC NO 326573   **ESTABLISHED** 1984

■ The Maud Elkington Charitable Trust

WHERE FUNDING CAN BE GIVEN Northamptonshire and Leicestershire (especially Desborough and Kettering).

WHO CAN BENEFIT Registered charities, particularly local, and local branches of UK charities and local social services.

WHAT IS FUNDED General charitable purposes including local educational establishments, and health and welfare, especially of older people, youth and community.

WHAT IS NOT FUNDED No grants to individuals.

TYPE OF GRANT One-off and recurrent. No loans will be made.

SAMPLE GRANTS In 1998–99: £34,000 to Heart of the National Forest Foundation for a visitor centre; £28,732 to Northants Social Services for general purposes; £24,600 to Desborough Town Cricket Club for a pavilion; £20,000 to Desborough Community Transport for general purposes; £19,560 to Leicester Grammar School for bursaries; £15,000 each to Northampton & District Mind and University of Leicester for a children's asthma centre; £13,000 to British Red Cross – Northants; £12,000 each to Kettering General Hospital for a pulmonary rehabilitation programme and Care & Repair – Northants for general purposes.

FINANCES *Year* 2000–01 *Income* £582,651 *Grants* £554,205

TRUSTEES Roger Bowder, Chair; Allan Veasey; Caroline Macpherson.

HOW TO APPLY In writing to the correspondent. There is no application form or guidelines. The trustees meet every eight or nine weeks.

WHO TO APPLY TO The Clerk to the Trust, c/o Messrs Harvey Ingram Owston, 20 New Walk, Leicester LE1 6TX *Tel* 0116 254 5454 *Fax* 0116 255 4559

CC NO 263929   **ESTABLISHED** 1972

■ Ellador Ltd

WHERE FUNDING CAN BE GIVEN UK.

WHO CAN BENEFIT Jewish people.

WHAT IS FUNDED The trust supports organisations benefiting Jewish people and also Jewish individuals.

FINANCES *Year* 1999–2000 *Income* £35,000 *Grants* £47,000 *Assets* £167,000

TRUSTEES J Schrieber; S Schrieber; Mrs H Schrieber; Mrs R Schrieber.

HOW TO APPLY In writing to the correspondent.

WHO TO APPLY TO J Schrieber, Trustee & Governor, Ellador Ltd, 20 Ashstead Road, London E5 9BH *Tel* 020 7242 3580

CC NO 283202   **ESTABLISHED** 1981

■ The John Ellerman Foundation

WHERE FUNDING CAN BE GIVEN Unrestricted.

WHO CAN BENEFIT UK registered charities only, which operate nationally; local charities should not apply.

WHAT IS FUNDED Community development and social welfare: including children, youth work, substance abuse, housing and homelessness, disadvantaged people and communities; the arts; conservation; medical and disability: including preventive medicine, treatment, relief of suffering, care and support, physical and learning disability, mental illness.

WHAT IS NOT FUNDED Grants are made only to registered charities, and are not made for the following purposes: medical research; for or on behalf of individuals; individual hospices; local branches of national organisations; 'Friends of' groups; education or educational establishments; religious causes; conferences and seminars; sports and leisure facilities; purchase of vehicles; the direct replacement of public funding; deficit funding; domestic animal welfare.

Circulars will not receive a reply. The foundation cannot make donations to the continents of America south of the USA.

TYPE OF GRANT One-off or recurring. Core costs, project, running costs, salaries, and start-up costs. Funding may be given for up to three years.

RANGE OF GRANTS £10,000 minimum.

SAMPLE GRANTS £150,000 to Help the Hospices towards the major grants programme; £100,000 each to British Museum towards restoring the King's Library and Natural History Museum (first of two payments) towards phase two construction costs of the centre; £80,000 to British Heart Foundation towards £10 subsidy on 8,000 resource packs to be distributed to agencies working with older people; £65,000 to Depaul Trust (first of three payments) towards a new unit to promote new initiatives, co-ordinate mergers and acquisitions, and offer consultancy services to charities in difficulty; £57,000 to Scope (first of three payments) towards employing an education programme manager; £50,000 each to English National Opera towards core funding, Mencap (first of two payments) towards development of a national advocacy framework, Refuge (first of two payments) towards development funding to cover internal infrastructure costs and Soil Association (first payment of three) towards employing a business and finance director.

FINANCES *Year* 2001–02 *Income* £3,926,000 *Grants* £4,505,000 *Assets* £105,205,000

TRUSTEES Angela Boschi; Richard Edmunds; John Hemming; Sue MacGregor; David Martin-Jenkins;

Peter Pratt, Chair; Vice-Admiral Anthony Revell; Lady Sarah Riddell; Mrs Beverley Stott.

HOW TO APPLY See the Guidelines above. In the first instance, send a letter of not more than one or two pages of A4 without enclosures. From this, trustees will decide whether they want to invite a formal application. If so an application form and further details will be sent. All letters will receive a reply. 'We are happy to discuss potential applications by telephone; please ask for the appeals manager' (Eileen Terry). The trustees meet regularly throughout the year and there are no deadlines.

WHO TO APPLY TO Eileen Terry, Appeals Manager, Aria House, 23 Craven Street, London WC2N 5NS *Tel* 020 7930 8566 *Fax* 020 7839 3654 *E-mail* enquiries@ellerman.org.uk *Website* www.ellerman.org.uk

CC NO 263207   **ESTABLISHED** 1971

■ The Ellinson Foundation Ltd

WHERE FUNDING CAN BE GIVEN Worldwide.

WHO CAN BENEFIT Jewish organisations, especially boarding schools teaching the Torah. The trust usually supports the same organisations each year.

WHAT IS FUNDED Hospitals, education and homelessness, usually with a Jewish teaching aspect.

WHAT IS NOT FUNDED No grants to individuals.

TYPE OF GRANT Capital and recurring grants.

SAMPLE GRANTS £50,000 to North West London Communal Mikvah; £20,000 each to Friends of United Institution of Arad and Ruzin Sadagora Trust; £17,500 to Friends of Neve Yerusholayim Seminary Trust; £12,000 to Friends of Yeshivas Brisk; £7,000 to British Friends of the Chazon Ish Institutions; £6,000 to Friends of Ohr Elchonon; £5,000 each to Talmud Torah Chavos Da'as and Yeshivat Ateral Israel; £3,000 each to Etz Chaim Yeshiva.

FINANCES *Year* 2000–01 *Income* £295,475 *Grants* £186,161 *Assets* £551,898

TRUSTEES C O Ellinson; Mrs E Ellinson; A Ellinson; A Z Ellinson; U Ellinson.

HOW TO APPLY In writing to the correspondent. However, the trust generally supports the same organisations each year and unsolicited applications are not welcome.

WHO TO APPLY TO Gerry Crichton, Messrs Robson Laidler & Co, Fernwood House, Fernwood Road, Jesmond, Newcastle upon Tyne NE2 1TJ *Tel* 0191 281 8191 *E-mail* ellinsonestates@aol.com

CC NO 252018   **ESTABLISHED** 1967

■ The Ellis Campbell Charitable Foundation

WHERE FUNDING CAN BE GIVEN Hampshire, Perth and Kinross/Tayside.

WHO CAN BENEFIT Organisations benefiting young disadvantaged people. Maintenance and preservation of buildings is also considered.

WHAT IS FUNDED Education of disadvantaged people under 25; preservation/protection/improvement of items of architectural/structural/horticultural/ mechanical heritage; encouragement of community based projects. An annual grant of £20,000 is made to the Scottish Community Foundation who vet Perthshire/Tayside applications and make grants on the foundation's behalf.

WHAT IS NOT FUNDED No grants to individuals. Other than the grants made annually over a period, no grants will be made more regularly than every other year. No funding for annual running costs.

TYPE OF GRANT One-off funding, though grants may be given for over three to five years.

RANGE OF GRANTS £25–£10,000; typical grant £500–£1,000.

SAMPLE GRANTS A grant of £20,000 a year is awarded to the Scottish Community Foundation who vet Perthshire/Tayside applications and make grants on the trust's behalf. £10,000 a year is committed to the Jubilee Sailing Trust until April 2003, and a grant of about £10,000 was made to the Countryside Foundation for Education.

FINANCES *Year* 2001 *Income* £63,000 *Grants* £70,000 *Assets* £1,000,000

TRUSTEES Michael Campbell, Chair; Mrs Linda Campbell; Mrs Doris Campbell; Jamie Campbell; Mrs Alexandra Andrew; Laura Campbell; Trevor Aldridge.

HOW TO APPLY In writing to the correspondent. Trustees meet in March, July and October. Applications should be submitted before the preceding month and they will not necessarily be acknowledged.

WHO TO APPLY TO Michael Campbell, Chair, Shalden Park Steading, Shalden, Alton, Hampshire GU34 4DS *Tel* 01256 381821 *Fax* 01256 381921 *E-mail* ellis.campbell@virgin.net

CC NO 802717   **ESTABLISHED** 1989

■ The Edith M Ellis 1985 Charitable Trust

WHERE FUNDING CAN BE GIVEN UK, Ireland and overseas.

WHO CAN BENEFIT Registered charities benefiting Quakers, at risk groups, and people who are disadvantaged by poverty or socially isolated. Support is also given to victims of disasters, famine and war, and refugees.

WHAT IS FUNDED General charitable purposes including religious and educational projects (but not personal grants for religious or secular education nor grants for church buildings) and projects in international fields especially related to economic, social and humanitarian aid to developing countries. Ecumenical and Quaker interests.

WHAT IS NOT FUNDED No grants to individuals.

FINANCES *Year* 1996–97 *Income* £49,000 *Grants* £30,000

TRUSTEES A P Honigmann; E H Milligan.

OTHER INFORMATION Accounts are on file at the Charity Commission only up to 1996–97.

HOW TO APPLY In writing to the correspondent. Telephone enquiries are not invited.

WHO TO APPLY TO The Clerk, c/o Field Fisher Waterhouse, 35 Vine Street, London EC3N 2AA *Tel* 020 7481 4841

CC NO 292835   **ESTABLISHED** 1985

■ James Ellis Charitable Trust

WHERE FUNDING CAN BE GIVEN UK.

WHO CAN BENEFIT Registered medical research charities and organisations involved with health issues.

WHAT IS FUNDED The trust gives in the areas of medical research and the relief of serious illness.

RANGE OF GRANTS £500–£5,000.

SAMPLE GRANTS £3,000 each to Association for Spina Bifida and Hydrocephalus, British Neurological Research Trust, Fight for Sight and Manningford Trust (Transplant Research); £2,000 each to Arthritis Research Campaign, Foundation for Conductive Education, National Meningitis Trust and Progressive Supranuclear Palsy Association.

FINANCES *Year* 2000–01 *Income* £21,500 *Grants* £23,250 *Assets* £551,000

TRUSTEES S J Ellis; J N Sheard; E Lord.

HOW TO APPLY In writing to the correspondent.

WHO TO APPLY TO S J Ellis, Settlor, Barn Cottage, Botany Lane, Lepton, Huddersfield HD8 0NE *Tel* 01484 602066

CC NO 1055617   **ESTABLISHED** 1996

■ Elman Charitable Trust

WHERE FUNDING CAN BE GIVEN UK and Israel.

WHO CAN BENEFIT Jewish charities and organisations benefiting Jewish people.

WHAT IS FUNDED Most grants are given to schools and hospitals in Israel. Also general Jewish purposes in the UK.

WHAT IS NOT FUNDED Grants are not usually given to individuals.

TYPE OF GRANT Mostly recurrent.

SAMPLE GRANTS £50,000 to Wish Care; £25,000 to Friends of Assaf Harofeh Medical Care; £16,750 to Save a Child's Heart; £12,000 to Emunah National Religious Women's organisation in Israel; £10,000 to Atidenu Fund; £7,500 to Ohel Moshe Synagogue; £7,000 to Shai Society for Rehabilitation and Support of Handicapped Children; £6,000 to Norwood Ltd; £5,000 each to Aleh Charitable Trust, Friends of the Israel Opera and Holocaust Educational Trust.

FINANCES *Year* 2000 *Grants* £300,000

TRUSTEES Charles Elman; Kenneth Elman; Colin Elman.

HOW TO APPLY In writing to the correspondent.

WHO TO APPLY TO Kenneth Elman, Trustee, Laurence Homes Eastern Limited, 14 Ruskin Close, Chilton Hall, Stowmarket, Suffolk IP14 1TY *Tel* 01449 771177

CC NO 261733   **ESTABLISHED** 1970

■ The Elmgrant Trust

WHERE FUNDING CAN BE GIVEN UK, with a preference for Devon and Cornwall.

WHO CAN BENEFIT Individuals and organisations.

WHAT IS FUNDED Encouragement of local life through education, the arts and the social sciences.

WHAT IS NOT FUNDED The following are not supported: large scale UK organisations; postgraduate study, overseas student grants, expeditions and travel and study projects overseas; counselling courses; also renewed requests from the same (successful) applicant within a two-year period.

TYPE OF GRANT Primarily one-off, occasionally recurring (but not within a two-year period); core funding; no loans.

RANGE OF GRANTS £50–£2,000 (very occasionally over this). Typically £500.

SAMPLE GRANTS In 1999–2000: £13,000 to Institute of Community Studies; £4,000 to Park School; £2,800 to Dartington Hall Trust; £2,000 each to Fight Against Addiction Dependency and Special Trustees of Middlesex Hospital for a teenage cancer ward; £1,300 to University of Plymouth.

FINANCES *Year* 2000–01 *Income* £75,389 *Grants* £117,887 *Assets* £2,054,066
TRUSTEES Marian Ash, Chair; Sophie Young; Paul Elmhirst; David Young.
HOW TO APPLY In writing to the correspondent, giving full financial details and, where possible, a letter of support. Initial telephone call if advice is needed. There are no application forms, except for the fellowship scheme. Guidelines are issued. An sae would be very helpful, although this is not obligatory. Currently, meetings are held three times a year in March, June and October. Applications need to be received one clear month prior to meeting.
WHO TO APPLY TO The Secretary, The Elmhirst Centre, Dartington Hall, Totnes, Devon TQ9 6EL *Tel* 01803 863160
CC NO 313398   **ESTABLISHED** 1936

■ The Dorothy Whitney Elmhirst Trust

WHERE FUNDING CAN BE GIVEN Somerset.
WHO CAN BENEFIT Inner city children.
WHAT IS FUNDED Speech and drama and providing multi-activity courses for inner city children.
SAMPLE GRANTS £8,000 to West Somerset Community College; £3,500 to Laban Centre; £2,000 each to Charlton Park School, Hermes Trust and Matthew Trust; £1,000 each to CATCH, Headway, Trinity College and Youth at Risk.
FINANCES *Year* 1999 *Income* £27,000 *Grants* £41,000 *Assets* £17,000
TRUSTEES William Knight Elmhirst; Heather Anne Elmhirst; Andrew Osbourne; Isabelle Kingston.
HOW TO APPLY This trust has stated that it does not respond to unsolicited applications.
WHO TO APPLY TO William K Elmhirst, Trustee, Applegreen, Bossington Lane, Porlock, Somerset TA24 8HD
CC NO 1064069   **ESTABLISHED** 1997

■ The Elmley Foundation

WHERE FUNDING CAN BE GIVEN Herefordshire and Worcestershire.
WHO CAN BENEFIT Individuals and organisations benefiting: actors and entertainment professionals; musicians; writers and poets; and textile workers and designers.
WHAT IS FUNDED Arts activity.
WHAT IS NOT FUNDED No grants for endowments, loans or general appeals.
TYPE OF GRANT Buildings, capital, core costs, feasibility studies, one-off, project, research, recurring costs, running costs, salaries and start-up costs. Funding of up to three years will be considered.
RANGE OF GRANTS £500–£20,000.
FINANCES *Year* 2001–02 *Income* £285,000 *Grants* £170,000 *Assets* £5,000,000
TRUSTEES John de la Cour; Diana Johnson; S Driver White.
OTHER INFORMATION The trustees also control a private charitable trust whose income goes to The Elmley Foundation.
HOW TO APPLY In writing to the correspondent, including a budget and showing other possible or existing sources of funding.
WHO TO APPLY TO J de la Cour, Trustee, West Aish, Morchard Bishop, Crediton, Devon EX17 6RX *Tel* 01363 877433 *Fax* 01363 877433
CC NO 1004043   **ESTABLISHED** 1991

■ Elshore Ltd

WHERE FUNDING CAN BE GIVEN Worldwide.
WHO CAN BENEFIT Jewish organisations.
WHAT IS FUNDED Advancement of religion and relief of poverty.
FINANCES *Year* 2000–01 *Income* £111,900 *Grants* £87,390
TRUSTEES H M Lerner; A Lerner; S Yanofsky.
HOW TO APPLY In writing to the correspondent.
WHO TO APPLY TO H Lerner, Trustee, 10 West Avenue, London NW4 2LY *Tel* 020 8203 1726
CC NO 287469   **ESTABLISHED** 1983

■ The Vernon N Ely Charitable Trust

WHERE FUNDING CAN BE GIVEN Worldwide, with a preference for London borough of Merton.
WHO CAN BENEFIT Organisations.
WHAT IS FUNDED Christian causes, welfare, disability, children, young people and overseas grants.
WHAT IS NOT FUNDED No grants to individuals.
FINANCES *Year* 2000–01 *Income* £93,396 *Grants* £89,999 *Assets* £1,307,493
TRUSTEES J S Moyle; D P Howorth; R S Main.
HOW TO APPLY In writing to the correspondent. Please note that the trust has previously stated that no funds are available.
WHO TO APPLY TO Derek Howorth, Trustee, Grosvenor Gardens House, 35–37 Grosvenor Gardens, London SW1W 0BY *Tel* 020 7828 3156 *Fax* 020 7630 7451
CC NO 230033   **ESTABLISHED** 1962

■ The Emerging Markets Charity for Children

WHERE FUNDING CAN BE GIVEN Worldwide, with a preference for the developing world.
WHO CAN BENEFIT Organisations benefiting people disadvantaged by poverty, deprivation and distress; education institutions.
WHAT IS FUNDED The relief of poverty, deprivation and distress; advancement of education and training in all aspects of knowledge by means of (but not limited to) grants, including the establishment of scholarships and prizes, and other like awards; other general charitable purposes.
FINANCES *Year* 2001 *Income* £310,227 *Grants* £252,976 *Assets* £47,819
TRUSTEES S Field; E Littlefield; H Snell; A McLeod.
HOW TO APPLY In writing to the correspondent.
WHO TO APPLY TO Stephanie Field, Director, 13 Clareville Grove, London SW7 5AU
CC NO 1030666   **ESTABLISHED** 1993

■ The Emerton-Christie Charity

WHERE FUNDING CAN BE GIVEN UK.
WHO CAN BENEFIT Registered charities only.
WHAT IS FUNDED General charitable purposes. Preference is given to assist older and younger people, particularly those who are disabled and disadvantaged.
WHAT IS NOT FUNDED Generally no grants to individuals; religious organisations; restoration or extension of buildings; start-up costs; animal welfare and research; cultural heritage; or environmental projects.
TYPE OF GRANT Donations for capital projects and/or income requirements.
RANGE OF GRANTS £1,000–£15,000.

SAMPLE GRANTS £5,000 each to Eastleach PCC to help fund a youth worker, and Knights of the Round Table Benevolent Fund for general purposes; £4,000 to Royal Academy of Music for general purposes; £3,500 to Royal College of Music for educational bursaries; £2,000 each to Cambridge Arthritis Research, Hope and Homes for Children, Missions to Seafarers, RNLI, and Sue Ryder Home – Ely, all for general purposes.

FINANCES *Year* 2002 *Income* £68,704 *Grants* £74,000 *Assets* £2,111,460

TRUSTEES A F Niekirk; D G Richards; Dr N A Walker.

HOW TO APPLY In writing to the correspondent. A demonstration of need based on budgetary principles is required and applications will not be acknowledged unless accompanied by an sae. Trustees normally meet once a year in the autumn to select charities to benefit.

WHO TO APPLY TO The Trustees, c/o Cartmell Shepherd, Viaduct House, Carlisle CA3 8EZ *Tel* 01228 516666

CC NO 262837   **ESTABLISHED** 1971

·····

■ The Emmandjay Charitable Trust

WHERE FUNDING CAN BE GIVEN UK, with a special interest in West Yorkshire.

WHO CAN BENEFIT Charities and individuals.

WHAT IS FUNDED General charitable purposes, with particular favour given to helping disadvantaged people. Many projects are supported; for example, caring for people who are physically and mentally disabled or terminally ill, work with young people and medical research. Projects which reach a lot of people are favoured.

WHAT IS NOT FUNDED 'The trust does not pay debts, does not make grants to individual students, and does not respond to circulars.' Grants are only given, via social services, to individuals if they live in Bradford.

RANGE OF GRANTS Usually £50–£10,000 (higher grants are exceptional).

SAMPLE GRANTS £50,000 to Marie Curie Cancer Centre for a new hospice in Bradford; £20,000 to West Yorkshire Youth Association; £10,000 each to Abbeyfield Bradford Society for sheltered housing, Cancer Support Centre in Bradford for care, and Research into Ageing for medical research; £5,000 each to Bradford's War on Cancer for its annual appeal, British Heart Foundation, British Red Cross for appeals in Mozambique and Turkey, and Caring for Life – Leeds.

FINANCES *Year* 1999–2000 *Income* £235,000 *Grants* £231,000 *Assets* £2,905,000

TRUSTEES Mrs Sylvia Clegg; John A Clegg; Mrs S L Worthington; Mrs E A Riddell.

HOW TO APPLY In writing to the correspondent.

WHO TO APPLY TO Mrs A E Bancroft, Administrator, PO Box 88, Otley, West Yorkshire LS21 3TE

CC NO 212279   **ESTABLISHED** 1962

·····

■ The Mayor of the London Borough of Enfield Appeal Fund

WHERE FUNDING CAN BE GIVEN The borough of Enfield.

WHO CAN BENEFIT People who are disabled. Some individuals may receive welfare grants, though primarily local organisations are supported.

WHAT IS FUNDED Special needs and welfare organisations.

SAMPLE GRANTS £2,000 each to Chicken Shed Theatre and Enfield Disability Action; £1,250 each to Enfield Arts Support Services and

Enfield Age Concern; £1,000 each to Alzheimer's Society, Oaktree School and Waverly School.

FINANCES *Year* 1999–2000 *Income* £37,000 *Grants* £29,000 *Assets* £559

TRUSTEES London Borough of Enfield Council.

HOW TO APPLY In writing to the correspondent.

WHO TO APPLY TO London Borough of Enfield, PO Box 50, Civic Centre, Silver Street, Enfield, Middlesex EN1 3XA *Tel* 020 8379 4119

CC NO 283320   **ESTABLISHED** 1981

·····

■ The Englass Charitable Trust

WHERE FUNDING CAN BE GIVEN Leicestershire.

WHO CAN BENEFIT Englass Group employees, ex-employees and their dependants.

WHAT IS FUNDED The main objective is the relief of hardship of Englass Group employees, ex-employees and their dependants. The trustees are prepared to make a limited amount of grants for the relief of people in need outside that group, but favour local rather than national charities. Funding is given to charity or voluntary umbrella bodies.

WHAT IS NOT FUNDED No grants to individuals unconnected with the company.

TYPE OF GRANT Usually an annual grant payable by instalments over the year. Buildings, capital, core costs, one-off, project and research will also be considered. Funding may be given for up to one year.

SAMPLE GRANTS £3,000 to Loros; £1,000 to Leicester Business Partnership (or business education for people with learning difficulties); £900 to Folville School.

FINANCES *Year* 2001 *Income* £26,000 *Grants* £20,000 *Assets* £463,000

TRUSTEES T J Lawson; R J Piasecki; S E Case; M Marvel; J W Spencer.

HOW TO APPLY In writing to the correspondent giving details of past residence and current financial circumstances. The trustees meet in June so applications should arrive between March and May.

WHO TO APPLY TO S E Case, Trustee, Rieke Packaging Systems Ltd, Scudamore Road, Leicester LE3 1UG *Tel* 0116 233 1133

CC NO 291786   **ESTABLISHED** 1985

·····

■ The Englefield Charitable Trust

WHERE FUNDING CAN BE GIVEN Worldwide, with a special interest in Berkshire.

WHO CAN BENEFIT Charitable organisations.

WHAT IS FUNDED Particularly charities working in the fields of: infrastructure development; religion; residential facilities and services; arts, culture and recreation; health; conservation; education and training; and various community facilities and services.

WHAT IS NOT FUNDED Individual applications for study or travel are not supported.

TYPE OF GRANT Buildings, capital, interest-free loans, research, running costs, salaries and start-up costs. Funding for one year or less will be considered.

RANGE OF GRANTS £250–£50,000. Average grants £1,000.

FINANCES *Year* 2001–02 *Income* £372,333 *Grants* £323,017 *Assets* £9,836,841

TRUSTEES Sir William Benyon; James Shelley; Lady Elizabeth Benyon; Richard H R Benyon; Mrs Catherine Haig.

OTHER INFORMATION Finances: funds are being withheld in addition to the figure for grants, as match funding for applications for National Lottery and other grants.

HOW TO APPLY In writing to the correspondent stating the purpose for which the money is to be used and accompanied with the latest accounts. All applicants should have charitable status. Applications are considered in March and September. Only applications going before the trustees will be acknowledged.

WHO TO APPLY TO A S Reid, Secretary to the Trustees, Englefield Estate Office, Theale, Reading RG7 5DU *Tel* 0118 930 2504 *Fax* 0118 932 3748 *E-mail* benyon@englefields.co.uk

CC NO 258123   **ESTABLISHED** 1968

....

■ The English Schools' Football Association

WHERE FUNDING CAN BE GIVEN England.

WHO CAN BENEFIT Members of the association, and organisations benefiting children and young adults, sportsmen and women and teachers.

WHAT IS FUNDED Mental, moral and physical development of schoolboys through association football. Assistance to teacher charities. General charitable purposes.

WHAT IS NOT FUNDED Grants are restricted to membership and teacher charities.

FINANCES *Year* 2001 *Income* £977,016 *Grants* £153,500

TRUSTEES D J Lailey, Chair; M R Duffield; G Lee.

PUBLICATIONS Referees' Charts; *Guide to Teaching Soccer in Schools;* International Honours List; handbooks.

OTHER INFORMATION A total of £152,000 was spent on sponsorships and tournament expenses, with £1,500 being given in grants to teachers for training courses.

HOW TO APPLY In writing to the correspondent.

WHO TO APPLY TO Mrs A Miller, 1–2 Eastgate Street, Stafford ST16 2NQ *Tel* 01785 251142 *E-mail* amiller@esfa.demon.co.uk *Website* www.esfa.co.uk

CC NO 306003   **ESTABLISHED** 1904

....

■ The Enkalon Foundation

WHERE FUNDING CAN BE GIVEN Northern Ireland.

WHO CAN BENEFIT Grants made only to organisations for projects inside Northern Ireland.

WHAT IS FUNDED Improving the quality of life in Northern Ireland. Funding is given to cross-community groups, self help, assistance to unemployed people and groups helping people who are disadvantaged.

WHAT IS NOT FUNDED No grants to individuals unless ex-employees. No grants are given outside Northern Ireland or for travel outside Northern Ireland. Normally grants are not made to playgroups or sporting groups outside the Antrim borough area or for medical research.

TYPE OF GRANT Mainly for starter finance, single projects or capital projects.

RANGE OF GRANTS Up to £6,000 maximum.

SAMPLE GRANTS £1,000 each to Dungiven Community Resource Centre, Steeple Community Association, and Youth Initiatives Northern Ireland; £500 each to Council for the Homeless – Northern Ireland and Tools for Solidarity for a Northern Ireland project.

FINANCES *Year* 1999–2000 *Income* £79,000 *Grants* £127,000 *Assets* £1,300,000

TRUSTEES Dr R L Schierbeek, Chair; J A Freeman; D H Templeton.

HOW TO APPLY In writing to the correspondent. Applications should provide the following information: description of the organisation and a copy of the constitution and rules; proposed budget and details of the project; audited accounts (if available) or statement of accounts for the most recent completed financial year and a copy of the latest annual report; details of charitable status; other sources of finance for the organisation at present and for the proposed project; experience and/or qualifications of staff and committee members; a list of officers and committee members; contact address and telephone number. Trustees meet four times a year and applicants will be advised as soon as practical after a meeting has taken place. All applicants, successful or unsuccessful, will be advised of the trustees' decision. Applications will not be acknowledged unless accompanied by a sae.

WHO TO APPLY TO J W Wallace, Secretary, 25 Randalstown Road, Antrim, Northern Ireland BT41 4LJ *Tel* 028 9446 3535 *Fax* 028 9446 5733 *E-mail* enkfoundation@lineone.net

IR NO XN62210   **ESTABLISHED** 1985

....

■ Entindale Ltd

WHERE FUNDING CAN BE GIVEN Unrestricted.

WHO CAN BENEFIT Organisations benefiting orthodox Jews.

WHAT IS FUNDED Orthodox Jewish charitable organisations.

TYPE OF GRANT Capital.

SAMPLE GRANTS £32,000 to Achisomoch Aid Co; £30,000 each to Kahal Chassidim Bobov and Yesodei Hatorah Schools.

FINANCES *Year* 2000–01 *Income* £1,500,000 *Grants* £747,000 *Assets* £7,600,000

TRUSTEES A C Becker; Mrs B A Sethill; Mrs B L Bridgeman; S J Goldberg.

HOW TO APPLY In writing to the correspondent.

WHO TO APPLY TO Mrs B L Bridgeman, Trustee, 14 Mayfield Gardens, London NW4 2QA

CC NO 277052   **ESTABLISHED** 1978

....

■ The Epigoni Trust

WHERE FUNDING CAN BE GIVEN Mainly UK.

WHO CAN BENEFIT Registered UK charities with a national remit benefiting people of all ages, homeless people, those with addictions, physical disabilities, cancer, diabetes, and underprivileged children.

WHAT IS FUNDED Support is given to projects including hostels, hospices, holiday accommodation, respite care, care in the community, health counselling and some environmental issues.

WHAT IS NOT FUNDED No grants to individuals, expeditions, research, scholarships, charities with a local focus, local branches of UK charities or towards running costs.

TYPE OF GRANT Project and one-off. Funding for one year or less.

RANGE OF GRANTS £500–£10,000.

SAMPLE GRANTS £14,000 to Royal Commonwealth Society for the Blind; £10,000 each to New Bridge, St Richard's Hospital Charitable Trust, St Wilfrid's Hospice – Chichester, Council of Milton Abbey School Ltd and Who Cares Trust; £9,700 to Shelter – Work Opportunities Project; £8,000 to Womankind Worldwide; £7,600 to Cabi Trust; £7,500 to Schizophrenia Association of Great Britain; £6,000 to Tree Aid.

FINANCES *Year* 2000 *Income* £164,560
Grants £162,500 *Assets* £3,173,482
TRUSTEES H Peacock; Mrs Bettine Bond; A M Bond.
HOW TO APPLY On an application form available from
the correspondent. Applications should include
a copy of the latest audited annual report and
accounts. They are considered twice a year in
mid-summer and mid-autumn. Organisations
which have received grants from this trust,
Cleopatra Trust or Dorus Trust should not
reapply in the following two years. Usually,
funding will be considered from only one of
these trusts.
WHO TO APPLY TO Mrs Sue David, Donor Grants
Officer, Charities Aid Foundation, King's Hill,
West Malling, Kent ME19 4TA *Tel* 01732
520083 *Fax* 01732 520001
CC NO 328700   **ESTABLISHED** 1990

....

■ Epilepsy Research Foundation

WHERE FUNDING CAN BE GIVEN UK.
WHO CAN BENEFIT Researchers conducting studies
that will benefit people with epilepsy.
WHAT IS FUNDED Grants are available only for basic
and clinical scientific research in the field of
epilepsy.
WHAT IS NOT FUNDED Research not undertaken within
a recognised institute in the UK.
TYPE OF GRANT Projects, fellowship, research and
equipment. Funding is for up to three years.
RANGE OF GRANTS Up to £60,000.
SAMPLE GRANTS £57,252 to an individual at King's
College for research into neuronal discharge
patterns in human symptomatic epilepsy;
£52,000 (over two years) to an individual at the
Institute of Child Health, London for research
into speech and language after
hemispherectomy in childhood; £3,000 to Great
Ormond Street Hospital for equipment to enable
a comparison of wireless protocols with cable-
based techniques for EEG telemetry for
epilepsy.
FINANCES *Year* 2002 *Income* £349,695
Grants £191,870 *Assets* £524,205
TRUSTEES B Akin; Prof. F Besag; Prof. C Binnie;
Prof. S Brown; Mrs J Cochrane; Dr H Cross;
Prof. G Harding; Dr J Mumford; Dr J Oxley; Prof.
A Richens; M Stevens.
PUBLICATIONS Newsletter; synopsis of research
funded to date.
OTHER INFORMATION For research enquiries tel: 020
8400 6108.
HOW TO APPLY Applications for the annual grant
round are invited in October. Full details are
available on www.erf.org.uk
WHO TO APPLY TO Ms Camilla Barrett, Research and
Information Executive, PO Box 3004, London
W4 4XT *Tel* 020 8995 4781 *Fax* 020 8995
4781 *E-mail* info@erf.org.uk
Website www.erf.org.uk
CC NO 326836   **ESTABLISHED** 1985

....

■ The Equitable Charitable Trust

WHERE FUNDING CAN BE GIVEN UK.
WHO CAN BENEFIT Schools and other organisations
benefiting disabled or disadvantaged children.
WHAT IS FUNDED Specific projects for the educational
needs of disabled or disadvantaged young
people. The trustees will also fund interesting
and educational projects of all kinds, especially
if they are capable of being introduced into a
large number of schools to supply needs not
adequately met at present.
WHAT IS NOT FUNDED No grants to individuals.

TYPE OF GRANT Capital and revenue.
RANGE OF GRANTS £2,000–£200,000.
SAMPLE GRANTS £135,000 to Palace for All for
running and expanding this north London special
needs project; £96,000 to Winged Horse Trust
for a basic education project in Brazil; £94,000
to Anna Freud Centre; £90,000 each to St
Christopher's Fellowship for a home tutoring
service in London and Newham Conflict and
Change Project; £75,000 each to Battersea
Fields Saturday School, British Stammering
Association, Changing Faces for supporting in
school children with disfigurements, Life
Education Centres and Orrell Youth Project in
Liverpool.
FINANCES *Year* 2001 *Grants* £2,184,000
TRUSTEES Brian McGeough; Roy Ranson; Peter
Goddard.
HOW TO APPLY In writing to the correspondent. The
charity does not use application forms but
offers the following guidelines to applicants for
grants: Applications should be no longer than
four A4 sides (plus budget and accounts) and
should incorporate a short (half page) summary.
Applications should state clearly who the
applicant is, what it does and whom it seeks to
help; give the applicant's status (e.g. registered
charity); describe the project for which a grant is
sought clearly and succinctly – explain the need
for it, say what practical results it is expected to
produce, state the number of people who will
benefit from it, show how it will be cost
effective, and say what stage the project has so
far reached; enclose a detailed budget for the
project together with a copy of the applicant's
most recent audited accounts (if those accounts
show a significant surplus or deficit of income,
please explain how this has arisen); name the
applicant's trustees/patrons and describe the
people who will actually be in charge of the
project giving details of their qualifications for
the job; describe the applicant's track record
and, where possible, give the names and
addresses of two independent referees to whom
the Equitable Charitable Trust may apply for a
recommendation if it wishes to do so; state
what funds have already been raised for the
project and name any other sources of funding
to whom the applicant has applied; explain
where the ongoing funding (if required) will be
obtained when the charity's grant has been
used; state what plans have been made to
monitor the project and wherever possible to
evaluate it and, where appropriate, to make its
results known to others; ask, where possible,
for a specific amount. Please keep the
application as simple as possible and avoid the
use of technical terms and jargon. The trustees
are in regular contact with each other and deal
with applications as and when received.
WHO TO APPLY TO Brian McGeough, Joint Managing
Trustee, 5 Chancery Lane, Clifford's Inn, London
EC4A 1BU *Tel* 020 7320 6292 *Fax* 020 7320
3842
CC NO 289548   **ESTABLISHED** 1984

....

■ The Equity Trust Fund

WHERE FUNDING CAN BE GIVEN UK.
WHO CAN BENEFIT Individuals and organisations in
the acting or entertainment industry.
WHAT IS FUNDED To help professional performers in
genuine need, with special reference to
members, past and present, of the Union
Equity; to provide bursaries for the retraining of
professional performers with at least 10 years

Think carefully about every application. Is it justified?

....

455

experience to enable them to pursue a new career.

WHAT IS NOT FUNDED No grants to non-professional performers, drama students, non-professional theatre companies, multi arts venues, community projects or projects with no connection to the professional theatre.

TYPE OF GRANT Building projects.

RANGE OF GRANTS £1–£2,000 for welfare; £1–£10,000 for bursaries.

SAMPLE GRANTS £5,000 to a two-year MSc Speech and Language Sciences Course.

FINANCES *Year* 2001–02 *Income* £373,632 *Grants* £354,673 *Assets* £7,888,355

TRUSTEES Hugh Manning; Milton Johns; Jeffry Wickham; Nigel Davenport; Gillian Raine; Peter Plouviez; Derek Bond; Frank Williams; Ian McGarry; John Barron; Colin Baker; Barbara Hyslop; Roy Marsden; Annie Bright; Graham Hamilton; Harry Landis; Frederik Pyne; Rosalind Shanks; Johnny Worthy; Frank Hitchman; James Bolam; Imogen Claire; Peter Finch; John Rubinstein; Ian Talbot; Josephine Tewson.

HOW TO APPLY In the first instance please call the office to ascertain if the application is relevant. Failing that, submit a brief letter outlining the application. A meeting takes place about every six to eight weeks. Ring for precise dates. Applications are required at least two weeks beforehand.

WHO TO APPLY TO Keith Carter, Secretary, 222 Africa House, 64 Kingsway, London WC2B 6AH *Tel* 020 7404 6041 *Fax* 020 7831 4953 *E-mail* keith@equitytrustfund.freeserve.co.uk
CC NO 328103   **ESTABLISHED** 1989

■ The Eranda Foundation

WHERE FUNDING CAN BE GIVEN UK.

WHO CAN BENEFIT Registered charities.

WHAT IS FUNDED The promotion of original research, and the continuation of existing research into medicine and education; fostering of the arts; and promotion of social welfare.

TYPE OF GRANT Capital, project, running costs and recurring costs for up to three years.

FINANCES *Year* 2001–02 *Income* £1,800,000 *Grants* £1,270,000 *Assets* £6,500,000

TRUSTEES Sir Evelyn de Rothschild; Mrs Renée Robeson; Leopold de Rothschild; Miss Jessica de Rothschild; Antony de Rothschild; Sir Graham Hearne.

HOW TO APPLY In writing to the correspondent. Trustees usually meet in March, July and November and applications should be received two months in advance.

WHO TO APPLY TO Rebecca Mellotte, Secretary, New Court, St Swithin's Lane, London EC4P 4DU *Tel* 020 7280 5301
CC NO 255650   **ESTABLISHED** 1967

■ The Ericson Trust

WHERE FUNDING CAN BE GIVEN UK, developing countries, Eastern and Central Europe.

WHO CAN BENEFIT Registered charities only, benefiting: middle-aged and older people; researchers; people disadvantaged by poverty; ex-offenders and those at risk of offending; homeless people; immigrants and refugees.

WHAT IS FUNDED Older people; community projects/local interest groups, including arts; prisons, prison reform, mentoring projects, and research in this area; refugees; mental health; environmental projects and research; aid to developing countries only if supported and

represented or initiated and administered by a UK registered charity.

WHAT IS NOT FUNDED No grants to individuals or to non-registered charities. Applications from the following areas are generally not considered unless closely connected with one of the above: children's and young people's clubs, centres, etc.; schools; charities dealing with illness or disability (except psychiatric); or religious institutions, except in their social projects.

TYPE OF GRANT Project. Requests for core funding, running costs or particular items are considered.

RANGE OF GRANTS Maximum £2,000.

SAMPLE GRANTS £2,000 each to Anti-Slavery International for a bonded labour campaign, Ashram International for a milk chilling plant in Nepal, Development Organisations of Rural Sichuan for projects in China, The Howard League for education and prevention projects, International Service for agro-forestry projects in Bolivia, One World Action for staff training courses, Psychiatric Rehabilitation Association for running costs and Refugee Council for running costs.

FINANCES *Year* 1999–2000 *Income* £35,031 *Grants* £42,000 *Assets* £662,777

TRUSTEES Miss R C Cotton; Mrs V J Barrow; Mrs A M C Cotton.

OTHER INFORMATION The trust is unable to consider new appeals for the foreseeable future.

HOW TO APPLY In writing to the correspondent. The trust stated that it can no support new applications.

WHO TO APPLY TO Ms C Cotton, Trustee, Flat 2, 53 Carleton Road, London N7 0ET *Tel* 020 7607 8333
CC NO 219762   **ESTABLISHED** 1962

■ The Erskine Cunningham Hill Trust

WHERE FUNDING CAN BE GIVEN Scottish registered charities and projects/appeals.

WHO CAN BENEFIT Organisations registered in Scotland benefiting older people, young people, ex-service men and women, seamen, and the Church of Scotland.

WHAT IS FUNDED The Church of Scotland is the largest single focus of the trust's interest (50% of annual income). Other grants are restricted to charitable work with older people; young people; ex-servicemen and women; seamen; Scottish interests; with priority given to charities administered by voluntary or honorary officials.

WHAT IS NOT FUNDED No grants to individuals.

TYPE OF GRANT Recurring grants to the Church of Scotland; one-off grants to individual charities.

RANGE OF GRANTS £1,000 each to individual charities.

SAMPLE GRANTS Beneficiaries have included Boys and Girls Clubs of Scotland and University of Edinburgh.

FINANCES *Year* 2000 *Income* £51,000 *Grants* £50,000 *Assets* £1,138,485

TRUSTEES G W Burnett; H Cole; A C E Hill; R M Maiden; D F Ross; D F Stewart.

HOW TO APPLY In writing to the correspondent at the above address. There is a two-year time bar on repeat grants.

WHO TO APPLY TO Fred Marsh, Secretary, 121 George Street, Edinburgh EH2 4YN *Tel* 0131 225 5722 *Fax* 0131 220 3113 *E-mail* fmarsh@cofscotland.org.uk
SC NO SC001853   **ESTABLISHED** 1955

■ Esher House Charitable Trust

WHERE FUNDING CAN BE GIVEN UK.

WHO CAN BENEFIT Organisations benefiting children, young adults, older people and Jews.

WHAT IS FUNDED Advancement of religion, health, and educational Jewish charitable causes.

WHAT IS NOT FUNDED No grants to individuals.

RANGE OF GRANTS £10–£5,000.

SAMPLE GRANTS £5,000 to Nightingale House for a home for older people; £3,550 to Norwood Ravenswood for general purposes; £1,000 to Kosovo Appeal for refugees.

FINANCES *Year* 1998–99 *Income* £43,271 *Grants* £23,459 *Assets* £313,341

TRUSTEES Michael B Conn; Mrs Hadassa R Conn; Douglas Conn.

HOW TO APPLY In writing to the correspondent.

WHO TO APPLY TO Michael Conn, Trustee, 845 Finchley Road, London NW11 8NA *Tel* 020 8455 1111 *Fax* 020 8455 9191

CC NO 276183   **ESTABLISHED** 1978

■ The Mihran Essefian Charitable Trust (also known as The Mihran & Azmir Essefian Charitable Trust)

WHERE FUNDING CAN BE GIVEN UK and overseas.

WHO CAN BENEFIT Individuals, universities, institutions and organisations benefiting Armenians, especially children, young adults and students.

WHAT IS FUNDED Scholarship grants to university students of Armenian origin and grants to organisations and institutions to promote specific educational, cultural and charitable activities for the benefit of the Armenian community throughout the world.

SAMPLE GRANTS £2,000 each to Hayastan All-Armenian Charitable Fund, Armenian Musical Assembly and St Tarkmanchat's School – Jerusalem; £1,000 to Surp Prigic Hospital – Istanbul.

FINANCES *Year* 2000–01 *Income* £88,900 *Grants* £68,800 *Assets* £1,366,890

TRUSTEES M Kalindjian; E Kurkdjian; H Abadjian; P Gulbenkian.

OTHER INFORMATION The grant total shown is for organisations and individuals. In 2000–01 organisations received £7,000.

HOW TO APPLY In writing to the correspondent, by 30 June each year.

WHO TO APPLY TO Stephen Ovanessoff, Administrator, 15 Elm Crescent, Ealing, London W5 3JW *Tel* 020 8567 1210

CC NO 275074   **ESTABLISHED** 1977

■ Essex Community Foundation

WHERE FUNDING CAN BE GIVEN Essex, Southend and Thurrock.

WHO CAN BENEFIT Any voluntary and community organisations, or any non-profit making organisation working for the benefit of people living in Essex, Southend and Thurrock.

WHAT IS FUNDED General charitable purposes, in particular, the advancement of education, the protection of mental and physical health and the relief of poverty and sickness.

WHAT IS NOT FUNDED No grants for projects outside Essex, political or religious activities, animal welfare, statutory bodies, general appeals or individuals.

TYPE OF GRANT One-off, capital, support costs, project costs, core costs, research, running

costs, salaries and start-up costs will be considered. Funding may be given for up to one year.

RANGE OF GRANTS £50–£10,000.

SAMPLE GRANTS £10,000 each to SWANS, Maldon towards day centre costs, IT training and other courses for people with disabilities, Maldon (Essex) Mind, for costs towards recruiting and training young adult volunteers on BroSis mentoring scheme (the organisation also received a further £3,000 towards running the scheme), Chelmsford Agency for Volunteering to fund the Youth Action Project which encourages and supports volunteering among young people aged 14 to 18, In Focus Essex to develop support work for families of children with special needs, Essex Association of Boy's Clubs towards the costs of extending Project Respect aimed at young people at risk; Uttlesford Community Travel, towards the cost of replacing a community vehicle; £9,000 to Realife Trust; £8,500 to Essex Disabled Peoples Association; £6,000 to Uttlesford Carers; £5,000 each to Furniture Project Thurrock, Kingsway Hall, Bridge Counselling Service and Interact Chelmsford.

FINANCES *Year* 2001–02 *Income* £744,659 *Grants* £383,879 *Assets* £3,799,534

TRUSTEES John Burrow; Charles Clark; Robert Erith; Revd Dr Laurie Green; Ian Marks; Annie Ralph; Caroline Stanger; Wilfrid Tolhurst; Peter Heap; David Price.

HOW TO APPLY Applicants can just apply to the foundation with a general application form. The foundation then finds the most appropriate fund. Application forms are available from the foundation's office. Deadlines are twice a year; please contact the trust for exact dates. Grants are awarded within three months of the deadlines. Trustees usually meet around the end of January, April, July and October.

WHO TO APPLY TO The Administrator, 52A Moulsham Street, Chelmsford, Essex CM2 0JA *Tel* 01245 355947 *Fax* 01245 251151 *E-mail* general@essexcf.freeserve.co.uk *Website* www.essexcommunityfoundation.org.uk

CC NO 1052061   **ESTABLISHED** 1996

■ The Essex Fairway Charitable Trust

WHERE FUNDING CAN BE GIVEN South east England, with a preference for Essex.

WHO CAN BENEFIT Registered charities, particularly those directly benefiting people in need. Small charities in south east England, particularly Essex, will be favoured.

WHAT IS FUNDED General charitable purposes.

WHAT IS NOT FUNDED No grants to large UK charities. Individuals are only considered in exceptional circumstances.

TYPE OF GRANT £250–£10,000.

SAMPLE GRANTS £5,000 to SNAP for core costs; £3,000 to Starlight Children's Foundation to purchase a fun centre for a children's ward in an Essex hospital; £2,000 each to Hamelin Trust for sensory equipment at an Essex residential respite care home, Action for Kids towards mobility equipment for Essex children, Mid-Essex Respite Care Association for core costs and Headway Essex for ongoing support for their brain injury centre; £1,000 each to Lady Hoare Truust to help support children with physical disabilities living in the county of Essex and Chicks to help fund holidays for inner city children; and £500 to Children Today towards equipment and aids to help young people and children overcome disabilities.

FINANCES Year 2001 Income £2,131,482 Grants £53,280 Assets £2,604,005

TRUSTEES P W George; K H Larkman.

HOW TO APPLY In writing to the correspondent with accounts. There are no application forms.

WHO TO APPLY TO K H Larkman, c/o Birkett Long, Essex House, 42 Crouch Street, Colchester, Essex CO3 3HH Tel 01206 217300 Fax 01206 711355 E-mail keithl@birkettlong.co.uk

CC NO 1066858   **ESTABLISHED** 1997

■ The Essex Heritage Trust

WHERE FUNDING CAN BE GIVEN Essex.

WHO CAN BENEFIT Any organisation, body or individual whose project will be to the benefit of the people of Essex.

WHAT IS FUNDED Grants to bodies or individuals undertaking specific work in accord with the objects of the trust, including publication or preservation of Essex history and restoration of monuments, significant structures, artefacts and church decorations and equipment.

WHAT IS NOT FUNDED 'At this stage in the trust's development the trustees are not in a position to make awards towards the repair of the fabric of churches or to what might be construed as the routine maintenance of buildings. The object of the grant must be to benefit the public in Essex. Applications will not be considered retrospective of the work being completed.'

TYPE OF GRANT Usually one-off starter finances for specific heritage. These may include a contribution to capital expenses or buildings.

RANGE OF GRANTS £300–£10,000.

SAMPLE GRANTS £10,000 to Saffron Walden Town Library for refurbishment and improvements; £8,000 to Salvation Army, Hadleigh for heritage/visitor centre equipment; £3,000 each to Gosfield Hall for refurbishments and St Mary's Hatfield Br Oak to create a treasury in the gallery; £2,500 each to Ashdon Windmill Trust for restoration of windmill and Royal Anglian Regiment for a memorial in France to 'Pompadours'; £2,000 each to Church of St James – Saling for Elizabeth Yeldham monument, Myddlyton House for Bridge Street elevation restoration and Southend Council Museum Service for a geophysical survey of Priory Park.

FINANCES Year 2001–02 Income £93,000 Grants £45,000 Assets £1,200,000

TRUSTEES Mrs K M Nolan, Chair; Lord Petre, H M Lord Lieutenant of Essex; Sir Terence Beckett; R J L Watson; Mrs H Rendle; K W S Ashurst; A Peel; R Wollaston; M Pertwee.

HOW TO APPLY In writing to the correspondent by letter in the first instance. An application form will be returned for detailed completion with estimates if it is considered that the project falls within the trust's objectives. Where appropriate, the project is inspected before submission to the trustees who usually meet three times a year in March, July and November. Emergency applications may be considered.

WHO TO APPLY TO Mrs E A Crouch, Administrator, Cressing Temple, Braintree, Essex CM77 8PD Tel 01376 584903 Fax 01376 584864 E-mail EHT@dial.pipex.com Website www.eht.dial.pipex.com

CC NO 802317   **ESTABLISHED** 1989

■ Essex Provincial Charity Fund

WHERE FUNDING CAN BE GIVEN Essex.

WHO CAN BENEFIT Essex Freemasons; their dependants; central masonic charities, and other charites.

WHAT IS FUNDED Preference for charities with a medical bias and, primarily in Essex, that assist the community in general.

WHAT IS NOT FUNDED No grants to individuals, other than those who are dependants of Essex Freemasons.

SAMPLE GRANTS In 1998–99: £5,000 each to Grand Charity, Masonic Trust for Boys and Girls, and New Masonic Samaritan Fund; £4,000 to London Chest Hospital; £3,500 to Broomfield Hospital, St Andrews Centre; £3,000 to Association of Friends – Prince Edward, Duke of Kent Court; £1,000 each to Essex Air Ambulance, St Francis Hospice in Havering, and St Helena Hospice in Colchester; £750 to St Luke's Hospice in Basildon.

FINANCES Year 2000–01 Income £121,459 Grants £93,000

TRUSTEES J P Rundlett; F A D Harris; A E Kemp; C G Williams; A P Bishop.

HOW TO APPLY In writing to the correspondent.

WHO TO APPLY TO K Harvey, 2 Station Court, Station Approach, Wickford, Essex SS11 7AT Tel 01268 571610

CC NO 215349   **ESTABLISHED** 1932

■ The Essex Youth Trust

WHERE FUNDING CAN BE GIVEN Essex.

WHO CAN BENEFIT Beneficiaries include schools, youth clubs and organisations giving advice, help and information.

WHAT IS FUNDED The trust aims to help prevent young people become involved in crime, especially through training and education and particularly in the field of drug abuse.

SAMPLE GRANTS In 1998–99: £37,287 to Royals; £28,875 to EABC; £25,000 to Cirden Sailing Club; £22,931 to Stubbes Adventure; £20,000 to Open Door Thurrock; £16,000 to Barking & Dagenham Volunteer Bureau; £10,000 to Barking & Dagenham Young Persons Project 2000; £5,000 to Basildon Boys' Club.

FINANCES Year 1999–2000 Income £364,000 Grants £302,000 Assets £7,200,000

TRUSTEES Mrs Enid Edwards; Richard Francis Wenley; Thomas Gepp; Julien Courtauld; Michael Dyer; Raymond Knappett; Revd Duncan Green; Mrs G Perry; W D Robson.

HOW TO APPLY On a form available from the correspondent.

WHO TO APPLY TO J P Douglas-Hughes, Clerk, Gepp & Sons, 58 New London Road, Chelmsford, Essex CM2 0PA Tel 01245 493939 Fax 01245 493940

CC NO 225768   **ESTABLISHED** 1963

■ Euro Charity Trust

WHERE FUNDING CAN BE GIVEN Worldwide.

WHO CAN BENEFIT Registered charities.

WHAT IS FUNDED The relief of poverty; to assist the vulnerable; and to assist in the advancement of education in the UK and the rest of the world.

FINANCES Year 2000 Income £3,000,000 Grants £1,405,000

TRUSTEES Abdul Majid Alimahomed; Afzal Majid Alimahomed; Shabir Majid Alimahomed.

HOW TO APPLY In writing to the correspondent.

WHO TO APPLY TO Afzal Majid Alimahomed, Chair, Unit M, Waterloo Road, Yardley, Birmingham B25 8AE *Tel* 0121 706 6181
CC NO 1058460   ESTABLISHED 1996

■ The Euroclydon Trust

WHERE FUNDING CAN BE GIVEN UK and worldwide.
WHO CAN BENEFIT Mostly Christian organisations.
WHAT IS FUNDED General charitable purposes.
RANGE OF GRANTS £300–£21,300.
SAMPLE GRANTS £12,100 to Missionary Aviation Fellowship; £5,800 to Convenanters; £2,600 to Timothy Trust; £2,500 to Ambassadors for Christ (India); £1,800 to London Institute; £1,500 to Langham Trust; £1,200 each to Millgrave Children's Home and Prison Fellowship; £1,100 to Yeldall Christian Centers.
FINANCES *Year* 2000–01 *Income* £52,535 *Assets* £1,000,000
TRUSTEES UKET.
HOW TO APPLY The trust states that applications are not invited.
WHO TO APPLY TO The Stewardship Services, UKET, PO Box 99, Loughton, Essex LG10 3QJ
CC NO 290382   ESTABLISHED 1977

■ The Alan Evans Memorial Trust

WHERE FUNDING CAN BE GIVEN UK.
WHO CAN BENEFIT Registered charities only.
WHAT IS FUNDED The purchase of land and the planting of trees, shrubs and plants. The restoration of cathedrals, churches and other buildings of beauty or historical interest, to which the public can have access.
WHAT IS NOT FUNDED No grants to individuals or for management or running expenses, although favourable consideration is given in respect of the purchase of land and restoration of buildings. Grants are given to registered charities only. Appeals will not be acknowledged.
RANGE OF GRANTS £1,000–£6,000.
SAMPLE GRANTS £6,000 to Northumberland Wildlife Trust; £5,000 to Essex Wildlife Trust; £4,000 each to Gaia Trust and John Muir Birthplace Trust; £3,500 to Lincolnshire Wildlife Trust; £3,000 each to Dorset Wildlife Trust and Yorkshire Wildlife Trust; £2,250 to National Trust; £2,100 to WWF; £2,000 each to Gwent Wildlife Trust, Ironbridge Gorge Museum Trust, Merchant's House Trust and Woodland Trust.
FINANCES *Year* 2000–01 *Income* £105,430 *Grants* £130,050 *Assets* £3,200,406
TRUSTEES Coutts & Co.; D J Halfhead; Mrs D Moss.
HOW TO APPLY There is no formal application form, but appeals should be made in writing to the correspondent, stating why the funds are required, what funds have been promised from other sources (for example, English Heritage) and the amount outstanding. Trustees normally meet four times a year, although in urgent cases decisions can be made between meetings.
WHO TO APPLY TO The Trust Manager, Coutts & Co., Trustee Department, 440 Strand, London WC2R 0QS *Tel* 020 7663 6758
CC NO 326263   ESTABLISHED 1979

■ Sir John Evelyn's Charity

WHERE FUNDING CAN BE GIVEN Ancient parish of St Nicholas Deptford and St Luke Deptford.
WHO CAN BENEFIT Charities benefiting people disadvantaged by poverty.
WHAT IS FUNDED Pensions and grants to organisations working to relieve poverty.
SAMPLE GRANTS £18,000 to Deptford Churches Crypt; £6,500 to Exodus Youth Project (after-school club); £4,000 to Deptford Discovery Team; £3,800 to Exodus Youth Project (summer scheme) and Lewisham Refugee; £2,000 to Deptford Summer Action; £1,900 to Deptford Methodist Mission.
FINANCES *Year* 1999 *Income* £116,000 *Grants* £44,000 *Assets* £3,900,000
TRUSTEES Maureen Vitler; Revd J K Lucas; Revd G Corneck; Jasmin Barnett; Bridget Perry; Janet Miller; Elaine O'Connor; Kate Ingledew.
HOW TO APPLY In writing to the correspondent.
WHO TO APPLY TO The Clerk, 11 Bladindon Drive, Bexley, Kent DA5 3BS *Tel* 020 8303 5260 *Fax* 020 8303 5260
CC NO 225707   ESTABLISHED 1974

■ The Eventhall Family Charitable Trust

WHERE FUNDING CAN BE GIVEN Preference for north west England.
WHO CAN BENEFIT Institutions and individuals.
WHAT IS FUNDED General charitable purposes.
WHAT IS NOT FUNDED No grants to students.
SAMPLE GRANTS In 1998–99: £72,000 to Heathlands Village (UK) for a home for older people; £10,000 to Nave Mitchael Village – Israel for a building project; £3,200 to Guide Dogs for the Blind for general purposes; £2,000 to Red Nose Day for general purposes; £1,650 to Sale Hebrew Congregation for maintenance; £1,500 to FED for relief of need; £250 each to King David's School for equipment and Norwood Ravenswood for an orphanage; £200 each to Childrens Food Fund for general purposes and Imperial Cancer Research Fund for general purposes.
FINANCES *Year* 2000–01 *Income* £293,549 *Grants* £96,970 *Assets* £1,368,369
TRUSTEES Leon Eventhall; Corinne Eventhall; David Eventhall.
HOW TO APPLY In writing to the correspondent, however, please note that the trust stated it only has a very limited amount of funds available. Telephone calls are not accepted by the trust. Trustees meet monthly to consider grants. A pre-addressed envelope is appreciated (stamp not necessary). Unsuccessful applicants will not receive a reply.
WHO TO APPLY TO L H Eventhall, Chair, PO Box 194, Sale M33 5XA
CC NO 803178   ESTABLISHED 1989

■ The Everard Foundation

WHERE FUNDING CAN BE GIVEN Leicestershire.
WHO CAN BENEFIT Local organisations of all sizes. Grants to UK-wide organisations must be to fund something tangibly local.
WHAT IS FUNDED General charitable purposes.
WHAT IS NOT FUNDED No grants to individuals.
TYPE OF GRANT One-off.
SAMPLE GRANTS £7,500 to Countryside Alliance; £5,700 to Age Concern – Leicestershire; £5,000 to Leicester Cathedral Millennium Appeal; £2,400 to Common Purchase UK;

£1,100 to Whizz-Kidz; £1,000 each to Home Start UK, Parish of Upper Weake and South Leicestershire Council for Voluntary Service.

FINANCES *Year* 1999–2000 *Income* £83,000 *Grants* £33,000 *Assets* £1,100,000

TRUSTEES R A S Everard; Mrs S A Richards; N W Smith.

HOW TO APPLY In writing to the correspondent at any time.

WHO TO APPLY TO R A S Everard, Trustee, Castle Acres, Narborough, Leicester LE19 1BY *Tel* 0116 201 4100

CC NO 272248   **ESTABLISHED** 1976

■ The Evergreen Foundation

WHERE FUNDING CAN BE GIVEN UK and North America.

WHAT IS FUNDED General charitable purposes.

SAMPLE GRANTS £13,000 each to St Stephen's Aids Research and Sioux Humane Society; £10,000 each to Action on Addiction and Chelsea Old Church for the Russian Orphanage Appeal; £5,000 each to British Red Cross and Balkan Crisis Appeal; £2,000 to Putney Samaritans; £1,000 to Invalids at Home.

FINANCES *Year* 1998–2000 *Income* £908,000 *Grants* £78,000 *Assets* £929,000

TRUSTEES Ms S K Warner, Chair; N Losse.

OTHER INFORMATION The financial data represents the period between December 1998 – April 2000.

HOW TO APPLY In writing to the correspondent.

WHO TO APPLY TO Ms S K Warner, Chair, 14 Park Place Villas, London W2 1SP *Tel* 020 7724 9285 *E-mail* warner@shonda.demon.co.uk

CC NO 1072519   **ESTABLISHED** 1998

■ The Norman Evershed Trust

WHERE FUNDING CAN BE GIVEN UK and overseas.

WHO CAN BENEFIT Christians and victims of famine.

WHAT IS FUNDED Christian work and famine relief. Primarily causes personally known to the trustees.

TYPE OF GRANT Various.

SAMPLE GRANTS In 1997–98: £2,000 each to London Bible College and Royal Commonwealth Society for the Blind; £1,500 to Gideons International; £1,000 each to Crusaders and Romanian Missionary Society.

FINANCES *Year* 1999–2000 *Income* £22,431 *Grants* £33,312 *Assets* £1,000,000

TRUSTEES Mrs J S Evershed; R J Evershed; Mrs C A Evershed.

HOW TO APPLY In writing to the correspondent. However, the trust states: 'No applications should be made: the funds are all committed'.

WHO TO APPLY TO Mrs C A Evershed, Trustee, 35 Lemsford Road, St Albans, Hertfordshire AL1 3PP *Tel* 01727 852019

CC NO 271318   **ESTABLISHED** 1976

■ Douglas Heath Eves Charitable Trust

WHERE FUNDING CAN BE GIVEN UK and occasionally overseas.

WHO CAN BENEFIT Organisations benefiting: people of all ages; actors and entertainment professionals; musicians; textile workers and designers; writers and poets; students; and people who are disabled.

WHAT IS FUNDED Charities supporting medical and paramedical projects, young people (particularly

educational), older people, the arts and the environment.

WHAT IS NOT FUNDED Grants are given to registered charities only and not to individuals.

TYPE OF GRANT One-off.

RANGE OF GRANTS £75–£250.

FINANCES *Year* 2001 *Income* £28,231 *Grants* £16,000

TRUSTEES D H Eves, Chair; P J Sheahan; Mrs B Way.

HOW TO APPLY In writing to the correspondent. The trustees met four times in 2000, in March, June, August and December.

WHO TO APPLY TO Mrs R Ziebart, 15 Hazel Road, Purley on Thames, Reading, Berkshire RG8 8BB *Tel* 01189 431048 *Fax* 01189 425608

CC NO 248003   **ESTABLISHED** 1964

■ The Eveson Charitable Trust

WHERE FUNDING CAN BE GIVEN Herefordshire, Worcestershire and the county of the West Midlands (covering Birmingham, Coventry, Dudley, Sandwell, Solihull, Walsall and Wolverhampton).

WHO CAN BENEFIT Registered charities benefiting children and older people, and people who are disabled or homeless. Organisations benefiting children in care, fostered and adopted may also be considered.

WHAT IS FUNDED Support for: people who are elderly, homeless, physically or mentally diabled; socially disadvantaged children; medical research; hospitals and hospices; special schools.

WHAT IS NOT FUNDED Grants are not made to individuals, even if such a request is submitted by a charitable institution.

TYPE OF GRANT Capital, recurring, one-off.

RANGE OF GRANTS From a few hundred pounds to £80,000; average grant around £8,000.

SAMPLE GRANTS £69,000 to Islet Research Laboratory – Worcester; £36,000 to Malvern Women's project towards running costs; £30,000 each to Herefordshire MIND, St Michael's Hospice Hereford and Workmatch, Hereford; £28,000 to Herefordshire Action for Conductive Education; £26,000 to Age Concern, Hereford and Worcester; £25,000 each to Acorns Children's Hospice, and Hereford and Worcester Advisory Service for an alcohol-related service; £20,000 to Kemp Hospice in Kidderminster.

FINANCES *Year* 2001–02 *Income* £2,200,000 *Grants* £2,016,000 *Assets* £64,000,000

TRUSTEES Bruce Maughfling, Chair; Rt. Revd John Oliver, Bishop of Hereford; J Martin Davies; David Pearson; Bill Wiggin MP.

HOW TO APPLY The trustees meet quarterly, usually at the end of March and June and the beginning of October and January. Applications can only be considered if they are on the trust's standard, but very simple, 'application for support' form which can be obtained from the administrator at the offices of the trust in Gloucester. The form must be completed and returned (together with a copy of the latest accounts and annual report of the organisation) to the trust's offices at least six weeks before the meeting of trustees at which the application is to be considered, in order to give time for necessary assessment procedures, including many visits to applicants. Before providing support to statutory bodies (such as hospitals and schools for people with learning difficulties), the trustees require written confirmation that no statutory funds are available to meet the need for which funds are being requested. In the case of larger grants to hospitals, the trustees ask the district health authority to confirm that no statutory funding is available. Where applications are submitted that clearly fall outside the grantmaking parameters of the trust, the applicant is advised that the application cannot be considered and reasons are given. All applications that are going to be considered by the trustees are acknowledged in writing. Applicants are advised of the reference number of their application and of the quarterly meeting at which their application is going to be considered. The decisions are advised to applicants in writing soon after these meetings.

WHO TO APPLY TO Alex D Gay, Administrator, 45 Park Road, Gloucester GL1 1LP *Tel* 01452 501352 *Fax* 01452 302195

CC NO 1032204   **ESTABLISHED** 1994

■ The Beryl Evetts & Robert Luff Animal Welfare Trust

WHERE FUNDING CAN BE GIVEN UK.

WHO CAN BENEFIT Animal charities. The trust supports the same beneficiaries each year.

WHAT IS FUNDED Veterinary research and the care and welfare of animals.

TYPE OF GRANT Priority to research projects and bursaries.

SAMPLE GRANTS £100,000 to Blue Cross; £35,000 in two grants to Animal Health Trust; £26,000 to Royal Veterinary College; £10,000 each to ARC Addington and Eden Animal Rescue; £1,000 to National Equine Defence League.

FINANCES *Year* 2000–01 *Income* £79,740 *Grants* £182,100 *Assets* £1,458,395

TRUSTEES Sir R Johnson; Revd M Tomlinson; Mrs J Tomlinson; R P J Price; B Nicholson; Lady Johnson; Ms G Favot.

HOW TO APPLY 'No applications, thank you.' The trust gives grants to the same beneficiaries each year and funds are often allocated two years in advance.

WHO TO APPLY TO The Administrator, 294 Earls Court Road, London SW5 9BB *Tel* 020 8954 2727

CC NO 283944   **ESTABLISHED** 1981

■ The Exilarch's Foundation

WHERE FUNDING CAN BE GIVEN Mainly UK.

WHO CAN BENEFIT Jewish people, at risk groups, and people who are disabled, disadvantaged by poverty or socially isolated.

WHAT IS FUNDED Mainly Jewish organisations; some medical and welfare charities.

FINANCES *Year* 1999 *Income* £494,362

TRUSTEES N E Dangoor; D A Dangoor; E B Dangoor; R D Dangoor; M J Dangoor.

HOW TO APPLY The trust stated that it does not respond to unsolicited applications for grants.

WHO TO APPLY TO His Highness the Exilarch, 4 Carlos Place, Mayfair, London W1K 3AW *Tel* 020 7399 0850 *Fax* 020 7399 0860

CC NO 275919   **ESTABLISHED** 1978

■ The G F Eyre Charitable Trust

WHERE FUNDING CAN BE GIVEN South west England.

WHO CAN BENEFIT Charitable organisations.

WHAT IS FUNDED General charitable purposes.

RANGE OF GRANTS £200–£3,000.

SAMPLE GRANTS £3,000 each to British Heart Foundation, St Mary's Church Thorncombe and Bottom Village Appeals Fund; £2,500 each to

Bottom Village Appeals Fund, Cowal Hospice Trust, Wessex Autistic Society, Lyme Town Mill Trust and Lyme Town Mill Trust; £2,000 each to CLIC and National Library for the Blind.

FINANCES *Year* 1999–2000 *Income* £44,000 *Grants* £44,000 *Assets* £151,000

TRUSTEES Mrs C A Eyre; Mrs E M Frost; C G S Eyre.

HOW TO APPLY In writing to the correspondent.

WHO TO APPLY TO T J Brigden, Wilkins Kennedy Hugill, Hugill House, Swanfield Road, Waltham Cross, Hertfordshire EN8 7JR *Tel* 01992 629144

CC NO 216040   **ESTABLISHED** 1960

■ F C Charitable Trust

WHERE FUNDING CAN BE GIVEN Worldwide, but mainly the UK.

WHO CAN BENEFIT Christian and welfare organisations.

WHAT IS FUNDED The trust gives support in the areas of Christian churches, missionary societies, ministers, missionaries and welfare.

SAMPLE GRANTS Emmanuel Church Wimbledon received £53,000 (given in 12 grants).

FINANCES *Year* 1999–2000 *Income* £64,000 *Grants* £60,000

TRUSTEES J C Vernor Miles; Revd Jonathan James Molyneux Fletcher.

HOW TO APPLY In writing to the correspondent.

WHO TO APPLY TO J C Vernor Miles, Trustee, Vernor Miles & Noble, 5 Raymond Buildings, Grays Inn, London WC1R 5DD *Tel* 020 7242 8688

CC NO 277686   **ESTABLISHED** 1978

■ The F P Limited Charitable Trust

WHERE FUNDING CAN BE GIVEN UK, with a possible preference for Greater Manchester.

WHO CAN BENEFIT Registered charities.

WHAT IS FUNDED The trust supports educational causes, giving most of its funds to regular beneficiaries although a few applicants are supported each year.

FINANCES *Year* 1999–2000 *Income* £26,000 *Grants* £29,000 *Assets* £10,000

TRUSTEES Joshua Pine; Simon Pine.

HOW TO APPLY In writing to the correspondent.

WHO TO APPLY TO Simon Pine, Trustee, Crown Mill, 1 Crown Street, Salford M3 7DH *Tel* 0161 834 0456

CC NO 328737   **ESTABLISHED** 1990

■ The Fairbairn Charitable Trust

WHERE FUNDING CAN BE GIVEN UK and overseas.

WHO CAN BENEFIT Organisations benefiting children, older people and Christians.

WHAT IS FUNDED Mainly Christian mission and education, churches and Christian umbrella bodies.

WHAT IS NOT FUNDED No grants to individuals, or for maintenance or repair of existing buildings or artefacts.

TYPE OF GRANT One-off grants, projects, research, and recurring costs will be considered. Funding may be given for up to three years.

RANGE OF GRANTS £100–£4,000.

SAMPLE GRANTS £4,000 to Sailors', Soldiers' & Airmen's Centres; £3,000 each to Church Army and Wycliffe Hall Development Fund; £2,500 each to Crosslinks, South American Missionary Society and Tearfund; £2,000 each to Christ Church Amsterdam, Church Society, Mission Aviation Fellowship and Scripture Union.

FINANCES *Year* 1999–2000 *Income* £17,000 *Grants* £46,000 *Assets* £367,000

TRUSTEES Revd John A Fairbairn, Chair; Susan P Fairbairn; Avril Saunders.

HOW TO APPLY In writing to the correspondent, enclosing an sae.

WHO TO APPLY TO Revd J A Fairbairn, Trustee, 36 Gunton Church Lane, Lowestoft, Suffolk NR32 4LF *Tel* 01502 580707

CC NO 1059697   **ESTABLISHED** 1996

■ Esmée Fairbairn Foundation

WHERE FUNDING CAN BE GIVEN UK.

WHO CAN BENEFIT Voluntary and charitable organisations working in the areas outlined below.

WHAT IS FUNDED There are four programmes: social development, education, environment, and arts and heritage. Applicants are encouraged to obtain a copy of the foundation's guidelines, either by post or on the website, www.esmeefairbairn.org.uk, where they are updated regularly. New guidelines are published in June 2003.

WHAT IS NOT FUNDED The foundation will not support the following: applications from individuals or which benefit one individual; applications from organisations which have applied within the previous 12 months; work which has already taken place; work which does not directly benefit people in the UK; work which directly replaces statutory funding; medical research; standard health services and day/residential care; animal welfare; expeditions and overseas travel; endowment funds; general appeals or circulars. The foundation will not fund routine work in the areas, or from the organisations, listed below. The only exception is that it may make occasional grants in these areas, if the work is developmental or preventive, and fulfils specific funding priorities in one or more of the sectors. If your work comes under one of these categories, telephone the foundation first to talk through whether making an application will be worthwhile: Large national charities which enjoy wide support; branches, members and affiliates of large national charities; after-school clubs; capital projects – building or major refurbishment costs; citizens' advocacy; community-based transport schemes; conferences and seminars; counselling services; furniture recycling projects; holidays/respite care; hospices; individual schools, nurseries and playgroups; information and advice service; items of equipment; maintenance of individual religious buildings (including parish churches) or projects that promote religious beliefs; rent guarantee schemes; sport; vocational training; work in prisons (unless the project is unique, or develops a new model capable of replication, or brings people without previous experience of prison into contact with an aspect of the prison system) ; and youth clubs.

TYPE OF GRANT Primarily core and project grants. Funding can be given for up to or over three years.

RANGE OF GRANTS £500 to in excess of £1 million; average grant £33,728.

SAMPLE GRANTS £520,000 to Peers Early Education Partnership for continued funding of early years work in Oxford; £433,000 to The Wordsworth Trust over three years to implement its development plan and launch its fundraising strategy; £350,000 to Farming and Wildlife Advisory group over three years to set up and run a farm conservation advice service in Wales; £289,000 to Plantlife for a campaign to reverse the decline of wild plants; £223,000 to Bio-Regional Development Group over three years for salaries; £197,000 to Marine Stewardship Council to promote certified seafood produce in the UK and Europe; £195,000 to Aldeburgh

Productions for the core costs of the Britten-Pears Orchestra; £180,000 to Foundation for International Environmental Law and Development; £175,000 to Welsh National Opera for the touring programme; £166,000 to Forest Stewardship Council for core costs.

FINANCES *Year* 2001 *Income* £32,326,000 *Grants* £24,894,000 *Assets* £639,251,000

TRUSTEES John S Fairbairn, Chair; Jeremy Hardie, Treasurer; Sir Antony Acland; Ashley G Down; Felicity Fairbairn; Rod Kent; Kate Lampard; Martin Lane-Fox; Baroness Linklater; Lord Rees-Mogg; William Sieghart.

PUBLICATIONS Policy guidelines.

HOW TO APPLY You can apply at any time as we do not set deadlines for applications. We have regular trustees' meetings and you do not need to time your application to coincide with any of these. We aim to make decisions on grants within the following target times: grants up to £20,000 – within two months of receipt; grants over £100,000 – within five months of receipt. We do our utmost to meet these target times and in order to assess your application within these times it is important that you send us all the information we request. Complex proposals may take longer and if this applies to you we will let you know. In order to apply for funding you must read our guidelines. You can read them online. If you decide to apply, you will need a hard copy of the guidelines in order to complete the application form which is at the back. You can order the guidelines by post or download them from the website. The sectors do not have separate guidelines. The guidelines tell you what information we need. If you do not send us all the information we need the decision on your application could be delayed.

WHO TO APPLY TO Margaret Hyde, Director, 11 Park Place, London SW1A 1LP *Tel* 020 7297 4700 *Fax* 020 7297 4701 *E-mail* info@esmeefairbairn.org.uk *Website* www.esmeefairbairn.org.uk

CC NO 200051   **ESTABLISHED** 1961

....

■ The Fairway Trust

WHERE FUNDING CAN BE GIVEN Worldwide, with a slight preference for north west England.

WHO CAN BENEFIT Charities, universities, colleges and schools.

WHAT IS FUNDED Support of charities, universities, colleges, and schools in UK and abroad; scholarships, grants and loans to postgraduates and undergraduates; grants to help religious purposes; support of clubs and recreational facilities for children and young people; preservation and maintenance of buildings of particular interest; and social welfare.

RANGE OF GRANTS £1,000–£10,000.

SAMPLE GRANTS In 1998–99: £10,000 each to British and International Sailors Society, Family Education Trust, and Riverside Housing Association; £2,500 to Boys and Girls Clubs of Northern Ireland; £2,400 to Kingston Arts Council; £2,000 each to Ex-Service Mental Welfare Society, Newham College – Cambridge, St John the Baptist Romanian Account, and Textile Conservation Centre; £1,600 to Welsh National Opera.

FINANCES *Year* 2001–02 *Income* £35,914

TRUSTEES Mrs Janet Grimstone; Mrs K V M Suenson-Taylor.

HOW TO APPLY In writing to the correspondent.

WHO TO APPLY TO Mrs J Grimstone, Trustee, The Gate House, Coombe Wood Road, Kingston-upon-Thames, Surrey KT2 7JY

CC NO 272227   **ESTABLISHED** 1976

....

■ The Family Foundations Trust

(also known as Mintz Family Foundation)

WHERE FUNDING CAN BE GIVEN UK.

WHO CAN BENEFIT Organisations benefiting Jewish people.

WHAT IS FUNDED Jewish causes; general charitable purposes.

TYPE OF GRANT Mainly one-off.

RANGE OF GRANTS £30–£10,300.

SAMPLE GRANTS £50,000 to JFS General Charitable Trust; £20,700 to Jewish Care; £20,100 to United Jewish Israel Appeal; £6,800 to Children of the East; £5,850 to Norwood Ltd; £5,750 to to Roundhouse Trust; £5,500 each to Bar Ilan University and National Autistic Society; £5,000 each to Community Development Trust, Friends of Hebrew, University of Jerusalem and Wellbeing.

FINANCES *Year* 2000–01 *Income* £141,028 *Grants* £162,997 *Assets* £592,837

TRUSTEES R B Mintz; P G Mintz.

HOW TO APPLY In writing to the correspondent.

WHO TO APPLY TO Simon Hosier, Accountant to the Trustees, Gerald Edelman, 25 Harley Street, London W1G 9BR *Tel* 020 7299 1400

CC NO 264014   **ESTABLISHED** 1972

....

■ The Family Rich Charities Trust

WHERE FUNDING CAN BE GIVEN UK and overseas, with a preference for Asia and Israel.

WHO CAN BENEFIT Medical and welfare organisations.

WHAT IS FUNDED Beneficiaries include hospitals; organisations specialising in disease research such as epilepsy, leukaemia, cancer, Parkinson's disease and diabetes; care of disabled people; and disaster relief.

RANGE OF GRANTS £50–£3000; generally £100.

SAMPLE GRANTS In 1998–99: £1,000 to Imperial College School of Medicine.

FINANCES *Year* 2000–01 *Income* £56,228 *Grants* £18,000

TRUSTEES Barbara Anderman; Margaret Fruchter; Tessa Goldstein; Jean Kitty Rich.

HOW TO APPLY In writing to the correspondent.

WHO TO APPLY TO Sidney Rich, Hon. Treasurer, Taylor House, 39 High Street, Marlow, Bucks SL7 1AF *Tel* 01628 890224 *Fax* 01628 478920

CC NO 264192   **ESTABLISHED** 1972

....

■ Famos Foundation Trust

WHERE FUNDING CAN BE GIVEN UK and overseas.

WHO CAN BENEFIT Small local projects and established organisations benefiting children, young adults, clergy and Jewish people.

WHAT IS FUNDED Education, religion, international organisations, and general charitable purposes. The trust will consider funding: the advancement of the Jewish religion; synagogues; Jewish umbrella bodies; church schools; cultural and religious teaching and religious studies.

WHAT IS NOT FUNDED No grants to individuals.

TYPE OF GRANT One-off, core costs and running costs. Funding is given for one year or less.

RANGE OF GRANTS Up to £5,000.

FINANCES *Year* 1998–99 *Income* £69,000 *Grants* £66,000 *Assets* £738,000

Think carefully about every application. Is it justified?

463

TRUSTEES Rabbi S M Kupetz; Mrs F Kupetz.

HOW TO APPLY In writing to the correspondent, at any time. The trust does not accept telephone enquiries.

WHO TO APPLY TO Rabbi S M Kupetz, Trustee, 4 Hanover Gardens, Salford, Lancashire M7 4FQ

CC NO 271211   ESTABLISHED 1976

■ The Lord Faringdon Charitable Trust

WHERE FUNDING CAN BE GIVEN UK.

WHAT IS FUNDED Educational grants and scholarships; hospitals and the provision of medical treatment for people who are ill; purchase of antiques and artistic objects for museums and ollections which have public access; care and assistance of people who are elderly or infirm; community and economic development and housing; development and assistance of arts and sciences, physical recreation and drama; research into matters of public interest; relief of poverty; support of matters of public interest; animal care and conservation; maintaining and improving the Faringdon Collection.

TYPE OF GRANT Core, capital and project support considered.

SAMPLE GRANTS £15,000 to Oxfordshire Youth Music Trust; £10,000 each to St Ethelburga's Appeal and the Prayer Book Society; £7,000 to MS Society; £6,300 to Royal Opera House; £6,250 to Brighton Dome Appeal; £5,000 each to Countryside Foundation, Jubilee Sailing Trust, Oxfordshire Community Trust, Prior's Court and St John's Ambulance.

FINANCES Year 2000–01 Income £153,755 Grants £155,720 Assets £6,085,618

TRUSTEES H S S Trotter; A D A W Forbes; Hon. J H Henderson; R P Trotter.

HOW TO APPLY In writing to the correspondent.

WHO TO APPLY TO J R Waters, Secretary to the Trustees, The Estate Office, Buscot Park, Oxfordshire SN7 8BU Tel 01367 240786 Fax 01367 241794

CC NO 1084690

■ Samuel William Farmer's Trust

WHERE FUNDING CAN BE GIVEN Mainly Wiltshire.

WHO CAN BENEFIT Registered charities benefiting children and older people.

WHAT IS FUNDED Charities working in the fields of residential facilities and services, infrastructure development, churches, hospices, healthcare, medical studies and research, conservation, environmental and animal sciences, education and various community facilities and services.

WHAT IS NOT FUNDED No grants to students, or for schools and colleges, endowments, inner city welfare or housing.

TYPE OF GRANT One-off and recurrent. Buildings, project, research, running costs, salaries and start-up costs. Funding is available for up to three years.

RANGE OF GRANTS £100–£10,000.

SAMPLE GRANTS £10,000 each to ILC and Wiltshire Community Foundation; £8,000 to Ramsbury School; £5,200 to St Francis School; £3,000 each to Royal Agricultural Benevolent Institution, RUKBA and Wiltshire Air Ambulance; £2,500 each to Devizes Museum and Merchants House Trust; £2,000 to Old Dauntseians Association.

FINANCES Year 1999 Income £75,000 Grants £56,000 Assets £2,100,000

TRUSTEES D Gauntlett; W J Rendell; P G Fox-Andrews; V H Rendell; D Brockis.

HOW TO APPLY In writing to the correspondent. Trustees meet in April and October.

WHO TO APPLY TO Mrs J Simpson, Tanglewood, 33 The Fairway, Devizes, Wiltshire SN10 5DX

CC NO 258459   ESTABLISHED 1929

■ The Farmers Company Charitable Fund

WHERE FUNDING CAN BE GIVEN UK.

WHO CAN BENEFIT Individuals and organisations benefiting students, and members of the Farmers' Company who are disadvantaged by poverty or distress, socially isolated or at risk.

WHAT IS FUNDED Promotion of agriculture research and education, including scholarships; providing relief to members of the Farmers' Company in hardship or distress; providing funds for UK students travelling abroad to study agriculture; environmental issues.

RANGE OF GRANTS Normally £100–£2,000.

SAMPLE GRANTS £42,200 to Wye College for the agricultural management course; £4,994 to Seale Hayne College for the agricultural management course; £2,000 to Royal Agricultural Benevolent Institution to assist farmers in need; £1,000 to Lord Mayor's Appeal for various city charities.

FINANCES Year 1999 Income £97,642 Grants £77,745 Assets £1,114,317

TRUSTEES The Court of Assistants of the Worshipful Company of Farmers.

HOW TO APPLY In writing to the correspondent.

WHO TO APPLY TO The Clerk, Worshipful Company of Farmers, Chislehurst Business Centre, 1 Bromley Lane, Chislehurst, Kent BR7 6LH Tel 020 8467 2255 Fax 020 8467 2666

CC NO 258712   ESTABLISHED 1969

■ The Thomas Farr Charitable Trust

WHERE FUNDING CAN BE GIVEN UK, especially Nottinghamshire.

WHO CAN BENEFIT Registered charities only.

WHAT IS FUNDED General charitable purposes.

WHAT IS NOT FUNDED No grants to individuals.

RANGE OF GRANTS £250–£25,000; mostly under £5,000.

SAMPLE GRANTS £25,000 to Nottingham High School for Girls; £10,000 to Macmillan Cancer Relief – Nottinghamshire; £8,000 to Edwards Lane Community Centre – Nottingham; £5,000 each to Bramcote Hills Comprehensive School, National Trust – Greet Workhouse, Sargent Cancer Care for Children – Nottingham and Sports Aid East Midlands – Loughborough; £4,500 to National Association of Child Contact Centres Nottingham; £3,000 each to Friends of Moorfields Eye Hospital, Nottingham Community Transport and REACT – Richmond.

FINANCES Year 2000–01 Income £208,583 Grants £163,788 Assets £5,514,931

TRUSTEES H J P Farr; Mrs E M Astley-Arlington; Mrs P K Myles; Mrs A M Chisholm; Rathbones Trust Co.

HOW TO APPLY In writing to the correspondent. Applications are considered in March and September.

Does the trust you have chosen match your needs? Haphazard applications waste postage and time

WHO TO APPLY TO Kevin Custis, Administrator, Rathbones Trust Co., 159 New Bond Street, London W1S 2UD *Tel* 020 7399 0807 *Fax* 020 7399 0013
CC NO 328394   **ESTABLISHED** 1989

■ Farthing Trust

WHERE FUNDING CAN BE GIVEN UK and overseas.
WHO CAN BENEFIT Individuals and charitable organisations which are personally known to the trustees.
WHAT IS FUNDED General charitable purposes.
TYPE OF GRANT One-off and recurring grants.
RANGE OF GRANTS £905–£27,750.
SAMPLE GRANTS £37,880 to UK churches; £22,230 to overseas Christian missions; £18,937 to overseas Christian causes; £15,850 to UK Christian causes; £12,500 to UK education; £7,545 to overseas education; £7,234 to local causes; £3,000 to overseas general charities.
FINANCES *Year* 2000–01 *Income* £343,694 *Grants* £191,494 *Assets* £2,080,684
TRUSTEES C H Martin; Mrs E Martin; Miss J Martin; Mrs A White.
HOW TO APPLY Applications and enquiries should be made in writing to the correspondent. Applicants, and any other requests for information, will only receive a response if an sae is enclosed. There would seem little point in applying unless a personal contact with a trustee is established.
WHO TO APPLY TO The Trustees, 48 Ten Mile Bank, Littleport, Ely, Cambridgeshire CB6 1EF
CC NO 268066   **ESTABLISHED** 1974

■ Walter Farthing (Trust) Limited

WHERE FUNDING CAN BE GIVEN Essex.
WHO CAN BENEFIT Organisations enlarging the range (including innovative projects) and/or volume of charitable services provided in the locality.
WHAT IS FUNDED Initiation or assistance of the development of projects by undertaking or grant aiding the acquisition, erection or adaptation of buildings and the provision of initial equipment.
WHAT IS NOT FUNDED The council does not ordinarily support headquarters organisations of national charities, services which public authorities are empowered to provide, individuals or current expenditure of any nature or description.
RANGE OF GRANTS £250–£20,000.
SAMPLE GRANTS In 1997–98: £50,000 to Farleigh Hospice; £5,000 to Family in Trust; £4,000 to Christchurch in Chelmsford; £3,500 to Braintree Womens' Aid; £3,000 to Mid-Essex Hospice; £1,000 to Essex Scouts; £500 to Essex Wildlife Trust.
FINANCES *Year* 2000–01 *Income* £36,954
TRUSTEES R A Knappett, Chair; R Fleming; Mrs B J Goldsmith; Mrs M E Hanley; J B Sharpe; P H Stunt; Revd Millington; G Chivas; D V Collins.
HOW TO APPLY In writing to the correspondent. Please note that the trust states that it receives many applications which fall outside its area of interest which cannot be considered.
WHO TO APPLY TO R A Knappett, Chair, Coval Hall, Chelmsford, Essex CM1 2QF *Tel* 01245 266744
CC NO 220114   **ESTABLISHED** 1957

■ The Fassnidge Memorial Trust

WHERE FUNDING CAN BE GIVEN London borough of Hillingdon, especially the former urban district of Uxbridge.
WHO CAN BENEFIT Individuals and organisations benefiting children, older people, parents and children, carers, people with disabilities, people disadvantaged by poverty, and victims of domestic violence.
WHAT IS FUNDED Welfare of older people and families, particularly charities working in the fields of care in the community, day centres and meals provision.
WHAT IS NOT FUNDED Applications from people or organisations outside the London borough of Hillingdon are not considered.
TYPE OF GRANT Small one-off grants and start-up costs. Funding of one year or less will be considered.
RANGE OF GRANTS £100–£3,000.
SAMPLE GRANTS In 1999–2000: £7,500 to Uxbridge Old Peoples' Welfare Association for a day centre for older people; £2,000 towards Christmas hampers for older people in Hillingdon; £1,855 to Hillingdon Open Door Project for kitchen equipment; £1,500 to Bell Farm Church Dining Centre for kitchen equipment; £1,000 to Northwood Youth Project for legal advice and start-up costs; £905 to Northwood Live at Home Scheme for office equipment.
FINANCES *Year* 2001–02 *Income* £50,200 *Grants* £37,300 *Assets* £824,300
TRUSTEES John Bebbington; David Horne; Andrew Retter; David Williams; Alfred Langley.
HOW TO APPLY In writing to the correspondent.
WHO TO APPLY TO Frazine Johnson, Clerk and Legal Adviser, 7 Park Place, Newdigate Road, Hareford, Middlesex UB9 6EJ *Tel* 01895 821818 *Fax* 01895 821819 *E-mail* frazinejohnson@lawyer.com
CC NO 303078   **ESTABLISHED** 1963

■ Fast Track Trust Limited

WHERE FUNDING CAN BE GIVEN Bristol.
WHO CAN BENEFIT Individuals and community groups in particular areas of Bristol.
WHAT IS FUNDED The trust exists to 'enable people to make informed choices, overcome barriers, fulfil their potential and to participate more fully in the wider economy'. It awards small grants to eligible individuals (and to a lesser extent community organisations working with individuals) for vocational training costs and expenses such as college fees, books and childcare.
SAMPLE GRANTS £7,000 each to Easton Community Nursery and Silai Project Creche; £3,400 to Dhek Bhal; £2,200 to St Paul's Asian Women's Group; £1,600 to St Werburgh's Asian Women's Group.
FINANCES *Year* 1999–2000 *Income* £159,000 *Grants* £71,000 *Assets* £66,000
TRUSTEES R Maggs; Z Haq; D Austin; F Scott; I Moon.
HOW TO APPLY In writing to the correspondent, but first contact the correspondent to find out whether you live/your organisation is based in an eligible area.
WHO TO APPLY TO Roscoe Jones, Trust Manager, Brunswick Court, Brunswick Square, St Paul's, Bristol BS2 8QU *Tel* 0117 942 8211 *E-mail* info@fasttracktrust.org *Website* www.fasttracktrust.org
CC NO 1009688   **ESTABLISHED** 1988

■ Joseph Fattorini Charitable Trust 'B' Account

WHERE FUNDING CAN BE GIVEN UK, including Guernsey.

WHO CAN BENEFIT Roman Catholic, older and younger people.

WHAT IS FUNDED General charitable purposes.

SAMPLE GRANTS £6,600 Stonyhurst College (half the fee of a scholarship for a pupil); £2,000 each to CHAS and Crisis – London; £1,700 each to St Gemma's Hospice – Leeds and St Joseph's Hospice – London; £1,500 to Jesuit Music; £1,100 to Sue Ryder Foundation – Suffolk; £1,000 each to St John's Raise the Roof Appeal and YDMT; 3500 each to Roses Charitable Trust, Marie Curie Memorial Fund and Loros.

FINANCES *Year* 1998–99 *Income* £29,000 *Grants* £27,000

TRUSTEES Joseph Fattorini; Peter Fattorini.

HOW TO APPLY In writing to the correspondent.

WHO TO APPLY TO Peter Fattorini, Trustee, White Abbey, Linton, Skipton, North Yorkshire BD23 5HQ

CC NO 200032   **ESTABLISHED** 1960

■ The Fawcett Charitable Trust

WHERE FUNDING CAN BE GIVEN UK, but preference given to Hampshire and West Sussex.

WHO CAN BENEFIT Work aimed at increasing the quality of life of people with disabilities by facilitating and providing recreation opportunities.

WHAT IS FUNDED The trust is presently commited to RYA Sailability. This is exclsuive and will continue for the foreseeable future.

WHAT IS NOT FUNDED Large national charities are excluded as a rule.

SAMPLE GRANTS £150,000 to RYA Sailability; £10,000 St Richard's MRI Appeal.

FINANCES *Year* 2000–01 *Income* £92,669 *Grants* £160,000 *Assets* £1,897,598

TRUSTEES D J Fawcett; Mrs F P Fawcett; D W Russell.

HOW TO APPLY Until further notice the trust is closed to new applications for the reasons given above.

WHO TO APPLY TO Sandra Evans, Blake Lapthorn, Harbour Court, Compass Road, North Harbour, Portsmouth, Hampshire PO6 4ST *Tel* 023 9222 1122

CC NO 1013167   **ESTABLISHED** 1990

■ The Guy Fawkes Charitable Trust

WHERE FUNDING CAN BE GIVEN UK.

WHO CAN BENEFIT Charities known to the trustees.

WHAT IS FUNDED General charitable purposes.

RANGE OF GRANTS £50–£30,000.

SAMPLE GRANTS 1997–98: £13,000 to Christian International Peace Service; £7,000 to Women's Career Foundation; £5,000 to Council for Music in Hospitals; £2,000 each to Finton House Educational Trust and HAPA Ltd; £1,000 each to Iris Fund for the Prevention of Blindness, National Eye Research Centre, and Royal Hospital for Neuro-disability.

FINANCES *Year* 2000–01 *Income* £28,188

TRUSTEES Miss Y V Calvocoressi; R St George Calvocoressi.

HOW TO APPLY In writing to the correspondent.

WHO TO APPLY TO Miss Y Calvocoressi, Trustee, 26 Quarrenden Street, Fulham, London SW6 3SU

CC NO 258045   **ESTABLISHED** 1969

■ Federation of Jewish Relief Organisations

WHERE FUNDING CAN BE GIVEN Mainly Israel.

WHO CAN BENEFIT Jewish people, particularly those disadvantaged by poverty, socially isolated or in at risk groups, and those who are victims of war.

WHAT IS FUNDED Relief of Jewish victims of war and persecution; help wherever Jewish need exists.

SAMPLE GRANTS £129,938 in grants to Israel, etc. towards kindergartens, youth centres, education and medical equipment; £30,450 for clothing and relief goods shipped to Israel; £10,430 for collection, packaging, insurance and freight of clothing, food, medicaments and other relief supplies.

FINANCES *Year* 1998–99 *Income* £154,033 *Grants* £129,938 *Assets* £732,276

TRUSTEES Dr W Schindler, Chair; M Katz; A Garfield; Mrs I Katz.

OTHER INFORMATION Founded in 1919 to assist victims of war and persecution in Europe and the Eastern Bloc. Since 1948 it has been concerned mainly in Israel with the rehabilitation, clothing, feeding and education of children of immigrant families.

HOW TO APPLY In writing to the address below.

WHO TO APPLY TO Alfred Garfield, Trustee, 143 Brondesbury Park, London NW2 5JL

CC NO 250006   **ESTABLISHED** 1919

■ Feed the Minds

WHERE FUNDING CAN BE GIVEN Developing countries and Eastern Europe.

WHO CAN BENEFIT Christian organisations.

WHAT IS FUNDED Grants are given to support Christian literature and communication programmes.

WHAT IS NOT FUNDED No grants to individuals.

TYPE OF GRANT Capital and project grants to develop new work and increase overall potential of organisations, for periods from one to three years.

RANGE OF GRANTS Most grants in the range of £1,000–£5,000 a year.

SAMPLE GRANTS £11,000 to Christian Commission for Development in Bangladesh – Dhaka for literacy primers; £10,100 to Elam Ministries – Iran for a magazine; £7,500 to Literacy and Evangelism Fellowship – Nairobi for a vehicle to enable staff to visit more literacy classes, give advice and follow-up encouragement to teachers and learners; £7,000 to Africa Inland Church AIDS Division – Nairobi for an AIDS awareness programme; £6,000 to Scripture Union – Rondebosch, South Africa for a Bible reading guide for teenagers; £5,000 to SERVE – Jalaabad, Afghanistan for printing a series of books, leaflets and games for children; £4,600 to Comunidad Teologica Evangelica de Chile – Santiago for production of two publications.

FINANCES *Year* 2001–02 *Income* £636,276

TRUSTEES Revd Canon John Lowe; Christopher Bayne; John Clark; Dr Pauline Webb.

PUBLICATIONS *Theological Book Review.*

HOW TO APPLY On a form available from the correspondent.

WHO TO APPLY TO The Trustees, 1 Marylebone Road, London NW1 4AQ *Tel* 0845 121 2102 *Fax* 020 7643 0388 *E-mail* info@feedtheminds.org *Website* www.feedtheminds.org

CC NO 291333   **ESTABLISHED** 1964

■ The John Feeney Charitable Bequest

WHERE FUNDING CAN BE GIVEN Birmingham.
WHO CAN BENEFIT Artists and residents of Birmingham.
WHAT IS FUNDED Benefit of public charities in Birmingham only; promotion of art in Birmingham only; acquisition and maintenance of open spaces near Birmingham.
WHAT IS NOT FUNDED No support for causes which could be considered as political or denominational.
TYPE OF GRANT Capital.
RANGE OF GRANTS £200–£5,000.
SAMPLE GRANTS £20,000 to Birmingham Royal Ballet; £5,000 each to Castle Bromwich Hall Gardens Trust and Birmingham Settlement; £2,500 each to Midlands Art Centre, and Symphony Hall Organ Appeal; £2,000 each to Birmingham Civic Society, University of Birmingham, and St Paul's Church – Hockley (for their restoration appeal for heritage and community work); £1,000 each to St Matthews – Perry Beeches, and Ironbridge Gorge Museum.
FINANCES *Year* 2000 *Grants* £57,000
TRUSTEES Mrs M Martineau; Charles R King-Farlow; Ranjit Sondhi; Derek M P Lea; S J Lloyd; P W Welch; Mrs M F Lloyd; H B Carslake; Ms A Bhalla; J R Smith; M S Darby; Mrs S R Wright.
HOW TO APPLY In writing to the correspondent by March of each year. There is no application form and no sae is required.
WHO TO APPLY TO M J Woodward, Secretary, Messrs Lee Crowder, 39 Newhall Street, Birmingham B3 3DY *Tel* 0121 236 4477
CC NO 214486   **ESTABLISHED** 1906

■ The George Fentham Birmingham Charity

WHERE FUNDING CAN BE GIVEN City of Birmingham.
WHO CAN BENEFIT Individuals and organisations benefiting young adults and people disadvantaged by poverty.
WHAT IS FUNDED Educational grants to bona fide residents of Birmingham (three-year minimum) under 25 years of age (September to April, i.e. academic year). Particularly charities working in the fields of tertiary and higher education, and various community services and facilities, will be considered.
FINANCES *Year* 1999 *Income* £124,377 *Grants* £106,850
TRUSTEES Four appointed by the City Council; two appointed by Birmingham Voluntary Service Council; four co-opted.
HOW TO APPLY In writing to the correspondent. There is an application form available for educational grants. Allocations for general grants are made following the annual meeting of trustees. General grants are made in April and October, while education grants are made from September to April.
WHO TO APPLY TO Mrs Anne E Holmes, Messrs Lee Crowder, 39 Newhall Street, Birmingham B3 3DY *Tel* 0121 236 4477
CC NO 214487   **ESTABLISHED** 1907

■ The A M Fenton Trust

WHERE FUNDING CAN BE GIVEN UK, preference for North Yorkshire, and overseas.
WHO CAN BENEFIT Registered charities.
WHAT IS FUNDED General charitable purposes.
WHAT IS NOT FUNDED The trust is unlikely to support local appeals, unless they are close to where the trust is based.
TYPE OF GRANT Mostly one-off.
RANGE OF GRANTS £100–£20,000.
SAMPLE GRANTS In 1999: £20,000 to Yorkshire County Cricket Club Charitable Youth Trust; £10,000 to Hipperholme Grammar School; £5,500 to Harrogate Community Transport; £5,000 to Dewsbury and District League of Friendship for Disabled Persons; £3,000 to Tweed Foundation; £2,500 each to Horticap and Winksley Organ Appeal at St Cuthbert's Church; £2,000 each to an individual and Yorkshire Association for the Disabled; £1,500 to Drake Music Project.
FINANCES *Year* 2001 *Income* £132,766
TRUSTEES J L Fenton; C M Fenton.
HOW TO APPLY In writing to the correspondent.
WHO TO APPLY TO J L Fenton, Trustee, 14 Beech Grove, Harrogate, North Yorkshire HG2 0EX
CC NO 270353   **ESTABLISHED** 1975

■ Allan and Nesta Ferguson Charitable Settlement

WHERE FUNDING CAN BE GIVEN Unrestricted, with a local interest in Birmingham and Bishop's Stortford.
WHO CAN BENEFIT Organisations and individuals.
WHAT IS FUNDED In the fields of peace, education and overseas development. Grants towards the fees of postgraduate students who are in their final year of a postgraduate course, subject to evidence of financial hardship.
SAMPLE GRANTS £2,500,000 to Birmingham University for a chair of Global Ethics; £500,000 to Birmingham University Department of Theology for a UNESCO Chair of Jewish and Interfaith Studies; £120,000 to United Nations Association; £58,000 to Human City Institute at Birmingham University; £50,000 to International Broadcasting Trust; £13,000 to Kings World Trust; £12,000 to UKCCSG; £10,000 each to International Health Association, Orien Organisation and Partners for Child Education.
FINANCES *Year* 2000 *Income* £564,000 *Grants* £3,389,000 *Assets* £39,000,000
TRUSTEES Elnora Ferguson; David Banister; Anne Roff; Richard Tee.
HOW TO APPLY In writing to the correspondent. Simple applications are dealt with on a monthly or bi-monthly basis. More complicated ones are decided at trustees' meetings in January and July each year.
WHO TO APPLY TO Richard Tee, Trustee, Stanley Tee, High Street, Bishops Stortford, Herts CM23 2LU *Tel* 01279 755200 *E-mail* jrt@stanleytee.co.uk
CC NO 275487   **ESTABLISHED** 1977

■ Ferguson Benevolent Fund Ltd

WHERE FUNDING CAN BE GIVEN Manchester and surrounding towns, Jersey and overseas.
WHO CAN BENEFIT Relief of social, medical and educational need, usually through charitable bodies working in fields of social and medical need in the areas specified. Organisations benefiting: people of all ages; unemployed people; those in care, fostered and adopted;

Methodists; at risk groups; carers; people disadvantaged by poverty; homeless people; people living in rural and urban areas; victims of domestic violence; and people with Alzheimer's disease, asthma, diabetes, hearing loss, heart disease, leprosy or polio.

WHAT IS FUNDED General, with a preference for Methodist causes. Preference to charities which the trust has special interest in, knowledge of or association with. These include: residential facilities; respite and sheltered accommodation; information technology and computers; infrastructure development; Methodist umbrella bodies; acute healthcare; respite care and care for carers; support and self-help groups; special schools; education and training; and community services.

WHAT IS NOT FUNDED No help is available for individuals for first degree or postgraduate studies, medical electives, private schooling, holidays or expeditions.

TYPE OF GRANT Buildings, capital, endowments, one-off, project, research and start-up costs. All funding is for up to two years.

RANGE OF GRANTS £500–£10,000.

FINANCES *Year* 1999–2000 *Grants* £74,000

TRUSTEES Mrs E Higginbottom, Chair; Ms S Ferguson; Mrs C M A Metcalfe; P A L Holt; Mrs P M Dobson; S M Higginbottom.

HOW TO APPLY In writing to the correspondent. Appeals are not acknowledged. Meetings to decide donations are held in March and October; applications should be received in the preceding month. No telephone calls are accepted.

WHO TO APPLY TO Mrs E Higginbottom, Chair of the Trustees, PO Box 27, Crewkerne, Somerset TA18 7YL

CC NO 228746   **ESTABLISHED** 1963

■ The Ferguson Bequest Fund

WHERE FUNDING CAN BE GIVEN South west Scotland.

WHO CAN BENEFIT Churches in south west Scotland and individuals connected with the church.

WHAT IS FUNDED Grants are given to churches for repairs, educational activities and for the benefit of individuals connected with the church.

TYPE OF GRANT Buildings. Funding for up to one year.

FINANCES *Year* 2000 *Income* £171,000 *Grants* £163,000 *Assets* £4,000,000

TRUSTEES D L M McNicol, Chair; R B Copleton; W S Carswell; S Bell; Revd R W M Johnston; I F Mackay; A D Maclaurin; J Boyle; T G Fielding; D Macrae; Revd D Kay.

HOW TO APPLY Written requests for application forms should be sent to the correspondent. Applications can be considered at any time.

WHO TO APPLY TO Ronald D Oakes, Secretary, 182 Bath Street, Glasgow G2 4HG *Tel* 0141 332 0476

SC NO SC009305   **ESTABLISHED** 1869

■ Elizabeth Hardie Ferguson Charitable Trust Fund

WHERE FUNDING CAN BE GIVEN UK, with some interest in Scotland.

WHO CAN BENEFIT Organisations benefiting children and young people, particularly those who are sick.

WHAT IS FUNDED The welfare and wellbeing of children and young people. Also charities involved in medical research and hospitals where special medical equipment is needed.

WHAT IS NOT FUNDED Non-registered charities and individuals are not supported. The trust does not make grants overseas.

RANGE OF GRANTS £250–£10,000.

FINANCES *Year* 1998–99 *Grants* £46,000

TRUSTEES Sir Alex Ferguson; Cathy Ferguson; Huw Roberts; Ted Way; Les Dalgarno.

HOW TO APPLY An application form and guidelines should be requested in writing from the correspondent. The committee meets to consider grants at the end of January and July. Applications should be received by December and June respectively.

WHO TO APPLY TO Ted Way, Secretary, c/o 11a Craig Street, Peterborough PE1 2EJ

SC NO SC026240   **ESTABLISHED** 1988

■ Fiat Auto (UK) Charity

WHERE FUNDING CAN BE GIVEN UK.

WHO CAN BENEFIT Organisations benefiting: people of all ages; people with disabilities; those in care, fostered and adopted; and widows and widowers.

WHAT IS FUNDED General charitable purposes including: children; older people; people with physical and mental disabilities; the advancement of education; relief of poverty and sickness; and elimination of social and religious discrimination.

WHAT IS NOT FUNDED No grants to individuals, religious or political appeals, expeditions or scholarships.

TYPE OF GRANT Buildings; capital; core costs; feasibility studies, one-off; project; research; running costs; recurring costs; salaries; and start-up costs. Funding may be given for more than three years.

RANGE OF GRANTS £5,000–£100,000 per annum.

SAMPLE GRANTS £100,000 to Children's Society; £40,000 to BEN; £6,000 each to Macmillan Nurses, Sick Kids Friends Foundation, and York Hill Royal Hospital for Sick Children.

FINANCES *Year* 2000 *Grants* £151,000

TRUSTEES L Osbourne; D Birch; A Dopudi.

OTHER INFORMATION Only long-term donations are given.

HOW TO APPLY In writing to the correspondent.

WHO TO APPLY TO Mark Pressburg, Secretary, c/o Fiat House, 266 Bath Road, Slough, Berkshire SL1 4HJ *Tel* 01753 786400

CC NO 1059498   **ESTABLISHED** 1996

■ The Fidelity UK Foundation

WHERE FUNDING CAN BE GIVEN Particular preference is given to projects in Kent, Surrey, London and Continental Europe, where Fidelity Investments has an office.

WHAT IS FUNDED General, giving is primarily allocated to the following sectors: community development, health, arts and culture and education. The trust seeks to support projects undertaken by organisations to increase proficiency, achieve goals and reach long-term self-sufficiency. Most often, funding is given for projects such as capital improvements, technology upgrades, organisational development and planning initiatives.

WHAT IS NOT FUNDED Grants are not made for sponsorships or benefit events, scholarships, corporate membership, advertising and promotional projects or exhibitions. Grants are not generally made to: start-up, sectarian, or political organisations; private schools and colleges or universities; or individuals. Generally grants are not made for running costs, but may be considered on an individual basis through the foundation's small grant scheme. Grants will not normally cover the entire cost of a project, or support an organisation in successive years.

TYPE OF GRANT Buildings, capital, IT development, one-off grants to develop infrastructure. Funding for less than one year is considered.

FINANCES *Year* 2001 *Income* £4,830,859 *Grants* £456,728 *Assets* £8,721,927

TRUSTEES Edward C Johnson; Barry Bateman; Anthony Bolton; Martin Cambridge; Robert Milotte; Richard Millar.

HOW TO APPLY In writing to the correspondent. Applications should include the Fidelity UK summary form, organisation history and objectives, itemised project budget, a list of other funders and the status of each request, a list of directors and trustees with their backgrounds, current operating budget and most recently audited financial statements. A description of the request and rationale should also be included addressing the following: how the project fits into the larger strategic plan of the organisation; what a grant will allow the organisation to achieve; how a grant will change or improve the long-term potential of the organisation; what the implementation plan and timeline for the project is and who is responsible; how the project will be evaluated. Applications will receive an initial response within three months. The foundation receives many more applications for grants than it is able to fund so not all applications that fall within the guidelines will receive grants.

WHO TO APPLY TO Miss Jacqueline Guthrie, Oakhill House, 130 Tonbridge Road, Hildenborough, Tonbridge, Kent TN11 9DZ *Tel* 01732 361144 *Fax* 01732 838300

CC NO 327899   **ESTABLISHED** 1988

■ The Doris Field Charitable Trust

WHERE FUNDING CAN BE GIVEN UK, with a preference for Oxfordshire.

WHO CAN BENEFIT Large UK and small local organisations benefiting children and young adults; at risk groups; people who are disadvantaged by poverty or socially isolated.

WHAT IS FUNDED Medical, welfare, education and general charitable purposes.

WHAT IS NOT FUNDED It is unlikely that grants would be made for overseas projects or to individuals for higher education.

TYPE OF GRANT One-off and recurrent.

RANGE OF GRANTS £50–£50,000, mostly £5,000 or less.

SAMPLE GRANTS £50,000 to Sobell House Hospice; £34,000 to Nuffield Orthopaedic Centre; £14,303 for work on a memorial field; £12,500 to Cystic Fibrosis Trust; £5,000 each to Headway Oxford and Oxfordshire Historic Churches Trust; £2,500 each to Marie Curie Cancer Relief, Pathway Workshop, Sixteen Ltd and Wildfowl and Wetlands Trust.

FINANCES *Year* 2000–01 *Income* £252,359 *Grants* £208,299 *Assets* £4,949,458

TRUSTEES N A Harper; J Cole; Mrs W Church.

HOW TO APPLY On a form available from the correspondent. Applications are considered three times a year.

WHO TO APPLY TO Helen Fanyinka, Morgan Cole Solicitors, Buxton Court, 3 West Way, Oxford OX2 0SZ *Tel* 01865 262183 *Fax* 01865 200962

CC NO 328687   **ESTABLISHED** 1990

■ The Fifty Fund

WHERE FUNDING CAN BE GIVEN Nottinghamshire and surrounding area.

WHO CAN BENEFIT Individuals and organisations benefiting retired people; unemployed people; those in care, fostered and adopted; parents and children; one-parent families; widows and widowers; carers; disabled people; and people disadvantaged by poverty.

WHAT IS FUNDED Relief of poverty, infrastructure development, charity or voluntary umbrella bodies, advice and information on housing, respite care, and various community services.

WHAT IS NOT FUNDED No grants for education, expeditions or travel.

TYPE OF GRANT Capital, core costs, interest-free loans, one-off, project, research and start-up costs. Funding of up to and over three years will be considered.

RANGE OF GRANTS £100–£8,000.

SAMPLE GRANTS £8,000 to Nottinghamshire Hospice; £6,000 to Macedon Trust; £5,000 to Macmillan Cancer Relief; £4,676 to Assarts Charity; £3,500 each to East Nottingham Boys' Club, Oliver Hind Club, Russell Club for Youth, Parents' Association for Seriously Ill Children, and Lenton Community Link; £3,000 to Southwell Care Project.

FINANCES *Year* 1999 *Income* £160,597 *Grants* £134,787 *Assets* £1,010,741

TRUSTEES D R Pell; M A Foulds; E A Randall; Revd Canon G B Barrodale.

OTHER INFORMATION Individuals have priority in allocation of funds. £67,576 in total went to charities in 1999.

HOW TO APPLY In writing to the correspondent.

WHO TO APPLY TO S J Moore, Clerk, Nelsons, Pennine House, 8 Stanford Street, Nottingham NG1 7BQ

CC NO 214422   **ESTABLISHED** 1963

■ Dixie Rose Findlay Charitable Trust

WHERE FUNDING CAN BE GIVEN UK.

WHO CAN BENEFIT Charitable organisations.

WHAT IS FUNDED General charitable purposes.

SAMPLE GRANTS £2,500 each to 10 organisations including Cassel Hospital, The Children's Society, Glen Arun, Mission to Seamen and St Johns Wood Church.

FINANCES *Year* 2000–01 *Grants* £25,000

TRUSTEES HSBC Trust Co. (UK) Ltd; Miss D R Findlay.

HOW TO APPLY In late 2002 this trust stated that it was not accepting appeals from any source.

WHO TO APPLY TO Colin Bould, HSBC Trust Co. (UK) Ltd, 15–17 Cumberland House, Southampton SO15 2UY *Tel* 023 8053 1352

CC NO 251661   **ESTABLISHED** 1967

■ Finnart House School Trust

WHERE FUNDING CAN BE GIVEN Worldwide.

WHO CAN BENEFIT Jewish children and young adults who are delinquent, deprived, sick, neglected and in need of care or education.

WHAT IS FUNDED Jewish children in need; respite accommodation; special needs education; speech therapy; playgrounds and recreation grounds; holidays and outings; and care in the community.

Bursaries and scholarships are given to Jewish secondary school pupils and university entrants who are capable of achieving, but would probably not do so because of family and economic pressures.

TYPE OF GRANT Buildings, capital, one-off and project. Funding is available for up to two years.

RANGE OF GRANTS £1,970–£20,000; typical grant £5,000.

SAMPLE GRANTS £20,000 to Keshet – Remedial Kindergarten; £15,000 to Nitzan; £10,000 to Ashalim Children's Village; £6,500 to Hasmonean High School; £5,000 each to Association for Research into Stammering in Childhood, Binoh of Manchester, Cosgrove Care, Gimmel Foundation, Institute for the Advancement of Deaf Persons in Israel, and JFS School.

FINANCES *Year* 2001–02 *Income* £168,556 *Grants* £154,588 *Assets* £4,275,982

TRUSTEES Dr Louis Marks, Chair; Robert Cohen; Lady Grabiner; Hilary Norton; David Fobel; Lilian Hochhauser; Jane Leaver; Dr Amanda Kirby; Mark Sebba; Linda Peterson; Sue Leifer.

HOW TO APPLY There is an application form, which needs to be submitted together with a copy of the latest annual report and accounts.

WHO TO APPLY TO Peter Shaw, Clerk, 5th Floor, 707 High Road, North Finchley, London N12 0BT *Tel* 020 8445 1670 *Fax* 020 8446 7370 *E-mail* finnart@anjy.org

CC NO 220917   **ESTABLISHED** 1901

■ The David Finnie & Alan Emery Charitable Trust

WHERE FUNDING CAN BE GIVEN UK.

WHO CAN BENEFIT Individuals and organisations.

WHAT IS FUNDED Support is mainly for national organisations working in the medical, health, welfare, and education and training fields, together with a number of benevolent funds which are regular beneficiaries. A few local organisations are also supported together with individuals for temporary relief of hardship and advancement of education, personal achievement and development.

WHAT IS NOT FUNDED No grants where alternative funding was or should be made available by other agencies, government or otherwise. No support for: loans and non-specific cash sums; expeditions, conference attendance and seminars; general cases of hardship falling outside the stated criteria; requests for holiday trips, family reunions and the like; debts of any kind; house removal or funeral expenses; TV, car and animal licences; nursing and/or residential care fees (including for homeless people); furniture and fixtures; treatment that should be provided by the NHS; or overseas funding.

TYPE OF GRANT One-off and recurrent (where circumstances warrant). Capital, project and research. Funding for up to three years will be considered.

RANGE OF GRANTS £500–£3,000.

SAMPLE GRANTS £3,000 to Youth at Risk; £2,500 each to Salvation Army and Samaritans.

FINANCES *Year* 2001–02 *Income* £95,000 *Grants* £74,000 *Assets* £2,000,000

TRUSTEES J A C Buck; R J Emery; Mrs S A Hyde.

HOW TO APPLY In writing to the correspondent. Trustees usually meet in April, July and October each year to consider grants. Replies will be sent to applicants who include an sae and cases considered of merit will generally be forwarded a grant application form for completion.

WHO TO APPLY TO J A C Buck, Trustee, 4 De Grosmont Close, Abergavenny, Monmouthshire NP7 9JN *Tel* 01873 851048

CC NO 258749   **ESTABLISHED** 1969

■ Gerald Finzi Charitable Trust

WHERE FUNDING CAN BE GIVEN UK.

WHO CAN BENEFIT Organisations and individuals.

WHAT IS FUNDED The trustees aim to reflect the ambitions and philosophy of the composer Gerald Finzi (1901–56), which included the general promotion of 20th century British music through assisting and promoting festivals, recordings and performances of British music. A limited number of modest grants are also offered to young musicians towards musical training.

FINANCES *Year* 1998–99 *Income* £71,128

TRUSTEES Christopher Finzi; Nigel Finzi; Jean Finzi; Andrew Burn; Robert Gower; J Dale Roberts; Paul Spicer; Michael Salmon; Christian Alexander.

HOW TO APPLY In writing to the correspondent.

WHO TO APPLY TO R Gower, Skrines, Glenalmond College, Glenalmond, Perth PH1 3RY

CC NO 313047   **ESTABLISHED** 1969

■ The Sir John Fisher Foundation

WHERE FUNDING CAN BE GIVEN UK, with a preference for the Furness peninsula and Merseyside.

WHO CAN BENEFIT UK and local charities and local branches.

WHAT IS FUNDED General charitable purposes, with a preference for the shipping industry, medicine, the navy or military, and music and theatre.

WHAT IS NOT FUNDED Grants are not given to students.

RANGE OF GRANTS £100–£25,000.

SAMPLE GRANTS £25,000 to Sir John Fisher Chair; £20,000 each to Friends of Wordsworth Trust, Hospice of St Mary of Furness and Merseside Maritime Museum; £12,000 to Worshipful Company of Shipwrights; £10,000 each to Foundation of Coagualtion, Brewery Arts Centre and Thrombosis – Dundee University; £8,000 to Downdales School; £6,500 each to Furness Drug and Alcohol Concern and Samaritans – Furness; £5,000 each to Abbot Hall, Croft Care Trust and Handel House Trust.

FINANCES *Year* 2000–01 *Income* £440,998 *Grants* £304,993 *Assets* £6,922,331

TRUSTEES D P Tindall; R F Hart Jackson; Mrs D S Meacock.

HOW TO APPLY In writing to the correspondent. Trustees usually meet in May and November.

WHO TO APPLY TO R F Hart Jackson, Trustee, 8–10 New Market Street, Ulverston, Cumbria LA12 7LW *Tel* 01229 583291

CC NO 277844   **ESTABLISHED** 1979

■ The Fishmongers' Company's Charitable Trust

WHERE FUNDING CAN BE GIVEN UK, with a slight special interest in the City of London and adjacent boroughs.

WHO CAN BENEFIT Registered charities benefiting people who are disabled, disadvantaged by poverty, homeless or socially isolated, seafarers and fishermen; charities involved with education, the environment, heritage and fishery matters; individuals in education.

WHAT IS FUNDED The relief of hardship and disability, education, the environment, heritage and fishery-related charities.

WHAT IS NOT FUNDED No grants are made to individual branches of national charities or to regional or local charities, other than those in the City of London and adjacent boroughs. No grants are awarded to individuals except for education. Ad hoc educational grants are not awarded to applicants who are over 19 years-old.

TYPE OF GRANT One-off.

RANGE OF GRANTS £500–£10,000; typical grant £1,000–£2,000.

SAMPLE GRANTS £350,000 to Fishmongers' Company's Fisheries Charitable Trust; £309,000 to Gresham's School for scholarships and bursaries; £146,000 to Jesus Hospital Almshouses; £51,000 to Harrietsham Almshouse; £25,000 to City & Guilds of London Art School; £13,000 to Marine Biological Association; £12,000 to Voluntary Service Overseas; £10,000 each to Handicapped Angler's Trust, Migratory Salmon Fund and Motor Neurone Disease Association.

FINANCES Year 2001 *Income* £4,700,000 *Grants* £1,370,000 *Assets* £10,300,000

TRUSTEES The Wardens and Court of the Fishmongers' Company.

HOW TO APPLY In writing to the clerk. Meetings take place three times a year, in March, July and November, and applications should be received a month in advance. No applications are considered within three years of a previous grant application being successful. Unsuccessful applications are not acknowledged.

WHO TO APPLY TO K S Waters, Clerk, The Fishmongers' Company, Fishmongers' Hall, London Bridge, London EC4R 9EL *Tel* 020 7626 3531 *Website* www.fishhall.co.uk

CC NO 263690   **ESTABLISHED** 1972

■ Marc Fitch Fund

WHERE FUNDING CAN BE GIVEN UK.

WHO CAN BENEFIT Both individual or societies benefiting young adults, research workers and students.

WHAT IS FUNDED Publication and research in archaeology, historical geography, history of art and architecture, heraldry, genealogy, surnames, catalogues and use of archives (especially ecclesiastical) and other antiquarian, archaeological or historical studies.

WHAT IS NOT FUNDED No grants are given towards foreign travel or for research outside Great Britain, unless the circumstances are very exceptional; or people reading full-time higher degrees.

TYPE OF GRANT Loans, guarantees or grants.

RANGE OF GRANTS Institutions: £120–£28,250.

SAMPLE GRANTS £28,250 to Manorial Documents Register; £5,000 to AHRB Centre for North-east England History; £3,000 to Bowes Museum; £2,100 to Oxford Archaeology; £1,000 to St Albans Architectural and Archaeological Society.

FINANCES *Year* 2001–02 *Income* £293,000 *Grants* £195,000 *Assets* £4,000,000

TRUSTEES A S Bell, Chair; Hon. Nicholas Assheton; Prof. J P Barron; A J Camp; Prof. C R Elrington; Dr J I Kermode; Prof. D M Palliser; J Porteous; Dr J Blair; Dr H Forde; A Murison; Dr G Worsley.

HOW TO APPLY In writing to the correspondent. The trustees meet twice a year to consider applications.

WHO TO APPLY TO Elaine M Paintin, Executive Secretary, 10 Market Street, Charlbury OX7 3PH *Tel* 01608 811944 *E-mail* admin@marcfitchfund.org.uk *Website* www.marcfitchfund.org.uk

CC NO 313303   **ESTABLISHED** 1956

■ The Fitton Trust

WHERE FUNDING CAN BE GIVEN UK.

WHO CAN BENEFIT Registered charities only.

WHAT IS FUNDED General charitable purposes.

WHAT IS NOT FUNDED No grants to individuals.

RANGE OF GRANTS £100–£250; occasionally £1,000 or more.

SAMPLE GRANTS 1999: £4,000 to St Mary's Hospital Medical School for medical research; £2,000 to Winnicott Foundation for medical research; £1,500 each to Berwick Village Hall Trust millennium project and King's Medical Research Trust for research; £1,050 to Save the Children – a special donation; £1,000 each to Movement for Non-mobile Children – a special donation, Royal College of Obstetricians & Gynaecologists for a special appeal, St Piers Lingfield special appeal, and Young People's Trust for the Environment for general purposes.

FINANCES *Year* 2001–02 *Income* £106,707

TRUSTEES Dr R P A Rivers; D M Lumsden; D V Brand.

HOW TO APPLY In writing to correspondent. The trust states: 'No application considered unless accompanied by fully audited accounts. No replies will be sent to unsolicited applications whether from individuals, charities or other bodies.'

WHO TO APPLY TO The Secretary, PO Box 649, London SW3 4LA *E-mail* Fitton.Trust@virgin.net

CC NO 208758   **ESTABLISHED** 1928

■ The Earl Fitzwilliam Charitable Trust

WHERE FUNDING CAN BE GIVEN UK, with a preference for areas with historical family connections, chiefly in Cambridgeshire, Northamptonshire and Yorkshire.

WHO CAN BENEFIT Organisations benefiting: children and young adults; clergy; ex-service and service people; volunteers; Christians; Church of England; at risk groups; disabled people; people living in rural areas; victims of abuse and crime; victims of man-made or natural disasters; and people with cancer, diabetes, head and other injuries, leprosy, mental illness, spina bifida and hydrocephalus. Projects and charities connected in some way with or which will benefit rural life and communities including churches.

WHAT IS FUNDED Preference for charitable projects in areas with historical family connections, chiefly in Cambridgeshire, Northamptonshire and Yorkshire. Particularly charities working in the fields of: accommodation and housing; infrastructure, support and development; Christian outreach; churches; religious umbrella bodies; arts, culture and recreation; health facilities and buildings; cancer research; conservation and environment; schools and colleges; and various community facilities and services.

WHAT IS NOT FUNDED No grants to individuals.

TYPE OF GRANT Buildings, capital, endowments, one-off, project and research. Funding of one year or less will be considered.

RANGE OF GRANTS Usually £250–£5,000.

Think carefully about every application. Is it justified?

471

FINANCES *Year* 2001–02 *Income* £190,000
Grants £60,000 *Assets* £5,100,000
TRUSTEES Sir Philip Naylor-Leyland Bart; Lady
Isabella Naylor-Leyland.
HOW TO APPLY In writing to the correspondent.
Trustees meet about every three months.
WHO TO APPLY TO J M S Thompson, Secretary to the
Trustees, Estate Office, Milton Park,
Peterborough PE6 7AH *Tel* 01733 267740
CC NO 269388   **ESTABLISHED** 1975

■ Bud Flanagan Leukaemia Fund

WHERE FUNDING CAN BE GIVEN UK.
WHO CAN BENEFIT Hospitals and similar
organisations carrying out research, diagnosis
and treatment of leukaemia and allied diseases;
people with leukaemia and their families and
dependants.
WHAT IS FUNDED Promotion of clinical research into
the treatment and possible cure of leukaemia
and allied diseases and the publication of the
results of all such research. Relief of people
with leukaemia and allied diseases and the
relief of poverty and distress among their
families and dependants. The policy is to make
donations to hospitals and similar institutions
for equipment or research into leukaemia and
allied diseases so that as many people as
possible benefit.
WHAT IS NOT FUNDED The fund does not normally
make grants to other charities or to individuals.
TYPE OF GRANT Capital (including buildings), project
and research. Funding can be for up to three
years.
RANGE OF GRANTS Usually up to £10,000.
SAMPLE GRANTS Recent beneficiaries include Royal
Marsden Hospital, Institute of Cancer Research,
Fergus Maclay Leukaemia Database and Bath
Cancer Research.
FINANCES *Year* 2001 *Income* £141,704
Grants £149,142 *Assets* £519,731
TRUSTEES B Coral; S Coventry; R Powles; B Jones;
The Countess of Normanton; K Kaye; A Rowden;
A Kitcherside; J Goodman; A Kingston; G Till.
HOW TO APPLY In writing to the correspondent.
WHO TO APPLY TO J Bernard Jones, 40 Redwood
Glade, Leighton Buzzard, Bedfordshire LU7 3JT
Tel 01525 376550 *Fax* 01525 376550
Website www.bflf.org.uk
CC NO 259670   **ESTABLISHED** 1969

■ The Rose Flatau Charitable Trust

WHERE FUNDING CAN BE GIVEN UK.
WHO CAN BENEFIT Registered charities.
WHAT IS FUNDED General charitable purposes,
particularly health, older people and Jewish
people. Funds are fully committed to the
support of charities which are of special interest
to the trustees.
WHAT IS NOT FUNDED No grants to individuals.
RANGE OF GRANTS £100–£15,000.
SAMPLE GRANTS £15,000 to Norwood; £10,000 to
Cherry Trees; £5,000 each to Anglo-Jewish
Association, Crisis, Jewish Aged Needy Pension
Trust, Jewish Care, Jewish Children's Day,
Queen Elizabeth Foundation for the Disabled,
Samaritans and Winged Fellowship.
FINANCES *Year* 2000–01 *Income* £60,457
Grants £118,614 *Assets* £1,261,531
TRUSTEES M E G Prince; A E Woolf; N L Woolf.
HOW TO APPLY The trust states: 'No further
applications can be accepted as the income
available is fully committed.'

WHO TO APPLY TO M E G Prince, Trustee, 5 Knott
Park House, Wrens Hill, Oxshott, Leatherhead
KT22 0HW *Tel* 01372 843082
CC NO 210492   **ESTABLISHED** 1959

■ The Ian Fleming Charitable Trust

WHERE FUNDING CAN BE GIVEN UK.
WHO CAN BENEFIT Individual musicians, and
registered charities benefiting medical
professionals, research workers and scientists.
Support is also given to at risk groups, and
people who are disabled, disadvantaged by
poverty or socially isolated.
WHAT IS FUNDED Income is allocated equally
between: national charities actively operating for
the support, relief and welfare of men, women
and children who are disabled or otherwise in
need of help, care and attention, and charities
actively engaged in research on human
diseases; and music education awards under a
scheme administered by the Musicians
Benevolent Fund and advised by a committee of
experts in the field of music.
WHAT IS NOT FUNDED No grants to individuals except
under the music education award scheme. No
grants to purely local charities.
RANGE OF GRANTS £1,000–£3,000.
SAMPLE GRANTS £3,000 to Breakthrough Breast
Cancer; £2,500 to SSAFA Forces Help; £2,000
each to Botton Village, British Heart Foundation,
British Red Cross, Council for Music in
Hospitals, Crisis, Help the Hospices, Multiple
Sclerosis Trust and Royal Star and Garter
Home.
FINANCES *Year* 2000–01 *Income* £109,796
Grants £129,875 *Assets* £2,262,928
TRUSTEES A A I Fleming; N A M McDonald; A W W
Baldwin; A H Isaacs.
HOW TO APPLY In writing to the correspondent.
WHO TO APPLY TO A A I Fleming, Trustee,
haysmacintyre, Southampton House, 317 High
Holborn, London WC1V 7NL *Tel* 020 7969
5500
CC NO 263327   **ESTABLISHED** 1971

■ The Joyce Fletcher Charitable Trust

WHERE FUNDING CAN BE GIVEN England, with a
preference for the south west.
WHO CAN BENEFIT National and south west charities.
This trust will consider funding for the benefit of
all ages; musicians; volunteers; those in care,
fostered and adopted; one-parent families;
parents and children; people with disabilities;
those living in rural areas; and socially isolated
people.
WHAT IS FUNDED Music in the community and in a
special needs context; children's welfare; and
charities in the south west. Currently main
areas of interest are institutions and
organisations specialising in music education
and performance, special needs education and
performance involving music, and charities for
children's welfare. Arts, culture and recreation;
art galleries and cultural centres; community
centres and village halls; theatres' and opera
houses' education programmes; and other
charitable purposes are all considered for
funding.
WHAT IS NOT FUNDED Grants to individuals are very
rarely considered. No grants are given towards
purely commercial music performances or to

areas which are primarily a statutory body responsibility.

TYPE OF GRANT Recurring expenses; capital; or new projects.

RANGE OF GRANTS £250–£10,000. Usually £500–£1,000.

SAMPLE GRANTS £10,000 to Live Music Now! for community concerts; £6,000 Share Music towards music courses for people with disabilities; £2,000 each to Drake Music Project towards music technology for people with disabilities and Jackdaws Educational Trust for music education; £1,000 each to Bath Area Play project for child and family support, Bath Festival for community outreach, National Library for the Blind for a music library, Project Trust for student gap years, and Wiltshire Music Centre towards a concert and education centre.

FINANCES *Year* 2002 *Income* £65,000 *Grants* £64,000 *Assets* £1,800,000

TRUSTEES R A Fletcher; W D R Fletcher.

HOW TO APPLY In writing to the correspondent by November each year. Applications should include the purpose for the grant, an indication of the history and viability of the organisation and a summary of accounts. Preliminary telephone calls are accepted. Acknowledgements are only given if the application is being considered or if an sae is sent.

WHO TO APPLY TO R A Fletcher, Trustee, 17 Westmead Gardens, Upper Weston, Bath BA1 4EZ *Tel* 01225 314355

CC NO 297901   **ESTABLISHED** 1987

■ The Roy Fletcher Charitable Trust

WHERE FUNDING CAN BE GIVEN Shropshire.

WHO CAN BENEFIT Local organisations.

WHAT IS FUNDED Children and young people; older people; disadvantage. The trust also established The Roy Fletcher Centre to house caring agencies and provide office space, meeting and counselling rooms; this is now run independently of the trust.

WHAT IS NOT FUNDED The trust is unlikely to fund projects eligible for statutory funding, applicants not seeking funds from elsewhere, UK charities, operating costs, building repairs or educational grants. The trust no longer supports individuals.

SAMPLE GRANTS £40,500 to Mayfair Centre; £5,000 to Relate; £3,000 to Bridge School; £1,500 to Vision Homes Association.

FINANCES *Year* 2001–02 *Income* £52,859 *Grants* £73,582

TRUSTEES Mrs R A Coles; Mrs G M Mathias; Mrs E J Fletcher Cooper; D N Fletcher.

OTHER INFORMATION At time of publication, the trustees were considering at least one major project which if they decide to go ahead may result in the restriction of their ability to fund many additional projects in the near future.

HOW TO APPLY In writing to the correspondent only. The trustees meet three times a year in early January, May and October, and requests for funding should be received at least four weeks before each meeting. The trust does not welcome telephone enquiries to The Roy Fletcher Centre (which is a separate organisation).

WHO TO APPLY TO The Trust Administrator, c/o Roy Fletcher Centre, 12–17 Cross Hill, Shrewsbury, Shropshire SY1 1JE

CC NO 276498   **ESTABLISHED** 1978

■ Florence's Charitable Trust

WHERE FUNDING CAN BE GIVEN UK, with a preference for Rossendale in Lancashire.

WHO CAN BENEFIT Mainly local organisations, or local branches of UK organisations, benefiting employees or former employees of the shoe trade and people who are elderly or disadvantaged by poverty. Support may be given to children and young adults.

WHAT IS FUNDED General charitable purposes, especially establishment, maintenance and support of places of education; relief of sickness of infirmity for older people; and relief of poverty of anyone employed or formerly employed in the shoe trade.

WHAT IS NOT FUNDED No grants to individual, educational costs, exchange visits or gap year activities.

TYPE OF GRANT Mainly recurrent grants.

RANGE OF GRANTS £50–£25,000.

SAMPLE GRANTS £15,000 to Rossendale Borough Council; £7,466 to Cardiac Services; £7,100 to Britannia Country Primary School; £6,000 to Age Concern; £3,500 to Lancashire Badger Group; £3,360 to Burnley Health Trust; £3,000 each to Lanchashire Constabulary – Fair Chance and Life Education Trust for Lancashire; £2,500 each to Lancaster Royal Grammar School and Stafford University; £2,025 to British Red Cross.

FINANCES *Year* 2000–01 *Income* £99,769 *Grants* £142,197 *Assets* £1,410,766

TRUSTEES C C Harrison, Chair; R Barker; A Connearn; G D Low; J Mellows; R D Uttley; K Duffy.

HOW TO APPLY In writing to the correspondent. The trust stated that funds are fully committed until 2006. To save on administration costs, unsuccessful applications will not be acknowledged even if an sae is provided.

WHO TO APPLY TO R Barker, Secretary to the Trustees, E Suttons & Sons, PO Box 2, Riverside, Bacup, Lancashire OL13 0DT *Tel* 01706 874961 *Fax* 01706 879268 *E-mail* ronnie@esutton.co.uk

CC NO 265754   **ESTABLISHED** 1973

■ The Florian Charitable Trust

WHERE FUNDING CAN BE GIVEN UK.

WHO CAN BENEFIT Individuals and organisations.

WHAT IS FUNDED General charitable purposes.

SAMPLE GRANTS In 1998–99: £2,000 to Sussex Autistic Society; £1,500 each to Action for ME, Brainwave, Canine Partners for Independence, Cystic Fibrosis Holiday Fund and Vision Aid; £1,000 each to Cancer Research Campaign, Children Nationwide, Fibromyalgia Support Group, International Spinal Research Trust and The Migraine Trust.

FINANCES *Year* 2000–01 *Income* £37,135 *Grants* £32,000 *Assets* £1,000,000

TRUSTEES V J Treasure; Mrs G W Treasure; G A Treasure; R W Wood.

HOW TO APPLY In writing to the correspondent. The trust says: 'Whilst the trustees have been prepared to look at all applications received during the six months prior to the biannual trustees meeting, particular emphasis has been placed on funding specific projects.'

WHO TO APPLY TO Richard Wood, Trustee, Lawrence Graham, 190 Strand, London WC2R 1JN *Tel* 020 7379 0000 *Fax* 020 7393 6854

CC NO 1043523   **ESTABLISHED** 1995

■ The Flow Foundation

WHERE FUNDING CAN BE GIVEN UK.

WHO CAN BENEFIT Registered charities.

WHAT IS FUNDED The trust makes grants to support child welfare, education, environment, Jewish, and medical causes.

SAMPLE GRANTS £14,000 to World Hope; £12,000 to Weizmann Institute Fund; £8,600 to Barnardos; £5,500 to Joint Jewish Charitable Trust; £2,000 to Tommy's Campaign; £1,800 to British Red Cross; £1,300 each to After Adoption and British Friends of Haifa University; £1,000 each to Children's Society and Millennium Bridge.

FINANCES *Year* 1999–2000 *Income* £68,000 *Grants* £50,000 *Assets* £896,000

TRUSTEES Mrs N Shashou; H Woolf; Mrs J Woolf.

HOW TO APPLY In writing to the correspondent on one sheet of paper only.

WHO TO APPLY TO Mrs Nita Sowerbutts, Suite A, 15 Portman Square, London W1H 6LJ *Tel* 020 7224 0077

CC NO 328274   **ESTABLISHED** 1989

■ The Gerald Fogel Charitable Trust

WHERE FUNDING CAN BE GIVEN UK.

WHO CAN BENEFIT Mainly headquarters organisations benefiting: children and older people, those in care, fostered and adopted, Jewish people and homeless people.

WHAT IS FUNDED Charities working in the fields of: the advancement of the Jewish religion; synagogues; and cultural and religious teaching. The trust may also fund residential facilities, arts activities, care in the community, hospices, hospitals, cancer research and campaigning on health issues.

WHAT IS NOT FUNDED No grants to individuals or non-registered charities.

TYPE OF GRANT One-off and recurrent.

SAMPLE GRANTS Previous beneficiaries include Jewish Care, Jewish Child's Day, Constable Educational Trust, Jewish Marriage Council, Imperial Cancer Research Fund, Jack's Pack, King Edward VII's Hospital for Officers, Macmillan Cancer Relief, Norwood and Variety Club.

FINANCES *Year* 2001–02 *Income* £48,000

TRUSTEES J G Fogel; B Fogel; S Fogel; D Fogel.

HOW TO APPLY In writing to the correspondent.

WHO TO APPLY TO J Clay, Accountant, Morley & Scott, Lynton House, 7–12 Tavistock Square, London WC1H 9LT *Tel* 020 7387 5868 *E-mail* clayj@morley-scott.co.uk

CC NO 1004451   **ESTABLISHED** 1991

■ The Row Fogo Charitable Trust

WHERE FUNDING CAN BE GIVEN Edinburgh, Lothians and Dunblane.

WHO CAN BENEFIT Funding primarily goes to research workers and people with neurological diseases, but other medical research and charitable purposes are considered.

WHAT IS FUNDED Grants are given to organisations which carry out medical research, particularly in the field of neuroscience; also to local charity projects and to small charities mostly in Central Scotland.

WHAT IS NOT FUNDED No grants to individuals.

SAMPLE GRANTS £187,000 to SHEFC Brain Imaging Research Centre; £8,000 to Macmillan Cancer Relief; £6,000 to RNLI; £5,000 each to Alzheimer Scotland Action on Dementia, Age Concern and Salvation Army; £4,500 each to Multiple Sclerosis Society, Muscular Dystrophy Campaign and The Wishbone Trust; £4,000 each to Drum Riding for the Disabled, Invalids at Home and Stobhill Kidney Patients Association; £3,500 to The Sandpiper Trust; £3,000 each to Erskine Hospital and Tak Tent.

FINANCES *Year* 2001–02 *Income* £141,652 *Grants* £288,000 *Assets* £3,000,000

TRUSTEES E J Cuthbertson; A W Waddell; Dr C Brough.

HOW TO APPLY In writing to the correspondent.

WHO TO APPLY TO Andrew M C Dalgleish, Messrs Brodies WS, 15 Atholl Crescent, Edinburgh EH3 8HA *Tel* 0131 228 3777 *Fax* 0131 228 3878 *E-mail* mailbox@brodies.co.uk *Website* www.brodies.co.uk

SC NO SC009685   **ESTABLISHED** 1970

■ The Follett Trust

WHERE FUNDING CAN BE GIVEN UK and overseas.

WHO CAN BENEFIT Individuals and organisations benefiting children and young adults, actors and entertainment professionals, musicians, textile workers and designers, writers and poets, at risk groups and people disadvantaged by poverty; medical research and hospital projects; people with disabilities.

WHAT IS FUNDED Education; individual students in higher education (including theatre); disability and health; trusts for writers and publishers; and international relief work.

RANGE OF GRANTS £50–£20,000.

SAMPLE GRANTS Beneficiaries included Canon Collins Trust, Dyslexia Institute, Stevenage Citizens Advice Bureau, Oxfam and University College London Development Fund.

FINANCES *Year* 2001–02 *Income* £71,835 *Grants* £70,000

TRUSTEES Martin Follett; Ken Follett; Barbara Follett.

HOW TO APPLY The trust states, 'A high proportion of donees come to the attention of the trustees through personal knowledge and contact rather than by written application. Where the trustees find it impossible to make a donation they rarely respond to the applicant unless a stamped addressed envelope is provided'.

WHO TO APPLY TO M D Follett, Trustee, 17 Chescombe Road, Yatton, North Somerset BS49 4EE *Tel* 01934 838337

CC NO 328638   **ESTABLISHED** 1990

■ The Football Association National Sports Centre Trust

WHERE FUNDING CAN BE GIVEN UK.

WHO CAN BENEFIT Hard surface play area schemes at clubs, schools and community centres.

WHAT IS FUNDED Provision of community sports facilities.

TYPE OF GRANT One-off.

RANGE OF GRANTS £5,000–£25,000.

SAMPLE GRANTS Iin 1996 , all for provision of hard surface play areas: £25,000 each to Alumwell Community Association, Bexhill College, Devon County Council, Lancashire County Council, LB Bromley, Middlewich Ground Trust, North Teesside Sports Complex and Radcliffe Borough FC; £20,000 to Shenley Lane Community Association; £15,000 to Ashford Amateurs FC.

FINANCES *Year* 2001 *Income* £231,159 *Grants* £356,313 *Assets* £769,794

TRUSTEES K St J Wiseman, Chair; W T Annable; A W Brett; A D McMullen; E M Parry.

HOW TO APPLY In writing to the correspondent.

WHO TO APPLY TO Mike Appleby, Secretary to the Trustees, 25 Soho Square, London W1D 4FA *Tel* 020 7745 4589 *Fax* 020 7745 5589 *E-mail* mike.appleby@TheFA.com

CC NO 265132   **ESTABLISHED** 1972

....

■ The Football Association Youth Trust

WHERE FUNDING CAN BE GIVEN UK.

WHO CAN BENEFIT County associations, schools and universities benefiting young people who play football or other sports.

WHAT IS FUNDED The furtherance of education of schools and universities encouraging football or other sports to ensure that due attention is given to the physical education and character development of pupils.

TYPE OF GRANT One-off.

RANGE OF GRANTS £1,123–£50,621.

SAMPLE GRANTS £50,621 to English Schools FA; £11,984 as payments to other institutions; £7,500 each to Independent Schools FA and British University Sports Association; £4,000 each to Cambridge University FC and Oxford University FC; £1,825 each to Birmingham FA, Cheshire FA, Essex FA, and Essex Happening Back.

FINANCES *Year* 2001–02 *Income* £1,142,050 *Grants* £1,692,256 *Assets* £10,011,491

TRUSTEES W T Annable; R G Berridge; B W Bright; G Thomson; M Armstrong.

HOW TO APPLY In writing to the correspondent. Grants are made throughout the year. There are no application forms, but a copy of the most recent accounts should be sent.

WHO TO APPLY TO M Appleby, Secretary, Football Association Ltd, 25 Soho Square, London W1D 4FA *Tel* 020 7745 4589 *Fax* 020 7745 5589 *E-mail* mike.appleby@thefa.org

CC NO 265131   **ESTABLISHED** 1972

....

■ The Football Foundation

WHERE FUNDING CAN BE GIVEN UK.

WHAT IS FUNDED The foundation was set up in 2000 to revitalise the grass roots of football. It also funds educational and community projects. Funding is mainly coordinated through a grass roots advisory group and a community and education panel.

The grass roots advisory group works at an infrastructure level to deliver modern facilities in parks, local leagues and schools throughout the country. Local football partnerships have been established to ensure that all relevant groups have a voice in how football is delivered in their communities. Members include representatives of the County FA, local authorities and local sports organisations.

The community and education panel aims to promote community and education initiatives and enhance football's role as a positive force in society.

SAMPLE GRANTS £897,000 to Long Lane Junior Football Club; £819,000 to Princes's Trust; £450,000 to City of Stoke of Trent; £438,000 to Street Football League; £271,000 to Bolton Metro Leisure Services; £137,000 to Springfield Football Club; £109,000 to National Literacy Trust; £108,000 to Trafford Borough Council;

£100,000 to National Football Museum – Preston.

FINANCES *Year* 2001–02 *Income* £53,000,000

TRUSTEES Rt Hon Lord Pendry; T D Brooking; D G Richards; R C Scudamore; G Thompson; F Pattison.

OTHER INFORMATION The foundation also runs a Junior Kit Scheme. Grants are available for FA affiliated under-16 teams and can be used for the purchase of kit. The maximum award is £300 and the club would normally receive only one grant every three years. The grant will be given in the form of vouchers which can be exchanged with a nominated supplier. A total of £250,000 has been distributed.

In addition to its grant-making activities the foundation has set up the Register of English Football Facilities. By creating a definitive database, it hopes to be able to identify the quality, quantity and demand for facilities in every part of the country and identify areas of need.

HOW TO APPLY Application forms and guidance notes are available on request from the foundation's helpline (tel: 0800 027 7766) or on their website.

WHO TO APPLY TO 25 Soho Square, London W1D 4FF *Tel* 020 7534 4210 *Fax* 020 7287 0459 *E-mail* enquiries@footballfoundation.org.uk *Website* www.footballfoundation.org.uk

CC NO 1079309   **ESTABLISHED** 1999

....

■ The Forbes Charitable Trust

WHERE FUNDING CAN BE GIVEN UK.

WHO CAN BENEFIT Charities benefiting people with learning disabilities.

SAMPLE GRANTS £50,000 to CARE Fund; £10,000 to Downs Syndrome Association; £5,000 to L'Arche; £2,000 to Hansel Foundation; £1,000 each to Brainwave, Break, Holm, Anthony Toby Holmes Trust and Merseyside Tuesday and Thursday Club.

FINANCES *Year* 2000–01 *Income* £73,863 *Grants* £72,028 *Assets* £1,743,630

TRUSTEES Colonel R G Wilkes, Chair; Major Gen. R L S Green; J C V Lang; E J Townsend; N J Townsend; C G Packham; J M Waite.

HOW TO APPLY In writing to the correspondent.

WHO TO APPLY TO J B Shepherd, Secretary to the Trustees, 9 Weir Road, Kibworth, Leicestershire LE8 0LQ *Tel* 0116 279 3225 *Fax* 0116 279 6384 *E-mail* jbscarecentral@freeuk.com

CC NO 326476   **ESTABLISHED** 1983

....

■ Forbesville Limited

WHERE FUNDING CAN BE GIVEN UK and overseas.

WHO CAN BENEFIT Children, young adults, students and Jewish people will be considered.

WHAT IS FUNDED Support for orthodox Jewish organisations, educational and charitable institutions.

FINANCES *Year* 2001 *Income* £38,276 *Grants* £58,000

TRUSTEES M Berger, Chair; Mrs J S Kritzler; D B Kritzler.

HOW TO APPLY In writing to the correspondent.

WHO TO APPLY TO M Berger, Chair, Holborn House, 219 Golders Green Road, London NW11 9DD *Tel* 020 8209 0355

CC NO 269898   **ESTABLISHED** 1975

■ The Oliver Ford Charitable Trust

WHERE FUNDING CAN BE GIVEN UK.

WHO CAN BENEFIT Neighbourhood-based community projects, students and institutions. People with mental illness will be considered for funding.

WHAT IS FUNDED The trust aims to educate the general public and advance knowledge of the history and techniques of interior decoration, the design of fabrics and other decorative materials and landscape gardening. Mental disability is also supported.

TYPE OF GRANT One-off.

RANGE OF GRANTS £200–£25,000.

SAMPLE GRANTS £11,820 to Victoria & Albert Museum for student scholarships for people on the MA in the history of design course; £5,800 to Cambridge Mencap; £5,500 to Aldingbourne Trust; £5,000 each to Camphill Communities East Anglia, Fortune Centre of Riding Therapy, Mencap and Wirral Autistic Society; £4,000 to Network; £3,000 to Stockdales; £2,000 to Autism Independent UK and Yarrow Housing Ltd; £1,892 to Scope – Dorset; £1,300 to L'Arche; £1,000 to Norman Laud Association.

FINANCES *Year* 2000–01 *Income* £94,773 *Grants* £89,142 *Assets* £1,648,816

TRUSTEES Derek Hayes; Lady Wakeham; Martin Levy.

HOW TO APPLY In writing to the correspondent. Trustees meet in March and October.

WHO TO APPLY TO Matthew Pintus, Messrs Macfarlanes, 10 Norwich Street, London EC4A 1BD *Tel* 020 7831 9222

CC NO 1026551   **ESTABLISHED** 1993

■ Ford of Britain Trust

WHERE FUNDING CAN BE GIVEN Local to the areas where the company is situated, namely South Wales, Northern Ireland, Merseyside, Southampton, Midlands, Essex and East London.

WHO CAN BENEFIT Organisations benefiting: children; young adults; older people; unemployed people; volunteers; at risk groups; carers; disabled people; people disadvantaged by poverty; ex-offenders and those at risk of offending; homeless people; and victims of crime, domestic violence and abuse.

WHAT IS FUNDED Currently the main areas of interest are children and young people (with emphasis on education, special needs children, youth organisations); community service; disability; social welfare; community arts and recreation; cultural heritage; accommodation and housing; respite care for carers; support and self-help groups; ambulances and mobile units; hospices; and social advice centres.

WHAT IS NOT FUNDED Organisations outside the beneficial area and national charities are rarely assisted, except for specific projects in Ford areas. Applications in respect of individuals (including students), charities requiring funds for overseas projects, and wholly religious or politically orientated projects are ineligible. Major building projects and research projects (including medical) are rarely assisted.

TYPE OF GRANT Capital, buildings, one-off, and start-up costs. Funding is available for one year or less.

RANGE OF GRANTS Most grants range between £100 and £5,000.

SAMPLE GRANTS Recent benficiaries include REACH and sponsorships at Faculty of Engineering – Cambridge University.

FINANCES *Year* 2001–02 *Income* £689,000 *Grants* £454,015 *Assets* £1,200,000

TRUSTEES R G Putnam, Chair; W G F Brooks; M J Callaghan; Prof. S Hochgreb; S McIlveen; I G McAllister; J H M Norris; P G Knight.

HOW TO APPLY In writing to the correspondent. Applications should include the following: purpose of the project; whom it is intended to help and how; why the project is important and necessary (how were things done before); how the project is to be carried out; the project's proposed starting time and time of completion; total cost of the project; how much has been raised so far, sources of funding obtained and expected; examples of fundraising activities by the organisation for the project; the amount being asked for. A brief resumé of the background of the charity is appreciated. Where appropriate copies of accounts should be provided. Trustees meet in March, July and November each year. Applications are considered in order of receipt and it may take several months before an application is considered. The trust receives many more applications than it can help; it received 1,300 in 2001–02.

WHO TO APPLY TO K D Jones, Room 1/602, Ford Motor Company, Central Office, Eagle Way, Brentwood, Essex CM13 3BW *Tel* 01277 252551

CC NO 269410   **ESTABLISHED** 1975

■ Fordeve Ltd

WHERE FUNDING CAN BE GIVEN UK.

WHO CAN BENEFIT Organisations benefiting Jews, at risk groups and people who are unemployed, disadvantaged by poverty or socially isolated. Support may also be given to people who are disabled, homeless, immigrants or refugees.

WHAT IS FUNDED Jewish causes and relief of need.

FINANCES *Year* 1999–2000 *Income* £305,020 *Grants* £413,619 *Assets* £468,665

TRUSTEES J Kon; Mrs H Kon.

HOW TO APPLY In writing to the correspondent.

WHO TO APPLY TO J Kon, Trustee, c/o Gerald Kreditor & Co., Tudor House, Llanvanor Road, London NW2 2AQ *Tel* 020 8209 1535 *Fax* 020 8209 1923

CC NO 1011612   **ESTABLISHED** 1992

■ The Forest Hill Charitable Trust

WHERE FUNDING CAN BE GIVEN UK and overseas.

WHO CAN BENEFIT Organisations and individuals.

WHAT IS FUNDED Christian causes.

SAMPLE GRANTS £5,600 to Great Parks Chapel; £1,000 each to Barnabas Fund, Bethany Ministries, Christ Response, Hope Now, Linx and Treasures in Heaven.

FINANCES *Year* 2001 *Income* £55,000 *Grants* £60,000 *Assets* £1,500,000

TRUSTEES H F Pile, Chair; Mrs P J Pile; R S Pile; Mrs M S Tapper; M Thomas.

HOW TO APPLY In writing to the correspondent; however, the trust has stated that new applications are 'unlikely to succeed'.

WHO TO APPLY TO Mrs P J Pile, Secretary to the Trustees, 104 Summercourt Way, Brixham, Devon TQ5 0RB *Tel* 01803 872857

CC NO 1050862   **ESTABLISHED** 1995

■ The Foresters' Charity Stewards UK Trust

WHERE FUNDING CAN BE GIVEN UK.

WHO CAN BENEFIT Individuals and institutions benefiting older people, disabled people and communities as a whole.

WHAT IS FUNDED To improve quality of life and the environment of the community at large.

RANGE OF GRANTS £50–£750.

SAMPLE GRANTS Previous beneficiaries include AOF Yorkshire Convalescent Home, AOF Foresters' Home, AOF Education Awards Fund, Marwood Guest House, Eastbourne, RNLI, Taste for Adventure, Abbeyfield, Potters Bar, Mayor of Scarborough's Charity and North Middlesex Hospital.

FINANCES *Year* 2001 *Income* £40,728

TRUSTEES A H W Overington; R J Overington; M F Penfold; F G Miller; M Prechner; M S Miller; G Penfold.

HOW TO APPLY In writing to the correspondent.

WHO TO APPLY TO A H W Overington, Springfield, 6 Halstead Road, Winchmore Hill, London N21 3EH

CC NO 328604   ESTABLISHED 1990

■ The Forman Hardy Charitable Trust

WHERE FUNDING CAN BE GIVEN Mostly Nottinghamshire.

WHO CAN BENEFIT Arts, Christian, medical, and welfare organisations.

WHAT IS FUNDED The trust exists to benefit a wide range of charitable activities but primarily focuses on the charitable needs of the city of Nottingham and the county of Nottinghamshire.

WHAT IS NOT FUNDED No grants are made to individuals.

SAMPLE GRANTS £75,000 to Nottingham University; £25,000 to Aysgarth School; £5,000 to Concert 2000; £2,000 to Mencap; £1,600 to Millennium Millions; £1,000 to Galleries of Justice.

FINANCES *Year* 2001–02 *Income* £34,495 *Grants* £89,520 *Assets* £1,530,798

TRUSTEES N J Forman Hardy; J M Forman Hardy; C R Bennion; Canon J E M Neale.

HOW TO APPLY In writing to the correspondent.

WHO TO APPLY TO N J Forman Hardy, Trustee, 64 St James' Street, Nottingham NG1 6FJ *Tel* 0115 950 8580

CC NO 1000687   ESTABLISHED 1990

■ The Donald Forrester Trust

WHERE FUNDING CAN BE GIVEN UK and overseas.

WHO CAN BENEFIT Charities benefiting people who are sick or disabled, particularly older people and children.

WHAT IS FUNDED Mainly health and disability, also animal welfare, heritage and conservation, the arts and overseas aid.

RANGE OF GRANTS £1,000–£10,000.

SAMPLE GRANTS £50,000 to the India Earthquake Appeal; £15,000 to HEAL (Herts, Essex and London) Cancer Charity; £10,000 each to British Heart Foundation, Crossroads – Caring for Carers, Deafblind UK, Help the Aged, League of Friends of the Middlesex Hospital, Motability, NSPCC, and the Samaritans.

FINANCES *Year* 2000–01 *Income* £754,000 *Grants* £720,000 *Assets* £10,000,000

TRUSTEES Anthony Smee; Michael Jones; Wendy Forrester, Chair.

HOW TO APPLY 'Regrettably, applications for aid cannot be considered as this would place an intolerable strain on administrative resources ...'

WHO TO APPLY TO Ms Brenda Ward, 231 Linen Hall, 156–170 Regent Street, London W1R 5TA *Tel* 020 7434 4021

CC NO 295833   ESTABLISHED 1986

■ The Forte Charitable Trust

WHERE FUNDING CAN BE GIVEN UK and overseas.

WHO CAN BENEFIT Community-based projects and national organisations and institutions benefiting primarily children, young adults, disabled people, Roman Catholics and Jewish people.

WHAT IS FUNDED Education, disability, Roman Catholic, Jewish and other charitable purposes.

TYPE OF GRANT One-off.

SAMPLE GRANTS £16,424 to University of Houston; £9,600 to English National Ballet School; £5,700 to Strathclyde University Foundation; £5,000 each to British Sports Trust and Jerusalem Foundation; £2,500 to KIDS; £2,000 each to Ampleforth Abbey Trustees, Dame Vera Lynn Trust for Children with Cerebral Palsey, Royal Hospital for Neuro Disability and World Vision; £1,000 each to CHICKS, Commonwealth Jewish Trust and Holocaust Education Trust.

FINANCES *Year* 2000–01 *Income* £63,092 *Grants* £57,984 *Assets* £2,554,701

TRUSTEES Hon. Sir Rocco Forte; Hon. Mrs Olga Polizzi di Sorrentino; G F L Proctor.

HOW TO APPLY In writing to the correspondent.

WHO TO APPLY TO Mrs Sarah Syborn, Lowndes House, Lowndes Place, Belgrave Square, London SW1X 8DB *Tel* 020 7235 6244 *Fax* 020 7259 5149

CC NO 326038   ESTABLISHED 1982

■ Lord Forte Foundation

WHERE FUNDING CAN BE GIVEN UK.

WHO CAN BENEFIT Educational establishments benefiting those carrying out research in the fields defined below.

WHAT IS FUNDED Educational establishments providing training courses or carrying out research in the field of hotel management and training, and the travel and tourism industries.

SAMPLE GRANTS £35,000 to The Butlers Wharf Chef School; £15,000 to Springboard UK.

FINANCES *Year* 2000–01 *Income* £49,000 *Grants* £51,000 *Assets* £1,600,000

TRUSTEES Lord Janner; Hon. Sir Rocco Forte; Hon. Mrs Olga Polizzi di Sorrentino; Lord Montagu of Beaulieu; Viscount Montgomery; Sir Chips Keswick; G F L Proctor.

HOW TO APPLY In writing to the correspondent.

WHO TO APPLY TO Mrs Sarah Syborn, Lowndes House, Lowndes Place, Belgrave Square, London SW1X 8DB *Tel* 020 7235 6244 *Fax* 020 7259 5149

CC NO 298100   ESTABLISHED 1987

■ The Fortuna Charitable Trust

WHERE FUNDING CAN BE GIVEN South west of England, especially Avon area.

WHO CAN BENEFIT Small local projects, newly established and national organisations benefiting children, young adults, and people with Alzheimer's disease, cancer, hearing loss and heart disease.

WHAT IS FUNDED General charitable purposes for children and youth, including arts, health, community facilities and Christian education.

WHAT IS NOT FUNDED No grants to individuals.

TYPE OF GRANT Small grants.

SAMPLE GRANTS £7,110 to Avon Youth Association; £6,000 each to Greater Bristol Foundation for youth and Valerie Peet Memorial for medical reserach.

FINANCES *Year* 1999 *Income* £6,900 *Grants* £38,620

TRUSTEES A V Tidmarsh; J N Tidmarsh.

HOW TO APPLY Unsolicited applications will not be acknowledged. The funds of this trust are fully committed and further applications are not requested.

WHO TO APPLY TO T Makorby, 8 Prince's Buildings, Clifton, Bristol BS8 4LB *Tel* 0117 973 0462 *Fax* 0117 970 6649

CC NO 291741   **ESTABLISHED** 1984

■ Foundation for Management Education

WHERE FUNDING CAN BE GIVEN UK.

WHO CAN BENEFIT UK business schools and management studies departments benefiting young adults, older people and students.

WHAT IS FUNDED Improvement of quality and relevance of management education and development, by encouraging and supporting innovation in management education in the leading UK business schools and colleges; enhancing the supply and quality of management teachers; encouraging the development of research into management education and teaching methods; and supporting innovative developments in management education for managers operating within a highly competitive environment.

WHAT IS NOT FUNDED Individual applications for further studies cannot be entertained.

SAMPLE GRANTS In 1998–99: £10,000 to Durham University; £9,820 to Bristol University; £6,668 to Leeds University.

FINANCES *Year* 2000–01 *Income* £69,444

HOW TO APPLY Unsolicited applications are not encouraged.

WHO TO APPLY TO Dr Brian A W Redfern, Director & Secretary, 29 Beaumont Street, Oxford OX1 2NP *Tel* 01865 310570 *E-mail* fme@online.net

CC NO 313388   **ESTABLISHED** 1960

■ Four Acre Trust

WHERE FUNDING CAN BE GIVEN Worldwide.

WHO CAN BENEFIT Charities benefiting at risk groups and carers, and people who are disadvantaged by poverty, disabled, homeless, socially isolated people or living in urban areas.

WHAT IS FUNDED Supporting charities that provide a service to individuals, including holiday and respite care, respite care and care for carers, vocational training, holidays and outings. Funding is given to property infrastructure costs, specific programme costs and core costs.

WHAT IS NOT FUNDED The trust does not support the following: animal welfare; arts; basic services (as opposed to imaginative new projects) for people who are disabled or elderly; commercial publications; conferences or seminars; direct replacement of statutory funding; establishing funds for scholarships or loans; expeditions;

general appeals; heritage; hospices; individual; individual parish churches; large UK-charities which enjoy wide support, including local branches of UK-charities; medical (including research), general healthcare or costs of individual applicants; night shelters; overseas travel, conference attendance or exchanges; performances, exhibitions or festivals; projects concerning drug abuse or alcoholism; religious activities; science; sports; stage, film or television production costs; university or similar research. The trust does not make loans, or give grants retrospectively. Grants are not given towards any large capital, endowment or widely distributed appeal. It would consider a specific item, or project, making part of a large appeal.

TYPE OF GRANT Provision of premises; project; capital; interest-free loans; and one-off funding.

RANGE OF GRANTS £1,000–£120,000.

SAMPLE GRANTS £121,590 to Brighton YMCA for provision of premises; £25,000 each to Prince's Royal Trust for Carers and Young Carers Home Start; £10,000 to YHA for 'Give Us A Break' scheme; £6,000 to Northam Lodge for holidays for adults with learning difficulties; £5,530 to BREAK to update facilities at a holiday centre; £5,000 each to Ashoka (UK) Trust towards support for social entrepreneur in Sotuh Africa, and Raleigh International; £3,100 to Barnstonddale Centre (for outdoor centre facilities).

FINANCES *Year* 2001–02 *Income* £411,863 *Grants* £418,964 *Assets* £2,778,414

TRUSTEES Mary A Bothamley; Jennifer J Bunner; John P Bothamley; Robert L Carruthers.

HOW TO APPLY In writing to the correspondent. Trustees meet in March, June, September and December. Applications should be kept brief and received one month before the meeting. The trust does not welcome telephone calls.

WHO TO APPLY TO The Trustees, 56 Leslie Grove, Croydon CRO 6TG *Tel* 020 8680 3100 *E-mail* info@fouracretrust.org.uk *Website* www.fouracretrust.org.uk

CC NO 1053884   **ESTABLISHED** 1996

■ The Four Lanes Trust

WHERE FUNDING CAN BE GIVEN Basingstoke and Deane District Council area.

WHO CAN BENEFIT Organisations benefiting people of all ages; actors and entertainment professionals; musicians; textile workers and designers; writers and poets; at risk groups; those disadvantaged by poverty; and socially isolated people.

WHAT IS FUNDED Charities working in the fields of information technology and computers; publishing and printing; community development; support to voluntary and community organisations and volunteers; professional bodies; charity or voluntary umbrella bodies; arts, culture and recreation; health facilities and buildings; schools and colleges; community issues; development proposals; various community facilities and services; and other charitable purposes will be considered. Personal and small initiatives are particularly welcomed.

WHAT IS NOT FUNDED No grants to individuals or for general appeals.

TYPE OF GRANT Buildings, capital, core costs, one-off, project, running costs, recurring costs, salaries and start-up costs. Funding for up to three years will be considered.

RANGE OF GRANTS £100–£2,000.

FINANCES *Year* 1999 *Income* £44,000
Grants £61,000 *Assets* £1,158,000
TRUSTEES Hon. Dwight Makins; Hon. Virginia
Shapiro; E I Roberts; Mrs G Evans.
HOW TO APPLY In writing to the correspondent. There
is no application form. Initial telephone calls
welcome.
WHO TO APPLY TO Bob Carr, 5 Ferguson Close,
Basingstoke, Hampshire RG21 3JA *Tel* 01256
477990 *Fax* 01256 477990
E-mail bobcarr@fourlt.fsnet.org.uk
Website www.fourlanestrust.org.uk
CC NO 267608   **ESTABLISHED** 1974

■ Four Winds Trust

WHERE FUNDING CAN BE GIVEN UK.
WHO CAN BENEFIT National and local, registered
charities.
WHAT IS FUNDED Conservation of the countryside and
to give those living in cities a better chance to
enjoy nature and the countryside.
WHAT IS NOT FUNDED No grants for individuals,
capital projects, buildings, expeditions or
overseas projects.
TYPE OF GRANT Project.
RANGE OF GRANTS £300–£6,300.
SAMPLE GRANTS In 1999: £1,500 to Harvest Trust;
£1,000 each to Birmingham PHAB, Community
Link Newham, Bedford Nursery School Farm,
Farms for City Children, National Trust and
Steatham Youth Centre; £800 to Scottish
Wildlife Trust; £750 each to Calvert Trust, Eden
Community Outdoors, National Trust for
Scotland and Rockingham Estate Play
Association.
FINANCES *Year* 2001 *Income* £23,102
TRUSTEES Mrs Libby Insall, Chair; Mrs Jane
Simmons; Mrs Elizabeth Hambly; Mrs Katharine
Charity; Jonathan Gillett; Mrs Loveday Craig-
Woods; Mrs L Holmes.
HOW TO APPLY In writing to the correspondent. This
entry was not confirmed by the trust, but the
information was correct according to the trust's
file at the Charity Commission.
WHO TO APPLY TO Mrs Jane Simmons, Secretary,
Woodlands, Park Lane, Alston, Cumbria CA9
3AB *Tel* 01434 381338
E-mail mail@theraise.freeserve.co.uk
CC NO 223794   **ESTABLISHED** 1943

■ The Four Winds Trust

WHERE FUNDING CAN BE GIVEN Worldwide.
WHAT IS FUNDED Christian and overseas aid
organisations, but grants are also given to
retired evangelists and to missionaries and their
dependants.
SAMPLE GRANTS £4,400 to Counties; £2,300 to
Impact; £1,900 to Action Partners; £1,200 to
Tearfund.
FINANCES *Year* 2000–01 *Income* £125,000
Grants £23,000 *Assets* £629,000
TRUSTEES P A Charters; M E Charters; P J Charters;
S V Charters; J Charters; F M Charters.
HOW TO APPLY The trust was set up for purposes in
which the trustees have a personal interest and
the funds are earmarked for these purposes.
Unsolicited requests are unlikely to be
considered.
WHO TO APPLY TO P A Charters, Trustee, Four Winds,
Church Lane, Ashbury, Swindon SN6 8LZ
Tel 01793 710431
CC NO 262524   **ESTABLISHED** 1971

■ The Fowler Memorial Trust

WHERE FUNDING CAN BE GIVEN Essex.
WHO CAN BENEFIT Essex registered charities.
WHAT IS FUNDED General charitable purposes.
WHAT IS NOT FUNDED No grants outside Essex. No
grants to individuals.
RANGE OF GRANTS £1,000–£5,400.
SAMPLE GRANTS In 1998–99: £5,400 to Raleigh
International; £3,000 to Imperial Cancer
Research Fund and RNLI; £2,000 to The
Salvation Army and Royal Agricultural
Benevolent Association; £1,175 to Royal
Thames Youth Training; £1,000 to Eastwood
Parochial Church Council and St David's
Parochial Church Council.
FINANCES *Year* 2001–02 *Income* £110,838
Grants £65,000
TRUSTEES W J Tolhurst, Chair; P J Tolhurst.
OTHER INFORMATION No recent information was
available on beneficiaries.
HOW TO APPLY In writing to the correspondent.
WHO TO APPLY TO Mrs Alix Mason, 3rd Floor,
Marlborough House, Victoria Road South,
Chelmsford, Essex CM1 1LN *Tel* 01245
216100
CC NO 269782   **ESTABLISHED** 1975

■ The Fox Memorial Trust

WHERE FUNDING CAN BE GIVEN UK.
WHO CAN BENEFIT General charities benefiting:
people of all ages who are carers; disabled
people; people disadvantaged by poverty; at risk
groups; disaster victims; ex-offenders and those
at risk of offending; victims of crime and abuse;
animals and wildlife, birds, ecology.
WHAT IS FUNDED Support will be given to
conservation and environment, health and
various community facilities and services.
Grants may be given towards costs of study and
voluntary organisations. Other general charitable
purposes will be considered.
RANGE OF GRANTS £250–£3,000; typical grant £500.
SAMPLE GRANTS £5,000 to City of London Sinfonia;
£1,400 to Follifoot Park Disabled Riders Group.
FINANCES *Year* 2001–02 *Income* £128,722
Grants £119,403 *Assets* £1,526,081
TRUSTEES Mrs S M F Fitton; Mrs F M F Le Masurier;
Miss A M Fox.
HOW TO APPLY In writing to the correspondent. Initial
telephone calls are not necessary. An sae will
guarantee a response.
WHO TO APPLY TO Mrs C Hardy, Administrator,
Hangover House, 3 Burford Lane, East Ewell,
Surrey KT17 3EY
CC NO 262262   **ESTABLISHED** 1970

■ The Foyle Foundation

WHERE FUNDING CAN BE GIVEN Unrestricted.
WHO CAN BENEFIT Registered charities and state
schools.
WHAT IS FUNDED Learning; the arts; and health.
WHAT IS NOT FUNDED Once a major award has been
made the trust will not normally accept any
further applications from the same charity for
three years. No grants to individuals. No
retrospective funding.
RANGE OF GRANTS Usually £5,000–£50,000.
SAMPLE GRANTS £500,000 to King's College part of
a four -year commitment of £2 million for the
creation of the Foyle Special Collections Library;
£200,000 to the Book Trade Benevolent Society
for its King's Langley Estate; £98,000 to the
Royal Geographical Society; £75,000 to English

Think carefully about every application. Is it justified?

479

National Opera; £70,000 to Spitalfields Festival; £50,000 each to Almeida Theatre, Deaf/Blind UK and Wessex Autistic Society; £40,000 to Motor Neurone Disease Association; £20,000 to Cystic Fibrosis Trust.

FINANCES Year 2001–02 Grants £1,800,000 Assets £50,000,000

TRUSTEES Silas Krendel, Chair; Michael Smith; Kathryn Skoyles.

HOW TO APPLY Application forms are available from the correspondent and via the foundation's website, as are checklists and guidelines for applicants. All applications will be acknowledged within two weeks and all eligible applications should be processed within four months.

WHO TO APPLY TO David Hall, Chief Executive, First Floor Rugby Chambers, 2 Rugby Street, London WC1N 3QU *Tel* 020 7430 9119 *Website* www.foylefoundation.org.uk

CC NO 1081766   **ESTABLISHED** 2000

■ The Charles Henry Foyle Trust

WHERE FUNDING CAN BE GIVEN UK, particularly south west Birmingham and north east Worcestershire.

WHO CAN BENEFIT Registered charities for new projects, benefiting children and adults, students, at risk groups, and people who are disadvantaged by poverty or sickness.

WHAT IS FUNDED General charitable purposes, particularly to encourage new forms of social work, research into social conditions and education and improvement of educational facilities. Also the provision of medical, dental and nursing facilities for the working classes, the assistance of junior or adult education, and the encouragement of educational travel.

WHAT IS NOT FUNDED Generally no grants are given outside the beneficial area with the exception of medical degrees which are considered nationally (for two years pre-clinical/intercalated/elective periods only).

TYPE OF GRANT Project, research and start-up costs.

RANGE OF GRANTS Below £500–£6,000.

SAMPLE GRANTS £6,000 to Friends of Victoria School; £2,000 each to Advance Housing & Support Ltd, Birmingham Conservation Trust, Huntington's Disease Association, Pershore Theatre Arts Association, and Whizz-Kidz; £1,090 to Relate – Birmingham; £1,000 each to Birmingham Botanical, Birmingham Habitat for Humanity, Big Brum Theatre in Education and Volunteer Reading Help – Birmingham Branch.

FINANCES Year 2001–02 Income £102,197 Grants £71,649 Assets £943,112

TRUSTEES Michael Francis, Chair; Roger K Booth; Mrs Bridget Morris; Prof. Rae Mackay; Paul R Booth.

HOW TO APPLY In writing to the correspondent.

WHO TO APPLY TO Mrs P Elvins, Trust Administrator, c/o Boxfoldia Ltd, Merse Road, Redditch, Worcestershire B98 9HB *Tel* 01527 64191 *Fax* 01527 68810 *E-mail* admin@foyletrust.org.uk

CC NO 220446   **ESTABLISHED** 1940

■ The Timothy Franey Charitable Foundation

WHERE FUNDING CAN BE GIVEN Mainly UK, although approximately 10% goes on overseas support. There is a small preference for south east London.

WHO CAN BENEFIT Organisations benefiting: children and young adults; people who are unemployed or disadvantaged by poverty; victims of abuse; victims of war; and people with cancer, hearing loss, HIV and AIDs, motor neurone disease and sight loss.

WHAT IS FUNDED Charities working in the fields of: music; arts education and activities; hospices; hospitals; cancer research; and holidays and outings.

WHAT IS NOT FUNDED No grants to individuals. The trust stated 'we mainly support registered charities, or work with them in funding specific situations and projects'.

TYPE OF GRANT One-off, core costs and running costs. Funding for up to two years will be considered.

RANGE OF GRANTS £100–£10,000.

SAMPLE GRANTS £44,000 to Anita Goulden Trust to for work in Peru caring for underprivileged and disabled children.

FINANCES Year 2001–02 Income £28,645 Grants £82,392 Assets £393,437

TRUSTEES Timothy Franey; Wendy Ann Franey; Samantha Richmond.

HOW TO APPLY Application by e-mail only. Further information will be requested by the trust if required. Applications in writing or by phone will not be considered.

WHO TO APPLY TO T Franey, Trustee, 32 Herne Hill, London SE24 9QS *E-mail* info@franeyfoundation.com

CC NO 802189   **ESTABLISHED** 1987

■ The Isaac and Freda Frankel Memorial Charitable Trust

WHERE FUNDING CAN BE GIVEN UK and overseas, particularly Israel.

WHO CAN BENEFIT Established organisations benefiting children, young adults and people disadvantaged by poverty. People of many different religions and cultures will be funded, but preference is given to Jewish people.

WHAT IS FUNDED Jewish charities, medicine and health, education, religion and the relief of poverty.

WHAT IS NOT FUNDED No grants to individuals or students, for expeditions or scholarships.

TYPE OF GRANT One-off and recurrent grants.

RANGE OF GRANTS £1,000 or less.

FINANCES Year 2001–02 Income £87,906

TRUSTEES M D Frankel; G Frankel; G J Frankel.

OTHER INFORMATION No information was available on beneficiaries.

HOW TO APPLY In writing to the correspondent.

WHO TO APPLY TO M D Frankel, Secretary, c/o Messrs Davis Frankel Mead, 33 Welbeck Street, London W1G 8LX *Tel* 020 7872 0023

CC NO 1003732   **ESTABLISHED** 1991

■ The Jill Franklin Trust

WHERE FUNDING CAN BE GIVEN Worldwide.

WHO CAN BENEFIT Charitable organisations, not necessarily registered charities, benefiting: disabled people; carers; ex-offenders and those at risk of offending; people with a mental illness; refugees.

WHAT IS FUNDED Current concerns are: advice, training and employment and self-help groups to support people with a mental illness or learning difficulties and their carers; respite care and holidays (in the UK only); special development projects in the Commonwealth with low overheads; organisations helping and supporting refugees coming to or in the UK – organisations based outside the UK should have a contact in the UK which can be approached; restoration (not improvement) of churches of architectural importance.

WHAT IS NOT FUNDED Grants are not given to: both branches of a UK organisation and its centre (unless it is a specific grant, probably for training in the branches); building appeals or endowment funds; encourage the 'contract culture', particularly where authorities are not funding the contract adequately; religious organisations set up for welfare, education and so on, of whatever religion, unless the users of the service are from all denominations, and there is no attempt whatsoever to conduct any credal propaganda or religious rituals; restoration; 'heritage schemes'; animals; students or any individuals or for overseas travel; medical research.

TYPE OF GRANT One-off, project, recurring costs, running costs and start-up costs. Funding for up to three years will be considered.

RANGE OF GRANTS Generally £500.

SAMPLE GRANTS In 2000–01: £9,000 to Camden City Islington and Westminister Bereavement Services; £1,000 each to Asylum Aid, BIA/ Quaker Social Action, Live Music Now!, Medical Foundation for Victims of Torture, Oxfam, Regugee Council and Scottish Refugee Council; £500 each to Book Aid International, and Sefton Children's Trust.

FINANCES *Year* 2001–02 *Income* £65,620 *Grants* £57,000 *Assets* £1,427,000

TRUSTEES Andrew Franklin; Norman Franklin; Sally Franklin; Sam Franklin; Tom Franklin.

PUBLICATIONS *Guidelines.*

HOW TO APPLY In writing to the correspondent, including the latest annual report, accounts and budget, and a clear statement of purpose. The trustees tend to look more favourably on an appeal which is simply and economically prepared rather than glossy, 'prestige' and mailsorted brochures. Many worthy applications are rejected simply due to a lack of funds. No acknowledgement is given to unsolicited enquiries, except where an sae is enclosed.

WHO TO APPLY TO N Franklin, Trustee, 78 Lawn Road, London NW3 2XB *Tel* 020 7722 4543 *Fax* 020 7722 4543 *E-mail* lawnroad@blueyonder.co.uk

CC NO 1000175   **ESTABLISHED** 1988

■ Sydney E Franklin Deceased's New Second Charity

WHERE FUNDING CAN BE GIVEN Worldwide. Priority, but not exclusively, to developing world projects.

WHO CAN BENEFIT Smaller charities with low overheads dealing with third world self-help projects or endangered species. Funding may be given to people disadvantaged by poverty and victims of famine, man-made or natural disasters and war.

WHAT IS FUNDED Mainly small charities with low overheads; focusing on third world self-help projects, endangered species and people disadvantaged by poverty.

WHAT IS NOT FUNDED No grants to individuals or for scholarships. No grants to large or umbrella charities. No grants to religious sectarism specfic charities.

TYPE OF GRANT One-off and project grants.

RANGE OF GRANTS £500–£7,000; typical grant £500–£3,000.

SAMPLE GRANTS £4,000 to Kerala Federation for the Blind for a South Indian group helping people who are blind; £2,500 to Womenkind Worldwide to support women's rights globally; £2,000 to Water for Kids for water/sanitation to third world children; £1,000 each to Survival International to support indigenous peoles, Tree Aid, Children of the Andes, Approriate Technology for Tibet, and Books Abroad – all supporting developing world projects to improve life of poverty.

FINANCES *Year* 2001–02 *Income* £27,500 *Grants* £32,000 *Assets* £632,000

TRUSTEES Dr R C G Franklin; Ms T N Franklin; Ms C Holliday.

HOW TO APPLY Donations may only be requested by letter, and these are placed before the trustees at their meeting which is normally held at the end of each year. Applications are not acknowledged.

WHO TO APPLY TO Dr R C G Franklin, Trustee, c/o 39 Westleigh Avenue, London SW15 6RQ

CC NO 272047   **ESTABLISHED** 1973

■ The Emily Fraser Trust

WHERE FUNDING CAN BE GIVEN UK with a preference for Scotland.

WHO CAN BENEFIT Funding is primarily given to individuals and organisations benefiting older people and people disadvantaged by poverty.

WHAT IS FUNDED Grants are made primarily to individuals connected to the drapery and allied trades and printing, publishing and allied trades in Scotland, but are also given to small charities which are dedicated to relieving poverty, illness and the condition of older people. Other charitable purposes are considered.

WHAT IS NOT FUNDED Applicants already receiving grants from the Hugh Fraser Foundation (see separate entry) will not be eligible.

SAMPLE GRANTS £7,000 to Sue Ryder Foundation; £5,000 each to Communicability and Manic Depression Fellowship Scotland; £3,000 to Brainwave; £2,500 to Age Concern Orkney; £2,000 each to Springburn Youth and Community Project (the final one of these grants), and Govan Society of Weavers (the second one of three)

FINANCES *Year* 1999–2000 *Income* £89,660 *Grants* £81,000 *Assets* £2,308,258

TRUSTEES Dr Kenneth Chrystie, Chair; Hon. Ann Fraser; Patricia Fraser; Blair Smith.

HOW TO APPLY In writing to the correspondent. The trustees meet quarterly to consider applications. In 2000 the meetings were held in July/August and the end of January, April and October. The trustees of this trust are also the trustees of the Hugh Fraser Foundation and applications are allocated to one or other of the trusts as appears appropriate.

WHO TO APPLY TO Heather Thompson, Trust Administrator, Turcan Connell, Princes Exchange, 1 Earl Grey Street, Edinburgh EH3 9EE *Tel* 0131 228 8111 *Fax* 0131 228 8118 *E-mail* lk@turcanconnell.com
SC NO SC007288   ESTABLISHED 1971

■ The Gordon Fraser Charitable Trust

WHERE FUNDING CAN BE GIVEN UK, with some preference for Scotland.
WHO CAN BENEFIT Registered charities.
WHAT IS FUNDED At present the trustees are particularly interested in help for children and young people, the environment and in assisting organisations associated with the arts. Other charitable purposes will also be considered.
WHAT IS NOT FUNDED No grants are made to organisations which are not recognised charities, or to individuals.
TYPE OF GRANT Grants are usually one-off, though funding for up to three years may be considered.
RANGE OF GRANTS £100–£12,000, typical grant £250–£750.
SAMPLE GRANTS £12,000 to Dulwich Picture Gallery; £6,000 each to Ballet West and MacRobert Arts Centre; £5,000 each to Scottish Museums Council and Lochaber Music Charitable Trust; £4,000 to National Library of Scotland; £3,000 each to Royal Botanic Garden Edinburgh and Royal Scottish National Orchestra; £2,000 to Scottish Opera; £1,000 each to Queen Margaret University College, Scottish National Portrait Gallery and Waverley Care Trust.
FINANCES *Year* 2001–02 *Income* £100,596 *Grants* £149,160 *Assets* £2,538,974
TRUSTEES Mrs M A Moss; W F T Anderson.
HOW TO APPLY In writing to the correspondent. Applications are considered in January, April, July and October. Grants towards national or international emergencies can be considered at any time. All applicants are acknowledged; an sae would therefore be appreciated.
WHO TO APPLY TO Mrs M A Moss, Trustee, Holmhurst, Westerton Drive, Bridge of Allan, Stirling FK9 4QL
CC NO 260869   ESTABLISHED 1966

■ The Hugh Fraser Foundation

WHERE FUNDING CAN BE GIVEN UK, especially western or deprived areas of Scotland.
WHO CAN BENEFIT Registered charities.
WHAT IS FUNDED Medical facilities and research; relief of poverty and assistance for older and infirm people; education and learning; provision of better opportunities for people who are disadvantaged; music and the arts; encouragement of personal development and training of young people.
WHAT IS NOT FUNDED Grants are not awarded to individuals. Major highly publicised appeals are rarely supported.
TYPE OF GRANT One-off, project, recurring costs and start-up costs.
RANGE OF GRANTS Largest £100,000.
SAMPLE GRANTS £100,000 each to the Scottish Science Trust and South Ayrshire Council for Alexander Goudie paintings; £50,000 to Capability Scotland.
FINANCES *Year* 2000–01 *Income* £1,255,381 *Grants* £1,178,000 *Assets* £31,246,202

TRUSTEES Dr Kenneth Chrystie, Chair; Hon. Ann Fraser; Miss Patricia Fraser; Blair Smith.
OTHER INFORMATION The trustees are also trustees of the Emily Fraser Trust. Applications are allocated to one or other of the trusts as appears appropriate, whichever trust receives the application.
HOW TO APPLY In writing to the correspondent. The trustees meet on a quarterly basis to consider applications.
WHO TO APPLY TO Heather Thompson, Turcan Connell, Princes Exchange, 1 Earl Grey Street, Edinburgh EH3 9EE *Tel* 0131 228 8111 *Fax* 0131 228 8118
E-mail enquiries@turcanconnell.com
SC NO SC009303   ESTABLISHED 1960

■ The Joseph Strong Frazer Trust

WHERE FUNDING CAN BE GIVEN England and Wales only.
WHO CAN BENEFIT Registered charities only.
WHAT IS FUNDED General charitable purposes.
WHAT IS NOT FUNDED No grants to individuals.
TYPE OF GRANT One-off, capital and recurring costs.
SAMPLE GRANTS £30,000 to Royal Agricultural Benevolent Institution; £10,000 to Childrens Hospice in Wales Appeal Limited; £8,000 to Royal Merchant Navy School Foundation; £6,000 each to Bearwood College Charitable Bursary Fund and Boar Bank Nursing Home; £5,500 to MHOSLJ Charitable Trust; £5,000 each to Downside Settlement, LXIX Charitable Trust, MS Multiple Sclerosis Society and National Botanic Garden of Wales.
FINANCES *Year* 2000–01 *Income* £516,201 *Grants* £643,550 *Assets* £9,297,296
TRUSTEES Sir William A Reardon Smith, Chair; D A Cook; R M H Read; W N H Reardon Smith.
HOW TO APPLY In writing to the correspondent. Trustees meet twice a year, usually in March and September. Application forms are not necessary. It is helpful if applicants are concise in their appeal letters, which must include an sae if acknowledgement is required.
WHO TO APPLY TO The Correspondent, Scottish Provident House, 31 Mosley Street, Newcastle Upon Tyne NE1 1HX *Tel* 0191 232 8065 *Fax* 0191 222 1554
CC NO 235311   ESTABLISHED 1940

■ The Louis Freedman Charitable Settlement

WHERE FUNDING CAN BE GIVEN UK, especially Burnham in Buckinghamshire.
WHO CAN BENEFIT National and local (Burnham in Buckinghamshire) charities.
WHAT IS FUNDED Health, welfare and equine interests in which the Freedman family have a particular interest. Local education and youth charities are also supported.
WHAT IS NOT FUNDED No grants to individuals. Only registered charities are considered for support.
RANGE OF GRANTS £50–£5,000.
SAMPLE GRANTS £15,000 each to Tavistock Trust for Aphasia and Winged Fellowship.
FINANCES *Year* 2001–02 *Income* £95,000 *Grants* £47,000 *Assets* £2,900,000
TRUSTEES M A G Ferrier; F H Hughes.
HOW TO APPLY There is no application form. Applications should be in writing to the correspondent and they will not be acknowledged.

■ The Thomas Freke & Lady Norton Charity

WHERE FUNDING CAN BE GIVEN The parishes of
Hannington, Inglesham, Highworth, Stanton
Fitzwarren, Blunsdon St Leonards and Castle
Eaton.

WHO CAN BENEFIT Local communities and
organisations benefiting children, young adults
and Christians.

WHAT IS FUNDED Buildings or equipment for
churches, schools, youth and community
facilities. The trust is willing to consider
emergency or unforeseen expenditure. Funding
may also be given to community centres, village
halls, recreation grounds and sports centres.

WHAT IS NOT FUNDED No grants are given for ordinary
running expenses. No applications from outside
the beneficial area can be considered.

TYPE OF GRANT Capital.

SAMPLE GRANTS In 1998–99: £45,000 to St
Andrew's Primary School, Blunsden towards
school redevelopment; £15,000 to St Michael's
Church, Highworth for church hall improvements;
£11,250 to Warneford School, Highworth
towards computer work stations; £9,500 to
Warneford School towards a new minibus;
£5,670 to Westrop School, Highworth towards a
school library; £4,980 to St John the Baptist
Church, Hannington for church and churchyard
maintenance; £2,753 to Westrop School for a
computer bay; £1,276 to Stanton Fitzwarren
Village Hall for door and drainage repairs; £796
to Southfield School, Highworth towards
furniture for the school library; £183 to
Southfield School towards fitments for the
school library.

FINANCES Year 2000–01 Income £109,703
Grants £100,000 Assets £2,550,560

TRUSTEES Mrs M G Hussey-Freke; Mrs V J Davies;
Dr K T Scholes; J M E Scott; E R Cole.

HOW TO APPLY In writing to the correspondent for
help with capital projects such as buildings or
equipment, or with emergency or unforeseen
expenditure. Clear outline details of the project
or circumstances are required, together with a
reliable estimate of the cost and a statement of
the funds in hand or anticipated from other
sources. The trustees meet at least four times
a year at irregular intervals.

WHO TO APPLY TO B T Compton, Century House,
Hannington, Swindon, Wiltshire SN6 7RT
Tel 01793 762088
CC NO 200824   ESTABLISHED 1990

■ The Anne French Memorial Trust

WHERE FUNDING CAN BE GIVEN Diocese of Norwich.

WHO CAN BENEFIT Christians, clergy and local
charities.

WHAT IS FUNDED Any charitable purpose in the
beneficial area, especially church-related
causes.

TYPE OF GRANT One-off, project, research and
feasibility.

RANGE OF GRANTS £30–£15,000.

SAMPLE GRANTS £21,000 was given to Norwich and
Norfolk charities; the rest was given to
members of the clergy as holiday gifts,
parsonages for repairs and maintenance,

members of the clergy for general purposes,
and for other church-related purposes.

FINANCES Year 2001–02 Income £214,000
Grants £182,000 Assets £4,273,000

TRUSTEES Lord Bishop of Norwich.

HOW TO APPLY In writing to the correspondent. The
trust states: 'In no circumstances does the
Bishop wish to encourage applications for
grants other than those which are dealt with
locally.'

WHO TO APPLY TO C H Dicker, c/o Lovewell Blake,
Sixty Six, North Quay, Great Yarmouth, Norfolk
NR30 1HE Tel 01493 335100 Fax 01493
335133 E-mail chd@lovewell-blake.co.uk
CC NO 254567   ESTABLISHED 1963

■ The Charles S French Charitable Trust

WHERE FUNDING CAN BE GIVEN UK, in practice north
east London and south west Essex.

WHO CAN BENEFIT Charities, especially children's
charities, and charities in Essex, East Anglia
and north east London area. Also charities
benefiting older people, disabled people, people
who are homeless, victims of abuse and victims
of crime.

WHAT IS FUNDED General purposes, including
community services and facilities, hospices and
hospitals, heritage.

WHAT IS NOT FUNDED Registered charities only.

TYPE OF GRANT Capital including buildings.

FINANCES Year 2000–01 Income £201,404
Grants £177,350 Assets £5,858,966

TRUSTEES W F Noble; R L Thomas; D B Shepherd.

HOW TO APPLY In writing to the correspondent,
including a copy of the latest accounts.

WHO TO APPLY TO R L Thomas, Trustee, 169 High
Road, Loughton, Essex IG10 4LF Tel 020 8502
3575
CC NO 206476   ESTABLISHED 1959

■ The Freshfield Foundation

WHERE FUNDING CAN BE GIVEN UK.

WHO CAN BENEFIT All applications considered.

WHAT IS FUNDED General charitable purposes.

SAMPLE GRANTS £3,000,000 to Formby Land Trust
for the purchase of land to house a swimming
pool for local residents; £191,421 to Centre for
Tomorrow's Children; £94,000 to Osteopathic
Centre for Children; £60,000 to Soil Associaton;
£40,000 each to Friends of the Earth and
Sustrans; £38,102 to Cree Valley Community
Woodland Trust; £27,500 to New Economic
Foundation; £10,000 each to Formby High
School and Southport Pier; £2,000 to
Architecture Foundation.

FINANCES Year 2000–01 Grants £3,513,000

TRUSTEES P A Moores; A Moores; Mrs E J Potter.

HOW TO APPLY In writing to the correspondent.

WHO TO APPLY TO Peter Turner, 2nd Floor ,
MacFarlane and Co., Cunard Building, Water
Street, Liverpool L3 1DS Tel 0151 236 6161
CC NO 1003316   ESTABLISHED 1991

■ The Freshgate Trust Foundation

WHERE FUNDING CAN BE GIVEN Mainly Sheffield and
South Yorkshire.

WHO CAN BENEFIT Organisations benefiting: people of
all ages; actors and entertainment
professionals; musicians; textile workers and
designers; writers and poets; at risk groups;

Think carefully about every application. Is it justified?

483

people disadvantaged by poverty and socially isolated people. Both innovatory and established bodies may be considered.

WHAT IS FUNDED Local appeals working in the fields of: education (including travel and training); medical (both psychological and physical); recreation; music and arts; welfare and social care; heritage.

WHAT IS NOT FUNDED The trust restricts its grants to UK charitable organisations and does not deal with applications from individuals, national appeals or for church fabric unless used for a wider community purpose.

TYPE OF GRANT Capital (including buildings), core costs, endowments, feasibility studies, interest free loans, one-off, project, research, running costs, recurring costs, salaries and start-up costs. Funding for up to three years will be considered.

SAMPLE GRANTS £6,000 each to St Mary's Community Centre and Sheffield Botanical Gardens Trust; £3,700 to Boys' Club of South Yorkshire and Humberside; £3,300 each to Brown Bayleys Steel Ltd – Pensioners and Sheffield Family Holiday Fund; £2,500 each to Enable, Relate and Sheffield Family Service Unit and £2,000 to Sheffield & District YMCA.

FINANCES *Year* 2000 *Income* £121,000 *Grants* £95,000 *Assets* £3,100,000

TRUSTEES M P W Lee, Chair; H Bull; Dr F P A Garton; Mrs J Haigh; J F B Hopkins; J E Parkin; A J Coombe; Miss E Murray; D R Stone.

HOW TO APPLY In writing to the correspondent, by early February, June and October each year. Applications are not normally acknowledged.

WHO TO APPLY TO Jonathan Robinson, Secretary, 346 Glossop Road, Sheffield, South Yorkshire S10 2HW *Tel* 0114 273 8551 *Fax* 0114 276 0934 **CC NO** 221467 **ESTABLISHED** 1962

■ The Friarsgate Trust

WHERE FUNDING CAN BE GIVEN UK, with a strong preference for East and West Sussex, especially Chichester.

WHO CAN BENEFIT UK and East and West Sussex organisations, especially those already supported by the trust.

WHAT IS FUNDED General charitable purposes, especially education and welfare of children and young people and care of people who are elderly or in need.

WHAT IS NOT FUNDED Local organisations outside Sussex are unlikely to be supported.

RANGE OF GRANTS £200–£3,000.

SAMPLE GRANTS £2,600 each to Arthritis and Rheumatism Council, Children Family's Trust, Friends of Chichester Hospitals, Institute of Ophtalmology, and St Christopher's Fellowship.

FINANCES *Year* 1998–99 *Income* £60,000 *Grants* £52,000 *Assets* £2,500,000

TRUSTEES R F Oates; Miss Amanda King-Jones.

HOW TO APPLY In writing to the correspondent. Applicants are welcome to telephone first to check they fit the trust's criteria.

WHO TO APPLY TO Miss Amanda King-Jones, Trustee, The Corn Exchange, Bassins Lane, Chichester, West Sussex PO19 1EG *Tel* 01243 786111 **CC NO** 220762 **ESTABLISHED** 1955

■ Friends of Biala Ltd

WHERE FUNDING CAN BE GIVEN UK and overseas.

WHO CAN BENEFIT Jewish organisations and registered charities.

WHAT IS FUNDED Religious institutions of the orthodox Jewish faith, and the relief of poverty.

FINANCES *Year* 2001–02 *Income* £564,552 *Grants* £70,000

TRUSTEES B Z Rabinovitch; Mrs T Weinberg.

OTHER INFORMATION Up to date information on beneficiaries was not available.

HOW TO APPLY In writing to the correspondent. This entry was not confirmed by the trust but the information was correct according to the Charity Commission.

WHO TO APPLY TO The Secretary, c/o 5 Rodsley Avenue, Gateshead NE8 4JY **CC NO** 271377 **ESTABLISHED** 1964

■ The Friends of Essex Churches

WHERE FUNDING CAN BE GIVEN The diocese of Chelmsford.

WHO CAN BENEFIT Any Christian church.

WHAT IS FUNDED Churches, irrespective of denomination, where the repairs necessary are beyond parish resources.

WHAT IS NOT FUNDED Grants are only permitted by charter for fabric repairs; thus work on decorations, bells and organs cannot be helped. No grants to individuals or for new work.

TYPE OF GRANT One-off (but may apply again in subsequent years) and buildings.

RANGE OF GRANTS £250–£20,000 (from Special Projects Fund).

FINANCES *Year* 2001 *Income* £242,800 *Grants* £194,650 *Assets* £511,800

PUBLICATIONS *Essex Churches and Chapels.*

HOW TO APPLY In writing to the correspondent. Application forms will be sent to those applying for a grant.

WHO TO APPLY TO Mrs M S Blaxall, 5 Brookhurst Close, Springfield Road, Chelmsford, Essex CM2 6DX *Tel* 01245 354745 *Website* www.foec.org.uk **CC NO** 236033 **ESTABLISHED** 1952

■ The Friends of Kent Churches

WHERE FUNDING CAN BE GIVEN County of Kent, particularly the dioceses of Canterbury and Rochester.

WHO CAN BENEFIT Churches of architectural merit and historical interest.

WHAT IS FUNDED The upkeep of their fabric and the preservation of fixtures of importance.

WHAT IS NOT FUNDED No grants towards redecoration, heating, lighting or organ repairs.

TYPE OF GRANT Building. Interest-free loans are considered.

RANGE OF GRANTS £250–£8,000.

SAMPLE GRANTS In 1999: £5,000 to St Mary the Blessed Virgin (Woodbesborough); £4,000 to St Mary of Charity (Faversham); £3,500 to All Saints (Iwade); £3,000 each to All Saints (Wouldham), All Saints (Boughton), Holy Cross (Goodnestone), St Mary (Goudhurst) and St Peter (Bekesbourne).

FINANCES *Year* 2001 *Income* £125,493 *Grants* £92,500

TRUSTEES R Anderson; C Banks; Mrs G Bracher; Mrs L M Clark; L M Clark; G Colvile; Canon Redman; T Monckton; P Morrish; Mrs A Neame; C Oliver; Dr J Physick; Hon. Mrs J Raikes; P Smallwood; A Wells; A Parish; N B Whitehead.

HOW TO APPLY In writing to the correspondent.
WHO TO APPLY TO Mrs Alysoun Carey, Coldharbour Farm, Rosemary Lane, Smarden, Kent TN27 8PF
CC NO 207021   **ESTABLISHED** 1950

....

■ Friends of Wiznitz Limited
WHERE FUNDING CAN BE GIVEN UK and overseas.
WHO CAN BENEFIT Registered charities.
WHAT IS FUNDED General support to charitable institutions.
SAMPLE GRANTS £220,000 to Yeshivath Wiznitz; £46,000 to Ahavas Israel Synagogue; £22,000 to CMA Trust.
FINANCES *Year* 1999–2000 *Income* £410,644 *Grants* £288,050 *Assets* £307,793
TRUSTEES H Feldman; E Kahan; R Bergmann; S Feldman.
HOW TO APPLY In writing to the correspondent.
WHO TO APPLY TO E Gottesfeld, 8 Jessam Avenue, London E5 9UD
CC NO 255685   **ESTABLISHED** 1948

....

■ The Frognal Trust
WHERE FUNDING CAN BE GIVEN UK.
WHO CAN BENEFIT Registered charities benefiting older people and people with disabilities or sight loss.
WHAT IS FUNDED The trustees current grant-making policy is to make relatively small grants to as many qualifying charities as possible. Particularly charities working in the fields of: residential facilities and services; cultural heritage; hospices; nursing homes; ophthalmological research; conservation; heritage; parks; and community services. Other charitable purposes will be considered.
WHAT IS NOT FUNDED The trust does not support: any animal charities; the advancement of religion; charities for the benefit of people outside the UK; educational or research trips; branches of national charities; general appeals; individuals.
TYPE OF GRANT Buildings, capital, one-off, research and start-up costs will be considered.
RANGE OF GRANTS £200–£3,500.
SAMPLE GRANTS £3,500 to Climb; £3,000 to Camphill Community Clanabogan; £2,625 to Cystic Fibrosis Trust; £2,000 each to Enham Trust, Norman Laud Association, and Who Cares Trust; £1,550 each to Herefordshire Nature Trust Ltd and Rockingham Forest Trust; £1,500 each to Arthritis Care, and Umbrella.
FINANCES *Year* 2001–02 *Income* £54,446 *Grants* £77,339 *Assets* £108,254
TRUSTEES Philippa Blake-Roberts; J P Van Montagu; P Fraser.
HOW TO APPLY In writing to the correspondent. Applications should be received by January, April, August or October, for consideration at the trustees' meeting the following month.
WHO TO APPLY TO Mrs Sue David, Donor Grants Officer, Charities Aid Foundation, King's Hill, West Malling, Kent ME19 4TA *Tel* 01732 520083 *Fax* 01732 520001
CC NO 244444   **ESTABLISHED** 1964

....

■ The Patrick Frost Foundation
WHERE FUNDING CAN BE GIVEN Worldwide, but only through UK charities.
WHO CAN BENEFIT Registered charities.
WHAT IS FUNDED The relief and welfare of people of small means and the less fortunate members of society, and assistance for small organisations

where a considerable amount of self-help and voluntary effort is required.
WHAT IS NOT FUNDED No grants to individuals or non-UK charities.
TYPE OF GRANT One-off donations.
RANGE OF GRANTS Mainly £5,000 or less.
SAMPLE GRANTS £15,000 each to Acorn Christian Foundation, Family Holiday Association and Universities Settlement in East London; £10,000 each to Action for Blind People, Intermediate Technology, Lifestyle, Medical Foundation for the Care of Victims of Torture, Naomi House, Opportunity International and Tools for Self Reliance.
FINANCES *Year* 2000–01 *Income* £174,954 *Grants* £201,500 *Assets* £1,386,975
TRUSTEES Mrs Helena Frost; Donald Jones; Luke Valner; John Chedzoy.
HOW TO APPLY In writing to the correspondent, accompanied by the last set of audited accounts. The trustees regret that due to the large number of applications they receive, they are unable to acknowledge unsuccessful applications.
WHO TO APPLY TO Mrs H Frost, Trustee, c/o Trowers & Hamlins, Sceptre Court, 40 Tower Hill, London EC3N 4DX *Tel* 020 7423 8000 *Fax* 020 7423 8001
CC NO 1005505   **ESTABLISHED** 1991

....

■ T F C Frost Charitable Trust
WHERE FUNDING CAN BE GIVEN UK and overseas.
WHO CAN BENEFIT Research associates of recognised centres of excellence in ophthalmology.
WHAT IS FUNDED Research in ophthalmology by establishing research fellowships and supporting specific projects.
WHAT IS NOT FUNDED There are no available resources for the relief of blind people or people suffering from diseases of the eye.
RANGE OF GRANTS £6,000–£38,000.
SAMPLE GRANTS In 1999–2000: £38,016 to Jules Stein Eye Institute, Los Angeles; £37,853 to Bascom Palmer Eye Institute, Florida; £34,179 to UMDS Guy's & St Thomas's Hospital; £15,587 to Moorfields Eye Hospital; £13,125 to Salisbury Health Care NHS Trust; £12,725 to Institute of Ophthalmology & Schepens Eye Research Institute, Boston; £10,000 to University of Bristol; £6,385 to Nuffield Laboratory of Ophthalmology.
FINANCES *Year* 2000–01 *Income* £116,000
TRUSTEES Mrs S E Frost; T A F Frost; M D Sanders; M H Miller.
HOW TO APPLY In writing to the correspondent. Trustees meet twice a year.
WHO TO APPLY TO Holmes & Co Accountants, 10 Torrington Road, Claygate, Esher, Surrey KT10 0SA *Tel* 01372 465378
CC NO 256590   **ESTABLISHED** 1966

....

■ Maurice Fry Charitable Trust
WHERE FUNDING CAN BE GIVEN UK and overseas.
WHO CAN BENEFIT Registered charities benefiting at risk groups, and people disadvantaged by poverty or socially isolated. Support is given to medical professionals, research workers, scientists, academics and writers and poets. Support may also be given to refugees, and victims of famine, man-made or natural disasters and war.
WHAT IS FUNDED General charitable purposes. Currently the main areas of interest are welfare,

....

humanities, environmental resources, and international causes.
WHAT IS NOT FUNDED No grants to individuals.
RANGE OF GRANTS £250–£2,500.
SAMPLE GRANTS £2,500 each to Intermediate Technology and Marie Stopes International; £2,000 each to ChildLine, Friends of the Earth, The Link Camden, Medical Foundation for the Care of Victims of Torture and National Childbirth Trust; £1,000 each to Amnesty International UK Section Charitable Trust, Children's Country Holidays Fund and The Island Trust.
FINANCES *Year* 2000–01 *Income* £23,932 *Grants* £40,000
TRUSTEES L E A Fry; Miss A Fry; Mrs F Cooklin; Mrs L Weaks.
HOW TO APPLY The trust states that it does not respond to unsolicited applications.
WHO TO APPLY TO L Fry, Trustee, 98 Savernake Road, London NW3 2JR *Tel* 020 7267 4969
CC NO 327934   **ESTABLISHED** 1988

....

■ Mejer and Gertrude Miriam Frydman Foundation

WHERE FUNDING CAN BE GIVEN UK and overseas.
WHO CAN BENEFIT Organisations benefiting children, young adults, students, teachers and governesses. Support is given to Jewish people, and particular favour is given to Jewish charities.
WHAT IS FUNDED New and established charitable projects for study and research, including scholarships, fellowships, professorial chairs, lectureships, prizes, awards and the cost of purchasing or erecting any building or land required for such projects. Support in these areas is given to organisations and institutions only. Individuals are not supported under any circumstances.
WHAT IS NOT FUNDED Applications from individuals for scholarships or any other type of grant.
RANGE OF GRANTS £300–£6,500.
SAMPLE GRANTS £6,500 to Friends of Ohel Torah Trust; £5,000 to British Friends of Lanaido Hospital Sanz Medical Centre; £4,000 to North West London Jewish Day School; £3,000 to Medical Aid Fund for Israel; £2,000 each to Classic Charitable Trust and Friends of Yeshiva Keren B'Yaunah; £1,000 each to Pardes House Grammar School and Yeshivath Meharash Engel Radomishl; £800 to Joint Jewish Charitable Trust; £750 to Kesser Torah.
FINANCES *Year* 1999–2000 *Income* £30,507 *Grants* £26,050 *Assets* £76,578
TRUSTEES L J Frydman; G B Frydman; D H Frydman.
HOW TO APPLY In writing to the correspondent.
WHO TO APPLY TO G Frydman, Trustee, c/o Messrs Westbury Schotness & Co., 145–157 St John Street, London EC1V 4PY
CC NO 262806   **ESTABLISHED** 1971

....

■ The Fulmer Charitable Trust

WHERE FUNDING CAN BE GIVEN Worldwide, especially the developing world and Wiltshire.
WHO CAN BENEFIT Registered charities worldwide, especially in the developing world and Wiltshire.
WHAT IS FUNDED General charitable purposes.
WHAT IS NOT FUNDED No support for gap year requests.
RANGE OF GRANTS £500–£5,000, but mostly £1,000–£3,000.

SAMPLE GRANTS £5,000 to European Children's Trust; £3,500 to Ethiopiaid; £3,300 to UFM; £3,000 to Jacorander Home Appeal; £2,800 each to ITDG, Sight Savers International, SOS Children's Village, Tearfund, UNICEF and Wiltshire Community Foundation.
FINANCES *Year* 2000–01 *Income* £110,479 *Grants* £117,844 *Assets* £1,639,518
TRUSTEES S A Reis; C M Mytum.
HOW TO APPLY In writing to the correspondent.
WHO TO APPLY TO J S Reis, Chair, Estate Office, Street Farm, Compton Bassett, Calne, Wiltshire SN11 8SW *Tel* 01249 760410
CC NO 1070428   **ESTABLISHED** 1998

....

■ Fund for Human Need

WHERE FUNDING CAN BE GIVEN Overseas.
WHO CAN BENEFIT Organisations benefiting: victims of famine; refugees; people who are socially isolated and disadvantaged by poverty; and at risk groups. Support may also be given to disaster victims, homeless people and victims of war.
WHAT IS FUNDED The relief of hunger, distress, poverty, deprivation and oppression in any part of the world without consideration of creed, race or politics.
WHAT IS NOT FUNDED No grants for UK projects.
RANGE OF GRANTS Project support for a limited number of organisations; distress grants of up to £100 which will solve a particular problem.
SAMPLE GRANTS £6,000 to Church Commission for Overseas Students; £5,150 to Colon School – Panama for scholarship.
FINANCES *Year* 2001–02 *Income* £37,886 *Grants* £33,431 *Assets* £90,680
HOW TO APPLY In writing to the correspondent.
WHO TO APPLY TO The Secretary, 25 Marylebone Road, London NW1 5TR
CC NO 208866   **ESTABLISHED** 1960

....

■ Furlongs Fund

WHERE FUNDING CAN BE GIVEN UK and overseas.
WHO CAN BENEFIT Charitable organisations.
WHAT IS FUNDED General charitable purposes.
SAMPLE GRANTS £3,000 to Eating Disorders Association; £2,500 to Psychiatric Rehabilitation Association; £2,000 each to Christian Outreach and Prison Reform Trust; £1,250 each to Albion Kids Show, B I A Quaker Social Action and Invalids at Home.
FINANCES *Year* 2000 *Income* £26,000 *Grants* £26,000
TRUSTEES Diana Cavendish, Chair; Jonathan Cavendish; Lesley Cavendish; Nicholas Crace; Brigid Crace; Christopher Crace; Louise Hutley.
HOW TO APPLY Please note, this trust's policy is to give to charities known to the trustees, which over the years has been refined to a regular list of beneficiaries. It would therefore appear to be pointless for you to apply. It states: 'We rarely accept unsolicited applications, simply because we do not have the money, and any new grant means that an existing beneficiary has to be thrown out.'
WHO TO APPLY TO Nicholas Crace, Secretary, Shadwells, The Lynch, Overton, Hampshire RG25 3DQ *Tel* 01256 770797
CC NO 260029   **ESTABLISHED** 1969

....

486

....

■ Worshipful Company of Furniture Makers Charitable Fund

WHERE FUNDING CAN BE GIVEN UK.

WHAT IS FUNDED Causes directly connected to furniture, such as running high quality courses to bring together and train people in the industry, funding design competitions, prototypes and visits to exhibitions or factories and offering bursaries to students at colleges.

SAMPLE GRANTS £34,000 to Castle Howard Arboretum for the furniture makers' walk and visitor centre; £10,000 to Wallace Collection Design Prize; £8,500 to Retail Management Development Course; £7,000 to Student Industrial Tour; £4,125 to Rycote College Residential Course for young manufactors; £3,315 to Craft Guildmark Seminar; £2,500 to Hans Jourdan Management Course for Manufacturing Excellence; £2,000 towards a seminar guildmark holders; £1,500 to London Guildhall University for a travel award; £1,000 to Design Trust.

FINANCES *Year* 1999–2000 *Income* £167,776 *Grants* £82,254 *Assets* £1,208,616

TRUSTEES Patrick V Radford; R B C Waring; Sir John Perring.

HOW TO APPLY In writing to the correspondent.

WHO TO APPLY TO Mrs J A Wright, Painters' Hall, 9 Little Trinity Lane, London EC4V 2AD *Tel* 020 7248 1677 *Fax* 020 7248 1688 *E-mail* clerk@furnituremkrs.co.uk *Website* www.furnituremkrs.co.uk

CC NO 270483   **ESTABLISHED** 1975

Think carefully about every application. Is it justified?

487

■ Gableholt Limited

WHERE FUNDING CAN BE GIVEN UK.

WHO CAN BENEFIT Jewish organisations.

WHAT IS FUNDED Advancement of the orthodox Jewish faith.

FINANCES *Year* 1999–2000 *Income* £343,638 *Grants* £70,618 *Assets* £3,491,478

TRUSTEES S Noe; Mrs E Noe; C Lerner; P Noe.

HOW TO APPLY In the past this trust has stated that 'in the governors' view, true charitable giving should always be coupled with virtual anonymity' and for this reason they are most reluctant to be a party to any publicity. Along with suggesting that the listed beneficiaries might also want to remain unidentified, they also state that the nature of the giving (to orthodox Jewish organisations) means the information is unlikely to be of much interest to anyone else. Potential applicants would be strongly advised to take heed of these comments.

WHO TO APPLY TO M A Vemitt, Governor, 115 Craven Park Road, London N15 6BL

CC NO 276250   **ESTABLISHED** 1978

■ The Horace & Marjorie Gale Charitable Trust

WHERE FUNDING CAN BE GIVEN UK, mainly Bedfordshire.

WHO CAN BENEFIT Registered charities, with a preference for Bedfordshire-based charities.

WHAT IS FUNDED Churches and church ministries, community life in Bedfordshire and general charitable purposes.

WHAT IS NOT FUNDED Grants are rarely given to individuals.

RANGE OF GRANTS £500–£11,000.

SAMPLE GRANTS £9,000 to Bunyan Meeting Free Church; £3.000 to Bedford Hospital Department of Rheumatology; £2,000 each to Bedford Hospital Trust Endowment Fund – Primrose Oncology Appeal, Bedford Modern School – Gale Prize Fund, St Peter's Church – Bedford; £1,500 to Baptist Union – Home Mission Fund; £1,000 each to Bedfordshire Victim Support, Brainwave, British Kidney Patients Association, Cancer Research UK, Children's Heart Foundation, Leukaemia Research, Mayday Trust, National Asthma Campaign, National Autistic Society and Whizz Kids.

FINANCES *Year* 2000–01 *Income* £231,233 *Grants* £50,300 *Assets* £1,803,865

TRUSTEES G D Payne, Chair; J Tyley; J Williams; P H Tyley; K Fletcher.

HOW TO APPLY In writing to the correspondent. Grants are distributed once a year and applications should be made by September; for consideration in November.

WHO TO APPLY TO Gerry Garner, Garner Associates, 138 Bromham Road, Bedford MK40 2QW *Tel* 01234 354508

CC NO 289212   **ESTABLISHED** 1984

■ The Angela Gallagher Memorial Fund

WHERE FUNDING CAN BE GIVEN UK and international organisations based in the UK.

WHO CAN BENEFIT Registered charities benefiting: children; Christians; Roman Catholics; and those suffering from paediatric diseases. Support will also go to people disadvantaged by poverty; people with disabilities; victims famine and disasters; and victims of abuse.

WHAT IS FUNDED The aim of the fund is to help children within the UK. The fund will also consider Christian, humanitarian and educational projects worldwide. Particularly charities working in the fields of: special needs education; day centres; holidays and outings; and Catholic bodies. Small charities which do not have access to large corporate donors are given priority. International disasters are aided by way of CAFOD and Red Cross only.

WHAT IS NOT FUNDED Donations will not be made to the following: older people; scientific research; hospitals and hospices; artistic and cultural appeals; animal welfare; or building and equipment appeals. No grants to individuals.

TYPE OF GRANT One-off grants for core costs.

RANGE OF GRANTS Usually £500–£1,000.

SAMPLE GRANTS In 1999: Three grants of £1,000 to CAFOD for disasters and emergencies; £3,000 to Grace & Compassion Benedictines for Indian project; £1,000 each to AMREF for general work in Africa, Autism – Bedfordshire for general funding, C-Far for general funding, Lady Hoare Trust, Christina Noble Children's Fund for general funding, Novo Futuro for Portuguese Child Project, St Loyes Foundation, and Uganda Disabled Children.

FINANCES *Year* 2001 *Income* £39,157 *Grants* £30,500 *Assets* £1,011,000

TRUSTEES N A Maxwell-Lawford; P Mostyn; P A Wolrige Gordon; A Swan.

HOW TO APPLY In writing to the correspondent, for consideration at trustees' meetings twice a year. Applicants must include a set of accounts or the appeal will not be considered. Applications are not acknowledged without an sae.

WHO TO APPLY TO Mrs D R Moss, Secretary, Church Cott, The Green, Mirey Lane, Woodbury, Nr Exeter, Devon EX5 1LT

CC NO 800739   **ESTABLISHED** 1989

■ The Gamma Trust

WHERE FUNDING CAN BE GIVEN UK, with a possible preference for Scotland.

WHO CAN BENEFIT Registered charities.

WHAT IS FUNDED General charitable purposes, especially cultural heritage, healthcare and medical research.

WHAT IS NOT FUNDED No grants to individuals.

TYPE OF GRANT Project, research and recurring costs.

FINANCES *Year* 1998 *Grants* £54,000

HOW TO APPLY In writing to the correspondent for consideration quarterly.

WHO TO APPLY TO The Manager, Clydesdale Bank, Trust & Executry Unit, Brunswick House, 51 Wilson Street, Glasgow G1 1UZ *Tel* 0141 223 2507

SC NO SC004330

■ The Gannochy Trust

WHERE FUNDING CAN BE GIVEN Scotland, with a preference for the Perth area.

WHO CAN BENEFIT Primarily charities (must be recognised as charitable by the Inland Revenue) benefiting children and young adults, but also older people, at risk groups, and people who are disabled, disadvantaged by poverty or socially isolated.

WHAT IS FUNDED The main object is the needs of youth and recreation, with grants categorised as social welfare, recreation, education, arts, health, and environment.

WHAT IS NOT FUNDED No grants to individuals. Donations are confined to organisations recognised by the Inland Revenue as charitable.

TYPE OF GRANT One-off, capital, revenue, loans.

SAMPLE GRANTS £617,000 to Perth & Kinross Recreational Facilities for development of the Gannochy sports centre, other capital costs and for sports coaching; £250,000 to Stirling University for the pool at its new national swimming academy; £190,000 to Kincarrathie Home for the Elderly, Perth to upgrade the facilities; £150,000 to Maggie Jencks Cancer Centre, Dundee; £115,000 to Perth Theatre for refurbishment; £100,000 each to Dementia Services Development Trust for a building at Stirling University, Salvation Army to redevelop their Perth citadel, Dundee University for a microscope at the Tayside Institute of Child Health, Perth and Kinross Heritage Trust, Pitlochry Festival Theatre for a plant collectors garden and Glasgow University for its new medical school building.

FINANCES *Year* 2000–01 *Income* £4,700,000 *Grants* £4,164,000 *Assets* £129,000,000

TRUSTEES Dr Russell Leather, Chair; Mark Webster; James A McCowan; Dr James H F Kynaston; Dr James Watson.

HOW TO APPLY In writing to the correspondent, confined to two pages of A4 including a general statement on the objects of the applicant's charity; the specific nature of the application; the estimated cost and how this is arrived at; the contribution of the applicant's charity towards the cost; the contributions of others, actual and promised; estimated shortfall; details of previous appeals to the trust – whether accepted or rejected; a copy of the latest audited accounts. It is the practice of the trustees to scrutinise accounts before making donations. The trustees meet frequently, generally monthly, to consider appeals.

WHO TO APPLY TO Mrs Jean Gandhi, Secretary, or Murdoch M MacKenzie, Administrator, Kincarrathie House Drive, Pitcullen Crescent, Perth PH2 7HX *Tel* 01738 620653

SC NO SC003133 **ESTABLISHED** 1937

■ The Ganzoni Charitable Trust

WHERE FUNDING CAN BE GIVEN Mainly Suffolk.

WHO CAN BENEFIT Registered charities.

WHAT IS FUNDED General charitable purposes.

WHAT IS NOT FUNDED Grants to individuals will not be considered. Applications from outside Suffolk are not normally considered and will not be acknowledged.

TYPE OF GRANT A number of the grants are recurring, the remainder will normally be one-off.

RANGE OF GRANTS £50–£12,000.

SAMPLE GRANTS £25,000 to the Friends of St Mary-le-Tower Church; £12,000 to St Mary-le-Tower Church (including £5,000 to the organist); £10,000 each to St Luke's Hospital for the Clergy and Suffolk Scouts for Sparks Appeal; £2,000 to St Elizabeth Hospice.

FINANCES *Year* 2001–02 *Income* £98,000 *Grants* £83,000 *Assets* £1,977,000

TRUSTEES Hon. Mary Jill Ganzoni, Lord Belstead; Stephen Wilson; Hon. Charles Boscawen.

HOW TO APPLY In writing to the correspondent. Telephone calls not encouraged. There are no application forms, guidelines or deadlines. No sae is required unless material is to be returned.

WHO TO APPLY TO S R M Wilson, Trustee, Messrs Birketts, 24–26 Museum Street, Ipswich IP1 1HZ *Tel* 01473 232300

CC NO 263583 **ESTABLISHED** 1971

■ The Gapper Trust

WHERE FUNDING CAN BE GIVEN UK.

WHO CAN BENEFIT Organisations previously selected by the trustees.

WHAT IS FUNDED The trust gives 'education' and 'community' donations.

WHAT IS NOT FUNDED No support for individuals or organisations not previously selected by the trustees.

FINANCES *Year* 2001–02 *Income* £26,300

TRUSTEES R P Gapper; Mrs R F Gapper; Mrs M C Gapper.

HOW TO APPLY **This trust states that it does not respond to unsolicited applications.**

WHO TO APPLY TO R P Gapper, Trustee, 12 Officers Terrace, Historic Dockyard, Chatham, Kent ME4 4LJ

CC NO 328623 **ESTABLISHED** 1990

■ The Worshipful Company of Gardeners of London

WHERE FUNDING CAN BE GIVEN Mainly City of London.

WHO CAN BENEFIT Horticultural organisations.

WHAT IS FUNDED The fund supports charitable activities connected with horticulture in all its forms and within the City of London.

RANGE OF GRANTS £200–£10,000.

SAMPLE GRANTS £2,600 to Society for Horticultural Therapy; £2,500 to London Children's Flower Society; £2,300 to City & Guilds of London Institution; £1,900 to the Lord Mayor's Appeal; £1,500 each to Metropolitan Public Gardens Association and Gardening for the Disabled; £1,200 to Flowers in the City.

FINANCES *Year* 1999–2000 *Income* £55,700 *Grants* £47,300 *Assets* £324,000

TRUSTEES Alan D Wiltshire; Alan K Edwards; Thomas Hugh Edwards; Mrs Janet Owens.

HOW TO APPLY In writing to the correspondent.

WHO TO APPLY TO Col. N G S Gray, 25 Luke Street, London EC2A 4AR *Tel* 020 7739 8200

CC NO 222079 **ESTABLISHED** 1962

■ The Garnett Charitable Trust

WHERE FUNDING CAN BE GIVEN South west England and Northern Ireland.

WHO CAN BENEFIT Registered charities.

WHAT IS FUNDED Health, hospices, environmental causes and animal welfare groups, arts, culture and recreation.

WHAT IS NOT FUNDED No grants to individuals.

RANGE OF GRANTS £5–£10,000.

SAMPLE GRANTS £2,500 each to Irish Youth Foundation and Irish Fund GB; £2,000 to Royal Opera House Trust; £1,500 to Schumacher

College; £1,000 each to Irish Studies Centre, Design Museum and DLRM.
FINANCES *Year* 2001 *Income* £16,000 *Grants* £44,000 *Assets* £291,000
TRUSTEES A J F Garnett; Mrs P Garnett; Mrs S Brown.
HOW TO APPLY In writing to the correspondent.
WHO TO APPLY TO Mrs Sandra Brown, Osborne Clarke Solicitors, 2 Temple Back East, Bristol BS1 6EG *Tel* 0117 917 3022
CC NO 327847   **ESTABLISHED** 1988

■ Garrick Charitable Trust

WHERE FUNDING CAN BE GIVEN UK.
WHO CAN BENEFIT Registered charities.
WHAT IS FUNDED Institutions which are seeking to further theatre (including dance), literature or music.
FINANCES *Grants* £300,000
OTHER INFORMATION The trust was established by the members of the Garrick Club in London in 1998. It was expected to be endowed with about £4 million from the proceeds of selling the Winnie the Pooh copyright to the Disney organisation. The trust is able to spend interest on capital.
HOW TO APPLY Initial approaches should be made in writing to the correspondent.
WHO TO APPLY TO The Secretary, 15 Garrick Street, London WC2E 9AY *Tel* 020 7836 1737 *Fax* 020 7379 5966
CC NO 1071279   **ESTABLISHED** 1998

■ Garthgwynion Charities

WHERE FUNDING CAN BE GIVEN Primarily the parishes of Isygarreg and Uwchygarreg at Machynlleth, Powys.
WHO CAN BENEFIT Organisations benefiting people who are ill, at risk groups and people who are disadvantaged by poverty or socially isolated.
WHAT IS FUNDED Main areas of interest are: (a) the leading national charities conducting research into cancer, sight or disorders of the nervous system; (b) community projects or individuals with a Welsh (better still, Mid-Wales) link, having either a social or artistic purpose.
RANGE OF GRANTS £250–£30,000.
SAMPLE GRANTS £30,000 to Machynlleth Tabernacle Trust.
FINANCES *Year* 2001–02 *Income* £53,000 *Grants* £73,000
TRUSTEES Mrs E R Lambert; D H O Owen; E C O Owen.
HOW TO APPLY In writing to the correspondent.
WHO TO APPLY TO The Secretary, 13 Osborne Close, Hanworth, Middlesex TW13 6SR *Tel* 020 8890 0469
CC NO 229334   **ESTABLISHED** 1963

■ Garvan Limited

WHERE FUNDING CAN BE GIVEN UK.
WHO CAN BENEFIT Jewish organisations.
FINANCES *Year* 2000–01 *Income* £235,598 *Grants* £170,480 *Assets* £339,324
TRUSTEES A Ebert; L Ebert.
HOW TO APPLY In writing to the correspondent.
WHO TO APPLY TO S Ebert, Flat 9, Windsor Court, Golders Green Road, London NW11 9PP
CC NO 286110   **ESTABLISHED** 1980

■ The Gatsby Charitable Foundation

WHERE FUNDING CAN BE GIVEN Unrestricted.
WHO CAN BENEFIT Registered charities only.
WHAT IS FUNDED Technical education – to support improvement in educational opportunity in the UK for a workforce which can better apply technology for wealth creation and to encourage effective technology transfer from universities and other research centres to productive industry; plant science – to develop basic research in fundamental processes of plant growth and development and molecular plant pathology and to encourage young researchers in this field in the UK and support improved introduction to the world of plants within school science teaching; cognitive neuroscience – to support world-class research in UK centres of excellence; mental health – to improve the quality of life for people with long-term problems by improved delivery of services; disadvantaged children – to explore new approaches to identifying and removing barriers to personal development; social renewal – to support new approaches to problems which can create social exclusion; developing countries – to promote environmentally sustainable development and poverty alleviation through selected programmes aimed at supporting basic agriculture and other enterprise in selected African countries; the arts – to support the fabric and programming of institutions with which Gatsby's founding family has long connections; economic and social research – to support institutions and individual studies which can help to understand and improve our society. Occasionally support is given to other charitable work which falls outside these main fields of interest.
WHAT IS NOT FUNDED Generally, the trustees do not make grants in response to unsolicited applications or to individuals.
TYPE OF GRANT One-off and recurring grants.
SAMPLE GRANTS £3,407,000 to the Sainsbury Laboratory at the John Innes Centre in Norwich; £2,289,618 to Sainsbury Centre for Mental Health; £1,544,671 to Royal Academy of Engineering towards the best programme, industrial studentships and the development of other training opportunities in engineering, science and life science programmes; £1,500,000 to Better Engineering Students Today programme administered by the Royal Academy of Engineering; £1,352,645 to Gatsby Technical Education Projects towards the science enhancement programme, mathematics primary programme, Gatsby teacher fellowships, teacher effectiveness enhancement programme, early years programme ad core costs; £1,309,000 to National Children's Bureau; £1,031,000 to Gatsby Computational Neuroscience Unit at University College London; £464,259 to Sainsbury Centre for the Visual Arts; £450,000 to the Schools Learning Together Programme run by the City of York Council; £338,380 to International Centre of Insect Physiology.
FINANCES *Year* 2000–01 *Income* £30,419,000 *Grants* £30,550,000 *Assets* £487,839,000
TRUSTEES Christopher Stone; Andrew Cahn; Miss Judith Portrait.
OTHER INFORMATION The trust is one of the Sainsbury Family Charitable Trusts which share a common administration. An application to one is taken as an application to all.
HOW TO APPLY Proposals are generally invited by the trustees or initiated at their request. Unsolicited

applications are nort encouraged and are unlikely to be successful.

WHO TO APPLY TO Michael Pattison, Director, Allington House, 1st Floor, 150 Victoria Street, London SW1E 5AE *Tel* 020 7410 0330 *Website* www.gatsby.org.uk

CC NO 251988   **ESTABLISHED** 1967

....

■ **Gatwick Airport Community Trust**

WHERE FUNDING CAN BE GIVEN Sussex, Surrey and Kent from Reigate in the north to Haywards Heath in the south and Tunbridge Wells in the east to Cranleigh in the west.

WHO CAN BENEFIT Environmental and community projects in the area of benefit.

WHAT IS FUNDED Projects funded could include: projects that are of special help to different sections of the community such as people who are young, disabled or elderly; projects which benefit community life or improve community facilities; arts, cultural or sports projects; or environmental and conservation schemes.

WHAT IS NOT FUNDED No grants to individuals.

TYPE OF GRANT Preference for project or capital, or development aspect.

RANGE OF GRANTS £250–£5,000. Average £1,000.

SAMPLE GRANTS Major grants ranging from £2,500 to £3,500 went to: a local residents association for a skateboard park and youth shelter; a cancer contact organisation for furniture and equipment; YMCA towards a gym for people with physical/learning disabilities; a local primary school for computers; a heritage school for an outdoor leisure project for children with physical/learning disabilities; a day centre for a physical and mental health improvement project for people with learning difficulties; Crimestoppers for drug awareness presentations to 11–14 year olds; a children's nursery towards relocation/survival costs; community transport for Dial-a-Ride facilities for people with disabilities; and a trust for young people for extension to campsite sanitary facilities.

FINANCES *Year* 2002 *Income* £120,000 *Grants* £100,000

TRUSTEES Christopher Lowe, Chair; Kay Hammond; Andy Kynoch; Neil Matthewson; John Mortimer; Marian Myland; George Pixley; Mike Roberts.

HOW TO APPLY Application forms are available by contacting the trust in writing or by telephone. Applications are considered once a year.

WHO TO APPLY TO P O Box 102, Crawley, West Sussex RH10 9WX *Tel* 01293 449147

CC NO 1089683   **ESTABLISHED** 2001

....

■ **The Robert Gavron Charitable Trust**

WHERE FUNDING CAN BE GIVEN UK.

WHO CAN BENEFIT Small charities for children and adults with mental or physical disabilities, ethnic minority groups, and those promoting the arts for young/underprivileged people.

WHAT IS FUNDED The principal fields of interest continue to include the arts, education, social policy and research and charities for people with disabilities. Much of the funding follows the trustees' own charitable involvement. The trust generally makes a small number of substantial grants together with a larger number of smaller donations.

WHAT IS NOT FUNDED The trust does not give donations to individuals or to large national charities.

TYPE OF GRANT One-off; project; research; recurring cost; and salaries. Funding can be given for up to three years.

SAMPLE GRANTS £200,000 to Royal Opera House – the last instalment of a five-year grant; £100,000 to the National Gallery – the fourth instalment of a five-year grant; £50,000 to London School of Economics – the first instalment of a five-year grant; £35,000 to Runnymede Trust; £20,000 each to National Film & TV School Foundation and One World Action; £17,642 to Ashten Trust; £13,423 to New Israel Fund; £11,000 to Open College of the Arts; £10,000 to Breathlessness Research Charitable Trust.

FINANCES *Year* 2000–01 *Income* £562,290 *Grants* £675,235 *Assets* £9,062,538

TRUSTEES Lord Gavron; Charles Corman; Dr. Katharine Gavron; Jessica Gavron; Sarah Gavron.

HOW TO APPLY In writing only to the correspondent. Please enclose a stamped addressed envelope and latest accounts. However, the trust has said that it is fully committed to its existing areas of interest and the trustees would have difficulty in considering further appeals. There are are no regular dates for trustees' meetings, but they take place about six times a year.

WHO TO APPLY TO Mrs Dilys Ogilvie-Ward, Secretary, 44 Eagle Street, London WC1R 4FS *Tel* 020 7400 4300 *Fax* 020 7400 4245

CC NO 268535   **ESTABLISHED** 1974

....

■ **Gederville Ltd**

WHERE FUNDING CAN BE GIVEN UK.

WHAT IS FUNDED Advancement of the orthodox Jewish faith and for general charitable purposes.

FINANCES *Year* 2000–01 *Income* £62,052 *Grants* £300,050 *Assets* £218,985

TRUSTEES Joseph Benedikt; C Benedikt; Jacob Benedikt.

HOW TO APPLY In writing to the correspondent.

WHO TO APPLY TO Y Benedikt, 40 Fontayne Road, London N16 7DT

CC NO 265645   **ESTABLISHED** 1973

....

■ **Jacqueline and Michael Gee Charitable Trust**

WHERE FUNDING CAN BE GIVEN UK.

WHAT IS FUNDED Almost exclusively health and educational charities, including many Jewish organisations. Arts and social welfare causes may be considered.

TYPE OF GRANT Project grants, one-off or long-term.

SAMPLE GRANTS £10,000 to Purcell School; £6,700 to British ORT; £6,000 each to Children's Classic Concerts and Garsington Opera; £3,900 to Nightingale House; £2,500 to Dementia Relief Trust; £2,000 each to Royal Opera House and UJIA.

FINANCES *Year* 2000–01 *Income* £96,736 *Grants* £72,488 *Assets* £38,000

TRUSTEES M J Gee; J S Gee.

HOW TO APPLY In writing to the correspondent.

WHO TO APPLY TO Michael J Gee, Trustee, Flat 27, Berkeley House, 15 Hay Hill, London W1J 8NS *Tel* 020 7493 1904 *Fax* 020 7499 1470 *E-mail* trust@sherman.co.uk

CC NO 1062566   **ESTABLISHED** 1997

■ The General Charities of the City of Coventry

WHERE FUNDING CAN BE GIVEN Within the city boundary of Coventry.

WHO CAN BENEFIT People in need and elderly people; organisations benefiting such people.

WHAT IS NOT FUNDED No grants to organisations outside Coventry, or for holidays unless of a recuperative nature.

SAMPLE GRANTS £42,500 to Coventry Sports Foundation; £10,200 to Coventry Boys' Club.

FINANCES *Year* 2002 *Income* £1,500,000 *Grants* £394,734

TRUSTEES Cllr H Richards; W P Thomson; Mrs E M Rosher; Mrs E Eaves; Cllr Mrs M Lancaster; R Barker; Cllr D S Ewart; T D McDonnell.

HOW TO APPLY In writing to the correspondent. Applications are not accepted directly from the general public for relief in need (individuals).

WHO TO APPLY TO The Clerk, Old Bablake, Hill Street, Coventry CV1 4AN *Tel* 024 7622 2769

CC NO 216235   **ESTABLISHED** 1983

■ The General Nursing Council for England and Wales Trust

WHERE FUNDING CAN BE GIVEN England and Wales.

WHO CAN BENEFIT Universities and other public bodies benefiting nurses.

WHAT IS FUNDED Public bodies undertaking research into matters directly affecting nursing or the nursing profession.

WHAT IS NOT FUNDED No grants to individuals.

TYPE OF GRANT One-off or annually towards research costs.

FINANCES *Year* 2001–02 *Income* £121,338 *Assets* £2,304,693

TRUSTEES Prof. J E Hooper, Chair; Prof. W de Witt; Prof. Rosemary Pope; Prof. Paul Lewis; Mrs Angela Roberts.

HOW TO APPLY In writing to the correspondent, by 30 April for June meeting, by 30 September for November meeting.

WHO TO APPLY TO Mrs P A Bovington, 36 Sunningdale Avenue, Eastcote, Ruislip, Middlesex HA4 9SR *Tel* 020 8868 6259

CC NO 288068   **ESTABLISHED** 1983

■ The Gertner Charitable Trust

WHERE FUNDING CAN BE GIVEN Worldwide.

WHO CAN BENEFIT Jewish people.

WHAT IS FUNDED Jewish organisations and individuals.

TYPE OF GRANT One-off.

SAMPLE GRANTS £250,000 to Kingsley Way Charitable Trust; £87,250 to Yesodey Hatorah – Beth Jacob; £65,500 to RS Trust; £55,136 to American Friends of Yad Aharon; £40,000 to Amuta Lekidum Emtzei Lemida; £39,350 to Kollel Bais Yechiiel; £36,650 to Menorah Grammar School; £36,000 to Gmach Bais Halachmi; £31,700 to Friends of Mir; £30,000 each to Commitee of Holy Sites and Mosdos Ohr Hatorah.

FINANCES *Year* 2000–01 *Income* £1,044,833 *Grants* £1,576,355 *Assets* £1,045,290

TRUSTEES Moises Gertner; Mrs Michelle Gertner; Mendi Gertner; Michael Wechsler; Simon Jacobs.

HOW TO APPLY In writing to the correspondent.

WHO TO APPLY TO Mrs Michelle Gertner, Trustee, Fordgate House, 1 Allsop Place, London NW1 5LF *Tel* 020 7224 1234

CC NO 327380   **ESTABLISHED** 1987

■ J Paul Getty Jr Charitable Trust

WHERE FUNDING CAN BE GIVEN UK.

WHO CAN BENEFIT Charities benefiting mentally ill people; offenders and ex-offenders; people addicted to drugs and alcohol; disadvantaged communities; homeless people; unemployed people; and ethnic minorities.

Priority is likely to be given to projects in the less prosperous parts of the country, particularly outside London and the south east, and to those which cover more than one beneficial area.

WHAT IS FUNDED Projects to do with poverty and misery in general, and unpopular causes in particular. The emphasis is on self-help, building esteem, and enabling people to reach their potential. The trustees favour small community and local projects which make good use of volunteers. Grants are given in the following categories: social welfare, including mental health, offenders, disadvantaged communities, homelessness, job creation projects, and ethnic minorities; arts – therapeutic use of the arts for the long-term benefit of the groups listed under social welfare and projects which enable people in the above groups to feel welcome in arts venues, and which enable them to make long-term constructive use of their leisure time; conservation – with an emphasis upon ensuring that fine buildings, landscapes and collections remain or become available to the general public or scholars, and training and conservation skills; the environment – mainly gardens, historic landscape and wilderness.

WHAT IS NOT FUNDED Grants are not given for: older people; children; education; research; animals; music or drama (except therapeutically); conferences or seminars; medical care (including hospices) or health; medical equipment; churches or cathedrals; holidays or expeditions; sports or leisure facilities (including cricket pitches); residential or large building projects; replacement of Lottery or statutory funds; national appeals; grantmaking trusts or community foundations; individuals; headquarters of national organisations and 'umbrella' organisations; projects outside the UK; or non-registered charities. Past recipients are not encouraged to re-apply.

TYPE OF GRANT Capital or recurrent; core funding and salaries are considered. Grants for salaries or running costs are for a maximum of three years. Some small grants of up to £1,000 can be made between meetings of the trustees.

RANGE OF GRANTS Usually £5,000–£30,000 (over three years).

SAMPLE GRANTS £22,000 to Survivors Poetry for 'rescue' grants to stay in operation until problems had been sorted out and further funding obtained; £20,000 a year for three years to Asylum Welcome in Oxford for its work with families to help them access healthcare and schooling; £20,000 a year for three years to the Hackfall Trust in Yorkshire towards the restoration of an 18th century landscaped wilderness; £19,000 a year for three years to Boscombe Family Drop-In in Bournemouth; £18,000 a year for three years to The Lantern in Weymouth for a new worker to find more daytime occupations or part-time work for their clients; £18,000 a year for two years to the Sycamore Project's Zac's Bar; £16,000 a year for three years to SPLITZ in Trowbridge for extra staff to support lone parents during the early difficult days alone; £16,000 a year for three years to YP2 Clay Action for Young People in St. Dennis to help set up a new challenge for young people from the clay area in Cornwall; £15,000 a year for three years to Community Projects Trust in Bodmin to promote and support self-help groups and encourage village-hall committees and Parish Councils to work with the disadvantaged; £15,000 to Electronic Information Network (EIN) towards updating and expanding its website.

FINANCES *Year* 2001 *Income* £1,556,800 *Grants* £2,395,000 *Assets* £41,957,738

TRUSTEES Sir Paul Getty; Lady Getty; Christopher Gibbs; James Ramsden; Vanni Treves.

PUBLICATIONS *Unpopular Causes. The First Five Years of the J Paul Getty Jr Charitable Trust.*

OTHER INFORMATION This trust has no connection with the Getty Foundation in the USA.

HOW TO APPLY 'We only accept applications by post. A letter no more than two sides long is all that is necessary at first, giving an outline of the project, who will benefit, a detailed costing, the existing sources of finance of the organisation, and what other applications, including those to statutory sources and the Lottery, have been made. Please also say if you have applied to or received a grant previously from this trust. Please read the 'exclusions' section carefully first before applying, as it is possible that the particular aspect of your application, rather than the general purpose of your organisation, may be excluded. 30% of the applications we received in 2001 were outside our guidelines. Please do not send videos, tapes or bulky reports. They will not be returned. Annual accounts will be asked for if your application is going to be taken further. Applications can be made to the administrator at any time. There are no 'closing dates', and all letters of appeal will be answered, we hope within six weeks. But please remember to submit only two sides in the first instance. And don't shrink the application – edit it! If a project is short-listed for taking forward for a grant over £2,000, it will also have to be visited by the administrator before an application can be considered by the trustees. This may mean a delay, as it is only possible to visit a small part of the country between each quarterly trustees' meeting. The trustees usually meet around the end of March, June, September and December. There is a short-listing process, and not all applications are taken forward. Not all those taken forward will necessarily be put to the next trustees' meeting as the administrator may not be visiting their area in that particular quarter. Three months is the least it usually takes to award a grant. Some small grants of up to £2,000 can be made in between meetings without a visit, but only for specific purposes.'

WHO TO APPLY TO Ms Bridget O'Brien Twohig, Administrator, 1 Park Square West, London NW1 4LJ *Tel* 020 7486 1859 *Website* www.jpgettytrust.org.uk

CC NO 292360   **ESTABLISHED** 1985

....

■ The Gibbs Charitable Trusts

WHERE FUNDING CAN BE GIVEN UK, particularly Avon and South Wales, and overseas.

WHO CAN BENEFIT Organisations benefiting Methodists are given particular attention.

WHAT IS FUNDED Primarily to support Methodist charities; also areas of social or educational concern. Grants are normally made to projects of which the trustees have personal knowledge. Also supported are international causes and creative arts, especially those which use the arts for personal development.

WHAT IS NOT FUNDED A large number of requests are received by the trust from churches undertaking improvement, refurbishment and development projects, but only a few of these can be helped. In general, Methodist churches are selected, sometimes those the trustees have particular knowledge of. Individuals and animal charities are not supported.

TYPE OF GRANT Buildings, capital and project will be considered.

RANGE OF GRANTS Almost all grants in range £500–£10,000.

SAMPLE GRANTS £30,000 to Methodist Church Fund for Ministerial Training; £18,000 to Christian Aid; £5,000 each to Cliff College, Genesis, and Tradescraft Exchange – Malawi; £4,500 to Child to Child; £3,000 each to Hope and Homes for Children, Jasperian Theatre Company and Penarth and Dinas Powys Circuit; £2,600 to International Planned Parenthood Federation.

FINANCES *Year* 2000–01 *Income* £76,784 *Grants* £116,950 *Assets* £2,190,875

TRUSTEES Mrs S M N Gibbs; Dr J N Gibbs; A G Gibbs; Dr J M Gibbs; W M Gibbs; Dr J E Gibbs; Mrs C Gibbs; Mrs E Gibbs; Mrs P Gibbs; Ms R N Gibbs; Ms J F Gibbs; J W K Gibbs.

HOW TO APPLY The trust has no application forms; requests should be made in writing to the correspondent. The trustees meet three times a year, at Christmas, Easter and late summer. Unsuccessful applicants are not normally notified. The trustees do not encourage telephone enquiries or speculative applications. They also state that they are not impressed by applicants that send a huge amount of paperwork.

WHO TO APPLY TO Dr James M Gibbs, Trustee, 8 Victoria Square, Clifton, Bristol BS8 4ET *Tel* 0117 973 6615 *Fax* 0117 974 4137

CC NO 207997   **ESTABLISHED** 1946

....

■ The G C Gibson Charitable Trust

WHERE FUNDING CAN BE GIVEN UK, with interests in East Anglia, Wales and Scotland.

WHO CAN BENEFIT Registered charities only.

WHAT IS FUNDED General charitable purposes.

WHAT IS NOT FUNDED No grants to individuals. Only registered charities are supported.

TYPE OF GRANT Capital, research, running and core costs.

RANGE OF GRANTS £1,000–£20,00; mostly £1,000–£3,000.

SAMPLE GRANTS £15,000 to Welsh College of Music and Drama; £13,000 to The Haven Trust; £10,000 each to King Edward VII Hospital, Parochial Church Council, St Nicholas Hospice – Bury St Edmonds, St Michael's Hospice – Hereford, Glenalmond College and Weston Spirit.

FINANCES *Year* 2001–02 *Income* £565,000 *Grants* £620,000 *Assets* £14,500,000

TRUSTEES R D Taylor; Mrs J M Gibson; George S C Gibson.

HOW TO APPLY In writing to the correspondent in October/November each year. Trustees meet in December/January. Successful applicants will receive their cheques during January. Organisations that have already received a grant should re-apply describing how the previous year's grant was spent and setting out how a further grant would be used. In general, less detailed information is required from national charities with a known track record than from small local charities that are not known to the trustees. 'Due to the volume of applications, it is not possible to acknowledge each application,

......

nor is it possible to inform unsuccessful applicants.'

WHO TO APPLY TO Karen Griffin, Deloitte & Touche, Blenheim House, Fitzalan Court, Newport Road, Cardiff CF24 0TS *Tel* 029 2048 1111

CC NO 258710   **ESTABLISHED** 1969

....

■ Simon Gibson Charitable Trust

WHERE FUNDING CAN BE GIVEN UK, with a preference for Norfolk, Suffolk, south Wales or central London.

WHO CAN BENEFIT Registered charities and other organisations tax exempt under Charity Commission schemes benefiting seafarers and fishermen; volunteers; children in care, fostered and adopted; and people who have a disease or medical condition or are homeless, unemployed or otherwise socially disadvantaged.

WHAT IS FUNDED Welfare, children and young people; medical; churches; animal welfare; arts and culture; international, and general.

WHAT IS NOT FUNDED No grants for individuals.

TYPE OF GRANT One-off or recurring, core costs, running costs, project, research, buildings and capital. Funding may be given for up to three years.

RANGE OF GRANTS £1,000–£50,000; normally £2,000–£5,000.

SAMPLE GRANTS £20,000 to the Royal Welsh Agricultural Society; £10,000 each to Cancer Relief Macmillan, Ely Cathedral, Ewing Foundation, Falkland Memorial Chapel, King's School – Ely, Mid-Anglia Health Trust's Gibson Centre, The Military and Hospitaller Order of St Lazarus, Orbit Theatre, Prostate Cancer Charity, Hospice of St Nicholas – Bury St Edmunds and the Prince's Trust.

FINANCES *Year* 2001–02 *Income* £472,700 *Grants* £461,000

TRUSTEES Bryan Marsh; Angela Homfray; George Gibson.

HOW TO APPLY In writing to the correspondent. Telephone calls should not be made. The trust has no application forms. It acknowledges all applications but does not enter into correspondence with applicants unless they are awarded a grant. The trustees meet in May and applications should be received by March in order to be considered at that meeting.

WHO TO APPLY TO Bryan Marsh, Trustee, Wild Rose House, Llancarfan, Vale of Glamorgan CF62 3AD *Tel* 01446 781004 *Fax* 01446 781004 *E-mail* bryan@marsh66.fsnet.co.uk

CC NO 269501   **ESTABLISHED** 1975

....

■ The Harvey and Hilary Gilbert Charitable Trust

WHERE FUNDING CAN BE GIVEN UK.

WHO CAN BENEFIT Registered charities.

WHAT IS FUNDED General charitable purposes.

SAMPLE GRANTS £20,000 to Sidney Gold Trust; £7,500 to King Solomon School; £2,500 to Parry Charitable Foundation; £1,000 each to Chigwell Sunset Committee, Cancer BACUP, Community Security Trust and King Solomon Brochure; £400 each to Teenage Cancer Trust and Hillel Foundation.

FINANCES *Year* 1998–99 *Income* £33,000 *Grants* £35,000

TRUSTEES Harvey Gilbert; Hilary Gilbert.

HOW TO APPLY In writing to the correspondent.

WHO TO APPLY TO Harvey Gilbert, Trustee, Kempton Mews, Kempton Road, London E6 2LD

CC NO 296293   **ESTABLISHED** 1986

....

■ Gilchrist Educational Trust

WHERE FUNDING CAN BE GIVEN UK and overseas, but the trust's power to apply funds outside the UK is never exercised for the benefit of individuals.

WHO CAN BENEFIT Individual students, university expeditions and organisations. The trust also offers the biennial Gilchrist Fieldwork Award of £10,000 for the best overseas research proposal by a small team of qualified scientists or academics, most of British nationality.

WHAT IS FUNDED Completion of a degree course by students who have almost finished and are facing unexpected financial difficulties; short study visits overseas which are an essential part of a degree course. British university expeditions with teams of three or more who are proposing to carry out research of a scientific nature. Organisations wishing to undertake projects which will fill educational gaps or make more widely available a particular aspect of education or learning.

WHAT IS NOT FUNDED Part-time students; courses for students who are eligible for student loans or an NHS bursary; intercalated degrees; maintenance of dependants; a whole year spent studying overseas as part of a UK course. British University Expeditions which have as their sole or main aim an adventurous activity such as caving or mountaineering. Primary or secondary schools, parochial organisations or groups, medical research, building or renovation of buildings, administrative or running costs.

TYPE OF GRANT One-off.

SAMPLE GRANTS 39 individual students were awarded adult study grants – average £633; 14 individual students were awarded travel study grants – average £378; 19 university expeditions were awarded grants – average £697; 8 organisations received awards – average £1,750.

FINANCES *Year* 2001–02 *Income* £82,596 *Grants* £62,650 *Assets* £1,591,722

TRUSTEES Lord Shuttleworth, Chair; Miss J M Sims; Dr John Hemming; Edmund Marsden; Prof. F L Pearce.

OTHER INFORMATION All applicants are advised to write in preference to telephoning, as the office is staffed part-time only.

HOW TO APPLY Individual grant seekers should send a brief description of their circumstances, enclosing an sae. Those who appear to be eligible will be sent a list of information needed to enable an application to be considered in detail. Applications from individuals are considered throughout the year. University expeditions should write requesting an application form, which must be completed and returned by 28 February. The deadline for applications from organisations is 31 March. Applications for the Gilchrist Fieldwork Award must be submitted by 15 March in even-numbered years; guidelines are available.

WHO TO APPLY TO The Secretary, Mary Trevelyan Hall, 10 York Terrace East, London NW1 4PT

CC NO 313877   **ESTABLISHED** 1865

■ The L & R Gilley Charitable Trust

WHERE FUNDING CAN BE GIVEN Primarily Devon and Birmingham.

WHO CAN BENEFIT Registered charities benefiting people who are elderly, retired or have disabilities.

WHAT IS FUNDED Preference for care of older people, people who are ill and people with disabilities.

WHAT IS NOT FUNDED No grants to individuals.

RANGE OF GRANTS Up to £5,000.

SAMPLE GRANTS £5,500 to Age Concern; £5,000 each to Cancer Research Campaign, Macmillan Cancer Relief, Midland Spastic Association and Sidmouth Inshore Rescue; £4,000 to RNLI; £3,000 each to Hospice of the Valleys, St Mary's Hospice, and Shakespeare Hospice.

FINANCES *Year* 2002 *Income* £50,000 *Grants* £53,000

TRUSTEES John Richard Bettinson; Richard Anthony Bettinson; Yvonne Garfield-Smith.

HOW TO APPLY In writing to the address below for consideration in July. Applications are not acknowledged.

WHO TO APPLY TO Miss C M Tempest, Secretary, c/o John Bettinson, 6 The Farthings, Metchley Lane, Harborne, Birmingham B17 0HQ *Tel* 0121 244 3258 *Fax* 0121 244 3269

CC NO 297127   **ESTABLISHED** 1987

■ The Girdlers' Company Charitable Trust

WHERE FUNDING CAN BE GIVEN UK, with a preference for City of London, Hammersmith and Peckham, overseas.

WHO CAN BENEFIT Registered charities benefiting children, young adults, academics, students and teachers.

WHAT IS FUNDED Welfare, medicine, education, youth, heritage, environment and religion.

WHAT IS NOT FUNDED No grants to individuals.

TYPE OF GRANT One-off and recurrent.

RANGE OF GRANTS £1,000–£30,000.

SAMPLE GRANTS £30,000 to London Youth; £15,000 to Surrey County Cricket Club Youth Scheme; £12,000 to Gordon's School; £10,000 each to Stoke Manderville Research Nurse and Sports Aid London; £8,000 to London College of Fashion for scholarships and bursaries; £5,000 each to St Paul's Choir School Foundation, Macmillan Cancer Relief and Dorothy House Hospice; £4,000 to Marchant Holiday School.

FINANCES *Year* 2001–02 *Income* £732,127 *Grants* £499,225 *Assets* £2,238,223

TRUSTEES C E Grace; Sir Gordon Pirie; D R L James; A R Westall; Sir David Burnett; Sir Michael Newton; N K Maitland; B D Moul; Dr D N Seaton; A J R Fairclough; Rt Hon. Viscount Brentford; I P R James; Capt. G M A James; T J Straker; P F D Trimingham; J S Maitland; P V Straker; Sir Thomas Crawley-Boevey; I W Fairclough; J P F Reeve; S V Straker; J M Westall; F M French; J O Udal.

HOW TO APPLY In writing to the correspondent.

WHO TO APPLY TO The Clerk to The Girdlers' Company, Girdlers' Hall, Basinghall Avenue, London EC2V 5DD *Tel* 020 7638 0488 *Fax* 020 7628 4030 *E-mail* margaret@girdlers.co.uk

CC NO 328026   **ESTABLISHED** 1988

■ Glasgow Conservation Trust – West

WHERE FUNDING CAN BE GIVEN The west end of Glasgow.

WHO CAN BENEFIT Conservation/heritage schemes.

WHAT IS FUNDED The trust's principle aim is to conserve and improve the physical environment of the west end of Glasgow, thus promoting wider interest and confidence in the area. Its objectives stating as being to: coordinate investment in the improvement and renewal of the area through public and private agencies; pool and extend knowledge and experience of methods of conserving the townscape and architectural heritage of the area; set new and higher standards of maintenance, decoration and preservation of the buildings of the west end; encourage the conservation and re-use of existing vacant buildings; generate employment by the wider use of local specialised tradesmen in conservation works; publicise the quality of the west end and its potential as a major tourist attraction; and show by example the possibility of regenerating other parts of the city.

WHAT IS NOT FUNDED Grants are only given for external repairs.

FINANCES *Year* 2001–02 *Income* £91,378 *Grants* £230,982 *Assets* £89,258

TRUSTEES Mrs Jean Charsley; Joseph Logan; Russell Logan; David Martin; Prof. David Green; Brian Park; James Dickson; Philip Schreiber; Ms Lesley Kerr; John McGee.

HOW TO APPLY Applications are subject to detailed technical approval. The trust recommends that potential applicants contact the trust to discuss eligibility and the availability of funds before submitting an application.

WHO TO APPLY TO Dr John Russell, Technical Director, 30 Cranworth Street, Glasgow G12 8AG *Tel* 0141 339 0092 *Fax* 0141 339 0092 *E-mail* glasgowwest@cqm.co.uk *Website* http://users.colloquium.co.uk/~glasgowwest/home.htm

SC NO SC012183

■ The Glass-House Trust

WHERE FUNDING CAN BE GIVEN Unrestricted, but UK in practice.

WHO CAN BENEFIT The trust is concentrating all its resources on housing design, with a big new initiative being developed by the Architecture Foundation and the National Tenants Resource Centre.

WHAT IS FUNDED Work aiming to bring about social change, with an emphasis on the importance of the built environment rather than the promotion of psychological welfare. The trust prefers to support innovative schemes that can be successfully replicated or become self-sustaining. The aim is to ensure tenants living in social housing have access to high quality independent design advice, assistance and technical aid, either to help initiate and realise local projects or give residents an effective say in development schemes that affect their lives.

WHAT IS NOT FUNDED Grants are not normally made to individuals.

RANGE OF GRANTS £300–£66,050.

SAMPLE GRANTS £634,058 to start up the new programme funded by the trust organised jointly by the Architecture Foundation and National Tenants Resource Centre; £90,000 to Kingsland School in Hackney for A Space After School project; £27,000 to Royal Free Hospital School of Medicine/ Oxford University

Department of Education to cover additional research costs on the 'Families, Children and Childcare' project; £5,000 to Matts Gallery for the production of educational materials based on an exhibition of the artist Matthew Tickle's work.

FINANCES *Year* 2001–02 *Income* £595,101 *Grants* £756,000

TRUSTEES Alexander Sainsbury; James Sainsbury; Jessica Sainsbury; Camilla Woodward; Miss Judith Portrait.

OTHER INFORMATION The trust is one of the Sainsbury Family Charitable Trusts which share a common administration. An application to one is taken as an application to all.

HOW TO APPLY Proposals are generally invited by the trustees or initiated at their request. Unsolicited applications are nort encouraged and are unlikely to be successful.

WHO TO APPLY TO Michael Pattison, Director, Allington House, 1st Floor, 150 Victoria Street, London SW1E 5AE *Tel* 020 7410 0330

CC NO 1017426   **ESTABLISHED** 1993

■ The B & P Glasser Charitable Trust

WHERE FUNDING CAN BE GIVEN UK and worldwide.

WHO CAN BENEFIT Registered charities.

WHAT IS FUNDED General charitable purposes, particularly health and disability charities, and Jewish organisations.

WHAT IS NOT FUNDED No grant to individuals or students.

RANGE OF GRANTS £500–£8,000.

SAMPLE GRANTS Abbeyfield (Buckinghamshire) Society, Barnardos, British Heart Foundation Appeal, Central British Fund for Jewish World Relief, Friends of Boys' Town Jerusalem, Great Ormond Street Childrens Hospital Fund, Jewish Care, Nightingale House, Relate and RNLI.

FINANCES *Year* 2000–01 *Income* £83,815 *Grants* £115,000

TRUSTEES H Glasser; J C Belfrage; J D H Cullingham; M J Glasser; J A Glasser.

HOW TO APPLY In writing to the correspondent.

WHO TO APPLY TO B S Christer, Stafford Young Jones, The Old Rectory, 29 Martin Lane, London EC4R 0AU *Tel* 020 7623 9490

CC NO 326571   **ESTABLISHED** 1984

■ The Glaziers' Trust

WHERE FUNDING CAN BE GIVEN UK.

WHO CAN BENEFIT Those involved in the craft of stained glass.

WHAT IS FUNDED The support of artists studying the craft of stained glass and the conservation of stained glass of historic importance.

RANGE OF GRANTS £250–£5,000; exceptionally more.

SAMPLE GRANTS £10,000 to various churches for the restoration and conservation of stained glass and a grant of £1,000 to the British Society of Master Glass Painters for the publication of a journal. There were further donations of over £15,000 in support of individuals studying the craft of stained glass, including a £9,000 Award for Excellence.

FINANCES *Year* 2001 *Income* £88,110 *Grants* £31,000 *Assets* £284,296

TRUSTEES Glaziers' Company.

HOW TO APPLY In writing to the correspondent. Application forms and conditions for grant-aid are available online.

WHO TO APPLY TO The Clerk, The Glaziers' Company, Glaziers' Hall, 9 Montague Close, London Bridge, London SE1 9DD *Tel* 020 7403 6652 *Fax* 020 7403 6652 *E-mail* info@worshipfulglaziers.com *Website* www.worshipfulglaziers.com/ glaziers_trust.asp

CC NO 1080279   **ESTABLISHED** 1966

■ The Glencore Foundation for Education and Welfare

WHERE FUNDING CAN BE GIVEN Mainly Israel.

WHO CAN BENEFIT Organisations.

WHAT IS FUNDED General charitable purposes, with the principal area of activity currently education and welfare, especially in Israel.

TYPE OF GRANT Generally one-off and project.

SAMPLE GRANTS $223,000 Chabad/Children of Chernobyl; $100,000 to the Society for the Advancement of Education in Israel, Jerusalem; $86,900 to SAD Schweiz; $80,000 to Israel Association of Community Centres; $50,000 each to Ashkelon Foundation, Beit Moria; Mandel Community Centre and Yitzhak Rabin leadership Development Programme for High School Graduates; $49,800 to Chabad Lubawitsch; $45,000 to Henrew Scouts Association.

FINANCES *Year* 2001 *Income* £2,564,000 *Grants* £2,559,000 *Assets* £1,304,640

TRUSTEES Danny Dreyfuss; M D Paisner; L M Weiss; C Smith.

OTHER INFORMATION The figures given for the sample grants are in US dollars.

HOW TO APPLY In writing to the correspondent.

WHO TO APPLY TO C Smith, Secretary, c/o Glencore UK Ltd, 50 Berkeley Street, London W1J 8HD *Tel* 020 7629 3800 *Fax* 020 7499 5555

CC NO 1041859   **ESTABLISHED** 1994

■ Global Care

WHERE FUNDING CAN BE GIVEN Overseas.

WHO CAN BENEFIT Children and families in poorest countries through relief and development. People of many religions, cultures and social circumstances will be supported.

WHAT IS FUNDED Trustees favour children's charities already supported by them working in the poorest countries and the advancement of Christian education.

FINANCES *Year* 2002 *Income* £628,732 *Grants* £388,986

TRUSTEES S D Wood; J Bull; N Lochhead; A C Cryer; M R Cryer.

PUBLICATIONS News updates.

HOW TO APPLY Applications are not recommended.Trustees seek out projects to support, as appropriate, and new grants cannot be considered.

WHO TO APPLY TO R F Newby, Trust Secretary and Chief Executive, 2 Dugdale Road, Coventry CV6 1PB *Tel* 024 7660 1800 *Fax* 024 7660 1444 *E-mail* hs@globalcare.org.uk *Website* www.globalcare.org.uk

CC NO 1054008   **ESTABLISHED** 1996

■ The Gloucestershire Historic Churches Trust

WHERE FUNDING CAN BE GIVEN Gloucestershire, including south Gloucestershire.

WHO CAN BENEFIT The Church of England or other religious body using for worship a church, chapel or other building.

WHAT IS FUNDED The restoration, preservation, repair and improvement of churches, including monuments, fittings and furniture, and possessing notable architectural features or historic associations within the area.

WHAT IS NOT FUNDED No grants are made for routine maintenance and decorations.

TYPE OF GRANT One-off, but repeat applications will be considered.

RANGE OF GRANTS £250–£10,000, typical grant £2,500.

SAMPLE GRANTS £5,000 to Lydney United Reformed Church for repairs to roof, rainwater goods and floor; £4,000 to Holy Trinity, Kingswood for restoration of tower stonework and leadwork.

FINANCES *Year* 2001 *Income* £123,000 *Grants* £77,500 *Assets* £970,000

TRUSTEES D W Turner, Chair; B C Woods; R H J Steel; S Ward.

HOW TO APPLY A detailed application form is available by writing to Peter Duxbury, Chairman of Grants Committee, Painters Cottage, Middle Duntisbourne, Cirencester, GL7 7AR.

WHO TO APPLY TO B C Woods, Chairman of Grants Committee, 2 Shepherds Way, Cirencester, Gloucestershire GL7 2EY *Tel* 01285 659159

CC NO 280879   **ESTABLISHED** 1980

■ Worshipful Company of Glovers of London Charity Fund

WHERE FUNDING CAN BE GIVEN UK with a preference for the City of London.

WHO CAN BENEFIT Glovers and glove-related projects; general charitable purposes.

WHAT IS FUNDED The trust makes grants mainly towards the provision of gloves, or to causes that are related to the City of London.

SAMPLE GRANTS General grants included: £4,000 to Glove Collection Trust Fund; £2,500 to City of London Girls' School; £2,000 to Guildhall School of Music & Drama; £1,000 to Salvation Army.

FINANCES *Year* 1999–2000 *Income* £38,000 *Grants* £36,000 *Assets* £606,000

TRUSTEES Margaret M Linton; James D H Clarke; Alan Howarth; John H Spanner; William Loach.

HOW TO APPLY In writing to the correspondent.

WHO TO APPLY TO The Trustees, 73 Clapham Manor Street, London SW4 6DS

CC NO 269091   **ESTABLISHED** 1975

■ GMC Trust

WHERE FUNDING CAN BE GIVEN UK, predominantly in the West Midlands.

WHO CAN BENEFIT Organisations benefiting children, young adults and older people.

WHAT IS FUNDED Primarily medical research, also causes related to inner city deprivation. Income is substantially committed to a range of existing beneficiaries.

WHAT IS NOT FUNDED No grants to individuals, or to local or regional appeals outside the West Midlands. The trust does not respond to national appeals, except where there are established links.

TYPE OF GRANT One-off.

RANGE OF GRANTS Grants of up to £10,000; typically £500.

SAMPLE GRANTS £15,000 to CRAB Appeal for cancer research in Birmingham; £10,000 to Mental Health Foundation; £5,000 each to Acorns Children's Hospice – Birmingham and Birmingham Settlement; £2,500 to Runnymede Trust for race relations; £1,000 each to Alzheimer's Research Trust, Cantab Millennium Fund for scholarships, Listening Books for books for deaf people, and Royal Birmingham Society of Artists; £750 to Dodford Children's Holiday Farm towards holidays for disadvantaged children.

FINANCES *Year* 2002 *Income* £59,000 *Grants* £62,000 *Assets* £2,322,000

TRUSTEES Sir Adrian Cadbury; B E S Cadbury.

HOW TO APPLY In writing to the correspondent. The trust will only consider written applications, and applications outside the trust's remit will not be acknowledged.

WHO TO APPLY TO Rodney Pitts, Secretary, 4 Fairways, 1240 Warwick Road, Knowle, Solihull, West Midlands B93 9LL *Tel* 01564 779971 *Fax* 01564 770499

CC NO 288418   **ESTABLISHED** 1965

■ The GNC Trust

WHERE FUNDING CAN BE GIVEN UK, with preferences for Midlands, Cornwall and Hampshire.

WHO CAN BENEFIT Charitable bodies.

WHAT IS FUNDED To support those charities which the trustees have special interest in, knowledge of or association with, particularly of a medical or educational nature.

WHAT IS NOT FUNDED Only very occasionally are grants made to individuals. National appeals are not favoured, nor are most London-based charities.

RANGE OF GRANTS £20–£14,000; mostly for £500 or less.

SAMPLE GRANTS £40,000 in two grants to National Institite of Conductive Education; £33,244 to Charney Manor – Society of Friends; £10,000 to Sibford School; £7,000 in two grants to Reece School; £5,000 each to British Kidney Patients Association, Refugee Council and Squire Resource; £2,500 to UNICEF; £2,000 each to Association for Spinabifida and Hydrocephalus and Symphony Hall Organ Fund; £1,500 to Birmingham Royal Ballet Trust and Hampshire Wildlife Trust.

FINANCES *Year* 2001 *Income* £87,565 *Grants* £142,021 *Assets* £2,472,429

TRUSTEES R Hardy; G T E Cadbury; Mrs J E B Yelloly.

HOW TO APPLY In writing to the correspondent. There is no application form. Applications are not acknowledged.

WHO TO APPLY TO R Hardy, Agent to the Trustees, c/o Messrs PricewaterhouseCoopers, Temple Court, Bull Street, Birmingham B4 6JT *Tel* 0121 265 5000 *Fax* 0121 265 5450

CC NO 211533   **ESTABLISHED** 1960

■ The Mrs Godfrey-Payton Trust

WHERE FUNDING CAN BE GIVEN Warwick only.

WHO CAN BENEFIT Registered charities benefiting people of all ages, retired people and people disadvantaged by poverty.

WHAT IS FUNDED Particular interests are: projects that benefit Warwick and the inhabitants thereof, for example, arts, almshouses and youth clubs; projects (non-medical) designed to help older people retain their independence; and projects known to the trustees.

WHAT IS NOT FUNDED Grants are not given for medical purposes or to individuals.

TYPE OF GRANT Usually one-off. Buildings, capital, core costs, feasibility studies, projects and funding for up to one year will be considered.

FINANCES *Year* 2001 *Income* £60,000 *Grants* £60,000 *Assets* £1,500,000

TRUSTEES Richard David Creed; Cornelius Brendan Moynihan.

HOW TO APPLY In writing to the correspondent. The trustees will accept unsolicited applications but cannot and will not support or reply to them all.

WHO TO APPLY TO Richard D Creed, Southfield, Sherston, Malmesbury, Wiltshire SN16 0PU *Tel* 01666 840843 (am only)

CC NO 1005851   **ESTABLISHED** 1991

■ The Godinton Charitable Trust

WHERE FUNDING CAN BE GIVEN UK.

WHO CAN BENEFIT Registered charities.

WHAT IS FUNDED Local general charitable purposes. A regular payment is made to the Godinton House Preservation Trust.

WHAT IS NOT FUNDED No grants to individuals.

TYPE OF GRANT One-off and recurrent.

RANGE OF GRANTS Up to £10,000.

SAMPLE GRANTS £5,000 to a local village hall committee; £4,000 to a local secondary school; £2,500 to a local primary school; £2,200 to a local church. A further £10,000 was donated in recurrent grants including: £750 each to a local church and a local parish committee; £500 each to Kent Wildlife Trust and a children's hospice.

FINANCES *Year* 2002 *Income* £170,000 *Grants* £23,700 *Assets* £4,700,000

TRUSTEES W G Plumtre; Hon. J D Leigh-Pemberton; M F Jennings; L H Parsons.

HOW TO APPLY In writing to the correspondent.

WHO TO APPLY TO N G Sandford, Godinton, Godinton Lane, Ashford, Kent EC4M 8SH *Tel* 01233 632 652 *Fax* 01233 647 351 *E-mail* ghpt@godinton.fsnet.co.uk

CC NO 268321   **ESTABLISHED** 1974

■ The Joseph & Queenie Gold Charitable Trust

WHERE FUNDING CAN BE GIVEN UK.

WHO CAN BENEFIT Jewish organisations; occasionally other charities.

WHAT IS NOT FUNDED No grants to individuals.

SAMPLE GRANTS £30,000 to JJCT towards a classroom; £3,000 to Norwood Ravenswood; £2,000 to Aly Hospital; £1,000 each to JJCT towards the Kol Midre Appeal and SCOPUS.

FINANCES *Year* 1998–99 *Income* £47,000 *Grants* £48,000 *Assets* £563,000

TRUSTEES Mrs Queenie Gold; Mrs Carol Djanogly.

HOW TO APPLY In writing to the correspondent. This entry was not confirmed by the trust, but the information was correct according to the trust's file at the Charity Commission.

WHO TO APPLY TO Mrs Queenie Gold, Trustee, Phredella House, Hyver Hill, Mill Hill, London NW7 4HU *Tel* 020 8959 2300

CC NO 286351   **ESTABLISHED** 1983

■ The Meir Golda Trust

WHERE FUNDING CAN BE GIVEN UK.

WHO CAN BENEFIT Particular favour is given to Jewish charities, but charities benefiting followers of all faiths are considered. People suffering from illnesses of all kinds are a priority.

WHAT IS FUNDED General charitable purposes; the arts; conservation; animal facilities and services; synagogues and Jewish bodies.

RANGE OF GRANTS £18–£40,500.

SAMPLE GRANTS In 1997: £41,000 to British Friends of Laniade Hospital.

FINANCES *Year* 1999–2000 *Income* £16,000 *Grants* £22,000 *Assets* £21,000

TRUSTEES J Glatt, Chair; Mrs G Glatt.

HOW TO APPLY In writing to the correspondent. This entry was not confirmed by the trust, but the information was correct according to the trust's file at the Charity Commission.

WHO TO APPLY TO J Glatt, 97 Leeside Crescent, London NW11 0JL

CC NO 1041256   **ESTABLISHED** 1994

■ The Sydney & Phyllis Goldberg Memorial Charitable Trust

WHERE FUNDING CAN BE GIVEN UK.

WHO CAN BENEFIT Organisations benefiting, research workers, at risk groups, and people who are disabled, disadvantaged by poverty or socially isolated.

WHAT IS FUNDED Medical research, welfare and disability.

TYPE OF GRANT One-off, some recurrent.

SAMPLE GRANTS £11,000 to Children of St Mary's Intensive Care Department of Child Health; £7,500 to Dystonia Society for research into the relief of sickness; £7,000 to Institute of Child Health for research into child leukaemia at Great Ormond Street Hospital; £6,000 to Elliott Comprehensive School to fund a library for children with disabilities; £5,000 to Handicapped Adventure Playground Association Limited.

FINANCES *Year* 1998–99 *Income* £56,000 *Grants* £57,000 *Assets* £1,800,000

TRUSTEES H G Vowles; M J Church; C J Pexton.

HOW TO APPLY In writing to the correspondent. Telephone requests are not appreciated. Applicants are advised to apply towards the end of the calendar year.

WHO TO APPLY TO M J Church, Trustee, Coulthards Mackenzie, 17 Park Street, Camberley, Surrey GU15 3PQ *Tel* 01276 65470

CC NO 291835   **ESTABLISHED** 1985

■ The Golden Bottle Trust

WHERE FUNDING CAN BE GIVEN UK.

WHO CAN BENEFIT Registered charities.

WHAT IS FUNDED General charitable purposes.

WHAT IS NOT FUNDED No grants for individuals or organisations that are not registered charities.

FINANCES *Year* 2000–01 *Income* £973,281 *Grants* £506,450 *Assets* £6,405,531

TRUSTEES Messrs Hoare Trustees.

HOW TO APPLY In writing to the correspondent, who stated 'trustees meet on a monthly basis, but the funds are already largely committed and, therefore, applications from sources not already known to the trustees are unlikely to be successful'.

WHO TO APPLY TO The Secretariat, C Hoare & Co, 37 Fleet Street, London EC4P 4DQ *Tel* 020 7353 4522
CC NO 327026   ESTABLISHED 1985

■ Golden Charitable Trust

WHERE FUNDING CAN BE GIVEN UK with a preference for West Sussex.
WHO CAN BENEFIT Registered charities.
WHAT IS FUNDED Literature, English Literature, the conservation of printed books and manuscripts, and libraries and museums.
WHAT IS NOT FUNDED No grants to individuals.
TYPE OF GRANT Endowment, sometimes recurring.
RANGE OF GRANTS £50–£100,000; typically under £1,000.
SAMPLE GRANTS £100,000 to Westminster Synagogue; £5,000 to British ORT; £1,500 to Petworth Festival; £1,350 to Friends of King Edward Hospital – Midhurst; £1,000 to National Trust; £700 to Chichester Cathedral Restoration and Development Trust; £500 to Whizz-Kidz; £450 to Petworth Cottage Nursing Home; £200 to Parish Church of St Mary the Virgin – Petworth; £100 each to Iris Fund, Motor Neurone Disease Association and Pallant House Gallery Trust.
FINANCES *Year* 2001–02 *Income* £100,429 *Grants* £111,050 *Assets* £389,904
TRUSTEES Mrs S J F Solnick; J M F Golden.
HOW TO APPLY In writing to the correspondent.
WHO TO APPLY TO Lewis Golden, Secretary to the Trustees, Little Leith Gate, Angel Street, Petworth, West Sussex GU28 0BG *Tel* 01798 342434
CC NO 263916   ESTABLISHED 1972

■ The Teresa Rosenbaum Golden Charitable Trust

WHERE FUNDING CAN BE GIVEN UK.
WHO CAN BENEFIT Independent vetted medical research projects, especially if departmentally backed and peer reviewed.
WHAT IS FUNDED Medical research only.
WHAT IS NOT FUNDED No support for individuals, or for non-medical research.
TYPE OF GRANT Project and research funding for up to three years will be considered.
RANGE OF GRANTS £200–£61,000.
SAMPLE GRANTS £61,000 to The Tissue Engineering Centre at Imperial College – Chelsea and Westminster and Hammersmith Hospitals to fund a researcher in a specific area of developing bone cells; £25,000 to Research into Ageing towards five different projects; £21,000 to Kings Medical Research Trust for a clinical trial into the treatment of advanced liver cancer; £15,000 to Oncology Trust at Royal Free Hospital into clinical trials in patients using new antibodies; £12,000 each to Arthritis Research Campaign for two research projects and a study project, and Immunotherapy at University College Hospital for research into bone marrow transplantation by culturing cells immune to specific viruses and putting them back into the body; £10,000 each to Alzheimer's Society for research into the role of TAU protein in the development of tangles leading to the death of brain cells, Hearing Research Trust for research at Institute of Otology – London and Institute of Hearing Research – Nottingham into regenerating hair cells and understanding more about possible

self-repair mechanisms by studying reptiles and birds, Institute of Psychiatry for two research projects, and Royal Free Hospital for a trial into islet transplantation as a treatment for diabetes which will obviate the need for insulin injections
FINANCES *Year* 2001–02 *Income* £885,805 *Grants* £399,838 *Assets* £740,560
TRUSTEES T Rosenbaum; R A Ross; R M Abbey.
OTHER INFORMATION Six-monthly progress reports in layman's terms are a condition of any grant made. These should give the trustees a quick and clear picture of whether anticipated targets have been achieved. Peer review and endorsement are required. Seed corn funding is available for good ideas requiring initial funding for a preliminary or pilot report which could lead to funding from a major trust.
HOW TO APPLY In writing to the correspondent. Applicants must complete a simple pro forma which sets out briefly in clear layman's terms the reason for the project, the nature of the research, its cost, its anticipated benefit and how and when people will be able to benefit. Proper reports in this form will be required at least six-monthly and funding will be conditional on these being satisfactory. 'The trustees are not medical experts and require short clear statements in plain English setting out the particular subject to be researched, the objects and likely benefits, the cost and the time-scale. Unless a charity will undertake to provide two concise progress reports each year, they should not bother to apply as this is a vital requirement. It is essential that the trustees are able to follow the progress and effectiveness of the research they support.'
WHO TO APPLY TO John Samuels, Trust Administrator, 140 High Street, Edgware, Middlesex HA8 7LW *Tel* 020 8952 1414 *Fax* 020 8952 2424 *E-mail* goldentrust@regentsmead.com
CC NO 298582   ESTABLISHED 1987

■ The Jack Goldhill Charitable Trust

WHERE FUNDING CAN BE GIVEN UK.
WHO CAN BENEFIT Registered charities benefiting those in need.
WHAT IS FUNDED Human need causes and visual arts.
WHAT IS NOT FUNDED No support for individuals or new applications.
RANGE OF GRANTS £30–£27,000.
SAMPLE GRANTS Recent beneficiaries have included: £20,000 to Jack Goldhill Sculpture Award Fund; £17,000 to Prince's Foundation; £6,000 to Norwood Ravenswood; £3,500 to CST; £3,000 to Royal London Hospital; £2,000 each to Inclusion, Tate Gallery, and Tricycle Theatre Co.; £1,000 to Atlantic College; £500 to Story of Christmas.
FINANCES *Year* 1999 *Income* £79,540 *Grants* £84,285 *Assets* £596,480
TRUSTEES G Goldhill; J A Goldhill.
HOW TO APPLY The trustees have a restricted list of charities to whom they are committed and no unsolicited applications can be considered.
WHO TO APPLY TO Jack Goldhill, Trustee, 85 Kensington Heights, Campden Hill Road, London W8 7BD
CC NO 267018   ESTABLISHED 1974

Think carefully about every application. Is it justified?

499

■ The Goldschmied Charitable Settlement

WHERE FUNDING CAN BE GIVEN UK.
WHO CAN BENEFIT Organisations.
WHAT IS FUNDED Culture, education and general charitable purposes.
SAMPLE GRANTS In 1997–98: £4,400 to Architectural Association Building Fund; £2,300 to Egyptian Cultural Centre; £1,500 to St James Bursary Fund; £114 to St James Independent School.
FINANCES *Year* 1999–2000 *Income* £17,000 *Grants* £37,000 *Assets* £124,000
TRUSTEES A Goldschmied; M L S Goldschmied.
HOW TO APPLY In writing to the correspondent. This entry was not confirmed by the trust, but the information was correct according to the trust's file at the Charity Commission.
WHO TO APPLY TO K A Hawkins, Lee Associates, 5 Southampton Place, London WC1A 2DA *Tel* 020 7025 4600
CC NO 283250   **ESTABLISHED** 1981

■ The Goldsmiths' Company's Charity

WHERE FUNDING CAN BE GIVEN UK, with a special interest in London charities.
WHO CAN BENEFIT Registered charities and individuals connected with the trade of goldsmithing, silversmithing and jewellery, or for Londoners in need. People of all ages can benefit, and the trust will consider charities benefiting clergy, medical professionals, volunteers, parents and children, carers, people with disabilities, refugees, service and ex-service people, homeless people, ex-offenders and those at risk of offending, and people disadvantaged by poverty.
WHAT IS FUNDED Support of the goldsmiths' craft, education, and general charitable purposes. The trust will consider funding churches and historic buildings, and conservation of heritage; some aspects of infrastructure and technical support, and infrastructure development; arts and arts facilities, including community arts and recreation; some aspects of education and training, schools and colleges; and community facilities and services.
WHAT IS NOT FUNDED Applications are not normally considered on behalf of medical research; memorials to individuals; overseas projects; animal welfare; individuals, except those who have been resident in certain inner London boroughs for at least ten years; these are made through Social Services or similar. Applications from any organisation, including those previously successful, are not considered more frequently than once every three years.
TYPE OF GRANT Buildings, capital, salaries, core, start-up and running costs; one-off and recurring, for up to three years.
RANGE OF GRANTS £500 upwards.
SAMPLE GRANTS £50,000 each to Acton (Middlesex) Relief in Need Charity and Cornwall Independent Trust Fund; £25,000 to Museum of London for the building of its new medieval gallery; £17,625 to Civic Music Society for six concerts; £8,500 to St Christopher's Hospice; £5,500 to Raleigh International; £5,000 to National Museum of Wales to enable it to buy part of the Jackson collection; £4,000 to National Youth Orchestra; £3,000 to CLIC and Dulwich Picture Gallery.

FINANCES *Year* 2000–01 *Income* £2,531,362 *Grants* £1,717,000 *Assets* £67,885,262
TRUSTEES The members of the Court of Assistants of the Goldsmiths' Company.
Charity committee: Lord Cunliffe, chair; Sir Edward Ford; S A Shepherd; Miss J A Lowe; Dr M P Godfrey; Revd P D Watherston; G P Blunden.
HOW TO APPLY Applications for all of the charities applying for general charitable support should be made on an application form available from the charity. This form requires detailed information about the purpose of the grant (including a budget for the proposed activity; the methods by which the success of the project will be evaluated; the income/expenditure projection for the organisation for the current year; other grantmaking organisations appealed to for the same project and with what result). The form should be accompanied by the following: a letter stating the aims and objectives of the charity, including an outline of the current work and details of staffing, organisational structure and use of volunteer; the specific purpose for which the grant is requested; the organisation's most recent annual report and audited accounts. Trustees meet monthly except during August and September.
WHO TO APPLY TO R D Buchanan-Dunlop, Clerk, Goldsmiths' Hall, Foster Lane, London EC2V 6BN *Tel* 020 7606 7010
Website www.thegoldsmiths.co.uk
CC NO 1088699   **ESTABLISHED** 1961

■ The Golsoncott Foundation

WHERE FUNDING CAN BE GIVEN UK.
WHO CAN BENEFIT Arts organisations.
WHAT IS FUNDED The trust states its objects as follows: 'to promote, maintain, improve and advance the education of the public in the arts generally and in particular ... the fine arts and music. The fostering of the practice and appreciation of the arts, especially amongst young people and new audiences, is a further specific objective.'
WHAT IS NOT FUNDED No grants to individuals.
TYPE OF GRANT One-off and some recurring grants.
RANGE OF GRANTS £25–£5,000.
SAMPLE GRANTS £5,000 each to Horniman Museum, National Youth Orchestra, Royal National Theatre – Education Department, London Suzuki Group and Haringey Young Musicians; £4,100 to Jessie's Fund, £4,000 to London Sinfonietta; £3,900 to the Rachel Reckitt retrospective exhibition; and £3,000 to Pandit Ram Sahai Sangit Vidyalaya.
FINANCES *Year* 2000–01 *Income* £64,000 *Grants* £60,000 *Assets* £1,800,000
TRUSTEES Penelope Lively, Chair; Josephine Lively; Stephen Wick; Diana Hinds; Dr Harriet Harvey Wood.
HOW TO APPLY In writing to the correspondent, including an annual report, accounts and any other relevant supporting information. Applications are considered inFebruary, May, August and November and need to be received by the end of the preceding month.
WHO TO APPLY TO Hal Bishop, Administrator, 31 Danes Road, Exeter EX4 4LS *Tel* 01392 252855 *Fax* 01392 252855
CC NO 1070885   **ESTABLISHED** 1998

■ The Good Neighbours Trust

WHERE FUNDING CAN BE GIVEN UK, with preference for Bristol, Somerset and Gloucestershire.

WHO CAN BENEFIT Registered charities whose principal activity is to assist people with physical or mental disabilities.

WHAT IS FUNDED Principally in respect of specific projects on behalf of people who are mentally or physically disabled.

WHAT IS NOT FUNDED Support is not given for overseas projects; general community projects*; individuals; general education projects*; religious and ethnic projects*; projects for unemployment and related training schemes*; projects on behalf of offenders and ex-offenders; projects concerned with the abuse of drugs and/or alcohol; wildlife and conservation schemes*; and general restoration and preservation of buildings, purely for historical and/or architectural. * If these projects are mainly or wholly for the benefit of people who have disabilities then they will be considered. Ongoing support is not given, and grants are not usually given for running costs, salaries, research and items requiring major funding. Loans are not given.

TYPE OF GRANT One-off for specific projects. Ongoing, research, core funding, and major funding appeals are not favoured.

RANGE OF GRANTS £50–£1,000; exceptionally higher.

SAMPLE GRANTS £3,000 to Help the Hospices; £1,000 each to Joseph Clarke School for the Blind, DeadBlind UK, Holidays With Help, PACE Centre, Royal Schools for the Deaf and St Peter's Hospice – Bristol.

FINANCES *Year* 2002 *Income* £76,000 *Grants* £69,900 *Assets* £1,754,000

TRUSTEES G V Arter, Chair; J C Gurney; R T Sheppard; P S Broderick.

HOW TO APPLY The trust does not have an official application form. Appeals should be made in writing to the secretary, at any time. The trust asks that the following is carefully considered before submitting an application: Appeals must be from registered charities; include a copy of the latest audited accounts available (for newly registered charities a copy of provisional accounts showing estimated income and expenditure for the current financial year); show that the project is 'both feasible and viable' and, if relevant, give the starting date of the project and the anticipated date of completion; include the estimated cost of the project, together with the appeal's target-figure and details of what funds have already been raised and any fundraising schemes for the project.

WHO TO APPLY TO P S Broderick, Secretary, 16 Westway, Nailsea, Bristol BS48 2NA

CC NO 201794　　　**ESTABLISHED** 1960

■ Nicholas & Judith Goodison's Charitable Settlement

WHERE FUNDING CAN BE GIVEN UK.

WHO CAN BENEFIT Registered charities.

WHAT IS FUNDED Arts and arts education; mostly commitments to previously supported charities. Other causes may be considered.

WHAT IS NOT FUNDED No grants to individuals.

TYPE OF GRANT Recurrent capital grants. One-off grants may be considered.

RANGE OF GRANTS £200–£40,000, although most grants are for £2,000 or less.

SAMPLE GRANTS £40,000 to Marlborough College; £25,000 each to English National Opera and Tate Gallery; £15,000 to Victoria and Albert Museum; £11,000 in total to Courtauld Institute; £10,000 to Handel House Trust; £8,000 in total to Fitzwilliam Museum; £2,000 each to Cambridge Foundation, National Art Collections Fund and Clockmaker's Company.

FINANCES *Year* 2001–02 *Income* £280,288 *Grants* £166,800 *Assets* £1,229,950

TRUSTEES Sir Nicholas Goodison; Lady Judith Goodison; Miss Katharine Goodison.

HOW TO APPLY The trust states that it cannot respond to unsolicited applications.

WHO TO APPLY TO Sir N Goodison, Trustee, PO Box 2512, London W1A 5ZP

CC NO 1004124　　　**ESTABLISHED** 1991

■ The Everard & Mina Goodman Charitable Foundation

WHERE FUNDING CAN BE GIVEN UK.

WHO CAN BENEFIT Jewish; general charitable purposes.

WHAT IS FUNDED As well as supporting causes related to the Jewish faith, this trust also makes grants for: the relief of poverty; the advancement of education; children and youth; medicine and health; and rehabilitation and training.

RANGE OF GRANTS £100–£12,000.

SAMPLE GRANTS £12,000 to Joint Jewish Charitable Trust; £10,000 to Prostate Research Campaign; £5,500 to Child Resettlement Fund; £4,800 to Western Marble Arch Synagogue; £3,300 to Balfour Diamond Jubilee Trust; £3,000 to Royal Opera House Trust; £1,500 to British Wizo.

FINANCES *Year* 2000–01 *Income* £34,000 *Grants* £45,000

TRUSTEES E N Goodman; M Goodman; M P Goodman; S J Goodman.

HOW TO APPLY In writing to the correspondent.

WHO TO APPLY TO E N Goodman, Trustee, Flat 5, 5 Bryanston Court, London W1H 7HA

CC NO 220474　　　**ESTABLISHED** 1962

■ Mike Gooley Trailfinders Charity

WHERE FUNDING CAN BE GIVEN UK.

WHO CAN BENEFIT Charitable organisations.

WHAT IS FUNDED Medical research, particularly cancer research.

WHAT IS NOT FUNDED Grants are not made to overseas charities or to individuals.

RANGE OF GRANTS £100–£600,000.

SAMPLE GRANTS £1,500,000 to Cancer Research UK.

FINANCES *Year* 2001–02 *Grants* £1,510,000

TRUSTEES M D W Gooley; Mrs B M Gooley; T P Gooley; M Bannister.

HOW TO APPLY In writing to the correspondent.

WHO TO APPLY TO Louise Breton, Trailfinders Ltd, 9 Abingdon Road, London W8 6AH *Tel* 020 7938 3143 *Fax* 020 7937 6059

CC NO 1048993　　　**ESTABLISHED** 1995

■ The Goshen Trust

WHERE FUNDING CAN BE GIVEN North east England and overseas.

WHO CAN BENEFIT Mostly Christian organisations.

WHAT IS FUNDED Evangelical Christian work.

TYPE OF GRANT One-off.

SAMPLE GRANTS In 1997–98: £3,500 to Whitchester House; £3,000 to Walsall Community Church; £2,000 to Lightfoot Grove Baptist Church; £1,000 each to Benny Hinn Media Ministries,

Kirroko Hospital – Uganda, and United Christian Broadcasters.

FINANCES *Year* 2001–02 *Income* £1,026,489

TRUSTEES A G Dicken; P B Dicken; J R Dicken; A Dicken; R Oliver.

HOW TO APPLY In writing to the correspondent. Applications are considered in March, June, September and December. An sae is needed if a reply in required. Initial applications should include minimum information as further information from potential beneficiaries will be requested.

WHO TO APPLY TO R Oliver, Administrator, PO Box 367, Stockton-on-Tees TS16 9YR

CC NO 274910   **ESTABLISHED** 1977

■ The Gosling Foundation Ltd

WHERE FUNDING CAN BE GIVEN UK.

WHO CAN BENEFIT Registered charities benefiting children, young adults, older people and people disadvantaged by poverty.

WHAT IS FUNDED The relief of poverty, suffering and distress; provision of facilities for recreation and other leisure-time occupation (in the interests of social welfare); naval charities; advancement of education; furtherance of other charitable purposes.

RANGE OF GRANTS Mainly £100–£5,000, but up to £55,000.

SAMPLE GRANTS £260,000 to Westminster Christmas Appeal; £200,000 each to Island Race Trust and John Groom Association for the Disabled; £192,000 to Fleet Air Arm Memorial Appeal; £150,000 to Parachute Regimental Central Fund; £100,000 each to Jubilee Sailing Trust, Liver Research Trust, Memorial Gates Trust and Outward Bound Trust; £76,000 to King George's Fund for Sailors.

FINANCES *Year* 2000–01 *Income* £4,300,000 *Grants* £2,320,000 *Assets* £30,000,000

TRUSTEES Sir Donald Gosling; Ronald Hobson.

HOW TO APPLY To the correspondent in writing.

WHO TO APPLY TO A Yusof, Secretary, 21 Bryanston Street, London W1A 4NH *Tel* 020 7499 7050

CC NO 326840   **ESTABLISHED** 1962

■ The Gough Charitable Trust

WHERE FUNDING CAN BE GIVEN UK, with a possible preference for Scotland.

WHO CAN BENEFIT Registered charities only, usually working in the areas outlined below, benefiting children, young adults and the Church of England.

WHAT IS FUNDED Youth projects; Episcopal or Church of England projects; preservation of the countryside.

WHAT IS NOT FUNDED No support for non-registered charities and individuals including students.

TYPE OF GRANT Usually one-off but some ongoing.

SAMPLE GRANTS £10,000 to Venture Trust; £5,000 each to RSPB Scotland, Women Caring Trust Wykeham Crown and Manor Trust; £2,000 each to Gordon Foundation and Irish Guards – Lieutenant Colonel's Charity; £1,000 each to Charlton Society, Christ's College, St Laxarus of Jerusalem and St James' and St Anne's Episcopal Churches.

FINANCES *Year* 2000–01 *Income* £47,553 *Grants* £37,600

TRUSTEES Lloyds Bank plc; N de L Harvie.

HOW TO APPLY In writing to the correspondent at any time. No application forms are available; no acknowledgements are sent. Applications are considered quarterly.

WHO TO APPLY TO Mrs E Osborn-King, Trust Manager, Lloyds TSB Private Banking Ltd, UK Trust Centre, 22–26 Ock Street, Abingdon OX14 5SW

CC NO 262355   **ESTABLISHED** 1970

■ The Gould Charitable Trust

WHERE FUNDING CAN BE GIVEN UK.

WHO CAN BENEFIT Registered charities only.

WHAT IS FUNDED General charitable purposes.

WHAT IS NOT FUNDED No support for non-registered charities. No grants to individuals.

RANGE OF GRANTS £24–£22,000.

SAMPLE GRANTS £20,000 to JPAIME; £6,600 to Childhope; £2,000 each to Centrepoint and NSPCC; £1,500 to Save the Children.

FINANCES *Year* 1999–2000 *Income* £45,200 *Grants* £41,551 *Assets* £736,449

TRUSTEES Mrs J B Gould; L J Gould; M S Gould; S Gould; S H Gould.

HOW TO APPLY In writing to the correspondent, although the trust states: 'We never give donations to unsolicited requests on principle.'

WHO TO APPLY TO S Gould, Trustee, Cervantes, Pinner Hill, Pinner, Middlesex HA5 3XU

CC NO 1035453   **ESTABLISHED** 1993

■ Grace Baptist Trust Corporation

WHERE FUNDING CAN BE GIVEN Throughout the UK, but most of the trusts administered by the corporation are restricted to a certain specified geographical area in which they can make grants.

WHO CAN BENEFIT Strict and Particular Baptist Chapels and their pastors, itinerant ministers, members and regular attenders, including their children.

WHAT IS FUNDED Advancement of the Christian religion, particularly in accordance with the principles of the Strict and Particular Baptist Churches. Grants and loans are made to Strict and Particular Baptist Churches for the maintenance and improvement of their premises and properties. Grants are made from three small funds to needy pastors, itinerant ministers, members and regular attenders of the Strict and Particular Baptist Church and their children. Male members of the Strict and Particular Baptist Church called to enter the ministry are assisted.

TYPE OF GRANT Usually one-off, but it depends upon the circumstances of the appeal. Interest-free loans are also made.

FINANCES *Year* 2001 *Income* £410,645 *Grants* £350,000

TRUSTEES Directors: J N Broome; D J Bucknall; J A Burch, Chair; N R Clarkson; A R Copeman; S D T Condy; D J Hollands; M C Penton; J A H Risbridger; D Schwier; D W J Skull; A J Symonds; M S Wright; H R Sayers; D J Steere; A B Keen; G D Hawkins.

HOW TO APPLY By application form, although the trust states that unsolicited applications are not accepted.

WHO TO APPLY TO E Cousins, General Secretary, 19 Croydon Road, Caterham, Surrey CR3 6DP *Tel* 01883 345488 *Fax* 01883 345129 *E-mail* admin@gbtc.org.uk

CC NO 251675   **ESTABLISHED** 1957

■ The Grace Charitable Trust

WHERE FUNDING CAN BE GIVEN UK.
WHO CAN BENEFIT Registered charities, including Christian organisations.
WHAT IS FUNDED General charitable purposes.
RANGE OF GRANTS £1,000–£10,000.
FINANCES *Year* 2000–01 *Income* £312,997 *Grants* £367,650 *Assets* £5,137,615
TRUSTEES Mrs G J R Payne; E Payne; Mrs G M Snaith; R B M Quayle.
HOW TO APPLY The trust states: 'Grants are made only to charities known to the settlors and unsolicited applications are, therefore, not considered.'
WHO TO APPLY TO Mrs G J R Payne, Trustee, Rhuallt House, Rhuallt, St Asaph, Sir Ddinbych LL17 0TG *Fax* 01745 585243
CC NO 292984   **ESTABLISHED** 1985

■ The Graff Foundation

WHERE FUNDING CAN BE GIVEN UK and worldwide.
WHO CAN BENEFIT Charitable organisations.
WHAT IS FUNDED General charitable purposes.
TYPE OF GRANT One-off and recurrent.
SAMPLE GRANTS £10,000 to Red Hot AIDS Charitable Trust; £1,500 to Friends of Beis Yisroel Trust; £959 to Gemological Institute of America; £250 to Nightingale House; £200 each to Barnardos, Cancer Vaccine Institute and Teenage Cancer Trust.
FINANCES *Year* 2000 *Income* £95,081 *Grants* £13,309 *Assets* £1,254,306
TRUSTEES Laurence Graff; Francois Xavier Graff; Anthony D Kerman.
HOW TO APPLY In writing to the correspondent.
WHO TO APPLY TO Anthony D Kerman, Trustee, 5 St James Square, London SW1Y 4JU
CC NO 1012859   **ESTABLISHED** 1991

■ E C Graham Belford Charitable Settlement

WHERE FUNDING CAN BE GIVEN Northumberland.
WHO CAN BENEFIT Organisations based in Northumberland.
WHAT IS FUNDED General charitable purposes.
TYPE OF GRANT One-off.
RANGE OF GRANTS £3,000–£10,000.
SAMPLE GRANTS £5,000 to Berwick Youth Project; £3,000 to Youth Against Crime for an awards scheme.
FINANCES *Year* 2001–02 *Income* £103,287 *Grants* £56,029
TRUSTEES A I Thompson.
HOW TO APPLY Please note, the trust states: 'There is only a limited amount of income available for distribution and there are local projects which the trustees already favour.' It is unlikely, therefore, that unsolicited applications will be successful.
WHO TO APPLY TO A I Thompson, Trustee, Lawrence Graham, 190 Strand, London WC2R 1JN *Tel* 020 7379 0000
CC NO 1014869   **ESTABLISHED** 1991

■ The Reginald Graham Charitable Trust

WHERE FUNDING CAN BE GIVEN UK.
WHO CAN BENEFIT Registered charities benefiting children and young adults; academics; sportsmen and women; at risk groups; victims of abuse and domestic violence; and people with cancer, cystic fibrosis and muscular dystrophy.
WHAT IS FUNDED Currently the main area of interest is cancer care; fine art; literature; music; special schools; and tertiary and higher education.
WHAT IS NOT FUNDED No grants to individuals; only charitable organisations are supported.
TYPE OF GRANT One-off, core costs, buildings and capital. Funding is available for up to and over three years.
RANGE OF GRANTS £25–£30,000.
SAMPLE GRANTS £30,000 to Pembroke College.
FINANCES *Year* 1997–98 *Income* £64,000 *Grants* £62,000
TRUSTEES Reginald Graham; Mrs Melanie Boyd; George Josselyn; Michael Wood.
OTHER INFORMATION In 2000–01 the trust had an income of £62,000 and a total expenditure of £78,000. Unfortunately we were unable to get any further information for this year.
HOW TO APPLY The trust stated that it currently has a number of charities which receive regular support and they are not considering new applications at present. It was anticipated in January 2003 that no new grants would be made in the next two years.
WHO TO APPLY TO Michael Wood, Trustee, Bircham Dyson Bell, 50 Broadway, London SW1H 0BL *Tel* 020 7227 7000
CC NO 212428   **ESTABLISHED** 1957

■ The Grahame Charitable Foundation

WHERE FUNDING CAN BE GIVEN UK and worldwide.
WHO CAN BENEFIT Organisations benefiting: children, young adults, older people and Jewish people.
WHAT IS FUNDED The advancement of the Jewish religion; health facilities and buildings, medical studies and research; special schools; cultural and religious teaching; and community services.
WHAT IS NOT FUNDED No grants to individuals.
TYPE OF GRANT Capital, core costs, interest-free loans, one-off, recurring costs and start-up costs. Funding for up to two years may be considered.
RANGE OF GRANTS £100–£50,000.
FINANCES *Year* 2001 *Income* £345,428 *Grants* £278,536 *Assets* £360,789
TRUSTEES Gitte Grahame; Jeffrey Greenwood.
HOW TO APPLY In writing to the correspondent. Funds are fully committed for the next four to five years. The trustees allocate funds on a long-term basis and therefore have none available for other applicants.
WHO TO APPLY TO Mrs S Brooks, 5 Spencer Walk, Hampstead High Street, London NW3 1QZ *Tel* 020 7794 5281 *Fax* 020 7794 0094
CC NO 259864   **ESTABLISHED** 1969

■ The Granada Foundation

WHERE FUNDING CAN BE GIVEN North west England.
WHAT IS FUNDED The study, practice and appreciation of the fine arts, including drawing, architecture and landscape architecture, sculpture, literature, music, opera, drama,

cinema and the methods and means of their dissemination.

From time to time the advisory council may take an initiative by offering, for instance, a specialist prize, a residency or even a university chair. In general, however, the council looks for imaginative proposals from organisations (preferably with charity status) which will in some way make the north-west in particular a richer and more attractive place in which to live and work.

There is a clear preference for new projects; although the foundation will support festivals and other annual events, it is on the understanding that such support should not be regarded as automatically renewable.

WHAT IS NOT FUNDED No grants will be given for general appeals, individuals (including for courses of study), expeditions, overseas travel or youth clubs/community associations.

RANGE OF GRANTS £500–£15,000.

SAMPLE GRANTS 1998–99: £15,000 to University of Manchester towards Arboretum project; £13,000 each to Empire Theatre, Liverpool (the second of two grants towards restoration and refurbishment), Royal Exchange Theatre (the second of two grants to help with the return to the exchange after the Manchester bomb), and the Tate Gallery, Liverpool for phase 4 of the development plan; £10,000 each to Buxton Festival (1999) and CAPE UK (and North West Arts Board) – the second of three grants towards creative arts partnership in four Manchester schools; £7,500 to Bolton Museum & Art Gallery towards acquisition of work by Thomas Moran; £6,500 to Liverpool Architect & Design Trust towards core costs and the Super Lamb Banana Tour; £5,000 each to Bluecoat Display Centre towards 'Countdown' – a series of live art commissions and Brouhaha International Festival (1998).

FINANCES *Year* 2001–02 *Grants* £164,000

TRUSTEES Advisory Council: Sir Robert Scott, Chair; Lord Bernstein; Lady Manduell; Prof. Denis McCaldin; Mrs Margaret Kenyon; Philip Ramsbottom; Miss Kathy Arundale; Viv Tyler; Christopher Kerr.

HOW TO APPLY Write for an application form, giving an outline of the project. Detailed information can be added when the formal application is submitted. Details of the next trustees' meeting will be given when an application form is sent (trustees meet three to four times a year at irregular intervals). All letters are acknowledged, whether possible successful applicants or immediate rejections. 'The Advisory Council interprets the guidelines in a flexible way, realising that it cannot hope to achieve a true balance across all the areas of activity. The council does, however, examine the context of each application and tries to make grants in areas where the benefit will be most widely felt.'

WHO TO APPLY TO Mrs Irene Langford, Administrator, c/o Bridgegate House, 5 Bridge Place, Lower Bridge Street, Chester CH1 1SA *Tel* 01244 403305
E-mail irene.langford@granadamedia.com
CC NO 241693   **ESTABLISHED** 1965

■ Grand Charitable Trust of the Order of Women Freemasons

WHERE FUNDING CAN BE GIVEN UK and overseas.
WHO CAN BENEFIT Registered charities.
WHAT IS FUNDED General charitable purposes.
SAMPLE GRANTS £50,000 in grants to outside charities; £54,000 to Adelaide Litten Charitable Trust; £1,800 to individuals in need (who have connections with the Order).
FINANCES *Year* 1999–2000 *Income* £167,000 *Grants* £50,000 *Assets* £492,000
TRUSTEES B I Fleming-Taylor; M J P Masters; B I Whittingham; H I Naldrett; J S Brown; I M Boggia-Black.
HOW TO APPLY In writing to the correspondent. Applications should be submitted by the end of July each year for consideration by the trustees.
WHO TO APPLY TO Mrs Joan Sylvia Brown, Trustee, 27 Pembridge Gardens, London W2 4EF *Tel* 020 7229 2368
CC NO 1059151   **ESTABLISHED** 1996

■ The Grand Charity of Freemasons

WHERE FUNDING CAN BE GIVEN England and Wales, with a local interest in London.
WHO CAN BENEFIT Individuals who are elderly or distressed; charities benefiting Freemasons of the United Grand Lodge of England and their dependants; other charities concerned with general welfare, especially of young and older people.
WHAT IS FUNDED Consideration is only given to charities whose work covers the whole of England and Wales; London charities (no other local charities should apply); and indigent Freemasons of the United Grand Lodge of England, their widows and certain other dependants. Welfare and medical charities, and some emergency aid charities, will be considered.
WHAT IS NOT FUNDED Local charities, except those serving London, are not eligible for funding. Grants are not normally given to individuals (other than for the relief of 'poor and distressed Freemasons' and their poor and distressed dependants); organisations not registered with the Charity Commission; activities that are primarily the responsibility of central or local government or some other responsible body; organisations or projects outside of England and Wales; animal welfare; the arts; the environment; charities with sectarian (religious) or political objectives.
RANGE OF GRANTS £500–£500,000.
SAMPLE GRANTS £160,000 to Help the Aged; £150,000 to Scope; £135,000 to CRISIS; £103,900 to the National Asthma Campaign; £100,000 each to the Buttle Trust and Refuge; £99,700 to Tommy's Campaign; £99,100 to Abbeyfield; £70,000 to Homestart; £45,000 to the Wishbone Trust.
FINANCES *Year* 2000–01 *Income* £4,612,400 *Grants* £2,795,000 *Assets* £21,000,000
TRUSTEES The council, consisting of a president and at least 26 council members, listed in the annual reports.
PUBLICATIONS Booklet, *Information on Masonic Charities*.
OTHER INFORMATION The grant figure given above is for grants to non-masonic charities. In addition, over £2 million was spent helping Freemasons and their dependants in need, and in support for other Masonic causes.

HOW TO APPLY Application forms are available from the Grand Charity office. They must be completed in full, either typed or written in block capitals, and accompanied by a copy of the latest annual report and full audited accounts; these must be less than 18 months old. Hospice grant applications are made on a separate form, available from either the appropriate Provincial Grand Lodge (listed in telephone directories, usually under 'Freemasons' or 'Masons') or the Grand Charity office. Applications may be submitted to the office of the Grand Charity at any time throughout the year.

WHO TO APPLY TO The Chief executive, 60 Great Queen Street, London WC2B 5AZ *Tel* 020 7395 9293 *Fax* 020 7831 6021 *E-mail* info@the-grand-charity.org

CC NO 281942   **ESTABLISHED** 1980

■ The Grand Order of Water Rats Charities Fund

WHERE FUNDING CAN BE GIVEN UK.

WHO CAN BENEFIT Organisations benefiting: actors and entertainment professionals and their dependants.

WHAT IS FUNDED Assistance to members of the variety and light entertainment profession who are in need. Also supplying medical equipment to certain hospitals and institutions.

WHAT IS NOT FUNDED No grants to students.

TYPE OF GRANT One-off and recurrent.

FINANCES *Year* 2001 *Income* £130,081 *Grants* £88,203 *Assets* £895,675

TRUSTEES Wyn Calvin; Declan Cluskey; Roy Hudd; Paul Daniels; Keith Simmons.

HOW TO APPLY In writing to the correspondent. The trustees meet once a month.

WHO TO APPLY TO John Adrian, Secretary, 328 Gray's Inn Road, London WC1X 8BZ *Tel* 020 7407 8007 *Fax* 020 7403 8610 *E-mail* gowr4adrian@aol.com

CC NO 292201   **ESTABLISHED** 1889

■ Grantham Yorke Trust

WHERE FUNDING CAN BE GIVEN West Midlands, in particular the Birmingham area.

WHO CAN BENEFIT People under the age of 25 who are in need and were born within the old West Midlands metropolitan county area, and youth organisations benefiting such people.

WHAT IS FUNDED Education, including providing outfits, clothing, tools, instruments, equipment or books to help such people on leaving school, university and so on, to prepare for, or enter a profession or trade.

RANGE OF GRANTS £50–£5,000.

SAMPLE GRANTS £12,000 to Foundation for Conductive Education; £10,000 each to BID Centre for Deaf People, Dudley Health Authority and Fairbridge; £6,000 each to Starlight Children's Foundation and Symphony Hall – Birmingham; £5,000 each to Avoncroft Musuem, Birmingham Community Association Youth Project, Carpenters Arms, Dodford Children's Holiday Farm, SENSE and Welford Community Trust.

FINANCES *Year* 1998–99 *Income* £351,114 *Grants* £316,000 *Assets* £4,751,479

TRUSTEES P Varcoe; H Belton; P Jones; P Smiglarski; L Cox; B Welford; D Macdonald; E Insch; Revd Chris Feak.

HOW TO APPLY In writing to the correspondent. The trustees meet four times a year, in March, June, November and December.

WHO TO APPLY TO Miss Lucy Chatt and David L Turfrey, Appeals Clerks, Martineau Johnson, St Philips House, St Philips Place, Birmingham B3 2PP *Tel* 0121 200 3300

CC NO 228466   **ESTABLISHED** 1975

■ The J G Graves Charitable Trust

WHERE FUNDING CAN BE GIVEN Mainly Sheffield.

WHO CAN BENEFIT Registered charities.

WHAT IS FUNDED Charities working in the fields of: provision of parks and open spaces; libraries and art galleries; advancement of education; general benefit of people who are sick or poor; and such other charitable purposes as the trustees see fit. The income is mainly applied to local (Sheffield) charities for capital purposes rather than running costs.

WHAT IS NOT FUNDED Grants are generally not made to or for the benefit of individuals.

TYPE OF GRANT Mainly for capital and one-off for start-ups. Some for running costs.

SAMPLE GRANTS £10,000 to Friends of the General Cemetary – Sheffield Botanical Gardens Trust for restoration work; £5,000 each to Stannington Scouts Group, Cavendish Fellowship on Hip Surgery for a research fellowship and St Mary's 2000 for community facilities.

FINANCES *Year* 2001 *Income* £174,000 *Grants* £130,000 *Assets* £4,000,000

TRUSTEES G F Young; R S Sanderson; T H Reed; R T Graves; S Hamilton; D S W Lee; Mrs A C Womack; G W Bridge; P Price; Mrs J Lee; Dr D R Cullen.

HOW TO APPLY In writing to the correspondent, to reach the secretary by 31 March, 30 June, 30 September or 31 December. Applications should indicate whether the applicant is a registered charity, include audited accounts and include a statement giving such up-to-date information as is available with regard to the income and any commitments the organisation has.

WHO TO APPLY TO R H M Plews, Secretary, Knowle House, 4 Norfolk Park Road, Sheffield S2 3QE *Tel* 0114 276 7991

CC NO 207481   **ESTABLISHED** 1930

■ The Gray Trust

WHERE FUNDING CAN BE GIVEN Nottinghamshire.

WHO CAN BENEFIT Organisations benefiting older people, retired people, ex-service and service people, and people who are disadvantaged by poverty or disability.

WHAT IS FUNDED General purposes for the benefit of three parishes set out in the deed; care of older people, especially in Nottinghamshire; Christian churches, especially in the diocese of Southall; county and national charities connected with the armed forces; specified repeat grants.

WHAT IS NOT FUNDED Grants are not made to individuals and seldom for applications from outside Nottinghamshire.

FINANCES *Year* 2002 *Grants* £70,000

TRUSTEES John D Radford; Bella St Clair Harlow; Clare Hardstaff; K H Turner; R B S Stringfellow.

HOW TO APPLY In writing to the correspondent by letter of application together with most recent accounts.

WHO TO APPLY TO The Trustees, 309–329 Haydn Road, Sherwood, Nottingham NG5 1HG
Tel 0115 960 7111
CC NO 210914   **ESTABLISHED** 1962

■ The Great Britain Sasakawa Foundation

WHERE FUNDING CAN BE GIVEN UK, Japan.
WHO CAN BENEFIT Voluntary, charitable, educational and cultural organisations benefiting citizens of UK and Japan. Emphasis on younger people and on projects benefiting groups of people rather than individuals.
WHAT IS FUNDED Advancement of the education of the citizens of the UK and Japan in each other's institutions, people, history, language, culture, and society and in each other's intellectual, artistic and economic life. Research, exchanges, seminars, courses, publications and cultural events may all be funded. The foundation has a special scheme for joint research in medicine and health.
WHAT IS NOT FUNDED Grants are not made to individuals applying on their own behalf. The foundation can, however, consider proposals from organisations that support the activities of individuals, provided they are citizens of the UK or Japan. No grants can be made for the construction, conservation or maintenance of land and buildings. The foundation will not support activities involving politics, legislation or election to public office. Grants are not normally made for medical research.
TYPE OF GRANT Mainly one-off; also project and research, maximum term three years. Funding for feasibility studies and start-up costs will also be considered
RANGE OF GRANTS £500–£15,000; average grant £2,000.
SAMPLE GRANTS £13,000 to British Association for Japanese Studies as part of a three-year commitment for UK-Japan research initiatives, including workshops and publications on regional governance and the Japanese political economy; £4,000 to London Sinfonietta towards the UK premier of one act music theatre work 'Hagoromo'; £3,000 to Asia House, London to fund six free lectures on contemporary Japan looking at design, architecture, film, society and lifestyle; £3,000 to Cardiff Japanese Studies Centre for a one-day conference on Japanese railways; £2,000 to St Catherine's College, Oxford to enable four speakers to travel to the Oxford-Kobe seminar on language change and historical linguistics in Kobe; £1,000 to Tokei Martial Arts Centre, London to enable members to participate in the International Karate Championships in Tokyo.
FINANCES *Year* 2001 *Income* £766,019 *Grants* £346,285 *Assets* £19,387,194
TRUSTEES Council: Prof. Peter Mathias, Chair; Hon. Yoshio Sakurauchi; Michael French, Treasurer; Baroness Brigstocke; Jeremy Brown; Baroness Park of Monmouth; Earl of St Andrews; Kazuo Chiba; Prof. Harumi Kimura; Yohei Sasakawa; Akira Iriyama; Prof. Shoichi Watanabe; Sir John Boyd.
OTHER INFORMATION The foundation is rarely able to consider grants for the total cost of any project and encourages applicants to seek additional support from other donors.
HOW TO APPLY In advance of formal applications, foundation staff welcome telephone enquiries or personal visits to their office to discuss eligibility. The awards committee meets in London in February, May and October. Applications should be received by December, March and August. Awards meetings in Tokyo are held in April and October, with applications to be submitted by February and September. Applicants should request an application form either from the London headquarters or from the Tokyo liaison office; however, the foundation expresses a strong preference for e-mailed applications. A form will be e-mailed on request, and is also available on their website. Applications should contain the following information: a summary of the proposed project and its aims, including its likely impact and long-term benefits; total cost of the project and the amount of the desired grant, together with a note of other expected sources of funds, including estimated period for research projects, visits or study; a description of the applicant's organisation and, where relevant, brief career details of the main participants in any project, and where appropriate the ages of those individuals who may be the recipients.
WHO TO APPLY TO The Administrator, Dilke House, 1 Malet Street, London WC1E 7JN *Tel* 020 7436 9042 *Fax* 020 7355 2230
E-mail grants@gbsf.org.uk
Website www.gbsf.org.uk
CC NO 290766   **ESTABLISHED** 1985

■ The Great Stone Bridge Trust of Edenbridge

WHERE FUNDING CAN BE GIVEN The parish of Edenbridge.
WHO CAN BENEFIT Organisations, and individuals under 25 for educational purposes.
WHAT IS FUNDED Education and general charitable purposes in the parish of Edenbridge.
TYPE OF GRANT Some recurrent.
SAMPLE GRANTS In 1998–99: £31,468 to Eden Valley School; £10,000 to Edenbridge Parish Council; £6,500 to Edenbridge Primary School; £5,000 to Eden Valley Museum Trust; £3,500 to Edenbridge Holiday Activity Scheme; £2,500 each to Edenbridge Community Care for the Elderly and Edenbridge Volunteer Bureau; £2,000 each to Bridges Trust, Edenbridge Mencap, and Marsh Primary School.
FINANCES *Year* 2001–02 *Income* £113,956
TRUSTEES N Young; T Smith; A Dell; J Harris; D Leigh; Mrs R Parsons; Mrs C Burgess; R Drew; Dr A Russell.
HOW TO APPLY In writing to the correspondent.
WHO TO APPLY TO W M Ross, Clerk, 8 Church Lane, East Grinstead, West Sussex RH19 3BA
Tel 01342 323687
CC NO 224309   **ESTABLISHED** 1964

■ Greater Bristol Foundation

WHERE FUNDING CAN BE GIVEN Former Avon area – Bristol, north Somerset, Bath, north east Somerset and south Gloucestershire.
WHO CAN BENEFIT Any charity aimed at increasing opportunities and enhancing the quality of life in the area; particularly smaller, low-profile community groups and people at a particular disadvantage through discrimination.
WHAT IS FUNDED Express Fund: Up to £1,000 to small, local voluntary and community organisations, with a priority for organisations which reach people who are disadvantaged or isolated. Catalyst Service: larger grants than the Express Fund (generally up to £5,000) for the

same criteria. Arts Access Fund: up to £1,000 for access issues and £3,000 for project work for artists who are disabled in the city of Bristol to help them develop their work. Bristol and West Charitable Trust: up to £1,000 to organisations in the south west supporting the education and development of young people, the welfare of young people with disabilities and homeless projects. Bristol Collection Box Scheme: up to £3,000 to Bristol organisations which support the resettlement of homeless people. Bristol Kidz Fund: up to £2,000 to organisations which work with school-aged children and young people within a ten-mile radius of the centre of Bristol. Bristol Youth Community Action (BYCA): for young people-led community safety projects in Bristol, and funding for locally-based groups providing summer activities for young people in Bristol. Churngold Environmental Fund: up to £5,000 for environmental and educational projects. Local Network Fund: up to £7,000 for voluntary organisations in Bristol, Bath and North East Somerset, South Gloucestershire and North Somerset which help children (aged 0 to 19) living in poverty to achieve their full potential. Neighbourhood Renewal Community Chest and Community Learning Chest: up to £5,000 for community organisations in the Neighbourhood Renewal area, other pockets of need in Bristol and some other communities of interrest. North Somerset Fund: up to £1,000 to small, local voluntary organisations where a small amount of funding can make a difference in disadvantaged areas of North Somerset. Safer Communities Fund: up to £2,000 to organisations aiming to make their communities safer. University of Bristol Students Rag Fund: up to £1,000 to organisations which work with children, homeless people or support people with long-term illness.

WHAT IS NOT FUNDED The foundation's own grants programme does not fund general appeals; statutory organisations or direct replacement of statutory funding; promotion of religious causes; overseas travel; medical research, equipment or treatment; sports without an identifiable charitable element; arts projects with limited community benefit; animal charities; individuals. Vehicles, conferences and exhibitions will be given low priority.

SAMPLE GRANTS From unrestricted funds: £5,000 to SARI; £3,000 to Children's Scrapstore; £1,800 to St Paul's Advice Centre; £1,167 to Shirehampton Public Hall; £1,000 each to Bannerman Road Primary School, Current Account Theatre, Dove Street Action Group, Parkway Parent and Child Project, Pop Inn Cafe and Stockwood Community Council.

FINANCES *Year* 2001–02 *Income* £1,800,000 *Grants* £1,008,000 *Assets* £6,000,000

TRUSTEES Trevor Smallwood, Chair; Will Bee; Norman Biddle; Gillian Camm; Steve Egginton; Jos Harrison; Alfred Morris; John Pontin; Simon Speirs; Tim Stevenson; Simon Storvik; Jay Tidmarsh; Heather Wheelhouse; Sir David Wills.

HOW TO APPLY There is a separate information sheet (detailing criteria, closing dates and maximum amount given) available for each fund. Please contact Alice Meason or Ronnie Brown at the foundation either to discuss the funding that you need, or to receive further information and assistance. Guidelines and application forms can be downloaded from the foundation's website. Most grants are made on an ongoing basis; however, some funds have deadlines. Please check the website for details.

WHO TO APPLY TO Helen Moss, Director, Royal Oak House, Royal Oak Avenue, Bristol BS1 4GB *Tel* 0117 989 7700 *Website* www.gbf.org.uk
CC NO 1080418   **ESTABLISHED** 1987

....

■ The Barry Green Memorial Fund

WHERE FUNDING CAN BE GIVEN UK, with a preference for Yorkshire and Lancashire.

WHO CAN BENEFIT There is a preference towards smaller charities working at grassroots level.

WHAT IS FUNDED Preference for smaller charities rescuing and caring for cruelly treated animals; animal homes; animal welfare; cats, catteries and other facilities for cats; dogs, kennels and other facilities for dogs; and horses, stables and other facilities for horses.

WHAT IS NOT FUNDED No expeditions, scholarships, work outside the UK or individuals.

TYPE OF GRANT Buildings, core costs, one-off, recurring costs, running costs and start-up costs. Funding available for more than three years.

RANGE OF GRANTS £100–£30,000.

SAMPLE GRANTS £5,000 to Winslade Wildlife Sanctuary; £3,000 each to Assisi Animal Sanctuary and Wildlife in Need; £2,500 each to Royal Veterinary College – North Mymms, Ty-Agored Open House Animal Sanctuary and Widewalls Animal Sanctuary; £2,000 each to BARK, Berwick Swan and Wildlife Trust, Cats Paws Sanctuary, Furness Cat Shelter, Mare and Foal Sanctuary, Mid Cheshire Animal Welfare and Thoroughbred Rehabilitation Centre.

FINANCES *Year* 2000–01 *Income* £169,606 *Grants* £68,250 *Assets* £1,247,064

TRUSTEES Richard Fitzgerald-Hart; Mark Fitzgerald-Hart.

HOW TO APPLY In writing to the correspondent including a copy of the accounts.

WHO TO APPLY TO The Clerk to the Trustees, Claro Chambers, Horsefair, Boroughbridge, York YO51 9LD
CC NO 1000492   **ESTABLISHED** 1990

....

■ The Constance Green Foundation

WHERE FUNDING CAN BE GIVEN England, with a preference for West Yorkshire.

WHO CAN BENEFIT Registered charities, and organisations recognised as charitable, benefiting children; young adults and older people; service and ex-service people; seafarers and fishermen; unemployed people; those in care, fostered and adopted; at risk groups; disabled people; people disadvantaged by poverty; homeless people; victims of famine and war; and people with autism, cancer, epilepsy, head and other injuries, multiple sclerosis, prenatal conditions, terminal illness or tropical diseases.

WHAT IS FUNDED Some preference is given to charities operating in Yorkshire. In previous years grants have been made mainly, but not exclusively, to national organisations in the fields of social welfare and medicine, with special emphasis on support of young people in need and mentally and physically disabled people. Preference for charities working in the fields of residential facilities and services, health and social care professional bodies, councils for voluntary service, special schools and special needs education, medical research and various community facilities and services.

Think carefully about every application. Is it justified?

507

WHAT IS NOT FUNDED Sponsorship of individuals is not supported.

TYPE OF GRANT Capital, special project, buildings and one-off funding of one year or less.

RANGE OF GRANTS £800–£125,000.

SAMPLE GRANTS £250,000 to Martin House Hospice – Wetherby; £5,000 each to BLESMA, Croft Community – Camphill Village Trust, Clow Beck Children's Farm, MERLIN, Orbis Charitable Trust, Park House Trust, Royal Agricultural Benevolent Institution, St Martin-in-the-Fields Social Care Unit, Salvation Army, Shelter and YMCA – England.

FINANCES *Year* 2001–02 *Income* £363,155 *Grants* £389,000 *Assets* £7,493,931

TRUSTEES M Collinson; Col. H R Hall; Mrs M L Hall; Mrs S Collinson.

HOW TO APPLY At any time in writing to the correspondent (no special form of application required). Applications should include clear details of the need the intended project is designed to meet, plus an outline budget. All applications meeting the foundation's criteria are acknowledged.

WHO TO APPLY TO ASL Management Services, Bel Royal House, Hilgrove Street, St Helier, Jersey JE2 4SL *Tel* 01534 726506 *Fax* 01534 720625 *E-mail* management@asl-jersey.com

CC NO 270775   **ESTABLISHED** 1976

■ The J C Green Charitable Settlement

WHERE FUNDING CAN BE GIVEN International, with a preference for Cornwall.

WHO CAN BENEFIT Local good causes in Cornwall.

WHAT IS FUNDED Leadership, environment, and local community initiatives.

TYPE OF GRANT Cash and loans.

RANGE OF GRANTS £10–£5,000.

SAMPLE GRANTS £5,155 to Institute of Agricultural Management; £1,000 each to Port Navis Village Hall Appeal, Kinfisher's Bridge Wetland Creation Trust; £600 to Nuffield Farm School JCG; £500 to Grange Park Opera; £200 each to Diocese of Truro, ACR Addington Fund, Zimbabwe Farmer's Trust Fund; £150 each to Ely Cathedral Tour Fund and Friends of Cornish Churches.

FINANCES *Year* 2001–02 *Income* £24,000 *Grants* £21,000 *Assets* £260,000

TRUSTEES J C Green; Mrs M C Green.

HOW TO APPLY Initial applications by email. Postal applications will not be responded to.

WHO TO APPLY TO J C Green, Trustee, Calamansac House, Port Navas, Constantine, Falmouth, Cornwall TR11 5RN *Tel* 01326 341042 *Fax* 01326 341043 *E-mail* j.green@eidosnet.co.uk

CC NO 291254   **ESTABLISHED** 1984

■ The Greencard Charitable Trust

WHERE FUNDING CAN BE GIVEN UK and overseas.

WHO CAN BENEFIT Local, regional and international environmental charities and credible projects.

WHAT IS FUNDED Purchase of equipment and materials for environmental projects.

WHAT IS NOT FUNDED No grants to individuals.

RANGE OF GRANTS Usually up to £5,000.

SAMPLE GRANTS In 1996–97: £21,000 to Biodiversity Challenge as payments to various wildlife trusts; £10,000 to Herpetological Conservation Trust; £5,000 to Royal Geographical Society; £3,300 to London Wildlife Trust; £3,000 to RSPB; £1,750 to Farm Africa.

FINANCES *Year* 2000–01 *Income* £35,428

TRUSTEES Dr J Hemming; Dr N Chalmers.

HOW TO APPLY In writing to the correspondent. Guidelines are available from the trust.

WHO TO APPLY TO Caroline Snowdon, Transnational Financial Services Ltd, 33 Blagrave Street, Reading RG1 1PW

CC NO 803506   **ESTABLISHED** 1990

■ The Mrs H R Greene Charitable Settlement

WHERE FUNDING CAN BE GIVEN UK, with a preference for Wistanstow in Shropshire and Norfolk.

WHO CAN BENEFIT Individuals and institutions, particularly those benefiting at risk groups, and people who are disadvantaged by poverty or socially isolated.

WHAT IS FUNDED Welfare and general charitable purposes.

SAMPLE GRANTS In 1997–98: £6,000 to St Michael's Hospital Bartestree; £2,500 each to Norfolk and Norwich Clergymens Widows and Children's Charity; £2,000 each to Brittle Bone Society, Children's Food Fund, Landau, Macmillan Cancer Relief, Muscular Dystrophy Group and Orbis.

FINANCES *Year* 1999–2000 *Income* £61,000 *Grants* £57,500

TRUSTEES A C Boston; Revd J B Boston; D A Moore.

HOW TO APPLY The trust states that it does not respond to unsolicited applications.

WHO TO APPLY TO N G Sparrow, Eversheds, Paston House, 11–13 Princes Street, Norwich NR3 1BD

CC NO 1050812   **ESTABLISHED** 1845

■ Greenham Common Community Trust Limited

WHERE FUNDING CAN BE GIVEN West Berkshire and northern Hampshire.

WHO CAN BENEFIT Community organisations and individuals.

WHAT IS FUNDED General charitable purposes.

SAMPLE GRANTS £23,000 to Watermill Theatre; £15,000 to East Garston Amenities; £9,000 to Compton Pre-school Playgroup; £7,000 to Age Concern – Newbury & District Old Peoples' Association; £2,500 to All Saints Church – Burghclere; £2,000 to Greeham After School Club; £1,500 each to Cruse Bereavement and Greenham Churchyard Wildlife Garden; £1,000 each to Alzheimer's Disease Society – West Berks and Bishop's Green Community Association.

FINANCES *Year* 2001–02 *Grants* £100,000

TRUSTEES Sir P C Michael; David Bailey; Tony Ferguson; Graham Mather; Malcolm Morris; Penrhyn Pockney; John Webb.

HOW TO APPLY Grants are usually decided once a year, at the end of June. Potential applicants can phone the trust to have their name put on a list and will be sent an application form to complete before June.

WHO TO APPLY TO Stuart Tagg, Chief Executive, Liberty House, The Enterprise Centre, New Greenham Park, Newbury, Berkshire RG19 6HW *Tel* 01635 817444 *Fax* 01635 817555 *E-mail* enquiries@greenham-common-trust.co.uk *Website* www.greenham-common-trust.co.uk

CC NO 1062762   **ESTABLISHED** 1997

■ Naomi & Jeffrey Greenwood Charitable Trust

WHERE FUNDING CAN BE GIVEN UK.

WHO CAN BENEFIT Mainly Jewish organisations.

WHAT IS FUNDED General charitable purposes.

RANGE OF GRANTS £25–£10,000.

SAMPLE GRANTS £10,000 to Jewish Care (in two grants); £840 to United Synagogue; £720 to Child Resettlement Foundation.

FINANCES *Year* 1999–2000 *Income* £35,000 *Grants* £18,000 *Assets* £17,000

HOW TO APPLY In writing to the correspondent.

WHO TO APPLY TO J Greenwood, Flat 6 Summit Lodge, 9 Lower Terrace, London NW3 6RF *Tel* 020 7794 5281

CC NO 275633   **ESTABLISHED** 1978

■ Greggs Trust

WHERE FUNDING CAN BE GIVEN Northumberland, Tyne and Wear, County Durham and Teesside.

WHO CAN BENEFIT The trustees are committed to equal opportunities and anti-discriminatory practice and wish to encourage applications from disadvantaged groups of all kinds including ethnic minorities, people with disabilities and other minorities, without prejudice as to racial origin, religion, age, gender or sexual orientation. Recent grants have included support for work with homeless people, older people, young people, children and women, including unemployed people, for people with disabilities and ethnic and multi-cultural groups.

WHAT IS FUNDED Applications from small community-led organisations and self-help groups are more likely to be successful than those from larger and well-staffed organisations and those which have greater fundraising capacity. Exceptions may be made where innovative work is being developed by established agencies or where such agencies are providing services to smaller or local groups. Projects in the fields of the arts, the environment, conservation, education and health will be considered so long as they have a social welfare focus and/or are located in areas of deprivation.

WHAT IS NOT FUNDED Grants will not be made to: individuals, other than for hardship grants; national appeals and, other than in exceptional circumstance, appeals of national organisations for work at regional or local level; activities which are primarily the responsibility of statutory agencies or which are likely to get funding from such agencies on a contractual basis; appeals of charities set up to support statutory agencies; fundraising organisations; general fundraising appeals; fundraising events and sponsorship; hospitals, health service trusts, medically-related appeals and medical equipment; school appeals other than for projects at LEA schools in areas of greater social need, such as after-school clubs and activities promoting parental and community involvement; advancement of religion or religious buildings (community aspects of church-based or religious projects may be considered if projects show outreach into the community or particularly to disadvantaged or at-risk groups); restoration and conservation of historic buildings and the purchase or conservation of furnishings, paintings, other artefacts or historic equipment; purchase, conversion and restoration of buildings other than community-based projects serving areas of greater social need and/or particularly disadvantaged or at-risk groups; capital appeals or running costs of fee-charging residential homes, nurseries and other such care facilities; appeals from organisations associated with the armed services; minibuses and vehicles, other than community transport schemes which serve a combination of groups in a wide geographical area; foreign travel and expeditions – including holidays and outings, other than in exceptional circumstances for children, young people or adults from areas of greater social need, or other disadvantaged groups; sports buildings, equipment and sporting activities other than where disadvantaged groups are involved and the activity is ongoing rather than one-off; academic and medical research; conferences, seminars, exhibitions, publications and events other than where they are closely related to the trust's main areas of interest; festivals, performances and other arts and entertainment activity, unless of specific educational value and involving groups from areas disadvantaged by low income, disability or other factor; appeals for projects or from organisations working abroad; animal welfare; loans or repayment of loans; or retrospective funding.

TYPE OF GRANT Core costs, running costs, project, start-up costs, buildings, capital other than building (computers, etc.), recurring costs, salaries, one-off. Funding may be given for up to three years.

RANGE OF GRANTS Major grants: more than £1,000 approved by trustees at meetings held in May and November. Small grants: in most cases to a maximum of £500, approved monthly. Hardship payments: to families and individuals in need through the Hardship Fund scheme – £50 per individual and a maximum of £200 per family. Applications must be made via a welfare agency on an application form which is available from the trust.

SAMPLE GRANTS £15,000 each to Escape Family Support – Blyth, and Walker Health Project – Newcastle upon Tyne; £13,000 as the second year of a two-year grant to Mea Trust to refurbish their building; £12,000 each to Newcastle Advocacy Centre and North Tyneside Disability; £10,000 each to Consett Churches Detached Youth Project and West End Refugee; £9,500 each to Cleveland Rape and Abuse Counselling Service; £5,000 each to Berwick Family Centre and Workers Educational Trust – Hartlepool; £2,500 each to North East Prison Aftercare Service and Trinity Youth Association – Bedlington; £2,000 to Tynedale Citizens Advice Bureau.

FINANCES *Year* 2000 *Income* £534,000 *Grants* £511,000 *Assets* £5,900,000

TRUSTEES Ian Gregg; Jane Gregg; Peter McKendrick; Fiona Nicholson; Felicity Deakin; Andrew Davison.

OTHER INFORMATION Funds for 2000 were allocated as follows (approximate figures only): (a) £200,000 in large grants, approved at twice yearly meetings of the trustees; (b) £75,000 in small grants mostly of £500 or less approved on a monthly basis; (c) £60,000 for 'hardship' grants distributed on a continuous basis; (d) £120,000 for the Charity Committees in Greggs Divisions (for distribution to local charitable causes) which includes funds to match what is contributed by employees through the Give As You Earn scheme and for the Challenge Grant award.

HOW TO APPLY In writing to the correspondent. Applicants for major grants are asked to set out their application briefly in a letter, giving full address, phone/fax number and a contact name, the purpose of the application, the amount requested, and details of other applications for the same purposes. More information about the project may be provided in supporting documents. The following should be included: latest audited accounts or financial report required by the Charity Commission and, if a period of three months or more has passed since the end of the year of the accounts/report, a certified statement of income and expenditure for the period; latest annual report or, if not available, summary of current work; the applicant organisation's equal opportunities policy and practice; details of constitutional status; charity registration number if applicable; organisational structure; composition of management; arrangements for the project for which application has been made; if support for a salaried post or posts is requested, the job description for the post(s); details of the organisation's policy and provision for training of management body, staff and volunteers; details of how it is intended to evaluate the work for which the grant is requested. The trustees meet twice a year to assess major grants applications, usually in May and November. Applications should be be sent no later than mid-March or mid-September. The trust aims to respond to applications for small grants within approximately two months and to acknowledge applications for major grants in the same period. Applicants will be informed if their applications have not been selected for further consideration.

WHO TO APPLY TO Jenni Wagstaff, Trust Officer, Fernwood House, Clayton Road, Jesmond, Newcastle upon Tyne NE2 1TL *Tel* 0191 212 7626 *Fax* 0191 281 1444 *E-mail* jenniw@greggs.co.uk

CC NO 296590 **ESTABLISHED** 1987

■ The Gretna Charitable Trust

WHERE FUNDING CAN BE GIVEN UK, with a preference for Hertfordshire.

WHO CAN BENEFIT Registered charities.

WHAT IS FUNDED Seedcorn grants to local causes.

TYPE OF GRANT On-going and one-off.

RANGE OF GRANTS £100–£3,000.

SAMPLE GRANTS £10,000 to Commonswood Welwyn Garden Charities; £5,000 to St Alban's Abbey Trust; £3,000 to Isabel Hospice; £2,600 to Hertfordshire University; £2,500 to St Mary's Essenda; £2,000 to Action for Blind People; £1,500 each to Action on Addiction and Museum of Garden History.

FINANCES *Year* 1999–2000 *Income* £269,000 *Grants* £51,000 *Assets* £642,000

TRUSTEES H R Walduck; Mrs S M C Walduck; A H E P Walduck; C B Bowles.

HOW TO APPLY This trust does not encourage applications.

WHO TO APPLY TO Hugh R Walduck, Trustee, c/o Director's Office, Imperial Hotel, Russell Square, London WC1 B5BB *Tel* 020 7837 3655 *Fax* 020 7278 0469

CC NO 1020533 **ESTABLISHED** 1993

■ The Griffith UK Foundation

WHERE FUNDING CAN BE GIVEN UK and overseas, with a preference for Derbyshire.

WHO CAN BENEFIT Christian organisations.

WHAT IS FUNDED Religious, charitable and educational purposes, with a preference for Christian witness in a variety of forms,

especially creative and innovative endeavours which advance the Holy Catholic Church.

SAMPLE GRANTS 1998–99: £9,300 to Raynes Park Methodist Church; £6,800 to New Testament Church of God; £4,600 Chapel Hill Retreat Centre; £3,000 to Springboard; £1,400 to Disabled Midland Games; £1,000 to Derby Hospital; £500 to Children's Asthmatic Trust; £300 to Stonebroom Playgroup; £100 to Basford Community; £50 each to Eastwood Amateur Boxing and First Crich Brownies.

FINANCES *Year* 2001–02 *Income* £34,813 *Grants* £40,307

TRUSTEES D L Griffith; B G Dinsmore; J Maslick; C C Hodson.

OTHER INFORMATION The trust receives its income from Griffith Laboratories Ltd and Griffith Micro Science Ltd through Gift Aid. The chair and finance manager of the former company are both trustees of the trust.

HOW TO APPLY In writing to the correspondent.

WHO TO APPLY TO Ian Bolton, Griffith Laboratories Ltd, Cotes Park Estate, Somercotes, Derbyshire DE55 4NN *Tel* 01773 837034

CC NO 1005300 **ESTABLISHED** 1991

■ The Grimley Charity

WHERE FUNDING CAN BE GIVEN Worcestershire.

WHO CAN BENEFIT Registered charities benefiting young adults, and older and disabled people.

WHAT IS FUNDED Charities working with older and disabled people, hospices and nursing homes.

WHAT IS NOT FUNDED No grants to individuals.

SAMPLE GRANTS £4,000 (in two grants) to The Baldwin Bewdley Trust; £2,000 to Worcestershire and Dudley Historic Churches; £1,500 to Universal Beneficent Society.

FINANCES *Year* 1999–2000 *Income* £33,549 *Grants* £27,463 *Assets* £792,209

TRUSTEES H B Carslake; J M G Fea; Mrs A R M Carter.

HOW TO APPLY On a form available from the correspondent.

WHO TO APPLY TO J M G Fea, Trustee, Messrs Martineau Johnson, St Philips House, St Philips Place, Birmingham B3 2PP *Tel* 0121 200 3300

CC NO 254250 **ESTABLISHED** 1967

■ Grimmitt Trust

WHERE FUNDING CAN BE GIVEN Birmingham and district and areas where trustees have a personal interest.

WHO CAN BENEFIT Local charities and local branches of UK charities.

WHAT IS FUNDED Culture and education, disability, community, children and youth, medical and health, overseas, and older people.

SAMPLE GRANTS £56,000 to Sense; £10,000 to St Basil's Centre; £7,500 to CBSO – Taking Music into Schools; £5,000 to Royal Birmingham Society of Artists; £4,100 to Getting Older Dressage Society; £3,500 to WaterAid; £2,500 to Canterbury Festival; £2,200 to Triangle Day Centre; £2,000 each to Black Country Museum and City of Birmingham Symphony Orchestra.

FINANCES *Year* 2000–01 *Income* £270,000 *Grants* £211,000 *Assets* £564,000

TRUSTEES P W Welch; Mrs M E Welch; P B Hyland; M G Fisher; C Hughes Smith; C Humphreys; Dr C Kendrick; Dr A D Owen; Mrs C E Chase.

HOW TO APPLY In writing to the correspondent.

WHO TO APPLY TO Catherine E Chase, c/o Grimmitt Holdings, Woodgate Business Park, Kettles Wood Drive, Birmingham B32 3GH *Tel* 0121 421 7000 *Fax* 0121 421 9848
CC NO 801975   **ESTABLISHED** 1989

....

■ The Grimsdale Charitable Trust

WHERE FUNDING CAN BE GIVEN UK and overseas.
WHO CAN BENEFIT Aid charities and religious charities benefiting at risk groups, people who are disadvantaged by poverty or socially isolated, and Christians.
WHAT IS FUNDED Aid and religious causes. The trust also states that it has a preference for supporting 'reasonably local things' – it will therefore probably not support local organisations outside of Somerset and the surrounding area. It appears, however, mainly to support national charities.
WHAT IS NOT FUNDED No grants to individuals.
RANGE OF GRANTS £1,000–£6,000.
SAMPLE GRANTS £7,500 to various Methodist church charities; £5,000 to Intermediate Technology; £2,000 to Christian Aid; £1,000 each to Shelter, Tearfund, VSO, WaterAid and YMCA.
FINANCES *Year* 1999–2000 *Income* £36,100 *Grants* £24,000 *Assets* £1,000,000
TRUSTEES Mrs M Grimsdale, Chair; B Holt; Martin Grimsdale.
HOW TO APPLY In writing to the correspondent.
WHO TO APPLY TO Martin Grimsdale, Trustee, 25 The Uplands, Gerrards Cross, Buckinghamshire SL9 7JQ
CC NO 327118   **ESTABLISHED** 1985

....

■ The Grocers' Charity

WHERE FUNDING CAN BE GIVEN UK.
WHO CAN BENEFIT Registered charities only.
WHAT IS FUNDED Within the broad aims which are reflected in the wide pattern of grants, the trustees currently have a special interest in the relief of poverty (including youth) and disability, and favour smaller charities. Accommodation and housing; charity or voluntary umbrella bodies; arts, culture and recreation; health; conservation; heritage; and community services and facilities will be considered.
WHAT IS NOT FUNDED Only UK-registered charities are supported. Individuals cannot receive grants directly, although grants can be given to organisations on their behalf. Support is rarely given to the following unless there is a specific or long-standing connection with the Grocers' Company: cathedrals, churches and other ecclesiastical bodies; hospices; schools and other educational establishments; research projects.
TYPE OF GRANT Both capital and revenue projects. Non-recurring grants of limited size. Core costs, one-off, running costs and salaries will be considered. Funding may be given for up to one year.
SAMPLE GRANTS £50,000 each to Community Links – East London for their children and youth work programme and Kids Company – South London for 100 Lives Project; £42,000 for Oundle Bursaries; £24,309 for Oundle Scholarships; £19,605 to Grocers' Company Livings; £13,625 for Oundle Day Bursaries; £10,950 in bursaries for children of freemen and others; £8,471 for The Elms Bursary Fund; £7,000 to VSO to sponsor seven volunteers; £6,954 for Oundle Day Scholarships.

FINANCES *Year* 2000–01 *Income* £484,000 *Grants* £502,000 *Assets* £6,700,000
TRUSTEES Directors of The Grocers' Trust Company Ltd (about 30).
HOW TO APPLY In writing to the correspondent on the charity's official headed notepaper. Full details of the project or projects referred to in the application and a copy of the latest audited accounts and annual report should be included. The receipt of applications is not acknowledged but all receive notification of the outcome. They are considered in January, April, June and November and should be received two months before the relevant meeting. Informal enquiries are welcome by telephone or e-mail to the correspondent. Unsuccessful applicants are advised to wait a year before re-applying. Successful applicants should wait for at least two years before re-applying.
WHO TO APPLY TO Miss Anne Blanchard, Charity Administrator, Grocers' Hall, Princes Street, London EC2R 8AD *Tel* 020 7606 3113 *Fax* 020 7600 3082 *E-mail* anne@grocershall.co.uk
CC NO 255230   **ESTABLISHED** 1968

....

■ The M & R Gross Charities Limited

WHERE FUNDING CAN BE GIVEN UK and overseas.
WHO CAN BENEFIT Jewish organisations benefiting Jewish people, in particular children and young adults. Support may be given to rabbis.
WHAT IS FUNDED Establishments set up to assist the Jewish religion and Jewish education.
SAMPLE GRANTS £987,000 to United Talmudical Associates; £100,000 to Notzar Chesed; £45,000 to KSH.
FINANCES *Year* 2000–01 *Income* £1,800,000 *Grants* £1,266,000 *Assets* £15,400,000
TRUSTEES Milton Gross; Mrs Rifka Gross; Mrs Sarah Padwa; Michael Saberski.
HOW TO APPLY In writing to the organisation.
WHO TO APPLY TO The Trustees, Messrs Cohen, Arnold and Co., Accountants/Auditors, 13–17 New Burlington Place, London W1X 2JP
CC NO 251888   **ESTABLISHED** 1967

....

■ The GRP Charitable Trust

WHERE FUNDING CAN BE GIVEN UK.
WHO CAN BENEFIT Organisations already known to the trust.
WHAT IS FUNDED Jewish, general.
WHAT IS NOT FUNDED No grants to individuals.
RANGE OF GRANTS £50–£125,000.
SAMPLE GRANTS £125,000 to Oxford Centre for Hebrew and Jewish Studies; £24,000 to Jerusalem Foundation; £10,000 to Jewish Care; £7,650 to Anglo-Israel Association; £5,000 each to British Technion Society, Council of Christians and Jews and National Gallery Trust; £3,000 to Friends of Boys Town Jerusalem; £2,500 each to Community Security Trust and World London Synagogue.
FINANCES *Year* 2000–01 *Income* £212,863 *Grants* £202,200 *Assets* £4,822,444
TRUSTEES Kleinwort Benson Trustees Ltd.
OTHER INFORMATION The GRP of the title is George Richard Pinto, a London banker who established the trust.
HOW TO APPLY In writing to the correspondent. However, the trustees prefer to provide medium-term support for a number of charities already known to them, and unsolicited applications are

not acknowledged. Trustees meet annually in March.

WHO TO APPLY TO The Secretary, Kleinwort Benson Trustees Ltd, PO Box 191, 10 Fenchurch Street, London EC3M 3LB *Tel* 020 7475 5086 *Fax* 020 7475 5558

CC NO 255733 **ESTABLISHED** 1968

■ The David & Marie Grumitt Foundation

WHERE FUNDING CAN BE GIVEN UK, with a preference for London.

WHO CAN BENEFIT Registered charities, with a preference for charities supporting homeless people.

WHAT IS FUNDED General charitable purposes.

RANGE OF GRANTS £500–£5,000.

SAMPLE GRANTS £5,900 to Diocese of Arundel & Brighton; £5,000 to Wimbledon College; £3,000 each to Jesuit Missions and Passage Day Centre; £2,000 each to Cardinal Hume Centre and St Thomas Fund for the Homeless; £1,000 to Cardinal Hume Centre.

FINANCES *Year* 1999 *Income* £26,000 *Grants* £22,000 *Assets* £675,000

TRUSTEES The Governor & Company of the Bank of Scotland; David Grumitt; Marie Grumitt.

HOW TO APPLY This trust has stated that the income of the foundation is fully committed for the foreseeable future and it does not respond to unsolicited applications.

WHO TO APPLY TO The Trustees, c/o Bank of Scotland, Apex House, 9 Haddington Place, Edinburgh EH7 4AL

CC NO 288826 **ESTABLISHED** 1984

■ N and R Grunbaum Charitable Trust

WHERE FUNDING CAN BE GIVEN UK and Israel.

WHO CAN BENEFIT Welfare; Jewish organisations.

WHAT IS FUNDED General charitable purposes.

FINANCES *Year* 1999–2000 *Income* £13,000 *Grants* £35,000 *Assets* £92,000

TRUSTEES N Grunbaum; Mrs R Grunbaum; D Grunbaum.

HOW TO APPLY In writing to the correspondent.

WHO TO APPLY TO Norman Grunbaum, Trustee, 7 Northdene Gardens, London N15 6LX *Tel* 020 8800 9974

CC NO 1068524 **ESTABLISHED** 1998

■ The Guardian Foundation

WHERE FUNDING CAN BE GIVEN UK and overseas.

WHO CAN BENEFIT To benefit children, young adults, students and journalists.

WHAT IS FUNDED Education, international. To promote the development of journalism particularly in Eastern European countries and to support free speech.

TYPE OF GRANT One-off.

FINANCES *Year* 2001–02 *Income* £97,500

TRUSTEES H J S Young; H J Roche; M J Scott; P J Preston; M R Unger; J P Scott; A W Phillips; A Sampson; J M Dean; A Lapping.

HOW TO APPLY In writing to the address below.

WHO TO APPLY TO P Boardman, Secretary to the Foundation, 164 Deansgate, Manchester M60 2RR

CC NO 1027893 **ESTABLISHED** 1993

■ Mrs Margaret Guido's Charitable Trust

WHERE FUNDING CAN BE GIVEN UK and overseas.

WHO CAN BENEFIT Organisations involved in archaeological or historical work; those benefiting musicians, actors and entertainment professionals; those concerned with nature and the environment. Famine relief and medical research are also considered.

WHAT IS FUNDED The preservation of the built and natural environment and the promotion of the arts, especially music.

WHAT IS NOT FUNDED No grants to individuals.

RANGE OF GRANTS £100–£1,000.

FINANCES *Year* 1999–2000 *Income* £34,400 *Grants* £29,100 *Assets* £683,449

TRUSTEES Coutts & Co.

HOW TO APPLY In writing to the correspondent.

WHO TO APPLY TO The Manager, Coutts & Co. Trustee Department, PO Box 1236, 6 High Street, Chelmsford, Essex CM1 1BQ *Tel* 01245 292459

CC NO 290503 **ESTABLISHED** 1984

■ The Bishop of Guildford's Foundation

WHERE FUNDING CAN BE GIVEN The Diocese of Guildford.

WHO CAN BENEFIT Independent organisations whose aims are charitable and help other people in need. Volunteers, unemployed people and others in a wide range of social circumstances will be considered.

WHAT IS FUNDED The relief of poverty and isolation, the advancement of education and other charitable purposes beneficial to the community.

WHAT IS NOT FUNDED The total cost of the project will not be funded. No grants to individuals.

TYPE OF GRANT Buildings, capital, core costs, one-off, project, recurring costs, running costs and start-up costs. Funding may be given for up to three years.

RANGE OF GRANTS £500–£5,000.

SAMPLE GRANTS £5,000 to The Rainbow Trust; £3,600 to Through the Roof (Disabilities); £500 to Say What Affects You.

FINANCES *Year* 1999–2000 *Income* £216,000 *Grants* £72,000

TRUSTEES Bishop of Guildford; Lord Lane of Horsell; Michael Young; Brian Elliott; Nick Neill.

OTHER INFORMATION Beneficiaries must have a bank or building society account.

HOW TO APPLY An information pack with guidelines for applicants is issued by the trust.

WHO TO APPLY TO Jane Schofield, Campaign Director, Diocesan House, Quarry Street, Guildford, Surrey GU1 3XG *Tel* 01483 304000 *Fax* 01483 790333 *E-mail* jane.schofield@cofeguildford.org.uk *Website* www.bgf.co.uk

CC NO 1017385 **ESTABLISHED** 1993

■ The Guildry Incorporation of Perth

WHERE FUNDING CAN BE GIVEN Perth.

WHO CAN BENEFIT Members of the Guildry; non-members; recipients are nominated by schools in Perth.

WHAT IS FUNDED The main purpose of the trust is to provide educational bursaries. Pensions and donations for general charitable purposes are also made.

FINANCES *Year* 2000–01 *Income* £174,000 *Grants* £91,000

TRUSTEES Roger Ward; Colin Carrie; David Donaldson; Alastair H Anderson; Richard W Frenz; Kenneth Darling; Louis Flood; Michael Norval; Neil Dewar.

OTHER INFORMATION Grants were broken down as follows: (i) weekly pensions £14,000; (ii) quarterly pensions £11,000; (iii) coal allowances £5,200; (iv) school prizes £1,800; (v) charitable donations £34,000; (vi) bursaries £19,000.

HOW TO APPLY In writing to the correspondent. The trust meets to consider grants on the last Tuesday of every month.

WHO TO APPLY TO Lorna Peacock, Secretary, 42 George Street, Perth PH1 5JL

SC NO SC008072

■ The Walter Guinness Charitable Trust

WHERE FUNDING CAN BE GIVEN UK and overseas, with a preference for Wiltshire and Hampshire.

WHO CAN BENEFIT Charitable organisations only.

WHAT IS FUNDED The trust is unlikely to be able to support anything it is not already in touch with, but would be interested to hear from charities concerned with research, education, communities and ecology.

WHAT IS NOT FUNDED No grants to individuals.

TYPE OF GRANT Normally one-off.

RANGE OF GRANTS £50–£10,000.

SAMPLE GRANTS £10,000 each to Enham Trust and St James' Church Ludgershall Restoration Fund; £9,000 to UNIPAL; £5,000 to Marlborough College Appeal; £3,000 to Project Ability; £2,500 to Royal Academy Trust.

FINANCES *Year* 1999 *Income* £154,491 *Grants* £121,723 *Assets* £1,900,000

TRUSTEES Hon. F B Guinness; Hon. Mrs R Mulji; Hon. Catriona Guinness.

HOW TO APPLY In writing to the correspondent. Replies are only sent when there is a positive decision. Initial telephone calls are not welcome. There are no application forms, guidelines or deadlines. No sae is required.

WHO TO APPLY TO The Secretary, Biddesden House, Andover, Hampshire SP11 9DN

CC NO 205375   **ESTABLISHED** 1961

■ The Gulbenkian Foundation

WHERE FUNDING CAN BE GIVEN UK and the Republic of Ireland.

WHO CAN BENEFIT Registered charities or tax exempt organisations concerned with the arts, education, social welfare or Anglo-Portuguese cultural relations.

WHAT IS FUNDED The foundation has four grants programmes which are arts; education; social welfare; and Anglo-Portuguese cultural relations.

WHAT IS NOT FUNDED The foundation gives grants only for proposals of a charitable kind, usually from organisations, which should normally be registered charities or otherwise tax-exempt. It does not give grants for the education, training fees, maintenance or medical costs of individual applicants; the purchase, construction, repair or furnishing of buildings; performances, exhibitions or festivals; conferences or seminars; university or similar research; science; medicine or related therapies; holidays of any sort; religious activities; establishing funds for scholarships or loans; projects concerning drug-abuse or alcoholism; animal welfare; sports; equipment, including vehicles or musical instruments; stage, film or television production costs; commercial publications; basic services or core costs (as opposed to imaginative new projects); overseas travel, conference attendance or exchanges; housing. The foundation never make loans or retrospective grants, nor help to pay off deficits or loans, nor can it remedy the withdrawal or reduction of statutory funding. It does not give grants in response to any large capital, endowment or widely distributed appeal.

TYPE OF GRANT Generally one-off grants, occasionally recurring for a maximum of three years.

RANGE OF GRANTS Average £5,000, with notional limit of £10,000.

SAMPLE GRANTS £61,000 to Atlantic Waves 2001; £30,000 each to Arts Catalyst; £25,000 to Children's Discovery Centre in East London; £20,000 each to Living Archive Project for young people to explore the effects of text messaging on the way they use words, Poetry Archive and Sciat Consortium; £15,000 each to Clinks to enable prison staff to work more effectively with the voluntary sector, Forum on Children and Violence, Nurture Group Network and Traverse Theatre.

FINANCES *Year* 2002 *Grants* £2,152,612

TRUSTEES The foundation's Board of Administration in Lisbon. UK resident trustee: Mikhael Essayan.

PUBLICATIONS *Advice to Applicants for Grants; publications catalogue.* The UK Branch commissions and publishes a number of reports and books connected with its programmes of work in the arts, education and social welfare.

HOW TO APPLY Apply to the relevant programme director. Please bear in mind the size of grant the UK branch of the foundation is normally able to make. At present there is a notional limit of £10,000 to any one grant. Please apply in writing to the UK branch, not by telephone, e-mail nor in person. There is no standard application form, nor does the foundation ask for any specified format or length (though succinctness is welcomed). Certain information, however, should be included: the exact purpose for which the proposed grant is sought and what difference a grant from the foundation would make; the amount required, with details of how the budget has been arrived at; information about other sources of income, if any: those that are firm commitments as well as those you are exploring; information about the aims and functions of your organisation and about its legal status. If your organisation is a registered charity, it is essential to send its charity registration number; if it has an official tax exemption number or letter, please send the reference. The foundation sometimes makes a grant available to an organisation which does not yet have charitable status through an organisation which does, when there is a suitable association between them. If you are uncertain, consult the foundation; your last annual report and any available audited accounts; any plans for monitoring and evaluating the work.

WHO TO APPLY TO Paula Ridley, Director, 98 Portland Place, London W1B 1ET *Tel* 020 7636 5313 *Fax* 020 7908 7580 *E-mail* info@gulbenkian.org.uk *Website* www.gulbenkian.org.uk

CC NO Y00046   **ESTABLISHED** 1956

■ The Gunter Charitable Trust

WHERE FUNDING CAN BE GIVEN UK.

WHO CAN BENEFIT Local and UK organisations.

WHAT IS FUNDED General charitable purposes including the countryside, medical and wildlife causes.

WHAT IS NOT FUNDED No support for unsolicited applications.

SAMPLE GRANTS £9,500 to Liverpool School of Tropical Medicine; £5,070 to Friends of Doctor Pearay Lal Hospital; £5,068 to Dandelion Trust; £4,000 to Hunter Trust; £3,760 to VSO; £2,350 to Scottish Wildlife Trust; £2,162 to Refugee Council; £2,000 each to Marie Stopes International, New Bridge and Sustrans Ltd; £1,000 each to Corrymeela Community, Jesus College Oxford, Multiple Sclerosis Society and Oxfam.

FINANCES *Year* 2000–01 *Income* £102,485 *Grants* £61,282 *Assets* £2,310,625

TRUSTEES J de C Findlay; H R D Billson.

HOW TO APPLY No unsolicited applications are accepted by the trustees. All such applications are immediately returned to the applicant.

WHO TO APPLY TO Miss L J Fay, c/o Forsters, 67 Grosvenor Street, London W1K 3JN

CC NO 268346   **ESTABLISHED** 1974

■ The Gur Trust

WHERE FUNDING CAN BE GIVEN Worldwide.

WHO CAN BENEFIT Individuals and organisations benefiting children, young adults, students and Jewish people.

WHAT IS FUNDED Advancement of education and the orthodox Jewish religion.

SAMPLE GRANTS £193,000 to Gur Talmudical College; £116,000 to Ichud Mosdor Gur.

FINANCES *Year* 1999–2000 *Income* £714,000 *Grants* £623,000 *Assets* £1,300,000

TRUSTEES J Schreiber; M Mandel; S Morgenstern.

HOW TO APPLY In writing to the correspondent. The brief annual report also states the following: 'Funds are raised by the trustees. All calls for help are carefully considered and help is given according to circumstances and funds then available.'

WHO TO APPLY TO J Schreiber, Trustee, 16 Grangecourt Road, London N16 5EG *Tel* 020 8800 4140

CC NO 283423   **ESTABLISHED** 1961

■ Gurunanak

WHERE FUNDING CAN BE GIVEN North west England.

WHO CAN BENEFIT Individuals and organisations.

WHAT IS FUNDED The relief of poverty in north west England; welfare; and general charitable purposes.

TYPE OF GRANT One-off and recurrent.

RANGE OF GRANTS £25–£1,500.

SAMPLE GRANTS £1,500 to Sikh Association in Manchester; £100 to Cliffdon Place; £25 each to Children with Leukaemia and Hope Hospital Special Care Baby Unit.

FINANCES *Year* 1999–2000 *Income* £66,000 *Grants* £66,000 *Assets* £23,000

TRUSTEES J S Kohli; B S Kohli; A S Dhody; H S Chadha.

HOW TO APPLY In writing to the correspondent at any time.

WHO TO APPLY TO J S Kohli, Trustee, 12 Sherborne Street, Manchester M3 1FE *Tel* 0161 831 7879

CC NO 1017903   **ESTABLISHED** 1993

■ Dr Guthrie's Association

WHERE FUNDING CAN BE GIVEN Scotland.

WHO CAN BENEFIT Charities benefiting disadvantaged children and young people under 21 years of age.

WHAT IS FUNDED Running costs of outreach services; residential weekends.

RANGE OF GRANTS £500–£4,000.

FINANCES *Year* 1999–2000 *Income* £59,000 *Grants* £59,000 *Assets* £1,554,000

HOW TO APPLY In writing to the correspondent. Trustees meet to consider grants in February, June and October.

WHO TO APPLY TO R Graeme Thom, c/o Scott-Moncrieff, 17 Melville Street, Edinburgh EH3 7PH *Tel* 0131 473 3500 *Fax* 0131 473 3535 *E-mail* smedin@scott-moncrieff.co.uk

SC NO SC009302

■ The GWR Community Trust

WHERE FUNDING CAN BE GIVEN The transmission area of GWR FM Wiltshire.

WHO CAN BENEFIT Registered charities.

WHAT IS FUNDED Furtherance of the work of charitable organisations, voluntary groups and community groups. Encouragement of new initiatives within local communities.

WHAT IS NOT FUNDED No grants to individuals or for operating costs.

TYPE OF GRANT For specific projects rather than revenue.

RANGE OF GRANTS Normally between £75 and £500.

FINANCES *Year* 2000–01 *Income* £198,139 *Grants* £163,954

TRUSTEES Nicky Morrison; Susanna Jones; Granville Gray; Geoff Hicks; Rob Harman; Neil Heavans; Neil Cooper.

HOW TO APPLY By e-mail on the website www.koko.com. Local charities and community groups are invited to apply for a grant in between 15 December and 15 February each year.

WHO TO APPLY TO Jackie Kent, Appeals Manager, PO Box 2000, Swindon, Wiltshire SN4 7EX *Tel* 01793 842600 *Fax* 01793 842602 *E-mail* trust@gwrfm.musicradio.com *Website* www.koko.com

CC NO 291284   **ESTABLISHED** 1985

■ Gwynedd Council Welsh Church Fund

WHERE FUNDING CAN BE GIVEN The county of Gwynedd.

WHO CAN BENEFIT Local organisations, local branches of national organisations, or specific local projects run by national organisations.

WHAT IS FUNDED General charitable purposes. It prefers to support organisations where a small grant can make a lot of difference. It supports all the Eisteddfodau in the county.

WHAT IS NOT FUNDED No grants to individuals or non-registered charities.

RANGE OF GRANTS £50–£2,500.

SAMPLE GRANTS £1,600 to a drug advice centre; £1,500 for restoration of a medieval window in a church; £1,000 for restoration of a church bell; £900 for a video to be made of a children's dance performance; £500 each for a piano for a community hall and to buy instruments for a sea cadets group; £300 to a mid-summer village arts festival.

FINANCES *Grants* £30,000

TRUSTEES Gwynedd County Council.

HOW TO APPLY An application form and guidelines
are available from the trust.
WHO TO APPLY TO Eirian Roberts, Gwynedd Council,
Council Offices, Caenarfon, Gwynedd LL55 1SH
Tel 01286 679018
E-mail maireirianroberts@gwynedd.gov.uk
Website www.gwynedd.gov.uk
CC NO 1055596   **ESTABLISHED** 1974

Think carefully about every application. Is it justified?

515

■ The H & M Charitable Trust

WHERE FUNDING CAN BE GIVEN UK, with some preference for Kent.

WHO CAN BENEFIT Charities concerned with seamanship, including welfare education.

WHAT IS FUNDED 'Resources are committed on a regular annual basis to organisations who have come to rely upon [the trust] for their funding'.

FINANCES *Year* 1999–2000 *Income* £45,000 *Grants* £13,000 *Assets* £726,000

TRUSTEES I C S Lewis, Chair; Mrs P M Lister; D Harris.

HOW TO APPLY The trustees said they do not wish their trust to be included in this guide since it leads to disappointment for applicants. Unsolicitied applications will not be successful.

WHO TO APPLY TO D Harris, Trustee, c/o Brooks Green, Chartered Accountants, Abbey House, 342 Regents Park Road, London N3 2LJ
CC NO 272391   **ESTABLISHED** 1976

■ H C D Memorial Fund

WHERE FUNDING CAN BE GIVEN UK, Ireland and worldwide.

WHO CAN BENEFIT Organisations benefiting people who are in need, homeless, unemployed, disadvantaged by poverty, sick or disabled, victims of natural disasters and war; and children, especially overseas.

WHAT IS FUNDED Health and development aid abroad, especially through appropriate technology and education; residential facilities and services, disability, and other social and educational work in the UK and the Irish Republic. Support may also be given towards economic regeneration schemes, job creation, small enterprises, support to voluntary and community organisations, woodlands and the environment.

WHAT IS NOT FUNDED The following are unlikely to be supported: evangelism or missionary work; individuals; nationwide emergency appeals; animal charities.

TYPE OF GRANT Can be one-off or recurring, including core costs, buildings and start-up costs. Funding may be given for up to three years.

RANGE OF GRANTS £1,000–£150,000; typical grant £20,000.

SAMPLE GRANTS £67,000 to San Carlos Hospital, Mexico; £40,000 to Arpana Charitable Trust and ITDG; £30,000 to Impact Foundation; £25,000 to Sussex Emmaus; £20,036 to Concern America; £20,000 each to Angels International, Camfed and Arrupe Society; £15,060 to SADEC.

FINANCES *Year* 2001–02 *Income* £516,360 *Grants* £446,972

TRUSTEES Bill Flinn; Dr Millie Sherman; Jeremy Debenham; Catherine Debenham; Nicholas Debenham, Chair.

HOW TO APPLY In writing to the correspondent, although please note that the trust has a preference for seeking out its own projects and only very rarely responds to general appeals. 'Unsolicited applications are not encouraged. They are acknowledged, but extremely rarely receive a positive response. No telephone enquiries, please.' Note that the trust does not have any employed staff.

WHO TO APPLY TO Jeremy Debenham, Secretary, Reeds Farm, Sayers Common, Hassocks, West Sussex BN6 9JQ *Tel* 01273 832 173 *Fax* 01273 832 146 *E-mail* debenham@reedsfarm.fslife.co.uk
CC NO 1044956   **ESTABLISHED** 1995

■ The H P Charitable Trust

WHERE FUNDING CAN BE GIVEN UK.

WHO CAN BENEFIT Orthodox Jewish charities.

FINANCES *Year* 1999–2000 *Income* £372,486 *Grants* £133,015 *Assets* £1,127,541

TRUSTEES A Piller; Mrs H Piller.

HOW TO APPLY In writing to the correspondent.

WHO TO APPLY TO Aron Piller, Trustee, 26 Lingwood Road, London E5 9BN *Tel* 020 8806 2432
CC NO 278006   **ESTABLISHED** 1979

■ D K A Hackney Charitable Trust

(also known as Katharine Hackney Trust)

WHERE FUNDING CAN BE GIVEN UK.

WHO CAN BENEFIT Registered charities only.

WHAT IS FUNDED General charitable purposes.

SAMPLE GRANTS £7,100 to South American Missionary Society; £5,600 each to eight beneficiaries, including those to Barnardos, Save the Children Fund and Shelter; £4,100 to Oxfam.

FINANCES *Year* 1999–2000 *Income* £10,000 *Grants* £61,000 *Assets* £179,000

TRUSTEES Mrs D K A Hackney; Mrs D P M Schiffer; J C Passmore.

HOW TO APPLY In writing to the correspondent, but the trust states that it does not respond to unsolicited applications.

WHO TO APPLY TO Mrs Janet Mills, Thomson Snell & Passmore, 3 Lonsdale Gardens, Tunbridge Wells, Kent TN1 1NX *Tel* 01892 510000
CC NO 1021109   **ESTABLISHED** 1993

■ The Hackney Parochial Charities

WHERE FUNDING CAN BE GIVEN The London borough of Hackney.

WHO CAN BENEFIT Organisations benefiting children, young adults and people disadvantaged by poverty may be considered. Community organisations can also benefit.

WHAT IS FUNDED Community and education projects which benefit people in Hackney who are poor.

TYPE OF GRANT One-off and recurrent.

SAMPLE GRANTS £21,000 to Hackney Quest; £13,000 to Clapton Sea Cadet Unit; £6,000 to Hackney Mission Circuit; £5,000 to Homerton Youth Project; £4,500 to Bishop of Stepney; £4,000 to Hackney Free and Parochial Schools Foundation; £3,000 each to Hackney Summer Camp, Hackney Victim Support, St Matthias Youth Club and Sutton Home Music.

FINANCES *Year* 1999–2000 *Income* £229,000 *Grants* £297,060 *Assets* £6,300,000

TRUSTEES Revd W R Hurdman, Chair; Revd J S Pridmore; Mrs A J Seabrook; Mrs J M Byrd; G R Bell; Lady Sherman; Miss A Esdaile; P O L Field.

HOW TO APPLY In writing to the correspondent.

WHO TO APPLY TO A D M Sorrell, Messrs Craigen Wilders Sorrell, 2 The Broadway, High Street, Chipping Ongar, Essex CM5 9JD
CC NO 219876   **ESTABLISHED** 1904

■ The Hadfield Trust

WHERE FUNDING CAN BE GIVEN Cumbria.

WHO CAN BENEFIT Organisations benefiting children, young adults and older people; unemployed people; parents and children; one parent families; and widows and widowers.

WHAT IS FUNDED Charities concerned with social needs, youth employment, help for older people, the arts and the environment. Particularly supported are those working in the fields of accommodation and housing; support and development; arts, culture and recreation; health; conservation; education and training; and social care and development.

WHAT IS NOT FUNDED 'The following would not normally be considered for a grant: applicants from outside the county of Cumbria; individuals; any form of sponsorship; religious bodies; political organisations; pressure groups; feasibility studies; where funding from statutory bodies is, or should be, available.'

TYPE OF GRANT Capital projects preferred; buildings will be considered and funding is generally for one year or less.

RANGE OF GRANTS Minimum £500.

SAMPLE GRANTS £10,000 each to Community Action Furness and Jibcraft; £5,000 each to Lakeland Housing, Life Education Centre Cumbria, Princes Trust, Salterbeck Residents Association and St John Ambulance Kendal; £4,000 each to Council Agriculture & Rural Life, Haigpit Restoration Society and South Lakes Support Disabled Kids.

FINANCES *Year* 2001 *Income* £246,000 *Grants* £226,000 *Assets* £6,196,000

TRUSTEES R A Morris; A T Morris; W Rathbone; A W Forsyth.

PUBLICATIONS A leaflet setting out the aims and objectives of the trust (available on request).

HOW TO APPLY Write for an application form and further details to the correspondent. The trustees normally meet at the end of March, July and November, although the dates can vary, and applicants are advised of the result within 10 days. Applications need to be with the administrator not later than 1 February, June or October to enable him to circulate the papers in time.

WHO TO APPLY TO Michael Hope, Administrator, c/o Rathbone Bros Co. & Ltd, Port of Liverpool Building, Pierhead, Liverpool L3 1NW *Tel* 0151 236 6666 *Fax* 0151 243 7001

CC NO 1067491   **ESTABLISHED** 1998

■ The Hadley Trust

WHERE FUNDING CAN BE GIVEN UK, especially London.

WHO CAN BENEFIT Registered charities.

WHAT IS FUNDED The trust's objects allow it to assist in creating opportunities for people who are disadvantaged as a result of environmental, educational or economic circumstances or physical or other handicap to improve their situation, either by direct financial assistance, involvement in project and support work, or research into the causes of and means to alleviate hardship.

FINANCES *Year* 1998–99 *Income* £2,000,000 *Grants* £925,000 *Assets* £36,000,000

TRUSTEES Mrs J Hulme; P W Hulme.

HOW TO APPLY In writing to the correspondent.

WHO TO APPLY TO P Hulme, Trustee, Gransmuir, Hadley Green Road, Barnet, Hertfordshire EN5 5QE

CC NO 1064823   **ESTABLISHED** 1997

■ The Hadrian Trust

WHERE FUNDING CAN BE GIVEN Within the boundaries of the old counties of Northumberland and Durham, this includes Tyne and Wear and the former county of Cleveland (north of the Tees).

WHO CAN BENEFIT Organisations benefiting people of all ages; unemployed people; volunteers; people in care, or who are fostered or adopted; one-parent families; and widows and widowers. Typical grants in 2002 were to councils of voluntary service, advice and counselling services, women's projects, youth clubs and schools, charities for people who are disabled, older people, arts and environmental projects, church restoration and block grants for individuals in need.

WHAT IS FUNDED Social welfare and other charitable projects within the boundaries of the old counties of Northumberland and Durham (this includes Tyne and Wear). The main headings under which applications are considered are: social welfare; youth; women; the elderly; the disabled; ethnic minorities; the arts; the environment; education and churches.

WHAT IS NOT FUNDED General appeals from large UK organisations and smaller bodies working outside the beneficial area are not considered.

TYPE OF GRANT Usually one-off for a special project or part of a project. The average grant is £1,000. Buildings, capital, project, research, recurring costs, as well as running costs, salaries and start-up costs will be considered. Funding of up to three years will be considered.

RANGE OF GRANTS £250–£5,000.

SAMPLE GRANTS £16,000 to Greggs Trust for the combined hardship fund for individuals; £15,000 in three grants to Mea Trust for the refurbishment of Mea House; £6,000 to Newcastle CVS towards a salary; £5,000 each to Calvert Trust – Kielder for holiday accommodation for people with disabilities, and Beamish North of England Open Air Museum; £2,000 to Newcastle Community Transport; £250 each to Summerhill Bird Club – Hartlepool, and Sunshine Panners Steel Band – Haltwhistle.

FINANCES *Year* 2001–02 *Income* £168,000 *Grants* £162,350 *Assets* £4,000,000

TRUSTEES Richard Harbottle; Brian J Gillespie; John B Parker.

PUBLICATIONS Information sheet.

HOW TO APPLY In writing to the correspondent setting out details of the project, the proposed funding, a list of any other applications being made (with the result if known) and a copy of the latest annual report/accounts. Applications are considered at meetings usually held in October, January, March and July each year, or as otherwise required. There is no application form but an information sheet is available on request. Eligible applications will be acknowledged and given a date when the application will be considered. Successful applicants will hear within two weeks of the meeting; no further correspondence is sent to unsuccessful applicants. To help assess the effectiveness of their grantmaking the trustees welcome reports from successful applicants on how the grant has been spent and how it has helped the project, especially if a repeat application is being considered. Applications for individuals should be sent to: Greggs Charitable Trust, Fernwood House, Clayton Road, Jesmond, Newcastle upon Tyne NE2 1TL.

WHO TO APPLY TO John Parker, 36 Rectory Road, Gosforth, Newcastle upon Tyne NE3 1XP *Tel* 0191 285 9553
CC NO 272161   **ESTABLISHED** 1976

■ The Alfred Haines Charitable Trust

WHERE FUNDING CAN BE GIVEN Birmingham and West Midlands (including Staffordshire and Warwickshire).
WHO CAN BENEFIT Community action including homelessness and young people.
WHAT IS FUNDED Christian social action. The trustees prefer to support specific projects rather than general running costs. They concentrate mainly on smaller charities based in the West Midlands.

The trusts grant giving was categorised as follows: family support and counselling (including salaries, training costs, centres, families at risk); humanitarian and Christian overseas aid (including healthcare, childcare, water provision, education, literacy); youth work, workers and support activities (including salaries, expenses of voluntary workers, educational literature); care for the elderly and disabled (including equipment, transport, life skills training, salaries and expenses); holidays for disadvantaged children and teenagers (including disabled and deprived children and one parent families); activities for and care of underprivileged children (including playschemes, after-school clubs, salaries, training counsellors).
WHAT IS NOT FUNDED No support for activities which are primarily the responsibility of central or local government or some other responsible body; animal welfare; church buildings – restoration, improvements, renovations or new ones; environmental – conservation and protection of wildlife and landscape; expeditions and overseas trips; hospitals and health centres; individuals, including students (on the rare occasions that individuals are supported, the person has to be recommended by someone known to the trustees and the funding should be of long-term benefit to others); large national charities; it is unusual for the trust to support large national charities even where there is a local project; loans and business finance; medical research projects; overseas appeals (see above); promotion of any religion other than Christianity; or school, universities and colleges.
TYPE OF GRANT Normally project-based, one-off grants, occasionally funding is given for up to three years.
RANGE OF GRANTS £200–£5,000.
FINANCES *Year* 2001–02 *Income* £59,057 *Grants* £194,416 *Assets* £1,808,523
TRUSTEES A L Gilmour; G H Moss.
HOW TO APPLY In writing to the trustees, quoting ref: INF. Applications should include a brief description of the activities of the organisation; details of the project and its overall cost; what funds have already been raised and how the remaining funds are to be raised; a copy of the latest accounts including any associated or parent organisation; any other leaflets or supporting documentation. When considering whether to apply for funding, advice (if needed) can be obtained from the administrator prior to writing. Replies are only sent where further information is required. No telephone calls or correspondence will be entered into for any

proposed or declined applications. Successful applicants are required to complete an official receipt and produce a report on the project, usually after 10 months. Successful applicants are advised to leave at least 10 months before applying for further support.
WHO TO APPLY TO Mrs J A Gilmour, Administrator, Dale Farm, Worcester Lane, Sutton Coldfield B75 5PR *Tel* 0121 323 3236 *Fax* 0121 323 3237
CC NO 327166   **ESTABLISHED** 1986

■ The Hale Trust

WHERE FUNDING CAN BE GIVEN Surrey, Sussex, Kent and Greater London.
WHO CAN BENEFIT Individuals and registered charities in the area defined above. It will consider children and young adults (up to the age of 25) who are disabled, and students for recognised courses who are disadvantaged by poverty, unemployed people and volunteers will be considered.
WHAT IS FUNDED There is a tendency to support local efforts where they can see the use the money is put to. Donations mainly to organisations for children deprived or disabled for capital works. Education is also funded.
WHAT IS NOT FUNDED The trust will not fund unspecified expenditure; deficit funding or the repayment of loans; projects which take place before applications can be processed; projects which are unable to start within 12 months; distribution to other organisations; general or nationwide appeals; on-going salaries; and second degrees or postgraduate work.
TYPE OF GRANT One-off grants funded for up to one year.
RANGE OF GRANTS £50–£2,000.
SAMPLE GRANTS £2,000 to an individual for equipment; £1,700 to Edenbridge Holiday Activities Scheme.
FINANCES *Year* 2000–01 *Income* £67,000 *Grants* £40,000 *Assets* £1,100,000
TRUSTEES Capt. M T Prest, Chair; Mrs J M Broughton; J E Tuke; Mrs S A Henderson; N K Maitland; A Stephens; Mrs D Whitmore.
OTHER INFORMATION Grants to individuals cannot exceed £1,200 each year or last for more than three years and the total amount allocated from the income of the trust for this purpose in any one year is strictly limited.
HOW TO APPLY In writing to the correspondent. The trustees meet in February, June and October so it is advisable to apply in time for these meetings. The correspondent for bursaries is Mrs S A Henderson, Crouch House, Edenbridge, Kent TN8 8LQ.
WHO TO APPLY TO Mrs J M Broughton, Secretary, Rosemary House, Woodhurst Park, Oxted, Surrey RH8 9HA
CC NO 313214   **ESTABLISHED** 1970

■ E F & M G Hall Charitable Trust

WHERE FUNDING CAN BE GIVEN South east England.
WHO CAN BENEFIT Charities concerned with children and older people; disability and medical charities; churches; and others.
WHAT IS FUNDED General charitable purposes.
WHAT IS NOT FUNDED No grants to individuals.
TYPE OF GRANT One-off and recurrent.
FINANCES *Year* 2000 *Income* £86,000 *Grants* £21,000 *Assets* £50,000
TRUSTEES E F Hall; Mrs M G Hall; I F Hall; R H L Brettle.

HOW TO APPLY This trust stated that its funds were already allocated to selected charities.

WHO TO APPLY TO Mrs Moira Hall, Trustee, Holmsley House, Holtye Common, Cowden, Edenbridge, Kent TN8 7ED

CC NO 256453 **ESTABLISHED** 1968

■ The Edith Winifred Hall Charitable Trust

WHERE FUNDING CAN BE GIVEN UK.

WHO CAN BENEFIT Registered charities.

WHAT IS FUNDED General charitable purposes.

SAMPLE GRANTS £150,000 each to Loros and Peterborough Cathedral; £50,000 to Shaftesbury; £20,000 to Friends of St Paul's Church Bedford; £19,000 to St Marys Little Harrowden Heritage Trust; £1,000 for computer equipment to Maplefields School.

FINANCES *Year* 1999–2000 *Income* £131,000 *Grants* £390,000 *Assets* £3,600,000

TRUSTEES D Reynolds; D Endicott; J R N Lowe.

HOW TO APPLY In writing to the correspondent.

WHO TO APPLY TO D Endicott, Trustee, Shoosmiths, 52–54 The Green, Banbury, Oxfordshire OX16 9AB *Tel* 01295 267971

CC NO 1057032 **ESTABLISHED** 1996

■ Robert Hall Charity

WHERE FUNDING CAN BE GIVEN West Walton and St Augustine's area of Wisbech.

WHO CAN BENEFIT Organisations benefiting children and young adults.

WHAT IS FUNDED General charitable purposes, including charities working with hospices and hospitals, medical research, conservation and campaigning, education and various community services and facilities.

WHAT IS NOT FUNDED No grants to individuals.

TYPE OF GRANT Range of grants including buildings, capital, recurring costs and start-up costs. Funding for up to three years may be available.

RANGE OF GRANTS £500–£10,000.

SAMPLE GRANTS The trust supplied the following details regarding recent beneficiaries (year in brackets): £6,000 to Wisbech Sea Cadets (2002–03); £10,000 to West Walton PCC; £5,000 to Duke of Edinburgh Award Scheme; £2,000 to Rural Youth Bus Project (all 2001–02); £22,000 to Walsoken Village Hall, £4,085 to Relate – King's Lynn & West Norfolk (both 2000–01); £2,000 to Friends of Wisbech Hospital (annually).

FINANCES *Year* 1999–2000 *Income* £41,356 *Grants* £42,161 *Assets* £811,768

TRUSTEES David Ball; Colin Arnold; David Burall; Eileen Plater.

HOW TO APPLY In writing to the correspondent. Applications are considered at twice yearly trustees' meetings.

WHO TO APPLY TO D Ball, Trustee, Frasers, Solicitors, 29 Old Market, Wisbech, Cambridgeshire PE13 1ND *Tel* 01945 468700 *Fax* 01945 468709 *E-mail* d.ball@frasers-solicitors.com

CC NO 1015493 **ESTABLISHED** 1992

■ Hallam FM – Help a Hallam Child Appeal (Money Mountain Trust)

WHERE FUNDING CAN BE GIVEN South Yorkshire and north Midlands.

WHO CAN BENEFIT Individuals and organisations benefiting children and young adults.

WHAT IS FUNDED Children and youth charities and organisations in South Yorkshire and north Midlands; also individual children and young people.

WHAT IS NOT FUNDED No grants for salaries.

SAMPLE GRANTS In 1996–97: £15,000 to Robert Ogden School for funding for a sensory room; £4,000 to Child Helpline towards the phone bill; £3,000 to Starlight Children's Foundation; £2,200 to Kelford School; £2,000 to White Rose Children's Charity; £1,000 each to Whirlow Hall Farm for equipment for children who are disabled, Brainwave for respite care, and North Derbyshire Handicapped Association; £900 to Sheffield Autistic Society; £850 to St Giles School for equipment.

FINANCES *Year* 1999–2000 *Income* £88,203

TRUSTEES Bill MacDonald; Tony Parsons; Howard Culley; Peter Flint; Jason Gill; Howard Pressman; D McKenzie; Anthony Hinchcliffe.

OTHER INFORMATION Nearly all the charity's income comes from donations.

HOW TO APPLY In writing to the correspondent, for consideration at quarterly meetings.

WHO TO APPLY TO Alison Ward, Charity Director, 900 Herries Road, Sheffield S6 1RH *Tel* 0114 209 1000 *Fax* 0114 285 5472 *E-mail* alison.ward@hallamfm.co.uk

CC NO 513377 **ESTABLISHED** 1982

■ The Hamamelis Trust

WHERE FUNDING CAN BE GIVEN UK, but with a special interest in the Godalming and Surrey areas.

WHO CAN BENEFIT UK charities involved in medical research or conservation projects.

WHAT IS FUNDED Medical research in the UK; and specific projects for conservation of the countryside in the UK.

WHAT IS NOT FUNDED Projects outside the UK are not considered. No grants to individuals.

TYPE OF GRANT Project.

RANGE OF GRANTS Up to £10,000.

SAMPLE GRANTS £10,000 to Chase; £2,500 each to Association for Spina Bifida and Hydrocephalus, BTCV, DEBRA, Defeating Blindness, Dorset Wildlife Trust, Gaia Trust, Help the Hopsices, Woodland Trust and Yorkshire Wildlife Trust.

FINANCES *Year* 2000–01 *Income* £80,808 *Grants* £70,660 *Assets* £2,950,000

TRUSTEES Michael Fellingham; Dr A F M Stone; Mr R Rippengal.

HOW TO APPLY In writing to the correspondent. All applicants are asked to include a short summary of the application along with any published material and references. Unsuccessful appeals will not be acknowledged. Medical applications are assessed by Dr Adam Stone, one of the trustees, who is medically qualified.

WHO TO APPLY TO Mrs Joanne Baddeley, c/o Penningtons, Highfield, Brighton Road, Godalming, Surrey GU7 1NS *Tel* 01483 791800

CC NO 280938 **ESTABLISHED** 1980

■ Eleanor Hamilton Educational and Charitable Trust

WHERE FUNDING CAN BE GIVEN UK, with some preference for Stockport and Hartlepool.

WHO CAN BENEFIT Organisations benefiting children and young adults up to the age of 30, students, people who are disadvantaged, deaf, homeless, disabled or who have a mental illness, young offenders, people with alcohol and solvent abuse problems, and families.

WHAT IS FUNDED The trust is currently focusing on children and young people in their second year of GCSEs or A-levels, whose parents are unable to pay for their education. About three-quarters of the grant total went to students. A range of welfare and disability charities are also supported.

RANGE OF GRANTS £1,000 or less.

SAMPLE GRANTS £1,000 each to Emmanuel Community, Royal Alfred Seafarers Socety, Southwark Community Educational Council and Women's Link; £500 each to Ace of Clubs, After Adoption, Brent Adolescent Club, Brick by Brick, Cerebral Palsy Children's Society and Express Linkup.

FINANCES *Year* 2000 *Income* £136,000 *Grants* £140,000 *Assets* £4,700,000

TRUSTEES G Miskin; Mrs J N Nyiri, Chair; R D D Orr; E Ribchester; The Hon. William Brandon; Dr P Brandon.

HOW TO APPLY In writing to the correspondent. The trustees meet once a year to consider applications. Re-applications for grants are invited.

WHO TO APPLY TO Mrs A Khadr, Secretary, 1 Cheyne Mews, London SW3 5RH *Tel* 020 7351 5226 *Fax* 020 7352 0224

CC NO 309997   **ESTABLISHED** 1957

■ Hamilton Wallace Trust

WHERE FUNDING CAN BE GIVEN UK.

WHO CAN BENEFIT Registered charities.

WHAT IS FUNDED General charitable purposes.

RANGE OF GRANTS £500 – £1,000.

SAMPLE GRANTS £5,000 to Queen Elizabeth Foundation for the Disabled; £1,500 to Shelter; £1,400 to South London Mission; £1,300 each to Pearson's Holiday Fund and Great Ormond Street Hospital; £1,000 each to Action Against Breast Cancer, Aidis Trust, Ataxia-Telangiectasia Society, Brainwave, British Neurological Research Trust, Marie Curie Cancer Care, Spencer Dayman Meningitis Laboratory, DELTA, Royal Hospital for Neuro-disability, Saint Loye's Foundation Exeter and Salvation Army

FINANCES *Year* 2000–01 *Income* £21,000 *Grants* £37,000 *Assets* £607,000

TRUSTEES Timothy James Lindsay Calder; Bryan James Weir.

HOW TO APPLY In writing to the correspondent. Trustees meet twice a year to consider appeals, in November and May of each year, and it would be helpful for any appeals to be received about a month before the meetings.

WHO TO APPLY TO B J Weir, Trustee, Travers Smith & Braithwaite & Co., 10 Snow Hill, London EC1A 2AL *Tel* 020 7295 3000 *Fax* 020 7295 3500 *E-mail* Bryan.Weir@TraversSmith.com

CC NO 1052453   **ESTABLISHED** 1996

■ The Paul Hamlyn Foundation

WHERE FUNDING CAN BE GIVEN UK and overseas (mainly India).

WHO CAN BENEFIT Those experiencing inequality and disadvantage, especially the young.

WHAT IS FUNDED The foundation aims to address issues of inequality and disadvantage, particularly in relation to young people. Its main areas of interest are divided into four categories: (a) the arts, (b) education, (c) India, and (d) Small Grants Programme.

WHAT IS NOT FUNDED General appeals or endowments; capital projects; buying, maintaining or refurbishing property or equipment; support for individuals, except where the Foundation has established a special scheme; production costs and exhibitions; education projects concerned with particular issues such as the environment or health; large national charities; applications for retrospective funding; organisations which do not have charitable purposes.

TYPE OF GRANT Grants are usually one-off, for a specific project or for a specific part of a project, and funding is normally given for one year only.

SAMPLE GRANTS £101,000 for emergency relief programmes in Nicaragua; £100,000 to the British Museum for the Paul Hamlyn Library in the Round Reading Room; £60,000 to the National Theatre for its Paul Hamlyn Nights; £53,000 to Tate Modern for education programmes; £51,000 to Institute for Public Policy Research; £48,000 to Kids Company; £40,000 for continued support of the Jaipur Foot programme, a scheme for the provision of low cost artificial limbs which has been supported by the foundation for some years; £38,000 to Refresh for a carers training programme; £35,000 for Newcastle's Centre for the Children's Book.

FINANCES *Year* 2001–02 *Income* £3,400,000 *Grants* £4,734,000 *Assets* £109,000,000

TRUSTEES Sue Mitchell, chair; Michael Hamlyn; Jane Hamlyn; Lord Gavron; Mike Fitzgerald; Robert Boas. Adviser, Arts: Sir Claus Moser; Adviser, Penal Reform: Roger Graef.

OTHER INFORMATION The foundation's support for projects in the developing world is currently limited to direct support for local projects in India.

HOW TO APPLY If you want to make an application talk to us first and ask to be sent a copy of our project details form if you wish to make an application. Applications by fax or e-mail will not be considered. Write not more than five single sides of A4 (unbound), with a further page for the budget. Supporting information may be supplied in appendices, but the main statement should be self-contained and provide the essential information required by the trustees. This should include: what sort of organisation you are; the general aim of the project and its specific objectives; how it is to be done and by whom; what problems you anticipate in doing it; whom it is intended to benefit and how many; when it will start and how long it will take; how much money you need and for what purposes (salaries, rent, administration and so forth); how other interested parties will be informed of the outcome; how you will know whether or not it has succeeded; which other funders you have approached and with what success; if you will need funding beyond the period of the grant, where it is to come from. Please enclose with your application a copy of your most recent accounts and details of the management and staffing structure, including trustees.

Applications will be acknowledged when, but it may take some time to assess them. This may involve correspondence and meetings between staff and applicants and will involve consultation with the trustees, advisers and independent referees. Applications for sums of £5,000 or less are handled by a small grants committee which meets monthly, except August and December. Grants will be made for one year only and applications in consecutive years from the same organisation will not normally be considered. Applications received by the first Friday of each month, except August and December, will be dealt with in the same month; otherwise the following month. Ideally, applications should be submitted at least two months before the commencement date of the project. A second grant committee, which meets four times a year, deals with applications for sums from £5,000 to £30,000. In 2003 these meetings will take place in January, April, July and October. Applications should reach the foundation in the first week of the preceding month, but we cannot guarantee that they will be considered at the next meeting. Applications for sums above £30,000 will be considered at the quarterly trustees' meetings. In 2003 these will take place in February, May, September and December. The closing date for applications is the first week of the preceding month but we cannot guarantee that they will be considered at the next meeting.

Applications in excess of £100,000 should also be submitted six weeks before each trustees' meeting. They will be considered in two stages. Trustees will look at an application principle at a first meeting and, if they wish to take it further, the full application will be considered at the next meeting.

WHO TO APPLY TO Faye Williams, Director, 18 Queen Anne's Gate, London SW1H 9AA *Tel* 020 7227 3500 *Website* www.phf.org.uk
CC NO 327474   **ESTABLISHED** 1987

■ Sue Hammerson's Charitable Trust

WHERE FUNDING CAN BE GIVEN UK.
WHO CAN BENEFIT Registered charities benefiting people disadvantaged by poverty, medical professionals, research workers and scientists.
WHAT IS FUNDED General charitable purposes. Particular consideration is given to the advancement of medical learning and research and to the relief of sickness and poverty. Substantial support is given to The Lewis W Hammerson Memorial Home.
WHAT IS NOT FUNDED No grants to individuals.
RANGE OF GRANTS £50–£150,000, most grants are under £500.
SAMPLE GRANTS £150,000 to Lewis W Hammerson Memorial Home; £6,000 to English National Opera; £5,650 to Royal Academy Trust; £4,000 to Royal Opera House Trust; £3,000 to National Theatre; £2,750 to Magen David Adom; £2,500 to UK Friends of AWIS; £2,000 to Institute for Jewish Policy Research; £1,950 to Friends of V & A; £1,500 to Royal Academy of Arts; £1,250 to West London Synagogue.
FINANCES *Year* 2001–02 *Income* £225,126 *Grants* £212,120 *Assets* £7,426,578
TRUSTEES Sir Gavin Lightman; A J Thompson; A J Bernstein; Mrs P A Beecham; D B Hammerson; P S Hammerson.

HOW TO APPLY In writing to the correspondent. The trust states, however, that its funds are fully committed.
WHO TO APPLY TO T D Brown, H W Fisher & Co, Acre House, 11–15 William Road, London NW1 3ER *Tel* 020 7388 7000
CC NO 235196   **ESTABLISHED** 1957

■ The Hammond Suddards Edge Charitable Trust

WHERE FUNDING CAN BE GIVEN Mainly Birmingham, London, Leeds, Bradford and Manchester.
WHO CAN BENEFIT Registered charities only with a preference for those local to Leeds and Birmingham.
WHAT IS FUNDED General charitable purposes.
SAMPLE GRANTS 1998–99: £10,000 to St Mary's Hospice; £2,000 each to Business in the Community and Edward's Trust; £1,150 each to After Adoption and Parents for Children; £1,000 each to Holborn Scout and Guide Group and Sense; £500 each to Acorn Children's Hospice Trust, KIDS, Barnardos Trek Trust, and The Home Farm Trust.
FINANCES *Year* 2000–01 *Income* £70,475
TRUSTEES Paul Cliff; Stephen Tupper; Noel Hutton; Chris Marks; John Heller; Mike Shepherd; Simon Gordon.
HOW TO APPLY In writing to the correspondent.
WHO TO APPLY TO The Trustees, c/o Hammond Suddards Edge, 2 Park Lane, Leeds LS3 1ES
CC NO 1064028   **ESTABLISHED** 1997

■ The Hampshire & Islands Historic Churches Trust

WHERE FUNDING CAN BE GIVEN Hampshire, Isle of Wight and the Channel Islands.
WHO CAN BENEFIT Churches.
WHAT IS FUNDED The restoration, preservation, repair, maintenance and improvement of churches, including monuments, fittings and furniture, in the area specified above.
SAMPLE GRANTS £5,000 to St Mary – Portsea; £3,500 to All Saints' – Farringdon; £2,500 to All Saints' – Botley; £2,000 each to St Denys – Chilworth and All Saints' – Hannington; £1,000 each to St John – Bashley, All Saints' – Compton, St Mary – Micheldever, St Michael – North Waltham, Jesus Chapel – Peartree, Southampton, and St John the Baptist – Rowlands Castle.
FINANCES *Year* 2001 *Grants* £40,466
TRUSTEES Sir Hugh Beach, Chair; Ven. Adrian Harbidge; Canon Alan Griffiths; Corinne Bennett; John Steel.
HOW TO APPLY In writing to the correspondent. Grants are paid out only on submission of architects' certificates and receipted fee accounts, so there is sometimes a considerable delay between the trust offering a grant and actually making the payment.
WHO TO APPLY TO Mrs L P Sawtell, Secretary, 19 St Peter Street, Winchester, Hampshire SO23 8BU *Tel* 023 9248 6093 *Website* www.hampshirehistoricchurches.org.uk
CC NO 299633   **ESTABLISHED** 1988

■ The Hampstead Wells and Campden Trust

WHERE FUNDING CAN BE GIVEN The former metropolitan borough of Hampstead; organisations covering a wider area but whose activities benefit Hampstead residents among others may also apply.

WHO CAN BENEFIT Organisations, institutions and individuals in Hampstead and Camden, benefiting children, young adults and older people, parents and children, ethnic minority groups, at risk groups, people who are disabled or disadvantaged by poverty, ex-offenders and those at risk of offending, refugees, homeless people, socially isolated people, and victims of abuse and domestic violence.

WHAT IS FUNDED The relief of people in need who are sick, convalescent, disabled or infirm, and the relief generally of people in need or distress.

WHAT IS NOT FUNDED Grants may not be made towards the payment of rates or taxes, or in principle where statutory bodies have the liability to help.

TYPE OF GRANT One-off to individuals and organisations, some recurring.

RANGE OF GRANTS £100–£15,000.

SAMPLE GRANTS £15,000 each to Central and Cecil Housing Trust and Royal Free Hospital; £12,000 to CCABX Trustees; £7,000 to Camden Community Transport; £6,000 to London Marriage Guidance Council; £5,500 to Kingsgate Community Association; £5,000 to Camden Arts Centre; £4,000 to Counsel and Care Advice; £3,900 to Brent Adolescent Centre; £3,500 to Family Holiday Association; £3,000 Camden Mediation Service; £2,600 to Prince Arthur House Limited; £2,500 to Camden Women's Aid £2,400 to Henna Asian Women's Group; £1,000 to Medical Foundation for the Care of Victims of Torture.

FINANCES *Year* 1999–2000 *Income* £575,000 *Grants* £499,000 *Assets* £114,000,000

TRUSTEES Up to 20 trustees including the vicar of Hampstead Parish Church and five trustees appointed by the London Borough of Camden. Ian Harrison, Chair.

HOW TO APPLY At any time. The trustees meet eight times a year and in addition requests for smaller grants are considered at more frequent intervals. There is no application form (for organisations), but 'it is imperative to show, preferably with statistical information, how many people in the former Metropolitan Borough of Hampstead have been or will be helped by the project .... Applications may be discussed with the staff of the trust prior to their submission'.

WHO TO APPLY TO Mrs Sheila A Taylor, Director/Clerk to the Trustees, 62 Rosslyn Hill, London NW3 1ND *Tel* 020 7435 1570 *Fax* 020 7435 1571 *E-mail* hwct@ndirect.co.uk

CC NO 208787 **ESTABLISHED** 1971

■ The Hampton Fuel Allotment Charity

WHERE FUNDING CAN BE GIVEN Hampton, the former borough of Twickenham, and the borough of Richmond (in that order).

WHO CAN BENEFIT Community groups, voluntary organisations and individuals.

WHAT IS FUNDED A percentage of fuel bills of individuals in need; to provide essential equipment for individuals in need or distress; to support organisations which deliver services for

people in need; general medical support; organisations supporting people who are mentally disabled; organisations which support social or medical welfare and housing needs; educational, youth and community projects; and organisations which provide recreation and leisure activities.

WHAT IS NOT FUNDED The charity is unlikely to support grants to individuals for private and post-compulsory education; adaptations or building alterations for individuals; holidays, except in cases of severe medical need; decoration, carpeting or central heating; anything which is the responsibility of a statutory body; national general charitable appeals; animal welfare; religious groups, unless offering a non-religious service to the community; commercial and business activities; endowment appeals; political projects; retrospective capital grants. The trustees have decided for the present to limit grants towards major 'one-off' projects generally to £30,000. Applicants are advised to contact the clerk prior to formally submitting such applications. The trustees are also reluctant to support ongoing revenue costs of organisations unless they can show clearly that within the area of benefit a substantial number of people are being charitably assisted. They also expect organisations to show that other support will be forthcoming and that the organisation will become self-reliant over an identified period of years.

TYPE OF GRANT Various including capital, one-off and loans.

RANGE OF GRANTS £200–£300,000; average grant £2,000.

SAMPLE GRANTS £48,000 to Richmond Citizens Advice Bureau for running costs; £45,000 to LBRuT Children with Disabilities for continuing support; £30,000 to Princess Alice Hospice for running costs; £25,000 to SPEAR for moving and refurbishing offices and IT facilities; £21,000 to Richmond Borough Association for Mental Health for running costs; £20,000 to Hampton and Hampton Hill Voluntary Care Group for the conversion of a bus into a mobile youth café and activity centre; £19,000 to Richmond upon Thames Music Trust towards remission of instrumental tuition fees; £18,000 to Age Concern – Richmond upon Thames for the provision of an advocacy service; £15,000 to St Edmund's Primary School – Whitton towards renovation of a pavilion.

FINANCES *Year* 2001–02 *Income* £1,607,989 *Grants* £1,049,100 *Assets* £38,696,792

TRUSTEES John Webb, Chair; Mrs M J M Woodriff; Dr R A Millis; Mrs M T Martin; M Gill; R Ellis; Revd D Winterburn; G Hunter; J Mortimer; Mrs A Woodward; Revd G Clarkson.

HOW TO APPLY The charity provides an application form for organisations seeking financial assistance. On receipt of your application form the clerk to the trustees will review it and may wish to ask further questions before submitting it to the trustees for consideration. All eligible applications will be put before the trustees. The general grants panel meets every two months and considers all project grants. For grants over £20,000, it makes a recommendation to a meeting of all the trustees. There is a meeting of the full trustees every three months. The clerk to the trustees will be pleased to inform organisations about the dates of meetings when their applications are to be considered. Organisations are advised to lodge their applications well in advance of meeting dates. A version of the application form is available in electronic form. Copies can be obtained by supplying a clean 3.5 inch diskette 1.44 MB. The version will be Windows 95, Microsoft Word 97. All applications must be submitted in printed form.

WHO TO APPLY TO M J Ryder, Clerk, 15 Hurst Mount, High Street, Hampton, Middlesex TW12 2SA Tel 020 8941 7866

CC NO 211756   **ESTABLISHED** 1811

■ **The Handicapped Children's Aid Committee**

WHERE FUNDING CAN BE GIVEN Worldwide.

WHO CAN BENEFIT Organisations supporting children who are disabled, such as hospitals, homes, special schools and so on. Individuals and their families in London and the Home Counties.

WHAT IS FUNDED To assist children who are disabled by means of equipment and services.

WHAT IS NOT FUNDED Building projects, research grants and salaries will not be funded.

TYPE OF GRANT Equipment purchased by the trust. No cash grants are given.

RANGE OF GRANTS Maximum of £2,000 for individuals.

FINANCES Year 2000 Income £863,589 Grants £270,940 Assets £863,589

TRUSTEES J Bonn; R Adelman; P Maurice.

HOW TO APPLY Initial telephone calls from applicants are not welcome. Application forms and guidelines are available from the correspondent.

WHO TO APPLY TO Mrs B Emden, Flat D, Mount Tyndal, Spaniards Road, Hampstead NW3 7JH

CC NO 200050   **ESTABLISHED** 1961

■ **The W A Handley Charitable Trust**

WHERE FUNDING CAN BE GIVEN Northumberland and Tyneside.

WHO CAN BENEFIT Registered charities only.

WHAT IS FUNDED General charitable purposes with preference for the alleviation of distress, crisis funding, pump-priming finance and operating expenses.

WHAT IS NOT FUNDED No grants to individuals.

TYPE OF GRANT Buildings; capital; core costs; endowments; feasibility studies; one-off; project; research; running costs; recurring costs; salaries; and start-up costs. Funding is available for up to one year.

RANGE OF GRANTS £200–£25,000.

SAMPLE GRANTS £25,000 each to Cancer Bridge, Gateshead Dispensary, The Mea Trust (which received two of such grants), St John Ambulance and St Oswald's Children Hospice; £5,000 each to Whitley Bay YMCA and Womens Cancer Detection Society; £3,400 to Chester-le-Street Sea Cadet Corp; £3,300 each to Leonard Cheshire in Northumbria and Tyneside Foyer.

FINANCES Year 1999–2000 Income £399,000 Grants £362,000 Assets £8,200,000

TRUSTEES Anthony Glenton; David Milligan; Douglas Errington.

HOW TO APPLY In writing to the correspondent, quoting the applicant's official charity number and providing full back-up information. Grants are made quarterly in March, June, September and December.

WHO TO APPLY TO The Secretaries to the Trustees, c/o Ryecroft Glenton, 27 Portland Terrace, Jesmond, Newcastle upon Tyne NE2 1QP Tel 0191 281 1292

CC NO 230435   **ESTABLISHED** 1963

■ **Beatrice Hankey Foundation Ltd**

WHERE FUNDING CAN BE GIVEN UK and overseas.

WHO CAN BENEFIT Institutions benefiting Christians.

WHAT IS FUNDED The advancement of the Christian religion, especially training missionaries. Study and training courses in Eastern Europe.

TYPE OF GRANT Recurrent.

RANGE OF GRANTS £50–£5,000.

SAMPLE GRANTS In 1998: £2,500 each to St Alphege School Project – Greenwich and Village Services Trust; £2,000 each to Community Meeting Point, Whizz-Kidz, Sudan Church Association, and College of Christian Theology Bangladesh; £1,500 to Beacon Christian Fellowship; £1,000 each to Mission to Romania, Kaloko Trust, and Medical Foundation for the Care of Victims of Torture.

FINANCES Year 2001 Income £65,403

TRUSTEES Prof. E G Wedell; Mrs A M Dawe; Revd J Elliott; Mrs A C Lethbridge; Mrs I Mentincke-Zuiderweg; Mrs N Starosta; Mrs H Pawson; Revd Mother L Morris; Revd D Savill; Revd Canon J W D Simonson; Mrs D Sampson.

HOW TO APPLY In writing to the correspondent.

WHO TO APPLY TO The Trustees, c/o Bates Wells & Braithwaite, Cheapside House, 138 Cheapside, London EC2V 6BB

CC NO 211093   **ESTABLISHED** 1949

■ **The Hanley Trust (1987)**

WHERE FUNDING CAN BE GIVEN UK.

WHO CAN BENEFIT Registered charities benefiting at risk groups, people disadvantaged by poverty and socially isolated people.

WHAT IS FUNDED Organisations concerned with social welfare and disadvantage.

WHAT IS NOT FUNDED Grants are not made to individuals or to non-registered charities.

RANGE OF GRANTS £100–£4,000.

SAMPLE GRANTS £2,500 to the Butler Trust (the prison service annual award scheme); £2,000 to Shelter; £1,000 each to Irene Taylor Trust (Music in Prisons), Howard League for Penal Reform, Helen Arkell Dyslexia Centre, Help the Hospices, MIND and Mental Health Foundation.

FINANCES Year 2001–02 Income £33,000 Grants £32,000 Assets £980,000

TRUSTEES The Hon. Sarah Price, Chair; The Hon. James Butler; Nicholas Smith.

HOW TO APPLY In writing to the correspondent.

WHO TO APPLY TO The Hon. Mrs Sarah Price, Chair, Brook House, 15 Spring Back Way, Uppingham, Rutland LE15 9TT Tel 01572 821831 Fax 01572 821831

CC NO 299209   **ESTABLISHED** 1987

■ **The Kathleen Hannay Memorial Charity**

WHERE FUNDING CAN BE GIVEN UK.

WHO CAN BENEFIT Registered charities benefiting people of all ages, clergy, medical professionals, musicians, people in care, or who are fostered or adopted, parents and children, one-parent families, widows and widowers, Baptists, Christians, Church of England, evangelists and Methodists, at risk groups, disabled people and people with mental illness.

WHAT IS FUNDED General charitable purposes but trustees favour religious causes. The trust will consider funding community development; support to voluntary and community organisations; support to volunteers; social care professional bodies; the advancement of the

Think carefully about every application. Is it justified?

523

Christian religion; churches including conservation of church buildings; Anglican and Free Church umbrella bodies; music; health; church schools; special schools; education and training; medical research; religion; social sciences; specialist research; and social care and development.

WHAT IS NOT FUNDED No grants to individuals or non-registered charities.

TYPE OF GRANT Capital, core costs, one-off, project and research. All funding is for one year or less.

RANGE OF GRANTS £800 – £25,000.

SAMPLE GRANTS £25,000 to Amnesty International UK Charitable Trust; £20,000 each to Friends of Russian Children and Handel House Ltd; £16,500 to Network Counselling; £15,000 to NSPCC; £14,000 to The Helen House Hospice; £12,000 to The Schizophrenia Association of Great Britain; £11,000 to Children's Aid Direct; £10,000 each to Barnados, Childline Charitable Trust, The Life of the World Trust and The Torch Trust for the Blind; £7,000 to Save the Children Fund; £5,000 each to The Red Hall Christian Centre and The Order of the Holy Paraclete.

FINANCES *Year* 2000–01 *Income* £475,000 *Grants* £407,000 *Assets* £1,550,000

TRUSTEES Enid A C Hannay; Simon P Weil; Mrs Christian A K Ward.

HOW TO APPLY In writing to the correspondent. Applications need to be received by February as trustees meet in March.

WHO TO APPLY TO G Fincham, c/o RF Trustee Co Ltd, Ely House, 37 Dover Street, London W1S 4NJ *Tel* 020 7409 5685

CC NO 299600   **ESTABLISHED** 1988

■ **The Lennox Hannay Charitable Trust**

WHERE FUNDING CAN BE GIVEN UK.

WHO CAN BENEFIT Registered charities benefiting people of all ages, ex-service and service people, medical professionals, retired people, people in care, or who are fostered or adopted, parents and children, widows and widowers, at risk groups, people who are disabled, homeless people, people living in rural areas, disaster victims and victims of domestic violence.

WHAT IS FUNDED This trust will consider funding accommodation and housing; community development; health professional bodies; volunteer bureaux; churches; health; conservation; animal welfare; agriculture; ecology; endangered species; environmental issues; heritage; special needs education; speech therapy; training for community development; medical research and research institutes; and social care and development.

WHAT IS NOT FUNDED No grants to individuals or non-registered charities.

TYPE OF GRANT Capital, core costs, one-off and research.

RANGE OF GRANTS £200–£30,000.

SAMPLE GRANTS £30,000 to Health Unlimited; £20,000 to The British Deaf Association; £15,000 to The Royal London Society for the Blind; £14,000 to Fight for Sight; £12,000 to Help the Aged; £10,000 each to The Sue Ryder Foundation, Margaret Pike Foundation and International Planned Parenthood Federation; £7,000 to The Childrens Family Trust; £5,000 each to NCH Action for Children, Triumph Over Phobia and The Holy Island Project.

FINANCES *Year* 2000–01 *Income* £955,000 *Grants* £529,000 *Assets* £28,500,000

TRUSTEES RF Trustee Co Ltd; Walter L Hannay; Caroline F Wilmot-Sitwell.

HOW TO APPLY In writing to the correspondent. Applications need to be received by February as trustees meet in March.

WHO TO APPLY TO The Trust Manager, c/o RF Trustee Co Ltd, Ely House, 37 Dover Street, London W1S 4NJ *Tel* 020 7409 5685

CC NO 299099   **ESTABLISHED** 1988

■ **The Haramead Trust**

WHERE FUNDING CAN BE GIVEN UK and overseas, with a preference for Leicestershire.

WHO CAN BENEFIT Organisations benefiting children, disadvantaged and socially excluded people, victims and oppressed people.

WHAT IS FUNDED Welfare generally, children's welfare and education about health.

TYPE OF GRANT Core support, building/renovation, equipment, vehicles and project support will all be considered.

RANGE OF GRANTS £1,000–£50,000.

SAMPLE GRANTS £50,000 to DePaul Trust; £33,000 to YMCA; £25,000 to British Red Cross; £20,000 each to Crisis, NSPCC, Rainbows and Shelter; £15,000 to Menphys; £13,000 to Royal Leicestershire Rutland and Wycliffe; £10,000 each to 28th Leicester (Wigston) Scout Group, Dawn Vann Leukaemia Fund and Save the Children.

FINANCES *Year* 1998–99 *Income* £16,000 *Grants* £284,000 *Assets* £120,000

TRUSTEES Mrs W M Linnett; M J Linnett; R H Smith; D L Tams.

HOW TO APPLY In writing to the correspondent.

WHO TO APPLY TO M J Linnett, Trustee, Park House, Park Hill, Gaddesby, Leicestershire LE7 4WH *Tel* 01664 840908

CC NO 1047416   **ESTABLISHED** 1995

■ **Harbo Charities Limited**

WHERE FUNDING CAN BE GIVEN UK.

WHO CAN BENEFIT Charities, and scholastic and religious institutions

WHAT IS FUNDED General charitable purposes.

FINANCES *Year* 1998–99 *Income* £48,000 *Grants* £32,000 *Assets* £346,000

TRUSTEES Harry Stern; Barbara J Stern; Harold Gluck.

HOW TO APPLY In writing to the correspondent.

WHO TO APPLY TO J Schwarz, Cohen Arnold & Co., Auditors, 13–17 New Burlington Place, Regent Street, London W1S 2HL *Tel* 020 8731 0777

CC NO 282262   **ESTABLISHED** 1981

■ **The Harborne Parish Lands Charity**

WHERE FUNDING CAN BE GIVEN The ancient parish of Harborne, which includes parts of Harborne, Smethwick, Bearwood and Quinton.

WHO CAN BENEFIT All grants must benefit people living within the parish. Local organisations and local branches of UK organisations benefiting students, unemployed people, at risk groups, carers, people who are disabled, people disadvantaged by poverty, disaster victims, ex-offenders and people at risk of offending, homeless and socially isolated people, people living in urban areas and victims of abuse, crime and domestic violence.

WHAT IS FUNDED Charities working in the fields of: accommodation and housing; infrastructure and technical support; infrastructure development; healthcare; health facilities and buildings; physical and mental disability organisations; schools; education and training; community centres and village halls; playgrounds and community services; individual need and other charitable purposes will be considered.

TYPE OF GRANT Buildings, capital, core costs, interest-free loans, one-off, project, running costs, salaries and start-up costs. Funding for up to one year will be considered.

RANGE OF GRANTS £200–£10,000.

SAMPLE GRANTS £21,000 to Home Farm Hospital Care; £10,000 to Little Sisters of the Poor; £7,000 to Smethwick ASRA's Day Centre.

FINANCES *Year* 2001–02 *Income* £495,000 *Grants* £316,000 *Assets* £10,900,000

TRUSTEES Cllr J E C Alden; Cllr P Hollingworth; Miss N M Williams; G W B Austin; P W Lawrence; D McKerracher; S Gregory; I McArdle; Cllr S Eling; Mrs V Montague-Smith; F Jephcott; Cllr R Horton.

HOW TO APPLY In writing to the correspondent.

WHO TO APPLY TO L J Bending, Clerk to the Trustees, 7 Harborne Park Road, Harborne, Birmingham B17 0DE *Tel* 0121 426 1600 *E-mail* theclerk@hplc.fednet.org.uk *Website* www.harborneparishlandscharity.org.uk

CC NO 219031   **ESTABLISHED** 1699

■ The Harbour Charitable Trust

WHERE FUNDING CAN BE GIVEN UK.

WHO CAN BENEFIT Organisations benefiting children, young adults and students. Support may also be given to teachers and governesses, medical professionals, research workers, parents and children and one-parent families.

WHAT IS FUNDED Childcare, education and health research, and other charitable organisations.

WHAT IS NOT FUNDED Grants are given to registered charities only.

SAMPLE GRANTS Grants were broken down as follows: Healthcare – £29,000; Joint Jewish Charitable Trust – £29,000; Education – £77,000; Other – £35,000; Childcare – £2,900.

FINANCES *Year* 2000–01 *Income* £277,253 *Grants* £179,015 *Assets* £2,996,109

TRUSTEES Mrs B B Green; Mrs Z S Blackman; Mrs T Elsenstat; Mrs E Knobil.

HOW TO APPLY In writing to the correspondent.

WHO TO APPLY TO The Trustees, c/o Blevins Frank, Barbican House, 26–34 Old Street, London EC1V 9QQ *Tel* 020 7935 7422

CC NO 234268   **ESTABLISHED** 1962

■ The Harbour Foundation

WHERE FUNDING CAN BE GIVEN Worldwide, with a preference for London.

WHO CAN BENEFIT There is a preference for at risk groups, people disadvantaged by poverty, people who are homeless, refugees and people who are socially isolated. Support may also be given to research workers and students.

WHAT IS FUNDED The relief of poverty and distress amongst refugees, homeless people, and displaced people throughout the world. The advancement of education, learning and research of persons and students of all ages and nationalities throughout the world and to disseminate the results of this research. General charitable purposes. In particular the

foundation is focusing on technology-based education for the community and on improving the physical environment of deprived areas in the inner London boroughs.

TYPE OF GRANT Recurring costs.

FINANCES *Year* 1999–2000 *Income* £307,692 *Grants* £92,779 *Assets* £6,465,984

TRUSTEES S R Harbour; A C Humphries; Mrs Z S Blackman; S Green; B B Green.

HOW TO APPLY In writing to the correspondent. Applications need to be received by February, as trustees meet in March.

WHO TO APPLY TO The Trustees, The Courtyard Building, 11 Curtain Road, London EC2A 3LT *Tel* 020 7456 8180

CC NO 264927   **ESTABLISHED** 1970

■ The Harding Trust

WHERE FUNDING CAN BE GIVEN Mainly, but not exclusively, north Staffordshire and surrounding areas.

WHO CAN BENEFIT To benefit actors and entertainment professionals; musicians; textile workers and designers; writers and poets; at risk groupsp; people disadvantaged by poverty; and socially isolated people. Consideration will be given to national charities if there is a good reason for doing so.

WHAT IS FUNDED To give to smaller rather than larger charities. Charities supported are in most cases connected with music and the arts but local welfare charities are also given support.

TYPE OF GRANT One-off and recurrent.

RANGE OF GRANTS £500–£6,000.

SAMPLE GRANTS £6,000 each to London Mozart Players and Stoke and Newcastle Festival; £3,000 each to BBC Philharmonic Education Project and English Haydn Festival at Bridgnorth; £2,000 each to Civit Hills Opera, Cloner Farm Music Trust, Katherine House Hospice, and Zenith Ensemble; £1,000 each to Orchestra de Camera and Staffs County Youth Orchestra.

FINANCES *Year* 1999–2000 *Grants* £40,000

TRUSTEES J S McAllester; G G Wall; J P C Fowell; M N Lloyd.

HOW TO APPLY In writing to the correspondent. The trustees meet annually in spring/early summer. Accounts are needed for recurrent applications.

WHO TO APPLY TO The Administrator, Brabners Chaffe Street, 1 Dale Street, Liverpool L2 2ET *Tel* 0151 236 5821 *Fax* 0151 600 3333

CC NO 328182   **ESTABLISHED** 1989

■ Matthew Harding Charitable Trust

WHERE FUNDING CAN BE GIVEN UK.

WHO CAN BENEFIT Registered charities.

WHAT IS FUNDED General charitable purposes.

SAMPLE GRANTS £40,000 to Emmaus UK, an ongoing beneficiary.

FINANCES *Year* 2000–01 *Income* £40,000

TRUSTEES The Charity Service Limited.

HOW TO APPLY The trust states: 'There are no funds available for grants, and applications cannot be considered.'

WHO TO APPLY TO The Secretary, The Charity Service Limited, 6 Great Jackson Street, Manchester M15 4AX *Tel* 0161 839 3291 *Fax* 0161 839 3298

CC NO 1041224   **ESTABLISHED** 1994

■ William Harding's Charity

WHERE FUNDING CAN BE GIVEN Aylesbury in Buckinghamshire.

WHO CAN BENEFIT Older people, those in the charity's almshouse accommodation and young people under the age of 25 to further their education.

WHAT IS FUNDED To assist young people in education, including at an individual level, by providing scholarships, maintenance allowances, travel awards and grants for equipment. At a wider level, grants are made to the LEA for Aylesbury schools to fund equipment in addition to that which can be provided by the authority. The charity also provides relief in need and for the general benefit of Aylesbury residents.

WHAT IS NOT FUNDED 'All persons and organisations not based in Aylesbury Town.'

TYPE OF GRANT One-off and capital.

RANGE OF GRANTS £6,000–£200,000 (organisations)

SAMPLE GRANTS £200,000 to Sir Henry Floyd Grammar School to enable it to attain Performing Arts College status; £192,000 to High School to enable it to attain Language and ICT College status; £50,000 each to Southcourt Baptist Church, Chamberlain Road Enterprises; £43,000 to Church of the Good Shepherd; £30,000 to Agency for Supported Employment; £20,000 to Multi-Cultural Centre; £15,000 each Addiction Counselling Trust and Broughton Infant School

FINANCES *Year* 2000 *Income* £526,000 *Grants* £415,000 *Assets* £20,500,000

TRUSTEES Mrs Zena Williams; William Chapple; Mrs Freda Roberts; Bernard Griffin, Chair ; Leslie Sheldon; Chester Jones; Betty Foster; Michael Sheffield; John Vooght.

OTHER INFORMATION Grants were given to 770 individuals totalling £19,250. Grants to organisations were categorised as follows: equipment and tools for young people – £8,573; travel costs for voluntary clubs and societies – £19,114; individual pupil support – £28,653; youth groups – £56,686; schools and educational establishments – £547,293; and general benefit – £26,072.

HOW TO APPLY In writing to the correspondent. Trustees meet regularly to consider applications.

WHO TO APPLY TO J Leggett, c/o Parrott & Coales (Solicitors), 14 Bourbon Street, Aylesbury, Buckinghamshire HP20 2RS *Tel* 01296 318500

CC NO 310619   **ESTABLISHED** 1978

■ The Hare of Steep Charitable Trust

WHERE FUNDING CAN BE GIVEN UK, with preference for the South, especially Petersfield and East Hampshire.

WHO CAN BENEFIT Registered charities only.

WHAT IS FUNDED Charities which benefit the community, in particular the advancement of social, cultural, medical, educational and religious projects.

WHAT IS NOT FUNDED No funding for overseas charities, students, visits abroad or political causes.

TYPE OF GRANT Mainly annual contributions but one-off grants are made for special projects.

RANGE OF GRANTS £250–£2,000.

SAMPLE GRANTS In 2000: £1,500 each to Alzheimer's Disease Society, Arthritis and Rheumatism Council – Petersfield, British Heart Foundation, Rainbow House Trust, and Soldiers, Sailors, Airmen & Families Association.

FINANCES *Year* 2002 *Income* £62,000 *Grants* £54,000 *Assets* £964,000

TRUSTEES P L F Baillon; V R Jackson; J R F Fowler; S E R Johnson-Hill.

HOW TO APPLY Unsolicited requests are not acknowledged.

WHO TO APPLY TO Mrs S M Fowler, Honeycritch, Froxfield, Petersfield, Hampshire GU32 1BQ

CC NO 297308   **ESTABLISHED** 1987

■ The Harebell Centenary Fund

WHERE FUNDING CAN BE GIVEN UK.

WHO CAN BENEFIT UK and small charitable organisations benefiting children, older people, carers, people who are disabled and animals.

WHAT IS FUNDED Neurological research and animal welfare. This includes charities working in fields of health, medical studies and research, conservation, heritage, special needs education and holidays and outings.

WHAT IS NOT FUNDED No grants are made towards infrastructure or to individuals.

TYPE OF GRANT One-off, core costs, research, recurring costs, running costs and funding for one year or less will be considered.

RANGE OF GRANTS £500–£2,500.

SAMPLE GRANTS £7,500 to Hebridean Trust for the Treshnish Idles; £5,000 each to AbilityNet, The Blackie Foundation, Canine Partners for Independence, DEMAND, Ferriers Barn, Motor Neurone Disease Society, National Library for the Blind, REMAP and Royal Hospital for Neuro-disability – Putney.

FINANCES *Year* 2001 *Income* £84,709 *Grants* £62,500 *Assets* £1,972,654

TRUSTEES J M Denker; M I Goodbody; F M Reed.

HOW TO APPLY In writing to the correspondent. Unsolicited applications are not requested, as the trustees prefer to make donations to charities whose work they have come across through their own research. As trustees meet in March and November, any applications made need to be received by February or October.

WHO TO APPLY TO Ms P J Chapman, 50 Broadway, London SW1H 0BL *Tel* 020 7227 7000

CC NO 1003552   **ESTABLISHED** 1991

■ The Kenneth Hargreaves Charitable Trust

WHERE FUNDING CAN BE GIVEN UK, with a preference for Wetherby, Yorkshire.

WHO CAN BENEFIT Registered charities benefiting children, young adults, students, medical professionals, community workers, research workers, teachers and project workers.

WHAT IS FUNDED Health, social welfare, arts, education, the environment and conservation.

WHAT IS NOT FUNDED No grants to individuals. Applications for core funding or salaries are rarely considered.

TYPE OF GRANT Preference is given to capital rather than revenue funding.

RANGE OF GRANTS £50–£2,000.

SAMPLE GRANTS £2,000 each to Opera North for community access to opera, Selby Abbey for refurbishment, and Children with Leukaemia for medical research; £1,000 to Elizabeth Foundation for new medical project in Bradford for young people who are profoundly deaf.

FINANCES *Year* 2000 *Income* £31,000 *Grants* £28,000 *Assets* £575,000

TRUSTEES Dr Ingrid Roscoe; Mrs M Hargreaves-Allen; Mrs Sheila Holbrook; P R P Chadwick.
HOW TO APPLY In writing to the correspondent including clear details of the intended project, an outline budget and an annual report. The trustees meet quarterly. Only successful applicants will be acknowledged.
WHO TO APPLY TO Mrs Sheila Holbrook, Hon. Treasurer, The Hollies, 28 Hookstone Drive, Harrogate HG2 8TT *E-mail* Holbrook58@aol.com
CC NO 223800   **ESTABLISHED** 1957

■ Harnish Trust

WHERE FUNDING CAN BE GIVEN Worldwide.
WHO CAN BENEFIT Christian organisations.
WHAT IS FUNDED To support Christian activity and education.
RANGE OF GRANTS £50–£10,000.
SAMPLE GRANTS £15,000 to St Mary's Church – Ealing; £10,000 to Lambeth Partnership; £4,692 to All Nations; £4,300 to Scripture Union; £3,448 to Jerusalem 2000; £2,500 to Lacock Church PCC; £2,000 each to Church Pastoral Aid Society, Jubilee Centre, Open Theological Seminary, and Pakistan Fellowship of Evangelical Students.
FINANCES *Year* 2000–01 *Income* £14,475 *Grants* £85,088 *Assets* £347,688
TRUSTEES Jill Dann; Jennifer R Paynter.
HOW TO APPLY Unsolicited applications are not considered.
WHO TO APPLY TO Jill Dann, Trustee, The Cottage, 21 St Mary Street, Chippenham, Wiltshire SN15 3JW
CC NO 293040   **ESTABLISHED** 1985

■ The Harris Charitable Trust

WHERE FUNDING CAN BE GIVEN UK, with a preference for Merton.
WHO CAN BENEFIT Registered charities known to the trustees.
WHAT IS FUNDED General charitable purposes.
SAMPLE GRANTS £5,000 to the Royal College of Music; £3,000 to Merton Crossroads Care Attendance Scheme; £2,000 to Multiple Sclerosis Society Merton; £1,500 to Leukaemia Research Fund.
FINANCES *Year* 2001–02 *Income* £36,000 *Grants* £32,000 *Assets* £483,000
TRUSTEES Diana Harris; Colin Harris; Dr Andrew Harris; Thomas Harris.
HOW TO APPLY The trust cannot respond to unsolicited applications; they are simply thrown in the bin.
WHO TO APPLY TO Mrs Diana Harris, Trustee, 101 Church Road, Wimbledon, London SW19 5AL
CC NO 292652   **ESTABLISHED** 1966

■ The Harris Charity

WHERE FUNDING CAN BE GIVEN Lancashire, with a preference for the Preston district.
WHO CAN BENEFIT Young people.
WHAT IS FUNDED Charities benefiting individuals, children and young people under 25, in the Lancashire area.
TYPE OF GRANT Capital projects and provision of equipment are preferred.
FINANCES *Year* 2001–02 *Income* £136,885 *Grants* £69,491 *Assets* £2,740,897
TRUSTEES W S Huck, Chair; E C Dickson; E J Booth; J Cotterall; S Huck; S R Fisher; Mrs S Jackson;

Mrs A Scott; S B R Smith; Mrs R Jolly; Miss B Banks; K Mellalieu.
HOW TO APPLY Application forms can be obtained from the correspondent. Appeals received before 31 March are considered by July each year. Appeals received before 30 September are considered by the following January.
WHO TO APPLY TO P R Metcalf, Secretary, Richard House, 9 Winckley Square, Preston PR1 3HP *Tel* 01772 821021 *Fax* 01772 259441
CC NO 526206   **ESTABLISHED** 1883

■ The R J Harris Charitable Settlement

WHERE FUNDING CAN BE GIVEN UK, with a preference for west Wiltshire, with particular emphasis on Trowbridge, north Wiltshire, south of the M4, and Bath and environs.
WHO CAN BENEFIT Local organisations within the area Where Funding Can Be Given are given precedence.
WHAT IS FUNDED Applications are generally categorised under the following headings: education; the arts; medical and mental health; young people's projects; conservation; and social welfare.
FINANCES *Year* 2001–02 *Income* £52,468 *Grants* £81,022 *Assets* £1,633,025
TRUSTEES H M Newton-Clare, Chair; T C M Stock; J L Rogers; A Pitt.
HOW TO APPLY In writing to the correspondent. Trustees meet three times each year. An sae is required.
WHO TO APPLY TO J J Thring, Secretary, Messrs Thring Townsend, Midland Bridge, Bath BA1 2HQ *Tel* 01225 340099
CC NO 258973   **ESTABLISHED** 1969

■ The Harrison & Potter Trust

WHERE FUNDING CAN BE GIVEN Leeds (pre-1974 boundary).
WHO CAN BENEFIT Individuals, or organisations supporting people in need who are resident in Leeds.
WHAT IS FUNDED Individuals can be given grants for heat, lighting, equipment, clothing and holidays. Organisations or projects concerned with homeless, older people, young mothers and unemployed people are supported.
WHAT IS NOT FUNDED No grants for certain equipment such as computers or washing machines unless there is a special medical need. The trust cannot commit to repeat grants.
TYPE OF GRANT One-off and project.
RANGE OF GRANTS Individuals: £100–£200. Organisations: £1,000–£30,000.
SAMPLE GRANTS £50,000 to Emmaus; £30,000 (in two grants) to Caring for Life; £10,000 to PHAB; £5,000 each to Leeds and Moortown Furniture, Bramley Elderly Action, CARE; £4,000 (in two grants) to BARCA; £2,000 to Cardigan Community Action; £1,000 each to Christians Against Poverty, Leeds Simon Community and Shaftsbury Society.
FINANCES *Year* 2001 *Grants* £104,000 *Assets* £3,900,000
HOW TO APPLY In writing to the correspondent to be considered in February, May, August and November. Individuals must write requesting an application form and these will be considered monthly.

WHO TO APPLY TO Miss A S Duchart, Clerk, Wrigleys Solicitors, 19 Cookridge Street, Leeds LS2 3AG *Tel* 0113 204 6100 *Fax* 0113 244 6101 *E-mail* ann.duchart@wrigleys.co.uk
CC NO 224941   ESTABLISHED 1970

....

■ The Peter Harrison Foundation

WHERE FUNDING CAN BE GIVEN UK.

WHO CAN BENEFIT Registered charities or friendly or provident societies.

WHAT IS FUNDED Charitable activities capable of demonstrating an existing high level of committed voluntary members with strong self-help activities together with well-planned and thought out projects under the following categories: Opportunities Through Sport Programme – support for sporting activities or projects which provide opportunities for disabled people or those who are disadvantaged to fulfil their potential, and for other personal and life skills to be developed; Special Needs and Care Programme for Children and Young People – only for organisations in south east England; Opportunities Through Education Programme – applications not invited; Small Grants Programme – only for organisations in south east England, grants of £500 to £5,000 for projects that fit within the first two categories; Trustees Discretionary Programme (applications not invited).

WHAT IS NOT FUNDED Buildings – capital costs of any buildings, either in part or in whole, but the trustees may consider applications for the refurbishment of buildings, the equipping of new or refurbished buildings, and the creation or restoration of indoor and outdoor sports pitches for projects within our guidelines; outdoor activity projects such as camping, expeditions, outward-bound, outdoor education and 'holiday' type excursions; building, repair, renewal, or restoration of any kind of swimming pool including hydrotherapy pools; animal welfare; preservation of churches and buildings; vehicles; retrospective funding; individuals; holidays in the UK or abroad and expeditions; overseas projects; projects solely for the promotion of religion; general appeals; projects that replace statutory funding.

SAMPLE GRANTS £250,000 to RYA Sailability; £500,000 to Children's Trust – Tadworth; £220,000 to Queen Elizabeth's Foundation for the Disabled; £192,000 to Reigate Grammar School to support scholars and students of limited means; £100,000 to Technology Colleges Trust for funding specialist schools in art, sport, language and technology; £75,000 to Reigate and Redhill YMCA to extend its gym; £50,000 to Priory School Portsmouth for an ICT suite; £40,000 to Fairbridge to refit a sail training yacht; £25,000 for an inshore lifeboat at Cowes; £23,000 to Sense towards a salary.

FINANCES *Year* 2000–01 *Grants* £1,661,000

TRUSTEES Peter Harrison, Chair; Joy Harrison; Julia Harrison-Lee; Peter Lee.

HOW TO APPLY Use the application form available from the foundation or downloadable from its website. No applications will be accepted by fax or e-mail. All applications will be acknowledged. You can only apply to one of the programmes. If your application has been refused then we cannot accept a further application from your organisation for 12 months for the same project. If your application is successful then we cannot accept a further application from your organisation for two years.

Local branches of national charities may apply only if they have the endorsement of their national head office or they are a local branch with a separate legal constitution. All applications should be sent to the director and not addressed to the individual trustees. For the Special Needs and Care Programme for Children and Young People and the Small Grants Programme the south east is defined as Surrey, West Sussex, East Sussex, Oxfordshire, Hampshire, Buckinghamshire, Kent, Berkshire, Isle of Wight. The definition of the south east excludes the London and Greater London area.

WHO TO APPLY TO John Ledlie, Director, Foundation House, 2–48 London Road, Reigate, Surrey RH2 9QQ *Tel* 01737 228 000 *Website* www.peterharrisonfoundation.org
CC NO 1076579   ESTABLISHED 1999

....

■ The Harrow Community Trust

WHERE FUNDING CAN BE GIVEN Harrow and its neighbourhood.

WHO CAN BENEFIT Registered charities.

WHAT IS FUNDED The preferred categories of support are advancement of education; protection of health (mental or physical); relief of poverty, distress, disability, disadvantage or sickness; advancement of the arts; assistance with leisure and cultural activities.

TYPE OF GRANT One-off, not normally repeatable for several years.

RANGE OF GRANTS £200–£2,000.

SAMPLE GRANTS £1,750 to Woodlands Community Association; £1,000 to Harrow Church Bereavement Visiting Scheme; £800 to YMCA; £500 each to Ealing and Harrow Citizen Advocacy and Harrow Recreation Ground Users Association; £250 to Wolstenholme Sheltered Housing; £200 to Harrow Environment Week.

FINANCES *Year* 1999–2000 *Income* £65,000 *Grants* £76,000 *Assets* £36,000

TRUSTEES Peter Lomax, Chair; Zoe Stavrinidis; Stephen Bantin; Dr Iain Farrell; David Wood; Marie Harrison; Kanti Nagda; Rajnicant Shan; Allen Bergson; Graham Zeitlan.

HOW TO APPLY On a form available from the correspondent.

WHO TO APPLY TO Malcolm Churchill, Director, Central Depot, (Unit 4), Forward Drive, Wealdstone, Middlesex HA3 8NT *Tel* 020 8424 1167 *Fax* 020 8909 1407
CC NO 299491   ESTABLISHED 1994

....

■ The Spencer Hart Charitable Trust

WHERE FUNDING CAN BE GIVEN UK and overseas.

WHO CAN BENEFIT Registered charities.

WHAT IS FUNDED General charitable purposes.

RANGE OF GRANTS £100–£5,000.

SAMPLE GRANTS £5,000 each to Lord William's Association, The League of the Helping Hand, Norwood Ravenswood, and Concern; £1,000 to The Interlink Foundation; £2,000 each to The Wigmore Hall Trust and The Friends of Neve Shalom; £1,000 each to Leicester Charity Organisation Society, UNICEF, and The British Council of the Shaare Zedac Medical Centre.

FINANCES *Year* 1999–2000 *Income* £57,082 *Grants* £39,100 *Assets* £596,092

TRUSTEES J S Korn; I A Burman.

HOW TO APPLY In writing to the correspondent.

WHO TO APPLY TO J S Korn, Trustee, c/o Beachcroft Wansbroughs, 100 Fetter Lane, London EC4A 1BN *Tel* 020 7242 1011
CC NO 800057   **ESTABLISHED** 1988

■ The Hartley Charitable Trust

WHERE FUNDING CAN BE GIVEN UK and overseas.
WHO CAN BENEFIT Organisations.
WHAT IS FUNDED General charitable purposes.
WHAT IS NOT FUNDED No grants to individuals.
TYPE OF GRANT One-off and recurrent grants for core costs, projects, research and salaries, for one year or less.
SAMPLE GRANTS 1998–99: £20,000 to University of Nottingham; £15,000 each to Peter Le Marchant Trust and Alzheimer's Disease Society, £10,000 to Marie Curie Cancer Care £5,000 to Henshaw's College; £2,000 each to Clarendon College BND and Guideposts Trust.
FINANCES *Year* 2001–02 *Income* £53,740
TRUSTEES Richard Hartley; Jane Hartley; Peta Hyland.
HOW TO APPLY In writing to the correspondent. Telephone requests are not considered. Aggressive or expensive 'glossy' funding requests are not considered.
WHO TO APPLY TO The Trustees, 42 Hallfields, Edwalton, Nottinghamshire NG12 4AA
CC NO 800968   **ESTABLISHED** 1989

■ Gay & Peter Hartley's Hillards Charitable Trust

WHERE FUNDING CAN BE GIVEN Areas served by a former Hillards store, mainly the north of England, especially Yorkshire.
WHO CAN BENEFIT Local and regional organisations benefiting children, young adults and older people. Beneficiaries by social circumstances include at risk groups, people disadvantaged by poverty, ex-offenders and people at risk of offending, homeless people, people living in urban areas and victims of abuse and crime.
WHAT IS FUNDED To give aid to people who are poor, in need or sick who live in the areas which were served by a Hillards store. Churches with a community outreach element and community centres within those areas may also be beneficiaries but it is preferable if they have charitable status themselves.
WHAT IS NOT FUNDED No grants are made to: unregistered charities; national charities unless with own autonomy in a relevant area; animal welfare and wildlife causes; trips/holiday schemes; individuals for education, holidays or any other purposes; activities that receive substantial support from statutory sources; local authority day centres and health centres; community-based projects run or managed by local authority workers; uniformed groups (such as dance troupes and bands); musical/artistic productions or touring companies (including as sponsorship); medical research; minibuses (unless shared transport, or occasional maintenance or driver training); major capital projects, such as building works (unless all other funding has been obtained and a small identifiable part of the project is apparent); church roof/spire restoration.
TYPE OF GRANT One-off.
RANGE OF GRANTS Generally £500–£1,000, although two grants of £10,000 are given each year.
SAMPLE GRANTS £1,000 each to Age Concern Lincolnshire, and Sycamore Project – Bolton;

£500 each to Dial-a-Ride Scarborough and Leeds Women's Aid.
FINANCES *Year* 2001 *Income* £87,306 *Grants* £80,661
TRUSTEES P A H Hartley; Mrs R C Hartley; S R H Hartley; Miss S J H Hartley; A C H Hartley.
HOW TO APPLY On a form available from the correspondent, upon written request. Completed forms must be returned by 31 December for consideration in the following spring. Applications are not acknowledged, and if no reply has been received by 1 May applicants should assume they have been unsuccessful.
WHO TO APPLY TO Mrs Julia J Peers, Secretary to the Trustees, 400 Shadwell Lane, Leeds LS17 8AW
CC NO 327879   **ESTABLISHED** 1988

■ The N & P Hartley Memorial Trust

WHERE FUNDING CAN BE GIVEN Principally West Yorkshire, although the rest of the north of England will be considered.
WHO CAN BENEFIT Organisations benefiting people who are disabled, elderly or terminally ill, children and young people, medical research and the environment.
WHAT IS FUNDED Individuals and community organisations benefiting people who are disabled, older people, young people and people who are sick including the provision of medical facilities and care for all age groups. Particular attention is given to smaller charities and individuals in need. It will support both old and new causes.
WHAT IS NOT FUNDED The trust does not support the arts or animal welfare. Grants are not made for non-vocational higher education.
TYPE OF GRANT One-off and recurring.
RANGE OF GRANTS £100–£5,000.
SAMPLE GRANTS £500 each to Childline Yorkshire to counsel 156 children, Leeds and Bradford Association for Spina Bifida and Hydrocephalus for Young Adults Social Activities Group to promote independent living and Youth Base – Bradford; £330 to Michael Palin Centre for Stammering Children to assess a child from the Yorkshire region;
FINANCES *Year* 2001 *Income* £46,617 *Grants* £63,688 *Assets* £902,871
TRUSTEES Mrs V B Watson; Jason Procter; John Kirman.
HOW TO APPLY In writing to the correspondent. Applications are considered at meetings held twice a year, although urgent cases can be considered outside these meetings. Relevant accounts or budget should be enclosed. Reapplications from previous beneficiaries are welcomed.
WHO TO APPLY TO J E Kirman, Trustee, c/o Monkgate House, 44 Monkgate, York YO31 7HF *Tel* 01904 34200 *Fax* 01904 341201 *E-mail* jkirman@garbutt-elliott.co.uk
CC NO 327570   **ESTABLISHED** 1987

■ William Geoffrey Harvey's Discretionary Settlement

WHERE FUNDING CAN BE GIVEN Some preference for north west England.
WHO CAN BENEFIT Registered charities.
WHAT IS FUNDED Animal facilities and services to promote the well-being of, and prevent cruelty to, animals and birds.

TYPE OF GRANT Running costs and capital expenditure.

RANGE OF GRANTS £20,000–£35,000.

SAMPLE GRANTS £35,000 to Three Owls Bird Sanctuary & Reserve; £30,000 each to National Canine Defence League and People's Dispensary for Sick Animals; £15,000 to Wildfowl & Wetlands Trust.

FINANCES *Year* 2001–02 *Income* £109,409 *Grants* £110,000 *Assets* £3,723,115

TRUSTEES F R Shackleton; F A Sherring; G J Hull.

HOW TO APPLY Please note, the trustees state that the settlor Mrs Harvey gave them 'a clear indication of the causes she favoured and [they] are guided by that for the moment at least'. New applicants will not be considered.

WHO TO APPLY TO F A Sherring, Trustee, 1A Gibsons Road, Stockport, Cheshire SK4 4JX *Tel* 0161 432 8307

CC NO 800473   ESTABLISHED 1968

....

■ The Edward Harvist Trust Fund

WHERE FUNDING CAN BE GIVEN The London boroughs of Barnet, Brent, Camden, Harrow and the City of Westminster.

WHO CAN BENEFIT Registered charities.

WHAT IS FUNDED General charitable purposes

SAMPLE GRANTS City of Westminster – (25%) £49,000; London borough of Barnet – (31%) £61,000; London borough of Brent – (28%) £54,000; London borough of Camden – (11%) £21,000; London borough of Harrow – (6%) £11,000.

FINANCES *Year* 2001–02 *Income* £186,000 *Grants* £186,000 *Assets* £6,100,000

TRUSTEES Cllr L Sussman (London borough of Barnet); Cllr Mrs J Prendergast (City of Westminster); Cllr N Nerva (London borough of Brent); F Broughton (London borough of Camden); Cllr H Bluston (London borough of Harrow).

OTHER INFORMATION Income is distributed to the local authorities in proportion to the length of the Edgware Road passing through their area.

HOW TO APPLY In writing to the relevant local authority. Do not write to the correspondent.

WHO TO APPLY TO John Fenwick, London Borough of Harrow, PO Box 2, Civic Centre, Station Road, Harrow, Middlesex HA1 2UH *Tel* 020 8863 5611 *Minicom* 020 8863 1527

CC NO 211970   ESTABLISHED 1994

....

■ The Lord and Lady Haskel Charitable Foundation

WHERE FUNDING CAN BE GIVEN UK.

WHO CAN BENEFIT Jewish people and research workers.

WHAT IS FUNDED The charity is currently funding projects concerned with social policy research and Jewish communal life.

RANGE OF GRANTS £500–£11,100.

SAMPLE GRANTS £25,000 to Kingston Synagogue; £22,000 to Institute for Jewish Policy Research; £3,500 to Britten-Pears Bursary Fund; £2,000 to Orange Tree Theatre; £1,000 to Chronic Disease Research Foundation; and £500 each to Holocaust Education Trust, New Israel Fund and Science Line.

FINANCES *Year* 2000 *Income* £313,000 *Grants* £55,000

TRUSTEES A M Davis; J Haskel; M Nutman; Lord Haskel.

HOW TO APPLY This trust states that it does not respond to unsolicited applications.

WHO TO APPLY TO J Lent, Auerbach Hope, 58–60 Berners Street, London W1T 3JS *Tel* 020 7637 4121

CC NO 1039969   ESTABLISHED 1993

....

■ The Hathaway Trust

WHERE FUNDING CAN BE GIVEN Barnet, Manchester and Tyne and Wear.

WHO CAN BENEFIT Registered charities.

WHAT IS FUNDED The trust tends to support Jewish organisations and causes.

FINANCES *Year* 1999–2000 *Income* £26,000 *Grants* £38,000 *Assets* £9,100

TRUSTEES N Younger; Mrs M Younger; S Schwalbe.

HOW TO APPLY The trustees have recently adopted a proactive approach to funding and now only fund projects with which they have a personal connection. Unsolicited requests will not be considered.

WHO TO APPLY TO The Trustees, 12 Hereford Drive, Prestwich, Manchester M25 0JA

CC NO 1064086   ESTABLISHED 1997

....

■ The Maurice Hatter Foundation

WHERE FUNDING CAN BE GIVEN Unrestricted.

WHO CAN BENEFIT Educational bodies, particularly those with Jewish links, and health.

WHAT IS FUNDED Education and health.

TYPE OF GRANT Grants, often recurring; loans.

RANGE OF GRANTS £760–£1,000,000.

SAMPLE GRANTS £198,000 to British Friends of Haifa University, part of a total grant of £500,000 to the Hatter School of Marine Studies; £99,000 to World ORT of a total grant of £500,000 for new technology courses; £50,000 to Group Relations Education Trust; £48,500 to The Hatter Institute of Cardiology at UCH, London as part of an ongoing £2 million commitment; £20,200 to the Anguilla Education Foundation.

FINANCES *Year* 2000–01 *Income* £502,000 *Grants* £658,000 *Assets* £7,600,000

TRUSTEES Sir Maurice Hatter; H I Connick; Jeremy Newman; Richard Hatter.

HOW TO APPLY Unsolicited applications will not be considered.

WHO TO APPLY TO J S Newman, Trustee, BDO Stoy Hayward, 8 Baker Street, London W1U 3LL *Tel* 020 7486 5888

CC NO 298119   ESTABLISHED 1987

....

■ The M A Hawe Settlement

WHERE FUNDING CAN BE GIVEN UK, with a preference for the north west of England, particularly the Flyde coast area.

WHO CAN BENEFIT UK and local organisations and schemes benefiting people of all ages, women, at risk groups, and people who are disabled, socially isolated, homeless or disadvantaged by poverty.

WHAT IS FUNDED Welfare of older people, women and children, education, disability, homelessness and other charitable purposes.

TYPE OF GRANT One-off, some recurrent.

SAMPLE GRANTS £320,000 to Kensington House Trust Ltd; £1,200 to Holy Cross Church and Soup Kitchen; £860 to Women's Refuge; £550 to DVU; £500 to Change for Charity; £270 to Mereside School; £250 each to Foetal Anti-

Convulsent Syndrome Association and Home-Start.

FINANCES *Year* 1999–2000 *Income* £291,000 *Grants* £327,000 *Assets* £5,400,000

TRUSTEES M A Hawe; Mrs G Hawe; Marc G Hawe.

OTHER INFORMATION The trust established the Kensington House Trust Ltd which provides accommodation for young homeless people; it receives substantial support from the trust.

HOW TO APPLY In writing to the correspondent.

WHO TO APPLY TO M A Hawe, Trustee, 94 Park View Road, Lytham St Annes, Lancashire FY8 4JF *Tel* 01253 796888

CC NO 327827   **ESTABLISHED** 1988

■ Mrs J E Hawes Charitable Trust

WHERE FUNDING CAN BE GIVEN UK.

WHO CAN BENEFIT Registered charities.

WHAT IS FUNDED General charitable purposes.

SAMPLE GRANTS £6,500 to Cancer Relief Macmillan Fund; £5,000 each to Marie Curie Cancer Care, Not Forgotten Association and Sulgrave Manor Appeal.

FINANCES *Year* 1999–2000 *Income* £27,000 *Grants* £21,500 *Assets* £717,000

TRUSTEES Robert Anthony Dolman; John Edgar Grande; John Christopher Frederick Magnay.

HOW TO APPLY In writing to the correspondent.

WHO TO APPLY TO Robert A Dolman, Trustee, 16 Bedford Street, Covent Garden, London WC2E 9HF *Tel* 020 7395 3000

CC NO 1059893   **ESTABLISHED** 1996

■ The Hawthorne Charitable Trust

WHERE FUNDING CAN BE GIVEN UK, especially Hereford and Worcester.

WHO CAN BENEFIT Organisations benefiting young people and older people, medical professionals and people disadvantaged by poverty.

WHAT IS FUNDED The trustees make donations, generally on an annual basis, to a large number of charities mainly concerned with the care of young people and older people, the relief of pain, sickness and poverty, the advancement of medical research, particularly into the various forms of cancer, research into animal health, the arts, disability and heritage.

WHAT IS NOT FUNDED Grants are given to registered charities only. No grants to individuals.

TYPE OF GRANT Often recurring.

RANGE OF GRANTS £500–£5,250.

SAMPLE GRANTS 2000–01: £5,250 to Birmingham Hippodrome Theatre Development Trust; £3,000 each to Avoncroft Museum, Downside Abbey Trustees for St Wulstan's, Friends of Little Malvern Priory, Malvern Festival Theatre Trust Limited and Worcester Association for the Blind; £2,500 each to Ability Net, Canine Partners for Independence, National Deaf Children's Society, Princes's Trust, St Michael's Hospice – Hereford and Toynbee Hall.

FINANCES *Year* 2001–02 *Income* £165,791 *Grants* £106,800 *Assets* £5,804,017

TRUSTEES Mrs A S C Berington; R J Clark.

HOW TO APPLY In writing to the correspondent, including up-to-date accounts. Applications should be received by October for consideration in November.

WHO TO APPLY TO Roger Clark, Trustee, c/o Messrs Baker Tilly, 2 Bloomsbury Street, London WC1B 3ST *Tel* 020 7413 5100

CC NO 233921   **ESTABLISHED** 1964

■ The Dorothy Hay-Bolton Charitable Trust

WHERE FUNDING CAN BE GIVEN UK and overseas.

WHO CAN BENEFIT Charities working with people who are blind or deaf, particularly children and young people.

WHAT IS NOT FUNDED The trust states that it does not generally give to individuals.

TYPE OF GRANT One-off and ongoing.

RANGE OF GRANTS £1,000–£3,300.

SAMPLE GRANTS £3,300 to Action for Blind People; £2,500 to Pattaya Orphanage; £2,000 to Falconer Trust; £1,300 to Darrickwood Impaired Hearing Support Group; £1,000 each to Country Holidays for Inner City Kids, NCH Action for Children – Pastens, Brainwave, and Tarabai Desai Eye Hospital and Research Centre.

FINANCES *Year* 1998–99 *Income* £47,000 *Grants* £27,000 *Assets* £1,100,000

TRUSTEES Brian E Carter; Stephen J Gallico.

HOW TO APPLY In writing to the correspondent.

WHO TO APPLY TO Brian E Carter, Trustee, F W Stephens & Co., 10 Charterhouse Square, London EC1M 6LQ *Tel* 020 7251 4434

CC NO 1010438   **ESTABLISHED** 1992

■ The Haydan Charitable Trust

WHERE FUNDING CAN BE GIVEN UK.

WHAT IS FUNDED General charitable purposes.

WHAT IS NOT FUNDED No grants are given for projects overseas.

TYPE OF GRANT Mainly recurrent.

SAMPLE GRANTS £50,000 to Nordoff Robbins Music Therapy Centre; £25,000 to Cedar School; £10,000 to Tommy's Campaign; £8,200 to Centrepoint; £8,000 to Babes in Arms; £5,000 each to Wessex Children's Heart Circle, Wessex Heartbeat and Whizz Kidz; £2,500 each to Children with Leukaemia, Leukaemia Research Fund and Nightingale House; £1,000 each to Beating Bowel Cancer, Nightegale House and Sheffield Children's Hospital.

FINANCES *Year* 2000 *Income* £157,648 *Grants* £136,300 *Assets* £445

TRUSTEES Christopher Smith; Irene Smith; Anthony Winter.

HOW TO APPLY Unsolicited applications are not considered.

WHO TO APPLY TO Neil Bradley, 4th Floor, 1 Knightsbridge, London SW1X 7LX *Tel* 020 7823 2200

CC NO 1003801   **ESTABLISHED** 1991

■ The Hayden Charitable Trust

WHERE FUNDING CAN BE GIVEN Preference for Hampshire.

WHO CAN BENEFIT Registered charities.

WHAT IS FUNDED Charities dealing with marital issues.

SAMPLE GRANTS £30,000 to The Grubb Institute in four grants; £1,600 R P Chester Memorial Trust Company; £1,000 to The Haberdasher's Donations; £370 to St Mary's Church, Twyford; £150 each to Marie Curie Cancer Care and Falklands Islands Memorial Appeal; £50 to The Christian Blind Mission.

FINANCES *Year* 1998–99 *Income* £33,633 *Grants* £33,250

TRUSTEES Michael Robert Macfadyen.

HOW TO APPLY In writing to the correspondent.

Think carefully about every application. Is it justified?

531

WHO TO APPLY TO Chris Monington, Secretary, Tenon, Clifton House, Bunnian Place, Basingstoke RG21 7JE *Tel* 01256 351521
CC NO 247961   **ESTABLISHED** 1990

■ The Haymills Charitable Trust

WHERE FUNDING CAN BE GIVEN UK, but particularly the west of London and Suffolk, where the Haymills group is sited.

WHO CAN BENEFIT Organisations benefiting children and young adults; former employees of Haymills; at risk groups, people who are disadvantaged by poverty and socially isolated people.

WHAT IS FUNDED The trust seeks to support projects which are not widely known, and therefore likely to be inadequately funded. Main support is given to registered charities operating in areas lying in and to the west of London and in Suffolk. Grants fall into four main categories: education – schools colleges and universities; medicine – hospitals, associated institutions and medical research; welfare – primarily to include former Haymills staff, people in need, or who are otherwise distressed or disadvantaged; and youth – support for schemes to assist in the education, welfare and training of young people. A limited number of applications will be considered which can show they are committed to further education and training, preferably for employment in the construction industry.

WHAT IS NOT FUNDED No personal applications will be considered unless endorsed by a university, college or other appropriate authority.

RANGE OF GRANTS £250–£10,000.

FINANCES Year 2000–01 *Income* £161,530 *Grants* £85,250 *Assets* £1,851,377

TRUSTEES E F C Drake; I W Ferres; A M H Jackson; K C Perryman; J A Sharpe; J L Wosner; W G Underwood.

HOW TO APPLY In writing to the correspondent, but note the comments in the general section. Trustees meet at least twice a year, usually in March and October. Applications are not acknowledged.

WHO TO APPLY TO I W Ferres, Secretary, Wesley House, 1–7 Wesley Avenue, London NW10 7BZ *Tel* 020 8951 9823
CC NO 277761   **ESTABLISHED** 1979

■ The Charles Hayward Foundation

WHERE FUNDING CAN BE GIVEN Most grants are made in the UK, with an emphasis on areas away from London and the south east. There is also a small grants programme.

WHO CAN BENEFIT UK-based registered national and regional charities; smaller local charities; churches and religious organisations; and community organisations which are responsible for their own management, finances and fundraising.

WHAT IS FUNDED Predominantly capital costs for organisations undertaking projects which are preventative or provide early intervention; developmental or innovative; promote or continue good practice and add value to existing services. Priority areas: older people, community facilities, medical research and art, preservation and the environment. Standard areas: under fives and early intervention, young people at risk, special needs, hospices, overseas projects. Minor areas: criminal justice, social research, homelessness, other charitable objects.

WHAT IS NOT FUNDED Grants are not made towards revenue costs; to individuals; to pay off loans; for fundraising activities; for transport, travel or holidays; for general repairs; for computers, video or sound equipment; for church restoration; for academic chairs, endowment funds or bursaries; to animal welfare organisations or sports clubs; to other grantmaking organisations.

Grants are not made in replacement of government or lottery funding or towards activities primarily the responsibility of central or local government or some other responsible body.

In an effort to ensure that funds are only distributed on the basis of need, organisations that restrict their benefit to one section of society are not supported.

Organisations that have large reserves or endowment funds and well established funding streams are given a lower priority.

TYPE OF GRANT Capital cost of buildings, extensions, adaptations, equipment and furnishings. Occasionally project funding for start-up or development.

RANGE OF GRANTS Generally £1,000–£50,000.

SAMPLE GRANTS £105,000 over three years to Youth at Risk for a programme in Wolverhampton; £75,000 over three years to the Children's Liver Disease Foundation in Birmingham for research on steroid use following liver surgery; £50,000 each to Abbeyfield in Ilkley towards an integrated care scheme and Peper Harow School in Surrey for renovations; £31,000 each to Missing persons Helpline for fitting out the new HQ and the Royal Hospital for Disability in London to refurbish two of its wards; £30,000 to Centre '81 in Norfolk to extend its premises; £25,000 each to the Royal Agricultural Benevolent Institution, St Andrew's community centre in Brockley and the Black Country Museum for the conservation of lime kilns.

FINANCES Year 2001 *Income* £2,042,530 *Grants* £1,537,000 *Assets* £45,607,640

TRUSTEES I F Donald, Chair; Sir William Asscher; Prof. Mrs A M Chamberlain; Sir Jack Hayward; Mrs S J Heath; B D Insch; J N van Leuven; A D Owen; Miss A T Rogers; Ms J Streather.

OTHER INFORMATION 'The trustees amend their policy from time to time. Up-to-date guidelines for applicants can be downloaded from our website. They may also be obtained by sending an sae to the foundation's offices specifying either "General Guidelines" or "Overseas Guidelines".'

HOW TO APPLY Applications should be made in writing to the administrator, although applicants may telephone to discuss their project before submitting a formal application. It is generally best to start by sending a short résumé of the project, together with a set of your latest audited accounts. The trust will advise if more information is required. All applications will receive an acknowledgement. However, as there is often a waiting list, and trustees meet only four times a year (usually in January, April, July and October) to consider applications, it may be several months before a decision is made. Information required: the official name of the organisation and its location; the name and position of person submitting the application, together with a contact telephone number and address; a description of your present work and the priorities you are addressing – quantify the scale of your operation: how many people do you help and how; a description of the project you are undertaking, detailing the number of people and groups who will benefit and how:

specify how life will be improved for the target group; a breakdown of the costs for the full project. Capital and revenue costs should be kept separate: for a capital project include only information on the capital costs; a breakdown of the funds raised to date towards your target, separating capital and revenue, where applicable – include the amount of any of your own funds or reserves going into the project, and also any money you intend to borrow: specify the amount of money you still need for capital and revenue; a timetable for the project – when it will start and be finished. In addition, for overseas projects, briefly describe the political and economic situation in the country where the project will be located. Explain how this may impact the project.

WHO TO APPLY TO David Brown, Administrator, Hayward House, 45 Harrington Gardens, London SW7 4JU *Tel* 020 7370 7063/7067 *Website* www.charleshaywardfoundation.org.uk

CC NO 1078969   **ESTABLISHED** 1961

....

■ The Headley Trust

WHERE FUNDING CAN BE GIVEN Unrestricted.

WHO CAN BENEFIT Registered charities working in the areas listed. The trust prefers to support innovative schemes that can be successfully replicated or become self-sustaining.

WHAT IS FUNDED Arts and heritage – UK: support for a wide variety of built conservation or heritage projects. Arts and heritage – overseas – : support for art conservation projects of outstanding artistic or architectural importance; particularly the restoration of buildings, statuary or paintings, primarily in the countries of Central and Eastern Europe. Medical: in recent years support has been given towards ageing and osteoporosis, although it is unlikely the trust will continue making medical grants. Developing countries: priority is given to projects in sub-Saharan Africa, and Central and Eastern Europe (except the Visegrad four), Baltic States and the former Soviet Union. Focus areas include water/sanitation projects, environmental projects, education and literacy projects, health projects and Community and voluntary sector development. Education: provision of bursary support, particularly for artistic or technical skills training. Health and social welfare: support for a broad range of health and social welfare projects, particularly supporting carers of a relative who is ill or disabled, and those that support older people of limited means. Support is also given towards educational (e.g. literacy) and psychological support for pre-school children and their families as well as parenting education programmes, promoting the wellbeing of the family, homelessness and welfare of children with autism.

TYPE OF GRANT One-off, capital and project over three years or less.

SAMPLE GRANTS £250,000 to Victoria and Albert Museum for the completion of the British Galleries project; £108,736 to Coram Family for a research programme; £100,000 each to Fitzwilliam Museum for the new courtyard development, Somerset House Trust for the Tudor Palace Exhibition Gallery, and Southwark Cathedral for the millennium development appeal; £90,000 to St Thomas Lupus Trust towards the salary of a researcher to look into the relationship between alternations in the immune system and the development of early arterial disease in people with Lupus and Hughes' syndrome; £85,000 to Allavida for core

funding; £66,000 to Rural Outreach Programme to help local communities to restore and protect natural springs in Western Kenya; £60,000 each to Academia Istropolitana Nova for 10 bursaries to train conservators from central and eastern Europe, and Yorkshire Sculpture Park for improvements to the visitor facilities and restoration of the integrity of the Bretton estate.

FINANCES *Year* 2001 *Grants* £3,412,000

TRUSTEES Sir Timothy Sainsbury; Lady Susan Sainsbury; T J Sainsbury; J R Benson; Miss Judith Portrait.

OTHER INFORMATION The trust is one of the Sainsbury Family Charitable Trusts which share a common administration. An application to one is taken as an application to all.

HOW TO APPLY Proposals are generally invited by the trustees or initiated at their request. Unsolicited applications are nort encouraged and are unlikely to be successful.

WHO TO APPLY TO Michael Pattison, Director, Allington House, 1st Floor, 150 Victoria Street, London SW1E 5AE *Tel* 020 7410 0330 *Fax* 020 7410 0332

CC NO 266620   **ESTABLISHED** 1973

....

■ Heagerty Charitable Trust

WHERE FUNDING CAN BE GIVEN UK.

WHO CAN BENEFIT Catholic organisations and registered charities.

RANGE OF GRANTS £1,000–£10,000.

SAMPLE GRANTS £10,000 to The Bridge Trust; £7,000 to Hope in the Valley Riding Group; £5,000 each to CAFOD, The Child Health Research Appeal Trust and The Haven Trust.

FINANCES *Year* 1999–2000 *Income* £131,000 *Grants* £50,000 *Assets* £911,000

TRUSTEES J S Heagerty; Miss P Smith; P J P Heagerty; Mrs V C M Heagerty.

HOW TO APPLY The trust says it identifies causes it wishes to support itself and unsolicited applications are not considered.

WHO TO APPLY TO J S Heagerty, Trustee, Walstead Grange, Lindfield, Surrey RH16 2QQ

CC NO 1033543   **ESTABLISHED** 1994

....

■ Healthsure Group Ltd *(formerly known as Manchester & Salford Hospital Saturday & Convalescent Homes Fund)*

WHERE FUNDING CAN BE GIVEN Manchester and surrounding areas, Northampton and Norwich.

WHO CAN BENEFIT Health authorities and welfare charities benefiting disabled people, at risk groups, people disadvantaged by poverty, and socially isolated people.

WHAT IS FUNDED Priority is given to health authorities and NHS trusts, with hospices, homes for people with disabilities and welfare organisations also within the trust's scope.

RANGE OF GRANTS £400–£15,000.

SAMPLE GRANTS £10,460 to Salford Royal Hospitals; £8,595 to Children's Hospital; £8,500 to South Manchester NHS Trust; £6,648 to Central Manchester Healthcare; £6,500 to North Manchester Healthcare; £5,000 to Clairehouse Children's Hospice; £4,650 to Bury Healthcare Trust; £4,500 each to Blackpool Victoria Hospital and Bolton NHS Trust; £4,200 to St Ann's Hospital.

FINANCES *Year* 1999 *Income* £125,000 *Grants* £156,369 *Assets* £118,686

HOW TO APPLY In writing to the correspondent.

WHO TO APPLY TO S Jellands, 43–45 Lever Street, Manchester M60 7HP *Tel* 0161 234 2827 CC NO 260031 ESTABLISHED 1969

■ May Hearnshaw's Charity

WHERE FUNDING CAN BE GIVEN UK, particularly north Midlands and South Yorkshire.

WHO CAN BENEFIT Registered charities concerned with the relief of poverty and sickness, advancement of religion and education.

WHAT IS NOT FUNDED No grants to individuals, except those recommended by known charities.

TYPE OF GRANT One-off, with grants for buildings, core costs, research, recurring costs, running costs and salaries all considered. Funding may be given for up to three years.

RANGE OF GRANTS £500–£10,000.

SAMPLE GRANTS £10,000 to Masonic Trust for Boys and Girls; £7,000 in two grants to Children's Appeal; £5,000 to NCH Action for Children; £4,000 to Cavendish Centre; £3,550 to Ashgate Hospice; £3,000 each to Home for Incurables, NSPCC, National Trust, Neurodegenerative Support Group, Parkinson's Disease Society and St John's Hospice.

FINANCES *Year* 2000–01 *Income* £91,945 *Grants* £96,050 *Assets* £2,003,138

TRUSTEES David Law; Jack Rowan.

HOW TO APPLY 'The trustees usually decide on and make grants to charitable organisations twice a year but may decide to make grants at any time. They do not include in their consideration appeals received direct from individuals.'

WHO TO APPLY TO David Law, Trustee, 35–47 North Church Street, Sheffield S1 2DH *Tel* 0114 275 2888 *Fax* 0114 273 0108 CC NO 1008638 ESTABLISHED 1992

■ The Heart of England Community Foundation

WHERE FUNDING CAN BE GIVEN The city of Coventry and Warwickshire.

WHO CAN BENEFIT Community-based groups and activities benefiting a wide range of social circumstances.

WHAT IS FUNDED General charitable purposes, in particular for the benefit of the local community in Warwickshire and the city of Coventry and people who are disabled, and to promote social and economic development. This includes residential facilities and services, community arts and recreation, respite care and care for carers, support and self-help groups, community services, social issues advice and information and health advocacy.

WHAT IS NOT FUNDED Grants will not usually be considered for the following: general and major fundraising; individuals; educational institutions except where the institution or project is aimed at the relief of disadvantage; promotion of religious causes except where the institution or the project is aimed at relief of disadvantage; medical research; organisations with no permanent presence in the beneficial area; animal welfare; political activity; organisations with substantial reserves relative to turnover; sport's clubs except where the institution or the project is aimed at relief of disadvantage; salaries and other core costs.

TYPE OF GRANT Buildings, capital, core costs, feasibility studies, one-off, project, research, development costs, salaries, and start-up costs. Funding is available for up to one year.

RANGE OF GRANTS £100–£7,000.

SAMPLE GRANTS £2,200 to Shipston Deanery Youth Project for forward planning and a feasibility study; £2,000 each to Atherstone Parents' Centre for a survey of families in need, Escape – Warwickshire to extend an arts project for people with mental health problems, Ansley Common & Ansty Village Community Project for bridge funding and Chatterbox Club at Allesley Primary School – Coventry to resurface a play area; £1,900 to Friends of Tiverton School – Coventry for fencing; £1,700 each to Bidford Community Group for IT training for volunteers and Rugby Youth Access Project for a portable computer; £1,500 to Atherstone Theatre Workshop to train members in circus skills; £1,400 to Coventry Boys' Club to replace their kitchen tent and equipment.

FINANCES *Year* 2000–01 *Income* £346,000 *Grants* £70,000 *Assets* £579,000

TRUSTEES John Towers, Chair; Mrs Margaret Backhouse; Peter Bell; Laurie Cooke; Peter Deeley; Richard Drew; Spencer Fenn; Stewart Fergusson; Prof. Harry Goulbourne; Lady Jean Liggins; Mrs Dorette McAuslan; Ven. Michael Paget Wilkes; Peter Shearing; Mrs Beth Towers.

OTHER INFORMATION The priorities of the trustees are reviewed annually; applicants are encouraged to contact the foundation by telephone to obtain up-to-date information on current priorities. Only one grant will be given to an organisation in any one year from the foundation.

HOW TO APPLY In writing to the correspondent. Organisations are encouraged to telephone the foundation to discuss their project in advance of applying.

WHO TO APPLY TO Ms Alison McCall, Director, Aldermoor House, PO Box 227, Aldermoor Lane, Coventry CV3 1LT *Tel* 024 7688 4386 *Fax* 024 7688 4726 *E-mail* info.hoe@virgin.net *Website* www.heartofengland.co.uk CC NO 1045304 ESTABLISHED 1995

■ Heart of England Radio Charitable Trust

WHERE FUNDING CAN BE GIVEN Warwickshire and West Midlands.

WHO CAN BENEFIT Organisations providing relief in need, medical research, and education.

WHAT IS FUNDED General charitable purposes.

SAMPLE GRANTS £25,000 to NSPCC to help develop an educational pack; £10,000 each to Foundation for Conductive Education to buy the freehold on their premises and Kids Like Us; £8,400 to Stow Heath Infants School – Wolverhampton to construct a playground; £7,400 to Acorn's Children's Hospice Trust for the purchase of equipment; £6,000 to Freshwinds Charitable Trust; £3,800 to The Birth Defects Foundation for a probe. The trust also committed £10,000 to Left Heart Matters and £3,400 to West Midlands Autistic Society.

FINANCES *Year* 1999 *Income* £132,000 *Grants* £116,000 *Assets* £42,000

TRUSTEES Penny Viscountess Cobham, Chair; Jill Lyndon Husselby; Paul Martin Fairburn; Mark Roy Evans; David Michael Allen; Dianne Teresa Hall; Wade Lyn.

HOW TO APPLY In writing to the correspondent.

WHO TO APPLY TO Paul Fairburn, 1 The Square, 111 Broad Street, Birmingham B15 1AS *Tel* 0121 607 7247 CC NO 1054689 ESTABLISHED 1996

■ The Heathcoat Trust

WHERE FUNDING CAN BE GIVEN Tiverton, Devon and Cornwall.

WHO CAN BENEFIT Employees and past employees of the Heathcoat Group of companies, and their relatives or dependants. Organisations working with people who are disabled will be considered.

WHAT IS FUNDED To help employees of the Heathcoat Companies and their relatives or dependants, who may be in need, and to contribute to their education and training. The trust will also build or make grants to health institutions in Tiverton and East Devon. Grants are made to organisations which benefit the people of Tiverton and its neighbourhood and other areas where John Heathcoat and Company Ltd and Lowman Manufacturing Ltd carry on business.

TYPE OF GRANT Recurring and one-off.

RANGE OF GRANTS Usually less than £1,000.

SAMPLE GRANTS £30,000 to Marie Curie Cancer Care for a local nurse; £10,000 to MS Society for a local nurse; £8,000 to Tiverton Volunteer Centre; £7,000 to Age Concern – Tiverton and District.

FINANCES *Year* 2001–02 *Income* £537,000 *Grants* £726,107 *Assets* £16,700,000

TRUSTEES Sir Ian Heathcoat Amory; M J Gratton; Mrs B Hill; J Smith; Mrs N J Green.

HOW TO APPLY In writing to the correspondent. There are application forms for certain education grants.

WHO TO APPLY TO E W Summers, Secretary, The Factory, Tiverton, Devon EX16 5LL *Tel* 01884 254949

CC NO 203367   **ESTABLISHED** 1945

■ Heathside Charitable Trust

WHERE FUNDING CAN BE GIVEN UK.

WHAT IS FUNDED General charitable purposes, with a preference for Jewish organisations.

RANGE OF GRANTS £1,000–£141,100.

SAMPLE GRANTS £141,100 to Joint Jewish Charitable Trust; £35,000 to Raft; £25,000 to Jewish Education Defence Trust; £21,300 to Community Security Trust; £15,000 to Jewish Care; £10,000 each to British Friends of Jaffa Institute, GRET, and Motivation; £8,500 to Holocaust Educational Trust; £8,000 to Norwood.

FINANCES *Year* 2000 *Income* £82,530 *Grants* £394,407 *Assets* £3,476,430

TRUSTEES Sir Harry Solomon; Lady Judith Solomon; G R Jayson; R C Taylor.

HOW TO APPLY In writing to the correspondent, at any time.

WHO TO APPLY TO Sir Harry Solomon, Trustee, Hillsdown House, 32 Hampstead High Street, London NW3 1QD *Tel* 020 7431 7739

CC NO 326959   **ESTABLISHED** 1985

■ The Hedgcock Bequest

WHERE FUNDING CAN BE GIVEN Brighton and Hove.

WHO CAN BENEFIT Small community groups.

WHAT IS FUNDED The trust states: 'It is our policy to look at all applications on their merits. However, there are certain criteria used that are useful guidelines for potential applicants: only applications that demonstrate a clear and direct benefit to people who are residents of Brighton and Hove will be considered; grants are only normally made to small community organisations that are based in Brighton and Hove or conduct identifiable local activities. Generally grants will not be made to larger organisations (turnover £20,000 a year or more) or those covering a more diffuse, wider area with no quantifiable benefit to Brighton and Hove residents.

'The trustees cannot commit to annual grants. Therefore one-off projects or purchases may be more suitable than ongoing commitments. Any applications for renewal of a grant will be considered on their merits and assessed against other competing bids in the light of the income available.'

WHAT IS NOT FUNDED Grants will not be made to organisations already in receipt of funding from Brighton and Hove Council. Grants are only very exceptionally made to individuals and then only where they will result in some general public gain rather than purely individual benefit.

FINANCES *Year* 2000–01 *Income* £24,000 *Grants* £24,000

HOW TO APPLY In writing to the Grants Office, Culture and Regeneration, at the address above. 'Applications for funding from the bequest can be made at any time of the year. They will normally be considered within eight weeks of being received and applicants will be informed of the result shortly afterwards. A copy of the constitution should be enclosed if you have one; the address of its headquarters or main centre of activities; the name, address and position in the organisation or the person who is to act as the council's contact point; the number of members and the subscription payable (if any); the number of people attending each meeting/ session/lesson/performance and so on, and/or the number of people likely to benefit; the geographical area which the organisation aims to benefit; the purpose for which the grant is being sought; whether the organisation is a registered charity or not. If so, please quote the number; details of the organisation's recent finances, together with an income and expenditure budget for the financial year in which assistance is sought; details of the organisation's bank account and who cheques should be made payable to; an indication whether grant aid has been sought from East Sussex County Council, Brighton and Hove Health Authority or any other public body, together with details of other fundraising initiatives undertaken by the organisation.'

WHO TO APPLY TO Jonathon Best, Grants Officer, Brighton and Hove Council, Room 428, King's House, Grand Avenue, Hove BN3 2LS *Tel* 01273 291114

CC NO 230147   **ESTABLISHED** 1903

■ The Hedley Denton Charitable Trust

WHERE FUNDING CAN BE GIVEN North east England.

WHO CAN BENEFIT Registered charities.

WHAT IS FUNDED General charitable purposes,

TYPE OF GRANT One-off grants are considered for core, capital and project support.

RANGE OF GRANTS £250–£2,000.

SAMPLE GRANTS In 1998–99: £3,000 (in two grants) to Tearfund; £2,000 each to Intermediate Technology and North East Promenades Against Cancer Limited; £1,000 each to Northumberland Association of Clubs for Young People, Young Sinfonia (Northern Sinfonia Concert Society Limited), Headway, NSPCC, CARE International UK, VSO and Stephenson Engineering Centre.

Think carefully about every application. Is it justified?

535

FINANCES *Year* 2001–02 *Income* £39,838
TRUSTEES Miss D M Wild; C M Watts; I H Nicholson, Chair.
HOW TO APPLY In writing to the correspondent.
WHO TO APPLY TO I H Nicholson, Trustee, 5 West Road, Ponteland, Newcastle upon Tyne NE20 9ST *Tel* 01661 823863 *Fax* 01661 823724 *E-mail* law@iainnicholson.co.uk
CC NO 1060725   **ESTABLISHED** 1996

■ The Hedley Foundation
WHERE FUNDING CAN BE GIVEN UK.
WHO CAN BENEFIT Registered charities benefiting young people, their education, training, health and welfare; disabled people and the terminally-ill.
WHAT IS FUNDED Organisations working with young people, local church and community projects, organisations concerned with people who are disabled or seriously ill, medical equipment and research.
WHAT IS NOT FUNDED Grants are made only to UK registered charities.
No grants to overseas charities; individuals, under any circumstances; national and very large appeals; vehicles and transport.
TYPE OF GRANT Grants for specific projects only, usually fostering change or development, mostly one-off but a limited number of recurring grants for up to three are given. No revenue or salary funding.
RANGE OF GRANTS £1,000–£20,000; average grant £3,000.
SAMPLE GRANTS £15,000 each to Queen Elizabeth's Foundation for the Disabled in memory of Philip Byam-Cook, World Conservation Monitoring Centre, St Chad's Wood End and Fairbridge for a school exclusion project; £11,000 to Raleigh International; £10,000 each to Camden School for Girls, Deafblind UK, Emmaus UK, Fortune Centre for Riding Therapy, Nigel Clare Network Trust, and Wellington School.
FINANCES *Year* 2001–02 *Grants* £1,002,000
TRUSTEES J F Rodwell, Chair; C H Parish; P R Holcroft; G R Broke; P G Chamberlin; Miss L B Wace.
OTHER INFORMATION The trust pointed out that the 'Top Ten' grants listed 'are very much the exception ... our standard grants are in the order of £2–£3,000 and the list above have been plucked from several previous years. It gives quite the wrong impression of the sort of foundation we are'.
From the information we have, all the listed grants refer to 2001–02. No alternative 'correct' list was provided by the trust.
HOW TO APPLY Applications should be made in writing to Mrs M Kitto, appeals secretary. The trustees meet about every six weeks, so applications receive prompt attention. They should be accompanied by the latest available accounts, and a note of the present state of the appeal and its future prospects; in the case of buildings, it should also outline plans and details of planning status. Although Hedley staff are happy to deal with questions from applicants, consulting the website will normally answer 90 per cent of them and save both time and money. For community schemes it would be helpful to have a brief description of the community, its history, present make-up and aspirations, what is going for and against it and so on to put flesh on the application. Trustees individually have visited many charities to which the foundation might make or had made grants.

WHO TO APPLY TO Mrs Mary Kitto, Appeals Secretary, 9 Dowgate Hill, London EC4R 2SU *Tel* 020 7489 8076 *Website* hedleyfoundation.org.uk
CC NO 262933   **ESTABLISHED** 1971

■ The H J Heinz Company Limited Charitable Trust
WHERE FUNDING CAN BE GIVEN UK.
WHO CAN BENEFIT Organisations benefiting children and young adults, at risk groups, people disadvantaged by poverty and socially isolated people.
WHAT IS FUNDED The trust typically supports medicine, welfare, education (food technology and nutrition in particular), conservation, community relations and the arts. UK bodies are more likely to be favoured than local groups unless local applicants operate in the immediate vicinity of the company's main operating locations.
WHAT IS NOT FUNDED No grants to individuals. Requests for political or denominational causes or for advertising are not considered.
TYPE OF GRANT One-off.
RANGE OF GRANTS £250–£5,000, but mainly for smaller amounts.
SAMPLE GRANTS £5,000 to The Royal Manchester Children's Hospital (for research equipment); £4,500 to David Baum Memorial Appeal; £3,000 each to The Mayor's Charity Appeal 2002/03, The Royal Liverpool School for the Blind and Whizz-Kidz; £1,600 to I CAN; £1,200 to Daisy's Dream.
FINANCES *Year* 1999 *Income* £115,000 *Grants* £66,170 *Assets* £296,486
TRUSTEES Dr A J F O'Reilly; Mrs D Heinz; B R Purgavie; M Cook; A G M Ritchie.
HOW TO APPLY In writing to the address below, no follow-up telephone calls. Applications are considered once or twice a year. Applicants whether successful or unsuccessful are informed of the trustees' decisions.
WHO TO APPLY TO The c/o Consumer Contact, Spring Road, Kitt Green, Wigan, Lancashire WN5 0JL *Tel* 0800 528 5757 *Website* www.heinz.co.uk
CC NO 326254   **ESTABLISHED** 1982

■ The Hellenic Foundation
WHERE FUNDING CAN BE GIVEN UK.
WHO CAN BENEFIT Organisations and individuals, to advance education in the cultural tradition and heritage of Greece, particularly in the subjects of education, philosophy, the arts and science.
WHAT IS FUNDED Projects involving education, research, music and dance, books and library facilities, and university symposia.
SAMPLE GRANTS £5,700 to Hellenic Fellowship; £1,500 to University of Warwick for Conference Mousike; £1,300 to Royal Albert Memorial Museum; £1,000 each to AGENDA Magazine – Greek Edition, Anglo Hellenic League and Theatro Technis; £500 to The Actors of Dionysos; £300 to Lyra Greek Dancers.
FINANCES *Year* 1999 *Income* £55,000 *Grants* £38,000 *Assets* £502,000
TRUSTEES George A Tsavliris, Chair; Nicos H Sideris; Irene M Monios; Edmee C Leventis; Stamos J Fafalios; Tryphon Kedros; Dr Eleni Yannakaki; Michael C Peraticos; Louisa Leventis; Zenon K Mouskos; Constantinos I Caroussis; Mary Bromley; Irene J Fafalios; Costas N Hadjipateras; Angela K Kulukundis; George A Lemos; George D Lemos.

HOW TO APPLY In writing to the correspondent.
WHO TO APPLY TO S J Fafalios, Honorary Secretary, St Paul's House, Warwick Lane, London EC4P 4BN *Tel* 020 7251 5100
CC NO 326301   **ESTABLISHED** 1982

■ The Michael & Morven Heller Charitable Foundation

WHERE FUNDING CAN BE GIVEN Worldwide.
WHO CAN BENEFIT Organisations benefiting academics, medical professionals, research workers, scientists, students and teachers.
WHAT IS FUNDED Medical, education and scientific research.
WHAT IS NOT FUNDED No support for individuals.
RANGE OF GRANTS £5,000–£100,000.
SAMPLE GRANTS In 2000–01: £28,994 in four grants to St Catherine's College; £15,000 each to Hampstead Theatre and London Jewish Cultural Centre; £12,000 to Norwood Ltd; £7,500 to Beth Shalom; £5,000 each to Community Security Trust, FMRC Charitable Trust, Jewish Marriage Council L'Chaim Independent Charitable Trust and Prostate Cancer Research Centre.
FINANCES *Year* 2001–02 *Income* £242,358 *Grants* £263,318 *Assets* £3,250,000
TRUSTEES Michael Heller; Morven Heller; Pearl Livingstone.
HOW TO APPLY In writing to the correspondent.
WHO TO APPLY TO The Trustees, 8–10 New Fetter Lane, London EC4A 1NQ *Tel* 020 7415 5000 *Fax* 020 7415 0611
CC NO 327832   **ESTABLISHED** 1988

■ The Simon Heller Charitable Settlement

WHERE FUNDING CAN BE GIVEN Worldwide.
WHO CAN BENEFIT Organisations benefiting academics, medical professionals, research workers, scientists, students and teachers.
WHAT IS FUNDED Medical research and scientific and educational research
WHAT IS NOT FUNDED No grants to individuals.
SAMPLE GRANTS In 2000–01: £35,000 each to Institute of Policy Research and UJIA; £30,000 to Jewish Care; £15,000 to Aish Hatora £12,500 to Spiro institute; £11,500 to Scopus; £10,000 to Chief Rabbinate Charitable Trust; £5,000 each to British ORT, Common Denominator and Community Charity Trust; £2,500 to Shvut Ami; £2,000 to Israel Diaspora Trust.
FINANCES *Year* 2001–02 *Income* £294,399 *Grants* £199,533 *Assets* £4,656,000
TRUSTEES M A Heller; Morven Heller; W S Trustee Company Limited.
HOW TO APPLY In writing to the correspondent.
WHO TO APPLY TO The Trustees, 8–10 New Fetter Lane, London EC4A 1NQ *Tel* 020 7415 5000 *Fax* 020 7415 0611
CC NO 265405   **ESTABLISHED** 1972

■ Help a London Child

WHERE FUNDING CAN BE GIVEN London, specifically the 95.8 Capital FM transmission area.
WHO CAN BENEFIT Disadvantaged and deprived children living in the Greater London area.
WHAT IS FUNDED Community groups; cultural groups; educational clubs; playgroups; refuge/homeless projects; social/leisure groups; special needs/ health projects; youth.
WHAT IS NOT FUNDED Help a London Child will not fund individual children or families; retrospective funding; statutory funding – funding for schools or health projects that would otherwise be covered by designated statutory funding from the local authority; salaried posts; deficit funding or repayment of loans; medical research; purchase of a minibus; trips abroad; distribution to other organisations; religious activities; general structural changes to buildings.
TYPE OF GRANT Capital; core costs; one-off; project; running costs; and salaries. Funding is available for one year or less.
RANGE OF GRANTS Typical grant £2,000.
SAMPLE GRANTS £6,400 to Ealing Women's Aid for their after-school project; £6,240 to Community Links, Newham for standing camp equipment; £5,600 to Whizz Kidz, London-wide for mobility equipment; £5,300 each to Queen's Park Bangladesh Association and Soho Family Centre Trust to support children's special needs in pre-school group; £5,100 to Film and Video Workshop, Islington for 'Hungerford gets animated!'; £5,000 to Teddington, Twickenham and Hampton NHS Trust for a project for exceptional children in their early development.
FINANCES *Year* 2002 *Grants* £1,013,000
TRUSTEES Richard Eyre; Alan Schaffer; David Mansfield, Chair; David Briggs.
HOW TO APPLY Grants are awarded once a year, in November. Application forms (with full guidelines and useful tips to improve your chances of success) are available from January and require an A4 stamped addressed envelope. HALC encourages potential applicants to call the office (number below) should they have any questions about filling in the form. Completed forms must be sent or delivered by hand to the contact address. Photocopies or faxes cannot be accepted. The closing date for 2003 has still to be confirmed but is likely to be in late April. Applicants will receive an acknowledgement in late June along with a reference number.
WHO TO APPLY TO Rich Hornsell, Allocations Manager, c/o Capital Radio, 30 Leicester Square, London WC2H 7LA *Tel* 020 7766 6203/6536 *Website* www.capitalfm.com/ helpalondonchild
CC NO 1091657   **ESTABLISHED** 1978

■ Help the Aged

WHERE FUNDING CAN BE GIVEN UK.
WHO CAN BENEFIT Voluntary and charitable groups which offer a range of resources to support vulnerable or disadvantaged older people live independently in thier communities. This includes minority ethnic groups, carers, homeless people, and people living in urban and rural areas.
WHAT IS FUNDED Local projects providing services which are needed in their communities, where the services in question (a) meet needs that are defined by older people themselves, and (b) clearly target disadvantage.
WHAT IS NOT FUNDED Funding for loans, or to reduce deficits already incurred by projects, or to make up a shortfall due to underbidding for a service contract; commercial companies or statutory agencies; organisations artificially created as trusts, designed to meet the needs of community care proposals or to realise European funding; holidays; residential or nursing homes, except to support independent

living of older people and where the benefits extend to the wider community; registered social landlords except where there is a clearly defined project focusing on a vulnerable group, e.g. homeless older people. Grants towards individuals, outings, general entertainment, leisure clubs and festive celebrations are generally excluded except where they may be supported with funds specifically donated to us for that particular purpose or within a geographical area.

TYPE OF GRANT Capital; one-off; running costs; salaries; and start-up costs. Funding is available for up to three years.

RANGE OF GRANTS £200–£50,000; typical grant £10,000.

SAMPLE GRANTS £200,000 to Oxford Centre on Ageing; £50,000 to St Mungo's; £40,000 each to Cheadle Live at Home and Gullane Day Centre, both for minibuses; £36,000 to Age Concern Ceredigion over three years to expand a rural lunch club service; £25,000 to British Commonwealth Ex-servicemen; £23,000 to Salvation Army in Bristol; £15,000 each to Age Concern West Glamorgan, CAN homelessness team in Northampton and Holborn Community Association.

FINANCES *Year* 2001–02 *Grants* £2,269,000

TRUSTEES John D Mather, Chair; Philip Ashfield; Henry Bowrey; Peter Bowring; Priscilla Campbell Allen; Jo Connell; Brian Fox; Vera Harley; Anne Harris; William Hastings; Rosemary Kelly; Trevor Larman; William Menzies-Wilson; Kevin Williams; Christopher Woodbridge; Angus Young.

PUBLICATIONS Publications include *Pensioners Transport Survey, A Life Worth Living – Summary: The independence and inclusion of older people* and *Housing Priorities of Older People*. A full list of publications is available on request.

OTHER INFORMATION The grants programme is only one aspect of Help the Aged's work, which can include seconding trained fundraisers to projects which need to raise large capital sums.

HOW TO APPLY In the first instance contact the regional distributions department on 020 7253 0253 or by fax on 020 7239 1849. The distributions committee meets approximately every other month, usually in March, June, September and December. In between meetings, grants can be agreed for up to £5,000, but only out of funds earmaked for specific local areas or subjects.

WHO TO APPLY TO Michael Lake, Director General, 207 – 221 Pentonville Road, London N1 9UZ *Tel* 020 7278 1114 *Website* www.helptheaged.org.uk

CC NO 272786   **ESTABLISHED** 1977

....

■ Help the Homeless Ltd

WHERE FUNDING CAN BE GIVEN UK.

WHO CAN BENEFIT Voluntary agencies benefiting single homeless people.

WHAT IS FUNDED To help any voluntary residential project which has made every endeavour, unsuccessfully, to raise funds from other known sources.

WHAT IS NOT FUNDED Charities with substantial funds are not supported. No grants for revenue expenditure such as ongoing running costs or salaries, and so on.

TYPE OF GRANT Usually one-off for buildings, capital and projects. Some beneficiaries have previously been supported.

RANGE OF GRANTS Up to £2,000.

SAMPLE GRANTS £33,333 to St Mungo's; £25,000 to Emmaus UK; £2,000 each to Chester Aid to the Homeless, Finsbury Park Street Drinkers, Kennet Action for Single Homeless, Lighthouse Outreach, Parish of East Ham, and St Edmund's Society; £1,982 to Bedford Housing Link; £1,964 to Good Shepherd Trust.

FINANCES *Year* 2001–02 *Income* £58,336 *Grants* £79,722 *Assets* £1,048,556

TRUSTEES F J Bergin; T S Cookson; L A Bains; M McIntyre; T Rogers; R Reed; P Fullerton.

HOW TO APPLY The trust has a specific application form that must be completed, which states that: 'you need to provide us with information about your organisation, its aims, how it works and how it intends to continue to meet those aims in the future. You will also be asked to send us a copy of your most recent audited reports and accounts'. Unformatted applications will not be considered. Trustees meet to consider grants four times a year. There should be a minimum period of two years between the receipt of a grant and a subsequent application.

WHO TO APPLY TO T Kenny, 5th Floor, Babmaes House, 2 Babmaes Street, London SW1Y 6HD *Tel* 020 7925 2725 *Fax* 020 7925 2583

CC NO 271988   **ESTABLISHED** 1975

....

■ Help the Hospices

WHERE FUNDING CAN BE GIVEN UK.

WHO CAN BENEFIT Organisations benefiting people who are disabled, and medical professionals in hospices.

WHAT IS FUNDED Grants are given to local voluntary hospices, in-patient, day care and home care teams, and for equipment for patient care and improved services; training for hospice staff (NHS and voluntary); research funding and advisory services to hospices.

TYPE OF GRANT One-off and recurrent.

RANGE OF GRANTS £75–£15,000.

SAMPLE GRANTS In 1997–98: £43,200 in two grants to Association for Hospice Management; £43,000 to IMPACT; £35,000 to National Council for Hospice and Specialist Palliative Care Services; £21,000 to Hth/Cruse; £20,000 to Association of Hospice Voluntary Service Coordinators.

FINANCES *Year* 2000–01 *Income* £2,217,955 *Grants* £1,121,358 *Assets* £3,583,872

TRUSTEES Rt Hon. Lord Newton of Braintree, Chair; Ron Giffin; John Cherry; Dr Helen Clayson; Ms Suzy Croft; Robin Eve; Dr Andrew Hoy; Mrs Ann Lee; Ms Terry Maggee; Miss Agnes Malone; Mrs Hilary McNair; George Miall; Hugh Scurfield.

HOW TO APPLY Generally on a form available from Karl Benn, Grants Officer, from whom further information is also available. For major grant programmes, potential applicants should request details first as policies change. The trust's website contains detailed information of the grant-making policy and should be viewed before an application is considered. For emergency grants, applicants should write directly to the chief executive.

WHO TO APPLY TO David Praill, Chief Executive, 34–44 Britannia Street, London WC1 9JG *Tel* 020 7520 8200 *Fax* 020 7278 1021 *E-mail* grants@helpthehospices.org.uk *Website* www.helpthehospices.org.uk

CC NO 1014851   **ESTABLISHED** 1984

....

■ The Hemby Trust

WHERE FUNDING CAN BE GIVEN Merseyside and Wirral.

WHAT IS FUNDED This trust will consider funding social needs, community facilities and services, youth and employment, schools and colleges, help for older people, health, the arts, culture and recreation, the environment and church buildings.

WHAT IS NOT FUNDED Grants will not be given to political organisations, pressure groups or individuals, feasibility studies, organisations outside Merseyside or Wirral, or to replace statutory funding.

TYPE OF GRANT Capital grants.

RANGE OF GRANTS £500 to £3,000.

SAMPLE GRANTS £10,000 to The Prince's Trust; £5,000 to Liverpool Women's Hospital; £4,000 to Merseyside Outward Bound; £3,500 to Litherland Youth Centre; £3,500 each to Liverpool & Merseyside Theatres Trust and Sefton Children's Trust; £2,500 to 4th Crosby Scouts; £2,000 each to Royal Liverpool Philharmonic, Invalids at Home, Formby & Southport Riding for the Disabled, Disabled Children's Holiday Fund, Leasowe Adventure Playground and British Red Cross St Helens.

FINANCES *Year* 2001–02 *Income* £104,375 *Grants* £114,502 *Assets* £2,380,241

TRUSTEES R A Morris; P T Furlong; A T Morris; N A Wainwright.

HOW TO APPLY Applicants should write to the correspondent for a leaflet which sets out the aims and objectives of the trust and an application form which should be returned with a copy of the applicant's latest accounts. A date will be given for the return of the form if it is to be discussed by the trustees at their next meeting. The trustees meet at the end of March, July and November. Applications are not acknowledged, but the applicant is welcome to telephone the administrator (01704 834887) to check it has been received.

WHO TO APPLY TO Michael Hope, c/o Rathbone Bros & Co. Ltd, Port of Liverpool Building, Pier Head, Liverpool L3 1NW *Tel* 0151 243 7350 *Fax* 0151 243 7019

CC NO 1073028   **ESTABLISHED** 1998

■ The Christina Mary Hendrie Trust for Scottish & Canadian Charities

WHERE FUNDING CAN BE GIVEN Scotland and Canada.

WHO CAN BENEFIT Charities benefiting young people and older people.

WHAT IS FUNDED Charities connected with young people and older people. Cancer charities are also supported.

WHAT IS NOT FUNDED Grants are not given to individuals.

RANGE OF GRANTS Typical grants £1,000–£5,000.

FINANCES *Year* 1999 *Grants* £81,000

TRUSTEES Mrs A D H Irwin; C R B Cox; J K Scott Moncrieff; Miss C Irwin; Maj. Gen. A S H Irwin; R N Cox; A G Cox.

HOW TO APPLY In writing to the correspondent. The trustees meet twice a year to consider grants, usually in March and November.

WHO TO APPLY TO George R Russell, 48 Castle Street, Edinburgh EH2 3LX *Tel* 0131 220 2345

SC NO SC014514   **ESTABLISHED** 1975

■ The Henley Educational Charity

WHERE FUNDING CAN BE GIVEN Henley-on-Thames and the parishes of Bix and Rotherfield Greys in Oxfordshire and Remenham in Berkshire.

WHO CAN BENEFIT Individuals and organisations concerned with the education of children, young adults and people who are disadvantaged. State maintained schools and colleges in the area defined above.

WHAT IS FUNDED Grants are given to alleviate financial hardship, to support particular educational initiatives and courses and to help meet the cost of educational visits, books and equipment at a local school or college.

WHAT IS NOT FUNDED Applicants must be under 25 years of age, and must either be resident in the area defined above or have/attended a state maintained school in the area for at least two years.

TYPE OF GRANT Mainly one-off grants for core and capital support; also project funding.

RANGE OF GRANTS All applications considered individually.

SAMPLE GRANTS Grants were given towards pre-school fees, sports club fees, music lessons, school study trips, and book grants of £75 in first year of higher education.

FINANCES *Year* 2000–01 *Income* £100,000 *Grants* £90,000

TRUSTEES Rector of Henley; Mayor of Henley; nine others nominated by councils.

HOW TO APPLY Apply in writing to the correspondent for an application form. The head of the local schools/colleges may be able to help potential applicants determine whether an application will be successful.

WHO TO APPLY TO Mrs M Clarke, Clerk, 16 Church Street, Henley-on-Thames, South Oxfordshire RG9 1SE *Tel* 01491 576058 *E-mail* hedcharity@hotmail.com

CC NO 309237   **ESTABLISHED** 1604

■ Philip Henman Trust

WHERE FUNDING CAN BE GIVEN Worldwide.

WHO CAN BENEFIT UK-registered charities.

WHAT IS FUNDED Long-term grants are aimed at large UK-based overseas aid organisations. One-off grants are given to projects benefiting young people in the UK.

WHAT IS NOT FUNDED 'There are no restrictions on which organisations can apply as long as they are a UK-registered charity.'

TYPE OF GRANT One-off and long-term grants.

RANGE OF GRANTS £3,000–£5,000 per year for long-term grants. One-off grants up to £1,000.

SAMPLE GRANTS Beneficiaries were Winged Fellowship, Jubilee Sailing Trust, Wateraid, NCH Action for Children, Anti Slavery, AMIE, Traidcraft Exchange, Sight Savers, International Care and Relief and Childhope.

FINANCES *Year* 2001–02 *Income* £65,000 *Grants* £50,000

TRUSTEES J C Clark; D J Clark; J Duffy.

HOW TO APPLY The trust asks that a small form is completed and sent with a description of your project to the correspondent. To apply for a one-off grant or long-term grant you should write a one or two page description of the project respectively, with an attached budget. The trust says: 'Any other information about your organisation and annual accounts is useful for an assessment of your organisation carried out by our secretary, but will not be forwarded to our trustees for consideration of the grant.' The trustees meet twice a year in March and

Think carefully about every application. Is it justified?

539

October. Applications for long-term grants should be sent before 10 September for consideration at the October meeting, and applications for one-off grants should be sent before 10 February for consideration at the March meeting. The trust prefers charities to look at its website where its guidelines for applications are published, before applying.

WHO TO APPLY TO D J Clark, Trustee, 17 Victoria Avenue, Lancaster LA1 4SY
E-mail info@pht.org.uk *Website* www.pht.org.uk
CC NO 1054707   **ESTABLISHED** 1986

....

■ The G D Herbert Charitable Trust

WHERE FUNDING CAN BE GIVEN UK.
WHO CAN BENEFIT Registered charities.
WHAT IS FUNDED The trust supports medicine, health, welfare and environmental resources. It mainly gives regular grants to a set list of charities, with a few one-off grants given each year.
TYPE OF GRANT Mainly recurrent.
SAMPLE GRANTS In 1997–98: £5,000 to Kent Youth Trust; £3,400 to National Trust; £1,700 each to Aged in Distress, Children's Country Holiday Fund, PDSA, Prostate Cancer Charity and Shelter; £500 each to Ogbourne St George PCC and Wiltshire Wildlife Trust.
FINANCES *Year* 2000–01 *Income* £66,441
TRUSTEES M E Beaumont; J J H Burden.
HOW TO APPLY In writing to the correspondent. No applications are invited other than from those charities currently supported by the trust.
WHO TO APPLY TO J J H Burden, Trustee, Tweedie & Prideaux Solicitors, 5 Lincoln's Inn Fields, London WC2A 3BT *Tel* 020 7405 1234
CC NO 295998   **ESTABLISHED** 1986

....

■ The Joanna Herbert-Stepney Charitable Settlement (also known as

The Paget Charitable Trust)

WHERE FUNDING CAN BE GIVEN Worldwide, with an interest in Loughborough.
WHO CAN BENEFIT Normally only British registered charities.
WHAT IS FUNDED Sheer need is paramount, and, in practice, nothing else can be considered. There is a preference for the unglamorous, for maximum achievement with minimal resources. Priorities include the developing world, deprived children, old age, 'green' projects, and animal welfare. The trust does sometimes give ongoing support, thus leaving fewer funds for new applicants.
WHAT IS NOT FUNDED The trust states that 'sheer need is paramount, in practice, nothing else is considered'. Grants are only given to registered UK charities. Overseas projects can only be funded via UK charities; no money can be sent overseas. The trust does not support individuals (including students), projects for people with mental disabilities, medical research or AIDS/HIV projects.
RANGE OF GRANTS £50–£7,000.
SAMPLE GRANTS £7,000 to Oxfam; £5,000 each to Peper Harrow Foundation, Leicestershire Food Links Ltd and Manacare Foundation; £4,000 each to CIWF and Royal Agricultural Benevolent Institute; £3,500 to Children's Aid Direct; £3,000 each to Dentaid, Ockenden International, Soil Association and Stepney Children's Fund.

FINANCES *Year* 2000–01 *Income* £183,148 *Grants* £253,325 *Assets* £3,666,171
TRUSTEES Joanna Herbert-Stepney; Lesley Mary Blood; Mrs Joy Pollard.
HOW TO APPLY In writing to the correspondent; there is no application form. The trustees meet in spring and autumn. The trust regrets that it cannot respond to all applications.
WHO TO APPLY TO Joanna Herbert-Stepney, Trustee, Old Village Stores, Dippenhall Street, Crondall, Farnham, Surrey GU10 5NZ *Tel* 01252 850253
CC NO 327402   **ESTABLISHED** 1986

....

■ The Anne Herd Memorial Trust

WHERE FUNDING CAN BE GIVEN Scotland, with a preference for Tayside, the City of Dundee and Broughty Ferry.
WHO CAN BENEFIT Visually impaired individuals.
WHAT IS FUNDED Organisations working in the beneficial area with visually impaired individuals.
SAMPLE GRANTS £20,000 to Dundee Society for the Visually Impaired for its new Herd building, the first instalment of a total of £100,000 committed over five years; £10,000 to Sense Scotland; 39,000 to RNIB Talking Book Service.
FINANCES *Year* 2000–01 *Income* £30,000 *Grants* £78,000
TRUSTEES B N Bowman; Mrs P M M Bowman; Mrs E N McGillivray; R W H Hudson; Mrs Elizabeth M Breckon; Robert J Wild.
HOW TO APPLY In writing to the correspondent. Trustees meet once a year to consider grants, usually in June. Applications should be received by March/April.
WHO TO APPLY TO The Trustees, Bowman Scottish Lawyers, 27 Bank Street, Dundee DD1 1RP *Tel* 01382 322267
SC NO SC014198

....

■ The Herefordshire Historic Churches Trust

WHERE FUNDING CAN BE GIVEN Old county of Herefordshire.
WHO CAN BENEFIT All Christian places of worship.
WHAT IS FUNDED The restoration, preservation, repair, maintenance and improvement of churches, their contents and their churchyards in Herefordshire.
TYPE OF GRANT Buildings.
RANGE OF GRANTS £500–£5,000.
SAMPLE GRANTS In 1999: £5,000 each to churches in Byford, Hampton Bishop, Ledbury, Much Cowarne, and Stretton Sugwas; £3,000 each to Eignbrook URC in Hereford, Kilpeck, Kington RC, Leominster New Life Church, and Monkland.
FINANCES *Year* 2000 *Income* £60,000 *Grants* £50,000
TRUSTEES Rear-Admiral P B Hogg, Chair; D M Annett; Archdeacon of Hereford; Miss Susan Bond; Peter Brown; C J N Dalton; Earl of Darnley; H C Moore; Miss R Munford; R Peers.
HOW TO APPLY In writing to the correspondent. Deadlines for applications are 15 March and 15 September.
WHO TO APPLY TO Peter Brown, Trustee, Lawton Lea, Eardisland, Near Leominister, Herefordshire HR6 9AS *Tel* 01544 388389
CC NO 511181   **ESTABLISHED** 1954

....

■ The Heritage of London Trust Ltd

WHERE FUNDING CAN BE GIVEN The London boroughs.
WHO CAN BENEFIT Listed buildings in London.
WHAT IS FUNDED The restoration of buildings of architectural importance. Grants are mainly given for skilled restoration of notable features of listed buildings, generally (though not exclusively) external work. Examples of buildings assisted are churches, community centres, almshouses, theatres, hospitals, museums and educational establishments.
RANGE OF GRANTS Grants rarely exceed £5,000.
FINANCES *Year* 2001–02 *Income* £89,000 *Grants* £75,000 *Assets* £579,000
TRUSTEES William Bell, President; Sir John Lambert, Vice-President; Giles Shepard, Chair; Miss Sophie Andreae; Hon. Nicholas Assheton, Vice-Chair; Ronald Barden; Mrs Bridget Cherry; Martin Drury; Kevin Gardner; Jonathan Gestetner; Norman Howard; Michael Medlicott; Ron Peet; Sir William Whitfield; Clarence Eng; Dame Valerie Strachan.
PUBLICATIONS Map: *Historic Buildings in Covent Garden.*
HOW TO APPLY Initial contact should be by telephone. If the project seems eligible, guidance notes will be sent to the applicant who should make a formal application in writing. Board meetings are held in January, May and September.
WHO TO APPLY TO Julian Spicer, Director, 55 Blandford St, 23 Savile Row, London W1H 3AF *Tel* 020 7208 8232 *Fax* 020 7208 8246 *E-mail* info@heritageoflondon.com
CC NO 280272   **ESTABLISHED** 1980

■ The Hertfordshire Community Foundation

WHERE FUNDING CAN BE GIVEN Hertfordshire.
WHO CAN BENEFIT Individuals and organisations benefiting: children; young adults; older people; parents and children; one-parent families; and widows and widowers. Any locally based charity or voluntary group benefiting local people. Many are smaller, less well-known groups or less 'popular' causes that often find it extremely difficult to obtain funds elsewhere.
WHAT IS FUNDED To support the work of local charities and voluntary groups for the benefit of the community, with the following particular concerns: disadvantaged children and families; developing young people; access to education, training and employment; the needs of older people. This includes: residential facilities and services; infrastructure support and development; religious ancillary buildings; pre-school education; special schools; education and training; community centres and village halls; playgrounds; recreation grounds; community services; equal opportunities; and social advice and information.
WHAT IS NOT FUNDED No grants are made towards: UK or general appeals, or those with no specific Hertfordshire focus; statutory or public bodies, or to replace withdrawn statutory funding; religious or political causes, medical research, holidays, overseas travel or full-time education; individuals, except within the terms of special funds, e.g. the Children's Fund.
TYPE OF GRANT Major grants, revenue or capital, not long-term funding or as part of a large building project. Maximum £5,000 for one-off grants, or £15,000 over three years; usually smaller

amounts. Project grants up to £500 for specific purpose, start-up or development. Small grants up to £200 for children within very specific areas.
RANGE OF GRANTS £100–£5,000 per year for up to three years.
SAMPLE GRANTS £4,500 to Buntingfor Youth Council for catering equipment; £4,300 to Hertfordshire Association for the Care and Resettlement of Offenders for a resettlement project for ex-offenders serving sentences of less than 12 months; £5,000 to Hertfordshire Care Trust for a preventative programme for children who play truant; £1,600 to Reach Out Project for a new fridge and cookers for narrow boats used by people with special needs; £1,450 to Age Concern, Dacorum for a handyperson scheme.
FINANCES *Year* 2000–01 *Income* £802,000 *Grants* £175,000 *Assets* £2,900,000
TRUSTEES Roland Everington, Chair; Elizabeth Allen; Kate Bellinis; David Cansdale; Betty Globe; Caroline McCaffrey; Bob Richardson; John Usher; Richard Walduck.
PUBLICATIONS Leaflets; newsletter; guidelines for applicants.
HOW TO APPLY An informal discussion with one of the grants staff is encouraged at an early stage. If appropriate, an application form will be issued. Major grants are considered quarterly, with deadlines at the end of February, May, August and November. Other requests are considered when received.
WHO TO APPLY TO Christine Mills, Grants Officer, Sylvia Adams House, 24 The Common, Hatfield, Hertfordshire AL10 0NB *Tel* 01707 251351 *Fax* 01707 251133 *E-mail* hcf@care4free.net
CC NO 299438   **ESTABLISHED** 1988

■ The Hesed Trust

WHERE FUNDING CAN BE GIVEN UK and overseas.
WHO CAN BENEFIT Christian charities benefiting children, young people, older people, clergy, students, Christians and evangelists.
WHAT IS FUNDED Christian charitable purposes. The trust will consider funding the advancement of religion and the Free Church umbrella bodies.
WHAT IS NOT FUNDED No support for expeditions and individual requests.
TYPE OF GRANT One-off grants, for one year or less.
RANGE OF GRANTS Not exceeding £500.
FINANCES *Year* 1997–98 *Income* £48,026 *Grants* £49,034 *Assets* £23,506
TRUSTEES P Briggs; R Eagle; G Rawlings; J C Smith.
HOW TO APPLY The trsut states that no applications are now being considered.
WHO TO APPLY TO G Rawlings, Secretary, 14 Chiltern Avenue, Cosby, Leicestershire LE9 1UF *Tel* 0116 286 2990
CC NO 1000489   **ESTABLISHED** 1990

■ Michael Heseltine Charitable Trust

WHERE FUNDING CAN BE GIVEN UK.
WHO CAN BENEFIT Registered charities.
WHAT IS FUNDED General charitable purposes.
RANGE OF GRANTS £4–£2,500.
SAMPLE GRANTS £2,500 to The Victoria and Albert Museum; £2,000 to Elias Ashmore Group; £1,700 to Royal Collection Studies; £1,500 to The Hillier Aboretum; £1,000 each to International Spinal Research Trust, Royal Holloway University of London and Tusk Trust.

FINANCES *Year* 1998–99 *Income* £26,000 *Grants* £29,000
TRUSTEES The Rt Hon. Michael Ray Dibdin Heseltine; Mrs Anne Heseltine.
HOW TO APPLY In writing to the correspondent.
WHO TO APPLY TO Mrs C Steans, Thenford House, Thenford, Banbury, Oxfordshire OX17 2BX
CC NO 266958   **ESTABLISHED** 1974

■ The Hesslewood Children's Trust (Hull Seamen's & General Orphanage)

WHERE FUNDING CAN BE GIVEN East Yorkshire and North Lincolnshire.
WHO CAN BENEFIT Individuals and organisations in the area defined above, benefiting children and young adults under 25. Support will be given to people in care, or who are fostered or adopted; people who are disabled; people disadvantaged by poverty; ex-offenders and people at risk of offending; homeless people; people living in both rural and urban areas; socially isolated people; and victims of abuse and crime.
WHAT IS FUNDED To provide aid for young individuals in need and to support youth organisations for holidays. Particularly supported are charities working in the fields of education, housing and accommodation, and arts, culture and recreation.
WHAT IS NOT FUNDED No grants to benefit people over the age of 25 will be made.
TYPE OF GRANT One-off. Funding may be given for up to one year.
SAMPLE GRANTS £15,000 to Hull Compact Ltd for grants and bursaries; £6,000 to Hull Resettlement Project for furniture and household goods for the homeless; £5,000 to Riding for the Disabled; £3,000 to Sebrief Project to enable disadvantaged youngsters to go sailing; £2,000 to St Michael's Youth Project for youth residential holidays; £1,000 to Sail Training Association for youngsters to go sailing; £750 to Duke of Edinburgh Awards for help for youngsters; £600 to Withernsea Out of School Club for equipment; £300 to Coltman Area Community Association for equipment for children.
FINANCES *Year* 2000 *Income* £91,500 *Grants* £70,000 *Assets* £1,600,000
TRUSTEES I D Graham; Dr J Alexander; R M S Allenby; Dr G Cameron; Capt. E Howlett; Mrs F J Turner; A A Croft; Mrs G Munn; Canon K David; Mrs M Fox; C I P Roberts; Dr D Nicholas; M Mitchell.
HOW TO APPLY On a form available from the correspondent, with a telephone number if possible. Deadlines are 16 February, 16 June and 16 September. No replies are given to ineligible organisations. This trust informed us that it promotes its work through its own avenues, receiving more applications than it can support, and asked not to be included in this guide.
WHO TO APPLY TO R E Booth, Secretary, 66 The Meadows, Cherry Barton, Beverley, East Yorkshire HU17 7SP
CC NO 529804   **ESTABLISHED** 1982

■ The Bernhard Heuberger Charitable Trust

WHERE FUNDING CAN BE GIVEN Worldwide.
WHO CAN BENEFIT Jewish organisations benefiting Jewish people.
WHAT IS FUNDED Jewish charitable purposes.
SAMPLE GRANTS £5,250 to Beis Brucha; £5,000 each to BH Gur, Bridge Lane Beth Hamerdrash and Jewish Free School; £2,000 to United Jewish Israel Appeal; £1,000 each to British Friends of Shalva, CST, Imrey Chaim Synagogue and World Emunah.
FINANCES *Year* 2000–01 *Income* £728,467 *Grants* £70,000 *Assets* £2,884,347
TRUSTEES D H Heuberger; S N Heuberger.
HOW TO APPLY In writing to the correspondent.
WHO TO APPLY TO H Heuberger, Secretary, 12 Sherwood Road, London NW4 1AD
CC NO 294378   **ESTABLISHED** 1986

■ The P & C Hickinbotham Charitable Trust

WHERE FUNDING CAN BE GIVEN UK, with a preference for Leicestershire and Rutland.
WHO CAN BENEFIT Registered charities only. Particular favour is given to Quakers.
WHAT IS FUNDED The trust generally supports local (Leicester, Leicestershire and Rutland) charities and Quaker activities in a wider field.
WHAT IS NOT FUNDED No grants to individuals applying for bursary-type assistance or to large UK charities.
TYPE OF GRANT Usually one-off grants.
SAMPLE GRANTS In 1999–2000: £15,000 to Royal Leicestershire, Rutland and Wycliffe Society for the Blind; £5,000 to National Trust; £1,700 to Age Concern; £1,100 to Society of Friends – Leicester; £1,000 each to Belgrave Playhouse and Leicester General Hospital NHS Trust; £450 to Music in Lyddington; £100 to Croxton Kerriel Parochial Church Council; £50 each to Ashby Parva Village Hall Committee and Rowena Fund – Oakham School; £25 to Uppingham Community College.
FINANCES *Year* 2001–02 *Income* £59,416 *Grants* £77,645
TRUSTEES Mrs C R Hickinbotham; P F J Hickinbotham; R P Hickinbotham.
HOW TO APPLY In writing to the correspondent, giving a brief outline of the purpose of the grant. Replies will not be sent to unsuccessful applicants.
WHO TO APPLY TO Mrs C R Hickinbotham, Trustee, 69 Main Street, Bushby, Leicester LE7 9PL *Tel* 0116 243 1152
CC NO 216432   **ESTABLISHED** 1947

■ The Higgs Charitable Trust

WHERE FUNDING CAN BE GIVEN UK, with a preference for the former county of Avon.
WHO CAN BENEFIT Mostly medical research trusts or foundations. Organisations benefiting children, young adults, older people and people who are disadvantaged by poverty or homeless.
WHAT IS FUNDED Mainly research into deafness carried out by private charitable foundations. Also considered are charities working in the fields of religious buildings; housing and accommodation; animal facilities and services; conservation and campaigning; and education and training.

TYPE OF GRANT One-off and research. Funding for more than three years will be considered.
SAMPLE GRANTS In 1999: £25,000 to TWJ Foundation; £10,000 to Skinners Company (Lord Mannesbury Bounty); £2,000 to Jobson Foundation.
FINANCES Year 2000–01 Income £33,404
TRUSTEES D W M Campbell; T W Higgs; Mrs L Humphris.
HOW TO APPLY In writing to the correspondent, not less than two months before the annual general meeting in November.
WHO TO APPLY TO A C Nash, Messrs Mogers, 24 Queen Square, Bath BA1 2HY Tel 01225 750000 Fax 01225 445208 E-mail anthonynash@mogers.co.uk
CC NO 267036   **ESTABLISHED** 1982

■ Alan Edward Higgs Charity

WHERE FUNDING CAN BE GIVEN Within 25 miles of the centre of Coventry only.
WHO CAN BENEFIT Registered charities where their activity will benefit young people either directly, through their family, or through the provision of facilities or services to the community.
WHAT IS FUNDED Activities or projects that contribute to the amelioration of deprivation.
WHAT IS NOT FUNDED Applications from individuals are not entertained. No grants for the funding of services usually provided by statutory services, medical research, travel outside the UK or evangelical or worship activities.
TYPE OF GRANT One-off capital for buildings and equipment; will consider both core and revenue funding of projects.
RANGE OF GRANTS £500–£45,000.
SAMPLE GRANTS £40,000 in two grants to Common Purpose; £35,000 in two grants to Myton Family Hospice; £30,000 each to Acorns Children's Hospice and Warwickshire Association of Boys Clubs (two grants); £25,000 each to Coventry and Warwickshire Awards Trust, Heartlands Cystic Fibrosis Appeal and West Bromwich and District YMCA; £20,000 to St Martin in the Bullring; £19,335 to Warwick Arts Centre; £18,300 to Royal Shakespeare Company; £17,500 to Family Holiday Association; £15,552 to Coventry School Education Trust; £10,000 each to Birmingham St Mary's Hospice, Coventry Cathedral Development Trust and Midland Sports Centre.
FINANCES Year 2001–02 Income £1,000,371 Grants £661,921 Assets £25,312,187
TRUSTEES P J Davis; D A Higgs; M F Knatchbull-Hugessen; the Law Debenture Trustee for Charities.
HOW TO APPLY In writing to the clerk to the trustees, along with a copy of the latest audited accounts; charity number (if registered); a detailed description of the local activities for the benefit of which the grant would be applied; the specific purpose for which the grant is sought; a copy of the organisation's policy that ensures the protection of young or vulnerable people and a clear description of how it is implemented and monitored.
WHO TO APPLY TO The Clerk, 5 Queen Victoria Road, Coventry CV1 3JL Tel 024 7622 1311 E-mail clerk@higgscharity.org.uk
CC NO 509367   **ESTABLISHED** 1979

■ The Walter Higgs Charitable Trust

WHERE FUNDING CAN BE GIVEN Preference for the Midlands.
WHO CAN BENEFIT Registered charities only.
WHAT IS FUNDED General charitable purposes.
WHAT IS NOT FUNDED No grants to individuals.
SAMPLE GRANTS £47,790 to DEBRA for medical research; £15,000 to Arkleton Trust for rural research; £1,200 to The Prince of Wales' Charitable Foundation for general charitable purposes.
FINANCES Year 1998–99 Income £21,000 Grants £68,000 Assets £961,000
TRUSTEES D C Y Higgs; Mrs A J Higgs; Lady Higgs; Miss C A Higgs; K J S Knott; Mrs N J Knott.
HOW TO APPLY In writing to the correspondent. The trust often has no funds available and unsolicited applications will not always receive a reply.
WHO TO APPLY TO K J S Knott, Trustee, Litchfield Farm, Enstone, Chipping Norton, Oxon OX7 4HH Tel 01608 677665 Fax 01608 677276 E-mail KNOTT@litchfield-farm.freeserve.co.uk
CC NO 229861   **ESTABLISHED** 1952

■ Highcroft Charitable Trust

WHERE FUNDING CAN BE GIVEN UK and overseas.
WHO CAN BENEFIT Organisations benefiting Jewish people, especially people disadvantaged by poverty.
WHAT IS FUNDED The advancement and study of the Jewish faith and the Torah. The relief of poverty and advancement of education among people of the Jewish faith.
RANGE OF GRANTS £148–£5,000.
FINANCES Year 1998–99 Income £31,967 Grants £65,037 Assets £195,415
TRUSTEES Rabbi R Fischer; S L Fischer.
HOW TO APPLY In writing to the correspondent.
WHO TO APPLY TO Rabbi R Fischer, 15 Highcroft Gardens, London NW11 0LY
CC NO 272684   **ESTABLISHED** 1975

■ Highmoor Hall Charitable Trust

WHERE FUNDING CAN BE GIVEN UK and overseas.
WHO CAN BENEFIT Registered charities benefiting: Christians; at risk groups; and victims of famine, man-made and natural disasters and war.
WHAT IS FUNDED Christian mission societies and relief agencies.
WHAT IS NOT FUNDED No grants to non-registered charities.
TYPE OF GRANT One-off.
SAMPLE GRANTS Home missions – £100,000; overseas missions – £32,000; other charities – £214,000.
FINANCES Year 2001–02 Income £155,539 Grants £159,000
TRUSTEES P D Persson; Mrs A D Persson; J P G Persson; A S J Persson.
HOW TO APPLY The trust states that it does not respond to unsolicited applications. Telephone calls are not welcome. The correspondent has now moved from the above address, although mail will be forwarded.
WHO TO APPLY TO P D Persson, Trustee, Highmoor Hall, Highmoor, Henley-on-Thames, Oxfordshire RG9 5DH
CC NO 289027   **ESTABLISHED** 1984

Think carefully about every application. Is it justified?

543

■ The Hilden Charitable Fund

WHERE FUNDING CAN BE GIVEN UK, overseas.

WHO CAN BENEFIT Charities and voluntary organisations that broadly meet the fund's criteria.

WHAT IS FUNDED Homelessness (especially among young people), minorities and race relations, penal affairs and overseas aid/developing world.

WHAT IS NOT FUNDED No grants to or on behalf of individuals and no circular appeals.

TYPE OF GRANT Capital, revenue and recurring. Also running costs and project.

RANGE OF GRANTS Average grant £4,000. Grants rarely exceed £5,000.

SAMPLE GRANTS £26,250 to Scottish Community Foundation; £20,000 each to Care UK and Mutual Aid Centre/Institute of Community Studies; £14,000 in total to Tanzania Development Trust; £11,500 in total to Zenzele in South Africa; £10,000 each to Baynard's Zambia Trust and Joint Council for the Welfare of Immigrants; £6,000 to Farm Africa; £5,000 each to Ashram International, Womankind Worldwide, Rhodes House Library, Youth at Risk, Southall Black Sisters and Bondway Housing Association.

FINANCES *Year* 2000–01 *Income* £440,147 *Grants* £537,755 *Assets* £12,843,655

TRUSTEES Mrs A M A Rampton; Prof. D S Rampton; Mrs G J S Rampton; J R A Rampton; A J M Rampton; C S L R Rampton; Dr M B H Rampton; Prof. C H Rodeck; Mrs E K Rodeck; C H Younger; Ms M E Baxter.

HOW TO APPLY All applicants are required to complete a very brief summary form outlining their request before they are considered. Otherwise all applications will be regarded as enquiries. Potential applicants should contact the office for guidelines and forms. Trustees meet approximately every three months.

WHO TO APPLY TO Rodney Hedley, Secretary, 34 North End Road, London W14 0SH *Tel* 020 7603 1525 *Fax* 020 7603 1525 *E-mail* hildencharity@hotmail.com *Website* www.hildencharitablefund.org.uk

CC NO 232591   **ESTABLISHED** 1963

■ The Joseph & Mary Hiley Trust

WHERE FUNDING CAN BE GIVEN The West Riding of Yorkshire.

WHO CAN BENEFIT Registered charities.

WHAT IS FUNDED General charitable purposes.

WHAT IS NOT FUNDED No grants to individuals, expeditions or travel bursaries. Grants to churches are usually only given to those once attended by Joseph or Mary Hiley.

TYPE OF GRANT Capital, core costs, research and recurring costs.

RANGE OF GRANTS Usually £100–£250.

FINANCES *Year* 2002 *Grants* £30,000

TRUSTEES Elizabeth Hjort; Mary Browning; Anne Palmer.

HOW TO APPLY In writing to the correspondent. Rejected applications are not notified unless an sae is enclosed.

WHO TO APPLY TO Anne Palmer, Trustee, Old Vicarage House, Vicarage Lane, Bramham, Wetherby, Leeds LS23 6QG *Tel* 01937 842850 *E-mail* annepalmer@hotmail.com

CC NO 248301   **ESTABLISHED** 1966

■ The Charles Littlewood Hill Trust

WHERE FUNDING CAN BE GIVEN UK, with a preference for Nottinghamshire and Norfolk.

WHO CAN BENEFIT Charitable organisations in the UK, particularly those in Norfolk and Nottinghamshire.

WHAT IS FUNDED General charitable purposes.

WHAT IS NOT FUNDED Applications from individuals are not considered. Grants are seldom made for repairs of parish churches outside Nottinghamshire.

TYPE OF GRANT Applications for starter finance are encouraged. Grants are seldom made to endowment or capital funds.

RANGE OF GRANTS £1,000–£13,000, but usually of £5,000 or less.

SAMPLE GRANTS £13,000 to Norwich Cathedral for the choir endowment; £10,000 each to The Great Hospital and Nottingham City Hospital for the breast unit fund; £5,700 to Norwich Cathedral; £5,000 each to Great Ormond Street Hospital, Norfolk Churches Trust, Norwich and Norfolk Far East POWs, and St Peters Church; £4,000 to Nottinghamshire Hospice; £3,500 to St John Ambulance.

FINANCES *Year* 2001 *Income* £156,017 *Grants* £146,000 *Assets* £3,231,145

TRUSTEES C W L Barratt; W F Whysall; T H Farr; N R Savory.

HOW TO APPLY In writing to the correspondent, including the latest set of audited accounts, at least one month before trustees' meetings in March, July and November. Unsuccessful applications will not be notified.

WHO TO APPLY TO W F Whysall, Trustee, Eversheds, 1 Royal Standard Place, Nottingham NG1 6FZ *Tel* 0115 950 7000 *Fax* 0115 950 7111

CC NO 286350   **ESTABLISHED** 1978

■ The Holly Hill Charitable Trust

WHERE FUNDING CAN BE GIVEN UK.

WHO CAN BENEFIT Registered charities.

WHAT IS FUNDED Environmental conservation work and education for environmental conservation. Most grants are made directly to educational institutions which accounts for most of the income – little is available for other applications.

WHAT IS NOT FUNDED No grants to individuals.

RANGE OF GRANTS £2,000–£40,000.

SAMPLE GRANTS £40,000 to Kasanka Trust, which manages the Kasanka National Park in Zambia; £35,000 to Rainforest Concern; £25,000 to Wildlife Conservation Research Unit (WildCRU); £13,000 to Sussex Wildlife Trust; £9,000 to Soil Association; £6,000 to Oxford University; £4,000 to Berkshire Buckinghamshire and Oxfordshire Wildlife Trust; £2,000 to Plymouth University.

FINANCES *Year* 2001–02 *Income* £43,000 *Grants* £133,600 *Assets* £1,261,826

TRUSTEES M D Stanley; A Lewis.

HOW TO APPLY In writing to the correspondent. Applications need to be received in April and September, and trustees meet in June and November.

WHO TO APPLY TO M D Stanley, Trustee, Flat 5, 89 Onslow Square, London SW7 3LT *Tel* 020 7589 2651

CC NO 1044510   **ESTABLISHED** 1994

■ M V Hillhouse Trust

WHERE FUNDING CAN BE GIVEN Ayrshire and Gloucestershire.

WHO CAN BENEFIT Local organisations known personally to the trustees.

WHAT IS FUNDED General charitable purposes. Grants are divided equally between Scotland and England.

FINANCES *Year* 2000 *Grants* £50,000

TRUSTEES G E M Vernon; H R M Vernon.

OTHER INFORMATION The trust anticipates that around £70,000 will be available in future years, spread evenly between Ayrshire and Gloucestershire.

HOW TO APPLY The trust states that unsolicited applications are not welcome and cannot be responded to. All available funds are allocated each year to organisations previously supported.

WHO TO APPLY TO Bowldown, Tetbury, Gloucestershire GL8 8UD

SC NO SC012904

■ The Hillingdon Partnership Trust

WHERE FUNDING CAN BE GIVEN The borough of Hillingdon.

WHO CAN BENEFIT Organisations benefiting people of all ages, at risk groups, people disadvantaged by poverty and socially isolated people.

WHAT IS FUNDED The trust aims: to build links between the local community and the business sector to secure funding for community initiatives and projects; to relieve people resident in Hillingdon who are sick, disabled, elderly, poor or in other social and economic circumstances; to provide, or assist in providing, equipment and facilities not normally provided by the local authority for the purpose of advancing education or relieving people in need.

FINANCES *Year* 2000–01 *Grants* £7,080,000

TRUSTEES K Musgrave, Chair; M J Taylor; J H Crowe; Air Commodore P Thomas; Prof. E Billett; J A Watts; M A Wisdom; Prof. H S Wolff; A R Woodbridge; T Phillips; H Volland; Dr D Neave; M Temple.

HOW TO APPLY On a form available from the correspondent.

WHO TO APPLY TO John Matthews, Chief Executive, Room 22–25, Building 219, Epsom Square, London Heathrow Airport, Hillingdon, Middlesex TW6 2BW *Tel* 020 8897 3611 *Fax* 020 8897 3613 *E-mail* johnmatthewshpt@lineone.net

CC NO 284668   **ESTABLISHED** 1982

■ R G Hills Charitable Trust

WHERE FUNDING CAN BE GIVEN UK and overseas.

WHO CAN BENEFIT Registered charities.

WHAT IS FUNDED General charitable purposes.

SAMPLE GRANTS £25,000 each to Barnardos, British Executive Service Overseas (BESO), The Injured Jockeys Fund, RNIB and St John Ambulance; £20,000 to National Society for Epilepsy; £15,000 each to Canterbury Oast Trust, Cruse Bereavement Trust, Federation for Artistic & Creative Therapy and Water Aid; £10,000 to Kent Music School.

FINANCES *Year* 1999–2000 *Income* £136,000 *Grants* £215,000 *Assets* £3,200,000

TRUSTEES D J Pentin; V E Barton.

HOW TO APPLY In writing to the correspondent.

WHO TO APPLY TO Mr Barton, Furley Page, 39 St Margaret's Street, Canterbury, Kent CT1 2TX *Tel* 01227 763939

CC NO 1008914   **ESTABLISHED** 1982

■ Hinchley Charitable Trust

WHERE FUNDING CAN BE GIVEN UK and overseas.

WHO CAN BENEFIT Mainly evangelical Christian organisations.

WHAT IS FUNDED General charitable purposes, with particular reference to evangelical Christian work.

TYPE OF GRANT One-off and recurring, usually for projects, but capital and core costs are considered.

RANGE OF GRANTS £100–£12,000.

SAMPLE GRANTS £12,000 to Tearfund for Christian relief and development work; £10,500 each to Associated Bus Ministries for evangelistic work and Mildmay Hospital for general expenses; £10,250 to Crusader's Union for Christian youth work; £5,000 each to Epsom and Ewell Boys' Club for youth work and Spurgeon's College for theological training; £2,500 to Arbury Road Baptist Church, Cambridge for church work; £1,500 to Church Pastoral Aid Society for church work.

FINANCES *Year* 2001 *Income* £1,382,919 *Grants* £98,650 *Assets* £1,898,096

TRUSTEES Dr B Stanley; J D Levick; B Levick; S P Dengate.

HOW TO APPLY The trust states that it does not respond to unsolicited applications. Replies will rarely, if ever, be made to applications for grants by post or on the telephone, as existing funds are all fully committed to charities which are regularly supported.

WHO TO APPLY TO Dr Brian Stanley, Trustee, Watersmeet, 56 Barton Road, Haslingfield, Cambridge CB3 7LL *Tel* 01223 741120 *E-mail* bs217@cam.ac.uk

CC NO 281178   **ESTABLISHED** 1973

■ Lady Hind Trust

WHERE FUNDING CAN BE GIVEN England and Wales only, with a preference for Nottinghamshire and Norfolk.

WHO CAN BENEFIT Charitable organisations in England and Wales, particularly those in Nottinghamshire and Norfolk.

WHAT IS FUNDED General charitable purposes.

WHAT IS NOT FUNDED Grants are seldom made for parish church appeals unless they are within Nottinghamshire. Applications from individuals are not considered.

TYPE OF GRANT Core and project support.

RANGE OF GRANTS £1,000 to £20,000, but mostly £5,000 or less.

SAMPLE GRANTS £20,000 to Macmillan Cancer Relief for the Nottinghamshire Appeal; £15,000 to Nottingham City Hospital for the breast unit fund; £13,500 to St John Ambulance; £12,500 to St Peter's Church, Nottingham Tower Appeal; £10,000 each to Cancer Care Society and 2nd Reepham Scout Group; £9,000 to Norfolk and Norwich Association for the Blind; £7,500 to Nottingham Dyslexia Association; £7,000 to Heydon Church – Norfolk; £5,500 to St Martin's Housing Trust.

FINANCES *Year* 2001 *Income* £337,895 *Grants* £308,958 *Assets* £9,152,587

TRUSTEES C W L Barratt; W F Whysall; T H Farr; N R Savory.

HOW TO APPLY Applications, in writing and with latest accounts, must be submitted at least one month in advance of meetings in March, July and November. Unsuccessful applicants are not notified.

WHO TO APPLY TO W F Whysall, Trustee, c/o Eversheds, 1 Royal Standard Place, Nottingham

NG1 6FZ _Tel_ 0115 950 7000 _Fax_ 0115 950 7111
cc no 208877   ESTABLISHED 1951

■ Stuart Hine Trust

WHERE FUNDING CAN BE GIVEN UK and overseas.

WHO CAN BENEFIT Evangelical Christian organisations, supported by Stuart K Hine during his lifetime or by the trustees since his death.

WHAT IS FUNDED The support of Christian ministry.

FINANCES _Year_ 2001–02 _Income_ £147,000 _Grants_ £118,000

TRUSTEES Raymond Bodkin; Nigel Coltman; Amelia Gardner; Philip Johnson.

PUBLICATIONS _The Story of 'How Great Thou Art'._

HOW TO APPLY In writing to the correspondent, although please note, the trust states that 'unsolicited requests for funds will not be considered'. Funds are basically distributed in accordance with the wishes of the settlor.

WHO TO APPLY TO Raymond Bodkin, Trustee, 'Cherith', 23 Derwent Close, Hailsham, East Sussex BN27 3DA _Tel_ 01323 843948
cc no 326941   ESTABLISHED 1985

■ The Hinrichsen Foundation

WHERE FUNDING CAN BE GIVEN UK.

WHO CAN BENEFIT Organisations benefiting musicians; individual musicians.

WHAT IS FUNDED Assisting contemporary composition and its performance, and musicological research. The trustees are aware that financial assistance is often necessary to create the opportunities for both composition and research. They are equally aware that the results of composition or research need to be made known and that financial assistance is often necessary for the production of performance materials, for the publication of the results of research and for performances of new compositions to take place.

WHAT IS NOT FUNDED The trust does not support study courses, including those at postgraduate level. Grants are not given for instruments, equipment or recordings.

TYPE OF GRANT Usually one-off for a specific project or part of a project.

RANGE OF GRANTS Variable, generally between £500 and £2,000.

SAMPLE GRANTS Grants either paid or approved in 2000–01 included: £15,000 to Huddersfield Contemporary Music Festival; £10,000 to Wingfield Arts for the Hinrichsen Composition Bursary; £3,000 each to Almeida Theatre/ Hoxton New Music Days and London Sinfonietta; £2,000 each to Bath Festival, Bromsgrove Concerts, Dartington Summer School and Rainbow Over Bath; £1,750 to Psappha; £1,500 to Spitalfields Festival.

FINANCES _Year_ 2001 _Income_ £89,063 _Grants_ £52,672 _Assets_ £89,302

TRUSTEES Mrs C E Hinrichsen; P Strang; K Potter; P Standford; S Walsh; Dr J Cross; Miss Linda Hirst; M Williams; T Berg; S Lubbock; T Bowers-Broadbent.

HOW TO APPLY On a form available from the correspondent. Grants are paid after the completion of the project, whenever that is. The trustees meet to consider grants four times a year, usually in February, April, July and October.

WHO TO APPLY TO Mrs Lesley E Adamson, Secretary, 10–12 Baches Street, London N1 6DN
cc no 272389   ESTABLISHED 1976

■ The Hiscox Foundation

WHERE FUNDING CAN BE GIVEN Worldwide.

WHO CAN BENEFIT Registered charities or individuals.

WHAT IS FUNDED Only charities known to the trustees.

WHAT IS NOT FUNDED Funds are fully committed.

TYPE OF GRANT Usually one-off.

RANGE OF GRANTS £50–£4,000.

SAMPLE GRANTS £4,000 to Virginia Primary School; £1,000 each to Hayward Gallery, Millennium Bridge Trust, Princes Youth Business Trust, Royal British Legion, Tate Gallery and Wiltshire Bobby Van.

FINANCES _Year_ 1999–2000 _Income_ £32,000 _Grants_ £19,000 _Assets_ £184,000

TRUSTEES Robert Hiscox; Alexander Foster; Rory Barker; Joanne Kenney.

HOW TO APPLY The trust states that it does not respond to unsolicited applications.

WHO TO APPLY TO Mrs Maureen Price, 1 Great St Helen's, London EC3A 6HX _Tel_ 020 7448 6022 _Fax_ 020 7448 6599 _Website_ www.hiscox.com
cc no 327635   ESTABLISHED 1987

■ Historic Churches Preservation Trust

WHERE FUNDING CAN BE GIVEN England and Wales.

WHO CAN BENEFIT Christian churches in need of repair which are over 100 years old and where the parish council has insufficient funds. The church should be of architectural or historical importance.

WHAT IS FUNDED To assist, with grants and loans, the efforts of congregations – mostly in rural areas – with the carrying out of essential repairs to the fabric of historic churches. Beneficiaries must be churches and chapels in regular use as places of public worship. Repairs should be carried out where possible in traditional material.

WHAT IS NOT FUNDED The HCPT and ICBS will not fund new amenities (other than worship area enlargement); re-ordering; church clocks; heating and lighting; stained glass; furniture and fittings; organ repair; murals; monuments; decoration (except after repairs); rewiring; churchyards and walls; work that has already been started or completed; Non-Anglican churches below 100 years of age. Churches must be open for public worship and properly insured.

SAMPLE GRANTS £80,000 to St Mary the Great in Sawbridgeworth; £60,000 to St James', Stedham in Sussex; £50,000 each to the Serbian Orthodox church of the Holy Trinity in Bradford, St Brandon – Brancepeth in Durham, St John the Evangelist in Cheetham and Christ Church, Denton, both in Lancashire, St Mary in Banbury and St Mary the Virgin in Ingestre.

FINANCES _Year_ 2001 _Income_ £1,400,000 _Grants_ £1,787,000

TRUSTEES Joint Presidents: the Archbishops of Canterbury and York. Chair: Lord Nicholas Gordon Lennox. Grants Secretary: Valerie Varley. Grants committee: Patrick Lepper, Chair; Tony Wedgewood, Treasurer; Hester Agate; Andrew Argyrakis; Sarah Bracher; Very Revd Christopher Campling; Robin Cotton; Lady Evans Lombe; Dr Jenny Freeman; Stephen Johnson; Ian Lockhart; Peter Sharp; Very Revd Henry Stapleton; John Worsley.

OTHER INFORMATION The grants figure given comprises both grants and loans. The trust also administers the smaller Incorporated Church Building Society.

HOW TO APPLY An electronic application form is available and this can also be downloaded from the website or obtained from the trust; however, it is helpful if a written approach is made in the first instance though a look at the website will give a clearer idea of whether the proposed work is eligible. 'We still receive a very large number of applications from churches for ineligible work.' The trust will not consider grant applications for those churches that qualify for aid from English Heritage/Heritage Lottery Fund until a response has been received from those organisations and all churches are encouraged to apply there first. In addition, where a faculty process exists, the church will be expected to demonstrate that a faculty has been granted by the Diocesan Advisory Committee, or, in the case of other denominations, the relevant authority. Note that churches will need to demonstrate that they cannot complete the work by applying free funds available as shown in their latest financial accounts.

WHO TO APPLY TO James Blott, Director, Fulham Palace, London SW6 6EA *Tel* 020 7736 3054 *Fax* 020 7736 3880 *Website* www.historicchurchespt.org.uk

CC NO 207402   **ESTABLISHED** 1953

■ The Hitachi Europe Charitable Trust

WHERE FUNDING CAN BE GIVEN In practice primarily the royal borough of Windsor and Maidenhead.

WHO CAN BENEFIT Registered charities.

WHAT IS FUNDED Set up in 1991, the trust established a fund for donations received from Hitachi Europe Ltd (General Fund). Support is given in the fields of education and training, health, social welfare, arts and culture, environmental education and research, natural environment, science and technology.

TYPE OF GRANT One-off.

FINANCES *Year* 2001 *Grants* £27,000

TRUSTEES A Tolan; M Tsukada; K Kosugi.

HOW TO APPLY In writing to the correspondent.

WHO TO APPLY TO Mrs Joanna MacGovern, Hitachi Europe Ltd, Whitebrook Park, Lower Cookham Road, Maidenhead, Berkshire SL6 8YA *Tel* 01628 585421 *Website* www.hitachi-eu.com

CC NO 1006169   **ESTABLISHED** 1991

■ The Hitchin Educational Foundation

WHERE FUNDING CAN BE GIVEN The former urban district of Hitchin.

WHO CAN BENEFIT Individuals and local organisations benefiting children, young adults and students under the age of 25 years.

WHAT IS FUNDED The advancement of education and training.

WHAT IS NOT FUNDED No support for second degrees or the purchase of certain books.

TYPE OF GRANT One-off.

RANGE OF GRANTS £50–£200.

FINANCES *Year* 2000–01 *Income* £72,000 *Grants* £79,000 *Assets* £362,000

OTHER INFORMATION Applicants must have lived in Hitchin or attended a Hitchin school for at least two years.

HOW TO APPLY Apply in writing to the correspondent for an application form.

WHO TO APPLY TO Brian Frederick, Herts Association, Icknield House, Eastcheap, Letchworth, Hertfordshire SG6 3YY *Tel* 01462 631717

CC NO 311024   **ESTABLISHED** 1965

■ The Hobart Charitable Trust

WHERE FUNDING CAN BE GIVEN UK, prioritising Hampshire.

WHO CAN BENEFIT Institutions benefiting people of any age.

WHAT IS FUNDED The advancement of education and religion, the relief of poverty and charitable purposes for the benefit of the community.

WHAT IS NOT FUNDED No grants to individuals.

SAMPLE GRANTS £136,410 to Cliddesden School; £5,000 to North Hampshire Medical Foundation.

FINANCES *Year* 2001–02 *Income* £37,000 *Grants* £141,000 *Assets* £350,000

TRUSTEES N G McNair Scott; Hon. Mrs Denise Berry; Mrs Gillian Williams; Mrs Kate Andrews.

HOW TO APPLY In writing to the correspondent. Unsuccessful applications will not be acknowledged.

WHO TO APPLY TO The Trustees, 140 Trustee Company, 36 Broadway, London SW1H 0BH *Tel* 020 7933 8044

CC NO 800750   **ESTABLISHED** 1986

■ The Eleemosynary Charity of William Hobbayne

WHERE FUNDING CAN BE GIVEN The borough of Ealing with priority given to Hanwell.

WHO CAN BENEFIT Specific beneficiaries as stated in the trust's deed; Organisations and individuals in (a) Hanwell, then (b) borough of Ealing.

WHAT IS FUNDED General charitable purpses.

SAMPLE GRANTS £3,500 to Educational Charity of William Hobbayne.

FINANCES *Year* 2000 *Grants* £40,000

HOW TO APPLY In writing to the correspondent.

WHO TO APPLY TO Barber, Clerk, 25 Golden Manor, Hanwell, London W7 3EE *Tel* 020 8579 2921 *Fax* 020 8579 2921

CC NO 211547   **ESTABLISHED** 1962

■ Hobson Charity Ltd

WHERE FUNDING CAN BE GIVEN UK.

WHO CAN BENEFIT Registered charities only, particularly those benefiting people of all ages, students, teachers, at risk groups, people disadvantaged by poverty and socially isolated people.

WHAT IS FUNDED Relief of poverty and distress among people who are elderly and poor. The provision of recreation and leisure facilities. The advancement of education and other charitable purposes.

RANGE OF GRANTS £500–£252,500.

SAMPLE GRANTS £252,500 to John Grooms Association for the Disabled; £225,000 to Westminster Council Christmas Appeal Building Trust; £135,000 to Samuel Johnson Prize; £132,000 to CSV People for People; £100,000 each to Churchill College Archives Fund, Health Foundation and Prince's Trust; £55,000 to St Mary and St Anne School; £50,000 each to Oriel College Oxford and University College.

FINANCES *Year* 2000–01 *Income* £134,820 *Grants* £1,512,200 *Assets* £1,998,388

TRUSTEES R F Hobson; Mrs P M Hobson; Sir Donald Gosling; Mrs Deborah Clarke.

Think carefully about every application. Is it justified?

547

HOW TO APPLY In writing to the correspondent.

WHO TO APPLY TO Mrs Deborah Clarke, Trustee & Secretary, 21 Bryanston Street, Marble Arch, London W1H 7PR *Tel* 020 7495 5599

CC NO 326839   ESTABLISHED 1985

■ The Hockerill Educational Foundation

WHERE FUNDING CAN BE GIVEN UK, with a preference for the dioceses of Chelmsford and St Albans.

WHO CAN BENEFIT Organisations benefiting young adults, older people, academics, students, teachers and educational support staff Christians and the Church of England.

WHAT IS FUNDED The advancement of education in accordance with the doctrines, rites and practices of the Church of England. Preference is given to teachers and prospective teachers of RE. It will also support other people involved in religious education; young people in need of financial assistance to attend an establishment of higher or further education; bodies engaged in research and development of religious education; the provision of chapels and chaplaincy for students; and the provision of instruction, classes, lectures, books, libraries and reading rooms.

WHAT IS NOT FUNDED Grants are not given for general appeals for funds, 'bricks and mortar' building projects or purposes that are the clear responsibility of another body. With regard to individuals, grants will not normally be considered from teachers who intend to move out of the profession; those in training for ordination or for other kinds of mission; clergy who wish to improve their own qualifications, unless they are already engaged in teaching in schools and/or intend to teach in the future; students of counselling, therapy or social work; undergraduates or people training for other professions, such as accountancy, business, law or medicine; people doing courses or visits abroad, including 'gap' year courses (except as an integral part of a course, or a necessary part of research); children at primary or secondary school.

TYPE OF GRANT For individuals: assistance with fees or maintenance. Corporate bodies: one-off grants. Funding can be given for up to three years. Grants for research or projects to enhance the Church's educational work will be considered.

RANGE OF GRANTS £500–£10,000.

SAMPLE GRANTS £61,000 to Chelmsford Diocesan Board of Finance in six grants towards employment and travel costs of FE Officer, salary of children's officer and related costs, expenses of children's work advisor, salary costs of staff at St Mark's College, resources for school visits and towards costs of Diocesan early years advisor; £49,090 to St Albans Diocesan Board of Education in five grants towards salaries of a RE support teacher and youth outreach worker, resources for the Diocesan RE Centre in Welwyn Garden City and children's projects concerned with IT and spirituality; £5,000 to Faculty of Initial Education – St Andrew's Paraguay for student bursaries (second of five annual grants); £4,455 to Luton Grassroots Programme to promote interfaith dialogue (third of three annual grants); £3,000 St Albans Cathedral Music Trust to help develop the choirs at the cathedral (second of three grants); £2,000 each to Bedford Chaplaincy Committee to support the

ecumenical chaplaincy at de Montfort (Bedford) University (third of three annual grants) and St Albans DBF Youth Services Account to subsidise the provision of 'Enable Holidays' canal boat holidays for young people with special needs.

FINANCES *Year* 2001–02 *Income* £205,783 *Grants* £157,199 *Assets* £5,110,027

TRUSTEES Dr S Hunter, Chair; Rt Revd Lord Bishop of Chelmsford; Rt Revd Lord Bishop of St Albans; Rt Revd Bishop of Bedford; Rt Revd Bishop of Bradwell; Ven. T P Jones; Ven. P Taylor; Prof. B J Aylett; Revd P Hartley; Mrs M L Helmore; H Marsh; Mrs H Potter; J O Reynolds; R Woods.

PUBLICATIONS *Annual Hockerill Lecture.*

HOW TO APPLY On a form available from the correspondent and submitted by 1 March each year. Results of applications will be communicated in early April. Receipt of applications are not acknowledged. Applications which do not fit the criteria would not normally receive a reply. Further information on the grants to individuals can be found in The Educational Grants Directory published by DSC.

WHO TO APPLY TO C R Broomfield, Secretary, 16 Hagsdell Road, Hertford, Hertfordshire SG13 8AG *Tel* 01992 303053 *Fax* 01992 425950

CC NO 311018   ESTABLISHED 1977

■ Matthew Hodder Charitable Trust

WHERE FUNDING CAN BE GIVEN Worldwide.

WHO CAN BENEFIT Organisations and individuals.

WHAT IS FUNDED The trust's charitable concern is with: book publishing; literacy and literature; the book trade (including the provision of books); arts education (including music); Christian endeavour.

TYPE OF GRANT One-off only.

RANGE OF GRANTS Typically £250–£500.

FINANCES *Year* 2001–02 *Income* £29,000 *Grants* £33,000 *Assets* £804,000

TRUSTEES Philip Attenborough; Mark Hodder-Williams; Roger Spurling; Timothy Ford; Anthony Brown.

HOW TO APPLY In writing to the correspondent.

WHO TO APPLY TO P J Attenborough, Trustee, Coldhanger, Seal Chart, Nr Sevenoaks, Kent TN15 0EJ *Tel* 01732 761516

CC NO 1042741   ESTABLISHED 1994

■ The Jane Hodge Foundation

WHERE FUNDING CAN BE GIVEN Unrestricted, but with a preference for Wales.

WHO CAN BENEFIT UK registered charities only, especially voluntary organisations. In particular organisations benefiting Christians, people disadvantaged by poverty and homeless people.

WHAT IS FUNDED Medical and surgical science, studies and research; education; religion; and general charitable purposes.

WHAT IS NOT FUNDED The foundation makes grants to registered or exempt charities only. No grants to individuals.

TYPE OF GRANT One-off and recurring grants and loans.

SAMPLE GRANTS £207,000 to Velindre NHS Trust for a palliative care training suite; £130,000 to Cardiff University Social Services for their New Road, Rumney project; £100,000 to Cardiff Business School for applied macroeconomics; £50,000 each to Cardiff 2001–02 Special Olympics Trust, George Thomas Memorial Trust,

Sisters of St Joseph of Annecy for their hospice appeal and Salvation Army as part of a £100,000 donation for their hostel in Cardiff; £36,850 to Poor Sisters of Nazareth; £25,000 each to Red Dragon Radio Trust and University of Wales Swansea; £20,000 to St Joseph's Society for Foreign Missions.

FINANCES *Year* 2000–01 *Income* £1,210,761 *Grants* £1,435,000 *Assets* £26,265,360

TRUSTEES Sir Julian Hodge; Lady Moira Hodge; Teresa Hodge; Robert Hodge; Joyce Harrison; Derrek Jones; Ian Davies; Margaret Cason.

HOW TO APPLY In writing to the correspondent. The foundation says that every application is acknowledged, despite the volume of requests.

WHO TO APPLY TO Mrs Margaret Cason, Secretary, Ty-Gwyn, Lisvane Road, Lisvane, Cardiff CF14 0SG *Tel* 029 2076 6521

CC NO 216053   **ESTABLISHED** 1962

■ The Sir Julian Hodge Charitable Trust

WHERE FUNDING CAN BE GIVEN UK.

WHO CAN BENEFIT Registered charities benefiting people of all ages. Support may also be given to people who are disabled, medical professionals, research workers, scientists, students and teachers and governesses. Support may also be given to people with cancer, paediatric diseases, polio and tuberculosis.

WHAT IS FUNDED General charitable purposes, especially medical research in cancer, polio, tuberculosis and diseases of children. General advancement of medical and surgical science, the advancement of education, religion, and the relief of older people and people who are disabled.

WHAT IS NOT FUNDED Individuals and companies.

RANGE OF GRANTS £500–£5,000.

FINANCES *Year* 2001 *Income* £24,263 *Grants* £24,000 *Assets* £322,000

TRUSTEES Sir Julian Hodge; Lady Moira Hodge; J J Hodge; R J Hodge; Joyce Harrison; Derrek L Jones.

HOW TO APPLY In writing to the correspondent.

WHO TO APPLY TO Mrs M Cason, Ty-Gwyn, Lisvane Road, Lisvane, Cardiff CF14 0SG *Tel* 029 2076 6521

CC NO 234848   **ESTABLISHED** 1964

■ The Edward Sydney Hogg Charitable Settlement

WHERE FUNDING CAN BE GIVEN UK.

WHO CAN BENEFIT Individuals and organisations benefiting ex-service and service people, at risk groups, and people who are disabled, disadvantaged by poverty or socially isolated.

WHAT IS FUNDED Service and ex-service organisations, conservation, welfare, disability and medical charities.

TYPE OF GRANT Buildings, capital, one-off, project, research and recurring costs funded for one year or less will be considered.

RANGE OF GRANTS £500–£6,000.

SAMPLE GRANTS In 1998–99: £5,000 each to Not Forgotten Association, Tusk Trust, Farms for City Children, Game Conservancy, and Joint Educational Trust; £3,000 each to Refugee Studies Programme, St Catherine's Hospice, and The Grubb Institute; £2,500 to Sussex Young Cricketers' Association.

FINANCES *Year* 2001–02 *Income* £90,000 *Grants* £47,500 *Assets* £3,100,000

TRUSTEES Messrs Hoare Trustees; John G Hogg.

HOW TO APPLY In writing to the correspondent. Trustees meet monthly.

WHO TO APPLY TO The Secretary, Messrs Hoare Trustees, 37 Fleet Street, London EC4P 4DQ *Tel* 020 7353 4522

CC NO 280138   **ESTABLISHED** 1980

■ The J G Hogg Charitable Trust

WHERE FUNDING CAN BE GIVEN Worldwide.

WHO CAN BENEFIT To benefit people in need and animals in need.

WHAT IS FUNDED Humanitarian causes, overseas charities, wild and domestic animal welfare causes.

WHAT IS NOT FUNDED No grants to individuals. Registered charities only are supported.

FINANCES *Year* 2000–01 *Income* £196,000 *Grants* £115,000 *Assets* £634,000

TRUSTEES Sarah Jane Houldsworth; Joanna Wynfreda Hogg.

HOW TO APPLY In writing to the correspondent.

WHO TO APPLY TO C M Jones, Trustees' Accountant, Chantrey Vellacott DFK, Russell Square House, 10–12 Russell Square, London WC1B 5LF *Tel* 020 7509 9000

CC NO 299042   **ESTABLISHED** 1987

■ The Holden Charitable Trust

WHERE FUNDING CAN BE GIVEN UK, with a preference for the Manchester area.

WHO CAN BENEFIT Organisations benefiting Jewish people. Children, young adults and students may benefit.

WHAT IS FUNDED Jewish charitable purposes with emphasis on the advancement of education.

FINANCES *Year* 1998–99 *Income* £69,000 *Grants* £49,000 *Assets* £343,000

TRUSTEES David Lopian; Marion Lopian.

HOW TO APPLY In writing to the correspondent.

WHO TO APPLY TO The Clerk, c/o Lopian Gross Barnett & Co., Harvester House, 37 Peter Street, Manchester M2 5QD *Tel* 0161 832 8721

CC NO 264185   **ESTABLISHED** 1972

■ The Hollick Family Charitable Trust

WHERE FUNDING CAN BE GIVEN UK and overseas.

WHO CAN BENEFIT Registered charities.

WHAT IS FUNDED General charitable purposes.

TYPE OF GRANT One-off and recurrent.

RANGE OF GRANTS £100–£5,000.

SAMPLE GRANTS £5,000 to Gateway Technology Centre; £2,500 each to Young Minds and Tunbridge Wells Citizens Advice Bureau; £2,000 to The Contemporary Dance Trust; £1,500 each to The Women's Therapy Centre, WSET for Index and The Spitalfields Centre.

FINANCES *Year* 1999–2000 *Income* £54,000 *Grants* £30,000 *Assets* £1,000,000

TRUSTEES Lord Hollick; Lady Hollick; C D Hollick; C M Kemp; D W Beech; G L Hollick; A M Hollick.

HOW TO APPLY In writing to the correspondent.

WHO TO APPLY TO D W Beech, Solicitor, 30 St James's Street, London SW1A 1HB *Tel* 020 7930 6225

CC NO 1060228   **ESTABLISHED** 1997

■ The Dorothy Holmes Charitable Trust

WHERE FUNDING CAN BE GIVEN UK, with a preference for Dorset.

WHO CAN BENEFIT UK registered charities benefiting young adults and older people; people who are sick; clergy; ex-service and service people; legal professionals; unemployed people; volunteers; parents and children; one-parent families; widows and widowers; at risk groups; carers; and people who are disabled.

WHAT IS FUNDED Charities working in the fields of advice and information on housing; emergency and short-term housing; residential facilities; respite and sheltered accommodation; information technology and computers; civil society development; support of voluntary and community organisations; health professional bodies; and religion will be considered. Support is also given to healthcare; hospices and hospitals; cancer research; church buildings; heritage; secondary schools and special schools; counselling on social issues; and income support and maintenance.

WHAT IS NOT FUNDED Only applications from registered charities will be considered.

TYPE OF GRANT Buildings; capital; core costs; one-off; project; research; recurring costs; running costs; salaries; and start-up costs. Funding for up to and over three years will be considered.

RANGE OF GRANTS £100–£1,000.

SAMPLE GRANTS In 1998: £1,000 to St Wilfrid's Hospice, Chichester; £750 each to St John's School, Wallingford and Crisis at Christmas; £700 to Friends of Stansted School; £600 to RAFT; £360 to National Children's Safety Books.

FINANCES *Year* 2000 *Grants* £36,660

TRUSTEES D G Roberts; B M Cody; Miss M E A Cody; S C Roberts.

HOW TO APPLY In writing to the correspondent.

WHO TO APPLY TO Margaret Cody, Moorfield Cody & Co, 5 Harley Place, Harley Street, London W1G 8QD *Tel* 020 7631 4574

CC NO 237213   **ESTABLISHED** 1964

■ The Holst Foundation

WHERE FUNDING CAN BE GIVEN UK.

WHO CAN BENEFIT Mainly musicians.

WHAT IS FUNDED To promote public appreciation of the musical works of Gustav and Imogen Holst and to encourage the study and practice of the arts. Funds are almost exclusively for the performance of music by living composers.

WHAT IS NOT FUNDED No support for the recordings or works of Holst that are already well supported. No grants to individuals for educational purposes.

SAMPLE GRANTS £144,000 to the recording label NMC to fund major recording projects.

FINANCES *Year* 2000–01 *Income* £288,011 *Grants* £317,023 *Assets* £1,951,468

TRUSTEES Rosamund Strode, Chair; Noel Periton; Prof. Arnold Whittall; Peter Carter; Andrew Clements; Julian Anderson.

HOW TO APPLY In writing to: The Grants Administrator, 43 Alderbrook Road, London SW12 8AD. Trustees meet four times a year. There is no application form. Seven copies of the application should be sent. Applications should contain full financial details and be as concise as possible. Funding is not given retrospectively.

WHO TO APPLY TO Peter Carter, Secretary, c/o Finers Stephens Innocent, 179 Great Portland Street, London W1W 5LS *Tel* 020 7323 4000 *E-mail* pcarter@fsilaw.co.uk

CC NO 283668   **ESTABLISHED** 1981

■ The Edward Holt Trust

WHERE FUNDING CAN BE GIVEN Greater Manchester.

WHO CAN BENEFIT Individuals and organisations benefiting older people and people with Alzheimer's disease; autism; cancers; epilepsy; head and other injuries; strokes; mental illness; motor neurone disease and muscular dystrophy.

WHAT IS FUNDED Primarily the maintenance of a block of 10 flats in Didsbury, Manchester, for retired gentlefolk. Preference to charities which the trustees have special interest in, knowledge of or association with, including cancer, neurological and ageing research.

TYPE OF GRANT Buildings, capital, project and research. Funding is available for up to two years.

SAMPLE GRANTS £30,000 to Christie Hospital NHS Trust; £14,000 to Disabled Living.

FINANCES *Year* 2002 *Income* £205,000 *Grants* £116,000 *Assets* £5,900,000

TRUSTEES R Kershaw, Chair; H W E Thompson; D J Tully; H Tudor-Evans.

HOW TO APPLY In writing to the correspondent. The trust is often oversubscribed.

WHO TO APPLY TO Bryan Peak, Secretary, 22 Ashworth Park, Knutsford, Cheshire WA16 9DE *Tel* 01565 651086 *E-mail* bryan.peak@btinternet.com

CC NO 224741   **ESTABLISHED** 1955

■ P H Holt Charitable Trust

WHERE FUNDING CAN BE GIVEN UK, with a preference for Merseyside.

WHAT IS FUNDED General charitable purposes in the UK, especially Merseyside, particularly when original work or work of special excellence is being undertaken.

WHAT IS NOT FUNDED No grants to individuals. Grants are not usually given to organisations outside Merseyside (see above for exceptions to this).

TYPE OF GRANT One-off and recurrent.

SAMPLE GRANTS £100,000 to University of Liverpool for its centenary foundation, management school, faculty of engineering and environmental works; £10,000 to PSS; £5,000 each to Liverpool Biennial for core costs and Local Solutions; £4,750 to Liverpool Council of Social Service for a programme of events and publications; £4,600 to North West Arts Board for a range of projects; £4,000 each to Brouhaha International for a street festival, St Helens Millennium Centre for development costs and Social Partnership for strategic and business plans.

FINANCES *Year* 2001–02 *Income* £393,053 *Grants* £257,910 *Assets* £11,258,496

TRUSTEES K Wright, Chair; John Utley; Derek Morris; Tilly Boyce; Neil Kemsley.

HOW TO APPLY In writing to the correspondent at any time.

WHO TO APPLY TO Roger Morris, Secretary, India Buildings, Liverpool L2 0RB *Tel* 0151 473 4693

CC NO 217332   **ESTABLISHED** 1955

■ The Holywood Trust

WHERE FUNDING CAN BE GIVEN Dumfries and Galloway.

WHO CAN BENEFIT Young people resident in Dumfries and Galloway who are mentally, physically or socially disadvantaged. Support may be for homeless and unemployed young people and people living in rural and urban areas.

WHAT IS FUNDED The trust is particularly keen to provide grants to young people, within the target group, of approximately 15 to 25 years of age, who produce proposals aimed at setting up self-help activities which contribute to their personal development or training, help other young people and benefit the wider community. Consideration is given to projects or organisations concerned with: (i) homeless young people (Nithsdale Trust); (ii) youth work (YMCA, Youth Clubs Scotland); (iii) personal development of young people; (iv) detached youth work; (v) drop in centres for young people; (vi) counselling support of young people involved with drug and solvent abuse; (vii) other trusts supporting young people (BBC Children in Need, Rank Foundation).

WHAT IS NOT FUNDED Grants are not given to political parties, as a substitute for statutory funding, for landlord's deposits or for retrospective applications.

TYPE OF GRANT One-off, capital and recurring (usually limited to three years) depending on need.

RANGE OF GRANTS £10–£50,000.

FINANCES *Year* 1999–2000 *Income* £559,000 *Grants* £326,000 *Assets* £6,500,000

TRUSTEES C A Jencks; J J G Brown; A M Macleod; A D Scott; Mrs E Nelson.

HOW TO APPLY On a form available from the correspondent. Applications are considered by the trustees at least four time a year.

WHO TO APPLY TO Peter O Robertson, Director, Mount St Michael, Craigs Road, Dumfries DG1 4UT *Tel* 01387 269176 *Fax* 01387 269175

SC NO SC009942　　　**ESTABLISHED** 1981

■ The Homelands Charitable Trust

WHERE FUNDING CAN BE GIVEN UK.

WHO CAN BENEFIT Registered charities benefiting children, particularly people in at risk groups, or who are victims of abuse or domestic violence. Support may also be given to clergy, medical professionals and research workers.

WHAT IS FUNDED General charitable purposes in accordance with the settlor's wishes. Special emphasis is given to the General Conference of the New Church, medical research and the care and protection of children. Hospices are also supported.

WHAT IS NOT FUNDED No grants to individuals.

RANGE OF GRANTS £500–£18,500.

FINANCES *Year* 2001–02 *Income* £266,181 *Grants* £242,304 *Assets* £5,774,254

TRUSTEES D G W Ballard; N J Armstrong; Revd C Curry.

HOW TO APPLY In writing to the correspondent.

WHO TO APPLY TO N J Armstrong, Trustee, c/o Alliotts, Ingersoll House, 5th Floor, 9 Kingsway, London WC2B 6XF *Tel* 020 7240 9971

CC NO 214322　　　**ESTABLISHED** 1962

■ Homeless International

WHERE FUNDING CAN BE GIVEN Overseas, particularly Asia, Africa, Latin America and the Caribbean.

WHO CAN BENEFIT International organisations, local community organisations and non-governmental organisations benefiting children, young adults, older people, homeless people and those disadvantaged by poverty.

WHAT IS FUNDED International poverty relief. Long-term community housing and housing-related projects in Asia, Africa, Latin America and the Caribbean.

WHAT IS NOT FUNDED No grants to individuals. No grants to organisations based in the north of England.

TYPE OF GRANT One-off and on-going capital, core and project support.

SAMPLE GRANTS The Namibian Housing Action Group, People's Dialogue – South Africa, Dialogue on Shelter – Zimbabwe, Alliance of SPARC – India, Solidarity for the Urban Poor Federation – Cambodia, Prohabitat – Bolivia, Intergrated Village Development Project – Southern India, YCO – India, National Slum Dwellers Federation – India, Mahila Milan and Indian Alliance.

FINANCES *Year* 2001–02 *Income* £1,024,000 *Grants* £688,000 *Assets* £1,135,000

TRUSTEES D J Alexander; P J Archer; J Bangerh; R Cashell; J Davies; A Farakish; J Harris; M Hudson; G A Lemos; C J Levy; R Newcombe; W Payne; M Prater; D Satterthwaite; R I Upton.

HOW TO APPLY In writing to correspondent, although the trust states that unsolicited applications are not accepted.

WHO TO APPLY TO Ms R McLeod, Chief Executive, Queens House, 16 Queens Road, Coventry CV1 3DF *Tel* 024 7663 2802

CC NO 1017255　　　**ESTABLISHED** 1989

■ The Homestead Charitable Trust

WHERE FUNDING CAN BE GIVEN UK.

WHO CAN BENEFIT Actors and entertainment professionals, musicians, textile workers and designers, writers and poets, Christians, at risk groups, people disadvantaged by poverty, and socially isolated people.

WHAT IS FUNDED Medical, health and welfare, animal welfare, Christianity and the arts.

TYPE OF GRANT Some recurring.

RANGE OF GRANTS £100–£5,000.

SAMPLE GRANTS In 1997–98: £5,000 each to ActionAid and NSPCC; £3,000 to The White Fathers Malawi; £1,000 each to RSPCA, St Joseph's Roman Catholic Church and Providence Row – Westminster.

FINANCES *Year* 1999–2000 *Income* £245,819

TRUSTEES Sir C Bracewell-Smith; Lady N Bracewell-Smith.

HOW TO APPLY In writing to the correspondent

WHO TO APPLY TO Lady Nina Bracewell-Smith, Trustee, Flat 7, Clarence Gate Gardens, Glentworth Street, London NW1 6AY

CC NO 293979　　　**ESTABLISHED** 1986

■ Mary Homfray Charitable Trust

WHERE FUNDING CAN BE GIVEN UK with some preference for Wales.

WHO CAN BENEFIT Registered charities.

WHAT IS FUNDED General charitable purposes.

SAMPLE GRANTS £5,000 to Penllyn Church Roof Fund; £2,000 each to Age Concern, Alzheimer's Disease Society, British Heart Foundation,

Centrepoint, Danybryn Cheshire Home, Marie Curie Cancer Care, NSPCC, PDSA, Salvation Army, Shelter, Urdd Gobaith Cymru, YMCA and Wildfowl and Wetlands Trust.

FINANCES *Year* 2000–01 *Income* £209,511 *Grants* £53,600 *Assets* £2,166,376

TRUSTEES Mrs A M Homfray; G C S Gibson.

HOW TO APPLY In writing to the correspondent. Applications should be made towards the end of the year, for consideration at the trustees' meeting in February or March each year.

WHO TO APPLY TO Mrs A M Homfray, Trustee, c/o Deloitte and Touche, Private Clients Ltd, Blenheim House, Fitzalan Court, Newport Road, Cardiff CF24 0TS *Tel* 029 2048 1111

CC NO 273564   **ESTABLISHED** 1977

■ Sir Harold Hood's Charitable Trust

WHERE FUNDING CAN BE GIVEN Worldwide.

WHO CAN BENEFIT Roman Catholic charities in the UK and overseas.

WHAT IS FUNDED Charities dealing with the advancement of the Roman Catholic religion through religious buildings, religious umbrella bodies and other Roman Catholic organisations.

WHAT IS NOT FUNDED No grants for individuals.

TYPE OF GRANT Recurring.

RANGE OF GRANTS £2,000–£33,000.

SAMPLE GRANTS £33,000 to Bourne Trust; £20,000 each to Craig Lodge and Duchess of Leeds Foundation; £18,000 each to Downside Settlement and Hospital of St John and St Elizabeth – NW8; £10,000 each to Coming Home Appeal – Clapham, and Redemptorists – Zimbabwe; £9,000 to Downside Abbey; £8,000 each to Our Lady's Church – Queensway and Venerable English College Rome.

FINANCES *Year* 2001–02 *Income* £152,954 *Grants* £396,000 *Assets* £7,977,378

TRUSTEES Sir Harold J Hood; Lady Ferelith R Hood; Kevin P Ney; Mrs Margaret Gresslin; Nicholas E True; Mrs A M True; James Hood.

HOW TO APPLY In writing to the correspondent. Applications are considered in late November and need to be received by October.

WHO TO APPLY TO Sir Harold Hood, Trustee, 31 Avenue Road, St John's Wood, London NW8 6DS *Tel* 020 7722 9088

CC NO 225870   **ESTABLISHED** 1962

■ The Hoover Foundation

WHERE FUNDING CAN BE GIVEN UK, but with a special interest in South Wales, Glasgow and Bolton.

WHO CAN BENEFIT UK registered charities, universities and small local charities working in South Wales, Glasgow and Bolton. There is a preference for organisations benefiting young adults and students.

WHAT IS FUNDED Wide range of charities including education (mainly supported through grants to universities, normally for research in the engineering subjects), welfare, medical research and small local charities.

WHAT IS NOT FUNDED The trustees do not make grants to individuals, including students.

FINANCES *Year* 1998–99 *Income* £121,000 *Grants* £150,000

TRUSTEES D J Lunt; A Bertali; C Jones.

HOW TO APPLY In writing to the correspondent.

WHO TO APPLY TO Mrs Marion Heaffey, Hoover plc, Pentrebach, Merthyr Tydfil, Mid Glamorgan CF48 4TU

CC NO 200274   **ESTABLISHED** 1961

■ The Hope Trust

WHERE FUNDING CAN BE GIVEN Worldwide, with a preference for Scotland.

WHO CAN BENEFIT Individuals and organisations benefiting Christians; Church of England; evangelists; Methodists; Quakers; Unitarians and people with a substance addiction.

WHAT IS FUNDED The provision of education and the distribution of literature to combat the misuse and effects of drink and drugs and to promote the principles of Reformed Churches; charities concerned with the advancement of the Christian religion, Anglican bodies, Free Church, rehabilitation centres and health education.

WHAT IS NOT FUNDED No grants to gap year students, scholarship schemes or to any individuals, with the sole exception of PhD students of theology studying at Scottish universities. No grants for the refurbishment of property.

TYPE OF GRANT Core costs, one-off funding, project, research, recurring costs, running costs, salaries, start-up costs and funding for more than three years will be considered.

RANGE OF GRANTS £100–£6,000.

SAMPLE GRANTS £11,000 to Church of Scotland Priority Areas Fund; £10,000 to World Alliance of Reformed Churches; £4,000 to National Bible Society for Scotland; £3,000 each to Feed the Minds and Waldensian Mission Aid.

FINANCES *Year* 2000 *Income* £174,000 *Grants* £119,000

TRUSTEES Revd Prof. D W D Shaw; Prof. G M Newlands; Prof. D A S Ferguson; Revd G R Barr; Revd Dr Lylal; Carole Hope.

HOW TO APPLY In writing to the correspondent. The trustees meet to consider applications in June and December each year. Applications should be submitted by mid-May or mid-November each year.

WHO TO APPLY TO Robert P Miller, Secretary, Drummond Miller, 32 Moray Place, Edinburgh EH3 6BZ *Tel* 0131 226 5151

SC NO SC000987   **ESTABLISHED** Late nineteenth century

■ The Joseph Hopkins Charity

WHERE FUNDING CAN BE GIVEN City of Birmingham.

WHO CAN BENEFIT Organisations relieving need, particularly for older people and children.

WHAT IS FUNDED Relief of people resident in the city of Birmingham who are in conditions of need, hardship or distress; small local charities.

WHAT IS NOT FUNDED Grants are only given to registered charities.

RANGE OF GRANTS Up to £1,000.

SAMPLE GRANTS £1,000 each to B-MAG, CAB – Castle Vale, and CAB – Northfield; £600 to Deafax Trust; £550 to Inter City Camp Trust; £500 each to Birmingham City Mission, BYV Adventure Camps, Leonard Cheshire Services in Birmingham, and Family Holiday Association; £400 to Pearson's Holiday Fund.

FINANCES *Year* 1999–2000 *Income* £35,000 *Grants* £30,000 *Assets* £794,000

TRUSTEES A T Argyle; Miss A M Grove; Mrs J R Jaffa; R J Sarjeant; R Sheldon; R Blyth; Mrs F M Collins; Miss D Goss; J Jones; T J Lunt; J Russell.

Does the trust you have chosen match your needs? Haphazard applications waste postage and time

OTHER INFORMATION Clothing vouchers were given to individuals totalling £6,750.

HOW TO APPLY In writing to the correspondent. Trustees meet twice a year.

WHO TO APPLY TO David Nightingale, Clerk, Martineau Johnson, St Philips House, St Philips Place, Birmingham B3 2PP *Tel* 0121 200 3300

CC NO 217303   **ESTABLISHED** 1681

■ HopMarket Charity

WHERE FUNDING CAN BE GIVEN The city of Worcester.

WHO CAN BENEFIT 'Needy' people in the city of Worcester. 'Needy' is defined as those 'who, by reason of poverty, sickness or infirmity, whether young or old, are in need of financial assistance, care or attention'. People of all ages, volunteers, and people who are disabled or disadvantaged by poverty.

WHAT IS FUNDED The trust has adopted the following guidelines: 'That as a general principle the funds should be allocated to either capital or revenue projects which fall within the purposes of the charity and which will generate further support for the community. Where revenue funding is made, such support should not imply any ongoing commitment except where the trustees specifically indicate otherwise. Emphasis should be placed on assisting applications which have an affinity to matters which are within the council's sphere of activity.'

WHAT IS NOT FUNDED No grants to, or on behalf of, individuals.

RANGE OF GRANTS £500–£11,900.

SAMPLE GRANTS £11,900 to Worcester Play Council for playscheme running costs; £11,400 to CAB for running costs; £10,350 to Worcester Welfare Rights Centre for running costs; £5,175 to Perdiswell Young People's Leisure Club; £1,000 each to Rainbow for equipment to support community worker in providing support and advice to young offenders and their families; £500 each to Council of British Pakistanis for a building extension and Worcestershire Relate for provision of outreach facilities; £250 to Worcestershire Rape and Sexual Abuse Support Centre for the operation of telephone services and a helpline.

FINANCES *Year* 2001–02 *Grants* £42,000

TRUSTEES The City Council.

HOW TO APPLY On a form available from the correspondent.

WHO TO APPLY TO Dave Clifford, Community Development Manager, Worcester City Council, Orchard House, Farrier Street, Worcester WR1 3BW *Tel* 01905 722325 *Fax* 01905 722350 *E-mail* dclifford@cityofworcester.gov.uk

CC NO 244569   **ESTABLISHED** 1964

■ The Cuthbert Horn Trust

WHERE FUNDING CAN BE GIVEN UK.

WHO CAN BENEFIT Organisations benefiting older people and the environment.

WHAT IS FUNDED Older people, the environment and general charitable purposes.

WHAT IS NOT FUNDED No grants are made to individuals.

TYPE OF GRANT One-off and recurrent.

RANGE OF GRANTS £1,000–£10,000.

SAMPLE GRANTS In 1998: £10,000 to Council & Care for the Elderly; £5,000 to Centre for Alternative Technology; £4,000 to Africa Educational Trust; £3,000 each to The Soil Association, Elm Farm Research Centre, Cotswold Canals Trust, The Island Trust,

Foundation for Communication for the Disabled, Farms for City Children, and The Safe Charitable Trust.

FINANCES *Year* 2001 *Income* £69,471

TRUSTEES Alliance Assurance Company Ltd; A H Flint.

HOW TO APPLY There are no application forms to complete; applicants should provide in writing as much background about their charity or cause as possible. Applications need to be received by September as the trustees meet in October. Only successful applications will be notified.

WHO TO APPLY TO S P Martin, Royal & Sun Alliance Trust Co. Ltd, Phoenix House, 18 King William Street, London EC4N 7HE *Tel* 020 7800 4188 *Fax* 020 7800 4180

CC NO 291465   **ESTABLISHED** 1985

■ The Antony Hornby Charitable Trust

WHERE FUNDING CAN BE GIVEN London and the Home Counties.

WHO CAN BENEFIT Organisations benefiting people of all ages, medical professionals, people involved in the arts and people who are disabled.

WHAT IS FUNDED Flexible, but mainly medical research and the arts. Support is also given for homes and holidays and to benefit people who are elderly, sick or disabled and disadvantaged young people.

WHAT IS NOT FUNDED No grants to individuals. Only registered charities are supported. No grants to localised building projects for the arts and so on.

RANGE OF GRANTS £200–£3,000.

SAMPLE GRANTS £3,000 to St Francis' Children's Society; £2,000 to Hertfordshire Association for Young People; £1,500 to New Shakespeare Company; £1,000 each to Alzheimer's Research Trust, Atlantic College, Game Conservancy Trust, Roundhouse Trust and Tommy's Campaign; £750 each to London Orphan Asylum – Reed School and Metropolitan Hospital Sunday Fund.

FINANCES *Year* 1999–2000 *Income* £49,000 *Grants* £38,000 *Assets* £1,400,000

TRUSTEES Mariette Hall; Mark Loveday; Michael Wentworth-Stanley; Jane Wentworth-Stanley.

HOW TO APPLY In writing to the correspondent, enclosing an sae. The trust has stated that it is fully committed and does not usually add new names to its list of beneficiaries unless it is a charity known to the trustees, or a very special appeal.

WHO TO APPLY TO Michael Wentworth-Stanley, Trustee, c/o 12 Tokenhouse Yard, London EC2R 7AN

CC NO 263285   **ESTABLISHED** 1971

■ Mrs E G Hornby's Charitable Settlement

WHERE FUNDING CAN BE GIVEN UK, with some preference for London.

WHO CAN BENEFIT Registered charities only. Preference is given to people who are disabled or elderly.

WHAT IS FUNDED General charitable purposes, with particular interest in the fields of animal welfare, disability, welfare of older people and hospices.

WHAT IS NOT FUNDED Individuals are not supported.

RANGE OF GRANTS £250–£17,000.

SAMPLE GRANTS £14,000 to Countryside Foundation; £10,000 to Friends of the Elderly and Gentlefolk's Help; £5,000 to World Transport Games; £2,500 each St Richard's Hospice and Macmillan Cancer Relief; £1,800 to Irish Draught Horse Society; £1,500 to Martin House Children's Hospice.

FINANCES *Year* 2000–01 *Income* £39,000 *Grants* £57,000 *Assets* £1,400,000

TRUSTEES N J M Lonsdale; Mrs P M W Smith-Maxwell; Rathbone Trust Company Ltd.

HOW TO APPLY In writing to the correspondent. The trust's current policy is to accumulate all the written appeals received, and to consider them on their individual merits when they meet annually, for distribution in April. Only successful applicants are notified.

WHO TO APPLY TO The Secretary, Rathbone Trust Company Ltd, 159 New Bond Street, London W1S 2UD *Tel* 020 7399 0823 *Fax* 020 7399 0050

CC NO 243516   **ESTABLISHED** 1965

■ The Horne Foundation

WHERE FUNDING CAN BE GIVEN Probably mainly Northamptonshire.

WHO CAN BENEFIT Preference is given to local organisations benefiting young adults, children and older people, especially people disadvantaged by poverty, with occasional grants also made to UK organisations.

WHAT IS FUNDED Education, the arts and youth-orientated organisations in the Northampton area. Predominantly large grants towards building projects in which the foundation is the major contributor.

WHAT IS NOT FUNDED The foundation has said in the past that it 'does not respond to appeals from charities providing local services in communities located outside Northamptonshire'. It prefers organisations without religious affiliation.

TYPE OF GRANT Capital and project grants.

FINANCES *Year* 2000–01 *Income* £282,000 *Grants* £637,000

TRUSTEES E J Davenport; Mrs R M Harwood; C A Horne.

HOW TO APPLY In writing to the correspondent at any time.

WHO TO APPLY TO Mrs R M Harwood, Secretary, Suite 33, Burlington House, 369 Wellingborough Road, Northampton NN1 4EU *Tel* 01604 629748

CC NO 283751   **ESTABLISHED** 1981

■ The Thomas J Horne Memorial Trust

WHERE FUNDING CAN BE GIVEN UK.

WHO CAN BENEFIT Homeless and disabled people; environmental initiatives; victims of international disasters.

WHAT IS FUNDED Charities and hospices benefiting the homeless; general charitable purposes.

SAMPLE GRANTS In 1998–99: £5,000 to Shelter; £1,500 to Intermediate Technology; £1,000 each to Sustrans, Church Housing Trust and New Crisis.

FINANCES *Year* 1999–2000 *Income* £45,000 *Grants* £43,000

TRUSTEES Mrs M Horne; J T Horne; J L Horne; N J Camamile.

HOW TO APPLY Normally in writing to the correspondent, but for the coming year the

trustees requested that no unsolicited applications for grants be made.

WHO TO APPLY TO J T Horne, Trustee, Kingsdown, Warmlake Road, Chart Sutton, Maidstone, Kent ME17 3RP

CC NO 1010625   **ESTABLISHED** 1992

■ The Hornsey Parochial Charities

WHERE FUNDING CAN BE GIVEN Ancient parish of Hornsey in part of the boroughs of Hackney and Haringey.

WHO CAN BENEFIT Individuals and organisations benefiting people disadvantaged by poverty.

WHAT IS FUNDED General benefit of poor people residing in Old Hornsey.

WHAT IS NOT FUNDED Residential qualification needed. No commitment to continuous grants.

FINANCES *Year* 2002 *Grants* £100,000

HOW TO APPLY In writing to the correspondent

WHO TO APPLY TO Lorraine Fincham, Clerk, PO Box 22895, London N10 3XB *Tel* 020 8352 1601 *Fax* 020 8352 1601 *E-mail* hornseypc@aol.com

CC NO 229410   **ESTABLISHED** 1890

■ The Hospital of God at Greatham

WHERE FUNDING CAN BE GIVEN Darlington, Durham, Gateshead, Hartlepool, Newcastle upon Tyne, Northumberland, North Tyneside, South Tyneside, Stockton on Tees and Sunderland.

WHO CAN BENEFIT Charities, voluntary organisations and individuals. Grants are only made to individuals when the application originates from social service offices. The trust supports children, young adults, older people, at risk groups, carers, people who are disabled, disadvantaged by poverty, homeless or socially isolated, victims of abuse and domestic violence, and people with Alzheimer's disease, epilepsy and hearing loss.

WHAT IS FUNDED Preference is given to projects concerned with local initiatives aimed at disadvantaged people, particularly charities working in the field of social care and with local communities.

WHAT IS NOT FUNDED No grants for: capital projects; building work; education, travel or adventure projects; hospices; work outside the beneficial area; UK organisations based outside the north east of England; training, conferences or feasibility studies.

TYPE OF GRANT One-off, capital, core funding, running costs and salaries. Funding for one year or more will be considered.

SAMPLE GRANTS £10,000 each to North East Council on Addictions and Second Crop; £9,500 to Lazarus Centre; £9,200 to West View Family Support.

FINANCES *Year* 1999–2000 *Income* £675,000 *Grants* £150,000 *Assets* £22,000,000

TRUSTEES Ven. P Elliott; Ven. S Conway; N D Abram; C Porter; Mrs J Thomas; Dr H Welsh; Ven. I Jagger; Miss M Jones; P Davies; F Williams.

OTHER INFORMATION The charity's main work is the provision of almshouse accommodation and residential care. Grants are made from surplus funds.

HOW TO APPLY Applications should be made to the correspondent in writing. The grants committee meets three times a year. Applications should include: the objects of the charity; a description of, and budget, for the project and the specific work for which funding is sought; a copy of the latest audited accounts. The correspondent is happy to answer initial telephone enquiries.

WHO TO APPLY TO David Granath, The Estate Office, Greatham, Hartlepool TS25 2HS *Tel* 01429 870247 *E-mail* david.granath@greatham.co.uk
CC NO 228571   ESTABLISHED 1273

■ Hospital Saturday Fund Charitable Trust

WHERE FUNDING CAN BE GIVEN UK, the Republic of Ireland and overseas.
WHO CAN BENEFIT Hospitals, hospices, medically-associated charities and welfare organisations providing similar services worldwide, but mostly in the UK and Republic of Ireland. Individuals can also be directly supported.
WHAT IS FUNDED Medical care and research to organisations; specialist equipment, welfare and scholarships to individuals.
WHAT IS NOT FUNDED Unless there are exceptional circumstances, organisations are not supported in successive years.
TYPE OF GRANT One-off grants. Organisations are rarely supported in successive years.
RANGE OF GRANTS Usually £650 in Republic of Ireland and £500 elsewhere, although up to £1,000 can be given.
SAMPLE GRANTS £1,000 to Glasgow Royal Infirmary; £650 each to Marymount Hospice – Cork and DeafBlind Foundation; £500 each to Colon Cancer Concern, Stroke Association and Willen Hospice – Milton Keynes.
FINANCES *Year* 2001–02 *Income* £149,499 *Grants* £139,729 *Assets* £136,780
TRUSTEES K R Bradley, Chair; D C Barnes; L I Fellman; P P Groat; Miss I Racher; A F Tierney; Mrs L M C Warner.
HOW TO APPLY Hospitals, hospices and medically-related charities are invited to write detailed letters or to send a brochure with an accompanying letter. There is a form for individuals to complete available from the personal assistant to the trust administrator.
WHO TO APPLY TO K R Bradley, Administrator, 24 Upper Ground, London SE1 9PD *Tel* 020 7928 6662 *Fax* 020 7928 0446 *E-mail* trust@hsf.co.uk
CC NO 327693   ESTABLISHED 1987

■ Houblon-Norman Fund

WHERE FUNDING CAN BE GIVEN UK.
WHO CAN BENEFIT Organisations benefiting academics and research workers.
WHAT IS FUNDED Research into the interaction and function of financial and business institutions, the economic conditions affecting them, and the dissemination of knowledge thereof. Fellowships are tenable at the Bank of England. The research work to be undertaken is intended to be full-time work, and teaching or other paid work must not be undertaken during the tenure of the fellowship, without the specific consent of the trustees. In considering applications the trustees will pay particular regard to the relevance of the research to current problems in economics and finance.
TYPE OF GRANT Research fellowship.
RANGE OF GRANTS £27,000–£61,250.
FINANCES *Year* 2000–01 *Income* £87,833 *Grants* £126,149 *Assets* £1,517,823
TRUSTEES Deputy Governor of The Bank of England; Sir Jeremy Morse; Ms Kathleen O'Donovan.
HOW TO APPLY On an application form available from the website.

WHO TO APPLY TO Ms Jay Begum, MA Division 2 HO-2, Bank of England, Threadneedle Street, London EC2R 8AH *Tel* 020 7601 3377 *Fax* 020 7601 5953 *E-mail* jay.begum@bankofengland.co.uk *Website* www.bankofengland.co.uk/houblonnorman/
CC NO 213168   ESTABLISHED 1944

■ The House of Industry Estate

WHERE FUNDING CAN BE GIVEN The borough of Bedford.
WHO CAN BENEFIT People who are in need and local organisations.
WHAT IS FUNDED Willing to support local organisations concerned with unemployed people, youth, counselling and housing.
WHAT IS NOT FUNDED Funds are not given in relief of taxes or other public funds. No recurrent grants are given.
TYPE OF GRANT One-off.
FINANCES *Year* 1999–2000 *Income* £55,000 *Grants* £50,000
HOW TO APPLY In writing to the correspondent.
WHO TO APPLY TO Sue Audin, Customer Services Manager, Bedford Borough Council, Town Hall, Bedford MK40 1SJ
CC NO 257079   ESTABLISHED 1968

■ The Housing Associations Charitable Trust (Hact)

WHERE FUNDING CAN BE GIVEN UK.
WHO CAN BENEFIT People with support needs; people with special needs; older people; refugee-led groups; and black and minority ethnic communities.
WHAT IS FUNDED Work with funders, social housing organisations and communities to develop creative, local solutions for people with acute housing and related social need.
WHAT IS NOT FUNDED Projects which are eligible for statutory funding, including furniture and building costs of housing schemes; ongoing revenue funding, including items which would normally be included in an organisation's annual budget; individuals; well-resourced organisations.
TYPE OF GRANT Developmental and start-up revenue grants; loans; and rarely capital grants.
RANGE OF GRANTS £1,000–£20,000.
SAMPLE GRANTS £40,000 to Bath & North East Somerset Care & Repair to develop a culturally relevant service; £38,000 to Lintel Trust to be distributed as small grants for older people's projects in Scotland; £37,000 to Lancashire Agencies Forum to develop, support and co-ordinate the HIAs throughout Lancashire; £35,000 to Mendip Care and Repair to develop a gardening and decorating service for older people; £30,000 to Preston Care and Repair to support development of a handyperson service for older people and disabled homeowners with limited means; £25,320 to North Tyneside Advocacy project to provide an advocacy service to older people living in residential or nursing care; £23,000 to Remisus to support capacity building within a new refugee community organisation; £22,500 to Iranian Centre North East to provide community development anbd housing advice for refugees; £22,000 each to Pitsmoor Somali Youth Association to provide housing advice to young Somali people in

Think carefully about every application. Is it justified?

555

Sheffield and Safe Haven to support community development work with refugees in Yorkshire.

FINANCES *Year* 2001 *Income* £1,309,755 *Grants* £704,000

TRUSTEES Paul Tennant, chair; Matthew Bennett; Rosalind Brooke; Nicholas Gage; Trevor Hendy; Peter Molyneaux; Philip Richardson; Prof. Bert Rima; Dawn Stephenson; Peter Stevenson; Janis Wong.

PUBLICATIONS Evaluation reports, available in six areas of funding.

HOW TO APPLY The trust says that it is committed to making the process of applying for funding as straightforward as possible.

The application process is as follows: Hact sends you an application pack; you read the grant guidelines and decide whether your project fits; you complete and return the form; at any point during the above you can phone or e-mail the grants team for advice or clarification. The decision-making process is as follows: Hact receives and acknowledges your application; it is assessed by a member of the grants and programme team; Hact aims to make a decision according to the following timetable. Grants up to £5,000 – six weeks; all other grants – two months. Potential applicants are invited to contact the programme team for further help and guidance. The grantmaking committee meets in February, April, June, September, October and December.

WHO TO APPLY TO Heather Petch, Director, 78 Quaker Street, London E1 6SW *Tel* 020 7247 7800 *Website* www.hact.org.uk

CC NO 256160   **ESTABLISHED** 1960

■ The John & Ruth Howard Charitable Trust

WHERE FUNDING CAN BE GIVEN England.

WHO CAN BENEFIT Organisations benefiting young adults and students.

WHAT IS FUNDED The trust divides its support into four categories which are supported equally. They are archaeology, church music, preservation and protection of public buildings, and general charitable purposes.

WHAT IS NOT FUNDED No grants to large appeals or to individuals.

TYPE OF GRANT Funding for single projects.

RANGE OF GRANTS The maximum grant is £5,000.

SAMPLE GRANTS £4,000 to Wakefield Museum and Arts; £3,500 to St Edmunds School, Canterbury; £3,000 to Meridian Trust Association; £2,500 each to East Sussex Arch and Trimonium Trust; £2,400 to Ampleforth College.

FINANCES *Year* 2000–01 *Income* £38,794

TRUSTEES Alec S Atchison, Chair; John H Hillier; Miss Nina Feldman; Richard Hobson.

HOW TO APPLY In writing to the correspondent. Trustees meet every three to six months.

WHO TO APPLY TO Alec S Atchison, Chair, 111 High Road, Willesden Green, London NW10 2TB *Tel* 020 8459 1125

CC NO 1005072   **ESTABLISHED** 1991

■ The Rita Lila Howard Foundation

WHERE FUNDING CAN BE GIVEN UK and Republic of Ireland.

WHO CAN BENEFIT Children up to the age of 16.

WHAT IS FUNDED Innovative projects that benefit children, and projects concerned with 'the education of young people or to ameliorate their physical and emotional envrionment'.

WHAT IS NOT FUNDED Grants are not given to individuals, organisations which are not registered charities, or towards operating expenses, budget deficits, (sole) capital projects, annual charitable appeals, general endowment funds, fundraising drives or events, conferences, or student aid.

FINANCES *Year* 2000–01 *Grants* £566,000

TRUSTEES Gretchen Bauta; Alannah Weston; Geordie Dalglish; Mark Mitchell; Tamara Rebanks; Galvin Weston; Melissa Baron.

HOW TO APPLY The trust states that it does not accept unsolicited applications, since the trustees seek out and support projects they are interested in.

WHO TO APPLY TO The Company Secretary, Jamestown Investments Ltd, 4 Felstead Gardens, Ferry Street, London E14 3BS *Tel* 020 7537 1118

CC NO 1041634   **ESTABLISHED** 1994

■ The Clifford Howarth Charity Settlement

WHERE FUNDING CAN BE GIVEN UK, with a preference for Lancashire (Burnley/Rossendale).

WHO CAN BENEFIT Local and UK-registered charities which were supported by the founder.

WHAT IS FUNDED General charitable purposes.

WHAT IS NOT FUNDED Only registered charities will be supported. No grants to individuals, for scholarships or for non-local special projects.

TYPE OF GRANT One-off.

RANGE OF GRANTS £1,000–£20,000.

SAMPLE GRANTS £18,000 to Rossendale Players for a new theatre; £10,000 to Chorley Scouts for a minibus; £5,000 each to Alzheimer's Society, Whalley Church for roof restoration, Salford RCD for general upkeep, and Macmillan Cancer Care; £4,000 to ELMBI (local maons); £3,000 each to St Mary's – Rossendale – for roof repair and Royal National Lifeboat Institution for a lifeboat appeal.

FINANCES *Year* 2000 *Income* £82,000 *Grants* £80,000 *Assets* £750,000

TRUSTEES James Clifford Howarth; Miss Elizabeth Howarth; Mary Fenton.

HOW TO APPLY In writing to the correspondent. Grants are distributed in February/March.

WHO TO APPLY TO James Howarth, Trustee, Lambert Howarth, Healey Royd Works, Healey Royd Road, Burnley, Lancashire BB11 2HL *Tel* 01282 471202 *Fax* 01282 471279

CC NO 264890   **ESTABLISHED** 1972

■ The James Thom Howat Charitable Trust

WHERE FUNDING CAN BE GIVEN Scotland, in particular Glasgow.

WHO CAN BENEFIT Individuals and organisations benefiting ex-service and service people, musicians, research workers, seafarers and fishermen, sportsmen and women, students, unemployed people, volunteers and writers and poets. Funding may also be given to at risk groups; carers; disabled people; those disadvantaged by poverty; homeless people; refugees; victims of abuse, crime and domestic violence; and people with Alzheimer's disease, autism, cancer, cystic fibrosis, head and other injuries, mental illness and multiple sclerosis.

WHAT IS FUNDED Grants are given to a range of organisations, including universities, cultural bodies and those caring for people who are

556

Does the trust you have chosen match your needs? Haphazard applications waste postage and time

sick. Support may also be given to charities working in the fields of community services, community centres and village halls, special needs education, voluntary and community organisations and volunteers.

WHAT IS NOT FUNDED The following are not usually supported: medical electives, second or further qualifications, payment of school fees or costs incurred at tertiary educational establishments.

TYPE OF GRANT Some grants are made to individuals for educational purposes. Core costs, one-off, project, research, running costs and start-up costs will be considered.

SAMPLE GRANTS £10,000 each to Crossroads (Scotland) Care Attendant Schemes and East Park Home for Infirm Children; £8,000 each to University of Glasgow and University of Strathclyde; £5,000 to Royal Blind Asylum and School; £4,000 each to Glasgow Old People's Welfare Council, Alzheimer's Scotland, National Youth Orchestra, Scottish Spina Bifida Association, and Glasgow Royal Infirmary Renal Unit.

FINANCES *Year* 1999–2000 *Income* £253,813 *Grants* £247,550 *Assets* £4,789,000

TRUSTEES Leslie Duncan; James Thom Howat; Russell Howat; Gordon Wyllie; Christine Howat.

HOW TO APPLY In writing to the correspondent. There is no application form for organisations. Applications should contain a summary not longer than one side of A4, backed up as necessary with schedules. A copy of the latest accounts and/or business plan should be included. Costs and financial needs should be broken down where possible. It should be clear what effect the grant will have and details of other grants applied for or awarded should be given. Evidence that the project will enhance the quality of life of the clients and that they are involved in the decision making must be included. Successful applicants should not reapply in the following year. Unsuccessful applicants are not acknowledged due to the large number of applications received by the trust. The trustees meet to consider grants in March, June, September and December. Applications should be received in the preceding month.

WHO TO APPLY TO Mrs Jean Lane, Biggart Baillie, Dalmore House, 310 St Vincent Street, Glasgow G2 5QR

SC NO SC000201

■ The HSA Charitable Trust

WHERE FUNDING CAN BE GIVEN UK.

WHO CAN BENEFIT Preference for smaller charities delivering treatment and clinical (not social) support to patients.

WHAT IS FUNDED The treatment of sickness and the furtherance of medical research.

WHAT IS NOT FUNDED Applicants, other than those for scholarships, must have charitable status. Other than for scholarships, there are no grants for individuals. Applicant organisations must be based in the UK. The trustees of the charity which receives the grant must have clear responsibility for the work which is being funded. The trust does not normally make grants to non-charitable umbrella organisations, such as most 'friends' groups; charities whose operational area extends outside the UK; very large national charities which enjoy wide support.

TYPE OF GRANT Capital and project. Equipment rather than buildings.

RANGE OF GRANTS £500–£10,000.

SAMPLE GRANTS £210,000 to Institute of Ophthalmology for a training centre for microscopic eye surgery in London; £62,000 to the Migraine Trust; £45,000 to St John Ambulance, Surrey; £42,000 to the National Centre for People with Epilepsy; £33,000 each to Action Research and Institute of Child Health; £30,000 to Brain Research Trust; £25,000 to Council of Midwife Teaching; £20,000 to Barts Cancer Centre for Excellence; £15,000 to Multiple Sclerosis Society.

FINANCES *Year* 2000–01 *Income* £984,531 *Grants* £1,000,000 *Assets* £422,359

TRUSTEES Mrs Carolyn Lemon, chair; Maj. Gen. B Pennicott; J A Elliott; K F Richardson.

PUBLICATIONS Guidance Notes for Applicants.

HOW TO APPLY Trustee meetings are held four times a year: March, June, September and December. There is no standard application form. Applications should be made in writing to the correspondent. The trust asks you to confine your application to two sides of A4 paper, and provide the following information: Please tell us what sort of organisation you are (i.e. what your legal status is) and its general aims and objectives. Are you part of a larger national organisation, and if so what is its name? An outline of the proposed project, including: its specific aims and objectives; how the project is to be organised and by whom; where the project is to take place; when it will start and how long it will take; whom it is intended to benefit and how many. How much money you need and for what purpose (e.g. equipment, building works, research, running costs, etc.) In addition state clearly how much you are asking the HSA Charitable Trust for and when you require it. We would also like to know which other funders you have approached and with what success. If you will need funding beyond the period of the proposed grant where is it to come from? Please tell us how you will know whether the project has succeeded. In particular, what are the measurable specific objectives and how will you publicise the outcome of the project to other interested parties? You must include: the most recent set of your annual accounts – if your accounts show apparently large reserves, attach a note explaining why you hold them and why they cannot be used to fund the project for which you are seeking funds; your most recent annual report; a detailed budget for the project.

WHO TO APPLY TO Sir Guy Acland, Administrator, Hambleden House, Waterloo Court, Andover, Hampshire SP10 1LQ *Tel* 01264 353 211 *Website* www.hsa.co.uk

CC NO 263521   **ESTABLISHED** 1972

■ The Huddersfield Common Good Trust

WHERE FUNDING CAN BE GIVEN South Kirklees.

WHO CAN BENEFIT Organisations benefiting people of all ages, at risk groups, carers, people who are disabled, people who are disadvantaged by poverty or who are homeless and victims of domestic violence.

WHAT IS FUNDED Youth and community groups, children, older people and general welfare organisations.

WHAT IS NOT FUNDED No grants to individuals, central/local government departments, religious bodies or national organisations.

TYPE OF GRANT One-off buildings and capital grants will be considered.

RANGE OF GRANTS £50–£5,000.

SAMPLE GRANTS Previous beneficiaries include Netherton Cottage Homes, Brockholes Village Trust, Huddersfield Scout Sailing, Linthwaite Band, Huddersfield Model Engineers, Scholes Cricket Club, Netherton Scouts, Kirklees Friends of the Earth and Paddock Young Persons.

FINANCES *Year* 2001–02 *Income* £25,767 *Grants* £20,000 *Assets* £350,000

TRUSTEES R Butterworth, Chair; J A Russell; Miss S Stott; Miss V Javin; G C Grimwood; J Ashworth; J Lockwood.

PUBLICATIONS Information leaflet.

HOW TO APPLY In writing to the correspondent.

WHO TO APPLY TO A Haigh, Secretary, PO Box 382, Huddersfield HD1 2YN *Tel* 01484 688688 *E-mail* cgtrust@ichuddersfield.co.uk

CC NO 231096   **ESTABLISHED** 1964

■ The Hudson Foundation

WHERE FUNDING CAN BE GIVEN UK, with a preference for the Wisbech area.

WHO CAN BENEFIT Individuals and organisations benefiting older people and those who are infirm, especially in the Wisbech area.

WHAT IS FUNDED The relief of people who are elderly or infirm.

SAMPLE GRANTS £157,436 to Ely Diocesan School Fund; £34,800 to Wisbech Grammar School; £15,200 to Alexandra House; £8,593 to Methodist Homes for the Aged; £8,036 to Wisbech Swimming Club, £5,200 to Wisbech St Mary PCC; £4,000 to Royal Fleet Club; £1,500 to Royal Naval Football Association; £1,000 to St Augustine's Parish Centre; £300 to Wisbech and Fenland Museum.

FINANCES *Year* 1999–2000 *Income* £132,012 *Grants* £240,035 *Assets* £1,879,412

TRUSTEES P A Turner, Chair; M A Bunting; H A Godfrey; A D Salmon.

HOW TO APPLY In writing to the correspondent. Applications are considered throughout the year.

WHO TO APPLY TO A D Salmon, Trustee, 12–13 The Crescent, Wisbech, Cambridge PE13 1EP *Tel* 01945 584113

CC NO 280332   **ESTABLISHED** 1980

■ The Huggard Charitable Trust

WHERE FUNDING CAN BE GIVEN UK, with a preference for south Wales.

WHO CAN BENEFIT Older people, people who are disabled, people who are disadvantaged by poverty.

WHAT IS FUNDED Advancement of religion, the relief of poverty, disability and the welfare of older people.

SAMPLE GRANTS £63,000 to Amelia Methodist Trust in Llancarfan; £2,000 each to Holme Tower Marie Curie Cancer Centre in Penarth and Ty Olwen Hospice in Morriston. Grants of less than £2,000 each totalled £30,000.

FINANCES *Year* 2000–01 *Income* £93,341 *Grants* £97,350 *Assets* £1,700,000

TRUSTEES Mrs E M Huggard; T R W Davies; S J Thomas.

HOW TO APPLY The trustees are not inviting applications for funds.

WHO TO APPLY TO S J Thomas, Trustee, Blacklands Farm, Five Mile Lane, Bonvilston, Cardiff CF5 6TQ

CC NO 327501   **ESTABLISHED** 1987

■ The Geoffrey C Hughes Charitable Trust

WHERE FUNDING CAN BE GIVEN UK.

WHO CAN BENEFIT Actors and entertainment professionals and musicians.

WHAT IS FUNDED This trust is essentially interested in two areas: nature conservation/environment and performing arts, particularly ballet or opera with a bias towards modern work.

WHAT IS NOT FUNDED No grants to individuals.

TYPE OF GRANT Small and large grants.

FINANCES *Year* 1999–2000 *Income* £50,172

TRUSTEES J R Young; P C M Solon; R Hillman.

HOW TO APPLY In writing to the correspondent.

WHO TO APPLY TO P C M Solon, Trustee, Beachcroft Wansbroughs, 100 Fetter Lane, London EC4A 1BN *Tel* 020 7242 1011

CC NO 1010079   **ESTABLISHED** 1992

■ The Hull & East Riding Charitable Trust

WHERE FUNDING CAN BE GIVEN Hull and the East Riding of Yorkshire.

WHO CAN BENEFIT Registered charities only, with a possible preference for organisations working with children/youth, medical/disability and welfare.

WHAT IS FUNDED General charitable purposes.

WHAT IS NOT FUNDED Grants are not normally given to individuals. No grants to organisations or causes of a political nature, or for religious purposes, although requests for maintenance of significant religious buildings may be considered. If a donation has been made the trustees would not expect to receive a further request from the recipient in the immediate future.

TYPE OF GRANT The trust prefers to fund the capital costs of a project, but will consider funding revenue costs over a limited period of time.

RANGE OF GRANTS £100–£20,000.

SAMPLE GRANTS £20,000 to Dove House Hospice; £10,000 each to Giroscope Ltd and Sobriety Project; £5,000 each to County History Trust, Eagle House, Guide Association, Hull Independent Housing Aid Centre, Humberside Probation, Kosovo Crisis Appeal, Ocean Youth Trust and others.

FINANCES *Year* 1999–2000 *Income* £268,000 *Grants* £223,000 *Assets* £6,100,000

TRUSTEES M J Hollingbery; Mrs M R Barker; A M Horsley.

PUBLICATIONS Trust guidelines.

HOW TO APPLY In writing to the correspondent, including the aims of the project and benefits hoped for, the costs involved with budgets/accounts as appropriate, the contribution sought from the trust and details of other funds raised. The trustees meet in May and November and requests for donations will only be considered at those meetings. Applications must be received by 30 April and 31 October.

WHO TO APPLY TO J R Barnes, Secretary and Administrator, Greenmeades, Kemp Road, Swanland, East Yorkshire HU14 3LY *Tel* 01482 634664 *Fax* 01482 631700 *E-mail* johnr@barnes1939.freeserve.co.uk

CC NO 516866   **ESTABLISHED** 1985

■ Hulme Trust Estates (Educational)

WHERE FUNDING CAN BE GIVEN Greater Manchester.

WHO CAN BENEFIT Educational establishments.

SAMPLE GRANTS £94,000 to Brasenose College; £47,000 to Manchester University; £32,000 (in two grants) to William Hulmes Grammar School; £5,900 to Bury Grammar School; £4,900 to Manchester High School for Girls; £980 to Manchester Grammar School.

FINANCES *Year* 1999 *Income* £225,000 *Grants* £222,000 *Assets* £8,000,000

TRUSTEES J R Leigh, Chair; Prof. S A Moore; D J Claxton; Lord Windlesham; Dr R P H Gasser; A J Burden; J M Walker; T A Hoyle.

HOW TO APPLY In writing to the correspondent.

WHO TO APPLY TO J M Shelmerdine, Secretary, Taylor, Kirkham and Mainprice, 205 Moss Lane, Bramhall, Cheshire SK7 1BA *Tel* 0161 439 8228

CC NO 532297   **ESTABLISHED** 1964

■ Human Relief Foundation

WHERE FUNDING CAN BE GIVEN Somalia, Bosnia, Iraq, Bangladesh, Lebanon and other regions requiring urgent relief/aid.

WHO CAN BENEFIT Organisations benefiting at risk groups, carers, people who are disabled, people disadvantaged by poverty, refugees, victims of famine, man-made or natural disasters and war. Medical professionals, scientists, unemployed people and volunteers will be supported.

WHAT IS FUNDED General charitable purposes for the relief of poverty, sickness and to protect and preserve good health, and advance education of those in need from impoverished countries, in particular Somalia, Bosnia, Iraq, Bangladesh and Lebanon. Infrastructure, support and development and cultural activity are also funded.

WHAT IS NOT FUNDED No grants to individuals, or for medical expenses, tutors or examination fees.

SAMPLE GRANTS In 1999: £139,173 to Red Cressent U A E; £73,349 to Qatar Charitable Society, £31,188 to Muslim Aid; £27,188 to Islamic Trust; £18,564 to Elrahm Trust; £15,253 to Saudi Arabia (Muslim World League).

FINANCES *Year* 2001 *Income* £1,187,405

TRUSTEES Dr Nabeel Al Rahmadhani, Chair; Dr Saad Mustafa; Dr Ali Al-Quirbi; Dr Haytham Al-Kaffaf; Wael Musabbah; Anas Osam Tawfeek; Farid Sabri; Osama Abdulla; Sultan Al-Qassime.

HOW TO APPLY In writing to the correspondent.

WHO TO APPLY TO The Chair, PO Box 194, Bradford BD7 1BQ *Website* www.hrf.co.uk

CC NO 1043676   **ESTABLISHED** 1995

■ The Humanitarian Trust

WHERE FUNDING CAN BE GIVEN Worldwide, mainly Israel.

WHO CAN BENEFIT Organisations benefiting people with disabilities, refugees, young adults, academics and students (graduate and postgraduate level only).

WHAT IS FUNDED Main fields of support are educational, medical and social welfare. Individual applicants for educational grants must hold a basic grant; any support given is a top-up only and is given through the educational institution. Particularly supported are charities working in the fields of hospices, medical centres, schools and colleges, IT training, speech therapy, archaeology, economics, engineering, law, medicine, physics, science and technology and libraries and museums.

WHAT IS NOT FUNDED Awards are not given for travel, overseas courses, fieldwork or the arts (such as theatre, dance, music, fashion, journalism and so on), but for academic purposes only. They are intended only as one-off grants to individuals up to a maximum of £200 as a final top-up for fees, not as domestic funding.

TYPE OF GRANT One-off grants.

RANGE OF GRANTS Average £200.

SAMPLE GRANTS £10,000 to Friends of the Hebrew University of Jerusalem; £5,000 to Jerusalem Foundation; £3,000 to Michaelson Institute for the Prevention of Blindness; £2,000 to Ben Gurion University; £1,500 to Shaare Zedek Medical Centre.

FINANCES *Year* 2000–01 *Income* £76,350 *Grants* £61,970 *Assets* £584,037

TRUSTEES M Jacques Gunsbourg; P Halban; A Lerman.

HOW TO APPLY In writing to the correspondent for consideration at trustees' meetings in March and November.

WHO TO APPLY TO Mrs M Myers, Secretary, 27 St James' Place, London SW1A 1NR

CC NO 208575   **ESTABLISHED** 1946

■ The Albert Hunt Trust

WHERE FUNDING CAN BE GIVEN UK.

WHO CAN BENEFIT UK registered charities.

WHAT IS FUNDED Projects that enhance the physical and mental welfare of individuals, or group of individuals.

WHAT IS NOT FUNDED No grants for research or overseas work.

RANGE OF GRANTS Typical grant for regular beneficiaries: £8,000; for new applicants: £2,000.

SAMPLE GRANTS £7,000 each to Help the Aged, NSPCC and St Gemma's Hospice; £6,000 to Royal Star and Garter; £5,000 each to British Home and Hospital for Incurables, Hestia Housing and Support, Leukaemia Research, Sons of Divine Providence and YMCA.

FINANCES *Year* 2000–01 *Income* £593,000 *Grants* £1,267,000 *Assets* £20,000,000

TRUSTEES Coutts & Co; R J Collis; Mrs B McGuire.

HOW TO APPLY The correspondent states that no unsolicited correspondence will be acknowledged, unless an application receives favourable consideration. Trustees meet in March, July and November although appeals are considered on an ongoing basis.

WHO TO APPLY TO Steve Harvey, Senior Trust Manager, Coutts & Co., Trustee Department, 440 Strand, London WC2R 0QS *Tel* 020 7663 6814 *Fax* 020 7663 6794

CC NO 277318   **ESTABLISHED** 1979

■ The Michael and Shirley Hunt Charitable Trust

WHERE FUNDING CAN BE GIVEN UK and overseas.

WHO CAN BENEFIT Prisoners and/or their families, and people charged with criminal offences and held in custody. Also, animals which are unwanted, sick or ill-treated.

WHAT IS FUNDED Relief of need, hardship or distress of prisoners and/or their families; animal welfare.

WHAT IS NOT FUNDED No grants for fines, bail, legal costs, rent deposits, and so on.

Think carefully about every application. Is it justified?

559

TYPE OF GRANT One-off.

RANGE OF GRANTS £50–£10,000; typical grant £1,300.

SAMPLE GRANTS £8,500 to Brighton YMCA for an emergency room for use by East Sussex Probation Service; £5,127 to the HMP Send Play Project; £5,000 to Prisoners Abroad; £3,000 each to The Bourne Trust towards its Holloway All Day Children's Visits Project and NCH Action for Children for its Wessex Community Remand Project; £2,000 each to Federation of Prisoners' Families Support Groups to provide grants to prisoners' families, and Canine Partners for Independence who train guide dogs for disabled people; £1,500 to New Bridge in support of its newspaper *Inside Time*; c.£1,000 each to various animal charities.

FINANCES *Year* 2001–02 *Income* £218,875 *Grants* £64,045 *Assets* £3,477,000

TRUSTEES W J Baker; C J Hunt; S E Hunt; D S Jenkins; K D Maybury.

HOW TO APPLY In writing to the correspondent.

WHO TO APPLY TO Mrs D S Jenkins, Trustee, Ansty House, Henfield Road, Small Dole, West Sussex BN5 9XH *Tel* 01903 817116 *Fax* 01903 879995

CC NO 1063418   **ESTABLISHED** 1997

■ Miss Agnes H Hunter's Trust

WHERE FUNDING CAN BE GIVEN UK, with a preference for Scotland.

WHO CAN BENEFIT Organisations benefiting people of all ages, including unemployed people, volunteers, people who are in care, fostered or adopted, parents and children, and one-parent families. Also supported are carers, people who are disabled, people disadvantaged by poverty, homeless people, socially isolated people and people who are ill.

WHAT IS FUNDED Charities assisting people who are blind in Scotland; people who are disabled; training and education for disadvantaged people; those working towards an established cause, relief or cure for cancer, tuberculosis or rheumatism. These aims are also pursued in the fields of children and family support; youth development; older people; homelessness; mental illness; and the environment.

WHAT IS NOT FUNDED No grants to individuals, or to organisations under the control of the UK government.

TYPE OF GRANT Mainly one-off, buildings, capital, core costs, feasibility studies, projects, research and start-up costs will be considered.

RANGE OF GRANTS £500–£8,000; typical grant £500–£5,000.

FINANCES *Year* 1997–98 *Income* £267,000 *Grants* £223,750 *Assets* £3,480,000

HOW TO APPLY Applicants should write, in the first instance, to request the trust's guidance notes. The closing dates for final applications are 15 January and 1 September every year.

WHO TO APPLY TO Mrs Jane Paterson, Grants Administrator, Robson McLean WS, 28 Abercromby Place, Edinburgh EH3 6QF *Tel* 0131 556 0556

SC NO SC004843   **ESTABLISHED** 1954

■ The Huntingdon Foundation

WHERE FUNDING CAN BE GIVEN Jewish communities in the UK.

WHO CAN BENEFIT Organisations benefiting Jewish people.

WHAT IS FUNDED Jewish organisations, particularly schools.

TYPE OF GRANT One-off.

FINANCES *Year* 2000–01 *Income* £1,200,000 *Grants* £1,159,000 *Assets* £7,000,000

TRUSTEES Benjamin Perl, Chair; S Perl; Mrs S Perl; Mrs R Perl.

HOW TO APPLY In writing to the correspondent.

WHO TO APPLY TO Mrs S Perl, Secretary, Forframe House, 35–37 Brent Street, London NW4 2EF *Tel* 020 8202 2282

CC NO 286504   **ESTABLISHED** 1984

■ Hurdale Charity Limited

WHERE FUNDING CAN BE GIVEN Worldwide.

WHO CAN BENEFIT Organisations benefiting Jewish people.

WHAT IS FUNDED Jewish organisations that promote the Orthodox Jewish way of life.

FINANCES *Year* 1999–2000 *Income* £1,442,768 *Grants* £387,894 *Assets* £1,215,289

TRUSTEES M Oestreicher; Mrs E Oestreicher.

HOW TO APPLY In writing to the trustees.

WHO TO APPLY TO The Trustees, 54–56 Euston Street, London NW1 2ES *Tel* 020 7387 0155 *Fax* 020 7388 4758

CC NO 276997   **ESTABLISHED** 1978

■ The Huxham Charitable Trust

WHERE FUNDING CAN BE GIVEN UK and Eastern Europe, especially Albania and Kosova.

WHO CAN BENEFIT Registered UK charities; Christian organisations, refugees.

SAMPLE GRANTS The trust divided its grants as follows: £12,000 to individuals for Christian and development work; £15,000 to UK charities; £3,100 towards UK education; £960 towards UK older people and poor people; £3,100 to humanitarian and medical aid mission to Eastern Europe; £3,700 towards costs incurred by a young refugee fleeing Albania; £6,700 to an Albanian church; £6,800 to other programmes in Albania and Kosova.

FINANCES *Year* 1999–2000 *Income* £55,000 *Grants* £51,360 *Assets* £191,000

TRUSTEES Revd Deryck Markham.

HOW TO APPLY In writing to the correspondent.

WHO TO APPLY TO Adrian W Huxham, Thatcher Brake, 37 Whidborne Avenue, Torquay TQ1 2PG *Tel* 01803 380399

CC NO 1000179   **ESTABLISHED** 1990

■ The P Y N & B Hyams Trust

WHERE FUNDING CAN BE GIVEN Worldwide.

WHO CAN BENEFIT Organisations, especially those benefiting Jewish people.

WHAT IS FUNDED Jewish organisations and general charitable purposes.

FINANCES *Year* 2000–01 *Income* £73,755 *Grants* £27,539 *Assets* £1,020,916

TRUSTEES N Hyams; Mrs M Hyams; D Levy.

HOW TO APPLY In writing to the correspondent, but please note, the trust states that funds are fully committed and unsolicited applications are not welcomed.

WHO TO APPLY TO N J Hyams, Trustee, 610 Clive Court, Maida Vale, London W9 1SG *Tel* 020 7266 5747
CC NO 268129 ESTABLISHED 1974

■ The Hyde Charitable Trust

WHERE FUNDING CAN BE GIVEN UK, with a preference for the south of England including Greater London.
WHO CAN BENEFIT Registered charities.
WHAT IS FUNDED The trust works closely with organisations addressing the needs of children and young people who are disadvantaged in the areas in which the Hyde Group operates.
WHAT IS NOT FUNDED No grants to individuals, medical research, hospices, residential homes for older people, and any other projects the trustees decide fall outside the main criteria.
TYPE OF GRANT One-off grants will be considered for core, capital and project costs; funding available for three years or more.
SAMPLE GRANTS £28,000 Deptford Youth Project; £15,000 to Respond; £11,000 to NACRO; £10,000 to Islington Women's Aid; £4,100 Learning to be Local.
FINANCES *Year* 2001–02 *Income* £82,000 *Grants* £71,000 *Assets* £686,000
TRUSTEES D Small, Chair; B Bishop; P Breathwick; R Finlinson; J Fitzmaurice; V Stead; R Collins.
HOW TO APPLY In writing to the correspondent.
WHO TO APPLY TO Scott McKinven, Youth Plus London Regional Office, Hollingsworth House, 181 Lewisham High Street, London SE13 6AA *Tel* 020 8297 7575 *Fax* 020 8297 7565 *E-mail* Scott.mckinven@hyde-housing.co.uk *Website* www.hyde-housing.co.uk
CC NO 289888 ESTABLISHED 1984

■ The Hyde Park Place Estate Charity – civil trustees

WHERE FUNDING CAN BE GIVEN City of Westminster.
WHO CAN BENEFIT Individuals and voluntary organisations benefiting children, young adults and students; volunteers; at risk groups; people who are disadvantaged by poverty, homeless or socially isolated.
WHAT IS FUNDED Community facilities and services; advice and information provision; residential and housing services; education and training, particularly books, equipment and travel costs; conservation; health care and medical research; community development and support to voluntary and community organisations.
WHAT IS NOT FUNDED No educational grants to foreign students. Grants will not be given in aid of campaigning activities, academic research, animal charities, or the furtherance of religious causes.
TYPE OF GRANT One-off or recurring. The trust will consider capital costs, core costs, start-up costs, running costs, salaries or project costs.
FINANCES *Year* 2001–02 *Income* £304,750 *Grants* £200,000
TRUSTEES Revd J Slater; Hugo H Summerson; M Lothian; Cllr Mrs T S Mallinson; Mrs R M Botting; Cllr Mrs J Prendergast; A F Shannon; Lady Rees-Mogg; D Harvey.
HOW TO APPLY By letter to the correspondent.
WHO TO APPLY TO Mrs J Roberts, Clerk, St George's Vestry, 2a Mill Street, London W1S 1FX *Tel* 020 7629 0874
CC NO 212439 ESTABLISHED 1914

■ The Ibbett Trust

WHERE FUNDING CAN BE GIVEN UK, in particular
Bedford, and overseas.

WHO CAN BENEFIT Registered charities only.

WHAT IS FUNDED General charitable purposes to
favour local causes.

FINANCES *Year* 1999–2000 *Income* £67,000
Grants £10,000 *Assets* £2,700,000

TRUSTEES C J C Ibbett; J C Ibbett; Mrs S Ibbett; Mrs
B Plumbly.

OTHER INFORMATION The trust is accruing funds for a
local home for older people.

HOW TO APPLY In writing to the correspondent.

WHO TO APPLY TO Mrs B Plumbly, Secretary, c/o
Estate Office, Milton House, Milton Ernest,
Bedford MK44 1YU *Tel* 01234 825081

CC NO 234329   **ESTABLISHED** 1964

■ IBM United Kingdom Trust

WHERE FUNDING CAN BE GIVEN UK, but preference is
given to organisations in areas in which the
company is based and/or where there is
employee involvement.

WHO CAN BENEFIT The trust gives preference to
organisations concerned with people
disadvantaged by poverty and / or at risk of
digital exclusion.

WHAT IS FUNDED The focus areas for IBM's
community investment are the strategic and
innovative use of Information & Communication
Technology (ICT) in education and training and
the promotion of digital inclusion, with the broad
objective of raising standards of achievement.
Most activity is within the compulsory education
phase. The vast majority of IBM's community
investment is delivered through specific
programmes initiated and developed by IBM in
partnership with organisations with appropriate
professional expertise.

WHAT IS NOT FUNDED The trust does not provide core
funding or contribute to appeals for building
projects, religious or sectarian organisations,
animal charities, individuals (including
students), overseas activities or expeditions,
recreational and sports clubs, appeals by third
parties on behalf of charities or individuals. The
company does not currently offer full-time
secondments of employees to voluntary
organisations.

SAMPLE GRANTS KidSmart – donations of purpose-
designed computer units for young children in
nursery schools to enable access to to ICT for
children from disadvantaged areas and to
research appropriate use of technology in the
early years curriculum
(www.kidsmartearlylearning.org). Donations to
nurseries are through selection via LEA's.
TryScience – a web based virtual science centre
(www.tryscience.org.uk) designed to encourage
interest in science and technology in 8–14 year
olds, an associated in service training
programme for teachers of science and
donations of TryScience 'kiosks' to science and
technology centres.
Used equipment: there is very limited availability
of used PCs and Thinkpads.

FINANCES *Year* 2001 *Income* £982,129

TRUSTEES Larry Hirst; Stephen Wilson; Kevin
Bishop; Richard Atkins; Brendan Dineen.

HOW TO APPLY Very few unsolicited requests are
considered. If requests are submitted then
these should be by e-mail or in writing and
include a brief resumé of the aims of the
organisation and details of what assistance is
required. Those considering making an
application are advised to telephone first for
advice.

WHO TO APPLY TO Valerie Ward, Trust Administrator,
76 Upper Ground, London SE1 9PZ *Tel* 020
7202 3608 *E-mail* wakefim@uk.ibm.com
Website www.uk.ibm.com/ibm.ibmgives

CC NO 290462   **ESTABLISHED** 1984

■ The Idlewild Trust

WHERE FUNDING CAN BE GIVEN UK.

WHO CAN BENEFIT Registered charities only.

WHAT IS FUNDED The encouragement of excellence in
the performing and fine arts and the
preservation for the benefit of the public of
buildings and items of historical interest or
national importance. Occasional support is given
to bodies for educational bursaries in these
fields and for conservation of the natural
environment.

WHAT IS NOT FUNDED Grants to registered charities
only. No grants are made to individuals. The
trust will not give to: repetitive UK-wide appeals
by large charities; appeals where all, or most, of
the beneficiaries live outside the UK; local
appeals unless the artistic significance of the
project is of more than local importance;
appeals whose sole or main purpose is to make
grants from the funds collected; endowment or
deficit funding.

TYPE OF GRANT Buildings, core costs, endowments,
feasibility studies, one-off, projects, research
and start-up costs.

RANGE OF GRANTS £500–£5,000. Average grant
£2,000.

SAMPLE GRANTS £5,000 each to St Mary's Church –
Banbury and Moggerhanger House Preservation
Trust; £4,000 each to Council for Music in
Hospitals, Courtauld Institute of Art, Great
Hospital – Norwich, Natural History Museum,
Reading University Library and Verulanium
Museums Trust; £3,000 each to Dorset Opera,
National Trust, Norfolk Wildlife Trust, Sinfonietta
Productions Limited, Wey & Arun Canal Trust
and Youth Brass 2000.

FINANCES *Year* 2001 *Income* £155,596
Grants £136,150 *Assets* £3,664,401

TRUSTEES Lady Judith Goodison, Chair; Mrs A S
Bucks; M H Davenport; J C Gale; Mrs A C
Grellier; A Ford; M Wilson.

PUBLICATIONS Guidelines leaflet available.

HOW TO APPLY On a form available from the
correspondent, which can be sent via post or e-
mailed as a Microsoft Word file. Applications
should include the following information: budget
breakdown (one page); most recent audited
accounts; a list of other sponsors, including
those applied to; other relevant information.
Trustees meet twice a year in March and
November.

WHO TO APPLY TO Mrs Angela Freestone,
Administrator, 54–56 Knatchbull Road, London
SE5 9QY *Tel* 020 7274 2266 *Fax* 020 7274
5222 *E-mail* idlewildtrust@lineone.net

CC NO 268124   **ESTABLISHED** 1974

■ IFAW Charitable Trust (The International Fund for Animal Welfare Charitable Trust)

WHERE FUNDING CAN BE GIVEN International.

WHO CAN BENEFIT Animal welfare and conservation organisations.

WHAT IS FUNDED The trust's mission is (a) to conserve and protect animals including wildlife and its habitats and the natural environment; and (b) to prevent cruelty to and the suffering of animals, including wildlife.

WHAT IS NOT FUNDED No grants for individual undergraduate courses.

SAMPLE GRANTS £374,000 to International Marine Mammal Association Inc.; £316,000 to South Africa National Parks Board; £155,000 to Animals Asia Foundation; £66,000 to Uganda Wildlife Authority; £47,000 to Food & Agriculture of the United Nations.

FINANCES *Year* 1999–2000 *Income* £1,200,000 *Grants* £1,100,000 *Assets* £1,400,000

TRUSTEES Frederick O'Regan; Stijn Albregts; Anne Fitzgerald; Karen Cotton; David White; Sally Banks.

HOW TO APPLY In writing to the correspondent. Although applications can be submitted at any time, it is best to apply between July and September.

WHO TO APPLY TO The IFAW UK Grant Co-ordinator, 87–90 Albert Embankment, London SE1 7UD *Tel* 020 7587 6761 *Fax* 020 7587 6720 *E-mail* cjeffery@ifaw.org *Website* www.ifaw.org

CC NO 1024806   **ESTABLISHED** 1992

■ The Iliffe Family Charitable Trust

WHERE FUNDING CAN BE GIVEN UK.

WHO CAN BENEFIT The majority of donations are made to charities already known to the trustees. Thereafter, preference is given to charities in which the trust has a special interest.

WHAT IS FUNDED Medical, activities for people who are disabled, heritage organisations, and education.

WHAT IS NOT FUNDED No grants to individuals and rarely to non-registered charities.

SAMPLE GRANTS £25,000 to Sherborne School Foundation; £15,000 to Arthur Rank Centre General Fund; £10,000 each to National and Cornwall Maritime Museum Trust, Royal Naval Museum – Portsmouth, The Jim and Olga Lloyd Trust, Game Conservancy Trust, Coventry Cathedral Development Trust and the University of Reading; £8,800 to Berkshire Community Foundation; £6,000 to Heartlands Cystic Fibrosis Centre Appeal.

FINANCES *Year* 2000–01 *Income* £124,821 *Grants* £195,760 *Assets* £1,585,747

TRUSTEES N G E Petter; G A Bremner; Lord Iliffe; The Hon. Edward Iliffe.

HOW TO APPLY In writing to the correspondent. Only successful applications will be acknowleged. Grants are considered at ad hoc meetings of the trustees, held throughout the year.

WHO TO APPLY TO Miss Julia Peel, Secretary to the Trustees, Barn Close, Yattendon, Berkshire RG18 0UY

CC NO 273437   **ESTABLISHED** 1977

■ Imerys South West Charitable Trust (formerly English China Clays Group Charitable Trust)

WHERE FUNDING CAN BE GIVEN Preference for Berkshire, south west England and Staffordshire.

WHO CAN BENEFIT Regional and local organisations benefiting children, young adults, students and people with disabilities.

WHAT IS FUNDED Large grants are regularly given to the St Austell China Clay Museum; other grants are made in the areas of youth, community, schools, education and disability.

SAMPLE GRANTS £70,000 to Wheal Martyn Museum; £5,000 to Berkshire Community Trust; £1,500 to an individual; £1,300 to West of England Bandmen's Festival; £1,200 to Playhouse Oxford Trust; £1,000 each to Abbots Kerswell Festival of Music Arts, Buges CP School, Friends of Sunningwell Church, and St Austell District Chamber of Commerce; £500 to Daphne Du Maurier Festival.

FINANCES *Year* 1998 *Income* £96,260 *Grants* £96,917 *Assets* £195,540

TRUSTEES P M Elliott; D Leadbeater; W Verrall; H Daniels.

HOW TO APPLY In writing to the correspondent.

WHO TO APPLY TO Ivor Bowditch, ECC International Ltd, John Keay House, St Austell, Cornwall PL25 4SJ *Tel* 01726 74482

CC NO 326184   **ESTABLISHED** 1982

■ The Inchrye Trust

WHERE FUNDING CAN BE GIVEN Mainly Scotland.

WHO CAN BENEFIT Small projects starting up. Organisations benefiting people of all ages, at risk groups, carers, people who are disabled or disadvantaged by poverty, ex-offenders and people at risk of offending; people living in rural areas, socially isolated people, and victims of man-made or natural disasters.

WHAT IS FUNDED Grants are given to cultural, social and humanitarian organisations. Charities working in the fields of accommodation and housing, arts and arts facilities, arts education, music groups and healthcare and hospices will be considered. Funding may also be given to special schools, care in the community, counselling on social issues and crime prevention schemes.

WHAT IS NOT FUNDED No funding for expeditions, scholarships, large existing charities, animal charities or campaigns.

TYPE OF GRANT One-off grants and recurring funding may be considered.

RANGE OF GRANTS £100–£3,000.

SAMPLE GRANTS £2,000 to Bield Housing Trust; £2,000 to Contact the Elderly; £3,000 to North Edinburgh Arts.

FINANCES *Year* 2001–02 *Income* £23,000 *Grants* £21,500

TRUSTEES Miss R Finlay; Mrs J David; N McLeod.

HOW TO APPLY In writing to the correspondent.

WHO TO APPLY TO The Trustees, Turcan Connell, Princes Exchange, 1 Earl Grey Street, Edinburgh EH3 9EE *Tel* 0131 228 8111 *Fax* 0131 228 8118

SC NO SC013382

Think carefully about every application. Is it justified?

563

■ The Incorporated Church Building Society

WHERE FUNDING CAN BE GIVEN England, Wales, Isle of Man and the Channel Islands.

WHO CAN BENEFIT Living churches benefiting Anglicans.

WHAT IS FUNDED Grants and interest-free loans repayable over four years to eligible churches. Larger loans may be made towards the building of Anglican churches.

WHAT IS NOT FUNDED Aid is limited to actual church and chapel buildings. Repairs are limited to essential fabric repairs. Enlarging is restricted to the worship area.

SAMPLE GRANTS £6,000 each to St Nicholas-on-the-Hill, Swansea and St Lawrence – Revesby; £4,000 each to Christ Church – Gretton, St Anne – Brislington, St Mary – Hampden Park.

FINANCES *Year* 2001 *Income* £79,900 *Grants* £60,500 *Assets* £1,210,700

TRUSTEES The Committee of Clergy and Laymen.

HOW TO APPLY In writing to the correspondent.

WHO TO APPLY TO The Historic Churches Preservation Trust, Fulham Palace, London SW6 6EA *Tel* 020 7736 3054 *Fax* 020 7736 3880 *E-mail* grants@historicchurchespt.org.uk *Website* www.historicchurchespt.org.uk

CC NO 212752   **ESTABLISHED** 1818

■ The Incorporated Leeds Church Extension Society

WHERE FUNDING CAN BE GIVEN The archdeaconry of Leeds.

WHO CAN BENEFIT Church of England. Churches and community projects.

WHAT IS FUNDED Capital projects, major repairs and reordering of churches and church halls. Outreach and community projects of the Church of England.

WHAT IS NOT FUNDED No support is given to appeals for church organs or for appeals from outside the Church of England (Leeds archdeaconry).

TYPE OF GRANT One-off grants and low-cost loans. Occasionally grants are given for projects lasting more than one year.

RANGE OF GRANTS £500–£6,000.

SAMPLE GRANTS £6,000 each to St John – Wortley-de-Leeds, and St Mary the Less – Allerton Bywater; £5,000 to St Michael's – Headingley; £5,000 in two grants each to Christ Church – Lofthouse, and St Hilda's – Cross Green; £2,500 each to St John – Oulton, and St Philip – Osmondthorpe; £2,000 each to The Epiphany – Leeds, and St Philip – Osmondthorpe; £1,500 to St Mary – Whitkirk.

FINANCES *Year* 2001 *Income* £32,796 *Grants* £30,700 *Assets* £1,208,913

TRUSTEES Ven. J Oliver; G D Breton; Revd P J Brindle; H G Paget; S Rawling; G Lancaster; R Hardy; K Endersby; Miss C E Walker; G Bass; A Nicholls; A B Menzies; Canon G Smith; Mrs D M Evans; Revd A F Bundock; Revd C A James; Revd T Lipscomb; M Bell.

HOW TO APPLY In writing to the correspondent for an application form. The trustees meet in March, June and October to consider applications which should be accompanied by accounts and quotations/plans as appropriate.

WHO TO APPLY TO G D Breton, Hon. Secretary, Holbeck Cottage, 10 Carr Bank Bottom, Otley LS21 2AJ *Tel* 01943 465753

CC NO 504682   **ESTABLISHED** 1863

■ The India Foundation (UK)

WHERE FUNDING CAN BE GIVEN UK and India.

WHO CAN BENEFIT People in need.

WHAT IS FUNDED School for Children in India who are deaf and dumb; rebuilding of a community centre subject to an arson attack in West Bromwich, UK. Academic subjects, sciences and research focusing on ethnicity and health issues.

WHAT IS NOT FUNDED No grants to individuals.

TYPE OF GRANT Project, research and recurring costs. Funding may be given for more than three years. Grants are given for financial assistance and moral support for research projects on ethnicity and health issues.

SAMPLE GRANTS £60,000 to West Bromwich Community Hall Project; £4,000 to Manav Kalyan Trust for a school for deaf children.

FINANCES *Year* 1999–2000 *Income* £93,758 *Grants* £72,648 *Assets* £20,782

TRUSTEES Dr Kiran C R Patel, Chair; Dr Pankaj Sharma; Mahesh Kothari; Chandrakant D Patel.

HOW TO APPLY In writing to the correspondent.

WHO TO APPLY TO Dr Kiran C R Patel, Chair, 26 Lightwoods Hill, Warley, West Midlands B67 5EA *E-mail* drkiranpatel@hotmail.com

CC NO 1073178   **ESTABLISHED** 1999

■ The Ingram Trust

WHERE FUNDING CAN BE GIVEN Surrey and Greater London, UK and overseas.

WHO CAN BENEFIT Established registered charities only.

WHAT IS FUNDED General charitable purposes. The trust prefers to support specific projects including special services and equipment. It will support major UK charities together with some local ones in the county of Surrey. Normal the policy is to support a limited number of charities (usually less than 20), but with a longer-term commitment to each.

WHAT IS NOT FUNDED No grants to non-registered charities or to individuals. No charities specialising in overseas aid are considered except those dedicated to encouraging self help or providing more permanent solutions. No animal charities except those concerned with wildlife conservation.

RANGE OF GRANTS £500–£8,000.

SAMPLE GRANTS £10,000 to Shelter; £7,000 to NSPCC; £5,000 each to Queen Elizabeth Foundation for Disabled People, LEPRA, ActionAid, Alzheimer's Society, Royal National Theatre, and Prince's Trust; £3,000 each to English Touring Opera and WWF-UK.

FINANCES *Year* 1999–2000 *Income* £71,165 *Grants* £61,500 *Assets* £5,800,000

TRUSTEES C J Ingram; Ms J E Ingram; Ms C M Maurice.

HOW TO APPLY In writing to the correspondent, although the trust states that it receives far more worthy applications than it is able to support.

WHO TO APPLY TO Joan Major, Administrator, c/o 8th Floor, 101 Wigmore Street, London W1U 1QU

CC NO 1040194   **ESTABLISHED** 1994

■ The Inland Waterways Association

WHERE FUNDING CAN BE GIVEN UK and Ireland.

WHO CAN BENEFIT Organisations promoting the restoration of inland waterways (such as canal and river navigations).

WHAT IS FUNDED (a) Construction, especially works relating to the restoration of navigation such as locks, bridges, aquaducts, culverts, weirs, pumps, excavation, dredging, lining, and so on; (b) administration – support for a particular purpose, such as a project officer, a funding appeal or for promotional literature or events; (c) professional services, such as funding of feasibility studies or detailed work on engineering, economic or environmental issues; (d) land purchase; (e) research on matters affecting waterway restoration, including original research, reviews of research undertaken by others and literature reviews; (f) education, such as providing information to local authorities or agencies to promote the nature and benefits of waterway restoration.

WHAT IS NOT FUNDED No grants to individuals. No retrospective grants for projects where expenditure has already been incurred or committed.

TYPE OF GRANT Capital, feasibility studies, one-off grants, project and research grants. Funding can be given over a number of years.

RANGE OF GRANTS Up to £20,000. In exceptional cases, larger grants can be made.

SAMPLE GRANTS In 2000: £20,000 to Wey & Arun Canal Trust towards the rebuilding of Drungewick Lane Canal Bridge; £4,500 to Lancaster Canal Northern Reaches Group for repairs to bridges near Holme and dredging at Millness; £3,000 to North Cornwall District Council towards essential repairs to the sea lock at Bude; and £1,000 each to a study into the impacts of user disturbance on wildlife led by British Waterways and to Worcester & Birmingham Canal Society. Grants were made to Lichfield & Hatherton Canals Restoration Trust and Wiltshire & Berkshire Canal Amenity Group for replacement and repair of working party machinery.

FINANCES *Year* 2001 *Income* £1,000,000 *Grants* £110,000 *Assets* £1,600,000

TRUSTEES The Council of the Association.

HOW TO APPLY In writing to the correspondent. Applications should comply with the association's guidelines for applicants, available from the correspondent. Each applicant should provide a full description of its proposal, show that the organisation can maintain a satisfactory financial position and demonstrate that it is capable of undertaking the proposed project. Applications for up to £2,000 are assessed under a simplified procedure – each application should demonstrate that the grant would be used to initiate or sustain a restoration scheme or significantly benefit a specific small project. Applications for over £2,000 should demonstrate that the grant would be applied to one of the types of projects (a–f).

WHO TO APPLY TO The Chairman of the IWA Restoration Committee, c/o IWA Head Office, P O Box 114, Rickmansworth WD3 1ZY *Tel* 01923 711114 *Fax* 01923 897000 *E-mail* iwa@waterways.org.uk *Website* www.waterways.org.uk

CC NO 212342   **ESTABLISHED** 1946

■ The Inlight Trust

WHERE FUNDING CAN BE GIVEN UK.

WHO CAN BENEFIT Registered charities benefiting people from many different religions.

WHAT IS FUNDED Donations are made on a non-denominational basis to charities providing valuable contributions to spiritual development and charities concerned with spiritual healing and spiritual growth through religious retreats. Note: The trustees of the Inlight Trust are only allowed under their trust deed to give donations for the advancement of religion.

WHAT IS NOT FUNDED Core funding or salaries are rarely considered. Non-registered charities are not supported. No grants are made to individuals, including students, or to general appeals from large UK organisations. Grants for church buildings are seldom made.

TYPE OF GRANT Usually one-off for a specific project or part of a project. Bursary schemes eligible. Core funding and/or salaries are rarely considered.

SAMPLE GRANTS In 2001–02: £67,000 to White Eagle Lodge; £40,000 to Holy Island Project – Dumfriesshire; £5,000 each to Emmaus House, Great Ocean Dharma Refuge and Vairochara Buddist Centre; £3,000 to International Interfaith Centre – Oxford; £2,000 to Jamyang Buddist Centre – London.

FINANCES *Year* 2001–02 *Income* £139,509 *Grants* £134,711 *Assets* £3,761,677

TRUSTEES Sir Thomas Lucas; Michael Collishaw; Michael Meakin; Stuart Neil; Richard Wolfe; Wendy Collett.

HOW TO APPLY In writing to the correspondent including details of the need the intended project is designed to meet plus an outline budget and the most recent available annual accounts of the charity. Only applications from eligible bodies are acknowledged. Applications must be accompanied by a copy of your trust deed or of your entry in the Charity Commission register. Only successful applicants are informed. Grants are considered at trustees' meetings four times a year in March, June, September and December and applications should be submitted two months before those meetings.

WHO TO APPLY TO Mrs Judy Hayward, P O Box 2, Liss, Hampshire GU33 6YP

CC NO 236782   **ESTABLISHED** 1957

■ The Inman Charity

WHERE FUNDING CAN BE GIVEN UK.

WHO CAN BENEFIT Registered charities benefiting older people and people who are ill or disabled.

WHAT IS FUNDED The main areas of interest are older people, medical research, hospices and disability.

WHAT IS NOT FUNDED No grants to individuals.

RANGE OF GRANTS Most grants were of £3,000 or less.

SAMPLE GRANTS £14,000 to Uppingham School – Victor Inman Bursary Fund; £10,500 to Deafblind UK; £7,500 to Counsel and Care for the Elderly, Gurkha Welfare Trust, National Benevolent Fund for the Aged, Queen Elizabeth's Foundation for the Disabled, Samaritans and Winged Fellowship.

FINANCES *Year* 2000 *Income* £227,849 *Grants* £252,000 *Assets* £5,345,715

TRUSTEES A L Walker; Miss B M A Strother; M R Matthews; Prof. J D Langdon.

HOW TO APPLY In writing only to the correspondent, including up-to-date reports and accounts.

Trustees meet half-yearly, usually in March and September.

WHO TO APPLY TO The Trustees, Payne Hicks Beech, 10 New Square, Lincoln's Inn, London WC2A 3QG

CC NO 261366   **ESTABLISHED** 1970

■ The Worshipful Company of Innholders General Charity Fund

WHERE FUNDING CAN BE GIVEN UK.

WHO CAN BENEFIT Registered charities and voluntary organisations.

WHAT IS FUNDED General charitable purposes.

WHAT IS NOT FUNDED No grants to individuals.

TYPE OF GRANT Mainly one-off, but also recurrent.

SAMPLE GRANTS £45,167 to Research into Ageing; £32,090 to City of London Schools Scholarships; £12,000 to Tommy's Campaign; £6,670 to Commanding Officers Fund for the 3rd Signals Regiment; £6,000 to Community Health South London NHS Trust; £5,701 to Master Innholder Scholarship; £5,000 to Treloar Trust; £3,957 to Sail Training Association; £3,000 to Master Innholders Charitable Trust; £2,000 to Corporation of the Sons of the Clergy.

FINANCES *Year* 1999–2000 *Income* £119,202 *Grants* £132,055 *Assets* £488,911

TRUSTEES J R Edwardes Jones; Brian W Hall; Anthony C Lorkin; Sir Malcolm Chaplin.

HOW TO APPLY In writing to the correspondent, including the reason for applying and current financial statements, and so on.

WHO TO APPLY TO The Clerk, 30 College Street, Dowgate Hall, London EC4R 2RH *Tel* 020 7236 6703 *Fax* 020 7236 0059 *E-mail* mail@innholders.co.uk

CC NO 270948   **ESTABLISHED** 1976

■ INTACH (UK) Trust

WHERE FUNDING CAN BE GIVEN India. Grants to be used in India.

WHO CAN BENEFIT UK postgraduates and university projects in India.

WHAT IS FUNDED Postgraduate study by UK nationals in India; the preservation of the art, cultural and national heritage of India; conservation projects in India.

WHAT IS NOT FUNDED No funding for expeditions, undergraduates, school projects or UK charities.

TYPE OF GRANT One-off and recurring; some to individuals to visit India in connection with projects relating to the trust's aims. Research is funded.

RANGE OF GRANTS £500–£6,000.

SAMPLE GRANTS 1997–98: £12,420 was given in stipends, travel of students and scholars; £8,049 to Museum Project; £816 to Charles Wallace Trust; £500 to Calcutta Trecentenary Trust; £167 to Vrajbumi Project.

FINANCES *Year* 2000–01 *Income* £114,774

TRUSTEES Martand Singh, Chair; Sir B M Feilden; Sir J Thomson; R W Skelton; Cyrus Guzder; Dr D W MacDowell; Saman Haider.

OTHER INFORMATION INTACH stands for the Indian National Trust for Art and Cultural Heritage.

HOW TO APPLY In writing to the correspondent. Applications are considered in January and June each year.

WHO TO APPLY TO Susan Denyer, Secretary, 10 Barley Mow Passage, London W4 4PH *Tel* 020 8994 6477

CC NO 298329   **ESTABLISHED** 1987

■ International Bar Association Educational Trust

WHERE FUNDING CAN BE GIVEN UK and developing countries.

WHAT IS FUNDED To advance legal education, to promote the study of law, and to promote research into common legal problems and disseminate useful results, with an emphasis on grants to developing countries.

WHAT IS NOT FUNDED No grants to individuals.

SAMPLE GRANTS £10,500 to its Intern Programme; £10,000 each to Terrorism Task Force 2001, Terrorism Task Force 2002 and GPP Fiji; £5,000 each to Human Rights Institute Contempt of Court Study, Caribbean Law Centres and IBA Distance Based Learning Programme and Book Aid International; £1,680 to IBA Hague Child Abduction Task Force; £1,500 to Shipping of Legal Books.

FINANCES *Year* 2002 *Income* £86,365 *Grants* £59,332 *Assets* £138,819

TRUSTEES Francis Neate; Andrew Primrose; Christopher Rees; Julie Onslow-Cole; Keith Baker; Emilio Cardenas; Tomas Lindholm.

HOW TO APPLY In writing to the correspondent.

WHO TO APPLY TO Elaine Owen, Executive Assistant, 271 Regent Street, London W1R 7PA

CC NO 287324   **ESTABLISHED** 1983

■ International Spinal Research Trust

WHERE FUNDING CAN BE GIVEN UK and overseas.

WHO CAN BENEFIT Academic institutions undertaking research into spinal cord injury.

WHAT IS FUNDED A wide range of research activities are funded, with the sole aim of ending the permanence of paralysis caused by spinal cord injury, such as clinical-based programmes and PhD studentships. Grants are given for specific scientific assistants (technical, pre-doctorate and post-doctorate), consumables, equipment for qualified scientific personnel and for collaboration between laboratories. Salaries may be considered.

WHAT IS NOT FUNDED No commercial organisations or private individuals are funded.

TYPE OF GRANT Recurring grants, generally for up to three years.

FINANCES *Year* 1999 *Income* £1,553,488 *Grants* £1,483,760 *Assets* £2,360,081

TRUSTEES M P Curtis, Chair; P Edmond; Miss H Faulls; Mrs P Herbert; J W A Hick; Dr L S Illis; Sir Christophor Laidlaw; Dr P C Sharpe; Dr D Short; Prof P D Wall; S Yesner.

PUBLICATIONS Annual research review; annual review: *'Move'*.

HOW TO APPLY The trust advertises in publications such as the *British Medical Journal*, *The Lancet*, and *Nature* and *Science* for people to apply to work on specific research topics. Applications should be made in the form of a letter of intent, of approximately two sides of A4 in length. All applications are reviewed by the Scientific Committee, assisted where appropriate by other scientists in the field. Some applicants will then be invited to make a full application. Unsolicited applications will not be considered.

WHO TO APPLY TO The Head of Research, Unit 8a Bramley Business Centre, Station Road, Bramley, Guildford, Surrey GU5 0AZ *Tel* 01483 898786 *Fax* 01483 898763 *E-mail* isrt@spinal-research.org *Website* www.spinal-research.org

CC NO 281325   **ESTABLISHED** 1980

■ The Inverclyde Bequest Fund

WHERE FUNDING CAN BE GIVEN UK and USA, with a preference for Glasgow and the west of Scotland.

WHO CAN BENEFIT Merchant seamen.

WHAT IS FUNDED Grants are given to seamen's missions, especially long-established ones.

WHAT IS NOT FUNDED The fund does not give grants to individuals.

RANGE OF GRANTS £300–£4,000.

FINANCES *Year* 2000 *Grants* £61,500

TRUSTEES The Directors of the Merchants House of Glasgow.

OTHER INFORMATION Grants are given through two district committees based in Liverpool/Manchester and in Belfast.

HOW TO APPLY In writing to the correspondent, including your annual report and audited accounts.

WHO TO APPLY TO Jimmy Dykes, Assistant Collector, Merchants House of Glasgow, 7 West George Street, Glasgow G2 1BA *Tel* 0141 221 8272

CC NO Y00126

■ The Inverforth Charitable Trust

WHERE FUNDING CAN BE GIVEN UK (as a whole).

WHO CAN BENEFIT UK-wide charities only, benefiting the arts, heritage, physical and mental health, youth and education, people who are disabled, older people, seafarers and fishermen, carers, homeless people and victims of abuse and crime.

WHAT IS FUNDED To support smaller UK-wide charities, in the areas of music, the arts, religion, heritage, health, youth, older people, education, disability and other areas of need.

WHAT IS NOT FUNDED No grants are made to local churches, village halls, schools and so on; animal charities; branches, affiliates or subsidiary charities; individuals; advertisers or fundraising events; organisations that have been supported in the last 12 months; charities which are not registered in the UK. Note: charities with the word 'community' or a relevant place name in their title (which are unlikely to be considered by the trust as a national charity).

TYPE OF GRANT General grants, including core costs. Projects and specific items are not normally funded.

RANGE OF GRANTS £500.

SAMPLE GRANTS £1,000 to Spitalfields Festival; £750 each to Donmar Warehouse, Live Music Now!, Music for Youth, national Youth Orchestra of Great Britain; £500 each to Abbeyfield Society, BREAK, Crisis, English National Opera, Inside Out Trust, Peper Harrow Foundation, Quaker Social Action Second Chance, Trinity Hospice and Woodland Trust.

FINANCES *Year* 2002 *Income* £56,346 *Grants* £44,000 *Assets* £2,895,069

TRUSTEES Elizabeth Lady Inverforth; Lord Inverforth; Hon. Mrs Jonathan Kane; Michael Gee.

HOW TO APPLY In writing to the correspondent at least one month before meetings. No special forms are necessary, although accounts are desirable. A summary is prepared for the trustees, who meet quarterly in March, June, September and early December. Replies are normally sent to all applicants; allow up to four months for an answer or grant. Over 1,000 applications are received each year, producing a high failure rate for new applicants. The trust has stated that nearly half of all applicants are ineligible for support, so potential applicants should read 'exclusions' above carefully.

Telephone calls are discouraged, particularly from ineligible applicants or people enquiring to see if they are eligible.

WHO TO APPLY TO E A M Lee, Secretary and Treasurer, The Farm, Northington, Alresford, Hampshire SO24 9TH

CC NO 274132   **ESTABLISHED** 1977

■ The Invicta Trust

WHERE FUNDING CAN BE GIVEN Worldwide.

WHO CAN BENEFIT Jewish organisations.

WHAT IS FUNDED Orthodox Jewish educational and general purposes.

SAMPLE GRANTS £4,000 each to Friends of Horim, Kolel Shomre Hachomoth, Torah V'Emunah and Yad Eliezer; £3,000 each to Achiezer Va'Achisomoch, Craven Walk Charities Trust, Hachzokas Torah, Holmleigh Trust and TYY Institution Trust; £2,000 each to Beth Hamedrash Ponevez and Yeshiva D'Chasidei Belz London.

FINANCES *Year* 1998–99 *Income* £40,000 *Grants* £37,000 *Assets* £355,000

TRUSTEES Mrs F H Hirsch; E H Feingold; Mrs N Silber.

HOW TO APPLY In writing to the correspondent.

WHO TO APPLY TO Mrs F H Hirsch, Trustee, 817 Finchley Road, London NW11 8AJ

CC NO 327039   **ESTABLISHED** 1985

■ The IPE Charitable Trust

WHERE FUNDING CAN BE GIVEN UK, with some preference for London.

WHAT IS FUNDED General charitable purposes, with the specific aims of relieving poverty and advancing education.

WHAT IS NOT FUNDED Grants are not made to overseas causes.

RANGE OF GRANTS £250–£1,030.

SAMPLE GRANTS £1,030 to Access Partnership; £1,025 to Arsenal Charitable Trust; £1,000 each to Evelina Children's Hospital Appeal and NHVS; £800 to Jeans for Genes; £500 each to British Heart Foundation, Children's Aid Direct, Kids 2 Care 4, Milton and Denton Football Club, and Toynbee Hall.

FINANCES *Year* 2000–01 *Income* £118,801 *Grants* £9,116 *Assets* £312,433

TRUSTEES P Hole; J Maidman; P Ottino; Sir Bob Read; R C Ward; D A Whiting.

HOW TO APPLY In writing to the correspondent, although the funds available for unsolicited applications are minimal.

WHO TO APPLY TO Miss Alison Jane Herring, c/o IPE, International House, 1 St Katharine's Way, London E1W 1UY *Tel* 020 7481 0643

CC NO 1048724   **ESTABLISHED** 1995

■ The Ireland Fund of Great Britain

WHERE FUNDING CAN BE GIVEN Ireland and Great Britain.

WHO CAN BENEFIT Organisations benefiting people disadvantaged by poverty.

WHAT IS FUNDED Peace, reconciliation, cultural activity and the alleviation of poverty among Irish communities north and south of the border and in the UK.

WHAT IS NOT FUNDED Grants are generally not given for: general appeals; purchase of buildings or land; major construction or repairs to buildings; other grant-making trusts; individuals; purchase of vehicles; debt repayment; tuition or student expenses; travel or transport costs; commercial trading businesses; replacement of statutory funding; medical research; or general administration.

RANGE OF GRANTS £500–£50,000.

SAMPLE GRANTS £50,000 to Newman Institute; £42,178 to Tyrrell Trust; £38,462 to All Hallows College; £30,000 to CORE; £6,000 each to Culra na nog, Leicester Irish Forum, and London Irish Elders Forum; £5,000 each to Foreglen Youth Club, Smurfit Archive of the Irish in Britain, and Upper Anderstown Community Forum.

FINANCES *Year* 2000 *Income* £728,094 *Grants* £441,546 *Assets* £156,473

TRUSTEES Bryan Hayes, Chair; Josephine Hart; Hon. Kevin Pakenham; Dr Anthony O'Reilly; John Riordan; Gavin O'Reilly; Stanley Watson.

HOW TO APPLY On a form available from the correspondent. In Ireland, applications are welcome between 1 October and 31 January, with successful applicants notified in early June. In Great Britain, the deadline for receipt of applications is 15 August with grants distributed in December/January. 'Notification of outcome will be by letter. In the meantime we would ask you not to contact the office, due to our small staff number. Lobbying will disqualify.' There is a stringent application of the guidelines and exclusions criteria. Applicants must submit copies of their constitution and audited accounts before receiving funding. Projects supported must make regular reports of progress and monitoring as well as providing promotional material and publicity.

WHO TO APPLY TO Aileen Ross, Director, 158 Regent Street, London W1B 5SW *Tel* 020 7439 4299 *Fax* 020 7439 4298 *E-mail* irelandfundgb@btclick.com

CC NO 327889   **ESTABLISHED** 1988

■ **The Irish Youth Foundation (UK) Ltd**

WHERE FUNDING CAN BE GIVEN UK.

WHO CAN BENEFIT Community-based organisations working directly with young Irish people.

WHAT IS FUNDED Projects benefiting young Irish people or enhancing their personal and social development, especially if they are disadvantaged or in need.

WHAT IS NOT FUNDED The foundation generally does not support: projects which cater for people over 25 years of age; individuals; general appeals; work in the arts, museums, or of an environmental nature; grants for academic research; educational bursaries; to substitute state support; alleviation of deficits already incurred; services run by statutory/public authorities; and major capital appeals.

TYPE OF GRANT Programme development grants; seeding grants; grants to upgrade premises and/or equipment and small grants.

SAMPLE GRANTS In 2001–02: £20,000 to Irish Community Care – Manchester for the salary of a youth development coordinator; £13,000 to Irish Community Centre – Merseyside for a full-time worker's salary; £10,000 to London Irish Centre for the youth resettlement project; £9,000 to Irish Commission for Prisoners Overseas for the salary of an administration assistant; £8,500 to Solas Anois – London for the children's playscheme and annual holiday; £8,141 to Solas Anois – London for a part-time children's worker's salary; £8,000 to Bristol Playbus for a junior youth community

development worker's salary; £7,000 to An Teach for the salary of a life skills coordinator; £6,000 to London Irish Women's Centre for a coordinator's salary; £5,000 to Ardoyne Youth Club for a development sports programme for 10 to 12 year olds.

FINANCES *Year* 2000–01 *Income* £196,343 *Grants* £203,952 *Assets* £57,200

TRUSTEES J O'Hara, Chair; Mary Clancy; F Hucker; P Kelly; D Murray; John O'Neill; Nessa O'Neill; John Power; Colin McNicholas; Sean O'Neill.

HOW TO APPLY In writing to the correspondent, requesting an application form. The application period is short, with forms being available at the end of August to be returned by the third week of September. Applicants should photocopy and send six copies of the completed form if they are in Northern Ireland and eight copies if they work elsewhere. Applications are considered in November and all applicants notified in January. Applications are assessed on the following requirements: need; continuity; track record/ evaluation; disadvantaged young people; innovativeness; funding sources; and budgetary control. Faxed applications are not considered.

WHO TO APPLY TO Linda Tanner, Administrator, The Irish Centre, Blacks Road, Hammersmith, London W6 9DT *Tel* 020 8748 9640 *Fax* 020 8748 7386 *E-mail* info@iyf.org.uk *Website* www.iyf.org.uk

CC NO 328265   **ESTABLISHED** 1989

■ **The Ironmongers' Quincentenary Charitable Fund**

WHERE FUNDING CAN BE GIVEN UK.

WHO CAN BENEFIT Organisations benefiting research workers.

WHAT IS FUNDED The trust supports community work, iron work and research connected to ferrous metallurgy and crafts. Other charitable purposes are also supported.

TYPE OF GRANT One-off.

RANGE OF GRANTS Up to amounts of £5,000 each.

SAMPLE GRANTS £19,000 to the National Trust; £7,200 to Surrey Institite of Design towards travel bursaries, equipment and an artist in residence; £5,000 each to Lord Mayor's Appeal and St John's School – Leatherhead; £4,500 to Ashburnham Christian Trust; £3,800 to Arkwright Scholarship; £2,700 each to Imperial College, University of Birmingham, University of Cambridge and University of Shelffield; £2,100 to Guildhall Scool of Music and Drama.

FINANCES *Year* 2000–01 *Income* £176,960 *Grants* £72,603 *Assets* £1,879,502

TRUSTEES Worshipful Ironmongers' Company.

HOW TO APPLY Applicants should send a brief outline of their work, including an sae. The trust will send an application form to those which fit its criteria. The committee meets twice a year in March and October; applications should be received before the end of January and the end of August.

WHO TO APPLY TO Ms H Sant, Charities Administrator, Ironmongers' Hall, Barbican, London EC2Y 8AA *Tel* 020 7776 2311 *Website* www.ironhall.co.uk

CC NO 238256   **ESTABLISHED** 1964

568

Does the trust you have chosen match your needs? Haphazard applications waste postage and time

■ The Charles Irving Charitable Trust

WHERE FUNDING CAN BE GIVEN Mainly Gloucestershire.

WHO CAN BENEFIT People who are older, disabled or homeless; victims of abuse, crime and domestic violence; and people with mental illness.

WHAT IS FUNDED Disability, mental health, older people in the community, local community projects, homelessness and victim support.

WHAT IS NOT FUNDED Research, expeditions, computers or equipment are not supported unless benefiting people who are disabled.

TYPE OF GRANT Capital, project and recurring.

RANGE OF GRANTS £50–£5,000. Larger grants are rarely given.

SAMPLE GRANTS £24,615 to Gloucestershire Association for Mental Health as a one-off grant; £2,000 each to Eye Therapy Trust, Gloucestershire Cloud 9 Project, New Bridge, and Sue Ryder Care; £1,275 to Marie Curie Cancer Care; £1,200 to Guild of Disabled Homeworkers; £1,000 each to National Meningitis Trust, National Star Centre, and Stroud and District Mentally Handicapped Society.

FINANCES *Year* 2000–01 *Income* £64,000 *Grants* £84,000 *Assets* £1,300,000

TRUSTEES A P Hilder; Mrs J E Lane; D J Oldham; P W Shephard.

HOW TO APPLY In writing to the correspondent, giving details of the proposed project, its total cost and the amount (if any) already raised or promised from other sources.

WHO TO APPLY TO Mrs J E Lane, Trustee, Wood End, Sandy Lane Road, Charlton Kings, Cheltenham, Gloucestershire GL53 9DA *Tel* 01242 572116 *Fax* 01242 263736

CC NO 297712   **ESTABLISHED** 1987

■ Irwin Trust

WHERE FUNDING CAN BE GIVEN UK and overseas.

WHO CAN BENEFIT Charities concerned with Christianity, relief of sickness, promotion of health, advancement of education and benefit to the community.

WHAT IS FUNDED General charitable purposes.

SAMPLE GRANTS £25,000 to Mount Sandel Christian Fellowship; £10,000 to Relief for Oppressed People Everywhere; £5,000 to Goldhill Baptist Church, Chalfont St Peter; £1,000 to Gioventu in Missione (YWAM) Italy; £250 to CMC Pensarn Harbour.

FINANCES *Year* 1998–99 *Income* £64,000 *Grants* £42,000 *Assets* £255,000

TRUSTEES T R Irwin; Mrs E J Irwin.

HOW TO APPLY In writing to the correspondent.

WHO TO APPLY TO T R Irwin, Trustee, Beechcroft, Camp Road, Gerrards Cross, Bucks SL9 7PG *Tel* 01753 883756 *Fax* 01753 893689

CC NO 1061646   **ESTABLISHED** 1997

■ The ISA Charity

WHERE FUNDING CAN BE GIVEN UK.

WHO CAN BENEFIT Registered charities only.

WHAT IS FUNDED General charitable purposes.

FINANCES *Year* 1999–2000 *Income* £25,457 *Grants* £52,000 *Assets* £557,880

TRUSTEES R Paice; Mrs M Paice; A Paice.

HOW TO APPLY The trust states that all funds have been allocated for several years ahead. The trust states that unsolicited applications cannot be considered nor responded to.

WHO TO APPLY TO R Paice, Trustee, ISA (Holdings) Ltd, 29–35 Rathbone Street, London W1P 1NJ *Tel* 020 7636 4301

CC NO 326882   **ESTABLISHED** 1985

■ The Isaacs Charitable Trust

WHERE FUNDING CAN BE GIVEN UK and Israel.

WHO CAN BENEFIT Registered charities.

WHAT IS FUNDED Jewish charities and general charitable purposes, particularly medical causes. The trustees tend to support favoured projects.

TYPE OF GRANT Recurrent and one-off.

RANGE OF GRANTS £500–£6,000.

SAMPLE GRANTS £6,000 to Jewish Care; £2,500 each to British Friends of Laniado Hospital and Child Resettlement Fund; £2,000 each to British Friends of the New Synagogue of Netanya and Norwood Ravenswood; £1,500 each to British Heart Foundation, Marie Curie Foundation and Scope.

FINANCES *Year* 1999–2000 *Income* £36,000 *Grants* £35,000 *Assets* £208,000

TRUSTEES J E Isaacs; N D Isaacs; M C Sefton-Green.

HOW TO APPLY This trust's income is fully committed to its current list of donees. New applications are not considered.

WHO TO APPLY TO Nathan David Isaacs, Trustee, 11 Grantham Close, Edgware, Middlesex HA8 8DL *Tel* 020 8958 7854

CC NO 264590   **ESTABLISHED** 1972

■ The Isle of Anglesey Charitable Trust

WHERE FUNDING CAN BE GIVEN The Isle of Anglesey only.

WHO CAN BENEFIT Charitable, sporting and voluntary organisations benefiting residents of the Isle of Anglesey. Particularly children and young adults, students, teachers, and sportsmen and women.

WHAT IS FUNDED Leisure and heritage; social services; education; and churches and chapels. Half the funds go to the Isle of Anglesey County Council.

WHAT IS NOT FUNDED Individuals; projects based outside Anglesey.

TYPE OF GRANT One-off and recurring.

SAMPLE GRANTS £67,000 to Holyhead CAB.

FINANCES *Year* 2000–01 *Income* £601,000 *Grants* £431,000

TRUSTEES The County Council. George Alun Williams is chair of the trust.

HOW TO APPLY In writing to the correspondent, following advertisements in the local press. The trust considers applications once a year.

WHO TO APPLY TO David Elis-Williams, Treasurer, Isle of Anglesey County Council, County Offices, Llangefni LL77 7TW *Tel* 01248 752603 *Fax* 01248 752696

CC NO 1000818   **ESTABLISHED** 1990

■ Isle of Dogs Community Foundation

WHERE FUNDING CAN BE GIVEN The Isle of Dogs (i.e. the pre-2002 wards of Blackwall and Millwall) in the London borough of Tower Hamlets.

WHO CAN BENEFIT Community organisations serving the area defined above or having direct impact on the area. Organisations benefiting people of all ages, unemployed people, volunteers, parents and children and people living in urban areas.

WHAT IS FUNDED Organisations working in the fields of community development; education and youth; and training and employment. Support may also be given to arts activities and education; voluntary organisations; cultural activities; health counselling; support and self-help groups; and health education and health promotion.

WHAT IS NOT FUNDED IDCF will not fund: individuals; projects with primarily religious activities; projects with primarily political activities; projects/activities that are a statutory service; activities that are the responsibility of the local or health authorities; activities that have already taken place.

TYPE OF GRANT The foundation's current policy is to offer: 'Fastrack' grants up to £800 – normally for one-off projects or capital needs; 'Standard' grants up to £10,000 per annum for three years – normally for revenue costs and depending on funds available; and training grants of up to £100.

RANGE OF GRANTS £100–£10,000; typical grant £2,000.

SAMPLE GRANTS £10,000 to Splash for a senior youth worker; £8,000 to Quaystone Christian Church for a family project; £7,000 each to the Cedar Centre for computer training, Digital Artwave for equipment and Trees for London for equipment; £6,000 to Tower Hamlets Chinese Association for an employment project; £5,000 each to East London Schools Fund for a home school support worker and Woolmore School for playground enhancment; £4,000 to Training Trust for specialist IT classes; £3,000 to Tower Hamlets Age Concern for a handyperson project.

FINANCES *Year* 2001–02 *Income* £985,579 *Grants* £1,874,000 *Assets* £3,600,000

TRUSTEES Richard Haeyes, Chair; Christine Frost, Chair of Grants; Mark Bensted; David Chesterton; Jonathan Davie; Adrian Greenwood; Helen Jenner; Zinnat Ahmed; Mohammad Shahid Ali; Heather Bird; Dermot O'Brien; Ric Papineau; Anthony Partington; Martin Young; Alan Amos.

PUBLICATIONS *Regenerating the Isle of Dogs: A Consultation and Baseline Study 2002.*

HOW TO APPLY Application procedures for the three types of grant awarded are as follows: Training grants – By letter, no more than one page of A4; Fast track grants – Through a two-page application form, available from the foundation; Standard grants – After discussion with the director, by using the 'single application form' currently being piloted by some London funders. This is available from the foundation. The grants committee meets every month, except August. Trustees consider the committees' standard grant recommendations at meetings in January, March, May, July, September and November. Fast track and training grant applications do not go to the main board and these grants are usually paid shortly after the meeting.

WHO TO APPLY TO Janet Kennedy, Director, Jack Dash House, 2 Lawn House Close, Isle of Dogs, London E14 9YQ *Tel* 020 7345 4444 *Fax* 020 7538 4671 *Website* www.idcf.org
CC NO 802942   **ESTABLISHED** 1990

■ The ITF Seafarers Trust

WHERE FUNDING CAN BE GIVEN UK and overseas.

WHO CAN BENEFIT Seafarers of all nations and their dependants.

WHAT IS FUNDED Seafaring organisations; and the social welfare of seafarers of all nations, their families and dependants.

TYPE OF GRANT Buildings, capital, one-off, project, training and education.

RANGE OF GRANTS Up to £1,500,000.

SAMPLE GRANTS £1,174,376 to Japan Seamen's Relief Association; £816,591 in 3 grants to Scandinavian Seamen's Services; £609,013 in 11 grants to (B) ISS; £578,847 in 11 grants to Ministry to Seafarers in Indonesia; £537,404 to Apostleship of the Sea; £397,993 in 7 grants to German Seamen's Mission; £367,060 in 19 grants to Mission to Seafarers; £246,652 in 2 grants to United Seamen's Service; £181,681 in 5 grants to Scandinavian Seamen's Mission; £81,599 in 4 grants to Seamen's Church Institute; £68,700 in 4 grants to Baptist agencies in USA; £51,828 in 4 grants to Les Amis des Marins agency; £25,819 in 2 grants to Confederation of Independent Seafarers' Clubs in Ukraine; £20,702 to Lide – ISCM; £19,289 in 3 grants to Seamen's Christain Friend Society.

FINANCES *Year* 2000–01 *Income* £8,695,000 *Grants* £11,583,852 *Assets* £40,799,000

TRUSTEES J Bowers; David Cockroft; W M Morris; T R M Thomas; Bob Baete; U Purdhit; B Orrell; Thomas Tay.

HOW TO APPLY On a form available from the correspondent. Applications must be supported by an ITF affiliated seafarers' or dockers' trade union and have a proven record of dealing with seafarers' welfare.

WHO TO APPLY TO David Cockroft, Secretary, 49–60 Borough Road, London SE1 1DS *Tel* 020 7403 2733 *Fax* 020 7357 7871 *E-mail* trust@itf.org.uk *Website* www.itf.org.uk
CC NO 281936   **ESTABLISHED** 1981

■ J A R Charitable Trust

WHERE FUNDING CAN BE GIVEN Worldwide.

WHO CAN BENEFIT Organisations benefiting older people, students, Roman Catholics, missionaries, and people disadvantaged by poverty.

WHAT IS FUNDED The advancement of the Roman Catholic religion; education for people under 30; and the provision of food, clothing and accommodation for people in need over 55.

TYPE OF GRANT One-off and recurring.

RANGE OF GRANTS £200–£5,000.

SAMPLE GRANTS 1998–99: £10,000 to Westminster Cathedral 1995 Charitable Trust; £8,000 each to Diocese of Brentwood, Schools at Somerhill Charitable Trust, Ursuline Convent, and Ursuline Sisters; £1,000 each to Archdiocese of Liverpool, Cardinal Hume Centre, Diocese of Middlesbrough, Dyslexia Association, LIFE, and Westminster Cathedral Night Shelter.

FINANCES *Year* 2001–02 *Income* £58,745

TRUSTEES Philip R Noble; Revd William Young; Revd Paschal Ryan.

HOW TO APPLY In writing to the correspondent. Please note that the trust's funds are fully committed to regular beneficiaries and it states that there is very little, if any, for unsolicited appeals.

WHO TO APPLY TO Philip R Noble, Trustee, c/o Vernor Miles & Noble, 5 Raymond Buildings, Gray's Inn, London WC1R 5DD *Tel* 020 7242 8688

CC NO 248418   **ESTABLISHED** 1966

■ The J J Charitable Trust

WHERE FUNDING CAN BE GIVEN Unrestricted.

WHO CAN BENEFIT Charities benefiting children with learning difficulties particularly dyslexia, ex-offenders and people at risk of offending.

WHAT IS FUNDED Literacy: to improve the effectiveness of literacy teaching in the primary and secondary education sectors for children with general or specific learning difficulties, including dyslexia, and to do the same through agencies working with ex-offenders or people at risk of offending. Also helping those who have become disaffected from education and who now find themselves homeless or in prison. Environment UK: to support environmental education, particularly supporting projects displaying practical ways of involving children and young adults. Support is rarely given to new educational resource packs in isolation from the actual process of learning and discovering. More interest is shown to programmes which help pupils and teachers develop a theme over a time, perhaps combining IT resources for data gathering and communication, with exchange visits and the sharing of information and ideas between schools. There is also an interest in the sustainable transport, energy efficiency and renewable energy in the wider society. Environment overseas: to support community-based agriculture projects which aim to help people to help themselves in an environmentally sustainable way. General: especially the education and social welfare of children who are disadvantaged.

RANGE OF GRANTS £500–£100,000.

SAMPLE GRANTS £120,000 to St Mungo's for employment costs of a literacy teacher in the 'Make it Work' scheme in five London hostels for people who are homeless; £59,250 to Inside Out Trust for the establishment and extension of literacy training in its prison work programmes; £50,000 to Envolve for expansion of the staff capacity for environmental education outreach work in Bath and North East Somerset schools (£30,000 over three years) and establishing and launching a travel club in Bath (£20,000); £48,262 to Henry Doubleday Research Association for the schools organic network project; £48,000 over three years to FARM Africa for a community training programme for the conservation of the Nou Forest in Tanzania; £45,000 to SOS Sahel International for the support of Meru dryland communities as they improve farming and natural resources management to avoid environmental degradation; £36,000 to Old Ford Housing Association for a CD-ROM to promote literacy skills among trainees in the construction industry for use initially in east London colleges and then throughout the UK; £35,950 to Springboard for Children for the extension of literacy learning support to a school in Southwark and two schools in Lambeth; £30,000 over two years each to Environ for salary costs and Transport 2000 Trust for core costs.

FINANCES *Year* 2001–02 *Income* £2,520,314 *Grants* £748,000 *Assets* £18,169,268

TRUSTEES Julian Sainsbury; Mark Sainsbury; Miss Judith Portrait.

OTHER INFORMATION The trust is one of the Sainsbury Family Charitable Trusts which share a common administration. An application to one is taken as an application to all.

HOW TO APPLY Proposals are generally invited by the trustees or initiated at their request. Unsolicited applications are nort encouraged and are unlikely to be successful.

WHO TO APPLY TO Michael Pattison, Director, Allington House, 1st Floor, 150 Victoria Street, London SW1E 5AE *Tel* 020 7410 0330 *Fax* 020 7410 0332

CC NO 1015792   **ESTABLISHED** 1992

■ The J R S S T Charitable Trust

WHERE FUNDING CAN BE GIVEN UK.

WHO CAN BENEFIT Organisations or individuals undertaking research or action in fields which relate directly to the non-charitable work of the Joseph Rowntree Reform Trust Ltd. Academics and research workers may benefit.

WHAT IS FUNDED The trust works in close association with the Joseph Rowntree Reform Trust Ltd, which is a non-charitable trust of which all the trustees of The JRSST Charitable Trust are directors, in supporting the development of an increasingly democratic and socially just UK.

WHAT IS NOT FUNDED No student grants are funded.

TYPE OF GRANT Specific project finance in particular fields of trust interest.

RANGE OF GRANTS £50–£25,000.

SAMPLE GRANTS £354,167 to Institute for Citizenship for the Democracy through Citizenship Project; £38,121 to Investigation in Private Finance Initiative; £33,840 to Future of Philanthropy Project; £25,000 to UK Noise Association.

FINANCES *Year* 2001 *Income* £181,776 *Grants* £466,947 *Assets* £3,134,890

Think carefully about every application. Is it justified?

571

TRUSTEES Archibald J Kirkwood, Chair; Trevor A Smith (Lord Smith of Clifton); David A Currie (Lord Currie of Marylebone); Christine J Day; Christopher J Greenfield; Diana E Scott; Pam Giddy.
HOW TO APPLY The trustees meet quarterly. They do not invite applications.
WHO TO APPLY TO Tina Walker, The Garden House, Water End, York YO30 6WQ *Tel* 01904 625744 *Website* www.jrrt.org.uk
CC NO 247498   **ESTABLISHED** 1955

■ **The Sir Barry Jackson Trust and County Fund (incorporating Horton Trust)**

WHERE FUNDING CAN BE GIVEN West Midlands.
WHO CAN BENEFIT Organisations benefiting actors and entertainment professionals and those involved in theatre production.
WHAT IS FUNDED Theatrical productions, particularly those touring in the West Midlands; training of disadvantaged young people in the performing arts.
WHAT IS NOT FUNDED No grants to individuals. Support is only given to established touring companies.
RANGE OF GRANTS £5,000–£42,500.
SAMPLE GRANTS £38,000 to Birmingham Repertory Theatre Limited; £9,000 to Big Brum TIE Company Limited.
FINANCES *Year* 2002 *Income* £73,000 *Grants* £53,000 *Assets* £2,000,000
TRUSTEES R S Burman, Chair; L A Chorley; D B Edgar; Ms J Hytch; Prof. J H Kaplan; Ms K Horton; Cllr J E C Alden; B W Tanner; A Allan; A Collins.
HOW TO APPLY In writing to the correspondent. Trustees meet three to four times a year.
WHO TO APPLY TO Ian A King, Secretary, c/o Baker Tilly, City Plaza, Temple Row, Birmingham B2 5AF *Tel* 0121 214 3100 *Fax* 0121 214 3101
CC NO 517306   **ESTABLISHED** 1935

■ **The Jacksons Charitable Trust**

WHERE FUNDING CAN BE GIVEN UK, with a preference for London.
WHO CAN BENEFIT Jewish organisations, and a range of other charities.
WHAT IS FUNDED Advancement of the Jewish faith and general charitable purposes.
RANGE OF GRANTS £200–£9,200.
SAMPLE GRANTS £8,500 to Community Security Trust; £7,650 to Norwood Ravensworth; £6,600 to Teenage Cancer Trust; £3,100 to Western Marble Arch Synagogue; £3,000 to Nightingale House; £2,500 to Variety Club; £2,300 to Raleigh International Trust; £1,000 each to St Christopher's School, North London College School and Donmar.
FINANCES *Year* 1999–2000 *Income* £58,000 *Grants* £44,000 *Assets* £482,000
TRUSTEES Michael Goldhill; Dr David Goldhill; Simon Goldhill.
HOW TO APPLY In writing to the correspondent.
WHO TO APPLY TO Mark Green, Leigh Saxton Green, No. 1 Marylebone High Street, London W1U 4NQ *Tel* 020 7486 5553
CC NO 328114   **ESTABLISHED** 1989

■ **Jacobs Charitable Trust**

WHERE FUNDING CAN BE GIVEN Unrestricted.
WHAT IS FUNDED Jewish charities and arts organisations are supported.
SAMPLE GRANTS £209,000 to Haifa University; £175,000 to Tate Gallery; £65,000 to Royal Opera House; £35,000 to Jewish Care Association; £12,000 to Israel Philharmonic Orchestra; £10,000 each to Central Synagogue, Imperial War Museum, National Theatre and Ravenswood.
FINANCES *Year* 2000–01 *Income* £926,000 *Grants* £573,000
TRUSTEES Lord Jacobs, Chair; Lady Jacobs.
HOW TO APPLY In writing to the correspondent.
WHO TO APPLY TO The Rt Hon Lord Jacobs, Chair, 9 Nottingham Terrace, London NW1 4QB *Tel* 020 7486 6323
CC NO 264942   **ESTABLISHED** 1972

■ **The Dorothy Jacobs Charity**

WHERE FUNDING CAN BE GIVEN UK.
WHO CAN BENEFIT Charities nominated in the trust deed.
WHAT IS FUNDED The trust supports medical causes, including medical research and Jewish organisations. It supports 15 nominated charities.
TYPE OF GRANT Recurrent.
SAMPLE GRANTS 15 nominated charities are listed in the trust deed – three hospitals, four Jewish charities, three cancer-related charities, and five others: Arthritis and Rheumatism Council, BBC Children in Need, British Red Cross, Oxfam and Scope.
FINANCES *Year* 2001 *Income* £19,570 *Grants* £62,000 *Assets* £592,000
TRUSTEES R H Moss; A M Alexander.
HOW TO APPLY The trust states that it cannot accept unsolicited applications.
WHO TO APPLY TO R H Moss, Trustee, Heywards, St George's House, 15 Hanover Square, London W1R 0HE *Tel* 020 7629 7826
CC NO 328430   **ESTABLISHED** 1989

■ **The J P Jacobs Charitable Trust**

WHERE FUNDING CAN BE GIVEN UK, with a preference for Merseyside, and overseas.
WHO CAN BENEFIT Registered charities concerned with health, older people and young people, overseas development (usually through a Jewish or Christian organisation).
WHAT IS NOT FUNDED No support for individuals.
RANGE OF GRANTS £50–£7,500, typically £1,000 or less. Some income is accumulated each year to enable the trust to make larger donations.
SAMPLE GRANTS £110,000 to Actors Professional Centre Ltd; £10,000 to Actors Professional Centre Ltd; £7,500 to Lake District Art Gallery; £5,000 each to Liverpool Jewish Youth Centre and New Israel Fund of Great Britain; £3,000 to Cumbria Rivers Foundation; £2,500 each to Cambridge Foundation and Handel House Trust; £1,000 each to Eden Project and Stonewall Lobby Group.
FINANCES *Year* 2000–01 *Income* £108,021 *Grants* £178,000 *Assets* £1,705,938
TRUSTEES David Swift; Paula Swift.
HOW TO APPLY The trust stated that funds are fully committed and new applications cannot be considered.

WHO TO APPLY TO G Young, 9 Southwood Park, Southwood Lawn Road, London N6 5SG *Tel* 020 8348 4287 *Fax* 020 8348 4287
CC NO 263161   ESTABLISHED 1971

■ The Ruth & Lionel Jacobson Trust (Second Fund) No 2

WHERE FUNDING CAN BE GIVEN UK, with a preference for north east England.
WHO CAN BENEFIT Organisations benefiting people of all ages, medical professionals, parents and children, people who are disabled, people who are sick, people who have had strokes or who are terminally ill, homeless people, refugees and victims of famine.
WHAT IS FUNDED Organisations working in the fields of holiday accommodation and residential facilities, support for voluntary organisations, the Jewish religion, health, animal/bird sanctuaries and nature reserves, special needs education and speech therapy and various community facilities and services.
WHAT IS NOT FUNDED No grants for individuals. Only registered charities will be supported.
TYPE OF GRANT One-off, project and research. Funding is available for one year or less.
RANGE OF GRANTS £50–£10,000; typical grant £100–£500.
SAMPLE GRANTS £15,000 to Northumbria Calvert Trust for a holiday complex for people who are disabled; £12,500 to Joint Jewish Charitable Trust; £5,000 to Cancer Bridge for cancer care; £2,000 each to Classworks Theatre for theatre in education, Spinal Injuries Association, Rehab UK, and Sunderland Talmudical College; £1,000 each to Redcar and Cleveland Museums for acquisition and UNICEF.
FINANCES *Year* 1999–2000 *Income* £77,582 *Grants* £72,597 *Assets* £1,141,912
TRUSTEES Irene Ruth Jacobson; Malcolm Jacobson.
HOW TO APPLY In writing to the correspondent. Please enclose an sae. Applications are considered every other month.
WHO TO APPLY TO Mrs I R Jacobson, Trustee, High Wray, 35 Montagu Avenue, Newcastle upon Tyne NE3 4JH
CC NO 326665   ESTABLISHED 1984

■ The Yvette and Hermione Jacobson Charitable Trust

WHERE FUNDING CAN BE GIVEN London and North Yorkshire.
WHO CAN BENEFIT Registered charities working with young people, people who are disabled and older people.
WHAT IS NOT FUNDED No grants to individuals.
TYPE OF GRANT £20–£19,000; mostly under £500.
SAMPLE GRANTS 1997–98: £19,000 to JPAIME; £3,000 to Jewish Care; £1,000 to West London Synagogue; £500 each to St Mary's Hospital, World Jewish Relief, Wizo Charitable Trust, and JNF Charitable Trust; £400 to Cystic Fibrosis; £200 each to Norwood Ravenswood and Nightingale House.
FINANCES *Year* 2001–02 *Income* £26,780
TRUSTEES Mrs H Allen; Miles Allen.
HOW TO APPLY In writing to the correspondent.
WHO TO APPLY TO Mrs Hermione Allen, Trustee, 5 Cotman Close, London NW11 6QD
CC NO 264491   ESTABLISHED 1972

■ John James Bristol Foundation

WHERE FUNDING CAN BE GIVEN UK, mainly Bristol.
WHO CAN BENEFIT Usually only charitable bodies who can clearly show that they are benefiting Bristol residents.
WHAT IS FUNDED Educational and medical causes and the welfare of older people are the key focus areas.
WHAT IS NOT FUNDED No grants to individuals.
SAMPLE GRANTS £259,530 to United Bristol Health Care Trust – Bristol Royal Hospital for Children; £85,000 to Bristol Light Opera Company; £74,559 to University of Bristol – Bowel Cancer Research; £50,000 each to Industrial Therapy Organisation and Leonard Cheshire Cossham Gardens; eight grants of £30,000 each including those to Bristol Cathedral School, Clifton High School, Colston Girls' School, Queen Elizabeth Hospital and Red Maids' School.
FINANCES *Year* 2001–02 *Grants* £1,130,496 *Assets* £27,000,000
TRUSTEES Joan Johnson; David Johnson; Elizabeth Chambers; Jacqueline Marsh; Michael Cansdale; John Evans.
HOW TO APPLY In writing to the correspondent.
WHO TO APPLY TO Julia Norton, Administrator, 7 Clyde Road, Redland, Bristol BS6 6RG *Tel* 0117 923 9444 *Fax* 0117 923 9470
CC NO 288417   ESTABLISHED 1983

■ The James Pantyfedwen Foundation

WHERE FUNDING CAN BE GIVEN Wales.
WHO CAN BENEFIT Welsh people; and organisations in Wales benefiting children, young adults, clergy, musicians, students, Christians, at risk groups, people disadvantaged by poverty and homeless people.
WHAT IS FUNDED Church buildings; religious purposes; students (mainly for postgraduate study); registered charities; local Eisteddfodau; and Sunday Schools. Charities working in the field of Christian education; religious umbrella bodies; infrastructure, support and development; cultural activity; academic research; and various community services and facilities will be considered.
WHAT IS NOT FUNDED Revenue funding of any kind.
TYPE OF GRANT Variable, one-off for registered charities and churches; recurrent for students. Buildings, capital, interest-free loans, projects, and start-up costs will also be considered.
RANGE OF GRANTS Up to a maximum of £8,000 in special cases; lower maximum in other cases.
SAMPLE GRANTS £8,000 to National Eisteddfod, Denbigh; £5,000 each to Woodville Baptist Church – Cardiff and Eaton Road Methodist Church – Swansea; £4,000 to Urdd Gobaith Cymru; £3,000 each to St Mary the Virgin Church – Troedrhiwgarth, St Michael Church – Maesteg and Unitarian Churches Ministerial Training Fund; £2,000 each to a range of local churches.
FINANCES *Year* 2001–02 *Income* £424,686 *Grants* £347,660 *Assets* £8,282,183
TRUSTEES There are 24 trustees in all. A full list is available in the annual report. It includes Emrys Wynn Jones, Chair.
HOW TO APPLY Applications should be made on a form available from the correspondent. Applications from churches and registered charities can be submitted at any time (trustees meet about five times a year in March, May, July, September and December); student

applications should be submitted before 31 July in the academic year for which the application is being made. All unsuccessful applicants receive a reply.

WHO TO APPLY TO Richard H Morgan, Executive Secretary, Pantyfedwen, 9 Market Street, Aberystwyth SY23 1DL *Tel* 01970 612806 *Fax* 01970 612806
E-mail pantyfedwen@btinternet.com
CC NO 1069598   **ESTABLISHED** 1998

■ The Susan and Stephen James Charitable Settlement (also known as the Stephen James Charitable Trust)

WHERE FUNDING CAN BE GIVEN UK.
WHO CAN BENEFIT Registered charities; Jewish organisations.
WHAT IS FUNDED General charitable purposes.
SAMPLE GRANTS £7,700 to Norwood Ravenswood; £7,400 to Jewish Care; £2,500 to Community Security Trust; £1,100 to Breakaway; £1,000 each to Joint Jewish Charitable Trust and Ramot Shapira – British Friends.
FINANCES *Year* 1999 *Income* £30,000 *Grants* £28,000
TRUSTEES S M James; Mrs S R James.
HOW TO APPLY In writing to the correspondent.
WHO TO APPLY TO S M James, Trustee, 4 Turner Drive, London NW11 6TX
CC NO 801622   **ESTABLISHED** 1988

■ The James Trust

WHERE FUNDING CAN BE GIVEN UK and overseas.
WHO CAN BENEFIT Principally Christian organisations benefiting Christians, young adults, older people, people disadvantaged by poverty, disaster victims, and refugees.
WHAT IS FUNDED Churches, Christian organisations and individuals. Support is primarily to Christian causes, the advancement of Christian religion and Anglican diocesan and Free Church umbrella bodies.
WHAT IS NOT FUNDED No grants to individuals not personally known to the trustees.
TYPE OF GRANT One-off, capital, projects, recurring costs, salaries and start-up costs. Funding is available for up to three years.
SAMPLE GRANTS £23,160 to Tearfund; £7,650 to Christian Aid; £3,575 to Bible Society; £3,500 to London City Mission; £2,000 to Scripture Union; £1,400 to Frontier Youth Trust.
FINANCES *Year* 2001 *Income* £7,000 *Grants* £125,000 *Assets* £26,000
TRUSTEES R J Todd; P Smith.
HOW TO APPLY In writing to the correspondent. Unsolicited applications are not acknowledged.
WHO TO APPLY TO R J Todd, Trustee, 27 Radway Road, Upper Shirley, Southampton, Hampshire SO15 7PL *Tel* 023 8078 8249
CC NO 800774   **ESTABLISHED** 1989

■ Lady Eda Jardine Charitable Trust

WHERE FUNDING CAN BE GIVEN Scotland.
WHO CAN BENEFIT Charitable organisations.
WHAT IS FUNDED General charitable purposes.
FINANCES *Grants* £55,000
HOW TO APPLY In writing to the correspondent by the end of April for consideration in July.

WHO TO APPLY TO Mrs L E Pennell, Trustees, Anderson Strathern, 48 Castle Street, Edinburgh EH2 3LX *Tel* 0131 220 2345
SC NO SC011599

■ The Jarman Charitable Trust

WHERE FUNDING CAN BE GIVEN Birmingham and district.
WHO CAN BENEFIT Organisations benefiting children, young adults, older people, one parent families, at risk groups, people who are disabled and homeless people. Also supported are people with Alzheimers's disease, arthritis and rheumatism, asthma, autism, cancer, cystic fibrosis, diabetes, head and other injuries, heart disease, multiple sclerosis, muscular dystrophy, spina bifida and hydrcepholus and people who have had strokes.
WHAT IS FUNDED Welfare work, church building extension schemes and general social services in the Birmingham district. This includes convalescent homes, hospices, hospitals, nursing homes, rehabilitation centres, cancer research, community centres and village halls, day centres, holidays and outings, youth work and playschemes.
WHAT IS NOT FUNDED There is a preference for registered charities. No grants to individuals.
TYPE OF GRANT Annual donations and one-off payments.
RANGE OF GRANTS £30–£250.
FINANCES *Year* 2001–02 *Income* £37,000 *Grants* £34,000 *Assets* £768,000
TRUSTEES Dr G M Jarman; Mrs S Chilton; Mrs B J Jarman; Mrs I Jarman.
HOW TO APPLY In writing to the correspondent by the third week in February or the third week in September. Trustees meet in spring and autumn. The trust does not want telephone calls and will not acknowledge applications even if an sae is enclosed. Accounts and/or budgets should be included.
WHO TO APPLY TO Mrs S M Chilton, Trustee, 52 Lee Cresceny, Edgbaston, Birmingham, West Midlands B15 2BJ
CC NO 239198   **ESTABLISHED** 1964

■ The John Jarrold Trust

WHERE FUNDING CAN BE GIVEN UK and overseas, but mostly Norfolk.
WHO CAN BENEFIT Organisations benefiting academics, research workers and students.
WHAT IS FUNDED General charitable purposes of all kinds and in particular of education and research in all or any of the natural sciences. Funds fully committed for a long time ahead.
WHAT IS NOT FUNDED Educational purposes that should be supported by the state will not be helped by the trust. Local groups outside of Norfolk are very unlikely to be supported unless there is a personal connection to the trust.
TYPE OF GRANT One-off.
RANGE OF GRANTS £50–£12,000.
SAMPLE GRANTS £12,000 to Norwich Cathedral Trust; £11,000 to Northern Ballet Theatre; £10,000 to Broadland Music Festival; £5,000 to Christopher Hepworth Organs Trust; £8,000 to UEA Sports Park; £5,000 each to East Anglian Air Ambulance and Norfolk Wildlife Trust; £3,000 to The Hamlet Centre; £2,000 each to King's Lynn Festival and National Asthma Campaign.
FINANCES *Year* 2001–02 *Income* £106,509 *Grants* £172,537 *Assets* £1,467,129

TRUSTEES A C Jarrold, Chair; R E Jarrold; P J Jarrold; Mrs D J Jarrold; Mrs J Jarrold; Mrs A G Jarrold; Mrs W A L Jarrold.

HOW TO APPLY Applications should be in writing and reach the correspondent before the trustees' meetings in January and July. Grants of up to £250 can be made between meetings.

WHO TO APPLY TO Brian Thompson, Secretary, Messrs Jarrold & Sons, Whitefriars, Norwich NR3 1SH *Tel* 01603 660211

CC NO 242029 **ESTABLISHED** 1965

....

■ JCA Charitable Foundation

WHERE FUNDING CAN BE GIVEN Israel.

WHO CAN BENEFIT Projects benefiting Jewish people, particularly children and those living in rural areas.

WHAT IS FUNDED The foundation helps the development of new settlements in Israel, the Kibbutzim and Moshavim, contributes to the resettlement of Jewish people in need, fosters viable agricultural and rural life to support them, and encourages other trusts and foundations to join it in partnership to fulfil its ideals. New projects in education and agricultural research are now the main interests of the JCA.

WHAT IS NOT FUNDED Grants are not awarded for individual students' tuition fees in Israel or elsewhere.

TYPE OF GRANT Loans, grants and feasibility studies. Funding may be given for one year or less.

SAMPLE GRANTS $250,000 to Volcani Centre; $110,000 each to The Agricultural Company of Galilee and The Centre Arava Development & Building Company; $100,000 to Kibbutz Ketura; $99,500 to Migal; $85,000 to Ramat Negev R & D; $80,000 to Kibbutz Neot Smadar; $70,000 to Eshkol Regional Council; $60,000 to Israel Oceanographic & Limnological Research; $58,000 to Ben Gurion University of the Negev.

FINANCES *Year* 1999 *Income* £1,257,000 *Grants* £990,000 *Assets* £37,874,000

TRUSTEES Sir Stephen Waley-Cohen, President; A Philippson; A Wormser; Y Admoni; J Jakobi; M Sebba; G Witkon; R Brickner; H Smouha; M Benhamou; G Wallier.

OTHER INFORMATION The amounts given in Sample Grants relate to US dollars.

HOW TO APPLY Full proposals should be sent to the office in Israel. Contact the address below for further information.

WHO TO APPLY TO T R Martin, Company Secretary, The Victoria Palace Theatre, Victoria Street, London SW1E 5EA *Tel* 020 7828 0600 *Fax* 020 7828 6882

CC NO 207031 **ESTABLISHED** 1891

....

■ The Jeffrey Charitable Trust

WHERE FUNDING CAN BE GIVEN Scotland and elsewhere.

WHO CAN BENEFIT Organisations benefiting seafarers and fishermen, volunteers, and people in care, or who are fostered or adopted.

WHAT IS FUNDED Primarily this trust is concerned with medical research, and carer organisations. It also considers holiday and respite accommodation; health; conservation; independent and special schools; tertiary, higher and special needs education; community facilities and transport; and emergency care for refugees and their families.

WHAT IS NOT FUNDED Animal-related charities, medical electives and projects eligible for statutory support are not considered.

TYPE OF GRANT One-off and recurring grants are most commonly made for capital, buildings, core costs, endowment, project, research, running costs, salaries and start-up costs. Funding is available for up to three years.

RANGE OF GRANTS £250–£20,000; typical grant £1,000–£1,500.

SAMPLE GRANTS £20,000 to Glasgow Royal Infirmary for HTR project – diabetes centre; £5,000 to Dunstans Home for the War-blinded for general purposes; £2,500 each to Morrison's Academy Appeal for bursary provision and Donaldson School for the Deaf for a development project; £2,000 each to Erskine Hospital for general purposes, Princess Royal Trust for Carers for general purposes, and Edinburgh Breast Cancer Foundation for general purposes; £1,359 to Salvation Army for general purposes; £1,000 each to Capability Scotland for general purposes and Crieff Parish Church for hall refurbishment.

FINANCES *Year* 2000 *Income* £68,000 *Grants* £53,000

TRUSTEES R B A Bolton; R S Waddell; Mrs M E Bolton.

HOW TO APPLY In writing to the correspondent, although due to continuing support to long-term projects and anticipated repeat grants to other organisations, new requests for assistance are unlikely to be successful in the short to medium term.

WHO TO APPLY TO R B A Bolton, Trustee, 29 Comrie Street, Crieff, Perthshire PH7 4BD *Tel* 01764 652224 *Fax* 01764 653999

SC NO SC015990 **ESTABLISHED** 1972

....

■ Rees Jeffreys Road Fund

WHERE FUNDING CAN BE GIVEN UK.

WHO CAN BENEFIT Universities, research bodies, academic staff and students, as well as proposers of roadside rest projects.

WHAT IS FUNDED The trustees will consider funding university teaching and postgraduate bursaries; research projects; roadside rests; and transport and alternative transport. Only subjects directly related with road and transportation will be considered.

WHAT IS NOT FUNDED Operational and administrative staff costs are rarely considered. Grants are not given to environmental projects not related to highways, individual works for cycle tracks or works of only local application.

TYPE OF GRANT Some one-off capital, some bursaries and others for research and lectureships including salaries and, in some cases, running costs and endowments. Funding is available for up to five years.

RANGE OF GRANTS £450–£30,000.

SAMPLE GRANTS £30,000 each to Leeds University towards the development of an International Knowledgebase on Urban Transport Instruments, Independent Transport Commission for research on transport pricing, taxation and investment and National Urban Forestry Unit to extend the Road Corridor Greening Programme; £25,000 each to Transport Research laboratory towards a study into demand for public transport and National Retail Planning Forum for research into the 'missing link' between town centre arrival points and key attractions; £15,000 to Nottingham University for research in to the design and maintenance of lightly trafficked roads; £12,000 to PACTS towards study into best value and

Think carefully about every application. Is it justified?

575

road safety; £10,000 each to the Greensand Trust for facilities at layby A6 south of Bedford, Highways Agency for a picnic site at Haggerston Castle – Northumberland, National Children's Bureau towards IT programmes, training for developing and linking school to 'Young Transnet' and Salford University for development for a distance learning module for transport MScs.

FINANCES *Year* 2002 *Income* £206,834 *Grants* £318,453 *Assets* £5,118,810

TRUSTEES P W Bryant, Chair; D Bayliss; Prof. S Glaister; M N T Cottell; Mrs June Bridgeman; Sir James Duncan; M J Kendrick; Prof. J Wootton.

HOW TO APPLY There is no set form of application for grants. Brief details should be submitted initially. Replies are sent to all applicants. A preliminary telephone call is helpful but not essential. The trustees meet five times in the year, usually in January, April, July, September and November.

WHO TO APPLY TO B Fieldhouse, Secretary, 13 The Avenue, Chichester, West Sussex PO19 4PX *Tel* 01243 787013 *Fax* 01243 790622 *E-mail* fieldhouse@reesjeffreys.co.uk

CC NO 217771 **ESTABLISHED** 1950

....
■ The Jenour Foundation

WHERE FUNDING CAN BE GIVEN UK, with a special interest in Wales.

WHO CAN BENEFIT Registered charities only.

WHAT IS FUNDED General charitable purposes. Both UK charities and local charities in Wales are supported.

WHAT IS NOT FUNDED No support for individuals.

RANGE OF GRANTS £500–£8,000.

SAMPLE GRANTS £8,000 to Red Cross International; £6,000 each to Atlantic College and Wales National Opera; £5,000 each to British Heart Foundation, Cancer Research Campaign, and Children's Hospital for Wales; £4,000 each to Princess of Wales Macmillan Cancer Care Centre, and Save the Children; £3,500 each to NSPCC for Cardiff Central Committee and Wales Council for the Blind.

FINANCES *Year* 2000–01 *Income* £99,584 *Grants* £96,500 *Assets* £2,370,764

TRUSTEES Sir P J Phillips; G R Camfield; D M Jones.

HOW TO APPLY Applications should be in writing and reach the correspondent by February for the trustees' meeting in March.

WHO TO APPLY TO Sir Peter Phillips, Trustee, Deloitte & Touche, Blenhein House, Fitzalan Court, Newport Road, Cardiff CF24 0TS *Tel* 029 2048 1111

CC NO 256637 **ESTABLISHED** 1968

....
■ The Jephcott Charitable Trust

WHERE FUNDING CAN BE GIVEN UK, developing countries overseas.

WHO CAN BENEFIT Organisations benefiting people of all ages, including research workers, carers, people who are disabled, disadvantaged by poverty or living in rural areas, and victims of domestic violence and victims of war. Preference is given to smaller projects (i.e. under £500,000 a year). New projects are favoured.

WHAT IS FUNDED The trust is concerned with the alleviation of poverty in developing countries. Priorities are population control, education, health and the environment. The policy is reviewed regularly. Other charitable purposes will be considered.

WHAT IS NOT FUNDED No grants to individuals, including students, or for medical research. No response to general appeals from large, UK organisations nor from organisations concerned with poverty and education in the UK. Core funding and/or salaries are rarely considered.

TYPE OF GRANT Usually one-off for a specific project or part of a project. Core funding and/or salaries are rarely considered. Start-up costs and funding of up to three years will be considered.

RANGE OF GRANTS £750–£16,000.

SAMPLE GRANTS £16,000 to Dorothea School in South Africa; £9,400 to Bazaruto Archipelago – Mozambique; £7,800 to Get It While You Can; £6,600 to Speakeasy Advice Centre; £6,500 to Inroads; £6,300 to HOESO – Uganda; £6,000 to Kindu Trust and St Lukes' Khayelitsha Day Hospice – South Africa; £5,500 to Friends of Swanirvar; £5,000 to St Michaels Church.

FINANCES *Year* 2000–01 *Income* £197,645 *Grants* £97,076 *Assets* £4,631,869

TRUSTEES Mrs M Jephcott, Chair; Dr P Davis; Judge A North; H Wolley; K Morgan; J Bunnell; Mrs C Thomas.

HOW TO APPLY Guidelines and application forms are available on request and receipt of an sae. Applications can be made in writing at any time to the correspondent. Trustees meet twice a year (in April and October) and must have detailed financial information about each project before they will make a decision. Only applications from eligible bodies are acknowledged, when further information about the project may be requested. Monitoring of grant expenditure is usually required.

WHO TO APPLY TO Mrs Meg Harris, Secretary, Cotley, Streatham Rise, Exeter EX4 4PE

CC NO 240915 **ESTABLISHED** 1965

....
■ The Jerusalem Trust

WHERE FUNDING CAN BE GIVEN Unrestricted.

WHO CAN BENEFIT Organisations working for the promotion of Christianity in the fields detailed below.

WHAT IS FUNDED Christian evangelism and relief work overseas, particularly for indigenous training and support and production of appropriate literature and resource materials for Christians in Anglophone Africa, central and eastern Europe, and the former Soviet Union; Christian media, particularly supporting training and networking projects for Christians working professionally in all areas of the media and for those considering media careers; Christian education, particularly the development of Christian school curriculum resource materials for RE and other subjects, support and training of Christian teachers of all subjects and lay training; Christian art, focused mainly on a small number of pro-active commissions of works of art for places of worship; Christian evangelism and social responsibility work at home, particularly Christian projects which develop new ways of working with children and young people and projects which promote Christian marriage and family life. Also church planting and evangelistic projects and those which undertake Christian work with prisoners, ex-prisoners and their families.

WHAT IS NOT FUNDED Trustees do not normally make grants towards building or repair work for churches. Grants are not normally made to individuals.

SAMPLE GRANTS £507,000 to Jerusalem Productions; £120,000 to Tearfund for relief and development work in Pakistan, Sierra Leone, Sudan and Yemen; £110,000 to Lambeth Partnership for the springboard evangelistic initiative; £90,000 to Evangelical Alliance for a bursary fund providing scholarships for overseas students studying in the UK who have leadership potential as Bible college principals or similar; £75,780 to Church Pastoral Aid Society to develop children's work within the churches; £75,000 to Walk Thru' the Bible to support the coordinator of the Junior Walk for Schools project; £72,220 to Keston College for developing the central Asian office; £72,000 to Langley House Trust for development work; £67,500 each to Reaching the Unchurched Network to support the development director, and Salmon Youth Centre for support to the director.

FINANCES *Year* 2000 *Income* £3,114,000 *Grants* £3,569,000 *Assets* £82,844,000

TRUSTEES Sir Timothy Sainsbury; Lady Susan Sainsbury; Dr V E Hartley Booth; Canon Gordon Bridger; Mrs Diana Wainman.

OTHER INFORMATION The trust is one of the Sainsbury Family Charitable Trusts which share a common administration. An application to one is taken as an application to all.

HOW TO APPLY Proposals are generally invited by the trustees or initiated at their request. Unsolicited applications are not encouraged and are unlikely to be successful.

WHO TO APPLY TO Michael Pattison, Director, Allington House, 1st Floor, 150 Victoria Street, London SW1E 5AE *Tel* 020 7410 0330 *Fax* 020 7410 0332

CC NO 285696   **ESTABLISHED** 1982

■ The Jerwood Foundation and the Jerwood Charitable Foundation

WHERE FUNDING CAN BE GIVEN UK, but with a limited special interest in UK organisations operating in Nepal.

WHO CAN BENEFIT Organisations benefiting young adults, actors, artists, medical professionals, musicians, research workers, writers, dancers and choreographers and directors and filmmakers.

WHAT IS FUNDED Principally education in its broadest sense and the visual and performing arts, but the trust also funds conservation, environment, medicine, film, literature, museums, science and engineering.

WHAT IS NOT FUNDED The Jerwood Charitable Foundation will not consider applications on behalf of individuals; building or capital costs (including purchase of equipment); projects in the fields of religion or sport; animal rights or welfare; general fundraising appeals which are likely to have wide public appeal; appeals to establish endowment funds for other charities; appeals for matching funding for National Lottery applications; grants for the running and core costs of voluntary bodies; projects which are of mainly local appeal or identified with a locality; medical research without current clinical applications and benefits; social welfare, particularly where it may be considered a government or local authority responsibility; retrospective awards. The trustees may, where there are very exceptional circumstances, decide to waive the exclusion.

TYPE OF GRANT Principally one-off, usually incorporating challenge funding, but will sometimes be prepared to maintain support if consistency will secure better results.

RANGE OF GRANTS Lower range will be around £5,000–£10,000, and the more substantial grants between £10,000–£50,000.

FINANCES *Year* 2001 *Grants* £5,600,000

TRUSTEES The Jerwood Foundation: Alan Grieve, Chair; Dr Peter Marxer; Dr Peter Marxer Jnr. The Jerwood Charitable Foundation: Alan Grieve, Chair; Edward Paul, Vice-chair; Viscount Chilston; Lady Harlech; Andrew Knight; Dr Kerry Parton; Julia Wharton; Anthony Palmer; Barbara Kalman; Tim Eyles.

HOW TO APPLY Applications should be by letter, outlining the aims and objectives of the organisation and the specific project for which assistance is sought. With the application the foundation needs a detailed budget for the project, identifying administrative, management and central costs; details of funding already in place for the project, including any other trusts or sources which are being or have been approached for funds: if funding is not in place, the foundation requires details of how the applicant plans to secure the remaining funding; details of the management and staffing structure, including trustees; the most recent annual report and audited accounts of the organisation, together with current management accounts if relevant to the project.

WHO TO APPLY TO Roanne Dods, Director, 22 Fitzroy Square, London W1T 6EN *Tel* 020 7388 6287 *Website* www.jerwood.org.uk

CC NO 1074036   **ESTABLISHED** 1999

■ Sir Charles Jessel Charitable Trust

WHERE FUNDING CAN BE GIVEN UK, particularly east Kent.

WHO CAN BENEFIT Individuals and registered charities.

WHAT IS FUNDED The trustees' particular interests are charities in east Kent, alternative holistic and non-toxic medicine and mental and emotional health. Grants are also occasionally given for animal welfare. Applications should be restricted to charities, groups or individuals who come within these categories. Requests from patients are best dealt with through their practitioners.

WHAT IS NOT FUNDED No educational grants for students, even those studying complementary and alternative therapies. No grants for expeditions.

TYPE OF GRANT One-off and annual grants.

SAMPLE GRANTS £5,000 to Nutritional Cancer Therapy Trust; £1,000 each to Bristol Cancer Help Centre and Environmental Research Association; £500 each to Hastingleigh Parochial Church Council and Psionic Medical Society.

FINANCES *Year* 2000–01 *Income* £33,000 *Grants* £17,000 *Assets* £824,000

TRUSTEES Sir Charles J Jessel; G E Jessel; M D Rust; Mrs D I V Jessel.

HOW TO APPLY In writing to the correspondent. Requests from patients are best dealt with through their practitioners.

WHO TO APPLY TO M N Tod, Hunters, 9 New Square, Lincoln's Inn, London WC2A 3QN

CC NO 263159   **ESTABLISHED** 1971

■ Jesus Hospital Charity

WHERE FUNDING CAN BE GIVEN Barnet, East Barnet and Friern Barnet Prior.

WHO CAN BENEFIT Individuals; and local organisations benefiting people of all ages, academics, research workers, scientists, students, unemployed people, volunteers, families, at risk groups, carers, people who are disabled, people with a medical condition or disease, people who are disadvantaged by poverty or who are socially isolated, and victims of abuse, crime and domestic violence.

WHAT IS FUNDED This trust will consider funding: almshouses; support to voluntary and community organisations; support to volunteers; respite care and care for carers; support and self-help groups; ambulances and mobile units; special needs education; training for work; costs of study; academic subjects, sciences and research; and community services.

WHAT IS NOT FUNDED No grants for relief of rates, taxes or other public funds.

TYPE OF GRANT Capital and one-off. Funding is available for one year or less. Each case is considered on its merits.

RANGE OF GRANTS Up to £5,850.

SAMPLE GRANTS £5,850 to Friends in Need for transport, rent, and relief-in-need; £3,625 to Chipping Barnet Day Centre for older people for transport, rent and relief-in-need; £3,200 each to Dollis Valley Project and Barnet College Educational Trust for relief-in-need for students; £2,295 to Chipping Barnet Trust Good Neighbour Scheme for general, relief-in-need and food vouchers; £1,440 to New Barnet Community Association for transport and general purposes; £1,325 to Dollis Valley Playscheme for needy children during school holidays; £1,270 to Friern Barnet Voluntary Care for older people for transport, rent and relief-in-need; £1,265 to Barnet Old People's Welfare Association for transport, rent and relief-in-need; £1,215 to Barnet Care Attendant Scheme for general purposes.

FINANCES *Year* 1999 *Income* £321,143 *Grants* £65,443 *Assets* £6,956,744

HOW TO APPLY In writing to the correspondent. Trustees meet six times a year to consider grants.

WHO TO APPLY TO The Clerk to the Visitors, Ravenscroft Lodge, 37 Union Street, Barnet, Hertfordshire EN5 4HY *Tel* 020 8440 4374

CC NO 1075889   **ESTABLISHED** 1679

■ Jewish Child's Day

WHERE FUNDING CAN BE GIVEN Worldwide.

WHO CAN BENEFIT Organisations caring for Jewish children.

WHAT IS FUNDED Specific purposes of direct benefit to Jewish children.

WHAT IS NOT FUNDED Individuals are not supported. Grants are not given towards general services, building or maintenance of property or staff salaries. No grants are made in response to general appeals from large UK organisations or to smaller bodies working in fields other than those set out above.

TYPE OF GRANT For medical or scientific equipment, educational material, playthings, clothing, medical supplies and so on of direct benefit to Jewish children with special needs. Grants are not made towards salaries or capital costs.

RANGE OF GRANTS £400–£102,230.

SAMPLE GRANTS £143,634 to Ashalim; £37,952 to Manchester Jewish Federation; £15,195 to

Merchavia; £12,200 to Micha Society for Deaf Children – Tel Aviv; £10,000 each to Cystic Fibrosis Foundation of Israel and Youth Aliya; £8,900 to Youth Aliya; £8,500 to Stamford Hill Community Centre; £8,000 to British Friends of Ramban Medical Centre; £7,919 to Eliya.

FINANCES *Year* 2001–02 *Income* £632,177 *Grants* £483,518 *Assets* £613,693

TRUSTEES The National Council.

PUBLICATIONS Newsletter published two or three times per annum; *50th Anniversary Commemorative Book.*

HOW TO APPLY There is an application form which needs to be submitted together with a copy of the latest annual report and accounts and any supporting information. The trustees meet to consider applications twice a year, usually in March and September/October; applications should be submitted two months earlier.

WHO TO APPLY TO P Shaw, Executive Director, 5th Floor, 707 High Road, North Finchley, London N12 0BT *Tel* 020 8446 8804 *Fax* 020 8446 7370 *E-mail* info@jewishchildsday.co.uk *Website* www.jewishchildsday.co.uk

CC NO 209266   **ESTABLISHED** 1947

■ The Jewish Youth Fund

WHERE FUNDING CAN BE GIVEN UK.

WHO CAN BENEFIT Jewish youth clubs, centres, movements and groups.

WHAT IS FUNDED Jewish youth work projects, equipment and premises.

WHAT IS NOT FUNDED Grants are not made in response to general appeals. Formal education is not supported.

TYPE OF GRANT Grants are made for a whole variety of Jewish youth work projects. Loans are sometimes offered towards the cost of building.

RANGE OF GRANTS £700–£15,000.

SAMPLE GRANTS £10,000 to Liverpool Jewish Youth and Community Centre; £7,500 to Habonim Dror; £5,400 to Redbridge Jewish Youth and Community Centre; £5,000 each to Friends of Bnei Akiva, Jewish Lads and Girls Brigade, Noam Masorti Youth, SPEC Jewish Youth and Community Centre, and Union of Maccabi Associations; £4,000 each to Kenton Maccabi Jewish Youth Club, and North Manchester Jewish Youth Project.

FINANCES *Year* 2000–01 *Income* £113,620 *Grants* £72,400 *Assets* £1,982,664

TRUSTEES Jonathan Gestetner; Richard McGratty; Lady Morris of Kenwood; Miss Wendy F Pollecoff.

HOW TO APPLY On an application form available from the correspondent, enclosing a copy of the latest accounts and an annual report.

WHO TO APPLY TO Peter Shaw, Secretary, 5th Floor, 707 High Road, North Finchley, London N12 0BT *Tel* 020 8445 1670 *Fax* 020 8446 7370 *E-mail* jyf@anjy.org

CC NO 251902   **ESTABLISHED** 1937

■ The JMK Charitable Trust

WHERE FUNDING CAN BE GIVEN Worldwide.

WHO CAN BENEFIT Registered charities only, benefiting children, particularly children who are sick.

WHAT IS FUNDED There is a preference for charities concerned with children's health.

RANGE OF GRANTS £500–£10,000.

SAMPLE GRANTS 1998–99: £10,000 each to Harefield Hospital and Royal Academy; £5,000

to Diana, Princess of Wales Memorial Fund;
£2,000 to Friends of Philharmonia.

FINANCES *Year* 2001–02 *Income* £74,476

TRUSTEES Mrs J M Karaviotis; J Karaviotis; R S
Parker.

HOW TO APPLY In writing to the correspondent. No
acknowledgement of receipt is given.

WHO TO APPLY TO The Trustees, Messrs Chantrey
Vellacott DFK, Prospect House, 58 Queen's
Road, Reading, Berkshire RG1 4RP *Tel* 0118
959 5432

CC NO 274576   **ESTABLISHED** 1977

■ The Harold Joels Charitable Trust

WHERE FUNDING CAN BE GIVEN UK and overseas.

WHO CAN BENEFIT Jewish organisations only, with a
possible preference for USA.

WHAT IS FUNDED General charitable purposes.

RANGE OF GRANTS £10–£15,000.

SAMPLE GRANTS £6,300 to Temple Beth Shalon;
£5,800 to World Jewish Relief; £2,500 each to
Jewish Care, Women's America Organisation
and Sarasota Manatee Jewish Federation;
£1,100 to US Holocaust Memorial Museum.

FINANCES *Year* 1999–2000 *Income* £40,000
Grants £24,000 *Assets* £648,000

TRUSTEES H Joels; Dr N Joels; Mrs V Joels; N E
Joels.

HOW TO APPLY In writing to the correspondent. This
entry was not confirmed by the trust, but the
information was correct according to the trust's
file at the Charity Commission.

WHO TO APPLY TO R A Lipman, Grunberg & Co, 13
Accommodation Road, London NW11 8ED
Tel 020 8458 0083

CC NO 206326   **ESTABLISHED** 1957

■ The Jonathan Joels Charitable Trust

WHERE FUNDING CAN BE GIVEN UK and overseas.

WHO CAN BENEFIT Registered charities only.

WHAT IS FUNDED General charitable purposes.

RANGE OF GRANTS $5–$17,336.

SAMPLE GRANTS In 1996: $17,336 to U J A
Federation of Bergen County & North Hudson;
$12,500 to Ramaz 2000 Fund; $6,635 to
Moriah School of Engelwood; $2,893 to
Congregation Ahavath Torah; $2,400 to Ramaz
Scholarship and Special Needs Fund; $2,000 to
Ramaz Scholarship Fund; $1,120 to Jewish
Community Center on the Pallisades; $575 to
Beit Yisrael Synagogue – Yemin Moshe; $360 to
Sinai Special Needs Institute; $300 to Yeshiva
Chanoch Lennar.

FINANCES *Year* 2000–01 *Income* £38,002

TRUSTEES J Joels; N E Joels; H Joels.

OTHER INFORMATION The figures in the Range of
Grants and Sample Grants are in US dollars.

HOW TO APPLY In writing only, to the address below.

WHO TO APPLY TO The Trustees, EBK Partnership,
311 Ballards Lane, Finchley, London N12 8LY

CC NO 278408   **ESTABLISHED** 1978

■ The Nicholas Joels Charitable Trust

WHERE FUNDING CAN BE GIVEN UK and overseas.

WHO CAN BENEFIT Registered charities only, with a
preference for Jewish charities.

WHAT IS FUNDED General charitable purposes.

RANGE OF GRANTS £10–£5,000.

SAMPLE GRANTS 1998–99: £5,000 to Norwood
Ravenswood; £1,800 to Joint Jewish Charitable
Trust; £1,100 to Scope; £950 to World Jewish
Relief; £850 to British Heart Foundation; £825
to Northwood United Synagogue; £525 to
Jewish Care; £500 to Youth Aliyah Child
Rescue; £370 to Great Ormond Street Hospital;
£350 to Barnardos; £300 each to Jewish Aid
Committee and Multiple Sclerosis Society.

FINANCES *Year* 2000–01 *Income* £22,581

TRUSTEES N E Joels; J Joels; H Joels.

HOW TO APPLY In writing to the correspondent.

WHO TO APPLY TO N Joels, Trustee, 20 Copse Wood
Way, Northwood, Middlesex HA6 2UF

CC NO 278409   **ESTABLISHED** 1978

■ The Norman Joels Charitable Trust

WHERE FUNDING CAN BE GIVEN UK, Israel and the
Middle East.

WHO CAN BENEFIT Registered charities only.

WHAT IS FUNDED General charitable purposes.

RANGE OF GRANTS £100–£3,500.

SAMPLE GRANTS £3,500 to Jewish Philanthropic
Association for Israel and the Middle East;
£1,400 to Friends of the Hebrew University of
Jerusalem; £1,100 to New London Synagogue.

FINANCES *Year* 1999–2000 *Income* £49,000
Grants £11,000 *Assets* £858,000

TRUSTEES Jessica L Joels; Norman Joels; Harold
Joels; Myriam Joels.

HOW TO APPLY In writing to the correspondent. This
entry was not confirmed by the trust, but the
information was correct according to the trust's
file at the Charity Commission.

WHO TO APPLY TO R A Lipman, Grunberg & Co, 13
Accommodation Road, London NW11 8ED
Tel 020 8458 0083

CC NO 206325   **ESTABLISHED** 1957

■ J G Joffe Charitable Trust

WHERE FUNDING CAN BE GIVEN Mainly the third world.

WHO CAN BENEFIT Registered charities only.

WHAT IS FUNDED Funds are fully committed to
charities of special interest to the trustees.
There is no intention to widen the range and
normally no applications will be considered.

TYPE OF GRANT One-off.

RANGE OF GRANTS £2,500–£66,000.

SAMPLE GRANTS £50,000 each to New Economics
Foundation (in two grants), and Basic Needs UK
Trust; £38,350 to The Green House Trust;
£25,000 each to Cambridge Female Education
Trust, Oxford University – Department for
Continuing Education, and Opportunity
International UK; £20,000 to Krotoa Science
Scholarship (South Africa); £15,305 to People's
Family Law Centre (South Africa); £15,000 each
to UK One World Linking Association, and
Students Partnership Worldwide.

FINANCES *Year* 2001–02 *Income* £278,000
Grants £452,000 *Assets* £10,869,414

TRUSTEES Mrs V L Joffe; Lord Joffe.

HOW TO APPLY Applications will not normally be
considered or acknowledged as the trustees
have a wide network of contacts in the voluntary
sector and the trust's resources are largely
committed for the foreseeable future.

WHO TO APPLY TO Joel Joffe, Liddington Manor, The
Street, Liddington, Swindon SN4 0HD

CC NO 270299   **ESTABLISHED** 1968

Think carefully about every application. Is it justified?

579

The Elton John Aids Foundation

WHERE FUNDING CAN BE GIVEN UK and overseas.
WHO CAN BENEFIT Organisations helping those people living with HIV/AIDS, or running AIDS prevention programmes.
WHAT IS FUNDED Projects concerned with the alleviation of the physical, mental and emotional hardship of people living with HIV/AIDS, and AIDS prevention programmes.
WHAT IS NOT FUNDED For both UK and international grants the foundation will not fund: capital costs; conferences or educational courses; drug treatment costs; individual grants; repatriation costs; research programmes; retrospective funding.
TYPE OF GRANT Revenue and specific projects. Core costs; one-off, running costs; and salaries. Funding may be given for one year or up to three years.
RANGE OF GRANTS £250–£150,000; average £20,000.
SAMPLE GRANTS £217,000 to Crusaid; £180,000 to EJAF USA; £169,000 to Sihanouk Hospital, Cambodia; £100,000 to IMIFAP, Mexico; £91,000 to St Francis Health Care, Uganda; £66,000 to International Family Health (Africa-wide); £62,000 to Wolfson Institute of Biomed; £60,000 to Community AIDS Response, South Africa; £56,000 to Food Chain; £50,000 each to CARE India, Laos HIV/AIDS Trust and Naz Foundation, India.
FINANCES *Year* 2001 *Income* £2,500,000 *Grants* £2,574,000 *Assets* £948,294
TRUSTEES Sir Elton John, chair; Robert Key; John Scott; David Furnish; Lynette Jackson; Neil Tennant; Frank Presland; Colin Bell; Anne Aslett; Margaret Littman; Johnny Bergius; James Locke; Tim Cohen, treasurer.
HOW TO APPLY Potential applicants should obtain a copy of the appropriate guidelines, either for the UK or international grants. Organisations applying to the foundation for funds must provide full information about their work, including their objectives and evaluation plan. Those applying to the UK small grants fund should include a copy of the latest annual report or accounts.
WHO TO APPLY TO Robert Key, Executive director, 1 Blythe Road, London W14 0HG *Tel* 020 7603 9996 *Website* www.ejaf.org
CC NO 1017336 **ESTABLISHED** 1993

Miss A M Johns Charitable Trust

WHERE FUNDING CAN BE GIVEN Beckenham.
WHO CAN BENEFIT Institutions in the area of Beckenham, Kent.
WHAT IS FUNDED General charitable purposes.
FINANCES *Year* 1998–99 *Income* £21,000 *Grants* £102,000 *Assets* £797,000
TRUSTEES S J Fraser; P J Castledine.
HOW TO APPLY In writing to the correspondent.
WHO TO APPLY TO P J Castledine, Trustee, 225–235 High Street, Beckenham, Kent BR3 1BN *Tel* 020 8663 0503
CC NO 1060135 **ESTABLISHED** 1990

The Miss E M Johnson Charitable Trust

WHERE FUNDING CAN BE GIVEN UK and overseas.
WHO CAN BENEFIT Welfare charities.
TYPE OF GRANT One-off and recurrent.
RANGE OF GRANTS £500–£3,000.
SAMPLE GRANTS £3,000 to Prison Reform Trust; £2,500 to Wolfson College Cambridge; £2,000 each to Amnesty International – UK Section Charitable Trust, London Detainee Support Group, Medical Foundation, Mind, St Christopher's Fellowship, The Samaritans and Simon Community.
FINANCES *Year* 1998–99 *Income* £31,000 *Grants* £22,000 *Assets* £407,000
TRUSTEES C F D Moore; Dr C J Kitching.
HOW TO APPLY In writing to the correspondent.
WHO TO APPLY TO David Gold, c/o Hunters, 9 New Square, Lincoln's Inn, London WC2A 3QN *Tel* 020 7412 0050
CC NO 267381 **ESTABLISHED** 1972

The Johnson Foundation

WHERE FUNDING CAN BE GIVEN Merseyside.
WHO CAN BENEFIT Registered charities benefiting medical professionals, carers, people who are disabled or disadvantaged by poverty, and victims of abuse.
WHAT IS FUNDED Medicine and health, welfare, education, environmental resources, infrastructure development and professional bodies.
WHAT IS NOT FUNDED Grants are not normally given to individuals.
TYPE OF GRANT One-off, recurrent, core costs, project and research. Funding is available for up to two years.
RANGE OF GRANTS £250–£500.
SAMPLE GRANTS In 1999–2000: £10,000 to Roy Castle Cancer Foundation; £5,000 to Merseyside Police & High Sherriffs' Trust.
FINANCES *Year* 2001–02 *Income* £166,079 *Grants* £68,000 *Assets* £3,600,000
TRUSTEES P R Johnson; C W Johnson.
OTHER INFORMATION The trust stated: 'Whilst this trust is prepared to help larger charities, it prefers to support small, local organisations unable to afford professional fundraisers with grants from about £250 to £500.'
HOW TO APPLY In writing to the correspondent. The trustees meet monthly.
WHO TO APPLY TO P R Johnson, Chair of the Council, Westmount, Vyner Road South, Birkenhead CH43 7PN *Tel* 0151 653 0566
CC NO 518660 **ESTABLISHED** 1987

The Johnson Group Cleaners Charity

WHERE FUNDING CAN BE GIVEN Merseyside only.
WHO CAN BENEFIT Registered local charities benefiting: children, young adults and older people; at risk groups; carers; people disadvantaged by poverty; ex-offenders and those at risk of offending; homeless people; victims of abuse and domestic violence; and people with substance misuse problems.
WHAT IS FUNDED Merseyside charities, including Councils for Voluntary Service, care in the community and holidays and outings.
WHAT IS NOT FUNDED No grants to national charities or individuals.

TYPE OF GRANT Core costs, one-off, project and running costs.

RANGE OF GRANTS £100–£49,000; usually £1,000 or less.

SAMPLE GRANTS £49,000 to Johnson Group Welfare Charity; £8,000 to Merseyside Council for Voluntary Services – second grant of a three-year commitment; £5,000 each to Acorn Venture Urban Farm – third grant of a three-year commitment and Fairbridge in Merseyside – first grant of a new three-year commitment; £2,500 each to sail Training Association, Sefton Women's and Children's Aid – first grant of a new three-year commitment, and Personal Services Society (Sefton Young Carers) – first grant of a new three-year commitment; £2,000 to Ocean Youth Club; £1,000 each to Liverpool Motorists' Annual Outing and Bootle YMCA.

FINANCES *Year* 1998–99 *Income* £112,162 *Grants* £901,526 *Assets* £2,013,732

TRUSTEES Johnson Group Cleaners Trustee Co. (No. 1) Ltd.

HOW TO APPLY In writing only to the correspondent.

WHO TO APPLY TO The Trustees, c/o Johnson Group Management Services Ltd, Mildmay Road, Bootle, Merseyside L20 5EW *Tel* 0151 933 6161

CC NO 802959   **ESTABLISHED** 1990

....

■ The H F Johnson Trust

WHERE FUNDING CAN BE GIVEN Worldwide, but mainly the UK.

WHO CAN BENEFIT The trust only supports organisations and individuals known to the trustees.

WHAT IS FUNDED Christian education.

RANGE OF GRANTS Christian books to schools.

SAMPLE GRANTS In 1999: £46,000 to School Bible and Book Project; £5,000 to Tearfund; £2,000 each to Manna Trust and Scripture Union; £1,500 each to Crusade for World Revival and St Paul's Church Kingston Hill; £1,000 each to Elim Pentecostal Church, CRIBS Trust, London Emmanuel Choir, and Saltmine Trust.

FINANCES *Year* 2001 *Income* £130,746 *Grants* £43,228 *Assets* £1,050,468

TRUSTEES Keith Danby; Janet Busk; Libby Kelly; Ian Waterfield.

HOW TO APPLY The trust stated that it only supports organisations and individuals which are personally known to the trustees and requests that you do not write in.

WHO TO APPLY TO Miss Janet Busk, PO Box 300, Kingstown Broadway, Carlisle, Cumbria CA3 0QS

CC NO 1050966   **ESTABLISHED** 1995

....

■ The Johnnie Johnson Trust

WHERE FUNDING CAN BE GIVEN UK, with a preference for the West Midlands.

WHO CAN BENEFIT To benefit children and young adults.

WHAT IS FUNDED Heritage and training/adventure breaks for children, youth and welfare organisations.

FINANCES *Year* 2002 *Grants* £102,000

TRUSTEES P V Johnson; P E T Johnson; Mrs J S Fordham; G W Ballard.

OTHER INFORMATION Over the last few years, the trust's funds have mostly been given to Johnnie Johnson Adventure Trust, which provides adventure/training for children.

HOW TO APPLY In writing to the correspondent. Please note that most funds go to the trust's sister charity.

WHO TO APPLY TO Carol Johnson, Newtown House, Hewell Road, Enfield, Redditch, Worcestershire B97 6AY *Tel* 01527 584458

CC NO 200351   **ESTABLISHED** 1961

....

■ The Lillie Johnson Charitable Trust

WHERE FUNDING CAN BE GIVEN UK, with a preference for the West Midlands.

WHO CAN BENEFIT Charities concerned with children, young people and medical causes.

WHAT IS NOT FUNDED No support for individuals.

SAMPLE GRANTS £40,000 to Birmingham Heartlands Hospital for their vascular disease project; £29,000 to University of Birmingham for tinitus research; £22,000 to Webb Care Services; £8,500 to Primrose Hospice; £7,000 to Edwards Trust; £6,700 to BMOS Youth Theatre; £6,000 to Scouts Association; £5,000 to Queen Alexander College; £3,500 to Pulse; £2,000 each to Birmingham Dogs Home and Warwickshire Junior Tennis Foundation.

FINANCES *Year* 1998–99 *Income* £183,000 *Grants* £230,000 *Assets* £1,600,000

TRUSTEES Victor Lyttle; Peter Adams.

HOW TO APPLY Applications are only considered from charities which are traditionally supported by the trust.

WHO TO APPLY TO Victor M C Lyttle, Trustee, Heathcote House, 136 Hagley Road, Edgbaston, Birmingham B16 9PN *Tel* 0121 454 4141

CC NO 326761   **ESTABLISHED** 1985

....

■ The N B Johnson Charitable Settlement

WHERE FUNDING CAN BE GIVEN UK, with a preference for Greater Manchester.

WHO CAN BENEFIT Mainly registered charities.

WHAT IS FUNDED General charitable purposes, particularly Jewish causes. Individuals are only considered in very special cases.

SAMPLE GRANTS In 1998–99: £5,000 to Heathlands; £4,250 to Manchester Jewish Federation; £4,000 to Joint Jewish Charitable Trust; £2,500 each to Community Security Trust and Lubavitch; £2,000 to Bolton Hebrew Congregation; £1,800 each to Manchester Charitable Trust and Manchester B'nai B'rith; £1,500 to Manchester Jewish Community; £1,250 each to Whitefield Hebrew Congregation and Langdon College.

FINANCES *Year* 2000–01 *Income* £32,357

HOW TO APPLY In writing to the correspondent. The trust has previously stated that unsolicited applications are not invited.

WHO TO APPLY TO Leslie Hyman, PO Box 165, Manchester M45 7XD

CC NO 277237   **ESTABLISHED** 1978

....

■ The Joicey Trust

WHERE FUNDING CAN BE GIVEN The county of Northumberland and the old metropolitan county of Tyne & Wear.

WHO CAN BENEFIT Registered charities operating in Northumberland and Tyne & Wear or groups with a specific project within the area defined above. The trust will consider funding organisations benefiting people of all ages, seafarers and fishermen, people who are in care, fostered or adopted and one-parent families.

WHAT IS FUNDED This trust will consider funding activities within the following fields: residential facilities and services; a range of infrastructure, technical support and development; charity or voluntary umbrella bodies; religious buildings; music, dance and theatre; healthcare, facilities and buildings; conservation; education and training; and community facilities and services. UK appeals are not normally supported unless there is specific evidence of activity benefiting the local area.

WHAT IS NOT FUNDED The trust states that it will not support 'bodies not having registered charitable status; personal applications; individuals; groups that do not have an identifiable project within the beneficial area'.

TYPE OF GRANT One-off for capital and revenue projects, with preference for discrete projects over running costs. Also start-up costs, buildings, core costs, projects and salaries.

RANGE OF GRANTS Up to £2,500 with very occasional larger grants.

SAMPLE GRANTS £10,000 to Border Union Agricultural Society; £6,000 to Newcastle Diocesan Repair Fund; £5,000 each to Centre for the Childrens Book, Community Council of Northumberland, The Maltings (Berwick) Trust, Salvation Army, Society of St Francis at Alnmouth Priory, St Anthony of Padua Community Association, St Cuthbert's Church – Bedlington, and Wear Body Positive.

FINANCES *Year* 2002 *Income* £207,000 *Grants* £212,000 *Assets* £6,086,000

TRUSTEES Rt Hon. Lord Joicey; Rt Hon. Lady Joicey; Elisabeth Lady Joicey; Hon. A H Joicey; R H Dickinson.

HOW TO APPLY There is no application form and applications should be made in writing to the correspondent. Trustees' meetings are held in January and July and applications should be received not later than the end of November and the end of May respectively.

WHO TO APPLY TO N A Furness, Appeals Secretary, c/o Dickinson Dees, St Ann's Wharf, 112 Quayside, Newcastle upon Tyne NE99 1SB *Tel* 0191 279 9662 *Fax* 0191 279 9905

CC NO 244679 ESTABLISHED 1965

....

■ The Jones 1986 Charitable Trust

WHERE FUNDING CAN BE GIVEN UK, mostly Nottinghamshire.

WHO CAN BENEFIT Registered charities.

WHAT IS FUNDED Medical research; relief of sickness or disability; community; animal welfare; welfare; relief of poverty.

WHAT IS NOT FUNDED No grants to individuals.

TYPE OF GRANT One-off grants.

RANGE OF GRANTS £1,000–£237,000; typical grant £3,000–£12,000.

SAMPLE GRANTS £174,000 to Nottingham University for medical research on behalf of Nottingham Health Authority; £50,000 to Nottingham High School; £40,000 to Cope Children's Trust; £35,000 each to Nottinghamshire Age Concern and NSPCC; £32,000 to Nottinghamshire Leukaemia Appeal; £26,000 to Ruddington Framework Knitters Museum.

FINANCES *Year* 2000–01 *Income* £595,000 *Grants* £573,000

TRUSTEES J O Knight; R B Stringfellow.

HOW TO APPLY The trustees identify their own target charities and do not wish to receive applications.

WHO TO APPLY TO N R P Smith, Shacklocks Mansfield, St Peter's House, Bridge Street, Mansfield, Nottinghamshire NG18 1AL *Tel* 01623 626141

CC NO 327176 ESTABLISHED 1986

....

■ The Edward Cecil Jones Settlement

WHERE FUNDING CAN BE GIVEN Local to Essex.

WHO CAN BENEFIT Local registered charities.

WHAT IS FUNDED General charitable purposes.

WHAT IS NOT FUNDED The trustees have stated that they will not fund activities that they believe are the responsibility of social services or the state. No grants to individuals.

TYPE OF GRANT Recurrent and one-off.

RANGE OF GRANTS £1,000–£25,000.

SAMPLE GRANTS £60,000 to Essex Community Foundation; £24,000 to CAFOD.

FINANCES *Year* 1999–2000 *Income* £142,497 *Grants* £148,000 *Assets* £3,125,287

TRUSTEES P J Tolhurst; W J Tolhurst; E C Watson.

HOW TO APPLY In writing to the correspondent.

WHO TO APPLY TO Mrs Alix Mason, Messrs Tolhurst & Fisher, Victoria Road South, Chelmsford, Essex CM1 1LN *Tel* 01245 216123

CC NO 216166 ESTABLISHED 1957

....

■ The Marjorie and Geoffrey Jones Charitable Trust

WHERE FUNDING CAN BE GIVEN UK, preference south west of England.

WHO CAN BENEFIT Registered charities.

WHAT IS FUNDED General charitable purposes.

RANGE OF GRANTS £1,000–£7,000.

SAMPLE GRANTS £7,000 to Torquay Museum for repairs to a roof; £6,000 to Dartmoor Rescue Group; £5,000 each to Dame Hannah Rogers School, Golden Vanity Trust, League of Friends of Paignton Hospital, Macmillan Cancer Relief, National Trust – Monk's Path – Buckland, Robert Owen Foundation, West of England School for Children of Little or No Sight, and West of England School for the Deaf.

FINANCES *Year* 1999–2000 *Income* £91,731 *Grants* £85,000 *Assets* £1,714,841

TRUSTEES N J Wollen; W F Coplestone Boughey; P M Kay.

HOW TO APPLY In writing to the correspondent. The trustees meet four times a year to consider applications.

WHO TO APPLY TO The Trustees, Carlton House, 30 The Terrace, Torquay, Devon TQ1 1BS *Tel* 01803 213251 *Fax* 01803 296871

CC NO 1051031 ESTABLISHED 1995

....

■ The Jordan Charitable Foundation

WHERE FUNDING CAN BE GIVEN Unrestricted, but strong local interests in Herefordshire and the Scottish highlands.

WHO CAN BENEFIT Organisations.

WHAT IS FUNDED General charitable purposes.

TYPE OF GRANT One-off, capital and core costs will be considered.

SAMPLE GRANTS £1,200,000 to Hereford Hospital for an MRI scanner; £30,000 to Highland Hospice; £28,000 to Harvard Medical School Library; £20,000 to Royal National College for the Blind; £10,000 each to Herefordshire Lifestyles and Northlands Creative Glass;

£6,000 to St John's Ambulance; £5,000 each to Herefordshire MIND, Herefordshire Nature Trust and Riding for the Disabled.

FINANCES *Year* 2001 *Income* £1,200,000 *Grants* £1,576,000 *Assets* £34,000,000

TRUSTEES Sir Ronald Miller; Sir George Russell; Ralph Stockwell; Snowport Ltd; Parkdove Ltd.

HOW TO APPLY In writing to the correspondent.

WHO TO APPLY TO Brian Scrivener, Secretary, Rawlinson and Hunter, Eagle House, 110 Jermyn Street, London SW1Y 6RH *Tel* 020 7451 9000 *Fax* 020 7451 9090

CC NO 1051507   **ESTABLISHED** 1995

■ The Lady Eileen Joseph Foundation

WHERE FUNDING CAN BE GIVEN UK.

WHO CAN BENEFIT Mainly UK organisations benefiting at risk groups and people who are disadvantaged by poverty or socially isolated.

WHAT IS FUNDED Largely welfare and medical causes. General charitable purposes are also supported.

TYPE OF GRANT One-off.

SAMPLE GRANTS £10,000 to Help the Hospices; £5,000 to Cancer BACUP; £2,500 to Community Security Trust.

FINANCES *Year* 2000–01 *Income* £52,000 *Grants* £34,000 *Assets* £1,029,000

TRUSTEES Mrs J Sawdy; T W P Simpson; Mrs N J Thornton.

HOW TO APPLY In writing to the correspondent, although the trust states that unsolicited requests will not be considered.

WHO TO APPLY TO Mrs J M S Sawdy, Trustee, BDO Stoy Hayward, 8 Baker Street, London W1M 1DA *Tel* 020 7486 5888 *Fax* 020 7893 2601

CC NO 327549   **ESTABLISHED** 1987

■ The J E Joseph Charitable Fund

WHERE FUNDING CAN BE GIVEN UK, with a preference for London, the Far East, Israel and Palestine.

WHO CAN BENEFIT Jewish people who are poor and in need, in certain cities and places in the area defined above, priority is given to those of Sephardi extraction.

WHAT IS FUNDED Jewish community organisations, especially those catering for people who are socially disadvantaged and young people. Only exceptionally individuals.

WHAT IS NOT FUNDED Grants to individuals in exceptional cases only and are usually made to assist towards education and in particular further and higher education. No application from an organisation will be considered without a copy of its most recent set of accounts. Only Jewish individuals or organisations need apply.

TYPE OF GRANT Outright cash grants frequently on an annual basis. Very occasionally loans.

RANGE OF GRANTS £500–£10,000.

FINANCES *Year* 2000–01 *Income* £112,000 *Grants* £93,000 *Assets* £3,700,000

TRUSTEES F D A Mocatta, Chair; D Silas; J H Corre; P S Gourgey; J S Horesh; S Frosh.

HOW TO APPLY In writing to the correspondent. The trustees respond to all applications which are first vetted by the secretary. The trust stated that many applications are unsuccessful as the number of application exceeds the amount available from limited income.

WHO TO APPLY TO Roger J Leon, Secretary, 6 Lyon Meade, Stanmore, Middlesex HA7 1JA *Fax* 020 7289 8780

CC NO 209058   **ESTABLISHED** 1946

■ The Judge Charitable Foundation

WHERE FUNDING CAN BE GIVEN UK, with a local interest in Cambridge and Worcestershire.

WHO CAN BENEFIT Registered charities benefiting young adults and students.

WHAT IS FUNDED The Judge Institute of Management Studies at the University of Cambridge and other organisations, mainly linked to management education. Grants are given to colleges and registered charities such as Prince's Trust and the British Food Heritage Trust.

WHAT IS NOT FUNDED No grants to individuals or medical causes.

TYPE OF GRANT One-off and recurring.

FINANCES *Year* 2000–01 *Income* £435,333

TRUSTEES Sir Paul Judge.

HOW TO APPLY In writing to the correspondent.

WHO TO APPLY TO Sir Paul Judge, Trustee, 88 The Panoramie, 152 Grosvenor Road, London SW1V 3JL *Tel* 020 7834 9041

CC NO 1009919   **ESTABLISHED** 1992

■ The Judith Trust

WHERE FUNDING CAN BE GIVEN UK.

WHO CAN BENEFIT Organisations concerned with people with a learning disability and mental health needs.

WHAT IS FUNDED Multi-disciplinary preventative and innovative approaches to help those with learning disabilities and mental health problems, especially women, children and Jewish people.

WHAT IS NOT FUNDED No grants to individuals.

TYPE OF GRANT One-off, project and research. Funding may be given for up to three years.

SAMPLE GRANTS In 1997–98: £25,000 to Department of Psychiatry of Disability – St George's Medical School; £15,000 to Leeds Jewish Welfare Board Rainbow Project; £10,000 to Consultant's Good Practice Report.

FINANCES *Year* 1999–2000 *Grants* £40,000

TRUSTEES Dr Annette Lawson; Peter Lawrence; George Lawson.

PUBLICATIONS *Joined Up Care*: good practice in services for people with learning disabilities and mental health needs.

OTHER INFORMATION In 1998–99 grants were approved to the first two beneficiaries in the previous year's list, but not paid during the year.

HOW TO APPLY In writing to the correspondent; however, please note that most grants are made through experts and advisors.

WHO TO APPLY TO Dr A R Lawson, Trustee, 5 Carriage House, 88–90 Randolph Avenue, London W9 1BD *Tel* 020 7266 1073 *E-mail* judith.trust@lineone.net

CC NO 1063012   **ESTABLISHED** 1997

■ The Jungels-Winkler Charitable Foundation

WHERE FUNDING CAN BE GIVEN UK.

WHO CAN BENEFIT People who are visually impaired.

WHAT IS FUNDED Projects for the benefit of the above, with some preference for arts-related charities.

Think carefully about every application. Is it justified?

583

RANGE OF GRANTS £2,000–£50,000.

SAMPLE GRANTS £500,000 to Royal Academy Trust; £9,650 to University of London for the Courtauld Institute of Art; £2,000 to Committee of Hackney Carriage Drivers Charitable Trust.

FINANCES *Year* 2000 *Income* £1,290,412 *Grants* £511,650 *Assets* £783,681

TRUSTEES Gabrielle Jungels-Winkler; Jonathan Wood; Alexandra Jungels-Winkler; Christophe Jungels-Winkler.

HOW TO APPLY In writing to the correspondent.

WHO TO APPLY TO Nicole Aubin-Parvu, Herbert Smith, Exchange House, Primrose Street, London EC2A 2HS *Tel* 020 7374 8000 *Fax* 020 7374 0888

CC NO 1073523 **ESTABLISHED** 1999

....

■ The Anton Jurgens Charitable Trust

WHERE FUNDING CAN BE GIVEN UK

WHO CAN BENEFIT UK registered charities.

WHAT IS FUNDED The welfare of children and young people; youth organisations; centres, clubs and institutions; community organisations; day centres and nurseries; and general welfare organisations.

TYPE OF GRANT Generally one-off.

RANGE OF GRANTS £500–£10,000.

SAMPLE GRANTS £12,000 to Tommy's Campaign at St Thomas Hospital; £10,000 each to Combat Stress, Fairbridge Mission, Gabbijas Truman and Tring Educational Trust, Hyperbaric Oxygen Trust, and International Social Service of UK; £7,500 to Treloar Trust; £7,000 to Downside Clubs for Young People; £5,000 each to Countess Moutbatten House and YMCA.

FINANCES *Year* 1999–2000 *Income* £405,569 *Grants* £308,600 *Assets* £7,995,698

TRUSTEES C V M Jurgens, Chair; J Jurgens; B W M Jurgens; E Deckers; M J Jurgens; F A V Jurgens.

HOW TO APPLY In writing to the correspondent. The trustees meet twice a year in the spring and the autumn. It is recommended that applications be submitted by 31 March for consideration at the spring meeting and by 31 August for the autumn meeting. The trustees do not enter into correspondence concerning grant applications beyond notifying successful applicants.

WHO TO APPLY TO Michael J Jurgens, Trustee, Saffrey Champness, Lion House, 72–75 Red Lion Street, London WC1R 4GB *Tel* 020 7841 4000 *Fax* 020 7841 4100

CC NO 259885 **ESTABLISHED** 1969

The Bernard Kahn Charitable Trust

WHERE FUNDING CAN BE GIVEN UK and Israel.

WHO CAN BENEFIT Organisations benefiting Jewish people, children and young adults, people disadvantaged by poverty, teachers, governesses and rabbis.

WHAT IS FUNDED Relief of, and assistance to, Jewish people to alleviate poverty; the advancement of religion and education.

SAMPLE GRANTS £60,000 to Yeshivat Margenita d'avrohom; £25,000 each to Ohr Somayach College and Orthodox Council of Jerusalem; £20,000 each to Gevurath Ari Academy and Tels Academy; £7,000 to Gateshead Jewish High School; £5,000 to Friends of Religious Settlement; £1,750 to Hasmonean High School; £800 to Woodstock Sinclair Trust; £250 to Enuno EC.

FINANCES *Year* 1998–99 *Income* £299,000 *Grants* £236,000 *Assets* £2,300,000

TRUSTEES Mrs C B Kahn; S Fuehrer.

HOW TO APPLY In writing to the correspondent.

WHO TO APPLY TO The Trustees, 18 Gresham Gardens, London NW11 8PD

CC NO 249130   **ESTABLISHED** 1965

The Stanley Kalms Foundation

WHERE FUNDING CAN BE GIVEN UK and overseas.

WHO CAN BENEFIT Organisations and individuals involved with: orthodox Jewish education in the UK and Israel; the arts; medicine; and other secular and religious programmes.

WHAT IS FUNDED Encouragement of orthodox Jewish education in the UK and Israel, particularly by providing scholarships, fellowships and research grants. Other areas supported include the arts, medicine and other programmes, both secular and religious.

TYPE OF GRANT One-off, research, project, bursaries and scholarships.

SAMPLE GRANTS £75,373 to Shalom Hartman Institute; £34,000 to Jewish Educational Development Trust; £32,000 to Royal Opera House Trust; £28,430 to Pluto Productions; £25,000 to Group Relations Education Trust; £20,000 to Institute for Policy Research; £15,000 each to Community Security Trust and Nightingale House; £10,000 to Jewish Association for Business Ethics and Oxford Centre for Jewish and Hebrew Studies.

FINANCES *Year* 2000–01 *Income* £46,445 *Grants* £314,255 *Assets* £1,444,230

TRUSTEES Sir Stanley Kalms; Pamela Kalms; Stephen Kalms.

HOW TO APPLY In writing to the correspondent, but note that most of the trust's funds are committed to projects supported for a number of years.

WHO TO APPLY TO Mrs Jane Hunt-Cooke, Dixons Group plc, 29 Farm Street, London W1J 5RL *Tel* 020 7499 3494

CC NO 328368   **ESTABLISHED** 1989

The Boris Karloff Charitable Foundation

WHERE FUNDING CAN BE GIVEN Worldwide.

WHO CAN BENEFIT UK and local charities benefiting actors, musicians and people disadvantaged by mental or physical illness.

WHAT IS NOT FUNDED Charities with large resources are not supported.

RANGE OF GRANTS £100–£10,000.

SAMPLE GRANTS £20,000 to Green Croft New Alliance; £10,000 to Royal Theatrical Fund; £5,000 to Bromley CAB, Cinema and Television Benevolent Fund, and Rose Road Association; £1,000 each to Action for Blind People, Amnesty International, Cancer Bacup, Cancer Vaccine Institute, Mental Health Foundation, and Royal Blind Asylum and School.

FINANCES *Year* 2001–02 *Income* £62,048 *Grants* £49,000 *Assets* £1,745,132

TRUSTEES Ian D Wilson; P A Williamson; O M Lewis.

HOW TO APPLY In writing to the correspondent.

WHO TO APPLY TO The Trustees, Peachey & Co., 95 Aldwych, London WC2B 4JF

CC NO 326898   **ESTABLISHED** 1985

The Ian Karten Charitable Trust

WHERE FUNDING CAN BE GIVEN Great Britain and Israel, with some local interest in Surrey and London.

WHO CAN BENEFIT People with disabilities attending CTEC Centres, and students who have been awarded Karten Scholarships by universities or conservatoires.

WHAT IS FUNDED The establishment by suitable charities of centres for computer-aided training, education and communication (CTEC Centres) for people with severe physical, sensory or cognitive disabilities, or with mental health problems; scholarships for postgraduate study and research in selected subjects at selected universities and for postgraduate training of musicians of outstanding talent at selected conservatoires; and the trust makes occasional small donations to some charities, mainly UK or local (based in Surrey) ones.

WHAT IS NOT FUNDED No grants to individuals.

TYPE OF GRANT Projects: sometimes funded over a period of two years; charities: normally one-off, but in some cases repeated annually; universities: scholarships.

RANGE OF GRANTS £50–£150,000.

SAMPLE GRANTS £120,000 to National Star Centre in Cheltenham; £107,000 to the Shaw Trust in Neath; £106,000 to Share Community in Wandsworth; £100,000 each to the RNIB in Torquay and Queen Alexandra School for the Blind in Birmingham; £92,000 to Brighton Society for the Blind; £85,000 to SCOPE, Cwmbran; £84,000 to University of Derby, Cromford Mill; £81,000 to Derby College for Deaf People; £80,000 to OUTSET Bedford.

FINANCES *Year* 2000–01 *Income* £352,888 *Grants* £1,895,000 *Assets* £4,109,911

TRUSTEES Ian H Karten, Chair; Mrs Mildred Karten; Tim Simon; Ellen Fraenkel.

HOW TO APPLY Those interested in the CTEC programme should contact Angela Hobbs. Students should approach their university. Applications for other grants should be accompanied by recent accounts and other material about the charity's activity.

WHO TO APPLY TO Angela Hobbs, The Mill House, Newark Lane, Ripley, Surrey GU23 6DP
Tel 01483 225425 *Fax* 01483 222420
E-mail iankarten@aol.com
CC NO 281721   ESTABLISHED 1980

■ The Kasner Charitable Trust

WHERE FUNDING CAN BE GIVEN UK and Israel.
WHAT IS FUNDED Jewish organisations.
SAMPLE GRANTS £51,000 to Gevurath Ari Academy Trust; £35,000 to Telz Academy Trust; £20,000 each to Beis Eliyahu and Law of Trust Talmudical College; £10,000 to Torath Moshe Moshe Educational and Charitable Trust; £7,000 to Menorah Primary School; £5,500 to Gateshead Talmudical College; £5,000 each to Menovah Grammar School and North London Communal Mikveh.
FINANCES *Year* 2000–01 *Income* £82,363 *Grants* £227,251 *Assets* £936,312
TRUSTEES Mrs Elfreda Erlich; Baruch Erlich; Josef Kasner.
HOW TO APPLY In writing to the correspondent.
WHO TO APPLY TO Josef Kasner, Trustee, Kimberley House, 172 Billet Road, London E17 5DT
Tel 020 8342 0211
CC NO 267510   ESTABLISHED 1974

■ The Kass Charitable Trust

WHERE FUNDING CAN BE GIVEN UK.
WHO CAN BENEFIT Organisations concerned with: welfare, nursing homes, older people, education, cancer, and Jewish causes.
WHAT IS FUNDED The trust supports: welfare; nursing homes and other facilities for older and infirm people; research into the causes of and cure for cancer and similar diseases; and promotion and advancement of the Jewish religion including the preservation and maintenance of Jewish cemeteries.
FINANCES *Year* 1999–2000 *Income* £49,000 *Grants* £30,000 *Assets* £20,000
TRUSTEES David Elliot Kass; Mrs Margaret Kathleen Kass.
HOW TO APPLY In writing to the correspondent.
WHO TO APPLY TO D E Kass, Trustee, 13 Haslemere Avenue, London NW4 2PU
CC NO 1006296   ESTABLISHED 1991

■ The Kathleen Trust

WHERE FUNDING CAN BE GIVEN UK, with a preference for London.
WHO CAN BENEFIT Organisations benefiting young musicians.
WHAT IS FUNDED Typically course fees or instrument costs for outstanding young musicians.
SAMPLE GRANTS £7,400 to Trinity College of Music; £7,000 to Dulwich College; £5,000 to Jackdaws Education Trust; £3,000 to Young Concert Artists' Trust.
FINANCES *Year* 1999–2000 *Income* £31,000 *Grants* £31,000 *Assets* £1,500,000
TRUSTEES E R H Perks; Sir O C A Scott; Lady P A Scott; Mrs C N Withington.
HOW TO APPLY In writing to the correspondent.
WHO TO APPLY TO E R H Perks, Trustee, Currey & Co, 21 Buckingham Gate, London SW1E 6LS
Tel 020 7828 4091
CC NO 1064516   ESTABLISHED 1997

■ The Michael & Ilse Katz Foundation

WHERE FUNDING CAN BE GIVEN Worldwide.
WHO CAN BENEFIT International and UK schemes and organisations benefiting Jewish people, at risk groups, and people who are disadvantaged by poverty or socially isolated.
WHAT IS FUNDED Primarily Jewish organisations. Medical/disability and welfare charities are also supported.
TYPE OF GRANT One-off and recurring.
SAMPLE GRANTS £56,495 to Royal Bournemouth Hospital; £21,005 to Bournemouth Orchestral Society; £16,000 to Jewish Care; £10,000 each to Norwood Ltd and UK Friends of the Well Being of Israel's Soldiers; £8,000 to Community Security Trust; £5,000 each to Leo Baeck College, Federation of Jewish Relief Organisations and Hillel Foundation; £4,823 to Poole Hospital for the Ladybird appeal.
FINANCES *Year* 2000–01 *Income* £27,647 *Grants* £175,390 *Assets* £1,700,930
TRUSTEES Norris Gilbert; Osman Azis.
HOW TO APPLY In writing to the correspondent.
WHO TO APPLY TO Osman Azis, Trustee, The Counting House, Trelill, Bodmin, Cornwall PL30 3HZ
Tel 01208 851814 *Fax* 01208 851813
E-mail osman.azis@virgin.net
CC NO 263726   ESTABLISHED 1971

■ The Katzauer Charitable Settlement

WHERE FUNDING CAN BE GIVEN UK, but mainly Israel.
WHO CAN BENEFIT Jewish people.
WHAT IS FUNDED Jewish organisations, predominantly in Israel.
SAMPLE GRANTS £3,300 to Institute Limudei Hashen Forae; £3,000 to Moria Synagogue; £2,000 to Mevkaz Ora V'Simncha; £1,500 World Jewish Relief; £1,000 each to Kollel Ra'anana and Lubavitch Zodnana Special Child.
FINANCES *Year* 1998–999 *Income* £114,000 *Grants* £31,000 *Assets* £622,000
TRUSTEES G C Smith; A Katzauer.
HOW TO APPLY In writing to the correspondent.
WHO TO APPLY TO Gordon Smith, Trustee, c/o Devonshire House, 1 Devonshire Street, London W1W 5DR *Tel* 020 7304 2000
CC NO 275110   ESTABLISHED 1977

■ The C S Kaufman Charitable Trust

WHERE FUNDING CAN BE GIVEN UK.
WHO CAN BENEFIT Organisations benefiting Jewish people.
WHAT IS FUNDED Mainly Jewish organisations.
WHAT IS NOT FUNDED No grants to individuals.
RANGE OF GRANTS £50–£13,000.
SAMPLE GRANTS in 1998–99: £13,000 to Society of Friends of Torah; £7,000 to Friends of Harim; £6,600 to Craven Walks; £6,000 to Friends of Knesset Yehuda; £3,100 to Gateshead Foundation for Torah.
FINANCES *Year* 2000–01 *Income* £46,279
TRUSTEES I I Kaufman; J Kaufman.
HOW TO APPLY In writing to the correspondent.
WHO TO APPLY TO C S Kaufman, 162 Whitehall Road, Gateshead, Tyne & Wear NE8 1TP
CC NO 253194   ESTABLISHED 1967

■ The Geoffrey John Kaye Charitable Foundation

WHERE FUNDING CAN BE GIVEN UK and overseas.
WHO CAN BENEFIT Jewish people.
WHAT IS FUNDED Jewish organisations and other charitable purposes.
WHAT IS NOT FUNDED The funds for the charity are fully committed for the forseeable future.
TYPE OF GRANT Largely recurrent.
SAMPLE GRANTS Grants were made to Friends of Nightingale House, The Ashten Trust, Holocaust Educational Trust, Zion Orphanage, Ila Escuela Para Sordos De Jacotepec, Lake Chapala Humane Society, Programa Pro Ninos Incapacados Del Lago.
FINANCES *Year* 2000–01 *Income* £75,047 *Grants* £82,567
TRUSTEES G J Kaye; Mrs S Rose; Miss J Kaye.
HOW TO APPLY In writing to the correspondent, but note the comments above.
WHO TO APPLY TO R J Freebody, Accountant, PEG, 54 Welbeck Street, London W1G 9XS *Tel* 020 7935 1339
CC NO 262547   **ESTABLISHED** 1971

■ The Emmanuel Kaye Foundation

WHERE FUNDING CAN BE GIVEN UK and overseas.
WHO CAN BENEFIT Organisations benefiting medical professionals, research workers, scientists, Jewish people, at risk groups, people who are disadvantaged by poverty and socially isolated people.
WHAT IS FUNDED Medical research, welfare and Jewish organisations.
WHAT IS NOT FUNDED Organisation not registered with the Charity Commission.
RANGE OF GRANTS £50–£25,000.
FINANCES *Year* 2000–01 *Income* £107,867 *Grants* £126,000
TRUSTEES David Kaye; Lady Kaye; John Forster; Michael Cutler.
HOW TO APPLY In writing to the correspondent.
WHO TO APPLY TO John Forster, Hart House, Hartley Wintney, Hampshire RG27 8PE *Tel* 01252 843773
CC NO 280281   **ESTABLISHED** 1980

■ Kelsick's Educational Foundation

WHERE FUNDING CAN BE GIVEN Lakes parish (Ambleside, Grasmere, Langdale and part of Troutbeck).
WHO CAN BENEFIT Organisations and individuals under 25 years of age.
WHAT IS FUNDED The trust supports educational establishments and educational community groups in the beneficial area. About a third of the grant total is usually given to the three church schools in the area, especially for special needs, about a third to organisations and a third to individuals.
TYPE OF GRANT Capital and project support, for longer than three years.
RANGE OF GRANTS £400–£2,000.
FINANCES *Year* 2001–02 *Income* £250,000 *Grants* £150,000 *Assets* £3,000,000
TRUSTEES N M Tyson, Chair; N Hutchinson; Mrs E M Braithwaite; Mrs L A Dixon; Mrs H M Fuller; P Jackson; R Sutton; Revd R Coke; P Collins; R Curphey; J O Halstead.
HOW TO APPLY Application forms are available from the correspondent.

WHO TO APPLY TO P G Frost, Clerk, Kelsick Centre, St Mary's Lane, Ambleside, Cumbria LA22 9DG *Tel* 01539 431289 *Fax* 01539 431292
CC NO 526956   **ESTABLISHED** 1723

■ The Kay Kendall Leukaemia Fund

WHERE FUNDING CAN BE GIVEN Unrestricted.
WHO CAN BENEFIT Organisations conducting research into and treatment of leukaemia.
WHAT IS FUNDED Medical research into and treatment of leukaemia.
WHAT IS NOT FUNDED Circular appeals for general support are not funded.
TYPE OF GRANT Research, capital, equipment.
SAMPLE GRANTS £396,000 to Medical Research Council – Cambridge, consisting of £203,922 over three years for the salary and expenses of two postdoctoral researchers on the development of intracellular reagents for leukaemia treatment and £192,209 over three years for a research fellowship studying the structure and function of the leukaemia-associated AML1/CBFÔ transcription factor complex; £331,545 to University College London, consisting of £169,204 over three years for a research fellowship to evaluate the effects of an indolcarbazole Jak tyrosine kinase inhibitor on the survival and proliferation of acute leukaemias and £162,431 over three years for a research fellowship to elucidate the full function of a cell cycle inhibitor and better understanding of cell cycle dysregulation in lymhomas; £196,677 to Institute of Cancer Research – London, consisting of £166,667 over three years for a research fellowship to study the molecular mechanisms of transcriptional deregulation by fusion proteins in acute leukaemia and £30,000 continued support for a chromosome/DNA bank of lymphoproliferative diseases; £170,000 to University of Wales College for three-year salary support and costs for a researcher to produce animal models for gene targeted immunotherapy for leukaemia, including £20,000 towards capital costs; £53,867 to Royal Bournemouth Hospital for salary and expenses for an initial year for a clinical scientist to characterise and determine the clinical significance of a candidate tumour suppressor gene; £3,250 to University of Manchester.
FINANCES *Year* 2000–01 *Income* £1,903,000 *Grants* £1,529,000 *Assets* £50,496,000
TRUSTEES Judith Portrait; T J Sainsbury; Christopher Stone.
OTHER INFORMATION The trust is one of the Sainsbury Family Charitable Trusts which share a common administration. An application to one is taken as an application to all.
HOW TO APPLY In writing to the corrspondent.
WHO TO APPLY TO Michael Pattison, Director, Allington House, 1st Floor, 150 Victoria Street, London SW1E 5AE *Tel* 020 7410 0330 *Fax* 020 7410 0332
CC NO 290772   **ESTABLISHED** 1984

■ William Kendall's Charity (Wax Chandlers' Company)

WHERE FUNDING CAN BE GIVEN Greater London and the London borough of Bexley.
WHO CAN BENEFIT Charitable organisations in Greater London working for relief of need; in Bexley, charitable organisations generally.

Think carefully about every application. Is it justified?

587

WHAT IS FUNDED Most donations are for relief of need in London.

WHAT IS NOT FUNDED Grants are not normally made to large charities, charities whose accounts disclose substantial reserves or non-registered charities.Grants are not made to replace cuts in funding made by local authorities or others, schemes or activities which would be regarded as relieving central or local government of their statutory responsibilities or cover deficits already incurred.

TYPE OF GRANT One-off or recurring.

RANGE OF GRANTS £500–£20,000, typical grant £5,000.

SAMPLE GRANTS £24,000 (in 8 grants) to individuals; £17,500 to London Connection to provide a year's funding for a basic literacy and training programme; £12,000 to Thamesmead Community College for a project to increase attainment, reduce truancy and reduce the level of school exclusions; £10,000 to Centrepoint for training and life-skills work with young people; £4,000 for the Sheriffs' and Recorder's Fund to fund training and education for prisoners approaching their release dates; £2,300 to the Hoxton Health Group to bring alternative medical therapies to the housebound elderly in the City of London and Hoxton; £2,500 to the St Lawrence Charitable Trust towards the cost of welfare grants; £2,000 to Age Chncern – Bexley towards the cost of holidays for people who are housebound.

FINANCES *Year* 2001–02 *Income* £107,000 *Grants* £97,000 *Assets* £2,339,000

TRUSTEES Wax Chandlers' Company.

HOW TO APPLY In writing to the correspondent, but note the comments in the general section. The committee meets four times a year. Information guidelines entitled 'Advice to Applicants' are available from the charity.

WHO TO APPLY TO The Clerk to the Wax Chandlers' Company, Wax Chandlers' Hall, Gresham Street, London EC2V 7AD *Tel* 020 7606 3591 *Fax* 020 7600 5462 *E-mail* info@waxchandlershall.co.uk *Website* www.waxchandlershall.co.uk
CC NO 228361   **ESTABLISHED** 1964

....

■ **The Kennedy Charitable Foundation**

WHERE FUNDING CAN BE GIVEN Unrestricted, but mainly Ireland with a preference for County Mayo and County Sligo.

WHO CAN BENEFIT Registered charities and individuals.

WHAT IS FUNDED Predominantly organisations connected with the Roman Catholic faith, mainly in Ireland.

RANGE OF GRANTS £200–£150,000; typical grant £1,000.

SAMPLE GRANTS £400,000 in two grants to Newman Institute Mayo Ireland Ltd; £50,000 to Restoration Ministries; £25,000 each to Diocese of Achonry, Diocese of Elphin and Diocese of Salford; £21,000 in three grants to Francis House Children's Hospice; £20,000 to St Vincent de Paul Society; £18,000 to Diocese of Killala; £10,000 each to Convent of Jesus & Mary and Diocese of Shrewsbury.

FINANCES *Year* 2000–01 *Income* £1,784,280 *Grants* £752,000 *Assets* £1,635,987

TRUSTEES Patrick Kennedy; Kathleen Kennedy; John Kennedy; Brown Street Nominees Ltd; Patrick Joseph; Francis Kennedy.

HOW TO APPLY In writing to the correspondent, but the foundation says that 'unsolicited applications are not accepted'.

WHO TO APPLY TO M Baines, Brown Street Nominees Ltd, Deloitte & Touche Private Clients Ltd, PO Box 500, 201 Deansgate, Manchester M60 2AT *Tel* 0161 455 8380 *Fax* 0161 829 3803
CC NO 1052001   **ESTABLISHED** 1996

....

■ **The Mathilda and Terence Kennedy Charitable Trust**

WHERE FUNDING CAN BE GIVEN UK.

WHO CAN BENEFIT Registered charities.

WHAT IS FUNDED General charitable purposes.

RANGE OF GRANTS £1,000–£20,000.

SAMPLE GRANTS £20,000 to Royal Ballet School; £7,500 to Royal National Theatre; £5,000 each to Mathilda Marks Kennedy School and Young Vic; £4,500 to Mathilda & Terence Kennedy Institute of Rheumatology; £3,000 each to Stonewall Iris Trust and University College of London; £2,500 each to Alternative Theatre Company Limited (Bush Theatre) and The Arc Dance Company; £2,000 each to Albert Kennedy Trust, The Terrence Higgins Charity Trust and Weizmann Institute Foundation; £1,500 to CRUSAID.

FINANCES *Year* 1999–2000 *Income* £47,027 *Grants* £61,000 *Assets* £722,701

TRUSTEES Hon. Amanda Sieff; John O'Neill; Mrs L Sieff; J Henderson.

HOW TO APPLY Grants are mainly made to charities known personally to the trustees, rather than as a result of unsolicited applications. Unsuccesful applications will not receive a reply.

WHO TO APPLY TO The Trustees, H W Fisher & Co., Acre House, 11–15 William Road, London NW1 3ER *Tel* 020 7388 7000
CC NO 206330   **ESTABLISHED** 1956

....

■ **The Kennel Club Charitable Trust**

WHERE FUNDING CAN BE GIVEN UK.

WHO CAN BENEFIT Registered charities or research bodies benefiting dogs; research workers and vets; and people who are disabled, blind or deaf, where dogs are involved (e.g in support of human beings).

WHAT IS FUNDED The trust supports research into canine diseases and disorders and assists charities for canine welfare and disadvantaged humans aided by dogs.

WHAT IS NOT FUNDED The trust does not give grants directly to individuals, veterinary nurses can apply to the British Veterinary Nursing Assoiciation where bursaries are available. The trustees tend not to favour funding the costs of building work.

TYPE OF GRANT One-off and recurring for set periods.

RANGE OF GRANTS Generally up to £25,000 a year for research; up to £10,000 for support of dogs and those who care for them, train them or benefit from them.

SAMPLE GRANTS £217,000 to Animal Health Trust (£135,000 to support the work of the KC Genetics Coordinator, £50,000 for epidemiology and £32,000 towards the cost of setting up a canine tumour registry); £14,000 to University of Bristol for canine gastro-enterology research; £13,000 to University of Glasgow for a molecular genetic study of canine cancer; £10,000 to Greyhound Rescue; £7,000 each to Blue Cross, Canine Partners for Independence

and Royal College of Veterinary Surgeons; £5,000 each to NCDL and Support Dogs.
FINANCES *Year* 2000–01 *Income* £617,759 *Grants* £308,229 *Assets* £838,223
TRUSTEES Brig. R J Clifford; W R Irving; M Townsend, Chair; M Herrtage.
OTHER INFORMATION Further information is available at the trust's website.
HOW TO APPLY In writing to the correspondent, including latest accounts. Please state clearly details of the costs for which you are requesting funding, and for what purpose and over what period the funding is required. The trustees meet three or four times a year.
WHO TO APPLY TO Mrs Mary Wetherell, Secretary, 1–5 Clarges Street, Piccadilly, London W1J 8AB *Tel* 020 7518 1029 *Fax* 020 7518 1050 *E-mail* mwetherell@the-kennel-club.org.uk *Website* www.the-kennel-club.org.uk
CC NO 327802   **ESTABLISHED** 1988

■ The Kensington District Nursing Trust

WHERE FUNDING CAN BE GIVEN The former borough of Kensington.
WHO CAN BENEFIT Welfare organisations; needy older people and individuals.
WHAT IS FUNDED General welfare needs and winter heating allowances and Christmas gifts to some of the needy older people in the borough.
WHAT IS NOT FUNDED No grants to pay rents, court orders or fines.
SAMPLE GRANTS £6,800 to Pembridge Palliative Care Centre; £5,500 to Avon House Nursing Home; £2,600 to Kensington Day Centre; £2,500 to Alexander House; £1,500 each to Age Concern and Alan Morkill House; £1,200 to Harrison Homes; £1,000 each to League of Friends of St Mary's Abbot's, Open Age Clinic, Marie Curie Cancer Care, St Charles Hospital Leg Ulcer Clinic and Winged Fellowship Trust.
FINANCES *Year* 2000–01 *Grants* £76,000
TRUSTEES Mrs S C D Jaffe, Chair; K J Kelman; M W F Jenkin; Mrs V J Thornhill; Mrs V Stanton; Dr A Hamilton; P Kraus.
HOW TO APPLY In writing to the correspondent.
WHO TO APPLY TO Margaret Rhodes, Clerk to the Trustees, 27a Pembridge Villas, London W11 3EP *Tel* 020 7229 3538 *Fax* 020 7229 4920 *E-mail* kdnt@btinternet.com
CC NO 210931   **ESTABLISHED** 1974

■ The Nancy Kenyon Charitable Trust

WHERE FUNDING CAN BE GIVEN UK.
WHO CAN BENEFIT Registered charities only.
WHAT IS FUNDED General charitable purposes. Primarily for people and causes known to the trustees.
WHAT IS NOT FUNDED No grants to individuals.
RANGE OF GRANTS £150–£21,500.
SAMPLE GRANTS Regular beneficiaries include: Nancy Oldfield Trust, Cheltenham Youth for Christ, Chanty Search, Rett Syndrome Association, Midland Narrowboat Association, ABC Wales, No Panic, Help an Orphan, Christchurch Cheltenham and Thorne House.
FINANCES *Year* 2000–01 *Income* £46,995 *Grants* £40,000 *Assets* £1,250,000
TRUSTEES C M Kenyon; R B Kenyon; R G Brown.
OTHER INFORMATION Applications for causes not known to the trustees are considered annually in December.

HOW TO APPLY In writing to the correspondent at any time. Applications for causes not known to the trustees are considered annually in December.
WHO TO APPLY TO R G Brown, Trustee, c/o Mercer and Hole, Gloucester House, 72 London Road, St Albans, Hertfordshire AL1 1NS *Tel* 01727 869141 *Fax* 01727 869149
CC NO 265359   **ESTABLISHED** 1972

■ Keren Association

WHERE FUNDING CAN BE GIVEN UK.
WHO CAN BENEFIT Organisations benefiting children, young adults and Jewish people.
WHAT IS FUNDED The advancement of education; the provision of religious instruction and training in traditional Judaism; general charitable purposes.
FINANCES *Year* 1998–99 *Income* £3,171,651 *Grants* £2,901,239 *Assets* £12,197,356
TRUSTEES E Englander, Chair; Mrs S Englander; P N Englander; S Z Englander; B Englander; J S Englander; Mrs H Z Weiss; Mrs N Weiss.
HOW TO APPLY In writing to the correspondent.
WHO TO APPLY TO Mrs S Englander, 136 Clapham Common, London E5 9AG
CC NO 313119   **ESTABLISHED** 1961

■ Kermaville Ltd

WHERE FUNDING CAN BE GIVEN UK.
WHO CAN BENEFIT Organisations benefiting Jewish people.
WHAT IS FUNDED Advancement of religion according to the orthodox Jewish faith and general charitable purposes.
FINANCES *Year* 2000–01 *Income* £156,593
TRUSTEES S Orenstein; J Orenstein.
HOW TO APPLY In writing to the correspondent.
WHO TO APPLY TO Mr Sugarwhite, 5 Windus Road, London W16 6UT *Tel* 020 8880 8910
CC NO 266075   **ESTABLISHED** 1973

■ E & E Kernkraut Charities Limited

WHERE FUNDING CAN BE GIVEN UK.
WHAT IS FUNDED General charitable purposes, Jewish orgnisations and education.
FINANCES *Year* 2001–02 *Income* £145,000 *Grants* £174,646 *Assets* £111,095
TRUSTEES E Kernkraut, Chair; Mrs E Kernkraut; Joseph Kernkraut; Jacob Kernkraut.
HOW TO APPLY In writing to the correspondent.
WHO TO APPLY TO E Kernkraut, Chair, The Knoll, Fountayne Road, London N16 7EA *Tel* 020 8806 7947
CC NO 275636   **ESTABLISHED** 1978

■ The Peter Kershaw Trust

WHERE FUNDING CAN BE GIVEN Manchester and the surrounding district only.
WHO CAN BENEFIT Registered charities benefiting young adults and older people, carers and people who are disadvantaged by poverty, homeless or socially isolated.
WHAT IS FUNDED Medical research, grants to medical and other institutions, bursaries for schools.
WHAT IS NOT FUNDED No grants to individuals.
TYPE OF GRANT One-off or core costs. Also research, running costs, salaries and start-up costs. Funding may be given for up to three years.

RANGE OF GRANTS £5,000–£40,000.

SAMPLE GRANTS £35,872 to John Charnley Research Institute for hip replacement surgery research; £25,000 to Prestwich Methodist Youth Association for a youth worker; £18,200 to Withington Girls' School for bursaries; £15,000 to Burnage Multi-Agency Group for a youth worker; £10,000 each to After Adoption for a social worker, and Relate for a social worker; £5,000 to Mustard Tree for a training officer.

FINANCES *Year* 2001–02 *Income* £321,579 *Grants* £454,263 *Assets* £5,958,275

TRUSTEES H F Kershaw; M L Rushbrooke; R P Kershaw; H W E Thompson; D Tully.

HOW TO APPLY In writing to the correspondent.

WHO TO APPLY TO B Peak, Secretary, 22 Ashworth Park, Knutsford, Cheshire WA16 9DE *Tel* 01565 651086 *E-mail* brian_peak@compuserve.com

CC NO 268934   ESTABLISHED 1974

■ The Kessler Foundation

WHERE FUNDING CAN BE GIVEN UK.

WHAT IS FUNDED The foundation will assist organisations which may be devoted to: the advancement of Jewish religion, learning, education and culture; the improvement of inter-faith, community and race relations, and the combating of prejudice; the alleviation of the problems of minority and disadvantaged groups; the protection, maintenance and monitoring of human rights; the promotion of health and welfare; the protection and preservation of records and objects with special significance to the Jewish and general community; or the encouragement of arts, literature and science including archaeology, natural history and protection of the environment with special reference to the Jewish community.

WHAT IS NOT FUNDED In general the foundation will not support the larger well-known charities with an income in excess of £100,000, and will not provide grants for social, medical and welfare projects which are the responsibility of local or national government.

RANGE OF GRANTS Up to £1,000.

SAMPLE GRANTS £1,000 each to the Brighton Jewish Film Festival, International Postgraduate Jewish Studies Conference and the Institute of Multicultural Education for Israel; £950 each to Counselling in the Community and Herzliya Museum; £850 to the Anglo-Israel Archaeological Society.

FINANCES *Year* 1999–2000 *Income* £293,000 *Grants* £22,500 *Assets* £578,000

TRUSTEES Mrs J Jacobs; L Blackstone, Chair; R A Fass; Prof. M Geller; Lady Susan Gilbert; Mrs J F Mayers; P Morgenstern; E J Temko.

HOW TO APPLY Applications will be accepted only on the foundation's application form which is available from the secretary at the above address. The trustees meet at least twice a year in June and December. Applicants will be notified of decisions as soon as possible after then.

WHO TO APPLY TO Richard A Fass, Secretary, The Jewish Chronicle, 25 Furnival Street, London EC4A 1JT *Tel* 020 7415 1500 *Fax* 020 7405 0278 *E-mail* kesslerfoundation@thejc.com

CC NO 290759   ESTABLISHED 1984

■ The Ursula Keyes Trust

WHERE FUNDING CAN BE GIVEN Chester, but occasionally other areas.

WHO CAN BENEFIT Individuals and institutions benefiting at risk groups, and people who are disadvantaged by poverty, socially isolated or sick.

WHAT IS FUNDED Ranges from medical research to practical support, e.g. purchase of equipment, wheelchairs and funding for a hospice to a wide range of activities in the medical/social field with an emphasis on medical research, welfare and care work.

WHAT IS NOT FUNDED No support for students or political groups.

TYPE OF GRANT Small and large grants.

RANGE OF GRANTS £1,000–£120,000, although most are for under £10,000.

SAMPLE GRANTS £50,000 to Kings School Bursary Fund; £48,000 to The Countess of Chester Hospital NHS Trust for the endovascular graft fund; £30,000 to Barrowmore; £25,000 to Hospice of the Good Shepherd; £10,000 each to Chester in Concert and Claire House Children's Hospice; £9,900 to Countess of Chester Hospital NHS Trust for the women's and children's directorate; £5,000 each to Cheshire Military Museum and St James Church Yard – Christleton; £2,300 to Chester Crossroads Limited; £2,000 each to Cheshire Literature Festival and Cheshire – Deesside Committee for the Deaf; £1,000 to Dial House for the 1999 Chester Disability Arts Festival.

FINANCES *Year* 1999 *Income* £272,000 *Grants* £232,000 *Assets* £4,500,000

TRUSTEES J F Kane, Chair; Dr R A Owen; H M Shaw; P R Wise; Dr A E Elliot; J R Leaman.

HOW TO APPLY In writing to the correspondent.

WHO TO APPLY TO P R Wise, Trustee, c/o Hillyer McKeown, 90–92 Telegraph Road, Heswall, Wirral CH60 0AQ *Tel* 0151 342 6136

CC NO 517200   ESTABLISHED 1985

■ The Kidani Memorial Trust

WHERE FUNDING CAN BE GIVEN UK and Japan.

WHO CAN BENEFIT Cancer related charities, organisations and associations.

WHAT IS FUNDED Organisations in the field of research, support, care, advice or activity relating to cancer, people who are disabled and older people, the education and training of young Japanese and English people, and training and care of guide dogs and rescue dogs.

TYPE OF GRANT One-off grants for capital and project research. Funding for longer periods is at the discretion of the trustees.

RANGE OF GRANTS £6,000–£50,000.

SAMPLE GRANTS £10,500 to the Momiji Project, an Anglo-Japanese Young People's Exchange Programme. The contribution represented one third of the total cost incurred in funding a trip to Japan by a team of five wheelchair bound football players to compete in an Anglo-Japanese football tournament.

FINANCES *Year* 2002 *Income* £800,000 *Grants* £130,000 *Assets* £2,800,000

TRUSTEES DW Trustees Limited; Peter Milner; James Howes.

HOW TO APPLY In writing to the correspondent.

WHO TO APPLY TO Peter Milner, Trustee, Galsworthy & Stones, PO Box 145, Hawksford House,

Caledonia Place, St Helier, Jersey JE4 8QP
Tel 01534 836800 *Fax* 01534 836999
E-mail mail@galsworthy.com
Website www.galsworthy.com
cc no Y00177

....

■ The Robert Kiln Charitable Trust

WHERE FUNDING CAN BE GIVEN UK, with a special interest in Hertfordshire and Bedfordshire. Occasionally overseas.

WHO CAN BENEFIT Organisations benefiting archaeologists, small environmental organisations and small local music projects..

WHAT IS FUNDED General charitable purposes with a preference for small organisations.

WHAT IS NOT FUNDED Applications from individuals, churches, schools, artistic projects (such as theatre groups) or large national appeals will not be considered.

TYPE OF GRANT Usually one-off, or instalments for particular projects.

RANGE OF GRANTS £250–£3,500. Mostly £500.

SAMPLE GRANTS £3,500 to Uper Nene Archaeological Society; £2,500 to Rescue British Archeological Trust; £2,000 to Hertford Symphony Orchestra; £1,550 to East Hertfordshire Archeological Society; £1,500 to University College London; £1,000 each to British Archeological Awards 2002, Kilmartin House Trust, Shropshire Union Canal Society, and Sussex Archaeological Society; £750 to Rainforest Concern – London.

FINANCES *Year* 2001–02 *Income* £42,000 *Grants* £27,650

TRUSTEES Mrs S F Chappell; S W J Kiln; Mrs B Kiln; Dr N P Akers; Mrs J Akers; G M Kiln.

OTHER INFORMATION The trust stated: 'Most of the income is allocated to regular beneficiaries, where relationship has been built up over many years (60%). The trustees are keen to support new projects, particularly those from small local organisations. The trustees support many charities where they have a particular interest.'

HOW TO APPLY In writing to the correspondent, setting out as much information as seems relevant and, if possible, costings and details of any other support. Two distribution meetings are held each year, usually in January and July. The trust will no longer acknowledge receipt of applications unless an sae is enclosed.

WHO TO APPLY TO Mrs Margaret Archer, 15a Bull Plain, Hertford SG14 1DX

cc no 262756   **ESTABLISHED** 1970

....

■ King George's Fund for Sailors

WHERE FUNDING CAN BE GIVEN UK and Commonwealth.

WHO CAN BENEFIT Organisations caring for seafarers whether these are officers or ratings, men or women, past or present of the Royal Navy, the Merchant Navy, the Fishing Fleets and their dependants.

WHAT IS FUNDED Registered nautical charities and other registered charities which assist seafarers and their dependants in distress, provide training for young people to become sailors, provide training for sailors and support for other institutions which promote safety at sea.

WHAT IS NOT FUNDED The fund does not make any grants direct to individuals but rather helps other organisations which do this. However, the fund may be able to advise in particular cases about a suitable organisation to approach. Full details of such organisations are to be found in

the companion volume, *Guide to Grants for Individuals in Need.*

TYPE OF GRANT Annual grants for general purposes; capital grants for specific projects such as new buildings, modernisations, conversions, etc.; and interim grants may be considered at any time. Core costs, feasibility studies, recurring and running costs will also be considered.

RANGE OF GRANTS £300–£500,000.

SAMPLE GRANTS £910,000 to Royal Naval Benevolent Trust for grants to seafarers; £599,000 to Shipwrecked Mariners' Society for grants to seafarers; £400,000 to Royal Naval & Royal Marines' Childrens' Fund for education and other support for seafarers' children; £88,000 to Royal National Mission to Deep Sea Fishermen for support for Fishermens' Mission; £81,000 to Merchant Seamen's War Memorial Society; £60,000 to Ex-Services Mental Welfare Society for support for medical and other care for ex-seafarers; £55,000 to Broughton House.

FINANCES *Year* 2001 *Grants* £3,627,000

TRUSTEES The General Council, of which Admiral Sir Brian Brown is chair and Captain D C Glass is deputy chairman.

PUBLICATIONS *Directory of Nautical Charities* published every two to three years (£5). *Flagship* quarterly newsletter.

HOW TO APPLY Applications from organisations should be addressed to 'the director, finance and grants'. Trustees meet in July and November.

WHO TO APPLY TO Commodore Barry Bryant, Director General, 8 Hatherley Street, London SW1P 2YY *Tel* 020 7932 0000 *Website* www.kgfs.org.uk
cc no 226446   **ESTABLISHED** 1917

....

■ The King's Fund (King Edward's Hospital Fund for London)

WHERE FUNDING CAN BE GIVEN London.

WHO CAN BENEFIT Voluntary or statutory organisations in the health sector in or serving Greater London. Funding is available to organisations that wish to improve the health of Londoners. Beneficiaries might including people who are homeless, refugees and people living with specific health conditions. The fund will also consider funding health related projects for people with mental ill health or who are disabled and their carers, lesbians and gay men and people who are disadvantaged by poverty or who are socially isolated.

WHAT IS FUNDED Projects which tackle inequalities in health and social injustice; projects which promote cultural diversity in health; projects which encourage public, patient and user involvement in healthcare; projects which promote co-operation across service and professional boundaries.

WHAT IS NOT FUNDED No support for medical or clinical research; general appeals; long-term funding (maximum length of funding is three years); capital projects (buildings and equipment, including medical equipment and vehicles); holidays and outings; individuals; initiatives in complementary therapies which have no strategic significance; local projects based outside London; projects where the work has already started; projects that are seeking ongoing funding after a statutory grant has run out.

TYPE OF GRANT Development grants are revenue grants for up to three years.

....

591

RANGE OF GRANTS The average size of a development grant is £25,000 per year. The average length of a grant is two years.

SAMPLE GRANTS £150,000 to Research Council for Complementary Medicine; £90,000 each to the Metropolitan Hospital Sunday Fund and Newham Asian Women's Project; £87,000 to Refugee Education and Training Advisory Service; £64,000 to Cruse Bereavement Care; £52,000 to Health Initiatives for Youth; £31,000 to Alcohol Recovery Project.

FINANCES *Year* 2001 *Income* £8,400,000 *Grants* £2,496,000 *Assets* £141,000,000

TRUSTEES The management committee under the authority of the president and general council, including Sir Graham Hart, Chair.

OTHER INFORMATION The King's Fund also provides leadership development programmes which aims to raise management standards in the health care fields through seminars, courses and field-based consultancy; policy and development which aims to support innovations in the NHS and related organisations, to learn from them, and to encourage the use of good new ideas and practices; and conference facilities and a library service for those interested in health care.

HOW TO APPLY Applicants should request a copy of the full guidelines for development or small grants, available from the fund or downloadable from its website www.kingsfund.org.uk. Applications for the development grants programme are considered five times a year, in February, May, July, October and December, but they need to be submitted at least three months before the meeting concerned, and at least four months before the project starts. Applications for the small grants programme are considered by a panel which looks at applications every two months; these must be received at least a month in advance.

WHO TO APPLY TO The The Grants Department, 11–13 Cavendish Square, London W1G 0AN *Tel* 020 7307 2495 *Fax* 020 7307 2621 *E-mail* grants@kingsfund.org.uk *Website* www.kingsfund.org.uk
CC NO 207401   **ESTABLISHED** 1897

■ The Mary Kinross Charitable Trust

WHERE FUNDING CAN BE GIVEN UK.

WHO CAN BENEFIT Registered charities benefiting research workers, students and people disadvantaged by poverty.

WHAT IS FUNDED General charitable purposes. Donations confined to projects which the trust promotes and manages, particularly in the areas of medical research, to benefit the communities of which trustees have direct knowledge: youth; mental health and penal affairs. Grants made under the heading of youth are often made with crime prevention in mind.

WHAT IS NOT FUNDED No grants to individuals.

TYPE OF GRANT Capital projects, core costs and recurring.

SAMPLE GRANTS £630,000 to Moseley Community Development Trust; £305,000 to support the work carried out by Professor Raymond Dolan who holds the Kinross Chair of Neuropsychiatry at the Institute of Neurology; £205,000 to National Schizophrenia Fellowship (now Rethink) to develop a 'social firm'; £60,000 over three years to the Inside Out Trust; £55,000 to Manic Depression Fellowship over four years; £35,000 to Chinnbrook Children and Parent's Project;

£22,000 to Youthwise – the Warstock and Billesley Detached Youth Project; £20,000 to Barry and Martin's Trust for HIV/AIDS care and education work in China; £16,000 to Newpin.

FINANCES *Year* 2001–02 *Income* £561,000 *Grants* £1,548,000

TRUSTEES Elizabeth Shields, Chair; Fiona Adams; Neil E Cross; H Jon Foulds; Robert McDougall.

HOW TO APPLY 'Neither written applications nor telephone calls are welcome. There is no application form or timetable and procedure for assessing applications.' Trustees meet quarterly.

WHO TO APPLY TO Fiona Adams, Trustee, 36 Grove Avenue, Moseley, Birmingham B13 9RY
CC NO 212206   **ESTABLISHED** 1957

■ The Kintore Charitable Trust

WHERE FUNDING CAN BE GIVEN Scotland with a preference for Grampian.

WHO CAN BENEFIT Organisations benefiting young people.

WHAT IS FUNDED Environmental groups, schemes which involve young people and local projects are all supported by the trust.

WHAT IS NOT FUNDED No grants to individuals.

FINANCES *Year* 2001–02 *Income* £19,800 *Grants* £40,000

TRUSTEES The Earl of Kintore; Turcan Connell.

HOW TO APPLY In writing to the correspondent. The trustees are not in a position to acknowledge individual applications.

WHO TO APPLY TO The Trustees, Turcan Connell, Princes Exchange, 1 Earl Grey Street, Edinburgh EH3 9EE *Tel* 0131 228 8111 *Fax* 0131 228 8118
SC NO SC000702   **ESTABLISHED** 1984

■ The Kirby & West Charitable Trust

WHERE FUNDING CAN BE GIVEN Leicestershire.

WHO CAN BENEFIT Registered charities only.

WHAT IS FUNDED General charitable purposes.

WHAT IS NOT FUNDED No grants to individuals.

SAMPLE GRANTS £22,000 to Emily Forte School – Leicester; £5,000 each to Lord Mayor's Appeal, Rainbow's, Willoughby Waterleys Village Hall Trust and Leicester Mosaic; £1,000 to Leicester Education-Business Co. Ltd.; £500 each to National Dairyman's Benevolent Institution (Inc), LORUS, NSPCC, British Red Cross, Council Order of St. John, Royal Society for the Blind and WRVS.

FINANCES *Year* 2002 *Income* £23,671 *Grants* £59,000 *Assets* £667,687

TRUSTEES I M Grundy; J C Smith; M J Smith.

HOW TO APPLY In writing to the correspondent. Apply at any time.

WHO TO APPLY TO J C Smith, Trustee, Kirby & West Ltd, Richard III Road, Leicester LE3 5QU *Tel* 0116 222 0000 *Fax* 0116 222 0011
CC NO 700119   **ESTABLISHED** 1988

■ The Graham Kirkham Foundation

WHERE FUNDING CAN BE GIVEN UK and Ireland.

WHO CAN BENEFIT Organisations benefiting children and young adults, armed service personnel, students and people disadvantaged by poverty.

WHAT IS FUNDED The promotion or development of the study and/or appreciation of literature, art, music or science; the advancement of education of people of any age and the advancement of physical education of young people; relief of hardship or poverty by providing financial assistance and accommodation; relief of illness and disease, including research into treatment and prevention; welfare of birds and animals through the support of rescue homes, hospitals, sanctuaries and other organisations; relief of poverty and hardship and the promotion of well being of people connected to the armed forces; the provision of support and protection to those dependent upon or in danger of becoming dependent on drugs; to provide public recreation facilities in the interest of social welfare; and to protect and preserve buildings of architectural interest or sites of historical interest or natural beauty.

TYPE OF GRANT One-off.

RANGE OF GRANTS £5,000–£50,000.

SAMPLE GRANTS £50,000 to The Presidents Award; £20,000 to NSPCC; £15,000 to Charlotte Beadle Italia Conti School; £10,000 to Martin House Children's Hospice; £5,000 each to Cancer Bacup and London Immunotherapy Cancer Trust.

FINANCES *Year* 2000–01 *Income* £122,712 *Grants* £105,000 *Assets* £41,090

TRUSTEES Lord G Kirkham; Lady P Kirkham; M Kirkham.

HOW TO APPLY In writing to the correspondent.

WHO TO APPLY TO Barry Todhunter, Bentley Moor Lane, Adwick-le-Street, Doncaster, South Yorkshire DN6 7BD *Tel* 01302 330365

CC NO 1002390   **ESTABLISHED** 1991

■ Kirkley Poor's Land Estate

WHERE FUNDING CAN BE GIVEN The parish of Kirkley.

WHO CAN BENEFIT Individuals and organisations benefiting people who are of pensionable age, students, former Kirkley High School pupils, at risk groups, and people who are disabled, disadvantaged by poverty, socially isolated or in conditions of need, hardship or distress.

WHAT IS FUNDED Welfare and disability. The trust administers a grocery voucher scheme enabling people of pensionable age in Kirkley to receive a grant each winter to purchase groceries. It cooperates with Kirkley High School to make grants to former pupils whose parents have low incomes to help with their expenses at university or other further education establishments. All funding has to be calculated to reduce identified need, hardship or distress.

TYPE OF GRANT One-off.

RANGE OF GRANTS £10–£3,250.

SAMPLE GRANTS £3,250 each to St John's Housing Trust and Waveney Women's Refugee; £2,500 to Waveney Counselling; £1,869 to Suffolk County Council; £1,500 each to Kirkley Church Hall, Kirkley Salvation Army, Waveney Counselling and Waveney Rape Crisis.

FINANCES *Year* 2001–02 *Income* £58,421 *Grants* £78,768 *Assets* £1,100,000

OTHER INFORMATION £4,677 was awarded to individuals in 2001–02.

HOW TO APPLY In writing to the correspondent.

WHO TO APPLY TO Ian R Walker, Clerk, 4 Station Road, Lowestoft, Suffolk NR32 4QF *Tel* 01502 514964

CC NO 210177   **ESTABLISHED** 1976

■ The Richard Kirkman Charitable Trust

WHERE FUNDING CAN BE GIVEN UK, with a preference for Hampshire.

WHO CAN BENEFIT Registered charities and individuals.

WHAT IS FUNDED The trustees are considering financing various plans for alleviating drug addiction.

RANGE OF GRANTS £250–£500.

SAMPLE GRANTS £3,500 to BLESMA; £1,000 each to Wessex Children's Hospice Trust, Aidis Trust and Salvation Army; £500 each to Hampshire and Isle of Wight Association for the Deaf, Leukaemia Busters, NSPCC and Rose Road Association.

FINANCES *Year* 2001–02 *Income* £42,008 *Grants* £44,400

TRUSTEES M Howson-Green; Mrs F O Kirkman.

HOW TO APPLY The trust carries out its own research for beneficiaries and does not respond to applications by post or telephone.

WHO TO APPLY TO M Howson-Green, Trustee, Charter Court, Third Avenue, Southampton SO15 0AP *Tel* 023 8070 2345

CC NO 327972   **ESTABLISHED** 1988

■ Kirschel Foundation

WHERE FUNDING CAN BE GIVEN UK.

WHO CAN BENEFIT Registered charities.

WHAT IS FUNDED The trust states that its aims and objectives are 'to provide benefits to underprivileged persons, who may be either handicapped or lacking resources'. In practice this includes many Jewish organisations.

SAMPLE GRANTS £25,000 to Jewish Educational Trust; £19,000 to Friends of Ohr Somayach; £11,000 to Lubavitch Foundation of Scotland; £2,500 to Variety Club of Great Britain.

FINANCES *Year* 1999–2000 *Grants* £61,000 *Assets* £430

TRUSTEES Laurence Grant Kirschel; John Hoare.

HOW TO APPLY In writing to the correspondent.

WHO TO APPLY TO John Hoare, Trustee, 171 Wardour Street, London W1V 3TA *Tel* 020 7437 4372

CC NO 1067672   **ESTABLISHED** 1998

■ Robert Kitchin (Saddlers' Company)

WHERE FUNDING CAN BE GIVEN City of London and Greater London.

WHO CAN BENEFIT Organisations and student welfare.

WHAT IS FUNDED Education and general charitable purposes.

FINANCES *Year* 2001–02 *Income* £134,000

TRUSTEES Saddlers' Company.

OTHER INFORMATION Each year the charity gives a fixed percentage to two organisations – City University receives 50 per cent of net income, while St Ethelburga Centre for Reconciliation and Peace receives 15 per cent of net income. The remaining 35 per cent is distributed at the discretion of the trustees.

HOW TO APPLY In writing to the correspondent, but note the comments above.

WHO TO APPLY TO The Clerk to the Trustees, Saddlers' Company, Saddlers' Hall, 40 Gutter Lane, London EC2V 6BR *Tel* 020 7726 8661

CC NO 211169   **ESTABLISHED** 1891

■ Kleinwort Benson Charitable Trust

WHERE FUNDING CAN BE GIVEN UK, and local projects in the City of London and east London.

WHO CAN BENEFIT Registered UK charities.

WHAT IS FUNDED Education and outreach through the arts, environmental regeneration, welfare (including disabilities) and health.

WHAT IS NOT FUNDED No grants to individuals or local church appeals.

TYPE OF GRANT One-off; long-term initiatives up to a maximum of three years; projects, including those needing funding to access government funds; core costs in some cases.

RANGE OF GRANTS £250–£50,000. Mostly for £1,000 or less.

SAMPLE GRANTS £25,000 to East London Small Business Charity; £18,000 to Leyton Orient Community Sports Programme; £14,000 each to Atlantic College and Marie Curie Cancer Care; £13,000 each to British Heart Foundation and Queen Elizabeth Children's Hospital Fund; £10,000 to English Martyrs School.

FINANCES *Year* 2000 *Income* £283,000 *Grants* £240,000

TRUSTEES Kleinwort Benson Trustees Ltd.

OTHER INFORMATION The website now refers to the trust as Dresdner Kleinwort Wasserstein's Charitable Trust.

HOW TO APPLY In writing to the correspondent. Trustees meet quarterly in March, June, September and December.

WHO TO APPLY TO Dresdner Kleinwort Benson, 20 Fenchurch St, London EC3P 3DB *Tel* 020 7475 5088 *Fax* 020 7475 9710 *Website* www.drkw.com

CC NO 278180   **ESTABLISHED** 1979

■ Ernest Kleinwort Charitable Trust

WHERE FUNDING CAN BE GIVEN UK and overseas, especially Sussex.

WHO CAN BENEFIT Charities efficiently organised and managed by people of proven business ability.

WHAT IS FUNDED The main fields of work are wildlife and environmental conservation, disability, medical research, welfare of older people and welfare of young people.

WHAT IS NOT FUNDED Individuals and local charities outside Sussex are normally excluded.

TYPE OF GRANT Donations towards specific projects and annual subscriptions until further notice (mostly confined to Sussex).

SAMPLE GRANTS £105,000 to Little Black Bag Housing Association; £100,000 to River Trust; £55,000 to South of England Agricultural Society; £48,000 to East Sussex Disability Association; £30,000 each to Marie Stopes International, St Michael's Hospice and WWF UK; £25,000 each to Chichester Cathedral and Royal Agricultural Benevolent Fund; £23,000 each to Hazel Court School Parents Association and Wildfowl and Wetlands Trust.

FINANCES *Year* 2001–02 *Income* £1,276,000 *Grants* £1,520,000 *Assets* £43,064,000

TRUSTEES Kleinwort Benson Trustees Ltd; Madeleine, Lady Kleinwort; Earl of Limerick; Sir Richard Kleinwort; Miss M R Kleinwort; R M Ewing; Sir Christopher Lever; S M Robertson.

HOW TO APPLY In writing to the correspondent, enclosing a copy of the most recent annual report and financial statements. Trustees meet in March and October, but applications are considered throughout the year, normally within

two to three months of receipt. Only successful applicants are notified of the trustees' decision.

WHO TO APPLY TO The Secretary, PO Box 191, 10 Fenchurch Street, London EC3M 3LB *Tel* 020 7475 6246

CC NO 229665   **ESTABLISHED** 1963

■ The Marina Kleinwort Charitable Trust

WHERE FUNDING CAN BE GIVEN UK.

WHO CAN BENEFIT Dance organisations.

SAMPLE GRANTS £20,000 to Rambert Dance Company; £14,000 to Dancer's Career Development Fund; £2,500 to Royal Ballet School; £1,300 to Dance Teacher's Benevolent Fund .

FINANCES *Year* 2000–01 *Grants* £41,000

TRUSTEES Miss Marina Rose Kleinwort, Chair; David James Roper Robinson; Mrs Clare Elizabeth Louise McCullouch.

HOW TO APPLY In writing to the correspondent.

WHO TO APPLY TO The Secretary, PO Box 31337, London SW11 5GS

CC NO 1081825   **ESTABLISHED** 2000

■ The Sir James Knott Trust

WHERE FUNDING CAN BE GIVEN Northumberland, County Durham (including Hartlepool) and Tyne and Wear.

WHO CAN BENEFIT Registered charities only, benefiting people of all ages, with little restriction as to their religion or social circumstance.

WHAT IS FUNDED Grants to registered charities only, for the benefit of the community and particularly in the areas of education/expeditions, children and youth, community welfare, disability, service charities, heritage/museums, housing/homeless, conservation, medical care and research, the arts, older people, and maritime charities.

WHAT IS NOT FUNDED No applications are considered from individuals or from non-registered charities. Grants are only made to charities from within the north east of England, and from UK charities either operating within, or where work may be expected to be of benefit to, the north east of England.

TYPE OF GRANT One-off and core costs for one year or less. Buildings, capital, endowments, project, recurring costs, salaries and start-up costs for up to three years.

RANGE OF GRANTS From £100 to over £10,000 (average grant £5,000).

SAMPLE GRANTS £30,000 to maritime and associated charities; £20,000 each to High Sheriff Awards and various young people's associations; £10,000 each to Phoenix House for substance rehabilitation, and Widdrington Regeneration for a foot and mouth disease disposal site; £5,000 to Victim Support branches.

FINANCES *Year* 2002–03 *Income* £1,050,000 *Grants* £909,500

TRUSTEES Viscount Ridley; Mark Cornwall-Jones; Prof, Oliver James; Charles Baker-Cresswell.

HOW TO APPLY In writing to the correspondent, giving a brief description of the need, with relevant consideration to the following points: Who are you? How are you organised/managed? What is your aim? What co-ordination do you have with other organisations with similar aims? What do you do and how does it benefit the community?

How many people use or take advantage of your facilities? How have you been funded in the past, how will you be funded in the future? Enclose summary of last year's balance sheet. How much do you need, what for and when? Have you thought about depreciation/running costs/replacement? If your project is not funded in full, what do you propose to do with the money you have raised? What is the overall cost, what is the deficit and how are you planning to cover the deficit? Is it an open-ended commitment, or when will you become self-supporting? If you will never be self-supporting, what is your long-term fundraising strategy? Who else have you asked for money, and how have they responded? What are you doing yourselves to raise money? Have you applied to the National Lottery? When will you get the result? If you have not applied, are you eligible and when will you apply? What is your registered charity number, or which registered charity is prepared to administer funds on your behalf? How can you be contacted by telephone, fax or email? Trustees normally meet in spring, summer and autumn. Applications need to be submitted up to two months in advance.

WHO TO APPLY TO Vivien Stapley, Secretary, 16–18 Hood Street, Newcastle upon Tyne NE1 6JQ *Tel* 0191 230 4016 *Fax* 0191 230 4016
CC NO 1001363   **ESTABLISHED** 1990

■ The Knowles Charitable Trust

WHERE FUNDING CAN BE GIVEN Barnet, Brent, Camden, Hackney, Harrow and City of Westminster. Applications from within London, but outside these specific boroughs, will be considered in exceptional circumstances.

WHO CAN BENEFIT Smaller organisations benefiting people in need arising from their age or physical or mental disabilities. Due to limited funds available the needs of older people are given preference.

WHAT IS FUNDED The provision of housing and any associated amenities and services.

WHAT IS NOT FUNDED Any projects not concerned with the provision of housing and any associated amenities and services.

TYPE OF GRANT One-off projects and start-up costs will be considered. Funding for capital or revenue costs is available for up to two years.

RANGE OF GRANTS Up to £15,000.

SAMPLE GRANTS In 2000–01: £16,000 to Paddington Churches Housing Association (who also administer the trust) for support services for older people; £5,000 to Central and Cecil Housing Trust towards an arts and education programme for older people; £3,000 to Councel and Care for the Elderly for a risk and restraint project concerning the care of people with dementia; £2,500 to Umbrella for a warm winter appeal for people with severe mental health needs; £2,000 to Staying Put – City of Westminster for a care and repair service; and £1,000 to Red Brick Housing Group to help fund a part-time development worker.

FINANCES *Year* 2001–02 *Income* £35,000 *Grants* £37,000 *Assets* £850,000

TRUSTEES Margaret Hepburn; Jacqueline Cannon; Dame Simone Prendergast; Judith Allen; Ann Vedi; Eric Witchell; Daniel Pross.

HOW TO APPLY In writing to the correspondent at any time; however, trustees meet quarterly, usually in March, June, September and December.

WHO TO APPLY TO Robert Smith, Secretary, Paddington Churches Housing Association, Canterbury House, Canterbury Road, London NW6 5SQ *Tel* 020 8537 4171 *Fax* 020 8537 4198 *Minicom* 020 8537 4181 *E-mail* info@ghg.org.uk *Website* www.ghg.org.uk
CC NO 293017   **ESTABLISHED** 1984

■ The Kobler Trust

WHERE FUNDING CAN BE GIVEN UK.

WHO CAN BENEFIT Charitable organisations benefiting people of all ages, relating to the arts, education or health.

WHAT IS FUNDED General charitable purposes with emphasis on the arts, healthcare and education.

WHAT IS NOT FUNDED Grant are only given to individuals in exceptional circumstances.

TYPE OF GRANT No restrictions. These vary from small grants on a one-off basis for a specific project to a continuing relationship.

RANGE OF GRANTS £200–£100,000.

SAMPLE GRANTS £25,000 to Crusaid for general purposes; £20,000 each to Covent Garden Festival for general purposes, Chicken Shed Theatre Company for subsidised child fees, and Jewish Care for general funds; £15,000 to Cancer Bacup for general purposes; £12,500 to Tricycle Theatre for 'Colour of Justice'; £12,000 to Pavilion Trust for opera in schools; £7,300 to Hotel and Catering Benevolent Society for Christmas Hampers; £5,000 to New Tabernacle Trust.

FINANCES *Year* 1999 *Income* £217,474 *Grants* £309,814 *Assets* £4,814,185

TRUSTEES A Xuereb; A H Stone; Ms J L Evans; J W Israelsohn.

OTHER INFORMATION The policy of the trust is to help where resources are not generally otherwise available. It tends to steer clear of assisting established organisations and prefers to deal with smaller charitable organisations.

HOW TO APPLY In writing to the correspondent.

WHO TO APPLY TO Ms J L Evans, Trustee, Lewis Silkin, 12 Gough Square, London EC4A 3DN
CC NO 275237   **ESTABLISHED** 1963

■ The Kohn Foundation

WHERE FUNDING CAN BE GIVEN UK.

WHO CAN BENEFIT Registered charities.

WHAT IS FUNDED General charitable purposes, especially education, Jewish religion, relief of poverty, care of people who are sick or who have a mental illness, medical research, and the arts (particularly music).

SAMPLE GRANTS £145,000 to Monteverdi Choir and Orchestra Ltd; £50,000 to Royal Society; £25,000 to Wigmore Hall International Song Contest; £10,000 each to National Osteoporosis Society and Vega Science Trust; £6,000 to Hasmonean High School; £5,000 each to Jewish Music Institute and Liver Research Trust; £2,000 to Rudolf Kempe Society; £1,250 to United Jewish Israel Appeal.

FINANCES *Year* 2000 *Income* £78,403 *Grants* £270,125 *Assets* £3,352,477

TRUSTEES Dr Ralph Kohn, Chair; Zahava Kohn; Anthony A Forwood.

HOW TO APPLY In writing to the correspondent.

WHO TO APPLY TO Dr R Kohn, Chair to the Trustees, 100 Fetter Lane, London EC4A 1BN
CC NO 1003951   **ESTABLISHED** 1991

■ KPR Charitable Trust

WHERE FUNDING CAN BE GIVEN UK.
WHO CAN BENEFIT Medical organisations.
SAMPLE GRANTS £10,000 each to The Ronald Raven Chair in Clinical Oncology and The Temenos Academy; £2,000 to NEST (UK).
FINANCES *Year* 1998–99 *Income* £25,000 *Grants* £22,000 *Assets* £52,000
TRUSTEES Alan Parker; Caroline Louise Parker; Andrew Fenwick.
OTHER INFORMATION In 2001–02 the income was £50,000, but no further information was available for this year.
HOW TO APPLY In writing to the correspondent.
WHO TO APPLY TO Graham Chambers, Rotherwick House, PO Box 900, 3 Thomas More Street, London E1W 1YX *Tel* 020 7628 4321
CC NO 1058058   **ESTABLISHED** 1996

■ Krattiger Rennison Charitable Trust

WHERE FUNDING CAN BE GIVEN Devon and the UK.
WHAT IS FUNDED The advancement of education specifically relating to artistic subjects, and work with AIDS including research into the disease, assistance to those suffering from AIDS and the promotion of information relating to AIDS.
SAMPLE GRANTS £27,000 to Crusaid; £20,500 to British Youth Opera; £20,000 to London East Aids Network; £17,500 to Grandma's; £15,000 to Bristol Old Vic Theatre School; £2,200 to National HIV Nurses Association.
FINANCES *Year* 2000–01 *Income* £24,698 *Grants* £102,200
TRUSTEES A L Banes; Ruth M Blaug; Prof. Robert J Pratt.
HOW TO APPLY In writing to the correspondent.
WHO TO APPLY TO Professor Robert J Pratt, Trustee, 35 Sherbrooke Road, London SW6 7QJ
CC NO 1015838   **ESTABLISHED** 1992

■ The Kreditor Charitable Trust

WHERE FUNDING CAN BE GIVEN UK, with preferences for London and north east England.
WHO CAN BENEFIT Jewish organisations and UK welfare organisations benefiting Jewish people, at risk groups, and people who are disadvantaged by poverty or socially isolated.
WHAT IS FUNDED Jewish organisations working in education and social and medical welfare.
SAMPLE GRANTS Previous beneficiaries include Fordeve Ltd, London Academy of Jewish Studies, Jerusalem Ladies Society, NW London Talmudical College, Ravenswood, Academy for Rabbinical Research, British Friends of Israel War Disabled, Kosher Meals on Wheels, Jewish Marriage Council and Jewish Care. Non-Jewish organisations supported included RNID, UNICEF UK and British Diabetic Association.
FINANCES *Year* 1998–99 *Income* £74,000 *Grants* £38,000 *Assets* £90,000
TRUSTEES P M Kreditor; Merle Kreditor.
OTHER INFORMATION This information is reprinted from the last edition of this guide.
HOW TO APPLY In writing to the correspondent.
WHO TO APPLY TO P M Kreditor, Trustee, Gerald Kreditor & Co., Chartered Accountants, Tudor House, Llanvanor Road, London NW2 2AQ *Tel* 020 8209 1535 *Fax* 020 8209 1923
CC NO 292649   **ESTABLISHED** 1985

■ The Kreitman Foundation

WHERE FUNDING CAN BE GIVEN UK and Israel.
WHO CAN BENEFIT Registered charities benefiting carers, people who are disadvantaged by poverty, disabled or have a mental illness, and Jewish people.
WHAT IS FUNDED Education, health, disability, culture, Jewish religion, the arts, and the environment.
WHAT IS NOT FUNDED No grants to individuals.
TYPE OF GRANT Project, buildings, capital, core costs, endowments and one-off. Funding may be given for up to and over three years.
RANGE OF GRANTS £100–£500,000.
SAMPLE GRANTS £2,623,000 to Ben-Gurion University Foundation; £82,000 to Joint Jewish Charitable Trust; £38,000 to Friends of the Hebrew University of Jerusalem; £32,000 to Royal National Theatre.
FINANCES *Year* 1999–2000 *Income* £1,100,000 *Grants* £2,831,000 *Assets* £31,700,000
TRUSTEES Hyman Kreitman; Mrs Irene Kreitman; Eric Charles.
HOW TO APPLY Grants are only given to charities of which the trustees have a personal knowledge. The trust is unable to respond to applications.
WHO TO APPLY TO Eric Charles, Trustee, Citroen Wells (Chartered accountants), 1 Devonshire Street, London W1N 2DR
CC NO 261195   **ESTABLISHED** 1970

■ The Neil Kreitman Foundation

WHERE FUNDING CAN BE GIVEN UK and Israel.
WHO CAN BENEFIT Registered charities and other tax exempt charitable organisations benefiting children and young adults, students, at risk groups and people who are disadvantaged by poverty or socially isolated.
WHAT IS FUNDED Culture, education, health and welfare.
WHAT IS NOT FUNDED No grants to individuals.
TYPE OF GRANT Primarily general funds with some small capital grants and core costs.
RANGE OF GRANTS Generally £500–£30,000.
SAMPLE GRANTS £137,384 to Ashmolean Museum; £30,000 to British Library; £15,000 to Ancient India and Iran Trust; £13,500 to Corpus Inscriptionium Iranicarum; £10,000 each to British Museum, Onaway Trust, Release Legal Emergency and Drugs Service, SE Cross College Development Fund, and Victoria and Albert Museum.
FINANCES *Year* 2000–01 *Income* £277,986 *Grants* £277,134 *Assets* £5,799,587
TRUSTEES N R Kreitman; Mrs S I Kreitman; Eric Charles.
HOW TO APPLY In writing to the correspondent.
WHO TO APPLY TO Eric Charles, Trustee, Citroen Wells (Chartered Accountants), Devonshire House, 1 Devonshire Street, London W1W 5DR *Tel* 020 7304 2000
CC NO 267171   **ESTABLISHED** 1974

■ The Heinz & Anna Kroch Foundation

WHERE FUNDING CAN BE GIVEN UK.
WHO CAN BENEFIT Individuals with chronic illnesses; disabled people; people who are disadvantaged by poverty; homeless people; victims of abuse and domestic violence; and victims of war.
WHAT IS FUNDED The foundation exists to further medical research, support people who have

suffered injustice and relieve hardship amongst people with medical conditions.

WHAT IS NOT FUNDED No grants are made to students or for holidays. Overseas applications or projects are not considered.

TYPE OF GRANT Grants do not exceed £10,000. Research and funding of up to three years will be considered.

RANGE OF GRANTS £500–£7,000 to organisations.

SAMPLE GRANTS £9,000 in total to University College London; £7,000 to Breakthrough Breast Cancer; £2,000 each to Eyeless Trust, VISCERAL and Bath Institute of Medical Engineering; £1,000 each to Hearing Research Trust, Northern Friends of ARMS and Iris Fund; £500 to Brainwave.

FINANCES *Year* 2000–01 *Income* £143,888 *Grants* £84,000 *Assets* £2,117,473

TRUSTEES Ms Ann Carol Kroch; Christopher Richardson; Daniel Lang; Dr Amatsia Kashti; John Seagrim; Mrs Margaret Cottam.

HOW TO APPLY Appeals are considered monthly. Applications on behalf of individuals must be submitted through a recognised body, i.e. social services, GP/consultant, CAB or welfare rights. Applications for medical research should include details of the research, cost of the project and any further relevant information, which should be no more than four pages long. Research applications are considered April/May and October/November. Applications always receive a reply. Please include an sae.

WHO TO APPLY TO Mrs H Astle, PO Box 5, Bentham, Lancaster LA2 7XA *Tel* 01524 263001 *Fax* 01524 263001 *E-mail* HAKF50@hotmail.com

CC NO 207622   **ESTABLISHED** 1962

....

■ The Kyte Charitable Trust

WHERE FUNDING CAN BE GIVEN UK.

WHO CAN BENEFIT Organisations benefiting medical professionals and research workers. Support may go to at risk groups, and people who are disadvantaged by poverty or socially isolated.

WHAT IS FUNDED Medical research, community services.

FINANCES *Year* 2000–01 *Income* £60,995 *Grants* £99,470 *Assets* £117

TRUSTEES D M Kyte; T M Kyte; A H Kyte.

HOW TO APPLY In writing to the correspondent.

WHO TO APPLY TO The Trustees, Business Design Centre, 52 Upper Street, London N1 0QH *Tel* 020 7390 7777

CC NO 1035886   **ESTABLISHED** 1994

■ Labone Charitable Trust

WHERE FUNDING CAN BE GIVEN UK.
WHO CAN BENEFIT Roman Catholics and registered charities.
WHAT IS FUNDED General charitable purposes.
SAMPLE GRANTS £5,000 each to The Columban Fathers and The Church in Need; £1,000 to Mary Magdalen Foundation.
FINANCES *Year* 1998–99 *Income* £100,000 *Grants* £12,500
TRUSTEES A Stiegler; Mrs A B Stiegler; C J Young.
HOW TO APPLY In writing to the correspondent.
WHO TO APPLY TO Mrs Stiegler, Trustee, 17 Eskdale Drive, Aspley, Nottingham NG8 5GZ *Tel* 0115 929 4700
CC NO 1042836 **ESTABLISHED** 1994

■ Lacims-Maclis Charitable Trust

WHERE FUNDING CAN BE GIVEN UK.
WHO CAN BENEFIT Charitable organisations.
WHAT IS FUNDED General charitable purposes.
RANGE OF GRANTS £100–£1,000.
SAMPLE GRANTS £1,000 each to Barnardos, Community Links, Epsom College Foundation, Fairbridge, Health Unlimited, Prince's Youth Business Trust, RSABI, St Botolph's Project and St Patricks Missionary Society.
FINANCES *Year* 1999–2000 *Income* £24,000 *Grants* £21,000 *Assets* £274,000
TRUSTEES R P Tullett; A H Bartlett; M N C Kerr-Dineen; R Leigh Wood.
HOW TO APPLY In writing to the correspondent.
WHO TO APPLY TO R P Tullett, Trustee, Laing & Cruikshank Investment Management Ltd, Broadwalk House, 5 Appold Street, London EC2A 2DA *Tel* 020 7588 2800
CC NO 265596 **ESTABLISHED** 1973

■ The Late Sir Pierce Lacy Charity Trust

WHERE FUNDING CAN BE GIVEN UK and overseas.
WHO CAN BENEFIT The trust only supports the Roman Catholic Church or associated institutions which are registered charities.
WHAT IS FUNDED Medicine and health, welfare, education, religion and general charitable purposes. Particularly charities working in the field of infrastructure development, residential facilities and services, Christian education, Christian outreach, Catholic bodies, charity or voluntary umbrella bodies, hospices, rehabilitation centres, advocacy, education and training, community services and community issues.
WHAT IS NOT FUNDED The trust only supports the Roman Catholic Church or associated institutions.
TYPE OF GRANT Recurrent small grants of £1,000 or less, buildings, capital, core costs, project, research, start-up costs and funding for more than three years may be considered.
RANGE OF GRANTS Most less than £500.
SAMPLE GRANTS £1,400 to Crusade of Rescue; £920 to St Francis Children's Society; £810 to Poor Mission Fund; £800 to St Cuthberts Mayne

RC School as a special donation; £720 to Society of St Vincent De Paul; £610 to Poor Mission Fund; £550 to Catholic Children's Society; £530 to St Francis Leprosy Guild.
FINANCES *Year* 2000–01 *Income* £53,000 *Grants* £28,000 *Assets* £583,000
TRUSTEES CGU Insurance PLC.
HOW TO APPLY In writing to the correspondent, at any time.
WHO TO APPLY TO P Burke, Head of Trustee Management, Norwich Union, Trustee Department, Pitheavlis, Perth PH2 0NH *Tel* 01738 895590 *Fax* 01738 895903
CC NO 1013505 **ESTABLISHED** 1992

■ Laing's Charitable Trust

WHERE FUNDING CAN BE GIVEN UK.
WHO CAN BENEFIT Existing and former employees of John Laing plc who are in need; UK registered charities or exempt charities.
WHAT IS FUNDED Projects and organisations working with homelessness, young people who are disadvantaged, education and the environment.
WHAT IS NOT FUNDED No grants to individuals (other than to Laing employees and/or their dependants).
TYPE OF GRANT Recurring and one-off.
SAMPLE GRANTS £25,000 to Homeless Link; £20,000 to Children's Society; £14,450 to Atlantic College; £11,000 to Northampton County Records Office; £10,000 each to Crime Concern, Prince's Trust, and WWF UK; £7,500 each to Business in the Community, Emmaus UK, and Hertfordshire Groundwork.
FINANCES *Year* 2002 *Income* £1,600,000 *Grants* £250,000 *Assets* £32,500,000
TRUSTEES C Laing; Sir Martin Laing; D C Madden; R I Sumner; G D Gibson.
OTHER INFORMATION A further £800,000 was distributed to former and present employees of the Laing building company.
HOW TO APPLY In writing to the correspondent. No particular application form is required. The trust says that all applications are acknowledged.
WHO TO APPLY TO Michael Hamilton, Secretary, The Waterfront, Elstree Road, Elstree, Herts WD6 3BS *Tel* 020 8236 8821
CC NO 236852 **ESTABLISHED** 1962

■ The Beatrice Laing Trust

WHERE FUNDING CAN BE GIVEN UK and overseas.
WHO CAN BENEFIT UK and local charities serving disadvantaged sections of the community, and UK and overseas missionary societies. Beneficiaries include missionaries, at risk groups, and people who are disabled, disadvantaged by poverty or socially isolated.
WHAT IS FUNDED The welfare of people who are homeless, older people, socially excluded and people with disabilities; agencies providing aid or involved in capacity building in developing countries.
WHAT IS NOT FUNDED No grants to individuals; no travel grants; no educational grants.
TYPE OF GRANT Usually capital costs or project funding on a one-off or recurrent basis. A few core cost grants to national organisations (rarely local).
RANGE OF GRANTS Most grants are between £1,000 and £5,000, occasionally larger.
SAMPLE GRANTS £28,000 to Echoes of Service in support of Echoes' evangelical missionary work; £20,000 each to Deafblind UK towards

construction of a national centre, Grove House Hospice towards a building extension, Royal National College for the Blind for refurbishment and Vassall Centre Trust for a disabled people's centre; £15,000 each to Africa Now – the first of three grants towards a land and water management programme, Calvert Trust Northumbria for new respite care facilities, Community Links Trust for a soft play area/ multi-sensory room and Riders for Health – first of three grants towards the cost of employing a fundraiser; £12,000 to Help the Hospices for a pilot purchasing project.

FINANCES *Year 2001–02 Income £1,290,660 Grants £951,000 Assets £25,000,000*

TRUSTEES Sir Maurice Laing; Sir Martin Laing; David E Laing; Christopher M Laing; John H Laing; Charles Laing; Paula Blacker.

HOW TO APPLY One application only is needed to apply to this or the Kirby Laing Foundation, Maurice Laing Foundation or Maurice and Hilda Laing Charitable Trust. Multiple applications will still only elicit a single reply; even then applicants are asked to accept non-response as a negative reply on behalf of all three trusts, unless a stamped addressed envelope is enclosed. Applications are considered monthly. These trusts make strenuous efforts to keep their overhead costs to a minimum. As they also make a very large number of grants each year, in proportion to their income the staff must rely almost entirely on the written applications submitted in selecting appeals to go forward to the trustees. Each application should contain all the information needed to allow such a decision to be reached, in as short and straightforward a way as possible. Specifically, each application should say what the money is for; how much is needed; how much has already been found; where the rest is to come from. Unless there is reasonable assurance on the last point the grant is unlikely to be recommended.

WHO TO APPLY TO Miss Elizabeth Harley, 33 Bunns Lane, London NW7 2DX *Tel* 020 8238 8890 *Fax* 020 8238 8897

CC NO 211884　　　　　**ESTABLISHED** 1952

....

■ The Christopher Laing Foundation

WHERE FUNDING CAN BE GIVEN UK, with an interest in Hertfordshire.

WHO CAN BENEFIT Applications from headquarters organisations and local organisations will be considered.

WHAT IS FUNDED General charitable purposes, with a preference for local projects.

WHAT IS NOT FUNDED Donations are only made to registered charities.

TYPE OF GRANT Recurrent and one-off. Grants are given for core support, capital funding and project, seed and feasibility funding. Loans may be given.

SAMPLE GRANTS £101,918 to Tyingham Foundation; £40,000 to Charities Aid Foundation to be distributed to other charities; £25,000 each to NPFA and The Lords Taverners; £10,000 to High Sheriff's Fund; £5,000 to Bunbury ESCA Festival; £3,000 to Royal Veterinary College Animal Care Trust; £2,500 each to Hertfordshire Action on Disability and Marie Curie Cancer Care; £2,000 to Stevenage Sea Cadets.

FINANCES *Year 2001–02 Income £171,439 Grants £234,143 Assets £4,599,204*

TRUSTEES Donald G Stradling; Peter S Jackson; Christopher M Laing; Diana C Laing.

HOW TO APPLY In writing to the correspondent.

WHO TO APPLY TO Mrs Margaret R White, Senior Trust Consultant, c/o Ernst & Young, 400 Capability Green, Luton LU1 3LU *Tel* 01582 643128

CC NO 278460　　　　　**ESTABLISHED** 1979

....

■ The David Laing Foundation

WHERE FUNDING CAN BE GIVEN Worldwide.

WHO CAN BENEFIT Organisations benefiting children, including those who are in care, fostered or adopted; one-parent families; and people who are disabled.

WHAT IS FUNDED The policy is to support charities aiding children, people from broken homes, and people who are physically and mentally disabled; with further donations to bodies supporting the improvement of the environment, the arts and animal welfare.

WHAT IS NOT FUNDED No grants to individuals.

TYPE OF GRANT Grants are not normally recurrent on a regular annual basis unless forming phases of a larger donation. Some charities are closely associated with the foundation and would benefit more frequently. Starter finance, recurring expenses or single projects are considered. Sometimes a small grant plus an interest-free loan.

SAMPLE GRANTS £55,000 to Charities Aid Foundation for disbursement as smaller grants; £8,700 to Emmanus St Albans; £5,000 each to DEMAND, Harpenden Music Foundation, and London Pro Arte Orchestra; £500 to RLEK.

FINANCES *Year 2000–01 Income £125,731 Grants £79,200 Assets £4,982,886*

TRUSTEES David Eric Laing; John Stuart Lewis; Richard Francis Dudley Barlow; Frances Mary Laing.

OTHER INFORMATION Where supporting larger charities, the support will be at both headquarters and local levels, as for instance in support of Save the Children Fund where donations to headquarters will aid the African famine appeal, but support is also given to local branches.

HOW TO APPLY In writing to the correspondent. Trustees meet in March, June, October and December, although applications are reviewed weekly. Due to the large number of applications received, and the relatively small number of grants made, the trust is not able to respond to all requests.

WHO TO APPLY TO David E Laing, Trustee, The Studio, Mackerye End, Harpenden, Hertfordshire AL5 5DR *Tel* 01582 461606 *Fax* 01582 461232

CC NO 278462　　　　　**ESTABLISHED** 1979

....

■ The Kirby Laing Foundation

WHERE FUNDING CAN BE GIVEN Unrestricted.

WHO CAN BENEFIT Registered charities benefiting disadvantaged sections of the community including people with disabilities or mental illness, people disadvantaged by poverty, and socially isolated people; UK and overseas mission societies.

WHAT IS FUNDED Advancement of the Christian faith, youth development, medical research, care and health organisations, social welfare.

WHAT IS NOT FUNDED No grants to individuals; no travel grants; no educational grants. The foundation rarely gives grants for the running costs of local organisations.

TYPE OF GRANT Usually capital costs or project funding on a one-off or recurring basis. A few grants towards the core costs of national organisations.

RANGE OF GRANTS Most grants are between £1,000 and £10,000, some larger grants.

SAMPLE GRANTS £67,000 to St Lawrence College towards IT infrastructure; £55,000 to Tyndale House in continuing support for fellowships in Christian scholarship; £50,000 to Cumbria Community Foundation towards combating the effects of foot and mouth disease; £40,000 to Hertfordshire University for the National Centre for Tactile Diagrams; £35,000 each to SAT-7 in continuing support for Christian broadcasts to the Middle East and Oriel College for the bursary endowment fund; £30,000 each to Restoration of Appearance and Function Trust (RAFT), Armonia UK Trust and Coventry Cathedral; £25,000 each to Cord Blood Charity, London City Mission, Mines Advisory Group and the National Society for Epilepsy.

FINANCES *Year* 2001 *Income* £1,651,000 *Grants* £1,191,000 *Assets* £35,499,798

TRUSTEES Sir Kirby Laing; Lady Isobel Laing; David E Laing; Simon Webley.

HOW TO APPLY One application only is needed to apply to this or the Maurice Laing Foundation, the Beatrice Laing Trust or Maurice and Hilda Laing Charitable Trust. Multiple applications will still only elicit a single reply. These trusts make strenuous efforts to keep their overhead costs to a minimum. As they also make a very large number of grants each year, in proportion to their income, the staff must rely almost entirely on the written applications submitted in selecting appeals to go forward to the trustees. Each application should contain all the information needed to allow such a decision to be reached, in as short and straightforward a way as possible. Specifically, each application should say: what the money is for; how much is needed; how much has already been found; and where the rest is to come from.

Unless there is reasonable assurance on the last point the grant is unlikely to be recommended. The trusts ask applicants, in the interest of reducing costs, to accept a non-response as a negative reply; if more is sought, a stamped addressed envelope must be sent with the application. Decisions are made on an ongoing basis.

WHO TO APPLY TO Miss Elizabeth Harley, 33 Bunns Lane, London NW7 2DX *Tel* 020 8238 8890

CC NO 264299   **ESTABLISHED** 1972

■ The Martin Laing Foundation

WHERE FUNDING CAN BE GIVEN UK and worldwide.

WHO CAN BENEFIT Registered charities.

WHAT IS FUNDED General charitable purposes, but most grants go to charities and projects which the trustees have a personal connection to.

RANGE OF GRANTS £75–£10,000 for smaller grants given through CAF. Similar for grants made directly by the trust.

SAMPLE GRANTS £30,000 to CAF to make 62 smaller grants to organisations; £12,500 to Ponds Conservation Trust; £10,000 each to Action for ME, British Executive Service Overseas, Business in the Community, and Princess Helena College; £5,500 to Westminster Pastoral Foundation; £5,000 to Macmillan Cancer Relief.

FINANCES *Year* 2001–02 *Income* £194,887 *Grants* £93,000 *Assets* £4,325,863

TRUSTEES Sir John Martin Laing; Donald Stradling; Brian O Chilver; Edward Charles Laing.

HOW TO APPLY The trust states: 'The trustees receive an enormous and increasing number of requests for help. Unfortunately the trustees are only able to help a small proportion of the requests and consequently they limit their support to those charities where they have a personal connection or interest in their activities.'

WHO TO APPLY TO Mrs Margaret R White, Senior Trust Consultant, c/o Ernst & Young, 400 Capability Green, Luton LU1 3LU *Tel* 01582 643128 *Fax* 01582 643006

CC NO 278461   **ESTABLISHED** 1979

■ The Maurice Laing Foundation

WHERE FUNDING CAN BE GIVEN Unrestricted.

WHO CAN BENEFIT Registered charities only.

WHAT IS FUNDED Mainly environment and conservation and research into complimentary medicine; support is also given for youth development and welfare and to development work in developing countries.

WHAT IS NOT FUNDED No grants to groups or individuals for education or travel purposes, including attendance at conferences and overseas exchange programmes or for voluntary work. Support is rarely given to the running costs of local organisations

TYPE OF GRANT Usually capital costs or project funding on a one-off or recurrent basis. A few grants towards core costs of national organisations.

RANGE OF GRANTS Most grants are between £1,000 and £10,000.

SAMPLE GRANTS £150,000 to World Wide Fund for Nature – second of three grants towards WWF's forestry programme; £108,000 to University of Southampton towards the core administrative costs of the Complementary Medicine Department; £50,000 each to Global Canopy Foundation – last of two grants for its research programme and Royal Geographical Society towards refurbishment of the lecture theatre; £30,000 to Whitley Awards Foundation to cover sponsorship of the Award for Nature Conservation and Education and some administration costs; £29,000 to Marine Stewardship Council to fund the post of UK development officer; £25,000 each to Commonwealth Society for the Deaf for a second mobile clinic and Cord Blood Charity – last of two grants for the London Cord Blood Bank.

FINANCES *Year* 2001 *Income* £6,384,000 *Grants* £1,614,000 *Assets* £65,329,000

TRUSTEES David Edwards, Chair; Sir Maurice Laing; Thomas D Parr; John H Laing; Peter J Harper; Andrea Gavazzi.

OTHER INFORMATION The foundation expects to merge with the Rufford Foundation in the course of 2003; administration will then pass to the Rufford Foundation office.

HOW TO APPLY One application only is needed to apply to this or the Kirby Laing Foundation, the Beatrice Laing Trust or the Maurice and Hilda Laing Charitable Trust. Multiple applications will only receive a single reply. The trusts ask applicants, in the interest of reducing costs, to accept a non-response as a negative reply; if more is sought, a stamped addressed envelope must be sent with the application. Each application should contain all the information needed to allow a decision to be reached, in as short and straightforward a way as possible. Specifically, they should cover: what the money is for; how much is needed; how much has already been found; and where the rest is to come from (unless there is reasonable assurance on this point the grant is unlikely to be recommended). A copy of the charity's latest annual accounts should also be enclosed. Applications for smaller amounts are considered on an ongoing basis; larger grants are considered quarterly; the exact dates of meetings vary from year to year.

WHO TO APPLY TO Miss Elizabeth Harley, 33 Bunns Lane, London NW7 2DX *Tel* 020 8238 8890 *Fax* 020 8238 8897

CC NO 264301   **ESTABLISHED** 1972

....

■ Maurice and Hilda Laing Charitable Trust

WHERE FUNDING CAN BE GIVEN UK and overseas.

WHO CAN BENEFIT Registered charities helping children (especially street children) and young people or people who are disabled, disadvantaged by poverty or socially isolated. Also Christian organisations seeking to advance the Christian faith or to apply Christian principles to those in need.

WHAT IS FUNDED The advancement of the Christian religion and the relief of poverty both in the UK and overseas.

WHAT IS NOT FUNDED No grants to groups or individuals for the purpose of education, travel, attendance at conferences or participation in overseas exchange programmes. No grants towards church restoration or repair.

TYPE OF GRANT Usually one-off grants to capital costs or project funding on a one-off or recurring basis. A few grants towards the core costs of national organisations.

RANGE OF GRANTS Most grants are between £1,000 and £10,000 but occasionally larger.

SAMPLE GRANTS £250,000 to Lambeth Fund, last of two grants towards evangelistic initiatives undertaken by the Archbishop of Canterbury; £100,000 towards the cost of connecting the Theodor Schneller School in Amman, Jordan to the main water authority sewage system; £50,000 each to Alpha International, first of two grants towards the Alpha in Prisons project, Dorothy Kerin Trust towards rebuilding the hospital wing and Philo Trust towards the production of a video series 'Back to Basics'; 49,000 to Culham College Institute towards the production of a video using material from the Faith Zone of the Millennium Dome for distribution to schools; £35,000 to SAT-7 in continued support for Christian satellite broadcasts to the middle east; £25,000 each to Coventry Cathedral towards installing fire devices, Douglas House – Oxford towards the cost of constructing a hospice for teenagers and London City Mission towards a new volunteer base.

FINANCES *Year* 2001 *Income* £1,816,000 *Grants* £1,384,000 *Assets* £1,482,000

TRUSTEES Sir Maurice Laing; Lady Hilda Laing; Peter Harper; Robert M Harley; Thomas D Parr; Ewan Harper.

HOW TO APPLY The trust is administered alongside the Beatrice Laing Trust, the Maurice Laing and the Kirby Laing Foundations. None of the trusts issue application forms and an application to one is seen as an application to all. In general the trusts rarely make grants towards the running costs of local organisations, which they feel have to be raised from local sources. An application for a grant towards a specific capital project should be in the form of a short letter

giving details of the project, its total cost, the amount raised and some indication of how it is to be financed. A copy of the organisation's latest annual report and accounts, together with a stamped addressed envelope, should be enclosed. Unless a stamped addressed envelope is enclosed applicants are asked to accept non-response as a negative reply. Trustees meet quarterly to consider applications for larger grants (above £10,000). Applications for smaller amounts are considered on an ongoing basis.

WHO TO APPLY TO Miss Elizabeth Harley, 33 Bunns Lane, London NW7 2DX *Tel* 020 8238 8890

CC NO 1058109   **ESTABLISHED** 1996

....

■ The Lambert Charitable Trust

WHERE FUNDING CAN BE GIVEN UK and Israel.

WHO CAN BENEFIT There is a preference for Jewish people.

WHAT IS FUNDED Each year one half of the income is given to organisations in Israel, one third to Jewish organisations based in the UK and one sixth to health and welfare charities in the UK.

RANGE OF GRANTS £250–£10,000.

SAMPLE GRANTS £12,000 to Jewish Care; £3,232 to Royal Opera House Trust; £2,500 to THET; £2,000 to Jewish Museum; £1,750 to British Friends of the Rambah Medical Centre; £1,500 each to Ben Gurion University, CFS Research Foundation, Facing the Future Together, Friends of Magen David Adom, and Norwood.

FINANCES *Year* 2000–01 *Income* £107,278 *Grants* £110,332 *Assets* £2,502,602

TRUSTEES M Lambert; Prof. H P Lambert; H Alexander-Passe; Jane Lambert.

HOW TO APPLY In writing to the correspondent before July for payment by 1 September.

WHO TO APPLY TO M Lambert, Trustee, Messrs Mercer & Hole, 76 Shoe Lane, London EC4A 3JB *Fax* 020 7353 1748

CC NO 257803   **ESTABLISHED** 1968

....

■ Lambeth Endowed Charities

WHERE FUNDING CAN BE GIVEN London borough of Lambeth.

WHO CAN BENEFIT Organisations as well as students and individuals with urgent needs.

WHAT IS FUNDED Schools, social and educational welfare.

WHAT IS NOT FUNDED No grants to: UK charities, unless the work is for the direct and specific benefit to Lambeth residents; revenue funding; replacement of statutory funds; or to meet the costs of debts already incurred.

SAMPLE GRANTS £13,000 to Lambeth Voluntary Action Council for the salary of a small groups officer; £10,000 each to Brixton Advice Centre towards new premises, Furniture Aid South Thames for a driver/workshop engineer salary, High Trees Community Development Project for IT project running costs, Immanuel Youth Centre towards a new minibus, Lambeth Welcare for the costs of a parenting group, Roots and Shoots for materials and equipment and The Spires Centre for building refurbishment; £8,000 to Lambeth Summer Projects Trust for summer playschemes; £7,000 to Courthouse Community Cafe for equipment.

FINANCES *Year* 2000 *Grants* £945,000

TRUSTEES 14 co-optive trustees and governors, and two representative trustees and two representative governors appointed by Lambeth

Borough Council. Dr C Gerada, Chair, Hayle's Charity. B R Holland, Chair, Walcot Charities.
OTHER INFORMATION The Lambeth Endowed Charities, with roots dating back to the seventeenth century, is an 'umbrella' title for what are now three charities: the Walcot Educational Foundation, Hayle's Charity and the Walcot Non-Educational Charity.
HOW TO APPLY All applications must be made on an application form, available on request from the office. Applicants are welcome to contact the office for further information and advice on how to apply. The trustees meet quarterly, usually in early March, June, October and December, and applications must be received at least six weeks before the date of the relevant meeting. Please ring the office to check deadlines for applications. Once your application has been received you will be contacted by the director or the fieldworker, who will usually arrange to visit your project to discuss your application in more detail. Successful applicants will be asked to give a report about how a grant has been used within 12 months of receiving it.
WHO TO APPLY TO Robert Dewar, Director and Clerk, 127 Kennington Road, London SE11 6SF
Tel 020 7735 1925 *Fax* 020 7735 7048
CC NO 206462

■ Bryan Lancaster's Charity

WHERE FUNDING CAN BE GIVEN North west England, especially Cumbria.
WHO CAN BENEFIT Organisations benefiting people of all ages, unemployed people and Quakers.
WHAT IS FUNDED This is a Quaker trust. It supports the setting up, repairs, running costs and new ventures in community and welfare. Priority is given to projects with Quaker involvement and preference is given to smaller and newer charities in north west England. Particularly supported are charities working in the fields of accommodation and housing; Quaker umbrella bodies; alternative healthcare; health counselling; respite care; care for carers; support and self help groups; Quaker church buildings; peace campaigning; advice centres; law centres; and various community facilities and services.
WHAT IS NOT FUNDED Applications from students and large charities are not considered. No grants to individuals.
TYPE OF GRANT Usually one-off grants towards a specific object and to local, not national, bodies. Buildings, capital, core costs, project costs, feasibility studies; running costs; and start-up costs. Funding for one year or less will be considered.
RANGE OF GRANTS £100–£5,000.
SAMPLE GRANTS £1,000 to Aberystwyth Quaker meeting house; £500 each to Emmaus Lancaster and Young People Counselling; £300 to Furniture Rehab, Stockport; £200–300 to village halls.
FINANCES *Year* 2000–2001 *Income* £26,000 *Grants* £21,000
HOW TO APPLY In writing to the correspondent; no telephone enquiries. Trustees meet every six to eight weeks. Applicants should enclose an sae for a reply.
WHO TO APPLY TO D M Butler, 9 Greenside, Kendal, Cumbria LA9 5DU
CC NO 222902   **ESTABLISHED** 1719

■ The John and Rosemary Lancaster Charitable Foundation

WHERE FUNDING CAN BE GIVEN UK, with a local interest in Clitheroe.
WHO CAN BENEFIT Only charities personally known to the trustees.
WHAT IS FUNDED Christian charities only.
SAMPLE GRANTS £1,224,000 to NGM; £240,000 to Clitheroe St James PCC; £174,000 to Soul Survivor; £100,000 to East Lancashire Hospice Fund; £142,000 to Message to Schools; £72,000 to Love and Joy Ministries; £61,000 to Salvation Army; £55,000 to Sparrow Ministries, South Africa; £52,000 to MAF; £45,000 to Annalena Tonelli, Somaliland.
FINANCES *Year* 2000–01 *Grants* £2,249,000
TRUSTEES Mrs R Lancaster, Chair; J E Lancaster; S J Lancaster; J R Broadhurst.
HOW TO APPLY The trust says: 'We do not consider applications made to us from organisations or people unconnected with us. All our donations are instigated because of personal associations. Unsolicited mail is, sadly, a waste of the organisation's resources.'
WHO TO APPLY TO Mrs R Lancaster, Chair, c/o Text House, 152 Edisford Road, Clitheroe BB7 2LA
Tel 01200 444404
CC NO 1066850   **ESTABLISHED** 1997

■ The Allen Lane Foundation

WHERE FUNDING CAN BE GIVEN UK, and a small programme in Ireland.
WHO CAN BENEFIT Organisations whose work is with groups who may be perceived as unpopular such as refugees and asylum seekers, black and ethnic minority communities, travellers, people with mental health problems and offenders, those experiencing violence or abuse, gay, lesbian or bi-sexual people.
WHAT IS FUNDED The provision of advice, information and advocacy; community development; neighbourhood mediation, conflict resolution and alternatives to violence; research and education aimed at changing public attitudes or policy; social welfare aimed at making a long-term difference and empowering users. The foundation also has a small funding programme for work on penal reform in the Republic of Ireland.
WHAT IS NOT FUNDED The foundation does not currently make grants for academic research; addiction, alcohol or drug abuse; animal welfare or animal rights; arts or cultural or language projects or festivals; work with children and young people; disability issues; endowments or contributions to other grantmaking bodies; holidays or holiday play schemes, sports and recreation; housing and homelessness; individuals; large appeals from charities which enjoy widespread public support; medical care, hospices and medical research; museums or galleries; overseas travel; private and/or mainstream education; promotion of sectarian religion; publications; purchase costs of property, building or refurbishment; restoration or conservation of historic buildings or sites; vehicle purchase; work relating to particular medical conditions of illness; work which the trustees believe is rightly the responsibility of the state; work outside the United Kingdom; work which will already have taken place before a grant is agreed; work by local organisations with an income of more than £150,000 per annum or those working over a wider area with an income of more than £350,000. The

Every application represents a cost to you and to the trust

foundation will not normally make grants to organisations which receive funding (directly or indirectly) from commercial sources where conflicts of interest for the organisation and its work are likely to arise.

TYPE OF GRANT Generally for one year only, although longer term funding of up to three years may be offered sometimes. Project or core costs. Also research, running costs and start-up costs.

RANGE OF GRANTS £500–£10,000 for one-off grants; £1,000–£5,000 per annum. Local projects rarely receive more than £3,000.

SAMPLE GRANTS £20,000 to Respect for start up costs; £15,000 each to Prisoners' Advice Service, the Geese Theatre Company, North Yorkshire Rehabilitation and Support Service, CLINKS – Prisons Community Links and Partners of Prisoners and Families Support Group; £12,000 each to Association of Visitors to Immigration Detainess, Centre for Crime & Justice Studies, Mediation Oxfordshire and Nottinghamshire Domestic Violence Forum.

FINANCES *Year* 2001–02 *Income* £467,000 *Grants* £511,000 *Assets* £14,860,000

TRUSTEES Clare Morpurgo; John Hughes; Christine Teale; Zoe Teale; Guy Dehn; Juliet Walker; Jane Walsh.

OTHER INFORMATION The trustees regret that applications far outstrip the funds available and not all good or appropriate projects can be offered funding, even though they may fall well within current funding priorities. A rejection may be no reflection on the value of the project. Trustees meet three times a year so applicants should allow up to four months for a positive decision

HOW TO APPLY Eligibility: If you are in any doubt please ring and discuss the matter, but if you are not eligible you will only be wasting your own time, and ours, by making an application. There is no formal application form but when sending in an application we ask you to complete the registration form (available from the foundation or downloadable from the website). An application should be no more than four sides of A4 but the project budget may be on extra pages. It should be accompanied by your last annual report and accounts if you produce such documents and the budget for the whole organisation (if this is different from the project budget) for the current year. Closing dates for each trustees' meeting are on the website or can be had from the foundation, but applicants are urged not to wait until the last minute before a closing date to make their application.

WHO TO APPLY TO Heather Swailes, Executive Secretary, 90 The Mount, York YO24 1AR *Tel* 01904 613223 *E-mail* enquiries@allenlane.demon.co.uk *Website* www.allenlane.demon.co.uk

CC NO 248031   **ESTABLISHED** 1966

■ The Langdale Trust

WHERE FUNDING CAN BE GIVEN Worldwide, but with a special interest in Birmingham.

WHO CAN BENEFIT Registered charities.

WHAT IS FUNDED Youth organisations, medical, environment and social needs.

TYPE OF GRANT Annual for general and specific use.

RANGE OF GRANTS £2,000–£5,000.

SAMPLE GRANTS £5,000 to British & Foreign Bible Society; £4,000 each to The Leprosy Mission and United Christian Broadcasters Ltd; £3,000 each to Addaction, Mental Health Foundation, National Trust, Samaritans, Save the Children, YMCA Birmingham and Y Care International.

FINANCES *Year* 2000–01 *Income* £118,442 *Grants* £96,000 *Assets* £3,306,563

TRUSTEES T R Wilson; Mrs T Whiting; M J Woodward.

HOW TO APPLY In writing to the correspondent. The trustees meet in September/October.

WHO TO APPLY TO M J Woodward, Trustee, c/o Lee Crowder, 39 Newhall Street, Birmingham B3 3DY *Tel* 0121 236 4477

CC NO 215317   **ESTABLISHED** 1960

■ The Richard Langhorn Trust

WHERE FUNDING CAN BE GIVEN UK and overseas.

WHO CAN BENEFIT Children who are underprivileged, disadvantaged or disabled.

WHAT IS FUNDED Sporting opportunities for children who are underprivileged and disabled, particularly in the areas of rugby, sailing, basketball and skiing.

TYPE OF GRANT Buildings, interest free loans, one-off and recurring costs will be considered. Funding may be given for more than three years

FINANCES *Year* 1997 *Income* £150,000 *Grants* £50,000 *Assets* £350,000

TRUSTEES Ms G Bell; K Bray; S Langhorn; P Winterbottom; T York.

PUBLICATIONS *Forward* published twice a year.

HOW TO APPLY Applications to the correspondent by e-mail, or in writing (e-mail is preferred).

WHO TO APPLY TO The Trustees, Harlequins Rugby Football Club, Stoop Memorial Ground, Langhorn Drive, Twickenham, Middlesex TW2 7SX

CC NO 1046332   **ESTABLISHED** 1995

■ The Langley Charitable Trust

WHERE FUNDING CAN BE GIVEN UK, with a preference for the West Midlands, and worldwide.

WHO CAN BENEFIT Individuals and groups benefiting Christians, at risk groups, people who are disadvantaged by poverty, socially isolated or sick.

WHAT IS FUNDED Advancement of the gospel and Christianity; welfare and health.

WHAT IS NOT FUNDED No grants to animal or bird charities.

RANGE OF GRANTS £20–£3,000.

FINANCES *Year* 1999 *Income* £190,000 *Grants* £21,000 *Assets* £1,200,000

TRUSTEES J P Gilmour; Mrs S S Gilmour.

HOW TO APPLY In writing to the correspondent. 'The trustees only reply where they require further information and so on. No telephone calls nor correspondence will be entered into concerning any proposed or declined applications.'

WHO TO APPLY TO J P Gilmour, Trustee, Wheatmoor Farm, 301 Tamworth Road, Sutton Coldfield, West Midlands B75 6JP

CC NO 280104   **ESTABLISHED** 1980

■ The Langtree Trust

WHERE FUNDING CAN BE GIVEN Gloucestershire.

WHO CAN BENEFIT Organisations benefiting the local community; occasionally to individuals if then of direct benefit to the community.

WHAT IS FUNDED General charitable purposes in Gloucestershire only. Priority is given to church projects, youth groups and people who are disabled or disadvantaged. The arts have a lower priority.

WHAT IS NOT FUNDED No grants are given in response to general appeals from large UK organisations. No grants to individuals for higher education.

Think carefully about every application. Is it justified?

603

TYPE OF GRANT Usually one-off for a specific project.
RANGE OF GRANTS £50–£1,000.
FINANCES *Year 1999–2000* *Income* £51,000
Grants £54,645 *Assets* £1,400,000
TRUSTEES R H Mann; Col P Haslam; Mrs J
Humpidge; G J Yates; Mrs A M Shepherd; Mrs
M E Hood.
HOW TO APPLY In writing to the correspondent giving
a simple, clear statement of the need with the
costs of the project, what funding has so far
been achieved and/or a recent copy of the
annual accounts. Expensive, extensive, glossy
appeal brochures are not appreciated. The
trustees meet four or five times a year to decide
the grant allocation. In exceptional
circumstances a grant may be made between
meetings. Please note that the address is an
accommodation address and Randall & Payne
cannot answer any telephone queries.
WHO TO APPLY TO The Secretary, c/o Messrs Randall
& Payne, Rodborough Court, Stroud,
Gloucestershire GL5 3LR
CC NO 232924   **ESTABLISHED** 1963

....

■ The Lankelly Foundation

WHERE FUNDING CAN BE GIVEN UK, except London.
WHO CAN BENEFIT Registered charities, with
preference given to enabling small organisations
to grow.
WHAT IS FUNDED The foundation's eight areas of
support are penal affairs – to encourage strong
links between prisons and local communities
and to promote good practice among voluntary
agencies working within prisons, support to
projects that contribute to the rehabilitation of
those in prison and those leaving prison and to
the support of their families and friends;
families and children – support of people and
younger children (under 13s) who are
marginalised because of poverty, unemployment
or crime, including domestic violence and sexual
abuse. Work funded may be in support of either
adults or children but needs to show a
preventative element; mental health – projects
which: promote independence and reintegration
into society; combat isolation whether
geographical or cultural; support those who are
particularly vulnerable such as the elderly, the
homeless, and those in secure accommodation;
neighbourhood work – support of communities
who are working to create a positive
environment in which people can flourish.
Grants will be targeted at small voluntary
agencies with a strong user involvement,
particularly in areas of high levels of poverty and
disadvantage; elderly people – projects that
clearly demonstrate the promotion of improved
quality of life, independent living and user
involvement, particularly innovative projects that
broaden choices and promote well-being;
homelessness – focus on preventative work with
young people and support to the older homeless
who need long-term support in resettlement,
particularly the most vulnerable groups, such as
ex-offenders, refugees, elderly homeless and
those with multiple problems; physical and
learning disabilities – support of people with
mental and physical disabilities, particularly
projects aimed at promoting independent living
and social inclusion, through advocacy, training,
sheltered and supported work opportunities;
young people – support work with young people
aged 14–25 years, and projects that support
vulnerable young people through the difficult
transition to adulthood, particularly those living
in deprived neighbourhoods, at risk of school

exclusion or offending, including youngsters
leaving local authority care.
WHAT IS NOT FUNDED We do not contribute to large,
widely circulated appeals, nor will we consider
retrospective funding for work that has already
taken place.
More particularly, we do not make grants in
support of adaptations to improve access to
buildings; the advancement of religion; animal
welfare; arts and heritage; conferences or
seminars; endowment funds; festivals or theatre
productions; hospices; individual needs;
individual youth club; large capital projects;
medical research; other grantmaking bodies;
publications, film or video; schools for people
with special needs; sport; travel, expedition or
holidays; vehicles. We do not support formal
education including institutes of further and
higher education, NHS hospital trusts and those
emanating from associated charities concerned
with medical projects.
If in doubt, it is probably advisable to contact
the office for an informal discussion before
spending time putting together a detailed
application.
TYPE OF GRANT One-off and recurring grants, which
must always be for a specific purpose. Capital
and revenue grants are considered, as are
buildings, core costs, project, running and start-
up costs, and salaries.
RANGE OF GRANTS £5,000 upwards.
SAMPLE GRANTS £250,000 to The Chase Charity to
be disbursed in the fields of arts and heritage
(this is an annual grant for the foreseeable
future); £112,500 to Family Welfare Association
to be disbursed in small amounts to individuals
in need; £75,500 over five years to Royston
Youth Action – Glasgow for salaries; £75,000
over three years to The Depaul Trust at HMP
Brinsford for salary costs, Partners of Prisoners
and Families Support Group – Manchester for
core costs; £72,000 over three years to
Wintercomfort for the Homeless – Cambridge for
the Ely supported housing project; £70,500 over
three years to Walsall Street Teams to
developing a drugs project working in schools
and on the streets; £70,000 to KIDS South
West for salary costs; £67,000over three years
to Easterhouse Carers Development Unit –
Glasgow for a young carers project; £66,300
over three years to HALOW – Birmingham for
salaries; £66,000 over three years to
Emmanuel House day Centre – Nottingham for
salaries.
FINANCES *Year 2001–02* *Income* £4,260,991
Grants £5,684,000 *Assets* £100,286,938
TRUSTEES Shirley Turner, chair; Leo Fraser-
Mackenzie; W J Mackenzie; Georgina Campbell;
Colleen Merlyn-Rees; Simon Raybould; Nicholas
Tatman.
HOW TO APPLY Your initial letter (by post) should
describe who you are; what you do; why you are
seeking our help; how you will measure
success; how much money you need to raise;
how soon you need it; who else you have asked
to help; what support you have already
attracted. You should attach brief information
about the origins and current company/
charitable status of your organisation; a copy of
your most recent annual report and full audited
accounts; an itemised income and expenditure
budget for your organisation; an itemised
income and expenditure budget for the work to
be funded; equal opportunities policy. The
trustees meet quarterly, in January, April, July
and October. Applications may be submitted at
any time but you should be aware that agendas
are planned well ahead and you should expect a

period of six months between an initial application and formal consideration by the trustees.

WHO TO APPLY TO Peter Kilgarriff, 2 The Court, High Street, Harwell, Oxfordshire OX11 0EY *Tel* 01235 820044 *Website* www.lankelly-foundation.org.uk

CC NO 256987   **ESTABLISHED** 1968

■ The R J Larg Family Charitable Trust

WHERE FUNDING CAN BE GIVEN UK but generally Scotland, particularly Tayside.

WHO CAN BENEFIT Organisations benefiting children, young adults, students and people who are disabled or who have a disease or medical condition.

WHAT IS FUNDED Grants are made for cancer research, amateur music and youth organisations including university students' associations. Funding may also be given to churches, conservation, respite care, hospices, MS and neurological research, care in the community and other community facilities. Other charitable purposes will be considered.

WHAT IS NOT FUNDED Grants are not available for individuals.

TYPE OF GRANT Generally one-off, some recurring. Buildings, core costs, running costs, salaries and start-up costs will be considered. Funding may be given for up to two years.

RANGE OF GRANTS £250–£5,000; typical grant £1,000–£2,000.

FINANCES *Year* 1997–98 *Income* £124,300 *Grants* £126,300 *Assets* £3,442,000

TRUSTEES R W Gibson; D A Brand; Mrs S A Stewart.

HOW TO APPLY In writing to the correspondent. Trustees meet to consider grants in February and August.

WHO TO APPLY TO N Barclay, Messrs Thorntons WS, 50 Castle Street, Dundee DD1 3RU

SC NO SC004946   **ESTABLISHED** 1970

■ Largsmount Ltd

WHERE FUNDING CAN BE GIVEN UK and overseas.

WHO CAN BENEFIT Jewish people.

WHAT IS FUNDED Jewish charitable purposes.

SAMPLE GRANTS £95,000 to Yetev Lev Jerusalem; £45,000 to Shaarei Zion Turda; £27,126 to A & H Pillar Charitable Trust; £25,000 to Dushinsky Trust; £14,308 to Gateshead Foundation for Torah; £4,075 each to Kollel Sha'rei Shlomo Kiryat Sefer and Tomechi Torah Family Relief; £3,480 to Bluzow Trust; £2,200 to Emmunah Education Centre; £1,740 to Gateshead Jewish High School.

FINANCES *Year* 2000–01 *Income* £409,365 *Grants* £237,141 *Assets* £2,430,773

TRUSTEES Z M Kaufman; Mrs I R Kaufman; S Kaufman.

HOW TO APPLY In writing to the correspondent.

WHO TO APPLY TO Mrs I R Kaufman, Trustee, Cohen Arnold & Co Accountants, 13–17 New Burlington Place, Regent Street, London W1S 2HL

CC NO 280509   **ESTABLISHED** 1979

■ The Lark Trust

WHERE FUNDING CAN BE GIVEN UK, but mainly in the Bristol locality.

WHO CAN BENEFIT Registered charities benefiting people of all ages; Quakers.

WHAT IS FUNDED Support in the areas of counselling, psychotherapy and the visual arts.

WHAT IS NOT FUNDED No grants to individuals.

TYPE OF GRANT One-off.

RANGE OF GRANTS £100–£1,000, but mostly for £500.

SAMPLE GRANTS Around £20,000 was paid in relation to work carried out by Avon Counselling and Psychotherapy Service at 11 Orchard Street, Bristol; £1,500 to The Harbour; £1,000 to Relate Avon; £500 to Bridge Foundation.

FINANCES *Year* 2002–03 *Income* £35,000 *Grants* £40,000

TRUSTEES Iris Tute; George Tute; Martin Mitchell.

OTHER INFORMATION Most grant money goes to projects the trust is already committed to.

HOW TO APPLY Initially in writing to the correspondent, who will check eligibility and then send a form which must be completed. Trustees do not accept information from charities wishing to build a relationship with them. Applications should be received by the end of January for consideration in March.

WHO TO APPLY TO Alice Meason, c/o Greater Bristol Foundation, Royal Oak House, Royal Oak Avenue, Bristol BS1 4GB *Tel* 0117 989 7700 *Fax* 0117 989 7701

CC NO 327982   **ESTABLISHED** 1988

■ Laslett's (Hinton) Charity

WHERE FUNDING CAN BE GIVEN Mainly the City and County of Worcester.

WHO CAN BENEFIT Children, older people, people who are disadvantaged by poverty and clergy.

WHAT IS FUNDED Church repairs; general benefit of people who are poor, including homes for older people and educating children; relief of sickness, hospitals and general charitable purposes in Worcester and surrounding area.

RANGE OF GRANTS £240–£10,000.

SAMPLE GRANTS In 1995: £20,050 to charities and church repairs; £400 to Rector of Hinton's expenses.

FINANCES *Year* 2001 *Income* £206,610 *Grants* £115,524 *Assets* £4,572,590

TRUSTEES J B Henderson, Chair; J S B Bennett; Miss E W Bonnett; D A E Finch; Mrs N Marshall; Mrs E A Pugh-Cook; A D J Scott; R A F Smith; J C Snell; Mrs J Webb; R J R Young.

HOW TO APPLY In writing to the correspondent.

WHO TO APPLY TO I C Pugh, 4 & 5 Sansome Place, Worcester WR1 1UQ *Tel* 01905 726600 *Fax* 01905 743366

CC NO 233696   **ESTABLISHED** 1879

■ Rachel & Jack Lass Charities Ltd

WHERE FUNDING CAN BE GIVEN England, Scotland and Wales.

WHO CAN BENEFIT Preference is given to children.

WHAT IS FUNDED General charitable purposes, with particular favour given to children's charities. Medical research is also supported.

WHAT IS NOT FUNDED No grants to individuals or for educational purposes. Only registered charities are considered.

SAMPLE GRANTS £35,750 to Yeshiva Horomo Talmudical College; £20,000 each to Friends of

Ilan, and Ravenswood Foundation; £15,100 to Tevini Ltd; £10,000 each to Gevurath Ari Torah Academy Trust and Yesodey Hatdlah; £5,000 each to Beth Hamedrash Ponovez and Yad Eliezer.

FINANCES *Year* 2000–01 *Income* £81,872 *Grants* £170,909 *Assets* £167,340

TRUSTEES Leonard Lass; Rachelle Lass; Sally Lass.

HOW TO APPLY In writing to the correspondent. Grants are paid annually during July/August/September.

WHO TO APPLY TO Mrs R Lass, Governor, 43 Linden Lea, London N2 0RF

CC NO 256514   **ESTABLISHED** 1968

■ Lauchentilly Charitable Foundation 1988

WHERE FUNDING CAN BE GIVEN UK and Republic of Ireland.

WHO CAN BENEFIT Small local projects, UK and established organisations benefiting children, young adults and people disadvantaged by poverty.

WHAT IS FUNDED Advancement of education, religion, relief of poverty and general charitable purposes.

WHAT IS NOT FUNDED No grants to individuals, including students, or to non-registered charities.

TYPE OF GRANT One-off and recurrent.

RANGE OF GRANTS £50–£10,000, usually £2,500 or less.

SAMPLE GRANTS £5,278 to Iveagh Trust; £5,000 each to Coombe Hospital – Dublin, and Elvenden PCC; £2,055 to Trust; £1,000 each to Ross McWhirter Foundation, Sir John Soane's Museum, and Zandra Rhodes Foundation; £500 each to Macmillan Cancer Relief, Wiltshire Wildlife Trust, and Zandra Rhodes Foundation.

FINANCES *Year* 2001–02 *Income* £28,625 *Grants* £24,688 *Assets* £689,142

TRUSTEES Countess of Iveagh; Cowdray Trust Ltd.

HOW TO APPLY In writing to the correspondent including an sae. Only successful applications will be acknowledged.

WHO TO APPLY TO Alan John Winborn, Cowdray Trust Ltd, 10–12 Cork Street, London W1S 3LW *Tel* 020 7439 9061

CC NO 299793   **ESTABLISHED** 1988

■ The Laufer Charitable Trust

WHERE FUNDING CAN BE GIVEN UK.

WHAT IS FUNDED Only charities personally known to the trustees will be considered. Other applications will not be acknowledged.

WHAT IS NOT FUNDED No grants to individuals, as grants are only made to registered charities.

TYPE OF GRANT Core costs for up to one year.

RANGE OF GRANTS Any new grants made would not exceed £50 as the trust has a number of outstanding commitments which will absorb its income for the foreseeable future.

SAMPLE GRANTS In 1999–2000: £1,000 each to Marbeh Torah Trust, Brook Foundation, and Hadassan Medical Relief Association; £675 to United Synagogue; £500 each to Scopus Jewish Educational Trust and British Friends of Ramot Shapiro; £400 to British Friends of Magen David Adam; £250 each to Jewish Learning Exchange, Friends of Religious Settlements, and British Friends of Shaare Zedek.

FINANCES *Year* 2001–02 *Income* £74,100

TRUSTEES S W Laufer; Mrs D D Laufer.

OTHER INFORMATION As this is a small charity, new beneficiaries are only considered in exceptional circumstances as the income is already allocated for some years to come.

HOW TO APPLY New beneficiaries are only considered by the trust in exceptional circumstances, as the income is already allocated for some years to come. In view of this it is suggested that no applications be made.

WHO TO APPLY TO S W Laufer, Trustee, 15 Leys Gardens, Cockfosters, Herts EN4 9NA *Tel* 020 8449 3432 *Fax* 020 8449 3432

CC NO 275375   **ESTABLISHED** 1961

■ The Lauffer Family Charitable Foundation

WHERE FUNDING CAN BE GIVEN Commonwealth countries, Israel and USA.

WHO CAN BENEFIT Educational and medical charities benefiting students.

WHAT IS FUNDED Education, medical and cultural causes.

WHAT IS NOT FUNDED No support for individuals.

TYPE OF GRANT Starter finance and recurrent for five years.

RANGE OF GRANTS £100–£15,000.

SAMPLE GRANTS £15,000 each to British Friends of Ariel and Spiro Ark; £12,500 to British Friends of Ohr Somayach; £11,750 to United Jewish Israel Appeal; £10,000 to British Friends of Sarah Herzog Memorial Hospital; £7,000 to Jewish Learning Experience; £6,250 to Jewish Deaf Association; £5,000 each to Aish Hatorah, B'nai B'rith Hillel Foundation, and Jerusalem Foundation.

FINANCES *Year* 2000–01 *Income* £151,010 *Grants* £171,748 *Assets* £2,868,150

TRUSTEES Mrs R R Lauffer; J S Lauffer; G L Lauffer; R M Lauffer.

HOW TO APPLY In writing to the correspondent; applications are considered once a year.

WHO TO APPLY TO J S Lauffer, Trustee, 18 Norrice Lea, London N2 0RE *E-mail* bethlauffer@lineone.net

CC NO 251115   **ESTABLISHED** 1965

■ The Mrs F B Laurence Charitable Trust

WHERE FUNDING CAN BE GIVEN Worldwide.

WHO CAN BENEFIT Organisations benefiting ex-service and service people, retired people, unemployed people and volunteers.

WHAT IS FUNDED The aid and support of people who are chronically ill and people who are disabled. The support of justice and human rights organisations and the protection of the environment and wildlife. Charities working in the fields of accommodation and housing legal services, publishing and printing, support to voluntary and community organisations, volunteer bureaux, community arts and recreation, community facilities, special schools and special needs education and literacy will also be considered.

WHAT IS NOT FUNDED No support for individuals. The following applications are unlikely to be considered: appeals for endowment or sponsorship; overseas projects, unless overseen by the charity's own fieldworkers; maintenance of buildings or landscape; provision of work or materials that are the responsibility of the state; where administration expenses, in all their guises, are considered by

the trustees to be excessive; or where the fundraising costs in the preceding year have not resulted in an increase in the succeeding years donations in excess of these costs.
TYPE OF GRANT Core costs, one-off, project and start-up costs. Funding is for one year or less.
RANGE OF GRANTS £250–£3,000.
SAMPLE GRANTS £2,000 each to Marie Curie Cancer Care, RNID, WWF- UK, SSAFA, Médecins Sans Frontières (UK); £1,500 each to Dreams Come True, Ghurka Welfare Trust, Fairtrade Foundation.
FINANCES *Year* 2001–02 *Income* £87,000 *Grants* £91,000 *Assets* £2,300,000
TRUSTEES M Tooth; G S Brown; D A G Sarre.
HOW TO APPLY In writing to the correspondent on not more than two pages of A4. Trustees meet twice a year, deadlines are 1 February for the April meeting and by 1 September for the November meeting. Only successful applicants are notified.
WHO TO APPLY TO The Trustees, PO Box 28927, London SW14 7WL
CC NO 296548   **ESTABLISHED** 1976

■ The Kathleen Laurence Trust

WHERE FUNDING CAN BE GIVEN UK.
WHO CAN BENEFIT General charities with specific projects and events.
WHAT IS FUNDED General charitable purposes. The trust particularly favours smaller organisations and those raising funds for specific requirements such as medical research, associations connected with disability and learning difficulties, and organisations helping people who are sick.
WHAT IS NOT FUNDED No donations are made for running costs, management expenses or to individuals.
RANGE OF GRANTS £350–£5,000.
SAMPLE GRANTS £4,000 each to British Kidney Patients Association and IVCS; £3,000 each to Dreams Come True and Rinoht Special Trustees; £2,000 each to Hope House, Imperial Cancer Research, National Asthma Campaign, Papworth Trust, Prince's Trust, Rainbow Trust and Wildside Trust.
FINANCES *Year* 1998–99 *Income* £100,383 *Grants* £86,500 *Assets* £3,160,641
TRUSTEES Coutts & Co.
HOW TO APPLY In writing to the correspondent. Trustees meet quarterly, usually in February, May, August and November.
WHO TO APPLY TO David Breach, Assistant Trust Manager, Trustee Department, Coutts & Co, 440 Strand, London WC2R 0QS *Tel* 020 7753 1000 *Fax* 020 7663 6794
CC NO 296461   **ESTABLISHED** 1987

■ The Law Society Charity

WHERE FUNDING CAN BE GIVEN Worldwide.
WHAT IS FUNDED Charitable activities in the furtherance of law and justice. This includes: charitable educational purposes for lawyers and would-be lawyers; legal research; promotion of an increased understanding of the law; and charities concerned with the provision of advice, counselling, mediation services connected with the law, welfare directly/indirectly of solicitors, trainee solicitors and other legal and Law Society staff and their families.
SAMPLE GRANTS £1,646,341 to The Law Society for educational purposes; £75,000 each to The Citizenship Foundation, LawCare Limited, and

Solicitors Benevolent Fund; £15,000 to Common Purpose; £12,000 to Trainee Solicitors' Group; £10,000 each to Galleries of Justice and Speakeasy Advise Service; £8,000 to Accis; £7,500 to National Centre for Volunteering; £6,000 to Fair Trials Abroad.
FINANCES *Year* 2001–02 *Income* £2,492,473 *Grants* £1,984,280 *Assets* £1,099,580
TRUSTEES The Law Society Trustees Ltd.
OTHER INFORMATION The income included a donation of £2,400,000 from The Law Society of England and Wales.
HOW TO APPLY In writing to the correspondent. Applications are considered at quarterly trustees' meetings, usually held in April, July, September and December.
WHO TO APPLY TO The Trustees, 113 Chancery Lane, London WC2A 1PL *Tel* 020 7320 5899
CC NO 268736   **ESTABLISHED** 1974

■ The Edgar E Lawley Foundation

WHERE FUNDING CAN BE GIVEN UK, with a preference for the West Midlands.
WHO CAN BENEFIT Medical, elderly and children's charities.
WHAT IS FUNDED Charities involved in the provision of medical care and services to older people, children's charities, and those involved with the advancement of medicine and medical research.
WHAT IS NOT FUNDED No grants to individuals.
TYPE OF GRANT One-off.
RANGE OF GRANTS £500 upwards; typical grant £1,000–£1,500.
SAMPLE GRANTS £30,000 to Imperial College School of Medicine; £28,685 to St Mary's Hospital, Paddington; £23,100 to The King's Fund; £5,000 to Walsall Society for the Blind; £1,500 each to Gateway Playgroup, Friends of Florence Nightingale House, Compton Hospice Wolverhampton, Acorns Children's Hospice Trust, Primrose Hospice Bromgrove and Prospect Hospice North Wiltshire.
FINANCES *Year* 2000–01 *Income* £161,479 *Grants* £153,785 *Assets* £3,540,861
TRUSTEES Mrs M D Heath, Chair; J H Cooke; Mrs G V H Hilton; P J Cooke; F S Jackson; Mrs E E Sutcliffe.
HOW TO APPLY In writing to the correspondent in April.
WHO TO APPLY TO Philip J Cooke, Trustee, Hollyoak, 1 White House Drive, Barnt Green, Birmingham B45 8HF *Tel* 0121 445 3536 *Fax* 0121 445 3536 *E-mail* philipjcooke@aol.com
CC NO 201589   **ESTABLISHED** 1961

■ The Lawlor Foundation

WHERE FUNDING CAN BE GIVEN Principally Northern Ireland, also Republic of Ireland, London, the home counties and Avon.
WHO CAN BENEFIT Individuals and organisations benefiting young adults, older people, students, parents and children, at risk groups, people disadvantaged by poverty, ex-offenders, people at risk of offending and victims of domestic violence.
WHAT IS FUNDED The current emphasis is on education, the principal beneficiaries being Irish educational establishments and individual students, UK organisations which support Irish immigrants and vulnerable young people. Particularly supported are Irish charities working in the fields of rehabilitation centres, support and self-help groups, well women clinics, postgraduate education, secondary schools,

tertiary and higher education, training for work, bursaries and fees, the purchase of books, and projects that underpin the peace process.

WHAT IS NOT FUNDED No grants are made in response to general appeals from large organisations or from organisations outside the geographical areas of Ireland, London and the Home Counties. Grants are not normally made to the arts, medicine, the environment, building projects, expeditions, children's projects or national causes.

TYPE OF GRANT Core costs, one-off, projects, recurring costs, running costs and start-up costs. Funding of up to and over three years will be considered.

RANGE OF GRANTS £250–£10,000.

SAMPLE GRANTS £10,000 each to Brent Adolescent Centre – London for core costs and St Louise's College – Belfast; £7,500 to Jesus College Cambridge for bursaries for Northern Irish students; £6,000 each to La Salle Boys' Secondary School – Belfast, St Cecilia's College – Derry, St Mary's Christian Brothers' Grammar School – Belfast, St Mary's College – Derry and St Mary's Christian Brothers' Grammar School – Belfast, all towards travel, books and course materials to allow young people who are disadvantaged to take up university places and additional school services such as breakfast clubs; £5,000 each to Young Minds – London and Belfast Royal Academy; £3,000 to Brandon Centre – London.

FINANCES *Year* 2001–02 *Income* £138,977 *Grants* £120,880 *Assets* £140,955

TRUSTEES Virginia Lawlor; Kelly Lawlor; Frank Baker; K R P Marshall; Blanca Fernadez Drayton; Patricia Manning.

HOW TO APPLY By letter to the correspondent at any time, with a description of the project and a copy of the latest accounts. Preliminary telephone enquiries are welcomed. Applications will only be acknowledged if they relate to the trust's general interests. The trustees normally meet in January, April, July and October. Please note that the trust has many ongoing commitments, which restrict the funds available for new applicants.

WHO TO APPLY TO Virginia Lawlor, Chairman, Traceys Farm, Stanford Rivers, Ongar, Essex CM5 9QD *Tel* 01277 364805 *Fax* 01277 364805

CC NO 297219   **ESTABLISHED** 1987

■ The Carole & Geoffrey Lawson Foundation

WHERE FUNDING CAN BE GIVEN UK.

WHAT IS FUNDED Jewish organisations and general charitable purposes.

WHAT IS NOT FUNDED No grants to local charities or individuals.

RANGE OF GRANTS £500–£135,000.

SAMPLE GRANTS £135,000 to World ORT Trust; £56,820 to Royal Opera House; £40,000 to Central Synagogue; £17,500 to London Symphony Orchestra; £10,000 each to British Council of Shaare Zedek, Central Cecil Housing Trust, Community Security Trust, and Jewish Care; £5,000 each to British ORT, and London Marriage Guidance Council.

FINANCES *Year* 2000–01 *Income* £347,257 *Grants* £309,820 *Assets* £628,009

TRUSTEES Geoffrey C H Lawson; Hon. Carole Lawson; Harold I Connick; E C S Lawson.

HOW TO APPLY In writing to the correspondent.

WHO TO APPLY TO Geoffrey Lawson, Trustee, Stilemans, Munstead, Godalming, Surrey GU8 4AB *Tel* 01483 420757

CC NO 801751   **ESTABLISHED** 1989

■ The Lawson Charitable Foundation

WHERE FUNDING CAN BE GIVEN South of England.

WHO CAN BENEFIT Organisations benefiting children, adults, students, people disadvantaged by poverty, and people involved in the arts, culture and Jewish religion.

WHAT IS FUNDED The advancement of education, Judaism, relief of poverty, the arts and general charitable purposes. In 1998–99, grants were distributed under three categories: health and welfare, education and culture, and the arts and humanities.

WHAT IS NOT FUNDED No grants to individuals.

SAMPLE GRANTS £8,544 to Central Synagogue; £6,825 to Norwood Ravenswood School; £4,690 to Perfect Technologies; £3,000 to Eugenia Chudonovich; £2,000 to The Speech Language & Hearing Centre; £1,500 each to Joint Jewish Charitable Trust and London Symphony Orchestra; £1,250 to Nightingale House; £1,219 to Jewish Federation Palm Beach; £1,100 to British ORT.

FINANCES *Year* 1998–99 *Income* £23,145 *Grants* £44,071 *Assets* £296,369

TRUSTEES G C H Lawson; M R Lawson; Mrs C Lawson.

HOW TO APPLY In writing to the correspondent, preferably with an sae.

WHO TO APPLY TO G C H Lawson, Trustee, Stilemans, Munstead, Godalming, Surrey GU8 4AB

CC NO 259468   **ESTABLISHED** 1969

■ The Herd Lawson Charitable Trust

WHERE FUNDING CAN BE GIVEN Mainly Cumbria.

WHAT IS FUNDED Organisations benefiting older people in need, particularly those who are members of evangelical or Christian brethren churches.

SAMPLE GRANTS £20,000 ongoing support to the Christian Workers' Fund (formerly the Homeworkers' Fund); £6,000 each to Lake District Cheshire Home and West Cumbria Hospice; £4,500 to Ambleside Baptist Church; £3,000 to Ambleside Welfare; £2,000 to Universal Beneficent Society (£2,000).

FINANCES *Year* 2000–01 *Income* £73,000 *Grants* £53,000 *Assets* £1,300,000

TRUSTEES John Scott; Peter Matthews.

HOW TO APPLY The trust receives more applications than it can deal with and does not seek further unsolicited appeals.

WHO TO APPLY TO The Trustees, The Estates Office, Church Street, Ambleside, Cumbria LA22 0BS

CC NO 272921   **ESTABLISHED** 1975

■ The Raymond & Blanche Lawson Charitable Trust

WHERE FUNDING CAN BE GIVEN UK, with an interest in west Kent and East Sussex.

WHO CAN BENEFIT Registered charities benefiting children, young adults and older people, including people with disabilities.

WHAT IS FUNDED This trust will consider funding: arts activities and education; hospice at home;

nursing service; hospices; hospitals; cancer research; community centres and village halls; guide dogs for the blind; care in the community; and armed service charities and benevolent associations.

WHAT IS NOT FUNDED No support for churches or individuals.

TYPE OF GRANT One-off, project and research. Funding is available for up to one year.

RANGE OF GRANTS £100–£10,055. Typically £1,000.

SAMPLE GRANTS £10,055 to Age Concern – Tonbridge; £5,000 each to Hospice in the Weald and Maidstone Trust; £4,000 to Kent Music School; £3,000 to Royal British Legion Poppy Appeal; £2,000 each to Cancer Research, Heart of Kent Trust, Maidstone Hospital League of Friends, Royal Society for the Blind and Worldwide Volunteering for Young People.

FINANCES *Year* 2000–01 *Income* £94,915 *Grants* £77,355 *Assets* £1,268,471

TRUSTEES John V Banks; John A Bertram; Mrs P E V Banks; Mrs Sarah Hill.

HOW TO APPLY In writing to the correspondent.

WHO TO APPLY TO Mrs P E V Banks, Trustee, 28 Barden Road, Tonbridge, Kent TN9 1TX *Tel* 01732 352183 *Fax* 01732 352621

CC NO 281269   **ESTABLISHED** 1980

■ The Lawson-Beckman Charitable Trust

WHERE FUNDING CAN BE GIVEN UK.

WHO CAN BENEFIT Mainly headquarters organisations.

WHAT IS FUNDED Jewish organisations, welfare, education, the arts and general purposes.

WHAT IS NOT FUNDED No grants to individuals.

RANGE OF GRANTS £200–£8,000.

SAMPLE GRANTS £23,000 to Jewish Care; £8,000 each to British ORT and Nightingale House; £6,750 to Norwood Ltd; £3,000 to Centrepoint; £2,500 each to Community Security Trust and UCH; £2,200 to Cystic Fibrosis Holiday Fund; £2,000 each to British Technion Society, Friends of Hebrew University and Who Cares Trust.

FINANCES *Year* 2000–01 *Income* £126,810 *Grants* £77,500 *Assets* £1,760,088

TRUSTEES M A Lawson; J N Beckman.

HOW TO APPLY In writing to the correspondent, but please note that grants are allocated two years in advance.

WHO TO APPLY TO Maurice Lawson, A Beckman plc, P O Box 1ED, London W1A 1ED *Tel* 020 7637 8412 *Fax* 020 7436 8599

CC NO 261378   **ESTABLISHED** 1970

■ Lazard Charitable Trust

WHERE FUNDING CAN BE GIVEN London.

WHO CAN BENEFIT Small, inner-city self-help charities benefiting: people of all ages; people who are in care, or who are fostered or adopted; people disadvantaged by poverty; homeless people; and victims of abuse. Funding may also go to people with various diseases and medical conditions. Prenatal care is also considered.

WHAT IS FUNDED Charities working in the fields of: accommodation and housing; supporting volunteers; respite care; support and self-help groups; and hospices will be considered. Funding may also be given for special needs education, speech therapy, training for work and various community facilities and services.

WHAT IS NOT FUNDED No grants for medical research, overseas charities, large UK/international charities or to individuals.

TYPE OF GRANT One-off, capital, recurring, core costs, buildings, project, running costs, salaries and start-up costs will be considered. Funding may be given for over three years.

RANGE OF GRANTS £100–£2,500.

FINANCES *Year* 1999 *Income* £209,000 *Grants* £212,000

TRUSTEES M C Baugham; Ms F A Heaton; P Gismondi; Ms J Field; D Wainwright; Ms T Stone.

HOW TO APPLY In writing to the correspondent. There are no application forms or guidelines.

WHO TO APPLY TO Fiona McGowan, Lazard Brothers & Co. Ltd, 21 Moorfields, London EC2P 2HT *Tel* 020 7588 2721

CC NO 1048043   **ESTABLISHED** 1995

■ The Mason Le Page Charitable Trust

WHERE FUNDING CAN BE GIVEN London area.

WHO CAN BENEFIT Organisations benefiting people with cancer and medical research.

WHAT IS FUNDED General charitable purposes, with a preference for supporting charities working in cancer research and care in the London area.

RANGE OF GRANTS £1,000–£10,000.

SAMPLE GRANTS £10,000 to St Bartholomews & London School of Medicine. Smaller amounts to Meadow House, Covent Garden Cancer Research Trust, Royal Hospital for Neuro-Disability, Breast Cancer Campaign, Sergeant Cancer Care for Children, St Christophers Hospice and KC Carers.

FINANCES *Year* 2001–02 *Income* £28,700 *Grants* £30,000 *Assets* £757,000

TRUSTEES David Morgan; Andrew John Francis Stebbings.

HOW TO APPLY In writing to the correspondent. The trust has an adviser who recommends charities for grants – Professor Malpas.

WHO TO APPLY TO Andrew Stebbings, Trustee, 45 Pont Street, London SW1X 0BX *Tel* 020 7591 3333 *Fax* 020 7591 3300

CC NO 1054589   **ESTABLISHED** 1996

■ The Eric and Dorothy Leach Charitable Trust

WHERE FUNDING CAN BE GIVEN UK, with a slight preference for North Wales.

WHO CAN BENEFIT Registered charities.

WHAT IS FUNDED General charitable purposes.

SAMPLE GRANTS £1,000 each to Kosovo Crisis and Landmark Trust; £500 each to Guide Dogs for the Blind, RSPCA, PDSA, North Wales Wildlife Trust, North Wales Youth Project and Royal School for the Blind.

FINANCES *Year* 1999–2000 *Income* £141,000 *Grants* £5,000 *Assets* £405,000

TRUSTEES R C Chamberlain; M D Blankstone; Mrs D M Leach.

HOW TO APPLY In writing to the correspondent.

WHO TO APPLY TO R Chamberlain, Trustee, Swayne Johnson & Wright, High Street, St Asaph, Clwyd LL17 0RF *Tel* 01745 582535

CC NO 1070041   **ESTABLISHED** 1998

■ The Leach Fourteenth Trust

WHERE FUNDING CAN BE GIVEN UK, with some preference for south west England and the home counties, and overseas.

WHO CAN BENEFIT Grants to registered charities only.

WHAT IS FUNDED Charities working in the fields of: residential facilities and services; missionary work; conservation and environment; and community services. Support may be given to: information technology and computers; professional bodies; councils for voluntary service; hospice at home; respite care; ambulances and mobile units; medical equipment; medical research; alternative medicine; professional and specialist training; and special needs education. Trustees mainly seek out their own ventures to support.

WHAT IS NOT FUNDED Only registered charities based in the UK are supported (the trust only gives overseas via a UK-based charity). No grants to: individuals, including for gap years or trips abroad; private schools, unless for people with disabilities or learning difficulties; or for pets.

TYPE OF GRANT Buildings, capital, core costs, one-off, project, research, running costs, recurring costs, salaries and start-up costs will be considered. Funding may be given for more than three years.

RANGE OF GRANTS £500–£10,000.

SAMPLE GRANTS £15,000 to Fosse Way School; £10,000 to Middlesex Hospital Special Trustees RYMD; £5,000 each to Deafblind UK, Isles of Scilly Environment Trust, Orbis and Royal College of Radiologists; £3,500 each to Mobility Trust and Countryside Restoration Fund; £3,000 to RUH Forever Friends Appeal; £2,250 to Lymphoma Association.

FINANCES *Year* 2000–01 *Income* £99,587 *Grants* £96,600 *Assets* £2,384,149

TRUSTEES W J Henderson; M A Hayes; Mrs J M M Nash; Roger Murray-Leach.

HOW TO APPLY In writing to the correspondent. Applications for a specific item or purpose are favoured. Only successful appeals can expect a reply. A representative of the trust occasionally visits potential beneficiaries. There is an annual meeting of trustees in the autumn, but not necessarily to consider grants. Grants tend to be distributed twice a year.

WHO TO APPLY TO Roger Murray-Leach, Trustee, Nettleton Mill, Castle Combe, Nr Chippenham, Wiltshire SN14 7NJ

CC NO 204844   **ESTABLISHED** 1961

■ The Leathersellers' Company Charitable Fund

WHERE FUNDING CAN BE GIVEN UK, particularly London.

WHO CAN BENEFIT Registered charities only.

WHAT IS FUNDED Charities associated with the Leathersellers' Company, the leather and hide trades, education in leather technology and for the welfare of poor and sick former workers in the industry and their dependants. Thereafter financial support is provided to registered charities associated with the City of London and its environs.

TYPE OF GRANT One-off grants for capital appeals. Occasionally recurrent grants for up to four years.

SAMPLE GRANTS £225,000 to Emmaus UK for capital costs; £165,000 to Rainbow Trust mainly for capital costs; £105,000 to the Leathersellers' University Exhibition; £64,000 to Colfe's Educational Foundation; £50,000 each

to Prendergast School and British School of Leather Technology, Northampton; £44,000 to Centrepoint Soho; £31,000 each to ChildLine and Society of Mary and Martha; £25,000 to Woodland Centre Trust.

FINANCES *Year* 2000–01 *Income* £1,200,000 *Grants* £1,479,000 *Assets* £35,400,000

TRUSTEES 'The Warden and Society of the Mystery and Art of the Leathersellers of the City of London.'

HOW TO APPLY In writing to the correspondent. The fund does not publish guidelines due to the wide range of causes it supports. Applicants should send a one-page letter describing their background and explaining what funds they require and their purpose. If interested, the charity will then request further information or conduct a visit as appropriate. Penny Burtwell, the charities administrator, is happy to speak to potential applicants before they write in and can be contacted on the number below.

WHO TO APPLY TO Penny Burtwell, Charities Administrator, 15 St Helen's Place, London EC3A 6DQ *Tel* 020 7330 1451 *Fax* 020 7330 1461 *Website* www.leathersellers.co.uk

CC NO 278072   **ESTABLISHED** 1979

■ The Leche Trust

WHERE FUNDING CAN BE GIVEN UK.

WHO CAN BENEFIT Individuals and organisations benefiting: musicians and overseas students during last six months of PhD courses.

WHAT IS FUNDED (a) preservation of buildings and furniture of the Georgian period; (b) assistance to organisations concerned with music and drama; (c) assistance to students from overseas during the final six months of PhD study in the UK; (d) assistance to postgraduate music students of outstanding ability; and (e) art galleries and cultural centres, libraries and museums and theatre and opera houses.

WHAT IS NOT FUNDED No grants are made for: religious bodies; overseas missions; schools and school buildings; social welfare; animals; medicine; expeditions; British students other than music students.

TYPE OF GRANT Grants for a specific purpose and not recurrent, including building costs.

RANGE OF GRANTS £500–£5,000.

SAMPLE GRANTS £15,000 to London Academy of Music and Dramatic Arts for bursaries; £10,000 each to Chiswick House – London for restoration of urns and St Andrew's Church – Presteigne for restoration of tapestry; £8,500 to St Cuthbert's Church in Widworthy for restoration of amonument; £6,000 to National Opera Studio for bursaries; £5,040 to Central School of Ballet for bursaries; £5,000 each to Dulwich Picture Gallery for restoration of painting, Leeds Art Gallery for purchase of secretaire and Tate Gallery for restoration of painting.

FINANCES *Year* 2000–01 *Income* £251,860 *Grants* £261,085 *Assets* £6,267,062

TRUSTEES Mrs Primrose Arnander, Chair; Simon Jervis; John Porteous; Dr Ian Bristow; Sir John Riddell; Mrs Felicity Guinness; Simon Wethered.

HOW TO APPLY In writing to the secretary. Trustees meet three times a year, in February, June and October; applications need to be received the month before.

WHO TO APPLY TO Mrs Louisa Lawson, Secretary, 84 Cicada Road, London SW18 2NZ *Tel* 020 8870 6233 *Fax* 020 8870 6233

CC NO 225659   **ESTABLISHED** 1963

■ The Arnold Lee Charitable Trust

WHERE FUNDING CAN BE GIVEN UK.

WHO CAN BENEFIT Organisations benefiting children, young adults and Jewish people. Support may also be given to rabbis, medical professionals, students, teachers and governesses. Very occasional grants may be made to individuals.

WHAT IS FUNDED Established charities of high repute working in the fields of education, health and religious purposes.

WHAT IS NOT FUNDED Grants are rarely made to individuals.

SAMPLE GRANTS In 1997–98: £34,000 to Joint Jewish Charitable Trust; £7,500 to Project SEED; £6,500 to Jewish Care; £5,000 to Lubavich Foundation; £2,500 to The Home of Aged Jews; £2,400 each to Friends of Akim and Yesodey Hatorah School.

FINANCES *Year* 2001–02 *Income* £97,796 *Grants* £85,150 *Assets* £1,364,943

TRUSTEES Arnold Lee; Helen Lee; Alan Lee.

HOW TO APPLY In writing to the correspondent.

WHO TO APPLY TO A Lee, Trustee, 47 Orchard Court, Portman Square, London W1H 9PD

CC NO 264437   **ESTABLISHED** 1972

■ The William Leech Charity

WHERE FUNDING CAN BE GIVEN Northumberland, Tyne and Wear, Durham and overseas.

WHO CAN BENEFIT Young people, disadvantaged people, volunteers and Christians.

WHAT IS FUNDED Small charities with a high proportion of unpaid volunteers, organisations working in deprived areas for the benefit of local people, particularly those which encourage people to help themselves, the promotion of community involvement and Christian charitable purposes. About a third of the trust's funds went to the University of Newcastle.

WHAT IS NOT FUNDED No grants for: community centres and similar (exceptionally, those in remote country areas may be supported); running expenses of youth clubs (as opposed to capital projects); running expenses of churches (this includes normal repairs, but churches engaged in social work, or using their buildings largely for 'outside' purposes, may be supported); sport; the arts; individuals or students; organisations which have been supported in the last 12 months (it would be exceptional to support an organisation in two successive years, unless we had promised such support in advance); holidays, travel, outings; minibuses (unless over 10,000 miles a year is expected); schools; and housing associations.

TYPE OF GRANT One-off and recurring grants, loans, running costs and salaries.

RANGE OF GRANTS Usual maximum grant is £5,000.

SAMPLE GRANTS £1,000,000 to University of Newcastle upon Tyne Mouse Genetics; £142,424 to University of Newcastle upon Tyne Medical School Projects; £80,000 to St Oswald's Hospice Children's Wing; £35,000 each to Institute of Ethics at Centre for Life and Mercy Ships; £30,000 to Breathe North; £25,000 to Second Crop Fund; £12,250 to Durham St John's College; £10,000 each to People's Kitchen and WaterAid.

FINANCES *Year* 2000–01 *Income* £653,293 *Grants* £1,536,000 *Assets* £13,478,000

TRUSTEES R E Leech, chair; Prof. P Baylis; C Davies; A Gifford; R D Leech; N Sherlock; D Stabler; B Wallace.

HOW TO APPLY In writing to the correspondent. The trustees meet every other month. For applications of £1,000 or over, one or more of the trustees may make further enquiries.

WHO TO APPLY TO Mrs Kathleen M Smith, Secretary, 4 St James Street, Newcastle upon Tyne NE1 4NG *Tel* 0191 232 7940

CC NO 265491   **ESTABLISHED** 1972

■ The Lord Mayor of Leeds Appeal Fund

WHERE FUNDING CAN BE GIVEN Leeds Metropolitan District.

WHO CAN BENEFIT The single charity selected by the Lord Mayor during his/her year of office.

WHAT IS FUNDED A charitable cause as identified by the Lord Mayor prior to their taking up office.

SAMPLE GRANTS In 1998–99: £164,157 to ChildLine (approved in the previous year, paid this year); £95,119 to Royal National Institute for the Blind (approved); £31,706 to The John Westmorland Trust (approved).

FINANCES *Year* 2000–01 *Income* £161,085 *Grants* £100,000

TRUSTEES Cllr Malcom James Bedford; Cllr William Winlow; Cllr Andrew Carter; Cllr Graham Peter Kirkland; Peter Rogerson.

OTHER INFORMATION In 2002, all money raised was given in support of Sue Ryder, Wheatfileds Hospice.

HOW TO APPLY In writing to the correspondent. However, it is usual for the Mayor to have decided before taking office.

WHO TO APPLY TO The Lord Mayor's Secretary, Lord Mayor's Office, Civic Hall, Leeds LS1 1UR *Tel* 0113 247 4055

CC NO 512441   **ESTABLISHED** 1982

■ Leeds & Holbeck Building Society Charitable Foundation

WHERE FUNDING CAN BE GIVEN Areas where the society's branches are located.

WHO CAN BENEFIT Organisations benefiting the homeless, local community centres, younger people, older people, individuals with disabilities, and deaf and/or blind people.

WHAT IS FUNDED Projects the society has supported include: provision of shelter, support and resettlement programmes for the homeless; centres offering facilities for the local community with emphasis on younger and older people; provision of work experience and skills training for young adults with special needs; educational projects for people who are deaf or blind; provision of transport for people with physical disabilities; winter warmth project for older people; arts project for a special needs group; play area for children with multiple disabilities; and hospices.

TYPE OF GRANT One-off for capital projects.

RANGE OF GRANTS £100–£500.

FINANCES *Year* 2001 *Income* £69,500 *Grants* £60,000 *Assets* £21,000

TRUSTEES Peter A H Hartley, Chair; Tony Burden; Christopher Holland; Peter J D Marshall; Victor H Watson.

HOW TO APPLY In writing to the correspondent. The trustees meet four times a year.

WHO TO APPLY TO Joy Baldry, Secretary, 105 Albion Street, Leeds, West Yorkshire LS1 5AS *Tel* 0113 216 7296 *E-mail* jbaldry@leeds-holbeck.co.uk

CC NO 1074429   **ESTABLISHED** 1999

Think carefully about every application. Is it justified?

611

■ The Leeds Hospital Fund Charitable Trust

WHERE FUNDING CAN BE GIVEN Yorkshire, especially Leeds.

WHO CAN BENEFIT Organisations involved with hospitals and local health-related charities including those working with people who are disabled.

WHAT IS FUNDED Hospitals, hospices, medical and disability charities.

WHAT IS NOT FUNDED No grants to individuals.

TYPE OF GRANT One-off and recurring.

SAMPLE GRANTS £75,000 each to Leeds Teaching Hospitals NHS Trust for various items of equipment and Leeds Teaching Hospitals Trust for specialist equipment; £72,000 in two grants to Martin House Hospice for patient care and provision of facilities for young adults; £35,000 to Bluebell Children's Hospital Doncaster; £30,000 each to St Gemma's Hospice for patient care and Wheatfield Hospice for patient care; £20,000 each to Pinderfields & Pontefract NHS Trust for equipment and Stepping Stones Appeal for equipment; £10,000 to Salvation Army for a new caravan to enable young children to have holidays; £5,000 to PHAB towards holidays and outings.

FINANCES *Year* 2001 *Income* £669,576 *Grants* £618,000 *Assets* £281,574

TRUSTEES Mrs P J Dobson, Chair; C Asquith; C S Bell; T Hardy; R T Strudwick.

HOW TO APPLY In writing to the correspondent. The trustees meet in February, May, July and November to consider applications.

WHO TO APPLY TO Mrs Lysanne MacCallion, Managing Director, Riverside House, 7 Canal Wharf, Leeds LS11 5WA *Tel* 0113 245 0813 *Website* www.lhfhealthplan.org.uk

CC NO 253861 **ESTABLISHED** 1967

■ The Leicester and Leicestershire Historic Churches Preservation Trust

WHERE FUNDING CAN BE GIVEN Diocese of Leicester.

WHAT IS FUNDED The restoration, preservation, repair, maintenance and improvement of churches and chapels, their churchyards and contents.

WHAT IS NOT FUNDED No grants for extensions of churches or chapels.

SAMPLE GRANTS £3,500 to St Paul's Church – Leicester for re-slating roofs, work on gutters and so on; £2,500 to Market Bosworth Parish Church for drainage system and repairs to tower; £1,820 to Hose Parish Church for roof, tower and wall repairs; £1,404 to Catthorpe Parish Church for stonework and flooring; £1,318 to Wigtoft Parish Church for walls, roof and ceiling repairs; £1,282 to Rotherby Parish Church for re-leading the roof and repairs to windows and stonework; £1,170 to Thornton Parish Church for tower and spire repairs; £1,104 to Thorpe Satchville Parish Church for re-flooring; £916 to Billesden Baptist Chapel for masonry and window repair; £690 to Thurnby United Reformed Church for roof, walls and woodwork repairs.

FINANCES *Year* 1999–2000 *Income* £41,000 *Grants* £36,000 *Assets* £37,000

TRUSTEES Dr A McWhirr; Rt Revd Timothy Stevens; M L Gardiner; Miss Y P Adams; Mrs J Arthur; R H Bloor; Hon. Mrs A Brooks; C B Byford; P Clifton; T Y Cocks; R Gill; Revd D H Hole; T H

Patrick; R J Wood; Rt Revd C J F Scott; Revd I Clarke.

HOW TO APPLY In writing to the correspondent. The trustees meet twice a year, in March and October. Applications should be by 1 September and 1 February to allow time for the trustees to visit the churches before the meetings.

WHO TO APPLY TO T Y Cocks, Hon. Secretary, 24 Beresford Drive, Leicester LE2 3LA *Tel* 0116 270 3424

CC NO 233476 **ESTABLISHED** 1964

■ Leicester Charity Link (formerly The Leicester Charity Organisation Society)

WHERE FUNDING CAN BE GIVEN The city of Leicester and its immediate vicinity.

WHO CAN BENEFIT Individuals and organisations.

WHAT IS FUNDED General charitable purposes.

FINANCES *Year* 1999–2000 *Income* £957,000 *Grants* £517,000 *Assets* £499,000

TRUSTEES S C F Vaughan, Chair; T G M Brooks, Lord Lieutenant of Leicestershire; E Watts; K Baddiley; Mrs A M Brennan; Mrs R Freer; Revd D N Hole; R J Hudson; C B L Murray; C E Smith; Mrs C M Wessel.

HOW TO APPLY In writing to the correspondent.

WHO TO APPLY TO M A Marvell, Chief Executive, 20a Millstone Lane, Leicester LE1 5JN *Tel* 0116 222 2200 *Fax* 0116 222 2201

CC NO 209464 **ESTABLISHED** 1876

■ The Leigh Trust

WHERE FUNDING CAN BE GIVEN Unrestricted, but with some apparent London interest.

WHO CAN BENEFIT Registered charities benefiting children; young adults; older people; unemployed people; volunteers; people who are in care, fostered or adopted; ethnic minority groups; at risk groups; people disadvantaged by poverty; ex-offenders and those at risk of offending; refugees; socially isolated people; people living in urban areas; victims of abuse and crime; and people with substance abuse problems.

WHAT IS FUNDED Grants can be given to legal services, support to voluntary and community organisations, support to volunteers, health counselling, support and self-help groups, drug and alcohol rehabilitation, education and training, social counselling, crime prevention schemes, community issues, international rights of the individual, advice and information (social issues), asylum seekers, racial equality and other charitable causes.

WHAT IS NOT FUNDED The trust does not make grants to individuals.

TYPE OF GRANT Buildings, capital, core costs, one-off, project, recurring costs, running costs, salaries and start-up costs. Funding is available for up to three years.

SAMPLE GRANTS £25,000 each to Ashdown Charitable Settlement, Chemical Dependency Centre, Inquest, Joint Council for the Welfare of Immigrants and Medical Foundation for the Care of Victims of Torture; £15,000 each to Prisoners Abroad, Public Concern and Who Cares Trust; £12,500 to European Association for the Treatment of Addictions – UK; £12,000 each to Children's Music Workshop and Paddington Development Trust.

FINANCES *Year* 2000–01 *Grants* £453,000

TRUSTEES Hon. David Bernstein; Dr R M E Stone; Caroline Moorehead.

HOW TO APPLY Initial applications should be made in writing to the registered office of the trust. Organisations should enclose the most recent audited accounts, a registered charity number, a cash flow statement for the next 12 months, and a stamped addressed envelope. Applicants should state clearly on one side of A4 what their charity does and what they are requesting funding for. They should provide a detailed budget and show other sources of funding for the project. The charity may be requested to complete an application form. It is likely that an officer of the trust will wish to visit the project before any grant is made. Trustees' meetings are held quarterly.

WHO TO APPLY TO The Trustees, Clive Marks and Company , 44a New Cavendish Street, London W1G 8TR *Tel* 020 7486 4663 *Fax* 020 7224 2942

CC NO 275372   **ESTABLISHED** 1976

■ The Kennedy Leigh Charitable Trust

WHERE FUNDING CAN BE GIVEN Israel and UK.

WHO CAN BENEFIT Registered charities only.

WHAT IS FUNDED Medical research, promotion of racial understanding in Israel, education, causes which will improve and enrich the lives of people who are underprivileged and young people who are disadvantaged.

WHAT IS NOT FUNDED No grants for individuals.

RANGE OF GRANTS £1,000–£500,000.

SAMPLE GRANTS £250,000 to Jewish Care for a home care service; £100,000 to University of Cambridge for educational purposes; £80,000 to St Mark's Hospital for the endoscopy unit.

FINANCES *Year* 2000–01 *Income* £1,000,000 *Grants* £606,000 *Assets* £17,500,000

TRUSTEES A M Sorkin, Chair; Mr G Goldkorn; Mrs Lesley D Berman; Leila I Foux; Carole Berman Sujo; Angela L Sorkin; Michele Foux.

HOW TO APPLY 'None considered. Funds fully committed for all non-Israel distributions.'

WHO TO APPLY TO Naomi Shoffman, Administrator, Suite 402, 258 Belsize Road, London NW6 4BT *Tel* 020 7316 1854 *Fax* 020 7316 1891

CC NO 288293   **ESTABLISHED** 1983

■ Morris Leigh Foundation

WHERE FUNDING CAN BE GIVEN Worldwide.

WHAT IS FUNDED The trust supports Jewish organisations and general charitable purposes, including the arts and humanities, education, culture and health and welfare causes.

TYPE OF GRANT Grants and long-term loans.

RANGE OF GRANTS £50–£6,000.

SAMPLE GRANTS £15,000 to Jewish Policy Research; £6,000 to Rycotwood College; £5,232 to Royal Opera House; £5,150 to Community Security Trust; £5,000 each to Board of Deputies, Jerusalem Academy of Music and Dance, London Business School, and St Mary's Hospital Special Trustees; £4,000 to Israel Philharmonic Orchestra; £3,000 to Pavilion Opera Educational Trust.

FINANCES *Year* 2000–01 *Income* £79,605 *Grants* £98,002 *Assets* £1,661,200

TRUSTEES Mrs Manja T Leigh; Martin D Paisner; Howard J Leigh.

HOW TO APPLY In writing to the correspondent.

WHO TO APPLY TO M D Paisner, Trustee, Berwin Leighton Paisner, Bouverie House, 154 Fleet Street, London EC4A 2JD *Tel* 020 7353 0299

CC NO 280695   **ESTABLISHED** 1980

■ Mrs Vera Leigh's Charity

WHERE FUNDING CAN BE GIVEN UK.

WHO CAN BENEFIT Organisations only.

WHAT IS FUNDED General charitable purposes.

WHAT IS NOT FUNDED No grants to individuals.

TYPE OF GRANT One-off.

RANGE OF GRANTS £100–£750.

SAMPLE GRANTS £1,000 each to CHASE (for Guildford Children's Hospice) and The Gauntlet Trust.

FINANCES *Year* 1999–2000 *Income* £47,000 *Grants* £43,000

TRUSTEES V R de A Woollcombe; T A Cole.

HOW TO APPLY In writing to the correspondent, although the trust states that unsolicited applications are not considered.

WHO TO APPLY TO D M King, Penningtons, Phoenix House, 9 London Road, Newbury, Berks RG14 1DH *Tel* 01635 571009

CC NO 274872   **ESTABLISHED** 1976

■ The P Leigh-Bramwell Trust 'E'

WHERE FUNDING CAN BE GIVEN UK, with a preference for Bolton.

WHO CAN BENEFIT Registered charities, schools, universities and churches benefiting children, young adults, students and Methodists.

WHAT IS FUNDED Specific regular allocations, leaving little opportunity to add further charities. Support is particularly given to Methodist churches and Bolton School Boys' and the Bolton School Girls' Division.

WHAT IS NOT FUNDED No grants to individuals.

RANGE OF GRANTS £100–£13,000.

SAMPLE GRANTS The same beneficiaries are supported each year; these are Leigh-Bramwell Scholarship Fund, for educational purposes, Circuit Methodist Church, Delph Hill Methodist Church, Bolton Hospice, Delph Hill Methodist Church, Breightmet Methodist Church, International Scientific Support Trust, West London Mission and RNLI.

FINANCES *Year* 2001–02 *Income* £62,189 *Grants* £76,000

HOW TO APPLY In writing to the correspondent; however, please note that there is only a small amount of funds available for unsolicited applications and therefore success is unlikely.

WHO TO APPLY TO P Morrison, Secretary, W & J Leigh & Co., Tower Works, Kestor Street, Bolton BL2 2AL *Tel* 01204 521771

CC NO 267333   **ESTABLISHED** 1973

■ Leng Charitable Trust

WHERE FUNDING CAN BE GIVEN UK, but with virtually exclusive preference for Scotland, and that very much in Tayside.

WHO CAN BENEFIT Registered charities.

WHAT IS FUNDED General charitable purposes including the arts, education, health, social welfare and the environment.

WHAT IS NOT FUNDED Grants are not given to individuals, overseas projects, political or religious appeals or for sports or recreation.

RANGE OF GRANTS Typically £500–£2,500.

FINANCES *Year* 2000 *Income* £151,000 *Grants* £140,000 *Assets* £4,800,000

TRUSTEES A F McDonald; J S Fair; Dr J Wood; Thorntons Trustees Ltd.

HOW TO APPLY In writing to the correspondent. Trustees meet to consider grants in January.

WHO TO APPLY TO A F McDonald, Trustee, Messrs Thorntons, 50 Castle Street, Dundee DD1 3RU *Tel* 01382 229111 *Fax* 01382 202288 *E-mail* afmcdonald@thorntonsws.co.uk *Website* www.thorntonsws.co.uk

SC NO SC009285

■ The Erica Leonard Trust

WHERE FUNDING CAN BE GIVEN Mainly Surrey and occasionally overseas.

WHO CAN BENEFIT Registered charities only.

WHAT IS FUNDED General charitable purposes.

SAMPLE GRANTS In 1998–99: £13,700 to Phoenix Trust for general purposes; £5,000 to Leonard Trust for general purposes; £4,000 to Third World Link for relief of poverty in Rajastan; £3,000 to P S W Belem Mission for street children in Belem; £2,000 to Footsteps Guildford for relief of poverty; £1,000 each to King's World Trust for a child project in South India, Surrey University for an education project, Bishop and Guildford Foundation for local social needs, Catholic Bible School for spiritual and religious needs, and Argentinian Homes Foundation for an orphanage in Buenos Aires.

FINANCES *Year* 1999–2000 *Income* £40,000 *Grants* £56,000 *Assets* £750,000

TRUSTEES R C E Grey; A C Kemp; R Beeston.

HOW TO APPLY In writing to the correspondent.

WHO TO APPLY TO R C E Grey, Trustee, Old Farmhouse, Elstead, Surrey GU8 6DB *Tel* 01252 702230

CC NO 291627   **ESTABLISHED** 1985

■ The Leonard Trust

WHERE FUNDING CAN BE GIVEN Overseas and UK, with a preference for Hampshire.

WHO CAN BENEFIT Registered charities. The trust looks favourably on special one-off appeals.

WHAT IS FUNDED Christian, overseas aid and medical research.

WHAT IS NOT FUNDED No grants to individuals.

TYPE OF GRANT Usually one-off.

RANGE OF GRANTS £1,000–£5,000.

SAMPLE GRANTS In 1997–98: £5,000 to Tearfund; £3,000 each to LEPRA, Church Missionary Society, and Winchester Cancer Research Trust; £2,000 each to Westminster Chapel, British Red Cross, The Salvation Army, The Samaritans, The Children's Society, and The Bible Society.

FINANCES *Year* 2000 *Grants* £30,000

TRUSTEES Tessa Feilden; Dominic Gold; Carol Gold.

HOW TO APPLY In writing to the correspondent.

WHO TO APPLY TO Mrs Tessa Feilden, Trustee, Manor Farm, Bramdean, Alresford, Hampshire SO24 0JS *Tel* 01962 771344

CC NO 1031723   **ESTABLISHED** 1993

■ The Mark Leonard Trust

WHERE FUNDING CAN BE GIVEN Worldwide, but mainly UK.

WHO CAN BENEFIT Organisations benefiting children, young adults and volunteers.

WHAT IS FUNDED Environment: environmental education, particularly supporting projects displaying practical ways of involving children and young adults, as well as sustainable transport, energy efficiency and renewable energy. Youth work: the rehabilitation of young people who have become marginalised and involved in anti-social or criminal activities, as well as extending and adding value to the existing use of school buildings and encouraging greater involvement of parents, school leavers and volunteers in extra-curricular activities. General charitable purposes.

WHAT IS NOT FUNDED Grants are not normally made to individuals.

SAMPLE GRANTS £25,000 to Envolve for the expansion of staff capacity for environmental outreach work in Bath and North East Somerset schools (£15,000) and establishing a travel club in Bath (£10,000); £15,206 to Clerkenwell Detached Youth Project for various salary costs; £14,000 to Worldwide Volunteering for Youth for salary costs over two years; £10,000 each to Milton Keynes Citischool for a re-cycle project for developing community business and service in the school's first year, Transport 2000 Trust for core costs over two years and Youth at Risk to help overcome a large deficit; £9,750 to BioRegional Development Group for seed funding for a project developing a new zero energy settlement by identifying a site and bringing in construction and planning partners; £7,500 to Youth Entertainment Studios for training people in performance, production and business skills in North Hammersmith; £5,000 each to Envision for an award scheme to encourage environmental awareness and education among 16 to 18 year olds and LATCH Housing for a self-help home improvement for a tenants self-build scheme in Leeds.

FINANCES *Year* 2001–02 *Income* £1,127,763 *Grants* £132,710 *Assets* £7,063,821

TRUSTEES Mrs Z Sainsbury; Miss Judith Portrait; J J Sainsbury; Mark Sainsbury.

OTHER INFORMATION The trust is one of the Sainsbury Family Charitable Trusts which share a common administration. An application to one is taken as an application to all.

HOW TO APPLY Proposals are generally invited by the trustees or initiated at their request. Unsolicited applications are not encouraged and are unlikely to be successful.

WHO TO APPLY TO Michael Pattison, Director, Addlington House, 1st Floor, 150 Victoria Street, London SW1E 5AE *Tel* 030 7410 0330 *Fax* 020 7410 0332

CC NO 1040323   **ESTABLISHED** 1994

■ Lesley Lesley and Mutter Trust

WHERE FUNDING CAN BE GIVEN Devon only.

WHO CAN BENEFIT Registered charities in Devon.

WHAT IS FUNDED Recipients are named and do not vary from year to year: Parkinson's Disease Association, the Chest Heart and Stroke Association, Multiple Sclerosis Society, Muscular Dystrophy Group of Great Britain, Royal National Institute for the Blind, Rowcroft Hospice for Torbay and the Guide Dogs for the Blind (Devon Area Branch).

TYPE OF GRANT Recurrent.

FINANCES *Year* 1999–2000 *Income* £44,743 *Grants* £40,566

TRUSTEES Lloyds TSB Private Banking Ltd.

HOW TO APPLY Applications are not welcome.

WHO TO APPLY TO Lloyds Private Banking Limited, A/C 215195, UK Trust Centre, The Clock House, 22–26 Ock Street, Abingdon, Oxfordshire OX14 5SW

CC NO 1018747   **ESTABLISHED** 1989

■ The Lethendy Charitable Trust

WHERE FUNDING CAN BE GIVEN Scotland, with a preference for Tayside.

WHO CAN BENEFIT Priority is given to children and young adults in Tayside.

WHAT IS FUNDED The chief interests of the trustees are in the development of young people and supporting worthwhile causes in Tayside.

WHAT IS NOT FUNDED Individuals for purely academic purposes such as school, university or college fees.

TYPE OF GRANT One-off.

RANGE OF GRANTS £50–£10,000.

SAMPLE GRANTS £10,000 each to Dundee Cancer Treatment Appeal and Game Conservancy Scottish Lowlands Research Project; £5,000 each to Links Overseas and Princes Royal Trust for Carers; £1,500 to The University of St Andrews – saving the stained glass of St Salvator's Chapel; £1,000 to the Byre Theatre Appeal. Grants to individuals ranged from £50 to £350.

FINANCES Year 2001 Income £49,000 Grants £49,000 Assets £1,600,000

TRUSTEES N M Sharp, Chair; W R Alexander; D L Laird; I B Rae; A Thomson.

HOW TO APPLY In writing to the correspondent. Trustees meet once a year in July to consider grants.

WHO TO APPLY TO George Hay, Henderson Loggie, Chartered Accountants, Royal Exchange, Panmure Street, Dundee DD1 1DZ Tel 01382 200055 Fax 01382 221240 E-mail ghay@hendersonloggie.co.uk

SC NO SC003428   **ESTABLISHED** 1979

■ Leukaemia Research Fund

WHERE FUNDING CAN BE GIVEN UK.

WHO CAN BENEFIT Hospitals and university medical centres which benefit medical professionals, nurses and doctors; students; and people with leukaemia.

WHAT IS FUNDED Improving treatments, finding the cures and preventing all forms of leukaemia, Hodgkin's disease and other lymphomata, myelomata, the myelodysplasias and aplastic anaemia.

TYPE OF GRANT Capital (equipment), feasibility study, recurring costs, research and salaries.

RANGE OF GRANTS £1,000–£4,000,000.

SAMPLE GRANTS £3,591,300 to University of Newcastle-upon-Tyne; £1,555,442 to Imperial College School of Medicine, London; £1,435,431 to University of Oxford; £1,063,686 to University College London; £983,695 to University of Dundee; £927,153 to Medical Research Council, London; £844,825 to University of Birmingham; £821,332 to Southampton General Hospital; £623,559 to Institute of Cancer Research, London; £481,080 to University of Bristol; £452,684 to Kings College School of Medicine, London.

FINANCES Year 2001–02 Income £19,489,166 Grants £16,655,813 Assets £36,009,500

TRUSTEES Earl Cadogan, Chair; J A C Barrington; K S Carmichael; Mrs P Bassett; Mrs I Burrage; R Delderfield; P C Hart; B Haynes; Mrs D Hensby; D Holliday; K Lomas; Mrs M Naddell; D Payne; W A Plummer; C G F Sharp; Mrs K A Smedley; Mrs H Potter; G Brodzlebantz.

PUBLICATIONS Yearbook, newsletters, *Making a Difference – 40 years of LRF Achievement*, *Directory of Research*, patient information booklets.

HOW TO APPLY On an application form available from the trust.

WHO TO APPLY TO Dr David Grant, Scientific Director, 43 Great Ormond Street, London WC1N 3JJ Tel 020 7405 0101 Fax 020 7242 1488 E-mail lrf@leukaemia.demon.co.uk Website www.leukaemia-research.org.uk

CC NO 216032   **ESTABLISHED** 1960

■ The Lord Leverhulme Charitable Trust

WHERE FUNDING CAN BE GIVEN UK, especially Cheshire, Merseyside and surrounding areas.

WHO CAN BENEFIT Registered and exempt charities.

WHAT IS FUNDED General charitable purposes. Priority is given to certain charitable organisations and trusts in Cheshire and Merseyside, particularly educational organisations, welfare charities, youth organisations, the arts, churches, and organisations benefiting older people and people with disabilities.

WHAT IS NOT FUNDED No grants to non-charitable organisations.

TYPE OF GRANT Recurrent, one-off and capital.

RANGE OF GRANTS £5–£10,000 and above.

SAMPLE GRANTS £250,000 to University of Liverpool Development Trust; £85,000 to Hammond School; £80,000 to SAM Appeal; £50,000 each to Dean and Chapter of Chester Cathedral and the Royal College of the Surgeons of England; £25,000 to Extra Care Charitable Trust; £20,000 to the Norwich Cathedral Trust; £15,000 to Lichfield Cathedral Music Camp; £10,000 each to Ability Net, Northamptonshire Association of Youth Clubs, St Magnus Parochial Church and Lambeth Partnership Fund.

FINANCES Year 2000–01 Income £646,000 Grants £942,000 Assets £19,400,000

TRUSTEES A E H Heber-Percy; A H S Hannay.

HOW TO APPLY By letter addressed to the trustees setting out details of the appeal, and including the most recent accounts.

WHO TO APPLY TO The Trustees, Leverhulme Estate Office, Thornton Hough, Wirral CH63 1JD

CC NO 212431   **ESTABLISHED** 1957

■ The Leverhulme Trade Charities Trust

WHERE FUNDING CAN BE GIVEN UK.

WHAT IS FUNDED Charities connected with and benefiting commercial travellers, grocers or chemists, their wives, widows and children, especially those disadvantaged by poverty.

WHAT IS NOT FUNDED No capital grants. No response is given to general appeals.

TYPE OF GRANT For a limited period only, usually one to three years.

SAMPLE GRANTS £160,000 to Commercial Travellers' Benevolent Institution; £94,000 to The Girls' Public Day School Trust; £80,000 to Royal Pinner School Foundation; £45,000 to UCTA Samaritan Fund; £30,000 to Royal Pharmaceutical Society; £17,000 to Provision Trade Benevolent Institution; £13,000 to Commercial Travellers of Scotland Benevolent Fund; £10,000 to United Reformed Church Schools.

FINANCES Year 2001 Income £987,000 Grants £612,000 Assets £31,119,000

Think carefully about every application. Is it justified?

615

TRUSTEES Sir Michael Angus, Chair; Sir Michael Perry; N W A Fitzgerald; Dr J I W Anderson; A S Ganguly.

OTHER INFORMATION Over £160,000 was disbursed in undergraduate bursaries.

HOW TO APPLY By letter to the correspondent. All correspondence is acknowledged. The trustees meet in February and applications need to be received by the preceding October. Undergraduate bursary applications should be directed to the relevant institution.

WHO TO APPLY TO The Secretary, 1 Pemberton Row, London EC4A 3BG *Tel* 020 7822 6915
CC NO 288404   **ESTABLISHED** 1983

■ The Leverhulme Trust

WHERE FUNDING CAN BE GIVEN UK and developing countries

WHO CAN BENEFIT Universities and other institutions of higher and further education; registered charities; and individuals.

WHAT IS FUNDED Grants are made to institutions for specific research undertakings, for schemes of international academic interchange and, exceptionally, for education.

TYPE OF GRANT One-off, project, research, recurring, running costs and salaries.

SAMPLE GRANTS £2,017,000 over six years to Nottingham University; £1,997,305 over nine years to Institute for Fiscal Studies – University of London; £1,997,220 over six years to Bristol University; £1,835,962 over nine years to School of Advanced Study – University of London; £1,000,000 each over 10 years to London School of Economics, University of Warwick, University of Durham and University of Exeter.

FINANCES *Year* 2000 *Income* £29,968,000 *Grants* £17,405,000 *Assets* £111,603,3000

TRUSTEES Sir Kenneth Durham, Chair; Sir Michael Angus; N W A Fitzgerald; Sir Michael Perry; Viscount Leverhulme; Dr J I W Anderson; Dr A S Ganguly.

PUBLICATIONS *Policies and Procedures: A guide for applicants* (published annually).

HOW TO APPLY The trust has detailed and specific requirements and procedures which applicants must meet, both as to timing and to content. All applicants should first ask for the trust's current 'Policies and Procedures' brochure before attempting to submit an application. The website may also be consulted.

WHO TO APPLY TO Prof. Barry Supple, Director, 1 Pemberton Row, London EC4A 3BG *Tel* 020 7822 6938 *Fax* 020 7822 5084 *E-mail* policies@leverhulme.org.uk *Website* www.leverhulme.org.uk
CC NO 288371   **ESTABLISHED** 1925

■ The Levy Foundation

WHERE FUNDING CAN BE GIVEN UK and Israel.

WHO CAN BENEFIT Registered charities benefiting children and young people, older people, health, medical research, Jewish causes.

WHAT IS FUNDED Arts, culture & sport, education, health and community care, religion and social welfare.

WHAT IS NOT FUNDED No grants to individuals, under any circumstances.

TYPE OF GRANT Project, research, salaries and start-up costs. Funding may be given for up to and over three years.

RANGE OF GRANTS £250–£200,000.

SAMPLE GRANTS £269,031 (in two grants) to London Youth; £203,340 to Dementia Relief Trust; £67,500 to Ashkelon Foundation (Cerebral Palsy Centre); £40,000 to English Blind Golf Association; £37,000 to Cystic Fibrosis Trust; £30,000 each to Cystic Fibrosis Holiday Fund for Children and Jewish Care; £25,000 to Tarleton Junior Rugby Development Project; £16,000 to Benei Arazim; £15,000 to Jewish Policy Research.

FINANCES *Year* 2001–02 *Income* £1,060,600 *Grants* £911,785 *Assets* £19,253,329

TRUSTEES Mrs N F Levy; Mrs Jane Jason; Peter L Levy; Silas Krendel.

HOW TO APPLY In writing to the grants manager at any time. 'The trust has always welcomed enquiries and I personally am happy to talk to any potential applicant'. (Sue Nyfield, Grants Manager)

WHO TO APPLY TO Sue Nyfield, Grants Manager, 6 Camden High Street, Camden Town, London NW1 0JH *Tel* 020 7874 7200 *Fax* 020 7874 7206 *E-mail* info@levyfoundation.org.uk
CC NO 245592   **ESTABLISHED** 1961

■ The Ralph Levy Charitable Company Ltd

WHERE FUNDING CAN BE GIVEN UK, occasionally overseas.

WHO CAN BENEFIT Registered charities only, in the field of education.

WHAT IS FUNDED Advancement of education, especially in the science of medicine, or any charitable purpose.

WHAT IS NOT FUNDED No educational grants to individuals.

FINANCES *Year* 1999–2000 *Income* £56,448 *Grants* £133,477 *Assets* £1,046,674

TRUSTEES S M Levy; D S Levy; C J F Andrews.

HOW TO APPLY In writing to the correspondent. Written applications must be received three clear months before the commencement of the proposed project.

WHO TO APPLY TO Christopher Andrews, Trustee, 14 Chesterfield Street, London W1J 5JN *Tel* 020 7408 9333 *Fax* 020 7408 9346
CC NO 200009   **ESTABLISHED** 1961

■ Lewis Family Charitable Trust

WHERE FUNDING CAN BE GIVEN UK and overseas.

WHO CAN BENEFIT Charitable bodies and research institutions.

WHAT IS FUNDED Research into cancer, head injuries and birth defects; health; education; and Jewish charities.

WHAT IS NOT FUNDED No grants to individuals.

TYPE OF GRANT Recurring, one-off, capital and salaries.

SAMPLE GRANTS £58,500 to King's College Hospital; £57,000 to Birth Defects Foundation; £42,000 to Association for the Advancement of Cancer Therapy; £40,000 to British Council for the Lewis Fellowship Fund; £21,000 to UJIA/Joint Jewish Charitable Trust; £19,000 each to University of Nottingham and Queen Mary and Westfield College Hospital; £17,000 to Imperial Cancer Research.

FINANCES *Year* 1998–99 *Income* £679,000 *Grants* £399,000 *Assets* £3,304,000

TRUSTEES David Lewis; Bernard Lewis.

HOW TO APPLY To the correspondent in writing. Grants are normally made only once a year. The trust states: 'Grants are not made on the basis of applications received.'

WHO TO APPLY TO David Lewis, Trustee, Chelsea House, West Gate, London W5 1DR

CC NO 259892   **ESTABLISHED** 1962

■ The Sir Edward Lewis Foundation

WHERE FUNDING CAN BE GIVEN UK and overseas, with a preference for Surrey.

WHO CAN BENEFIT Registered charities.

WHAT IS FUNDED General charitable purposes.

WHAT IS NOT FUNDED Grants are only given to charities, projects or people known to the trustees. No grants are given to individuals.

SAMPLE GRANTS £25,000 to Gurkha Welfare Trust; £10,000 to Accord International; £4,000 to St Bartholomew's Church – Leigh; £3,000 each to Institute of Economic Affairs and Progressive Supranuclear Palsy Association; £2,000 each to Great Ormnd Street Children's Hospital, King Edward's VII's Hospital, RYA Sailability, See Ability and Sports Aid London.

FINANCES *Year* 2000–01 *Income* £190,169 *Grants* £114,450 *Assets* £8,074,709

TRUSTEES R A Lewis; K W Dent; Christine Lewis; Sarah Dorin.

OTHER INFORMATION The trust makes one substantial donation every two or three years, as well as smaller donations each year.

HOW TO APPLY In writing to the correspondent. The trustees meet every six months.

WHO TO APPLY TO The Trustees, Messrs Rawlinson & Hunter, Eagle House, 110 Jermyn Street, London SW1Y 6RH *Tel* 020 7451 9000

CC NO 264475   **ESTABLISHED** 1972

■ John Lewis Partnership General Community Fund

WHERE FUNDING CAN BE GIVEN UK.

WHO CAN BENEFIT Registered charities.

WHAT IS FUNDED UK and local registered charities benefiting children and young adults, at risk groups, people who are sick or disabled, people disadvantaged by poverty and socially isolated people. Medical professionals and research workers may be considered for funding.

WHAT IS NOT FUNDED Loans are not made and sponsorship is not undertaken. Grants are not made for the promotion of religion, political organisations, advertising or to individuals.

TYPE OF GRANT One-off and recurring grants.

RANGE OF GRANTS £500 upwards.

SAMPLE GRANTS £60,000 to Cottage Homes; £10,000 to Anchor Trust; £8,000 to Barnardos; £5,000 each to Eyeless Trust and The Landmark Trust; £3,500 to Mobility Trust; £3,000 to Support Dogs; £2,000 to National Autistic Society; £1,000 to Jack Charlton Disabled Anglers' Trust.

FINANCES *Year* 1999 *Income* £850,000 *Grants* £850,000

TRUSTEES The Central Council.

HOW TO APPLY In writing to the correspondent, accompanied by the latest annual report and accounts.

WHO TO APPLY TO Mrs C Jones, Secretary, Central Charities Committee, 171 Victoria Street, London SW1E 5NN *Tel* 020 7592 5464 *Fax* 020 7592 5929 *E-mail* chris_l_jones@johnlewis.co.uk

CC NO 209128   **ESTABLISHED** 1961

■ The John Spedan Lewis Foundation

WHERE FUNDING CAN BE GIVEN UK.

WHO CAN BENEFIT The focus is on applications for small projects connected with the natural sciences, in particular ornithology, entomology and horticulture, from organisations benefiting, in the first instance, children, young adults and research workers.

WHAT IS FUNDED Charitable purposes, in the first instance reflecting the particular interests of John Spedan Lewis, namely horticulture, ornithology, entomology and associated educational and research projects. The trustees will also consider applications from organisations for imaginative and original educational projects aimed at developing serious interest and evident talent, particularly among young people.

WHAT IS NOT FUNDED No grants to individuals (including students), local branches of national organisations, or for medical research, welfare projects or building works.

TYPE OF GRANT Mostly straight donations. Salaries not funded.

FINANCES *Year* 2001–02 *Income* £55,198 *Grants* £48,752 *Assets* £1,932,981

TRUSTEES Sir Stuart Hampson; C W F Redmond; G K Atkins; Dr Vaughan Southgate; Simon Fowler.

HOW TO APPLY In writing to the correspondent with latest report and accounts and a budget for the proposed project.

WHO TO APPLY TO Ms B M F Chamberlain, Secretary, 171 Victoria Street, London SW1E 5NN *Tel* 020 7828 1000 *E-mail* bmfchamberlain@johnlewis.co.uk

CC NO 240473   **ESTABLISHED** 1964

■ The Licensed Trade Charities Trust

WHERE FUNDING CAN BE GIVEN England and Wales.

WHO CAN BENEFIT For charitable institutions connected to the licensed trade only.

WHAT IS NOT FUNDED No grants to individuals.

SAMPLE GRANTS £54,000 to Hospitality Action; £44,000 to Licensed Victuallers National Homes; £63,000 to Society of Licensed Victuallers; £40,000 to Wine and Spirit Trades Benevolent Society.

FINANCES *Year* 2001 *Income* £131,000 *Grants* £332,000 *Assets* £5,005,000

TRUSTEES A G Eadie, Chair; W L Page; S Williams; W P Catesby; T G Cockerell; C Cox; M Curnock Cook; C J Eld; J J Madden; J C Overton; G B Richardson.

HOW TO APPLY New applications are not considered.

WHO TO APPLY TO Nicholas Harry Block, The Brows, Sutton Place, Dorking, Surrey RH5 6RL *Tel* 01306 731223 *Fax* 01306 731169

CC NO 282161   **ESTABLISHED** 1981

■ The Life Insurance Association Charitable Foundation

WHERE FUNDING CAN BE GIVEN UK.

WHAT IS FUNDED General charitable purposes.

FINANCES *Year* 2000 *Income* £69,000 *Grants* £65,000

TRUSTEES K Carby, Chair; M Clarke; S Myers; J Travis; F Weisinger; S Sprung; M Bousfield.

HOW TO APPLY Beneficiaries are elected by local LIA regions.

WHO TO APPLY TO The Trustees, LIA House, Station Approach, Chorleywood, Rickmansworth, Herfordshire WD3 5PF *Tel* 01923 285333 *Website* www.lia.co.uk
CC NO 1071492   **ESTABLISHED** 1998

■ The Thomas Lilley Memorial Trust

WHERE FUNDING CAN BE GIVEN UK.
WHO CAN BENEFIT Individuals and organisations.
WHAT IS FUNDED General charitable purposes.
RANGE OF GRANTS £100–£5,000.
SAMPLE GRANTS In 1997–98: £5,000 to an individual; £2,500 to Stonar Development Fund; £1,500 each to All Saints church PCC Cuddeston, Cancer Relief Macmillan Fund (Isle of Man), and Riding for the Disabled; £1,200 to Samaritans.
FINANCES *Year* 2001–02 *Income* £22,122 *Assets* £1,000,000
TRUSTEES J F Luke; P T A Lilley.
HOW TO APPLY The trust has previously stated that its funds are fully committed and no new applications are considered.
WHO TO APPLY TO N Buckley Sharp, FAO Trustees, Cooper Lancaster Brewers, Accountants, Aldwych House, 81 Aldwych, London WC2B 4HP *Tel* 020 7242 2444
CC NO 1039529   **ESTABLISHED** 1960

■ Limoges Charitable Trust

WHERE FUNDING CAN BE GIVEN UK, with a preference for Birmingham.
WHO CAN BENEFIT Registered charities.
WHAT IS FUNDED Preference for animal and service organisations.
RANGE OF GRANTS £50–£15,000; mostly £200–£1,000.
SAMPLE GRANTS £15,000 to Symphony Hall Organ Appeal; £14,700 to Blue Coat School for the piano appeal; £5,000 each to Symphony Hall (Birmingham) Ltd and University of Birmingham; £3,270 to an individual; £3,000 to Birmingham Parish Church (St Martin's) Renewal Campaign; £2,650 to Elizabeth Svendsen Trust; £2,000 each to Birmingham Early Music Fund, KGFS, and Web Care Services.
FINANCES *Year* 2000–01 *Income* £21,206 *Grants* £93,748 *Assets* £115,342
TRUSTEES Catherine Harriet Mary Bligh St George; Albert Kenneth Dyer; Judy Ann Dyke; Andrew Miller.
HOW TO APPLY In writing to the correspondent.
WHO TO APPLY TO Ms J A Dyke, Trustee, Tyndall Woods Solicitors, 5 Greenfield Crescent, Edgbaston, Birmingham B15 3BE *Tel* 0121 243 3025
CC NO 1016178   **ESTABLISHED** 1991

■ The Linbury Trust

WHERE FUNDING CAN BE GIVEN Unrestricted.
WHO CAN BENEFIT Charities working in the fields listed below.
WHAT IS FUNDED Arts and arts education, especially support for dance and dance education. Medical research into chronic fatigue syndrome, and occasionally other 'unfashionable' areas. Drug abuse, provision of hands-on care to treat and rehabilitate drug users, particularly those which work with young people and the families of drug users. Education, especially support for best practice in the identification and teaching of children and young people with literacy problems, especially dyslexia. Environment and heritage, particularly historical buildings and major art institutions. Social welfare, especially for work helping young people disadvantaged by poverty, educational achievement or difficult family backgrounds, or who are involved in the criminal justice system. Also support for initiatives that improve quality of life of older people and through which they are helped to continue living in their own home. Developing countries, including humanitarian aid, social welfare and educational opportunities.
TYPE OF GRANT Running costs, project.
SAMPLE GRANTS £1,250,000 to Said Business School – University of Oxford as part of a £4,125,000 contribution towards the Sainsbury Library; £1,000,000 to Tate Britain as part of a £3,000,000 contribution for the new Linbury Galleries; £600,000 to Museum of London as part of a £1,200,000 contribution towards a new gallery for temporary exhibitions; £250,000 to Sir Harold Hillier and Arboretum Gardens for a new visitor centre; £200,000 to British Empire and Commonwealth Museum – Bristol for an education programme; £151,422 to Linbury Biennial Prize for Stage Design; £150,000 each to St George's House – Windsor Castle for refurbishment, and Stowe House Preservation Trust as part of a £600,000 contribution for a restoration project; £148,556 to University of Cape Town for postgraduate scholarships; £125,000 to Southampton General Hospital for rebuilding and re-equipping the paediatric cardiac facilities; £100,000 to Queen's Golden Jubilee Weekend Trust towards the celebrations.
FINANCES *Year* 2001–02 *Income* £7,216,000 *Grants* £4,472,000 *Assets* £181,726,000
TRUSTEES Lord Sainsbury of Preston Candover; Lady Sainsbury; Miss Judith Portrait.
OTHER INFORMATION The trust is one of the Sainsbury Family Charitable Trusts which share a common administration. An application to one is taken as an application to all.
HOW TO APPLY Because of the trustees' proactive approach, unsolicited applications are usually unsuccessful, although applications are considered on their merits. Applicants are always required to provide a detailed budget for their proposals and up-to-date audited accounts with a copy of their most recently published annual report.
WHO TO APPLY TO Michael Pattison, Director, Allington House, 1st Floor, 150 Victoria Street, London SW1E 5AE *Tel* 020 7410 0330 *Fax* 020 7410 0332
CC NO 287077   **ESTABLISHED** 1973

■ The Lincolnshire Old Churches Trust

WHERE FUNDING CAN BE GIVEN The old Anglican Diocese of Lincoln and former County to the Humber.
WHO CAN BENEFIT Churches, principally Christian churches, of any denomination.
WHAT IS FUNDED The preservation, repair and maintenance of churches over 100 years old in the area defined above, to exclude wind and weather, achieve safety and security and to ensure the preservation of those features which make old churches unique.
WHAT IS NOT FUNDED No grants for ritual, heating, lighting or gravestone repair.
RANGE OF GRANTS £500–£10,000.

FINANCES *Year* 2001 *Income* £188,278 *Grants* £185,197 *Assets* £222,533
TRUSTEES P Sandberg, Chair; Rt Hon. Lady Willoughby; Nevile Camamile; Mrs B Cracroft-Eley; Ven. Dr David Griffiths; Lt Cdr C Rodwell; R Stanley; Mrs K Walter; Mrs J Ware; D Wellman; J Healage; D Lawrence; Mrs R Lindop; A Seton; C Hammant.
HOW TO APPLY On a form available from the correspondent.
WHO TO APPLY TO The Secretary, PO Box 195, Lincoln LN6 9XR *Tel* 01522 868959 *Fax* 01522 868958
CC NO 509021   **ESTABLISHED** 1953

■ Lindale Educational Foundation

WHERE FUNDING CAN BE GIVEN UK and overseas.
WHO CAN BENEFIT Roman Catholic organisations benefiting children, young adults and students.
WHAT IS FUNDED Charities which aim to advance education in accordance with Christian principles and ideals within the Roman Catholic tradition, in particular those organisations that train priests. Most grants are already allocated to specific charities.
WHAT IS NOT FUNDED No grants to individuals.
TYPE OF GRANT Recurrent.
RANGE OF GRANTS £1,000–£60,000.
SAMPLE GRANTS £60,000 in four grants to Collegio Romano della Santa Croce for the training of priests; £55,000 in two grants to Fondation Belmont for the training of priests; £41,395 to Wickenden Manor, the Natherhall Educational Association Centre for Retreats and Study Activites; £12,000 each to Brixton Baytree Centre, and Dawliffe Hall Educational Foundation, which are connected organisations; £10,000 to Fundacion para el desarrollo integral (FUDI) for an humanitarian/educational project in Guatemala; £6,123 to Thornycroft Hall; £2,000 to Collegio Mayor de Humanidades to support seminiarians; £1,000 to a school project in Ghana.
FINANCES *Year* 2001–02 *Income* £179,870 *Grants* £199,538 *Assets* £6,438
TRUSTEES Netherhall Educational Association; Dawliffe Hall Educational Foundation; Greygarth Association.
HOW TO APPLY In writing to the correspondent, but note that most funds are already committed.
WHO TO APPLY TO J Valero, 1 Leopold Road, London W5 3PB
CC NO 282758   **ESTABLISHED** 1981

■ The Linden Charitable Trust

WHERE FUNDING CAN BE GIVEN UK, with a preference for West Yorkshire.
WHO CAN BENEFIT Organisations benefiting medical professionals.
WHAT IS FUNDED The trustees favour medical and healthcare charities.
WHAT IS NOT FUNDED No grants to individuals.
SAMPLE GRANTS £15,000 to Leeds International Pianoforte Competition; £10,000 each to Elizabeth Foundation and Leeds University School of Medicine; £5,000 each to Marie Curie Cancer Care, DEC Mozambique Flood Appeal, Leeds City Council – Art Gallery, Little Sisters of the Poor, Macmillan Cancer Relief and SENSE.
FINANCES *Year* 2000–01 *Income* £95,853 *Grants* £122,570 *Assets* £2,485,721
TRUSTEES G L Holbrook; M H Pearson; J F H Swales.
HOW TO APPLY In writing to the correspondent.

WHO TO APPLY TO The Trustees, Addleshaw Booth & Co., Sovereign House, PO Box 8, Sovereign Street, Leeds LS1 1HQ *Tel* 0113 209 2000
CC NO 326788   **ESTABLISHED** 1985

■ Enid Linder Foundation

WHERE FUNDING CAN BE GIVEN Unrestricted.
WHO CAN BENEFIT Registered charities benefiting children, older people and people who are disabled.
WHAT IS FUNDED Medical research; teaching hospitals and universities; and other charitable purposes including care for people who are disabled, older people, children, the arts, young people, sports and hospices. Local (normally London and the south of England), UK and international charities are supported.
TYPE OF GRANT One-off.
SAMPLE GRANTS £35,000 to Royal College of Surgeons; £25,000 to Médecins sans Frontières; £15,000 to Victoria and Albert Museum; £12,000 to Cancer Research; £10,000 each to Intermediate Technology and Stroke Association; £7,000 to Age Concern; £5,000 each to Friends of Sudbury and Iris Fund.
FINANCES *Year* 2000–01 *Income* £470,000 *Grants* £547,000 *Assets* £8,800,000
TRUSTEES Jack Ladeveze; Audrey Ladeveze; M Butler; G Huntly; J Stubbings.
OTHER INFORMATION Direct charitable expenditure, other than the trust's normal grantmaking, included £112,000 to 'teaching hospitals and universities'.
HOW TO APPLY In writing to the correspondent.
WHO TO APPLY TO Brian Billingham, Secretary, Studio 4, Chartwell Business Centre, The Avenue, Bromley, Kent BR1 2BS
CC NO 267509   **ESTABLISHED** 1974

■ The Lindeth Charitable Trust

WHERE FUNDING CAN BE GIVEN UK and overseas.
WHO CAN BENEFIT Registered charities benefiting scientists and research workers.
WHAT IS FUNDED The trustees propose to make grants to charities operating in the fields of ecological and biological research and related research of an educational nature.
WHAT IS NOT FUNDED No grants are given to individuals. Registered UK charities only.
RANGE OF GRANTS £50–£3,000.
SAMPLE GRANTS £3,000 to Childcare Trust; £1,800 to Azafady; £1,300 to University of Manchester; £1,000 each to Fauna and Flora International, Oxfam, Rainforest Concern, Winchester Parish Church Trust Fund and The Woodland Trust.
FINANCES *Year* 1999–2000 *Income* £20,000 *Grants* £20,000 *Assets* £574,000
TRUSTEES Christopher J Scott; Mrs Emma J Scott; E R H Perks.
HOW TO APPLY In writing to the correspondent.
WHO TO APPLY TO E R H Perks, Trustee, Currey & Co. Solicitors, 21 Buckingham Gate, London SW1E 6LS *Tel* 020 7802 2700
CC NO 802665   **ESTABLISHED** 1989

■ The Linmardon Trust

WHERE FUNDING CAN BE GIVEN UK, with a preference for the Nottingham area.
WHO CAN BENEFIT Registered charities.
WHAT IS FUNDED General charitable purposes.
WHAT IS NOT FUNDED Grants are made to registered charities only. No support to individuals.
FINANCES *Year* 1997–98 *Income* £31,000 *Grants* £36,000 *Assets* £854,000
TRUSTEES HSBC Trust Company Limited.
HOW TO APPLY In writing to the correspondent. The trustees meet quarterly, in February, May, August and November.
WHO TO APPLY TO Barry Sims, Trust Manager, HSBC Trust Company Limited, Norwich House, Nelson Gate, Commercial Road, Southampton SO15 1GX *Tel* 023 8072 2244
CC NO 275307   **ESTABLISHED** 1977

■ The Lintel Trust

WHERE FUNDING CAN BE GIVEN Scotland.
WHO CAN BENEFIT Housing and community projects in Scotland.
WHAT IS FUNDED The trust funds organisations in Scotland which work with: single homeless people; older people; people with support needs or disabilities of all kinds; people of ethnic minorities; refugees.
It makes grants or interest-free loans, for the following, to: provide or promote accommodation and support for people in housing need; promote volunteering in housing-related projects; promote participation in housing activities within communties; help social housing providers with activities which benefit their tenants and local communities; promote innovative ideas in housing provision.
WHAT IS NOT FUNDED The trust does not fund individuals, large capital projects, large UK organisations, holidays or vehicles.
FINANCES *Year* 2000–01 *Grants* £100,000
TRUSTEES Andrew Robertson; David Orr; Neil Hall; David Chalmers; Stewart Kinsman; Robert McDowell; Margaret Richards; Eileen Shand; Lynne Carr; Dinesh Joshi; Isabel Moore; Kate Dewar.
HOW TO APPLY On a form available from the correspondent. The trustees meet four times a year. Applicants are encouraged to telephone the administrator beforehand for a general discussion.
WHO TO APPLY TO Karen Jackson, Director, 38 York Place, Edinburgh EH1 3HU *Tel* 0131 556 5777 *Fax* 0131 557 6028 *E-mail* lintel@sfha.co.uk *Website* www.sfha.co.uk
SC NO SC024763

■ The Ruth & Stuart Lipton Charitable Trust

WHERE FUNDING CAN BE GIVEN UK and overseas.
WHO CAN BENEFIT Organisations benefiting Jewish people.
WHAT IS FUNDED Jewish charitable purposes.
WHAT IS NOT FUNDED No grants to individuals.
RANGE OF GRANTS £25–£23,000.
SAMPLE GRANTS In 1998–99: £23,000 to Royal Opera House.
FINANCES *Year* 2001–02 *Income* £105,073
TRUSTEES N W Benson; S Lipton; Mrs R Lipton.
HOW TO APPLY In writing to the correspondent.

WHO TO APPLY TO N W Benson, Trustee, Lewis Golden & Co., 40 Queen Ann Street, London W1M 0EL *Tel* 020 7580 7313
CC NO 266741   **ESTABLISHED** 1973

■ The Lister Charitable Trust

WHERE FUNDING CAN BE GIVEN UK.
WHO CAN BENEFIT Registered charities which work with young people in sailing and other water-based activities.
WHAT IS FUNDED The advancement and the educational, physical, mental and spiritual development of children and young people under the age of 25, by providing or assisting in providing facilities for training in sailing and seamanship of children and young people who have need of such facilities by reason of poverty, social or economic circumstances (so that they may grow to full maturity as individuals and members of society). Also to provide or assist in the provision of facilities for recreation and other leisure time occupation of the general public with the object of improving their conditions of life.
WHAT IS NOT FUNDED Applications from individuals, including students, are ineligible. No grants are made in response to general appeals from large UK organisations or to smaller bodies working in areas outside its criteria.
TYPE OF GRANT Usually one-off for specific project or part of a project. Core funding and/or salaries rarely considered. Funding may be given for up to one year.
SAMPLE GRANTS £125,000 to Miami Project; £100,000 to Bobath Centre; £38,005 to UK Sailing Academy; £1,420 to Treasury Cay Community Centre.
FINANCES *Year* 2002 *Income* £277,793 *Grants* £264,425 *Assets* £9,503,000
TRUSTEES Noel A V Lister; Benjamin Piers Cussons; Stephen John Chipperfield; D A Collingwood; David J Lister.
HOW TO APPLY In writing to the correspondent. Applications should include clear details of the need the intended project is designed to meet, plus an outline budget. Only applications from eligible bodies are acknowledged, when further information may be requested.
WHO TO APPLY TO Mrs S J Sharkey, Windyridge, The Close, Totteridge, London N20 8PT *Fax* 020 8445 3156
CC NO 288730   **ESTABLISHED** 1981

■ Frank Litchfield Charitable Trust

WHERE FUNDING CAN BE GIVEN Mostly in and around Cambridge.
WHAT IS FUNDED Medical services in and around the Cambridge area as well as relieving poverty amongst those involved in agriculture.
RANGE OF GRANTS £500–£25,000.
SAMPLE GRANTS £25,000 to University of Cambridge; £10,000 each to Royal Agricultural Benevolent Fund and Royal Star and Garter Home; £5,000 to Camsight.
FINANCES *Year* 2000–01 *Income* £150,560 *Grants* £50,000 *Assets* £975,470
TRUSTEES M T Womack; D M Chater; P Gooderham.
HOW TO APPLY In writing to the correspondent.
WHO TO APPLY TO M T Womack, Trustee, Taylor Vinters, Merlin Place, Milton Road, Cambridge CB4 0DP *Tel* 01223 423444
CC NO 1038943   **ESTABLISHED** 1994

■ The Little Foundation

WHERE FUNDING CAN BE GIVEN UK.

WHO CAN BENEFIT Established research bodies which will benefit future generations of children with neurodevelopmental disorders.

WHAT IS FUNDED The foundation favours research projects recommended by its own scientific advisory committee. These projects directly reflect the aims of foundation to find the primary causes of neurodevelopmental disorders and set up research with a view to prevention.

WHAT IS NOT FUNDED No grants for individuals, training grants or scholarships.

TYPE OF GRANT Research. Staged payments as agreed in advance.

RANGE OF GRANTS £12,000 or more.

SAMPLE GRANTS In 1999: £53,800 to Imperial College for European Cerebral Palsy Study.

FINANCES *Year* 2001 *Income* £82,472 *Grants* £62,578 *Assets* £85,907

TRUSTEES C Robinson, Chair; Prof. M Crawford; Dr K Hameed; Prof. D Harvey; Prof. N Morris; Sara Cooke.

PUBLICATIONS Scientific findings are published in appropriate journals/books.

HOW TO APPLY All available funds are committed.

WHO TO APPLY TO C Robinson, Chair, c/o Mac Keith Press, High Holborn House, 52–54 High Holborn, London WC1V 6RL *Tel* 020 7831 4918 *Fax* 020 7405 5365

CC NO 803551   **ESTABLISHED** 1990

■ The Second Joseph Aaron Littman Foundation

WHERE FUNDING CAN BE GIVEN UK.

WHO CAN BENEFIT Registered charities only.

WHAT IS FUNDED General charitable purposes with special preference for academic and medical research.

WHAT IS NOT FUNDED Applications from individuals are not considered.

FINANCES *Year* 2001 *Income* £180,000 *Grants* £180,000

TRUSTEES Mrs C C Littman; R J Littman.

HOW TO APPLY The trust's funds are fully committed and no new applications are considered.

WHO TO APPLY TO Barry Lock, 190 Strand, London WC2R 1JN *Tel* 020 7379 0000 *Fax* 020 7379 6854

CC NO 201892   **ESTABLISHED** 1961

■ The George John Livanos Charitable Trust

WHERE FUNDING CAN BE GIVEN UK.

WHO CAN BENEFIT Registered charities.

WHAT IS FUNDED Medical research and equipment, health, medical charities for children or older people, marine charities and general charitable purposes.

WHAT IS NOT FUNDED No grants to individuals or non-registered charities.

TYPE OF GRANT One-off and recurring grants. Capital grants.

SAMPLE GRANTS £100,000 to Abbeyfield Society; £30,000 each to Crimestoppers and Maritime Volunteer Service; £25,000 each to Macmillan Cancer Relief and Trinity Hospice; £20,000 to WhizzKidz for work in Wales; £10,000 to Sunrise Cornwall; £5,000 each to Alder Hey Children's Hospital and Wandsworth Cancer Research Centre.

FINANCES *Year* 2001 *Income* £297,000 *Grants* £479,000 *Assets* £5,000,000

TRUSTEES Mrs S D Livanos; P N Harris; A S Holmes; P D Powell.

HOW TO APPLY Unsolicited applications are not requested. Trustees meet about every three months and applications received right up to a day or two before the meeting are considered.

WHO TO APPLY TO Philip Harris, Secretary, c/o Jeffrey Green Russell, Apollo House, 56 New Bond Street, London W1S 1RG *Tel* 020 7339 7000

CC NO 1002279   **ESTABLISHED** 1985

■ The Liverpool Queen Victoria District Nursing Association (LCSS)

WHERE FUNDING CAN BE GIVEN Merseyside.

WHO CAN BENEFIT Organisations benefiting people who are sick or disabled people; also individuals who are sick and disabled.

WHAT IS FUNDED The trust gives grants to people who are in need, hardship or distress due to sickness, disability or convalescence. It can provide trained nurses to attend to people who are sick and will support organisations which provide and encourage the education and training of nurses and other helpers to look after and assist people who are sick. Also supported are other charitable organisations working with people who are sick or disabled.

SAMPLE GRANTS Mencap St Helens & District, Merseyside Holiday Service, Merseyside Tuesday Club, Old Swan Youth Club, Sefton Children's Trust, Sightline and Southport Stroke Club.

FINANCES *Year* 2001 *Income* £36,000 *Grants* £51,000 *Assets* £677,000

TRUSTEES G F Appleton, Chair; R P Bradshaw; Cllr Karen Afford; Ms Delia Cartlidge; R Currie; Canon Nicholas Frayling; Cllr Dot Gavin; Neil Malley; Mrs L M Newsome; Mrs I Nightingale; Mrs J Pickett; M Rathbone; Ken Wright.

HOW TO APPLY In writing to the correspondent setting out aims, activities, the particular purpose of a grant and enclosing a copy of accounts if possible. Applications are considered in January, May and September and should be received by the middle of the previous month.

WHO TO APPLY TO The Company Secretaries, Liverpool Council of Social Service (Inc.), 14 Castle Street, Liverpool L2 0NJ *Tel* 0151 236 7728 *Fax* 0151 258 1153 *E-mail* info@liverpoolcss.org

CC NO 501196   **ESTABLISHED** 1898

■ Liverpool Sailors' Home Trust

WHERE FUNDING CAN BE GIVEN Merseyside.

WHO CAN BENEFIT Organisations benefiting seafarers and fishermen and ex-service and service people.

WHAT IS FUNDED Nautical charities in Merseyside.

WHAT IS NOT FUNDED No grants to individuals.

TYPE OF GRANT One-off and capital grants will be considered.

SAMPLE GRANTS £8,615 to The Royal Merchant Navy School Foundation; £4,000 each to Sail Training Association and Fairbridge Merseyside; £2,000 to Sea Cadet Corps – Ellesmere Port; £1,500 each to RNLI – New Brighton and RNLI – Hoylake and West Kirby; £1,000 each to BISS and Sea Cadet Corps – Liverpool Mersey Unit.

FINANCES *Year* 2001–2002 *Income* £8,719
Grants £30,595 *Assets* £276,323

TRUSTEES D G Beazley, Chair; F D M Lowry; P O Copland; M Crowson; M A Seaford.

HOW TO APPLY In writing to the correspondent. Trustees meet to consider grants in March, applications should be sent by 20 January.

WHO TO APPLY TO Mrs L Gidman, Secretary, Unit 3a, Ground Floor, Tower Building, 22 Water Street, Liverpool L3 1AB *Tel* 0151 227 3417 *Fax* 0151 227 3417

CC NO 515183   **ESTABLISHED** 1984

■ Harry Livingstone Charitable Trust

WHERE FUNDING CAN BE GIVEN UK.

WHO CAN BENEFIT Registered charities benefiting Jewish people, at risk groups, and people who are disadvantaged by poverty or socially isolated.

WHAT IS FUNDED Welfare and Jewish charities and general charitable purposes.

FINANCES *Year* 2000–01 *Income* £80,000
Grants £63,000 *Assets* £1,200,000

TRUSTEES J Livingstone; Mrs H Bloom.

HOW TO APPLY The trust does not respond to unsolicited applications.

WHO TO APPLY TO Jack Livingstone, Trustee, Westholme, The Springs, Park Road, Bowdon, Altrincham, Cheshire WA14 3JH *Tel* 0161 928 3232

CC NO 263471   **ESTABLISHED** 1970

■ Jack Livingstone Charitable Trust

WHERE FUNDING CAN BE GIVEN UK and worldwide, with a preference for Manchester.

WHO CAN BENEFIT Registered charities benefiting Jewish people, at risk groups, and people who are ill, disadvantaged by poverty or socially isolated.

WHAT IS FUNDED Jewish charities and general charitable purposes.

RANGE OF GRANTS £100–£50,000.

SAMPLE GRANTS £10,700 to Christie's Against Cancer; £10,000 to UJIA; £7,500 to Royal Exchange Theatre Appeal Fund; £5,000 to Jerusalem Foundation; £3,500 to Community Security Trust; £2,500 to National Councl of YMCAs; £2,250 to Heathlands Village; £1,450 to Manchester Balfour Trust; £1,000 each to Ashten Trust, Brookvale Royal Schools for the Deaf and Manchester Jewish Federation.

FINANCES *Year* 2000–01 *Income* £88,652
Grants £52,665 *Assets* £1,432,329

TRUSTEES Mrs J V Livingstone; Brian White.

HOW TO APPLY The trust does not respond to unsolicited applications.

WHO TO APPLY TO Mrs Janice Livingstone, Trustee, Westholme, The Springs, Park Road, Bowdon, Altrincham, Cheshire WA14 3JH *Tel* 0161 928 3232 *Fax* 0161 928 3232

CC NO 263473   **ESTABLISHED** 1971

■ Lloyd's Charities Trust

WHERE FUNDING CAN BE GIVEN UK, with some interest in London.

WHO CAN BENEFIT General fund – registered charities. Other funds – education, training and enterprise initiatives.

WHAT IS NOT FUNDED No grants for any appeal where it is likely that the grant would be used for sectarian purposes or to local or regional branches of charities where it is possible to support the UK organisation. Support is not given to individuals.

SAMPLE GRANTS £250,000 split between Alzheimer's Research Trust, British Trust for Conservation Volunteers, Care International, Crimestoppers Trust (London) and Save the Children Fund; £28,000 to Tower Hamlets Education Business Partnership (£10,000 towards core funding and £10,000 in respect of Lloyd's sponsorship of the business mentoring scheme and £8,000 for school travel bursaries); £15,000 to the East London Small Business Centre (£10,000 towards the cost of administering Lloyd's Loan Fund and £5,000 to fund training courses); £10,000 to Business in the Community.

FINANCES *Year* 2000 *Income* £709,000
Grants £386,000 *Assets* £2,800,000

TRUSTEES J L Stace, Chair; P Barnes; Lady Delves Broughton; G Morgan; M J Wade: H Richie; R A Fleming-Williams; E Gilmour; N Gooding; Ms B Merry.

HOW TO APPLY In writing to the correspondent including a copy of the latest annual report and accounts.

WHO TO APPLY TO Mrs Linda Harper, Secretary, One Lime Street, London EC3M 7HA *Tel* 020 7327 1000 ext. 5925 *Fax* 020 7327 6368 *Website* www.lloyds.com

CC NO 207232   **ESTABLISHED** 1953

■ The Elaine & Angus Lloyd Charitable Trust

WHERE FUNDING CAN BE GIVEN UK. There may be a preference for Surrey, Kent and the south of England.

WHO CAN BENEFIT Individuals, local, regional and UK organisations benefiting children, young adults, at risk groups, people disadvantaged by poverty and socially isolated people.

WHAT IS FUNDED Health and welfare organisations, churches and education.

WHAT IS NOT FUNDED No support for overseas aid.

TYPE OF GRANT Recurrent and one-off.

RANGE OF GRANTS Below £1,000–£6,500.

FINANCES *Year* 2001–02 *Income* £75,321

TRUSTEES C R H Lloyd; A S Lloyd; J S Gordon; Sir Michael C Cooper.

HOW TO APPLY In writing to the correspondent. The trustees meet regularly to consider grants.

WHO TO APPLY TO R Badger, Messrs Badger Hakim Chartered Accountants, 10 Dover Street, London W1X 3PH

CC NO 237250   **ESTABLISHED** 1964

■ The W M & B W Lloyd Trust

WHERE FUNDING CAN BE GIVEN The old borough of Darwen.

WHO CAN BENEFIT Individuals and organisations benefiting children, young adults and students, and support for individual emergencies and disasters.

WHAT IS FUNDED A range of support is given for individual emergencies and disasters; equipment for schools welfare; the advancement of education, medical science and provision of medical equipment and facilities; and the provision and improvement of public amenities.

TYPE OF GRANT One-off grants.

FINANCES *Year* 2001–02 *Income* £69,297 *Grants* £50,510 *Assets* £1,500,000

TRUSTEES J N Jacklin; David G Watson; E Aspin.

OTHER INFORMATION The trust has four committees: emergency, education, social amenities and medical. Each committee considers requests specific to its areas of remit.

HOW TO APPLY In writing to the correspondent. Trustees meet in March, June, July and December.

WHO TO APPLY TO The Secretary, 10 Borough Road, Darwen, Lancashire BB3 1PL *Tel* 01254 702111

CC NO 503384   **ESTABLISHED** 1974

....

■ Lloyds TSB Foundation for England and Wales

WHERE FUNDING CAN BE GIVEN England and Wales. See separate entries for the Lloyds TSB Foundations for Scotland and Northern Ireland.

WHO CAN BENEFIT Registered charities benefiting people who are disabled or disadvantaged.

WHAT IS FUNDED Education and training and social and community needs.

WHAT IS NOT FUNDED No grants to: non-registered charities; activities which a statutory body is responsible for; activities which collect funds to give to other charities or to individuals or to other organisations; animal welfare; corporate subscriptions or membership of a charity; endowment funds; environment – conserving and protecting plants and animals, geography and scenery; expeditions or overseas travel; fabric appeals for places of worship – including capital projects to comply with the Disability Discrimination Act; fundraising events or activities; hospitals and medical centres; individuals, including students; loans or business finance; promoting religion; mainstream schools and colleges; universities – mainstream teaching activities; sponsorship or marketing appeals; or overseas work.

TYPE OF GRANT One-off for a specific project, core funding, two or three year funding. Also capital, recurring costs, running costs and salaries.

RANGE OF GRANTS Average local or regional grant in 2002 was £5,750. Average England and Wales - wide grant in 2002 was £19,500.

SAMPLE GRANTS In 2002: £52,000 Samaritans; £50,000 each to Women's Aid Federation of England, and English National Opera; £45, 511 to Blind Business; £42,160 to National Association of Citizens Advice Bureaux; £40,361 to Shaw Trust; £40,000 each to Contact a Family, National Council of Voluntary Child Care Organisations, and Help the Hospices; £39,000 to Dyslexia Institute.

FINANCES *Year* 2001 *Income* £25,661,000 *Grants* £24,342,000 *Assets* £3,870,000

TRUSTEES Joanna Foster, Chair; Prof. Murray Stewart (South West); Revd Rachel Benson (North East and Yorkshire); Virginia Burton (South East); Ann Curno (Greater London); Gareth Roberts, (West Midlands); Dr Pauleen Lane (North West); John Penny; Howard Phillips (East of England and East Midlands); Linda Quinn (Wales); Karamjit Singh; Colin Webb.

OTHER INFORMATION Applicants are strongly advised to seek advice from the foundation: (a) before applying for sums in excess of the average grant amounts; (b) before applying for funding over two or more years; and (c) before submitting an application for support on a England and Wales-wide basis.

HOW TO APPLY On a form available from the correspondent, or the website. Applicants are strongly advised to contact the trust in the initial stages and before the form is completed. For advice about local and regional funding, please contact the appropriate regional office (details are available on the website or from central office). Please send your completed application form to the appropriate regional office. The trustees meet every three months, although small grants are often approved within six weeks.

WHO TO APPLY TO Kathleen Duncan, Director General, 3rd Floor, 4 St Dunstan's Hill, London, EC3R 8UL *Tel* 0870 4111223 *Fax* 0870 411 1224 *E-mail* guidelines@lloydstsbfoundations.org.uk *Website* www.lloydstsbfoundations.org.uk

CC NO 327114   **ESTABLISHED** 1986

....

■ Lloyds TSB Foundation for Northern Ireland

WHERE FUNDING CAN BE GIVEN Northern Ireland.

WHO CAN BENEFIT Organisations benefiting children, young adults, older people, volunteers and people who are unemployed, homeless, living in rural communities, disabled or disadvantaged by poverty.

WHAT IS FUNDED Underfunded voluntary organisations which enable people who are disabled and people who are disadvantaged through social and economic circumstances, to make a contribution to the community. The trustees regret that, as the funds available are limited, they cannot support all fields of voluntary and charitable activity. The two main objectives to which funds are allocated are: (a) social and community needs; (b) education and training. Charities working in the field of housing and accommodation, infrastructure and technical support, infrastructure development, social care professional bodies, healthcare, health facilities and buildings, health promotion, social campaigning and advocacy and advice and law centres may be considered.

WHAT IS NOT FUNDED No grants for: organisations who have received three years consecutive funding must leave at least two years before re-applying: only in exceptional circumstances will the trustees consider a further application within this two year period; organisations which are not recognised as charities by the Inland Revenue (in exceptional circumstances the trustees may make donations up to a maximum of £1,000 to organisations not recognised as a charity, where the annual income of the applicant organisation is less than £2,000); individuals, including students; animal welfare; environmental projects, including projects which deal with geographic and scenic issues – however the trustees may consider projects improve the living conditions of disadvantaged individuals and groups; activities which are normally the responsibility of central or local government or some other responsible body; schools, universities and colleges (except for projects specifically to benefit people with disabilities); hospitals and medical centres; sponsorship or marketing appeals; fabric appeals for places of worship; promotion of religion; activities which collect funds for subsequent redistribution to others; endowment funds; fundraising events or activities; corporate affiliation or membership of a charity; loans or business finance; expeditions or overseas travel (except for projects specifically benefiting disadvantaged young people from Northern Ireland); or construction of and extensions to buildings.

TYPE OF GRANT Capital, core costs, one-off, project, recurring costs, salaries, and start-up costs. Funding of up to three years may be considered.

RANGE OF GRANTS Normally a maximum of £5,000, but larger amounts are considered.

FINANCES *Year* 2002 *Income* £1,949,474 *Grants* £1,923,146

TRUSTEES Mrs Ann Shaw; Lady McCollum; Roy MacDougall; Mrs Brenda Callaghan; Mrs Breige Gadd; Mrs Dawn Livingstone; David Magill; Denis Wilson; Mrs Angela McShane; David Patton; Mrs Janice Doherty; Peter Morrow.

HOW TO APPLY On a form available from the correspondent, to be returned with one additional page of supporting text. Trustees meet quarterly to review applications.

WHO TO APPLY TO The Gate Lodge, 73A Malone Rd, Belfast BT9 6SB *Tel* 028 9038 2864 *Fax* 028 9038 2839 *E-mail* info@lloydstsbfoundationni.org *Website* www.lloydstsbfoundations.org

IR NO XN72216   **ESTABLISHED** 1986

....

■ Lloyds TSB Foundation for Scotland

WHERE FUNDING CAN BE GIVEN Scotland and overseas.

WHO CAN BENEFIT Recognised charities which provide support to the Scottish community, enabling people, primarily those in need, to become active members of society and to improve their quality of life.

WHAT IS FUNDED Social and community needs, education and training, and scientific, medical and social research. There are also two other grant schemes: a capacity building grants scheme and a partnership drugs initiative. For 2003–2005, the foundation has established priorities for particular projects within the following areas: children; young people; ageing population; parenting; physical and mental disability; support for people at risk; substance misuse; development of people and resource. There is also an overseas grants scheme for charities with a Scottish base working overseas.

WHAT IS NOT FUNDED The trustees regret they cannot support all fields of voluntary and charitable activity. To focus funding on the foundation's priority areas, the following purposes will not be considered organisations which are not recognised as a charity by the Inland Revenue/ Charity Commission; individuals – including students; animal welfare; environment – projects entirely of an environmental nature, e.g. geographic and scenic, conservation and protection of flora and fauna; mainstream activities and statutory requirements of schools, universities and colleges; mainstream activities and statutory requirements of hospitals and medical centres; sponsorship or marketing appeals; activities which collect funds for subsequent redistribution to others; the establishment/preservation of endowment funds; expeditions or overseas travel; building projects for places of worship, other than where such buildings provide accommodation to community groups; building projects for visitor centres, heritage centres, museums and theatres; historic restoration; retrospective funding; the one year rule – applicants will not be eligible for further consideration until at least one year has elapsed from their original application. In the case of a multi-year award

having been granted, no further application will be considered until 12 months has elapsed from the final scheduled payment, e.g. an organisation granted a three-year award in April 2003 may not re-apply until April 2006.

TYPE OF GRANT Mostly one-off. However the foundation will consider grants over two or three years. Grants are made for buildings, capital, core costs, feasibility studies, project, research, recurring costs, running costs, salaries and start-up costs.

RANGE OF GRANTS £400–£120,000; typical £10,000. There is no minimum or maximum.

SAMPLE GRANTS £111,000 to Glasgow University for research; £75,000 to Deafblind Scotland for a salary; £65,000 to Royal Hospital for Sick Children for research; £54,000 to Scottish Throughcare for a salary and West Lothian Theatre for the SNAP project coordinator; £53,000 to Oxfam for work in Sudan; £50,000 to Glasgow YMCA for a salary; £38,000 to Interminds programme for resource packs and training; £35,000 to Christian Aid Scotland for revenue costs; £34,000 to Scottish World Exchange Trust for training for Rwandan women.

FINANCES *Year* 2002 *Income* £8,595,832 *Grants* £6,814,483 *Assets* £3,928,963

TRUSTEES Revd Norman Drummond, Chair; Prof. Sir Michael Bond; Mrs Sandra E Brydon; Mrs Fiona Crighton; Ms Rani Dhir; Revd Ronald Ferguson; Ms Elaine Ross; Ms Susan Robinson; Prof. Joyce Lishman.

PUBLICATIONS *A Foundation for the Future;* comprehensive application pack.

HOW TO APPLY Application forms for all grants schemes, complete with comprehensive guidance notes, are available from the foundation. These can be requested by telephone, by e-mail, or through the website. Foundation staff are always willing to provide additional help. Surgery dates for all the schemes are finalised in December of the preceding year and details can be obtained from the foundation after that date.

WHO TO APPLY TO Andrew Muirhead, Chief Executive, Riverside House, 502 Gorgie Road, Edinburgh EH11 3AF *Tel* 0870 902 1201 *Fax* 0870 902 1202 *E-mail* enquiries@ltsbfoundationfor scotland.org.uk *Website* www.ltsbfoundationforscotland.org.uk

SC NO SC009481   **ESTABLISHED** 1986

....

■ Lloyds TSB Foundation for the Channel Islands

WHERE FUNDING CAN BE GIVEN The Channel Islands.

WHO CAN BENEFIT Registered charities benefiting young adults; older people; volunteers; at risk groups; people who are unemployed, carers, disabled, disadvantaged by poverty or homeless; and victims of abuse and domestic violence.

WHAT IS FUNDED The main aims of the foundation are to assist disadvantaged and disabled people and to promote social and community welfare within the Channel Islands, including support to volunteers; residential facilities and services; respite care; self-help groups; hospices; campaigning for health issues; health-related volunteer schemes; advice centres; and various community services. Training and education for managers and staff of charities is also funded.

WHAT IS NOT FUNDED Registered charities only. Applications from individuals, including

624

Does the trust you have chosen match your needs? Haphazard applications waste postage and time

students, are ineligible. Animal welfare and overseas appeals are not funded.

TYPE OF GRANT Depends on merit, but usually one-off for a specific project, operational costs, salaries and start-up costs. Funding of up to three years may be considered.

SAMPLE GRANTS £150,000 over three years to Jersey Addiction Group for salary costs; £80,000 over three years to Les Amis Incorporated for a day care service; £51,000 over three years to Guernsey Women's Refuge for operational costs; £50,000 to Sarnia Housing Association for fitting out self-contained flats; £45,000 each, both over three years to Jersey Hospice Care for salary costs of administrator and Drug Concern Guernsey for educational project; £32,115 over three years to Jersey Cheshire Home for a physio service; £26,400 over three years to Ace of Clubs for an after-school club; £25,000 to Information Exchange – Guernsey – for operational costs; £22,000 to Grow Limited for a new packing shed.

FINANCES *Year* 2001 *Assets* £358,000

TRUSTEES Mrs C Jeune, Deputy Chair; E A Le Maistre; A L Ozanne, Deputy Chair; D J Watkins; P Mourant; D Rowland; Wendy Hurford.

HOW TO APPLY In writing at any time. The trustees meet three times a year, in March, July and November. Application form and guidelines are available from the administrator.

WHO TO APPLY TO David Beaugeard, Administrator, PO Box 160, 25 New Street, St Helier, Jersey JE4 8RG *Tel* 01534 503052 *Fax* 01534 864570 *E-mail* foundationCl@Lloydstsb-offshore.com *Website* www.ltsbfoundationCl.org

CC NO 327113   **ESTABLISHED** 1986

■ The Llysdinam Trust

WHERE FUNDING CAN BE GIVEN Wales.

WHO CAN BENEFIT Registered charities.

WHAT IS FUNDED General charitable purposes.

WHAT IS NOT FUNDED No grants to individuals.

RANGE OF GRANTS £500–£30,000.

SAMPLE GRANTS In 1998–99: £30,000 to All Saints Church Restoration Fund; £5,000 each to Radnorshire Macmillan Nurse Appeal and University of Wales; £3,000 to Llandovery College 150th Anniversary Fund; £2,500 to Swansea Rugby Foundation; £2,000 each to Brecon & District Disabled Club and Friends of St Andrews Church; £1,500 to Penclacwydd Wildlife & Wetlands Centre; £1,000 each to Bobath Cymru and Brecon and Radnor Samaritans.

FINANCES *Year* 2001–02 *Income* £154,000 *Grants* £74,900 *Assets* £3,938,000

HOW TO APPLY The trust stated that it was overloaded with applications and does not welcome unsolicited applications.

WHO TO APPLY TO The Trustees, Rees Richards & Partners, Managing Agents, Druslyn House, De La Beche Street, Swansea, West Glamorgan SA1 3HH *Tel* 01792 650705 *Fax* 01792 468384 *E-mail* post@reesrichards.co.uk

CC NO 255528   **ESTABLISHED** 1968

■ Localtrent Ltd

WHERE FUNDING CAN BE GIVEN UK, with some preference for Manchester.

WHO CAN BENEFIT Charities benefiting Jewish people, children, young adults, students and people disadvantaged by poverty.

WHAT IS FUNDED The trustees will consider applications from organisations concerned with orthodox Jewish faith education and the relief of poverty.

SAMPLE GRANTS £27,000 to Chasday Yoel; £4,500 to Charity Association Limited; £1,000 to Manchester Jewish Grammar School.

FINANCES *Year* 1999–2000 *Income* £58,000 *Grants* £73,000 *Assets* £324,000

TRUSTEES Mrs M Weiss; B Weiss; J L Weiss; P Weiss; Mrs S Feldman.

HOW TO APPLY In writing to the correspondent.

WHO TO APPLY TO A Kahan, Accountant, Lopian Gross Barnett & Co., Harvester House, 37 Peter Street, Manchester M2 5QD *Tel* 0161 832 8721

CC NO 326329   **ESTABLISHED** 1982

■ The Locker Foundation

WHERE FUNDING CAN BE GIVEN UK and overseas.

WHO CAN BENEFIT Organisations benefiting Jewish people, children and young adults, students and teachers.

WHAT IS FUNDED Jewish charities, Synagogues, schools and colleges and Jewish education studies.

RANGE OF GRANTS £100–£33,000.

SAMPLE GRANTS £33,000 to Jewish National Fund; £15,000 each to Society of Friends of Torah and Kahal Cassidim Bobov.

FINANCES *Year* 1998–99 *Income* £276,000 *Grants* £76,000 *Assets* £1,500,000

TRUSTEES I Carter; M Carter; Miss S Carter.

HOW TO APPLY In writing to the correspondent.

WHO TO APPLY TO The Trustees, 28 High Road, East Finchley, London N2 9PJ *Tel* 020 8455 9280

CC NO 264180   **ESTABLISHED** 1972

■ Lockerbie Trust

WHERE FUNDING CAN BE GIVEN Lockerbie.

WHO CAN BENEFIT Registered charities.

WHAT IS FUNDED General charitable purposes including the arts, children/young people, conservation, disability, education/training, heritage, social welfare and sports/recreation.

TYPE OF GRANT Pump-priming grants, only for up to 50% of the total cost.

SAMPLE GRANTS £18,000 for Lockerbie Christmas Lights; £7,000 to South of Scotland Ice Rink Club; £1,000 to Lockerbie Jazz Festival; £500 to Lockerbie Scout Group.

FINANCES *Year* 1998–99 *Income* £27,000 *Grants* £28,000 *Assets* £402,000

TRUSTEES Local MP; chair of Lockerbie and District Community Council; two Lockerbie councillors.

HOW TO APPLY On a form available from the correspondent. Trustees meet to consider grants in February, July and December. Applications should be sent in the month prior to the meetings.

WHO TO APPLY TO Alex Haswell, Clerk, Dumfries and Galloway Council, Council Offices, High Street, Annan, Dumfriesshire DG12 6AQ *Tel* 01461 207012 *Fax* 01461 207029

SC NO SC019796

■ Lofthouse Foundation

WHERE FUNDING CAN BE GIVEN Fleetwood and the surrounding area.

WHO CAN BENEFIT The people of Fleetwood only.

WHAT IS FUNDED The provision of amenities and facilities.

WHAT IS NOT FUNDED Grants are now limited to projects which will benefit the whole community.
SAMPLE GRANTS In 1996–97: £61,000 to Welcome Homed Memorial; £10,000 to Fleetwood Hospital.
FINANCES Year 2001 Income £127,411
TRUSTEES Mrs D W Lofthouse; J A Lofthouse; D C Lofthouse.
HOW TO APPLY In writing to the correspondent.
WHO TO APPLY TO Mrs D W Lofthouse, Trustee, Lofthouse of Fleetwood, Maritime Street, Fleetwood, Lancashire FY7 7LP Tel 01253 872435
CC NO 1038728   **ESTABLISHED** 1994

■ The Loftus Charitable Trust

WHERE FUNDING CAN BE GIVEN UK and overseas.
WHO CAN BENEFIT Jewish organisations benefiting children, young adults and students.
WHAT IS FUNDED Jewish organisations working in the areas of welfare, education and religion.
SAMPLE GRANTS £28,480 to Jewish Care; £25,500 to Lubavitch Foundation; £10,100 to Community Security Trust; £10,000 to Chief Rabbinate Trust; £6,500 to Habad Orphan Aid; £6,000 to Chief Rabbinate Council; £5,000 to British ORT; £4,000 to United Jewish Israel Appeal; £3,747 to United Synagogue; £3,200 to Norwood.
FINANCES Year 2000–01 Income £225,515 Grants £139,775 Assets £716,387
TRUSTEES R I Loftus; A L Loftus; A D Loftus.
HOW TO APPLY The trustees state that all funds are committed and unsolicited applications are not welcome.
WHO TO APPLY TO A Loftus, Trustee, 48 George Street, London W1U 7DY Tel 020 7486 2969
CC NO 297664   **ESTABLISHED** 1987

■ The Lolev Charitable Trust

WHERE FUNDING CAN BE GIVEN Worldwide
WHO CAN BENEFIT Individuals and organisations benefiting Jewish people.
WHAT IS FUNDED Jewish charitable purposes.
SAMPLE GRANTS £5,590 to Yeshivat Knesset Hagdola; £4,556 to Or Avraham; £3,970 to Yad Harashaz; £2,860 to Chajdey Shalom; £2,820 to Ateres Chachomin; £2,772 to Ezer Nissuin Fund; £2,770 to Zidit Shov; £2,420 to Mishcan Rephael; £2,200 to Mifal Oseh Chayil; £2,140 to Talmud Torah RMA.
FINANCES Year 2001 Income £573,082 Grants £569,846 Assets £2,513
TRUSTEES A Tager; E Tager; M Tager.
HOW TO APPLY In writing to the correspondent.
WHO TO APPLY TO A Tager, Trustee, 14a Gilda Crescent, London N16 6JP
CC NO 326249   **ESTABLISHED** 1982

■ London Law Trust

WHERE FUNDING CAN BE GIVEN UK.
WHO CAN BENEFIT Registered charities benefiting children and young people.
WHAT IS FUNDED The prevention and cure of illness and disability in children and young people; the alleviation of illness and disability in children and young people; and the encouragement in young people of the qualities of leadership and service to the community. The trust may also support charities working in the fields of education and residential facilities and services.
WHAT IS NOT FUNDED Applications from individuals, including students, are ineligible.

TYPE OF GRANT Usually one-off grants for or towards specific projects. Buildings, capital, core costs, research, running costs, recurring costs, salaries and start-up costs will also be considered. Funding may be given for up to three years.
RANGE OF GRANTS £500–£5,000; typical grant £2,500.
SAMPLE GRANTS £5,000 to Michael Palin Center; £3,000 to Young Minds; £2,500 each to Association of Wheelchair Users, Soundabout, and West Wiltshire Portage Service; £1,000 each to Angus Special Play Scheme, Circus Eruption, and Hereditary Extosis Support Group.
FINANCES Year 2001–02 Income £135,043 Grants £144,000 Assets £3,442,058
TRUSTEES Prof. Anthony R Mellows; R A Pellant; Sir Michael Hobbs; Sir Ian Gainsford.
HOW TO APPLY In writing to the correspondent. The trustees employ a grant advisor whose job is to evaluate applications. Grant applicants are requested to supply detailed information in support of their applications. The grant advisor makes on-site visits to almost all applicants. The trustees meet twice a year to consider the grant advisor's reports. Most grants are awarded in the autumn.
WHO TO APPLY TO G D Ogilvie, Secretary, Messrs Hunters, 9 New Square, Lincoln's Inn, London WC2A 3QN Tel 020 7412 0050
CC NO 255924   **ESTABLISHED** 1968

■ London North East Community Foundation

WHERE FUNDING CAN BE GIVEN London boroughs of Redbridge, Newham, and Barking and Dagenham.
WHO CAN BENEFIT The community in north east London, including people who are disabled, older people and people disadvantaged by poverty; people involved in arts and cultural activities and multi-cultural groups.
WHAT IS FUNDED Projects working with people who are disabled, older people, arts organisations, sports, and multi-cultural groups through the development of closer links between corporate supporters and local organisations. The advancement of education, protection of physical and mental health, and relief of poverty and sickness are all considered, and other charitable purposes.
WHAT IS NOT FUNDED No grants to individuals or to activities that are primarily religious or party political.
TYPE OF GRANT One-off small grants.
RANGE OF GRANTS £200–£1,000.
SAMPLE GRANTS £1,000 to Training for Transition towards recruiting and training volunteers and support of a student placement; £950 to MS Action towards maintenance of their hyperbaric chamber; £760 to African Caribbean Community Resource Fund towards equipment and promotional work; £750 to Focus Club of Redbridge towards replacing radio microphones; £725 to Disabled Muslim Women's Association for transport, stationery, postage and equipment; £700 to Redbridge Tinnitus Group for costs of an open meeting to promote current developments; £640 to Derby Road Playgroup for training costs; £600 to Redbridge Stroke Club towrads costs of an outing for members; £570 each to Barnabas Workshops for a pilot intervention providing job search skills and Epping Forest Centenary Trust
FINANCES Year 2000–01 Grants £32,000

TRUSTEES John Hogben, Chair; David Harris; Marcus Selmon; Robert Sidley; Mark Sweetingham; John D'Abbro.

HOW TO APPLY Application forms are available on request.

WHO TO APPLY TO Phil Miller, PO Box 77, Ilford, Essex IG1 1EB *Tel* 020 8554 7922

CC NO 1000540   **ESTABLISHED** 1990

■ The London Youth Trust (W H Smith Memorial)

WHERE FUNDING CAN BE GIVEN Greater London.

WHO CAN BENEFIT Local community initiatives and street organisations benefiting children and young adults, at risk groups and people disadvantaged by poverty.

WHAT IS FUNDED The trustees aim to support projects which: support detached youth workers in the inner city; encourage the development of young people physically, mentally and spiritually through carefully planned experiences which lead to positive achievements and growth skills; take account of individual differences and needs, and give priority to people with learning difficulties, physical disabilities, people who are poor, who have been abused, or who are dependent on drugs; allow young people to gain an understanding of issues relating to race, culture, sex and religious beliefs; foster and develop good community relationships; and encourage young people to accept responsibility in planning and developing their own programmes. Particularly local community initiatives working with young people to provide training and an atmosphere in which social development is encouraged.

WHAT IS NOT FUNDED No grants to individuals or for overseas activities.

TYPE OF GRANT Project and salaries. Up to a maximum of £5,000 per annum for three years. Recurring costs, salaries and start-up costs are also considered.

RANGE OF GRANTS £100–£5,000.

FINANCES *Year* 2001–02 *Income* £66,207 *Grants* £67,207 *Assets* £494,898

TRUSTEES D Howe, Chair; R K Cobley; Mrs J Clay; L W Lockhart; C Miers; A H N Molesworth; M Pearce; Brigadier P R Wildman.

HOW TO APPLY In writing to the correspondent.

WHO TO APPLY TO Revd Brian Walshe, 10 Warrior Court, 16 Warrior Square, St Leonards-on-Sea, East Sussex TN37 6BS *Tel* 01424 720061

CC NO 224484   **ESTABLISHED** 1909

■ The William & Katherine Longman Trust

WHERE FUNDING CAN BE GIVEN UK.

WHO CAN BENEFIT Registered charities.

WHAT IS FUNDED General charitable purposes. The trustees believe in taking a proactive approach in deciding which charities to benefit and it is their policy not to respond to unsolicited appeals.

WHAT IS NOT FUNDED Grants are only made to registered charities.

FINANCES *Year* 2000–01 *Income* £148,000 *Grants* £240,000 *Assets* £5,100,000

TRUSTEES W P Harriman; J B Talbot; A C O Bell.

HOW TO APPLY The trustees believe in taking a proactive approach in deciding which charities to support and it is their policy not to respond to unsolicited appeals.

WHO TO APPLY TO W P Harriman, Trustee, Charles Russell, 8–10 New Fetter Lane, London EC4A 1RS *Tel* 020 7203 5000 *Fax* 020 75203 5301 *E-mail* grainnef@cr-law.co.uk

CC NO 800785   **ESTABLISHED** 1988

■ John Longwill's Agricultural Scheme

WHERE FUNDING CAN BE GIVEN Leicestershire.

WHO CAN BENEFIT Young farmers.

WHAT IS FUNDED The trust's objects are to promote agriculture in Leicestershire through the provision of grants and loans to farmers in need, supporting Young Farmers' Clubs and other agricultural groups, and sponsoring education at an agricultural college.

SAMPLE GRANTS £7,000 to FWAG; £6,000 each to Brooksby College and Leicestershire and Rutland Young Farmers Clubs.

FINANCES *Year* 1999 *Income* £59,000 *Grants* £75,000 *Assets* £1,500,000

TRUSTEES Lord John Manners, Chair; O D Lucas; R T Thomas; C Winterton.

HOW TO APPLY In writing to the correspondent. The trustees meet to consider grants twice a year.

WHO TO APPLY TO Mrs H A M Lander, Clerk, 3 Wycliffe Street, Leicester LE1 5LR *Tel* 0116 262 6052

CC NO 215278   **ESTABLISHED** 1982

■ The Lord's Taverners

WHERE FUNDING CAN BE GIVEN UK.

WHO CAN BENEFIT Charitable and voluntary organisations benefiting young people, particularly those with special needs.

WHAT IS FUNDED Providing incentives to play cricket and other team games in schools and clubs. Encouraging people with disabilities to participate in sport. Giving mobility to special needs youngsters through the Lord's Taverners' minibus scheme. The provision of grants for sports and recreation for youngsters with special needs.

WHAT IS NOT FUNDED Youth cricket: the following is not normally grant aided: building or renovation of pavilions; sight screens; bowling machines; mowers/rollers; overseas tours; helmets. Sport for young people with special needs: the following will not normally be considered for a grant: capital costs; general grants; running costs including salaries; individuals; holidays/overseas tours; retrospective grants. Minibuses: homes, schools and organisations catering for young people with special needs under the age of 25 years, are entitled to only one minibus per location, although applications are accepted for a replacement.

TYPE OF GRANT One-off grants.

RANGE OF GRANTS £200–£25,000.

SAMPLE GRANTS £367,538 to ECB; £100,000 to English Schools Cricket Association; £25,000 to National Playing Fields Association.

FINANCES *Year* 2001 *Income* £4,640,000 *Grants* £2,016,000 *Assets* £2,121,000

TRUSTEES The Council of The Lord's Taverners comprising John Ayling, chair, and 17 others. Roger Smith is chair of the grantmaking foundation committee.

PUBLICATIONS *Disbursement of Grant Aid: Policy and Guidelines.*

HOW TO APPLY Cricket grants are normally considered by the foundation on the recommendation of the ECB (England and Wales

---

Cricket Board) and the necessary application forms are available from local county cricket boards. The foundation committee meets quarterly to review applications for grant aid. All applications must be presented on the appropriate application forms and should be submitted to the foundation secretary no later than one month before the foundation committee meeting. Application forms with detailed application instructions are available from the foundation secretary or on the website.
WHO TO APPLY TO Nicky Atkinson, Chief executive, 10 Buckingham Place, London SW1E 6HX *Tel* 020 7821 2828 *Fax* 020 7821 2829 *E-mail* nicky.atkinson@lordstaverners.org *Website* www.lordstaverners.org.uk
CC NO 306054   **ESTABLISHED** 1950

■ The Loseley & Guildway Charitable Trust

WHERE FUNDING CAN BE GIVEN International and UK, with an interest in Guildford.
WHO CAN BENEFIT Organisations benefiting people with Alzheimer's disease, cancer, epilepsy, HIV and AIDS, leprosy, mental illness, motor neurone disease, multiple sclerosis, Parkinson's disease, sight loss, spina bifida and hydrocephalus and terminal illness. Victims of natural disasters are also considered.
WHAT IS FUNDED Compassionate causes, mainly local or causes with which the family and members of the Loseley & Guildway firm are associated, including health and animal welfare.
WHAT IS NOT FUNDED No grants to individuals or non-registered charities.
RANGE OF GRANTS £25–£5,000. Typically £100.
SAMPLE GRANTS £5,000 to Challengers (Disability Challenge); £1,000 to Cherry Trees; £500 to International League for the Protection of Horses.
FINANCES *Year* 2000–01 *Income* £97,000 *Grants* £67,000 *Assets* £1,000,000
TRUSTEES Maj. James More-Molyneux, Chair; Mrs Susan More-Molyneux; Michael More-Molyneux; Adrian Abbott; Glye Hodson.
HOW TO APPLY In writing to the correspondent. The trustees meet in February, May and September to consider applications. However, due to commitments, new applications for any causes are unlikely to be successful.
WHO TO APPLY TO Miss Nicola Cheriton-Sutton, Secretary, The Estate Offices, Loseley Park, Guildford, Surrey GU3 1HS *Tel* 01483 304440 *Fax* 01483 302036
CC NO 267178   **ESTABLISHED** 1973

■ Lotus Foundation

WHERE FUNDING CAN BE GIVEN UK and overseas.
WHO CAN BENEFIT Established or newly-formed charities.
WHAT IS FUNDED The primary objectives of the trust are 'to offer financial aid and assistance to facilitate family and child welfare, women's issues, animal protection, addiction recovery and education'.
SAMPLE GRANTS Variety Club of Great Britain Children's Charity, Kids Company (London), UCLA Intervention Programme (Los Angeles) and British Red Cross for the Kosovo appeal.
FINANCES *Year* 1999 *Income* £281,000 *Grants* £290,000 *Assets* £43,000
TRUSTEES Mrs B Starkey; R Starkey.

HOW TO APPLY In writing to the correspondent. This trust is proactive in examining requests that meet with its criteria: in 1999 the trustees visited various organisations requiring funding, seeing first hand the type of assistance required and where the trust could best help.
WHO TO APPLY TO Mrs B Starkey, Trustee, Startling Music Limited, 90 Jermyn Street, London SW1Y 6JD *Tel* 020 7930 5133
CC NO 1070111   **ESTABLISHED** 1998

■ Michael Lowe's & Associated Charities

WHERE FUNDING CAN BE GIVEN The city of Lichfield.
WHO CAN BENEFIT Primarily individuals in need; some organisations benefiting people in need.
WHAT IS FUNDED Relief of need, hardship or distress.
RANGE OF GRANTS £270–£20,000.
SAMPLE GRANTS In 1998–99: £20,000 to Lichfield Methodist Church; £7,500 to Age Concern; £2,000 to St Mary's Centre; £1,250 to Relate; £1,000 each to Saxon Hill School and Shaw Trust; £700 to Lichfield Victim Support; £470 to Winged Fellowship Trust; £200 to Friary Drop In Centre.
FINANCES *Year* 2001–02 *Income* £99,316
TRUSTEES Mrs A Hall; E J Ashley, Chair; P C Boggis; Revd J Atkinson; Mrs G M Eagland; Mrs D Godfrey; C P Greatorex; M B Johnson; G T Kemp; N G Sedgwick; A D Thompson; Revd R Bull; A J Wilkins; A Wilson; Mrs P Brooks.
OTHER INFORMATION Fuel grants were given to 459 individuals totalling £22,950; other grants went to 151 individuals totalling £52,269.
HOW TO APPLY In writing to the correspondent. Trustees usually meet every two months.
WHO TO APPLY TO C P Kitto, Clerk, Hinckley Birch & Brown, 20 St John Street, Lichfield, Staffordshire WS13 6PD *Tel* 01543 262491
CC NO 214785   **ESTABLISHED** 1593

■ The C L Loyd Charitable Trust

WHERE FUNDING CAN BE GIVEN UK, with a preference for Berkshire and Oxfordshire.
WHO CAN BENEFIT Neighbourhood-based community projects and UK organisations benefiting at risk groups, and people who are disabled, disadvantaged by poverty or socially isolated.
WHAT IS FUNDED General charitable purposes. Local charities in Berkshire and Oxfordshire, UK health and welfare charities and UK animal welfare charities.
WHAT IS NOT FUNDED No support for individuals or medical research.
TYPE OF GRANT One-off and recurring.
RANGE OF GRANTS Up to £25,000; mostly £1,000 or less.
SAMPLE GRANTS In 2000–01: £25,000 to Coldstream Regimental Charity; £15,000 to Country Building Protection Trust; £10,000 to Country Building Protection Trust; £5,000 to Injured Jockey's Fund, Holy Trinity – West Hendred, and West Hendred Playground and Management Group; £3,630 to Country Building Protection Trust; £3,500 to Ardington and Lockinge Church; £3,000 to King Alfred's Educational Charity; £2,500 to Royal Agricultural Benevolent Institution.
FINANCES *Year* 2001–02 *Income* £115,355 *Grants* £73,190 *Assets* £2,347,619
TRUSTEES C L Loyd; T C Loyd.
HOW TO APPLY In writing to the correspondent. Grants are made several times each month.

WHO TO APPLY TO C L Loyd, Trustee, Lockinge, Wantage, Oxfordshire OX12 8QL *Tel* 01235 833265

CC NO 265076 **ESTABLISHED** 1973

■ LSA Charitable Trust

WHERE FUNDING CAN BE GIVEN UK.

WHO CAN BENEFIT Individuals and institutions benefiting horticultural researchers, students and people working in horticulture, and former tenants and employees of the former Land Settlement Association Ltd, who are in need.

WHAT IS FUNDED Horticultural research, the promotion of horticultural knowledge, and the relief of poverty.

RANGE OF GRANTS For organisations: £5,000–£20,000. For individuals: £1,000–£8,000.

SAMPLE GRANTS £28,709 to RABI for the support of 20 older people in need; £20,000 to the Department of Plant Sciences, Cambridge University, for research studentships; £8,550 to Reading University for an MSc studentship in horticulture; £5,653 to Nuffield Farm Scholarship Trust; £5,000 to Northern Horticultural Society for a studentship.

FINANCES *Year* 2001–2002 *Income* £43,000 *Grants* £61,000 *Assets* £1,328,587

TRUSTEES A R Eden; B E G Howe; P Hadley; C F Woodhouse; A M M Ross; S R V Pomeroy.

HOW TO APPLY For organisations: in writing to the correspondent. Grants to individuals are made through the Royal Agricultural Benefit Institution.

WHO TO APPLY TO Cheryl Boyce, Messrs Farrer & Co, 66 Lincoln's Inn Fields, London WC2A 3LH *Tel* 020 7242 2022

CC NO 803671 **ESTABLISHED** 1989

■ The Luck-Hille Foundation

WHERE FUNDING CAN BE GIVEN UK.

WHO CAN BENEFIT Registered charities and other tax exempt charitable organisations benefiting children, young adults and older people, people who are disabled and people disadvantaged by poverty.

WHAT IS FUNDED Education, health and welfare.

WHAT IS NOT FUNDED No grants to individuals.

TYPE OF GRANT Capital and core costs.

RANGE OF GRANTS Generally £200–£8,500.

SAMPLE GRANTS £36,848 to Middlesex University; £8,500 to King Alfred School Appeal Fund; £3,575 to Norwood; £500 to Project Trust; £250 each to The National Hospital and Raleigh International; £200 to Children with Aids Charity.

FINANCES *Year* 2000–01 *Income* £201,723 *Grants* £50,123 *Assets* £4,390,525

TRUSTEES Mrs Jill Luck-Hille; P M Luck-Hille; J W Prevezer.

HOW TO APPLY To the correspondent in writing. The trustees seem to have a list of regular beneficiaries and it may be unlikely that any new applications will be successful.

WHO TO APPLY TO J W Prevezer, Trustee, c/o Citroen Wells, Devonshire House, 1 Devonshire Street, London W1N 2DR *Tel* 020 7304 2000

CC NO 269046 **ESTABLISHED** 1975

■ The Marie Helen Luen Charitable Trust

WHERE FUNDING CAN BE GIVEN UK, with a preference for Wimbledon.

WHO CAN BENEFIT Charitable organisations.

WHAT IS FUNDED The trust supports both UK and local charities concerned with cancer relief, homelessness and the relief of hardship, pain and suffering. Grants are also given to relieve developing world poverty.

RANGE OF GRANTS £350–£5,000.

SAMPLE GRANTS £5,000 to University of Durham Student Hardship Fund; £2,700 to Merton Volunteer Bureau; £2,000 each to Wimbledon Guild of Social Welfare and St Mungo's; £1,000 to Lee House – Wimbledon; £780 to Deen City Farm; £500 to Winston's Wish.

FINANCES *Year* 1999 *Income* £41,000 *Grants* £35,000 *Assets* £1,300,000

TRUSTEES S V Perera; R R Littleton; M G Whitehead.

HOW TO APPLY In writing to the correspondent.

WHO TO APPLY TO R R Littleton, Trustee, Hillcroft, 57 Langley Avenue, Surbiton, Surrey KT6 6QR

CC NO 291012 **ESTABLISHED** 1984

■ Robert Luff Foundation Ltd

WHERE FUNDING CAN BE GIVEN UK.

WHO CAN BENEFIT Medical research charities.

RANGE OF GRANTS £12,500–£530,000.

SAMPLE GRANTS £530,000 to Cystic Fibrosis Trust for a five-year research project into finding a cure for the condition; £50,000 to Harpur Trust; £45,000 to National Heart and Lung Institute; £30,000 to St John Ambulance; £26,500 to British Lung Foundation; £20,000 to St Briavels Centre; £16,250 each to Sheffield Health Authority Trust Fund and University College London Medical School; £15,000 to National Asthma Campaign; £12,500 to British Scoliosis Research Foundation.

FINANCES *Year* 2000–01 *Income* £551,022 *Grants* £761,500 *Assets* £19,344,143

TRUSTEES Sir Robert Johnson; Lady Johnson; R P J Price; Gynia Favot; Mrs J Tomlinson.

HOW TO APPLY The foundation makes its own decisions about what causes to support. It has stated that 'outside applications are not considered, or replied to'.

WHO TO APPLY TO Ms R Jessop, Secretary, 294 Earls Court Road, Kensington, London SW5 9BB *Tel* 020 7373 7003 *Fax* 020 7373 8634

CC NO 273810 **ESTABLISHED** 1977

■ Paul Lunn-Rockliffe Charitable Trust

WHERE FUNDING CAN BE GIVEN UK with a preference for Hampshire.

WHO CAN BENEFIT Organisations of UK significance and charities which may be known to the trustees, or members of their family, benefiting: people of all ages, unemployed people, Christians, at risk groups, carers, people who are disabled, people disadvantaged by poverty, ex-offenders and people at risk of offending, homeless people, people living in urban areas, victims of famine and disasters and people with cerebral palsy or Parkinson's disease.

WHAT IS FUNDED It is the trustees' policy not to raise income through public and private appeals. The trust's sole source of income is the dividends received from the trust's capital investments. As far as grant making is concerned the trustees' policy is to give first but not exclusive consideration to charities likely to further Christianity; to give support to charities concerned with the relief of poverty, helping the aged, supporting the infirm and disaster relief; to consider charities connected with prisons and prisoners, medical research, rehabilitation of drug addicts and youth organisations; housing and accommodation. It will also support training for work; bursaries and fees; neurological research; and holidays and outings. Finally, the trustees should not accept such new commitments that will significantly dilute the size of current grants.

WHAT IS NOT FUNDED The trustees will not fund individuals; for example, students expenses and travel grants. Repair and maintenance of historic buildings are also excluded for support.

TYPE OF GRANT Core costs, one-off and start-up costs. Funding for more than three years will be considered.

RANGE OF GRANTS £100–£1,000.

SAMPLE GRANTS £1,000 to TAP; £800 to Bible Society; £700 to AIM; £600 each to Help the Aged, NSPCC, Christians Against Poverty, Christian Aid and Churban Urban Fund; £500 each to Children Family Trust, Spastics India, Care, Samaritans, Prison Fellowship, British Red Cross (Kosovo) and King Alfred Youth Activity Centre.

FINANCES *Year* 1999–2000 *Income* £30,000 *Grants* £31,000 *Assets* £643,000

TRUSTEES Mrs Jacqueline Lunn-Rockliffe; Victor Lunn-Rockliffe; James Lunn-Rockliffe.

HOW TO APPLY The trust encourages preliminary phone calls to discuss applications. It will generally only reply to written correspondence if an sae has been included.

WHO TO APPLY TO Mrs J M Lunn-Rockliffe, Secretary, 4a Barnes Close, Winchester, Hampshire SO23 9QX *Tel* 01962 852949 *Fax* 01962 852949

CC NO 264119   **ESTABLISHED** 1972

- - - - - - - -

■ C F Lunoe Trust Fund

WHERE FUNDING CAN BE GIVEN UK.

WHO CAN BENEFIT Grants from the fund are limited to ex-employees (and their dependants) of Norwest Holst Group Ltd, in needy circumstances, and to universities associated with the construction industry.

WHAT IS FUNDED Assistance to ex-employees (and their dependants), in needy circumstances, of Norwest Holst Group Ltd.

FINANCES *Year* 1999–2000 *Income* £46,000 *Grants* £40,000

TRUSTEES D R Huntingford; J A Bosdet; P H Lunoe; R F Collins; J E Ellis; M B Watson.

HOW TO APPLY Almost all the funds go to registered charities already known to the trustees so most new applications are unsuccessful.

WHO TO APPLY TO The Trustees, 4 Woodstock Road, Walthamstow, London E17 4BJ

CC NO 214850   **ESTABLISHED** 1960

- - - - - - - -

■ The Ruth & Jack Lunzer Charitable Trust

WHERE FUNDING CAN BE GIVEN UK.

WHO CAN BENEFIT Organisations benefiting children, young adults and students are given priority.

WHAT IS FUNDED Educational institutions. Other charitable purposes will be considered.

RANGE OF GRANTS £150–£5,900.

SAMPLE GRANTS £5,900 to Bobov Foundation; £5,000 each to KKL Executor & Trustee Co. and Lubavitch Foundation; £3,100 to Vaad Hatzdokoh; £3,000 to Chai Lifeline; £2,500 to GGBH Ladies Guild; £2,300 to SOFT; £2,000 to Service to the Aged; £500 to Project Seed; £150 to Friends of the Sick.

FINANCES *Year* 1999–2000 *Income* £61,000 *Grants* £56,000 *Assets* £204,000

TRUSTEES J V Lunzer; M D Paisner.

HOW TO APPLY In writing to the correspondent.

WHO TO APPLY TO M D Paisner, Trustee, c/o BDO Stoy Hayward, 8 Baker Street, London W1U 3LL *Tel* 020 7893 2499

CC NO 276201   **ESTABLISHED** 1978

- -

■ Lord and Lady Lurgan Trust

WHERE FUNDING CAN BE GIVEN UK and South Africa.

WHO CAN BENEFIT Medical charities, older people and the arts.

WHAT IS FUNDED The registered objects of this trust are: the relief and medical care of older people; medical research, in particular cancer research and the publication of the useful results of such research; the advancement of education including education in the arts for the public benefit by the establishment of educational and artistic bursaries; other charitable purposes at the discretion of the trustees.

FINANCES *Year* 2000–01 *Income* £45,800 *Grants* £42,700 *Assets* £1,215,000

TRUSTEES Simon David Howard Ladd Staughton; Andrew John Francis Stebbings; Diana Sarah Graves (partners Pemberton Greenish).

HOW TO APPLY In writing to the correspondent.

WHO TO APPLY TO Pemberton Greenish (Ref MDB), 45 Pont Street, London SW1X 0BX *Tel* 020 7591 3333 *Fax* 020 7591 3300

CC NO 297046   **ESTABLISHED** 1987

- -

■ The Lyndhurst Settlement

WHERE FUNDING CAN BE GIVEN Usually UK, but overseas applications are considered if there is a strong civil liberty component.

WHO CAN BENEFIT Registered charities benefiting: young adults, older people, people who are in care, or who are fostered or adopted; one parent families; ethnic minority groups; at risk groups; carers; ex-offenders and people at risk of offending; gays and lesbians; homeless people; immigrants and refugees; travellers; victims of abuse, crime or domestic violence and victims of war; people with HIV and AIDs; and people with substance misuse problems.

WHAT IS FUNDED The policy of the Lyndhurst Settlement is to encourage research into social problems with specific emphasis on safeguarding civil liberties, maintaining the rights of minorities and protecting the environment which the trustees regard as an important civil liberty. The trustees prefer to support charities (both innovatory and long established) that seek to prevent as well as alleviate hardship. In response to the pressing needs of today, the continuing policy of the trustees is to make grants in excess of income. Whilst supporting some larger organisations, the settlement tries to encourage smaller local groups. It is the view of the trustees that an essential element in the protection of the environment is the discouragement of population growth. The settlement was one of the first trusts to be concerned about the civil rights of prisoners. Minority groups, both here and abroad, are also a continuing concern. Also supported are: community development; support to voluntary and community organisations; residential facilities and services; family planning clinics; respite care and care for carers; health education and population control; libraries and museums; community centres; parks; community services; campaigning, advocacy advice and information on social issues; conservation; bird and wildlife sanctuaries; ecology; and conservation campaigning.

WHAT IS NOT FUNDED No grants to non-registered charities or individuals. Medical or religious charities are not normally supported.

TYPE OF GRANT Core costs, feasibility studies, one-off, projects, research, running costs, salaries and start-up costs. Grants are normally given on a one-off basis. They are usually for the general purposes of the registered charities supported.

RANGE OF GRANTS £500–£9,000.

SAMPLE GRANTS £9,000 to Education for Choice; £6,000 to Release; £5,000 to Prison Reform Trust; £4,500 to Prisoners Abroad; £4,000 each to Civil Liberties Trust, Common Ground, EHSH, Federation of Prisoners Families Support Group, Quaker Social Action, London Detainees Support Group, Sheffied Vietnamese Community Association and Sustrans.

FINANCES *Year* 2001–02 *Income* £45,765 *Grants* £175,000 *Assets* £632,975

TRUSTEES Michael Isaacs; Anthony Skyrme; Kenneth Plummer.

OTHER INFORMATION It is the trustees' policy to maintain a level of distribution in excess of income. With this in mind, they stated the following: 'The trustees anticipate that the work of the Settlement will be concluded soon after 31/12/2004.'

HOW TO APPLY Requests for grants should include a brief description of the aims and objects of the charity and must be in writing and not by telephone. Unsuccessful applications will not be acknowledged unless an sae is enclosed. Applications are considered throughout the year.

WHO TO APPLY TO Michael Isaacs, Administrative Trustee, The Lyndhurst Settlement, 2nd Floor, 15–19 Cavendish Place, London W1G 0DD **CC NO** 256063   **ESTABLISHED** 1968

■ The Lyndhurst Trust

WHERE FUNDING CAN BE GIVEN UK and overseas, with preferences for north east England and the developing world.

WHO CAN BENEFIT Evangelistic Christian organisations, especially those operating where people have never had the opportunity of hearing the gospel. Those involved in difficult areas for Christian witness. Charities ministering to the needs of the disadvantaged in society are also funded.

WHAT IS FUNDED Charities connected with the propagation of the gospel or the promotion of the Christian religion; the distribution of bibles and other Christian religious works; the support of Christian missions; the provision of clergy; the maintenance of churches and chapels; work with disadvantaged people in society. Funds are given worldwide; there is a preference for the developing world, and in the UK a preference for the north east of England. It tends to support specific charities on a regular basis.

WHAT IS NOT FUNDED No support for individuals or buildings.

TYPE OF GRANT Recurring.

RANGE OF GRANTS £800–£10,000, with most grants for £800.

FINANCES *Year* 2000–01 *Income* £58,613 *Grants* £97,975 *Assets* £1,546,940

TRUSTEES W P Hinton; J A L Hinton; Dr W J Hinton.

OTHER INFORMATION The grants were divided into the following areas: UK – north east England: 42%; third world countries: 30%; UK – general: 19%; Europe and the rest of the world: 9%.

HOW TO APPLY In writing to the correspondent, enclosing an sae if a reply is required. Requests are considered quarterly.

WHO TO APPLY TO W P Hinton, Trustee, 66 High Street, Swainby, Northallerton, North Yorkshire DL6 3DG **CC NO** 235252   **ESTABLISHED** 1964

■ The Lynn Foundation

WHERE FUNDING CAN BE GIVEN UK and overseas.

WHO CAN BENEFIT Registered charities, institutions benefiting musicians, textile workers and designers, and artists. Older people and people who are disabled will also benefit.

WHAT IS FUNDED Promotion and encouragement of music, art, masonic charities, disability, and charities concerned with children and older people.

TYPE OF GRANT One-off grants for core, capital and project support. Loans are also made.

RANGE OF GRANTS Usually £500–£1,000.

SAMPLE GRANTS Recent beneficiaries include Wigmore Hall, Discover – Children's Discovery Centre, London Master Classes, Awards for Young Musicians, The Young Vic, Bath International Music Festival, Northern Rock Festival Group, Oratorio and Jazz Choirs, Bampton Classical Opera, Abbotsbury Music and Listening Books.

FINANCES *Year* 2002 *Income* £303,513 *Grants* £118,550 *Assets* £5,500,641

TRUSTEES Guy Parsons, Chair; J F Emmott; Dr P E Andry; P R Parsons; Ian Fair.

HOW TO APPLY In writing to the correspondent.

WHO TO APPLY TO Guy Parsons, Trustee, Blackfriars, 17 Lewes Road, Haywards Heath, West Sussex RH17 7SP *Tel* 01444 454773 *Fax* 01444 456192 **CC NO** 326944   **ESTABLISHED** 1985

■ The Lynwood Trust

WHERE FUNDING CAN BE GIVEN UK and overseas.

WHO CAN BENEFIT Organisations benefiting children, older people and people who are disabled.

WHAT IS FUNDED Advancement of religion and other charitable purposes including churches and missionary organisations.

WHAT IS NOT FUNDED No grants to individuals.

TYPE OF GRANT One-off and recurrent.

SAMPLE GRANTS Previous beneficiaries include Scripture Union for purchase of land in Uganda and for schools and Christian work, Africa Inland Mission for evangelism, CARE for Christian social concerns and TearFund for overseas aid.

FINANCES *Year* 2001–02 *Income* £22,944

TRUSTEES J S Barling; C R Harmer.

HOW TO APPLY In writing to the correspondent.

WHO TO APPLY TO C R Harmer, Trustee, Harmer Slater, Quoin House, Alfred Road, Sutton, Surrey SM1 4RR *Tel* 020 8652 2700 *Fax* 020 8652 2719 **CC NO** 289535   **ESTABLISHED** 1984

■ John Lyon's Charity

WHERE FUNDING CAN BE GIVEN The London boroughs of Barnet, Brent, Camden, Ealing, Kensington and Chelsea, Hammersmith and Fulham, Harrow and the Cities of London and Westminster.

WHO CAN BENEFIT Young people, homeless people, unemployed people and other disadvantaged groups. Also the provision of childcare, support for parents and for children where parental support is lacking, and the promotion of activities to broaden cultural horizons and enhance recreation and leisure.

WHAT IS FUNDED Organisations benefiting children and young adults living in the areas defined above.

WHAT IS NOT FUNDED The charity cannot give grants to individuals; for research, unless it is action research designed to lead directly to the advancement of practical activities in the community; for feasibility studies; for medical care and resources; in response to general charitable appeals, unless they can be shown to be of specific benefit to children and young people in one or more of the geographical areas listed; as direct replacements for the withdrawal of funds by statutory authorities for activities which are primarily the responsibility of central or local government; to umbrella organisations to distribute to projects which are already in receipt of funds from the charity; for the promotion of religion or politics; for telephone helplines; as core funding for national charities; for advice and information services; to housing associations.

TYPE OF GRANT Capital costs, revenue costs and recurring costs up to three years. Buildings, core costs, project, salaries and start-up costs.

SAMPLE GRANTS £100,000 to Punch and Judy Drop in; £90,000 each to National Theatre for Back Stage Pass over three years – a rolling programme of ticket subsidies and workshops for school students and teachers and English National Opera over three years for a similar programme; £70,000 to Paddington Development Trust; £50,000 each to Local Employment Access Projects, Oakleigh School Parent Staff Association, Roundhouse Trust and Soho Green.

FINANCES *Year* 2001–02 *Grants* £2,512,000

TRUSTEES The keepers and governors of the possessions revenues and goods of the Free Grammar School of John Lyon. Grants committee: Nick Stuart, Chair; Prof. D M P Mingos; Mrs G Baker; F Singer.

HOW TO APPLY You should put in a letter the following information: a summary of the main purpose of the project; details of the overall amount requested; over what time scale; some indication of how funds from the charity would be allocated. If your first proposal is assessed positively, you will be sent an application form. This must be completed and returned (not by e-mail or fax) by the deadline date in order for your project to be considered for funding. The grants committee meets three times a year, in March, June and November. Closing dates are about two months in advance of these meetings.

WHO TO APPLY TO The Grants Director, 45 Pont Street, London SW1X 0BX *Tel* 020 7591 3330 *Fax* 020 7589 0807 *E-mail* jlc@glaw.co.uk *Website* www.johnlyonscharity.org.uk

CC NO 237725   **ESTABLISHED** 1578

■ The Lyons Charitable Trust

WHERE FUNDING CAN BE GIVEN UK.

WHO CAN BENEFIT Registered charities.

WHAT IS FUNDED Health, medical research, children in need and charities concerned with people who are homeless.

RANGE OF GRANTS Average £12,000.

FINANCES *Year* 1999–2000 *Income* £86,567 *Grants* £70,000 *Assets* £1,534,615

TRUSTEES M S Gibbon; Nick Noble.

HOW TO APPLY In writing to the correspondent.

WHO TO APPLY TO Mrs H Fuff, Field Fisher Waterhouse, 35 Vine Street, London EC3N 2AA

CC NO 1045650   **ESTABLISHED** 1995

■ The Sir Jack Lyons Charitable Trust

WHERE FUNDING CAN BE GIVEN UK and overseas.

WHO CAN BENEFIT Charities benefiting children and young people; actors and entertainment professionals; musicians; students; textile workers and designers; writers and poets; at risk groups; those disadvantaged by poverty, and people who are socially isolated.

WHAT IS FUNDED Relief in need, arts, education and humanities. Jewish charities are also supported.

WHAT IS NOT FUNDED No grants to individuals.

RANGE OF GRANTS £40–£10,000.

SAMPLE GRANTS £10,000 each to Jewish Music Institute at SOAS and University of York; £6,000 to Jewish Community Foundation; £5,500 to Community Security Trust; £5,000 each to UJIA and Joint Jewish Charitable Trust; £3,500 to York Early Music Festival; £2,500 each to City University London, Royal Academy of Arts and The Jewish Museum; £1,500 each to Amnesty International and London String Quartet Foundation. Seven grants of £1,000 or less were also made.

FINANCES *Year* 2000–01 *Income* £138,000 *Grants* £58,000 *Assets* £2,300,000

TRUSTEES Sir Jack Lyons; Lady Roslyn Marion Lyons; M J Friedman; J E Lyons; D S Lyons.

HOW TO APPLY In writing to the correspondent. In the past the trust has stated: 'In the light of increased pressure for funds, unsolicited appeals are less welcome and would waste much time and money for applicants who were looking for funds which were not available.'

WHO TO APPLY TO M J Friedman, Trustee, Sagars, 3rd Floor, Elizabeth House, Queen Street, Leeds LS1 2TW *Tel* 0113 297 6789

CC NO 212148   **ESTABLISHED** 1960

■ Malcolm Lyons Foundation

WHERE FUNDING CAN BE GIVEN UK.

WHO CAN BENEFIT Jewish and Israeli organisations.

SAMPLE GRANTS £75,000 to Friends of Horim Establishments; £37,000 to Mesorah Heritage Foundation; £10,000 to Jewish Care; £2,100 to Jewish Learning Council; £1,163 to Mesoral Publications Limited ; £1,120 to United Synagogue; £1,000 to Friends of Adereth Yaakov; £639 to Finchley Synagogue; £500 to United Jewish Appeal; £375 to Friends of Bnei Akiva; £200 to Kisharon.

FINANCES *Year* 2000–01 *Income* £91,845 *Grants* £131,241 *Assets* £23,787

TRUSTEES M S Lyons; Mrs J Lyons; D Mendoza; J S Newman.

HOW TO APPLY The trust states that it will not consider unsolicited applications.

WHO TO APPLY TO J S Newman, Trustee, BDO Stoy
Hayward, 8 Baker Street, London W1U 3LL
Tel 020 7893 2318
CC NO 1050689   ESTABLISHED 1995

WHO TO APPLY TO N A M Smith, c/o Messrs
Rowberry Morris, Morroway House, Station
Road, Gloucester GL1 1DW *Tel* 01452 301903
CC NO 202939   ESTABLISHED 1980

■ The Lyras Family Charitable Trust

WHERE FUNDING CAN BE GIVEN UK, Greece, worldwide.
WHO CAN BENEFIT Organisations working in the areas
outlined above, including people disadvantaged
by poverty and members of the Greek Orthodox
religion.
WHAT IS FUNDED (a) Disaster funds worldwide; (b)
the relief of poverty; (c) the advancement of
religion, in particular within the country of
Greece; and (d) other charitable purposes.
RANGE OF GRANTS £200–£10,000, usually £2,000 or
less.
SAMPLE GRANTS £10,000 to National Deaf
Children's Society; £5,000 to International
Religious & Scientific Community for the
Environmental Activities of the Ecumenical
Patriarchate; £2,900 to Lyreio Paidiko Idryma –
Greece; £3,000 to Royal Free Hospital Special
Trustees; £2,000 each to Archdiocese of
Albania, and Institute of Advanced Neuromotor
Rehabilitation; £1,260 to Friends of Oinoussai
Society; £1,000 each to Athens College, Royal
Marsden Hospital Charity, and Salvation Army.
FINANCES *Year* 2001 *Income* £58,015
Grants £48,900 *Assets* £818,377
TRUSTEES John C Lyras; John M Lyras; Richard
Moore.
HOW TO APPLY In writing to the correspondent,
although the trust states that its funds are fully
committed and unsolicited applications are not
requested.
WHO TO APPLY TO T Cripps, Secretary, Snow Hill
Trustees Ltd, 1 Snow Hill, London EC1A 2EN
Tel 020 7334 9191 *Fax* 020 7334 7973
CC NO 328628   ESTABLISHED 1990

■ Sylvanus Lyson's Charity

WHERE FUNDING CAN BE GIVEN Gloucester diocese.
WHO CAN BENEFIT Individuals and organisations
benefiting people of all ages, clergy, and Church
of England.
WHAT IS FUNDED Religious and charitable work in the
areas of youth, community, relief for widows,
clergy and people in need.
WHAT IS NOT FUNDED The trustees' present policy is
to make no grants for the repair or maintenance
and improvement of churches or other buildings,
other than in very exceptional circumstances.
TYPE OF GRANT Recurrent and one-off.
SAMPLE GRANTS £31,000 to the Diocesan Board of
Finance; £25,000 to Pentecost 2000; £10,000
each to Emmaus Gloucester and Dean &
Chapter – Cathedral Youth Choir; £5,000 each
to Matson Youth Centre (Spurgeons Childcare)
and Winchcombe Abbey School; £4,000 each to
St Paul's Youth & Community Centre, St
Stephens – Bristol Road, St David – Moreton in
Marsh and St Mary – Newent.
FINANCES *Year* 1999–2000 *Income* £224,000
Grants £160,000 *Assets* £5,300,000
TRUSTEES B V Day; G V Doswell; Rt Revd J S Went;
Revd Canon Michael Page; Ven. Hedley
Ringrose.
HOW TO APPLY In writing to the correspondent.

■ The M B Foundation

WHERE FUNDING CAN BE GIVEN Some preference for Greater Manchester.

WHO CAN BENEFIT Registered charities.

WHAT IS FUNDED General charitable purposes.

FINANCES *Year* 2001–02 *Income* £848,000

TRUSTEES Rabbi W Kaufman; Rabbi M Bamberger; S B Bamberger.

HOW TO APPLY In writing to the correspondent, although the trust states that its funds are already committed.

WHO TO APPLY TO The Trustees, c/o CTL Estates, Newhaven Business Park, Barton Lane, Eccles, Manchester M30 0HH

CC NO 222104   **ESTABLISHED** 1965

■ The M & C Trust

WHERE FUNDING CAN BE GIVEN UK.

WHO CAN BENEFIT Mainly Jewish organisations benefiting Jewish people, at risk groups, people disadvantaged by poverty, and socially isolated people.

WHAT IS FUNDED Primarily Jewish and welfare organisations.

WHAT IS NOT FUNDED No grants to individuals.

TYPE OF GRANT Normally one-off grants.

SAMPLE GRANTS £35,000 to Jerusalem Foundation; £10,000 each to Action for Kids, Connect, CSV, Friends of Israel Education Trust, Helen House, Jewish Children's Holiday Fund, Jewish Women's Aid, Nightingale House, Tree House and World Jewish Relief.

FINANCES *Year* 2000–01 *Income* £150,215 *Grants* £187,500 *Assets* £5,354,141

TRUSTEES A Bernstein; Mrs J B Kemble; A C Langridge; Elizabeth J Marks; Rachel J Lebus.

HOW TO APPLY In writing to the correspondent, but the trust states that funds are currently earmarked for existing projects. In order to keep administration costs to a minimum, they are unable to reply to any unsuccessful applications.

WHO TO APPLY TO A C Langridge, Trustee, c/o Chantrey Vellacott DFK, Russell Square House, 10–12 Russell Square, London WC1B 5LF *Tel* 020 7509 9000 *Fax* 020 7509 9219

CC NO 265391   **ESTABLISHED** 1973

■ The M D & S Charitable Trust

WHERE FUNDING CAN BE GIVEN UK and Israel.

WHO CAN BENEFIT Organisations benefiting Jewish people. Support is given to rabbis, children and young adults, students, teachers and people disadvantaged by poverty.

WHAT IS FUNDED Trustees are primarily interested in Jewish causes for either the relief of poverty or the advancement of education or religion.

RANGE OF GRANTS Below £1,000–18,000.

SAMPLE GRANTS £12,500 to Ichud Mosdos Gur; £11,250 to Yeshivat Gaon Yaakov; £11,000 to Yeshivat Dromah; £9,750 to Mosdos Kaliv; £8,000 to Yeshivat Magen Aurohom; £7,000 to Yeshivat Kolel Zecher Yaakov; £6,100 to Yeshivat Ponevez; £5,500 to Yeshivat

Nechomos Isa Yisroel; £5,000 each to Telz Academy Trust and Yeshivat Tomchey Temimen.

FINANCES *Year* 2000–01 *Income* £233,415 *Grants* £146,005 *Assets* £645,328

TRUSTEES M D Cymerman; Mrs S Cymerman.

HOW TO APPLY In writing to the correspondent.

WHO TO APPLY TO Martin D Cymerman, Trustee, 22 Overlea Road, London E5 9BG *Tel* 020 7272 2255

CC NO 273992   **ESTABLISHED** 1977

■ The M K (Mendel Kaufman) Charitable Trust

WHERE FUNDING CAN BE GIVEN UK, especially the north east of England.

WHO CAN BENEFIT Organisations benefiting Jewish people.

WHAT IS FUNDED Jewish organisations.

FINANCES *Year* 1999–2000 *Income* £553,000 *Grants* £912,000 *Assets* £4,000,000

TRUSTEES Z M Kaufman; C S Kaufman; S Kaufman; A Piller; D Katz.

HOW TO APPLY In writing to the correspondent.

WHO TO APPLY TO Mr R Gill, c/o Cohen Arnold & Co., 13–17 New Burlington Place, Regent Street, London W1X 2JP *Tel* 020 7734 1362

CC NO 260439   **ESTABLISHED** 1966

■ M N R Charitable Trust

WHERE FUNDING CAN BE GIVEN UK, overseas.

WHO CAN BENEFIT Organisations with charitable purposes.

WHAT IS FUNDED Support is normally only given to projects which are nominated to the management committee by the partners and staff of Mazars (chartered accountants).

WHAT IS NOT FUNDED Support is not given to an organisation within three years of an earlier grant, and, as such, recurrent grants are not made. No grants are made to individuals.

TYPE OF GRANT Single strategic projects; one-off; research; building; and capital. Funding is for one year or less.

SAMPLE GRANTS £15,000 each to Indian Earthquake Appeal via Christian Aid and London City Mission; £10,000 each to Bonny Downs Community Association, Primary Immunodeficiency Association, Saltmine, and Scriptural Knowledge Institution regarding Mercy Ships; £7,000 to Sight Savers International; £5,000 each to Chartered Accountants' Benevolent Fund, Miscarriage Association, and Operation Mobilisation – India.

FINANCES *Year* 2002 *Income* £119,225 *Grants* £99,725 *Assets* £44,670

TRUSTEES Peter R Hyatt, Chair; John S Mellows; David E Ryan.

HOW TO APPLY Unsolicited applications will rarely be considered or acknowledged. Applications will generally only be considered in respect of charities nominated to the management committee by partners or staff of Mazars.

WHO TO APPLY TO Bryan K H Rogers, Mazars, 24 Bevis Marks, London EC3A 7NR

CC NO 287735   **ESTABLISHED** 1983

■ The Madeline Mabey Trust

WHERE FUNDING CAN BE GIVEN UK, and UK registered international charities.

WHO CAN BENEFIT Registered charities, including UK registered charities and international charities.

WHAT IS FUNDED Principally medical research and children's welfare.

FINANCES *Year* 2000–01 *Income* £296,541 *Grants* £242,131 *Assets* £167,630

TRUSTEES Alan G Daliday; Bridget A Nelson; Joanna L Singeisen.

HOW TO APPLY In writing to the correspondent. Please note, unsuccessful applications are not acknowledged.

WHO TO APPLY TO Joanna Singeisen, Trustee, Mabey House, Floral Mile, Twyford, Reading RG10 9SQ

CC NO 326450   **ESTABLISHED** 1983

■ The Robert McAlpine Foundation

WHERE FUNDING CAN BE GIVEN UK.

WHO CAN BENEFIT Registered charities and hospitals.

WHAT IS FUNDED Children with disabilities, older people, medical research, social welfare.

WHAT IS NOT FUNDED The trust does not like to fund overheads. No grants to individuals.

RANGE OF GRANTS £100–£40,000.

SAMPLE GRANTS £40,000 to Ewing Foundation; £35,000 to Fairbridge; £16,527 to Stoke Mandeville Burns and Reconstruction Surgery; £10,000 each to Devas Club and H & F Skills Centre; £7,500 to Brittle Bone Society; £5,000 each to Beamsley Project, Community Development Project, Kith & Kids, and Thrift Urban Housing.

FINANCES *Year* 1999–2000 *Income* £265,702 *Grants* £249,500 *Assets* £6,334,024

TRUSTEES Hon. David McAlpine; M H D McAlpine; Kenneth McAlpine; Cullum McAlpine; Adrian N R McAlpine.

HOW TO APPLY In writing to the correspondent at any time. Considered annually, normally in November.

WHO TO APPLY TO Graham Prain, Eaton Court, Maylands Avenue, Hemel Hempstead, Hertfordshire HP2 7TR *Tel* 01442 233444

CC NO 226646   **ESTABLISHED** 1963

■ The E M MacAndrew Trust

WHERE FUNDING CAN BE GIVEN UK.

WHAT IS FUNDED Trustees are primarily interested in medical and children's charities.

SAMPLE GRANTS £7,000 in two grants to Stoke Manderville Burns and Reconstructive Surgery Research Trust; £4,000 in two grants to MERLIN.

FINANCES *Year* 2001–02 *Income* £46,923 *Grants* £35,800 *Assets* £993,113

TRUSTEES A R Nicholson; E P Colquhoun.

HOW TO APPLY The trustees state that they do not respond to any unsolicited applications under any circumstances, as they prefer to make their own decisions as to which charities to support.

WHO TO APPLY TO J P Thornton, Administrator, J P Thornton & Co., The Old Dairy, Adstockfields, Adstock, Buckingham MK18 2JE *Tel* 01296 714886 *Fax* 01296 714711

CC NO 290736   **ESTABLISHED** 1984

■ The R S MacDonald Charitable Trust

WHERE FUNDING CAN BE GIVEN Scotland.

WHO CAN BENEFIT Charities benefiting people with cerebral palsy, people who are visually impaired, children and animals at risk of cruelty.

WHAT IS FUNDED Grants are made to charities which focus on research into the origins, prevention or alleviation of visual impairment and cerebral palsy or similar conditions; also to those which care for people affected by either or both of those conditions. Grants are also made to charities which work to prevent cruelty to children and animals.

WHAT IS NOT FUNDED Grants are not given to non-registered charities or individuals.

TYPE OF GRANT One-off, recurring costs, project and research will be considered. Funding may be given for up to three years.

RANGE OF GRANTS Average grants are about £25,000.

SAMPLE GRANTS £50,000 to Royal Blind Asylum and School; £35,000 each to Sense Scotland and Deafblind Scotland; £34,000 to Children's Fund; £33,000 to Capability Scotland; £25,000 each to Children 1st, St Dunstans and SSPCA; £25,000 to Eyeless Trust; £20,000 to RNLI; £18,000 to Glasgow & West of Scotland Society for the Blind; £10,000 to Visually Impaired Services South East of Scotland.

FINANCES *Year* 2001 *Income* £415,000 *Grants* £310,000 *Assets* £18,000,000

TRUSTEES E D Buchanan; D W A MacDonald; Ms Sheila C MacDonald; Donald G Sutherland; Richard K Austin.

PUBLICATIONS Information is available from the trust.

HOW TO APPLY In writing to the correspondent, including a copy of the latest audited accounts and constituting documents. Applications should be received by March/April to be considered in the summer. Trustees usually want to meet new applicants requesting a larger grant. Successful applicants are asked for a follow-up report and are often visited by a trustee.

WHO TO APPLY TO Richard K Austin, Trustee, 27 Cramond Vale, Edinburgh EH4 6RB *Tel* 0131 312 6766

SC NO SC012710   **ESTABLISHED** 1978

■ Ronald McDonald Children's Charities Limited

WHERE FUNDING CAN BE GIVEN UK.

WHO CAN BENEFIT Organisations benefiting children and the families of sick children.

WHAT IS FUNDED Ronald McDonald Houses and Ronald McDonald Family Rooms. Equipment grants for children's charities, hospitals, hospices and schools, focusing on special needs.

WHAT IS NOT FUNDED No grants to individuals or for salaries, administration costs or holidays.

TYPE OF GRANT Capital, including buildings; and one-off. Funding may be given for more than three years.

RANGE OF GRANTS £500–£500,000; typically £2,000.

SAMPLE GRANTS For Ronald McDonald Family Rooms: £250,000 to Southport Hospital, £187,000 to Southampton Hospital, £87,500 to Hammersmith Hospital, £81,250 to Frenchay Hospital, and £10,250 to Frimley Park Hospital; £10,000 each to Friends of Westfield School for multi-sensory equipment, League of Friends of

Crawley Hospital for multi-sensory equipment, and Winchester Healthcare Trust for a family room; £7,150 to Acorns Children's Hospice Trust for specialist furniture.
FINANCES *Year* 1999 *Income* £1,881,000 *Grants* £1,028,000 *Assets* £2,917,000
TRUSTEES C Aronson; J Lebus; A Taylor; M Wellwood; C Bowring.
HOW TO APPLY On an application form available from the address below. An initial telephone call is welcomed.
WHO TO APPLY TO Wendy Ayling, 11–59 High Road, East Finchley, London N2 8AW *Tel* 020 8700 7331 *Fax* 020 8700 7417 *E-mail* wayling@uk.mcd.com
CC NO 802047   **ESTABLISHED** 1989

■ Macdonald-Buchanan Charitable Trust

WHERE FUNDING CAN BE GIVEN UK, with a slight preference for Northamptonshire.
WHO CAN BENEFIT Registered charities, with a preference for those benefiting young people in Northamptonshire.
WHAT IS FUNDED General charitable purposes with a preference for charities which the trust has special interest in, knowledge of or association with.
WHAT IS NOT FUNDED No grants to individuals.
RANGE OF GRANTS Generally £25–£500.
SAMPLE GRANTS £30,000 to Carrie Jo Charitable Trust; £22,500 to Orrin Charitable Trust; £1,500 to Queen Margaret's School; £500 each to British Heart Foundation, Cot Death Society, Marie Curie Cancer Care, National Asthma Campaign, Anthony Nolan Bone Marrow Trust, Northamptonshire Association of Youth Clubs, and NSPCC.
FINANCES *Year* 2001 *Income* £123,181 *Grants* £106,205 *Assets* £2,912,743
TRUSTEES Capt. John Macdonald-Buchanan; A J Macdonald-Buchanan; A R Macdonald-Buchanan; H J Macdonald-Buchanan; Mrs M C A Philipson.
HOW TO APPLY In writing to the correspondent, for consideration once a year. Appeals will not be acknowledged.
WHO TO APPLY TO Miss Linda Cousins, Rathbone Trust Ltd, 159 New Bond Street, London W1S 2UD *Tel* 020 7399 0820
CC NO 209994   **ESTABLISHED** 1952

■ The McDougall Trust

WHERE FUNDING CAN BE GIVEN UK and overseas.
WHO CAN BENEFIT Organisations or individuals 'carrying out charitable work including research in accord with the trust's objects'.
WHAT IS FUNDED The knowledge, study and research of: political or economic science and functions of government and the services provided to the community by public and voluntary organisations; methods of election of and the selection and government of representative organisations whether national, civic, commercial, industrial or social; and representative democracy, its forms, functions and development and also its associated institutions. Special priority is given to electoral research projects.
WHAT IS NOT FUNDED No grants to any political party or commercial organisation, for an individual's education, for social welfare matters, or for general appeals, expeditions or scholarships.

TYPE OF GRANT Usually one-off for a specific project or part of a project or work programme. Applications for small 'pump-priming' grants are welcomed. Feasibility studies and research grants are also considered.
RANGE OF GRANTS Minimum grant £250.
SAMPLE GRANTS In 1999: £112,988 to Electoral Reform Society; £2,418 to University of Strathclyde.
FINANCES *Year* 2000 *Income* £206,100 *Grants* £117,700 *Assets* £540,500
TRUSTEES Prof. David M Farrell, Chair; Elizabeth Bee; Elizabeth Collingridge; Michael Meadowcroft; Nigel Siedever; John Ward; Prof. Paul Webb.
PUBLICATIONS *Representation: Journal of Representative Democracy*, (quarterly).
OTHER INFORMATION The trustees have established a library called the Lakeman Library for Electoral Studies at the address below. This is available for the use of research workers and the public generally on conditions laid down by the trustees. The trustees also sponsor several prizes in conjunction with the Political Studies Association and the Politics Association
HOW TO APPLY In writing to the correspondent, including annual accounts. Trustees normally meet quarterly. Brief details of proposal needed. Initial enquiries by telephone accepted. Two deadlines for receipt of applications: 1 May and 1 October. Applications received after a deadline may be held over for consideration at the trustees' discretion.
WHO TO APPLY TO Paul Wilder, Trust Secretary, 6 Chancel Street, London SE1 0UX *Tel* 020 7620 1080 *Fax* 020 7928 1528 *E-mail* admin@mcdougall.org.uk
CC NO 212151   **ESTABLISHED** 1959

■ The Macfarlane Walker Trust

WHERE FUNDING CAN BE GIVEN UK, with priority for Gloucestershire.
WHO CAN BENEFIT Individuals, registered charities and institutions benefiting: former employees of Walker, Crosweller and Co Ltd; musicians; actors and entertainment professionals; artists; students; and scientists.
WHAT IS FUNDED Grants to former employees, and their families, of Walker, Crosweller & Co Ltd; provision of educational facilities particularly for scientific research; encouragement of music, drama and the fine arts. Also support for community facilities and services, and charities in the fields of conservation, alternative transport, and recreation.
WHAT IS NOT FUNDED No grants for expeditions, medical expenses, or nationwide appeals, or animal charities.
TYPE OF GRANT Feasibility studies, one-off, project, research, running costs and start-up costs. Funding for up to and over three years will be considered.
RANGE OF GRANTS £100–£5,000.
SAMPLE GRANTS £5,000 each to Cheltenham Transport for the Disabled, Forum for the Future and Second World War Experience Centre; £3,000 to European Association of Teachers; £2,400 to Lilian Faithful Homes; £2,000 each to Gloucester Society and Gloucester Playing Fields Association.
FINANCES *Year* 1999–2000 *Income* £29,000 *Grants* £56,000 *Assets* £446,000
TRUSTEES D F Walker; N G Walker; D A Launchbury.
HOW TO APPLY In writing to the correspondent giving the reason for applying, and an outline of the

project with a financial forecast. An sae must accompany the initial application.

WHO TO APPLY TO Mrs S V Walker, Secretary, 50 Courthope Road, London NW3 2LD

CC NO 227890   **ESTABLISHED** 1963

■ The A M McGreevy No 5 Charitable Settlement

WHERE FUNDING CAN BE GIVEN UK, with a preference for the Bristol and Bath area.

WHO CAN BENEFIT Registered charities.

WHAT IS FUNDED General charitable purposes.

WHAT IS NOT FUNDED No support for individuals.

SAMPLE GRANTS £10,000 each to Childline and NSPCC; £7,500 to Grateful Society; £7,000 to Theo Moorman Charitable Trust; £5,000 to Camerton Church; £2,500 to National Missing Persons Helpline; £1,000 to National Osteoporosis Society; £998 to Edward James Foundation; £250 each to Alzheimer's Society and Stroke Association.

FINANCES *Year* 2000–01 *Income* £51,222 *Grants* £44,498 *Assets* £1,661,856

TRUSTEES Avon Executor & Trustee Co.; Anthony M McGreevy; Elise McGreevy-Harris; Katrina McGreevy.

HOW TO APPLY In writing to the correspondent.

WHO TO APPLY TO Matthew Bird, KPMG, 100 Temple Street, Bristol BS1 6AG *Tel* 0117 905 4000

CC NO 280666   **ESTABLISHED** 1979

■ The Mackintosh Foundation

WHERE FUNDING CAN BE GIVEN UK, with a slight interest in western Scotland, and overseas.

WHO CAN BENEFIT Registered charities benefiting children, students and young adults, theatres and theatrical production companies, dramatists, writers, poets, actors, musicians, entertainment professionals, and medical professionals. Also people disadvantaged by poverty, homeless people, refugees, and victims of abuse, domestic violence, famine, man-made or natural disasters, war, and HIV/AIDS.

WHAT IS FUNDED Priority is given to the theatre and the performing arts. Also funded are children and education; medicine; homelessness; community projects; the environment; refugees; and other charitable purposes.

WHAT IS NOT FUNDED Religious or political activities are not supported. Apart from the foundation's drama award and some exceptions, applications from individuals are discouraged.

TYPE OF GRANT Capital, project and recurring costs; up to three years.

RANGE OF GRANTS £100–100,000.

SAMPLE GRANTS £100,000 to the Arts Council of England, for reallocation to specified theatres; £30,000 to National Student Drama Festival Ltd; £20,000 to Mallaig & Morar Community Centre Association; £16,000 to Christ's Hospital; £15,000 to Regional Theatre Young Director's Scheme; £12,000 to Tricycle Theatre; £10,000 each to Crusaid, Centrepoint, Comic Relief and National Aids Trust.

FINANCES *Year* 2001–02 *Income* £948,000 *Grants* £818,000 *Assets* £11,800,000

TRUSTEES Sir Cameron Mackintosh, Chair; Nicholas Mackintosh; Martin McCallum; Nicholas Allott, Appeals Director; D Michael Rose; Patricia Macnaughton; Alain Boublil.

PUBLICATIONS Information sheet.

HOW TO APPLY In writing to the correspondent. The trustees meet in May and November in plenary

session, but a grants committee meets weekly to consider grants of up to £10,000.

WHO TO APPLY TO Nicholas Mackintosh, Appeals Director, 1 Bedford Square, London WC1B 3RA *Tel* 020 7637 8866

CC NO 327751   **ESTABLISHED** 1988

■ Martin McLaren Memorial Trust

WHERE FUNDING CAN BE GIVEN UK.

WHO CAN BENEFIT Horticulture students.

WHAT IS FUNDED Horticultural scholarships.

SAMPLE GRANTS £10,000 each to Horticultural Scholarships Fund and Memorial Trust Foundation.

FINANCES *Year* 1999–2000 *Income* £30,000 *Grants* £20,000 *Assets* £682,000

TRUSTEES Mrs Nancy Gordon McLaren; Nicholas Durlacher; Michael Robert Macfadyen; Revd Richard Francis McLaren.

HOW TO APPLY In writing to the correspondent.

WHO TO APPLY TO Michael Macfadyen, Trustee, 8–10 New Fetter Lane, London EC4A 1RS *Tel* 020 7203 5000

CC NO 291609   **ESTABLISHED** 1985

■ The Helen Isabella McMorran Charitable Foundation

WHERE FUNDING CAN BE GIVEN UK and overseas.

WHO CAN BENEFIT Registered charities benefiting children, young adults and older people; those in care, fostered and adopted; Christians, Church of England; people with disabilities; people disadvantaged by poverty; homeless and socially isolated people.

WHAT IS FUNDED Older people's welfare, Christian education, churches, the arts, residential facilities and services, social and moral welfare, special schools, cultural and religious teaching, special needs education, health, medical and religious studies, conservation, animal welfare, bird sanctuaries and heritage.

WHAT IS NOT FUNDED No grants to individuals.

TYPE OF GRANT One-off.

RANGE OF GRANTS £500–£2,000.

SAMPLE GRANTS Christian Aid, Marine Conservation, Moon Bear Rescue, National Association for Crohn's Disease, National Children's Bureau, React, St Matthews PCC, St Nicholas Church, Sense International, and Stoneham Housing Association.

FINANCES *Year* 2001–02 *Income* £18,600 *Grants* £26,000 *Assets* £556,547

TRUSTEES NatWest Bank plc.

HOW TO APPLY In writing to the correspondent. Brief guidelines are available. The closing date for applications is February each year.

WHO TO APPLY TO John Feeney, NatWest Private Banking, 153 Preston Road, Brighton BN1 6BD *Tel* 01273 545035

CC NO 266338   **ESTABLISHED** 1973

■ D D McPhail Charitable Settlement

WHERE FUNDING CAN BE GIVEN UK.

WHO CAN BENEFIT Registered charities, especially those benefiting people who are elderly or disabled.

WHAT IS FUNDED Medical research and welfare.

SAMPLE GRANTS Condover Hall School for the Blind, Harrow Blind Social Club, The Barbara Bus Fund, International League for the Protection of

Horses, Invalid Children's Aid Association, National Society for Epilepsy, RADAR, Cancer Relief Macmillan Fund, and The National Meningitis Trust.

FINANCES *Year* 1999–2000 *Income* £873,000 *Grants* £177,000 *Assets* £10,000,000
TRUSTEES I McPhail; P Cruddas; J K Noble.
HOW TO APPLY In writing to the correspondent.
WHO TO APPLY TO Mrs Sheila Watson, Administrator, PO Box 285, Pinner, Middlesex HA5 3FB
CC NO 267588   **ESTABLISHED** 1974

■ The MacRobert Trust

WHERE FUNDING CAN BE GIVEN UK, mainly Scotland.
WHO CAN BENEFIT Recognised charitable organisations benefiting children, young adults and older people, ex-service and service people, seafarers and fishermen, and volunteers. Also artists, musicians, textile workers and designers, and writers and poets. At risk groups, carers, disabled people, people disadvantaged by poverty, and socially isolated people will also be considered.
WHAT IS FUNDED Major categories: science and technology; ex-servicemen's hospitals and homes; youth; education; services and sea; community welfare; disability. Minor categories: agriculture and horticulture; medical care; arts and music; Tarland and Deeside.
WHAT IS NOT FUNDED Grants are not normally provided for: religious organisations (but not including youth/community services provided by them, or projects of general benefit to the whole community, or local churches); organisations based outside the UK; individuals; endowment or memorial funds; general appeals or mail shots; political organisations; student bodies (as opposed to universities); fee-paying schools (apart from an educational grants scheme for children who are at, or need to attend, a Scottish independent secondary school and for which a grant application is made through the headteacher); expeditions; retrospective grants; or departments within a university (unless the appeal gains the support of, and is channelled through, the principal).
TYPE OF GRANT Core/revenue costs, project. Capital including buildings, feasibility studies, one-off, research, recurring and running costs, and salaries. Funding may be given for one year or more.
RANGE OF GRANTS Mostly £5,000–£10,000.
SAMPLE GRANTS £110,000 to Princess Louise Scottish Hospital (Erskine Hospital); £50,000 to National Galleries Of Scotland; £25,000 to Glasgow Science Centre; £20,000 in two grants to Leukaemia Research Fund; £20,000 to Moredun Research Institute; £10,000 each to Barnardo's Scotland, Liberating Scots Trust, Maritime Volunteer Service, Prince and Princess of Wales Hospice and Quarriers – Bridge of Weir.
FINANCES *Year* 2001–02 *Grants* £580,000 *Assets* £49,000,000
TRUSTEES Mrs C J Cuthbert; D M Heughan; J Mackie; W G Morrison; Group Capt. D A Needham; R M Sherriff; A M Summers; Cromar Nominees Ltd; J Swan; H Woodd.
PUBLICATIONS Leaflet – *Advice to Applicants for Grants.*
HOW TO APPLY The application form and full guidelines can be downloaded from the website, although applications must be posted. The trustees meet to consider applications twice a year in March and October. To be considered, applications must be received for the March

meeting by the end of October previously and for the October meeting by early June previously.
WHO TO APPLY TO Maj. Gen. J A Barr, Administrator, Cromar, Tarland, Aboyne, Aberdeenshire AB34 4UD *Tel* 01339 881444
Website www.themacroberttrust.org.uk
SC NO SC031346   **ESTABLISHED** 1943

■ Ian Mactaggart Fund

WHERE FUNDING CAN BE GIVEN UK, with a possible preference for Scotland.
WHO CAN BENEFIT Charitable organisations.
WHAT IS FUNDED The trust supports education and training, culture, the relief of people who are poor, sick, in need or disabled.
FINANCES *Year* 1999 *Income* £410,000 *Grants* £60,000
TRUSTEES Sir John Mactaggart; P A Mactaggart; R Rogerson Easton Pender; Jane L Mactaggart; Fiona M Mactaggart; Lady Caroline Mactaggart.
HOW TO APPLY In writing to the correspondent. This entry was not confirmed by the trust.
WHO TO APPLY TO Ms H Warren, 63a South Audley Street, London W1K 2QS
SC NO SC012502

■ Magdalen Hospital Trust

WHERE FUNDING CAN BE GIVEN UK.
WHO CAN BENEFIT Organisations benefiting: deprived children and young adults up to 25 years; those in care, fostered and adopted; parents and children; one-parent families; people disadvantaged by poverty; and people with HIV/AIDS.
WHAT IS FUNDED Projects for deprived and disabled children and young people, with priority for IT training, literacy, special needs education, training for work and personal development, clubs, crime prevention, emergency care, playschemes, and counselling.
WHAT IS NOT FUNDED No grants to non-registered charities, individuals, charities with an income in excess of £150,000 or national charities.
TYPE OF GRANT One-off; project; start-up funding; one year or less.
RANGE OF GRANTS £500–£2,000; typically £1,000.
SAMPLE GRANTS £2,000 to Rainbow Charity for Homeless Children (Nepal); £1,500 each to Camp & Trek, Churches in Action (Bargoed), Romanian Challenge Appeal and Wandsworth Wel-care (Karibu Project); £1,300 to Hull Lighthouse Project; £1,000 each to Caring for Life (Leeds), CCTL (Suffolk), Christ Church Primary School (Shine Project), Edinburgh Sitters, St Chad's (Coventry), Southwark and Camberwell Wel-care, Yeovil Opportunity Group and Youth at Risk.
FINANCES *Year* 2000–01 *Income* £27,000 *Grants* £25,000 *Assets* £783,000
TRUSTEES Mrs M Gregory; Lady Holderness; Mrs B Lucas; Mrs S Gibson; J Martin; Revd R Mitchell; Ven. F R Hazell; Miss D Lazenby; Hon. E Wood; Mrs D Hinton.
HOW TO APPLY An application form and guidelines are available and deadlines for applications are given. An sae is required. Initial telephone calls from applicants are welcome.
WHO TO APPLY TO Mrs Norma Hazell, Cotswold Cottage, School Lane, Alvechurch, Worcestershire B48 7SA *Tel* 0121 445 1318
CC NO 225878   **ESTABLISHED** 1963

■ The Magdalen & Lasher Charity

WHERE FUNDING CAN BE GIVEN Hastings.
WHO CAN BENEFIT Individuals, and organisations benefiting elderly and young people, and people disadvantaged by poverty.
WHAT IS FUNDED Pensions for elderly people in Hastings; playschemes; primary, secondary and special schools; purchase of books, travel and maintenance in schools; literacy; health care, facilities and buildings; community services.
TYPE OF GRANT One-off; one year or less.
SAMPLE GRANTS £30,000 to St Michael's Hospice; £10,000 to Seaview Project; £6,100 to Salvation Army; £6,000 to Hollington Residents Association; £3,500 to St Clement's and All Saints; £3,000 to Addaction; £2,000 to Art Works; £1,500 to St Mary Star of the Sea.
FINANCES *Year* 1999–2000 *Income* £787,000 *Grants* £110,000 *Assets* £8,300,000
TRUSTEES A Slack, Chair; G L Dengate; G R Douglas-Kellie; M J Foster; J S Hayward; Daphne Hughes; C R Morris; I M Steel; Cllr R D Stevens; C N Bendon; M Bigg; K L L Boorman; J H Dengate; R J B Guy; D Kent; I E Morrison.
HOW TO APPLY In writing to the correspondent.
WHO TO APPLY TO Christopher Langdon, Clerk to the Trustees, Langham House, Albert Road, Hastings, East Sussex TN34 1QT *Tel* 01424 437878
CC NO 211415   **ESTABLISHED** 1951

■ The Magen Charitable Trust

WHERE FUNDING CAN BE GIVEN UK.
WHO CAN BENEFIT Registered charities.
WHAT IS FUNDED Jewish organisations.
FINANCES *Year* 1999–2000 *Income* £152,548 *Grants* £115,610 *Assets* £562,477
TRUSTEES Jacob Halpern; Mrs Rose Halpern.
HOW TO APPLY In writing to the correspondent.
WHO TO APPLY TO The Trustees, Lopian Gross Barnett & Co., Harvester House, 37 Peter Street, Manchester M2 5QD *Tel* 0161 832 8721
CC NO 326535   **ESTABLISHED** 1984

■ Mageni Trust

WHERE FUNDING CAN BE GIVEN UK.
WHO CAN BENEFIT Arts organisations; registered charities.
WHAT IS FUNDED General charitable purposes.
RANGE OF GRANTS £500–£50,000.
SAMPLE GRANTS £50,000 to CAF as a Gift Aid donation; £10,000 to National Youth Orchestra; £1,000 to National Theatre; and £500 to London Philharmonic Orchestra School Appeal.
FINANCES *Year* 1998–99 *Income* £646,000 *Grants* £62,000
TRUSTEES G L Collins; Mrs G L Collins; S J Hoare.
HOW TO APPLY In writing to the correspondent.
WHO TO APPLY TO G L Collins, Trustee, 17 Hawthorne Road, Bromley, Kent BR1 2HN
CC NO 1070732   **ESTABLISHED** 1998

■ Man Group plc Charitable Trust

WHERE FUNDING CAN BE GIVEN East London.
WHO CAN BENEFIT Registered charities.
WHAT IS FUNDED General charitable purposes, with preference for causes near to or linked to the business of E D & F Man Plc, particularly enterprise initiatives and charities concerned with underprivileged and disabled young people.
RANGE OF GRANTS £150–£12,000.
SAMPLE GRANTS £8,000 to London Philharmonic; £5,300 to Royal Opera House Trust; £2,500 to Home Start UK; £2,000 each to London First Trust and Tower Hamlets Education Business Partnership; £1,800 to City of London Festival; £1,000 to Southwark Cathedral Millennium Appeal and Victim Support London; £500 each to British Red Cross, Children's Aid Direct and North East London Cancer Help Centre.
FINANCES *Year* 1999–2000 *Income* £253,000 *Grants* £246,000
TRUSTEES M J C Stone, Chair; D Boehm; C Brumpton; K R Davis; H A McGrath; S J Nesbitt; A H Scott.
HOW TO APPLY The trust has stated that it does not accept unsolicited applications.
WHO TO APPLY TO Ann Simpkin, Administrator, Man Group Plc, Sugar Quay, Lower Thames Street, London EC3R 6DU *Tel* 020 7285 3040
CC NO 275386   **ESTABLISHED** 1978

■ Manchester Airport Community Trust Fund

WHERE FUNDING CAN BE GIVEN The area which is most affected by the Manchester Airport. This includes South Manchester and Tameside, Trafford, Stockport, the borough of Macclesfield and the borough of Congleton up to but not including the towns of Macclesfield and Congleton, Vale Royal, and up to but not including Northwich.
WHO CAN BENEFIT Established groups or charities able to demonstrate clear financial records.
WHAT IS FUNDED Projects which: encourage tree planting, forestation, landscaping and other environmental improvements or heritage conservation; promote social welfare through recreation, sport and leisure; provide better appreciation of the natural and urban environment; and promote the use of the natural environment as a safe habitat for flora and fauna. Projects must be for the benefit of the whole community or a substantial section of it, with preference given to those that have considered needs of people who are disabled or elderly.
WHAT IS NOT FUNDED Grants will not be awarded to organisations which have statutory responsibilities such as hospitals or schools unless it is for a project which is clearly not a statutory responsibility. No grants for the purchase of land or buildings. No grants are given for staffing costs or project running. Grants are not normally recurrent. Organisations cannot apply for a second three-year grant within three years of the first grant. An organisation can reapply only if the project is entirely different. No grants are given to individuals. Organisations must be established groups or charities. Branches of large UK organisations will have lower priority. Organisations which are in receipt of, or with access to, substantial support from elsewhere will also have lower priority.
RANGE OF GRANTS Limited number of £5,001– £25,000; remainder up to £5,000.
FINANCES *Year* 2000–01 *Income* £242,000 *Grants* £260,000
TRUSTEES There is one trustee from each of the following: the metropolitan boroughs of Stockport and Trafford; Manchester City Council, Congleton, Macclesfield and Vale Royal Borough Council; Cheshire County Council; Manchester Airport Company Board.

HOW TO APPLY On a form available from the correspondent. Applicants should obtain the fund's brochure to make sure they fit the criteria. The administrator may also visit the project or proposed site or applicants may be asked to visit Manchester Airport to provide further details. The administrator will liaise with local environmental organisations such as Cheshire Wildlife Trust, Cheshire Landscape Trust, Manchester Wildlife Trust and Groundwork Trust Network. The trustees meet four times a year in the first weeks of April, July, October and January. Applications should be received no later than the first Friday of the preceding month. It is advisable to send applications early. This will ensure that any queries can be dealt with before the trustees' meeting.
WHO TO APPLY TO The Trust Fund Administrator, The Community Relations Department, Manchester Airport Plc, 3rd Floor, Olympic House, Manchester M90 1QX *Tel* 0161 489 5281 *Fax* 0161 489 3647
E-mail trust.fund@manairport.co.uk
Website www.manchesterairport.co.uk
CC NO 1071703   ESTABLISHED 1997

....
■ **The Manchester Guardian Society Charitable Trust**
WHERE FUNDING CAN BE GIVEN Greater Manchester.
WHO CAN BENEFIT Preference is usually shown to smaller charities.
WHAT IS FUNDED General charitable purposes. The emphasis is very much on helping the Greater Manchester area.
WHAT IS NOT FUNDED Generally the trust does not give to individuals.
TYPE OF GRANT Primarily small, single, capital projects.
RANGE OF GRANTS £100–£5,000.
SAMPLE GRANTS £2,000 each to Beechwood Cancer Care Centre, North West Drug Treatment Commission, and Woodside Junior School; £1,500 each to Stroke Association and Victim Support – Greater Manchester; £1,400 to Dobcross Youth Band; £1,000 to Fairbridge – Salford; £840 to Gingerbread – Heywood; £500 to Greater Manchester Play Resources.
FINANCES *Year* 2000–01 *Income* £108,000 *Grants* £95,000 *Assets* £2,800,000
TRUSTEES P R Green; D A Sutherland; W R Lees-Jones; W J Smith; P Goddard; Mrs J Powell; D G Wilson; Mrs J Harrison; J P Wainwright; K Ahmed; K Hardinge; J A H Fielden.
HOW TO APPLY On a form available from the correspondent. Applications are considered on the first Monday in March, June, September and December; they must arrive 14 days before these dates. The trustees do not welcome repeat applications within 18 months.
WHO TO APPLY TO Miss K A Graham, Cobbetts, Ship Canal House, King Street, Manchester M2 4WB *Tel* 0161 833 3333 *Fax* 0161 833 3030 *E-mail* kathryn.graham@corbetts.co.uk
CC NO 515341   ESTABLISHED 1984

....
■ **Lord Mayor of Manchester's Charity Appeal Trust**
WHERE FUNDING CAN BE GIVEN The City of Manchester.
WHO CAN BENEFIT Registered charities.
WHAT IS FUNDED General charitable purposes.
RANGE OF GRANTS Up to £500.
FINANCES *Year* 2000–01 *Grants* £53,000

TRUSTEES Cllr G Conquest; Cllr P Conquest; Cllr G Carroll; Richard Paver; Howard Bernstein; Fred Marks; Anthony Baldwin.
HOW TO APPLY In writing to the correspondent. Applications are considered quarterly.
WHO TO APPLY TO Anita Scallan, Lord Mayor's Office, Town Hall, Albert Square, Manchester M60 2LA *Tel* 0161 234 3375 *Fax* 0161 234 3230 *Minicom* 0161 234 3230
E-mail lord.mayor's.office@notes.manchester.gov.uk
CC NO 1066972   ESTABLISHED 1997

....
■ **Mandeville Trust**
WHERE FUNDING CAN BE GIVEN UK.
WHO CAN BENEFIT Organisations.
WHAT IS FUNDED General charitable purposes.
SAMPLE GRANTS £18,000 to Sindlesham School; £14,000 to breast cancer research at Charing Cross Hospital; £2,000 each to Berkshire Community Trust and Career Best Ltd.
FINANCES *Year* 1997–98 *Income* £38,000 *Grants* £45,000 *Assets* £60,000
TRUSTEES Robert Cartwright Mandeville; Pauline Maude Mandeville; Peter William Murcott; Justin Craigie Mandeville.
HOW TO APPLY In writing to the correspondent.
WHO TO APPLY TO R C Mandeville, Trustee, The Hockett, Hockett Lane, Cookham Dean, Berkshire SL6 9UF *Tel* 01628 484272
CC NO 1041880   ESTABLISHED 1994

....
■ **The Manifold Trust**
WHERE FUNDING CAN BE GIVEN UK.
WHO CAN BENEFIT UK registered charities only.
WHAT IS FUNDED Almost all grants are given to charities concerned with: the conservation of historic churches and other buildings, but a few are also given for waterways; arts and education; community centres and village halls; libraries and museums; and campaigning on conservation and social issues.
WHAT IS NOT FUNDED The trust does not give grants to churches for 'improvements'; nor, with regret, to individuals for any purpose.
TYPE OF GRANT One-off..
RANGE OF GRANTS £500–£160,000.
SAMPLE GRANTS In 2001: £357,000 to the Historic Churches Preservation Trust; £100,000 to Institute for Policy Research; £40,000 to Magdalene College, Cambridge; £32,000 to Coastal Forces Heritage Trust; £20,000 each to British School at Rome and HMS Trincomalee Trust; £15,000 each to Countryside Foundation, Empress Eugenie Memorial Trust, Scottish Churches Architectural Heritage Trust and Waterways Trust.
FINANCES *Year* 2002 *Income* £840,000 *Grants* £1,356,000
TRUSTEES Sir John Smith; Lady Smith; Miss Christine Gilbertson.
HOW TO APPLY In writing to the correspondent. Applications are considered twice a month, and a reply is sent to most applicants (whether successful or not) who have written a letter rather than sent a circular.
WHO TO APPLY TO Miss Christine Gilbertson, Shottesbrooke House, Maidenhead SL6 3SW *Fax* 01628 820159
CC NO 229501   ESTABLISHED 1962

■ R W Mann Trustees Limited

WHERE FUNDING CAN BE GIVEN UK, but grants are practically all confined to organisations in Tyne and Wear, with a preference for North Tyneside.

WHO CAN BENEFIT Local activities or local branches of national charities benefiting children, young adults, older people, academics, seafarers and fishermen, students, teachers and governesses, unemployed people, volunteers, those in care, fostered and adopted, parents and children, one-parent families, widows and widowers, at risk groups, carers, people with disabilities, people disadvantaged by poverty, ex-offenders and those at risk of offending, homeless people, people living in urban areas, and victims of abuse, crime and domestic violence. People with Alzheimer's disease, autism, cancer, cerebral palsy, Crohn's disease, mental illness, motor neurone disease, multiple sclerosis, muscular dystrophy, sight loss and all terminal diseases will be considered.

WHAT IS FUNDED Charities working in the fields of: accommodation and housing; information technology and computers; infrastructure development; professional bodies; charity and umbrella bodies; arts and art facilities; theatre; the visual arts; arts activities and education; cultural activity; health; conservation and environment; education and training; and social care and development. Other charitable purposes will be considered.

WHAT IS NOT FUNDED 'No grants to individuals, except in the form of particular educational scholarships through an agency.'

TYPE OF GRANT Recurrent expenditure, capital or single expenditure. Core costs, feasibility studies, interest-free loans, one-off and project funding, recurring costs, running costs, and salaries up to two years will be considered.

RANGE OF GRANTS £250–£10,000.

SAMPLE GRANTS £10,000 to Community Foundation Serving Tyne and Wear for the Millennium Awards scheme; £9,000 to Sea Cadets, Wallsend for a minibus and running costs; £5,000 to Cancer Bridge for a new building appeal, Churches Acting Together for homelessness action, and Fairbridge in Tyne and Wear for work with young people; £3,600 to University of Newcastle for engineering prizes and bursaries; £3,000 to Mea Trust towards a new building.

FINANCES *Year* 1999–2000 *Income* £168,875 *Grants* £143,835 *Assets* £2,529,388

TRUSTEES Directors: Mrs Judy Hamilton, Chair; Guy Javens; Mrs Monica Heath.

HOW TO APPLY In writing to the correspondent, with an sae. The trustees meet quarterly at no set times.

WHO TO APPLY TO John Hamilton, PO Box 119, Gosforth, Newcastle upon Tyne NE3 4WF *Tel* 0191 284 2158 *Fax* 0191 285 8617 *E-mail* john.hamilton@onyx.octacon.co.uk

CC NO 259006   **ESTABLISHED** 1959

■ The Victor Mann Trust (also known as The Wallsend Charitable Trust)

WHERE FUNDING CAN BE GIVEN The borough of Wallsend.

WHO CAN BENEFIT Individuals and local organisations benefiting older people, and people who are disadvantaged by poverty or homeless.

WHAT IS FUNDED The welfare and provision of accommodation for older poor people within the borough of Wallsend.

SAMPLE GRANTS In 1999: £1,225 to Age Concern; £686 to Diabetes Foundation; £500 to Wallsend Voluntary Committee for the Blind; £200 to Eden Court; £64 to Community Transport.

FINANCES *Year* 2001 *Income* £32,540

TRUSTEES Cllr M J Huscroft, Chair; B Springthorne; Ms S Watson; Cllr T Cruikshanks; Cllr D Charlton; Cllr M Mulgrove; Cllr R Usher; Mrs M Kelly; Mrs M Lavery.

HOW TO APPLY On a form available from the correspondent. Applications are considered in April, June, September and December.

WHO TO APPLY TO Ms Sheila Watson, Secretary, Adult Services, 126 Great Lime Road, West Moor, Newcastle upon Tyne NE12 7DQ *Tel* 0191 200 8181

CC NO 215476   **ESTABLISHED** 1956

■ W M Mann Foundation

WHERE FUNDING CAN BE GIVEN Scotland.

WHO CAN BENEFIT Organisations based in Scotland or serving the Scottish community.

WHAT IS FUNDED The arts, education, medical research, and music.

SAMPLE GRANTS £4,000 to Trades House of Glasgow. Other larger grants of £1,000 to £2,300 included those to City of Glasgow Chorus, East Park Home, Macmillan Cancer Relief and St Margaret's Hospice. There were 21 smaller grants of £50 to £1,000, including those to Ayrshire Hospice Appeal, Children 1st, Garelochhead Primary School and Scottish Down's Syndrome Association.

FINANCES *Year* 2000–01 *Income* £381,000 *Grants* £24,000 *Assets* £1,700,000

TRUSTEES W M Mann; B M Mann; A W Mann; S P Hutcheon.

HOW TO APPLY In writing to the trustees.

WHO TO APPLY TO Bruce M Mann, Trustee, 201 Bath Street, Glasgow G2 4HY *Tel* 0141 248 4936 *Fax* 0141 221 2976

SC NO sc010111

■ The Leslie & Lilian Manning Trust

WHERE FUNDING CAN BE GIVEN The north east of England.

WHO CAN BENEFIT Principally charities with local affinities benefiting at risk groups, and people who are disadvantaged by poverty, socially isolated, sick or disabled.

WHAT IS FUNDED Principally medicine, health and welfare.

WHAT IS NOT FUNDED No grants to individuals.

TYPE OF GRANT Annual – but not necessarily recurrent.

RANGE OF GRANTS Usually £500–£2,000.

SAMPLE GRANTS In 1998–99: £4,000 to Salvation Army Foyer Appeal; £1,200 to St Oswald's Hospice; £1,000 each to Children's Foundation, Leukaemia Research Fund, Northumberland Scouts, Percy Hedley Spastic School, Phillip Cussins House, Save the Children Fund (North East), and Salvation Army.

FINANCES *Year* 2001–02 *Income* £34,805

TRUSTEES D Jones; P Jones; N Sherlock.

HOW TO APPLY In writing to the correspondent by January for consideration in March.

WHO TO APPLY TO Kristian Leif Andersen, Watson Burton, 20 Collingwood Street, Newcastle upon Tyne NE99 1YQ *Tel* 0191 244 4444

CC NO 219846   **ESTABLISHED** 1960

■ Maranatha Christian Trust

WHERE FUNDING CAN BE GIVEN UK and worldwide.
WHO CAN BENEFIT Individuals and institutions.
WHAT IS FUNDED The advancement of the Christian gospel.
RANGE OF GRANTS £200–£35,000.
SAMPLE GRANTS £35,000 to CARE Trust; £10,000 each to Riding Lights and Stewards Trust; £9,000 to Prison Fellowship; £8,000 to Nairobi Cathedral Primary School; £7,500 to Portman House Trust; £7,000 to Ashburnham Thanksgiving Trust; £5,000 each to InterHealth, Oasis Media, and Kingston Charitable Trust (Ukraine).
FINANCES *Year* 1997–98 *Income* £65,000 *Grants* £368,000 *Assets* £2,000,000
TRUSTEES A C Bell; Revd L Bowring; Rt Hon. Viscount Brentford.
HOW TO APPLY In writing to the correspondent, but please note, the trust does not consider unsolicited applications.
WHO TO APPLY TO G P Ridsdale, 208 Cooden Drive, Bexhill-on-Sea, East Sussex TN39 3AH *Fax* 01424 844741
CC NO 265323   **ESTABLISHED** 1972

■ Marbeh Torah Trust

WHERE FUNDING CAN BE GIVEN UK and Israel.
WHO CAN BENEFIT Jewish charities.
WHAT IS FUNDED Furtherance of orthodox Jewish religious education and relief of poverty.
SAMPLE GRANTS In 1999–2000: £69,500 to Yeshiva Marbeh Torah; £25,850 to Sharei Shimon Aryeh; £25,000 to Yeshiva Beis Meir; £15,000 to Mishkenos Yakov; £13,000 to Ezer Mitzion; £12,700 to Nachalat Avrohom; £10,150 to Knessess Hatorah; £10,000 to Nechomas Isser Yisoroel; £7,500 to Nachalet Binyahu; £6,000 to Beis David.
FINANCES *Year* 2000–01 *Income* £213,703 *Grants* £208,000 *Assets* £19,508
TRUSTEES Moishe Chaim Elzas; Jacob Naftoli Elzas; Simone Elzas.
HOW TO APPLY In writing to the correspondent.
WHO TO APPLY TO M C Elzas, Trustee, 116 Castlewood Road, London N15 6BE
CC NO 292491   **ESTABLISHED** 1985

■ The Marchday Charitable Fund

WHERE FUNDING CAN BE GIVEN UK, with a preference for south east England.
WHO CAN BENEFIT Organisations benefiting children, young adults, older people, those in care, fostered and adopted, parents and children, one-parent families, carers, disabled people, people disadvantaged by poverty, ex-offenders and those at risk of offending, homeless people, immigrants and refugees, victims of abuse, victims of famine and war, people with Alzheimer's disease, autism, cystic fibrosis, HIV and AIDs, mental illness, multiple sclerosis, paediatric disease, psoriasis, substance abuse and terminal illness.
WHAT IS FUNDED Smaller charities where a contribution will make a noticeable difference covering advice and information (housing); emergency and short-term housing; respite; arts education; economic regeneration schemes; support to voluntary and community organisations; support to volunteers; health care; convalescent homes; hospices; rehabilitation centres; special schools and special needs education; literacy; training for work; vocational training; care in the community; counselling; crime prevention; day centres; emergency care.
WHAT IS NOT FUNDED The trust prefers not to support local organisations outside the south east of England. No grants to individuals or towards building projects.
TYPE OF GRANT Capital, core costs, one-off, project, recurring costs, salaries and start-up costs. All funding is up to three years.
RANGE OF GRANTS £1,000–£7,500.
SAMPLE GRANTS £7,500 to the Core Trust for a holistic drug rehabilitation centre; £7,000 to the Refugee Council for a volunteer coordinator; £5000 each to Red R for volunteer engineers and so on to help in developing countries, Children in Touch for support to families with autistic children, National Missing Person's Helpline, Remap for specialist wheelchairs and aids for disabled people, Down's Syndrome Educational Trust for assisting families with Down's Syndrome children, Weston Spirit for a drop-in facility for young people and Domestic Violence Matters for a support service for victims of domestic violence.
FINANCES *Year* 2001 *Income* £76,055 *Grants* £80,300
TRUSTEES Alan Mann; Lyndsey Mann; Dudley Leigh; Rose Leigh; Maureen Postles; Graham Smith; John Orchard; Priyen Gudka.
HOW TO APPLY In writing to the correspondent. Replies cannot be sent to all requests. Trustees meet quarterly.
WHO TO APPLY TO Mrs Rose Leigh, c/o Marchday Group plc, Allan House, 10 John Princes Street, London W1M 0AH *Tel* 020 7629 8050 *Fax* 020 7629 9204
CC NO 328438   **ESTABLISHED** 1989

■ Marchig Animal Welfare Trust

WHERE FUNDING CAN BE GIVEN Worldwide.
WHO CAN BENEFIT Organisations and individuals that make positive contributions in protecting animals and promoting and encouraging practical work in preventing animal cruelty and suffering.
WHAT IS FUNDED Organisations and individuals preventing cruelty to animals, relieving their suffering and encouraging the preservation of the environment in which they live. Awards are given in either of the following two categories: the development of an alternative method to the use of animals in experimental procedures and the practical implementation of such an alternative resulting in a significant reduction in the number of animals used in experiments; practical work in the field of animal welfare resulting in significant improvements for animals either nationally or internationally.
WHAT IS NOT FUNDED Applications which fail to meet the above criteria will be rejected. Additionally, those relating to: educational studies or other courses; expeditions; payment of salaries; support of conferences and meetings; and activities that are not totally animal welfare related.
TYPE OF GRANT Based on project.
RANGE OF GRANTS Based on project.
SAMPLE GRANTS US$25,000 each to Cat Welfare Society of Israel, and CHAI – Israel; £10,000 each to Blue Cross of India, Compassion Unlimited Plus Action – India and Fethiye Friends of Animals Association; £5,000 each to Foundation for the Protection of Community Dogs – Romania, and Society for Protection of Stray Animals – Turkey; £4,500 to Puss in

Boots; £4,016 to Asociacion Nacional para la Defensa de los Animales (ANDA) – Spain; £4,000 to Advocates for Animals; £3,500 to Brooke Hospital for Animals (Delhi).
FINANCES *Year* 2001 *Income* £243,738 *Grants* £119,669 *Assets* £2,369,223
TRUSTEES Madame Jeanne Marchig; Trevor Scott; Les Ward, Bill Jordan; Jenny Palmer.
HOW TO APPLY In writing to the correspondent.
WHO TO APPLY TO The Administrator, 10 Queensferry Street, Edinburgh EH2 4PG *Tel* 0131 225 6039 *Fax* 0131 220 6377 *E-mail* marchigtrust@marchigawt.org
Website www.marchigawt.org
CC NO 802133   **ESTABLISHED** 1989

■ The Linda Marcus Charitable Trust

WHERE FUNDING CAN BE GIVEN Worldwide.
WHO CAN BENEFIT Charities benefiting: children; young adults; actors and entertainment professionals; musicians; textile workers and designers; and writers and poets.
WHAT IS FUNDED Education; welfare; the arts; and health. Particularly Jewish causes.
TYPE OF GRANT Recurrent and one-off.
SAMPLE GRANTS £60,000 (in four grants) to Tel Aviv University – Porter Super Centre; £32,000 to Arava Institute – New Israel Fund; £20,000 to Israel Family Therapy Advancement Centre; £16,000 to British Friends of Israel Philharmonic Orchestra; £9,300 to Tel Aviv Foundation – IVAI; £6,000 to World Jewish Relief – Metuna; £5,200 to British Friends of Hebrew University; £5,000 each to International Scholarship Foundation and Open Air Theatre
FINANCES *Year* 1999–2000 *Grants* £188,000
TRUSTEES Dame Shirley Porter; Mrs Linda Streit; Peter Green; Steven Nigel Porter.
HOW TO APPLY In writing to the correspondent.
WHO TO APPLY TO Mrs Sarah Hunt, Seymour Pierce Advisory Limited, 79 Mount Street, London W1Y 5HJ *Tel* 020 7616 4700
CC NO 267173   **ESTABLISHED** 1974

■ The Margaret Foundation

WHERE FUNDING CAN BE GIVEN UK.
WHO CAN BENEFIT Organisations benefiting medical research, older people, children who are disadvantaged, and welfare generally.
SAMPLE GRANTS Allergy Induced Autism, Children National Medical Research Fund, Cystic Fibrosis Trust, NSPCC, and The Rainbow Centre.
FINANCES *Year* 2000–01 *Income* £22,109 *Grants* £22,000
TRUSTEES Royal Bank of Canada Trust Corporation Limited.
HOW TO APPLY In writing to the correspondent.
WHO TO APPLY TO Miss Anita Carter, Royal Bank of Canada Trust Corporation Limited, 71 Queen Victoria Street, London EC4V 4DE *Tel* 020 7653 4756 *Fax* 020 7329 3484 *E-mail* anita.carter@rbc.com
CC NO 1001583   **ESTABLISHED** 1990

■ The Stella and Alexander Margulies Charitable Trust

WHERE FUNDING CAN BE GIVEN UK.
WHO CAN BENEFIT Institutions benefiting Jews.
WHAT IS FUNDED Jewish charities; general charitable purposes.
RANGE OF GRANTS Generally £100–£3,000.
SAMPLE GRANTS £90,000 to UJIA for Alma and other projects; £20,000 to Royal Opera House Trust for the development appeal; £3,064 to Central Synagogue; £2,500 to British Red Cross; £2,000 each to British Friends of Y Meharash Engel Radomishl, Community Security Trust, and Nightingale House; £1,750 to Heal the World Foundation; £1,500 to Prince's Trust; £1,000 to Royal Albert Hall Trust.
FINANCES *Year* 2000–01 *Income* £332,862 *Grants* £131,824 *Assets* £6,325,025
TRUSTEES Marcus J Margulies; Martin D Paisner; Sir Stuart Lipton.
HOW TO APPLY In writing to the correspondent.
WHO TO APPLY TO M J Margulies, Trustee, 23 Grosvenor Street, London W1K 4QL *Tel* 020 7416 4160
CC NO 220441   **ESTABLISHED** 1970

■ Market Harborough and The Bowdens Charity

WHERE FUNDING CAN BE GIVEN The parishes of Market Harborough, Great Bowden and Little Bowden.
WHO CAN BENEFIT Organisations and individuals.
WHAT IS FUNDED The trust supports a wide range of large and small projects, giving towards the improvement of the environment, the arts, healthcare, heritage and relief-in-need.
WHAT IS NOT FUNDED No grants towards sporting projects or to replace statutory funding.
SAMPLE GRANTS St Luke's Hospital Palliative Care Unit, Market Harborough Union Wharf, Market Harborough Parish Church for clock repairs, Great Bowden Parish Church for general repairs, Life Education Centre for facilities at local schools, Harborough in Bloom project, Market Harborough Theatre, Millennium Mile project, Market Harborough Shopmobility Scheme and Market Harborough Cricket Club for enhanced coaching facilities.
FINANCES *Year* 1999 *Income* £285,000 *Grants* £225,000 *Assets* £10,000,000
TRUSTEES T Banks; Dr A Bowles; R Burden; R J Clarke; J C Clare; Mrs A V Dowley; T W Duckham; Mrs J Hefford; B R Johnson; Mrs S King; D Kemp; B Marshall; O de Rousset-Hall; G Stamp; M Stamp; F Trotter; I Wells; Mrs J A Williams.
OTHER INFORMATION The trust works in informal administrative partnerships with organisations and other funding bodies to pursue schemes in line with its main areas of work.
HOW TO APPLY On a form available from the correspondent. Potential applicants are welcome to contact the correspondent directly for further guidance.
WHO TO APPLY TO J G Jacobs, Steward, 149 St Mary's Road, Market Harborough, Leicestershire LE16 7DZ *Tel* 01858 462467 *Fax* 01858 431898 *E-mail* mhbc@godfrey-payton.co.uk or enquiries@godfrey-payton.co.uk
CC NO 1041958   **ESTABLISHED** 1994

■ The Hilda & Samuel Marks Foundation

WHERE FUNDING CAN BE GIVEN UK and Israel.

WHO CAN BENEFIT Voluntary organisations and charitable groups benefiting Jewish people of all ages. Support is given to those helped by the Jewish Blind Society.

WHAT IS FUNDED General charitable purposes; the relief and assistance of poor and needy persons; education; advancement of Judaism and assistance to synagogues and Jewish bodies; community facilities and services; health. Otherwise the trust fund shall be held upon trust for the Jewish Blind Society.

WHAT IS NOT FUNDED No grants to individuals.

TYPE OF GRANT Buildings and other capital; core costs; project; start-up costs.

FINANCES *Year* 2000–01 *Income* £383,000 *Grants* £172,000 *Assets* £2,600,000

TRUSTEES S Marks; Mrs H Marks; D L Marks; Mrs R D Selby.

HOW TO APPLY In writing to the correspondent. However, the trust primarily supports projects known to the trustees and its funds are fully committed.

WHO TO APPLY TO D L Marks, Trustee, 1 Ambassador Place, Stockport Road, Altrincham, Cheshire WA15 8DB *Tel* 0161 941 3183 *Fax* 0161 927 7437 *E-mail* davidmarks@mutleyproperties.co.uk

CC NO 245208   **ESTABLISHED** 1965

■ Michael Marks Charitable Trust

WHERE FUNDING CAN BE GIVEN UK and overseas.

WHO CAN BENEFIT Registered charities.

WHAT IS FUNDED Conservation, environment and the arts.

WHAT IS NOT FUNDED Grants are given to registered charities only. No grant to individuals or profit organisations.

RANGE OF GRANTS Generally £150–£25,000.

SAMPLE GRANTS £50,000 to Walton-on-Thames Community Arts Trust; £35,900 to British Museum; £27,000 to Christchurch College – Oxford; £24,750 to Arc Dance Company; £24,551 to Victoria and Albert Museum; £20,000 each to British Institute of Florence, British School at Rome, Mauritshuis, and Vivat Trust; £15,000 to Early English Organ Project.

FINANCES *Year* 2000–01 *Income* £176,580 *Grants* £370,542 *Assets* £3,511,472

TRUSTEES Martina, Lady Marks; Prof. Sir Christopher White; Dr D MacDiarmid.

HOW TO APPLY In writing to the correspondent before July. Applications should include audited accounts, information on other bodies approached and details of funding obtained. Requests will not receive a response unless they have been successful.

WHO TO APPLY TO The Secretary, 5 Elm Tree Road, London NW8 9JY *Tel* 020 7286 4633 *Fax* 020 7289 2173

CC NO 248136   **ESTABLISHED** 1966

■ The Erich Markus Charitable Foundation

WHERE FUNDING CAN BE GIVEN UK.

WHO CAN BENEFIT Registered charities and institutions benefiting at risk groups and people who are disadvantaged by poverty or socially isolated.

WHAT IS FUNDED The trustees are primarily interested in social welfare causes.

WHAT IS NOT FUNDED No grants to individuals.

RANGE OF GRANTS £250–£14,750.

SAMPLE GRANTS £14,750 to Magen David Adom; £5,250 to World Jewish Relief; £4,750 to St Francis Hospice; £4,500 to St Christopher's Hospice; £4,000 each to Chai Lifeline Cancer Care, In Kind Direct, Jewish Blind & Disabled, Jewish Care, Kisharon, Lady Hoare Trust, Nightingale House, Norwood Ravenswood, RABI, Samaritans, Spanish & Portuguese Jews Home for the Aged and Trinity Hospice.

FINANCES *Year* 2001 *Income* £100,000 *Grants* £138,000

TRUSTEES Erich Markus Charity Trustees Ltd.

HOW TO APPLY In writing to the correspondent. Applications will only be considered if accompanied by a copy of the latest report and accounts. Trustees meet twice a year, usually in April and October. No telephone enquiries please.

WHO TO APPLY TO Payne Hicks Beach, 10 New Square, Lincoln's Inn, London WC2A 3QG

CC NO 283128   **ESTABLISHED** 1981

■ Marr-Munning Trust

WHERE FUNDING CAN BE GIVEN Worldwide, mainly developing world.

WHO CAN BENEFIT Organisations benefiting refugees, people disadvantaged by poverty, and victims of famine, war and man-made or natural disasters.

WHAT IS FUNDED Overseas aid projects, particularly those likely to improve economic and educational work. Provision of water supplies and general medical care. Refugee works and language schools are also supported.

WHAT IS NOT FUNDED No grants to individuals.

TYPE OF GRANT Recurrent and one-off.

SAMPLE GRANTS Beneficiaries have previously included Health Unlimited, Sense, Sound Seekers, UNICEF – North Korea, Marr-Munning Ashram, Impact India, Cambodia Trust and Save the Children – Vietnam.

FINANCES *Year* 1999–2000 *Income* £291,756 *Grants* £59,145 *Assets* £2,772,768

TRUSTEES W Macfarlane; Mary Herbert; J O'Brien; C A Alam; Margaret Lorde; Richard Tomlinson.

HOW TO APPLY In writing to the correspondent.

WHO TO APPLY TO D Gleeson, 9 Madeley Road, Ealing, London W5 2LA

CC NO 261786   **ESTABLISHED** 1970

■ The Marsh Christian Trust

WHERE FUNDING CAN BE GIVEN UK.

WHO CAN BENEFIT Registered charities only.

WHAT IS FUNDED General charitable purposes; housing advice and information; holiday accommodation; sheltered accommodation; arts, culture and recreation; schools and colleges; education and training; day centres; emergency care; community holidays and outings; family planning clinics; support and self-help groups; well woman clinics; Christian education; missionaries and evangelicals; Quakerism; conservation of flora and fauna, historic buildings, nature reserves and woodlands; animal facilities and services; environmental and animal sciences; conservation and campaigning.

WHAT IS NOT FUNDED No grants can be made to individuals or for sponsorships. No start-up grants. No support for building funds, ordinary schools, colleges, universities or hospitals, or research.

TYPE OF GRANT Annual; more than three years.

RANGE OF GRANTS £250–£5,000.

FINANCES *Year* 2000–01 *Income* £167,527 *Grants* £122,990 *Assets* £4,335,183

TRUSTEES B P Marsh; R J C Marsh; N C S Marsh.

HOW TO APPLY In writing to the correspondent, including a copy of the most recent accounts. The trustees currently receive about 8,000 applications every year, of which 7,800 are new. Decisions are made at monthly trustee meetings.

WHO TO APPLY TO Lorraine McMorrow, Administrator, Granville House, 132–135 Sloane Street, London SW1X 9AX *Tel* 020 7730 2626 *Fax* 020 7823 5225

CC NO 284470   **ESTABLISHED** 1981

■ The Michael Marsh Charitable Trust

WHERE FUNDING CAN BE GIVEN Birmingham, Staffordshire, Worcestershire, Warwickshire, Coventry, Wolverhampton and associated towns in the Black Country.

WHO CAN BENEFIT Organisations benefiting childen and young people, people who are elderly, at risk groups and people who are disabled, disadvantaged by poverty or socially isolated.

WHAT IS FUNDED Health and welfare charities, community-based organisations, education and training and religious activities.

WHAT IS NOT FUNDED No grants towards animals, medical research, disaster relief or entertainment charities. Grants to individuals are only given through charitable institutions on their behalf.

TYPE OF GRANT Largely recurrent.

RANGE OF GRANTS £300–£6,500.

SAMPLE GRANTS £6,500 to East Birmingham Family Service Unit; £5,000 to Birmingham Settlement; £3,000 to St Anne's Hostel; £2,500 each to Jobs Close Residential Home for the Elderly, Sunfield Family Research Centre and Reach; £2,250 to Saltley Neighbourhood Pensioners; £2,000 each to Children at Risk Project, Phoenix Sheltered Workshop, St Community Project, St Luke's Community Project and Bethel Chapel; £1,500 each to Sense and Youth at Risk; £1,000 each to Care and Repair Project, Carr-Gomm Society, Birmingham Foster Care Association, BREAK, Norman Land Association, Salvation Army and Wolverhampton Grammar School.

FINANCES *Year* 2000–01 *Income* £80,000 *Grants* £76,450 *Assets* £2,333,272

TRUSTEES G B G Hingley; P G Barker; L Nuttall.

HOW TO APPLY In writing to the correspondent. Trustees meet in May and November, considering all applications received in the preceding six months. However, they will consider on an ad-hoc basis any applications which they consider should not be retained until their next scheduled meeting.

WHO TO APPLY TO Tony Evans, Clerk to the Trust, c/o Messrs Wragge & Co., 55 Colmore Row, Birmingham B3 2AS *Tel* 0121 233 1000 *Fax* 0121 214 1099

CC NO 220473   **ESTABLISHED** 1958

■ The Charlotte Marshall Charitable Trust

WHERE FUNDING CAN BE GIVEN UK.

WHO CAN BENEFIT Registered charities, institutions benefiting Roman Catholics, children, young adults and students.

WHAT IS FUNDED Educational and religious objects for Roman Catholics.

WHAT IS NOT FUNDED No grants are given to individuals.

RANGE OF GRANTS £200–£15,000.

SAMPLE GRANTS £15,000 to St Mary Magdalenes Church; £11,260 to St Michael's Hospice; £10,000 to Cardinal Hume Centre; £9,000 each to St Augustine of Canterbury Roman Catholic School and St Gregory Youth Project; £6,450 to Depaul Trust; £5,600 to St Mary Star of the Sea; £5,000 each to Festival of Hope 2001, St Patricks Missionary Society, and Shaftesbury Society.

FINANCES *Year* 2000–01 *Income* £164,175 *Grants* £141,000 *Assets* £750,691

TRUSTEES Miss C C Cirket; T P Cirkett; K B Page; J M Russell.

HOW TO APPLY On a form available from the correspondent. Completed forms must be returned by 31 December for consideration in March.

WHO TO APPLY TO S Roy, c/o C & C Marshall Limited, 55–65 Castleham Road, Castleham Industrial Estate, Hastings, East Sussex TN38 9NU *Tel* 01424 856020

CC NO 211941   **ESTABLISHED** 1962

■ The D G Marshall of Cambridge Trust

WHERE FUNDING CAN BE GIVEN Predominantly Cambridge and Cambridgeshire.

WHO CAN BENEFIT Community projects, local appeals and local charities benefiting disabled people and people disadvantaged by poverty.

WHAT IS FUNDED Charitable causes in and around Cambridge. Priorities are primary and secondary schools, tertiary and higher education and hospices. Arts, culture and recreation and community facilities and services are considered.

WHAT IS NOT FUNDED Unsolicited applications are not supported.

RANGE OF GRANTS £100–£10,000, usually less than £1,000.

SAMPLE GRANTS £10,000 to RAF Benevolent Fund Enterprises; £5,000 each to Ely Cathedral Restoration Fund, Magdalene College for theBernard Rose Appeal and Air League; £3,500 to Cambridge University Science in Schools; £1,000 to Horningsea Village Hall; £500 each to Cambridge Gilding Club, Cambridge Samaritans and Cambridge University Athletics Club; £300 each to Cambridge Talking News and Cambridge Society for the Blind.

FINANCES *Year* 1999–2000 *Income* £73,000 *Grants* £71,000 *Assets* £1,500,000

TRUSTEES M J Marshall; J D Barker; W C M Dastur.

HOW TO APPLY The trust has stated that it does not respond to unsolicited applications.

WHO TO APPLY TO J D Barker, Secretary, Airport House, The Airport, Newmarket Road, Cambridgeshire CB5 8RY *Tel* 01223 373737 *Fax* 01223 373562

CC NO 286468   **ESTABLISHED** 1982

■ The Jim Marshall Charitable Trust

WHERE FUNDING CAN BE GIVEN UK.

WHO CAN BENEFIT Charitable organisations.

WHAT IS FUNDED General charitable purposes, mainly for the benefit of children, young people, families and people who are disabled or sick.

FINANCES *Year* 2000 *Income* £228,401 *Grants* £284,698 *Assets* £115,288

TRUSTEES J Marshall; K W J Saunders; B Charlton; S B Marshall; L Hack.

HOW TO APPLY In writing to the correspondent at any time.

WHO TO APPLY TO Mr Graham, Simpson Wreford and Co, 62 Beresford Street, London SE18 6BG *Tel* 020 8854 9552

CC NO 328118   **ESTABLISHED** 1989

■ Marshall's Charity

WHERE FUNDING CAN BE GIVEN England and Wales.

WHO CAN BENEFIT Clergy.

WHAT IS FUNDED Improvement work to parsonages in England and Wales, repairs to existing churches in Kent, Surrey and Lincolnshire.

WHAT IS NOT FUNDED No grants to churches outside the counties of Kent, Surrey and Lincolnshire, as defined in 1855.

TYPE OF GRANT Building and other capital works; interest-free loans.

RANGE OF GRANTS Up to £20,000.

FINANCES *Year* 2001 *Grants* £717,000

TRUSTEES D M Lang; Mrs A. Nicholson; and others.

HOW TO APPLY To the correspondent in writing. Trustees meet in January, April, July and October. Applications need to be sent by the end of January, April, July and October for consideration at the next meeting.

WHO TO APPLY TO R Goatcher, Clerk to the Trustees, Marshall House, 66 Newcomen Street, London SE1 1YT *Tel* 020 7407 2979 *Fax* 020 7403 3969 *E-mail* richard@marshalls.org.uk

CC NO 206780   **ESTABLISHED** 1627

■ The Martin Charitable Trust

WHERE FUNDING CAN BE GIVEN Scotland, particularly Glasgow and the west of Scotland.

WHO CAN BENEFIT Charitable organisations.

WHAT IS FUNDED General charitable purposes.

WHAT IS NOT FUNDED No grants to individuals.

FINANCES *Year* 2000 *Income* £69,000 *Grants* £75,000

TRUSTEES A C Fyfe; N A Fyfe; G H W Waddell.

HOW TO APPLY In writing to the correspondent, including up-to-date accounts.

WHO TO APPLY TO Norman A Fyfe, Trustee, c/o Miller Beckett & Jackson, 190 St Vincent Street, Glasgow G2 5SP *Tel* 0141 204 2833 *Fax* 0141 248 7185

SC NO SC028487

■ Sir George Martin Trust

WHERE FUNDING CAN BE GIVEN Largely north and west Yorkshire and occasionally in Cumbria.

WHO CAN BENEFIT Organisations benefiting children, young adults and older people; dance and ballet; music; theatre; opera companies; schools and colleges; education and training; community facilities and services; religious buildings; conservation.

WHAT IS FUNDED Education, social welfare, general charitable purposes, especially in Yorkshire. The trust assists a very wide range of charitable causes with a number of awards to schools and groups working with young people. Emphasis is placed on projects located in north and west Yorkshire and occasionally in Cumbria.

WHAT IS NOT FUNDED Full guidelines detailing what is and is not funded by the trust is available from the correspondent.

TYPE OF GRANT Grants for capital rather than revenue projects; reluctant to support general running costs. Grants are not repeated to any charity in any one year; the maximum number of consecutive grants is three, though a one-off approach to grant applications is preferred. Average donation is just over £1,230.

SAMPLE GRANTS £28,000 to St Gemma's Hospice – Leeds towards a refurbishing scheme; £25,000 to Woodhouse Grove School for capital developments of the school; £20,000 to RABI to assist farmers in severe distress in the Yorkshire Area; £12,500 to Leeds Grammar School to assist with a language laboratory; £10,150 to Dales Recovery Appeal via the Craven Trust; £10,000 to the Square Chapel Appeal – Halifax to help with their refurbishing scheme; £7,500 to Captain Cook Museum – Whitby towards their development scheme; £5,000 each to the Georgian Theatre Royal – Richmond towards development costs and the Roses Charitable Trust to help with ongoing activities of Hebridean Pursuits in Oban; £4,500 to Harrogate Festival.

FINANCES *Year* 2001–02 *Income* £170,543 *Grants* £258,143 *Assets* £5,423,234

TRUSTEES T D Coates, Chair; M Bethel; R F D Marshall; P D Taylor; Miss Janet Martin.

HOW TO APPLY The trust meets in March, July and December each year to consider applications. These should be made in writing to the secretary in good time for the meetings, which take place in the middle of the month. Applications that are not within the guidelines cannot be answered due to substantial increase in costs. Applications that are relevant will be acknowledged and, following meetings, successful applicants will be told of the grants they are to receive. Unsuccessful applicants will not be informed.

WHO TO APPLY TO Peter Marshall, Secretary, Netherwood House, Ilkley, West Yorkshire LS29 9RP *Tel* 01943 831019 *Fax* 01943 831570 *E-mail* sirgeorgemartintrust@care4free.net

CC NO 223554   **ESTABLISHED** 1956

■ John Martin's Charity

WHERE FUNDING CAN BE GIVEN The town of Evesham only.

WHO CAN BENEFIT Individuals and charitable or voluntary organisations benefiting the residents of Evesham.

WHAT IS FUNDED Grants are made to every state school in Evesham, and to students at schools, colleges and universities. Help is given to charitable and voluntary organisations and needy individuals. Grants are given to further religious and educational work and maintain church buildings in the parishes of Hampton, Bengeworth and Evesham; also to contribute towards the costs of the vicars in the parishes of Hampton and Bengeworth and to provide special benefits to Hampton Parochial First School. Grants may be made for music, visual arts, community arts and recreation, community facilities and services, support to voluntary organisations and volunteers, advocacy, advice and information, health care, some health facilities and buildings, and animal welfare.

WHAT IS NOT FUNDED No grants for the payment of rates or taxes.

TYPE OF GRANT One-off, buildings, capital, core costs, start-up costs and running costs funded for one year or less. No loans are made.

RANGE OF GRANTS Individuals £5–£1,500; organisations £50–£50,000.

SAMPLE GRANTS In 2000–01: £12,000 to St Richard's Hospice; £6,000 to Riverside Shop Mobility; £5,200 to ExtraCare; £5,000 to MIND.

FINANCES *Year* 2001–02 *Income* £728,110 *Grants* £622,364 *Assets* £17,130,702

TRUSTEES N J Lamb, Chair; J K Icke, Vice Chair; Revd J Bomyer; Revd B Collins; Mrs M Stephenson; A W Bennett; Mrs J Turner; G Robbins; Revd R Armitage; J H Smith; R G Gould; C Scorse; R G Emson; Mrs D Raphael.

HOW TO APPLY On a form available from the correspondent on written request. Initial telephone calls are welcomed. The trustees normally meet on the second and fourth Thursday in each month, with one meeting in June and December. The charity can make urgent grants in exceptional circumstances. Applicants for education grants should supply an sae and may obtain details of deadlines from the charity.

WHO TO APPLY TO Phil Woodcock, Clerk, 16 Queen's Road, Evesham, Worcestershire WR11 4JP *Tel* 01386 765440 *Fax* 01386 765340 *E-mail* enquiries@johnmartins.org.uk *Website* www.johnmartins.org

CC NO 527473   **ESTABLISHED** 1714

■ Mervyn Martin Charitable Trust

WHERE FUNDING CAN BE GIVEN UK and overseas.

WHO CAN BENEFIT Institutions.

WHAT IS FUNDED General charitable purposes.

TYPE OF GRANT One-off grants.

RANGE OF GRANTS Up to £3,000.

SAMPLE GRANTS £35,000 to Aid to the Church in Need; £2,000 each to Alzheimer's Disease Society, British Red Cross, The Healing Research Trust, The Mental Health Foundation and Salvation Army; £1,000 to Ethiopiaid.

FINANCES *Year* 1999–2000 *Income* £25,000 *Grants* £16,000

TRUSTEES M H A Martin; A M Martin.

HOW TO APPLY In writing to the correspondent.

WHO TO APPLY TO N J Barker, Trustees' Solicitor, Dawson & Co., 2 New Square, Lincoln's Inn, London WC2A 3RZ *Tel* 020 7421 4800

CC NO 327682   **ESTABLISHED** 1987

■ The Mason Porter Charitable Trust

WHERE FUNDING CAN BE GIVEN UK.

WHO CAN BENEFIT Grants are made only to charities known to the settlor.

WHAT IS FUNDED General charitable purposes, particularly Christian causes.

SAMPLE GRANTS £66,000 to Personal Service Society; £14,000 to Abernethy Trust; £13,000 to Cliff College; £11,000 to New Creations; £6,000 to Just Care; £4,000 to Worldwide Christian Outreach; £2,500 to Philo Trust; £1,500 each to International Youth Exchange of Methodist Church, Life Changing Ministries, Liverpool Hope University, St Luke's Methodist Church in Hoylake and the University of Lincolnshire and Humberside.

FINANCES *Year* 2000–01 *Income* £101,000 *Grants* £140,000 *Assets* £1,800,000

TRUSTEES Liverpool Council of Social Services (Inc.).

HOW TO APPLY The trust states that it only makes grants to charities known to the settlor and unsolicited applications are not considered.

WHO TO APPLY TO The Secretary, Liverpool Council of Social Service (Inc.), 14 Castle Street, Liverpool L2 0NJ *Tel* 0151 236 7728

CC NO 255545   **ESTABLISHED** 1968

■ Masonic Trust for Girls and Boys

WHERE FUNDING CAN BE GIVEN UK.

WHO CAN BENEFIT Charities and individual children of Freemasons.

WHAT IS FUNDED This trust predominantly makes grants to individual children of Freemasons who are in need. However grants are also made to UK organisations working with children and young people; it also supports bursaries at cathedrals and collegiate chapels.

SAMPLE GRANTS £100,000 to Caldecott Foundation; £25,000 to Fountaindale Trust Communication Project; £23,000 to Dame Hannah Rogers School; £20,050 to Royal Wolverhampton School; £10,000 to Gordon's School; £7,500 each to Blue Cross and Brainwave Trust; £5,050 to Reed's School; £5,000 each to Girls Guild of Good Life, Nigel Clare Network Trust and Winston's Wish.

FINANCES *Year* 2000 *Income* £8,534,000 *Grants* £352,041 *Assets* £153,260,000

TRUSTEES Col G S H Dicker; Rt Hon. the Lord Swansea; M B Jones; P A Marsh.

OTHER INFORMATION The grant total shown in this entry only refers to the funds distributed to non-Masonic charities.

The trust marked the millennium with 'Lifelites', a special commitment of £7.5 million for children's hospices throughout England and Wales. Half of this was to pay for IT equipment, the other half was set aside to fund future upgrading of the systems.

HOW TO APPLY In writing to the correspondent.

WHO TO APPLY TO Lt Col J C Chambers, Secretary, 31 Great Queen Street, London WC2B 5AG *Tel* 020 7405 2644 *Fax* 020 7831 4094 *Website* www.mtgb.org

CC NO 285836   **ESTABLISHED** 1982

■ The Nancie Massey Charitable Trust

WHERE FUNDING CAN BE GIVEN Scotland, particularly Edinburgh and Leith.

WHO CAN BENEFIT Charitable groups only.

WHAT IS FUNDED Income split between five areas: young people; elderly people; education; the arts; and medical research.

WHAT IS NOT FUNDED Grants are not given to individuals.

RANGE OF GRANTS £500–£2,000, but can be larger.

SAMPLE GRANTS £25,000 to Donaldson's Trust; £11,550 to Royal Zoological Society of Scotland; £5,000 each to Edinburgh Community Trust, Edinburgh and Lothian Council on Alcohol, L'Arche, and Scottish Opera; £4,000 to Scotland Yard Adventure Centre.

FINANCES *Year* 2000–01 *Income* £179,134 *Grants* £135,400 *Assets* £4,617,103

TRUSTEES J G Morton; M F Sinclair; Ann Trotman.

OTHER INFORMATION There was also £14,000 in provision for future grants: £10,000 to

Edinburgh and Lothian Council on Alcohol; £4,000 to Edinburgh Headway Group.

HOW TO APPLY Write to the correspondent requesting an application form. Trustees meet three times a year in February, June and October. Applications need to be received by January, May or September.

WHO TO APPLY TO J G Morton, Trustee, 61 Dublin Street, Edinburgh EH3 6NL *Tel* 0131 558 5800 *Fax* 0131 558 5899

SC NO SC008977 **ESTABLISHED** 1989

■ The Leonard Matchan Fund Ltd

WHERE FUNDING CAN BE GIVEN UK.
WHO CAN BENEFIT Registered charities.
WHAT IS FUNDED General charitable purposes.
WHAT IS NOT FUNDED No grants to individuals.
SAMPLE GRANTS £5,000 to Exmoor Calvert Trust; £3,000 each to Alzheimer's Disease Society, Attlee Foundation, Children's Society, Helen House, Roy Kinnear Charitable Trust, Relate, Weston Spirit, Willow Trust, and YMCA Croydon.
FINANCES *Year* 1998–99 *Income* £60,000 *Grants* £53,000 *Assets* £767,000
TRUSTEES Ms B A Thompson; Ms S D Groves; Ms J E M Sutherland; K H Thompson; P A Rosenthal.
HOW TO APPLY In writing to the correspondent.
WHO TO APPLY TO Ms Jeanne Sutherland, 5 Connaught Way, Huntington, York YO32 9QX
CC NO 257682 **ESTABLISHED** 1968

■ The Mathew Trust

WHERE FUNDING CAN BE GIVEN Dundee and district.
WHO CAN BENEFIT Charities benefiting young adults and older people.
WHAT IS FUNDED The advancement of education of adults; advancement of vocational and professional training; relief of poverty by providing assistance in the recruitment of people who are unemployed, or who are likely to become unemployed in the near future.
TYPE OF GRANT Salaries for up to one year.
SAMPLE GRANTS £75,000 (£50,000 capital, £25,000 revenue grant) to Dundee Repertory Theatre; £25,000 to NineWells Cancer Campaign; £20,000 to Dundee College 'The Space' Theatre Project; £15,000 to Dundee Heritage Trust; £13,000 to Dundee Science Centre.
FINANCES *Year* 1999–2000 *Income* £197,000 *Grants* £243,000 *Assets* £6,900,000
TRUSTEES D B Grant, Chair; G S Lowden; A F McDonald.
HOW TO APPLY Contact the correspondent at the address given.
WHO TO APPLY TO Fiona Bullions, Henderson Logie, Royal Exchange, Panmure Street, Dundee DD1 1DZ *Tel* 01382 201234
SC NO SC016284 **ESTABLISHED** 1935

■ Matliwala Family Charitable Trust

WHERE FUNDING CAN BE GIVEN UK and overseas, especially Bharuch – India.
WHAT IS FUNDED The advancement of education for pupils at Matliwala School Of Baruch in Gujerat – India, and other schools, including assisting with the provision of equipment and facilities; advancement of the Islamic religion; relief of sickness and poverty; advancement of education.

SAMPLE GRANTS £14,050 to Jamia Faizanul Quran; £5,000 each to Bharuch Muslim Medical and Welfare Trust, and Munshi (Manubarwaia) Educational Trust; £3,360 to Dar-ul-aloom Jamia Habibia; £2,500 each to Islamic Research Institute of Great Britain and Preston Muslim Girl's School.
FINANCES *Year* 2001–02 *Income* £279,323 *Grants* £114,238 *Assets* £1,713,087
TRUSTEES Ayub Vali Bux; Usman Salya; Abdul Aziz Vali Patel; Yousuf Bux; Ibrahim Vali Patel.
HOW TO APPLY In writing to the correspondent.
WHO TO APPLY TO A V Bux, Trustee, 9 Brookview, Fulwood, Preston PR2 8FG *Tel* 01772 706501
CC NO 1012756 **ESTABLISHED** 1992

■ The Violet Mauray Charitable Trust

WHERE FUNDING CAN BE GIVEN UK and overseas.
WHO CAN BENEFIT Registered charities.
WHAT IS FUNDED General charitable purposes, particularly medical charities and Jewish organisations.
WHAT IS NOT FUNDED No grants to individuals.
RANGE OF GRANTS Usually £50–£1,500.
SAMPLE GRANTS Regular beneficiaries include Jewish Care, Meningitis Research Foundation, Royal National Institute for the Deaf, Joint Jewish Charitable Trust, JAMI, Jewish Child's Day, Susy Lamplugh Trust, World Jewish Relief, Extra Care Charitable Trust.
FINANCES *Year* 2001–02 *Income* £40,157 *Grants* £20,000
TRUSTEES Mrs J Stephany; Mrs A Karlin; J D Stephany; R K Stephany.
HOW TO APPLY In writing to the correspondent.
WHO TO APPLY TO Mrs J Stephany, Trustee, c/o Febeson and Arbeid, 3 Albemarle Street, London W1S 4AU *Tel* 020 7499 7558
CC NO 1001716 **ESTABLISHED** 1990

■ The Maxwell Family Foundation

WHERE FUNDING CAN BE GIVEN UK.
WHO CAN BENEFIT Registered charities in the fields of health, medical research, and the relief of people who are elderly, disabled or sick.
WHAT IS FUNDED An established list of charities is supported.
WHAT IS NOT FUNDED The trust states explicitly that there is no support for unsolicited applications. It clearly abides by this policy and we would urge readers who do not know the trustees personally not to write to the trust.
SAMPLE GRANTS £22,116 to Home Farm Trust, £7,800 to Royal International Air Tatoo Flying Scholarships for the Disabled; £3,500 to Deafblind UK; £1,500 to Newcastle Society for Blind People; £1,000 each to and Mental Health Foundation, MRI Scanner Appeal – Southmead Hospital and Multiple Sclerosis Nerve Centre Appeal.
FINANCES *Year* 2000–01 *Income* £126,345 *Grants* £46,226 *Assets* £2,219,450
TRUSTEES E M Maxwell; P M Maxwell; R P Spicer.
HOW TO APPLY Applications are neither sought nor acknowledged. There appears little purpose in applying to this trust as no application will be supported unless accompanied by a personal request from someone known by the trustees.
WHO TO APPLY TO E M Maxwell, Trustee, 181 Whiteladies Road, Clifton, Bristol BS8 2RY
CC NO 291124 **ESTABLISHED** 1965

■ The Pamela and Jack Maxwell Foundation

WHERE FUNDING CAN BE GIVEN UK.

WHO CAN BENEFIT Registered charities, Jewish organisations.

WHAT IS FUNDED General charitable purposes.

WHAT IS NOT FUNDED No grants to individuals or for expeditions.

RANGE OF GRANTS Up to £5,000.

SAMPLE GRANTS £5,000 each to Commonwealth Jewish Trust and Education Holocaust Trust; £2,000 each to London Symphony Trust and Royal Academy Trust; £1,500 to MDA UK.

FINANCES *Year* 2000–01 *Income* £13,259 *Grants* £23,000

TRUSTEES Mrs P H Maxwell; Jack Maxwell.

HOW TO APPLY In writing to the correspondent. Only successful applicants will be replied to.

WHO TO APPLY TO Andrew Tappin, 18 East Sheen Avenue, London SW14 8AS *Tel* 020 8287 8825 *Fax* 020 8287 8747 *E-mail* andrew.tappin@ukgateway.net

CC NO 209618   **ESTABLISHED** 1957

■ Evelyn May Trust

WHERE FUNDING CAN BE GIVEN Worldwide.

WHO CAN BENEFIT Registered charities, mainly headquarters organisations, especially those benefiting elderly people, children, medical professionals, research workers, and people disadvantaged by sickness and poverty.

WHAT IS FUNDED Currently the main areas of interest are elderly people, children, medical projects and natural disaster relief, but support is given to a variety of registered charities.

WHAT IS NOT FUNDED No grants to individuals, including students, or to general appeals.

TYPE OF GRANT Often one-off for a specific project, but support for general purposes is also given.

SAMPLE GRANTS £8,000 to Tearfund for the relief of earthquake victims in India; £2,000 to Hearing Dogs for the Deaf; £1,000 each to REACT, Richard House Children's Hospice and Teen Talk drop-in centre for young people.

FINANCES *Year* 2001 *Income* £22,784 *Grants* £20,496 *Assets* £596,888

TRUSTEES Mrs E Tabersham; Ms K Gray; Mrs J Smyth.

HOW TO APPLY **This trust states that it does not respond to unsolicited applications.**

WHO TO APPLY TO Ms Kim Gray, c/o Jansons, 21–23 Kew Road , Richmond, Surrey TW9 2NQ *Tel* 020 8332 2310 *Fax* 020 8948 5629

CC NO 261038   **ESTABLISHED** 1970

■ Mayfair Charities Ltd

WHERE FUNDING CAN BE GIVEN UK and overseas.

WHO CAN BENEFIT Registered charities benefiting orthodox Jews, particularly children and young adults.

WHAT IS FUNDED Education, religion and medical welfare charities which support orthodox Judaism.

TYPE OF GRANT Capital and running costs.

RANGE OF GRANTS Typically £500–£2,500.

SAMPLE GRANTS £5,300,000 to Raphael Freshwater Memorial Association; £610,000 to Beth Jacob Grammar School.

FINANCES *Year* 2000–01 *Income* £4,200,000 *Grants* £9,331,000 *Assets* £31,000,000

TRUSTEES B S E Freshwater, Chair; D Davis.

HOW TO APPLY In writing to the correspondent.

WHO TO APPLY TO Mark Jenner, Secretary, Freshwater House, 158–162 Shaftesbury Avenue, London WC2H 8HR *Tel* 020 7836 1555 *E-mail* mark.jenner@highdorn.co.uk

CC NO 255281   **ESTABLISHED** 1968

■ The Mayfield Valley Arts Trust

WHERE FUNDING CAN BE GIVEN Unrestricted, but with a special interest in Sheffield and South Yorkshire.

WHO CAN BENEFIT Charities concerned with music and the promotion and presentation of musical events and activities.

WHAT IS FUNDED Support is concentrated on certain beneficiaries, with remaining funds to established chamber music venues.

WHAT IS NOT FUNDED No grants to students.

TYPE OF GRANT Up to three years for core costs.

RANGE OF GRANTS £2,000–£16,000, although more than one grant can be made to an organisation in each year.

SAMPLE GRANTS £44,500 to Sheffield Chamber Music in the Round for festivals and concert series; £27,500 to York Early Music Foundation for a festival; £18,000 to Live Music Now!; £10,000 to Wigmore Hall for concerts.

FINANCES *Year* 2000–01 *Income* £119,335 *Grants* £115,000 *Assets* £2,345,467

TRUSTEES A Thornton; J R Thornton; P M Thornton; D Whelton; D Brown; J R Rider.

HOW TO APPLY The trust states that no unsolicited applications are considered.

WHO TO APPLY TO J M Jelly, Administrator, Irwin Mitchell, St Peter's House, Hartshead, Sheffield S1 2EL *Tel* 0870 1500 100 *Fax* 0114 275 3306

CC NO 327665   **ESTABLISHED** 1988

■ Maypride Ltd

WHERE FUNDING CAN BE GIVEN UK.

WHO CAN BENEFIT Institutions benefiting Jewish people and people disadvantaged by poverty.

WHAT IS FUNDED The advancement of religion in accordance with the orthodox Jewish faith, relief of poverty and general charitable purposes.

RANGE OF GRANTS £100–£5,000.

SAMPLE GRANTS £5,000 to Society of Friends of the Torah; £2,000 each to Kollel Reb Yechiel and Yeshiva L'zeirim Tiferes Yaacor; £1,000 each to Collel Chibath Yerushalayim and Yeshiva Horomo; £300 each to Buyit Lepletot and ZSV Trust; £200 to Holmleigh Trust; £120 to Jewish Rescue and Relief Committee; £100 to Orthodox Council of Jerusalem.

FINANCES *Year* 1997–98 *Income* £87,956 *Grants* £12,020 *Assets* £211,738

TRUSTEES A Sternlicht; Mrs E Sternlicht.

HOW TO APPLY In writing to the correspondent.

WHO TO APPLY TO The Trustees, Martin & Heller, 5 North End Road, London NW11 7RJ *Tel* 020 8455 6789

CC NO 289394   **ESTABLISHED** 1984

■ The James Frederick & Ethel Anne Measures Charity

WHERE FUNDING CAN BE GIVEN The West Midlands.

WHO CAN BENEFIT All categories within the West Midlands area.

WHAT IS FUNDED General charitable purposes. Applicants must usually originate in the West Midlands and show evidence of self-help in their application. Trustees have a preference for disadvantaged people.

WHAT IS NOT FUNDED Trustees will not consider funding students who have a full local authority grant and want finance for a different course of study. Applications by individuals in cases of hardship will not usually be considered unless sponsored by a local authority, health professional or other welfare agency.

TYPE OF GRANT Recurrent grants are occasionally considered. The trustees favour grants towards the cost of equipment.

RANGE OF GRANTS £100–£1,600.

SAMPLE GRANTS £25,000 to Nepal Fellowship; £8,000 to Snitterfield Tennis Club; £5,000 to Electronic Aids for the Blind; £2,800 (in three grants) to Wolverhampton School; £750 to St Martin's in the Bullring; £500 each to Edwards Trust and Farms for City Children; £300 each to Brockmoore and District Community Association and Lapel Scout Group; £250 each to Heartland Harriers Football Club and TS Dolphin Sea Cadets; £200 each to Castle Bromwich Hall Gardens Trust, Warwickshire Association for the Blind and YMCA – Wolverhampton.

FINANCES *Year* 1999–2000 *Income* £58,000 *Grants* £74,000 *Assets* £1,300,000

TRUSTEES D J K Nichols; C H Lees; Dr I Durie-Kerr; R S Watkins; M P Green.

HOW TO APPLY In writing to the correspondent. No reply is sent to unsuccessful applicants unless an sae is enclosed. The trustees meet quarterly.

WHO TO APPLY TO Mrs S E Darby, 2nd Floor, 33 Great Charles Street, Birmingham B3 3JN

CC NO 266054   **ESTABLISHED** 1973

■ Charity of Mary Jane, Countess of Meath

WHERE FUNDING CAN BE GIVEN UK.

WHO CAN BENEFIT Organisations benefiting older people, and people who are disadvantaged by poverty, sick or infirm.

RANGE OF GRANTS £1,000–£2,000.

SAMPLE GRANTS £1,500 each to Age Concern, British Red Cross, NSPCC and Royal Commonwealth Society for the Blind; £1,000 each to St Andrews Society, Meath Homes and World Emergency Relief; £750 each included those to Friends of the Elderly, National Benevolent Fund, Passage Day Centre and Trinity Hospice.

FINANCES *Year* 1999–2000 *Income* £23,000 *Grants* £19,000 *Assets* £498,000

TRUSTEES Mrs C E Forrester; Mrs E M Poole.

HOW TO APPLY In writing to the correspondent. This entry was not confirmed by the trust, but the information was correct according to the trust's file at the Charity Commission.

WHO TO APPLY TO Mrs C E Forrester, Trustee, Copper Beeches, Sikeside, Kirlington, Carlisle, Cumbria CA6 6DR

CC NO 238101   **ESTABLISHED** 1919

■ Medical Research Council

WHERE FUNDING CAN BE GIVEN UK and overseas.

WHO CAN BENEFIT Organisations benefiting medical professionals, research workers and scientists.

WHAT IS FUNDED The endowment funds are used to supplement existing research carried out by the council. The trust's aims are to promote the development of medical and related biological

research and to advance knowledge that will lead to improved health care.

TYPE OF GRANT Medical research and fellowships.

FINANCES *Year* 2001–02 *Income* £419,096,000 *Grants* £146,010,000 *Assets* £272,745,000

TRUSTEES Sir Anthony Cleaver, Chair; Prof. Sir G K Radda; Dr E M Armstrong; Prof. J I Bell; Sir William Castell; Prof. R M Denton; Dr Peter Fellner; Prof. R Fitzpatrick; Derek Flint; Dr Ruth Hall; Prof. E Johnstone; Prof. Ian MacLennan; Prof. Alan North; Prof. Sir John Pattison; Prof. Genevra Richardson; Prof. Nancy Rothwell; Dr Chris Henshall.

OTHER INFORMATION The charity also gave research studentships, advanced course studentships and postdoctoral fellowships totalling £45,768,000.

HOW TO APPLY **This trust states that it does not respond to unsolicited applications.** Funds are only used to supplement existing activities.

WHO TO APPLY TO The Grants Department, 20 Park Crescent, London W1B 1AL *Tel* 020 7636 5422 *Fax* 020 7436 6179 *Website* www.mrc.ac.uk

CC NO 250696   **ESTABLISHED** 1920

■ The Medlock Charitable Trust

WHERE FUNDING CAN BE GIVEN Overwhelmingly the areas of Bath and Boston, Lincolnshire.

WHO CAN BENEFIT Small local projects and established organisations benefiting children, adults and young people.

WHAT IS FUNDED General charitable purposes, especially medicine, health, welfare and education. Also publishing and printing, support to volunteers, CVS and volunteer bureaux, and community services and facilities.

WHAT IS NOT FUNDED No grants to individuals or students.

TYPE OF GRANT One-off capital and research grants, and interest-free loans for up to three years.

SAMPLE GRANTS £109,000 to Boston Grammar School for the first stage of a bursary scheme for students who will go on to further education; £100,000 each to Bath University, Boston College towards a management centre and Boston Borough Council Sports Iniative; £50,000 each to All Saints Centre and Royal United Hospital; £30,000 each to Boston West Childcare Project, City Hospital NHS Trust and St Bartholomew; £25,000 to Kennet and Avon Canal Partnership.

FINANCES *Year* 2000–01 *Income* £1,300,000 *Grants* £1,142,000 *Assets* £22,500,000

TRUSTEES Leonard Medlock; Brenda Medlock; David Medlock; P H Carr.

HOW TO APPLY In writing to the correspondent.

WHO TO APPLY TO David Medlock, Trustee, St George's Lodge, 33 Oldfield Rd, Bath BA2 3NE *Tel* 01225 428221 *Fax* 01225 789262

CC NO 326927   **ESTABLISHED** 1985

■ The Anthony and Elizabeth Mellows Charitable Settlement

WHERE FUNDING CAN BE GIVEN UK.

WHO CAN BENEFIT UK bodies benefiting: children and young adults; actors and entertainment professionals; musicians; textile workers and designers; and writers and poets.

WHAT IS FUNDED The acquisition of objects to be used or displayed in houses of the National Trust or churches of the Church of England; the encouragement of hospices and medical research; support of the arts; the training and development of children and young people. The trustees can only consider projects recommended to them by those UK institutions with whom they are in close cooperation.

WHAT IS NOT FUNDED Applications from individuals, including students, are ineligible.

TYPE OF GRANT Generally single projects.

SAMPLE GRANTS £24,102 to Order of St John; £14,220 to Royal Opera House Trust; £1,490 to St John Ambulance; £1,350 to National Art Collections Fund; £1,080 to Arc Dance Company; £1,010 to National History Museum; £1,000 each to Great Hospital – Norwich and The Sixteen; £800 to Matlock PCC for the preservation of 18th century crances; £500 to King Edward VII Hospital for Officers

FINANCES *Year* 2001–02 *Income* £45,746 *Grants* £61,641 *Assets* £546,732

TRUSTEES Prof. Anthony R Mellows; Mrs Elizabeth Mellows.

HOW TO APPLY Applications are considered when received, but only from UK institutions. No application forms are used. Grants will be made three times a year when the trustees meet to consider applications.

WHO TO APPLY TO Prof. A R Mellows, Trustee, 22 Devereux Court, Temple Bar, London WC2R 3JR *Tel* 020 7353 6221

CC NO 281229   **ESTABLISHED** 1980

■ Melodor Ltd

WHERE FUNDING CAN BE GIVEN UK and overseas.

WHO CAN BENEFIT Organisations benefiting Jewish people.

WHAT IS FUNDED Jewish causes, particularly the advancement of religion in accordance with the orthodox Jewish faith.

RANGE OF GRANTS £100–£15,235.

SAMPLE GRANTS £15,235 to Chasdei Yoel; £10,400 to Beis Michas Yitchok; £7,930 to Yeshivas Ohel Shimon; £7,857 to Yeshiva of Nitra; £4,600 to Shaarei Torah; £3,185 to Belz – Manchester; £3,000 to Beth Yaakov Seminary – Manchester; £2,500 to Jewish High School for Girls; £2,220 to Beth Soroh Schemirer Seminary; £2,150 to Tzedoko Charity.

FINANCES *Year* 1999–2000 *Income* £148,883 *Grants* £82,256 *Assets* £764,112

TRUSTEES B Weiss; M Weiss; P Weiss; S Weiss; J L Weiss; H Weiss; R Sofer; F Neuman; H Neuman; M Neuman; E Neuman; M Friedlander; P Neumann; J Bleier; E Henry; R De Lange.

HOW TO APPLY In writing to the correspondent.

WHO TO APPLY TO The Trustees, 148 Bury Old Road, Manchester M7 4SE

CC NO 260972   **ESTABLISHED** 1970

■ Melow Charitable Trust

WHERE FUNDING CAN BE GIVEN UK and overseas.

WHO CAN BENEFIT Jewish charities.

RANGE OF GRANTS £1,200–£31,000.

SAMPLE GRANTS £31,000 to Shalom Torah Centre – USA; £30,000 to Yeshivas Chidushei Harim; £23,000 to United Talmudical Associates; £15,000 to Mosdos Toledos Aharon; £12,000 to Yeshiva Horomoh Talmudical College; £11,000 to Dushinsky Trust; £10,000 to Satmar Gemach; £8,000 each to Congregation Letev Lev and Rabbi Pinet Memorial Fund; £7,000 to Craven Walk Charitable Trust.

FINANCES *Year* 2000–01 *Income* £529,593 *Grants* £323,608 *Assets* £1,014,077

TRUSTEES M Spitz; E Weiser.

HOW TO APPLY In writing to the correspondent.

WHO TO APPLY TO J Low, 21 Warwick Grove, London E5 9HX *Tel* 020 8806 1549

CC NO 275454   **ESTABLISHED** 1978

■ Melville Trust for Care and Cure of Cancer

WHERE FUNDING CAN BE GIVEN Lothian, Borders or Fife only.

WHO CAN BENEFIT Universities, medical schools, scientific bodies, research workers, medical professionals, and people with cancer.

WHAT IS FUNDED Scientific or clinical investigations on cancer.

WHAT IS NOT FUNDED Grants are not given for other causes.

TYPE OF GRANT Fellowships, research assistantships, grants for equipment.

RANGE OF GRANTS £2,000–£42,000 per year.

FINANCES *Year* 2002 *Income* £126,284 *Grants* £42,353 *Assets* £2,440,118

TRUSTEES Melville Estate Trustees.

HOW TO APPLY Application forms are available from the correspondent. They must be submitted no later than 31 March each year.

WHO TO APPLY TO Tods Murray WS, 66 Queen Street, Edinburgh EH2 4NE *Tel* 0131 226 4771 *Fax* 0131 225 3078 *E-mail* maildesk@todsmurray.co.uk

SC NO SC032409   **ESTABLISHED** 1922

■ Mental Health Foundation

WHERE FUNDING CAN BE GIVEN UK.

WHO CAN BENEFIT Voluntary organisations, research departments and statutory organisations promoting well-being and supporting people with learning disabilities. Medical professionals and research workers may be considered for funding.

WHAT IS FUNDED Treatment, service and support for people with mental health issues and people with learning difficulties. Innovative, ground-breaking projects under specific programmes of work.

WHAT IS NOT FUNDED No grants for: individual hardship, education and training; travel; attendance at conferences; capital; expenses such as vehicles or property; general appeals; general running costs; overseas events.

TYPE OF GRANT Salaries; project grants; and revenue costs.

RANGE OF GRANTS £400–£70,000.

SAMPLE GRANTS In 1998: £68,918 over two years to Sharing Caring Project, Sheffield for continuation of 'Planning Ahead' project to provide support for families with an older person with learning disabilities; £65,806 over three years to School of Psychology, University of Birmingham for evaluation of benefits of psychosocial intervention for adults with Down's Syndrome who develop dementia; £54,288 over three years to East Lothian Care and Accommodation Project, Prestonpans to promote the inclusion of older people with learning disabilities as active members of their local communities; £53,140 over two years to British Institute of Learning Disabilities, Kidderminster for support for family carer groups; £43,000 over three years to Surrey Oaklands NHS Trust and Oxleas NHS Trust for development of a resource pack for supporting and planning services for adults with Down's Syndrome and Alzheimer's Disease; £36,728 over two years to the Tizard Centre,

Think carefully about every application. Is it justified?

651

University of Kent for study of menopause and women with learning disabilities; £26,178 over two years to Wandsworth Rathbone, London for support of project 'Making plans for the future with people with mild learning disabilities'; £24,150 over one year to the Housing and Support Partnership, Witney for project to identify the options for families to use house equity to assure a future for adult children with learning disabilities; £4,672 over two years to Enable Services, Edinburgh to develop a self-sustaining allotment club; £4,312 over two years to St Marylebone School for Girls, towards implementation of a whole school approach to positive mental health.

The nine largest grants were made under the foundation's Growing Older with Learning Disabilities (GOLD) programme.

FINANCES *Year* 2001–02 *Income* £3,973,225 *Grants* £1,014,292 *Assets* £949,661

TRUSTEES Christopher S Martin, Chair; Jane Carter; Lady Clare Euston; Abel Hadden; Prof. Rachel Jenkins; Dr Zenobia Nadirshaw; Giles Ridley; Philippa Russell; David Sachon; Daphne Statham; Lady Weston.

PUBLICATIONS *Awards Schemes 1998–99: Applicants Handbook.* List of grants made. A list of other publications is available from the foundation.

OTHER INFORMATION Grants are available only under special programmes.

HOW TO APPLY Please contact the foundation offices for current grant priorities, guidelines and closing dates.

WHO TO APPLY TO 83 Victoria Street, London SW1H OHW *Tel* 020 7802 0300 *Fax* 020 7802 0301 *E-mail* mhf@mhf.org.uk *Website* www.mentalhealth.org.uk

CC NO 801130   **ESTABLISHED** 1949

■ Menuchar Ltd

WHERE FUNDING CAN BE GIVEN UK.

WHO CAN BENEFIT Jewish organisations.

WHAT IS FUNDED Advancement of religion in accordance with the orthodox Jewish faith, and relief of people in need.

WHAT IS NOT FUNDED No grants to non-registered charities or to individuals.

TYPE OF GRANT Primarily one-off.

FINANCES *Year* 2000–01 *Income* £232,379 *Grants* £300,725 *Assets* £369,527

TRUSTEES N Bude; G Bude.

HOW TO APPLY In writing to the correspondent.

WHO TO APPLY TO The Trustees, Equity House, 128–136 High Street, Edgware HA8 7EL

CC NO 262782   **ESTABLISHED** 1971

■ The Mercers' Charitable Foundation

WHERE FUNDING CAN BE GIVEN UK; in practice mainly London and the southern half of England.

WHO CAN BENEFIT Registered charities benefiting carers, disabled people, people disadvantaged by poverty, ex-offenders and those at risk of offending, homeless people, socially isolated people, victims of abuse, women, and people with Alzheimer's disease, asthma, autism, diabetes, head and other injuries, and Parkinson's disease, and people who are terminally ill.

WHAT IS FUNDED Arts, culture and recreation, including community arts; art galleries; theatres and opera houses; community development and

support to volunteers; community services; schools and colleges; education and training; science and technology studies; playgrounds; respite care for carers; support and self-help groups; hospices; rehab centres; advancement of Christianity; religious umbrella bodies; conservation; bird sanctuaries; ecology, natural history, ornithology and zoology; heritage.

WHAT IS NOT FUNDED The company does not respond to circular (mail shot) appeals, nor does it provide sponsorship. Generally, funds are only available to charities registered with the charity commission or exempt from registration. The primary area of activity is Greater London but other worthy applications will be considered.

TYPE OF GRANT Building and other capital grants; feasibility studies; one-off grants; project and research grants; recurring and start-up costs. Grants given for up to three years.

RANGE OF GRANTS Usually no more than £7,500.

SAMPLE GRANTS In 2000–01: £175,000 to Community Health South London NHS Trust; £174,600 to Peter Symond's College; £145,000 to Gresham College; £100,000 to Royal Ballet School; £60,000 to Royal Institute; £50,000 each to Royal Geographical Society and Royal Society; £33,750 to Ridley Hall for Theology through the Arts; £33,000 to Coram Family; £30,000 to Paternoster Centre.

FINANCES *Year* 2001–02 *Grants* £3,567,000

TRUSTEES The Mercers' Company.

HOW TO APPLY Initial applications should be in the form of a letter (no more than two sides of A4), giving details of the charity, its activities, and the proposed project, with some idea of costs, and sent to the grants manager. Please note that this should be accompanied by a copy of the latest audited accounts. The company's grants department staff are happy to give advice. Qualifying applicants will then be sent an application form and guidelines. The charity committee meets every six weeks; the education, heritage and church committees meet quarterly.

WHO TO APPLY TO Katherine Payne, Grants Manager, Mercers' Hall, Ironmonger Lane, London EC2V 8ME *Tel* 020 7726 4991 *Website* www.mercers.co.uk

CC NO 326340   **ESTABLISHED** 1982

■ The Merchant Taylors' Company Charities Fund

WHERE FUNDING CAN BE GIVEN UK.

WHO CAN BENEFIT Organisations benefiting children, older people, actors and entertainment professionals, medical professionals, musicians, substance misusers, carers, people who are disabled, and homeless people.

WHAT IS FUNDED Areas that may be considered are the arts, social care and community development, disability, older people, poverty, medical studies and research, chemical dependency, homelessness, children, and education, with priority for special needs.

TYPE OF GRANT One-off grants or three-year tapering grants.

RANGE OF GRANTS £500–£25,000.

SAMPLE GRANTS Grants included money for training awards, prizes and other awards made via nine schools associated with Merchant Taylors' Company. The schools include Merchant Taylors' School Northwood, Merchant Taylors' School for Boys and Girls Crosby, St Helen's Girls School Northwood, Wolverhampton

Grammar School, Foyle & Londonderry College and Willingford School, Oxford.
FINANCES *Year* 2001–02 *Income* £366,000 *Grants* £153,000 *Assets* £546,000
TRUSTEES The Master and warden of the Merchant Taylor's Company
HOW TO APPLY In writing to the correspondent.
WHO TO APPLY TO T J Maroney, Clerk to the Trustees, 30 Threadneedle Street, London EC2R 8JB *Tel* 020 7450 4440 *E-mail* tmaroney@merchant_taylors.co.uk *Website* www.merchant-taylors.co.uk
CC NO 1069124   **ESTABLISHED** 1941

■ The Merchant Venturers' Charity

WHERE FUNDING CAN BE GIVEN Bristol.
WHO CAN BENEFIT Local and regional organisations; local branches of national organisations; and some individuals.
WHAT IS FUNDED Any charitable purpose at the trustees' discretion.
TYPE OF GRANT Some recurrent.
SAMPLE GRANTS £60,000 to the Harbourside Foundation; £20,000 to Bristol University SMV Building; £18,000 to Greater Bristol Foundation; £15,000 each to SS Great Britain and Bristol University Campaign for Resources.
FINANCES *Year* 2000–01 *Income* £251,000 *Grants* £230,000 *Assets* £4,000,000
TRUSTEES The Society of Merchant Venturers of Bristol.
HOW TO APPLY In writing to the correspondent. A sub-committee of the trustees meets quarterly while the trustees meet monthly and can, if necessary, consider any urgent business at that meeting.
WHO TO APPLY TO Brig H W K Pye, Treasurer, The Society of Merchant Venturers, Merchants' Hall, The Promenade, Clifton , Bristol BS8 3NH *Tel* 0117 973 8058 *E-mail* smvbristol@btinternet.com
CC NO 264302   **ESTABLISHED** 1972

■ The Merchants House of Glasgow

WHERE FUNDING CAN BE GIVEN Glasgow and the West of Scotland.
WHO CAN BENEFIT Registered charities benefiting seamen, pensioners and young people (aged 10 to 30) in full-time education.
WHAT IS FUNDED Seamen's missions, general charitable purposes, and grants to pensioners and young people in education.
WHAT IS NOT FUNDED No grants to individuals or churches other than Glasgow Cathedral.
TYPE OF GRANT Capital projects.
SAMPLE GRANTS £4,925 to Erskine Hospital; £2,000 each to Citizens Theatre, and Salvation Army – Glasgow; £1,500 each to National Youth Orchestra of Scotland and Strathclyde Youth Club Association; £1,000 each to CLIC, Canniesburn Research Trust, East Glasgow School of Music, Lodging House Mission, and Safety Zone Community Project.
FINANCES *Year* 2001 *Income* £615,182 *Grants* £51,043 *Assets* £5,422,069
HOW TO APPLY In writing to the correspondent at any time, supported by copy of accounts.
WHO TO APPLY TO Jimmy Dykes, Assistant Collector, 7 West George Street, Glasgow G2 1BA *Tel* 0141 221 8272 *Fax* 0141 226 2275 *E-mail* enquiries@merchantshouse.org.uk
SC NO SC008900   **ESTABLISHED** 1605

■ Mercury Phoenix Trust

WHERE FUNDING CAN BE GIVEN Worldwide.
WHO CAN BENEFIT Registered charities benefiting people with AIDS and the HIV virus.
WHAT IS FUNDED Relief of poverty, sickness and distress of people affected by AIDS and the HIV virus, and to stimulate awareness of the virus throughout the world.
TYPE OF GRANT One-off, capital, project, running costs.
FINANCES *Year* 1998–99 *Income* £259,000 *Grants* £601,000 *Assets* £1,400,000
TRUSTEES M Austin; Jim Beach; B H May; R M Taylor.
HOW TO APPLY In writing to the correspondent.
WHO TO APPLY TO Peter Chant, The Mill, Mill Lane, Cookham, Berkshire SL6 9QT *Tel* 01628 527874
CC NO 1013768   **ESTABLISHED** 1992

■ Merseyside Police and High Sheriff's Charitable Trust

WHERE FUNDING CAN BE GIVEN Merseyside.
WHO CAN BENEFIT The local community on Merseyside.
WHAT IS FUNDED The trust was established in March 1998. Its objectives are: to promote for the public benefit on Merseyside a safer and increased quality of life through the prevention of crime and the protection of people and property from criminal acts; and to secure the advancement of education for the public benefit in all areas relating to public safety.
FINANCES *Year* 2000–01 *Income* £126,000 *Grants* £55,000
TRUSTEES Ex-officio: Brian Thaxter (Chair), Past High Sheriff of Merseyside; Cllr Ms Carol Gustafson, Chair of Merseyside Police Authority; B Hogan-Howe, High Sheriff of Merseyside Police; Paul Stephenson, Assistant Chief Constable Merseyside Police. Co-opted: Richard Banks; Michael Chapman; Leo Coligan; Colette Connell; Jennifer Grundy; Leslie Howell; Peter Johnson; Neil Kemsley; Philip Love; Roy Morris; Robert Mottram; Lady Kirsty Pilkington; Roy Swainson.
HOW TO APPLY In writing to the correspondent.
WHO TO APPLY TO The Trust Administrator, Canning Place, Liverpool L69 1JD
CC NO 1068806   **ESTABLISHED** 1998

■ Merthyr Charitable Trust

WHERE FUNDING CAN BE GIVEN England and Wales.
WHO CAN BENEFIT Organisations.
WHAT IS FUNDED General charitable purposes.
SAMPLE GRANTS £3,000 to Disasters Emergency Committee; £1,000 each to Aberglasney Restoration Trust and Llandeilo Graban Village; £500 each included those to One Parent Families, Pembrokeshire Wildlife Trust, Woodland Trust, Radnorshire Wildlife Trust, RNLI and Shelter Cymru.
FINANCES *Year* 1999–2000 *Income* £42,000 *Grants* £34,000 *Assets* £775,000
TRUSTEES The trust informed us that this information was confidential.
HOW TO APPLY In writing to the correspondent. The trust does not respond to unsuccessful applications.
WHO TO APPLY TO Hon. Antony Thomas Lewis, Trustee, The Skreen, Llandilo Graban, Builth Wells, Powys LD2 3SJ *Tel* 01982 560210
CC NO 262630   **ESTABLISHED** 1971

■ The Zachary Merton & George Woofindin Convalescent Trust

WHERE FUNDING CAN BE GIVEN Preference for Sheffield and Lincoln including the following areas: north Nottinghamshire, north Derbyshire and South Yorkshire.

WHO CAN BENEFIT Organisations benefiting carers, disabled people and people disadvantaged by poverty.

WHAT IS FUNDED Convalescent homes, travelling expenses of convalescent poor people, respite care for carers, people in need through illness, and community medicine.

WHAT IS NOT FUNDED No grants to individuals.

TYPE OF GRANT Recurring costs; up to two years.

RANGE OF GRANTS £500–£3,500.

FINANCES *Year* 2001 *Income* £44,000 *Grants* £36,000 *Assets* £478,000

TRUSTEES M G S Frampton; G Connell; Dr G A B Davies-Jones; J S Ibberson; N J A Hutton; C J Jewitt; Mrs P M Perriam; M P Newton.

HOW TO APPLY In writing to the correspondent, by the middle of March or September.

WHO TO APPLY TO G J Smallman, Secretary, Wrigleys, Fountain Precinct, Balm Green, Sheffield S1 2GZ *Tel* 0114 267 5596

CC NO 221760   **ESTABLISHED** 1956

■ The Tony Metherell Charitable Trust

WHERE FUNDING CAN BE GIVEN UK, especially Hertfordshire and Worcestershire.

WHO CAN BENEFIT Particularly older people and people who have cancer or disabilities.

WHAT IS FUNDED General charitable purposes, including hospices, cancer charities and the care and welfare of people who are elderly or have disablities.

WHAT IS NOT FUNDED No grants to overseas causes.

RANGE OF GRANTS £50–£5,000

SAMPLE GRANTS In 1998–99: £5,000 to Relate; £2,900 to Arthritis Research Council; £2,700 to St John Opthalmic Hospital; £1,000 to Break.

FINANCES *Year* 2001–02 *Income* £31,000 *Grants* £28,000 *Assets* £600,000

TRUSTEES B R M Fox; Ms C J Good.

HOW TO APPLY In writing to the correspondent.

WHO TO APPLY TO B R M Fox, Trustee, Jenningsbury, London Road, Hertford, Herts SG13 7NS *Tel* 01992 583978

CC NO 1046899   **ESTABLISHED** 1992

■ The Methodist Relief and Development Fund

WHERE FUNDING CAN BE GIVEN Overseas and UK.

WHO CAN BENEFIT Development – indigenous NGOs in the developing world; emergency relief – Action by Churches Together (ACT) and existing partner NGOs/organisations in the developing world; and development education – NGOs implementing development education programmes in the UK.

WHAT IS FUNDED Emergency relief in disasters and long-term refugee assistance; overseas development, including agroforestry (organic farming, permaculture etc.), literacy (particularly non-formal education), water (for drinking and agricultural use), health, disability and community development (skills training, micro enterprise and capacity building); development education in the UK, including campaigns, publications and support for development education organisations which resource MRDF supporters.

WHAT IS NOT FUNDED No grants to individuals or to organisations without charitable status; UK-based charity NGO work; scholarships for studies or voluntary work overseas; church-building or evangelism; capital costs, or for individual development education centres affiliated to the development education association.

TYPE OF GRANT Project costs. Funding for up to three years will be considered.

RANGE OF GRANTS £1,000–£20,000; average £5,000–£15,000.

SAMPLE GRANTS £63,000 to ACT for famine relief in southern Africa; £14,755 to Voluntary Action for Development in Uganda for water and sanitation; £12,504 to Westnell Nursaries in Peru for disadvantaged children; £10,570 to J&D in Mali for community literacy; £8,670 to Harvest Help in Zambia for sustainable agriculture; £5,875 to GROWS in India for mother and child health; £5,000 to Fairtrade Foundation for development education work in the UK.

FINANCES *Year* 2001–02 *Income* £1,214,000 *Grants* £939,759 *Assets* £458,464

TRUSTEES Revd Dr Peter Byass (Chair); Ms Fiona Bidnell (Vice Chair); Luis Algorta; Revd Inderjit Bhogal; Richard Hide; Revd Henry Keys; Robert Mortimer; Martin Nthakomwa; Ms Selina Oppong-Asare; Ms Ellie O'Malley; Rev John Parkin; Mrs Pamela Stone; Rev Peter Sulston.

PUBLICATIONS *Funds in Focus* (quarterly publication), development education resources (*Harvest Pack and Six Actions for Lent*); country information sheets, MDRF newsletter.

HOW TO APPLY Applications should be sent to the correspondent. Applicants should ask for guidance on funding criteria for humanitarian aid and development if they are unsure about their application to the MRDF. Applications are by pro forma, accompanied by a proposal of no more than 10 pages, including a detailed budget. Trustees' meetings are held quarterly, but MRDF may not be able to consider applications for several months.

WHO TO APPLY TO Kirsty Smith, Director, 25 Marylebone Road, London NW1 5JR *Tel* 020 7467 5158 *Fax* 020 7467 5233 *E-mail* mrdf@methodistchurch.org.uk *Website* www.mrdf.org.uk

CC NO 291691   **ESTABLISHED** 1985

■ The Metropolitan Drinking Fountain and Cattle Trough Association

WHERE FUNDING CAN BE GIVEN UK, mainly London, and overseas.

WHAT IS FUNDED Projects working to provide clean water supplies in developing countries, the provision of drinking fountains in schools and the restoration of disused drinking fountains. The preservation of the association's archive materials, artefacts, drinking fountains, cattle troughs and other installations.

SAMPLE GRANTS Natural History Museum, North Aston Village Foundation and Sustrans 'Flora Garden'.

FINANCES *Year* 1999 *Income* £39,147 *Grants* £19,009 *Assets* £565,628

TRUSTEES Executive committee: A E Buxton; J E Mills; I Evans; R P Baber; Mrs I De Pelet; J King; R Sheridan-White; Sir J Smith; M W Elliott; J Barrett; R E T Gurney.

PUBLICATIONS *The Drinking Fountain Association.*

OTHER INFORMATION As at 1999 the total of fountains and troughs supplied, for use both in the UK and overseas by the association were: 4,063 drinking fountains; 927 cattle troughs; 3,721 water wells; and 24 tanks.

HOW TO APPLY In writing to the correspondent.

WHO TO APPLY TO R P Baber, Secretary and Treasurer, Oaklands, 5 Queenborough Gardens, Chislehurst, Kent BR7 6NP *Tel* 020 8467 1261 *E-mail* ralph.baber@tesco.net

CC NO 207743   **ESTABLISHED** 1960

····················

■ The Metropolitan Hospital-Sunday Fund

WHERE FUNDING CAN BE GIVEN Greater London, within the boundaries of the M25.

WHO CAN BENEFIT Hospitals, homes and medical charities outside the NHS who are themselves registered charities; NHS hospitals throughout London; clients of social workers.

WHAT IS FUNDED Capital Grants (formerly known as Specific Purpose Grants): 'For registered charities, hospitals, homes and other organisations providing care for sick and disabled people. These grants will be distributed on a three times per year cycle, and interested organisations may make an application at any time during the year.' Samaritan Grants (formerly known as the Samaritan Fund and Special Reserve Grants) 'There are two types of Samaritan grants – block and individual. Block grants are available to social work teams to allocate to in-patients and out-patients of NHS and NHS Trust hospitals who have immediate personal needs that cannot be met from statutory sources. Individual grants are provided through social workers who make a separate application when the amount required exceeds the delegation level of the social work team. Items funded by these awards include clothes, household equipment and convalescent or respite holidays.
'Social workers holding a Samaritan Grant may apply for renewal of the grant at the end of their financial year. Additional funding may be obtained during the year, providing there is evidence of need.'

WHAT IS NOT FUNDED No grants to individuals, except through NHS hospital social workers. Organisation grants to registered charities only.

TYPE OF GRANT Project and one-off. Capital grants to hospitals, homes and other medical organisations outside the NHS. 'Samaritan grants' for use by social workers in NHS hospitals and local authorities to assist individual clients.

RANGE OF GRANTS Normally £50–£25,000.

SAMPLE GRANTS £25,000 each to Anglican Diocese of Rochester and Salvation Army; £10,000 to Trustees of the Home of Compassion; £12,500 to Roman Catholic Diocese of Westminster; £6,500 to Bromley Ablement; £6,925 to Oasis Trust; £6,000 to Children's Trust; £5,100 to Federation for Artistic and Creative Therapy; £5,0000 each to Norwood, Princess Trust for Carers, Refugee Support Centre, Shaftesbury Society and Umbrella.

FINANCES *Year* 2001 *Income* £385,288 *Grants* £325,536 *Assets* £9,793,547

TRUSTEES The board of the fund, which is divided between clerical and lay members. Robin Holland-Martin, Chair.

OTHER INFORMATION 2000 saw the launch of the Ministers' Grant Scheme, which relieves hardship among disadvantaged individuals via places of worship.

HOW TO APPLY Application forms are available from the grants administrator and must be returned by the end of March (for new applications) or June (for existing applicants). Awards are made annually in December. There is no restriction on the number of successive years that the same charity may submit an application, or on the number of years that an applicant may be awarded a grant. Hospital social workers may apply at any time for Samaritan grants.

WHO TO APPLY TO The Trustees, 45 Westminster Bridge Road, London SE1 7JB *Tel* 020 7922 0200 *Fax* 020 7401 3641 *E-mail* mhsf@peabody.org.uk *Website* www.mhsf.org.uk

CC NO 1066739   **ESTABLISHED** 1872

····················

■ The Mickel Fund

WHERE FUNDING CAN BE GIVEN UK, with a preference for Scotland.

WHO CAN BENEFIT Voluntary organisations and charitable groups benefiting people of all ages, especially at risk groups. The trust prefers local charities but does give to UK charities.

WHAT IS FUNDED General charitable purposes including: health and social care professional bodies; hospices; cancer research; immunology, MS and neurological research; health-related volunteer schemes; church and historical buildings; zoos; heritage; art galleries, libraries and museums; sports centres; care in the community; and holidays and outings.

WHAT IS NOT FUNDED Unsolicited applications from individuals will not be acknowledged.

TYPE OF GRANT One-off and recurrent, capital including buildings, project and research. Funding is available for more than three years.

RANGE OF GRANTS £100–£10,000.

SAMPLE GRANTS In 1996–97: £52,000 to Edinburgh Old Town Housing Association for special one-off renovations; £26,200 to Scottish Sports Aid Trust; £10,000 to National Trust for Scotland; £5,000 to Bo'ness Old Kirk; £2,500 to Dunbar John Muir Museum; £1,000 to Cancer Research.

FINANCES *Year* 1998 *Income* £50,000 *Grants* £50,000

TRUSTEES J C Craig; D A Mickel; B G A Mickel; A Smith; A L Bassi.

HOW TO APPLY In writing to the correspondent.

WHO TO APPLY TO A Smith, 126 West Regent Street, Glasgow G2 2BH *Tel* 0141 332 0001 *Fax* 0141 248 4921

SC NO SC003266   **ESTABLISHED** 1970

····················

■ Gerald Micklem Charitable Trust

WHERE FUNDING CAN BE GIVEN UK, especially Hampshire.

WHO CAN BENEFIT Registered charities benefiting at risk groups and people who are disadvantaged by poverty or socially isolated.

WHAT IS FUNDED Medicine and health, welfare and general charitable purposes.

WHAT IS NOT FUNDED No grants to non-registered charities or to individuals.

TYPE OF GRANT One-off and recurrent.

RANGE OF GRANTS £500–£2,000.

SAMPLE GRANTS £3,000 each to BRACE, Fight for Sight, Mencap and Sustrans (of nine grants); £2,000 each to Arthritis Care, Disabilities Trust, Hawk and Owl Trust, Harvest Trust (Holidays for Children) and Treloar Trust (of 13 grants).

FINANCES *Year* 2000 *Income* £80,000 *Grants* £58,000 *Assets* £485,000

TRUSTEES Susan J Shone; Joanna L Scott-Dalgleish; Helen Ratcliffe.

HOW TO APPLY In writing to the correspondent. Interested applicants should note that the organisations which have received grants in the past should not be taken as indicative of a geographical or other bias. The trustees meet informally a few times each year, but the dates are not fixed. They usually meet once only to decide on grants in January or February. Applications can be sent at any time, but preferably not later the the preceding November.

WHO TO APPLY TO Mrs S J Shone, Trustee, Bolinge Hill Farm, Buriton, Petersfield, Hampshire GU31 4NN *Tel* 01730 264207 *Fax* 01730 268515 *E-mail* ghmicklem.charitabletrust@btinternet.com *Website* www.peter.shone.btinternet.co.uk

CC NO 802583   **ESTABLISHED** 1988

■ Middlesex County Rugby Football Union Memorial Fund

WHERE FUNDING CAN BE GIVEN UK.

WHO CAN BENEFIT Preference is given to participants or former participants in sport. Organisations benefiting people of all ages who are at risk, disabled, or disadvantaged by poverty are also considered.

WHAT IS FUNDED Relief of poverty, physical education of children and young people with disabilities, and health. Charities working in the fields of acute health care, support and self help groups, health facilities and buildings, and various community facilities and services may be supported.

TYPE OF GRANT Mainly one-off sums for capital projects. Project, research, recurring costs and running costs funded for one year or less will be considered.

RANGE OF GRANTS £250–£5,000, average grant £750.

FINANCES *Year* 2001–02 *Income* £36,000 *Grants* £25,000 *Assets* £750,000

TRUSTEES M J Christie; C D L Hogbin; Sir Peter Yarranton; K L King; R H B Jones; D Wellman; M J Foxwell; H Hiles; D C Mann.

HOW TO APPLY In writing to the correspondent.

WHO TO APPLY TO C D L Hogbin, Chestnut Cottage, 20a Stubbs Wood, Chesham Bois, Buckinghamshire HP6 6EY *Tel* 01494 729220 *Fax* 01494 729220 *E-mail* charles@hogbin.com

CC NO 209175   **ESTABLISHED** 1947

■ Midhurst Pensions Trust

WHERE FUNDING CAN BE GIVEN UK and overseas.

WHO CAN BENEFIT Registered charities and individuals.

WHAT IS FUNDED General charitable purposes and pensions to older people in need in Midhurst – West Sussex.

WHAT IS NOT FUNDED No grants to individuals, other than those detailed above.

FINANCES *Year* 2001–02 *Income* £141,989 *Grants* £61,906 *Assets* £3,928,182

TRUSTEES The Cowdray Trust Limited and Rathbone Trust Company Ltd.

OTHER INFORMATION No distributions were made to organisations during 2001–02.

HOW TO APPLY In writing to the correspondent. Acknowledgements will be sent to unsuccessful applicants if an sae is enclosed with the application.

WHO TO APPLY TO Alan J Winborn, The Cowdray Trust Limited, Pollen House, 10–12 Cork Street, London W1S 3LW *Tel* 020 7439 9061

CC NO 245230   **ESTABLISHED** 1965

■ The Migraine Trust

WHERE FUNDING CAN BE GIVEN UK and overseas.

WHO CAN BENEFIT Organisations benefiting people suffering from migraines, medical professionals, research workers and scientists.

WHAT IS FUNDED Research grants, fellowships and studentships (studentships are applied for by host institution only) for the study of migraine. Funds provide for research into migraine at recognised institutions, e.g. hospitals and universities.

FINANCES *Year* 1999 *Income* £779,806 *Grants* £228,924 *Assets* £1,196,050

TRUSTEES A Jordan, Chair; Lady Schiemann; Prof. C Kennard; H Mitchell; J Ames; J P S Wolff-Ingham; Prof. P J Goadsby; Ms S Hammond; Harvey McGregor.

PUBLICATIONS Migraine News, *Migraine: Understanding and coping with migraine.*

OTHER INFORMATION The trust holds the Migraine Trust International Symposia, funds research into migraine, and has a full sufferer service.

HOW TO APPLY By application form available from trust. Applications will be acknowledged.

WHO TO APPLY TO The Trustees, 45 Great Ormond Street, London WC1N 3HZ *E-mail* research@migrainetrust.org *Website* www.migrainetrust.org

CC NO 1081300   **ESTABLISHED** 1965

■ Miles Trust for the Putney and Roehampton Community

WHERE FUNDING CAN BE GIVEN The borough of Wandsworth.

WHO CAN BENEFIT Organisations benefiting people of all ages, people disadvantaged by poverty and homeless people.

WHAT IS FUNDED Schools, youth organisations, and social welfare organisations caring for people who are poor, homeless, elderly or sick.

WHAT IS NOT FUNDED No grants to individuals.

TYPE OF GRANT Often recurring.

RANGE OF GRANTS £100–£4,000.

SAMPLE GRANTS £9,000 to All Saints' Church of England School; £5,000 to Wandsworth MIND; £3,000 each to Putney Poor Relief Committee, Wandsworth Bereavement Service and Regenerate.com; £2,100 to National Schizophrenia Fellowship; £2,000 each to St Mary's Church of England School and Housebound Learners.

FINANCES *Year* 1999–2000 *Income* £38,000 *Grants* £54,000 *Assets* £889,000

TRUSTEES A R Collender, Chair; R J G Holman; T J E Marwood; Dr Giles Fraser; Mrs L P Paiba; Mrs A Raikes; Mrs L Moir; Mrs J Maxwell; Mrs J Walters; P Kitchen; Mrs A Stevens; Mrs C V Davey.

OTHER INFORMATION The trust donated £20,250 to community projects; £14,610 to youth causes; and £5,100 to the Church.

HOW TO APPLY In writing to the correspondent.

WHO TO APPLY TO Mrs Angela Holman, Secretary to the Trust, 11 Genoa Avenue, Putney, London SW15 6DY *Tel* 020 8789 0953 *Fax* 020 8789 2984

CC NO 246784   **ESTABLISHED** 1967

■ The Miller Foundation

WHERE FUNDING CAN BE GIVEN UK, with a preference for Scotland, especially the West of Scotland.

WHO CAN BENEFIT Charities benefiting children and young adults; students; at risk groups; disabled groups; those disadvantaged by poverty; and socially isolated people.

WHAT IS FUNDED Grants are given to educational projects, especially at tertiary level. Organisations working for the welfare of humans and animals are also supported, as are schemes working with people who are disabled.

WHAT IS NOT FUNDED No grants to individuals.

RANGE OF GRANTS £1,000–£2,000.

FINANCES *Year* 1999 *Grants* £161,000

TRUSTEES C Fleming-Brown; G R G Graham; J Simpson; G F R Fleming-Brown.

HOW TO APPLY On a form available from the secretary. Trustees meet once a year to consider grants in April. Applications should be received by the end of March.

WHO TO APPLY TO A Biggart, Secretary to the Foundation, c/o Maclay Murray & Spens, 151 St Vincent Street, Glasgow G2 5NJ *Tel* 0141 248 5011 *Fax* 0141 248 5819

SC NO SC008798   **ESTABLISHED** 1979

■ The Hugh and Mary Miller Bequest Trust

WHERE FUNDING CAN BE GIVEN Mainly Scotland.

WHO CAN BENEFIT Registered charities.

WHAT IS FUNDED Healthcare and disability.

WHAT IS NOT FUNDED Only registered charities are supported. No grants to individuals.

TYPE OF GRANT Capital including buildings, core costs, project, research, recurring costs, running costs and salaries. Funding is available for more than three years.

FINANCES *Year* 1999–2000 *Income* £96,000 *Grants* £85,360 *Assets* £1,800,000

TRUSTEES G R G Graham; H C Davidson.

HOW TO APPLY In writing to the correspondent. Trustees meet in spring and autumn to consider grants; applications should be received by March and October respectively.

WHO TO APPLY TO Andrew J Biggart, Maclay Murray & Spens, 151 St Vincent Street, Glasgow G2 5NJ *Tel* 0141 248 5011 *Fax* 0141 248 5819 *E-mail* andrew.biggart@mms.co.uk *Website* www.mms.co.uk

SC NO SC014950

■ The M Miller Charitable Trust

WHERE FUNDING CAN BE GIVEN UK.

WHO CAN BENEFIT Jewish causes.

WHAT IS FUNDED General charitable purposes.

FINANCES *Year* 1998–99 *Income* £43,000 *Grants* £42,000

TRUSTEES Matthew Miller; Renee B Miller; Richard Ellis.

HOW TO APPLY In writing to the correspondent.

WHO TO APPLY TO Richard Ellis, Trustee, 41 Harrogate Road, Chapel Allerton, Leeds, West Yorkshire LS7 3PD *Tel* 0113 228 4000

CC NO 1014957   **ESTABLISHED** 1992

■ The Millfield House Foundation

WHERE FUNDING CAN BE GIVEN North east England particularly Tyne and Wear.

WHO CAN BENEFIT Applicants should be voluntary agencies and other bodies with charitable objectives working with socially and economically disadvantaged people. Bodies undertaking policy research and advocacy should have close links with or voluntary or community organisations in the region.

WHAT IS FUNDED Applications should have any of the following aims: to seek to influence the policy of national, regional or local government and other public bodies, and to inform and educate opinion on social, economic and political issues; to enable the voluntary sector as a whole, individual voluntary and community organisations and those who benefit from their services to contribute to policy and debate from first-hand experience of social need and current conditions, by campaigning for the improvement of policy and public provision; and to develop activities which may have been proven in other parts of the UK but have not been developed in Tyne and Wear or, which through being tested in Tyne and Wear, could provide models for practice and development elsewhere, particularly activities which empower people and communities to meet their own needs and exploit their own resources.

Please note, there will be a review of policy in 2003.

WHAT IS NOT FUNDED The trust does not make grants: unrelated to the needs of people in Tyne and Wear; to large, well-established UK charities or in response to general appeals; towards arts, medicine, conservation or purely academic; research; for buildings; for debts already incurred; to replace statutory funding or provide funding which should be the responsibility of statutory agencies; to individuals; for travel/ adventure projects or educational bursaries; to causes likely to receive statutory, EU or Community Fund support or very likely to be successful from other trusts and sources (although contributions may be made towards a part of an otherwise popular project which other sources are unlikely to fund); or for the delivery of a service unless in the trust's priority areas of support.

TYPE OF GRANT Significant and medium-term support (alone or in partnership with other funders) to a relatively few carefully selected projects or organisations. Since MHF can only afford to have six to eight such grants in payment at the same time, it will be able to approve only one or two new applications in any year. In some cases MHF may consider a small grant to support work needed in preparation for an application for a major grant.

RANGE OF GRANTS Mostly between £5,000 and £20,000.

SAMPLE GRANTS £26,260 to University of Northumbria for the Sustainable Cities Research Institute; £16,000 to Newcastle Healthy City Project; £11,350 to Alzheimer's Society for the Newcastle branch; £7,500 to North East Family Centre Network; £5,000 to Crime Concern for the Neighbourhood Safety Project – Blyth; £2,000 each to Cedarwood Trust – Meadow Well, NACAB and Total Learning Challenge; £1,615 to Willan Trust; £500 to Voluntary Organisations' Network North East; £450 to Newcastle CVS.

FINANCES *Year* 2001–02 *Income* £141,811 *Grants* £76,786 *Assets* £5,389,669

TRUSTEES Grigor McClelland; Rosemary Chubb; Jenifer McClelland; Stephen McClelland; George Hepburn.

PUBLICATIONS *Guidelines for Applicants. Report on Grant-making 1989–96. Summary of Political Activities and Campaigning by Charities (CC9, Charity Commission 1995).*

HOW TO APPLY In writing to the correspondent. If the application meets the stated guidelines the administrator may request further information or arrange a meeting. Applications unconnected to Tyne and Wear are not acknowledged. The trustees meet twice a year, in May/June and November so completed applications should arrive by the end of March or end of September. The administrator is willing to provide guidance for the preparation of final applications, but not without first receiving an outline proposal.

WHO TO APPLY TO The Administrator, 19 The Crescent, Benton Lodge, Newcastle upon Tyne NE7 7ST *Tel* 0191 266 9429 *Fax* 0191 266 9429 *E-mail* finley@lineone.net *Website* www.newnet.org.uk/mhf

CC NO 271180 **ESTABLISHED** 1976

■ The Millfield Trust

WHERE FUNDING CAN BE GIVEN UK and worldwide.

WHO CAN BENEFIT Individuals, and organisations benefiting elderly people, Christians, and people in need.

WHAT IS FUNDED Support of religious or other charitable institutions or work. Advancement of the Protestant and Evangelical tenets of the Christian faith and encouragement of missionary activity. Relief of need. Preference to charities of which the trust has special interest, knowledge or association. Funds fully allocated or committed.

RANGE OF GRANTS £40–£12,000.

SAMPLE GRANTS £15,000 to Gideons International; £10,000 to Mission to Europe; £6,000 to Mark Gillingham Charitable Trust; £3,300 to Tear Fund; £3,200 to Ashbury Evangelical Free Church; £3,200 to Ashbury Evangelical Free Church; £2,000 to Overseas Council; £1,800 to Scripture Union, £1,400 to OMF International; £1,000 each to British Red Cross, Leprosy Mission, Prospect Hospice and Schools Outreach.

FINANCES *Year* 2000–01 *Income* £79,303 *Grants* £67,400 *Assets* £142,021

TRUSTEES D Bunce; Mrs R Bunce; P W Bunce; S D Bunce; A C Bunce.

HOW TO APPLY No replies to unsolicited applications.

WHO TO APPLY TO D Bunce, Trustee, Millfield House, Bell Lane, Liddington, Swindon, Wiltshire SN4 0HE *Tel* 01793 790181

CC NO 262406 **ESTABLISHED** 1971

■ The Millhouses Charitable Trust

WHERE FUNDING CAN BE GIVEN UK and overseas.

WHO CAN BENEFIT Registered charities benefiting Christians, at risk groups, people disadvantaged by poverty, socially isolated people, victims of famine, disasters and war.

WHAT IS FUNDED Overseas aid, social welfare and community services (with a Christian emphasis). A preference is shown for Baptist charities.

WHAT IS NOT FUNDED Grants are made to registered charities only; no grants to individuals.

TYPE OF GRANT One-off.

RANGE OF GRANTS £250–£5,000.

SAMPLE GRANTS In 1996–97: £10,000 to Batah Foundation; £5,000 each to Christian Aid, Home

Mission, Medical Foundation, NSPCC, Amnesty UK Section, and Baptist Missionary Society; £2,000 each to Barnston Dale Centre, Bible Society, and Child Hope UK.

FINANCES *Year* 1997–98 *Income* £72,000 *Grants* £78,000 *Assets* £539,000

TRUSTEES Revd J S Harcus; Dr A W Harcus.

HOW TO APPLY In writing to the correspondent, but note that most of the grants given by this trust are recurrent. If new grants are made, they are usually to organisations known to the trustees.

WHO TO APPLY TO Dr A W Harcus, Trustee, Medicos House, 79 Beverly Road, Hull HU3 1XR

CC NO 327773 **ESTABLISHED** 1988

■ The Millichope Foundation

WHERE FUNDING CAN BE GIVEN UK, especially the West Midlands and Shropshire.

WHO CAN BENEFIT Registered charities, some grants to UK and international organisations; local applications limited to the West Midlands and Shropshire.

WHAT IS FUNDED Social and health funding which is not covered by government programmes; the arts and conservation.

WHAT IS NOT FUNDED No grants to individuals or non-registered charities.

TYPE OF GRANT Normally an annual commitment for a period of five years.

RANGE OF GRANTS Usually £100–£5,000.

SAMPLE GRANTS £12,800 in two grants to Fauna and Flora Preservation Society; £7,500 in two grants to Moor Park School; £5,000 each to Midlands Centre for Spinal Injuries Appeal, National Trust, Oxfam Bangladesh, Oxfam Hurricane Appeal, and Save the Children; £3,500 to Royal Opera House Covent Garden; £2,500 each to St Paul's Community Project and National Institute of Conductive Education.

FINANCES *Year* 1998–99 *Income* £253,000 *Grants* £186,000 *Assets* £4,200,000

TRUSTEES L C N Bury; Mrs S A Bury; Mrs B Marshall.

HOW TO APPLY In writing to the correspondent.

WHO TO APPLY TO Mrs S A Bury, Trustee, Millichope Park, Munslow, Craven Arms, Shropshire SY7 9HA *Tel* 01584 841234 *Fax* 01584 841445

CC NO 282357 **ESTABLISHED** 1981

■ The Clare Milne Trust

WHERE FUNDING CAN BE GIVEN Unrestricted, but Devon and Cornwall in practice.

WHAT IS FUNDED Disability projects in Devon and Cornwall, especially small and well-run local and regional charities with strong support from volunteers and with only modest expenditure on fundraising and administration.

WHAT IS NOT FUNDED No grants directly to or for individuals.

RANGE OF GRANTS Typically £1,000–£25,000.

FINANCES *Grants* £400,000

TRUSTEES Michael Coyne; Lesley Milne; Michael Brown.

HOW TO APPLY If you think your project meets the trust's criteria, you should write summarising your request on one side of an A4 sheet if possible, with minimal supporting literature; the trust will request a copy of your annual report and accounts later on if necessary. Potential applicants may call Roger Jefcoate on 01296 720 533 (weekdays before 7pm) if wishing to discuss a proposal before writing. The trustees meet three time annually, in January, May and October, and to save unnecessary administration only applications which fit the trust's criteria will be responded to.

WHO TO APPLY TO Roger Jefcoate, Administrator, 2 Swanbourne Road, Mursley, Milton Keynes MK17 0JA *Tel* 01296 720533

CC NO 1084733   **ESTABLISHED** 1999

■ Milton Keynes Community Foundation

WHERE FUNDING CAN BE GIVEN Milton Keynes unitary authority.

WHO CAN BENEFIT Organisations benefiting people of all ages, volunteers, at risk groups, carers, disabled people, those disadvantaged by poverty, homeless people, and victims of abuse, crime and domestic violence. The foundation will only make grants to voluntary groups with a local-based committee whose work is in Milton Keynes. Through its arts fund it does occasionally make grants to individuals and other less formally constituted groups.

WHAT IS FUNDED The foundation's main priority is to help those in the Milton Keynes Council area who miss out because of poverty, ill health, disability or disadvantage. It also supports important initiatives in the spheres of the arts and leisure. Charities working in the following fields will be considered: information technology and computers; publishing and printing; community development; economic regeneration schemes; support to voluntary and community organisations; charity or voluntary umbrella bodies; family planning clinics; respite care, care for carers; support and self-help groups; community centres and village halls; training for community development; counselling on social issues; playschemes and advice centres.

WHAT IS NOT FUNDED Grants are normally not given to proposals chiefly focused upon the following: musical instruments; travel expenses; commercial publications; conferences or seminars; university or similar research, formal education or training; retrospective grants, nor grants to pay off deficits; projects connected with promoting a religious message of any kind.

TYPE OF GRANT Small grants of up to £1,500; general grants from £1,500 to £7,500 to cover equipment costs, projects and minor building work, training, publicity and one-off activity costs; arts grants awarded for artistic and cultural activities, particularly of high quality and originality, up to a maximum of £5,000; development grants, up to a maximum, exceptionally, of £25,000 and typically from £9,000 to £20,000 per year for each of three years, generally for discrete project work (can include salaries, rents and other overheads).

RANGE OF GRANTS £100–£25,000, depending on grant type.

SAMPLE GRANTS £55,000 to Home Start Milton Keynes to provide support and meet the needs of young ethnic minority families and families who have a carer or child who is disabled; £40,000 to SNAP (Milton Keynes Special Needs Advancement Project) for a woodwork project for young adults with special needs; £31,000 to MK Chinese School and Community Centre for a development officer to work in the community; £7,500 each to Newport Pagnell Old People's Welfare Committee, Safety Centre, PEACE (People Establishing a Caring Environment), Al Karam Trust Community Centre, Willen Hospital, MK Division Guide Association and Extracare Charitable Trust – Pagnell Grange; £5,500 to SSAFA Forces Help; £5,000 each to Living

Archive and Bletchley Rugby Union Football Club – Mini Junior Section; £4,000 each to MK Lesbian, Gay and Bisexual Youthline and Headway MK; £2,000 to The Open Door Charity; £1,500 each to City Counselling Centre, MK Brook Advisory Centre, Woughton Parish, The Ark Charity, MK Athletic Club, Two Villages Archive Trust and MK Mind.

FINANCES *Year* 2000–01 *Income* £597,000 *Grants* £393,000

TRUSTEES Philippa Eccles; Walter Greaves; Brian Hocken; Simon Ingram; Andrew Jones; Peter Kara; Eleanor Milburn; Juliet Murray; Michael Murray; Stephen Norrish; Francesca Skelton; Lady Tudor Price; Dr Anthony Walton.

PUBLICATIONS *What is the Community Trust?*, quarterly newsletter, Guide to Grants, annual report.

HOW TO APPLY Application forms and guidelines are available, but the trust advises applicants to phone them to discuss the proposal with a relevant grants co-ordinator.

WHO TO APPLY TO The Grants Manager, Acorn House, 381 Midsummer Boulevard, Central Milton Keynes MK9 3HP *Tel* 01908 690276 *Fax* 01908 233635 *E-mail* information@mkcommunityfoundation. co.uk *Website* www.mkcommunityfoundation.co.uk

CC NO 295107   **ESTABLISHED** 1987

■ The Edgar Milward Charity

WHERE FUNDING CAN BE GIVEN Worldwide, with a preference for Reading and the surrounding area.

WHO CAN BENEFIT Causes known to the trustees, particularly those supported by the settlor.

WHAT IS FUNDED A limited number of Christian and humanitarian causes. The trustees currently have an established interest in a range of charities. Few new charities will be added to this list.

WHAT IS NOT FUNDED No new applications will be supported.

SAMPLE GRANTS £3,000 to Four Lanes Infant and Junior Schools – Reading; £2,500 to Reading Blue Coat School; £2,000 each to Avenue School – Reading and Greyfriars Church; £1,000 each to Billy Graham Evangelistic Association, Frontiers, Global Care – Mozambique, JC 2000, Premier Radio and St John and St James Church – Bootle.

FINANCES *Year* 2000–01 *Income* £63,635 *Grants* £54,425 *Assets* £1,219,363

TRUSTEES J S Milward, Chair; T Pittom; Mrs M V Roberts; G M Fogwill; Mrs J C Austin; Mrs E M Smuts; M O L Fogwill.

HOW TO APPLY Unsolicited applications cannot be considered.

WHO TO APPLY TO Mrs J C Austin, Trustee, 16 Cufelle Close, Sherfield Park, Chineham, Basingstoke, Hampshire RG24 8RH *Tel* 01256 359590

CC NO 281018   **ESTABLISHED** 1980

■ The Keith and Joan Mindelsohn Charitable Trust

WHERE FUNDING CAN BE GIVEN Birmingham and West Midlands.

WHO CAN BENEFIT Organisations and individuals preferably West Midlands based.

WHAT IS FUNDED General charitable purposes.

Think carefully about every application. Is it justified?

659

TYPE OF GRANT Preferably for a defined project or individual.

RANGE OF GRANTS £100–£500

FINANCES *Year* 2001–02 *Grants* £25,000

TRUSTEES Jane Jaffa; Jill Amiss; Sue Bowman.

HOW TO APPLY In writing to the correspondent.

WHO TO APPLY TO Richard Jaffa, Administrator, 32 Malcolmson Close, Edgbaston, Birmingham B15 3LS *Fax* 0121 605 4737 *E-mail* rjaffa3266@aol.com

CC NO 1075174   ESTABLISHED 1998

■ The Peter Minet Trust

WHERE FUNDING CAN BE GIVEN Mainly south east London boroughs, particularly Lambeth and Southwark.

WHO CAN BENEFIT Registered charities benefiting at risk groups, and people who are disabled, sick or disadvantaged by poverty.

WHAT IS FUNDED Registered charities, particularly those working in the fields of environment, health, disability, social welfare, youth, community and with people who are young, sick, disabled, disadvantaged or elderly.

WHAT IS NOT FUNDED Grants to registered charities only. No grants are made to individuals. The trust will not give to: local appeals, other than those within or directly affecting the trust's immediate locality; repetitive nationwide appeals by large charities for large sums of money; appeals where all, or most of the beneficiaries live outside the UK; appeals whose sole purpose is to make grants from collected funds; endowment or deficit funding; or medical or other research.

TYPE OF GRANT Usually one-off for a specific project or part of a project.

RANGE OF GRANTS Average grant £1,000.

SAMPLE GRANTS £5,000 each to India Earthquake Appeal and Southwark Bereavement Care; £4,000 to Springfield Community Flat; £3,500 to Southwark Churches Care; £3,000 each to Cancer Resource Centre, Frankie Miller Songwriting Project and Riverpoint; £2,500 each to 198 Gallery and Pegasus Opera Company; £2,000 each to Adfam National, Brixton Society, Charterhouse in Southwark, Nehemiah Project, Single Homeless Project, Toucan Employment, Trinity Hospice and Vauxhall Community Childrens Projects.

FINANCES *Year* 2000–01 *Income* £154,684 *Grants* £120,535 *Assets* £3,210,950

TRUSTEES J C B South, Chair; N McGregor-Wood; Mrs R L C Rowan; Ms P C Jones; R Luff; Revd Bruce Stokes.

PUBLICATIONS Guidelines leaflet available.

OTHER INFORMATION If you require further information or would like to discuss your project, please contact the administrator at the address below on Tuesday or Wednesday between 10am and 4pm.

HOW TO APPLY A form is available from the correspondent with a leaflet giving guidelines for applicants, either by post or via e-mail as a Microsoft Word file. The form should be submitted including audited accounts, details of the project (no more than two sides of A4), a budget breakdown, money raised so far, and a list of other bodies to whom you have applied for funding. Meetings are usually held in January, June and October. Unsuccessful applicants will not be acknowledged unless an sae is enclosed.

WHO TO APPLY TO Angela Freestone, Administrator, 54–56 Knatchbull Road, London SE5 9QY *Tel* 020 7274 2266 *Fax* 020 7274 5222 *E-mail* peterminet@lineone.net

CC NO 259963   ESTABLISHED 1969

■ Minge's Gift

WHERE FUNDING CAN BE GIVEN UK.

WHO CAN BENEFIT Registered charities only.

WHAT IS FUNDED General charitable purposes as directed by the Master and Wardens of the Cordwainers Company. The income of Minge's Gift is generally allocated for the long-term support of medical and educational establishments and towards disabled and/or disadvantaged young people. Currently there is no surplus income available for distribution.

WHAT IS NOT FUNDED No grants to individuals.

TYPE OF GRANT Grants of up to three years for core costs, projects, research, and recurring costs; start-up costs are considered.

FINANCES *Year* 2001 *Income* £88,000 *Grants* £59,000 *Assets* £581,000

TRUSTEES The Master and Wardens of the Worshipful Company of Cordwainers.

HOW TO APPLY In writing to the correspondent.

WHO TO APPLY TO Lt Col. J R Blundell, Clerk, The Worshipful Company of Cordwainers, 8 Warwick Court, Gray's Inn, London WC1R 5DJ *Tel* 020 7242 4411 *Fax* 020 7242 3366

CC NO 266073   ESTABLISHED 1972

■ The Minos Trust

WHERE FUNDING CAN BE GIVEN UK and overseas.

WHO CAN BENEFIT Organisations.

WHAT IS FUNDED General charitable purposes, especially Christian causes.

RANGE OF GRANTS £25–£2,000, exceptionally higher.

SAMPLE GRANTS £10,000 each to Chichester Cathedral Trust and Tigers Club Project; £2,500 to Care Trust; £2,000 to Tearfund; £1,500 to Ashburnham Christian Trust; £1,000 each to Bible Society, Friends of the Elderly, and Youth with a Mission.

FINANCES *Year* 1998–99 *Income* £29,000 *Grants* £72,000

TRUSTEES K W Habershon; E M Habershon; Mrs D Irwin-Clark.

HOW TO APPLY In writing to the correspondent, for consideration on an ongoing basis.

WHO TO APPLY TO The Trustees, Kleinwort Benson Trustees Ltd, PO Box 191, 10 Fenchurch Street, London EC3M 3LB

CC NO 265012   ESTABLISHED 1972

■ The Mirfield Educational Charity

WHERE FUNDING CAN BE GIVEN The urban district of Mirfield.

WHO CAN BENEFIT Individuals and organisations.

WHAT IS FUNDED Schools; youth groups; and educational expenses for individuals.

SAMPLE GRANTS £35,000 to Gearstones Lodge for improvement; £12,000 to Castle Hall School for a minibus; £3,600 to Mirfield Free Grammar and Sixth Form College for a biology trip, music equipment and A-level physical education course; £3,500 to Crossley Fields School for printers, software and books; £3,300 to Battyeford C of E Junior and Infants School to replace portable staging; £2,400 to Crowlees C of E Junior and Infants School for IT equipment and a trampolining competition; £500 to

Wellhouse Playgroup for improvements; £350 to Phoenix Karate Club for mats and equipment.
FINANCES *Year* 1999–2000 *Income* £40,000 *Grants* £72,000 *Assets* £1,300,000
TRUSTEES Dr H G Grason, Chair; S R Garnett; D B Brook; R Goodall; D S Metcalfe; Mrs S Beetham; D Beetham; B Nicholson; B C Whitaker.
HOW TO APPLY In writing to the correspondent. Trustees meet three times a year in February, May and October.
WHO TO APPLY TO M G Parkinson, 7 Kings Road, Mirfield WF14 8AW
CC NO 529334   **ESTABLISHED** 1961

━━━━━━━━━━━━━━━━━━━━━━━━━━

■ **The Laurence Misener Charitable Trust**

WHERE FUNDING CAN BE GIVEN UK.
WHO CAN BENEFIT There is a tendency to benefit those charities in which the settlor was interested.
WHAT IS FUNDED General charitable purposes, particularly Jewish organisations and medical causes.
RANGE OF GRANTS £1,350–£10,000.
SAMPLE GRANTS £10,000 to Richard Dimbleby Cancer Fund; £7,500 to Home for Aged Jews, Jewish Association for Physically Handicapped and Jewish Care; £6,000 to Robert Owen Foundation; £5,000 to Royal College of Surgeons of England; £4,500 to Imperial Cancer Research Fund; £4,200 to Jews' Temporary Shelter; £4,000 to SGHMS Haematology Research Fund; £3,500 to Great Ormond Street Children's Hospital Fund.
FINANCES *Year* 2000–01 *Income* £96,286 *Grants* £107,800 *Assets* £2,865,291
TRUSTEES J E Cama; P M Tarsh; Mrs J M Cama.
HOW TO APPLY In writing to the correspondent.
WHO TO APPLY TO C A Letts, Messrs Bourner Bullock, Sovereign House, 212–224 Shaftesbury Avenue, London WC2H 8HQ
CC NO 283460   **ESTABLISHED** 1981

━━━━━━━━━━━━━━━━━━━━━━━━━━

■ **The Victor Mishcon Charitable Trust**

WHERE FUNDING CAN BE GIVEN UK.
WHO CAN BENEFIT Registered charities, particularly Jewish organisations.
WHAT IS FUNDED General charitable purposes. Within the limited funds available each application is considered on its merits with preference given to applications for the relief of poverty from recognised organisations.
TYPE OF GRANT One-off.
RANGE OF GRANTS £5–£35,000. Generally £5,000 or less.
SAMPLE GRANTS £35,000 to British Council of Shaare Zedak; £13,620 to UJIA; £12,500 to Joint Jewish Charitable Trust; £4,630 to Friends of Alyn; £3,500 to S & P A Cohen Charitable Trust; £2,575 to United Synagogue; £1,500 to Nightingale House; £1,388 to Central Synagogue; £1,000 each to Life Neurological Research Trust, and Maccabi Union.
FINANCES *Year* 2000–01 *Income* £89,887 *Grants* £106,078 *Assets* £1,635,375
TRUSTEES Lord Mishcon; P A Cohen; P Mishcon; R Mishcon; J Landau.
HOW TO APPLY In writing to the correspondent.

WHO TO APPLY TO Miss M Grant, Summit House, 12 Red Lion Square, London WC1R 4QD *Tel* 020 7440 7000
CC NO 213165   **ESTABLISHED** 1961

━━━━━━━━━━━━━━━━━━━━━━━━━━

■ **Mary Miskin Charitable Trust**

WHERE FUNDING CAN BE GIVEN UK and overseas.
WHO CAN BENEFIT Registered charities.
WHAT IS FUNDED General charitable purposes.
RANGE OF GRANTS £400 on average.
SAMPLE GRANTS £600 to Countryside Workshop Charitable Trust; £500 each to Friends of the Elderly, Guildford Undetected Tumour Screening, Jubilee Sailing Trust, NSPCC, Royal Alfred Seafarers Society, SABC Clubs for Young People, Sail Training Association, St Christopher's Hospice, Wytham Hall, Yand MCA.
FINANCES *Year* 1999–2000 *Income* £35,000 *Grants* £17,000 *Assets* £612,000
TRUSTEES John C Vernor Miles; Michael Bridges Webb; Gloria Taviner.
HOW TO APPLY In writing to the correspondent. The trust reviews applications once a year.
WHO TO APPLY TO J C Vernor Miles, Trustee, Vernor Miles & Noble, 5 Raymond Buildings, Gray's Inn, London WC1R 5DD *Tel* 020 7242 8688
CC NO 235972   **ESTABLISHED** 1964

━━━━━━━━━━━━━━━━━━━━━━━━━━

■ **Misselbrook Trust**

WHERE FUNDING CAN BE GIVEN UK with a preference for the Wessex area.
WHO CAN BENEFIT Registered charities.
WHAT IS FUNDED General charitable purposes.
SAMPLE GRANTS £2,000 to Aidis Trust; £1,000 each to The Enham Trust, Haemophilia Society, Jubilee Sailing Trust and Wessex Childrens Hospice Trust.
FINANCES *Year* 1999–2000 *Income* £27,000 *Grants* £25,000 *Assets* £503,000
TRUSTEES Miss M J Misselbrook; M Howson-Green.
HOW TO APPLY In writing to the correspondent.
WHO TO APPLY TO M Howson-Green, Trustee, Charter Court, Third Avenue, Southampton SO15 0AP *Tel* 023 8070 2345
CC NO 327928   **ESTABLISHED** 1988

━━━━━━━━━━━━━━━━━━━━━━━━━━

■ **The Mitchell Charitable Trust**

WHERE FUNDING CAN BE GIVEN UK, with a preference for London.
WHO CAN BENEFIT Organisations benefiting: people of all ages; volunteers; Jews; at risk groups; people disadvantaged by poverty; homeless people; and victims of abuse and domestic violence.
WHAT IS FUNDED Jewish organisations, social welfare, child welfare, homelessness, voluntary organisations.
WHAT IS NOT FUNDED No grants to individuals or for research, education, overseas appeals or non-Jewish religious appeals. Applicants from small charities outside London are unlikely to be considered.
TYPE OF GRANT Some recurring.
RANGE OF GRANTS £16–£25,000.
SAMPLE GRANTS £25,000 to Jewish Care; £20,000 to World Jewish Relief; £15,000 to Refuge; £5,000 each to Action for ME and London School of Economics.
FINANCES *Year* 2001–02 *Income* £65,000 *Grants* £78,000 *Assets* £191,800
TRUSTEES Ashley Mitchell; Parry Mitchell; Elizabeth Mitchell; Hannah Lowy.

HOW TO APPLY In writing to the correspondent. Applications must include financial information. The trust does not reply to any applications unless they choose to support them. Trustees do not meet on a regular basis, thus applicants may not be advised of a grant for a considerable period.
WHO TO APPLY TO Ashley Mitchell, Trustee, 28 Heath Drive, London NW3 7SB *Tel* 020 7794 5668 *Fax* 020 7794 5680
CC NO 290273   ESTABLISHED 1984

■ The Mitchell Trust (also known as Mrs
M A Lascelles' Charitable Trust)

WHERE FUNDING CAN BE GIVEN Scotland and the developing world.
WHO CAN BENEFIT Registered Scottish charities.
WHAT IS FUNDED General charitable purposes.
WHAT IS NOT FUNDED Only recognised Scottish charities are supported.
SAMPLE GRANTS £4,900 to Scottish Youth Dance Festival; £4,000 to SITA; £4,000 (in three grants) to Seer Centre; £1,300 to Intermediate Technology; £1,200 to Oxfam; £1,000 each to British Red Cross, Byre Theatre, Kirkmichael, Straloch & Glenshee Church, Marie Stopes International and Children 1st.
FINANCES *Year* 1999–2000 *Income* £86,000 *Grants* £53,000 *Assets* £1,700,000
TRUSTEES Mrs M A Lascelles; C W Pagan.
HOW TO APPLY In writing to the correspondent. Applications should be received by 30 April and 31 October 31.
WHO TO APPLY TO Mrs M A Lascelles, c/o Pagan Osborne, 12 St Catherine Street, Cupar KY15 4HN *Tel* 01334 653777 *Fax* 01334 655063
SC NO SC003495

■ The Esmé Mitchell Trust

WHERE FUNDING CAN BE GIVEN Ireland, but mainly Northern Ireland.
WHO CAN BENEFIT Organisations, and individuals who are involved in the arts and cultural activities.
WHAT IS FUNDED General charitable purposes in Ireland as a whole but principally in Northern Ireland with a particular interest in cultural and artistic objects. Part of the trust fund is only available to assist certain heritage bodies as set out in Schedule 3 to the Capital Transfer Act 1984.
WHAT IS NOT FUNDED Grants are not usually given to individuals wishing to undertake voluntary service or further education.
TYPE OF GRANT No time limits have generally been set on grants. The trust has on occasions given grant assistance over a period of two to three years but in general tries not to become involved in commitments of a long-term nature.
FINANCES *Year* 1999 *Income* £125,000 *Grants* £122,000
TRUSTEES P J Rankin; Mrs F Jay-O'Boyle; R P Blakiston-Houston.
OTHER INFORMATION In previous years the trust has had both an income of, and made grants totalling, around £120,000. Further information was not available.
HOW TO APPLY In writing to the correspondent. Applicants should submit three copies of the following: a concise description of the proposed project; a recent statement of accounts and balance sheet; a copy of the constitution; details of tax and legal or charitable status; a list of committee officers; information on other

sources of finance; a contact address and telephone number. Trustees meet about five or six times a year. Guidelines for applicants are available from the trust.
WHO TO APPLY TO The Northern Bank Executor & Trustee Co. Ltd, PO Box 183, Donegall Square West, Belfast BT1 6JS *Tel* 028 9024 5277 *Fax* 028 9024 1790
IR NO XN48053   ESTABLISHED 1965

■ Mitsubishi Corporation Fund for Europe and Africa

WHERE FUNDING CAN BE GIVEN UK, Africa and Europe.
WHAT IS FUNDED Grants are given to conserve and protect for the benefit of the public the environment as a whole, and its animal, forest and plant life in particular, and to educate the public in natural history and ecology and the importance of conservation of the environment. Also to advance the education of the public and in particular to: promote education and research in the field of ecology and conservation of natural resources and the environment; promote the study and appreciation of flora and fauna with particular emphasis on endangered species; promote the study and appreciation of agriculture, horticulture, silviculture, and land and estate management; carry out research into the sustainable development of forest lands; and relieve poverty in any part of the world.
SAMPLE GRANTS £50,000 to Wildcru Big Cats Project; £24,000 to Zoological Society of London; £23,250 to Earthwatch Europe; £5,000 to Botanic Gardens Conservation.
FINANCES *Year* 2000–01 *Income* £125,334 *Grants* £103,542 *Assets* £679,663
TRUSTEES D Pownall; M Miyaji; Y Otani; J Brumm; Y Hirota; H Nomura.
HOW TO APPLY In writing to the address below. However, it should be noted that funds are committed a year in advance.
WHO TO APPLY TO Mrs J Rogers, Secretary to the Fund, Mid City Place, 71 High Holborn, London WC1V 6BA *Tel* 020 7025 3034 *Fax* 020 7025 3039 *E-mail* julie.rogers@mitsubishicorp.com *Website* www.mitsubishicorp.com/europe
CC NO 1014621   ESTABLISHED 1992

■ Keren Mitzvah Trust

WHERE FUNDING CAN BE GIVEN UK.
WHO CAN BENEFIT Registered charities.
WHAT IS FUNDED General charitable purposes.
TYPE OF GRANT One-off and recurrent.
FINANCES *Year* 2001 *Income* £225,670
TRUSTEES C J Smith; M Weiss; M Weisss.
OTHER INFORMATION Total expenditure for the year was £272,638. No information was available on beneficiaries.
HOW TO APPLY The trust stated that the trustees support their own personal charities.
WHO TO APPLY TO P Willoughby, c/o Manro Haydan Trading, 1 Knightsbridge, London SW1X 7LX *Tel* 020 7823 2200
CC NO 1041948   ESTABLISHED 1994

■ The Mizpah Trust

WHERE FUNDING CAN BE GIVEN UK.

WHO CAN BENEFIT Registered charities.

WHAT IS FUNDED General charitable purposes, especially Christian organisations.

SAMPLE GRANTS £10,000 each to CARE, H & B Alpha Partners and Relationships Foundation; £7,500 to Downe House 21st Century Appeal; £6,000 to Stewards Trust; £5,000 to Action for ME; £1,750 to Cloud Trust; £1,000 to Love for the Family; £500 each to Harvester Trust and Timothy Trust.

FINANCES *Year* 2000–01 *Income* £129,000 *Grants* £165,000 *Assets* £134,000

TRUSTEES A C O Bell; J E Bell.

HOW TO APPLY The trust has stated that 'no applications will be considered'.

WHO TO APPLY TO A C O Bell, Trustee, Foresters House, Humbly Grove, South Warnborough, Hook, Hampshire RG29 1RY

CC NO 287231   **ESTABLISHED** 1983

■ The Mobbs Memorial Trust Ltd

WHERE FUNDING CAN BE GIVEN Stoke Poges and district within a 35-mile radius of St Giles Church.

WHO CAN BENEFIT Organisations benefiting: people of all ages; ex-service and service people; volunteers; unemployed; those in care, fostered and adopted; parents and children; at risk groups; people with disabilities; those disadvantaged by poverty; ex-offenders and those at risk of offending; homeless people; those living in rural areas; socially isolated people; victims of abuse, crime and domestic violence.

WHAT IS FUNDED St Giles Church and other charitable purposes including: almshouses; sheltered accommodation; community development; support to voluntary and community organisations; combined arts; community arts and recreation; health; conservation and environment; schools and colleges; and community facilities and services.

WHAT IS NOT FUNDED No grants to individuals.

TYPE OF GRANT Buildings and project. Funding is given for up to three years.

SAMPLE GRANTS £14,000 each to Church House Trust and St John Ambulance; £5,000 each to Buckinghamshire Foundation, Reading YMCA, and Stoke Mandeville Hospital.

FINANCES *Year* 2000 *Income* £61,700 *Grants* £117,000

TRUSTEES M R Mobbs; Sir Nigel Mobbs; Dr C N A Mobbs.

HOW TO APPLY In writing to the correspondent.

WHO TO APPLY TO Nick Hamilton, Slough Estates House, 234 Bath Road, Slough, Berkshire SL1 4EE *Tel* 01753 537171 *Fax* 01753 820585 *E-mail* nickh@sloughestates.co.uk

CC NO 212478   **ESTABLISHED** 1963

■ The Moette Charitable Trust

WHERE FUNDING CAN BE GIVEN UK.

WHO CAN BENEFIT People educationally disadvantaged through poverty.

WHAT IS FUNDED 'The principal activity of the trust is the provision of support of the poor and needy for educational purposes.'

FINANCES *Year* 1998–99 *Income* £82,000 *Grants* £30,000

TRUSTEES Simon Lopian; Pearl Lopian; David Haffner.

HOW TO APPLY In writing to the correspondent.

WHO TO APPLY TO Simon Lopian, Trustee, 1 Holden Road, Salford M7 4NL *Tel* 0161 832 8721

CC NO 1068886   **ESTABLISHED** 1998

■ The Mole Charitable Trust

WHERE FUNDING CAN BE GIVEN UK, with a preference for Manchester.

WHO CAN BENEFIT Individuals, registered charities and institutions benefiting children, young adults, Jews and people disadvantaged by poverty.

WHAT IS FUNDED Jewish causes, educational institutions and organisations to relieve poverty.

RANGE OF GRANTS £600–£200,000.

SAMPLE GRANTS £200,000 to Shaarei Torah Buildings Ltd; £55,250 to Manchester Jewish Grammar School; £50,000 each to Bar Yochai Charitable Trust and Broom Foundation; £25,000 to Binoh of Manchester; £15,000 to Shaarei Chested Trust; £11,400 to Manchester Charitable Trust; £5,000 each to Beis Ruchel D'Satmar Girls School Ltd, Kollel Rabbi Yechiel and Ner Yisrael Education Trust.

FINANCES *Year* 2001–02 *Income* £42,266 *Grants* £467,886 *Assets* £2,135,215

TRUSTEES M Gross; Mrs L P Gross.

HOW TO APPLY In writing to the correspondent.

WHO TO APPLY TO Martin Gross, 2 Okeover Road, Salford M7 4JX *Tel* 0161 832 8721

CC NO 281452   **ESTABLISHED** 1980

■ The D C Moncrieff Charitable Trust

WHERE FUNDING CAN BE GIVEN UK and worldwide, with a preference for Norfolk and Suffolk.

WHO CAN BENEFIT Registered charities only.

WHAT IS FUNDED General charitable purposes. Trustees already have a list of donees whose requirements outweigh the trustees' ability to help.

WHAT IS NOT FUNDED No grants for individuals.

RANGE OF GRANTS Usually £500–£1,000. Larger grants for larger one-off projects or certain regularly supported local charities.

SAMPLE GRANTS £6,000 to The Church Army (Harleston House); £3,000 each to All Hallows Hospital and Friends of Lothlingland; £2,500 each to Ashby Church, Lound Church, and Lowestoft Girl Guides.

FINANCES *Year* 2000–01 *Income* £55,000 *Grants* £48,000 *Assets* £738,000

TRUSTEES D J Coleman; L G Friston; A S Cunningham.

HOW TO APPLY In writing to the correspondent. The trust stated in October 2002 that demand for funds exceeded available resources, therefore no further requests are currently invited.

WHO TO APPLY TO L G Friston, Trustee, 8 Quinnell Way, Lowestoft, Suffolk NR32 4WL

CC NO 203919   **ESTABLISHED** 1965

■ Monmouthshire County Council Welsh Church Act Fund

WHERE FUNDING CAN BE GIVEN In practice, Monmouthshire.

WHO CAN BENEFIT Students, at risk groups, and people who are disadvantaged by poverty, socially isolated, disaster victims, or sick.

WHAT IS FUNDED Education, relief in sickness and need, people who are blind or elderly, medical and social research, probation, social and recreational, libraries, museums and art galleries and protection of historic buildings relating to Wales, places of worship and burial grounds, emergencies and disasters.

TYPE OF GRANT Mostly for provision, upkeep and repair of religious buildings and community halls.

RANGE OF GRANTS Up to £1,000.

SAMPLE GRANTS Beneficiaries included Hanover United Reformed Church, Christian Lewis Children's Cancer Care, Rogiet Methodist Church, Llansoy Parochial Church Council, North Wales Society for the Blind, Mathern & District Club, Marie Curie Cancer Care, Sound Affairs and St Arvans Memorial Hall.

FINANCES *Year* 2001–02 *Grants* £15,118 *Assets* £2,000,000

TRUSTEES Two trustees from each of the following councils: Monmouthshire Borough Council, Blaenau Gwent Borough Council, Caerphilly County Borough Council, Newport County Borough Council and Torfaen County Borough Council.

HOW TO APPLY In writing to the correspondent. Applicants can only apply once a year.

WHO TO APPLY TO S K F Greenslade, Treasurer's Department, Monmouthshire County Council, County Hall, Cwmbran, Monmouthshire NP44 2XH

CC NO 507094　　　**ESTABLISHED** 1996

■ The Monument Trust

WHERE FUNDING CAN BE GIVEN Unrestricted, but UK in practice.

WHO CAN BENEFIT Registered charities working in the fields outlined below.

WHAT IS FUNDED Health and community care; AIDS; environment; arts; social development; general. Preference is given to new ideas or methods which can be replicated widely or become self-sustaining.

WHAT IS NOT FUNDED Grants are not normally made to individuals.

TYPE OF GRANT No set pattern.

SAMPLE GRANTS £1,000,000 to Victoria and Albert Museum for refurbishment of the British Galleries; £252,000 over three years to Royal College of Arts/University of Cambridge towards establishing a centre of excellence in design innovation; £250,000 each to the Roundhouse in London for redevelopment and Royal Ballet School for new premises; £150,000 over three years to English National Opera for redevelopment of the Coliseum; £120,000 each to Crime Concern for work with Sir Henry Cooper School in Hull (over two years) and Meadow Well Community Resource Centre in South Shields for a business manager (over three years); £100,000 over two years to Hackney Empire for renovation; £90,000 to HIV i-base towards a new information service; £89,000 over three years to Tavistock Trust for Aphasia for research on treatment of aphasia; £75,500 to Judge Institute of Management Studies for the establishment of a diploma and masters course.

FINANCES *Year* 2000–01 *Income* £4,524,000 *Grants* £4,014,000 *Assets* £119,007,000

TRUSTEES S Grimshaw; Linda Heathcoat-Amory; R H Gurney; Sir Anthony Tennant.

OTHER INFORMATION The trust is one of the Sainsbury Family Charitable Trusts which share a common administration. An application to one is taken as an application to all.

HOW TO APPLY Proposals are generally invited by the trustees or initiated at their request. Unsolicited applications are nort encouraged and are unlikely to be successful.

WHO TO APPLY TO Michael Pattison, Director, Allington House, 1st Floor, 150 Victoria Street, London SW1E 5AE *Tel* 020 7410 0330

CC NO 242575　　　**ESTABLISHED** 1965

■ George A Moore Foundation

WHERE FUNDING CAN BE GIVEN Principally Yorkshire and the Isle of Man but also some major UK appeals.

WHO CAN BENEFIT Only registered charities are considered and the foundation rarely contributes seedcorn finance to newly established organisations. Projects for young people (teenagers/young adults) are favoured, as are community care projects. Organisations benefiting: ex-service and service people; medical professionals; seafarers and fishermen; and widows and widowers. Support may also be given to carers, disabled people, those living in rural areas, victims of crime, and people with various diseases and medical conditions.

WHAT IS FUNDED The trustees select causes and projects from the applications received during the year and also independently research and identify specific objectives where they wish to direct assistance. The type of grants made can vary quite widely from one year to another and care is taken to maintain a rough parity among the various fields covered so that one sphere of activity does not benefit unduly at the expense of another. Areas which are not or cannot be covered by official sources are favoured. The foundation will also consider charities working in the fields of: respite and sheltered accommodation; infrastructure support and development; special needs education; respite care; first aid; self-help groups; and health facilities and buildings. Support may also go to memorials, monuments, special schools, care in the community, cancer research, crime prevention schemes and day centres.

WHAT IS NOT FUNDED No assistance will be given to individuals, courses of study, expeditions, overseas travel, holidays, or for purposes outside the UK. Local appeals for UK charities will only be considered if in the area of interest. Because of present long-term commitments, the foundation is not prepared to consider appeals for religious property or institutions, or for educational purposes.

TYPE OF GRANT Grants are generally non-recurrent and the foundation is reluctant to contribute to revenue appeals.

RANGE OF GRANTS £20–£170,000; average grant £500. Approximately 75 % of the grants made are £500 or below.

SAMPLE GRANTS £21,730 to HMS Illustrious Central Fund; £10,000 each to Duke of Edinburgh Award, Marie Curie Cancer Care and RNLI; £5,000 to Second World War Experience Centre; £3,000 to Dyslexia Institute Bursary Fund; £2,750 to Outward Bound Trust; £2,600 to British Red Cross; £2,000 each to Bradford Bears Wheelchair Sports Club, Haig Homes, St John Ambulance and Tockwith Show.

FINANCES *Year* 2001–02 *Income* £475,410 *Grants* £105,150 *Assets* £7,472,462

TRUSTEES George A Moore; Mrs E Moore; J R Moore; Mrs A L James.

HOW TO APPLY In writing to the correspondent. No guidelines or application forms are issued. The trustees meet approximately four times a year,

on variable dates, and an appropriate response is sent out after the relevant meeting.
WHO TO APPLY TO Miss L P Oldham, Mitre House, North Park Road, Harrogate, North Yorkshire HG1 5RX
CC NO 262107   **ESTABLISHED** 1970

■ The Henry Moore Foundation

WHERE FUNDING CAN BE GIVEN UK and overseas.
WHO CAN BENEFIT Charitable organisations and institutions benefiting the general public.
WHAT IS FUNDED Financial support is given to a broad range of institutions, public visual art and educational bodies, and to activities, including exhibitions, acquisitions, conservation, research and publishing.
WHAT IS NOT FUNDED The foundation does not give grants to individual applicants and cannot fund on a regular basis the revenue expenditure of galleries and other publicly-supported institutions.
TYPE OF GRANT One-off.
FINANCES *Year* 2001–02 *Income* £2,098,000 *Grants* £1,052,000 *Assets* £89,300,000
TRUSTEES Sir Ewen Fergusson, Chair; Sir Alan Bowness; Marianne Brouwer; Joanna Drew; Patrick Gaynor; Henry Wrong; Prof. Andrew Causey; Margaret McLeod; Greville Worthington; Sir Rex Richards.
PUBLICATIONS *The Henry Moore Foundation Review.*
HOW TO APPLY In writing to the correspondent. Applications are usually considered at quarterly meetings of the donations sub-committee, which makes recommendations to the management committee of the trustees. Applications should not be made by telephone or in person.
WHO TO APPLY TO Timothy Llewellyn, Director, Dane Tree House, Perry Green, Much Hadham, Herts SG10 6EE *Tel* 01279 843333 *Fax* 01279 843647 *Website* www.henry-moore-fdn.co.uk/hmf
CC NO 271370   **ESTABLISHED** 1977

■ The Horace Moore Charitable Trust

WHERE FUNDING CAN BE GIVEN UK.
WHO CAN BENEFIT Registered charities benefiting: children; actors and entertainment professionals; ex-service and service people; musicians; seafarers and fishermen; C of E and Roman Catholic Christians; disabled people; and victims of abuse.
WHAT IS FUNDED The priorities of the trust are: dance and ballet, music, opera and theatre; church buildings; animal homes, animal welfare and horse facilities; and heritage. The trust will consider funding: information technology and computers; Christian education and churches; hospices and hospice at home; conservation and environment; purchase of books for education; and community facilities and day centres.
SAMPLE GRANTS £4,000 to Macmillan Cancer Relief; £2,000 to The British Forces Foundation; £1,000 each to NSPCC, Motor Neurone Disease Association, The Mark Davies Injured Riders Fund, Children's Promise and Friends of St Michaels Bray.
FINANCES *Year* 1999–2000 *Income* £29,000 *Grants* £24,000
TRUSTEES J A G Leighton; J E A Leighton.
HOW TO APPLY The trust states that funds are fully committed. Donations are only given to

charitable organisations and to those of personal interest to the trustees.
WHO TO APPLY TO J A G Leighton, Trustee, Mallows Studio, Warreners Lane, Weybridge, Surrey KT13 0LH
CC NO 262545   **ESTABLISHED** 1962

■ The Moore Stephens Charitable Foundation

WHERE FUNDING CAN BE GIVEN Greater London.
WHO CAN BENEFIT Registered charities. Preference is given to charities operating within, or affecting, the City of London.
WHAT IS FUNDED General charitable purposes.
SAMPLE GRANTS £3,000 each to CHASE Children's Hospitals in the South East and Oinoussai Benevolent Fund; £1,000 to Children in Need.
FINANCES *Year* 1999–2000 *Income* £32,000 *Grants* £20,000 *Assets* £59,000
TRUSTEES Richard Moore; Nicholas Hilton; Timothy Cripps.
HOW TO APPLY 'Unsolicited applications are not requested as the trustees prefer to make donations to charities whose causes they have identified through their own research.'
WHO TO APPLY TO Nicholas Hilton, Trustee, St Paul's House, Warwick Lane, London EC4P 4BN
CC NO 297194   **ESTABLISHED** 1987

■ John Moores Foundation

WHERE FUNDING CAN BE GIVEN Merseyside (plus Skelmersdale, Ellesmere Port and Halton), Northern Ireland, South Africa, overseas.
WHO CAN BENEFIT Voluntary organisations and community groups in the UK benefiting people who are marginalised as a result of social, educational, physical, economic, cultural, geographical or other disadvantage. South Africa and international relief organisations are also supported, but only organisations proactively selected by the trustees rather than applicants.
WHAT IS FUNDED Women, including girls; black and other racial organisations; race, gender and disability awareness; advice and information to alleviate poverty; second chance learning; and grass roots community groups. In addition, the following are supported in Merseyside only: people with disabilities; carers; support and training for voluntary organisations; homeless people; childcare; complementary therapy; people in crisis; cooperative working/trust building; small appeals from charitable organisations whose work does not fall into these categories.
WHAT IS NOT FUNDED The foundation does not give grants for individuals; academic or medical research; animal charities; arts, heritage or local history projects; new buildings; churches for church-based or church-run activities (although community groups running activities in church premises which come within the foundation's policy guidelines will be considered); children and young people, except via the South Moss Foundation (administered by JMF); conservation and the environment; employment creation schemes; festivals; holidays, expeditions and outings; individuals; medicine or health; national organisations or organisations based outside of Merseyside or Northern Ireland, even if working within those areas; overseas projects, unless initiated by the foundation; schools, universities or colleges; sponsorship, including fundraising events; sport;

statutory bodies; vehicles; victims of crime –
other than rape crisis and domestic violence
projects.

TYPE OF GRANT Core costs, one-off, revenue, project,
recurring costs, capital and start-up costs.
Funding for up to three years. Volunteers
expenses and help towards salaries.

RANGE OF GRANTS In 2001–02, 75% of grants were
for £5,000 or less, and a little over 12% for
£1,000 or less.

SAMPLE GRANTS £88,564 to Merseyside Information
and Advice Project; £50,000 to Themba Health
Trust – South Africa; £40,000 to Women's
Education Fund for Southern Africa; £25,000
each to British Red Cross for the Afghan Crisis
Appeal and Christian Aid for the Goma Volcano
Appeal; £17,000 to Bronte Youth and
Community centre – Liverpool; £15,000 to
Sheila Kay Fund and Merseyside Sexual Assault
Projec for the EVA project; £14,950 to
Roundabout Centre – Wirral; £10,000 to West
Lancashire Crisis and Information Centre –
Skelmersdale.

FINANCES *Year* 2001–02 *Income* £863,000
Grants £678,000 *Assets* £16,300,000

TRUSTEES Mrs Jane Moores; Barnaby Moores;
Sister M McAleese; Peter Bassey.

PUBLICATIONS *Applying For A Grant.*

HOW TO APPLY Applications should be in writing and
accompanied by an application form, copies of
which are obtainable from the foundation.
Applications are expected to contain the
following information: a description of your
organisation, its work and existing sources of
funding; a description of the project for which
you are applying for funds; detailed costings of
the project, including details of funds already
raised or applied for, if any; details of how the
project will benefit people within the
foundation's target groups. Applicants should
also send, if possible: latest accounts; latest
annual report; list of management committee
members; equal opportunities policy. Trustees
meet five to six times a year and all applications
are acknowledged.

WHO TO APPLY TO Tara Parveen, Grants Director, 7th
Floor, Gostins Building, 32–36 Hanover Street,
Liverpool L1 4LN *Tel* 0151 707 6077
Fax 0151 707 6066 *E-mail* jmf@dial.pipex.com
Website www.jmf.org.uk

CC NO 253481   **ESTABLISHED** 1963

....

■ **The Nigel Moores Family
Charitable Trust**

WHERE FUNDING CAN BE GIVEN UK, but mostly Wales
and Liverpool.

WHO CAN BENEFIT Institutions benefiting children and
young adults, actors and entertainment
professionals, musicians, students and textile
workers and designers.

WHAT IS FUNDED Principal objective should be the
raising of the artistic taste of the public whether
in relation to music, drama, opera, painting,
sculpture or otherwise in connection with the
fine arts, the promotion of education in the fine
arts and academic education, the promotion of
the environment, the provision of recreation and
leisure facilities and the advancement of
religion.

RANGE OF GRANTS Generally £250–£3,600.

SAMPLE GRANTS £486,037 to A Foundation; £3,600
to Bellan House School Parents Association;
£2,250 to Llantysilio School Fund; £2,000 to
Pentrdwr Community Association; £1,000 each
to Llangollen Pre School Playgroup, Nightingale

Appeal and Wrexham Maelor Hospital for its
cancer and maternity wards; £500 each to the
Llangollen and Glenafron branches of Cylch
Meithrin Llangollen and Glenrafon; £250 to
Millennium Seedbank Appeal.

FINANCES *Year* 2000–01 *Income* £1,608,214
Grants £498,137 *Assets* £2,410,509

TRUSTEES J C S Moores; Mrs L M White; Mrs P M
Kennaway.

HOW TO APPLY In writing to the correspondent.

WHO TO APPLY TO P Kurthausen, Accountant, c/o
Macfarlane & Co., 2nd Floor, Cunard Building,
Water Street, Liverpool L3 1DS *Tel* 0151 236
6161 *Fax* 0151 236 1095

CC NO 1002366   **ESTABLISHED** 1991

....

■ **The Peter Moores Foundation**

WHERE FUNDING CAN BE GIVEN UK and Barbados.

WHO CAN BENEFIT Organisations benefiting children
and young adults, artists, actors, musicians,
textile workers and designers, writers and
poets, teachers and sportsmen and women.

WHAT IS FUNDED Projects which come to the
attention of the patron or the trustees, that: (a)
raise the artistic taste of the public whether in
relation to music, drama, opera, painting,
sculpture or otherwise, in connection with the
fine arts; (b) promote education in the fine arts;
(c) promote academic education; (d) promote
the Christian religion; or (e) provide facilities for
recreation or other leisure-time occupation.

TYPE OF GRANT One-off or recurring, for buildings,
revenue costs, capital costs and running costs.

SAMPLE GRANTS £272,000 for a recording of
Rossini's Bianca e Falliero; £166,000 to
English National Opera; £102,000 to Peter
Moores Barbados Trust; £100,000 to Almeida
Opera; £78,000 to Welsh National Opera;
£58,000 to Royal Northern College of Music for
scholarships; £50,000 each to Game
Conservancy Trust and Rossini Opera Festival;
£40,000 to Ampleforth College.

FINANCES *Year* 2000–01 *Grants* £5,000,000

TRUSTEES Barbara Johnstone; Peter Egerton-
Warburton; Eileen Ainscough; Ludmilla Andrew.

HOW TO APPLY In writing to the correspondent, but
applicants should be aware that its 1999 report
states that the foundation: 'will normally
support projects which come to the attention of
its patron or trustees through their interests or
special knowledge. General applications for
sponsorship are not encouraged and are
unlikely to succeed.'

WHO TO APPLY TO Peter Saunders, Wallwork Nelson
and Johnson, Derby House, Lytham Road,
Fulwood, Lancashire PR2 4JF *Tel* 01772
712000 *E-mail* moores@pmf.org.uk

CC NO 258224   **ESTABLISHED** 1964

....

■ **The Morel Charitable Trust**

WHERE FUNDING CAN BE GIVEN UK and the developing
world.

WHO CAN BENEFIT Grants are normally made to
projects of which the trustees have personal
knowledge. Organisations benefiting people
disadvantaged by poverty are prioritised, but
those benefiting volunteers, people living in
inner city areas, and victims of famine will be
considered.

WHAT IS FUNDED The arts, particularly drama;
organisations working for improved race
relations; inner city projects and developing
world projects. Charities working in the fields of
arts, culture and recreation; health;

conservation and environment; education and training; and social care and development.

WHAT IS NOT FUNDED No grants to individuals.

TYPE OF GRANT Project.

SAMPLE GRANTS In 1998–99: £7,500 to Child to Child for health education in the developing world; £7,000 to Oxfam for three separate appeals; £4,200 to International Network for the Availability of Scientific Publications; £4,000 to VSO; £2,000 to Ghana School Aid.

FINANCES *Year* 1999–2000 *Grants* £51,000

TRUSTEES J M Gibbs, Chair; W M Gibbs; S E Gibbs; B M O Gibbs; S Gibbs; E Gibbs; Thomas Gibbs.

HOW TO APPLY In writing to the correspondent. The trustees meet three times a year to consider applications. In 1999–2000 they met on 10 April, 30 October and 13 February.

WHO TO APPLY TO S E Gibbs, Trustee, 34 Durand Gardens, London SW9 0PP *Tel* 020 7582 6901

CC NO 268943   **ESTABLISHED** 1972

■ The Morgan Crucible Company plc Charitable Trust

WHERE FUNDING CAN BE GIVEN Primarily Wirral, Leeds, South Wales, South London, Worcester, Thames Valley.

WHO CAN BENEFIT People with physical or mental disabilities; young people in deprived or undesirable circumstances; and people disadvantaged by poverty. Medical professionals and research workers will be considered.

WHAT IS FUNDED Medical development and research; care (including holidays) of people with disabilities; care (including holidays) of disadvantaged young people; adventure or training holidays or courses for character development of young people; local (Windsor area) good causes; character reform; arts; education; community services.

WHAT IS NOT FUNDED Grants are not made to individuals, parish churches or youth clubs. The following causes are not usually supported: overseas appeals, armed forces, restoration of buildings, travel, wildlife and countryside.

TYPE OF GRANT Donations are made to the same charities for a period of years. One payment per annum.

FINANCES *Year* 1999–2000 *Income* £53,000 *Grants* £61,000 *Assets* £36,000

TRUSTEES Dr E B Farmer; David Coker.

HOW TO APPLY In writing to the correspondent.

WHO TO APPLY TO D J Coker, The Morgan Crucible Company plc, Morgan House, Madeira Walk, Windsor, Berkshire SL4 1EP *Tel* 01753 837000

CC NO 273507   **ESTABLISHED** 1977

■ The J P Morgan Fleming Educational Trust and Foundation (formerly Save & Prosper Educational Trust and Foundation)

WHERE FUNDING CAN BE GIVEN UK, with a special interest in Islington, Havering, east London generally, Bournemouth and the regions of Edinburgh and Glasgow in Scotland.

WHAT IS FUNDED UK-based educational projects, with an emphasis on special needs, which generally fit into one of the following categories: special needs education including youngsters disadvantaged by disability, background or lack of opportunity; children's projects that offer education and training that widen the opportunities for youngsters, particularly those

children who are in trouble or 'at risk'; rimary and secondary schools, universities and museums; supporting school age children and students in all art forms, helping them to gain access to the arts and to better appreciate them; some scholarships and bursaries are made to organisations supporting educational fees and maintenance; New and innovative ways of advancing education in the UK.

The J P Morgan Fleming Foundation has a modest unrestricted portion of its budget that is generally used for donations to children's charities

WHAT IS NOT FUNDED Projects not usually supported include: pen appeals from national charities; building appeals; charity gala nights and similar events; or appeals by individuals for study grants, travel scholarships or charity sponsorships.

SAMPLE GRANTS £67,000 over four years to Wiltshire Community Foundation for a fund for tackling rural deprivation through education; £60,000 over three years to Multiple Sclerosis Charitable Trust for the development of a Bsc in professional nursing practice; £45,000 over three years to both Community Foundation (in north east England) for a training project for 'at risk' youngsters and Maidstone YMCA for a detached youth worker and playgroup; £30,000 each over three years to KIDS Birmingham for a salary, ProShare Education Trust for a competition and Edinburgh Royal College of Surgeons for bursaries; £30,000 over two years to Marine Aquarium for schools equipment.

FINANCES *Year* 2001 *Grants* £903,000

TRUSTEES J P Morgan Fleming Marketing Ltd, who have appointed the following managing committee: M Garvin, chair; D Grant; J White; R Kaye; E Banks; M Ridley; G Lindey; D MacIntyre; C Machell; L Filby; D Williams; C Lake; A Roughead; C Eardley.

HOW TO APPLY To apply for funding please write a brief letter (not more than two sides of A4) to Duncan Grant, the director. Please avoid bulky items such as cassettes in the original request. Applications are always acknowledged, and will be reviewed within eight weeks. Final approval for funding must come from trustees who meet four times a year, in January, March, July and October.

WHO TO APPLY TO Duncan Grant, Director, 10 Aldermanbury, London EC2Y 7RF *Tel* 020 7325 8771

CC NO 291617   **ESTABLISHED** 1985

■ The Mr and Mrs J T Morgan Foundation

WHERE FUNDING CAN BE GIVEN Mainly Wales.

WHO CAN BENEFIT Churches, and national and local charities benefiting children, young people, students and Christians.

WHAT IS FUNDED Preference is given to the support of charities in Wales and to the promotion of education and religion in Wales.

WHAT IS NOT FUNDED No grants to individuals.

TYPE OF GRANT One-off.

SAMPLE GRANTS £1,000 each to Cambrian Educational Charity, Morriston Orpheus Choir, Overton Studio Trust, St Teilo Church Bishopston and South Gower & Swansea West Fundraisers; £500 to Books Abroad; £250 to Play Right; £200 each to British Red Cross, Chicks and Ysgol Gymraeg Lon Las.

FINANCES *Year* 1999–2000 *Income* £23,000 *Grants* £20,000 *Assets* £283,000

Think carefully about every application. Is it justified?

667

TRUSTEES J A Lloyd, Chair; J Aylward; R Morgan.

HOW TO APPLY In writing to the correspondent. All applications are acknowledged, but funds only permit that one in twelve applicants receive a grant.

WHO TO APPLY TO Richard Morgan, Beor Wilson and Lloyd, Calvert House, Calvert terrace, Swansea SA1 6AP *Tel* 01792 655178

CC NO 241835   **ESTABLISHED** 1965

■ Morgan Stanley International Foundation

WHERE FUNDING CAN BE GIVEN London boroughs of Tower Hamlets and Newham.

WHO CAN BENEFIT UK registered charities benefiting unemployed people, at risk groups, carers, and people who are disabled, disadvantaged by poverty or homeless.

WHAT IS FUNDED Grants are focused in the following areas, with a particular emphasis on education, training and employment: (a) services for youth: organisations of which the primary mission is providing educational and leadership activities for young people; (b) job training/remedial education/disabled and homeless support: for adults and young people in order to prepare these people to become self-supporting; (c) hospitals/health: support for hospitals and innovative healthcare projects in the East End of London. As a rule, the foundation does not support organisations involved in the research of specific diseases.

WHAT IS NOT FUNDED 'As a rule, grants will not be made to either international or UK charitable organisations unless they have a project in this local area. In addition, grants will not be made to either political or evangelistic organisations, "pressure groups", or individuals who are seeking sponsorship either for themselves (e.g. to help pay for education) or for onward transmission to a charitable organisation.'

TYPE OF GRANT Capital or revenue costs, but not loans.

RANGE OF GRANTS £1,000–£50,000, average grant £5,000.

SAMPLE GRANTS £71,000 each to the foundation's 'charities of the year', Community Links and Royal London Hospital; £68,556 to Community Links; £28,000 to Fulcrum Challenge; £25,000 to Woodland Centre Trust; £21,672 to George Green School; £20,000 each to Newtec and Tower Hamlets Education Business Partnership; £18,296 to Providence Row; £16,000 to Stephen Hawking School Trust; £15,476 to Comic Relief; £15,000 to East-Side Educational Trust, Spitalfields Festival and Good Shepherd Mission.

FINANCES *Year* 2001 *Income* £1,208,376 *Grants* £518,000 *Assets* £2,680,859

TRUSTEES Jerker Johansson, Chair; Jonathan Chenevix-Trench; John Crompton; Amelia Fawcett; Richard Heyes; David Nicol; Tamsin Rowe; Charles Scott; Peter Stott; John Studzinski.

HOW TO APPLY In writing to the correspondent. However please note that the trust has a 'proactive approach to its funding programme and thus rarely will a grant be made in response to an unsolicited application or proposal'.

WHO TO APPLY TO Mrs Heather Bird, Secretary, 25 Cabot Square, Canary Wharf, London E14 4QA *Tel* 020 7425 6221 *Fax* 020 7425 4949

CC NO 1042671   **ESTABLISHED** 1994

■ Morgan Williams Charitable Trust

WHERE FUNDING CAN BE GIVEN UK.

WHO CAN BENEFIT Christian organisations.

WHAT IS FUNDED Charities with which the trustees have some connection.

RANGE OF GRANTS Generally up to £5,000.

SAMPLE GRANTS £179,708 to Holy Trinity Church; £5,791 to Oasis Trust; £5,000 each to Chasah Trust, New Life Outreach, and Philo Trust; £2,500 to Church of the Holy Spirit; £2,180 to Youth for Christ; £2,000 each to St Eterburgha's Centre and Salvation Army.

FINANCES *Year* 1999–2000 *Income* £137,343 *Grants* £237,678 *Assets* £2,905

TRUSTEES K J Costa; Mrs A F Costa.

HOW TO APPLY The trust states that only charities personally connected with the trustees are supported and absolutely no applications are either solicited or acknowledged.

WHO TO APPLY TO K J Costa, Trustee, 2 Finsbury Avenue, London EC2M 2PP *Tel* 020 7568 2569 *Fax* 020 7568 0912 *E-mail* sally.baker@ubsw.com

CC NO 221604   **ESTABLISHED** 1964

■ The Oliver Morland Charitable Trust

WHERE FUNDING CAN BE GIVEN UK.

WHO CAN BENEFIT Registered charities usually chosen through personal knowledge of the trustees.

WHAT IS FUNDED Most of the funds are given to Quaker projects or Quaker-related projects.

WHAT IS NOT FUNDED No grants to individuals.

TYPE OF GRANT Grants are given for core, capital and project support for up to three years.

RANGE OF GRANTS £200–£22,000.

SAMPLE GRANTS £26,000 to Quaker Peace and Service; £7,400 to Quaker Home Service – Children and Young People; £5,000 to Woodbrooke; £2,500 to Pakistan Environmental Protection Foundation; £1,500 to Sightsavers International; £1,000 to Uganda Peace Education; £800 to SOS Sahel International; £300 to Tools for Self Reliance; £200 to Stoneham Housing Association Yeovil.

FINANCES *Year* 2001–02 *Income* £89,000 *Grants* £104,000

TRUSTEES Priscilla Khan; Stephen Rutter; Joseph Rutter; Jennifer Pittard; Kate Lovell; Charlotte Jones.

HOW TO APPLY The trustees meet twice a year, probably in May and November. The trust tends to support the same charities each year and only limited funds are available for unsolicited applications.

WHO TO APPLY TO J M Rutter, Trustee, Thomas's House, Stower Row, Shaftesbury, Dorset SP7 0QW *Tel* 01747 853524

CC NO 1076213   **ESTABLISHED** 1999

■ S C and M E Morland's Charitable Trust

WHERE FUNDING CAN BE GIVEN UK.

WHO CAN BENEFIT Quaker, local and UK charities which have a strong social bias and also some UK-based international charities.

WHAT IS FUNDED Support to Quaker charities and others which the trustees have special interest in, knowledge of or association with, including

religious groups, relief of poverty and ill-health, promotion of peace and development overseas.
WHAT IS NOT FUNDED The trust does not usually give to animal welfare, individuals or medical research.
TYPE OF GRANT Project.
RANGE OF GRANTS Up to £3,000.
SAMPLE GRANTS In 1998–99: £3,000 to Responding to Conflict; £2,500 to Britain Yearly Meeting; £2,000 to Quaker Housing Trust.
FINANCES *Year* 2001–02 *Income* £36,362 *Grants* £36,000
TRUSTEES J C Morland; Ms J E Morland; Ms E Boyd; H N Boyd.
HOW TO APPLY In writing to the correspondent. The trustees meet three times a year to make grants, in March, July and December. Applications should be submitted in the month before each meeting.
WHO TO APPLY TO J C Morland, Trustee, Gable House, Parbrook, Glastonbury, Somerset BA6 8PB *Tel* 01458 850804
CC NO 201645　　　**ESTABLISHED** 1957

■ The Morris Charitable Trust

WHERE FUNDING CAN BE GIVEN UK and overseas, with a preference for Islington.
WHO CAN BENEFIT Small local projects and national organisations.
WHAT IS FUNDED General charitable purposes. National, international and local community projects, particularly causes within the community of the London borough of Islington.
WHAT IS NOT FUNDED No grants for individuals.
TYPE OF GRANT One-off grants for recurring costs for one year or less are priorities. Building and other capital grants, core costs, research grants, running costs, salaries and start-up costs are considered.
RANGE OF GRANTS £50–£35,000; average grant £250.
SAMPLE GRANTS £15,000 to Harborough School; £13,000 to Holloway School; £6,000 to Pavilion Opera Trust; £5,000 each to Anne Frank Trust and Hackney Empire; £3,750 to Youth Aliyah Child Rescue; £2,500 to Finsbury Park Action Group.
FINANCES *Year* 2000–01 *Income* £82,829 *Grants* £144,240 *Assets* £88,556
TRUSTEES Mrs G Morris; J A Morris; P B Morris; A R Stenning.
PUBLICATIONS Information pamphlet.
HOW TO APPLY By application form available from the trust.
WHO TO APPLY TO Julie Davies, Chairman's PA, Management Office, Business Design Centre, 52 Upper Street, Islington Green, London N1 0QH *Tel* 020 7359 3535
CC NO 802290　　　**ESTABLISHED** 1989

■ Morris Family Israel Trust

WHERE FUNDING CAN BE GIVEN UK and Israel.
WHO CAN BENEFIT General charitable purposes, but mainly Jewish organisations.
SAMPLE GRANTS £25,000 to Karliver Rebbe; £23,000 to Bet Haggi; £14,000 to Keren Le Pituach; £5,000 to Elad and Jewish Community of Hebron; £3,000 to Palestine Media Watch; £2,800 to Mosdot Neu Zvia; £1,800 to Keren Miarachit Ie Israel. Beneficiaries receiving grants of under £500 included Beer Avraham, Bet Yisrael, Galrinai, Keren Klita and Ohr Semeach.
FINANCES *Year* 2000–01 *Income* £73,192 *Grants* £93,162 *Assets* £17,483

TRUSTEES Conrad Morris; Ruth Morris; Sara Jo Ben Zvi; Elisabeth Pushett; David Morris.
HOW TO APPLY In writing to the correspondent.
WHO TO APPLY TO Conrad J Morris, Trustee, Flat 90, North Gate, Prince Albert Road, London NW8 7EJ
CC NO 1004976　　　**ESTABLISHED** 1991

■ Ruth and Conrad Morris Charitable Trust

WHERE FUNDING CAN BE GIVEN UK and Israel.
WHO CAN BENEFIT Jewish organisations; registered charities.
WHAT IS FUNDED Advancement of the Jewish faith; general charitable purposes.
RANGE OF GRANTS £600–£46,271.
SAMPLE GRANTS £46,271 to Morris Family Israel Trust; £36,600 to Lubavitch; £25,000 to Hertsmere; £22,000 to Friends of Bar Ilan; £12,000 to Aish Hatorah Jerusalem Fellowship; £10,000 each to Safe and UJIA; £7,500 to SAJFID; £7,000 to Remembering the Future; £6,000 to Immanuel College.
FINANCES *Year* 2000–01 *Income* £272,890 *Grants* £302,132
TRUSTEES R S Morris; C J Morris.
HOW TO APPLY In writing to the correspondent.
WHO TO APPLY TO Conrad Morris, Trustee, c/o Paul Maurice, MRI Moores Rowland, 3 Sheldon Square, Paddington, London W2 6PS *Tel* 020 7470 0000
CC NO 276864　　　**ESTABLISHED** 1978

■ The Willie & Mabel Morris Charitable Trust

WHERE FUNDING CAN BE GIVEN UK.
WHO CAN BENEFIT Registered charities benefiting people who are ill, particularly with cancer, heart trouble, cerebral palsy, arthritis or rheumatism.
WHAT IS FUNDED Welfare and disability.
WHAT IS NOT FUNDED No grants for individuals or non-registered charities.
RANGE OF GRANTS £250–£4,000.
SAMPLE GRANTS £4,000 each to Association for International Cancer Research and British Lung Foundation; £2,500 each to Arthritis Research Campaign and British Heart Foundation; £2,000 each to Back Care, Bedford Hospital NHS Trust, Brain Research Trust, Changing Faces, DEBRA, High Blood Pressure Foundation and David Tolkien Trust for Stoke Mandeville.
FINANCES *Year* 1999–2000 *Income* £116,047 *Grants* £107,541 *Assets* £3,504,664
TRUSTEES Michael Macfadyen; Joyce Tether; Peter Tether; Andrew Tether; Angela Tether; Suzanne Marriott.
HOW TO APPLY The trustees 'formulate an independent grants policy at regular meetings so that funds are already committed'.
WHO TO APPLY TO Angela Tether, Bramfield Place, Church Road, Sutton, Sandy, Bedfordshire SG19 2NB
CC NO 280554　　　**ESTABLISHED** 1980

■ G M Morrison Charitable Trust

WHERE FUNDING CAN BE GIVEN UK and worldwide charities registered in the UK.
WHO CAN BENEFIT Registered charities only.
WHAT IS FUNDED General charitable purposes. The trustees give priority to those charities already

supported. Very few charities are added to the list each year.

WHAT IS NOT FUNDED No support for individuals, non-registered charities, schemes or activities which are generally regarded as the responsibility of statutory authorities, short-term projects or one-off capital grants.

TYPE OF GRANT Normally annual.

RANGE OF GRANTS £250–£10,000, average £550.

SAMPLE GRANTS £10,000 to University of Aberdeen Development Appeal; £6,000 to Wolfson College for the Wolfson Course; £2,500 to Rugby School for the science schools appeal fund; £2,200 to Royal College of Surgeons; £2,000 each to Royal Institution and Royal Society of Arts endowment fund; £1,500 each to Royal College of Paediatrics and Child Health and Rugby School Head Master's Fund; £1,200 each to Kurt Hahn Trust (Cambridge German Students) and UCL Phoenix Appeal (plastic surgery).

FINANCES *Year* 2001–02 *Income* £230,325 *Grants* £144,850 *Assets* £5,717,240

TRUSTEES G M Morrison; N W Smith; A E Cornick.

HOW TO APPLY In writing to the correspondent. However, grants are normally selected on the basis of trustees' personal knowledge and recommendation. As the trust's grantmaking is of a long-term recurring nature and is restricted by available income, very few new grant applications can be accepted each year. Applications are not acknowledged. Grants are distributed once a year in January. Please note, telephone applications are not considered. Monitoring is undertaken by assessment of annual reports and accounts which are required from all beneficiaries, and by occasional trustee visits.

WHO TO APPLY TO A E Cornick, Trustee, Currey & Co, 21 Buckingham Gate, London SW1E 6LS

CC NO 261380   **ESTABLISHED** 1970

■ The Peter Morrison Charitable Foundation

WHERE FUNDING CAN BE GIVEN UK.

WHO CAN BENEFIT Registered charities benefiting at risk groups and people who are disadvantaged by poverty and socially isolated.

WHAT IS FUNDED A wide range of social welfare causes.

RANGE OF GRANTS £38–£3,000.

SAMPLE GRANTS £3,000 to West London Synagogue; £2,300 to World Jewish Relief; £2,000 to Norwood Ravenswood; £1,400 to Royal Horticultural Society; £1,300 to Maccabi Union; £1,100 each to Royal Academy Trust and Andover District Medical Fund; £1,000 to Educare Small School; £900 to National Horse Retirement Programme; £850 to Music at Winchester.

FINANCES *Year* 1998–99 *Income* £58,000 *Grants* £35,000 *Assets* £1,200,000

TRUSTEES M Morrison; I R Morrison.

HOW TO APPLY In writing to the correspondent.

WHO TO APPLY TO J Payne, Hope Agar, Chartered Accountants, Epworth House, 25 City Road, London EC1Y 1AR *Tel* 020 7628 5801

CC NO 277202   **ESTABLISHED** 1978

■ The Stanley Morrison Charitable Trust

WHERE FUNDING CAN BE GIVEN The west coast of Scotland, with a preference for Glasgow and Ayrshire.

WHO CAN BENEFIT Organisations benefiting young adults, and sportsmen and women.

WHAT IS FUNDED Sporting activities in Scotland, with particular emphasis on the encouragement of youth involvement; charities which have as their principal base of operation and benefit the west coast of Scotland, in particular the Glasgow and Ayrshire areas; charities whose funds arise from or whose assistance is provided to people having connection with the licensed trades and in particular the whisky industry; Scottish educational establishments.

TYPE OF GRANT Buildings, project and recurring costs. Grants and funding for up to and over three years will be considered.

RANGE OF GRANTS £100–£10,000.

SAMPLE GRANTS £11,000 to Scottish Cricket Union; £10,000 each to Princess Royal Trust for Carers, Riding for the Disabled and Mark Scott Foundation; £6,000 to Glasgow University Sports Sponsorship; £5,000 each to Grange Cricket Club for its youth section and Cancer UK Scotland; £4,000 Scottish Schools Badminton Union.

FINANCES *Year* 2002 *Income* £38,000 *Grants* £72,000 *Assets* £1,600,000

TRUSTEES S W Morrison; J H McKean; Mrs M E Morrison; T F O'Connell; G L Taylor; A S Dudgeon.

HOW TO APPLY In writing to the correspondent. Applicants should include details on the purpose of the grant, what funding has already been secured and the actual sum that they are looking for.

WHO TO APPLY TO Tom O'Connell, O'Connell Consulting, McGregor House, Southbank Business Park, Kirkintilloch, Glasgow G66 1XF *Tel* 0141 578 2252 *Fax* 0141 578 2248 *E-mail* tom@oconnell-consulting.com

SC NO SC006610   **ESTABLISHED** 1989

■ The Morton Charitable Trust

WHERE FUNDING CAN BE GIVEN Scotland, especially the Lothian region.

WHO CAN BENEFIT Registered charities.

WHAT IS FUNDED General charitable purposes.

FINANCES *Year* 2001 *Grants* £90,000

HOW TO APPLY In writing to the correspondent. The trust stated it is not in a position to acknowledge individual applicants.

WHO TO APPLY TO Turcan Connell, Princes Exchange, 1 Earl Grey Street, Edinburgh EH3 9EE *Tel* 0131 228 8111 *Fax* 0131 228 8118

SC NO SC004507

■ Moshal Charitable Trust

WHERE FUNDING CAN BE GIVEN UK.

WHO CAN BENEFIT Jewish causes.

WHAT IS FUNDED General charitable purposes.

FINANCES *Year* 1998–99 *Income* £23,000 *Grants* £48,000 *Assets* £23,000

TRUSTEES D Halpern; L Halpern.

HOW TO APPLY In writing to the correspondent.

WHO TO APPLY TO D Z Lopian, Accountant, c/o Lopian Barnett & Co., Harvester House, 37 Peter Street, Manchester M2 5QP

CC NO 284448   **ESTABLISHED** 1981

■ Vyoel Moshe Charitable Trust

WHERE FUNDING CAN BE GIVEN UK and overseas.
WHO CAN BENEFIT Registered charities.
WHAT IS FUNDED Education and relief of poverty.
FINANCES *Year* 2001–02 *Income* £430,502
Grants £400,000 *Assets* £35,000
TRUSTEES Rabbi M Teitelbaum; Rabbi J Meisels; Y Frankel; B Berger; S Seidenfeld.
OTHER INFORMATION There was very little information on file at the Charity Commission for this trust.
HOW TO APPLY In writing to the correspondent.
WHO TO APPLY TO J Weinberger, Secretary, 2–4 Chardmore Road, London N16 6HX *Tel* 020 8806 2598
CC NO 327054   **ESTABLISHED** 1986

■ The Moss Charitable Trust

WHERE FUNDING CAN BE GIVEN Worldwide, with an interest in Dorset, Hampshire and Sussex.
WHO CAN BENEFIT Registered charities, especially Christian.
WHAT IS FUNDED General charitable purposes, specifically for the benefit of the community in the county borough of Bournemouth, and Hampshire, Dorset and Sussex; advancement of religion either UK or overseas; advancement of education; and relief of poverty, disease and sickness.
TYPE OF GRANT Outright grant or interest-free loan.
RANGE OF GRANTS Up to £10,000, but mostly less than £5,000.
SAMPLE GRANTS £8,600 to Christ Church – Westbourne; £7,913 to Tearfund; £7,500 to Slavic Gospel Association Limited; £5,440 to Scripture Union; £5,000 each to Albanians Orphans, Outreach to Kenya, and Youth for Christ.
FINANCES *Year* 2001–02 *Income* £144,742
Grants £228,662 *Assets* £729,053
TRUSTEES J H Simmons; A F Simmons; P L Simmons; D S Olby.
HOW TO APPLY No funds are available by direct application. Because of the way in which this trust operates it is not open to external applications for grants.
WHO TO APPLY TO P D Malpas, 7 Church Road, Parkstone, Poole, Dorset BH14 8UF *Tel* 01202 730002
CC NO 258031   **ESTABLISHED** 1969

■ Moss Family Charitable Trust

WHERE FUNDING CAN BE GIVEN England.
WHO CAN BENEFIT Jewish organisations.
WHAT IS FUNDED Religious and welfare purposes.
SAMPLE GRANTS £3,450 (in four grants) to WLS; £1,850 (in four grants) to the Jewish Museum; £1,500 to Jewish Care; £1,000 to Barnardos 2000.
FINANCES *Year* 2000–01 *Income* £22,000
Grants £25,000
TRUSTEES S D Moss; R S Moss; Mrs V J Campus.
HOW TO APPLY In writing to the correspondent. The trust is unlikely to respond to unsolicited applications.
WHO TO APPLY TO S D Moss, Trustee, 28 Bolton Street, Mayfair, London W1J 8BP *Tel* 020 7629 9933
CC NO 327529   **ESTABLISHED** 1987

■ The Moulton Charitable Trust

WHERE FUNDING CAN BE GIVEN UK, with a preference for Kent.
WHO CAN BENEFIT Established organisations benefiting people with asthma.
WHAT IS FUNDED Medicine and health.
WHAT IS NOT FUNDED No grants for individuals, students or animal charities.
TYPE OF GRANT One-off grants of £5,000 or more. Buildings, capital, core costs, project, research, recurring costs and running costs will be considered.
FINANCES *Year* 2000–01 *Income* £69,000
Grants £205,000 *Assets* £347,000
TRUSTEES J P Moulton; P M Moulton.
HOW TO APPLY In writing to the correspondent.
WHO TO APPLY TO J P Moulton, Trustee, The Mount, Church Street, Shoreham, Sevenoaks, Kent TN14 7SD *Tel* 01959 524008
CC NO 1033119   **ESTABLISHED** 1993

■ The Mount 'A' Charitable Trust

WHERE FUNDING CAN BE GIVEN UK, with a preference for Bristol and Jersey; and Italy.
WHO CAN BENEFIT Registered charities benefiting children and young adults.
WHAT IS FUNDED General charitable purposes. Grants are made at the request of the settlor and her family.
SAMPLE GRANTS £10,000 to Famiglia Bordigaiana; £2,000 to NSPCC; £1,625 to Men of the Trees; £1,150 to Cancer Bacup Jersey; £1,000 each to ACET Jersey, British Heart Foundation, Jersey Blind Society, Lion's Club Swimarathon, South Hampstead High School and Wellbeing.
FINANCES *Year* 1999–2000 *Income* £41,651
Grants £33,250 *Assets* £956,421
TRUSTEES The Barbinder Trust.
HOW TO APPLY In writing to the correspondent. Presumably a letter to either the Mount 'A' or Mount 'B' Charitable Trusts will be considered by both.
WHO TO APPLY TO The Trustees, PricewaterhouseCoopers, 9 Greyfriars Road, Reading RG1 1JG *Tel* 0118 9597111
CC NO 264127   **ESTABLISHED** 1971

■ The Mount 'B' Charitable Trust

WHERE FUNDING CAN BE GIVEN UK, with a preference for Bristol and Jersey; and Italy.
WHO CAN BENEFIT Registered charities benefiting children and young adults.
WHAT IS FUNDED General charitable purposes. Grants are made at the request of the settlor and her family.
SAMPLE GRANTS £10,000 to Famiglia Bordigaiana; £2,000 to NSPCC; £1,625 to Men of the Trees; £1,150 to Cancer Bacup Jersey; £1,000 each to ACET Jersey, British Heart Foundation, Jersey Blind Society, Lion's Club Swimarathon, South Hampstead High School and Wellbeing.
FINANCES *Year* 1999–2000 *Income* £41,651
Grants £33,050 *Assets* £966,285
TRUSTEES The Barbinder Trust.
HOW TO APPLY In writing to the correspondent. Presumably a letter to either the Mount 'A' or Mount 'B' Charitable Trusts will be considered by both.
WHO TO APPLY TO The Trustees, PricewaterhouseCoopers, 9 Greyfriars Road, Reading RG1 1JG *Tel* 0118 9597111
CC NO 264129   **ESTABLISHED** 1971

Think carefully about every application. Is it justified?

671

■ The Mount Everest Foundation

WHERE FUNDING CAN BE GIVEN Expeditions from Great Britain and New Zealand.

WHO CAN BENEFIT Organisations, young adults and older people.

WHAT IS FUNDED Support of expeditions for exploration and research in high mountain regions only.

WHAT IS NOT FUNDED Youth, training and commercial expeditions are not eligible.

TYPE OF GRANT Project.

RANGE OF GRANTS £600–£2,500.

SAMPLE GRANTS £1,200 in two grants to West Gyundi 2002 – India; £950 to British-Indian Suitilla – India; £900 each to Borkoldoy 2002 – Kyrgyzstan, British Great Walls of China – China, Khrebet Kyokkiar 2002 – Kyrgyzstan and West Buttress of Mount Hunter – USA; £850 to British Siguniang – China, East Face Denali 2002 – USA, Ramjak Peak 2002 – India, Scottish West Face of Kizer Asker – Kyrgyzstan and Sharks Finn – India.

FINANCES *Year* 2001–02 *Income* £32,400 *Grants* £26,300 *Assets* £851,700

TRUSTEES The Committee of Management.

PUBLICATIONS A map of Central Asia has been produced in collaboration with the Royal Geographical Society.

HOW TO APPLY Applications should be made on the appropriate forms obtainable from the address below. Deadlines for receipt of completed application forms are 31 August and 31 December for the following year's expeditions.

WHO TO APPLY TO W H Ruthven, Hon. Secretary, Gowrie, Cardwell Close, Warton, Preston PR4 1SH *Tel* 01772 635346 *Fax* 01772 635346 *E-mail* bill.ruthven@ukgateway.net *Website* www.mef.org.uk

CC NO 208206   **ESTABLISHED** 1955

■ The Edwina Mountbatten Trust

WHERE FUNDING CAN BE GIVEN UK and overseas.

WHO CAN BENEFIT Medical organisations, particularly those benefiting children and nurses.

WHAT IS FUNDED Save the Children Fund (for children who are sick, distressed or in need), the promotion and improvement of the art and practice of nursing, and St John Ambulance.

WHAT IS NOT FUNDED No grants for research or to individual nurses working in the UK for further professional training.

TYPE OF GRANT Project grants.

RANGE OF GRANTS £500–£30,000.

SAMPLE GRANTS £35,000 each to St John Ambulance and Save the Children; £10,000 each to Countess Brecknock Hospice, Demelza Hospice, Edwina Mountbatten House, Pilgrims House and 40th Anniversary Grant of St John Ophthalmic Hospital for a capital project; £5,000 each to Changing Faces and Soma Project.

FINANCES *Year* 2000 *Income* £91,047 *Grants* £227,000 *Assets* £3,099,831

TRUSTEES Countess Mountbatten of Burma, Chair; Noel Cunningham-Reid; Lord Faringdon; Lord Romsey; Peter H T Mimpriss; Mrs Mary Fagan.

HOW TO APPLY In writing to the correspondent. The trustees meet once a year, generally in September/October.

WHO TO APPLY TO John Moss, Secretary, Estate Office, Broadlands, Romsey, Hampshire SO51 9ZE *Tel* 01794 518885

CC NO 228166   **ESTABLISHED** 1960

■ Mountbatten Festival of Music

WHERE FUNDING CAN BE GIVEN UK.

WHO CAN BENEFIT Registered charities benefiting (ex) servicemen/women.

WHAT IS FUNDED Charities connected with the Royal Marines and Royal Navy.

WHAT IS NOT FUNDED Charities/organisations unknown to the trustees.

TYPE OF GRANT One-off and recurrent.

SAMPLE GRANTS £17,000 to Malcolm Sargent Cancer Fund; £16,000 to The 1939 War Fund; £9,000 to RN Benevolent Trust; £8,000 to RM Museum; £4,000 each to St Loye's Foundation and RM/RN Children's Home; £3,000 each to St Dunstan's Home and The Mountbatten Trust; £2,500 to Metropolitan Police Benevolent Fund; £1,000 each to St John Ambulance, Erskine Hospital and Royal British Legion. Grants of £500 each included those to 3 Cdo Bde Memorial Fund and Pembroke House.

FINANCES *Year* 2000–01 *Income* £213,000 *Grants* £88,000 *Assets* £103,000

TRUSTEES Commandant General Royal Marines; Chief of Staff; Chief Staff Officer Personnel.

HOW TO APPLY Unsolicited applications are not considered as the trust's income is dependent upon the running and success of various musical events. Any money raised by this means is then disbursed to a set of regular beneficiaries.

WHO TO APPLY TO Lt. Col. A J F Noyes, Corps Secretary, HMS Excellent, Whale Island, Portsmouth PO2 8ER

CC NO 1016088   **ESTABLISHED** 1993

■ The Mountbatten Memorial Trust

WHERE FUNDING CAN BE GIVEN Worldwide.

WHO CAN BENEFIT Registered charities.

WHAT IS FUNDED Grants restricted to technological research in aid of disabilities.

WHAT IS NOT FUNDED No grants are made towards the purchase of technology to assist people with disabilities.

TYPE OF GRANT Technological research projects.

RANGE OF GRANTS £5,000–£15,000.

SAMPLE GRANTS In 1999: £21,000 to the Disabled Living Foundation; £11,000 to Hearing Concern; £7,400 to Cassel Hospital; £2,500 to NACRO.

FINANCES *Year* 2001 *Income* £58,486 *Grants* £37,679 *Assets* £598,324

TRUSTEES HRH The Prince of Wales, Chair; Lord Brabourne; Lady Pamela Hicks; Hon. Michael-John Knatchbull; Countess Mountbatten of Burma; Lord Romsey.

HOW TO APPLY In writing to the correspondent, at any time.

WHO TO APPLY TO John Moss, Secretary, The Estate Office, Broadlands, Romsey, Hampshire SO51 9ZE *Tel* 01794 518885

CC NO 278691   **ESTABLISHED** 1979

■ The Gweneth Moxon Charitable Trust

WHERE FUNDING CAN BE GIVEN UK, particularly Exeter and east Devon.

WHO CAN BENEFIT Registered charities.

WHAT IS FUNDED General charitable purposes.

WHAT IS NOT FUNDED No grants can be given to individuals.

RANGE OF GRANTS £500–£2,500.

SAMPLE GRANTS In 1996–97: £2,415 to Welsh National Opera; £2,000 each to Blond McIndoe Centre, Mental Health Foundation, Plymouth Age

Concern, and St Margaret's Somerset Hospice; £1,000 each to Bristol Cancer Scanner Appeal, British Bach Choir, SS Great Britain, Radar South West, and Foundation for the Study of Infant Deaths.
FINANCES *Year* 1999–2000 *Income* £25,000 *Grants* £36,000 *Assets* £793,000
HOW TO APPLY In writing to the correspondent. Distributions are considered in February and August.
WHO TO APPLY TO The Secretary, NatWest Private Banking, 153 Preston Road, Brighton, East Sussex BN1 6BD
CC NO 266672   **ESTABLISHED** 1971

■ The Mugdock Children's Trust

WHERE FUNDING CAN BE GIVEN Scotland.
WHO CAN BENEFIT Charities benefiting children up to the age of about 14 who are ill or disabled.
WHAT IS FUNDED Poor children from Glasgow or other districts of Scotland who are in need of convalescent treatment for sickness or any other disability; organisations of a charitable nature whose objects either consist of or include the provision in Scotland of rehabilitation, recreation or education for children convalescing or still suffering from the effects of illness, injury or disability; organisations of a charitable nature whose objects either consist of or include the provision in Scotland of accommodation or facilities for children who are in need of care or assistance.
FINANCES *Year* 1999–2000 *Income* £47,000 *Grants* £40,000 *Assets* £540,000
TRUSTEES Rosamund Blair; Joyce Duguid; Anne Leask; Avril Meighan; G M Philips; A J Struthers; Moira Bruce.
HOW TO APPLY On a form available from the correspondent. Trustees meet in March and November.
WHO TO APPLY TO L J McIntyre, 135 Wellington Street, Glasgow G2 2XE *Tel* 0141 248 3904 *Fax* 0141 226 5047
SC NO SC006001

■ The F H Muirhead Charitable Trust

WHERE FUNDING CAN BE GIVEN UK.
WHO CAN BENEFIT Hospitals/medical research institutes.
WHAT IS FUNDED Specific items of medical equipment for use in research by hospitals and universities. Priority is given to applications from smaller organisations.
WHAT IS NOT FUNDED No grants to non-charitable bodies. No grants for equipment for diagnostic or clinical use.
TYPE OF GRANT Capital grants; research grants considered.
RANGE OF GRANTS Up to £10,000.
FINANCES *Year* 2000 *Grants* £730,000 *Assets* £780,000
TRUSTEES J H Purves; M J Harding; S J Gallico; C N Mallinson.
HOW TO APPLY On a form available from the address below. This should be returned with details of specific items of equipment for which a grant is required. Trustees meet twice a year in March and October. Application forms to be received at least three weeks before the meeting.

WHO TO APPLY TO S J Gallico, Chatham Court, Lesbourne, Reigate, Surrey RH2 7FN *Tel* 01403 214500 *Fax* 01403 241457
E-mail teca@argonet.co.uk
CC NO 327605   **ESTABLISHED** 1987

■ The Mulberry Trust

WHERE FUNDING CAN BE GIVEN UK, with an interest in Harlow, Essex and surrounding areas, including London.
WHO CAN BENEFIT Charitable organisations.
WHAT IS FUNDED General charitable purposes.
RANGE OF GRANTS £100–£100,000.
SAMPLE GRANTS £100,000 to Cambridge University for a psychology and Christianity project; £50,000 to Knoydart Foundation; £45,000 to St Clare West Essex Hospice Care Trust; £30,000 to Gibberd Garden Trust; £25,000 each to Credit Action, Pioneer Sailing Trust, Royal Agricultural Benevolent Institution and Royal Engineers Museum Foundation; £22,000 to Harlow Parochial Church Council; £20,000 to Leadership Institute.
FINANCES *Year* 2000–01 *Income* £229,000 *Grants* £538,000 *Assets* £5,900,000
TRUSTEES John G Marks; Mrs Ann M Marks; Charles F Woodhouse; Timothy J Marks.
HOW TO APPLY The trust has stated that it 'will not, as a matter of policy, consider favourably applications which are unsolicited'. However, some of the successful applicants are unaware of this; perhaps the 'application' format should be avoided in favour of an individual letter.
WHO TO APPLY TO Charles Woodhouse, Trustee, Messrs Farrer & Co, 66 Lincoln's Inn Fields, London WC2A 3LH *Tel* 020 7242 2022
CC NO 263296   **ESTABLISHED** 1971

■ The Edith Murphy Foundation

WHERE FUNDING CAN BE GIVEN UK.
WHO CAN BENEFIT Organisations benefiting people in need, and animals.
WHAT IS FUNDED Relief for people suffering hardship/distress due to their age, youth, infirmity, disability, poverty or social and economic circumstances. Relief of suffering of animals and provision for the care of unwanted or sick animals. Other general charitable purposes.
SAMPLE GRANTS £110,000 to Leicester Animal Aid Association; £54,000 to Winged Fellowship Trust; £50,000 to National Kidney Research Fund; £10,000 each to Leicester Children's Holiday Centre, Lord Mayor Scanner Appeal, and Mainline Steam Trust; £1,500 to Burleigh Houses for the Elderly; £500 to Glenfield Hospital Breast Care Appeal; £300 to Aylestone Park Youth Football Club; £250 to Dr Hadwen's Trust.
FINANCES *Year* 1998–99 *Income* £55,000 *Grants* £247,000 *Assets* £749,000
TRUSTEES Edith A Murphy; David L Tams; Pamela M Breakwell; Freda Kesterton; Jack Kesterton.
HOW TO APPLY In writing to the correspondent.
WHO TO APPLY TO D L Tams, Solicitor, c/o Crane & Walton, 113–117 London Road, Leicester LE2 0RG
CC NO 1026062   **ESTABLISHED** 1993

■ Murphy-Newmann Charity Company Limited

WHERE FUNDING CAN BE GIVEN UK, predominantly the south and the south east.

WHO CAN BENEFIT Registered charities only.

WHAT IS FUNDED Financial relief of people who are elderly, very young or disabled.

WHAT IS NOT FUNDED No grants to individuals.

TYPE OF GRANT Recurrent

RANGE OF GRANTS £250–£2,500.

SAMPLE GRANTS In 1999–2000: £2,500 to Ormiston Charitable Trust; £2,000 each to Haemophilia Society, Contact the Elderly, Malcolm Sargent Cancer Care for Children and Invalids at Home Trust; £1,000 each to Barnardos and London Association for the Blind.

FINANCES *Year* 2001–02 *Income* £36,000 *Grants* £29,500 *Assets* £730,000

TRUSTEES M J Lockett; Mrs T R Lockett; M Richman.

HOW TO APPLY In writing to the correspondent, in a letter outlining the purpose of the required charitable donation. Telephone calls are not welcome. There are no application forms, guidelines or deadlines. No sae required. Grants are usually given in November and December.

WHO TO APPLY TO Mrs T R Lockett, Director, Hayling Cottage, Upper Street, Stratford-St-Mary, Colchester, Essex CO7 6JW *Tel* 01206 323685 *Fax* 01206 323686

CC NO 229555   **ESTABLISHED** 1963

■ The Mushroom Fund

WHERE FUNDING CAN BE GIVEN UK and overseas, with a preference for St Helens.

WHO CAN BENEFIT Registered charities. Donations are made only to charities known to the trustees.

WHAT IS FUNDED General charitable purposes.

WHAT IS NOT FUNDED No grants to individuals or to organisations which are not registered charities.

SAMPLE GRANTS £10,000 each to Cambridge University and St Helens Housing for the retirement village project; £5,000 each to Refraid and Roy Castle Lung Cancer Foundation; £1,000 each to Children's Trust, Médecins Sans Frontières, Drugs Initiative Group, Halo Trust, Macmillan Cancer Relief, Marie Curie Cancer Care, Merseyside Police and High Sheriff's Charitable Trust, Middlefield Community School – Gainsborough, Sherbourne School, The National Trust for the foot and mouth crisis appeal, Urolink and Walesby Village Hall.

FINANCES *Year* 2000–01 *Income* £25,865 *Grants* £61,900 *Assets* £975,553

TRUSTEES Liverpool Council of Social Services (Inc.); D F Pilkington; Lady K Pilkington; Mrs R Christian; Mrs J Wailing.

HOW TO APPLY In writing to the correspondent. Please note, the trust does not respond to unsolicited applications.

WHO TO APPLY TO Marjorie Staunton, Liverpool Council of Social Services (Inc.), 14 Castle Street, Liverpool L2 0NJ *Tel* 0151 236 7728

CC NO 259954   **ESTABLISHED** 1969

■ The Music Sales Charitable Trust

WHERE FUNDING CAN BE GIVEN Preference for Bury St Edmunds and London.

WHO CAN BENEFIT Registered charities benefiting children and young adults, musicians, disabled people and people disadvantaged by poverty.

WHAT IS FUNDED The trust supports the education of children attending schools in the UK, relief of need, and other charitable purposes. The trustees are particularly interested in helping to promote music and musical education for young people.

WHAT IS NOT FUNDED No grants to individuals.

RANGE OF GRANTS £75–£12,000.

FINANCES *Year* 2000 *Income* £61,000 *Grants* £41,000

TRUSTEES Robert Wise; Frank Johnson; Ian Morgan; Malcolm Graham; Christopher Butler; David Rockberger; Mrs Mildred Wise.

HOW TO APPLY In writing to the correspondent.

WHO TO APPLY TO Neville Wignall, Clerk, Music Sales Ltd, Newmarket Road, Bury St Edmunds, Suffolk IP33 3YB *Tel* 01284 702600

CC NO 1014942   **ESTABLISHED** 1992

■ The Music Sound Foundation

WHERE FUNDING CAN BE GIVEN UK.

WHO CAN BENEFIT Individuals and organisations benefiting: children and young adults; musicians; music students; and music teachers.

WHAT IS FUNDED The Music Sound Foundation gives grants to individuals and schools for the purchase of instruments and equipment and for music courses for teachers. Assistance with sponsorship for art college status can be provided, although this is co-ordinated through the Technology Colleges Trust. The foundation has agreed to sponsor a minimum of 15 schools over the next five years to become art colleges, totalling £1.5 million.

WHAT IS NOT FUNDED Community projects, student fees/living expenses and music therapy are not funded.

TYPE OF GRANT Capital, core costs, one-off, project, and salaries for schools. Bursaries may be given initially for up to three years but are decided by each college.

RANGE OF GRANTS Average grant size: £750; maximum award: £2,000 (for schools, individuals and music teachers). Bursaries: annual donation of £5,000 to each college.

SAMPLE GRANTS Bursary funds have been made to Royal Scottish Academy of Music & Drama – Glasgow, Royal Welsh College of Music & Drama – Cardiff, Royal Academy – London, Institute of Popular Music – University of Liverpool, Birmingham Conservatoire and Drumtech Drum and Percussion School – London.
Previous beneficiaries include North Leamington School, Churchfield School, Brentwood Ursulie Convent, Egglescliffe School, Guthlaxton College, Focus Events for the String of Pearls Millennium Festival, King William's College, Young Persons Concert Foundation and Music Wheel.

FINANCES *Year* 2001 *Income* £467,734 *Grants* £499,903 *Assets* £6,291,614

TRUSTEES Sir Colin Southgate, Chair; Jim Beach; Jason Berman; John Deacon; Leslie Hill; David Hughes; Steve O'Rourke; Rupert Perry; Richard Holland; John Hutchinson.

OTHER INFORMATION The Music Sound Foundation is the working name of the EMI Sound Foundation.

It was established in 1997 by EMI Records. It is an independent charity dedicated to the improvement of music education.

HOW TO APPLY On a form available from the correspondent. Application for Music Sound Foundation funds from students are considered by the colleges themselves. Applicants must come from within the UK and be able to show evidence of severe financial hardship.

WHO TO APPLY TO Ms Janie Orr, Administrator, 4 Tenterden Street, Hanover Square, London W1A 2AY *Tel* 020 7355 4848 *Fax* 020 7495 1424 *E-mail* orrj@emigroup.com
Website www.emigroup.com/msf

CC NO 1055434   **ESTABLISHED** 1996

■ Muslim Hands

WHERE FUNDING CAN BE GIVEN Overseas.

WHO CAN BENEFIT Organisations benefiting people disadvantaged by poverty and victims of man-made or natural disasters and war.

WHAT IS FUNDED The relief of poverty and sickness in the event of natural disasters and areas of war; help to people in need, particularly orphans; advancement of the Islamic faith and distribution of Islamic literature; provision of schools, training colleges, safe water schemes, medical centres, and orphan sponsorship schemes.

FINANCES *Year* 2001 *Income* £2,159,010 *Grants* £1,868,987 *Assets* £409,692

TRUSTEES S L Hassnain; N Ahmed; A A Parwaz; K A Minhas; M I Qureshi; Dr M Hussain; S G Gillani; Dr Z Nawaz; M Ilyas.

HOW TO APPLY In writing to the correspondent.

WHO TO APPLY TO The Trustees, 148–164 Gregory Boulevard, Nottingham NG7 5JE *Tel* 0115 911 7222 *Fax* 0115 911 7220 *E-mail* contact@muslimhands.org
Website www.muslimhands.org

CC NO 1029742   **ESTABLISHED** 1993

■ The Mutual Trust Group

WHERE FUNDING CAN BE GIVEN UK.

WHO CAN BENEFIT Organisations benefiting Jewish people and people disadvantaged by poverty.

WHAT IS FUNDED General charitable purposes. In particular, for the relief of poverty and the advancement of orthodox Jewish religious education.

FINANCES *Year* 2001 *Income* £96,000 *Grants* £60,000

TRUSTEES A Weisz; B Weisz; M Weisz.

HOW TO APPLY In writing to the correspondent.

WHO TO APPLY TO B Weisz, Trustee, 12 Dunstan Road, London NW11 8AA *Tel* 020 8458 7549

CC NO 1039300   **ESTABLISHED** 1994

■ MYA Charitable Trust

WHERE FUNDING CAN BE GIVEN Worldwide.

WHO CAN BENEFIT Children, young adults and Jewish people.

WHAT IS FUNDED Advancement of orthodox Jewish religion and education.

SAMPLE GRANTS £20,000 to Torah Ve-emuno; £10,400 to Society of Friends of the Torah; £10,000 each to Beis Avrohom Trust and Torah Vachesed Leezrah Vesaad; £7,000 each to Friends of Nachalas Osher and Yad Eliezer; £6,100 to Friends of Ponevezh; £6,000 to Beis Ruzin Trust; £5,000 each to Beis Yaakov

Institution, Dushinsky Trust and Friends of Horim.

FINANCES *Year* 1999–2000 *Income* £271,794 *Grants* £147,458 *Assets* £540,125

TRUSTEES M Rothfeld; Mrs E Rothfeld; Mrs H Schraiber.

HOW TO APPLY In writing to the correspondent.

WHO TO APPLY TO M Rothfeld, Trustee, 4 Amhurst Parade, Amhurst Park, London N16 5AA *Tel* 020 8800 3582

CC NO 299642   **ESTABLISHED** 1987

Think carefully about every application. Is it justified?

675

■ The Kitty and Daniel Nabarro Charitable Trust

WHERE FUNDING CAN BE GIVEN UK.

WHO CAN BENEFIT Registered charities.

WHAT IS FUNDED Relief of poverty, advancement of medicine and advancement of education. This trust will consider funding: information technology and computers; support and self-help groups; environmental issues; IT training; literacy; training for work; vocational training; and crime prevention schemes.

WHAT IS NOT FUNDED No grants to individuals.

FINANCES *Year* 1999–2000 *Income* £20,000 *Grants* £30,000 *Assets* £600,000

TRUSTEES D J N Nabarro; Katherine Nabarro; Elizabeth Cohen.

HOW TO APPLY In writing to the correspondent. However, the trustees allocate grants on an annual basis to an existing list of charities. The trustees do not at this time envisage grants to charities which are not already on the list. **This trust states that it does not respond to unsolicited applications.**

WHO TO APPLY TO D J N Nabarro, Trustee, PO Box 7491, London N20 8LY *Fax* 020 8906 4030

CC NO 1002786   **ESTABLISHED** 1991

■ The Willie Nagel Charitable Trust

WHERE FUNDING CAN BE GIVEN UK.

WHO CAN BENEFIT Registered charities.

WHAT IS FUNDED General charitable purposes.

FINANCES *Year* 2000–01 *Income* £65,016 *Grants* £71,306 *Assets* £14,644

TRUSTEES W Nagel; A L Sober.

OTHER INFORMATION In January 2003, no grants list was available at the Charity Commission since that for 1989–90.

HOW TO APPLY In writing to the correspondent, but note that the trust stated in its report that 'all income is fully spoken for'.

WHO TO APPLY TO A L Sober, Trustee, Lubbock Fine, Russell Bedford House, City Forum, 250 City Road, London EC1V 2QQ *Tel* 020 7490 7766

CC NO 275938   **ESTABLISHED** 1978

■ The Naggar Charitable Trust

WHERE FUNDING CAN BE GIVEN Worldwide.

WHO CAN BENEFIT Jews.

WHAT IS FUNDED Jewish organisations.

TYPE OF GRANT Some recurrent.

RANGE OF GRANTS £500–£98,972, mostly for 500 or less.

SAMPLE GRANTS £99,000 to Jerusalem Foundation; £60,000 to Society of the Friends of Torah; £38,000 to BFAMI; £10,000 to Community Security Trust; £3,300 to British Friends of Hebrew University; £2,500 to Israel Philharmonic Orchestra Fund; £2,000 to British Aid Committee; £1,000 to Tate Gallery Foundation.

FINANCES *Year* 2000–01 *Income* £169,000 *Grants* £228,000 *Assets* £79,000

TRUSTEES Guy Naggar; Hon. Marion Naggar.

HOW TO APPLY In writing to the correspondent.

WHO TO APPLY TO Mr & Mrs Naggar, Trustees, 15 Grosvenor Gardens, London SW1W 0BD *Tel* 020 7834 8060

CC NO 265409   **ESTABLISHED** 1973

■ The Elani Nakou Foundation

WHERE FUNDING CAN BE GIVEN Worldwide, mostly Continental Europe.

WHAT IS FUNDED Advancement of education of the peoples of Europe in each other's culture, history, literature, language, institutions, art, science, religion, music and folklore, and promotion of the exchange of knowledge about the cultures of northern and southern Europe in order to bridge the divide between these cultures and promote international understanding.

RANGE OF GRANTS £15–£12,906.

SAMPLE GRANTS £12,906 to Danish Institute at Athens; £7,240 to Archanes Museum; £3,629 to Danish Greek Cultral Association – Copenhagen; £3,500 to Greek Notos Theatre Co.; £3,03 to Eliamap Institute – Athens; £3,057 to University Copenhagen; £2,419 to Ny Carlsberg Glyptotek – Copenhagen; £1,820 to Institute of Mediterreanan Studies; £16 to University of Aarhus; £15 to Charlemange Trust.

FINANCES *Year* 2000–01 *Income* £56,462 *Grants* £37,695 *Assets* £6,175

TRUSTEES E Holm; Y A Sakellarakis; L St John T Jackson; H Moller.

HOW TO APPLY In writing to the correspondent. Applications are considered in May.

WHO TO APPLY TO Dr E Holm, Trustee, c/o Kleinwort Benson Trustees, PO Box 191, 10 Fenchurch Street, London EC3M 3LB *Tel* 020 7475 5093

CC NO 803753   **ESTABLISHED** 1990

■ NAM Charitable Trust

WHERE FUNDING CAN BE GIVEN Mainly the USA.

WHO CAN BENEFIT Medical, educational and cultural institutions, mainly on recommendations of settlor.

WHAT IS FUNDED Education, health, and community arts and recreation.

WHAT IS NOT FUNDED No travel or education bursaries; no grants to individuals.

TYPE OF GRANT Recurrent.

FINANCES *Year* 1998–99 *Income* £47,304 *Grants* £49,740 *Assets* £1,130,000

TRUSTEES M Cohen; D S Watson.

HOW TO APPLY In writing to the correspondent.

WHO TO APPLY TO M Cohen, Trustee, Saffery Champness, Lion House, Red Lion Street, London WC1R 4GB *Tel* 020 7841 4000

CC NO 265830   **ESTABLISHED** 1973

■ The Janet Nash Charitable Trust

WHERE FUNDING CAN BE GIVEN UK.

WHO CAN BENEFIT Institutions and individuals.

WHAT IS FUNDED General charitable purposes.

SAMPLE GRANTS £33,000 to Vail Valley Foundation; £18,700 to Croix-Rouge Monegasque; £17,291 to Northwestern University Medical School; £15,000 to Duke of Edinburgh's Award International Foundation; £10,000 to Acorn's Children's Hospice Trust; £5,000 to Ovingdean Hall School; £4,000 to Dyslexia Institute; £3,771 to Child Advocacy International; £1,000 to Headway Coventry and Warwickshire.

FINANCES *Year* 2000–01 *Income* £327,471 *Grants* £355,722 *Assets* £117,942

TRUSTEES Ronald Gulliver; M S Jacobs.
OTHER INFORMATION In 2000–01, £109,776 was given to organisations and £245,946 to individuals.
HOW TO APPLY In writing to the correspondent. The trustees meet monthly.
WHO TO APPLY TO R Gulliver, Trustee, Ron Gulliver and Co. Ltd, The Old Chapel, New Mill, Eversley, Hampshire RG27 0RA *Tel* 0118 973 0300 *Fax* 0118 973 0022
CC NO 326880   **ESTABLISHED** 1985

■ Nathan Charitable Trust

WHERE FUNDING CAN BE GIVEN UK and overseas.
WHO CAN BENEFIT Christian organisations.
SAMPLE GRANTS £6,000 to Open Doors; £5,000 each to Leprosy Mission, Operation Mobilisation and Tearfund; £3,000 each to Christian Outreach, Mission Aviation Fellowship and Care; £2,000 each to African Inland Mission and Christian Friends of Israel; £1,000 to Riding Lights.
FINANCES *Year* 1999–2000 *Income* £31,000 *Grants* £35,000
TRUSTEES T R Worth; Mrs P J Worth; G A Jones.
HOW TO APPLY In writing to the correspondent including an sae, although please note, most of the trust's funds are already fully allocated.
WHO TO APPLY TO T R Worth, Trustee, Trewardreva Farm, Constantine, Falmouth, Cornwall TR11 5QQ
CC NO 251781   **ESTABLISHED** 1967

■ The National Art Collections Fund

WHERE FUNDING CAN BE GIVEN UK.
WHO CAN BENEFIT Any museum, gallery or other institution in the UK with a permanent art collection on public display, providing it is registered with the Museums and Galleries Commission.
WHAT IS FUNDED The purchase of works of art of all kinds. It also: presents works of art, which it has received as gifts or bequests, to museums and galleries; works to promote greater awareness of the visual arts; and campaigns to safeguard public art collections.
WHAT IS NOT FUNDED Grants are restricted to establishments which are constantly open to the public.
TYPE OF GRANT One-off grants.
RANGE OF GRANTS There is no fixed upper or lower limit to the size of grant the committee may offer.
SAMPLE GRANTS £300,000 to Tate Gallery (towards John Constable 'Fen Lane, East Bergholt'); £294,029 to Nostell Priory – National Trust (for William Hogarth 'Ferdinand Paying Court to Miranda...[The Tempest]').
FINANCES *Year* 2002 *Grants* £5,585,808
TRUSTEES Committee: Professor Brian Allen, Chair; David Barrie, Director; Rupert Hambro, Treasurer, and 14 others.
PUBLICATIONS *Review, Art Quarterly*, Information notes for grant applicants.
HOW TO APPLY To the correspondent. A basic information leaflet is available for applicants, and an application form. Applicants are expected to have approached other sources of help, and, except in very special circumstances, museums are expected to make a contribution to the purchase from their own funds. The trustees meet monthly, apart from January and

August. Meeting dates are available from the Grants Office, and the deadline for applications is two weeks before the meeting.
WHO TO APPLY TO Mary Yule, Assistant Director and Head of Grants, Millais House, 7 Cromwell Place, London SW7 2JN *Tel* 020 7225 4800 *Fax* 020 7225 4850 *E-mail* myule@artfund.org *Website* www.artfund.org
CC NO 209174   **ESTABLISHED** 1903

■ National Asthma Campaign

WHERE FUNDING CAN BE GIVEN UK.
WHO CAN BENEFIT Organisations benefiting scientists, clinicians, general practitioners, research workers, and people with asthma.
WHAT IS FUNDED Research into and the provision of information and education on asthma and allied respiratory disorders.
TYPE OF GRANT Project grants and fellowships.
SAMPLE GRANTS In 2002: £166,173 to University of Aberdeen; £156,159 to National Heart and Lung Institute; £142,199 to Guy's, King's and St Thomas' – London; £129,934 to Imperial College London; £84,155 to University of Portsmouth; £44,115 to City Hospital – Nottingham; £40,021 to Southampton General Hospital; £14,242 to The Box Surgery – Wiltshire.
FINANCES *Year* 2000–01 *Income* £10,872,000 *Grants* £2,251,000 *Assets* £4,898,000
TRUSTEES Prof. Duncan Geddes, Chair; Sir Stuart Burgess; Andrew Gairdner; Tom Garrett; Chris Griffiths; John Griffiths; Christopher McLaren; Delyth Morgan; Howard Ridley; Dr Rebecca Rosen; Dr Martyn Partridge; Michael Pillans; Prof. John Price; Brian Schirn; Kay Sonneborn; Dr Madge Vickers; Mrs Patricia Weller.
HOW TO APPLY The application process opens in September and closes in November each year; during this period application forms are downloadable from the charity's website.
WHO TO APPLY TO The Research Team, Providence House, 8 Providence Place, London N1 0NT *Tel* 020 7226 2260 *Fax* 020 7704 0740 *Website* www.asthma.org.uk
CC NO 802364   **ESTABLISHED** 1990

■ The National Catholic Fund

WHERE FUNDING CAN BE GIVEN England and Wales.
WHO CAN BENEFIT Organisations and projects which are both national and Catholic benefiting Roman Catholics.
WHAT IS FUNDED The national work of the Catholic Church only. Most of its income is spent on running the Catholic Bishops' Conference General Secretariat and Catholic Communications Service.
WHAT IS NOT FUNDED No grants to individuals, local projects or projects not immediately advancing the Roman Catholic religion in England and Wales.
SAMPLE GRANTS £30,000 to Young Christian Workers; £18,000 to National Board of Catholic Women; £16,000 each to Diocesan Vocational Service and Movement of Christian Workers; £11,000 to National Conference of Priests; £10,000 to Linacre Centre.
FINANCES *Year* 2001 *Income* £1,600,000 *Grants* £165,618 *Assets* £1,800,000
TRUSTEES Archcardinal Cormac Murphy O'Connor; Archbishop Michael Bowen; Archbishop Vincent Nicholls; Archbishop Peter Smith; Robin Smith; Monsignor Michael McKenna; John Gibbs.

HOW TO APPLY In writing to the correspondent before June.

WHO TO APPLY TO Monsignor Andrew Summersgill, 39 Eccleston Square, London SW1V 1BX *Tel* 020 7901 4810 *Fax* 020 7901 4819 *E-mail* secretariat@cbcew.org.uk *Website* www.catholic-ew.org.uk

CC NO 257239   **ESTABLISHED** 1968

■ National Committee of The Women's World Day of Prayer for England, Wales, and Northern Ireland

WHERE FUNDING CAN BE GIVEN UK and worldwide.

WHO CAN BENEFIT Christian literature societies.

WHAT IS FUNDED Charitable Christian educational projects and Christian literature societies, including audio-visual materials.

WHAT IS NOT FUNDED No grants to individuals.

TYPE OF GRANT Annual, regular or one-off.

RANGE OF GRANTS £100–£20,000.

SAMPLE GRANTS £20,000 each to Bible Society, Feed the Minds and United Society for Christian Literature; £10,000 each to Scripture Gift Mission and World Day of Prayer International Committee – Annual; £7,500 each to Bible Reading Fellowship, International Bible Reading Association and Society for Promoting Christian Knowledge; £4,000 to World Day of Prayer National Committee – Samoa; £3,000 each to The Salvation Army Missionary Literature Fund and Scripture Union.

FINANCES *Year* 2001 *Income* £292,690 *Grants* £130,000

TRUSTEES The Officers of the National Committee.

PUBLICATIONS Order of service for the Day of Prayer; children's service; Bible study notes on theme for year; annual booklet, *Together in Prayer*; meditation cards; prayer cards.

HOW TO APPLY In writing to the correspondent, before the end of June. Grants are made in November.

WHO TO APPLY TO Mrs Lynda Lynam, Commercial Road, Tunbridge Wells, Kent TN1 2RR *Tel* 01892 541411 *Fax* 01892 541745 *E-mail* office@wwdp-natcomm.org

CC NO 233242   **ESTABLISHED** 1932

■ The National Kidney Research Fund Limited

WHERE FUNDING CAN BE GIVEN UK.

WHO CAN BENEFIT Recognised renal research establishments supporting medical professionals, research workers and students, and for the benefit of people with kidney and renal diseases.

WHAT IS FUNDED The fund provides grants for medical research into: kidney and renal disease generally; the acute failure of the kidneys and chronic renal failure, including the causes, effects and prevention of such disease and failure; and the congenital malformations of the kidneys and the bladder. Grants are also provided for: post-doctoral studentships and fellowships for the training of individuals, and thereby the advancement and promotion of kidney and renal research; patient welfare and care; and awareness and education. The fund also promotes and distributes the Donor Card.

TYPE OF GRANT Research grants may be awarded for between one and five years. Patient grants are mostly one-off. Loans are not made.

RANGE OF GRANTS Project grants of up to £100,000 are awarded for a maximum of three years; start-up grants of up to £30,000 are awarded for up to one year; programme grants of up to £500,000 are awarded for up to five years.

SAMPLE GRANTS £125,708 over three years to University of Manchester for proximal tubular integration of calcium and phosphate homeostasis; £125,555 over two years to Addenbrooke's Hospital – Cambridge for investigation of AE1 cell biology in health and disease; £102,918 over two years to Imperial College London for complement, CD59 and renal injury; £99,711 to University College London and Middlesex Hospital for endosomal trafficking and the fanconi syndrome: the relationship between megalin recyclin and tublicar transport dysfunction; £99,449 to Imperial College London for the regulation of mesangial cell phenotype by phophoniositol 3-kinase enzyme activity; £99,117 to Addenbrookes Hospital for the regulation of TNF receptors in patients undergoing renal transplantation; £97,708 to University of Dundee for disease modifying loci and malignant hypertension; £96,672 to Institute of Child Health – London for angiopetin-2 and kidney vascular development; £96,169 to National Heart and Lung Institute and Imperial College London for the role of notch/notch-ligand signalling in activity of human regulatory T-cells; £93,993 to South Manchester University for identification of factors important in urolithiasis using an in-vitro model of kidney stone formation.

FINANCES *Year* 2000–01 *Income* £3,050,377 *Grants* £2,552,317 *Assets* £4,637,409

TRUSTEES Prof. David N S Kerr, Chair; Prof. Graham Badley; Dr John R Bradley; Very Revd Michael Bunker; Rupert Caldecott; Emeritus Prof. J Stewart Cameron; Pevd Dr Judy Craig; Peter W Phillips; Prof. Kathryn Wood; Prof. Charles D Pusey.

PUBLICATIONS Research review; *Kidney News* (quarterly magazine); leaflets for patients; guidelines for applicants.

HOW TO APPLY Application forms and guidelines for applicants may be obtained from the grants administrator by telephone, fax or e-mail and from the fund's website. Adverts will be posted in January and July each year inviting applications for project grants, studentship grants, training fellowships, and senior fellowships. Research grants are awarded twice-yearly, in May and November. Applications for kidney patient grants are made on behalf of a patient and are supported by a renal social worker. The Patient Grants Committee will meet twice a year and will also review grants monthly via e-mail.

WHO TO APPLY TO A A Pinchera, Chief Executive, Kings Chambers, Priestgate, Peterborough PE1 1FG *Tel* 01733 704650; Helpline: 0845 300 1499 *Fax* 01733 704699 *E-mail* enquiries@nkrf.org.uk *Website* www.nkrf.org.uk

CC NO 252892   **ESTABLISHED** 1967

■ The National Manuscripts Conservation Trust

WHERE FUNDING CAN BE GIVEN UK.

WHO CAN BENEFIT Grants are made to record offices, libraries, other similar publicly funded institutions including local authority, university and specialist record repositories, and owners of manuscript material which is conditionally exempt from capital taxation or owned by a charitable trust and where reasonable public access is allowed, suitable storage conditions are available, and there is a commitment to continuing good preservation practice.

WHAT IS FUNDED Conservation of manuscripts and archives.

WHAT IS NOT FUNDED The following are not eligible: public records within the meaning of the Public Records Act; official archives of the institution or authority applying except in the case of some older records; loan collections which are exempt from capital taxation or owned by a charitable trust; and photographic, audio-visual or printed materials.

TYPE OF GRANT The grants cover the cost of repair, binding and other preservation measures including reprography, but not cost of equipment. Funding is for up to three years.

RANGE OF GRANTS To match the applicants contribution, up to 50% of the total estimated cost. Grants are not normally considered for projects costing less than £1,000.

SAMPLE GRANTS £20,936 to complete the conservation and microfilming of the Berkeley Castle muniments; £12,500 to University of Nottingham Library towards the conservation of the Wollaton Antiphonal, a service book from the fifteenth century; £11,000 to Staffordshire and Stoke on Trent Archive Service towards a project to conserve the Staffordshire Tithe maps; £9,211 to London Metropolitan Archives towards the conservation of architectural plans of three London theatres: the Theatre Royal at Drury Lane, the Savoy and the Gaiety; £8,600 to The Royal Institute of British Architects Architectural Library towards the Architects' Papers Conservation Project; £5,500 to York City Archives towards the repair and rebinding of volume A/Y, which contains material from the fourteenth to the sixteenth centuries on the life and customs of York; £3,944 to the University of Surrey Library towards the conservation of the manuscript letters of E H Shepard; £2,500 to D'Oyly Opera Company to conserve their archives; and £1,900 to Glasgow University Archive Services towards the conservation of the Blackhouse charters.

FINANCES *Year* 2001 *Income* £107,227 *Grants* £76,091 *Assets* £1,658,639

TRUSTEES Lord Egremont; B Naylor; C Sebag-Montefiore.

PUBLICATIONS *Guide for Applicants.*

HOW TO APPLY Applications must be submitted on a form in the Guide to Applicants, which is available from the trust. Deadlines are 1 April and 1 October each year. The trustees are prepared to be flexible and each application is considered on its own merits; the trust encourages potential applicants to contact the secretary for further advice and an informal discussion about eligibility.

WHO TO APPLY TO The Secretary, The British Library, Co-operation and Partnership Programme, 96 Euston Road, London NW1 2DB *Tel* 020 7412 7052 *Fax* 020 7412 7155 *E-mail* nmct@bl.uk *Website* www.bl.uk/concord/nmct-about.html

CC NO 802796   **ESTABLISHED** 1990

■ The National Power Charitable Trust

WHERE FUNDING CAN BE GIVEN England, Wales, Europe, Asia, Africa and America, preference for areas local to company sites.

WHO CAN BENEFIT Charitable organisations.

WHAT IS FUNDED A wide range of community, health and social causes, particularly initiatives which aim to alleviate need. It is keen to support community initiatives, especially self-help programmes and voluntary work. The trust also continues to support a number of UK charities including health, welfare and medical causes.

WHAT IS NOT FUNDED Support is not given to the following: advertising in charity brochures, animal welfare charities, individuals, the arts, environment/heritage, fundraising events, political appeals, religious appeals, science/technology, or sport.

TYPE OF GRANT Buildings, capital, core costs, one-off, project, research and recurring costs. Funding is available for up to three years.

FINANCES *Year* 1999 *Income* £423,254 *Grants* £361,248

TRUSTEES Mrs A Ferguson; J W Baker; G A W Blackman; M G Herbert.

OTHER INFORMATION National Power plc has changed its name to Innogy.

HOW TO APPLY In writing to the correspondent.

WHO TO APPLY TO Catherine Springett, Innogy, Trigonos, Windmill Hill Business Park, Whitehill Way, Swindon, Wiltshire SN5 6PB

CC NO 1002358   **ESTABLISHED** 1991

■ Nazareth Trust Fund

WHERE FUNDING CAN BE GIVEN UK and developing countries.

WHO CAN BENEFIT Young adults, Christian missionaries and victims of famine, war, and man-made or natural disasters – both individually and through registered institutions.

WHAT IS FUNDED Churches, Christian missionaries, Christian youth work, and overseas aid. Grants are only made to people or causes known personally to the trustees.

WHAT IS NOT FUNDED No support for individuals not known to the trustees.

RANGE OF GRANTS £50–£5,000.

SAMPLE GRANTS £10,000 (in four grants) to Harnham Free Church; £1,800 to Crusaders; £1,000 to SAT 7.

FINANCES *Year* 2001–02 *Income* £33,000 *Grants* £29,000 *Assets* £33,700

TRUSTEES Robert Gainer Hunt; Eileen Mary Hunt; David Gainer Hunt; Elma Lilburn Hunt; Philip Hunt; Nicola Mhairi Hunt.

HOW TO APPLY In writing to the correspondent, although the trust tends to only support organisations it is directly involved with.

WHO TO APPLY TO Mrs E M Hunt, Trustee, Barrowpoint, 18 Millennium Close, Salisbury, Wiltshire SP2 8TB *Tel* 01722 349322

CC NO 210503   **ESTABLISHED** 1956

■ The Nchima Trust

WHERE FUNDING CAN BE GIVEN Malawi.

WHO CAN BENEFIT Individuals and established local organisations benefiting children and young adults, at risk groups, and people who are disadvantaged by poverty or living in rural areas.

WHAT IS FUNDED Initiation and help in schemes aimed at advancing education, health, welfare standards and the provision of clean water, with particular emphasis on self-help schemes and assisting people with disabilities.

SAMPLE GRANTS The trust had a total expenditure of £56,588.

FINANCES *Year* 2000–01 *Income* £71,109

TRUSTEES Ms M Gardiner; Ms A Scarborough; Mrs G Legg; Ms R Richards; K Legg.

OTHER INFORMATION The trust makes fixed grants of approximately £5,000 a year plus other discretionary grants.

HOW TO APPLY In writing to the correspondent.

WHO TO APPLY TO Konrad P Legg, Trustee, Tudeley Hall, Tudeley, Tonbridge, Kent TN11 0PQ

CC NO 1072974   **ESTABLISHED** 1962

■ The Neighbourly Charitable Trust

WHERE FUNDING CAN BE GIVEN Bedfordshire, Hertfordshire and occasionally areas close by.

WHO CAN BENEFIT Organisations benefiting disabled people.

WHAT IS FUNDED Leisure/adventure trips for people who are disabled.

WHAT IS NOT FUNDED No grants to national charities (except occasionally a local branch) or individuals.

SAMPLE GRANTS £2,400 to Borough of Luton Social Services; £2,000 each to Families United Network, Lady Hoare Trust and Happy Days Childrens Charity; £1,400 to Bedfordshire County Council Services; £1,300 to Victim Support Bedfordshire; £1,000 each to MS Society Bedfordshire and Bedfordshire and Northamptonshire MS Therapy Centre; £500 each to Rugby Mayday Trust in Bedford, Family Welfare Association and Beds Garden Carers; £400 to Reach Out Projects.

FINANCES *Year* 1999–2000 *Income* £64,000 *Grants* £18,000 *Assets* £1,600,000

TRUSTEES John Sell; Emma Simpson; Jane Wade.

HOW TO APPLY In writing to the correspondent, for consideration at trustees' meetings three or four times a year.

WHO TO APPLY TO John Byrnes, Secretary, Ground Floor, 52–58 London Road, St Albans, Hertfordshire AL1 1NG *Tel* 01727 843603 *Fax* 01727 843663

CC NO 258488   **ESTABLISHED** 1969

■ The James Neill Trust Fund

WHERE FUNDING CAN BE GIVEN Within 20 miles of Sheffield Cathedral.

WHO CAN BENEFIT Voluntary organisations.

WHAT IS FUNDED Voluntary work for the benefit of people in the area specified above.

TYPE OF GRANT Ongoing support for established organisations and one-off grants to meet start-up costs or unexpected expenses.

RANGE OF GRANTS £100–£2,000.

SAMPLE GRANTS £13,806 on Christmas hampers for older people; £2,000 each to Cavendish Centre and South Yorkshire Community Foundation; £1,500 to Relate – South Yorkshire and Wakefield ; £1,100 each to South Yorkshire and Hallamshire Club for Young People and Voluntary Action – Sheffield; £1,000 to Emmaus Sheffield Ltd; £850 to CRUSE Bereavement Care – Rotherham; £750 to National Probation Service – South Yorkshire; £600 each to Guide Association – Sheffield County, Sheffield Scout Resources Charity and YMCA – Sheffield.

FINANCES *Year* 2001–02 *Income* £39,653 *Grants* £37,356 *Assets* £1,091,407

TRUSTEES Sir Hugh Neill; G H N Peel; Lady Neill.

HOW TO APPLY In writing to the correspondent in July for consideration in August/September.

WHO TO APPLY TO Sir Hugh Neill, Trustee, Barn Cottage, Lindrick Common, Worksop, Nottinghamshire S81 8BA

CC NO 503203   **ESTABLISHED** 1974

■ Nemoral Ltd

WHERE FUNDING CAN BE GIVEN Unrestricted.

WHO CAN BENEFIT Orthodox Jewish communities.

WHAT IS FUNDED Religious, educational and other charitable institutions serving orthodox Jewish communities.

TYPE OF GRANT One-off, recurring, capital and occasionally loans.

SAMPLE GRANTS £250,000 to Friends of Torim; £140,000 to Gemach Tzedaka Vachesed; £100,000 to Friends of Yeshiva Shaar Hashomayim; £96,000 to United Talmudical Associates.

FINANCES *Year* 2000 *Grants* £1,200,000

TRUSTEES C D Schlaff; M Gross; Mrs Z Schlaff; Mrs R Gross; Michael Saberski.

HOW TO APPLY In writing to the correspondent.

WHO TO APPLY TO The Trustees, 13–17 New Burlington Place, Regent Street, London W1X 2JP *Tel* 020 7734 1362

CC NO 262270   **ESTABLISHED** 1971

■ Nesswall Ltd

WHERE FUNDING CAN BE GIVEN Worldwide.

WHO CAN BENEFIT Jewish organisations.

WHAT IS FUNDED Jewish organisations, including education.

FINANCES *Year* 1998–99 *Income* £48,000 *Grants* £48,000 *Assets* £279,000

TRUSTEES I Teitelbaum, Chair; Mrs R Teitelbaum; I Chersky.

HOW TO APPLY In writing to the correspondent, at any time.

WHO TO APPLY TO Mrs R Teitelbaum, Trustee, 28 Overlea Road, London E5 9BG *Tel* 020 8806 2965

CC NO 283600   **ESTABLISHED** 1981

■ The Nestlé Rowntree York Employees Community Fund Trust

WHERE FUNDING CAN BE GIVEN The Yorkshire area; mainly York.

WHO CAN BENEFIT Organisations benefiting: people who are disabled; those disadvantaged by poverty; homeless people; victims of abuse and crime; and victims of famine, man-made or natural disasters and war.

WHAT IS FUNDED Health and community services. The fund supports charities in other parts of the UK which are involved in supporting people who are deaf, blind or disabled, disadvantaged children, relief and research organisations and some international relief organisations.

WHAT IS NOT FUNDED No grants to: capital projects; individuals; government-funded organisations; umbrella organisations whose purpose is to collect funds to disburse themselves; or religious or political organisations for overtly or covertly religious or political aims.

TYPE OF GRANT Core costs, one-off, recurring costs, research, running costs and start-up costs are priorites.

RANGE OF GRANTS £50–£2,000

SAMPLE GRANTS In 1998: £2,000 each to St Leonard's Hospice – York, and British Legion Poppy Appeal – York; £1,500 each to Confectioners Benevolent Fund, Martin House Hospice – Boston Spa, and York CVS; £1,300 to Christian Aid; £1,100 to Macmillan Cancer Relief – York; £1,000 each to NSPCC – York, York Citizens Advice Bureau, and Age Concern – York.

FINANCES *Year* 2001 *Income* £65,000 *Grants* £56,420

TRUSTEES Miss Vivien Tweddell; Miss Catherine Wainwright; Miss Julia Hudson.

HOW TO APPLY In writing to the correspondent. Initial telephone calls are welcomed and simple one-paged applications are preferred.

WHO TO APPLY TO The Secretary, Nestlé Rowntree, Haxby Road, York YO91 1XY *Tel* 01904 602163

CC NO 516702   **ESTABLISHED** 1985

■ The Network for Social Change

WHERE FUNDING CAN BE GIVEN UK and overseas.

WHO CAN BENEFIT Smaller schemes.

WHAT IS FUNDED The Network for Social Change is a group of givers who actively seek out projects that they want to fund, rather than responding to applications, in the areas of arts for change, education, health and wholeness, human rights and peace and planet.

TYPE OF GRANT Smaller projects.

RANGE OF GRANTS Up to £25,000.

SAMPLE GRANTS £50,000 to Jubilee Plus; £41,000 to Oxford Research Group; £15,000 each to Cardboard Citizens for a regional development project, Dance United for development, Ecological Foundation, Gaia Foundation, Medical Foundation towards conflict resolution in Guatemala and NMP Anti-Racist Trust for a monitoring project in Newham.

FINANCES *Year* 2000–01 *Grants* £838,000

TRUSTEES Ingrid Broad; Linda Chase Broda; Candia Carolan; Chris Marks; Ed Ross; Philip Sanders.

HOW TO APPLY The network chooses the projects it wishes to support and does not solicit applications. Unsolicited applications cannot expect to receive a reply. Information for potential members is provided by contacting the Network for Social Change at BM 2063, London WC1N 3XX.

WHO TO APPLY TO The Administrator, BM 2063, London WC1N 3XX

CC NO 295237   **ESTABLISHED** 1986

■ The New Appeals Organisation for the City & County of Nottingham

WHERE FUNDING CAN BE GIVEN Nottinghamshire.

WHO CAN BENEFIT Individuals and organisations benefiting at risk groups and people who are disabled, disadvantaged by poverty or socially isolated.

WHAT IS FUNDED Help which is not available from any other source.

WHAT IS NOT FUNDED Appeals to cover debts or arrears will not be considered.

TYPE OF GRANT One-off.

RANGE OF GRANTS £50–£4,584.

SAMPLE GRANTS In 1997–98: £4,584 to Kilton Municipal Golf Course for a disabled buggy; £4,175 to Col. F Seeley School for a swimming pool hoist; £2,975 to an individual for an electric wheelchair; £2,583 to Nottingham

Rugby Football Club for two sports wheelchairs; £2,146 to an individual for an electric scooter; £2,000 each to Aspley Wood School for a garden for children who are disabled, a playscheme for minibus equipment, a sports team for two wheelchairs for bowls, and an individual for a scooter.

FINANCES *Year* 1999–2000 *Grants* £72,000

TRUSTEES P Everett, Joint Chairman; Mrs E Litman, Joint Chairman; Hon. Ald. B Bateman; David Jones; L S Levin.

HOW TO APPLY In writing to the correspondent. An initial telephone call from the applicant is welcome.

WHO TO APPLY TO The Joint Chairmen, 4 Rise Court, Hamilton Road, Sherwood Rise, Nottingham NG5 1EU *Tel* 0115 960 9644

CC NO 502196   **ESTABLISHED** 1973

■ The New Durlston Trust

WHERE FUNDING CAN BE GIVEN UK and developing countries.

WHO CAN BENEFIT Christian organisations/individuals.

WHAT IS FUNDED General charitable purposes.

WHAT IS NOT FUNDED No grants for work other than for Christian-based work. Overseas grants are only given through UK-based charities.

TYPE OF GRANT Usually one-off, for core costs, capital or project funding.

RANGE OF GRANTS £100–£500.

FINANCES *Year* 2000–01 *Income* £122,000 *Grants* £72,000 *Assets* £226,000

TRUSTEES Nigel Austen Hewitt Pool; Alister John Mogford; Alexandra Louise Mayne.

HOW TO APPLY In writing to the correspondent.

WHO TO APPLY TO N A H Pool, Trustee, 95 Fleet Road, Fleet, Hants GU51 3PJ *Tel* 01252 620444

CC NO 1019028   **ESTABLISHED** 1993

■ Newby Trust Limited

WHERE FUNDING CAN BE GIVEN UK.

WHO CAN BENEFIT Registered charities; social services for their clients; hospitals; and students. People from differing professional and economic groups will be considered.

WHAT IS FUNDED Within the general objects of the trust (medical welfare, relief of poverty, training and education) one category for special support is selected each year. In 2002–03 the theme is supporting families with health care problems and in 2003–04 the homeless. Previous themes have included children under the age of 11 with particular educational needs (2000–01) and regeneration of the urban community (2001–02). Alongside the special category, funding is available each year for relief of poverty, medical welfare and educational grants.

WHAT IS NOT FUNDED Funding is not provided for the following: CPE Law Exam; BSc intercalated with a medical degree; postgraduate medical/veterinary degrees in the first or second years; courses which are outside of the UK; adventure or volunteer courses, including gap-year projects. In addition, first degrees are generally excluded. For medical welfare and relief of poverty, grant applications from individuals are not considered (see How to Apply).

TYPE OF GRANT Usually one-off for part of a project. Buildings, capital, core costs and salaries may be considered.

RANGE OF GRANTS Normally £150–£5,000; the majority for under £1,000.

SAMPLE GRANTS £25,000 to Hampshire Rose Bowl Appeal; £10,000 each to Academy of Ancient Music Trust, Hanley Crouch Community Association, Sheffield Cathedral Development Project, St Cuthbert Copnor Regeneration Project, and Voluntary Action Leicester; £5,000 each to Camphill Village Trust and Medical Foundation for the Care of Victims of Torture.

FINANCES *Year* 2001–02 *Income* £350,426 *Grants* £331,579 *Assets* £8,801,759

TRUSTEES Mrs S A Charlton; Mrs J M Gooder; Dr R D Gooder; Mrs A S Reed; R B Gooder; Mrs A L Foxell.

HOW TO APPLY The secretary takes principal responsibility for most of the smaller grants for relief of poverty and medical welfare, the directors being responsible for the remaining grants, either at the twice-yearly meetings in November and March or in response to specific applications, especially educational grants. Relief of poverty and medical welfare: applications on behalf of individuals are only acceptable if they are made by the social services or other similar bodies on an individual's behalf. Grants are restricted to a maximum of two per household. Special category: applications are invited from registered charities by way of two A4 pages giving full particulars of the project, supported by annual report and/or budget together with any photographs if relevant. The directors will award grants at their meetings in November and March each year. Education: The trust's general policy is to make grants available to those taking second degrees, to mature students, and to students from abroad whose circumstances have been affected by adverse events beyond their control (but not including students whose funds have been cut off by their own government). Individuals (students) should submit the following paperwork, in duplicate and by post: a full cv, statement of financial situation, two letters of reference (preferably academic), and an sae. No reply is made without an sae. Awards usually range from £150 to £1,000 (maximum). Cheques are made out to the educational institution and not to the individual student. It is recommended that applications intended for the start of a new academic year should be submitted at least four months in advance, preferably earlier.

WHO TO APPLY TO Miss W Gillam, Secretary, Hill Farm, Froxfield, Petersfield, Hampshire GU32 1BQ *Tel* 01730 827557 *Fax* 01730 827938 *Website* www.newbytrust.org.uk

CC NO 227151   **ESTABLISHED** 1938

■ The Newcastle Diocesan Society

WHERE FUNDING CAN BE GIVEN Diocese of Newcastle.

WHO CAN BENEFIT Religious organisations.

WHAT IS FUNDED The trust stated: 'The society is a registered charity acting as trustee and custodian trustee responsible for trust funds and properties held upon trust for the diocese and parochial church councils.'

SAMPLE GRANTS £23,000 to Newcastle Diocesan Education Board for their millennium project and governor support project officer; £17,000 to Newcastle Diocesan Board of Finance for stipends.

FINANCES *Year* 1999 *Income* £313,000 *Grants* £299,000 *Assets* £6,900,000

HOW TO APPLY In writing to the correspondent.

WHO TO APPLY TO P Davies, St John's Terrace, North Shields NE29 6HS *Tel* 0191 270 4125 *Fax* 0191 270 4101

CC NO 247234   **ESTABLISHED** 1950

■ The Newcomen Collett Foundation

WHERE FUNDING CAN BE GIVEN The London borough of Southwark.

WHO CAN BENEFIT Individuals and small local projects benefiting children, young adults and students under 25.

WHAT IS FUNDED Education of young people under 25 years of age, including community arts and recreation, with priority for dance and ballet, music and theatre.

WHAT IS NOT FUNDED The trust can only help young people living in the London borough of Southwark. People on courses of further education should have lived in Southwark for at least two years before starting their course.

TYPE OF GRANT One-off.

SAMPLE GRANTS £5,000 each to London Coaching Foundation and the Cathedral School in Southwark.

FINANCES *Year* 2001 *Income* £193,000 *Grants* £116,000 *Assets* £2,500,000

TRUSTEES Prof. C Jennings; E H C Bowman; Mrs S Hase; Miss M Jackson; R Edwards; A G H Stocks; Revd M Johnson; Canon H Cunliffe; R Lovell; A Covell; Miss J Archer.

HOW TO APPLY By application form, available by writing to the clerk. The governors consider requests four times a year.

WHO TO APPLY TO Richard Goatcher, Clerk, Marshall House, 66 Newcomen Street, London Bridge, London SE1 1YT *Tel* 020 7407 2967 *Fax* 020 7403 3969 *E-mail* richard@marshalls.org.uk

CC NO 312804   **ESTABLISHED** 1988

■ The Richard Newitt Fund

WHERE FUNDING CAN BE GIVEN UK.

WHO CAN BENEFIT Organisations and institutions benefiting students who are disadvantaged by poverty. The help is for the advancement of a person's further education rather than the financing of a project.

WHAT IS FUNDED The trustees have designated a small number of educational institutions and awards will be made direct to their student hardship funds.

WHAT IS NOT FUNDED No grants to individuals.

TYPE OF GRANT Non-recurring bursaries to students.

RANGE OF GRANTS £1,500–£40,000.

SAMPLE GRANTS £41,000 to University of Southampton towards bursaries and £3,500 towards prizes; £5,000 each to Bristol Old Vic Theatre Company and Royal Northern College of Music; £38,500 to Southampton University for bursaries, prize awards, and hardship awards; £4,400 each to University of Durham and University of Newcastle upon Tyne; £4,000 to North London University; £3,300 to Winchester School of Art; £2,750 each to Imperial College School of Medicine, Royal Free Hospital School of Medicine, Royal Northern College of Music, and Royal Veterinary College; £2,200 to Bristol Old Vic Theatre School.

FINANCES *Year* 2000–01 *Income* £71,409 *Grants* £55,420 *Assets* £2,449,703

TRUSTEES Kleinwort Benson Trustees Ltd; D A Schofield; Prof. D Holt; Baroness Diana Maddock.

HOW TO APPLY Requests for application forms should be submitted by 1 April in any one year; applicants will be notified of the results in August. Unsolicited applications are unlikely to be considered, educational institutional applications by invitation only.

WHO TO APPLY TO Chris Gilbert, Kleinwort Benson Trustees Ltd, PO Box 191, 10 Fenchurch Street, London EC3M 3LB *Tel* 020 7475 5093

CC NO 276470   **ESTABLISHED** 1978

■ The Newman Charitable Trust

WHERE FUNDING CAN BE GIVEN UK and overseas.

WHO CAN BENEFIT Registered charities.

WHAT IS FUNDED General charitable purposes, with support given to charities known personally to the trustees.

WHAT IS NOT FUNDED No grants to individuals.

RANGE OF GRANTS £250–£25,000.

SAMPLE GRANTS £5,000 to Amnesty International; £2,000 each to ChildLine, Chailey Heritage School and Crisis; £1,000 each to AFASIC, Ethiopiaid, Oxfam and YMCA; £800 to Save the Children; £750 to Sight Savers.

FINANCES *Year* 1999–2000 *Income* £32,000 *Grants* £26,000 *Assets* £518,000

TRUSTEES Newman Trustees Ltd.

HOW TO APPLY In writing to the correspondent.

WHO TO APPLY TO C S Jones, Secretary, Newman Trustees Ltd, Irwin House, 118 Southwark Street, London SE1 0SW *Tel* 020 7928 7252

CC NO 264032   **ESTABLISHED** 1972

■ Mr and Mrs F E F Newman Charitable Trust

WHERE FUNDING CAN BE GIVEN UK, Republic of Ireland and overseas.

WHO CAN BENEFIT Charities benefiting children, young adults and older people. At risk groups, people disadvantaged by poverty, socially isolated people, clergy, students, teachers and governesses may also be considered.

WHAT IS FUNDED Primarily local religious purposes; welfare and educational purposes; and other charitable purposes.

WHAT IS NOT FUNDED No grants to individuals.

RANGE OF GRANTS £100–£3,000.

SAMPLE GRANTS £3,000 each to Bible Society, Children's Society, CMS, and Tearfund; £2,000 to African Enterprise; £1,600 in two donations to St John's Church; £1,000 each to Amnesty International, Credit Action (in two donations), and Novi Most International (in two donations); £750 to Christian Aid.

FINANCES *Year* 1999–2000 *Income* £45,000 *Grants* £42,200 *Assets* £123,000

TRUSTEES G S Smith; F E F Newman.

HOW TO APPLY In writing to the correspondent.

WHO TO APPLY TO S P Weil, Bircham Dyson Bell, 50 Broadway, London SW1H 0BL

CC NO 263831   **ESTABLISHED** 1972

■ The Frances and Augustus Newman Foundation

WHERE FUNDING CAN BE GIVEN UK and overseas.

WHO CAN BENEFIT Mainly professorials working in teaching hospitals and academic units.

WHAT IS FUNDED Mainly, but not exclusively, medical research projects and equipment including Fellowships of The Royal College of Surgeons of England.

WHAT IS NOT FUNDED Applications are not normally accepted from overseas. Requests from other charities seeking funds to supplement their own general funds to support medical research in a particular field are seldom supported.

TYPE OF GRANT One-off and recurring. Research and salaries will also be considered. Funding may be given for up to three years.

RANGE OF GRANTS £2,000–£45,000 per year.

SAMPLE GRANTS £40,000 each to three individuals for research fellowships re. vascular disease, wound healing following bowel cancer and prostate cancer; £36,189 to the Muscular Dystrophy Campaign for a Fellowship for the study of mitochondrial myopathies); £30,000 to an individual at the University of Cambridge for research into breast epithelium changes following pregnancy; £28,277 to an individual at the University of Bristol for research into oral cancer; £27,473 to Breakthrough Breast Cancer; £23,396 to an individual at the University of Oxford, Nuffield Dept of Orthopaedic Surgery for study into breast cancer; £18,000 to an individual at Wolfson Unit for Endoscopy St. Mark's Hospital for research into flat colorectal neoplasms; £17,000 to an individual at the Royal College of Surgeons for research into the provision of care for the critically ill surgical patient.

FINANCES *Year* 2001–02 *Income* £484,000 *Grants* £374,000 *Assets* £9,800,000

TRUSTEES Sir Rodney Sweetnam, Chairman; Mrs Frances Moody Newman; Lord Rathcavan; John Ll. Williams.

HOW TO APPLY Applications should include a detailed protocol and costing and be sent to the secretary. They may then be peer-reviewed. The foundation awards for surgical research fellowships should be addressed to the Royal College of Surgeons of England which evaluates each application. The trustees meet in June and December each year and applications must be received at the latest by the end of April or October respectively.

WHO TO APPLY TO Miss Elizabeth Yeo, Secretary, c/o Baker Tilly (Chartered Accountants), 33 Wine Street, Bristol BS1 2BQ *Tel* 0117 925 2255 *Fax* 0117 925 2679 *E-mail* elizabeth.yeo@bakertilly.co.uk

CC NO 277964   **ESTABLISHED** 1978

■ Newpier Charity Ltd

WHERE FUNDING CAN BE GIVEN UK.

WHO CAN BENEFIT Jewish organisations.

WHAT IS FUNDED Advancement of the orthodox Jewish faith and the relief of poverty.

RANGE OF GRANTS £100–£22,500.

SAMPLE GRANTS In 1997–98: £22,500 to SOFT for redistribution to other charities; £17,000 to KID; £7,000 to Mesdos Wiznitz; £6,100 to BML Benityashvut; £5,000 to Friends of Biala; £3,000 to Gateshead Yeshiva.

FINANCES *Year* 1998–99 *Income* £412,000 *Grants* £129,000

TRUSTEES C Margulies; H Knopfler; R Margulies; S Margulies; M Margulies.

HOW TO APPLY In writing to the correspondent. The address given is effectively a PO Box, from where letters are passed on to the trustees and telephone calls are not invited.

WHO TO APPLY TO Charles Margulies, Trustee & Secretary, Wilder Coe, Auditors, 233–237 Old Marylebone Road, London NW1 5QT

CC NO 293686   **ESTABLISHED** 1985

Think carefully about every application. Is it justified?

683

■ Newport County Borough Welsh Church Fund

WHERE FUNDING CAN BE GIVEN The area administered by Newport City Council.
WHO CAN BENEFIT Registered charities and community organisations.
WHAT IS FUNDED Arts, buildings, children and young people, disability, older people and sports or recreation (for young people only).
WHAT IS NOT FUNDED Grants are not given to the same organisation in successive years. It is rare that support will be given for running costs or to cover the full cost of a project. Individuals cannot receive grants for education, health, sporting, artistic or other personal development matters. The following areas are not supported: animal welfare, education/training, conservation, medical or health causes, overseas projects and political or religious appeals.
TYPE OF GRANT Usually one-off.
SAMPLE GRANTS Beneficiaries included Alway Community Association, Bettws Youth Football Club, Castleton Village Hall, Duffryn Community Link, Maindee Festival Association, National Eisteddfod, Newport Credit Union, St Thomas Church, St Mark's Church, Underwood Village Association and Wales in Bloom.
FINANCES *Year* 2001–02 *Income* £35,000 *Grants* £30,430
HOW TO APPLY An application form and guidelines are available from the trust.
WHO TO APPLY TO Mrs Joyce Steven, Head of Financial Services, Newport County Borough Council, Civic Centre, Newport NP20 4YR *Tel* 01633 232202 *Fax* 01633 232116 *E-mail* joyce.steven@newport.gov.uk
CC NO 218169   **ESTABLISHED** 1914

■ J F Newsome Charitable Trust

WHERE FUNDING CAN BE GIVEN UK, with a preference for the north west of England.
WHO CAN BENEFIT Charitable organisations.
WHAT IS FUNDED Educational and child-based projects.
FINANCES *Year* 1999–2000 *Income* £41,000 *Grants* £59,000 *Assets* £760,000
TRUSTEES J F Newsome; W J Hughes; C Bowen.
HOW TO APPLY In writing to the correspondent.
WHO TO APPLY TO C Bowen, Trustee, Kingsleigh, 13 Carrwood Avenue, Bramhall, Stockport, Cheshire SK7 2PX *Tel* 01565 651176
CC NO 1071690   **ESTABLISHED** 1998

■ The Newstead Charity

WHERE FUNDING CAN BE GIVEN UK, with a preference for Merseyside and North Wales.
WHO CAN BENEFIT Organisations benefiting sick and disabled people.
WHAT IS FUNDED Health, disability and community facilities.
WHAT IS NOT FUNDED No grants to individuals.
TYPE OF GRANT One-off, project and research. Funding for up to one year will be considered.
RANGE OF GRANTS £500–£1,500.
SAMPLE GRANTS £1,500 each to British Lung Foundation and Wirral Schools Brass Band; £1,000 each to British Dyslexics and Cruse Bereavement Care.
FINANCES *Year* 1998–99 *Income* £21,000 *Grants* £21,000 *Assets* £717,000
TRUSTEES K E B Clayton; G D Tasker; W F Glazebrook.

HOW TO APPLY In writing to the correspondent. Trustees meet in March to consider applications.
WHO TO APPLY TO The Clerk to the Trustees, Rathbones, Port of Liverpool Building, Pier Head, Liverpool L3 1NW *Tel* 0151 236 6666 *Fax* 0151 243 7003
CC NO 327244   **ESTABLISHED** 1986

■ Alderman Newton's Educational Foundation

WHERE FUNDING CAN BE GIVEN The City of Leicester.
WHO CAN BENEFIT Individuals and organisations such as schools and so on.
WHAT IS FUNDED Education.
FINANCES *Year* 1999–2000 *Income* £120,000 *Grants* £73,000 *Assets* £2,000,000
HOW TO APPLY On a form available from the correspondent. Applications may be made at any time.
WHO TO APPLY TO Mrs H A M Lander, Clerk, Salusburys, 3 Wycliffe Street, Leicester LE1 5LR *Tel* 0116 262 6052
CC NO 527881   **ESTABLISHED** 1983

■ The Laurie Nidditch Foundation

WHERE FUNDING CAN BE GIVEN UK.
WHO CAN BENEFIT Registered charities only, benefiting: children, young adults and older people; medical professionals; research workers; musicians; students; blind people; orphans; people with Alzheimer's disease, arthritis and rheumatism, cancer, and kidney disease; people who are terminally ill.
WHAT IS FUNDED Advancement of medical and surgical studies and research; homes for older people, blind people and orphans; education and religious learning (particularly Judaism).
TYPE OF GRANT One-off.
SAMPLE GRANTS £13,000 to British Friends Israel Free Loan Association; £5,000 to British Aid Committee Jewish Blind in Israel; £3,750 to Shalom Hartman Educational Institute, Jerusalem; £1,800 to Shaare Zedek Hospital, Jerusalem; £1,350 to United Synagogue; £1,000 to Keren Klita; £500 each to Council of Christians and Jews, Jewish Blind and Physically Handicapped Society and Jews College; £250 to Camp Simcha.
FINANCES *Year* 1999 *Income* £27,000 *Grants* £19,000 *Assets* £366,000
TRUSTEES Dr J Saper; K C Keller.
HOW TO APPLY In writing to the correspondent.
WHO TO APPLY TO Dr J Saper, Trustee, Flat 1 High Sheldon, Sheldon Avenue, London N6 4NJ *Tel* 020 8348 3553
CC NO 209668   **ESTABLISHED** 1960

■ Ninesquare Charitable Trust

WHERE FUNDING CAN BE GIVEN Central Somerset.
WHO CAN BENEFIT Major charitable projects.
WHAT IS FUNDED General national charities.
FINANCES *Year* 2000–2001 *Income* £138,000 *Grants* £0 *Assets* £753,000
TRUSTEES A T Clothier; J C Clothier; G O Edwards.
HOW TO APPLY In writing to the correspondent.
WHO TO APPLY TO KPMG, 100 Temple Street, Bristol BS1 6AG *Tel* 0117 905 4694
CC NO 1048447   **ESTABLISHED** 1995

■ The Chevras Ezras Nitzrochim Trust

WHERE FUNDING CAN BE GIVEN UK, with a preference for London.

WHO CAN BENEFIT Organisations benefiting Jewish people who are disadvantaged by poverty.

WHAT IS FUNDED Orthodox Jewish organisations set up to raise money to help the poor in Jewish communities.

FINANCES *Year* 2001 *Income* £197,000 *Grants* £190,000 *Assets* £4,500

TRUSTEES H Kahan; J Stern.

HOW TO APPLY In writing to the correspondent.

WHO TO APPLY TO H Kahan, Trustee, 53 Heathland Road, London N16 5PQ

CC NO 275352   **ESTABLISHED** 1978

■ The Noel Buxton Trust

WHERE FUNDING CAN BE GIVEN UK, eastern and southern Africa.

WHO CAN BENEFIT Registered charities, although grants are not made to large popular national charities or in response to general appeals. Smaller local bodies and less popular causes are preferred, which benefit: children under 12 in disadvantaged families; prisoners and their families and young people at risk of offending; and education and development in eastern and southern Africa.

WHAT IS FUNDED Welfare of children in disadvantaged families and children in care; prevention of crime, especially among young people; the rehabilitation of prisoners and the welfare of their families; education and development in eastern and southern Africa.

WHAT IS NOT FUNDED The trust does not give to: academic research; advice centres; animals; the arts of any kind; buildings; conferences; counselling; development education; drug and alcohol work; the elderly; the environment; expeditions, exchanges, study tours, visits, and so on, or anything else involving fares; housing and homelessness; human rights; anything medical or connected with illness or mental or physical disability; anywhere overseas except eastern and southern Africa; peace and disarmament; race relations; youth (except for the prevention of offending); and unemployment. Grants are not made to individuals for any purpose.

TYPE OF GRANT One-off or recurrent. Not for buildings or salaries.

RANGE OF GRANTS £50–£4,000. Most grants are below £1,000.

SAMPLE GRANTS £4,000 each to APT Enterprise Development – Zimbabwe and Family Rights Group – UK; £3,300 to WaterAid – Tanzania; £3,000 to Howard League for Penal Reform – UK; £2,500 each to Harvest Help – Zambia, Center for Crime and Justice – UK and Prisoners Abroad – UK.

FINANCES *Year* 2001 *Income* £119,000 *Grants* £82,000 *Assets* £2,100,000

TRUSTEES Richenda Wallace, Chair; Joyce Morton; Simon Buxton; Paul Buxton; David Birmingham; Angelica Mitchell; Jon Snow; Jo Tunnard, Vice Chair; John Littlewood; Brendan Gormley.

HOW TO APPLY There is no application form and applications may be submitted at any time. They should include the organisation's charity registration number and the name of the organisation to which grants should be paid if different from that at the head of the appeal letter. The following should be included with applications: budget for current and following year; details of funding already received, promised, or applied for from other sources and the last available annual report/accounts in their shortest available form.

WHO TO APPLY TO Ray Waters, Secretary, PO Box 393, Farnham, Surrey GU9 8WZ

CC NO 220881   **ESTABLISHED** 1919

■ The Noon Foundation

WHERE FUNDING CAN BE GIVEN England and Wales.

WHAT IS FUNDED General charitable purposes including, education, relief of poverty, community relations and alleviation of racial discrimination

SAMPLE GRANTS £41,000 to Tower Hamlets College; £26,000 to Southhall Young Adults Centre; £10,000 to Royal College of Organists; £3,500 to Asian Business Association; £2,400 to Tamasha Theatre Company; £2,000 each to Friends of Life and Music for Youth; £1,100 to the Lions Club; £1,000 each to Akedemi, Muslim News, Thames Community Foundation and the Arpana Charitable Trust.

FINANCES *Year* 2000 *Income* £161,000 *Grants* £102,000 *Assets* £3,800,000

TRUSTEES Gulam Kanderbhoy Noon; Akbar Shirazi; Mrs Zeenat Harnal; Mrs Zarmin Noon Sekhon; Jehangir Jamshed Mehta.

HOW TO APPLY In writing to the correspondent.

WHO TO APPLY TO The Trustees, 25 Queen Anne's Gate, St James' Park, London SW1H 9BU *Tel* 020 7654 1600

CC NO 1053654   **ESTABLISHED** 1995

■ The Norfolk Churches Trust Ltd

WHERE FUNDING CAN BE GIVEN The Diocese of Norwich – Norfolk and part of Suffolk.

WHO CAN BENEFIT Churches and places of Christian worship with particular regard to country churches still in the parochial system and needing help.

WHAT IS FUNDED The advancement of religion to preserve, repair, maintain, improve, beautify and reconstruct churches or chapels of any Christian denomination, the monuments, fittings, fixtures, stained glass, furniture, ornaments and chattels in such churches and chapels; and the churchyards belonging to such churches. Also disused or redundant churches or chapels of historic interest or architectural importance.

WHAT IS NOT FUNDED Currently, no grants for heating, interior decoration, organs, kitchen facilities or lavatories.

TYPE OF GRANT Buildings and feasibility studies.

RANGE OF GRANTS £100–£20,000.

SAMPLE GRANTS In 1999–2000: £10,000 each to All Saints, Sharrington and St Margaret, King's Lynn; £8,500 to St Andrew, Kilverstone; £7,000 each to All Saints, Crostwight, St Margaret, Paston, St Mary, Whinburgh, St Peter, Mattishall Burgh, and St Peter & St Paul Burgh Castle; £6,500 to All Saints, Santon; £6,000 to St John the Baptist, Trimingham.

FINANCES *Year* 2001–02 *Income* £355,786 *Grants* £288,194 *Assets* £801,683

PUBLICATIONS *Treasures for the Future – A Celebration: The Norfolk Churches Trust 1976–2001. The Brasses of Norfolk Churches* by Roger Greenwood and Malcolm Norris. *Sculptured Monuments in Norfolk Churches* by Noel Spencer, ARCA. Occasional papers on the rural church.

OTHER INFORMATION The trust is leasee for 99 years of the following redundant churches: Barmer All

Saints, Cockthorpe All Saints, Snetterton All Saints, Dunton St Mary, Illington St Andrew, Hargham All Saints, West Rudham St Peter, Bagthorpe St Mary, Morton-on-the-Hill St Margaret, Rackheath All Saints, West Bilney St Cecilia.

HOW TO APPLY Initially contact the secretary to discuss your application. The application form consists of one-side of A4. Accounts giving up-to-date financial information will also be required.

WHO TO APPLY TO Malcolm Fisher, Secretary, 9 The Old Church, St Matthews Road, Norwich NR1 1SP *Tel* 01603 767576 *Fax* 01986 798776

CC NO 271176　　　**ESTABLISHED** 1976

····················

■ Lavinia Norfolk's Family Charitable Trust

WHERE FUNDING CAN BE GIVEN Mostly West Sussex.

WHO CAN BENEFIT Registered charities only.

WHAT IS FUNDED General charitable purposes, with preference to charities already known to the trustees.

WHAT IS NOT FUNDED No grants to individuals.

SAMPLE GRANTS £1,000 each to Chichester Festival Theatre and HCPT Handicap Children's Pilgrimage.

FINANCES *Year* 2000–01 *Income* £16,700 *Grants* £28,450 *Assets* £609,000

TRUSTEES Lady Mary Mumford; Lady Sarah Clutton.

HOW TO APPLY The funds of the trust are fully committed.

WHO TO APPLY TO Christopher J Holmes, Norfolk Estate Office, 1 London Road, Arundel, West Sussex BN18 9BH *Tel* 01903 882213

CC NO 280730　　　**ESTABLISHED** 1994

····················

■ The Alderman Norman's Foundation

WHERE FUNDING CAN BE GIVEN Norwich and Old Catton.

WHO CAN BENEFIT Individuals who are descendants of Alderman Norman, and organisations benefiting children, young adults and students.

WHAT IS FUNDED The trust primarily supports the education of the descendants of Alderman Norman, but also supports young people, local schools and educational establishments in the area.

WHAT IS NOT FUNDED No grants to non-registered charities. No applications from outside of Norwich and Old Catton will be considered.

RANGE OF GRANTS £500–£5,000.

SAMPLE GRANTS £5,000 each to Norwich Cathedral Choir Endowment Fund, Norfolk County Council for a musical festival, and Young Citizen's Guild; £3,750 to EWS (Norwich) Holiday Fund; £3,000 to Norfolk Splash; £2,000 each to Magdalene Group and Victim Support; £1,874 to Assist Trust; £1,000 each to Musical Keys and Welesley First School.

FINANCES *Year* 1998–99 *Income* £234,371 *Grants* £176,697 *Assets* £4,711,408

TRUSTEES Revd J Boston; G H Drake; C D Brown; T Boore; Dr W Roy; Canon M W Smith; C I H Mawson; R Sandall; D Armes.

OTHER INFORMATION 495 descendants of Alderman Norman received a total of £134,000. 14 Old Catton residents received a total of £3,962. £6,000 went to LEA Grants Committee for 12 Norman's exhibitions. Special Awards totalled £32,375 as shown above.

HOW TO APPLY In writing to the correspondent. The trustees meet twice each year, in June and October.

WHO TO APPLY TO N F Saffell, Clerk, Brown & Co, Old Bank of England Court, Queen Street, Norwich NR2 4TA *Tel* 01603 629871

CC NO 313105　　　**ESTABLISHED** 1962

····················

■ The Duncan Norman Trust Fund

WHERE FUNDING CAN BE GIVEN UK, with a preference for Merseyside.

WHO CAN BENEFIT Registered charities which are known to the trustees.

WHAT IS FUNDED General charitable purposes.

WHAT IS NOT FUNDED No grants to individuals.

SAMPLE GRANTS £10,000 to Petrus; £5,000 each to St Judes-on-the-Hill Parish Church Organ Appeal, The Children's Society and The Royal Agricultural Benevolent Institution; £3,800 to Christ Church Youth and Community Centre; £2,500 to Personal Service Society; £2,000 each to Hereford College and Oundel School Foundation; £1,500 to Merseyside Drugs Council; £1,000 each to All Saints DCC Special Projects, Banbury District Housing Connection, Imagine, Marie Curie Cancer Care, Motor Neurone Disease Association, PCC of St Paul's Banbury, Sahir House, St Nicholas Church PCC and The Spring Centre.

FINANCES *Year* 2000–01 *Income* £62,714 *Grants* £69,140 *Assets* £2,109,006

TRUSTEES J A H Norman; R K Asser; Mrs V S Hilton; Mrs C E Lazar.

HOW TO APPLY The trust states that it only makes grants to charities known to the settlor and unsolicited applications are not considered.

WHO TO APPLY TO The Trustees, Liverpool Council of Social Service (Inc.), 14 Castle Street, Liverpool L2 0NJ *Tel* 0151 236 7728

CC NO 250434　　　**ESTABLISHED** 1996

····················

■ The Norman Family Charitable Trust

WHERE FUNDING CAN BE GIVEN Primarily south west England.

WHO CAN BENEFIT Registered charities only.

WHAT IS FUNDED Grants are made at the trustees' discretion, mostly in south west England.

WHAT IS NOT FUNDED No support will be given to projects involving experiments on live animals or the maintenance of churches, or to overseas projects. No grants to individuals.

TYPE OF GRANT One-off, interest-free loans, project, research and start-up costs will be considered. Funding may be given for up to one year.

RANGE OF GRANTS £250–£10,000.

FINANCES *Year* 2001–02 *Income* £333,321 *Grants* £288,457 *Assets* £5,691,240

TRUSTEES R J Dawe, Chairman; Mrs M H Evans; M B Saunders; Mrs M J Webb; Mrs C E Houghton.

HOW TO APPLY In writing to the trustees, who meet regularly to agree the distribution of grants.

WHO TO APPLY TO R J Dawe, Chairman of the Trustees, 14 Fore Street, Budleigh Salterton, Devon EX9 6NG *Tel* 01395 446699 *Fax* 01395 446698 *E-mail* enquiries@nfct.org *Website* www.nfct.org

CC NO 277616　　　**ESTABLISHED** 1979

■ The Normanby Charitable Trust

WHERE FUNDING CAN BE GIVEN UK, with a special interest in north east England.
WHO CAN BENEFIT Registered charities.
WHAT IS FUNDED General charitable purposes.
WHAT IS NOT FUNDED No grants to individuals, or to non-UK charities.
RANGE OF GRANTS £50–£30,000.
SAMPLE GRANTS £10,000 each to Lythe Village Hall Committee, Northumberland Aged Mineworkers' Home Association, Rainbow Trust; Redcar Literacy Institute, Royal Free Hospital and University College Medical School, St Mary's Church – Clymping, and Teesside Hospital Care Foundation; £6,522 to Fryup Village Hall; £5,000 each to Albion Trust, and Fairbridge Teesside.
FINANCES *Year* 2000–01 *Income* £312,663 *Grants* £197,013 *Assets* £8,453,184
TRUSTEES The 5th Marquis of Normanby; The Dowager Marchioness of Normanby; Lady Lepel Kornicka; Lady Evelyn Buchan; Lady Peronel Phipps de Cruz; Lady Henrietta Burridge.
HOW TO APPLY In writing to the correspondent. Only successful applications will be acknowledged. Telephone calls are not encouraged. There are no regular dates for trustees' meetings.
WHO TO APPLY TO Lady Henrietta Burridge, Morgan Intakes, Great Fryup Dale, Lealholm, Whitby, North Yorkshire YO21 2AT
CC NO 252102   **ESTABLISHED** 1966

■ The North British Hotel Trust

WHERE FUNDING CAN BE GIVEN UK, but mainly Scotland.
WHO CAN BENEFIT Any recognised and registered charity (although this does not preclude special donations) benefiting mainly disabled people.
WHAT IS FUNDED General charitable purposes, with some favour given to appeals for disabled, sick and needy.
WHAT IS NOT FUNDED No grants to individuals.
TYPE OF GRANT One-off or recurrent; buildings and capital costs; not normally for salaries or running costs.
RANGE OF GRANTS £240–£60,000.
SAMPLE GRANTS £47,000 to Scarborough Homeless Support Services; £40,000 to CLIC, Glasgow; £19,000 to D R Welfare; £15,000 to Hazel Court Primary School; £14,500 to Mountain Rescue; £10,000 to Highland Counselling; £8,498 to Oban Disability Forum; £6,000 to Puffin Port, Dingwall.
FINANCES *Year* 2001–02 *Income* £522,938 *Grants* £734,288 *Assets* £5,759,449
TRUSTEES W G Crerar, Chair; I C Fraser.
HOW TO APPLY In writing to the correspondent.
WHO TO APPLY TO C Leivesley, Secretary to the Council, 1 Queen Charlotte Lane, Edinburgh EH6 6BL *Tel* 0131 554 7173
CC NO 221335   **ESTABLISHED** 1903

■ North London Charities Limited

WHERE FUNDING CAN BE GIVEN North London.
WHO CAN BENEFIT Registered charities.
WHAT IS FUNDED General charitable purposes.
FINANCES *Year* 1998–99 *Income* £257,000 *Grants* £256,000 *Assets* £7,500
TRUSTEES H Feldman; S Feldman.
OTHER INFORMATION We were not able to update the information on this trust either from the trust itself, or from the file at the Charity Commission.

HOW TO APPLY In writing to the correspondent.
WHO TO APPLY TO H Feldman, Trustee, 23 Overlea Road, Springfield Park, London E5 9BG *Tel* 020 8209 1535
CC NO 312740   **ESTABLISHED** 1964

■ North London Islamic Association Trust

WHERE FUNDING CAN BE GIVEN Finchley area.
WHO CAN BENEFIT Children and young adults, Muslims, and people who are disabled, disadvantaged by poverty and victims of famine and man-made or natural disasters.
WHAT IS FUNDED The advancement of religion according to the tenets and teaching of Islam and the relief of poverty, sickness and distress, in particular: providing and maintaining premises in or near the Finchley area for Muslims for worship and to provide facilities for children's religious education; teaching and educating young members of the Muslim community in the Muslim religion; providing transport for children with disabilities attending classes; and providing relief to people in need as a result of local, national or international disaster.
FINANCES *Year* 1999–2000 *Income* £114,021 *Grants* £67,139 *Assets* £30,783
TRUSTEES Y K Oguz; F Kaldi; H Sevkat; H Gok.
HOW TO APPLY In writing to the correspondent.
WHO TO APPLY TO The Trustees, 90 Evelyn Court, Amhurst Road, London E8 2BG
CC NO 1037896   **ESTABLISHED** 1994

■ North West Cancer Research Fund

WHERE FUNDING CAN BE GIVEN North west England and north and mid Wales.
WHO CAN BENEFIT Those undertaking fundamental cancer research approved by and under the direction of the North West Cancer Research Fund Scientific Committee.
WHAT IS FUNDED Fundamental research into the causes of cancer, including the cost of associated equipment.
WHAT IS NOT FUNDED Funding is not given for research whose primary aim is to develop new forms of treatment or evaluate existing ones, e.g. drug development, nor for clinical trials or building projects.
TYPE OF GRANT Project; research; running and start-up costs; and salaries. Usually for three-year periods subject to review. Fellowships are also available.
RANGE OF GRANTS Average grant size is £45,000 per annum, awarded for three years.
FINANCES *Year* 2001–02 *Grants* £760,000
TRUSTEES J C Lewys-Lloyd, Chair; Mrs H Dring; A P Farmer; P H Kennedy.
HOW TO APPLY Applications must be limited to 2,000 words. Relevant papers in print or submitted should be included as an appendix. Applications must be submitted in triplicate to the secretary by 1 April or 1 October. They will be considered approximately eight weeks later. Late applications will be held over to the following meeting.
WHO TO APPLY TO A W Renison, General Secretary, 22 Oxford Street, Liverpool L7 7BL *Tel* 0151 709 2919 *Fax* 0151 708 7997 *E-mail* nwcrf@btclick.com *Website* www.cancerresearchnorthwest.co.uk
CC NO 223598   **ESTABLISHED** 1948

Think carefully about every application. Is it justified?

687

■ The Northampton Municipal Church Charities

WHERE FUNDING CAN BE GIVEN The borough of Northampton.

WHO CAN BENEFIT Organisations and individuals in need.

WHAT IS NOT FUNDED No grants to individuals.

RANGE OF GRANTS Usually between £1,000 and £20,000 for organisations.

SAMPLE GRANTS £100,000 fo YMCA for their mobile youth work project.

FINANCES *Year* 1999–2000 *Income* £277,000 *Grants* £124,000 *Assets* £4,300,000

TRUSTEES K T Davidson, Chair; J W Buckby; W R Gates; Mrs V A Holmes; B C May; Mrs J Lineker; Mrs I Abbott; Mrs R Hampson; P Haddon; P Wain; Mrs J Vowden.

HOW TO APPLY In writing to the correspondent.

WHO TO APPLY TO The Clerk, Wilson Browne, 60 Gold Street, Northampton NN1 1RS *Tel* 01604 628131

CC NO 259593   **ESTABLISHED** 1969

■ The Northampton Queen's Institute Relief in Sickness Fund

WHERE FUNDING CAN BE GIVEN The borough of Northampton.

WHO CAN BENEFIT Organisations benefiting children and young adults, at risk groups, and people who are disadvantaged by poverty or socially isolated.

WHAT IS FUNDED Youth groups, welfare organisations, hospitals and health organisations.

RANGE OF GRANTS £1,000–£3,000.

SAMPLE GRANTS £3,000 each to Bethany Homestead and St John Ambulance; £2,000 each to British Red Cross, Dystonia Society, Manna House Counselling Service, Maple Healthcare, Nazareth House, Northants Association for the Blind, Northants Association of Youth Clubs, and Talbot Butler Ward.

FINANCES *Year* 1998–99 *Income* £35,352 *Grants* £24,000 *Assets* £931,764

TRUSTEES D M Orton-Jones, Chair; C F N Pedley; P W Wilkinson; J A Cooper; S Jackson; Mrs J Bradshaw; J Mackaness; Dr R Marshall.

HOW TO APPLY In writing to the correspondent. There are one or two main meetings where applications are considered during the year, although decisions can be made in between.

WHO TO APPLY TO Mrs Susan Peet, Shoosmiths, The Lakes, Bedford Road, Northampton NN4 7SH *Tel* 01604 543000

CC NO 208583   **ESTABLISHED** 1971

■ The Northamptonshire Historic Churches Trust

WHERE FUNDING CAN BE GIVEN Northamptonshire.

WHO CAN BENEFIT Churches.

WHAT IS FUNDED The preservation, improvement, repair and restoration of churches and their fixtures and fittings.

RANGE OF GRANTS £100–£2,000.

SAMPLE GRANTS £2,500 to St Matthew's; £2,000 each to St Andrew's Spratton and St Mary Virgin, East Haddon; £1,500 to Corby Baptist Church; £1,000 each to St Helen's Sibberloft, St Mary Virgin, St Michael & All Angels Winwick, St Nicholas Overstone, and St Peter & St Paul Cosgrove; £750 to St John the Baptist Corby.

FINANCES *Year* 2000 *Income* £39,000 *Grants* £25,000 *Assets* £107,000

TRUSTEES Mrs B Lancaster; Sir John Lowther; Revd P Moseling; J S Shuttleworth; J A White; B Bailey; Mrs M Bland; Bishop of Brixworth; P W Dunn; P F Haddon; M F Hawkins; Revd Canon W Kentigern-Fox; Bishop of Peterborough; F Sitwell; Mrs H Collings; Lady Juliet Townsend; William de Croz; N Gold; Mrs S A Parkinson.

HOW TO APPLY In writing to the correspondent. Trustees meet to consider grants in April.

WHO TO APPLY TO John White, Secretary, c/o Hewitson Becke & Shaw, 7 Spencer Parade, Northampton NN1 5AB *Tel* 01604 233233

CC NO 1021632   **ESTABLISHED** 1993

■ The Northcott Devon Foundation

WHERE FUNDING CAN BE GIVEN Devon.

WHO CAN BENEFIT Individuals, families or registered charities benefiting: students; unemployed people; volunteers; at risk groups; carers; disabled people; those disadvantaged by poverty; ex-offenders and those at risk of offending; gays and lesbians; those living in rural areas and socially isolated people; victims of abuse, crime and domestic violence; and victims of famine, man-made or natural disasters and war.

WHAT IS FUNDED (a) Individuals or families living in Devon who are experiencing distress and hardship deriving from disability, illness, injury, bereavement or exceptional disadvantage, in circumstances where such assistance offers long-term benefit. (b) Registered charities operating primarily within Devon, whose objects are broadly in sympathy with those of the foundation, and who seek to improve the living conditions or life experiences of people who are disabled or disadvantaged living in Devon. (c) Young people of limited means undertaking philanthropic activity which is not part of a formal education or training programme and who live in Devon.

WHAT IS NOT FUNDED The foundation is unable to enter into longer term financial commitments. Assistance will not be given to statutory agencies, including self-governing National Health Service Trusts in the performance of their duties. Assistance will not be given to clear any debts owed to statutory agencies or to financial institutions. Other debts will not formally be considered unless agreement has been reached with the creditors for full and final settlement in a substantially reduced sum.

TYPE OF GRANT Usually one-off for a specific purpose or project. Research, capital and buildings will be considered. Core funding is not considered.

RANGE OF GRANTS £40–£25,000, average grant £300.

SAMPLE GRANTS £5,000 each to Exeter Leukaemia Association, Multiple Sclerosis Society and St John Ambulance; £3,000 to West of England School for the Deaf; £2,000 to RNIB.

FINANCES *Year* 1999–2000 *Income* £246,000 *Grants* £199,000 *Assets* £5,400,000

TRUSTEES P Burdick, Chair; M Horwood; Maj. Gen. J St J Grey; P D Egan; M Pentreath.

OTHER INFORMATION Assistance will not be given unless applicants or their sponsors have checked thoroughly that assistance or benefit is not available from the Department of Social Security or other public funds.

HOW TO APPLY Initially in writing to the correspondent enclosing an sae, who will supply an application form and statement of policy.

WHO TO APPLY TO G G Folland, Secretary, 1b Victoria Road, Exmouth, Devon EX8 1DL *Tel* 01395 269204
CC NO 201277   **ESTABLISHED** 1960

■ The Northcott Devon Medical Foundation

WHERE FUNDING CAN BE GIVEN Devon.
WHO CAN BENEFIT Academics, medical professionals, research workers and postgraduate students.
WHAT IS FUNDED Support of postgraduate, medical research and the improvement of medical practice. Provision of schools, research laboratories, libraries and so on for the promotion of medicine, surgery and other subjects.
WHAT IS NOT FUNDED Tuition fees for medical/nursing undergraduates; living expenses.
SAMPLE GRANTS Five grants to two institutions – University of Exeter: characterisation of normal and reactive sub-ventricular human astrocytes and reactive astrocytosis in multiple sclerosis (£31,497), an investigation into the role of inducible nitric oxide synthase in insulin-stimulated nitric oxide production (£1,298) and localisation of the gene causing Autosomal Dominant Duanes Syndrome in a four generation family (£800). University of Plymouth's The Honiton Group Practice for the implications of teenage motherhood for primary care (£11,069); genetic 'fingerprinting' of markers used to predict childhood diabetes (£1,000).
FINANCES *Year* 2001–02 *Income* £44,000 *Grants* £45,664 *Assets* £1,000,000
TRUSTEES Prof. D Partridge; Prof. P P Anthony; Dr A P Warin; Dr C Gardener-Thorpe.
HOW TO APPLY In writing to the correspondent.
WHO TO APPLY TO R E T Borton, Secretary, 1 Barnfield Crescent, Exeter EX1 1QY *Tel* 01392 278436 *Fax* 01392 413617 *E-mail* tborton@bishopfleming.co.uk
CC NO 204660   **ESTABLISHED** 1961

■ The Northern Electric Employees Charity Association

WHERE FUNDING CAN BE GIVEN North east England.
WHO CAN BENEFIT Charitable organisations.
WHAT IS FUNDED General charitable purposes.
WHAT IS NOT FUNDED Grants are only given to registered charities.
SAMPLE GRANTS £16,000 to Children's Promise; £1,500 to Cot Death Society; £1,000 each to North of England Children's Cancer Research and NorthEast Helplink; £750 each to Headstart Newcastle and Teesside Hospice; £500 each to The Peoples Kitchen and Streets Ahead Youth Project; £400 to Stephen Lamb Memorial Fund; £370 to Newcastle General Hospital; £250 to Northumberland County Blind Association; £200 to Northumberland Hospital Radio; £100 to Kids & Us.
FINANCES *Year* 2000 *Income* £31,000 *Grants* £34,000
TRUSTEES Angela Miller, Chair; David Anderson; Ashley Shotton; Jill Ayre; Jill Jones.
HOW TO APPLY In writing to the correspondent for consideration every two months.
WHO TO APPLY TO The Secretary, Kepier Farm Training Centre, Durham DH1 1LB *Tel* 0191 333 5922 *Fax* 0191 333 5932 *E-mail* jill.jones@nedl.co.uk
CC NO 1026188   **ESTABLISHED** 1993

■ The Northern Rock Foundation

WHERE FUNDING CAN BE GIVEN Cumbria, Durham, Northumberland, the Tees Valley and Tyne and Wear. Organisations in Scotland, Lancashire and north Yorkshire are no longer supported.
WHO CAN BENEFIT Organisations helping disadvantaged people and arts, cultural and heritage organisations benefit
WHAT IS FUNDED Grant programmes are: prevention of social decline; regeneration through local initiatives; basics – day to day services; exploration and experiment; a better, stronger voluntary sector; and aspirational, cultural, environmental, heritage and sporting activities.
WHAT IS NOT FUNDED No grants for: organisations which do not have purposes recognised as charitable in law; charities which appear to have excessive unrestricted or free reserves (up to 12 months' expenditure is normally acceptable) or are in serious deficit; national charities which do not have a regional office or other representation in the north east; grantmaking bodies seeking to distribute grants on the foundation's behalf; open-ended funding agreements; general appeals, sponsorship and marketing appeals; corporate applications for founder membership of a charity; retrospective grants; replacement of statutory funding; activities primarily the responsibility of central or local government or health authorities; individuals and organisations that distribute funds to individuals; animal welfare; mainstream educational activity, schools and educational establishments; medical research, hospitals, hospices and medical centres; medical treatments and therapies including art therapy; fabric appeals for places of worship; promotion of religion; expeditions or overseas travel; minibuses, other vehicles and transport schemes except where they are a small and integral part of a larger scheme; holidays and outings; playgrounds and play equipment; private clubs or those with such restricted membership as to make them not charitable; capital bids purely towards compliance with the Disability Discrimination Act; amateur arts organisations; musical instruments; and sports kit and equipment.
TYPE OF GRANT Capital, core or project funding and for up to three years (sometimes renewable for another three).
RANGE OF GRANTS £1,000–£250,000; typical grant £5,000–£60,000.
SAMPLE GRANTS In 2001: £203,000 to Ulverston and North Lonsdale CAB over three years for money advice connected with foot and mouth disease; £200,000 over two years to Northumberland Community Council towards the Northumberland Rural Stress Initiative; £200,000 for a further two years to Inside Out Trust for work in prisons in the north east; £200,000 to King's College, London to continue research into restorative justice in north east prisons; £180,000 over three years to Debt Advice Within Northumberland; £150,000 over three years to Brinkburn Music for artistic and education programmes in Northumberland; £125,000 over three years to Durham Community Council for its community involvement programme; £111,000 over three years to Berwick CAB for benefits advice work.
FINANCES *Year* 2002 *Income* £16,885,000 *Grants* £13,068,000 *Assets* £24,302,000
TRUSTEES Richard Harbottle, Chair; David Chapman; David Faulkner; Leo Finn; Charles Howick; Chris Jobe; Frank Nicholson; Dorothy Russell; Julie Shipley; John Ward.

HOW TO APPLY Applications must be made on the foundation's two-page application form. This comes with full instructions and guidance. The form will have to be accompanied by: brief supporting statement (not more than two pages); current budget and recent management accounts; most recent annual report and accounts (or equivalent for very small organisations); the 'objects' and 'dissolution' parts of the constitution; and a budget for the project, how much you are asking for and how you hope to get the rest. There should normally be a response within four months (for the small organisations scheme, two months).The foundation receives ve many more requests than they can help and has to turn down many good applications.

WHO TO APPLY TO Fiona Ellis, Director, The Old Chapel, Woodbine Road , Gosforth, Newcastle upon Tyne NE3 1DD *Tel* 0191 284 8412 *Minicom* 0191 284 5411 *Website* www.nr-foundation.org.uk

CC NO 1063906   **ESTABLISHED** 1997

■ The Northmoor Trust

WHERE FUNDING CAN BE GIVEN UK.

WHO CAN BENEFIT Local, regional and UK charitable organisations benefiting people who are disadvantaged.

WHAT IS FUNDED The direct or indirect relief of poverty, hardship or distress.

WHAT IS NOT FUNDED Grants are only made to organisations which one or more of the trustees have direct personal knowledge. No grants to individuals, or organisations concerned with religion, medicine or the arts. Occasionally grants are made to educational charities where the guiding criteria are met. The trust does not respond to general appeals.

TYPE OF GRANT Some recurrent.

RANGE OF GRANTS £1,000–£9,000.

SAMPLE GRANTS Previous grants include £9,000 to FARE; £4,000–£5,000 each to ATD Fourth World, Inquest, Kings Cross Homeless Project, St John's Wood Terrace Adventure Playground, and Vietnamese Mental Health Project.

FINANCES *Year* 2000–01 *Income* £33,000 *Grants* £25,000 *Assets* £2,500,000

TRUSTEES Viscount Runciman; Viscountess Runciman; Frances Bennett.

HOW TO APPLY In writing to the correspondent, including the latest accounts and annual report, a list of the main sources of funding and a budget for the current year including details of other grant applications made. For first time applicants, a general description of aims and achievements to date and an outline of plans for future development. Applications should arrive by 31 January for preliminary consideration in March, decisions are made in May. Applicants may be visited or asked to provide additional information for the May meeting. The trustees may also visit applicants between the two meetings. The trustees expect to receive a short report confirming how the grant was spent. No grants for more than one year can be made in the first instance, although the trust may extend grants over a period of several years where their criteria has been sufficiently met and repeat applications are accompanied by an account of how the previous grant was spent.

WHO TO APPLY TO Mrs Hilary Edwards, Secretary, 44 Clifton Hill, London NW8 0QG *Tel* 020 7372 0698 *Fax* 020 7327 4668

CC NO 256818   **ESTABLISHED** 1968

■ The Northumberland Village Homes Trust

WHERE FUNDING CAN BE GIVEN North east England.

WHO CAN BENEFIT Individuals and youth organisations benefiting those under 18 years of age who are disadvantaged by poverty.

WHAT IS FUNDED Education and training and the relief of poverty and sickness among young people.

WHAT IS NOT FUNDED No personal applications will be considered unless supported by a letter from a registered charity or local authority, or unless the applicant is personally known to one of the trustees. No applications will be considered for 'gap year' projects or for work relating to medical research or such matters.

RANGE OF GRANTS £200–£8,000; mostly under £800.

SAMPLE GRANTS £14,000 to Children North East; £5,000 to Barnardos North East; £3,000 to St Cuthberts Care; £2,000 each to ChildLine – Yorkshire/Tyne Tees and NCH Action for Children; £1,000 to Mea Trust; £800 to National Blind Children's Society; £500 each to Alnwick Young People Association, Heaton and Wallsend Methodist Circuit, Second Crop and Whitley Bay Baptist Church.

FINANCES *Year* 2000–01 *Income* £65,739 *Grants* £49,000 *Assets* £1,232,064

TRUSTEES D Welch; B Porter; Richard Baron Gisborough, Chair; Mrs E P Savage; K Hunt; D McCoy.

HOW TO APPLY Applications should be made by 30 September for consideration in November. Applications should be in writing and state: whether the applicant is an individual, private charity or registered charity; the objects (if a charity); the amount required and what it is for; any other sources of funding.

WHO TO APPLY TO Derek McCoy, Trustee, c/o Savages, Bellwood Buildings, 36 Mosley Street, Newcastle upon Tyne NE1 1DL *Tel* 0191 221 2111 *Fax* 0191 222 1712

CC NO 225429   **ESTABLISHED** 1880

■ The Northumbria Historic Churches Trust

WHERE FUNDING CAN BE GIVEN The dioceses of Durham and Newcastle.

WHO CAN BENEFIT Churches that are at least 100 years old.

WHAT IS FUNDED The restoration, preservation, repair, maintenance, reconstruction, improvement and beautification of churches, their contents and their churchyards.

WHAT IS NOT FUNDED 'The trust is unable to help with work on bells, organs, church halls, decoration (unless consequential), notice boards, publications, heating, re-orderings, new facilities or routine maintenance.'

TYPE OF GRANT One-off, feasibility studies and buildings. Funding for one year or less.

RANGE OF GRANTS £250–£5,000.

SAMPLE GRANTS £5,000 each to St Helen's – Auckland for renewal of stone floor in conjuction with new heating, St Mary's – South Hylton for stabilisation of west elevation and stone repairs, and St Mary's – Whickham for renewal of the aisle roof; £3,000 each to St Mary's – Morpeth for stonework and glazing, and Hunstanworth for major roof repairs and reslating; £2,500 to Easington for restoration of the south aisle capital and other stone work; £2,000 each to Norham for window pointing and reroofing and St Mary's – Seaham for reslating of the south roof; £1,000 each to St Thomas Stanley for reslating and guttering, and St James' – Darlington for restoration and reglazing of nave windows.

FINANCES *Year* 2000–01 *Income* £40,000 *Grants* £33,900 *Assets* £140,000

TRUSTEES Dr R A Lomas, Chair; Rt Hon. A Beith; G Bell; P O R Bridgeman; C Downs; T R Fenwick; G E R Heslop; Mrs M Hindmarsh; J B Kendall; Lady Sarah Nicholson; J H N Porter; Canon J E Ruscoe; Canon C P Unwin; Lord Vinson; Mrs G Walker; C H L Westmacott; R R V Nicholson; Revd R Firth; Elizabeth Norris; Ivy Ferguson.

PUBLICATIONS *The Northumbria Historic Churches Trust – The First Fifteen Years.*

HOW TO APPLY In writing to the correspondent requesting an application form and guidelines. Initial telephone calls are welcomed.

WHO TO APPLY TO Canon J E Ruscoe, Secretary, The Vicarage, South Hylton, Sunderland SR4 0QB *Tel* 0191 534 2325

CC NO 511314   **ESTABLISHED** 1980

■ The Northwood Charitable Trust

WHERE FUNDING CAN BE GIVEN Scotland, especially Dundee and Tayside.

WHO CAN BENEFIT Organisations.

WHAT IS FUNDED General charitable purposes. In the past, grants have been given to a university and to medical and educational projects.

TYPE OF GRANT One-off and recurring grants.

SAMPLE GRANTS £418,000 to Tenovus Medical Projects; £62,000 to Tayside Orthopaedic and Rehabilitation Technology Centre; £33,000 to Dundee University in five separate grants; £30,000 to Dundee Repertory Theatre in two grants; £27,000 to D C Thompson Charitable Trust; £25,000 to Strathmore Hospice; £11,000 each to Brittle Bone Society and MacMillan Cancer Relief Scotland.

FINANCES *Year* 2001–02 *Income* £1,400,000 *Grants* £1,415,000 *Assets* £47,000,000

TRUSTEES Brian Harold Thomson; Andrew Francis Thomson; Lewis Murray Thomson.

HOW TO APPLY The trust's funds are fully committed and it states that no applications will be considered or acknowledged.

WHO TO APPLY TO Mr Brian McKernie, Secretary, 22 Meadowside, Dundee DD1 1LN *Tel* 01382 201534 *Fax* 01382 227654

SC NO SC014487   **ESTABLISHED** 1972

■ The Norton Foundation

WHERE FUNDING CAN BE GIVEN UK, with a preference for Birmingham, Coventry and Warwickshire.

WHO CAN BENEFIT Young people under 25 years of age.

WHAT IS FUNDED The trust was created in 1990. Its objects are to help children and young people under 25 who are in 'need of care or rehabilitation or aid of any kind, particularly as a result of delinquency, deprivation, maltreatment or neglect or who are in danger of lapsing or relapsing into delinquency'.

WHAT IS NOT FUNDED No grants for the payment of debts that have already been incurred.

RANGE OF GRANTS Individuals: £50–£500; institutions: £500–£5,000.

SAMPLE GRANTS £5,000 each to Cornerstone – Birmingham and First Kineton Scout Group; £3,000 each to Coventry Boys Club, Crisis Fareshare – Birmingham, Family & Friends – Leamington Spa, Hockley Church Sunday

Special – Birmingham, Trescott School, Birmingham and Wood End Family Project – Coventry; £2,500 each to Furnace Fields Parents Centre – Bedworth and React – Richmond (for West Midlands children).

FINANCES *Year* 2001–02 *Income* £144,000 *Grants* £133,000 *Assets* £3,400,000

TRUSTEES P S Birdi; Mrs E Corney; Mrs P Francis; Mrs J Gaynor; Mrs S V Henderson; J R Kendrick; B W Lewis; D F Perkins; R H G Suggett; Mrs L Singh; J Gardener; P Adkins.

HOW TO APPLY On a form available from the correspondent or the website. Applications from organisations are normally processed by the trustees at their meeting in July each year. Applications should be sent by the end of April.

WHO TO APPLY TO The Clerk to the Trustees, PO Box 10282, Redditch, Worcestershire B97 5ZA *E-mail* clerk@nortonfoundation.org *Website* www.nortonfoundation.org

CC NO 702638   **ESTABLISHED** 1990

■ The Norwich Consolidated Charities

WHERE FUNDING CAN BE GIVEN Norwich, within the city boundary.

WHO CAN BENEFIT Individuals, and charities benefiting young adults, older people, parents and children, one-parent families, unemployed people, at risk groups, carers, and people who are disabled or disadvantaged by poverty, living in Norwich.

WHAT IS FUNDED Social welfare including community centres, clubs, respite care, and alternative healthcare.

TYPE OF GRANT One-off, capital, project and research.

SAMPLE GRANTS £177,000 to Marion Road Centre Trust; £10,000 to Mancroft Advice Project; £8,000 to Disabled Access Floating Trust; £7,200 to Norwich and District MIND; £7,000 to Norwich Community Co-Op Credit Union Ltd; £6,000 to Norwich and District Legal Services.

FINANCES *Year* 2001 *Income* £1,365,000 *Grants* £277,000 *Assets* £15,600,000

TRUSTEES Roger Pearson, Chair; Anthony Batty Shaw; David Fullman; Ronald Round; Roger Rowe; Ronald Barrett; Brenda Ferris; Susan Gale; Pamela Scutter; Philip Blanchflower; Joyce Hopwood; Geoffrey Loades; Glennes Rolph; Sarah Barham.

HOW TO APPLY In writing to the correspondent.

WHO TO APPLY TO The Clerk, 10 Golden Dog Lane, Magdalen Street, Norwich NR3 1BP *Tel* 01603 621023 *Fax* 01603 767025

CC NO 209224   **ESTABLISHED** 1910

■ The Norwich Historic Churches Trust Ltd

WHERE FUNDING CAN BE GIVEN Norwich.

WHO CAN BENEFIT Churches.

WHAT IS FUNDED The preservation, repair and maintenance of disused churches of all denominations which have particular architectural or historic value.

FINANCES *Year* 1998–99 *Income* £155,113 *Grants* £117,292 *Assets* £84,462

TRUSTEES C J Pordham, Chair; Cllr D C Bradford; D B Colman; Mrs S Curran; K S Dugdale; Mrs A V Fenner; Cllr T Gordon; J W Knight; J H Pogson; Cllr R E N Quinn; K Rowe; P Tolley; A C Whitwood.

HOW TO APPLY In writing to the correspondent.

WHO TO APPLY TO Mrs J Jones, Hall Farm, Great Plumstead, Norwich NR13 5EF
CC NO 266686   ESTABLISHED 1973

■ The Norwich Town Close Estate Charity

WHERE FUNDING CAN BE GIVEN Within a 20-mile radius of the Guildhall of the city of Norwich.

WHO CAN BENEFIT Only charities based in the area specified and carrying out educational activities will be supported.

WHAT IS FUNDED Primarily Freemen of Norwich, for education, pensions, TV licences, and relief in need. Surplus monies may be used for grants to educational charities.

WHAT IS NOT FUNDED No grants to: individuals who are not Freemen (or dependants of Freemen) of the city of Norwich; charities more than 20 miles from Norwich; or charities which are not educational. Revenue funding for educational charities is not generally given.

TYPE OF GRANT Buildings, capital, one-off and project. Funding for up to one year will be considered.

SAMPLE GRANTS £50,000 to Norfolk & Norwich Heritage Trust (Dragon Hall); £15,000 to City of Norwich School Association; £10,000 each to BREAK and Hewett School Association.

FINANCES Year 2000–01 Income £677,000 Grants £466,000 Assets £11,551,000

TRUSTEES M G Quinton, Chairman; N B Q Back; P J Colby; T C Eaton; R E T Gurney; A P Hansell; J S Livock; H W Watson; R H Pearson; A B Shaw; R G Round; D Fullman; Mrs S Gale; Lady J Hopwood; P R Blanchflower; Mrs B Ferril.

HOW TO APPLY After a preliminary enquiry, in writing to the clerk.

WHO TO APPLY TO The Clerk, 10 Golden Dog Lane, Magdalen Street, Norwich NR3 1BP Tel 01603 621023 Fax 01603 767025
CC NO 235678   ESTABLISHED 1892

■ Norwood & Newton Settlement

WHERE FUNDING CAN BE GIVEN England and Wales.

WHO CAN BENEFIT Methodist and other mainstream non-conformist churches. Church of England only in exceptional circumstances.

WHAT IS FUNDED New building work in Methodist and other Free Churches. Smaller national charities in which the Settlor expressed a particular interest and other charitable causes which commend themselves to the trustees.

WHAT IS NOT FUNDED Projects will not be considered where an application for National Lottery funding has been made or is contemplated. No grants to individuals, rarely to large UK charities and not for staff/running costs, equipment, repairs or general maintenance.

TYPE OF GRANT Normally one-off.

RANGE OF GRANTS £1,500–£10,000.

SAMPLE GRANTS £10,000 each to Blackheath Methodist Church – Birmingham, Chichester Baptist Church, Faversham Baptist Church – Kent, Hawkwell Baptist Church – Essex, Kenilworth Methodist Church – Warwickshire, Port St Mary Baptist Church – Isle of Man and Yatton Methodist Church – Bristol; £7,500 each to Ashby Methodist Church – Leicestershire, Dovercourt Central Church – Essex, Nuthall Methodist Church – Nottingham and Wesley Methodist Church – Manchester.

FINANCES Year 2001–02 Income £285,194 Grants £239,500 Assets £6,641,423

TRUSTEES P Clarke; D M Holland; W W Leyland.

HOW TO APPLY In writing to the correspondent. In normal circumstances, the trustees' decision is communicated to the applicant within seven days (if a refusal), and if successful, immediately after the trustees' quarterly meetings.

WHO TO APPLY TO David M Holland, Trustee, 126 Beauly Way, Romford, Essex RM1 4XL Tel 01708 723670
CC NO 234964   ESTABLISHED 1952

■ The Noswad Charity

WHERE FUNDING CAN BE GIVEN UK.

WHO CAN BENEFIT Emphasis is on charities which benefit the arts and people who are disabled, particularly ex-service people.

WHAT IS FUNDED Currently the trustees are supporting those charitable bodies which they have hitherto supported.

WHAT IS NOT FUNDED No grants to individuals.

RANGE OF GRANTS £600–£2,600.

SAMPLE GRANTS Typically grants are made to Douglas Bader Foundation, Royal Air Force Benevolent Fund, BLESMA, RADAR, Macmillan Cancer Relief and National Arts Collections Fund. It also supports scholarships for postgraduate piano students at London music colleges.

FINANCES Year 2001–02 Income £21,329 Grants £29,600 Assets £505,422

TRUSTEES J A Mills; C N Bardswell; H E Bromley Davenport.

HOW TO APPLY In writing to the correspondent.

WHO TO APPLY TO C N Bardswell, Trustee, c/o Messrs Belmont & Lowe, Solicitors, Henrietta House, 93 Turnmill Street, London EC1M 5TQ Tel 020 7608 4600
CC NO 282080   ESTABLISHED 1981

■ The Noswal Charitable Trust

WHERE FUNDING CAN BE GIVEN UK and overseas.

WHO CAN BENEFIT Organisations benefiting Jewish people. At risk groups, and people who are disadvantaged by poverty, ill or socially isolated will be considered.

WHAT IS FUNDED Generally Jewish charities and synagogues but some general health and welfare groups will be considered.

TYPE OF GRANT One-off and recurrent grants.

RANGE OF GRANTS Up to £5,000.

SAMPLE GRANTS £8,900 to Ben Gurion University Foundation; £1,700 to West London Synagogue; £1,000 to British Red Cross.

FINANCES Year 1999–2000 Income £24,000 Grants £13,000 Assets £879,000

TRUSTEES S S Lawson; Ms B V Lawson.

HOW TO APPLY In writing to the correspondent.

WHO TO APPLY TO Dr S S Lawson, 12a Chelwood House, Gloucester Square, London W2 2SY Tel 020 7724 5714
CC NO 326341   ESTABLISHED 1983

■ The Notgrove Trust

WHERE FUNDING CAN BE GIVEN Generally in the Gloucestershire area.

WHO CAN BENEFIT Local or special interests of the trustees.

WHAT IS FUNDED Any local charities can be considered.

WHAT IS NOT FUNDED No grants to individuals.

TYPE OF GRANT Except in special circumstances, single donations only will be considered.
RANGE OF GRANTS £1,000–£5,000.
SAMPLE GRANTS £10,000 to University of Gloucestershire; £1,000 each to Farms for City Children, Cotswold School, Notgrove PCC, Starlight Childrens Foundation and Care Share.
FINANCES *Year* 2001–2002 *Income* £50,000 *Grants* £51,000 *Assets* £1,500,000
TRUSTEES David Acland; Elizabeth Acland.
HOW TO APPLY Applications are considered from Gloucestershire charities or from an organisation having an established connection with the trustees. Applicants should include a copy of their latest accounts. Speculative appeals from outside of Gloucestershire are strongly discouraged and unlikely to get a positive response. Past donations to charities outside Gloucestershire should not be taken as an indication of likely future support.
WHO TO APPLY TO David Acland, Trustee, The Manor, Notgrove, Cheltenham, Gloucestershire GL54 3BT *Tel* 01451 850239
CC NO 278692   **ESTABLISHED** 1979

■ The Nottingham General Dispensary

WHERE FUNDING CAN BE GIVEN Nottinghamshire.
WHO CAN BENEFIT Individuals or other organisations.
WHAT IS FUNDED The alleviation of need or aid in recovery through the provision of items and services not readily available from ordinary channels. Charities working in the fields of: respite; professional bodies; councils for voluntary service; and health will be considered.
TYPE OF GRANT One-off preferred. Capital, project, research, recurring costs, running costs and salaries. Funding for up to three years will be considered.
RANGE OF GRANTS £25–£4,000; mostly under £500.
SAMPLE GRANTS £4,000 to District Nurse Network; £3,000 to Radford Visiting Scheme; £2,500 to Elizabeth Fitzroy Home; £2,000 to Emmanuel House; £1,750 to Electronic Aids for the Blind; £1,500 to an individual for a stairlift; £1,000 each to The A Team – Arthritis Care and an individual for building work.
FINANCES *Year* 2001–02 *Income* £49,000 *Grants* £30,000 *Assets* £1,200,000
TRUSTEES Ingle Dawson, Chair; Dr I McLauchlan; Mrs P Johnston; J Bendall; R Batterbury; Dr S Harris; J Williams; A Hopwood.
HOW TO APPLY In writing to the correspondent.
WHO TO APPLY TO D S Corder, Secretary, Bramley House, 1 Oxford Street, Nottingham NG1 5BH *Tel* 0115 935 0350 *Fax* 0115 859 9652
CC NO 228149   **ESTABLISHED** 1963

■ Nottinghamshire Community Foundation

WHERE FUNDING CAN BE GIVEN Nottinghamshire.
WHO CAN BENEFIT The communities of Nottinghamshire.
WHAT IS FUNDED General charitable purposes, particularly the improvement of social conditions, protection of good health (both mental and physical) and relief of poverty and sickness.
SAMPLE GRANTS The foundation's total expenditure was £99,095.
FINANCES *Year* 2000–01 *Income* £93,523

TRUSTEES Revd Alan Morgan, Chair; Cllr Sally Higgins; Chris Sowman; Corri Van de Stege; Fran Walker.
HOW TO APPLY The foundation has a number of different forms, all of which have different application procedures. Contact the foundation, or visit its website, for further information.
WHO TO APPLY TO The Trustees, Dunham House, Westgate, Southwell, Nottinghamshire NG25 0JL *Tel* 01636 819219 *E-mail* enquiries@nottscommunityfoundation. org.uk *Website* www.nottscommunityfoundation.org.uk
CC NO 1069538   **ESTABLISHED** 1998

■ The Nottinghamshire Historic Churches Trust

WHERE FUNDING CAN BE GIVEN Nottinghamshire.
WHO CAN BENEFIT Churches and chapels.
WHAT IS FUNDED The trust gives grants for the preservation, repair and improvement of historic churches and chapels in Nottinghamshire and of the monuments, fittings and furniture and so on, of such churches.
RANGE OF GRANTS Up to £5,000.
FINANCES *Year* 1999–2000 *Income* £76,000 *Grants* £112,000
HOW TO APPLY In writing to the correspondent.
WHO TO APPLY TO Dr C Brooke, 3 Woodland View, Halam Road, Southwell, Nottinghamshire NG25 0AG
CC NO 518335   **ESTABLISHED** 1985

■ The Nottinghamshire Miners' Welfare Trust Fund

WHERE FUNDING CAN BE GIVEN Nottinghamshire.
WHO CAN BENEFIT Miners or ex-miners who are retired, redundant or unemployed.
WHAT IS FUNDED The trust supports miners or ex-miners in need living in Nottinghamshire, who are retired or redundant and still unemployed, and their dependants.
SAMPLE GRANTS £20,000 to Mansfield Miners' Welfare Scheme for a roof; £18,000 (in two grants) to CISWO for a UK-wide relief-in-need scheme and a Nottinghamshire bowls competition; £13,000 to Cotgrave Miners' Welfare for a new fence and disabled toilets; £7,500 to East Kirkby Miners' Welfare Scheme for a central heating boiler; £5,000 each to Bestwood Miners' Welfare for repairs to the pavilion roof and Notts and District Miners' Pension Scheme for heating; £3,000 to Medical Welfare Scheme for running costs; £1,000 to Church Warsop Miners' Welfare Scheme to install ladies toilets; £80 to Blidworth Brass Band to play at Southwell Minster.
FINANCES *Year* 1999 *Income* £93,000 *Grants* £103,000 *Assets* £1,900,000
TRUSTEES J C H Longden; M F Ball; N Greatrex; M L Stevens.
HOW TO APPLY In writing to the correspondent.
WHO TO APPLY TO E R Andrews, Coal Industry Social Welfare Organisation, Berry Hill Lane, Mansfield NG18 4JR *Tel* 01623 625767
CC NO 1001272   **ESTABLISHED** 1990

■ The Nova Charitable Trust

WHERE FUNDING CAN BE GIVEN UK and overseas.
WHO CAN BENEFIT Children in need of medical or social assistance.
WHAT IS FUNDED General charitable purposes, in particular, to assist children who are in need or hardship.
TYPE OF GRANT One-off payments and recurring annual payments.
FINANCES *Year* 1998–99 *Income* £55,000 *Grants* £55,000
TRUSTEES Heather Kneller; Graham Kneller; Robert Turton.
HOW TO APPLY In writing to the correspondent.
WHO TO APPLY TO R P Turton, Trustee, BDO Stoy Hayward, Mander House, Wolverhampton, West Midlands WV1 3NF *Tel* 01902 714828
CC NO 1068293   **ESTABLISHED** 1998

■ Novi Most International

WHERE FUNDING CAN BE GIVEN Bosnia-Herzegovina and Bosnian people in exile.
WHO CAN BENEFIT Bosnians disadvantaged and displaced by war, especially children and young people.
WHAT IS FUNDED Evangelical Christian ministry to meet physical, spiritual, emotional and social needs, with particular emphasis on long-term support of children and young people traumatised by war. Reconciliation and community development initiatives are also supported.
WHAT IS NOT FUNDED Grants seldom given to projects not connected with evangelical churches or where the trust's own staff or partners are not involved.
TYPE OF GRANT One-off and recurring.
RANGE OF GRANTS £50–£20,000.
FINANCES *Year* 1998–99 *Income* £319,753 *Grants* £302,832 *Assets* £55,630
TRUSTEES W Beech; D Birch; R Egner; J Parkin; T Stone; G O'Neill.
PUBLICATIONS *New Bridge* and *Bosnia Prayer Briefing*.
HOW TO APPLY Funds fully committed for the foreseeable future. Unsolicited applications are not encouraged or acknowledged.
WHO TO APPLY TO P H Brooks, Brushell House, 118–120 Broad Street, Chesham, Buckinghamshire HP5 3ED *Website* www.novimost.org
CC NO 1043501   **ESTABLISHED** 1995

■ The Nuffield Foundation

WHERE FUNDING CAN BE GIVEN UK and Commonwealth.
WHO CAN BENEFIT Charitable and voluntary organisations, and universities benefiting children, young adults and older people; research workers; students; legal professionals; those in care, fostered and adopted; parents and children; one-parent families; at risk groups; carers; disabled people; those disadvantaged by poverty; refugees; travellers; and people suffering from arthritis and rheumatism. Grants are not made to individuals except under the fellowship schemes.
WHAT IS FUNDED Research, experiment or practical development in the fields of: child protection, family ustice; access to justice; educational provision and children's needs; curriculum innovation; older people and their families; Commonwealth; miscellaneous.

WHAT IS NOT FUNDED No grants for: general appeals; buildings or capital costs; projects which are mainly of local interest; research that is mainly of theoretical interest; day to day running costs or accommodation needs; the provision of health or social services; grants to replace statutory funding; healthcare (outside mental health); the arts, religion; museums, exhibitions, performances; sports and recreation; conservation, heritage or environmental projects; animal rights or welfare; attendance at conferences; expeditions, travel, adventure/ holiday projects; business or job creation projects; academic journals; or medical research (other than in rheumatism and arthritis research). Grants are not made for the following purposes except when the activity is part of a project that is otherwise acceptable: work for degrees or other qualifications; production of films, videos or television programmes; orpurchase of equipment, including computers.
TYPE OF GRANT One-off grants for projects.
RANGE OF GRANTS £20,000–£250,000.
SAMPLE GRANTS £195,000 to Edinburgh University for a study of youth transitions and crime; £188,000 to Link Community Development UK for educational development in the eastern Cape, South Africa; £179,000 to Reproduction Health Alliance for training teachers in Zambia to provide sexuality and life skills education to pupils aged 8 to 14 years; £142,000 to York University for a study of unaccompanied immigrant children and the social work services; £118,000 each to the Constitution Unit for an independent commission to review Britain's experience of proportional voting systems and York University for a new curriculum for key stage 4 science; £113,000 to De Montfort University School of Law for a study of unfitness to plead insanity and diminished responsibility; £100,000 to Central London Law Centre to produce five practical publications relating to the law on discrimination in employment; £98,000 to Thomas Coram Research Unit for an evaluation of a clinical programme for enhancing placement stability after adoption or placement for adoption; £93,000 to Leeds University Centre for Criminal Justice Studies for a study of plural policing and the market for a visible patrolling presence.
FINANCES *Year* 2002 *Grants* £6,250,000
TRUSTEES Baroness O'Neill, chair; Sir Tony Atkinson; Prof. Genevra Richardson; Prof. Lord Robert May; Prof. Sir Michael Rutter; Mrs Anne Sofer; Dr Peter Doyle.
PUBLICATIONS Guidelines.
HOW TO APPLY Initially in a written outline proposal so trust staff can assess if it is eligible. The outline should describe: the issue or problem you wish to address; the expected outcome(s); what will happen in the course of the project; (for research projects) an outline of the methods to be employed; and an outline of the budget and the timetable. The outline must not exceed three sides of A4, but you are welcome to include additional supporting information about yourself and your organisation. Prosposals which appear suitable will be either advised to submit a full application or meet with trust staff. Extensive guidance on how to prepare the fuller application is available.
WHO TO APPLY TO 28 Bedford Square, London WC1B 3EG *Tel* 020 7631 0566 *Fax* 020 7232 4877 *Website* www.nuffieldfoundation.org
CC NO 206601   **ESTABLISHED** 1943

■ The Nuffield Trust

WHERE FUNDING CAN BE GIVEN UK.

WHO CAN BENEFIT Organisations undertaking health services research and policy studies in health.

WHAT IS FUNDED The work is centred on four main areas: health policy futures; the changing role of the state in health care; public health; quality. For other trust interests, see the website.

WHAT IS NOT FUNDED Grants are not awarded to individuals for personal studies, nor to meet the core costs of other organisations.

TYPE OF GRANT One year or recurring (for normally not more than three years), including salaries of staff, associated expenses and equipment costs. The trust does not meet the overhead costs of other organisations.

SAMPLE GRANTS £142,000 to Professor Peter Donnelly, University of Oxford, for a three-year research fellowship in medical mathematics; £125,000 over 18 months to a professor at University College London for a project on health care quality; £92,000 to Professor Martin McKee, London School of Hygiene, for three year research fellowship in international benchmarking; £19,151 to a professor at University College London for analysing divergence, stability and change.

FINANCES *Year* 2001–02 *Income* £1,970,000 *Grants* £611,000 *Assets* £58,110,000

TRUSTEES Sir Maurice Shock, Chair; Prof. Sir Leszek Borysiewicz; Prof. Sir Denis Pereira Gray; Prof. Sir Keith Peters; Dame Fiona Caldicott; Sir Christopher France; Lord Carlile; Baroness Cox; Prof. Don Detmer.

PUBLICATIONS See the trust's website, or contact the trust, for recent, current and forthcoming publications.

OTHER INFORMATION The trust is currently reviewing its grant making policy; for details please see website.

HOW TO APPLY In writing to the correspondent, giving a brief outline of the study for which they seek funding. The trustees meet in March, July and November and applications should be submitted will in advance of the month it is intended to be considered in. However, the trust has moved from being primarily a grant making body to one working mainly on the basis of commissioned work in support of priority programmes. In the current difficult financial climate there is little scope for funding unsolicited applications. Potential applicants are strongly advised, therefore, to obtain up-to-date guidelines for applicants before approaching the trust.

WHO TO APPLY TO John Wyn Owen, Secretary, 59 New Cavendish Street, London W1G 7LP *Tel* 020 7631 8450 *Fax* 202 7631 8451 *E-mail* mail@nuffieldtrust.org.uk *Website* www.nuffieldtrust.org.uk

CC NO 209201   **ESTABLISHED** 1940

■ The Father O'Mahoney Memorial Trust

WHERE FUNDING CAN BE GIVEN Developing countries.

WHO CAN BENEFIT Organisations benefiting 'impotent people and those disadvantaged by poverty'.

WHAT IS FUNDED The relief of 'impotent and poor' people in all parts of the world except the UK.

WHAT IS NOT FUNDED UK organisations; individual requests.

RANGE OF GRANTS Depends on finances; maximum usually £5,000.

SAMPLE GRANTS In 1998–99: £4,000 to Father Veasey Clinic, Ecuador for medicines; £3,000 each to Child in Need Institute, Calcutta for healthcare, Santi TB Centre, Calcutta for healthcare, and Bushmen Project, Namibia for primary healthcare; £2,500 to St Bridget, Rwanda for health, agriculture and medicines; £2,000 each to CAFOD Nicaragua Appeal, and Lar das Criancos Orphanage, Brazil; £1,500 to Medical Foundation for the Victims of Torture for rehabilitation of torture victims.

FINANCES *Year* 2000 *Grants* £36,000

TRUSTEES C Carney-Smith; Ms C A Hearn; D M Maclean; M A Moran; Fr G Murray; A H Sanford; Mrs P Hirons; Mrs M Jennings; Mrs B Carney.

HOW TO APPLY In writing to the correspondent. The trustees meet every two months to consider applications.

WHO TO APPLY TO The Trustees, Our Lady of the Wayside Church, 566 Stratford Road, Shirley, Solihull, West Midlands B90 4AY

CC NO 1039288   **ESTABLISHED** 1993

■ O-Regen

WHERE FUNDING CAN BE GIVEN Waltham Forest.

WHO CAN BENEFIT Local communities.

WHAT IS FUNDED The charitable company supports 'communities in neighbourhoods where unemployment and other problems are damaging community wellbeing'.

FINANCES *Year* 1999–2000 *Income* £2,000,000 *Grants* £40,000 *Assets* £2,900,000

TRUSTEES Monica Tyler, Chair; Michael Polledri; Lucia Bird; Simon Bartlett; Tony Buckley; Mike Pettit; Stephen Thake; Sheila Bass; Peter Brokenshire; Diana Murray; Milton Martin; Kathy Francis; Godwin Poi; Susan Nwalema; Afzal Akram.

HOW TO APPLY The charity works through four community development officers based in Chingford, Walthamstow, Leyton and Leytonstone.

WHO TO APPLY TO Beverley McKenzie, 7 Kirkdale Road, Leytonstone, London E11 1HP *Tel* 020 8539 5533 *Fax* 020 8539 8074 *Website* www.o-regen.co.uk

CC NO 1066883   **ESTABLISHED** 1997

■ The Oak Trust

WHERE FUNDING CAN BE GIVEN UK.

WHO CAN BENEFIT Registered charities. Preference to charities which the trust has special interest in, knowledge of or association with.

WHAT IS FUNDED General charitable purposes.

WHAT IS NOT FUNDED No support to individuals.

SAMPLE GRANTS £5,000 to Christian Aid; £3,000 each to Cardan Sailing Trust, Red Cross, and Save the Children; £2,000 each to Ocean Youth Trust, Prader-Willi Syndrome Association (UK), Refugee Council, and St Mungo Community Housing Association Ltd.

FINANCES *Year* 1999–2000 *Income* £45,154 *Grants* £54,000 *Assets* £704,446

TRUSTEES Revd A C C Courtauld; J Courtauld; Dr E Courtauld.

HOW TO APPLY In writing to the correspondent. Trustees meet twice a year. Unsuccessful applications are not replied to.

WHO TO APPLY TO Richard Long, Clerk, Birkett Long, Red House, Colchester Road, Halstead, Essex CO9 2DZ *Tel* 01787 272200

CC NO 231456   **ESTABLISHED** 1963

■ The Oakdale Trust

WHERE FUNDING CAN BE GIVEN Worldwide, especially Wales.

WHO CAN BENEFIT Organisations doing social and medical work benefiting at risk groups, carers, disabled people, those disadvantaged by poverty, ex-offenders and those at risk of offending, homeless people, refugees, and victims of crime, famine and war.

WHAT IS FUNDED The trust gives preference to Welsh charities engaged in social work, medical support groups and medical research. Some support is given to UK charities working overseas and to conservation projects at home and abroad. Some arts and community arts activities, infrastructure support and development, community facilities and services, mediation, peace and disarmament will also be considered. The trust also supports Quaker activities.

WHAT IS NOT FUNDED No grants to individuals, holiday schemes, sport activities or expeditions.

TYPE OF GRANT Single outright grants. Buildings, capital, core costs, feasibility studies, one-off, project, research, recurring costs, salaries and start-up costs will be considered. Funding may be given for up to one year.

RANGE OF GRANTS Typical grant around £750.

SAMPLE GRANTS £10,000 each to The Brandon Centre and Concern Universal; £5,000 each to The Bracken Trust, CARAD, Howard League for Penal Reform and Medical Foundation for the Care of Victims of Torture; £4,000 to Youth Hostel Association; £3,000 to Survivors Fund; £2,000 each to Cambridge Female Education Trust, Gwent Wildlife Trust, Radnorshire Wildlife Trust and WaterAid.

FINANCES *Year* 2001–02 *Income* £187,690 *Grants* £161,437

TRUSTEES B Cadbury; Mrs F F Cadbury; R A Cadbury; F B Cadbury; Mrs O Tatton-Brown; Dr R C Cadbury.

HOW TO APPLY An application form is available from the trust; however, applicants are free to submit requests in any format, providing they are clear and concise, covering aims, achievements, plans and needs, and supported by a budget. Applications for grants in excess of £1,000 are asked to submit a copy of a recent set of audited accounts (these can be returned on request). The trustees meet twice a year in April and October to consider applications. The deadline for these meetings is 1 March and 1 September respectively; no grants are awarded between meetings. Unsuccessful applicants are not normally notified and similarly applications are not acknowledged even when accompanied by an sae.

WHO TO APPLY TO Rupert Cadbury, Tansor House, Tansor, Oundle, Peterborough PE8 5HS
E-mail oakdale@tanh.demon.co.uk
CC NO 218827   **ESTABLISHED** 1950

■ The Oakley Charitable Trust

WHERE FUNDING CAN BE GIVEN Predominantly the Midlands, south west of England and the channel Isles.

WHO CAN BENEFIT Registered charities.

WHAT IS FUNDED Predominantly welfare; health; education; arts, culture and recreation; conservation and environment.

WHAT IS NOT FUNDED No grants to individuals can be considered. Grants are only made to registered charities.

TYPE OF GRANT One-off, core costs, project, research, recurring costs and buildings. Funding is available for one year or less.

RANGE OF GRANTS Average grant £500–£2,000.

SAMPLE GRANTS £20,000 to St Mary' s Hospice; £2,000 to Birmingham Hippodrome Vital Stage Appeal; £1,100 to Acorn Children' s Hospice; £1,000 each to Coventry Cathedral Development Trust, Edgbaston Old Church, Symphony Hall Organ Appeal and West Midlands Stammering in School Appeal; £500 each to James Beattie House Appeal, Birmingham Institute for the Deaf, Citizen Advocacy – Solihull, Handsworth Grammar School and St Giles Hospice.

FINANCES *Year* 2001–02 *Income* £66,000 *Grants* £66,000 *Assets* £1,400,000

TRUSTEES Mrs C M Airey; G M W Oakley; S M Sharp.

HOW TO APPLY In writing to the correspondent. Trustees usually meet in March, July and November.

WHO TO APPLY TO G M W Oakley, Trustee, c/o Gerrard, Temple Court, 35 Bull Street, Birmingham B4 6ES *Tel* 0121 200 2244
CC NO 233041   **ESTABLISHED** 1963

■ The Oakmoor Trust

WHERE FUNDING CAN BE GIVEN UK.

WHO CAN BENEFIT Registered charities.

WHAT IS FUNDED General charitable purposes.

WHAT IS NOT FUNDED No grants to individuals.

SAMPLE GRANTS £10,000 to Trustees of the Wakes Museum; £7,500 to Save Britain's Heritage; £3,800 to Charterhouse School; £2,500 to the Institute of Economic Affairs; £2,000 each to Friends of Westminster Cathedral, Medical Foundation and St Mary's Witon.

FINANCES *Year* 2000 *Income* £48,000 *Grants* £44,000 *Assets* £1,600,000

TRUSTEES Rathbone Trust Company Ltd; P M H Andreae; R J Andreae.

HOW TO APPLY The trust states that it does not respond to unsolicited applications.

WHO TO APPLY TO Rathbone Trust Company Limited, 159 New Bond St, London W1Y 9PA *Tel* 020 7399 0000 *Fax* 020 7399 0050
CC NO 258516   **ESTABLISHED** 1969

■ The Odin Charitable Trust

WHERE FUNDING CAN BE GIVEN UK.

WHO CAN BENEFIT Registered charities.

WHAT IS FUNDED General charitable purposes with preference for: the arts; care for people who are disabled and disadvantaged people; hospices, homeless people, prisoners' families, refugees, gypsies and 'tribal groups'; research into false memories and dyslexia.

WHAT IS NOT FUNDED Applications from individuals are not considered.

RANGE OF GRANTS £300–£35,000.

SAMPLE GRANTS Recurrent grants were given to Crisis Fairshare (£9,000 in total to 2003), Dorothy House (£15,000 in total to 2004), Helen Arkell Dyslexia Centre (£17,000 in total to 2004), Mustard Tree (£9,000 in total to 2003) and New Bridge (£15,000 in total to 2003).

Other beneficiaries included Detention Advice Centre, Finsbury Park Street Drinkers Initiative, Bath Recital Artists' Trust, Pearson's Holiday Fund, Neighbourly Care Southall and Southwark Children's Foundation, Friends of Style Acre and The PACE Centre.

FINANCES *Year* 2001–02 *Income* £123,000 *Grants* £135,000 *Assets* £4,181,637

TRUSTEES Mrs S G P Scotford; Mrs A H Palmer; Mrs M Mowinckel.

HOW TO APPLY In writing to the correspondent.

WHO TO APPLY TO Mrs M Mowinckel, Trustee, PO Box 1898, Bradford on Avon, Wiltshire BA15 1YS
CC NO 1027521   **ESTABLISHED** 1993

■ The Ofenheim Charitable Trust

WHERE FUNDING CAN BE GIVEN UK.

WHO CAN BENEFIT Registered charities.

WHAT IS FUNDED General charitable purposes, usually in the fields of health, the arts and the environment. The trust usually supports well known and established charitable organisations of personal interest and concern to the the trustees.

SAMPLE GRANTS £12,000 each to Barnardos, Musicians' Benevolent Fund, NSPCC, St Wilfred's Hospice, Salvation Army, Save the Children Fund and World Wildlife Fund; £7,500 each to British Stroke Association, King Edward VII Hospital and National Youth Orchestra of Great Britain.

FINANCES *Year* 2000–01 *Income* £51,097 *Grants* £70,000 *Assets* £1,461,151

TRUSTEES Roger J Clark; Rory McLeod.

HOW TO APPLY In writing to the correspondent. Unsuccessful applications will not be acknowledged. Trustees meet in November and applications need to be received by October.

WHO TO APPLY TO G Wright, Baker Tilly, 1st Floor, 4b Clarendon Road, Watford, Hertfordshire WD17 1HE *Tel* 01923 816400
CC NO 263751   **ESTABLISHED** 1972

■ Ogilvie Charities Deed 2 (including the Charity of Mary Catherine Ford Smith)

WHERE FUNDING CAN BE GIVEN Primarily London, Essex and Suffolk.

WHO CAN BENEFIT Individuals or organisations benefiting female teachers and governesses, homeless people and those disadvantaged by poverty.

WHAT IS FUNDED Specific philanthropic work. Assistance to present or former governesses or female teachers in straitened circumstances. Country holidays for London children. Support of the charity's own homes and almshouses and residents living in them. Aid to other charitable institutions in Metropolitan London, Essex and Suffolk or, if situated beyond, serving the needs of people living in those areas. Support may also be given to infrastructure and technical support and religious ancillary buildings.

WHAT IS NOT FUNDED No payment of debts.

TYPE OF GRANT One-off usually. Grants for individuals must be made through medical and other social workers who are already aware of what is available. Buildings, core costs, project, running costs, salaries and start-up costs will be considered. Funding may be given for up to one year.

RANGE OF GRANTS Individual grants £100, organisation grants £2,500.

FINANCES *Year* 2001 *Income* £88,000 *Grants* £113,800 *Assets* £129,000

HOW TO APPLY Applications must be made through official sources, not by personal application. Preliminary telephone enquiries are acceptable. Applicant organisations must send copies of annual accounts.

WHO TO APPLY TO T Last, General Manager, The Gate House, 9 Burkitt Road, Woodbridge, Suffolk IP12 4JJ *Tel* 01394 388746 *Fax* 01394 388746 *E-mail* ogilviecharities@btconnect.com

CC NO 211778   **ESTABLISHED** 1890

■ The Ogle Christian Trust

WHERE FUNDING CAN BE GIVEN Worldwide.

WHO CAN BENEFIT Registered charities benefiting Bible students, pastors, Christians, evangelists and victims of famine.

WHAT IS FUNDED The trust's main concern is the promotion of Biblical Christianity. Currently it includes: new initiatives in evangelism; support for the publishing and distribution of Scriptures and Christian literature; training of Bible students and pastors; and Christian social enterprise and famine relief.

WHAT IS NOT FUNDED Applications from individuals are discouraged; those granted require accreditation by a sponsoring organisation. No grants are made for building projects. Grants will not be offered in response to general appeals from large national organisations.

TYPE OF GRANT Normally one-off or short-term commitments only. Salaries will not be funded.

RANGE OF GRANTS £150–£10,000.

FINANCES *Year* 2001 *Income* £161,951 *Grants* £146,256 *Assets* £2,373,334

TRUSTEES D J Harris, Chair; S Procter; Mrs F J Putley; C A Fischbacher; Mrs L M Quanrud.

HOW TO APPLY In writing to the correspondent, accompanied by documentary support and an sae. Trustees meet in May and November, but applications can be made at any time.

WHO TO APPLY TO Chris Fischbacher, Secretary, 2 Park Farm Stables, Stopham Rd, Pulborough, West Sussex RH20 1DR *Tel* 01798 874692 *E-mail* oglectrust@aol.com

CC NO 1061458   **ESTABLISHED** 1938

■ Oglesby Trust

WHERE FUNDING CAN BE GIVEN The north west of England.

WHAT IS FUNDED Charitable activities across a broad spectrum reflecting the beliefs and interests of the founding trustee family.

RANGE OF GRANTS £200–£25,000.

SAMPLE GRANTS £250,000 to Fitzwilliam Museum – Cambridge for a portrait by Sir Anthony Van Dyck; £232,997 to National Library of Scotland – Edinburgh for an album of 206 calotype prints; £130,000 to York City Art Gallery for a painting by Paret; £80,000 to Captain Cook Memorial Museum – Whitby for a painting by William Hodges; £75,000 to Ulster Museum – Belfast for two ribbon torcs; £62,852 to Tate – London for a collection by Anslem Kiefer; £50,000 to Wiltshire Heritage Museum – Devizes for 1,196 coins; £25,000 to Penlee House Gallery and Museum – Penzance for a painting by Fredrick Hall; £23,300 to Brecknock Museum and Art Gallery – Brecon for three paintings; £2,587 to Williamson Art Gallery and Museum – Birkenhead for a Minton punch bowl.

FINANCES *Grants* £500,000

TRUSTEES Jean Oglesby; Michael Oglesby; Robert Kilson; Roger Groarke; Kate Vokes; Jane Oglesby.

HOW TO APPLY On a form available from the correspondent, or the website. An initial response is given within four weeks, usually within two. For applications up to £200, this is all that is needed. For larger applications a more comprehensive application form is sent and they may be interviewed by the trustees.

WHO TO APPLY TO The Trustees, PO Box 336, Altrincham, Cheshire WA14 3XD *Website* www.oglesbycharitabletrust.co.uk

CC NO 1026669   **ESTABLISHED** 1993

■ The Oikonomia Trust

WHERE FUNDING CAN BE GIVEN UK and overseas.

WHO CAN BENEFIT Organisations benefiting evangelists.

WHAT IS FUNDED The trust is not looking for new outlets as those it has knowledge of are sufficient to absorb its available funds.

WHAT IS NOT FUNDED No grants made in response to general appeals from large national organisations.

TYPE OF GRANT Evangelical work, famine and other relief through Christian agencies, particularly when accompanied with the offer of the Gospel.

SAMPLE GRANTS £7,000 to Bethel Church; £6,000 to Association of Evangelists; £5,000 to Africa Inland Mission; £4,000 each to Asia Link, Japan Mission, Caring for Life and Leeds City Mission; £3,000 each to The Faith Mission, Slavic Gospel Association and Drumchapel Church; £2,000 each to Arab World Ministries and Africa International.

FINANCES *Year* 1999–2000 *Income* £24,000 *Grants* £58,000 *Assets* £523,000

TRUSTEES D H Metcalfe; R H Metcalfe; S D Metcalfe; R O Owens.

HOW TO APPLY In writing to the correspondent, although the trust has previously stated that known needs are greater than the trust's supplies. If an applicant desires an answer, an sae should be enclosed. Applications should arrive in January.

WHO TO APPLY TO D H Metcalfe, Trustee, Westoaks, St John's Close, Sharow, Ripon, North Yorkshire HG4 5BB *Tel* 01765 602829

CC NO 273481   **ESTABLISHED** 1977

■ The Oizer Charitable Trust

WHERE FUNDING CAN BE GIVEN Preference for Greater Manchester.
WHO CAN BENEFIT Registered charities.
WHAT IS FUNDED Education and welfare.
FINANCES *Year* 1996–97 *Income* £39,000 *Grants* £26,000
TRUSTEES J Halpern; Mrs C Halpern.
HOW TO APPLY In writing to the correspondent.
WHO TO APPLY TO Joshua Halpern, Trustee, 35 Waterpark Road, Salford M7 0FT
CC NO 1014399   **ESTABLISHED** 1992

■ The Old Broad Street Charity Trust

WHERE FUNDING CAN BE GIVEN UK and overseas.
WHO CAN BENEFIT Registered charities benefiting children, young adults, students, people working in a bank or financial institution, actors and entertainment professionals, musicians, textile workers and designers, and writers and poets.
WHAT IS FUNDED General charitable purposes with an emphasis on arts and education. Funding scholarships for people serving in a bank or financial institution in the UK to spend time in any seat of learning (principally INSEAD) to attain the highest level of executive management.
WHAT IS NOT FUNDED The trustees only support organisations of which they personally have some knowledge.
TYPE OF GRANT One-off and project grants for one year or less.
RANGE OF GRANTS £385–£9,531.
SAMPLE GRANTS £9,531 to L'Hopital Intercommunal de Cretei; £8,830 to Bezirksfursorge – Sannen; £8,195 to Pour Que L'Espirit Vive; £5,000 Grange Park Opera Society; £2,133 to Fondation de Bellerive; £2,500 each to Royal Academy of Arts, Treloar Trust and Victoria & Albert Museum; £650 each to Tate Gallery Foundation and Serpentine Galley Trust; £455 to Whitechapel Art Gallery Trust; £385 to Artangel.
FINANCES *Year* 2001–02 *Income* £90,587 *Grants* £83,029 *Assets* £1,988,342
TRUSTEES P A Hetherington; A T J Stanford; Mrs M Cartier-Bresson; C J Sheridan; Mrs E J Franck.
OTHER INFORMATION This charity includes the Louis Franck Scholarship Fund.
HOW TO APPLY In writing to the correspondent. Unsolicited applications are not considered.
WHO TO APPLY TO S P Jennings, Secretary to the Trustees, Eagle House, 110 Jermyn Street, London SW1Y 6RH *Tel* 020 7451 9000 *Fax* 020 7451 9090
CC NO 231382   **ESTABLISHED** 1964

■ The Old Enfield Charitable Trust

WHERE FUNDING CAN BE GIVEN The ancient parish of Enfield (old borough of Enfield).
WHO CAN BENEFIT Charities and individuals in need including: children; young adults and older people; parents and children; one-parent families; widows and widowers; disabled people and people disadvantaged by poverty.
WHAT IS FUNDED Education and training, community projects and social development for those in need. Particularly: support to voluntary and community organisations; training for work; vocational training; costs of study including fees, purchase of books and travel costs; almshouses for residents of the ancient parish of Enfield; and general grants for household goods, clothing and so on. Postgraduateor pre-school education and community clubs or transport are considered.
WHAT IS NOT FUNDED No scholarships, loans, national charity appeals, public school fees or support for anything where central or local government funding is available.
TYPE OF GRANT One-off, core costs, project, running costs, salaries and start-up costs. Funding is available for up to and over three years and assessed according to need.
RANGE OF GRANTS £200–£20,000.
SAMPLE GRANTS £29,000 to Nightingale Trust for start-up costs; £20,000 (over three years) to Age Concern Enfield to fund a drop-in centre/ luncheon club; £3,200 to Enfield Baptist Church; £3,000 to MS Society; £2,500 to Enfield Preservation Society; £2,200 to Ponders End United Reform Church; £1,000 each to Enfield Rangers, Good Neighbour Scheme, and Winged Fellowship; £800 to Enfield Caribbean Association.
FINANCES *Year* 2002 *Income* £553,490 *Grants* £238,546 *Assets* £4,540,543
TRUSTEES Mrs S Attwood; S Bell; C Bond; M Braithwaite; H Brown; R Cross; J Eustance; C Griffiths; J Little; Miss P Oborn; Dr P O'Mahony; C Parker; G Smith; Mrs A Thacker; Mrs A Webb.
OTHER INFORMATION This charity was formed in 1994 via the merger of The Enfield Parochial Charity and the Hundred Acres Charity.
HOW TO APPLY In writing to the correspondent. Application forms and guidelines are available. Initial telephone calls are welcome. There is no deadline for applications and no sae is required.
WHO TO APPLY TO The Trust Administrator, The Old Vestry Office, 22 The Town , Enfield, Middlesex EN2 6LT *Tel* 020 8367 8941 *Fax* 020 8366 7898 *E-mail* toect@ic24.net *Website* www.toect.org.uk
CC NO 207840   **ESTABLISHED** 1962

■ Old Possum's Practical Trust

WHERE FUNDING CAN BE GIVEN UK and overseas.
WHO CAN BENEFIT Registered charities and individuals of all ages.
WHAT IS FUNDED The increase of knowledge and appreciation of any matters of historic, artistic, architectural, aesthetic, literary, musical, theatrical or scientific interest; human and animal welfare.
WHAT IS NOT FUNDED No grants towards sports or to students for academic studies or overseas trips, unless special circumstances apply.
RANGE OF GRANTS £10–£10,500.
SAMPLE GRANTS £10,500 to The Arvon Foundation; £10,000 each to Parkinson's Disease Society, Poetry Book Society, St Stephen's Organ Appeal, and Victoria and Albert Museum; £5,000 each to Anglican Centre – Rome, Handel House Trust, Hearing Dogs for Deaf People, RNIB, and Vale Of Elham Trust.
FINANCES *Year* 2000/01 *Income* £355,027 *Grants* £160,940 *Assets* £2,837,096
TRUSTEES Mrs Esme Eliot; Judith Hooper; Brian Stevens.
HOW TO APPLY In writing to the correspondent. The 2000–01 annual report stated: 'The trustees wish to continue the policy of using the trust's income to support a few carefully chosen cases, generally located in the UK, rather than make a large number of small grants. The emphasis will be on continued support of those institutions and individuals who have received support in the past. Unfortunately we have to disappoint

the great majority of applicants who nevertheless continue to send appeal letters. The trustees do not welcome telephone calls from applicants soliciting funds.'

WHO TO APPLY TO Judith Hooper, Trustee, Baker Tilly, 5th Floor, Exchange House, 446 Midsummer Boulevard, Milton Keynes MK9 2EA *Tel* 01908 687800 *Fax* 01908 687801

CC NO 328558   **ESTABLISHED** 1990

■ The John Oldacre Foundation

WHERE FUNDING CAN BE GIVEN UK.

WHO CAN BENEFIT Universities, agricultural colleges and innovative projects benefiting students and research workers.

WHAT IS FUNDED Research and education in agricultural sciences.

WHAT IS NOT FUNDED No grants towards tuition fees.

TYPE OF GRANT One-off, recurrent, feasibility, project, research and funding of up to three years will be considered.

RANGE OF GRANTS £5,000–£10,000.

SAMPLE GRANTS £35,000 to Royal Agricultural College; £12,000 to Arable Research Centre; £11,705 to University of Bristol; £7,500 to Nuffield Farming Scholarship Trust; £6,000 to Wye College; £3,000 to Writtle College; £2,740 to Cranfield University; £2,500 to Paignton Zoo.

FINANCES *Year* 2000–01 *Income* £93,686 *Grants* £90,445 *Assets* £3,126,161

TRUSTEES H B Shouler; S J Charnock; D G Stevens.

HOW TO APPLY In writing to the correspondent.

WHO TO APPLY TO Henry Shouler, Trustee, Hazleton House, Hazleton, Cheltenham, Gloucestershire GL54 4EB *Tel* 01453 835486

CC NO 284960   **ESTABLISHED** 1981

■ The Oldham Foundation

WHERE FUNDING CAN BE GIVEN North west and south west of England.

WHO CAN BENEFIT Organisations benefiting children, young adults, ex-service and service people, Church of England and former employees of Oldham Batteries (employed before 1971). Funding is considered for people disadvantaged by poverty, victims of man-made or natural disasters, and people with cancer, HIV and AIDs and mental illness.

WHAT IS FUNDED Main donations to former employees of Oldham Batteries (employed before 1971) and charitable activities where trustees give personal service or where they know people who do so. Charities working in the fields of arts, culture and recreation; conservation and environment; and churches will be considered. Support may also be given to hospices, nursing services, cancer research, libraries and museums, day centres, holidays and outings.

WHAT IS NOT FUNDED No grants for UK appeals or individuals.

TYPE OF GRANT Annual grant to former employees. Grants usually one-off. Does not provide core funding. General charitable grants with bias towards active participation by trustees.

RANGE OF GRANTS £40–£5,000; typical grant £250/£500/£1,000.

SAMPLE GRANTS In 1999–2000: £20,245 to Oldham Batteries former employees; £5,000 each to Cheltenham Festival of Music and Cheltenham Festival of Literature; £4,000 to Felsted School; £2,000 each to Mid-Cheshire Sheltered Workshop, International Red Cross for the

Kosovo Appeal, SSAFA Sussex, East Cheshire Hospice, Multi A Project Bristol, and CABE.

FINANCES *Year* 2000/01 *Income* £69,600

TRUSTEES Mrs D R Oldham; J H Oldham; Prof. R Thomas; S T Roberts; John Sharpe; John Bodden.

HOW TO APPLY In writing to the correspondent. Applications should include clear details of projects, budgets and/or accounts where appropriate. Telephone calls are not welcomed. The trustees meet annually but applications can be considered between meetings. Inappropriate appeals are not acknowledged.

WHO TO APPLY TO Mrs D R Oldham, Swift House, 62 North St, Winchcombe, Gloucestershire GL54 5PS

CC NO 269263   **ESTABLISHED** 1974

■ The Kate Wilson Oliver Trust

WHERE FUNDING CAN BE GIVEN Preference for the West Midlands.

WHO CAN BENEFIT Charitable institutions benefiting: at risk groups; people disadvantaged by poverty; disaster victims; homeless people; victims of abuse, crime and domestic violence.

WHAT IS FUNDED Assistance to deserving gentlefolk and to charitable institutions for the relief of human suffering.

WHAT IS NOT FUNDED No grants to individuals.

TYPE OF GRANT Lump sum payments.

RANGE OF GRANTS £500–£2,500.

SAMPLE GRANTS £2,500 to St Mary's Hospice, Birmingham; £2,000 each to Leonard Cheshire Service in Birmingham and RUKBA; £1,500 to Circumstances; £1,000 each to British Home & Hospital for Incurables, Cancer Relief Macmillan Fund, CRUSE, Friends of the Elderly, Help the Aged, and National Benevolent Fund for the Aged.

FINANCES *Year* 2001–02 *Income* £27,961 *Grants* £26,000 *Assets* £726,177

TRUSTEES W M Colacicchi; C R S Clutterbuck; Mrs C E V Colacicchi.

HOW TO APPLY In writing to the correspondent. Applications are considered in September/October.

WHO TO APPLY TO W M Colacicchi, Trustee, Putsman.wlc, Britannia House, 50 Great Charles Street, Birmingham B3 2LT *Tel* 0121 237 3000

CC NO 211968   **ESTABLISHED** 1940

■ Onaway Trust

WHERE FUNDING CAN BE GIVEN UK, USA and worldwide.

WHO CAN BENEFIT Registered charities benefiting indigenous peoples, in the main, Native Americans, and animal welfare.

WHAT IS FUNDED Trustees like to provide seed funds for self-generating, self-sufficiency projects based upon indigenous traditional beliefs and practices. The trustees concentrate mainly on Native Americans. The Onaway Trust's wide remit is to relieve poverty and suffering. This is expressed in many areas: the environment, child and animal welfare, world refugees and human rights.

WHAT IS NOT FUNDED No grants for administration costs, travel expenses or projects considered unethical or detrimental to the struggle of indigenous people.

TYPE OF GRANT Small, start-up costs.

SAMPLE GRANTS £19,000 to PISIL – Honduras; £10,000 to Rainy Mountain Society for Indigenous Peoples; £8,700 to Compassion in

World Farming; £8,528 to Forest Peoples Programme – Africa; £8,150 to Simon Community; £8,000 each to British Red Cross, Academy for Development Science – India and Jeel Al Amal – Middle East; £6,550 to the Society for the Welfare of Horses and Ponies; £5,000 each to Care International – Central America and Friends of Conservation; £4,000 Drukpa Kargyud Trust – India.

FINANCES *Year* 2001 *Income* £206,000 *Grants* £199,000 *Assets* £5,275,000

TRUSTEES J Morris; Ms B J Pilkinton; A Breslin; Annie Smith; Elaine Fearnside; C Howles; D Watters.

HOW TO APPLY In writing to the correspondent, enclosing an sae.

WHO TO APPLY TO David Watters, Trust Administrator, 275 Main Street, Shadwell, Leeds LS17 8LH *Tel* 0113 265 9611 *E-mail* david@onaway.org *Website* www.onaway.org

CC NO 268448   **ESTABLISHED** 1974

■ Oppenheim Foundation

WHERE FUNDING CAN BE GIVEN UK.

WHO CAN BENEFIT Registered charities.

WHAT IS FUNDED Not known.

FINANCES *Year* 2000–01 *Income* £9,086 *Grants* £108,383 *Assets* £267,895

TRUSTEES J N Oppenheim; T S Oppenheim; P A Smith.

HOW TO APPLY The trust stated that it does not consider applications from organisations with whom it has had no previous contact.

WHO TO APPLY TO Peter Smith, Trustee, 39 King Street, London EC2V 2DQ *Tel* 020 7623 9021

CC NO 279246   **ESTABLISHED** 1980

■ Oppenheimer Charitable Trust

WHERE FUNDING CAN BE GIVEN UK.

WHO CAN BENEFIT Registered charities only, benefiting children, young adults and older people, at risk groups, and people who are sick, disadvantaged by poverty or socially isolated.

WHAT IS FUNDED General charitable purposes for the well-being and benefit of people living in areas where companies of the De Beers group operate. The following areas are particularly supported: medicine and health; children and youth; older people; general welfare; and the arts.

WHAT IS NOT FUNDED No educational grants are given.

FINANCES *Year* 2000–01 *Income* £62,200 *Grants* £63,873

TRUSTEES Sir Christopher Collet; Michael Farmiloe; G I Watson.

HOW TO APPLY In writing to the correspondent. Trustees meet in January, April, July and October.

WHO TO APPLY TO The Secretary to the Trust, 17 Charterhouse Street, London EC1N 6RA *Tel* 020 7404 4444

CC NO 200395   **ESTABLISHED** 1961

■ The Raymond Oppenheimer Foundation

WHERE FUNDING CAN BE GIVEN UK and worldwide.

WHO CAN BENEFIT National organisations and localised institutions' appeals.

WHAT IS FUNDED General charitable purposes, including conservation, education, the arts and medical research.

TYPE OF GRANT One-off.

SAMPLE GRANTS US$100,000 to Stichting Mario Montessori 75 Fund; US$25,000 to African Medical & Research Foundation; £5,000 to York Minister Fund; £500 to Imperial Cancer Research.

FINANCES *Year* 2000–01 *Income* £28,478 *Grants* £86,756 *Assets* £733,967

TRUSTEES Alec G Berber; David Murphy; Clifford T Elphick.

HOW TO APPLY In writing to the correspondent.

WHO TO APPLY TO D Murphy, Trustee, 40 Holborn Viaduct, London EC1N 2PB *Tel* 020 7404 0069

CC NO 326551   **ESTABLISHED** 1984

■ The Ormsby Charitable Trust

WHERE FUNDING CAN BE GIVEN UK, London and the South East.

WHO CAN BENEFIT Registered charities.

WHAT IS FUNDED Mainly organisations concerned with people who are sick, older people and young people.

WHAT IS NOT FUNDED No grants to individuals, animals or religious causes.

SAMPLE GRANTS In 1997–98: £9,200 to Child Health; £1,000 to NSPCC.

FINANCES *Year* 2000–01 *Grants* £30,000

TRUSTEES Rosemay David; Angela Chiswell; Katrina McCrossan.

HOW TO APPLY In writing to the correspondent.

WHO TO APPLY TO Mrs K McCrossan, Trustee, 85 Ravenscourt Road, London W6 0UJ *Tel* 020 8741 9077

CC NO 1000599   **ESTABLISHED** 1990

■ Orrin Charitable Trust

WHERE FUNDING CAN BE GIVEN Mainly Scotland.

WHO CAN BENEFIT Registered charities.

WHAT IS FUNDED General charitable purposes including conservation, hospitals, community projects, and galleries.

WHAT IS NOT FUNDED Grants are not given overseas or to individuals.

RANGE OF GRANTS £250–£13,000.

SAMPLE GRANTS £13,000 to Wester Ross Fishing Trust; £8,000 to National Galleries of Scotland; £4,000 to Highland Hospice; £2,000 each to Macmillan Cancer Relief Scotland and National Trust for Scotland.

FINANCES *Year* 1999–2000 *Income* £44,613 *Grants* £46,750 *Assets* £581,685

TRUSTEES Mrs E V MacDonald-Buchanan; J MacDonald-Buchanan; H MacDonald-Buchanan.

HOW TO APPLY The trust tends to mainly support organisations known to the trustees rather than supporting unsolicited applications. The trustees meet twice a year.

WHO TO APPLY TO The Secretary, c/o Hedley Foundation Limited, 9 Dowgate Hill, London EC4R 2SU *Tel* 020 7489 8076

CC NO 274599   **ESTABLISHED** 1977

■ The Ouseley Trust

WHERE FUNDING CAN BE GIVEN England, Wales and Ireland.

WHO CAN BENEFIT Cathedrals, choirs, parish churches, and choir schools. Children who are members of choirs of recognised choral foundations. Funding is only given to individuals through institutions.

WHAT IS FUNDED Projects that promote and maintain to a high standard the choral services of the Church of England, the Church in Wales or the Church of Ireland. These may include contributions to endowment funds, courses, fees, repairs of organs, and the purchase of music.

WHAT IS NOT FUNDED Grants will not be awarded to help with the cost of fees for ex-choristers, for chant books, hymnals or psalters. Grants will not be made for the purchase of new instruments nor for the installation of an instrument from another place of worship where this involves extensive reconstruction. Under normal circumstances, grants will not be awarded for buildings, cassettes, commissions, compact discs, furniture, pianos, robes, tours or visits.

TYPE OF GRANT One sum – for specific project or contribution to endowment fund.

RANGE OF GRANTS Up to £50,000.

SAMPLE GRANTS £10,000 each to St Michael & All Angels – Croydon, Norwich Cathedral Choir Endowment Fund and Bangor Cathedral; £7,000 to Worcester Cathedral; £6,000 in total to Salisbury Cathedral School; £5,000 each to St Bartholomew the Great – Smithfield and St Patrick's Cathedral – Armagh; £3,000 in total to Wells Cathedral School; £2,000 in total to Holy Trinity –Stroud.

FINANCES *Year* 2001 *Income* £121,326 *Grants* £66,280 *Assets* £2,934,173

TRUSTEES Dr Christopher Robinson, Chair; Dr J A Birch; Rev Canon Mark Boyling; Dr R J Shephard; N E Walker; Revd A F Walters; Mrs Gillian Perkins; Sir David Willcocks; N A Ridley; Dr S M Darlington; Dr J Rutter.

HOW TO APPLY Applicants are strongly advised to obtain a copy of the trust's guidelines (either from the correspondent or their website, currently under construction at the time of writing) before drafting an application. Applications must be submitted by an institution on a form available from the correspondent. Closing dates for applications are 31 January for the March meeting and 30 June for the October meeting.

WHO TO APPLY TO Martin Williams, Clerk, 127 Coleherne Court, London SW5 0EB *Tel* 020 7373 1950 *Fax* 020 7341 0043 *E-mail* clerk@ouseleytrust.org.uk *Website* www.ouseleytrust.org.uk

CC NO 527519   ESTABLISHED 1989

■ The Owen Family Trust

WHERE FUNDING CAN BE GIVEN UK, with a preference for Midlands, Gwynedd and Wrexham.

WHO CAN BENEFIT Schools (independent and church), Christian youth centres, churches, community associations, national organisations benefiting people of all ages, and people with Alzheimer's disease, cancer and strokes.

WHAT IS FUNDED Mainly support for projects known personally by the trustees. Christian outreach projects are supported, with consideration also given to the arts, conservation, cancer research,

Christian education, church and related community buildings.

WHAT IS NOT FUNDED The trust states 'no grants to individuals unless part of a charitable request'.

TYPE OF GRANT Buildings, capital, and recurring costs will be considered. Funding may be given for more than three years.

RANGE OF GRANTS £50–£25,000.

SAMPLE GRANTS £5,000 each to Black Country Museum Development Trust, Emmanuel Church – Sutton Coldfield, Grubb Institute, Lichfield Cathedral Trust Music Campaign, Pioneer Centre, St Martin's Parish Church – Oswestry and Symphony Hall Organ Appeal; £3,000 to Youth for Christ – Rock Solid; £2,000 to NSPCC; £1,500 to Lichfield International Arts Festival.

FINANCES *Year* 2000–01 *Income* £414,000 *Grants* £61,000 *Assets* £1,300,000

TRUSTEES Mrs H G Jenkins; A D Owen.

HOW TO APPLY In writing to the correspondent including brochures. Only a small number of grants can be given each year and unsuccessful applications are not acknowledged unless an sae is enclosed.

WHO TO APPLY TO A D Owen, Trustee, Mill Dam House, Mill Lane, Aldridge, Walsall WS9 0NB *Tel* 0121 526 3131

CC NO 251975   ESTABLISHED 1967

■ Oxfam (GB)

WHERE FUNDING CAN BE GIVEN Africa, Asia, Caribbean, Central America, Eastern Europe, countries of the former Soviet Union, Great Britain, Middle East, South America.

WHO CAN BENEFIT Organisations which benefit people of all ages who are disadvantaged by poverty, disabled or victims of famine, disasters or war.

WHAT IS FUNDED Organisations worldwide working for the relief of hunger, disease, exploitation and poverty. Organisations working in public education in the UK and Ireland.

WHAT IS NOT FUNDED Applications for individuals are not considered.

TYPE OF GRANT Majority are one-off cash grants.

SAMPLE GRANTS £524,000 to Service Formation Action pour le Développement Economiqe et Social; £411,000 to Union de Cooperatives Agropecuaries de Siuna; £275,000 to Assocation Nationale des maisons familiales Rurales; £255,000 to Centre for Research and Training on Development; £180,000 to Association of Handicapped People of Kosovo; £169,000 to Fundacion para la Cooperacion con Desplazados y Repoblados Salvadorenos; £167,000 to Association Nationale de Formation des Adultes; £149,000 to Yayasen Nen Mas II; £130,000 to Ugandan Participatory Poverty Assessment Project; £126,000 to Centro de Estudios para el Desarrollo Laboral y Agrario.

FINANCES *Year* 2001–02 *Income* £189,398,000 *Grants* £15,309,000 *Assets* £68,873,000

TRUSTEES Dr Rosemary Thorp, Chair; Dino Adriano, Vice Chair; Amartya Sen, Honorary Adviser; Frank Kirwan, Honorary Treasurer; Michael Behr; Jackie Gunn; Sir Richard Jolly; Michael Rowntree; Norman Sanson; Angela Sealey; Hugo Slim; Scarlett McGwire; Matthew Sparrow; Stan Thekaekara; Shriti Vadera.

HOW TO APPLY Applications should be made to the Regional Management Centre in the region concerned.

WHO TO APPLY TO 274 Banbury Road, Oxford OX2 7DZ *Tel* 01865 313600 *Fax* 01865 312452 *E-mail* oxfam@oxfam.org.uk *Website* www.oxfam.org.uk
CC NO 202918   **ESTABLISHED** 1958

■ The Oxford Preservation Trust

WHERE FUNDING CAN BE GIVEN Oxford and the green belt around it.

WHO CAN BENEFIT Projects must be of public benefit.

WHAT IS FUNDED Environmental enhancement and conservation projects within Oxford and the green belt and works to preserve, repair or restore historic buildings in the Oxford area. This includes charities working in the fields of religious buildings, support to voluntary and community organisations, support to volunteers, architecture and community facilities.

WHAT IS NOT FUNDED No support for any project not publicly visible. No educational grants.

TYPE OF GRANT One-off and recurring grants; interest-free loans.

RANGE OF GRANTS £390–£10,000.

SAMPLE GRANTS 2000 and 2001: £10,000 to Oxfordshire Historic Churches Trust; £7,000 to Oxfordshire Victoria County History Trust; £5,000 to Friends of the Cathedral (St Frideswide Shrine); £1,500 to Centre for Oxfordshire Studies (purchase of photographs); £1,000 each to Oxford Conservation Volunteers; Oxfordshire Woodland Trust.

FINANCES *Year* 2001 *Income* £314,000 *Grants* £57,000 *Assets* £5,514,000

TRUSTEES Sir David Yardley, Chair and 26 others.

HOW TO APPLY In writing to the correspondent. Initial telephone calls are welcome. Trustees meet bi-monthly.

WHO TO APPLY TO Mrs D Dance, Secretary, 10 Turn Again Lane, St Ebbe's, Oxford OX1 1QL *Tel* 01865 242918 *Fax* 01865 251022 *E-mail* info@oxfordpreservation.org.uk *Website* www.oxfordpreservation.org.uk
CC NO 203043   **ESTABLISHED** 1927

■ The Oxfordshire Community Foundation

WHERE FUNDING CAN BE GIVEN Oxfordshire.

WHO CAN BENEFIT Community-based non-profit organisations constituted in Oxfordshire. Beneficiaries of all ages, social circumstances, family situations and medical conditions will be considered, although the following are prioritised: parents and children; at risk groups; carers; disabled people; people disadvantaged by poverty; homeless people; immigrants; those living in rural areas; socially isolated people; victims of domestic violence; those with hearing loss, mental illness, and sight loss; and substance misusers.

WHAT IS FUNDED Specific projects up to one year with outputs related to poverty, unemployment, education and health promotion, including charities working in the fields of infrastructure and technical support, infrastructure development, charity or voluntary umbrella bodies, residential facilities and services, self-help groups, campaigning for health issues, health related volunteer schemes, equal opportunities and various community facilities and services.

WHAT IS NOT FUNDED The grants panel would not consider departments or divisions of public bodies; sports groups for people without

disabilities; organisations whose principal concern is animal welfare; medical research; religious organisations (unless it can be clearly demonstrated that the particular project for which grant aid is sought will be of benefit to the community at large); organisations whose principal concern is the provision of overseas aid; organisations whose principal activity is the protection or improvement of the natural environment (except where it can be demonstrated that the particular project for which grant aid is sought also meets the primary objectives set out in eligibility criteria above); or UK charities and appeals. Grants are not given to charities with a turnover of more than £200,000 or towards recurrent expenditure, ongoing core costs, large building projects or fundraising costs.

TYPE OF GRANT One-off; capital. One year start-up for projects, training and equipment.

RANGE OF GRANTS Up to £6,000; average £900.

SAMPLE GRANTS In 2000–01: £6,500 to Focus; £6,200 to Bicester & District Citizens Advice Bureau; £4,300 to Greenshoots; £3,500 to Energy and Vision; £2,600 to The Courtyard Youth Arts Centre, Bicester; £1,900 to Banbury Young Homeless Project; £1,200 to Kidlington and District Information Centre; £1,000 to Campaign Against Institutional Racism in Oxon.

FINANCES *Year* 2001–02 *Income* £308,333 *Grants* £108,000 *Assets* £801,142

TRUSTEES Simon Stubbings, Chair; Anna Moon; Jane Wates; Peter Jay; Nigel Hamway; Nigel Talbot-Rice; Gavin Isle.

PUBLICATIONS *The Other Oxfordshire.*

HOW TO APPLY On a form available from the correspondent or on the foundation's website, to be submitted by a certain date each year. To be eligible for a grant you must demonstrate the following: that you are a properly constituted not-for-profit organisation based in Oxfordshire; that your organisation aims to serve the needs of people in Oxfordshire; that the activity for which funding is sought will result in an improvement in the quality of life for people in Oxfordshire by alleviating the effects of poverty, addressing the needs of disabled people, promoting good health, promoting educational attainment; that the activities for which the grant is sought are capable of being implemented within a specified period of time.

WHO TO APPLY TO Philippa McAllister, Grants Manager, Vanbrugh House, 20 St Michael's Street, Oxford OX1 2EB *Tel* 01865 798666 *Fax* 01865 245385 *E-mail* ocf@oxfordshire.org *Website* www.oxfordshire.org
CC NO 1046432   **ESTABLISHED** 1995

■ The Oxfordshire Historic Churches Trust

WHERE FUNDING CAN BE GIVEN Oxfordshire.

WHO CAN BENEFIT Churches and chapels of all denominations which are open for public worship.

WHAT IS FUNDED The preservation, repair and restoration of churches.

WHAT IS NOT FUNDED No grants for conversions (e.g. kitchens), re-ordering or new-build projects.

TYPE OF GRANT One-off grants.

RANGE OF GRANTS £500–£10,000.

SAMPLE GRANTS £10,000 each to St Helen's Abingdon (spire repairs), St Leonard, Sunningwell (repairs to 16th century porch) and Witney Methodist church (stonework repairs); £9,000 to Friends Meeting House, Wallingford (window and door lintel repairs); £7,000 to St Birinus Roman Catholic Church, Dorchester (roof reslating); £5,000 to SS Peter and Paul, Aston Rowant (stonework repairs to nave); £3,000 to St Nicholas and Swithun, Yelford (heating repairs).

FINANCES *Year* 2001–02 *Income* £174,000 *Grants* £223,000 *Assets* £598,931

TRUSTEES C H Walton; R C Cotton; H L J Brunner; R H Lethbridge; H Sandilands.

HOW TO APPLY On a form available from the correspondent. The trustees meet three times a year, normally in January, May and September.

WHO TO APPLY TO R H Lethbridge, Hon. Secretary, The Dower House, Westhall Hill, Fulbrook, Oxfordshire OX18 4BJ *Tel* 01993 824196 *Fax* 01993 824196

CC NO 235644   **ESTABLISHED** 1964

■ The P F Charitable Trust

WHERE FUNDING CAN BE GIVEN Unrestricted, with local interests in Oxfordshire and Scotland.

WHO CAN BENEFIT Voluntary organisations and charitable groups only.

WHAT IS FUNDED General charitable purposes.

WHAT IS NOT FUNDED No grants to individuals or non-registered charities.

TYPE OF GRANT One-off and recurring, buildings, core costs, project, research and running costs. Funding may be given for up to three years.

SAMPLE GRANTS £3,500,000 to buy from Flemings Bank, and establish a new gallery, that organisation's collection of Scottish art; £1,160,000 to St Paul's Cathedral Appeal; £740,000 to Amaryllis Fleming Foundation; £550,000 to Dorchester Abbey; £500,000 each to Oxfordshire Community Foundation and the Playfair Project; £60,000 to 'Isaac Newton for mathematical sciences'; £50,000 each to Abbeyfield in Ballachulish, Douglas House and Prince's Trust; £42,000 to Cancer Research Campaign in Oxford.

FINANCES *Year* 2000–01 *Income* £3,177,992 *Grants* £8,619,925 *Assets* £106,646,058

TRUSTEES Robert Fleming; Valentine P Fleming; Philip Fleming; Rory D Fleming.

HOW TO APPLY Applications to the correspondent in writing. Trustees usually meet monthly to consider applications and approve grants.

WHO TO APPLY TO D H Pocknee, Secretary, or Geoffrey Fincham, Ely House, 37 Dover Street, London W1S 4NJ *Tel* 020 7409 5685

CC NO 220124   **ESTABLISHED** 1951

■ Padwa Charitable Foundation

WHERE FUNDING CAN BE GIVEN UK.

WHO CAN BENEFIT Organisations and individuals.

WHAT IS FUNDED The trust has the following aims: the relief of poverty; the advancement of religion and education; charitable purposes beneficial to the community. Donations are given to both individuals and organisations.

FINANCES *Year* 1999–2000 *Income* £34,000 *Grants* £17,000

TRUSTEES Meyer Padwa; K O'Sullivan; J Randall; N A Fulton; T Chandler.

HOW TO APPLY In writing to the correspondent.

WHO TO APPLY TO John A Benns, Secretary, Walpole Group Plc, 18 Rosebery Avenue, London EC1R 4TD *Tel* 020 7843 1635

CC NO 1019274   **ESTABLISHED** 1992

■ The Pallant Charitable Trust

WHERE FUNDING CAN BE GIVEN UK, with emphasis to date on work currently being carried out in central southern England.

WHO CAN BENEFIT Church musicians and choristers.

WHAT IS FUNDED Chorister's scholarships and musician's salaries.

SAMPLE GRANTS 1999–2000: £24,000 to Sarum College for a church musician; £22,000 to Church Music Advisor Project towards salary costs; £16,000 to Prebendal School for chorister's scholarships; £3,000 to St Peter's

Brighton Choral Foundation; £2,000 to Dean and Chapter of Chichester for awards to the organ scholar.

FINANCES *Year* 2001–02 *Income* £59,309 *Grants* £69,198 *Assets* £1,241,904

TRUSTEES W A Fairbairn; R F Ash; A J Thurlow; S A E Macfarlane.

HOW TO APPLY In writing to the correspondent.

WHO TO APPLY TO The Clerk to the Trustees, c/o Thomas Eggar, The Corn Exchange, Baffins Lane, Chichester, West Sussex PO19 1GE *Tel* 01243 786111 *Fax* 01243 532001

CC NO 265120   **ESTABLISHED** 1972

■ The Palmer Foundation

WHERE FUNDING CAN BE GIVEN London.

WHO CAN BENEFIT Selected registered charities chosen by the trustees. Children and young adults at Coopers' Company and Coborn School and Strode's College will be considered.

WHAT IS FUNDED Grants and donations to charitable organisations and payments for educational scholarships, bursaries and prizes at Coopers' Company and Coborn School and Strode's College.

TYPE OF GRANT Recurrent grants for up to three years will be considered.

FINANCES *Year* 1998–99 *Income* £81,214 *Grants* £55,395 *Assets* £407,959

TRUSTEES The Master Wardens or Keepers of the Commonalty of Freeman of the Mystery of Coopers of the City of London and suburbs (commonly known as the Coopers' Company), including J B Holden; J A Newton; J R Lawes.

HOW TO APPLY The trust conducts its own research and does not respond to unsolicited applications.

WHO TO APPLY TO Adrian Carroll, Clerk to the Trustees, Coopers Hall, 13 Devonshire Square, London EC2M 4TH *Tel* 020 7247 9577

CC NO 278666   **ESTABLISHED** 1979

■ The Eleanor Palmer Trust

WHERE FUNDING CAN BE GIVEN Former urban districts of Chipping Barnet and East Barnet.

WHO CAN BENEFIT Charities benefiting young adults and older people and people disadvantaged by poverty.

WHAT IS FUNDED Charities working in the fields of: relief in need; the provision of almshouses, amenities and grants for its housing association residents; support to voluntary and community organisations; clubs; day centres; and people on income support and maintenance.

WHAT IS NOT FUNDED Anything other than relief-in-need is not considered.

TYPE OF GRANT One-off, project and capital. Funding for one year or less will be considered.

RANGE OF GRANTS £100–£4,000.

SAMPLE GRANTS £22,000 to residents of the trust's properties towards outings, holidays and a lunch club; £4,000 to the local Good Neighbour Scheme for running costs; £3,000 each to the local Friend in Need Scheme for running costs and transport, and a local day centre for running costs; £2,500 to a local charity for electrical vouchers for people in need; £1,500 each to a care attendant scheme and Alzheimer's Society.

FINANCES *Year* 2002 *Income* £81,000 *Grants* £53,500 *Assets* £3,500,000

TRUSTEES Laurence Adams; Pauline Coakley-Webb; Pamela Coleman; Anthony Grimwade; Stephen Lane; Peter Mellows; Joan Nicholson; Catherine Older; Martyn Woolf; Sheila Elkin.

HOW TO APPLY In writing to the correspondent.
WHO TO APPLY TO R W Peart, Clerk, 106b Wood Street, Barnet, Herts EN5 4BY *Tel* 020 8441 3222 *Fax* 020 8364 8279
CC NO 220857 **ESTABLISHED** 1558

■ The Gerald Palmer Trust

WHERE FUNDING CAN BE GIVEN UK, especially Berkshire.
WHO CAN BENEFIT Organisations benefiting Christians, and people who are disadvantaged by poverty or sick.
WHAT IS FUNDED (a) The advancement of the Christian religion, more particularly according to the teaching and usage of the Orthodox Churches of the East. (b) The advancement of medical research and the study of medicine. (c) The relief of sickness and/or poverty. (d) The furtherance of education particularly with a Christian ethic. (e) General charitable purposes locally in Berkshire.
WHAT IS NOT FUNDED No grants to individuals or to local charities geographically remote from Berkshire.
RANGE OF GRANTS £100–£20,000.
FINANCES *Year* 2000–01 *Income* £712,000 *Grants* £147,500 *Assets* £16,082,636
TRUSTEES J M Clutterbuck; D R W Harrison; J N Abell; R Broadhurst.
HOW TO APPLY In writing to the correspondent.
WHO TO APPLY TO The Clerk, Eling Estate Office, Hermitage, Thatcham, Berkshire RG18 9UF *Tel* 01635 200268 *Fax* 01635 201077
CC NO 271327 **ESTABLISHED** 1968

■ Panahpur Charitable Trust

WHERE FUNDING CAN BE GIVEN UK, overseas (see below).
WHO CAN BENEFIT Christian charities and individuals, especially Christian missionary organisations.
WHAT IS FUNDED Scripture distribution/reading encouragement, relief work, missionary work, education and retreats.
RANGE OF GRANTS £15–£11,222.
SAMPLE GRANTS £11,222 to Interserve; £10,000 each to Himlit and Word for Life Trust; £9,600 to Relationships Foundation; £8,000 to Penhurst Retreat Centre; £6,000 to EHA UK; £5,400 to Outlook Trust; £4,980 to Christian Outreach; £4,100 to SIM International; £4,000 to Evangelical Missionary Alliance.
FINANCES *Year* 2000–01 *Income* £187,659 *Grants* £139,447 *Assets* £4,822,002
TRUSTEES P East; Miss D Haile; Mrs E R M Myers; A E Perry; R Moffett.
HOW TO APPLY In writing to the correspondent, although the trust informed us that applicants will not be successful unless they are already known to the trust.
WHO TO APPLY TO The Trust Department, Jacob Cavenagh and Skeet, 6–8 Tudor Court, Brighton Road, Sutton, Surrey SM2 5AE *Tel* 020 8643 1166
CC NO 214299 **ESTABLISHED** 1911

■ Panton Trust

WHERE FUNDING CAN BE GIVEN UK and overseas.
WHO CAN BENEFIT Worldwide organisations concerned with animal wildlife; UK: the environment.
WHAT IS FUNDED The trust states that it is 'concerned with any animal or animals or with wildlife in any part of the world, or with the environment of the UK or any part thereof. ... The trustees consider applications from a wide variety of sources and favour smaller charities which do not have the same capacity for large-scale fundraising as major charities in this field'.
TYPE OF GRANT Grants are made for strategic planning and project funding and can be for up to three years.
SAMPLE GRANTS £7,600 to Gonville & Caius College; £6,000 to Whale & Dolphin Society; £4,000 to Flora and Fauna International; £3,000 each to Cambridge Mpingo Project and St Tiggywinkles Wildlife Hospital; £2,000 to Emmanuel College and IPPL.
FINANCES *Year* 1999–2000 *Income* £25,000 *Grants* £33,000 *Assets* £177,000
TRUSTEES L M Slavin; R Craig.
HOW TO APPLY In writing to the correspondent.
WHO TO APPLY TO Laurence Slavin, Trustee, Ramsay House, 18 Vera Avenue, Grange Park, London N21 1RB *Tel* 020 8370 7700
CC NO 292910 **ESTABLISHED** 1983

■ The Paragon Trust

WHERE FUNDING CAN BE GIVEN UK.
WHO CAN BENEFIT Charities and occasionally certain individuals but only those known to the trustees.
WHAT IS FUNDED A wide range of charitable bodies.
TYPE OF GRANT The majority of donations are standing orders.
RANGE OF GRANTS Mostly £500 each.
SAMPLE GRANTS £3,000 to British Red Cross; £1,100 to Crisis; £1,000 to National AIDS Trust; £910 to Children's Society; £500 each to Action Health, Friends of National Libraries, Church of England Pensions Board, L'Arche, Leprosy Relief Association and RNIB.
FINANCES *Year* 1999–2000 *Income* £93,000 *Grants* £47,000 *Assets* £1,400,000
TRUSTEES Rt Hon. J B B Wrenbury; Revd Canon R F Coppin; Miss L J Whistler; P Cunningham; P Bagwell-Purefoy.
HOW TO APPLY The trust states that it does not respond to unsolicited applications; all beneficiaries 'are known personally to the trustees and no attention is paid to appeal literature, which is discarded on receipt. Fundraisers are therefore urged to save resources by not sending literature'.
WHO TO APPLY TO Kathy Larter, c/o Thomson Snell & Passmore, Solicitors, 3 Lonsdale Gardens, Tunbridge Wells, Kent TN1 1NX *Tel* 01892 510000
CC NO 278348 **ESTABLISHED** 1979

■ The Parivar Trust

WHERE FUNDING CAN BE GIVEN UK, with a preference for the West Midlands.
WHO CAN BENEFIT Individuals and local projects are priorities, but national organisations are also considered. Support is given to children, women; those in care, fostered and adopted; and parents and children. The following may also be considered: at risk groups, and people who are disabled, disadvantaged by poverty, socially isolated, or victims of abuse and domestic violence.
WHAT IS FUNDED Relief of sickness and poverty, provision of education, preservation and protection of good health. Grants are for the benefit of children, young people and women.

WHAT IS NOT FUNDED No grants to individuals for further education or vocational courses nor for sponsored trips.

TYPE OF GRANT Capital (including buildings), core costs, one-off, project, recurring costs, running costs, salaries and start-up costs will be considered. Funding may be given for up to three years.

RANGE OF GRANTS £50–£750 in UK.

FINANCES *Year* 2001 *Income* £31,095 *Grants* £24,296 *Assets* £475,000

TRUSTEES N A Rogers; Dr P Ramani; R O Walters.

HOW TO APPLY In writing to the correspondent at any time.

WHO TO APPLY TO N A Rogers, Trustee, 62 Symphony Court, Birmingham B16 8AF

CC NO 1032529   **ESTABLISHED** 1993

■ The Park Hill Charitable Trust

WHERE FUNDING CAN BE GIVEN UK, with a preference for the Midlands, particularly Coventry and Warwickshire.

WHAT IS FUNDED General charitable purposes, with preference towards social welfare and Christian causes.

WHAT IS NOT FUNDED No grants to individuals.

TYPE OF GRANT Normally one-off for general funds.

RANGE OF GRANTS Normally £1,000–£5,000.

SAMPLE GRANTS £5,000 each to Cambridge Nazareth Trust and Society for the Protection of Urban Children; £2,000 each to Coventry Homes and Myton Hamlet Hospice.

FINANCES *Year* 2001 *Income* £392,900 *Grants* £132,000 *Assets* £862,000

TRUSTEES N P Bailey; M M Bailey; P Bailey; J Hill; Mrs I A Creffield.

HOW TO APPLY In writing to the correspondent. The trust stated in May 2002 that it did not expect to have surplus funds available to meet the majority of applications.

WHO TO APPLY TO Paul Varney, Daffern & Co, Queen's House, Queen's Road, Coventry CV1 3DR *Tel* 024 7622 1046

CC NO 1077677   **ESTABLISHED** 1999

■ The Park Hill Trust

WHERE FUNDING CAN BE GIVEN UK.

WHO CAN BENEFIT Registered charities (but not major well-known organisations) benefiting older people and retired people.

WHAT IS FUNDED Imaginative new projects which aim to improve the quality of life of older people in retirement and to relieve loneliness by helping them to use their knowledge and experience for the benefit of the community. Particularly charities working in the fields of community facilities, conservation, the arts, support and self-help groups, health-related volunteer schemes and health promotion.

WHAT IS NOT FUNDED The trust aims to encourage new ideas rather than existing work. No project will be considered unless older people play an active rather than a passive role. Funding is not available to meet the costs of paid staff or professional contractors.

TYPE OF GRANT One-off for a specific project or start-up costs. Not to be used for payment of salaries. Funding for one year or less will be considered.

FINANCES *Year* 2001–02 *Income* £43,000 *Grants* £42,000 *Assets* £485,000

TRUSTEES A M Pilch; Mrs B C Pilch; Mrs R A Gill; P D Salter; Ms N D G Pendrigh.

HOW TO APPLY No applications can be considered unless they satisfy the criteria above. Applications falling outside these guidelines will not be acknowledged. Apply in writing to the correspondent. There is no application form.

WHO TO APPLY TO A M Pilch, Trustee, Miller Centre, 30 Godstone Road, Caterham, Surrey CR3 6RA

CC NO 258420   **ESTABLISHED** 1969

■ The Frank Parkinson Agricultural Trust

WHERE FUNDING CAN BE GIVEN UK.

WHO CAN BENEFIT Mainly corporate entities benefiting the improvement of agriculture and horticulture.

WHAT IS FUNDED The improvement and welfare of British agriculture, primarily to agricultural colleges and affiliated institutions.

WHAT IS NOT FUNDED Grants are given to corporate bodies and the trust is not able to assist with financial help to any individuals undertaking postgraduate studies or degree courses.

TYPE OF GRANT Short-term: two to four years preferred. One-off will also be considered.

RANGE OF GRANTS One-off at chairman's discretion: smallest £200; largest over three years £100,000; typical grants (over two years) £40,000.

SAMPLE GRANTS In 1999: £30,000 to Royal Agricultural College, Cirencester – Information and Communications Centre; £25,000 to Hartpury College, Gloucester – Learning Resources Centre; £1,600 for publishing costs of 'A Tale of Two Trusts'.

FINANCES *Year* 2001 *Income* £48,855

TRUSTEES Prof. P N Wilson; Prof. J D Leaver; W M Hudson; J S Sclanders; C Bourchier; A D S Robb.

HOW TO APPLY In writing to the correspondent. A detailed Guidelines for Grant Applications is available from the trust. The trustees meet annually in April. 'The Chairman has the authority to approve small grants between annual meetings, but these are only for minor sums and minor projects.'

WHO TO APPLY TO Miss Janet Smith, Secretary to the Trustees, c/o Grant Thornton, St John's Centre, 110 Albion Street, Leeds LS2 8LA *Tel* 0113 245 5514 *Fax* 0113 246 5055

CC NO 209407   **ESTABLISHED** 1943

■ The Samuel & Freda Parkinson Charitable Trust

WHERE FUNDING CAN BE GIVEN UK.

WHO CAN BENEFIT Registered charities specified by the founder of the trust.

SAMPLE GRANTS 2000–01: £25,000 to Leonard Cheshire Foundation; £23,000 each to Salvation Army and Church Army; £10,000 each to RNLI and RSPCA; £5,000 each to Animal Rescue and Animal Concern. A 'special distribution' of £10,000 was paid to RSPCA – Foot and Mouth Appeal.

FINANCES *Year* 2001–02 *Income* £103,654 *Grants* £100,000 *Assets* £2,356,651

TRUSTEES D E G Roberts; Miss J A Todd; J F Waring.

HOW TO APPLY The founder of this charity restricted the list of potential beneficiaries to named charities of his choice and accordingly the trustees do not have discretion to include further beneficiaries, although they do have complete discretion within the stated beneficiary list.

Think carefully about every application. Is it justified?

707

WHO TO APPLY TO J R M Crompton, Solicitor, Thomson Wilson Pattinson, Trustees' Solicitors, Stonecliffe, Lake Road, Windermere, Cumbria LA23 3AR *Tel* 01539 442233 *Fax* 01539 488810
CC NO 327749   **ESTABLISHED** 1987

■ The Parthenon Trust

WHERE FUNDING CAN BE GIVEN Unrestricted

WHO CAN BENEFIT Organisations which: benefit war and famine victims, older people, homeless people and the long-term unemployed; organisations which support long-term development in third world countries; people who are physically or mentally disabled; and medical research.

WHAT IS FUNDED (a) Children in need, refugees and famine victims; (b) older, homeless and long-term unemployed people; (c) long-term development in the third world; (d) medical research in areas which appear to be underfunded in relation to the likelihood of achieving progress; (e) supporting patient care, hospices and rehabilitation; and (f) helping people who are disabled.

WHAT IS NOT FUNDED No grants for individuals, scientific/geographical expeditions or projects which promote religious beliefs.

TYPE OF GRANT Normally one-off grants for general purposes.

RANGE OF GRANTS Wide range: there is no typical grant.

SAMPLE GRANTS £2,050,000 to Save the Children; £1,000,000 to Médecins sans Frontières (UK); £634,000 to Cancer Research Campaign; £627,000 to Association Voix Libres; £575,000 to EORTC (European Organisation for Research and Treatment of Cancer Foundation); £250,000 each to British Red Cross, Fundacion Promotora del Desarrollo de la Boquilla and Prince of Wales International Business Leaders Forum; £225,000 to Action Against Hunger UK; £207,000 to People's Committee of Son-La Province, Vietnam.

FINANCES *Year* 2001 *Income* £15,270,000 *Grants* £12,142,000

TRUSTEES Geraldine Whittaker, Chair; Dr J M Darmady; Prof. C N Hales.

HOW TO APPLY Anyone proposing to submit an application should telephone the secretary. Unsolicited written applications are not normally acknowledged.

WHO TO APPLY TO John E Whittaker, Secretary, Saint-Nicolas 9, 2000 Neuchatel, Switzerland *Tel* 00 41 32 724 8130 *Fax* 00 41 32 724 8131
CC NO 1051467   **ESTABLISHED** 1995

■ The Alan Pascoe Charitable Trust

WHERE FUNDING CAN BE GIVEN UK.

WHO CAN BENEFIT Organisations benefiting children and people who are sick.

WHAT IS FUNDED Medical and children's charities.

TYPE OF GRANT One-off and recurrent.

FINANCES *Year* 1999–2000 *Income* £11,000 *Grants* £22,000 *Assets* £229,000

TRUSTEES E P S Leesk; A P Pascoe.

HOW TO APPLY In writing to the correspondent.

WHO TO APPLY TO Bill Arnold, Morley & Scott, Old Treasury, 7 Kings Road, Portsmouth, Hampshire PO5 4DJ *Tel* 023 9275 4820
CC NO 296552   **ESTABLISHED** 1986

■ Pastoral Care Trust

WHERE FUNDING CAN BE GIVEN Scotland.

WHO CAN BENEFIT Community and local organisations working with people in need.

WHAT IS FUNDED The 1999/2000 annual report stated: 'The Pastoral Care Trust was set up in 1992 to mark the 500th anniversary of the Archdiocese of Glasgow. It was founded to establish in a modern context the traditions of five centuries of Christian life and action here in Scotland. In particular it was established to offer small grants to groups, agencies and projects working for the common good of all Glasgow's people.'

WHAT IS NOT FUNDED No grants to individuals or to fund salaries.

RANGE OF GRANTS Up to £15,000.

SAMPLE GRANTS £25,000 to Scottish Churches Community Trust; £5,500 to Milton Volunteer and Care Project; £5,000 each to 1 in 100 Theatre Company and St Matthew's Centre; £3,500 to Spinal Injuries Scotland; £3,000 to Govan Churches Elderpark Project; £2,900 to Pathway; £2,000 to Ruchill Summer Outreach and Wee Care Group; £1,300 to St Pius X Church; £1,200 to Our Lady of Fatima Family Resource Centre to develop a community resource for young people and families; £1,000 each to Glasgow YWCA Family Centre and Starters Packs Glasgow.

FINANCES *Year* 1999–2000 *Grants* £86,000

TRUSTEES Monsignor Maguire; Mrs Kathleen McConville; Frank McCormick; Miss Angus Malone; Revd Mario Joseph Conti, Archbishop of Glasgow; John McHugh; John Geggan; Michael Fitzpatrick; Sarah Fitzpatrick.

HOW TO APPLY On a form available from the correspondent.

WHO TO APPLY TO Elizabeth M McQuade, Development Officer, 196 Clyde Street, Glasgow G1 4JY *Tel* 0141 226 5898 *Fax* 0141 225 2600 *E-mail* pctrust@rcag.org.uk *Website* www.rcag.org.uk
SC NO SC029832

■ Arthur James Paterson Charitable Trust

WHERE FUNDING CAN BE GIVEN UK.

WHO CAN BENEFIT Organisations benefiting children, older people, retired people, at risk groups, socially isolated people and those disadvantaged by poverty.

WHAT IS FUNDED Medical research, welfare of older people and children.

TYPE OF GRANT One-off.

RANGE OF GRANTS Usually £250–£5,000.

SAMPLE GRANTS £9,500 each to Glenalmond College for a scholarship and Worcester College, Oxford; £5,000 each to Children Nationwide and Islet Research Laboratories for diabetes research; £4,000 to NSPCC; £3,100 to Children's Liver Disease Fund; £3,000 each to Age Concern Edinburgh, Parkinson's Disease Society, and Royal College of Surgeons; £2,400 to Children First.

FINANCES *Year* 2001–02 *Income* £116,806

TRUSTEES Royal Bank of Canada Trust Corporation Ltd.

HOW TO APPLY There are no application forms. Send your application with a covering letter and include latest set of report and accounts. Deadlines are February and August. This entry was not confirmed by the trust, but the information was correct according to the trust's file at the Charity Commission.

WHO TO APPLY TO Miss Anita Carter, Royal Bank of Canada Trust Corporation Limited, 71 Queen Victoria Street, London EC4V 4DE *Tel* 020 7653 4756 *E-mail* anita.carter@rbc.com
CC NO 278569   ESTABLISHED 1979

■ The Constance Paterson Charitable Trust

WHERE FUNDING CAN BE GIVEN UK.
WHO CAN BENEFIT Organisations benefiting children, older people, retired people, ex-service and service people, at risk groups, socially isolated people and those disadvantaged by poverty. Carers, disabled people, homeless people, victims of abuse, crime or domestic violence and people with dyslexia are also considered.
WHAT IS FUNDED Medical research, health care, welfare of older people and children (including accommodation and housing) and service people's welfare.
WHAT IS NOT FUNDED No grants to individuals.
TYPE OF GRANT One-off grants, which can be for capital costs (including buildings), core or running costs, project or research funding, or salaries.
RANGE OF GRANTS £250–£5,000.
SAMPLE GRANTS £3,000 to Weston Spirit; £2,500 each to Myasthemia Gravis Association, DEBRA, Contact the Elderly and Elderly Accommodation Counsel; £2,000 each to Cystic Fibrosis Holiday Fund for Children, Motability, Inkerman Community Support, Kidscape, and Dogs for the Disabled.
FINANCES Year 2001–02 Income £50,647
TRUSTEES Royal Bank of Canada Trust Corporation Ltd.
HOW TO APPLY In writing to the correspondent, including covering letter and latest set of annual report and accounts. The trust does not have an application form. Deadlines for applications are June and December.
WHO TO APPLY TO Miss Anita Carter, Royal Bank of Canada Trust Corporation Limited, 71 Queen Victoria Street, London EC4V 4DE *Tel* 020 7653 4756 *E-mail* anita.carter@rbc.com
CC NO 249556   ESTABLISHED 1966

■ Mrs M E S Paterson's Charitable Trust

WHERE FUNDING CAN BE GIVEN Scotland.
WHO CAN BENEFIT Organisations benefiting Christians and young people.
WHAT IS FUNDED Support to the Church of Scotland and other Christian groups in the maintenance of church buildings and in their work with young people.
WHAT IS NOT FUNDED No grants to individuals.
TYPE OF GRANT Average about £1,000.
FINANCES Year 2001 Income £40,000
Grants £35,000
HOW TO APPLY In writing to the correspondent. Trustees meet once a year in July to consider grants.
WHO TO APPLY TO Callam S Kennedy, Lindsays Solicitors, 11 Atholl Crescent, Edinburgh EH3 8HE *Tel* 0131 477 8721
SC NO SC004835   ESTABLISHED 1989

■ The Patients' Aid Association Hospital & Medical Charities Trust

WHERE FUNDING CAN BE GIVEN Generally in the East and West Midlands, Staffordshire and Shropshire and other areas where the association operates.
WHO CAN BENEFIT Mainly NHS hospitals and registered, medically related charities benefiting: children; young adults; older people; ex-service and service people; medical professionals, nurses and doctors; research workers; volunteers; people in care; at risk groups; carers; disabled people; those disadvantaged by poverty; homeless people; victims of abuse and domestic violence.
WHAT IS FUNDED Provision of equipment and patient amenities to NHS hospitals, hospices, convalescent homes and other medically related charities in the area where the parent association operates. These include: support to volunteers; health professional bodies; councils for voluntary service; advancement of religion; churches; respite; sheltered accommodation; health; special schools; speech therapy; special needs education; scholarships; medical research; specialist research; and community services.
WHAT IS NOT FUNDED Appeals must be from officials of the appealing body and submitted on official stationery. Appeals are not accepted from, or on behalf of, individuals or for provision of vehicles.
TYPE OF GRANT Mainly medical equipment. Grants are not made towards running costs or administration.
RANGE OF GRANTS Usually £200–£3,000.
SAMPLE GRANTS £2,500 each to Walsall Hospital Radio and Royal Wolverhampton Hospitals NHS Trust; £2,045 to North Staffordshire Combined Healthcare; £1,398 to Warwickshire Ambulance Service; £1,230 to St Edmund's School – Wolverhampton; £1,150 to Dove Cottage Day Hospice – Leicester; £1,000 to St Giles Hospice – Litchfield; £863 to Salvation Army – Wolverhampton.
FINANCES Year 2001 Income £84,000
Grants £65,700 Assets £89,000
TRUSTEES E P Booth; D Bradley; J Dickie; G F Lewis; H Reynolds; D Kent; D Clegg.
PUBLICATIONS A brochure concerning the trust.
HOW TO APPLY Application forms are available from the correspondent. Any hospital or registered charity may apply for a grant and all such applications are considered by the trustees who meet four times a year. '[The] reason for the rejection of appeals is due usually to an excessive amount involved, [or] to the appeal being outside the trust's permitted area of donations.'
WHO TO APPLY TO Ms P M Stokes, Secretary, Paycare House, George Street, Wolverhampton WV2 4DX *Tel* 01902 371000 *Fax* 01902 371030
CC NO 240378   ESTABLISHED 1964

■ Andrew Paton's Charitable Trust

WHERE FUNDING CAN BE GIVEN Unrestricted but with a preference for the west of Scotland.
WHO CAN BENEFIT Organisations benefiting children and young adults.
WHAT IS FUNDED A range of charitable activities such as Christian missionary and youth work, support for a hospice, children's charities and medical research.
WHAT IS NOT FUNDED No grants to individuals.

RANGE OF GRANTS £500–£5,000.

SAMPLE GRANTS £5,000 to St Andrew's Hospice; £4,000 to David Cargill House; £3,000 to Church of Scotland Mission Aid Fund; £2,000 to Scottish Motor Neurone Disease Association; £1,500 to Salvation Army; 15 recipients of £1,000 each, including Children 1st, Glasgow Old People's Welfare Association, King George's Fund for Sailors, Sense Scotland and West of Scotland Deaf Children Society.

FINANCES *Year* 1999–2000 *Income* £44,000 *Grants* £61,000 *Assets* £1,000,000

TRUSTEES G A Maguire; N A Fyfe; R G Dingwall.

HOW TO APPLY In writing to the correspondent.

WHO TO APPLY TO G A Maguire, Trustee, 190 St Vincent Street, Glasgow G2 5SP *Tel* 0141 204 2833

SC NO SC017502

■ The Patrick Charitable Trust

WHERE FUNDING CAN BE GIVEN UK, with a special interest in the Midlands.

WHO CAN BENEFIT Organisations.

WHAT IS FUNDED General charitable purposes.

WHAT IS NOT FUNDED No grants to individuals.

TYPE OF GRANT One-off or recurrent.

SAMPLE GRANTS £500,000 designated loan to Muscular Dystrophy Campaign; £100,000 to Sir Josiah Mason Trust; £10,000 each to Martha Trust – Hereford and Symphony Hall Organ Appeal; £6,000 to Peckwood Centre; £4,750 to Black Country Museum; £4,000 to Make A Wish Foundation; £3,000 to Muscular Dystrophy Campaign.

FINANCES *Year* 2001–02 *Income* £1,537,390 *Grants* £650,450 *Assets* £6,150,000

TRUSTEES J A Patrick, Chair; M V Patrick; Mrs H P Cole; W Bond-Williams; N Duckitt; G Wem.

OTHER INFORMATION The trust also has future commitments to Black Country Museum totalling £1 million.

HOW TO APPLY In writing to the correspondent at any time.

WHO TO APPLY TO J A Patrick, Chair, The Lakeside Centre, 180 Lifford Lane, Kings Norton, Birmingham B30 3NU

CC NO 213849   **ESTABLISHED** 1962

■ The Jack Patston Charitable Trust

WHERE FUNDING CAN BE GIVEN Preferably Leicestershire and Cambridgeshire.

WHAT IS FUNDED The trust supports in particular preservation of wildlife and the environment, advancement of religion and preservation of rural church fabric. Primarily organisations in Leicestershire and Cambridgeshire are supported.

WHAT IS NOT FUNDED No grants to individuals.

TYPE OF GRANT Single payments.

RANGE OF GRANTS £1,000–£10,000.

SAMPLE GRANTS £10,000 to RSPB – Hope Farm; £5,000 each to the Countryside Restoration Trust, East Anglia's Children's Hospices, Freeby Church Restoration Fund, Friends of St Luke's – Laughton, Leicester & Leicestershire Historic Churches Preservation Trust and St Andrew Church – Easton; £3,000 to the Badminton Trust; £2,500 each to Care Fund – Shangton and Peterborough Cathedral Trust.

FINANCES *Year* 2001–02 *Income* £92,000 *Grants* £95,500 *Assets* £2,100,000

TRUSTEES Allan Arthur Veasey; Charles John Urquhart Applegate.

HOW TO APPLY In writing to the correspondent.

WHO TO APPLY TO C J U Applegate, Trustee, Buckle Mellows, 35/45/51 Priestgate, Peterborough PE1 1LB *Tel* 01733 888888 *Fax* 01733 553043 *E-mail* charles.applegate@bucklemellows.co.uk

CC NO 701658   **ESTABLISHED** 1989

■ The Late Barbara May Paul Charitable Trust

WHERE FUNDING CAN BE GIVEN East Anglia and UK-wide.

WHO CAN BENEFIT Registered charities benefiting older people needing care. Research workers and medical professionals will be considered.

WHAT IS FUNDED Suffolk-based charities are given priority but national charities considered, with emphasis on care for the elderly and medical research.

WHAT IS NOT FUNDED No grants to overseas charities.

TYPE OF GRANT Research grants are a priority.

RANGE OF GRANTS £150–£10,000.

SAMPLE GRANTS In 1998–99: £5,000 to Whizz Kids; £3,000 each to Norfolk Millennium Trust for Carers and Suffolk Preservation Society; £2,000 each to the Bus Project, Cancer Research Campaign, East Anglian Autistic Support Trust, Essex County Youth Service, Norfolk Guide & Scout Association, Norfok & Norwich Scope, and Shelter.

FINANCES *Year* 2000–01 *Income* £19,984 *Grants* £62,100 *Assets* £13,715

TRUSTEES Lloyds TSB Bank plc.

HOW TO APPLY In writing to the correspondent at any time.

WHO TO APPLY TO Chris Shambrook, Trust Manager, Lloyds TSB Private Banking Ltd, UK Trust Centre, The Clock House, 22–26 Ock Street, Abingdon, Oxfordshire OX14 5SW *Tel* 01235 232731

CC NO 256420   **ESTABLISHED** 1968

■ Paul Charitable Trust

WHERE FUNDING CAN BE GIVEN Balfron and Killearn and the surrounding area.

WHO CAN BENEFIT Community organisations and individuals in need.

WHAT IS FUNDED The trust makes grants for the provision of sports and recreation facilities, adult education and drama and music or other recreational activities. It gives grants to people in need and also to voluntary organisations or clubs with similar objects.

RANGE OF GRANTS £1,000–£50,000.

FINANCES *Year* 2001 *Income* £38,363 *Grants* £35,500

TRUSTEES W G Davidson; G A Murray; J N P Ford; J F Bisset.

HOW TO APPLY In writing to the correspondent. The trustees meet quarterly.

WHO TO APPLY TO James Millar, c/o Morrison Bishop, 2 Blythswood Square, Glasgow G2 4AD *Tel* 0141 248 4672 *Fax* 0141 221 9270 *E-mail* jamie.millar@bishopslaw.biz

SC NO SC023880   **ESTABLISHED** 1995

■ Charity Fund of the Worshipful Company of Paviors

WHERE FUNDING CAN BE GIVEN UK, especially the City of London.

WHO CAN BENEFIT Registered charities.

WHAT IS FUNDED General charitable purposes, including charities operating in the City of London; charities in the UK related to the construction industry and industrial archaeology; educational grants for postgraduate study and research in the UK in highway and pavement engineering; and awards for excellence in the craft of paving, i.e. the design, construction, maintenance and management of paved areas wherever they occur.

WHAT IS NOT FUNDED Charities with several years' reserves and high administration costs.

TYPE OF GRANT Annual – up to a maximum of three years.

RANGE OF GRANTS £200–£5,000.

SAMPLE GRANTS £5,000 to University of Birmingham – bursary for postgraduate study; £4,000 to University of Nottingham; £2,500 to Tower Hamlets Education Business Partnership; £1,500 to Lord Mayor's Appeal; £1,300 to Amberley Museum; £1,000 to Lighthouse Benevolent Fund.

FINANCES *Year* 2001 *Grants* £37,000

TRUSTEES Masters and Wardens in office.

PUBLICATIONS *The Pavior* three times a year.

HOW TO APPLY In writing to the correspondent by 31 May.

WHO TO APPLY TO John White, Clerk, 3 Ridgemount Gardens, Enfield, Middlesex EN2 8QL *Tel* 020 8366 1566 *Fax* 020 8366 1566 *E-mail* jlwhite@talk21.com

CC NO 257671　　　**ESTABLISHED** 1934

■ The Payne Charitable Trust

WHERE FUNDING CAN BE GIVEN UK and overseas.

WHO CAN BENEFIT Missionaries, churches, and people engaged in the propagation of the Christian gospel.

WHAT IS FUNDED To support religious and charitable objects. The main area of interest is the support of evangelical Christians in the promotion and proclamation of the Christian gospel.

WHAT IS NOT FUNDED No grants for repairs to church buildings or towards education.

TYPE OF GRANT One-off grants and loans; capital support.

SAMPLE GRANTS In 1997–98: £24,000 to the Andrew League Trust; £5,000 to Westwood League; £3,500 to Crusaders; £2,300 to SASRA; £1,000 each to Association of Military Christian Fellowships and Newark Evangelical Church; £750 to Kingsway Chapel; £250 to Bloomsbury Evangelical Church.

FINANCES *Year* 2000–01 *Income* £51,000 *Grants* £34,000 *Assets* £556,000

TRUSTEES John Payne; Eric Payne.

OTHER INFORMATION Due to the large number of applications, some considerable time can elapse before communication can be sent.

HOW TO APPLY In writing to the correspondent. Applications should be submitted between 1 January and 21 March only, for grants made from the following 1 May. The trustees regret that they cannot support many of the deserving organisations which apply for a grant. Due to the large number of applications, some considerable time can elapse before communication can be sent.

WHO TO APPLY TO J Payne, Trustee, Copthorne House, The Broadway, Abergele LL22 7DD *Tel* 01745 825779 *Fax* 01745 833161 *E-mail* jpayne99@aol.com

CC NO 241816　　　**ESTABLISHED** 1965

■ The Harry Payne Trust

WHERE FUNDING CAN BE GIVEN Birmingham and the immediately surrounding areas of the West Midlands.

WHO CAN BENEFIT Voluntary organisations and charitable groups only, benefiting: older people; those in care, fostered and adopted; parents and children; children who are disabled or disadvantaged; victims, offenders and their families; and people undergoing alcohol and drug abuse rehabilitation. Support will be considered for a wide variety of medical conditions, but particularly where there is evidence of social disadvantage. The trust operates a non-discriminatory policy as regards race and religion.

WHAT IS FUNDED Priority is given to charitable work in Birmingham, where the trust was founded. Funding may be given to: churches, synagogues and religious ancillary buildings; family planning and well woman clinics; hospices and hospitals; pre-school and special needs education; advice centres and community services; and the advancement of Quakerism.

WHAT IS NOT FUNDED Applications from outside the beneficial area will not be acknowledged. No grants to individuals.

TYPE OF GRANT Capital (including buildings), one-off, research, running costs (including salaries), recurring costs and start-up costs will be considered. Funding may be given for up to three years.

RANGE OF GRANTS £100–£6,000, typical grant £250.

SAMPLE GRANTS £4,000 to Care of the Elderly in Balsall Heath; £1,500 each to Birmingham Settlement, St Mary's Settlement, St Mary's Hospice and MSA; £1,000 each to Woodbrooke Quaker Study Centre and Carrs Lane Homes.

FINANCES *Year* 2001–02 *Income* £50,633 *Grants* £46,125 *Assets* £1,221,087

TRUSTEES Mrs B J Major, Chair; R King, President; Mrs A K Burnett; D F Dodd; R C King; R I Payne; D J Cadbury; Mrs V C Dub.

PUBLICATIONS Notes on the trust are available from the secretary by post or e-mail. Alternatively they can be downloaded from the trust's website.

HOW TO APPLY On a form available from the correspondent. Applications should include the organisation's most recent set of audited accounts and must be submitted by the end of May for the summer meeting and the end of November for the winter meeting. Successful applications will be acknowledged as soon as possible after the meeting at which they are considered.

WHO TO APPLY TO Robert C King, Secretary, 1 Matthews Close, Rushton, Kettering, Northamptonshire NN14 1QJ *Tel* 01536 418905 *E-mail* robcking@harrypayne.org.uk *Website* www.harrypaynetrust.org.uk

CC NO 231063　　　**ESTABLISHED** 1939

■ The Peabody Community Fund

WHERE FUNDING CAN BE GIVEN London.

WHO CAN BENEFIT The majority of those benefiting from a grant must be Londoners in the lower income groups.

WHAT IS FUNDED Community schemes that benefit Londoners on low incomes, usually the refurbishment or improvement of premises or for items of equipment. Grants are given under the headings: investing in community support; overcoming disabilities; employment initiatives.

WHAT IS NOT FUNDED political or religious purposes; the direct provision of housing accommodation; to support ordinary ongoing revenue activity; purposes already catered for by statutory bodies, unless the project aims to promote further action by central and local authorities, rather than to relieve them of their responsibilities; general appeals; the arts; medical charities unless projects overcome handicaps; intermediate bodies for redistribution to other organisations; individuals, except for registered unemployed Peabody tenants who require assistance for vocational training or those who qualify for the PCF's Champions for Change Millennium Awards. This programme is funded by the Millennium Commission and was introduced in April 2001. It aims to tackle social exclusion and will benefit 1,000 individuals over the next three years. An average grant of £2,000 will be given to realise a personal ambition and enrich local communities.

TYPE OF GRANT One-off grants.

RANGE OF GRANTS Up to £10,000.

SAMPLE GRANTS 1999–2000: £40,000 to Interchange for disabled lift; £30,000 to The Passage for refurbishment; £13,000 to Safestart for IT equipment; £10,000 to Homerton Grove Adventure Playground for re-equipment; £8,000 to Open Doors for wheelchairs; £6,000 to Field Lane Community Centre for refurbishment; £5,000 to West London Action for Children for project costs; £4,500 to Bangladesh Welfare Association for equipment; £3,500 to Waltham Forest Mencap for IT equipment.

FINANCES *Year* 2001–02 *Grants* £570,000

TRUSTEES Sir Hugh Cubitt; Pam Alexander; Teddy Bourne; Anne Chan; Tim Cook; J Dudley Fishburn; M G M Haines; James Hambro; Hattie Llewelyn-Davies; Ken Olisa; Sir Idris Pearce; Shamit Saggar; Geoffrey Wilson; William S Farish.

PUBLICATIONS *Guidelines for Applicants*; and *Peabody Trust Millennium Awards: Guidance to Applicants*.

OTHER INFORMATION The fund also adminstered the Champions for Change – Millennium Awards Scheme and the Local Network Fund in Westminster, Kensington and Chelsea, Hammersmith and Fulham, Wandsworth, Merton, Sutton and Tower Hamlets.

HOW TO APPLY All applications must be made using the application form available from the trust. The trust requests that all questions are answered in as much detail as possible, and that replies such as 'please see attached' be avoided. Applicants will be notified of a decision made by the trust as soon as is reasonably possible. Applications from organisations are considered three times a year (usually in June, October and March).

WHO TO APPLY TO Everton Counsell, Peabody Community Fund Manager, 45 Westminster Bridge Road, London SE1 7JB *Tel* 020 7928 7811 *Fax* 020 7261 9187 *Website* www.peabody.org.uk

CC NO 206061 **ESTABLISHED** 1981

■ The Peacock Charitable Trust

WHERE FUNDING CAN BE GIVEN UK.

WHO CAN BENEFIT Registered charities benefiting children and young adults, ex-service and service people, disabled people, ex-offenders, at risk groups and carers. Also people with Alzheimer's disease, arthritis and rheumatism, cancer, hearing loss, heart disease, mental illness, multiple sclerosis, and substance abuse.

WHAT IS FUNDED Charities which the trustees have special knowledge of, interest in or association with, in the fields of medical research, disability, and some youth work.

WHAT IS NOT FUNDED No donations are made to individuals and only in rare cases are additions made to charities already being supported.

TYPE OF GRANT Capital, project and some recurring.

RANGE OF GRANTS £150–£125,000.

SAMPLE GRANTS £130,000 to Cancer Research Campaign; £100,000 each to Fairbridge and Marie Curie Cancer Care; £60,000 each to Cancer BACUP and YMCA; £52,000 to Macmillan Cancer Relief; £50,000 each to Alzheimer Research Trust, Jubilee Sailing Trust and St Wilfred's Hospice; £40,000 to Mental Health Foundation.

FINANCES *Year* 2001–02 *Grants* £2,364,000

TRUSTEES W M Peacock; Mrs S Peacock; C H Peacock; K R Burgin.

HOW TO APPLY In 2002 the trust stated that its funds were fully committed, and with the big reduction in interest rates it was unlikely to be able to help any new causes. Registered charities only can apply in writing, preferably early in the year and accompanied by full accounts. Applications should include clear details of the need the intended project is designed to meet, plus any outline budget.

WHO TO APPLY TO Mrs Barbara Davis, The Charities Aid Foundation, Kings Hill, West Malling, Kent ME19 4TA *Tel* 01732 520081 *Fax* 01732 520001 *E-mail* bdavis@cafonline.org *Website* www.cafonline.org

CC NO 257655 **ESTABLISHED** 1968

■ The Michael Peacock Charitable Foundation

WHERE FUNDING CAN BE GIVEN UK.

WHO CAN BENEFIT Organisations benefiting older people, research workers and postgraduate students from the former Soviet Union and eastern Europe.

WHAT IS NOT FUNDED No grants to individuals, non-registered charities, or local or regional projects.

TYPE OF GRANT Project and research grants will be considered.

FINANCES *Year* 2001 *Income* £62,858 *Grants* £40,000 *Assets* £470,000

TRUSTEES Michael Peacock, Chair; R Wheeler-Bennett; Gillian Baverstock; Michael Croft Baker; Sir John Maddox; Daphne Peacock.

HOW TO APPLY In writing to the correspondent.

WHO TO APPLY TO Michael Peacock, Chair, 21 Woodlands Road, Barnes, London SW13 0JZ *Tel* 020 8876 2025 *E-mail* peacock@truly.demon.co.uk
CC NO 801441   **ESTABLISHED** 1989

....

■ The Susanna Peake Charitable Trust

WHERE FUNDING CAN BE GIVEN UK.
WHO CAN BENEFIT Registered charities.
WHAT IS FUNDED General charitable purposes.
WHAT IS NOT FUNDED No grants to individuals.
TYPE OF GRANT Usually one-off grants.
RANGE OF GRANTS £100–£5,000.
SAMPLE GRANTS £5,000 each to North Cotswolds Voluntary Help Centre, Longborough Primary School, Parents and Friends Association and Royal Agricultural Institution; £4,000 to PCC St James Longborough; £3,000 to Chipping Norton Theatre Trust; £2,500 to APT Enterprise Development; £2,000 including those to Alzheimer's Society, Charing Cross Hospital, and Deafblind UK.
FINANCES *Year* 1999–2000 *Income* £78,080 *Grants* £65,850 *Assets* £1,975,000
TRUSTEES Susanna Peake; David Peake.
HOW TO APPLY In writing to the correspondent.
WHO TO APPLY TO The Secretary, Rathbone Trust Company Limited, 159 New Bond St, London W1Y 9PA *Tel* 020 7399 0820 *Fax* 020 7399 0050 *E-mail* linda.cousins@rathbones.com
CC NO 283462   **ESTABLISHED** 1981

....

■ The Joseph and Sarah Pearlman Jewish Charitable Trust

WHERE FUNDING CAN BE GIVEN UK and Israel.
WHO CAN BENEFIT Jewish causes.
RANGE OF GRANTS £50–£5,000.
SAMPLE GRANTS £5,000 to Mannny Cussins Home; £3,000 to Centre for Advanced Rabbinics; £2,900 to Sunderland Tahmudical College; £1,400 UHC Newcastle.
FINANCES *Year* 1999–2000 *Income* £20,000 *Grants* £22,000
TRUSTEES M L Pearlman; S D Pearlman; H H Pearlman; H A Davis.
HOW TO APPLY In writing to the correspondent.
WHO TO APPLY TO H Pearlman, Trustee, 10 Murton Street, Sunderland, Tyne and Wear SR1 2RB
CC NO 232082   **ESTABLISHED** 1957

....

■ The Frank Pearson Foundation

WHERE FUNDING CAN BE GIVEN Principally Yorkshire.
WHO CAN BENEFIT Registered charities, particular preference is given to local causes concerned with children, older people, and people disadvantaged by poverty.
WHAT IS FUNDED General charitable purposes.
WHAT IS NOT FUNDED No grants to individuals.
TYPE OF GRANT Where possible, specific projects.
RANGE OF GRANTS £250–£1,500.
SAMPLE GRANTS In 1996: £1,500 to Botton Village; £1,100 to National Kidney and Lung Fund; £1,000 each to Multiple Sclerosis Society, NSPCC, Plastic Surgery and Burns Research Unit, Macmillan Cancer Relief, British Red Cross for the Former Yugoslavia, Tusk Force, and Leukaemia Fund.
FINANCES *Year* 1999–2000 *Income* £25,000 *Grants* £25,000 *Assets* £511,000

TRUSTEES Mrs I I Pearson; D A F Pearson; Wheawill & Sudworth Trustees Ltd.
HOW TO APPLY In writing to the correspondent.
WHO TO APPLY TO R G Warrington, PO Box B30, 35 Westgate, Huddersfield HD1 1PA *Tel* 01484 423691
CC NO 278884   **ESTABLISHED** 1979

....

■ The Pedmore Sporting Club Trust Fund

WHERE FUNDING CAN BE GIVEN West Midlands.
WHO CAN BENEFIT Registered charities.
WHAT IS FUNDED General charitable purposes.
TYPE OF GRANT Capital projects, not general funding.
SAMPLE GRANTS £2,100 to Primrose Hospice – Bromsgrove; £1,000 each to Netherend Neighbourhood Association – Cradley and Lisa Potts Romanian Orphans Appeal; £500 each to Friends of Poplars – Brierley Hill and Hagley Theatre Group Youth Section; £100 to Mary Stevens Hospice – Stourbridge.
FINANCES *Year* 2000 *Income* £72,000 *Grants* £31,000 *Assets* £271,000
TRUSTEES N A Hickman; R Herman-Smith; R Williams; T J Hickman; J M Price; P J E Harley.
OTHER INFORMATION £25,000 has been committed for future years.
HOW TO APPLY In writing to the correspondent. The trustees meet to consider grants in January, May, September and November.
WHO TO APPLY TO B W Mann, Secretary, Pedmore House, Ham Lane, Stourbridge, West Midlands DY9 0YA *Tel* 01384 372727 *Fax* 01384 440359 *E-mail* psclub@pedmorehouse.co.uk
CC NO 263907   **ESTABLISHED** 1973

....

■ The Pedmore Trust

WHERE FUNDING CAN BE GIVEN Worldwide.
WHO CAN BENEFIT Causes related to the Christian faith, benefiting Christians.
WHAT IS FUNDED Advancement of the Christian Gospel.
WHAT IS NOT FUNDED No support for students on short-term projects (gap years).
TYPE OF GRANT Capital and recurring grants, and loans in exceptional circumstances.
FINANCES *Year* 2000–01 *Income* £32,250 *Grants* £36,315 *Assets* £600,000
TRUSTEES W R Cossham; D R Meek; J Hutchinson; D M John; L R Meek; W E John; A M Fordyce.
HOW TO APPLY Please note, the trust states that it carries out its own research and is unable to accept any applications for grants.
WHO TO APPLY TO L R Meek, Secretary, Fallow Croft, Meadow Road, Torquay, Devon TQ2 6PR
CC NO 266644   **ESTABLISHED** 1961

....

■ The Dowager Countess Eleanor Peel Trust

WHERE FUNDING CAN BE GIVEN UK, with an apparent interest in the Lancaster area.
WHO CAN BENEFIT Registered charities.
WHAT IS FUNDED General charitable purposes, particularly medical charities, charities for older people, and 'those who have fallen on evil days through no fault of their own'. Medical research accounts for about 50% of the grants made.
WHAT IS NOT FUNDED No grants to children's charities, individuals or charitable bodies substantially under the control of central or local government.

TYPE OF GRANT Mostly one-off, capital, project.

SAMPLE GRANTS 2001–02: £120,000 to Nottingham Trent University; £114,000 Lancaster University (Department of Biological Sciences); £86,225 to the Peel Medical Research Trust; £50,000 to St George's Hospital Medical School; £20,003 to WaterAid; £20,000 each to Birmingham City Hospital and Covent Garden Cancer Research Fund; £12,708 to The Wishbone Trust; £10,000 to The British Brain and Spinal Foundation and Age Concern – Salford.

FINANCES *Year* 2001–02 *Income* £562,000 *Grants* £651,000 *Assets* £13,374,000

TRUSTEES R M Parkinson; Anthony G Trower; J W Parkinson; R L Rothwell Jackson; L H Valner.

HOW TO APPLY In writing to the correspondent.

WHO TO APPLY TO L H Valner, Trustee, Sceptre Court, 40 Tower Hill, London EC3N 4DX *Tel* 020 7423 8000 *Fax* 020 7423 8001

CC NO 214684   **ESTABLISHED** 1951

■ **The J B Pelly Charitable Settlement**

WHERE FUNDING CAN BE GIVEN UK, with some prefeence for south Devon.

WHO CAN BENEFIT Quakers and other adults.

WHAT IS FUNDED Tree planting, nature conservation and environment; support to voluntary and community organisations; arts activities.

WHAT IS NOT FUNDED No support for illness, disease, Church of England, accommodation, infrastructure, technical support, religion, children, older people, hospitals, conventional education, social care and development, and young people doing gap year projects.

TYPE OF GRANT One-off; project; research,; and start-up costs. Funding is available for up to three years.

RANGE OF GRANTS Usually £50–£1,000.

SAMPLE GRANTS £25,000 to Cathy Pelly Maungaronga Trust; £3,000 to The Woodland Trust; £800 to RSPB; £500 each to Carrifran Wildwood, Devon Wildlife Trust, St Luke's Hospice and Peaceworks.

FINANCES *Year* 1998–99 *Income* £84,000 *Grants* £33,000 *Assets* £2,000,000

TRUSTEES G M Rossetti; G L Price.

HOW TO APPLY In writing to the correspondent, with supporting information if available.

WHO TO APPLY TO Malcolm D Franke, c/o Bromhead & Co., Britton House, 10 Fore Street, Kingsbridge, Devon TQ7 1NY *Tel* 01548 852599

CC NO 285565   **ESTABLISHED** 1987

■ **Peltz Trust**

WHERE FUNDING CAN BE GIVEN UK and Israel.

WHAT IS FUNDED Arts, cultural and educational initiatives; health and welfare projects; religion.

WHAT IS NOT FUNDED No grants to individuals for research or educational awards.

SAMPLE GRANTS £7,500 to Joint Jewish Charitable Trust; £5,000 to British Friends of the Council for a Beautiful Israel; £3,000 to Drive for Youth; £1,500 each to British Ort and Good Relations Educational Trust; £1,000 to Jerusalem Foundation; £500 each to Cardiac Risk in the Young, Child Psychotherapy Trust, Edward Lerman Environmental Trust, and St John's Hospice.

FINANCES *Year* 1998–99 *Income* £203,000 *Grants* £27,000

TRUSTEES M D Paisner; Daniel Peltz; Elizabeth Julia Natasha Wolfson Peltz.

HOW TO APPLY In writing to the correspondent. The trustees meet at irregular intervals during the year to consider appeals from appropriate organisations.

WHO TO APPLY TO M D Paisner, Trustee, Berwin Leighton, Paisner & Co., Bouverie House, 154–160 Fleet Street, London EC4A 2JD *Tel* 020 7353 0299

CC NO 1002302   **ESTABLISHED** 1991

■ **Penny in the Pound Fund Charitable Trust**

WHERE FUNDING CAN BE GIVEN Northern England, southern Scotland, Wales and Northern Ireland, but mostly around the Merseyside area.

WHO CAN BENEFIT NHS hospitals and health authorities.

WHAT IS FUNDED NHS hospitals amenities for patients.

WHAT IS NOT FUNDED No grants towards medical equipment.

TYPE OF GRANT Capital.

SAMPLE GRANTS £9,775 to Aintree Hospitals NHS Trust; £9,000 to Wirral Hospitals NHS Trust; £7,945 to Royal Liverpool and Broadgreen University Hospitals NHS Trust; £5,371 to Cardiothoracic Centre – Liverpool NHS Trust; £5,000 to Wirral NHS Trust for the SAM Appeal; £4,196 to St Helens and Knowsley Hospitals NHS Trust; £3,500 to KIND; £3,329 to Southport and Ormskirk Hospital NHS Trust; £2,074 to Liverpool Women's Hospital NHS Trust; £2,000 to Beechwood Cancer Care Centre.

FINANCES *Year* 2001 *Income* £85,646 *Grants* £82,637 *Assets* £106,138

TRUSTEES P B Teare; K W Monti; K Arnold; W Gaywood; J E Brown.

HOW TO APPLY In writing to the correspondent. Applications need to be received in July and trustees meet in October.

WHO TO APPLY TO K Arnold, Finance Officer, Medicash Health Benefits Limited, Merchants Court, 2–12 Lord Street, Liverpool L2 1TS *Tel* 0151 702 0202 *Fax* 0151 702 0250 *E-mail* karnold@medicash.org *Website* www.medicash.org

CC NO 257637   **ESTABLISHED** 1968

■ **The Pennycress Trust**

WHERE FUNDING CAN BE GIVEN UK, with a preference for Cheshire and Norfolk.

WHO CAN BENEFIT Voluntary organisations and charitable groups only.

WHAT IS FUNDED General charitable purposes. Support is given to a restricted list of registered charities only, principally in Cheshire and Norfolk, in the fields of: arts and cultural heritage; education; infrastructure, support and development; science and technology; community facilities; campaigning on health and social issues; health care and advocacy; medical studies and research; and animal welfare.

WHAT IS NOT FUNDED No support for individuals.

TYPE OF GRANT Recurrent and one-off.

RANGE OF GRANTS Usually £200–£500.

SAMPLE GRANTS In 1997–98: £5,000 to Chopin Society towards the cost of a piano; £2,500 each to Norwich Cathedrals Trust towards preservation work and North Sea Havens for a millennium project; £2,000 to King's College, Cambridge to replace sets of music; £1,000 each to Great Ormond St Hospital, Macclesfield Museum for purchase and refurbishment of premises, Royal Academy Trust, and St Wenefrede's Church towards re-wiring; £500 each to ApTibeT for practical help to Tibetan refugees and Children's Country Holiday Fund.

FINANCES *Year* 2001–02 *Income* £82,075

TRUSTEES Lady Aline Cholmondeley; Anthony J M Baker; C G Cholmondeley.

HOW TO APPLY In writing to the correspondent. 'No telephone applications please.' Trustees meet twice during the year, usually in July and December. Applications need to be received by June or November.

WHO TO APPLY TO Mrs Doreen Howells, Secretary to the Trustees, 25 North Row, London W1K 6DJ *Tel* 020 7404 0145

CC NO 261536   **ESTABLISHED** 1970

■ The Mrs C S Heber Percy Charitable Trust

WHERE FUNDING CAN BE GIVEN Worldwide, with a preference for Gloucestershire.

WHO CAN BENEFIT Registered charities.

WHAT IS FUNDED General charitable purposes.

WHAT IS NOT FUNDED No grants to individuals.

RANGE OF GRANTS £200–£10,000, but mostly less than £1,000.

SAMPLE GRANTS In 1997–98: £15,000 to Health Unlimited; £12,500 to Friends of the Aphrodisias Trust; £5,000 each to Leukaemia Research Fund and Shakespeare Hospice Trust; £3,000 each to Bequia Society, British Light Horse Breeding Society, and Mark Davies Injured Riders Fund; £1,000 each to Berkshire Buckinghamshire and Oxfordshire Naturalist Trust, League of Friends of Macintyre Tall Trees, and Macmillan Cancer Relief.

FINANCES *Year* 2000–01 *Income* £80,000 *Grants* £65,000 *Assets* £2,000,000

TRUSTEES Mrs C S Heber Percy; Mrs J A Prest.

HOW TO APPLY The correspondent stated that unsolicited applications are not required.

WHO TO APPLY TO Miss L J Cousins, Rathbones, 159 New Bond Street, London W1S 2UD *Tel* 020 7399 0823

CC NO 284387   **ESTABLISHED** 1981

■ B E Perl Charitable Trust

WHERE FUNDING CAN BE GIVEN UK.

WHO CAN BENEFIT Orthodox Jewish organisations.

WHAT IS FUNDED General charitable purposes.

FINANCES *Year* 1998–99 *Income* £426,000 *Grants* £25,000 *Assets* £907,000

TRUSTEES B Perl, Chair; Mrs S Perl; S Perl; J Koval; Jonathan Perl; Mrs R Reidel; Joseph Perl.

HOW TO APPLY In writing to the correspondent.

WHO TO APPLY TO B Perl, Chair, Fofoane House, 35–37 Brent Street, Hendon, London NW4 2EF

CC NO 282847   **ESTABLISHED** 1981

■ The Personal Assurance Charitable Trust

WHERE FUNDING CAN BE GIVEN Mainly UK with a preference for the Milton Keynes area, overseas considered.

WHO CAN BENEFIT Health and related charities preferred.

WHAT IS FUNDED Medicine and health, welfare, education, environmental resources and general charitable purposes. This includes residential facilities and services; infrastructure, support and development; religion; arts, culture and recreation; conservation and environment; and social care and development.

WHAT IS NOT FUNDED Individuals or groups who are not policy holders with, or employees of, Personal Assurance PLC.

TYPE OF GRANT Capital (including buildings), core costs, endowments, feasibility studies, interest-free loans, one-off, project, research, running costs, recurring costs, salaries and start-up costs. Funding is for up to and over three years.

SAMPLE GRANTS £29,000 to BBC Children in Need; £22,500 to St John Ambulance for a national schools competition; £6,000 to NCH Action for Children; £5,000 to Milton Keynes Community Foundation.

FINANCES *Year* 2000 *Income* £53,000 *Grants* £87,000

TRUSTEES C W T Johnston; Dr John Barber.

OTHER INFORMATION Applications restricted to charities nominated by policyholders of Personal Assurance plc or their employees.

HOW TO APPLY The trust invites Personal Assurance policyholders and their employees to nominate beneficiaries. Other applicants will not be considered.

WHO TO APPLY TO Dr J Barber, Trustee, Personal Assurance plc, John Ormond House, 899 Silbury Boulevard, Milton Keynes MK9 3XL *Tel* 01908 605000

CC NO 1023274   **ESTABLISHED** 1993

■ The Persula Foundation

WHERE FUNDING CAN BE GIVEN Predominantly UK; overseas grants are given, but this is rare.

WHO CAN BENEFIT Mainly small registered charities benefiting at risk groups, people who are socially isolated, disadvantaged by poverty or homeless, people with cancer or disabilities, including visual impairment, deafness, spinal injuries and multiple sclerosis, and animals.

WHAT IS FUNDED Original and unique projects of national benefit in the areas of homelessness, disability, and human and animal welfare.

WHAT IS NOT FUNDED No grants to individuals, including sponsorship, for core costs, buildings/ building work or to statutory bodies.

TYPE OF GRANT Up to two years.

SAMPLE GRANTS 1999: £20,000 to Royal National Institute for the Deaf for the safer sound campaign; £6,000 to Kidscape for assertiveness training for bullied children; £5,000 each to Wandle Valley Animal Hospital for new enclosures for wildlife and National Missing Persons Helpline towards a case manager for Message Home service; £4,500 to New Forest Drag Hunt; £2,000 to Irwell Valley Housing Association for Gold Service project; £1,750 to Bridge Housing Association for a rent deposit scheme for homeless people; £1,500 to National Information Forum towards a conference and brochure; £1,000 each to Mayhew Animal Home for a neutering project and League Against Cruel Sports.

FINANCES *Year* 2001 *Income* £207,300 *Grants* £133,879

TRUSTEES Julian Richer; David Robinson; David Highton; Mrs R Richer; Mrs H Oppenheim.

PUBLICATIONS Guidelines.

HOW TO APPLY In writing to the correspondent.

WHO TO APPLY TO Mrs Fiona Brown, Chief Executive, Richer House, Hankey Place, London SE1 4BB *Tel* 020 7357 9298 *Fax* 020 7357 8685 *E-mail* info@persula.org *Website* www.persula.org
CC NO 1044174   ESTABLISHED 1994

....

■ The Pet Plan Charitable Trust

WHERE FUNDING CAN BE GIVEN UK.
WHO CAN BENEFIT Animal charities and organisations benefiting students, research workers and veterinarians.
WHAT IS FUNDED Veterinary research, animal welfare, education in animal welfare, and other charitable purposes. Help is limited to dogs, cats and horses only, those being the animals insured by Pet Plan. Rabbits will be considered.
WHAT IS NOT FUNDED No grants to individuals or non-registered charities. The trust does not support or condone invasive procedures, vivisection or experimentation of any kind.
RANGE OF GRANTS £1,000–£150,000.
SAMPLE GRANTS £38,721 to Animal Health Trust for research into the cause of cancer in dogs; £21,480 to University of Cambridge Veterinary School to investigate joint disease in horses; £19,523 to Royal Veterinary College for a study investigating insulin resistance in diabetic cats; £12,000 to Paws for Kids for its pet fostering service; £8,000 each to Ada Cole Rescue Stables for a replacement van and Ty-Agored Animal Sanctuary for neutering and veterinary assistance.
FINANCES Year 2000–01 Income £488,000 Grants £563,000 Assets £850,000
TRUSTEES David Simpson, Chair; Clarissa Baldwin; Patsy Bloom; John Bower; Dave Bishop; Nicholas Mills; George Stratford; Michael Tucker.
HOW TO APPLY In writing, or by telephone or e-mail, to the correspondent. Closing dates for scientific and welfare applications vary so please check first. Grants are generally announced at the end of the year.
WHO TO APPLY TO Roz Hayward-Butt, Administrator, Great West Road, Brentford, Middlesex TW8 9EG *Tel* 020 8580 8013 *Fax* 020 8580 8186 *E-mail* roz-hb-petplanct@allianzcornhill.co.uk
CC NO 1032907   ESTABLISHED 1994

....

■ The Jack Petchey Foundation

WHERE FUNDING CAN BE GIVEN East London and west Essex, i.e. the boroughs/districts of Barking and Dagenham, Brentwood, Epping Forest, Hackney, Harlow, Havering, Newham, Redbridge, Tower Hamlets, Thurrock, Uttlesford and Waltham Forest, but see below.
WHO CAN BENEFIT Young people aged between 11 and 25.
WHAT IS FUNDED Project grants and achievement awards to give young people the opportunity to help themselves. Project grants are available to: promote community involvement and personal responsibility within society; provide financial assistance to clubs, youth groups, schools, etc. that demonstrate that they are enabling individuals to achieve their potential, take control of their lives and contribute to society as a whole; support the training of youth leaders; support other youth projects. Achievement awards of £200 a month are given to young people who make a 'wholehearted contribution' to their club, group or community. The grant must be spent on a community project chosen

by the winner. Organisations may select award candidates each month, making a possible £2,400 grant total available to clubs/schools/ projects each year. For other, smaller programmes, (including sponsorship of up to £200 for young people on gap year programmes or undertaking fundraising initiatives for other people or charities), see the foundation's website.
WHAT IS NOT FUNDED The foundation does not support: organisations who have applied within the last 12 months; the replacement of statutory funding; individuals; except through the sponsorship programme; work that has already taken place; work that does not directly benefit people in the UK; medical research; animal welfare; endowment funds; general appeals or circulars. The foundation is also unlikely to support: building or major refurbishment projects; conferences or seminars; religious projects. Applications from outside the foundation's catchment area will not be supported.
SAMPLE GRANTS In 2001: £164,000 to London Youth; £74,000 to Essex Association of Boys Clubs; £64,000 to Community Links; £50,000 each to Leeds Grammar School, Leeds University Business School, and Community Service Volunteers; £31,200 to Scouts – Greater London N/E County; £30,000 each to British Sports Trust and Medical Foundation for the Victims of Torture; £20,000 each to Centrepoint and Endeavour School.
FINANCES Year 2002 Income £2,500,000 Grants £2,500,000
TRUSTEES Ron Mills; Ray Rantell; Graham Adams; Barbara Staines.
OTHER INFORMATION The budget for 2003 is expected to be divided as follows: Projects grants – £2 million; Achievement awards – £1.4 million; Sponsorship – £144,000.
HOW TO APPLY Application forms for each of the grant schemes are available from the foundation and can be downloaded from its website. There are no deadlines for applications but they should be made in 'good time' before the money is needed. The foundation holds monthly management meetings and aims to give a decision within six weeks.
WHO TO APPLY TO Andrew Billington, Director, Exchange House, 13–14 Clements Court, Ilford, Essex IG1 2QY *Tel* 020 8252 8000 *Fax* 020 8252 7892 *E-mail* mail@jackpetcheyfoundation.org.uk *Website* www.jackpetcheyfoundation.org.uk
CC NO 1076886   ESTABLISHED 1999

....

■ Peugeot Charity Trust (formerly The Peugeot Talbot Motor Company Charity Trust)

WHERE FUNDING CAN BE GIVEN Coventry and Rugby.
WHO CAN BENEFIT Local voluntary organisations and charitable groups only.
WHAT IS FUNDED General charitable purposes. Causes are often associated with the motor industry.
WHAT IS NOT FUNDED No grants to individuals or outside the beneficial area. Sponsorships and charitable advertising are not given.
TYPE OF GRANT One-off grants.
RANGE OF GRANTS £50–£10,000 (average grant £50–£100).
SAMPLE GRANTS In 1998–99: £20,000 to Heart of England Community Foundation; £8,000 to Warwick University; £4,300 to Crow Recycling; £2,400 to Rugby NHS; £2,000 each to Exhall

Grange School and St Anne's and All Saints Church; £1,500 to Horticultural Therapy; £1,200 to Mylot Hamlet Hospice; £1,000 to Auto Express Charity Appeal and Baby Lifeline.
FINANCES *Year* 2001–02 *Income* £79,931
TRUSTEES T L Evans; A Didlick; R Lewis.
HOW TO APPLY In writing to the correspondent.
WHO TO APPLY TO Maureen Barnes, Secretary, PO Box 227, Aldermoor Lane, Coventry CV3 1LT *Tel* 024 7688 4000
CC NO 266182   **ESTABLISHED** 1970

■ The Philanthropic Trust

WHERE FUNDING CAN BE GIVEN UK, Africa, Asia.
WHO CAN BENEFIT Registered charities benefiting unemployed people and volunteers of all ages. Overseas projects must apply through UK-registered charities.
WHAT IS FUNDED Projects to alleviate homelessness in the UK and poverty in the developing world. The trust also has an interest in: fauna; animal welfare; wildlife sanctuaries; campaigning for peace, the rights of the individual and racial equality; and conservation.
WHAT IS NOT FUNDED No grants for the arts, education, religious organisations, expeditions or individuals. Grants are given to UK registered charities only.
TYPE OF GRANT Recurring, core costs and projects.
RANGE OF GRANTS £100–£5,000.
SAMPLE GRANTS £20,000 to Crisis; £10,000 each to Medical Foundation for the Care of Victims of Torture and Samaritans; £5,000 to National Centre for Conductive Education; £3,000 each to St Basil's and St Mungo's; £2,500 to Shelter; £2,000 each to Mental Health Foundation, National Homeless Alliance and Refugee Council.
FINANCES *Year* 2000–01 *Income* £174,797 *Grants* £199,990 *Assets* £2,351,413
TRUSTEES Paul H Burton; Jeremy J Burton; Amanda C Burton.
HOW TO APPLY In writing to the correspondent. Unsuccessful appeals will not necessarily be acknowledged.
WHO TO APPLY TO The Trust Administrator, Trustee Management Limited, 19 Cookridge Street, Leeds LS2 3AG
CC NO 1045263   **ESTABLISHED** 1995

■ The Phillips Charitable Trust

WHERE FUNDING CAN BE GIVEN UK, with a preference for the Midlands, particularly Northamptonshire.
WHAT IS FUNDED The trust gives grants to seafarer organisations in Great Britain and Ireland, animal welfare organisations, the National Trust and English Heritage, and smaller one-off grants for national or local projects.
SAMPLE GRANTS £13,500 to The National Trust; £5,500 to RNLI; £3,000 to PDSA; £2,000 to The Extracare Charitable Trust; £1,000 each to Wildlife Trust and Northamptonshire Scout Council.
FINANCES *Year* 2000–01 *Income* £77,000 *Grants* £26,000 *Assets* £1,800,000
TRUSTEES M J Ford; M J Percival; Mrs A M Marrum; P R Saunderson; S G Schanschieff.
HOW TO APPLY In writing to the correspondent.
WHO TO APPLY TO M J Percival, Trustee, Oxford House, Cliftonville, Northampton NN1 5PN *Tel* 01604 230400 *Fax* 01604 604164 *E-mail* mjp@howes-percival.co.uk
CC NO 1057019   **ESTABLISHED** 1995

■ The Phillips Family Charitable Trust

WHERE FUNDING CAN BE GIVEN UK.
WHO CAN BENEFIT Registered charities only.
WHAT IS FUNDED General charitable purposes, mainly Jewish organisations, and those concerned with older people, children, refugees and education.
WHAT IS NOT FUNDED No grants to individuals.
TYPE OF GRANT Grants are given for core, capital and project support.
RANGE OF GRANTS Usually £50–£2,000.
FINANCES *Year* 1999–2000 *Income* £30,000 *Grants* £39,000 *Assets* £363,000
TRUSTEES M L Phillips; Mrs R Phillips; M D Paisner; P S Phillips; G M Phillips.
HOW TO APPLY In writing to the correspondent. Please note, the trust informed us that there is not much scope for new beneficiaries.
WHO TO APPLY TO Paul S Phillips, Trustee, Berkeley Square House, Berkeley Square, London W1J 6BY *Tel* 020 7491 3763 *Fax* 020 7491 0818 *E-mail* psphillipsbsh@aol.com
CC NO 279120   **ESTABLISHED** 1979

■ The Ruth & Michael Phillips Charitable Trust

WHERE FUNDING CAN BE GIVEN UK.
WHO CAN BENEFIT Registered charities, especially Jewish causes.
WHAT IS FUNDED Jewish organisations, especially those in the fields of education, children's charities, the arts, and medical groups.
WHAT IS NOT FUNDED No grants are made to individuals.
TYPE OF GRANT Recurrent and one-off.
SAMPLE GRANTS £36,000 to Jewish Care; £25,000 to Community Security Trust; £10,000 to London School of Jewish Studies; £6,420 to Marble Arch Synagogue; £6,000 to Norwood; £5,232 to Royal Opera House Benevolent Fund; £5,000 each to British ORT, Immanuel College, and Naima Jewish Prep School; £4,000 to Lubavitch Foundation.
FINANCES *Year* 2000–01 *Income* £201,230 *Grants* £135,281 *Assets* £1,009,286
TRUSTEES M L Phillips; Mrs R Phillips; M D Paisner.
HOW TO APPLY In writing to the correspondent at any time.
WHO TO APPLY TO M L Phillips, Trustee, Berkeley Square House, Berkeley Square, London W1J 6BY *Tel* 020 7491 3763 *Fax* 020 7491 0818
CC NO 260378   **ESTABLISHED** 1970

■ Philological Foundation

WHERE FUNDING CAN BE GIVEN The City of Westminster and the London borough of Camden.
WHO CAN BENEFIT Schools in the City of Westminster and the borough of Camden, and their pupils and ex-pupils under 25 years of age.
WHAT IS FUNDED Individuals may receive grants for educational expenses and tuition fees; schools in the area may benefit over a wide range of purposes.
WHAT IS NOT FUNDED No support for schools not in Westminster or Camden and individuals who did not attend school in the City of Westminster or London borough of Camden. The foundation does not give bursaries, scholarships or loans.
RANGE OF GRANTS £200–£2,000.
SAMPLE GRANTS £2,000 each to a drama student for course fees, a school for musical

equipment, a performing arts student for fees, a school for library books, and a fashion student for expenses; £1,900 each to two schools for library books; £1,000 to an economics student for fees; £1,300 to a school for teaching materials; £650 to an information technology student for expenses; £200 to a student for books.

FINANCES *Year* 2001–02 *Income* £54,000 *Grants* £56,000 *Assets* £773,000

TRUSTEES P E Sayers, Chair; Dr R Philpot; Mrs R Brightmore; Mrs G Hampson; S Briddes; Mrs J Keen; D Jones; G Margolis; A Leys.

HOW TO APPLY In writing to the clerk. Trustees meet typically in January, March, June, September and December. Apply several weeks before. One application per student or school. Can apply again after one year.

WHO TO APPLY TO Mrs Audrey Millar, Clerk, 24 Carlton Hill, St John's Wood, London NW8 0JY

CC NO 312692   **ESTABLISHED** 1982

■ The David Pickford Charitable Foundation

WHERE FUNDING CAN BE GIVEN UK, with a preference for Kent and London

WHO CAN BENEFIT Mainly, but not solely, young people and Christian evangelism.

WHAT IS FUNDED Support of a residential Christian youth centre in Kent for those in the 15 to 25 age group and other similar activities, mainly Christian youth work.

WHAT IS NOT FUNDED No grants to individuals. No building projects.

SAMPLE GRANTS £6,000 to Philo Trust; £5,800 to Oasis Trust; £2,500 to Chasar Trust; £1,500 to Saltmine Trust.

FINANCES *Year* 2001–02 *Income* £48,208 *Grants* £38,400 *Assets* £808,862

TRUSTEES D M Pickford; Mrs E G Pickford.

HOW TO APPLY In writing to the correspondent. Trustees meet every other month from January. Applications will not be acknowledged. Those falling outside the criteria mentioned above will be ignored.

WHO TO APPLY TO D M Pickford, Trustee, Elm Tree Farm, Mersham, Ashford, Kent TN25 7HS *Tel* 01233 720200 *Fax* 01233 720522

CC NO 243437   **ESTABLISHED** 1965

■ The Bernard Piggott Trust

WHERE FUNDING CAN BE GIVEN North Wales and Birmingham.

WHO CAN BENEFIT Organisations benefiting children, young adults, medical, actors and entertainment professionals, and Church of England and Wales.

WHAT IS FUNDED Church of England; Church of Wales; education; medical charities, both care and research; drama and the theatre; youth and children.

WHAT IS NOT FUNDED No grants to individuals.

TYPE OF GRANT Usually one-off capital. No further grants within two years.

RANGE OF GRANTS £250–£4,000. Average about £1,000.

SAMPLE GRANTS Previous beneficiaries include St Rhedgw Church in Llanllyfni, CMC, Retired and Senior Volunteers Programme, St Martin's in the Bull Ring – Birmingham, St Mary's Church – Beddgelert and Salvation Army.

FINANCES *Year* 2001–02 *Income* £56,000 *Grants* £44,000 *Assets* £836,000

TRUSTEES D M P Lea; N J L Lea; R J Easton; Ven. Arfon Williams.

HOW TO APPLY The trustees meet in May/June and November. Applications should be in writing to the secretary including annual accounts and details of the specific project including running costs and so on.

WHO TO APPLY TO Miss J P Whitworth, Secretary, 4 Streetsbrook Road, Shirley, Solihull, West Midlands B90 3PL *Tel* 0121 744 1695 *Fax* 0121 744 1695

CC NO 260347   **ESTABLISHED** 1970

■ The Claude & Margaret Pike Charity

WHERE FUNDING CAN BE GIVEN Devon.

WHO CAN BENEFIT Individuals and organisations.

WHAT IS FUNDED General charitable purposes. Particularly by making small donations to many people to encourage and advance their leadership qualities and gain experience through organisations such as the Projects Trust, Operation Raleigh, British Schools Exploration Society and the Duke of Edinburgh Gold Award Scheme.

WHAT IS NOT FUNDED No appeals from outside Devon will be considered.

TYPE OF GRANT One-off grants.

SAMPLE GRANTS £12,000 to Exeter Cathedral; £1,500 each to Devon Conservation Forum, and Hospicare – Exeter; £1,000 each to Bovy Tracey Activities Trust, Sight Savers International, Wolborough PCC, and Wydicombe PCC.

FINANCES *Year* 2002 *Grants* £54,000

TRUSTEES J D Pike; Dr P A D Holland.

HOW TO APPLY In writing to the correspondent.

WHO TO APPLY TO J D Pike, Trustee, Dunderdale Lawn, Penshurst Road, Newton Abbey, Devon TQ12 1EN *Tel* 01626 354404 *Fax* 01626 333582

CC NO 247657   **ESTABLISHED** 1965

■ The Claude & Margaret Pike Woodlands Trust

WHERE FUNDING CAN BE GIVEN Devon and Cornwall.

WHO CAN BENEFIT People living in Devon.

WHAT IS FUNDED To protect, improve or foster an appreciation of the landscape, natural beauty and amenity of woodlands, copses or other areas of land and the flora and fauna therein for the benefit of the public. To foster the growth of specimen trees and shrubs and the establishment of woodlands or copses which by their location will be an inspiration to people in the environment in which they live and a demonstration of people's faith in nature.

WHAT IS NOT FUNDED Support is rarely given to appeals outside Devon. General national appeals are rarely supported, and appeals from outside Devon are not acknowledged.

SAMPLE GRANTS £1,000 each to Devon Wildlife Trust and Royal Horticultural Society; £500 each to Devon County Agricultural Association, Greenacre Farm, National Trust, Plantlife, and Teigbridge District Council Tree Council.

FINANCES *Year* 2002 *Income* £70,000 *Grants* £7,000

TRUSTEES C D Pike; J D Pike; Dr P A D Holland.

HOW TO APPLY In writing to the correspondent.

WHO TO APPLY TO J D Pike, Trustee, Dunderdalae Lawn, Penshurst Road, Newton Abbot, Devon TQ12 1EN *Tel* 01626 354404 *Fax* 01626 333582

CC NO 266072 **ESTABLISHED** 1973

■ The Pilgrim Trust

WHERE FUNDING CAN BE GIVEN UK, but not the Channel Islands and the Isle of Man.

WHO CAN BENEFIT Local and UK charities, and recognised public bodies.

WHAT IS FUNDED Preservation (covering ecclesiastical buildings, secular buildings), art and learning and social welfare.

WHAT IS NOT FUNDED The purpose of the application must be charitable. Normally applications will only be considered from UK-registered charities except where the applicant is exempt from registration, is a recognised public body or is registered as a Friendly Society. The project must be based within the UK. Organisations from the Channel Islands and the Isle of Man are not eligible to apply. No grants can be made to private individuals.

Currently, the Pilgrim Trust does not make grants for: major capital projects and major appeals, particularly where ' partnership' funding is required and where any contribution from the Pilgrim Trust would not make a significant difference; activities that the trustees consider to be primarily the responsibility of central or local government; medical research, hospices, residential homes for the elderly and people with learning disabilities; projects which offer training or employment for people with learning disabilities; projects for people with physical disabilities and schemes specifically to give access to public buildings for people with physical disabilities; drop-in centres, unless the specific work within the centre falls within one of the trustees' current priorities, youth and sports clubs, travel or adventure projects, community centres or children' s play groups; drop-in centres or hostels for people who are homeless; re-ordering of churches or places of worship for wider community use; education, assistance to individuals for degree or post-degree work, school, university and college development; trips abroad; one-off events such as exhibitions, festivals, seminars, conferences and theatrical and musical productions; commissioning of new works of art; general appeals.

TYPE OF GRANT Infrastructure costs for specific projects (salary and running costs up to a maximum of three years), capital projects. Also buildings, one-off, research and start-up costs.

FINANCES *Year* 2001 *Income* £1,656,292 *Grants* £1,987,000 *Assets* £51,550,609

TRUSTEES Mary Moore, chair; Sir Richard Carew Pole; Neil MacGregor; Nicolas Barker; Lord Bingham; Dame Ruth Runciman; Eugenie Turton; Lord Cobbold; Lady Jay.

HOW TO APPLY An application form, and guidelines for applicants, are available from the correspondent or the trust's website. You can make an application at any time during the year. The full board of trustees meets quarterly, normally in late January, April, July and October. Applications will normally be placed before trustees at the next quarterly meeting following submission, so long as the application and all the necessary supporting information is received at least six weeks before the date of that meeting. You should read the guidelines carefully to make sure that your organisation and your project is eligible. You should then complete the application form, which is attached to the guidelines, and send it to the trust with all the relevant supporting information from the checklist at the end of the form. Trustees run a small grants fund and have set aside an annual sum of £200,000 for applications of £5,000 or less. These applications normally require less detailed assessment, whereas a site visit or meeting may be required for larger applications. Applicants for sums of less than £5,000 should include the names of two referees from organisations with whom they work. For larger projects, the average grant from the Pilgrim Trust is in the region of £20,000.

WHO TO APPLY TO Georgina Nayler, Director, Cowley House, 9 Little College Street, London SW1P 3SH *Tel* 020 7222 4723 *Fax* 020 7976 0461 *Website* www.thepilgrimtrust.org.uk

CC NO 206602 **ESTABLISHED** 1930

■ A M Pilkington's Charitable Trust

WHERE FUNDING CAN BE GIVEN UK, with a preference for Scotland.

WHO CAN BENEFIT Registered charities.

WHAT IS FUNDED General charitable purposes, including conservation/environment, health and social welfare.

WHAT IS NOT FUNDED Grants are not given to overseas projects or political appeals.

RANGE OF GRANTS £500–£1,500.

FINANCES *Year* 1999–2000 *Income* £172,000 *Grants* £129,000 *Assets* £3,000,000

HOW TO APPLY The trustees state that, regrettably, they are unable to make grants to new applicants since they already have more than enough causes to support. Trustees meet in June and December; applications should be received by April and October.

WHO TO APPLY TO The Trustees, Carters, Chartered Accountants, Pentland House, Saltire Centre, Glenrothes, Fife KY6 2AH *Tel* 01592 630055 *Fax* 01592 630555 *E-mail* cartersca@sol.co.uk

SC NO SC000282

■ The Pilkington Charities Fund

WHERE FUNDING CAN BE GIVEN Unrestricted, but with a strong preference for Merseyside.

WHO CAN BENEFIT Registered charities, including local and national organisations benefiting disadvantaged and disabled people; older people; sick people, including those with cancer; victims of abuse, crime and domestic violence; victims of natural disasters and war.

WHAT IS FUNDED Local community projects and facilities; medical research; science and technology research; support for those listed under Who Can Benefit.

WHAT IS NOT FUNDED No grants to individuals.

TYPE OF GRANT Capital (including buildings), core costs, one-off, project, research, recurring costs. Funding for more than three years will be considered.

RANGE OF GRANTS £500–£45,000.

SAMPLE GRANTS £117,000 to C & A Pilkington Trust Fund; £110,000 to Cancer Research Campaign; £50,000 each to Cystic Fibrosis Trust and Psychiatry Research Trust; £41,000 to Alder Hey Hospital; £30,000 each to Liverpool Personal Service Society, Macmillan Cancer Relief, Oxfam and Refugee Council; £25,000 to Merseyside Prostate Cancer Trust.

Think carefully about every application. Is it justified?

719

FINANCES *Year* 2000–01 *Income* £505,000 *Grants* £1,262,000 *Assets* £17,000,000
TRUSTEES Neil Jones; Mrs Jennifer Jones; Arnold Pilkington.
HOW TO APPLY In writing to the correspondent.
WHO TO APPLY TO The Trustees, Rathbones, Port of Liverpool Building, Pier Head, Liverpool L3 1NW *Tel* 0151 236 6666 *Fax* 0151 243 7003
CC NO 225911   ESTABLISHED 1964

■ The Austin & Hope Pilkington Trust

WHERE FUNDING CAN BE GIVEN Unrestricted, but see below.
WHO CAN BENEFIT Registered charities only; national organisations preferred. In 2000, communities and those disadvantaged by poverty and in needy circumstances were supported; in 2001, children, young people, the elderly and those with various medical conditions were supported; in 2002, musicians, artists, and victims of famine.
WHAT IS FUNDED The trust has a three year cycle of funding. In 2002, it focused on music and the arts, famine and overseas projects. In 2003 the theme is community, poverty and religion; in 2004 medical; children and youth; elderly. Then the cycle repeats with 2005 being music and the arts; overseas.
WHAT IS NOT FUNDED Grants only to registered charities. No grants to individuals. National organisations are more likely to be supported than purely local organisations.
TYPE OF GRANT Building and other capital costs, core costs, feasibility studies, one-off, project, research, running costs and start-up costs will be considered. Funding may be given for up to three years.
RANGE OF GRANTS Up to £5,000, occasional grants of £10,000–£20,000.
SAMPLE GRANTS £20,000 each to Campaign, Centrepoint and National Asthma Campaign; £10,000 to Breakthrough Breast Cancer and Imperial Cancer Research Fund; £5,000 each to Addaction, Corda, Help the Hospices, Maternity Alliance and RNID.
FINANCES *Year* 2000–01 *Income* £251,892 *Grants* £646,000 *Assets* £7,537,000
TRUSTEES Jennifer Jones; Deborah Nelson; Penny Shankar.
HOW TO APPLY In writing to the correspondent. There is no application form. Applications should include a one- or two-page summary of their project, full budget and annual accounts. No telephone calls, please. Please note the selected areas for each year as given above. Grants are made in June and November each year. Applications should be received by 1 June and 1 November to be considered.
WHO TO APPLY TO Karen Frank, PO Box 124, Stroud, Gloucestershire GL6 7YN
CC NO 255274   ESTABLISHED 1967

■ The Cecil Pilkington Charitable Trust

WHERE FUNDING CAN BE GIVEN UK, particularly Sunningwell in Oxfordshire and St Helens.
WHO CAN BENEFIT Registered charities only.
WHAT IS FUNDED Environmental and conservation projects; advancement of education in agriculture and forestry; the arts and humanities; other charitable purposes.

WHAT IS NOT FUNDED No grants to individuals or non-registered charities.
RANGE OF GRANTS £500–£50,000.
SAMPLE GRANTS £10,000 each to Liverpool School of Medicine, Sunningwell Church Appeal, and Willowbreak Hospice – St Helens; £8,000 to Exeter University Postgraduate School of Medicine; £7,000 each to BBONT, and Richmond Fellowship; £5,000 each to Bristol Cancer Help Centre, Citadel Arts Centre – St Helens, Providence Row Housing Association, Royal School of the Blind – Liverpool, and Soil Association.
FINANCES *Year* 1999–2000 *Income* £179,123 *Grants* £177,300 *Assets* £6,854,203
TRUSTEES A P Pilkington; R F Carter Jones.
HOW TO APPLY In writing to the correspondent.
WHO TO APPLY TO A P Pilkington, Trustee, PO Box 8162, London W2 1JG
CC NO 249997   ESTABLISHED 1966

■ The Elsie Pilkington Charitable Trust

WHERE FUNDING CAN BE GIVEN UK.
WHO CAN BENEFIT Organisations benefiting people who are elderly, infirm or poor, or horses.
WHAT IS FUNDED Welfare and relief work as well as prevention of cruelty.
SAMPLE GRANTS £145,000 to prevent cruelty to equine animals; £105,000 to relieve suffering and distress amongst such equine animals, and to care for and protect such equines in need of care and attention; £100,000 to provide social services and help for the relief of older people, and people who are infirm or poor.
FINANCES *Year* 2000–01 *Income* £112,000 *Grants* £350,000 *Assets* £3,300,000
TRUSTEES Mrs Caroline Doulton; Mrs Tara Economakis; Richard Scott.
HOW TO APPLY In writing to the correspondent.
WHO TO APPLY TO Lord Brentford, Taylor Johnson Garrett, Carmelite, 50 Victoria Embankment, London EC4Y 0DX
CC NO 278332   ESTABLISHED 1979

■ The Sir Harry Pilkington Trust

WHERE FUNDING CAN BE GIVEN UK and worldwide, with a preference for the St Helens area.
WHAT IS FUNDED General charitable purposes.
RANGE OF GRANTS Generally £100–£10,000.
SAMPLE GRANTS £80,000 to Liverpool Council for Social Service; £15,000 to Colden Children's Club; £10,000 each to Roy Castle Foundation and Guy Pilkington Benefit Fund; £9,150 to United Reformed Church – St Helens; £5,000 each to Southport Flower Show and Willow Brook Hospice; £4,000 to Weston Spirit; £2,000 to St Helens and District Crossroads; £1,500 to PSS for St Helens Young Carers.
FINANCES *Year* 2000–01 *Income* £146,557 *Grants* £144,392 *Assets* £5,114,388
TRUSTEES Liverpool Council of Social Service (Inc.).
HOW TO APPLY In writing to the correspondent.
WHO TO APPLY TO The Trustees, Liverpool Council of Social Service (Inc.), 14 Castle Street, Liverpool, Merseyside L2 0NJ *Tel* 0151 236 7728 *Fax* 0151 258 1153
CC NO 206740   ESTABLISHED 1962

■ The Col W W Pilkington Will Trusts – The General Charity Fund

WHERE FUNDING CAN BE GIVEN UK, with a preference for Merseyside.

WHO CAN BENEFIT Local and regional registered charities.

WHAT IS FUNDED The welfare of disadvantaged people, especially the young, and the encouragement of their involvement in the community.

WHAT IS NOT FUNDED No support for non-registered charities, building projects, animal charities or individuals.

TYPE OF GRANT Generally annual.

RANGE OF GRANTS £500–£1,000.

SAMPLE GRANTS £12,000 to Exeter University Postgraduate Medical School; £6,000 to support a research fellowship in complimentary medicine; £2,500 to Handel House Museum; £1,000 each to Merseyside Drugs Council, Drugscope, Monkbeggar Theatre Company, Re-solv and Marie Stopes International.

FINANCES *Year* 2000–01 *Income* £43,000 *Grants* £45,000 *Assets* £1,500,000

TRUSTEES Dr Lawrence Pilkington; Arnold Pilkington; Hon. Mrs Jennifer Pilkington; Neil Pilkington Jones.

HOW TO APPLY In writing to the correspondent. Grant distributions are made in January and July.

WHO TO APPLY TO A P Pilkington, PO Box 8162, London W2 1GF

CC NO 234710   **ESTABLISHED** 1964

■ The John Pitman Charitable Trust

WHERE FUNDING CAN BE GIVEN UK, with a preference for London and the south east of England.

WHO CAN BENEFIT Organisations benefiting Christians, at risk groups, carers, people who are disabled, disadvantaged by poverty or socially isolated.

WHAT IS FUNDED Charities which provide services to individuals to enable them to live their lives more fully. Particularly charities working in the fields of accommodation and housing; infrastructure and technical support; Anglican bodies; health care; health facilities and buildings; community facilities; and various community services.

WHAT IS NOT FUNDED Grants are not normally made to educational or research charities. No grants are made to individuals, including for Raleigh International projects and so on.

TYPE OF GRANT No restriction – either capital or revenue. Buildings, core costs, endowments, one-off, recurring costs and running costs. Funding of up to three years will be considered.

RANGE OF GRANTS £250–£2,500; typical grant £1,000.

SAMPLE GRANTS £2,500 to Shooting Star Trust to set up a children's hospice in West Middlesex; £1,000 each to Macmillan Cancer Relief, Ramblers' Association, VSO, Roy Kinnear Foundation, Woodland Trust, Church Housing Trust, and Dawcliffe Hall Educational Trust; £850 to First Eastnor Brownies.

FINANCES *Year* 1998–99 *Income* £41,686 *Grants* £17,350 *Assets* £462,816

TRUSTEES V M S Browne; J L McKenzie; J M Pitman; Miss M R Pitman; B H Tan; N A R Winckless.

OTHER INFORMATION The trust has no staff and therefore no correspondence can be entered into.

HOW TO APPLY In writing to the correspondent. Applications are considered periodically. Please note, the trust has no employed staff and therefore correspondence is kept to a minimum. Unsuccessful applicants are not informed.

WHO TO APPLY TO J M Pitman, Trustee, Parkgate House, 27 High Street, Hampton Hill, Middlesex TW12 1NB

CC NO 803018   **ESTABLISHED** 1988

■ The Platinum Trust

WHERE FUNDING CAN BE GIVEN UK.

WHO CAN BENEFIT Charities benefiting people with disabilities.

WHAT IS FUNDED Representative organisations of people with disabilities, with which the trust has an established relationship.

WHAT IS NOT FUNDED No grants for services run by statutory or public bodies, or from mental health organisations. No grants for: medical research/ treatment or equipment; mobility aids/ wheelchairs; community transport/disabled transport schemes; holidays/exchanges/holiday playschemes; special needs playgroups; toy and leisure libraries; special Olympic and Paralympics groups; sports and recreation clubs for people with disabilities; residential care/ sheltered housing/respite care; carers; conservation schemes/city farms/horticultural therapy; sheltered or supported employment/ community business/social firms; purchase/ construction/repair of buildings; and conductive education/other special educational programmes.

RANGE OF GRANTS Usually £5,000–£40,000.

SAMPLE GRANTS £500,000 to Kosovo Appeal; £38,500 to BCODP; £20,000 each to Alliance for Inclusive Education and Parents for Inclusion; £17,500 to CSIE; £10,900 to DPPI; £5,000 each to Disability Equality in Education, Muscle Power, and Regard.

FINANCES *Year* 1999–2000 *Income* £604,673 *Grants* £621,900 *Assets* £86,317

TRUSTEES G K Panayiotou; A D Russell; C D Organ.

HOW TO APPLY The trust does not accept unsolicited applications; all future grants will be allocated by the trustees to groups they have already made links with.

WHO TO APPLY TO The Secretary, 19 Victoria Street, St Albans, Hertfordshire AL1 3JJ

CC NO 328570   **ESTABLISHED** 1990

■ G S Plaut Charitable Trust

WHERE FUNDING CAN BE GIVEN Predominantly UK.

WHO CAN BENEFIT Voluntary organisations and charitable groups only.

WHAT IS FUNDED General charitable purposes.

WHAT IS NOT FUNDED No grants to individuals or for repeat applications.

TYPE OF GRANT Some annual, others one-off.

RANGE OF GRANTS £100–£750.

SAMPLE GRANTS In 1999–2000: £750 each to C M Jacobs Home and Friends of Meals on Wheels Service (Liverpool); £600 each to Nightingale Home for Aged Jews, RNIB Talking Book Services and St Dunstans.

FINANCES *Year* 2000–01 *Income* £34,000 *Grants* £37,000 *Assets* £582,000

TRUSTEES Dr G S Plaut, Chair; T N Wheldon; Mrs A D Wrapson; Dr H M Liebeschuetz; K A Sutcliffe; W E Murfett; Miss T A Warburg.

HOW TO APPLY In writing to the correspondent. Applications are reviewed twice a year. An sae should be enclosed. Applications will not be acknowledged.

WHO TO APPLY TO Dr R Speirs, c/o 3 Princess Gardens, Grove, Wantage, Oxon OX12 0QN
CC NO 261469   **ESTABLISHED** 1970

■ Frederic William Plaxton Charitable Trust

WHERE FUNDING CAN BE GIVEN Scarborough
WHO CAN BENEFIT The town of Scarborough and its citizens.
WHAT IS FUNDED General charitable purposes.
FINANCES *Year* 1999–2000 *Grants* £200,000
HOW TO APPLY In writing to the correspondent at any time.
WHO TO APPLY TO J C Parkinson, Albermarle Chambers, Albermarle Crescent, Scarborough, North Yorkshire YO11 1LA *Tel* 01723 360001
CC NO 1073208   **ESTABLISHED** 1996

■ The J D Player Endowment Fund

WHERE FUNDING CAN BE GIVEN Nottinghamshire and surrounding areas.
WHO CAN BENEFIT Individuals, and organisations benefiting: retired people; unemployed people; those in care, fostered and adopted; parents and children; one-parent families; widows and widowers; carers; disabled people; and those disadvantaged by poverty.
WHAT IS FUNDED Relief of poverty and various community services.
WHAT IS NOT FUNDED No grants for educational purposes, expedition or travel.
TYPE OF GRANT Capital, core costs, interest-free loans, one-off, project, research, and start-up costs. Funding of up to and over three years will be considered.
RANGE OF GRANTS £100–£5,500.
SAMPLE GRANTS £5,500 to Salvation Army Nottingham Region; £4,500 to Council for Family Care; £4,000 each to Army Benevolent Fund Nottingham, Nottingham Mencap, and SSAFA Nottingham Region; £3,500 each to Cheshire Home – Holme Lodge, Elizabeth Fry Day Centre, and Radford Care Group; £3,000 to Abbeyfield Society; £2,000 to Centre for Conus and Spirit.
FINANCES *Year* 1998–99 *Income* £92,790 *Grants* £74,480 *Assets* £776,151
TRUSTEES D R Pell, Chair; M A Foulds; E A Randall; Revd Canon G B Barrodale.
OTHER INFORMATION The trust gives most of its support to individuals and families, and the surplus to organisations. In 1998–99 this amounted to £49,040.
HOW TO APPLY In writing to the correspondent at any time.
WHO TO APPLY TO S J Moore, Clerk, c/o Nelsons, Pennine House, 8 Stanford Street, Nottingham NG1 7BQ *Tel* 0115 958 6262
CC NO 214421   **ESTABLISHED** 1963

■ The Charles Plimpton Foundation

WHERE FUNDING CAN BE GIVEN North west England.
WHO CAN BENEFIT Registered charities.
WHAT IS FUNDED General charitable purposes.
WHAT IS NOT FUNDED No grants to individuals or non-registered charities.
SAMPLE GRANTS £29,000 to British Heart Foundation – North West Region; £10,000 each

to Age Concern – Newton-le-Willows, Heswell Centre and Merseyside Police for Viking Youth Centre; £9,000 to Cardiothoracic Centre – Liverpool; £5,000 each to Petrus Neighbourhood Centre – Liverpool, Staffordshire University School of Art and Design and Wirral Narrowboat Appeal; £2,500 to Wirral Victim Support; £2,000 to Raynauds and Scleroderma Association.
FINANCES *Year* 1999–2000 *Income* £68,000 *Grants* £92,000 *Assets* £235,000
TRUSTEES HSBC Trust Company (UK) Ltd.
HOW TO APPLY In writing to the correspondent. Trustees meet in May and November.
WHO TO APPLY TO The Secretary, HSBC Trust Company (UK) Ltd, 3rd Floor, 4 Dale Street, Liverpool L69 2BZ *Tel* 0151 801 2190
CC NO 519461   **ESTABLISHED** 1987

■ Plymouth Sound Trust – The Magic Appeal

WHERE FUNDING CAN BE GIVEN Plymouth, South Hams, south east Cornwall and west Devon.
WHO CAN BENEFIT Charities benefiting children and young people.
FINANCES *Year* 1999 *Grants* £25,000
TRUSTEES Louise Churchill; Derek Laycock; Revel Arnold; Roger Collins; John Brewer; Jason Ryder; Lynn Adams; Roy Gosling; Linda Quick; Miss Rachel Haile.
HOW TO APPLY In writing to the correspondent.
WHO TO APPLY TO Jason Ryder, Chair, Earls Acre, Plymouth, Devon PL3 4HX *Tel* 01752 227272
CC NO Y00090

■ Polden-Puckham Charitable Foundation

WHERE FUNDING CAN BE GIVEN UK and overseas.
WHO CAN BENEFIT Registered charities only.
WHAT IS FUNDED Peace and conflict resolution, ecological issues, and human rights work related to peace, ecological and women's issues.
WHAT IS NOT FUNDED The trust does not support: individuals; travel bursaries (including overseas placements and expeditions); study; academic research; capital projects (e.g. building projects or purchase of nature reserves); community or local projects (except innovative prototypes for widespread application); general appeals; or organisations based overseas.
TYPE OF GRANT Core costs and project funding for up to three years.
RANGE OF GRANTS Normally £1,000 to £15,000.
SAMPLE GRANTS £20,000 each to Responding to Conflict and Quaker Peace and Service; £15,000 each to New Economics Foundation and Oxford Research Group; £13,000 to Sustain; £10,000 to Food Ethics Council; £7,450 to Lansbury House Trust Fund for disbursement to Peaceworkers UK; £7,000 to Peace Research and Education Trust for disbursement to Peace Pledge Union; £6,000 to Food Commission.
FINANCES *Year* 2001–02 *Income* £299,359 *Grants* £348,233 *Assets* £9,868,902
TRUSTEES Carol Freeman; David Gillett; Harriet Gillett; Jenepher Gordon; Heather Swailes; Anthony Wilson.
PUBLICATIONS *Review of Grant Making* – for copy please send 9 x 6 sae.
HOW TO APPLY The trustees meet twice a year in spring and autumn; applications should be

submitted by 15 February and 15 September respectively. Decisions can occasionally be made on smaller grants between these meetings. The foundation will not send replies to applications outside its area of interest. Up-to-date guidelines will be sent on receipt of an sae. Applications should be no longer than two pages and should include the following: a short outline of the project, its aims and methods to be used; the amount requested (normally between £500 and £5,000 over one to three years), the names of other funders and possible funders, and expected sources of funding after termination of PPCF funding; information on how the project is to be monitored, evaluated, and publicised; background details of the key persons in the organisation. Please also supply: latest set of audited accounts; a detailed budget of the project; list of trustees or board of management; names of two referees; charity registration number; annual report.

WHO TO APPLY TO The Secretary, BM PPCF, London WC1N 3XX *Website* www.polden-puckham.org.uk
CC NO 1003024   **ESTABLISHED** 1970

■ The Carew Pole Charitable Trust

WHERE FUNDING CAN BE GIVEN Mainly Cornwall.
WHO CAN BENEFIT Donations normally made only to registered charities, but applications will be considered from individuals for non-full-time education purposes.
WHAT IS FUNDED General charitable purposes principally in Cornwall. In the case of support to churches and village halls, donations are in practice only made to those in the immediate vicinity to Antony House, Torpoint or to those with connections to the Carew Pole Family.
WHAT IS NOT FUNDED The trustees do not support applications from individuals for full-time education.
RANGE OF GRANTS £100–£31,000.
SAMPLE GRANTS £31,000 to Carew Pole Garden Trust; £10,000 to The National Trust; £5,000 each to Rural Horticultural Society and National Maritime Museum Cornwall; £1,000 each to The Tate Gallery, Kingston Hospital NHS Trust and Antony Parochial Church Council.
FINANCES *Year* 2001 *Income* £61,000 *Grants* £65,000 *Assets* £1,425,000
TRUSTEES J C Richardson; J R Cooke-Hurle.
OTHER INFORMATION This charitable trust was founded by Sir John Gawen Carew Pole, Bt, DSO, whose family has both lived in and been connected with Cornwall for many years.
HOW TO APPLY In writing to the correspondent. Applications are considered six-monthly in March and September.
WHO TO APPLY TO J C Richardson, Dawsons Solicitors, 2 New Square, Lincoln's Inn, London WC2A 3RZ *Tel* 020 7421 4800 *Fax* 020 7421 4848 *E-mail* j.richardson@dawsons-legal.com
CC NO 255375   **ESTABLISHED** 1968

■ The Poling Charitable Trust

WHERE FUNDING CAN BE GIVEN Mainly Sussex.
WHO CAN BENEFIT Organisations.
WHAT IS FUNDED General charitable purposes.
WHAT IS NOT FUNDED No support for individuals or medical causes.
RANGE OF GRANTS £25–£5,600.
SAMPLE GRANTS In 1996–97: £5,500 to Arundel Festival which had received grants in previous years; £1,500 to Chichester Cathedral Development Trust; £1,300 to Parochial Church

Council of St Nicholas; £1,000 each to 14 organisations including Royal Academy of Music, Sherborne Abbey, Sussex Association for Rehabilitation of Offenders and Wave Heritage Trust. Other grants given were mostly under £500 and recipients included City Music Society, Friends of Covent Garden, RAF Escapers, Sussex Association for the Deaf and Sussex Trust for Nature Conservation.
FINANCES *Year* 1999–2000 *Income* £46,000 *Grants* £42,000 *Assets* £828,000
HOW TO APPLY In writing to the correspondent; however, the trust stated that it has no spare income as it is all fully committed.
WHO TO APPLY TO D H L Hopkinson, St John's Priory, Poling, Arundel, West Sussex BN18 9PS
CC NO 240066   **ESTABLISHED** 1964

■ The George & Esme Pollitzer Charitable Settlement

WHERE FUNDING CAN BE GIVEN UK.
WHO CAN BENEFIT Registered charities, particularly Jewish organisations.
WHAT IS FUNDED General charitable purposes.
TYPE OF GRANT Normally for single, specific projects.
RANGE OF GRANTS £500–£10,000.
SAMPLE GRANTS £10,000 each to Big Issue Foundation, Jewish Museum, Nightingale House, and Prince's Youth Business Trust; £5,000 to Breast Cancer Care; £2,000 each to AFASIC, Crisis, NSPCC, Royal Free and University College Medical School, and United World College of the Atlantic.
FINANCES *Year* 1999–2000 *Income* £111,512 *Grants* £123,000 *Assets* £2,415,205
TRUSTEES J Barnes; B G Levy; R F C Pollitzer.
HOW TO APPLY In writing to the correspondent.
WHO TO APPLY TO J Barnes, Trustee, Saffery Champness, Courtyard House, Oakfield Grove, Clifton, Bristol BS8 2AE *Tel* 0117 915 1617
CC NO 212631   **ESTABLISHED** 1960

■ The J S F Pollitzer Charitable Settlement

WHERE FUNDING CAN BE GIVEN UK and overseas.
WHO CAN BENEFIT Registered charities only, benefiting: children and older people; academics; actors and entertainment professionals; artists; service and ex-service people; medical professionals; musicians; scientists; seafarers and fishermen; sportsmen and women; textile workers and designers; Jews; carers; disabled people; people in rural areas; and victims of crime and man-made or natural disasters.
WHAT IS FUNDED General charitable purposes including: the arts; infrastructure development; independent and special schools; pre-school education; travel and maintenance costs for education; vocational training; community facilities; health; the advancement of Judaism; Jewish umbrella bodies; and conservation and environment. Particular favour is given to neighbourhood-based community projects.
WHAT IS NOT FUNDED No grants to individuals or students, i.e. those without charitable status.
TYPE OF GRANT One-off.
RANGE OF GRANTS £250–£2,000; typical grant £1,000.
SAMPLE GRANTS £1,000 each included Artists First, Chipping Norton Theatre, Dulwich Picture Gallery, Easy Go, International Rescue Corps,

London Master Classes, Newcastle Community School, Sick Children's Trust and WaterAid.

FINANCES *Year* 1999–2000 *Income* £44,000 *Grants* £49,000

TRUSTEES Mrs J F A Davis; Mrs S C O'Farrell; R F C Pollitzer; J S Challis.

HOW TO APPLY In writing to the correspondent. Grants are distributed twice a year, usually around April/May and November/December.

WHO TO APPLY TO P Samuel, Accountant, c/o H W Fisher & Co., 11–15 William Road, London NW1 3ER *Tel* 020 7388 7000

CC NO 210680   **ESTABLISHED** 1960

■ The Pontin Charitable Trust

WHERE FUNDING CAN BE GIVEN Mainly Bristol.

WHO CAN BENEFIT The beneficiary is almost always an organisation well-known to the trustees.

WHAT IS FUNDED General charitable purposes. The trustees are already in touch with the organisations which they wish to support and further applications are not considered.

WHAT IS NOT FUNDED No grants to UK appeals.

TYPE OF GRANT Buildings, capital, core costs, endowments, feasibility studies, interest-free loans, one-off, project, research, running costs, recurring costs, salaries and start-up costs will be considered. Funding may be given for more than three years.

RANGE OF GRANTS £500–£25,000.

SAMPLE GRANTS £8,400 to Bristol Initiative Charitable Trust for general funds; £6,000 to VOSCUR; £5,000 to St Peter's Hospice towards a sculpture and water feature; £1,600 to RSA for general funding; £1,000 to Seed Co.

FINANCES *Year* 2001–02 *Income* £7,488 *Grants* £74,688 *Assets* £915,044

TRUSTEES David Johnstone, Chair; Christopher Zealley; Benjamin Pontin.

HOW TO APPLY Unsolicited applications are not considered or acknowledged.

WHO TO APPLY TO D W R Johnstone, Chair, Bush House, 72 Prince Street, Bristol BS1 4HU *Tel* 0117 924 7276 *E-mail* DavidJohnstone@westend5.freeserve.co.uk

CC NO 271409   **ESTABLISHED** 1976

■ The Ponton House Trust

WHERE FUNDING CAN BE GIVEN Lothians.

WHO CAN BENEFIT Organisations benefiting disadvantaged groups, principally young and elderly people.

WHAT IS FUNDED Grants are given mainly to support small charities working with young people, elderly people and disadvantaged groups.

WHAT IS NOT FUNDED No grants to individuals or non-charitable organisations.

TYPE OF GRANT One-off.

RANGE OF GRANTS £300–£2,000.

FINANCES *Year* 2000 *Income* £36,000 *Grants* £32,000 *Assets* £1,088,000

TRUSTEES G Gemmell; Hon. Lord Grieve; Mrs G Russell; Mrs J Gilliat; Revd J Munro; Mrs F Meikle; A Dobson.

HOW TO APPLY In writing to the correspondent. Trustees usually meet in January, April, July and October. Applications should include a full explanation of the project for which funding is sought plus annual reports and accounts.

WHO TO APPLY TO David S Reith, Secretary, 11 Atholl Crescent, Edinburgh EH3 8HE *Tel* 0131 477 8708 *Fax* 0131 229 5611

SC NO SC021716   **ESTABLISHED** 1993

■ Edith & Ferdinand Porjes Charitable Trust

WHERE FUNDING CAN BE GIVEN UK and overseas.

WHO CAN BENEFIT Jewish organisations; registered charities.

WHAT IS FUNDED General charitable purposes, particularly Jewish causes.

SAMPLE GRANTS £51,845 to Jerusalem Foundation for Bikar Cholim; £27,588 to Jerusalem Foundation for Beit Harinar; £17,606 to Jerusalem Foundation for YMCA; £12,000 to Oxford Centre for Hebrew and Jewish Studies; £10,563 to Jerusalem Foundation for Beit David; £10,000 each to Jewish Book Council, and Manor House Trust; £6,000 each to British Friends of Rabbi Steinsaltz and Friends of Rabbi Steinsaltz Aleph Society Trust; £5,000 to Centre for Jewish-Christian Relations.

FINANCES *Year* 2000–01 *Income* £88,526 *Grants* £203,602 *Assets* £1,987,160

TRUSTEES M D Paisner; A H Freeman; A S Rosenfelder.

HOW TO APPLY In writing to the correspondent.

WHO TO APPLY TO M D Paisner, Trustee, Berwin Leighton Paisner, Bouverie House, 154 Fleet Street, London EC4A 2JD *Tel* 020 7353 0299 *Fax* 020 7583 8621

CC NO 274012   **ESTABLISHED** 1973

■ The Porter Foundation

WHERE FUNDING CAN BE GIVEN Israel and the UK

WHO CAN BENEFIT Registered charities and community organisations benefiting: children and young adults; academics; research workers; teachers; students; artists; musicians; textile workers and designers; writers and poets; medical professionals; and carers.

WHAT IS FUNDED Practical projects to enhance the quality of people's lives and environment. Priorities are health, education, the environment and humanities.

WHAT IS NOT FUNDED The foundation makes grants only to registered charitable organisations or to organisations with charitable objects that are exempt from the requirement for charitable registration. Grants will not be made to: individuals; general appeals such as direct mail circulars; charities which redistribute funds to other charities; third-party organisations raising money on behalf of other charities; or cover general running costs.

TYPE OF GRANT Usually project-based and capital.

SAMPLE GRANTS £511,677 to Tel Aviv University Trust; £162,933 to JPAIME for the Daniel Amichai Education Centre; £120,000 to TAUT for the Porter Super-center for Ecological and Environmental Studies; £18,336 to New Israel Fund; £17,881 to New Israel Opera; £17,153 to United Jewish Israel Appeal for a bursary; £17,109 to Friends of the Israel Educational Trust; £12,698 to British Friends of the Art Museums of Israel; £12,224 to New Israel Fund for Shatil Environmental Justice; £10,000 to Oxford Centre for Hebrew and Jewish Studies for the Porter Fellowship in Yiddish Language and Literature.

FINANCES *Year* 2000–01 *Income* £1,400,000 *Grants* £786,000 *Assets* £40,000,000

TRUSTEES Dame Shirley Porter; Sir Leslie Porter; Steven Porter; David Brecher; Abbey Castle.

HOW TO APPLY In writing to the correspondent, with basic costings and background details, such as the annual report and accounts. Speculative approaches containing expensive publicity material are not encouraged! Applicants who appear suitable will be contacted for further information, and possibly visited. The trustees meet three times a year, usually in March, July and November. Only applications with an sae are guaranteed a response.

WHO TO APPLY TO Paul Williams, Director, PO Box 229, Winchester, Hampshire SO23 7WF

CC NO 261194   **ESTABLISHED** 1970

■ The John Porter Charitable Trust

WHERE FUNDING CAN BE GIVEN Worldwide, but mainly UK and Israel.

WHO CAN BENEFIT Registered and exempt charities.

WHAT IS FUNDED Education, culture, environment, health and welfare.

WHAT IS NOT FUNDED No grants to individuals.

SAMPLE GRANTS £40,000 to Tel Aviv University Trust for Porter Super-Centre for Environmental and Ecological Studies; £10,000 to Institute for Jewish Policy Research; £7,000 to JPAIME for Daniel Amichai Education Centre; £3,000 each to Israel Music Foundation and Wiener Library.

FINANCES *Year* 1998–99 *Income* £172,000 *Grants* £63,000 *Assets* £5,800,000

TRUSTEES Sir Leslie Porter; John Porter; Steven Porter; Peter Green.

HOW TO APPLY In writing to the correspondent.

WHO TO APPLY TO The Trustees, 79 Mount Street, London W1Y 5HJ

CC NO 267170   **ESTABLISHED** 1974

■ The Portishead Nautical Trust

WHERE FUNDING CAN BE GIVEN Bristol and North Somerset.

WHO CAN BENEFIT People under 25 years of age who are disadvantaged or at risk; voluntary and charitable groups working with such people, with young offenders and with people with addictions.

WHAT IS FUNDED Projects with young people who are disadvantaged; educational support for such people; counselling services; and youth groups.

WHAT IS NOT FUNDED No grants for further education costs of non-disadvantaged people.

TYPE OF GRANT One-off, project, recurring costs and running costs will be considered. Funding may be given for up to three years.

RANGE OF GRANTS Usually £100–£5,000.

SAMPLE GRANTS £24,000 to Dyslexic Institute for classes for 15 students; £5,000 to Filton Sea Cadets; £1,000 each to Avon Outward Bound, Cruse Bereavement Care – Bristol, Jessie May Trust, and No Way Trust; £500 each to Bristol Youth Bus Project, North Somerset Under 8's Playscheme, and Young Mothers' Group Trust.

FINANCES *Year* 2001–02 *Income* £75,000 *Grants* £50,000

TRUSTEES Miss S Belk; Revd T White; H J Crossman; M R Cruse; G Russ; Mrs S Haysom; Mrs M Hosking; Mrs A F Kay; Mrs T Kirby; Mrs D P Netcott; Dr R B Pardoe; S P Gillingham.

HOW TO APPLY In writing to the correspondent.

WHO TO APPLY TO P C Dingley-Brown, Secretary, 108 High Street, Portishead, Bristol BS20 6AJ

CC NO 228876   **ESTABLISHED** 1964

■ The J E Posnansky Charitable Trust

WHERE FUNDING CAN BE GIVEN UK and overseas.

WHO CAN BENEFIT Voluntary organisations and charitable groups only, predominantly Jewish. Beneficiaries include Jews and people with a range of diseases and medical conditions, especially HIV and AIDS. Charities benefiting at risk groups, homeless people and those disadvantaged by poverty are also considered.

WHAT IS FUNDED Primarily Jewish charitable organisations, some in the medical and education fields; also child health; homelessness; AIDS charities; work with victims of torture and freedom for people unjustly imprisoned.

WHAT IS NOT FUNDED No grants to individuals.

TYPE OF GRANT One-off.

RANGE OF GRANTS £300–£29,000, although one grant of £110,000 was made.

SAMPLE GRANTS £110,000 to WaterAid; £29,000 to Friends of Magen David Adom; £25,000 to JPAIME; £15,000 to British Wizo; £13,000 to Friends of the Hebrew University of Jerusalem; £10,000 each to Oxfam and Norwood Ravenswood; £5,000 to Medecins Sans Frontieres; £2,500 each to The Sue Ryder Foundation, Leukaemia Research Fund and The Jewish Aid Committee; £2,000 each to B'nai B'rith Hillel Foundation and National Head Injuries Association; £1,000 each to PHAB and St Martin In The Fields Christmas Appeal Fund; £500 each to Action for Kids, Age Concern, Eaves Housing for Women, Greater London Fund for the Blind, Jewish Bereavement Counselling Service, Riding for the Disabled Association, The Samaritans and Toynbee Hall.

FINANCES *Year* 2000–01 *Income* £241,563 *Grants* £398,204 *Assets* £5,619,464

TRUSTEES Lord Mishcon; Philip A Cohen; Gillian Raffles; Anthony Victor Posnansky; P A Mishcon; E J Feather; N S Ponansky.

HOW TO APPLY In writing to the correspondent. The trustees meetings are held in May.

WHO TO APPLY TO The Trustees, c/o Baker Tilly, 2 Bloomsbury Street, London WC1B 3ST *Tel* 020 7413 5100 *Fax* 020 7413 5101

CC NO 210416   **ESTABLISHED** 1962

■ The Mary Potter Convent Hospital Trust

WHERE FUNDING CAN BE GIVEN Nottinghamshire.

WHO CAN BENEFIT Organisations and individuals.

WHAT IS FUNDED The trust makes grants towards the relief of medical and health problems.

WHAT IS NOT FUNDED No grants to non-registered charities, or for capital/building costs.

TYPE OF GRANT Mainly one-off grants, but payments over two or three years may be considered.

RANGE OF GRANTS Up to £25,000.

SAMPLE GRANTS £20,000 each to Mary Magdalen Foundation, Nottinghamshire Hospice and Radford Care Group; £15,000 each to NSPCC Full Stop Appeal, Macmillan Cancer Relief and Sargent Cancer Care; £5,000 each to Age Concern, Headway and Winged Fellowship.

FINANCES *Year* 2000–01 *Income* £187,000 *Grants* £51,000 *Assets* £2,579,793

TRUSTEES John E F Bruce; Sister Jeannette Connell; Mrs Jennifer M Farr; Dr Glyn D Flowerdew; John R M Garratt; Christopher J Howell; Michael F Mason; Frederick T C Pell; Rupert A L Roberts; Sister Colette White.

HOW TO APPLY In writing to the correspondent. Unsuccessful applicants will not be notified.

WHO TO APPLY TO Michael F Mason, Administrator, Massers Solicitors, 15 Victoria Street, Nottingham NG1 2JZ *Tel* 0115 851 1666 *E-mail* michaelm@masser.co.uk

CC NO 1078525   **ESTABLISHED** 1999

■ The Powell Foundation

WHERE FUNDING CAN BE GIVEN Within the Milton Keynes Council area.

WHO CAN BENEFIT Individuals and local organisations benefiting older people and people of any age with disabilities.

WHAT IS FUNDED Grants for the benefit of older people and mentally and physically disabled people. Localised charities working in the fields of community development including supporting voluntary organisations, community arts and recreation, community facilities and services for people with disabilities, healthcare and special needs education.

TYPE OF GRANT One-off grants up to £5,000. Longer term funding for specific projects can be considered. Buildings, capital, feasibility studies, project and start-up costs. One, two and three year funding will also be considered.

SAMPLE GRANTS £192,000 to Milton Keynes Centre for Integrated Living; £100,000 to Milton Keynes Community Trust, an annual grant for distribution to voluntary groups that meet the foundation's criteria; £30,000 to Milton Keynes MIND; £10,000 to Milton Keynes Theatre Pantomime Trip; £8,400 to Pace Centre; £7,500 was distributed to small groups for Christmas parties.

FINANCES *Year* 1999–2000 *Income* £162,000 *Grants* £374,000 *Assets* £3,500,000

TRUSTEES R W Norman; R Hill.

OTHER INFORMATION All grant applications are handled by the Community Trust Milton Keynes on behalf of the foundation.

HOW TO APPLY In writing to the correspondent.

WHO TO APPLY TO Stephanie Gallagher, Grants Manager, c/o Milton Keynes Community Foundation, Acorn House, 381 Midsummer Boulevard, Central Milton Keynes MK9 3HP *Tel* 01908 690276 *Fax* 01908 233635 *E-mail* information@mkcommunityfoundation.co.uk *Website* www.mkcommunityfoundation.co.uk

CC NO 1012786   **ESTABLISHED** 1992

■ Powys Welsh Church Fund

WHERE FUNDING CAN BE GIVEN Powys.

WHO CAN BENEFIT Charitable organisations, churches, chapels, students and apprentices within or having some connection with the county of Powys. Particular preference is given to children and young adults.

WHAT IS FUNDED Community facilities; various community services; advice and information on social issues; health facilities and buildings; and health advocacy. The following are also considered: arts and arts facilities; community arts and recreation; cultural heritage; the conservation of church and historical buildings; the purchase of educational books; community development; support to voluntary and community organisations; and charity or voluntary umbrella bodies. The fund provides grant-aid to assist organisations, bodies and individuals within Powys or providing services or facilities of benefit to its residents in accordance with these areas of interest.

WHAT IS NOT FUNDED Grants are not made to organisations outside Powys or to those that provide services or benefit to residents outside the county. Grants to churches are not given for running costs, interior work, including redecoration and repair/installation of heating systems or for the construction of new buildings. Applications from churches for buildings and for community projects will be considered separately. Individuals may only apply if resident in, or natives of, Powys. Salaries or other employment costs are not funded. The trustees will not make grants of over £100 to organisations which are not registered as a charity with the Charity Commissioners.

TYPE OF GRANT Cash payments paid on a pro rata basis of estimated expenditure. Donations of income of charity only – mainly one-off for a specific project (or part). Core funding rarely considered.

RANGE OF GRANTS Generally up to £3,000.

SAMPLE GRANTS Beriew Methodist Church for external repairs to the chapel; Coleg Trefeca for the 250th anniversary celebrations; Meifod Village Institution and Recreation Association for a replacement bowling pavilion and new green's mower; Montgomeryshire Genealogical society for the publishing of memorial inscriptions from churches and chapels in Montgomeryshire; Radnorshire Wildlife Trust for a computer; Reactive for theatrical events at Powys Special School; St Mary's Church – Llwydiarth for repairs to corbel stones, roof repairs and replacement guttering; St Peter's Church – Machynlleth for the rebuilding of the east wall; and Trefedlwys Eisteddfod Committee for the 2001 annual Eisteddfod.

FINANCES *Year* 2001–02 *Income* £38,023 *Grants* £79,904 *Assets* £1,336,430

TRUSTEES Powys County Council Board.

OTHER INFORMATION Commencement of projects/building works: the committee will very rarely consider applications which are submitted after the project/building works have been commenced. Churches and chapels: repair and restoration work of the main fabric of the building of places of worship will be considered for grant-aid but day to day running costs, constituting maintenance, interior work, including redecoration and repair/installation of heating systems, will not be grant aided. Applications in respect of churches and chapels used for public worship and wider community purposes will be considered separately, and on the same basis as applications in respect of village halls/community centres.

HOW TO APPLY On a form available from the correspondent. Applicant organisations must be able to demonstrate that they are properly constituted and keep proper accounts and financial records. All projects or facilities for which a grant is requested must be open to inspection by appropriate officers. If it is a new project then the applicants should 'demonstrate, if required, that the facility when completed can be viably operated'. Trustees meet to consider grants throughout the year. Applications should be received one month prior to being considered by the trustees.

WHO TO APPLY TO The Director, Economic and Community Regeneration Directorate, Powys County Council, Llandrindod Wells, Powys LD1 5LG

CC NO 507967   **ESTABLISHED** 1974

■ PPP Foundation (formerly PPP Healthcare Medical Trust)

WHERE FUNDING CAN BE GIVEN Unrestricted.

WHO CAN BENEFIT Research organisations, educational institutions, charities, NHS bodies and individuals.

WHAT IS FUNDED Following a recent review of its funding programme, the foundation now aims to improve healthcare delivery by supporting innovative ways of improving health services and the development of healthcare leadership. Funding priorities are: supporting the development of leadership amongst healthcare professionals; capacity building in educational institutions; encouraging health service improvement and redesign initiatives; and supportinig health improvement in the developing world.

WHAT IS NOT FUNDED The foundation has a different list of exclusions for each scheme it runs.

TYPE OF GRANT Typically project grants for up to three years.

RANGE OF GRANTS Varies for each programme, but typically £15,000–£30,000.

SAMPLE GRANTS £290,000 over two years to National Deaf Children's Society to develop family services for deaf children; £268,000 over two and half years for York NHS Trust for a study on whether occupation or activity reduces depression in care homes; £163,000 over three years to Dundee University for a trial of exercise training in older people with heart failure; £105,000 over two years to the Mental Health Foundation looking at the effectiveness of early interventions for children with / or at risk of developing mental health problems; £88,000 to Guys, Kings and St Thomas' Hospitals for a joint study on the effect of ageing; £48,000 to Enuresis Resource and Information Centre to establish a national information service about acquiring bladder and bowel control for children with learning disabilities; £36, 927 to the University of Manchester to produce a website for teenagers promoting self-help for physical and psychological problems; £25,000 to St George's Hospital for a study into prevention of early onset anorexia.

FINANCES *Year* 2001 *Income* £14,305,000 *Grants* £25,811,000 *Assets* £537,286,000

TRUSTEES Sir David Carter, Chairman; Bernard Asher; Lawrence Banks; Prof. Yvonne Carter; Prof. Richard Cooke; Ram Gidoomal; Prof. Mary Marshall; Dr Harry McNeilly; Sir Peter Morris; Prof. Brian Pentecost; Michael Sayers; Dr Elizabeth Vallance; Prof. Sally Macintyre; Prof. Klim McPherson; Prof. John Savill; John Roques.

PUBLICATIONS Guidelines for each grant programme.

HOW TO APPLY In writing to the correspondent.

WHO TO APPLY TO Stephen Thornton, Chief Executive, 13 Cavendish Square, London W1G 0PQ *Tel* 020 7307 2622 *Website* www.pppfoundation.org.uk
CC NO 286967　　　　**ESTABLISHED** 1983

■ Prairie Trust

WHERE FUNDING CAN BE GIVEN Worldwide.

WHO CAN BENEFIT Organisations benefiting those disadvantaged by poverty and victims of war.

WHAT IS FUNDED A small number of organisations working on issues of third world development, the environment, and conflict prevention, and particularly to support policy and advocacy work in these areas.

WHAT IS NOT FUNDED No grants to individuals, for expeditions or for capital projects.

TYPE OF GRANT Core costs and project funding for up to three years will be considered.

RANGE OF GRANTS £250–£10,000. Typical grants £1,000–£5,000, rarely more.

SAMPLE GRANTS £5,500 to Network Foundation; £5,100 to New Economics Foundation; £5,000 each to Lincoln Charitable Trust and UK Social Investment Forum; £3,250 to Oxfam; £2,900 to RESULTS Education; £2,500 each to Oxford Research Group and Pilotlight; £2,250 to Network for Social Change.

FINANCES *Year* 1999–2000 *Income* £27,000 *Grants* £48,000 *Assets* £497,000

TRUSTEES Dr R F Mulder; James Sinclair Taylor; Fenella Rouse.

HOW TO APPLY The trust states: 'As we are a proactive trust with limited funds and administrative help, we are unable to consider unsolicited applications'.

WHO TO APPLY TO The The Administrator, 83 Belsize Park Gardens, London NW3 4NJ *Tel* 020 7722 2105 *Fax* 020 7483 4228
CC NO 296019　　　　**ESTABLISHED** 1987

■ The W L Pratt Charitable Trust

WHERE FUNDING CAN BE GIVEN UK, particularly York, and overseas.

WHO CAN BENEFIT Organisations with worldwide scope; UK welfare organisations and organisations for disabled people; certain local religious and social organisations. This includes those benefiting children and older people, and people who are terminally ill, disabled, disadvantaged by poverty, homeless, and victims of man-made and natural disasters, war and famine.

WHAT IS FUNDED Overseas: to help the developing world by assisting in food production and relief of famine and disease. In the UK: to support religious and social objectives with priority for York and district, including health and community services.

WHAT IS NOT FUNDED UK and overseas grants are restricted to well-known registered charities. No grants to individuals. No grants for buildings or for upkeep and preservation of places of worship.

TYPE OF GRANT One-off for core costs, project and research.

RANGE OF GRANTS £100–£4,600. Average grant £1,000.

SAMPLE GRANTS £4,600 to York Diocesan Board of Finance for the ministry of the Church of England; £2,000 to York Minster Fund; £2,500 to St Leonard's Hospice; £2,400 each to Christian Aid for overseas aid, Royal Commonwealth Society for the Blind for overseas aid, and Wilberforce Home for the Multiple Handicapped; £1,200 each to York CVS and Barnardo's; £1,500 each to York Samaritans and Yorkshire Cancer Relief.

FINANCES *Year* 2001–02 *Income* £52,700 *Grants* £41,600 *Assets* £1,500,000

TRUSTEES J L C Pratt; C M Tetley; C C Goodway.

HOW TO APPLY In writing to the correspondent. Applications will not be acknowledged unless an sae is supplied. Telephone applications are not accepted.

WHO TO APPLY TO C C Goodway, Trustee, Messrs Grays, Duncombe Place, York YO1 7DY *Tel* 01904 634771 *Fax* 01904 610711 *E-mail* christophergoodway@grayssolicitors.co.uk
CC NO 256907　　　　**ESTABLISHED** 1968

■ Premierquote Ltd

WHERE FUNDING CAN BE GIVEN Worldwide.

WHO CAN BENEFIT Jews and people disadvantaged by poverty.

WHAT IS FUNDED Jewish charitable purposes, relief of poverty, general charitable purposes.

FINANCES *Year* 1997–98 *Income* £439,000 *Grants* £236,000 *Assets* £3,500,000

TRUSTEES D Last; Mrs L Last; H Last; M Weisenfeld.

HOW TO APPLY In writing to the correspondent.

WHO TO APPLY TO D Last, Trustee, Harford House, 101–103 Great Portland Street, London W1N 6BH *Tel* 020 8203 0665

CC NO 801957   **ESTABLISHED** 1985

■ Premishlaner Charitable Trust

WHERE FUNDING CAN BE GIVEN UK and worldwide.

WHO CAN BENEFIT Jewish people and people disadvantaged by poverty.

WHAT IS FUNDED To advance orthodox Jewish education; to advance the religion of the Jewish faith in accordance with the orthodox practice; to relieve poverty; other general charitable purposes.

SAMPLE GRANTS £20,000 to a Jewish educational organisation; £1,600 to Lev Efraim; £1,500 to SOFT; £1,000 to Beth Jacob Primary School; £620 to Yeshuos Chaim Synagogue; £250 to Beis Ruzhim Trust.

FINANCES *Year* 1999–2000 *Income* £75,311 *Grants* £47,000

TRUSTEES H C Freudenberger; S Honig; C M Margulies.

HOW TO APPLY In writing to the correspondent.

WHO TO APPLY TO C M Margulies, Trustee, 186 Lordship Road, London N16 5ES

CC NO 1046945   **ESTABLISHED** 1995

■ Simone Prendergast Charitable Trust

WHERE FUNDING CAN BE GIVEN UK, Israel.

WHO CAN BENEFIT Registered charities benefiting: children; older people; ex-service and service people; medical professionals; Christians; Jews; ethnic minority groups; disabled people; victims of abuse; people with Alzheimer's disease, cancer, diabetes, HIV and AIDS, Parkinson's disease and strokes.

WHAT IS FUNDED There is no specific policy. Particular preference is given to charities working in the fields of: religion; arts, culture and recreation; hospices; immunology; historic buildings; pre-school education; theatres and opera houses; crime prevention schemes; play schemes; and campaigning for racial equality, for better relations and against discrimination.

WHAT IS NOT FUNDED No grants to non-registered charities or to individuals.

TYPE OF GRANT Core costs, one-off and research. Funding up to three years will be considered.

SAMPLE GRANTS £6,700 to WIZO Charitable Foundation; £5,100 to East Grinstead Medical Research Trust; £5,000 to Jewish Lads' and Girls' Brigade; £3,000 to World Jewish Relief; £1,000 each to Anglo-Israel Association and Royal College of Surgeons; £750 to British ORT.

FINANCES *Year* 1999–2000 *Income* £36,000 *Grants* £39,350 *Assets* £664,000

TRUSTEES Dame Simone Prendergast; C H Prendergast; Mrs J Skidmore.

HOW TO APPLY In writing to the correspondent, at any time. Trustees meet twice a year. Clear details of the project are required – no acknowledgements will be sent.

WHO TO APPLY TO Dame Simone Prendergast, Trustee, Flat C, 52 Warwick Square, London SW1V 2AJ *Tel* 020 7821 7653

CC NO 242881   **ESTABLISHED** 1961

■ The Nyda and Oliver Prenn Foundation

WHERE FUNDING CAN BE GIVEN UK, with a preference for London.

WHO CAN BENEFIT Registered charities, especially those in London.

WHAT IS FUNDED Arts, education, and health. The trustees prefer to make donations to charities whose work they have come across through their own research.

WHAT IS NOT FUNDED Local projects outside London are unlikely to be considered.

TYPE OF GRANT Various.

RANGE OF GRANTS Mostly £500–£10,000.

SAMPLE GRANTS £100,000 to Tate Gallery Foundation; £30,000 to UCL Development Fund; £10,000 each to Rambert Dance Company, and Union Dance Trust, £3,216 to SOS Poland; £3,000 each to Amadeus Scholarship Fund, British Red Cross and Contemporary Art Society; £2,500 each to Hearing Dogs for the Deaf and University of Sussex.

FINANCES *Year* 2000–01 *Income* £244,752 *Grants* £192,416 *Assets* £623,979

TRUSTEES O S Prenn; Mrs N M McDonald Prenn; S Lee; Mrs C P Cavanagh; A D S Prenn; N C N Prenn.

HOW TO APPLY Unsolicited applications are not acknowledged.

WHO TO APPLY TO T Cripps, Moore Stephens, Chartered Accountants, 1 Snow Hill, London EC1A 2EN

CC NO 274726   **ESTABLISHED** 1977

■ The Douglas Prestwich Charitable Trust

WHERE FUNDING CAN BE GIVEN UK, with a possible preference for the south of England.

WHO CAN BENEFIT Hospices and other organisations benefiting older people and people with disabilities.

WHAT IS FUNDED Help to older people, especially through hospices, and help for people with disabilities, especially through mechanical and other aids.

RANGE OF GRANTS Income grants usually £5,0000; capital grants up to £50,000.

FINANCES *Year* 2001–02 *Income* £100,515

TRUSTEES Mrs M M Prestwich; D J Duthie; D D C Monro.

OTHER INFORMATION The income figure for 2001–02 was exceptionally high. In the years between 1996 and 2001 it had been in the range of £17,774 and £31,329. Total expenditure for 2001/02 was £45,000.

HOW TO APPLY In writing to the correspondent; however, please note the trust stated that its 'present policy ... is only to consider grants to institutions which it has already assisted and where the need continues to be shown'.

WHO TO APPLY TO D D C Monro, Trustee, 8 Great James Street, London WC1N 3DF *Tel* 020 7636 8701

CC NO 1017597   **ESTABLISHED** 1993

■ The William Price Charitable Trust

WHERE FUNDING CAN BE GIVEN Fareham's town parishes of St Peter & St Paul, Holy Trinity with St Columba and St John the Evangelist. Please note this area is that of the Fareham town parishes and not the borough of Fareham.

WHO CAN BENEFIT Individuals and schools benefiting children, young people (under 25) and the Church of England.

WHAT IS FUNDED Schools for educational benefits not normally provided by the local education authority, and individuals for help with fees, travel, outfits, clothing, books and so on. Also promoting education in the doctrines of the Church of England.

WHAT IS NOT FUNDED Grants cannot be given to those living outside the Fareham town parishes.

TYPE OF GRANT One-off.

SAMPLE GRANTS In 2001–02 grant expenditure mainly went to the 20 schools in the beneficial area. The sum of £9,080 was disbursed to 79 young people in need.

FINANCES *Year* 2001–02 *Income* £158,000 *Grants* £141,125 *Assets* £4,100,000

TRUSTEES William Price Trust Company.

HOW TO APPLY Whenever possible applications should be made through the establishment concerned. Application forms are available from the correspondent. Larger grants are considered by trustees on a six monthly basis. Closing dates are 1 March and 1 September. Smaller grants for individual assistance are considered quickly, and normally in less than one month.

WHO TO APPLY TO Cdr J A Bagg, Clerk, 59 Kiln Road, Fareham, Hampshire PO16 7UH *Tel* 01329 280636

CC NO 307319   **ESTABLISHED** 1989

■ Sir John Priestman Charity Trust

WHERE FUNDING CAN BE GIVEN County borough of Sunderland and historic counties of Durham and York.

WHO CAN BENEFIT Local organisations benefiting children and older people, clergy, people of the Church of England and people disadvantaged by poverty.

WHAT IS FUNDED The trust includes a clothing fund to provide clothing for poor children resident in Sunderland who attend churches and Sunday school; and a general fund to provide for the relief of people who are poor, elderly or infirm. Also the establishment of hospitals and convalescent homes; the advancement of education of candidates for Holy Orders who after ordination will work in Durham for not less than six years; the benefit of the Church of England.

SAMPLE GRANTS £7,500 to Dean & Chapter of Durham Cathedral; £6,940 to Durham Diocesan Board of Finance; £6,308 to Outward Bound Trust; £6,000 to St Peter's Bishopton; £5,000 each to Durham Association of Boys Clubs, Friends of All Saints Parish Church Northallerton, St Mary's Ebberston, St Matthew's Newbottle, St Peter's Driffield, and St Peter and St Felix Ravensworth.

FINANCES *Year* 1999 *Income* £354,479 *Grants* £286,116 *Assets* £8,799,875

TRUSTEES J R Heslop; R W Farr; T R P S Norton; P W Taylor.

OTHER INFORMATION Grants were broken down as follows: for the aged and infirm £4,300; establishment and maintenance of hospitals for the poor of Durham £2,000; charitable

organisations £132,848; maintenance of churches and church buildings £110,900; relief and maintenance of clergy £25,240; and other £10,328.

HOW TO APPLY In writing to the correspondent. The trustees meet in January, April, July and October. Applications should include clear details of the need the project is designed to meet plus estimates, where appropriate, and details of amounts subscribed to date.

WHO TO APPLY TO P W Taylor, Trustee, McKenzie Bell, 19 John Street, Sunderland SR1 1JG *Tel* 0191 567 4857

CC NO 209397   **ESTABLISHED** 1931

■ The Primrose Hill Trust

WHERE FUNDING CAN BE GIVEN UK and worldwide.

WHO CAN BENEFIT People detained at Her Majesty's pleasure.

WHAT IS FUNDED The trust currently supports matters relating to prison welfare.

SAMPLE GRANTS In 1998–99: £48,000 to Prison Video Trust; £5,000 to The Brandon Centre; £2,500 to Asylum Aid.

FINANCES *Year* 2000–01 *Income* £28,660 *Grants* £20,000

TRUSTEES Richard Astor; Mrs Sarah Astor; Stuart Kemp.

HOW TO APPLY In writing to the correspondent.

WHO TO APPLY TO Stuart G Kemp, Trustee, Sayers Butterworth, 18 Bentink Street, London W1U 2AR *Tel* 020 7935 8504

CC NO 326957   **ESTABLISHED** 1985

■ The Primrose Trust

WHERE FUNDING CAN BE GIVEN UK.

WHO CAN BENEFIT Registered charities.

WHAT IS FUNDED General charitable purposes.

WHAT IS NOT FUNDED Grants are given to registered charities only.

RANGE OF GRANTS £1,000–£20,000.

SAMPLE GRANTS £20,000 each to Bluebell Charitable Trust and Langford Trust; £15,000 to National Federation of Badger Groups; £10,000 each to Fovant Youth Club, Gloucestershire Wildlife Rescue and Raptor Rescue; £5,000 each to Clwyd Special Riding Centre, Sail Training Centre Association, Splitz and Warwickshire Scout Council; £2,000 to Children's Transplant Centre.

FINANCES *Year* 2000–01 *Income* £146,938 *Grants* £112,000 *Assets* £3,237,850

TRUSTEES M G Clark; Susan Boyes-Korkis.

HOW TO APPLY In writing to the correspondent, including a copy of the most recent accounts. The trust does not wish to receive telephone calls.

WHO TO APPLY TO M Clark, Trustee, 5 South View, Horton, Wiltshire SN10 3NA

CC NO 800049   **ESTABLISHED** 1986

■ The Prince Foundation

WHERE FUNDING CAN BE GIVEN Southern England.

WHO CAN BENEFIT Organisations benefiting people with cancer and heart disease.

WHAT IS FUNDED General charitable purposes. Particularly charities working in the fields of churches, cancer research and training for community development. Funding for schools and colleges and scholarships will also be considered.

WHAT IS NOT FUNDED No grants to individuals.

TYPE OF GRANT Capital, core costs and research. Funding for up to and over three years will be considered.

SAMPLE GRANTS £6,000 to Kosovo Crisis Appeal (for costs); £5,000 to sponsor two students at the Royal Academy of Dramatic Arts (for annual fees); over £2,000 each to Wessex Cardiac Trust and Minstead Training Project; £1,000 each to Rose Road Childrens Appeal, Romsey Hospital Appeal and Brohenhurst Manor Golf Club Lady Captains Charity.

FINANCES *Year* 2000 *Income* £126,000 *Grants* £25,000 *Assets* £9,035

TRUSTEES A C Prince; Mrs S J Prince; D L Morgan.

HOW TO APPLY The trust's funds are committed for the foreseeable future and applications are therefore not invited.

WHO TO APPLY TO Mrs C Cox, Accountant, c/o Messrs Rothman Pantall & Co, 10 Romsey Road, Eastleigh, Hampshire SO50 9AL *Tel* 023 8061 4555

CC NO 328024   **ESTABLISHED** 1988

■ The Prince of Wales's Charitable Foundation

WHERE FUNDING CAN BE GIVEN UK.

WHO CAN BENEFIT Registered charities in which the Prince of Wales has a particular interest.

WHAT IS FUNDED Particularly the fields of environment, architecture, heritage and health.

WHAT IS NOT FUNDED No grants to individuals.

TYPE OF GRANT One-off grants for capital or core expenditure.

RANGE OF GRANTS Usually £100–£15,000, typical grant £500.

SAMPLE GRANTS £302,100 to Phoenix Trust; £104,500 to Foundation for Integrated Medicine; £100,000 to Rare Breed Survival Trust; £70,000 to Soil Association; £62,699 to United World colletges; £30,000 to dancebase; £25,000 to Mihai Eminnescu Trust; £13,000 to Bristol Cancer Help Centre; £10,000 each to National Osteoporosis Society and Tetbury Hospital Trust.

FINANCES *Year* 2001–02 *Income* £1,179,000 *Grants* £923,000 *Assets* £4,548,000

TRUSTEES Rt Hon. Earl Peel; Sir Michael Peat; Mrs Fiona Shackleton.

HOW TO APPLY In writing to the correspondent, with full details of the project including financial data.

WHO TO APPLY TO David Hutson, The Prince of Wales's Office, St James's Palace, London SW1A 1BS *Tel* 020 7930 4832 *Fax* 020 7930 0119

CC NO 277540   **ESTABLISHED** 1979

■ The Prince Philip Trust Fund

WHERE FUNDING CAN BE GIVEN The royal borough of Windsor and Maidenhead.

WHO CAN BENEFIT Individuals and organisations.

WHAT IS FUNDED The promotion of artistic appreciation, knowledge and understanding of literature, the fine arts and sciences; the training of young people through undertaking voluntary work; the provision of recreational facilities.

TYPE OF GRANT On-going revenue funding; grants to maintained schools for building improvements, equipment or school activities; grant-aid to activities or items that should properly be funded by local authorities e.g. social services.

RANGE OF GRANTS £100–£5,000.

SAMPLE GRANTS In 1999–2000: £4,000 to Paul Bevan Foundation; £2,800 to Pact House Windsor; £2,500 to St George's School; £2,000 each to All Saints Church Bedworth, Methodist Church Maidenhead, Old Windsor Youth Club, Relate Middle Thames, Sea Cadets Corps, Sunningdale Women's Institute, and Windsor and Maidenhead District Sports Association for the Disabled.

FINANCES *Year* 1999–2000 *Income* £68,898 *Grants* £48,685 *Assets* £947,558

TRUSTEES HRH Prince Philip; Mayor of Windsor & Maidenhead; Lord Lieutenant of Berkshire; Headteacher of Eton College; Governor of Windsor Castle; J E Handcock; K McGarry; A R Wilson; P B Everett; Lady Palmer; G B Blackler; Mrs R Ussher.

HOW TO APPLY In writing to the correspondent.

WHO TO APPLY TO Kevin M McGarry, Secretary, 10 Cadogan Close, Holyport, Maidenhead, Berkshire SL6 2JS *Tel* 01628 639577

CC NO 272927   **ESTABLISHED** 1977

■ Princess Anne's Charities

WHERE FUNDING CAN BE GIVEN UK.

WHO CAN BENEFIT Registered charities, especially charities in which Princess Anne has a particular interest.

WHAT IS FUNDED Social welfare, medical research and care, children and youth, wildlife.

WHAT IS NOT FUNDED No grants to individuals.

TYPE OF GRANT Core, capital and project support all considered.

SAMPLE GRANTS £54,100 towards children and youth; £48,000 towards social welfare; £23,275 to medical causes; £22,850 towards education; £7,000 towards animals; £6,500 towards the armed forces; £5,000 towards environment; £2,000 for general charitable purposes.

FINANCES *Year* 2000–01 *Income* £113,506 *Grants* £168,725 *Assets* £4,197,246

TRUSTEES Hon. M T Bridges; Commodore T J H Laurence; B Hammond.

HOW TO APPLY Trustees meet to consider applications in January, and applications need to be received by November. 'The trustees are not anxious to receive unsolicited general applications as these are unlikely to be successful and only increase the cost of administration of the charity.'

WHO TO APPLY TO Capt. N Wright, Buckingham Palace, London SW1A 1AA

CC NO 277814   **ESTABLISHED** 1979

■ The Priory Foundation

WHERE FUNDING CAN BE GIVEN UK.

WHO CAN BENEFIT Registered charities, especially those benefiting children.

WHAT IS FUNDED General charitable purposes.

FINANCES *Year* 1998 *Grants* £198,000 *Assets* £4,500,000

TRUSTEES N W Wray; L E Wray; M Kelly; T W Bunyard.

HOW TO APPLY In writing to the correspondent.

WHO TO APPLY TO The Trustees, 20 Thayer Street, London W10 2DD

CC NO 295919   **ESTABLISHED** 1986

■ The Priory of Scotland of the Order of St John of Jerusalem

WHERE FUNDING CAN BE GIVEN Scotland.

WHO CAN BENEFIT Hospitals, hospices, charities concerned with health, welfare, mountain rescue, and disability.

WHAT IS FUNDED Local initiatives providing services and supplies for people who are ill or disabled; vehicles and bases for mountain rescue teams; vehicles for other charities.

FINANCES *Year* 1999–2000 *Income* £1,100,000 *Grants* £314,000 *Assets* £14,000,000

HOW TO APPLY In writing to the correspondent. Trustees meet in November and December; applications should be received the preceding two months.

WHO TO APPLY TO Mrs Joan Blair, 21 St John Street, Edinburgh EH8 8DG *Tel* 0131 556 8711 *Fax* 0131 558 3250 *E-mail* scotstj@aol.com

SC NO SC000262

■ Prison Service Charity Fund

WHERE FUNDING CAN BE GIVEN UK.

WHO CAN BENEFIT Organisations only through prison staff.

WHAT IS FUNDED The trust does not accept outside applications – the person making the application has got to be a member of staff.

FINANCES *Year* 2001 *Income* £115,631 *Grants* £70,000 *Assets* £430,000

TRUSTEES A N Joseph, Chair; D Magill; C F Smith; Revd P Beaman; P McFall; R Howard.

HOW TO APPLY The trust does not accept outside applications – the person making the application has to be a member of staff.

WHO TO APPLY TO The Trustees, 68 Hornby Road, Walton, Liverpool L9 3DF *Tel* 0151 524 0537

CC NO 801678   **ESTABLISHED** 1989

■ The Privy Purse Charitable Trust

WHERE FUNDING CAN BE GIVEN UK.

WHO CAN BENEFIT Registered charities.

WHAT IS FUNDED General charitable purposes.

RANGE OF GRANTS Mostly up to £10,000.

SAMPLE GRANTS £72,000 to Choristers' School for fees; £38,000 to Hampton Court Place for the Chapel Royal; £35,000 to St James's Place for the Chapel Royal; £21,000 to Sandringham Group of Parishes; £11,000 to The Queen's Chorister for scholarships.

FINANCES *Year* 2000–01 *Income* £337,985 *Grants* £293,160 *Assets* £2,371,619

TRUSTEES Sir M C Peat; G N Kennedy; I McGregor.

HOW TO APPLY The trust makes donations to a wide variety of charities, but does not respond to applications.

WHO TO APPLY TO Ian McGregor, Trustee, Buckingham Palace, London SW1A 1AA *Tel* 020 7930 4832 *E-mail* privpurse@royal.gov.uk

CC NO 296079   **ESTABLISHED** 1987

■ The Proven Family Trust

WHERE FUNDING CAN BE GIVEN Cumbria, Halton, Knowsley, Liverpool, St Helens, Sefton, Warrington and Wirral.

WHO CAN BENEFIT Organisations benefiting children and older people; those in care, fostered and adopted; and animals. Support may be given to at risk groups and people who are disabled, disadvantaged by poverty, homeless, victims of abuse or domestic violence or who have Alzheimer's disease, arthritis and rheumatism, asthma, cancer, motor neurone disease, multiple sclerosis, Parkinson's disease or sight loss.

WHAT IS FUNDED Charities working in the fields of holiday and respite accommodation; volunteer bureaux; religious and historic buildings; health; community facilities and services; and animal welfare. Other charitable purposes will be considered.

WHAT IS NOT FUNDED No grants to individuals.

TYPE OF GRANT One-off grants for up to three years. Research grants will be considered.

RANGE OF GRANTS Up to £5,000.

SAMPLE GRANTS In 1998: £5,000 to Zoe's Hospice for an indoor pool; £2,500 each to Calvert Trust for a pool for people who are disabled and Stainburn School towards a minibus for disabled children; £1,372 to Arthritis Care for an outreach visitor; £1,350 to Harvest Trust for a week's holiday for poor children; £1,000 each to Cumbria Hospice at Home and Parish of Cockermouth and Embleton for church repairs; £500 each to Rising Sun for a 24-hour drugs helpline, All Saints Primary School for help with children with autism, and Sequal Trust for help to a child with cerebral palsy.

FINANCES *Year* 2001–02 *Income* £38,733

TRUSTEES G R Quigley; Ms D R Proven; M C Taxman; C J Worthington.

HOW TO APPLY In writing to the correspondent, for consideration twice a year.

WHO TO APPLY TO Dorothy Proven, Trustee, 35 The Mount, Papcastle, Cockermouth, Cumbria CA13 0JY *Tel* 01900 822307

CC NO 1050877   **ESTABLISHED** 1995

■ The Provincial Grand Charity of the Province of Derbyshire

WHERE FUNDING CAN BE GIVEN Derbyshire.

WHO CAN BENEFIT Masons and dependants; other charitable organisations.

WHAT IS FUNDED Masonic charities and general charitable purposes.

FINANCES *Year* 1999–2000 *Income* £230,000 *Grants* £49,000 *Assets* £1,100,000

TRUSTEES J T Clewes; S Evans; J G R Rudd.

HOW TO APPLY In writing to the correspondent.

WHO TO APPLY TO Graham Sisson, The Masonic Hall, 457 Burton Road, Littleover, Derby DE23 6XX *Tel* 01332 769702

CC NO 701963   **ESTABLISHED** 1989

■ The John Pryor Charitable Trust

WHERE FUNDING CAN BE GIVEN UK.

WHO CAN BENEFIT Medical research and homelessness charities.

WHAT IS FUNDED At present the trustees are concentrating on a number of charities personally known to them. These include medical research and homeless charities. No new applications can therefore be entertained.

WHAT IS NOT FUNDED No grants to individuals.

TYPE OF GRANT Recurrent and one-off.

RANGE OF GRANTS £500–£1,000, exceptionally higher.

SAMPLE GRANTS 1997–98: £10,000 to Help the Hospices; £5,000 to Whale and Dolphin Conservation Society; £1,000 each to Research into Ageing, Institute of Orthopaedics, National Osteoporosis Society, Marie Curie Cancer Care, Imperial Cancer Research Fund, Multiple Sclerosis Research Trust, Multiple Sclerosis

Think carefully about every application. Is it justified?

731

Society, and Liverpool School of Tropical Medicine.

FINANCES *Year* 2000–01 *Income* £26,424

TRUSTEES Mrs J H Pryor; M F Cook; A W Cook; Mrs E Dixon.

HOW TO APPLY In writing to the correspondent. Initial telephone calls are not welcome. However, the trust advises that no applications from new charities can be considered as all funds are going to charities already supported.

WHO TO APPLY TO Mrs J H Pryor, Trustee, The Old Cricketers, Passfield, Nr Liphook, Hampshire GU30 7RU

CC NO 275605 **ESTABLISHED** 1977

■ The Ronald & Kathleen Pryor Charitable Trust

WHERE FUNDING CAN BE GIVEN Sheffield and surrounding areas.

WHO CAN BENEFIT Registered charities only. Organisations benefiting children and older people, victims of crime and people with arthritis and rheumatism, cancers, cerebral palsy and sight loss.

WHAT IS FUNDED Sickness, disability, youth institutions, cancer research. Particularly charities working in the fields of: music and theatre; acute healthcare; hospices and hospitals; conservation; zoos and parks; care in the community; crime prevention schemes; and holidays and outings.

WHAT IS NOT FUNDED No grants to individuals.

TYPE OF GRANT One-off funding for up to and over three years will be considered.

RANGE OF GRANTS £250–£5,000.

SAMPLE GRANTS £10,000 each to North of England Zoological Society and RNLI.

FINANCES *Year* 2001 *Income* £32,000
Grants £30,000

TRUSTEES P W Lee; J D Grayson; R D Littlewood.

HOW TO APPLY In writing to the correspondent for consideration in May and October.

WHO TO APPLY TO J A Douglas, Edward Pryor & Son Ltd, Egerton Street, Sheffield S1 4JX *Tel* 0114 276 6044
E-mail thepryorcharity@pryormarking.com

CC NO 276868 **ESTABLISHED** 1979

■ The Puebla Charitable Trust

WHERE FUNDING CAN BE GIVEN Worldwide.

WHO CAN BENEFIT Organisations benefiting people disadvantaged by poverty living in both urban and rural areas.

WHAT IS FUNDED 'At present, the council limits its support to charities which assist the poorest sections of the population and community development work – either of these may be in urban or rural areas, both in the UK and overseas.'

WHAT IS NOT FUNDED No grants for capital projects, religious institutions, research or institutions for people who are disabled. Individuals are not supported and no scholarships are given.

RANGE OF GRANTS Normally £5,000–£20,000, over a number of years where possible.

SAMPLE GRANTS £20,000 to Wandsworth and Merton Law Centre; £15,000 each to Child Poverty Action Group and Shelter; £10,000 each to Action on Development, Cambodian Trust, Immigrants Aid and Medical Foundation for the Victims of Torture.

FINANCES *Year* 2000–01 *Income* £108,373
Grants £90,000 *Assets* £2,447,901

TRUSTEES J Phipps; M A Strutt.

HOW TO APPLY In writing to the correspondent. The trustees meet in July. The trust is unable to acknowledge applications.

WHO TO APPLY TO The Clerk, Ensors, Cardinal House, 46 St Nicholas Street, Ipswich IP1 1TT

CC NO 290055 **ESTABLISHED** 1984

■ The Puri Foundation

WHERE FUNDING CAN BE GIVEN Nottinghamshire, India (particularly the towns of Mullan Pur near Chandigarh and Ambala).

WHO CAN BENEFIT Organisations benefiting: children; young adults; students; Hindus; at risk groups; those disadvantaged by poverty; and socially isolated people.

WHAT IS FUNDED Welfare, community centres and the furtherance of Hinduism. The trust aims to: relieve those in conditions of need, hardship or distress; advance education; provide facilities for recreation; and relieve and rehabilitate young unemployed people in the Nottinghamshire area.

WHAT IS NOT FUNDED No grants are given for holidays.

RANGE OF GRANTS Minimum of £50.

SAMPLE GRANTS £299,000 for a new school building in Mullan Pur; £50,000 each to British Council for a library in Chandigarh and University of Nottingham for a scholarship endowment fund; £35,765 to National Defence Fund – India to assist the families of soldiers killed in the Kargil Sector; £5,000 each to University of Nottingham for a charity cricket match, Labour Friends of India for assistance to send Labour MPs to India, and Mozambique Appeal for disaster relief; £4,739 to City of London School for Girls for school fees; £2725 to Queen's College – London for school fees; £2,500 to Nottingham Racial Equality Council for a seminar arranged by Nottinghamshire Police following the Lawrence Inquiry.

FINANCES *Year* 1999–2000 *Income* £765,000
Grants £475,000 *Assets* £3,100,000

TRUSTEES N R Puri; A Puri; U Puri; Arwind Puri.

HOW TO APPLY In writing to the correspondent.

WHO TO APPLY TO N R Puri, Trustee, Environment House, 6 Union Road, Nottingham NG3 1FH *Tel* 0115 901 3000 *Fax* 0115 901 3100

CC NO 327854 **ESTABLISHED** 1988

■ The Pye Foundation

WHERE FUNDING CAN BE GIVEN Cambridgeshire and the immediate surrounding area.

WHO CAN BENEFIT Organisations benefiting older, retired, ex-service and service people, and people who are disadvantaged. Preference is given to retired employees of the former Pye group of companies.

WHAT IS FUNDED Young and older people; welfare; housing; education and outreach; hospices; day centres; and other charitable purposes.

WHAT IS NOT FUNDED No grants to individuals or students.

TYPE OF GRANT Capital including buildings, one-off, project, running costs, recurring costs and start-up costs. Funding is available for up to three years.

RANGE OF GRANTS £10–£5.000; usually £1,000 or less.

SAMPLE GRANTS In 2000–01: £7,000 (in two grants) to Cambridge Work Relations Group; £5,000 to St Andrew's Church in Chesterton; £2,300 (in two grants) to Cambridge Hospice for the Eastern Region; £2,000 to Castle Project;

£1,100 to Cambridge Housing Trust; £1,000 each to Cambridgeshire Association of Youth Clubs and Ely Cathedral Restoration Trust, and three branches of Age Concern; £900 to Cambridge Cyrenians; £900 (in two grants) to Biggleswade Sea Cadet Unit; £800 to Cancer Relief – Cambridge.

FINANCES *Year* 2001–02 *Income* £86,000 *Grants* £77,000 *Assets* £24,000

TRUSTEES F Keys; A B Dasgupta; J A House; D M J Ball; R R Pascoe; R D Crabtree; J H Hemming; D J Roebuck; M R Pine; R C Ketland.

HOW TO APPLY In writing to the correspondent. The trustees meet regularly to consider applications.

WHO TO APPLY TO The Trustees, Philips House, Cambridge Business Park, Cowley Road, Cambridge CB4 0HF *Tel* 01954 253130

CC NO 267851   **ESTABLISHED** 1974

··

■ Mr and Mrs J A Pye's Charitable Settlement

WHERE FUNDING CAN BE GIVEN UK, with a special interest in the Oxford area and, to a lesser extent, in Reading, Cheltenham and Bristol.

WHO CAN BENEFIT Organisations benefiting children and young adults are given priority, although those benefiting older people will also be funded.

WHAT IS FUNDED General charitable purposes at the trustees' discretion. Of particular interest are: environmental – this subject particularly deals with organic farming matters, conservation generally and health related matters such as pollution research and some wildlife protection; adult health and care – especially causes supporting: post natal depression, schizophrenia, mental health generally and research into the main causes of early death; children's health and care – for physical, mental and learning disabilities, respite breaks and so on; youth organisations – particularly projects encouraging self reliance or dealing with social deprivation; education – nursery, primary, secondary or higher/institutions (not individuals); regional causes around Oxford, Reading, Cheltenham and Bristol – under this category the trustees will consider academic and arts projects.

WHAT IS NOT FUNDED No grants for: organisations that are not recognised charities; activities which are primarily the responsibility of government or some other responsible body; activities which collect funds for subsequent re-distribution to other charities; corporate affiliation or membership of charities; endowment funds; expeditions or overseas charities; fabric appeals for places of worship, other than in geographical locations indicated above; fundraising events or activities; hospitals or medical centres (except for projects that are clearly additional to statutory responsibilities); individual, including students; overseas appeals; promotion of religion.

TYPE OF GRANT One-off, core costs, projects, research, recurring, running and start-up costs, and salaries. Capital costs may be considered. Funding may be given for up to or more than three years. Also interest-free loans.

RANGE OF GRANTS £250–£25,000.

SAMPLE GRANTS £134,000 to Elm Farm Research Centre; £100,000 to Music at Oxford; £50,000 to University College, Oxford; £33,000 to Magdalen College, Oxford; £22,000 to Association for Post Natal Illness; £20,000 to Harris Manchester College, Oxford.

FINANCES *Year* 2001–02 *Income* £634,000 *Grants* £615,000 *Assets* £8,000,000

TRUSTEES G C Pye; J S Stubbings; D S Tallon.

PUBLICATIONS Guidelines for applicants.

HOW TO APPLY There are no application forms but the following information is essential: registered charity number or evidence of an organisation's tax exempt status; brief description of the activities of the charity; the names of the trustees and chief officers (this is more important than patrons); details of the purpose of the application and where funds will be put to use; details of the funds already raised and the proposals for how remaining funds are to be raised; the latest trustees report and full audited or independently examined accounts (which must comply with Charity Commission guidelines and requirements). Trustees meet quarterly to take decisions. Any decision can therefore take up to four months before it is finally taken. However, all applicants are informed of the outcome of their applications and all applications are acknowledged. Telephone contact will usually be counter-productive, as the trust only wishes to respond to written applications.

WHO TO APPLY TO The Administrator, c/o Mercer and Hole, International Press Centre, 76 Shoe Lane, London EC4A 3JB *Tel* 020 7353 1597 *Fax* 020 7353 1748

CC NO 242677   **ESTABLISHED** 1965

··

■ The Pyke Charity Trust

WHERE FUNDING CAN BE GIVEN UK, but mostly local to the trust.

WHO CAN BENEFIT Registered charities only.

WHAT IS FUNDED General charitable purposes, 'whatever inspires the trustees'.

TYPE OF GRANT Annual donations are considered.

RANGE OF GRANTS Up to £15,000.

FINANCES *Year* 2000 *Income* £87,000 *Grants* £114,000 *Assets* £3,700,000

TRUSTEES R van Zwanenberg; J Macpherson; T Harvie Clark.

HOW TO APPLY The trust told us in July 2001 that 'it no longer accepts speculative applications and instead its trustees approach charities that they know well and respect'.

WHO TO APPLY TO Tom Harvie Clark, Trustee, 11 Fountain Close, 22 High Street, Edinburgh EH1 1TF *Tel* 0131 557 2995

CC NO 296418   **ESTABLISHED** 1960

Queen Elizabeth's Charitable Trust

WHERE FUNDING CAN BE GIVEN UK.
WHO CAN BENEFIT Registered charities.
WHAT IS FUNDED General charitable purposes.
FINANCES *Year* 1999–2000 *Income* £49,000 *Grants* £35,000 *Assets* £1,900,000
TRUSTEES The Rt Hon. The Earl of Home; Sir Angus Ogilvy; M H Boyd-Carpenter; Hon. Nicholas Assheton.
HOW TO APPLY In writing to the correspondent.
WHO TO APPLY TO Mrs J Cannon, Farrer & Co., 66 Lincoln's Inn Fields, London WC2A 3LH *Tel* 020 7242 2022
CC NO 1059721   **ESTABLISHED** 1996

Queen Mary's Roehampton Trust

WHERE FUNDING CAN BE GIVEN UK.
WHO CAN BENEFIT Ex-servicemen or women who were disabled in war and their dependants.
WHAT IS FUNDED Grants are made to ex-service and other charities who provide welfare services, or residential or nursing homes for needy men and women who were disabled in war service in the armed services and their widows and dependants; and ex-Merchant Navy and Civil Defence personnel disabled during the 1914–1918 and 1939–1945 wars and their dependants.
WHAT IS NOT FUNDED No grants to individuals.
TYPE OF GRANT Annual recurring, one-off. Also capital and project. Funding may be given for up to two years.
RANGE OF GRANTS Usually £1,000–£50,000.
SAMPLE GRANTS £50,000 to Erskine Hospital for redevelopment; £42,000 to Royal Patriotic Fund Corporation for the TV scheme for war widows; £40,000 each to Army Benevolent Fund, Broughton House for redevelopment, and Ex-Services Mental Welfare Society for Tyrwhitt House; £30,000 to Haig Homes for accommodation improvements; £25,000 to British Limbless Ex-Service Men's Association for a new coach and Royal Naval Benevolent Trust; £20,000 each to Gurkha Welfare Trust and 'Not Forgotten' Association for the TV scheme for war widows.
FINANCES *Year* 2001–02 *Income* £557,000 *Grants* £564,000 *Assets* £10,000,000
TRUSTEES Maj. Gen. R P Craig, Chair; Dr J Watkinson, Vice-Chair; J J Macnamara; Col. S D Brewis; Col. A W Davis; Brig. A K Dixon; Col. T E English; R R Holland; Brig. J O E Moriarty; Dr J G Paterson; R D Wilson.
HOW TO APPLY In writing to the correspondent (seven copies), to be submitted in April or September annually. Details must be given of the number of war disabled and their widows assisted during a recent period of 12 months. In the case of nursing/residential homes, information concerning occupancy will be required under a number of headings (complement, residents, respite holidays, waiting list). Three copies of the latest annual report and accounts should be enclosed.
WHO TO APPLY TO Alan H Baker, Clerk to the Trustees, 13 St George's Road, Wallington, Surrey SM6 OAS *Tel* 020 8395 9980 *Fax* 020 8255 1457 *E-mail* alanbaker13@hotmail.com
CC NO 211715   **ESTABLISHED** 1928

Quercus Trust

WHERE FUNDING CAN BE GIVEN UK.
WHO CAN BENEFIT Established organisations and registered charities.
WHAT IS FUNDED Mainly the arts, and other purposes which seek to further public knowledge, understanding and appreciation of any matters of artistic, aesthetic, scientific or historical interest.
WHAT IS NOT FUNDED No grants to individuals.
TYPE OF GRANT One-off and recurring grants.
RANGE OF GRANTS £375–£100,000.
SAMPLE GRANTS £100,000 to Old Vic Theatre Trust; £31,000 to Tate Gallery Foundation; £15,000 to Gate Theatre; £12,500 to Royal Court Theatre; £10,500 to Young Vic Theatre Company; £7,000 to Royal Opera House Trust; £4,500 to Royal National Theatre; £2,500 each to Guggenheim Foundation and Jazz Xchange Music & Dance Company; £2,000 to British Friends of the Art Museums of Israel; £1,500 to National Gallery Trust; £1,000 each to Royal Academy of Art and Donmar Warehouse Projects Ltd; £500 to Resources for Autism; £375 each to Artangel and Kirov Opera and Ballet.
FINANCES *Year* 2000–01 *Income* £158,532 *Grants* £192,000 *Assets* £6,096,157
TRUSTEES Lord Bernstein of Craigwell; A C Langridge; Kate E Bernstein; Lady Bernstein.
HOW TO APPLY In writing to the correspondent, but please note, the trust states: 'All of the trust's funds are currently earmarked for existing projects. The trust has a policy of not making donations to individuals and the trustees regret that, in order to keep administrative costs to a minimum, they are unable to reply to any unsuccessful applicants.'
WHO TO APPLY TO A C Langridge, Trustee, Chantrey Vellacott, Russell Square House, 10–12 Russell Square, London WC1B 5LF *Tel* 020 7509 9000
CC NO 1039205   **ESTABLISHED** 1993

R

■ R S Charitable Trust

WHERE FUNDING CAN BE GIVEN UK.
WHO CAN BENEFIT Registered charities.
WHAT IS FUNDED Jewish causes and the relief of poverty.
FINANCES *Year* 2000–01 *Income* £517,028 *Grants* £158,828 *Assets* £3,831,024
TRUSTEES M Freudenberger; Mrs M Freudenberger; H C Freudenberger; S N Freudenberger; C Margulies.
HOW TO APPLY In writing to the correspondent.
WHO TO APPLY TO Max Freudenberger, Trustee, 138 Stamford Hill, London N16 6QT
CC NO 1053660   **ESTABLISHED** 1996

■ The R V W Trust

WHERE FUNDING CAN BE GIVEN UK.
WHO CAN BENEFIT Organisations and individuals, particularly composers, musicians and music students.
WHAT IS FUNDED The present policy is to concentrate on young British composers and neglected British music of the past.
WHAT IS NOT FUNDED No grants for local authority or other government-funded bodies, nor degree courses, except first Masters degrees in musical composition. No support for dance or drama courses. No grants for workshops without public performance, private vocal or instrumental tuition or the purchase or repair of musical instruments. No grants for concerts that do not include music by 20th and 21st century composers or for musicals, rock, pop, ethnic, jazz or dance music. No grants for the construction or restoration of buildings.
RANGE OF GRANTS Usually £250–£15,000.
SAMPLE GRANTS In 2001: £87,500 to British Music Information Centre; £60,000 to Society for the Promotion of New Music; £22,000 to BBC Philharmonic Orchestra; £20,000 to Huddersfield Contemporary Music Festival; £18,000 to Royal Philharmonic Society; £15,000 to Sinfonia 21; £8,000 to Oxford Bach Choir; £5,000 each to Bath Festival, Classico Records, Goldberg Ensemble, London Sinfonietta and Birmingham Contemporary Music Festival.
FINANCES *Year* 2002 *Income* £290,687 *Grants* £286,554 *Assets* £1,380,945
TRUSTEES Michael Kennedy, Chair; Lord Armstrong of Ilminster; Sir John Manduell; Mrs Ralph Vaughan Williams; Hugh Cobbe.
HOW TO APPLY In writing to the correspondent, giving project details, at least two months before the trustees meet. Trustees' meetings are held in February, June and October. Masters in Music Composition applicants will only be considered at the June meeting; applications must be received by the middle of April. Further details are available from the trust.
WHO TO APPLY TO Helen Faulkner, Secretary/ Administrator, 16 Ogle Street, London W1W 6JA *Tel* 020 7255 2590 *Fax* 020 7255 2591
CC NO 1066977   **ESTABLISHED** 1958

■ The RAC Foundation for Motoring and the Environment Ltd

WHERE FUNDING CAN BE GIVEN UK.
WHO CAN BENEFIT Organisations benefiting academics and research workers.
WHAT IS FUNDED Promotion for the public benefit, awareness and understanding of the environmental problems of the use of motor vehicles, and to research and investigate solutions to these problems. Research projects undertaken so far include examining the concept of 'car dependence' and the impact of traffic on the North York Moors National Park. Research programme undertaken to examine the impacts of the Okehampton Bypass. Major research project into the future of transport entitled 'Motoring towards 2050'.
TYPE OF GRANT Research.
FINANCES *Year* 2001 *Income* £700,782
TRUSTEES Sir Trevor Chinn; David Liebling; Tim McKeown; Sir Brian McGivern; Sir Christopher Foster; Prof. T M Ridley.
OTHER INFORMATION Charitable expenditure concerns consultancy fees for the research projects. No grants were given in 1995.
HOW TO APPLY In writing to the correspondent.
WHO TO APPLY TO Edmund King, Secretary, 89–91 Pall Mall, London SW1Y 5HS *Website* www.racfoundation.org
CC NO 1002705   **ESTABLISHED** 1991

■ The Mr & Mrs Philip Rackham Charitable Trust

WHERE FUNDING CAN BE GIVEN Norfolk including Norwich.
WHO CAN BENEFIT Registered charities.
WHAT IS FUNDED General charitable purposes, although there is some preference for asthma charities and Samaritans.
WHAT IS NOT FUNDED No grants to individuals.
RANGE OF GRANTS £400–£6,000.
SAMPLE GRANTS In previous years the largest beneficiary has been Samaritans. Other beneficiaries have included Norwich Cathedral Trust, Norfolk Millennium Trust for Carers, Barnham Broom Village Hall, Barnham Broom PCC, Grove Cheshire Home, National Asthma Campaign and Norwich & Norfolk Asthma Society.
FINANCES *Year* 2000–01 *Income* £44,929 *Grants* £30,000 *Assets* £1,000,000
TRUSTEES Neil G Sparrow; C W L Barratt; Ann E S Rush.
HOW TO APPLY In writing to the correspondent.
WHO TO APPLY TO Neil G Sparrow, Trustee, Eversheds, Holland Court, The Close, Norwich NR1 4DX *Tel* 01603 272727 *Fax* 01603 610535 *E-mail* neilsparrow@eversheds.com
CC NO 1013844   **ESTABLISHED** 1992

■ Richard Radcliffe Charitable Trust

WHERE FUNDING CAN BE GIVEN UK.
WHO CAN BENEFIT Charitable organisations.
WHAT IS FUNDED The trust stated its policy as being to support, through making grants to other organisations, the following charitable activities: to assist physically disabled people; to provide technical training to give young people a start in life; to support hospice care for people who are

Think carefully about every application. Is it justified?

735

terminally ill; to provide help for people who are severely deaf and/or blind.

FINANCES *Year* 1998–99 *Income* £27,000 *Grants* £25,000

TRUSTEES Miss I M R Radcliffe; Miss P Radcliffe; A M Bell.

HOW TO APPLY In writing to the correspondent.

WHO TO APPLY TO Adrian Bell, Griffith Smith Solicitors, 32 Keymer Road, Hassocks, West Sussex BN6 8AL *Tel* 01273 843405

CC NO 1068930   **ESTABLISHED** 1998

■ The Radcliffe Trust

WHERE FUNDING CAN BE GIVEN UK.

WHO CAN BENEFIT Organisations and schemes benefiting musicians and those involved in the crafts.

WHAT IS FUNDED Classical music; craft training among young people both at the level of apprenticeships (mostly, but not exclusively, in cathedral workshops) and also at the postgraduate and post-experience levels; the repair and conservation of church furniture, including bells and monuments (such grants are made in England through the Council for the Care of Churches and in Scotland through the Scottish Churches Architectural Heritage Trust – direct applications are not accepted and grants are not made for structural repairs to church buildings, nor for organs); general charitable purposes (where funds permit), except buildings, sponsoring of musical and theatrical performances, medical research, social welfare, support of excellence, or any capital projects to create or improve buildings.

WHAT IS NOT FUNDED No grants to individual applicants. No grants to non-registered charities, or to clear or reduce past debts.

TYPE OF GRANT The trustees do not make grants for longer than a three-year period except in very exceptional circumstances.

RANGE OF GRANTS £15–£25,500.

SAMPLE GRANTS £25,500 to West Dean College; £18,088 to Allegri String Quartet; £17,975 to Birmingham Conservatoire; £12,500 to University of Cambridge for the Faculty of Music; £11,250 to Iona Cathedral Trust; £10,750 to Meridian Trust Association; £10,000 each to Dance Research Committee, Green Wood Trust, and Stained Glass Museum; £9,500 to Textile Conservation Centre.

FINANCES *Year* 1999–2000 *Income* £327,319 *Grants* £354,828 *Assets* £10,700,000

TRUSTEES Lord Cottesloe, Chair; Lord Quinton; Lord Balfour of Burleigh; Christopher J Butcher; Dr Ivor F Guest.

PUBLICATIONS *Dr John Radcliffe and his Trust* by Ivor Guest.

HOW TO APPLY 'Applications for music grants are short-listed for consideration by a panel of musicians who make recommendations, where appropriate; recommended applications are then placed before the trustees for decision. The music panel usually meets in March and October in advance of the trustees' meetings in June and December, and applications should be submitted by the end of January and the end of August respectively to allow time for any further particulars (if so required) to be furnished.' Applications for miscellaneous grants should be in writing and received by the end of April for consideration at the June meeting, or by October for consideration at the December meeting.

WHO TO APPLY TO John Burden, Secretary to the Trustees, 5 Lincoln's Inn Fields, London WC2A 3BT *Tel* 020 7405 1234

CC NO 209212   **ESTABLISHED** 1714

■ Radio Forth Help a Child Appeal

WHERE FUNDING CAN BE GIVEN East central Scotland.

WHO CAN BENEFIT Children only, especially those with special needs (i.e. disability or disadvantage).

WHAT IS FUNDED Grants are given to local children's charities and individual children with special needs in East central Scotland. Support will be given to children requiring healthcare. Funding will also be considered for holiday accommodation, respite, arts activities, community centres and village halls, playgrounds, clubs, holidays, outings and playschemes.

TYPE OF GRANT Capital grants for other than buildings.

FINANCES *Year* 1999 *Grants* £100,000

TRUSTEES B Malcolm; T Gallagher; D Mackinlay; A Wilkie; M Scott; Lady Dunpak; J Kennedy.

HOW TO APPLY Contact the correspondent. Initial telephone calls are welcome and application forms and guidelines are available. No sae required.

WHO TO APPLY TO Lesley Fraser, Charity Coordinator, Forth House, Forth Street, Edinburgh EH1 3LF *Tel* 0131 556 9255 *Fax* 0131 475 1221 *E-mail* lesley.fraser@srh.co.uk *Website* www.forthonline.co.uk

SC NO SC005626   **ESTABLISHED** 1980

■ The Ragdoll Foundation

WHERE FUNDING CAN BE GIVEN UK and worldwide.

WHO CAN BENEFIT Children.

WHAT IS FUNDED The arts.

WHAT IS NOT FUNDED Grants are not given for: work that has already started or will have been completed while the application is being considered; promotion of religion; animal welfare charities; vehicles; emergency relief work; general fundraising or marketing appeals; open-ended funding arrangements; loans or business finance; retrospective grants; replacement of statutory funding; charities which are in serious deficit; holidays of any sort; any large capital, endowment or widely distributed appeal.

RANGE OF GRANTS Typically £500–£20,000, although large-scale grants will be considered.

SAMPLE GRANTS £105,000 to Coram Family London for their Listening to Children Project; £16,000 to Hope and Homes for Children – Sarajevo Children's Home; £10,000 to Sibford School, Oxfordshire for Arts Development Project; £5,000 each to The Drama Practice in Edinburgh to fund Clowndoctors' hospital visits, and Gellideg Infant School in Merthyr Tydfil to fund a nursery garden creative play area; £2,500 to Unicef Colour for Kosovo colouring book project; £1,500 to Tibet Relief Fund of the UK; £950 to Parenting, Education and Support Forum, Romania; £600 to National Youth Theatre.

FINANCES *Year* 1999–2001 *Income* £614,456 *Grants* £155,000 *Assets* £387,592

TRUSTEES Anne Wood; Mark Hollingsworth; Katherine Wood; Ann Burdus.

OTHER INFORMATION The foundation is currently undergoing a review of its grant giving policies. New guidelines will be available in 2004.

HOW TO APPLY A leaflet detailing guidelines and the application process is available in standard and large-scale print, and on audio cassette. Applications should be in writing and should include: the precise purpose for the grant and how it will make a difference; full budget details (including how the budget has been determined); total grant required; information about potential partners from whom other sources of income are being sought, where relevant, including any firm commitments of support; full information about the aims and purposes of your organisation or project including your legal status and registered charity number; latest annual report and audited accounts; and a clear indication of how the project will be monitored and evaluated. The trustees meet in April and October to review applications: applications should be submitted by 1 March for a decision by 1 July, and by 1 September for a decision by 1 December. The trust aims to issue a letter of acknowledgement within 14 days of receipt of an application.

WHO TO APPLY TO Russell House, Ely Street, Stratford upon Avon CV37 6LW *Tel* 01789 404100 *E-mail* info@ragdollfoundation.org.uk *Website* www.ragdollfoundation.org.uk

CC NO 1078998   **ESTABLISHED** 2000

■ **The Rainford Trust**

WHERE FUNDING CAN BE GIVEN Worldwide, with a preference for areas in which Pilkington plc have works and offices, especially St Helens and Merseyside.

WHO CAN BENEFIT Individuals, charitable and voluntary organisations benefiting people of all ages.

WHAT IS FUNDED The trust considers applications from organisations that aim to enhance the quality of community life and helps initiate and promote special projects by charitable organisations which seek to provide new kinds of employment. Assistance is given to programmes whose objects are the provision of medical care, including holistic medicine, the advancement of education and the arts and the improvement of the environment. Applications from religious bodies and individuals will be considered if they fall within the scope of these aims.

WHAT IS NOT FUNDED Funding for the arts is restricted to St Helens only. Applications from individuals for grants for educational purposes will be considered only from applicants who are normally resident in St Helens.

TYPE OF GRANT Buildings, capital, core costs, project, research, salaries and start-up costs will be considered. Only exceptionally will grants be given in consecutive years, up to a maximum of three years.

RANGE OF GRANTS £100–£8,000 ; but mainly for £1,000 or under.

SAMPLE GRANTS £6,000 to Clonter Opera for All; £5,000 each to Citadel Arts Centre and Clonter Opera for All; £2,000 each to Foundation for the Prevention of Blindness and VSO; £1,200 to Farm Africa; £1,000 each to British Blind Sport Royal School of the Blind – Liverpool, St Helens and District Women's Aid, and The Willow Trust.

FINANCES *Year* 2001–02 *Income* £283,169 *Grants* £101,075 *Assets* £4,712,156

TRUSTEES Mrs J Graham; A L Hopkins; Mrs A J Moseley; H Pilkington; Lady Pilkington; R E Pilkington; R G Pilkington; Mrs I Ratiu.

HOW TO APPLY On a form available from the correspondent. Applications should be accompanied by latest accounts and cost data on projects for which funding is sought. Applicants may apply at any time. Only successful applications will be acknowledged.

WHO TO APPLY TO W H Simm, Secretary, c/o Pilkington plc, Prescot Road, St Helens, Merseyside WA10 3TT *Tel* 01744 20574 *Fax* 01744 20574

CC NO 266157   **ESTABLISHED** 1973

■ **The Peggy Ramsay Foundation**

WHERE FUNDING CAN BE GIVEN British Isles.

WHO CAN BENEFIT Individuals and organisations benefiting playwrights. Also playwrights' family members disadvantaged by poverty.

WHAT IS FUNDED The assistance of theatre and television writers and the encouragement of new playwriting. Relief of poverty for writers' families.

WHAT IS NOT FUNDED No grants are made for productions or writing not for the theatre. Commissioning costs are often considered as part of production costs. Course fees are not considered. Aspiring writers without some production record are not usually considered.

TYPE OF GRANT Grants awarded for projects, recurring costs and salaries, for up to three years.

RANGE OF GRANTS £500–£20,000. Maximum of £1,000 for word processors and £5,000 for individuals.

SAMPLE GRANTS £20,000 to Theatre Centre Limited; £10,000 to Paines Plough; £6,500 to Contact Theatre; £6,000 to Eastern Angles Theatre Company Limited; £6,000 in total to Warehouse Theatre Company Limited; £5,000 each to UK Arts Explore/Festcep, TAPS and The George Devine Memorial Fund; £4,000 each to The Ashton Group Contemporary Theatre Limited and Magnetic North Theatre Productions Limited; £3,000 each to Wilson Wilson Company and Production Line; £2,000 each to Artists in Exile – Gog Theatre, New Perspectives Theatre Company, PMA Award, Stellar Quines, Theatre & Beyond and Union Theatre.

FINANCES *Year* 2001 *Income* £357,000 *Grants* £202,000 *Assets* £5,049,250

TRUSTEES Laurence Harbottle; Simon Callow; John Welch; Michael Codron; Sir David Hare; John Tydeman; Baroness McIntosh of Hudnall; Harriet Walker.

HOW TO APPLY Applications should be made by writing a short letter, when there is a promising purpose not otherwise likely to be funded and which will help writers or writing for the stage. Grants are considered at four or five meetings during the year, although urgent appeals can be considered at other times. All appeals are usually acknowledged.

WHO TO APPLY TO G Laurence Harbottle, Trustee, Harbottle & Lewis Solicitors, Hanover House, 14 Hanover Square, London W1S 1HP *Tel* 020 7667 5000 *Fax* 020 7667 5100 *E-mail* laurence.harbottle@harbottle.com *Website* www.peggyramsayfoundation.org

CC NO 1015427   **ESTABLISHED** 1992

■ The Elise Randall Educational Trust

WHERE FUNDING CAN BE GIVEN UK, with a preference for East Sussex.

WHO CAN BENEFIT Schools and colleges and individuals.

WHAT IS FUNDED Promotion of food and textile technology. Support is given to schools and colleges towards equipment and facilities for food and textile technology; students wishing to follow post-16 courses in food and nutrition, childcare, fashion or other aspects of food or fashion technology at college, university or similar educational institution in the UK; men and women wishing to retrain in a career as teachers in food and textile technology; special projects or research programmes into the subjects; and the promotion of the food and textile technology tuition in schools by accredited organisations.

WHAT IS NOT FUNDED Grants are not given as a substitute for funding that should be provided from other sources.

TYPE OF GRANT Matched funding as a one-off or start-up payment.

SAMPLE GRANTS £9,300 to Kids Cookery School; £5,000 each to Blanchedale Girls School, Brooklands School and Falmer High School.

FINANCES *Year* 1999–2000 *Income* £19,000 *Grants* £42,000 *Assets* £458,000

TRUSTEES Mrs A Morris, Chairman; Mrs M Patten; Miss M C Todd; M J Boella; Miss A Ladbury; Mrs A Hudson; Mrs H Osmer.

PUBLICATIONS Leaflet and guidelines.

HOW TO APPLY There is no application form. Applications should be by letter and include: full details of your organisation or group, together with a copy of your constitution, activities and last set of accounts; nature of the request; any information from a third party which should be considered in support of the application. Individuals should provide full details of the applicant including date and place of birth. Also a brief summary of educational qualifications and courses completed, along with the nature of the request and any information from a third party which should be considered in support of the application. All applications will be acknowledged. They are discussed by the trustees three times a year and applicants will be informed of the decision as soon as possible after the relevant meeting. No discussion or correspondence will be entered into concerning any refusal of an application. Where any application is for support over a period of time, the trustees may decide to make a grant for only part of that time and to consider the application again at a future date.

WHO TO APPLY TO C J Middleton, Price & Co., 30–32 Gildredge Road, Eastbourne, East Sussex BN21 4SH *Tel* 01323 639661

CC NO 306380   **ESTABLISHED** 1948

■ The Joseph & Lena Randall Charitable Trust

WHERE FUNDING CAN BE GIVEN Worldwide.

WHO CAN BENEFIT Registered charities (mainly headquarters organisations) benefiting at risk groups and people who are disadvantaged by poverty or socially isolated.

WHAT IS FUNDED Regular support to a selection of charities, providing medical, educational and cultural facilities.

WHAT IS NOT FUNDED No grants to individuals.

TYPE OF GRANT Recurrent and capital grants.

RANGE OF GRANTS £500 upwards.

SAMPLE GRANTS Aldenham School 400 Development Appeal, Diabetes UK, Glyndebourne Festival Opera, Imperial Cancer Research Campaign, London School of Economics and Political Science, and Royal Opera House Development Fund.

FINANCES *Year* 2001–02 *Income* £105,196 *Grants* £129,038 *Assets* £1,745,171

TRUSTEES D A Randall; B Y Randall.

HOW TO APPLY In writing to the correspondent. The trust stated in its 2001–02 report that funds were fully committed, and that it was 'unable to respond to the many worthy appeals'.

WHO TO APPLY TO D A Randall, Trustee, Europa Residence, Place des Moulins, Monte-Carlo, 98000 Monaco *Tel* 00 377 93 50 03 82 *Fax* 00 377 93 25 82 85

CC NO 255035   **ESTABLISHED** 1967

■ The Rank Foundation

WHERE FUNDING CAN BE GIVEN UK.

WHO CAN BENEFIT Organisations working in the areas of promoting Christianity, promoting education and general charitable purposes.

WHAT IS FUNDED (a) Youth programmes: projects in this area are mainly identified by staff who have considerable experience and contacts within the field. The four programmes are Youth or Adult?, Investing in Success, Key Workers, and Rank Volunteer (Gap) Awards. (b) Welfare organisations: especially those concerned with support for people who are elderly or disabled. (c) Promotion of Christianity, substantial and continuing support to an associated charity, the Foundation for Christian Communication Ltd, which means that the funds available for this purpose are effectively committed. (d) Education: primarily concerned with supplementing the fees of pupils at independent schools whose families have become unable to meet all the costs involved. Occasional support is given to health and medical groups, and for environmental and cultural organisations.

WHAT IS NOT FUNDED No grants to: individuals; registered charities on behalf of individuals; non-registered charities; or overseas projects, regardless of whether carried out by a UK charity. Grants are generally not given for: agriculture and farming; cathedrals and churches (except where community facilities are involved); culture; university and school building and bursary funds; or medical research.

TYPE OF GRANT One-off, recurrent, core costs (costs of running the organisation as a whole), capital, research, salaries, buildings.

RANGE OF GRANTS For unsolicited appeals: £250–£10,000.

SAMPLE GRANTS £213,000 to West Yorkshire Youth Association; £193,000 to YMCA Scotland; £90,000 to Disability Wales; £75,000 to Home Farm Trust; £60,000 to Ryedale Special Families; £53,000 to Dundee Drugs and AIDS Project; £52,000 to Scarman Trust; £47,000 to Llanelli Centre; £30,000 to Seven Springs Play and Support Centre; £26,000 a year for three years to Caradon Housing Youth Project.

FINANCES *Year* 2000 *Income* £8,287,000 *Grants* £7,412,000 *Assets* £209,446,000

TRUSTEES F A Packard, chair; M D Abrahams; J A Cave; A E Cowen; M E Davies; Mrs L G Fox; J R Newton; ; D R Peppiatt; V A Powell; Lord Shuttleworth; D R Silk; Earl St Aldwyn; Dr M J Scurr.

OTHER INFORMATION In general, the directors are active in identifying initiatives where they provide substantial support and the vast majority of unsolicited appeals do not receive a grant.

HOW TO APPLY In writing to the correspondent, on one or two sides of A4 with accounts and supporting material. Preliminary enquiries are welcomed. Unsolicited appeals are considered in March, June, September and December. All appeals are acknowledged and applicants advised as to when a decision can be expected.

WHO TO APPLY TO Mrs S Gant, Grants administrator, PO Box 2862, Whitnash, Leamington Spa CV31 2YH *Tel* 01926 744 550
Website www.rankfoundation.com
CC NO 276976   **ESTABLISHED** 1953

■ The Joseph Rank Trust

WHERE FUNDING CAN BE GIVEN UK and Ireland.

WHO CAN BENEFIT Registered charities benefiting Methodists, children, young adults, older people, and people with disabilities.

WHAT IS FUNDED The building, maintenance or adaptation of Methodist Church properties; support for Christian-based social work, categorised under youth projects, community service, religious education and disabled, elderly, health.

WHAT IS NOT FUNDED No grants to individuals, or for charities on behalf of individuals, or for unregistered organisations.

TYPE OF GRANT One-off and recurring.

RANGE OF GRANTS £1,000–£100,000.

SAMPLE GRANTS £149,000 over five years to Chrysalis Youth Project in Castleford, Manchester; £53,000 over three years to Methodist Homes for the Aged; £48,000 over four years to International Student Christian Services; £45,000 over four years to RADICLE; £30,000 to Walworth Methodist Church; £25,000 each to Dorothy Kerin Trust for Christian medical healing, Lee Abbey for a youth centre and Westminster Experiment and Research in Evangelism; £20,000 to Queen Victoria's Seamen's Rest for minibuses.

FINANCES *Year* 2001 *Income* £2,933,000
Grants £2,946,000 *Assets* £65,458,000

TRUSTEES Colin Rank, chair; Revd David Cruise; Revd Paul Hulme; Dr Jean Moon; Ms Gay Moon; Anthony Reddall; Revd Dr R John Tudor; Sue Warner.

OTHER INFORMATION On 31 December 2002, The Joseph Rank Benevolent Trust (CC No. 233099) ceased to operate. As of this date its assets and liabilities were transferred to this new trust which has no additional resources.

HOW TO APPLY Unsolicited appeals are considered although the chance of a grant being made is small. General appeals should be addressed to the correspondent and include full details of the appeal and a copy of the most recent audited accounts. Appeals from within Methodism should only be put forward after consultation with the relevant division of the church.

WHO TO APPLY TO John A Wheeler, 11a Station Road West, Oxted, Surrey RH8 9EE *Tel* 01883 717919 *Fax* 01883 717411
E-mail ranktrust@btopenworld.com
CC NO 1093844   **ESTABLISHED** 1929

■ Ranworth Trust

WHERE FUNDING CAN BE GIVEN UK and developing countries, with a preference for Norfolk.

WHO CAN BENEFIT Registered charities.

WHAT IS FUNDED General including medical research, local community, health and welfare and social charities in the Norfolk area, and national and international charities.

SAMPLE GRANTS £10,000 to Ranworth PCC; £5,000 each to Children's Hospice for the Eastern Region and Norfolk Wildlife Trust; £2,000 each to East Anglian Arts Foundation, Norfolk & Norwich Families House and Norfolk Youth Projects; £1,000 to South Walsham Millennium Group.

FINANCES *Year* 1999–2000 *Income* £121,000
Grants £118,000 *Assets* £4,500,000

TRUSTEES Hon. Mrs J Cator; F Cator; Mrs E A Thistlewayte; C F Cator.

OTHER INFORMATION The trust underwent tremendous growth in 1999–2000, due to the receipt of a donation of £2.9 million from one of the trustees in the form of shares. A substantial one-off donation of over £1.2 million was made to Jubilee Sailing Trust from the sales proceeds of these shares.

HOW TO APPLY In writing to the correspondent.

WHO TO APPLY TO Hon. Mrs J Cator, Trustee, The Old House, Ranworth, Norwich NR13 6HS
Tel 01603 270300
CC NO 292633   **ESTABLISHED** 1985

■ The Fanny Rapaport Charitable Settlement

WHERE FUNDING CAN BE GIVEN North west England.

WHO CAN BENEFIT Registered charities only.

WHAT IS FUNDED General charitable purposes; advancement of Judaism.

WHAT IS NOT FUNDED No grants to individuals.

TYPE OF GRANT One-off and recurring.

RANGE OF GRANTS £50–£10,000. Only in exceptional circumstances do grants exceed £1,000; most grants are in the region of £50–£250.

SAMPLE GRANTS £2,000 to Christie Hospital NHS Trust; £1,000 to Delamere Forest School; £500 to Manchester Charitable Trust; £250 to Disabled Living; £100 to Derian House Children's Hospice.

FINANCES *Year* 2000–01 *Income* £48,700
Grants £36,900 *Assets* £1,150,000

TRUSTEES J S Fidler; N Marks.

HOW TO APPLY Trustees hold meetings twice a year in March/April and September/October with cheques for donations issued shortly thereafter. If the applicant does not receive a cheque by the end of April or October, the application will have been unsuccessful. No applications acknowledged. Copy of applicant's annual accounts not necessary (unless it forms part of a package).

WHO TO APPLY TO J S Fidler, Trustee, Kuit Steinart Levy, 3 St Mary's Parsonage, Manchester M3 2RD *Tel* 0161 832 3434 (C J Tyldesley)
Fax 0161 832 6650 *E-mail* janfidler@kuits.com
CC NO 229406   **ESTABLISHED** 1963

■ The Ratcliff Foundation

WHERE FUNDING CAN BE GIVEN UK, with a preference for local charities in the Midlands, north Wales and Gloucestershire.

WHO CAN BENEFIT Any organisation which has charitable status for tax purposes.

WHAT IS FUNDED General charitable purposes.

Think carefully about every application. Is it justified?

739

WHAT IS NOT FUNDED No grants to individuals.

RANGE OF GRANTS £1,000–£23,000; most are for £5,000 or less.

SAMPLE GRANTS £23,000 to Holy Trinity Belfry Appeal – Conway; £11,000 to CRAB Appeal for Cancer Research – Birmingham; £10,000 to Birmingham Parish Church Renewal Campaign; £6,300 to Acorn Children's Hospice Trust; £5,000 each to Cancer Research Campaign – Kemerton and St Nicholas Church – Kemerton; £4,000 to YMCA Birmingham; £3,500 to British Blind Sport; £3,300 to Birmingham Federation of Clubs for Young People; £3,000 each to Extra Care, Hearing Dogs for Deaf People, Myton Hamlet Hospice, Soil Association, Tewkesbury Welfare & Volunteer Centre and Warwickshire Wildlife Trust.

FINANCES *Year* 2001–2 *Income* £211,605 *Grants* £180,550 *Assets* £2,994,384

TRUSTEES Miss C M Ratcliff; E H Ratcliff; D M Ratcliff; J M G Fea; Mrs G M Thorpe; C J Gupwell.

HOW TO APPLY In writing to the correspondent, by 30 November for consideration by trustees in following January. Grants made once a year only, by 31 March.

WHO TO APPLY TO C J Gupwell, Secretary, Felton & Co, 36 Great Charles Street, Birmingham B3 3RQ *Tel* 0121 236 8181 *Fax* 0121 200 1614 *E-mail* chris.gupwell@feltonandco.co.uk

CC NO 222441 **ESTABLISHED** 1959

■ The Ratcliffe Charitable Trust

WHERE FUNDING CAN BE GIVEN UK.

WHO CAN BENEFIT Registered charities.

WHAT IS FUNDED General charitable purposes.

SAMPLE GRANTS In 1998–99: £1,500 each to Barnardos, Family Holiday Association, New Martin Community Youth Trust, Motor Neurone Disease Association, Orchdale Vale Trust Limited, VSO, Cancer Care Dorset, GUTS, British Council for the Prevention of Blindness, British Laser Appeal, Save the Children, Brainwave, Compaid Trust, Chicks (camping for inner city kids) and South West Thames Kidney Fund.

FINANCES *Year* 1999–2000 *Grants* £37,000 *Assets* £816,000

TRUSTEES James Arthur Brett; Timothy Christopher James Adams.

HOW TO APPLY In writing to the correspondent.

WHO TO APPLY TO Messrs Barlows, 55 Quarry Street, Guildford, Surrey GU1 3UE *Tel* 01483 562901

CC NO 802320 **ESTABLISHED** 1989

■ The E L Rathbone Charitable Trust

WHERE FUNDING CAN BE GIVEN UK, with a strong preference for Merseyside.

WHO CAN BENEFIT Charities benefiting at risk groups, older people, women, and people who are disadvantaged by poverty or socially isolated.

WHAT IS FUNDED General charitable purposes, especially social work charities. Preference to charities which the trust has special interest in, knowledge of, or association with.

WHAT IS NOT FUNDED No grants to individuals seeking support for second degrees.

RANGE OF GRANTS £250–£5,000.

FINANCES *Year* 1999–2000 *Income* £81,698 *Grants* £74,580

TRUSTEES Miss E J Cotton; Mrs S K Rathbone; Mrs V P Rathbone; R S Rathbone.

HOW TO APPLY In writing to the correspondent.

WHO TO APPLY TO The Trustees, Rathbones, Port of Liverpool Building, Pier Head, Liverpool L3 1NW *Tel* 0151 236 6666

CC NO 233240 **ESTABLISHED** 1921

■ The Eleanor Rathbone Charitable Trust

WHERE FUNDING CAN BE GIVEN UK, with the major allocation for Merseyside; also women-focused international projects.

WHO CAN BENEFIT Organisations benefiting general charitable projects in Merseyside; women; and unpopular and neglected causes.

WHAT IS FUNDED The trustees concentrate their support largely on: charities and charitable projects focused on Merseyside; charities benefiting women; and unpopular and neglected causes (while avoiding those of a sectarian nature). Special consideration is given to charities with which any of the trustees have a particular knowledge of or association with, or in which it is thought Eleanor Rathbone or her father William Rathbone VI had a special interest.

WHAT IS NOT FUNDED Grants are not made in support of: any activity which relieves a statutory authority of its obligations; individuals, unless (and only exceptionally) it is made through a charity and it also fulfils at least one of the other positive objects mentioned above; overseas organisations without a sponsoring charity based in the UK. The trust does not generally favour grants for running costs, but prefers to support specific projects, services or to contribute to specific developments.

TYPE OF GRANT Mostly one-off, although longer-term commitments are considered.

RANGE OF GRANTS £100–£3,000, but exceptionally for larger amounts.

SAMPLE GRANTS £10,000 to The Merseybeat Appeal – Liverpool Cardiothoracic Centre; £8,100 each to Liverpool CSS and Thornhill Neighbourhood Project; £6,000 to Eleanor Rathbone Holiday Fund; £5,000 each to Canon Collins Educational Trust for South Africa, NMGN Development Trust and Young Persons Advisory Service; £4,700 to Sheila Kay Fund; £4,000 to I Can; £4,000 to PSS.

FINANCES *Year* 2001–02 *Income* £215,593 *Grants* £216,200 *Assets* £6,193,391

TRUSTEES W Rathbone; Ms Jenny Rathbone; P W Rathbone; Lady Morgan.

HOW TO APPLY No application form. The trust asks for a brief proposal for funding including costings, accompanied by the latest available accounts and any relevant supporting material. It is useful to know who else is supporting the project. Trustees currently meet three times a year, dates vary.

WHO TO APPLY TO Lindsay Keenan, 3 Sidney Avenue, Wallasey, Merseyside CH45 9JL *E-mail* eleanor.rathbone.trust@tinyworld.co.uk *Website* www.eleanorrathbonetrust.org

CC NO 233241 **ESTABLISHED** 1947

■ The Märit and Hans Rausing Charitable Foundation

WHERE FUNDING CAN BE GIVEN UK and worldwide.

WHO CAN BENEFIT The arts and national heritage, children's charities, medicine, the sciences and British wildlife.

WHAT IS FUNDED Medical research, children who are disabled, science, economics, architecture and social science. The conservation of fauna, flora and nature reserves.

WHAT IS NOT FUNDED No grants to individuals. No deficit funding.

TYPE OF GRANT Buildings, endowments, one-off, project and research.

SAMPLE GRANTS £100,000 each to Changing Faces, and National Gallery; £85,000 to Alzheimer's Society; £50,000 to Burrswood; £30,000 each to Canterbury Oast Trust, European Science and Environment Forum, and Kinder Archive Project; £25,000 to Friends of Sussex Hospices.

FINANCES *Year* 2002 *Grants* £659,500

TRUSTEES Peter Hetherington; Prof. Anthony R Mellows; Sir John Sparrow; Philippa Blake-Roberts.

HOW TO APPLY In writing to the trustees (but note that the foundation, which is lightly staffed, already reports that it is receiving an 'overwhelming' number of applications).

WHO TO APPLY TO Andrea Poole, Administrator, c/o 39 Sloane Street, London SW1X 9LP *Tel* 020 7235 3064 *Fax* 020 7235 9580

CC NO 1059714   **ESTABLISHED** 1996

■ The Ruben and Elisabeth Rausing Trust

WHERE FUNDING CAN BE GIVEN Unrestricted.

WHO CAN BENEFIT Charitable or voluntary organisations.

WHAT IS FUNDED Human rights, women's causes, environmental protection and economic and social development.

WHAT IS NOT FUNDED No grants are made to individuals.

TYPE OF GRANT One-off, buildings, core costs, project, research, recurring costs, salaries, and start-up costs. Funding may be given for up to one year.

RANGE OF GRANTS £1,000–£750,000; average grant £110,000.

SAMPLE GRANTS £750,000 to Human Rights Watch; £500,000 to Medical Foundation for the Care of Victims of Torture; £400,000 to Oxfam; £200,000 each to International Crisis Group and International Institute for Environment and Development; £175,000 to Women Living under Muslim Law; £150,000 to International Human Rights Law Group; £140,000 to Rainforest Action Network.

FINANCES *Year* 2001 *Income* £52,700,000 *Grants* £9,134,655 *Assets* £95,000,000

TRUSTEES Dr Sigrid Rausing; Joshua Mailman; Dr Lisbet Rausing; Robert Bernstein.

HOW TO APPLY In writing to the correspondent, but unsolicited applications cannot normally be considered or acknowledged. There is a very simple initial two-page application form for invited applicants.

WHO TO APPLY TO Jo Andrews, Director, 39 Sloane Street, London SW1X 9LP *Tel* 020 7235 9560

CC NO 1046769   **ESTABLISHED** 1995

■ The Ravensdale Trust

WHERE FUNDING CAN BE GIVEN Merseyside, particularly St Helens.

WHO CAN BENEFIT Registered charities benefiting: people of all ages; Christians, Church of England and Unitarians; at risk groups; people who are disabled, homeless or disadvantaged by poverty; and victims of abuse, crime and domestic violence.

WHAT IS FUNDED The trustees' policy is to make donations to charitable institutions they believe the settlor, the late Miss M Pilkington, would have wished to fund, with particular reference to charities dealing with education, health, the arts, religion, social welfare and the environment.

WHAT IS NOT FUNDED No grants to individuals.

TYPE OF GRANT Generally one-off.

RANGE OF GRANTS Usually £100–£3,000.

SAMPLE GRANTS In 1997–98: £4,000 to Newtown United Reform Church; £3,000 to URC St Helens; £2,000 to Scarisbrick Girl Guides; £1,500 each to YMCA Lakeside Appeal and Youth Clubs UK; £1,000 to St Helens Scout Association; £750 each to Liverpool Family Service Unit and YWCA St Helens (Nunn Street project).

FINANCES *Year* 2001–2002 *Income* £86,000 *Grants* £62,000 *Assets* £2,000,000

TRUSTEES J Wailing; J L Fagan; M R Feeny.

HOW TO APPLY In writing to the correspondent. No application form. No acknowledgement of applications are made. Grants are paid in May and October.

WHO TO APPLY TO Mrs J L Fagan, Secretary, Messrs Chaffe Street, 1 Dale Street, Liverpool L2 2ET *Tel* 0151 600 3000

CC NO 265165   **ESTABLISHED** 1973

■ The Rawdon-Smith Trust

WHERE FUNDING CAN BE GIVEN Coniston and those parishes bordering Coniston Water.

WHO CAN BENEFIT Local organisations.

WHAT IS FUNDED The preservation of the area called the 'Bed of Coniston Water' for the benefit of the public; other charitable purposes including education, welfare, animal welfare and preservation of churches.

WHAT IS NOT FUNDED No support for individuals.

FINANCES *Year* 2000 *Grants* £33,000

HOW TO APPLY In writing to the correspondent. The trustees meet in February, May and November.

WHO TO APPLY TO I Stancliffe, Secretary, Campbell House, Coniston, Cumbria LA21 8EF *Tel* 01539 441707

CC NO 500355   **ESTABLISHED** 1964

■ The Rawlings Charitable Trust

WHERE FUNDING CAN BE GIVEN UK.

WHAT IS NOT FUNDED No grants to individuals.

SAMPLE GRANTS £10,000 to Friends of St Andrews; £4,000 to British Epilepsy Association; £2,000 each to Save Britain's Heritage and Médecins Sans Frontières; £1,000 each to Jubilee Sailing Trust and Prince's Youth Business Trust; £500 each, including those to Countryside Alliance, Rehab, Study of Infant Deaths and Turning Point.

FINANCES *Year* 1999–2000 *Income* £42,000 *Grants* £24,000 *Assets* £1,200,000

TRUSTEES Rathbone Trust Company Limited.

HOW TO APPLY In writing to the correspondent.

WHO TO APPLY TO The Administrator, Rathbone Trust Company Limited, 159 New Bond Street, London W1S 2UD *Tel* 020 7399 0823

CC NO 287483   **ESTABLISHED** 1983

■ The Raydan Charitable Trust

WHERE FUNDING CAN BE GIVEN UK.

WHO CAN BENEFIT Jewish organisations.

WHAT IS FUNDED General charitable purposes.

SAMPLE GRANTS £7,800 to Or Chadash; £7,300 to Naima JPS; £4,100 to UK Friends for Further Education in Israel; £2,500 to Western Marble Arch Synagogue; £2,000 to Nightingale House; £1,600 to Yesoday Hatorah School; £1,400 each to LWCJDS and Norwood Ravenswood; £1,300 to L'Chaim Society.

FINANCES *Year* 2000–01 *Income* £50,000 *Grants* £49,000 *Assets* £10,600

TRUSTEES S Raydan; C Raydan; P Raydan.

HOW TO APPLY In writing to the correspondent.

WHO TO APPLY TO Clive Raydan, Trustee, 9 Harley Street, London W1G 9QF *Tel* 020 7436 3323

CC NO 294446   **ESTABLISHED** 1985

■ The Roger Raymond Charitable Trust

WHERE FUNDING CAN BE GIVEN UK (and very occasionally large, well-known overseas organisations).

WHO CAN BENEFIT Mainly headquarters organisations. Overseas grants are only made to large, well-known organisations (such as Sight Savers International and UNICEF).

WHAT IS FUNDED Older people, education, medical.

WHAT IS NOT FUNDED Grants are rarely given to individuals.

TYPE OF GRANT One-off and recurrent.

RANGE OF GRANTS Up to £5,000, although most for £1,000 or less.

SAMPLE GRANTS £126,000 to Bloxham School; £5,000 each to King Edward VII Hospital and Macmillan Cancer Relief; £3,000 each to National Trust and Royal Commonwealth Society for the Blind; £2,000 each to Putney Animal Hospital and Salvation Army; £1,000 each to Huntington's Disease Society, Defeating Deafness and Children with Leukaemia.

FINANCES *Year* 2001–02 *Income* £231,300 *Grants* £205,861 *Assets* £7,023,968

TRUSTEES R W Pullen; P F Raymond; M G Raymond.

HOW TO APPLY The trust stated that applications are considered throughout the year, although funds are not always available.

WHO TO APPLY TO R W Pullen, Trustee, Suttondene, 17 South Border, Purley, Surrey CR8 3LL *Tel* 020 8660 9133 *E-mail* russell@pullen.cix.co.uk

CC NO 262217   **ESTABLISHED** 1971

■ The Rayne Foundation

WHERE FUNDING CAN BE GIVEN UK.

WHO CAN BENEFIT Registered charities benefiting children, young adults, older people, or society's most vulnerable people.

WHAT IS FUNDED Work of national importance in medicine, education, social welfare and the arts.

WHAT IS NOT FUNDED No grants to individuals.

TYPE OF GRANT Capital expenditure and recurrent expenses.

RANGE OF GRANTS £250–£100,000.

SAMPLE GRANTS £250,000 to Edinburgh University; £100,000 to Rayne Trust; £50,000 each to King's College, London and Technology Colleges Trust; £25,000 to Academy of Medical Sciences; £20,000 each to Caldecott Foundation and Modern Art Oxford.

FINANCES *Year* 2001–02 *Income* £1,799,000 *Grants* £1,736,000 *Assets* £3,689,200

TRUSTEES Lord Max Rayne, Chair; Lord Tom Bridges; Lord Claus Moser; Lady Jane Rayne; R A Rayne; Prof. Dame Margaret Turner-Warwick.

HOW TO APPLY In writing (ideally less than two pages) to the correspondent at any time, enclosing a copy of the most recent annual report and full audited accounts.

WHO TO APPLY TO Robert Dufton, Director, 33 Robert Adam Street, London W1U 3HR *Tel* 020 7487 9650 *Website* www.raynefoundation.org.uk

CC NO 216291   **ESTABLISHED** 1962

■ The Rayne Trust

WHERE FUNDING CAN BE GIVEN UK.

WHO CAN BENEFIT Registered charities benefiting children, older and young people, at risk groups, and people disadvantaged by poverty or socially isolated.

WHAT IS FUNDED Social welfare and arts.

WHAT IS NOT FUNDED No grants to individuals or non-registered charities.

TYPE OF GRANT Capital expenditure and recurrent expenses.

RANGE OF GRANTS £200–£25,500.

SAMPLE GRANTS £25,000 to Home for Aged Jews; £20,000 to Yehudi Menuhin School; £15,000 to The Centre for Jewish-Christian Relations; £10,250 to Community Security Trust; £10,000 each to Jewish Care and Royal Academy of Dramatic Art; £6,000 each to Royal Opera House Trust and West London Synagogue; £5,600 to Jewish Association for the Mentally Ill; £5,165 to Finchley Reform Trust.

FINANCES *Year* 2000–01 *Income* £234,090 *Grants* £166,630 *Assets* £2,155,776

TRUSTEES Lord Rayne, Chair; Lady Rayne; Hon. R A Rayne.

HOW TO APPLY In writing to the correspondent at any time, enclosing annual report and accounts.

WHO TO APPLY TO Robert Dufton, Director, 33 Robert Adam Street, London W1U 3HR *Tel* 020 7487 9650

CC NO 207392   **ESTABLISHED** 1958

■ The John Rayner Charitable Trust

WHERE FUNDING CAN BE GIVEN UK, with a preference for Merseyside.

WHO CAN BENEFIT Charities, especially those supporting children, medical research, youth projects, older people and drug addiction. The trust will also consider charities benefiting ex-service and service people; musicians; seafarers and fishermen; unemployed people; and volunteers. Support may be given to carers; people who are disabled, disadvantaged by poverty, homeless or socially isolated; those living in urban areas: and victims of abuse, crime and domestic violence.

WHAT IS FUNDED There is a preference for small charities in the UK to receive the largest donations. The trust supports charities working in the fields of accommodation and housing; arts, culture and recreation; health; and community facilities and services. Support may also be given to voluntary and community organisations and special schools.

WHAT IS NOT FUNDED No grants to individuals or non-registered charities.

TYPE OF GRANT Single donations given annually in February/March for buildings, capital, core costs, one-off, project, research and start-up costs. Funding may be given for up to three years.

RANGE OF GRANTS £1,000–£5,000.

SAMPLE GRANTS £5,000 to Uphill Ski Club for skiing for people who are disabled; £3,000 each to Merseyside Drugs Council for continuing support, Live Music Now! North West for music for people of all ages with special needs, Marie Curie Cancer Care, Gifts in Kind, and Médecins Sans Frontières; £2,500 to Child Death Helpline for a helpline for anyone affected by the death of a child; £2,000 each to Leuka 2000, Shrewsbury School Foundation for the music centre, and Community Selfbuild Agency for core funding.

FINANCES *Year* 1999 *Income* £31,726 *Grants* £30,000 *Assets* £1,606,000

TRUSTEES Mrs J Wilkinson; Dr J M H Rayner; Mrs A L C de Boinville.

HOW TO APPLY In writing to the correspondent by 31 January each year. Trustees meet to allocate donations in February/March. Only successful applicants will be contacted. There are no application forms or guidelines.

WHO TO APPLY TO Mrs J Wilkinson, Trustee, Manor Farmhouse, Church St, Gt Bedwyn, Marlborough, Wiltshire SN8 3PE *Tel* 01672 870362 *Fax* 01672 870750

CC NO 802363   **ESTABLISHED** 1989

■ Reading St Laurence Church Lands & John Johnson's Estate Charities

WHERE FUNDING CAN BE GIVEN The borough of Reading.

WHO CAN BENEFIT Welfare organisations and individuals.

SAMPLE GRANTS £74,000 to St Laurence Ecclesiastical Charities; £58,000 to St Laurence Charities for the Poor.

FINANCES *Year* 2000 *Income* £156,000 *Grants* £132,000 *Assets* £3,100,000

TRUSTEES Three ex-officio and two representative trustees.

HOW TO APPLY In writing to the correspondent. The trustees meet twice a year in April and November.

WHO TO APPLY TO I G Hammond, Clerk, Oak Lodge, Wyfold Lane, Peppard Common, Henley-on-Thames, Oxfordshire RG9 5LR *Tel* 01491 628456

CC NO 272566   **ESTABLISHED** 1941

■ The Albert Reckitt Charitable Trust

WHERE FUNDING CAN BE GIVEN UK.

WHO CAN BENEFIT UK registered charities including those which benefit the Society of Friends.

WHAT IS FUNDED General charitable purposes (excluding political or sectarian) including charities connected with the Society of Friends.

WHAT IS NOT FUNDED No support to individuals. No grants for political or sectarian charities, except for Quaker organisations.

TYPE OF GRANT One-off donations or yearly subscriptions.

RANGE OF GRANTS £250–£750.

FINANCES *Year* 2001–02 *Income* £67,439 *Grants* £67,050 *Assets* £22,034,962

TRUSTEES Mrs S C Bradley, Chair; Sir Michael Colman; Mrs G M Atherton; D F Reckitt; J Hughes-Reckitt; P C Knee; Dr A Joy.

HOW TO APPLY In writing to the correspondent. Trustees meet in June/July and applications need to be received by March.

WHO TO APPLY TO J Barrett, Secretary, Southwark Towers, 32 London Bridge Street, London SE1 9SY

CC NO 209974   **ESTABLISHED** 1946

■ The Sir James Reckitt Charity

WHERE FUNDING CAN BE GIVEN Hull and the East Riding of Yorkshire, UK and occasionally overseas.

WHO CAN BENEFIT Registered charities covering a wide range of causes, including Quaker causes and occasional relief for victims of overseas distasters.

WHAT IS FUNDED Charitable organisations submitting applications within the framework of the following priorities. General charitable purposes, with priority in descending order: The Society of Friends (Quakers) in all localities; Hull and the East Riding of Yorkshire, which excludes York; registered charities where work affects the UK as a whole; regional charities whose work extends to include the Hull area; and international in special circumstances only, e.g. major disasters. Those not meeting any of the criteria, for example, purely local organisations outside the Hull area are not considered for support.

WHAT IS NOT FUNDED Grants are normally made only to registered charities. Local organisations outside the Hull area are not supported, unless their work has regional implications. Grants are not normally made to individuals other than Quakers and residents of Hull and the East Riding of Yorkshire.

TYPE OF GRANT Annual subscription and/or donation for special projects or towards running costs. Innovatory or long-established projects receive equal consideration.

RANGE OF GRANTS £50–£20,000; typical grant £500.

SAMPLE GRANTS £73,000 to Britain Yearly Meeting (a Quaker organisation); £29,000 to The Retreat – York for a Quaker care home for older people; £24,000 to Dove House Hospice – Hull; £20,000 to Addington Fund.

FINANCES *Year* 2002 *Income* £646,500 *Grants* £622,000 *Assets* £14,500,000

TRUSTEES J H Holt, Chair and 11 others, mainly descendants of the founder.

PUBLICATIONS *A History of the Sir James Reckitt Charity 1921–1979* by B N Reckitt; *A History of the Sir James Reckitt Charity 1921–1999* by G M Atherton.

HOW TO APPLY In writing to the correspondent, giving details of the project, the costs involved and the benefits it will bring. Guidelines are available on request. Decisions are taken at the twice-yearly meeting of trustees.

WHO TO APPLY TO J McGlashan, Administrator, 7 Derrymore Road, Willerby, East Yorkshire HU10 6ES *Tel* 01482 655861 *E-mail* charity@derrymore.karoo.co.uk *Website* www.sirjamesreckitt.co.uk

CC NO 225356   **ESTABLISHED** 1921

■ Red Dragon Radio Trust

WHERE FUNDING CAN BE GIVEN The broadcast area of Red Dragon FM.

WHO CAN BENEFIT Charities benefiting children and young people under 18.

WHAT IS FUNDED Equipment, therapy and items that would benefit disadvantaged children.

WHAT IS NOT FUNDED No grants for items that should be government funded, salaries, transport and holidays.

RANGE OF GRANTS Up to £5,000.

SAMPLE GRANTS In 1997–98: £5,000 each to Torfaen Opportunity and Wallach Clifford; £3,800 to Newport Women's Aid; £2,400 to Living Proof; £1,500 to Marie Curie Holme Trust; £1,400 to Cwn Clydach Activity; £360 to Lower Rhymney Youth.

FINANCES *Year* 1998–99 *Income* £34,000 *Grants* £35,000 *Assets* £43,000

HOW TO APPLY In writing to the correspondent. The trustees meet four times a year, in March, June, September and December, to consider grant applications.

WHO TO APPLY TO Kath Snell, Red Dragon FM, Atlantic Wharf Leisure Park, Hemingway Road, Cardiff CF10 4DJ *Tel* 029 2066 2066

CC NO 1062035   **ESTABLISHED** 1997

■ The C A Redfern Charitable Foundation

WHERE FUNDING CAN BE GIVEN UK.

WHO CAN BENEFIT Registered UK charities.

WHAT IS FUNDED General charitable purposes.

WHAT IS NOT FUNDED No grants for building works or individuals.

TYPE OF GRANT Core costs, one-off, project and research. Funding is available for one year or less.

SAMPLE GRANTS In 1998–99: £30,000 to South Buckinghamshire Riding for the Disabled; £25,000 to Saints and Sinners Club; £10,000 to Motor and Allied Trades Benevolent Fund; £5,000 each to Cancer Support Centre Wandsworth, Canine Partners for Independence, Seven Springs Play and Support Centre, and Farms for City Children.

FINANCES *Year* 2001–02 *Income* £239,597 *Grants* £188,500 *Assets* £4,577,135

TRUSTEES C A G Redfern; T P Thornton; S R Ward; Sir R A Clark; D S Redfern.

HOW TO APPLY The trust does not accept unsolicited applications.

WHO TO APPLY TO The Trustees, PricewaterhouseCoopers, 9 Greyfriars Road, Reading, Berkshire RG1 1JG

CC NO 299918   **ESTABLISHED** 1989

■ The Christopher H R Reeves Charitable Trust

WHERE FUNDING CAN BE GIVEN UK.

WHO CAN BENEFIT Organisations benefiting young adults and older people, academics, research workers, students and people with special dietary needs. Donations will largely be made to charities already associated with this trust.

WHAT IS FUNDED The trustees are holding about 75% of the trust's income and capital for application in the limited area of food allergy and related matters. Nearly all the income in this sector has already been committed to Allergy Research and Environmental Health at King's College, London and to the production and distribution of a database of research references under the title of 'Allergy and Environmental Medicine Database'. New appeals related to food allergy and intolerance are invited and a response will be made to the applicants. The remaining 25% of the trust's income and capital will be held for general

donations. The main area of interest is disability.

WHAT IS NOT FUNDED No grants for individuals, overseas travel and expeditions, animal charities, church/community hall/school appeals outside the north Bedfordshire area, overseas aid, children's charities, drugs/alcohol charities, mental health charities, or education.

TYPE OF GRANT Income and capital.

RANGE OF GRANT Mostly for under £5,000.

SAMPLE GRANTS £65,000 to University College London; £50,000 to King's College; £10,000 to Uppingham School; £5,000 each to Western Australia Cancer Foundation, seeAbility and RASE; £2,000 to Solicitors Benevolent Fund; £1,000 each to Centrepoint, Clergy Orphan Corporation, Countryside Foundation for Education, East of England Agricultural Society, London Youth Clubs, Malcolm Sargent Children Cancer Fund, NSPCC, Papworth Trust, Project Trust, Red Poll Cattle Society, Salvation Army, Schizophrenia Society of Great Britain, SSAFA and Uppingham Church Refurbishment.

FINANCES *Year* 2001 *Income* £156,000 *Grants* £157,669 *Assets* £4,000,000

TRUSTEES E M Reeves; V Reeves; M Kennedy.

HOW TO APPLY In writing to the correspondent. Trustees meet five times a year in March, May, July, September and November.

WHO TO APPLY TO E M Reeves, Trustee, Hinwick Lodge, Nr Wellingborough, Northamptonshire NN29 7JQ *Tel* 01234 781090 *Fax* 01234 781090

CC NO 266877   **ESTABLISHED** 1973

■ The Max Reinhardt Charitable Trust

WHERE FUNDING CAN BE GIVEN UK.

WHO CAN BENEFIT Organisations benefiting medical professionals or people who are deaf.

WHAT IS FUNDED Medical schools and research.

SAMPLE GRANTS £57,818 to St George's Medical School; £1,000 each to Diamond Blackfan Anaemia Support Group and Sense; £500 to RNID; £100 to Sound Seekers.

FINANCES *Year* 2000–01 *Income* £75,045 *Grants* £62,370 *Assets* £529,478

TRUSTEES Joan Reinhardt; Alexandra Reinhardt; Veronica Reinhardt; Belinda McGill.

HOW TO APPLY In writing to the correspondent.

WHO TO APPLY TO The Secretary, Flat 2, 43 Onslow Square, London SW7 3LR

CC NO 264741   **ESTABLISHED** 1973

■ REMEDI

WHERE FUNDING CAN BE GIVEN UK.

WHO CAN BENEFIT Hospitals and universities.

WHAT IS FUNDED The support of pioneering research into all aspects of disability in the widest sense of the word, with special emphasis on disability and the way in which it limits the activities and lifestyle of all ages. Preference for applicants who wish to carry out innovative and original research and experience difficulty in attracting funding from the larger and better-known organisations. Collaboration with other charities working in the same field is encouraged.

WHAT IS NOT FUNDED Cancer and cancer-related diseases are not normally supported.

TYPE OF GRANT Grants are usually given for one year, occasionally for two and exceptionally for three years. Projects, equipment and therapy research are supported.

RANGE OF GRANTS £1,000–£50,000. Average grant £10,000.

SAMPLE GRANTS £53,900 towards the research project 'Can functional magnetic resonance imaging (MRI) studies help to develop effective therapy interventions for stroke patients?'; £49,250 towards research into some underlying causes of autism; £40,000 towards research into prostate cancer; £37,800 towards early intensive home-based intervention for the treatment of autism and analysis of tutor performance; £33,500 over two years towards evaluation of the effects of radiotherapy for pituitary tumours on cognitive function; £32,000 towards further development of intensive single-case methods for investigation of recovery after stroke; £29,500 towards research into the mechanisms underlying the loss of muscle mass in old age; £27,000 towards a study into an association between autism and Cohen Syndrome; £25,750 towards the clinical trial of ossointegrated prostheses for Transfemoral amputees; £25,000 towards reseach in the control of prosthetic wrist rotation from residual rotation of the amputated forearm.

FINANCES *Year* 2001–02 *Income* £309,981 *Grants* £226,980 *Assets* £337,527

TRUSTEES Brian Winterflood, President; Dr A K Clarke, Chair; Alan Line; Dr A H M Heagerty; Dr A St J Dixon; Dr I T Stuttaford; David Hume; Rosie Wait; Michael Hines.

HOW TO APPLY By e-mail to the correspondent. Applications are received throughout the year. They should initially include a summary of the project on one side of A4 with costings. The chair normally examines applications on the third Tuesday of each month with a view to inviting applicants to complete an application form by e-mail.

WHO TO APPLY TO Lt Col Patrick Mesquita, Director, The Old Rectory, Stanton Prior, Bath BA2 9HT *Tel* 01761 472662 *Fax* 01761 470662 *E-mail* director.remedi@btinternet.com *Website* www.remedi.org.uk
CC NO 1063359   **ESTABLISHED** 1973

■ The Rest Harrow Trust

WHERE FUNDING CAN BE GIVEN UK.

WHO CAN BENEFIT Registered charities benefiting people who are disabled, disadvantaged by poverty or homeless.

WHAT IS FUNDED Main areas of interest are older people, education, disability, housing, poverty, and youth. Particularly Jewish organisations.

WHAT IS NOT FUNDED No grants to non-registered charities or to individuals.

TYPE OF GRANT Occasionally one-off for part or all of a particular project.

RANGE OF GRANTS £100–£2,000.

SAMPLE GRANTS £2,000 each to Assembly of Masorti Synagogues, Jewish Museum, Jewish National Fund, Nightingale House and St Hilda's East Community Centre; £1,000 each to British Technion Society, Institute of Jewish Affairs, Jewish Care, Pinhas Rutenberg Educational Trust and Weizmann Institute Foundation.

FINANCES *Year* 1999–2000 *Income* £36,000 *Grants* £31,000

TRUSTEES Miss Ethel Wix; HON & V Trustee Limited.

OTHER INFORMATION Grants are usually made to national bodies rather than local branches, or local groups.

HOW TO APPLY In writing to the correspondent. Appeals are considered quarterly. Only applications from eligible bodies are acknowledged.

WHO TO APPLY TO Mr T Miles, c/o Portrait Solicitors, 1 Chancery Lane, London WC2A 1LF *Tel* 020 7320 3890
CC NO 238042   **ESTABLISHED** 1964

■ Reuters Foundation

WHERE FUNDING CAN BE GIVEN UK and overseas.

WHO CAN BENEFIT Charitable causes actively supported by Reuters staff.

WHAT IS FUNDED International journalism, educational, humanitarian and environmental causes.

WHAT IS NOT FUNDED Political, religious, sports and animal causes are not supported. No grants to individuals.

TYPE OF GRANT One-off, project, recurring costs, research and start-up costs.

FINANCES *Year* 2000 *Grants* £3,200,000

TRUSTEES David Ure, Chair; Stephen Somerville; Geoffrey Weetman; Mark Wood; Sir Crispin Tickell.

PUBLICATIONS *Reuterlink.* The foundation also runs *AlertNet*, an internet-based news and communications service for international relief agencies.

OTHER INFORMATION Applications must be supported by a member of Reuters staff. Unsolicited applications are not accepted.

HOW TO APPLY Application forms for journalism training are found on the foundation's website. Other unsolicited requests for funding are not considered.

WHO TO APPLY TO The Director, 85 Fleet Street, London EC4P 4AJ *Tel* 020 7542 7015 *Fax* 020 7542 8599 *E-mail* foundation@reuters.com *Website* www.foundation.reuters.com
CC NO 803676   **ESTABLISHED** 1982

■ The Nathaniel Reyner Trust Fund

WHERE FUNDING CAN BE GIVEN Merseyside area.

WHO CAN BENEFIT Registered charities and Christian organisations helping children, young adults, older people, clergy, Baptists, Church of England, Christians, evangelists and Methodists.

WHAT IS FUNDED The promotion of evangelical Christianity and also general charitable purposes, particularly the advancement of Christian religion and Christian religious buildings.

WHAT IS NOT FUNDED No grants to individuals, medical research, the arts or denominations other than URC or Baptist unless there is a clear and overriding ecumenical or community objective.

RANGE OF GRANTS £100–£3,000.

SAMPLE GRANTS £3,000 to Lord Street West United Church; £2,500 to North Western Baptist Association; £2,000 to Moreton Baptist Church.

FINANCES *Year* 1999–2000 *Income* £38,588 *Grants* £30,000 *Assets* £847,070

TRUSTEES D E G Faragher, Chair; G C Lindsay; G C Dickie; J R Watson; W B Howarth; Miss M Proven.

HOW TO APPLY In writing to the correspondent. Trustees meet in April and November.

WHO TO APPLY TO Lawrence Downey, Secretary, Drury House, 19 Water Street, Liverpool L2 0RP *Tel* 0151 236 8989
CC NO 223619   **ESTABLISHED** 1965

■ The Rhodes Trust Public Purposes Fund

WHERE FUNDING CAN BE GIVEN UK and overseas.

WHO CAN BENEFIT Educational organisations benefiting young adults and students.

WHAT IS FUNDED Educational purposes in Oxford University and Commonwealth countries in Africa and the Caribbean.

WHAT IS NOT FUNDED Grants to institutions only. No grants to individuals.

TYPE OF GRANT One-off and recurring.

SAMPLE GRANTS In 1998–99: £862,000 to Rothermere America Institute; £517,000 to University of Witwatersan Foundation; £274,000 to Rhodes University, Eden Grove Centre; £250,000 to Oxford University Scholarships for overseas students; £100,000 to University of Cape Town; £90,000 to Oxford University Sports Committee; £61,000 to Liverpool University's Diabetes Education; £51,000 to Valley Trust; £50,000 to Erasmus Exchange Scheme; £25,000 to British School in Rome.

FINANCES *Year* 2000–01 *Income* £2,114,620

TRUSTEES Rt Hon. William Waldegrave of North Hill; Sir John Kerr; Sir Colin Lucas; Rt Hon Lord Fellowes; Lord Butler of Brockwell; J Ogilvie Thompson; Prof. J I Bell; Dame Ruth Deech; Miss R Hedley-Miller.

HOW TO APPLY To the correspondent in writing. Trustees meet in June and November.

WHO TO APPLY TO Dr John Rowett, Rhodes House, Oxford OX1 3RG *Tel* 01865 270902 *Fax* 01865 270914 *E-mail* admin@rhodeshouse.ox.ac.uk *Website* www.rhodeshouse.ox.ac.uk

CC NO 232492　　　**ESTABLISHED** 1946

■ The Rhododendron Trust

WHERE FUNDING CAN BE GIVEN UK and overseas.

WHO CAN BENEFIT Registered charities.

WHAT IS FUNDED Overseas charities, UK social welfare charities and UK cultural charities.

WHAT IS NOT FUNDED No grants to individuals, or for expeditions, scholarships or research work.

TYPE OF GRANT Preferably project-based.

RANGE OF GRANTS £500–£1,000.

SAMPLE GRANTS 71 grants of £500 each, including those to Ashram International, Ethiopiaid, Farm Africa, Nepal Leprosy Trust, St George's Romania Appeal, Family Service Units, Kings Cross Homelessness Project, the Multiple Sclerosis Society, The Refugee Support Centre and Parasol Theatre for Children Ltd.

FINANCES *Year* 2000–01 *Income* £39,000 *Grants* £35,000 *Assets* £1,009,000

TRUSTEES Peter Edward Healey; Dr Ralph Walker; Mrs Sarah Ray; Dr David Michael Smith.

HOW TO APPLY In writing to the correspondent. The majority of donations are made in February. Applications are not acknowledged.

WHO TO APPLY TO P E Healey, Trustee, Lewis House, 1c Smith Street, Rochdale OL16 1TX *Tel* 01706 355505

CC NO 267192　　　**ESTABLISHED** 1974

■ The Rhondda Cynon Taff Welsh Church Acts Fund

WHERE FUNDING CAN BE GIVEN Rhondda-Cynon-Taff, Brigend and Merthyr Tydfil County Borough Councils, i.e. the former county of Mid Glamorgan, with the exception of Rhymney Valley which is now outside the area of benefit.

WHO CAN BENEFIT Churches, youth organisations and musical groups benefiting children, young adults, Christians, at risk groups, and people who are disadvantaged by poverty or socially isolated.

WHAT IS FUNDED Churches; youth activities; and welfare.

WHAT IS NOT FUNDED No grants to students, individuals, or projects of other local authorities. Grants are not given for running costs.

FINANCES *Year* 2001–02 *Grants* £225,000 *Assets* £7,887,000

TRUSTEES Rhondda-Cynon-Taff County Borough Council.

HOW TO APPLY On a form available from Mrs Susan Robinson, Development and Regeneration Unit, Chief Executive's Department, Valley Innovation Centre, Navigation Park, Abercynon CF45 4SN (tel. 01443 665744). Applications are sent out between April and July. The closing date for applications is 31 July each year.

WHO TO APPLY TO George Sheldrick, Accounts Section, Bronwydd House, Porth, Mid Glamorgan CF39 9DL *Tel* 01443 680573 *Fax* 01443 680555

CC NO 506658　　　**ESTABLISHED** 1977

■ The Tim Rice Charitable Trust

WHERE FUNDING CAN BE GIVEN UK.

WHO CAN BENEFIT Individuals and organisations.

WHAT IS FUNDED General charitable purposes.

WHAT IS NOT FUNDED Applications from postgraduates are given lower priority. No grants are made towards computers.

RANGE OF GRANTS £240–£10,000.

SAMPLE GRANTS In 1996–97: £10,000 each to Countryside Movement and England Schools Cricket Association; £5,000 to Save the Children for the Equality Learning Centre; £2,700 to Institute for the Advancement of Journalism; £2,500 each to Sir Geoffrey de Havilland Memorial Fund and Peter May Memorial Appeal; £2,000 to Nelson Mandela's Children's Fund; £1,800 to Saints and Sinners Trust Ltd; £1,000 to Child Bereavement Trust; £550 to Phoenix Players Ltd.

FINANCES *Year* 1998–99 *Income* £26,000 *Grants* £30,000

TRUSTEES N W Benson; Mrs E Heinink; Sir Tim Rice.

HOW TO APPLY In writing to the correspondent, at any time.

WHO TO APPLY TO Mrs E Heinink, Trustee, 31 The Terrace, Barnes, London SW13 0NR *Tel* 020 8878 7950

CC NO 1049578　　　**ESTABLISHED** 1995

■ Daisy Rich Trust

WHERE FUNDING CAN BE GIVEN UK, with a priority for the Isle of Wight.

WHAT IS FUNDED General charitable purposes.

FINANCES *Year* 2000–01 *Income* £86,000 *Grants* £95,000 *Assets* £2,300,000

HOW TO APPLY In writing to the correspondent.

WHO TO APPLY TO Mrs J Williams, Secretary, The Cranbourn Suite, 61 Upper James Street, Newport, Isle of Wight PO30 1LQ *Tel* 01983 521236

CC NO 236706　　　**ESTABLISHED** 1964

■ Cliff Richard Charitable Trust

WHERE FUNDING CAN BE GIVEN UK.

WHO CAN BENEFIT Registered charities only, benefiting a broad spectrum, including: children, adults and young people; Baptists, Methodists, Anglicans and Evangelists; people who are disabled or have a medical condition.

WHAT IS FUNDED Smaller, grass-roots projects are often preferred, for general charitable purposes that reflect the support, Christian commitment and interest of Sir Cliff Richard, including: special schools, special needs education and vocational training; community centres, village halls, playgrounds and playschemes; care in the community and community transport; respite care and care for carers; cancer, MS and neurological research; Christian education and outreach; missionaries and evangelicals; and animal homes and welfare.

WHAT IS NOT FUNDED Capital building projects, church repairs and renovations are all excluded. No support for individuals.

TYPE OF GRANT Usually small one-off sums for operational needs.

SAMPLE GRANTS 2000–01: £50,000 each to British Lung Foundation, and Cliff Richard Tennis Development Trust; £6,500 to Genesis Art Trust; £5,000 to Arts Centre Group.

FINANCES *Year* 2001–02 *Income* £127,107 *Grants* £150,320 *Assets* £994,225

TRUSTEES William Latham; Malcolm Smith.

HOW TO APPLY Applications should be from registered charities only, in writing, and for one-off needs. All applications are acknowledged. Grants are made quarterly in January, April, July and October.

WHO TO APPLY TO Bill Latham, Trustee, Harley House, 94 Hare Lane, Claygate, Esher, Surrey KT10 0RB *Tel* 01372 467752 *Fax* 01372 462352

CC NO 259056   **ESTABLISHED** 1969

■ The Clive Richards Charity Ltd

WHERE FUNDING CAN BE GIVEN Preference for Herefordshire.

WHO CAN BENEFIT Individuals and registered charities benefiting children and older people, musicians, Roman Catholics, people who are disabled or disadvantaged by poverty and victims of crime.

WHAT IS FUNDED The assistance of social welfare, people with disabilities, the arts, conservation and religion, mostly in the county of Herefordshire, especially in church schools.

WHAT IS NOT FUNDED No grants for political causes.

TYPE OF GRANT One-off, project and buildings. Interest-free loans are considered. Grants may be for up to two years.

SAMPLE GRANTS £11,000 to Everest 2000 Reserve Forces North Ridge Expedition; £10,000 to Premanda Orphanage Centre; £5,840 to Royal Opera House Trust; £4,000 to Bromyard Sports Foundation; £2,500 to Rural Britain 2006.

FINANCES *Year* 2001–02 *Income* £21,259 *Grants* £64,688 *Assets* £408,645

TRUSTEES W S C Richards; Mrs S A Richards.

HOW TO APPLY In writing to the correspondent. However, the trust states that 'due to the generally low interest rates that have been available over the last few months, the charity's resources are fully committed and thus it is extremely selective in accepting any requests for funding'.

WHO TO APPLY TO John Manby, 40 Great James Street, London WC1N 3HB *Tel* 020 7831 3310

CC NO 327155   **ESTABLISHED** 1986

■ The Violet M Richards Charity

WHERE FUNDING CAN BE GIVEN UK, with a preference for East and West Sussex and Kent.

WHO CAN BENEFIT Organisations benefiting: older people; medical professionals; researchers; medical students; and people with a medical condition.

WHAT IS FUNDED The relief of older people, the relief of sickness and the advancement of medical education to support particularly: medical research and research into geriatric problems, homes for people who are sick, facilities for the relief of older people and medical education. The trustees would prefer to be associated with a programme of research and are prepared to commit themselves to support over a given period.

WHAT IS NOT FUNDED No support for individuals.

TYPE OF GRANT Applications for grants of all types will be considered.

SAMPLE GRANTS £25,000 to University of Cambridge for the Huntington's Disease Promoter Project; £10,000 to Imperial College of Science, Technology and Medicine; £5,000 each to Brain Research Trust, British Neurological Research Trust, DISCS, Islet Research Laboratory, Raynauld's Scleroderma Association, St Christopher's Hospice, and Stroke Association; £2,000 to Fight for Sight.

FINANCES *Year* 2001–02 *Income* £79,229 *Grants* £76,000 *Assets* £2,040,185

TRUSTEES Mrs E H Hill; G R Andersen; C A Hicks; Miss M Davies; Mrs M Burt; Dr J Clements.

HOW TO APPLY In writing to the correspondent. There is no set format for applying. The trustees generally meet to consider grants approximately twice a year. Only successful applications are acknowledged.

WHO TO APPLY TO Charles Hicks, c/o Wedlake Bell (ref CAH), 16 Bedford Street, London WC2E 9HF *Tel* 020 7395 3000 *Fax* 020 7395 3118

CC NO 273928   **ESTABLISHED** 1977

■ The Richmond Parish Lands Charity

WHERE FUNDING CAN BE GIVEN Richmond, Kew, North Sheen, East Sheen, Ham, Petersham and central Mortlake.

WHO CAN BENEFIT Charitable organisations and individuals. Children, young adults and older people; musicians; sportsmen and women; artists; people with disabilities, disadvantaged by poverty or with mental illness.

WHAT IS FUNDED Grants are given for the relief of poverty; social and medical welfare; physical and mental disability and illness; sport; youth and community; music and the arts; older people; education; pre-school children's welfare; community centres; and general charitable purposes.

WHAT IS NOT FUNDED Projects and organisations located outside the benefit area, unless it can be demonstrated that a substantial number of residents from the benefit area will gain from their work. UK charities (even if based in the benefit area), except for that part of their work which caters specifically for the area.

TYPE OF GRANT One-off and recurring.

SAMPLE GRANTS £39,000 to Richmond CAB; £35,000 to RABMIND; £19,000 to SPEAR: Single Persons' Emergency Accommodation in Richmond; £17,000 to Princess Alice Hospice; £16,000 to Crossroads; £15,000 each to Grey Court School for an outreach worker, St Michael

Think carefully about every application. Is it justified?

747

and All Angels towards building a new community centre and Vineyard Church.

FINANCES *Year* 2001–02 *Income* £1,302,043 *Grants* £799,593 *Assets* £34,500,000

TRUSTEES The mayor of Richmond ex-officio; three nominated by the borough of Richmond (not necessarily councillors or officials); five nominated by local voluntary organisations; up to five co-opted.

OTHER INFORMATION A further £76,000 (£85,000) was awarded to individuals from the charity's education fund; £42,000 (£40,000) in heating vouchers to older people through its WARM campaign, and £66,000 (£50,000) in small grants to individuals in severe need.

HOW TO APPLY If you would like some clarification on whether your organisation would qualify for a grant, please contact the clerk to the trustees (020 8948 5701) who will be able to give you guidance. You will also be given an application form. On receipt of your application the clerk to the trustees will evaluate it and may wish to ask further questions before submitting it to the trustees for their consideration. Trustees' meetings are held eight times a tear, when eligible applications received 14 days beforehand are considered by the trustees (a schedule of meetings and deadlines is provided in the guidance pack). They may decide that they need further information before they can make a decision regarding a grant. You will be advised by letter within 10 days of the meeting whether or not your application has been successful. If you wish to know before that you may of course telephone the clerk.

WHO TO APPLY TO Mrs Penny Rkaina, Clerk to the trustees, The Vestry House, 21 Paradise Road, Richmond, Surrey TW9 1SA *Tel* 020 8948 5701 *Website* www.rplc.org.uk

CC NO 200069 **ESTABLISHED** 1786

■ The Muriel Edith Rickman Trust

WHERE FUNDING CAN BE GIVEN UK.

WHO CAN BENEFIT Hospitals and research organisations benefiting people with cancer or sight loss.

WHAT IS FUNDED Emphasis on cancer and blindness but other areas are not excluded. Normally research equipment is funded.

WHAT IS NOT FUNDED The trustees will not respond to individual students, clubs, community projects or expeditions.

TYPE OF GRANT Research and one-off payments on specified equipment.

RANGE OF GRANTS £250–£24,000.

SAMPLE GRANTS £23,820 to Kings College London; £17,900 to Elimination of Leukaemia Fund; £15,000 each to Cardiothoracic Centre NHS Trust and Spencer Dayman Meningitis Laboratories; £13,597 to Muscular Dystrophy Campaign; £13,000 to Colon Cancer Concern; £7,863 to Christie Hospital NHS Trust; £7,000 to Myasthenia Gravis Association; £5,655 to Salford Royal Hospitals NHS Trust; £3,467 to Motor Neurone Disease Association.

FINANCES *Year* 2000–01 *Income* £44,659 *Grants* £126,652 *Assets* £40,787

TRUSTEES H P Rickman, Chair; M D Gottlieb; Raymond Tallis.

HOW TO APPLY There are no guidelines for applications and the trust only replies if it is interested at first glance; it will then ask for further details. Trustees meet as required.

WHO TO APPLY TO H P Rickman, Trustee, 12 Fitzroy Court, 57–59 Shepherds Hill, London N6 5RD

CC NO 326143 **ESTABLISHED** 1982

■ Ridgesave Limited

WHERE FUNDING CAN BE GIVEN UK.

WHO CAN BENEFIT Individuals and organisations benefiting Jews and people disadvantaged by poverty.

WHAT IS FUNDED The advancement of religion in accordance with the orthodox Jewish faith; the relief of poverty; and other charitable purposes.

FINANCES *Year* 1999–2000 *Income* £440,000 *Grants* £413,000 *Assets* £2,700,000

TRUSTEES J L Weiss; Mrs H Z Weiss; E Englander.

HOW TO APPLY In writing to the correspondent.

WHO TO APPLY TO The Trustees, 13–17 New Burlington Place, Regent Street, London W1S 2HL *Tel* 020 7734 1362

CC NO 288020 **ESTABLISHED** 1983

■ The Ripple Effect Foundation

WHERE FUNDING CAN BE GIVEN UK.

WHO CAN BENEFIT Registered charities.

WHAT IS FUNDED General charitable purposes, particularly the broad fields of environmental work, third world development and empowering young people in the UK.

SAMPLE GRANTS £49,600 to Network Foundation; £11,572 to Devon Community Foundation; £250 to Breakthrough.

FINANCES *Year* 2000–01 *Income* £30,147 *Grants* £61,422 *Assets* £1,471,820

TRUSTEES Miss Caroline D Marks; I R Marks; I S Wesley.

HOW TO APPLY The trust states that it does not respond to unsolicited applications.

WHO TO APPLY TO Miss Caroline D Marks, Trustee, Marlborough Investment Consultants Ltd, Wessex House, Oxford Road, Newbury, Berkshire RG14 1PA *Tel* 01635 814470

CC NO 802327 **ESTABLISHED** 1989

■ The Rivendell Trust

WHERE FUNDING CAN BE GIVEN UK only.

WHO CAN BENEFIT Individuals and organisations benefiting children, young adults and students, people who are disabled or mentally ill, and families in need.

WHAT IS FUNDED Small charities that benefit people, particularly children, who are sick, disabled, mentally ill or with family problems. Consideration will also be given to applications from individuals for educational purposes – particularly music.

WHAT IS NOT FUNDED Applications for the construction, restoration or purchase of buildings are not normally considered. Grants to individuals are limited to those in the above categories, and children and bona fide students within the UK in connection with education in music. Further grants to charities or individuals will normally be considered once every three years.

TYPE OF GRANT Usually single cash payments, although more than one will be considered, depending on the circumstances of the grantee. Monthly allowances.

RANGE OF GRANTS Individuals: £100–£500; organisations: £50–£1,000.

FINANCES *Year* 2000–01 *Income* £37,811 *Grants* £65,570 *Assets* £1,299,208

TRUSTEES Mrs S D Caird; Miss M J Verney; E R Verney; A W Layton; Dr I Laing; S P Weil; G Caird.

HOW TO APPLY Charities should send comprehensive details including a statement of the previous two years' accounts. Individuals apply in writing with an sae to the correspondent for an application form. Because of the number of grants received, failure to supply an sae could result in an application failing. Trustees meet three times a year (usually March, July and November) to consider applications. The list of applications is closed six weeks before the date of each meeting, and any applications received after the closing date are carried forward.

WHO TO APPLY TO Jayne Buchanan, PO Box 19375, London W4 2GH

E-mail jayne@rivendelltrust.freeserve.co.uk

CC NO 271375 **ESTABLISHED** 1976

■ The River Trust

WHERE FUNDING CAN BE GIVEN UK, with a preference for Sussex.

WHO CAN BENEFIT Organisations benefiting Christians.

WHAT IS FUNDED Christian charities.

WHAT IS NOT FUNDED Only appeals for Christian causes will be considered. No grants to individuals. The trust does not support 'repairs of the fabric of the church' nor does it give grants for capital expenditure.

TYPE OF GRANT Certain charities are supported for more than one year.

RANGE OF GRANTS £400 – £16,000.

SAMPLE GRANTS £16,000 to Youth with a Mission; £12,000 to Timothy Trust; £10,000 to London Bible College; £9,000 to Barcombe Parochial Church Council; £8,000 each to Genesis Arts Trust and Care Trust; £6,000 to St Luke's Prestonville Church; £5,000 to St Peter & James Hospice; £4,000 each to Scripture Union and Chasah Trust; £3,000 each to Tear Fund and Ashburnham Christian Trust; £750 to St Barnabus Church; £400 to St Margaret's PCC.

FINANCES *Year* 2000–01 *Income* £191,316 *Grants* £127,000 *Assets* £492,674

TRUSTEES Kleinwort Benson Trustees Ltd.

HOW TO APPLY In writing to the correspondent. Unsolicited appeals are considered as well as causes which have already been supported and are still regarded as commitments of the trust. Only successful applicants are notified of the trustees' decision. Some charities are supported for more than one year, although no commitment is usually given to the recipients.

WHO TO APPLY TO Chris Gilbert, Secretary, c/o Kleinwort Benson Trustees Ltd, PO Box 191, 10 Fenchurch Street, London EC3M 3LB *Tel* 020 7475 5093

CC NO 275843 **ESTABLISHED** 1977

■ Riverside Charitable Trust Limited

WHERE FUNDING CAN BE GIVEN Mainly Lancashire.

WHO CAN BENEFIT Individuals and organisations benefiting people disadvantaged by poverty and illness, older people, and people employed or formerly employed in the shoe trade.

WHAT IS FUNDED Relief of need, education, healthcare, and other charitable purposes.

WHAT IS NOT FUNDED No grants for political causes.

TYPE OF GRANT Recurring costs.

SAMPLE GRANTS £10,000 each to Macmillan Cancer Relief – Burnley and Macmillan Cancer Relief – London; £6,000 each to Rossendale Valley Mencap and St Mary's Hospice; £5,000 each to Rossendale After Care Society and Rossendale Society for the Blind; £3,000 each to British

Dyslexics Association, British Heart Foundation and Royal Northern College of Music; £2,500 each to Derian Hose Hospice – Bolton, East Lancashire Contact Centre and Furness Lions' Club.

FINANCES *Year* 2000–01 *Income* £124,537 *Grants* £201,674 *Assets* £2,261,274

TRUSTEES B J Lynch; I B Dearing; J A Davidson; F Drew; H Francis; A Higginson; G Maden.

HOW TO APPLY In writing to the correspondent.

WHO TO APPLY TO Jackie Davidson, Trustee, c/o E Suttons & Sons, Riverside, New Church Ward, Bacup, Lancashire OL13 0DT *Tel* 01706 874961

CC NO 264015 **ESTABLISHED** 1972

■ The Daniel Rivlin Charitable Trust

WHERE FUNDING CAN BE GIVEN UK.

WHO CAN BENEFIT Jewish organisations.

SAMPLE GRANTS £10,000 to UJIA; £6,000 in two grants to Holly Bank Trust; £5,000 each to British Technion Society and Beth Shalom; £3,000 to JPAIME; £2,500 to JNFCT; and £2,000 to JJCT.

FINANCES *Year* 1999–2000 *Income* £36,000 *Grants* £34,000 *Assets* £36,000

TRUSTEES D R Rivlin; N S Butler; M Miller.

HOW TO APPLY The trust states that funds are fully committed and does not welcome unsolicited applications.

WHO TO APPLY TO D R Rivlin, Trustee, Manor House, Northgate Lane, Linton, Wetherby, West Yorkshire LS22 4HN

CC NO 328341 **ESTABLISHED** 1989

■ The E E Roberts Charitable Trust

WHERE FUNDING CAN BE GIVEN Preference for East Sussex and Kent.

WHO CAN BENEFIT Registered charities benefiting children and young people, people with disabilities or learning difficulties and older people.

WHAT IS FUNDED There is no specific category of support, but the emphasis is on youth, musical education, disability, people with learning difficulties and the elderly.

WHAT IS NOT FUNDED No support for large UK charities and church or village appeals outside the area. No grants to individuals.

TYPE OF GRANT Mainly recurrent. Occasional one-off grants.

RANGE OF GRANTS Up to £1,000.

SAMPLE GRANTS Previous beneficiaries include Kent Music School, Chailey Heritage School, South East Farming & Wildlife Advisory Group, Church of St Albans – Frant, South of England Agricultural Society and East Sussex Association for the Blind.

FINANCES *Year* 2001–02 *Income* £40,000 *Grants* £44,000 *Assets* £784,000

TRUSTEES Mrs E E Roberts; Ms E F Roberts; N B C Evelegh.

HOW TO APPLY In writing to the correspondent. The trustees meet twice a year in April and October. Unsuccessful applications will not be acknowledged.

WHO TO APPLY TO Robert B McKillop, Clerk to the Trustees, Messrs Cripps Harries Hall, Wallside

House, 12 Mount Ephraim Road, Tunbridge Wells, Kent TN1 1EG *Tel* 01892 506010 *Fax* 01892 506059 *E-mail* rbm@crippslaw.com *Website* www.crippslaw.com
cc no 273697   **established** 1977

■ Thomas Roberts Trust

where funding can be given UK.
who can benefit Organisations benefiting people with a disability or illness.
what is funded The trust mainly makes grants to medical, disability and welfare organisations.
sample grants £1,500 to Multiple Sclerosis Society; £1,000 each to Alzheimer's Society, Dermatrust, Harvest Trust Holidays for Children, Prison Reform Trust and Stroke Association .
finances *Year* 2000–01 *Income* £21,000 *Grants* £29,000 *Assets* £921,000
trustees R E Gammage; J Roberts; P M Roberts; Mrs G Hemmings.
how to apply In writing to the correspondent.
who to apply to Mrs G Hemmings, Trustee, 5–6 The Square, Winchester, Hampshire SO23 9WE *Tel* 01962 843211 *Fax* 01962 843223
cc no 1067235   **established** 1997

■ The Robertson Trust

where funding can be given Scotland.
who can benefit Registered charities only.
what is funded Priority areas: education, medical, care (especially of older and young people), drugs prevention and treatment. Other areas supported: community service, disability, heritage/conservation, research into alcoholism, arts, sport, animal welfare, and environmental issues.
what is not funded The trust does not support: individuals or organisations which are not recognised as charities by the Inland Revenue or the Charity Commission; general appeals or circulars, including contributions to endowment funds; local charities whose work takes place outside Scotland; projects which are exclusively or primarily intended to promote political beliefs; organisations which have applied within the last 12 months; or students or organisations for personal study, travel or for expeditions, whether in Scotland or not. The trust is unlikely to support: projects which are properly the subject of statutory funding; or projects which collect funds to distribute to others.
type of grant One-off, annual, pledges (to give grants if a target figure is raised), and recurring.
sample grants £750,000 to Stirling University for a new swimming pool and fitness centre; £284,000 to Glasgow University to carry out research into prevention and treatment of drug addiction; £250,000 to Drumchapel Opportunities for new playing fields; £104,000 to Cancer Research Campaign towards equipment for the Beatson Institute in Glasgow; £100,000 each to Abbeyfield Ballachulish for a new integrated care building and East Park towards the opening of four community houses for residential care for young people who are disabled in Glasgow.
finances *Year* 2001–02 *Income* £5,600,000 *Grants* £5,794,000 *Assets* £215,000,000
trustees Ian J G Good, chair; Thomas M Lawrie; Sir Lachlan Maclean; Richard J A Hunter; David D Stevenson; Mrs Barbara M Kelly.
how to apply In writing to the correspondent, with a recent annual report and full set of accounts. If the request is for a donation towards salary

costs, a job description will also be required. The trustees meet every two months, in May, July, September, November, February and March. A decision is usually made within three months and applicants may be contacted for more information or to arrange an assessment visit.
who to apply to Sir Lachlan Maclean, Secretary, 85 Berkeley Street, Glasgow G3 7DX *Tel* 0141 221 3151 *Website* www.therobertsontrust.org.uk
sc no SC002970   **established** 1961 and 1963

■ The Edwin George Robinson Charitable Trust

where funding can be given UK and developing countries.
who can benefit Disabled and older people; charitable organisations.
what is funded The trust makes grants to a range of charities, with a preference for those charities which care for people who are disabled or older people. The trustees favour applications from smaller organisations for specific research projects.
what is not funded No grants for general running costs for small local organisations.
range of grants £50 upwards.
sample grants 1998–99: £5,000 each to Brainwave, British Diabetic Association, British Red Cross – Hurricane Appeal, Marie Curie Cancer Care, Princess Alice Hospital and RNLI; £2,500 each to National Osteoporosis Society and Shaw Trust; £1,500 to the Dyslexia Institute; £750 to The Listening Library.
finances *Year* 2001–02 *Grants* £45,000
trustees E C Robinson; Mrs S C Robinson.
how to apply In writing to the correspondent.
who to apply to E C Robinson, Trustee, 71 Manor Road South, Hinchley Wood, Surrey KT10 0QB *Tel* 020 8398 6845
cc no 1068763   **established** 1998

■ The Rochester Bridge Trust

where funding can be given Kent.
who can benefit Charitable bodies.
what is funded The maintenance and reconstruction of the Rochester bridges, Medway tunnel and any other crossings of the River Medway. After this has been achieved, grants can be made for other general charitable purposes.
what is not funded No grants to individuals. No funding for revenue.
type of grant Capital including equipment, buildings and one-off.
range of grants Up to £50,000.
sample grants £215,878 to Bridge Wardens College; £23,000 to Master Ropemakers; £16,508 to Wye College; £5,000 each to Kent History Project and New College of Cobham.
finances *Year* 2000–01 *Income* £2,054,312 *Grants* £290,546 *Assets* £40,624,799
trustees The trust is administered by the Court of Wardens and Assistants of Rochester Bridge in the county of Kent, consisting of 12 members who are in office for 4 or 5 years.
publications Policy synopsis available on request.
other information Around £100,000 is available for charities each year.
how to apply In writing to the correspondent, with the latest accounts. Applications should be

submitted by 30 June each year and grants are decided by August.

WHO TO APPLY TO Michael Lewis, Bridge Clerk, The Bridge Chamber, 5 Esplanade, Rochester, Kent ME1 1QE *Tel* 01634 846706 *Fax* 01634 840125 *E-mail* lewis@rochester-bridge-trust.freeserve.co.uk

CC NO 207100 **ESTABLISHED** 1399

■ Rock House Foundation

WHERE FUNDING CAN BE GIVEN Worldwide.
WHO CAN BENEFIT Charitable organisations.
WHAT IS FUNDED General charitable purposes.
FINANCES *Year* 2000–01 *Income* £41,375
TRUSTEES M E Rossiter; Mrs F G Tovee; W G Hilton.
HOW TO APPLY Unsolicited applications are not welcomed by the trust. Charities making such applications will not receive a reply.
WHO TO APPLY TO The Clerk, Rock House, Byrons Lane, Gurnett, Macclesfield SK11 0HA
CC NO 1068343 **ESTABLISHED** 1998

■ The Rock Solid Trust

WHERE FUNDING CAN BE GIVEN Worldwide.
WHAT IS FUNDED Christian charitable institutions and the advancement of Christian religion; the maintenance, restoration and repair of the fabric of Christian church; the education and training of individuals; relief of need.
SAMPLE GRANTS £50,000 to Christ Church – Clifton; £10,000 to Christ Church School; £1,400 to Hope Community Church; £1,000 to Tearfund.
FINANCES *Year* 1999–2000 *Income* £249,000 *Grants* £62,000 *Assets* £166,000
TRUSTEES J D W Pocock; A J Pocock; T P Wicks; T G Bretell.
OTHER INFORMATION £18,000 was given to organisations.
HOW TO APPLY In writing to the correspondent.
WHO TO APPLY TO J D W Pocock, Trustee, 7 Belgrave Place, Clifton, Bristol B58 3DD
CC NO 1077669 **ESTABLISHED** 1999

■ Richard Rogers Charitable Settlement

WHERE FUNDING CAN BE GIVEN UK.
WHAT IS FUNDED Homelessness and housing projects.
SAMPLE GRANTS A grant of £100,000 was made to National Tenants Resource Centre. No further information was available.
FINANCES *Year* 1999–2000 *Income* £21,000 *Grants* £165,000 *Assets* £401,000
TRUSTEES Lord R G Rogers; P Rogers; G H Camamile.
HOW TO APPLY In writing to the correspondent.
WHO TO APPLY TO K A Hawkins, Lee Associates, 5 Southampton Place, London WC1A 2DA *Tel* 020 7831 3609
CC NO 283252 **ESTABLISHED** 1981

■ Rokach Family Charitable Trust

WHERE FUNDING CAN BE GIVEN UK.
WHO CAN BENEFIT Jewish organisations; registered charities.
WHAT IS FUNDED Advancement of the Jewish religion; general charitable purposes.
SAMPLE GRANTS £32,739 to Finchley Road Synagogue; £20,668 to Beth Hamedrash

Ponovez; £10,036 to Adath Israel Synagogue; £10,032 to Woodstock Sinclair Trust; £7,598 to Cosmon (Belz) Ltd; £2,390 to Moreshet Hatorah Ltd; £2,000 to Jewish Education Trust; £1,462 to Institute of Rabbinical Studies D'Chasidei Belz London; £941 to Before Trust; £806 to Beis Yaakov Primary School.

FINANCES *Year* 2000–01 *Income* £155,404 *Grants* £103,260 *Assets* £1,274,969
TRUSTEES N Rokach; Mrs H Rokach; Mrs E Hoffman; Mrs M Feingold; Mrs A Gefilhaus; Mrs N Brenig.
HOW TO APPLY In writing to the correspondent.
WHO TO APPLY TO Norman Rokach, Trustee, 20 Middleton Road, London NW11 7NS *Tel* 020 8455 6359
CC NO 284007 **ESTABLISHED** 1981

■ The Helen Roll Charitable Trust

WHERE FUNDING CAN BE GIVEN UK.
WHO CAN BENEFIT Registered charities only, including universities, schools, colleges, research institutions, groups helping disadvantaged people, theatres, animal welfare charities, and environmental and wildlife organisations.
WHAT IS FUNDED General charitable purposes, particularly: education, especially higher education; libraries and museums; the arts; and health and welfare.
WHAT IS NOT FUNDED No support for individuals or non-registered charities.
TYPE OF GRANT Generally one-off for specific projects, but within a framework of charities whose work is known to the trustees.
RANGE OF GRANTS £500–£10,000.
SAMPLE GRANTS £10,000 to Trinity College of Music; £9,000 to Pembroke College Oxford; £8,000 to Friends of Home Farm Trust; £6,000 each to Oxford University Bodleian Library, Purcell School and Sick Children's Trust Cambridge; £5,500 to Stroud Court Community Trust; £5,000 to European Men's Health Development Foundation; £4,000 each to Canine Partners for Independence, Greenhouse Trust, Michael Sobell House and Notting Hill Housing Trust.
FINANCES *Year* 2001–02 *Income* £51,125 *Grants* £98,178 *Assets* £1,722,829
TRUSTEES Jennifer Williamson; Dick Williamson; Paul Strang; Christine Chapman; Terry Jones; Christine Reid.
HOW TO APPLY In writing to the correspondent during the first fortnight in February. Applications should be kept short, ideally on one sheet of A4. Further material will then be asked of those who are short-listed. The trustees normally make their distribution in March.
WHO TO APPLY TO F R Williamson, Trustee, Manches, 3 Worcester Street, Oxford OX1 2PZ
CC NO 299108 **ESTABLISHED** 1988

■ The Sir James Roll Charitable Trust

WHERE FUNDING CAN BE GIVEN UK.
WHO CAN BENEFIT Registered charities.
WHAT IS FUNDED Mainly the promotion of mutual tolerance, commonality and cordiality in major world religions; furtherance of access to computer technology as a teaching medium at primary school level; promotion of improved access to computer technology in community-based projects other than political parties or local government; funding of projects aimed at early identification of specific learning disorders.

SAMPLE GRANTS £15,000 to DEC India Earthquake Appeal; £10,000 to Crisis at Christmas; £6,000 each to Howard League for Penal Reform and Prison Reform Trust; £5,000 each to The Community Self Build Agency and Frontline Community Project; £3,000 each to National Missing Persons Helpline and Mission in Houndslow; £2,000 each to The National Autistic Society and The Dyslexia Institute; £1,000 each to Alzheimers Disease Society and Battersea Dogs Home; £500 each to Five Ways School, MIND and NatureWatch.
FINANCES *Year* 2000–01 *Income* £178,875 *Grants* £149,000 *Assets* £3,828,507
TRUSTEES N T Wharton; B W Elvy; J M Liddiard.
HOW TO APPLY In writing to the correspondent.
WHO TO APPLY TO N T Wharton, Trustee, 5 New Road Avenue, Chatham, Kent ME4 6AR *Tel* 01634 830111 *Fax* 01634 408891
CC NO 1064963   **ESTABLISHED** 1997

■ The Roman Catholic Diocese of Hexham and Newcastle

WHERE FUNDING CAN BE GIVEN Diocese of Hexham and Newcastle.
WHO CAN BENEFIT Roman Catholic organisations.
WHAT IS FUNDED This trust supports the advancement of the Roman Catholic religion in Hexham and Newcastle by both initiating its own projects and giving grants to other organisations.
SAMPLE GRANTS £340,000 to CAFOD; Sick and Retired Priests NBF; £94,000 to Retired Priests NBF; £56,000 to National Catholic Fund; £50,000 to Catholic Educational Services; £25,000 to Holy Places; £8,000 to Catholic Youth; £6,000 to Comboni Missions.
FINANCES *Year* 1999–2000 *Income* £18,000,000 *Grants* £820,000 *Assets* £44,000,000
TRUSTEES Right Revd Michael Ambrose Griffiths (Bishop of Hexham and Newcastle); Very Revd Canon Alexander H Barrass; Very Revd Canon Robert Spence; Revd John B Coyle; Revd William O'Gorman.
HOW TO APPLY Apply via a parish priest or Bishop Ambrose.
WHO TO APPLY TO Mrs Kathleen M Smith, Treasurers Office, St Vincents, Roman Way, West Denton, Newcastle upon Tyne NE12 7LT *Tel* 0191 229 3300
CC NO 234071   **ESTABLISHED** 1867

■ The Roman Research Trust

WHERE FUNDING CAN BE GIVEN UK, but preference given to Wiltshire and neighbouring counties to the west.
WHO CAN BENEFIT Individuals and organisations benefiting postgraduate students, professional archaeologists and non-professionals of equivalent standing.
WHAT IS FUNDED Excavation, recording, analysis and publication of Romano-British archaeological research not otherwise funded or for which existing funds are insufficient. Romano-British archaeological exhibitions in museums and other places accessible to the public; educational programmes related to Roman Britain.
WHAT IS NOT FUNDED Undergraduate or postgraduate courses.
TYPE OF GRANT Project and research. Funding is for one year or less.

RANGE OF GRANTS £200–£10,000. Typical grant £2,000.
SAMPLE GRANTS £5,000 each to University of Oxford for excavation of the amphitheatre at Frilford, and Wiltshire Archaeology and Natural History Scoiety for work on the Littlecoat excavation archive; £2,000 to University of Sheffield for excavation and geophysical survey at Chedworth Villa; £1,500 to Primary Latin Project for illustrations for 'Minimus 2'; £1,000 to Liverpool Musum for analysis of Roman artefacts from the Wirral; £500 to Yorkshire Archaeological Society for publication of excavations at Newton Kyme.
FINANCES *Year* 2001–02 *Income* £51,660 *Grants* £25,843 *Assets* £1,045,466
TRUSTEES A K Bowman, Chair; P Johnson; A C King; P Salway; Sir John Sykes; L Allason-Jones; R Birch; A S Esmonde Cleary; C Johns.
HOW TO APPLY By 15 November and 15 April annually. Application forms and guidelines available from the address below.
WHO TO APPLY TO Dr John Pearce, Hon. Secretary, Centre for the Study of Ancient Documents, 67 St Giles, Oxford OX1 3LU *Tel* 01865 288266 *E-mail* john.pearce@classics.ox.ac.uk
CC NO 800983   **ESTABLISHED** 1990

■ Rooke Atlay Charitable Trust

WHERE FUNDING CAN BE GIVEN Northallerton and its surrounding districts.
WHO CAN BENEFIT Young people, older people and people who are sick.
WHAT IS FUNDED Young people, the elderly and health.
SAMPLE GRANTS £22,000 to Northdale Horticulte Society; £3,800 to Friarage Hospital; £2,600 to Mowbray School; £2,500 to Dales Care Millennium Appeal; £2,000 to St Leonard's Church – Welbury; £1,000 each to Riding for the Disabled and Youth Clubs of North Yorkshire.
FINANCES *Year* 1999–2000 *Income* £71,000 *Grants* £35,000 *Assets* £672,000
TRUSTEES R H Renwick; D R Moore.
OTHER INFORMATION £4,682 was given to six individual beneficiaries.
HOW TO APPLY Unsolicited applications will not be acknowledged.
WHO TO APPLY TO R H Renwick, Trustee, 121 High Street, Northallerton, North Yorkshire DL7 8PQ *Tel* 01609 776200
CC NO 1032546   **ESTABLISHED** 1993

■ The C A Rookes Charitable Trust

WHERE FUNDING CAN BE GIVEN South Warwickshire, especially Stratford-upon-Avon.
WHO CAN BENEFIT Small local projects, innovative projects and UK organisations benefiting older people in particular, but also children and young adults.
WHAT IS FUNDED Medicine and health, welfare and humanities.
WHAT IS NOT FUNDED No grants to individuals for educational purposes.
TYPE OF GRANT One-off and recurrent.
RANGE OF GRANTS £150–£10,000.
FINANCES *Year* 2000 *Income* £50,000 *Grants* £30,000 *Assets* £500,000
TRUSTEES C J B Flint; Christopher Ironmonger.
HOW TO APPLY In writing to the correspondent at any time.

■ The Rootstein Hopkins Foundation

WHERE FUNDING CAN BE GIVEN UK.

WHO CAN BENEFIT The arts.

WHAT IS FUNDED The trust's objects are described as follows: to promote fine and applied arts by providing grants, bursaries and other financial assistance to schools of art, other art educational establishments, arts organisations, artists or groups of artists, and students or groups of them, art teachers and lecturers and groups of them, and any body which runs a school or arts school or otherwise promotes or develops for public benefit the development, study, research and practice of art in all its branches, but in particular painting, drawing, sculpture, photography and fine and applied art; to promote and develop the study and research of fine arts in all branches (particularly painting and drawing); to promote and develop the study and research into improved methods of display and visual mechanisms.

SAMPLE GRANTS £30,000 to Glasgow School of Art; £10,000 to Kingston University.

FINANCES *Year* 1999 *Income* £155,000 *Grants* £71,000

TRUSTEES M J Southgate, Chair; G L Feldman; Ms J Hartwell; Mrs D Hopkins; Mrs J Morreau.

HOW TO APPLY In writing to the correspondent.

WHO TO APPLY TO The Trustees, PO Box 14720, London W3 7ZG *Tel* 020 8746 2136
CC NO 1001223   **ESTABLISHED** 1990

■ Mrs L D Rope Third Charitable Settlement

WHERE FUNDING CAN BE GIVEN UK and overseas, with a particular interest in Suffolk.

WHO CAN BENEFIT For unsolicited applications, charities who work at grassroots level within their community, generally small in size, that are little catered for from other sources, or those that are based in particularly deprived areas. Charities with a large and committed volunteer base and those that have relatively low administration costs, in terms of staff salaries.

WHAT IS FUNDED Relief of poverty, advancement of education, advancement of religion and other charitable purposes.

WHAT IS NOT FUNDED The following are the main categories of exclusion for unsolicited applications; they are spelt out in more detail in the guidelines than is possible here: overseas projects; national charities; replacement of statutory funding; requests for core funding; buildings; medical research/health care, except in the immediate local area; students, except for a few overseas postgraduat science students in the last stages of their studies; schools, except in the local area; environmental charities and animal welfare; the arts; 'matched' funding except on a small scale; individuals – repayment of debts.

TYPE OF GRANT For unsolicited requests, grants are usually one-off and small scale. Also interest-free loans, project and start-up costs. Funding is given for one year or less.

RANGE OF GRANTS Generally £100–£750.

SAMPLE GRANTS £80,000 to Roman Catholic Diocese of East Anglia for the advancement of Christianity and education, and the relief of poverty; £40,000 to Science/Human Dimension Project for the advancement of education; £35,000 to Worth Abbey for the advancement of Christianity and education, and the relief of poverty; £31,000 to Westminster Diocese – Depaul Trust for the relief of poverty; £30,000 to Mrs L D Rope's Second Charity; £25,000 each to CAFOD for the relief of poverty and Mrs L D Rope Fourth Charity; £24,000 to St Stephen's Hospital, Kampala; £20,000 each to 1st Kesgrave Scout Group Troop and Kesgrave Town Council – Pavilion.

FINANCES *Year* 2001–02 *Income* £1,071,646 *Grants* £894,948 *Assets* £24,349,861

TRUSTEES Mrs Lucy D Rope, Jeremy P W Heal; Crispin M Rope.

HOW TO APPLY Please send a concise letter (preferably one side of A4) explaining the main details of your request. Please always send your most recent accounts and a budgeted breakdown of the sum you are looking to raise. The trust will also need to know whether you have applied to other funding sources and whether you have been successful elsewhere. Your application should say who your trustees are and include a daytime telephone number. Individuals should write a concise letter including details of household income and expenses, daytime telephone number and the name of at least one personal referee.

WHO TO APPLY TO Crispin M Rope, Crag Farm, Boyton, Near Woodbridge, Suffolk IP12 3LH *Tel* 01473 288 987 (office hours) *Fax* 01473 217182
CC NO 290533   **ESTABLISHED** 1984

■ The Rosca Trust

WHERE FUNDING CAN BE GIVEN The boroughs of Southend-on-Sea, Castle Point and Rochford District Council.

WHO CAN BENEFIT Registered charities benefiting: one-parent families; parents and children; those of various Christian denominations; ethnic minorities; at risk groups; people who are disabled; those disadvantaged by poverty; refugees; those living in urban areas; and victims of domestic violence.

WHAT IS FUNDED Preference given to charities catering for the needs of those under the age of 20 or over 65, medical (in the widest sense) charities or religious causes.

WHAT IS NOT FUNDED Grants are not given outside the beneficial area or to individuals.

TYPE OF GRANT Special consideration is given to one-off donations for capital projects. Regular donations are also given to other local charities for projects, buildings and start-up costs.

RANGE OF GRANTS Usually £250–£5,000.

SAMPLE GRANTS £5,000 to Southend Night Shelter for the Homeless; £3,000 to Southend Churches and Refugees Together; £1,500 each to Starlight Children's Foundation, Milton Community Partnership, Childline (local branch), an infant school breakfast club and three local Citizen's Advice Bureaux; £1,000 to a special needs scout group.
A total of £3,700 was also donated to several voluntary run residential homes for the elderly.

FINANCES *Year* 2001–02 *Income* £84,000 *Grants* £55,600 *Assets* £531,000

TRUSTEES K J Crowe; T T Ray; Mrs D A Powell; Mrs M Frewin.

HOW TO APPLY In writing to the correspondent. Applications are reviewed in March and September. An sae is appreciated. Preliminary telephone calls are considered unnecessary.
WHO TO APPLY TO K J Crowe, Trustee, 19 Avenue Terrace, Westcliff-on-Sea, Essex SS0 7PL *Tel* 01702 307840 *Fax* 01702 319390
CC NO 259907   **ESTABLISHED** 1966

■ The Rose Foundation

WHERE FUNDING CAN BE GIVEN In and around London.
WHO CAN BENEFIT Registered charities.
WHAT IS FUNDED The main emphasis is on financing building projects for other charities, where the trust cost is less than £200,000. A policy of seeking small self-contained projects usually in London or the Home Counties has been adopted. The trustees' policy is to offer assistance where needed with the design and construction process, ensuring wherever possible that costs are minimised and the participation of other contributing bodies can be utilised to maximum benefit.
WHAT IS NOT FUNDED The foundation can support any type of building project (decoration, construction, repairs, extensions, adaptations) but not the provision of equipment (such as computers, transportation and so on). Items connected with the finishes, such as carpets, curtains, wallpaper and so on, should ideally comprise a part of the project not financed by the foundation.
TYPE OF GRANT Part-funding building projects.
RANGE OF GRANTS Usually £5,000–£30,000.
SAMPLE GRANTS £50,000 to Hampstead Theatre for the landscaping of the terraces and gardens; £37,500 to Royal St George's Church – Kemp Town for the construction of a new entrance to, and a glass roof over, a newly formed community centre within the crypt of the church; £30,000 to St John's Hospice at Hospital of St John and St Elizabeth – St John's Wood for the conversion of a number of rooms into a day centre for both patients and visitors; £25,000 to Childs Hill School – Hendon for the construction of an amphitheatre; £20,000 to Friends of Reflection – Feltham for an adventure playgroup for hyperactive children; £15,000 to Beis Malka Girls' School – Tottenham for disabled and standard toilet cubicles; £13,000 to YWCA – Tonbridge for a fire alarm system and internal emergency lighting; £11,000 to Queen Elizabeth's Foundation for Disabled People towards the refurbishment and re-equipping of two bedrooms; £10,000 to Almeida Theatre for the fitting out of the foyer, ticket office and toilets; £6,000 to Hope House – Finchley for the refurbishment of a large open area on the first floor as a multi-function amenity.
FINANCES *Year* 2000–01 *Income* £938,807 *Grants* £1,022,000 *Assets* £27,225,987
TRUSTEES Martin Rose; Alan Rose; John Rose; Paul Rose.
OTHER INFORMATION The trust made two exceptional grants during the year: £342,800 to Crawford Street Centre ; and £115,078 to The New Amsterdam Charitable Foundation, a connected charitable trust in the USA.
HOW TO APPLY In writing to the correspondent. Applications should be received by the end of March for building projects starting between January and August of the following year.
WHO TO APPLY TO Martin Rose, Trustee, 28 Crawford Street, London W1H 1LN *Tel* 020 7262 1155 *Fax* 020 7724 2044
CC NO 274875   **ESTABLISHED** 1977

■ E J B Rose Charitable Trust

WHERE FUNDING CAN BE GIVEN UK.
WHO CAN BENEFIT Organisations who benefit the sick and disabled.
WHAT IS FUNDED General charitable purposes.
SAMPLE GRANTS £10,000 to Runneymede; £4,600 to The Times Talents Association; £2,200 to Writers and Scholars Education Trust; £2,100 to NSPCC; £1,100 to UNICEF; £1,000 to St Martins-in-the-Fields; £500 to Stroke Association; £150 to Canon Collins Educational Trust for South Africa.
FINANCES *Year* 1998–99 *Income* £34,000 *Grants* £36,000 *Assets* £133,000
TRUSTEES Susan Rose; Michael Prince.
HOW TO APPLY In writing to the correspondent, although with the expected decrease in income, no new applications can be accepted.
WHO TO APPLY TO M E G Prince, Trustee, 5 Knott Park House, Wrens Hill, Oxshott, Leatherhead, Surrey KT22 0HW
CC NO 258878   **ESTABLISHED** 1969

■ The M K Rose Charitable Trust

WHERE FUNDING CAN BE GIVEN UK, mostly West Midlands, and Israel.
WHO CAN BENEFIT Registered charities.
WHAT IS FUNDED Jewish causes and general charitable purposes.
SAMPLE GRANTS £330,000 to Friends of Nahariya Hospital; £101,000 to Diana Princess of Wales Childrens' Hospital – Birmingham; £100,700 to United Jewish Israel Appeal; £100,000 each to ALDEMI, The Jerusalem Foundation, and KDRE&I; £80,000 to Solihull and District Hebrew Congregation; £50,000 each to Jewish National Fund and World Jewish Relief; £21,000 to Beth Shalom Holocaust Memorial Centre.
FINANCES *Year* 2000 *Grants* £1,346,800 *Assets* £265,000
TRUSTEES M K Rose; Mrs I W Rose; H Aron; S Gould.
OTHER INFORMATION 2000 was an exceptional year when the trust decided to realise all its investments and give most of the proceeds in grants, thus greatly reducing the income for future years although this was seen as a positive thing in view of the financial situation during the year.
HOW TO APPLY In writing to the correspondent.
WHO TO APPLY TO M K Rose, Trustee, 20 Coppice Close, Dovehouse Lane, Solihull, West Midlands B91 2ED *Tel* 0121 706 6558
CC NO 1039857   **ESTABLISHED** 1994

■ The Cissie Rosefield Charitable Trust

WHERE FUNDING CAN BE GIVEN UK.
WHO CAN BENEFIT Registered charities.
WHAT IS FUNDED General charitable purposes, particularly Jewish causes.
SAMPLE GRANTS £3,300 to World Jewish Relief; £3,000 to Richard House Trust; £1,200 to LEVKA 2000; £500 to British Emunah; £450 to Friends of the Jerusalem Rubin Academy; £300 to The Lord Mayor's Appeal.
FINANCES *Year* 1999–2000 *Income* £23,000 *Grants* £25,000 *Assets* £392,000
TRUSTEES John Rosefield; Stephen Rosefield; Peter Rough; M D Paisner.
HOW TO APPLY In writing to the correspondent.
WHO TO APPLY TO M D Paisner, Trustee, Berwin Leighton Paisner & Co., Bouverie House, 154–

160 Fleet Street, London EC4A 2JD *Tel* 020 7353 0299
cc no 293177　　　　established 1985

■ The Cecil Rosen Foundation

where funding can be given UK.
who can benefit Organisations benefiting people who are disabled or have diabetes, hearing and sight loss, heart disease or mental illness. Medical professionals and research workers are also considered.
what is funded General charitable purposes especially to assist people who are blind, deaf, physically or mentally disabled; also for research into causes of heart disease, diabetes and mental illness.
what is not funded No grants to individuals.
type of grant Research is considered.
sample grants £80,000 to Jewish Blind and Disabled; £50,000 to The Cecil Rosen Charitable Trust.
finances *Year* 2000–01 *Income* £304,438 *Grants* £216,243 *Assets* £2,894,065
trustees Mrs L F Voice; M J Ozin; J A Hart.
how to apply The correspondent stated that 'no new applications can be considered'. Unsuccessful applications are not acknowledged.
who to apply to M J Ozin, Trustee, 118 Seymour Place, London W1H INP *Tel* 020 7262 2003
cc no 247425　　　　established 1966

■ The Rothermere Foundation

where funding can be given UK and overseas.
who can benefit Registered charities and individual graduates of the Memorial University of Newfoundland.
what is funded Establishment and maintenance of 'Rothermere Scholarships' to be awarded to graduates of the Memorial University of Newfoundland to enable them to undertake further periods of study in the UK; and general charitable causes.
type of grant Fellowship grants, scholarships, other educational grants.
sample grants £320,000 to London City Ballet; £62,781 to Oxford Institute of American Studies to support students of Drake University attending programmes at Oxford University; £5,000 to Coram Field Harmsworth Memorial Playing Field; £1,175 to St Bride's Church; £250 to St Peter's Church, Paylesford.
finances *Year* 1998–99 *Income* £382,000 *Grants* £469,093
trustees Rt Hon. Viscount Rothermere; V P W Harmsworth; J G Hemingway; Hon. Esme Countess of Cromer.
other information £78,387 was given in fellowship grants; £390,706 in donations.
how to apply In writing to the correspondent.
who to apply to V P W Harmsworth, Director of Corporate Affairs, Associated Newspapers, Northcliffe House, 2 Derry Street, London W8 5TT *Tel* 020 7938 6682
cc no 314125　　　　established 1964

■ The Rotherwick Foundation

where funding can be given Within a 20-mile radius of: Wither Ashdown Park Hotel, Wych Cross, East Sussex; Grand Hotel, Eastbourne, East Sussex; or Tynley Hall Hotel, Rotherwick, Hampshire.

who can benefit Individuals and organisations benefiting students and Protestant Christians.
what is funded The provision of scholarships, bursaries and maintenance allowances and educational grants tenable at any school, university or other educational establishment to people under 25 who, or whose parents or guardians, are resident in the specified localities or have for not less than five years attended a school or other educational establishment within those localities; the provision of financial assistance, equipment, books and clothing to such people on leaving school, university or other educational establishment for entry into a trade or profession; the provision of amenities and facilities including public recreation and sports grounds for public benefit; the advancement of religion and other charitable works of, and the maintenance of, Protestant churches; the provision, maintenance, improvement and equipment of hospitals, nursing homes, hospices and clinics; and such other charitable purposes as the trustees in their absolute discretion think fit to support or establish.
type of grant Funding is available for over to two years.
finances *Year* 2001–02 *Income* £2,506,525
how to apply In writing to the correspondent.
who to apply to G C Bateman, Trustee and General Manager, Ashdown Park, Wych Cross, Forest Row, East Sussex RH18 5JR *Tel* 01342 820227
cc no 1058900　　　　established 1996

■ The Rothley Trust

where funding can be given Northumberland, North and South Tyneside, Newcastle upon Tyne, Gateshead and the former counties of Cleveland and Durham.
who can benefit Registered charities only.
what is funded Children, community, education, disability, medical, third world and youth. Apart from a few charities with which the trust has been associated for many years, its activities are now directed exclusively towards north east England (Northumberland to Cleveland inclusive). Developing world appeals, arising from this area only, will be considered.
what is not funded No grants for further education, the promotion of religion, the repair of buildings used primarily for worship, older people, ex-services, art, feasibility studies, environmental projects, animals, sponsorship of medical conferences or to individuals.
type of grant Mainly one-off donations towards specific projects and not running costs. Start-up costs, buildings, equipment, resources and capital grants will be considered.
range of grants Typical grant £200.
sample grants £300 each to Hebburn Neighbourhood Advice Centre and Parkinson's Disease Society; £250 each to Air Cadets – County Durham, Deckham Community Centre – Gateshead, Revive Youth Project, and Tools for Self Reliance – Middlesbrough; £200 each to Mencap – Hartlepool, Mind Sunderland, South Benwall Play Group – Newcastle, and Stranton Toddler Group – Hartlepool.
finances *Year* 2001–02 *Income* £145,000 *Grants* £90,500 *Assets* £3,000,000
trustees Dr H A Armstrong, Chair; Mrs R V Barkes; Mrs J Brown; C Bucknall; Mrs A Galbraith; R P Gordon; R R V Nicholson; C J Pumphrey; G Salvin.

OTHER INFORMATION The trust has a list of charities it has always supported, giving large grants each year. This policy is being reviewed and it is possible that these grants will stop and more new applicants will receive funding. The sample grants in this entry relate to grants typical of new applicants rather than the largest 10 made during the year.

HOW TO APPLY By letter to the secretary explaining the charitable status and the constitution of the applicant body and enclosing a budget of proposed expenditure and the latest annual report/accounts. E-mail applications are not considered, although e-mailed enquiries are welcomed. Trustees meet quarterly to 'consider applications for capital costs and equipment'. Only applications from the preferred area (the north east of England) will be acknowledged. The trust states that an sae is appreciated.

WHO TO APPLY TO Diane Lennon, Secretary, Mea House, Ellison Place, Newcastle upon Tyne NE1 8XS *Tel* 0191 232 7783 *Fax* 0191 232 7783 *E-mail* diane_lennon@rothley-trust.fsnet.co.uk
CC NO 219849 **ESTABLISHED** 1959

■ The Rothschild Foundation (formerly Caritas)

WHERE FUNDING CAN BE GIVEN Unrestricted, but mainly UK.
WHO CAN BENEFIT Registered charities.
WHAT IS FUNDED General charitable purposes.
TYPE OF GRANT Generally one-off.
RANGE OF GRANTS £11–£481,000.
SAMPLE GRANTS £200,000 to National Trust for the restoration of Waddesdon Manor; £106,000 towards the restoration and development of the Butrint site in Southern Albania; £50,000 each to British Museum and Institute of Historic Research; £15,000 each to Botanic Gardens Conservation International and the Prince's Foundation.
FINANCES *Year* 2000–01 *Income* £2,300,000 *Grants* £574,000 *Assets* £23,600,000
TRUSTEES Sir Edward Cazalet; Lord Rothschild; Lady Rothschild; Hannah Rothschild; SJP Trustee Company Ltd.
HOW TO APPLY In writing to the correspondent.
WHO TO APPLY TO Fiona Sinclair, The Dairy, Queen Street, Waddesdon, Aylesbury, Buckinghamshire HP18 0JW
CC NO 230159 **ESTABLISHED** 1956

■ The Roughley Charitable Trust

WHERE FUNDING CAN BE GIVEN Mainly Birmingham and surrounding area.
WHO CAN BENEFIT Registered charities.
WHAT IS FUNDED General charitable purposes. Funds are mostly committed to projects known to the trustees.
WHAT IS NOT FUNDED No support for animal charities.
RANGE OF GRANTS Mostly £1,000 or less. Larger grants to projects where trustees have special knowledge.
SAMPLE GRANTS £12,000 each to Midlands Art Centre for New Work Trust and Rehabilitation for Addicted Prisoners Trust; £10,000 to Emmaus UK; £3,000 each to St James Church – Hill, and St Paul's Church Appeal; £2,000 to Medical Foundation for the Care of Victims of Torture; £1,500 to Relate; £1,000 each to Amnesty International UK Section Charitable Trust and Birmingham Citizens Advice Bureau.

FINANCES *Year* 2000–01 *Income* £130,000 *Grants* £202,380 *Assets* £3,247,364
TRUSTEES Mrs M K Smith; Mrs D M Newton; M C G Smith; J R L Smith.
HOW TO APPLY This trust states that it does not normally respond to unsolicited applications. The annual meeting is held in September.
WHO TO APPLY TO J R L Smith, Correspondent, 90 Somerset Road, Edgbaston, Birmingham B15 2PP
CC NO 264037 **ESTABLISHED** 1972

■ The Rowan Charitable Trust

WHERE FUNDING CAN BE GIVEN UK, especially Merseyside, and overseas.
WHO CAN BENEFIT Registered charities benefiting children and young adults, medical professionals, students, teachers, and unemployed people. Also carers, and people who are disabled, homeless, living in rural areas or blind.
WHAT IS FUNDED Overseas: agriculture (especially crop and livestock production and settlement schemes); community development (especially appropriate technology and village industries); health (especially preventative medicine, water supplies, blindness); education (especially adult education and materials); environment (especially protecting and sustaining ecological systems at risk); human rights (especially of women, children and people with disabilities); and fair trade (especially relating to primary producers and workers). UK: housing and homelessness; social and community care; education; employment/unemployment; after-care; welfare rights; community development; and environmental improvement.
WHAT IS NOT FUNDED The trust does not give grants for: individuals; buildings, building work or office equipment (including IT hardware); academic research and medical research or equipment; expeditions; bursaries or scholarships; vehicle purchases; or animal welfare charities.
TYPE OF GRANT One-off, recurring.
SAMPLE GRANTS £50,000 each to Christian Aid and ITDG; £30,000 to UNICEF; £20,000 to Personal Service Society in Liverpool; £15,000 to Children's Society; £10,000 each to Church Action on Poverty, Crossroads Centre, Liverpool Family Service Unit and Rurcon; £8,000 to Opportunity International.
FINANCES *Year* 2000–01 *Income* £315,000 *Grants* £516,000 *Assets* £5,000,000
TRUSTEES C R Jones; Mrs H E Russell.
PUBLICATIONS Guidelines for applicants.
HOW TO APPLY In writing to the correspondent. Trustees meet twice a year. The closing dates for applications are 30 June and 15 December. 'Unfortunately the volume of applications received precludes acknowledgement on receipt or notifying unsuccessful applicants. The trust emphasises that is unable to make donations to applicants who are not, or do not have links with, a UK-registered charity.'
WHO TO APPLY TO Keith Westran, c/o PricewaterhouseCoopers, 9 Greyfriars Road, Reading RG1 1JG *Tel* 0118 959 7111 *Fax* 0118 960 7700
CC NO 242678 **ESTABLISHED** 1964

■ Rowanville Ltd

WHERE FUNDING CAN BE GIVEN UK and Israel.

WHO CAN BENEFIT Jewish organisations.

WHAT IS FUNDED Established organisations for the advancement of religion in accordance with the orthodox Jewish faith.

SAMPLE GRANTS £109,000 to Lerose Charitable Trust; £48,000 to Yesodei Hatorah School for general funding; £34,500 to Memoral Grammar School for general funding; £26,500 to KKL Executor & Trustee Co. for general charitable purposes; £20,000 each to Achisomoch Aid Society for general charitable purposes and Noyzar Chesed for relief of poverty; £14,900 to Yeshivas Shaarei Torah for advanced education; £13,075 to Centre for Advanced Rabbinical Study; £11,600 to Toral Va Chesed for relief of poverty; £11,000 to Telz Talmudical Academy for advanced education.

FINANCES *Year* 1999–2000 *Income* £506,000 *Grants* £428,000 *Assets* £1,700,000

TRUSTEES J Pearlman; Mrs R Pearlman; M Neuberger; M D Frankel.

HOW TO APPLY The trust states that applications are unlikely to be successful unless one of the trustees has prior personal knowledge of the cause, as this charity's funds are already very heavily committed.

WHO TO APPLY TO J Pearlman, Governor, 8 Highfield Gardens, London NW11 9HB *Tel* 020 8458 9266

CC NO 267278   **ESTABLISHED** 1973

■ The Christopher Rowbotham Charitable Trust

WHERE FUNDING CAN BE GIVEN Bolton, Cheshire, Gateshead, Lancashire, Newcastle upon Tyne, North Tyneside and Northumberland.

WHO CAN BENEFIT Organisations benefiting: children; young adults; older people; people with disabilities and their carers; ex-service and service people; retired people; sportsmen and women who are disabled; unemployed people; and volunteers.

WHAT IS FUNDED Selected UK charities with branches in north west or north east England and local charities. Priority given to smaller charities with low overheads. This trust will consider funding: infrastructure and development; health care; health education; education and training; and community services.

WHAT IS NOT FUNDED Grants are only given to registered charities. No grants to individuals or overseas charities and no grants for capital building costs. The trust prefers to give regular grants but does not fund salaries.

TYPE OF GRANT Core costs, one-off, recurring costs, running costs and start-up costs. Funding can be given for up to and over three years. Salaries never considered.

RANGE OF GRANTS £50–£3,500; usually £250–£750.

SAMPLE GRANTS £3,500 to Shiplake College to support an individual during their A-levels; £2,000 to Winged Fellowship for respite care; £1,250 each to Fairbridge branches in Greater Manchester and Tyne & Wear; £1,000 each to Calvert Trust – Kielder for respite holidays, Disabled Living Foundation for general purposes, and Royal Star and Garter Homes for general purposes; £750 each to Jubilee Sailing Trust to allow people with disabilities to go sailing, Raleigh International for their North East Youth Development Programme, and Friends of Stamfordham First School to support their music teaching and library.

FINANCES *Year* 2002 *Income* £41,000 *Grants* £35,000 *Assets* £859,000

TRUSTEES Mrs C A Jackson, Chair; Mrs E J Wilkinson; R M Jackson.

HOW TO APPLY In writing: for north east England to the correspondent; for north west England to: Mrs Wilkinson, PO Box 43, Bolton, Lancashire BL1 5EZ. There are no application forms, guidelines or deadlines. Telephone calls are not welcome. No sae is required; applications are not acknowledged. Trustees meet annually in autumn. Applications can be sent at any time.

WHO TO APPLY TO Mrs C A Jackson, Chair, 18 Northumberland Square, North Shields, Tyne & Wear NE30 1PX

CC NO 261991   **ESTABLISHED** 1970

■ Joshua and Michelle Rowe Charitable Trust

WHERE FUNDING CAN BE GIVEN UK and worldwide.

WHAT IS FUNDED Jewish organisations.

SAMPLE GRANTS £28,515 to King David School; £17,000 to Chief Rabbi Charitable Trust; £15,378 to Manchester Great and New Synagogue; £12,000 to Aish Hatorah; £10,000 to Friends of Yeshivat Kerem B'yavneh; £9,000 to Midreshet Lindenbaum; £8,200 to Manchester Jewish Grammar; £4,105 to Manchester Jewish Federation; £3,000 to Manchester Talmudical College; £2,100 to Community Security Trust.

FINANCES *Year* 2000–01 *Income* £232,083 *Grants* £247,261 *Assets* £123,967

TRUSTEES J Rowe; Mrs M B Rowe.

HOW TO APPLY In writing to the correspondent.

WHO TO APPLY TO J Rowe, Trustee, 84 Upper Park Road, Salford M7 0JA

CC NO 288336   **ESTABLISHED** 1983

■ The Rowlands Trust

WHERE FUNDING CAN BE GIVEN UK, but primarily the West Midlands and South Midlands, and Gloucestershire.

WHO CAN BENEFIT People of all ages, research workers, disabled people and those disadvantaged by poverty.

WHAT IS FUNDED Medical and scientific research; the welfare of elderly, infirm, poor and disabled people; support for the arts and conservation; the encouragement of education and training for individuals to better themselves.

WHAT IS NOT FUNDED No support for individuals or to charities for the benefit of animals.

TYPE OF GRANT One-off, capital including buildings, project and research.

RANGE OF GRANTS Up to £20,000.

SAMPLE GRANTS £20,000 to National Trust Nimmings Wood, £15,000 to Shenley Court School; £10,000 each to City Technology College, Hereford Hospitals NHS Trust – new medical equipment, Kemp Hospice, Colwall Millennium Room Trust and Herefordshire Historic Churches Trust; £8,500 to Baverstock School; £7,500 to St Mark's Church, Tipton; £6,800 to Symphony Hall; £5,000 each to Extracare Charitable Trust, Herefordshire Mind, Jobs Close Residential Home, St Martin's Church – Bradley, Pershore Theatre Arts Association and Royal Agricultural Benevolent Association.

FINANCES *Year* 2001 *Income* £207,107 *Grants* £289,835 *Assets* £6,239,135

TRUSTEES A C S Hordern, Chair; G B G Hingley; K G Mason; Mrs A M I Harris; Mrs F J Burman.
HOW TO APPLY On a form available from the correspondent, to be returned with a copy of the most recent accounts. The trustees meet to consider grants four times a year.
WHO TO APPLY TO Mrs T Priest, Clerk to the Trustees, c/o Wragge & Co., 55 Colmore Row, Birmingham B3 2AS *Tel* 0121 233 1000
CC NO 1062148   **ESTABLISHED** 1997

■ The Rowley Trust

WHERE FUNDING CAN BE GIVEN Preference for Staffordshire and adjacent counties.
WHO CAN BENEFIT Individuals and organisations.
WHAT IS FUNDED Grants are made for the benefit of women and girls.
TYPE OF GRANT Various.
RANGE OF GRANTS Normally up to about £2,000.
SAMPLE GRANTS £5,000 to Stafford Furniture Exchange; £4,000 to Stafford Womens Aid; £2,600 to Newcastle Volunteer Bureau; £2,000 each to Staffordshire Probation Services and Staffordshire Social Services; £1,600 to Stoke on Trent District Gingerbread; £500 to Burntwood Pathway Project; £200 to Knutton Playgroup; £150 to East Staffordshire Borough Council.
FINANCES *Year* 1998–99 *Income* £60,000 *Grants* £50,000 *Assets* £980,000
HOW TO APPLY On a form available from the correspondent. Applications may be made at any time.
WHO TO APPLY TO J G Langford, Clerk, 7–8 St Mary's Grove, Stafford ST16 2AT *Tel* 01785 252377
CC NO 508630   **ESTABLISHED** 1988

■ The Joseph Rowntree Charitable Trust

WHERE FUNDING CAN BE GIVEN UK, Republic of Ireland and southern (mainly South) Africa.
WHO CAN BENEFIT Voluntary organisations and charitable groups benefiting people of all ages, ethnic minority groups, Quakers, those disadvantaged by poverty, immigrants and refugees. If the trustees decide to meet you to find out more about your application they will be looking to see if you know where you are heading, and how to get there; know about wider policy matters which might affect your work; know about work being done by others which is relevant to your work; are planning to do work which could be a useful example to others; have thought about the impact of your work upon the world's resources; and have thought about whether a grant from the trust may help you fundraising elsewhere.
WHAT IS FUNDED The following areas: peace – work towards the control or elimination of all forms of warfare, the development of effective peace work and the creation of a culture of peace; democratic process – work which strengthens democracy and upholds the rights of the citizen; racial justice – work towards the creation of a harmonious multi-racial and multi-cultural society, based on principles of justice, equality and respect; corporate responsibility – work to encourage corporations to behave with integrity, transparency and social responsibility; justice and reconciliation in South Africa and in Ireland (north and south); Quaker concerns.
WHAT IS NOT FUNDED Generally, the trust does not make grants for: work in larger, older national

charities which have an established constituency of supporters; general appeals; local work (except in Northern Ireland or parts of Yorkshire); building, buying or repairing buildings; providing care for elderly people, children, people with learning difficulties, people with physical disabilities, or people using mental health services; work in mainstream education, including schools and academic or medical research; work on housing and homelessness; travel or adventure projects; business development or job creation; paying off debts; work which should be funded by the state, or has been in the recent past; work which has already been done; work which tries to make a problem easier to live with, rather than getting to the root of it; the personal benefit of individuals in need; or the arts, except where they are used in the context of the kinds of work which the trust does support. The trust can only support work which is legally charitable.
TYPE OF GRANT Initial funding, usually short-term and interest-free loans.
RANGE OF GRANTS A few hundred pounds to over £100,000.
SAMPLE GRANTS £270,000 to Democratic Audit of the UK; £250,000 to 1990 Trust; £161,000 to International Security Information Service Europe; £140,000 to Fawcett Society; £120,000 to the Acronym Institute; £105,000 to Statewatch; £99,000 to Peaceworkers UK; £90,000 to Immigrants Aid Trust; £85,000 to Runnymede Trust; £84,000 to Educating and Acting for a Better World.
FINANCES *Year* 2001 *Grants* £3,960,000
TRUSTEES Andrew Gunn, Chair; Ruth McCarthy, vice-chair; Margaret Bryan; Christine Davis; Beverley Meeson; Marion McNaughton; Roger Morton; Vas Shend' ge; David Shutt; Tom Allport; Emily Miles; John Guest.
OTHER INFORMATION The Joseph Rowntree Charitable Trust is a Quaker trust and the value base of the trustees, as of the founder Joseph Rowntree (1836–1925), reflects the religious convictions of the Society of Friends.
HOW TO APPLY The trust expects all applicants to have made themselves familiar with the relevant funding programmes, summarised above but set out in full on the website and available in leaflet form.
They then require a letter and a completed registration form (also on the website). The details expected in the letter are set out in detail on the website and leaflet, at a length too great to be reprinted here. There is a deadline for receipt of applications ten weeks before the quarterly meeting of trustees. It is helpful if applications arrive well before the deadline. The trust tries its best to deal with applications which arrive before the deadline in the quarter they arrive, but sometimes this proves impossible. Occasionally it is possible to deal with applications which arrive after the deadline, but there have to be exceptional reasons for this to be considered. Future deadlines (and corresponding trust meeting dates) are: 31 March 2003 (14 June 2003); 7 July 2003 (13 September 2003); 22 September 2003 (29 November 2003).
WHO TO APPLY TO Stephen Pittam, Secretary, The Garden House, Water End, York YO30 6WQ *Tel* 01904 627810 *Fax* 01904 651990 *E-mail* info@jrct.org.uk *Website* www.jrct.org.uk
CC NO 210037   **ESTABLISHED** 1904

■ The Joseph Rowntree Foundation

WHERE FUNDING CAN BE GIVEN UK.

WHO CAN BENEFIT Organisations carrying out social science research.

WHAT IS FUNDED The foundation is not a grant-making body in the normal sense. Instead it works in partnership with projects once grants are awarded. The foundation initiates projects as well as considering unsolicited proposals in its areas of interest. Most of the projects funded fall into one of three areas, each having its own priorities for any given year. The areas are: housing; social policy; and social care.

WHAT IS NOT FUNDED With the exception of funds for particular projects in York and the surrounding area, the foundation does not generally support: projects outside the topics within its current priorities; development projects which are not innovative; development projects from which no general lessons can be drawn; general appeals, for example from national charities; core or revenue funding, including grants for buildings or equipment; conferences and other events, websites or publications, unless they are linked with work which the foundation is already supporting; grants to replace withdrawn or expired statutory funding, or to make up deficits already incurred; educational bursaries or sponsorship for individuals for research or further education and training courses; grants or sponsorship for individuals in need; or work that falls within the responsibility of statutory bodies.

TYPE OF GRANT Project and research. Funding can be given for up to two years.

SAMPLE GRANTS Approved in 2001: £275,000 to South Bank University; £245,823 to York University; £212,270 to Policy Studies Institute; £167,952 to Glasgow University; £166,180 to Institute of Psychiatry; £163,829 to Southampton University; £162,500 to Joseph Rowntree Housing Trust; £154,629 to Luton University; £132,008 to National Children's Bureau; £98,233 to National Centre for Social Research.

FINANCES *Year* 2001 *Income* £7,827,000 *Grants* £6,614,000 *Assets* £218,551,000

TRUSTEES Dame Margaret Booth; Kenneth Dixon; Robert Maxwell; J Nigel Naish; Sir William Utting; Catherine Graham-Harrison; Susan V Hartshorne; Dame Ann Bowtell; Debby Ounsted.

PUBLICATIONS *Findings* – short briefing papers summarising the main findings of projects in the Research and Development Programme (approximately 100 issued each year); *Special Reports* (approximately 20 in a year) designed to present research results with clarity and impact; *Search* – a magazine published two or three times a year featuring recent work of the foundation. For publication orders, ring: 01904 654328.

HOW TO APPLY Proposers are advised to obtain a copy of the most recent Research and Development information before making a proposal. A draft proposal or short outline covering the main headings identified below, received early, is welcome and usually better than a telephone call. Two unbound copies of the proposal should be provided, presented as follows: a succinct but clear proposal of a maximum 3,000 words; a summary of the proposal of not more than 600 words; completed copies of the foundation's project budget forms, with supporting details; and a curriculum vitae for the project proposer (and worker/s if known). Any proposal not submitted in this way may be returned for revision and thus delayed for consideration by the relevant committee. Further details on how the proposal should look are available on the foundation's website, or the correspondent.

WHO TO APPLY TO Lord Richard Best, Director, The Homestead, 40 Water End, York YO30 6WP *Tel* 01904 629241 *Website* www.jrf.org.uk

CC NO 210169 **ESTABLISHED** 1904

■ Royal British Legion

WHERE FUNDING CAN BE GIVEN UK, excluding Scotland.

WHO CAN BENEFIT People who have served in the Armed Forces, their widow(er) s and dependants, and those organisations which help them. Beneficiaries include those who have served in a hostile area with bodies such as the Mercantile Marines, the Allied Civil Police forces, the Home Guard, the Voluntary Aid Society and the Polish Resettlement Corp.

WHAT IS FUNDED The welfare of men and women who have served in the armed forces.

WHAT IS NOT FUNDED Funding is not given to people who have served with the Women's Land Army, National or Auxiliary Fire Service, Civil Defence organisations, or NAAFI.

TYPE OF GRANT One-off and recurring costs.

RANGE OF GRANTS £10–£800,000.

SAMPLE GRANTS £1,012,000 to The Officers Association; £330,000 to Royal British Legion Industries Ltd; £101,000 to St Dunstans; £50,000 to Sir Oswald Stoll Foundation; £40,000 to Ex-Service Mental Welfare Society; £30,000 to Earl Haig Fund – Scotland; £29,000 to Alcohol Recovery Project; £27,000 to British Ex-services Wheelchair Sports Association; £25,000 to British Commonwealth Ex-Services League; £18,000 to 'Not Forgotten' Association.

FINANCES *Year* 2000–01 *Income* £54,644,000 *Grants* £1,780,000 *Assets* £124,822,000

TRUSTEES J G H Champ, Chair; J J Brookes; C W Broughton; T B Buckby; I P Cannell; R I Glendinning; J Hawthornthwaite; M Hammond; E R Jobson; J H Lawrence; A I V Lyon; N Rogers; D P Smith; R E Swabey; J A Tedder; M E W Tidman; J B Tuckey; J E Williamson.

PUBLICATIONS *The Legion* magazine.

OTHER INFORMATION A further £7,357,000 was given to individuals.

HOW TO APPLY Societies should apply in writing to the secretary of the Benevolent and Strategy Committee.

WHO TO APPLY TO The Grants Department, 48 Pall Mall, London SW1Y 5JY *Tel* 020 7973 7200 *Fax* 020 7973 7399 *Website* www.britishlegion.org.uk

CC NO 219279 **ESTABLISHED** 1921

■ Royal Docks Trust (London)

WHERE FUNDING CAN BE GIVEN Part of the London borough of Newham (see below).

WHO CAN BENEFIT Community organisations in the stated area.

WHAT IS FUNDED The trust supports the community in that part of the London borough of Newham which lies to the south of the London – Tilbury Trunk Road (A13) known as Newham Way.

WHAT IS NOT FUNDED No grants to individuals.

RANGE OF GRANTS £40–£25,000.

FINANCES *Year* 2001–02 *Income* £138,105 *Grants* £108,348

TRUSTEES Eric Sorenson, Chair; Steve Nicholas; Sid Keys; Richard Gooding; Mubin Haq; Cllr Pat

Think carefully about every application. Is it justified?

759

Holland; Cllr Marie Collier; Michael Grier; Dennis Hone; John Ringwood; Andrea Miller-Chan.

OTHER INFORMATION The trust operates an annual joint grant programme with the London borough of Newham. Applications are invited in the autumn for grants from the following year's programme. However, there is ongoing provision throughout the year for minor grants not exceeding £1,000.

HOW TO APPLY In writing to the correspondent.

WHO TO APPLY TO John Parker, Church Cottage, Darenth Hill, Darenth DA2 7QY *Tel* 01322 226336 *Fax* 01322 226882 *E-mail* john.parker@royaldockstrust.org *Website* www.royaldockstrust.org.uk

CC NO 1045057   **ESTABLISHED** 1995

■ The Royal Eastern Counties Schools Limited

WHERE FUNDING CAN BE GIVEN UK – preference will normally be given to Essex, Suffolk, Norfolk, Cambridgeshire and Hertfordshire.

WHO CAN BENEFIT Those with special educational needs, particularly those under 25 who have emotional and behavioural difficulties.

WHAT IS FUNDED Activities and projects which will assist the above.

WHAT IS NOT FUNDED Normally no grants are given for recurring costs and no grants to non-registered charities.

TYPE OF GRANT Cash.

RANGE OF GRANTS £500–£10,000.

FINANCES *Year* 2001–02 *Income* £62,480 *Grants* £19,453 *Assets* £1,561,104

TRUSTEES Mrs A R Boyle; Mrs C Edey; G M H McLoughlin; Mrs V L d'Angibau; P G Glossop; L M Lepper; F V Morgan; Mrs K E Norman-Butler; A J Willis.

HOW TO APPLY An application form should be obtained from the correspondent. This provides details of information to be submitted with it. Unsuccessful applicants will not be informed unless an sae is provided.

WHO TO APPLY TO A H Corin, Company Secretary, Brook Farm, Wet Lane, Boxted, Colchester, Essex CO4 5TN *Tel* 01206 273295 *Fax* 01206 273295

CC NO 310038   **ESTABLISHED** 1922

■ The Royal London Aid Society

WHERE FUNDING CAN BE GIVEN UK.

WHO CAN BENEFIT Individuals and organisations benefiting ex-offenders and those at risk of offending.

WHAT IS FUNDED Prisoners and ex-prisoners for art and craft materials, vocational training and work tools after release. Similar projects carried out by groups are also supported.

WHAT IS NOT FUNDED No grants for the benefit of non-offenders.

TYPE OF GRANT Core costs and recurring costs. Funding may be given for up to one year.

SAMPLE GRANTS £370 to inmates at HMP Sudbury for fork lift truck driving lessons; £250 to a self supporting group at HMP Dartmoor for art materials.

FINANCES *Year* 2001 *Income* £64,654 *Grants* £19,126 *Assets* £967,061

TRUSTEES Miss I O D Harrison; A G F Young; G E Mitchell; Revd P Timms; I R C Bieber; Miss E A Day; I M Kirk; J B H Martin; R Kissin.

HOW TO APPLY In writing to the correspondent for an application form. Applications are considered

each quarter in March, June, September and December.

WHO TO APPLY TO Jude Cohen, 69 Felhampton Road, London SE9 3NT *Tel* 020 8851 7209 *Fax* 020 8851 7209 *Minicom* jude@rlas.evesham.net

CC NO 214695   **ESTABLISHED** 1863

■ The Royal Victoria Hall Foundation

WHERE FUNDING CAN BE GIVEN Greater London.

WHO CAN BENEFIT Professional theatre groups (including youth and children's theatre).

WHAT IS FUNDED Encouragement of organisations devoted to the development of and education in theatrical pursuits, infrastructure and technical support, opera and theatre.

WHAT IS NOT FUNDED Grants are made for theatrical pursuits only, not for the fine arts and music, or dance which is not in a theatrical context. No grants to individuals. No repeat applications within two years and no retrospective grants.

TYPE OF GRANT Buildings, capital, feasibility studies, one-off, projects, recurring costs, running costs and salaries are all considered for one year or less.

RANGE OF GRANTS Usually between £500 and £1,000.

SAMPLE GRANTS £2,500 to Polka Theatre for Children towards their first-timers' scheme; £1,500 each to Balagan Theatre Company, Mirage Children's Theatre Company and Soho Theatre and Writers Centre; £1,400 each to 12 individuals.

FINANCES *Year* 2002 *Income* £96,858 *Grants* £47,800 *Assets* £947,587

TRUSTEES Valerie Colgan, Chair; Dilys Gane; Anne Stanesby; Michael Redington; David Collier, Vice Chair; Annie Castledine; Gerald Lidstone; Annabel Arden; Vivienne Rochester.

HOW TO APPLY In writing by 1 February and 1 August prior to trustees' meetings. No replies without an sae.

WHO TO APPLY TO Mrs C Cooper, Clerk, 111 Green Street, Sunbury-on-Thames, Middlesex TW16 6QX *Tel* 01932 782341 *E-mail* rvhfoundation@ntlworld.com

CC NO 211246   **ESTABLISHED** 1891

■ The Alfred and Frances Rubens Charitable Trust

WHERE FUNDING CAN BE GIVEN UK.

WHO CAN BENEFIT Registered charities only.

WHAT IS FUNDED General charitable purposes.

TYPE OF GRANT Recurrent.

RANGE OF GRANTS £25–£5,000.

SAMPLE GRANTS £5,000 to Jewish Museum; £3,300 to West London Synagogue; £2,000 each to Jewish Care and Norwood Ravenswood.

FINANCES *Year* 2000 *Income* £30,000 *Grants* £30,000 *Assets* £510,000

TRUSTEES J F Millan; A E Gutwin; W C Lambros.

HOW TO APPLY The trust states that it does not respond to unsolicited applications.

WHO TO APPLY TO J F Millan, Trustee, 4 Court Close, St John's Wood Park, London NW8 6NN *Tel* 020 7586 5509

CC NO 264430   **ESTABLISHED** 1972

■ The J B Rubens Charitable Foundation

WHERE FUNDING CAN BE GIVEN UK, Israel, USA, India, Sri Lanka, Pakistan, South Africa, New Zealand, Australia, Canada.

WHO CAN BENEFIT Children and younger and older people.

WHAT IS FUNDED Education and social welfare of children and young people, social welfare of older people and medical care.

WHAT IS NOT FUNDED No grants are made to individuals.

TYPE OF GRANT Capital costs, general support.

SAMPLE GRANTS £140,000 to Ruth and Michael Phillips Charitable Trust; £16,845 to Simon Weisenthal Centre; £10,000 to Charities Aid Foundation; £7,695 to Jerusalem Foundation; £500 to Jewish Blind and Physically Handicapped Society.

FINANCES *Year* 2000–01 *Income* £370,677 *Grants* £175,040 *Assets* £8,687,737

TRUSTEES Michael Phillips; J B Rubens Charity Trustees Limited.

HOW TO APPLY In writing to the correspondent, at any time.

WHO TO APPLY TO Michael Phillips, Trustee, Berkeley Square House, Berkeley Square, London W1J 6BY *Tel* 020 7491 3763 *Fax* 020 7491 0818

CC NO 218366　　　**ESTABLISHED** 1959

■ The Rubin Foundation

WHERE FUNDING CAN BE GIVEN UK and overseas.

WHO CAN BENEFIT Organisations benefiting Jewish people, students and people who are sick.

WHAT IS FUNDED Primarily, but not exclusively, Jewish charities. Also, medical charities, museums and universities.

RANGE OF GRANTS Up to £150,000; exceptionally higher.

SAMPLE GRANTS £236,000 to Joint Jewish Charitable Trust.

FINANCES *Year* 2000–01 *Income* £507,000 *Grants* £507,000

TRUSTEES Alison Mosheim; Angela Rubin; R Stephen Rubin; Carolyn Kubetz; Andrew Rubin.

HOW TO APPLY The trust has committed its funds for the next few years, and it uses the remainder for chosen charities known to members of the family, and those associated with the Pentland Group plc. Unsolicited applications are very unlikely to succeed.

WHO TO APPLY TO A McMillan, Secretary, The Pentland Centre, Squires Lane, Finchley, London N3 2QL *Tel* 020 8346 2600

CC NO 327062　　　**ESTABLISHED** 1986

■ William Arthur Rudd Memorial Trust

WHERE FUNDING CAN BE GIVEN In practice UK and Spain.

WHO CAN BENEFIT UK and certain Spanish charities.

WHAT IS FUNDED General charitable purposes.

RANGE OF GRANTS £500–£5,000.

SAMPLE GRANTS £5,000 to Providence Row Night Refuge; £4,000 to the Wallace Collection; £3,000 each to St Thomas' Fund for the Homeless and Holy Trinity Church Las Palmas; £2,000 each to Divert, Koestler Awards Trust, San Juan de Dios, Nuevo Futro and Trinity Hospice.

FINANCES *Year* 2000–01 *Income* £46,000 *Grants* £38,500

TRUSTEES Miss A A Sarkis; D H Smyth; R G Maples.

HOW TO APPLY As the trust's resources are fully committed, the trustees do not consider unsolicited applications.

WHO TO APPLY TO Miss A A Sarkis, Trustee, 12 South Square, Gray's Inn, London WC1R 5HH *Tel* 020 7405 8932 *Fax* 020 7831 0011 *Minicom* mmm@elawuk.com

CC NO 326495　　　**ESTABLISHED** 1983

■ The Rufford Foundation

WHERE FUNDING CAN BE GIVEN Developing countries, UK.

WHO CAN BENEFIT Registered charities only, mainly in developing countries.

WHAT IS FUNDED The focus is on conservation, environmental and sustainable development projects in developing countries. UK organisations supporting social welfare may also receive support.

WHAT IS NOT FUNDED The foundation cannot consider proposals for: building or construction projects; non-charitable organisations; grants to individuals; projects which seek to exclusively benefit local communities, such as playgroups, youth clubs, luncheon clubs and so on; loans; endowment funds; general appeals or circulars; student conservation expeditions.

RANGE OF GRANTS Usually £500 to £5,000.

SAMPLE GRANTS £271,184 to Conservation International to fund various AquaRAP projects in South America, aquatic expeditions in Botswana and transfrontier conservation initiatives in southern Africa; £248,197 to Whitley Awards Foundation to fund various awards for grassroots conservation and sustainable development projects worldwide; £110,000 to WWF-UK for aspects of their international campaigns; £109,035 to TRAFFIC UK to fund various conservation related projects in the developing world; £87,000 to Global Canopy Foundation (GCP) towards the establishment of a Global Forest Company research programme and for the production of a Global Canopy Handbook; £70,000 to Attivecomeprima (an Italian breast cancer charity) towards core costs of the organisation; £68,500 to the Wildlife Protection Society of India to fund various projects and elements of core costs; £60,920 to EIA Charitable Trust in support of their CFC campaign. A percentage of these funds were allocated towards the organisation's communication core costs; £54,465 to Fauna and Flora International towards core costs; £50,000 to Earthwatch Institute to fund an international programmes fundraiser for the Global Programmes Initiative.

FINANCES *Year* 2001–02 *Income* £2,600,000 *Grants* £2,299,630 *Assets* £59,000,000

TRUSTEES J H Laing; A Gavazzi; C R Barbour; A J Johnson; K W Scott; M I Smailes; V Lees.

HOW TO APPLY All applications must be received by post and meet with the following criteria: All applicants must be charities registered in the UK. Applications must include: a comprehensive plan outlining the project for which funding is being sought; a full budget; a covering letter with contact details; a copy of the charity's most recent accounts; a copy of the latest annual report (if available).

Applications are assessed monthly. Gifts over £5,000 will be considered at trustees' meetings held twice a year. Each application is assessed individually and while the trust strives to respond quickly, it only has one full-time member of staff, so please be patient. Any incomplete applications received, or applications which fail to meet with the trust's criteria, as outlined above, will immediately be rejected.

WHO TO APPLY TO Terry Kenny, Director, Babmaes House, 2 Babmaes Street, London SW1Y 6RF *Tel* 020 7925 2582 *Website* www.rufford.org

CC NO 326163 **ESTABLISHED** 1982

■ The Rural Trust

WHERE FUNDING CAN BE GIVEN UK.

WHO CAN BENEFIT Registered charities.

WHAT IS FUNDED The protection, maintenance or preservation of the countryside, and to educate the public and promote any object that will benefit the countryside.

WHAT IS NOT FUNDED No support for non-charitable bodies or individuals.

RANGE OF GRANTS £250–£9,000.

SAMPLE GRANTS £9,000 to Centurion Press for an educational video 'Our Countryside Matters'; £2,000 to Rural Buildings Trust for barn restoration in North Yorkshire; £1,500 to Oxenhope Millennium Green for the creation of a green in the Pennines; £1,000 each to Blake Shield BNA Trust for conservation projects for 7–16 year olds, Second Chance towards angling for children with special needs, and Wildlife Trust Cumbria for red squirrel protection; £500 to Chicks towards country holidays for inner city kids; £250 each to Burnbake Trust for river bank restoration in Wiltshire, and North Wales Wildlife Trust for a water vole survey.

FINANCES *Year* 1999–2000 *Grants* £30,000

TRUSTEES Dr C Goodson-Wickes; The Earl of Stockton; H B E van Cutsem.

HOW TO APPLY In writing to the correspondent.

WHO TO APPLY TO Dr Charles Goodson-Wickes, Chairman, Fraser House, Albemarle Street, London W1S 4JB *Tel* 020 7409 1447 *Fax* 020 7409 1449

CC NO 1060040 **ESTABLISHED** 1996

■ The Frank Russell Charitable Trust

WHERE FUNDING CAN BE GIVEN Not known.

WHO CAN BENEFIT Charities known to the trust.

WHAT IS FUNDED General charitable purposes.

FINANCES *Year* 1999–2000 *Income* £18,000 *Grants* £40,000 *Assets* £274,000

TRUSTEES F Russell; J Russell; A Levy.

HOW TO APPLY In writing to the correspondent. Unsolicited applications are not considered.

WHO TO APPLY TO A Levy, Trustee, Richard Anthony & Co., 13–15 Station Road, London N3 2SB *Tel* 020 8349 0353

CC NO 327548 **ESTABLISHED** 1987

■ The Russell Trust

WHERE FUNDING CAN BE GIVEN UK, especially Scotland.

WHO CAN BENEFIT Registered charities.

WHAT IS FUNDED General charitable purposes.

WHAT IS NOT FUNDED Only registered charities are supported.

TYPE OF GRANT One-off for projects or start-up costs.

RANGE OF GRANTS £250–£10,000.

SAMPLE GRANTS In 1998–99: £10,000 each to Edinburgh Green Belt Trust for an educational initiative, National Galleries of Scotland to set up a 'friends' scheme, National Trust for

Scotland for Hew Lorimer project at Kellie Castle, Royal Society of Edinburgh, and St Andrews University for PhD awards; £6,000 to Liberating Scots Trust for a military museum to commemorate Scots in the second world war; £5,000 each to Clovenstone Primary School for a new playground and Craighead Institute.

FINANCES *Year* 2000–01 *Income* £287,515 *Grants* £232,000 *Assets* £5,100,000

TRUSTEES Mrs Cecilia Croal; Fred Bowden; Duncan Ingram; David Erdal; Mrs Margaret Russell Granelli.

HOW TO APPLY On a form available from the correspondent.

WHO TO APPLY TO Mrs Cecilia Croal, Secretary, Markinch, Glenrothes, Fife KY7 6PB *Tel* 01592 753311

SC NO SC004424

■ Willy Russell Charitable Trust

WHERE FUNDING CAN BE GIVEN Worldwide.

WHO CAN BENEFIT Mainly arts organisations.

WHAT IS FUNDED General charitable purposes.

RANGE OF GRANTS £1,000–£8,000.

SAMPLE GRANTS £8,000 to Avron Foundation; £5,000 each to Liverpool Lunchtime Theatre, JMU Trust, London Lighthouse, Khulani Literary Centre, and Production Line; £2,500 to Rahma Kingfisher Scholarship; £2,000 to Merseyside Drugs Council; £1,000 to The Library Company.

FINANCES *Year* 1999–2000 *Income* £62,000 *Grants* £51,000

TRUSTEES William M Russell; Ann Russell; John C Malthouse.

HOW TO APPLY In writing to the correspondent.

WHO TO APPLY TO J Malthouse, Trustee, Malthouse & Co., America House, Rumford Court, Rumford Place, Liverpool L3 9DD *Tel* 0151 284 2000

CC NO 1003546 **ESTABLISHED** 1991

■ Rycroft Children's Fund

WHERE FUNDING CAN BE GIVEN Cheshire, Derbyshire, Greater Manchester, Lancashire, Staffordshire and West Yorkshire.

WHO CAN BENEFIT Individuals and organisations benefiting children and young adults.

WHAT IS FUNDED Welfare of children and young adults.

WHAT IS NOT FUNDED Grants are not given to individuals for education, holidays or computers.

SAMPLE GRANTS £5,000 each to Family Welfare Assocation and Manchester & Salford Family Service Unit; £1,000 each to NSPCC, Rainbow Family Trust and Vision Aid (Bolton branch); £750 to Salford Lads Club; £700 each to Greater Manchester Federation of Boys Clubs and Norbrook; £400 to Catholic Children's Rescue.

FINANCES *Year* 1998–99 *Income* £43,060 *Grants* £42,927 *Assets* £710,987

HOW TO APPLY In writing to the correspondent. Trustees meet four times a year.

WHO TO APPLY TO J N Smith, Secretary, 10 Heyridge Drive, Northenden, Manchester M22 4HB *Tel* 0161 998 3127

CC NO 231771 **ESTABLISHED** 1985

■ **The J S & E C Rymer Charitable Trust**

WHERE FUNDING CAN BE GIVEN East Yorkshire.

WHO CAN BENEFIT People who have retired from rural industry or agriculture.

WHAT IS FUNDED Housing for retired people who have spent the major part of their working lives in rural industry or agriculture; general charitable purposes in the specified area.

WHAT IS NOT FUNDED No grants to charities outside East Yorkshire.

RANGE OF GRANTS £10–£1,000.

SAMPLE GRANTS In 1996: £10,000 to York Minster for bells to commemorate the Queen Mother's 100th birthday; £5,110 to NFU Trust for Education for agricultural education for children; £5,000 to Sue Ryder Foundation for Holme Hall Hospice; £500 each to NSPCC for local green spot committee and NCH Action for Children; £320 to Sailors' Families Society for local Hull orphanage; £250 each to Bishop Willon Agricultural Show, Mobility Trust, Alzheimer's Society for local care, Hull and East Riding Digestive Foundation for medical equipment needed locally, and Macmillan Cancer Relief for local care.

FINANCES *Year* 1999–2000 *Income* £62,000 *Grants* £23,000 *Assets* £910,000

HOW TO APPLY In writing to the correspondent.

WHO TO APPLY TO Mrs E C Rymer, Trustee, Southburn Offices, Southburn, Driffield, East Yorkshire YO25 9ED *Tel* 01377 229264 *Fax* 01377 229253 *E-mail* charitable.trust@jsr.co.uk

CC NO 267493   **ESTABLISHED** 1974

■ The Audrey Sacher Charitable Trust

WHERE FUNDING CAN BE GIVEN UK.
WHO CAN BENEFIT Registered charities.
WHAT IS FUNDED General charitable purposes. Requests are generally only considered if they are from organisations that are personally known to the trustees.
WHAT IS NOT FUNDED No grants to individuals or organisations which are not registered charities.
RANGE OF GRANTS £250–£30,000.
SAMPLE GRANTS £123,000 to Royal Opera House; £25,000 to National Gallery.
FINANCES *Year* 2000–01 *Income* £65,175 *Grants* £198,452 *Assets* £2,274,460
TRUSTEES Mrs Nicola Shelley Sacher; Michael Harry Sacher.
HOW TO APPLY In writing to the correspondent.
WHO TO APPLY TO P Samuel, H W Fisher & Co, 11–15 William Road, London NW1 3ER *Tel* 020 7388 7000
CC NO 288973   **ESTABLISHED** 1984

■ The Michael Sacher Charitable Trust

WHERE FUNDING CAN BE GIVEN UK and Israel.
WHO CAN BENEFIT There are no restrictions; however, non-Jewish organisations will only receive small grants.
WHAT IS FUNDED General charitable purposes; Jewish organisations.
RANGE OF GRANTS £200–£40,000.
FINANCES *Year* 2000–01 *Income* £647,274 *Grants* £161,347 *Assets* £5,107,921
TRUSTEES Simon John Sacher; Jeremy Michael Sacher; Hon. Mrs Rosalind E C Sacher; Mrs Elisabeth J Sacher.
OTHER INFORMATION In 1997–98: £40,000 to Israel Disapora Trust; £32,500 to British Friends of the Art Museums of Israel; £30,000 to J'Paime; £7,500 to Community Security Trust; £4,500 to Friends of the Hebrew University of Jerusalem; £2,500 to Jewish Care; £2,000 each to New Israel Fund and Norwood; £1,000 to CBF World Jewish Relief; £889 to West London Synagogue.
HOW TO APPLY In writing to the correspondent at any time.
WHO TO APPLY TO Mrs Irene Wiggins, Secretary, 16 Clifton Villas, London W9 2PH *Tel* 020 7289 5873
CC NO 206321   **ESTABLISHED** 1957

■ Dr Mortimer and Theresa Sackler Foundation

WHERE FUNDING CAN BE GIVEN UK.
WHO CAN BENEFIT Large institutions benefiting actors and entertainment professionals, musicians, textile workers and designers, and writers and poets.
WHAT IS FUNDED The arts; hospitals.
TYPE OF GRANT Some recurring; others one-off.
SAMPLE GRANTS £105,000 to Dulwich Picture Gallery; £50,000 each to Kings College London and London University – Courtauld Institute;

£46,000 to Tate Modern; £30,000 to University Of Reading; £25,000 each to National Maritime Museum and Royal National Theatre Board; £15,000 to St Thomas' Schools Foundation; £10,000 each to Serpentine Trust and Stoke Manderville Hospital.
FINANCES *Year* 2000 *Income* £214,559 *Grants* £420,979 *Assets* £3,945,284
TRUSTEES Mortimer Sackler; Theresa Sackler; Christopher Mitchell; Robin Stormonth-Darling; Raymond Smith.
OTHER INFORMATION With the expiry of the original deed of covenant, donations are likely to fall so that the foundation's previously large commitments must be curtailed. New applicants are unlikely to be successful.
HOW TO APPLY To the correspondent in writing.
WHO TO APPLY TO Christopher B Mitchell, Trustee, 15 North Audley Street, London W1K 6WZ *Tel* 020 7493 3842
CC NO 327863   **ESTABLISHED** 1988

■ The Raymond & Beverley Sackler Foundation

WHERE FUNDING CAN BE GIVEN UK.
WHO CAN BENEFIT The trust has a list of regular beneficiaries.
WHAT IS FUNDED Grants are given to the arts, sciences and medical research.
TYPE OF GRANT Annual grants.
FINANCES *Year* 2000 *Income* £14,886 *Grants* £31,250 *Assets* £356,778
TRUSTEES Dr Raymond Sackler; Dr Richard Sackler; Jonathan Sackler; Christopher Mitchell; Dr Ronald Miller; Paul Manners; Raymond Smith.
HOW TO APPLY Grants are not open to application.
WHO TO APPLY TO Christopher Mitchell, Solicitor, 15 North Audley Street, London W1K 6WZ
CC NO 327864   **ESTABLISHED** 1988

■ The Ruzin Sadagora Trust

WHERE FUNDING CAN BE GIVEN UK, Israel.
WHO CAN BENEFIT Charities benefiting Jewish people.
WHAT IS FUNDED Preference for Jewish charities.
FINANCES *Year* 2000–01 *Income* £344,739 *Grants* £290,289
TRUSTEES Israel Friedman; Sara Friedman.
HOW TO APPLY In writing to the correspondent.
WHO TO APPLY TO I M Friedman, Trustee, 269 Golders Green Road, London NW11 9JJ
CC NO 285475   **ESTABLISHED** 1982

■ The Saddlers' Company Charitable Fund

WHERE FUNDING CAN BE GIVEN UK, but mainly England in practice.
WHO CAN BENEFIT Organisations working in the areas listed below.
WHAT IS FUNDED Grants are made by the company in four main categories: City of London; the equestrian world; education; and general charitable purposes.
WHAT IS NOT FUNDED Appeals by individuals for educational grants cannot be considered.
TYPE OF GRANT Cash grants, normally one-off for one year or less.
SAMPLE GRANTS £130,000 to Alleyn's School; £27,500 to Riding for the Disabled; £24,000 to British Horse Society; £5,000 to Lord Mayor's Appeal for the Square Smile; £4,000 to Leather Conservation Centre; £3,000 to City & Guilds;

£2,000 each to Museum of Leathercraft; Combined Services Equitation Association, Middlesex & NW London ACF, London Area Sea Cadets, London Wing ATC, London Youth, Army Benevolent Fund and RAF Benevolent Fund.

FINANCES *Year* 2001–02 *Income* £320,513 *Grants* £300,704 *Assets* £7,913,480

TRUSTEES The Saddlers' Company. The company is directed by the court of assistants consisting of the master, three wardens, a number of past masters and up to four junior assistants. There shall be a minimum of 12 and a maximum of 24.

HOW TO APPLY By letter, with supporting background information. Grants are made in January and July, following trustees' meetings. Charities are asked to submit reports at the end of the following year on their continuing activities and the use of any grant received.

WHO TO APPLY TO W S Brereton-Martin, Saddlers' Hall, 40 Gutter Lane, London EC2V 6BR *Tel* 020 7726 8661 *Fax* 020 7600 0386 *E-mail* clerk@saddlersco.co.uk *Website* www.saddlersco.co.uk

CC NO 261962 **ESTABLISHED** 1970

■ The Karim Rida Said Foundation

WHERE FUNDING CAN BE GIVEN Middle East, with a focus on Lebanon, Syria, Jordan, Palestine and Iraq.

WHO CAN BENEFIT Institutions working with very poor people and focusing on children and young people. Scholarships, to individuals from the Middle East in financial need, for postgraduate study in the UK. Also at risk groups, people who are disabled and those disadvantaged by poverty.

WHAT IS FUNDED To relieve poverty and suffering in the Arab world by the provision of assistance in the fields of health, disability, education and children at risk. To promote understanding in the West of Arabic language and culture.

WHAT IS NOT FUNDED No support for general appeals, sponsorship events, conferences, newsletters or individuals (except through its scholarship programme).

TYPE OF GRANT Capital, core costs, endowments, one-off, project, research, recurring and running costs, salaries, and start-up costs. Donations to projects whose progress can be monitored and which can become self-sustaining, and scholarships.

RANGE OF GRANTS Variable for up to three years.

SAMPLE GRANTS £190,000 to Syria Disability Programme; £17,323 to Medical Aid to Iraqi Children; £15,512 to South Society for Special Education; £15,000 each to Save the Children – Lebanon and Union of Palestine Medical Relief Committees; £14,814 to Care International; £12,696 to British Museum – Arab World Education Programme; £11,975 to Jofeh Community-Based Rehabilitation Programme; £10,884 to Young Women's Christian Association – Family Counselling Centre; £9,076 to the Family Friends Society in Jordan; £7,925 to Spafford Children's Centre – Jerusalem; £7,500 to Quaker Peace and Social Witness – Lebanon; and £1,778 to Kanafani Habilitation to Pre-School In Lebanon.

FINANCES *Year* 2000–01 *Income* £1,172,991 *Grants* £973,821 *Assets* £24,814,686

TRUSTEES Wafic R Said, Chair; A Rosemary Said; Mr Ghayth Armanazi; Dr Peter Clark; Mrs Sirine Idilby; Lord Powell; Ms Catherine Roe; Khaled Said.

PUBLICATIONS Information brochure; *KRSF News*(termly newsletter).

HOW TO APPLY On a form available from the address below. If the proposed project is eligible for a grant, it will be visited. To apply for a scholarship apply through the offices of the British Council in Damascus, Amman, Beirut, East Jerusalem or Gaza City (by 28 February); apply direct to the foundation if you are already in the UK (by 1 May); apply direct to Oxford (by 31 March) and Cambridge (by 30 September) Universities if these are the universities at which you wish to study.

WHO TO APPLY TO Marc Long, Director, 4 Bloomsbury Place, Second Floor, London WC1A 2QA *Tel* 020 7691 2772 *Fax* 020 7691 2780 *E-mail* admin@krsf.org *Website* www.krsf.org

CC NO 1073096 **ESTABLISHED** 1982

■ The Alan and Babette Sainsbury Charitable Fund

WHERE FUNDING CAN BE GIVEN Unrestricted.

WHO CAN BENEFIT Charities operating in the fields summarised below.

WHAT IS FUNDED Education, health and social welfare, overseas, scientific and medical research, the arts.

WHAT IS NOT FUNDED Grants are not normally made to individuals.

TYPE OF GRANT One-off, core costs, capital, project and running costs.

RANGE OF GRANTS £100–£100,000.

SAMPLE GRANTS £100,000 to Pestalozzi Children's Village Trust; £64,800 to Interights; £45,000 to World ORT Union; £30,000 to Minority Rights Group; £25,000 each to Canon Collins Educational Trust for Southern Africa and Global Cancer Concern; £21,510 to British Friends of Neve Shalom; £20,000 each to Council of Christians and Jews, Jewish Children's Holiday Fund and Evelyn Oldfield Unit.

FINANCES *Year* 2000–01 *Income* £600,562 *Grants* £638,835 *Assets* £14,091,819

TRUSTEES Simon Sainsbury; Miss Judith Portrait.

OTHER INFORMATION The trust is one of the Sainsbury Family Charitable Trusts which share a common administration.

HOW TO APPLY Proposals are generally invited by the trustees or initiated at their request. Unsolicited applications are nort encouraged and are unlikely to be successful.

WHO TO APPLY TO Michael Pattison, Director, Allington House, 1st Floor, 150 Victoria Street, London SW1E 5AE *Tel* 020 7410 0330 *Fax* 020 7410 0332

CC NO 292930 **ESTABLISHED** 1953

■ The Jean Sainsbury Animal Welfare Trust

WHERE FUNDING CAN BE GIVEN Mainly the UK, but overseas charities are considered.

WHO CAN BENEFIT National and international animal welfare organisations.

WHAT IS FUNDED To support smaller charities concerned with animal welfare and wildlife.

WHAT IS NOT FUNDED No grants are made to individuals or non-registered charities and no loans can be given.

TYPE OF GRANT Capital, buildings, core costs, project, running costs and recurring costs. Funding for up to one year is available.

RANGE OF GRANTS £200–£10,000; typical grant £500.

SAMPLE GRANTS £10,000 each to Celia Hammond Animal Rescue, The Blue Cross and North Clwyd Animal Rescue; £7,500 each to Donkey Sanctuary and Royal Veterinary College Small Animals Hospital, Beaumont; £7,000 to Three Owls Bird Sanctuary & Rescue; £7,000 in total to Remus Memorial Horse Sanctuary; £6,000 each to Worcestershire Animal Rescue Shelter and Brent Lodge Bird & Wildlife Trust; £5,000 each to Hull & East Riding Boxer Rescue, Society for the Welfare of Horses & Ponies and Vidanimal Colombia.

FINANCES Year 2001 Income £262,287 Grants £218,000 Assets £7,328,318

TRUSTEES Jean Sainsbury; Cyril Sainsbury; Colin Russell; Gillian Tarlington; James Keliher; Mark Spurdens; Jane Winship; Audrey Lowrie.

HOW TO APPLY In writing to the correspondent, including a copy of accounts. There are three trustees meetings every year, usually in March, July and November.

WHO TO APPLY TO Miss Ann Dietrich, Administrator, PO Box 469, London W14 8PJ Fax 020 7371 4918

CC NO 326358   ESTABLISHED 1982

■ The Robert and Lisa Sainsbury Charitable Trust

WHERE FUNDING CAN BE GIVEN Unrestricted.

WHO CAN BENEFIT Organisations benefiting students, actors and entertainment professionals, textile workers and designers, musicians, and writers and poets.

WHAT IS FUNDED Medical research charities and caring charities; education in art, the humanities and other branches of learning; general charitable purposes.

WHAT IS NOT FUNDED No grants to individuals.

TYPE OF GRANT Largely capital.

SAMPLE GRANTS £1,300,000 to University of East Anglia; £500,000 to The Sainsbury Institute for the Study of Japanese Art and Culture; £242,000 to Norwich Cathedral; £15,000 to Community Health South London NHS Trust.

FINANCES Year 2000–01 Grants £2,061,000

TRUSTEES Sir Robert Sainsbury; Lady Lisa Sainsbury; Christopher Stone; Miss Judith Portrait.

HOW TO APPLY In writing to the correspondent.

WHO TO APPLY TO David Walker, c/o Horwarth Clark Whitehill, 25 New Street Square, London EC4A 3LN Tel 020 7353 1577 Fax 020 7583 1720

CC NO 276923   ESTABLISHED 1978

■ St Andrew Animal Fund Ltd

WHERE FUNDING CAN BE GIVEN UK and overseas, with a preference for Scotland.

WHO CAN BENEFIT Registered charities and individuals concerned with animal welfare.

WHAT IS FUNDED Priorities are: support for the development of non-animal research techniques; funding farm animal, companion animal and wildlife studies to improve welfare; supporting projects which will enhance the welfare of animals.

WHAT IS NOT FUNDED No support for routine day-to-day expenses.

TYPE OF GRANT The trust will consider grants for buildings and other capital, projects, research and start-up costs, for up to three years.

SAMPLE GRANTS £1,000 each to Crosskennan Lane Animal Sanctuary, Norwegian School of Veterinary Science, Hessilhead Wildlife Rescue

Trust, World Animal Net and Orkney Seal Rescue.

FINANCES Year 2000 Income £113,000 Grants £17,000

TRUSTEES Prof. Timothy Sprigge; Murray McGrath; Christopher Mylne; Eileen Aitken; David Martin; Dr Jane Goodall; Heather Petrie; Rebecca Ford; Shona McManus; Stephen Blakeway; Ginny Hay; Emma Law.

HOW TO APPLY In writing to the correspondent. The trustees meet in April and applications must reach the fund by 31 December for consideration at the next meeting. Applications should include a copy of the latest accounts, the name and address of a referee (e.g. veterinary surgeon, bank manager, pet food supplier and so on), the purpose for which any grant will be used and, where relevant, two estimates. Receipts for work carried out may be requested and the fund states that visits by representatives of the fund to those organisations receiving grants will be made at random.

WHO TO APPLY TO Les Ward, 10 Queensferry Street, Edinburgh EH2 4PG Tel 0131 225 2116 Fax 0131 220 6377 E-mail advocates.animals@virgin.net Website www.advocatesforanimals.org.uk

SC NO SC005337   ESTABLISHED 1969

■ St Andrews Conservation Trust

WHERE FUNDING CAN BE GIVEN Preference for the south west of England.

WHAT IS FUNDED The conservation, restoration and preservation of monuments, sculptures and artefacts of historic or public interest which are upon or attached to property owned by any charitable organisation.

WHAT IS NOT FUNDED No support is given for conservation or restoration of churchyard table tombs except in very restricted circumstances.

RANGE OF GRANTS £100–£7,500.

SAMPLE GRANTS £3,125 to an organisation in East Pennard – Somerset for conservation of a wall painting; £3,000 to an organisation in Meeth – Devon for the conservation of Royal Arms; £2,500 to an organisation in Slafton – Devon for the conservation of Royal Arms; £2,000 each to an organisation in Widworth – Devon for the conservation of seventeenth/eighteenth century monuments, and an organisation in Muchelney – Somerset for the conservation of medieval tomb; £1,500 to an organisation in Great Wisherd – Wiltshire for the conservation of a 1629 monument; £1,250 to an organisation in Caerhays – Cornwall for the conservation of 1767 monument; £1,000 each to an organisation in Keinton Mandeville – Somerset for the conservation of relief boards and an organisation in Wedmere – Somerset for the conservation of tower statues.

FINANCES Year 1999 Income £28,784 Grants £43,603 Assets £506,704

TRUSTEES S R V Pomeroy, Chair; Ven. R F Acworth; J Coales; H G M Leighton; Very Revd R Lewis; H G L Playfair; A W G Thomas.

HOW TO APPLY On a form available from the correspondent.

WHO TO APPLY TO S R V Pomeroy, Chair, Duddle Farm, Nr Bockhampton, Dorchester, Dorset DT2 8QL

CC NO 282157   ESTABLISHED 1980

■ St Christopher's College Educational Trust

WHERE FUNDING CAN BE GIVEN UK.

WHAT IS FUNDED Organisations and individuals connected to the Church of England.

TYPE OF GRANT Small grants, usually one-off; some part-funded projects.

SAMPLE GRANTS £10,300 to National Society Religious Education Centre; £5,000 to Welsh Religious Education Centre; £1,000 to Craven Development; £246 to Six Pilgrims Group of Parishes.

FINANCES *Year* 2001 *Income* £34,662 *Grants* £20,446 *Assets* £685,564

TRUSTEES Revd Canon D Isaac, Chair; Miss M Braithwaite; Miss M Code; Revd Prof. L Francis; Revd Canon J R Hall; Mrs B Harvey; Mrs D Murrie; Dr M D L Sellick; J P Swallow; Ven. P Wheatley.

HOW TO APPLY In writing to the correspondent.

WHO TO APPLY TO David S Grimes, c/o The National Society, Church House, Great Smith Street, Westminster, London SW1P 3NZ *Tel* 020 7898 1492 *Fax* 020 7898 1493 *E-mail* info@natsoc.c-of-e.org.uk

CC NO 313864   **ESTABLISHED** 1971

■ The Saint Edmund, King & Martyr Trust

WHERE FUNDING CAN BE GIVEN London diocese.

WHO CAN BENEFIT Registered charities connected to the Church of England.

WHAT IS FUNDED Charitable work connected to the Church of England.

WHAT IS NOT FUNDED The trustees do not usually consider: repairs to buildings and church organs, or non-Anglican or secular work.

TYPE OF GRANT One-off and recurrent grants.

RANGE OF GRANTS £250–£2,500.

SAMPLE GRANTS £8,700 to St Edmund King & Martyr and St Mary Woolnoth PCC; £10,000 to Lord Bishop of London Float Account; £7,000 to Archdeacon of London Float Account; £2,000 each to Christ Church – Isle of Dogs, Old St Pancras parishes, St Anne's Church – Hoxton and Tower Hamlets Old Peoples Welfare Trust; £1,500 to The Passage.

FINANCES *Year* 2001 *Income* £59,000 *Grants* £46,000 *Assets* £1,400,000

TRUSTEES The Lord Bishop of London; The Archdeacon of London; Revd A Walker; R Hepburn; P Wilson.

OTHER INFORMATION The trustees have entered into a major financial committment for the development of St Edmund the King Church, Lombard Street. This will result in a substantial reduction in the trust's assets and income generated.

HOW TO APPLY In writing to the correspondent.

WHO TO APPLY TO James Kennedy, Secretary, 43 Trinity Square, London EC3N 4DJ *Tel* 020 7488 2335 *Fax* 020 7488 2648

CC NO 1032116   **ESTABLISHED** 1963

■ St Francis Leprosy Guild

WHERE FUNDING CAN BE GIVEN Developing countries.

WHO CAN BENEFIT People with leprosy or affected by leprosy, leprosy workers and medical staff.

WHAT IS FUNDED Leprosy treatment and care programmes, social, economic and physical rehabilitation, leprosy training and education, medical elective projects related to leprosy.

WHAT IS NOT FUNDED Centres not run by Catholic missionaries or not approved by the local bishop.

TYPE OF GRANT Money for running costs or for specific projects. Capital grants.

RANGE OF GRANTS Average grant: £3,500.

FINANCES *Year* 2001 *Income* £687,079 *Grants* £325,708 *Assets* £652,795

TRUSTEES Mrs G Sankey; T G R Lawrence; T Grobel; Miss V Melia; P Wurr; Ms M Hood; E Marshall

OTHER INFORMATION In 2000 a total of £281,000 was given in maintenance grants, £59,000 for special projects, £13,600 in educational grants and £1,800 for elective students.

HOW TO APPLY In writing to the correspondent in November. Applications for revenue grants should enclose most recent accounts. Applications for capital grants should specify the total cost and anticipated start date. In all cases, charity registration title and number should be given. The committee regrets that applications cannot be acknowledged.

WHO TO APPLY TO The President, 73 St Charles Square, London W10 6EJ *Tel* 020 8969 1345 *Fax* 020 8969 3272 *E-mail* enquiries@stfrancisleprosy.org *Website* www.stfrancisleprosy.org

CC NO 208741   **ESTABLISHED** 1895

■ St Gabriel's Trust

WHERE FUNDING CAN BE GIVEN Mainly in the UK, with an interest in the diocese of Southwark.

WHO CAN BENEFIT Institutions engaged in higher or further religious education, with a view to training school RE teachers. Young adults and members of the Church of England may benefit.

WHAT IS FUNDED Higher and further religious education with the purpose of training RE teachers and encouraging good practice in RE.

WHAT IS NOT FUNDED Grants are not normally available for: any project for which local authority money is available, or which ought primarily to be funded by the church – theological study, parish or missionary work – unless school RE is involved; and research projects where it will be a long time before any benefit can filter down into RE teaching. No grants are made to schools as such; higher and further education must be involved.

TYPE OF GRANT Recurring, one-off, project, research and start-up will be considered.

SAMPLE GRANTS £10,000 to the National Society; £7,348 to Millennium Development Programme and College Centenary; £7,100 to University of Exeter; £6,600 to Lambeth Place Symposium; £2,000 to Churches' Action for Racial Equality; £1,750 to St Pierre International Youth Trust; £840 to Ignite Anglican Church; £500 to Goldsmiths' College; £380 to Rochester Diocese.

FINANCES *Year* 2001 *Income* £220,538 *Grants* £141,081 *Assets* £5,413,958

TRUSTEES General Secretary of the National Society; nine co-optative trustees and two nominated trustees.

HOW TO APPLY In writing to the correspondent with an sae. Applicants are asked to describe their religious allegiance and to provide a reference from their minister of religion. Applications need to be received by the beginning of January, April or September as trustees meet in February, May and October.

WHO TO APPLY TO Peter Duffell, Clerk, Ladykirk, 32 The Ridgeway, Enfield, Middlesex EN2 8QH *Tel* 020 8363 6474

CC NO 312933   **ESTABLISHED** 1977

■ St Hilda's Trust

WHERE FUNDING CAN BE GIVEN The diocese of Newcastle (Newcastle upon Tyne, North Tyneside and Northumberland).

WHO CAN BENEFIT Young people, generally and in particular today's equivalent of the original clientele of St Hilda's School (an approved school and community home); and people whose needs are not met by state social welfare provisions.

WHAT IS FUNDED Organisations working with young people and people in need (as specified above). Also considered are community businesses and development, support to voluntary and community groups, training for work, community centres and village halls, and community services.

TYPE OF GRANT Wide-ranging; sometimes recurring. The trustees prefer to support projects involving the employment of staff qualified to provide care and support to those in need rather than to provide buildings, equipment or motor vehicles.

RANGE OF GRANTS £100–£5,000.

FINANCES *Year* 2000 *Income* £50,000 *Grants* £50,000 *Assets* £1,500,000

TRUSTEES Bishop of Newcastle; Archdeacon of Northumberland; R P Gordon; Mrs R Nicholson; Dr M J Wilkinson; E Wright.

HOW TO APPLY Application forms will be sent on request. Completed forms should be returned by the last day of March, June, September and December.

WHO TO APPLY TO Philip Davies, Secretary, Church House, St John's Terrace, North Shields NE29 6HS *Tel* 0191 270 4100 *Fax* 0191 270 4101

CC NO 500962   **ESTABLISHED** 1904

■ St James's Place Foundation

WHERE FUNDING CAN BE GIVEN UK.

WHO CAN BENEFIT Registered charities supporting children and young people (up to the age of 25) with mental or physical conditions, life threatening or degenerative illnesses. Hospices are also supported, regardless of the ages of their clients.

WHAT IS FUNDED The small grants programme gives grants of up to £5,000 to organisations with a turnover of less than £200,000 a year. The major grants programme gives up to £25,000 for a maximum of two years to organisations with a turnover of less than £2 million. These turnover limitations do not apply to hospices.

WHAT IS NOT FUNDED The foundation will not consider applications in relation to holidays. It has a policy of not considering an application from any charity within two years of receiving a previous application. The trust does not provide support for: political, sectarian, religious and cultural organisations; research projects; sponsorship or advertising; building projects; running costs, administration or salaries.

TYPE OF GRANT One-off.

RANGE OF GRANTS £500–£10,000; average grant £3,600.

SAMPLE GRANTS £8,137 to Get Kids Going! for four specially built sports wheelchairs; £8,000 to St Christopher's School towards a new hydrotherapy pool; £7,200 to Clearvision for 2,400 Braille books for children; £5,988 to Wessex Children's Hospice Trust for a ceiling hoist for one of the adapted bathrooms; £5,480 to Devon and Exeter Spastics Society for equipment; £5,000 each to Bromley Hall School for their Personal Passport scheme which ensures all its children with physical disabilities

or sensory impairment have an ongoing record as their carers change in mainstream schools, Daisy's Dream for a residential weekend for 25 children aged 5 to 16 who have been bereaved, Percy Hedley Foundation for specialist furniture and equipment, Riding for the Disabled – Muirfield for mounting facilities, and St Andrew's Hospice – Grimsby for an interactive sensory mural in the children's unit.

FINANCES *Year* 2002 *Income* £1,092,400 *Grants* £855,641

TRUSTEES M Cooper-Smith; J Newman; Sir Mark Weinberg; M Wilson; D Bellamy.

HOW TO APPLY All applications must be submitted on a fully completed application form and be accompanied by the latest audited report and accounts, together with any supporting explanatory documents as appropriate. The trustees meet quarterly.

WHO TO APPLY TO Gail Mitchell-Briggs, Secretary, St James's Place House, Dollar Street, Cirencester, Gloucestershire GL7 2AQ *Tel* 01285 640302 *Fax* 01285 640436

CC NO 1031456   **ESTABLISHED** 1994

■ St James' Trust Settlement

WHERE FUNDING CAN BE GIVEN Worldwide.

WHO CAN BENEFIT Registered charities benefiting children, young adults, older people, parents and children, ethnic minority groups, homeless people and immigrants.

WHAT IS FUNDED Educational facilities and services; personnel and human resource services; community development; support to voluntary and community organisations; pre-school education; bursaries and fees; day centres; international rights of the individual; racial equality, discrimination and relations; and other charitable purposes.

WHAT IS NOT FUNDED No grants to individuals.

TYPE OF GRANT Core costs, one-off, project, research, recurring costs, salaries and start-up costs. Funding is for up to three years.

SAMPLE GRANTS £25,000 each to Elizabeth House and Yakar Educational Foundation; £15,000 to Lord Ashdown Charitable Settlement; £10,000 each to Children of Chernobyl, Community Security Trust, In Kind Direct, Marchant-Holliday School, Matthew Trust and Norwood Ltd; £7,500 to Family Welfare Association.

FINANCES *Year* 2001–02 *Income* £117,968 *Grants* £453,761 *Assets* £3,941,522

TRUSTEES Jane Wells; Cathy Ingram; Simon Taffler.

HOW TO APPLY 'The trust does not seek unsolicited applications to grants, the trustees do not feel justified in allocating administrative costs to responding to applications. If you do send an application you must send a stamped addressed envelope.'

WHO TO APPLY TO Edwin Green, Secretary, 44a New Cavendish Street, London W1G 8TR *Tel* 020 7486 4663

CC NO 280455   **ESTABLISHED** 1980

■ Sir Walter St John's Educational Charity

WHERE FUNDING CAN BE GIVEN The boroughs of Wandsworth and Lambeth, with a preference for Battersea.

WHO CAN BENEFIT Young people under 25 who are resident in Wandsworth and Lambeth and who are in financial need. Grants are awarded both to individuals and local schools, colleges, youth clubs, and voluntary and community organisations. Special consideration is given to meeting the educational needs of young people who are disabled.

WHAT IS FUNDED The education of young people under 25 who are resident in Wandsworth and Lambeth. The charity has a special interest in the education of young people excluded from school, in early years education, and in young refugees and asylum seekers. The charity also supports the development of new educational initiatives and projects, curriculum enrichment programmes, and short holiday projects. Student grants are made only to individuals on approved or recognised courses.

WHAT IS NOT FUNDED The charity does not normally fund expenditure involving ongoing salary or premises costs or donations to general fund-raising appeals. School pupils under 16, full-time students on postgraduate courses or gap-year travel are not normally supported.

TYPE OF GRANT One-off, buildings, capital, projects and start-up costs. Funding is for up to three years. Student grants are normally awarded yearly to meet the cost of books and equipment, travel to college, and childcare.

RANGE OF GRANTS £200–£15,000; typically less than £5,000. Most student grants are in the range £350–£600.

SAMPLE GRANTS £16,282 to Wandsworth & Merton Law Centre Ltd for Year 3 of the Education Rights Project; £8,000 to Wandsworth Primary Play Association for Out of School Care Childcare Adviser; £2,528 to Battersea Churches Housing Trust for a Digital Photography and Homework Learning Plus Project; £3,000 to Number One Performing Arts for an Ear Training Programme for Choral Singers; £1,500 to English Pocket Opera Company for the Opera-tastic project in Lambeth Primary Schools; £950 to Christ Church Primary School, Battersea for the purchase of African instruments.

FINANCES *Year* 2001–02 *Income* £136,000 *Grants* £152,000 *Assets* £3,500,000

TRUSTEES Dr D Lewis, Chair; Revd P Kennington; Cllr G Passmore; J O Malley; A Crellin; Ms D Daytes; Prof. M Naylor; Ms J Rackham; A Tuck; C Blackwood; Ms J Scribbins; P Dyson; B Fairbank; Ms S Webb; Cllr S Wilkie; J Radcliffe; A Patel; Ms R Trim.

HOW TO APPLY Individuals: Students attending courses at Lambeth College, South Thames College or St Francis Xavier College should apply to their college student advice service. Students attending other colleges should provide the following information by letter or telephone call: name, date and place of birth, present address and length of residence there, college/school and course of study or training for which support is being requested, including start and finish dates. Applicants who appear to be eligible for an award will then be asked to complete an application form. Organisations: In writing to the correspondent. Organisations and individuals who wish to apply for grants are welcome to contact the charity's office by letter or telephone for further information and advice. The office is usually open on Tuesdays, Wednesday mornings and Thursdays.

WHO TO APPLY TO Philip Barnard, Administrator, Unit 11, Culvert House, London SW11 5AP *Tel* 020 7498 8878 *E-mail* swsjcharity@hotmail.com

CC NO 312690   **ESTABLISHED** 1992

■ St Jude's Trust

WHERE FUNDING CAN BE GIVEN UK, with a possible preference for London.

WHO CAN BENEFIT Organisations, both local and national, benefiting children, young adults, students and people disadvantaged by poverty. Exceptionally funding will be given to individuals.

WHAT IS FUNDED Relief of poverty; the advancement of religion and education; other charitable purposes.

TYPE OF GRANT Both recurrent and one-off. Grants made towards both capital and revenue expenditure. May be recurrent for up to 10 years.

RANGE OF GRANTS £550–£3,000.

SAMPLE GRANTS £3,000 each to Ability Net and St John's Roman Catholic School – Woodford; £2,000 to NSPCC; £1,000 each to Oundle School, PACE Centre, St Luke's Hospital for the Clergy, and St Mungo's.

FINANCES *Year* 1998–99 *Income* £32,000 *Grants* £30,000 *Assets* £701,000

TRUSTEES J M A Paterson; Mrs R K Duckett.

HOW TO APPLY In writing to the correspondent. Applications are considered twice a year. Acknowledgements are not given. This entry was not confirmed by the trust, but the information was correct according to the trust's file at the Charity Commission.

WHO TO APPLY TO Anthony Mao, Arnolds Fooks Chadwick, 15 Bolton Street, Piccadilly, London W1J 8AR *Tel* 020 7499 3007

CC NO 222883   **ESTABLISHED** 1961

■ St Katharine & Shadwell Trust

WHERE FUNDING CAN BE GIVEN The St Katharine & Shadwell wards in the borough of Tower Hamlets.

WHO CAN BENEFIT Organisations providing a benefit for residents of the St Katharine and Shadwell wards of the London Borough of Tower Hamlets.

WHAT IS FUNDED The objects of the trust include: the promotion of education and learning, including training in employment skills; the provision of facilities for recreation or other leisure-time occupations; the relief of poverty and sickness; the advancement of public education in the arts; and the provision of housing accommodation for the needy or those suffering from physical or mental disability. Up to and including 2005, priority is given to the education and training of children and adults with a particular emphasis on literacy projects. Applications relating to activities for pensioners or events that can bring together different sections of the community will also be considered.

WHAT IS NOT FUNDED The trust will not normally make grants: to individuals; for travel or study outside the area; where funds are available from statutory sources; towards buying, repairing or maintaining buildings or vehicles; to support religious groups unless they offer a non-religious service to the whole community; to support projects of a political nature; towards research, other than action research studies complying with the trust's aims. Nor does it sponsor fundraising events or make retrospective grants, or pay off mortgages, deficits or loans.

TYPE OF GRANT Capital (not vehicles), core costs, one-off, project, running costs, salaries, and start-up costs. Funding is available for up to and over three years.

RANGE OF GRANTS Variable.

SAMPLE GRANTS £14,428 to Tower Hamlets Playgroups and Under 5s Association; £12,000

each to Shadwell Basin Outdoor Activity Centre, Tower Hamlets Education Business Partnership and Youth Outreach; £10,000 each to £10,000 to Age Concern – Tower Hamlets and Leyton Orient Community Sports Programme; £8,500 to Tower Hamlets Community Transport; £8,000 to Tower Hamlets Summer University; £7,200 each Pensioners' Summer Programme and Summer Holiday Programme; £6,000 to Children's Music Workshop; £5,000 to New Generation Youth Club.

FINANCES Year 2001 *Income* £237,322 *Grants* £174,869 *Assets* £6,517,311

TRUSTEES The trust is run by a board of governors: Sir Robin Mountfield, Chair; Sir David Hardy; Les Hinton; Sylvia McAtee; Mary Nepstad; Vicky O'Cuneff; Jane Reed; Richard Roberts; Cllr Abdul Shukur; Eric Sorensen; Peter Stehrenberger; Revd Ronald Swan; Maj. Gen. Geoffrey Field; Peter Rimmel; Dan Jones; Vaugn Williams; Cllr. Shafiqul Haque.

HOW TO APPLY No application forms. Applicants are asked to write a letter giving details of their request and of their organisation. Applicants are usually visited by the director, and grant decisions are made by the governors who meet four times a year, although urgent requests for small grants may be considered at any time. Successful applicants are asked to help the trust monitor its work by making a simple report on how the grant was spent and how effective the trust's contribution really was.

WHO TO APPLY TO Jenny Dawes, Director, PO Box 1779, London E1W 2BY *Tel* 020 7782 6962 *Fax* 020 7782 6963

CC NO 1001047   **ESTABLISHED** 1990

■ The St Laurence Charities for the Poor

WHERE FUNDING CAN BE GIVEN The ancient parish of St Laurence, then the borough of Reading.

WHO CAN BENEFIT Persons resident generally, or individually, in the area of the ancient parish of St Laurence in Reading and, thereafter, persons resident generally, or individually, in the county borough of Reading.

WHAT IS FUNDED Persons, generally or individually, who are in conditions of need, hardship or distress.

WHAT IS NOT FUNDED No grants to individuals outside the ancient parish of St Laurence, Reading or the county borough of Reading, even when supported by social services or similar agencies.

TYPE OF GRANT One-off or annual.

RANGE OF GRANTS £1,000 annual to £10,000 one-off.

SAMPLE GRANTS £5,000 to St. John Ambulance; £1,000 to Reading PHAB Club.

FINANCES Year 2001 *Income* £66,000 *Grants* £85,000 *Assets* £15,000

TRUSTEES Revd Cannon B Shenton, Chair; Mrs T Thomas; K Monger; M D H Nicholls; Cllr Rose Williams.

HOW TO APPLY In writing to the correspondent, supplying latest accounts or details of bank balances etc., together with reason for application. The trustees meet twice a year in April and November.

WHO TO APPLY TO John M James, Vale & West, 26 Queen Victoria Street, Reading RG1 1TG

CC NO 205043   **ESTABLISHED** 1962

■ St Luke's College Foundation

WHERE FUNDING CAN BE GIVEN UK and overseas, with some preference for Exeter and Truro.

WHO CAN BENEFIT Individual or corporate applications for studies or research in theology or religious education, including the provision of these subjects for colleges and universities.

WHAT IS FUNDED Encouraging original work and imaginative new projects by educational and training bodies. Postgraduate education and various study costs are also supported.

WHAT IS NOT FUNDED Grants are not made for studies or research in fields other than religious studies, or for buildings or schools (except indirectly through courses or research projects undertaken by RE teachers). Block grants to support schemes or organisations are not made. Grants are not normally made for periods in excess of three years.

TYPE OF GRANT Normally for a specific project or part of a project, or for a specific course or research. Grants can be made for periods of up to three years.

RANGE OF GRANTS £120–£4,000.

FINANCES Year 2000–01 *Income* £149,790

TRUSTEES The Bishop of Exeter; The Dean of Exeter; Diocesan Director of Education; Chairman of Diocesan Board of Finance; one nominated by the Bishop of Exeter; three nominated by the University of Exeter; four co-optative trustees.

OTHER INFORMATION The trust's scheme requires that the first charge on the foundation's income is the maintenance of a chapel and a chaplaincy: grants can be made from the residue. The trust stated that about £50,000 is given in grants each year.

HOW TO APPLY Requests for application packs, and all other correspondence, should be sent to Professor M Bond. Applications are considered once a year and should be received by 1 May.

WHO TO APPLY TO Professor Michael Bond, Heathayne, Colyton, Devon EX24 6RS *Tel* 01297 552281 *Fax* 01297 552281

CC NO 306606   **ESTABLISHED** 1977

■ St Martin-in-the-Fields' Vicar's General Charity

WHERE FUNDING CAN BE GIVEN St Martin-in-the-Fields.

WHO CAN BENEFIT Organisations and individuals.

WHAT IS FUNDED The trust gives grants for the relief of poverty and the furtherance of Christianity normally only where there is a direct connection with St Martin-in-the-Fields. It has also undertaken a major commitment to the planning and building redevelopment at St Martin-in-the-Fields.

FINANCES Year 2001 *Income* £143,000 *Grants* £390,000 *Assets* £2,000,000

TRUSTEES Revd N R Holtam; N A B Anson; C F Chan; A Stewart.

HOW TO APPLY In writing to the correspondent.

WHO TO APPLY TO The Vicar, 6 St Martin's Place, London WC2N 4JJ

CC NO 273004   **ESTABLISHED** 1977

■ The St Mary-le-Strand Charity

WHERE FUNDING CAN BE GIVEN City of Westminster.

WHO CAN BENEFIT Residents of Westminster who are in need and have lived in the area for at least one year. Also to organisations benefiting these residents. This includes those who are unemployed, volunteers, parents and children, one parent families, widows and widowers.

WHAT IS FUNDED Relief of need, community development, health projects, youth clubs and educational institutions, including accommodation and housing; infrastructure, support and development; Christian outreach; religious ancillary buildings; religious umbrella bodies; arts education; health; schools and colleges; education and training; community centres and village halls; community services and advice centres.

TYPE OF GRANT One-off grants for capital, buildings, core costs, feasibility studies, projects, running costs, salaries and start-up costs. Funding is available for up to one year.

RANGE OF GRANTS Organisations: £500–£5,000; individuals: £100.

SAMPLE GRANTS In 1999: £5,500 to St Marylebone Health Society for grants to those in need; £5,000 to St John's Hospice; £3,000 each to Church Street Drop-in Centre and St Clement Danes Primary School for music and library facilities; £2,500 to Charing Cross Holiday Dialysis; £2,400 to All Soul's Clubhouse; £2,000 to St Augustine's Primary School for educational trip costs for children from disadvantaged families; £1,800 to Dutch Pot Lunch and Social Club; £1,500 to Contact the Elderly; £1,300 to Westminster Sports Unit.

FINANCES *Year* 2001 *Income* £86,259

TRUSTEES S Harrow, Chair; M F Cayley; D J Harvey; Miss A Kavanagh; J A Maycock; T Sheppard; P D Symmons; J Stevenson; P Maplestone.

HOW TO APPLY In writing to the correspondent including a set of accounts and background information.

WHO TO APPLY TO F Brenchley-Brown, Clerk, St Mary-le-Strand Office, 169 Strand, London WC2R 2LS *Tel* 020 7836 3205

CC NO 208631   **ESTABLISHED** 1962

··

■ The Saint Marylebone Educational Foundation

WHERE FUNDING CAN BE GIVEN City of Westminster.

WHO CAN BENEFIT Young people.

WHAT IS FUNDED The education of young people in the City of Westminster (i.e. people between the ages of 8 and 25 who are resident in, or educated in, the St Marylebone/Westminster area).

RANGE OF GRANTS £1,000–£10,000.

SAMPLE GRANTS £21,000 to St Marylebone School for a maintenance grant; £15,000 each to St Peter's Primary School and St Matthew's School Orchard Appeal; £14,000 to Westminster St Margaret's Deanery Synod for a maintenance grant.

FINANCES *Year* 1999–2000 *Income* £95,000 *Grants* £81,000 *Assets* £753,000

HOW TO APPLY In writing to the correspondent.

WHO TO APPLY TO Mrs P J le Gassick, Clerk, c/o St Peter's Church, 119 Eaton Square, London SW1W 9AL

CC NO 312378   **ESTABLISHED** 1750

··

■ St Olave, St Thomas and St John United Charity

WHERE FUNDING CAN BE GIVEN Former metropolitan borough of Bermondsey.

WHO CAN BENEFIT Older people; students; at risk groups; those disadvantaged by poverty; and socially isolated people.

WHAT IS FUNDED Relief in need, education for people under 24 years of age and general welfare purposes.

WHAT IS NOT FUNDED No grants towards political causes.

SAMPLE GRANTS £115,176 for holidays and outings; £77,315 for educational grants; £13,514 individual grants; £12,850 for Christmas gifts.

FINANCES *Year* 1998–99 *Income* £413,231 *Grants* £218,855 *Assets* £11,792,381

HOW TO APPLY In writing to the correspondent.

WHO TO APPLY TO Mrs S Broughton, Secretary, 6–8 Druid Street, Off Tooley Street, London SE1 2EU *Tel* 020 7407 2530

CC NO 211763   **ESTABLISHED** 1892

··

■ The Late St Patrick White Charitable Trust

WHERE FUNDING CAN BE GIVEN UK, with a possible preference for Hampshire.

WHO CAN BENEFIT Registered charities.

WHAT IS FUNDED Large UK charities catering for people who are elderly or disabled, and local groups in Hampshire. The trust has a list of regular beneficiaries, although grants are available to other organisations.

RANGE OF GRANTS Up to £10,000, usually £1,000 or less.

SAMPLE GRANTS £9,800 to Age Concern; £8,800 to Arthritis Research Campaign; £8,200 each to Guide Dogs for the Blind Association and Salvation Army; £6,200 to Barnardos; £6,000 to National Eye Research Centre; £4,100 to 2Care; £4,000 to Institute of Cancer Research; £2,600 to Extra Care Charitable Trust; £2,200 to Pramacare.

FINANCES *Year* 1999–2000 *Income* £96,198 *Grants* £104,415 *Assets* £2,621,857

TRUSTEES HSBC Trusts Co. (UK) Ltd.

HOW TO APPLY In writing to the correspondent. Applications are considered in February, May, August and November.

WHO TO APPLY TO Barry Stubbs, Trust Manager, HSBC Trusts, Cumberland House, 15–17 Cumberland Place, Southampton SO15 2UY *Tel* 023 8053 1378

CC NO 1056520   **ESTABLISHED** 1995

··

■ St Peter's Saltley Trust

WHERE FUNDING CAN BE GIVEN The dioceses of Worcester, Hereford, Lichfield, Birmingham and Coventry.

WHO CAN BENEFIT Organisations benefiting people of all ages, teachers, governors, unemployed people and volunteers.

WHAT IS FUNDED The advancement of education and religion via projects in the dioceses named above. Infrastructure development will also be considered.

WHAT IS NOT FUNDED No grants to individuals.

TYPE OF GRANT Project funding for up to three years will be considered.

FINANCES *Year* 2001–02 *Income* £127,449

TRUSTEES The Bishops of the five dioceses covered by the trust; Miss J A Price; T D R Jenkins; Revd P Lister; Ven. J Duncan; Canon J Eardley; Miss H Haines; Revd Jackies Hughes; Mrs A Turner.

HOW TO APPLY In writing to the correspondent.

WHO TO APPLY TO Mrs J E Jones, Clerk, Grays Court, 3 Nursery Road, Edgbaston, Birmingham B15 3JX *Tel* 0121 427 6800 *Fax* 0121 428 3392 *E-mail* saltru@aol.com
CC NO 528915   ESTABLISHED 1980

■ Saint Sarkis Charity Trust

WHERE FUNDING CAN BE GIVEN UK and overseas.
WHO CAN BENEFIT Smaller registered charities benefiting Christians, disabled people and victims of abuse.
WHAT IS FUNDED Primarily charitable objectives with an Armenian connection including Armenian religious buildings; and other small charities catering for disadvantaged groups in response to applications.
WHAT IS NOT FUNDED No grants to individuals.
TYPE OF GRANT Mainly confined to one-off grants for capital projects or operational expenses.
SAMPLE GRANTS £138,920 to Armenian Church of St Sarkis; £110,620 to Surp Pirgic Hospital in Turkey; £70,000 to University of Cambridge; £5,500 to Trama After Care; £3,417 to Armenian General Benevolent Fund; £3,000 to Christian Solidarity Worldwide; £2,800 to Armenian 17th Century Concert; £2,000 to Noah's Ark Community Venture and People First (Self Advocacy); £1,450 to Wavendon All Music Plan.
FINANCES *Year* 2000–01 *Income* £296,795 *Grants* £345,707 *Assets* £6,894,372
TRUSTEES Mikhael Essayan; Boghos Parsegh Gulbenkian; Paul Curno.
HOW TO APPLY In writing to the correspondent. Trustees meet monthly.
WHO TO APPLY TO Mrs Christine Lewis, Secretary, c/o Economic & General Secretariat Ltd, 98 Portland Place, London W1N 4ET *Tel* 020 7636 5313
CC NO 215352   ESTABLISHED 1954

■ St Thomas' Dole Charity

WHERE FUNDING CAN BE GIVEN The ancient parish of Aston.
WHO CAN BENEFIT Local organisations, local branches of UK organisations.
WHAT IS FUNDED Children and young people, community projects, churches, disability and welfare.
TYPE OF GRANT One-off.
RANGE OF GRANTS Up to £2,000.
SAMPLE GRANTS £2,000 to Age Concern Kingstanding; £1,900 to St Paul & St Silas PCC Playgroup; £1,500 each to Aston Parish Church and Friends of Bertram Road Day Nursery; £1,000 each to Birmingham Rathbone Society, Birmingham Settlement, Hodge Hill Carers Support Group, Cornerstone Christian Charity, St Andrew's Sport & Community Centre and St Martin's Church Centre.
FINANCES *Year* 1999–2000 *Income* £42,000 *Grants* £37,000 *Assets* £1,200,000
TRUSTEES Revd G K Sinclair, Chair; Ven. Archdeacon of Aston; F Jephcott; Mrs P Oakes; Mrs S Ordridge; M Duddy; G Engledow; Mrs B Price.
HOW TO APPLY On a form available from the correspondent. Trustees meet in April and November, applications should be sent in March and October respectively.
WHO TO APPLY TO J F M Fea, Joint Clerk, Martineau Johnson, St Philips House, St Philips Place, Birmingham B3 2PP *Tel* 0121 200 3300
CC NO 244053   ESTABLISHED 1965

■ St Thomas Ecclesiastical Charity

WHERE FUNDING CAN BE GIVEN Bristol, with preference for the parish of St Mary Redcliffe with Temple and St John the Baptist, Bedminster.
WHO CAN BENEFIT Charities benefiting the Church of England in the city of Bristol.
WHAT IS FUNDED The religious and charitable work of the Church of England, including social welfare and community projects.
WHAT IS NOT FUNDED No grants for scholarships or expeditions, or to individuals.
TYPE OF GRANT One-off, recurring costs, project, salaries and start-up costs. Funding for up to and over three years will be considered.
SAMPLE GRANTS £13,000 to Industrial and Social Responsibility for a commercial sector chaplaincy (Diocese of Bristol); £7,000 to Easton Christian Family Centre towards the salaries of a youth worker and centre manager; £5,000 to St Stephen's Community Work Project towards the salary of an administrative worker; £4,000 to SPACE (Space for Parents and Children to Enjoy) towards funding a project leader; £3,500 to One 25 Limited to assist the work of this charitable company which helps women working in street prostitution; £3,000 to Bishop's Urban Fund – Withywood Project; £1,000 to Bristol Cathedral Organ Project towards the cost of a scholarship; £700 to Easton CE VA School.
FINANCES *Year* 2000 *Income* £80,000 *Grants* £37,000 *Assets* £1,200,000
TRUSTEES D J Yabsley, Chair; Ven. T E McClure; Canon S A N Darley; Mrs L Goodridge; B B Richards; K F Shattock; J Smith; C Tippetts.
HOW TO APPLY In writing to the correspondent.
WHO TO APPLY TO J M Haddrell, Clerk to the Trustees, Messrs Harris & Harris Solicitors, Diocesan Registry, 14 Market Place, Wells, Somerset BA5 2RE *Tel* 01749 674747 *Fax* 01749 676585 *E-mail* hh.wells@virgin.net
CC NO 229807   ESTABLISHED 1989

■ The Saintbury Trust

WHERE FUNDING CAN BE GIVEN Gloucestershire, West Midlands and Worcestershire; UK in exceptional circumstances.
WHO CAN BENEFIT Registered charities.
WHAT IS FUNDED General charitable purposes.
WHAT IS NOT FUNDED No grants to individuals or to animal charities. The trust stated that they do not respond to 'cold-calling' from organisations outside its main beneficial area, and groups from other parts of the UK are only considered if personally known to one of the trustees.
RANGE OF GRANTS £500–£30,000.
SAMPLE GRANTS £30,000 to Fortune Riding Centre; £25,000 to University of Birmingham; £20,000 to Emmaus – Gloucester; £15,000 each to RAPt and St Paul's Church – Birmingham; £10,000 each to Avoncroft Museum, MAC, Merton House, St Paul's Church – Birmingham; £5,000 each to Queen Alexandra College, RSAS Age Care and St Basils.
FINANCES *Year* 2000 *Income* £163,870 *Grants* £210,000 *Assets* £3,688,723
TRUSTEES Victoria K Houghton; Anne R Thomas; Jane P Lewis; Amanda E Atkinson-Willes; Harry O Forrester.
HOW TO APPLY In writing to the correspondent. Applications are considered in April and November and should be received one month earlier.

WHO TO APPLY TO Mrs V K Houghton, Trustee, Hawnby House, Hawnby, Nr Helmsley, York YO62 5QS
CC NO 326790   **ESTABLISHED** 1985

■ The Saints & Sinners Trust

WHERE FUNDING CAN BE GIVEN Mostly UK.
WHO CAN BENEFIT Registered charities.
WHAT IS FUNDED General charitable purposes. Priority is given to requests for grants sponsored by members of Saints and Sinners.
WHAT IS NOT FUNDED No grants to individuals or non-registered charities.
RANGE OF GRANTS £500–£10,000 but generally in the range of £1,000 – £3,000.
SAMPLE GRANTS £10,000 to Outward Bound Trust; £7,000 to University of Sheffield; £5,000 each to Help the Aged – Royal Buckinghamshire, Riding for the Disabled – South Buckinghamshire, and White Ensign Association Limited; £3,000 each to Advancement for Jewish Education Trust, Crusaid, Marine Conservation Society, Reform Foundation Trust, and Sight Savers International.
FINANCES *Year* 2000–01 *Income* £92,061 *Grants* £91,500 *Assets* £198,744
TRUSTEES N W Benson; Sir Donald Gosling; P Moloney; N C Royds; I A N Irvine.
HOW TO APPLY Applications are not considered unless nominated by members of the club.
WHO TO APPLY TO N W Benson, Trustee, Lewis Golden & Co., 40 Queen Anne Street, London W1G 9EL *Tel* 020 7580 7313
CC NO 200536   **ESTABLISHED** 1961

■ The Salamander Charitable Trust

WHERE FUNDING CAN BE GIVEN Worldwide.
WHO CAN BENEFIT Registered charities benefiting children, young adults, people disadvantaged by poverty and people who are disabled.
WHAT IS FUNDED The trust has a list of charities, in the fields of advancement of education and religion, and relief of poverty or physical disability, to which it gives on an annual basis. No other charities are funded.
WHAT IS NOT FUNDED No grants to individuals. Only registered charities are supported.
RANGE OF GRANTS £100–£1,500, generally £1,000 or less.
SAMPLE GRANTS £1,500 to SAT-7 Trust; £1,000 each to Birmingham Bible Institute, Christian Aid, FEBA Radio, International Christian College, Maltersey Hall Bible College, Moorlands College, Saint James' PCC – Poole, SAMS, and Trinity College.
FINANCES *Year* 2000–01 *Income* £69,030 *Grants* £73,650 *Assets* £2,295,659
TRUSTEES J R T Douglas; Mrs Sheila M Douglas.
HOW TO APPLY The trust's income is fully allocated each year, mainly to regular beneficiaries. The trustees do not wish to receive any further new requests.
WHO TO APPLY TO John R T Douglas, Trustee, Threave, 2 Brudenell Avenue, Canford Cliffs, Poole, Dorset BH13 7NW
CC NO 273657   **ESTABLISHED** 1977

■ The Salt Foundation

WHERE FUNDING CAN BE GIVEN Saltaire and Shipley.
WHO CAN BENEFIT Individuals and schools benefiting children, young adults, older people and students.
WHAT IS FUNDED Education.
WHAT IS NOT FUNDED No grants to replace statutory funding.
TYPE OF GRANT One-off grants (although applicants may reapply), capital, project and recurring costs for funding of one year or less.
RANGE OF GRANTS £150–£10,000.
SAMPLE GRANTS In 1997–98: £10,000 to Salt Grammar School for establishment of Education Action Zone; £5,000 each to Hirst Wood Nursery for educational equipment and Low Ash Primary School for a computer learning programme; £1,300 to Oakdale Primary School for equipment for a child with special needs; £1,220 to Shipley Church of England Primary School for two computers; £1,000 each to High Crags Primary School for a computer and printer and Redbeck Press for publishing costs of an educational text; £755 to Glenaire Primary School for books; £570 to Nabwood Grammar School for equipment; £466 to Temple Bank Special School for a large tricyle.
FINANCES *Year* 2000–01 *Income* £90,000 *Grants* £50,000 *Assets* £220,000
HOW TO APPLY In writing to the correspondent.
WHO TO APPLY TO The Clerk, Directorate of Legal and Democratic Services, First Floor, City Hall, Bradford BD1 1HY *Tel* 01274 434287 *Fax* 01274 728260 *E-mail* tracey.sugden@bradford.co.uk
CC NO 511978   **ESTABLISHED** 1981

■ Salters' Charities

WHERE FUNDING CAN BE GIVEN Greater London or UK.
WHO CAN BENEFIT As a matter of general policy, the company supports those charities where Salters are involved. As part of the need to take a more detailed interest in those charities which are supported, liverymen are encouraged to make personal enquiries regarding charities which they had initially introduced prior to a subsequent donation being considered. Visits should also be made to supported charities by liverymen and members of staff.
WHAT IS FUNDED General charitable purposes, spread as widely as possible over the charitable fields. Smaller contributions to major UK charities will be discontinued and the focus will be towards a smaller number of charities with specific projects and/or anniversaries.
WHAT IS NOT FUNDED Grants are not normally made to charities working with people who are homeless unless there is some connection with a liveryman of the company or with the Salters' City Foyer and the charities therein involved.
SAMPLE GRANTS £18,000 to Christ's Hospital; £7,000 to World Conservation Monitoring Centre; £2,500 to Tearfund.
FINANCES *Year* 1999–2000 *Income* £150,000 *Grants* £153,960
TRUSTEES The Salters' Company: Master, Upper Warden and Clerk.
HOW TO APPLY In writing to the correspondent.
WHO TO APPLY TO The Charities Administrator, The Salters' Company, Salters' Hall, 4 Fore Street, London EC2Y 5DE *Tel* 020 7588 5216 *Fax* 020 7638 3679 *E-mail* diane@salters.co.uk
CC NO 328258   **ESTABLISHED** 1989

■ The Saltire Society

WHERE FUNDING CAN BE GIVEN Scotland.

WHO CAN BENEFIT Arts and cultural organisations.

WHAT IS FUNDED The trust describes itself as 'looking to the future as well as the past encouraging creativity in Scotland as well as cultural heritage'. Its aims and objectives are to 'increase public awareness of Scotland's distinct natural and cultural heritage in all its richness and diversity and foster the cherishing and enrichment of all aspects of this heritage, including the Scots and Gaelic languages, enhance the quality of Scotland's contribution to all of the arts and sciences by encouraging creativity, inventiveness and the achievement of the highest standards of excellence in these fields, build on the achievements of the past to advance Scotland's standing as a vibrant, creative force in European civilisation, improve all aspects of Scottish life and letters at home and abroad and strengthen Scotland's cultural links with other countries and people'.

FINANCES *Year* 1999 *Grants* £30,000 *Assets* £130,000

TRUSTEES Revd A Black, Chair; S Aitken; Marillyn Gray; I M Hume; Madame May MacKerrell of Hillhouse; C Rankin; Moria Stratton; Dr D Wilkie; Anne Warren; Dr D Purves; J Gibson.

HOW TO APPLY In writing to the correspondent.

WHO TO APPLY TO The Trustees, 9 Fountain Close, 22 High Street, Edinburgh EH1 1TF *Tel* 0131 556 1836 *Fax* 0131 557 1675 *E-mail* saltire@saltiresociety.org.uk *Website* www.saltiresociety.org.uk

SC NO SC004962

■ The Andrew Salvesen Charitable Trust

WHERE FUNDING CAN BE GIVEN UK, with a preference for Scotland.

WHO CAN BENEFIT Organisations benefiting children who are ill and people who are disabled or homeless.

WHAT IS FUNDED Grants are made to a variety of charitable organisations who work for sick children, people who are disabled, homeless people and a range of other causes.

WHAT IS NOT FUNDED No grants to individuals.

SAMPLE GRANTS In 1994: £7,500 to Royal Zoological Society of Scotland; £5,000 to Sick Kids Appeal; £3,500 each to Bield Housing Trust and Scottish Down's Syndrome Association; £3,000 to Sail Training Association; £2,400 to Multiple Sclerosis Society in Scotland; £1,500 to William Higgins Marathon Account.

FINANCES *Year* 2000 *Grants* £100,000

TRUSTEES A C Salvesen; Ms K Turner; V Lall.

HOW TO APPLY The trustees only support organisations known to them through their personal contacts. The address holders told us that all applications sent to them are thrown in the bin.

WHO TO APPLY TO Mark Brown, c/o Meston Reid & Co., 12 Carden Place, Aberdeen AB10 1UR *Tel* 01224 625554

SC NO SC008000 **ESTABLISHED** 1989

■ The Sammermar Trust

WHERE FUNDING CAN BE GIVEN UK and overseas.

WHAT IS FUNDED General charitable purposes.

SAMPLE GRANTS £5,000 each to Oxfordshire Community Foundation and Whitley Awards Foundation; £4,000 each to BAAF, and Cystic Fibrosis Trust; £3,600 to St John Ambulance; £3,000 each to All Saints Farnborough PCC, Queen Mary's Clothing Guild, Royal Marsden Research Fund, and St Clement Danes Resident Chaplain's Discretionary Fund; £2,500 to Spitfire Society.

FINANCES *Year* 2001 *Income* £135,016 *Grants* £68,504 *Assets* £3,306,010

TRUSTEES Lady Judith Swire; M Dunne; B N Swire; Sir Kerry St Johnson.

HOW TO APPLY In writing to the correspondent. The trustees meet.

WHO TO APPLY TO Mrs D Omar, Swire House, 59 Buckingham Gate, London SW1E 6AJ *Tel* 020 7834 7717

CC NO 800493 **ESTABLISHED** 1988

■ Basil Samuel Charitable Trust

WHERE FUNDING CAN BE GIVEN UK and overseas.

WHO CAN BENEFIT Registered charities only, benefiting people of any age including carers, and people who are disadvantaged by poverty or disabled.

WHAT IS FUNDED Medical, socially supportive, educational and cultural charities.

WHAT IS NOT FUNDED Grants are given to registered charities only.

TYPE OF GRANT One-off funding for research and feasibility studies is considered, for one year or less. No loans are made.

SAMPLE GRANTS In 2000–01: £50,000 each to GRET, Old Vic Theatre – London, Royal Academy of Arts, Royal Horticultural Society, and St Paul's School. Coram Foundation, Macmillan Cancer Relief, and Prince's Trust received between £25,000 and £30,000 each.

FINANCES *Year* 2001–02 *Income* £466,000 *Grants* £372,000

TRUSTEES Coral Samuel; Richard Peskin.

HOW TO APPLY In writing to the correspondent. 'The trustees meet on a formal basis annually and regularly on an informal basis to discuss proposals for individual donations.'

WHO TO APPLY TO Mrs Coral Samuel, c/o Great Portland Estates Plc, Knighton House, 56 Mortimer Street, London W1N 8BD *Tel* 020 7580 3040

CC NO 206579 **ESTABLISHED** 1959

■ The Camilla Samuel Fund

WHERE FUNDING CAN BE GIVEN UK.

WHO CAN BENEFIT Medical research projects in a discipline agreed by the trustees at their annual meetings. Funding may be given to medical professionals and research workers.

WHAT IS FUNDED The promotion, encouragement, assistance, support, conduct and accomplishment of any research or inquiry into any matters relating to the causes, prevention, diagnosis, incidence, treatment, cure or effects of any form of illness, injury or disability requiring medical or dental treatment.

WHAT IS NOT FUNDED No grants to individuals, general appeals or any other charitable institution.

TYPE OF GRANT Agreed expenses of research only. Maximum period three years, subject to satisfactory annual report and review by trustees.

FINANCES *Year* 1999 *Income* £30,000 *Grants* £30,000 *Assets* £680,000

TRUSTEES Sir Ronald Grierson; Hon. Mrs Waley-Cohen; Dr Hon. J P H Hunt; J Grierson.

HOW TO APPLY The trustees will request written applications following the recommendation of a suitable project by the medical trustees. However, please note as all the money available, together with the fund's future income, has been earmarked for four years for an important research project, the fund will not be in a position to consider any applications for grants during this period.

WHO TO APPLY TO The Secretary to the Trustees, Upton Viva, Banbury, Oxfordshire OX15 6HT

CC NO 235424   **ESTABLISHED** 1964

■ Coral Samuel Charitable Trust

WHERE FUNDING CAN BE GIVEN UK.

WHO CAN BENEFIT Registered charities only.

WHAT IS FUNDED General charitable purposes, including arts, culture and recreation, and literacy. Grants of £10,000 or more go to educational, cultural and socially supportive charities and smaller donations are made to other charities.

WHAT IS NOT FUNDED Grants are only made to registered charities.

RANGE OF GRANTS £250–£50,000.

SAMPLE GRANTS £25,000 each to British Museum Development Trust and Natural History Museum Development Trust; £20,000 to Royal Opera House Trust; £10,000 to Brighton Festival Society; £6,000 to Norwood Ltd; £5,000 each to Godolphin & Latymer School, Jackdaws Educational Trust, RNLI and Weizmann Institute Foundation; £1,250 to Friends of the MDA; £1,000 each to the Costume Society, IM Prussia Cove, Nightingale House and Sick Children's Trust.

FINANCES *Year* 2000–01 *Income* £226,414 *Grants* £122,250 *Assets* £4,300,294

TRUSTEES Coral Samuel; P Fineman.

HOW TO APPLY In writing to the correspondent.

WHO TO APPLY TO Mrs Coral Samuel, Trustee, c/o Great Portland Estates plc, Knighton House, 56 Mortimer Street, London W1N 8BD *Tel* 020 7580 3040

CC NO 239677   **ESTABLISHED** 1962

■ The Peter Samuel Charitable Trust

WHERE FUNDING CAN BE GIVEN UK, with a preference for local organisations in Berkshire.

WHO CAN BENEFIT Registered charities benefiting medical professionals, scientists, at risk groups and people disadvantaged by poverty.

WHAT IS FUNDED Medical sciences, the quality of life in local areas, heritage and land/forestry restoration.

WHAT IS NOT FUNDED No grants to local charities outside Berkshire or to individuals.

TYPE OF GRANT Single and annual donations.

RANGE OF GRANTS £250–£30,000.

SAMPLE GRANTS In 1999–2000: £65,000 to Pippin; £20,000 to ULPS Lord Goodman Appeal; £18,720 to The Game Conservancy Trust; £10,000 to British Red Cross; £5,000 each to Jewish Care and Child Bereavement Trust; £3,000 each to Barkingside Jewish Youth Centre, Norwood Ravenswood and World Jewish

Relief; £2,500 to Chicken Shed Theatre Company.

FINANCES *Year* 2000–01 *Income* £101,259 *Grants* £195,817 *Assets* £3,686,802

TRUSTEES Hon. Viscount Bearsted; Hon. Michael Samuel.

HOW TO APPLY In writing to the correspondent. Trustees meet twice-yearly.

WHO TO APPLY TO Keith Morris, Secretary, Bridge Farm, Reading Road, Arborfield, Berkshire RG2 9HT *Tel* 0118 976 0412 *Fax* 0118 976 0147

CC NO 269065   **ESTABLISHED** 1975

■ The Sandford Trust

WHERE FUNDING CAN BE GIVEN Preference for in and around north Oxfordshire.

WHO CAN BENEFIT Registered charities.

WHAT IS FUNDED Appeals to which the trust's donation will make a material difference.

RANGE OF GRANTS £100–£1,000.

SAMPLE GRANTS £1,000 each to Teenage Cancer Trust, Oxford Home Start, Farm Africa, Oxfordshire Family Mediation Service, Society for Mucopolysaccharide Diseases, and Hanborough Freeland Scout Group; £735 to Kingham Hill School; £500 each to Oxford Community Mediation, Chicks, and British Blind Sport.

FINANCES *Year* 2000 *Income* £24,000 *Grants* £28,000 *Assets* £861,000

TRUSTEES Lady E H M Wills, Chair; Mrs S K A Loder; C A Ponsonby.

HOW TO APPLY In writing to the correspondent.

WHO TO APPLY TO Lady Wills, Trustee, Sandford Park, Sandford St Martin, Chipping Norton, Oxfordshire OX7 7AJ

CC NO 1044615   **ESTABLISHED** 1995

■ The Sandra Charitable Trust

WHERE FUNDING CAN BE GIVEN UK, with a preference for the south east of England.

WHO CAN BENEFIT Organisations benefiting: medical professionals; research workers; at risk groups; people disadvantaged by poverty; socially isolated people; and veterinary students.

WHAT IS FUNDED Medical research; animal welfare and research; environmental protection; childcare.

WHAT IS NOT FUNDED No grants to individuals other than nurses.

SAMPLE GRANTS £42,400 to VIRART; £25,000 to Dorchester Abbey Preservation Trust; £19,000 to Stoke Row Pavillion Fund; £15,500 to Barnados; £15,000 to the Florence Nightingale Foundation; £11,600 to Youth Sport Trust; £10,105 to Junior League of Friends of the Royal Marsden Hospital; £10,000 to Museum of London; £7,500 to Cancer Research Campaign; £6,000 to Lloyds Officer Cadet Scholarship.

FINANCES *Year* 2000–01 *Income* £429,750 *Grants* £381,616 *Assets* £13,074,836

TRUSTEES Richard Moore; M Macfayden.

HOW TO APPLY The trust states that 'unsolicited applications are not requested, as the trustees prefer to support charities whose work they have researched ... funds are largely committed'.

WHO TO APPLY TO K Lawrence, Moore Stephens, St Paul's House, Warwick Lane, London EC4P 4BN *Tel* 020 7334 9191 *Fax* 020 7528 9934

CC NO 327492   **ESTABLISHED** 1987

Think carefully about every application. Is it justified?

775

■ Sandringham Estate Cottage Horticultural Society Trust

WHERE FUNDING CAN BE GIVEN King's Lynn and the west Norfolk area.

WHO CAN BENEFIT Local charities benefiting the people of Kings Lynn and the west Norfolk area.

WHAT IS FUNDED The trust supports general charitable purposes especially health and welfare.

SAMPLE GRANTS £4,500 to Air Ambulance East Anglia; £2,500 to Alderman Jackson School; £2,400 to Queen Elizabeth Hospital for Radio Lynn; £2,000 each to Colon Cancer Detection Appeal, BREAK Hunstanton, Alzheimer's Group King's Lynn and Multiple Sclerosis King's Lynn; £1,400 to Sue Ryder Home Snettisham; £1,000 each to Friends in Bereavement and Victim Support.

FINANCES *Year* 2000 *Grants* £26,000

TRUSTEES T Murrell; Sir Edmund Grove; Mrs J Jackson; M O' Lone; D Reeve; F Waite.

OTHER INFORMATION The trust supports the promotion of horticulture and floriculture by the holding of an annual show on the Sandringham Estate for the benefit of the public for the exhibition of flowers, fruit and vegetables.

HOW TO APPLY In writing to the correspondent.

WHO TO APPLY TO P Murrell, Hon. Treasurer, 46 Dodds Hill Road, Dersingham, Norfolk PE31 6LP *Tel* 01485 541501

CC NO 1037268   **ESTABLISHED** 1994

■ The Sarnia Charitable Trust

WHERE FUNDING CAN BE GIVEN UK, with an interest in the Channel Islands, particularly Guernsey.

WHO CAN BENEFIT Registered charities only.

WHAT IS FUNDED Interest in wildlife and conservation projects in the Channel Islands especially Guernsey.

WHAT IS NOT FUNDED No support for expeditions and scholarships. No grants to individuals.

RANGE OF GRANTS £200–£6,100.

SAMPLE GRANTS £6,100 to George Adamson Wildlife Trust; £5,000 to La Société Guernesiase; £2,300 to Norfolk Wildlife Trust; £1,000 each to Action Bethlehem Children with Disability and Tropical Health and Education Trust.

FINANCES *Year* 2001–02 *Income* £32,394 *Grants* £18,900 *Assets* £585,245

TRUSTEES Dr T N D Peet; R Harriman; Mrs C V E Benfield.

HOW TO APPLY In writing to the correspondent, although unsolicited applications are unlikely to be successful. They are, however, considered quarterly.

WHO TO APPLY TO Roger Harriman, Trust Administrator, New Guild House, 45 Great Charles Street, Queensway, Birmingham B3 2LX *Tel* 0121 212 2222

CC NO 281417   **ESTABLISHED** 1979

■ The Sarum St Michael Educational Charity

WHERE FUNDING CAN BE GIVEN The diocese of Salisbury.

WHO CAN BENEFIT Individuals, parishes, schools and corporate bodies.

WHAT IS FUNDED Advancement of education in accordance with the principles and doctrines of the Church of England. This includes funding for: schools; individuals in further, higher and postgraduate education; and training.

WHAT IS NOT FUNDED The trust does not: 'encourage the perpetual student'; normally contribute towards maintenance, unless an integral part of a residential course; make grants for buildings, fixtures or fittings; make retrospective grants; and contribute to the general funds of any organisation.

TYPE OF GRANT One-off, project and research will be considered. Funding may be given for up to three years.

RANGE OF GRANTS £100–£2,000 (except some larger corporate grants).

SAMPLE GRANTS In 2000: £25,000 to Young Sarum for Diocesan children and youth work; £16,000 to Sarum College towards the salary of the principal; £15,000 to Salisbury Diocese for a religious education advisor to schools; £8,000 to Weymouth College for a chaplaincy service; £3,000 to Salisbury Diocese for a further and higher education advisor.

FINANCES *Year* 2001 *Income* £170,000 *Grants* £150,000 *Assets* £4,000,000

TRUSTEES M Marriott; J Roseaman; Revd Dr D Hart; Mrs D Arundale; Revd K Curnock; Rt Revd Dr D S Stancliffe; Brig. C C Owen; S Tong; Ms S O'Sullivan; Cdr M Chamberlain.

HOW TO APPLY Only on a form available from the correspondent. Applications for the academic year should be received by 1 June.

WHO TO APPLY TO The Clerk, 2nd Floor, 13 New Canal, Salisbury, Wiltshire SP1 2AA *Tel* 01722 422296

CC NO 309456   **ESTABLISHED** 1980

■ Jimmy Savile Charitable Trust

WHERE FUNDING CAN BE GIVEN UK.

WHO CAN BENEFIT Registered charities.

WHAT IS FUNDED General charitable purposes.

TYPE OF GRANT One-off grants.

SAMPLE GRANTS £5,000 to Nightingale Breast Cancer Foundation; £1,000 each to Bedford Hospital and DHC National Health Trust; £500 each to Apostleship of the Sea, Children's Wonderland Appeal, Disability Aid Foundation, New May Lodge Appeal and St John's Hospice; and £200 each to RNIB and Stocks Hill Day Centre.

FINANCES *Year* 1999–2000 *Income* £134,000 *Grants* £11,000 *Assets* £2,600,000

TRUSTEES Sir James Savile; James Collier; Harold Gruber; Luke Lucas.

HOW TO APPLY The trust does not respond to unsolicited applications.

WHO TO APPLY TO Harold Gruber, Trustee, 4 Valley Close, Cheadle, Cheshire SK8 1HZ *Tel* 0161 428 7111

CC NO 326970   **ESTABLISHED** 1984

■ The Henry James Sayer Charity

WHERE FUNDING CAN BE GIVEN Birmingham.

WHO CAN BENEFIT Charitable organisations and, but only in exceptional cases, individuals.

WHAT IS FUNDED General charitable purposes. To support small local charities who apply for help towards specific projects.

TYPE OF GRANT Cash – normally not recurrent.

FINANCES *Year* 2001–02 *Income* £27,000 *Grants* £15,000 *Assets* £641,000

TRUSTEES M B Shaw; Miss A M Grove; J M G Fea.

HOW TO APPLY On a form available from the correspondent. Applications must be returned by 1 March or 1 September and include accounts.

WHO TO APPLY TO The Clerk, Martineau Johnson, St Philips House, St Philips Place, Birmingham B3 2PP *Tel* 0121 200 3300
CC NO 222438 **ESTABLISHED** 1944

■ The Rosemary Scanlan Charitable Trust

WHERE FUNDING CAN BE GIVEN Glasgow.
WHO CAN BENEFIT Projects supported by the office of the Roman Catholic Archbishop of Glasgow.
WHAT IS FUNDED It gives grants for the 'up-keep and maintenance' of the Archdiocese of Glasgow and for Catholic educational purposes.
TYPE OF GRANT The trust is committed to providing long-term funding.
SAMPLE GRANTS In 1999 over 95 per cent of funds (£87,000) went to various projects run by the Archdiocese including educational grants to priests. Other beneficiaries included Catholic Education Commission and Glasgow University Catholic Chaplaincy.
FINANCES *Year* 1999 *Grants* £91,000
TRUSTEES Archbishop of Glasgow; K Sweeny.
HOW TO APPLY In writing to the correspondent. The trust stated that most funds are fully committed.
WHO TO APPLY TO The Trustees, Grant Thornton, 95 Bodwell Street, Glasgow G2 7JZ *Tel* 0141 223 0000 *Fax* 0141 223 0001
SC NO SC000360

■ The Scarfe Charitable Trust

WHERE FUNDING CAN BE GIVEN UK, with an emphasis on Suffolk.
WHO CAN BENEFIT Individuals and organisations benefiting: actors and entertainment professionals; musicians; writers and poets; and people with multiple sclerosis.
WHAT IS FUNDED This trust will consider funding: conservation; environmental interests; medical research into multiple sclerosis; hospices; arts and arts facilities; churches; religious ancillary buildings; art galleries and cultural centres; libraries and museums; and theatres and opera houses.
TYPE OF GRANT Capital, core costs, one-off, project, research, recurring costs and running costs. Funding is normally for one year or less.
RANGE OF GRANTS £150–£2,000.
SAMPLE GRANTS £20,000 to Institute of Neurology for research into multiple sclerosis; £10,000 to Aldeburgh Productions; £4,000 to Norfolk Museums Service; £1,000 to Wingfield Arts.
FINANCES *Year* 2001–02 *Income* £70,000 *Grants* £78,000 *Assets* £1,000,000
TRUSTEES N Scarfe; E E Maule.
HOW TO APPLY In writing to the correspondent.
WHO TO APPLY TO Eric Maule, Salix House, Falkenham, Ipswich, Suffolk IP10 0QY *Tel* 01394 448 339 *Fax* 01394 448 339 *E-mail* ericmaule@hotmail.com
CC NO 275535 **ESTABLISHED** 1978

■ The Schapira Charitable Trust

WHERE FUNDING CAN BE GIVEN UK.
WHO CAN BENEFIT Organisations benefiting Jewish people.
WHAT IS FUNDED Jewish charitable purposes.
SAMPLE GRANTS £27,000 in 13 grants to Society of Friends of the Torah; £9,000 in 3 grants to Keren Association; £6,000 in 4 grants to the

Gur Trust; £3,800 to New Rachmistrvke; £2,000 to Toldos Aharon; £1,000 to Gateshead Talmudical College.
FINANCES *Year* 1999 *Income* £125,000 *Grants* £121,000
TRUSTEES Issac Y Schapira; Michael Neuberger; Suzanne L Schapira.
HOW TO APPLY In writing to the correspondent.
WHO TO APPLY TO The Trustees, 2 Dancastle Court, 14 Arcadia Avenue, Finchley, London N3 2JU
CC NO 328435 **ESTABLISHED** 1989

■ The Annie Schiff Charitable Trust

WHERE FUNDING CAN BE GIVEN UK, overseas.
WHO CAN BENEFIT Orthodox Jewish institutions supporting religious, educational and relief of poverty aims.
WHAT IS FUNDED The relief of poverty generally and payment to needy individuals of the Jewish faith, for the advancement of education and religion. General charitable purposes.
WHAT IS NOT FUNDED No support for individuals and non-recognised institutions.
RANGE OF GRANTS £50–£20,000.
SAMPLE GRANTS £11,000 to Beis Yaacov Primary School; £8,000 to Be'er Avrohom (UK) Trust; £7,500 to Friends of Nachalat Osher Charitable Trust; £7,000 to Gevurath Ari Torah Academy Trust; £6,000 to Telz Talmudical Academy and Talmud Torah Trust; £5,500 to Torah Teminah Primary School; £5,000 to Friends of Beis Yisroel Trust; £4,000 to Friends of Ohel Moshe; £2,000 to Choshen Mishpat Centre; £1,500 to Yeshivo Horomo Talmudical College.
FINANCES *Year* 2001–02 *Income* £62,290 *Grants* £71,500 *Assets* £255,550
TRUSTEES J Pearlman; Mrs R Pearlman.
HOW TO APPLY In writing to the correspondent, but grants are generally made only to registered charities. The trust states that presently all funds are committed.
WHO TO APPLY TO J Pearlman, Trustee, 8 Highfield Gardens, London NW11 9HB *Tel* 020 8458 9266
CC NO 265401 **ESTABLISHED** 1973

■ The Schmidt-Bodner Charitable Trust

WHERE FUNDING CAN BE GIVEN Worldwide.
WHO CAN BENEFIT Jewish organisations; registered charities concerned with health and welfare.
SAMPLE GRANTS £21,000 to United Synagogue; £6,200 to Yesodey Hatorah Schools; £6,000 to Norwood Ltd; £5,000 to Institute of Cancer Research; £4,000 to World Jewish Relief Fund; £3,360 to Torah Terminah; £3,250 to Gateshead Talmudical College; £3,000 each to British Friends of Chadash, British Friends of Laniado Hopsital and James Menzies-Kitchin Memorial Trust.
FINANCES *Year* 2000–01 *Income* £40,625 *Grants* £73,160 *Assets* £802,603
TRUSTEES Mrs E Schmidt-Bodner; Marion Diner; Linda Rosenblatt.
HOW TO APPLY In writing to the correspondent.
WHO TO APPLY TO Harvey Rosenblatt, 3 Wyndham Place, London W1H 1AP *Tel* 020 7724 4044
CC NO 283014 **ESTABLISHED** 1981

■ The R H Scholes Charitable Trust

WHERE FUNDING CAN BE GIVEN England.

WHO CAN BENEFIT Registered charities benefiting children and young adults, Church of England, and people who are disabled or disadvantaged by poverty.

WHAT IS FUNDED Preference is given to charities which the trustees have a special interest in, knowledge of, or association with. New charities to be supported will be in the fields helping children and young people who are disadvantaged or disabled. Particularly charities working in the fields of: residential facilities; respite and sheltered accommodation; Anglican bodies; music and opera; special schools and special needs education; training for community development; care in the community; day centres; holidays and outings; playschemes; and research into medicine.

WHAT IS NOT FUNDED Grants only to registered charities. No grants to individuals, animal charities, expeditions or scholarships. The trust tries not to make grants to more than one charity operating in a particular field, and does not make grants to charities outside England.

TYPE OF GRANT Both recurrent and one-off grants are made depending upon needs of beneficiary. Core costs, project and research. Funding for more than three years will be considered.

RANGE OF GRANTS £100–£1,000, average grant £300.

SAMPLE GRANTS £1,000 each to Children's Country Holidays Fund, Church of England Pensions Board, Friends of Lancing Church, Historic Churches Preservation Trust, St Luke's Hospital for the Clergy, and Southwater Parish Church.

FINANCES Year 2001–02 Income £34,834 Grants £37,150

TRUSTEES R H C Pattison; Mrs A J Pattison.

HOW TO APPLY In writing to the correspondent, with the latest annual report and account, at any time. The trustees prefer to increase grants to existing beneficiaries when funds are available rather than take on new charities and unsuccessful applications are not acknowledged.

WHO TO APPLY TO R H C Pattison, Trustee, Fairacre, Bonfire Hill, Southwater, Horsham, West Sussex RH13 7BU *E-mail* roger_pattison@msn.com

CC NO 267023   **ESTABLISHED** 1974

■ The Schreib Trust

WHERE FUNDING CAN BE GIVEN UK.

WHO CAN BENEFIT Jewish people, especially those disadvantaged by poverty.

WHAT IS FUNDED Relief of poverty and advancement of religious education of Jewish people.

FINANCES Year 1999–2000 Income £899,817 Grants £2,146,828 Assets £2,839,134

TRUSTEES Mrs I Schreiber; J Schreiber; A Green; Mrs R Niederman.

HOW TO APPLY In writing to the correspondent.

WHO TO APPLY TO Mrs R Niederman, Trustee, 147 Stamford Haill, London N16 5LG

CC NO 275240   **ESTABLISHED** 1977

■ The Schreiber Charitable Trust

WHERE FUNDING CAN BE GIVEN UK.

WHO CAN BENEFIT Registered charities benefiting Jewish people.

WHAT IS FUNDED Jewish causes are preferred.

RANGE OF GRANTS £1,000–£50,000.

SAMPLE GRANTS £23,000 to Friends of Rabbinical College Kol Torah; £7,500 to Gateshead Talmudical College; £7,000 each to Aish Hatorah UK and Conference of European Rabbis; £6,100 to Friends of Ohr Somayach; £5,470 to Friends of Ohr Torah Limited; £3,700 to British Friends of Israel Museums; £3,500 to British Friends of Gesher; £2,706 to Finchley Road Synagogue; £1,710 to Yesodeh Hatorah Grammar School.

FINANCES Year 2000–01 Income £140,842 Grants £96,521 Assets £2,368,986

TRUSTEES Graham S Morris; David A Schreiber; Mrs Sara Schreiber.

HOW TO APPLY The trust states that all funds are currently committed. No applications are therefore considered or replied to.

WHO TO APPLY TO G S Morris, Trustee, PO Box 35547, The Exchange, 4 Brent Cross Gardens, London NW4 3WH

CC NO 264735   **ESTABLISHED** 1972

■ Schroder Charity Trust

WHERE FUNDING CAN BE GIVEN UK, occasionally overseas.

WHO CAN BENEFIT Preference for UK-registered charities and charities in which the Schroder family (the board) has a special interest.

WHAT IS FUNDED Medical charities, international relief, social welfare, heritage, environment and the arts. Preference is given to UK-registered charities and charities in which the trust has a special interest.

WHAT IS NOT FUNDED No grants to individuals.

TYPE OF GRANT Single payments or regular recurrent payments with preference given to headquarters organisations and established charities.

SAMPLE GRANTS £27,500 to Old People's Home; £5,000 each to Atlantic Council for the UK, British Urological Foundation, Lambeth Palace Library – Sion College, Lord Mayor Appeal – St Barts Hospital and Motor Neurone Disease Association.

FINANCES Year 2001 Income £128,553 Grants £280,005 Assets £4,801,578

TRUSTEES Directors: Mrs C L Fitzalan Howard; Mrs C B Mallinckrodt; B L Schroder; T B Schroder; Mrs L K E Schroder-Fane; Mrs J Schroder.

OTHER INFORMATION Following the sale of the investment banking arm of Schroder plc in 2000, the Schroder Charity Trust is no longer a vehicle for the company's charitable giving. Consequently, the scale and culture of the trust has changed. We were advised that: 'The charitable giving policy is now reactive rather than a proactive ethos and is concentrated on specific 'family' projects and appeals received personally (e.g. at home) by the directors of the trust.

HOW TO APPLY In writing to the address below, at any time. Trustees meet every six months to consider appeals.

WHO TO APPLY TO Mrs S Robertson, Secretary, 31 Gresham Street, London EC2V 8AS *Tel* 020 7698 6578

CC NO 214050   **ESTABLISHED** 1944

■ Scopus Jewish Educational Trust

WHERE FUNDING CAN BE GIVEN UK.

WHO CAN BENEFIT Jewish day schools, associations, societies and institutions, calculated to benefit directly or indirectly Jewish education.

WHAT IS FUNDED To advance and maintain Jewish day schools and Jewish education in any part of Great Britain and Northern Ireland.

SAMPLE GRANTS 1997–98: £12,985 to Brodetsky – Leeds; £11,059 to North Cheshire Jewish Primary School; £6,000 to King David – Birmingham; £2,000 to Bournemouth Jewish Day School.

FINANCES *Year* 2001 *Income* £132,293

TRUSTEES P Ohrenstein, Chair; J Kramer; S Cohen; S Ronson.

PUBLICATIONS *Scopus Nation Jewish Studies Curriculum; Scopus National Hebrew Curriculum.*

HOW TO APPLY In writing to the address below.

WHO TO APPLY TO 52 Queen Anne Street, London W1G 8HL

CC NO 313154 **ESTABLISHED** 1956

■ The Scotbelge Charitable Trust

WHERE FUNDING CAN BE GIVEN UK, with a preference for Scotland.

WHO CAN BENEFIT Registered charities.

WHAT IS FUNDED Charities working in the fields of: accommodation and housing; arts, culture and recreation; health; conservation; and community facilities.

WHAT IS NOT FUNDED No grants to individuals, expeditions or travel bursaries.

TYPE OF GRANT Buildings, core costs, one-off and recurring costs. Funding of up to three years will be considered.

RANGE OF GRANTS £500–£2,500.

SAMPLE GRANTS £1,500 to Dynamic Earth Charitable Trust; £1,000 each to National Library of Scotland and Scottish International Children's Festival.

FINANCES *Year* 1999–2000 *Income* £23,000 *Grants* £26,000 *Assets* £298,000

TRUSTEES Mrs A Wetherall; S L Keswick; K H Galloway; A J J Stanford.

HOW TO APPLY In writing to the correspondent. Telephone calls are not welcome.

WHO TO APPLY TO K H Galloway, Trustee, Bank of Butterfield (UK) Ltd, St Helens, 1 Undershaft, London EC3A 8JX *Tel* 020 7816 8300

CC NO 802962 **ESTABLISHED** 1990

■ The Scots Trust

WHERE FUNDING CAN BE GIVEN Preference for Hull and the East Riding of Yorkshire.

WHO CAN BENEFIT Registered charities.

WHAT IS FUNDED General charitable purposes, with a preference for animals, education and welfare.

SAMPLE GRANTS £5,000 to Barnardos; £1,300 to Royal British Legion; £1,000 to Hull Animal Welfare Trust; £500 to Salmon and Trout Association; £250 each to Dog Aid Society and Peta Vanguard Society.

FINANCES *Year* 1999–2000 *Income* £29,000 *Grants* £20,000

TRUSTEES D T C Caldow; Mrs M R Caldow; Mrs R Finstoy.

HOW TO APPLY In writing to the correspondent.

WHO TO APPLY TO D T C Caldow, Trustee, Kirkella House, Church Lane, Kirkella, Hull HU10 7TG

CC NO 297659 **ESTABLISHED** 1987

■ The Scott Bader Commonwealth Ltd

WHERE FUNDING CAN BE GIVEN UK and overseas.

WHO CAN BENEFIT Projects, activities or charities which: find difficulty raising funds; are innovative, imaginative and pioneering; or are initiated and/or supported by local people. Each year there is a particular area of focus, so applicants should check current focus before applying.

WHAT IS FUNDED Assistance of distressed and needy people of all nationalities. Establishment and support of charitable institutions whose objects may include the advancement of education. The commonwealth looks for projects, activities or charities which: respond to the needs of those who are most underprivileged, disadvantaged, poor or excluded; encourage the careful use and protection of the earth's resources (those which assist poor rural people to become self reliant are particularly encouraged); or promote peace-building and democratic participation. The commonwealth also supports the research, development and advancement of education and advancement of education in industrial participation of a nature beneficial to the community.

WHAT IS NOT FUNDED No support for charities concerned with the well-being of animals, individuals in need or organisations sending volunteers abroad. It does not respond to general appeals or support the larger well-established national charities. It does not provide educational bursaries or grants for academic research. It does not make up deficits already incurred, or support the arts, museums, travel/adventure or sports clubs.

TYPE OF GRANT One-off and funding over a period (3–5 years).

SAMPLE GRANTS £8,763 to Harvest Help for work with farmers in Zambia; £7,997 to Kettering Centre for the Unemployed to upgrade IT equipment; £5,000 each to Service Six for administration costs for a youth drop-in service, and Peper Harow Foundation for work with traumatized children; £6,570 to VSO towards a training programme on sustainable farming in Tanzania; £7,500 to Northants Probation Service towards education programme for young offenders; £3,000 to Joe Homan Charitable Trust for a child labour prevention scheme in India; £1,000 to Dublin Rape Crisis Centre.

FINANCES *Year* 2001 *Income* £128,575 *Grants* £122,046 *Assets* £391,782

TRUSTEES The Board of Management: S Carter; S Inman; M Waters; N Kegg; D Johnson; P Ganfield; A Gunn; J Deamer.

HOW TO APPLY In writing to the correspondent. Trustees meet quarterly.

WHO TO APPLY TO Denise Sayer, Secretary, Wollaston, Wellingborough, Northamptonshire NN29 7RL *Tel* 01933 666755 *Fax* 01933 666608 *E-mail* commonwealth_office@scottbader.com

CC NO 206391 **ESTABLISHED** 1951

■ The Francis C Scott Charitable Trust

WHERE FUNDING CAN BE GIVEN Cumbria and Lancashire, especially the northern part.

WHO CAN BENEFIT Social welfare organisations working with disadvantaged people.

WHAT IS FUNDED Registered charities in Cumbria and north Lancashire that assist disadvantaged

Think carefully about every application. Is it justified?

779

people. There is an emphasis on community services, support and development for youth organisations, family support services and community development projects.

WHAT IS NOT FUNDED Church restoration; medical appeals; expeditions; scholarships; applications from schools. Normally only registered charities receive grants.

TYPE OF GRANT Capital including buildings, revenue, recurrent, core costs, feasibility studies, one-off, project, research, salaries and start-up costs. Funding for up to three years may be given.

SAMPLE GRANTS £140,000 to Cumbria Association of Clubs for Young People (CACYP) for director/training organisers costs; £104,167 to CACYP for a training development worker; £82,070 to Cumbria Outdoors for an outdoor education officer; £76,318 to YWCA for a counselling scheme; £67,445 to CACYP for the bursary awards scheme; £60,000 to Barnardos – North East Ewanrigg; £36,000 to Barnardos – South Lakeland for family support; £30,000 each to Furness Homeless Support Group and West Cumbria Rape Crisis – Cockermouth; £27,500 to Howgill.

FINANCES *Year* 2001–02 *Income* £832,382 *Grants* £1,162,248 *Assets* £27,331,996

TRUSTEES Mrs S E Bagot, chair; R W Sykes; D Shaw; Miss M M Scott; F A Scott; W Dobie; I H Pirnie; F J R Boddy; C C Spedding.

HOW TO APPLY We are always pleased to hear from charities who need help. If you consider that your organisation comes within our criteria: you are invited to write to the director to request an application form; if you wish, you are welcome to telephone the director or one of his colleagues for an informal discussion before submitting an application; please make your initial application on our standard form which should be completed and returned with your latest set of accounts. The trustees meet three times a year, usually in March, July and November. The whole process of application to receipt of a grant may take up to four months. An application form is available from the correspondent and should be returned with the latest set of audited accounts.

WHO TO APPLY TO Donald Harding, Director, 3 Lambrigg Terrace, Kendal, Cumbria LA9 4BB *Tel* 01539 741610 *Fax* 01539 741611 *Website* www.fcsct.org.uk

CC NO 232131   **ESTABLISHED** 1963

....

■ The Frieda Scott Charitable Trust

WHERE FUNDING CAN BE GIVEN Old county of Westmorland and the area covered by South Lakeland District Council.

WHO CAN BENEFIT Small local charities, church restoration for community benefit, parish halls, youth groups and occasionally locally based work of larger charities.

WHAT IS FUNDED A very wide range of registered charities concerned with social welfare, community projects, the upkeep of village halls and voluntary sector infrastructure support and development.

WHAT IS NOT FUNDED Applications are not considered if they are from outside the beneficial area. No grants to individuals or school appeals.

TYPE OF GRANT Capital including building costs, core costs, one-off, project, research, recurring costs, running costs, salaries and start-up costs. Funding of up to three years may be considered.

RANGE OF GRANTS £200–£5,000 with occasional larger grants.

SAMPLE GRANTS £5,000 each to Cumbria Association of Clubs for Young People, Kirkby Lonsdale Methodist Church and Royal Agricultural Benevolent Institution; £4,000 to Kendal St George Community Project; £3,000 to Broughton Community Transport Trust; £2,000 to Postnatal Illness Support Group; £1,500 to Kirkby Thore Safe Play Project; and £1,000 to Grasmere Reading Rooms.

FINANCES *Year* 2001–02 *Income* £203,816 *Grants* £265,600 *Assets* £6,200,000

TRUSTEES Mrs C E Brockbank, Chair; Mrs O Clarke; R A Hunter; P R W Hensman; Mrs M G Wilson; Mrs S J H Barker; P V Hoyle.

HOW TO APPLY An application form is available from the correspondent and should be returned with the latest set of audited accounts. Potential applicants are welcome to ring for an informal discussion before submitting an application.

WHO TO APPLY TO J Sharpe, Secretary, 3 Lambrigg Terrace, Kendal, Cumbria LA9 4BB *Tel* 01539 741610 *Fax* 01539 741611 *Website* www.friedascotttrust.org.uk

CC NO 221593   **ESTABLISHED** 1962

....

■ The Sir James & Lady Scott Trust

WHERE FUNDING CAN BE GIVEN The borough of Bolton.

WHO CAN BENEFIT Registered charities offering social welfare services to disadvantaged people.

WHAT IS FUNDED To support the settlor's servants and dependants or others connected with him and his family and who are in need, and local charities. The latter includes: residential facilities and services; infrastructure development; charity or voluntary umbrella bodies; religion; arts, culture and recreation; health care; conservation; animal welfare; environmental issues; heritage; education and training; social care and development; and other charitable purposes.

WHAT IS NOT FUNDED No grants to schools or for medical appeals or expeditions. No grants to individuals.

TYPE OF GRANT Recurring costs; one-off; capital costs including buildings; core costs; endowment; feasibility studies; project research; running costs; salaries; and start-up costs. Funding is available for one year or less

RANGE OF GRANTS £200–£5,000.

SAMPLE GRANTS £4,300 to Bolton Lads and Girls Club; £3,000 each to Bolton Association and Network of Drop-ins, and Bolton YMCA; £2,000 each to Relate – Bolton Marriage Guidance, and Society of St Vincent de Paul, Bolton; £1,500 to Step by Step Project; £1,000 each to Christ Church – Little Lever, Oriel College Oxford for a bursary, St Catherine's Church, Highfield, and Guide Association, Bolton Division.

FINANCES *Year* 2000 *Income* £58,125 *Grants* £39,946 *Assets* £2,692,075

TRUSTEES C J Scott; W L G Swann; M M Scott.

HOW TO APPLY On a form available from the correspondent together with a latest set of audited accounts. An initial telephone call is welcomed.

WHO TO APPLY TO D J Harding, Secretary, 3 Lambrigg Terrace, Kendal, Cumbria LA9 4BB *Tel* 01539 741610 *Fax* 01539 741611

CC NO 231324   **ESTABLISHED** 1907

■ The John Scott Trust

WHERE FUNDING CAN BE GIVEN Scotland.

WHO CAN BENEFIT Registered charities only.

WHAT IS FUNDED Grants are awarded to a variety of organisations whose concerns include Scotland's heritage, recreation for young people and care for people who are disadvantaged.

WHAT IS NOT FUNDED No grants to individuals.

FINANCES *Year* 1999–2000 *Income* £98,489 *Grants* £90,500 *Assets* £1,059,438

TRUSTEES J D Scott.

HOW TO APPLY Applications are not invited.

WHO TO APPLY TO John W Laighland, Trustee, Kiloran, 8 Carrick Avenue, Ayr KA7 2SN *Tel* 01560 320092

SC NO SC003297

■ Sir Samuel Scott of Yews Trust

WHERE FUNDING CAN BE GIVEN UK.

WHO CAN BENEFIT Medical research bodies benefiting medical professionals and research workers.

WHAT IS FUNDED Medical research.

WHAT IS NOT FUNDED No grants for: core funding; purely clinical work; individuals (although research by an individual may be funded if sponsored by a registered charity through which the application is made); research leading to higher degrees (unless the departmental head concerned certifies that the work is of real scientific importance); medical students' elective periods; or expeditions (unless involving an element of genuine medical research).

TYPE OF GRANT One-off, project.

SAMPLE GRANTS £1,000,000 each to Gray Cancer Research Laboratory at Mount Vernon Hospital and Marie Curie Research Fund; £129,000 to Moredun Research Institute; £20,000 to Queen Charlotte's Appeal; £5,000 each to International LH Gray Conference, Breakthrough Breast Cancer, DEBRA and International Spinal Research Trust; £4,000 each to Brain Research Trust and Iris Fund for Prevention of Blindness.

FINANCES *Year* 2000–01 *Income* £197,000 *Grants* £2,217,000 *Assets* £9,000,000

TRUSTEES Lady Phoebe Scott; Sir Oliver Scott; Hermione Stanford; Camilla Withington; Edward Perks.

HOW TO APPLY In writing to the correspondent. Trustees hold their half-yearly meetings in April and October and applications have to be submitted two months before. There are no special forms, but applicants should give the following information: the nature and purpose of the research project or programme; the names, qualifications and present posts of the scientists involved; reference to any published results of their previous research; details of present funding; and, if possible, the budget for the next 12 months or other convenient period. All applications are acknowledged and both successful and unsuccessful applicants are notified after each meeting of the trustees. No telephone calls.

WHO TO APPLY TO The Secretary, c/o Currey & Co, 21 Buckingham Gate, London SW1E 6LS

CC NO 220878   **ESTABLISHED** 1951

■ The Storrow Scott Will Trust

WHERE FUNDING CAN BE GIVEN Preference for the north east of England.

WHO CAN BENEFIT Charitable organisations.

WHAT IS FUNDED General charitable purposes.

WHAT IS NOT FUNDED Grants for individuals and for the purchase of depreciating assets such as mini-buses will not be considered.

SAMPLE GRANTS £5,000 each to Anaphylaxis Campaign, Camphill Village Trust, Northumberland Association of Clubs for Young People, Natural History Society of Northumbria, St Oswald's Hospice and Samaritans Newcastle; £2,000 each to Calvert Trust and Northumberland Wildlife Trust; £1,000 each to British Red Cross – North East branch and Sunderland University.

FINANCES *Year* 1999–2000 *Income* £24,000 *Grants* £36,000 *Assets* £458,000

TRUSTEES G W Meikle; J S North Lewis.

HOW TO APPLY In writing to the correspondent. There are no formal application forms.

WHO TO APPLY TO The Trustees, c/o Dickinson Dees, St Anne's Wharf, 112 Quayside, Newcastle upon Tyne NE99 1SB

CC NO 328391   **ESTABLISHED** 1989

■ The Scottish Arts Council

WHERE FUNDING CAN BE GIVEN Scotland.

WHO CAN BENEFIT Individuals and arts organisations.

WHAT IS FUNDED Scotland's indigenous arts; the encouragment of international links and artistic innovation; the creation of greater access to the arts; the improvment of arts marketing.

WHAT IS NOT FUNDED No full-time education courses or individual children are funded.

TYPE OF GRANT Revenue and project grants; one-off and recurring grants; and capital grants.

RANGE OF GRANTS Generally £750–£5,000.

SAMPLE GRANTS £6,902,759 to Scottish Opera; £2,591,585 to Scottish Ballet Limted; £2,555,613 to Royal Scottish National Orchestra Society Limited; £1,414,835 to Scottish Chamber Orchestra Limited; £935,000 to Scottish Opera; £875,000 to Edinburgh International Festival Society Limited; £730,297 to Citizens Theatre Company Limited; £604,089 to Royal Lyceum Theatre Company Limited; £500,000 to Royal Scottish National Orchestra Society Limited for core funding in the following year; £473,330 to Traverse Theatre (Scotland) Limited.

FINANCES *Year* 2001–02 *Income* £39,767,000 *Grants* £33,706,000 *Assets* £4,236,000

TRUSTEES SAC Council Members: Sam Ainsley; Hugh Buchanan; Elizabeth Cameron; Richard Chester; Bill English; Jim Faulds; Dale Idiens; Magnus Linklater, Chair; Maud Marshall; Dr Ann Matheson; John Scott Moncrieff; Robin Presswood; Bill Spiers; Jean Urquhart.

OTHER INFORMATION Grants in 2001–02 were broken down as follows: combined arts £3,717,000; crafts £356,000; cross-council artforms £756,000; dance £3,637,000; drama £6,555,000; Literature £1,417,000; music £14,064,000; planning and development £373,000; traditional arts £348,000; visual arts £2,483,000.

HOW TO APPLY Applicants should telephone the help desk for advice and an application form.

■ The Scottish Churches Architectural Heritage Trust

WHERE FUNDING CAN BE GIVEN Scotland.

WHO CAN BENEFIT Scottish churches.

WHAT IS FUNDED Care of Scottish church buildings in use for public worship, principally by raising funds for their repair and restoration and by acting as a source of technical advice and assistance on maintenance and repair.

WHAT IS NOT FUNDED Repairs to halls or manse; electrical work; interior decoration.

TYPE OF GRANT Buildings.

RANGE OF GRANTS £1,000–£8,000.

SAMPLE GRANTS £5,000 each to Cambeltown – Lorne and Lowland for general repairs, Dunfermline Abbey – Fife for general repairs, Edinburgh – Liberton for stonework restoration, Firth – Orkney for general repairs, Fowlis Easter – Liff for stonework repairs, Glasgow – Bargeddie for urgent repairs to the steeple, Tingwall – Shetland for general repairs, St Michael and all Saints – Edinburgh for repairs to the roof and rainwater goods.

FINANCES *Year* 2000–01 *Income* £163,000 *Grants* £115,000 *Assets* £570,000

TRUSTEES Lord Penrose, Chair; Donald S Erskine; Magnus Magnusson; Lady Marion Fraser; John Gerrard; Revd Malcolm Grant; Ivor Guild; Revd Kenneth Nugent; Prof. Frank Willett; Revd Douglas Galbraith.

HOW TO APPLY On a form available from the correspondent. The grants committee meets four times a year in February, May, October and November.

WHO TO APPLY TO Mrs Florence MacKenzie, Director, 15 North Bank Street, The Mound, Edinburgh EH1 2LP *Tel* 0131 225 8644
SC NO SC000819 ESTABLISHED 1978

■ Scottish Churches Community Trust

WHERE FUNDING CAN BE GIVEN Scotland.

WHO CAN BENEFIT People living in areas of greatest disadvantage.

WHAT IS FUNDED Work developed by churches and community groups meeting real and identified needs in either a local community or among groups of disadvantaged people.

WHAT IS NOT FUNDED No funding for: work developed by organisations working in isolation from others; building work being done solely in compliance with legislation or not in direct support of a project for community benefit; one-off short-term activities such as trips or excursions, holiday clubs, mission events and festivals; work developed by organisations whose primary purpose is the promotion of abortion, euthanasia or artificial contraception; or work not carried out by recognised charities or properly constituted groups.

TYPE OF GRANT One-off or for a period of between one and four years.

RANGE OF GRANTS Normally in the range £3,000 to £5,000. Maximum normally available will be £20,000 over four years; or up to one third of the total costs.

SAMPLE GRANTS £20,000 each to Bridge Project – Lanark for a community cafe, Orbiston Neighbourhood Centre – Bellshill for places on an out of school care programme for people with special needs, Richmond Outreach Child Support – Edinburgh for a play therapy unit, St Matthew's Centre – Glasgow for a community centre, and Whitburn Churches for out-of-school care; £15,000 each to Drumchapel Emmaus – Glasgow for family support drop-in, Lochaber Health for All – Fort William for youth outreach, PEEK – Glasgow for a children's project, Viewpark Family Centre – Uddingston for community care, and YWCA – Glasgow for a family centre.

FINANCES *Year* 2001 *Income* £1,058,487 *Grants* £304,117

TRUSTEES Gordon Armour; Sandra Carter; Nena Dinnes; William Edgar; Alan Grist; Irene Hudson; Elizabeth McQuade; Frank Maxwell; Ian Moir; Robert Owens; Richard Toller.

HOW TO APPLY Guidelines are available from the correspondent.

WHO TO APPLY TO John Dornan, Development Coordinator, 200 Balmore Road, Possilpark, Glasgow G22 6LJ *Tel* 0141 336 3766 *Fax* 0141 336 3771 *E-mail* admin@scct.org.uk *Website* www.scct.org.uk
CC NO SC0030315 ESTABLISHED 2000

■ Scottish Coal Industry Special Welfare Fund

WHERE FUNDING CAN BE GIVEN Scotland.

WHO CAN BENEFIT Miners.

WHAT IS FUNDED The fund was set up to improve the conditions of people employed in the mining industry and their families. It supports individuals in need and also the provision of recreational facilities, youth clubs and courses.

FINANCES *Year* 2000 *Income* £200,000 *Grants* £90,000

HOW TO APPLY In writing to the correspondent.

WHO TO APPLY TO The Trustees, Second Floor, 50 Hopetoun Street, Bathgate, West Lothian EH48 4EU *Tel* 01506 635550
SC NO SC001200

■ The Scottish Community Foundation

WHERE FUNDING CAN BE GIVEN Scotland.

WHO CAN BENEFIT Organisations benefiting people of all ages and family and social circumstances; through Millennium Awards (Chase Awards) young people aged 14 to 25 who are disadvantaged, disaffected or socially excluded and (You and Your Community Awards) individuals over the age of 12 who have a project idea which will benefit themselves and their community.

WHAT IS FUNDED Local charitable activity, including: accommodation and housing; arts, culture and recreation; infrastructure, support and development; education and training; community facilities and services; advice and information; health; and conservation.

WHAT IS NOT FUNDED The community grants programme will not fund: individuals; the advancement of religion or a political party; major fundraising appeals; the purchase of secondhand vehicles; debts or other retrospective funding; payments towards areas generally understood to be the responsibility of statutory authorities.

TYPE OF GRANT Capital and revenue.

RANGE OF GRANTS Small grants up to £1,000, larger grants up to £5,000 but rarely at the top of that scale.

FINANCES *Year* 2001–02 *Grants* £3,010,000

TRUSTEES Rev Bobby Anderson; Alastair Balfour; Anne Boyd; Hamish Buchan; Alastair Dempster; John Frame; Michael Gray; Alan Hobbett; Iain Johnston; Helen Mackie; George Menzies; Graeme Millar; Allan Munro; Martin Sime; Graeme Simmers.

OTHER INFORMATION Roughly two-thirds of the above total was earmarked for specific statutory and lottery grant programmes including Millennium Awards for individuals, while around £1 million was spent on general community grants.

HOW TO APPLY On an application form available from the correspondent, along with guidelines. There is no closing date for applications. Completed from must be returned with a constitution, up-to-date accounts and an sae. As assessor will then conduct a short telephone interview before giving a report to the funders committee.

WHO TO APPLY TO Jackie Scutt, Chief Executive, 126 Canongate, Edinburgh EH8 8DD *Tel* 0131 524 0300
Website www.scottishcommunityfoundation.com
SC NO SC022910   **ESTABLISHED** 1995

....

■ The Scottish Hospital Endowments Research Trust

WHERE FUNDING CAN BE GIVEN Scotland.

WHO CAN BENEFIT Organisations benefiting research workers.

WHAT IS FUNDED Grants are awarded for individual or group research, scholarships and fellowships, travel and visitors, capital.

WHAT IS NOT FUNDED Grants are only for projects carried out in Scotland.

SAMPLE GRANTS £85,505 to Edinburgh University; £76,860 to Glasgow University; £59,722 to St Andrews University; £58,833 to Aberdeen University; £50,374 to Glasgow University; £49,678 to Glasgow University; £41,276 to Royal Dick Veterinary School; £39,687 to Edinburgh University; £38,355 to Aberdeen University; £36,925 to Aberdeen University.

FINANCES *Year* 2001–02 *Income* £1,274,875 *Grants* £658,450 *Assets* £21,048,855

TRUSTEES Lord Kilpatrick of Kincraig, Chair; Prof. Margaret Alexander; Prof. William Bowman; Alastair Dempster; Prof. Kevin Docherty; Dr Alexander Proudfoot; Mrs Brenda Rennie.

HOW TO APPLY Contact the correspondent for further information.

WHO TO APPLY TO The Secretaries to the Trust, Turcan Connell, Prince's Exchange, 1 Earl Grey Street, Edinburgh EH3 9EE *Tel* 0131 228 8111 *Fax* 0131 228 8118
E-mail sshert4578@aol.com
Website www.shert.com
SC NO SC014959   **ESTABLISHED** 1953

....

■ The Scottish International Education Trust

WHERE FUNDING CAN BE GIVEN Scotland.

WHO CAN BENEFIT Scots (by birth or upbringing) taking advanced studies for which support from public funds is not available. Funding may be given to young adults; musicians; writers and poets; and people disadvantaged by poverty.

WHAT IS FUNDED Grants are given to organisations and individuals whose concerns lie in education,

the arts or the areas of economic or social welfare.

WHAT IS NOT FUNDED No grants to commercial organisations, for capital work, general maintenance, or for courses (e.g. undergraduate study) for which there is support from statutory bodies/public funds.

TYPE OF GRANT Normally one-off.

RANGE OF GRANTS £400–£2,000.

SAMPLE GRANTS £15,000 was distributed in travel grants to students made through Scottish universities; £9,000 to Royal Scottish Academy of Music and Drama; £2,500 to National Youth Choir of Scotland; £2,380 to Fruit Market Gallery; £2,000 each to Apex – Scotland, Ballet West, Edinburgh Youth Orchestra and Scottish Mathematics Council; £1,000 to Alexander Gibson Awards (made through RSAMD); £625 to University of Strathclyde Music Society.

FINANCES *Year* 2001–02 *Income* £174,000 *Grants* £125,000 *Assets* £1,472,000

TRUSTEES J D Houston, Chair; W Menzies Campbell; Sir Sean Connery; Tom Fleming; Lady Gibson; Alexander Goudie; Andy Irvine; Prof. Alistair Macfarlane; Kenneth McKellar; Jackie Stewart; John F McClellan.

PUBLICATIONS A brochure is available from the trust.

HOW TO APPLY In writing to the director. There is an application form.

WHO TO APPLY TO E C Davison, Director, 22 Manor Place, Edinburgh EH3 7DS *Tel* 0131 225 1113 *Fax* 0131 225 1113 *E-mail* siet@ukonline.co.uk
SC NO SC009207   **ESTABLISHED** 1970

....

■ The Scouloudi Foundation

WHERE FUNDING CAN BE GIVEN UK charities working domestically or overseas.

WHO CAN BENEFIT (a) The Institute of Historical Research, University of London, for the sponsorship of graduates with honours degrees in history to undertake historical research; publications; and fellowships ('Historical Awards'), (b) registered charities in the fields of elderly people; children and youth; environment; famine relief and overseas aid; disability; the humanities (archaeology, art, history, libraries, museums, records); medicine and health; natural disasters; and social welfare.

WHAT IS FUNDED Candidates fulfilling the Institute of Historical Research's criteria may apply to the Institute for their research and publication costs to be funded; successful fellows will have a quarterly grant paid for a six or twelve month period. 'Special Donations' are made for extraordinary appeals and capital projects, and not day-to-day expenditure or staff costs. No applications for 'Regular Donations' are invited as these are specially selected.

WHAT IS NOT FUNDED Donations are not made to individuals, and are not normally made for welfare activities of a purely local nature. The trustees do not make loans or enter into deeds of covenant.

TYPE OF GRANT There are three categories of grant: an annual donation for historical research and fellowships to the Institute of Historical Research at the University of London; recurring grants to a regular list of charities; and 'special donations' which are one-off grants in connection with capital projects.

RANGE OF GRANTS Typically £1,000–£2,000.

SAMPLE GRANTS £72,847 to University of London for Institute of Historical Research, including £67,847 as the historical award; £3,000 to Merlin; £1,500 each to ACE Centre Advisory Trust, Bath Institute of Medical Engineering,

British Museum, Down's Syndrome Association for teacher training, Federation of Artistic and Creative Therapy, Get it While You Can, Hartlepool and District Hospice, and Neighbourly Care – Southall.

FINANCES *Year* 2001–02 *Income* £225,571 *Grants* £209,347 *Assets* £5,173,784

TRUSTEES Miss Sarah E Stowell, Chair; David J Marnham; James R Sewell.

PUBLICATIONS Notes for the guidance of applicants for 'Special Donations' and 'Historical Awards' .

HOW TO APPLY Applications for 'Special Donations', giving full but concise details, should be sent to the administrators at the above address by 1 March for consideration in April. Copies of the regulations and application forms for 'Historical Awards' can be obtained from: The Secretary, The Scouloudi Foundation Historical Awards Committee, c/o Institute of Historical Research, University of London, Senate House, London WC1E 7HU.

WHO TO APPLY TO The Administrators, c/o Haysmacintyre, Southampton House, 317 High Holborn, London WC1V 7NL *Tel* 020 7969 5500 *Fax* 020 7969 5529

CC NO 205685   **ESTABLISHED** 1962

························

■ **Seamen's Hospital Society**

WHERE FUNDING CAN BE GIVEN UK.

WHAT IS FUNDED Medical, care and welfare organisations working with seafarers and to individual seafarers and their dependants.

SAMPLE GRANTS £55,000 to Royal Alfred Seafarers' Society; £25,000 each to NUMAST Welfare Fund and Merchant Seamen's War Memorial Society; £15,000 to Queen Victoria Seamen's Rest; £12,000 to Royal National Mission to Deep Sea Fishermen; £5,000 each to International Seafarers' Centre at Great Yarmouth and Royal Merchant Navy School Foundation; £4,000 to Glasgow Veterans Seafarers' Association.

FINANCES *Year* 2001 *Income* £360,000 *Grants* £231,000 *Assets* £9,000,000

TRUSTEES Capt. S T Smith, Chair; A P J Lydekker; J C Jenkinson; J Allen; J D Guthrie; Capt. P M Hambling; P McEwan; Capt. G W S Miskin; A R Nairne; Capt. A G Russell; T Santamera; Capt. A J Speed; A F D Williams; Mr G P Ellis; Dr J F Leonard; Capt. A J R Tyrrell.

OTHER INFORMATION In 2001 the sum of £70,000 was given to 168 individuals.

HOW TO APPLY On a form available from the correspondent.

WHO TO APPLY TO Peter Coulson, General Secretary, 29 King William Walk, Greenwich, London SE10 9HX *Tel* 020 8858 3696 *E-mail* shs@btconnect.com *Website* www.seahospital.org.uk

CC NO 231724   **ESTABLISHED** 1999

························

■ **Search**

WHERE FUNDING CAN BE GIVEN UK, with a possible preference for the south of England.

WHO CAN BENEFIT Established medical research institutions, organisations benefiting people who are sick and disabled. Children and young adults may be considered.

WHAT IS FUNDED Medical research, medicine and health. Provision of equipment, materials or grants for people with disabling conditions or diseases and to educational projects.

WHAT IS NOT FUNDED No grants to individuals or students.

TYPE OF GRANT One-off grants.

RANGE OF GRANTS £1,500–£60,000.

SAMPLE GRANTS £40,000 to the Institute of Child Health; £29,000 to Brunel University.

FINANCES *Year* 2002 *Income* £114,681 *Grants* £104,400 *Assets* £252,891

TRUSTEES Dr R Leach; Prof. H Wolff; Prof S Glickman.

HOW TO APPLY Application forms are available from the correspondent, however all funds are currently committed.

WHO TO APPLY TO A Farquhar, 22 City Business Centre, 6 Brighton Road, Horsham, West Sussex RH13 5BB *Tel* 01403 211252 *Fax* 01403 271553 *E-mail* search@snowdonawardscheme.org.uk

CC NO 1038477   **ESTABLISHED** 1994

························

■ **The Searchlight Electric Charitable Trust**

WHERE FUNDING CAN BE GIVEN UK, with a preference for Manchester.

WHO CAN BENEFIT Registered charities. In the past the trustees have stated that it is their policy to only support charities already on their existing list of beneficiaries, or those already known to them.

WHAT IS FUNDED General charitable purposes.

WHAT IS NOT FUNDED No grants for individuals.

SAMPLE GRANTS £30,000 to UJIA; £10,300 to OHR Yerusalem; £5,000 to British Friends of Laniado Hospital; £4,900 to VHT; £2,500 each to King David Schools and Shaare Torah Yeshiva; £2,000 each to Bachad Fellowship, and Young Israel Synagogue – Netanya; £1,980 to Lubavitch; £1,864 to Manchester Great and New Synagogue.

FINANCES *Year* 2000–01 *Income* £73,065 *Grants* £75,414 *Assets* £749,559

TRUSTEES H E Hamburger; D M Hamburger; M E Hamburger; J S Fidler.

HOW TO APPLY In writing to the correspondent, but note that in the past the trustees have stated that it is their policy to only support charities already on their existing list of beneficiaries or those already known to them.

WHO TO APPLY TO H E Hamburger, Trustee, Searchlight Electric Ltd, 900 Oldham Road, Manchester M40 2BS *Tel* 0161 203 3300

CC NO 801644   **ESTABLISHED** 1988

························

■ **The Searle Charitable Trust**

WHERE FUNDING CAN BE GIVEN UK.

WHO CAN BENEFIT Established youth organisations benefiting those disadvantaged by poverty.

WHAT IS FUNDED Projects/organisations connected with sailing for youth development.

WHAT IS NOT FUNDED No grants for individuals or for appeals not related to sailing.

TYPE OF GRANT One-off, recurring costs, project and core costs. Funding is available for up to three years.

SAMPLE GRANTS £53,000 to RONA Trust; £500 to Wooden Spoon Society; £360 to Cancer Research Campaign; £250 each to ICRF and Scope.

FINANCES *Year* 2000–01 *Income* £75,338 *Grants* £55,667 *Assets* £2,965,571

TRUSTEES Andrew D Searle; Victoria C Searle.

OTHER INFORMATION The trust funds the 'Donald Searle' sail training yacht which is part of a fleet of vessels run and operated by the London Sailing Project based at Southampton. The main aim of the trust is youth development within a nautical environment.

HOW TO APPLY In writing to the correspondent.

WHO TO APPLY TO A D Searle, Trustee, 20 Kensington Church Street, London W8 4EP

CC NO 288541   **ESTABLISHED** 1982

■ The Helene Sebba Charitable Trust

WHERE FUNDING CAN BE GIVEN UK, Canada and Israel.

WHO CAN BENEFIT Organisations involved in medical research or benefiting people with disabilities or people of the Jewish faith.

WHAT IS FUNDED Support for: medical research; people who are disabled; and people of the Jewish faith.

RANGE OF GRANTS £200–£15,000.

SAMPLE GRANTS The second of three grants of £43,412 each to Norwood Ltd to fund the running of a hydrotherapy pool; £15,000 each to Akim and the Ehlers-Danlos and Connective Tissue Disorders Fund; £5,000 each to the Bridge Project and Edward L Erdman Environmental Fund; £2,000 each to Sayser, Norwood Ltd and We Care 2000 – Norfolk Millennium Trust for Carers; £1,000 to AdFam – Suffolk; £200 to Break.

FINANCES *Year* 2000–01 *Income* £43,728 *Grants* £90,612 *Assets* £2,782,950

TRUSTEES Mrs N C Klein; Mrs J C Sebba; L Sebba.

HOW TO APPLY In writing to the correspondent.

WHO TO APPLY TO David L Hull, PO Box 326, Bedford MK40 3XU *Tel* 01234 266657

CC NO 277245   **ESTABLISHED** 1978

■ The Samuel Sebba Charitable Trust

WHERE FUNDING CAN BE GIVEN UK and Israel.

WHO CAN BENEFIT Jewish organisations.

WHAT IS FUNDED The four main areas are: general communal matters including youth clubs and community centres; Jewish education, schools and the training of future rabbis; hospices and older people; and medical aid and hospitals.

WHAT IS NOT FUNDED No grants to individuals.

SAMPLE GRANTS £40,000 to Community Security Trust; £25,000 each to Cyril and Betty Stein Charitable Trust for underprivileged children at the Jaffa Institute, Israel Institute for Talmudic Publications and JFS General Charitable Trust; £22,000 to Jewish Care; £20,000 each to British Council of Shaare Zedek Medical Centre, Hawthorne Trust and Ruth and Conrad Morris Charitable Trust.

FINANCES *Year* 2000–01 *Grants* £805,000

TRUSTEES Leigh Sebba; Stanley Sebba; Leslie Sebba; Victor Klein; Clive Marks.

HOW TO APPLY In writing to the correspondent, on one page of A4, with a set of accounts, an sae and, most importantly, a cash flow statement for the next 12 months. Because of ongoing support to so many organisations already known to the trust, it is likely that unsolicited applications will, for the foreseeable future, be unsuccessful.

WHO TO APPLY TO Clive Marks, Trustee, 44a New Cavendish Street, London W1M 7LG

CC NO 253351   **ESTABLISHED** 1967

■ Second Quothquan Charitable Trust

WHERE FUNDING CAN BE GIVEN Preference for projects in Birmingham and immediate surrounding areas.

WHO CAN BENEFIT Projects known to the trustees, usually Christian organisations benefiting the community.

WHAT IS FUNDED Usually local Christian projects. Any project outside the West Midlands must be known to the trustees, whether in the UK or abroad.

WHAT IS NOT FUNDED No grants are given towards: anything that does not have the promotion of Christianity as part of its ethos; activities that are the primarily responsibility of central or local government; animal welfare; church buildings for restorations, improvements, renovations or new building; environmental projects such as conservation and protection of wildlife and landscape; expeditions and overseas trips; hospitals and health centres; individuals; large UK charities are not normally supported, even for local projects; loans and business finance; medical research projects; overseas appeals, unless there is a recommendation from someone known personally to the trustees; promotion of any non-Christian religion; schools, universities and colleges.

TYPE OF GRANT Normally one-off, but further applications after ten months have elapsed are considered.

RANGE OF GRANTS £50–£50,000.

SAMPLE GRANTS £147,000 in nine grants to Christian centres and promoting prayer; £32,000 in 27 grants to full-time UK Christian workers; £28,000 in 23 grants to evangelism, education, books and bibles; £18,000 in 25 grants to overseas Christian missions; £6,200 in 18 grants to low income, unemployed and one-parent families; £6,000 in 22 grants to bible college students; £4,900 in 7 grants to welfare; £4,400 in 4 grants to churches; £1,600 in 8 grants to volunteers.

FINANCES *Year* 2000 *Income* £50,000 *Grants* £246,000 *Assets* £1,300,000

TRUSTEES A L Gilmour; Mrs J A Gilmour.

PUBLICATIONS Information sheet available.

OTHER INFORMATION No appeals are acknowledged or replies made unless grants are made.

HOW TO APPLY In writing to the correspondent, including a brief description of the organisation, details of the project and its overall cost, details of funds already raised and remaining funds to be raised, a copy of the latest accounts (including any associated or parent organisations) and any other leaflets or supporting documentation. The trust does not acknowledge applications or enter into correspondence unless they require further information. Unsuccessful applicants are not notified. The trust stated that advice to potential applicants on whether to apply can be obtained by telephoning Mrs Janet Gilmour on 0121 323 3236 prior to applying.

WHO TO APPLY TO A L Gilmour, Trustee, Dale Farm, Worcester Lane, Four Oaks, Sutton Coldfield, West Midlands B75 5PR *Tel* 0121 323 3236 *Fax* 0121 323 3237 *E-mail* appeals@qouthquan.org

CC NO 273229   **ESTABLISHED** 1977

■ Second Sidbury Trust

WHERE FUNDING CAN BE GIVEN UK, with some preference for Devon.

WHO CAN BENEFIT Organisations and institutions addressing education, the relief of poverty and sickness, and medical research.

WHAT IS FUNDED The trust makes grants to institutions established for educational purposes or for the relief of poverty or sickness and especially the investigation and cure of arthritis and rheumatic diseases.

RANGE OF GRANTS £500–£20,000.

SAMPLE GRANTS £20,000 to Disabled Living Foundation; £3,000 each to Sail Training Association and University of Manchester; £2,800 to Child Psychotherapy Trust; £2,300 to Wytham Hall; £2,000 to Winged Fellowship; £1,600 to Abbeyfield Sidmouth Society; £1,500 each to Devonian Orthopaedic Association and Royal Alfred Seafarers Society; £1,300 to Devon Archaeological Society; £1,200 to British Red Cross Devon branch; and £1,100 each to Sid Vale Heritage Centre (Sidmouth Museum) and International Tree Foundation.

FINANCES *Year* 1999–2000 *Income* £46,000 *Grants* £49,000 *Assets* £925,000

TRUSTEES Lady Hamilton; Gilian Frank Hubert Glover; J C Vernor Miles; George William Semark Miskin; Mrs J N Nyiri.

HOW TO APPLY In writing to the correspondent.

WHO TO APPLY TO J C Vernor Miles, Trustee, Vernor Miles & Noble, 5 Raymond Buildings, Gray's Inn, London WC1R 5DD *Tel* 020 7242 8688

CC NO 239432   **ESTABLISHED** 1964

■ The Securicor Charitable Trust

WHERE FUNDING CAN BE GIVEN Mainly UK but occasionally overseas where the Securicor group has local operations.

WHO CAN BENEFIT Registered charities.

WHAT IS FUNDED General charitable purposes, with a preference for specific charitable projects rather than large general appeals.

WHAT IS NOT FUNDED No educational grants, expeditions, travel or wildlife. No advertising.

RANGE OF GRANTS Typical grant £250. Occasionally up to £1,000.

FINANCES *Year* 2001 *Income* £55,530 *Grants* £57,750

TRUSTEES Mrs A Munson, Chair; Mrs I Cowden; P V David; R K Davies; N C Youngman.

HOW TO APPLY Trustees meet every two months, and consider only written applications. No application form. No telephone calls please.

WHO TO APPLY TO The Chairman, Sutton Park House, 15 Carshalton Road, Sutton, Surrey SM1 4LD *Fax* 020 8661 0204

CC NO 274637   **ESTABLISHED** 1977

■ The Sedbury Trust

WHERE FUNDING CAN BE GIVEN Gloucestershire.

WHO CAN BENEFIT Organisations benefiting people who have been in care, at risk groups, people disadvantaged by poverty and socially isolated people.

WHAT IS FUNDED General welfare especially concerned with children and young people who have been in care.

FINANCES *Year* 2000–01 *Income* £93,000 *Grants* £10,000 *Assets* £2,100,000

TRUSTEES N F C Smith; Dame Janet Trotter; D Morris; Mavis Lady Dunrossil; K Edwards.

HOW TO APPLY In writing to the correspondent. Any application falling outside of the trust's area of work will not be considered.

WHO TO APPLY TO Mrs J Lane, Clerk to the Trustees, Wood End, Sandy Lane Road, Cheltenham, Gloucestershire GL53 9DA *Tel* 01242 572116 *Fax* 01242 263736

CC NO 1012875   **ESTABLISHED** 1992

■ The Seedfield Trust

WHERE FUNDING CAN BE GIVEN Worldwide.

WHO CAN BENEFIT Registered charities benefiting: Christians; evangelists; victims of famine, man-made and natural disasters, and war; people disadvantaged by poverty; retired clergy; and missionaries.

WHAT IS FUNDED To support the preaching and teaching of the Christian faith throughout the world, including publication and distribution of Scripture, Christian literature and audio-visual aids. To assist in the relief of human suffering and poverty, including retired ministers and missionaries.

WHAT IS NOT FUNDED No grants to individuals.

TYPE OF GRANT Capital, interest free loans, one-off, project and start-up costs. Funding is for up to three years.

RANGE OF GRANTS £250–£12,500.

SAMPLE GRANTS £21,700 to European Christian Mission; £11,000 to Dorothea Trust; £10,000 each to Overseas Missionary Fellowship and Thana Trust; £7,500 to Restorers Trust; £7,000 to Gideons International; £6,000 to Muller Homes; £4,000 to Pentecostal Child Care Association; £3,000 to Operation Mobilisation; £2,500 each to Cosmo Club and The Message – Manchester.

FINANCES *Year* 2000 *Income* £107,771 *Grants* £103,250 *Assets* £2,412,757

TRUSTEES John Atkins; Keith Buckler; David Ryan; Revd Lionel Osborn; Janet Buckler; D Heap.

HOW TO APPLY In writing to the correspondent, for consideration by the trustees who meet twice each year. Please enclose an sae for acknowledgement.

WHO TO APPLY TO David Ryan, Trustee, Regent House, Heaton Lane, Stockport, Cheshire SK4 1BS *Tel* 0161 477 4750

CC NO 283463   **ESTABLISHED** 1981

■ Sefton Community Foundation

WHERE FUNDING CAN BE GIVEN Merseyside, with a special interest in Sefton.

WHO CAN BENEFIT Children, young adults, older people, those in any family and social circumstances, and those with an illness.

WHAT IS FUNDED General charitable purposes for the benefit of the community, in particular, the advancement of education, the protection of mental and physical health and the relief of poverty and sickness. Accommodation and housing; arts, culture and recreation; infrastructure, support and development; religious buildings; and conservation and the environment will also be considered.

RANGE OF GRANTS £70–£1,000.

SAMPLE GRANTS £1,000 each included Sefton's Children's Trust, Sightline, Sefton Opera, Adult Dyslexia Access, NCT – Southport & Formby, Crosby Young Mothers and Formby Family Association.

FINANCES *Year* 2001–02 *Grants* £646,000

TRUSTEES A. White; R. Swainson; J. Flynn; L. Barnett; I. Chapman; A. McCombe.

PUBLICATIONS Range of leaflets.

OTHER INFORMATION The foundation manages funds on behalf of parent donors. Funding priorities will vary considerably depending on the requirements of these donors.

HOW TO APPLY Applicants are advised to consult the foundation's website or phone the foundation on 0151 9664604 or 9664609 for information or to request an application pack. Alternatively, applicants can e-mail the foundation, stating which fund(s) they are interested in.

WHO TO APPLY TO Dave Roberts, Executive Director, c/o Alliance & Leicester, Administration Block, West Wing, Bridle Road, Bootle GIR OAA
Tel 0151 966 4604
Website www.seftoncf.org.uk
CC NO 1068887   **ESTABLISHED** 1998

■ Leslie Sell Charitable Trust

WHERE FUNDING CAN BE GIVEN UK and worldwide.

WHO CAN BENEFIT Scout and Guide Associations.

WHAT IS FUNDED Assistance for Scout and Guide Associations, mainly but not exclusively in Bedfordshire, Hertfordshire, and Buckinghamshire area.

TYPE OF GRANT Usually one-off payments for a specific project.

FINANCES *Year* 2001–02 *Income* £178,160 *Grants* £147,815 *Assets* £2,265,104

TRUSTEES P S Sell, Chair; Mrs M R Wiltshire; A H Sell.

HOW TO APPLY In writing to the correspondent. Applications should include clear details of the project or purpose for which funds are required, together with an estimate of total costs and total funds raised by the group or individual for the project.

WHO TO APPLY TO J Byrnes, Ground Floor Offices, 52/58 London Road, St Albans, Hertfordshire AL1 1NG *Tel* 01727 843603 *Fax* 01727 843663
CC NO 258699   **ESTABLISHED** 1969

■ The Sellafield Charity Trust Fund

WHERE FUNDING CAN BE GIVEN The local authority areas of Copeland and Allerdale in West Cumbria.

WHO CAN BENEFIT NHS, local community groups, youth groups, and clubs for disabled people.

WHAT IS FUNDED General charitable purposes.

WHAT IS NOT FUNDED The trust does not deal directly with individuals. If, for example, an individual wanted a nebuliser, the trust would consider supplying the equipment to an agency such as social services, local surgery or hospital, which would then 'loan' the equipment to the individual. The trust will not support the following: sports clubs; churches (except in the case of community halls and so on) or other religious organisations; private nursing facilities or any other profit-making body; UK appeals; improvements to private dwellings; or any group outside West Cumbria.

TYPE OF GRANT The trust does not give money, only equipment.

RANGE OF GRANTS £150–£23,000.

SAMPLE GRANTS In 2000: £52,000 in six grants to West Cumberland Hospital; between £1,000–£3,000 went to 15 organisations including Age Concern, Broughton First Responders, Centre for Complementary Care, Cumbria Cerebral Palsy Society, Seascale Health Centre and West Cumbria Society for the Blind.

FINANCES *Year* 2001 *Income* £57,500 *Grants* £70,000

TRUSTEES J W Reid; I Withycombe; J Fleming.

HOW TO APPLY In writing to the correspondent.

WHO TO APPLY TO J W Reid, Hon. Secretary, Human Resources B444, British Nuclear Fuels plc, Sellafield, Seascale, Cumbria CA20 1PG *Tel* 01946 771742
CC NO 517829   **ESTABLISHED** 1978

■ Sellata Ltd

WHERE FUNDING CAN BE GIVEN UK.

WHAT IS FUNDED The advancement of religion and the relief of poverty.

FINANCES *Year* 1999–2000 *Income* £192,000 *Grants* £75,000 *Assets* £532,000

TRUSTEES E S Benedikt; Mrs N Benedikt; P Benedikt.

HOW TO APPLY In writing to the correspondent.

WHO TO APPLY TO E S Benedikt, Trustee, 29 Fontayne Road, London N16 7EA
CC NO 285429   **ESTABLISHED** 1980

■ SEM Charitable Trust

WHERE FUNDING CAN BE GIVEN Mainly South Africa, Israel and UK.

WHO CAN BENEFIT Mainly educational institutions benefiting disabled people, children and young adults.

WHAT IS FUNDED Mainly recommendations of the settlor, particularly charities working in the fields of the education of disadvantaged and disabled people; and the empowerment of grassroots people in developing countries.

WHAT IS NOT FUNDED No grants to individuals.

TYPE OF GRANT Recurring.

SAMPLE GRANTS £17,000 to Together in Notre Dame; £10,000 each to Beth Shalon, CET, HAFAD and KWA Zulu National Philharmonic Orchestra; £8,000 to Sea World.

FINANCES *Year* 2000–01 *Income* £73,000 *Grants* £110,000 *Assets* £776,000

TRUSTEES Mrs Sarah E Radomir; Michael Cohen.

HOW TO APPLY In writing to the correspondent.

WHO TO APPLY TO M Cohen, Trustee, Saffery Champness, Red Lion Street, London WC1R 4GB *Tel* 020 7841 4000
CC NO 265831   **ESTABLISHED** 1973

■ The Ayrton Senna Foundation

WHERE FUNDING CAN BE GIVEN Worldwide, with a preference for Brazil.

WHO CAN BENEFIT Children's health and education charities.

WHAT IS FUNDED 'The objectives seek to provide education, healthcare and medical support for children.'

WHAT IS NOT FUNDED No grants to individuals.

SAMPLE GRANTS £342,000 to Instituto Ayrton Senna; £3,000 to Cancer Bacup.

FINANCES *Year* 1998 *Income* £433,000 *Grants* £345,000

TRUSTEES Viviane Lalli, President; Milton Guerado Theodoro da Silva; Neyde Joanna Senna da Silva; Leonardo Senna da Silva; Fabio da Silva Machado; Christopher Bliss; Julian Jakobi.

HOW TO APPLY In writing to the correspondent.

WHO TO APPLY TO Julian Jakobi, Trustee, 34–43 Russell Square, London WC2B 5HA
CC NO 1041759   **ESTABLISHED** 1994

■ Servite Sisters' Charitable Trust Fund

WHERE FUNDING CAN BE GIVEN UK and Worldwide.

WHO CAN BENEFIT Marginalised women; refugees and other disadvantaged migrants.

WHAT IS FUNDED The support of activities intended primarily to help women who are marginalised physically, spiritually or mentally; the support of activities intended to alleviate the distress of refugees and other disadvantaged migrants.

WHAT IS NOT FUNDED No grants to individuals. No grants towards building projects and no recurring grants.

TYPE OF GRANT One-off, project, running costs, salaries and start-up costs. Funding may be given for one year or less.

RANGE OF GRANTS Average £1,000.

SAMPLE GRANTS £1,886 to Indo American Refugee & Migrant Organisation (UK) for their interpreting and advocacy services; £1,500 to Addaction (UK) towards support for women prostitutes who are using drugs; £1,550 to South Africa Enterprises Foundation for office equipment and sewing machines; £1,000 to Quilon Social Service Society (India) for their new coir manufacturing project for widows; £850 to Rukira Women's Group (Uganda) for sewing and horticulture women's income-generation projects; £600 to Sisters of St Joseph of Cluny (Philippines) for working capital to support women's tailoring income-generation project; £500 to St Mary Magdalen Centre for Asylum Seekers (UK) for their befriending service.

FINANCES *Year* 2002 *Grants* £220,000

TRUSTEES Sister Joyce Mary Fryer OSM; Sister Ruth Campbell OSM; Sister Eugenia Geraghty OSM; Sister Catherine Ryan OSM.

HOW TO APPLY In writing to the correspondent with brief details of your organisation, project and needs.

WHO TO APPLY TO Michael J W Ward, Secretary, Parkside, Coldharbour Lane, Dorking, Surrey RH4 3BN *Tel* 01306 875756 *Fax* 01306 889339 *E-mail* m@servite.demon.co.uk

CC NO 241434   **ESTABLISHED** 1993

■ The Seven Fifty Trust

WHERE FUNDING CAN BE GIVEN UK and worldwide.

WHO CAN BENEFIT Registered charities benefiting Christians.

WHAT IS FUNDED Trustees mainly give to causes they have supported for many years.

WHAT IS NOT FUNDED No support for unsolicited requests.

RANGE OF GRANTS £350–£7,110.

SAMPLE GRANTS £42,005 to All Saints Church – Crowbridge for the Faith in the Future Fund; £21,200 to Care for the Family; £7,556 to All Saints Church – Crowbridge; £3,800 to St Mathew's Fulham; £3,750 to Aquila; £2,800 to Universities and Colleges Christian Fellowship; £2,621 to Coalition for Christian Outreach; £2,400 to Langham Trust; £2,200 to Tearfund; £2,000 to International Fellowship of Evangelical Students.

FINANCES *Year* 2000–01 *Income* £65,282 *Grants* £101,027 *Assets* £1,399,887

TRUSTEES Revd Andrew C J Cornes; Katherine E Cornes; Peter N Collier; Susan M Collier.

HOW TO APPLY It should be noted that the trust's funds are fully committed and unsolicited requests are not entertained. No reply is sent unless an sae is included with the application, but even then the reply will only say that the trust does not respond to unsolicited applications.

WHO TO APPLY TO Revd Andrew C J Cornes, Trustee, All Saints Vicarage, Chapel Green, Crowborough, East Sussex TN6 1ED *Tel* 01892 667384

CC NO 298886   **ESTABLISHED** 1988

■ The Severn Trent Water Charitable Trust

WHERE FUNDING CAN BE GIVEN The area covered by the Severn Trent Water Ltd, which stretches from Wales to east Leicestershire and from the Humber estuary down to the Bristol Channel.

WHAT IS FUNDED Relief of poverty, money advice, debt counselling.

WHAT IS NOT FUNDED People who do not have a liability to pay water charges to Severn Trent Water Ltd.

TYPE OF GRANT Revenue grants and capital grants up to £1,500.

FINANCES *Year* 2001–02 *Income* £2,700,000 *Grants* £320,000

TRUSTEES Dr Derek W Harris, Chair; John R A Crabtree; Mrs L Pusey; Mrs Edna Sadler; Roy Simpson; Mrs Mary Milton; Mrs Sheila Barrow; Andrew D Peet.

HOW TO APPLY On a form available from advice agencies or direct from the trust at a freepost address: Severn Trent Trust Fund, FREEPOST MID 16999, Sutton Coldfield B72 1BR. Further details can be found on the website.

WHO TO APPLY TO S Braley, Director, Emmanuel Court, 12–14 Mill Street, Sutton Coldfield, West Midlands B72 1TJ *Tel* 0121 355 7766 *Fax* 0121 354 8485 *E-mail* office@sttf.org.uk *Website* www.sttf.org.uk

CC NO 1064005   **ESTABLISHED** 1997

■ The Cyril Shack Trust

WHERE FUNDING CAN BE GIVEN UK.

WHO CAN BENEFIT Voluntary organisations and charitable groups only.

WHAT IS FUNDED General charitable purposes.

WHAT IS NOT FUNDED No grants for expeditions, travel bursaries, scholarships or to individuals.

TYPE OF GRANT Capital; recurring.

RANGE OF GRANTS £25–£9,600.

SAMPLE GRANTS £9,600 in four grants to Finchley Road Synagogue; £3,100 in five grants to St John's Wood Synagogue; £1,300 in four grants to Nightingale House.

FINANCES *Year* 1999–2000 *Income* £22,000 *Grants* £69,000 *Assets* £315,000

TRUSTEES J Shack; C C Shack.

HOW TO APPLY In writing to the correspondent.

WHO TO APPLY TO The Clerk, c/o Lubbock Fine, Chartered Accountants, Russell Bedford House, City Forum, 250 City Road, London EC1V 2QQ *Tel* 020 7490 7766

CC NO 264270   **ESTABLISHED** 1972

■ The Shaftoe Educational Foundation

WHERE FUNDING CAN BE GIVEN Parish of Haydon.

WHO CAN BENEFIT Residents of the parish of Haydon only. The three schools (First, Middle & High) serving Haydon children.

WHAT IS FUNDED Schools serving the area specified, local organisations and individuals for educational purposes.

TYPE OF GRANT Usually one-off revenue support.

788

Does the trust you have chosen match your needs? Haphazard applications waste postage and time

RANGE OF GRANTS Can be up to £10,000. Typical size of grant in range £300–£600.

SAMPLE GRANTS £34,651 to local schools (First – £14,789; Middle – £12,000; High – £7,862); £21,864 to individuals for educational purposes; £11,193 to local organisations for educational purposes; £3,145 to the John Shafton Almshouses Charity.

FINANCES *Year* 2001–02 *Income* £108,775 *Grants* £70,853 *Assets* £2,431,705

TRUSTEES T A Bates, Chair; B L Bates; J W Clarkson; J J Drydon; T J Stephenson; J C Wardle; Mrs E Garrow; Mrs L A Gilhespy; Mrs L A Philp.

HOW TO APPLY In writing to the correspondent for consideration at March, July and November meetings. Initial telephone calls are welcomed.

WHO TO APPLY TO R A D Snowdon, Clerk, The Office, Shaftoe Terrace, Haydon Bridge, Hexham NE47 6BW *Tel* 01434 688871 *E-mail* News4shaftoe@aol.com

CC NO 528101   **ESTABLISHED** 1685

■ The Shakespeare Temperance Trust

WHERE FUNDING CAN BE GIVEN Durham City.

WHO CAN BENEFIT Organisations benefiting young, older and disabled people.

WHAT IS FUNDED Support for youth clubs and organisations; the welfare of people who are disabled and older people.

TYPE OF GRANT Primarily recurrent.

SAMPLE GRANTS 1998–99: £2,500 to Durham Samaritans; £1,000 to Durham Woman's Refuge; £750 to North East Council on Addictions; £450 each to Salvation Army – Durham Corps and Salvation Army – Sherburn Hill Corps; £400 to Relate; £300 each to Durham District Crime Prevention, Durham Nightstop, Durham County Schools Benevolent Fund, and 5th Durham Scout Group.

FINANCES *Year* 2001–02 *Income* £51,554

TRUSTEES C W Beswick, Chair; J B Young; J M Hitchman; E Clarke; I McIntyre; P J Storey; E Beaumont; R Lund.

HOW TO APPLY This trust is not seeking unsolicited applications.

WHO TO APPLY TO J M Hitchman, Trustee, Hedley & Hitchman, Palatine Studio, Palatine View, Durham DH1 4QQ *Tel* 0191 386 2170

CC NO 224895   **ESTABLISHED** 1974

■ The Shanti Charitable Trust

WHERE FUNDING CAN BE GIVEN UK, with preference for West Yorkshire and developing countries.

WHAT IS FUNDED General, Christian, international development.

WHAT IS NOT FUNDED No grants to gap year students, or political or animal welfare causes.

SAMPLE GRANTS £50,000 to International Nepal Fellowship; £5,000 each to Sue Ryder Foundation, Tear Fund, All Nations Christian College and CBRS; £3,000 each to Marie Curie Cancer Care, The Corinthian Trust and St John's Church; £1,000 to Foundation for Conductive Education; £500 to The Gate Christian Outreach.

FINANCES *Year* 2000–01 *Income* £54,500 *Grants* £80,500 *Assets* £213,000

TRUSTEES Miss J B Gill; T F X Parr; R K Hyett.

HOW TO APPLY In writing to the correspondent. Please note, most beneficiaries are those the trustees already have contact with.

WHO TO APPLY TO J E Brown, 53 Kirkgate, Silsden, Keighley, West Yorkshire BD20 0AQ *Tel* 01535 653094

CC NO 1064813   **ESTABLISHED** 1997

■ ShareGift (The Orr Mackintosh Foundation)

WHERE FUNDING CAN BE GIVEN Unrestricted

WHO CAN BENEFIT UK registered charities.

WHAT IS FUNDED General charitable purposes, guided by the wishes of the donors of shares, from where its income derives.

WHAT IS NOT FUNDED Grants to UK registered charities only.

SAMPLE GRANTS £102,000 to Hackney Empire; £75,500 to Marie Curie Cancer Care; £75,000 to Cancer Research UK; £50,000 to Help the Hospices; £45,000 to Camphill Village Trust; £36,500 to NSPCC; £32,000 to Landmark Trust; £30,500 to Shelter; £27,000 to Tearfund; £26,000 to Victim Support.

FINANCES *Year* 2001–02 *Income* £1,827,245 *Grants* £1,300,000 *Assets* £450,144

TRUSTEES Viscount Mackintosh of Halifax; Charles Moore; Matthew Orr.

HOW TO APPLY No applications can be considered. Charities wishing to benefit from the scheme should contact ShareGift to discuss how they might promote the concept to their and everyone else's advantage.

WHO TO APPLY TO Bridget Roe, Director, 46 Grosvenor Street, London W1K 3HN *Tel* 020 7337 0501 *Website* www.sharegift.org

CC NO 1052686   **ESTABLISHED** 1995

■ The Sharon Trust

WHERE FUNDING CAN BE GIVEN England, Scotland and overseas.

WHO CAN BENEFIT Christian missions, Christian camps, elderly Christian rest homes and organisations benefiting young Christians.

WHAT IS FUNDED To help where needed, especially Christian work and missions. Cultural and religious teaching will be considered. Printing Gospel tracts.

WHAT IS NOT FUNDED Usually no grants to individuals.

TYPE OF GRANT Generally recurrent.

SAMPLE GRANTS In 1996: £6,000 to Mount Pleasant Gospel Hall for new building; £1,500 to Lord's Work Trust for missionary support; £1,400 to Foreign Missionary Fund for foreign missions; £1,200 to Slavic Gospel Association; £925 to Young People's Christian Conference; £750 to Filey Gospel Camp; £700 to Bradford Christian School; £500 each to Home Labourer's Fund for bibles, etc, and Albanian Christian Fund; £300 to Gideon International.

FINANCES *Year* 2000–01 *Income* £47,053

TRUSTEES J F Warnes; F W Warnes; Mrs H G Taylor; Miss M H Warnes; W R Warnes.

HOW TO APPLY In writing to the correspondent. The trustees meet to consider applications in January.

WHO TO APPLY TO Miss N Warnes, 1 Mount Pleasant, Lowestoft, Suffolk NR32 4JB *Tel* 01502 574849

CC NO 268742   **ESTABLISHED** 1974

■ The Shaw Lands Trust

WHERE FUNDING CAN BE GIVEN Barnsley.

WHO CAN BENEFIT Organisations and individuals who have not attained the age of 25 years, who live in the former county borough of Barnsley, or are, or have been for not less than two years, in attendance at any school within the former borough and who are in need.

WHAT IS FUNDED Youth groups; welfare organisations; individuals for scholarships, bursaries, maintenance allowances or grants at any place of learning, and for outfits, clothing, tools, instruments or books to help beneficiaries on leaving school, university or other educational establishments.

SAMPLE GRANTS £3,000 each to Barnsley Girl Guides and Barnsley Sea Cadets Corps; £1,500 each to Barnsley Blind and Partial Sight Association and Riding for the Disabled; £1,100 to RAF Association; £1,000 each to Hoyle Mill Boys and Rockley House Trust; £850 to Samaritans Barnsley; £750 to Scope; £550 to British Legion (Men's Section) Barnsley; £500 each to Barnsley Dyslexia and Friends of Holden House.

FINANCES *Year* 1999–2000 *Income* £43,000 *Grants* £37,000 *Assets* £1,300,000

TRUSTEES Cllr Mrs J Watts; S Henshaw; Mrs P J Adcock; Cllr Mrs M Wilby; Cllr R Warden; Cllr W Denton; Cllr S Birkinshaw; Cllr J R Bostwick; R J Casken; M Bird; Mrs C Carrington; D Eade; N P Goodyear; C L Sutherland; Miss L A Field; H A Leigh; A W Sherriff.

HOW TO APPLY In writing to the correspondent for consideration in April and October.

WHO TO APPLY TO Gill Leece, Newman & Bond, 35 Church Street, Barnsley S70 2AP *Tel* 01226 213434

CC NO 224590   **ESTABLISHED** 1915

■ The Linley Shaw Foundation

WHERE FUNDING CAN BE GIVEN UK.

WHO CAN BENEFIT Registered charities in rural locations.

WHAT IS FUNDED The conservation, preservation and restoration of the natural beauty of the countryside of the UK for the public benefit. In particular, charities that organise voluntary workers to achieve these objectives.

WHAT IS NOT FUNDED No grants to non-charitable organisations, or to organisations whose aims or objects do not include conservation, preservation or restoration of the natural beauty of the UK countryside, even if the purpose of the grant would be eligible. No grants to individuals.

RANGE OF GRANTS £500–£8,000.

SAMPLE GRANTS £6,600 to British Trust for Conservation Volunteers; £5,000 each to Carfare Winnowed, Trees for Life, West Country Rivers, Wildfowl and Wetlands Trust, and Worcestershire Wildlife Trust.

FINANCES *Year* 2000 *Income* £97,289 *Grants* £60,000 *Assets* £1,509,824

TRUSTEES National Westminster Bank plc.

HOW TO APPLY In writing to the correspondent. All material will be photocopied by the trust so please avoid sending 'bound' copies of reports and so on. Evidence of aims and objectives are needed, usually in the forms of accounts, annual reports or leaflets, which cannot be returned. Applications are considered in February/early March and should be received by December/early January.

WHO TO APPLY TO The Trust Section, National Westminster Bank plc, Natwest Private Banking, 153 Preston Road, Brighton BN1 6BD *Tel* 01273 545035 *Fax* 01273 545075

CC NO 1034051   **ESTABLISHED** 1993

■ The Shears Charitable Trust

WHERE FUNDING CAN BE GIVEN Northumberland, Tyne & Wear, Durham and West Yorkshire.

WHO CAN BENEFIT Registered charities only.

WHAT IS FUNDED Funding may be given to health education; children's charities; arts, culture and recreation; heritage; conservation and environment.

WHAT IS NOT FUNDED No grants for domestic animal welfare.

TYPE OF GRANT One-off.

RANGE OF GRANTS Up to £5,000; typical grant £1,000.

SAMPLE GRANTS £40,000 to Community Foundation of Tyne and Wear and Northumberland; £30,000 each to the Ear Trust, Royal College of Surgeons and St Oswald's Hospice; £26,000 to National Tramway Museum; £5,000 each to BTCV, RSPB, WWF-UK and Woodland Trust; and £1,000 to Karuna Trust.

FINANCES *Year* 2001–02 *Income* £182,000 *Grants* £136,000 *Assets* £7,031,000

TRUSTEES L G Shears; T H Shears; P J R Shears.

HOW TO APPLY In writing to the correspondent.

WHO TO APPLY TO T H Shears, Trustee, 35 Elmfeld Road, Gosforth, Newcastle upon Tyne NE3 4BA

CC NO 1049907   **ESTABLISHED** 1994

■ The Sheepdrove Trust

WHERE FUNDING CAN BE GIVEN UK, but especially north Lambeth, London, where applicable.

WHO CAN BENEFIT Registered charities only.

WHAT IS FUNDED General charitable purposes, particulary child education, organic farming and biodiversity.

WHAT IS NOT FUNDED No grants to students or other individuals, nor for building projects or medical research.

TYPE OF GRANT One-off and recurrent.

SAMPLE GRANTS £150,000 to the Soil Association; £60,000 to Elm Farm Research Centre; £45,000 to Forum for the Future; £30,000 to Hawk & Owl Trust; £23,000 each to British Trust for Ornithology and Kids Company; £15,000 to Pesticide Action Network; £12,000 to Roots and Shoots.

FINANCES *Year* 2001 *Income* £770,000 *Grants* £875,000 *Assets* £18,052,000

TRUSTEES Mrs Juliet E Kindersley; Peter D Kindersley; Mrs Harriet R Treuille; Barnabas G Kindersley.

HOW TO APPLY In writing to the correspondent.

WHO TO APPLY TO Sarah Manasseh, 2 Methley Street, London SE11 4AJ

CC NO 328369   **ESTABLISHED** 1989

■ The Sheffield Bluecoat & Mount Pleasant Educational Foundation

WHERE FUNDING CAN BE GIVEN Sheffield.

WHO CAN BENEFIT Individuals under 25 and schools.

WHAT IS FUNDED Education and training, church schools, independent schools, language schools, primary and secondary schools, further education and special schools. Also bursaries and fees, scholarships and the purchase of books.

TYPE OF GRANT Core costs, one-off and running costs. Funding may be given for up to three years.

FINANCES *Year* 2001–02 *Grants* £46,000

TRUSTEES Mrs M Neill, Chair; Mrs M Roberts; J P Toomey; J C V Hunt; R G Grayson; Mrs K Lamb; Mrs M Barker; M Robertson; Mrs A Hunter.

HOW TO APPLY In writing to the correspondent.

WHO TO APPLY TO G J Smallman, c/o Wrigleys, 4th Floor, Fountain Precinct, Sheffield S1 2GZ *Tel* 0114 267 5596

CC NO 529351   **ESTABLISHED** 1962

■ The Sheffield Church Burgesses Trust

WHERE FUNDING CAN BE GIVEN Sheffield.

WHO CAN BENEFIT Voluntary organisations and registered charities benefiting at risk groups and people who are disadvantaged by poverty or socially isolated.

WHAT IS FUNDED Ecclesiastical purposes, education, and other charitable purposes. Specifically, Sheffield Cathedral, four Anglican deaneries, and the local community, including local health and welfare charities.

TYPE OF GRANT One-off and recurring.

SAMPLE GRANTS 1997: £125,000 to All Saints Ecclesall; £40,000 to Saint Catherine's of Siena; £13,500 to an individual (ex gratia pension package); £10,648 to Brightside (Saint Thomas, Saint Margaret); £10,621 to Saint Mary's PCC; £10,000 to Saint Thomas Wincobank; £9,000 to St Luke's Hospice; £8,421 to Saint Mark's Mosborough; £8,000 each to Saint John's PCC (rent grant) and Saint Aidans PCC.

FINANCES *Year* 2000–01 *Grants* £1,600,000

TRUSTEES P W Lee; Canon Dr G Tolley; D L Fletcher; J F W Peters; S McK Hamilton; Prof. G D Sims; N J A Hutton; S A P Hunter; A G Johnson; D F Booker; M P W Lee; I G Walker.

HOW TO APPLY In writing to the correspondent. The trustees meet in January, April, July and October.

WHO TO APPLY TO G J Smallman, c/o Wrigleys, 4th Floor, Fountain Precinct, Sheffield S1 1GZ *Tel* 0114 267 5594

CC NO 221284   **ESTABLISHED** 1554

■ Sheffield and District Hospital Services Charitable Fund

WHERE FUNDING CAN BE GIVEN Mostly South Yorkshire, also UK.

WHO CAN BENEFIT NHS hospitals and trusts; registered charities.

WHAT IS FUNDED Medical equipment and general charitable purposes.

SAMPLE GRANTS £40,000 to Age Concern – Sheffield; £25,000 each to Alzheimer's Disease Society – Sheffield for a home respite care service and Cherrytree Children's Home – Sheffield towards extensions; £20,000 to PACES – Sheffield for a classroom refurbishment; £15,000 to Fieldfare Trust – Sheffield for the Kielder Challenge; £13,000 to Barnsley (St Peter's) Hospice for a minibus; £11,000 to National Centre for Popular Music for a vibrating seat; £10,000 to Speakup – Rotherham for a DV camera/playback machine; £6,000 to Porterbrook Clinic – Sheffield for

video/audio equipment; £5,000 each to British Red Cross – Sheffield for a mobile first aid unit and Phoenix Association – Sheffield for health, fitness and educational resources.

FINANCES *Year* 1999 *Income* £800,000 *Grants* £810,000

TRUSTEES G Moore, Chair; K N Ibbotson; K Bardsley; A Birt; M Foster; J D S Hammond; N J A Hutton; A Matthews; I Taylor; P Watson.

HOW TO APPLY In writing to the correspondent.

WHO TO APPLY TO Graham Moore, Chair, Westfield House, 87 Division Street, Sheffield S1 1HT *Tel* 0114 272 9521

CC NO 246057   **ESTABLISHED** 1965

■ The Sheffield Town Trust

WHERE FUNDING CAN BE GIVEN Sheffield.

WHO CAN BENEFIT Mainly local charities.

WHAT IS FUNDED General charitable purposes in the Sheffield area.

RANGE OF GRANTS £250–£10,000.

SAMPLE GRANTS £10,000 to Four Weirs Walk; £8,000 to Nomad Homeless Advice and Support Unit; £7,500 to Salvation Army; £6,500 each to Sheffield Galleries and Museum Trust and Voluntary Action Sheffield; £6,000 to Youth Association South Yorkshire; £5,000 each to Cherry Tree, Crisis Fare Share, Mencap Blue Sky Appeal, and Mental Health Action Group.

FINANCES *Year* 1999 *Income* £321,000 *Grants* £312,000 *Assets* £5,800,000

TRUSTEES Clifford Talbot; Gerard Young; Robert Gordon Grayson; Charles Murray; Walter Jenkinson; Sir Hugh Neill; Christopher Barker; Adrian Staniforth; John Stephenson; Jonathan Brayshaw; Jennifer Ann Lee; Penelope Jewitt; James Fulton.

HOW TO APPLY In writing to the correspondent for consideration in February, May, August and November. A brochure titled 'Information for Applicants' is available from the correspondent.

WHO TO APPLY TO G Connell, Law Clerk, Old Cathedral Vicarage, St James' Row, Sheffield S1 1XA *Tel* 0114 272 2061

CC NO 223760   **ESTABLISHED** 1297

■ The Sheldon Trust

WHERE FUNDING CAN BE GIVEN West Midlands.

WHO CAN BENEFIT Registered charities.

WHAT IS FUNDED The funding priorities of the trustees are the relief of poverty and distress in society, concentrating on community projects. Aftercare, hospice at home, respite care, self-help and support groups, and rehabilitation centres are also considered. Facilities for disadvantaged and disabled people. Encouragement of local voluntary groups, recreational facilities, youth, community, rehabilitation for drugs, alcohol, and solvent abuse, religion, the elderly, mental health, learning difficulties.

WHAT IS NOT FUNDED 'The trustees will not consider appeals in respect of the cost of buildings, but will consider appeals where buildings have to be brought up-to-date to meet health, safety and fire regulations.' No grants to individuals.

TYPE OF GRANT Core costs, project, running costs, salaries and start-up costs will be considered. Funding may be given for up to two years.

SAMPLE GRANTS £11,000 to Birmingham Money Advice and Grants for grants for individuals in need in the Midlands; £10,000 to St Basil's Centre Birmingham for salary of project worker; £7,500 each to National Asthma and

Think carefully about every application. Is it justified?

791

Respiratory – Warwick for a bursary fund and Amelia Methodist Trust – Barry for salary of workshop manager; £6,000 to Methodist Homes for the Aged for outreach in the Midlands; £5,700 to Edwards Trust – Birmingham for running costs of family room; £5,000 each to Bethany Project – Birmingham for running costs, Cascade – Solihull for core funding, and John Grooms for equipment and housing in the Midlands; £2,000 to KIDS for Saturday and Siblings Clubs.

FINANCES *Year* 1999–2000 *Income* £165,070 *Grants* £208,050 *Assets* £3,386,934

TRUSTEES Revd R S Bidnell; J K R England; R V Wiglesworth; J C Barratt; Mrs R M Bagshaw.

HOW TO APPLY On a form available from the correspondent. The trustees meet three times a year, in March, July and November, considering 10 to 15 applicants depending on income. The trust's report stated that they will 'for the present be committing a good proportion of their income to continuing grants which means that they will have less income for other charitable purposes'.

WHO TO APPLY TO The Trust Administrator, Box S, White Horse Court, 25c North Street, Bishop's Stortford, Hertfordshire CM23 2LD *Fax* 01279 657626 *E-mail* charities@pothecary.co.uk

CC NO 242328   **ESTABLISHED** 1965

....

■ The David Shepherd Wildlife Foundation

WHERE FUNDING CAN BE GIVEN Africa and Asia.

WHO CAN BENEFIT Endangered wild flora and fauna and their dependent species, including people.

WHAT IS FUNDED The conservation of endangered mammals worldwide. Particular focus is given to direct funding for field work for tigers, elephants and rhinos in Africa and Asia. The foundation assists official law enforcement agencies to combat wildlife crime.

WHAT IS NOT FUNDED Applications for grants must be related to the conservation of the world's major endangered mammals and to field projects.

TYPE OF GRANT Direct grants to field projects.

RANGE OF GRANTS £200–£20,000.

SAMPLE GRANTS £30,500 to Save the Rhino, Namibia for field equipment for anti-poaching, monitoring and tracking rhinos and desert elephants; £30,000 each to The Prakratik Society, Ranthambhore – India to provide healthcare, education and alternative farming techniques, and Wildlife Trust of India for life insurance for Indian forest staff; £27,000 to Lusaka Agreement Task Force (LAFT) for vehicles, other equipment, undercover operations and training; £25,000 to Khao Yai Project and Border Patrol Training Programme, Thailand, for training, equipment and a community outreach project creating alternative income sources in the area around the park; £24,000 to Anti-poaching and Investigations, Zambia towards undercover operations, and work with regional enforcement agencies, in the fight against wildlife criminals; £23,500 to Alaungdaw Kathapa National Park Project, Myanma towards 30 rangers; £20,000 each to Asian Conservation Awareness Programme for a campaign to stop the trade in body parts of endangered animals, The Sunderbans Tiger Project – India to provide training and basic anti-poaching kits to the team of 400 forest rangers, and a Siberian tiger project towards anti-poaching operations, monitoring and an educational outreach programme;

FINANCES *Year* 2000–01 *Income* £733,416 *Grants* £357,877

TRUSTEES Bruce Norris, Chair; Peter Giblin; David Gower; Avril Shepherd; Nigel Colne; Nigel Keen.

HOW TO APPLY In writing to the correspondent.

WHO TO APPLY TO Ms Melanie Shepherd, Director, 61 Smithbrook Kilns, Cranleigh, Surrey GU8 6JJ *Tel* 01483 272323 *Fax* 01483 272427 *E-mail* dswf@davidshepherd.org *Website* www.davidshepherd.org

CC NO 289646   **ESTABLISHED** 1984

....

■ The Patricia and Donald Shepherd Trust

WHERE FUNDING CAN BE GIVEN Worldwide, particularly the north of England.

WHO CAN BENEFIT Mainly local organisations – particularly those in the north of England.

WHAT IS FUNDED General charitable purposes. Local charities or charities with which the trustees have personal knowledge of, interest in or association with.

TYPE OF GRANT Mainly one-off.

SAMPLE GRANTS £5,000 each to St Leonard's Hospice, Macmillan Cancer Relief and Yorkshire Air Museum; £2,800 to York Archaeolgical Trust; £2,000 to St Gemma's Hospice; £1,000 each to York Early Music Festival and NCH Action for Children.

FINANCES *Year* 2000–01 *Income* £98,000 *Grants* £71,000 *Assets* £515,368

TRUSTEES Mrs P Shepherd; Mrs J L Robertson; Patrick M Shepherd; D R Reaston; I O Robertson; Mrs C M Shepherd.

HOW TO APPLY In writing to the correspondent.

WHO TO APPLY TO Mrs Patricia Shepherd, Trustee, PO Box 10, York YO1 1XU

CC NO 272948   **ESTABLISHED** 1973

....

■ The Shepherd Street Trust

WHERE FUNDING CAN BE GIVEN Within 50 miles of Preston, although there is a preference for Preston.

WHO CAN BENEFIT Individuals and organisations. Grants must benefit people under 21.

WHAT IS FUNDED The relief of poverty and distress; provision of medical equipment and specialist medical attention; provision of educational training and recreation and leisure facilities.

SAMPLE GRANTS £7,000 to an individual; £5,355 to an individual; £5,000 to Royal Preston Hospital Children's Ward; £3,000 each to two individuals; £2,500 to Lostock Hall Guide Association towards the costs of a new hut; £2,000 each to Grimsargh Playground Action Group towards the cost of play equipment, Hillside Centre for Children with Autism, and an individual; £1,500 to Avenger Corps towards costs for musical instruments.

FINANCES *Year* 1998–99 *Income* £58,161 *Grants* £66,981 *Assets* £1,155,465

TRUSTEES W W M Margerison, Chair; Miss L M Margerison; Mrs I D S C Dickson; J T Smith; Mrs G Whalley; Mrs D Swarbrick; Mrs B Smales; T Scott; J Brandwood.

HOW TO APPLY The trust advertises in the local newspaper twice a year in May and November. The closing dates for applications are 30 June and 31 December; the meetings to consider grants are in the following September and March respectively. Grants can be made at other times where there is a 'real need'.

WHO TO APPLY TO Mrs J Bate, Secretary, 119 Oxford Street, Preston PR1 3QY *Tel* 01772 734263
CC NO 222922 ESTABLISHED 1973

■ The Sylvia & Colin Shepherd Charitable Trust

WHERE FUNDING CAN BE GIVEN North east England, but mostly within a 25-mile radius of York.

WHO CAN BENEFIT Registered charities only, benefiting children and older people, retired people and people who are disabled.

WHAT IS FUNDED In the medium-term the policy is to build up the trust's capital base. Currently the main areas of interest are community initiatives, care of older people, childcare, people who are mentally or physically disabled, conservation, and medical support and equipment.

WHAT IS NOT FUNDED Applications from individuals will not be considered and support does not extend to organisations working outside the areas defined above and excludes overseas activities.

TYPE OF GRANT Usually for specific projects on an enabling basis. Core funding or ongoing support will not normally be provided.

RANGE OF GRANTS £100–£5,000, typically £250–£1,000.

SAMPLE GRANTS £5,000 each to Mount School – York for a sports hall and York Childcare Ltd for its 10th anniversary; £3,000 to Catholic Childcare for counselling service in York; £2,000 to St Leonard's Hospice York for millennium appeal (new buildings); £1,000 each to Expanding Boundaries of Music Therapy (University of York) for music therapy for disturbed children, Stagecoach Youth Theatre York for a new arts and community centre, Friends of the University of York Library to develop the library collection, NSPCC for York child protection team, British Epilepsy Association for work in the York area, and York Cemetery for the chapel bell.

FINANCES *Year* 2000–01 *Income* £76,000 *Grants* £76,000 *Assets* £496,000

TRUSTEES Mrs S Shepherd; Mrs S C Dickson; D Dickson.

HOW TO APPLY In writing to the correspondent. The trustees meet frequently. Applications should include details of the need to be met, achievements and a copy of the latest accounts.

WHO TO APPLY TO The Trustees, 15 St Edward's Close, York YO24 1QB
CC NO 272788 ESTABLISHED 1973

■ Sherburn House Charity

WHERE FUNDING CAN BE GIVEN The ancient Diocese of Durham (the north east of England between the rivers Tweed and Tees).

WHO CAN BENEFIT Individuals and registered charities benefiting residents and former residents of the area specified, either suffering need, hardship or distress, or in need of care or sheltered accommodation.

WHAT IS FUNDED The following are areas of interest: health (including mental health); learning disabilities; physical disabilities; substance abuse; community needs; homelessness; special needs; effects of long-term unemployment.

WHAT IS NOT FUNDED Organisations which have substantial reserves or are in serious deficit; grantmaking bodies seeking to distribute grants on the trust's behalf; activities which are the responsibility of central/local government or other statutory body; fabric appeals for places of worship per se; fabric appeals for halls except those which demonstrate service/ activities for the whole community; fundraising events or activities; general appeals; sponsorship; expeditions or overseas travel; mainstream educational activity; national charities except those which have a strong representation within the trust's area; hospitals and medical centres (except hospices); retrospective grants; applications from organisations who have received a grant or have been refused a grant within the preceding two years; those who do not fully complete the application form.

TYPE OF GRANT Capital including buildings, core costs, one-off, running costs, salaries and start-up costs will be considered. Funding may be given for up to three years.

RANGE OF GRANTS Individual: £100–£1,000, typical grant £400. Organisations: £175–£15,000, typical grant £5,000.

SAMPLE GRANTS £34,000 to Action on Pain, Durham; £25,000 each to Churches Acting Together, Linton Co-operative Association and Westhelp; £20,000 each to Hartlepool Alzheimers Trust and Tyneside Cyrenians; £15,000 to Tynedale CAB.

FINANCES *Year* 2001–02 *Income* £1,912,670 *Grants* £747,100 *Assets* £4,871,089

TRUSTEES Canon G Miller; Margaret Bozic; William Brooks; David Forbes; Dorothy Hale; Mary Hawgood; Lindsay Perks; Graham Rodmell; Leslie B Smith; Ron Wilson; Gene Hill; Peter Thompson; Margaret L Rushford; Ian Stewart; Steve Laverick.

HOW TO APPLY On the application forms available from the correspondent. This is a straightforward four-page document. Applications for summer activities should ideally be submitted to the charity by the beginning of April to allow the process to give an answer well before the summer.

WHO TO APPLY TO Stephen Hallett, Chief Officer, Ramsey House, Sherburn House, Durham DH1 2SE *Tel* 0191 372 2551
Website www.sherburnhouse.org
CC NO 217652 ESTABLISHED 1181

■ The Archie Sherman Cardiff Charitable Foundation

WHERE FUNDING CAN BE GIVEN UK, Canada, Australia, New Zealand, Pakistan, Sri Lanka, South Africa, India, Israel, USA and other parts of the British Commonwealth.

WHAT IS FUNDED General charitable purposes.

WHAT IS NOT FUNDED No grants to individuals.

RANGE OF GRANTS £1,394–£36,000.

SAMPLE GRANTS £36,000 to the British Council of the Shaare Zedek Medical Centre; £1,394 to the Joint Jewish Charitable Trust.

FINANCES *Year* 2000–01 *Income* £133,213

TRUSTEES Rothschild Trust Corporation Ltd Directors: D L Harris; D N Allison; R F A Balfour; A J H Penney; Hon. J B Soames.

HOW TO APPLY In writing to the correspondent.

WHO TO APPLY TO Rothschild Trust Corporation Limited, P O Box 58, St Julian's Court, Guernsey GY1 3BP, Channel Islands
CC NO 272225 ESTABLISHED 1976

■ The Archie Sherman Charitable Trust

WHERE FUNDING CAN BE GIVEN UK and overseas.
WHO CAN BENEFIT Charitable organisations.
WHAT IS FUNDED Most grants are to Jewish organisations. Other causes supported are the arts, health, welfare and to assist children worldwide.
TYPE OF GRANT Capital, buildings and project. Funding may be given for more than three years.
SAMPLE GRANTS £192,000 to Friends of the Hebrew University of Jerusalem; £141,000 to Assaf Harofeh Medical Centre; £115,000 to Jacqueline and Michael Gee Charitable Trust; £106,000 to Diana and Allan Morgenthau Charitable Trust; £90,000 to Rosalyn and Nicholas Springer Charitable Trust; £70,000 to Youth Aliyah Child Rescue; £66,000 to Royal Opera House; £27,000 to Imperial War Museum; £25,000 each to the Ear Foundation and Royal Academy.
FINANCES *Year* 2000–01 *Income* £1,300,000 *Grants* £1,256,000 *Assets* £16,000,000
TRUSTEES Michael Gee; Allan Morgenthau; E Charles.
HOW TO APPLY In writing to the correspondent. Trustees meet every month except August and December.
WHO TO APPLY TO Michael Gee, Trustee, 27 Berkeley House, Hay Hill, London W1X 7LG *Tel* 020 7493 1904 *Fax* 020 7499 1470 *E-mail* trust@sherman.co.uk
CC NO 256893   **ESTABLISHED** 1967

■ The R C Sherriff Rosebriars Trust

WHERE FUNDING CAN BE GIVEN The borough of Elmbridge.
WHO CAN BENEFIT Local individuals for art training bursaries (short courses only) and local amateur and professional organisations planning arts activities of a developmental nature.
WHAT IS FUNDED The trust is primarily concerned with arts development projects and funds charities, schools and constituted organisations working with one or more art form for the benefit of members of the local community, especially where a professional artist is involved. The trust has funded projects concerned with music, dance, drama, visual arts, crafts, literature, film and new media.
WHAT IS NOT FUNDED Any project taking place outside Elmbridge cannot be supported unless the principal beneficiaries are Elmbridge residents. The trust rarely sole funds projects and does not give retrospective grants. Individuals may only apply for training bursaries for short course of up to one month in length, not for longer-term educational needs.
TYPE OF GRANT Capital, one-off, event underwriting, project and school funds. Funding of up to three will years be considered.
RANGE OF GRANTS £32–£12,000; typical grant £1,000.
SAMPLE GRANTS £10,000 over three years to Riverhouse Community Arts Centre for a new art gallery; £2,000 to Elmbridge Youth Theatre for a professional orchestra for its production of West Side Story; £1,000 to Cleves Junior School for an artist in residence programme; £570 to Cobham Players for storage for props and costumes; £180 to Walton and Weybridge Advocacy Group for drama sessions for people with mental health problems.
FINANCES *Year* 2000 *Income* £211,000 *Grants* £65,800
TRUSTEES Elmbridge Borough Council.
HOW TO APPLY On a form available from the correspondent. The trustees meet at least six times a year to consider applications. Applicants must telephone first to check eligibility.
WHO TO APPLY TO The Director, Case House, 85–89 High Street, Walton on Thames KT12 1DZ *Tel* 01932 235990 *E-mail* beccy@rosebriars.org.uk *Website* www.rosebriars.org.uk
CC NO 272527   **ESTABLISHED** 1976

■ Shetland Amenity Trust

WHERE FUNDING CAN BE GIVEN Shetland.
WHO CAN BENEFIT Conservation and heritage organisations benefitting the Shetland Isles.
WHAT IS FUNDED The trust's objectives are: 'The protection, improvement and enhancement of buildings and artefacts of architectural, historical, educational or other interest in Shetland with a view to securing public access to such buildings and the permanent display for the benefit of the public of such artefacts for the purposes of research, study or recreation; The provision, development and improvement of facilities for the enjoyment by the public of the Shetland countryside and its flora and fauna, the conservation and enhancement for the benefit of the public of its natural beauty and amenity and the securing of public access to the Shetland countryside for the purposes of research, study or recreation; Such other purpose or purposes charitable in law as the trustees shall from time to time determine'.
SAMPLE GRANTS £34,000 to Old Scatness Broch; £7,500 to Whalsay History Group; £7,300 to University of Glasgow; £4,800 to Scottish Conservation Volunteers; £3,000 to Shetland Ranger Service; £2,200 to SAT Viking Legacy; £2,000 each to SAT Delting Disaster Fund and Scalloway Waterfront Trust; £1,500 to Fetlar Museum Trust; £1,000 to Auld Skule Recycling Centre; £840 to Lunnasting History Group; £750 to Quarff Primary School; £420 to Unst Heritage Centre.
FINANCES *Year* 2000–01 *Income* £2,000,000 *Grants* £102,000 *Assets* £2,500,000
TRUSTEES Andrew Blackadder; William A Cumming; Cecil Eunson; Florence Grains; Brian Gregson; Martin Heubeck; Roger Riddington; Frank Robertson; Douglas Sinclair; John Scott; P Brian Smith.
HOW TO APPLY In writing to the correspondent.
WHO TO APPLY TO The Trustees, Garthspool, Lerwick, Shetland ZE1 0NY *Tel* 01595 694688 *Fax* 01595 693956 *E-mail* shetamenity.trust@zetnet.co.uk *Website* www.shetland-heritage.co.uk/ amenitytrust
SC NO SC017505

■ The Shetland Islands Council Charitable Trust

WHERE FUNDING CAN BE GIVEN Shetland.
WHO CAN BENEFIT Self-help and voluntary organisations benefiting the inhabitants of Shetland.
WHAT IS FUNDED Social need, leisure, environment, education, artistic and cultural activities, traditional and new industries.

WHAT IS NOT FUNDED Funds can only be used to benefit the inhabitants of Shetland.

TYPE OF GRANT Project, one-off, capital, running and recurring costs, agricultural ten-year loan scheme.

SAMPLE GRANTS £2,020,000 to Shetland Recreational Trust; £1,935,000 to Shetland Welfare Trust – day care and running costs; £1,805,000 to Shetland Recreational Trust – West Mainland Leisure Centre; £1,071,000 to Shetland Amenity Trust; £1,015,000 to Isleburgh Trust; £552,000 to Shetland Recreational Trust for special projects; £500,000 to Shetland Welfare Trust – Unst Care Centre construction; £352,000 to Shetland Arts Trust; £152,000 to Walter and Joan Gray Eventide Home for construction and running costs; £139,000 to Shetland Alcohol Trust.

FINANCES *Year* 2000–01 *Income* £13,033,000 *Grants* £12,801,000 *Assets* £44,292,000

TRUSTEES 24 trustees, being the elected Shetland councillors (acting as individuals), the lord lieutenant and the headmaster of Anderson High School. The chair is Robert Irvine Black.

HOW TO APPLY Applications from the general public are not considered. Projects are recommended by the various committees of Shetland Islands Council. The trustees meet every six to eight weeks.

WHO TO APPLY TO Jeff Goddard, Finance Department, Breiwick House, 15 South Road, Lerwick, Shetland ZE1 0TD *Tel* 01595 744681 *Fax* 01595 744667

SC NO SC027025   **ESTABLISHED** 1976

■ SHINE (Support and Help in Education)

WHERE FUNDING CAN BE GIVEN London and the south east.

WHO CAN BENEFIT Organisations working with underachieving 7 to 18 year olds living in disadvantaged areas.

WHAT IS FUNDED (a) Projects involving children starting from age seven to nine, research convinced the trust that early intervention is the most effective. (b) Projects tackling the problems of transition from primary to secondary school – extra support at this crucial period can prevent serious problems later on. (c) Projects targeting school age children who are disaffected, have been excluded or are at risk of exclusion – it is important to reengage these children and young people in the learning process in a meaningful way.

WHAT IS NOT FUNDED Shine will not fund: individuals; the direct replacement of statutory funding; schools or other educational establishments, except where funding is for activities which are clearly additional; short-term programmes; programmes targeted at specific subjects or beneficiary groups; parenting programmes where the primary focus is the parent; activities promoting particular political or religious beliefs.

SAMPLE GRANTS £145,506 to CSV; £80,00 to All Nations Centre; £79,060 to Lift; £62,747 to Real Action; £48,211 to Lighthouse Supplementary School; £34,871 to Springboard; £22,400 to Newham Gifted and Talented Association; £10,030 to Tower Hamlets EBP.

FINANCES *Year* 2001–02 *Income* £1,376,962 *Grants* £483,000 *Assets* £2,867,444

TRUSTEES Gavin Boyle, chair; Gerry Boyle; Mark Heffernan (founder); Jim O'Neill; Richard Rothwell.

HOW TO APPLY All potential applicants must initially speak to a member of the grants team by telephoning 020 8393 1880. The trustees meet about three times a year, but not at fixed intervals.

WHO TO APPLY TO Stephen Shields, 1 Cheam Road, Ewell Village, Surrey KT17 1SP *Tel* 020 8393 1880 *Website* www.shinetrust.org.uk

CC NO 1082777   **ESTABLISHED** 1999

■ J Shine Charities Ltd

WHERE FUNDING CAN BE GIVEN Manchester.

WHO CAN BENEFIT Organisations.

WHAT IS FUNDED Jewish educational purposes.

RANGE OF GRANTS £100–£10,000.

SAMPLE GRANTS In 1997–98: £9,500 to Zdoko Charity; £5,000 each to The Manchester and District Mikva and AIHA; £4,500 to The Chinock N'orim School; £3,000 to The Rabbinical Research Campaign; £2,000 each to Peyilim Manchester and Brios Yisroel School Manchester.

FINANCES *Year* 1999–2000 *Income* £119,000 *Grants* £52,000 *Assets* £550,000

TRUSTEES W Brunner; M Brunner.

HOW TO APPLY In writing to the correspondent. The trust states that unsolicited applications are not considered since new clients cannot be taken on.

WHO TO APPLY TO W Brunner, Trustee, 21 Stanley Road, Salford M7 4FR

CC NO 251283   **ESTABLISHED** 1967

■ The Barnett & Sylvia Shine No 1 Charitable Trust

WHERE FUNDING CAN BE GIVEN Worldwide.

WHO CAN BENEFIT Registered charities.

WHAT IS FUNDED General charitable purposes.

WHAT IS NOT FUNDED No grants to individuals.

SAMPLE GRANTS £5,000 to Tzedek; £3,000 to St Joseph's Hospital; £1,000 to Commonwealth Institute.

FINANCES *Year* 1999–2000 *Income* £74,000 *Grants* £9,000 *Assets* £2,000,000

TRUSTEES M D Paisner; S S Shine.

HOW TO APPLY In writing to the correspondent.

WHO TO APPLY TO M D Paisner, Trustee, Berwin Leiton Paisner, Bouverie House, 154 Fleet Street, London EC4A 2JD *Tel* 020 7353 0299

CC NO 270025   **ESTABLISHED** 1975

■ The Barnett & Sylvia Shine No 2 Charitable Trust

WHERE FUNDING CAN BE GIVEN Worldwide.

WHO CAN BENEFIT Organisations benefiting children and young adults.

WHAT IS FUNDED General charitable purposes.

WHAT IS NOT FUNDED No grants to individuals.

FINANCES *Year* 1999–2000 *Income* £55,000 *Grants* £3,500 *Assets* £1,400,000

TRUSTEES M D Paisner; B J Grahame; R Grahame.

HOW TO APPLY In writing to the correspondent.

WHO TO APPLY TO M D Paisner, Trustee, Berwin Leiton Paisner, Bouverie House, 154 Fleet Street, London EC4A 2JD *Tel* 020 7353 0299

CC NO 281821   **ESTABLISHED** 1980

Think carefully about every application. Is it justified?

795

■ The Bassil Shippam and Alsford Trust

WHERE FUNDING CAN BE GIVEN UK, with a preference for West Sussex; international.

WHO CAN BENEFIT Organisations benefiting children, young adults and Christians.

WHAT IS FUNDED General charitable purposes. Support is concentrated on local charities located in West Sussex rather than on UK appeals, with emphasis on Christian objects and youth.

SAMPLE GRANTS £50,000 to Lodge Hill Residential Care; £15,000 to Christian Youth Enterprises; £10,000 to St Anthony's School; £8,000 in two grants to St Wilfrid's Hospice; £5,500 to Chichester Eventide Housing Association; £5,000 to St Richard's Hospice Appeal; £2,000 each to Bishop Otter Centre for Theology and Ministry, Chichester Counselling Services, Chichester Christian Care Association, and West Sussex Association for the Blind.

FINANCES *Year* 1998–99 *Income* £255,000 *Grants* £209,000 *Assets* £4,100,000

TRUSTEES J H S Shippam; C W Doman; D S Olby; S W Young; Mrs M Hanwell; R Tayler; Mrs S Trayler.

HOW TO APPLY In writing to the correspondent. Applications are considered in May and November.

WHO TO APPLY TO C W Doman, Trustee Administrator, Messrs Thomas Eggar, The Corn Exchange, Bassins Lane, Chichester, West Sussex PO19 1GE *Tel* 01243 786111 *Fax* 01243 775640

CC NO 256996   **ESTABLISHED** 1967

■ The Shipwrights Company Charitable Fund

WHERE FUNDING CAN BE GIVEN UK.

WHO CAN BENEFIT Individuals and organisations benefiting children, young adults and older people, ex-service and service people, seafarers and fishermen, parents and children, and victims of war.

WHAT IS FUNDED Maritime training, sailors' welfare and maritime heritage. Churches and Anglican bodies are also supported.

WHAT IS NOT FUNDED Any application without a clear maritime connection. Outdoor activities bursaries are awarded only to young people sponsored by liverymen in response to an annual invitation.

TYPE OF GRANT Annual donations, general donations and outdoor activity bursaries. Buildings, capital, core costs, one-off, project and start-up costs. Funding for one year or less will be considered.

RANGE OF GRANTS £250–£4,000. Larger grants can be made from unspent surpluses from previous years.

SAMPLE GRANTS £27,763 to George Green's School for a minibus with wheelchair hoisting and securing facilities; £19,852 to Jubilee Sailing Trust for a ships' carpenter on the Lord Nelson and Tenacious for one year.

FINANCES *Year* 2001–02 *Income* £161,028 *Grants* £131,868 *Assets* £1,480,543

TRUSTEES The Wardens of the Shipwrights' Company.

HOW TO APPLY In writing to the correspondent. Applications are considered in February, June and November.

WHO TO APPLY TO Capt. R F Channon, Worshipful Company of Shipwrights, Ironmongers' Hall, Barbican, London EC2Y 8AA *Tel* 020 7606 2376 *Fax* 020 7600 8117 *E-mail* clerk@shipwrights.co.uk *Website* www.shipwrights.co.uk

CC NO 262043   **ESTABLISHED** 1971

■ The Shirley Foundation

WHERE FUNDING CAN BE GIVEN UK.

WHAT IS FUNDED Future focus will be mainly on Autism Spectrum Disorders and, within that, on larger projects that can clearly have strategic impact on the sector as a whole. Particularly collaborative medical research to explore the causes of autism and to lever extra resources for this area. Most of the annual grant total goes to organisations with which the foundation has close connections or at least an established relationship.

WHAT IS NOT FUNDED No grants to individuals, or for non autism-specific work.

SAMPLE GRANTS £10,000,000 to Oxford Internet Institute for start up; £1,800,000 to Autism Cymru; £568,000 to Prior's Court Foundation; £400,000 to Wirral Autistic Society; £270,000 to the Foundation for People with Learning Disabilities.

FINANCES *Year* 2001–02 *Grants* £13,127,000

TRUSTEES Dame Stephanie Shirley, Chair; Prof. Michael Gelder; Michael Robert Macfadyen; Anne McCartney Menzies.

HOW TO APPLY In writing (less than two pages) or by e-mail to the correspondent.Trustees meet quarterly. The trust stated: 'applicants should note that with £4 million grants planned for 2002–03 and £5 million thereafter, current resources are fully committed'.

WHO TO APPLY TO Elizabeth Lake, Administrator, Rotherfield House, 7 The Fairmile, Henley-on-Thames, Oxfordshire RG9 2JR *Tel* 01491 579004 *Website* www.steveshirley.com/ shirley_foundation.asp

CC NO 1057662   **ESTABLISHED** 1996

■ Shlomo Memorial Fund Limited

WHERE FUNDING CAN BE GIVEN Worldwide.

WHO CAN BENEFIT Individuals and organisations, particularly those benefiting Jewish people.

WHAT IS FUNDED Jewish charitable purposes.

FINANCES *Year* 1999–2000 *Income* £1,404,000 *Grants* £1,299,000 *Assets* £11,300,000

TRUSTEES E Kleineman; G Nadel; I D Lopian; H Y Hoffner; M S Lebanon Weisfish; A Toporowitz.

HOW TO APPLY In writing to the correspondent.

WHO TO APPLY TO I Lopian, Secretary, Cohen Arnold & Co, 13–17 New Burlington Place, Regent Street, London W1X 2JP

CC NO 278973   **ESTABLISHED** 1980

■ The J A Shone Memorial Trust

WHERE FUNDING CAN BE GIVEN Merseyside and overseas.

WHO CAN BENEFIT Registered charities known to the trustees.

WHAT IS FUNDED Christian and local causes in Merseyside and mission work overseas.

FINANCES *Year* 1999–2000 *Income* £43,000 *Grants* £60,000 *Assets* £802,000

HOW TO APPLY In writing to the correspondent. The trust has stated that it does not respond to unsolicited applications.

WHO TO APPLY TO A W Shone, Trustee, c/o Wilson Foods Ltd, 412 Corn Exchange, Fenwick Street, Liverpool L2 7QS
CC NO 270104   **ESTABLISHED** 1974

■ The Charles Shorto Charitable Trust

WHERE FUNDING CAN BE GIVEN UK.
WHO CAN BENEFIT Registered charities.
WHAT IS FUNDED General charitable purposes; projects related to the late Charles Shorto which the trustees investigate themselves.
RANGE OF GRANTS £1,000–£314,539.
SAMPLE GRANTS £314,539 to Rugby School Charitable Trust for a organ; £269,500 to Optimum for the Wharf Project in Coventry to acquire premises on the canal system to allow access and work experience to people who are disadvantaged; £33,000 to Cumnor PCC; £15,000 to League of Friends – Budleigh Salterton; £14,000 to Oxford Youth Works; £9,000 to Usk House; £7,000 to Optimum for Conner Cottage for fixtures and fittings; £5,000 each to Balnain House and Catherdine PCC; £4,605 to Age Concern – Budliegh Salterton.
FINANCES *Year* 2000–01 *Income* £197,724 *Grants* £686,394 *Assets* £4,094,926
TRUSTEES Joseph A V Blackham; Brian M Dent.
HOW TO APPLY In writing to the correspondent at any time.
WHO TO APPLY TO T J J Baxter, Blackhams, King Edward House, 135a New Street, Birmingham B5 4HG *Tel* 0121 643 7070
CC NO 1069995   **ESTABLISHED** 1998

■ The Shropshire Historic Churches Trust

WHERE FUNDING CAN BE GIVEN Shropshire.
WHO CAN BENEFIT Churches.
WHAT IS FUNDED The restoration, preservation, repair, maintenance and improvement of churches and their contents in Shropshire.
WHAT IS NOT FUNDED No grants for repairing churchyard walls, organs, furniture, fittings and redecoration.
TYPE OF GRANT Buildings costs.
SAMPLE GRANTS £2,000 each to Jackfield Church, Darrington Church, Marville Church (all for general repairs) and St Giles' Church – Shrewsbury for window repairs; £1,500 to Knowbury Church for general repairs; £1,000 each to Cheswordine Church for repairs to steps, Hedley Church for woodworm treatment, Ironbridge Church for repairs to tower roof, Ludford Church for window repairs and Shrewsbury Church for general repairs.
FINANCES *Year* 2000 *Income* £30,000 *Grants* £18,000 *Assets* £300,000
TRUSTEES Archdeacon John Hall, Chair; Leonard Baart; Michael Charlesworth; Dr David Harding; Marian Haslam; Harvey James; Dr John Leonard; Bishop Michael Hooper; Mrs Jean Morris-Eyton; David Taylor; Mrs Ruth Taylor.
HOW TO APPLY On a form available from: Preb. David Austerberry, Chad Cottage, Dovaston, Kinnerley, Oswestry SY10 8DT. Completed forms should be sent to the correspondent. The trustees meet in March/April, July, September/October and December.
WHO TO APPLY TO Archdeacon John Hall, Chair, Tong Vicarage, Shifnal, Shropshire TF11 8PW *Tel* 01902 372622
CC NO 1010690   **ESTABLISHED** 1991

■ The Shuttlewood Clarke Foundation

WHERE FUNDING CAN BE GIVEN Leicestershire.
WHO CAN BENEFIT Individuals and organisations benefiting older and retired people, people who are housebound and disabled people.
WHAT IS FUNDED Charitable purposes for the relief of need, hardship or distress. Funding is given to the foundation's two day centres. Particularly charities supporting voluntary and community organisations, and also support and self-help groups.
TYPE OF GRANT One-off.
RANGE OF GRANTS £100–£5,000, depending on the level of funding available for the particular year.
FINANCES *Year* 2001–02 *Income* £224,000 *Grants* £10,200 *Assets* £6,000,000
TRUSTEES M Freckelton; A V Norman; K P Byass.
HOW TO APPLY In writing to the correspondent for consideration quarterly. As grants are made from surplus income, check availability before making an application.
WHO TO APPLY TO Alan Norman, Trustee, Ulverscroft Grange, Ulverscroft, Markfield, Leicester LE67 9QB *Tel* 01530 244914 *Fax* 01530 249484
CC NO 803525   **ESTABLISHED** 1990

■ The Barbara A Shuttleworth Memorial Trust

WHERE FUNDING CAN BE GIVEN UK, with a preference for West Yorkshire.
WHO CAN BENEFIT Organisations benefiting, in particular, children who are disabled, such as special schools.
WHAT IS FUNDED Charities working with children who are disabled and associated causes. Grants are given especially for equipment, but holidays and outings, respite care, and other needs are also considered.
WHAT IS NOT FUNDED No grants to individuals.
TYPE OF GRANT Capital grants.
SAMPLE GRANTS In 1997 grants included: £14,524 to Heaton Royds School; £3,853 to Shipley Leisure; £2,895 to an individual for a wheelchair; £2,496 to Friends of Airedale Child Development Centre; £2,000 to Meanwood Valley Urban Farm; £1,700 to the Haaris Qureshi Appeal; £500 to Bradford City Farm; £200 to Bradford Toy Library.
FINANCES *Year* 2000 *Income* £30,059 *Grants* £37,350 *Assets* £521,158
HOW TO APPLY In writing to the correspondent.
WHO TO APPLY TO John Baty, Chair, Baty Casson Long, Provincial House, 26 Albion Street, Leeds LS1 6HX *Tel* 0113 242 5848 *Fax* 0013 242 5848 *E-mail* baty@btinternet.com
CC NO 1016117   **ESTABLISHED** 1992

■ The Mary Elizabeth Siebel Charity

WHERE FUNDING CAN BE GIVEN Within a 12-mile radius of Newark Town Hall.
WHO CAN BENEFIT Individuals and some organisations benefiting older people, people who are disabled, people disadvantaged by poverty and carers.
WHAT IS FUNDED Hospice at home, respite care for carers and care in the community. Preference is given to assisting people who wish to live independently in their own homes.
TYPE OF GRANT Flexible, but one-off grants preferred for buildings, capital and core costs.

RANGE OF GRANTS £50–£15,000.

SAMPLE GRANTS In 1998–99: £16,000 to Crossroads Care.

FINANCES *Year* 1999–2000 *Income* £102,980

TRUSTEES P Blatherwick; Mrs A Hine; Mrs R White; Mrs A Austin; Mrs S Watson; Miss G Moore; I Mathews.

OTHER INFORMATION The trustees have a policy to prefer to assist those who wish to continue to live independently in their own homes.

HOW TO APPLY In writing to the correspondent, requesting an application form.

WHO TO APPLY TO Mrs Frances C Kelly, Tallents Godfrey, 3 Middlegate, Newark, Nottinghamshire NG24 1AQ *Tel* 01636 671881 *Fax* 01636 700148 *E-mail* fck@tallents.co.uk

CC NO 1001255 **ESTABLISHED** 1990

■ David and Jennifer Sieff Charitable Trust

WHERE FUNDING CAN BE GIVEN UK.

WHO CAN BENEFIT Registered charities.

WHAT IS FUNDED General charitable purposes.

SAMPLE GRANTS £10,000 to Racing Welfare Charities; £3,600 to Audrey Sacher Charitable Trust; £1,000 each to Glyndebourne Arts Trust, Imperial Society of Knights Bachelor, Macmillan Cancer Relief and Royal Festival Hall – South Bank Foundation.

FINANCES *Year* 2000–01 *Income* £9,100 *Grants* £23,000 *Assets* £220,000

TRUSTEES Hon. Sir David Daniel Sieff; Lady Jennifer Riat Sieff; Lord Wolfson of Sunningdale.

HOW TO APPLY In writing to the correspondent.

WHO TO APPLY TO The Trustees, H W Fisher, Acre House, 11–15 William Road, London NW1 3ER *Tel* 020 7388 7000

CC NO 206329 **ESTABLISHED** 1970

■ The Julius Silman Charitable Trust

WHERE FUNDING CAN BE GIVEN UK.

WHAT IS FUNDED Charities benefiting at risk groups and humanitarian causes.

WHAT IS NOT FUNDED No grants to individuals.

TYPE OF GRANT One-off and recurrent.

SAMPLE GRANTS £2,500 to New London Synagogue; £1,400 to Hope Charity; £1,000 each to Jewish National Fund, Pembroke College and New Israel Fund

FINANCES *Year* 2000–01 *Income* £50,000 *Grants* £29,000 *Assets* £943,000

TRUSTEES S A Silman; Mrs C Smith; Mrs W Silman.

HOW TO APPLY In writing to the correspondent. The trustees meet about four times a year.

WHO TO APPLY TO S A Silman, Trustee, Roselands, 2 High Street, Steeple Ashton BA14 6EL

CC NO 263830 **ESTABLISHED** 1971

■ L H Silver Charitable Trust

WHERE FUNDING CAN BE GIVEN UK, but mostly West Yorkshire.

WHO CAN BENEFIT Small local projects, new organisations and established organisations primarily benefiting children and young adults, and Jewish causes.

WHAT IS FUNDED Medicine and health; welfare; sciences and humanities; the advancement of the Jewish religion, synagogues, Jewish religious umbrella bodies; arts, culture and recreation; community facilities; and other charitable purposes.

WHAT IS NOT FUNDED No grants to individuals or students.

TYPE OF GRANT One-off grants.

RANGE OF GRANTS £500–£50,000.

SAMPLE GRANTS £50,000 to United Jewish Israel Appeal; £38,000 to Imperial Cancer Research; £10,000 each to Brodetsky Primary School and West Yorkshire Playhouse; £5,000 each to Beth Shalom and Yorkshire Women of the Century Project; £4,000 each to Donisthorpe Hall and Leeds Judean Club for Boys and Girls; £3,000 each to Leed Metropolitan University and Leeds Wizo Council; £2,500 to Commmunity Security Trust; £2,000 each to British Friends of Laniado Hospital, Emmaus and Leeds Education 2000.

FINANCES *Year* 2000–01 *Income* £49,229 *Grants* £150,100 *Assets* £762,569

TRUSTEES Leslie H Silver; Mark S Silver; Ian J Fraser.

HOW TO APPLY The trustees state that 'the recipients of donations are restricted almost exclusively to the concerns in which the trustees take a personal interest and that unsolicited requests from other sources, although considered by the trustees, are rejected almost invariably'.

WHO TO APPLY TO I J Fraser, Trustee, Wilson Braithwaite Scholey, 21–27 St Paul's Street, Leeds LS1 2ER *Tel* 0113 244 5451 *Fax* 0113 242 6308

CC NO 1007599 **ESTABLISHED** 1991

■ The Bishop Simeon CR Trust

WHERE FUNDING CAN BE GIVEN South Africa, particularly Gauteng, Mpumalanga and the north west provinces.

WHO CAN BENEFIT The trust seeks to help people whose lives have been, and continue to be, affected by the inequalities and injustices of apartheid. Working with partners rooted in their communities, it aims to benefit younger people whose education and welfare is at a disadvantage.

WHAT IS FUNDED Guided by its partners' recommendations, the trust funds education and welfare projects in deprived rural and urban areas.

WHAT IS NOT FUNDED Educational grants for individuals in South Africa are already provided for at the discretion of the trust's partners. The trust therefore will not respond to unsolicited applications for grants from individuals. Trustees are presently not looking for new initiatives to support and applications from organisations are very unlikely to be successful.

TYPE OF GRANT Capital and revenue costs funded. Bursary programmes are run by local partners.

RANGE OF GRANTS Typically £500–£5,000.

SAMPLE GRANTS 1999–2000: £7,000 to Highveld Education Trust for discretionary educational bursaries; £5,800 to Trevor Huddleston CR Memorial Centre for educational upgrading programmes; £5,500 to Pre-schools – Klerksdorp for development and running costs; £4,400 to Nothemba Children's Centre for education and social care of street children; £4,000 to Klerksdorp Education Fund for discretionary education bursaries; £3,000 each to Ekukhanyeni Community Counselling Centre for youth work, literacy and community advice, Daggakraal Pre-school for primary healthcare and education, Masakane Trust for Pre-school development and HIV Hospice, Highveld for AIDS terminal care; £2,000 to Johannesburg College of Education for a teacher upgrading programme.

FINANCES *Year* 2001–02 *Income* £127,114 *Grants* £60,900 *Assets* £85,881

TRUSTEES Revd Canon Geoffrey Brown, Chair; Patricia Sibbons; Joan Antcliff, Angela Cunningham; Christopher Lintott; Solomon Motsiri; Peter Roberts; Father Superior Community of the Resurrection; Clive Scott; Julie Williams; Sian Slater; Thabo Nkoane; Scott Morrish.

HOW TO APPLY In writing to the correspondent, however the trust stated that funds are already committed to existing organisations in South Africa and unsolicited applications are unlikely to be successful.

WHO TO APPLY TO Mrs S McDowell, Administrator, Otter House, Ingsdon, Newton Abbot, Devon TQ12 6NW *Tel* 01626 821739 *Fax* 01626 821739 *E-mail* bstlsam@freeuk.com

CC NO 106122 **ESTABLISHED** 1989

■ The Simpson Education & Conservation Trust

WHERE FUNDING CAN BE GIVEN UK and overseas, with a preference for the neotropics (South America).

WHAT IS FUNDED Advancement of education, including medical and scientific research; the conservation and protection of the natural environment and endangered species of plants and animals with special emphasis on the protection of forests and endangered avifauna in the neotropics (South America).

WHAT IS NOT FUNDED No grants to individuals.

TYPE OF GRANT One-off or up to three years, for development or project funding.

RANGE OF GRANTS Usually £500–£5,000.

SAMPLE GRANTS £56,000 to Jocotoco Conservation Foundation; £7,000 to Association Armonia for a conservation needs project in Bolivia; £3,000 each to World Lands Trust towards a training and education project to encourage sustainable use of tropical forests and BirdLife International; and £1,000 each to Caius College Cambidge University, Sound Seekers – Royal Commonwealth Institute for the Deaf and Treloar Trust.

FINANCES *Year* 2001–02 *Income* £77,556 *Grants* £72,000

TRUSTEES Dr R N F Simpson, Chair; Prof. D M Broom; Dr J M Lock; Prof. S Chang; Dr K A Simpson.

HOW TO APPLY In writing to the correspondent. The day-to-day activities of this trust are carried out by e-mail, telephone and circulation of documents, since the trustees do not all live in the UK.

WHO TO APPLY TO N Simpson, Acting Chair, Honeysuckle Cottage, Tidenham Chase, Chepstow, Gwent NP16 7JW *Tel* 01291 689423 *Fax* 01291 689803

CC NO 1069695 **ESTABLISHED** 1998

■ The Simpson Foundation

WHERE FUNDING CAN BE GIVEN UK and overseas.

WHO CAN BENEFIT Registered charities only, particularly those benefiting Roman Catholics.

WHAT IS FUNDED The support of charities favoured by the founder in his lifetime and others with similar objects; mainly Catholic charities.

WHAT IS NOT FUNDED No grants to non-registered charities or individuals.

FINANCES *Year* 2001 *Income* £19,300 *Grants* £76,300 *Assets* £472,700

TRUSTEES C E T Bellord; P J M Hawthorne; P J O Herschan.

HOW TO APPLY In writing to the correspondent, at any time. No telephone applications will be considered. Please note, however, the trust states funds are already fully committed.

WHO TO APPLY TO C E T Bellord, Trustee, Messrs Witham Weld, 70 St George's Square, London SW1V 3RD *E-mail* postmaster@wwlaw.co.uk

CC NO 231030 **ESTABLISHED** 1961

■ Sinclair Charitable Trust

WHERE FUNDING CAN BE GIVEN UK.

WHO CAN BENEFIT Jewish charities.

WHAT IS FUNDED Education and welfare causes.

FINANCES *Year* 2000 *Income* £189,940 *Grants* £149,224 *Assets* £37,197

TRUSTEES Dr M J Sinclair; Mrs P K Sinclair; E J Gold.

HOW TO APPLY In writing to the correspondent.

WHO TO APPLY TO Dr M J Sinclair, Trustee, Apect Gate, 166 College Road, London HA1 1BH

CC NO 289433 **ESTABLISHED** 1984

■ The Huntly & Margery Sinclair Charitable Trust

WHERE FUNDING CAN BE GIVEN UK.

WHO CAN BENEFIT Generally to registered charities.

WHAT IS FUNDED Well-established charities in particular.

SAMPLE GRANTS £45,000 to Royal Agricultural Benevolent Institution; £25,000 to Rendcombe College.

FINANCES *Year* 2001–02 *Income* £71,601 *Grants* £90,000 *Assets* £1,241,317

TRUSTEES Mrs A M H Gibbs; Mrs M A H Windsor; Mrs J Floyd.

HOW TO APPLY This trust does not respond to unsolicited applications.

WHO TO APPLY TO Wilfrid Vernor-Miles, c/o Vernor-Miles & Noble Solicitors, 5 Raymond Buildings, Gray's Inn, London EC1R 5DD *Tel* 020 7423 8000 *Fax* 020 7423 8001 *E-mail* wilfridvm@vmn.org.uk

CC NO 235939 **ESTABLISHED** 1964

■ Sino-British Fellowship Trust

WHERE FUNDING CAN BE GIVEN UK and China.

WHO CAN BENEFIT Institutions benefiting individual postgraduate students.

WHAT IS FUNDED Scholarships to Chinese citizens to enable them to pursue their studies in Britain. Grants to British citizens in China to educate/train Chinese citizens in any art, science, profession or handicraft. Grants to Chinese citizens associated with charitable bodies to promote their education and understanding of European methods.

TYPE OF GRANT Fees; fares; and allowances.

FINANCES *Year* 2001 *Income* £376,123 *Grants* £428,192 *Assets* £10,827,398

TRUSTEES P Ely; Mrs A E Ely; Dr J A Langton; K Mostyn; Prof. M N Naylor; Prof. Sir David Todd; Lady Pamela Youde.

HOW TO APPLY On a form available by writing to the address below. Trustees meet twice a year to consider grants in spring and autumn.

WHO TO APPLY TO Mrs Anne Ely, 23 Bede House, Manor Fields, London SW15 3LT
CC NO 313669 **ESTABLISHED** 1948

■ The Skelton Bounty

WHERE FUNDING CAN BE GIVEN Lancashire (as it existed in 1934).
WHO CAN BENEFIT Registered charities benefiting young, older and infirm people.
WHAT IS FUNDED Restricted to Lancashire charities (not national ones unless operating in Lancashire from a permanent establishment within the county predominantly for the benefit of residents from that county) assisting young, elderly and infirm people.
WHAT IS NOT FUNDED No grants to individuals, religious charities, medical or scientific research or minibus appeals.
TYPE OF GRANT Capital expenditure preferred.
RANGE OF GRANTS £200–£4,000.
SAMPLE GRANTS £4,000 each to Blackpool Sea Cadets Corps to buy a rescue boat and equipment, Fazakerly Community Federation for respite for carers, and YMCA Lytham for equipment for children's activities; £3,500 each to Light for Life Southport for refurbishment and decoration of house and St Ann's Parish Charity Manchester to build a counselling and advice room; £3,250 to Meteors WBC St Helens for sports wheelchairs and equipment; £3,000 each to Francis House Children's Hospice towards equipment for a music therapy room, Heart of Lancashire for cardiac emergency equipment, and Liverpool Special Needs Athletic Club for funding to attend Cardiff games; £2,500 to Derian House Children's Hospice for bedroom furniture.
FINANCES *Year* 2000 *Income* £76,925 *Grants* £78,311
TRUSTEES S R Fisher; Lord Shuttleworth; Lady M Towneley; Mrs Avril Fishwick; Alan Waterworth; K A Gledhill; Sir David Trippier; William D Fulton; Mrs M H C Pitt.
HOW TO APPLY On a form available from the correspondent. Requests for application forms should be made as soon as possible after 1 January each year. The completed form should be returned before 31 March immediately following. Applications received after this date will not be considered. The trustees meet annually in July, with successful applicants receiving their grant cheques in late July/early August. Applications should include the charitable registration number of the organisation, or, where appropriate, a letter confirming charitable status, or a letter from the Chief Inspector of Taxes confirming the organisation's income is tax exempt.
WHO TO APPLY TO The Trustees, Cockshott Peck Lewis, 24 Hoghton Street, Southport, Merseyside PR9 0PA *Tel* 01704 534034
CC NO 219370 **ESTABLISHED** 1934

■ The Skerritt Trust

WHERE FUNDING CAN BE GIVEN Within a 10-mile radius of Nottingham market square.
WHO CAN BENEFIT Older people.
WHAT IS FUNDED Trustees consider applications for housing and amenities for older people including various residential facilities and services; council of voluntary services; nursing homes; care in the community; and day centres.

TYPE OF GRANT Capital, core costs, interest-free loans; one-off, project, research, recurring and running costs, salaries and startup costs.
SAMPLE GRANTS £20,000 to Age Concern; £16,000 to Joint Homes Committee; £10,800 in two grants to Radford Care Group(£9,400 for a new roof for the main building and £1,400 for annexe roof repairs); £3,700 to Help the Aged for their senior safety project; £3,000 to Age Concern for their home maintenance service.
FINANCES *Year* 2000–01 *Income* £62,000 *Grants* £70,000 *Assets* £585,000
TRUSTEES Mrs P Davies, Chair; Ms J Sterck; I W Dawson; H Vernon; D Hancock; N Cutts; R Costa; J Corder; Miss M Guttridge; M Reece.
HOW TO APPLY In writing to the correspondent. All applications are acknowledged and considered quarterly.
WHO TO APPLY TO D S Corder, Clerk, Bramley House, 1 Oxford Street, Nottingham NG1 5BH *Tel* 0115 936 9369 *Fax* 0115 901 5500
CC NO 1016701 **ESTABLISHED** 1992

■ The Charles Skey Charitable Trust

WHERE FUNDING CAN BE GIVEN UK.
WHAT IS FUNDED General charitable purposes. The trustees do their own research and unsolicited applications are not considered.
TYPE OF GRANT Grants are given on a one-off and recurring basis for core and capital support.
RANGE OF GRANTS £500–£10,000.
SAMPLE GRANTS £10,000 to Lloyds Patriotic Fund; £7,500 to Trinity Hospice; £5,000 to Million for Millennium; £4,500 each to Careforce and Stepping Stones Trust; £3,000 each to The Abbeyfield (Reading) Society and Camphill Village Trust; £2,500 each to Cleft Lip and Palate Trust Fund and St James Church, Ryde; £2,000 was given to seven different organisations including Christian Care Association.
FINANCES *Year* 1999–2000 *Income* £76,000 *Grants* £65,000 *Assets* £2,200,000
TRUSTEES C H A Skey, Chair; J M Leggett; C B Berkeley; Revd J H A Leggett.
HOW TO APPLY No written or telephoned requests for support will be entertained.
WHO TO APPLY TO J M Leggett, Trustee, Flint House, Park Homer Road, Colehill, Wimborne, Dorset BH21 2SP
CC NO 277697 **ESTABLISHED** 1979

■ Skinners' Company Lady Neville Charity

WHERE FUNDING CAN BE GIVEN UK.
WHO CAN BENEFIT Registered charities with less than four full-time paid staff or equivalent.
WHAT IS FUNDED This trust will consider funding: activities for people who are disabled; the environment; improving the facilities or quality of life for deprived neighbourhoods; and performing and visual arts.
WHAT IS NOT FUNDED Grants will not be made to: organisations working in similar areas as the Skinners' Company and its other charities. These include schools, education and vocational training, care of older people, and sheltered housing; individuals; organisations which are not registered charities working in the UK; organisations with more than four full-time paid staff.

TYPE OF GRANT Items of non-recurring expenditure (e.g. equipment, building works, events).
RANGE OF GRANTS £500–£1,000.
FINANCES *Year* 1999–2000 *Income* £370,000 *Grants* £29,500 *Assets* £726,000
TRUSTEES The Worshipful Company of Skinners.
PUBLICATIONS *Guidelines on Grant Making'* leaflet is available.
HOW TO APPLY By application form enclosing a copy of the latest audited accounts and annual report. Applications need to be received in March and September, for consideration in May and November. Successful applicants will hear the outcome and be sent a cheque in early January and late June. Please note, in order to keep administrative costs to a minimum, applications are not acknowledged nor are unsuccessful applicants informed. Organisations that receive a grant from the charity may not re-apply until three years have elapsed.
WHO TO APPLY TO The Charities Administrator, Skinners' Hall, 8 Dowgate Hill, London EC4R 2SP *Tel* 020 7213 0562 *Fax* 020 7236 6590 *E-mail* charities@skinners.org.uk
CC NO 277174 **ESTABLISHED** 1978

....

■ The John Slater Foundation

WHERE FUNDING CAN BE GIVEN UK, with a preference for the north west of England especially West Lancashire.
WHO CAN BENEFIT Registered charities.
WHAT IS FUNDED Welfare, including animal welfare, and general charitable purposes.
WHAT IS NOT FUNDED No grants to individuals.
SAMPLE GRANTS Bispham Parish Church, Blackpool and Fylde Society for the Blind, Blue Cross Hospital, Guide Dogs for the Blind, Liverpool School of Tropical Medicine, RNLI, Samaritans, Wildlife Hospital Trust, and Duchess of York Hospital for Babies.
FINANCES *Year* 2000–01 *Grants* £170,000
TRUSTEES HSBC Trust Co. Ltd.
HOW TO APPLY Send general information with accounts to the correspondent. Applications are considered twice a year on 1 May and 1 November.
WHO TO APPLY TO Colin Bould, HSBC Trust Services, Norwich House, Nelson Gate, Commercial Road, Southampton SO15 1GX *Tel* 023 8072 2230
CC NO 231145 **ESTABLISHED** 1963

....

■ The Ernest William Slaughter Charitable Trust

WHERE FUNDING CAN BE GIVEN Worldwide.
WHO CAN BENEFIT Organisations benefiting people who are elderly or chronically sick.
WHAT IS FUNDED General charitable purposes.
WHAT IS NOT FUNDED No grants for explorations or expeditions.
RANGE OF GRANTS £500–£5,000.
SAMPLE GRANTS In 1996–97 grants included: £5,000 each to Little Sisters of the Poor and Foetal Medicine Foundation; £4,000 each to Vision Aid, Medical Foundation for the Care of the Victims of Torture, Tommy's Campaign, Médecins Sans Frontières, and Medilink; £3,000 to Motivation; £2,000 each to The Passage and Environmental Investigation Agency.
FINANCES *Year* 1999–2000 *Income* £61,000 *Grants* £32,000 *Assets* £1,000,000
TRUSTEES Mrs J Harris; Mrs M A Matthews.
HOW TO APPLY In writing to the correspondent.

WHO TO APPLY TO R A R Evans, c/o Ozannes, PO Box 186, 1 Le Marchant Street, St Peter Port, Guernsey GY1 4HP *Tel* 01481 723466 *Fax* 01481 713491
CC NO 256684 **ESTABLISHED** 1968

....

■ Rita and David Slowe Charitable Trust

WHERE FUNDING CAN BE GIVEN UK and overseas.
WHO CAN BENEFIT Registered charities.
WHAT IS FUNDED General charitable purposes.
SAMPLE GRANTS £20,000 to Motivation Charitable Trust; £5,000 to Africa Equipment for Schools; £3,000 to Brooks Abroad.
FINANCES *Year* 2000–01 *Income* £77,732 *Grants* £73,500 *Assets* £364,387
TRUSTEES R L Slowe; Ms E H Slowe; J L Slowe; G Weinberg.
HOW TO APPLY In writing to the correspondent.
WHO TO APPLY TO R L Slowe, Trustee, 32 Hampstead High Street, London NW3 1JQ
CC NO 1048209 **ESTABLISHED** 1995

....

■ The SMB Trust

WHERE FUNDING CAN BE GIVEN UK and overseas.
WHO CAN BENEFIT Organisations for the advancement of the Christian religion and the relief of need, hardship or distress.
WHAT IS FUNDED Christian and welfare organisations. Accommodation and housing, various community services, healthcare, health facilities and buildings, medical studies and research, and environmental campaigning will also be considered.
WHAT IS NOT FUNDED Grants to individuals are not normally considered.
TYPE OF GRANT One-off grants, project grants and grants for recurring costs are prioritised. Also considered are building and other capital grants, funding for core and running costs, funding for salaries and start-up costs.
RANGE OF GRANTS £250–£4,000.
SAMPLE GRANTS £4,000 each to London City Mission and Pilgrim Homes; £3,000 to Salvation Army.
FINANCES *Year* 2001–02 *Income* £227,000 *Grants* £175,900 *Assets* £5,100,000
TRUSTEES E D Anstead; P J Stanford; Mrs B O'Driscoll; J A Anstead.
HOW TO APPLY In writing to the correspondent. Trustees meet quarterly.
WHO TO APPLY TO Mrs B M O'Driscoll, Trustee, 15 Wilman Rd, Tunbridge Wells, Kent TN4 9AJ *Tel* 01892 537301 *Fax* 01892 618202
CC NO 263814 **ESTABLISHED** 1962

....

■ The Smith Charitable Trust

WHERE FUNDING CAN BE GIVEN UK and overseas.
WHO CAN BENEFIT Registered charities, usually large, well-known UK organisations, which are on a list of regular beneficiaries.
WHAT IS FUNDED General charitable purposes.
WHAT IS NOT FUNDED No grants to animal charities or to individuals.
RANGE OF GRANTS £1,500–£6,500.
SAMPLE GRANTS £6,500 to Sue Ryder Foundation; £2,000 to RNIB; £1,500 each to Artists General Benevolent Institute, British Red Cross, Macmillan Cancer Relief, NCH Action for Children, RNLI, Sea Cadet Association,

Salvation Army, and St Mary's Convent and Nursing Home.

FINANCES *Year* 1998–99 *Income* £54,500 *Grants* £29,900 *Assets* £1,900,000

TRUSTEES A G F Fuller; J W H Carey; C R L Coubrough; R I Turner.

HOW TO APPLY In writing to the correspondent. Unsolicited applications are not considered.

WHO TO APPLY TO Paul Shields, Messrs Moon Beever, Solicitors, 24 Bloomsbury Square, London WC1A 2PL *Tel* 020 7637 0661

CC NO 288570   **ESTABLISHED** 1983

■ The Smith (Haltwhistle & District) Charitable Trust

WHERE FUNDING CAN BE GIVEN The Tyne Valley area of Northumberland, especially the parish of Haltwhistle.

WHO CAN BENEFIT Local organisations and charities together with UK charities primarily with local interest.

WHAT IS FUNDED General charitable purposes.

WHAT IS NOT FUNDED No grants to individuals.

TYPE OF GRANT Recurrent and capital expenditure.

RANGE OF GRANTS £200–£3,150, mostly under £500.

SAMPLE GRANTS In 1999–2000: £3,500 to Beltingham with Henshaw PCC; £1,200 to Samaritans of Tyneside; £910 each to St Oswald's Hospice and SSAFA; £810 to Salvation Army; £730 to Northumberland Theatre Company; £660 each to Friends of the Hospital League – Haltwhistle branch and St Cutberts PCC – Allendale; £400 each to Bardon Mill Women's Institute and Hardley Bank Under Fives Group.

FINANCES *Year* 2000–01 *Income* £50,218

TRUSTEES Mrs Isabel M Smith; Peter D Pattrick; Dr Richard A D Pattrick; Nigel C N Clayburn; John M Clark; Revd Vincent Ashwin.

HOW TO APPLY In writing to the correspondent. Trustees meet once a year in July to consider grants, applications should be sent in March/April.

WHO TO APPLY TO J Y Luke, Secretary, Hay & Kilner, Merchant House, 30 Cloth Market, Newcastle upon Tyne NE1 1EE *Tel* 0191 232 8345 *Fax* 0191 261 8191

CC NO 200520   **ESTABLISHED** 1961

■ The Albert & Florence Smith Memorial Trust

WHERE FUNDING CAN BE GIVEN UK, with a strong emphasis on Essex.

WHO CAN BENEFIT New grants limited to Essex based projects.

WHAT IS FUNDED Churches, some UK organisations, overseas charities.

WHAT IS NOT FUNDED No grants to individuals.

TYPE OF GRANT One-off and limited recurrent grants.

SAMPLE GRANTS £60,000 to Farleigh Hopsice; £30,000 to Macmillan Cancer Relief; £22,548 to Essex Community Foundation; £10,000 each to Hedway Essex, Raleigh International, and St John's Bartish Church – Danbury; £6,000 to Royal British Legion; £5,484 to NSPCC; £5,000 to Basildon Citizens Advice Bureau and Scope.

FINANCES *Year* 2001–02 *Income* £332,143 *Grants* £252,652 *Assets* £4,255,596

TRUSTEES W J Tolhurst, Chair; P J Tolhurst; E C Watson.

HOW TO APPLY In writing to the correspondent.

WHO TO APPLY TO Mrs A Mason, Secretary, Messrs Tolhurst Fisher, Marlborough House, Victoria Road South, Chelmsford, Essex CM1 1LN *Tel* 01245 216123

CC NO 259917   **ESTABLISHED** 1969

■ The Amanda Smith Charitable Trust

WHERE FUNDING CAN BE GIVEN UK.

WHO CAN BENEFIT Registered charities.

WHAT IS FUNDED General charitable purposes.

SAMPLE GRANTS £19,000 to Cedar School; £5,000 to Cancer Bacup.

FINANCES *Year* 1999 *Income* £159,000 *Grants* £24,000 *Assets* £1,200,000

TRUSTEES C Smith, Chair; P Bennett; Ms A Smith.

HOW TO APPLY In writing to the correspondent.

WHO TO APPLY TO Christopher Smith, Chair, c/o Manro Haydan Trading, 1 Knightsbridge, London SW1X 7LX *Tel* 020 7823 2200

CC NO 1052975   **ESTABLISHED** 1996

■ The E H Smith Charitable Trust

WHERE FUNDING CAN BE GIVEN UK, some preference for the Midlands.

WHO CAN BENEFIT Organisations.

WHAT IS FUNDED General charitable purposes.

WHAT IS NOT FUNDED No grants to political parties. Grants are not normally given to individuals.

SAMPLE GRANTS £3,500 (in four grants) to Betel International; £2,400 (in two grants) to CRASH; £1,500 to Fox Hollies Community Association; £1,400 (in two grants) to Elgar Birthplace Museum; £1,300 (in three grants) to Knowle FC; £640 to Acorns Children's Trust; £500 to Bovingdon Evergreen Club; £150 each to City of Birmingham YMCA, Cottesbrooke School Parents Association, Midlands Refugee Council and Rotaract Club of Solihull.

FINANCES *Year* 1999–2000 *Income* £38,000 *Grants* £30,000 *Assets* £267,000

TRUSTEES K H A Smith; Mrs B M Hodgskin-Brown; D P Ensell.

HOW TO APPLY In writing to the correspondent. Apply at any time.

WHO TO APPLY TO K H A Smith, Trustee, 1 Sherbourne Road, Acocks Green, Birmingham B27 6AB *Tel* 0121 706 6100

CC NO 328313   **ESTABLISHED** 1989

■ Harold Smith Charitable Trust

WHERE FUNDING CAN BE GIVEN UK.

WHO CAN BENEFIT Organisations

WHAT IS FUNDED General charitable purposes.

SAMPLE GRANTS £3,000 to Princess Royal Hospital Surgical Research Fund; £2,000 to Scope; £1,200 to Maidstone & Tunbridge Wells NHS Trust – Haematology Research Fund; £1,000 each, to Lewis-Manning House Cancer Trust, Lord's Taverners, National Trust, RNLI, SIMCAS, St Catherine's Hospice and St Peter's Church of England Primary School in Cowfold.

FINANCES *Year* 2000–01 *Income* £12,000 *Grants* £32,000 *Assets* £575,000

TRUSTEES B V Norgan; Mrs S E Norgan; Mrs E C Selby.

HOW TO APPLY In writing to the correspondent.

WHO TO APPLY TO B V Norgan, Trustee, Keepers, 3 Oakland Close, Horsham, West Sussex RH13 6RU

CC NO 277172   **ESTABLISHED** 1978

■ The Henry Smith Charity

WHERE FUNDING CAN BE GIVEN UK. Specific local programmes in east and west Sussex, Hampshire, Kent, Gloucestershire, Leicestershire, Suffolk and Surrey.

WHO CAN BENEFIT Charitable organisations.

WHAT IS FUNDED Grants are given in the categories of: community service; hospitals and medical care; hospices and palliative care; medical research; physical, mental and multiple disability; older people; young people; drugs and alcohol projects; community service; counselling; family support services; homelessness; homeless people; rehabilitation of offenders; refugees; and general in Merseyside.

WHAT IS NOT FUNDED No grants to: individuals; charities applying on behalf of individuals; arts or educational projects, except those specifically for the rehabilitation and/or training of people with disabilities; leisure or recreational activities, except those specifically and solely for the rehabilitation and/or training of people with disabilities, or those in areas of considerable disadvantaged, or trips to the county for disadvantaged children; environmental projects; projects which promote a particular point of view, or a particular organisation; Church projects or community centres except those in areas of considerable disadvantage, where those served are primarily those in special need of help (such as older people, those prone to drug or alcohol abuse or the homeless), and where the staff involved in the project have proper professional qualifications; capital appeals for places of worship; youth clubs, except those situated in areas of considerable disadvantage; playgrounds, except where a substantial element of need is involved, such as children who are disabled or disadvantaged; local council projects; NHS hospitals and NHS Trust hospitals for operational or building costs; umbrella or grantmaking organisations; universities and colleges, and grant maintained, private or local education authority schools or their parent-teachers associations, except if those schools are for students with disabilities; appeals for general financial support which resemble ' a shopping list' and are unfocused; core costs under £10,000 per annum (except in the case of small grants in the traditional counties); training of professionals; overseas projects; expeditions or overseas travel; campaigning , advocacy organisations or citizens advice projects; and animal welfare.

TYPE OF GRANT One-off, recurring, capital and core costs.

RANGE OF GRANTS For special list and general list: £5,000–£500,000; for small grants programme: £100–£10,000.

SAMPLE GRANTS £500,000 to TreeHouse Trust towards the capital costs of their new school; £450,000 (payable over 3 years) to the Moorfields Eye Hospital major appeal for the new children' s eye centre; £400,000 to HACT (Housing Association Charitable Trust) for projects identified as meeting the various housing needs of the elderly; £250,000 towards St Mungo Community Housing Association Sanctuary Appeal; £150,000 for Faith Together in Leeds 11 towards the capital costs of a new Healthy Living Centre; £150,000 to the Winged Fellowship Trust towards the redevelopment and modernisation of the Sandpiper' s Holiday Centre for the Disabled in Southport.

FINANCES *Year* 2002 *Grants* £23,000,000

TRUSTEES Julian Sheffield, Chair; Mrs A E Allen; Lord Egremont; Countess of Euston; Viscount Nicholas Gage; Mrs C Godman Law; Marilyn J Gallyer; J D Hambro; Lord Hamilton of Dalzell; T D Holland-Martin; Sir John James; G E Lee-Steere; M Lowther; T J Millington-Drake; Mark Newton; Ronnie Norman; P W Smallridge; P W Urquhart; Mrs Diana Barran.

PUBLICATIONS *Henry Smith's Charities – A Brief Introduction*; guidelines for applicants.

OTHER INFORMATION The trust runs a small grants programme for organisations with an income of under £250,000 in the areas of preference above.

HOW TO APPLY In writing to the correspondent.For small grants on no more than two sides of A4 with accounts at any time for a decision within two weeks. For standard grants, on no more than four sides of A4 for consideration in March, June, September or December. The charity welcomes telephone enquiries about its guidelines.

WHO TO APPLY TO Richard Hopgood, Director, 5 Chancery Lane, Clifford's Inn, London EC4A 1BU *Tel* 020 7320 6216/6277 *Fax* 020 7320 3842 *Website* www.henrysmithcharity.org.uk

CC NO 230102   **ESTABLISHED** 1628

■ The Leslie Smith Foundation

WHERE FUNDING CAN BE GIVEN UK.

WHO CAN BENEFIT Small, local charities benefiting unemployed people, volunteers, clergy, at risk groups, carers, people who are disabled, and people living in rural areas. People with arthritis, rheumatism, asthma or addiction problems are also supported.

WHAT IS FUNDED Preference is given to charities which the trust has special interest in, knowledge of, or association with, but with an emphasis on: research into and the treatment of addiction, arthritis/rheumatism, and asthma; childcare and treatment; the care of older people and people who are bereaved; work with children and youth, including schools; and marriage guidance. Also considered for funding are: historic buildings; nature reserves; playgrounds; theatre and opera houses; film, video and multi-media broadcasting; and hospices, rehabilitation centres and counselling.

WHAT IS NOT FUNDED Grants are given to registered charities only; no grants are available to individuals.

TYPE OF GRANT Buildings, capital, one-off, research and recurring costs. Funding is available for up to one year.

RANGE OF GRANTS £1,000–£100,000; typical grant £3,000–£5,000.

SAMPLE GRANTS £25,000 to Music for Living; £20,000 to Greenford Willow Tree Lions Club; £10,000 each to Gaddum Centre, Kings College Chapel Foundation, Paul Strickland Scanner Centre Appeal, Joseph Weld Hospice, Wessex Children's Hospice Trust and Wiltshire Community Foundation; £6,000 to Relate; £5,000 each to the College of St Barnabas, Cystic Fibrosis Holiday Fund for Children, Royal British Legion and Theatre Royal Training School.

FINANCES *Year* 2000–01 *Income* £867,595 *Grants* £154,500 *Assets* £3,441,168

TRUSTEES M D Willcox; E A Rose; H L Young Jones.

HOW TO APPLY In writing to the correspondent. Only successful applications are acknowledged.

WHO TO APPLY TO M D Willcox, Trustee, The Old Coach House, Sunnyside, Bergh Apton, Norwich NR15 1DD
CC NO 250030 **ESTABLISHED** 1964

■ The Mrs Smith & Mount Trust

WHERE FUNDING CAN BE GIVEN London and south east England, i.e. Norfolk, Suffolk, Cambridgeshire, Hertfordshire, Essex, Kent and Surrey.

WHO CAN BENEFIT Organisations benefiting people with mental illness or learning difficulties, homeless people and families.

WHAT IS FUNDED The trust has three main areas of interest mental illness/learning difficulties, family support and homelessness.

WHAT IS NOT FUNDED This trust no longer supports individuals. The trustees do not consider building costs, only refurbishment or alterations necessary to bring them up to health and safety/fire regulations.

TYPE OF GRANT One-off and continuing capital and revenue grants are considered.

SAMPLE GRANTS £3,000 to Watford New Hope; £10,000 each to Institute of Family Therapy, Housing the Homeless, and Leicester Charity Organisation; £7,500 each to Penrose Housing Association and Interact; £5,000 each to The Bridge Project Eaves Housing for Women, Wintercomfort and National Foster Care Association; £4,000 to Alone in London.

FINANCES *Year* 1999–2000 *Income* £246,976 *Grants* £264,000 *Assets* £8,300,000

TRUSTEES J C Barratt; R S Fowler; D J Mobsby; Mrs G M Gorell Barnes.

HOW TO APPLY Applications should be on a form available from the trust. Requests for running costs/salary should also provide: budget for the year in question; details of salary/job description; details of funding received and from what source i.e. statutory, charitable or other; details about outstanding appeals whether statutory or charitable. Requests for capital should also provide details about outstanding appeals, whether statutory or charitable. Applications should be submitted in January, May or September, for consideration at trustees' meetings in March, July or November.

WHO TO APPLY TO Mrs J Day, Box MST, White Horse Court, 25c North Street, Bishop's Stortford, Hertfordshire CM23 2LD *Fax* 01279 657626 *E-mail* charities@pothecary.co.uk
CC NO 1009718 **ESTABLISHED** 1992

■ The N Smith Charitable Trust

WHERE FUNDING CAN BE GIVEN Worldwide.
WHO CAN BENEFIT Registered charities.
WHAT IS FUNDED General charitable purposes.
WHAT IS NOT FUNDED Grants are only made to registered charities and not to individuals.
TYPE OF GRANT Appeals for capital equipment are preferred over salary costs.
RANGE OF GRANTS £500–£1,000.
SAMPLE GRANTS £1,000 each to Action Research, Action Water, Artlink, Dermatrust, European Children's Trust, Find Your Feet, Huntingdon Hall, Mercy Ships, Prostrate Cancer Appeal, and Tools for Self Reliance.
FINANCES *Year* 2000–01 *Income* £122,776 *Grants* £96,150 *Assets* £3,668,117
TRUSTEES T R Kendal; P R Green; J H Williams-Rigby; G Wardle.
HOW TO APPLY In writing to the correspondent. The trustees met in October and March.

WHO TO APPLY TO Anne E Merricks, Bullock Worthington & Jackson, 1 Booth Street, Manchester M2 2HA *Tel* 0161 833 9771 *Fax* 0161 832 0489 *E-mail* bulworjac@compuserve.com *Website* www.bulworjac.co.uk
CC NO 276660 **ESTABLISHED** 1978

■ Philip Smith's Charitable Trust

WHERE FUNDING CAN BE GIVEN UK, with a preference for Gloucestershire.
WHO CAN BENEFIT Registered charities.
WHAT IS FUNDED General charitable purposes in Gloucestershire; children, older people and UK welfare organisations.
SAMPLE GRANTS £10,900 to North Foreland Lodge Ltd; £10,000 to Cheltenham and Gloucester College of Further Education; £5,000 to Chipping Campden School.
FINANCES *Year* 2001 *Income* £31,000 *Grants* £74,000 *Assets* £782,000
TRUSTEES Hon. P R Smith; Mrs M Smith.
HOW TO APPLY In writing to the correspondent. The trustees meet regularly to consider grants. A lack of response can be taken to indicate that the trust does not wish to contribute to an appeal.
WHO TO APPLY TO M Wood, 50 Broadway, Westminster, London SW1H 0BL *Tel* 020 7227 7039 *Fax* 020 7222 3480
CC NO 1003751 **ESTABLISHED** 1991

■ Stanley Smith General Charitable Trust

WHERE FUNDING CAN BE GIVEN UK.
WHO CAN BENEFIT Any organisations or people who are in need.
WHAT IS FUNDED General charitable purposes.
SAMPLE GRANTS £8,000 to British Agencies for Adoption and Fostering.
FINANCES *Year* 1999–2000 *Income* £71,000 *Grants* £8,000 *Assets* £1,800,000
TRUSTEES John Norton; John Dilger; A de Brye.
OTHER INFORMATION The trust advised that further donations totalling £69,000 were made just after the end of its financial year. These were to the NSPCC (£21,000), British Agencies for Adoption and Fostering (£16,000), Fairbridge (£15,000), British Red Cross and Youth at Risk (£5,000 each), Salisbury and District Family Mediation Service (£3,000), and Chemical Dependency Centre and Strathfoyle Women's Activity Group (£2,000 each).
HOW TO APPLY In writing to the correspondent.
WHO TO APPLY TO John Norton, Trustee, Mercer & Hole Trustees Ltd, 72 London Road, St Albans, Hertfordshire AL1 1NS *Tel* 01727 869141
CC NO 326226 **ESTABLISHED** 1982

■ The Stanley Smith UK Horticultural Trust

WHERE FUNDING CAN BE GIVEN UK and, so far as it is charitable, outside the UK.
WHO CAN BENEFIT Grants are made to individuals or to institutions benefiting students of botany and horticulture.
WHAT IS FUNDED Grants are made to individual projects which involve the advancement of amenity horticulture and horticultural education. In the past, assistance has been given to the creation, preservation and development of

gardens to which the public is admitted, to the cultivation and wider distribution of plants derived by breeding or by collection from the wild, to research, and to the publication of books with a direct bearing on horticulture.

WHAT IS NOT FUNDED Grants are not made for projects in commercial horticulture (crop production) or agriculture, nor are they made to support students taking academic or diploma courses of any kind, although educational institutions are supported.

TYPE OF GRANT Capital (including buildings), core costs, feasibility studies, interest-free loans, one-off, research and start-up costs. Grants are normally made as a contribution to cover the costs of identified projects. In exceptional cases grants are made over a three-year period.

SAMPLE GRANTS £10,000 to the Conifer Conservation Programme operated from the Royal Botanic Garden Edinburgh; £5,700 to University of York; £5,000 to Curators of the University Parks Oxford; £4,500 to Chelsea Physic Garden; £3,500 to Flora for Fauna; £3,000 to The Pukeiti Rhododendron Trust in New Zealand; £2,000 each to University of Bangalore – India, and The Association of Garden Trusts; £1,200 to Marcher Apple Network; £1,000 to Landscape Design Trust.

FINANCES *Year* 1998–99 *Income* £143,000 *Grants* £84,000 *Assets* £3,200,000

TRUSTEES John Norton; Christopher Brickell; John Dilger; Lady Renfrew; J B E Simmons.

HOW TO APPLY In writing to the correspondent. Detailed *Guidelines for Applicants* are available from the trust. The director is willing to give advice on how applications should be presented. Grants are awarded twice a year, in spring and autumn. To be considered in the spring allocation, applications should reach the director before 15 February of each year; for the autumn allocation the equivalent date is 15 August. Potential recipients are advised to get their applications in early.

WHO TO APPLY TO James Cullen, Director, Cory Lodge, PO Box 365, Cambridge CB2 1HR *Tel* 01223 336299 *Fax* 01223 336278

CC NO 261925   **ESTABLISHED** 1970

■ The Snowball Trust

WHERE FUNDING CAN BE GIVEN Coventry and Warwickshire – the circulation area of the Coventry Evening Telegraph and the broadcasting area covered by Mercia Sound – the joint organisers.

WHO CAN BENEFIT Individuals or institutions for the benefit of children up to 21 years of age who are disabled.

WHAT IS FUNDED The provision of moveable equipment for sick and disabled children.

WHAT IS NOT FUNDED Applications for administration and maintenance costs, salaries, fees, short-term respite care and holidays are rejected.

TYPE OF GRANT Capital and one-off.

FINANCES *Year* 2000–01 *Income* £111,000 *Grants* £88,000 *Assets* £195,000

TRUSTEES D C Fitzhugh, Chair; A A Kirby; Alan Rhodes; C R Dale; Michael Tracey.

HOW TO APPLY On a form available from the correspondent.

WHO TO APPLY TO Mrs P Blackham, Clerk to the Trustees, 11 Rotherham Road, Holbrooks, Coventry CV6 4FF *Tel* 024 7672 9727

CC NO 702860   **ESTABLISHED** 1989

■ SO Charitable Trust

WHERE FUNDING CAN BE GIVEN Gateshead.

WHO CAN BENEFIT Jewish people.

WHAT IS FUNDED Jewish causes.

SAMPLE GRANTS £84,302 to Ram Hal Institute; £37,500 to Gateshead Foundation for Torah; £5,000 to Beis Hatalmund; £1,500 to Centre for Advanced Rabbis; £1,000 to Haskel; £300 to Gateshead Jewish Primary School.

FINANCES *Year* 1998–99 *Income* £63,721 *Grants* £160,635 *Assets* £596,449

TRUSTEES S O'Hayon; N O'Hayon; Mrs S O'Hayon.

HOW TO APPLY In writing to the correspondent.

WHO TO APPLY TO S O'Hayon, Trustee, 19 Oxford Terrace, Gateshead, Tyne and Wear NE8 1RQ

CC NO 326314   **ESTABLISHED** 1982

■ The Sobell Foundation

WHERE FUNDING CAN BE GIVEN England, Wales and Israel.

WHO CAN BENEFIT Registered Jewish charities (50%) and non-Jewish charities benefiting older people, people who are sick, in need or disabled, in particular children who are disabled (50%).

WHAT IS FUNDED Health or welfare causes (not research), specifically for sick people; adults and children with physical and mental disabilities; older people; children; homelessness.

WHAT IS NOT FUNDED No grants to individuals. Only registered charities or organisations registered with the Inland Revenue should apply.

TYPE OF GRANT One-off, capital, project, running costs, buildings, core costs and recurring costs. Funding may be given for up to and over three years.

RANGE OF GRANTS £250–£1,000,000. Average grant £1,000–£10,000.

SAMPLE GRANTS £226,000 to Sobell House Hospital Charity; £200,000 (in two grants) to Sobell House Hospice Charity; £175,000 to Jewish Care; £150,000 to Barnardos; £100,000 each to Tel Aviv Foundation, Reading Mental Health Resource Centre, Spring Centre Trust Fund, and St Loye's Foundation; Eleven grants of £50,000 including thosde to Prior's Court School Appeal and Thomley Hall Centre Ltd.

FINANCES *Year* 2001–02 *Income* £2,626,474 *Grants* £3,779,070 *Assets* £51,829,161

TRUSTEES Mrs Susan Lacroix; Roger K Lewis; Mrs Andrea Gaie Scouller.

HOW TO APPLY On a form available from the correspondent, or online. Completed forms should be returned with: an income and expenditure budget for the proposed document; current year's summary income and expenditure budget for the organisation; and most recent annual report and full accounts. It will generally be two to three months before applicants are notified of the trustees' decision. Trustees meet every three to four months and major grants are considered at these meetings. Requests for smaller amounts may be dealt with on a more frequent basis.

WHO TO APPLY TO Mrs P J Newton, P O Box 2137, Shepton Mallet, Somerset BA4 6YA *Tel* 01749 813135 *Website* www.sobellfoundation.org.uk

CC NO 274369   **ESTABLISHED** 1977

■ Social Education Trust

WHERE FUNDING CAN BE GIVEN UK.

WHO CAN BENEFIT Charities and not-for-profit organisations concerned with young people.

WHAT IS FUNDED Projects concerned with residential care and exploring alternative approaches from other countries such as the social pedagogy model. Support to help young people who have been in the public care to participate and communicate.

WHAT IS NOT FUNDED Support to individual young people – other than through the Travel Bursary Fund.

TYPE OF GRANT One-off funding.

RANGE OF GRANTS £500–£30,000.

SAMPLE GRANTS Grant commitments included £30,000 to fund a national survey of residential childcare to ascertain morale and job satisfaction; £25,000 to a charity to develop an electronic youth club; £9,600 to enable the development of a website and boost an advocacy service; £7,500 to to enable young people to attend a parliamentary group. A total of 40 bursaries of up to £500 a year were made from the Travel Bursary Fund.

FINANCES *Year* 2001–02 *Income* £24,000 *Grants* £48,000 *Assets* £450,000

TRUSTEES Phill Warrilow, Chair; David Crimmens; Jim Hyland; Kathleen Lane; Erinna McNeil.

PUBLICATIONS *Social Pedagogy* and *Social Education.*

OTHER INFORMATION The trust is especially interested in stimulating a debate about ideas and approach to residential care for young people, including concepts of social pedagogy and social education, common elsewhere in Europe.

HOW TO APPLY In writing to the correspondent. E-mail applications are welcomed. For details of the Travel Bursary Scheme see website: www.childrenuk.co.uk.

WHO TO APPLY TO Michael Tidball, PO Box 47, St Alban's AL1 4ZN *Tel* 01727 836624 *Fax* 01727 836624 *E-mail* tidballpartnership@btinternet.com

CC NO 297605 **ESTABLISHED** 2000

■ Society for the Assistance of Ladies in Reduced Circumstances

WHERE FUNDING CAN BE GIVEN UK.

WHO CAN BENEFIT Individuals and organisations.

WHAT IS FUNDED This trust mainly makes grants to individual women living on their own who are on a low income, but grants are also made to organisations supporting 'needy females'.

FINANCES *Year* 2001 *Income* £785,000 *Grants* £27,000 *Assets* £21,000

TRUSTEES N A Clifford, Chair; S D Ginn; Revd D F Gutteridge.

OTHER INFORMATION Grants to individuals in 2001 totalled £478,000.

HOW TO APPLY In writing to the correspondent.

WHO TO APPLY TO John Sands, General Secretary, Lancaster House, 25 Hornyold Road, Malvern WR14 1QQ *Tel* 01684 574645 *Fax* 01684 577212 *Website* www.salrc.org.uk

CC NO 205798 **ESTABLISHED** 1962

■ Solev Co Ltd

WHERE FUNDING CAN BE GIVEN UK.

WHO CAN BENEFIT Individuals and organisations benefiting Jewish people.

WHAT IS FUNDED Principally Jewish causes.

SAMPLE GRANTS £100,000 to Dina Perelman Trust Limited; £40,000 to Songdale Limited; £20,100 to Finchley Road Synagogue; £15,000 to Sage; £10,000 to Jewish Education Foundation for the Torah; £9,000 to Torah Terimah Primary School; £8,500 to Beis Yacov Institution.

FINANCES *Year* 1996–97 *Income* £489,000 *Grants* £313,000 *Assets* £1,600,000

TRUSTEES M Grosskopf; A E Perelman; R Tager.

HOW TO APPLY In writing to the correspondent.

WHO TO APPLY TO O Tager, Trustee, Romeo House, 160 Bridport Road, London N18 1SY

CC NO 254623 **ESTABLISHED** 1967

■ The Solo Charitable Settlement

WHERE FUNDING CAN BE GIVEN UK and Israel.

WHO CAN BENEFIT Organisations benefiting Jewish people, disabled people, research workers and medical professionals.

WHAT IS FUNDED Jewish organisations, medical research and disability.

TYPE OF GRANT Mostly recurrent.

RANGE OF GRANTS £50–£18,000, although most grants are for under £500.

SAMPLE GRANTS £18,000 to Ashten Trust; £17,000 to Joint Jewish Charitable Trust; £15,000 to Jewish Care; £12,000 to United Jewish Israel Appeal; £2,500 each to Children with Leukaemia and Norwood Ravenswood; £1,000 each to Spiro Institute, Spanish and Portuguese Congregation and Sutton Synagogue. Beneficiaries receiving £500 or under included Alyn Hospital, Breakthrough Breast Cancer, Dream Come True, Group House, Leukaemia Research, Royal Academy of Arts, St Nicholas Church, WIZO and World Jewish Relief.

FINANCES *Year* 1998–99 *Income* £103,035 *Grants* £76,128 *Assets* £5,193,730

TRUSTEES P D Goldstein; Edna Goldstein; R S Goldstein; H Goldstein.

HOW TO APPLY In writing to the correspondent.

WHO TO APPLY TO The Trustees, Rawlinson & Hunter, Eagle House, 110 Jermym Street, London SW1Y 6RH

CC NO 326444 **ESTABLISHED** 1983

■ David Solomons Charitable Trust

WHERE FUNDING CAN BE GIVEN UK.

WHO CAN BENEFIT UK and local charitable organisations benefiting people who have learning difficulties and their carers.

WHAT IS FUNDED Mostly capital projects for disability groups.

WHAT IS NOT FUNDED No grants to individuals.

TYPE OF GRANT Capital (including buildings), feasibility studies, one-off, project, research and start-up costs. Funding for up to or more than three years will be considered.

RANGE OF GRANTS £500–£4,000, but mostly £1,000–£2,000.

SAMPLE GRANTS In 1999–2000: £8,000 to Down's Syndrome Association; £5,000 to Ysgol Grug Glas; £3,500 to Keighley Mental Health; £3,000 each to Roy Kinnear Charitable Foundation, and The Development Trust.

FINANCES *Year* 2000–01 *Income* £64,334 *Grants* £47,850

TRUSTEES Mrs B J Taylor; J J Rutter; W H McBryde; J L Drewitt; Dr R E B Solomons; Dr Y V Wiley; M T Chamberlayne.

HOW TO APPLY In writing to the correspondent. Meetings are in May and November and applications should be received the previous month.

WHO TO APPLY TO Miss Glynis Jones, Administrator, 81 Chancery Lane, London WC2A 1DD *Tel* 020 7911 7209 *Fax* 020 7911 7105 *E-mail* glynis.jones@offsol.qsi.gov.uk

CC NO 297275   **ESTABLISHED** 1986

■ Friends of Somerset Churches & Chapels

WHERE FUNDING CAN BE GIVEN Somerset.

WHO CAN BENEFIT Churches and chapels.

WHAT IS FUNDED The repair of churches and chapels which are open for worship in Somerset.

WHAT IS NOT FUNDED No grants to individuals. No support for new work, reordering or repairs to moveable items.

RANGE OF GRANTS Usually £500 to £3,000.

FINANCES *Year* 1999–2000 *Income* £33,000 *Grants* £29,000 *Assets* £67,000

TRUSTEES Hugh Playfair; Peter Clackson; Gerald Leighton; John Wood; Dom Aiden Bellenger; Dr Robert Dunning; Richard Watts; Michael Fairbank; Jennifer Beazley; Roger Morris; Jane Venner-Pack.

HOW TO APPLY An application form is available from the correspondent. Trustees meet three times a year. This entry was not confirmed by the trust, but the address was correct according to the Charity Commission database.

WHO TO APPLY TO H G L Playfair, Trustee, c/o Harris & Harris, 14 Market Place, Wells, Somerset BA5 2RE

CC NO 1055840   **ESTABLISHED** 1996

■ Songdale Ltd

WHERE FUNDING CAN BE GIVEN UK and Israel.

WHO CAN BENEFIT People of the Orthodox Jewish faith.

WHAT IS FUNDED All which is in accordance with the Orthodox Jewish faith. Jewish general charitable purposes.

SAMPLE GRANTS £44,500 to Cosmon Belz Limited; £25,000 each to Kedushas Zion and Nevey Eretz; £10,500 to Toldos Avraham Bet Sh.; £7,000 each to Bnos Yroshalayim, B'H Govoha Lakewood and Yad Romoh; £6,000 to Yeshiva Belz, Jerusalem; £4,000 each to CWCT and Tora Vemuma; £3,500 to Ezras Yitchock Yisoe; £3,000 each to N W L Talmundical College and Yad Eliezer; £1,500 to Ponovez Rabbi Pinter Memorial; £1,000 to New Rachmestriuke Trust.

FINANCES *Year* 2000–01 *Income* £242,214 *Grants* £163,274 *Assets* £1,510,607

TRUSTEES M Grosskopf; Mrs M Grosskopf; Y Grosskopf.

HOW TO APPLY In writing to the correspondent.

WHO TO APPLY TO M Grosskopf, Governor, 6 Spring Hill, London E5 9BE

CC NO 286075   **ESTABLISHED** 1961

■ The E C Sosnow Charitable Trust

WHERE FUNDING CAN BE GIVEN UK, overseas.

WHO CAN BENEFIT Cultural institutions; UK and international organisations benefiting children, young people, students, older people and people who are disadvantaged.

WHAT IS FUNDED Education; medical organisations; emergency overseas aid; disability; the arts; and people who are underprivileged.

WHAT IS NOT FUNDED No grants are made to individuals.

TYPE OF GRANT One-off.

RANGE OF GRANTS £50–£15,000.

SAMPLE GRANTS £15,000 to London School of Economics; £5,000 to Chicken Shed (Theatre Co.); £2,500 to RNIB; £2,000 each to Jewish Care and Redbridge Youth and Community Centre; £1,000 each to Nightingale House and Norwood Ravenswood.

FINANCES *Year* 1997–98 *Income* £67,000 *Grants* £39,000 *Assets* £1,500,000

TRUSTEES E S Birk; E R Fattal; Mrs F I M Fattal.

HOW TO APPLY In writing to the correspondent.

WHO TO APPLY TO Ellis S Birk, Trustee, PO Box 13398, London SW3 6ZL

CC NO 273578   **ESTABLISHED** 1977

■ Souldern Trust

WHERE FUNDING CAN BE GIVEN Oxfordshire.

WHO CAN BENEFIT Small local projects and innovative projects.

WHAT IS FUNDED The advancement of education and general charitable purposes.

SAMPLE GRANTS £19,000 to Harris Manchester College; £5,000 each to Science Museum, SeeSaw Oxfordshire and Oxford Community Foundation; £1,500 to Ovingham Hall School; £1,000 to Katherine House Hospice; £500 to University College London.

FINANCES *Year* 1999–2000 *Income* £17,000 *Grants* £38,000 *Assets* £643,000

TRUSTEES Joseph C Pillman; Dr Rosemary S Sanders; Elaine Elliot-Smith.

OTHER INFORMATION In 2000–01 the trust had an income of £281,732, due to a large gift of shares donated by one of the trustees and given in a special grant. The income and level of giving has since returned to the 1999–2000 levels.

HOW TO APPLY Initially in writing to the correspondent, giving a brief outline of the reasons for a donation and the amount required. Telephone requests are not welcomed.

WHO TO APPLY TO Dr R Sanders, Trustee, Souldern Manor, Souldern, Bicester, Oxfordshire OX27 7JT

CC NO 1001488   **ESTABLISHED** 1990

■ The Souter Charitable Trust (and the Souter Foundation)

WHERE FUNDING CAN BE GIVEN UK, but with a preference for Scotland; overseas.

WHO CAN BENEFIT Grants are given to a variety of organisations concerned with the relief of human suffering, particularly those with a Christian emphasis. Through these organisations, support may be given to people of all ages; people who are in care, fostered or adopted; Christians; evangelists; carers; people disadvantaged by poverty; refugees; or victims of famine, man-made or natural disasters or war.

WHAT IS FUNDED Relief of human suffering, particularly projects with a Christian emphasis.

WHAT IS NOT FUNDED Building projects, personal education grants and expeditions are not supported.

TYPE OF GRANT One-off and recurring grants.

RANGE OF GRANTS Typically £200–£500; 240 grants out of the 378 awarded in 1998 were for £500 or less.

SAMPLE GRANTS £400,000 to Alpha International; £113,000 to Church of the Nazarene; £50,000 each to Sargent Cancer Care Scotland and Schools Enterprise Scotland; £30,000 each to Make a Wish Foundation and Operation Mobilisation's Afghanistan appeal; £25,000 to Family Education Trust; £20,000 to Save the Children.

FINANCES *Year* 2000–01 *Grants* £1,299,000

TRUSTEES Brian Souter; Betty Souter; Mrs Ann Allen.

HOW TO APPLY In writing to the correspondent. Please keep applications brief and no more than two sides of A4 paper: you may send audited accounts, but please do not send brochures, business plans, videos and so on. The trust states that it will request more information if necessary. The trustees meet every two months or so, and all applications will be acknowledged in due course, whether successful or not. A stamped addressed envelope would be appreciated. Subsequent applications should not be made within a year of the initial submission.

WHO TO APPLY TO Linda Scott, Secretary, PO Box 7412, Perth PH1 5YX *Tel* 01738 634745 *Fax* 01738 440275

SC NO sc029998   **ESTABLISHED** 1991

■ South Ayrshire Council Charitable Trusts

WHERE FUNDING CAN BE GIVEN South Ayrshire.

WHO CAN BENEFIT Organisations and individuals.

WHAT IS FUNDED General charitable purposes.

SAMPLE GRANTS £16,000 to North Ayr Resource Centre; £14,000 to SALVO – South Ayrshire Local Volunteer Organisation; £8,200 to Ayrshire Fiddle Orchestra; £6,000 to Council for Voluntary Organisations; £5,500 to Waverley Steam Navigation Co./Waverley Excursions Ltd., £5,100 to One Plus: One Parent Families; £5,000 each to Carrick Community Transport Group and South Ayrshire Sports Council; £4,600 to Arthritis Care in Scotland; £4,000 to Girvan Traditional Folk Festival.

FINANCES *Year* 2000–01 *Grants* £185,000

HOW TO APPLY On a form available from the correspondent with guidelines.

WHO TO APPLY TO Marion Young, Grants Officer, Development, Safety and Regulation, South Ayrshire Council, County Buildings, Wellington Square, Ayr KA7 1DR *Tel* 01292 612463 *Fax* 01292 612367 *E-mail* marion.young@south-ayrshire.gov.uk

SC NO sc025088

■ The South East London Community Foundation

WHERE FUNDING CAN BE GIVEN The London boroughs of Lambeth, Southwark, Lewisham, Greenwich, Bromley and Bexley.

WHO CAN BENEFIT Community organisations benefiting unemployed people, volunteers, people disadvantaged by poverty, refugees and people living in urban areas.

WHAT IS FUNDED Community based projects enhancing the quality of life of people in the community and addressing discrimination and disadvantage. Each scheme run by the foundation has its own local grant criteria and awards panel. The schemes operating in 2001–02 were: Children's Fund (supports projects working with children and young people aged 0–19 years); Healthy Communities Fund (grants to help community groups improve the health and welfare of young people); Deptford Challenge Trust (supporting families and young people); Connecting Stockwell (grants for community projects); Neighbourhood Renewal Community Chest; Other small grants.

WHAT IS NOT FUNDED No grants for individuals, political groups or activities which promote religion.

TYPE OF GRANT Normally one-off for core costs, feasibility studies, project, running costs, salaries and start up costs. Funding is available for up to two years on some programmes. Most are up to one year.

RANGE OF GRANTS Small grant programmes up to £5,000. Large grants up to £35,000.

SAMPLE GRANTS £30,000 to Federation of Vietnam Refugees in Lewisham; £28,100 to Deptford Advocacy Project; £25,700 to Albany Childcare Project/Dovetail; £25,600 to London Action Trust; £25,300 to Target 3; £20,000 to Southwark Bereavement Care; £19,900 to Lewisham CV Service; £16,000 to African Research Community Health; £14,785 to Stockwell Partnership; £14,700 to Vauxhall City Farm.

FINANCES *Year* 2001–02 *Income* £1,772,897 *Grants* £1,355,000 *Assets* £387,874

TRUSTEES Colin Roberts, Chair; Suhail Aziz; Rita Beckwith; Gillian Davies; Lady Hart; Maxine James; Peter Jefferson-Smith; Crawford Lindsay; Ade Sawyer; Carole Souter.

OTHER INFORMATION The foundation is primarily the local distributor of funds from a number of government programmes under a variety of different schemes.

HOW TO APPLY Application forms for the various programmes are available from the foundation.

WHO TO APPLY TO Lena Young, Director, Room 6, Winchester House, 11 Cranmer Road, London SW9 6EJ *Tel* 020 7582 5117 *Fax* 020 7582 4020 *E-mail* enquiries@selcf.globalnet.co.uk

CC NO 1091263   **ESTABLISHED** 2002

■ The South Square Trust

WHERE FUNDING CAN BE GIVEN UK.

WHO CAN BENEFIT The trust assists in two areas general donations to registered charities, and support of individual students undertaking full-time undergraduate or postgraduate courses connected with the fine and applied arts within the UK. Individuals are considered especially for courses related to goldsmithing, silversmithing, and metalwork but also for music, drama and dance. Preference is given to students commencing undergraduate studies – students must be at least 18 years old. The trust has established scholarships and bursaries with schools connected with the fine and applied arts and a full list of these schools can be obtained from the clerk to the trustees. Where a school is in receipt of a bursary, no further assistance will be given to individuals as the school will select candidates themselves.

WHAT IS FUNDED Annual income is allocated in awards to individuals for educational purposes, specifically help with tuition fees but living expenses will be considered for courses as specified above. Donations are also considered to registered charities working in the fields of arts, culture and recreation; health; conservation and environment; community facilities and services; and others.

WHAT IS NOT FUNDED No grants given to individuals under 18 or those seeking funding for expeditions, travel, courses outside UK, short courses or courses not connected with fine and applied arts.

TYPE OF GRANT Individual students: funding may be given for the duration of a course, for up to three years, payable in three termly instalments to help with tuition fees or living expenses. Registered charities: single donations to assist with specific projects, one-off expenses, buildings renovation, core costs and research.

RANGE OF GRANTS Individuals: £500–£1,500; charities: £300–£1,000.

FINANCES *Year* 2000–01 *Income* £187,891 *Grants* £238,820 *Assets* £3,764,870

TRUSTEES C R Ponter; A E Woodall; W P Harriman; C P Grimwade; D B Inglis.

HOW TO APPLY Registered charities – In writing to the correspondent with details about your charity, the reason for requesting funding, and enclosing a condensed copy of your accounts. Applications are considered three times a year, in spring, summer and winter. It is advisable to telephone the correspondent for up-to-date information about the criteria for funding. Individuals – Standard application forms are available from the correspondent. Forms are sent out between January and April only, to be returned by the end of April for consideration for the following academic year.

WHO TO APPLY TO Mrs Nicola Chrimes, Clerk to the Trustees, PO Box 67, Heathfield, East Sussex TN21 9ZR *Tel* 01435 830778 *Fax* 01435 830778

CC NO 278960   **ESTABLISHED** 1979

■ The South Yorkshire Community Foundation

WHERE FUNDING CAN BE GIVEN South Yorkshire.

WHO CAN BENEFIT Community and voluntary organisations benefiting people disadvantaged by poverty and people who are homeless.

WHAT IS FUNDED The policy is reviewed annually. Current priorities are: neighbourhood-based community development initiatives; the education and training needs of voluntary community groups; voluntary sector housing and homelessness initiatives; community information and advice services; community-based and self-help health projects; community-based environmental groups. Applications are encouraged from small, local groups who find it hard to raise money elsewhere for projects. Preference is given to projects where a grant of a few hundred pounds will make a significant difference, meaning that most projects helped are small ones.

WHAT IS NOT FUNDED No grants to: party political and religious activities; medical charities (except self-help groups); individuals (except through the Community Champions Fund); or branches of UK charities (unless with independent bank accounts, committees and constitution).

TYPE OF GRANT The main grants programme is for amounts under £1,000. Capital and revenue

costs. South Yorkshire Key Fund grants are for similar purposes for larger amounts.

RANGE OF GRANTS £50–£1,000 (main grants); £1,001–£25,000 for South Yorkshire Key Fund grants.

FINANCES *Year* 2001–02 *Income* £1,700,000 *Grants* £2,876,000

TRUSTEES Martin Lee, Chair; Isadora Aiken; David Clark; The Earl of Scarbrough; Pauline Acklam; Anthony Green; Galen Ives; Narendra Bajaria; Joseph Rowntree; Roger Viner; Christopher Jewitt; James Ogley.

HOW TO APPLY On a form available from the correspondent. Initial enquiries can be made using the internet, telephone or fax. The main foundation grants have four closing dates per year – the end of February, May, August and November. The applications received that fit the grant priorities are then sent out to the grant assessors of the district advisory committees for each local authority area, or the key fund advisory committee. The assessors visit the group and then meet as the advisory committee to make their recommendations to the trustees on the grants to be made and the sums given.

WHO TO APPLY TO The Grants Team, Clay Street, Sheffield S9 2PE *Tel* 0114 242 4294 *Website* www.sycf.org.uk

CC NO 517714   **ESTABLISHED** 1986

■ The Stephen R and Philippa H Southall Charitable Trust

WHERE FUNDING CAN BE GIVEN UK, but mostly Herefordshire.

WHO CAN BENEFIT Registered charities.

WHAT IS FUNDED General charitable purposes.

SAMPLE GRANTS In 1998–99: £11,000 to Hereford Waterworks Museum; £1,000 each to MIND Hereford and Relate – Hereford and Shropshire.

FINANCES *Year* 2000–01 *Income* £52,838

TRUSTEES S R Southall; Mrs P H Southall; Anna Catherine Southall; Candia Compton.

HOW TO APPLY The trust has previously stated: 'No applications can be considered or replied to'. This entry was not confirmed by the trust, but the address was correct according to the Charity Commission database.

WHO TO APPLY TO Mrs P H Southall, Trustee, Porking Barn, Clifford, Hereford HR3 5HE

CC NO 223190   **ESTABLISHED** 1947

■ The W F Southall Trust

WHERE FUNDING CAN BE GIVEN UK and overseas, with an interest in Birmingham.

WHO CAN BENEFIT Registered charities, especially imaginative new grassroots initiatives and smaller charities where funding will make a more significant difference.

WHAT IS FUNDED Work of Society of Friends; peace and reconciliation; alcohol, drug abuse and penal affairs; environmental action; homelessness; community action; overseas development.

WHAT IS NOT FUNDED No grants to individuals or large national charities.

TYPE OF GRANT Normally one-off payments.

RANGE OF GRANTS £15–£50,000; usually £100–£5,000.

SAMPLE GRANTS £50,000 to Sibford School Appeal; £45,000 to Britain Yearly Meeting; £7,500 each to Friends World Committee for Consultant and Woodbrooke (in two grants); £6,500 each to Leap Confronting Conflict (in two grants) and

Oxfam; £6,000 to Q S R & E Joint Bursaries Scheme; £5,450 to Responding to Conflict (in two grants); £5,000 each to Quaker Social Action, and South Belfast Friends Meeting
FINANCES *Year* 2000–01 *Income* £592,438 *Grants* £397,132 *Assets* £6,087,432
TRUSTEES Donald Southall, Chair; Joanna Engelkamp; Claire Greaves; Mark Holtom; Daphne Maw; Christopher Southall; Annette Wallis.
HOW TO APPLY In writing to, or e-mailing, the correspondent requesting an application form. Applications are considered in February/March and November. Applications received between meetings are considered at the next meeting.
WHO TO APPLY TO Stephen T Rutter, Secretary, c/o Rutters Solicitors, 2 Bimport, Shaftesbury, Dorset SP7 8AY *Tel* 01747 852377 *Fax* 01747 851989 *E-mail* southall@rutterslaw.co.uk
CC NO 218371   ESTABLISHED 1937

■ The Southover Manor General Education Trust

WHERE FUNDING CAN BE GIVEN Sussex
WHO CAN BENEFIT Schools, colleges and individuals under the age of 25.
WHAT IS FUNDED The trustees support the 'education of boys and girls under 25 by providing books and equipment, supporting provision of recreational and educational facilities, scholarships and awards'.
WHAT IS NOT FUNDED No grants for people over 25 years of age. Organisations and individuals outside Sussex are not supported.
TYPE OF GRANT Capital and projects.
FINANCES *Year* 2001–02 *Income* £106,629 *Grants* £110,550 *Assets* £2,361,504
TRUSTEES B J Hanbury, Chair; Mrs R Teacher; Miss S Aird; Brig. J B Birkett; P Cooper; Mrs M Forrest; G Furse; Mrs J Gordon-Lennox; Mrs M Postgate; D W Usherwood.
HOW TO APPLY In writing to the correspondent.
WHO TO APPLY TO The Secretary, Old Vicarage Cottage, Newhaven Road, Iford, Lewes, East Sussex BN7 3PL
CC NO 299593   ESTABLISHED 1988

■ The Southwold Trust

WHERE FUNDING CAN BE GIVEN Southwold and Reydon.
WHO CAN BENEFIT Registered charities.
WHAT IS FUNDED General charitable purposes.
RANGE OF GRANTS £250 to £25,000, but mostly between £1,000 and £5,000.
SAMPLE GRANTS £25,000 to Southwold Sailors' Reading Museum; £5,000 each to St Edmund's Hall, Southwold Museum and Southwold Methodist Church; £3,000 to St Barnabas; £1,500 each to East Sussex Association for the Blind, Reydon Village Hall and Southwold PCC; £1,000 to Southwold and Aldenburgh Theatre Trust and Southwold and District Day Centre; £250 to Sound of Wangford.
FINANCES *Year* 1999–2000 *Income* £95,000 *Grants* £55,000 *Assets* £1,300,000
TRUSTEES B T Selgrave Daly, Chair; G W Bumstead; D J Gaffney; G J Filby; W D Crick; J W Denny; R D James; D L Boult; R S Leach.
HOW TO APPLY In writing to the correspondent.
WHO TO APPLY TO David Gaffney, Treasurer, Margary and Miller, 73 High Street, Southwold, Suffolk IP18 6DS *Tel* 01502 723308
CC NO 206480   ESTABLISHED 1962

■ The Sovereign Health Care Charitable Trust (formerly known as The Charities Fund)

WHERE FUNDING CAN BE GIVEN UK.
WHO CAN BENEFIT Generally local organisations benefiting older people, at risk groups, and people with disabilities, disadvantaged by poverty or socially isolated.
WHAT IS FUNDED The provision of amenities for hospital patients. The making of grants to charitable associations. The making of grants to or for the relief and assistance of people who are in need, sick or elderly.
WHAT IS NOT FUNDED No grants to individuals.
TYPE OF GRANT Buildings, core costs, one-off or recurrent, project, research, running costs.
RANGE OF GRANTS £50–£58,000.
SAMPLE GRANTS £58,000 to Marie Curie Cancer Care for new premises; £12,500 to Cancer Support Centre for administration; £12,000 each to Sue Ryder Foundation for running costs and War on Cancer for research; £10,000 to Lord Mayor's Appeal; £8,000 to Bradford Bulls Study Centre for children's drug awareness and healthy lifestyle; £7,000 to Samaritans for premises; £6,000 each to Champion House for administration and York Conductive Education for various purposes; £5,000 to Bradford Sport & Recreation Association for People with Disabilities for administration and formation of new groups.
FINANCES *Year* 2000 *Income* £423,000 *Grants* £310,000 *Assets* £112,000
TRUSTEES G McGowan; S Benson; J Hellawell; M Austin; D Child; D J Lewis; M Bower; M Hudson; S W Johnson.
HOW TO APPLY In writing to the correspondent.
WHO TO APPLY TO The Secretary, Royal Standard House, 26 Manningham Lane, Bradford, West Yorkshire BD1 3DN *Tel* 01274 729472 *Fax* 01274 722252 *E-mail* postroom@sovereignhealth.co.uk
CC NO 1079024   ESTABLISHED 1955

■ Spar Charitable Fund

WHERE FUNDING CAN BE GIVEN UK.
WHO CAN BENEFIT Beneficiaries should be connected with the grocery industry.
WHAT IS FUNDED To provide financial assistance at the discretion of the Spar guilds. In practice, grants are only made to beneficiaries connected with the grocery industry.
SAMPLE GRANTS £240,000 to Macmillan Cancer Relief; £20,000 to Northwich Park Hospital Children's Ward; £5,000 to National Grocers Benevolent Fund; £1,250 to Scottish Grocers Benevolent Fund.
FINANCES *Year* 1999–2000 *Income* £40,000 *Grants* £206,250 *Assets* £650,000
TRUSTEES The National Guild of Spar Ltd.
HOW TO APPLY The trust responded to our request for accounts by sending a grant reject letter, which stated that applications cannot be considered. It appears they simply receive a rejection letter without being read.
WHO TO APPLY TO P W Marchant, Director and Company Secretary, Spar Landmark Ltd, 32–40 Headstone Drive, Harrow, Middlesex HA3 5QT *Tel* 020 8863 5511
CC NO 236252   ESTABLISHED 1964

■ Sparks Charity (Sport Aiding Medical Research For Kids)

WHERE FUNDING CAN BE GIVEN UK.

WHO CAN BENEFIT Research units at UK hospitals and universities.

WHAT IS FUNDED Medical research to enable children to be born healthy and to stay healthy.

RANGE OF GRANTS £50,000–£150,000. Applications outside this range will be considered.

SAMPLE GRANTS £122,187 to Aberdeeen University for research into the genes that cause club foot; £107,200 to Queen Charlotte's and Chelsea Hospital & The Institute of Child Health for research into the genes for spina bifida; £83,330 to The Instituute of Child Health for research into immune system recovery after stem-cell transplant for childhood arthritis; £44,988 to University College Hospital, London & the Institute of Child Health for the development of a clinical tool for optimising lung volume and gas mixing during high-frequency oscillatory ventilation in preterm infants; £43,784 to the University of Leeds for research into modelling neonatal ventalation for clinical decision support using a novel blood gas monitor.

FINANCES *Year* 2001–02 *Income* £1,887,127 *Grants* £897,389 *Assets* £1,240,075

TRUSTEES T Brooke-Taylor; T Brooking; J Buddle; B Cribbins; A Dwyer; R Haddingham; M Higgins; J Hill; M Kelly; D Lockyear; D Metcalfe; D Mills; G Morgan; R Pierce; Lady Ann Redgrave; K Tubby; R Uttley; M Stephens; S Waugh.

OTHER INFORMATION Grant-making guidelines are available on the SPARKS website. Renny Leach will be happy to talk through potential applications.

HOW TO APPLY Application forms can be downloaded from the SPARKS website or obtained fron Renny Leach.

WHO TO APPLY TO Renny Leach, Medical Research Consultant, Linden House, Ashdown Road, Forest Row, East Sussex RH18 5BN *Tel* 01342 825 390 *E-mail* info@sparks.org.uk *Website* www.sparks.org.uk

CC NO 1003825   **ESTABLISHED** 1991

■ Sparquote Limited

WHERE FUNDING CAN BE GIVEN A preference for north and west London, including Edgware in Middlesex.

WHO CAN BENEFIT Jewish charities.

WHAT IS FUNDED Education and welfare.

SAMPLE GRANTS £15,000 each to Beth Jacob Youth Movement, Woodstock Sinclair Trust and Yeshiva Arteret Yisrael – Rabbinical College; £10,000 to Sharei Ezrah Institute; £6,000 to Shatnez Centre Trust; £3,000 to Friends of Wiznitz Ltd; £2,300 to Edgware Foundation; £1,000 to Union of Orthodox Hebrew Congregations.

FINANCES *Year* 1999–2000 *Income* £260,000 *Grants* £134,000 *Assets* £723,000

TRUSTEES David Reichmann; Dov Reichmann; Mrs A M Reichmann.

HOW TO APPLY In writing to the correspondent.

WHO TO APPLY TO Mrs A M Reichmann, Secretary, Grosvenor House, 1 High Street, Edgware, Middlesex HA8 7TA

CC NO 286232   **ESTABLISHED** 1982

■ The Spear Charitable Trust

WHERE FUNDING CAN BE GIVEN UK.

WHO CAN BENEFIT Individuals and organisations, particularly employees and former employees of J W Spear & Sons plc, their families and dependants.

WHAT IS FUNDED Welfare of employees and former employees of J W Spear & Sons plc, their families and dependants; also general charitable purposes.

SAMPLE GRANTS £10,000 each to Enfield Baptist Church, Yehudi Menuhin School, and Purcell School; £6,000 to RSPCA Enfield; £5,000 each to Gutana Diocesan Association, Music for Living, Pesticide Action Network, Royal Agricultural Benevolent Institution, Sargent Cancer Care for Children, and Tree Aid.

FINANCES *Year* 2001 *Income* £174,828 *Grants* £197,286 *Assets* £4,402,467

TRUSTEES P N Harris; K B Stuart Crowhurst; F A Spear; H E Spear; N Gooch.

HOW TO APPLY In writing to the correspondent.

WHO TO APPLY TO Hazel E Spear, Secretary, Roughound House, Old Hall Green, Ware, Hertfordshire SG11 1HB *E-mail* franzel@farmersweekly.net

CC NO 1041568   **ESTABLISHED** 1962

■ Roama Spears Charitable Settlement

WHERE FUNDING CAN BE GIVEN Worldwide.

WHO CAN BENEFIT Registered charities.

WHAT IS FUNDED General charitable purposes, relief of poverty, Jewish causes, museums and arts organisations.

SAMPLE GRANTS £24,000 to Macmillan Cancer Relief; £14,000 to Royal Academy; £9,300 to Brooklyn Friends; £5,000 to WellBeing; £3,500 to Haven Trust; £2,000 to Variety Isreal; £1,000 to British Museum.

FINANCES *Year* 1998–99 *Income* £127,000 *Grants* £68,000 *Assets* £2,200,000

TRUSTEES Mrs R L Spears; P B Mendel.

HOW TO APPLY In writing to the correspondent.

WHO TO APPLY TO Robert Ward, Silver Altman, Chartered Accountants, 8 Baltic Street East, London EC1Y 0UP *Tel* 020 7251 2200

CC NO 225491   **ESTABLISHED** 1964

■ The Jessie Spencer Trust

WHERE FUNDING CAN BE GIVEN UK, with a preference for Nottinghamshire.

WHO CAN BENEFIT Registered charities, with a preference for those in Nottinghamshire.

WHAT IS FUNDED General charitable purposes.

WHAT IS NOT FUNDED Grants are rarely made for the repair of parish churches outside Nottinghamshire.

TYPE OF GRANT Grants are made towards both capital and revenue expenditure. They can be recurrent for up to 10 years.

RANGE OF GRANTS £100–£10,000.

SAMPLE GRANTS £100,000 to Mansfield Road (Nottingham) Baptist Housing Association Limited; £5,000 to Nottingham City Hospital for the Breast Unit Fund; £4,500 to Concert 2000; £3,750 each to Autonomic Disorders Association for the Sarah Matheson Trust, Nottinghamshire Historic Churches Trust, Rainbows Children's Hospices, and Winged Fellowship Trust; £2,500 to Nottinghamshire Hospice.

Think carefully about every application. Is it justified?

811

FINANCES *Year* 2001–02 *Income* £128,246 *Grants* £98,515 *Assets* £3,102,208

TRUSTEES V W Semmens; Mrs E K M Brackenbury; R S Hursthouse; Mrs J Galloway.

HOW TO APPLY In writing to the correspondent, including the latest set of audited accounts, at least three weeks before the trustees' meetings in March, June, September and December. Unsuccessful applications will not be notified.

WHO TO APPLY TO The Trustees, c/o Eversheds, 1 Royal Standard Place, Nottingham NG1 6FZ *Tel* 0115 950 7000 *Fax* 0115 950 7111

CC NO 219289   ESTABLISHED 1962

■ The Ralph and Irma Sperring Charity

WHERE FUNDING CAN BE GIVEN The parishes situated within a five-mile radius of the church of St John the Baptist, Midsomer Norton.

WHO CAN BENEFIT Organisations and individuals in the beneficial area.

WHAT IS FUNDED Grants are given to: provide or assist with the provision of residential accommodation for the relief of people who are elderly, disabled or in need; assist with the establishment of village halls, recreation grounds, charitable sports grounds and playing fields; and further the religious or other charitable work of the Anglican churches in the parishes.

FINANCES *Year* 1998–99 *Income* £101,000 *Grants* £42,000 *Assets* £1,000,000

TRUSTEES Revd C G Chiplin; E W L Hallam; Mrs R A Jones; J M Russell; K G W Saunders; Mrs M E Shearn.

HOW TO APPLY In writing to the correspondent.

WHO TO APPLY TO Mrs P Powell, Secretary, Thatcher and Hallam Solicitors, Island House, Midsomer Norton, Bath BA3 2HJ *Tel* 01761 414646

CC NO 1048101   ESTABLISHED 1995

■ SPIRAX – Sarco Engineering plc Group Charitable Trust

WHERE FUNDING CAN BE GIVEN UK and overseas with a preference for Gloucestershire and Cornwall.

WHO CAN BENEFIT Registered charities.

WHAT IS FUNDED General charitable purposes.

SAMPLE GRANTS £2,000 each to Leonard Cheshire Home – Gloucester, Lilian Faithful Homes and Sue Ryder Foundation; £1,500 to Winston's Wish; £1,000 to Cheltenham and District Spastic Association; £500 each to Gloucestershire County Scout Council, Gloucestershire Playing Fields Association and County Air Ambulance; £250 to Gloucestershire Outward Bound Association; £100 to Cheltenham Senior Citizens' Fuel Fund.

FINANCES *Year* 1999–2000 *Income* £30,000 *Grants* £31,000

TRUSTEES M J Steel; T B Fortune; M Townsend.

HOW TO APPLY In writing to the correspondent.

WHO TO APPLY TO P Aplin, Spirax Sarco, Charlton House, Cirencester Road, Charlton Kings, Cheltenham GL53 8ER *Tel* 01242 521361 *Fax* 01242 581470 *Website* www.spiraxsarcoengineering.com

CC NO 1082534   ESTABLISHED 1970

■ The Moss Spiro Will Charitable Foundation

WHERE FUNDING CAN BE GIVEN UK.

WHO CAN BENEFIT Jewish people.

WHAT IS FUNDED Grants are made towards Jewish welfare.

SAMPLE GRANTS £20,000 to American Friends of Yershivas Birchas Ha Torah; £16,000 to Lubavitch Foundation; £10,000 to J T Tannenbaum Jewish Cultural Centre; £4,000 to Friends of Neve Shalom; £2,500 to Jewish Care; £500 to HGS Emunah.

FINANCES *Year* 1999–2000 *Grants* £53,000 *Assets* £1,500,000

TRUSTEES Trevor David Spiro; Geoffrey Michael Davis; David Jeremy Goodman.

HOW TO APPLY In writing to the correspondent.

WHO TO APPLY TO Trevor Spiro, Trustee, Crowndean House, 26 Bruton Lane, London W1J 6JH *Tel* 020 7491 9817 *Fax* 020 7499 6850

CC NO 1064249   ESTABLISHED 1997

■ The Spitalfields Market Community Trust

WHERE FUNDING CAN BE GIVEN The London borough of Tower Hamlets, especially Bethnal Green.

WHO CAN BENEFIT Organisations benefiting the residents of Tower Hamlets, particularly children, young adults, older people and ethnic minorities.

WHAT IS FUNDED Support for education, youth, training, social welfare, housing, advice and information, art and culture, community development and the environment.

WHAT IS NOT FUNDED The trust does not fund: individuals; political parties and political activities; religious activities; grants which do not benefit people living in Tower Hamlets; activities or expenditure that has already taken place.

TYPE OF GRANT Two-thirds of grants for revenue costs, one-third for capital projects.

RANGE OF GRANTS £1,000–£500,000, but mostly up to £10,000.

SAMPLE GRANTS £500,000 to Rich Mix Centre for a new centre; £275,000 to Qualify for Employment for a graduate development programme; £125,000 to Kobi Nazrul Centre (Bengali Cultural and Education Centre) for refurbishment; £32,000 to City-side Regeneration Ltd in match funding towards a voluntary sector capacity building project; £30,000 to Keen Students School to fund a borough-wide study support programme aimed at GCSE students; £25,000 to East London Partnership for a fundraising consultant; £24,000 to Tower Hamlets Parents Centre for a full-time education project worker; £23,000 to Banglatown Arts and Cultural Trust towards Baishakhi Mela, a festival to celebrate the Bengali new year; £21,000 to Sports Network Council for start up funding.

FINANCES *Year* 2000–01 *Grants* £620,000

TRUSTEES Stella Currie, Chair; Jusna Begum; Sue Brown; Ghulam Mortuza; Ala Uddin.

OTHER INFORMATION This trust is consistently spending more than its income and will eventually wind up.

HOW TO APPLY On a form available from the correspondent, which is available on computer disc, for grants of £5,000 or more. For applications of less than £5,000, in writing to the correspondent on no more than three sides of A4, including: a job description, if the application concerns a post; a list of the names and addresses of the office holders of your management body; your organisation's constitution or governing documents; your organisation's latest accounts; and your organisation's bank account and account signatory details. The trust's directors meet every two months to consider applications. All applications will be acknowledged and applicants will be given the date when their funding request will be considered.

WHO TO APPLY TO Elaine Crush, Grants and monitoring officer, Attlee House, 28 Commercial Street, London E1 6LR *Tel* 020 7247 6689 *Fax* 020 7247 8748 *E-mail* smct.org@virgin.net

CC NO 1004003   **ESTABLISHED** 1991

■ Stanley Spooner Deceased Charitable Trust

WHERE FUNDING CAN BE GIVEN UK.

WHO CAN BENEFIT Organisations, particularly those benefiting children and people who are disadvantaged by poverty.

WHAT IS FUNDED General charitable purposes, in particular the Metropolitan Police Courts Poor Boxes (Drinan Bequest), the Docklands Settlements, and the Church of England Children's Society.

FINANCES *Year* 1999 *Income* £35,000 *Grants* £31,000

OTHER INFORMATION Included in the trust's objectives are percentages of the trust's income to go to the Drinan Bequest, the Dockland Settlements and the Church of England Children's Society.

HOW TO APPLY In writing to the correspondent.

WHO TO APPLY TO G Owen, Trust Officer, The Public Trustee Ref 65361, Official Solicitor and Public Trustee, 81 Chancery Lane, London WC2A 1DD *Tel* 020 7911 7068 *Fax* 020 7911 7230

CC NO 1044737   **ESTABLISHED** 1995

■ W W Spooner Charitable Trust

WHERE FUNDING CAN BE GIVEN UK, with a preference for Yorkshire especially West Yorkshire.

WHO CAN BENEFIT Specific causes reflecting the founder's interests; projects and welfare within the community; youth; education; assistance in the purchase of works of art for the benefit of the public. The trust responds to appeals from individuals, institutions, voluntary organisations and charitable groups. Preference given to Yorkshire-based appeals.

WHAT IS FUNDED The trustees invite appeals which broadly fall within the following selected fields: Youth – welfare, sport and education including school appeals and initiatives, clubs, scouting, guiding and adventure training; individual voluntary service overseas and approved expeditions. The community – including churches, associations, welfare and support groups. Healing – care of sick, disabled and underprivileged people; welfare organisations, victim support, hospitals, hospices and selected medical charities and research. The countryside – protection and preservation of the environment including rescue and similar services; preservation and maintenance of historic buildings. The arts – including museums, teaching, performing, musical and literary festivals; selective support for the purchase of works of art for public benefit.

WHAT IS NOT FUNDED 'No grants for high-profile appeals seeking large sums.' Most donations are for less than £500.

TYPE OF GRANT Recurring annual donations to a set list of charities. One-off to 50–60 single appeals a year.

RANGE OF GRANTS £200–£3,500; average £250–£350.

SAMPLE GRANTS £5,000 to Wordsworth Trust – Grasmere; £2,500 to Parish of Tong and Holme Wood; £1,700 to Guide Dogs for the Blind; £1,500 to St Margaret's PCC – Ilkley; £1,000 each to Abbeyfield Society, All Saints Church – Ilkley, Ardenlea, Hawksworth Church of England School, Leith School of Art, Martin House Hospice, North of England Christian Healing Trust, St Gemma's Hospice, St George's Crypt, Wheatfield House and Yorkshire Ballet Seminar.

FINANCES *Year* 2000–01 *Income* £77,779 *Grants* £89,000 *Assets* £1,873,406

TRUSTEES M H Broughton, Chair; Sir James F Hill; R Ibbotson; T J P Ramsden; Mrs J M McKiddie; J H Wright.

HOW TO APPLY In writing to the correspondent.

WHO TO APPLY TO M H Broughton, Trustee, Addleshaw Booth & Co., PO Box 8, Sovereign House, Sovereign Street, Leeds LS1 1HQ *Tel* 0113 209 2000

CC NO 313653   **ESTABLISHED** 1961

■ Foundation for Sport and the Arts

WHERE FUNDING CAN BE GIVEN UK.

WHAT IS FUNDED The foundation aims to support 'a lot with a little', it looks to encourage wide participation in sport and the arts rather than elite performers and the development of excellence. The money is divided two-thirds for sport and one-third for art. Grassroots activities with community benefit are the priority. Sports: most awards are for small voluntary sports clubs, capital funding is the main element of support, though revenue funding can be considered. Arts: both amateur and professional activities are supported, with categories including music, museums and galleries, festivals, theatres, drama, visual arts, film and television, dance, and crafts. Grants are made for capital projects, artistic productions, and to support individual students.

WHAT IS NOT FUNDED Fees, costs or expenses of non-UK performers and participants; croquet; playground equipment for pre-school play groups; commercial applicants. At present, there are no funds available for students on three-year courses in drama, music and dance.

TYPE OF GRANT Capital and revenue. Interest-free loans are considered.

RANGE OF GRANTS Up to £75,000, most grants are for less than £5,000.

SAMPLE GRANTS £20,000 to Margate Theatre Royal for equipment and other costs; £17,000 to Dartington Hall Trust for funding its festival orchestra; £14,000 to Northwich Rowing Club for a rowing eight; £10,000 to Mavericks Wheelchair Basketball Club for wheelchairs; £3,500 to Northampton Fencing Club for equipment.

FINANCES *Year* 2001–02 *Income* £4,851,000 *Grants* £7,249,000 *Assets* £31,647,000

TRUSTEES Sir Tim Rice, chair; Lord Brabazon; Lord Attenborough; Nicholas Allott; Dame Janet Baker; Sir Christopher Chataway; Lord Faulkner; Clive Lloyd; Lord Grantchester; Steve Roberts; Gary Speakman.

HOW TO APPLY Full application packs are available from the telephone number above. Grants are considered on a rolling basis. Owing to the way the foundation is funded, there may be time-lags between agreeing a grant and the cheque being sent. The FSA empties the funding barrel whenever pools income is received. Successful applications have therefore to wait their turn. This can be four to six months or more, depending on the size of the application.
WHO TO APPLY TO Grattan Endicott, Secretary, PO Box 20, Liverpool L13 1HB *Tel* 0151 259 5505 *Fax* 0151 230 0664
CC NO Y00104

■ The Sportsman's Charity

WHERE FUNDING CAN BE GIVEN Scotland.
WHO CAN BENEFIT Charities and community groups.
WHAT IS FUNDED Money is distributed to charities across Scotland, especially those which are successful in their aims, are perhaps less well known, or which focus on the disadvantaged, particularly children, or the sporting needs of people with disabilities. Infrastructure development, education and training, and community facilities and services will be considered.
WHAT IS NOT FUNDED Grants are not made to cover running costs. No grants to individuals.
TYPE OF GRANT Capital, one-off and project will be considered. Funding may be given for up to two years.
RANGE OF GRANTS £100–£5,000.
FINANCES *Year* 2001–02 *Income* £100,000 *Grants* £100,000
TRUSTEES D McLean; A Cubie.
OTHER INFORMATION Distribution of all the charity's funding is now managed by the Scottish Community Foundation.
HOW TO APPLY In writing to the correspondent.
WHO TO APPLY TO Louise Massara, c/o Scottish Community Foundation, 126 Canongate, Edinburgh EH8 8DD *Tel* 0131 524 0305 *Fax* 0131 524 0329 *E-mail* louise@scottishcommunityfoundation.com *Website* www.scottishcommunityfoundation.com
SC NO SC015424   **ESTABLISHED** 1983

■ The Spring Harvest Charitable Trust

WHERE FUNDING CAN BE GIVEN UK and overseas.
WHO CAN BENEFIT Organisations and individuals.
WHAT IS FUNDED Christian evangelism and welfare.
RANGE OF GRANTS £1,000 to £46,000, although almost half were for £1,000.
SAMPLE GRANTS £46,000 to Tear Fund; £40,000 each to Eurovangelism, Mildmay and World Relief; £16,000 to Oasis Trust; £13,500 to Signpost International; £10,892 to Release International; £10,000 each to British Youth for Christ, Care for the Family, Lambeth Fund and Scripture Union International; £9,000 to World Evangelical Fellowship; £8,000 to Bulgarian Evangelical Theological Institute; £7,000 to Saltmine Children Theatre Company.
FINANCES *Year* 2000–01 *Income* £791,000 *Grants* £752,000 *Assets* £215,000
TRUSTEES I C Coffey; J S Richardson; C A M Sinclair; Marion White.
HOW TO APPLY In writing to the correspondent.

WHO TO APPLY TO The Clerk to the Trustees, 14 Horsted Square, Bellbrook Industrial Estate, Uckfield, East Sussex TN22 1QG *Tel* 01825 746510 *Fax* 01825 769141 *E-mail* theclerk@shct.springharvest.org
CC NO 1042041   **ESTABLISHED** 1994

■ Rosalyn and Nicholas Springer Charitable Trust

WHERE FUNDING CAN BE GIVEN UK.
WHO CAN BENEFIT Organisations, particularly those supporting Jewish people, and individuals.
WHAT IS FUNDED The promotion of welfare, education and personal development, particularly amongst the Jewish community.
RANGE OF GRANTS £80–£32,7000, but mostly £1,000 or less.
SAMPLE GRANTS £32,700 to UJIA, £16,450 to King Alfred School; £10,575 to Jewish Care; £6,400 to Jewish Care; £6,000 to Shaare Zedek; £5,100 to Almeida Theatre; £3,700 to Chicken Shed Theatre Co.; £3,940 to Magen David Adom; £3,342 to Philharmonia Orchestra.
FINANCES *Year* 2000–01 *Income* £146,749 *Grants* £118,230 *Assets* £36,415
TRUSTEES Mrs R Springer; N S Springer; J Joseph.
HOW TO APPLY The trust states that it only supports organisations it is already in contact with. 99% of unsolicited applications are unsuccessful and because of the volume it receives, the trust is unable to reply to such letters. It would therefore not seem appropriate to apply to this trust.
WHO TO APPLY TO Nicholas Springer, Trustee, Flat 27, Berkeley House, 15 Hay Hill, London W1J 8NS *Tel* 020 7493 1904
CC NO 1062239   **ESTABLISHED** 1997

■ Spurrell Charitable Trust

WHERE FUNDING CAN BE GIVEN UK, with some preference for Norfolk.
WHO CAN BENEFIT Charities known personally to the trustees.
WHAT IS FUNDED General charitable purposes.
SAMPLE GRANTS £2,500 to British Red Cross, Norfolk branch; £1,000 to Cancer Research and Development for Norfolk and Norwich Trust Ltd.
FINANCES *Year* 2000–01 *Income* £24,000 *Grants* £27,000 *Assets* £506,000
TRUSTEES A T How; P M N Spurrell; R J K Spurrell.
HOW TO APPLY Unsolicited applications are not considered.
WHO TO APPLY TO A T How, Trustee, 16 Harescroft, Moat Farm, Tunbridge Wells, Kent TN2 5XE
CC NO 267287   **ESTABLISHED** 1960

■ The Staffordshire Historic Churches Trust

WHERE FUNDING CAN BE GIVEN Staffordshire, including that part of 'Old Staffordshire' now in West Midlands.
WHO CAN BENEFIT Churches and chapels.
WHAT IS FUNDED Structural repair/restoration to historic churches and chapels in Staffordshire.
WHAT IS NOT FUNDED Normally only churches/chapels built at least 100 years ago will be supported. Newer churches are only supported if of outstanding architectural significance.
FINANCES *Year* 2000–01 *Income* £23,000 *Grants* £21,000 *Assets* £97,000
TRUSTEES R D Birch; P B Clarke; D J Simkin.

HOW TO APPLY In writing to the correspondent.

WHO TO APPLY TO Dr Jane Benton, Secretary, 1 Yew Tree Cottage, Slindon, Stafford ST21 6LX *Tel* 01782 791514 *Website* www.shct.freewire.co.uk

CC NO 240854   **ESTABLISHED** 1953

■ Miss Doreen Stanford Trust

WHERE FUNDING CAN BE GIVEN UK.

WHO CAN BENEFIT Registered charities.

WHAT IS FUNDED General charitable purposes.

SAMPLE GRANTS £3,342 to Aidis Trust; £3,000 each to Deafblind UK and Motor Neurone Disease Association; £2,550 to Kent Association for the Blind; £2,000 to Church Army; £1,500 each to Aid for the Aged in Distress, Charity Search, and Harvester Trust; £1,200 to Invalids-at-Home; £1,000 each to Neuromuscular Centre and Talking Newspaper Association.

FINANCES *Year* 1999 *Income* £117,407 *Grants* £22,842 *Assets* £669,000

TRUSTEES J S Borner; R S Borner; T Butler.

HOW TO APPLY In writing to the correspondent. Trustees meet twice a year in March and October.

WHO TO APPLY TO Mrs G M B Borner, Secretary, 26 The Mead, Beckenham, Kent BR3 5PE *Tel* 020 8650 3368

CC NO 1049934   **ESTABLISHED** 1995

■ The Stanley Charitable Trust

WHERE FUNDING CAN BE GIVEN UK, with a preference for Greater Manchester.

WHAT IS FUNDED Jewish religious charities, with a preference for those in Greater Manchester and for projects and people known to the trustees.

WHAT IS NOT FUNDED Only registered charities are supported.

FINANCES *Year* 1998–99 *Grants* £100,000

TRUSTEES A M Adler; I Adler; J Adler.

HOW TO APPLY The trust has said that it gives regular donations and does not consider new applications.

WHO TO APPLY TO David Adler, 32 Waterpark Road, Salford M7 4ET *Tel* 0161 708 8090

CC NO 326220   **ESTABLISHED** 1982

■ The Stanley Foundation Ltd

WHERE FUNDING CAN BE GIVEN UK.

WHO CAN BENEFIT Organisations benefiting children and young adults, students, actors and entertainment professionals, musicians, students, textile workers and designers, writers and poets, and the sick.

WHAT IS FUNDED Medical, the arts and youth/education.

WHAT IS NOT FUNDED No grants to individuals.

FINANCES *Year* 1997 *Income* £100,374 *Grants* £110,414 *Assets* £3,053,001

TRUSTEES Nicholas Stanley, Chair; D J Aries; S R Stanley; Albert Rose; Mrs E Stanley; C Shale.

HOW TO APPLY In writing to the correspondent.

WHO TO APPLY TO The Secretary, Flat 3, 19 Holland Park, London W11 3TD

CC NO 206866   **ESTABLISHED** 1962

■ The Stanton Ballard Charitable Trust

WHERE FUNDING CAN BE GIVEN City of Oxford and the immediate neighbourhood.

WHO CAN BENEFIT Individuals, charities, institutions and organisations.

WHAT IS FUNDED Residents of the City of Oxford who are in conditions of need, hardship or stress; voluntary organisations providing services and facilities for such people; provision of leisure services; promotion of education; and ecclesiastical purposes and the advancement of religion.

WHAT IS NOT FUNDED No grants towards buildings or salaries.

TYPE OF GRANT Small grants.

FINANCES *Year* 1999–2000 *Grants* £43,000

TRUSTEES Mrs M J Tate; M G Ballard; Mrs J Kimberley; Mrs R Nicholson; J Martin; Revd D Pritchard; K Pawson; Miss A Layng; S Tate.

HOW TO APPLY On an application form available from the correspondent on receipt of an sae. The trustees meet about every eight weeks.

WHO TO APPLY TO The The Secretary, PO Box 81, Oxfordshire OX4 4ZA

CC NO 294688   **ESTABLISHED** 1986

■ The Staples Trust

WHERE FUNDING CAN BE GIVEN Overseas, UK.

WHO CAN BENEFIT Charities working in the fields of international development, environment and women's issues organisations benefiting victims of abuse and domestic violence, and ex-offenders.

WHAT IS FUNDED Overseas development: projects which contribute to the empowerment of women, the rights of indigenous people, improved shelter and housing, income-generation in disadvantaged communities and sustainable agriculture and forestry. There is a particular interest in development projects which take account of environmental sustainability and, in many cases, the environmental and developments benefits of the project are of equal importance. Environment: support for projects in developing countries, Central and Eastern Europe and the UK. Grants for renewable energy technology, training and skills upgrading and, occasionally, research. In Central and Eastern Europe, particular interest is given to providing training opportunities for community/business leaders and policy makers, and in contributing to the process of skill-sharing and information exchange. In the UK, there is an interest in helping communities protect, maintain and improve areas of land and to support work aimed at informing rural conservation policy. Women's issues: the interest is in domestic violence issues. The priority is for innovative or strategic programmes of support with a national focus (particularly work to tackle domestic violence from the male perpetrator perspective), also smaller grants to assist local refuge services and women's self-help groups. General: Frankopan Scholarship Fund, established to assist exceptionally talented students from Croatia to further or complete their studies (in any discipline) in the UK.

WHAT IS NOT FUNDED Normally, no grants to individuals.

TYPE OF GRANT One off and recurring for up to three years.

SAMPLE GRANTS £78,430 over three years to Womankind Worldwide for salary costs;

£53,721 to Domestic Violence Intervention Project for salary costs; £47,175 over three years to Female Prisoners' Welfare Project (FPWP) Hibiscus for salary costs; £40,000 over two years to Survival International Charitable Trust for core costs; £30,000 each to AMREF (African Medical and Research Foundation) for the establishment of a community banking system in Kitui – Kenya, CEE Bankwatch Network for development of its network and environmental lobbying service, Fairtrade Foundation for the costs of a manager, Global Witness for two-year funding for a campaign to research and disseminate information about the illegal timber trade in Cambodia, and Non-profit Enterprise and Self-Sustainability Team (NESsT) for the development of the venture fund; £20,000 to Pragya for a conservation and sustainable harvest programme in the Himalayas.

FINANCES *Year* 2000–01 *Income* £593,678 *Grants* £332,503 *Assets* £13,978,150

TRUSTEES Jessica Sainsbury; Alexander J Sainsbury; T J Sainsbury; P Frankopan; Miss Judith Portrait.

OTHER INFORMATION The trust is one of the Sainsbury Family Charitable Trusts which share a common administration.

HOW TO APPLY Proposals are generally invited by the trustees or initiated at their request. Unsolicited applications are nort encouraged and are unlikely to be successful.

WHO TO APPLY TO Michael Pattison, Director, Allington House, 1st Floor, 150 Victoria Street, London SW1E 5AE *Tel* 020 7410 0330

CC NO 1010656   **ESTABLISHED** 1992

■ The Starfish Trust

WHERE FUNDING CAN BE GIVEN Within a 25-mile radius of Bristol.

WHO CAN BENEFIT Individuals and charitable organisations in the Bristol area.

WHAT IS FUNDED Direct assistance is given to people who are disabled and people who have an illness or disease. Medical research and welfare are also supported.

WHAT IS NOT FUNDED Individuals and charitable organisations outside a 25-mile radius of Bristol or not working in the areas defined above.

TYPE OF GRANT Buildings, individual projects, research and recurring costs will be considered.

SAMPLE GRANTS £9,300 to an individual for the purchase of an adapted vehicle to aid mobility; £5,000 to Greenhill House Cheshire Home towards modernisation; £3,737 to an individual who is disabled; £3,135 to Chameleon Trust; £2,500 to Emergency Appeal for Young Homeless People; £1,457 to an individual who is disabled; £1,000 to Multiple Sclerosis Society.

FINANCES *Year* 1998–99 *Income* £4,310,457 *Grants* £30,186 *Assets* £4,814,888

TRUSTEES Charles E Dobson; Mary Dobson.

HOW TO APPLY In writing to the correspondent.

WHO TO APPLY TO Robert N Woodward, Chief Executive, PO Box 213, Patchway, Bristol BS32 4YY

CC NO 800203   **ESTABLISHED** 1988

■ The Educational Charity of the Stationers' and Newspaper Makers' Company

WHERE FUNDING CAN BE GIVEN Greater London and UK.

WHO CAN BENEFIT Individuals and organisations benefiting children and young adults under the age of 25.

WHAT IS FUNDED The education of people wishing to enter the printing, stationers' or newspaper makers' trades, the installation of printing departments in schools.

WHAT IS NOT FUNDED No grants towards anything not related to printing, stationery or papermaking.

TYPE OF GRANT One-off, capital and funding of one year or less.

RANGE OF GRANTS £200–£2,500.

FINANCES *Year* 2000–01 *Income* £110,000 *Grants* £94,000 *Assets* £2,500,000

TRUSTEES Stationers' and Newspaper Makers' Company.

HOW TO APPLY Application forms can be obtained from the correspondent.

WHO TO APPLY TO P Thornton, Secretary, The Old Dairy, Adstockfields, Adstock, Buckingham MK18 2JE *Tel* 01296 714886 *Fax* 01296 714711

CC NO 312633   **ESTABLISHED** 1985

■ The Peter Stebbings Memorial Charity

WHERE FUNDING CAN BE GIVEN UK and developing countries.

WHO CAN BENEFIT Registered charities.

WHAT IS FUNDED General charitable purposes. Job creation, community services, campaigning on social issues, health care, and medical studies and research are priorities. Also considered is funding for: accommodation and housing; information technology and computers; publishing and printing; job creation; special schools; special needs education; speech therapy; advocacy; advice and information; health facilities and buildings; health campaigning; conservation; and environmental campaigning.

WHAT IS NOT FUNDED No grants to individuals, non-registered charities or for salaries.

TYPE OF GRANT One-off grants only, for capital other than buildings, core costs, projects and start-up costs.

RANGE OF GRANTS £250–£2,000.

SAMPLE GRANTS £2,000 to Age Concern; £1,000 each to Alzheimer's Disease Society, Amnesty International, Brent Family Service Unit, Camden Society, MIND, Mozambique Flood Appeal, National Schizophrenic Society, SOS Childrens Villages, Wellcome Brent and Westminster School PHAB.

FINANCES *Year* 1999–2000 *Income* £31,000 *Grants* £24,000 *Assets* £2,100,000

TRUSTEES Mrs P M Cosin; N F Cosin; Mrs J A Clifford.

HOW TO APPLY **This trust states that it does not respond to unsolicited applications** and that its funds are fully committed.

WHO TO APPLY TO Andrew Stebbings, Secretary to the Trustees, 45 Pont Street, London SW1X 0BX *Tel* 020 7591 3333

CC NO 274862   **ESTABLISHED** 1977

■ The Steel Charitable Trust

WHERE FUNDING CAN BE GIVEN UK, with a local interest in Luton and the surrounding area.

WHO CAN BENEFIT Registered charities.

WHAT IS FUNDED Social services, health and medical research, environment and preservation, culture and recreation, and international aid. Thirty per cent of the grant total each year goes to charities in Luton and Bedfordshire.

WHAT IS NOT FUNDED Individuals, students and expeditions are not supported.

TYPE OF GRANT One-off.

RANGE OF GRANTS £200–£150,000; average grant £5,000.

SAMPLE GRANTS £150,000 each to Luton University for the Steel Memorial Bursary Fund and NYO Composers Course Fund; £100,000 to Pasque Hospice – Luton for a building extension; £25,000 each to Imperial Cancer Research Fund, National Deaf Children's Society, Salvation Army and St Albans Cathedral Music Trust; £20,000 each to Donkey Sanctuary, Foundation for Conductive Education and National Missing Persons Helpline.

FINANCES *Year* 2001–02 *Income* £935,022 *Grants* £1,300,000 *Assets* £24,105,905

TRUSTEES N E W Wright, Chair; A W Hawkins; J A Childs; J A Maddox.

HOW TO APPLY In writing to the correspondent, including: statement of purpose for which the grant is required; full latest accounts showing all other sources of funding; statement of existing funding for the purpose of the grant application. Grants are made at the end of January, April, July and October.

WHO TO APPLY TO The Secretary, Bullimores, 3 Boutport Street, Barnstaple, Devon EX31 1RH *Tel* 01271 375257

CC NO 272384   **ESTABLISHED** 1976

■ The Cyril & Betty Stein Charitable Trust

WHERE FUNDING CAN BE GIVEN UK and Israel.

WHO CAN BENEFIT Jewish organisations.

WHAT IS FUNDED Predominantly Jewish causes, including education, advancement of the Jewish religion and welfare.

TYPE OF GRANT One-off and recurring.

SAMPLE GRANTS £36,000 to The Institute for the Advancement of Education in Jaffa; £20,000 to Friends of Yeshivat Kerem B' Yavneh; £15,000 to Project Seed; £12,500 each to Friends of Bnei David and Friends of Bar Ilan University; £8,000 to Carmel College; £7,500 to L'Chaim Independent Charitable Trust; £6,500 to Friends of Mifal Hatorah; £5,000 each to The Hope Charity and Lubavitch Foundation; £2,000 to Friends of the Hebrew University of Jerusalem.

FINANCES *Year* 1999–2000 *Income* £143,311 *Grants* £152,615 *Assets* £324,567

TRUSTEES Cyril Stein; Betty Stein; David Clayton.

HOW TO APPLY In writing to the correspondent.

WHO TO APPLY TO The Trustees, c/o Clayton Stark & Co., 5th Floor, Charles House, 108–110 Finchley Road, London NW3 5JJ

CC NO 292235   **ESTABLISHED** 1985

■ The Steinberg Family Charitable Trust

WHERE FUNDING CAN BE GIVEN UK, with a preference for north west England.

WHAT IS FUNDED General charitable purposes.

SAMPLE GRANTS £20,000 to Crimestoppers Trust; £15,000 to The Heathlands Village; £10,000 to HaMesorah Institute; £8,500 to Jerusalem Foundation; £5,000 each to King David's Schools, North West Cancer Research Fund and Christie's Against Cancer; £2,000 each to Israel Guide Dogs for the Blind, and Hale Adult Education Trust; £1,000 to British Heart Foundation.

FINANCES *Year* 2001 *Income* £145,357 *Grants* £268,295 *Assets* £2,873,848

TRUSTEES D Burke, Chairman; Ms B Steinberg; J Steinberg; Ms L R Ferster; D K Johnston; M Sampson; B Davidson.

HOW TO APPLY In writing to the correspondent.

WHO TO APPLY TO L Steinberg, Trustee, Stanley House, 151 Dale Street, Liverpool L2 2JW

CC NO 1045231   **ESTABLISHED** 1995

■ Jack Steinberg Charitable Trust

WHERE FUNDING CAN BE GIVEN UK, Israel, USA, France, Jamaica.

WHO CAN BENEFIT Organisations, especially Jewish.

WHAT IS FUNDED General charitable purposes.

FINANCES *Year* 1999–2000 *Income* £18,000 *Grants* £37,000 *Assets* £181,000

TRUSTEES Hannah Anne Steinberg; Raymonde Joan Jay; Katherine Palmer.

HOW TO APPLY In writing to the correspondent.

WHO TO APPLY TO N D Ware, Baker Tilly, 2 Bloomsbury Street, London WC1B 3ST *Tel* 020 7413 5100

CC NO 222383   **ESTABLISHED** 1962

■ The Hugh Stenhouse Foundation

WHERE FUNDING CAN BE GIVEN Mainly Scotland, with an emphasis on the west coast.

WHO CAN BENEFIT Charities benefiting children; young adults; those in care, fostered and adopted; and people disadvantaged by poverty. The foundation had stated that it tends to support smaller charities.

WHAT IS FUNDED General charitable purposes, including welfare, young people, and nature reserves, woodlands and bird sanctuaries.

WHAT IS NOT FUNDED Grants are not given for political appeals.

TYPE OF GRANT Recurring, one-off and core costs. Funding is available for more than three years.

RANGE OF GRANTS Usually £100–£3,000.

SAMPLE GRANTS Beneficiaries included Boys Brigade – Glasgow battalion, Maxwelton House Trust and Tarbolton Mothers and Toddlers Group.

FINANCES *Year* 1998–99 *Income* £26,000 *Grants* £25,000 *Assets* £805,000

TRUSTEES Mrs P R H Irvine Robertson; M R L Stenhouse; P H A Stenhouse; R G T Stenhouse; Mrs R C L Stewart.

HOW TO APPLY In writing to the correspondent. Trustees meet in January and June. Applications should be received by December and May respectively.

WHO TO APPLY TO P D Bowman, Secretary and Treasurer, Lomynd, Knockbuckle Road, Kilmacolm, Renfrewshire PA13 4JT

SC NO SC015074   **ESTABLISHED** 1968

Have you read How to use the DGMT *on page xvi?*

■ The E J H Stephenson Deceased Charitable Trust

WHERE FUNDING CAN BE GIVEN UK charities or local to Hampshire and Dorset.

WHO CAN BENEFIT The trustees live in the New Forest and support a number of local causes known to them. In recent years support has increasingly been given locally. They also make grants elsewhere in Hampshire and Dorset and will consider supporting organisations UK-wide.

WHAT IS FUNDED Charities supported have included those working for people who are disabled, older people, children, youth, medical research and medical care – particularly cancer care.

WHAT IS NOT FUNDED No grants to individuals.

SAMPLE GRANTS £1,300 to the Fordingbridge Choral Society. Other beneficiaries included Sir Richards Hospice Appeal and Age Concern Hampshire.

FINANCES *Year* 1999–2000 *Income* £24,000 *Grants* £33,000 *Assets* £1,500,000

TRUSTEES A M B Butterworth, Chair; M T James.

HOW TO APPLY In writing to the correspondent.

WHO TO APPLY TO A M B Butterworth, Trustee, Moore & Blatch Solicitors, 48 High Street, Lymington, Hampshire SO41 9ZQ *Tel* 01590 625800 *Fax* 01590 671224

CC NO 295065   **ESTABLISHED** 1985

■ The Sir Sigmund Sternberg Charitable Foundation

WHERE FUNDING CAN BE GIVEN Worldwide.

WHO CAN BENEFIT Registered charities.

WHAT IS FUNDED Inter-faith projects.

WHAT IS NOT FUNDED No grants to individuals.

TYPE OF GRANT Usually one-off.

RANGE OF GRANTS Up to £50,000, although most grants are of £1,000 or less.

SAMPLE GRANTS £46,690 to Reform Foundation Trust; £45,096 to Manor House Trust; £33,419 to Friends of the Hebrew University of Jerusalem; £19,567 to International Council for Christians and Jews; £15,724 to Institute of Business Ethics; £13,750 to Institute of Jewish Policy Research; £12,000 to Interreligious Coordinating Council in Israel; £11,177 to Millennium World Peace Summit; £10,000 to Institute of Archaeo-Metallurgical Studies; £4,133 to Board of Deputies Charitable Foundation

FINANCES *Year* 2000–01 *Income* £255,748 *Grants* £305,745 *Assets* £3,064,004

TRUSTEES Sir S Sternberg; V M Sternberg; Lady Sternberg.

HOW TO APPLY The foundation has stated in the past that its funds are fully committed.

WHO TO APPLY TO Sir S Sternberg, Trustee, Star House, Grafton Road, London NW5 4BD *Tel* 020 7485 2538

CC NO 257950   **ESTABLISHED** 1968

■ Stervon Ltd

WHERE FUNDING CAN BE GIVEN UK.

WHO CAN BENEFIT Jewish people.

WHAT IS FUNDED Jewish causes and general charitable purposes.

SAMPLE GRANTS £45,000 to Chasdei Yoel; £32,000 to Bnos Yisroel; £12,000 to UTA; £9,700 to Machzikei Hadass; £8,000 to Talmud Torah Education; £6,100 to Shaarei Torah; £5,500 to Friends of Maase Tsedoko; £5,300 to Zedokoh Charity; £5,000 each to Assos Chessed and Kesser Charities.

FINANCES *Year* 1998 *Income* £237,000 *Grants* £209,000 *Assets* £146,000

TRUSTEES A Reich; G Rothbart.

HOW TO APPLY In writing to the correspondent.

WHO TO APPLY TO A Reich, Secretary, c/o Stervon House, 1 Seaford Road, Salford, Greater Manchester M6 6AS *Tel* 0161 737 5000

CC NO 280958   **ESTABLISHED** 1980

■ The Stevenage Community Trust

WHERE FUNDING CAN BE GIVEN The borough of Stevenage and immediate neighbourhood.

WHO CAN BENEFIT Organisations.

WHAT IS FUNDED General charitable purposes including community projects, disability, elderly, children and youth.

WHAT IS NOT FUNDED Religious, education and political appeals are not supported.

FINANCES *Year* 2000–01 *Income* £102,000

TRUSTEES Lord D Cobbold, Chair; M Addison; R Ball; J Bentley; R Gochin; G Gorham; Dr R Gomm; S Hollingsworth; Cllr Mrs H Lawrence; M Simpson; Cllr R Woodward; D Wall; D Ronksley; Andy Hughes; J Ireton; Marian Hurle; A Martin; J Murray; Miss D Woods.

HOW TO APPLY On a form available from the the following address: c/o MMS Space Systems Ltd, Gunnels Wood Road, Stevenage, Hertfordshire SG1 2AS (01483 773368). Grants are considered quarterly.

WHO TO APPLY TO M Addison, Secretary to the Trustees, Howe Roche Waller, Mindenhall, High Street, Stevenage, Hertfordshire SG1 3AY *Tel* 01438 728366

CC NO 1000762   **ESTABLISHED** 1990

■ The June Stevens Foundation

WHERE FUNDING CAN BE GIVEN Some preference for Gloucestershire.

WHO CAN BENEFIT Health and welfare charities benefiting children and older people, animal welfare and conservation and a few local causes in Gloucestershire.

WHAT IS NOT FUNDED No grants to individuals.

RANGE OF GRANTS £200–£1,000.

SAMPLE GRANTS £1,000 each for general purposes to Brooke Hospital for Animals, Greek Animal Welfare Fund, International League for the Protection of Horses and Royal British Legion.

FINANCES *Year* 2000–01 *Income* £23,000 *Grants* £30,000 *Assets* £482,000

TRUSTEES J D Stevens; A J Quinton; A R St C Tahourdin.

HOW TO APPLY In writing to the correspondent. However, no applications are being accepted at the present time.

WHO TO APPLY TO A Tahourdin, Herrington & Carmichael, 4 Station Rd, Aldershot GU11 1HU *Tel* 01252 322451 *Fax* 01252 311561

CC NO 327829   **ESTABLISHED** 1988

■ Stevenson Family's Charitable Trust

WHERE FUNDING CAN BE GIVEN Unrestricted.

WHO CAN BENEFIT UK, international and local charitable organisations.

WHAT IS FUNDED Education, medical and welfare, arts and heritage.

TYPE OF GRANT Some recurrent.

SAMPLE GRANTS £200,000 each to British Museum, St Hilda's College Oxford and University College, Oxford; £135,000 to London Millennium Bridge Trust; £100,000 each to English Ladies Golf Association and Institute of Child Health at Great Ormond Street Hospital; £20,000 to University of Oxford Development Trust; £12,500 to St Michael and All Angels, Sunninghill; £10,000 to Berkshire County Blind Society; £8,415 to Royal Botanic Gardens.

FINANCES *Year* 2000–01 *Income* £259,210 *Grants* £1,023,000 *Assets* £5,863,861

TRUSTEES Hugh A Stevenson; Mrs Catherine M Stevenson; Jeremy F Lever.

HOW TO APPLY 'No unsolicited applications can be considered as the charity's funds are required to support purposes chosen by the trustees.'

WHO TO APPLY TO H A Stevenson, 33 St Mary Axe, London EC3A 8LL *Tel* 020 7342 2630

CC NO 327148   ESTABLISHED 1986

■ The Steventon Allotments & Relief-in-Need Charity

WHERE FUNDING CAN BE GIVEN Steventon.

WHO CAN BENEFIT Individuals and local organisations benefiting people of all ages and Christians in the parish of Steventon.

WHAT IS FUNDED Projects benefiting the local community, churches, schools, older people and the maintenance of the allotments and St Michael's House.

FINANCES *Year* 1999 *Income* £79,000 *Grants* £32,000 *Assets* £2,800,000

TRUSTEES Robert Dunsdon; Howard Fuller; John Jarvis; Stephen Prior; Mary Wallis; David Otterburn; S Ward.

OTHER INFORMATION A further £12,000 was given in grants to individuals.

HOW TO APPLY In writing to the correspondent.

WHO TO APPLY TO Mrs Patrina Effer, 19 Lime Grove, Southmoor, Abingdon, Oxfordshire OX13 5DN

CC NO 203331   ESTABLISHED 1987

■ The Stewards' Charitable Trust

WHERE FUNDING CAN BE GIVEN Principally the UK.

WHO CAN BENEFIT Organisations and clubs benefiting sportsmen and women.

WHAT IS FUNDED Support of rowing at all levels, from grassroots upwards, beneficiaries should be in full-time education or training.

WHAT IS NOT FUNDED No grants to individuals or for building or capital costs.

TYPE OF GRANT Preferably one-off and especially where there are matched funds raised elsewhere.

RANGE OF GRANTS £1,000–£60,000.

SAMPLE GRANTS 2001: £40,000 to ARA – Project Oarsome; £25,000 to Biodynamics Project; £7,500 to Rowing Foundation; £7,000 to ARA Safety Video.

FINANCES *Year* 2002 *Income* £343,000 *Grants* £70,000 *Assets* £2,700,000

TRUSTEES M A Sweeney; C G V Davidge; C L Baillieu; R C Lester.

HOW TO APPLY In writing to the correspondent. Applications are usually first vetted by Amateur Rowing Association.

WHO TO APPLY TO R S Goddard, Secretary, Regatta Headquarters, Henley-on-Thames, Oxfordshire RG9 2LY

CC NO 299597   ESTABLISHED 1988

■ The Stewards Company (incorporating the J W Laing Trust and the J W Laing Biblical Scholarship Trust)

WHERE FUNDING CAN BE GIVEN Unrestricted.

WHO CAN BENEFIT Organisations involved with training people in religious education. About half the trust's funds are given for work overseas.

WHAT IS FUNDED Grants given overseas are made under the following categories: church buildings; scriptures and literature; educational and orphanages; education of missionaries' children; national evangelists and missionaries' vehicles. Grants given in the UK are categorised under: church buildings; evangelistic associations; scriptures and literature; teachers and evangelists and youth and children. Substantial funds are also transferred to the Beatrice Laing Trust (see separate entry).

TYPE OF GRANT Usually one-off, with a proportion of core regular giving to establish work.

SAMPLE GRANTS £1,025,000 to Myrtlefield Trust; £955,000 to Echoes of Service; £681,000 to UCCF; £655,650 to Beatrice Laing Trust; £350,000 to Scripture Gift Mission; £126,000 to to Interlink; £121,500 to Redcliffe College; £115,000 to IFES; £100,000 to RMAF (Retired Missionary Aid Fund); £80,000 to Belmont Chapel Exeter.

FINANCES *Year* 2000–01 *Income* £5,050,422 *Grants* £7,259,000 *Assets* £120,084,000

TRUSTEES Twenty-two directors, chaired by J G McEwen.

WHO TO APPLY TO B J Chapman, Secretary, PO Box 133, Bath BA1 2YU *Tel* 01225 427326 *Fax* 01225 427427

CC NO 234558   ESTABLISHED 1947

■ The Sir Halley Stewart Trust

WHERE FUNDING CAN BE GIVEN Unrestricted, but mainly UK and south and west Africa in practice.

WHO CAN BENEFIT Promising young researchers, either directly or through the organisations they work for.

WHAT IS FUNDED (a) Religion: theological training where there is a special or specific need (such as in Africa or Eastern Europe); teaching in the UK about Christianity outside the formal education system; encouragement of specific groups of people to explore their spiritual needs and strengths; and encouragement of appropriate people to develop their skills in communicating the Christian message through the media. (b) Social and educational: innovative projects which attempt to prevent and resolve conflicts, promote reconciliation and increase understanding within families and across racial, cultural, class, religious and professional divides; innovative projects which attempt to help people 'move beyond disadvantage'; projects which attempt to address the needs of vulnerable people in imaginative ways; and innovative projects overseas, especially in Africa, which are aimed at community development. (c) Medical: problems associated with older people such as Alzheimer's Disease, nutrition, osteporosis and incontinence; prevention of disease and disability in children; prevention, diagnosis and treatment of tropical infectious and parasitic diseases; innovative projects, involving any discipline, which are likely to improve healthcare; and ethical problems arising from advances in medical practice.

WHAT IS NOT FUNDED No grants for: general appeals of any kind; personal education fees or fees for taught courses – unless connected with research which falls within our current priority areas; educational or 'gap' year travel projects; the purchase, erection or conversion of buildings; capital costs; running costs of established organisations; or university overhead charges. The trustees do not favour grantmaking to enable the completion of a project or PhD.

TYPE OF GRANT One-off and project grants. Feasibility studies, research and salaries will also be considered. Funding may be given for up to three years.

SAMPLE GRANTS £150,000 to Sarum College – Salisbury for a three-year project looking at contemporary culture and the spirituality of young people; £51,000 to Clean Break Theatre Company – London towards the salary of the head of education for three years for a theatre company offering female ex-offenders training, educational and professional support; £33,152 to University of Cambridge Faculty of Divinity for the part-time salary for two years of a project director; £32,000 each to Margaret Beaufort Institute of Theology – University of Cambridge for scholarships to enable two overseas women to study for a two year certificate in theology for ministry and KwaZulu-Natal Programme for the Survivors of Violence for various groups and projects; £30,000 to Corrymeela Community – Northern Ireland for an interface community programme to develop appropriate models to build confidence and skills within communities; £27,878 to Religious Society of Friends in Britain to support a worker for the Quaker Peace Centre in Cape Town to train two new community mediators; £26,690 to National Museums and Galleries of Northern Ireland towards the salary of a citizenship education officer; £26,400 to Centre for Jewish-Christian Relations – Cambridge for the salary of a part-time flexible learning administrator; £19,700 to Ashoka (UK) Trust for a stipend in Burkina Faso.

FINANCES *Year* 2001–02 *Income* £995,000 *Grants* £1,006,000 *Assets* £22,143,000

TRUSTEES Prof John Lennard Jones, chair; Dr Duncan Stewart; William P Kirkman; Lord Stewartby; George Russell; Prof. Phyllida Parsloe (chair of social committee); Miss Barbara Clapham; Prof. J Wyatt; Michael Ross Collins; Brian Allpress; Prof. Philip Whitfield; Prof. C Hallett; Rev Dr Leslie Griffiths (chair of religious committee); Dr A Caroline Berry; Professor Gordon Willcock (chair of medical committee).

HOW TO APPLY The application should come, in the first instance, from the individual concerned, rather than the 'host' organisation. Applications can be received throughout the year and will be considered for the next available meeting. Assessment can take several weeks, so applicants should allow for this when submitting their proposals (which should not be faxed or e-mailed). Initial telephone enquiries are welcomed. Applications should include details of exactly how the grant will be spent and how long and where the project will take place. CV's and job descriptions are useful. Full trustees' meetings take place in February, June and October.

WHO TO APPLY TO Mrs Sue West, 22 Earith Rd, Willingham, Cambridge CB4 5LS *Tel* 01954 260707 *Website* www.sirhalleystewart.org
CC NO 208491   **ESTABLISHED** 1924

WHERE FUNDING CAN BE GIVEN England and Wales with a preference for the west of England, Bristol, Cornwall, Devon, Dorset and Somerset (especially west Somerset).

WHO CAN BENEFIT Methodist organisations benefiting children and young adults, people who are disabled and people disadvantaged by poverty. Community projects and small local innovatory projects with a strong emphasis on self-help are preferred.

WHAT IS FUNDED The broad categories the trust supported (in decreasing order of the amount spent under each category in 2001–02) were: medical and disability; churches (of which three-quarters are Methodist in the specified counties); youth and children; community projects; disadvantage; and environment.

WHAT IS NOT FUNDED Grants are not usually given towards general running expenses of charitable organisations, and never to individuals towards tuition fees, research projects and so on. Mail shot type appeals from large organisations are unlikely to be successful.

TYPE OF GRANT Usually one-off for a specific project or part of a project.

RANGE OF GRANTS £100–£2,500.

SAMPLE GRANTS £2,000 each to help renovate a church building, and towards a community support project in a deprived area; £1,000 each towards equipment in training establishments for people who are disabled, and to a village hall for an extension; £680 towards youth camps in Devon; £500 each to help set up a helpline for a medical research charity, to help fund a football initiative in a deprived area, and towards refurbishment costs for a Methodist church; £250 to a scout group for equipment.

FINANCES *Year* 2001–02 *Income* £61,000 *Grants* £78,000 *Assets* £1,650,000

TRUSTEES S R Duckworth; Mrs S Harnden; C Stoate; Dr P C Stoate; P J Stoate; The Chair of the Bristol Methodist District.

OTHER INFORMATION Although the trust does not want to rule out anywhere in England and Wales, it is a comparatively small trust and is forced to be very selective. Therefore, the further an applicant is from the trust's core area the less likely they are to be successful.

HOW TO APPLY In writing to the correspondent. Applications can be sent at any time, but to catch the main allocation meetings, April to June, or September to November is best. Unsuccessful applications cannot be acknowledged unless accompanied by an sae.

WHO TO APPLY TO Philip J Stoate, Secretary, 15 Sherwood Avenue, Ferndown, Dorset BH22 8JS *Tel* 01202 855992 *Fax* 01202 8855992 *E-mail* pjs@erminea.org.uk
CC NO 221325   **ESTABLISHED** 1950

■ **The Stobart Newlands Charitable Trust**

WHERE FUNDING CAN BE GIVEN Unrestricted.

WHO CAN BENEFIT Registered charities.

WHAT IS FUNDED General charitable purposes at the discretion of the trustees; mainly Christian organisations and missionary societies.

WHAT IS NOT FUNDED No grants for individuals.

SAMPLE GRANTS £205,000 to World Vision UK for Christian relief work; £160,000 to Operation Mobilisation for Christian outreach; £151,000 to Mission Aviation Fellowship for Christian relief work.

FINANCES *Year* 2000 *Grants* £944,000

TRUSTEES R J Stobart; M Stobart; R A Stobart; P J Stobart; L E Rigg.

HOW TO APPLY Unsolicited applications are most unlikely to be successful.

WHO TO APPLY TO Mrs M Stobart, Trustee, Newlands Mill, Hesket Newmarket, Wigton, Cumbria CA7 8HP *Tel* 01697 478261

CC NO 328464   **ESTABLISHED** 1989

■ The Stoller Charitable Trust

WHERE FUNDING CAN BE GIVEN UK, with a preference for the Greater Manchester area.

WHO CAN BENEFIT Established UK charities and local causes benefiting children and young adults.

WHAT IS FUNDED Healthcare, health facilities and buildings. Other charitable purposes will be considered.

WHAT IS NOT FUNDED No grants to individuals.

TYPE OF GRANT Buildings, capital, one-off, project, research, recurring costs and start-up costs will be considered. Funding may be given for up to three years.

SAMPLE GRANTS £25,000 each to Cancer Research UK, Emmaus – Bolton, Prince's Trust; £20,000 each to Hulme Grammar School, Manchester High School for Girls, Manchester Grammar School, The Message and On the Beat – Greater Manchester Police; £15,000 each to Imperial War Museum and Make A Difference; £14,400 to Duke of Edinburgh Foundation; £10,000 to NEARIS.

FINANCES *Year* 2001–02 *Income* £713,921 *Grants* £441,881 *Assets* £7,728,498

TRUSTEES Norman Stoller; Roger Gould; Jan Fidler.

HOW TO APPLY In writing to the correspondent. Applications need to be received by February, May, August or November and the trustees meet in March, June, September and December.

WHO TO APPLY TO Alison Ford, c/o SSL International plc, Tubiton House, Oldham OL1 3HS *Tel* 0161 621 2003 *Fax* 0161 627 0932

CC NO 285415   **ESTABLISHED** 1982

■ The Stone Ashdown Charitable Trust

WHERE FUNDING CAN BE GIVEN UK, mainly London, and, to a limited extent, overseas.

WHO CAN BENEFIT Registered charities.

WHAT IS FUNDED The areas of activities are: relief of poverty; education; inter-religious dialogue; asylum and immigration; black voluntary sector support; promoting equalities and anti-racism; outward looking Judaism in the UK; other charitable purposes.

WHAT IS NOT FUNDED The trust does not generally support individuals.

SAMPLE GRANTS £50,000 to the Institute for Jewish Policy Research – the last instalment of a four-year grant for a long-term planning project; £38,000 in two grants to Civil Liberties Trust; £33,000 to Ebony Steelband Trust; £32,000 to Kente; £31,000 to 1990 Trust; £24,000 to Community Links for a Bangladeshi Community Support Worker; £21,000 to Scarman Trust; £20,000 to Notting Hill Social Council for work with BME residents; £15,000 to Paddington Development Trust for a regeneration programme.

FINANCES *Year* 2001–02 *Grants* £698,000

TRUSTEES Richard Stone; Lutfur Ali; Francesca Klug; Leroy Logan.

OTHER INFORMATION Due to existing commitments the trust states that it is unable to respond to unsolicited applications. This position is likely to continue for at least two years.

HOW TO APPLY On a five-page application form, obtainable from the correspondent. Documents required along with the form will usually include several of the following: most recent audited accounts; annual report; business plan/ project work programme; constitution/ memorandum and articles of association; job descriptions for posts for which funding is sought.

WHO TO APPLY TO Steve Roberts, Grants Manager, 4th Floor, Barkat House, 116–118 Finchley Road, London NW3 5HT *Tel* 020 7472 6060 *Website* www.nonamegiven.com/stoneashdown

CC NO 298722   **ESTABLISHED** 2000

■ The Stone Foundation

WHERE FUNDING CAN BE GIVEN UK.

WHO CAN BENEFIT Organisations benefiting substance misusers.

WHAT IS FUNDED Charities dealing with drug and alcohol dependency, directing resources to the area of research, education and treatment of addiction to alcohol and drugs as well as focusing on the alleviation of other compulsive disorders. It supports 'Stone Workshops', which is committed to out patient therapeutic groups and educational workshops, and provides funding for the clinical application of Standards of Practice in treatment centres via EATA.

SAMPLE GRANTS £35,000 to Camden and Islington CHS to develop a dual diagnoses programme; £25,000 to Chemical Dependency Centre for a quality assurance programme in line with EATA UK standards; £17,500 to Cancer Bacup for a nurse of the information service; £10,000 to British Liver Trust for research into Hepatitis C; £8,750 to NAADAC for development; £5,137 to Glyndebourne; £5,000 to Broadway Trust towards setting up a fully endowed charity bed; £2,500 to WRVS Contact Centres; £1,000 each to The Passage Day Centre and Royal Court.

FINANCES *Year* 1999–2000 *Income* £119,276 *Grants* £110,897

TRUSTEES Lady Shauna Gosling; M J Kirkwood; Adam Gosling.

HOW TO APPLY In writing to the correspondent. Trustees meet in January, April, June, September and November.

WHO TO APPLY TO Lady Gosling, Chair of the Trustees, 24 Wilton Row, London SW1X 7NS *Tel* 020 7235 4871

CC NO 1084454   **ESTABLISHED** 1988

■ The M J C Stone Charitable Trust

WHERE FUNDING CAN BE GIVEN UK.

WHO CAN BENEFIT UK charities and smaller scale local organisations.

WHAT IS FUNDED Children, medicine and health, education and conservation.

RANGE OF GRANTS £100–£25,000.

SAMPLE GRANTS £25,000 to Bradfield Foundation; £20,000 each to Blue Coat C of E School and Game Conservancy; £13,500 to United World College of the Atlantic; £12,000 each to National Hospital Development Trust and Countryside Foundation for Education; £10,000 each to University of Gloucestershire and Winnicott Foundation; £5,700 to Macmillan Cancer Relief; £5,000 to British Wheelchair

Sports Foundation; £2,500 to NSPCC; £1,000 each to Tyndale Monument Appeal and Wildlife Trust Cumbria.

FINANCES *Year* 2000 *Income* £594,000 *Grants* £164,000 *Assets* £861,000

TRUSTEES M J C Stone; Mrs L Stone; C R H Stone; A J Stone; N J Farquhar.

HOW TO APPLY 'Unsolicited applications will not be replied to.'

WHO TO APPLY TO M J C Stone, Trustee, Estate Office, Ozleworth Park, Wotton-under-Edge, Gloucestershire GL12 7QA *Tel* 01453 845591

CC NO 283920　　　**ESTABLISHED** 1981

■ The Stone-Mallabar Charitable Foundation

WHERE FUNDING CAN BE GIVEN UK.

WHO CAN BENEFIT Registered charities.

WHAT IS FUNDED Particularly medical charities and educational establishments.

WHAT IS NOT FUNDED No grants to individuals.

SAMPLE GRANTS £100,000 each to Centrepoint Soho, English National Opera and St Christopher's Hospice; £53,000 to Alzheimer's Research Trust; £25,000 to Multiple Sclerosis Society; £15,000 to Big Issue in the North.

FINANCES *Year* 2000–01 *Grants* £491,000 *Assets* £661,000

TRUSTEES Jonathan Stone; Thalia Stone; Robin Paul.

HOW TO APPLY In writing to the correspondent. Due to the level of applications received, the trustees regret that they cannot respond to unsuccessful applications.

WHO TO APPLY TO Jonathan M Stone, Trustee, 41 Orchard Court, Portman Square, London W1H 6LF *Tel* 020 7839 3899

CC NO 1013678　　　**ESTABLISHED** 1992

■ The Stonewall Iris Trust

WHERE FUNDING CAN BE GIVEN UK.

WHO CAN BENEFIT Organisations, particularly those benefiting gays and lesbians.

WHAT IS FUNDED The trustees are interested in a wide range of charitable issues particularly those affecting lesbian and gay communities. The advancement of public education in relation to all aspects of discrimination in society whether by reason of sexual orientation, gender, race, mental or physical disability, social or economic circumstances or other reason.

WHAT IS NOT FUNDED Grants are not awarded: to individuals; for capital projects; for fundraising activities; to organisations, projects or activities that fall outside the charity's objects or the trustees' current priorities as shown above.

SAMPLE GRANTS £5,000 each to Macintosh Foundation, The Wates Foundation and The Woodward Charitable Trust; £3,000 to Allen Lane Foundation.

FINANCES *Year* 1999 *Income* £50,000 *Grants* £15,000 *Assets* £76,000

TRUSTEES Sir Ian McKellen, Chair; Olivette Cole-Wilson; Dr P H Rivas; S Fanshawe.

HOW TO APPLY In writing to the correspondent for consideration by the trustees at their quarterly meetings. Preferably applications should be no more than two sides of A4 and state clearly the purposes for which the grant is sought, the amount sought and the outcome the grant is intended to achieve.

WHO TO APPLY TO Max Manin, 46 Grosvenor Gardens, London SW1W 0EB *Tel* 020 7881 9440 *Fax* 020 7881 9444

CC NO 802664　　　**ESTABLISHED** 1989

■ Foundation of Edward Storey

WHERE FUNDING CAN BE GIVEN Cambridgeshire.

WHO CAN BENEFIT Projects should primarily benefit women in need, hardship or distress living in the county of Cambridgeshire or closely involved in the work of the Church of England.

WHAT IS FUNDED Priority is given firstly to the foundation's almshouses, and secondly to individuals. Women's welfare organisations are also considered.

WHAT IS NOT FUNDED No grants to males.

TYPE OF GRANT Funding for up to one year.

SAMPLE GRANTS In 1998–99: £10,000 to St Luke's Hospital for the Clergy; £9,175 to St Martin's Day Centre, Cambridge; £5,000 to Venn House (CMS).

FINANCES *Year* 2000–01 *Income* £786,834 *Grants* £165,345

TRUSTEES Stephen Fleet; John Marks; Richard Smith; Elizabeth Walser; Sue Young; Peter Brook; Nicky Blanning; William Johnson; Pam Gatrell.

HOW TO APPLY In writing to the correspondent. Organisations are required to provide information on what they do and who for e.g. breakdown of their clients showing the majority are women over 40 years of age etc.

WHO TO APPLY TO Mrs Diana Lindsay, Clerk, Storey's House, Mount Pleasant, Cambridge CB3 0BZ *Tel* 01223 364405 *Fax* 01223 321313

CC NO 203653　　　**ESTABLISHED** 1693

■ The Samuel Storey Family Charitable Trust

WHERE FUNDING CAN BE GIVEN Uk, with a preference for Yorkshire.

WHO CAN BENEFIT Registered charities.

WHAT IS FUNDED General charitable purposes.

WHAT IS NOT FUNDED The trust does not support non-registered charities or individuals.

RANGE OF GRANTS Generally £2–£5,000.

SAMPLE GRANTS £1,500,040 to Sir Harold Hillier Gardens and Arboretum; £5,000 each to Macmillan Cancer Relief, Florence Nightingale Aid in Sickness Trust, and Paxton Trust; £2,000 each to JC2000, and Trinity Hospice; £1,000 each to Anglican Centre in ome and Tukes; £750 each to Fondazione Caetani, and Foundation and Friends R B G Kew.

FINANCES *Year* 2000–01 *Income* £244,409 *Grants* £1,530,412 *Assets* £4,679,259

TRUSTEES Hon. Sir Richard Storey; Wren Hoskyns Abrahall; K Storey.

HOW TO APPLY In writing to the correspondent.

WHO TO APPLY TO Hon. Sir Richard Storey, Trustee, 21 Buckingham Gate, London SW1E 6LS *Tel* 020 7802 2700 *Fax* 020 7828 5049

CC NO 267684　　　**ESTABLISHED** 1974

■ Peter Stormonth Darling Charitable Trust

WHERE FUNDING CAN BE GIVEN UK.

WHO CAN BENEFIT Organisations benefiting children, young adults, and sportsmen and women.

WHAT IS FUNDED Preference for heritage, education, healthcare and sports facilities.

SAMPLE GRANTS In 1997: £35,000 to Winchester · College; £8,000 to King Edward VII Hospital for Officers; £5,000 to Royal Medical Benevolent Fund; £3,000 to National Trust for Scotland; £2,500 to Martin and Barry's Trust.
FINANCES *Year* 2001 *Income* £47,939
TRUSTEES Tom Colville; J F M Rodwell; Peter Stormonth Darling.
HOW TO APPLY This trust states that it does not respond to unsolicited applications.
WHO TO APPLY TO Peter Stormonth Darling, Trustee, 33 King William Street, London EC4R 9AS
CC NO 1049946   **ESTABLISHED** 1995

■ Peter Storrs Trust
WHERE FUNDING CAN BE GIVEN UK.
WHO CAN BENEFIT Registered charities.
WHAT IS FUNDED The advancement of education.
FINANCES *Year* 1999–2000 *Income* £74,000
TRUSTEES C V Adams; A R E Curtis; J A Fordyce.
HOW TO APPLY In writing to the correspondent. Applications are considered every three to six months. Please note, the trust receives far more applications than it is able to support, many of which do not meet the criteria outlined above. This results in a heavy waste of time and expense for both applicants and the trust itself.
WHO TO APPLY TO J A Fordyce, Trustee, Fordyce Curry & Co., 91–93 Charterhouse Street, London EC1M 6PN *Tel* 020 7253 3757
CC NO 313804   **ESTABLISHED** 1970

■ The Strangward Trust
WHERE FUNDING CAN BE GIVEN UK.
WHO CAN BENEFIT Small local projects in eastern England and UK organisations concerned with people with disabilities.
WHAT IS FUNDED Funding for care and treatment of people who are physically or mentally disabled, particularly charities working in the field of the nursing service, hospice in the home, special schools, and holidays and outings.
TYPE OF GRANT One-off, capital, core costs. Funding is for one year or less.
SAMPLE GRANTS In 1998–99: £4,000 each to Northamptonshire Country Centre, Marshfields School, Deafblind UK, Caring and Sharing Trust and BREAK; £3,000 to East Anglian Autistic Support Trust; £2,000 to an individual.
FINANCES *Year* 2001–02 *Income* £78,617
TRUSTEES Mrs T A Strangward; M Measures; J Higham Mrs E Conroy.
HOW TO APPLY In writing to the correspondent.
WHO TO APPLY TO Mrs L Davies, Vincent Sykes & Higham, Montague House, Chancery Lane, Thrapston, Northamptonshire NN14 4LN *Tel* 01832 732161 *E-mail* louise.davies@evslaw.co.uk
CC NO 1036494   **ESTABLISHED** 1993

■ The Strasser Foundation
WHERE FUNDING CAN BE GIVEN Staffordshire.
WHO CAN BENEFIT Organisations and individuals.
WHAT IS FUNDED General charitable purposes.
TYPE OF GRANT One-off.
RANGE OF GRANTS £100–£1,500.
SAMPLE GRANTS £2,500 to University of Keele for a building project; £1,500 to ARCH (North Staffordshire) for community projects; £1,000 each to Staffordshire Guides for a travel fund, Staffordshire Wildlife Trust for an environmental project, and Stoke-on-Trent Citizen's Advice

Bureau for allocation at their discretion; £750 to Queens Croft School, a local school for children who are disadvantaged.
FINANCES *Year* 2000 *Income* £32,673 *Grants* £34,877 *Assets* £610,737
TRUSTEES A F Booth; A P Bell.
HOW TO APPLY In writing to the correspondent. The trustees meet quarterly. Applications are only acknowledged if an sae is sent.
WHO TO APPLY TO A P Bell, c/o Knight & Sons, The Brampton, Newcastle-under-Lyme, Staffordshire ST5 0QW *Tel* 01782 619225
CC NO 511703   **ESTABLISHED** 1978

■ The W O Street Charitable Foundation
WHERE FUNDING CAN BE GIVEN UK, with local interests in the north west of England and Jersey.
WHO CAN BENEFIT Registered charities, mostly local branches of UK disability or welfare organisations.
WHAT IS FUNDED Support is given for education, relief of poverty, helping people in financial difficulties (particularly people who are elderly, blind or disabled), and the relief of ill health or sickness and social welfare generally.
WHAT IS NOT FUNDED No grants towards: schools, colleges or universities; running or core costs; religion or church buildings; medical research; animal welfare; hospices; overseas projects or charities; NHS trusts. Applications directly from individuals are not considered.
TYPE OF GRANT One-off grants for capital projects.
RANGE OF GRANTS Typically £2,500–£5,000.
SAMPLE GRANTS £50,000 each to Museum of Science and Industry and Prince's Trust; £46,000 to W O Street Jersey Charitable Trust; £37,000 to Independent Schools Information Service (in 21 grants to individual students); £35,000 to the Combined Trusts Sixth Form Scholarships Trust; £10,000 to Bury Hospice.
FINANCES *Year* 2001 *Grants* £463,000
TRUSTEES Barclays Bank Trust Co. Ltd; A Paines.
HOW TO APPLY In writing only, to the correspondent. Trustees aim to consider appeals on a quarterly basis, at the end of January, April, July and October.
WHO TO APPLY TO Miss M Bertenshaw, Trust Officer, c/o Barclays Bank Trust Company Ltd, PO Box 15, Osborne Court, Gadbrook Park, Rudheath, Northwich CW9 7UE
CC NO 267127   **ESTABLISHED** 1973

■ The A B Strom & R Strom Charitable Trust
WHERE FUNDING CAN BE GIVEN UK.
WHO CAN BENEFIT Registered charities.
WHAT IS FUNDED A set list of charities working with older people, schools/colleges, hospitals and Christian causes.
FINANCES *Year* 1999–2000 *Income* £57,018 *Grants* £37,000
TRUSTEES Mrs R Strom; M Weissbraun.
HOW TO APPLY In writing to the correspondent. Please note that the same organisations are supported each year.
WHO TO APPLY TO Mrs R Strom, Trustee, c/o 11 Gloucester Gardens, London NW11 9AB
CC NO 268916   **ESTABLISHED** 1971

Think carefully about every application. Is it justified?

823

■ The Sudborough Foundation

WHERE FUNDING CAN BE GIVEN Preference for Northamptonshire.

WHO CAN BENEFIT Educational establishments and other charities.

WHAT IS FUNDED Students in need or for scholarships; general charitable purposes.

WHAT IS NOT FUNDED No grants for expeditions or drama and dance courses.

SAMPLE GRANTS £4,300 to Nene University College; £3,000 to University of Sheffield; £2,000 to Leicester University; £1,800 to The Gordon Robinson Memorial Trust; £1,500 each to Northamptonshire Scout Council and Royal College of Music for scholarships; £1,000 each to Drake Charity Trust and Evelyn Hodgson Memorial Trust; £750 to St John's Home; £500 each to Homestart Northampton and Northampton Hebrew Congregation.

FINANCES *Year* 1999–2000 *Income* £48,000 *Grants* £30,000 *Assets* £322,000

TRUSTEES M D Engel, Chair; Mrs R E Engel; Sir J Lowther; G Pollard; S E Markham; Mrs E A Engel; W M Reason.

HOW TO APPLY In writing to the correspondent.

WHO TO APPLY TO Max D Engel, Chair, 8 Hazelwood Road, Northampton NN1 1LP

CC NO 272323   **ESTABLISHED** 1976

■ Sueberry Ltd

WHERE FUNDING CAN BE GIVEN UK and overseas.

WHO CAN BENEFIT Jewish organisations; UK welfare and medical organisations benefiting children and young adults; at risk groups; people who are disadvantaged by poverty, or socially isolated people.

WHAT IS FUNDED Jewish organisations, medical, educational and welfare charities.

TYPE OF GRANT Mostly recurrent.

FINANCES *Year* 1999–2000 *Income* £46,000 *Grants* £61,000 *Assets* £7,100

TRUSTEES J Davis, Chair; Mrs M Davis; Mrs H Davis.

HOW TO APPLY In writing to the correspondent.

WHO TO APPLY TO Mrs M Davis, Trustee, 11 Clapton Common, London E5 9AA

CC NO 256566   **ESTABLISHED** 1968

■ The Suffolk Historic Churches Trust

WHERE FUNDING CAN BE GIVEN Suffolk.

WHO CAN BENEFIT Churches and chapels of all denominations.

WHAT IS FUNDED The preservation, repair, maintenance, restoration and improvement of churches in Suffolk.

WHAT IS NOT FUNDED New buildings, electricity repair and redecoration.

RANGE OF GRANTS £200–£6,000.

SAMPLE GRANTS Grants were given to 59 churches and chapels.

FINANCES *Year* 2001–02 *Income* £259,255 *Grants* £141,780 *Assets* £417,721

TRUSTEES Mrs Diana Hunt, Chair; Alan Barker; Ven. John Cox; The Countess of Euston; Martin Favell; Hon. Jill Ganzoni; Ivan Howlett; Mrs Wendy Marchant; Mrs Frances Parkinson; Christopher Spicer; Robert Rous; Christina van Melzen; Robert Williams; Raymond Bedwell.

HOW TO APPLY In writing to the correspondent.

WHO TO APPLY TO Howard Stephens, Secretary, Brinkleys, Hall Street, Long Melford, Suffolk CO10 9JR *Tel* 01787 883884 *Fax* 01787 370685 *E-mail* shct@btconnect.com

CC NO 267047   **ESTABLISHED** 1973

■ The Alan Sugar Foundation

WHERE FUNDING CAN BE GIVEN UK.

WHO CAN BENEFIT Registered charities.

WHAT IS FUNDED Grants are made to causes of current and ongoing interest to the trustees.

WHAT IS NOT FUNDED No grants for individuals or to non-registered charities.

TYPE OF GRANT One-off and recurring, capital and project.

SAMPLE GRANTS £125,000 to Jewish Care; £100,000 each to Great Ormond Street Hospital and King Solomon School – Redbridge; £75,000 to Jewish Blind and Disabled; and £3,000 to Drugs Education in Schools.

FINANCES *Year* 2000–01 *Income* £425,000 *Grants* £403,000 *Assets* £45,000

TRUSTEES Sir Alan Sugar; Colin Sandy; Simon Sugar; Daniel Sugar; Mrs Louise Baron.

HOW TO APPLY **This trust states that it does not respond to unsolicited applications.** All projects are initiated by the trustees.

WHO TO APPLY TO Colin Sandy, Brentwood House, 169 Kings Road, Brentwood, Essex CM14 4EF *Tel* 01277 201333 *Fax* 01277 208006

CC NO 294880   **ESTABLISHED** 1986

■ The Summerfield Charitable Trust

WHERE FUNDING CAN BE GIVEN Gloucestershire.

WHO CAN BENEFIT Registered charities local to Gloucestershire. Private organisations and individuals are only very rarely supported, students being more likely to find favour than those with other needs. In any event, the trustees urge individuals to use a specialist charity to sponsor their application.

WHAT IS FUNDED The trustees are interested in hearing from those involved in helping older people, people in need and the arts. Viewed especially favourably are: the needs of people living in rural areas; ventures which make a point of using volunteers (and which train volunteers); applicants who show clear indications that they have assessed the impact of their project upon the environment; and joint appeals from groups working in similar areas, who wish to develop a partnership. The trustees particularly welcome innovative ideas from: small, voluntary groups; schemes that indicate planning for long-term self-sufficiency; and projects that demonstrate active involvement with the beneficiaries.

WHAT IS NOT FUNDED Donations are not given towards medical research, private education or animal welfare appeals. Individuals are only very rarely supported, students being more likely to find favour than those with other needs.

TYPE OF GRANT Usually one-off. The trustees prefer to award one-off grants to help fund specific projects rather than to make payments for revenue items. The trustees will occasionally consider start-up costs and grants for up to three years.

RANGE OF GRANTS £500–£5,000.

SAMPLE GRANTS £37,000 to Cheltenham & Gloucester College Development Trust Ltd; £25,000 to Gloucester Civic Trust, towards its commissioning of a statue to mark the city's 1900th anniversary; £17,000 to Gloucestershire Rural Community Council; £15,000 each to At Home Trust, for equipment for specialised housing for young people with physical disabilities, Gloucestershire Neighbourhood Projects Network, Everyman Youth Theatre (third of three grants) for the salary of its director, and Gloucestershire Dance Project (second of two grants) for core funding to enable the charity to develop a long-term strategy for its work; £12,000 to Cheltenham Community Projects; £10,000 each to Cheltenham Arts Festivals Ltd and Holst Birthplace Museum Trust.

FINANCES *Year* 2000 *Income* £367,000 *Grants* £436,000 *Assets* £10,000,000

TRUSTEES Charles Fisher, Chair; Dr The Hon. Gilbert Greenall; Mrs Rosaleen Kaye; Mrs Jamila Gavin; Richard Wakeford.

HOW TO APPLY In writing to the correspondent, enclosing a sae.The trustees meet quarterly, usually in January, April, July and October, when they consider all applications received by the end of the preceding month.

WHO TO APPLY TO Mrs Lavinia Sidgwick, Administrator, PO Box 4, Winchcombe, Cheltenham, Gloucs GL54 5ZD *Tel* 01242 676774 *Fax* 01242 677120 *E-mail* admin@summerfield.org.uk *Website* www.summerfield.org.uk

CC NO 802493   **ESTABLISHED** 1989

■ Sir John Sumner's Trust

WHERE FUNDING CAN BE GIVEN Mainly the Midlands.

WHAT IS FUNDED Mainly: (a) grants to people in need and (b) donations to charities concerned with community facilities and services, art, literature, archaeology and research (other than experiments involving animals). Some grants may be made for education in nursing and mental care, or training in medicine.

WHAT IS NOT FUNDED No support for politics or religion: 'though purely social efforts connected to religious denominations are not excluded'.

TYPE OF GRANT One-off grants to individuals plus occasional quarterly payments to fund education. Normally one-off amounts to charitable organisations.

FINANCES *Year* 2000–01 *Income* £39,000 *Grants* £36,000 *Assets* £796,000

TRUSTEES J B Sumner, Chair; Mrs E J Wood; J M G Fea; Lady Richard Wellesley; Mrs V J Mackie.

HOW TO APPLY In writing to the correspondent with full details including balance sheets if available. Individuals should apply on a form available from the correspondent, via social services or citizens advice bureaux, except students who should write directly with full details.

WHO TO APPLY TO A C Robson, Secretary, 8th Floor, Union Chambers, 63 Temple Row, Birmingham B2 5LT *Tel* 0121 643 3756

CC NO 218620   **ESTABLISHED** 1927

■ The Sumray Charitable Trust

WHERE FUNDING CAN BE GIVEN UK.

WHO CAN BENEFIT Jewish people.

WHAT IS FUNDED Principally Jewish charities.

RANGE OF GRANTS £250–£10,000.

SAMPLE GRANTS £10,000 to Jewish Care; £500 to Institute of Jewish Policy Research; £300 to UNICEF; £250 to Norwood Ravenswood.

FINANCES *Year* 1999–2000 *Income* £32,000 *Grants* £14,000 *Assets* £622,000

TRUSTEES M Sumray; Mrs C Sumray; M M Davis; M D Frankel.

HOW TO APPLY In writing to the correspondent.

WHO TO APPLY TO H Kramer, c/o Citroen Wells & Co, Devonshire House, 1 Devonshire Street, London W1W 5DR *Tel* 020 7304 2000

CC NO 270270   **ESTABLISHED** 1975

■ The Sunderland Trust

WHERE FUNDING CAN BE GIVEN UK.

WHO CAN BENEFIT Registered charities.

WHAT IS FUNDED General charitable purposes.

FINANCES *Year* 2001–02 *Income* £28,709

TRUSTEES Leslie Marr; Joanne Marr.

HOW TO APPLY As all its funds are totally committed for the foreseeable future the trust does not welcome unsolicited applications.

WHO TO APPLY TO Ward Mitchell Partnership Ltd, Investment Managers, 1 De Montfort Mews, Leicester LE1 7FW *Tel* 0116 247 1010

CC NO 265462   **ESTABLISHED** 1972

■ The Bernard Sunley Charitable Foundation

WHERE FUNDING CAN BE GIVEN Unrestricted, but mainly southern England.

WHO CAN BENEFIT Registered charities benefiting clergy, ex-service and service people, medical professionals, retired people, seafarers and fishermen, volunteers and Christians.

WHAT IS FUNDED General charitable purposes; with grants categorised under: education; culture; professional and public bodies; community; youth; elderly; religion; health; service charities; environment; and overseas.

WHAT IS NOT FUNDED 'We would reiterate that we do not make grants to individuals; we still receive several such applications each week. This bar on individuals applies equally to those people taking part in a project sponsored by a charity such as VSO, Duke of Edinburgh Award Scheme, Trekforce, Scouts and Girl Guides, etc., or in the case of the latter two to specific units of these youth movements.'

TYPE OF GRANT One-off, capital and recurring, for up to a maximum of five years.

RANGE OF GRANTS £100–£220,000; typical grant £5,000–£10,000.

SAMPLE GRANTS £150,000 to Dulwich Picture Gallery third of three instalments towards major renovations and refurbishment; £100,000 each to Pilrims Hospice towards building costs, Thatcher Foundation third grant of three towards the endowment of a chair of enterprise studies at Cambridge University School of Management Studies and Uppingham School first of two instalments to build an all-weather hockey pitch; £82,250 to London Youth for a climbing wall; £77,000 to Brunswick School in Greenwich (USA) second of two instalments towards the new Middle School project; £60,000 to National Gallery second of three instalments to fund a series of exhibitions in the Bernard and Mary Sunley Room; £50,000 each to Archdiocese of Westminster to buy tapes of 'Witness to Hope', based on the biography of Pope John Paul for distribution to local schools and churches and Friends of the Elderly first of two instalments to rebuild the residential home.

FINANCES *Year* 2000–01 *Income* £2,721,000 *Grants* £2,771,000 *Assets* £70,265,000

TRUSTEES John B Sunley; Mrs Joan M Tice; Mrs Bella Sunley; Sir Donald Gosling.

HOW TO APPLY There is no application form, but the covering letter to the Director should give the following details. A description of what the charity does and what its objectives are; an explanation of the need and purpose of the project for which the grant is required. How much will the project cost?; the costings should be itemised and supported with quotations etc. as necessary; the size of grant requested; how much has already been raised and from whom; how is it planned to raise the shortfall? If applicable, how the running costs of the project will be met, once the project is established; any other documentation that the applicant feels will help to support or explain the appeal.

WHO TO APPLY TO Dr Brian Martin, Director, 20 Berkeley Square, London W1J 6LH *Tel* 020 7408 2198 *Fax* 020 7499 5859 *E-mail* asstdirbsunleycharfund@ukgateway.net

CC NO 213362   ESTABLISHED 1960

■ The Surrey Historic Buildings Trust Ltd

WHERE FUNDING CAN BE GIVEN Surrey.

WHO CAN BENEFIT Individuals or groups.

WHAT IS FUNDED Preservation of the historical architectural and constructional heritage existing in Surrey.

WHAT IS NOT FUNDED No support for local authority-owned buildings or the general upkeep of places of worship (although specific artefacts or architectural features may attract a grant).

RANGE OF GRANTS Up to £1,000.

FINANCES *Year* 1999–2000 *Income* £40,000 *Grants* £22,000

TRUSTEES Mrs Cecilia Gerrard; H P Chetwynd-Stapylton; Mrs J Ash; D Morris; R Rothwell; Mrs P Adamson; D J Turner; Mrs Angela Fraser; Michael Gammon; John Griffiths; Cllr Tony Hayes Allen; Cllr T S Stewart; Cllr M Blower; R Phillips; Mrs N Westbury.

HOW TO APPLY On a form available from the correspondent and enclosing two estimates of the cost.

WHO TO APPLY TO Nicola Morris, Room 122, County Hall, Kingston-upon-Thames, Surrey KT1 2DN *Tel* 020 8541 9001/9019

CC NO 279240   ESTABLISHED 1979

■ The Surrey Square Charitable Trust

WHERE FUNDING CAN BE GIVEN UK and overseas.

WHO CAN BENEFIT Registered charities known to the settlor.

WHAT IS FUNDED General charitable purposes.

SAMPLE GRANTS £10,000 each to Bicycle Helmet Initiative Trust and Fitzwilliam Museum; £5,000 each to Extra Care Charitable Trust, Westminster Association for Mental Health and Young Vic Company; £1,500 to City of London School for Girls; and £1,000 each to Future Hope, the Passage, Prostate Cancer Research Centre and Royal Opera House.

FINANCES *Year* 2000–01 *Income* £7,049 *Grants* £41,260 *Assets* £236,646

TRUSTEES Liverpool Council of Social Service (Inc.).

HOW TO APPLY Unsolicited applications will not be considered.

WHO TO APPLY TO Carol Chapman, Liverpool Council of Social Services, 14 Castle Street, Liverpool L2 0NJ *Tel* 0151 236 7728 *Fax* 0151 258 1153

CC NO 1041062   ESTABLISHED 1994

■ The Sussex Historic Churches Trust

WHERE FUNDING CAN BE GIVEN Sussex.

WHO CAN BENEFIT Churches of any denomination over 100 years old and of some architectural or historical significance.

WHAT IS FUNDED Preservation, repair, maintenance and restoration of churches in Sussex.

WHAT IS NOT FUNDED No grants for bells.

TYPE OF GRANT Interest-free loans and buildings will be considered.

RANGE OF GRANTS £1,000–£10,000, typical grant £5,000.

FINANCES *Year* 2001 *Income* £74,193

TRUSTEES Countess De La Ware; Ven. M Brotherton; Ven. W C L Filby; Ven. N Reade; I V Askew; C Loveless.

HOW TO APPLY In writing to the correspondent.

WHO TO APPLY TO Steven Sleight, Hon. Secretary, Diocesan Church House, 211 New Church Road, Hove BN3 4ED *Tel* 01273 421021

CC NO 282159   ESTABLISHED 1981

■ The Adrienne and Leslie Sussman Charitable Trust

WHERE FUNDING CAN BE GIVEN UK, in practice Greater London, particularly Barnet.

WHO CAN BENEFIT Registered charities.

WHAT IS FUNDED General charitable purposes.

WHAT IS NOT FUNDED No grants to branches of UK charities outside Barnet, non-registered charities and individuals.

SAMPLE GRANTS In 1997: £10,425 to Children and Youth Aliyah; £4,000 to Norwood Ravenswood; £3,000 to Sidney Sussex CLL; £2,515 to Child Resettlement; £2,485 to Finchley Synagogue; £2,060 to Jewish Care; £1,500 to Nightingale House; £1,110 to Chai – Lifeline; £1,050 to B'nai B'rith Hillel Fund; £750 to BF Shvut Ami.

FINANCES *Year* 1999 *Income* £55,213 *Grants* £55,883 *Assets* £1,380,715

TRUSTEES A H Sussman; L Sussman; M D Paisner.

HOW TO APPLY In writing to the correspondent.

WHO TO APPLY TO Mrs A H Sussman, 25 Tillingbourne Gardens, London N3 3JJ

CC NO 274955   ESTABLISHED 1977

■ The Sutasoma Trust

WHERE FUNDING CAN BE GIVEN UK and overseas.

WHO CAN BENEFIT Individuals and organisations benefiting students.

WHAT IS FUNDED Assisting students with the cost of one-off projects related to their studies in the fields of the social sciences and humanities; general charitable purposes.

TYPE OF GRANT One-off and recurrent.

SAMPLE GRANTS In 1996–97: £12,500 to Lucy Cavendish College; £7,199 to Bina Antarburdaya (Indonesian Foundation for Inter-Cultural Learning); £5,000 to University College London; £5,000 in two grants to Royal Anthropology Society; £3,000 to Haverford College – USA; £2,000 each to Sideman School – Bali and Universitas Udayana; £1,018 to Spettabile Teatro San Materno; £1,000 to Goldsmith College.

FINANCES *Year* 2000–01 *Income* £97,927

TRUSTEES M K Hobart; Dr A R Hobart; M A Burgauer; J M Lichtenstein.

OTHER INFORMATION The trust incorporates the Sutasoma Small Projects Award Fund, which gives small single payments to full-time students for one-off projects related to their studies.

HOW TO APPLY In writing to the correspondent.

WHO TO APPLY TO Miss Lynn Wicks, Trust Administrator, Eversheds, Daedalus House, Station Road, Cambridge CB1 2RE *Tel* 01223 355933

CC NO 803301   **ESTABLISHED** 1990

....

■ Sutton Coldfield Municipal Charities

WHERE FUNDING CAN BE GIVEN The former borough of Sutton Coldfield, comprising three electoral wards: New Hall, Vesey and Four Oaks.

WHO CAN BENEFIT Individuals in need and organisations, without restriction, in Sutton Coldfield.

WHAT IS FUNDED The aims are: to help people who are aged, sick, have disabilities or living in poverty; to support facilities for recreational and leisure activities; to promote the arts and advance religion; the repair of historic buildings; and advancement of education through grants to schools for maintenance and equipment.

WHAT IS NOT FUNDED No awards are given to individuals or organisations outside the area of benefit, unless the organisations are providing essential services in the area.

TYPE OF GRANT The trustees will consider making grants for buildings, projects, research, start-up costs, and capital and running costs for up to three years or as one-off payments. No cash payments are made; payments are made via invoices or vouchers.

RANGE OF GRANTS £150–£220,000.

SAMPLE GRANTS £100,000 to Wylde Green United Reformed Church for repairs to church building, organ and church hall; £60,496 to Sutton Arts Theatre for improvements and upgrading of auditorium and stage; £50,000 to All Saints Church Centre for re-roofing and disabled facilities; £36,354 to The Friendship Club for set-up expenses of a holiday home; £31,410 to St Peter's Church for restoration work and legal costs at The Stone House; £30,000 each to Birmingham Specialist NHS Trust for refurbishment of the kitchen and dining room at The Cottage Hospital, and Penns Lane Tennis Club for four floodlit tennis courts; £26,496 to Acorns Children's Hospice Trust for home support for families; £25,000 to St Giles Hospice for an enlarged day care unit; £20,000 to S R S Urchin Sea Rangers for renovation and refurbishment of headquarters.

FINANCES *Year* 2000–01 *Income* £1,306,428 *Grants* £743,525 *Assets* £27,434,126

TRUSTEES Jean Millington; Rodney Kettel; John Gray; Cllr. David Roy; John Slater; Alfred David Owen; Dr Nigel Cooper, Chair; Cllr. J Whorwood; Sue Bailey; Cllr Susanna McCorry; Mr John Jordan; Rev J Langstaff; Mrs J Rothwell; Mr D Grove.

OTHER INFORMATION As well as providing grants, the charities maintains 46 almshouses and provides school clothing grants to individuals.

HOW TO APPLY In writing to the correspondent. The following applies to applications from groups and organisations. There are no forms, so applicants may provide information in a format which is most convenient for them but must include: a brief description of the organisation, its objects and its history; the number of members/users, their age range and any membership fees paid; a full account of the purpose of the project for which a grant is requested; accurate costs, showing reasonable estimates from a range of sources where appropriate and including VAT if payable – no additional sums will be granted if estimates prove to be inaccurate; other sources of funding – these must be shown; sixteen copies of the latest audited accounts or, for very small organisations, copies of bank statements. Notes of explanation may be included; for example, if accounts show a balance set aside for a particular project applicants may wish to point this out. Receipt of applications is not normally acknowledged unless a stamped addressed envelope is sent with the application. Applications may be submitted at any time. The grants committee meets eight or nine times a year. Requests for grants over £20,000 must be approved by the board of trustees, who meet four times a year.

At all stages, staff at the charities will give assistance to those making applications. For example, projects and applications can be discussed, either at the charity's office or on site. Advice about deadlines for submitting applications can also be given. (There are application forms for individuals, who must obtain them from the charity.)

WHO TO APPLY TO Andrew MacFarlane, Clerk to the trustees, Lingard House, Fox Hollies Road, Sutton Coldfield, West Midlands B76 2RJ *Tel* 0121 351 2262 *Fax* 0121 313 0615

CC NO 218627   **ESTABLISHED** 1898

....

■ The Sutton Trust

WHERE FUNDING CAN BE GIVEN UK only.

WHO CAN BENEFIT Educational institutions, and other groups that organise formal education projects or undertake educational research.

WHAT IS FUNDED Educational opportunities for children and young people from non-privileged backgrounds, with a particular emphasis on recognising the needs and raising the aspirations of the academically able. In particular projects in the following specific areas: access to university for under-represented groups; the development of able children, including independent/state school partnerships; enriching early learning for the under-three age group, including the involvement of parents in stimulating their children's early development; research and analysis surrounding these issues.

WHAT IS NOT FUNDED Individuals; scholarships; assisted places replacement schemes or independent school fees; sports and arts projects; capital projects; general appeals.

TYPE OF GRANT Core costs, feasibility studies, interest-free loans, one-off, project, research, recurring costs, running costs, salaries and start-up costs. Funding is available for up to three years. Capital and equipment grants are not considered.

RANGE OF GRANTS Average grant not yet established.

SAMPLE GRANTS £159,864 to Belveder School – Liverpool; £111,500 to University of Oxford Summer School; £85,000 to Technology Colleges Trust; £56,000 to University of Oxford Teacher INSET; £41,000 to Teacher Survey for a survey of teachers and their understanding of higher education; £35,325 to London School of Economics Saturday School; £35,180 to University of Bristol Summer School; £35,000 to Pathways to the Professions for an access programme at University of Edinburgh to encourage applications to law and medicine courses; £34,657 to University of Nottingham

Summer School; £30,635 to University of Cambridge Summer School.

FINANCES *Year* 2001 *Income* £1,330,384 *Grants* £1,006,000 *Assets* £611,462

TRUSTEES Peter Lampl; Karen Lampl; Glyn Morris.

HOW TO APPLY Before making a formal application, applicants are advised to write in with a brief outline of a project or to make an exploratory call to discuss their project. Applications must be no more than two pages and should include the following: Background – What sort of organisation you are and your legal status; your general aims and objectives; if you are part of a larger organisation, the same information for them. Project – An outline of the proposed project, including: specific aims and objectives; how the project is to be organised and by whom; where the project will take place; any anticipated problems in set up and operation of the project; when will it start and how long will it take; whom is it intended to benefit and how many; the names and addresses of two independent referees. Finance – How much money you will need; a budget breaking down what this will be spent on (e.g. salaries, rent, administration); state clearly how much are you asking the Sutton Trust for and when; your most recent annual report and accounts; which other funders have you approached and with what success; if you will need funding beyond the period of the grant, where is it to come from. Evaluation – What are the specific, measurable objectives and how will these be evaluated? ; How will you publicise the outcome of the project to other interested parties? To avoid applicants wasting their time, they are encouraged to understand that unsolicited applications are not generally considered.

WHO TO APPLY TO The Administrator, Heritage House, 21 Inner Park Road, London SW19 6ED *Tel* 020 8788 3223 *Website* www.suttontrust.com

CC NO 1067197   **ESTABLISHED** 1998

■ Swan Mountain Trust

WHERE FUNDING CAN BE GIVEN UK.

WHO CAN BENEFIT Organisations benefiting mental health patients and prisoners, ex-offenders and potential offenders.

WHAT IS NOT FUNDED No grants for annual holidays, debt replayment and large appeals.

TYPE OF GRANT One-off.

RANGE OF GRANTS Up to £1,000.

SAMPLE GRANTS £1,200 to Queens Cross Housing Association; £1,000 each to Care Dai Trust, Overstream Support Fund, Prisoners Advice Service, Rhoserchan Project and Verne Prison.

FINANCES *Year* 1999–2000 *Income* £28,000 *Grants* £26,000 *Assets* £386,000

TRUSTEES Dodie Carter; Jan Hargreaves; Peter Kilgarriff; Calton Younger.

HOW TO APPLY In writing to the correspondent, enclosing an up-to-date report on your fundraising, and a copy of your most recent annual report and accounts (or any financial information you have). The trustees meet in early February, June and October each year, but can occasionally reach decisions quickly in an emergency. Applications should be made at least four weeks before the trustees' next meeting. Applicants are welcome to telephone or fax the correspondent (below) to discuss a possible approach to the trust – be prepared to leave her a message to ring you back. The trust tries to be as responsive as it can be to appropriate applicants.

WHO TO APPLY TO Mrs J Hargreaves, Trustee, 7 Mount Vernon, London NW3 6QS *Tel* 020 7794 2486 *Fax* 020 7794 2486

CC NO 275594   **ESTABLISHED** 1977

■ The Swan Trust

WHERE FUNDING CAN BE GIVEN Overseas and the UK, with a preference for East Sussex, Kent, Surrey and West Sussex.

WHO CAN BENEFIT Registered charities.

WHAT IS FUNDED General charitable purposes, including: arts, culture and recreation; various community facilities; day centres; hospices and hospice at home; cancer research; conservation; and church buildings.

WHAT IS NOT FUNDED No grants to individuals or non-registered charities.

TYPE OF GRANT One-off capital grants; funding for up to two years are considered.

RANGE OF GRANTS £20–£60,000.

SAMPLE GRANTS £60,000 to Magdelen College Development Trust; £20,000 to Save the Children Fund; £5,000 each to British Museum Development Trust and Yehudi Menuhin School Ltd; £2,000 each to National Portrait Gallery and Sussex Heritage Trust Ltd; £1,500 each to Friends of Covent Garden and Royal Academy Trust; £1,200 to Lake District Art & Museum Trust; £1,000 each to Broomhill Trust, Lewes Millennium Gallery Trust, Royal National Theatre, Sussex Housing & Care, Victoria and Albert Museum and Withyham Parochial Church Council.

FINANCES *Year* 2001–02 *Income* £73,329 *Grants* £121,545 *Assets* £916,657

TRUSTEES The Cowdray Trust Limited.

OTHER INFORMATION Applications for grants will only be acknowledged if a donation is to be sent.

HOW TO APPLY In writing to the correspondent. Acknowledgements will only be sent if a grant is being made.

WHO TO APPLY TO A J Winborn, Pollen House, 10/12 Cork Street, London W1S 3LW *Tel* 020 7439 9061

CC NO 261442   **ESTABLISHED** 1970

■ The Swann-Morton Foundation

WHERE FUNDING CAN BE GIVEN South Yorkshire.

WHO CAN BENEFIT Individuals and organisations benefiting children, young adults, medical professionals, nurses and doctors, students; disabled people; and people who are disadvantaged by poverty.

WHAT IS FUNDED The advancement of education and the relief of poverty and suffering. Particularly the arts, culture and recreation; health; conservation and environment; and various community services.

RANGE OF GRANTS £50–£5,000. Average £750.

FINANCES *Year* 1999–2000 *Income* £61,000 *Grants* £61,000

TRUSTEES R Fell; J J McGinley; P B A Renshaw.

HOW TO APPLY In writing to the correspondent.

WHO TO APPLY TO R Fell, Trustee, Owlerton Green, Sheffield S6 2BJ *Tel* 0114 234 4231 *Fax* 0114 231 4966

CC NO 271925   **ESTABLISHED** 1976

■ The Walter Swindon Charitable Trust

WHERE FUNDING CAN BE GIVEN UK.

WHO CAN BENEFIT Registered charities benefiting people of all ages but with priority for children, including those in care, or who are fostered or adopted. Medical professionals, unemployed people, followers of most religions, people disadvantaged by poverty, immigrants, refugees, victims of domestic violence, victims of war, and people who are sick, are also prioritised.

WHAT IS FUNDED General charitable purposes. The trust makes contributions to charities and worthy causes.

WHAT IS NOT FUNDED No grants to individuals.

SAMPLE GRANTS In 1997: £4,000 to Child Health Research Appeal Trust; £3,000 to Alyn Hospital; £300 to Joint Jewish Charitable Trust; £250 each to Marie Curie Cancer Care and Norwood Ravenswood; £100 each to Fight for Life, Multiple Sclerosis Society, SCOPE, and Unicef.

FINANCES *Year* 2000–01 *Income* £25,000

TRUSTEES Mrs S R Swindon; Ruth Swindon.

HOW TO APPLY In writing to the correspondent.

WHO TO APPLY TO Apartment 93, Westfield, 15 Kidderpore Avenue, London NW3 7SG

CC NO 273105   **ESTABLISHED** 1977

■ The Swire Charitable Trust

WHERE FUNDING CAN BE GIVEN Worldwide.

WHO CAN BENEFIT Regional and UK organisations.

WHAT IS FUNDED Children, the arts and heritage, medical research, welfare, the environment and general charitable purposes.

SAMPLE GRANTS £60,000 to Neak and Neck Cancer Research Trust; £17,500 to Air League Educational Trust; £12,699 to GAPAN; £10,000 to University of Southampton – East Asia Centre; £7,500 to USO; £3,990 to Mission to Seafarers; £3,500 to London School of Hygiene and Tropical Medicine; £2,500 each to Book Aid International and CWGC; £1,500 each to KIDS and Maritime Volunteer Service.

FINANCES *Year* 2001 *Income* £228,520 *Grants* £270,822 *Assets* £191,527

TRUSTEES Sir J Swire; Sir Adrian Swire; B N Swire; M J B Todhunter; E J R Scott.

HOW TO APPLY In writing to the correspondent. Applications are considered throughout the year.

WHO TO APPLY TO B N Swire, Trustee, John Swire & Sons Ltd, Swire House, 59 Buckingham Gate, London SW1E 6AJ *Tel* 020 7834 7717

CC NO 270726   **ESTABLISHED** 1976

■ The John Swire (1989) Charitable Trust

WHERE FUNDING CAN BE GIVEN UK.

WHAT IS FUNDED General charitable purposes.

RANGE OF GRANTS £1,000–£25,000.

SAMPLE GRANTS £25,000 each to Caldecott Foundation, Demelza House Children's Hospice and Kent County Council for Selling C of E Primary School; £12,500 to Durrell Institute for Conservation and Ecology; £10,000 to Canterbury Open Centre; £6,000 to Toynbee Hall; £5,000 each to Canterbury Festival and Helen House; £2,500 each to Leigh School PTA and Royal Caledonian Ball Trust; £1,500 each to Ataxia-Telangiectasia Society and Orchid Cancer Society; £1,250 each to Selling Church Building Trust and Selling PCC.

FINANCES *Year* 2001 *Income* £303,930 *Grants* £225,310 *Assets* £7,435,367

TRUSTEES Sir John Swire; J S Swire; B N Swire; M C Robinson; Lady Swire.

HOW TO APPLY In writing to the correspondent.

WHO TO APPLY TO B N Swire, Trustee, John Swire & Sons Ltd, Swire House, 59 Buckingham Gate, London SW1E 6AJ *Tel* 020 7834 7717

CC NO 802142   **ESTABLISHED** 1989

■ The Charles and Elsie Sykes Trust

WHERE FUNDING CAN BE GIVEN UK and overseas. The trust stated that a preference is given towards applications 'from the northern part of the United Kingdom and in particular from Yorkshire'.

WHO CAN BENEFIT Registered charities only, benefiting people of all ages, especially people who are mentally ill and people with sensory impairments. There is a preference for service and ex-service people.

WHAT IS FUNDED Animals and birds; people who are blind or partially sighted; children and youth; cultural and environmental heritage; people who are deaf, hard of hearing or speech impaired; people who are disabled; education; hospices and hospitals; medical research; medical welfare; mental health and mental disability; welfare of older people; overseas aid; services and ex-services; social and moral welfare; trades and professions; and sundry.

WHAT IS NOT FUNDED The following applicants are unlikely to be successful: individuals; local organisations not in the north of England; and recently-established charities. Non-registered charities are not considered.

TYPE OF GRANT Usually one-off for a specific project or part of a project. The same regular grants are given.

RANGE OF GRANTS £500–£50,000

FINANCES *Year* 2001 *Income* £459,000 *Grants* £365,000 *Assets* £9,700,000

TRUSTEES John Ward, Chair; Mrs Anne E Brownlie; Martin P Coultas; Mrs G Mary Dance; John Horrocks; R Barry Kay; Dr Michael D Moore; Michael G H Garnett; Dr Michael W McEvoy.

HOW TO APPLY Applications from registered charities may be made with full details and an sae to the above address. Applications without up-to-date audited or examined accounts will not be considered. The trust regrets that it cannot conduct correspondence with applicants.

WHO TO APPLY TO David J Reah, Secretary, 6 North Park Road, Harrogate, Yorkshire HG1 5PA

CC NO 206926   **ESTABLISHED** 1954

■ The Hugh & Ruby Sykes Charitable Trust

WHERE FUNDING CAN BE GIVEN Principally South Yorkshire, also Derbyshire.

WHO CAN BENEFIT Registered charities.

WHAT IS FUNDED Principally local charities but some major UK charities are supported. The trust has major commitments with several medical charities. It is the policy of the trust to distribute income and preserve capital.

WHAT IS NOT FUNDED No grants are made to individuals. Most grants are made to organisations which have a connection to one of the trustees.

FINANCES *Year* 2000–01 *Income* £162,862 *Grants* £143,550 *Assets* £2,286,734

TRUSTEES Sir Hugh Sykes; Lady Sykes.

HOW TO APPLY Applications can only be accepted from registered charities and should be in writing to the correspondent. In order to save administration costs, replies are not sent to unsuccessful applicants. If the trustees are able to consider a request for support, they aim to express interest within one month.

WHO TO APPLY TO Sir Hugh Sykes, Trustee, Bamford Hall Holdings Ltd, Bamford Hall, The Hollow, Bamford, Hope Valley S33 0AU *Tel* 01433 651190

CC NO 327648   **ESTABLISHED** 1987

■ The Sylvanus Charitable Trust

WHERE FUNDING CAN BE GIVEN Europe and North America.

WHO CAN BENEFIT Organisations benefiting Roman Catholics and animals.

WHAT IS FUNDED The traditional Catholic church and animal welfare, including wildlife sanctuaries.

WHAT IS NOT FUNDED No grants for expeditions, scholarships or individuals.

TYPE OF GRANT One-off and recurring.

RANGE OF GRANTS £1,000–£30,000.

SAMPLE GRANTS In the sterling section: £30,000 to Fraternity of Saint Pius X – Switzerland; £15,000 to Mauritian Wildlife Trust; £7,500 to University College Oxford; £6,000 each to Frame, Oeuvre d'Assistance aux Betes d'Abattoirs, and World Society for the Protection of Animals; £4,000 each to Environmental Investigation Agency, and RSPCA; £3,000 each to Help in Suffering and Lynx Educational Trust.

FINANCES *Year* 2000 *Income* £65,273 *Grants* £90,000 *Assets* £2,151,803

TRUSTEES John C Vernor Miles; Alexander D Gemmill; Wilfred E Vernor Miles; Gloria Taviner

OTHER INFORMATION This trust has a sterling section for European grants and a dollar section for USA grants. The financial information in this entry relates to the Sterling section. In the dollar section, the assets were US$855,088, the income £52,500, the grants total US$1110,000 and the largest grants US$25,000 each to Montery Institute of International Studies and SPCA Horse Power Project.

HOW TO APPLY In writing to the correspondent. The trustees meet once a year.

WHO TO APPLY TO John C Vernor Miles, Trustee, Vernor Miles & Noble, 5 Raymond Buildings, Gray's Inn, London WC1R 5DD *Tel* 020 7242 8688

CC NO 259520   **ESTABLISHED** 1968

■ The Stella Symons Charitable Trust

WHERE FUNDING CAN BE GIVEN UK and overseas with reserved funds for Shipston on Stour.

WHO CAN BENEFIT Registered charities.

WHAT IS FUNDED Residential facilities and services; infrastructure, support and development; the advancement of religion; arts, culture and recreation; health; conservation and environment; education and training; and social care and development will be considered.

WHAT IS NOT FUNDED The trustees do not normally favour projects which substitute the statutory obligations of the state or projects which in their opinion should be commercially viable operations per se. No grants to individuals or politically biased organisations.

TYPE OF GRANT Outright gifts and larger sums on loan on beneficial terms. Buildings, capital, core costs, one-off, project, research, recurring and running costs, salaries, and start-up costs. Funding for up to and over three years will be considered.

RANGE OF GRANTS £10–£5,000, average grant £200.

SAMPLE GRANTS In 1997–98: £10,000 to Shakespeare Hospice; £200 each to Shipston Home Carers, Riverpoint, FARM Africa, BLISS, Hackney Quest, York Minister Fund, Sussex Association for Spina Bifida, Weston Spirit and VSO.

FINANCES *Year* 2000–01 *Income* £40,000 *Grants* £42,450 *Assets* £954,955

TRUSTEES Mrs M E Mitchell; J S S Bosley; Mrs K A Willis.

HOW TO APPLY In writing to the correspondent.

WHO TO APPLY TO J S S Bosley, Trustee, 20 Mill Street, Shipston on Stour, Warwickshire CV36 4AW

CC NO 259638   **ESTABLISHED** 1968

■ The Tabeel Trust

WHERE FUNDING CAN BE GIVEN Worldwide.
WHO CAN BENEFIT Evangelical Christian organisations.
WHAT IS FUNDED Christian charitable purposes, where the trustees have an existing interest.
SAMPLE GRANTS £9,000 to NEGST; £4,500 to Brentwood Schools' Christian Worker Trust; £3,625 to TWK; £3,500 each to Association of Christian Teachers and Interserve; £3,000 to Countess of Huntingdon Connection; £2,000 each to Bible Society, IFES, MAF and SFI.
FINANCES *Year* 2000–01 *Income* £30,762 *Grants* £55,125 *Assets* £1,005,290
TRUSTEES K A Brown, Chair; D K Brown; Mrs P M Brown; Mrs B J Carter; Dr M P Clark; Mrs J A Richardson; N T Davey; Mrs H M Corteen.
HOW TO APPLY In writing to 'the trustee who has an interest in the project', i.e. only charities with which a trustee already has contact should apply. Grants are considered at trustees' meetings in May and November.
WHO TO APPLY TO D K Brown, Secretary, Dairy House Farm, Great Holland, Frinton-on-Sea, Essex CO13 0EX *Tel* 01255 812130
CC NO 266645   **ESTABLISHED** 1974

■ The Tajtelbaum Charitable Trust

WHERE FUNDING CAN BE GIVEN Generally UK and Israel.
WHO CAN BENEFIT Jewish organisations benefiting children, young adults and students will be considered. Support may be given to older and sick people.
WHAT IS FUNDED Orthodox synagogues and education establishments generally in the UK and Israel; and hospitals and homes for older people generally in the UK and Israel.
RANGE OF GRANTS £1,000–£112,000.
FINANCES *Year* 2000–01 *Income* £398,985 *Grants* £312,590
TRUSTEES Mrs I Tajtelbaum; I Tajtelbaum; M Tajtelbaum; E Tajtelbaum; E Jaswon; H Frydenson.
HOW TO APPLY In writing to the correspondent.
WHO TO APPLY TO Mrs I Tajtelbaum, Trustee, 17 Western Avenue, London NW11 9EH
CC NO 273184   **ESTABLISHED** 1974

■ The Talbot Trusts

WHERE FUNDING CAN BE GIVEN Sheffield and immediate surrounding areas.
WHO CAN BENEFIT Organisations directly benefiting people who are sick, convalescent, disabled or infirm.
WHAT IS FUNDED Items, services or facilities which are calculated to relieve suffering or assist recovery.
WHAT IS NOT FUNDED No grants are given towards the direct relief of rates, taxes or other public funds and no commitment can be made to repeat or renew grants. Grants are not normally given to: non-registered charities or other organisations; individuals; appeal requests, research or educational costs; or to finance fundraising initiatives.
TYPE OF GRANT One-off, capital, core costs, running costs, salaries and start-up costs. Funding may be given for up to one year.
SAMPLE GRANTS £28,250 to hospital social workers for travelling expenses, meals and equipment; £5,500 to Sheffield Family Service Unit for operational costs; £5,000 to Alzheimer's Disease Society; £4,059 to Rockingham Drug Project for GP sessions; £3,500 each to Multiple Sclerosis Therapy Centre, North Sheffield Federation for the Disabled, and Trinity Day Centre; £3,080 to Winged Fellowship Trust; £3,000 each to Age Concern, St Luke's Hospice, and Whizz-Kidz.
FINANCES *Year* 2001–02 *Income* £105,413 *Grants* £102,517 *Assets* £1,918,000
TRUSTEES Dr B P Jackson, Chair; Dr L C Kershaw; Mrs K E Riddle; J Brassington; G J Smallman.
HOW TO APPLY On a form available from the correspondent, for consideration in July and December.
WHO TO APPLY TO Ron Jones, Clerk, c/o Community Health Sheffield Finance, Fulwood House, 5 Old Fulwood Road, Sheffield S10 3TG *Tel* 0114 271 1138
CC NO 221356   **ESTABLISHED** 1928

■ The Talbot Village Trust

WHERE FUNDING CAN BE GIVEN The boroughs of Bournemouth, Christchurch and Poole; the districts of east Dorset and Purbeck.
WHO CAN BENEFIT Community organisations (i.e. schools, churches, youth clubs, playgroups and so on).
WHAT IS FUNDED Youth, older people and church-related charities.
WHAT IS NOT FUNDED No grants for individuals.
RANGE OF GRANTS Usually £20,000–£50,000.
SAMPLE GRANTS £50,000 for a new village hall in Lytchett Minster; £40,000 to Streetscene to refurbish rehabilitation units; £35,000 each to Bearwood Young People's Centre, Hyped for a health clinic suite and Youth Cancer Trust; £30,000 each to Kinson Methodist Church and St Aldhelm's C of E School; £28,000 each to Salvation Army and St Philip's Church; £16,000 to Bournemouth Town Centre Parish.
FINANCES *Year* 2001 *Income* £1,100,000 *Grants* £356,000 *Assets* £28,000,000
TRUSTEES Sir Thomas Lees, Chair; Henry Plunkett-Ernle-Erle-Drax; Sir George Meyrick; Sir Thomas Salt; James Fleming; Christopher Lees.
HOW TO APPLY In writing to the correspondent.
WHO TO APPLY TO G Cox, Clerk, Dickinson Manser, 5 Parkstone Road, Poole, Dorset BH15 2NL *Tel* 01202 673071
CC NO 249349   **ESTABLISHED** 1867

■ Tallow Chandlers Benevolent Fund

WHERE FUNDING CAN BE GIVEN City of London and adjacent boroughs.
WHAT IS FUNDED Charities based in City of London and adjacent boroughs. Its main areas of interest include hospices, youth clubs, medical research and education.
FINANCES *Year* 2000–01 *Income* £277,000 *Grants* £147,000 *Assets* £2,600,000
TRUSTEES D Kirby Johnson; Lt Col P W S Boult; Sir Antony Driver; R A V Nicolle.

OTHER INFORMATION In 2000–01 a further £19,000 went on awards and £3,600 to individuals connected with the company and trade.
HOW TO APPLY The allocation of grants is determined by the committee.
WHO TO APPLY TO J H G Loch, Tallow Chandlers Hall, 4 Dowgate Hill, London EC4R 2SH *Tel* 020 7248 4726 *Fax* 020 7236 0844 *E-mail* clerk@tallowchandlers.org *Website* www.tallowchandlers.org
CC NO 246255 **ESTABLISHED** 1966

■ Talteg Ltd

WHERE FUNDING CAN BE GIVEN UK, with a preference for Scotland.
WHO CAN BENEFIT Registered charities benefiting Jewish people, children, young adults and people disadvantaged by poverty.
WHAT IS FUNDED To support the advancement of religion, especially Jewish, and the relief of poverty. Educational and other charitable purposes are also supported.
FINANCES *Year* 1999 *Income* £262,000 *Grants* £109,000 *Assets* £2,400,000
TRUSTEES F S Berkeley; M Berkeley; A Berkeley; A N Berkeley; M Berkeley; Miss D L Berkeley.
HOW TO APPLY In writing to the correspondent.
WHO TO APPLY TO F S Berkeley, Trustee, 90 Mitchell Street, Glasgow G1 3NA *Tel* 0141 221 3353
CC NO 283253 **ESTABLISHED** 1981

■ The Tangent Charitable Trust

WHERE FUNDING CAN BE GIVEN UK.
WHO CAN BENEFIT Registered charities and voluntary organisations.
WHAT IS FUNDED General charitable purposes.
SAMPLE GRANTS £5,000 to Jewish Policy Research; £2,100 to Eastern Grey Parochial Church Council; £2,000 each to Joint Jewish Charitable Trust, Israel Diaspora Trust, The National Gallery Trust and Badminton Dressage; £1,000 each to Teenage Cancer Trust, North West London Jewish Day School and Reform Foundation Trust.
FINANCES *Year* 1999–2000 *Income* £31,000 *Grants* £25,000 *Assets* £644,000
TRUSTEES M P Green; Mrs T M Green; R S Wolfson Green; C V Wolfson Green.
HOW TO APPLY In writing to the correspondent.
WHO TO APPLY TO Beverley Matthews, 25 Knightsbridge, London SW1X 7RZ *Tel* 020 7663 6363
CC NO 289729 **ESTABLISHED** 1984

■ The David Tannen Charitable Trust

WHERE FUNDING CAN BE GIVEN UK.
WHO CAN BENEFIT Jewish organisations.
WHAT IS FUNDED Advancement of the Jewish religion.
RANGE OF GRANTS £250–£15,000.
SAMPLE GRANTS £25,000 each to Huntington Foundation Limited and Northwest London Communal Mikveh; £20,000 to SOFT; £10,000 to Finchley Road Synagogue; £5,000 to Adath Yisroel Synagogue; £900 to Beth Hamedesh Hendon; £600 to Woodstock Sinclair Trust; £500 to Sparkle Children Charity.
FINANCES *Year* 1999–2000 *Income* £1,300,000 *Grants* £87,000 *Assets* £2,400,000
TRUSTEES J M Miller; S Jacobowitz.
HOW TO APPLY In writing to the correspondent.

WHO TO APPLY TO J M Miller, Trustee, Sutherland House, 70–78 West Hendon Broadway, London NW9 7BT *Tel* 020 8202 1066
CC NO 280392 **ESTABLISHED** 1974

■ The Tanner Trust

WHERE FUNDING CAN BE GIVEN UK and overseas.
WHO CAN BENEFIT Foundations, schools, societies, charities and projects.
WHAT IS FUNDED General charitable purposes.
WHAT IS NOT FUNDED No grants to individuals.
RANGE OF GRANTS £300–£5,000; exceptionally higher.
SAMPLE GRANTS £7,000 to Royal Agricultural Benevolent Fund; £6,500 to Kings College Body and Soul; £5,000 each to British Retinitis Pigmentosa Society, DEC India Earthquake Appeal, Voices Foundation, and Y Care International; £3,000 each to Miriam Dean Fund, Probus Gardens, Royal Scottish Agricultural Benevolent Fund, and Sunrise Appeal.
FINANCES *Year* 2000–01 *Income* £218,468 *Grants* £203,159 *Assets* £4,935,565
TRUSTEES Lucie Nottingham; Alice Williams; Peter Youatt.
HOW TO APPLY The trust states that unsolicited applications are, without exception, not considered. Support is only given to charities personally known to the trustees.
WHO TO APPLY TO Mrs L Whitcomb, Trust Administrator, PO Box 4207, Worthing, West Sussex BN11 1PW *Tel* 01903 709229 *Fax* 01903 709229
CC NO 1021175 **ESTABLISHED** 1993

■ The Lili Tapper Charitable Foundation

WHERE FUNDING CAN BE GIVEN UK.
WHO CAN BENEFIT Organisations benefiting Jewish people.
WHAT IS FUNDED Preference to charitable purposes or institutions which are for the benefit of Jewish people.
WHAT IS NOT FUNDED No grants to individuals.
SAMPLE GRANTS £5,000 each to JABE and Sargent Cancer Care for Children; £2,500 to JAMI, Jennifer Trust, Manchester Jewish Federation, British ORT, Weizmann Institute, and World Jewish Relief; £2,000 each to IDT and Manchester Jewish Soup Kitchen.
FINANCES *Year* 1998–99 *Income* £34,710 *Grants* £32,535 *Assets* £481,788
TRUSTEES Mrs L Tapper; M Webber; J Webber.
HOW TO APPLY The trust states that it does not respond to any unsolicited applications.
WHO TO APPLY TO Robert Luty, KPMG Tax, St James' Square, Manchester M2 6DS *Tel* 0161 246 4608
CC NO 268523 **ESTABLISHED** 1974

■ The Mrs A Lacy Tate Trust

WHERE FUNDING CAN BE GIVEN East Sussex.
WHO CAN BENEFIT Individuals and organisations benefiting at risk groups and people who are disabled, disadvantaged by poverty or socially isolated.
WHAT IS FUNDED Welfare, disability and medical charities.
TYPE OF GRANT Often recurrent.
RANGE OF GRANTS £250–£5,000.

SAMPLE GRANTS 1998–99: £5,000 to Herstmonceux Village Hall; £2,000 each to Fellowship of St Nicholas, Hazel Court School, Queen Alexandra Cottage Homes, Surviving Christmas and Sussex Autistic Community Trust; £1,500 to East Sussex Care for the Carers; £1,000 each to Eastbourne & District Police Court Mission, Hailsham Open Door and Talking Newspaper Association of the UK.

FINANCES *Year* 2001–02 *Income* £35,870

TRUSTEES I M Stewart; Ms J Roberts; Ms L A Macy; Ms L A Burgess.

HOW TO APPLY In writing to the correspondent.

WHO TO APPLY TO I Stewart, Trustee, Heringtons Solicitors, 39 Gildredge Road, Eastbourne, East Sussex BN21 4RY *Tel* 01323 411020

CC NO 803596   ESTABLISHED 1990

■ The Tay Charitable Trust

WHERE FUNDING CAN BE GIVEN UK, with a preference for Scotland, particularly Dundee.

WHO CAN BENEFIT Registered charities benefiting people of any age and Christians. A wide range of professional and economic groups are considered.

WHAT IS FUNDED General charitable purposes in the fields of: residential facilities; infrastructure support and development; Christian religion; arts, culture and recreation; health; conservation and environment; education and training; and community facilities and services.

WHAT IS NOT FUNDED Grants are only given to charities recognised by the Inland Revenue. No grants to individuals.

TYPE OF GRANT One-off and recurring.

RANGE OF GRANTS £250–£10,000, mostly £1,000 or less.

SAMPLE GRANTS £10,500 to University of Dundee; £10,000 to Maritime Volunteer; £5,500 to RNLI; £5,300 to Dundee Heritage Trust; £5,000 each to Bliss, Gather in the Isles, and Link; £3,000 each to Imperial Cancer Research Trust and Mansfield Traquair Trust; £2,000 to Scottish Seabirds.

FINANCES *Year* 2001–02 *Income* £198,949 *Grants* £188,650 *Assets* £4,605,536

TRUSTEES Mrs E A Mussen; Mrs Z C Martin; G C Bonar.

HOW TO APPLY No standard form; applications in writing to the correspondent, including a financial statement. An sae is appreciated.

WHO TO APPLY TO Mrs Elizabeth A Mussen, Trustee, 6 Douglas Terrace, Broughty Ferry, Dundee DD5 1EA

SC NO SC001004   ESTABLISHED 1951

■ A P Taylor Fund

WHERE FUNDING CAN BE GIVEN Ancient parishes of Hayes and Harlington.

WHO CAN BENEFIT The inhabitants of the parishes of Hayes and Harlington (as they existed on 9 January 1953) without distinction of political, religious or other opinion.

WHAT IS FUNDED Support is given to organisations providing recreational and leisure activities for people living in the ancient parishes of Hayes and Harlington.

SAMPLE GRANTS Previous beneficiaries include Charville Riding Club, Hayes and District Metal Detecting Club, Manor Clubs, Brookside Community Association, Botwell Tenants and Residents Association, Langwood Social Club, Claretian Missionaries, Harlington Hospice

Association, Hayes and Harlington Polio Fellowship and Social Action for MS.

FINANCES *Year* 2000–01 *Income* £47,207

TRUSTEES A J Tyrrell, Chair; T McCarthy; M J Fitzpatrick; A Woodhouse; W C Palmer.

HOW TO APPLY In writing to the correspondent.

WHO TO APPLY TO Tim McCarthy, Secretary, 14 Berwick Avenue, Hayes, Middlesex UB4 0NF *Tel* 020 8573 2598

CC NO 260741   ESTABLISHED 1969

■ The A R Taylor Charitable Trust

WHERE FUNDING CAN BE GIVEN UK, but with some emphasis on Hampshire.

WHO CAN BENEFIT Registered charities or similar bodies benefiting children, young adults and students.

WHAT IS FUNDED Preference is given to charities which the trustees have special interest in, knowledge of or association with, particularly service charities and educational organisations. Funds are fully committed or allocated.

WHAT IS NOT FUNDED No grants to individuals.

TYPE OF GRANT Both one-off and recurrent grants. There is no formal limit to the length of time for recurrent grants.

RANGE OF GRANTS £50–£7,000.

SAMPLE GRANTS £7,000 to Ex-services Mental Welfare Society; £4,000 to Winchester College; £2,500 to Regimental HQ 1st Grenadier Regimental Foot Guards Charity; £1,250 to RUKBA; £1,000 each to Bighton Church, Hampshire, Rainbow House, and Kosovo Crisis Appeal; £750 each to British Kidney Association and Brendon Care Foundation; £500 to Army Benevolent Fund.

FINANCES *Year* 2000 *Income* £20,881 *Grants* £25,950 *Assets* £653,834

TRUSTEES A R Taylor; Mrs E J Taylor.

HOW TO APPLY Applications may be made at any time but will only be considered periodically. The trust does not use an application form. Unsuccessful applications will generally not be acknowledged.

WHO TO APPLY TO J Bristol, c/o Birketts, Solicitors, 24–26 Museum Street, Ipswich IP1 1HZ *Tel* 01473 232300

CC NO 275560   ESTABLISHED 1978

■ C B & H H Taylor 1984 Trust

WHERE FUNDING CAN BE GIVEN West Midlands, Ireland and overseas.

WHO CAN BENEFIT Organisations benefiting Christians, ethnic minority groups and Quakers. Approximately 75% of funds available are currently given to the work and concerns of the Religious Society of Friends. The remaining funds are allocated to those charities in which the trustees have a special interest, particularly in the Midlands.

WHAT IS FUNDED General charitable purposes, particularly: religious buildings; arts and arts facilities; healthcare; medical studies and research; conservation; environmental and animal sciences; education and training; and community facilities and services.

WHAT IS NOT FUNDED The trust does not fund: individuals (whether for research, expeditions, educational purposes and so on); local projects or groups outside the West Midlands; or projects concerned with travel or adventure.

TYPE OF GRANT Regular annual donations and some single donations to special appeals.

SAMPLE GRANTS £31,600 to Warwickshire Monthly Meeting for Quaker work; £4,500 to QPS (Brussels); £3,000 each to Oxfam, Bryray House for the elderly, Bournville Village Trust, and Cape Town Quaker Peace Centre; £2,500 Birmingham Family Services Unit, South; £2,000 each to Responding to Conflict and The Salvation Army; £1,500 to FWCC Ramalla (Lebanon).

FINANCES *Year* 2000–01 *Income* £174,000 *Grants* £140,000 *Assets* £5,800,000

TRUSTEES Mrs C H Norton; Mrs E J Birmingham; J A B Taylor; Mrs C M Penny; T W Penny; R J Birmingham.

OTHER INFORMATION Grants should be acknowledged by an official receipt made out to C B & H H Taylor 1984 Trust.

HOW TO APPLY There is no formal application form. Applicants should write to the correspondent giving the charity's registration number, a brief description of the charity's activities, and details of the specific project for which the grant is being sought. Applicants should also include a budget of the proposed work, together with a copy of the charity's most recent accounts. Trustees will also wish to know what funds have already been raised for the project and how the shortfall will be met. Trustees meet twice-yearly in May and November.

WHO TO APPLY TO W J B Taylor, Trustee, c/o Home Farm, Abberton, Worcestershire WR10 2NR

CC NO 291363   ESTABLISHED 1946

....

■ The Connie and Albert Taylor Charitable Trust

WHERE FUNDING CAN BE GIVEN West Midlands.

WHO CAN BENEFIT Organisations concerned with medical research, hospices, education and recreation, and preservation.

WHAT IS FUNDED The trust was established by the will of Mrs Constance Iris Taylor in 1998 for the benefit of the West Midlands with the following object research into the cure and causes of cancer, blindness and heart disease provision and maintainance of nursing homes for people who are elderly or unable to look after themselves provision of maintainance of hospices for people with terminal illnesses facilities for the education and recreation of children and young people the preservation, protection and improvements of any amenity or land of beauty, scientific or of horticultural interest and any building of historical, architectural or artistic or scientific interest.

SAMPLE GRANTS £42,000 to University of Birmingham for a project analysing brain tumours in children (first of four yearly grants); £40,000 each to The Extra Care Charitable Trust for equipment for the James Beattie House, St Mary's Hospice for rebuilding and refurbishing, The National Star Centre for the completion of Centre for Acquired Brain Injury Rehabilitation, and Stafford District Scouts to buy a 25-acre site, including ancient woodlands, to use as a camp and which will be maintained and preserved for the local community and youth organisations.

FINANCES *Year* 1999 *Income* £323,000 *Grants* £222,000 *Assets* £5,500,000

TRUSTEES Alan Foster; Harry Grundy; Richard D Long.

HOW TO APPLY In writing to the correspondent. The trust may visit applicants/beneficiaries.

WHO TO APPLY TO A Foster, Trustee, 2 Millbank, Mill Street, Oxford OX2 0HJ

CC NO 1074785   ESTABLISHED 1998

....

■ Rosanna Taylor's 1987 Charity Trust

WHERE FUNDING CAN BE GIVEN UK and overseas, with a preference for Oxfordshire and West Sussex.

WHO CAN BENEFIT Registered charities only.

WHAT IS FUNDED General charitable purposes.

WHAT IS NOT FUNDED No grants to individuals or non-registered charities.

TYPE OF GRANT One-off.

RANGE OF GRANTS £500–£36,000.

SAMPLE GRANTS £36,000 to Pearson Taylor Trust; £30,000 to Charities Aid Foundation.

FINANCES *Year* 2001–02 *Income* £39,031 *Grants* £66,000 *Assets* £1,218,739

TRUSTEES The Cowdray Trust Limited.

HOW TO APPLY In writing to the correspondent. Acknowledgements are not sent to unsuccessful applicants.

WHO TO APPLY TO A J Winborn, Pollen House, 10–12 Cork Street, London W1S 3LW *Tel* 020 7439 9061 *Fax* 020 7437 2680

CC NO 297210   ESTABLISHED 1987

....

■ Tearfund

WHERE FUNDING CAN BE GIVEN UK and overseas, but mainly in poorer countries.

WHO CAN BENEFIT Evangelical Christian organisations which benefit at risk groups; people who are disabled, disadvantaged by poverty or socially isolated; and victims of famine, man-made or natural disasters, and war.

WHAT IS FUNDED Evangelical Christian ministry to meet all needs – physical, mental, social and spiritual. Funding is given to partner organisations only.

WHAT IS NOT FUNDED Applications for individuals will not be considered.

TYPE OF GRANT Project/partner.

RANGE OF GRANTS Smallest £1,000; typical £15,000.

SAMPLE GRANTS The top ten grants awarded in 1998 were as follows (all grants except the largest were made to several partner organisations): £4,007,000 to Compassion International for child development; £998,000 in India; £593,000 in Ethiopia; £563,000 in Sudan; £463,000 in Bangladesh; £362,000 in Uganda; £353,000 in Kenya; £338,000 in Rwanda; £321,000 in Nepal; £283,000 in Brazil.

FINANCES *Year* 2001–02 *Income* £33,151,000 *Grants* £17,079,000 *Assets* £13,405,000

TRUSTEES David White, Chair; Miles Buttrick; Ewan Cathcart; Ms Anne de Leyser; Revd Stephen Finamore; Ms Kim Hurst; Revd Ian Prior; Ms Margaret Smith; Revd John Smith; Ms Sarah Tillett; Prof. Andrew Tomkins.

PUBLICATIONS *Tear Times;* Tearcraft Catelogue; *Activ 1st; Footsteps; Gobstopper Gardens; Network; Uncovered.*

HOW TO APPLY Initial approaches by potential partner organisations should be made in writing.

WHO TO APPLY TO The International Director, 100 Church Road, Teddington, Middlesex TW11 8QE *Tel* 020 8977 9144 *Fax* 020 8943 3594 *E-mail* enquiries@tearfund.org *Website* www.tearfund.org

CC NO 265464   ESTABLISHED 1968

■ The Tedworth Trust

WHERE FUNDING CAN BE GIVEN Unrestricted, but UK in practice.

WHO CAN BENEFIT Organisations with charitable status working in the fields summarised below.

WHAT IS FUNDED Parenting, family welfare and child development; environment and the arts; general.

WHAT IS NOT FUNDED Grants are not normally made to individuals.

TYPE OF GRANT One-off and core costs.

RANGE OF GRANTS £1,000–£30,000.

SAMPLE GRANTS £127,800 to Royal Free Hospital/ University of Oxford Department of Education for research costs; £55,000 to INTACH UK Trust for salaries and training costs for a conservation project in Orccha – India; £47,466 over two years to Parenting Education and Support Forum for the part-time salary of a director; £38,935 to National Family and Parenting Institute for a national audit of parenting services; £31,064 over three years to William Tyndale Primary School for therapeutic group support for children with emotional and/or behavioural difficulties; £30,000 each to Navdanya International Centre for Sustainable Living to establish Bija Vidyapeeth, a college promoting education in sustainable farming, business and living near Delhi, and to Prisoners Abroad for survival grants for prisoners in custody overseas; £25,000 to David Baum International for bursary funds to train paediatricians for work in developing countries; £20,000 each to Bow Family Centre for core costs, and Dartington Hall Trust for establishment and subsidising a series of courses at Schumacher College aimed at teachers of all backgrounds.

FINANCES *Year* 2000–01 *Grants* £545,000

TRUSTEES James Sainsbury; Mrs M Sainsbury; Alexander Sainsbury; Jessica Sainsbury; Miss Judith Portrait.

OTHER INFORMATION The trust is one of the Sainsbury Family Charitable Trusts which share a common administration. An application to one is taken as an application to all.

HOW TO APPLY Proposals are generally invited by the trustees or initiated at their request. Unsolicited applications are nort encouraged and are unlikely to be successful.

WHO TO APPLY TO Michael Pattison, Director, Allington House, 1st Floor, 150 Victoria Street, London SW1E 5AE *Tel* 020 7410 0330

CC NO 328524   **ESTABLISHED** 1990

■ Tegham Limited

WHERE FUNDING CAN BE GIVEN UK.

WHO CAN BENEFIT Registered charities.

WHAT IS FUNDED Jewish Orthodox faith and the relief of poverty.

FINANCES *Year* 2000–01 *Income* £187,942 *Grants* £127,358 *Assets* £1,382,737

TRUSTEES Mrs S Fluss; Miss N Fluss.

HOW TO APPLY In writing to the correspondent, although the trust stated that it has enough causes to support and does not welcome other applications.

WHO TO APPLY TO Mrs S Fluss, Trustee, c/o Gerald Kreditor & Co., Tudor House, Llanvanor Road, London NW2 2AQ

CC NO 283066   **ESTABLISHED** 1981

■ The Templeton Goodwill Trust

WHERE FUNDING CAN BE GIVEN Glasgow and the West of Scotland (the Glasgow postal area).

WHO CAN BENEFIT Scottish registered charities.

WHAT IS FUNDED General charitable purposes.

WHAT IS NOT FUNDED Support is given to Scottish registered charities only. Individuals are not supported and grants are generally not given to arts or cultural organisations.

TYPE OF GRANT Discretionary, both continuing annual sums and ' one-off' , support grants.

RANGE OF GRANTS £250–£4,000.

FINANCES *Year* 2001–02 *Income* £105,000 *Grants* £100,000 *Assets* £1,700,000

TRUSTEES A D Montgomery; J H Millar; B Bannerman; W T P Barnstaple.

HOW TO APPLY In writing to the correspondent, preferably including a copy of accounts. Applications should be received by April as the trustees meet once a year, at the end of April or in May. Initial telephone calls are welcome. An sae is required from applicants if a reply is required.

WHO TO APPLY TO W T P Barnstaple, Trustee and Administrator, 12 Doon Street, Motherwell ML1 2BN *Tel* 01698 262202

SC NO SC004177

■ Tenovus Scotland

WHERE FUNDING CAN BE GIVEN Scotland.

WHO CAN BENEFIT Medical and dental professionals, and research workers.

WHAT IS FUNDED To 'prime the pump' especially for new and innovative research projects across the full spectrum of medicine carried out within Scotland.

WHAT IS NOT FUNDED Grants are not made to individuals other than as members of institutions engaged in research approved by such institutions and by the National Scientific Advisory Committee of Tenovus Scotland.

TYPE OF GRANT Usually a single grant with the emphasis on equipment and consumables. Only in exceptional circumstances would funding be considered for salaries and then only for a period of up to 12 months. One-off, project, research and start-up costs. Funding for up to three years will be considered.

SAMPLE GRANTS £12,000 to two doctors in Strathclyde for research into Huntington's Disease; £10,000 each to a doctor in Grampian for research into muscle wasting disorders, a team in Edinburgh working on research into eye development and disease, and a scientist in Tayside working on possible new treatments for multiple sclerosis; £9,500 to a group in Tayside working on a molecule that may be involved in the development of a range of cancers; £8,500 to a doctor in Grampian researching better treatments for asthma.

FINANCES *Year* 2001–02 *Income* £467,000 *Grants* £492,644 *Assets* £595,944

TRUSTEES The Committee: D G Brown; Mrs F Cutler; Dr S Duncan; Sir Malcolm MacNaughton; W M Mann; Mary Marquis; G M Philips; Lady Arbuthnott; Prof. I H Stevenson; Prof. S A M McLean; Prof. P W Howie; Prof. A A Calder; M McIver.

PUBLICATIONS Six-monthly newsletter and a video, *Today's Research – Tomorrow's Health.*

HOW TO APPLY At any time on a form available via e-mail from the correspondent or from the trust's website. Regional committees meet quarterly. Applications must be recieved by 15 May or 15 November; allow three months for notification.

Think carefully about every application. Is it justified?

835

WHO TO APPLY TO E R Read, General Secretary, 234 St Vincent Street, Glasgow G2 5RJ *Tel* 0141 221 6268 *Fax* 01292 311276 *E-mail* gen.sec@talk21.com *Website* www.tenovus-scotland.org.uk
SC NO SC009675   **ESTABLISHED** 1967

■ The Noel Goddard Terry Charitable Trust

WHERE FUNDING CAN BE GIVEN City of York.
WHO CAN BENEFIT Charities concerned with historic buildings.
WHAT IS FUNDED Grants mainly for the preservation and restoration of historic buildings.
WHAT IS NOT FUNDED No grants are made to individuals.
SAMPLE GRANTS £20,000 to York Early Music Foundation; £5,000 each to Stagecoach Youth Theatre and University of York – Kings Manor; £4,939 to York Civic Trust for statue of St Helena; £3,504 to York Civic Trust for annual report colourwork; £3,000 to York Civic Trust for a millennium exhibition at Fairfax House; £2,000 to Friends of York Cemetery; £1,000 to York Consortium for Conservation & Craftsmanship.
FINANCES *Year* 1999–2000 *Income* £14,858 *Grants* £44,500 *Assets* £154,053
TRUSTEES P N L Terry; J Shannon; A K N Terry; M Shannon; J M Hargreaves.
HOW TO APPLY In writing to the correspondent.
WHO TO APPLY TO K Sutcliffe, Harland & Co., 18 St Saviourgate, York YO1 8NS *Tel* 01904 655555
CC NO 209203   **ESTABLISHED** 1962

■ Tesco Charity Trust

WHERE FUNDING CAN BE GIVEN UK.
WHO CAN BENEFIT National and local charity appeals benefiting children's welfare and education, people who are elderly and people with disabilities.
WHAT IS FUNDED Main areas of interest are: local charities promoting welfare and education of children, people who are elderly and people who are disabled.
WHAT IS NOT FUNDED No grants to political organisations, individuals or towards new buildings. The trust will not make donations to other trusts or charities for onward transmission to other charitable organisations.
TYPE OF GRANT Generally one-off, or for one year or less.
SAMPLE GRANTS £30,000 to National Grocers' Benevolent Fund; £10,000 each to Save the Children Fund, Crime Concern Trust Limited, Isabel Hospice, Sense and Weston Spirit; £5,000 each to Bradford Foyer, Centrepoint, Life Education Centres Nottingham and Speenhamland Primary School; £3,500 to Archie Foundation; £3,000 to Brecon and District Disabled Club.
FINANCES *Year* 2002 *Income* £3,009,615 *Grants* £3,482,727 *Assets* £758,366
TRUSTEES R S Ager; T J R Mason; Miss L Neville-Rolfe; Mrs A Murray; P Smythe.
HOW TO APPLY In writing to the address below.
WHO TO APPLY TO Mrs L Marsh, Tesco House, Delamare Road, Cheshunt, Hertfordshire EN8 9SL *Tel* 01992 646768 *Fax* 01992 646794
CC NO 297126   **ESTABLISHED** 1987

■ The C Paul Thackray General Charitable Trust

WHERE FUNDING CAN BE GIVEN Yorkshire and overseas.
WHO CAN BENEFIT Organisations benefiting people with special needs, people from developing countries, and sick people.
WHAT IS FUNDED The trustees' areas of interest in Yorkshire are the care, rehabilitation and education of those with special needs, complementary medicine and the protection of the local environment. International interests lie in training and technology for developing countries, simple medical assistance of mass benefit, the protection of human rights, ecology and conservation.
WHAT IS NOT FUNDED Grants are not made for disaster appeals, appeals for medical or educational equipment, charities for domestic pets, politics, religion, the arts and heritage, unregistered charities and individuals.
TYPE OF GRANT Recurrent grants are made, although this list is reviewed annually and capital projects are considered and allocated a small proportion of the total funds available. Unfortunately, this leaves little funding for new applicants.
RANGE OF GRANTS £400–£18,750.
SAMPLE GRANTS £18,750 to Age Concern, Leeds; £2,000 to Marie Stopes International; £1,500 to Swarthmore Educational Centre; £1,200 to Camphill Village Trust; £1,000 to Salvation Army, Leeds; £600 each to Oxfam, Leeds, Shelter, Leeds, and Wheatfields Hospice, Leeds; £500 each to The Samaritans, Leeds and SENSE, Leeds.
FINANCES *Year* 1997–98 *Income* £98,256 *Grants* £48,150 *Assets* £1,185,981
TRUSTEES C P Thackray; W M Wrigley; Mrs L T Thackray; Ms R C Thackray; Mrs R L Lockie.
HOW TO APPLY 'The trustees add that the administration is carried out voluntarily. For this reason no further guidance can be given to applicants and only successful applications are acknowledged, following the trustees' annual meeting.'
WHO TO APPLY TO Mrs Ramona Lockie, Administrative Trustee, PO Box 2002, Pulborough, West Sussex RH20 2FR
CC NO 328650   **ESTABLISHED** 1990

■ Thackray Medical Research Trust

WHERE FUNDING CAN BE GIVEN Worldwide.
WHO CAN BENEFIT Charities providing medical supplies to the third world; charities, university departments and individuals researching the history of medicine, or organising conferences on the subject.
RANGE OF GRANTS Up to £10,000.
FINANCES *Year* 2001–02 *Income* £16,144 *Grants* £239,256 *Assets* £4,860,425
TRUSTEES Martin Schweiger, Chair; Richard Keeler; Christin Thackray; Paul Thackray; Stanley Warren; Matthew Wrigley.
HOW TO APPLY In writing to the correspondent, in duplicate. The trustees meet quarterly, in January, April, July and October; applications should be submitted no later than the start of the preceding month. Projects which are not supported cannot be resubmitted. All applications must include: names and addresses of applicant(s), with brief CVs; a description of the activity to be supported; a timetable against which progress can be

measured; a breakdown of the expected costs, with details of how any balance will be paid; details of requests made to other sources of funding; names and addresses of referees. For medical supply grants, accounts for the last three years, a copy of the trust deed, and a summary of the operational policy must be provided. For conference organisers grants, details must be provided of the applicant's experience in organising similar events and details of the intended speakers. For research grants, a list of any previously published work, details of intended publication and/or dissemination of the results of the research and, where appropriate, a letter from a supervisor confirming the details of the application and their support for the research must be included.

WHO TO APPLY TO Martin Schweiger, Chair of the Trustees, c/o Thackray Museum, Beckett Street, Leeds LS9 7LN *Website* www.tmrt.org

CC NO 702896   **ESTABLISHED** 1990

■ Thames Community Foundation

WHERE FUNDING CAN BE GIVEN London boroughs of Hounslow, Kingston and Richmond.
WHO CAN BENEFIT Local charitable and voluntary organisations providing welfare, working with young people, helping adults with disabilities or with all problems of addiction.
WHAT IS FUNDED Encouraging links between the local communities of the area and the business sector.
WHAT IS NOT FUNDED No grants to individuals, or for research or capital projects.
RANGE OF GRANTS Up to £7,000 a year.
FINANCES *Year* 2001–02 *Income* £105,800 *Grants* £90,672 *Assets* £24,164
TRUSTEES Monica Unwin, Chair; Sue Buller; Grant Gordon; Philip Ralph; Charlotte Bailey; Stephen Wilkinson; Iain Hadcroft; Dee Slater.
HOW TO APPLY In writing to the correspondent.
WHO TO APPLY TO The Business Development Development, NPL Buildings, Room 112, Teddington, Middlesex TW11 0LW *Tel* 020 8943 5525 *Fax* 020 8943 2319 *E-mail* tcf@thamescommunityfoundation.org.uk *Website* www.thamescommunityfoundation. org.uk
CC NO 1001994   **ESTABLISHED** 1992

■ The Thames Wharf Charity

WHERE FUNDING CAN BE GIVEN UK.
WHO CAN BENEFIT Charitable organisations.
WHAT IS FUNDED General charitable purposes.
WHAT IS NOT FUNDED No grants for the purchase of property, motor vehicles or holidays.
RANGE OF GRANTS £21–£9,100.
SAMPLE GRANTS 1996–97: £9,100 to Shelter; £4,781 to IUR; £4,000 to Architectural Association; £3,344 to Kent Air Ambulance; £2,770 to World Wildlife Fund; £2,180 to Satya SAI UK; £2,043 each to National Meningitis Fund and Clinical Science Foundation; £2,035 to Queen Charlotte's Hospital; £2,020 to Motivation.
FINANCES *Year* 1999–2000 *Income* £262,045
TRUSTEES P H Burgess; G H Camamile; J M Young; A Lotay.
HOW TO APPLY In writing to the correspondent.
WHO TO APPLY TO K Hawkins, Lee Associates, 5 Southampton Place, London WC1A 2DA
CC NO 1000796   **ESTABLISHED** 1990

■ The Theodore Trust

WHERE FUNDING CAN BE GIVEN UK.
WHO CAN BENEFIT Christian organisations.
WHAT IS FUNDED The trust aims to support the advancement of Christianity by way of education.
WHAT IS NOT FUNDED No grants to individuals.
SAMPLE GRANTS Between 1999 and 2001 grants included: £30,000 (in three grants) to Sarum College for Institute of Liturgy; £15,000 each to Anglican Centre in Rome for their library and to Catholic Central Library; £10,000 to Let the Children Live to help fund a Christian television station in South America; £5,000 to St Dimitry's Orphanage in Moscow; £3,000 to Catholic Student Council; £2,500 to International Theological Institute; and £1,400 to Newman Conference at Oxford for attenders' expenses.
FINANCES *Income* £40,000
TRUSTEES Revd D J Baker, Chair; Revd J E Barnes; Right Hon. J S Gummer MP; S P Smith; G W Woolsey Brown.
OTHER INFORMATION The trust's income is around £40,000 a year.
HOW TO APPLY In writing to the correspondent.
WHO TO APPLY TO G W Woolsey Brown, Trustee, 3 Upper King Street, Norwich NR3 1RL
CC NO 1008532   **ESTABLISHED** 1992

■ Third House Trust

WHERE FUNDING CAN BE GIVEN UK.
WHO CAN BENEFIT UK registered charities.
WHAT IS FUNDED 'The advancement of the education and training and the promotion of the moral and spiritual wellbeing of prisoners, which expression shall mean persons who are suffering or have suffered a legal restriction on their liberty in any penal or correctional establishment or through any means whatsoever, and shall include persons lately discharged from Norman House and Second House and secondly at the discretion of the trustees in the relief of persons in necessitous circumstances.'
WHAT IS NOT FUNDED Registered charities only. Applications from individuals are ineligible with the sole exception of ex-residents of Third House. No response to general appeals or appeals from large national organisations, nor to circular appeals of any kind.
TYPE OF GRANT Usually last resort one-off for a specific project. Core funding and/or salaries considered but rarely acceded to. Grants are made twice yearly in July and January.
FINANCES *Year* 2000–01 *Income* £43,401
TRUSTEES Currently five, with a maximum of eight.
HOW TO APPLY In the first instance a letter of application to the trust administrator. Appeals to be submitted by the end of April for consideration in July and by the end of October for consideration in January. Only applications short-listed for consideration will be acknowledged. Should further clarification be required an application form will be sent. N.B. Initial applications must include clear details of the need the project is designed to meet, plus a budget, annual report and accounts for the last two years.
WHO TO APPLY TO Ian Thomson, Director, PO Box 7398, Perth PH1 3ZS
CC NO 253794   **ESTABLISHED** 1966

■ The Loke Wan Tho Memorial Foundation

WHERE FUNDING CAN BE GIVEN Worldwide.
WHO CAN BENEFIT Registered charities only.
WHAT IS FUNDED Medical studies and research; conservation and environment; and overseas aid.
TYPE OF GRANT One-off project and research grants.
RANGE OF GRANTS £1,000–£13,000.
SAMPLE GRANTS In 1998–99: £13,000 to Bird Life International; £12,000 to Flora and Fauna International; £5,000 to World Wildlife Fund; £4,000 to Global Cancer Concern; £3,000 to Liverpool School of Tropical Medicine.
FINANCES *Year* 2001–02 *Income* £62,250 *Grants* £54,500 *Assets* £1,871,224
TRUSTEES Lady Y P McNeice; Mrs T S Tonkyn; A Tonkyn.
HOW TO APPLY In writing to the correspondent.
WHO TO APPLY TO The Administrator, c/o PricewaterhouseCoopers, 9 Greyfriars Road, Reading RG1 1JG
CC NO 264273   **ESTABLISHED** 1972

■ The Arthur & Margaret Thompson Charitable Trust

WHERE FUNDING CAN BE GIVEN The town or burgh of Kinross.
WHO CAN BENEFIT Registered charities in the beneficial area.
WHAT IS FUNDED General charitable purposes.
FINANCES *Year* 2000–01 *Income* £155,000 *Grants* £67,000 *Assets* £2,000,000
HOW TO APPLY The trustees meet to consider applications about every four months.
WHO TO APPLY TO Alastair Dorwood, Miller Hendry, 10 Blackfriars Street, Perth PH1 5NS *Tel* 01738 637311 *Fax* 01738 638685 *E-mail* info@miller-hendry.co.uk
SC NO SC012103

■ The Thompson Charitable Trust

WHERE FUNDING CAN BE GIVEN UK.
WHO CAN BENEFIT All registered charities and charitable purposes, including organisations benefiting: children, young adults and students; at risk groups; people disadvantaged by poverty; and socially isolated people.
WHAT IS FUNDED Preference for donations to lesser known charities in the fields of medicine, welfare and education.
WHAT IS NOT FUNDED No fixed restrictions but the trustees would tend to avoid giving to the major established national charities.
RANGE OF GRANTS £100–£16,545.
SAMPLE GRANTS In 1996–97: £16,545 to Special Trustees for St Thomas; £1,906 to Sidcot School; £1,100 to Red Maids School; £500 each to Salvation Army, SCARF, and Eccleshall All Saints Church; £300 to BRACE; £100 to Cancer Care Appeal.
FINANCES *Year* 1998–99 *Income* £38,800 *Grants* £23,564 *Assets* £294,160
TRUSTEES T P Thompson; Mrs J M Thompson; Mrs S Brown.
HOW TO APPLY In writing to the correspondent. Applications will not be acknowledged unless successful. No telephone applications considered.

WHO TO APPLY TO Sandra Brown, Osborne Clarke, 2 Temple Back East, Temple Quay, Bristol BS1 6EG *Tel* 0117 917 3000
CC NO 1003013   **ESTABLISHED** 1991

■ The Thompson Family Charitable Trust

WHERE FUNDING CAN BE GIVEN UK.
WHO CAN BENEFIT Registered charities only, with a preference for those with low administration costs such as charities staffed by volunteers.
WHAT IS FUNDED General charitable purposes, although the trustees are particularly interested in educational, medical and veterinary charities.
WHAT IS NOT FUNDED No grants to individuals.
TYPE OF GRANT The trust makes one-off grants, recurring grants and pledges.
RANGE OF GRANTS Generally £200–£5,000, occasionally larger.
SAMPLE GRANTS £74,050 in three grants to NSPCC; £12,000 to One to One Project; £10,000 each to Break Caring Homes for Special Children, Chicken Shed Theatre Company, and Totteridge Manor Association; £6,200 in three grants to North London Hospice; £5,000 each to Colon Cancer Concern and Countryside Alliance; £3,232 to Royal Opera House Trust; £1,800 to British Horse Society.
FINANCES *Year* 2000–01 *Income* £1,757,928 *Grants* £149,062 *Assets* £30,827,699
TRUSTEES D B Thompson; P Thompson; K P Thompson.
HOW TO APPLY In writing to the trustees.
WHO TO APPLY TO Roy Copus, Hillsdown Court, 15 Totteridge Common, London N20 8LR *Tel* 020 8445 4343
CC NO 326801   **ESTABLISHED** 1985

■ The Thompson Fund

WHERE FUNDING CAN BE GIVEN UK, with a preference for Sussex and the Brighton and Hove area.
WHO CAN BENEFIT Mainly charities.
WHAT IS FUNDED Support may be given to medical, welfare, education and general appeals.
WHAT IS NOT FUNDED No personal applications; grants only to other charitable and similar organisations.
TYPE OF GRANT One-off and recurrent grants.
RANGE OF GRANTS £50–£6,500.
SAMPLE GRANTS £6,500 to Scope – Hamilton House Hove; £5,000 to Disabled Living Foundation; £3,800 to Sussex Rehabilitation Centre; £3,000 to Hove Lagoon Splash and Paddle Appeal; £2,000 to WRVS – Brighton and Hove Caravan Account; £1,800 to Chichester Cathedral Restoration Trust; £1,500 to Samaritans; £1,000 to Motability; £500 each to Newhaven Volunteer Bureau and Sussex Emmaus.
FINANCES *Year* 1999–2000 *Income* £60,187 *Grants* £64,816 *Assets* £920,372
TRUSTEES P G Thompson; Patricia Thompson; M H de Silva.
HOW TO APPLY In writing to the correspondent. The trustees meet approximately every six to eight weeks.
WHO TO APPLY TO The Trustees, PO Box 104, Hove, East Sussex BN3 2XD
CC NO 327490   **ESTABLISHED** 1987

■ The Thomson Corporation Charitable Trust

WHERE FUNDING CAN BE GIVEN UK with some preference for London and the home counties.

WHO CAN BENEFIT Registered charities only.

WHAT IS FUNDED General charitable purposes.

WHAT IS NOT FUNDED No grants for advertisements in souvenir brochures, expeditions or to individuals.

RANGE OF GRANTS £500–£2,000.

SAMPLE GRANTS £2,000 each to Derwent House, Isabel Hospice, and Portland College; £1,350 to Northgate School; £1,000 each to Age Concern, British Diabetic Association, Covent Garden Cancer Research Trust, National Deaf Children's Society, REMEDI, and Sight Savers International.

FINANCES *Year* 2000 *Income* £98,973 *Grants* £100,000 *Assets* £99,966

TRUSTEES S J H Coles.

HOW TO APPLY In writing to the correspondent; trustees meet on an ad hoc basis.

WHO TO APPLY TO Sue Jenner, 1st Floor, The Quadrangle, 180 Wardour Street, London W1A 4YG

CC NO 1013317   **ESTABLISHED** 1992

■ The Len Thomson Charitable Trust

WHERE FUNDING CAN BE GIVEN Scotland.

WHO CAN BENEFIT Young people.

WHAT IS FUNDED Young people, local communities and organisations undertaking medical research.

RANGE OF GRANTS £1,000–£5,000.

SAMPLE GRANTS £5,000 to CHAS; £3,000 to Maggie's Centre; £1,000 to Newtowngrange Children's Gala Day.

FINANCES *Year* 2001–02 *Income* £28,000 *Grants* £26,000 *Assets* £620,000

TRUSTEES D A Connell; Mrs E Thomson.

HOW TO APPLY In writing to the correspondent.

WHO TO APPLY TO Lesley Kelly, Secretary, Turcan Connell, Princes Exchange, 1 Earl Grey Street, Edinburgh EH3 9EE *Tel* 0131 228 8111 *Fax* 0131 228 8118

SC NO SC000981   **ESTABLISHED** 1989

■ The Sue Thomson Foundation

WHERE FUNDING CAN BE GIVEN UK.

WHO CAN BENEFIT Small, usually self-help, low overhead organisations benefiting children and young adults.

WHAT IS FUNDED Advancement of education, especially of children in need. Trustees' main interest is in Christ's Hospital School, Horsham, and its children, especially those in need.

WHAT IS NOT FUNDED No grants to large charities or individuals, except as part of a specific scheme (see above).

TYPE OF GRANT Very few apart from Christ's Hospital, one-off grants.

RANGE OF GRANTS £25–£2,250 for other than Christ's Hospital.

SAMPLE GRANTS 2000–01: £120,000 to Christ's Hospital; £2,250 to Dechert Charitable Trust; £1,600 to Bridewell Royal Hospital; £1,500 to Publishing Training Centre. Less than £500: Sunfield & Community Arts Trust, Sequal Trust, Royal National Theatre, Mathieson Music School, Friends of Crawley Hospital, Friends of Covent Garden, Friends for Young Deaf and Finnish Children's Songs.

FINANCES *Year* 2001–02 *Income* £65,142 *Grants* £121,181 *Assets* £2,283,093

TRUSTEES Mrs S M Mitchell; C L Corman; J Gillham.

HOW TO APPLY No guidelines. Applications are acknowledged only if an sae is enclosed.

WHO TO APPLY TO Mrs S M Mitchell, Trustee, Furners Keep, Furners Lane, Henfield, West Sussex BN5 9HS *Tel* 01273 493461 *Fax* 01273 495139

CC NO 298808   **ESTABLISHED** 1988

■ The Thoresby Charitable Trust

WHERE FUNDING CAN BE GIVEN UK, with a preference for Nottinghamshire.

WHO CAN BENEFIT Organisations, often local branches and usually well established, but innovatory appeals considered.

WHAT IS FUNDED Nottinghamshire-based charities with the exception of a few national charities. Particularly those working in the fields of: churches; arts, culture and recreation; health facilities and buildings; medical studies and research; conservation and environment; education and training; and transport and community services. Other charitable purposes will be considered.

TYPE OF GRANT One-off and project. Funding for one year or less will be considered.

RANGE OF GRANTS £100–£1,000.

SAMPLE GRANTS £1,000 each to Portland College, Nottinghamshire for re-training for disabled people and ADASMT – autonomic disorders for medical research; £500 each to Kneesall Village Hall for building maintenance and Kneesall Church; £300 each to Wellow School, Woodard Schools, and St Mary's Church, Edwinstone.

FINANCES *Year* 2001 *Income* £34,500 *Grants* £23,462 *Assets* £780,138

TRUSTEES Lady Rozelle Raynes; H P Matheson; I D P Thorne.

HOW TO APPLY In writing to the correspondent. Decisions are usually made in January for distribution in March. Acknowledgements are only sent if an sae is enclosed.

WHO TO APPLY TO R P H McFerran, Thoresby Estate Management Ltd, Estate Office, Thoresby Park, Newark, Nottinghamshire NG22 9EF

CC NO 277215   **ESTABLISHED** 1978

■ The Sir Jules Thorn Charitable Trust

WHERE FUNDING CAN BE GIVEN UK.

WHO CAN BENEFIT Registered charities engaged in medical research (universities/hospitals only); medically related work; and humanitarian work.

WHAT IS FUNDED Medical research with strong clinical relevance, medicine generally, and small grants for humanitarian appeals.

WHAT IS NOT FUNDED The trust does not fund: research which is considered unlikely to provide clinical benefit within five years; research which could reasonably be expected to be supported by a disease specific funder, unless there is a convincing reason why the trust has been approached; research into cancer or AIDS, for the sole reason that they are relatively well funded elsewhere; 'top up' grants for ongoing projects; research which will also involve other funders, apart from the Institution itself; individuals – except in the context of a project undertaken by an approved institution which is in receipt of a grant from the trust; research or data collection overseas; third parties raising

Think carefully about every application. Is it justified?

839

resources to fund research themselves; research institutions which are not registered charities. Further details of exclusions for medically related and humanitarian appeals can be found on the trust's website.

TYPE OF GRANT Medical research projects usually covering a period of up to three years, plus one-off donations to other charities.

RANGE OF GRANTS (a) Humanitarian donations – £100 to £500; (b) research grants – depending upon the timescale and nature of investigation – up to £40,000 a year; (c) medically-related donations – generally not more than £300,000 in total in any one year; (d) the trust's annual 'special project' award – not normally more than £500,000.

SAMPLE GRANTS £993,138 to University College London's Institute of Ophthalmology and Institute of Child Health for a research project into gene therapy for x-linked retinitis pigmentosa; £750,000 to Moorfields Eye Hospital for the International Children's Eye Centre; £135,864 to Greenbank Sports Academy – Liverpool for a fitness and training suite at the sports academy for people with disabilities; £133,981 to University of Southampton for investigation of the role of xenobiotic disposition in the development of allergic contact hypersensitivity; £133,352 to University College London's Department of Chemical Pathology for development of a cellular model for the study of oxalate metabolism in normal and hyperoxaluric states; £129,000 to English Federation of Disability Sports – East Midlands for projects providing recreational and sporting opportunities for people with disabilities in isolated communities throughout the East Midlands; £100,000 each to Army Benevolent Fund over five years and Charlton School – South East London for hot tubs and indoor health facilities for children with special needs; £96,556 to Royal Free and University College for redox regulation of vascular function in liver disease; £83,789 to University of Glasgow's Department of Obstetrics and Gynaecology randomised comparison of the nitric oxide donor isosorbide mononitrate with prostaglandin E2 gel for cervical ripening prior to the induction of labour at term.

FINANCES *Year* 2001 *Income* £3,715,031 *Grants* £3,030,114 *Assets* £78,220,289

TRUSTEES Ann Rylands, chair; Christopher Sporborg; Prof. Frederick V Flynn; Sir Bruce MacPhail; Nicholas Wilson, Prof. J Richard Batchelor.

HOW TO APPLY For medical research, short-term project grants and 'seed corn' are the only categories of award for which unsolicited applications are considered. A short submission is requested initially to determine whether a detailed proposal is appropriate. For medically-related donations, appeals are considered by the trustees at their meetings in April and November each year. There is no specific application form. Proposals should be submitted to the trust's director. For the smaller donations programme, there are no specific dates for submitting applications. Appeals may be made at any time and will be considered by the trustees as soon as possible, depending on volume. There is no special application form. Applicants should submit their appeal to the director.

WHO TO APPLY TO David H Richings, Director, 24 Manchester Square, London W1U 3TH *Tel* 020 7487 5851 *Website* www.julesthorntrust.org.uk

CC NO 233838 **ESTABLISHED** 1964

■ The Thornton Foundation

WHERE FUNDING CAN BE GIVEN UK.

WHO CAN BENEFIT Charities which are personally known to the trustees.

WHAT IS FUNDED General charitable purposes.

RANGE OF GRANTS £1,000–£20,000.

SAMPLE GRANTS £109,792 to a major capital project; £60,000 to Peper Harrow Foundation; £35,000 to St Christopher's Hospice; £32,188 to a capital project; £30,000 each to 21st Learning Initiative and HMS Trincomlee Trust; £20,000 to Mary Rose Trust; £10,000 to Stowe House Preservation Trust; £7,500 to St Peter's Trust; £5,000 to Keble College – Oxford.

FINANCES *Year* 2001–02 *Income* £159,104 *Grants* £356,936 *Assets* £3,585,320

TRUSTEES R C Thornton, Chair; A H Isaacs; H D C Thornton; Mrs S J Thornton.

HOW TO APPLY The trust strongly emphasises that it does not accept unsolicited applications, and, as it states above, only organisations that are known to one of the trustees will be considered for support. Any unsolicited applications will not receive a reply.

WHO TO APPLY TO Richard Thornton, Chair, Stephenson Harwood, 1 St Paul's Churchyard, London EC4M 8SH *Tel* 020 7329 4422

CC NO 326383 **ESTABLISHED** 1983

■ The Thornton Trust

WHERE FUNDING CAN BE GIVEN UK and overseas.

WHO CAN BENEFIT Organisations benefiting Christians or people in need.

WHAT IS FUNDED 'Promoting and furthering education and the evangelical Christian faith and assisting in the relief of sickness, suffering and poverty.' The trust mainly supports churches, missionary societies, colleges/bible societies and non-Christian causes.

WHAT IS NOT FUNDED No grants to general appeals or individuals.

RANGE OF GRANTS £70–£46,400; mostly £500–£5,000.

SAMPLE GRANTS £24,250 to Africa Inland Mission; £15,400 to Saffron Walden Baptist Church; £7,000 to Redcliffe Missionary College; £5,000 each to Bible Society, Keswick Convention, and London City Mission.

FINANCES *Year* 2001–02 *Income* £88,429 *Grants* £152,225 *Assets* £1,563,056

TRUSTEES D H Thornton; Mrs B Y Thornton; J D Thornton.

HOW TO APPLY The trust states: 'Our funds are fully committed to charities which the trustees have supported for many years and we regret that we are unable to respond to the many calls for assistance we are now receiving.'

WHO TO APPLY TO D H Thornton, Trustee, Hunters Cottage, Hunters Yard, Debden Road, Saffron Walden, Essex CB11 4AA

CC NO 205357 **ESTABLISHED** 1962

■ The Three Guineas Trust

WHERE FUNDING CAN BE GIVEN Unrestricted.

WHO CAN BENEFIT Currently, organisations with charitable status working with people suffering from autism and Asperger's Syndrome.

WHAT IS FUNDED Initiatives related to autism and Asperger's Syndrome. Projects concerned with women's issues or the relief of poverty or homelessness may also be supported, but only on the initiative of the trustees.

WHAT IS NOT FUNDED No grants for individuals.

SAMPLE GRANTS £94,000 to West Midlands Autistic Society; £64,062 to National Autistic Society; £54,449 to Yarrow Housing Ltd; £42,544 to Alice Project; £40,912 to University of Cambridge; £17,700 to Kingwood Trust; £9,175 to St George's Hospital Medical School; £5,300 to Autistic Society of Trinidad; £5,000 to Autism Bedfordshire; £3,000 to Northamptonshire Society for Autism.

FINANCES *Year* 2000–01 *Income* £4,222,528 *Grants* £338,642 *Assets* £4,513,016

TRUSTEES Clare Sainsbury; Christopher Stone; Miss Judith Portrait.

OTHER INFORMATION The trust is one of the Sainsbury Family Charitable Trusts which share a common administration. An application to one is taken as an application to all.

HOW TO APPLY Proposals are generally invited by the trustees or initiated at their request. Unsolicited applications are nort encouraged and are unlikely to be successful. However, applications for research into autism or Asperger's Syndrome are welcomed.

WHO TO APPLY TO Michael Pattison, Director, Allington House, 1st Floor, 150 Victoria Street, London SW1E 5AE *Tel* 020 7410 0330 *Fax* 020 7410 0332
CC NO 1059652   **ESTABLISHED** 1996

■ The Three Oaks Trust

WHERE FUNDING CAN BE GIVEN Overseas, UK, with a preference for West Sussex.

WHO CAN BENEFIT Registered charities, voluntary organisations and individuals.

WHAT IS FUNDED Projects which aid people with psychological or emotional difficulties; educational projects where there is a special needs element; people with physical difficulties; medical research; environmental issues; welfare (illness); and organisations providing aid overseas.

SAMPLE GRANTS £15,000 each to Kaloko Trust – Zambia and Raynauds and Scleroderma Association for a welfare support worker's salary; £10,200 to Ceco – Sri Lanka for computer equipment and tuition for students to provide job opportunities; £10,000 each to Crawley Open House and Horsham Counselling Service for running costs; £5,000 each to Coventry Day Centre for Norton House, Visceral for research into gastro-intestinal disorders, West Midlands Post Adoption Service for counselling for adults, and YMCA Hove for the training of professionals; £4,000 to West Sussex County Council for a psychotherapeutic service for children.

FINANCES *Year* 2000–01 *Grants* £252,787

TRUSTEES The Three Oaks Family Trust Co. Ltd.

HOW TO APPLY The trust's 2000–01 annual report stated: 'The directors intend to continue supporting the organisations that they have supported in the past and are not planning to fund any new projects in the near future. To save administration costs, the directors do not respond to requests, unless they are considering making a donation. Requests from organisations for donations that exceed £2,000 are considered on a quarterly basis in meetings held in January, April, July and October.'

WHO TO APPLY TO The Trustees, The Three Oaks Family Trust Co. Ltd, PO Box 243, Crawley, West Sussex RH10 6YB
Website www.thethreeoakstrust.co.uk
CC NO 297079   **ESTABLISHED** 1987

■ The Thriplow Charitable Trust

WHERE FUNDING CAN BE GIVEN Preference for British institutions.

WHO CAN BENEFIT Universities, university colleges and other places of learning benefiting young adults and older people, academics, research workers and students.

WHAT IS FUNDED Advancement of higher and further education, the promotion of research and the dissemination of the results of such research.

WHAT IS NOT FUNDED Grants can only be made to charitable bodies or component parts of charitable bodies. In no circumstances can grants be made to individuals.

TYPE OF GRANT Research study funds, research fellowships, certain academic training schemes, computer facilities and building projects related to research.

RANGE OF GRANTS £2,000–£8,000

SAMPLE GRANTS £8,000 each to Cambridge Foundation to purchase papers by Isaac Newton and Kew Foundation for plant research; £7,000 to the University of Bath for research; £5,500 each to the British Museum to buy trays for cuneiform tablets and Quarriers for training costs; £5,000 each to Queen Alexandra College for accommodation for people who are blind, Chronic Fatigue Syndrome for research, the University of Edinburgh biology department for microarray facilities, Courtauld Institute of Art for scholarships, Stoke Mandeville Hospital for research into spinal injuries, Girton College towards archive building costs, Pembroke College towards student hardship funds, and the Early English Organ Project for research.

FINANCES *Year* 2000–01 *Income* £89,675 *Grants* £97,750 *Assets* £3,199,150

TRUSTEES Sir Peter Swinnerton-Dyer; Dr Harriet Crawford; Prof. Karen Sparck Jones; Prof. Christopher Bayly.

HOW TO APPLY There is no application form. A letter of application should specify the purpose for which funds are sought and the costings of the project. It should be indicated whether other applications for funds are pending and, if the funds are to be channelled to an individual or a small group, what degree of supervision over the quality of the work would be exercised by the institution. Trustee meetings are held twice a year – in spring and in autumn.

WHO TO APPLY TO Mrs E Mackintosh, Secretary, PO Box 243, Cambridge CB3 9PQ
CC NO 1025531   **ESTABLISHED** 1993

■ The Tilda Foundation

WHERE FUNDING CAN BE GIVEN UK and Asia.

WHO CAN BENEFIT Registered charities.

WHAT IS FUNDED General charitable purposes, particularly health, education and Asian charities.

RANGE OF GRANTS £30–£10,000.

SAMPLE GRANTS £15,700 to Sarvoday Yuvak Mandal; £5,000 to The Gujarat Hindu Society; £2,500 to Bharatiya Vidya Bhavan; £500 each to CYANA: Cancer – You Are Not Alone and Alzheimer's Disease Society; £200 each to Muscular Dystrophy Group and Age Concern; £100 each to Leukaemia Research Fund, Whizz-Kid, Saint Francis Hospice and The Children's Care Challenge.

FINANCES *Year* 1998–99 *Grants* £25,000 *Assets* £112,000

TRUSTEES S Thakrar; R Thakrar; V Thakrar; R Samani.

HOW TO APPLY In writing to the correspondent.

■ The Tillett Trust

WHERE FUNDING CAN BE GIVEN UK.

WHO CAN BENEFIT Young musicians of outstanding talent residing in the UK.

WHAT IS FUNDED Funds are directed towards assisting outstanding young classical musicians at the start of their professional solo careers and in the main to help them obtain performing experience. It is not available for those at student level, either undergraduate or postgraduate.

WHAT IS NOT FUNDED Funding for the purchase of musical instruments, for study courses, for commercial recordings or for the commissioning of new works. Applications for ordinary subsistence costs are also not considered.

TYPE OF GRANT Non-recurrent.

SAMPLE GRANTS £12,000 to YCAT for performances by young artists under their management; £4,000 to Young Songmakers for auditions and concerts; £500 each to two young musicians for travel to auditions in New York; £500 to a violinist for tuition; £480 each to three British Youth Opera singers; £500 to a conductor with Opera East.

FINANCES *Year* 2000–01 *Income* £49,209 *Grants* £49,355

TRUSTEES Paul Strang, Chair; Miss Fiona Grant; Miss Yvonne Minton; David Stiff; Miss Clara Taylor; Howard Davis.

OTHER INFORMATION The trust also runs a young artists' plaform recital scheme, for auditions and concerts, on which £14,000 was spent in 2001–02.

HOW TO APPLY In writing to the address below. No application form is used and there are no deadlines. Enclose a cv or biography and references, also a performance cassette and budget for project.

WHO TO APPLY TO Miss K Avey, Secretary to the Trust, Courtyard House, Neopardy, Crediton, Devon EX17 5EP *Fax* 01363 777845 *E-mail* tilletttrust@tiscali.co.uk
CC NO 257329   ESTABLISHED 1963

■ Tillotson Bradbery Charitable Trust

WHERE FUNDING CAN BE GIVEN Merseyside (and elsewhere at the trustees' discretion).

WHO CAN BENEFIT Registered charities.

WHAT IS FUNDED Special interest in social work, second-chance education and welfare of older people.

TYPE OF GRANT Usually one-off.

RANGE OF GRANTS Typically £250–£500.

SAMPLE GRANTS 1998–99: £1,000 to Duke of Edinburgh Award Scheme; £600 to Welsh National Opera; £500 each to Liverpool One Parent Families, West Kirby Residential School, PADA Wirral, YMCA Training, Special Gymnastics, Winged Fellowship, DELTA and Roundabout Centre.

FINANCES *Year* 2000–01 *Income* £24,732

TRUSTEES Mrs L J E Hudson-Davies, Chair; R C Hudson-Davies; Mrs K G Hume; Revd S Tillotson.

HOW TO APPLY In writing to the correspondent.

■ The Tinsley Foundation

WHERE FUNDING CAN BE GIVEN UK and overseas.

WHO CAN BENEFIT Charities which: promote human rights and democratisation and/or which educate against racism, discrimination and oppression; promote self-help in fighting poverty and homelessness; or provide reproductive health education in underdeveloped countries, but specifically excluding charities whose policy is against abortion or birth control.

WHAT IS FUNDED General charitable purposes.

TYPE OF GRANT Core support for up to two years.

RANGE OF GRANTS £500–£5,000.

SAMPLE GRANTS £3,500 to The Carter Centre; £1,400 to Santa Barbara Symphony.

FINANCES *Year* 2001–02 *Income* £53,761 *Grants* £4,892 *Assets* £142,452

TRUSTEES H C Tinsley; Mrs R C Tinsley; T A Jones.

HOW TO APPLY In writing to the correspondent.

WHO TO APPLY TO H C Tinsley, Trustee, The Office, West Deeping Manor, Peterborough PE6 9HR *Tel* 01778 342217 *Fax* 01778 346121 *E-mail* henrytinsley@compuserve.com
CC NO 1076537   ESTABLISHED 1999

■ The Tisbury Telegraph Trust

WHERE FUNDING CAN BE GIVEN UK and overseas.

WHO CAN BENEFIT Registered charities only, benefiting: children and young adults; medical professionals; those in care, fostered or adopted; parents and children; one-parent families; Christians and evangelists; disaster victims; homeless people; refugees; victims of war; and people who have a disease or medical condition.

WHAT IS FUNDED Most distributions are to charities of which the trustees have personal knowledge. Other applications are unlikely to be successful. There is a preference for organisations working in the fields of: charity or voluntary umbrella bodies; the advancement of Christianity; Anglican bodies and Free Church; hospices; multiple sclerosis research; flora and fauna, waterways, wildlife parks and sanctuaries, and zoos; ecology, environmental issues, renewable energy and power; transport and alternative transport; church schools and pre-school education; special schools, special needs education and playgrounds. Other charitable purposes may be considered.

WHAT IS NOT FUNDED No grants for individuals towards sponsoring expeditions or courses.

TYPE OF GRANT Core costs, one-off, project, research and running costs will be considered.

RANGE OF GRANTS £100–£4,000. Unsolicited applications will not receive more than about £400.

SAMPLE GRANTS £10,000 to Mid Hertfordshire Churches – Romania; £5,800 to St Mary's PCC; £5,000 to St Paul's PCC; £4,000 to Community of Celebration; £3,500 to Help the Aged; £3,000 to Ethiopaid; £2,500 to World Vision; £2,000 to Tearfund; £1,200 Christian Aid; £1,000 each to Crosslinks, Scope and Southwark Habitat for Humanity.

FINANCES *Year* 1998–99 *Income* £77,000 *Grants* £65,000 *Assets* £80,000

TRUSTEES John Davidson; Alison Davidson; Eleanor Orr; Roger Orr; Sonia Phippard.

HOW TO APPLY In writing to the correspondent.
However, it is extremely rare that unsolicited
applications are successful and the trust does
not respond to applicants unless an sae is
included. No telephone applications please.
WHO TO APPLY TO Mrs E Orr, Trustee, 35 Kitto Road,
Telegraph Hill, London SE14 5TW
E-mail ttt@howzatt.demon.co.uk
CC NO 328595   **ESTABLISHED** 1990

■ The Company of Tobacco Pipe Makers and Tobacco Blenders Benevolent Fund

WHERE FUNDING CAN BE GIVEN City of London, and
Sevenoaks School.
WHO CAN BENEFIT Educational establishments
benefiting children, young adults, students, and
people disadvantaged by poverty.
WHAT IS FUNDED To assist in the education of those
who would not otherwise be able to afford it. To
support only those charities with which the
company can have an active relationship.
WHAT IS NOT FUNDED No grants to individuals.
TYPE OF GRANT Ongoing scholarships.
RANGE OF GRANTS £1,000–£3,000.
SAMPLE GRANTS £33,000 to Sevenoaks School for
scholarships; £4,000 to Guildhall School for
Music for scholarships; £2,500 to Riding for the
Disabled for general purposes; £1,000 each to
St Bartholomew's Hospital for scholarships and
St Botolph's Project for food for the homeless;
£300 to Lord Mayor's Fund for Charities for
general purposes.
FINANCES *Year* 2000 *Income* £85,353
Grants £42,268 *Assets* £1,296,802
TRUSTEES J J Adler, Chair; J W Solomon; D P C
Harris; S L Preedy; J A G Murray.
HOW TO APPLY The trust has stated that it is not
seeking additional beneficiaries.
WHO TO APPLY TO J E Maxwell, 5 Cliffe House,
Radnor Cliff, Folkestone, Kent CT20 2TY
Tel 01303 248477
CC NO 200601   **ESTABLISHED** 1961

■ The Tolkien Trust

WHERE FUNDING CAN BE GIVEN UK, with a preference
for Oxfordshire.
WHO CAN BENEFIT Registered charities, with a
preference for Christian organisations,
especially Catholic; welfare; and organisations
in Oxfordshire.
WHAT IS FUNDED General charitable purposes.
WHAT IS NOT FUNDED No support for non-registered
charities.
RANGE OF GRANTS £250–£13,000.
SAMPLE GRANTS £13,000 to Find Your Feet Ltd;
£4,000 each to Catholic Housing Aid Society
and St Anthony's RC Church – Littlemore.
FINANCES *Year* 1998–99 *Income* £94,000
Grants £60,000
TRUSTEES John Tolkien; Christopher Tolkien; Priscilla
Tolkien.
HOW TO APPLY In writing to the correspondent.
WHO TO APPLY TO Mrs Cathleen Blackburn, Manches
Solicitors, 3 Worcester Street, Oxford OX1 2PZ
Tel 01865 722106 *Fax* 01865 813687
CC NO 273615   **ESTABLISHED** 1977

■ Tollemache (Buckminster) Charitable Trust

WHERE FUNDING CAN BE GIVEN UK.
WHO CAN BENEFIT Voluntary organisations and
charitable groups only.
WHAT IS FUNDED General charitable purposes.
WHAT IS NOT FUNDED No grants to individuals.
FINANCES *Year* 2002 *Income* £22,000
Grants £21,000 *Assets* £450,000
TRUSTEES Sir Lyonel Tollemache; H M Neal; W H G
Wilks.
HOW TO APPLY In writing to the secretary. No
acknowledgements sent.
WHO TO APPLY TO The Secretary, Estate Office,
Buckminster, Grantham, Lincolnshire NG33 5SD
CC NO 271795   **ESTABLISHED** 1976

■ Tomchei Torah Charitable Trust

WHERE FUNDING CAN BE GIVEN UK.
WHO CAN BENEFIT Jewish people and organisations.
WHAT IS FUNDED Jewish causes.
RANGE OF GRANTS £40–£22,000; average £5,000.
SAMPLE GRANTS £22,000 to Merkaz Hatorah;
£5,300 each to Chested Charity Trust and
Parsha Limited; £3,500 to Woodstock Sinclair
Trust; £2,500 to Notzer Chested.
FINANCES *Year* 1998–99 *Income* £81,000
Grants £70,000 *Assets* £58,000
TRUSTEES I J Kohn; S M Kohn; A Frei.
HOW TO APPLY In writing to the correspondent at any
time.
WHO TO APPLY TO A Frei, Trustee, Harold Everett
Wreford, Second Floor, 32 Wigmore Street,
London W1U 2RP *Tel* 020 7535 5900
CC NO 802125   **ESTABLISHED** 1989

■ The Tompkins Foundation

WHERE FUNDING CAN BE GIVEN UK.
WHO CAN BENEFIT UK and local organisations.
WHAT IS FUNDED The advancement of education,
learning and religion; the provision of facilities
for recreation and other purposes beneficial to
the community in the parishes of Hampstead
Norreys in Berkshire and of West Grinstead in
Sussex, and any other parishes with which the
patron may have a connection with from time to
time.
SAMPLE GRANTS £55,000 to Anna Freud Centre;
£50,000 each to Foundation of Nursing Studies,
Order os St John, St Mary's Hospital Coronary
Flow Trust and St Mary's Hospital trustees;
£30,000 each to Police Foundation and Variety
Club.
FINANCES *Year* 1999–2000 *Grants* £438,000
TRUSTEES Elizabeth Tompkins, Patron; John Sharp;
Colin Warburton.
HOW TO APPLY Applications are not sought.
WHO TO APPLY TO The Secretary, 31 St John's
Square, London EC1M 4DN *Tel* 020 7608
1369
CC NO 281405   **ESTABLISHED** 1980

■ Torchbearer Trust

WHERE FUNDING CAN BE GIVEN UK and overseas.
WHO CAN BENEFIT Young adults; students;
volunteers; Christians and evangelists.
WHAT IS FUNDED For the promotion and
encouragement of the Christian faith: enabling
or assisting people who are professing
Christians by the provision of bursaries or
grants to obtain full-time instruction and

training; and supporting people engaged in full-time Christian or Missionary work. Mainly grants are given to students or ex-students of Torchbearer. Support may also be given to people in full-time Christian work.

TYPE OF GRANT Single and recurring as required by the project. Funding is available for up to one year.

RANGE OF GRANTS Usually up to £200; Torchbearer students excepted.

FINANCES *Year* 2000 *Income* £61,696 *Grants* £71,228 *Assets* £261,154

TRUSTEES Ms A Mills; Ms J Thomas; M Thomas.

HOW TO APPLY In writing to the secretary. No form required.

WHO TO APPLY TO The Secretary, Capernwray Hall, Carnforth, Lancashire LA6 1AG *Tel* 01524 733908

CC NO 253607   **ESTABLISHED** 1956

····································

■ The Tory Family Foundation

WHERE FUNDING CAN BE GIVEN Worldwide, but principally Folkestone.

WHO CAN BENEFIT Registered charities only.

WHAT IS FUNDED Grants are given to benefit the community of east Kent, such as church halls, schools and so on. Grants are only given to UK organisations if the work benefits local people. A few overseas grants are also given.

WHAT IS NOT FUNDED Grants are given to registered charities only. Applications outside Kent are unlikely to be considered. No grants are given for further education.

RANGE OF GRANTS £200–£7,000, mostly £1,000 or less.

SAMPLE GRANTS £7,000 to Salvation Army for a worship and community centre; £6,000 to Atlantic Education for the Atlantic partnership; £5,000 to St Mary's Church for maintenance; £4,000 to Atlantic Education as an additional payment; £2,000 each to Apt Enterprise Development, Canterbury Festival for the production of Marriage of Figaro, Gateway Club for general purposes, Prisoners Abroad, and Weald Samaritans for an activity centre.

FINANCES *Year* 2000–01 *Income* £119,707 *Grants* £73,642 *Assets* £2,374,505

TRUSTEES P N Tory; J N Tory; Mrs S A Rice.

HOW TO APPLY In writing to the correspondent. Applications are considered throughout the year. To keep costs down, unsuccessful applicants will not be notified.

WHO TO APPLY TO P N Tory, Trustee, The Estate Office, Etchinghill Golf, Folkestone, Kent CT18 8FA *Tel* 01303 862280

CC NO 326584   **ESTABLISHED** 1984

····································

■ The Tower Hill Improvement Trust

WHERE FUNDING CAN BE GIVEN Tower Hill and St Katherine's ward in Tower Hamlets.

WHO CAN BENEFIT Community-based organisations and appeals benefiting children and young adults, at risk groups, people disadvantaged by poverty and socially isolated people.

WHAT IS FUNDED Organisations working for the relief of need or sickness, the provision of leisure and recreation facilities for social welfare and in support of education, and to provide and maintain gardens and open spaces.

WHAT IS NOT FUNDED No grants to individuals.

TYPE OF GRANT General and capital projects involving building renovation will be considered.

RANGE OF GRANTS £500–£30,000.

SAMPLE GRANTS £30,000 to All Hallows Development Appeal towards the construction of the Queen Mother Centre; £28,000 to John Grooms Association for the provision of a lift for disabled people; £27,490 to St Botolph's Project for the salary of an outreach worker; £5,775 to Volunteer Reading Help to provide school assistance for ethnic minority children; £3,176 to Wakefield Terrace for the provision of benches; £3,000 to SSAFA (ex-servicemen's fund); £1,250 to Working Support for an employment of disabled people project; £1,175 to Trinity Square Gardens for a garden design project; £1,000 to School Museum for a children's summer project.

FINANCES *Year* 1999–2000 *Income* £123,199 *Grants* £95,808 *Assets* £4,161,382

TRUSTEES Charles G A Parker, Chair; Maj. Gen. Christopher Tyler; David Palmer; Capt. John Burton-Hall; Mrs Davina Walter.

HOW TO APPLY In writing to the correspondent. The trustees meet every three months to consider applications.

WHO TO APPLY TO James Connelly, Secretary Treasurer, Attlee House, 28 Commercial Street, London E1 6LR *Tel* 020 7377 6614 *Fax* 020 7377 9822

CC NO 206225   **ESTABLISHED** 1938

····································

■ The Fred Towler Charity Trust

WHERE FUNDING CAN BE GIVEN Bradford diocese.

WHO CAN BENEFIT Local charities or local branches of national societies benefiting children and older people, retired people, people disadvantaged by poverty and people living in urban areas.

WHAT IS FUNDED To provide holidays for older people (one-third of income). To support charities devoted to sick, older or young people (two-thirds of income) and other charitable purposes.

WHAT IS NOT FUNDED No grants to individuals.

TYPE OF GRANT For recurrent operational expenses. Funding of up to three years will be considered.

SAMPLE GRANTS £8,000 to Tradesmen's Homes; £2,600 each to Bradford Sea Cadets and Riding for the Disabled; £1,600 each to Catholic Housing, Spinster's Endowment, Methodist's Home and Marlin House.

FINANCES *Year* 2000–01 *Income* £41,000 *Grants* £37,000 *Assets* £770,000

TRUSTEES 10 professional/business people in Bradford district.

HOW TO APPLY In writing to the correspondent. Trustees meet twice a year, usually in June and November.

WHO TO APPLY TO Peter G Meredith, Trustee, Pelican House, 10 Currer Street, Bradford BD1 5BA *Tel* 01274 732522 *Fax* 01274 390154 *E-mail* peter.meredith@horwath-yorks.co.uk

CC NO 225026   **ESTABLISHED** 1939

····································

■ The Towry Law Charitable Trust

WHERE FUNDING CAN BE GIVEN UK, with a slight preference for the south of England.

WHO CAN BENEFIT Organisations benefiting people of all ages and disabled people. Medical professionals and research workers may be considered.

WHAT IS FUNDED The trust's grant-making policy is currently under review. Only organisations previously supported by the trust will be considered for the foreseeable future.

WHAT IS NOT FUNDED No grants to individuals, bodies which are not UK-registered charities, local branches or associates of UK charities.

RANGE OF GRANTS £1,000–£12,000.

SAMPLE GRANTS £12,000 to Berkshire Community Trust; £10,000 each to RNIB Sunshine School for Blind Children, Sargent Cancer Care for Children, and University of Exeter; £9,500 to Children's Hospital School; £9,000 each to Break, and Imperial Cancer Research Campaign; £7,500 each to Evelina Children's Hospital Appeal, King Edward VII's Hospital for Officers, and National Star Centre for Disabled Youth.

FINANCES *Year* 2000–01 *Income* £237,362 *Grants* £296,250 *Assets* £2,227,254

TRUSTEES Hon. C T H Law, Chair; K H Holmes; D G Ainslie.

HOW TO APPLY In writing to the correspondent. Unsolicited applications are not considered.

WHO TO APPLY TO Mrs Merl Gurr, Towry Law House, Western Road, Bracknell, Berkshire RG12 1TL *Tel* 01344 828009

CC NO 278880   **ESTABLISHED** 1979

■ The Toy Trust

WHERE FUNDING CAN BE GIVEN UK.

WHO CAN BENEFIT Children and young adults.

WHAT IS FUNDED General charitable purposes for children and young people.

SAMPLE GRANTS £10,000 each to DEBRA, NATLL, Toy Box Charity, and Wexford Children Hospice; £9,000 to Kidscape; £7,835 to Diana Louise Trust; £5,000 each to Mildmay, Royal Liverpool Philharmonic Society, St Andrew's Hospice, and Speech Language and Learn Centre.

FINANCES *Year* 2001 *Income* £215,390 *Grants* £208,910 *Assets* £213,840

TRUSTEES The British Toy and Hobby Association; T G Willis; A Munn; J D Hunter; B Ellis.

HOW TO APPLY In writing to the correspondent.

WHO TO APPLY TO Ms Karen Baxter, British Toy & Hobby Association, 80 Camberwell Road, London SE5 0EG

CC NO 1001634   **ESTABLISHED** 1991

■ The Trades House of Glasgow

WHERE FUNDING CAN BE GIVEN Glasgow.

WHO CAN BENEFIT Organisations and individuals.

WHAT IS FUNDED General charitable purposes.

WHAT IS NOT FUNDED The funds are held primarily for the benefit of Glasgow and its citizens, if you fall outside those parameters you should not submit an application. Political, municipal, and ecclesiastical appeals cannot be entertained. Charities duplicating rather than complementing existing services and those with national purposes and/or large running surpluses normally cannot be helped. Applicants receiving help one year will normally be refused the next.

TYPE OF GRANT One-off, capital, core costs, recurring and running costs. Funding is only given for one year or less.

RANGE OF GRANTS Typically £2–£3,000.

SAMPLE GRANTS £35,000 to Queen Mother's Hospital; £8,012 to Fairbridge Trust; £7,806 to Glasgow Bute Benevolent Trust; £7,300 to Clyde Cruising Club; £7,000 to Children's Classic Concerts; £5,000 to Bridgeton Traditional Music Centre; £4,023 to Association of Deacons; £4,000 to Royal Scottish Academy of Music and Drama; £3,805 to University of Glasgow; £3,432 to Erskine Hospital.

FINANCES *Year* 2001–02 *Income* £895,689 *Grants* £182,152 *Assets* £12,597,210

OTHER INFORMATION A further £187,767 went to individuals.

HOW TO APPLY There is no set form of application for organisations seeking help. You should write a summary in your own words extending to not more than a single A4 sheet, backed as necessary by schedules and accompanied by your latest accounts and/or business plan. Evidence of need must be produced, as should evidence that client groups participate in decision making and that their quality of life and choice is enhanced. Where possible, costs and financial needs should be broken down, evidence of the difference which a grant would make be produced, and details given, with results, of other grants applied for. Applications should include evidence of charitable status, current funding and the use you are making of that. Projects should be demonstrated to be practical and business-like. It is a condition of any grant that a report be made as to how the funds have been used. Grants not used for the purposes stated must be returned.

WHO TO APPLY TO The Clerk, 310 St Vincent Street, Glasgow G2 5QR *Tel* 0141 228 8000

SC NO SC012507   **ESTABLISHED** 1920

■ The Mayoress of Trafford's Charity Fund

WHERE FUNDING CAN BE GIVEN The borough of Trafford.

WHO CAN BENEFIT Voluntary organisations and charitable groups only.

WHAT IS FUNDED The Mayoress chooses a single charity (occasionally two) to support the year before she takes office; the charity must benefit the inhabitants of the borough of Trafford.

TYPE OF GRANT Capital; one-off; one year or less.

SAMPLE GRANTS £47,000 to Trafford General Hospital for a piece of specialist equipment to treat prostate cancer.

FINANCES *Year* 2000–01 *Income* £47,000 *Grants* £47,000

HOW TO APPLY As the recipient charity is selected before the mayoress takes office, there is little point applying to this fund.

WHO TO APPLY TO The Mayor's Office, Trafford Town Hall, Talbot Road, Stretford, Trafford, Manchester M32 0YT *Tel* 0161 912 4106 *Fax* 0161 912 4209

CC NO 512299   **ESTABLISHED** 1982

■ TRAID (Textile Recycling for Aid and International Development)

WHERE FUNDING CAN BE GIVEN Developing countries.

WHO CAN BENEFIT Children and young people.

WHAT IS FUNDED Innovative international aid and development projects with an emphasis on health and educational projects targeting children and young people.

WHAT IS NOT FUNDED No grants to individuals.

TYPE OF GRANT One-off grant, paid in six monthly instalments over a one-two year period.

RANGE OF GRANTS £5,000–£30,000.

SAMPLE GRANTS £30,000 to rehabilitate street children in Sao Paulo – Brazil; £27,650 to a primary education project in Afghanistan; £25,000 to a water and sanitation project in Madagascar; £10,550 towards prevention of domestic violence in Costa Rica.

FINANCES *Year* 2001 *Income* £1,770,638 *Assets* £493,505

TRUSTEES Ian Hagg, Chairman; Julie Davies; Gillian Gee.

HOW TO APPLY An application form and guidelines are available from the charity. The closing date is August with funds allocated by December. Applicants may be invited to discuss their proposal in person with the project evaluation committee and successful applicants will be required to give TRAID staff a presentation on the progress of the project at head office.

WHO TO APPLY TO The Project Evaluation Committee, 5 Second Way, Wembley, Middlesex HA9 0YJ *Tel* 020 8733 2580 *Fax* 020 8903 9922 *E-mail* projects@traid.org.uk *Website* www.traid.org.uk

CC NO 297489   ESTABLISHED 1999

■ The Constance Travis Charitable Trust

WHERE FUNDING CAN BE GIVEN UK (national charities only); Northamptonshire (all sectors).

WHO CAN BENEFIT UK-wide organisations and local groups in Northamptonshire.

WHAT IS FUNDED General charitable causes.

WHAT IS NOT FUNDED No grants to individuals or non-registered charities.

TYPE OF GRANT One-off grants for core, capital and project support.

RANGE OF GRANTS Up to £30,000.

SAMPLE GRANTS 2000–01: £29,000 to NSPCC; £20,000 to Imperial Cancer Research Fund; £15,000 to Age Concern; £10,000 each to Macmillan Cancer Relief, and The Stroke Association; £8,100 to Quinton Village Hall Trust; £5,000 each to Colon Cancer Concern, Mental Health Foundation, Northamptonshire Association for the Blind, and Princes Trust.

FINANCES *Year* 2001–02 *Income* £247,369 *Grants* £262,000 *Assets* £12,310,343

TRUSTEES Mrs C M Travis; E R A Travis.

HOW TO APPLY In writing to the correspondent.

WHO TO APPLY TO A Travis, Quinton Rising, Quinton, Northampton NN7 2EF

CC NO 294540   ESTABLISHED 1986

■ The Treeside Trust

WHERE FUNDING CAN BE GIVEN UK, but mainly local.

WHO CAN BENEFIT Mainly local charities, and a few UK charities which are supported on a regular basis.

TYPE OF GRANT One-off.

RANGE OF GRANTS Maximum £10,000; mainly £500–£1,000.

FINANCES *Year* 2001–02 *Income* £47,000 *Grants* £97,500 *Assets* £915,000

TRUSTEES C C Gould; J R B Gould; J R W Gould; D M Ives; R J Ives; B Washbrook.

OTHER INFORMATION The trust states: 'In the main the trustees intend to make a limited number of substantial grants each year, rather than a larger number of smaller ones, in order to make significant contributions to some of the causes supported.'

HOW TO APPLY In writing to the correspondent, but unsolicited applications are unlikely to be supported.

WHO TO APPLY TO John Roger Beresford Gould, Trustee, 4 The Park, Grasscroft, Oldham OL4 4ES *Tel* 01457 876422

CC NO 1061586   ESTABLISHED 1997

■ The Triangle Trust (1949) Fund

WHERE FUNDING CAN BE GIVEN UK.

WHO CAN BENEFIT Individuals employed or who have been employed in the pharmaceutical industry and their dependants; organisations benefiting carers, people with disabilities, older people and disadvantaged people.

WHAT IS FUNDED Grants are given to: individuals who are employed or have been employed in the pharmaceutical industry and their dependants; also organisations and registered charities which have already been approached by the trust, particularly projects concerned with carers, community arts, disability, education, elderly and poverty.

WHAT IS NOT FUNDED Direct applications from individuals; overseas charities or projects outside the UK; charities for the promotion of religion; medical research; environmental, wildlife or heritage appeals.

TYPE OF GRANT One-off, educational, recurring, salaries and running costs.

RANGE OF GRANTS £250–£45,000.

SAMPLE GRANTS £50,000 to University of London; £45,000 to Family Welfare Association; £26,000 to East Anglia Children's Hospice; £10,000 each to ASHA, Family Service Units, Headway Essex, National Autistic Society and Ulverston and North Lonsdale CAB.

FINANCES *Year* 2001–02 *Income* £483,000 *Grants* £553,000 *Assets* £14,000,000

TRUSTEES J C Maisey, Chair; M Pearce; Mrs J Turner; Rt Revd D Urquhart; Dr Marjorie Walker; Mrs M Burfitt; M Powell; R Kathoke.

OTHER INFORMATION In addition to the figure given above, £53,000 was given in grants to individuals in need.

HOW TO APPLY Organisations should apply using the trust's application form, available from the correspondent. This should be returned to the trust by post. The accompanying guidance states that 'trustees prefer to initiate their own projects for funding, and do not normally respond to unsolicited applications'.

WHO TO APPLY TO Jill Hailey, Secretary, 28 Great James Street, London WC1N 3EY *Tel* 020 7831 5942 *E-mail* triang@triangletrust.org

CC NO 222860   ESTABLISHED 1949

■ Triodos Foundation

WHERE FUNDING CAN BE GIVEN UK and developing countries.

WHO CAN BENEFIT Registered charities.

WHAT IS FUNDED General charitable purposes. The objectives of the foundation are to support charitable needs which have been identified through, but which are unable to be fully supported by, the work of Triodos Bank in the UK. It works closely with individuals, organisations and depositors of the bank to support projects which work in charitable areas.

WHAT IS NOT FUNDED No grants to individuals or students.

FINANCES *Year* 1997 *Income* £136,000 *Grants* £36,000 *Assets* £128,000

TRUSTEES P Blom; M Robinson; M Bierman.

HOW TO APPLY In writing to the correspondent. Initial telephone enquiries are welcome.

WHO TO APPLY TO The Trustees, Brunel House, 11 The Promenade, Clifton, Bristol BS8 3NN *Tel* 0117 973 9339

CC NO 1052958   ESTABLISHED 1996

■ Mrs S H Troughton Charity Trust

WHERE FUNDING CAN BE GIVEN UK.

WHO CAN BENEFIT Registered charities.

WHAT IS FUNDED General charitable purposes.

WHAT IS NOT FUNDED No grants to individuals including students, or to non-registered charities.

TYPE OF GRANT One-off.

RANGE OF GRANTS £50–£20,000.

SAMPLE GRANTS £20,000 to Blair Charitable Trust; £12,000 to Charities Aid Foundation; £3,000 to The New School – Butterstone; £50 to Friends of Atholl Abbeyfield.

FINANCES *Year* 2001–02 *Income* £24,761 *Grants* £35,050 *Assets* £614,514

TRUSTEES The Dickinson Trust Ltd.

HOW TO APPLY In writing to the correspondent, including an sae. Only successful applications for a grant will be acknowledged.

WHO TO APPLY TO Alan John Winborn, The Dickinson Trust Limited, 10–12 Cork Street, London W1S 3LW *Tel* 020 7439 9061

CC NO 265957   **ESTABLISHED** 1972

■ Truedene Co. Ltd

WHERE FUNDING CAN BE GIVEN UK and overseas.

WHO CAN BENEFIT Organisations benefiting children, young adults, students and Jewish people.

WHAT IS FUNDED Educational, religious and other charitable institutions, principally Jewish.

FINANCES *Year* 1996–97 *Income* £5,500 *Grants* £184,000 *Assets* £5,000,000

TRUSTEES H Laufer; M Gross; S Berger; S Laufer; S Berger; Mrs Sarah Klein; Mrs Z Sternlicht.

HOW TO APPLY In writing to the correspondent.

WHO TO APPLY TO The Trustees, Cohen Arnold & Co., 13–17 New Burlington Place, London W1X 2HL

CC NO 248268   **ESTABLISHED** 1966

■ The Truemark Trust

WHERE FUNDING CAN BE GIVEN UK only.

WHO CAN BENEFIT Registered charities with preference for neighbourhood-based community projects and innovatory work with less popular groups.

WHAT IS FUNDED The trust favours small organisations with a preference for innovatory projects. Current main areas of interest are disability, older people and people otherwise disadvantaged and include counselling and community support groups in areas of unrest or deprivation; alternative or complementary health projects.

WHAT IS NOT FUNDED No grants to individuals, for scientific or medical research or for church buildings. General appeals from large UK organisations are not supported.

TYPE OF GRANT Usually one-off for a specific project or part of a project. Core funding and/or salaries rarely considered.

RANGE OF GRANTS Average grant £1,000.

SAMPLE GRANTS 2000–01: £5,000 each to Bristol Cancer Help Centre, Foundation for Integrated Medicine and Prison Phoenix Trust – Oxford; £3,500 to Bristol Stepping Stone; £3,000 each to Brainwave, Friends Fellowship of Healing, Hamlin Religious Trust, RAPT and White Eagle Lodge; £2,500 to Citizen's Advice Bureau – Teignbridge; £2,000 each to Brighton & Hove Federation of Disabled People, Freshwinds Charitable Trust – Birmingham, Katie Foxton's Holidays for Sick Children – Leicester, Sport

Forum for the Disabled, Step by Step Project and Wheelchairs to Go.

FINANCES *Year* 2001–02 *Income* £189,132 *Grants* £214,500 *Assets* £5,225,788

TRUSTEES Michael Collishaw; Michael Meakin; Richard Wolfe; Sir Thomas Lucas; Wendy Collett; Stuart Neil.

HOW TO APPLY In writing to the correspondent, including the most recent set of accounts, clear details of the need the project is designed to meet and an outline budget. Trustees meet four times a year (in March, June, September and December). Only successful applicants receive a reply.

WHO TO APPLY TO Mrs Judy Hayward, PO Box 2, Liss, Hampshire GU33 6YP

CC NO 265855   **ESTABLISHED** 1973

■ Trumros Limited

WHERE FUNDING CAN BE GIVEN UK.

WHO CAN BENEFIT Jewish institutions.

WHAT IS FUNDED Jewish religious and educational institutions.

RANGE OF GRANTS £100–£20,000; typical grant £1,000–£2,000.

SAMPLE GRANTS In 1999: £20,000 each to Beis Yoseph Zvi Institution, Centre for Torah Education Zichron Yaacov, and Memorah Primary School; £11,000 to SOFOT; £5,800 to General Cherra Kadish Jerusalem; £4,800 To Oldos Aharon.

FINANCES *Year* 2000 *Income* £539,117 *Grants* £138,989 *Assets* £2,460,885

TRUSTEES R S Hofbauer; Mrs H Hofbauer.

HOW TO APPLY In writing to the correspondent, but note that the trust states it is already inundated with applications.

WHO TO APPLY TO Mrs H Hofbauer, Trustee, 182 Finchley Road, London NW3 7AD

CC NO 285533   **ESTABLISHED** 1982

■ Trust for London

WHERE FUNDING CAN BE GIVEN The Metropolitan Police District of London and the City of London.

WHO CAN BENEFIT Organisations that: benefit local people and communities in London; are open to all members of the community; help local communities to identify and tackle local problems; do work that might be used to teach others; local people and communities have set up to help themselves; are open to all members of their community; and are set up to tackle a specific issue. Funding is mainly given to refugee and migrant groups; self-help groups, for example, children and groups, estate-based organisations, lesbian and gay groups, older people' s groups, organisations set up to tackle a specific issue, women' s groups and youth groups; and supplementary and mother-tongue schools.

WHAT IS FUNDED Identifying needs and deliver services; gaining access to training opportunities; and organise meetings, conferences, seminars and events which identify problems, raise awareness, explore solutions, or promote good practice.

WHAT IS NOT FUNDED No grants for: distribution by umbrella bodies; general appeals; holiday play schemes; individual members of the public; major expenses for buying or building premises; part of a full-time salary; replacing spending cuts made by local or central government; research; or trips abroad.

Think carefully about every application. Is it justified?

847

TYPE OF GRANT Core costs, part-time or sessional salaries (not full-time), equipment, capital purchases.

RANGE OF GRANTS Maximum grant available is £10,000 a year.

SAMPLE GRANTS This list includes grants made over several years: £20,000 to Haringey Standing Committee on Community Languages for operating costs; £14,000 each to Alborz School of Persian Language – Barnet for operating costs of the mother-tongue classes, Ealing Somali Welfare and Cultural Association for running costs and Rafidain Relief Association – Redbridge for salary costs; £13,900 to North West Saturday School – Brent for the Saturday School; £13,655 to Stoned Arts – Brent for running costs; £13,600 to Craig Park Business and Training Centre – Enfield for running costs; £12,620 to Afro-Caribbean People's Organisation – Brent for extension to the lunch club; £12,000 each to Corali Dance Company – Southwark for staffing and running costs and Enfield Bangladesh Welfare Association for a part-time advice worker.

FINANCES *Year* 2001 *Income* £680,000 *Grants* £695,000 *Assets* £17,290,000

TRUSTEES The trustee of Trust for London is City Parochial Foundation, whose trustees are: Prof. Gerald Manners, chair; Maggie Baxter, vice-chair; John Barnes; Bishop of Willesden; Peter Dale; William Dove; Prof. Julian Franks; Patrick Haynes; Edward Lord; Ian Luder; John Muir; Miss Jyoti Munsiff; Elahe Panahi; Nigel Pantling; Roger Payton; Gillian Roberts; Robin Sherlock; Lynda Stevens; Albert Tucker; Jane Wilmot.

OTHER INFORMATION The trust also works with other funding organisations and funded groups to identify emerging needs and to develop and make appropriate responses.

HOW TO APPLY In writing to the correspondent. Guidelines are available from the trust. Applications should be submitted in writing, on no more than two sides of A4, with a copy of the organisation's constitution and most recent report and accounts. Telephone discussions are welcomed and if the trust feels the application will be considered for funding, a field officer will arrange a meeting to give an application form and give advice on what to apply for. The field officer will then present the applicant's case to the trustees. The deadlines for receiving completed applications are: 31 January for the March meeting; 15 April for the June meeting; 31 July for the September Meeting; and 15 October for the December meeting.

WHO TO APPLY TO Bharat Mehta, Clerk, 6 Middle Street, London EC1A 7PH *Tel* 020 7606 6145 *Website* www.cityparochial.org.uk
CC NO 294710 **ESTABLISHED** 1986

■ Trust Sixty Three

WHERE FUNDING CAN BE GIVEN UK and overseas, with a preference for Bedfordshire and Hertfordshire.

WHO CAN BENEFIT There are no restrictions regarding beneficiaries other than that stated under What Is Not Funded below.

WHAT IS FUNDED General charitable purposes.

WHAT IS NOT FUNDED No grants to individuals.

TYPE OF GRANT General.

RANGE OF GRANTS £20–£10,000.

SAMPLE GRANTS £9,650 to North Hertfordshire Sanctuary; £7,000 to Christian Aid; £5,400 each to Bedfordshire Garden Carers and Rainbow School; £5,00 each to Pasque Hospital and Prebend Day Centre; £4,280 to St Mary's

Church; £3,189 to Ridgeway School; £2,500 each to Richmond School, and Scope.

FINANCES *Year* 2000–01 *Income* £21,888 *Grants* £106,188 *Assets* £579,160

TRUSTEES M W Tait; Mrs A F Tait; C G Nott; Mrs J Hobbs; Mrs D Staines.

HOW TO APPLY In writing to the correspondent.

WHO TO APPLY TO Mrs A F Tait, Trustee, 3 The Compasses, High Street, Clophill, Bedfordshire MK45 4AF *Tel* 01525 860777 *Fax* 01525 862246
CC NO 1049136 **ESTABLISHED** 1995

■ Trust Thamesmead Limited

WHERE FUNDING CAN BE GIVEN Thamesmead and Abbey Wood.

WHO CAN BENEFIT Community and voluntary groups.

WHAT IS FUNDED This trust administers the Abbey Wood & Thamesmead Community Chest project. The aim of the Community Chest is to provide community and voluntary groups, which often do not have the resources of larger organisations, with a means of accessing Single Regeneration Budget (SRB) funds.

WHAT IS NOT FUNDED Grants will not be awarded to organisations already receiving funds from the mainstream SRB funding, or to groups who have already received a grant from the Community Chest during the current financial year. No support for: individuals – only organised groups will be considered; grants to cover expenditure that has already been incurred; activities that are considered by the Awarding Panel to be predominantly for religious or political purposes, or the responsibility of a statutory authority; activities that do not meet community needs within the Thamesmead and Abbey Wood area.

RANGE OF GRANTS Usually £250 to £2,000.

FINANCES *Year* 2000–01 *Grants* £50,000

TRUSTEES E Claridge; G Reynolds; A Dixon.

HOW TO APPLY Application packs are available from the trust. Applicants for grants of £1,000 or more will be expected to show how their project relates to one or more objectives of the SRB document. Applicants will also have to provide comprehensive financial details of their project, with evidence that income targets are realistic and achievable.

WHO TO APPLY TO The Community Involvement Team, 19a Joyce Dawson Way, Thamesmead, London SE28 8RA *Tel* 020 8320 4470 *E-mail* jmartin@trust-thamesmead.co.uk *Website* www.trustthamesmead.co.uk
CC NO 271731 **ESTABLISHED** 1976

■ The Trusthouse Charitable Foundation

WHERE FUNDING CAN BE GIVEN Unrestricted.

WHO CAN BENEFIT Headquarters organisations rather than local branches.

WHAT IS FUNDED The six priority areas are: relief of hardship and disability; education; environment; heritage; the arts; sporting activities.

WHAT IS NOT FUNDED The foundation will not normally support: small local charities; applications from individuals; overseas charities, except those which are based in the UK and are operating overseas; other grantmaking bodies; or appeals received directly from local branches of national charities.

TYPE OF GRANT One-off for specific purposes.

SAMPLE GRANTS £60,000 to Ronald Raven Cancer Research Association; £50,000 each to Centre for the Children's Book, Children's Hospital of Wales and Victoria and Albert Museum; £10,000 each to Birmingham Hippodrome Development Centre, Martin House Children's Hopsice, MERLIN, Rehab UK, Royal Academy of Art and Yeovil Hospice Appeal.

FINANCES *Year* 2000–01 *Grants* £1,585,000

TRUSTEES Lord Peyton, chair; Sir Jeremy Beecham; Lord Alex Bernstein; Sir Richard Carew Pole; Baroness Cox; Earl of Gainsborough; Duke of Marlborough; Olga Polizzi; Sir Hugh Rossi.

HOW TO APPLY On brief application forms (one side of an A4 sheet) available on written request to the correspondent. Applicants are invited, if necessary, to add any additional information on the reverse of the form and enclose such supporting documentation as they feel will help the application. Please note the foundation does not generally accept telephone requests. The trustees meet quarterly.

WHO TO APPLY TO Derek Harris, Administrator, S G Hambro's Trust Co. Ltd, 41 Tower Hill, London EC3N 4SG *Tel* 020 7480 5000

CC NO 1063945   **ESTABLISHED** 1997

··

■ Tubney Charitable Trust

WHERE FUNDING CAN BE GIVEN Unrestricted, but mainly UK, with a local interest in the Oxfordshire area.

WHO CAN BENEFIT UK registered, exempt and excepted charities which undertake charitable activities where there is a demonstrable element of outward provision and benefit to the community at large, to ensure that as many people benefit as possible.

WHAT IS FUNDED (a) The environment, both built and natural. (b) Animal welfare. (c) Education, including the arts, literature, music and history. (d) Medical research and palliative care.

WHAT IS NOT FUNDED The trust does not generally make grants to the following: individuals; non-UK charities (although grants may be made to UK charities operating overseas); housing/homeless charities; refugees; non specific university appeals; projects that replace statutory funding and provision; retrospective funding; the promotion of sectarian religious interests; large national charities which already enjoy widespread public support; projects/work which cannot demonstrate a sufficiently wide degree of outward provision and benefit to the community at large; the repair and maintenance of historic buildings or the funding of new buildings, other than where such building works fall within another programme; medical research; or pure research, publications, public lectures or the development of websites.

TYPE OF GRANT Capital and revenue.

RANGE OF GRANTS £30,000–£250,000 a year. Small grants programmes exist in some areas, administrated by local community foundations.

SAMPLE GRANTS In first quarter of 2002–03: £466,450 to Volunteer Reading Help; £425,000 to Rare Breeds Survival Trust; £140,000 to Treloar Trust; £111,000 to BTCV; £100,000 each to Compassion in World Farming, and Douglas House a Respice for Young People; £75,000 each to Chicken Shed Theatre Company and Sick Children's Trust; £71,700 to National School Band Association; £66,785 to Rehab UK; £66,000 to Iain Rennie Hospice at Home.

FINANCES *Year* 2001–02 *Income* £26,696,599 *Grants* £550,577 *Assets* £27,247,175

TRUSTEES Jonathan Burchfield; Terry Collins; Jim Kennedy; René Olivieri.

OTHER INFORMATION The income for the year includes £26,000,000 in legacies received. It is anticipated the trust will have around £6,000,000 a year available.

HOW TO APPLY Applications will only be considered if made on the standard application form. The application form and full grant guidelines may be downloaded from the charity' s website, or may be obtained from the correspondent. Alternatively, you may request an application form by telephoning Catherine Small on 0118 925 4662 or e-mailing c.small@nabarro.com. Applications must be made by post and signed by a trustee or senior manager of the applicant charity. The application form is a straightforward four-page document. If you have any queries in relation to filling out the application form or if you are uncertain whether you are eligible for a grant you are welcome to contact Catherine Small, whose details are set out above, to discuss your application. The trustees meet every three months to consider the applications received in the previous quarter. The grant application periods close on 31 March, 30 June, 30 September and 31 December in each year. In each grant application period the Trustees will only consider applications which are received by the close of business on the final day of that grant application period.

WHO TO APPLY TO Catherine Small, Nabarro Nathanson, 34 Bridge Street, Reading RG1 2LU *Tel* 0118 925 4662 *Website* www.tubney.org.uk

CC NO 1061480   **ESTABLISHED** 1997

··

■ Tudor Rose Ltd

WHERE FUNDING CAN BE GIVEN UK.

WHO CAN BENEFIT Registered charities benefiting Jewish people and people disadvantaged by poverty.

WHAT IS FUNDED Advancement of religion (orthodox Jewish), relief of poverty and other charitable purposes.

SAMPLE GRANTS £28,700 to Ponovex; £18,100 to CWCT; £12,500 to Yetev Lev; £11,500 to Yad Eliezer; £4,125 to Torah Study Centre; £3,000 to Rihiliation Trust; £1,640 to NWL Synagogue; £1,000 to Gur Trust.

FINANCES *Year* 2000–01 *Income* £253,674 *Grants* £81,615 *Assets* £704,132

TRUSTEES M Lehrfield; M Taub; A Taub; S Taub; S L Taub.

HOW TO APPLY In writing to the correspondent.

WHO TO APPLY TO Samuel Taub, Secretary, Martin and Heller, Accountants, 5 North End Road, London NW11 7RJ *Tel* 020 8455 6789

CC NO 800576   **ESTABLISHED** 1987

··

■ The Tudor Trust

WHERE FUNDING CAN BE GIVEN UK and overseas.

WHO CAN BENEFIT Registered charities and other charitable organisations.

WHAT IS FUNDED For the period 2000-April 2003, applications were considered from charities/charitable organisations working in communities with significant need in rural and urban areas. This included support for people who are vulnerable or only just about managing, particularly young people aged 9–18 and elderly people. The trust also assisted charitable organisations working to help people with mental health problems and head injuries; people who are substance misusers; homeless people; offenders, ex-offenders, and others at risk such as young people coming out of care.

The trust sometimes helped organisations providing assistance with: (a) accommodation, e.g. rent deposit schemes and supported accommodation, and schemes offering integrated care for older people; (b) education, such as home/school links, core curriculum at supplementary schools, literacy and IT for the family; (c) health, such as work with people who are frail or have dementia, support for families under stress, including carers; (d) recreation, such as detached youth work, fun learning opportunities, encouragement of social interaction, green spaces in urban settings; (e) relationships including counselling and mediation for families and in schools, befriending, contact centres, work with fathers/young men, intergenerational work and parenting; (f) resources, such as centres and community buildings for the whole community, voluntary sector offices, advice for young people. Note: There are a lot of organisations/areas of work which cannot be funded and guidelines should be studied before applying.

WHAT IS NOT FUNDED No grants are made for: activity centres; advice; advocacy; after-school clubs; animal charities; arts; breakfast clubs; bursaries and scholarships; capacity building/technical support; church and hall fabric appeals; colleges; commercial organisations; community foundations; community transport; conferences/seminars; conservation of buildings/flora/fauna; Councils of Voluntary Service; counselling; disabilities (mental and physical); endowment appeals; expeditions/overseas travel; fabric; fundraising events/salaries of fundraisers; halls and church centres; healthy living centres; helplines; holidays/holiday centres; homework clubs; hospitals and hospices; illness (physical); individuals; large national charities enjoying widespread support; leisure clubs; medical care; medical research; minibuses; mother tongue classes/cultural activities; museums/places of entertainment; neighbourhood mediation; nurseries, crèches and pre-school childcare; play schemes and parent & toddler groups; playgrounds; research; religion; schools; scouts, guides and other uniformed youth groups; sponsorship and marketing appeals; sports; training and employment schemes; universities; victims of crime, domestic and sexual abuse, trauma or war; volunteer centres; or women's centres.

TYPE OF GRANT Capital and revenue grants.

RANGE OF GRANTS From £5,000 upwards. Average £23,000.

SAMPLE GRANTS £80,000 to Launceston Youth Partnership for a youth resource centre; £50,000 to Cornerstone for a residential unit for young care leavers; £30,000 to Brighton Unemployed Centre for running costs; £25,000 over three years to Inside Out Trust for operational costs; £20,000 to Banbury Young Homelessness Project for start-up supported lodgings scheme; £15,000 each to Greater Manchester Headway House for operational costs and Littlehay Prison Visitors Centre for operational costs; £10,000 over two years to Wishart Centre for core costs for people who are homeless; £7,500 over two years to Ascension Community Project; £5,000 to Citizen's Advice Bureau – Aberdeen for a hospital advice service.

FINANCES *Year* 2001–02 *Income* £12,727,000 *Grants* £21,361,000 *Assets* £329,000,000

TRUSTEES Grove Charity Management Ltd., of which the directors are: Mrs Mary Graves; Mrs Helen Dunwell; Dr Desmond Graves; Mrs Penelope Buckler; Christopher Graves* (also the present director of the trust); Ray Anstice; Mrs Catherine Antcliff; Mrs Louise Collins; Mrs Elizabeth Crawshaw; Matt Dunwell*; James Long*; Ben Dunwell*; Frances Runacres; Monica Barlow* (asterisks indicate membership of the grantmaking trustee committee).

PUBLICATIONS *Guidelines for Applicants*.

HOW TO APPLY Applications can only be made in writing and cannot be accepted by fax or e-mail. The trust does not use an application form. Information needed includes: a summary of the current work of the organisation, with the latest annual report; a description of the project/proposals/area of work for which funding is requested; an indication of the numbers of people involved/likely to be involved and how they will benefit; a breakdown of costs (for capital works, these might be building costs, VAT; fees, furniture and equipment; for revenue they might be salaries, premises, training, publicity, expenses, etc.) – retrospective grants are not available; details of funding raised or committed to date and steps being taken to raise the balance other than the approach to the Tudor Trust; any other relevant information such as catchment area served, numbers attending existing activities per month or per annum, how revenue implications of capital proposals will be met – for new buildings or major refurbishment schemes, drawings/plans and possibly a photo are helpful; and the latest annual accounts (or a copy of a recent financial/bank statement if the organisation is too new to have annual accounts). Some applicants will be told almost immediately that the trust cannot help. For the remainder, there is a continuous process of assessment, and applicants will usually be told the outcome eight weeks after all the information has been received by the trust. Please do not telephone for news of progress during this period. A letter will be sent giving the trustees' decision. If a grant has been approved, conditions relating to the release of the grant will be included in the letter. A visit may be made to the project; but this will be initiated by the trust and will not necessarily result in a grant being approved. Organisations are requested not to approach the trust again for at least 12 months after a grant has been paid or notification of an unsuccessful application has been given.

WHO TO APPLY TO Christopher Graves, Director, 7 Ladbroke Grove, London W11 3BD *Tel* 020 7727 8522 *Website* www.tudortrust.org.uk

CC NO 206260 **ESTABLISHED** 1955

....

■ The Tufton Charitable Trust

WHERE FUNDING CAN BE GIVEN UK.

WHO CAN BENEFIT Individuals and organisations benefiting Christians, Jews and evangelists.

WHAT IS FUNDED Christian activity supporting evangelism.

WHAT IS NOT FUNDED No grants for repair or maintenance of buildings.

TYPE OF GRANT One-off and project-related.

SAMPLE GRANTS £22,000 in nine grants to Church of England; £3,000 to Lambeth Partnership; £2,500 to Variety Club of Great Britain; £2,022 to charters Ancaster College; £2,000 each to Action Institute, Goodenough College, LICC and Regeneration Trust.

FINANCES *Year* 2001 *Income* £307,692 *Grants* £54,010 *Assets* £1,556,035

TRUSTEES Sir Christopher Wates; Lady Wates; J R F Lulham.

HOW TO APPLY In writing to the correspondent, including an sae.

WHO TO APPLY TO C Sadlow, Slater Maidment, 7 St James's Square, London SW1Y 4JU *Tel* 020 7930 7621

CC NO 801479   **ESTABLISHED** 1989

■ The Tunnell Trust

WHERE FUNDING CAN BE GIVEN UK, with a preference for Scotland.

WHO CAN BENEFIT British-based groups and societies of two to eight professional chamber music players aged 27 or under.

WHAT IS FUNDED The trust aims to promote chamber music, advance the education of young musicians and provide performance opportunities for talented young professional chamber musicians.

WHAT IS NOT FUNDED Awards are not available to singers or vocal groups, nor to instrumental duos consisting of a soloist with accompanist. Duos in which the players are equal partners, for example in violin and piano or cello and piano sonatas, are eligible.

FINANCES *Year* 2000–01 *Grants* £44,000

TRUSTEES C J Packard, Chair; C Abram; R Deakin; Carol Høgel; M Hunter; D McLellan; D Nicholson; K Robb; D W S Todd; J C Tunnell; O W Tunnell; P Tunnell.

HOW TO APPLY Application forms are available from the correspondent at the above address. The deadline is 30 June, with auditions for potential recipients held in November.

WHO TO APPLY TO The Secretary, 4 Royal Terrace, Edinburgh EH7 5AB *Tel* 0131 556 4043 *Fax* 0131 556 3969 *E-mail* tunnelltrust@aol.com

SC NO SC018408

■ The Douglas Turner Trust

WHERE FUNDING CAN BE GIVEN West Midlands, particularly Birmingham; UK.

WHO CAN BENEFIT Mainly local charities benefiting children, older people and people with disabilities.

WHAT IS FUNDED General charitable purposes, including the arts, education, older people, medical research, hospices, children and disabled people.

WHAT IS NOT FUNDED No grants to individuals or non-registered charities.

TYPE OF GRANT Recurring and one-off donations, capital and core costs.

SAMPLE GRANTS £40,333 to Age Concern – Birmingham for the TV fund; £30,000 to Acorn's Children's Hospice; £18,000 to Christian Aid; £15,000 to Merlin for the India Earthquake Appeal and as an annual donation; £12,000 each to Birmingham Dsylexia Association and Opportunity International; £10,000 each to British Red Cross, Compton Hospice, Historic Churches Preservation Trust, St Martin's Renewal Campaign, and St Mary's Hospice.

FINANCES *Year* 2001–02 *Income* £432,192 *Grants* £410,983 *Assets* £12,361,166

TRUSTEES W S Ellis; D P Pearson; T J Lunt; Sir Christopher Stuart-White.

HOW TO APPLY Telephone enquiries before formal applications are welcomed. Applications must include the latest annual report and accounts. There are no application forms.

WHO TO APPLY TO J E Dyke, Trust Administrator, 1 The Yew Trees, High Street, Henley-in-Arden, Solihull B95 5BN *Tel* 01564 793085

CC NO 227892   **ESTABLISHED** 1964

■ The Florence Turner Trust

WHERE FUNDING CAN BE GIVEN UK, but with a strong preference for Leicestershire.

WHO CAN BENEFIT Local charities and local branches of national charities benefiting people of all ages, at risk groups, and people who are disadvantaged by poverty, disabled or socially isolated.

WHAT IS FUNDED Local educational establishments, health and welfare, especially the elderly, youth and community. music and maintenance and preservation of buildings (including religious buildings) and and the countryside.

WHAT IS NOT FUNDED The trust does not support individuals for educational purposes.

TYPE OF GRANT Largely recurrent. No loans.

SAMPLE GRANTS £23,430 to Leicester Grammar School for bursaries, library and prizes; £11,650 to Leicester Charity Organisation Society; £5,000 to Barnardos – Leicester; £2,550 to Leicester and Lericestershire Historic Churches Preservation Trust; £2,400 to Royal Leicestershire, Rutland and Wycliffe Society for the Blind; £2,300 to EEIBA; £2,200 each to Age Concern Leicester, CARE Fund for the Mentally Handicapped, Leicester YMCA, and Leicestershire Scout Council.

FINANCES *Year* 2000–01 *Income* £158,898 *Grants* £151,635 *Assets* £4,319,949

TRUSTEES Roger Bowder; Allan A Veasey; Caroline A Macpherson.

HOW TO APPLY In writing to the correspondent. Trustees meet every eight or nine weeks.

WHO TO APPLY TO The Trustees, c/o Harvey Ingram Owston, 20 New Walk, Leicester LE1 6TX *Tel* 0116 254 5454 *Fax* 0116 255 3318

CC NO 502721   **ESTABLISHED** 1973

■ The R D Turner Charitable Trust

WHERE FUNDING CAN BE GIVEN UK, with a preference for Worcestershire.

WHO CAN BENEFIT Registered charities only.

WHAT IS FUNDED General charitable purposes.

WHAT IS NOT FUNDED No grants to non-registered charities or to individuals.

TYPE OF GRANT One-off and recurrent.

RANGE OF GRANTS £500–£50,000.

SAMPLE GRANTS £50,000 to Acorns Children's Hospice for the Worcester Appeal; £10,000 each to Cambridge Foundation, Ironbridge Gorge Museum Development Trust, Pioneer Centre, and Worcester and Dudley Historic Churches Trust; £5,000 each to Royal Agricultural Benevolent Institution, Sunfield School, Worcester Rural Stress Support Network, and Worcester Three Choirs Festival; £3,000 to Pattaya Orphanage.

FINANCES *Year* 2001–02 *Income* £344,182 *Grants* £150,250 *Assets* £15,458,701

TRUSTEES W S Ellis; D P Pearson; T J Lunt; Sir Christopher Stuart-White.

HOW TO APPLY In writing to the correspondent with a copy of your latest annual report and accounts. There are no application forms. The trustees meet in May, August, October and December to consider applications, which should be submitted in the month prior to each meeting. Telephone enquiries may be made before submitting an appeal.

Think carefully about every application. Is it justified?

851

WHO TO APPLY TO J E Dyke, Administrator, 1 The Yew Trees, High Street, Henley-in-Arden, Solihull, West Midlands B95 5BN *Tel* 01564 793085
CC NO 263556   ESTABLISHED 1971

■ Miss S M Tutton Charitable Trust

WHERE FUNDING CAN BE GIVEN UK.

WHO CAN BENEFIT The trust provides financial support to young singers through the Sybil Tutton Awards. In addition it makes grants to selected music colleges and training opera companies benefiting adults aged 20 to 30, students and musicians.

WHAT IS FUNDED Awards and grants for postgraduate opera studies and grants to music colleges, charities and opera companies. The trust has some funds available for occasional discretionary grants, but they are very limited.

TYPE OF GRANT Awards and grants.

SAMPLE GRANTS £15,000 to Sybil Tutton Awards; £5,000 to National Opera Studio; £3,000 to Clontor Farm Music Trust; £1,500 to Aldeburgh Foundation for Britten Pears School.

FINANCES *Year* 2002 *Income* £53,214 *Grants* £32,751 *Assets* £690,731

TRUSTEES P G G Miller; R Pickering; R Van Allen.

HOW TO APPLY Individuals seeking grants for opera studies should consider applying directly to the Musicians Benevolent Fund (charity no: 228089) which administers the Sybil Tutton Awards. Organisations should submit full details of projects to the address below. The trust has some funds available for occasional discretionary grants, but they are very limited. Assistance is generally provided only where students are recommended by organisations with which the trust has a close working relationship.

WHO TO APPLY TO Peter Raddenbury, BDO Stoy Hayward, 8 Baker Street, London W1U 3LL *Tel* 020 7893 2439
CC NO 298774   ESTABLISHED 1988

■ The TUUT Charitable Trust

WHERE FUNDING CAN BE GIVEN Worldwide.

WHO CAN BENEFIT Those supported by, or having close associations with, trade unions.

WHAT IS FUNDED General at trustees' discretion, with an overriding priority to charities with strong trade union connections or interests.

WHAT IS NOT FUNDED No grants to individuals.

TYPE OF GRANT One-off, recurrent, research and capital. Funding is for up to three years.

FINANCES *Year* 2001–02 *Income* £108,014 *Grants* £102,545 *Assets* £1,755,203

TRUSTEES Lord Christopher; J Monks; A Tuffin; M Walsh; M Bradley; E Chapman.

PUBLICATIONS Guidelines and newsletter.

HOW TO APPLY In writing to the correspondent. Applications should be submitted from a head office (where appropriate) and include latest accounts, purpose for donation and details of trade union links. Trustees meet three times a year.

WHO TO APPLY TO Ann Smith, Secretary, Congress House, Great Russell Street, London WC1B 3LQ *Tel* 020 7637 7116 *Fax* 020 7637 7087 *E-mail* info@tufm.co.uk
CC NO 258665   ESTABLISHED 1969

■ The Tyneside Charitable Trust

WHERE FUNDING CAN BE GIVEN Principally North Tyneside/Newcastle upon Tyne.

WHO CAN BENEFIT Registered charities.

WHAT IS FUNDED The relief of former employees of Swan Hunter Group Ltd or its subsidiary companies, or their dependants in need or such charitable bodies or institutions.

WHAT IS NOT FUNDED No grants to individuals.

TYPE OF GRANT Mostly one-off but there are some recurrent commitments.

RANGE OF GRANTS Average £1,000.

FINANCES *Year* 2000 *Income* £26,000 *Grants* £24,000 *Assets* £740,000

TRUSTEES R H Dickinson; R A Dickinson.

HOW TO APPLY In writing to the correspondent.

WHO TO APPLY TO S Lamb, Secretary, 43 Fairfield Drive, Cullercoats, North Shields, Tyne & Wear NE30 3AG *Tel* 0191 252 0663
CC NO 505758   ESTABLISHED 1976

■ Trustees of Tzedakah

WHERE FUNDING CAN BE GIVEN UK.

WHO CAN BENEFIT Mainly Jewish religious institutions and people disadvantaged by poverty.

WHAT IS FUNDED Funds are fully committed. Support is given for religious educational facilities and for poor families to supply their day-to-day facilities.

WHAT IS NOT FUNDED Grants only to registered charities. No grants to individuals.

RANGE OF GRANTS Generally £35–£25,000.

SAMPLE GRANTS £225,000 to Gevuras Ari Torah Academy; £100,000 to Telz Institutions; £26,431 to Woodstock Sinclair Trust; £26,213 to Friends of Poneviez Yeshiva; £25,790 to Hasmonean Girls School; £25,766 to Friends of Or Someach; £22,243 to Torah Temimoh; £17,252 to Lubavitch Foundation; £15,819 to Hendon Adath Yisroel Synagogue; £13,546 to Menorah Foundation School.

FINANCES *Year* 2000–01 *Income* £1,006,088 *Grants* £833,304 *Assets* £661,507

TRUSTEES Trustees of Tzedakah Ltd.

HOW TO APPLY **This trust states that it does not respond to unsolicited applications.**

WHO TO APPLY TO C Hollander, Brentmead House, Britannia Road, London N12 9RU *Tel* 020 8446 6767
CC NO 251897   ESTABLISHED 1966

■ The Ullmann Trust

WHERE FUNDING CAN BE GIVEN UK.

WHO CAN BENEFIT Individuals and organisations benefiting Jews and people who are disabled.

WHAT IS FUNDED Education and training, disability groups and the advancement of the Jewish religion.

RANGE OF GRANTS Usually £100–£2,000.

SAMPLE GRANTS £2,000 to Liberal Jewish Synagogue; £1,500 to Israel Disapora Trust; £1,000 to VPLS Lord Goodman Appeal; £500 to Staffordshire University.

FINANCES *Year* 1997–98 *Income* £336,000 *Grants* £8,600 *Assets* £468,000

TRUSTEES B W Lillymann; M Ullmann; C Ullmann.

HOW TO APPLY In writing to the correspondent.

WHO TO APPLY TO Michael Ullman, Trustee, Lathbury Park, Lathbury, Newport Pagnell, Bucks MK16 8LD *Tel* 01908 610316

CC NO 233630   **ESTABLISHED** 1970

■ Ultach Trust

WHERE FUNDING CAN BE GIVEN Northern Ireland only.

WHO CAN BENEFIT Generally voluntary Irish-language or cross-community groups based in Northern Ireland. Irish medium schools benefiting children and young adults.

WHAT IS FUNDED The trust normally funds new or established groups based in Northern Ireland involved in the promotion of the Irish language. Grants are normally aimed at specific projects and schemes rather than ongoing costs. Particular consideration is given to groups developing inter-community Irish-language activities. The trustees also, in exceptional cases, support projects aimed at improving the position of Irish people in the community and promoting knowledge of the language.

WHAT IS NOT FUNDED Generally the following are not supported: individuals, ongoing running costs, major capital programmes, to substitute cutbacks in statutory funding, travel expenses, publications or videos.

TYPE OF GRANT Except with regard to Irish-medium education, funding is generally restricted to starter finances and single projects.

TRUSTEES Ruairi O Bleine; Leslie Burnett; Sean O Coinn; Barry Kinghan; Ferdia Mac an Fhaili; Risteard Mac Gaghann; Sue MacGeown; Seamus de Napier; Sean Mac Giolla Cearra.

PUBLICATIONS Titles of publications and Irish courses available on request.

OTHER INFORMATION The trust has an annual budget of around £100,000 (when operating).

HOW TO APPLY This trust is currently dormant. It is dependent on the Northern Ireland Assembly for its grantmaking and this was not in operation at the time of publication. The trust stated that when the assembly is reconvened its grantmaking will resume.

WHO TO APPLY TO Róife Ní-Bhaoill, Room 202, Fountain House, 19 Donegall Place, Belfast BT1 5AB *Tel* 028 9023 0749 *Fax* 028 9023 0749 *E-mail* ultach@cinni.org *Website* www.cinni.org/ultach/uindex.htm

IR NO XN83581   **ESTABLISHED** 1989

■ Ulting Overseas Trust

WHERE FUNDING CAN BE GIVEN Worldwide, with preference for Asia, Africa and America.

WHO CAN BENEFIT Christian workers in the developing world undergoing further training for Christian service.

WHAT IS FUNDED The training in biblical and pastoral theology and mission of Christian workers in, and from, the developing world. Grants are made to training institutions, seminaries and other agencies involved in Christian ministry in the developing world, for the support of students in training for Christian service.

WHAT IS NOT FUNDED No grants are made towards the theological training of students from the developing world, nor to any training in subjects other than biblical, theological and missionary studies.

RANGE OF GRANTS £500–£18,000.

SAMPLE GRANTS £16,000 to Langham Trust; £6,000 each to Asian Theological Seminary – Manila, Discipleship Training College – Singapore, Nairobi Evangelical Graduate School of Theology, and Pan African Christian College; £1,000 each to Christian Service College – Kumasi, and Instituto Superior de Teologia Sicuani – Peru.

FINANCES *Year* 2001–02 *Income* £111,144 *Grants* £153,700 *Assets* £3,362,967

TRUSTEES Dr J B A Kessler; J S Payne; A J Bale; C Harland; Dr D G Osborne; Mrs M Brinkley; D Ford; Nigel Sylvester; Timothy Warren; John Heyward.

HOW TO APPLY The funds of the trust are already committed. Unsolicited applications cannot be supported.

WHO TO APPLY TO Dr Sue Brown, Projects Officer, 2 Bristol Avenue, Ashby-de-la-Zouch, Leicestershire LE65 2PA *Tel* 01530 417426 *Fax* 01530 417426 *E-mail* sue.brown22@btopenworld.com

CC NO 294397   **ESTABLISHED** 1986

■ The Ulverscroft Foundation

WHERE FUNDING CAN BE GIVEN Worldwide.

WHO CAN BENEFIT Organisations benefiting visually impaired people, sick and disabled people, academics, medical professionals, research workers and scientists in the field of opthalmology.

WHAT IS FUNDED To support sick and disabled people, particularly those with defective eyesight, and to promote or conduct medical research. Grants are given to hospitals for research, and to libraries and groups of visually impaired people for items such as computer equipment.

WHAT IS NOT FUNDED Applications from individuals are not encouraged. Generally, assistance towards salaries and general running costs are not given.

TYPE OF GRANT Annual for up to and more than three years. Buildings; capital; project and research; one-off and recurring grants.

SAMPLE GRANTS £146,000 to Great Ormond Street Children's Ophthalmology Unit; £57,000 to St Mary's Chair of Ophthalmology; £30,000 to Royal Australian College; £23,000 to Great Ormond Street Children's Hospital; £17,000 to National Library for the Blind; £2,150 to St Dunstans; £2,000 each to Action for Blind People, Electronic Aids for the Blind an Suffolk County Council; £1,600 to Stockport Libraries; £1,000 each to Calibre, Gladhand Foundation, Royal London Society for the Blind, Stirling Libraries and Vision Foundation.

FINANCES *Year* 2000–01 *Income* £16,379,989 *Grants* £311,691 *Assets* £7,410,241

TRUSTEES P H Carr; Allan Leach; Michael Down; A W Price; D Owen; R Crooks.

HOW TO APPLY In writing to the correspondent. Applicants are advised to make their proposal as detailed as possible, to include details of the current service to people who are visually impaired, if any, and how the proposed project will be integrated or enhanced. If possible the trust asks for an estimate of how many people who are visually impaired use/will use the service, the amount of funding obtained to date, if any, and the names of other organisations to whom they have applied. The success of any appeal is dependent on the level of funding at the time of consideration. The trustees meet four times a year to consider applications.

WHO TO APPLY TO Joyce Sumner, 1 The Green, Bradgate Road, Anstey, Leicester LE7 7FU *Tel* 0116 236 4325 *Fax* 0116 234 0205 *E-mail* foundation@ulverscroft.co.uk *Website* www.ulverscroft.co.uk

CC NO 264873   **ESTABLISHED** 1972

■ Ulverston Town Lands Charity

WHERE FUNDING CAN BE GIVEN The urban district of Ulverston.

WHO CAN BENEFIT Local organisations.

WHAT IS FUNDED Youth, health and welfare, disability, and schools.

WHAT IS NOT FUNDED No grants outside the beneficial area. Grants are generally given to organisations and not to individuals.

TYPE OF GRANT One-off, running costs.

SAMPLE GRANTS £3,400 each to St Mary's Hospice and Ulverston Ford Park Community Group; £2,000 each to Ulverston MIND and Kosovan families in Cumbria at Lower School – Ulverston; £1,500 to Cumbria County Council for a summer playscheme for children with learning difficulties; £1,400 to South Lakeland District Council; £1,000 each to Sir John Barrow School for the hardship fund, Cats and Kittens Playgroup, Church Walk School, Dale Street Infant School and Ulverston Heritage Centre.

FINANCES *Year* 1999–2000 *Income* £30,000 *Grants* £27,000

TRUSTEES Edward Twentyman, Chair; Cllr Robert Bolton; Cllr Ronald Marshall Creer; Cllr Valerie Miller; Cllr Philip Lister; Cllr Richard Scott; Cllr David Miller; Anthony Edmondson; Mrs Judith Wren.

HOW TO APPLY In writing to the correspondent. Trustees meet four or five times a year.

WHO TO APPLY TO J Going, Secretary to the Trustees, Messrs Hart Jackson & Sons, PO Box 2, 8 & 10 New Market Street, Ulverston, Cumbria LA12 7LW *Tel* 01229 583291 *Fax* 01229 581136

CC NO 215779   **ESTABLISHED** 1963

■ The Underwood Trust

WHERE FUNDING CAN BE GIVEN UK, especially London and Wiltshire.

WHO CAN BENEFIT Registered charities only, or bodies with equivalent status such as universities or churches.

WHAT IS FUNDED Support is given within four general sectors: medicine and health; welfare; education, sciences, humanities and religion; environmental resources. There is no particular preference for any one sector.

WHAT IS NOT FUNDED Individuals directly; political activities; commercial ventures or publications; the purchase of vehicles including minibuses; overseas travel or holidays; retrospective grants or loans; direct replacement of statutory funding or activities that are primarily the responsibility of central or local government; large capital, endowment or widely distributed appeals.

SAMPLE GRANTS £50,000 each to ARC Addington Fund, Frenchay Hospital Speech Therapy Unit, India Earthquake Appeal and National Eye Research Trust; £35,000 to Wiltshire Wildlife Trust; £25,000 each to Centrepoint, Friends of the Earth, International Centre for Child Studies, Royal Scottish Academy for Music and Drama and Trinity Hall, Cambridge.

FINANCES *Year* 2000–01 *Grants* £1,113,000

TRUSTEES Robin Clark; Patricia Clark.

HOW TO APPLY All applicants must complete an application form and send it by post to the trust's office. The trustees meet to consider applications once a year in the autumn. Applicants are informed of the trustees' decision and payments are made before Christmas. To be considered applications must be received by the end of August for the autumn meeting.

WHO TO APPLY TO Antony P Cox, Manager, 32 Haymarket, London SW1Y 4TP *Tel* 020 7930 8494 *Website* www.theunderwoodtrust.org.uk

CC NO 266164   **ESTABLISHED** 1973

■ Unemployed Voluntary Action Fund

WHERE FUNDING CAN BE GIVEN Scotland.

WHO CAN BENEFIT Voluntary organisations in Scotland which are properly constituted and recognised as charitable by the Inland Revenue.

WHAT IS FUNDED Projects must aim to meet needs in one or more of the fields of social and community development or health. The voluntary activity must develop a service which will positively assist those involved as volunteers and its beneficiaries. Projects should show how they will: (a) combat exclusion by reducing isolation, improving communication, increasing self-worth and independence; (b) provide ongoing, regular structured voluntary work; (c) enhance and improve skills which promote job readiness, educational opportunties and personal development. There is also an ethnic minority grant scheme which seeks to promote racial equality and reduce racial disadvantage by establishing projects which enable black and ethnic minority communities to access mainstream funding.

WHAT IS NOT FUNDED Schemes which cannot be considered include exhibitions, arts clubs and performances; business co-operatives; credit unions; food co-operatives; out-of-school care; housing and hostel welfare; formal educational or vocational courses and skills and training; clean-ups and one-off projects; holidays and camps; conservation schemes; building projects, including playgrounds; social clubs; sports centres and sports activities; campaigning and political activities.

TYPE OF GRANT Small Grants Scheme: starter grants for up to one year, which are not renewable. Main Grants Programme: three-year project grants. Feasibility studies, core costs, running costs and salaries will also be considered.

RANGE OF GRANTS Main Grants Programme: up to £31,000 a year. Small Grants Scheme: up to £5,000; average grant size is £2,000.

SAMPLE GRANTS £29,350 to CARD (Carers Action Renfrew District); £29,000 to Angus Mental

Health Association for a drop-in project; £28,252 to Volunteer Action – Dumfries and Galloway; £27,381 to Home-Start Deveron; £26,174 to National Schizophrenia Fellowship for the Fife Here You Are project; £26,060 to Gordon Disability Action for the Able to Volunteer Too project; £25,649 to Groundwork – Glasgow for a volunteer programme; £25,237 to Dundee Drugs and Aids Project for a befriending scheme; £25,025 to Pilton Central Association for the West Pilton Neighbourhood Centre in Edinburgh; £24,966 to Minority Learning Disability Initiative Ltd (MELDI); £24,052 to Ability Centre – Galashiels; £23,770 to Nari Kallyan Shangho.

FINANCES *Year* 2001–02 *Income* £1,393,483 *Grants* £1,214,883 *Assets* £56,337

TRUSTEES Susan Elsley, Convener; Farkhanda Chaudhry; Philomena de Lima; Carol Downie; Susan Elsley; John Hawthorne; John Knox; Stuart McGregor; Laurie Naumann.

HOW TO APPLY In writing to the correspondent. The trustees meet quarterly.

WHO TO APPLY TO Mrs Sandra Carter, Administrator, Comely Park House, 80 New Row, Dunfermline, Fife KY12 7EJ *Tel* 01383 620780 *Fax* 01383 626129 *E-mail* uvaf@uvaf.sagehost.co.uk *Website* www.uvaf.org.uk

SC NO SC005229   **ESTABLISHED** 1982

....

■ The Union of Orthodox Hebrew Congregation

WHERE FUNDING CAN BE GIVEN UK.

WHO CAN BENEFIT Jewish organisations.

WHAT IS FUNDED To protect and to further in every way the interests of traditional Judaism in Great Britain and to establish and support such institutions as will serve this object.

SAMPLE GRANTS £22,000 to Machne Israel Loan Fund; £20,500 to Keren Gemilus Chasodim; £14,400 to Yesuous Chaim Shul; £10,800 to Woodstock Sinclair Trust; £9,500 to Kolel Avrechim; £8,875 to Toldos Yacov Yoseph; £8,500 to Friends of Belz; £7,000 to Ponevez Yeshiva; £6,500 to Craven Walk Shul; £3,500 to Beth Samuel Schul.

FINANCES *Year* 1998 *Income* £791,419 *Grants* £170,892 *Assets* £771,790

TRUSTEES B S F Freshwater; I Cymerman; C Konig; Rabbi A Pinter.

HOW TO APPLY In writing to the correspondent.

WHO TO APPLY TO J R Conrad, Acting Administrator, 140 Stamford Hill, London N16 6QT *Tel* 020 8802 6226

CC NO 249892   **ESTABLISHED** 1966

....

■ The United Reformed Church (West Midlands) Trust Ltd

WHERE FUNDING CAN BE GIVEN West Midlands.

WHO CAN BENEFIT United Reformed Churches, their ministers and members.

WHAT IS FUNDED The promotion of the United Reformed Church in the West Midlands

FINANCES *Year* 1998 *Income* £323,000 *Grants* £168,000 *Assets* £4,300,000

TRUSTEES A Sheldon, Chair; M Allman; D Black; D Duffield; M Farnsworth; B Keeling; D MacDonald; R Pickering; F I Rose; S Rowntree; Revd E Welch.

HOW TO APPLY In writing to the correspondent.

WHO TO APPLY TO The Trustees, Provincial Office, Digbeth-in-the-Field URC, Moat Lane, Yardley, Birmingham B26 1TW *Tel* 0121 783 1177

CC NO 507027   **ESTABLISHED** 1977

....

■ The United Society for the Propagation of the Gospel

WHERE FUNDING CAN BE GIVEN Mainly churches in Africa, West Indies, South Pacific, South America, Pakistan, India, Indian Ocean, Myanmar (Burma), Bangladesh, East Asia.

WHO CAN BENEFIT Overseas Anglican provinces and dioceses and churches in communion with the Anglican Church which benefit Christians and other disadvantaged groups.

WHAT IS FUNDED The promotion of the Christian religion and related charitable works.

WHAT IS NOT FUNDED Direct applications from individuals are not considered.

TYPE OF GRANT One-off grants; bursaries; loans.

FINANCES *Year* 1999 *Income* £8,369,095 *Grants* £5,518,480 *Assets* £47,289,525

TRUSTEES Governors: Judge Francis Aglionby; Mrs Jane Arden; Deaconess Diane Clutterbuck; Revd Canon Helen Cunliffe, Chair; Revd Alan Moses; William Peters; Revd Canon Ivor Smith-Cameron; Revd David Tuck, Vice Chair; Douglas Yates; Revd Christopher Atkinson; Mrs Enid Powell; Revd Cannon Guy Smith.

PUBLICATIONS Governors' report and financial statements; Yearbook. Project information, educational books, religious pamphlets and visual aids are also available.

HOW TO APPLY Applications must be submitted by Anglican Archbishops or Bishops to the Finance in Mission Officer.

WHO TO APPLY TO Tony Bacon, Funding Officer, Partnership House, 157 Waterloo Road, London SE1 9XA *Tel* 020 7928 8681 *Fax* 020 7928 2371 *E-mail* enquiries@uspg.org.uk *Website* www.uspg.org.uk

CC NO 234518   **ESTABLISHED** 1701

....

■ United St Saviour's Charities

WHERE FUNDING CAN BE GIVEN North Southwark.

WHO CAN BENEFIT Organisations benefiting people disadvantaged by poverty.

WHAT IS FUNDED General benefit of poor people in the area stated above.

WHAT IS NOT FUNDED No support of individuals. No recurrent grants, nor relief of rates, taxes or other public funds nor support of running costs or salaries.

TYPE OF GRANT Equipment, repairs, interest-free loans, one-off, project and start-up costs. Funding is for one year or less.

RANGE OF GRANTS £300–£5,000.

SAMPLE GRANTS £5,242 to Eveline Children's Hospital Appeal for a child's heart and respiration monitor; £3,420 to Age Concern, Southwark to purchase chairs for a health centre; £3,245 to Time & Talents, Rotherhithe for wheelchairs and other equipment for young and disabled people; £2,600 to Surrey Docks Farm for the millennium breed festival for inner city children; £2,500 to St Giles Trust towards start-up costs of a youthwork project; £2,426 to Manna Centre for Homeless to buy a gas cooker; £2,320 to Prisoner's Families & Friends to refurbish a family room; £2,244 to Manna Centre for Homeless to replace showers and toilets; £2,089 to Walworth Newpin Centre to install blinds and enable expansion of the

Think carefully about every application. Is it justified?

855

centre; £2,000 to Lorrimore Drop-in Centre towards the cost of an annual holiday for people with mental health needs.

FINANCES *Year* 2001–02 *Income* £712,000 *Grants* £45,000 *Assets* £23,000,000

TRUSTEES Mrs G Domminney; E A C Tucker; C B Slee; Mrs S Chantler; S Kerbal.

HOW TO APPLY In writing to the correspondent. Initial telephone calls are welcome. Application forms are available, but no guidelines. No sae is required. Trustees usually meet monthly.

WHO TO APPLY TO Mrs M C O' Halloran, Director & Clerk, Thomas Cure House, 7 Park Street, London SE1 9AB *Tel* 020 7407 5961 *Fax* 020 7357 0452 *E-mail* enquiries@corporationofwardens.org.uk

CC NO 206767   **ESTABLISHED** 1960

....

■ United Trusts

WHERE FUNDING CAN BE GIVEN Mainly north west England.

WHO CAN BENEFIT Neighbourhood-based community projects tend to be major recipients.

WHAT IS FUNDED General charitable purposes. Distribution decisions are made by workplace charity committees or local trust committees.

WHAT IS NOT FUNDED 'Grants to individuals, called "top-up funds", are made through "umbrella charities" in cases where the government does not feel it has a responsibility.'

FINANCES *Year* 1999–2000 *Income* £422,000 *Grants* £503,000

TRUSTEES Up to 20 people elected by members.

HOW TO APPLY It is requested that applications should be made to the secretary of the local United Trust Fund or Workplace Trust concerned if the address is known. Otherwise applications may be made to the correspondent.

WHO TO APPLY TO John Hugh Pritchard, PO Box 14, 8 Nelson Road, Edge Hill, Liverpool L69 7AA *Tel* 0151 709 8252 *Fax* 0151 708 5621 *E-mail* information@unitedtrusts.org *Website* www.unitedtrusts.org

CC NO 327579   **ESTABLISHED** 1987

....

■ Unity Charitable Trust

WHERE FUNDING CAN BE GIVEN UK.

WHO CAN BENEFIT Registered charities.

WHAT IS FUNDED General charitable purposes.

FINANCES *Year* 1999–2000 *Income* £30,000 *Grants* £22,000

TRUSTEES J Endfield; R Baron; R Woolich.

HOW TO APPLY In writing to the correspondent.

WHO TO APPLY TO Jonathan Endfield, Trustee, 5 Accommodation Road, London NW11 8ED

CC NO 1057710   **ESTABLISHED** 1996

....

■ The David Uri Memorial Trust

WHERE FUNDING CAN BE GIVEN Worldwide.

WHO CAN BENEFIT Registered charities benefiting Jewish people, at risk groups and people who are disadvantaged by poverty or socially isolated.

WHAT IS FUNDED Mainly Jewish organisations; also welfare and education charities.

WHAT IS NOT FUNDED No grants to individuals.

TYPE OF GRANT One-off, capital, feasibility studies and research grants will be considered. Funding is available for up to three years.

RANGE OF GRANTS £250–£15,000.

FINANCES *Year* 1997–98 *Income* £196,000 *Grants* £44,000 *Assets* £1,600,000

TRUSTEES Mrs Z S Blackman.

HOW TO APPLY In writing to the correspondent.

WHO TO APPLY TO The Trustees, Suite 511, 78 Marylebone High Street, London W1U 5AP

CC NO 327810   **ESTABLISHED** 1988

■ Vale of Glamorgan Welsh Church Fund

WHERE FUNDING CAN BE GIVEN Vale of Glamorgan, city of Cardiff area.

WHO CAN BENEFIT Organisations benefiting children, young adults, students and local communities may all be considered.

WHAT IS FUNDED Restoration of churches and memorials; education and training, particularly vocational or religious; health; social welfare; arts and culture; recreation and sport; environment and animals; faith activities; science and technology; social sciences, policy and research; philanthropy and the voluntary sector.

WHAT IS NOT FUNDED No grants to individuals.

TYPE OF GRANT One-off.

RANGE OF GRANTS Wide-ranging.

FINANCES *Year* 2001–02 *Grants* £25,644 *Assets* £2,278,344

TRUSTEES Vale of Glamorgan County Borough Council.

HOW TO APPLY On a form available from the correspondent, or in the case of organisations based within the city and county of Cardiff, from Richard Anthony at Cardiff County Council (02920 872395).

WHO TO APPLY TO A D Williams, Director of Finance, ICT and Property, Vale of Glamorgan Council, Civic Offices, Holton Road, Barry, Vale of Glamorgan CF63 4RU *Tel* 01446 709250 *Fax* 01446 791729 *E-mail* adwilliams@valeofglamorgan.gov.uk

CC NO 506628   **ESTABLISHED** 1996

■ The Valentine Charitable Trust

WHERE FUNDING CAN BE GIVEN Dorset.

WHO CAN BENEFIT Registered charities.

WHAT IS FUNDED Trustees mainly restrict their giving to healthcare and environmental projects.

TYPE OF GRANT Core, capital and project support is given as well as loan finance. One-off grants are preferred, but funding can be for longer periods.

RANGE OF GRANTS Up to £30,000 but usually for about £5,000.

SAMPLE GRANTS £35,000 in three grants to British Red Cross Appeals; £30,000 each to Broadstone Methodist Church and Relate – Dorset; £5,000 each to Army Benevolent Fund, Marine Conservation Society, Motability, SSAFA and Samaritans.

FINANCES *Year* 2001–02 *Income* £779,615 *Grants* £696,300 *Assets* £18,993,799

TRUSTEES D J E Neville-Jones; S F Neville-Jones; Mrs P B N Walker; N E N Neville-Jones.

HOW TO APPLY In writing to the correspondent.

WHO TO APPLY TO D J E Neville-Jones, Trustee, Preston & Redman, Hinton House, Hinton Road, Bournemouth, Dorset BH1 2EN *Tel* 01202 292424

CC NO 1001782   **ESTABLISHED** 1990

■ The Albert Van Den Bergh Charitable Trust

WHERE FUNDING CAN BE GIVEN UK and overseas.

WHO CAN BENEFIT Local and UK organisations benefiting people of all ages, at risk groups and people disadvantaged by poverty.

WHAT IS FUNDED Welfare and medical charities, including research charities, and those concerned with young and older people.

RANGE OF GRANTS £500–£5,000.

FINANCES *Year* 1999–2000 *Income* £71,000 *Grants* £73,000 *Assets* £2,400,000

TRUSTEES P A Van Den Bergh; G R Oliver; Mrs J M Hartley.

HOW TO APPLY In writing to the correspondent, including accounts and budgets.

WHO TO APPLY TO G R Oliver, Trustee, Triggs Wilkinson Mann, Broadoak House, Horsham Road, Cranleigh, Surrey GU6 8DJ *Tel* 01483 273515

CC NO 296885   **ESTABLISHED** 1987

■ John and Lucille van Geest Foundation

WHERE FUNDING CAN BE GIVEN UK and overseas, with a special interest in south Lincolnshire and adjoining areas.

WHO CAN BENEFIT (a) Charities concerned with certain areas of medical research; (b) Charities concerned with the welfare of (i) people (particularly older and young people residing in south Lincolnshire and adjoining areas) in need through illness, infirmity or social circumstances and (ii) victims of natural and man-made disasters.

WHAT IS FUNDED There are no restrictions on the charitable purposes for which funds can be used. However, funds are normally applied by the trustees in providing support to charitable bodies concerned with medical research, the welfare of young and older people and disaster victims.

WHAT IS NOT FUNDED No grants to individuals.

TYPE OF GRANT Primarily one-off, although any type of grant is considered. Loans are not made.

RANGE OF GRANTS £1,000–£250,000; typical grant £5,000–£50,000.

SAMPLE GRANTS £250,000 to Deafblind UK; £125,000 to Nottingham Trent University; £100,000 to Orchid Cancer Appeal; £30,000 to Royal Brompton Hospital; £28,000 to Action Research; £27,000 to Huntingdon's Disease Association; £25,000 to Society for Mucopoly Saccharide Diseases; £24,000 to Lincolnshire and Nottinghamshire Air Ambulance; £20,000 each to Cystic Fibrosis Trust and Motor Neurone Disease Association.

FINANCES *Year* 2001–02 *Income* £740,810 *Grants* £775,000 *Assets* £22,877,700

TRUSTEES Lucille van Geest; Hilary P Marlowe; Stuart R Coltman; Tonie Gibson.

HOW TO APPLY To the correspondent in writing, but only if they are from other charities engaged in areas of work to which the trustees' policy extends. Telephone calls are not welcome. The trustees meet three to four times a year to consider applications, but there are no set dates. Every applicant will receive a reply.

WHO TO APPLY TO S R Coltman, Trustee, 42 Pinchbeck Road, Spalding, Lincolnshire PE11 1QF

CC NO 1001279   **ESTABLISHED** 1990

■ Baroness Van Heemstra's Charitable Trust

WHERE FUNDING CAN BE GIVEN UK.

WHO CAN BENEFIT Registered charities concerned with animal welfare.

WHAT IS FUNDED A list of regular beneficiaries is reviewed at the annual trustees' meeting.

WHAT IS NOT FUNDED Grants are given exclusively for animal welfare.

RANGE OF GRANTS Usually up to £10,000.

SAMPLE GRANTS £23,000 to Ferne Animal Sanctuary; £5,000 to Redwings Horse Sanctuary; £3,000 each to Blue Cross, Brooke Hospital for Animals, Cats Protection League, Celia Hamond Animal Trust, National Canine Defence League, PDSA, Society for the Protection of Animals Abroad and Wood Green Animal Shelters.

FINANCES *Year* 1999 *Income* £10,000 *Grants* £59,000 *Assets* £306,000

TRUSTEES R E MacWatt; A B V Hughes; Mrs M L MacWatt.

HOW TO APPLY In writing with full accounts, to the correspondent.

WHO TO APPLY TO A B V Hughes, Trustee, Payne Hicks Beach, 10 New Square, Lincoln's Inn, London WC2A 3QG *Tel* 020 7465 4300

CC NO 289249   **ESTABLISHED** 1983

■ Bernard Van Leer Foundation

WHERE FUNDING CAN BE GIVEN Worldwide.

WHO CAN BENEFIT Institutions such as educational authorities, universities, and private bodies clearly engaged in activities benefiting children up to the age of seven, and that are recognised charities.

WHAT IS FUNDED To enhance opportunities for children up to the age of seven growing up in circumstances of social and economic disadvantage, with the objective of developing their innate potential to the greatest possible extent.

WHAT IS NOT FUNDED Grants are not made to individuals, nor for the general support of organisations such as staffing/administrative costs. The foundation does not provide study, research or travel grants. No grants are made in response to general appeals.

FINANCES *Year* 2000 *Income* £297,564 *Assets* £4,131,345

TRUSTEES The Royal Bank of Scotland plc.

PUBLICATIONS Newsletter.

OTHER INFORMATION Grantmaking was suspended in the late 1990's. It was expected in 2000 to resume within a year, although it is unclear if it actually has.

HOW TO APPLY On a form available from the correspondent, which requires a brief, 50-word description of the project. Applications are considered in March and September. Due to the large number of applications received, no acknowledgements are given and unsuccessful appeals will not receive a reply.

WHO TO APPLY TO Mrs Claire Lundy, Senior Trust Administrator, The Royal Bank of Scotland plc, Private Trust and Taxation, 2 Festival Square, Edinburgh EH3 9SU *Tel* 0131 523 2657 *Fax* 0131 228 9889

CC NO 265186   **ESTABLISHED** 1972

■ The Van Neste Foundation

WHERE FUNDING CAN BE GIVEN UK, especially the Bristol area, and overseas.

WHO CAN BENEFIT Recognised charities benefiting people disadvantaged by poverty, disabled people, older people and Christians.

WHAT IS FUNDED Currently the main areas of interest are: developing world; people who are disabled and older; advancement of religion; community and Christian family life; and respect for the sanctity and dignity of life.

WHAT IS NOT FUNDED No grants to individuals or to large, well-known charities. Applications are only considered from registered charities.

TYPE OF GRANT Usually one-off for a specific project or part of a project. Core funding is rarely considered.

SAMPLE GRANTS £50,000 each to Clifton Diocese and Little Brother of Nazareth; £15,000 to Bristol Folk House; £5,000 each to Bristol City Southmead Project, St Peters Hospice – Bristol and Seven Springs; £3,000 to National Drug Prevention Alliance; £2,000 each to Bristol Childrens Help Society, Lincoln College – Oxford, Volunteer Reading Help and Whiteladies Health Project.

FINANCES *Year* 2001–02 *Income* £214,407 *Grants* £154,800 *Assets* £4,867,753

TRUSTEES M T M Appleby, Chair; F J F Lyons, Secretary; G J Walker.

HOW TO APPLY Applications should be in the form of a concise letter setting out the clear objectives to be obtained, which must be charitable. Information must be supplied concerning agreed funding from other sources together with a timetable for achieving the objectives of the appeal and a copy of the latest accounts. The foundation does not normally make grants on a continuing basis. To keep overheads to a minimum, only successful applications are acknowledged. Even then it may be a matter of months before any decision can be expected, depending on the dates of trustees' meetings.

WHO TO APPLY TO Fergus Lyons, Secretary, 15 Alexandra Road, Clifton, Bristol BS8 2DD *Tel* 0117 973 5167

CC NO 201951   **ESTABLISHED** 1959

■ Mrs Maud Van Norden's Charitable Foundation

WHERE FUNDING CAN BE GIVEN UK.

WHO CAN BENEFIT Generally registered UK charities benefiting children, older people, carers, people with disabilities and victims of war.

WHAT IS FUNDED General charitable purposes, particularly aid to younger or older people. Also preservation of the environment and heritage, disability and animal welfare.

WHAT IS NOT FUNDED No grants to individuals, expeditions or scholarships.

TYPE OF GRANT One-off and research.

RANGE OF GRANTS Up to £1,000.

SAMPLE GRANTS £2,000 each to Dockland Settlement, House of St Barnabas – Soho, Ian Rennie Hospice at Home, and Society for the Relief of the Homeless Poor.

FINANCES *Year* 2000 *Income* £44,000 *Grants* £35,000 *Assets* £1,000,000

TRUSTEES F C S Tufton; Mrs E M Dukler; Mrs E A Humphryes; N J Wingerath.

HOW TO APPLY The trustees will only consider applications if accompanied by a copy of the applicant's latest reports and accounts. The trustees make donations to registered charities only. The trustees meet to consider applications in May each year.

WHO TO APPLY TO N J Wingerath, Trustee, Messrs Payne Hicks Beach, 10 New Square, Lincoln's Inn, London WC2A 3QG *Tel* 020 7465 4300 *Fax* 020 7465 4393

CC NO 210844   **ESTABLISHED** 1962

■ The Vandervell Foundation

WHERE FUNDING CAN BE GIVEN UK.
WHO CAN BENEFIT Individuals and organisations.
WHAT IS FUNDED General charitable purposes.
RANGE OF GRANTS £1,000–£5,000.
FINANCES *Year* 2000 *Income* £826,416 *Grants* £530,809 *Assets* £4,904,948
TRUSTEES The Vandervell Foundation Limited Trustee Company.
HOW TO APPLY In writing to the correspondent. Trustees meet every two months to consider major grant applications; smaller grants are considered more frequently.
WHO TO APPLY TO Ms Sheila Lawler, Bridge House, 181 Queen Victoria Street, London EC4V 4DZ *Tel* 020 7248 9045
CC NO 255651   **ESTABLISHED** 1968

■ The Vardy Foundation

WHERE FUNDING CAN BE GIVEN UK.
WHO CAN BENEFIT Charitable organisations and individuals.
WHAT IS FUNDED General charitable purposes.
TYPE OF GRANT Recurrent.
SAMPLE GRANTS £100,000 to L Velez; £95,000 to Bethany Church; £60,000 to Christian Channel; £50,000 to Care Trust; £35,000 to Crusaders in the North East; £25,000 to County Durham Foundation.
FINANCES *Year* 1998–99 *Income* £267,000 *Grants* £617,000 *Assets* £5,400,000
TRUSTEES Sir Peter Vardy, Chair; Mrs M B Vardy.
HOW TO APPLY In writing to the correspondent.
WHO TO APPLY TO Sir Peter Vardy, Chair of the Trustees, Houghton House, Emperor Way, Doxford International Business Park, Sunderland SR3 3XR *Tel* 0191 516 3636
CC NO 328415   **ESTABLISHED** 1989

■ The Variety Club Children's Charity

WHERE FUNDING CAN BE GIVEN UK.
WHO CAN BENEFIT Hospitals, schools, charities and other organisations.
WHAT IS FUNDED The welfare of children up to the age of 19 who are disadvantaged or have disabilities.
WHAT IS NOT FUNDED For grants to organisations: trips abroad; medical treatment or research; administrative or salary costs; maintenance or ongoing costs; repayment of loans; distribution to other organisations; computers for mainstream schools or non-disabled children; basic cost of a family vehicle; non-specific appeals.
TYPE OF GRANT One-off and recurring. Money and equipment, including coaches, to organisations. Individual children have received money, electric wheelchairs, toys and holidays.
SAMPLE GRANTS £70,000 to Army Benevolent Fund; £55,000 to Sargent Cancer Trust; £48,000 to Royal United Hospital – Bath for the children's centre and neonatal unit; £40,000 to Ingfield

Manor School; £39,800 to Lineham Farm – Yorkshire; £39,000 to Royal Belfast Hospital for Sick Children; £38,650 to Bolton Lads' and Girls' Club; £33,603 to Variety Clubs International; £30,014 to Isebrook School – Kettering; £30,008 to Southampton General Hospital for the children's unit.

FINANCES *Year* 2001 *Income* £9,017,059 *Grants* £4,936,000 *Assets* £2,021,008
TRUSTEES Hugo Amaya-Torres; Jarvis Astaire; Hedy-Joy Babani; Lloyd Barr; Philip Burley; Stephen Crown; Raymond Curtis; Tony Frame; Richard Freeman; Anthony Harris; Tony Hatch; Paul Lawrence; Ronnie Nathan; Rod Natkiel; John Ratcliff; Angela Rippon; Pamela Sinclair; John Webber; Jim Whittell; Patricia Bloomfield; Tom O'Connor; Ivor Stocker; Jack Taylor.
HOW TO APPLY There are application forms for each programme, available from the charity or through its website.
WHO TO APPLY TO Pamela Robertson, Company Secretary, Variety Club House, 93 Bayham Street, London NW1 0AG *Tel* 020 7428 8100 *Website* www.varietyclub.org.uk
CC NO 209259   **ESTABLISHED** 1949

■ The VEC Acorn Trust

WHERE FUNDING CAN BE GIVEN The New Forest and south west Hampshire.
WHO CAN BENEFIT Individuals and organisations benefiting young adults, people disadvantaged by poverty and people living in rural and urban areas. The trustees support projects attached to well-established charitable organisations and are willing to consider joint ventures.
WHAT IS FUNDED Young people between the ages of 16 and 25 who are disadvantaged as a result of the environment in which they live to assist in developing their potential in skills which they would not otherwise be able to achieve. Support is given to projects which reach a number of people, but the emphasis is on self-help and, in particular, to charities working in the field of development of the individual.
WHAT IS NOT FUNDED Grants are only made towards young people who are environmentally disadvantaged.
TYPE OF GRANT The trustees are prepared to consider applications on their merit as to whether they involve single or recurring grants. Capital, project; salaries; and start-up costs. Funding of up to three years will be considered.
RANGE OF GRANTS £50–£5,000; average £1,530.
SAMPLE GRANTS £10,000 to The Quay Foyer; £8,000 to HYPED; £2,000 to Forest Forge Theatre Company; £1,500 each to Arkwright Scholarship, and Lighthouse (ex-Poole Arts Trust); £1,000 each to Pilley Youth Club, and St Thomas' Church; £250 to Lymington Sea Scouts.
FINANCES *Year* 2000–01 *Grants* £102,000
TRUSTEES Mrs V E Coates; K Newman; E N Heesom; Miss V L M Heesom.
HOW TO APPLY In writing to the correspondent. Trustees meet quarterly. If of interest to the trustees, arrangements would be made for further discussion to take place, possibly followed by a visit. The trustees think it important that any grant should be followed through and reported back as to the utilisation of funding and the degree of success.
WHO TO APPLY TO Kenneth Newman, Trustee, Pennington Chase, Lower Pennington Lane, Lymington, Hampshire SO41 8AN *Tel* 01590 672088 *Fax* 01590 672088
CC NO 1002997   **ESTABLISHED** 1991

■ Veneziana Fund

WHERE FUNDING CAN BE GIVEN Venice and the UK.

WHAT IS FUNDED This trust gives half its grant total to the Venice in Peril Fund, and in the UK or the preservation, restoration, repair and maintenance of: buildings originally constructed before 1750; the fixtures and fittings of such buildings; and works of art made before 1750 (including the purchase of such items).

TYPE OF GRANT £1,000–£22,500.

SAMPLE GRANTS £23,000 to Venice in Peril; £5,000 each to Sir William Turner's Hospital and University of St Andrews – Fife; £3,000 to Sir John Moore Building; £2,000 each to All Saints Church – Old Burghclere Trust, St Giles Church – Coberley, St James Church – Christow and St Mary's Church – Wilsford; £1,500 to St Botolph's Church – Lullingstone; £1,000 to Friends Meeting House – Wallingford.

FINANCES *Year* 2001–02 *Income* £137,148 *Grants* £47,000 *Assets* £33,867

HOW TO APPLY In writing to the correspondent to request an application form.

WHO TO APPLY TO The Trust Administrator, c/o White Horse Court, 25c North Street, Bishops Stortford, Hertfordshire CM23 2LD *Tel* 01279 506421 *E-mail* charities@pothecary.co.uk

CC NO 1061760   **ESTABLISHED** 1997

■ The Verdon-Smith Family Charitable Settlement

WHERE FUNDING CAN BE GIVEN South west England, mainly the former county of Avon, Somerset, Gloucestershire and Wiltshire.

WHO CAN BENEFIT Registered charities with emphasis on local activity and needs benefiting: people of all ages; ex-service and service people; seafarers and fishermen; musicians; widows and widowers; Church of England; disabled people; disaster victims; and homeless people.

WHAT IS FUNDED This trust will consider funding: almshouses and respite accommodation; architecture; music; visual arts; arts education; orchestras; cultural activities; religious buildings; acute health care; hospices and hospice at home; respite care for carers; cancer and MS research; conservation; animal welfare; church schools; independent schools; care in the community and day centres. There is a quarterly review of regular donations with occasional addition of new donations.

WHAT IS NOT FUNDED No grants to individuals, or for salaries or running costs.

TYPE OF GRANT Recurrent, occasional one-off, buildings, capital, core costs, project and research. Funding is available for one year or less.

RANGE OF GRANTS £50–£1,000; mostly £150 or less.

SAMPLE GRANTS £1,000 to Kosovan Crisis Appeal; £500 to St Thomas Church in Salisbury; £300 to Ex-services Mental Welfare Society; £275 each to Barnardos, Bristol & Avon Federation of Clubs for Young People, RNLI, Salvation Army (Western Region), Shrewsbury House, and Winged Fellowship Foundation; £250 each to Bath Preservation Trust and Greater Bristol Foundation.

FINANCES *Year* 1999–2000 *Income* £29,753 *Grants* £26,816 *Assets* £274,357

TRUSTEES Lady Verdon-Smith; W G Verdon-Smith; Lady E J White; Mrs D N Verdon-Smith.

HOW TO APPLY In writing to the correspondent. The trustees meet quarterly and applications will not be acknowledged unless successful.

WHO TO APPLY TO Lady E J White, Trustee, 94 Sydney Place, Bath BA2 6NE

CC NO 284919   **ESTABLISHED** 1983

■ Roger Vere Foundation

WHERE FUNDING CAN BE GIVEN UK and worldwide, with a special interest in High Wycombe.

SAMPLE GRANTS £200,000 to Trent Vineyard; £100,000 to Jubilee 2000 Coalition; £50,000 each to National Star Centre and YMCA; £20,000 each to Disaster Emergency Committee and Stepping Stones Trust; £15,000 to USPG ; £10,000 to CARE International; £7,000 to Church Army; £6,000 to BTCV.

FINANCES *Year* 1999–2000 *Income* £7,563,240 *Grants* £551,500 *Assets* £6,980,433

TRUSTEES Mrs Rosemary Vere, Chair; Mrs Marion Lyon; Peter Allen.

OTHER INFORMATION The above income relates to the first financial year, therefore the income includes the funds used to established the trust.

HOW TO APPLY In writing to the correspondent. The trustees meet quarterly, in March, June, September and December.

WHO TO APPLY TO Peter Allen, Trustee, 19 Berwick Road, Marlow, Buckinghamshire SL7 3AR, *Tel* 01628 471702

CC NO 1077559   **ESTABLISHED** 1999

■ Victoria Homes Trust

WHERE FUNDING CAN BE GIVEN Northern Ireland.

WHO CAN BENEFIT Registered charities benefiting children and young people.

WHAT IS FUNDED Voluntary projects in the fields of homelessness, alcohol and drug abuse and counselling.

WHAT IS NOT FUNDED Grants are not normally given to individuals.

FINANCES *Year* 2001–02 *Income* £56,000 *Grants* £50,000

HOW TO APPLY On a form available from the correspondent. A copy of the most recent audited accounts should be included. Applications should be typed or written in block capital letters using black ink. If the project requires work which involves planning permission, evidence that the permission has been granted should be enclosed. The trust asks that pamphlets or other printed matter should not be sent and also for 'as much information as possible about the project'. Trustees meet in February, June and October.

WHO TO APPLY TO Derek H Catney, Secretary, 2 Tudor Court, Rochester Road, Belfast BT6 9LB *Tel* 028 9079 4306 *E-mail* derek.catney@btclick.com

IR NO XN45474

■ The Eric W Vincent Trust Fund

WHERE FUNDING CAN BE GIVEN Within a 20-mile radius of Halesowen.

WHO CAN BENEFIT Local activities preferred.

WHAT IS FUNDED General charitable purposes. Particularly charities working in the fields of residential facilities and services, infrastructure development, professional bodies, religious umbrella bodies, arts, culture and recreation, education and training, and community facilities and services.

WHAT IS NOT FUNDED No grants towards salaries, debts or vehicles. Students are rarely funded.

TYPE OF GRANT Mainly one-off and capital grants.

RANGE OF GRANTS £50–£500; typical grant £200–£250.

FINANCES *Year* 1999–2000 *Income* £42,000 *Grants* £42,000 *Assets* £1,100,000

TRUSTEES Mrs D Williams, Chair; K E Symonds; C Jordan; A Birch; Ms J Turner; Revd D R M Smith; J M Jennings.

HOW TO APPLY In writing to the correspondent. Trustees meet six times a year. Applications for holiday schemes must be received by 1 April and will be considered at the May meeting. Applications from organisations should be accompanied by a copy of the latest accounts. Applications are considered on merit, subject to funds being available.

WHO TO APPLY TO Mrs J Stephen, Clerk, 4–5 Summer Hill, Halesowen, West Midlands B63 3BU

CC NO 204843   **ESTABLISHED** 1954

■ The Vincent Wildlife Trust

WHERE FUNDING CAN BE GIVEN UK.

WHO CAN BENEFIT Wildlife organisations.

WHAT IS FUNDED The trust aims to 'promote the study of, and research and education in relation to wildlife conservation and the establishment, control, development and maintenance of nature reserves'.

TYPE OF GRANT One-off or long-term, given for core support including development and strategic funding.

RANGE OF GRANTS £9,000–£233,000.

SAMPLE GRANTS £232,237 to Herpetological Conservation Trust; £131,563 to British Butterfly Conservation Trust; £50,000 to Plantlife; £16,894 to Nottingham University.

FINANCES *Year* 2000 *Income* £1,099,691 *Grants* £430,784 *Assets* £19,760,469

TRUSTEES Hon. Vincent Weir, Chair; Ronald Yarham; Terence O'Connor.

PUBLICATIONS Various.

HOW TO APPLY In writing to the correspondent. It appears unlikely that applications from charities without a relationship with the trust will be successful.

WHO TO APPLY TO Dr Johnny Birks, Secretary, 3–4 Bronsil Courtyard, Eastnor, Ledbury, Herefordshire HR8 1EP *Tel* 01531 636441 *Fax* 01531 636442 *E-mail* vwt@vwt.org.uk *Website* www.vwt.org.uk

CC NO 270679   **ESTABLISHED** 1975

■ The Nigel Vinson Charitable Trust

WHERE FUNDING CAN BE GIVEN UK, with a preference for north east England.

WHO CAN BENEFIT Individuals and organisations benefiting: actors and entertainment professionals; musicians; students; textile workers and designers; and writers and poets.

WHAT IS FUNDED The encouragement and development of business and industry, the arts and education.

TYPE OF GRANT Capital (including buildings), one-off, project and research. Funding is for one year or less.

RANGE OF GRANTS £25–£10,000.

SAMPLE GRANTS £10,000 to Institute of Economic Affairs; £3,000 to Institute for Policy Research; £2,500 to Hampden Trust.

FINANCES *Year* 2001–02 *Income* £90,000 *Grants* £37,000 *Assets* £2,100,000

TRUSTEES Rt Hon. Lord Vinson of Roddam Dene; Hon. Mrs Bettina Claire Witheridge; M F Jodrell; Mrs Rowena A Cowan; Thomas O C Harris.

HOW TO APPLY In writing to the correspondent. Applications are considered throughout the year.

WHO TO APPLY TO Messrs Hoare Trustees, 37 Fleet Street, London EC4P 4DQ *Tel* 020 7353 4522

CC NO 265077   **ESTABLISHED** 1973

■ The William and Ellen Vinten Trust

WHERE FUNDING CAN BE GIVEN UK, but mostly Bury St Edmunds.

WHO CAN BENEFIT Individuals, schools and colleges; and industrial firms and companies. There is a strong preference for Bury St Edmunds.

WHAT IS FUNDED Training and education of people for industry; scientific and technological training in schools and colleges. Welfare of people in industry.

FINANCES *Year* 2000–01 *Income* £82,812 *Grants* £70,085 *Assets* £1,768,496

TRUSTEES D J Medcalf, Chair; J V Crosher; M Shallow; A C Leacy; P M Tracey; A Grigg.

HOW TO APPLY The trust stated that as a proactive charity it does not seek unsolicited applications. Such applications are now so significant in number that the trust has decided not to respond to them, however discourteous this may seem.

WHO TO APPLY TO D J Medcalf, Chair, Greene & Greene Solicitors, 80 Guildhall Street, Bury St Edmunds, Suffolk IP33 1QB

CC NO 285758   **ESTABLISHED** 1982

■ The Vintners Company Charitable Trust

WHERE FUNDING CAN BE GIVEN London only.

WHO CAN BENEFIT Hospices, hospitals and organisations benefiting older people, people with disabilities and those who have experienced abuse or addiction.

WHAT IS FUNDED The trust supports smaller London charities, with a cycle of different causes supported every six months, as follows: Older people – May 2003; Abuse and addiction – November 2003; Disabled – May 2004; Hospices and hospitals – November 2004.

TYPE OF GRANT One-off.

RANGE OF GRANTS Around £2,000.

SAMPLE GRANTS £48,000 to Riverpoint Ltd; £5,000 each to Woodland Trust Centre and Wetland Centre; £3,000 each to Matthew Trust, The New Bridge, Ripple Down House and St Joseph's Pastoral Centre; £2,500 to The Swan Sanctuary; £2,000 each to Comeback, and Working Support.

FINANCES *Year* 1999–2000 *Income* £184,000 *Grants* £105,000 *Assets* £129,000

TRUSTEES The Master, Wardens, Freemen and commonalty of the Mystery of Vinters' of the City of London.

HOW TO APPLY In writing to the correspondent. The trustees meet twice a year to consider grant applications; applications from relevant causes (see above) should be submitted each year by the middle of March for consideration at the

May meeting, and by the middle of August for consideration at the November meeting.

WHO TO APPLY TO Brigadier Michael Smythe, Vinters Company, Vinters Hall, 68 and a half, Upper Thames Street, London EC4V 3BG *Tel* 020 7236 1863

CC NO 1015212   **ESTABLISHED** 1992

■ Vision Charity

WHERE FUNDING CAN BE GIVEN UK.

WHO CAN BENEFIT Preferably organisations, but also individuals.

WHAT IS FUNDED Welfare of people with dyslexia or visual difficulties.

TYPE OF GRANT Preferably equipment rather than core funding.

FINANCES *Year* 2001–02 *Income* £146,502

PUBLICATIONS *Vision Charity News* (published twice yearly).

OTHER INFORMATION The total expenditure was £150,411.

HOW TO APPLY A brief summary of the request should be sent to the correspondent. If the request is of interest to the trustees, further details will be requested. If the request has not been acknowledged within three months of submission, the applicant should assume that it has not been successful. The charity is interested to receive such applications but regrets that it is not able to acknowledge every unsuccessful submission.

WHO TO APPLY TO Mrs G Fitzpatrick, PO Box 260, Dorking, Surrey RH5 6WL *Tel* 01306 731781 *Fax* 01306 731791 *Website* www.visioncharity.org.uk

CC NO 1075630   **ESTABLISHED** 1976

■ Vivdale Ltd

WHERE FUNDING CAN BE GIVEN UK.

WHO CAN BENEFIT Jewish people.

WHAT IS FUNDED To advance religion in accordance with the orthodox Jewish faith and general charitable purposes.

RANGE OF GRANTS £20–£3,600.

FINANCES *Year* 1998–99 *Income* £83,000 *Grants* £46,000 *Assets* £421,000

TRUSTEES D H Marks; L Marks; F Z Sinclair.

HOW TO APPLY In writing to the correspondent.

WHO TO APPLY TO D H Marks, Trustee, 17 Cheyne Walk, London NW4 3QH

CC NO 268505   **ESTABLISHED** 1974

■ The Viznitz Foundation

WHERE FUNDING CAN BE GIVEN Worldwide.

WHO CAN BENEFIT Organisations, including schools and registered charities.

WHAT IS FUNDED General charitable purposes and religious activities, probably of benefit to those of the Jewish faith.

FINANCES *Year* 2000–01 *Income* £205,932

TRUSTEES H Feldman; E Kahan; E S Margulies.

HOW TO APPLY In writing to the correspondent.

WHO TO APPLY TO H Feldman, Trustee, 23 Overlea Road, London E5 9BG *Tel* 020 8557 9557

CC NO 326581   **ESTABLISHED** 1984

■ The Vodafone UK Foundation

WHERE FUNDING CAN BE GIVEN UK, especially Banbury, Birmingham, Croydon and Newbury.

WHO CAN BENEFIT Registered charities only.

WHAT IS FUNDED Enabling access to information and opportunities primarily via communications technology, support is considered for projects at a national level across most categories but must be within this area of focus; local communities near the company's offices (Banbury, Birmingham, Croydon and Newbury), especially secondary schools, and projects/ groups providing a broad benefit, or a specific need to the community; community activities carried out by Vodafone employees, regardless of the nature of the work.

WHAT IS NOT FUNDED No grants to individuals or bodies which are not a registered charity. Overseas organisations should apply through their local foundation in their own country.

TYPE OF GRANT Capital (including buildings), one-off, project and research will be considered. Funding is available for up to three years.

RANGE OF GRANTS Typical grant £15,000.

SAMPLE GRANTS £2,500,000 to Youth Net for a flagship programme to allow free access to a website through kiosks and an e-bus; £200,000 each to Big Brothers and Sisters for the opening of a centre in Birmingham and core costs, Get Connected for promotion of the charity's awareness amongst young people potentially needing its services, and Home-Start UK for organisational development; £50,000 each to Daily Mail Farm Appeal for farms affected by foot and mouth, and The Queen's Golden Jubille Weekend Trust; £33,000 to St Bartholomew's School – Newbury towards the lifelong learning centre; £30,000 to Sustrans for a five kilometre cycle route on the Kennet and Avon canal; £25,000 to NCVO for a trustee and governance briefing pack.

FINANCES *Year* 2001–02 *Grants* £5,376,722

TRUSTEES Gavin Darby, Chair; Nigel Brocklehurst; Mike Caldwell; Alan Harper.

OTHER INFORMATION The financial information in this entry includes donations made outside of the UK before December 2001, when a network of local foundations were created. An estimated £3,000,000 was expected to be available through the foundation to UK causes in 2002–03.

HOW TO APPLY No application forms are used. Applications should write, or e-mail, for consideration at the quarterly meetings.

WHO TO APPLY TO Sarah Shillito, Foundation Manager, The Courtyard, 2–4 London Road, Newbury, Berkshire RG14 1JX *Tel* 01635 33251 *Fax* 01635 581806 *E-mail* thevodafoneukfoundation@vodafone.co.uk *Website* www.vodafonefoundation.org

CC NO 1013850   **ESTABLISHED** 1992

■ Voluntary Action Luton

WHERE FUNDING CAN BE GIVEN Luton and district.

WHO CAN BENEFIT Organisations benefiting children, young adults and students, at risk groups, those disadvantaged by poverty, and socially isolated people.

WHAT IS FUNDED General charitable purposes, in particular the advancement of education and the relief of poverty, sickness and distress. Development of groups' capacity building to enable improvements in the delivery of services to beneficiaries.

RANGE OF GRANTS Under £500.

FINANCES *Year* 2000 *Income* £479,744
Grants £114,396 *Assets* £87,027

TRUSTEES Mrs M Deidrick; G Dillingham; I Feekins;
Mrs M Turton; R Licorish; M Heyland; D Tsiricos;
I Nancollar; C Harrison.

HOW TO APPLY Initial enquiries regarding any
proposal should be made by telephone.

WHO TO APPLY TO Ms A Laing, 15 New Bedford Road,
Luton LU1 1SA *Tel* 01582 733418 *Fax* 01582
733013 *E-mail* info@valuton.org.uk

CC NO 1059287   **ESTABLISHED** 1996

....

■ Marie-Louise Von Motesiczky Charitable Trust

WHERE FUNDING CAN BE GIVEN UK.

WHO CAN BENEFIT Organisations and individuals.

WHAT IS FUNDED (a) The advancement of education
of the public in the fine arts, particularly painting
and sculpture by any means but primarily by the
acquisition for exhibition to the public of
paintings and works of art and in particular
those by Marie-Louise von Motesiczky. (b) The
relief of diseases and other medical conditions
impairing vision by assisting with the payment of
medical and other expenses incurred by artists
in the treatment and care of their eyes. (c)
General charitable purposes.

FINANCES *Year* 2000–01 *Income* £65,740

TRUSTEES Jeremy David Adler; Richard Karplus;
Sean Rainbird; David Scrase.

HOW TO APPLY In writing to the correspondent.

WHO TO APPLY TO The Trust Secretary, 6 Chesterford
Gardens, London NW3 7DE *Tel* 020 7794 3394

CC NO 1059380   **ESTABLISHED** 1992

■ The Charity of Thomas Wade & Others

WHERE FUNDING CAN BE GIVEN Leeds, within the pre-1974 boundary of the city (approximately LS1 to LS17 postcodes).

WHO CAN BENEFIT Charities benefiting people of all ages and those living in urban areas. Mainly youth organisations and community centres. (Grants are only a part of the charity's activities.)

WHAT IS FUNDED Provision of open spaces, allotments, playing fields, facilities for recreation, amusement, entertainment, including establishment of community and youth centres and for the general social intercourse of inhabitants of the city of Leeds; or grants to any authority, association or body providing such facilities.

WHAT IS NOT FUNDED No grants to individuals or to schools (unless special needs). The trustees tend not to support medical/health orientated bodies. No grants are given for church repairs unless there is some other significant community use which is eligible.

TYPE OF GRANT Usually one-off capital grants. Core costs, recurring costs, running costs and start-up costs. Funding for up to three years may be considered.

RANGE OF GRANTS £200–£30,000; typical grant £1,000–£2,000.

SAMPLE GRANTS £15,000 to Hunslet Club for Boys' and Girls'; £4,000 each to Christ Church Armley Youth Project, St George's Crypt and Voluntary Action – Leeds; £3,000 to Market Place Project; £2,500 each to Bramley & Rodley Community Action, Central Yorkshire Scout Council and St Cyprians Parish Church; £2,000 each to Girls' Brigade and Youth Fellowship, Hyde Park Churches Detached Youth Project, South Leeds Youth Theatre.

FINANCES *Year* 2001 *Income* £154,000 *Grants* £100,000 *Assets* £3,800,000

TRUSTEES Lord Mayor; Rector of Leeds; J Roberts; E M Arnold; J Thorpe; A L Chadwick; P J D Marshall; I A Ziff; Dr A Cooke; M J Dodgson; Cllr A D Atkinson; J Tinker; M S Wainwright; J D M Stoddart-Scott; B T Braimah; Cllr A Gabriel; Cllr B Atha.

HOW TO APPLY In writing to the correspondent. Applicants must submit accounts, evidence of charitable status and a contact telephone number with the application. They should be submitted not later than one month before the trustees' meeting. Trustees consider applications in April, July and November. A charity adviser visits most of the applicants and gives them advice; a detailed report is then made on each application for consideration at the trustees' meetings. The charity adviser also reports on how grants have been used and successful applicants are encouraged to provide follow-up reports to help the trust with its future grantmaking (a note is made of organisations which do not do this).

WHO TO APPLY TO W M Wrigley, Wrigleys, 19 Cookridge Street, Leeds LS2 3AG *Tel* 0113 244 6100 *Fax* 0113 244 6101

CC NO 224939   **ESTABLISHED** 1530

■ The Albert Waghorn Charitable Trust

WHERE FUNDING CAN BE GIVEN UK and overseas.

WHO CAN BENEFIT Registered charities.

WHAT IS FUNDED Christian organisations. Some aid is given to overseas medical need charities, such as Water Aid, on a one-off basis.

WHAT IS NOT FUNDED No grants to students for gap year voluntary activities.

FINANCES *Grants* £29,000

TRUSTEES Dr B S Beardsworth, Chair; and others.

HOW TO APPLY In writing to the correspondent. Please note however that this trust is fully committed to ongoing beneficiaries and new applicants are very unlikely to receive a grant.

WHO TO APPLY TO Dr B S Beardsworth, Chair, 18 Springfield Road, Hinckley, Leicestershire LE10 1AN *Tel* 01455 446818

CC NO 254933   **ESTABLISHED** 1968

■ The Scurrah Wainwright Charity

WHERE FUNDING CAN BE GIVEN Preference for Yorkshire, South Africa and Zimbabwe.

WHO CAN BENEFIT Organisations benefiting: people of all ages; unemployed people; at risk groups; those disadvantaged by poverty; homeless people; those living in areas of social disadvantage; those in care, and fostered and adopted people; one-parent families; and widows and widowers.

WHAT IS FUNDED Preference for radical rather than palliative projects relating to the most disadvantaged in society and where possible involving them in management. Particularly charities working in the fields of: infrastructure and technical support; infrastructure development; accommodation and housing; education and training; and social care and development.

WHAT IS NOT FUNDED No grants for individuals, buildings, medical research or the welfare of animals.

TYPE OF GRANT One-off and recurring grants.

RANGE OF GRANTS £100–£50,000.

SAMPLE GRANTS £30,000 over three years to Chapeltown and Harehills Assisted Learning Computer School; £9,360 to Big Issue in the North for the Big Futures Programme; £7,000 to People and Planet; £6,000 each to YMCA Leeds and GIPSIL; £4,500 to Bradford Community Project; £3,000 each to Future Outlook and Liberatarian and Education Research; £1,000 to The Right Track (BMX) Foundation.

FINANCES *Year* 2001–02 *Income* £61,784 *Grants* £195,591 *Assets* £1,450,570

TRUSTEES J M Wainwright; H A Wainwright; M S Wainwright; T M Wainwright; P Wainwright; H Scott; R Bhaskar.

HOW TO APPLY In writing to the correspondent. Applicants are expected to provide background information about themselves and/or their organisation, the work they wish to pursue and their plans for its practical implementation, which will involve an outline budget and details of any other sources of finance. The most recent income and expenditure and balance sheets should be included. Trustees meet in March, July and November. Applications should be received by the first day of the preceding month.

WHO TO APPLY TO Kerry McQuade, Administrator, 16 Blenheim Street, Hebden Bridge, West Yorkshire HX7 8BU *Tel* 01422 845085 *E-mail* kerry@waintrust.fsnet.co.uk

CC NO 1002755   **ESTABLISHED** 1991

■ Wakefield Trust

WHERE FUNDING CAN BE GIVEN One mile radius of 42 Trinity Square, London.

WHO CAN BENEFIT Registered charities, particularly those benefiting adult women and older people.

WHAT IS FUNDED General charitable purposes for the development of Tower Hill and Trinity Square as a centre from which welfare work can be promoted. In particular, the following areas are supported: assistance to hostels for young men giving their time to welfare work; assistance to clubs for young men, boys, young women or girls, living or working in the trust's area; assistance to educational and recreational associations in connection with hostels or youth clubs.

WHAT IS NOT FUNDED No support for work/projects outside the beneficial area, full salary costs, applications from individuals, capital expenditure, foreign travel, commercial publications, establishing bursary or loan schemes, private education, lobbying – political or otherwise, replacement of statutory funding, business schemes, general appeals, research or umbrella bodies for redistribution.

TYPE OF GRANT General, although preference is given to revenue and salary costs.

RANGE OF GRANTS £100–£60,000.

SAMPLE GRANTS £58,000 to All Hallows Church for parish development; £42,000 to Toc H for an East End project; £20,000 to St Botolph's Homeless Project; £11,000 each to Heba Women's Project towards a worker's salary and Age Concern – Southwark; £9,000 to Spitalfields Care Worker service for salary costs; £7,500 to Tower Hamlets Old People's Welfare Trust; and £6,000 to Breakthrough Trust for social work with minority deaf people.

FINANCES *Year* 2000 *Income* £176,000 *Grants* £224,000 *Assets* £4,100,000

TRUSTEES Prof. Harry Allred; Ven. P J Peter Delaney; Peter Bowring; Jean Harris; Kenneth Prideaux-Brune; Bill Almond; Stuart Morganstein; Helal Rahman.

HOW TO APPLY In writing to the correspondent. Applications are considered four times a year in March, June, September and December.

WHO TO APPLY TO James Connelly, Clerk to the Trustees, Atlee House, 28 Commercial Street, London E1 6LR *Tel* 020 7377 6614 *Fax* 020 7377 9822

CC NO 209123   **ESTABLISHED** 1937

■ The Wakefield Trust

WHERE FUNDING CAN BE GIVEN UK, with a preference for Devon.

WHAT IS FUNDED Church restoration and provision of almshouses in Devon and Cornwall. The trustees intend to endow further almshouses in the Totnes area and will not consider new applications for a number of years.

WHAT IS NOT FUNDED No grants to individuals.

RANGE OF GRANTS £500–£3,000.

FINANCES *Year* 2000–01 *Income* £39,942

TRUSTEES Mrs M P Mitchell; Anne N Brain; C D Torlesse; M B Shaw; A J Harrison.

HOW TO APPLY In writing to the correspondent.

WHO TO APPLY TO C E White, Yarner Farm House, Dartington, Devon TQ9 6JH *Tel* 01803 732436

CC NO 800079   **ESTABLISHED** 1988

■ Wakeham Trust

WHERE FUNDING CAN BE GIVEN UK.

WHO CAN BENEFIT Organisations benefiting local communities and the development of young people.

WHAT IS FUNDED The trust makes grants to a wide range of community organisations, and for educational purposes. This includes grants towards community service carried out by young people and help with start-up projects by volunteers.

WHAT IS NOT FUNDED No grants to individuals or large, well-established charities, or towards buildings and transport.

RANGE OF GRANTS Usually £50–£250.

SAMPLE GRANTS £3,700 to Glebe Charitable Trust; £2,500 to Liverpool Council of Social Service; £1,000 each to Find Your Feet, Inner City Music, International Service, Lansalian Developing World Projects and Zion Congregational Church.

FINANCES *Year* 1999–2000 *Income* £46,000 *Grants* £37,000 *Assets* £2,200,000

TRUSTEES Harold Carter; Barnaby Newbolt; Tess Silkstone.

HOW TO APPLY In writing to the correspondent.

WHO TO APPLY TO Mrs Julie Austin, Wakeham Lodge, Rogate, Petersfield, Hampshire GU31 5EJ *Fax* 01730 821748 *E-mail* trust@wakeham.com

CC NO 267495   **ESTABLISHED** 1974

■ Wales Council for Voluntary Action

WHERE FUNDING CAN BE GIVEN Wales.

WHO CAN BENEFIT Registered charities and voluntary organisations only.

WHAT IS FUNDED Grants schemes are: (a) Enfys for the quality and quantity of playing fields and green spaces as well as sustainable projects; (b) Social Risk Fund for projects costing up to £10,000 which aim to take chances and do something innovative to regenerate local communities; (c) Traws Cymru – Across Wales which aims to foster greater understanding and friendship among people aged 11 to 25 by supporting sporting or cultural exchanges; (d) Community Buildings 2001–2004 which supports small-scale repairs and improvements of between £5,000 and £20,000 which are essential to maintain and sustain existing activities in village/community halls; (e) Communities First which aims to regenerate the most disadvantaged communities in Wales; (f) Agor Frysau – Opening Doors, which aims to support community buildings increase their accessibility, encourage the integration of people with hearing difficulties or encourage bilingualism in community buildings.

WHAT IS NOT FUNDED Grants are made to constituted voluntary organisations only.

TYPE OF GRANT Capital, core costs, one-off, project, recurring costs, running costs, start-up costs.

RANGE OF GRANTS (a) Up to £25,000; (b) Unknown; (c) Up to £500; (d) Up to £5,000; (e) Up to £2,500; (e) Unknown.

FINANCES *Year* 1997–98 *Income* £3,760,699 *Grants* £2,222,251 *Assets* £544,983

PUBLICATIONS Guidance notes for applicants available on request. *Directory of Voluntary Organisations in Wales, Evaluating Community Projects for European Funding, Wales Funding Handbook.* Handbooks, briefing papers, reports, information sheets are also available.

HOW TO APPLY There are separate application forms for each scheme. Contact the trust, or visit its website, for further information.

WHO TO APPLY TO Dave Maggs, Assistant Chief Executive, Baltic House, Mount Stuart Square, Cardiff CF10 5FH *Tel* 0870 607 1666 *Fax* 029 2043 1701 *Minicom* 029 2043 1702 *Website* www.wcva.org.uk

CC NO 218093 ESTABLISHED 1963

....

■ Robert and Felicity Waley-Cohen Charitable Trust

WHERE FUNDING CAN BE GIVEN London and Oxfordshire.

WHO CAN BENEFIT Charitable organisations, schools and those of the Jewish faith.

WHAT IS FUNDED The trust supports Jewish, education, fine arts, and health related appeals.

WHAT IS NOT FUNDED No grants to individuals.

RANGE OF GRANTS £50–£6,000.

SAMPLE GRANTS £6,000 to Warwickshire College (the fourth of four grants); £5,000 to Dragon School Trust Ltd; £3,000 to University of Oxford Development Charity; £2,500 to Community Security Trust (third of three grants); £1,500 to St Edwards School Endowment Fund; £1,200 to Action for Hunger UK; £1,000 each to Help the Hospices and Liberal Jewish Synagogue.

FINANCES *Year* 1999–2000 *Income* £14,000 *Grants* £23,000 *Assets* £428,000

TRUSTEES R Waley-Cohen; Mrs F Waley-Cohen.

HOW TO APPLY In writing to the correspondent.

WHO TO APPLY TO R Waley-Cohen, Trustee, 18 Gilston Road, London SW10 9SR *Tel* 020 7244 6022

CC NO 272126 ESTABLISHED 1976

....

■ Ruth Walker Charitable Trust

WHERE FUNDING CAN BE GIVEN South Yorkshire.

WHO CAN BENEFIT Registered charities.

WHAT IS FUNDED General charitable purposes.

SAMPLE GRANTS £5,000 to Janson Dean Nursing Home; £3,000 each to Cawthorpe Methodist Church and Cawthorpe Parish Church; £2,000 to Cawthorpe Jubilee Museum.

FINANCES *Year* 1999–2000 *Income* £29,000 *Grants* £21,000 *Assets* £71,000

TRUSTEES Michael J M Walker; Josephine R Lees; Helen E Porteous.

HOW TO APPLY In writing to the correspondent.

WHO TO APPLY TO The Trustees, c/o Britannic House, Regent Street, Barnsley S70 2EQ *Tel* 01226 733533

CC NO 271910 ESTABLISHED 1976

....

■ The Walker Trust

WHERE FUNDING CAN BE GIVEN Shropshire.

WHO CAN BENEFIT Individuals and organisations benefiting children and young adults who are in care, fostered and adopted.

WHAT IS FUNDED The establishment or towards maintenance of any hospital, infirmary, convalescent homes or other institution having for its object the relief of sickness or promoting convalescence; the provision of medical or surgical aid or appliance; any institution for the maintenance and education of orphans.

WHAT IS NOT FUNDED No grants to individuals for second degrees or postgraduate courses. Appeals from outside Shropshire will not be considered or replied to.

SAMPLE GRANTS £50,000 to Shrewsbury Postgraduate Centre for building works; £10,000 each to Macmillan Cancer Relief, Princess Royal Hospital, Shropshire Schools and Colleges Football Association and Shropshire Full Stop; £5,000 to Walford College; £3,200 to Burton Borough Scholarship; £3,000 to Keele University; £2,500 to Volunteer Reading Help; £2,000 each to British Red Cross – Shropshire for medical equipment and Severdale School Parents for nursery facilities.

FINANCES *Year* 1999–2000 *Income* £192,000 *Grants* £211,000 *Assets* £4,600,000

TRUSTEES A E Heber-Percy, Chair; M W Beardwell; N Bishop; Major A H Coales; Miss P Harrison; Mrs C Paton-Smith.

HOW TO APPLY In writing to the correspondent. Details of other assistance applied for must be given and, in the case of organisations, the latest annual report and accounts. The trustees meet in January, April, July and September each year, but arrangements can be made for urgent applications to receive consideration between meetings. Applications must reach the clerk not less than one month before a decision is required.

WHO TO APPLY TO E Hewitt, Clerk, The Shirehall, Abbey Foregate, Shrewsbury SY2 6ND *Tel* 01743 252725

CC NO 215479 ESTABLISHED 1897

....

■ The Thomas Wall Trust

WHERE FUNDING CAN BE GIVEN UK.

WHO CAN BENEFIT Adult students of all ages needing to gain a skill or qualification to earn a living; community-based organisations with practical schemes for helping young people. Organisations benefiting young adults, older peole, disabled people and people disadvantaged by poverty.

WHAT IS FUNDED Grants are given to UK individual students for educational, especially vocational, courses which will lead to paid employment. For medicine, dentistry, law and veterinary science interest-free loans are given, not grants. Grants are only given to schoolchildren if unexpected financial crisis occurs during their final A-level year. Grants to charitable organisations in education and social welfare will preferably be made to those that are small or pioneering, and for specific purposes.

WHAT IS NOT FUNDED No grants for: undergraduate study, unless not eligible for normal state support; postgraduate study or research for higher degrees, except short courses of vocational or professional training; travel or study abroad; elective or intercalated courses; attendance at conferences; building projects or large general appeals.

TYPE OF GRANT Students, for fees or maintenance: normal maximum grant £800. Charities, for capital, one-off, project, start-up or running costs: maximum grant £1,000. Grants are for one year or less.

SAMPLE GRANTS £1,000 each to Fellowship of St Nicholas -St Leonard's-on-sea for youth workshops, The Blind Business Association towards helping blind people into employment, Capital Carers – London SE22 for a young carers project, Horticap – Harrogate for new equipment, Weston Spirit – Liverpool for the provision of short courses.

FINANCES *Year* 2002 *Income* £85,874 *Grants* £65,960 *Assets* £2,208,462

TRUSTEES G M Copland, Chair; Mrs M A Barrie; P H Bolton; C R Broomfield; Miss A S Kennedy; Miss

A-M Martin; J Porteous; R Waller, and one vacancy. One representative each from Secondary Heads Association and Oxford, Cambridge and London Universities, and five co-opted.

HOW TO APPLY On a form available from the trust's website or by sending an sae to the correspondent. Applications from individuals may be made from January onwards preceding the start of the academic year for which the grant is sought, and will be considered for as long as the available funds allow. Eligible charitable organisations may submit applications by mid-May for decisions at the trustees' meeting in July, and by mid-October for December.

WHO TO APPLY TO Prof. G Holt, 64 Thomas More House, Barbican, London EC2Y 8BT *Tel* 020 7638 1753

CC NO 206121   **ESTABLISHED** 1920

■ The A F Wallace Charity Trust

WHERE FUNDING CAN BE GIVEN UK, with a preference for Aberdeenshire.

WHO CAN BENEFIT Older people in the Upper Donside area of West Aberdeen and former employees of Bombay Burmah Trading Corporation.

WHAT IS FUNDED Most appeals and charitable causes are considered. Currently the main call on the trust's funds is to provide enhanced housing, welfare and pension facilities for a number of older people in the UK who have been associated over many years with the Wallace family.

TYPE OF GRANT Mainly one-off.

RANGE OF GRANTS Registered charities: average £200.

FINANCES *Year* 1999–2000 *Income* £47,000 *Grants* £36,000 *Assets* £855,000

TRUSTEES Falconer Alexander Wallace; Alistair James Wishart Falconer Wallace.

HOW TO APPLY In writing to the correspondent.

WHO TO APPLY TO S J Thornton, NCL Investments Ltd, Bartlett House, 9–12 Basinghall Street, London EC2V 5NS *Tel* 020 7600 2801

CC NO 207110   **ESTABLISHED** 1912

■ Wallington Missionary Mart and Auctions

WHERE FUNDING CAN BE GIVEN Overseas.

WHO CAN BENEFIT Missionary societies working overseas benefiting Christians.

WHAT IS FUNDED Christian education and outreach.

WHAT IS NOT FUNDED Only registered charities may receive support. Applications from individuals are only considered if funds will go to a missionary society or Christian charity.

TYPE OF GRANT Usually one-off grants for core costs. Fully committed for charities selected by the trustees.

SAMPLE GRANTS £11,622 in 11 grants to OMF International (UK); £7,780 in 6 grants to Heath Evangelical Trust; £9,584 in 10 grants to Tearfund; £9,392 in 12 grants to Mission Aviation Fellowship; £8,687 in 4 grants to Crusaders; £7,000 to All Nations Christian College; £6,214 in 7 grants to SIM-UK; £5,552 in 4 grants to CORD; £5,478 in 6 grants to FEBA Radio; £5,302 in 7 grants to South American Mission Society.

FINANCES *Year* 2002 *Income* £279,852 *Grants* £200,525 *Assets* £174,000

TRUSTEES Council of Management: V W W Hedderly, Chair; B E Chapman; Mrs S P Collett; H F Curwood; D C Lewin; Mrs S M Symes; Mrs F L Willey; G C Willey.

HOW TO APPLY In writing to the correspondent, with an sae. The trustees meet to consider grants throughout the year.

WHO TO APPLY TO B E Chapman, Company Secretary, 99 Woodmansterne Road, Carshalton Beeches, Surrey SM5 4EG *Tel* 020 8643 3616 *Website* www.wallingtonmissionary.org.uk

CC NO 289030   **ESTABLISHED** 1965

■ The F J Wallis Charitable Settlement

WHERE FUNDING CAN BE GIVEN UK, with some interest in Hampshire and Surrey.

WHO CAN BENEFIT Charitable organisations, including both headquarters and branches of large UK charities.

WHAT IS FUNDED General charitable purposes. The policy is wide and could be said to be any deserving cause.

WHAT IS NOT FUNDED No grants to individuals or to local charities except those in Surrey or in Hampshire. The same organisation is not supported twice within a 24-month period.

TYPE OF GRANT Mostly one-off but there are some recurring grants.

RANGE OF GRANTS £500–£5,000.

SAMPLE GRANTS £5,000 each to Action Research, Children's Hospice for Naomi House, Reed's School Foundation Appeal, SANDS and World Trade Center Disaster Fund; £2,500 to Harlow and Area Stroke Support Group; £1,000 each to British Epilepsy Association, Headway, National Missing Persons Helpline and Save the Children Fund.

FINANCES *Year* 2001–02 *Income* £57,035 *Grants* £68,500 *Assets* £1,172,462

TRUSTEES Mrs D I Wallis; F H Hughes; A J Hills.

HOW TO APPLY In writing to the correspondent. No telephone calls. Applications are not acknowledged and unsuccessful applicants will only be contacted if an sae is provided. Trustees meet in March, June, September and December and applications need to be received the month prior to the trustees' meeting.

WHO TO APPLY TO F H Hughes, Trustee, Bridge House, 11 Creek Road, Hampton Court, East Molesey, Surrey KT8 9BE

CC NO 279273   **ESTABLISHED** 1979

■ The Walton Foundation

WHERE FUNDING CAN BE GIVEN West of Scotland.

WHO CAN BENEFIT Organisations benefiting: people disadvantaged by poverty; refugees; victims of man-made or natural disasters; and people with asthma, cancer, heart disease, mental illness, strokes or a terminal illness.

WHAT IS FUNDED General charitable purposes, especially education and medical causes.

WHAT IS NOT FUNDED No grants to individuals. No grants for political causes.

RANGE OF GRANTS £100–£25,000.

SAMPLE GRANTS £6,000 to British Council of SZMC; £4,000 to Lubavitch Foundation; £2,000 to Glasgow Jewish Education Foundation; £1,950 to Jewish National Fund; £1,730 to Queens Park Hebrew Congregation; £1,240 to Glasgow Maccabi.

FINANCES *Year* 1998 *Income* £121,000 *Grants* £76,000 *Assets* £2,100,000

Think carefully about every application. Is it justified?

867

TRUSTEES D Walton; Mrs C Walton; Prof. R A Lorimer; E Glen; Prof. L Blumgart; M Walton; J R Walton.

HOW TO APPLY In writing to the correspondent. Trustees meet to consider grants in June; applications should be received by March.

WHO TO APPLY TO Fiona Jamieson, Deloitte & Touche, 9 George Square, Glasgow G2 1QQ *Tel* 0141 204 2800

SC NO SC004005

■ War on Want

WHERE FUNDING CAN BE GIVEN Developing countries only.

WHO CAN BENEFIT Typically, War on Want directly funds the work of labour organisations and NGOs in developing countries, usually trade unions or similar workers' organisations, and women's organisations.

WHAT IS FUNDED Overseas development projects that address the root causes of poverty, oppression and injustice in developing countries. The current focus is on workers' rights.

WHAT IS NOT FUNDED War on Want is an overseas development agency and does not make grants to organisations in the UK.

TYPE OF GRANT Continuous project funding.

SAMPLE GRANTS In 1999: £138,040 to Landless Movement Capacity Building, Sao Paulo, Brazil; £63,858 to Association for the Realisation of Basic Needs, Dhaka, Bangladesh; £49,882 to Rubbish Collectors and Homeless People Project, Sao Paulo, Brazil; £49,579 to Mines Awareness Project, West Bank, Palestine; £40,660 Black Women's Cultural Centre, Santos, Brazil; £35,798 to Masisukumeni Women's Centre, South Africa; £28,000 to Women's Legal Aid, Rukwa, Tanzania; £19,852 to Bangladesh Association of Farm Labourers Federation, Bangladesh; £15,660 to Children's Education, Moiplaas, South Africa; £7,000 to Women Garment Workers Training, Indonesia.

FINANCES *Year* 2000 *Income* £1,200,174 *Grants* £795,174 *Assets* £629,036

TRUSTEES The Council of Management: L Philipson, Chair; A Boyle; S Branford; J Chowcat; M Hughes; P Ingram; F Awua-Kyrematen; M Luetchford; R Pearson; J Prudence; M Hindley; N Alam.

PUBLICATIONS *Upfront* (a regular newsletter); publications list – covering subjects such as health, women, trade, aid, Asia, Latin America and Africa.

HOW TO APPLY Unsolicited applications are not accepted and will not be acknowledged.

WHO TO APPLY TO The Director, Fenner Brockway House, 37–39 Great Guildford Street, London SE1 0ES *Tel* 020 7620 1111 *Fax* 020 7261 9291 *E-mail* mailroom@waronwant.org *Website* www.waronwant.org

CC NO 208724 **ESTABLISHED** 1959

■ Warbeck Fund Ltd

WHERE FUNDING CAN BE GIVEN UK and overseas, with a preference for London.

WHO CAN BENEFIT Charitable organisations, both headquarters and local organisations.

WHAT IS FUNDED General charitable purposes, but mostly Jewish, arts, medical and welfare.

WHAT IS NOT FUNDED No grants to individuals or non-UK registered charities.

RANGE OF GRANTS £15–£26,100.

SAMPLE GRANTS £26,100 to Westminster Society for People with Learning Difficulties; £21,300 to United Jewish Israel Appeal; £21,250 to Royal National Theatre; £10,600 to World Jewish Relief; £10,250 to Hampstead Theatre Trust; £10,000 to British ORT; £7,000 to British Friends of Haifa University; £6,850 to West London Synagogue; £5,300 to Wiezmann Institute Foundation; £4,250 to Chicken Shed Theatre Company.

FINANCES *Year* 2000–01 *Income* £256,614 *Grants* £178,744 *Assets* £188,896

TRUSTEES Michael Brian David; Jonathan Gestetner; Neil Sinclair.

OTHER INFORMATION The trust's funds are fully committed and it expects to spend both its income and assets over the next few years.

HOW TO APPLY According to the correspondent, it may not be worth writing to the trust as unsolicited applications tend to be unsuccessful.

WHO TO APPLY TO The Secretary, 2nd Floor, Pump House, 10 Chapel Place, Rivington Street, London EC2A 3DQ *Tel* 020 7739 2224 *Fax* 020 7739 5544

CC NO 252953 **ESTABLISHED** 1967

■ Sir Siegmund Warburg's Voluntary Settlement

WHERE FUNDING CAN BE GIVEN UK, especially London.

WHO CAN BENEFIT Research organisations.

WHAT IS FUNDED Medical studies and research; general charitable purposes.

WHAT IS NOT FUNDED No grants to individuals.

TYPE OF GRANT Recurring.

SAMPLE GRANTS £134,192 to University of Birmingham; £80,032 to Institute of Child Health; £74,150 to Natural Justice; £65,889 to King's College London; £60,000 to Institute of Cancer Research; £56,802 to Imperial College; £49,364 to Lewisham Hospital NHS Trust; £27,066 to St George's Hospital Medical School; £25,000 to Institute of Jewish Policy Research; £22,763 to Kennedy Institute of Rheumatology.

FINANCES *Year* 2000–01 *Income* £471,987 *Grants* £631,229 *Assets* £14,855,610

TRUSTEES Doris E Wasserman; Hugh A Stevenson; Dr Michael J Harding; Christopher Purvis.

HOW TO APPLY In writing to the correspondent.

WHO TO APPLY TO Robin Jessel, Secretary, 33 St Mary Ave, London EC3 8LL *Tel* 020 7342 2000

CC NO 286719 **ESTABLISHED** 1983

■ The Ward Blenkinsop Trust

WHERE FUNDING CAN BE GIVEN UK, with a special interest in Merseyside and surrounding counties.

WHO CAN BENEFIT Mainly research foundations and charitable organisations.

WHAT IS FUNDED General charitable purposes with emphasis on support for medical research, social welfare, arts and education.

WHAT IS NOT FUNDED No grants to individuals.

RANGE OF GRANTS Up to £10,000.

FINANCES *Year* 1998–99 *Income* £279,000 *Grants* £204,000

TRUSTEES A M Blenkinsop; J H Awdry; S J Blenkinsop; C A Blenkinsop; A F Stormer; H E Millin.

HOW TO APPLY In writing to the correspondent.

WHO TO APPLY TO Charlotte Blenkinsop, Trustee, PO Box 28840, London SW13 0WZ *Tel* 020 8878 9975

CC NO 265449 **ESTABLISHED** 1972

■ The John Warren Foundation

WHERE FUNDING CAN BE GIVEN Lincolnshire, then
Bedfordshire, Northamptonshire and
Nottinghamshire.

WHO CAN BENEFIT Churches.

WHAT IS FUNDED Church fabric repairs.

WHAT IS NOT FUNDED No support for major cathedral
appeals.

TYPE OF GRANT One-off grants.

FINANCES *Year* 1999–2000 *Income* £36,000
Grants £34,000 *Assets* £634,000

TRUSTEES J E Lamb; R H Lamb; B H Marshall.

HOW TO APPLY In writing to the correspondent.

WHO TO APPLY TO J E Lamb, Trustee, Lamb &
Holmes Solicitors, West Street, Kettering,
Northamptonshire NN16 0AZ *Tel* 01536
513195 *Fax* 01536 410191

CC NO 201522 **ESTABLISHED** 1949

■ The Warrington Church of England Educational Trust

WHERE FUNDING CAN BE GIVEN The borough of
Warrington.

WHO CAN BENEFIT Church of England schools.

WHAT IS FUNDED Educational purposes in the
Warrington area, including repairs to school
buildings.

WHAT IS NOT FUNDED No grants to individuals.

FINANCES *Year* 2000 *Income* £45,339
Grants £32,237 *Assets* £20,861,120

TRUSTEES About 20 trustees including the Rector of
Warrington and representatives from each of the
19 schools in the beneficial area.

HOW TO APPLY In writing to the correspondent. A
copy of the grant notification from the
government must be included.

WHO TO APPLY TO Chris Royle, Law Clerk, Ridgway
Greenall, 21 Palmyra Square, Warrington WA1
1BW *Tel* 01925 654221 *Fax* 01925 416527
E-mail law@ridgway.co.uk
Website www.ridgway.co.uk

CC NO 511469 **ESTABLISHED** 1952

■ The Warwick Municipal Charities – Charity of King Henry VIII, Warwick

WHERE FUNDING CAN BE GIVEN The former borough of
Warwick only.

WHO CAN BENEFIT Half the income goes to Warwick
churches, 30% to Kings School, Warwick and
20% for general charitable purposes for the
inhabitants of the town of Warwick.

WHAT IS FUNDED General charitable purposes.

SAMPLE GRANTS £100,000 to Warwick Hospital A &
E Appeal; £61,000 to Warwick Corps of Drums;
£50,000 to St Mary Immaculate Church;
£42,000 to Royal Regiment of Fusiliers;
£27,000 to Lord Leycester Hospital; £20,000
each to Aylesford School and Warwick
Apprenticing Charities.

FINANCES *Year* 2001 *Income* £1,600,000
Grants £440,000 *Assets* £22,000,000

TRUSTEES Prof. E W Ives, Chair; Mrs M Haywood; B
Gillitt; N F J Thurley; J P McCarthy; Mrs S
Rhodes; P Ritchie; D Cooke; P G Butler.

HOW TO APPLY In writing to the correspondent.
Trustees meet to make grants six times a year,
in February, April, May, July, September and
November.

WHO TO APPLY TO R J Wyatt, Clerk, 12 High Street,
Warwick CV34 4AP *Tel* 01926 495533
Fax 01926 401464

CC NO 232862 **ESTABLISHED** 1964

■ The Warwickshire Masonic Charitable Association Ltd

WHERE FUNDING CAN BE GIVEN Warwickshire and the
Midlands.

WHO CAN BENEFIT Local and regional organisations
and local branches of UK organisations
benefiting masons, at risk groups, and people
who are disabled, disadvantaged by poverty or
socially isolated.

WHAT IS FUNDED Masonic charities; and health and
welfare causes, especially hospices and
disability organisations.

SAMPLE GRANTS £6,000 to Mary Ann Evans Hospice;
£3,000 each to Acorn's Children's Hospice,
Myton Hamlet Hospice, St Giles Hospice, St
Mary's Hospice, Shakespeare Hospic and
Warren Pearl; £2,000 each to Bryony House and
Greenacres Cheshire Home; £1,500 to CRAB –
Cancer Research at Birmingham.

FINANCES *Year* 2001–02 *Income* £311,887
Grants £305,597 *Assets* £4,204,023

TRUSTEES D W Old; R V Willis; R S Mac; E J
Soderman; V W Keene; D C Hooker; D J F
Rawlins; M J Price; C J Grove; A C Taylor; W F
Aitken; I Jones; F Jephcott; P L Britton; R
Pitham; J G Blandford; P G Randon; M B
Squires; S Lewis; A J Wall; E Rymer; S T E Fenn.

HOW TO APPLY In writing to the correspondent.

WHO TO APPLY TO W F Aitken, Trustee, The Charity
Office, 2 Stirling Road, Edgbaston, Birmingham
B16 9SB *Tel* 0121 454 0554 *Fax* 0121 455
9822

CC NO 211588 **ESTABLISHED** 1945

■ Mrs Waterhouse Charitable Trust

WHERE FUNDING CAN BE GIVEN UK, with an interest in
Lancashire.

WHO CAN BENEFIT Registered charities only,
especially those working in Lancashire.

WHAT IS FUNDED Churches and medical; health;
welfare; environmental; wildlife; and heritage
charities.

WHAT IS NOT FUNDED No grants to individuals.

TYPE OF GRANT Cash grants, mostly recurring.
Occasional large grants for capital purposes.

RANGE OF GRANTS £1,000–£50,000; typical grant
£2,000–£5,000.

SAMPLE GRANTS £15,000 to Whalley Abbey
Restoration Fund; £10,000 each to Christie
Hospital NHS Trust, East Lancashire Hospice
Fund, National Trust for the Lake District
Appeal, and RSPB; £8,000 each to Marie Curie
Cancer Care, and Macmillan Cancer Relief;
£5,000 each to Arthritis Research Campaign,
British Diabetics Association and National
Eczema Society.

FINANCES *Year* 2000–01 *Income* £288,025
Grants £288,000 *Assets* £6,401,962

TRUSTEES D H Dunn; E Dunn.

HOW TO APPLY In writing to the correspondent. There
is no set time for the consideration of
applications, but donations are normally made
in March each year.

WHO TO APPLY TO D H Dunn, Trustee, 25 Clitheroe
Road, Whalley, Clitheroe BB7 9AD

CC NO 261685 **ESTABLISHED** 1967

■ G R Waters Charitable Trust 2000

WHERE FUNDING CAN BE GIVEN UK. Also North and Central America.

WHO CAN BENEFIT Registered charities.

WHAT IS FUNDED General charitable purposes.

RANGE OF GRANTS Usually £500–£10,000.

SAMPLE GRANTS £100,000 to Rhys Daniels Trust; £25,000 to Ovingdean Hall School; US$10,000 each to Barbados Welfare Charities, Millennium Kids Foundation, and Robin Hood Foundation; £5,000 each to Dove Cottage Day Hospice, Happy Days Children's Charity, NSPCC and React.

FINANCES *Year* 1999–2000 *Income* £67,809 *Grants* £185,713 *Assets* £723,530

TRUSTEES G R Waters; A Russell.

OTHER INFORMATION This trust has replaced The G R Waters 1989 Charitable Trust (cc number 328574). The financial information in this entry refers to the previous trust, although it stated this new one would operate in the same manner.

HOW TO APPLY In writing to the correspondent.

WHO TO APPLY TO Michael Lewis, Finers Stephens Innocent, 179 Great Portland Street, London W1W 5LS *Tel* 020 7323 4000 *Fax* 020 7344 7689

CC NO 1091525   **ESTABLISHED** 2000

■ The Waterside Trust

WHERE FUNDING CAN BE GIVEN Unrestricted.

WHO CAN BENEFIT Charitable organisations.

WHAT IS FUNDED Adult Christian formation and pastoral care, educational and recreational activities for disadvantaged young people and young offenders, care and support for older people and disadvantaged people and community development. Ethics and Church management and finance are also areas of interest.

WHAT IS NOT FUNDED No grants to: individuals; environmental projects; construction costs or purchase of buildings; arts organisations; conservation groups; endowment appeals; major research projects.

SAMPLE GRANTS £760,000 to Rathbone Jersey Ltd; £208,062 to Research Centre for Genetic Medicine – USA; £75,000 to Stitching Porticus – Netherlands; £70,022 to Philosophy and Theology – Netherlands; £55,918 to Pontificia Università San Tommaso d'Aquino – Italy; £54,200 to International Bureau of Solidarity – Philippines; £51,746 to International Study Commission on Media, Religion and Culture – USA; £49,931 to Salesian Society of St John Bosco – Philippines; £44,081 to Pontificia Facoltà Di Scienze Dell' Educazione Ausilium – Italy; £42,439 to University of Montreal Human Genetics and Social Policy Project – Canada.

FINANCES *Year* 2001 *Income* £110,326 *Grants* £1,689,239 *Assets* £1,290,284

TRUSTEES Irvine Bay Trustee Company.

OTHER INFORMATION The trust expected to spend its reserves in 2002 and will rely on donations received for its income, giving smaller grants and few, if any, for work overseas. Donations received in 2001 totalled £9,000.

HOW TO APPLY In writing, to the correspondent, for consideration on an ongoing basis.

WHO TO APPLY TO Robert Clark, 56 Palmerston Place, Edinburgh EH12 5AY *Tel* 0131 225 6366 *Fax* 0131 220 1041

SC NO SC003232

■ The Wates Foundation

WHERE FUNDING CAN BE GIVEN General, but no local grants outside Greater London and the south east of England.

WHO CAN BENEFIT Projects with charitable status. Practical projects involving people are preferred especially those benefiting young and disadvantaged people.

WHAT IS FUNDED (a) Community projects tackling disadvantage, such as substance addiction, mental and physical disability, homelessness, youth and the care of children, prostitution, penal reform and criminal justice, and vocational training and education for socially excluded or disadvantaged groups, refugee communities, people in therapy or institutional aftercare, and those for whom English is not a first language. (b) Arts projects where there is a mainstream aim to support socially excluded people such as inmates of institutions or schools in recognised deprived areas. This should not preclude grants to enhance the general quality of life through the support of cultural activities. (c) Education, science and health, particularly the promotion of work in areas directly addressing distress and disadvantage. (d) Environment, contributing to the maintenance and enhancement of the urban community. (e) Christianity and the promotion of moral values and inter-faith relations. The trust particularly likes to support: crime, prisons and resettlement; social enterprise; urban regeneration and community capacity building; and addiction and mental health therapies for those for whom English is not a first language.

WHAT IS NOT FUNDED The trust does not generally support: any work that is not legally charitable; sponsorship of individuals for any purpose; large well-established or UK charities; umbrella organisations or support to other grantmaking bodies; building projects including the repair of churches and church appeals; medical or disaster relief appeals; sporting, social or other events; foreign travel including expeditions; conferences; or overseas projects and projects outside Greater London.

TYPE OF GRANT Normally up to £25,000. Maximum length of support three years. Grants may be one-off and for salaries, although buildings, capital, project, research, start-up, core, running and recurring costs will also be considered.

SAMPLE GRANTS £30,000 to Unlock (National Association of Ex-offenders) for a salary; £25,000 each to Croydon Sports Partnership for core costs and Irene Taylor Trust for the London prisons collaboration project; £24,973 to Camden and Westminster Refugee Training Programme for an ESOL/IT training course for refugee groups in London; £22,000 to Domestic Violence Matters – Islington for core funding of a support worker; £20,000 each to Pepys Community Forum – Deptford for a salary, Prisoners' Advice Service for a salary, Sarum College – Salisbury for a lift for disabled access, Synergy Theatre Project for two drama productions at HMP Latchmere House and Who Cares? Trust for an interactive website for young people in care; £19,100 to Drug and Alcohol Foundation – Central London for a research project into the provision of substance abuse therapies for ethnic minorities for whom English is not a first language.

FINANCES *Year* 2001–02 *Income* £1,469,031 *Grants* £1,540,000 *Assets* £32,659,675

TRUSTEES Jane Wates, chair; Susan Wates; Ann Ritchie; Michael Wates; David Wates; William Wates. (The grants committee of the foundation also includes other members of the Wates family.)

HOW TO APPLY In writing to the correspondent, including a signed copy of the latest annual report and accounts. Applications should be on no more than four A4 pages and contain no additional publicity, although a breakdown of the budget may be included (including inflation and national insurance costs if appropriate). Formal application using an application questionnaire will only be invited after this process. The foundation is happy to hold telephone discussions with potential applicants to assess suitability.

WHO TO APPLY TO The Director, 1260 London Road, Norbury, London SW16 4EG *Tel* 020 8764 5000 *Website* www.watesfoundation.org.uk

CC NO 247941   **ESTABLISHED** 1966

■ The Perry Watlington Trust

WHERE FUNDING CAN BE GIVEN Essex.

WHO CAN BENEFIT Local and regional organisations, and local branches of national organisations benefiting people who are disabled or sick.

WHAT IS FUNDED Charities providing acute healthcare and aftercare, medical centres, hospices, hospice at home and nursing services for people who are disabled or chronically ill. Funding of medical research will also be considered.

WHAT IS NOT FUNDED Any cause unconnected with disabled/sick people in the county of Essex.

TYPE OF GRANT Recurrent, occasionally one-off.

SAMPLE GRANTS £4,300 each to Acorn Village and Pony Riding for the Disabled; £2,750 to Essex Clergy; £2,250 each to Essex Association for the Physically Handicapped and Trueloves (Shaftsbury Society); £1,750 each to Ferries Barn, St Francis Hospice, St Helen's Hospice – Colchester and Children's Hospice for Eastern Region; £1,650 Colchester and North East Essex Headway.

FINANCES *Year* 1999 *Income* £27,355 *Grants* £27,500

TRUSTEES R L H Lyster, Chair; Mrs A Ashton; Mrs M Judd; Mrs C Cottrell; R G Newman; J O Parker; T E Ruggles-Brise.

HOW TO APPLY In writing to the correspondent, but please note that funds are fully committed and grant seekers are highly unlikely to obtain financial support from the trust.

WHO TO APPLY TO R L H Lyster, Chair, Malting Green House, Layer De La Haye, Colchester CO2 0JE

CC NO 255014   **ESTABLISHED** 1968

■ The Bertie Watson Foundation

WHERE FUNDING CAN BE GIVEN UK and Portugal.

WHO CAN BENEFIT Organisations benefiting children and people who are disabled or have learning difficulties.

WHAT IS FUNDED Small hospitals, hospices, children's healthcare and welfare, mental illness, Portuguese charities.

WHAT IS NOT FUNDED No grants to individuals, including students. No grants will be made in response to general appeals from large organisations or to smaller bodies working in areas other than those set out above.

RANGE OF GRANTS Grants for £500, £1,000 or £2,000.

SAMPLE GRANTS Grants of £2,000 each were made to Berkshire Community Trust, Feathers Youth Clubs Association and King Edward VII Hospital for Officers –Sister Agnes Benevolent Fund.

Beneficiaries receiving £1,000 each were Alzheimer's Disease Society, Downs Syndrome Association, Elizabeth Finn Trust, HAPPY – Great Ormond Street, Institute for the Special Child, Motor Neurone Disease Association, Riding for the Disabled – Algarve and St Luke's Hospital for the Clergy.

FINANCES *Year* 2001–02 *Income* £21,140 *Grants* £18,000 *Assets* £547,272

TRUSTEES N S D Bulmer; Rt Hon. Viscountess Waverley; Graham Wedlake; Julian Wethered.

HOW TO APPLY Trustees meet annually in June to consider applications. Applications should be made to the correspondent in writing and should include clear details of the need, the project and the outline budget, including the amount of funds raised so far. Successful applications only will be acknowledged.

WHO TO APPLY TO N S D Bulmer, Trustee, Messrs Farrer & Co., 66 Lincoln's Inn Fields, London WC2A 3LH *Tel* 020 7242 2022 *Fax* 020 7242 9899 *E-mail* nsb@farrier.co.uk

CC NO 285523   **ESTABLISHED** 1982

■ Blyth Watson Charitable Trust

WHERE FUNDING CAN BE GIVEN UK.

WHAT IS FUNDED UK-based causes which may broadly be described as humanitarian in nature.

RANGE OF GRANTS £1,000–£7,300.

SAMPLE GRANTS £7,348 to Seaford College; £5,000 each to Alzheimer's Society, Brain Research Trust, Cancer BACUP, Deafblind UK, Development Foundation, Jessie May Trust, Princess Royal Trust for Carers, RUKBA and Society for the Relief of Distress.

FINANCES *Year* 2000–01 *Income* £96,201 *Grants* £103,148 *Assets* £3,384,950

TRUSTEES Edward William Nicholas Brown; Ian Hammond McCulloch.

HOW TO APPLY The trust will consider applications for grants at meetings usually held in June and December each year. The trustees will respond to a letter of application indicating the purpose for which the grant is sought. They do not generally require to see formal accounts. In order to save administration costs the trustees will not respond to applications that do not contain a reply paid envelope, unless the cause is awarded a grant. Applications may be addressed to the trustees or to Miss Helen Abbey, the administrator.

WHO TO APPLY TO Miss Helen Abbey, Administrator, 50 Broadway, Westminster, London SW1H 0BL *Tel* 020 7227 7000

CC NO 1071390   **ESTABLISHED** 1997

■ The Howard Watson Symington Memorial Charity

WHERE FUNDING CAN BE GIVEN The former urban district of Market Harborough.

WHO CAN BENEFIT Residents of Market Harborough.

WHAT IS FUNDED The trust has a particular interest towards relief of need, welfare, recreation, leisure and education.

SAMPLE GRANTS £28,000 to local district council; £25,000 from a committed £36,000 for the Millennium Mile; £8,600 committed to Symington's Recreation Ground for the pavillion refurbishment; £3,000 for the sundial project at the canal basin.

FINANCES *Year* 1999–2000 *Income* £13,000 *Grants* £48,000 *Assets* £267,000

TRUSTEES Harborough District Council.

HOW TO APPLY In writing to the correspondent. Applications are considered in early autumn.

WHO TO APPLY TO Peter Butcher, Harborough District Council, Council Offices, Adam and Eve Street, Market Harborough, Leicestershire LE16 7AG *Tel* 01858 821100

CC NO 512708   **ESTABLISHED** 1946

■ John Watson's Trust

WHERE FUNDING CAN BE GIVEN Scotland, with a preference for Lothian.

WHO CAN BENEFIT Individuals, charitable organisations, ad hoc groups, research bodies or individuals. Beneficiaries must be under 21 years of age. People in care, fostered or adopted; children of one-parent families; disabled people; and people disadvantaged by poverty will be considered.

WHAT IS FUNDED (a) Grants to children and young people under 21, physically or mentally disabled or socially disadvantaged, for further education and training, equipment, travel, and educational, social, recreational and cultural activities. Grants can be made to charitable organisations and ad hoc groups in this field and to bodies and individuals for educational research. (b) Grants for boarding education to orphans and children subject to some other special family difficulty. See the John Watson's Trust Scheme 1984 (SI 1984 No 1480).

WHAT IS NOT FUNDED No grants to people over 21, nor for overseas causes or medical courses. Grants are not available for day school fees.

TYPE OF GRANT Equipment, small capital expenditure, tuition, student support, personal equipment, (e.g. special wheelchairs, special typewriters), projects and activities including travel. One year only, but can be extended.

RANGE OF GRANTS Grants for What Is Funded (a) are likely to be around £100–£1,000 and are unlikely to exceed £10,000 (though there are some in the £5,000 range).

FINANCES *Year* 2000 *Income* £195,000 *Grants* £158,000 *Assets* £4,000,000

TRUSTEES Six representatives of the Society of Writers to Her Majesty's Signet: two from Lothian Regional Council – Councillor Ewan Aitken, Glen Rodger: one from the Lothian Association of Youth Clubs – Nancy L G Ovens: co-opted trustees – Fraser D Falconer; Dr David C Drummond; Pippa Snell; John Kerr; R Shaun Pringle.

PUBLICATIONS Background notes and application forms available.

HOW TO APPLY On a form available from the correspondent for individual applicants. By form or letter for organisations. Trustees meet five times a year (early February, late March, early June, middle of August, and late October). The trust is happy to receive telephone enquiries.

WHO TO APPLY TO Iola Wilson, Administrator, Signet Library, Parliament Square, Edinburgh EH1 1RF *Tel* 0131 220 1640 *E-mail* jwatson@signet.fsnet.co.uk

SC NO SC014004   **ESTABLISHED** 1984

■ The Weavers' Company Benevolent Fund

WHERE FUNDING CAN BE GIVEN UK.

WHO CAN BENEFIT Registered charities; preference to small, community-based groups, rather than larger, established charities.

WHAT IS FUNDED Trustees restrict their grants to projects concerned with helping young people at risk from criminal involvement, young offenders and with the rehabilitation of young prisoners and ex-prisoners.

WHAT IS NOT FUNDED No grants to individuals, or to non-registered charities – unless they are intending to apply for charitable status. Grants are not normally made in response to general appeals from large, well-established charities whose work does not fall within one of the company's chosen areas of interest. It does not often support central or umbrella bodies, but prefers assisting projects directly working in its chosen fields. It is not the company's policy to provide for running costs or deficit funding for established projects, nor to provide grants to replace start-up funding provided by other statutory or charitable funds.

TYPE OF GRANT Pump-priming grants for one to three years for new and innovatory projects.

RANGE OF GRANTS Usually £5,000–£15,000, but applications for smaller amounts from small or new organisations are welcomed.

SAMPLE GRANTS £15,000 to HMYOI Portland towards resettlement workshops; £10,000 each to Christ Church – Upper Armley for youth clubs, drop-in facilities and detached work, Sobriety Project for a training project for women prisoners, and St Peter's Community & Advice Centre for drugs education and outreach work; £6,000 to Streets Youth Project for computers; £5,000 each to Portobello Trust for Holland Park School exclusion project, and Youth Alive & Connections for the Foundry Project – youth cafe; £1,800 to Bourne Trust for mentoring for people leaving prison.

FINANCES *Year* 2001 *Grants* £165,283

TRUSTEES The Worshipful Company of Weavers.

PUBLICATIONS *Guidelines for Applicants.*

HOW TO APPLY In writing to the correspondent, with accounts. An application form will be sent if the application appears suitable. Detailed Guidelines for Applicants are available from the trust and applicants are urged to obtain these before making any appeal. The trustees meet three times a year in February, June and October, visiting potential applicants before each meeting.

WHO TO APPLY TO John Snowdon, Clerk, The Worshipful Company of Weavers', Saddlers' House, Gutter Lane, London EC2V 6BR *Tel* 020 7606 1155 *Fax* 020 7606 1119 *E-mail* charity@weaversco.co.uk

CC NO 266189   **ESTABLISHED** 1973

■ The Mary Webb Trust

WHERE FUNDING CAN BE GIVEN UK and overseas.

WHO CAN BENEFIT Registered charities only.

WHAT IS FUNDED Philanthropic organisations, health, religion, environment, culture and recreation, education and research, social services, development and housing, international.

WHAT IS NOT FUNDED No grants to individuals or non-registered charities.

TYPE OF GRANT One-off for projects or capital.

RANGE OF GRANTS Mostly under £500.

SAMPLE GRANTS £35,000 to The National Trust; £10,000 to RNLI; £5,000 each to Fenland

Archeological Trust and The Royal Agricultural Benevolent Institute; £3,000 to The Soil Association; £2,000 each to Friedrich's Ataxia Group, London Zoo and NSRA Apeldoorn Blind Shooting; £1,500 each to Arthritis Research Campaign, John Grooms, The RAF Benevolent Fund, The Sue Ryder Foundation and The Woodland Trust.

FINANCES *Year* 2000–01 *Income* £50,294 *Grants* £135,250 *Assets* £816,690

TRUSTEES Martin Ware; Mrs Jacqueline Fancett; Mrs Cherry Nash.

HOW TO APPLY The trust's annual report says that the trustees are 'concerned by the large number of appeals received during the year. They prefer to make their own enquiries and find it difficult to handle the large volume of documents and unsolicited accounts sent to them'. Trustees normally meet quarterly, in March, May, August and December; applications need to be received by the month prior to the trustees' meeting.

WHO TO APPLY TO Mrs C M Nash, Trustee, Cherry Cottage, Hudnall Common, Berkhamsted HP4 1QN

CC NO 327659   **ESTABLISHED** 1987

■ Webb Memorial Trust

WHERE FUNDING CAN BE GIVEN UK and Eastern Europe.

WHO CAN BENEFIT Individuals, universities and other organisations.

WHAT IS FUNDED Higher education (particularly economic and social sciences); the furthering of democracy and human rights; development in Eastern Europe; scholarships for students from Eastern Europe. The trust states that it distributes about £60,000 to £65,000 each year in grants, half of which goes towards 'June scholarships' from Eastern Europe and the other half on projects either within the UK or overseas in Europe.

WHAT IS NOT FUNDED No grants in support of any political party.

RANGE OF GRANTS £500–£10,000.

FINANCES *Grants* £60,000

TRUSTEES M D Bailey; D Gladwin; D Hayter; J Miller; M J Parker; R N Rawes.

HOW TO APPLY On a form available from the correspondent, outlining the nature of the project – costs, timing and how the project fits in with the trust's objectives as outlined above. Applications for grants in the trust's financial year, which begins on 1 August, must be submitted by 31 January in the previous financial year (i.e. in the same calendar year). A copy of your latest annual report and accounts should be submitted with the application form.

WHO TO APPLY TO Michael J Parker, Honorary Secretary, Mount Royal, Allendale Road, Hexham, Northumberland NE46 2NJ *Fax* 01434 601846

CC NO 313760   **ESTABLISHED** 1944

■ The William Webster Charitable Trust

WHERE FUNDING CAN BE GIVEN North east England.

WHO CAN BENEFIT Registered charitable organisations in the north east of England, or for the benefit of branches in the north east of England.

WHAT IS FUNDED General charitable purposes.

WHAT IS NOT FUNDED No grants to individuals or to non-charitable organisations. Core/running costs are not funded.

TYPE OF GRANT One-off only, for capital projects.

RANGE OF GRANTS £500–£2,800.

SAMPLE GRANTS £2,800 to Sir William Turners Almshouse; £2,500 each to Barnardos, Calvert Trust – Kielder, Newcastle Preparatory School Trust Ltd, Newcastle upon Tyne Church High School Trust, and North of England Cadet Forces Trust; £2,000 each to ADAPT, Hilltop PTA – Gateshead, Motor Neurone Disease Association, Royal National Mission to Deep Sea Fishermen, and Swaledale Outdoor Club.

FINANCES *Year* 2001 *Income* £106,382 *Grants* £72,800 *Assets* £2,000,000

TRUSTEES Barclays Bank Trust Company Ltd.

HOW TO APPLY Applications should be submitted by the end of May for consideration in July; by the end of September for consideration in November; and by January for consideration in March. They should include details of the costings of capital projects, of funding already raised, a set of the latest annual accounts and details of the current charity registration.

WHO TO APPLY TO Miss Bertenshaw, Barclays Bank Trust Company Ltd., Executorship & Trustee Service, Osborne Court, Gadbrook Park, Rudheath, Northwich, Cheshire CW9 7UE *Tel* 01606 313173

CC NO 259848   **ESTABLISHED** 1969

■ The Weetabix Charitable Trust

WHERE FUNDING CAN BE GIVEN UK, with a preference for Northamptonshire.

WHO CAN BENEFIT Registered charities.

WHAT IS FUNDED General charitable purposes.

RANGE OF GRANTS £3,000–£30,000.

SAMPLE GRANTS £425,000 to Prince's Trust; £30,000 to Northamptonshire Chamber of Commerce Training and Enterprise; £25,000 to Centenary Appeal; £10,000 to Northamptonshire County Council; £5,000 each to British Nutrition Foundation, Institute of Economic Affairs, Northamptonshire County History Trust, and Ronald Tree Nursery School; £3,200 to Wren Spinney School; £3,000 to Warmington Parish Council.

FINANCES *Year* 1998–99 *Income* £741,432 *Grants* £559,397 *Assets* £621,011

TRUSTEES J H Carver; I P Clarke; Sir R W George.

HOW TO APPLY In writing to the correspondent.

WHO TO APPLY TO Peter Davidson, Weetabix Ltd, Burton Latimer, Kettering, Northamptonshire NN15 5JR *Tel* 01536 722181

CC NO 1044949   **ESTABLISHED** 1995

■ The Weinberg Foundation

WHERE FUNDING CAN BE GIVEN UK and overseas.

WHO CAN BENEFIT Registered charities.

WHAT IS FUNDED General charitable purposes.

FINANCES *Year* 2000–01 *Income* £97,436 *Grants* £178,234 *Assets* £2,499,395

TRUSTEES N H Ablitt; C L Simon.

HOW TO APPLY In writing to the correspondent.

WHO TO APPLY TO N A Steinberg, 138 Park Lane, London W1K 7AS *Tel* 020 7436 6667

CC NO 273308   **ESTABLISHED** 1971

■ The Weinstein Foundation

WHERE FUNDING CAN BE GIVEN Worldwide.
WHO CAN BENEFIT Registered charities.
WHAT IS FUNDED General charitable purposes.
WHAT IS NOT FUNDED No grants to individuals.
TYPE OF GRANT Recurrent.
RANGE OF GRANTS £25–£20,500.
SAMPLE GRANTS £20,500 to Menorah Primary School; £10,500 to Lubavitch Foundation; £6,550 to Norwood; £5,000 to National Jewish Chaplaincy Board; £4,750 to Menorah Grammar School Trust; £3,700 to Gateshead Seminary; £2,750 to Kisharon; £2,680 to Woodstock Sinclair Charitable Trust; £2,320 to Jewish Care; £2,306 to Hachnosas Torah V'Chesed (HTCV).
FINANCES *Year* 1999–2000 *Income* £55,402 *Grants* £117,183 *Assets* £1,581,294
TRUSTEES E Weinstein; Mrs S R Weinstein; M L Weinstein; P D Weinstein; Mrs L A F Newman.
HOW TO APPLY In writing to the correspondent.
WHO TO APPLY TO M L Weinstein, Trustee, 32 Fairholme Gardens, Finchley, London N3 3EB *Tel* 020 8346 1257
CC NO 277779   **ESTABLISHED** 1979

■ The Stella & Ernest Weinstein Trust

WHERE FUNDING CAN BE GIVEN UK.
WHO CAN BENEFIT Jewish organisations.
RANGE OF GRANTS £15–£20,000, but generally less than £200.
SAMPLE GRANTS £20,000 to Menorah Primary School Building Fund; £10,000 to Lubavitch Foundation; £5,045 to Emunah – Child Resettlement Fund; £3,750 to Friends of Haifa University; £2,000 to Chevras Ezras Nitzrochim; £1,800 to Chai Lifeline; £1,000 to Wembley Care Society; £625 to Friends of Bnei Akiva; £610 to World Jewish Relief; £500 to HTCV.
FINANCES *Year* 2000–01 *Income* £7,460 *Grants* £49,694 *Assets* £159,750
TRUSTEES E Weinstein; Mrs S W Weinstein; M G Freeman; Mrs L A F Newman.
HOW TO APPLY In writing to the correspondent. Applications are considered at any time.
WHO TO APPLY TO M G Freedman, Trustee, 65 Northgate, St John's Wood, London NW8 7EH *Tel* 020 8903 5122
CC NO 1008280   **ESTABLISHED** 1992

■ The Weinstock Fund

WHERE FUNDING CAN BE GIVEN Unrestricted, but with some local interest in the Wiltshire and Newbury area.
WHO CAN BENEFIT Registered charities benefiting people of all ages and people who are disabled or disadvantaged.
WHAT IS FUNDED Mainly medical and disability, arts and heritage, overseas and Jewish organisations.
WHAT IS NOT FUNDED No grants to individuals or unregistered organisations.
RANGE OF GRANTS Usually £500–£5,000.
SAMPLE GRANTS £860,000 to the Weizmann Institute; £250,000 to the Sobell Trust; £200,000 to Royal Opera House; £20,000 to Community Security Trust; £16,000 to WWF; £15,000 to Handel House Trust; £10,000 each to Institute for Policy Research and Ravenna Festival; £7,000 to National Society for Epilepsy; £5,000 to Next Century Foundation.

FINANCES *Year* 2000–01 *Income* £528,000 *Grants* £1,703,000 *Assets* £11,147,000
TRUSTEES Susan Lacroix; Michael Lester; Laura Weinstock.
HOW TO APPLY In writing to the correspondent. There are no printed details or applications forms. 'Where nation wide charities are concerned, the trustees prefer to make donations centrally.' Donations can only be made to registered charities, and details of the registration number are required before any payment can be made.
WHO TO APPLY TO Miss Jacqueline Elstone, PO Box 17734, London SW18 3ZQ *Tel* 020 7493 8484
CC NO 222376   **ESTABLISHED** 1962

■ The Alfred and Beatrice Weintrop Charity

WHERE FUNDING CAN BE GIVEN UK.
WHO CAN BENEFIT Jewish people, people with disabilities and older people.
WHAT IS FUNDED Cancer, immunology and neurological research; the care of people who are sick, disabled or elderly; and Jewish causes.
WHAT IS NOT FUNDED No grants to individuals.
TYPE OF GRANT One-off.
FINANCES *Year* 2000–01 *Income* £46,000 *Grants* £20,000 *Assets* £641,000
TRUSTEES Mrs S Joseph; D Howells.
HOW TO APPLY In writing to the correspondent.
WHO TO APPLY TO Jamie Mathieson, c/o Fladgate Fielder, 25 North Row, London W1K 6DJ *Tel* 020 7462 2308
CC NO 296706   **ESTABLISHED** 1987

■ The James Weir Foundation

WHERE FUNDING CAN BE GIVEN UK, with a preference for Ayrshire and Glasgow.
WHO CAN BENEFIT Recognised charities in the UK, mainly Scottish charities benefiting people who are sick.
WHAT IS FUNDED National appeals and local Scottish appeals in the Glasgow and Ayrshire area in particular. Educational institution, welfare groups, hospices, hospice at home, health counselling and self-help groups will be considered.
WHAT IS NOT FUNDED Grants are given to recognised charities only. No grants to individuals.
TYPE OF GRANT Lump sum. Many biannually recurrent, or one-off.
RANGE OF GRANTS £500–£3,000.
SAMPLE GRANTS £3,000 each to Briitsh Association for the Advancement of Science, RAF Benevolent Fund, Royal College of Physicians England, Royal College of Surgeons of England, Royal Society, Royal Star & Garter Home, and University of Strathclyde; £2,000 each to Cot Death Society, Donaldson's Development Project, and Epilepsy Association of Scotland.
FINANCES *Year* 2000 *Income* £189,665 *Grants* £165,000 *Assets* £6,266,819
TRUSTEES Simon Bonham; William J Ducas; Elizabeth Bonham.
HOW TO APPLY In writing to the correspondent. Distributions are made twice-yearly in June and November when the trustees meet. Applications should be received by May or October.
WHO TO APPLY TO Louisa Lawson, Secretary, 84 Cicada Road, London SW18 2NZ *Tel* 020 8870 6233 *Fax* 020 8870 6233
CC NO 251764   **ESTABLISHED** 1967

■ The Barbara Welby Trust

WHERE FUNDING CAN BE GIVEN UK and overseas, with a small preference for Lincolnshire.

WHO CAN BENEFIT Normally limited to established charitable foundations and institutions.

WHAT IS FUNDED General charitable purposes. Preference is given to charities of which the founder had special knowledge or those with objects with which she was specially associated.

WHAT IS NOT FUNDED Applications for individual assistance are not normally considered unless made through an established charitable organisation.

RANGE OF GRANTS £250–£2,500.

SAMPLE GRANTS £2,500 to Countryside Foundation; £2,000 each to Braceby Church, Denton School, Lincoln Cathedral Fabric Fund, Newton Church, and Prince's Trust; £1,500 to Game Conservancy Trust; £1,000 each to CAFOD, Zibby Garnett Travelling Fellowship, and Ponies Association.

FINANCES *Year* 2000–01 *Income* £43,937 *Grants* £37,000 *Assets* £854,597

TRUSTEES N J Barker; C W H Welby; C N Roberston.

HOW TO APPLY In writing at any time to the above address, although the trustees meet to consider grants in March and October.

WHO TO APPLY TO C W H Robertson, Dawsons, 2 New Square, Lincoln's Inn, London WC2A 3RZ *Tel* 020 7421 4800 *Fax* 020 7421 4850 *E-mail* legal@dawsons-legal.com

CC NO 252973   **ESTABLISHED** 1967

■ The Weldon UK Charitable Trust

WHERE FUNDING CAN BE GIVEN UK.

WHO CAN BENEFIT Arts and educational institutions benefiting children, young adults and older people, academics, students, actors and entertainment professionals, musicians, and writers and poets.

WHAT IS FUNDED Trustees fund a very limited number of major projects normally associated with the arts or education.

WHAT IS NOT FUNDED No grants to individuals.

TYPE OF GRANT Capital grants.

SAMPLE GRANTS 1998–99: £50,000 to Royal Opera House Theatre; £3,900 to Yehudi Menuhin School.

FINANCES *Year* 2000 *Income* £26,554 *Grants* £69,041 *Assets* £324,576

TRUSTEES J M St J Harris; H J Fritze.

HOW TO APPLY In writing to the correspondent, although the trust stated that it is fully committed with existing projects.

WHO TO APPLY TO J M St J Harris, Trustee, 4 Grosvenor Place, London SW1X 7HJ *Tel* 020 7235 6146 *Fax* 020 7235 3081

CC NO 327497   **ESTABLISHED** 1987

■ The Wellcome Trust

WHERE FUNDING CAN BE GIVEN UK and overseas.

WHO CAN BENEFIT Academic researchers working in the fields of human and veterinary medicine, bio-ethics, public understanding of science and the history of medicine.

WHAT IS FUNDED The support of clinical and basic scientific research into human and veterinary medicine; support of research in tropical medicine; the social and ethical implications of medical advances; and the history of medicine. Grants to individuals are usually given via a university, although small grants for travel or developing public understanding of science may be given directly.

WHAT IS NOT FUNDED The trust does not normally consider support for the extension of professional education or experience, the care of patients or clinical trials. Contributions are not made towards overheads and not normally towards office expenses. The trust does not supplement support provided by other funding bodies, nor does it donate funds for other charities to use, nor does it respond to general appeals. For policy on funding cancer research (and other funding policies) please refer to 'Research Funding Policies' on the website (www.wellcome.ac.uk/en/1/biopolcan.html).

TYPE OF GRANT All types of grant including project grants, programme grants, fellowships, research expenses, travel grants, equipment and occasionally laboratory equipment for research in human and veterinary medicine and the history of medicine. Grants may last for more than three years.

RANGE OF GRANTS £800,000–£46,200,000.

SAMPLE GRANTS £57,500,000 to University of Oxford; £25,800,000 to University College London; £23,200,000 to University of Cambridge; £22,500,000 to University of Manchester; £21,000,000 to University of Bristol; £20,900,000 to University of Sheffield; £20,800,000 to Imperial College; £16,800,000 to University of Edinburgh; £13,900,000 to King's College London; £9,200,000 to University of Leeds.

FINANCES *Year* 2001 *Income* £332,000,000 *Grants* £388,000,000 *Assets* £120,000,00000

TRUSTEES Sir Dominic Cadbury, Chair; Prof. Sir Michael Rutter; Prof. Julian Jack; Prof. Christopher R W Edwards; Prof. Martin Bobrow; Prof. Adrian Bird; Prof. Jean Thomas; Prof. Mark Walport; Edward Walker-Arnott; Alistair Ross Goobey.

OTHER INFORMATION The Wellcome Trust is the world's largest medical research charity.

HOW TO APPLY Applicants are advised, in the first instance, to contact the grants section by telephone for further relevant information or to make a preliminary application in writing. A preliminary application should include: brief details of the proposed research (one A4 page maximum); a note of existing funding from all sources, including the source of the applicant's salary funding; a brief curriculum vitae; a list of relevant publications and an approximate costing. If applicants are eligible to apply, they are sent a full application form. A preliminary application can be submitted at any time, other than those for special schemes and initiatives with advertised closing dates. For UK-based project or programme grants a preliminary application is not necessary and an application form can be obtained via the trust's website. The trust has many funding schemes and therefore potential applicants are advised to refer to the website for information on meeting dates and application deadlines.

WHO TO APPLY TO Rebecca Christou, Grants information officer, Wellcome Building, 183 Euston Road, London NW1 2BE *Tel* 020 7611 8545 *Website* www.wellcome.ac.uk

CC NO 210183   **ESTABLISHED** 1936

Think carefully about every application. Is it justified?

875

■ The Wellfield Trust

WHERE FUNDING CAN BE GIVEN The parish of Hatfield.

WHO CAN BENEFIT People who are disadvantaged by poverty or socially isolated and organisations benefiting such people.

WHAT IS FUNDED General welfare purposes for projects or individuals in need.

WHAT IS NOT FUNDED No grants for the relief of rates, taxes or public funds.

SAMPLE GRANTS £10,000 to Foyer Project; £6,000 to Connect Club; £4,000 to Hertfordshire Young Homeless Group; £3,000 to Council for Voluntary Services.

FINANCES *Year* 2000–01 *Income* £58,000 *Grants* £50,000 *Assets* £177,000

TRUSTEES A Ashby, Chair.

HOW TO APPLY In writing to the correspondent. Individuals should apply via a third party, e.g. social services, citizens advice bureaux etc.

WHO TO APPLY TO The Secretary, Birchwood Centre, Longmead, Hatfield, Hertfordshire AL10 0AS *Tel* 01707 251018 *Fax* 01707 251018 *E-mail* wellfieldtrust@cs.com

CC NO 296205 **ESTABLISHED** 1987

■ Welsh Church Act Fund – Neath Port Talbot County Borough Council

WHERE FUNDING CAN BE GIVEN Neath Port Talbot County Borough area.

WHO CAN BENEFIT Registered charities.

WHAT IS FUNDED General charitable purposes.

WHAT IS NOT FUNDED Grants to individuals are only given in exceptional circumstances. Grants are not given where the service could be supported by the council or other public bodies. Running costs are not supported.

RANGE OF GRANTS Usually up to £1,000; exceptionally up to £5,000.

FINANCES *Year* 2000–01 *Income* £38,709

HOW TO APPLY In writing to the correspondent. Successful applicants should not reapply for a further grant within three years of the approval date of the last grant.

WHO TO APPLY TO The Director of Finance, The Civic Centre, Port Talbot, Neath Port Talbot SA13 1PS *Tel* 01639 763251 *Fax* 01639 763469

CC NO 1076440 **ESTABLISHED** 1999

■ Welsh Church Fund – Carmarthenshire area

WHERE FUNDING CAN BE GIVEN Carmarthenshire.

WHO CAN BENEFIT Churches, chapels, and registered charities, particularly those concerned with health and welfare. Grants are also given to individuals.

RANGE OF GRANTS To a maximum of £3,000.

SAMPLE GRANTS 1997–98: £5,000 to Prince Philip Hospital Hydrotherapy Pool; £3,000 each to Capel Dewi Community Association and Milford Haven Town Band; £2,400 to Aberystwyth & District Old People's Housing Society Ltd; £2,000 each to Bethel Eglwys y Bedyddwyr Defach and Cyngor Henoed Ceredogopm Age Concern.

FINANCES *Year* 2001–02 *Grants* £47,176

HOW TO APPLY In writing to the correspondent.

WHO TO APPLY TO Mrs S Doughton, Grants Officer, Department of Regeneration, Town Hall, Llanelli

SA15 3AH *Tel* 01554 742185 *Fax* 01554 742199 *E-mail* sdoughton@carmarthenshire.gov.uk *Website* www.carmarthenshire.gov.uk

CC NO 506583 **ESTABLISHED** 1977

■ The Welton Foundation

WHERE FUNDING CAN BE GIVEN UK.

WHO CAN BENEFIT Registered charities and voluntary organisations.

WHAT IS FUNDED Principally supports projects in medical fields. Other charitable purposes considered include education, welfare and arts organisations.

WHAT IS NOT FUNDED Grants only to registered charities, and not in response to general appeals.

TYPE OF GRANT Some recurrent funding and several small and large donations.

SAMPLE GRANTS £77,000 to Alleyn's School; £67,000 to Oxford University; £44,000 to Kings College London; £40,000 to Brain Research Trust; £38,000 each to Imperial College Medical School and Royal College of Physicians; £36,000 to Visceral; £30,000 to Institute of Child Health; £25,000 to Kidscape; £22,000 to Young Concert Artists Trust.

FINANCES *Year* 2000–01 *Income* £371,959 *Grants* £648,000 *Assets* £9,703,584

TRUSTEES D B Vaughan; H A Stevenson; Prof. J Newsom-Davis.

HOW TO APPLY In writing to the secretary, stating: what the charity does; what specific project the money is needed for, giving as much detail as possible; how much money is needed; the source of any other funding. Due to the number of appeals received, the foundation only replies to those that are successful.

WHO TO APPLY TO Robin R Jessel, Secretary, 33 St Mary Axe, London EC3A 8LL *Tel* 020 7280 2800 (for secretary)

CC NO 245319 **ESTABLISHED** 1965

■ Wentwood Education Trust

WHERE FUNDING CAN BE GIVEN UK, with an emphasis on the south west of England.

WHO CAN BENEFIT Organisations working with people with learning disabilities.

WHAT IS FUNDED The trust makes grants to advance the education of people with learning difficulties, with an emphasis on the 16–30 age group.

WHAT IS NOT FUNDED No grants to individuals.

RANGE OF GRANTS £100–£10,000.

SAMPLE GRANTS £10,000 to Bridge Project; £5,000 each to Croydon Contacts and Salisbury Lifestyle Project; £2,000 to Dorset Advocacy.

FINANCES *Year* 2000–01 *Income* £4,000 *Grants* £64,000 *Assets* £200,000

TRUSTEES G Carter; L Curbishley; J T Dalglish; M Morris; H Reynolds.

HOW TO APPLY Brief guidance and an application form is available from the correspondent.

WHO TO APPLY TO S A Reynolds, Secretary to the Trustees, Ty Carreg, Govilon, Abergavenny, Monmouthshire NP7 9PT *Tel* 01873 832220

CC NO 280831 **ESTABLISHED** 1980

■ The Alexander Pigott Wernher Memorial Trust

WHERE FUNDING CAN BE GIVEN UK and Commonwealth countries.

WHO CAN BENEFIT Charitable organisations benefiting research workers looking into the prevention or cure of blindness or deafness.

WHAT IS FUNDED Research into the causes or cure of blindness and deafness in the UK and the Commonwealth.

WHAT IS NOT FUNDED No grants to individuals.

TYPE OF GRANT Research work/fellowships.

RANGE OF GRANTS Up to £24,000.

SAMPLE GRANTS £35,000 to Medical Research Council for eye research equipment; £9,000 to the Foundation for the Prevention of Blindness for research and treatment of the causes of eye diseases in Malawi.

FINANCES *Year* 2001–02 *Income* £24,159 *Grants* £41,000 *Assets* £258,243

TRUSTEES Major Sir David Butter.

HOW TO APPLY In writing to the correspondent.

WHO TO APPLY TO Miss A Snow, 8 Meredyth Road, Barnes, London SW13 0DY *Tel* 020 8876 0791

CC NO 261362 **ESTABLISHED** 1946

■ The Wesleyan Charitable Trust

WHERE FUNDING CAN BE GIVEN Some preference for the Midlands.

WHO CAN BENEFIT Small local projects, established and national organisations benefiting children and older people; those in care, fostered and adopted; at risk groups; carers; people who are disadvantaged by poverty or homeless; victims of abuse, crime and domestic violence.

WHAT IS FUNDED Medicine and health, welfare. General preference given to causes associated with the Wesleyan Assurance Society's policy holders and staff.

TYPE OF GRANT Capital (including buildings), core costs, one-off, project, research, running costs and recurring costs. Funding is for one year or less.

RANGE OF GRANTS £50–£15,000, typical grant £250.

SAMPLE GRANTS In 1998–99: £5,000 each to Revive, Business in the Community, National Snowden Appeal, Rainbow Trust and Fund for Epilepsy; £3,000 each to Symphony Hall and Starlight Children's Foundation; £1,300 to Moseley Hall Hospital; £1,000 each to Medsick Cancer Care and Insurance Benefit Fund.

FINANCES *Year* 1999–2000 *Income* £63,000 *Grants* £58,000 *Assets* £24,000

TRUSTEES Derek Byfield, Chair; Clive Ward; Raymond Lowe; Joe Roderick; Neil Boast; Miss Chris Gibbons.

HOW TO APPLY In writing to the correspondent including accounts. The trustees meet quarterly.

WHO TO APPLY TO The Secretary to the Trustees, Colmore Circus, Birmingham B4 6AR *Tel* 0121 200 9101 *Fax* 0121 200 9120

CC NO 276698 **ESTABLISHED** 1978

■ Wessex Cancer Trust

WHERE FUNDING CAN BE GIVEN Dorset, Hampshire, Wiltshire, the Isle of Wight and the Channel Islands.

WHO CAN BENEFIT Cancer patients, families and carers.

WHAT IS FUNDED Improvement of cancer care, by promoting cancer prevention; supporting patients, families and carers; providing education and information for patients, families and professionals; and funding early detection and research.

FINANCES *Year* 2000–01 *Income* £751,390 *Grants* £489,428 *Assets* £853,070

TRUSTEES Hon. Mrs C M Villiers, Chair; M H Le Bas; C G Bashford; Dr C A Baughan; Mrs J E Beschi; Dr P M Gillam; D A Hoare; Mrs M J Kernick; Dr B Moran; P M Perry; P Robertson; Dr G Sharp; R Starr; Dr J Stutley; T Titheridge; N L Woodford.

HOW TO APPLY In writing to the correspondent.

WHO TO APPLY TO Nichola Jacobs, Bellis House, 11 Westwood Road, Southampton SO17 1DL *Tel* 023 8067 2200 *Minicom* 023 8067 2266 *E-mail* wct@wessexcancer.org *Website* www.wessexcancer.org

CC NO 280133 **ESTABLISHED** 1980

■ The Earl & Countess of Wessex Charitable Trust

WHERE FUNDING CAN BE GIVEN Worldwide.

WHO CAN BENEFIT Registered charities with which the Earl and Countess have a personal interest.

WHAT IS FUNDED General charitable purposes.

WHAT IS NOT FUNDED No grants are made to: non-registered charities or causes; individuals, including to people who are undertaking fundraising activities on behalf of a charity; organisations whose main objects are to fund or support other causes; organisations whose accounts disclose substantial financial resources and that have well-established and ample fundraising capabilities; fund research that can be supported by government funding or that is popular among trusts.

TYPE OF GRANT Mostly one-off grants. Substantial recurrent grants are also made.

SAMPLE GRANTS Delta, Family Heart Association, Four Lanes Regeneration Group, International Care and Relief, Northwick Park Hospital Childrens Centre Appeal, Michael Palin Centre for Stammering Children, Royal Liverpool Philharmonic Society, Rural Stress Network, Saddler's Wells Trust, and Side by Slde.

FINANCES *Year* 2000–01 *Income* £117,806 *Grants* £157,888 *Assets* £362,908

TRUSTEES Mark Foster-Brown; Abel Hadden; Denise Poulton; Sir Henry Boyd-Carpenter; Malcolm Cockren.

HOW TO APPLY In writing to the correspondent in the first instance. A response will be made within two weeks in the form of an application form and guidelines to eligible applicants or a letter of rejection if more appropriate. Completed forms, which are not acknowledged upon receipt, need to be submitted by 1 May or 1 November, for consideration by the end of the month. Clarity of presentation and provision of financial details are among the qualities which impress the trustees. Successful applicants will receive a letter stating that the acceptance of the funding is conditional on an update being received before the next meeting. The trust's criteria state other correspondence cannot be entered into, and organisations cannot reveal the size of any grants they receive.

WHO TO APPLY TO Jenny Cannon, Farrer & Co, 66 Lincoln's Inn Fields, London WC2A 3LH *Tel* 020 7242 2022

CC NO 1076003 **ESTABLISHED** 1999

■ The West Derby Wastelands Charity

WHERE FUNDING CAN BE GIVEN The ancient township of West Derby in Liverpool.

WHO CAN BENEFIT Local organisations and local branches of national organisations benefiting volunteers; at risk groups; carers; people disadvantaged by poverty; socially isolated people; and victims of abuse, crime or domestic violence.

WHAT IS FUNDED Health and welfare; carers organisations; victim support and volunteer organisations.

WHAT IS NOT FUNDED No grants to individuals.

RANGE OF GRANTS £250–£3,500.

SAMPLE GRANTS £3,000 each to Compass and Liverpool Voluntary Society for the Blind; £2,800 to Sandfield Park School; £2,000 each to Canal Boat Adventure Project and Crossroads Centre.

FINANCES *Year* 2000 *Income* £56,000 *Grants* £44,000 *Assets* £1,500,000

TRUSTEES Mrs J Holmes; Cllr D Gavin; Cllr S Ellison; Cllr P Moloney; J Ruddock; P H North; R H Owen; T B Flynn; D Lunt; Cllr G W Smith; Miss A Shacklady.

HOW TO APPLY In writing to the correspondent.

WHO TO APPLY TO Alan J Morris, Drury House, 19 Water Street, Liverpool L2 0RP *Tel* 0151 236 8989

CC NO 223623   **ESTABLISHED** 1964

■ Charity of John West & Others

WHERE FUNDING CAN BE GIVEN UK.

WHO CAN BENEFIT Charitable organisations benefiting people of all ages, retired people and people with visual impairment or dyslexia.

WHAT IS FUNDED The income of this charity is, first of all, used to provide pensions to people with visually impairment or dyslexia through recognised relief agencies. No new pension obligations are entered into. The balance of the income is used to make grants to charitable organisations concerned with helping visual impairment or dyslexia.

WHAT IS NOT FUNDED No grants to individuals.

TYPE OF GRANT One-off and capital.

RANGE OF GRANTS £1,000–£50,000.

FINANCES *Year* 1999 *Income* £192,780 *Grants* £202,192 *Assets* £7,013,700

TRUSTEES The Governors of Clothworkers' Foundation.

HOW TO APPLY In writing to the correspondent at any time.

WHO TO APPLY TO A C Blessley, Secretary, Clothworkers' Hall, Dunster Court, Mincing Lane, London EC3R 7AH *Tel* 020 7623 7041

CC NO 803660   **ESTABLISHED** 1987

■ West London Synagogue Charitable Fund

WHERE FUNDING CAN BE GIVEN UK.

WHO CAN BENEFIT Registered charities only.

WHAT IS FUNDED Grants are made to Jewish, Israeli, inter-faith and non-Jewish charities for general charitable purposes, at a national level and a local level within Westminster and Marylebone.

WHAT IS NOT FUNDED No grants to individuals.

SAMPLE GRANTS £10,000 each to RNIB Sunshine House School and Juvenile Diabetes Foundation.

FINANCES *Year* 2000 *Income* £61,000 *Grants* £57,000 *Assets* £68,000

OTHER INFORMATION The fund prefers to be involved with charities which synagogue members are involved with or helped by.

HOW TO APPLY In writing to the correspondent.

WHO TO APPLY TO Mrs Kay Colton, Coordinator, 33 Seymour Place, London W1H 6AT *Tel* 020 7723 4404 *E-mail* k.colton@wls.org.uk

CC NO 209778   **ESTABLISHED** 1959

■ Mrs S K West's Charitable Trust

WHERE FUNDING CAN BE GIVEN UK.

WHO CAN BENEFIT Registered charities selected by the trustees.

WHAT IS FUNDED General charitable purposes.

FINANCES *Year* 2000 *Income* £33,000 *Grants* £33,000

TRUSTEES P Schoon; Chris Blakeborough; J Grandage.

HOW TO APPLY The trust states that it does not respond to unsolicited applications.

WHO TO APPLY TO P J Schoon, Trustee, Davies & Crane Chartered Accountants, 5 Winckley Street, Preston PR1 2AA *Tel* 01772 253656 *Fax* 01772 202511

CC NO 294755   **ESTABLISHED** 1986

■ The Westcroft Trust

WHERE FUNDING CAN BE GIVEN Unrestricted, but with a special interest in Shropshire – causes of local interest outside Shropshire are rarely supported.

WHO CAN BENEFIT Organisations benefiting: people of all ages; medical professionals; Quakers; ex-offenders and those at risk of offending; victims of abuse; and victims of famine, man-made or natural disasters and war.

WHAT IS FUNDED Currently the trustees have five main areas of interest: international understanding, including conflict resolution and the material needs of the third world; religious causes, particularly of social outreach, usually of the Society of Friends (Quakers) but also for those originating in Shropshire; development of the voluntary sector in Shropshire; special needs of people with disabilities, primarily in Shropshire; development of community groups and reconciliation between different cultures in Northern Ireland. Woodlands and medical research into orthopaedics will be considered. Medical education is only helped by support for expeditions abroad which include pre-clinical students. Medical aid, education and relief work in developing countries are helped but mainly through UK agencies; international disasters may be helped in response to public appeals.

WHAT IS NOT FUNDED Grants to charities only. No grants to individuals or for medical electives, sport, the arts (unless specifically for people with disabilities in Shropshire) or armed forces charities. Requests for sponsorship are not supported. Annual grants are withheld if recent accounts are not available or do not satisfy the trustees as to continuing need.

TYPE OF GRANT Single or annual with or without specified time limit. Few grants for capital or endowment. One-off, research, recurring costs, running costs and start-up costs. Funding for up to and over three years will be considered.

SAMPLE GRANTS 2000–01: £5,725 to Britain Yearly Meeting; £5,000 to Silo Central Youth Project; £4,000 to University of Bradford for the Department of Peace Studies; £3,025 in two payments to Orbis International; £3,000 each to Derwen College, and Uganda Development Services; £2,780 in two grants to Friends World

Committee for Consultation; £2,200 to Northern Friends Peace Board; £2,000 each to Alternatives to Violence, and DEC India Earthquake Appeal

FINANCES *Year* 2001–02 *Income* £95,372 *Grants* £91,558 *Assets* £2,231,860

TRUSTEES Mary C Cadbury; Richard G Cadbury; James E Cadbury; Erica R Cadbury.

OTHER INFORMATION The trustees favour charities which carry low administrative overheads and which pursue clear policies of equal opportunity in meeting need. Printed letters signed by the great and good, and glossy literature are wasted on them.

HOW TO APPLY In writing to the correspondent. There is no application form or set format but applications should be restricted to a maximum of three sheets of paper, stating purpose, overall financial needs and resources together with previous years' accounts if appropriate. Printed letters signed by 'the great and good' and glossy literature do not impress the trustees, who prefer lower-cost applications. Applications are dealt with about every two months. No acknowledgement will be given. Replies to relevant but unsuccessful applicants will be sent only if a self-addressed envelope is enclosed. As some annual grants are made by Bank Telepay, details of bank name, branch, sort code, and account name and number should be sent in order to save time and correspondence.

WHO TO APPLY TO Mary Cadbury, Managing Trustee, 32 Hampton Road, Oswestry, Shropshire SY11 1SJ

CC NO 212931   **ESTABLISHED** 1947

■ Western Recreation Trust

WHERE FUNDING CAN BE GIVEN West of Scotland.

WHO CAN BENEFIT Organisations based in the west of Scotland working to improve recreational facilities for young people, older people and people who are unemployed.

WHAT IS FUNDED Grants towards the cost of equipment.

WHAT IS NOT FUNDED Grants are not normally given to individuals.

RANGE OF GRANTS £200, exceptionally up to £1,000.

FINANCES *Grants* £25,000

HOW TO APPLY In writing to the correspondent at any time.

WHO TO APPLY TO Ian Paterson, Scott-Moncrieff, 25 Bothwell Street, Glasgow G2 6NL *Tel* 0141 567 4500

SC NO SC002534

■ The Westminster Amalgamated Charity

WHERE FUNDING CAN BE GIVEN City of Westminster.

WHO CAN BENEFIT Organisations based in the City of Westminster, and individuals who reside in the old City of Westminster, including homeless people. The charity also seeks to benefit people affected by a range of social circumstances: at risk groups, disabled people, poor and homeless people, immigrants, refugees and socially isolated people.

WHAT IS FUNDED Relief of poverty and need, either by providing grants to organisations who share the same aim, or by supporting individuals in need directly. It will enable residents in need to go on holiday who would otherwise not be able to afford to do so.

WHAT IS NOT FUNDED Applications from outside the City of Westminster are not supported.

TYPE OF GRANT One-off grants.

RANGE OF GRANTS Individuals: £50–£350, typical grant £100. Organisations: £500–£10,000.

SAMPLE GRANTS 1999: £21,000 to St Martin-in-the-Fields Social Care Unit; £15,000 to West London Mission; £11,000 to National Children's Home; £10,000 each to the Avenue's Youth Project, Marylebone Bangladesh Society, St Christopher's Fellowship, Soho Family Centre Trust and Westminster Society for People with Learning Disabilities.

FINANCES *Year* 2001 *Income* £320,000 *Grants* £275,000 *Assets* £6,700,000

TRUSTEES P J M Prain, Chair; B C Burroughs; Mrs J Bianco; K Gardner; Miss J Jacob; Dr C Nemeth; B Parkin; Ms M Sykes; S H G Twining; A P Gardner; J P Miller; M E W Studer.

HOW TO APPLY Organisations should apply in writing to the correspondent, including a copy of the latest accounts. Applications are considered six times a year. Individuals should complete an application form and have a sponsor, in the form of a respected member of the community or a local organisation. Applications from individuals are considered on a continual basis.

WHO TO APPLY TO Mrs J A Turner, Clerk & Chief Executive, School House, Drury Lane, London WC2B 5SU *Tel* 020 7395 9460 *Fax* 020 7595 9479 *E-mail* wac@3chars.org.uk

CC NO 207964   **ESTABLISHED** 1961

■ The City of Westminster Charitable Trust

WHERE FUNDING CAN BE GIVEN City of Westminster.

WHO CAN BENEFIT Organisations only.

WHAT IS FUNDED General charitable purposes.

WHAT IS NOT FUNDED No grants to individuals.

TYPE OF GRANT One-off.

RANGE OF GRANTS Up to £2,000.

FINANCES *Year* 2000–01 *Income* £70,348 *Grants* £45,000

TRUSTEES Lord Mayor of City of Westminster; Cllr Jenny Bianco; Cllr Dr Cyril Nemeth; Colin Wilson; Peter Rogers; Cllr Alan Bradley.

HOW TO APPLY In writing to the correspondent at any time of the year, although applications are only considered in October/November.

WHO TO APPLY TO Colin Lodge, Overview and Scrutiny Department, Westminster City Hall, 64 Victoria Street, London SW1E 6QP *Tel* 020 7641 3255

CC NO 296091   **ESTABLISHED** 1987

■ The Westminster Foundation

WHERE FUNDING CAN BE GIVEN UK, and local interests in central London (SW1 and W1 and immediate environs), the north west of England, especially rural Lancashire and the Chester area, and the Sutherland area of Scotland.

WHO CAN BENEFIT Registered charities benefiting children, young adults and older people, ex-service and service people, homeless people, and those living in rural areas.

WHAT IS FUNDED General charitable purposes at the discretion of the trustees. Grants are categorised under: social welfare; education; conservation; youth; medical; arts; and church.

WHAT IS NOT FUNDED Only registered charities will be considered; charitable status applied for, or pending, is not sufficient. No grants to individuals, 'holiday' charities, student expeditions, or research projects.

TYPE OF GRANT Usually one-off, but any type is considered.

SAMPLE GRANTS £331,000 to Royal Agricultural Benevolent Institution; £265,000 to Cambridge Foundation; £200,000 to Pembroke College; £111,000 to Game Conservancy Trust; £100,000 each to NSPCC's north west appeal and Royal Scottish Benevolent Institution; £60,000 to Rural Stress Information Network; £56,000 to Royal United Service Institute; £50,000 each to Henry Doubleday Research Association and Samaritans.

FINANCES *Year* 2001 *Income* £2,043,608 *Grants* £2,182,000 *Assets* £28,826,655

TRUSTEES The Duke of Westminster, chair; J H M Newsum; R M Moyse.

HOW TO APPLY In writing to the secretary, enclosing an up-to-date set of accounts, together with a brief history of the project to date, and the current need.

WHO TO APPLY TO Colin Redman, Secretary, 70 Grosvenor Street, London W1K 3JP *Tel* 01252 722557

CC NO 267618   ESTABLISHED 1974

■ The Garfield Weston Foundation

WHERE FUNDING CAN BE GIVEN UK.

WHO CAN BENEFIT UK registered charities and churches.

WHAT IS FUNDED A broad range of activities in the fields of education, the arts, health (including research), welfare, the environment, religion and other areas of general benefit to the community.

WHAT IS NOT FUNDED Support cannot be considered for organisations or groups which are not UK registered charities. Applications from individuals or for individual research or study or from organisations outside the UK cannot be considered. The trustees do not support animal welfare charities. Charities are asked not to re-apply within a 12-month period of an appeal to the foundation, whether they have received a grant or not.

TYPE OF GRANT Usually small contributions to a specific project or part of a project. Capital (including buildings), core costs, endowments, one-off, research, recurring costs, running costs and start-up costs. Salaries are rarely considered. Funding is given by means of a single cash donation.

RANGE OF GRANTS £100–£10,000,000.

SAMPLE GRANTS £2,000,000 to National Galleries of Scotland for its Playfair project; £1,000,000 each to Courtauld Institute towards its endowment and renovation, Gateshead Music Centre for capital works, Imperial Cancer Research Fund in support of its merger with the Cancer Research Campaign, Royal College of Art for major redevelopment, Somerset House Arts Fund for restoration and refurbishment, St Paul's Cathedral for a major restoration programme, Technology Colleges Trust and Victoria and Albert Museum for new galleries.

FINANCES *Year* 2001–02 *Income* £29,927,000 *Grants* £32,961,000 *Assets* £228,684,4000

TRUSTEES Guy Weston, Chair; Galen Weston; Miriam Burnett; Eliza Mitchell; Nancy Baron; Camilla Dalglish; Jana R Khayat; Anna C Hobhouse; George G Weston; Sophia Mason.

HOW TO APPLY All applications are considered on an individual basis by a committee of trustees. Trustees meet monthly and there is no deadline for applications, which are considered in order of receipt. It normally takes three or four months for an application to be processed. All applicants are notified of the outcome by letter.

All applications are asked to include the following information: the charity's registration number; a copy of the most recent report and audited accounts; an outline description of the charity's activities; a synopsis of the project requiring funding, with details of who will benefit; a financial plan; details of current and proposed fundraising.

WHO TO APPLY TO Fiona Hare, Administrator, Weston Centre, Bowater House, 68 Knightsbridge, London SW1X 7LQ *Tel* 020 7589 6363 *Fax* 020 7584 5921 *E-mail* fhare@wittington-investment.co.uk

CC NO 230260   ESTABLISHED 1958

■ The Whitaker Charitable Trust

WHERE FUNDING CAN BE GIVEN UK, but mostly east Midlands, Northern Ireland and Scotland, particularly Bassetlaw.

WHO CAN BENEFIT Registered charities benefiting musicians, students and people in prison.

WHAT IS FUNDED The trust's resources are heavily committed and only very limited funds are available for charities not previously supported by the trust. The trustees are particularly interested in music education, agricultural education, countryside conservation, spiritual matters, prison-related charities and supporting charities in the localities stated above.

WHAT IS NOT FUNDED Support is given to registered charities only. No grants are given to individuals or for the repair or maintenance of individual churches.

RANGE OF GRANTS £500–£100,000.

SAMPLE GRANTS £100,000 to Atlantic College; £15,000 to Marlborough College; £10,000 each to Koppel Goodman Family Housing for a family support project, and Queen Margaret's School; £5,000 each to Harworth PCC, Opera North for education, Portland College, and Royal Forestry Society; £3,000 each to Game Conservancy and Leith School of Art.

FINANCES *Year* 2000–01 *Income* £210,872 *Grants* £211,800 *Assets* £5,842,165

TRUSTEES Edward Ronald Haslewood Perks; David W J Price; Lady Elizabeth Jane Ravenscroft Whitaker.

HOW TO APPLY In writing to the correspondent. Trustees meet half-yearly. Applications should include clear details of the need the intended project is designed to meet plus a copy of the latest accounts available and an outline budget. If an acknowledgement of the application, or notification in the event of the application not being accepted, is required, an sae should be enclosed.

WHO TO APPLY TO Edward Perks, Trustee, c/o Currey & Co., 21 Buckingham Gate, London SW1E 6LB *Tel* 020 7828 4091

CC NO 234491   ESTABLISHED 1964

■ The Whitbread 1988 Charitable Trust

WHERE FUNDING CAN BE GIVEN UK.

WHO CAN BENEFIT Registered charities.

WHAT IS FUNDED General charitable purposes.

WHAT IS NOT FUNDED No support given to individuals, international appeals or capital appeals.

RANGE OF GRANTS £1,200–£18,000.

SAMPLE GRANTS in 1998–99: £18,500 to National Centre for Volunteering; £10,000 each to Business in the Community, Charities Aid Foundation, Fairbridge Alliance Fund, and

Institute for Citizenship; £7,690 to Young People's Trust for the Environment and Nature Conservation; £5,300 to Children with Special Needs Foundation; £5,000 to YouthNet UK; £4,000 to Retired Executives Action Clearing House; £3,200 to National Association of Citizens Advice Bureau; £3,000 to Employers' Forum on Disability.

FINANCES *Year* 2001–02 *Income* £94,474
TRUSTEES S C Barratt; Sir John Banham; S J Ward.
HOW TO APPLY In writing to the correspondent.
WHO TO APPLY TO Paul D Patten, Administrator, Whitbread Plc, City Point, 1 Ropemaker Street, London EC2Y 9MY
CC NO 800501   **ESTABLISHED** 1988

■ The Simon Whitbread Charitable Trust

WHERE FUNDING CAN BE GIVEN UK, with a preference for Bedfordshire.
WHO CAN BENEFIT Registered charities, or bodies with similar status.
WHAT IS FUNDED General charitable purposes. Preference is given to charities which the trustees have special interest in, knowledge of, or association with.
WHAT IS NOT FUNDED Generally no support for local projects outside Bedfordshire.
TYPE OF GRANT Usually one-off, but dependent on circumstances.
RANGE OF GRANTS £50–£15,000.
SAMPLE GRANTS £30,000 to Bedford Hospitals Charity; £15,000 to Maytree; £5,000 each to British Brain and Spine Foundation, Canine Partners for Independence, Mencap – Luton and Bedfordshire, and Moorfields International Children's Eye Centre; £3,500 to Relate Bedford; £3,333 to Countryside Foundation for Education; £3,000 each to Mencap and RUKBA.
FINANCES *Year* 2001–02 *Income* £143,699 *Grants* £113,133 *Assets* £3,622,049
TRUSTEES Mrs H Whitbread; S C Whitbread; E C A Martineau.
HOW TO APPLY In writing to the correspondent. Acknowledgements are not given. Please do NOT telephone.
WHO TO APPLY TO E C A Martineau, Administrator, Dawsons, 2 New Square, Lincoln's Inn, London WC2A 3RZ *Fax* 020 7421 4850
CC NO 200412   **ESTABLISHED** 1961

■ The Colonel W H Whitbread Charitable Trust

WHERE FUNDING CAN BE GIVEN UK, with an interest in Gloucestershire.
WHO CAN BENEFIT Children and young adults, at risk groups, people disadvantaged by poverty, and socially isolated people.
WHAT IS FUNDED Primarily local health and welfare charities.
RANGE OF GRANTS £1,000–£5,000; occasionally larger amounts are given.
SAMPLE GRANTS £100,000 to ARC Addington Fund; £7,000 each in two payments to Animal Health Trust, and in three payments to Child Health Research Appeal Trust; £6,000 in two payments to Countryside Foundation for Education; £5,000 each to DSCF, Household Cavalry Museum Appeal, Hunt Servants Fund, Imperial Cancer Research Fund, Oval House Christchurch (Oxford) United Clubs, and St John Ambulance.
FINANCES *Year* 2001 *Income* £189,715 *Grants* £252,000 *Assets* £5,329,234

TRUSTEES M W Whitbread; J J Russell; R H J Steel; H F Whitbread.
HOW TO APPLY In writing to the correspondent. Trustees meet quarterly. Please note, successful applicants must cash their cheques within three months of receipt or, unless there are special circumstances, it is the trust's policy to cancel the cheque.
WHO TO APPLY TO R H A MacDougald, Winckworth Sherwood, 35 Great Peter Street, London SW1P 3LR *Tel* 020 7593 5000 *Fax* 020 7593 5099
CC NO 210496   **ESTABLISHED** 1953

■ White Rose Children's Aid International Charity

WHERE FUNDING CAN BE GIVEN UK and overseas.
WHO CAN BENEFIT Organisations benefiting young adults, and people who are disabled, disadvantaged by poverty or have emotional difficulties. Support may also be given to people who are unemployed, homeless or socially isolated, and at risk groups.
WHAT IS FUNDED Hospitals, respite homes, special needs schools and youth groups.
TYPE OF GRANT Small grants of £3,000 or less.
RANGE OF GRANTS £10–£1,449.
FINANCES *Year* 2000–01 *Income* £43,723
TRUSTEES J F Buttery; D Dawson; E Hewlett; R Rosser; J Sirrett; E Straw; R W Urie; A M Wright.
HOW TO APPLY In writing to the correspondent.
WHO TO APPLY TO A Wright, 23 Teesdale Road, Ridgeway, Sheffield S12 3XH
CC NO 1036377   **ESTABLISHED** 1994

■ The Whitecourt Charitable Trust

WHERE FUNDING CAN BE GIVEN UK and overseas, with a preference for Sheffield.
WHO CAN BENEFIT Organisations benefiting Christians.
WHAT IS FUNDED General charitable purposes. Trustees prefer to support Christian projects, especially near Sheffield.
WHAT IS NOT FUNDED No support for animal or conservation organisations or for campaigning on social issues.
RANGE OF GRANTS £25–£4,500.
FINANCES *Year* 2001–02 *Income* £73,000 *Grants* £40,000 *Assets* £434,000
TRUSTEES P W Lee; Mrs G W Lee; M P W Lee.
HOW TO APPLY In writing to the correspondent, at any time. However, the trust states very little money is available for unsolicited applications, due to advance commitments.
WHO TO APPLY TO Mrs P W Lee, Trustee, 48 Canterbury Avenue, Fulwood, Sheffield S10 3RU *Tel* 0114 230 5555
CC NO 1000012   **ESTABLISHED** 1990

■ A H and B C Whiteley Charitable Trust

WHERE FUNDING CAN BE GIVEN England, Scotland and Wales, with a special interest in Nottinghamshire.
WHO CAN BENEFIT Registered charities.
WHAT IS FUNDED General charitable purposes, particularly the arts and environment.
RANGE OF GRANTS £600–£35,000.
SAMPLE GRANTS £20,000 to Portland College; £15,000 to National Trust; £5,000 to Mansfield Cats Protection League; £3,000 each to Trinity Rebuild 2000, The Samaritans and Children

with Special Needs; £2,000 to Nottinghamshire Wildlife Trust.

FINANCES *Year* 1999–2000 *Income* £65,000 *Grants* £51,000 *Assets* £1,700,000

TRUSTEES E G Aspley; K E B Clayton.

HOW TO APPLY None are invited. The trust does not seek applications.

WHO TO APPLY TO E G Aspley, Trustee, Marchants, Regent Chambers, Regent Street, Mansfield, Nottinghamshire NG18 1SW *Tel* 01623 655111

CC NO 1002220 **ESTABLISHED** 1990

■ The Norman Whiteley Trust

WHERE FUNDING CAN BE GIVEN Worldwide, although in practice mainly Cumbria.

WHO CAN BENEFIT Christian charities. Organisations benefiting Christians and evangelists.

WHAT IS FUNDED To help evangelical Christian causes primarily.

WHAT IS NOT FUNDED Whilst certain overseas organisations are supported, applications from outside of Cumbria are not accepted.

TYPE OF GRANT One-off, recurrent, capital, running costs.

RANGE OF GRANTS Up to £45,000.

SAMPLE GRANTS £44,377 to Baptistenge; £34,432 to Bethsan Sheltered Housing Association; £30,000 to Luis Palau Lakes 2000; £15,831 to Kindersingkrien; £15,651 to Millom Methodist Church; £11,911 to Koinonia; £11,301 to Alpha Osterreich; £10,000 each to Lakes Christian Centre, The Potteries Trust and Sports Reach.

FINANCES *Year* 2000/01 *Income* £189,206 *Grants* £279,750 *Assets* £2,163,091

TRUSTEES Mrs B M Whiteley; P Whiteley; D Dickson; J Ratcliff.

HOW TO APPLY In writing to the correspondent. Trustees meet to consider applications twice a year.

WHO TO APPLY TO D Foster, 23 Brow Crescent, Windermere, Cumbria LA23 2EY

CC NO 226445 **ESTABLISHED** 1963

■ The Whitley Animal Protection Trust

WHERE FUNDING CAN BE GIVEN UK and overseas, with a preference for Scotland.

WHO CAN BENEFIT Registered charities only.

WHAT IS FUNDED Prevention of cruelty to animals and promoting their conservation and environment.

WHAT IS NOT FUNDED No grants to non-registered charities.

TYPE OF GRANT Core and project grants, one-off or for several years.

RANGE OF GRANTS Generally £1,000–£5,000, although larger amounts are often given.

SAMPLE GRANTS £85,000 to Whitley Awards Foundation; £50,400 to Hawk and Owl Trust; £17,000 to IPE – Brazil; £15,000 each to The Tweed Foundation for the Riparian Habitats Project and the Wildlife Conservation Research Unit of the Department of Zoology in the University of Oxford (Oxford WILDCRU); £10,000 each to Edinburgh Zoo, Fauna and Flora International, and Tusk Trust; £5,000 each to Awe Fisheries Trust and Spey Research Trust for the Findhorn Habitat survey.

FINANCES *Year* 2000 *Income* £303,508 *Grants* £262,400 *Assets* £9,393,660

TRUSTEES E Whitley, Chair; Mrs P A Whitley; E J Whitley; J Whitley.

HOW TO APPLY In writing to the correspondent. The correspondent stated: 'The trust honours

existing commitments and initiates new ones through its own contacts rather than responding to unsolicited applications.'

WHO TO APPLY TO Paul Rhodes, Edgbaston House, Walker Street, Wellington, Telford, Shropshire TF1 1HF *Tel* 01952 641651 *Fax* 01952 247441 *E-mail* info@gwynnes.com

CC NO 236746 **ESTABLISHED** 1964

■ The Sheila Whitley Trust

WHERE FUNDING CAN BE GIVEN UK with a preference for Shropshire.

WHO CAN BENEFIT Registered charities benefiting older people, at risk groups, and people who are disadvantaged by poverty, socially isolated or disabled.

WHAT IS FUNDED Assistance to sick, disabled, elderly or deprived people.

WHAT IS NOT FUNDED No grants to individuals.

RANGE OF GRANTS Variable.

FINANCES *Year* 2001 *Income* £28,269 *Grants* £20,000

TRUSTEES Mrs P A Whitley; E Whitley; Mrs V Thompson; E J Whitley; J Whitley.

HOW TO APPLY 'The trust honors existing commitments and initiates new ones through its own contacts rather than responding to unsolicited applications.'

WHO TO APPLY TO Paul Rhodes, Gwynne's Solicitors, Edgbaston House, Walker Street, Wellington, Telford TF1 1HF *Tel* 01952 641651 *Fax* 01952 247441 *E-mail* info@gwynnes.com

CC NO 253681 **ESTABLISHED** 1967

■ The Gladys Wightwick Charitable Trust

WHERE FUNDING CAN BE GIVEN UK.

WHO CAN BENEFIT Registered charities and voluntary organisations only.

WHAT IS FUNDED General charitable purposes.

TYPE OF GRANT One-off grants.

SAMPLE GRANTS In 1997–98: £2,500 to MIND, £2,000 each to The Bobby Appeal and Fulbrook PCC; £1,500 each to PHAB, and Hodgkins Disease and Lymphoma Association; £1,000 each to DEBRA, The Girls Public Day School Trust, St Lawrence Friends Heritage Trust and Watford CT Scanner Appeal.

FINANCES *Year* 2000–01 *Income* £26,000 *Grants* £25,000 *Assets* £615,000

TRUSTEES C A McLintock; K T C Arnold; D Harris; Miss P Smith.

HOW TO APPLY In writing to the correspondent. Grants are made in the spring and autumn each year.

WHO TO APPLY TO The Clerk, c/o Messrs Bird & Bird, 90 Fetter Lane, London EC4A 1JP *Tel* 020 7415 6000

CC NO 1024622 **ESTABLISHED** 1969

■ The Lionel Wigram Memorial Trust

WHERE FUNDING CAN BE GIVEN UK, with a preference for Greater London.

WHO CAN BENEFIT Registered charities and voluntary organisations.

WHAT IS FUNDED General charitable purposes.

TYPE OF GRANT One-off and recurrent.

SAMPLE GRANTS £12,000 to WAACIS Fund; £3,000 to Listening Books; £2,000 each to Newbury Spring Festival and Deafblind UK; £1,000 each to three individuals and Family Friends, International Spinal Research Trust and NSPCC.

FINANCES *Year* 1999–2000 *Income* £50,000 *Grants* £41,000 *Assets* £153,000

TRUSTEES A Wigram, Chair; Mrs S A Wigram.

HOW TO APPLY In writing to the correspondent.

WHO TO APPLY TO A Wigram, Chair, Highfield House, 4 Woodfall Street, London SW3 4DJ *Tel* 020 7730 6820

CC NO 800533   **ESTABLISHED** 1988

■ The Felicity Wilde Charitable Trust

WHERE FUNDING CAN BE GIVEN UK.

WHO CAN BENEFIT National organisations benefiting children. Research workers and medical professionals may be supported for research work.

WHAT IS FUNDED Children's charities and medical research, particularly into asthma.

WHAT IS NOT FUNDED No grants to individuals or non-registered charities.

RANGE OF GRANTS £1,000–£20,000.

SAMPLE GRANTS £40,000 in two grants to National Asthma Campaign; £5,000 each to Childrens Hospital Appeal Trust and Royal Alexandra Hospital for Sick Children for the Rocking Horse Appeal. £2,000 in two payments to Children Action Rocket Enterprise; £1,000 each to Breast Cancer Campaign, Derbyshire Children's Holiday Centre, North West Cancer Research Fund, React, Scottish Adoption Association, and Wirral Autistic Society.

FINANCES *Year* 2000–01 *Income* £80,110 *Grants* £75,000

TRUSTEES Barclays Bank Trust Co Ltd.

HOW TO APPLY In writing to the correspondent at any time. Applications are usually considered quarterly.

WHO TO APPLY TO Miss M Bertenshaw, Barclays Bank Trust Company Ltd, Executorship & Trustee Service, PO Box 15, Northwich, Cheshire CW9 7UR *Tel* 01606 313173

CC NO 264404   **ESTABLISHED** 1972

■ The Wilkinson Charitable Foundation

WHERE FUNDING CAN BE GIVEN UK.

WHO CAN BENEFIT Academic institutions benefiting young adults and older people, students, research workers and scientists.

WHAT IS FUNDED The advancement of scientific knowledge, especially in the fields of chemistry, virology and radiology through research, support of facilities and encouragement of promising students.

WHAT IS NOT FUNDED No grants to individuals.

FINANCES *Year* 1999–2000 *Grants* £65,000

TRUSTEES B D S Lock; Dr Anne M Hardy.

HOW TO APPLY In writing to the correspondent. Applications from individuals will not be considered.

WHO TO APPLY TO B D S Lock, Trustee, Lawrence Graham, 190 Strand, London WC2R 1JN

CC NO 276214   **ESTABLISHED** 1978

■ The Will Charitable Trust

WHERE FUNDING CAN BE GIVEN UK and overseas

WHO CAN BENEFIT Registered or exempt charities with a proven record in a relevant field benefiting people with cancer, mental illness, sight loss or other disabilities.

WHAT IS FUNDED (a) Countryside conservation including flora and fauna; (b) care of people with sight loss and prevention of blindness; (c) care of people with cancer and their families; (d) residential care of people with mental disabilities by making a life-long commitment to provide a family environment and maximum choice in lifestyle.

WHAT IS NOT FUNDED Grants are only given to registered charities.

TYPE OF GRANT As determined by needs of grantee or project.

RANGE OF GRANTS The trust does not normally give grants smaller than £5,000 or bigger than £50,000. Most grants are in the range of £15,000–£25,000.

SAMPLE GRANTS £40,000 each to Marie Curie Cancer Care and West of England School and College; £35,000 to RUKBA; £30,000 each to Essex Wildlife Trust and Woodland Trust; £25,000 to Dorset Wildlife Trust, L'Arche, Marlets Hospice, RNIB and Sandwell Community Caring Trust.

FINANCES *Year* 2001–02 *Income* £905,862 *Grants* £705,000 *Assets* £21,278,066

TRUSTEES H N Henshaw, chair; P Andras; A McDonald.

HOW TO APPLY The grants administrator is Ian McIntosh who has an office in Sunbury, Middlesex. Telephone enquiries should be made to him on 01932 724148. Unless advised to the contrary, applications should be submitted in writing to the correspondent. There are no application forms. The trust normally distributes income twice yearly. Grants are made in March to organisations whose activities fall within the fields of blindness and mental handicap with applications to be received by 31 January at the latest. Grants are made in October to organisations operating within the fields of conservation and cancer, with applications to be received by 31 August at the latest.

WHO TO APPLY TO Vanessa Reburn, Farrer & Co Solicitors, 66 Lincoln's Inn Fields, London WC2A 3LH *Tel* 01932 724148 (Sunbury office)

CC NO 801682   **ESTABLISHED** 1989

■ The Williams Family Charitable Trust

WHERE FUNDING CAN BE GIVEN Worldwide.

WHO CAN BENEFIT Jewish people.

WHAT IS FUNDED Organisations benefiting Jewish people.

RANGE OF GRANTS Generally less than £1,000.

SAMPLE GRANTS £65,000 to HaGemach Al-Shem Naheim Zeev Williams; £20,000 to Amutat El-Ad-Jerusalem; £18,000 to Yeshivat Hahesder Kiryat Arba; £10,000 to Child Resettlement Fund; £5,000 Joint Jewish Charitable Trust; £4,000 to Aerial Mifalei Torah; £2,000 to Seeing Eyes for the Blind; £1,000 to Beit Haggai Youth Village; £500 to Cambridge University; £400 to Victims of Arab Terror.

FINANCES *Year* 1998–99 *Income* £114,000 *Grants* £230,000 *Assets* £1,600,000

TRUSTEES Shimon Benison; Arnon Levy.

OTHER INFORMATION Please note, in January 2003 the trust stated that the correspondent was likely to change in the near future.

HOW TO APPLY In writing to the correspondent.
WHO TO APPLY TO The Trustees, 8 Holne Chase, London N2 0QN
CC NO 255452 **ESTABLISHED** 1959

■ The Kay Williams Charitable Foundation

WHERE FUNDING CAN BE GIVEN UK.
WHO CAN BENEFIT Registered charities.
WHAT IS FUNDED General charitable purposes.
RANGE OF GRANTS £250–£2,000.
SAMPLE GRANTS £2,500 to Royal Opera House Trust; £2,000 each in 19 grants including those to Action for Blind People, Cancer Research Campaign, Help the Aged, Cancer Relief Macmillan Fund, The Samaritans, VSO, World Cancer Research Fund and RSPCA.
FINANCES *Year* 1998–99 *Income* £33,000 *Grants* £50,000 *Assets* £1,000,000
TRUSTEES R M Cantor; D W Graham; Mrs M C Williams.
HOW TO APPLY In writing to the correspondent.
WHO TO APPLY TO R M Cantor, Trustee, BDO Stoy Hayward, Kings Wharf, 20–30 Kings Road, Reading, Berkshire RG1 3EX *Tel* 0118 925 4400
CC NO 1047947 **ESTABLISHED** 1995

■ The William Williams Charity

WHERE FUNDING CAN BE GIVEN The ancient parishes of Blandford Forum, Shaftesbury and Sturminster Newton.
WHO CAN BENEFIT Primarily individuals, also some local organisations benefiting people in need, children, young adults, at risk groups, and people disadvantaged by poverty or socially isolated.
WHAT IS FUNDED People in need, youth organisations, schools and welfare charities.
SAMPLE GRANTS £6,000 each to Shaftesbury Museum Trust and Yewstock School; £4,000 each to Age Concern – Sturminster Newton and Shaftesbury Club for Young People; £3,000 to Treads; £1,000 to Age Concern – Blandford Forum.
FINANCES *Year* 1999 *Income* £205,000 *Grants* £127,000 *Assets* £3,800,000
TRUSTEES Mrs J D Frampton, Chair; R J F Prideaux-Brune; L Williams; Cllr C Sharpe; Cllr R Gillam; Cllr G G Morgan; Cllr R Cowley.
OTHER INFORMATION Of the grant total, £98,000 was to or for the benefit of individuals, £29,000 was to institutions.
HOW TO APPLY In writing to the correspondent.
WHO TO APPLY TO Ian Windsor, Steward, Stafford House, 10 Prince of Wales Road, Dorchester, Dorset DT1 1PW *Tel* 01305 264573 *Fax* 01305 269873 *E-mail* wwc@kennedylegg.demon.co.uk
CC NO 202188 **ESTABLISHED** 1621

■ R H Willis Charitable Trust

WHERE FUNDING CAN BE GIVEN Birmingham, Staffordshire, Worcestershire, Coventry, Wolverhampton and associated towns in the Black Country.
WHO CAN BENEFIT Charities benefiting older people, children, people with disabilities, people in financial need and for educational needs.
WHAT IS NOT FUNDED No grants are given to: animal charities; medical research; relief of disease charities; entertainment charities; operating costs which could be met from statutory sources; charities receiving more than 50% public funding; individuals, unless the application is submitted by charitable institutions on behalf of individuals.
SAMPLE GRANTS £4,800 to Acafess Community Trust; £2,000 to National Institute of Conductive Education.
FINANCES *Year* 1999–2000 *Income* £30,000 *Grants* £21,000 *Assets* £901,000
TRUSTEES Gerald Hingley; Louise Woodhead.
HOW TO APPLY In writing to the correspondent.
WHO TO APPLY TO Gerald Hingley, Trustee, Wragge & Co., 55 Colmore Row, Birmingham B3 2AS *Tel* 0121 233 1000 *Fax* 0121 214 1099
CC NO 328525 **ESTABLISHED** 1989

■ The H D H Wills 1965 Charitable Trust

WHERE FUNDING CAN BE GIVEN UK and Ireland.
WHO CAN BENEFIT Registered or recognised charities only.
WHAT IS FUNDED General charitable purposes, with particular favour given to environmental projects.
WHAT IS NOT FUNDED No grants to individuals or national charities.
TYPE OF GRANT One-off grants.
RANGE OF GRANTS 90% of grants made from the General Fund total £500 or less.
SAMPLE GRANTS £7,000 to Royal Agricultural Benevolent Institution; £4,000 to Scottish Royal Agricultural Benevolent Institution; £2,070 to Rendcomb College for the summer term; £2,000 each to Ousden Parish Council and Royal Shakespeare Company; £1,500 each to ILPH and St John Ambulance – Oxfordshire; £1,200 to Moorcroft Racing Welfare Centre; £1,000 each to Canine Partners for Independence and Groundwork – Northern Ireland.
FINANCES *Year* 2000–01 *Income* £704,592 *Grants* £704,000 *Assets* £29,931,145
TRUSTEES John Carson; The Lord Killearn; Lady E H Wills; Dr Catherine Wills; Liell Francklin.
HOW TO APPLY In writing to the correspondent. The trust considers small appeals monthly and large ones bi-annually from the Martin Wills Fund. Only one application from a given charity will be considered in any one 18-month period.
WHO TO APPLY TO Mrs Wendy Cooper, Trust Secretary, Henley Knapp Barn, Fulwell, Chipping Norton, Oxfordshire OX7 4EN *Tel* 01608 678051 *Fax* 01608 678052 *E-mail* willsct@ukonline.co.uk
CC NO 244610 **ESTABLISHED** 1965

■ Dame Violet Wills Charitable Trust

WHERE FUNDING CAN BE GIVEN UK and overseas, but there may be a preference for Bristol.
WHO CAN BENEFIT Associations for evangelical religious purposes.
WHAT IS FUNDED General charitable purposes for evangelical associations.
WHAT IS NOT FUNDED Grants are not given to individuals.
TYPE OF GRANT One-off.
RANGE OF GRANTS £90–£14,000, but mostly £5,000 or less.
SAMPLE GRANTS £14,000 to Western Counties and SWE Trust for the Evangelists Fund; £6,400 to

Echoes of Service – Bristol Missionaries; £5,000 to Overseas Council; £3,500 to Philip Street Chapel for an Evangelist's house; £3,000 to Christian Ministries for general purposes; £2,500 each to Bristol International Students Centre, Open Air Campaigners – Bristol, and Living Waters Radio Ministry; £2,000 each to FEBA Radio and Univeristies and Colleges Christian Fellowship.

FINANCES Year 2000–01 *Income* £105,630 *Grants* £113,985 *Assets* £1,582,426

TRUSTEES D G Cleave, Chair; H E Cooper; A J G Cooper; S Burton; Dr D M Cunningham; J R Dean; Miss J R Guy; R Hill; G J T Landreth.

HOW TO APPLY In writing to the correspondent. The trust states 'whilst a vast number of appeals are received each year, grants are more likely to be made to those which are personally known to one or more of the trustees.' Trustees meet in March and in September; applications need to be received by January or June.

WHO TO APPLY TO H E Cooper, Secretary and Treasurer, Ricketts Cooper & Co., Thornton House, Richmond Hill, Bristol BS8 1AT *Tel* 0117 973 8441

CC NO 219485   **ESTABLISHED** 1955

■ The Dame Violet Wills Will Trust

WHERE FUNDING CAN BE GIVEN Bristol and Torbay areas.

WHO CAN BENEFIT Registered charities benefiting children.

WHAT IS FUNDED The support of homes established privately by the late Dame Violet Wills and charities active in Bristol and south Devon.

WHAT IS NOT FUNDED No support for individuals or for charities outside the area of benefit.

TYPE OF GRANT Single donations.

SAMPLE GRANTS 1998–99: £20,000 to Lord Mamhead Homes; £3,000 each to Brunelcave, DRIB and Rowcroft Hospice – Torquay; £2,000 each to Barnardos, Bristol Orthopaedic Trust, Changing Faces, Friends of Bristol Royal Hospital for Sick Children, Jessie May Trust and RNLI – Bristol Channel.

FINANCES Year 2001–02 *Income* £75,304

TRUSTEES H J Page; D P L Howe; P J Page.

HOW TO APPLY In writing to the correspondent.

WHO TO APPLY TO H J Page, Trustee, 33 Julian Road, Sneyd Park, Bristol BS9 1JY *Tel* 0117 968 1475

CC NO 262251   **ESTABLISHED** 1965

■ The Wilmcote Charitrust

WHERE FUNDING CAN BE GIVEN Birmingham and Midlands.

WHO CAN BENEFIT Registered charities and voluntary organisations.

WHAT IS FUNDED General charitable purposes.

SAMPLE GRANTS Previous beneficiaries have included Birmingham Children's Hospital, Birmingham Council for Old People, Birmingham Railway Museum, PDSA, Queen Elizabeth School, Stratford-upon-Avon Ambulance Association, Wilmcote Pre-school Playgroup and Wilmcote C of E Church.

FINANCES Year 2000–01 *Income* £66,013 *Grants* £20,000

TRUSTEES G C Allman; B W Frost; Mrs A L M Murphy; Mrs R J S Whiteside.

OTHER INFORMATION No recent information was available on beneficiaries.

HOW TO APPLY In writing to the correspondent.

WHO TO APPLY TO Douglas M King, Clerk, Warren Chase, Wilmcote, Stratford-upon-Avon CV37 9XG *Tel* 01789 298472

CC NO 503837   **ESTABLISHED** 1974

■ David Wilson Foundation

WHERE FUNDING CAN BE GIVEN Leicestershire.

WHO CAN BENEFIT Organisations.

WHAT IS FUNDED General charitable purposes.

SAMPLE GRANTS £50,000 to Oakham School; £25,000 to Dr Crowe & Partners; £1,000 each to Marlborough Square Methodist Church and St Denys Church; £500 to RNIB; £250 to Whizz-Kidz.

FINANCES Year 1999–2000 *Income* £176,000 *Grants* £78,000 *Assets* £1,400,000

TRUSTEES J D Wilson; T G Neiland; Mrs L I Wilson.

HOW TO APPLY In writing to the correspondent.

WHO TO APPLY TO J A Gillions, Fisher Solicitors, 6–8 Kilwardby Street, Ashby de la Zouch, Leicestershire LE65 2FU *Tel* 01530 412167

CC NO 1049047   **ESTABLISHED** 1995

■ J and J R Wilson Trust

WHERE FUNDING CAN BE GIVEN Mainly Scotland, particularly Glasgow and the west coast of Scotland.

WHO CAN BENEFIT Organisations benefiting older people, animals and birds.

WHAT IS FUNDED Grants are given to charitable bodies which are concerned with older people, or the care of both domestic and wild animals and birds.

WHAT IS NOT FUNDED No grants to individuals.

RANGE OF GRANTS £100–£8,000, but mostly £200–£2,000.

SAMPLE GRANTS £8,000 to Central Scotland Countryside Trust (West Quarter Glen); £6,000 to Crossroads (Scotland) Care Attendance Scheme; £5,000 each to Age Concern Scotland and Alzheimers Scotland; £3,000 each to Marie Curie Cancer Care for their home nursing service and Prince and Princess of Wales Hospice.

FINANCES Year 1999–2000 *Grants* £105,000

TRUSTEES Hugh M K Hopkins; John G L Robinson.

HOW TO APPLY In writing to the correspondent. The trustees meet once a year, usually in January, to consider grants.

WHO TO APPLY TO Hugh Hopkins, Trustee, Tho and J W Barty, 61 High Street, Dunblane, Perthshire FK15 0EH *Tel* 01786 822296

SC NO SC007411

■ The John Wilson Bequest Fund

WHERE FUNDING CAN BE GIVEN Mainly Edinburgh.

WHO CAN BENEFIT Charities which are concerned with people who are poor or unwell living in Edinburgh, especially those which make special provision for women. It also supports individuals in need in Edinburgh and foreign missionaries of any protestant church in Scotland while they are at home.

FINANCES Year 1999 *Income* £70,000 *Grants* £63,000 *Assets* £1,600,000

OTHER INFORMATION £28,000 of the grant total was given to organisations and the remainder to individuals.

HOW TO APPLY In writing to the correspondent.

WHO TO APPLY TO A D Sheperd, Messrs J & R A Robertson, 15 Great Stuart Street, Edinburgh EH3 7TS *Tel* 0131 225 5095
CC NO SC010651

■ Sumner Wilson Charitable Trust

WHERE FUNDING CAN BE GIVEN UK.
WHO CAN BENEFIT Registered charities.
WHAT IS FUNDED General charitable purposes.
FINANCES *Year* 2001–02 *Income* £54,363 *Grants* £172,270
TRUSTEES J G Joffe; A M W Wilson; M S Wilson.
HOW TO APPLY In writing to the correspondent, or to the trustees.
WHO TO APPLY TO N A Steinberg, 138 Park Lane, London W1K 7AS *Tel* 020 7436 6667
CC NO 1018852   **ESTABLISHED** 1992

■ Wiltshire and Swindon Community Foundation

WHERE FUNDING CAN BE GIVEN Wiltshire and Swindon only.
WHO CAN BENEFIT Voluntary and community groups in Wiltshire benefiting young adults and older people, one-parent families and ethnic minority groups.
WHAT IS FUNDED Main projects fund: supporting community care; tackling isolation; investing in young people. There are also two other funds: Community development fund and Initiatives fund. Support may also be given to accommodation and housing, health, infrastructure development and infrastructure and technical support.
WHAT IS NOT FUNDED No grants for projects operating outside Wiltshire or Swindon; large UK charities without local management groups; individuals; sponsored events; medical research and equipment; animal welfare; general/large appeals; promotion of religion; party political activity. The foundation normally only funds work with children and young people in the 12–25 age group, unless they have a special need or disability. Arts and environmental work is not supported unless its primary aim is to support, enable and include people in need.
TYPE OF GRANT Not normally for capital expenditure or to contribute to large appeals. Core costs, feasibility studies, project, research, running costs, recurring costs, salaries and start-up costs will be considered. Funding is given for up to three years.
RANGE OF GRANTS Main grants: £500–£3,000 per year for three years. Small grants: £50–£500 on a one-off basis.
SAMPLE GRANTS £8,100 (over three years) to Greencroft Centre (New Alliance) for production costs of a newsletter by members of this daycentre for people with ongoing mental health problems; £6,000 (over three years) to Harnham Youth Venture to enable the continuation of outreach support to young people; £5,000 (over two years) to Millen Advice Point towards costs of employment of an outreach worker to visit elderly, disabled and housebound clients of this Asian advice point; £4,500 (over three years) to Devizes & District Opportunity Centre to help towards the cost of employing a special needs playleader; £4,000 (over two years) to Anchor Staying Put towards the cost of running a handyman scheme for older people and those with disabilities in North Wiltshire; £3,000 each to Stepping Forward towards development costs of programme which supports disadvantaged young people in Parks area of Swindon and Fairfield Opportunity Farm to purchase a horse for this establishment which provides riding facilities for those with learning difficulties; £3,000 each (over two years) to Trussell Trust to cover costs of pilot project for development of a food-bank for those in need in Salisbury area and Cruse Bereavement Care towards costs of volunteer counselling; £3,000 (over three years) to Monday Wednesday Club Trowbridge to enable this club for people with disabilities to employ a craft tutor.
FINANCES *Year* 2000–01 *Income* £943,240 *Grants* £257,000 *Assets* £2,136,658
TRUSTEES John Manser, Chair; David Airey; David Bousfield; Lady Cairns; Caroline Caunter; Alice Cleland; Alan Fletcher; Elinor Goodman; Chapman Harrison; Alastair Muir; Jill Otley; John Rendell; Phil Smith; Jeremy del Srother; Marigold Treloar; Rhoddy Voremberg; Ian Wilson.
PUBLICATIONS Grants policy booklet. *Communities in Crisis in Wiltshire* (needs assessment report) and *The Future We All Want* (developing the strategy for the care of older people in eastern Wiltshire).
OTHER INFORMATION Applications are unlikely to succeed. Wiltshire Community Foundation aims to assist groups that are working very closely with their local community. The foundation also aims to allocate funds where they will make the most difference. For these reasons the following applications are unlikely to be supported. (a) Applications from national charities where there is no clear management structure based in Wiltshire. (b) Applications from organisations that have access to professional fund-raisers. (c) Applications for services that are closely associated with statutory provision. (d) Applications for contributions towards projects that are not being offered mainly in Wiltshire. (e) Applications for a contribution toward a major item where WCF's contribution would not make a significant difference.
HOW TO APPLY Application forms and guidelines are available from the foundation. All potential applicants are asked to make early contact, preferable by phone, with the Programme Director to discuss their project, prior to completing an application form. Details of main grants rounds, plus any other funding opportunities open during the year, are publicised via local Voluntary Action newsletters and the local press. Decisions on main grants usually take place twice a year in the autumn and spring.
WHO TO APPLY TO The Programme Director, 48 New Park Street, Devizes, Wiltshire SN10 1DS *Tel* 01380 729284 *Fax* 01380 729772 *E-mail* info@wscf.org.uk *Website* www.wscf.org.uk
CC NO 298936   **ESTABLISHED** 1991

■ The J L Wine Charitable Trust

WHERE FUNDING CAN BE GIVEN UK.
WHO CAN BENEFIT Registered charities.
WHAT IS FUNDED General charitable purposes.
RANGE OF GRANTS £50–£6,800.
SAMPLE GRANTS In 1997: £6,800 to Nightingale House; £600 to Jewish Care; £587 to Royal Court Theatre; £550 to Wimbledon and District Synagogue; £500 each to Wigmore Hall Trust and L'Chaim Independent Charitable Trust; £330 to Norwood Ravenswood; £250 to Thomas Coram Foundation for Children; £200 to

B'nai B'rith Hillel Foundation; £150 to Thames Valley Friends of Ravenswood.
FINANCES *Year* 1999 *Income* £25,639 *Grants* £16,365
TRUSTEES H M Wine; Ms C Goldbart; J S Korn.
HOW TO APPLY The trust does not welcome applications.
WHO TO APPLY TO Julian Korn, Trustee, 100 Fetter Lane, London EC4A 1BN *Tel* 020 7894 6589
CC NO 291209   **ESTABLISHED** 1985

■ The Benjamin Winegarten Charitable Trust

WHERE FUNDING CAN BE GIVEN UK.
WHO CAN BENEFIT Individuals and organisations benefiting Jewish people and people disadvantaged by poverty.
WHAT IS FUNDED Relief of poverty and the advancement of Jewish religion and religious education.
RANGE OF GRANTS £200–£5,000.
SAMPLE GRANTS £10,000 to Hechal Hatovah Institute; £8,000 to Merkaz Lechinuch Torani Zichron Ya'akov; £5,000 each to The Jewish Educational Trust and Ohr Someach Friends; £4,000 to Yeshivo Hovomo Talmudical College; £3,000 each to The Mechinah School, Ohr Akiva Community Centre and ZSVT.
FINANCES *Year* 1998–99 *Income* £74,000 *Grants* £57,600 *Assets* £147,000
TRUSTEES B A Winegarten; Mrs E Winegarten.
HOW TO APPLY In writing to the correspondent.
WHO TO APPLY TO B A Winegarten, Trustee, 25 St Andrew's Grove, Stoke Newington, London N16 5NF *Tel* 020 8800 6669
CC NO 271442   **ESTABLISHED** 1976

■ The Harold Hyam Wingate Foundation

WHERE FUNDING CAN BE GIVEN Mainly UK.
WHO CAN BENEFIT Organisations benefiting Jewish people, the performing arts, medical research and healthcare.
WHAT IS FUNDED Jewish charities, performing arts, medical research, healthcare and education where relevant to problems associated with social exclusion.
WHAT IS NOT FUNDED No grants to individuals. The Wingate Scholarship Fund, for students over the age of 24, is separately administered by Faith Clark at the above address. Obtain details direct from her or from *The Educational Grants Directory*. The trustees will not normally consider donations to the general funds of large charitable bodies, wishing instead to focus support on specific projects.
TYPE OF GRANT Either one-off or recurrent for a limited period. Also capital projects on a highly selective basis.
RANGE OF GRANTS £50–£250,000; generally £5,000 or less.
SAMPLE GRANTS £250,000 to The Caldercott Foundation; £35,000 to National Film and Television School; £30,000 to Israel Museum Jerusalem; £20,000 to Hampstead Theatre Trust; £16,763 to English Chamber Organisation; £15,000 each to English Touring Opera, and Oxford Centre for Hebrew and Jewish Studies; £12,899 to Wingate Book Prize; £12,000 to Leo Baeck College; £10,000 to New Israel Fund.
FINANCES *Year* 2001 *Income* £568,000 *Grants* £759,000 *Assets* £17,000,000

TRUSTEES R C Wingate; A J Wingate; R H Cassen; D L WIngate; W J Wingate.
OTHER INFORMATION The foundation also operates a scholarship scheme, under the name of Wingate Scholarships. Further details and an application form can be obtained by writing to the foundation. Alternatively, e-mail: clark@win-sch.demon.co.uk.
HOW TO APPLY In writing to the correspondent, giving financial statements where possible. Applications are only acknowledged if a stamped addressed envelope is enclosed or if the application is successful. They are considered about every three months.
WHO TO APPLY TO Karen Marshall, 2nd Floor, 20–22 Stukeley Street, London WC2B 5LR *Website* www.wingate.org.uk
CC NO 264114   **ESTABLISHED** 1960

■ Mrs Wingfield's Charitable Trust

WHERE FUNDING CAN BE GIVEN UK and overseas, with some preference for the Shrewsbury area.
WHO CAN BENEFIT Registered charities and bodies nurturing artistic individuals.
WHAT IS FUNDED General charitable purposes; fees towards supporting people with exceptional talent in the arts who do not have the financial means to progress – particularly opera and ballet.
FINANCES *Year* 1999–2000 *Income* £28,000 *Grants* £18,000
TRUSTEES John Malcolm Dodds; Denzil John Onslow.
HOW TO APPLY In writing to the correspondent. Applications are usually considered once a month. The trust receives many more applications than it is able to support. Only those applicants who include an sae will receive a reply.
WHO TO APPLY TO The Trustees, 1 Brassey Road, Old Pots Way, Shrewsbury SY3 7FA
CC NO 269524   **ESTABLISHED** 1974

■ The Francis Winham Foundation

WHERE FUNDING CAN BE GIVEN England.
WHO CAN BENEFIT Older people.
WHAT IS FUNDED Organisations, institutions and foundations benefiting older people.
SAMPLE GRANTS £63,000 to Age Concern; £43,000 to SSAFA; £41,000 to Care and Repair; £32,000 to Universal Beneficent Society; £22,000 to Charity Search; £10,000 each to Bedfordshire Advocacy, Camden Housebound Link, GAVS, Oak Lodge Residential Home and Shipwrecked Fishermen and Mariners Royal.
FINANCES *Year* 2000–01 *Income* £655,000 *Grants* £586,000 *Assets* £3,000,000
TRUSTEES Francine Winham; Dr John Norcliffe Roberts; Gwendoline Winham; Josephine Winham.
HOW TO APPLY In writing to the correspondent. The trust regrets it cannot send replies to applications outside its specific field of help for older people. Applications should be made through registered charities or social services departments only.
WHO TO APPLY TO The Secretary, 35 Pembroke Gardens, London W8 6HU *Tel* 020 7602 1261
CC NO 278092   **ESTABLISHED** 1979

■ The Mayor of Wirral's Charity Trust

WHERE FUNDING CAN BE GIVEN Wirral.

WHO CAN BENEFIT Local organisations, and local branches of UK organisations.

WHAT IS FUNDED A large variety of causes including welfare and medical charities, children and youth organisations, and disability groups. Many are community-based or local branches of UK charities.

FINANCES *Year* 2001 *Income* £88,316

TRUSTEES Stephen Maddox; Ian Coleman; the present and previous Mayor of Wirral.

HOW TO APPLY In writing to the correspondent.

WHO TO APPLY TO The Mayor of Wirral, The Mayor's Parlour, Town Hall, Brighton Street, Wallasey, Wirral CH44 8ED *Tel* 0151 691 8527

CC NO 518288   **ESTABLISHED** 1986

■ The James Wise Charitable Trust

WHERE FUNDING CAN BE GIVEN UK, but mainly Surrey and Hampshire.

WHO CAN BENEFIT Charitable organisations and individuals.

WHAT IS FUNDED General charitable purposes.

TYPE OF GRANT Generally one-off grants.

RANGE OF GRANTS Up to £25,000.

SAMPLE GRANTS £12,000 to Royal Surrey County Hospital; £5,000 each to Milford and Villages Day Care Centre, and Phyllis Tuckwell Memorial Hospice; £2,000 to Disability Challengers; £1,000 to Witley Scout and Guide PMC.

FINANCES *Year* 2000–01 *Income* £74,000 *Grants* £54,000 *Assets* £690,000

TRUSTEES D A S Dear; B Kilburn; Miss S C Coate.

HOW TO APPLY In writing to the correspondent.

WHO TO APPLY TO The Trustees, Marshalls Solicitors, 102 High Street, Godalming, Surrey GU7 1DS *Tel* 01483 416101

CC NO 273853   **ESTABLISHED** 1977

■ The Michael and Anna Wix Charitable Trust

WHERE FUNDING CAN BE GIVEN UK.

WHO CAN BENEFIT Registered charities (mainly UK) benefiting students, at risk groups, and people who are disabled, disadvantaged by poverty or socially isolated.

WHAT IS FUNDED Main areas of interest are older people, disability, education, medicine and health, poverty and welfare.

WHAT IS NOT FUNDED Applications from individuals are not considered. Grants are to national bodies rather than local branches or local groups.

TYPE OF GRANT 'Modest semi-regular' donations. Also one-off for part or all of a specific project.

RANGE OF GRANTS Normally between £100 and £2,000.

SAMPLE GRANTS £20,000 each to British Technion Society and Nightingale House; £1,500 to the Jewish Museum; £1,250 to Norwood Ravenswood; £1,000 each to Institute for Jewish Policy Research and World Jewish Relief; £500 to Jewish Care; £350 to Lilian Faithfull Homes; £250 each to Break and British ORT.

FINANCES *Year* 1999–2000 *Income* £54,574 *Grants* £18,700 *Assets* £1,636,448

TRUSTEES Miss E Wix; Mrs J B Bloch; Miss Judith Portrait.

HOW TO APPLY In writing to the trustees. Applications are considered half-yearly. Only applications

from registered charities are acknowledged. Frequent applications by a single charity are not appreciated.

WHO TO APPLY TO The Trustees, Portrait Solicitors, Trustees' Solicitors, 1 Chancery Lane, London WC2A 1LF *Tel* 020 7320 3883

CC NO 207863   **ESTABLISHED** 1955

■ The Wixamtree Trust

WHERE FUNDING CAN BE GIVEN Primarily Bedfordshire.

WHO CAN BENEFIT Local registered charities.

WHAT IS FUNDED Any registered charities based or operating within Bedfordshire.

WHAT IS NOT FUNDED No grants to non-registered charities, individuals or overseas projects.

TYPE OF GRANT One-off projects, capital, core costs and research. Single grants are usually given but successful applicants may reapply on an annual basis.

RANGE OF GRANTS On average £1,000–£5,000, although larger grants can be made.

SAMPLE GRANTS £50,000 to Moggerhanger House Preservation Trust; £25,00 to The Pasque Charity; £20,000 each to St Albans Cathedral Campaign and Home Farm Trust Bedfordshire Appeal; £18,000 to Cecil Higgins Art Gallery; £10,000 each to Bushmead Church Building Project, Friends of Bedford Child Development Centre and Victim Support Bedfordshire.

FINANCES *Year* 2001–02 *Income* £630,148 *Grants* £361,981 *Assets* £17,310,173

TRUSTEES S C Whitbread; Mrs J M Whitbread; H F Whitbread; C R Skottowe.

HOW TO APPLY On a form available from the correspondent, for consideration throughout the year. The trustees meet in January, April, July and October. An application form is available by e-mail and all requests for support must be accompanied by a current report and accounts, where available.

WHO TO APPLY TO Paul Patten, Administrator, c/o CCAS, 80 Croydon Road, Elmers End, Beckenham, Kent BR3 4DF *Tel* 020 8658 8902 *Fax* 020 8658 3292 *E-mail* wixamtree@ccas.globalnet.co.uk

CC NO 210089   **ESTABLISHED** 1949

■ The Woburn 1986 Charitable Trust

WHERE FUNDING CAN BE GIVEN Primarily Woburn.

WHO CAN BENEFIT Primarily pensioners; also welfare and medical charities.

WHAT IS FUNDED The main priority is the provision and maintenance of housing for Woburn estate pensioners in need.

TYPE OF GRANT Recurrent and single donations.

RANGE OF GRANTS £200 to £15,000.

SAMPLE GRANTS £15,000 to MacMillan Cancer Relief; £10,000 each to Foundling Museum and Racing Welfare Charities; £5,500 to British Red Cross.

FINANCES *Year* 2000–01 *Income* £81,000 *Grants* £55,000 *Assets* £1,200,000

TRUSTEES Marquess of Tavistock; Lord Howland; D H Fox; P R W Pemberton.

HOW TO APPLY In writing to the correspondent.

WHO TO APPLY TO The Trustees, Woburn Abbey, Woburn, Bedfordshire MK17 9WA *Tel* 01525 290666 *Fax* 01525 290731

CC NO 295525   **ESTABLISHED** 1986

■ The Maurice Wohl Charitable Foundation

WHERE FUNDING CAN BE GIVEN UK and Israel.

WHO CAN BENEFIT In practice, Jewish groups, and health, welfare and medical organisations.

WHAT IS FUNDED The main areas of interest include medicine and health, including research projects, organisations for people with physical and mental disabilities, sheltered housing, community welfare, including older people and children, education and the arts.

WHAT IS NOT FUNDED The trustees do not in general entertain applications for grants for ongoing maintenance projects. The trustees do not administer any schemes for individual awards or scholarships and they do not, therefore, entertain any individual applications for grants.

TYPE OF GRANT Specific projects or part of a project; variable annual donations or one-off donations.

RANGE OF GRANTS In general, £50–£10,000.

SAMPLE GRANTS £175,000 to The Royal Academy; £143,000 to Kings College; £83,333 to JFS; £66,903 to Bikur Cholim Hospital; £50,000 each to Friends of Bar-Ilan University, Lord Jakobovits Centre, and UCL; £16,546 to Yeshivat Hakotel; £12,000 to Medical Aid Trust; £10,000 to Jewish Care.

FINANCES *Year* 2000–01 *Income* £914,401 *Grants* £651,105 *Assets* £18,000,523

TRUSTEES Maurice Wohl; Mrs Vivienne Wohl; Mrs Ella Latchman; Prof. David Latchman; M D Paisner.

HOW TO APPLY In writing to the correspondent. The trustees meet regularly throughout the year.

WHO TO APPLY TO J Houri, 1st Floor, 7–8 Conduit Street, London W1S 2XF *Tel* 020 7493 3777

CC NO 244519   **ESTABLISHED** 1965

■ The Maurice Wohl Charitable Trust

WHERE FUNDING CAN BE GIVEN UK and Israel.

WHO CAN BENEFIT Jewish groups, and health, welfare and medical organisations.

WHAT IS FUNDED Jewish causes and general charitable purposes.

WHAT IS NOT FUNDED The trustees do not administer any schemes for individual awards or scholarships, and they do not, therefore, entertain any individual applications for grants.

TYPE OF GRANT Specific projects or part of project; variable annual donations or one-off donations.

RANGE OF GRANTS £25–£10,000; generally £1,000 or less.

SAMPLE GRANTS £9,934 to Communaute Israelite de Geneve; £3,510 to Society of Friends of the Torah; £3,500 to Mecial Aid Trust; £2,091 to Yad Sarah; £2,000 in two grants to Yesodey Hatorah School; £1,800 to Helensea Charities; £1,412 to Re'uth; £1,250 in two grants to Western Marble Arch Synagoge; £1,000 each to Friends of the Sick and Orthodox Jewish Aid Society.

FINANCES *Year* 2000–01 *Income* £146,730 *Grants* £39,513 *Assets* £2,552,995

TRUSTEES Maurice Wohl; Mrs Vivienne Wohl; Mrs Ella Latchman; Prof. David Latchman; Martin Paisner.

HOW TO APPLY To the correspondent in writing. Applications are regularly considered throughout the year.

WHO TO APPLY TO J Houri, 1st Floor, 7–8 Conduit Street, London W1S 2XF *Tel* 020 7493 3777

CC NO 244518   **ESTABLISHED** 1965

■ The Aviezer Wolfson Charitable Trust

WHERE FUNDING CAN BE GIVEN UK.

WHO CAN BENEFIT Registered charities and institutions, especially those benefiting Jewish people.

WHAT IS FUNDED Trustees mainly give to Jewish charities and organisations.

RANGE OF GRANTS £3,000–£10,000.

SAMPLE GRANTS £10,000 to Yad Eliezev; £5,000 to British Friends of Laniado Hospital; £4,000 to British Friends of Ezra Lamarpeh; £3,300 to Arachim; £3,000 to British Friends of Yad Sarah.

FINANCES *Year* 1999–2000 *Income* £54,539

TRUSTEES I S J Wolfson; Mrs A Wolfson; D Clayton; Mrs R R Lauffer.

HOW TO APPLY In writing to the correspondent.

WHO TO APPLY TO D Clayton, Trustee, c/o Clayton Stark & Co., 5th Floor, Charles House, 108–110 Finchley Road, London NW3 5JJ *Tel* 020 7431 4200

CC NO 275927   **ESTABLISHED** 1978

■ The Charles Wolfson Charitable Trust

WHERE FUNDING CAN BE GIVEN UK, Israel.

WHO CAN BENEFIT Organisations benefiting children and young adults, Jewish people, research workers, and medical professionals. At risk groups and people who are disabled, disadvantaged by poverty or socially isolated will also be considered.

WHAT IS FUNDED Medical research and facilities, education, welfare and ecology.

WHAT IS NOT FUNDED It is not the policy of the trust to make grants to individuals or to charities for running costs.

TYPE OF GRANT Grants, also some interest-free loans and the provision of rent-free premises. Grants may be made for up to three years.

SAMPLE GRANTS £344,000 to King's College – London University; £300,000 to Royal West Sussex NHS Trust; £250,000 each to Jewish Care and Nightingale House Home for Aged Jews; £220,000 to Princess Royal NHS Hospital – Telford; £200,000 to Jews Free School; £160,000 to Northwich Park NHS Hospital Children's Centre; £150,000 to Huntingdon Foundation; £125,000 each to CSV and Margaret Thatcher Fund.

FINANCES *Year* 2000–01 *Income* £6,700,000 *Grants* £3,222,000 *Assets* £80,000,000

TRUSTEES Lord Wolfson of Sunningdale; Simon Wolfson; John Franks; Andrew Wolfson.

HOW TO APPLY In writing to the correspondent. Grants are made in response to applications, and while all applications will be considered, the trustees cannot undertake to notify all unsuccessful applicants, because of the volume of appeals received.

WHO TO APPLY TO Mrs Cynthia Crawford, c/o 129 Battenhall Road, Worcester WR5 2BU

CC NO 238043   **ESTABLISHED** 1960

■ The Edith & Isaac Wolfson (Scotland) Trust

WHERE FUNDING CAN BE GIVEN Scotland.

WHO CAN BENEFIT Scottish organisations, especially those benefiting students.

WHAT IS FUNDED Building and equipment for special needs and higher education.

WHAT IS NOT FUNDED No grants to individuals.

TYPE OF GRANT Capital and buildings will be considered.

RANGE OF GRANTS £5,000–£50,000

SAMPLE GRANTS £20,000 each to Balnacraig School, Perth (for an extension to school for teenagers with special needs), Royal Blind Asylum and School, Edinburgh (for furniture for 20 bedrooms), and Beaconhurst School, Bridge of Allan (for IT equipment); £10,000 to Edinvar, Edinburgh (for technology for people with special needs).

FINANCES *Year* 1999 *Income* £75,000 *Grants* £88,000 *Assets* £919,000

TRUSTEES Lord Wolfson of Marylebone; Lord Quirk; Lord Quinton.

HOW TO APPLY Contact the correspondent at the above address for further information. The trustees meet annually in December. This charity works jointly with the Wolfson Foundation, to whom applicants should refer.

WHO TO APPLY TO Dr Victoria Harrison, Secretary, 8 Queen Anne Street, London W1G 9LD *Tel* 020 7323 5730 *Fax* 020 7323 3241

SC NO SC006281   **ESTABLISHED** 1976

····················

■ The Wolfson Family Charitable Trust

WHERE FUNDING CAN BE GIVEN Israel and UK.

WHO CAN BENEFIT Particularly Jewish groups and Israeli institutions.

WHAT IS FUNDED Science, technology and medicine; education; medical research and care and welfare; arts and humanities.

WHAT IS NOT FUNDED Grants are not made to individuals.

TYPE OF GRANT One-off for capital costs and equipment.

SAMPLE GRANTS £812,500 to Tel Aviv University for a new computer and software engineering building (£437,500) and computer hardware (£375,000); £700,000 to Chaim Sheba Medical Centre for an upgrade to the MRI system (£450,000) and Linear Accelerator for Oncology Institute (£250,000); £672,896 to Weizmann Institute for laboratory refurbishment (£475,000) and the Wolfson Institute for Functional Brain Injuring (£197,896); £500,000 to University College London for the Cruciform project; £425,000 each to Hadassah Medical Organisation for enlargement of the bone marrow transplantation department (£250,000), stealth frame stereotaxy for image guided brain surgery (£125,000) and gene therapy institute (£50,000), and to Tel Aviv Sourasky Medical Centre for interventional radiology machine (£250,000) and linear accelerator (£175,000); £230,000 to Edith Wolfson Medical Centre for equipment for the neonatal intensive care unit; £165,500 to Ben Gurion University for laboratory refurbishment (£133,000) and Herzog Archives Centre (£32,500); £136,550 to Technion Israel Institute of Technology for laboratory refurbishment; £125,000 to Rabin Medical Centre for equipment for the department of obstetrics and gynaecology.

FINANCES *Year* 2000–01 *Income* £2,716,000 *Grants* £4,755,000 *Assets* £36,522,000

TRUSTEES Lord Wolfson of Marylebone; Lady Wolfson; Mrs Janet Wolfson de Botton; Laura Wolfson Townsley; M D Paisner; Sir Martin Gilbert; Prof. Barrie Jay; Prof. Sir Eric Ash; Sir Bernard Rix.

HOW TO APPLY The trust shares its application procedure with the Wolfson Foundation. A brief explanatory letter, with organisation and project details, including costs and current shortfalls, will elicit an up-to-date set of guidelines in return, if the charity is able to consider the project concerned.

WHO TO APPLY TO Dr Victoria Harrison, 8 Queen Anne Street, London W1G 9LD *Tel* 020 7323 5730 *Fax* 020 7323 3241

CC NO 228382   **ESTABLISHED** 1958

····················

■ The Wolfson Foundation

WHERE FUNDING CAN BE GIVEN Mainly UK, but also Israel.

WHO CAN BENEFIT Registered charities and exempt charities (such as universities), benefiting people of all ages, especially academics, scientists and terminally ill people.

WHAT IS FUNDED Renovation of historic buildings; libraries; support for preventative medicine; science and technology; programmes for people with special needs, and education. Grants for university research awarded through competitive programmes.

WHAT IS NOT FUNDED No grants for: overheads, running or administrative costs, VAT or professional fees; non-specific appeals (including circulars), endowment funds or conduit organisations; costs of meetings, exhibitions, concerts, expeditions, etc.; the purchase of land; research involving live animals; or film or video production.

TYPE OF GRANT Capital, equipment.

SAMPLE GRANTS £4,000,000 to University College London; £2,500,000 to Imperial College of Science Technology and Medicine for the Chain Wolfson Building; £2,481,000 to Royal Society for the laboratory refurbishment programme; £1,800,000 to Imperial College of Science Technology and Medicine for the Department of Physics; £1,000,000 each to King's College London for the Centre for Age Related Diseases, Loughborough University, University of Durham and Victoria and Albert Museum; £500,000 each to University of Glasgow and Weizmann Institute – Israel for renovation of the Wolfson Buildings.

FINANCES *Year* 2000–01 *Income* £37,278,000 *Grants* £24,738,000 *Assets* £633,339,000

TRUSTEES Lord Wolfson of Marylebone, Chair; Lady Wolfson; Lord Quirk; Lord Quinton; Prof. Sir Eric Ash; Sir Derek Harry Roberts; Lord McColl; Prof. Lord Turnberg; Mrs Janet Wolfson de Botton; Mrs Laura Wolfson Townsley; Prof. Sir David Weatherall.

OTHER INFORMATION Eligible applications from registered charities will normally be considered only when at least 50% of the appeal has been raised.

HOW TO APPLY In writing to the correspondent, sent from head office and including nine copies suitable for photocopying. Applications should include a brief summary of the aims of the project and full contact details of an independent professional referee and a financial section giving: a detailed breakdown of the grant requested, stated as a percentage of the overall project cost; professional fees and VAT (indicated separately); estimates of the subsequent running and maintenance costs of the complete development and how these costs will be provided; where relevant, cost per room and cost of fixtures and fittings; and three written quotations should be obtained and submitted together with an artist's impression of the building. For historic buildings, please specify: category of building (listed building grade); date of current building; and enclose a recent photograph. Proposals involving research or scholarship should include a more detailed appendix, for assessment by expert referees. The applicant's one-page curriculum vitae (including a list of key publications) should be enclosed.

WHO TO APPLY TO Dr Victoria Harrison, Executive secretary, 8 Queen Anne Street, London W1G 9LD *Tel* 020 7323 5730 *Fax* 020 7323 3241
CC NO 206495　　　　**ESTABLISHED** 1955

....

■ Women at Risk

WHERE FUNDING CAN BE GIVEN UK.

WHO CAN BENEFIT Smaller projects that do not have well-developed fundraising campaigns, and which benefit: women; people disadvantaged by poverty; research workers; scientists; students; medical professionals; and teachers.

WHAT IS FUNDED The relief of poverty and sickness; the preservation of health and advancement of education among women who are in need.

WHAT IS NOT FUNDED No grants to individuals. Only charitable/not-for-profit organisations are supported on a long-term basis.

TYPE OF GRANT The charity wishes to enter into long-term partnership with organisations doing practical work, not research.

SAMPLE GRANTS £11,000 to Refuge; £10,000 each to Cleveland Rape & Sexual Abuse Counselling Service and Centre for Filipinos; £5,000 each to Action on Elder Abuse, Family Focus, and Shooting Star Trust; £2,500 to Womankind Worldwide.

FINANCES *Year* 2000 *Income* £118,000 *Grants* £44,000 *Assets* £21,000

TRUSTEES A Reed; A J Jewitt; Ms M Newham.

OTHER INFORMATION The trust seeks projects that meet its charitable objects, to work in partnership to fundraise and to then distribute the money raised to the partners.

HOW TO APPLY In writing to the correspondent.

WHO TO APPLY TO Alec Reed, Chair, PO Box 31055, London SW1X 9WD *Tel* 01753 830861 *Fax* 01753 841688 *E-mail* women.risk@reed.co.uk
CC NO 1059332　　　　**ESTABLISHED** 1996

....

■ Women Caring Trust

WHERE FUNDING CAN BE GIVEN Northern Ireland.

WHO CAN BENEFIT Integrated schools; community playgroups; play buses; youth clubs; women's groups; cross-community holiday schemes benefiting children and young adults.

WHAT IS FUNDED To give practical help to innocent families in the troubled areas of Northern Ireland; to promote integrated education and the support of groups and organisations working for peace and reconciliation among young people. 'A leg-up, not a hand-out.' Trustees are keen to encourage new projects, particularly cross-community, wherever possible.

WHAT IS NOT FUNDED No grants for individuals, large capital expenditure or salaries, organisations solely for the welfare of physically or mentally disabled people, or drug or alcohol related projects. No grants for holidays outside the island of Ireland.

TYPE OF GRANT Recurring costs funded for up to one year.

RANGE OF GRANTS £200–£2,000.

SAMPLE GRANTS £2,000 to Corrymeela Community (Belfast); £1,500 each to Women's Aid (Lisburn) and Northern Ireland Children's Holiday; £1,000 each to Interchange (Craigavon), Strathfoyle Women's Activity Group (Londonderry), Sion Mills Community Association, Centre Care, Women's Aid (Omagh), Foyle Women's Information Network (Londonderry), and North Down Volunteer Bureau (Bangor).

FINANCES *Year* 1999 *Income* £62,689 *Grants* £77,220 *Assets* £149,593

TRUSTEES Judge Hubert Dunn, Chair; Mrs G Darling; Mrs J Herdman; Mrs D Lindsay; Mrs M Mackie; Mrs A Mckenzie-Hill; Sven Tester; Anthony Watson; Mrs G Moriarty; Mrs C Nelson; J S Barber; Viscount Gough.

HOW TO APPLY In writing to the correspondent, providing full details of the project, with copies of accounts showing simple details of income and expenditure, and a daytime telephone number. The trustees meet four or five times a year and receive many more applications than can be accepted.

WHO TO APPLY TO The Secretary, c/o Voluntary Service Bureau, 24 Shaftesbury Square, Belfast BT2 7DB *Tel* 020 9020 0850 *Fax* 020 9020 0860
CC NO 264843　　　　**ESTABLISHED** 1972

....

■ The Woo Charitable Foundation

WHERE FUNDING CAN BE GIVEN UK.

WHO CAN BENEFIT Arts organisations and schools.

WHAT IS FUNDED Advancement of education through supporting, organising, promoting or assisting the development of the arts in England. Mainly through funding small projects in primary schools which aim to restore arts education (particularly drama and music) where it has been cut out of the national curriculum.

WHAT IS NOT FUNDED No grants for travel, building work and fundraising activities, especially abroad. Support is very rarely given to individuals, but note the above.

RANGE OF GRANTS £5,000–£15,000.

SAMPLE GRANTS £15,000 to Chicken Shed Theatre; £12,000 to Serpentine Gallery for educational activities focusing on the under-12 age group; £11,000 to the Royal Academy towards intensive education projects based on a specifc exhibition; £10,000 each to London Academy of Music and Dramatic Art for the student hardship fund, Greenwich Chinese School towards providing five extra teachers and classes, and Opera North towards workshops in primary and secondary schools; £8,500 to Citizens Theatre towards its youth group; £7,500 to the Centre for Arts and Disability towards the salary of a sculptor tutor; £5,000 each to The Orchesta towards expenses for volunteers, New Addington Musical Project, Poetry Archive and SPEC Jewish Youth & Community Orchestra.

FINANCES *Year* 2000–01 *Income* £406,330 *Grants* £392,973 *Assets* £13,957

TRUSTEES Nelson Woo, Chair; Countess Benckendorff; Nigel Kingsley; Michael Trask; Jackson Woo.

HOW TO APPLY In writing to the correspondent.

WHO TO APPLY TO The Administrator, 277 Green Lanes, London N13 4XS *Tel* 07974 570475 *Fax* 020 7383 5004
CC NO 1050790　　　　**ESTABLISHED** 1995

Think carefully about every application. Is it justified?

....
891

■ Miss Hazel M Wood Charitable Trust

WHERE FUNDING CAN BE GIVEN UK, with possible preferences for Edinburgh, London and the south east of England

WHO CAN BENEFIT Charities concerned with social services and the environment.

WHAT IS FUNDED 'Social services: the trustees have helped homeless people, children and older people. The trustees tend to support the smaller less well-known charities and, where possible, the trustees prefer to contribute towards some specific project or item of equipment. The environment: the trustees help charities working in the "great outdoors" and they also help with the renovation of historic buildings.'

SAMPLE GRANTS £2,500 each to National Trust for Scotland for the Newhailes Appeal and Whizz-Kidz towards a regional mobility scheme (third of four payments); £2,000 each to Amber Foundation towards a double decker bus, New Horizon Youth Centre, Princess Royal Trust for Carers and Sycamore Project for equipment; £1,000 each to The Hebridean Trust towards lighthouse keepers' cottages and Scottish Down's Syndrome Association towards information service costs; £500 to Campberwell Pocket Opera; £200 to Prison Phoenix Trust; £100 to John Muir Birthplace Trust.

FINANCES *Year* 2000–01 *Income* £19,000 *Grants* £35,000

TRUSTEES Miss Hazel M Wood; Ian N MacDonald; Mrs Vanessa J Vasey.

HOW TO APPLY In writing to the correspondent no later than May or November for consideration in June/July and December for payments in July and January.

WHO TO APPLY TO Callum Kennedy, Messrs Lindsays, 11 Atholl Crescent, Edinburgh EH3 8HE *Tel* 0131 229 1212

SC NO sc003658

■ The James Wood Bequest Fund

WHERE FUNDING CAN BE GIVEN Glasgow and the 'central belt of Scotland'.

WHO CAN BENEFIT Registered charities.

WHAT IS FUNDED General charitable purposes. Church of Scotland, historic buildings and other registered charities based in Scotland with preference being given to the central belt.

WHAT IS NOT FUNDED Registered charities only. Grants cannot be made to individuals.

TYPE OF GRANT Capital.

RANGE OF GRANTS £500–£5,000.

FINANCES *Year* 2000 *Grants* £67,000

HOW TO APPLY In writing to the correspondent, including if possible a copy of the latest accounts, a budget for the project, sources of funding received and other relevant financial information. Trustees meet in January, April, July and October. Applications should be received by the preceding month.

WHO TO APPLY TO The Trustees, Messrs Mitchells Roberton, George House, 36 North Hanover Street, Glasgow G1 2AD *Tel* 0141 552 3422

SC NO SC000459

■ The Woodcote Trust

WHERE FUNDING CAN BE GIVEN Woburn Sands and district.

WHO CAN BENEFIT Registered charities and selected individuals and groups, with particular reference to needs of Woburn Sands and district.

WHAT IS FUNDED General charitable purposes.

RANGE OF GRANTS £100–£5,000.

SAMPLE GRANTS £5,000 to Woburn Sands Bowling Club; £2,000 each to British Red Cross Appeals in Kosovo and Turkey; £1,500 to Blue Cross; £1,300 to Barnardos; £1,200 to Leukaemia Research Fund; £1,000 each to Cinnamon Trust, DEGA Project – Aspley Guise, and MS Therapy Centre – Bedford.

FINANCES *Year* 1999–2000 *Income* £47,036 *Grants* £48,400 *Assets* £1,069,804

TRUSTEES C S J Summerlin; M J Summerlin.

HOW TO APPLY In writing to the correspondent.

WHO TO APPLY TO Mrs P M Henstock, Woodcote, Woodside Aspley Guise, Nr Milton Keynes, Buckinghamshire MK17 8EB

CC NO 326090   **ESTABLISHED** 1982

■ Woodlands Green Ltd

WHERE FUNDING CAN BE GIVEN Worldwide.

WHO CAN BENEFIT Organisations benefiting Jewish people.

WHAT IS FUNDED Jewish charities performing educational projects.

WHAT IS NOT FUNDED No grants to individuals, or for expeditions or scholarships.

FINANCES *Year* 1998–99 *Income* £269,619 *Grants* £182,734 *Assets* £1,520,080

TRUSTEES A Ost; E Ost; D J A Ost; J A Ost; A Hepner.

HOW TO APPLY In writing to the correspondent.

WHO TO APPLY TO A Ost, Trustee, 19 Green Walk, London NW4 2AL

CC NO 277299   **ESTABLISHED** 1979

■ Woodlands Trust (1015942)

WHERE FUNDING CAN BE GIVEN Worldwide.

WHO CAN BENEFIT Organisations benefiting Christians.

WHAT IS FUNDED To support church and missionary work, preaching and teaching the gospel.

TYPE OF GRANT Non-recurring.

SAMPLE GRANTS £19,600 (in four grants) to The Living Well Trust; £10,000 to Borders Christian Fellowship; £3,000 to Highwood Theological College – Library Project; £2,700 to Nazarene Theological College; £1,000 to Borderline Pregnancy Counselling.

FINANCES *Year* 1999–2000 *Income* £142,000 *Grants* £39,000 *Assets* £138,004

TRUSTEES E Stobart; W Stobart; E P Stobart; Revd J McAllen; I B Thomas.

HOW TO APPLY In writing to the correspondent. Unsolicited applications will not receive a response.

WHO TO APPLY TO I B Thomas, 33 Longlands Road, Carlisle CA3 9AD

CC NO 1015942   **ESTABLISHED** 1992

■ Woodlands Trust (259569)

WHERE FUNDING CAN BE GIVEN West Midlands, Warwickshire, London within the boundaries of the M25.

WHO CAN BENEFIT Organisations benefiting young adults and older people; at risk groups; carers;

disabled people; people disadvantaged by poverty; ex-offenders and those at risk of offending; homeless people; people living in rural and urban areas; socially isolated people; refugees; victims of abuse, crime or domestic violence.

WHAT IS FUNDED Preference to charities which the trust has special interest in, knowledge of, or association with. Particularly charities working in the fields of hospice at home; respite care and care for carers; support and self-help groups; woodlands and horticulture.

WHAT IS NOT FUNDED No grant for the cost of buildings (only furnishings, equipment and alterations to existing buildings to comply with health and safety regulations). No grants to individuals.

TYPE OF GRANT Core costs, one-off, project, research, running costs, recurring costs, salaries and start-up costs. Funding of up to three years will be considered.

RANGE OF GRANTS £500–£4,000.

SAMPLE GRANTS £4,000 to Oasis – London SE1 towards the salary of a residential support worker and the running costs of the mobile unit; £3,000 to The Basement Project towards their drug awareness outreach work; £2,000 each to Fairbridge Midlands for bursaries to allow young black people to attend a programme to increase their education, employability and community involvement, Pravasi Mandal – Wellingborough to landscape the garden area surrounding the day centre, Extra-Care Coventry towards equipment and a greenhouse at a Wolverhampton home for older people, Addaction – Walthamstow for the Bank Day Programme, RNIB – Midlands and Anglia, Shaw Trust – Opening Doors and Rugby Mayday Trust; £1,500 each to Mencap Birmingham and Sense – Midlands for Kingstanding bungalows.

FINANCES *Year* 1999–2000 *Income* £103,000 *Grants* £74,000 *Assets* £2,300,000

TRUSTEES J D W Field; J C Barratt; Miss J M Steele; Mrs R M Bagshaw; Mrs J N Houston.

HOW TO APPLY In writing to the correspondent. The trust administrator will only enter into correspondence if: (a) further information is required concerning the appeal; and (b) the appeal has been placed on the trustees' next agenda. Notification will then be given as to the trustees' decision. The trustees meet to consider applications in March and September each year, and applications should be submitted in January and July.

WHO TO APPLY TO The Trust Administrator, Box W, White Horse Court, 25c North Street, Bishop's Stortford, Hertfordshire CM23 2LD *Fax* 01279 657626 *E-mail* charities@pothecary.co.uk

CC NO 259569   **ESTABLISHED** 1969

■ The Woodroffe Benton Foundation

WHERE FUNDING CAN BE GIVEN UK.

WHO CAN BENEFIT Registered charities only.

WHAT IS FUNDED Financial assistance in times of disaster on behalf of individuals in need within the UK through registered charitable bodies; accommodation and housing; promotion of education – especially through scholarships at Queen Elizabeth Grammar School in Ashbourne; conservation and environment; and community services and facilities.

WHAT IS NOT FUNDED Grants are not made outside the UK and are only made to registered charities. No grants to individuals. Branches of

UK charities should not apply as grants, if made, would go to the charity's headquarters.

TYPE OF GRANT Starter finances, recurrent, research, project, one-off, core costs, feasibility studies and running costs. Funding is available for one year or less.

RANGE OF GRANTS Normally between £500 and £1,500.

SAMPLE GRANTS Calibre, Community Links, Queen Elizabeth's Grammar School – Ashbourne, and Victim Support.

FINANCES *Year* 2002 *Income* £181,000 *Grants* £151,850 *Assets* £4,518,000

TRUSTEES James Hope; Kenneth Stoneley; Colin Russell; Miss Celia Clout; Peter Foster; Tony Shadrack.

HOW TO APPLY On a form available from the correspondent. Full guidance notes on completing the form and procedures for processing applications are sent with the form.

WHO TO APPLY TO Alan King, 16 Fernleigh Court, Harrow, London HA2 6NA *Tel* 020 8421 4120 *E-mail* alan.king3@which.net

CC NO 1075272   **ESTABLISHED** 1988

■ The Geoffrey Woods Charitable Foundation

WHERE FUNDING CAN BE GIVEN UK and overseas.

WHO CAN BENEFIT Grants are now only given to charities nominated by members of the Girdler's Company who are involved with that charity and who make a donation to the foundation.

WHAT IS FUNDED The objects of the foundation are the advancement of education and religion and the relief of poverty.

TYPE OF GRANT One-off and capital grants. Special projects preferred.

RANGE OF GRANTS From under £1,000–£30,000

SAMPLE GRANTS In 1996–97: £30,000 to London Federation of Clubs for Young People; £10,000 each to Garden School (third of three), Almshouse Association, Westminster Abbey Choir School; £6,000 to Surrey County Cricket Board, LCCA initiative; £5,600 to Cordwainers College; £5,000 each to Crown and Manor Boys Club (second of three), Kings College Cambridge, All Saints Cathedral – Nairobi, National Spinal Injuries Unit (fourth of five) and Queen Elizabeth Foundation for the Disabled (second of three).

FINANCES *Year* 2000–01 *Grants* £64,000

TRUSTEES The Girdlers Company; N K Maitland; A J R Fairclough.

HOW TO APPLY 'Beneficiaries are nominated by members of the company and outside applications are no longer considered.'

WHO TO APPLY TO The Clerk, The Girdlers Company, Girdlers Hall, Basinghall Avenue, London EC2V 5DD *Tel* 020 7638 0488

CC NO 248205   **ESTABLISHED** 1966

■ The Woodward Trust

WHERE FUNDING CAN BE GIVEN Unrestricted.

WHO CAN BENEFIT Registered charities.

WHAT IS FUNDED Arts, community and social welfare (including children's summer holiday schemes), disability, health, education, environment. Priority to a few charitable causes of which the trustees have personal knowledge, and smaller-scale, locally based initiatives.

WHAT IS NOT FUNDED The trustees are unable to respond to: standard appeals; general appeals from large national charities; requests for small contributions to large appeals; medical research; individuals; student support; course fees; expedition costs; hospices; parish facilities; homework clubs; overseas projects.

TYPE OF GRANT Usually one-off.

RANGE OF GRANTS £1,000 or less, rarely more than £5,000.

SAMPLE GRANTS £200,000 to English National Opera; £100,000 to National Portrait Gallery; £25,000 each to ChildLine, and Dragon School Trust Ltd; £10,500 to Oxfordshire Mind; £10,000 each to Home-Start UK, Trialogue Educational Trust, and Youth Sport Trust; £8,350 to Oxfordshire Association for Young People; £6,100 to Brandon Centre for Counselling and Psychotherapy for Young People.

FINANCES *Year* 2000–01 *Income* £506,437 *Grants* £548,813 *Assets* £11,187,779

TRUSTEES Camilla Woodward; Shaun A Woodward MP; Miss Judith Portrait.

OTHER INFORMATION The trust is one of the Sainsbury Family Charitable Trusts which share a common administration. An application to one is taken as an application to all.

HOW TO APPLY On simple application forms available from the trust, or downloadable from the website. Potential applicants are invited to telephone Karin Hooper in advance to discuss the advisability of making an application. Main grants are allocated following trustees' meetings in January and July each year, with the exception of summer schemes, which are considered at the beginning of May each year. All application forms are assessed on arrival and if additional information is required you will be contacted further. Applicants must make sure the trust receives a project budget and audited accounts.

WHO TO APPLY TO Michael Pattison, Director, Allington House, 1st Floor, 150 Victoria Street, London SW1E 5AE *Tel* 020 7410 0330 *Website* www.woodwardcharitabletrust.org.uk

CC NO 299963   **ESTABLISHED** 1988

■ The A & R Woolf Charitable Trust

WHERE FUNDING CAN BE GIVEN Worldwide; UK, mainly in Hertfordshire.

WHO CAN BENEFIT Registered charities and voluntary organisations only. Sundry charitable organisations and institutions which are registered charities or of similar standing and which are personally known, or of personal interest, to the trustees.

WHAT IS FUNDED General charitable purposes.

WHAT IS NOT FUNDED No grants to individuals or non-registered charities unless schools, hospices and so on.

RANGE OF GRANTS £100–£5,000.

SAMPLE GRANTS £20,000 to UNICEF; £6,000 to Anglo Israel Association; £5,000 each to University of Hertfordshire and the British Diabetic Association; £3,000 to Peace Hospital; £2,500 to Golf Foundation; £1,000 each to WWF UK, RSPCA, Council of Christians and Jews and Feltonfleet School Trust Ltd.

FINANCES *Year* 1999–2000 *Income* £66,000 *Grants* £58,000 *Assets* £2,100,000

TRUSTEES Mrs J D H Rose; C Rose; Dr G L Edmonds; S Rose; A Rose.

HOW TO APPLY Support is only given to projects/organisations/causes personally known to the trustees. The trust does not respond to unsolicited applications.

WHO TO APPLY TO Mrs J D H Rose, Trustee, 2 Oak House, 101 Ducks Hill Road, Northwood, Middlesex HA6 2WQ

CC NO 273079   **ESTABLISHED** 1977

■ The Woolnoth Society Charitable Trust

WHERE FUNDING CAN BE GIVEN Greater London.

WHO CAN BENEFIT Local organisations and smaller charities benefiting children, at risk groups, and people who are disadvantaged by poverty, homeless or socially isolated.

WHAT IS FUNDED Welfare, housing, relief in need, community health groups, facilities for children in their local communities.

RANGE OF GRANTS £500–£3,000.

SAMPLE GRANTS £5,000 to Barnardos; £3,600 to North Brixton Trust; £3,500 to Union Chapel; £3,000 to St Botolph's Project; £2,000 each to Hoxton Health, Tower Hamlets Opportunity Group and Motor Neurone Disease; £1,500 to Havering Women's Aid; £1,000 to First City of London Scout Group; £650 to Spitalfields City Farm.

FINANCES *Year* 2000 *Income* £51,000 *Grants* £45,000

TRUSTEES M Barnett; Dr D McMullan; I Cormack; J Howles; H M D Woolley; N De Berry; J Ruzicka; R Parkinson; J O'Driscoll.

HOW TO APPLY In writing to the correspondent.

WHO TO APPLY TO D J McMullan, Trustee, c/o Bank of America, 1 Alie Street, London E1 8DE *Tel* 020 7634 4282 *E-mail* skip.mcmullen@bankofamerica.com

CC NO 274008   **ESTABLISHED** 1977

■ Worcester Municipal Charities (incorporating Worcester Consolidated Municipal Charity and Worcester Municipal Exhibitions Foundation)

WHERE FUNDING CAN BE GIVEN The city of Worcester.

WHO CAN BENEFIT Poorer people, individually or generally, in Worcester City.

WHAT IS FUNDED Grants to relieve need. Purchase of household equipment, clothes, food and so on, help with bills. Donations to organisations who help poorer people. Grants to poorer students.

WHAT IS NOT FUNDED No grants to organisations of over 49% of their annual income. No grants to individuals unless all statutory sources have been exhausted. Requests for furniture (except bunk beds) are referred to the 'Armchair Project'. Requests for clothes are referred to the 'Lydia Project'.

TYPE OF GRANT Cheque or purchase of item.

RANGE OF GRANTS £1,000–£35,000 for running costs; £100–£100,000 for capital costs; £50–£1,000 for individuals.

SAMPLE GRANTS In 2000: £135,000 to Worcestershire Lifestyle for a new workshop; £107,000 to Age Concern for a new charity shop. (Both of these grants brought properties which remain an asset of the trust but provide low-cost premises for the organisation.); £35,000 (in two grants) to The Salvation Army for outreach projects; £30,000 to Citizens Advice Bureau; £25,000 to Worcestershire Association for the Blind towards a new resource centre; £12,000 to Perdiswell Young People's Leisure Club to extend the premises; £8,200 each to Ethnic Access Link Scheme and

Maggs Day Centre; £7,700 to Worcester Racial Equality Co; £6,500 to Shopmobility; £5,000 to Age Concern Handyman Service.

FINANCES *Year* 2001 *Income* £655,000 *Grants* £468,000 *Assets* £7,740,518

TRUSTEES Paul Griffith, Chair; Roger Berry; Dave Clifford; Philip Hytch; Margaret Jones; Bob Kington; Cliff Lord; Barry McKenzie-Williams; Irene Mapp; Rob Peachey; Martyn Saunders; Brenda Sheridan; Ray Turner; Brian Whitmore.

HOW TO APPLY In writing to the correspondent requesting an application form.

WHO TO APPLY TO Mrs Mary Barker, Hallmarks, 4–5 Sansome Place, Worcester WR1 1UQ *Tel* 01905 726600 *Fax* 01905 613302 *E-mail* mb@hallmarkslaw.co.uk

CC NO 205299   **ESTABLISHED** 1836

■ The Worcestershire & Dudley Historic Churches Trust

WHERE FUNDING CAN BE GIVEN The diocese and county of Worcester.

WHO CAN BENEFIT Christian churches.

WHAT IS FUNDED The trust gives grants for the preservation, repair and improvement of churches in the beneficial area and of the monuments, fittings and furniture etc., of such churches.

WHAT IS NOT FUNDED No grants for new building projects or bells.

TYPE OF GRANT £500–£5,000.

FINANCES *Year* 2001 *Income* £50,000 *Grants* £52,000

HOW TO APPLY In writing to the correspondent.

WHO TO APPLY TO J A Lakeman, Secretary, Westlyn Old Farm, Stockton Road, Abberley, Worcestershire WR6 6AS *Tel* 01299 896846 *Fax* 01299 896390 *E-mail* johnlakeman@abberley.co.uk

CC NO 1035156   **ESTABLISHED** 1993

■ The Fred & Della Worms Charitable Trust

WHERE FUNDING CAN BE GIVEN UK.

WHO CAN BENEFIT Jewish organisations, education and the arts.

WHAT IS FUNDED General charitable purposes, but in practice almost all of the money goes to Jewish organisations.

WHAT IS NOT FUNDED No grants to individuals.

TYPE OF GRANT One-off grants.

SAMPLE GRANTS £65,000 to British Friends of the Art Museums of Israel; £26,000 to Joint Jewish Charitable Trust; £20,700 to British Friends of the Hebrew University; £17,250 to Moccali Union; £17,000 to British Friends of Rabbi Steinsaltz; £7,000 to Child Resettlement Fund; £5,000 each to B'nai B'rith Hillel Foundation, and European Jewish Publication Society; £1,250 to Jewish National Fund; £1,150 to United Synagogue Hampstead Garden Suburb.

FINANCES *Year* 2001–02 *Income* £86,125 *Grants* £187,284 *Assets* £1,963,662

TRUSTEES Mrs D Worms; M D Paisner; F S Worms.

HOW TO APPLY In writing to the correspondent. The trust stated that its funds are fully committed.

WHO TO APPLY TO The Trustees, 23 Highpoint, North Hill, London N6 4BA *Tel* 020 8342 5360 *Fax* 020 8342 5359 *E-mail* fred@worms5.freeserve.co.uk

CC NO 200036   **ESTABLISHED** 1961

■ The Worshipful Company of Chartered Accountants General Charitable Trust (also known as CALC – Chartered Accountant Livery Charity)

WHERE FUNDING CAN BE GIVEN UK.

WHO CAN BENEFIT Registered charities and voluntary organisations.

WHAT IS FUNDED At least one theme directly or indirectly of relevance to the work of the profession (chosen by the master on their appointment in October of each year). Other recommendations and proposals put to the trustees by members of the Livery.

RANGE OF GRANTS Up to £20,000, but mostly £1,000–£5,000.

SAMPLE GRANTS £20,000 to The Place to Be; £10,000 to The Beacon Community Cancer Palliative Care Centre; £9,030 to Guildhall School of Music for scholarship; £9,000 to Jubilee Primary School; £6,200 to Royal Albert Dock Trust; £5,000 to Foxhill and Birley Carr Live at Home Scheme; £3,302 to VSO; £3,000 to Chartered Accountants in the Community; £2,600 to Windlesham Village Primary School – Surrey; £2,500 to Robert Ferguson School – Cumbria.

FINANCES *Year* 2000–01 *Income* £122,678 *Grants* £114,192 *Assets* £933,488

TRUSTEES D P J Ross; M N Peterson; J M Renshall; Sir Jeremy Hanley; Miss M A Yale; M J Richardson; A M C Staniforth; W I D Plaistowe.

HOW TO APPLY Applications must be sponsored by a liveryman of the company.

WHO TO APPLY TO M R Hardman, Oak House, 38 Botley Road, Chasham, Buckinghamshire HP5 1XG *Tel* 01494 783402 *Fax* 01494 793306 *E-mail* michael_hardman@bigfoot.com

CC NO 327681   **ESTABLISHED** 1988

■ The Worshipful Company of Founders Charities

WHERE FUNDING CAN BE GIVEN England.

WHO CAN BENEFIT Individuals (including needy dependants of members of the company or people in the foundry industry) and organisations. Medical professionals, students, volunteers, disabled people, Christians, Church of England and Quakers may also be supported.

WHAT IS FUNDED Appeals connected with the foundry industry, and the education and support of young or older people. Accommodation and housing, infrastructure development, hospice at home, respite care, hospices, holidays and outings will be considered.

WHAT IS NOT FUNDED No grants to national appeals and larger charities.

TYPE OF GRANT One-off. Funding is available for up to three years.

RANGE OF GRANTS £200–£1,000.

SAMPLE GRANTS £1,500 each in bursaries for studying materials engineering at the universities including Birmingham and Nottingham.

FINANCES *Year* 2001 *Income* £40,000 *Grants* £40,000

TRUSTEES The Master Wardens and Commonalty of the Founders.

HOW TO APPLY Before the end of May in each year.

WHO TO APPLY TO The Clerk, Founders' Hall, 1 Cloth Fair, London EC2Y 8DL

CC NO 222905   **ESTABLISHED** 1365

■ The Worwin UK Foundation

WHERE FUNDING CAN BE GIVEN UK and overseas.
WHO CAN BENEFIT Registered charities.
WHAT IS FUNDED General charitable purposes.
FINANCES *Year* 2000–01 *Income* £363,531
Grants £319,887 *Assets* £14,487
TRUSTEES William Hew John Hancock; Brian Moore;
Mark Musgrave; Andrew Jonathan Hughes
Penney; David John Marcus Ward.
HOW TO APPLY The foundation makes its own
arrangements for making grants and does not
seek applications.
WHO TO APPLY TO D J M Ward, Trustee, 6 St Andrew
Street, London EC4A 3LX *Tel* 020 7427 6400
CC NO 1037981   **ESTABLISHED** 1994

■ The Diana Edgson Wright Charitable Trust

WHERE FUNDING CAN BE GIVEN UK with some
preference for Kent.
WHO CAN BENEFIT Registered charities.
WHAT IS FUNDED General charitable purposes. The
policy is to support a small number of charities.
RANGE OF GRANTS £100–£12,000.
SAMPLE GRANTS 1999: £12,000 to Sustainable
London Trust; £3,000 to Charing Parochial
Church Council; £1,500 each to British Red
Cross – Ashford branch, Hospice on the Hill
Pilgrim's Appeal and Little Chart Village Hall;
£1,250 each to Little Chart (Kent) Parochial
Church Council and St Luke's Hospital for the
Clergy; £1,000 each to Dumfries & Galloway
Action, Mammal Society, National Coastwatch
Institution and St Dunstans.
FINANCES *Year* 2001 *Income* £40,996
TRUSTEES R H V Moorhead; P Edgson Wright; H C D
Moorhead.
HOW TO APPLY In writing to the correspondent.
WHO TO APPLY TO R H V Moorhead, Trustee, 2 Stade
Street, Hythe, Kent CT21 6BD *Tel* 01303
262525
CC NO 327737   **ESTABLISHED** 1987

■ Miss E B Wrightson's Charitable Settlement

WHERE FUNDING CAN BE GIVEN UK.
WHO CAN BENEFIT Individuals and organisations
involved in projects connected to music,
recreation and inshore rescue.
WHAT IS FUNDED The advancement of music
education and recreation; inshore rescue.
FINANCES *Year* 2000–01 *Income* £54,258
Grants £44,700 *Assets* £1,856,842
TRUSTEES A Callard; Mrs E Clarke; P Dorkings.
HOW TO APPLY In writing to the correspondent.
Trustees meet regularly to consider applications
and 'all properly completed applications are
acknowledged'. Guidelines are provided by the
trust for applications by individuals, but not
organisations.
WHO TO APPLY TO Mrs N Hickman, Swangles Farm,
Cold Christmas, Hertfordshire SG12 7SP
E-mail norahhickman@henryhickman.com
CC NO 1002147

■ The Matthews Wrightson Charity Trust

WHERE FUNDING CAN BE GIVEN UK and some
overseas.
WHO CAN BENEFIT Smaller charitable projects
concerned with young adults, students, ex-
offenders and those at risk of offending; and
church-based projects.
WHAT IS FUNDED The trustees favour smaller
charitable projects seeking to raise under
£25,000, with a bias towards youth, Christian
work and organisations helping the
disadvantaged reintegrate into the community,
including residential facilities and services,
crime prevention schemes, and training for
community and personal development for
individuals such as those going abroad to do
charitable work, and other charitable purposes.
Unusual ideas within the guidelines often catch
the trustees' eye. About 15% of up to 100
applicants a month receive grants.
WHAT IS NOT FUNDED No support for individuals
(other than visitors from abroad) seeking
education or adventure for personal character
improvement. No support for unconnected local
churches, village halls, schools and animal
charities. Charities with a turnover of over
£250,000 are generally not considered, most
grants are to organisations seeking, or with a
turnover of less than, £25,000. Individuals
seeking funding for 'self-improvement' education
are not favoured.
TYPE OF GRANT One-off cash grants, on annual
basis. Core costs are preferred to projects.
RANGE OF GRANTS Average grant size £400.
SAMPLE GRANTS £14,000 to Royal College of Arts
for the Hardship and Industrial Production
Awards; £1,200 each to Children's Family Trust,
Demand and Peper Harow Foundation; £1,000
to Garden History Society; £800 each to ITDG,
New Bridge, Penrose Housing Association, Pro
Corda Trust and Yeldall Christian Centres.
FINANCES *Year* 2002 *Income* £67,258
Grants £93,300 *Assets* £1,315,742
TRUSTEES Miss Priscilla W Wrightson; Anthony H
Isaacs; Guy D G Wrightson; Miss Isabelle S
White.
OTHER INFORMATION Gifts are made in small units
(£400 for 2003), with a few larger gifts deriving
specifically from old connections.
HOW TO APPLY In writing to the correspondent. No
special forms are used, although latest financial
accounts are desirable. One or two sheets
(usually the covering letter) are circulated
monthly to the trustees, who meet every six
months only for policy and administrative
decisions. Replies are only sent to successful
applicants; allow up to three months for an
answer. Please include an sae if an answer to
an unsuccessful application is required. The
trust receives over 1,000 applications a year;
'winners have to make the covering letter more
attractive than the 90 others received each
month'.
WHO TO APPLY TO Adam Lee, Secretary &
Administrator, The Farm, Northington, Alresford,
Hampshire SO24 9TH
CC NO 262109   **ESTABLISHED** 1970

■ Wychdale Ltd

WHERE FUNDING CAN BE GIVEN UK.
WHO CAN BENEFIT Jewish people.
WHAT IS FUNDED Jewish educational institutions.
WHAT IS NOT FUNDED Non-Jewish organisations are
not supported.

SAMPLE GRANTS £49,903 to Bobover Yeshiva Bnei Zion; £19,000 to UTA; £15,036 to Breslov Yeshiva; £8,000 to Kollel Bobover; £4,000 each to Slabodke Yeshiva Trust and Yetv Lev Jerusalem; £2,000 to Yetev Lev Synagogue; £1,650 to Yeshiva Shaar Hasomayim; £1,000 each to Achdut and Beis Nadvorne.

FINANCES *Year* 2000–01 *Income* £48,642 *Grants* £110,930 *Assets* £279,861

TRUSTEES C D Schlaff; J Schlaff; Mrs Z Schlaff.

HOW TO APPLY In writing to the correspondent.

WHO TO APPLY TO The Secretary, 4–6 Windus Mews, Windus Road, London N16 6UP

CC NO 267447   **ESTABLISHED** 1974

■ Wychville Ltd

WHERE FUNDING CAN BE GIVEN UK.

WHO CAN BENEFIT Organisations benefiting Jewish people.

WHAT IS FUNDED Jewish organisations and general charitable purposes.

FINANCES *Year* 2000–01 *Income* £173,606 *Grants* £167,415 *Assets* £100,174

TRUSTEES B Englander, Chair; Mrs S Englander; E Englander; Mrs B R Englander.

HOW TO APPLY In writing to the correspondent.

WHO TO APPLY TO Berisch Englander, Governor, 44 Leweston Place, London N16 6RH

CC NO 267584   **ESTABLISHED** 1973

■ The Wyndham Charitable Trust

WHERE FUNDING CAN BE GIVEN UK and developing countries.

WHO CAN BENEFIT Charitable organisations.

WHAT IS FUNDED General charitable purposes.

WHAT IS NOT FUNDED No grants to organisations not known to the trustees, or to any individuals.

RANGE OF GRANTS £10–£7,400.

SAMPLE GRANTS £7,400 to Anti-Slavery International; £1,500 to Christian Aid; £1,300 to Cancer Research UK; £700 to International Glaucoma Association; £250 each to Liverpool School of Tropical Medicine and Cord Blood Charity.

FINANCES *Year* 2001–02 *Income* £24,804 *Grants* £23,465

TRUSTEES John Gaselee; Juliet Gaselee.

HOW TO APPLY In writing to the correspondent. The trust stated that unsolicited applications are unlikely to be supported and they do not encourage requests.

WHO TO APPLY TO J Gaselee, Trustee, 16 Shouldham Street, London W1H 5FL
Website uk.geocities.com/wyndham_ct

CC NO 259313   **ESTABLISHED** 1969

■ The Wyseliot Charitable Trust

WHERE FUNDING CAN BE GIVEN UK.

WHO CAN BENEFIT Registered charities only.

WHAT IS FUNDED Medical, especially cancer research and care; welfare; arts organisations, including music, visual arts and literature.

WHAT IS NOT FUNDED Local charities are not supported. No support for individuals.

RANGE OF GRANTS £1,000–£5,000.

SAMPLE GRANTS £5,000 to Prostate Cancer Charity; £3,500 each to Enham Trust, Macmillan Cancer Relief, and Time and Talents Association; £3,000 each to Marie Curie Cancer Care, NH Church Homeless Concern, Notting Hill Housing Trust, St Mungo's, and Winged Fellowship; £2,500 to Avenues Youth Project.

FINANCES *Year* 2001–02 *Income* £89,109 *Grants* £92,500 *Assets* £2,114,324

TRUSTEES E A D Rose; J H Rose; A E G Raphael.

HOW TO APPLY In writing to the correspondent; however, note that the trust states that the same charities are supported each year, with perhaps one or two changes. It is unlikely new charties sending circular appeals will be supported and large UK charities are generally not supported.

WHO TO APPLY TO J H Rose, Trustee, 17 Chelsea Square, London SW3 6LF

CC NO 257219   **ESTABLISHED** 1968

■ The Xerox (UK) Trust

WHERE FUNDING CAN BE GIVEN UK.

WHO CAN BENEFIT Usually local or mid-sized organisations benefiting children, young adults, at risk groups, and people who are disabled, disadvantaged by poverty or socially isolated.

WHAT IS FUNDED The advancement of equality of opportunity, working with people who are disabled, disadvantaged or terminally ill; and young people.

WHAT IS NOT FUNDED No grants to individuals, religious or political organisations or national bodies.

TYPE OF GRANT One-off grants.

RANGE OF GRANTS £2,500–£20,000.

SAMPLE GRANTS £20,000 to Hillingdon Trust; £5,000 each to Asian Awareness of MS, South Buckinghamshire NHS Trust, and Watford Peace Memorial; £2,500 each to Detached Youth Work Project, Douglas House Children's Trust, Dream Holidays, Loch Lomond, Royal School for the Blind, and Royal School for the Deaf.

FINANCES *Year* 1999 *Income* £66,333 *Grants* £70,500 *Assets* £739,472

TRUSTEES S W Pantling; Mrs J M Robertson; J Hopwood.

HOW TO APPLY In writing to the correspondent, preferably supported by a Xerox employee. Applications are considered in April and October, for payment in June and December respectively.

WHO TO APPLY TO Jacqueline Robertson, Xerox Ltd, Bridge House, Oxford Road, Uxbridge UB8 1HS *Tel* 01895 251133

CC NO 284698   **ESTABLISHED** 1982

■ The Yamanouchi European Foundation

WHERE FUNDING CAN BE GIVEN Worldwide.

WHO CAN BENEFIT Scientific research institutes, universities, research workers and medical professionals.

WHAT IS FUNDED Long-term support of basic medical and related scientific programmes; selected short, medium and long-term projects aimed at integrating basic science and clinical research; the support of educational lectures and discussions to promote or sponsor exchange of views; general charitable purposes.

SAMPLE GRANTS US$75,000 to Departimento di Medicina Interna Universita di Pisa as the second of two grants; US$75,000 to Department of Oncology at Helsinki University Central Hospital as the first of two grants; US$30,000 to a doctor of SIU for a lectureship; US$10,000 each to Brauninger Stiftung GmbH Online Mouse Projekt, Connaître Les Syndromes Cérébelleux, and Chase Childrens Hospice; US$7,500 each to Foundation Sance for the Department of Hematooncology, Pediatric Faculty Hospital – Olomouc, Stichting VTV and Comitato Maria Letizia Verga.

FINANCES *Year* 2000–01 *Income* $774,300 *Grants* $265,020 *Assets* $11,865,039

TRUSTEES Dr Toichi Takenaka, Chair; Yasuo Ishii; Philippe Ballero; Masayoshi Onoda; Joseph F Harford; Dudley H Ferguson; Prof. Peter van Brummeley; Toshinari Tamura; Dr Nick Matthews.

HOW TO APPLY In writing to the correspondent.

WHO TO APPLY TO D Ferguson, Trustee, Yamanouchi House, Pyrford Road, West Byfleet, Surrey KT14 6RA *Tel* 01932 345535

CC NO 1036344　　　　**ESTABLISHED** 1993

■ The Yapp Charitable Trust

WHERE FUNDING CAN BE GIVEN UK.

WHO CAN BENEFIT It is the trustees' policy to focus their support on smaller charities (local rather than UK), and to offer grants only in situations where a small grant will make a significant difference. The trust therefore only considers applications from charities whose normal turnover is less than £75,000 in the year of application. Grants are only made to applicants who have charitable status. Applicants who do not have a Charity Registration Number (in England and Wales) or an Inland Revenue Approved Number (in Scotland and Northern Ireland) will need to provide evidence that they have charitable objectives.

WHAT IS FUNDED Older people; children and young people; people with disabilities or mental health problems; moral welfare, e.g. people trying to overcome life-limiting problems such as addiction, relationship difficulties, abuse or a history of offending; education and learning (including lifelong learning); and scientific or medical research.

WHAT IS NOT FUNDED Grants are only made to organisations with charitable status. The following are not supported: individuals, including students undertaking research, expeditions or gap year projects and charities raising funds to purchase equipment for individuals; groups that do not have their own charity registration number or exemption – students' hostels and youth hostels are therefore usually not eligible; fundraising groups raising money to benefit another organisation such as a hospital or school. In March 2002 the trust introduced the following exclusions due to a large number of applications. The trust hopes to lift these in the future: work with under-five's; childcare; holidays and holiday centres; core funding of general community facilities such as community centres and village halls; capital expenditure, such as buildings, renovations, extentions, furnishings, equipment or minibuses.

TYPE OF GRANT Grants are given towards running costs and salaries but not capital equipment. Recurrent grants for up to three years may be considered.

RANGE OF GRANTS Grants ranged from £800–£12,000 but on average were for around £2,000.

SAMPLE GRANTS £12,000 (over three years) to Three Churches Youth Project – Coventry; £9,000 (over three years) to Coventry Refugee Centre; £7,000 each (over three years) to Liveline, UK East African Women and Children Group, Youth Link and Africa People's Link; £6,000 each (over 2–3 years) to Sahara Communities Abroad, Soundabout, Rape and Abuse Line, and Agape Family Support.

FINANCES *Year* 2000–01 *Income* £319,000 *Grants* £299,000 *Assets* £5,300,000

TRUSTEES Revd Timothy C Brooke; Peter R Davies; Peter G Murray; Miss Alison J Norman; Peter M Williams.

OTHER INFORMATION The Yapp Welfare Trust (two-thirds share) and The Yapp Education and Research Trust (one-third share) merged in September 1999 to become The Yapp Charitable Trust.

HOW TO APPLY On a form available from the administrator. Applicants may request a form by e-mail in Word 97 format if preferred, although all applications must be sent by post. The only document that will be read by all the trustees is the application form. It is therefore important that applicants complete every section. Applicants uncertain whether they are eligible or how to complete the form should contact the administrator for advice. Applications must include most recent accounts, and annual reports and newsletters are also appreciated, although the trust does not like bulky reports or specialist or technical documents. Closing dates for applications are 31 January, 31 May and 30 September for consideration about six weeks later, and notification around two weeks after this. Applications are all acknowledged, and all applicants hear the outcome after the trustees' meeting. In the case of successful applicants, this normally takes about two weeks as the letters are accompanied by grant cheques which take a little time to prepare and circulate for signature. Late applications will be considered at the following meeting.

WHO TO APPLY TO Mrs Margaret Thompson, Administrator, 47a Paris Road, Scholes, Holmfirth HD9 1SY *Tel* 01484 683403 *Fax* 01484 683403 *E-mail* info@yappcharitabletrust.org.uk *Website* www.yappcharitabletrust.org.uk

CC NO 1076803　　　　**ESTABLISHED** 1999

■ The Yardley Great Trust

WHERE FUNDING CAN BE GIVEN The ancient parish of Yardley now part of the County of West Midlands. This includes the wards of Yardley, Acocks Green, Fox Hollies, Billesley, Hall Green and parts of the wards of Hodge Hill, Shard End, Sheldon, Small Heath, Sparkhill, Moseley, Stechford, Sparkbrook and Brandwood. (A map is available on request.)

WHO CAN BENEFIT Individuals and organisations benefiting people of all ages in the ancient parish of Yardley in Birmingham.

WHAT IS FUNDED Individuals in need, hardship or distress. Projects which benefit the community, particularly charities working in the fields of support for voluntary and community organisations, community centres and village halls, community transport, day centres, holidays and outings, meals provision and playschemes.

TYPE OF GRANT Usually one-off. Buildings, capital, feasibility studies, project and start-up costs funded for one year or less will be considered.

RANGE OF GRANTS No limit.

SAMPLE GRANTS £15,000 to St Christopher's Project to provide a community centre for disadvantaged people in the Springfield area; £2,200 to Yardley Grange Nursing Home for equipment for residents; £2,000 to Midlands Ethnic Albanian Foundation to help the needs of refugees in the area; £1,300 to Greswood House Leisure Fund to provide holidays for residents; £1,000 each to Brays School to assist young people who are severely disabled, Green Apple Crafts to help provide leisure activities for people in need and Youthwise to aid their work in reaching disaffected young people; £650 to Rathbone Society to help people with learning difficulties.

FINANCES *Year* 2000 *Income* £1,600,000 *Grants* £83,000 *Assets* £5,900,000

TRUSTEES Mrs I Aylin, Chair; A Beach; A J Boden; Revd J Ray; Mrs J Holt; C James; R B W Lowndes; K Rollins; Revd J Tyndall; Revd Canon R H Postill; Revd J Self; Revd J Richards; Revd D Senior; Cllr Mrs T J Stewart.

HOW TO APPLY On a form available from the correspondent. Applications from individuals should be via a third party.

WHO TO APPLY TO Mrs V K Slayter, Clerk to the Trustees, Old Brookside, Yardley Fields Road, Stechford, Birmingham B33 8QL *Tel* 0121 784 7889 *Fax* 0121 785 1386

CC NO 216082   **ESTABLISHED** 1300

■ The W Wing Yip & Bros Charitable Trust

WHERE FUNDING CAN BE GIVEN Birmingham, Manchester, Croydon and Cricklewood.

WHO CAN BENEFIT Chinese organisations benefiting children, young adults, students and people disadvantaged by poverty.

WHAT IS FUNDED Chinese organisations especially those concerned with education, relief of poverty, Chinese students, and education of Chinese children living in the above stated areas.

WHAT IS NOT FUNDED No grants to individuals.

TYPE OF GRANT One-off, project and start-up costs. Funding for up to two years will be considered.

RANGE OF GRANTS £50–£1,900; typically £250.

SAMPLE GRANTS In 1998–99: £11,000 to China Flood Relief; £2,468 for a medical student's tuition fees; £2,000 to the Birmingham Chinese School; £400 to CSV Environmental; £300 to The Mayor of Croydon Charity Appeal; £200 to Aston Community Youth Project; £200 to Whizz-Kidz.

FINANCES *Year* 1999–2000 *Income* £104,000 *Grants* £190,000 *Assets* £787,000

TRUSTEES R A Brittain; W Wing Yip; G Ying Yap; L Sing Yap; J C J Orchard.

HOW TO APPLY In writing to the correspondent.

WHO TO APPLY TO R A Brittain, Trustee, 375 Nechells Park Road, Nechells, Birmingham B7 5NT *Tel* 0121 327 6618 *Fax* 0121 327 6612

CC NO 326999   **ESTABLISHED** 1986

■ The York Children's Trust

WHERE FUNDING CAN BE GIVEN Within 20 miles of York City.

WHO CAN BENEFIT Individuals; group-based organisations; local groups and schools benefiting people under 25 years of age, parents and children; one-parent families; at risk groups; people with disabilities; people disadvantaged by poverty, and people fostering talents in music, drama and athletic activities.

WHAT IS FUNDED Voluntary groups helping in the care and development of young people through arts, culture and recreation, healthcare, education and community services; support of individuals with special needs.

WHAT IS NOT FUNDED The trust will not normally give grants for private education fees. Exceptions may be made where unforeseen circumstances, such as the death of a parent, would prevent a child completing the last year of a critical stage of education such as A-levels.

FINANCES *Year* 1999 *Income* £90,000 *Grants* £69,000

TRUSTEES J P Birch, Chair; and fifteen others.

HOW TO APPLY In writing to the correspondent.

WHO TO APPLY TO H G Sherriff, Secretary, 34 Lucombe Way, Hartrigg Oaks, New Earswick, York YO32 4DS *Tel* 01904 750705

CC NO 222279   **ESTABLISHED** 1976

■ The Yorkshire Agricultural Society

WHERE FUNDING CAN BE GIVEN Particularly Yorkshire and Humbershire, with some activity extending into Durham, Northumberland and the former county of Cleveland.

WHO CAN BENEFIT Primarily local activities and organisations, particularly those in farming and related industries, and those living in rural areas. Priority is given to charities in Yorkshire and former Cleveland, with some activities extending into Durham and Northumberland.

WHAT IS FUNDED (a) Promotion of agriculture and allied industries, related research and education. (b) Protection and safeguarding of the environment. (c) Holding of an annual agricultural show. (d) Appropriate charitable purposes. Environmental projects normally require relevance to agriculture to attract support. The trust will consider giving support to religious umbrella bodies, schools and colleges, and rural crime prevention schemes, all within the context of farming and the rural economy.

WHAT IS NOT FUNDED No support to students. Overseas projects are seldom supported.

TYPE OF GRANT Most usually once only or starter/pump priming finance. Buildings, capital, core costs, feasibility studies, projects, research, running costs, recurring costs and salaries will be considered. Funding may be given for up to three years.

RANGE OF GRANTS £200–£10,000, typical grant £1,000.

SAMPLE GRANTS In 2000: £12,000 each to two agricultural colleges; £6,750 to Nuffield Trust for a Farming & Travel Scholarship; seven grants ranging between £6,000 and £2,500 each to seven northern universities for research relevant to agriculture/forestry/horticulture; £2,000 each to four Farming and Wildlife Advisory Group branches towards administration costs.

FINANCES *Year* 2001 *Income* £2,053,000 *Grants* £182,000 *Assets* £21,413,000

PUBLICATIONS Quarterly newsletter.

HOW TO APPLY In writing to the correspondent, to be considered quarterly. Applications should include accounts, proposed budget, details of confirmed and anticipated funding and ongoing management and costs.

WHO TO APPLY TO N Pulling, Chief Executive, Great Yorkshire Showground, Harrogate HG2 8PW *Tel* 01423 541000 *Fax* 01423 541414 *E-mail* info@yas.co.uk *Website* www.yas.co.uk

CC NO 513238　　　**ESTABLISHED** 1837

....

■ The Yorkshire Bank Charitable Trust

WHERE FUNDING CAN BE GIVEN Within the area covered by branches of the Bank, i.e. from north of the Thames Valley to Newcastle upon Tyne.

WHO CAN BENEFIT Registered charities benefiting: young adults; at risk groups; people with physical or mental disabilities; people disadvantaged by poverty; socially isolated people, and those involved in the arts and education.

WHAT IS FUNDED Charities engaged in youth work; facilities for people with mental or physical disabilities; counselling and community work in depressed areas, with some support also being given for education and for the arts. The trustees would be unlikely to make more than one donation per organisation within any 12 month period.

WHAT IS NOT FUNDED Applications from individuals, including students, are ineligible. No grants made in response to general appeals from UK organisations.

TYPE OF GRANT Usually one-off for a specific project or part of a project.

FINANCES *Year* 2001 *Income* £41,581 *Grants* £63,000

TRUSTEES George Cookson; Geoff Greer; John C Hurst.

HOW TO APPLY In writing to the correspondent. Trustees meet every six to eight weeks.

WHO TO APPLY TO Nicola Ashcroft, Executive Security, Yorkshire Bank plc, 20 Merrion Way, Leeds, West Yorkshire LS2 8NZ *Tel* 0113 247 2104

CC NO 326269　　　**ESTABLISHED** 1982

....

■ Yorkshire Building Society Charitable Foundation

WHERE FUNDING CAN BE GIVEN UK, with a preference for grantmaking in branch localities.

WHO CAN BENEFIT Charitable organisations/good causes meeting foundation criteria.

WHAT IS FUNDED General charitable purposes/ specific items to maximum donation of £2,000.

WHAT IS NOT FUNDED No grants for: political or propagandist activities; support of religious activities or advancement (unless for a group or

community in social need); UK charities for ongoing fundings (local branches may apply for projects/specific costs); support which should be funded by local/central government including schools, unless special needs; sport; expeditions; proposals to raise funds for another cause (such as to take part in fundraising events); carnivals or shows for public entertainment where there is no control over the eventual destination of funds raised; any purpose concerned with 'friendship', such as town twinning associations.

TYPE OF GRANT Money for specific items.

RANGE OF GRANTS Maximum of £2,000.

SAMPLE GRANTS Since the foundation's launch 1,380 causes have benefited from grants totalling over £900,000.

FINANCES *Year* 2000–01 *Income* £224,000 *Grants* £276,000 *Assets* £232,000

TRUSTEES C J Faulkner; Miss L S Will; Mrs S Needham; Mrs J L Wesson; Prof. A Robards.

HOW TO APPLY In writing to the correspondent or through a local Yorkshire Building Society branch.

WHO TO APPLY TO Miss J Howarth, Campaign Manager, Yorkshire House, Yorkshire Drive, Bradford, West Yorkshire BD5 8LJ *Tel* 01274 472015 *Fax* 01274 735571 *E-mail* marketing@ybs.co.uk

CC NO 1069082　　　**ESTABLISHED** 1998

....

■ The Yorkshire County Cricket Club Charitable Youth Trust

WHERE FUNDING CAN BE GIVEN Yorkshire.

WHO CAN BENEFIT Schools and colleges benefiting children and young adults, students, sports people, teachers and coaches.

WHAT IS FUNDED The provision of facilities for young people in full-time education to play cricket.

FINANCES *Year* 2000 *Income* £95,000 *Grants* £27,000 *Assets* £593,000

TRUSTEES C M Fenton, Chair; H North; R Appleyard; B W Moss; W A R Boag; J P Honeysett; J C D Allen; R A Hutton.

HOW TO APPLY In writing to the correspondent.

WHO TO APPLY TO J P Honeysett, Secretary, 9 St Winifred's Road, Harrogate, North Yorkshire HG2 8LN *Tel* 01423 887978 *E-mail* peter@honeysett.totalserve.co.uk

CC NO 1001497　　　**ESTABLISHED** 1991

....

■ Yorkshire Dales Millennium Trust

WHERE FUNDING CAN BE GIVEN The Yorkshire Dales.

WHO CAN BENEFIT Voluntary organisations, community groups, farmers and other individuals, Yorkshire Dales National Park Authority, estates, National Trust, parish councils, district councils and English Nature.

WHAT IS FUNDED The conservation and regeneration of the natural and built heritage and community life of the Yorkshire Dales, for example, planting new and restoring old woods, the restoration of dry stone walls and field barns, conservation of historical features and community projects.

FINANCES *Year* 2001–02 *Grants* £613,000

TRUSTEES Roger Stott, Chair; Dorothy Fairburn; Brian Braithwaite-Exley; Heather Jane Hancock; Colin Speakman; Vicky Fattorini; Marquess of Hartington; David Anthony Welton Joy; Jane Roberts; Joseph Joshua Pearlman; Lord Shuttleworth; Robin Grove-White; Max Robinson; Steve Macaré.

HOW TO APPLY In writing to the correspondent.
WHO TO APPLY TO Iain Cag, Director, The Old Post Office, Main Street, Clapham, via Lancaster, North Yorkshire LA2 8DP *Tel* 01524 251002
CC NO 1061687 **ESTABLISHED** 1996

■ The Yorkshire Historic Churches Trust

WHERE FUNDING CAN BE GIVEN Yorkshire.
WHO CAN BENEFIT All Christian churches.
WHAT IS FUNDED The repair, restoration, preservation and maintenance of churches in the area stated above.
WHAT IS NOT FUNDED No grants for the reordering of churches or any other new work.
TYPE OF GRANT Capital building grants. Funding of up to three years will be considered.
RANGE OF GRANTS £500–£20,000.
SAMPLE GRANTS £20,000 to St James – Anston for repairs to tower parapet and spire; £11,000 to Goldthorpe Parish Church for restoration; £10,000 each to All Saints – Laughten en le Morthen for repairs to tower walls and bells, Christ Church – Doncaster for internal restoration, St Botolph – Knottingley for repairs to roofs and gutters, and St Peter's – Letwell for repairs to tower walls and gutters; £9,000 to St Pauls – Barnsley Old Town for re-roofing; £5,000 to St Helen's – Burghwallis for restoration; £4,000 to All Saints – Woodlands for repairs to windows; £2,500 to All Saints – Hooton Pagnell for repairs to windows.
FINANCES *Year* 2000 *Income* £139,000 *Grants* £117,000 *Assets* £124,000
TRUSTEES C Clarkson, Chair; Dr C Binfield; R Carr-Archer; Miss I Cunliffe; Ven. C J Hawthorne; Revd A Holmes; W Legard; Revd Canon E Newlyn; L Lennox; D A Quick; S Reynolds; D Rubinstein; B Smith; W J A Smith; Very Revd H E C Stapleton.
HOW TO APPLY In writing to the correspondent by 28 February. Applications should state dedication and locality of the church.
WHO TO APPLY TO Canon Edwin Newlyn, c/o The Parish Office, Whitby Mission and Seafarers Centre, Whitby, North Yorkshire YO21 3PP *Tel* 01947 825746 *Fax* 01947 602798
CC NO 700639 **ESTABLISHED** 1988

■ David Young Charitable Settlement

WHERE FUNDING CAN BE GIVEN UK.
WHO CAN BENEFIT Mainly Jewish organisations.
WHAT IS FUNDED General charitable purposes.
SAMPLE GRANTS £15,000 each to Jewish Care and Joint Jewish Charitable Trust; £5,000 to Community Security Trust; £1,000 each to UCL Development Fund and the Board of Deputies.
FINANCES *Year* 1999–2000 *Income* £43,000 *Grants* £41,000 *Assets* £40,000
TRUSTEES Lord Young; Lady Young; M S Mischon.
HOW TO APPLY In writing to the correspondent.
WHO TO APPLY TO R E Pond, Blick Rothenberg, Chartered Accountants, 12 York Gate, Regents Park, London NW1 4QS *Tel* 020 7486 0111
CC NO 265195 **ESTABLISHED** 1972

■ The John K Young Endowment Fund

WHERE FUNDING CAN BE GIVEN Edinburgh.
WHO CAN BENEFIT Organisations benefiting: people of all ages; chemists; research workers and medical professionals.
WHAT IS FUNDED Grants are given to support medical and surgical research and research in chemistry as an aid to UK industry. Also to fund charities which are concerned with the physical wellbeing of the youth of Edinburgh or with restoring people who are sick to health.
WHAT IS NOT FUNDED No grants to individuals or non-registered charities.
TYPE OF GRANT One-off grants are awarded. Funding is available for up to one year.
RANGE OF GRANTS £500–£2,000.
FINANCES *Year* 1997–98 *Income* £40,000 *Grants* £30,000 *Assets* £900,000
TRUSTEES T C Foggo; A J R Ferguson; R J S Morton; R I F Macdonald.
HOW TO APPLY In writing to the correspondent. Trustees meet to consider grants in the spring and autumn.
WHO TO APPLY TO Robin Morton, Partner/Trust Administrator, Skene Edwards WS, 5 Albyn Place, Edinburgh EH2 4NJ *Tel* 0131 225 6665 *Fax* 0131 220 1015
SC NO SC002264

■ The John Young Charitable Settlement

WHERE FUNDING CAN BE GIVEN UK and overseas.
WHO CAN BENEFIT Charitable organisations.
WHAT IS FUNDED General charitable purposes, with a preference for wildlife.
RANGE OF GRANTS £120–£10,000.
SAMPLE GRANTS In 1997–98: £8,000 to Refuge; £5,000 each to RSPB and Serious Road Trip; £3,500 to Edge Habitat Associates; £2,000 to Cape Clear Bird Observatory; £1,500 to Breakthrough Breast Cancer.
FINANCES *Year* 1999–2000 *Income* £7,300 *Grants* £42,000 *Assets* £178,000
TRUSTEES J M Young; G H Camamile.
HOW TO APPLY In writing to the correspondent.
WHO TO APPLY TO K A Hawkins, c/o Lee Associates, 5 Southampton Place, London WC1A 2DA *Tel* 020 7025 4600
CC NO 283254 **ESTABLISHED** 1981

■ The William Allen Young Charitable Trust

WHERE FUNDING CAN BE GIVEN UK, with a preference for south London.
WHO CAN BENEFIT Registered charities, churches and education-related organisations.
WHAT IS FUNDED General charitable purposes, with a preference for health and social welfare.
RANGE OF GRANTS £100–£11,000.
SAMPLE GRANTS £21,220 to National Hospital Development Foundation; £10,895 to St George's Ophthalmic Research Fund; £10,000 to British Benevolent Fund of Madrid; £9,000 to West Sussex Doctors on Call; £5,136 to Royal Hospital for Neuro-disability; £5,000 each to Brain Research Trust and St John Ambulance Somerset; £3,500 to National Hospital for Neurology and Neurosurgery; £3,000 to St George's Hospital for the Eye Department Research Fund; £2,000 to RNLI Taunton.

FINANCES *Year* 2000–01 *Income* £113,973
Grants £134,751 *Assets* £3,650,389
TRUSTEES J A Young; T F B Young; J G A Young.
HOW TO APPLY The trust does not support
unsolicited applications as funds are already
committed.
WHO TO APPLY TO J A Young, Trustee, The Ram
Brewery, Wandsworth, London SW18 4JD
Tel 020 8875 7000
CC NO 283102   **ESTABLISHED** 1978

■ Elizabeth & Prince Zaiger Trust

WHERE FUNDING CAN BE GIVEN UK, some preference for Somerset, Dorset and the south-west.

WHO CAN BENEFIT Registered charities benefiting people of all ages who are mentally and physically disabled and disadvantaged by poverty; registered charities providing care and protection for animals.

WHAT IS FUNDED Relief for elderly and disabled people; advancement of education; care and protection for animals; relief of poverty and general charitable purposes.

WHAT IS NOT FUNDED No grants to individuals.

TYPE OF GRANT One-off and recurrent.

RANGE OF GRANTS £1,000–£5,000.

SAMPLE GRANTS £30,000 to Variety Club of Great Britain; £5,000 each to British Heart Foundation, Cystic Fibrosis Trust, Juvenile Diabetes Trust, Royal Hospital for Neuro-disability and Yeovil Hospice; £4,000 each to ASBHA, National Animal Welfare Trust, Royal National Institute for the Blind and St Margaret – Somerset Hospice; £3,000 to British Institute for Brain-Injured Children.

FINANCES *Year* 2000–01 *Income* £293,000 *Grants* £306,305 *Assets* £9,500,000

TRUSTEES D W Parry; P J Harvey; D G Long.

HOW TO APPLY The trust does not respond to unsolicited applications, stating 'we have an ongoing programme of support for our chosen charities'.

WHO TO APPLY TO D W Parry, Trustee, 6 Alleyn Road, Dulwich, London SE21 8AL

CC NO 282096 **ESTABLISHED** 1981

■ Zephyr Charitable Trust

WHERE FUNDING CAN BE GIVEN UK and worldwide.

WHO CAN BENEFIT National help for organisations benefiting disabled people; homeless people; victims of famine, man-made or natural disasters and war.

WHAT IS FUNDED Housing, health, environment, third world projects.

WHAT IS NOT FUNDED No grants to individuals, expeditions or scholarships.

TYPE OF GRANT Varies.

RANGE OF GRANTS £500–£3,000.

SAMPLE GRANTS £3,000 each to DEC Mozambique Flood Appeal and Intermediate Technology; £2,100 to Pesticides Trust; £2,000 each to CRISIS, MIND, Medical Foundation for the Care of Victims of Torture; £1,900 each to Shelter and Survival International; £1,600 to Womankind UK; £1,500 to the Hearing Research Trust.

FINANCES *Year* 2000 *Income* £35,899 *Grants* £31,300 *Assets* £893,218

TRUSTEES Elizabeth Breeze; Roger Harriman; David Baldock; Donald I Watson.

OTHER INFORMATION The bulk of the trust's annual income is allocated by way of 15 annual subscriptions leaving a very small annual amount of £2,000 available for one-off grants. Unsolicited applications are therefore unlikely to be successful.

HOW TO APPLY In writing to the correspondent. The trustees meet to consider grants in June or July each year. Unsolicited applications are unlikely to be successful, since the trust makes annual donations to a list of beneficiaries.

WHO TO APPLY TO R Harriman, Trust Administrator, New Guild House, 45 Great Charles Street, Queensway, Birmingham B3 2LX *Tel* 0121 212 2222

CC NO 1003234 **ESTABLISHED** 1991

■ The I A Ziff Charitable Foundation

WHERE FUNDING CAN BE GIVEN UK, with a preference for Yorkshire, especially Leeds and Harrogate.

WHO CAN BENEFIT There are no restrictions regarding beneficiaries other than no grants to individuals.

WHAT IS FUNDED General charitable purposes, especially 'value for money' donations which will bring the most benefit to the largest number of people.

WHAT IS NOT FUNDED No grants to individuals.

TYPE OF GRANT One-off; no loans.

SAMPLE GRANTS £50,000 to University of Leeds to refurbish buildings to improve the working conditions for students; £13,000 to Joint Jewish Charitable Trust; £7,620 to Leeds Jewish Welfare Board; £6,340 to Leeds International Piano Competition; £4,000 to National Eye Research Centre – Yorkshire; £3,020 to United Jewish Israel Appeal; £2,303 to BHH; £2,000 each to Almshouse Association, St Gemma's Hospice, and Yorkshire Association of Boys Clubs.

FINANCES *Year* 2000–01 *Income* £248,203 *Grants* £130,810 *Assets* £2,017,295

TRUSTEES I Arnold Ziff; Marjorie E Ziff; Michael A Ziff; Edward M Ziff; Ann L Manning.

OTHER INFORMATION The charity has undertaken to finance two major projects which will consume its resources for the foreseeable future. It may make token gifts to requests outside its normal range of beneficiaries but the funds available are very strictly limited.

HOW TO APPLY In writing to the correspondent. Initial telephone calls are welcome, but please note the above comments.

WHO TO APPLY TO B Rouse, Secretary, Town Centre House, The Merrion Centre, Leeds LS2 8LY *Tel* 0113 222 1234 *Fax* 0113 242 1026

CC NO 249368 **ESTABLISHED** 1964

■ The Zochonis Charitable Trust

WHERE FUNDING CAN BE GIVEN UK, particularly Greater Manchester, and overseas, particularly Africa.

WHO CAN BENEFIT Registered charities only.

WHAT IS FUNDED General charitable purposes.

WHAT IS NOT FUNDED No grants for individuals.

TYPE OF GRANT One-off and recurrent.

SAMPLE GRANTS £57,000 to BESO (British Executive Services Overseas); £50,000 each to Chethams School of Music and Technology Colleges Trust; £50,000 each to Imperial War Museum, Manchester City Art Gallery and Withington Girls' School; £40,000 to North Manchester Jewish Youth Project; £35,000 to St George's House Trust; £25,000 to Waterford School Trust and VSO.

FINANCES *Year* 2000–01 *Income* £1,147,913 *Grants* £1,122,000 *Assets* £18,970,514

TRUSTEES John Zochonis; Richard B James; Alan Whittaker.

HOW TO APPLY In writing to the correspondent.

WHO TO APPLY TO Mrs J Lloyd, Deloitte & Touche, PO Box 500, 201 Deansgate, Manchester M60 2AT *Tel* 0161 455 8287 *Fax* 0161 829 3803
CC NO 274769   ESTABLISHED 1977

....

■ Zurich Financial Services Community Trust

WHERE FUNDING CAN BE GIVEN UK and overseas. Some preference for Dorset, Gloucestershire, Hampshire and Wiltshire for the Zurich Cares programme, and also around Birmingham, Cardiff and Leeds.

WHO CAN BENEFIT Voluntary organisations and registered charities.

WHAT IS FUNDED Zurich Cares Trust programmes focuses on the most disadvantaged groups of people in society and on less popular causes, such as dementia, older people and social exclusion issues, plus a programme in India. All fund capacity building and work in partnership with a combination of long-term funding and business skill transfer. Most of the projects in these programmes are researched and identified by the trust;

Zurich Cares employee charity fund supports local community organisations that are near the main offices plus some national partners and overseas projects. Local fundraising and regular giving by staff have funded this, which is then matched by company money. Local budgets are held for main locations in the UK, where the company has large numbers of staff and business units. Some of these areas are new and developing, whilst others are well established. Typically, these grants will range from £100–£10,000, but will vary depending on the location concerned;

Zurich Advice Network Foundation has a theme, currently Kids2Care4, helping disadvantaged children under 18 years of age. Capital grants are only given to those organisations that have been nominated by a member of the Zurich Advice Network or business centre staff. This fund is not open to direct applications.

WHAT IS NOT FUNDED The trust does not normally support the following: statutory organisations (including mainstream schools and hospitals) – unless exclusively for special needs unit; fundraising events including appeals or events for national charities; expeditions, exchanges or study tours; playgroups and mother and toddler groups, unless for special needs groups; medical research, animal welfare charities, conservation or environmental projects; sports clubs, village halls or religious organisations (including the upkeep and repair of places of worship); advertising or sponsorship connected with charitable events or appeals.

TYPE OF GRANT One-off and recurrent. Capital, core costs, project costs, revenue, salaries and seed funding. Partnerships are typically for three years.

RANGE OF GRANTS £100–£100,000.

SAMPLE GRANTS £100,000 each to Action Aid and Thames Valley Adventure Playground; £52,875 to Charities Management Consortium; £48,894 to Dove House in Belfast; £46,000 to Pinewood School; £43,250 to the Alzheimer's Society; £35,000 to Gloucestershire Neighbourhood Projects Network; £30,000 to Dementia Care Initiative and Royal National Institute for the Blind (RNIB); £27,000 to Dementia Relief Trust.

FINANCES *Year* 2001 *Income* £3,949,000 *Grants* £4,067,000 *Assets* £6,025,000

HOW TO APPLY Contact the trust, or visit its website, for further information on how to apply.

WHO TO APPLY TO Chris Staples, Zurich Financial Services (UKISA) Community Trust Ltd, PO Box 1288, Swindon SN1 1FL *Tel* 01793 511227 *Fax* 01793 506982 *Website* www.zurich.co.uk
CC NO 266983   ESTABLISHED 1973